Student Instructions for Registration and Login

Before you go online to register be sure you have:

- A valid **e-mail address**

- The MyMathLab **Course ID** from your instructor

- A **student access code**, which should have come packaged with your textbook

 Sample: `MMLST-TAROK-THOLE-PICON-SHRIK-PRAWN`

If you are using a computer <u>off campus</u> (at home or work) you will need to have administrative access so you can install the necessary plug-ins, and be connected to the internet. *(If you're not sure your computer meets the system requirements, go to <u>www.mymathlab.com/system.html</u>, visit the MyMathLab Installation Wizard in your course, or contact tech support at 1-800-677-6337).*

If you are using a computer <u>on campus</u> the necessary plug-ins may already be installed in the lab. If you aren't sure, check with the lab coordinator or your instructor.

Instructions:

1. Launch Internet Explorer. *If you are off campus and using AOL to connect to the Internet you will need to minimize AOL and then launch Internet Explorer.*

NOTE: Your MyMathLab course may be available on both PC and Mac platforms, using Internet Explorer, Firefox, and Safari. Check with your instructor for more information.

2. If necessary, clear the address field and enter <u>www.coursecompass.com</u>.

3. Click the **Register** button for students.

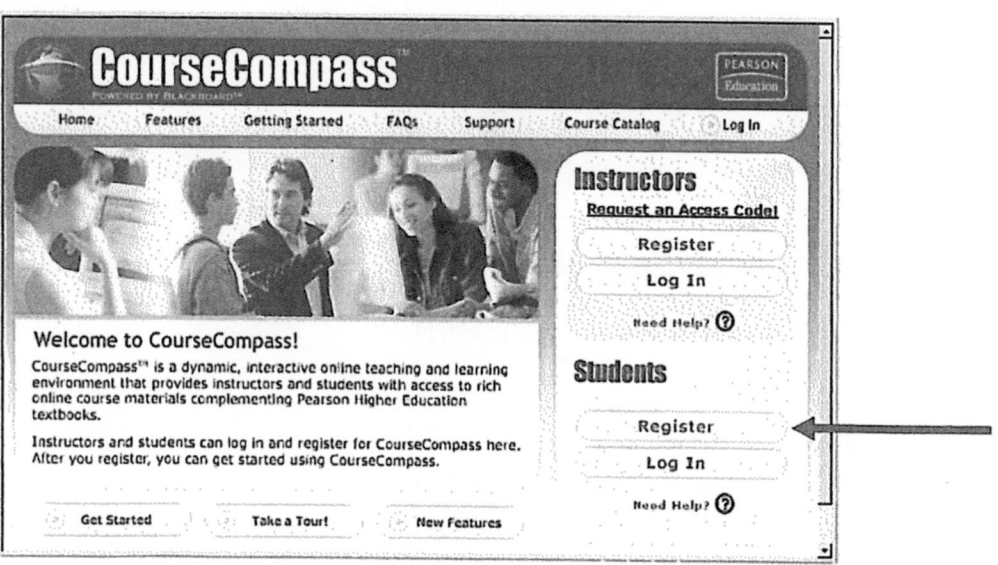

4. Confirm that you have the information necessary to continue and click **Next** on the "Before you Start..." page.

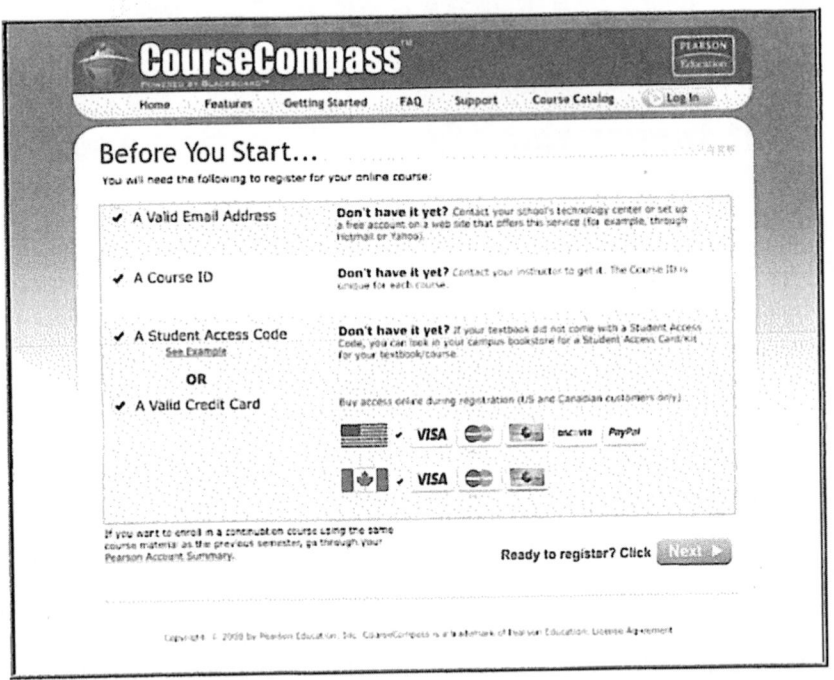

5. On the Product Selection page, enter the **course ID** your instructor gave you and click **Find Course**.

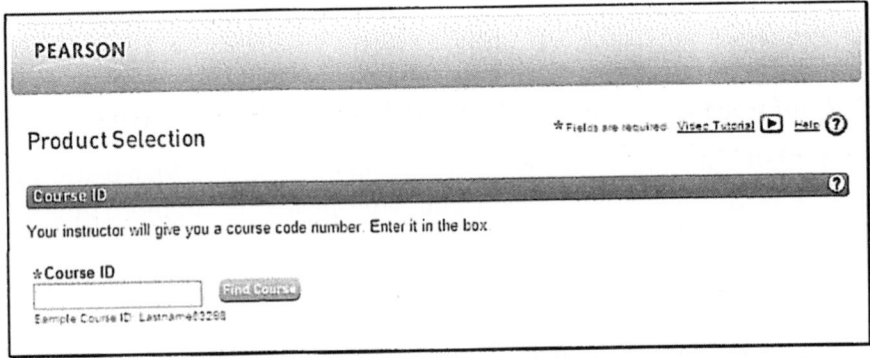

Your course information will appear. *Be sure to check that your instructor's course information is correct. If not, contact your instructor to verify the correct course ID.*

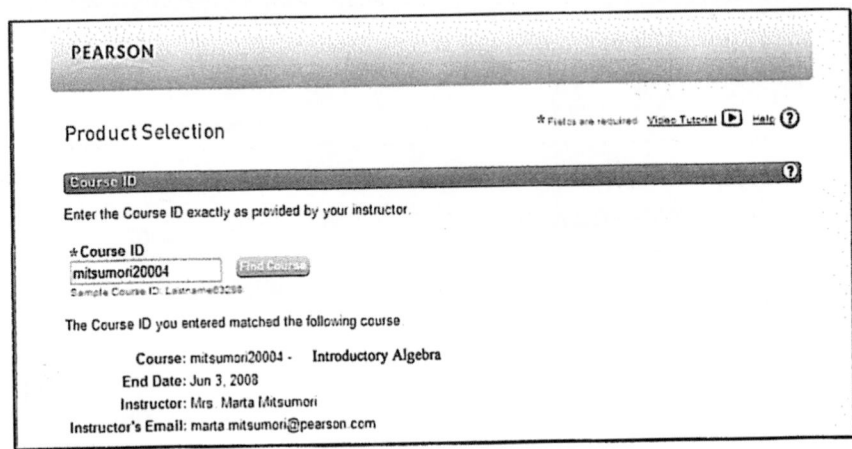

6. If your student access code came packaged with your textbook, select **Access Code**. If you do not have an access code and want to purchase access to your course with a credit card, select **Buy Now**.

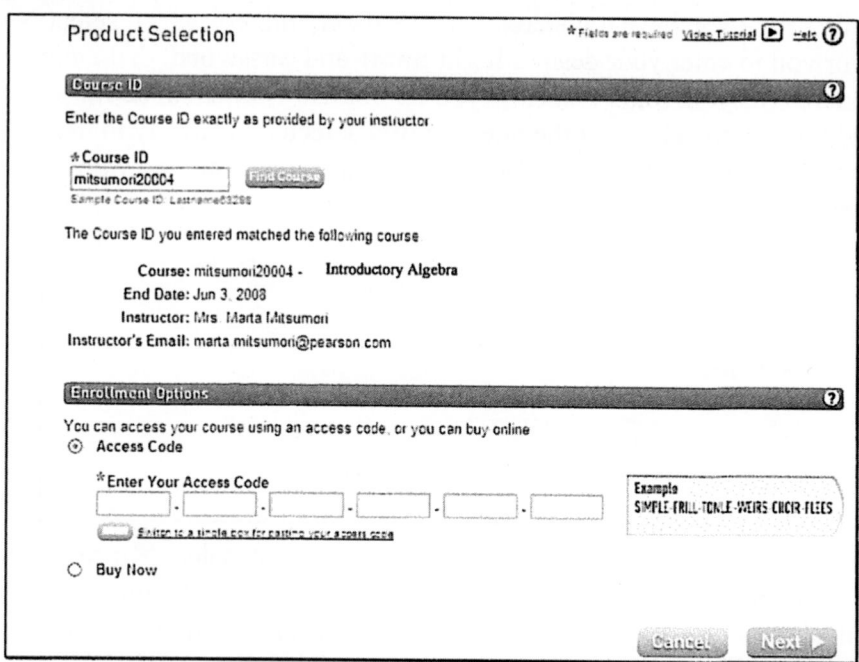

7. Type in your student access code using the tab key to move from one box to the next. Type letters in either all uppercase or all lowercase. Click **Next** after you have entered your code. *If you are buying access with a credit card, the on-screen instructions will guide you through the purchase process.*

8. Please read all information on the License Agreement and Privacy Policy page. Click on **Accept** if you agree to the terms of use.

9. On the Access Information Screen, you'll be asked whether you already have a Pearson Education Account.

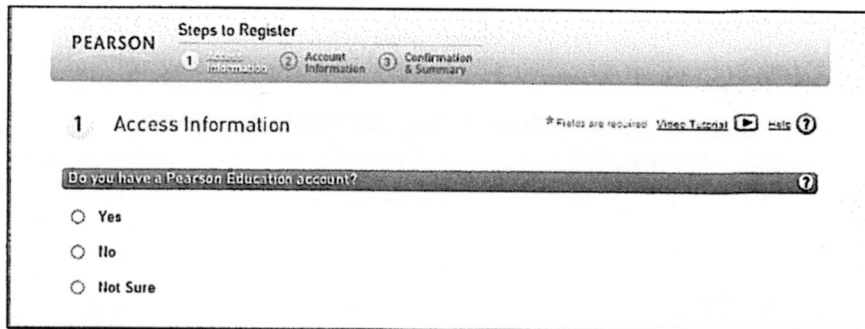

10. If you have registered for other Pearson online products and already have a login name and password, select **Yes**. Boxes will appear for you to enter your login information.

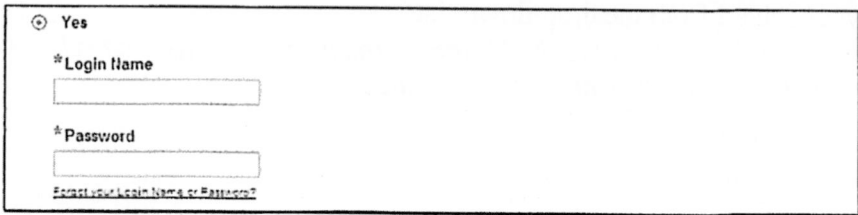

If you select Yes, you will see a Welcome Back screen, where you may be prompted to update your password and make changes to your account information as needed.

11. If this is the first time you have registered for a Pearson online product, select **No**. Boxes will appear for you to enter your desired **login name** and **password**. You may want to use your email address as your login name. If you do not use your email address, be prepared with a second login name choice if the one you first selected is already in use. Your login name must be at least 4 characters and cannot be the same as your password.

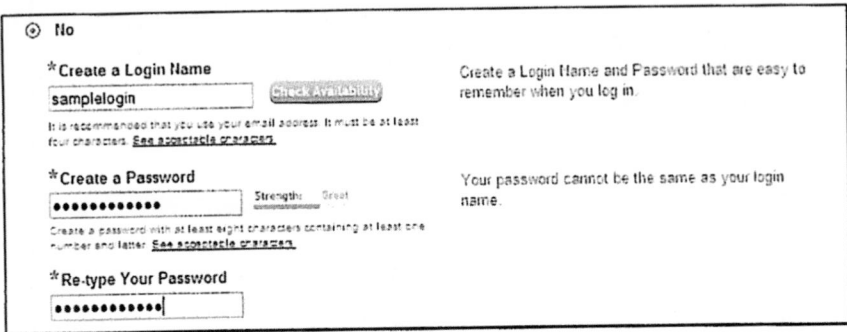

12. If you aren't sure whether you have a Pearson account or not, select **Not Sure**. Enter your email address and click **Search**. If you have an account, your login information will be sent to your email address within a few moments. Change your selection to Yes, and enter your login name and password as directed.

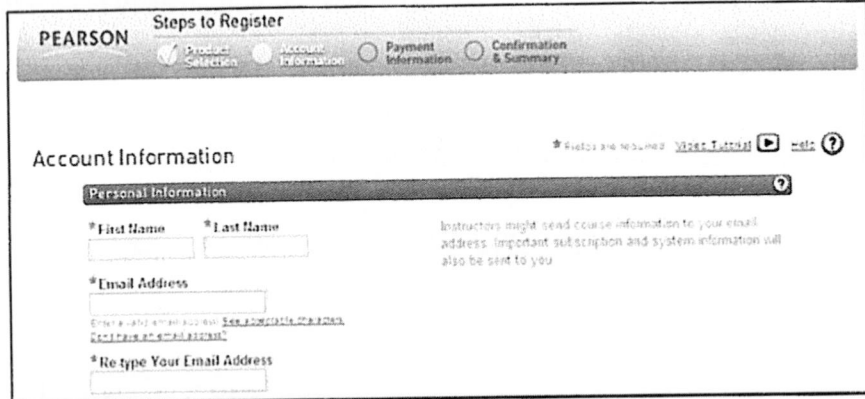

13. On the Account Information page, enter your first and last name and email address. Re-type your email address to make sure it is correct.

14. In the School Location section, select **United States** from the School Country drop-down menu (NOTE - United States appears at the top of this list). Enter your **school** zip code, and then select your school from the drop-down list.
 *If your school is not listed, scroll to the bottom of the drop-down list and select **Other**. Then enter your school name and city and select the state.*

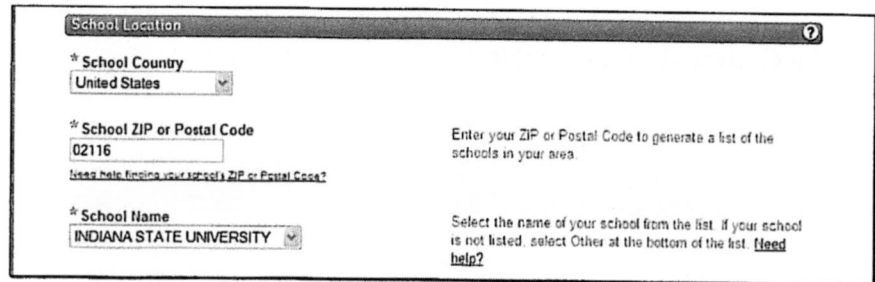

15. Select a security question and answer to ensure the privacy of your account. Then click **Next.**

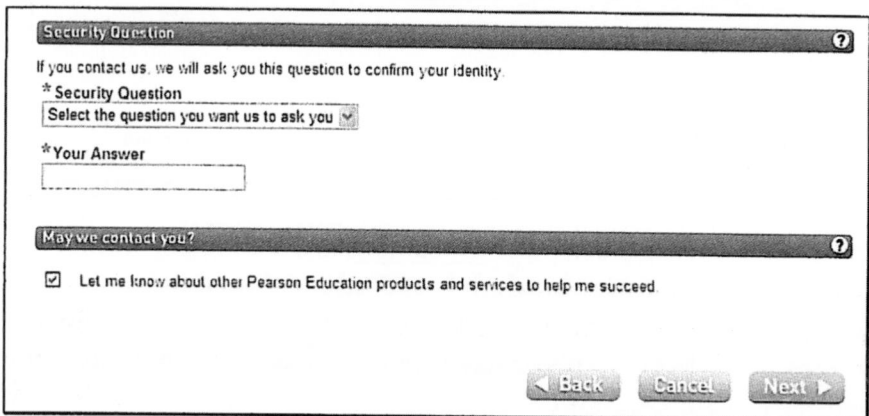

16. When your registration process is complete you will see a confirmation screen.

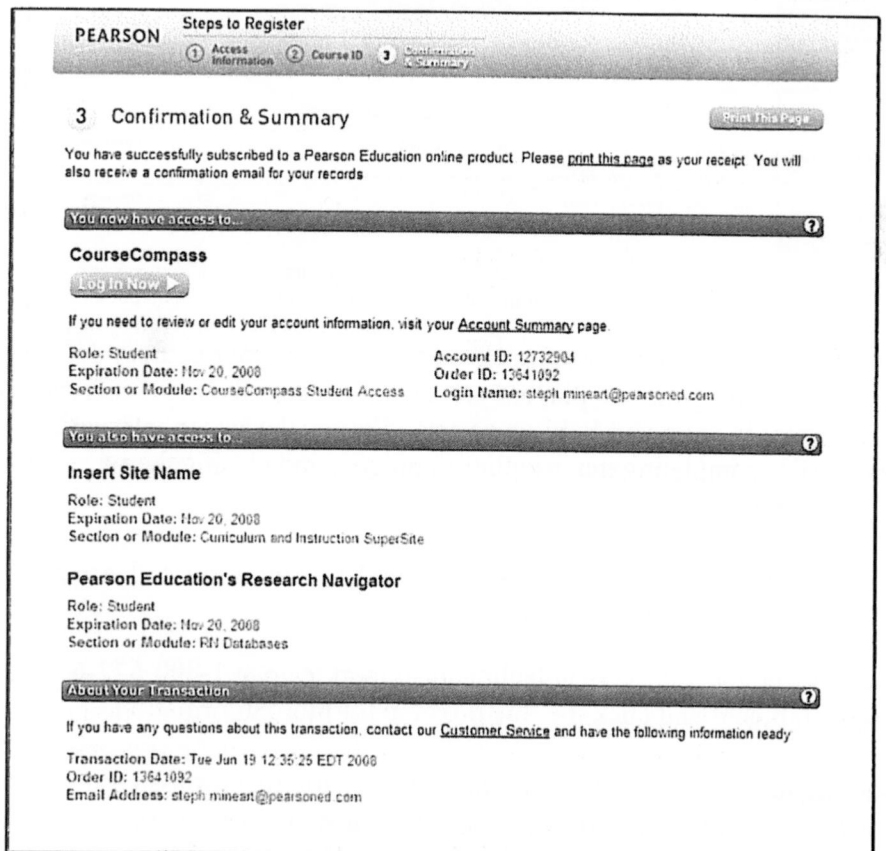

Congratulations – You have successfully registered for your MyMathLab course!

17. Print the Confirmation & Summary page so you will have a record of your login name and the email address used for your account. Be sure to keep the email confirmation sent to you.

18. Click **Log in Now** to reach your My CourseCompass page. You will see your MyMathLab course title in the **Courses** box on the left.

19. Click your course title to begin exploring MyMathLab!

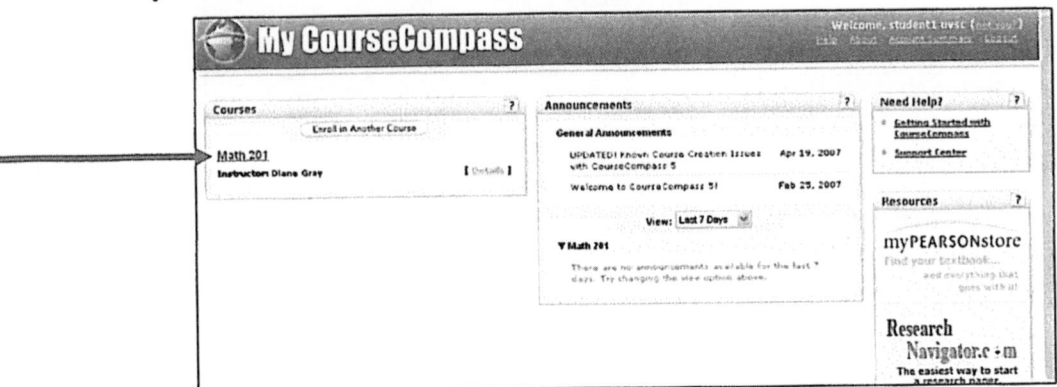

20. **Important!** If you are using a computer <u>off campus</u> and are logging into MyMathLab for the first time, you must click the **MyMathLab Installation Wizard** link now.

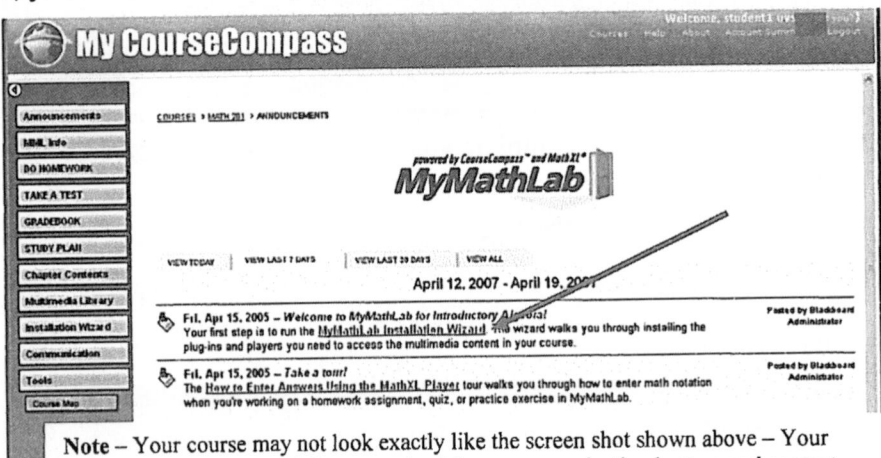

Note – Your course may not look exactly like the screen shot shown above – Your instructor may have specially customized the course navigation buttons and content.

21. The InstallationWizard (or Browser Check – depending on your course) detects and then helps you install the plug-ins and players you need to access the math exercises and multimedia content in your MyMathLab course. Follow the screen instructions to complete this process. After completing the installation process and closing the wizard you will be back on the Welcome page of your course.

22. Click the **How to Enter Answers Using the MathXL Player** link to learn how to enter answers when working within MyMathLab.

23. If you need help, contact the student technical support team at **1-800-677-6337**, or visit www.mymathlab.com and click the **Support** tab for more information.

24. When returning to work in MyMathLab, go to www.coursecompass.com. Click on the Log In button for students and log in using your login name and password.

25. **Important!** You will access your MyMathLab course from this site, so be sure to **bookmark this page!**

A BRIEF GUIDE TO GETTING THE MOST FROM THIS BOOK

1 Read the Book

Feature	Description	Benefit	Page
Section-Opening Scenarios	Every section opens with a scenario presenting a unique application of algebra in your life outside the classroom.	Realizing that algebra is everywhere will help motivate your learning.	101
Detailed Worked-Out Examples	Examples are clearly written and provide step-by-step solutions. No steps are omitted, and each step is thoroughly explained to the right of the mathematics.	The blue annotations will help you understand the solutions by providing the reason why every algebraic step is true.	104
Applications Using Real-World Data	Interesting applications from nearly every discipline, supported by up-to-date real-world data, are included in every section.	Ever wondered how you'll use algebra? This feature will show you how algebra can solve real problems.	238
Study Tips	The book's study tip boxes offer suggestions for problem solving, point out common errors to avoid, and provide informal hints and suggestions.	By seeing common mistakes, you'll be able to avoid them.	103
Explanatory Voice Balloons	Voice balloons help to demystify algebra. They translate algebraic language into plain English, clarify problem-solving procedures, and present alternative ways of understanding.	Does math ever look foreign to you? This feature often translates math into everyday English.	184
Learning Objectives	Every section begins with a list of objectives. Each objective is restated in the margin where the objective is covered.	The objectives focus your reading by emphasizing what is most important and where to find it.	116
Technology	The screens displayed in the technology boxes show how graphing utilities verify and visualize algebraic results.	Even if you are not using a graphing utility in the course, this feature will help you understand different approaches to problem solving.	105

2 Work the Problems

Feature	Description	Benefit	Page
Check Point Examples	Each example is followed by a similar matched problem, called a Check Point, that offers you the opportunity to work a similar exercise. The answers to the Check Points are provided in the answer section.	You learn best by doing. You'll solidify your understanding of worked examples if you try a similar problem right away to be sure you understand what you've just read.	260
Extensive and Varied Exercise Sets	An abundant collection of exercises is included in an exercise set at the end of each section. Exercises are organized within categories. Your instructor will usually provide guidance on which exercises to work. The exercises in the first category, Practice Exercises, follow the same order as the section's worked examples.	The parallel order of the Practice Exercises lets you refer to the worked examples and use them as models for solving these problems.	338-341
		NEW to This Edition The "make sense" exercises ask you to determine whether statements are sensible, and to explain why or why not. This enables you to test your conceptual understanding of the section's objectives.	136

A BRIEF GUIDE TO GETTING THE MOST FROM THIS BOOK

Feature	Description	Benefit	Page
Practice Plus Problems	This category of exercises contains more challenging problems that often require you to combine several skills or concepts.	It is important to dig in and develop your problem-solving skills. Practice Plus Exercises provide you with ample opportunity to do so.	362
Preview Problems	NEW to This Edition Each exercise set concludes with three problems to help you prepare for the next section.	These exercises let you review previously covered material that you'll need to be successful for the forthcoming section. Some of these problems will get you thinking about concepts you'll soon encounter.	252

③ Review for Quizzes and Tests

Feature	Description	Benefit	Page
Mid-Chapter Check Points	At approximately the midway point in the chapter, an integrated set of review exercises allows you to review the skills and concepts you learned separately over several sections.	By combining exercises from the first half of the chapter, the Mid-Chapter Check Points give a comprehensive review before you move on to the material in the remainder of the chapter.	253-254
Chapter Review Grids	Each chapter contains a review chart that summarizes the definitions and concepts in every section of the chapter. Examples that illustrate these key concepts are also included in the chart.	Review this chart and you'll know the most important material in the chapter!	474-475
Chapter Review Exercises	A comprehensive collection of review exercises for each of the chapter's sections follows the grid.	Practice makes perfect. These exercises contain the most significant problems for each of the chapter's sections.	191-194
Chapter Tests	Each chapter contains a practice test with approximately 25 problems that cover the important concepts in the chapter. Take the practice test, check your answers, and then watch the Chapter Test Prep Video CD to see worked-out solutions for any exercises you miss.	You can use the chapter test to determine whether you have mastered the material covered in the chapter.	479
Chapter Test Prep Video CDs	These video CDs found at the back of your text contain worked-out solutions to every exercise in each chapter test.	The videos let you review any exercises you miss on the chapter test.	479
Cumulative Review Exercises	Beginning with Chapter 2, each chapter concludes with a comprehensive collection of mixed cumulative review exercises. These exercises combine problems from previous chapters and the present chapter, providing an ongoing cumulative review.	Ever forget what you've learned? These exercises ensure that you are not forgetting anything as you move forward.	410

College Algebra
Robert Blitzer
Custom Edition for Anne Arundel Community College

Taken from:
College Algebra, Fifth Edition
by Robert Blitzer

Custom Publishing

New York Boston San Francisco
London Toronto Sydney Tokyo Singapore Madrid
Mexico City Munich Paris Cape Town Hong Kong Montreal

Taken from:

College Algebra, Fifth Edition
by Robert Blitzer
Copyright © 2010, 2007, 2004, 2001, 1998 by Pearson Education, Inc.
Published by Prentice Hall
Upper Saddle River, New Jersey 07458

This special edition published in cooperation with Pearson Custom Publishing.

Printed in the United States of America

10 9 8 7 6 5 4 3 2 1

2009360641

KC

**Pearson
Custom Publishing**
is a division of

www.pearsonhighered.com

ISBN 10: 0-558-22560-8
ISBN 13: 978-0-558-22560-5

CONTENTS

Preface

I've written **College Algebra, Fifth Edition**, to help diverse students, with different backgrounds and future goals, to succeed. The book has three fundamental goals:

1. To help students acquire a solid foundation in algebra, preparing them for other courses such as calculus, business calculus, and finite mathematics.

2. To show students how algebra can model and solve authentic real-world problems.

3. To enable students to develop problem-solving skills, while fostering critical thinking, within an interesting setting.

One major obstacle in the way of achieving these goals is the fact that very few students actually read their textbook. This has been a regular source of frustration for me and for my colleagues in the classroom. Anecdotal evidence gathered over years highlights two basic reasons that students do not take advantage of their textbook:

- "I'll never use this information."
- "I can't follow the explanations."

I've written every page of the Fifth Edition with the intent of eliminating these two objections. The ideas and tools I've used to do so are described for the student in "A Brief Guide to Getting the Most from This Book," which appears inside the front cover.

What's New in the Fifth Edition?

- **New Applications and Real-World Data.** I'm on a constant search for real-world data that can be used to illustrate unique algebraic applications. I researched hundreds of books, magazines, newspapers, almanacs, and online sites to prepare the Fifth Edition. Among the 261 worked-out examples and application exercises based on new data sets, you'll find models that describe changing attitudes of college students over time.

- **"Make Sense?" Classroom Discussion Exercises.** Each exercise set contains four Critical Thinking exercises intended for classroom discussion in order to engage participation in the learning process. These items test conceptual understanding by asking students to determine whether statements are sensible, and to explain why or why not. Although sample answers are provided,

students have skills and perspectives that frequently differ from those of math teachers, so answers and explanations may vary. The important part of this new feature is to let you ask students what they think about selected statements, determine whether they understand the concepts, and give them feedback to clarify any misunderstandings.

- **New Directions for the True/False Critical Thinking Exercises.** The Fifth Edition asks students to determine whether each statement in an itemized list is true or false. If the statement is false, students are then asked to make the necessary change or changes to produce a true statement.

- **Preview Exercises.** Each exercise set concludes with three problems to help students prepare for the next section. Some of these problems review previously covered material that students will need to be successful in the forthcoming section. Other problems are designed to get students thinking about concepts they will soon encounter.

- **More Detailed Directions When Comparing Mathematical Models with Actual Data.** The Fifth Edition asks students if values obtained from mathematical models understimate or overestimate data displayed by graphs, and, if so, by how much.

- **Increased Study Tip Boxes.** The book's Study Tip boxes offer suggestions for problem solving, point out common errors to avoid, and provide informal hints and suggestions. These invaluable hints appear in greater abundance in the Fifth Edition.

- **New Chapter-Opening and Section-Opening Scenarios.** Every chapter and every section open with a scenario based on an application, the majority of which are unique to the Fifth Edition. These scenarios are revisited in the course of the chapter or section in one of the book's new examples, exercises, or discussions. The often-humorous tone of these openers is intended to help fearful and reluctant students overcome their negative perceptions about math.

- **677 New Examples and Exercises.** The Fifth Edition contains 24 detailed worked-out examples involving new data, 237 new application exercises, 216 "make sense" discussion exercises, 159 preview exercises, and 41 new exercises that appear in the various other categories of the exercise sets.

What Content and Organizational Changes Have Been Made to the Fifth Edition?

- **Section P.1 (Algebraic Expressions and Real Numbers)** contains a more detailed number line that illustrates both rational and irrational numbers. A new essay based on humorist Garth Sundem's *Geek Logik* sets the stage for the book's engaging collection of unique applications.

- **Section 1.1 (Graphs and Graphing Utilities)** contains additional exercises that ask students to select the graph that best illustrates a given description or story.

- **Section 1.7 (Linear Inequalities and Absolute Value Inequalities)** presents a new example of an inequality that contains fractions.

- **Section 2.1 (Basics of Functions and Their Graphs)** adds to the discussion of identifying domain and range from a function's graph with a new example in which the range is not determined by looking at a graph's endpoints.

- **Section 2.2 (More on Functions and Their Graphs)** now opens with a discussion of intervals on which a function increases, decreases, or is constant. This serves as a fluid transition from the information on analyzing the graph of a function in the previous section, as well as an immediate connection to the section's introduction. With the revised order of objectives, the section closes with a discussion of the difference quotient. There is also a more detailed presentation on piecewise functions, including an example on graphing such a function.

- **Section 2.3 (Linear Functions and Slope)** contains a new modeling example on climate change that is connected to the chapter opener.

- **Section 3.2 (Polynomial Functions and Their Graphs)** follows the definition of a polynomial function with examples of functions that are polynomial functions and examples of functions that are not polynomial functions. There is a new example on the Leading Coefficient Test where a function's degree and leading coefficient are determined for an equation in factored form.

- **Section 4.5 (Exponential Growth and Decay; Modeling Data)** has a greater variety of exercises on half-life and exponential decay.

- **Section 8.3 (Geometric Sequences and Series)** has a more thoroughly developed example on determining the value of an annuity, supported by an essay on "Stashing Cash and Making Taxes Less Taxing." Finance problems have been expanded in the exercise set.

I hope that my passion for teaching, as well as my respect for the diversity of students I have taught and learned from over the years, is apparent throughout this new edition. By connecting algebra to the whole spectrum of learning, it is my intent to show students that their world is profoundly mathematical, and indeed, π is in the sky.

Robert Blitzer

Supplements

STUDENT RESOURCES	INSTRUCTOR RESOURCES
	Instructor Resources can be downloaded from http://www.pearsonhighered.com or hard copy instructor resources can be ordered from your sales representative.
• *Student's Solutions Manual* Fully worked solutions to odd-numbered exercises.	• *TestGen®* Enables instructors to build, edit, print, and administer tests using a computerized bank of questions developed to cover all the objectives of the text. TestGen is algorithmically based, allowing instructors to create multiple but equivalent versions of the same question or test with the click of a button. Instructors can also modify test bank questions or add new questions. Tests can be printed or administered online. The software and test bank are available for download from Pearson Education's online catalog.
• *Videos on DVD* A comprehensive set of DVDs, tied to the textbook, containing 10–13-minute lectures for each section of the textbook. Each lecture covers the key topics of the section including definitions and formulas when applicable. Videos also have optional English and Spanish subtitles.	
	• *Test Item File* A printed test bank derived from TestGen.
• *Chapter Test Prep CD* Students can watch instructors work through step-by-step solutions to all the Chapter Test exercises from the textbook. The Chapter Test Prep Videos CD is included with each new student text.	• *PowerPoint Lecture Slides* Fully editable slides that follow the textbook. Project in class or post to a website in an online course. Included in these presentations are slides designed to work with Classroom Response Systems (Clickers).
	• *Instructor's Solutions Manual* Fully worked solutions to all textbook exercises.
	• *Mini Lecture Notes* These include additional examples and helpful teaching tips, by section.
	Instructor's Edition Provides answers to *all* exercises in the back of the text.

MathXL®

MathXL® is a powerful online homework, tutorial, and assessment system that accompanies Pearson Education's textbooks in mathematics or statistics. With MathXL, instructors can create, edit, and assign online homework and tests using algorithmically generated exercises correlated at the objective level to the textbook. They can also create and assign their own online exercises and import TestGen tests for added flexibility. All student work is tracked in MathXL's online gradebook. Students can take chapter tests in MathXL and receive personalized study plans based on their test results. The study plan diagnoses weaknesses and links students directly to tutorial exercises for the objectives they need to study and retest. Students can also access supplemental animations and video clips directly from selected exercises. MathXL is available to qualified adopters. For more information, visit our website at www.mathxl.com, or contact your sales representative.

MyMathLab®

MyMathLab® is a series of text-specific, easily customizable online courses for Pearson Education's textbooks in mathematics and statistics. Powered by CourseCompass™ (our online teaching and learning environment) and MathXL® (our online homework, tutorial, and assessment system), MyMathLab gives you the tools you need to deliver all or a portion of your course online, whether your students are in a lab setting or working from home. MyMathLab provides a rich and flexible set of course materials, featuring free-response exercises that are algorithmically generated for unlimited practice and mastery. Students can also use online tools, such as video lectures, animations, and a multimedia textbook, to independently improve their understanding and performance. Instructors can use MyMathLab's homework and test managers to select and assign online exercises correlated directly to the textbook, and they can also create and assign their own online exercises and import TestGen tests for added flexibility. MyMathLab's online gradebook—designed specifically for mathematics and statistics—automatically tracks students' homework and test results and gives the instructor control over how to calculate final grades. Instructors can also add offline (paper-and-pencil) grades to the gradebook. MyMathLab also includes access to the **Pearson Tutor Center** (www.pearsontutorservices.com). The Tutor Center is staffed by qualified mathematics instructors who provide textbook-specific tutoring for students via toll-free phone, fax, email, and interactive Web sessions. MyMathLab is available to qualified adopters. For more information, visit our website at www.mymathlab.com or contact your sales representative.

Acknowledgments

An enormous benefit of authoring a successful series is the broad-based feedback I receive from the students, dedicated users, and reviewers. Every change to this edition is the result of their thoughtful comments and suggestions. I would like to express my appreciation to all the reviewers, whose collective insights form the backbone of this revision. In particular, I would like to thank the following people for reviewing *College Algebra, Algebra and Trigonometry*, and *Precalculus*.

Barnhill, Kayoko Yates, *Clark College*
Beaver, Timothy, *Isothermal Community College*
Best, Lloyd, *Pacific Union College*
Burgin, Bill, *Gaston College*
Chang, Jimmy, *St. Petersburg College*
Colt, Diana, *University of Minnesota-Duluth*
Davidson, Wendy, *Georgia Perimeter College-Newton*
Densmore, Donna, *Bossier Parish Community College*
Enegren, Disa, *Rose State College*
Fisher, Nancy, *University of Alabama*
Gerken, Donna, *Miami Dade College*
Glickman, Cynthia, *Community College of Southern Nevada*
Goel, Sudhir Kumar, *Valdosta State University*
Gordon, Donald, *Manatee Community College*
Gross, David L., *University of Connecticut*
Haack, Joel K., *University of Northern Iowa*
Haefner, Jeremy, *University of Colorado*
Hague, Joyce, *University of Wisconsin at River Falls*
Hall, Mike, *University of Mississippi*
Hayes, Tom, *Montana State University*
Hay-Jahans, Christopher N., *University of South Dakota*
Hernandez, Celeste, *Richland College*
Howard, Heidi, *FCCJ South*
Ihlow, Winfield A., *SUNY College at Oswego*
Johnson, Nancy Raye, *Manatee Community College*
Leesburg, Mary, *Manatee Community College*
Lehmann, Christine Heinecke, *Purdue University North Central*
Levichev, Alexander, *Boston University*
Lin, Zongzhu, *Kansas State University*
Marlin, Benjamin, *Northwestern Oklahoma State University*
Massey, Marilyn, *Collin County Community College*
McCarthy-Germaine, Yvelyne, *University of New Orleans*
Mertens, Owen, *Missouri State University-Springfield*
Miller, James, *West Virginia University*

Nega, Martha, *Georgia Perimeter College-Decatur*
Pharo, Debra A., *Northwestern Michigan College*
Phoenix, Gloria, *North Carolina Agricultural and Technical State University*
Platt, David, *Front Range Community College*
Pohjanpelto, Juha, *Oregon State University*
Quinlan, Brooke, *Hillsborough Community College*
Rech, Janice, *University of Nebraska at Omaha*
Rouhani, Behnaz, *Georgia Perimeter College-Dunwoody*
Salmon, Judith, *Fitchburg State College*
Schultz, Cynthia, *Illinois Valley Community College*
Shelton, Pat, *North Carolina Agricultural and Technical State University*
Spillman, Caroline, *Georgia Perimeter College-Clarkston*
Stump, Chris, *Bethel College*
Sykes, Scott, *University of Western Georgia*
Trim, Pamela, *Southwest Tennessee Community College*
Turner, Chris, *Arkansas State University*
Van Lommel, Richard E., *California State University-Sacramento*
Van Peursem, Dan, *University of South Dakota*
Van Veldhuizen, Philip, *University of Nevada at Reno*
White, David, *The Victoria College*
Wienckowski, Tracy, *University of Buffalo*

Additional acknowledgments are extended to Dan Miller and Kelly Barber, for preparing the solutions manuals, Brad Davis, for preparing the answer section and serving as accuracy checker, the Preparè, Inc. formatting team, for the book's brilliant paging, Brian Morris at Scientific Illustrators, for superbly illustrating the book, Sheila Norman, photo researcher, for obtaining the book's new photographs, and Barbara Mack, whose talents as production editor kept every aspect of this complex project moving through its many stages.

I would like to thank my editor at Pearson, Adam Jaworski, and sponsoring editor, Dawn Murrin, who guided and coordinated the book from manuscript through production. Thanks to Heather Scott for the beautiful covers and interior design. Finally, thanks to Katherine Greig, for your innovative marketing efforts, and to the entire Pearson sales force, for your confidence and enthusiasm about the book.

Robert Blitzer

To the Student

What unique insights can algebra offer me regarding

- whether or not I should apologize to a friend for a blunder I committed? (Chapter P, page 15)
- how my sense of humor might predict my response to difficult life events? (Chapter 1, pages 111–112)
- global warming and climate change? (Chapter 2, pages 238–239)
- becoming a safer driver? (Chapter 3, page 384 and pages 392–393)
- making my financial goals a reality? (Chapter 4, page 455, and Chapter 8, page 695)
- symptoms of physical illness among students who are procrastinators? (Chapter 5, pages 482 and 495)
- computer images in the forthcoming technology of tele-imersion? (Chapter 6, pages 586–588)
- the path on which humanity journeys through space? (Chapter 7, pages 631 and 635)

I've written this book so that you can learn about the power of algebra and how it relates directly to your life outside the classroom. A great deal of attention has been given to applying algebra to your life to make your learning experience both interesting and relevant.

Although the pages that follow are filled with unique applications, I understand that your primary goal in reading the book is to acquire a solid understanding of the required topics in your college algebra course. In order to achieve this goal, I've carefully explained each topic, using voice balloons to help you understand the objectives while avoiding dense paragraphs with an intimidating amount of information. Important definitions and procedures are set off in boxes, and worked-out examples that present solutions in a step-by-step manner appear in every section. Each example is followed by a similar matched problem, called a Check Point, for you to try so that you can actively participate in the learning process as you read the book. (Answers to all Check Points appear in the back of the book.) Study Tips offer hints and suggestions and often point out common errors to avoid.

As you begin your studies, I would like to offer some specific suggestions for using this book and for being successful in this course:

- **Attend all lectures.** No book is intended to be a substitute for valuable insights and interactions that occur in the classroom. In addition to arriving for lecture on time and being prepared, you will find it useful to read the section before it is covered in lecture. This will give you a clear idea of the new material that will be discussed.

- **Read the book.** Read each section with pen (or pencil) in hand. Move through the worked-out examples with great care. These examples provide a model for doing exercises in the exercise sets. As you proceed through the reading, do not give up if you do not understand every single word. Things will become clearer as you read on and see how various procedures are applied to specific worked-out examples.

- **Work problems every day and check your answers.** The way to learn mathematics is by doing mathematics, which means working the Check Points and assigned exercises in the exercise sets. The more exercises you work, the better you will understand the material.

- **Review for quizzes and tests.** After completing a chapter, study the chapter review chart, work the exercises in the Chapter Review, and work the exercises in the Chapter Test. Answers to all these exercises are given in the back of the book.

The methods that I've used to help you read the book, work the problems, and review for tests are described in "A Brief Guide to Getting the Most from This Book," which appears inside the front cover. Spend a few minutes reviewing the guide to familiarize yourself with the book's features and their benefits.

- **Use the resources available with this book.** Additional resources to aid your study are described on page x. These resources include a Solutions Manual; a Chapter Test Prep Video CD; MyMath-Lab®, an online version of the book with links to multimedia resources; MathXL®, an online homework, tutorial, and assessment system of the text; and tutorial support at the Pearson Tutor Services.

I wrote this book in Point Reyes National Seashore, 40 miles north of San Francisco. The park consists of 75,000 acres with miles of pristine surf-washed beaches, forested ridges, and bays bordered by white cliffs. It was my hope to convey the beauty and excitement of mathematics using nature's unspoiled beauty as a source of inspiration and creativity. Enjoy the pages that follow as you empower yourself with the algebra needed to succeed in college, your career, and in your life.

Regards,
Bob
Robert Blitzer

About the Author

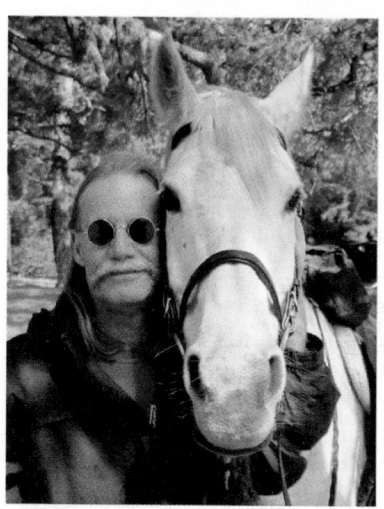

Bob and his horse Jerid

Bob Blitzer is a native of Manhattan and received a Bachelor of Arts degree with dual majors in mathematics and psychology (minor: English literature) from the City College of New York. His unusual combination of academic interests led him toward a Master of Arts in mathematics from the University of Miami and a doctorate in behavioral sciences from Nova University. Bob's love for teaching mathematics was nourished for nearly 30 years at Miami Dade College, where he received numerous teaching awards, including Innovator of the Year from the League for Innovations in the Community College and an endowed chair based on excellence in the classroom. In addition to *College Algebra*, Bob has written textbooks covering introductory algebra, intermediate algebra, algebra and trigonometry, precalculus, and liberal arts mathematics, all published by Prentice Hall. When not secluded in his Northern California writer's cabin, Bob can be found hiking the beaches and trails of Point Reyes National Seashore, and tending to the chores required by his beloved entourage of horses, chickens, and irritable roosters.

Applications Index

Prerequisites: Fundamental Concepts of Algebra

P

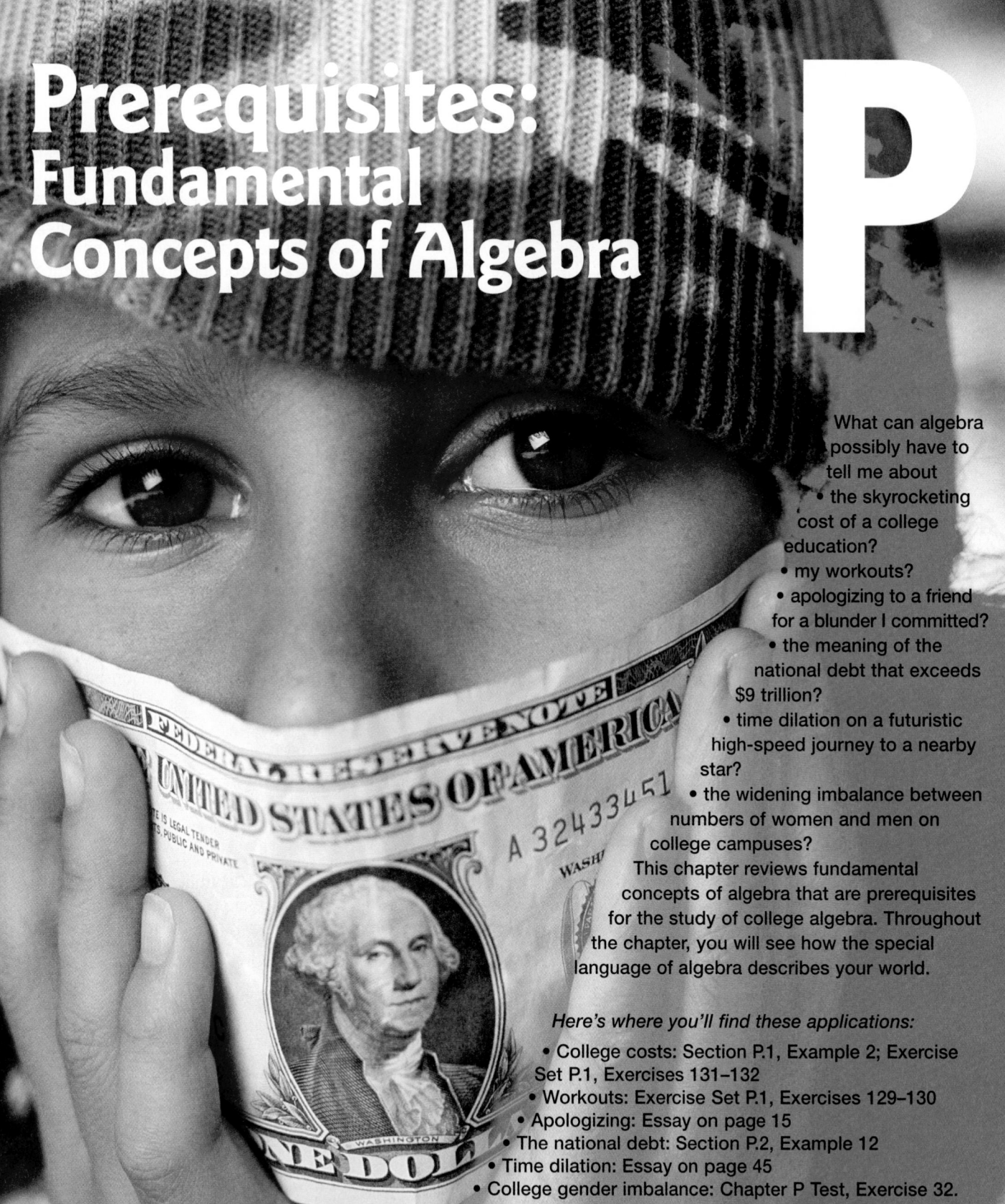

What can algebra possibly have to tell me about
• the skyrocketing cost of a college education?
• my workouts?
• apologizing to a friend for a blunder I committed?
• the meaning of the national debt that exceeds $9 trillion?
• time dilation on a futuristic high-speed journey to a nearby star?
• the widening imbalance between numbers of women and men on college campuses?

This chapter reviews fundamental concepts of algebra that are prerequisites for the study of college algebra. Throughout the chapter, you will see how the special language of algebra describes your world.

Here's where you'll find these applications:

• College costs: Section P.1, Example 2; Exercise Set P.1, Exercises 131–132
• Workouts: Exercise Set P.1, Exercises 129–130
• Apologizing: Essay on page 15
• The national debt: Section P.2, Example 12
• Time dilation: Essay on page 45
• College gender imbalance: Chapter P Test, Exercise 32.

1

Section **P.1**

Algebraic Expressions, Mathematical Models, and Real Numbers

Objectives

① Evaluate algebraic expressions.

② Use mathematical models.

③ Find the intersection of two sets.

④ Find the union of two sets.

⑤ Recognize subsets of the real numbers.

⑥ Use inequality symbols.

⑦ Evaluate absolute value.

⑧ Use absolute value to express distance.

⑨ Identify properties of the real numbers.

⑩ Simplify algebraic expressions.

How would your lifestyle change if a gallon of gas cost $9.15? Or if the price of a staple such as milk was $15? That's how much those products would cost if their prices had increased at the same rate college tuition has increased since 1980. (*Source*: Center for College Affordability and Productivity) In this section, you will learn how the special language of algebra describes your world, including the skyrocketing cost of a college education.

Algebraic Expressions

Algebra uses letters, such as x and y, to represent numbers. If a letter is used to represent various numbers, it is called a **variable**. For example, imagine that you are basking in the sun on the beach. We can let x represent the number of minutes that you can stay in the sun without burning with no sunscreen. With a number 6 sunscreen, exposure time without burning is six times as long, or 6 times x. This can be written $6 \cdot x$, but it is usually expressed as $6x$. Placing a number and a letter next to one another indicates multiplication.

Notice that $6x$ combines the number 6 and the variable x using the operation of multiplication. A combination of variables and numbers using the operations of addition, subtraction, multiplication, or division, as well as powers or roots, is called an **algebraic expression**. Here are some examples of algebraic expressions:

$$x + 6, \quad x - 6, \quad 6x, \quad \frac{x}{6}, \quad 3x + 5, \quad x^2 - 3, \quad \sqrt{x} + 7.$$

Many algebraic expressions involve *exponents*. For example, the algebraic expression

$$17x^2 + 261x + 3257$$

approximates the average cost of tuition and fees at public U.S. colleges for the school year ending x years after 2000. The expression x^2 means $x \cdot x$, and is read "x to the second power" or "x squared." The exponent, 2, indicates that the base, x, appears as a factor two times.

Exponential Notation

If n is a counting number (1, 2, 3, and so on),

Exponent or Power

$$b^n = \underbrace{b \cdot b \cdot b \cdot \cdots \cdot b}_{\substack{b \text{ appears as a} \\ \text{factor } n \text{ times.}}}$$

Base

b^n is read "the nth power of b" or "b to the nth power." Thus, the nth power of b is defined as the product of n factors of b. The expression b^n is called an **exponential expression**. Furthermore, $b^1 = b$.

For example,

$$8^2 = 8 \cdot 8 = 64, \quad 5^3 = 5 \cdot 5 \cdot 5 = 125, \quad \text{and} \quad 2^4 = 2 \cdot 2 \cdot 2 \cdot 2 = 16.$$

1 Evaluate algebraic expressions.

Evaluating Algebraic Expressions

Evaluating an algebraic expression means to find the value of the expression for a given value of the variable.

Many algebraic expressions involve more than one operation. Evaluating an algebraic expression without a calculator involves carefully applying the following order of operations agreement:

The Order of Operations Agreement

1. Perform operations within the innermost parentheses and work outward. If the algebraic expression involves a fraction, treat the numerator and the denominator as if they were each enclosed in parentheses.

2. Evaluate all exponential expressions.

3. Perform multiplications and divisions as they occur, working from left to right.

4. Perform additions and subtractions as they occur, working from left to right.

(**EXAMPLE 1**) **Evaluating an Algebraic Expression**

Evaluate $7 + 5(x - 4)^3$ for $x = 6$.

Solution

$$
\begin{aligned}
7 + 5(x - 4)^3 &= 7 + 5(6 - 4)^3 &&\text{Replace x with 6.}\\
&= 7 + 5(2)^3 &&\text{First work inside parentheses: } 6 - 4 = 2.\\
&= 7 + 5(8) &&\text{Evaluate the exponential expression:}\\
& &&2^3 = 2 \cdot 2 \cdot 2 = 8.\\
&= 7 + 40 &&\text{Multiply: } 5(8) = 40.\\
&= 47 &&\text{Add.}
\end{aligned}
$$

✓ Check Point **1** Evaluate $8 + 6(x - 3)^2$ for $x = 13$.

2 Use mathematical models.

Formulas and Mathematical Models

An **equation** is formed when an equal sign is placed between two algebraic expressions. One aim of algebra is to provide a compact, symbolic description of the world. These descriptions involve the use of *formulas*. A **formula** is an equation that uses variables to express a relationship between two or more quantities.

Here are two examples of formulas related to heart rate and exercise.

Couch-Potato Exercise

$$H = \frac{1}{5}(220 - a)$$

Heart rate, in beats per minute, is $\frac{1}{5}$ of the difference between 220 and your age.

Working It

$$H = \frac{9}{10}(220 - a)$$

Heart rate, in beats per minute, is $\frac{9}{10}$ of the difference between 220 and your age.

The process of finding formulas to describe real-world phenomena is called **mathematical modeling**. Such formulas, together with the meaning assigned to the variables, are called **mathematical models**. We often say that these formulas model, or describe, the relationships among the variables.

(**EXAMPLE 2**) **Modeling the Cost of Attending a Public College**

The bar graph in **Figure P.1** shows the average cost of tuition and fees for public four-year colleges, adjusted for inflation. The formula

$$T = 17x^2 + 261x + 3257$$

models the average cost of tuition and fees, T, for public U.S. colleges for the school year ending x years after 2000.

 a. Use the formula to find the average cost of tuition and fees at public U.S. colleges for the school year ending in 2007.

 b. By how much does the formula underestimate or overestimate the actual cost shown in **Figure P.1**?

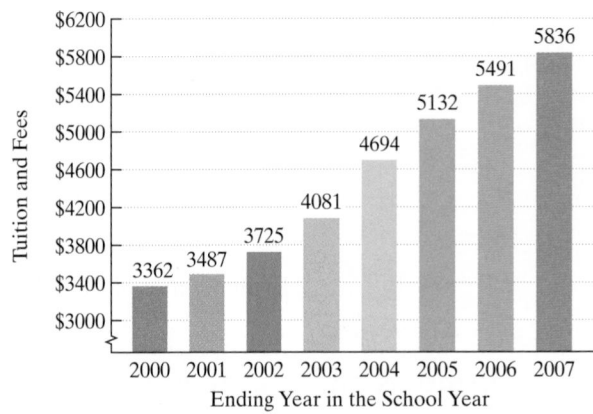

Average Cost of Tuition and Fees at Public Four-Year United States Colleges

Figure P.1
Source: The College Board

Solution

 a. Because 2007 is 7 years after 2000, we substitute 7 for x in the given formula. Then we use the order of operations to find T, the average cost of tuition and fees for the school year ending in 2007.

 $T = 17x^2 + 261x + 3257$ This is the given mathematical model.

 $T = 17(7)^2 + 261(7) + 3257$ Replace each occurrence of x with 7.

 $T = 17(49) + 261(7) + 3257$ Evaluate the exponential expression $7^2 = 7 \cdot 7 = 49$.

 $T = 833 + 1827 + 3257$ Multiply from left to right: $17(49) = 833$ and $261(7) = 1827$.

 $T = 5917$ Add.

 The formula indicates that for the school year ending in 2007, the average cost of tuition and fees at public U.S. colleges was $5917.

 b. **Figure P.1** shows that the average cost of tuition and fees for the school year ending in 2007 was $5836.

 The cost obtained from the formula, $5917, overestimates the actual data value by $5917 − $5836, or by $81.

⊘ Check Point **2** Assuming trends indicated by the data in **Figure P.1** continue, use the formula $T = 17x^2 + 261x + 3257$, described in Example 1, to project the average cost of tuition and fees at public U.S. colleges for the school year ending in 2010.

Sometimes a mathematical model gives an estimate that is not a good approximation or is extended to include values of the variable that do not make sense. In these cases, we say that **model breakdown** has occurred. For example, it is not likely that the formula in Example 2 would give a good estimate of tuition and fees in 2050 because it is too far in the future. Thus, model breakdown would occur.

Sets

Before we describe the set of real numbers, let's be sure you are familiar with some basic ideas about sets. A **set** is a collection of objects whose contents can be clearly determined. The objects in a set are called the **elements** of the set. For example, the set of numbers used for counting can be represented by

$$\{1, 2, 3, 4, 5, \dots \}.$$

The braces, { }, indicate that we are representing a set. This form of representation, called the **roster method**, uses commas to separate the elements of the set. The symbol consisting of three dots after the 5, called an *ellipsis*, indicates that there is no final element and that the listing goes on forever.

A set can also be written in **set-builder notation**. In this notation, the elements of the set are described, but not listed. Here is an example:

$$\{x|x \text{ is a counting number less than } 6\}.$$

<div align="center">

The set of all x such that x is a counting number less than 6.

</div>

The same set written using the roster method is

$$\{1, 2, 3, 4, 5\}.$$

If A and B are sets, we can form a new set consisting of all elements that are in both A and B. This set is called the *intersection* of the two sets.

Study Tip

Grouping symbols such as parentheses, (), and square brackets, [], are not used to represent sets. Only commas are used to separate the elements of a set. Separators such as colons or semicolons are not used.

3 Find the intersection of two sets.

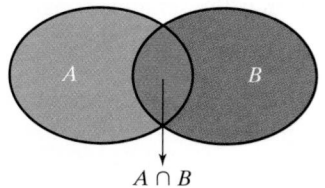

$A \cap B$

Figure P.2 Picturing the intersection of two sets

Definition of the Intersection of Sets

The **intersection** of sets A and B, written $A \cap B$, is the set of elements common to both set A **and** set B. This definition can be expressed in set-builder notation as follows:

$$A \cap B = \{x|x \text{ is an element of } A \text{ AND } x \text{ is an element of } B\}.$$

Figure P.2 shows a useful way of picturing the intersection of sets A and B. The figure indicates that $A \cap B$ contains those elements that belong to both A and B at the same time.

(EXAMPLE 3) **Finding the Intersection of Two Sets**

Find the intersection: $\{7, 8, 9, 10, 11\} \cap \{6, 8, 10, 12\}$.

Solution The elements common to $\{7, 8, 9, 10, 11\}$ and $\{6, 8, 10, 12\}$ are 8 and 10. Thus,

$$\{7, 8, 9, 10, 11\} \cap \{6, 8, 10, 12\} = \{8, 10\}. \qquad \bullet$$

⊘ Check Point **3** Find the intersection: $\{3, 4, 5, 6, 7\} \cap \{3, 7, 8, 9\}$.

If a set has no elements, it is called the **empty set**, or the **null set**, and is represented by the symbol Ø (the Greek letter phi). Here is an example that shows how the empty set can result when finding the intersection of two sets:

$$\{2, 4, 6\} \cap \{3, 5, 7\} = \varnothing.$$

These sets have no common elements.

Their intersection has no elements and is the empty set.

4 Find the union of two sets.

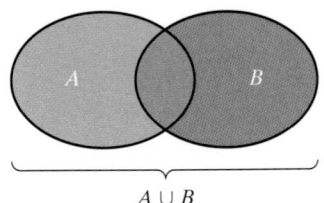

$A \cup B$

Figure P.3 Picturing the union of two sets

Another set that we can form from sets A and B consists of elements that are in A or B or in both sets. This set is called the *union* of the two sets.

Definition of the Union of Sets

The **union** of sets A and B, written $A \cup B$, is the set of elements that are members of set A **or** of set B or of both sets. This definition can be expressed in set-builder notation as follows:

$$A \cup B = \{x \,|\, x \text{ is an element of } A \text{ OR } x \text{ is an element of } B\}.$$

Figure P.3 shows a useful way of picturing the union of sets A and B. The figure indicates that $A \cup B$ is formed by joining the sets together.

We can find the union of set A and set B by listing the elements of set A. Then, we include any elements of set B that have not already been listed. Enclose all elements that are listed with braces. This shows that the union of two sets is also a set.

Study Tip

When finding the union of two sets, do not list twice any elements that appear in both sets.

(EXAMPLE 4) Finding the Union of Two Sets

Find the union: $\{7, 8, 9, 10, 11\} \cup \{6, 8, 10, 12\}$.

Solution To find $\{7, 8, 9, 10, 11\} \cup \{6, 8, 10, 12\}$, start by listing all the elements from the first set, namely 7, 8, 9, 10, and 11. Now list all the elements from the second set that are not in the first set, namely 6 and 12. The union is the set consisting of all these elements. Thus,

$$\{7, 8, 9, 10, 11\} \cup \{6, 8, 10, 12\} = \{6, 7, 8, 9, 10, 11, 12\}.$$ ●

⊘ Check Point **4** Find the union: $\{3, 4, 5, 6, 7\} \cup \{3, 7, 8, 9\}$.

5 Recognize subsets of the real numbers.

The Set of Real Numbers

The sets that make up the real numbers are summarized in **Table P.1**. We refer to these sets as **subsets** of the real numbers, meaning that all elements in each subset are also elements in the set of real numbers.

Notice the use of the symbol \approx in the examples of irrational numbers. The symbol means "is approximately equal to." Thus,

$$\sqrt{2} \approx 1.414214.$$

Technology

A calculator with a square root key gives a decimal approximation for $\sqrt{2}$, not the exact value.

We can verify that this is only an approximation by multiplying 1.414214 by itself. The product is very close to, but not exactly, 2:

$$1.414214 \times 1.414214 = 2.000001237796.$$

Table P.1 Important Subsets of the Real Numbers

Name	Description	Examples
Natural numbers \mathbb{N}	$\{1, 2, 3, 4, 5, \ldots\}$ These are the numbers that we use for counting.	$2, 3, 5, 17$
Whole numbers \mathbb{W}	$\{0, 1, 2, 3, 4, 5, \ldots\}$ The set of whole numbers includes 0 and the natural numbers.	$0, 2, 3, 5, 17$
Integers \mathbb{Z}	$\{\ldots, -5, -4, -3, -2, -1, 0, 1, 2, 3, 4, 5, \ldots\}$ The set of integers includes the negatives of the natural numbers and the whole numbers.	$-17, -5, -3, -2, 0, 2, 3, 5, 17$
Rational numbers \mathbb{Q}	$\left\{\frac{a}{b} \mid a \text{ and } b \text{ are integers and } b \neq 0\right\}$ This means that b is not equal to zero. The set of rational numbers is the set of all numbers that can be expressed as a quotient of two integers, with the denominator not 0. Rational numbers can be expressed as terminating or repeating decimals.	$-17 = \frac{-17}{1}, -5 = \frac{-5}{1}, -3, -2,$ $0, 2, 3, 5, 17,$ $\frac{2}{5} = 0.4,$ $\frac{-2}{3} = -0.6666\ldots = -0.\overline{6}$
Irrational numbers \mathbb{I}	The set of irrational numbers is the set of all numbers whose decimal representations are neither terminating nor repeating. Irrational numbers cannot be expressed as a quotient of integers.	$\sqrt{2} \approx 1.414214$ $-\sqrt{3} \approx -1.73205$ $\pi \approx 3.142$ $-\frac{\pi}{2} \approx -1.571$

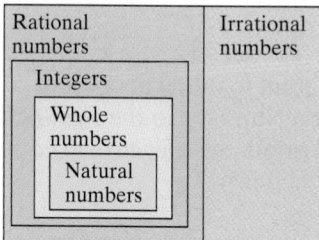

Real numbers

Figure P.4 Every real number is either rational or irrational.

Not all square roots are irrational. For example, $\sqrt{25} = 5$ because $5^2 = 5 \cdot 5 = 25$. Thus, $\sqrt{25}$ is a natural number, a whole number, an integer, and a rational number $\left(\sqrt{25} = \frac{5}{1}\right)$.

The set of *real numbers* is formed by taking the union of the sets of rational numbers and irrational numbers. Thus, every real number is either rational or irrational, as shown in **Figure P.4**.

Real Numbers

The set of **real numbers** is the set of numbers that are either rational or irrational:

$$\{x \mid x \text{ is rational or } x \text{ is irrational}\}.$$

The symbol \mathbb{R} is used to represent the set of real numbers. Thus,

$$\mathbb{R} = \{x \mid x \text{ is rational}\} \cup \{x \mid x \text{ is irrational}\}.$$

EXAMPLE 5 **Recognizing Subsets of the Real Numbers**

Consider the following set of numbers:

$$\left\{-7, -\frac{3}{4}, 0, 0.\overline{6}, \sqrt{5}, \pi, 7.3, \sqrt{81}\right\}.$$

List the numbers in the set that are

a. natural numbers. **b.** whole numbers. **c.** integers.

d. rational numbers. **e.** irrational numbers. **f.** real numbers.

Solution

a. Natural numbers: The natural numbers are the numbers used for counting. The only natural number in the set $\left\{-7, -\frac{3}{4}, 0, 0.\overline{6}, \sqrt{5}, \pi, 7.3, \sqrt{81}\right\}$ is $\sqrt{81}$ because $\sqrt{81} = 9$. (9 multiplied by itself, or 9^2, is 81.)

b. Whole numbers: The whole numbers consist of the natural numbers and 0. The elements of the set $\left\{-7, -\frac{3}{4}, 0, 0.\overline{6}, \sqrt{5}, \pi, 7.3, \sqrt{81}\right\}$ that are whole numbers are 0 and $\sqrt{81}$.

c. Integers: The integers consist of the natural numbers, 0, and the negatives of the natural numbers. The elements of the set $\left\{-7, -\frac{3}{4}, 0, 0.\overline{6}, \sqrt{5}, \pi, 7.3, \sqrt{81}\right\}$ that are integers are $\sqrt{81}$, 0, and -7.

d. Rational numbers: All numbers in the set $\left\{-7, -\frac{3}{4}, 0, 0.\overline{6}, \sqrt{5}, \pi, 7.3, \sqrt{81}\right\}$ that can be expressed as the quotient of integers are rational numbers. These include $-7\left(-7 = \frac{-7}{1}\right), -\frac{3}{4}, 0\left(0 = \frac{0}{1}\right)$, and $\sqrt{81}\left(\sqrt{81} = \frac{9}{1}\right)$. Furthermore, all numbers in the set that are terminating or repeating decimals are also rational numbers. These include $0.\overline{6}$ and 7.3.

e. Irrational numbers: The irrational numbers in the set $\left\{-7, -\frac{3}{4}, 0, 0.\overline{6}, \sqrt{5}, \pi, 7.3, \sqrt{81}\right\}$ are $\sqrt{5}\left(\sqrt{5} \approx 2.236\right)$ and $\pi\left(\pi \approx 3.14\right)$. Both $\sqrt{5}$ and π are only approximately equal to 2.236 and 3.14, respectively. In decimal form, $\sqrt{5}$ and π neither terminate nor have blocks of repeating digits.

f. Real numbers: All the numbers in the given set $\left\{-7, -\frac{3}{4}, 0, 0.\overline{6}, \sqrt{5}, \pi, 7.3, \sqrt{81}\right\}$ are real numbers. ●

✓ Check Point **5** Consider the following set of numbers:

$$\left\{-9, -1.3, 0, 0.\overline{3}, \frac{\pi}{2}, \sqrt{9}, \sqrt{10}\right\}.$$

List the numbers in the set that are

a. natural numbers. b. whole numbers. c. integers.

d. rational numbers. e. irrational numbers. f. real numbers.

The Real Number Line

The **real number line** is a graph used to represent the set of real numbers. An arbitrary point, called the **origin**, is labeled 0. Select a point to the right of 0 and label it 1. The distance from 0 to 1 is called the **unit distance**. Numbers to the right of the origin are **positive** and numbers to the left of the origin are **negative**. The real number line is shown in **Figure P.5**.

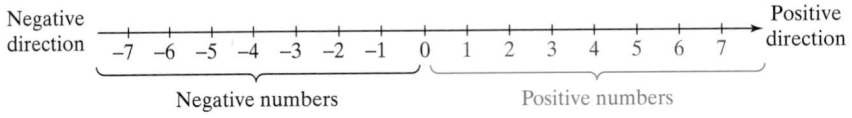

Figure P.5 The real number line

Study Tip

Wondering how we located $\sqrt{2}$ as a precise point on the number line in **Figure P.6**? We used a right triangle with both legs of length 1. The remaining side measures $\sqrt{2}$.

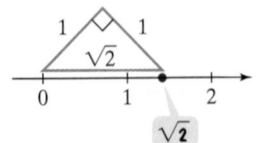

We'll have lots more to say about right triangles later in the book.

Real numbers are **graphed** on a number line by placing a dot at the correct location for each number. The integers are easiest to locate. In **Figure P.6**, we've graphed six rational numbers and three irrational numbers on a real number line.

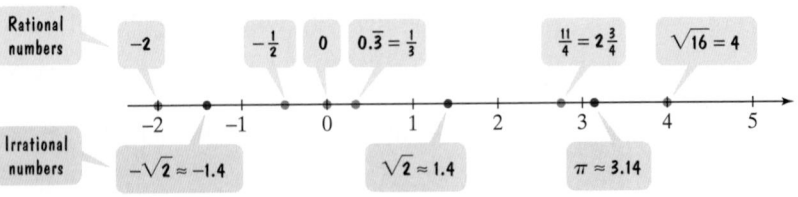

Figure P.6 Graphing numbers on a real number line

Every real number corresponds to a point on the number line and every point on the number line corresponds to a real number. We say that there is a **one-to-one correspondence** between all the real numbers and all points on a real number line.

⑥ Use inequality symbols.

Ordering the Real Numbers

On the real number line, the real numbers increase from left to right. The lesser of two real numbers is the one farther to the left on a number line. The greater of two real numbers is the one farther to the right on a number line.

Look at the number line in **Figure P.7**. The integers −4 and −1 are graphed.

Figure P.7

Observe that −4 is to the left of −1 on the number line. This means that −4 is less than −1.

$$-4 < -1$$ −4 is less than −1 because −4 is to the **left** of −1 on the number line.

In **Figure P.7**, we can also observe that −1 is to the right of −4 on the number line. This means that −1 is greater than −4.

$$-1 > -4$$ −1 is greater than −4 because −1 is to the **right** of −4 on the number line.

The symbols $<$ and $>$ are called **inequality symbols**. These symbols always point to the lesser of the two real numbers when the inequality statement is true.

−4 is less than −1. $-4 < -1$ The symbol points to −4, the lesser number.

−1 is greater than −4. $-1 > -4$ The symbol still points to −4, the lesser number.

The symbols $<$ and $>$ may be combined with an equal sign, as shown in the following table:

	Symbols	Meaning	Examples	Explanation
This inequality is true if either the < part or the = part is true.	$a \le b$	a is less than or equal to b.	$2 \le 9$ $9 \le 9$	Because 2 < 9 Because 9 = 9
This inequality is true if either the > part or the = part is true.	$b \ge a$	b is greater than or equal to a.	$9 \ge 2$ $2 \ge 2$	Because 9 > 2 Because 2 = 2

⑦ Evaluate absolute value.

Absolute Value

The **absolute value** of a real number a, denoted by $|a|$, is the distance from 0 to a on the number line. This distance is always taken to be nonnegative. For example, the real number line in **Figure P.8** shows that

$$|-3| = 3 \quad \text{and} \quad |5| = 5.$$

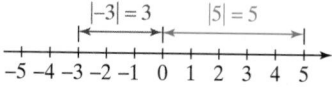
Figure P.8 Absolute value as the distance from 0

The absolute value of −3 is 3 because −3 is 3 units from 0 on the number line. The absolute value of 5 is 5 because 5 is 5 units from 0 on the number line. The absolute value of a positive real number or 0 is the number itself. The absolute value of a negative real number, such as −3, is the number without the negative sign.

We can define the absolute value of the real number x without referring to a number line. The algebraic definition of the absolute value of x is given as follows:

Definition of Absolute Value

$$|x| = \begin{cases} x & \text{if } x \geq 0 \\ -x & \text{if } x < 0 \end{cases}$$

If x is nonnegative (that is, $x \geq 0$), the absolute value of x is the number itself. For example,

$$|5| = 5 \qquad |\pi| = \pi \qquad \left|\frac{1}{3}\right| = \frac{1}{3} \qquad |0| = 0.$$

Zero is the only number whose absolute value is 0.

If x is a negative number (that is, $x < 0$), the absolute value of x is the opposite of x. This makes the absolute value positive. For example,

$$|-3| = -(-3) = 3 \qquad |-\pi| = -(-\pi) = \pi \qquad \left|-\frac{1}{3}\right| = -\left(-\frac{1}{3}\right) = \frac{1}{3}.$$

This middle step is usually omitted.

EXAMPLE 6 Evaluating Absolute Value

Rewrite each expression without absolute value bars:

a. $\left|\sqrt{3} - 1\right|$ **b.** $|2 - \pi|$ **c.** $\dfrac{|x|}{x}$ if $x < 0$.

Solution

a. Because $\sqrt{3} \approx 1.7$, the number inside the absolute value bars, $\sqrt{3} - 1$, is positive. The absolute value of a positive number is the number itself. Thus,

$$\left|\sqrt{3} - 1\right| = \sqrt{3} - 1.$$

b. Because $\pi \approx 3.14$, the number inside the absolute value bars, $2 - \pi$, is negative. The absolute value of x when $x < 0$ is $-x$. Thus,

$$|2 - \pi| = -(2 - \pi) = \pi - 2.$$

c. If $x < 0$, then $|x| = -x$. Thus,

$$\frac{|x|}{x} = \frac{-x}{x} = -1.$$

Check Point **6** Rewrite each expression without absolute value bars:

a. $\left|1 - \sqrt{2}\right|$ **b.** $|\pi - 3|$ **c.** $\dfrac{|x|}{x}$ if $x > 0$.

Listed below are several basic properties of absolute value. Each of these properties can be derived from the definition of absolute value.

Properties of Absolute Value

For all real numbers a and b,

1. $|a| \geq 0$ 2. $|-a| = |a|$ 3. $a \leq |a|$

4. $|ab| = |a||b|$ 5. $\left|\dfrac{a}{b}\right| = \dfrac{|a|}{|b|}, \quad b \neq 0$

6. $|a + b| \leq |a| + |b|$ (called the triangle inequality)

⑧ Use absolute value to express distance.

Distance between Points on a Real Number Line

Absolute value is used to find the distance between two points on a real number line. If a and b are any real numbers, the **distance between a and b** is the absolute value of their difference. For example, the distance between 4 and 10 is 6. Using absolute value, we find this distance in one of two ways:

$$|10 - 4| = |6| = 6 \quad \text{or} \quad |4 - 10| = |-6| = 6.$$

> The distance between 4 and 10 on the real number line is 6.

Notice that we obtain the same distance regardless of the order in which we subtract.

Distance between Two Points on the Real Number Line

If a and b are any two points on a real number line, then the distance between a and b is given by

$$|a - b| \quad \text{or} \quad |b - a|.$$

(EXAMPLE 7) Distance between Two Points on a Number Line

Find the distance between -5 and 3 on the real number line.

Solution Because the distance between a and b is given by $|a - b|$, the distance between -5 and 3 is

$$|-5 - 3| = |-8| = 8.$$

$a = -5$ $b = 3$

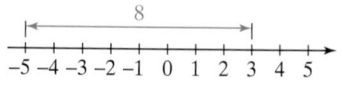

Figure P.9 The distance between -5 and 3 is 8.

Figure P.9 verifies that there are 8 units between -5 and 3 on the real number line. We obtain the same distance if we reverse the order of the subtraction:

$$|3 - (-5)| = |8| = 8.$$

✓ **Check Point 7** Find the distance between -4 and 5 on the real number line.

⑨ Identify properties of the real numbers.

Properties of Real Numbers and Algebraic Expressions

When you use your calculator to add two real numbers, you can enter them in any order. The fact that two real numbers can be added in any order is called the **commutative property of addition**. You probably use this property, as well as other

properties of real numbers listed in **Table P.2**, without giving it much thought. The properties of the real numbers are especially useful when working with algebraic expressions. For each property listed in **Table P.2**, a, b, and c represent real numbers, variables, or algebraic expressions.

Table P.2 Properties of the Real Numbers

Name	Meaning	Examples
Commutative Property of Addition	Changing order when adding does not affect the sum. $a + b = b + a$	• $13 + 7 = 7 + 13$ • $13x + 7 = 7 + 13x$
Commutative Property of Multiplication	Changing order when multiplying does not affect the product. $ab = ba$	• $\sqrt{2} \cdot \sqrt{5} = \sqrt{5} \cdot \sqrt{2}$ • $x \cdot 6 = 6x$
Associative Property of Addition	Changing grouping when adding does not affect the sum. $(a + b) + c = a + (b + c)$	• $3 + (8 + x) = (3 + 8) + x$ $= 11 + x$
Associative Property of Multiplication	Changing grouping when multiplying does not affect the product. $(ab)c = a(bc)$	• $-2(3x) = (-2 \cdot 3)x = -6x$
Distributive Property of Multiplication over Addition	Multiplication distributes over addition. $a \cdot (b + c) = a \cdot b + a \cdot c$	• $7(4 + \sqrt{3}) = 7 \cdot 4 + 7 \cdot \sqrt{3}$ $= 28 + 7\sqrt{3}$ • $5(3x + 7) = 5 \cdot 3x + 5 \cdot 7$ $= 15x + 35$
Identity Property of Addition	Zero can be deleted from a sum. $a + 0 = a$ $0 + a = a$	• $\sqrt{3} + 0 = \sqrt{3}$ • $0 + 6x = 6x$
Identity Property of Multiplication	One can be deleted from a product. $a \cdot 1 = a$ $1 \cdot a = a$	• $1 \cdot \pi = \pi$ • $13x \cdot 1 = 13x$
Inverse Property of Addition	The sum of a real number and its additive inverse gives 0, the additive identity. $a + (-a) = 0$ $(-a) + a = 0$	• $\sqrt{5} + (-\sqrt{5}) = 0$ • $-\pi + \pi = 0$ • $6x + (-6x) = 0$ • $(-4y) + 4y = 0$
Inverse Property of Multiplication	The product of a nonzero real number and its multiplicative inverse gives 1, the multiplicative identity. $a \cdot \dfrac{1}{a} = 1, \quad a \neq 0$ $\dfrac{1}{a} \cdot a = 1, \quad a \neq 0$	• $7 \cdot \dfrac{1}{7} = 1$ • $\left(\dfrac{1}{x - 3}\right)(x - 3) = 1, \quad x \neq 3$

The Associative Property and the English Language

In the English language, phrases can take on different meanings depending on the way the words are associated with commas.

Here are three examples.

- Woman, without her man, is nothing.
 Woman, without her, man is nothing.
- What's the latest dope?
 What's the latest, dope?
- Population of Amsterdam broken down by age and sex
 Population of Amsterdam, broken down by age and sex

The properties of the real numbers in **Table P.2** apply to the operations of addition and multiplication. Subtraction and division are defined in terms of addition and multiplication.

> ### Definitions of Subtraction and Division
>
> Let a and b represent real numbers.
>
> **Subtraction:** $a - b = a + (-b)$
> We call $-b$ the **additive inverse** or **opposite** of b.
>
> **Division:** $a \div b = a \cdot \frac{1}{b}$, where $b \neq 0$
> We call $\frac{1}{b}$ the **multiplicative inverse** or **reciprocal** of b. The quotient of a and b, $a \div b$, can be written in the form $\frac{a}{b}$, where a is the **numerator** and b the **denominator** of the fraction.

Because subtraction is defined in terms of adding an inverse, the distributive property can be applied to subtraction:

$$a(b - c) = ab - ac$$

$$(b - c)a = ba - ca.$$

For example,

$$4(2x - 5) = 4 \cdot 2x - 4 \cdot 5 = 8x - 20.$$

🔟 Simplify algebraic expressions.

Simplifying Algebraic Expressions

The **terms** of an algebraic expression are those parts that are separated by addition. For example, consider the algebraic expression

$$7x - 9y + z - 3,$$

which can be expressed as

$$7x + (-9y) + z + (-3).$$

This expression contains four terms, namely $7x$, $-9y$, z, and -3.

The numerical part of a term is called its **coefficient**. In the term $7x$, the 7 is the coefficient. If a term containing one or more variables is written without a coefficient, the coefficient is understood to be 1. Thus, z means $1z$. If a term is a constant, its coefficient is that constant. Thus, the coefficient of the constant term -3 is -3.

$$7x + (-9y) + z + (-3)$$

| Coefficient is 7. | Coefficient is −9. | Coefficient is 1; z means $1z$. | Coefficient is −3. |

The parts of each term that are multiplied are called the **factors** of the term. The factors of the term $7x$ are 7 and x.

Like terms are terms that have exactly the same variable factors. For example, $3x$ and $7x$ are like terms. The distributive property in the form

$$ba + ca = (b + c)a$$

enables us to add or subtract like terms. For example,

$$3x + 7x = (3 + 7)x = 10x$$
$$7y^2 - y^2 = 7y^2 - 1y^2 = (7 - 1)y^2 = 6y^2.$$

This process is called **combining like terms**.

An algebraic expression is **simplified** when parentheses have been removed and like terms have been combined.

Study Tip

To combine like terms mentally, add or subtract the coefficients of the terms. Use this result as the coefficient of the terms' variable factor(s).

EXAMPLE 8 Simplifying an Algebraic Expression

Simplify: $6(2x^2 + 4x) + 10(4x^2 + 3x)$.

Solution

$6(2x^2 + 4x) + 10(4x^2 + 3x)$

> $52x^2$ and $54x$ are not like terms. They contain different variable factors, x^2 and x, and cannot be combined.

$= 6 \cdot 2x^2 + 6 \cdot 4x + 10 \cdot 4x^2 + 10 \cdot 3x$ Use the distributive property to remove the parentheses.

$= 12x^2 + 24x + 40x^2 + 30x$ Multiply.

$= (12x^2 + 40x^2) + (24x + 30x)$ Group like terms.

$= 52x^2 + 54x$ Combine like terms.

⬤

☑ Check Point **8** Simplify: $7(4x^2 + 3x) + 2(5x^2 + x)$.

Properties of Negatives

The distributive property can be extended to cover more than two terms within parentheses. For example,

> This sign represents subtraction.

> This sign tells us that the number is negative.

$-3(4x - 2y + 6) = -3 \cdot 4x - (-3) \cdot 2y - 3 \cdot 6$

$= -12x - (-6y) - 18$

$= -12x + 6y - 18.$

The voice balloons illustrate that negative signs can appear side by side. They can represent the operation of subtraction or the fact that a real number is negative. Here is a list of properties of negatives and how they are applied to algebraic expressions:

Properties of Negatives

Let a and b represent real numbers, variables, or algebraic expressions.

Property	**Examples**
1. $(-1)a = -a$	$(-1)4xy = -4xy$
2. $-(-a) = a$	$-(-6y) = 6y$
3. $(-a)b = -ab$	$(-7)4xy = -7 \cdot 4xy = -28xy$
4. $a(-b) = -ab$	$5x(-3y) = -5x \cdot 3y = -15xy$
5. $-(a + b) = -a - b$	$-(7x + 6y) = -7x - 6y$
6. $-(a - b) = -a + b$ $\qquad\quad = b - a$	$-(3x - 7y) = -3x + 7y$ $\qquad\qquad\quad = 7y - 3x$

It is not uncommon to see algebraic expressions with parentheses preceded by a negative sign or subtraction. Properties 5 and 6 in the box, $-(a + b) = -a - b$ and $-(a - b) = -a + b$, are related to this situation. An expression of the form $-(a + b)$ can be simplified as follows:

$$-(a + b) = -1(a + b) = (-1)a + (-1)b = -a + (-b) = -a - b.$$

Do you see a fast way to obtain the simplified expression on the right at the bottom of the previous page? **If a negative sign or a subtraction symbol appears outside parentheses, drop the parentheses and change the sign of every term within the parentheses.** For example,

$$-(3x^2 - 7x - 4) = -3x^2 + 7x + 4.$$

EXAMPLE 9 Simplifying an Algebraic Expression

Simplify: $8x + 2[5 - (x - 3)]$.

Solution

$$8x + 2[5 - (x - 3)]$$

$= 8x + 2[5 - x + 3]$ Drop parentheses and change the sign of each term in parentheses: $-(x - 3) = -x + 3$.

$= 8x + 2[8 - x]$ Simplify inside brackets: $5 + 3 = 8$.

$= 8x + 16 - 2x$ Apply the distributive property:

$$2[\overset{\frown}{8 - x}] = 2 \cdot 8 - 2x = 16 - 2x.$$

$= (8x - 2x) + 16$ Group like terms.

$= (8 - 2)x + 16$ Apply the distributive property.

$= 6x + 16$ Simplify.

⊘ Check Point **9** Simplify: $6 + 4[7 - (x - 2)]$.

Using Algebra to Solve Problems in Your Everyday Life

In *Geek Logik* (Workman Publishing, 2006), humorist Garth Sundem presents formulas covering dating, romance, career, finance, everyday decisions, and health. On the right is a sample of one of his formulas that "takes the guesswork out of life, providing easier living through algebra."

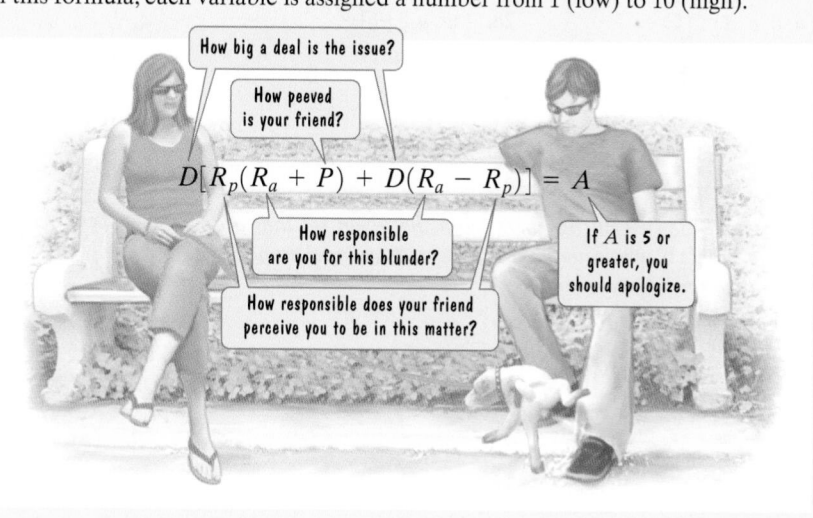

Should You Apologize to Your Friend?

In this formula, each variable is assigned a number from 1 (low) to 10 (high).

How big a deal is the issue?

How peeved is your friend?

$$D[R_p(R_a + P) + D(R_a - R_p)] = A$$

How responsible are you for this blunder?

How responsible does your friend perceive you to be in this matter?

If A is 5 or greater, you should apologize.

Exercise Set P.1

Practice Exercises

In Exercises 1–16, evaluate each algebraic expression for the given value or values of the variable(s).

1. $7 + 5x$, for $x = 10$

2. $8 + 6x$, for $x = 5$

3. $6x - y$, for $x = 3$ and $y = 8$

4. $8x - y$, for $x = 3$ and $y = 4$

5. $x^2 + 3x$, for $x = 8$

6. $x^2 + 5x$, for $x = 6$

7. $x^2 - 6x + 3$, for $x = 7$

8. $x^2 - 7x + 4$, for $x = 8$

9. $4 + 5(x - 7)^3$, for $x = 9$

10. $6 + 5(x - 6)^3$, for $x = 8$

11. $x^2 - 3(x - y)$, for $x = 8$ and $y = 2$

12. $x^2 - 4(x - y)$, for $x = 8$ and $y = 3$

13. $\dfrac{5(x + 2)}{2x - 14}$, for $x = 10$

14. $\dfrac{7(x - 3)}{2x - 16}$, for $x = 9$

15. $\dfrac{2x + 3y}{x + 1}$, for $x = -2$ and $y = 4$

16. $\dfrac{2x + y}{xy - 2x}$, for $x = -2$ and $y = 4$

The formula

$$C = \frac{5}{9}(F - 32)$$

expresses the relationship between Fahrenheit temperature, F, and Celsius temperature, C. In Exercises 17–18, use the formula to convert the given Fahrenheit temperature to its equivalent temperature on the Celsius scale.

17. 50°F

18. 86°F

A football was kicked vertically upward from a height of 4 feet with an initial speed of 60 feet per second. The formula

$$h = 4 + 60t - 16t^2$$

describes the ball's height above the ground, h, in feet, t seconds after it was kicked. Use this formula to solve Exercises 19–20.

19. What was the ball's height 2 seconds after it was kicked?

20. What was the ball's height 3 seconds after it was kicked?

In Exercises 21–28, find the intersection of the sets.

21. $\{1, 2, 3, 4\} \cap \{2, 4, 5\}$

22. $\{1, 3, 7\} \cap \{2, 3, 8\}$

23. $\{s, e, t\} \cap \{t, e, s\}$

24. $\{r, e, a, l\} \cap \{l, e, a, r\}$

25. $\{1, 3, 5, 7\} \cap \{2, 4, 6, 8, 10\}$

26. $\{0, 1, 3, 5\} \cap \{-5, -3, -1\}$

27. $\{a, b, c, d\} \cap \varnothing$

28. $\{w, y, z\} \cap \varnothing$

In Exercises 29–34, find the union of the sets.

29. $\{1, 2, 3, 4\} \cup \{2, 4, 5\}$

30. $\{1, 3, 7, 8\} \cup \{2, 3, 8\}$

31. $\{1, 3, 5, 7\} \cup \{2, 4, 6, 8, 10\}$

32. $\{0, 1, 3, 5\} \cup \{2, 4, 6\}$

33. $\{a, e, i, o, u\} \cup \varnothing$

34. $\{e, m, p, t, y\} \cup \varnothing$

In Exercises 35–38, list all numbers from the given set that are
a. *natural numbers,* **b.** *whole numbers,* **c.** *integers,* **d.** *rational numbers,*
e. *irrational numbers,* **f.** *real numbers.*

35. $\left\{-9, -\frac{4}{5}, 0, 0.25, \sqrt{3}, 9.2, \sqrt{100}\right\}$

36. $\left\{-7, -0.\overline{6}, 0, \sqrt{49}, \sqrt{50}\right\}$

37. $\left\{-11, -\frac{5}{6}, 0, 0.75, \sqrt{5}, \pi, \sqrt{64}\right\}$

38. $\left\{-5, -0.\overline{3}, 0, \sqrt{2}, \sqrt{4}\right\}$

39. Give an example of a whole number that is not a natural number.

40. Give an example of a rational number that is not an integer.

41. Give an example of a number that is an integer, a whole number, and a natural number.

42. Give an example of a number that is a rational number, an integer, and a real number.

Determine whether each statement in Exercises 43–50 is true or false.

43. $-13 \leq -2$

44. $-6 > 2$

45. $4 \geq -7$

46. $-13 < -5$

47. $-\pi \geq -\pi$

48. $-3 > -13$

49. $0 \geq -6$

50. $0 \geq -13$

In Exercises 51–60, rewrite each expression without absolute value bars.

51. $|300|$

52. $|-203|$

53. $|12 - \pi|$

54. $|7 - \pi|$

55. $|\sqrt{2} - 5|$

56. $|\sqrt{5} - 13|$

57. $\dfrac{-3}{|-3|}$

58. $\dfrac{-7}{|-7|}$

59. $\|-3| - |-7\|$

60. $\|-5| - |-13\|$

In Exercises 61–66, evaluate each algebraic expression for $x = 2$ and $y = -5$.

61. $|x + y|$

62. $|x - y|$

63. $|x| + |y|$

64. $|x| - |y|$

65. $\dfrac{y}{|y|}$

66. $\dfrac{|x|}{x} + \dfrac{|y|}{y}$

In Exercises 67–74, express the distance between the given numbers using absolute value. Then find the distance by evaluating the absolute value expression.

67. 2 and 17

68. 4 and 15

69. −2 and 5

70. −6 and 8

71. −19 and −4

72. −26 and −3

73. −3.6 and −1.4

74. −5.4 and −1.2

In Exercises 75–84, state the name of the property illustrated.

75. $6 + (-4) = (-4) + 6$

76. $11 \cdot (7 + 4) = 11 \cdot 7 + 11 \cdot 4$

77. $6 + (2 + 7) = (6 + 2) + 7$

78. $6 \cdot (2 \cdot 3) = 6 \cdot (3 \cdot 2)$

79. $(2 + 3) + (4 + 5) = (4 + 5) + (2 + 3)$

80. $7 \cdot (11 \cdot 8) = (11 \cdot 8) \cdot 7$

81. $2(-8 + 6) = -16 + 12$

82. $-8(3 + 11) = -24 + (-88)$

83. $\dfrac{1}{(x + 3)}(x + 3) = 1, x \neq -3$

84. $(x + 4) + [-(x + 4)] = 0$

In Exercises 85–96, simplify each algebraic expression.

85. $5(3x + 4) - 4$

86. $2(5x + 4) - 3$

87. $5(3x - 2) + 12x$

88. $2(5x - 1) + 14x$

89. $7(3y - 5) + 2(4y + 3)$

90. $4(2y - 6) + 3(5y + 10)$

91. $5(3y - 2) - (7y + 2)$

92. $4(5y - 3) - (6y + 3)$

93. $7 - 4[3 - (4y - 5)]$

94. $6 - 5[8 - (2y - 4)]$

95. $18x^2 + 4 - [6(x^2 - 2) + 5]$

96. $14x^2 + 5 - [7(x^2 - 2) + 4]$

In Exercises 97–102, write each algebraic expression without parentheses.

97. $-(-14x)$

98. $-(-17y)$

99. $-(2x - 3y - 6)$

100. $-(5x - 13y - 1)$

101. $\frac{1}{3}(3x) + [(4y) + (-4y)]$

102. $\frac{1}{2}(2y) + [(-7x) + 7x]$

Practice Plus

In Exercises 103–110, insert either $<$, $>$, or $=$ in the shaded area to make a true statement.

103. $|-6|$ ▨ $|-3|$

104. $|-20|$ ▨ $|-50|$

105. $\left|\dfrac{3}{5}\right|$ ▨ $|-0.6|$

106. $\left|\dfrac{5}{2}\right|$ ▨ $|-2.5|$

107. $\dfrac{30}{40} - \dfrac{3}{4}$ ▨ $\dfrac{14}{15} \cdot \dfrac{15}{14}$

108. $\dfrac{17}{18} \cdot \dfrac{18}{17}$ ▨ $\dfrac{50}{60} - \dfrac{5}{6}$

109. $\dfrac{8}{13} \div \dfrac{8}{13}$ ▨ $|-1|$

110. $|-2|$ ▨ $\dfrac{4}{17} \div \dfrac{4}{17}$

In Exercises 111–120, use the order of operations to simplify each expression.

111. $8^2 - 16 \div 2^2 \cdot 4 - 3$

112. $10^2 - 100 \div 5^2 \cdot 2 - 3$

113. $\dfrac{5 \cdot 2 - 3^2}{[3^2 - (-2)]^2}$

114. $\dfrac{10 \div 2 + 3 \cdot 4}{(12 - 3 \cdot 2)^2}$

115. $8 - 3[-2(2 - 5) - 4(8 - 6)]$

116. $8 - 3[-2(5 - 7) - 5(4 - 2)]$

117. $\dfrac{2(-2) - 4(-3)}{5 - 8}$

118. $\dfrac{6(-4) - 5(-3)}{9 - 10}$

119. $\dfrac{(5 - 6)^2 - 2|3 - 7|}{89 - 3 \cdot 5^2}$

120. $\dfrac{12 \div 3 \cdot 5|2^2 + 3^2|}{7 + 3 - 6^2}$

In Exercises 121–128, write each English phrase as an algebraic expression. Then simplify the expression. Let x represent the number.

121. A number decreased by the sum of the number and four

122. A number decreased by the difference between eight and the number

123. Six times the product of negative five and a number

124. Ten times the product of negative four and a number

125. The difference between the product of five and a number and twice the number

126. The difference between the product of six and a number and negative two times the number

127. The difference between eight times a number and six more than three times the number

128. Eight decreased by three times the sum of a number and six

Application Exercises

The maximum heart rate, in beats per minute, that you should achieve during exercise is 220 minus your age:

$$220 - a.$$

This algebraic expression gives maximum heart rate in terms of age, a.

The bar graph at the top of the next column shows the target heart rate ranges for four types of exercise goals. The lower and upper limits of these ranges are fractions of the maximum heart rate, $220 - a$. Exercises 129–130 are based on the information in the graph.

Target Heart Rate Ranges for Exercise Goals

Fraction of Maximum Heart Rate, $220 - a$

129. If your exercise goal is to improve cardiovascular conditioning, the graph shows the following range for target heart rate, H, in beats per minute:

Lower limit of range $H = \dfrac{7}{10}(220 - a)$

Upper limit of range $H = \dfrac{4}{5}(220 - a).$

 a. What is the lower limit of the heart range, in beats per minute, for a 20-year-old with this exercise goal?

 b. What is the upper limit of the heart range, in beats per minute, for a 20-year-old with this exercise goal?

130. If your exercise goal is to improve overall health, the graph shows the following range for target heart rate, H, in beats per minute:

Lower limit of range $H = \dfrac{1}{2}(220 - a)$

Upper limit of range $H = \dfrac{3}{5}(220 - a).$

 a. What is the lower limit of the heart range, in beats per minute, for a 30-year-old with this exercise goal?

 b. What is the upper limit of the heart range, in beats per minute, for a 30-year-old with this exercise goal?

The bar graph shows the average cost of tuition and fees at private four-year colleges in the United States.

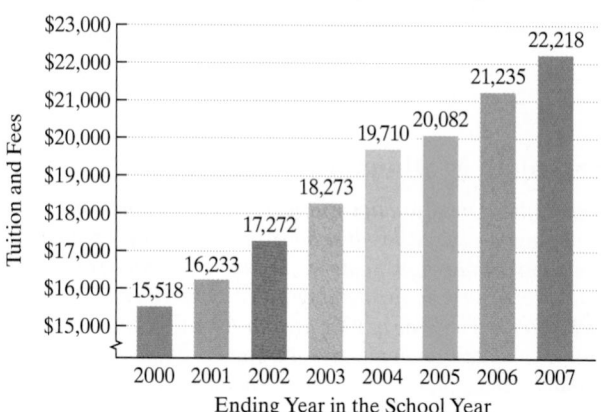

Average Cost of Tuition and Fees at Private Four-Year United States Colleges

Source: The College Board

The formula

$$T = 15,395 + 988x - 2x^2$$

models the average cost of tuition and fees, T, at private U.S. colleges for the school year ending x years after 2000. Use this information to solve Exercises 131–132.

131. a. Use the formula to find the average cost of tuition and fees at private U.S. colleges for the school year ending in 2007.

 b. By how much does the formula underestimate or overestimate the actual cost shown by the graph at the bottom of the previous page for the school year ending in 2007?

 c. Use the formula to project the average cost of tuition and fees at private U.S. colleges for the school year ending in 2010.

132. a. Use the formula to find the average cost of tuition and fees at private U.S. colleges for the school year ending in 2006.

 b. By how much does the formula underestimate or overestimate the actual cost shown by the graph at the bottom of the previous page for the school year ending in 2006?

 c. Use the formula to project the average cost of tuition and fees at private U.S. colleges for the school year ending in 2012.

133. You had $10,000 to invest. You put x dollars in a safe, government-insured certificate of deposit paying 5% per year. You invested the remainder of the money in noninsured corporate bonds paying 12% per year. Your total interest earned at the end of the year is given by the algebraic expression

$$0.05x + 0.12(10,000 - x).$$

 a. Simplify the algebraic expression.

 b. Use each form of the algebraic expression to determine your total interest earned at the end of the year if you invested $6000 in the safe, government-insured certificate of deposit.

134. It takes you 50 minutes to get to campus. You spend t minutes walking to the bus stop and the rest of the time riding the bus. Your walking rate is 0.06 mile per minute and the bus travels at a rate of 0.5 mile per minute. The total distance walking and traveling by bus is given by the algebraic expression

$$0.06t + 0.5(50 - t).$$

 a. Simplify the algebraic expression.

 b. Use each form of the algebraic expression to determine the total distance that you travel if you spend 20 minutes walking to the bus stop.

Writing in Mathematics

Writing about mathematics will help you learn mathematics. For all writing exercises in this book, use complete sentences to respond to the question. Some writing exercises can be answered in a sentence; others require a paragraph or two. You can decide how much you need to write as long as your writing clearly and directly answers the question in the exercise. Standard references such as a dictionary and a thesaurus should be helpful.

135. What is an algebraic expression? Give an example with your explanation.

136. If n is a natural number, what does b^n mean? Give an example with your explanation.

137. What does it mean when we say that a formula models real-world phenomena?

138. What is the intersection of sets A and B?

139. What is the union of sets A and B?

140. How do the whole numbers differ from the natural numbers?

141. Can a real number be both rational and irrational? Explain your answer.

142. If you are given two real numbers, explain how to determine which is the lesser.

143. Think of a situation where you either apologized or did not apologize for a blunder you committed. Use the formula in the essay on page 15 to determine whether or not you should have apologized. How accurately does the formula model what you actually did?

144. Read *Geek Logik* by Garth Sundem (Workman Publishing, 2006). Would you recommend the book to college algebra students? Were you amused by the humor? Which formulas did you find most useful? Apply at least one of the formulas by plugging your life data into the equation, using the order of operations, and coming up with an answer to one of life's dilemmas.

Critical Thinking Exercises

Make Sense? *In Exercises 145–148, determine whether each statement makes sense or does not make sense, and explain your reasoning.*

145. My mathematical model describes the data for tuition and fees at public four-year colleges for the past ten years extremely well, so it will serve as an accurate prediction for the cost of public colleges in 2050.

146. A model that describes the average cost of tuition and fees at private U.S. colleges for the school year ending x years after 2000 cannot be used to estimate the cost of private education for the school year ending in 2000.

147. The humor in this cartoon is based on the fact that the football will never be hiked.

148. Just as the commutative properties change groupings, the associative properties change order.

In Exercises 149–156, determine whether each statement is true or false. If the statement is false, make the necessary change(s) to produce a true statement.

149. Every rational number is an integer.

150. Some whole numbers are not integers.

151. Some rational numbers are not positive.

152. Irrational numbers cannot be negative.

153. The term x has no coefficient.

154. $5 + 3(x - 4) = 8(x - 4) = 8x - 32$

155. $-x - x = -x + (-x) = 0$

156. $x - 0.02(x + 200) = 0.98x - 4$

In Exercises 157–159, insert either $<$ or $>$ in the shaded area between the numbers to make the statement true.

157. $\sqrt{2}$ ▨ 1.5

158. $-\pi$ ▨ -3.5

159. $-\dfrac{3.14}{2}$ ▨ $-\dfrac{\pi}{2}$

Preview Exercises

Exercises 160–162 will help you prepare for the material covered in the next section.

160. In parts (a) and (b), complete each statement.

 a. $b^4 \cdot b^3 = (b \cdot b \cdot b \cdot b)(b \cdot b \cdot b) = b^?$

 b. $b^5 \cdot b^5 = (b \cdot b \cdot b \cdot b \cdot b)(b \cdot b \cdot b \cdot b \cdot b) = b^?$

 c. Generalizing from parts (a) and (b), what should be done with the exponents when multiplying exponential expressions with the same base?

161. In parts (a) and (b), complete each statement.

 a. $\dfrac{b^7}{b^3} = \dfrac{b \cdot b \cdot b \cdot b \cdot b \cdot b \cdot b}{b \cdot b \cdot b} = b^?$

 b. $\dfrac{b^8}{b^2} = \dfrac{b \cdot b \cdot b \cdot b \cdot b \cdot b \cdot b \cdot b}{b \cdot b} = b^?$

 c. Generalizing from parts (a) and (b), what should be done with the exponents when dividing exponential expressions with the same base?

162. If 6.2 is multiplied by 10^3, what does this multiplication do to the decimal point in 6.2?

Section **P.2** **Exponents and Scientific Notation**

Objectives

① Use the product rule.
② Use the quotient rule.
③ Use the zero-exponent rule.
④ Use the negative-exponent rule.
⑤ Use the power rule.
⑥ Find the power of a product.
⑦ Find the power of a quotient.
⑧ Simplify exponential expressions.
⑨ Use scientific notation.

Listening to the radio on the way to campus, you hear politicians discussing the problem of the national debt, which exceeds \$9 trillion. They state that it's more than the gross domestic product of China, the world's second-richest nation, and four times greater than the combined net worth of America's 691 billionaires. They make it seem like the national debt is a real problem, but later you realize that you don't really know what a number like 9 trillion means. If the national debt were evenly divided among all citizens of the country, how much would every man, woman, and child have to pay? Is economic doomsday about to arrive?

In this section, you will learn to use exponents to provide a way of putting large and small numbers in perspective. Using this skill, we will explore the meaning of the national debt.

① Use the product rule.

The Product and Quotient Rules

We have seen that exponents are used to indicate repeated multiplication. Now consider the multiplication of two exponential expressions, such as $b^4 \cdot b^3$. We are multiplying 4 factors of b and 3 factors of b. We have a total of 7 factors of b:

4 factors of b 3 factors of b

$$b^4 \cdot b^3 = (b \cdot b \cdot b \cdot b)(b \cdot b \cdot b) = b^7.$$

Total: 7 factors of b

The product is exactly the same if we add the exponents:

$$b^4 \cdot b^3 = b^{4+3} = b^7.$$

The fact that $b^4 \cdot b^3 = b^7$ suggests the following rule:

The Product Rule

$$b^m \cdot b^n = b^{m+n}$$

When multiplying exponential expressions with the same base, add the exponents. Use this sum as the exponent of the common base.

(EXAMPLE 1) Using the Product Rule

Multiply each expression using the product rule:

 a. $2^2 \cdot 2^3$ **b.** $(6x^4y^3)(5x^2y^7)$.

Solution

 a. $2^2 \cdot 2^3 = 2^{2+3} = 2^5$ or 32 $2^5 = 2 \cdot 2 \cdot 2 \cdot 2 \cdot 2 = 32$

 b. $(6x^4y^3)(5x^2y^7)$

$$= 6 \cdot 5 \cdot x^4 \cdot x^2 \cdot y^3 \cdot y^7 \quad \text{Use the associative and commutative properties. This step can be done mentally.}$$

$$= 30x^{4+2}y^{3+7}$$

$$= 30x^6y^{10}$$

✓ Check Point 1 Multiply each expression using the product rule:

 a. $3^3 \cdot 3^2$ **b.** $(4x^3y^4)(10x^2y^6)$.

② Use the quotient rule.

Now, consider the division of two exponential expressions, such as the quotient of b^7 and b^3. We are dividing 7 factors of b by 3 factors of b.

$$\frac{b^7}{b^3} = \frac{b \cdot b \cdot b \cdot b \cdot b \cdot b \cdot b}{b \cdot b \cdot b} = \boxed{\frac{b \cdot b \cdot b}{b \cdot b \cdot b}} \cdot b \cdot b \cdot b \cdot b = 1 \cdot b \cdot b \cdot b \cdot b = b^4$$

This factor is equal to 1.

The quotient is exactly the same if we subtract the exponents:

$$\frac{b^7}{b^3} = b^{7-3} = b^4.$$

This suggests the following rule:

The Quotient Rule

$$\frac{b^m}{b^n} = b^{m-n}, \quad b \neq 0$$

When dividing exponential expressions with the same nonzero base, subtract the exponent in the denominator from the exponent in the numerator. Use this difference as the exponent of the common base.

EXAMPLE 2 **Using the Quotient Rule**

Divide each expression using the quotient rule:

a. $\dfrac{(-2)^7}{(-2)^4}$ **b.** $\dfrac{30x^{12}y^9}{5x^3y^7}$.

Solution

a. $\dfrac{(-2)^7}{(-2)^4} = (-2)^{7-4} = (-2)^3 \text{ or } -8$ 　　$(-2)^3 = (-2)(-2)(-2) = -8$

b. $\dfrac{30x^{12}y^9}{5x^3y^7} = \dfrac{30}{5} \cdot \dfrac{x^{12}}{x^3} \cdot \dfrac{y^9}{y^7} = 6x^{12-3}y^{9-7} = 6x^9y^2$

⦿

✓ Check Point **2** Divide each expression using the quotient rule:

a. $\dfrac{(-3)^6}{(-3)^3}$ **b.** $\dfrac{27x^{14}y^8}{3x^3y^5}$.

③ Use the zero-exponent rule.

Zero as an Exponent

A nonzero base can be raised to the 0 power. The quotient rule can be used to help determine what zero as an exponent should mean. Consider the quotient of b^4 and b^4, where b is not zero. We can determine this quotient in two ways.

$$\dfrac{b^4}{b^4} = 1 \qquad\qquad \dfrac{b^4}{b^4} = b^{4-4} = b^0$$

Any nonzero expression divided by itself is 1.　　　Use the quotient rule and subtract exponents.

This means that b^0 must equal 1.

The Zero-Exponent Rule

If b is any real number other than 0,

$$b^0 = 1.$$

Here are examples involving simplification using the zero-exponent rule:

$$8^0 = 1, \quad (-6)^0 = 1, \quad -6^0 = -1, \quad (5x)^0 = 1, \quad 5x^0 = 5.$$

Only 6 is raised to the 0 power:
$-6^0 = -(6^0) = -1$.　　　Only x is raised to the 0 power:
$5x^0 = 5 \cdot 1 = 5$.

④ Use the negative-exponent rule.

Negative Integers as Exponents

A nonzero base can be raised to a negative power. The quotient rule can be used to help determine what a negative integer as an exponent should mean. Consider the quotient of b^3 and b^5, where b is not zero. We can determine this quotient in two ways.

$$\dfrac{b^3}{b^5} = \dfrac{b \cdot b \cdot b}{b \cdot b \cdot b \cdot b \cdot b} = \dfrac{1}{b^2} \qquad\qquad \dfrac{b^3}{b^5} = b^{3-5} = b^{-2}$$

After dividing common factors, we have two factors of b in the denominator.　　　Use the quotient rule and subtract exponents.

Notice that $\dfrac{b^3}{b^5}$ equals both b^{-2} and $\dfrac{1}{b^2}$. This means that b^{-2} must equal $\dfrac{1}{b^2}$. This example is a special case of the **negative-exponent rule**.

The Negative-Exponent Rule

If b is any real number other than 0 and n is a natural number, then

$$b^{-n} = \frac{1}{b^n}.$$

(**EXAMPLE 3**) **Using the Negative-Exponent Rule**

Use the negative-exponent rule to write each expression with a positive exponent. Simplify, if possible:

a. 9^{-2} **b.** $(-2)^{-5}$ **c.** $\dfrac{1}{6^{-2}}$ **d.** $7x^{-5}y^2$.

Solution

a. $9^{-2} = \dfrac{1}{9^2} = \dfrac{1}{81}$

b. $(-2)^{-5} = \dfrac{1}{(-2)^5} = \dfrac{1}{(-2)(-2)(-2)(-2)(-2)} = \dfrac{1}{-32} = -\dfrac{1}{32}$

> Only the sign of the exponent, −5, changes.
> The base, −2, does not change sign.

c. $\dfrac{1}{6^{-2}} = \dfrac{1}{\dfrac{1}{6^2}} = 1 \cdot \dfrac{6^2}{1} = 6^2 = 36$

d. $7x^{-5}y^2 = 7 \cdot \dfrac{1}{x^5} \cdot y^2 = \dfrac{7y^2}{x^5}$

⊘ **Check Point 3** Use the negative-exponent rule to write each expression with a positive exponent. Simplify, if possible:

a. 5^{-2} **b.** $(-3)^{-3}$ **c.** $\dfrac{1}{4^{-2}}$ **d.** $3x^{-6}y^4$.

In Example 3 and Check Point 3, did you notice that

$$\frac{1}{6^{-2}} = 6^2 \qquad \text{and} \qquad \frac{1}{4^{-2}} = 4^2?$$

In general, if a negative exponent appears in a denominator, an expression can be written with a positive exponent using

$$\frac{1}{b^{-n}} = b^n.$$

Negative Exponents in Numerators and Denominators

If b is any real number other than 0 and n is a natural number, then

$$b^{-n} = \frac{1}{b^n} \quad \text{and} \quad \frac{1}{b^{-n}} = b^n.$$

When a negative number appears as an exponent, switch the position of the base (from numerator to denominator or from denominator to numerator) and make the exponent positive. The sign of the base does not change.

⑤ Use the power rule.

The Power Rule for Exponents (Powers to Powers)

The next property of exponents applies when an exponential expression is raised to a power. Here is an example:

$$(b^2)^4.$$

> The exponential expression b^2 is raised to the fourth power.

There are 4 factors of b^2. Thus,

$$(b^2)^4 = b^2 \cdot b^2 \cdot b^2 \cdot b^2 = b^{2+2+2+2} = b^8.$$

> Add exponents when multiplying with the same base.

We can obtain the answer, b^8, by multiplying the original exponents:

$$(b^2)^4 = b^{2 \cdot 4} = b^8.$$

This suggests the following rule:

The Power Rule (Powers to Powers)

$$(b^m)^n = b^{mn}$$

When an exponential expression is raised to a power, multiply the exponents. Place the product of the exponents on the base and remove the parentheses.

EXAMPLE 4 **Using the Power Rule (Powers to Powers)**

Simplify each expression using the power rule:

a. $(2^2)^3$ **b.** $(y^5)^{-3}$ **c.** $(b^{-4})^{-2}$.

Solution

a. $(2^2)^3 = 2^{2 \cdot 3} = 2^6$ or 64 **b.** $(y^5)^{-3} = y^{5(-3)} = y^{-15} = \dfrac{1}{y^{15}}$

c. $(b^{-4})^{-2} = b^{(-4)(-2)} = b^8$

✓ Check Point 4 Simplify each expression using the power rule:

a. $(3^3)^2$ **b.** $(y^7)^{-2}$ **c.** $(b^{-3})^{-4}$.

⑥ Find the power of a product.

The Products-to-Powers Rule for Exponents

The next property of exponents applies when we are raising a product to a power. Here is an example:

$$(2x)^4.$$

> The product $2x$ is raised to the fourth power.

There are four factors of $2x$. Thus,

$$(2x)^4 = 2x \cdot 2x \cdot 2x \cdot 2x = 2 \cdot 2 \cdot 2 \cdot 2 \cdot x \cdot x \cdot x \cdot x = 2^4 x^4.$$

We can obtain the answer, $2^4 x^4$, by raising each factor within the parentheses to the fourth power:

$$(2x)^4 = 2^4 x^4.$$

The fact that $(2x)^4 = 2^4x^4$ suggests the following rule:

Products to Powers

$$(ab)^n = a^n b^n$$

When a product is raised to a power, raise each factor to that power.

(**EXAMPLE 5**) **Raising a Product to a Power**

Simplify: $(-2y^2)^4$.

Solution

$$\begin{aligned}
(-2y^2)^4 &= (-2)^4(y^2)^4 &&\text{Raise each factor to the fourth power.}\\
&= (-2)^4 y^{2\cdot4} &&\text{To raise an exponential expression to a power, multiply}\\
& &&\text{exponents: } (b^m)^n = b^{mn}.\\
&= 16y^8 &&\text{Simplify: } (-2)^4 = (-2)(-2)(-2)(-2) = 16. \quad\blacksquare
\end{aligned}$$

✅ Check Point **5** Simplify: $(-4x)^3$.

The rule for raising a product to a power can be extended to cover three or more factors. For example,

$$(-2xy)^3 = (-2)^3 x^3 y^3 = -8x^3 y^3.$$

7 Find the power of a quotient.

The Quotients-to-Powers Rule for Exponents

The following rule is used to raise a quotient to a power:

Quotients to Powers

If b is a nonzero real number, then

$$\left(\frac{a}{b}\right)^n = \frac{a^n}{b^n}.$$

When a quotient is raised to a power, raise the numerator to that power and divide by the denominator to that power.

(**EXAMPLE 6**) **Raising Quotients to Powers**

Simplify by raising each quotient to the given power:

a. $\left(-\dfrac{3}{x}\right)^4$ **b.** $\left(\dfrac{x^2}{4}\right)^3$.

Solution

a. $\left(-\dfrac{3}{x}\right)^4 = \dfrac{(-3)^4}{x^4} = \dfrac{(-3)(-3)(-3)(-3)}{x^4} = \dfrac{81}{x^4}$

b. $\left(\dfrac{x^2}{4}\right)^3 = \dfrac{(x^2)^3}{4^3} = \dfrac{x^{2\cdot3}}{4\cdot4\cdot4} = \dfrac{x^6}{64}$ \blacksquare

✅ Check Point **6** Simplify:

a. $\left(-\dfrac{2}{y}\right)^5$ **b.** $\left(\dfrac{x^5}{3}\right)^3$.

⑧ Simplify exponential
expressions.

Simplifying Exponential Expressions

Properties of exponents are used to simplify exponential expressions. An exponential expression is **simplified** when

- No parentheses appear.
- No powers are raised to powers.
- Each base occurs only once.
- No negative or zero exponents appear.

Simplifying Exponential Expressions

Example

1. If necessary, remove parentheses by using
$$(ab)^n = a^n b^n \quad \text{or} \quad \left(\frac{a}{b}\right)^n = \frac{a^n}{b^n}.$$

$(xy)^3 = x^3 y^3$

2. If necessary, simplify powers to powers by using
$$(b^m)^n = b^{mn}.$$

$(x^4)^3 = x^{4\cdot3} = x^{12}$

3. If necessary, be sure that each base appears only once by using
$$b^m \cdot b^n = b^{m+n} \quad \text{or} \quad \frac{b^m}{b^n} = b^{m-n}.$$

$x^4 \cdot x^3 = x^{4+3} = x^7$

4. If necessary, rewrite exponential expressions with zero powers as 1 $(b^0 = 1)$. Furthermore, write the answer with positive exponents by using
$$b^{-n} = \frac{1}{b^n} \quad \text{or} \quad \frac{1}{b^{-n}} = b^n.$$

$\dfrac{x^5}{x^8} = x^{5-8} = x^{-3} = \dfrac{1}{x^3}$

The following example shows how to simplify exponential expressions. Throughout the example, assume that no variable in a denominator is equal to zero.

EXAMPLE 7 **Simplifying Exponential Expressions**

Simplify:

a. $(-3x^4 y^5)^3$ **b.** $(-7xy^4)(-2x^5 y^6)$ **c.** $\dfrac{-35x^2 y^4}{5x^6 y^{-8}}$ **d.** $\left(\dfrac{4x^2}{y}\right)^{-3}.$

Solution

a. $(-3x^4 y^5)^3 = (-3)^3 (x^4)^3 (y^5)^3$ Raise each factor inside the parentheses to the third power.

$= (-3)^3 x^{4\cdot3} y^{5\cdot3}$ Multiply the exponents when raising powers to powers.

$= -27x^{12} y^{15}$ $(-3)^3 = (-3)(-3)(-3) = -27$

b. $(-7xy^4)(-2x^5 y^6) = (-7)(-2)xx^5 y^4 y^6$ Group factors with the same base.

$= 14x^{1+5} y^{4+6}$ When multiplying expressions with the same base, add the exponents.

$= 14x^6 y^{10}$ Simplify.

c. $\dfrac{-35x^2y^4}{5x^6y^{-8}} = \left(\dfrac{-35}{5}\right)\left(\dfrac{x^2}{x^6}\right)\left(\dfrac{y^4}{y^{-8}}\right)$ Group factors with the same base.

$= -7x^{2-6}y^{4-(-8)}$ When dividing expressions with the same base, subtract the exponents.

$= -7x^{-4}y^{12}$ Simplify. Notice that $4 - (-8) = 4 + 8 = 12$.

$= \dfrac{-7y^{12}}{x^4}$ Write as a fraction and move the base with the negative exponent, x^{-4}, to the other side of the fraction bar and make the negative exponent positive.

d. $\left(\dfrac{4x^2}{y}\right)^{-3} = \dfrac{(4x^2)^{-3}}{y^{-3}}$ Raise the numerator and the denominator to the -3 power.

$= \dfrac{4^{-3}(x^2)^{-3}}{y^{-3}}$ Raise each factor in the numerator to the -3 power.

$= \dfrac{4^{-3}x^{-6}}{y^{-3}}$ Multiply the exponents when raising a power to a power: $(x^2)^{-3} = x^{2(-3)} = x^{-6}$.

$= \dfrac{y^3}{4^3x^6}$ Move each base with a negative exponent to the other side of the fraction bar and make each negative exponent positive.

$= \dfrac{y^3}{64x^6}$ $4^3 = 4 \cdot 4 \cdot 4 = 64$ ●

○ Check Point **7** Simplify:

a. $(2x^3y^6)^4$ **b.** $(-6x^2y^5)(3xy^3)$ **c.** $\dfrac{100x^{12}y^2}{20x^{16}y^{-4}}$ **d.** $\left(\dfrac{5x}{y^4}\right)^{-2}$.

Study Tip

Try to avoid the following common errors that can occur when simplifying exponential expressions.

Correct	Incorrect	Description of Error
$b^3 \cdot b^4 = b^7$	$b^3 \cdot b^4 = b^{12}$	The exponents should be added, not multiplied.
$3^2 \cdot 3^4 = 3^6$	$3^2 \cdot 3^4 = 9^6$	The common base should be retained, not multiplied.
$\dfrac{5^{16}}{5^4} = 5^{12}$	$\dfrac{5^{16}}{5^4} = 5^4$	The exponents should be subtracted, not divided.
$(4a)^3 = 64a^3$	$(4a)^3 = 4a^3$	Both factors should be cubed.
$b^{-n} = \dfrac{1}{b^n}$	$b^{-n} = -\dfrac{1}{b^n}$	Only the exponent should change sign.
$(a+b)^{-1} = \dfrac{1}{a+b}$	$(a+b)^{-1} = \dfrac{1}{a} + \dfrac{1}{b}$	The exponent applies to the entire expression $a + b$.

⑨ Use scientific notation.

Table P.3 Names of Large Numbers

10^2	hundred
10^3	thousand
10^6	million
10^9	billion
10^{12}	trillion
10^{15}	quadrillion
10^{18}	quintillion
10^{21}	sextillion
10^{24}	septillion
10^{27}	octillion
10^{30}	nonillion
10^{100}	googol
10^{googol}	googolplex

Scientific Notation

As of December 2007, the national debt of the United States was about \$9.2 trillion. This is the amount of money the government has had to borrow over the years, mostly by selling bonds, because it has spent more than it has collected in taxes. A stack of \$1 bills equaling the national debt would rise to twice the distance from Earth to the moon. Because a trillion is 10^{12} (see **Table P.3**), the national debt can be expressed as

$$9.2 \times 10^{12}.$$

The number 9.2×10^{12} is written in a form called *scientific notation*.

Scientific Notation

A number is written in **scientific notation** when it is expressed in the form

$$a \times 10^n,$$

where the absolute value of a is greater than or equal to 1 and less than 10 $(1 \leq |a| < 10)$, and n is an integer.

It is customary to use the multiplication symbol, \times, rather than a dot, when writing a number in scientific notation.

Converting from Scientific to Decimal Notation

Here are two examples of numbers in scientific notation:

$$6.4 \times 10^5 \quad \text{means} \quad 640,000.$$
$$2.17 \times 10^{-3} \quad \text{means} \quad 0.00217.$$

Do you see that the number with the positive exponent is relatively large and the number with the negative exponent is relatively small?

We can use n, the exponent on the 10 in $a \times 10^n$, to change a number in scientific notation to decimal notation. If n is **positive**, move the decimal point in a to the **right** n places. If n is **negative**, move the decimal point in a to the **left** $|n|$ places.

EXAMPLE 8 **Converting from Scientific to Decimal Notation**

Write each number in decimal notation:

a. 6.2×10^7 **b.** -6.2×10^7 **c.** 2.019×10^{-3} **d.** -2.019×10^{-3}.

Solution In each case, we use the exponent on the 10 to determine how far to move the decimal point and in which direction. In parts (a) and (b), the exponent is positive, so we move the decimal point to the right. In parts (c) and (d), the exponent is negative, so we move the decimal point to the left.

a. $6.2 \times 10^7 = 62,000,000$

 $n = 7$ Move the decimal point 7 places to the right.

b. $-6.2 \times 10^7 = -62,000,000$

 $n = 7$ Move the decimal point 7 places to the right.

c. $2.019 \times 10^{-3} = 0.002019$

 $n = -3$ Move the decimal point $|-3|$ places, or 3 places, to the left.

d. $-2.019 \times 10^{-3} = -0.002019$

 $n = -3$ Move the decimal point $|-3|$ places, or 3 places, to the left.

✓ Check Point **8** Write each number in decimal notation:

a. -2.6×10^9 **b.** 3.017×10^{-6}.

Converting from Decimal to Scientific Notation

To convert from decimal notation to scientific notation, we reverse the procedure of Example 8.

Converting from Decimal to Scientific Notation

Write the number in the form $a \times 10^n$.

- Determine a, the numerical factor. Move the decimal point in the given number to obtain a number whose absolute value is between 1 and 10, including 1.
- Determine n, the exponent on 10^n. The absolute value of n is the number of places the decimal point was moved. The exponent n is positive if the decimal point was moved to the left, negative if the decimal point was moved to the right, and 0 if the decimal point was not moved.

EXAMPLE 9 **Converting from Decimal Notation to Scientific Notation**

Write each number in scientific notation:

a. 34,970,000,000,000
b. −34,970,000,000,000
c. 0.0000000000802
d. −0.0000000000802.

Solution

a. $34{,}970{,}000{,}000{,}000 = 3.497 \times 10^{13}$

> Move the decimal point to get a number whose absolute value is between 1 and 10.

> The decimal point was moved 13 places to the left, so $n = 13$.

b. $-34{,}970{,}000{,}000{,}000 = -3.497 \times 10^{13}$

c. $0.0000000000802 = 8.02 \times 10^{-11}$

> Move the decimal point to get a number whose absolute value is between 1 and 10.

> The decimal point was moved 11 places to the right, so $n = -11$.

d. $-0.0000000000802 = -8.02 \times 10^{-11}$

☑ Check Point **9** Write each number in scientific notation:

a. 5,210,000,000
b. −0.00000006893.

EXAMPLE 10 **Expressing the U.S. Population in Scientific Notation**

As of December 2007, the population of the United States was approximately 303 million. Express the population in scientific notation.

Solution Because a million is 10^6, the 2007 population can be expressed as

$$303 \times 10^6.$$

> This factor is not between 1 and 10, so the number is not in scientific notation.

Technology

You can use your calculator's $\boxed{\text{EE}}$ (enter exponent) or $\boxed{\text{EXP}}$ key to convert from decimal to scientific notation. Here is how it's done for 0.0000000000802.

Many Scientific Calculators

Keystrokes

.0000000000802 $\boxed{\text{EE}}$ $\boxed{=}$

Display

8.02 − 11

Many Graphing Calculators

Use the mode setting for scientific notation.

Keystrokes

.0000000000802 $\boxed{\text{ENTER}}$

Display

8.02E − 11

Study Tip

If the absolute value of a number is greater than 10, it will have a positive exponent in scientific notation. If the absolute value of a number is less than 1, it will have a negative exponent in scientific notation.

The voice balloon indicates that we need to convert 303 to scientific notation.

$$303 \times 10^6 = (3.03 \times 10^2) \times 10^6 = 3.03 \times 10^{2+6} = 3.03 \times 10^8$$

$$303 = 3.03 \times 10^2$$

In scientific notation, the population is 3.03×10^8.

⊘ Check Point **10** Express 410×10^7 in scientific notation.

Computations with Scientific Notation

Properties of exponents are used to perform computations with numbers that are expressed in scientific notation.

(**EXAMPLE 11**) **Computations with Scientific Notation**

Perform the indicated computations, writing the answers in scientific notation:

a. $(6.1 \times 10^5)(4 \times 10^{-9})$ **b.** $\dfrac{1.8 \times 10^4}{3 \times 10^{-2}}$.

Solution

Technology

$(6.1 \times 10^5)(4 \times 10^{-9})$
On a Calculator:

Many Scientific Calculators

6.1 \boxed{EE} 5 $\boxed{\times}$ 4 \boxed{EE} 9 $\boxed{+/-}$ $\boxed{=}$

Display

2.44 − 03

Many Graphing Calculators

6.1 \boxed{EE} 5 $\boxed{\times}$ 4 \boxed{EE} $\boxed{(-)}$ 9 \boxed{ENTER}

Display (in scientific notation mode)

2.44E − 3

a. $(6.1 \times 10^5)(4 \times 10^{-9})$

$= (6.1 \times 4) \times (10^5 \times 10^{-9})$ *Regroup factors.*

$= 24.4 \times 10^{5+(-9)}$ *Add the exponents on 10 and multiply the other parts.*

$= 24.4 \times 10^{-4}$ *Simplify.*

$= (2.44 \times 10^1) \times 10^{-4}$ *Convert 24.4 to scientific notation: $24.4 = 2.44 \times 10^1$.*

$= 2.44 \times 10^{-3}$ *$10^1 \times 10^{-4} = 10^{1+(-4)} = 10^{-3}$*

b. $\dfrac{1.8 \times 10^4}{3 \times 10^{-2}} = \left(\dfrac{1.8}{3}\right) \times \left(\dfrac{10^4}{10^{-2}}\right)$ *Regroup factors.*

$= 0.6 \times 10^{4-(-2)}$ *Subtract the exponents on 10 and divide the other parts.*

$= 0.6 \times 10^6$ *Simplify: $4 - (-2) = 4 + 2 = 6$.*

$= (6 \times 10^{-1}) \times 10^6$ *Convert 0.6 to scientific notation: $0.6 = 6 \times 10^{-1}$.*

$= 6 \times 10^5$ *$10^{-1} \times 10^6 = 10^{-1+6} = 10^5$*

⊘ Check Point **11** Perform the indicated computations, writing the answers in scientific notation:

a. $(7.1 \times 10^5)(5 \times 10^{-7})$ **b.** $\dfrac{1.2 \times 10^6}{3 \times 10^{-3}}$.

Applications: Putting Numbers in Perspective

Due to tax cuts and spending increases, the United States began accumulating large deficits in the 1980s. To finance the deficit, the government had borrowed $9.2 trillion as of December 2007. The graph in **Figure P.10** shows the national debt increasing over time.

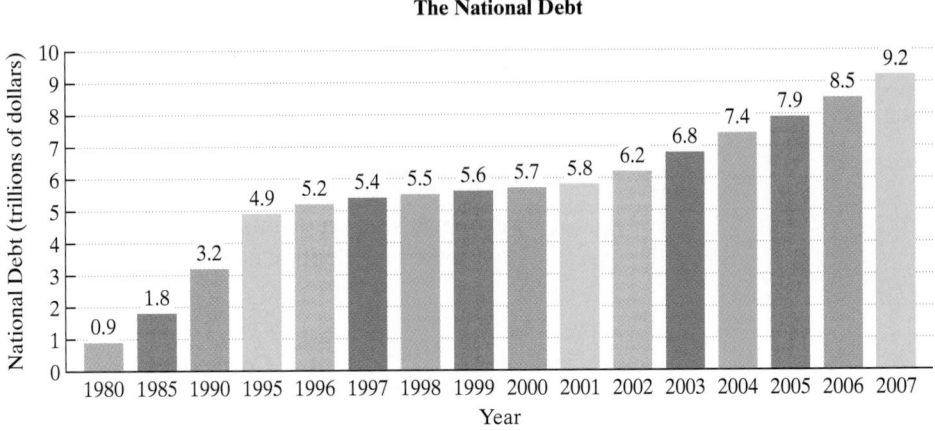

The National Debt

Figure P.10
Source: Office of Management and Budget

Example 12 shows how we can use scientific notation to comprehend the meaning of a number such as 9.2 trillion.

EXAMPLE 12 The National Debt

As of December 2007, the national debt was $9.2 trillion, or 9.2×10^{12} dollars. At that time, the U.S. population was approximately 303,000,000 (303 million), or 3.03×10^8. If the national debt was evenly divided among every individual in the United States, how much would each citizen have to pay?

Solution The amount each citizen must pay is the total debt, 9.2×10^{12} dollars, divided by the number of citizens, 3.03×10^8.

$$\frac{9.2 \times 10^{12}}{3.03 \times 10^8} = \left(\frac{9.2}{3.03}\right) \times \left(\frac{10^{12}}{10^8}\right)$$

$$\approx 3.04 \times 10^{12-8}$$

$$= 3.04 \times 10^4$$

$$= 30,400$$

Every U.S. citizen would have to pay approximately $30,400 to the federal government to pay off the national debt.

⊘ Check Point **12** Pell Grants help low-income undergraduate students pay for college. In 2006, the federal cost of this program was $13 billion ($13 \times 10^9$) and there were 5.1 million (5.1×10^6) grant recipients. How much, to the nearest hundred dollars, was the average grant?

Exercise Set P.2

Practice Exercises

Evaluate each exponential expression in Exercises 1–22.

1. $5^2 \cdot 2$ **2.** $6^2 \cdot 2$

3. $(-2)^6$ **4.** $(-2)^4$

5. -2^6 **6.** -2^4

7. $(-3)^0$ **8.** $(-9)^0$

9. -3^0 **10.** -9^0

11. 4^{-3} **12.** 2^{-6}

13. $2^2 \cdot 2^3$ **14.** $3^3 \cdot 3^2$

15. $(2^2)^3$ **16.** $(3^3)^2$

17. $\dfrac{2^8}{2^4}$ **18.** $\dfrac{3^8}{3^4}$

19. $3^{-3} \cdot 3$ **20.** $2^{-3} \cdot 2$

21. $\dfrac{2^3}{2^7}$ **22.** $\dfrac{3^4}{3^7}$

Simplify each exponential expression in Exercises 23–64.

23. $x^{-2}y$ **24.** xy^{-3}

25. $x^0 y^5$ **26.** $x^7 y^0$

27. $x^3 \cdot x^7$ **28.** $x^{11} \cdot x^5$

29. $x^{-5} \cdot x^{10}$ **30.** $x^{-6} \cdot x^{12}$

31. $(x^3)^7$ **32.** $(x^{11})^5$

33. $(x^{-5})^3$ **34.** $(x^{-6})^4$

35. $\dfrac{x^{14}}{x^7}$ **36.** $\dfrac{x^{30}}{x^{10}}$

37. $\dfrac{x^{14}}{x^{-7}}$ **38.** $\dfrac{x^{30}}{x^{-10}}$

39. $(8x^3)^2$ **40.** $(6x^4)^2$

41. $\left(-\dfrac{4}{x}\right)^3$ **42.** $\left(-\dfrac{6}{y}\right)^3$

43. $(-3x^2 y^5)^2$ **44.** $(-3x^4 y^6)^3$

45. $(3x^4)(2x^7)$ **46.** $(11x^5)(9x^{12})$

47. $(-9x^3 y)(-2x^6 y^4)$ **48.** $(-5x^4 y)(-6x^7 y^{11})$

49. $\dfrac{8x^{20}}{2x^4}$ **50.** $\dfrac{20x^{24}}{10x^6}$

51. $\dfrac{25a^{13}b^4}{-5a^2 b^3}$ **52.** $\dfrac{35a^{14}b^6}{-7a^7 b^3}$

53. $\dfrac{14b^7}{7b^{14}}$ **54.** $\dfrac{20b^{10}}{10b^{20}}$

55. $(4x^3)^{-2}$ **56.** $(10x^2)^{-3}$

57. $\dfrac{24x^3 y^5}{32x^7 y^{-9}}$ **58.** $\dfrac{10x^4 y^9}{30x^{12} y^{-3}}$

59. $\left(\dfrac{5x^3}{y}\right)^{-2}$ **60.** $\left(\dfrac{3x^4}{y}\right)^{-3}$

61. $\left(\dfrac{-15a^4 b^2}{5a^{10}b^{-3}}\right)^3$ **62.** $\left(\dfrac{-30a^{14}b^8}{10a^{17}b^{-2}}\right)^3$

63. $\left(\dfrac{3a^{-5}b^2}{12a^3 b^{-4}}\right)^0$ **64.** $\left(\dfrac{4a^{-5}b^3}{12a^3 b^{-5}}\right)^0$

In Exercises 65–76, write each number in decimal notation without the use of exponents.

65. 3.8×10^2 **66.** 9.2×10^2

67. 6×10^{-4} **68.** 7×10^{-5}

69. -7.16×10^6 **70.** -8.17×10^6

71. 7.9×10^{-1} **72.** 6.8×10^{-1}

73. -4.15×10^{-3} **74.** -3.14×10^{-3}

75. -6.00001×10^{10} **76.** -7.00001×10^{10}

In Exercises 77–86, write each number in scientific notation.

77. 32,000 **78.** 64,000

79. 638,000,000,000,000,000 **80.** 579,000,000,000,000,000

81. -5716 **82.** -3829

83. 0.0027 **84.** 0.0083

85. -0.00000000504 **86.** -0.00000000405

In Exercises 87–106, perform the indicated computations. Write the answers in scientific notation. If necessary, round the decimal factor in your scientific notation answer to two decimal places.

87. $(3 \times 10^4)(2.1 \times 10^3)$ **88.** $(2 \times 10^4)(4.1 \times 10^3)$

89. $(1.6 \times 10^{15})(4 \times 10^{-11})$ **90.** $(1.4 \times 10^{15})(3 \times 10^{-11})$

91. $(6.1 \times 10^{-8})(2 \times 10^{-4})$ **92.** $(5.1 \times 10^{-8})(3 \times 10^{-4})$

93. $(4.3 \times 10^8)(6.2 \times 10^4)$ **94.** $(8.2 \times 10^8)(4.6 \times 10^4)$

95. $\dfrac{8.4 \times 10^8}{4 \times 10^5}$ **96.** $\dfrac{6.9 \times 10^8}{3 \times 10^5}$

97. $\dfrac{3.6 \times 10^4}{9 \times 10^{-2}}$ **98.** $\dfrac{1.2 \times 10^4}{2 \times 10^{-2}}$

99. $\dfrac{4.8 \times 10^{-2}}{2.4 \times 10^6}$ **100.** $\dfrac{7.5 \times 10^{-2}}{2.5 \times 10^6}$

101. $\dfrac{2.4 \times 10^{-2}}{4.8 \times 10^{-6}}$ **102.** $\dfrac{1.5 \times 10^{-2}}{3 \times 10^{-6}}$

103. $\dfrac{480,000,000,000}{0.00012}$ **104.** $\dfrac{282,000,000,000}{0.00141}$

105. $\dfrac{0.00072 \times 0.003}{0.00024}$ **106.** $\dfrac{66,000 \times 0.001}{0.003 \times 0.002}$

Practice Plus

In Exercises 107–114, simplify each exponential expression. Assume that variables represent nonzero real numbers.

107. $\dfrac{(x^{-2}y)^{-3}}{(x^2y^{-1})^3}$

108. $\dfrac{(xy^{-2})^{-2}}{(x^{-2}y)^{-3}}$

109. $(2x^{-3}yz^{-6})(2x)^{-5}$

110. $(3x^{-4}yz^{-7})(3x)^{-3}$

111. $\left(\dfrac{x^3y^4z^5}{x^{-3}y^{-4}z^{-5}}\right)^{-2}$

112. $\left(\dfrac{x^4y^5z^6}{x^{-4}y^{-5}z^{-6}}\right)^{-4}$

113. $\dfrac{(2^{-1}x^{-2}y^{-1})^{-2}(2x^{-4}y^3)^{-2}(16x^{-3}y^3)^0}{(2x^{-3}y^{-5})^2}$

114. $\dfrac{(2^{-1}x^{-3}y^{-1})^{-2}(2x^{-6}y^4)^{-2}(9x^3y^{-3})^0}{(2x^{-4}y^{-6})^2}$

Application Exercises

The bar graph shows the total amount Americans paid in federal taxes, in trillions of dollars, and the U.S. population, in millions, from 2003 through 2006. Exercises 115–116 are based on the numbers displayed by the graph.

Federal Taxes and the United States Population

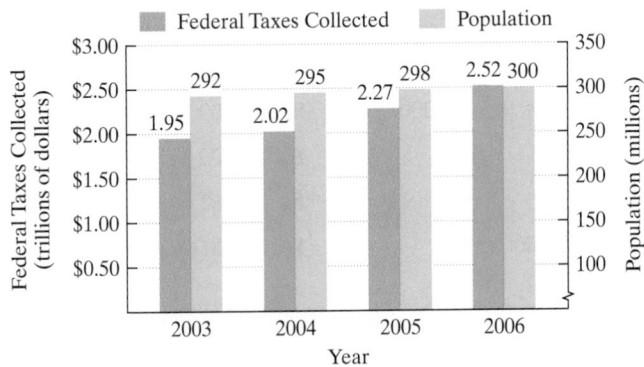

Sources: Internal Revenue Service and U.S. Census Bureau

115. a. In 2006, the United States government collected $2.52 trillion in taxes. Express this number in scientific notation.

 b. In 2006, the population of the United States was approximately 300 million. Express this number in scientific notation.

 c. Use your scientific notation answers from parts (a) and (b) to answer this question: If the total 2006 tax collections were evenly divided among all Americans, how much would each citizen pay? Express the answer in decimal notation.

116. a. In 2005, the United States government collected $2.27 trillion in taxes. Express this number in scientific notation.

 b. In 2005, the population of the United States was approximately 298 million. Express this number in scientific notation.

 c. Use your scientific notation answers from parts (a) and (b) to answer this question: If the total 2005 tax collections were evenly divided among all Americans, how much would each citizen pay? Express the answer in decimal notation, rounded to the nearest dollar.

In the dramatic arts, ours is the era of the movies. As individuals and as a nation, we've grown up with them. Our images of love, war, family, country—even of things that terrify us—owe much to what we've seen on screen. The bar graph quantifies our love for movies by showing the number of tickets sold, in billions, and the average price per ticket for five selected years. Exercises 117–118 are based on the numbers displayed by the graph.

United States Film Admissions and Admission Charges

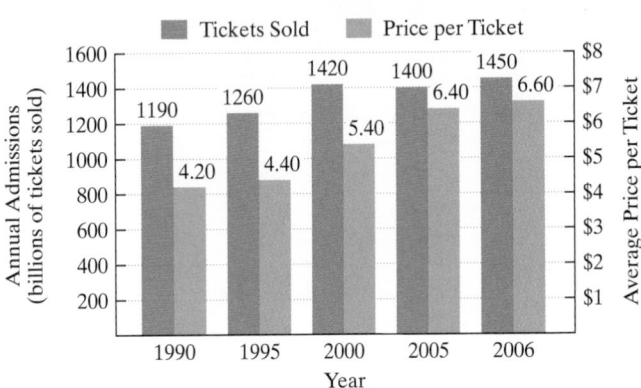

Source: National Association of Theater Owners

117. Use scientific notation to compute the amount of money that the motion picture industry made from box-office receipts in 2006. Express the answer in scientific notation.

118. Use scientific notation to compute the amount of money that the motion picture industry made from box office receipts in 2005. Express the answer in scientific notation.

119. The mass of one oxygen molecule is 5.3×10^{-23} gram. Find the mass of 20,000 molecules of oxygen. Express the answer in scientific notation.

120. The mass of one hydrogen atom is 1.67×10^{-24} gram. Find the mass of 80,000 hydrogen atoms. Express the answer in scientific notation.

121. In this exercise, use the fact that there are approximately 3.2×10^7 seconds in a year. According to the United States Department of Agriculture, Americans consume 127 chickens per second. How many chickens are eaten per year in the United States? Express the answer in scientific notation.

122. Convert 365 days (one year) to hours, to minutes, and, finally, to seconds, to determine how many seconds there are in a year. Express the answer in scientific notation.

Writing in Mathematics

123. Describe what it means to raise a number to a power. In your description, include a discussion of the difference between -5^2 and $(-5)^2$.

124. Explain the product rule for exponents. Use $2^3 \cdot 2^5$ in your explanation.

125. Explain the power rule for exponents. Use $(3^2)^4$ in your explanation.

126. Explain the quotient rule for exponents. Use $\dfrac{5^8}{5^2}$ in your explanation.

127. Why is $(-3x^2)(2x^{-5})$ not simplified? What must be done to simplify the expression?

128. How do you know if a number is written in scientific notation?

129. Explain how to convert from scientific to decimal notation and give an example.

130. Explain how to convert from decimal to scientific notation and give an example.

Critical Thinking Exercises

Make Sense? *In Exercises 131–134, determine whether each statement makes sense or does not make sense, and explain your reasoning.*

131. There are many exponential expressions that are equal to $36x^{12}$, such as $(6x^6)^2$, $(6x^3)(6x^9)$, $36(x^3)^9$, and $6^2(x^2)^6$.

132. If 5^{-2} is raised to the third power, the result is a number between 0 and 1.

133. The population of Colorado is approximately 4.6×10^{12}.

134. I just finished reading a book that contained approximately 1.04×10^5 words.

In Exercises 135–142, determine whether each statement is true or false. If the statement is false, make the necessary change(s) to produce a true statement.

135. $4^{-2} < 4^{-3}$

136. $5^{-2} > 2^{-5}$

137. $(-2)^4 = 2^{-4}$

138. $5^2 \cdot 5^{-2} > 2^5 \cdot 2^{-5}$

139. $534.7 = 5.347 \times 10^3$

140. $\dfrac{8 \times 10^{30}}{4 \times 10^{-5}} = 2 \times 10^{25}$

141. $(7 \times 10^5) + (2 \times 10^{-3}) = 9 \times 10^2$

142. $(4 \times 10^3) + (3 \times 10^2) = 4.3 \times 10^3$

143. The mad Dr. Frankenstein has gathered enough bits and pieces (so to speak) for $2^{-1} + 2^{-2}$ of his creature-to-be. Write a fraction that represents the amount of his creature that must still be obtained.

144. If $b^A = MN$, $b^C = M$, and $b^D = N$, what is the relationship among A, C, and D?

145. Our hearts beat approximately 70 times per minute. Express in scientific notation how many times the heart beats over a lifetime of 80 years. Round the decimal factor in your scientific notation answer to two decimal places.

Group Exercise

146. Putting Numbers into Perspective. A large number can be put into perspective by comparing it with another number. For example, we put the $9.2 trillion national debt (Example 12) and the $2.52 trillion the government collected in taxes (Exercise 115) by comparing these numbers to the number of U.S. citizens.

For this project, each group member should consult an almanac, a newspaper, or the World Wide Web to find a number greater than one million. Explain to other members of the group the context in which the large number is used. Express the number in scientific notation. Then put the number into perspective by comparing it with another number.

Preview Exercises

Exercises 147–149 will help you prepare for the material covered in the next section.

147. a. Find $\sqrt{16} \cdot \sqrt{4}$.
 b. Find $\sqrt{16 \cdot 4}$.
 c. Based on your answers to parts (a) and (b), what can you conclude?

148. a. Use a calculator to approximate $\sqrt{300}$ to two decimal places.
 b. Use a calculator to approximate $10\sqrt{3}$ to two decimal places.
 c. Based on your answers to parts (a) and (b), what can you conclude?

149. a. Simplify: $21x + 10x$.
 b. Simplify: $21\sqrt{2} + 10\sqrt{2}$.

Section P.3

Objectives

1. Evaluate square roots.
2. Simplify expressions of the form $\sqrt{a^2}$.
3. Use the product rule to simplify square roots.
4. Use the quotient rule to simplify square roots.
5. Add and subtract square roots.
6. Rationalize denominators.
7. Evaluate and perform operations with higher roots.
8. Understand and use rational exponents.

Radicals and Rational Exponents

This photograph shows mathematical models used by Albert Einstein at a lecture on relativity. Notice the radicals that appear in many of the formulas. Among these models, there is one describing how an astronaut in a moving spaceship ages more slowly than friends who remain on Earth. No description of your world can be complete without roots and radicals. In this section, in addition to reviewing the basics of radical expressions and the use of rational exponents to indicate radicals, you will see how radicals model time dilation for a futuristic high-speed trip to a nearby star.

① Evaluate square roots.

Square Roots

From our earlier work with exponents, we are aware that the square of both 5 and -5 is 25:

$$5^2 = 25 \quad \text{and} \quad (-5)^2 = 25.$$

The reverse operation of squaring a number is finding the *square root* of the number. For example,

- One square root of 25 is 5 because $5^2 = 25$.
- Another square root of 25 is -5 because $(-5)^2 = 25$.

In general, **if $b^2 = a$, then b is a square root of a.**
The symbol $\sqrt{}$ is used to denote the *positive* or *principal square root* of a number. For example,

- $\sqrt{25} = 5$ because $5^2 = 25$ and 5 is positive.
- $\sqrt{100} = 10$ because $10^2 = 100$ and 10 is positive.

The symbol $\sqrt{}$ that we use to denote the principal square root is called a **radical sign**. The number under the radical sign is called the **radicand**. Together we refer to the radical sign and its radicand as a **radical expression**.

Radical sign $\quad \sqrt{a} \quad$ Radicand

Radical expression

Definition of the Principal Square Root

If a is a nonnegative real number, the nonnegative number b such that $b^2 = a$, denoted by $b = \sqrt{a}$, is the **principal square root** of a.

The symbol $-\sqrt{}$ is used to denote the negative square root of a number. For example,

- $-\sqrt{25} = -5$ because $(-5)^2 = 25$ and -5 is negative.
- $-\sqrt{100} = -10$ because $(-10)^2 = 100$ and -10 is negative.

(**EXAMPLE 1**) Evaluating Square Roots

Evaluate:

a. $\sqrt{64}$ **b.** $-\sqrt{49}$ **c.** $\sqrt{\dfrac{1}{4}}$ **d.** $\sqrt{9 + 16}$ **e.** $\sqrt{9} + \sqrt{16}.$

Solution

a. $\sqrt{64} = 8$ The principal square root of 64 is 8. Check: $8^2 = 64$.

b. $-\sqrt{49} = -7$ The negative square root of 49 is -7. Check: $(-7)^2 = 49$.

c. $\sqrt{\dfrac{1}{4}} = \dfrac{1}{2}$ The principal square root of $\frac{1}{4}$ is $\frac{1}{2}$. Check: $\left(\frac{1}{2}\right)^2 = \frac{1}{4}$.

d. $\sqrt{9 + 16} = \sqrt{25}$ First simplify the expression under the radical sign.

$\phantom{\sqrt{9 + 16}} = 5$ Then take the principal square root of 25, which is 5.

e. $\sqrt{9} + \sqrt{16} = 3 + 4$ $\sqrt{9} = 3$ because $3^2 = 9$. $\sqrt{16} = 4$ because $4^2 = 16$.

$\phantom{\sqrt{9} + \sqrt{16}} = 7$

Study Tip

In Example 1, parts (d) and (e), observe that $\sqrt{9 + 16}$ is not equal to $\sqrt{9} + \sqrt{16}$. In general,

$$\sqrt{a + b} \neq \sqrt{a} + \sqrt{b}$$

and

$$\sqrt{a - b} \neq \sqrt{a} - \sqrt{b}.$$

⊘ Check Point I Evaluate:

a. $\sqrt{81}$ **b.** $-\sqrt{9}$ **c.** $\sqrt{\dfrac{1}{25}}$

d. $\sqrt{36 + 64}$ **e.** $\sqrt{36} + \sqrt{64}$.

A number that is the square of a rational number is called a **perfect square**. All the radicands in Example 1 and Check Point 1 are perfect squares.

- 64 is a perfect square because $64 = 8^2$. Thus, $\sqrt{64} = 8$.

- $\dfrac{1}{4}$ is a perfect square because $\dfrac{1}{4} = \left(\dfrac{1}{2}\right)^2$. Thus, $\sqrt{\dfrac{1}{4}} = \dfrac{1}{2}$.

Let's see what happens to the radical expression \sqrt{x} if x is a negative number. Is the square root of a negative number a real number? For example, consider $\sqrt{-25}$. Is there a real number whose square is -25? No. Thus, $\sqrt{-25}$ is not a real number. In general, **a square root of a negative number is not a real number**.

If a number a is nonnegative ($a \geq 0$), then $(\sqrt{a})^2 = a$. For example,

$$\left(\sqrt{2}\right)^2 = 2, \quad \left(\sqrt{3}\right)^2 = 3, \quad \left(\sqrt{4}\right)^2 = 4, \quad \text{and} \quad \left(\sqrt{5}\right)^2 = 5.$$

② Simplify expressions of the form $\sqrt{a^2}$.

Simplifying Expressions of the Form $\sqrt{a^2}$

You may think that $\sqrt{a^2} = a$. However, this is not necessarily true. Consider the following examples:

$$\sqrt{4^2} = \sqrt{16} = 4$$
$$\sqrt{(-4)^2} = \sqrt{16} = 4.$$

> The result is not -4, but rather the absolute value of -4, or 4.

Here is a rule for simplifying expressions of the form $\sqrt{a^2}$:

Simplifying $\sqrt{a^2}$

For any real number a,

$$\sqrt{a^2} = |a|.$$

In words, the principal square root of a^2 is the absolute value of a.

For example, $\sqrt{6^2} = |6| = 6$ and $\sqrt{(-6)^2} = |-6| = 6$.

③ Use the product rule to simplify square roots.

The Product Rule for Square Roots

A rule for multiplying square roots can be generalized by comparing $\sqrt{25} \cdot \sqrt{4}$ and $\sqrt{25 \cdot 4}$. Notice that

$$\sqrt{25} \cdot \sqrt{4} = 5 \cdot 2 = 10 \quad \text{and} \quad \sqrt{25 \cdot 4} = \sqrt{100} = 10.$$

Because we obtain 10 in both situations, the original radical expressions must be equal. That is,

$$\sqrt{25} \cdot \sqrt{4} = \sqrt{25 \cdot 4}.$$

This result is a special case of the **product rule for square roots** that can be generalized as follows:

The Product Rule for Square Roots

If a and b represent nonnegative real numbers, then

$$\sqrt{ab} = \sqrt{a} \cdot \sqrt{b} \quad \text{and} \quad \sqrt{a} \cdot \sqrt{b} = \sqrt{ab}.$$

> The square root of a product is the product of the square roots.

> The product of two square roots is the square root of the product of the radicands.

A square root is **simplified** when its radicand has no factors other than 1 that are perfect squares. For example, $\sqrt{500}$ is not simplified because it can be expressed as $\sqrt{100 \cdot 5}$ and 100 is a perfect square. Example 2 shows how the product rule is used to remove from the square root any perfect squares that occur as factors.

EXAMPLE 2 Using the Product Rule to Simplify Square Roots

Simplify: **a.** $\sqrt{500}$ **b.** $\sqrt{6x} \cdot \sqrt{3x}$.

Solution

a. $\sqrt{500} = \sqrt{100 \cdot 5}$ Factor 500. 100 is the greatest perfect square factor.

$\phantom{\sqrt{500}} = \sqrt{100}\sqrt{5}$ Use the product rule: $\sqrt{ab} = \sqrt{a} \cdot \sqrt{b}$.

$\phantom{\sqrt{500}} = 10\sqrt{5}$ Write $\sqrt{100}$ as 10. We read $10\sqrt{5}$ as "ten times the square root of 5."

b. We can simplify $\sqrt{6x} \cdot \sqrt{3x}$ using the product rule only if $6x$ and $3x$ represent nonnegative real numbers. Thus, $x \geq 0$.

$\sqrt{6x} \cdot \sqrt{3x} = \sqrt{6x \cdot 3x}$ Use the product rule: $\sqrt{a}\sqrt{b} = \sqrt{ab}$.

$\phantom{\sqrt{6x} \cdot \sqrt{3x}} = \sqrt{18x^2}$ Multiply in the radicand.

$\phantom{\sqrt{6x} \cdot \sqrt{3x}} = \sqrt{9x^2 \cdot 2}$ Factor 18. 9 is the greatest perfect square factor.

$\phantom{\sqrt{6x} \cdot \sqrt{3x}} = \sqrt{9x^2}\sqrt{2}$ Use the product rule: $\sqrt{ab} = \sqrt{a} \cdot \sqrt{b}$.

$\phantom{\sqrt{6x} \cdot \sqrt{3x}} = \sqrt{9}\sqrt{x^2}\sqrt{2}$ Use the product rule to write $\sqrt{9x^2}$ as the product of two square roots.

$\phantom{\sqrt{6x} \cdot \sqrt{3x}} = 3x\sqrt{2}$ $\sqrt{x^2} = |x| = x$ because $x \geq 0$. ●

Study Tip

When simplifying square roots, always look for the *greatest* perfect square factor possible. The following factorization will lead to further simplification:

$$\sqrt{500} = \sqrt{25 \cdot 20} = \sqrt{25}\sqrt{20} = 5\sqrt{20}.$$

25 is a perfect square factor of 500, but not the greatest perfect square factor.

Because 20 contains a perfect square factor, 4, the simplification is not complete.

$$5\sqrt{20} = 5\sqrt{4 \cdot 5} = 5\sqrt{4}\sqrt{5} = 5 \cdot 2\sqrt{5} = 10\sqrt{5}$$

Although the result checks with our simplification using $\sqrt{500} = \sqrt{100 \cdot 5}$, more work is required when the greatest perfect square factor is not used.

⌀ Check Point **2** Simplify:

a. $\sqrt{75}$ **b.** $\sqrt{5x} \cdot \sqrt{10x}$.

④ Use the quotient rule to simplify square roots.

The Quotient Rule for Square Roots

Another property for square roots involves division.

The Quotient Rule for Square Roots

If a and b represent nonnegative real numbers and $b \neq 0$, then

$$\sqrt{\frac{a}{b}} = \frac{\sqrt{a}}{\sqrt{b}} \qquad \text{and} \qquad \frac{\sqrt{a}}{\sqrt{b}} = \sqrt{\frac{a}{b}}.$$

The square root of a quotient is the quotient of the square roots.

The quotient of two square roots is the square root of the quotient of the radicands.

$\boxed{\text{EXAMPLE 3}}$ **Using the Quotient Rule to Simplify Square Roots**

Simplify: **a.** $\sqrt{\dfrac{100}{9}}$ **b.** $\dfrac{\sqrt{48x^3}}{\sqrt{6x}}$.

Solution

a. $\sqrt{\dfrac{100}{9}} = \dfrac{\sqrt{100}}{\sqrt{9}} = \dfrac{10}{3}$

b. We can simplify the quotient of $\sqrt{48x^3}$ and $\sqrt{6x}$ using the quotient rule only if $48x^3$ and $6x$ represent nonnegative real numbers and $6x \neq 0$. Thus, $x > 0$.

$$\dfrac{\sqrt{48x^3}}{\sqrt{6x}} = \sqrt{\dfrac{48x^3}{6x}} = \sqrt{8x^2} = \sqrt{4x^2}\sqrt{2} = \sqrt{4}\sqrt{x^2}\sqrt{2} = 2x\sqrt{2}$$

$\sqrt{x^2} = |x| = x$ because $x > 0$.

\oslash **Check Point 3** Simplify:

a. $\sqrt{\dfrac{25}{16}}$ **b.** $\dfrac{\sqrt{150x^3}}{\sqrt{2x}}$.

⑤ Add and subtract square roots.

Adding and Subtracting Square Roots

Two or more square roots can be combined using the distributive property provided that they have the same radicand. Such radicals are called **like radicals**. For example,

$$7\sqrt{11} + 6\sqrt{11} = (7 + 6)\sqrt{11} = 13\sqrt{11}.$$

7 square roots of 11 plus 6 square roots of 11 result in 13 square roots of 11.

$\boxed{\text{EXAMPLE 4}}$ **Adding and Subtracting Like Radicals**

Add or subtract as indicated:
a. $7\sqrt{2} + 5\sqrt{2}$ **b.** $\sqrt{5x} - 7\sqrt{5x}$.

Solution

a. $7\sqrt{2} + 5\sqrt{2} = (7 + 5)\sqrt{2}$ Apply the distributive property.

$= 12\sqrt{2}$ Simplify.

b. $\sqrt{5x} - 7\sqrt{5x} = 1\sqrt{5x} - 7\sqrt{5x}$ Write $\sqrt{5x}$ as $1\sqrt{5x}$.

$= (1 - 7)\sqrt{5x}$ Apply the distributive property.

$= -6\sqrt{5x}$ Simplify.

\oslash **Check Point 4** Add or subtract as indicated:

a. $8\sqrt{13} + 9\sqrt{13}$ **b.** $\sqrt{17x} - 20\sqrt{17x}$.

In some cases, radicals can be combined once they have been simplified. For example, to add $\sqrt{2}$ and $\sqrt{8}$, we can write $\sqrt{8}$ as $\sqrt{4 \cdot 2}$ because 4 is a perfect square factor of 8.

$$\sqrt{2} + \sqrt{8} = \sqrt{2} + \sqrt{4 \cdot 2} = 1\sqrt{2} + 2\sqrt{2} = (1 + 2)\sqrt{2} = 3\sqrt{2}$$

EXAMPLE 5 **Combining Radicals That First Require Simplification**

Add or subtract as indicated:

a. $7\sqrt{3} + \sqrt{12}$ **b.** $4\sqrt{50x} - 6\sqrt{32x}$.

Solution

a. $7\sqrt{3} + \sqrt{12}$

$= 7\sqrt{3} + \sqrt{4 \cdot 3}$ Split 12 into two factors such that one is a perfect square.

$= 7\sqrt{3} + 2\sqrt{3}$ $\sqrt{4 \cdot 3} = \sqrt{4}\sqrt{3} = 2\sqrt{3}$

$= (7 + 2)\sqrt{3}$ Apply the distributive property. You will find that this step is usually done mentally.

$= 9\sqrt{3}$ Simplify.

b. $4\sqrt{50x} - 6\sqrt{32x}$

$= 4\sqrt{25 \cdot 2x} - 6\sqrt{16 \cdot 2x}$ 25 is the greatest perfect square factor of 50x and 16 is the greatest perfect square factor of 32x.

$= 4 \cdot 5\sqrt{2x} - 6 \cdot 4\sqrt{2x}$ $\sqrt{25 \cdot 2x} = \sqrt{25}\sqrt{2x} = 5\sqrt{2x}$ and $\sqrt{16 \cdot 2x} = \sqrt{16}\sqrt{2x} = 4\sqrt{2x}$.

$= 20\sqrt{2x} - 24\sqrt{2x}$ Multiply: $4 \cdot 5 = 20$ and $6 \cdot 4 = 24$.

$= (20 - 24)\sqrt{2x}$ Apply the distributive property.

$= -4\sqrt{2x}$ Simplify.

⊘ Check Point 5 Add or subtract as indicated:

a. $5\sqrt{27} + \sqrt{12}$ **b.** $6\sqrt{18x} - 4\sqrt{8x}$.

⑥ Rationalize denominators.

```
1/√(3)
         .5773502692
√(3)/3
         .5773502692
```

Figure P.11 The calculator screen shows approximate values for $\dfrac{1}{\sqrt{3}}$ and $\dfrac{\sqrt{3}}{3}$.

Rationalizing Denominators

The calculator screen in **Figure P.11** shows approximate values for $\dfrac{1}{\sqrt{3}}$ and $\dfrac{\sqrt{3}}{3}$. The two approximations are the same. This is not a coincidence:

$$\frac{1}{\sqrt{3}} = \frac{1}{\sqrt{3}} \cdot \boxed{\frac{\sqrt{3}}{\sqrt{3}}} = \frac{\sqrt{3}}{\sqrt{9}} = \frac{\sqrt{3}}{3}.$$

Any number divided by itself is 1. Multiplication by 1 does not change the value of $\frac{1}{\sqrt{3}}$.

This process involves rewriting a radical expression as an equivalent expression in which the denominator no longer contains any radicals. The process is called **rationalizing the denominator**. If the denominator consists of the square root of a natural number that is not a perfect square, **multiply the numerator and the denominator by the smallest number that produces the square root of a perfect square in the denominator**.

EXAMPLE 6 **Rationalizing Denominators**

Rationalize the denominator:

a. $\dfrac{15}{\sqrt{6}}$ **b.** $\dfrac{12}{\sqrt{8}}$.

Study Tip

Rationalizing a numerical denominator makes that denominator a rational number.

Solution

a. If we multiply the numerator and the denominator of $\dfrac{15}{\sqrt{6}}$ by $\sqrt{6}$, the denominator becomes $\sqrt{6} \cdot \sqrt{6} = \sqrt{36} = 6$. Therefore, we multiply by 1, choosing $\dfrac{\sqrt{6}}{\sqrt{6}}$ for 1.

$$\frac{15}{\sqrt{6}} = \frac{15}{\sqrt{6}} \cdot \frac{\sqrt{6}}{\sqrt{6}} = \frac{15\sqrt{6}}{\sqrt{36}} = \frac{15\sqrt{6}}{6} = \frac{5\sqrt{6}}{2}$$

Multiply by 1. Simplify: $\frac{15}{6} = \frac{15 \div 3}{6 \div 3} = \frac{5}{2}$.

b. The *smallest* number that will produce the square root of a perfect square in the denominator of $\dfrac{12}{\sqrt{8}}$ is $\sqrt{2}$, because $\sqrt{8} \cdot \sqrt{2} = \sqrt{16} = 4$. We multiply by 1, choosing $\dfrac{\sqrt{2}}{\sqrt{2}}$ for 1.

$$\frac{12}{\sqrt{8}} = \frac{12}{\sqrt{8}} \cdot \frac{\sqrt{2}}{\sqrt{2}} = \frac{12\sqrt{2}}{\sqrt{16}} = \frac{12\sqrt{2}}{4} = 3\sqrt{2}$$

⊘ **Check Point 6** Rationalize the denominator:

a. $\dfrac{5}{\sqrt{3}}$ **b.** $\dfrac{6}{\sqrt{12}}$.

Radical expressions that involve the sum and difference of the same two terms are called **conjugates**. Thus,

$$\sqrt{a} + \sqrt{b} \quad \text{and} \quad \sqrt{a} - \sqrt{b}$$

are conjugates. Conjugates are used to rationalize denominators because the product of such a pair contains no radicals:

Multiply each term of $\sqrt{a} - \sqrt{b}$ by each term of $\sqrt{a} + \sqrt{b}$.

$$(\sqrt{a} + \sqrt{b})(\sqrt{a} - \sqrt{b})$$
$$= \sqrt{a}(\sqrt{a} - \sqrt{b}) + \sqrt{b}(\sqrt{a} - \sqrt{b})$$

Distribute \sqrt{a} over $\sqrt{a} - \sqrt{b}$. Distribute \sqrt{b} over $\sqrt{a} - \sqrt{b}$.

$$= \sqrt{a} \cdot \sqrt{a} - \sqrt{a} \cdot \sqrt{b} + \sqrt{b} \cdot \sqrt{a} - \sqrt{b} \cdot \sqrt{b}$$
$$= (\sqrt{a})^2 - \sqrt{ab} + \sqrt{ab} - (\sqrt{b})^2$$

$-\sqrt{ab} + \sqrt{ab} = 0$

$$= (\sqrt{a})^2 - (\sqrt{b})^2$$
$$= a - b.$$

Multiplying Conjugates

$$(\sqrt{a} + \sqrt{b})(\sqrt{a} - \sqrt{b}) = (\sqrt{a})^2 - (\sqrt{b})^2 = a - b$$

How can we rationalize a denominator if the denominator contains two terms with one or more square roots? **Multiply the numerator and the**

denominator by the conjugate of the denominator. Here are three examples of such expressions:

- $\dfrac{7}{5 + \sqrt{3}}$

 The conjugate of the denominator is $5 - \sqrt{3}$.

- $\dfrac{8}{3\sqrt{2} - 4}$

 The conjugate of the denominator is $3\sqrt{2} + 4$.

- $\dfrac{h}{\sqrt{x + h} - \sqrt{x}}$

 The conjugate of the denominator is $\sqrt{x + h} + \sqrt{x}$.

The product of the denominator and its conjugate is found using the formula

$$\left(\sqrt{a} + \sqrt{b}\right)\left(\sqrt{a} - \sqrt{b}\right) = \left(\sqrt{a}\right)^2 - \left(\sqrt{b}\right)^2 = a - b.$$

The simplified product will not contain a radical.

EXAMPLE 7 Rationalizing a Denominator Containing Two Terms

Rationalize the denominator: $\dfrac{7}{5 + \sqrt{3}}$.

Solution The conjugate of the denominator is $5 - \sqrt{3}$. If we multiply the numerator and denominator by $5 - \sqrt{3}$, the simplified denominator will not contain a radical. Therefore, we multiply by 1, choosing $\dfrac{5 - \sqrt{3}}{5 - \sqrt{3}}$ for 1.

$$\frac{7}{5 + \sqrt{3}} = \frac{7}{5 + \sqrt{3}} \cdot \frac{5 - \sqrt{3}}{5 - \sqrt{3}} = \frac{7(5 - \sqrt{3})}{5^2 - \left(\sqrt{3}\right)^2} = \frac{7(5 - \sqrt{3})}{25 - 3}$$

Multiply by 1. $\left(\sqrt{a} + \sqrt{b}\right)\left(\sqrt{a} - \sqrt{b}\right) = \left(\sqrt{a}\right)^2 - \left(\sqrt{b}\right)^2$

$$= \frac{7(5 - \sqrt{3})}{22} \quad \text{or} \quad \frac{35 - 7\sqrt{3}}{22}$$

In either form of the answer, there is no radical in the denominator.

⊘ **Check Point 7** Rationalize the denominator: $\dfrac{8}{4 + \sqrt{5}}$.

7 Evaluate and perform operations with higher roots.

Other Kinds of Roots

We define the **principal nth root** of a real number a, symbolized by $\sqrt[n]{a}$, as follows:

Definition of the Principal nth Root of a Real Number

$$\sqrt[n]{a} = b \text{ means that } b^n = a.$$

If n, the **index**, is even, then a is nonnegative ($a \geq 0$) and b is also nonnegative ($b \geq 0$). If n is odd, a and b can be any real numbers.

For example,

$$\sqrt[3]{64} = 4 \text{ because } 4^3 = 64 \quad \text{and} \quad \sqrt[5]{-32} = -2 \text{ because } (-2)^5 = -32.$$

The same vocabulary that we learned for square roots applies to nth roots. The symbol $\sqrt[n]{}$ is called a **radical** and the expression under the radical is called the **radicand**.

Study Tip

Some higher even and odd roots occur so frequently that you might want to memorize them.

Cube Roots	
$\sqrt[3]{1} = 1$	$\sqrt[3]{125} = 5$
$\sqrt[3]{8} = 2$	$\sqrt[3]{216} = 6$
$\sqrt[3]{27} = 3$	$\sqrt[3]{1000} = 10$
$\sqrt[3]{64} = 4$	

Fourth Roots
$\sqrt[4]{1} = 1$
$\sqrt[4]{16} = 2$
$\sqrt[4]{81} = 3$
$\sqrt[4]{256} = 4$
$\sqrt[4]{625} = 5$

Fifth Roots
$\sqrt[5]{1} = 1$
$\sqrt[5]{32} = 2$
$\sqrt[5]{243} = 3$

A number that is the nth power of a rational number is called a **perfect nth power**. For example, 8 is a perfect third power, or perfect cube, because $8 = 2^3$. Thus, $\sqrt[3]{8} = \sqrt[3]{2^3} = 2$. In general, one of the following rules can be used to find the nth root of a perfect nth power:

Finding nth Roots of Perfect nth Powers

If n is odd, $\sqrt[n]{a^n} = a$.
If n is even, $\sqrt[n]{a^n} = |a|$.

For example,

$$\sqrt[3]{(-2)^3} = -2 \quad \text{and} \quad \sqrt[4]{(-2)^4} = |-2| = 2.$$

Absolute value is not needed with odd roots, but is necessary with even roots.

The Product and Quotient Rules for Other Roots

The product and quotient rules apply to cube roots, fourth roots, and all higher roots.

The Product and Quotient Rules for nth Roots

For all real numbers a and b, where the indicated roots represent real numbers,

$$\sqrt[n]{ab} = \sqrt[n]{a} \cdot \sqrt[n]{b} \quad \text{and} \quad \sqrt[n]{a} \cdot \sqrt[n]{b} = \sqrt[n]{ab}$$

The nth root of a product is the product of the nth roots.

The product of two nth roots is the nth root of the product of the radicands.

$$\sqrt[n]{\frac{a}{b}} = \frac{\sqrt[n]{a}}{\sqrt[n]{b}}, b \neq 0 \quad \text{and} \quad \frac{\sqrt[n]{a}}{\sqrt[n]{b}} = \sqrt[n]{\frac{a}{b}}, b \neq 0.$$

The nth root of a quotient is the quotient of the nth roots.

The quotient of two nth roots is the nth root of the quotient of the radicands.

EXAMPLE 8 **Simplifying, Multiplying, and Dividing Higher Roots**

Simplify: **a.** $\sqrt[3]{24}$ **b.** $\sqrt[4]{8} \cdot \sqrt[4]{4}$ **c.** $\sqrt[4]{\dfrac{81}{16}}$.

Solution

a. $\sqrt[3]{24} = \sqrt[3]{8 \cdot 3}$ Find the greatest perfect cube that is a factor of 24. $2^3 = 8$, so 8 is a perfect cube and is the greatest perfect cube factor of 24.

$\phantom{\sqrt[3]{24}} = \sqrt[3]{8} \cdot \sqrt[3]{3}$ $\sqrt[n]{ab} = \sqrt[n]{a} \cdot \sqrt[n]{b}$

$\phantom{\sqrt[3]{24}} = 2\sqrt[3]{3}$ $\sqrt[3]{8} = 2$

b. $\sqrt[4]{8} \cdot \sqrt[4]{4} = \sqrt[4]{8 \cdot 4}$ $\sqrt[n]{a} \cdot \sqrt[n]{b} = \sqrt[n]{ab}$

$\phantom{\sqrt[4]{8} \cdot \sqrt[4]{4}} = \sqrt[4]{32}$ Find the greatest perfect fourth power that is a factor of 32.

$\phantom{\sqrt[4]{8} \cdot \sqrt[4]{4}} = \sqrt[4]{16 \cdot 2}$ $2^4 = 16$, so 16 is a perfect fourth power and is the greatest perfect fourth power that is a factor of 32.

$\phantom{\sqrt[4]{8} \cdot \sqrt[4]{4}} = \sqrt[4]{16} \cdot \sqrt[4]{2}$ $\sqrt[n]{ab} = \sqrt[n]{a} \cdot \sqrt[n]{b}$

$\phantom{\sqrt[4]{8} \cdot \sqrt[4]{4}} = 2\sqrt[4]{2}$ $\sqrt[4]{16} = 2$

c. $\sqrt[4]{\dfrac{81}{16}} = \dfrac{\sqrt[4]{81}}{\sqrt[4]{16}}$ $\quad\sqrt[n]{\dfrac{a}{b}} = \dfrac{\sqrt[n]{a}}{\sqrt[n]{b}}$

$= \dfrac{3}{2}$ $\quad\sqrt[4]{81} = 3$ because $3^4 = 81$ and $\sqrt[4]{16} = 2$ because $2^4 = 16$.

✓ Check Point **8** Simplify:

a. $\sqrt[3]{40}$ **b.** $\sqrt[5]{8} \cdot \sqrt[5]{8}$ **c.** $\sqrt[3]{\dfrac{125}{27}}$.

We have seen that adding and subtracting square roots often involves simplifying terms. The same idea applies to adding and subtracting nth roots.

(**EXAMPLE 9**) **Combining Cube Roots**

Subtract: $5\sqrt[3]{16} - 11\sqrt[3]{2}$.

Solution

$5\sqrt[3]{16} - 11\sqrt[3]{2}$

$= 5\sqrt[3]{8 \cdot 2} - 11\sqrt[3]{2}$ Factor 16. 8 is the greatest perfect cube factor: $2^3 = 8$ and $\sqrt[3]{8} = 2$.

$= 5 \cdot 2\sqrt[3]{2} - 11\sqrt[3]{2}$ $\sqrt[3]{8 \cdot 2} = \sqrt[3]{8}\sqrt[3]{2} = 2\sqrt[3]{2}$

$= 10\sqrt[3]{2} - 11\sqrt[3]{2}$ Multiply: $5 \cdot 2 = 10$.

$= (10 - 11)\sqrt[3]{2}$ Apply the distributive property.

$= -1\sqrt[3]{2}$ or $-\sqrt[3]{2}$ Simplify.

✓ Check Point **9** Subtract: $3\sqrt[3]{81} - 4\sqrt[3]{3}$.

8 Understand and use rational exponents.

Rational Exponents

We define rational exponents so that their properties are the same as the properties for integer exponents. For example, we know that exponents are multiplied when an exponential expression is raised to a power. For this to be true,

$$\left(7^{\frac{1}{2}}\right)^2 = 7^{\frac{1}{2}\cdot 2} = 7^1 = 7.$$

We also know that

$$\left(\sqrt{7}\right)^2 = \sqrt{7}\cdot\sqrt{7} = \sqrt{49} = 7.$$

Can you see that the square of both $7^{\frac{1}{2}}$ and $\sqrt{7}$ is 7? It is reasonable to conclude that

$$7^{\frac{1}{2}} \quad \text{means} \quad \sqrt{7}.$$

We can generalize the fact that $7^{\frac{1}{2}}$ means $\sqrt{7}$ with the following definition:

The Definition of $a^{\frac{1}{n}}$

If $\sqrt[n]{a}$ represents a real number, where $n \geq 2$ is an integer, then

$$a^{\frac{1}{n}} = \sqrt[n]{a}.$$

The denominator of the rational exponent is the radical's index.

Furthermore,

$$a^{-\frac{1}{n}} = \dfrac{1}{a^{\frac{1}{n}}} = \dfrac{1}{\sqrt[n]{a}}, \quad a \neq 0.$$

(**EXAMPLE 10**) **Using the Definition of $a^{\frac{1}{n}}$**

Simplify:

a. $64^{\frac{1}{2}}$ **b.** $125^{\frac{1}{3}}$ **c.** $-16^{\frac{1}{4}}$ **d.** $(-27)^{\frac{1}{3}}$ **e.** $64^{-\frac{1}{3}}$.

Solution

a. $64^{\frac{1}{2}} = \sqrt{64} = 8$

b. $125^{\frac{1}{3}} = \sqrt[3]{125} = 5$

The denominator is the index.

c. $-16^{\frac{1}{4}} = -(\sqrt[4]{16}) = -2$

The base is 16 and the negative sign is not affected by the exponent.

d. $(-27)^{\frac{1}{3}} = \sqrt[3]{-27} = -3$

Parentheses show that the base is −27 and that the negative sign is affected by the exponent.

e. $64^{-\frac{1}{3}} = \dfrac{1}{64^{\frac{1}{3}}} = \dfrac{1}{\sqrt[3]{64}} = \dfrac{1}{4}$

✓ Check Point **10** Simplify:

a. $25^{\frac{1}{2}}$ **b.** $8^{\frac{1}{3}}$ **c.** $-81^{\frac{1}{4}}$ **d.** $(-8)^{\frac{1}{3}}$ **e.** $27^{-\frac{1}{3}}$.

In Example 10 and Check Point 10, each rational exponent had a numerator of 1. If the numerator is some other integer, we still want to multiply exponents when raising a power to a power. For this reason,

$$a^{\frac{2}{3}} = \left(a^{\frac{1}{3}}\right)^2 \quad \text{and} \quad a^{\frac{2}{3}} = \left(a^2\right)^{\frac{1}{3}}.$$

This means $(\sqrt[3]{a})^2$. This means $\sqrt[3]{a^2}$.

Thus,

$$a^{\frac{2}{3}} = \left(\sqrt[3]{a}\right)^2 = \sqrt[3]{a^2}.$$

Do you see that the denominator, 3, of the rational exponent is the same as the index of the radical? The numerator, 2, of the rational exponent serves as an exponent in each of the two radical forms. We generalize these ideas with the following definition:

The Definition of $a^{\frac{m}{n}}$

If $\sqrt[n]{a}$ represents a real number and $\dfrac{m}{n}$ is a positive rational number, $n \geq 2$, then

$$a^{\frac{m}{n}} = \left(\sqrt[n]{a}\right)^m.$$

Also,

$$a^{\frac{m}{n}} = \sqrt[n]{a^m}.$$

Furthermore, if $a^{-\frac{m}{n}}$ is a nonzero real number, then

$$a^{-\frac{m}{n}} = \dfrac{1}{a^{\frac{m}{n}}}.$$

The first form of the definition of $a^{\frac{m}{n}}$, shown again below, involves taking the root first. This form is often preferable because smaller numbers are involved. Notice that the rational exponent consists of two parts, indicated by the following voice balloons:

The numerator is the exponent.

$$a^{\frac{m}{n}} = \left(\sqrt[n]{a}\right)^m.$$

The denominator is the radical's index.

(EXAMPLE 11) **Using the Definition of $a^{\frac{m}{n}}$**

Simplify: **a.** $27^{\frac{2}{3}}$ **b.** $9^{\frac{3}{2}}$ **c.** $81^{-\frac{3}{4}}$.

Solution

a. $27^{\frac{2}{3}} = \left(\sqrt[3]{27}\right)^2 = 3^2 = 9$

b. $9^{\frac{3}{2}} = \left(\sqrt{9}\right)^3 = 3^3 = 27$

c. $81^{-\frac{3}{4}} = \dfrac{1}{81^{\frac{3}{4}}} = \dfrac{1}{\left(\sqrt[4]{81}\right)^3} = \dfrac{1}{3^3} = \dfrac{1}{27}$

Technology

Here are the calculator keystroke sequences for $81^{-\frac{3}{4}}$:

Many Scientific Calculators

81 $\boxed{y^x}$ $\boxed{(}$ 3 $\boxed{+/_-}$ $\boxed{\div}$ 4 $\boxed{)}$ $\boxed{=}$

Many Graphing Calculators

81 $\boxed{\wedge}$ $\boxed{(}$ $\boxed{(-)}$ 3 $\boxed{\div}$ 4 $\boxed{)}$ $\boxed{\text{ENTER}}$.

✓ Check Point **11** Simplify:

a. $27^{\frac{4}{3}}$ **b.** $4^{\frac{3}{2}}$ **c.** $32^{-\frac{2}{5}}$.

Properties of exponents can be applied to expressions containing rational exponents.

(EXAMPLE 12) **Simplifying Expressions with Rational Exponents**

Simplify using properties of exponents:

a. $\left(5x^{\frac{1}{2}}\right)\left(7x^{\frac{3}{4}}\right)$ **b.** $\dfrac{32x^{\frac{5}{3}}}{16x^{\frac{3}{4}}}$.

Solution

a. $\left(5x^{\frac{1}{2}}\right)\left(7x^{\frac{3}{4}}\right) = 5 \cdot 7x^{\frac{1}{2}} \cdot x^{\frac{3}{4}}$ Group numerical factors and group variable factors with the same base.

$= 35x^{\frac{1}{2}+\frac{3}{4}}$ When multiplying expressions with the same base, add the exponents.

$= 35x^{\frac{5}{4}}$ $\frac{1}{2} + \frac{3}{4} = \frac{2}{4} + \frac{3}{4} = \frac{5}{4}$

b. $\dfrac{32x^{\frac{5}{3}}}{16x^{\frac{3}{4}}} = \left(\dfrac{32}{16}\right)\left(\dfrac{x^{\frac{5}{3}}}{x^{\frac{3}{4}}}\right)$ Group numerical factors and group variable factors with the same base.

$= 2x^{\frac{5}{3}-\frac{3}{4}}$ When dividing expressions with the same base, subtract the exponents.

$= 2x^{\frac{11}{12}}$ $\frac{5}{3} - \frac{3}{4} = \frac{20}{12} - \frac{9}{12} = \frac{11}{12}$

✓ Check Point **12** Simplify using properties of exponents:

a. $\left(2x^{\frac{4}{3}}\right)\left(5x^{\frac{8}{3}}\right)$ **b.** $\dfrac{20x^4}{5x^{\frac{3}{2}}}$.

Rational exponents are sometimes useful for simplifying radicals by reducing the index.

> (EXAMPLE 13) **Reducing the Index of a Radical**

Simplify: $\sqrt[9]{x^3}$.

Solution

$$\sqrt[9]{x^3} = x^{\frac{3}{9}} = x^{\frac{1}{3}} = \sqrt[3]{x}$$

✓ Check Point **13** Simplify: $\sqrt[6]{x^3}$.

A Radical Idea: Time Is Relative

Salvador Dali "The Persistence of Memory" 1931, oil on canvas, $9\frac{1}{2} \times 13$ in. (24.1 × 33 cm). The Museum of Modern Art/Licensed by Scala-Art Resource, N.Y. © 1999 Demart Pro Arte, Geneva/Artists Rights Society (ARS), New York.

What does travel in space have to do with radicals? Imagine that in the future we will be able to travel at velocities approaching the speed of light (approximately 186,000 miles per second). According to Einstein's theory of special relativity, time would pass more quickly on Earth than it would in the moving spaceship. The special-relativity equation

$$R_a = R_f\sqrt{1 - \left(\frac{v}{c}\right)^2}$$

gives the aging rate of an astronaut, R_a, relative to the aging rate of a friend, R_f, on Earth. In this formula, v is the astronaut's speed and c is the speed of light. As the astronaut's speed approaches the speed of light, we can substitute c for v.

$R_a = R_f\sqrt{1 - \left(\frac{v}{c}\right)^2}$ Einstein's equation gives the aging rate of an astronaut, R_a, relative to the aging rate of a friend, R_f, on Earth.

$R_a = R_f\sqrt{1 - \left(\frac{c}{c}\right)^2}$ The velocity, v, is approaching the speed of light, c, so let $v = c$.

$\quad = R_f\sqrt{1 - 1}$ $\left(\frac{c}{c}\right)^2 = 1^2 = 1 \cdot 1 = 1$

$\quad = R_f\sqrt{0}$ Simplify the radicand: $1 - 1 = 0$.

$\quad = R_f \cdot 0$ $\sqrt{0} = 0$

$\quad = 0$ Multiply: $R_f \cdot 0 = 0$.

Close to the speed of light, the astronaut's aging rate, R_a, relative to a friend, R_f, on Earth is nearly 0. What does this mean? As we age here on Earth, the space traveler would barely get older. The space traveler would return to an unknown futuristic world in which friends and loved ones would be long gone.

Exercise Set P.3

Practice Exercises

Evaluate each expression in Exercises 1–12, or indicate that the root is not a real number.

1. $\sqrt{36}$

2. $\sqrt{25}$

3. $-\sqrt{36}$

4. $-\sqrt{25}$

5. $\sqrt{-36}$

6. $\sqrt{-25}$

7. $\sqrt{25 - 16}$

8. $\sqrt{144 + 25}$

9. $\sqrt{25} - \sqrt{16}$

10. $\sqrt{144} + \sqrt{25}$

11. $\sqrt{(-13)^2}$

12. $\sqrt{(-17)^2}$

Use the product rule to simplify the expressions in Exercises 13–22. In Exercises 17–22, assume that variables represent nonnegative real numbers.

13. $\sqrt{50}$

14. $\sqrt{27}$

15. $\sqrt{45x^2}$

16. $\sqrt{125x^2}$

17. $\sqrt{2x} \cdot \sqrt{6x}$

18. $\sqrt{10x} \cdot \sqrt{8x}$

19. $\sqrt{x^3}$

20. $\sqrt{y^3}$

21. $\sqrt{2x^2} \cdot \sqrt{6x}$

22. $\sqrt{6x} \cdot \sqrt{3x^2}$

Use the quotient rule to simplify the expressions in Exercises 23–32. Assume that $x > 0$.

23. $\sqrt{\dfrac{1}{81}}$

24. $\sqrt{\dfrac{1}{49}}$

25. $\sqrt{\dfrac{49}{16}}$

26. $\sqrt{\dfrac{121}{9}}$

27. $\dfrac{\sqrt{48x^3}}{\sqrt{3x}}$

28. $\dfrac{\sqrt{72x^3}}{\sqrt{8x}}$

29. $\dfrac{\sqrt{150x^4}}{\sqrt{3x}}$

30. $\dfrac{\sqrt{24x^4}}{\sqrt{3x}}$

31. $\dfrac{\sqrt{200x^3}}{\sqrt{10x^{-1}}}$

32. $\dfrac{\sqrt{500x^3}}{\sqrt{10x^{-1}}}$

In Exercises 33–44, add or subtract terms whenever possible.

33. $7\sqrt{3} + 6\sqrt{3}$

34. $8\sqrt{5} + 11\sqrt{5}$

35. $6\sqrt{17x} - 8\sqrt{17x}$

36. $4\sqrt{13x} - 6\sqrt{13x}$

37. $\sqrt{8} + 3\sqrt{2}$

38. $\sqrt{20} + 6\sqrt{5}$

39. $\sqrt{50x} - \sqrt{8x}$

40. $\sqrt{63x} - \sqrt{28x}$

41. $3\sqrt{18} + 5\sqrt{50}$

42. $4\sqrt{12} - 2\sqrt{75}$

43. $3\sqrt{8} - \sqrt{32} + 3\sqrt{72} - \sqrt{75}$

44. $3\sqrt{54} - 2\sqrt{24} - \sqrt{96} + 4\sqrt{63}$

In Exercises 45–54, rationalize the denominator.

45. $\dfrac{1}{\sqrt{7}}$

46. $\dfrac{2}{\sqrt{10}}$

47. $\dfrac{\sqrt{2}}{\sqrt{5}}$

48. $\dfrac{\sqrt{7}}{\sqrt{3}}$

49. $\dfrac{13}{3 + \sqrt{11}}$

50. $\dfrac{3}{3 + \sqrt{7}}$

51. $\dfrac{7}{\sqrt{5} - 2}$

52. $\dfrac{5}{\sqrt{3} - 1}$

53. $\dfrac{6}{\sqrt{5} + \sqrt{3}}$

54. $\dfrac{11}{\sqrt{7} - \sqrt{3}}$

Evaluate each expression in Exercises 55–66, or indicate that the root is not a real number.

55. $\sqrt[3]{125}$

56. $\sqrt[3]{8}$

57. $\sqrt[3]{-8}$

58. $\sqrt[3]{-125}$

59. $\sqrt[4]{-16}$

60. $\sqrt[4]{-81}$

61. $\sqrt[4]{(-3)^4}$

62. $\sqrt[4]{(-2)^4}$

63. $\sqrt[5]{(-3)^5}$

64. $\sqrt[5]{(-2)^5}$

65. $\sqrt[5]{-\dfrac{1}{32}}$

66. $\sqrt[6]{\dfrac{1}{64}}$

Simplify the radical expressions in Exercises 67–74.

67. $\sqrt[3]{32}$

68. $\sqrt[3]{150}$

69. $\sqrt[3]{x^4}$

70. $\sqrt[3]{x^5}$

71. $\sqrt[3]{9} \cdot \sqrt[3]{6}$

72. $\sqrt[3]{12} \cdot \sqrt[3]{4}$

73. $\dfrac{\sqrt[5]{64x^6}}{\sqrt[5]{2x}}$

74. $\dfrac{\sqrt[4]{162x^5}}{\sqrt[4]{2x}}$

In Exercises 75–82, add or subtract terms whenever possible.

75. $4\sqrt[5]{2} + 3\sqrt[5]{2}$

76. $6\sqrt[5]{3} + 2\sqrt[5]{3}$

77. $5\sqrt[3]{16} + \sqrt[3]{54}$

78. $3\sqrt[3]{24} + \sqrt[3]{81}$

79. $\sqrt[3]{54xy^3} - y\sqrt[3]{128x}$

80. $\sqrt[3]{24xy^3} - y\sqrt[3]{81x}$

81. $\sqrt{2} + \sqrt[3]{8}$

82. $\sqrt{3} + \sqrt[3]{15}$

In Exercises 83–90, evaluate each expression without using a calculator.

83. $36^{\frac{1}{2}}$

84. $121^{\frac{1}{2}}$

85. $8^{\frac{1}{3}}$

86. $27^{\frac{1}{3}}$

87. $125^{\frac{2}{3}}$

88. $8^{\frac{2}{3}}$

89. $32^{-\frac{4}{5}}$

90. $16^{-\frac{5}{2}}$

In Exercises 91–100, simplify using properties of exponents.

91. $\left(7x^{\frac{1}{3}}\right)\left(2x^{\frac{1}{4}}\right)$

92. $\left(3x^{\frac{2}{3}}\right)\left(4x^{\frac{3}{4}}\right)$

93. $\dfrac{20x^{\frac{1}{2}}}{5x^{\frac{1}{4}}}$

94. $\dfrac{72x^{\frac{3}{4}}}{9x^{\frac{1}{3}}}$

95. $\left(x^{\frac{2}{3}}\right)^3$

96. $\left(x^{\frac{4}{5}}\right)^5$

97. $(25x^4y^6)^{\frac{1}{2}}$

98. $(125x^9y^6)^{\frac{1}{3}}$

99. $\dfrac{(3y^{\frac{1}{4}})^3}{y^{\frac{1}{12}}}$

100. $\dfrac{(2y^{\frac{1}{5}})^4}{y^{\frac{3}{10}}}$

In Exercises 101–108, simplify by reducing the index of the radical.

101. $\sqrt[4]{5^2}$

102. $\sqrt[4]{7^2}$

103. $\sqrt[3]{x^6}$

104. $\sqrt[4]{x^{12}}$

105. $\sqrt[6]{x^4}$

106. $\sqrt[9]{x^6}$

107. $\sqrt[9]{x^6y^3}$

108. $\sqrt[12]{x^4y^8}$

Practice Plus

In Exercises 109–110, evaluate each expression.

109. $\sqrt[3]{\sqrt[4]{16} + \sqrt{625}}$

110. $\sqrt[3]{\sqrt{\sqrt{169} + \sqrt{9}} + \sqrt{\sqrt[3]{1000} + \sqrt[3]{216}}}$

In Exercises 111–114, simplify each expression. Assume that all variables represent positive numbers.

111. $(49x^{-2}y^4)^{-\frac{1}{2}}(xy^{\frac{1}{2}})$

112. $(8x^{-6}y^3)^{\frac{1}{3}}(x^{\frac{5}{6}}y^{-\frac{1}{3}})^6$

113. $\left(\dfrac{x^{-\frac{5}{4}}y^{\frac{1}{3}}}{x^{-\frac{3}{4}}}\right)^{-6}$

114. $\left(\dfrac{x^{\frac{1}{2}}y^{-\frac{7}{4}}}{y^{-\frac{5}{4}}}\right)^{-4}$

Application Exercises

115. The bar graph shows spam as a percentage of e-mail for four selected years. The data can be modeled by

$$y = 20.8\sqrt{x} + 21,$$

where y is the percentage of e-mail that is spam and x is the number of years after 1999.

Spam as a Percentage of e-Mail

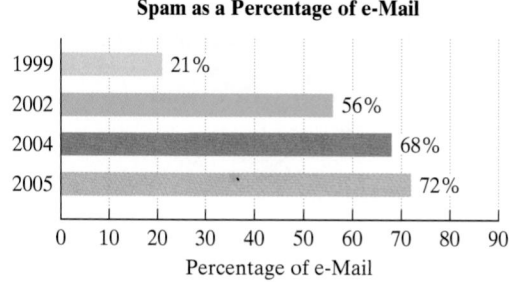

Source: IronPort

a. According to the model, what percentage of e-mail was spam in 2004? Use a calculator and round to the nearest tenth of a percent. Does this underestimate or overestimate the actual percentage given in the bar graph? By how much?

b. According to the model, what percentage of e-mail will be spam in 2011? Round to the nearest tenth of a percent.

116. America is getting older. The graph shows the projected elderly U.S. population for ages 65–84 and for ages 85 and older.

Projected Elderly United States Population

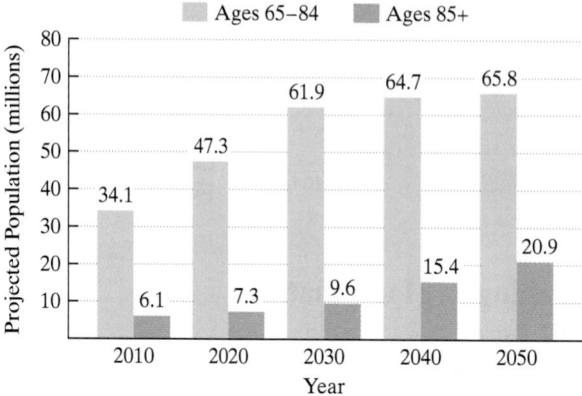

Source: U.S. Census Bureau

The formula $E = 5\sqrt{x} + 34.1$ models the projected number of elderly Americans ages 65–84, E, in millions, x years after 2010.

a. Use the formula to find the projected increase in the number of Americans ages 65–84, in millions, from 2020 to 2050. Express this difference in simplified radical form.

b. Use a calculator and write your answer in part (a) to the nearest tenth. Does this rounded decimal overestimate or underestimate the difference in the projected data shown by the bar graph? By how much?

117. The early Greeks believed that the most pleasing of all rectangles were **golden rectangles**, whose ratio of width to height is

$$\frac{w}{h} = \frac{2}{\sqrt{5} - 1}.$$

The Parthenon at Athens fits into a golden rectangle once the triangular pediment is reconstructed.

Rationalize the denominator of the golden ratio. Then use a calculator and find the ratio of width to height, correct to the nearest hundredth, in golden rectangles.

118. Use Einstein's special-relativity equation

$$R_a = R_f\sqrt{1 - \left(\frac{v}{c}\right)^2},$$

described in the essay on page 45, to solve this exercise. You are moving at 90% of the speed of light. Substitute $0.9c$ for v, your velocity, in the equation. What is your aging rate, correct to two decimal places, relative to a friend on Earth? If you are gone for 44 weeks, approximately how many weeks have passed for your friend?

The perimeter, P, of a rectangle with length l and width w is given by the formula P = 2l + 2w. The area, A, is given by the formula A = lw. In Exercises 119–120, use these formulas to find the perimeter and area of each rectangle. Express answers in simplified radical form. Remember that perimeter is measured in linear units, such as feet or meters, and area is measured in square units, such as square feet, ft², or square meters, m².

119. $\sqrt{125}$ feet

120. $4\sqrt{20}$ feet

$2\sqrt{20}$ feet

$\sqrt{80}$ feet

Writing in Mathematics

121. Explain how to simplify $\sqrt{10} \cdot \sqrt{5}$.

122. Explain how to add $\sqrt{3} + \sqrt{12}$.

123. Describe what it means to rationalize a denominator. Use both $\dfrac{1}{\sqrt{5}}$ and $\dfrac{1}{5 + \sqrt{5}}$ in your explanation.

124. What difference is there in simplifying $\sqrt[3]{(-5)^3}$ and $\sqrt[4]{(-5)^4}$?

125. What does $a^{\frac{m}{n}}$ mean?

126. Describe the kinds of numbers that have rational fifth roots.

127. Why must a and b represent nonnegative numbers when we write $\sqrt{a} \cdot \sqrt{b} = \sqrt{ab}$? Is it necessary to use this restriction in the case of $\sqrt[3]{a} \cdot \sqrt[3]{b} = \sqrt[3]{ab}$? Explain.

128. Read the essay on page 45. The future is now: You have the opportunity to explore the cosmos in a starship traveling near the speed of light. The experience will enable you to understand the mysteries of the universe in deeply personal ways, transporting you to unimagined levels of knowing and being. The down side: You return from your two-year journey to a futuristic world in which friends and loved ones are long gone. Do you explore space or stay here on Earth? What are the reasons for your choice?

Critical Thinking Exercises

Make Sense? *In Exercises 129–132, determine whether each statement makes sense or does not make sense, and explain your reasoning.*

129. The joke in this Peanuts cartoon would be more effective if Woodstock had rationalized the denominator correctly in the last frame.

PEANUTS © United Feature Syndicate, Inc.

130. Using my calculator, I determined that $6^7 = 279{,}936$, so 6 must be a seventh root of 279,936.

131. I simplified the terms of $2\sqrt{20} + 4\sqrt{75}$, and then I was able to add the like radicals.

132. When I use the definition for $a^{\frac{m}{n}}$, I usually prefer to first raise a to the m power because smaller numbers are involved.

In Exercises 133–136, determine whether each statement is true or false. If the statement is false, make the necessary change(s) to produce a true statement.

133. $7^{\frac{1}{2}} \cdot 7^{\frac{1}{2}} = 49$

134. $8^{-\frac{1}{3}} = -2$

135. The cube root of -8 is not a real number.

136. $\dfrac{\sqrt{20}}{8} = \dfrac{\sqrt{10}}{4}$

In Exercises 137–138, fill in each box to make the statement true.

137. $\left(5 + \sqrt{}\right)\left(5 - \sqrt{}\right) = 22$

138. $\sqrt{x^{}} = 5x^7$

139. Find exact value of $\sqrt{13 + \sqrt{2} + \dfrac{7}{3 + \sqrt{2}}}$ without the use of a calculator.

140. Place the correct symbol, $>$ or $<$, in the shaded area between the given numbers. *Do not use a calculator.* Then check your result with a calculator.

 a. $3^{\frac{1}{2}}$ ▨ $3^{\frac{1}{3}}$

 b. $\sqrt{7} + \sqrt{18}$ ▨ $\sqrt{7 + 18}$

141. a. A mathematics professor recently purchased a birthday cake for her son with the inscription

 Happy $\left(2^{\frac{5}{2}} \cdot 2^{\frac{3}{4}} \div 2^{\frac{1}{4}}\right)$th Birthday.

 How old is the son?

 b. The birthday boy, excited by the inscription on the cake, tried to wolf down the whole thing. Professor Mom, concerned about the possible metamorphosis of her son into a blimp, exclaimed, "Hold on! It is your birthday, so why not take $\dfrac{8^{-\frac{4}{3}} + 2^{-2}}{16^{-\frac{3}{4}} + 2^{-1}}$ of the cake? I'll eat half of what's left over." How much of the cake did the professor eat?

Preview Exercises

Exercises 142–144 will help you prepare for the material covered in the next section.

142. Multiply: $(2x^3y^2)(5x^4y^7)$.

143. Use the distributive property to multiply: $2x^4(8x^4 + 3x)$.

144. Simplify and express the answer in descending powers of x:

$$2x(x^2 + 4x + 5) + 3(x^2 + 4x + 5).$$

Section **P.4**

Objectives

1. Understand the vocabulary of polynomials.
2. Add and subtract polynomials.
3. Multiply polynomials.
4. Use FOIL in polynomial multiplication.
5. Use special products in polynomial multiplication.
6. Perform operations with polynomials in several variables.

Polynomials

Can that be Axl, your author's yellow lab, sharing a special moment with a baby chick? And if it is (it is), what possible relevance can this have to polynomials? An answer is promised before you reach the exercise set. For now, we open the section by defining and describing polynomials.

Old Dog ... New Chicks

How We Define Polynomials

More education results in a higher income. The mathematical models

$$M = -18x^3 + 923x^2 - 9603x + 48{,}446$$

$$\text{and} \quad W = 17x^3 - 450x^2 + 6392x - 14{,}764$$

describe the median, or middlemost, annual income for men, M, and women, W, who have completed x years of education. We'll be working with these models and the data upon which they are based in the exercise set.

The algebraic expressions that appear on the right sides of the models are examples of *polynomials*. A **polynomial** is a single term or the sum of two or more terms containing variables with whole-number exponents. The polynomials above each contain four terms. Equations containing polynomials are used in such diverse areas as science, business, medicine, psychology, and sociology. In this section, we review basic ideas about polynomials and their operations.

1 Understand the vocabulary of polynomials.

How We Describe Polynomials

Consider the polynomial

$$7x^3 - 9x^2 + 13x - 6.$$

We can express this polynomial as

$$7x^3 + (-9x^2) + 13x + (-6).$$

The polynomial contains four terms. It is customary to write the terms in the order of descending powers of the variable. This is the **standard form** of a polynomial.

Some polynomials contain only one variable. Each term of such a polynomial in x is of the form ax^n. If $a \neq 0$, the **degree** of ax^n is n. For example, the degree of the term $7x^3$ is 3.

Study Tip

We can express 0 in many ways, including $0x$, $0x^2$, and $0x^3$. It is impossible to assign a unique exponent to the variable. This is why 0 has no defined degree.

The Degree of ax^n

If $a \neq 0$, the degree of ax^n is n. The degree of a nonzero constant is 0. The constant 0 has no defined degree.

Here is an example of a polynomial and the degree of each of its four terms:

$$6x^4 - 3x^3 + 2x - 5.$$

degree 4 degree 3 degree 1 degree of nonzero constant: 0

Notice that the exponent on x for the term $2x$, meaning $2x^1$, is understood to be 1. For this reason, the degree of $2x$ is 1. You can think of -5 as $-5x^0$; thus, its degree is 0.

A polynomial is simplified when it contains no grouping symbols and no like terms. A simplified polynomial that has exactly one term is called a **monomial**. A **binomial** is a simplified polynomial that has two terms. A **trinomial** is a simplified polynomial with three terms. Simplified polynomials with four or more terms have no special names.

The **degree of a polynomial** is the greatest degree of all the terms of the polynomial. For example, $4x^2 + 3x$ is a binomial of degree 2 because the degree of the first term is 2, and the degree of the other term is less than 2. Also, $7x^5 - 2x^2 + 4$ is a trinomial of degree 5 because the degree of the first term is 5, and the degrees of the other terms are less than 5.

Up to now, we have used x to represent the variable in a polynomial. However, any letter can be used. For example,

- $7x^5 - 3x^3 + 8$ is a polynomial (in x) of degree 5. Because there are three terms, the polynomial is a trinomial.
- $6y^3 + 4y^2 - y + 3$ is a polynomial (in y) of degree 3. Because there are four terms, the polynomial has no special name.
- $z^7 + \sqrt{2}$ is a polynomial (in z) of degree 7. Because there are two terms, the polynomial is a binomial.

We can tie together the threads of our discussion with the formal definition of a polynomial in one variable. In this definition, the coefficients of the terms are represented by a_n (read "a sub n"), a_{n-1} (read "a sub n minus 1"), a_{n-2}, and so on. The small letters to the lower right of each a are called **subscripts** and are *not exponents*. Subscripts are used to distinguish one constant from another when a large and undetermined number of such constants are needed.

Definition of a Polynomial in x

A **polynomial in x** is an algebraic expression of the form

$$a_n x^n + a_{n-1} x^{n-1} + a_{n-2} x^{n-2} + \cdots + a_1 x + a_0,$$

where $a_n, a_{n-1}, a_{n-2}, \ldots, a_1$, and a_0 are real numbers, $a_n \neq 0$, and n is a non-negative integer. The polynomial is of **degree n,** a_n is the **leading coefficient**, and a_0 is the **constant term**.

② Add and subtract polynomials.

Adding and Subtracting Polynomials

Polynomials are added and subtracted by combining like terms. For example, we can combine the monomials $-9x^3$ and $13x^3$ using addition as follows:

$$-9x^3 + 13x^3 = (-9 + 13)x^3 = 4x^3.$$

These like terms both contain x to the third power.

Add coefficients and keep the same variable factor, x^3.

EXAMPLE 1 Adding and Subtracting Polynomials

Perform the indicated operations and simplify:

a. $(-9x^3 + 7x^2 - 5x + 3) + (13x^3 + 2x^2 - 8x - 6)$

b. $(7x^3 - 8x^2 + 9x - 6) - (2x^3 - 6x^2 - 3x + 9)$.

Solution

a. $(-9x^3 + 7x^2 - 5x + 3) + (13x^3 + 2x^2 - 8x - 6)$

$= (-9x^3 + 13x^3) + (7x^2 + 2x^2) + (-5x - 8x) + (3 - 6)$ Group like terms.

$= 4x^3 + 9x^2 + (-13x) + (-3)$ Combine like terms.

$= 4x^3 + 9x^2 - 13x - 3$ Simplify.

b. $(7x^3 - 8x^2 + 9x - 6) - (2x^3 - 6x^2 - 3x + 9)$

> Change the sign of each coefficient.

$= (7x^3 - 8x^2 + 9x - 6) + (-2x^3 + 6x^2 + 3x - 9)$ Rewrite subtraction as addition of the additive inverse.

$= (7x^3 - 2x^3) + (-8x^2 + 6x^2) + (9x + 3x) + (-6 - 9)$ Group like terms.

$= 5x^3 + (-2x^2) + 12x + (-15)$ Combine like terms.

$= 5x^3 - 2x^2 + 12x - 15$ Simplify. ●

Study Tip

You can also arrange like terms in columns and combine vertically:

$$7x^3 - 8x^2 + 9x - 6$$
$$\underline{-2x^3 + 6x^2 + 3x - 9}$$
$$5x^3 - 2x^2 + 12x - 15$$

The like terms can be combined by adding their coefficients and keeping the same variable factor.

⊘ Check Point **1** Perform the indicated operations and simplify:

a. $(-17x^3 + 4x^2 - 11x - 5) + (16x^3 - 3x^2 + 3x - 15)$

b. $(13x^3 - 9x^2 - 7x + 1) - (-7x^3 + 2x^2 - 5x + 9)$.

③ Multiply polynomials.

Study Tip

Don't confuse adding and multiplying monomials.

Addition:
$$5x^4 + 6x^4 = 11x^4$$

Multiplication:
$$(5x^4)(6x^4) = (5 \cdot 6)(x^4 \cdot x^4)$$
$$= 30x^{4+4}$$
$$= 30x^8$$

Only like terms can be added or subtracted, but unlike terms may be multiplied.

Addition:
$5x^4 + 3x^2$ cannot be simplified.

Multiplication:
$$(5x^4)(3x^2) = (5 \cdot 3)(x^4 \cdot x^2)$$
$$= 15x^{4+2}$$
$$= 15x^6$$

Multiplying Polynomials

The product of two monomials is obtained by using properties of exponents. For example,

$$(-8x^6)(5x^3) = -8 \cdot 5x^{6+3} = -40x^9.$$

> Multiply coefficients and add exponents.

Furthermore, we can use the distributive property to multiply a monomial and a polynomial that is not a monomial. For example,

$$3x^4(2x^3 - 7x + 3) = 3x^4 \cdot 2x^3 - 3x^4 \cdot 7x + 3x^4 \cdot 3 = 6x^7 - 21x^5 + 9x^4.$$

Monomial
Trinomial

How do we multiply two polynomials if neither is a monomial? For example, consider

$$(2x + 3)(x^2 + 4x + 5).$$

Binomial
Trinomial

One way to perform $(2x + 3)(x^2 + 4x + 5)$ is to distribute $2x$ throughout the trinomial

$$2x(x^2 + 4x + 5)$$

and 3 throughout the trinomial

$$3(x^2 + 4x + 5).$$

Then combine the like terms that result.

> **Multiplying Polynomials When Neither Is a Monomial**
>
> Multiply each term of one polynomial by each term of the other polynomial. Then combine like terms.

(**EXAMPLE 2**) **Multiplying a Binomial and a Trinomial**

Multiply: $(2x + 3)(x^2 + 4x + 5)$.

Solution

$(2x + 3)(x^2 + 4x + 5)$

$= 2x(x^2 + 4x + 5) + 3(x^2 + 4x + 5)$ Multiply the trinomial by each term of the binomial.

$= 2x \cdot x^2 + 2x \cdot 4x + 2x \cdot 5 + 3x^2 + 3 \cdot 4x + 3 \cdot 5$ Use the distributive property.

$= 2x^3 + 8x^2 + 10x + 3x^2 + 12x + 15$ Multiply monomials: Multiply coefficients and add exponents.

$= 2x^3 + 11x^2 + 22x + 15$ Combine like terms: $8x^2 + 3x^2 = 11x^2$ and $10x + 12x = 22x$. ●

Another method for performing the multiplication is to use a vertical format similar to that used for multiplying whole numbers.

$$
\begin{array}{r}
x^2 + 4x + 5 \\
2x + 3 \\
\hline
3x^2 + 12x + 15 \\
2x^3 + 8x^2 + 10x \\
\hline
2x^3 + 11x^2 + 22x + 15
\end{array}
$$

$3(x^2 + 4x + 5)$

$2x(x^2 + 4x + 5)$

Write like terms in the same column.

Combine like terms.

✓ Check Point **2** Multiply: $(5x - 2)(3x^2 - 5x + 4)$.

④ Use FOIL in polynomial multiplication.

The Product of Two Binomials: FOIL

Frequently, we need to find the product of two binomials. One way to perform this multiplication is to distribute each term in the first binomial through the second binomial. For example, we can find the product of the binomials $3x + 2$ and $4x + 5$ as follows:

$$(3x + 2)(4x + 5) = 3x(4x + 5) + 2(4x + 5)$$

Distribute $3x$ over $4x + 5$. Distribute 2 over $4x + 5$.

$$= 3x(4x) + 3x(5) + 2(4x) + 2(5)$$

$$= 12x^2 + 15x + 8x + 10.$$

We'll combine these like terms later. For now, our interest is in how to obtain *each* of these four terms.

We can also find the product of $3x + 2$ and $4x + 5$ using a method called FOIL, which is based on our work shown at the bottom of the previous page. Any two binomials can be quickly multiplied by using the FOIL method, in which **F** represents the product of the **first** terms in each binomial, **O** represents the product of the **outside** terms, **I** represents the product of the **inside** terms, and **L** represents the product of the **last**, or second, terms in each binomial. For example, we can use the FOIL method to find the product of the binomials $3x + 2$ and $4x + 5$ as follows:

first \qquad last

F \quad O \quad I \quad L

$$(3x + 2)(4x + 5) = 12x^2 + 15x + 8x + 10$$

inside

outside

| Product of First terms | Product of Outside terms | Product of Inside terms | Product of Last terms |

$$= 12x^2 + 23x + 10 \qquad \text{Combine like terms.}$$

In general, here's how to use the FOIL method to find the product of $ax + b$ and $cx + d$:

Using the FOIL Method to Multiply Binomials

first \qquad last

F \quad O \quad I \quad L

$$(ax + b)(cx + d) = ax \cdot cx + ax \cdot d + b \cdot cx + b \cdot d$$

inside

outside

| Product of First terms | Product of Outside terms | Product of Inside terms | Product of Last terms |

(**EXAMPLE 3**) **Using the FOIL Method**

Multiply: $(3x + 4)(5x - 3)$.

Solution

first \qquad last

F \quad O \quad I \quad L

$$(3x + 4)(5x - 3) = 3x \cdot 5x + 3x(-3) + 4 \cdot 5x + 4(-3)$$

inside

outside

$$= 15x^2 - 9x + 20x - 12$$

$$= 15x^2 + 11x - 12 \qquad \text{Combine like terms.}$$

✓ Check Point **3** Multiply: $(7x - 5)(4x - 3)$.

⑤ Use special products in polynomial multiplication.

Multiplying the Sum and Difference of Two Terms

We can use the FOIL method to multiply $A + B$ and $A - B$ as follows:

F \quad O \quad I \quad L

$$(A + B)(A - B) = A^2 - AB + AB - B^2 = A^2 - B^2.$$

Notice that the outside and inside products have a sum of 0 and the terms cancel. The FOIL multiplication provides us with a quick rule for multiplying the sum and difference of two terms, referred to as a *special-product formula*.

The Product of the Sum and Difference of Two Terms

$$(A + B)(A - B) = A^2 - B^2$$

| The product of the sum and the difference of the same two terms | is | the square of the first term minus the square of the second term. |

EXAMPLE 4 Finding the Product of the Sum and Difference of Two Terms

Multiply:

a. $(4y + 3)(4y - 3)$ **b.** $(5a^4 + 6)(5a^4 - 6)$.

Solution Use the special-product formula shown.

$$(A + B)(A - B) \quad = \quad A^2 \quad - \quad B^2$$

| | First term squared | − | Second term squared | = | Product |

a. $(4y + 3)(4y - 3) \quad = \quad (4y)^2 - 3^2 \quad = \quad 16y^2 - 9$

b. $(5a^4 + 6)(5a^4 - 6) \quad = \quad (5a^4)^2 - 6^2 \quad = \quad 25a^8 - 36$

○ Check Point **4** Multiply:

a. $(7x + 8)(7x - 8)$ **b.** $(2y^3 - 5)(2y^3 + 5)$.

The Square of a Binomial

Let us find $(A + B)^2$, the square of a binomial sum. To do so, we begin with the FOIL method and look for a general rule.

$$
\begin{array}{c}
\qquad\qquad\quad \text{F} \quad\quad \text{O} \quad\quad \text{I} \quad\quad \text{L} \\
(A + B)^2 = (A + B)(A + B) = A \cdot A + A \cdot B + A \cdot B + B \cdot B \\
= A^2 + 2AB + B^2
\end{array}
$$

This result implies the following rule, which is another example of a special-product formula:

The Square of a Binomial Sum

$$(A + B)^2 \quad = \quad A^2 \quad + \quad 2AB \quad + \quad B^2$$

| The square of a binomial sum | is | first term squared | plus | 2 times the product of the terms | plus | last term squared. |

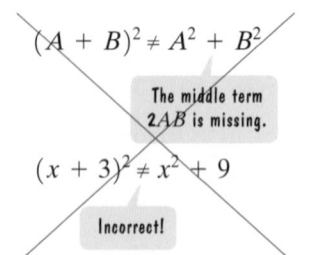

EXAMPLE 5 Finding the Square of a Binomial Sum

Multiply:

a. $(x + 3)^2$ **b.** $(3x + 7)^2$.

Solution Use the special-product formula shown.

$$(A + B)^2 = \quad A^2 \quad + \quad 2AB \quad + \quad B^2$$

	(First Term)²	+	2 · Product of the Terms	+	(Last Term)²	= Product
a. $(x + 3)^2 =$	x^2	+	$2 \cdot x \cdot 3$	+	3^2	$= x^2 + 6x + 9$
b. $(3x + 7)^2 =$	$(3x)^2$	+	$2(3x)(7)$	+	7^2	$= 9x^2 + 42x + 49$

Check Point **5** Multiply:

a. $(x + 10)^2$ **b.** $(5x + 4)^2$.

A similar pattern occurs for $(A - B)^2$, the square of a binomial difference. Using the FOIL method on $(A - B)^2$, we obtain the following rule:

The Square of a Binomial Difference

$$(A - B)^2 \quad = \quad A^2 \quad - \quad 2AB \quad + \quad B^2$$

| The square of a binomial difference | is | first term squared | minus | 2 times the product of the terms | plus | last term squared. |

EXAMPLE 6 Finding the Square of a Binomial Difference

Multiply:

a. $(x - 4)^2$ **b.** $(5y - 6)^2$.

Solution Use the special-product formula shown.

$$(A - B)^2 = \quad A^2 \quad - \quad 2AB \quad + \quad B^2$$

	(First Term)²	−	2 · Product of the Terms	+	(Last Term)²	= Product
a. $(x - 4)^2 =$	x^2	−	$2 \cdot x \cdot 4$	+	4^2	$= x^2 - 8x + 16$
b. $(5y - 6)^2 =$	$(5y)^2$	−	$2(5y)(6)$	+	6^2	$= 25y^2 - 60y + 36$

Check Point **6** Multiply:

a. $(x - 9)^2$ **b.** $(7x - 3)^2$.

Special Products

There are several products that occur so frequently that it's convenient to memorize the form, or pattern, of these formulas.

Special Products

Let A and B represent real numbers, variables, or algebraic expressions.

Special Product	Example
Sum and Difference of Two Terms	
$(A + B)(A - B) = A^2 - B^2$	$(2x + 3)(2x - 3) = (2x)^2 - 3^2$
	$\qquad\qquad\qquad\quad = 4x^2 - 9$
Squaring a Binomial	
$(A + B)^2 = A^2 + 2AB + B^2$	$(y + 5)^2 = y^2 + 2 \cdot y \cdot 5 + 5^2$
	$\qquad\qquad = y^2 + 10y + 25$
$(A - B)^2 = A^2 - 2AB + B^2$	$(3x - 4)^2$
	$\qquad = (3x)^2 - 2 \cdot 3x \cdot 4 + 4^2$
	$\qquad = 9x^2 - 24x + 16$
Cubing a Binomial	
$(A + B)^3 = A^3 + 3A^2B + 3AB^2 + B^3$	$(x + 4)^3$
	$\qquad = x^3 + 3x^2(4) + 3x(4)^2 + 4^3$
	$\qquad = x^3 + 12x^2 + 48x + 64$
$(A - B)^3 = A^3 - 3A^2B + 3AB^2 - B^3$	$(x - 2)^3$
	$\qquad = x^3 - 3x^2(2) + 3x(2)^2 - 2^3$
	$\qquad = x^3 - 6x^2 + 12x - 8$

Polynomials in Several Variables

⑥ Perform operations with polynomials in several variables.

A **polynomial in two variables**, x and y, contains the sum of one or more monomials in the form $ax^n y^m$. The constant, a, is the **coefficient**. The exponents, n and m, represent whole numbers. The **degree** of the monomial $ax^n y^m$ is $n + m$.

Here is an example of a polynomial in two variables:

The coefficients are 7, −17, 1, −6, and 9.

$$7x^2 y^3 \quad - \quad 17x^4 y^2 \quad + \quad xy \quad - \quad 6y^2 \quad + \quad 9.$$

| Degree of monomial: $2 + 3 = 5$ | Degree of monomial: $4 + 2 = 6$ | Degree of monomial $(1x^1 y^1)$: $1 + 1 = 2$ | Degree of monomial $(-6x^0 y^2)$: $0 + 2 = 2$ | Degree of monomial $(9x^0 y^0)$: $0 + 0 = 0$ |

The **degree of a polynomial in two variables** is the highest degree of all its terms. For the preceding polynomial, the degree is 6.

Polynomials containing two or more variables can be added, subtracted, and multiplied just like polynomials that contain only one variable. For example, we can add the monomials $-7xy^2$ and $13xy^2$ as follows:

$$-7xy^2 + 13xy^2 = (-7 + 13)xy^2 = 6xy^2.$$

These like terms both contain the variable factors x and y^2. Add coefficients and keep the same variable factors, xy^2.

(**EXAMPLE 7**) **Subtracting Polynomials in Two Variables**

Subtract:

$$(5x^3 - 9x^2y + 3xy^2 - 4) - (3x^3 - 6x^2y - 2xy^2 + 3).$$

Solution

$$(5x^3 - 9x^2y + 3xy^2 - 4) - (3x^3 - 6x^2y - 2xy^2 + 3)$$

Change the sign of each coefficient.

$$= (5x^3 - 9x^2y + 3xy^2 - 4) + (-3x^3 + 6x^2y + 2xy^2 - 3)$$

Add the opposite of the polynomial being subtracted.

$$= (5x^3 - 3x^3) + (-9x^2y + 6x^2y) + (3xy^2 + 2xy^2) + (-4 - 3)$$ Group like terms.

$$= 2x^3 - 3x^2y + 5xy^2 - 7$$

Combine like terms by adding coefficients and keeping the same variable factors.

✓ Check Point **7** Subtract: $(x^3 - 4x^2y + 5xy^2 - y^3) - (x^3 - 6x^2y + y^3).$

(**EXAMPLE 8**) **Multiplying Polynomials in Two Variables**

Multiply: **a.** $(x + 4y)(3x - 5y)$ **b.** $(5x + 3y)^2.$

Solution We will perform the multiplication in part (a) using the FOIL method. We will multiply in part (b) using the formula for the square of a binomial sum, $(A + B)^2.$

a. $(x + 4y)(3x - 5y)$ Multiply these binomials using the FOIL method.

F O I L

$$= (x)(3x) + (x)(-5y) + (4y)(3x) + (4y)(-5y)$$
$$= 3x^2 - 5xy + 12xy - 20y^2$$
$$= 3x^2 + 7xy - 20y^2$$ Combine like terms.

$$(A + B)^2 = A^2 + 2 \cdot A \cdot B + B^2$$

b. $(5x + 3y)^2 = (5x)^2 + 2(5x)(3y) + (3y)^2$
$$= 25x^2 + 30xy + 9y^2$$

✓ Check Point **8** Multiply:

a. $(7x - 6y)(3x - y)$ **b.** $(2x + 4y)^2.$

Labrador Retrievers and Polynomial Multiplication

The color of a Labrador retriever is determined by its pair of genes. A single gene is inherited at random from each parent. The black-fur gene, B, is dominant. The yellow-fur gene, Y, is recessive. This means that labs with at least one black-fur gene (BB or BY) have black coats. Only labs with two yellow-fur genes (YY) have yellow coats.

Axl, your author's yellow lab, inherited his genetic makeup from two black BY parents.

Second BY parent, a black lab with a recessive yellow-fur gene

	B	**Y**
B	BB	BY
Y	BY	YY

First BY parent, a black lab with a recessive yellow-fur gene

The table shows the four possible combinations of color genes that BY parents can pass to their offspring.

Because YY is one of four possible outcomes, the probability that a yellow lab like Axl will be the offspring of these black parents is $\frac{1}{4}$.

The probabilities suggested by the table can be modeled by the expression $\left(\frac{1}{2}B + \frac{1}{2}Y\right)^2$.

$$\left(\frac{1}{2}B + \frac{1}{2}Y\right)^2 = \left(\frac{1}{2}B\right)^2 + 2\left(\frac{1}{2}B\right)\left(\frac{1}{2}Y\right) + \left(\frac{1}{2}Y\right)^2$$

$$= \frac{1}{4}BB + \frac{1}{2}BY + \frac{1}{4}YY$$

The probability of a black lab with two dominant black genes is $\frac{1}{4}$.

The probability of a black lab with a recessive yellow gene is $\frac{1}{2}$.

The probability of a yellow lab with two recessive yellow genes is $\frac{1}{4}$.

Exercise Set P.4

Practice Exercises

In Exercises 1–4, is the algebraic expression a polynomial? If it is, write the polynomial in standard form.

1. $2x + 3x^2 - 5$

2. $2x + 3x^{-1} - 5$

3. $\dfrac{2x + 3}{x}$

4. $x^2 - x^3 + x^4 - 5$

In Exercises 5–8, find the degree of the polynomial.

5. $3x^2 - 5x + 4$

6. $-4x^3 + 7x^2 - 11$

7. $x^2 - 4x^3 + 9x - 12x^4 + 63$

8. $x^2 - 8x^3 + 15x^4 + 91$

In Exercises 9–14, perform the indicated operations. Write the resulting polynomial in standard form and indicate its degree.

9. $(-6x^3 + 5x^2 - 8x + 9) + (17x^3 + 2x^2 - 4x - 13)$

10. $(-7x^3 + 6x^2 - 11x + 13) + (19x^3 - 11x^2 + 7x - 17)$

11. $(17x^3 - 5x^2 + 4x - 3) - (5x^3 - 9x^2 - 8x + 11)$

12. $(18x^4 - 2x^3 - 7x + 8) - (9x^4 - 6x^3 - 5x + 7)$

13. $(5x^2 - 7x - 8) + (2x^2 - 3x + 7) - (x^2 - 4x - 3)$

14. $(8x^2 + 7x - 5) - (3x^2 - 4x) - (-6x^3 - 5x^2 + 3)$

In Exercises 15–58, find each product.

15. $(x + 1)(x^2 - x + 1)$

16. $(x + 5)(x^2 - 5x + 25)$

17. $(2x - 3)(x^2 - 3x + 5)$

18. $(2x - 1)(x^2 - 4x + 3)$

19. $(x + 7)(x + 3)$

20. $(x + 8)(x + 5)$

21. $(x - 5)(x + 3)$

22. $(x - 1)(x + 2)$

23. $(3x + 5)(2x + 1)$

24. $(7x + 4)(3x + 1)$

25. $(2x - 3)(5x + 3)$

26. $(2x - 5)(7x + 2)$

27. $(5x^2 - 4)(3x^2 - 7)$

28. $(7x^2 - 2)(3x^2 - 5)$

29. $(8x^3 + 3)(x^2 - 5)$

30. $(7x^3 + 5)(x^2 - 2)$

31. $(x + 3)(x - 3)$

32. $(x + 5)(x - 5)$

33. $(3x + 2)(3x - 2)$

34. $(2x + 5)(2x - 5)$

35. $(5 - 7x)(5 + 7x)$

36. $(4 - 3x)(4 + 3x)$

37. $(4x^2 + 5x)(4x^2 - 5x)$

38. $(3x^2 + 4x)(3x^2 - 4x)$

39. $(1 - y^5)(1 + y^5)$

40. $(2 - y^5)(2 + y^5)$

41. $(x + 2)^2$

42. $(x + 5)^2$

43. $(2x + 3)^2$

44. $(3x + 2)^2$

45. $(x - 3)^2$

46. $(x - 4)^2$

47. $(4x^2 - 1)^2$

48. $(5x^2 - 3)^2$

49. $(7 - 2x)^2$

50. $(9 - 5x)^2$

51. $(x + 1)^3$

52. $(x + 2)^3$

53. $(2x + 3)^3$

54. $(3x + 4)^3$

55. $(x - 3)^3$

56. $(x - 1)^3$

57. $(3x - 4)^3$

58. $(2x - 3)^3$

In Exercises 59–66, perform the indicated operations. Indicate the degree of the resulting polynomial.

59. $(5x^2y - 3xy) + (2x^2y - xy)$

60. $(-2x^2y + xy) + (4x^2y + 7xy)$

61. $(4x^2y + 8xy + 11) + (-2x^2y + 5xy + 2)$

62. $(7x^4y^2 - 5x^2y^2 + 3xy) + (-18x^4y^2 - 6x^2y^2 - xy)$

63. $(x^3 + 7xy - 5y^2) - (6x^3 - xy + 4y^2)$

64. $(x^4 - 7xy - 5y^3) - (6x^4 - 3xy + 4y^3)$

65. $(3x^4y^2 + 5x^3y - 3y) - (2x^4y^2 - 3x^3y - 4y + 6x)$

66. $(5x^4y^2 + 6x^3y - 7y) - (3x^4y^2 - 5x^3y - 6y + 8x)$

In Exercises 67–82, find each product.

67. $(x + 5y)(7x + 3y)$

68. $(x + 9y)(6x + 7y)$

69. $(x - 3y)(2x + 7y)$

70. $(3x - y)(2x + 5y)$

71. $(3xy - 1)(5xy + 2)$

72. $(7x^2y + 1)(2x^2y - 3)$

73. $(7x + 5y)^2$

74. $(9x + 7y)^2$

75. $(x^2y^2 - 3)^2$

76. $(x^2y^2 - 5)^2$

77. $(x - y)(x^2 + xy + y^2)$

78. $(x + y)(x^2 - xy + y^2)$

79. $(3x + 5y)(3x - 5y)$

80. $(7x + 3y)(7x - 3y)$

81. $(7xy^2 - 10y)(7xy^2 + 10y)$

82. $(3xy^2 - 4y)(3xy^2 + 4y)$

Practice Plus

In Exercises 83–90, perform the indicated operation or operations.

83. $(3x + 4y)^2 - (3x - 4y)^2$ **84.** $(5x + 2y)^2 - (5x - 2y)^2$

85. $(5x - 7)(3x - 2) - (4x - 5)(6x - 1)$

86. $(3x + 5)(2x - 9) - (7x - 2)(x - 1)$

87. $(2x + 5)(2x - 5)(4x^2 + 25)$

88. $(3x + 4)(3x - 4)(9x^2 + 16)$

89. $\dfrac{(2x - 7)^5}{(2x - 7)^3}$

90. $\dfrac{(5x - 3)^6}{(5x - 3)^4}$

Application Exercises

As you complete more years of education, you can count on a greater income. The bar graph shows the median, or middlemost, annual income for Americans, by level of education, in 2004.

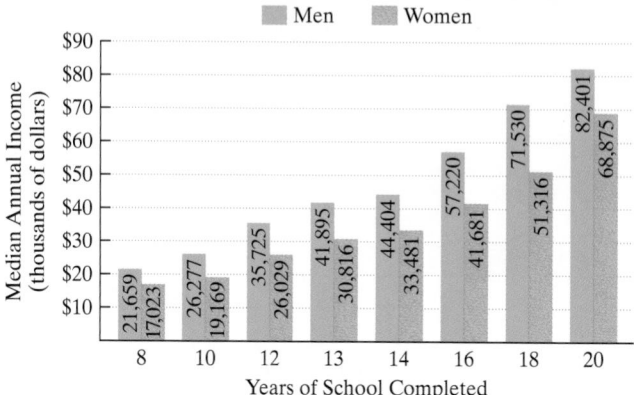

Median Annual Income, by Level of Education, 2004

Source: Bureau of the Census

Here are polynomial models that describe the median annual income for men, M, and for women, W, who have completed x years of education:

$$M = 177x^2 + 288x + 7075$$
$$W = 255x^2 - 2956x + 24{,}336$$

$$M = -18x^3 + 923x^2 - 9603x + 48{,}446$$
$$W = 17x^3 - 450x^2 + 6392x - 14{,}764.$$

Exercises 91–92 are based on these models and the data displayed by the graph.

91. a. Use the equation defined by a polynomial of degree 2 to find the median annual income for a man with 16 years of education. Does this underestimate or overestimate the median income shown by the bar graph? By how much?

 b. Use the equations defined by polynomials of degree 3 to find a mathematical model for $M - W$.

 c. According to the model in part (b), what is the difference in the median annual income between men and women with 14 years of education?

 d. According to the data displayed by the graph, what is the actual difference in the median annual income between men and women with 14 years of education? Did the result of part (c) underestimate or overestimate this difference? By how much?

92. a. Use the equation defined by a polynomial of degree 2 to find the median annual income for a woman with 18 years of education. Does this underestimate or over-estimate the median income shown by the bar graph? By how much?

 b. Use the equations defined by polynomials of degree 3 to find a mathematical model for $M - W$.

 c. According to the model in part (b), what is the difference in the median annual income between men and women with 16 years of education?

 d. According to the data displayed by the graph, what is the actual difference in the median annual income between men and women with 16 years of education? Did the result of part (c) underestimate or overestimate this difference? By how much?

The volume, V, of a rectangular solid with length l, width w, and height h is given by the formula V = lwh. In Exercises 93–94, use this formula to write a polynomial in standard form that models, or represents, the volume of the open box.

93.

$8 - 2x$

$10 - 2x$

x

94.

$8 - 2x$

$5 - 2x$

x

In Exercises 95–96, write a polynomial in standard form that models, or represents, the area of the shaded region.

95.

$x + 9$

$x + 5$

$x + 3$

$x + 1$

96.

$x + 4$

$x + 2$

$x + 3$

$x + 1$

Writing in Mathematics

97. What is a polynomial in x?

98. Explain how to subtract polynomials.

99. Explain how to multiply two binomials using the FOIL method. Give an example with your explanation.

100. Explain how to find the product of the sum and difference of two terms. Give an example with your explanation.

101. Explain how to square a binomial difference. Give an example with your explanation.

102. Explain how to find the degree of a polynomial in two variables.

Critical Thinking Exercises

Make Sense? *In Exercises 103–106, determine whether each statement makes sense or does not make sense, and explain your reasoning.*

103. Knowing the difference between factors and terms is important: In $(3x^2y)^2$, I can distribute the exponent 2 on each factor, but in $(3x^2 + y)^2$, I cannot do the same thing on each term.

104. I used the FOIL method to find the product of $x + 5$ and $x^2 + 2x + 1$.

105. Many English words have prefixes with meanings similar to those used to describe polynomials, such as *monologue*, *binocular*, and *tricuspid*.

106. Special-product formulas have patterns that make their multiplications quicker than using the FOIL method.

In Exercises 107–110, determine whether each statement is true or false. If the statement is false, make the necessary change(s) to produce a true statement.

107. $(3x^3 + 2)(3x^3 - 2) = 9x^9 - 4$

108. $(x - 5)^2 = x^2 - 5x + 25$

109. $(x + 1)^2 = x^2 + 1$

110. Suppose a square garden has an area represented by $9x^2$ square feet. If one side is made 7 feet longer and the other side is made 2 feet shorter, then the trinomial that models the area of the larger garden is $9x^2 + 15x - 14$ square feet.

In Exercises 111–113, perform the indicated operations.

111. $[(7x + 5) + 4y][(7x + 5) - 4y]$

112. $[(3x + y) + 1]^2$

113. $(x^n + 2)(x^n - 2) - (x^n - 3)^2$

114. Express the area of the plane figure shown as a polynomial in standard form.

x

x

$x - 1$

$x + 3$

Preview Exercises

Exercises 115–117 will help you prepare for the material covered in the next section. In each exercise, replace the boxed question mark with an integer that results in the given product. Some trial and error may be necessary.

115. $(x + 3)(x + \boxed{?}) = x^2 + 7x + 12$

116. $(x - \boxed{?})(x - 12) = x^2 - 14x + 24$

117. $(4x + 1)(2x - \boxed{?}) = 8x^2 - 10x - 3$

What You Know: We defined the real numbers $[\{x|x$ is rational$\} \cup \{x|x$ is irrational$\}]$ and graphed them as points on a number line. We reviewed the basic rules of algebra, using these properties to simplify algebraic expressions. We expanded our knowledge of exponents to include exponents other than natural numbers:

$$b^0 = 1; \quad b^{-n} = \frac{1}{b^n}; \quad \frac{1}{b^{-n}} = b^n; \quad b^{\frac{1}{n}} = \sqrt[n]{b};$$

$$b^{\frac{m}{n}} = \left(\sqrt[n]{b}\right)^m = \sqrt[n]{b^m}; \quad b^{-\frac{m}{n}} = \frac{1}{b^{\frac{m}{n}}}.$$

We used properties of exponents to simplify exponential expressions and properties of radicals to simplify radical expressions. Finally, we performed operations with polynomials. We used a number of fast methods for finding products of polynomials, including the FOIL method for multiplying binomials, a special-product formula for the product of the sum and difference of two terms $[(A + B)(A - B) = A^2 - B^2]$, and special-product formulas for squaring binomials $[(A + B)^2 = A^2 + 2AB + B^2;$ $(A - B)^2 = A^2 - 2AB + B^2]$.

In Exercises 1–25, simplify the given expression or perform the indicated operation (and simplify, if possible), whichever is appropriate.

1. $(3x + 5)(4x - 7)$

2. $(3x + 5) - (4x - 7)$

3. $\sqrt{6} + 9\sqrt{6}$

4. $3\sqrt{12} - \sqrt{27}$

5. $7x + 3[9 - (2x - 6)]$

6. $(8x - 3)^2$

7. $\left(x^{\frac{1}{3}}y^{-\frac{1}{2}}\right)^6$

8. $\left(\frac{2}{7}\right)^0 - 32^{-\frac{2}{5}}$

9. $(2x - 5) - (x^2 - 3x + 1)$

10. $(2x - 5)(x^2 - 3x + 1)$

11. $x^3 + x^3 - x^3 \cdot x^3$

12. $(9a - 10b)(2a + b)$

13. $\{a, c, d, e\} \cup \{c, d, f, h\}$

14. $\{a, c, d, e\} \cap \{c, d, f, h\}$

15. $(3x^2y^3 - xy + 4y^2) - (-2x^2y^3 - 3xy + 5y^2)$

16. $\dfrac{24x^2y^{13}}{-2x^5y^{-2}}$

17. $\left(\frac{1}{3}x^{-5}y^4\right)(18x^{-2}y^{-1})$

18. $\sqrt[12]{x^4}$

19. $\dfrac{24 \times 10^3}{2 \times 10^6}$ (Express the answer in scientific notation.)

20. $\dfrac{\sqrt[3]{32}}{\sqrt[3]{2}}$

21. $(x^3 + 2)(x^3 - 2)$

22. $(x^2 + 2)^2$

23. $\sqrt{50} \cdot \sqrt{6}$

24. $\dfrac{11}{7 - \sqrt{3}}$

25. $\dfrac{11}{\sqrt{3}}$

26. List all the rational numbers in this set:

$$\left\{-11, -\frac{3}{7}, 0, 0.45, \sqrt{23}, \sqrt{25}\right\}.$$

In Exercises 27–28, rewrite each expression without absolute value bars.

27. $|2 - \sqrt{13}|$

28. $x^2|x|$ if $x < 0$

29. If the population of the United States is approximately 3.0×10^8 and each person spends about \$140 per year on ice cream, express the total annual spending on ice cream in scientific notation.

30. A human brain contains 3×10^{10} neurons and a gorilla brain contains 7.5×10^9 neurons. How many times as many neurons are in the brain of a human as in the brain of a gorilla?

31. The number of TV channels is increasing. The bar graph shows the total channels available in the average U.S. household from 2000 through 2006.

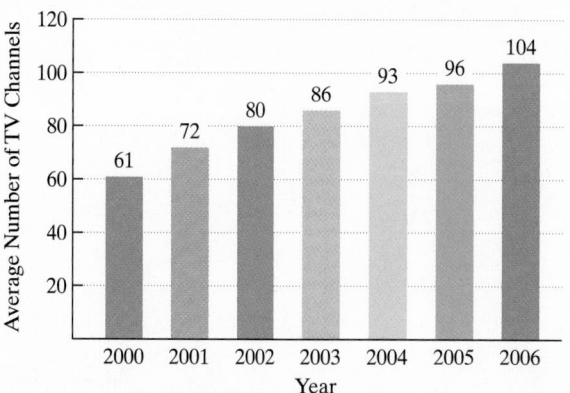

Number of TV Channels in the Average United States Household

Source: Nielsen Media Research

Here are two mathematical models for the data shown by the graph. In each formula, N represents the number of TV channels in the average U.S. household x years after 2000.

Model 1 — $N = 6.8x + 64$

Model 2 — $N = -0.5x^2 + 9.5x + 62$

a. Which model best describes the data for 2000?

b. Does the polynomial model of degree 2 underestimate or overestimate the number of channels for 2006? By how many channels?

c. According to the polynomial model of degree 1, how many channels will the average household have in 2010?

Section P.5 Factoring Polynomials

Objectives

1 Factor out the greatest common factor of a polynomial.

2 Factor by grouping.

3 Factor trinomials.

4 Factor the difference of squares.

5 Factor perfect square trinomials.

6 Factor the sum or difference of two cubes.

7 Use a general strategy for factoring polynomials.

8 Factor algebraic expressions containing fractional and negative exponents.

A two-year-old boy is asked, "Do you have a brother?" He answers, "Yes." "What is your brother's name?" "Tom." Asked if Tom has a brother, the two-year-old replies, "No." The child can go in the direction from self to brother, but he cannot reverse this direction and move from brother back to self.

As our intellects develop, we learn to reverse the direction of our thinking. Reversibility of thought is found throughout algebra. For example, we can multiply polynomials and show that

$$5x(2x + 3) = 10x^2 + 15x.$$

We can also reverse this process and express the resulting polynomial as

$$10x^2 + 15x = 5x(2x + 3).$$

Factoring a polynomial containing the sum of monomials means finding an equivalent expression that is a product.

Factoring $10x^2 + 15x$

Sum of monomials

Equivalent expression that is a product

$$10x^2 + 15x = 5x(2x + 3)$$

The factors of $10x^2 + 15x$ are $5x$ and $2x + 3$.

In this section, we will be **factoring over the set of integers**, meaning that the coefficients in the factors are integers. Polynomials that cannot be factored using integer coefficients are called **irreducible over the integers**, or **prime**.

The goal in factoring a polynomial is to use one or more factoring techniques until each of the polynomial's factors, except possibly for a monomial factor, is prime or irreducible. In this situation, the polynomial is said to be **factored completely**.

We will now discuss basic techniques for factoring polynomials.

1 Factor out the greatest common factor of a polynomial.

Common Factors

In any factoring problem, the first step is to look for the *greatest common factor*. The **greatest common factor**, abbreviated GCF, is an expression of the highest degree that divides each term of the polynomial. The distributive property in the reverse direction

$$ab + ac = a(b + c)$$

can be used to factor out the greatest common factor.

EXAMPLE 1 Factoring Out the Greatest Common Factor

Factor: **a.** $18x^3 + 27x^2$ **b.** $x^2(x + 3) + 5(x + 3)$.

Solution

a. First, determine the greatest common factor.

9 is the greatest integer that divides 18 and 27.

$$18x^3 + 27x^2$$

x^2 is the greatest expression that divides x^3 and x^2.

The GCF of the two terms of the polynomial is $9x^2$.

$$18x^3 + 27x^2$$
$$= 9x^2(2x) + 9x^2(3) \qquad \text{Express each term as the product of the GCF and its other factor.}$$
$$= 9x^2(2x + 3) \qquad \text{Factor out the GCF.}$$

b. In this situation, the greatest common factor is the common binomial factor $(x + 3)$. We factor out this common factor as follows:

$$x^2(x + 3) + 5(x + 3) = (x + 3)(x^2 + 5). \quad \text{Factor out the common binomial factor.}$$

○ Check Point **1** Factor:

a. $10x^3 - 4x^2$ **b.** $2x(x - 7) + 3(x - 7)$.

2 Factor by grouping.

Factoring by Grouping

Some polynomials have only a greatest common factor of 1. However, by a suitable grouping of the terms, it still may be possible to factor. This process, called **factoring by grouping**, is illustrated in Example 2.

EXAMPLE 2 Factoring by Grouping

Factor: $x^3 + 4x^2 + 3x + 12$.

Solution There is no factor other than 1 common to all terms. However, we can group terms that have a common factor:

$$\boxed{x^3 + 4x^2} \quad + \quad \boxed{3x + 12}.$$

Common factor is x^2. Common factor is 3.

We now factor the given polynomial as follows:

$$x^3 + 4x^2 + 3x + 12$$
$$= (x^3 + 4x^2) + (3x + 12) \qquad \text{Group terms with common factors.}$$
$$= x^2(x + 4) + 3(x + 4) \qquad \text{Factor out the greatest common factor from the grouped terms. The remaining two terms have } x + 4 \text{ as a common binomial factor.}$$
$$= (x + 4)(x^2 + 3). \qquad \text{Factor out the GCF, } x + 4.$$

Thus, $x^3 + 4x^2 + 3x + 12 = (x + 4)(x^2 + 3)$. Check the factorization by multiplying the right side of the equation using the FOIL method. Because the factorization is correct, you should obtain the original polynomial.

Discovery

In Example 2, group the terms as follows:

$$(x^3 + 3x) + (4x^2 + 12).$$

Factor out the greatest common factor from each group and complete the factoring process. Describe what happens. What can you conclude?

○ Check Point **2** Factor: $x^3 + 5x^2 - 2x - 10$.

③ Factor trinomials.

Factoring Trinomials

To factor a trinomial of the form $ax^2 + bx + c$, a little trial and error may be necessary.

A Strategy for Factoring $ax^2 + bx + c$

Assume, for the moment, that there is no greatest common factor.

1. Find two **First** terms whose product is ax^2:

$$(\Box x + \quad)(\Box x + \quad) = ax^2 + bx + c.$$

2. Find two **Last** terms whose product is c:

$$(\Box x + \Box)(\Box x + \Box) = ax^2 + bx + c.$$

3. By trial and error, perform steps 1 and 2 until the sum of the **O**utside product and **I**nside product is bx:

$$(\Box x + \Box)(\Box x + \Box) = ax^2 + bx + c.$$

$$\text{Sum of O + I}$$

If no such combination exists, the polynomial is prime.

Study Tip

The *error* part of the factoring strategy plays an important role in the process. If you do not get the correct factorization the first time, this is not a bad thing. This error is often helpful in leading you to the correct factorization.

EXAMPLE 3 **Factoring a Trinomial Whose Leading Coefficient Is 1**

Factor: $x^2 + 6x + 8$.

Solution

Step 1 Find two First terms whose product is x^2.

$$x^2 + 6x + 8 = (x \quad)(x \quad)$$

Step 2 Find two Last terms whose product is 8.

Factors of 8	8, 1	4, 2	−8, −1	−4, −2

Step 3 Try various combinations of these factors. The correct factorization of $x^2 + 6x + 8$ is the one in which the sum of the **O**utside and **I**nside products is equal to $6x$. Here is a list of the possible factorizations:

Possible Factorizations of $x^2 + 6x + 8$	Sum of Outside and Inside Products (Should Equal $6x$)	
$(x + 8)(x + 1)$	$x + 8x = 9x$	
$(x + 4)(x + 2)$	$2x + 4x = 6x$	This is the required middle term.
$(x - 8)(x - 1)$	$-x - 8x = -9x$	
$(x - 4)(x - 2)$	$-2x - 4x = -6x$	

Thus, $x^2 + 6x + 8 = (x + 4)(x + 2)$ or $(x + 2)(x + 4)$. ●

In factoring a trinomial of the form $x^2 + bx + c$, you can speed things up by listing the factors of c and then finding their sums. We are interested in a sum of b. For example, in factoring $x^2 + 6x + 8$, we are interested in the factors of 8 whose sum is 6.

Factors of 8	8, 1	4, 2	−8, −1	−4, −2
Sum of Factors	9	6	−9	−6

This is the desired sum.

Thus, $x^2 + 6x + 8 = (x + 4)(x + 2)$.

☑ Check Point **3** Factor: $x^2 + 13x + 40$.

(EXAMPLE 4) **Factoring a Trinomial Whose Leading Coefficient Is 1**

Factor: $x^2 + 3x - 18$.

Solution

Step 1 Find two First terms whose product is x^2.

$$x^2 + 3x - 18 = (x \quad)(x \quad)$$

To find the second term of each factor, we must find two integers whose product is -18 and whose sum is 3.

Step 2 Find two Last terms whose product is -18.

Factors of -18	18, -1	$-18, 1$	9, -2	$-9, 2$	6, -3	$-6, 3$

Step 3 Try various combinations of these factors. We are looking for the pair of factors whose sum is 3.

Factors of -18	18, -1	$-18, 1$	9, -2	$-9, 2$	6, -3	$-6, 3$
Sum of Factors	17	-17	7	-7	3	-3

This is the desired sum.

Thus, $x^2 + 3x - 18 = (x + 6)(x - 3)$ or $(x - 3)(x + 6)$.

☑ Check Point **4** Factor: $x^2 - 5x - 14$.

(EXAMPLE 5) **Factoring a Trinomial Whose Leading Coefficient Is Not 1**

Factor: $8x^2 - 10x - 3$.

Solution

Step 1 Find two First terms whose product is $8x^2$.

$$8x^2 - 10x - 3 \overset{?}{=} (8x \quad)(x \quad)$$
$$8x^2 - 10x - 3 \overset{?}{=} (4x \quad)(2x \quad)$$

Step 2 Find two Last terms whose product is -3. The possible factorizations are $1(-3)$ and $-1(3)$.

Step 3 Try various combinations of these factors. The correct factorization of $8x^2 - 10x - 3$ is the one in which the sum of the Outside and Inside products is equal to $-10x$. Here is a list of the possible factorizations:

Possible Factorizations of $8x^2 - 10x - 3$	Sum of Outside and Inside Products (Should Equal $-10x$)
$(8x + 1)(x - 3)$	$-24x + x = -23x$
$(8x - 3)(x + 1)$	$8x - 3x = 5x$
$(8x - 1)(x + 3)$	$24x - x = 23x$
$(8x + 3)(x - 1)$	$-8x + 3x = -5x$
$(4x + 1)(2x - 3)$	$-12x + 2x = -10x$
$(4x - 3)(2x + 1)$	$4x - 6x = -2x$
$(4x - 1)(2x + 3)$	$12x - 2x = 10x$
$(4x + 3)(2x - 1)$	$-4x + 6x = 2x$

These four factorizations use $(8x \quad)(x \quad)$ with $1(-3)$ and $-1(3)$ as factorizations of -3.

These four factorizations use $(4x \quad)(2x \quad)$ with $1(-3)$ and $-1(3)$ as factorizations of -3.

This is the required middle term.

Thus, $\quad 8x^2 - 10x - 3 = (4x + 1)(2x - 3)$ or $(2x - 3)(4x + 1)$.

Use FOIL multiplication to check either of these factorizations.

Study Tip

Here are some suggestions for reducing the list of possible factorizations for $ax^2 + bx + c$:

1. If b is relatively small, avoid the larger factors of a.

2. If c is positive, the signs in both binomial factors must match the sign of b.

3. If the trinomial has no common factor, no binomial factor can have a common factor.

4. Reversing the signs in the binomial factors reverses the sign of bx, the middle term.

⊘ Check Point **5** Factor: $6x^2 + 19x - 7$.

(EXAMPLE 6) **Factoring a Trinomial in Two Variables**

Factor: $2x^2 - 7xy + 3y^2$.

Solution

Step 1 Find two First terms whose product is $2x^2$.

$$2x^2 - 7xy + 3y^2 = (2x \quad)(x \quad)$$

Step 2 Find two Last terms whose product is $3y^2$. The possible factorizations are $(y)(3y)$ and $(-y)(-3y)$.

Step 3 Try various combinations of these factors. The correct factorization of $2x^2 - 7xy + 3y^2$ is the one in which the sum of the **O**utside and **I**nside products is equal to $-7xy$. Here is a list of possible factorizations:

Possible Factorizations of $2x^2 - 7xy + 3y^2$	Sum of Outside and Inside Products (Should Equal $-7xy$)
$(2x + 3y)(x + y)$	$2xy + 3xy = 5xy$
$(2x + y)(x + 3y)$	$6xy + xy = 7xy$
$(2x - 3y)(x - y)$	$-2xy - 3xy = -5xy$
$(2x - y)(x - 3y)$	$-6xy - xy = -7xy$

This is the required middle term.

Thus,

$$2x^2 - 7xy + 3y^2 = (2x - y)(x - 3y) \quad \text{or} \quad (x - 3y)(2x - y).$$

Use FOIL multiplication to check either of these factorizations.

⊘ Check Point **6** Factor: $3x^2 - 13xy + 4y^2$.

④ Factor the difference of squares.

Factoring the Difference of Two Squares

A method for factoring the difference of two squares is obtained by reversing the special product for the sum and difference of two terms.

The Difference of Two Squares

If A and B are real numbers, variables, or algebraic expressions, then

$$A^2 - B^2 = (A + B)(A - B).$$

In words: The difference of the squares of two terms factors as the product of a sum and a difference of those terms.

(EXAMPLE 7) **Factoring the Difference of Two Squares**

Factor: **a.** $x^2 - 4$ **b.** $81x^2 - 49$.

Solution We must express each term as the square of some monomial. Then we use the formula for factoring $A^2 - B^2$.

a. $x^2 - 4 = x^2 - 2^2 = (x + 2)(x - 2)$

$$A^2 - B^2 = (A + B) (A - B)$$

b. $81x^2 - 49 = (9x)^2 - 7^2 = (9x + 7)(9x - 7)$

⊘ Check Point **7** Factor:

a. $x^2 - 81$ **b.** $36x^2 - 25$.

We have seen that a polynomial is factored completely when it is written as the product of prime polynomials. To be sure that you have factored completely, check to see whether any factors with more than one term in the factored polynomial can be factored further. If so, continue factoring.

(EXAMPLE 8) **A Repeated Factorization**

Factor completely: $x^4 - 81$.

Study Tip

Factoring $x^4 - 81$ as

$$(x^2 + 9)(x^2 - 9)$$

is not a complete factorization. The second factor, $x^2 - 9$, is itself a difference of two squares and can be factored.

Solution

$x^4 - 81 = (x^2)^2 - 9^2$ Express as the difference of two squares.

$= (x^2 + 9)(x^2 - 9)$ The factors are the sum and the difference of the expressions being squared.

$= (x^2 + 9)(x^2 - 3^2)$ The factor $x^2 - 9$ is the difference of two squares and can be factored.

$= (x^2 + 9)(x + 3)(x - 3)$ The factors of $x^2 - 9$ are the sum and the difference of the expressions being squared.

⊘ Check Point **8** Factor completely: $81x^4 - 16$.

⑤ Factor perfect square trinomials.

Factoring Perfect Square Trinomials

Our next factoring technique is obtained by reversing the special products for squaring binomials. The trinomials that are factored using this technique are called **perfect square trinomials**.

Factoring Perfect Square Trinomials

Let A and B be real numbers, variables, or algebraic expressions.

1. $A^2 + 2AB + B^2 = (A + B)^2$ **2.** $A^2 - 2AB + B^2 = (A - B)^2$

Same sign Same sign

The two items in the box show that perfect square trinomials, $A^2 + 2AB + B^2$ and $A^2 - 2AB + B^2$, come in two forms: one in which the coefficient of the middle term is positive and one in which the coefficient of the middle term is negative. Here's how to recognize a perfect square trinomial:

1. The first and last terms are squares of monomials or integers.

2. The middle term is twice the product of the expressions being squared in the first and last terms.

(**EXAMPLE 9**) **Factoring Perfect Square Trinomials**

Factor: **a.** $x^2 + 6x + 9$ **b.** $25x^2 - 60x + 36$.

Solution

a. $x^2 + 6x + 9 = x^2 + 2 \cdot x \cdot 3 + 3^2 = (x + 3)^2$ The middle term has a positive sign.

$$\underbrace{A^2}_{} + \underbrace{2AB}_{} + \underbrace{B^2}_{} = \underbrace{(A + B)^2}_{}$$

b. We suspect that $25x^2 - 60x + 36$ is a perfect square trinomial because $25x^2 = (5x)^2$ and $36 = 6^2$. The middle term can be expressed as twice the product of $5x$ and 6.

$$25x^2 - 60x + 36 = (5x)^2 - 2 \cdot 5x \cdot 6 + 6^2 = (5x - 6)^2$$

$$\underbrace{A^2}_{} - \underbrace{2AB}_{} + \underbrace{B^2}_{} = \underbrace{(A - B)^2}_{}$$

✓ Check Point **9** Factor:

 a. $x^2 + 14x + 49$ **b.** $16x^2 - 56x + 49$.

6 Factor the sum or difference of two cubes.

Factoring the Sum or Difference of Two Cubes

We can use the following formulas to factor the sum or the difference of two cubes:

Study Tip

A Cube of SOAP

When factoring sums or differences of cubes, observe the sign patterns shown by the voice balloons in the box. The word *SOAP* is a way to remember these patterns:

S O A P.

| Same signs | Opposite signs | Always Positive |

> **Factoring the Sum or Difference of Two Cubes**
>
> **1.** Factoring the Sum of Two Cubes
>
> $$A^3 + B^3 = (A + B)(A^2 - AB + B^2)$$
>
> Same signs Opposite signs Always positive
>
> **2.** Factoring the Difference of Two Cubes
>
> $$A^3 - B^3 = (A - B)(A^2 + AB + B^2)$$
>
> Same signs Opposite signs Always positive

(**EXAMPLE 10**) **Factoring Sums and Differences of Two Cubes**

Factor: **a.** $x^3 + 8$ **b.** $64x^3 - 125$.

Solution

 a. To factor $x^3 + 8$, we must express each term as the cube of some monomial. Then we use the formula for factoring $A^3 + B^3$.

$$x^3 + 8 = x^3 + 2^3 = (x + 2)(x^2 - x \cdot 2 + 2^2) = (x + 2)(x^2 - 2x + 4)$$

$$\underbrace{A^3}_{} + \underbrace{B^3}_{} = \underbrace{(A + B)}_{} \underbrace{(A^2 - AB + B^2)}_{}$$

b. To factor $64x^3 - 125$, we must express each term as the cube of some monomial. Then we use the formula for factoring $A^3 - B^3$.

$$64x^3 - 125 = (4x)^3 - 5^3 = (4x - 5)[(4x)^2 + (4x)(5) + 5^2]$$

$$A^3 - B^3 = (A - B)(A^2 + AB + B^2)$$

$$= (4x - 5)(16x^2 + 20x + 25)$$

◉

⊘ Check Point **10** Factor:

 a. $x^3 + 1$ **b.** $125x^3 - 8$.

7 Use a general strategy for factoring polynomials.

A Strategy for Factoring Polynomials

It is important to practice factoring a wide variety of polynomials so that you can quickly select the appropriate technique. The polynomial is factored completely when all its polynomial factors, except possibly for monomial factors, are prime. Because of the commutative property, the order of the factors does not matter.

A Strategy for Factoring a Polynomial

1. If there is a common factor, factor out the GCF.

2. Determine the number of terms in the polynomial and try factoring as follows:

 a. If there are two terms, can the binomial be factored by using one of the following special forms?

 Difference of two squares: $A^2 - B^2 = (A + B)(A - B)$

 Sum of two cubes: $A^3 + B^3 = (A + B)(A^2 - AB + B^2)$

 Difference of two cubes: $A^3 - B^3 = (A - B)(A^2 + AB + B^2)$

 b. If there are three terms, is the trinomial a perfect square trinomial? If so, factor by using one of the following special forms:

$$A^2 + 2AB + B^2 = (A + B)^2$$
$$A^2 - 2AB + B^2 = (A - B)^2.$$

 If the trinomial is not a perfect square trinomial, try factoring by trial and error.

 c. If there are four or more terms, try factoring by grouping.

3. Check to see if any factors with more than one term in the factored polynomial can be factored further. If so, factor completely.

(**EXAMPLE 11**) **Factoring a Polynomial**

Factor: $2x^3 + 8x^2 + 8x$.

Solution

Step 1 If there is a common factor, factor out the GCF. Because $2x$ is common to all terms, we factor it out.

$$2x^3 + 8x^2 + 8x = 2x(x^2 + 4x + 4) \quad \text{Factor out the GCF.}$$

Step 2 Determine the number of terms and factor accordingly. The factor $x^2 + 4x + 4$ has three terms and is a perfect square trinomial. We factor using $A^2 + 2AB + B^2 = (A + B)^2$.

$$2x^3 + 8x^2 + 8x = 2x(x^2 + 4x + 4)$$

$$= 2x(x^2 + 2 \cdot x \cdot 2 + 2^2)$$

$$\underbrace{A^2}_{} \; + \; \underbrace{2AB}_{} \; + \; \underbrace{B^2}_{}$$

$$= 2x(x + 2)^2 \qquad\qquad A^2 + 2AB + B^2 = (A + B)^2$$

Step 3 Check to see if factors can be factored further. In this problem, they cannot. Thus,

$$2x^3 + 8x^2 + 8x = 2x(x + 2)^2.$$

⦿

✓ Check Point **11** Factor: $3x^3 - 30x^2 + 75x$.

⟮ **EXAMPLE 12** ⟯ **Factoring a Polynomial**

Factor: $x^2 - 25a^2 + 8x + 16$.

Solution

Step 1 If there is a common factor, factor out the GCF. Other than 1 or -1, there is no common factor.

Step 2 Determine the number of terms and factor accordingly. There are four terms. We try factoring by grouping. It can be shown that grouping into two groups of two terms does not result in a common binomial factor. Let's try grouping as a difference of squares.

$$x^2 - 25a^2 + 8x + 16$$

$$= (x^2 + 8x + 16) - 25a^2 \qquad \text{Rearrange terms and group as a perfect square trinomial minus } 25a^2 \text{ to obtain a difference of squares.}$$

$$= (x + 4)^2 - (5a)^2 \qquad \text{Factor the perfect square trinomial.}$$

$$= (x + 4 + 5a)(x + 4 - 5a) \qquad \text{Factor the difference of squares. The factors are the sum and difference of the expressions being squared.}$$

Step 3 Check to see if factors can be factored further. In this case, they cannot, so we have factored completely.

⦿

✓ Check Point **12** Factor: $x^2 - 36a^2 + 20x + 100$.

⑧ Factor algebraic expressions containing fractional and negative exponents.

Factoring Algebraic Expressions Containing Fractional and Negative Exponents

Although expressions containing fractional and negative exponents are not polynomials, they can be simplified using factoring techniques.

⟮ **EXAMPLE 13** ⟯ **Factoring Involving Fractional and Negative Exponents**

Factor and simplify: $x(x + 1)^{-\frac{3}{4}} + (x + 1)^{\frac{1}{4}}$.

Solution The greatest common factor of $x(x + 1)^{-\frac{3}{4}} + (x + 1)^{\frac{1}{4}}$ is $x + 1$ with the *smaller exponent* in the two terms. Thus, the greatest common factor is $(x + 1)^{-\frac{3}{4}}$.

$$x(x + 1)^{-\frac{3}{4}} + (x + 1)^{\frac{1}{4}}$$

$$= (x + 1)^{-\frac{3}{4}}x + (x + 1)^{-\frac{3}{4}}(x + 1) \qquad \text{Express each term as the product of the greatest common factor and its other factor.}$$

$$= (x + 1)^{-\frac{3}{4}}[x + (x + 1)] \qquad \text{Factor out the greatest common factor.}$$

$$= \frac{2x + 1}{(x + 1)^{\frac{3}{4}}} \qquad b^{-n} = \frac{1}{b^n}$$

⬤

✓ **Check Point 13** Factor and simplify: $x(x - 1)^{-\frac{1}{2}} + (x - 1)^{\frac{1}{2}}$.

Exercise Set P.5

Practice Exercises

In Exercises 1–10, factor out the greatest common factor.

1. $18x + 27$

2. $16x - 24$

3. $3x^2 + 6x$

4. $4x^2 - 8x$

5. $9x^4 - 18x^3 + 27x^2$

6. $6x^4 - 18x^3 + 12x^2$

7. $x(x + 5) + 3(x + 5)$

8. $x(2x + 1) + 4(2x + 1)$

9. $x^2(x - 3) + 12(x - 3)$

10. $x^2(2x + 5) + 17(2x + 5)$

In Exercises 11–16, factor by grouping.

11. $x^3 - 2x^2 + 5x - 10$

12. $x^3 - 3x^2 + 4x - 12$

13. $x^3 - x^2 + 2x - 2$

14. $x^3 + 6x^2 - 2x - 12$

15. $3x^3 - 2x^2 - 6x + 4$

16. $x^3 - x^2 - 5x + 5$

In Exercises 17–38, factor each trinomial, or state that the trinomial is prime.

17. $x^2 + 5x + 6$

18. $x^2 + 8x + 15$

19. $x^2 - 2x - 15$

20. $x^2 - 4x - 5$

21. $x^2 - 8x + 15$

22. $x^2 - 14x + 45$

23. $3x^2 - x - 2$

24. $2x^2 + 5x - 3$

25. $3x^2 - 25x - 28$

26. $3x^2 - 2x - 5$

27. $6x^2 - 11x + 4$

28. $6x^2 - 17x + 12$

29. $4x^2 + 16x + 15$

30. $8x^2 + 33x + 4$

31. $9x^2 - 9x + 2$

32. $9x^2 + 5x - 4$

33. $20x^2 + 27x - 8$

34. $15x^2 - 19x + 6$

35. $2x^2 + 3xy + y^2$

36. $3x^2 + 4xy + y^2$

37. $6x^2 - 5xy - 6y^2$

38. $6x^2 - 7xy - 5y^2$

In Exercises 39–48, factor the difference of two squares.

39. $x^2 - 100$

40. $x^2 - 144$

41. $36x^2 - 49$

42. $64x^2 - 81$

43. $9x^2 - 25y^2$

44. $36x^2 - 49y^2$

45. $x^4 - 16$

46. $x^4 - 1$

47. $16x^4 - 81$

48. $81x^4 - 1$

In Exercises 49–56, factor each perfect square trinomial.

49. $x^2 + 2x + 1$

50. $x^2 + 4x + 4$

51. $x^2 - 14x + 49$

52. $x^2 - 10x + 25$

53. $4x^2 + 4x + 1$

54. $25x^2 + 10x + 1$

55. $9x^2 - 6x + 1$

56. $64x^2 - 16x + 1$

In Exercises 57–64, factor using the formula for the sum or difference of two cubes.

57. $x^3 + 27$

58. $x^3 + 64$

59. $x^3 - 64$

60. $x^3 - 27$

61. $8x^3 - 1$

62. $27x^3 - 1$

63. $64x^3 + 27$

64. $8x^3 + 125$

In Exercises 65–92, factor completely, or state that the polynomial is prime.

65. $3x^3 - 3x$

66. $5x^3 - 45x$

67. $4x^2 - 4x - 24$

68. $6x^2 - 18x - 60$

69. $2x^4 - 162$

70. $7x^4 - 7$

71. $x^3 + 2x^2 - 9x - 18$

72. $x^3 + 3x^2 - 25x - 75$

73. $2x^2 - 2x - 112$

74. $6x^2 - 6x - 12$

75. $x^3 - 4x$

76. $9x^3 - 9x$

77. $x^2 + 64$

78. $x^2 + 36$

79. $x^3 + 2x^2 - 4x - 8$

80. $x^3 + 2x^2 - x - 2$

81. $y^5 - 81y$

82. $y^5 - 16y$

83. $20y^4 - 45y^2$

84. $48y^4 - 3y^2$

85. $x^2 - 12x + 36 - 49y^2$

86. $x^2 - 10x + 25 - 36y^2$

87. $9b^2x - 16y - 16x + 9b^2y$

88. $16a^2x - 25y - 25x + 16a^2y$

89. $x^2y - 16y + 32 - 2x^2$

90. $12x^2y - 27y - 4x^2 + 9$

91. $2x^3 - 8a^2x + 24x^2 + 72x$

92. $2x^3 - 98a^2x + 28x^2 + 98x$

In Exercises 93–102, factor and simplify each algebraic expression.

93. $x^{\frac{3}{2}} - x^{\frac{1}{2}}$

94. $x^{\frac{3}{4}} - x^{\frac{1}{4}}$

95. $4x^{-\frac{2}{3}} + 8x^{\frac{1}{3}}$

96. $12x^{-\frac{3}{4}} + 6x^{\frac{1}{4}}$

97. $(x + 3)^{\frac{1}{2}} - (x + 3)^{\frac{3}{2}}$

98. $(x^2 + 4)^{\frac{3}{2}} + (x^2 + 4)^{\frac{7}{2}}$

99. $(x + 5)^{-\frac{1}{2}} - (x + 5)^{-\frac{3}{2}}$

100. $(x^2 + 3)^{-\frac{2}{3}} + (x^2 + 3)^{-\frac{5}{3}}$

101. $(4x - 1)^{\frac{1}{2}} - \frac{1}{3}(4x - 1)^{\frac{3}{2}}$

102. $-8(4x + 3)^{-2} + 10(5x + 1)(4x + 3)^{-1}$

Practice Plus

In Exercises 103–114, factor completely.

103. $10x^2(x + 1) - 7x(x + 1) - 6(x + 1)$

104. $12x^2(x - 1) - 4x(x - 1) - 5(x - 1)$

105. $6x^4 + 35x^2 - 6$

106. $7x^4 + 34x^2 - 5$

107. $y^7 + y$

108. $(y + 1)^3 + 1$

109. $x^4 - 5x^2y^2 + 4y^4$

110. $x^4 - 10x^2y^2 + 9y^4$

111. $(x - y)^4 - 4(x - y)^2$

112. $(x + y)^4 - 100(x + y)^2$

113. $2x^2 - 7xy^2 + 3y^4$

114. $3x^2 + 5xy^2 + 2y^4$

Application Exercises

115. Your computer store is having an incredible sale. The price on one model is reduced by 40%. Then the sale price is reduced by another 40%. If x is the computer's original price, the sale price can be modeled by

$$(x - 0.4x) - 0.4(x - 0.4x).$$

 a. Factor out $(x - 0.4x)$ from each term. Then simplify the resulting expression.

 b. Use the simplified expression from part (a) to answer these questions. With a 40% reduction followed by a 40% reduction, is the computer selling at 20% of its original price? If not, at what percentage of the original price is it selling?

116. Your local electronics store is having an end-of-the-year sale. The price on a plasma television had been reduced by 30%. Now the sale price is reduced by another 30%. If x is the television's original price, the sale price can be modeled by

$$(x - 0.3x) - 0.3(x - 0.3x).$$

 a. Factor out $(x - 0.3x)$ from each term. Then simplify the resulting expression.

 b. Use the simplified expression from part (a) to answer these questions. With a 30% reduction followed by a 30% reduction, is the television selling at 40% of its original price? If not, at what percentage of the original price is it selling?

In Exercises 117–120,

 a. Write an expression for the area of the shaded region.

 b. Write the expression in factored form.

117. **118.**

119. **120.**

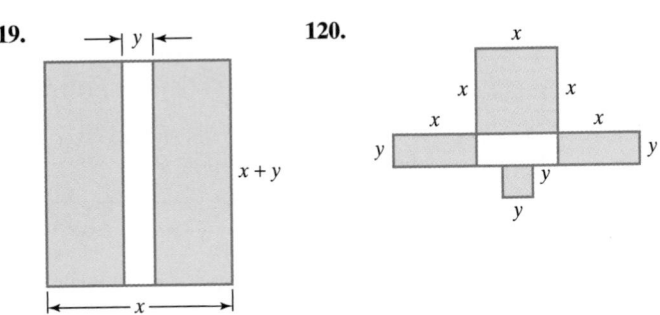

In Exercises 121–122, find the formula for the volume of the region outside the smaller rectangular solid and inside the larger rectangular solid. Then express the volume in factored form.

121.

122.

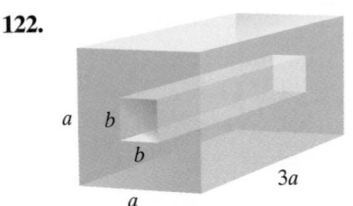

Writing in Mathematics

123. Using an example, explain how to factor out the greatest common factor of a polynomial.

124. Suppose that a polynomial contains four terms. Explain how to use factoring by grouping to factor the polynomial.

125. Explain how to factor $3x^2 + 10x + 8$.

126. Explain how to factor the difference of two squares. Provide an example with your explanation.

127. What is a perfect square trinomial and how is it factored?

128. Explain how to factor $x^3 + 1$.

129. What does it mean to factor completely?

Critical Thinking Exercises

Make Sense? *In Exercises 130–133, determine whether each statement makes sense or does not make sense, and explain your reasoning.*

130. Although $20x^3$ appears in both $20x^3 + 8x^2$ and $20x^3 + 10x$, I'll need to factor $20x^3$ in different ways to obtain each polynomial's factorization.

131. You grouped the polynomial's terms using different groupings than I did, yet we both obtained the same factorization.

132. I factored $4x^2 - 100$ completely and obtained $(2x + 10)(2x - 10)$.

133. First factoring out the greatest common factor makes it easier for me to determine how to factor the remaining factor, assuming that it is not prime.

In Exercises 134–137, determine whether each statement is true or false. If the statement is false, make the necessary change(s) to produce a true statement.

134. $x^4 - 16$ is factored completely as $(x^2 + 4)(x^2 - 4)$.

135. The trinomial $x^2 - 4x - 4$ is a prime polynomial.

136. $x^2 + 36 = (x + 6)^2$

137. $x^3 - 64 = (x + 4)(x^2 + 4x - 16)$

In Exercises 138–141, factor completely.

138. $x^{2n} + 6x^n + 8$ **139.** $-x^2 - 4x + 5$

140. $x^4 - y^4 - 2x^3y + 2xy^3$

141. $(x - 5)^{-\frac{1}{2}}(x + 5)^{-\frac{1}{2}} - (x + 5)^{\frac{1}{2}}(x - 5)^{-\frac{3}{2}}$

In Exercises 142–143, find all integers b so that the trinomial can be factored.

142. $x^2 + bx + 15$ **143.** $x^2 + 4x + b$

Preview Exercises

Exercises 144–146 will help you prepare for the material covered in the next section.

144. Factor the numerator and the denominator. Then simplify by dividing out the common factor in the numerator and the denominator.

$$\frac{x^2 + 6x + 5}{x^2 - 25}$$

In Exercises 145–146, perform the indicated operation. Where possible, reduce the answer to its lowest terms.

145. $\dfrac{5}{4} \cdot \dfrac{8}{15}$ **146.** $\dfrac{1}{2} + \dfrac{2}{3}$

(Section) P.6 **Rational Expressions**

Objectives

① Specify numbers that must be excluded from the domain of a rational expression.

② Simplify rational expressions.

③ Multiply rational expressions.

④ Divide rational expressions.

⑤ Add and subtract rational expressions.

⑥ Simplify complex rational expressions.

Discovery

What happens if you try substituting 100 for x in

$$\frac{250x}{100 - x}?$$

What does this tell you about the cost of cleaning up all of the river's pollutants?

How do we describe the costs of reducing environmental pollution? We often use algebraic expressions involving quotients of polynomials. For example, the algebraic expression

$$\frac{250x}{100 - x}$$

describes the cost, in millions of dollars, to remove x percent of the pollutants that are discharged into a river. Removing a modest percentage of pollutants, say 40%, is far less costly than removing a substantially greater percentage, such as 95%. We see this by evaluating the algebraic expression for $x = 40$ and $x = 95$.

$$\text{Evaluating } \frac{250x}{100 - x} \text{ for}$$

$x = 40$:

$$\text{Cost is } \frac{250(40)}{100 - 40} \approx 167.$$

$x = 95$:

$$\text{Cost is } \frac{250(95)}{100 - 95} = 4750.$$

The cost increases from approximately $167 million to a possibly prohibitive $4750 million, or $4.75 billion. Costs spiral upward as the percentage of removed pollutants increases.

Many algebraic expressions that describe costs of environmental projects are examples of *rational expressions*. First we will define rational expressions. Then we will review how to perform operations with such expressions.

Rational Expressions

① Specify numbers that must be excluded from the domain of a rational expression.

A **rational expression** is the quotient of two polynomials. Some examples are

$$\frac{x-2}{4}, \quad \frac{4}{x-2}, \quad \frac{x}{x^2-1}, \quad \text{and} \quad \frac{x^2+1}{x^2+2x-3}.$$

The set of real numbers for which an algebraic expression is defined is the **domain** of the expression. Because rational expressions indicate division and division by zero is undefined, **we must exclude numbers from a rational expression's domain that make the denominator zero.**

EXAMPLE 1 Excluding Numbers from the Domain

Find all the numbers that must be excluded from the domain of each rational expression:

a. $\dfrac{4}{x-2}$ **b.** $\dfrac{x}{x^2-1}.$

Solution To determine the numbers that must be excluded from each domain, examine the denominators.

a. $\dfrac{4}{x-2}$ **b.** $\dfrac{x}{x^2-1} = \dfrac{x}{(x+1)(x-1)}$

> This denominator would equal zero if $x = 2$.

> This factor would equal zero if $x = -1$.

> This factor would equal zero if $x = 1$.

For the rational expression in part (a), we must exclude 2 from the domain. For the rational expression in part (b), we must exclude both -1 and 1 from the domain. These excluded numbers are often written to the right of a rational expression:

$$\frac{4}{x-2}, x \neq 2 \qquad \frac{x}{x^2-1}, x \neq -1, x \neq 1$$

⬤

🗹 **Check Point 1** Find all the numbers that must be excluded from the domain of each rational expression:

a. $\dfrac{7}{x+5}$ **b.** $\dfrac{x}{x^2-36}.$

Simplifying Rational Expressions

② Simplify rational expressions.

A rational expression is **simplified** if its numerator and denominator have no common factors other than 1 or -1. The following procedure can be used to simplify rational expressions:

Simplifying Rational Expressions

1. Factor the numerator and the denominator completely.
2. Divide both the numerator and the denominator by any common factors.

(EXAMPLE 2) **Simplifying Rational Expressions**

Simplify:

a. $\dfrac{x^3 + x^2}{x + 1}$ **b.** $\dfrac{x^2 + 6x + 5}{x^2 - 25}$.

Solution

a. $\dfrac{x^3 + x^2}{x + 1} = \dfrac{x^2(x + 1)}{x + 1}$ Factor the numerator. Because the denominator is $x + 1, x \neq -1$.

$= \dfrac{x^2\cancel{(x + 1)}^{1}}{\cancel{x + 1}_{1}}$ Divide out the common factor, $x + 1$.

$= x^2, x \neq -1$ Denominators of 1 need not be written because $\frac{a}{1} = a$.

b. $\dfrac{x^2 + 6x + 5}{x^2 - 25} = \dfrac{(x + 5)(x + 1)}{(x + 5)(x - 5)}$ Factor the numerator and denominator. Because the denominator is $(x + 5)(x - 5), x \neq -5$ and $x \neq 5$.

$= \dfrac{\cancel{(x + 5)}^{1}(x + 1)}{\cancel{(x + 5)}_{1}(x - 5)}$ Divide out the common factor, $x + 5$.

$= \dfrac{x + 1}{x - 5}, \quad x \neq -5, \quad x \neq 5$ ●

⊘ Check Point **2** Simplify:

a. $\dfrac{x^3 + 3x^2}{x + 3}$ **b.** $\dfrac{x^2 - 1}{x^2 + 2x + 1}$.

③ Multiply rational expressions.

Multiplying Rational Expressions

The product of two rational expressions is the product of their numerators divided by the product of their denominators. Here is a step-by-step procedure for multiplying rational expressions:

Multiplying Rational Expressions

1. Factor all numerators and denominators completely.

2. Divide numerators and denominators by common factors.

3. Multiply the remaining factors in the numerators and multiply the remaining factors in the denominators.

EXAMPLE 3 Multiplying Rational Expressions

Multiply: $\dfrac{x-7}{x-1} \cdot \dfrac{x^2-1}{3x-21}$.

Solution

$\dfrac{x-7}{x-1} \cdot \dfrac{x^2-1}{3x-21}$

This is the given multiplication problem.

$= \dfrac{x-7}{x-1} \cdot \dfrac{(x+1)(x-1)}{3(x-7)}$

Factor as many numerators and denominators as possible. Because the denominators have factors of $x-1$ and $x-7$, $x \neq 1$ and $x \neq 7$.

$= \dfrac{\overset{1}{\cancel{x-7}}}{\underset{1}{\cancel{x-1}}} \cdot \dfrac{(x+1)\overset{1}{\cancel{(x-1)}}}{3\underset{1}{\cancel{(x-7)}}}$

Divide numerators and denominators by common factors.

$= \dfrac{x+1}{3},\ x \neq 1, x \neq 7$

Multiply the remaining factors in the numerators and denominators.

> **These excluded numbers from the domain must also be excluded from the simplified expression's domain.**

✓ **Check Point 3** Multiply:

$$\dfrac{x+3}{x^2-4} \cdot \dfrac{x^2-x-6}{x^2+6x+9}.$$

④ Divide rational expressions.

Dividing Rational Expressions

The quotient of two rational expressions is the product of the first expression and the multiplicative inverse, or reciprocal, of the second expression. The reciprocal is found by interchanging the numerator and the denominator. Thus, **we find the quotient of two rational expressions by inverting the divisor and multiplying**.

EXAMPLE 4 Dividing Rational Expressions

Divide: $\dfrac{x^2-2x-8}{x^2-9} \div \dfrac{x-4}{x+3}$.

Solution

$\dfrac{x^2-2x-8}{x^2-9} \div \dfrac{x-4}{x+3}$

This is the given division problem.

$= \dfrac{x^2-2x-8}{x^2-9} \cdot \dfrac{x+3}{x-4}$

Invert the divisor and multiply.

$= \dfrac{(x-4)(x+2)}{(x+3)(x-3)} \cdot \dfrac{x+3}{x-4}$

Factor as many numerators and denominators as possible. For nonzero denominators, $x \neq -3$, $x \neq 3$, and $x \neq 4$.

$= \dfrac{\overset{1}{\cancel{(x-4)}}(x+2)}{\underset{}{\cancel{(x+3)}}(x-3)} \cdot \dfrac{\overset{1}{\cancel{(x+3)}}}{\underset{1}{\cancel{(x-4)}}}$

Divide numerators and denominators by common factors.

$= \dfrac{x+2}{x-3},\ x \neq -3, x \neq 3, x \neq 4$

Multiply the remaining factors in the numerators and in the denominators.

⊘ Check Point **4** Divide:

$$\frac{x^2 - 2x + 1}{x^3 + x} \div \frac{x^2 + x - 2}{3x^2 + 3}.$$

⑤ Add and subtract rational expressions.

Adding and Subtracting Rational Expressions with the Same Denominator

We add or subtract rational expressions with the same denominator by (1) adding or subtracting the numerators, (2) placing this result over the common denominator, and (3) simplifying, if possible.

EXAMPLE 5 **Subtracting Rational Expressions with the Same Denominator**

Subtract: $\dfrac{5x + 1}{x^2 - 9} - \dfrac{4x - 2}{x^2 - 9}.$

Solution

Study Tip

Example 5 shows that when a numerator is being subtracted, we must subtract every term in that expression.

Don't forget the parentheses.

$$\frac{5x + 1}{x^2 - 9} - \frac{4x - 2}{x^2 - 9} = \frac{5x + 1 - (4x - 2)}{x^2 - 9}$$

Subtract numerators and include parentheses to indicate that both terms are subtracted. Place this difference over the common denominator.

$$= \frac{5x + 1 - 4x + 2}{x^2 - 9}$$

Remove parentheses and then change the sign of each term in parentheses.

$$= \frac{x + 3}{x^2 - 9}$$

Combine like terms.

$$= \frac{\overset{1}{\cancel{x + 3}}}{\underset{1}{\cancel{(x + 3)}}(x - 3)}$$

Factor and simplify ($x \neq -3$ and $x \neq 3$).

$$= \frac{1}{x - 3}, x \neq -3, x \neq 3$$

⊘ Check Point **5** Subtract: $\dfrac{x}{x + 1} - \dfrac{3x + 2}{x + 1}.$

Adding and Subtracting Rational Expressions with Different Denominators

Rational expressions that have no common factors in their denominators can be added or subtracted using one of the following properties:

$$\frac{a}{b} + \frac{c}{d} = \frac{ad + bc}{bd} \qquad \frac{a}{b} - \frac{c}{d} = \frac{ad - bc}{bd}, b \neq 0, d \neq 0.$$

The denominator, bd, is the product of the factors in the two denominators. Because we are considering rational expressions that have no common factors in their denominators, the product bd gives the least common denominator.

EXAMPLE 6 **Subtracting Rational Expressions Having No Common Factors in Their Denominators**

Subtract: $\dfrac{x + 2}{2x - 3} - \dfrac{4}{x + 3}$.

Solution We need to find the least common denominator. This is the product of the distinct factors in each denominator, namely $(2x - 3)(x + 3)$. We can therefore use the subtraction property given previously as follows:

$$\dfrac{a}{b} - \dfrac{c}{d} = \dfrac{ad - bc}{bd}$$

$\dfrac{x + 2}{2x - 3} - \dfrac{4}{x + 3} = \dfrac{(x + 2)(x + 3) - (2x - 3)4}{(2x - 3)(x + 3)}$

Observe that $a = x + 2$, $b = 2x - 3$, $c = 4$, and $d = x + 3$.

$= \dfrac{x^2 + 5x + 6 - (8x - 12)}{(2x - 3)(x + 3)}$

Multiply.

$= \dfrac{x^2 + 5x + 6 - 8x + 12}{(2x - 3)(x + 3)}$

Remove parentheses and then change the sign of each term in parentheses.

$= \dfrac{x^2 - 3x + 18}{(2x - 3)(x + 3)}, x \neq \dfrac{3}{2}, x \neq -3$

Combine like terms in the numerator.

⬤ **Check Point 6** Add: $\dfrac{3}{x + 1} + \dfrac{5}{x - 1}$.

The **least common denominator**, or LCD, of several rational expressions is a polynomial consisting of the product of all prime factors in the denominators, with each factor raised to the greatest power of its occurrence in any denominator. When adding and subtracting rational expressions that have different denominators with one or more common factors in the denominators, it is efficient to find the least common denominator first.

Finding the Least Common Denominator

1. Factor each denominator completely.
2. List the factors of the first denominator.
3. Add to the list in step 2 any factors of the second denominator that do not appear in the list.
4. Form the product of the factors from the list in step 3. This product is the least common denominator.

EXAMPLE 7 **Finding the Least Common Denominator**

Find the least common denominator of

$$\dfrac{7}{5x^2 + 15x} \quad \text{and} \quad \dfrac{9}{x^2 + 6x + 9}.$$

Solution

Step 1 Factor each denominator completely.

$$5x^2 + 15x = 5x(x + 3)$$
$$x^2 + 6x + 9 = (x + 3)^2 \quad \text{or} \quad (x + 3)(x + 3)$$

Factors are
5, *x*, and *x* + 3.
$$\frac{7}{5x^2 + 15x}$$
$$\frac{9}{x^2 + 6x + 9}$$
Factors are
x + 3 and *x* + 3.

Step 2 List the factors of the first denominator.

$$5, x, x + 3$$

Step 3 Add any unlisted factors from the second denominator. One factor of $x^2 + 6x + 9$ is already in our list. That factor is $x + 3$. However, the other factor of $x + 3$ is not listed in step 2. We add a second factor of $x + 3$ to the list. We have

$$5, x, x + 3, x + 3.$$

Step 4 The least common denominator is the product of all factors in the final list. Thus,

$$5x(x + 3)(x + 3) \quad \text{or} \quad 5x(x + 3)^2$$

is the least common denominator. ●

⊘ Check Point **7** Find the least common denominator of

$$\frac{3}{x^2 - 6x + 9} \quad \text{and} \quad \frac{7}{x^2 - 9}.$$

Finding the least common denominator for two (or more) rational expressions is the first step needed to add or subtract the expressions.

Adding and Subtracting Rational Expressions That Have Different Denominators

1. Find the LCD of the rational expressions.
2. Rewrite each rational expression as an equivalent expression whose denominator is the LCD. To do so, multiply the numerator and the denominator of each rational expression by any factor(s) needed to convert the denominator into the LCD.
3. Add or subtract numerators, placing the resulting expression over the LCD.
4. If possible, simplify the resulting rational expression.

(EXAMPLE 8) **Adding Rational Expressions with Different Denominators**

Add: $\dfrac{x + 3}{x^2 + x - 2} + \dfrac{2}{x^2 - 1}.$

Solution

Step 1 Find the least common denominator. Start by factoring the denominators.

$$x^2 + x - 2 = (x + 2)(x - 1)$$
$$x^2 - 1 = (x + 1)(x - 1)$$

The factors of the first denominator are $x + 2$ and $x - 1$. The only factor from the second denominator that is not listed is $x + 1$. Thus, the least common denominator is

$$(x + 2)(x - 1)(x + 1).$$

Step 2 Write equivalent expressions with the LCD as denominators. We must rewrite each rational expression with a denominator of $(x + 2)(x - 1)(x + 1)$. We do so by multiplying both the numerator and the denominator of each rational expression by any factor(s) needed to convert the expression's denominator into the LCD.

$$\frac{x + 3}{(x + 2)(x - 1)} \cdot \frac{x + 1}{x + 1} = \frac{(x + 3)(x + 1)}{(x + 2)(x - 1)(x + 1)} \qquad \frac{2}{(x + 1)(x - 1)} \cdot \frac{x + 2}{x + 2} = \frac{2(x + 2)}{(x + 2)(x - 1)(x + 1)}$$

Multiply the numerator and denominator by $x + 1$ to get $(x + 2)(x - 1)(x + 1)$, the LCD.

Multiply the numerator and denominator by $x + 2$ to get $(x + 2)(x - 1)(x + 1)$, the LCD.

Because $\dfrac{x + 1}{x + 1} = 1$ and $\dfrac{x + 2}{x + 2} = 1$, we are not changing the value of either rational expression, only its appearance.

Now we are ready to perform the indicated addition.

$$\frac{x + 3}{x^2 + x - 2} + \frac{2}{x^2 - 1}$$

This is the given problem.

$$= \frac{x + 3}{(x + 2)(x - 1)} + \frac{2}{(x + 1)(x - 1)}$$

Factor the denominators.

The LCD is $(x + 2)(x - 1)(x + 1)$.

$$= \frac{(x + 3)(x + 1)}{(x + 2)(x - 1)(x + 1)} + \frac{2(x + 2)}{(x + 2)(x - 1)(x + 1)}$$

Rewrite equivalent expressions with the LCD.

Step 3 Add numerators, putting this sum over the LCD.

$$= \frac{(x + 3)(x + 1) + 2(x + 2)}{(x + 2)(x - 1)(x + 1)}$$

$$= \frac{x^2 + 4x + 3 + 2x + 4}{(x + 2)(x - 1)(x + 1)}$$

Perform the multiplications in the numerator.

$$= \frac{x^2 + 6x + 7}{(x + 2)(x - 1)(x + 1)}, x \neq -2, x \neq 1, x \neq -1$$

Combine like terms in the numerator: $4x + 2x = 6x$ and $3 + 4 = 7$.

Step 4 If necessary, simplify. Because the numerator is prime, no further simplification is possible. ●

⊘ Check Point **8** Subtract: $\dfrac{x}{x^2 - 10x + 25} - \dfrac{x - 4}{2x - 10}$.

6 Simplify complex rational expressions.

Complex Rational Expressions

Complex rational expressions, also called **complex fractions**, have numerators or denominators containing one or more rational expressions. Here are two examples of such expressions:

$$\frac{1 + \dfrac{1}{x}}{1 - \dfrac{1}{x}}$$

Separate rational expressions occur in the numerator and the denominator.

$$\frac{\dfrac{1}{x + h} - \dfrac{1}{x}}{h}$$

Separate rational expressions occur in the numerator.

One method for simplifying a complex rational expression is to combine its numerator into a single expression and combine its denominator into a single expression. Then perform the division by inverting the denominator and multiplying.

EXAMPLE 9 Simplifying a Complex Rational Expression

Simplify: $\dfrac{1 + \dfrac{1}{x}}{1 - \dfrac{1}{x}}$.

Solution

Step 1 Add to get a single rational expression in the numerator.

$$1 + \frac{1}{x} = \frac{1}{1} + \frac{1}{x} = \frac{1 \cdot x}{1 \cdot x} + \frac{1}{x} = \frac{x}{x} + \frac{1}{x} = \frac{x + 1}{x}$$

The LCD is $1 \cdot x$, or x.

Step 2 Subtract to get a single rational expression in the denominator.

$$1 - \frac{1}{x} = \frac{1}{1} - \frac{1}{x} = \frac{1 \cdot x}{1 \cdot x} - \frac{1}{x} = \frac{x}{x} - \frac{1}{x} = \frac{x - 1}{x}$$

The LCD is $1 \cdot x$, or x.

Step 3 Perform the division indicated by the main fraction bar: Invert and multiply. If possible, simplify.

$$\frac{1 + \dfrac{1}{x}}{1 - \dfrac{1}{x}} = \frac{\dfrac{x + 1}{x}}{\dfrac{x - 1}{x}} = \frac{x + 1}{x} \cdot \frac{x}{x - 1} = \frac{x + 1}{\overset{1}{\cancel{x}}} \cdot \frac{\overset{1}{\cancel{x}}}{x - 1} = \frac{x + 1}{x - 1}$$

Invert and multiply.

✓ Check Point **9** Simplify: $\dfrac{\dfrac{1}{x} - \dfrac{3}{2}}{\dfrac{1}{x} + \dfrac{3}{4}}$.

A second method for simplifying a complex rational expression is to find the least common denominator of all the rational expressions in its numerator and denominator. Then multiply each term in its numerator and denominator by this least common denominator. Because we are multiplying by a form of 1, we will obtain an equivalent expression that does not contain fractions in its numerator or denominator. Here we use this method to simplify the complex rational expression in Example 9.

$$\frac{1 + \dfrac{1}{x}}{1 - \dfrac{1}{x}} = \frac{\left(1 + \dfrac{1}{x}\right)}{\left(1 - \dfrac{1}{x}\right)} \cdot \frac{x}{x}$$

The least common denominator of all the rational expressions is x. Multiply the numerator and denominator by x. Because $\dfrac{x}{x} = 1$, we are not changing the complex fraction $(x \neq 0)$.

$$= \frac{1 \cdot x + \dfrac{1}{x} \cdot x}{1 \cdot x - \dfrac{1}{x} \cdot x}$$

Use the distributive property. Be sure to distribute x to every term.

$$= \frac{x + 1}{x - 1}, \ x \neq 0, \ x \neq 1$$

Multiply. The complex rational expression is now simplified.

(**EXAMPLE 10**) **Simplifying a Complex Rational Expression**

Simplify: $\dfrac{\dfrac{1}{x+h}-\dfrac{1}{x}}{h}$.

Solution We will use the method of multiplying each of the three terms, $\dfrac{1}{x+h}, \dfrac{1}{x}$, and h, by the least common denominator. The least common denominator is $x(x+h)$.

$$\dfrac{\dfrac{1}{x+h}-\dfrac{1}{x}}{h}$$

$$=\dfrac{\left(\dfrac{1}{x+h}-\dfrac{1}{x}\right)x(x+h)}{hx(x+h)}$$

Multiply the numerator and denominator by $x(x+h)$, $h \neq 0$, $x \neq 0$, $x \neq -h$.

$$=\dfrac{\dfrac{1}{x+h}\cdot x(x+h)-\dfrac{1}{x}\cdot x(x+h)}{hx(x+h)}$$

Use the distributive property in the numerator.

$$=\dfrac{x-(x+h)}{hx(x+h)}$$

Simplify: $\dfrac{1}{x+h}x(x+h) = x$ and $\dfrac{1}{x}\cdot x(x+h) = x+h$.

$$=\dfrac{x-x-h}{hx(x+h)}$$

Subtract in the numerator. Remove parentheses and change the sign of each term in parentheses.

$$=\dfrac{-\overset{1}{\cancel{h}}}{\underset{1}{\cancel{h}}x(x+h)}$$

Simplify: $x - x - h = -h$.

$$=-\dfrac{1}{x(x+h)},\ h \neq 0,\ x \neq 0,\ x \neq -h$$ Divide the numerator and denominator by h. ●

⏺ Check Point **10** Simplify: $\dfrac{\dfrac{1}{x+7}-\dfrac{1}{x}}{7}$.

Exercise Set P.6

Practice Exercises

In Exercises 1–6, find all numbers that must be excluded from the domain of each rational expression.

1. $\dfrac{7}{x-3}$

2. $\dfrac{13}{x+9}$

3. $\dfrac{x+5}{x^2-25}$

4. $\dfrac{x+7}{x^2-49}$

5. $\dfrac{x-1}{x^2+11x+10}$

6. $\dfrac{x-3}{x^2+4x-45}$

In Exercises 7–14, simplify each rational expression. Find all numbers that must be excluded from the domain of the simplified rational expression.

7. $\dfrac{3x-9}{x^2-6x+9}$

8. $\dfrac{4x-8}{x^2-4x+4}$

9. $\dfrac{x^2-12x+36}{4x-24}$

10. $\dfrac{x^2-8x+16}{3x-12}$

11. $\dfrac{y^2+7y-18}{y^2-3y+2}$

12. $\dfrac{y^2-4y-5}{y^2+5y+4}$

13. $\dfrac{x^2 + 12x + 36}{x^2 - 36}$

14. $\dfrac{x^2 - 14x + 49}{x^2 - 49}$

In Exercises 15–32, multiply or divide as indicated.

15. $\dfrac{x - 2}{3x + 9} \cdot \dfrac{2x + 6}{2x - 4}$

16. $\dfrac{6x + 9}{3x - 15} \cdot \dfrac{x - 5}{4x + 6}$

17. $\dfrac{x^2 - 9}{x^2} \cdot \dfrac{x^2 - 3x}{x^2 + x - 12}$

18. $\dfrac{x^2 - 4}{x^2 - 4x + 4} \cdot \dfrac{2x - 4}{x + 2}$

19. $\dfrac{x^2 - 5x + 6}{x^2 - 2x - 3} \cdot \dfrac{x^2 - 1}{x^2 - 4}$

20. $\dfrac{x^2 + 5x + 6}{x^2 + x - 6} \cdot \dfrac{x^2 - 9}{x^2 - x - 6}$

21. $\dfrac{x^3 - 8}{x^2 - 4} \cdot \dfrac{x + 2}{3x}$

22. $\dfrac{x^2 + 6x + 9}{x^3 + 27} \cdot \dfrac{1}{x + 3}$

23. $\dfrac{x + 1}{3} \div \dfrac{3x + 3}{7}$

24. $\dfrac{x + 5}{7} \div \dfrac{4x + 20}{9}$

25. $\dfrac{x^2 - 4}{x} \div \dfrac{x + 2}{x - 2}$

26. $\dfrac{x^2 - 4}{x - 2} \div \dfrac{x + 2}{4x - 8}$

27. $\dfrac{4x^2 + 10}{x - 3} \div \dfrac{6x^2 + 15}{x^2 - 9}$

28. $\dfrac{x^2 + x}{x^2 - 4} \div \dfrac{x^2 - 1}{x^2 + 5x + 6}$

29. $\dfrac{x^2 - 25}{2x - 2} \div \dfrac{x^2 + 10x + 25}{x^2 + 4x - 5}$

30. $\dfrac{x^2 - 4}{x^2 + 3x - 10} \div \dfrac{x^2 + 5x + 6}{x^2 + 8x + 15}$

31. $\dfrac{x^2 + x - 12}{x^2 + x - 30} \cdot \dfrac{x^2 + 5x + 6}{x^2 - 2x - 3} \div \dfrac{x + 3}{x^2 + 7x + 6}$

32. $\dfrac{x^3 - 25x}{4x^2} \cdot \dfrac{2x^2 - 2}{x^2 - 6x + 5} \div \dfrac{x^2 + 5x}{7x + 7}$

In Exercises 33–58, add or subtract as indicated.

33. $\dfrac{4x + 1}{6x + 5} + \dfrac{8x + 9}{6x + 5}$

34. $\dfrac{3x + 2}{3x + 4} + \dfrac{3x + 6}{3x + 4}$

35. $\dfrac{x^2 - 2x}{x^2 + 3x} + \dfrac{x^2 + x}{x^2 + 3x}$

36. $\dfrac{x^2 - 4x}{x^2 - x - 6} + \dfrac{4x - 4}{x^2 - x - 6}$

37. $\dfrac{4x - 10}{x - 2} - \dfrac{x - 4}{x - 2}$

38. $\dfrac{2x + 3}{3x - 6} - \dfrac{3 - x}{3x - 6}$

39. $\dfrac{x^2 + 3x}{x^2 + x - 12} - \dfrac{x^2 - 12}{x^2 + x - 12}$

40. $\dfrac{x^2 - 4x}{x^2 - x - 6} - \dfrac{x - 6}{x^2 - x - 6}$

41. $\dfrac{3}{x + 4} + \dfrac{6}{x + 5}$

42. $\dfrac{8}{x - 2} + \dfrac{2}{x - 3}$

43. $\dfrac{3}{x + 1} - \dfrac{3}{x}$

44. $\dfrac{4}{x} - \dfrac{3}{x + 3}$

45. $\dfrac{2x}{x + 2} + \dfrac{x + 2}{x - 2}$

46. $\dfrac{3x}{x - 3} - \dfrac{x + 4}{x + 2}$

47. $\dfrac{x + 5}{x - 5} + \dfrac{x - 5}{x + 5}$

48. $\dfrac{x + 3}{x - 3} + \dfrac{x - 3}{x + 3}$

49. $\dfrac{3}{2x + 4} + \dfrac{2}{3x + 6}$

50. $\dfrac{5}{2x + 8} + \dfrac{7}{3x + 12}$

51. $\dfrac{4}{x^2 + 6x + 9} + \dfrac{4}{x + 3}$

52. $\dfrac{3}{5x + 2} + \dfrac{5x}{25x^2 - 4}$

53. $\dfrac{3x}{x^2 + 3x - 10} - \dfrac{2x}{x^2 + x - 6}$

54. $\dfrac{x}{x^2 - 2x - 24} - \dfrac{x}{x^2 - 7x + 6}$

55. $\dfrac{x + 3}{x^2 - 1} - \dfrac{x + 2}{x - 1}$

56. $\dfrac{x + 5}{x^2 - 4} - \dfrac{x + 1}{x - 2}$

57. $\dfrac{4x^2 + x - 6}{x^2 + 3x + 2} - \dfrac{3x}{x + 1} + \dfrac{5}{x + 2}$

58. $\dfrac{6x^2 + 17x - 40}{x^2 + x - 20} + \dfrac{3}{x - 4} - \dfrac{5x}{x + 5}$

In Exercises 59–72, simplify each complex rational expression.

59. $\dfrac{\dfrac{x}{3} - 1}{x - 3}$

60. $\dfrac{\dfrac{x}{4} - 1}{x - 4}$

61. $\dfrac{1 + \dfrac{1}{x}}{3 - \dfrac{1}{x}}$

62. $\dfrac{8 + \dfrac{1}{x}}{4 - \dfrac{1}{x}}$

63. $\dfrac{\dfrac{1}{x} + \dfrac{1}{y}}{x + y}$

64. $\dfrac{1 - \dfrac{1}{x}}{xy}$

65. $\dfrac{x - \dfrac{x}{x + 3}}{x + 2}$

66. $\dfrac{x - 3}{x - \dfrac{3}{x - 2}}$

67. $\dfrac{\dfrac{3}{x - 2} - \dfrac{4}{x + 2}}{\dfrac{7}{x^2 - 4}}$

68. $\dfrac{\dfrac{x}{x - 2} + 1}{\dfrac{3}{x^2 - 4} + 1}$

69. $\dfrac{\dfrac{1}{x + 1}}{\dfrac{1}{x^2 - 2x - 3} + \dfrac{1}{x - 3}}$

70. $\dfrac{\dfrac{6}{x^2 + 2x - 15} - \dfrac{1}{x - 3}}{\dfrac{1}{x + 5} + 1}$

71. $\dfrac{\dfrac{1}{(x + h)^2} - \dfrac{1}{x^2}}{h}$

72. $\dfrac{\dfrac{x + h}{x + h + 1} - \dfrac{x}{x + 1}}{h}$

Practice Plus

In Exercises 73–80, perform the indicated operations. Simplify the result, if possible.

73. $\left(\dfrac{2x + 3}{x + 1} \cdot \dfrac{x^2 + 4x - 5}{2x^2 + x - 3}\right) - \dfrac{2}{x + 2}$

74. $\dfrac{1}{x^2 - 2x - 8} \div \left(\dfrac{1}{x - 4} - \dfrac{1}{x + 2}\right)$

75. $\left(2 - \dfrac{6}{x + 1}\right)\left(1 + \dfrac{3}{x - 2}\right)$

76. $\left(4 - \dfrac{3}{x + 2}\right)\left(1 + \dfrac{5}{x - 1}\right)$

77. $\dfrac{y^{-1} - (y + 5)^{-1}}{5}$

78. $\dfrac{y^{-1} - (y + 2)^{-1}}{2}$

79. $\left(\dfrac{1}{a^3 - b^3} \cdot \dfrac{ac + ad - bc - bd}{1}\right) - \dfrac{c - d}{a^2 + ab + b^2}$

80. $\dfrac{ab}{a^2 + ab + b^2} + \left(\dfrac{ac - ad - bc + bd}{ac - ad + bc - bd} \div \dfrac{a^3 - b^3}{a^3 + b^3}\right)$

Application Exercises

81. The rational expression

$$\frac{130x}{100 - x}$$

describes the cost, in millions of dollars, to inoculate x percent of the population against a particular strain of flu.

a. Evaluate the expression for $x = 40$, $x = 80$, and $x = 90$. Describe the meaning of each evaluation in terms of percentage inoculated and cost.

b. For what value of x is the expression undefined?

c. What happens to the cost as x approaches 100%? How can you interpret this observation?

82. The average rate on a round-trip commute having a one-way distance d is given by the complex rational expression

$$\frac{2d}{\dfrac{d}{r_1} + \dfrac{d}{r_2}},$$

in which r_1 and r_2 are the average rates on the outgoing and return trips, respectively. Simplify the expression. Then find your average rate if you drive to campus averaging 40 miles per hour and return home on the same route averaging 30 miles per hour. Explain why the answer is not 35 miles per hour.

83. The bar graph shows the estimated number of calories per day needed to maintain energy balance for various gender and age groups for moderately active lifestyles. (Moderately active means a lifestyle that includes physical activity equivalent to walking 1.5 to 3 miles per day at 3 to 4 miles per hour, in addition to the light physical activity associated with typical day-to-day life.)

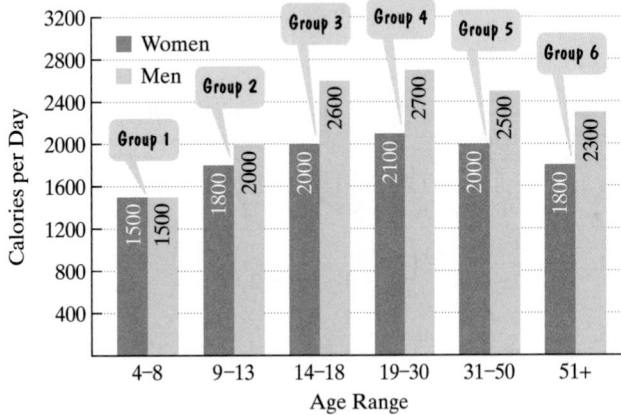

Calories Needed to Maintain Energy Balance for Moderately Active Lifestyles

Source: U.S.D.A.

a. The mathematical model

$$W = -66x^2 + 526x + 1030$$

describes the number of calories needed per day, W, by women in age group x with moderately active lifestyles. According to the model, how many calories per day are needed by women between the ages of 19 and 30, inclusive, with this lifestyle? Does this underestimate or overestimate the number shown by the graph? By how much?

b. The mathematical model

$$M = -120x^2 + 998x + 590$$

describes the number of calories needed per day, M, by men in age group x with moderately active lifestyles. According to the model, how many calories per day are needed by men between the ages of 19 and 30, inclusive, with this lifestyle? Does this underestimate or overestimate the number shown by the graph? By how much?

c. Write a simplified rational expression that describes the ratio of the number of calories needed per day by women in age group x to the number of calories needed per day by men in age group x for people with moderately active lifestyles.

In Exercises 84–85, express the perimeter of each rectangle as a single rational expression.

84.

85.

Writing in Mathematics

86. What is a rational expression?

87. Explain how to determine which numbers must be excluded from the domain of a rational expression.

88. Explain how to simplify a rational expression.

89. Explain how to multiply rational expressions.

90. Explain how to divide rational expressions.

91. Explain how to add or subtract rational expressions with the same denominators.

92. Explain how to add rational expressions having no common factors in their denominators. Use $\dfrac{3}{x + 5} + \dfrac{7}{x + 2}$ in your explanation.

93. Explain how to find the least common denominator for denominators of $x^2 - 100$ and $x^2 - 20x + 100$.

94. Describe two ways to simplify $\dfrac{\dfrac{3}{x} + \dfrac{2}{x^2}}{\dfrac{1}{x^2} + \dfrac{2}{x}}$.

Explain the error in Exercises 95–97. Then rewrite the right side of the equation to correct the error that now exists.

95. $\dfrac{1}{a} + \dfrac{1}{b} = \dfrac{1}{a + b}$

96. $\dfrac{1}{x} + 7 = \dfrac{1}{x + 7}$

97. $\dfrac{a}{x} + \dfrac{a}{b} = \dfrac{a}{x + b}$

Critical Thinking Exercises

Make Sense? *In Exercises 98–101, determine whether each statement makes sense or does not make sense, and explain your reasoning.*

98. I evaluated $\dfrac{3x - 3}{4x(x - 1)}$ for $x = 1$ and obtained 0.

99. The rational expressions

$$\frac{7}{14x} \quad \text{and} \quad \frac{7}{14 + x}$$

can both be simplified by dividing each numerator and each denominator by 7.

100. When performing the division

$$\frac{7x}{x + 3} \div \frac{(x + 3)^2}{x - 5},$$

I began by dividing the numerator and the denominator by the common factor, $x + 3$.

101. I subtracted $\frac{3x - 5}{x - 1}$ from $\frac{x - 3}{x - 1}$ and obtained a constant.

In Exercises 102–105, determine whether each statement is true or false. If the statement is false, make the necessary change(s) to produce a true statement.

102. $\frac{x^2 - 25}{x - 5} = x - 5$

103. The expression $\frac{-3y - 6}{y + 2}$ simplifies to the consecutive integer that follows -4.

104. $\frac{2x - 1}{x - 7} + \frac{3x - 1}{x - 7} - \frac{5x - 2}{x - 7} = 0$

105. $6 + \frac{1}{x} = \frac{7}{x}$

In Exercises 106–108, perform the indicated operations.

106. $\frac{1}{x^n - 1} - \frac{1}{x^n + 1} - \frac{1}{x^{2n} - 1}$

107. $\left(1 - \frac{1}{x}\right)\left(1 - \frac{1}{x + 1}\right)\left(1 - \frac{1}{x + 2}\right)\left(1 - \frac{1}{x + 3}\right)$

108. $(x - y)^{-1} + (x - y)^{-2}$

109. In one short sentence, five words or less, explain what

$$\frac{\dfrac{1}{x} + \dfrac{1}{x^2} + \dfrac{1}{x^3}}{\dfrac{1}{x^4} + \dfrac{1}{x^5} + \dfrac{1}{x^6}}$$

does to each number x.

Preview Exercises

Exercises 110–112 will help you prepare for the material covered in the first section of the next chapter.

110. If $y = 4 - x^2$, find the value of y that corresponds to values of x for each integer starting with -3 and ending with 3.

111. If $y = 1 - x^2$, find the value of y that corresponds to values of x for each integer starting with -3 and ending with 3.

112. If $y = |x + 1|$, find the value of y that corresponds to values of x for each integer starting with -4 and ending with 2.

Chapter P Summary, Review, and Test

Summary: Basic Formulas

Definition of Absolute Value

$$|x| = \begin{cases} x & \text{if } x \geq 0 \\ -x & \text{if } x < 0 \end{cases}$$

Distance between Points a and b on a Number Line

$$|a - b| \quad \text{or} \quad |b - a|$$

Properties of Real Numbers

Commutative	$a + b = b + a$
	$ab = ba$
Associative	$(a + b) + c = a + (b + c)$
	$(ab)c = a(bc)$
Distributive	$a(b + c) = ab + ac$
Identity	$a + 0 = a$
	$a \cdot 1 = a$
Inverse	$a + (-a) = 0$
	$a \cdot \dfrac{1}{a} = 1, a \neq 0$

Properties of Exponents

$$b^{-n} = \frac{1}{b^n}, \quad b^0 = 1, \quad b^m \cdot b^n = b^{m+n},$$

$$(b^m)^n = b^{mn}, \quad \frac{b^m}{b^n} = b^{m-n}, \quad (ab)^n = a^n b^n, \quad \left(\frac{a}{b}\right)^n = \frac{a^n}{b^n}$$

Product and Quotient Rules for nth Roots

$$\sqrt[n]{ab} = \sqrt[n]{a} \cdot \sqrt[n]{b}, \quad \sqrt[n]{\frac{a}{b}} = \frac{\sqrt[n]{a}}{\sqrt[n]{b}}$$

Rational Exponents

$$a^{\frac{1}{n}} = \sqrt[n]{a}, \quad a^{-\frac{1}{n}} = \frac{1}{a^{\frac{1}{n}}} = \frac{1}{\sqrt[n]{a}},$$

$$a^{\frac{m}{n}} = (\sqrt[n]{a})^m = \sqrt[n]{a^m}, \quad a^{-\frac{m}{n}} = \frac{1}{a^{\frac{m}{n}}}$$

Special Products

$$(A + B)(A - B) = A^2 - B^2$$
$$(A + B)^2 = A^2 + 2AB + B^2$$
$$(A - B)^2 = A^2 - 2AB + B^2$$
$$(A + B)^3 = A^3 + 3A^2B + 3AB^2 + B^3$$
$$(A - B)^3 = A^3 - 3A^2B + 3AB^2 - B^3$$

Factoring Formulas

$$A^2 - B^2 = (A + B)(A - B)$$
$$A^2 + 2AB + B^2 = (A + B)^2$$
$$A^2 - 2AB + B^2 = (A - B)^2$$
$$A^3 + B^3 = (A + B)(A^2 - AB + B^2)$$
$$A^3 - B^3 = (A - B)(A^2 + AB + B^2)$$

Review Exercises

You can use these review exercises, like the review exercises at the end of each chapter, to test your understanding of the chapter's topics. However, you can also use these exercises as a prerequisite test to check your mastery of the fundamental algebra skills needed in this book.

P.1

In Exercises 1–2, evaluate each algebraic expression for the given value or values of the variable(s).

1. $3 + 6(x - 2)^3$ for $x = 4$

2. $x^2 - 5(x - y)$ for $x = 6$ and $y = 2$

3. You are riding along an expressway traveling x miles per hour. The formula

$$S = 0.015x^2 + x + 10$$

models the recommended safe distance, S, in feet, between your car and other cars on the expressway. What is the recommended safe distance when your speed is 60 miles per hour?

In Exercises 4–7, let $A = \{a, b, c\}, B = \{a, c, d, e\}$, and $C = \{a, d, f, g\}$. Find the indicated set.

4. $A \cap B$ **5.** $A \cup B$

6. $A \cup C$ **7.** $C \cap A$

8. Consider the set:

$$\left\{-17, -\tfrac{9}{13}, 0, 0.75, \sqrt{2}, \pi, \sqrt{81}\right\}.$$

List all numbers from the set that are **a.** natural numbers, **b.** whole numbers, **c.** integers, **d.** rational numbers, **e.** irrational numbers, **f.** real numbers.

In Exercises 9–11, rewrite each expression without absolute value bars.

9. $|-103|$ **10.** $|\sqrt{2} - 1|$ **11.** $|3 - \sqrt{17}|$

12. Express the distance between the numbers -17 and 4 using absolute value. Then evaluate the absolute value.

In Exercises 13–18, state the name of the property illustrated.

13. $3 + 17 = 17 + 3$ **14.** $(6 \cdot 3) \cdot 9 = 6 \cdot (3 \cdot 9)$

15. $\sqrt{3}(\sqrt{5} + \sqrt{3}) = \sqrt{15} + 3$

16. $(6 \cdot 9) \cdot 2 = 2 \cdot (6 \cdot 9)$

17. $\sqrt{3}(\sqrt{5} + \sqrt{3}) = (\sqrt{5} + \sqrt{3})\sqrt{3}$

18. $(3 \cdot 7) + (4 \cdot 7) = (4 \cdot 7) + (3 \cdot 7)$

In Exercises 19–22, simplify each algebraic expression.

19. $5(2x - 3) + 7x$

20. $\frac{1}{5}(5x) + [(3y) + (-3y)] - (-x)$

21. $3(4y - 5) - (7y + 2)$

22. $8 - 2[3 - (5x - 1)]$

23. The bar graph shows the percentage of U.S. adults who have been tested for HIV, by age.

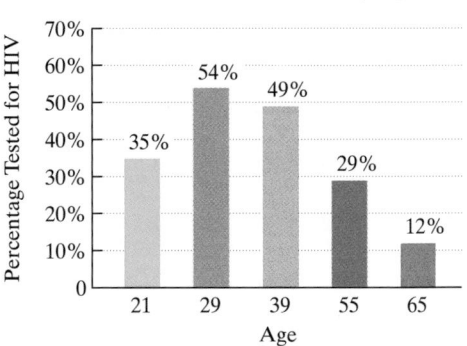

Percentage of Adults in the United States Tested for HIV, by Age

Source: National Center for Health Statistics

The data in the graph can be modeled by the formula

$$P = -0.05x^2 + 3.6x - 15,$$

where P represents the percentage of U.S. adults tested for HIV at age x. According to the formula, what percentage of U.S. adults who are 21 years old have been tested for HIV? Does the model underestimate or overestimate the percent displayed by the bar graph? By how much?

P.2

Evaluate each exponential expression in Exercises 24–27.

24. $(-3)^3(-2)^2$ **25.** $2^{-4} + 4^{-1}$

26. $5^{-3} \cdot 5$ **27.** $\dfrac{3^3}{3^6}$

Simplify each exponential expression in Exercises 28–31.

28. $(-2x^4y^3)^3$ **29.** $(-5x^3y^2)(-2x^{-11}y^{-2})$

30. $(2x^3)^{-4}$ **31.** $\dfrac{7x^5y^6}{28x^{15}y^{-2}}$

In Exercises 32–33, write each number in decimal notation.

32. 3.74×10^4 **33.** 7.45×10^{-5}

In Exercises 34–35, write each number in scientific notation.

34. 3,590,000 **35.** 0.00725

In Exercises 36–37, perform the indicated operation and write the answer in decimal notation.

36. $(3 \times 10^3)(1.3 \times 10^2)$ **37.** $\dfrac{6.9 \times 10^3}{3 \times 10^5}$

In Exercises 38–39, use 10^6 for one million and 10^9 for one billion to rewrite the number in each statement in scientific notation.

38. According to the Tax Foundation, in 2005, individuals and companies in the United States spent approximately $257 billion on tax preparation costs.

39. According to the Internal Revenue Service, in 2005, approximately 175 million tax returns were filed.

40. Use your scientific notation answers from Exercises 38 and 39 to answer this question: If the total 2005 tax preparation costs were evenly divided among all tax returns, how much would it cost to prepare each return? Express the answer in decimal notation, rounded to the nearest dollar.

P.3

Use the product rule to simplify the expressions in Exercises 41–44. In Exercises 43–44, assume that variables represent nonnegative real numbers.

41. $\sqrt{300}$

42. $\sqrt{12x^2}$

43. $\sqrt{10x} \cdot \sqrt{2x}$

44. $\sqrt{r^3}$

Use the quotient rule to simplify the expressions in Exercises 45–46.

45. $\sqrt{\dfrac{121}{4}}$

46. $\dfrac{\sqrt{96x^3}}{\sqrt{2x}}$ (Assume that $x > 0$.)

In Exercises 47–49, add or subtract terms whenever possible.

47. $7\sqrt{5} + 13\sqrt{5}$

48. $2\sqrt{50} + 3\sqrt{8}$

49. $4\sqrt{72} - 2\sqrt{48}$

In Exercises 50–53, rationalize the denominator.

50. $\dfrac{30}{\sqrt{5}}$

51. $\dfrac{\sqrt{2}}{\sqrt{3}}$

52. $\dfrac{5}{6 + \sqrt{3}}$

53. $\dfrac{14}{\sqrt{7} - \sqrt{5}}$

Evaluate each expression in Exercises 54–57 or indicate that the root is not a real number.

54. $\sqrt[3]{125}$

55. $\sqrt[5]{-32}$

56. $\sqrt[4]{-125}$

57. $\sqrt[4]{(-5)^4}$

Simplify the radical expressions in Exercises 58–62.

58. $\sqrt[3]{81}$

59. $\sqrt[3]{y^5}$

60. $\sqrt[4]{8} \cdot \sqrt[4]{10}$

61. $4\sqrt[3]{16} + 5\sqrt[3]{2}$

62. $\dfrac{\sqrt[4]{32x^5}}{\sqrt[4]{16x}}$ (Assume that $x > 0$.)

In Exercises 63–68, evaluate each expression.

63. $16^{\frac{1}{2}}$

64. $25^{-\frac{1}{2}}$

65. $125^{\frac{1}{3}}$

66. $27^{-\frac{1}{3}}$

67. $64^{\frac{2}{3}}$

68. $27^{-\frac{4}{3}}$

In Exercises 69–71, simplify using properties of exponents.

69. $\left(5x^{\frac{2}{3}}\right)\left(4x^{\frac{1}{4}}\right)$

70. $\dfrac{15x^{\frac{3}{4}}}{5x^{\frac{1}{2}}}$

71. $\left(125x^6\right)^{\frac{2}{3}}$

72. Simplify by reducing the index of the radical: $\sqrt[6]{y^3}$.

P.4

In Exercises 73–74, perform the indicated operations. Write the resulting polynomial in standard form and indicate its degree.

73. $(-6x^3 + 7x^2 - 9x + 3) + (14x^3 + 3x^2 - 11x - 7)$

74. $(13x^4 - 8x^3 + 2x^2) - (5x^4 - 3x^3 + 2x^2 - 6)$

In Exercises 75–81, find each product.

75. $(3x - 2)(4x^2 + 3x - 5)$ **76.** $(3x - 5)(2x + 1)$

77. $(4x + 5)(4x - 5)$

78. $(2x + 5)^2$

79. $(3x - 4)^2$

80. $(2x + 1)^3$

81. $(5x - 2)^3$

In Exercises 82–83, perform the indicated operations. Indicate the degree of the resulting polynomial.

82. $(7x^2 - 8xy + y^2) + (-8x^2 - 9xy - 4y^2)$

83. $(13x^3y^2 - 5x^2y - 9x^2) - (-11x^3y^2 - 6x^2y + 3x^2 - 4)$

In Exercises 84–88, find each product.

84. $(x + 7y)(3x - 5y)$

85. $(3x - 5y)^2$

86. $(3x^2 + 2y)^2$

87. $(7x + 4y)(7x - 4y)$

88. $(a - b)(a^2 + ab + b^2)$

P.5

In Exercises 89–105, factor completely, or state that the polynomial is prime.

89. $15x^3 + 3x^2$

90. $x^2 - 11x + 28$

91. $15x^2 - x - 2$

92. $64 - x^2$

93. $x^2 + 16$

94. $3x^4 - 9x^3 - 30x^2$

95. $20x^7 - 36x^3$

96. $x^3 - 3x^2 - 9x + 27$

97. $16x^2 - 40x + 25$

98. $x^4 - 16$

99. $y^3 - 8$

100. $x^3 + 64$

101. $3x^4 - 12x^2$

102. $27x^3 - 125$

103. $x^5 - x$

104. $x^3 + 5x^2 - 2x - 10$

105. $x^2 + 18x + 81 - y^2$

In Exercises 106–108, factor and simplify each algebraic expression.

106. $16x^{-\frac{3}{4}} + 32x^{\frac{1}{4}}$

107. $(x^2 - 4)(x^2 + 3)^{\frac{1}{2}} - (x^2 - 4)^2(x^2 + 3)^{\frac{3}{2}}$

108. $12x^{-\frac{1}{2}} + 6x^{-\frac{3}{2}}$

P.6

In Exercises 109–111, simplify each rational expression. Also, list all numbers that must be excluded from the domain.

109. $\dfrac{x^3 + 2x^2}{x + 2}$

110. $\dfrac{x^2 + 3x - 18}{x^2 - 36}$

111. $\dfrac{x^2 + 2x}{x^2 + 4x + 4}$

In Exercises 112–114, multiply or divide as indicated.

112. $\dfrac{x^2 + 6x + 9}{x^2 - 4} \cdot \dfrac{x + 3}{x - 2}$

113. $\dfrac{6x + 2}{x^2 - 1} \div \dfrac{3x^2 + x}{x - 1}$

114. $\dfrac{x^2 - 5x - 24}{x^2 - x - 12} \div \dfrac{x^2 - 10x + 16}{x^2 + x - 6}$

In Exercises 115–118, add or subtract as indicated.

115. $\dfrac{2x - 7}{x^2 - 9} - \dfrac{x - 10}{x^2 - 9}$

116. $\dfrac{3x}{x + 2} + \dfrac{x}{x - 2}$

117. $\dfrac{x}{x^2 - 9} + \dfrac{x - 1}{x^2 - 5x + 6}$

118. $\dfrac{4x - 1}{2x^2 + 5x - 3} - \dfrac{x + 3}{6x^2 + x - 2}$

In Exercises 119–121, simplify each complex rational expression.

119. $\dfrac{\dfrac{1}{x} - \dfrac{1}{2}}{\dfrac{1}{3} - \dfrac{x}{6}}$

120. $\dfrac{3 + \dfrac{12}{x}}{1 - \dfrac{16}{x^2}}$

121. $\dfrac{3 - \dfrac{1}{x + 3}}{3 + \dfrac{1}{x + 3}}$

CHAPTER
Test Prep VIDEOS

Chapter P TEST

In Exercises 1–18, simplify the given expression or perform the indicated operation (and simplify, if possible), whichever is appropriate.

1. $5(2x^2 - 6x) - (4x^2 - 3x)$

2. $7 + 2[3(x + 1) - 2(3x - 1)]$

3. $\{1, 2, 5\} \cap \{5, a\}$

4. $\{1, 2, 5\} \cup \{5, a\}$

5. $(2x^2y^3 - xy + y^2) - (-4x^2y^3 - 5xy - y^2)$

6. $\dfrac{30x^3y^4}{6x^9y^{-4}}$

7. $\sqrt{6r}\sqrt{3r}$ (Assume that $r \geq 0$.)

8. $4\sqrt{50} - 3\sqrt{18}$

9. $\dfrac{3}{5 + \sqrt{2}}$

10. $\sqrt[3]{16x^4}$

11. $\dfrac{x^2 + 2x - 3}{x^2 - 3x + 2}$

12. $\dfrac{5 \times 10^{-6}}{20 \times 10^{-8}}$ (Express the answer in scientific notation.)

13. $(2x - 5)(x^2 - 4x + 3)$

14. $(5x + 3y)^2$

15. $\dfrac{2x + 8}{x - 3} \div \dfrac{x^2 + 5x + 4}{x^2 - 9}$

16. $\dfrac{x}{x + 3} + \dfrac{5}{x - 3}$

17. $\dfrac{2x + 3}{x^2 - 7x + 12} - \dfrac{2}{x - 3}$

18. $\dfrac{\dfrac{1}{x} - \dfrac{1}{3}}{\dfrac{1}{x}}$

In Exercises 19–24, factor completely, or state that the polynomial is prime.

19. $x^2 - 9x + 18$

20. $x^3 + 2x^2 + 3x + 6$

21. $25x^2 - 9$

22. $36x^2 - 84x + 49$

23. $y^3 - 125$

24. $x^2 + 10x + 25 - 9y^2$

25. Factor and simplify:

$$x(x + 3)^{-\frac{3}{5}} + (x + 3)^{\frac{2}{5}}.$$

26. List all the rational numbers in this set:

$$\left\{-7, -\tfrac{4}{5}, 0, 0.25, \sqrt{3}, \sqrt{4}, \tfrac{22}{7}, \pi\right\}.$$

In Exercises 27–28, state the name of the property illustrated.

27. $3(2 + 5) = 3(5 + 2)$

28. $6(7 + 4) = 6 \cdot 7 + 6 \cdot 4$

29. Express in scientific notation: 0.00076.

30. Evaluate: $27^{-\frac{5}{3}}$.

31. In 2007, world population was approximately 6.6×10^9. By some projections, world population will double by 2040. Express the population at that time in scientific notation.

32. Big (Lack of) Men on Campus In 2007, 135 women received bachelor's degrees for every 100 men. According to the U.S. Department of Education, that gender imbalance will widen in the coming years, as shown by the bar graph.

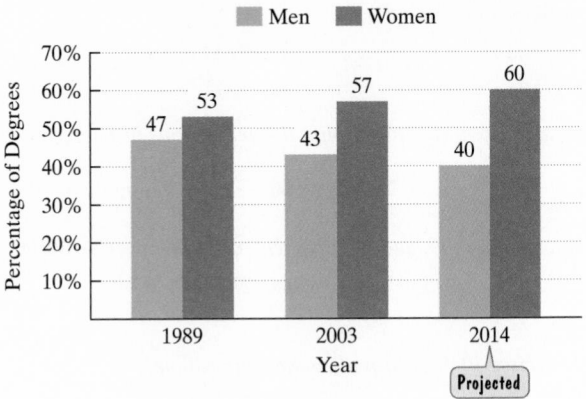

Percentage of Bachelor's Degrees Awarded to United States Men and Women

Source: U.S. Department of Education

The data for bachelor's degrees can be described by the following mathematical models:

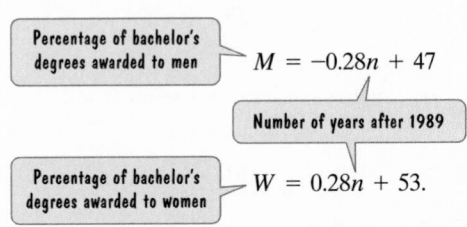

Percentage of bachelor's degrees awarded to men → $M = -0.28n + 47$

Number of years after 1989

Percentage of bachelor's degrees awarded to women → $W = 0.28n + 53$.

a. According to the first formula, what percentage of bachelor's degrees were awarded to men in 2003? Does this underestimate or overestimate the actual percent shown by the bar graph? By how much?

b. Use the given formulas to write a new formula with a rational expression that models the ratio of the percentage of bachelor's degrees received by men to the percentage received by women n years after 1989. Name this new mathematical model R, for ratio.

c. Use the formula for R to find the projected ratio of bachelor's degrees received by men to degrees received by women in 2014. According to the model, how many women will receive bachelor's degrees for every two men in 2014? How well does this describe the projections shown by the graph?

Equations and Inequalities

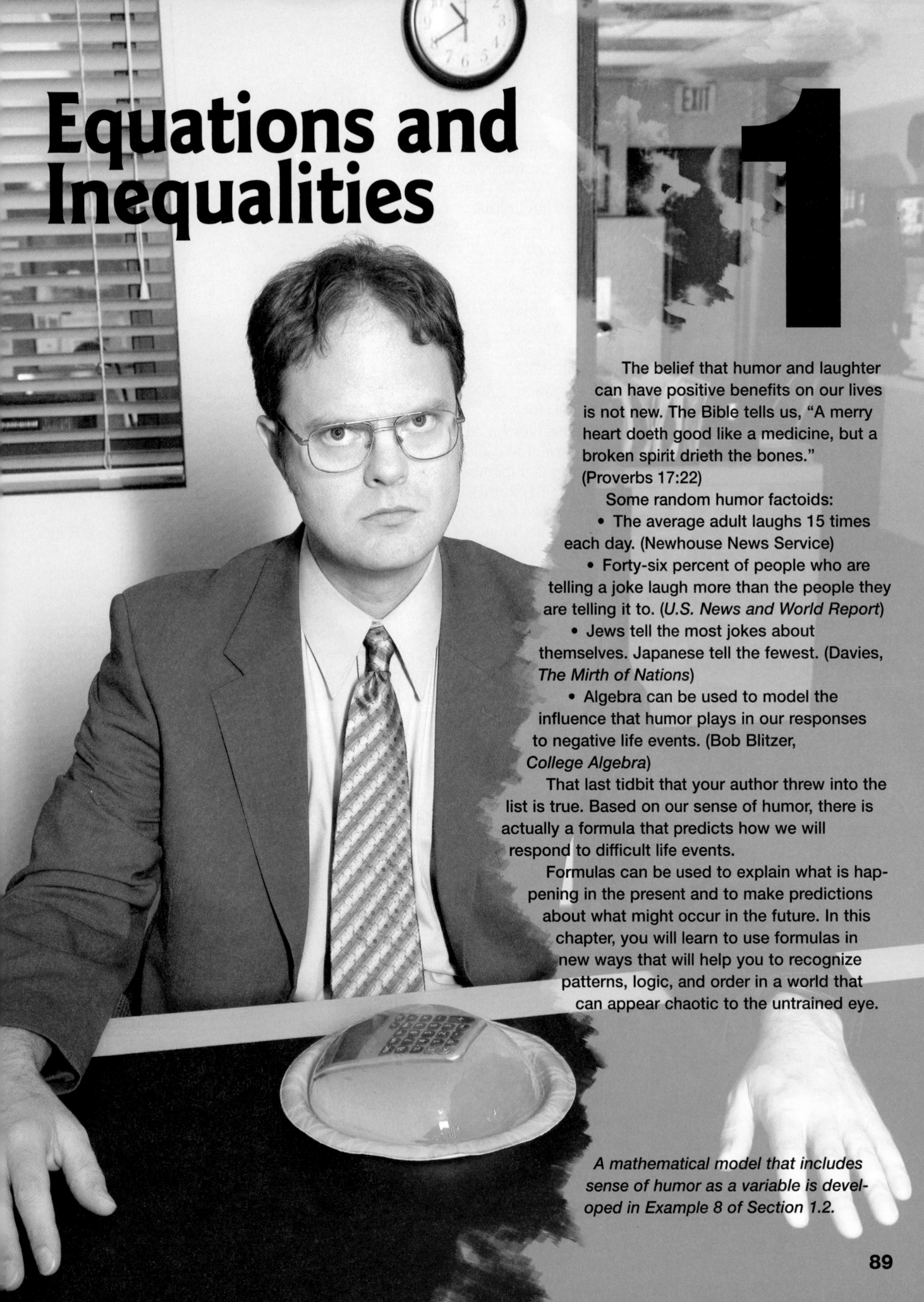

1

The belief that humor and laughter can have positive benefits on our lives is not new. The Bible tells us, "A merry heart doeth good like a medicine, but a broken spirit drieth the bones." (Proverbs 17:22)

Some random humor factoids:

• The average adult laughs 15 times each day. (Newhouse News Service)

• Forty-six percent of people who are telling a joke laugh more than the people they are telling it to. (*U.S. News and World Report*)

• Jews tell the most jokes about themselves. Japanese tell the fewest. (Davies, *The Mirth of Nations*)

• Algebra can be used to model the influence that humor plays in our responses to negative life events. (Bob Blitzer, *College Algebra*)

That last tidbit that your author threw into the list is true. Based on our sense of humor, there is actually a formula that predicts how we will respond to difficult life events.

Formulas can be used to explain what is happening in the present and to make predictions about what might occur in the future. In this chapter, you will learn to use formulas in new ways that will help you to recognize patterns, logic, and order in a world that can appear chaotic to the untrained eye.

A mathematical model that includes sense of humor as a variable is developed in Example 8 of Section 1.2.

Section 1.1

Graphs and Graphing Utilities

Objectives

1 Plot points in the rectangular coordinate system.

2 Graph equations in the rectangular coordinate system.

3 Interpret information about a graphing utility's viewing rectangle or table.

4 Use a graph to determine intercepts.

5 Interpret information given by graphs.

The beginning of the seventeenth century was a time of innovative ideas and enormous intellectual progress in Europe. English theatergoers enjoyed a succession of exciting new plays by Shakespeare. William Harvey proposed the radical notion that the heart was a pump for blood rather than the center of emotion. Galileo, with his new-fangled invention called the telescope, supported the theory of Polish astronomer Copernicus that the sun, not the Earth, was the center of the solar system. Monteverdi was writing the world's first grand operas. French mathematicians Pascal and Fermat invented a new field of mathematics called probability theory.

Into this arena of intellectual electricity stepped French aristocrat René Descartes (1596–1650). Descartes (pronounced "day cart"), propelled by the creativity surrounding him, developed a new branch of mathematics that brought together algebra and geometry in a unified way—a way that visualized numbers as points on a graph, equations as geometric figures, and geometric figures as equations. This new branch of mathematics, called *analytic geometry,* established Descartes as one of the founders of modern thought and among the most original mathematicians and philosophers of any age. We begin this section by looking at Descartes's deceptively simple idea, called the **rectangular coordinate system** or (in his honor) the **Cartesian coordinate system**.

1 Plot points in the rectangular coordinate system.

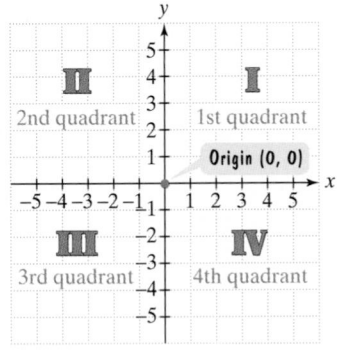

Figure 1.1 The rectangular coordinate system

Study Tip

The phrase *ordered pair* is used because order is important. The order in which coordinates appear makes a difference in a point's location. This is illustrated in **Figure 1.2**.

Points and Ordered Pairs

Descartes used two number lines that intersect at right angles at their zero points, as shown in **Figure 1.1**. The horizontal number line is the **x-axis.** The vertical number line is the **y-axis.** The point of intersection of these axes is their zero points, called the **origin.** Positive numbers are shown to the right and above the origin. Negative numbers are shown to the left and below the origin. The axes divide the plane into four quarters, called **quadrants.** The points located on the axes are not in any quadrant.

Each point in the rectangular coordinate system corresponds to an **ordered pair** of real numbers, (x, y). Examples of such pairs are $(-5, 3)$ and $(3, -5)$. The first number in each pair, called the **x-coordinate**, denotes the distance and direction from the origin along the x-axis. The second number in each pair, called the **y-coordinate**, denotes vertical distance and direction along a line parallel to the y-axis or along the y-axis itself.

Figure 1.2 shows how we **plot**, or locate, the points corresponding to the ordered pairs $(-5, 3)$ and $(3, -5)$. We plot $(-5, 3)$ by going 5 units from 0 to the left along the x-axis. Then we go 3 units up parallel to the y-axis. We plot $(3, -5)$ by going 3 units from 0 to the right along the x-axis and 5 units down parallel to the y-axis. The phrase "the points corresponding to the ordered pairs $(-5, 3)$ and $(3, -5)$" is often abbreviated as "the points $(-5, 3)$ and $(3, -5)$."

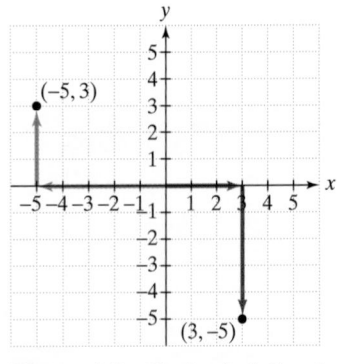

Figure 1.2 Plotting $(-5, 3)$ and $(3, -5)$

EXAMPLE 1 **Plotting Points in the Rectangular Coordinate System**

Plot the points: $A(-3, 5)$, $B(2, -4)$, $C(5, 0)$, $D(-5, -3)$, $E(0, 4)$, and $F(0, 0)$.

Solution See **Figure 1.3**. We move from the origin and plot the points in the following way:

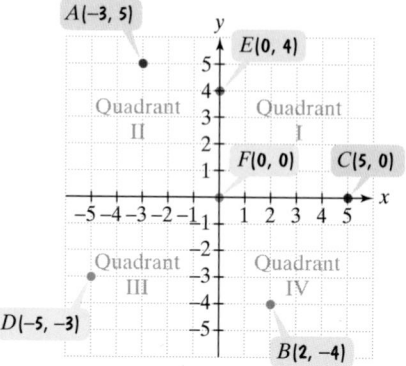

$A(-3, 5)$:	3 units left, 5 units up
$B(2, -4)$:	2 units right, 4 units down
$C(5, 0)$:	5 units right, 0 units up or down
$D(-5, -3)$:	5 units left, 3 units down
$E(0, 4)$:	0 units right or left, 4 units up
$F(0, 0)$:	0 units right or left, 0 units up or down

Notice that the origin is represented by (0, 0).

Figure 1.3 Plotting points

✓ **Check Point 1** Plot the points: $A(-2, 4)$, $B(4, -2)$, $C(-3, 0)$, and $D(0, -3)$.

2 Graph equations in the rectangular coordinate system.

Graphs of Equations

A relationship between two quantities can be expressed as an **equation in two variables**, such as

$$y = 4 - x^2.$$

A **solution of an equation in two variables**, x and y, is an ordered pair of real numbers with the following property: When the x-coordinate is substituted for x and the y-coordinate is substituted for y in the equation, we obtain a true statement. For example, consider the equation $y = 4 - x^2$ and the ordered pair $(3, -5)$. When 3 is substituted for x and -5 is substituted for y, we obtain the statement $-5 = 4 - 3^2$, or $-5 = 4 - 9$, or $-5 = -5$. Because this statement is true, the ordered pair $(3, -5)$ is a solution of the equation $y = 4 - x^2$. We also say that $(3, -5)$ **satisfies** the equation.

We can generate as many ordered-pair solutions as desired to $y = 4 - x^2$ by substituting numbers for x and then finding the corresponding values for y. For example, suppose we let $x = 3$:

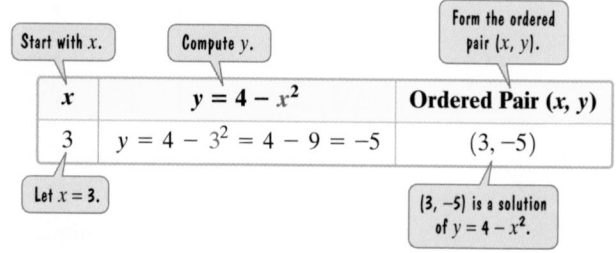

Start with x.	*Compute y.*	*Form the ordered pair (x, y).*
x	$y = 4 - x^2$	**Ordered Pair (x, y)**
3	$y = 4 - 3^2 = 4 - 9 = -5$	$(3, -5)$

Let $x = 3$. *$(3, -5)$ is a solution of $y = 4 - x^2$.*

The **graph of an equation in two variables** is the set of all points whose coordinates satisfy the equation. One method for graphing such equations is the **point-plotting method**. First, we find several ordered pairs that are solutions of the equation. Next, we plot these ordered pairs as points in the rectangular coordinate system. Finally, we connect the points with a smooth curve or line. This often gives us a picture of all ordered pairs that satisfy the equation.

EXAMPLE 2 **Graphing an Equation Using the Point-Plotting Method**

Graph $y = 4 - x^2$. Select integers for x, starting with -3 and ending with 3.

Solution For each value of x, we find the corresponding value for y.

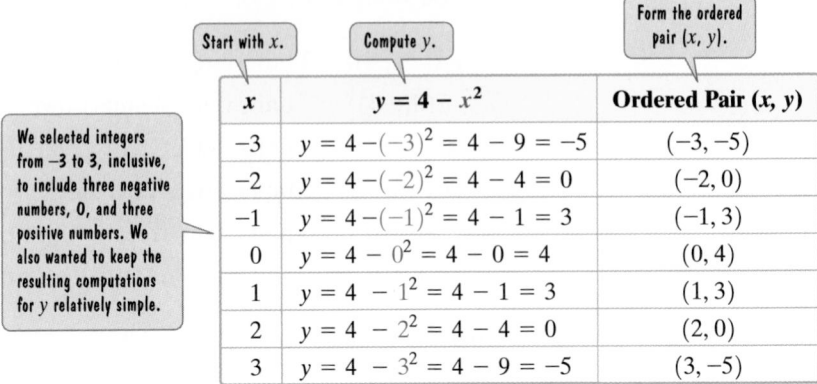

	Start with x.	Compute y.	Form the ordered pair (x, y).

We selected integers from -3 to 3, inclusive, to include three negative numbers, 0, and three positive numbers. We also wanted to keep the resulting computations for y relatively simple.

x	$y = 4 - x^2$	Ordered Pair (x, y)
-3	$y = 4 - (-3)^2 = 4 - 9 = -5$	$(-3, -5)$
-2	$y = 4 - (-2)^2 = 4 - 4 = 0$	$(-2, 0)$
-1	$y = 4 - (-1)^2 = 4 - 1 = 3$	$(-1, 3)$
0	$y = 4 - 0^2 = 4 - 0 = 4$	$(0, 4)$
1	$y = 4 - 1^2 = 4 - 1 = 3$	$(1, 3)$
2	$y = 4 - 2^2 = 4 - 4 = 0$	$(2, 0)$
3	$y = 4 - 3^2 = 4 - 9 = -5$	$(3, -5)$

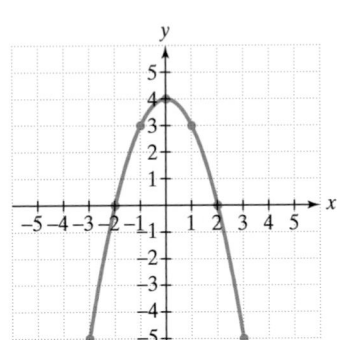

Figure 1.4 The graph of $y = 4 - x^2$

Now we plot the seven points and join them with a smooth curve, as shown in **Figure 1.4**. The graph of $y = 4 - x^2$ is a curve where the part of the graph to the right of the y-axis is a reflection of the part to the left of it and vice versa. The arrows on the left and the right of the curve indicate that it extends indefinitely in both directions.

Study Tip

In Chapters 2 and 3, we will be studying graphs of equations in two variables in which

$$y = \text{a polynomial in } x.$$

Do not be concerned that we have not yet learned techniques, other than plotting points, for graphing such equations. As you solve some of the equations in this chapter, we will display graphs simply to enhance your visual understanding of your work. For now, think of graphs of first-degree polynomials as lines and graphs of second-degree polynomials as symmetric U-shaped bowls that open upward or downward.

⊘ Check Point **2** Graph $y = 4 - x$. Select integers for x, starting with -3 and ending with 3.

EXAMPLE 3 **Graphing an Equation Using the Point-Plotting Method**

Graph $y = |x|$. Select integers for x, starting with -3 and ending with 3.

Solution For each value of x, we find the corresponding value for y.

| x | $y = |x|$ | Ordered Pair (x, y) |
|---|---|---|
| -3 | $y = |-3| = 3$ | $(-3, 3)$ |
| -2 | $y = |-2| = 2$ | $(-2, 2)$ |
| -1 | $y = |-1| = 1$ | $(-1, 1)$ |
| 0 | $y = |0| = 0$ | $(0, 0)$ |
| 1 | $y = |1| = 1$ | $(1, 1)$ |
| 2 | $y = |2| = 2$ | $(2, 2)$ |
| 3 | $y = |3| = 3$ | $(3, 3)$ |

We plot the points and connect them, resulting in the graph shown in **Figure 1.5**. The graph is V-shaped and centered at the origin. For every point (x, y) on the graph, the point $(-x, y)$ is also on the graph. This shows that the absolute value of a positive number is the same as the absolute value of its opposite.

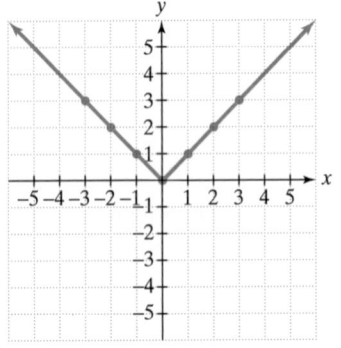

Figure 1.5 The graph of $y = |x|$

⊘ Check Point **3** Graph $y = |x + 1|$. Select integers for x, starting with -4 and ending with 2.

③ Interpret information about a graphing utility's viewing rectangle or table.

Graphing Equations and Creating Tables Using a Graphing Utility

Graphing calculators and graphing software packages for computers are referred to as **graphing utilities** or graphers. A graphing utility is a powerful tool that quickly generates the graph of an equation in two variables. **Figures 1.6(a)** and **1.6(b)** show two such graphs for the equations in Examples 2 and 3.

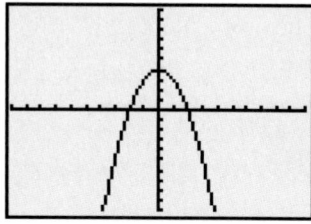

Figure 1.6(a) The graph of $y = 4 - x^2$

Figure 1.6(b) The graph of $y = |x|$

Study Tip

Even if you are not using a graphing utility in the course, read this part of the section. Knowing about viewing rectangles will enable you to understand the graphs that we display in the technology boxes throughout the book.

What differences do you notice between these graphs and the graphs that we drew by hand? They do seem a bit "jittery." Arrows do not appear on the left and right ends of the graphs. Furthermore, numbers are not given along the axes. For both graphs in **Figure 1.6**, the x-axis extends from -10 to 10 and the y-axis also extends from -10 to 10. The distance represented by each consecutive tick mark is one unit. We say that the **viewing rectangle**, or the **viewing window**, is $[-10, 10, 1]$ by $[-10, 10, 1]$.

To graph an equation in x and y using a graphing utility, enter the equation and specify the size of the viewing rectangle. The size of the viewing rectangle sets minimum and maximum values for both the x- and y-axes. Enter these values, as well as the values representing the distances between consecutive tick marks, on the respective axes. The $[-10, 10, 1]$ by $[-10, 10, 1]$ viewing rectangle used in **Figure 1.6** is called the **standard viewing rectangle.**

EXAMPLE 4 **Understanding the Viewing Rectangle**

What is the meaning of a $[-2, 3, 0.5]$ by $[-10, 20, 5]$ viewing rectangle?

Solution We begin with $[-2, 3, 0.5]$, which describes the x-axis. The minimum x-value is -2 and the maximum x-value is 3. The distance between consecutive tick marks is 0.5.

Next, consider $[-10, 20, 5]$, which describes the y-axis. The minimum y-value is -10 and the maximum y-value is 20. The distance between consecutive tick marks is 5.

Figure 1.7 illustrates a $[-2, 3, 0.5]$ by $[-10, 20, 5]$ viewing rectangle. To make things clearer, we've placed numbers by each tick mark. These numbers do not appear on the axes when you use a graphing utility to graph an equation.

Figure 1.7 A $[-2, 3, 0.5]$ by $[-10, 20, 5]$ viewing rectangle

⌀ Check Point **4** What is the meaning of a $[-100, 100, 50]$ by $[-100, 100, 10]$ viewing rectangle? Create a figure like the one in **Figure 1.7** that illustrates this viewing rectangle.

On most graphing utilities, the display screen is two-thirds as high as it is wide. By using a square setting, you can equally space the x and y tick marks. (This does not occur in the standard viewing rectangle.) Graphing utilities can also *zoom in*

and *zoom out.* When you zoom in, you see a smaller portion of the graph, but you do so in greater detail. When you zoom out, you see a larger portion of the graph. Thus, zooming out may help you to develop a better understanding of the overall character of the graph. With practice, you will become more comfortable with graphing equations in two variables using your graphing utility. You will also develop a better sense of the size of the viewing rectangle that will reveal needed information about a particular graph.

Graphing utilities can also be used to create tables showing solutions of equations in two variables. Use the Table Setup function to choose the starting value of x and to input the increment, or change, between the consecutive x-values. The corresponding y-values are calculated based on the equation(s) in two variables in the $\boxed{Y=}$ screen. In **Figure 1.8**, we used a TI-84 Plus to create a table for $y = 4 - x^2$ and $y = |x|$, the equations in Examples 2 and 3.

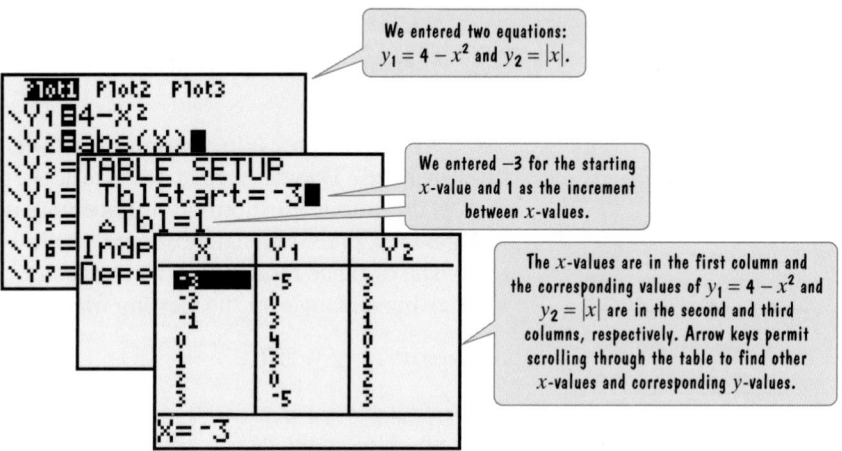

Figure 1.8 Creating a table for $y_1 = 4 - x^2$ and $y_2 = |x|$

④ Use a graph to determine intercepts.

Intercepts

An **x-intercept** of a graph is the x-coordinate of a point where the graph intersects the x-axis. For example, look at the graph of $y = 4 - x^2$ in **Figure 1.9**. The graph crosses the x-axis at $(-2, 0)$ and $(2, 0)$. Thus, the x-intercepts are -2 and 2. **The y-coordinate corresponding to an x-intercept is always zero.**

A **y-intercept** of a graph is the y-coordinate of a point where the graph intersects the y-axis. The graph of $y = 4 - x^2$ in **Figure 1.9** shows that the graph crosses the y-axis at $(0, 4)$. Thus, the y-intercept is 4. **The x-coordinate corresponding to a y-intercept is always zero.**

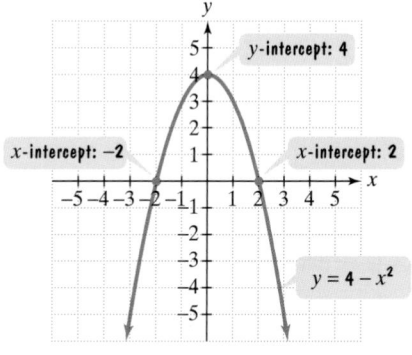

Figure 1.9 Intercepts of $y = 4 - x^2$

Study Tip

Mathematicians tend to use two ways to describe intercepts. Did you notice that we are using single numbers? If a is an x-intercept of a graph, then the graph passes through the point $(a, 0)$. If b is a y-intercept of a graph, then the graph passes through the point $(0, b)$.

Some books state that the x-intercept is the *point* $(a, 0)$ and the x-intercept is *at a* on the x-axis. Similarly, the y-intercept is the *point* $(0, b)$ and the y-intercept is *at b* on the y-axis. In these descriptions, the intercepts are the actual points where the graph intersects the axes.

Although we'll describe intercepts as single numbers, we'll immediately state the point on the x- or y-axis that the graph passes through. Here's the important thing to keep in mind:

x-intercept: The corresponding value of y is 0.

y-intercept: The corresponding value of x is 0.

(**EXAMPLE 5**) **Identifying Intercepts**

Identify the *x*- and *y*-intercepts.

a.

b.

c.

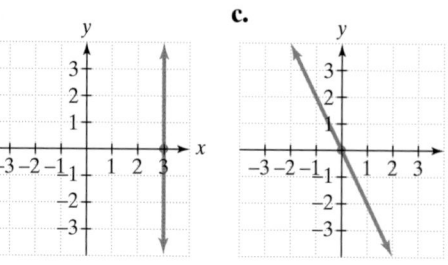

Solution

a. The graph crosses the *x*-axis at $(-1, 0)$. Thus, the *x*-intercept is -1. The graph crosses the *y*-axis at $(0, 2)$. Thus, the *y*-intercept is 2.

b. The graph crosses the *x*-axis at $(3, 0)$, so the *x*-intercept is 3. This vertical line does not cross the *y*-axis. Thus, there is no *y*-intercept.

c. This graph crosses the *x*- and *y*-axes at the same point, the origin. Because the graph crosses both axes at $(0, 0)$, the *x*-intercept is 0 and the *y*-intercept is 0. ●

⊘ Check Point **5** Identify the *x*- and *y*-intercepts.

a.

b.

c.

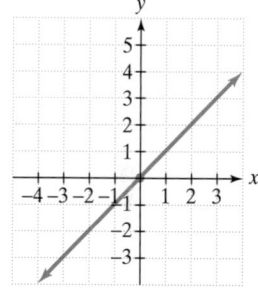

Figure 1.10 illustrates that a graph may have no intercepts or several intercepts.

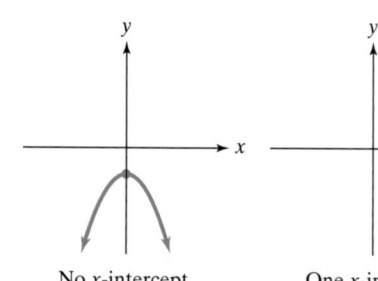

No *x*-intercept
One *y*-intercept

Figure 1.10

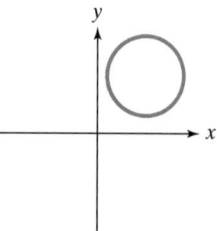

One *x*-intercept
No *y*-intercept

No intercepts

One *x*-intercept
Three *y*-intercepts

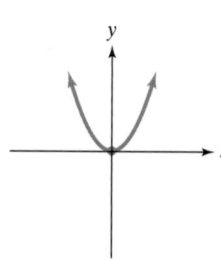

The same *x*-intercept
and *y*-intercept

5 Interpret information given by graphs.

Interpreting Information Given by Graphs

Line graphs are often used to illustrate trends over time. Some measure of time, such as months or years, frequently appears on the horizontal axis. Amounts are generally listed on the vertical axis. Points are drawn to represent the given information. The graph is formed by connecting the points with line segments.

A line graph displays information in the first quadrant of a rectangular coordinate system. By identifying points on line graphs and their coordinates, you can interpret specific information given by the graph.

EXAMPLE 6 Age at Marriage and the Probability of Divorce

Divorce rates are considerably higher for couples who marry in their teens. The line graphs in **Figure 1.11** show the percentages of marriages ending in divorce based on the wife's age at marriage.

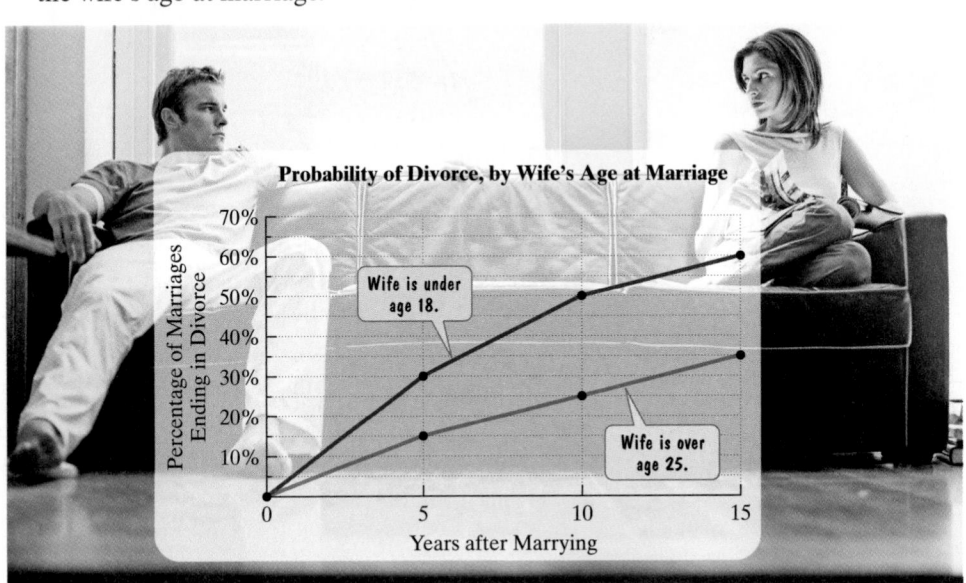

Figure 1.11
Source: B. E. Pruitt et al., *Human Sexuality*, Prentice Hall, 2007

Here are two mathematical models that approximate the data displayed by the line graphs:

Wife is under 18 at time of marriage.
$$d = 4n + 5$$

Wife is over 25 at time of marriage.
$$d = 2.3n + 1.5.$$

In each model, the variable n is the number of years after marriage and the variable d is the percentage of marriages ending in divorce.

 a. Use the appropriate formula to determine the percentage of marriages ending in divorce after 10 years when the wife is over 25 at the time of marriage.

 b. Use the appropriate line graph in **Figure 1.11** to determine the percentage of marriages ending in divorce after 10 years when the wife is over 25 at the time of marriage.

 c. Does the value given by the mathematical model underestimate or overestimate the actual percentage of marriages ending in divorce after 10 years as shown by the graph? By how much?

Solution

 a. Because the wife is over 25 at the time of marriage, we use the formula on the right, $d = 2.3n + 1.5$. To find the percentage of marriages ending in divorce after 10 years, we substitute 10 for n and evaluate the formula.

$$d = 2.3n + 1.5 \qquad \text{This is one of the two given mathematical models.}$$
$$d = 2.3(10) + 1.5 \qquad \text{Replace } n \text{ with 10.}$$
$$d = 23 + 1.5 \qquad \text{Multiply: } 2.3(10) = 23.$$
$$d = 24.5 \qquad \text{Add.}$$

The model indicates that 24.5% of marriages end in divorce after 10 years when the wife is over 25 at the time of marriage.

b. Now let's use the line graph that shows the percentage of marriages ending in divorce when the wife is over 25 at the time of marriage. The graph is shown again in **Figure 1.12**. To find the percentage of marriages ending in divorce after 10 years:

• Locate 10 on the horizontal axis and locate the point above 10.

• Read across to the corresponding percent on the vertical axis.

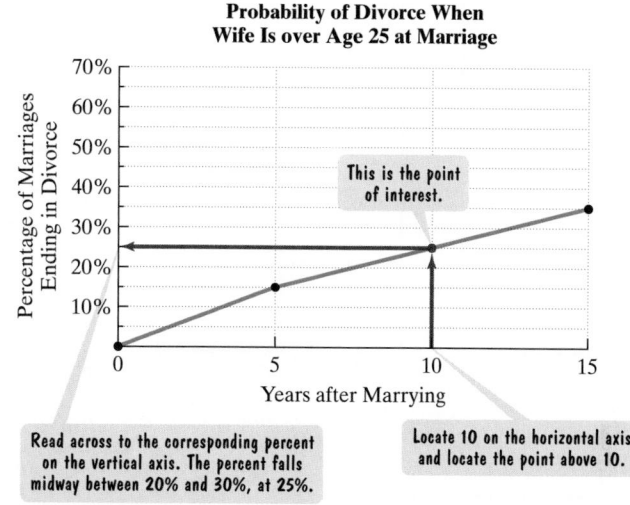

Figure 1.12

The actual data displayed by the graph indicate that 25% of these marriages end in divorce after 10 years.

c. The value obtained by evaluating the mathematical model, 24.5%, is close to, but slightly less than, the actual percentage of divorces, 25.0%. The difference between these percents is 25.0% − 24.5%, or 0.5%. The value given by the mathematical model, 24.5%, underestimates the actual percent, 25%, by only 0.5, providing a fairly accurate description of the data.

✅ Check Point **6**

a. Use the appropriate formula from Example 6 to determine the percentage of marriages ending in divorce after 15 years when the wife is under 18 at the time of marriage.

b. Use the appropriate line graph in **Figure 1.11** to determine the percentage of marriages ending in divorce after 15 years when the wife is under 18 at the time of marriage.

c. Does the value given by the mathematical model underestimate or overestimate the actual percentage of marriages ending in divorce after 15 years as shown by the graph? By how much?

Exercise Set 1.1

Practice Exercises

In Exercises 1–12, plot the given point in a rectangular coordinate system.

1. $(1, 4)$ **2.** $(2, 5)$ **3.** $(-2, 3)$

4. $(-1, 4)$ **5.** $(-3, -5)$ **6.** $(-4, -2)$

7. $(4, -1)$ **8.** $(3, -2)$ **9.** $(-4, 0)$

10. $(0, -3)$ **11.** $\left(\frac{7}{2}, -\frac{3}{2}\right)$ **12.** $\left(-\frac{5}{2}, \frac{3}{2}\right)$

Graph each equation in Exercises 13–28. Let $x = -3, -2, -1, 0, 1, 2,$ and 3.

13. $y = x^2 - 2$ **14.** $y = x^2 + 2$ **15.** $y = x - 2$

16. $y = x + 2$ **17.** $y = 2x + 1$ **18.** $y = 2x - 4$

19. $y = -\frac{1}{2}x$ **20.** $y = -\frac{1}{2}x + 2$ **21.** $y = 2|x|$

22. $y = -2|x|$ **23.** $y = |x| + 1$ **24.** $y = |x| - 1$

25. $y = 9 - x^2$ **26.** $y = -x^2$ **27.** $y = x^3$

28. $y = x^3 - 1$

In Exercises 29–32, match the viewing rectangle with the correct figure. Then label the tick marks in the figure to illustrate this viewing rectangle.

29. $[-5, 5, 1]$ by $[-5, 5, 1]$ **30.** $[-10, 10, 2]$ by $[-4, 4, 2]$

31. $[-20, 80, 10]$ by $[-30, 70, 10]$

32. $[-40, 40, 20]$ by $[-1000, 1000, 100]$

a. **b.**

c. **d.**

The table of values was generated by a graphing utility with a TABLE feature. Use the table to solve Exercises 33–40.

X	Y₁	Y₂
-3	9	5
-2	4	4
-1	1	3
0	0	2
1	1	1
2	4	0
3	9	-1

X = -3

33. Which equation corresponds to Y_2 in the table?

 a. $y_2 = x + 8$ **b.** $y_2 = x - 2$

 c. $y_2 = 2 - x$ **d.** $y_2 = 1 - 2x$

34. Which equation corresponds to Y_1 in the table?

 a. $y_1 = -3x$ **b.** $y_1 = x^2$

 c. $y_1 = -x^2$ **d.** $y_1 = 2 - x$

35. Does the graph of Y_2 pass through the origin?

36. Does the graph of Y_1 pass through the origin?

37. At which point does the graph of Y_2 cross the x-axis?

38. At which point does the graph of Y_2 cross the y-axis?

39. At which points do the graphs of Y_1 and Y_2 intersect?

40. For which values of x is $Y_1 = Y_2$?

In Exercises 41–46, use the graph to **a.** *determine the x-intercepts, if any;* **b.** *determine the y-intercepts, if any. For each graph, tick marks along the axes represent one unit each.*

41. **42.**

43. **44.**

45. **46.**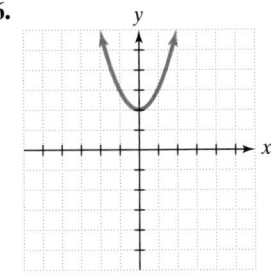

Practice Plus

In Exercises 47–50, write each English sentence as an equation in two variables. Then graph the equation.

47. The y-value is four more than twice the x-value.

48. The y-value is the difference between four and twice the x-value.

49. The y-value is three decreased by the square of the x-value.

50. The y-value is two more than the square of the x-value.

In Exercises 51–54, graph each equation.

51. $y = 5$ (Let $x = -3, -2, -1, 0, 1, 2,$ and 3.)

52. $y = -1$ (Let $x = -3, -2, -1, 0, 1, 2,$ and 3.)

53. $y = \dfrac{1}{x}$ (Let $x = -2, -1, -\dfrac{1}{2}, -\dfrac{1}{3}, \dfrac{1}{3}, \dfrac{1}{2}, 1,$ and 2.)

54. $y = -\dfrac{1}{x}$ (Let $x = -2, -1, -\dfrac{1}{2}, -\dfrac{1}{3}, \dfrac{1}{3}, \dfrac{1}{2}, 1,$ and 2.)

Application Exercises

The graphs show the percentage of high school seniors who used alcohol or marijuana during the 30 days prior to being surveyed for the University of Michigan's Monitoring the Future *study.*

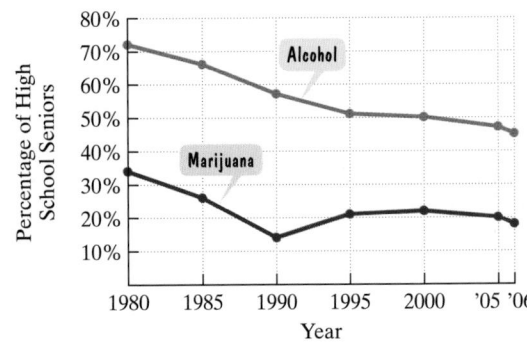

Alcohol and Marijuana Use by United States High School Seniors

Source: U.S. Department of Health and Human Services

The data can be described by the following mathematical models:

Percentage of seniors
using alcohol $A = -n + 70$

Number of years after 1980

Percentage of seniors
using marijuana $M = -0.4n + 28.$

Use this information to solve Exercises 55–56.

55. a. Use the appropriate line graph to determine the percentage of seniors who used marijuana in 2005.

b. Use the appropriate formula to determine the percentage of seniors who used marijuana in 2005. Does the formula underestimate or overestimate the actual percentage displayed by the graph? By how much?

c. Use the appropriate line graph to estimate the percentage of seniors who used alcohol in 2006.

d. Use the appropriate formula to determine the percentage of seniors who used alcohol in 2006. How does this compare with your estimate in part (c)?

e. For the period from 1980 through 2006, in which year was marijuana use by seniors at a minimum? Estimate the percentage of seniors who used marijuana in that year.

56. a. Use the appropriate line graph to determine the percentage of seniors who used alcohol in 2000.

b. Use the appropriate formula to determine the percentage of seniors who used alcohol in 2000. What do you observe?

c. Use the appropriate line graph to estimate the percentage of seniors who used marijuana in 2000.

d. Use the appropriate formula to determine the percentage of seniors who used marijuana in 2000. How does this compare with your estimate in part (c)?

e. For the period from 1980 through 2006, in which year was alcohol use by seniors at a maximum? Estimate the percentage of seniors who used alcohol in that year.

Contrary to popular belief, older people do not need less sleep than younger adults. However, the line graphs show that they awaken more often during the night. The numerous awakenings are one reason why some elderly individuals report that sleep is less restful than it had been in the past. Use the line graphs to solve Exercises 57–60.

**Average Number of Awakenings
During the Night, by Age and Gender**

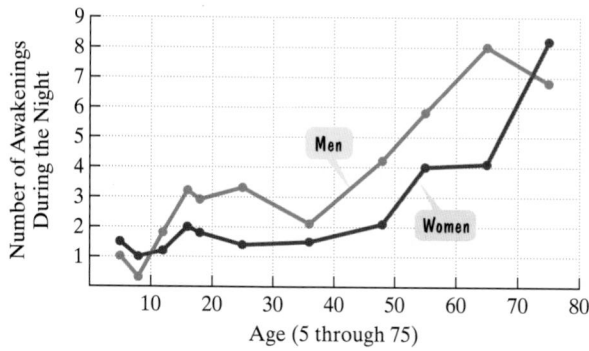

Source: Stephen Davis and Joseph Palladino, *Psychology*, 5th Edition, Prentice Hall, 2007

57. At which age, estimated to the nearest year, do women have the least number of awakenings during the night? What is the average number of awakenings at that age?

58. At which age do men have the greatest number of awakenings during the night? What is the average number of awakenings at that age?

59. Estimate, to the nearest tenth, the difference between the average number of awakenings during the night for 25-year-old men and 25-year-old women.

60. Estimate, to the nearest tenth, the difference between the average number of awakenings during the night for 18-year-old men and 18-year-old women.

Writing in Mathematics

61. What is the rectangular coordinate system?

62. Explain how to plot a point in the rectangular coordinate system. Give an example with your explanation.

63. Explain why $(5, -2)$ and $(-2, 5)$ do not represent the same point.

64. Explain how to graph an equation in the rectangular coordinate system.

65. What does a $[-20, 2, 1]$ by $[-4, 5, 0.5]$ viewing rectangle mean?

Technology Exercise

66. Use a graphing utility to verify each of your hand-drawn graphs in Exercises 13–28. Experiment with the size of the viewing rectangle to make the graph displayed by the graphing utility resemble your hand-drawn graph as much as possible.

Critical Thinking Exercises

Make Sense? *In Exercises 67–70, determine whether each statement makes sense or does not make sense, and explain your reasoning.*

67. The rectangular coordinate system provides a geometric picture of what an equation in two variables looks like.

68. There is something wrong with my graphing utility because it is not displaying numbers along the x- and y-axes.

69. I used the ordered pairs $(-2, 2)$, $(0, 0)$, and $(2, 2)$ to graph a straight line.

70. I used the ordered pairs

(time of day, calories that I burned)

to obtain a graph that is a horizontal line.

In Exercises 71–74, determine whether each statement is true or false. If the statement is false, make the necessary change(s) to produce a true statement.

71. If the product of a point's coordinates is positive, the point must be in quadrant I.

72. If a point is on the x-axis, it is neither up nor down, so $x = 0$.

73. If a point is on the y-axis, its x-coordinate must be 0.

74. The ordered pair $(2, 5)$ satisfies $3y - 2x = -4$.

In Exercises 75–78, match the story with the correct figure. The figures are labeled (a), (b), (c), and (d).

75. As the blizzard got worse, the snow fell harder and harder.

76. The snow fell more and more softly.

77. It snowed hard, but then it stopped. After a short time, the snow started falling softly.

78. It snowed softly, and then it stopped. After a short time, the snow started falling hard.

a.

b.

c.

d.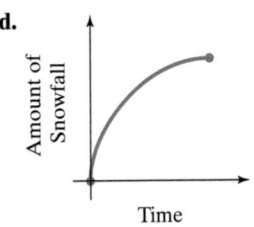

In Exercises 79–82, select the graph that best illustrates each story.

79. An airplane flew from Miami to San Francisco.

a.

b.

c.

d.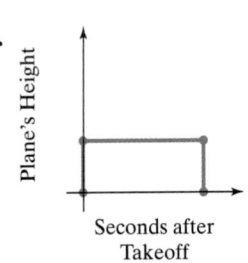

80. At noon, you begin to breathe in.

a.

b.

c.

d.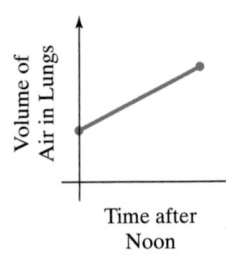

81. Measurements are taken of a person's height from birth to age 100.

a.

b.

c.

d.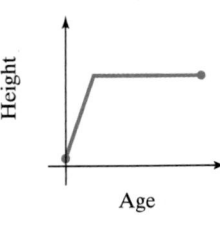

82. You begin your bike ride by riding down a hill. Then you ride up another hill. Finally, you ride along a level surface before coming to a stop.

a.

b.

c.

d.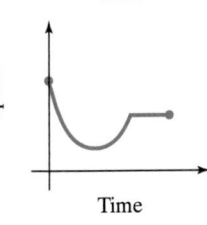

Preview Exercises

Exercises 83–85 will help you prepare for the material covered in the next section.

83. If 6 is substituted for x in the equation

$$2(x - 3) - 17 = 13 - 3(x + 2),$$

is the, resulting statement true or false?

84. Multiply and simplify: $12\left(\dfrac{x + 2}{4} - \dfrac{x - 1}{3}\right)$.

85. Multiply and simplify: $(x - 3)\left(\dfrac{3}{x - 3} + 9\right)$.

Linear Equations and Rational Equations

Objectives

1. Solve linear equations in one variable.
2. Solve linear equations containing fractions.
3. Solve rational equations with variables in the denominators.
4. Recognize identities, conditional equations, and inconsistent equations.
5. Solve applied problems using mathematical models.

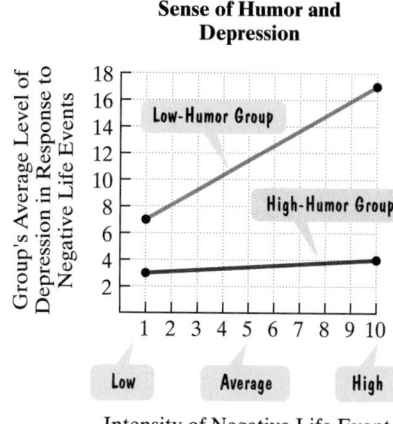

Sense of Humor and Depression

Low-Humor Group

High-Humor Group

Low Average High

Intensity of Negative Life Event

Figure 1.13
Source: Stephen Davis and Joseph Palladino, *Psychology*, 5th Edition, Prentice Hall, 2007

The belief that humor and laughter can have positive benefits on our lives is not new. The graphs in **Figure 1.13** indicate that persons with a low sense of humor have higher levels of depression in response to negative life events than those with a high sense of humor. These graphs can be modeled by the following formulas:

Low-Humor Group

High-Humor Group

$$D = \frac{10}{9}x + \frac{53}{9} \qquad D = \frac{1}{9}x + \frac{26}{9}.$$

In each formula, x represents the intensity of a negative life event (from 1, low, to 10, high) and D is the average level of depression in response to that event.

Suppose that the low-humor group averages a level of depression of 10 in response to a negative life event. We can determine the intensity of that event by substituting 10 for D in the low-humor model:

$$10 = \frac{10}{9}x + \frac{53}{9}.$$

The two sides of an equation can be reversed. So, we can also express this equation as

$$\frac{10}{9}x + \frac{53}{9} = 10.$$

Notice that the highest exponent on the variable is 1. Such an equation is called a *linear equation in one variable*. In this section, we will study how to solve linear equations.

1. Solve linear equations in one variable.

Solving Linear Equations in One Variable

We begin with a general definition of a linear equation in one variable.

Definition of a Linear Equation

A **linear equation in one variable** x is an equation that can be written in the form

$$ax + b = 0,$$

where a and b are real numbers, and $a \neq 0$.

An example of a linear equation in one variable is

$$4x + 12 = 0.$$

Solving an equation in x involves determining all values of x that result in a true statement when substituted into the equation. Such values are **solutions**, or **roots**, of the equation. For example, substitute -3 for x in $4x + 12 = 0$. We obtain

$$4(-3) + 12 = 0, \quad \text{or} \quad -12 + 12 = 0.$$

This simplifies to the true statement $0 = 0$. Thus, -3 is a solution of the equation $4x + 12 = 0$. We also say that -3 **satisfies** the equation $4x + 12 = 0$, because when we substitute -3 for x, a true statement results. The set of all such solutions is called the equation's **solution set**. For example, the solution set of the equation $4x + 12 = 0$ is $\{-3\}$ because -3 is the equation's only solution.

Two or more equations that have the same solution set are called **equivalent equations**. For example, the equations

$$4x + 12 = 0 \quad \text{and} \quad 4x = -12 \quad \text{and} \quad x = -3$$

are equivalent equations because the solution set for each is $\{-3\}$. To solve a linear equation in x, we transform the equation into an equivalent equation one or more times. Our final equivalent equation should be of the form

$$x = \text{a number}.$$

The solution set of this equation is the set consisting of the number.

To generate equivalent equations, we will use the following principles:

Generating Equivalent Equations

An equation can be transformed into an equivalent equation by one or more of the following operations:

Example

1. Simplify an expression by removing grouping symbols and combining like terms.

$$3(x - 6) = 6x - x$$
$$3x - 18 = 5x$$

2. Add (or subtract) the same real number or variable expression on *both* sides of the equation.

$$3x - 18 = 5x$$

$$3x - 18 - 3x = 5x - 3x$$

> Subtract $3x$ from both sides of the equation.

$$-18 = 2x$$

3. Multiply (or divide) by the same *nonzero* quantity on *both* sides of the equation.

$$-18 = 2x$$

$$\frac{-18}{2} = \frac{2x}{2}$$

> Divide both sides of the equation by 2.

$$-9 = x$$

4. Interchange the two sides of the equation.

$$-9 = x$$
$$x = -9$$

If you look closely at the equations in the box, you will notice that we have solved the equation $3(x - 6) = 6x - x$. The final equation, $x = -9$, with x isolated on the left side, shows that $\{-9\}$ is the solution set. The idea in solving a linear equation is to get the variable by itself on one side of the equal sign and a number by itself on the other side.

EXAMPLE 1 **Solving a Linear Equation**

Solve and check: $2x + 3 = 17$.

Solution Our goal is to obtain an equivalent equation with x isolated on one side and a number on the other side.

$2x + 3 = 17$	This is the given equation.
$2x + 3 - 3 = 17 - 3$	Subtract 3 from both sides.
$2x = 14$	Simplify.
$\dfrac{2x}{2} = \dfrac{14}{2}$	Divide both sides by 2.
$x = 7$	Simplify.

Now we check the proposed solution, 7, by replacing x with 7 in the original equation.

$2x + 3 = 17$	This is the original equation.
$2 \cdot 7 + 3 \overset{?}{=} 17$	Substitute 7 for x. The question mark indicates that we do not yet know if the two sides are equal.
$14 + 3 \overset{?}{=} 17$	Multiply: $2 \cdot 7 = 14$.
$17 = 17$	Add: $14 + 3 = 17$.

This statement is true.

Because the check results in a true statement, we conclude that the solution set of the given equation is $\{7\}$.

⬤

☑ **Check Point 1** Solve and check: $4x + 5 = 29$.

Study Tip

We simplify algebraic expressions. We solve algebraic equations. Notice the differences between the procedures:

Simplifying an Algebraic Expression

Simplify: $3(x - 7) - (5x - 11)$.

This is not an equation. There is no equal sign.

Solution $3(x - 7) - (5x - 11)$
$= 3x - 21 - 5x + 11$
$= (3x - 5x) + (-21 + 11)$
$= -2x + (-10)$
$= -2x - 10$

Stop! Further simplification is not possible. Avoid the common error of setting $-2x - 10$ equal to 0.

Solving an Algebraic Equation

Solve: $3(x - 7) - (5x - 11) = 14$.

This is an equation. There is an equal sign.

Solution $3(x - 7) - (5x - 11) = 14$
$3x - 21 - 5x + 11 = 14$
$-2x - 10 = 14$

Add 10 to both sides. $-2x - 10 + 10 = 14 + 10$
$-2x = 24$

Divide both sides by -2. $\dfrac{-2x}{-2} = \dfrac{24}{-2}$
$x = -12$

The solution set is $\{-12\}$.

Here is a step-by-step procedure for solving a linear equation in one variable. Not all of these steps are necessary to solve every equation.

Solving a Linear Equation

1. Simplify the algebraic expression on each side by removing grouping symbols and combining like terms.
2. Collect all the variable terms on one side and all the numbers, or constant terms, on the other side.
3. Isolate the variable and solve.
4. Check the proposed solution in the original equation.

$\boxed{\text{EXAMPLE 2}}$ **Solving a Linear Equation**

Solve and check: $2(x - 3) - 17 = 13 - 3(x + 2)$.

Solution

Step 1 Simplify the algebraic expression on each side.

> Do not begin with 13 − 3. Multiplication (the distributive property) is applied before subtraction.

$2(x - 3) - 17 = 13 - 3(x + 2)$ This is the given equation.

$2x - 6 - 17 = 13 - 3x - 6$ Use the distributive property.

$2x - 23 = -3x + 7$ Combine like terms.

Step 2 Collect variable terms on one side and constant terms on the other side. We will collect variable terms on the left by adding $3x$ to both sides. We will collect the numbers on the right by adding 23 to both sides.

$2x - 23 + 3x = -3x + 7 + 3x$ Add 3x to both sides.

$5x - 23 = 7$ Simplify: $2x + 3x = 5x$.

$5x - 23 + 23 = 7 + 23$ Add 23 to both sides.

$5x = 30$ Simplify.

Step 3 Isolate the variable and solve. We isolate the variable, x, by dividing both sides of $5x = 30$ by 5.

$$\frac{5x}{5} = \frac{30}{5}$$ Divide both sides by 5.

$x = 6$ Simplify.

Discovery

Solve the equation in Example 2 by collecting terms with the variable on the right and numerical terms on the left. What do you observe?

Step 4 Check the proposed solution in the original equation. Substitute 6 for x in the original equation.

$2(x - 3) - 17 = 13 - 3(x + 2)$ This is the original equation.

$2(6 - 3) - 17 \overset{?}{=} 13 - 3(6 + 2)$ Substitute 6 for x.

$2(3) - 17 \overset{?}{=} 13 - 3(8)$ Simplify inside parentheses.

$6 - 17 \overset{?}{=} 13 - 24$ Multiply.

$-11 = -11$ Subtract.

The true statement $-11 = -11$ verifies that the solution set is $\{6\}$.

Technology

Numeric and Graphic Connections

In many algebraic situations, technology provides numeric and visual insights into problem solving. For example, you can use a graphing utility to check the solution of a linear equation, giving numeric and geometric meaning to the solution. Enter each side of the equation separately under y_1 and y_2. Then use the table or the graphs to locate the x-value for which the y-values are the same. This x-value is the solution.

Let's verify our work in Example 2 and show that 6 is the solution of

$$2(x - 3) - 17 = 13 - 3(x + 2).$$

Enter $y_1 = 2(x - 3) - 17$
in the $\boxed{y=}$ screen.

Enter $y_2 = 13 - 3(x + 2)$
in the $\boxed{y=}$ screen.

Numeric Check

Display a table for y_1 and y_2.

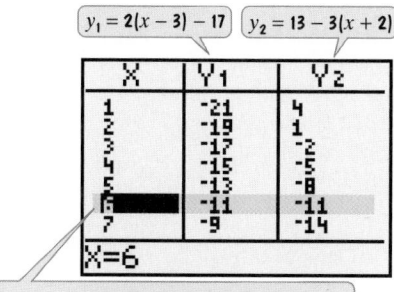

$y_1 = 2(x - 3) - 17$ $y_2 = 13 - 3(x + 2)$

When $x = 6$, y_1 and y_2 have the same value, namely −11. This verifies that 6 is the solution of $2(x - 3) - 17 = 13 - 3(x + 2)$.

Graphic Check

Display graphs for y_1 and y_2 and use the intersection feature. The solution is the x-coordinate of the intersection point.

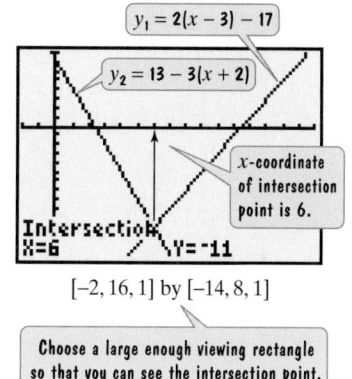

$[-2, 16, 1]$ by $[-14, 8, 1]$

Choose a large enough viewing rectangle so that you can see the intersection point.

✓ Check Point **2** Solve and check: $4(2x + 1) = 29 + 3(2x - 5)$.

2 Solve linear equations containing fractions.

Linear Equations with Fractions

Equations are easier to solve when they do not contain fractions. How do we remove fractions from an equation? We begin by multiplying both sides of the equation by the least common denominator of any fractions in the equation. The least common denominator is the smallest number that all denominators will divide into. Multiplying every term on both sides of the equation by the least common denominator will eliminate the fractions in the equation. Example 3 shows how we "clear an equation of fractions."

(**EXAMPLE 3**) **Solving a Linear Equation Involving Fractions**

Solve and check: $\dfrac{x + 2}{4} - \dfrac{x - 1}{3} = 2$.

Solution The fractional terms have denominators of 4 and 3. The smallest number that is divisible by 4 and 3 is 12. We begin by multiplying both sides of the equation by 12, the least common denominator.

$$\frac{x + 2}{4} - \frac{x - 1}{3} = 2 \qquad \text{This is the given equation.}$$

$$12\left(\frac{x + 2}{4} - \frac{x - 1}{3}\right) = 12 \cdot 2 \qquad \text{Multiply both sides by 12.}$$

$$12\left(\frac{x + 2}{4}\right) - 12\left(\frac{x - 1}{3}\right) = 24 \qquad \text{Use the distributive property and multiply each term on the left by 12.}$$

$$\overset{3}{\cancel{12}}\left(\frac{x + 2}{\underset{1}{4}}\right) - \overset{4}{\cancel{12}}\left(\frac{x - 1}{\underset{1}{3}}\right) = 24 \qquad \text{Divide out common factors in each multiplication on the left.}$$

$$3(x + 2) - 4(x - 1) = 24 \qquad \text{The fractions are now cleared.}$$

$$3x + 6 - 4x + 4 = 24 \qquad \text{Use the distributive property.}$$

$$-x + 10 = 24 \qquad \text{Combine like terms: } 3x - 4x = -x \text{ and } 6 + 4 = 10.$$

$$-x + 10 - 10 = 24 - 10 \qquad \text{Subtract 10 from both sides.}$$

$$-x = 14 \qquad \text{Simplify.}$$

> We're not finished. A negative sign should not precede the variable.

Isolate x by multiplying or dividing both sides of this equation by -1.

$$\frac{-x}{-1} = \frac{14}{-1} \qquad \text{Divide both sides by } -1.$$

$$x = -14 \qquad \text{Simplify.}$$

Check the proposed solution. Substitute -14 for x in the original equation. You should obtain $2 = 2$. This true statement verifies that the solution set is $\{-14\}$. ⬤

⊘ **Check Point 3** Solve and check: $\dfrac{x - 3}{4} = \dfrac{5}{14} - \dfrac{x + 5}{7}$.

❸ Solve rational equations with variables in the denominators.

Rational Equations

A **rational equation** is an equation containing one or more rational expressions. In Example 3, we solved a rational equation with constants in the denominators. This rational equation was a linear equation. Now, let's consider a rational equation such as

$$\frac{1}{x} = \frac{1}{5} + \frac{3}{2x}.$$

Can you see how this rational equation differs from the rational equation that we solved earlier? The variable, x, appears in two of the denominators. Although this rational equation is not a linear equation, the solution procedure still involves multiplying each side by the least common denominator. However, we must avoid any values of the variable that make a denominator zero. For example, examine the denominators in the equation

$$\frac{1}{x} = \frac{1}{5} + \frac{3}{2x}.$$

> This denominator would equal zero if $x = 0$.

> This denominator would equal zero if $x = 0$.

We see that x cannot equal zero. With this in mind, let's solve the equation.

EXAMPLE 4 Solving a Rational Equation

Solve: $\dfrac{1}{x} = \dfrac{1}{5} + \dfrac{3}{2x}$.

Solution The denominators are x, 5, and $2x$. The least common denominator is $10x$. We begin by multiplying both sides of the equation by $10x$. We will also write the restriction that x cannot equal zero to the right of the equation.

$$\dfrac{1}{x} = \dfrac{1}{5} + \dfrac{3}{2x}, \quad x \neq 0 \qquad \text{This is the given equation.}$$

$$10x \cdot \dfrac{1}{x} = 10x \left(\dfrac{1}{5} + \dfrac{3}{2x} \right) \qquad \text{Multiply both sides by 10x.}$$

$$10x \cdot \dfrac{1}{x} = 10x \cdot \dfrac{1}{5} + 10x \cdot \dfrac{3}{2x} \qquad \text{Use the distributive property. Be sure to multiply each term by 10x.}$$

$$10\,\cancel{x} \cdot \dfrac{1}{\cancel{x}} = \overset{2}{\cancel{10}}\,x \cdot \dfrac{1}{\cancel{5}} + \overset{5}{\cancel{10}}\,\cancel{x} \cdot \dfrac{3}{2\,\cancel{x}} \qquad \text{Divide out common factors in the multiplications.}$$

$$10 = 2x + 15 \qquad \text{Complete the multiplications.}$$

Observe that the resulting equation,

$$10 = 2x + 15,$$

is now cleared of fractions. With the variable term, $2x$, already on the right, we will collect constant terms on the left by subtracting 15 from both sides.

$$10 - 15 = 2x + 15 - 15 \qquad \text{Subtract 15 from both sides.}$$

$$-5 = 2x \qquad \text{Simplify.}$$

Finally, we isolate the variable, x, in $-5 = 2x$ by dividing both sides by 2.

$$\dfrac{-5}{2} = \dfrac{2x}{2} \qquad \text{Divide both sides by 2.}$$

$$-\dfrac{5}{2} = x \qquad \text{Simplify.}$$

We check our solution by substituting $-\frac{5}{2}$ into the original equation or by using a calculator. With a calculator, evaluate each side of the equation for $x = -\frac{5}{2}$, or for $x = -2.5$. Note that the original restriction that $x \neq 0$ is met. The solution set is $\left\{ -\frac{5}{2} \right\}$. ●

⊘ Check Point **4** Solve: $\dfrac{5}{2x} = \dfrac{17}{18} - \dfrac{1}{3x}$.

EXAMPLE 5 Solving a Rational Equation

Solve: $\dfrac{x}{x-3} = \dfrac{3}{x-3} + 9$.

Solution We must avoid any values of the variable x that make a denominator zero.

$$\dfrac{x}{x-3} = \dfrac{3}{x-3} + 9$$

These denominators are zero if $x = 3$.

We see that x cannot equal 3. With denominators of $x - 3$, $x - 3$, and 1, the least common denominator is $x - 3$. We multiply both sides of the equation by

$x - 3$. We also write the restriction that x cannot equal 3 to the right of the equation.

$$\frac{x}{x-3} = \frac{3}{x-3} + 9, \quad x \neq 3$$ This is the given equation.

$$(x - 3) \cdot \frac{x}{x-3} = (x-3)\left(\frac{3}{x-3} + 9\right)$$ Multiply both sides by x − 3.

$$(x - 3) \cdot \frac{x}{x-3} = (x-3) \cdot \frac{3}{x-3} + (x-3) \cdot 9$$ Use the distributive property.

$$\cancel{(x-3)} \cdot \frac{x}{\cancel{x-3}} = \cancel{(x-3)} \cdot \frac{3}{\cancel{x-3}} + 9(x-3)$$ Divide out common factors in two of the multiplications.

$$x = 3 + 9(x - 3)$$ Simplify.

The resulting equation is cleared of fractions. We now solve for x.

$$x = 3 + 9x - 27$$ Use the distributive property.

$$x = 9x - 24$$ Combine numerical terms.

$$x - 9x = 9x - 24 - 9x$$ Subtract 9x from both sides.

$$-8x = -24$$ Simplify.

$$\frac{-8x}{-8} = \frac{-24}{-8}$$ Divide both sides by −8.

$$x = 3$$ Simplify.

Study Tip

Reject any proposed solution that causes any denominator in an equation to equal 0.

The proposed solution, 3, is *not* a solution because of the restriction that $x \neq 3$. There is *no solution to this equation*. The solution set for this equation contains no elements. The solution set is \varnothing, the empty set.

✓ **Check Point 5** Solve: $\dfrac{x}{x-2} = \dfrac{2}{x-2} - \dfrac{2}{3}$.

EXAMPLE 6 **Solving a Rational Equation to Determine When Two Equations Are Equal**

Consider the equations

$$y_1 = \frac{3}{x+6} + \frac{1}{x-2} \quad \text{and} \quad y_2 = \frac{4}{x^2 + 4x - 12}.$$

Find all values of x for which $y_1 = y_2$.

Solution Because we are interested in one or more values of x that cause y_1 and y_2 to be equal, we set the expressions that define y_1 and y_2 equal to each other:

$$\frac{3}{x+6} + \frac{1}{x-2} = \frac{4}{x^2 + 4x - 12}.$$

To identify values of x that make denominators zero, let's factor $x^2 + 4x - 12$, the denominator on the right. This factorization is also necessary in identifying the least common denominator.

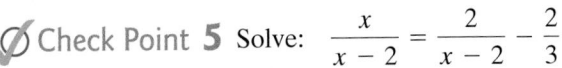

$$\frac{3}{x+6} + \frac{1}{x-2} = \frac{4}{(x+6)(x-2)}$$

| This denominator is zero if $x = -6$. | This denominator is zero if $x = 2$. | This denominator is zero if $x = -6$ or $x = 2$. |

We see that x cannot equal -6 or 2. The least common denominator is $(x+6)(x-2)$.

$$\frac{3}{x + 6} + \frac{1}{x - 2} = \frac{4}{(x + 6)(x - 2)}, \quad x \neq -6, \quad x \neq 2$$

This is the given equation with a denominator factored.

$$(x + 6)(x - 2)\left(\frac{3}{x + 6} + \frac{1}{x - 2}\right) = (x + 6)(x - 2) \cdot \frac{4}{(x + 6)(x - 2)}$$

Multiply both sides by $(x + 6)(x - 2)$, the LCD.

$$(x + 6)(x - 2) \cdot \frac{3}{x + 6} + (x + 6)(x - 2) \cdot \frac{1}{x - 2} = (x + 6)(x - 2) \cdot \frac{4}{(x + 6)(x - 2)}$$

Use the distributive property and divide out common factors.

$$3(x - 2) + 1(x + 6) = 4$$

Simplify. This equation is cleared of fractions.

$$3x - 6 + x + 6 = 4$$

Use the distributive property.

$$4x = 4$$

Combine like terms.

$$\frac{4x}{4} = \frac{4}{4}$$

Divide both sides by 4.

$$x = 1$$

Simplify. This is not part of the restriction that $x \neq -6$ and $x \neq 2$.

The value of x for which $y_1 = y_2$ is 1.

Check

Is $y_1 = y_2$ when $x = 1$? We use the given equations

$$y_1 = \frac{3}{x + 6} + \frac{1}{x - 2} \quad \text{and} \quad y_2 = \frac{4}{x^2 + 4x - 12}$$

to answer the question.

Checking by Hand

Substitute 1 for x in y_1 and y_2.

$$y_1 = \frac{3}{1 + 6} + \frac{1}{1 - 2} = \frac{3}{7} + \frac{1}{-1}$$

$$= \frac{3}{7} - 1 = \frac{3}{7} - \frac{7}{7} = -\frac{4}{7}$$

$$y_2 = \frac{4}{1^2 + 4 \cdot 1 - 12} = \frac{4}{1 + 4 - 12}$$

$$= \frac{4}{-7} = -\frac{4}{7}$$

When $x = 1$, y_1 and y_2 have the same value, namely, $-\frac{4}{7}$.

Checking with a Graphing Utility

Display a table showing values for y_1 and y_2. Enter the equations as y_1 and y_2, and be careful with parentheses.

$y_1 = 3 \div (x + 6) + 1 \div (x - 2)$ $y_2 = 4 \div (x^2 + 4x - 12)$

No matter how far up or down you scroll, $y_1 = y_2$ only when $x = 1$.

✓ Check Point **6** Consider the equations

$$y_1 = \frac{1}{x + 4} + \frac{1}{x - 4} \quad \text{and} \quad y_2 = \frac{22}{x^2 - 16}.$$

Find all values of x for which $y_1 = y_2$ and check.

④ Recognize identities, conditional equations, and inconsistent equations.

Types of Equations

Equations can be placed into categories that depend on their solution sets.

An equation that is true for all real numbers for which both sides are defined is called an **identity**. An example of an identity is

$$x + 3 = x + 2 + 1.$$

Every number plus 3 is equal to that number plus 2 plus 1. Therefore, the solution set to this equation is the set of all real numbers, expressed as $\{x | x \text{ is a real number}\}$.

Another example of an identity is

$$\frac{2x}{x} = 2.$$

Because division by 0 is undefined, this equation is true for all real number values of x except 0. The solution set is the set of nonzero real numbers, expressed as $\{x | x \text{ is a real number and } x \neq 0\}$.

An equation that is not an identity, but that is true for at least one real number, is called a **conditional equation**. The equation $2x + 3 = 17$ is an example of a conditional equation. The equation is not an identity and is true only if x is 7.

An **inconsistent equation** is an equation that is not true for even one real number. An example of an inconsistent equation is

$$x = x + 7.$$

There is no number that is equal to itself plus 7. The equation's solution set is \varnothing, the empty set. Some inconsistent equations are less obvious than this. Consider the equation in Example 5,

$$\frac{x}{x - 3} = \frac{3}{x - 3} + 9.$$

This equation is not true for any real number and has no solution. Thus, it is inconsistent.

Study Tip

If you are concerned by the vocabulary of equation types, keep in mind that there are three possible situations. We can state these situations informally as follows:

1. $x = $ a real number

 conditional equation

2. $x = $ all real numbers

 identity

3. $x = $ no real numbers.

 inconsistent equation

(EXAMPLE 7) **Categorizing an Equation**

Solve and determine whether the equation

$$2(x + 1) = 2x + 3$$

is an identity, a conditional equation, or an inconsistent equation.

Solution Begin by applying the distributive property on the left side. We obtain

$$2x + 2 = 2x + 3.$$

Does something look strange? Can doubling a number and increasing the product by 2 give the same result as doubling the same number and increasing the product by 3? No. Let's continue solving the equation by subtracting $2x$ from both sides.

$$2x - 2x + 2 = 2x - 2x + 3$$

Keep reading. 2 = 3 is not the solution. $2 = 3$

The original equation, $2(x + 1) = 2x + 3$, is equivalent to the statement $2 = 3$, which is false for every value of x. The equation is inconsistent and has no solution. The solution set is \varnothing, the empty set.

Technology

Graphic Connections

How can technology visually reinforce the fact that the equation

$$2(x + 1) = 2x + 3$$

has no solution? Enter $y_1 = 2(x + 1)$ and $y_2 = 2x + 3$. The graphs of y_1 and y_2 appear to be parallel lines with no intersection point. This supports our conclusion that $2(x + 1) = 2x + 3$ is an inconsistent equation with no solution.

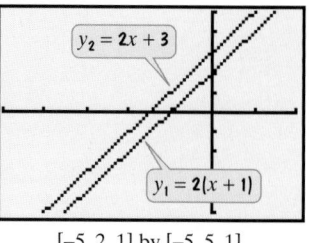

$[-5, 2, 1]$ by $[-5, 5, 1]$

⊘ Check Point **7** Solve and determine whether the equation

$$4x - 7 = 4(x - 1) + 3$$

is an identity, a conditional equation, or an inconsistent equation.

⑤ Solve applied problems using mathematical models.

Applications

Our next example shows how the procedure for solving linear equations can be used to find the value of a variable in a mathematical model.

(**EXAMPLE 8**) **An Application: Responding to Negative Life Events**

In the section opener, we introduced line graphs, repeated in **Figure 1.13**, indicating that persons with a low sense of humor have higher levels of depression in response to negative life events than those with a high sense of humor. These graphs can be modeled by the following formulas:

Low-Humor Group

High-Humor Group

$$D = \frac{10}{9}x + \frac{53}{9} \qquad D = \frac{1}{9}x + \frac{26}{9}.$$

In each formula, x represents the intensity of a negative life event (from 1, low, to 10, high) and D is the average level of depression in response to that event. If the high-humor group averages a level of depression of 3.5, or $\frac{7}{2}$, in response to a negative life event, what is the intensity of that event? How is the solution shown on the red line graph in **Figure 1.13**?

Solution We are interested in the intensity of a negative life event with an average level of depression of $\frac{7}{2}$ for the high-humor group. We substitute $\frac{7}{2}$ for D in the high-humor model and solve for x, the intensity of the negative life event.

Sense of Humor and Depression

Low-Humor Group

High-Humor Group

Group's Average Level of Depression in Response to Negative Life Events

Low Average High

Intensity of Negative Life Event

Figure 1.13 (repeated)

$$D = \frac{1}{9}x + \frac{26}{9} \qquad \text{This is the given formula for the high-humor group.}$$

$$\frac{7}{2} = \frac{1}{9}x + \frac{26}{9} \qquad \text{Replace } D \text{ with } \frac{7}{2}.$$

$$18 \cdot \frac{7}{2} = 18\left(\frac{1}{9}x + \frac{26}{9}\right) \qquad \text{Multiply both sides by 18, the least common denominator.}$$

$$18 \cdot \frac{7}{2} = 18 \cdot \frac{1}{9}x + 18 \cdot \frac{26}{9} \qquad \text{Use the distributive property.}$$

$$\overset{9}{\cancel{18}} \cdot \frac{7}{\underset{1}{2}} = \overset{2}{\cancel{18}} \cdot \frac{1}{\underset{1}{9}} x + \overset{2}{\cancel{18}} \cdot \frac{26}{\underset{1}{9}}$$ Divide out common factors in the multiplications.

$$63 = 2x + 52$$ Complete the multiplications. The fractions are now cleared.

$$63 - 52 = 2x + 52 - 52$$ Subtract 52 from both sides to get constants on the left.

$$11 = 2x$$ Simplify.

$$\frac{11}{2} = \frac{2x}{2}$$ Divide both sides by 2.

$$\frac{11}{2} = x$$ Simplify.

The formula indicates that if the high-humor group averages a level of depression of 3.5 in response to a negative life event, the intensity of that event is $\frac{11}{2}$, or 5.5. This is illustrated on the line graph for the high-humor group in **Figure 1.14**.

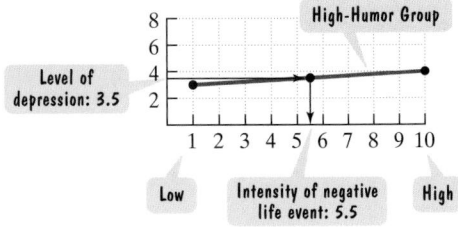

Figure 1.14

✓ Check Point **8** Use the model for the low-humor group given in Example 8 to solve this problem. If the low-humor group averages a level of depression of 10 in response to a negative life event, what is the intensity of that event? How is the solution shown on the blue line graph in **Figure 1.13**?

Exercise Set 1.2

Practice Exercises

In Exercises 1–16, solve and check each linear equation.

1. $7x - 5 = 72$

2. $6x - 3 = 63$

3. $11x - (6x - 5) = 40$

4. $5x - (2x - 10) = 35$

5. $2x - 7 = 6 + x$

6. $3x + 5 = 2x + 13$

7. $7x + 4 = x + 16$

8. $13x + 14 = 12x - 5$

9. $3(x - 2) + 7 = 2(x + 5)$

10. $2(x - 1) + 3 = x - 3(x + 1)$

11. $3(x - 4) - 4(x - 3) = x + 3 - (x - 2)$

12. $2 - (7x + 5) = 13 - 3x$

13. $16 = 3(x - 1) - (x - 7)$

14. $5x - (2x + 2) = x + (3x - 5)$

15. $25 - [2 + 5y - 3(y + 2)] =$
$-3(2y - 5) - [5(y - 1) - 3y + 3]$

16. $45 - [4 - 2y - 4(y + 7)] =$
$-4(1 + 3y) - [4 - 3(y + 2) - 2(2y - 5)]$

Exercises 17–30 contain linear equations with constants in denominators. Solve each equation.

17. $\frac{x}{3} = \frac{x}{2} - 2$

18. $\frac{x}{5} = \frac{x}{6} + 1$

19. $20 - \frac{x}{3} = \frac{x}{2}$

20. $\frac{x}{5} - \frac{1}{2} = \frac{x}{6}$

21. $\frac{3x}{5} = \frac{2x}{3} + 1$

22. $\frac{x}{2} = \frac{3x}{4} + 5$

23. $\frac{3x}{5} - x = \frac{x}{10} - \frac{5}{2}$

24. $2x - \frac{2x}{7} = \frac{x}{2} + \frac{17}{2}$

25. $\frac{x + 3}{6} = \frac{3}{8} + \frac{x - 5}{4}$

26. $\frac{x + 1}{4} = \frac{1}{6} + \frac{2 - x}{3}$

27. $\frac{x}{4} = 2 + \frac{x - 3}{3}$

28. $5 + \frac{x - 2}{3} = \frac{x + 3}{8}.$

29. $\frac{x + 1}{3} = 5 - \frac{x + 2}{7}$

30. $\frac{3x}{5} - \frac{x - 3}{2} = \frac{x + 2}{3}$

*Exercises 31–50 contain rational equations with variables in denominators. For each equation, **a.** Write the value or values of the variable that make a denominator zero. These are the restrictions on the variable. **b.** Keeping the restrictions in mind, solve the equation.*

31. $\frac{4}{x} = \frac{5}{2x} + 3$

32. $\frac{5}{x} = \frac{10}{3x} + 4$

33. $\frac{2}{x} + 3 = \frac{5}{2x} + \frac{13}{4}$

34. $\frac{7}{2x} - \frac{5}{3x} = \frac{22}{3}$

35. $\frac{2}{3x} + \frac{1}{4} = \frac{11}{6x} - \frac{1}{3}$

36. $\frac{5}{2x} - \frac{8}{9} = \frac{1}{18} - \frac{1}{3x}$

37. $\frac{x - 2}{2x} + 1 = \frac{x + 1}{x}$

38. $\frac{4}{x} - \frac{9}{5} = \frac{7x - 4}{5x}$

39. $\frac{1}{x - 1} + 5 = \frac{11}{x - 1}$

40. $\frac{3}{x + 4} - 7 = \frac{-4}{x + 4}$

41. $\frac{8x}{x + 1} = 4 - \frac{8}{x + 1}$

42. $\frac{2}{x - 2} = \frac{x}{x - 2} - 2$

43. $\frac{3}{2x - 2} + \frac{1}{2} = \frac{2}{x - 1}$

44. $\dfrac{3}{x+3} = \dfrac{5}{2x+6} + \dfrac{1}{x-2}$

45. $\dfrac{3}{x+2} + \dfrac{2}{x-2} = \dfrac{8}{(x+2)(x-2)}$

46. $\dfrac{5}{x+2} + \dfrac{3}{x-2} = \dfrac{12}{(x+2)(x-2)}$

47. $\dfrac{2}{x+1} - \dfrac{1}{x-1} = \dfrac{2x}{x^2-1}$

48. $\dfrac{4}{x+5} + \dfrac{2}{x-5} = \dfrac{32}{x^2-25}$

49. $\dfrac{1}{x-4} - \dfrac{5}{x+2} = \dfrac{6}{x^2-2x-8}$

50. $\dfrac{6}{x+3} - \dfrac{5}{x-2} = \dfrac{-20}{x^2+x-6}$

In Exercises 51–56, find all values of x satisfying the given conditions.

51. $y_1 = 5(2x-8) - 2$, $y_2 = 5(x-3) + 3$, and $y_1 = y_2$.

52. $y_1 = 7(3x-2) + 5$, $y_2 = 6(2x-1) + 24$, and $y_1 = y_2$.

53. $y_1 = \dfrac{x-3}{5}$, $y_2 = \dfrac{x-5}{4}$, and $y_1 - y_2 = 1$.

54. $y_1 = \dfrac{x+1}{4}$, $y_2 = \dfrac{x-2}{3}$, and $y_1 - y_2 = -4$.

55. $y_1 = \dfrac{5}{x+4}$, $y_2 = \dfrac{3}{x+3}$, $y_3 = \dfrac{12x+19}{x^2+7x+12}$, and $y_1 + y_2 = y_3$.

56. $y_1 = \dfrac{2x-1}{x^2+2x-8}$, $y_2 = \dfrac{2}{x+4}$, $y_3 = \dfrac{1}{x-2}$, and $y_1 + y_2 = y_3$.

In Exercises 57–60, find all values of x such that y = 0.

57. $y = 4[x - (3-x)] - 7(x+1)$

58. $y = 2[3x - (4x-6)] - 5(x-6)$

59. $y = \dfrac{x+6}{3x-12} - \dfrac{5}{x-4} - \dfrac{2}{3}$

60. $y = \dfrac{1}{5x+5} - \dfrac{3}{x+1} + \dfrac{7}{5}$

In Exercises 61–68, determine whether each equation is an identity, a conditional equation, or an inconsistent equation.

61. $4(x-7) = 4x - 28$

62. $4(x-7) = 4x + 28$

63. $2x + 3 = 2x - 3$

64. $\dfrac{7x}{x} = 7$

65. $4x + 5x = 8x$

66. $8x + 2x = 9x$

67. $\dfrac{2x}{x-3} = \dfrac{6}{x-3} + 4$

68. $\dfrac{3}{x-3} = \dfrac{x}{x-3} + 3$

The equations in Exercises 69–80 combine the types of equations we have discussed in this section. Solve each equation. Then state whether the equation is an identity, a conditional equation, or an inconsistent equation.

69. $\dfrac{x+5}{2} - 4 = \dfrac{2x-1}{3}$

70. $\dfrac{x+2}{7} = 5 - \dfrac{x+1}{3}$

71. $\dfrac{2}{x-2} = 3 + \dfrac{x}{x-2}$

72. $\dfrac{6}{x+3} + 2 = \dfrac{-2x}{x+3}$

73. $8x - (3x+2) + 10 = 3x$

74. $2(x+2) + 2x = 4(x+1)$

75. $\dfrac{2}{x} + \dfrac{1}{2} = \dfrac{3}{4}$

76. $\dfrac{3}{x} - \dfrac{1}{6} = \dfrac{1}{3}$

77. $\dfrac{4}{x-2} + \dfrac{3}{x+5} = \dfrac{7}{(x+5)(x-2)}$

78. $\dfrac{1}{x-1} = \dfrac{1}{(2x+3)(x-1)} + \dfrac{4}{2x+3}$

79. $\dfrac{4x}{x+3} - \dfrac{12}{x-3} = \dfrac{4x^2+36}{x^2-9}$

80. $\dfrac{4}{x^2+3x-10} - \dfrac{1}{x^2+x-6} = \dfrac{3}{x^2-x-12}$

In Exercises 81–84, use the Y= *screen to write the equation being solved. Then use the table to solve the equation.*

81.

82.

83.

84.

Practice Plus

85. Evaluate $x^2 - x$ for the value of x satisfying
$4(x - 2) + 2 = 4x - 2(2 - x)$.

86. Evaluate $x^2 - x$ for the value of x satisfying
$2(x - 6) = 3x + 2(2x - 1)$.

87. Evaluate $x^2 - (xy - y)$ for x satisfying $\dfrac{3(x + 3)}{5} = 2x + 6$
and y satisfying $-2y - 10 = 5y + 18$.

88. Evaluate $x^2 - (xy - y)$ for x satisfying $\dfrac{13x - 6}{4} = 5x + 2$
and y satisfying $5 - y = 7(y + 4) + 1$.

In Exercises 89–96, solve each equation.

89. $[(3 + 6)^2 \div 3] \cdot 4 = -54x$

90. $2^3 - [4(5 - 3)^3] = -8x$

91. $5 - 12x = 8 - 7x - [6 \div 3(2 + 5^3) + 5x]$

92. $2(5x + 58) = 10x + 4(21 \div 3.5 - 11)$

93. $0.7x + 0.4(20) = 0.5(x + 20)$

94. $0.5(x + 2) = 0.1 + 3(0.1x + 0.3)$

95. $4x + 13 - \{2x - [4(x - 3) - 5]\} = 2(x - 6)$

96. $-2\{7 - [4 - 2(1 - x) + 3]\} = 10 - [4x - 2(x - 3)]$

Application Exercises

The latest guidelines, which apply to both men and women, give healthy weight ranges, rather than specific weights, for your height. The further you are above the upper limit of your range, the greater are the risks of developing weight-related health problems. The bar graph shows these ranges for various heights for people between the ages of 19 and 34, inclusive.

Healthy Weight Ranges for Men and Women, Ages 19 to 34

Source: U.S. Department of Health and Human Services

The mathematical model

$$\frac{W}{2} - 3H = 53$$

describes a weight, W, in pounds, that lies within the healthy weight range for a person whose height is H inches over 5 feet. Use this information to solve Exercises 97–98.

97. Use the formula to find a healthy weight for a person whose height is 5′6″. (*Hint: H = 6* because this person's height is 6 inches over 5 feet.) How many pounds is this healthy weight below the upper end of the range shown by the bar graph?

98. Use the formula to find a healthy weight for a person whose height is 6′0″. (*Hint: H = 12* because this person's height is 12 inches over 5 feet.) How many pounds is this healthy weight below the upper end of the range shown by the bar graph?

The line graph shows the cost of inflation. What cost $10,000 in 1975 would cost the amount shown by the graph in subsequent years. (The symbol ⌁ on the horizontal axis shows that there is a break in values between 0 and 80. Thus, the first tick mark on the horizontal axis represents 1980.)

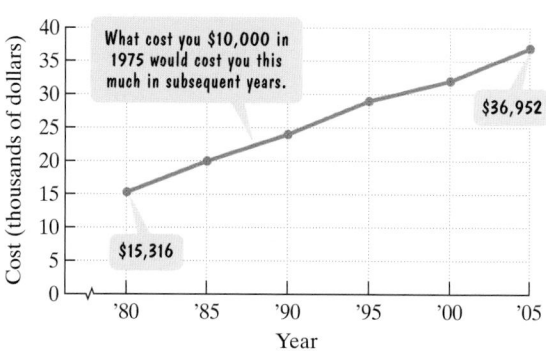

The Cost of Inflation

Source: Bureau of Labor Statistics

Here are two mathematical models for the data shown in the graph. In each formula, C represents the cost x years after 1980 of what cost $10,000 in 1975.

Model 1 $C = 865x + 15,316$

Model 2 $C = -2x^2 + 900x + 15,397$

Use these models to solve Exercises 99–102.

99. a. Use the graph to estimate the cost in 2000, to the nearest thousand dollars, of what cost $10,000 in 1975.

　b. Use model 1 to determine the cost in 2000 of what cost $10,000 in 1975. By how much does this differ from your estimate from part (a)?

　c. Use model 2 to determine the cost in 2000 of what cost $10,000 in 1975. By how much does this differ from your estimate from part (a)?

100. a. Use the graph to estimate the cost in 1990, to the nearest thousand dollars, of what cost $10,000 in 1975.

　b. Use model 1 to determine the cost in 1990 of what cost $10,000 in 1975. By how much does this differ from your estimate from part (a)?

　c. Use model 2 to determine the cost in 1990 of what cost $10,000 in 1975. By how much does this differ from your estimate from part (a)?

101. Use model 1 to determine in which year the cost will be $43,861 for what cost $10,000 in 1975.

102. Use model 1 to determine in which year the cost will be $54,241 for what cost $10,000 in 1975.

Formulas with rational expressions are often used to model learning. Many of these formulas model the proportion of correct responses in terms of the number of trials of a particular task. One such model, called a learning curve, is

$$P = \frac{0.9x - 0.4}{0.9x + 0.1},$$

where P is the proportion of correct responses after x trials. If P = 0, there are no correct responses. If P = 1, all responses are correct. The graph of the rational formula is shown. Use the formula to solve Exercises 103–104.

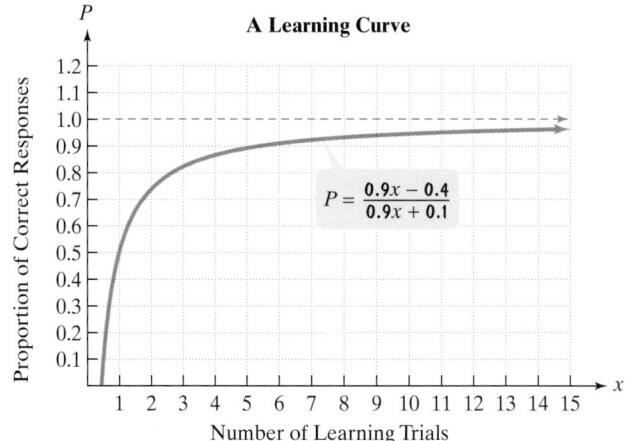

A Learning Curve

$$P = \frac{0.9x - 0.4}{0.9x + 0.1}$$

Number of Learning Trials

103. How many learning trials are necessary for 0.95 of the responses to be correct? Identify your solution as a point on the graph.

104. How many learning trials are necessary for 0.5 of the responses to be correct? Identify your solution as a point on the graph.

105. A company wants to increase the 10% peroxide content of its product by adding pure peroxide (100% peroxide). If x liters of pure peroxide are added to 500 liters of its 10% solution, the concentration, C, of the new mixture is given by

$$C = \frac{x + 0.1(500)}{x + 500}.$$

How many liters of pure peroxide should be added to produce a new product that is 28% peroxide?

106. Suppose that x liters of pure acid are added to 200 liters of a 35% acid solution.

 a. Write a formula that gives the concentration, C, of the new mixture. (*Hint:* See Exercise 105.)

 b. How many liters of pure acid should be added to produce a new mixture that is 74% acid?

Writing in Mathematics

107. What is a linear equation in one variable? Give an example of this type of equation.

108. Suppose that you solve $\frac{x}{5} - \frac{x}{2} = 1$ by multiplying both sides by 20, rather than the least common denominator of 5 and 2 (namely, 10). Describe what happens. If you get the correct solution, why do you think we clear the equation of fractions by multiplying by the *least* common denominator?

109. Suppose you are an algebra teacher grading the following solution on an examination:

$$-3(x - 6) = 2 - x$$
$$-3x - 18 = 2 - x$$
$$-2x - 18 = 2$$
$$-2x = -16$$
$$x = 8.$$

You should note that 8 checks, so the solution set is {8}. The student who worked the problem therefore wants full credit. Can you find any errors in the solution? If full credit is 10 points, how many points should you give the student? Justify your position.

110. Explain how to find restrictions on the variable in a rational equation.

111. Why should restrictions on the variable in a rational equation be listed before you begin solving the equation?

112. What is an identity? Give an example.

113. What is a conditional equation? Give an example.

114. What is an inconsistent equation? Give an example.

115. Describe the trend shown by the graph in Exercises 103–104 in terms of learning new tasks. What happens initially and what happens as time increases?

Technology Exercises

In Exercises 116–119, use your graphing utility to enter each side of the equation separately under y_1 and y_2. Then use the utility's TABLE *or* GRAPH *feature to solve the equation.*

116. $5x + 2(x - 1) = 3x + 10$

117. $2x + 3(x - 4) = 4x - 7$

118. $\frac{x - 3}{5} - 1 = \frac{x - 5}{4}$

119. $\frac{2x - 1}{3} - \frac{x - 5}{6} = \frac{x - 3}{4}$

Critical Thinking Exercises

Make Sense? *In Exercises 120–123, determine whether each statement makes sense or does not make sense, and explain your reasoning.*

120. The model $P = -0.18n + 2.1$ describes the number of pay phones, P, in millions, n years after 2000, so I have to solve a linear equation to determine the number of pay phones in 2006.

121. Although I can solve $3x + \frac{1}{5} = \frac{1}{4}$ by first subtracting $\frac{1}{5}$ from both sides, I find it easier to begin by multiplying both sides by 20, the least common denominator.

122. Because I know how to clear an equation of fractions, I decided to clear the equation $0.5x + 8.3 = 12.4$ of decimals by multiplying both sides by 10.

123. Because $x = x + 5$ is an inconsistent equation, the graphs of $y = x$ and $y = x + 5$ should not intersect.

In Exercises 124–127, determine whether each statement is true or false. If the statement is false, make the necessary change(s) to produce a true statement.

124. The equation $-7x = x$ has no solution.

125. The equations $\dfrac{x}{x-4} = \dfrac{4}{x-4}$ and $x = 4$ are equivalent.

126. The equations $3y - 1 = 11$ and $3y - 7 = 5$ are equivalent.

127. If a and b are any real numbers, then $ax + b = 0$ always has one number in its solution set.

128. If x represents a number, write an English sentence about the number that results in an inconsistent equation.

129. Find b such that $\dfrac{7x + 4}{b} + 13 = x$ has a solution set given by $\{-6\}$.

130. Find b such that $\dfrac{4x - b}{x - 5} = 3$ has a solution set given by \varnothing.

Preview Exercises

Exercises 131–133 will help you prepare for the material covered in the next section.

131. Jane's salary exceeds Jim's by $150 per week. If x represents Jim's weekly salary, write an algebraic expression that models Jane's weekly salary.

132. A long-distance telephone plan has a monthly fee of $20 with a charge of $0.05 per minute for all long-distance calls. Write an algebraic expression that models the plan's monthly cost for x minutes of long-distance calls.

133. If the width of a rectangle is represented by x and the length is represented by $x + 200$, write a simplified algebraic expression that models the rectangle's perimeter.

Section 1.3

Models and Applications

Objectives

1 Use linear equations to solve problems.

2 Solve a formula for a variable.

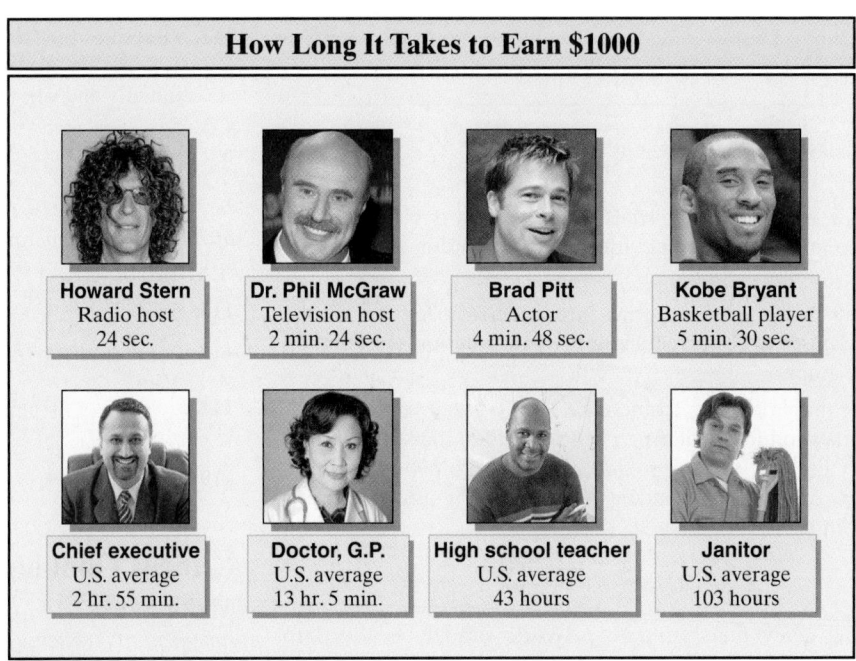

How Long It Takes to Earn $1000

Howard Stern
Radio host
24 sec.

Dr. Phil McGraw
Television host
2 min. 24 sec.

Brad Pitt
Actor
4 min. 48 sec.

Kobe Bryant
Basketball player
5 min. 30 sec.

Chief executive
U.S. average
2 hr. 55 min.

Doctor, G.P.
U.S. average
13 hr. 5 min.

High school teacher
U.S. average
43 hours

Janitor
U.S. average
103 hours

Source: Time

In this section, you'll see examples and exercises focused on how much money Americans earn. These situations illustrate a step-by-step strategy for solving problems. As you become familiar with this strategy, you will learn to solve a wide variety of problems.

1 Use linear equations to solve problems.

Problem Solving with Linear Equations

We have seen that a model is a mathematical representation of a real-world situation. In this section, we will be solving problems that are presented in English. This means that we must obtain models by translating from the ordinary language of English into the language of algebraic equations. To translate, however, we must understand the English prose and be familiar with the forms of algebraic language. On the next page are some general steps we will follow in solving word problems:

Study Tip

When solving word problems, particularly problems involving geometric figures, drawing a picture of the situation is often helpful. Label x on your drawing and, where appropriate, label other parts of the drawing in terms of x.

Strategy for Solving Word Problems

Step 1 Read the problem carefully. Attempt to state the problem in your own words and state what the problem is looking for. Let x (or any variable) represent one of the unknown quantities in the problem.

Step 2 If necessary, write expressions for any other unknown quantities in the problem in terms of x.

Step 3 Write an equation in x that models the verbal conditions of the problem.

Step 4 Solve the equation and answer the problem's question.

Step 5 Check the solution *in the original wording* of the problem, not in the equation obtained from the words.

(**EXAMPLE 1**) **Celebrity Earnings**

Forbes magazine published a list of the highest paid TV celebrities between June 2006 and June 2007. The results are shown in **Figure 1.15**.

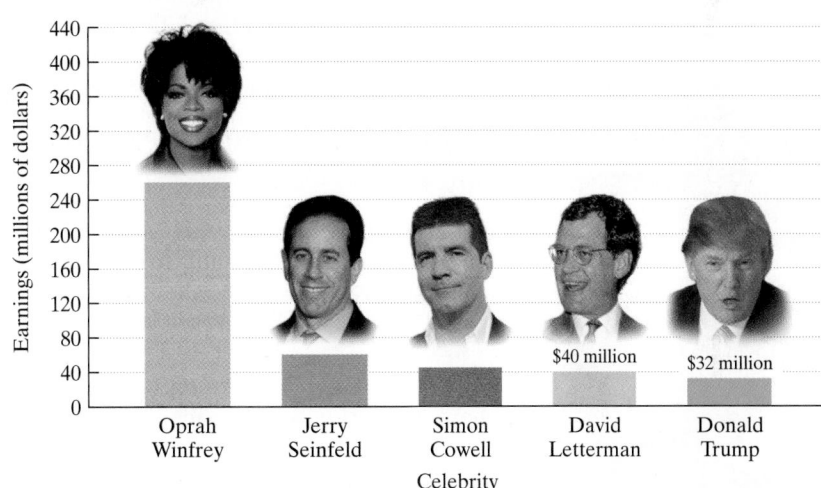

Highest Paid TV Celebrities between June 2006 and June 2007

Figure 1.15
Source: Forbes

The bar heights indicate that nobody came close to Oprah, who earned over four times more than any of the other TV stars. Although Seinfeld earned $15 million more than Cowell, Oprah's earnings exceeded Cowell's by $215 million. Combined, these three celebrities earned $365 million. How much did each of them earn?

Solution

Step 1 Let x represent one of the unknown quantities. We know something about Seinfeld's earnings and Oprah's earnings: Seinfeld earned $15 million more than Cowell, and Oprah's earnings exceeded Cowell's by $215 million. We will let

$$x = \text{Cowell's earnings (in millions of dollars)}.$$

Step 2 Represent other unknown quantities in terms of x. Because Seinfeld earned $15 million more than Cowell, let

$$x + 15 = \text{Seinfeld's earnings}.$$

Because Oprah's earnings exceeded Cowell's by $215 million, let

$$x + 215 = \text{Oprah's earnings}.$$

Step 3 **Write an equation in x that models the conditions.** Combined, the three celebrities earned $365 million.

$$(x + 215) + (x + 15) + x = 365$$

Step 4 **Solve the equation and answer the question.**

$$(x + 215) + (x + 15) + x = 365 \quad \text{This is the equation that models the problem's conditions.}$$
$$3x + 230 = 365 \quad \text{Remove parentheses, regroup, and combine like terms.}$$
$$3x = 135 \quad \text{Subtract 230 from both sides.}$$
$$x = 45 \quad \text{Divide both sides by 3.}$$

Thus,

$$\text{Cowell's earnings} = x = 45$$
$$\text{Seinfeld's earnings} = x + 15 = 45 + 15 = 60$$
$$\text{Oprah's earnings} = x + 215 = 45 + 215 = 260.$$

Between June 2006 and June 2007, Oprah earned $260 million, Seinfeld earned $60 million, and Cowell earned $45 million.

Step 5 **Check the proposed solution in the original wording of the problem.** The problem states that combined, the three celebrities earned $365 million. Using the earnings we determined in step 4, the sum is

$$\$45 \text{ million} + \$60 \text{ million} + \$260 \text{ million},$$

or $365 million, which verifies the problem's conditions.

Study Tip

Modeling with the word *exceeds* can be a bit tricky. It's helpful to identify the smaller quantity. Then add to this quantity to represent the larger quantity. For example, suppose that Tim's height exceeds Tom's height by a inches. Tom is the shorter person. If Tom's height is represented by x, then Tim's height is represented by $x + a$.

∅ Check Point **I** According to the U.S. Department of Education (2007 data), there is a gap between teaching salaries for men and women at private colleges and universities. The average salary for men exceeds the average salary for women by $14,037. Combined, their average salaries are $130,015. Determine the average teaching salaries at private colleges for women and for men.

EXAMPLE 2 **Modeling Attitudes of College Freshmen**

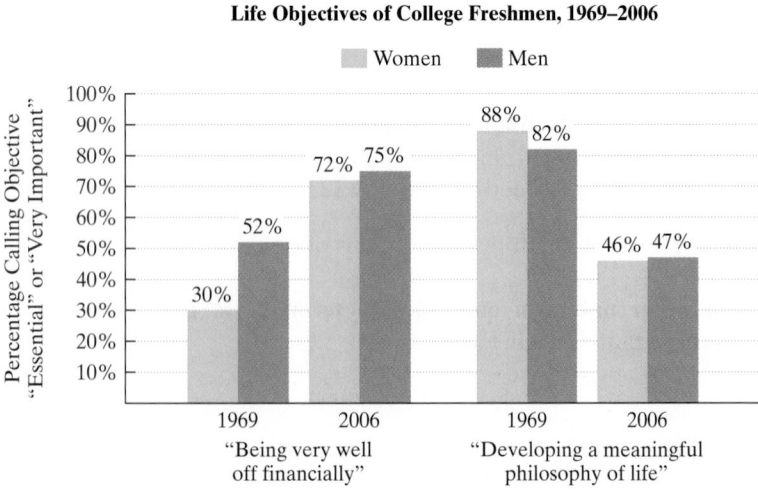

Life Objectives of College Freshmen, 1969–2006

Figure 1.16
Source: John Macionis, *Sociology,* Twelfth Edition, Prentice Hall, 2008

Researchers have surveyed college freshmen every year since 1969. **Figure 1.16** shows that attitudes about some life goals have changed dramatically. **Figure 1.16** shows that the freshmen class of 2006 was more interested in making money than the freshmen of 1969 had been. In 1969, 52% of first-year college men considered "being very well off financially" essential or very important. For the period from 1969 through 2006, this percentage increased by approximately 0.6 each year. If this trend

continues, by which year will all male freshmen consider "being very well off financially" essential or very important?

Solution

Step 1 Let *x* represent one of the unknown quantities. We are interested in the year when all male freshmen, or 100% of the men, will consider this life objective essential or very important. Let

> *x* = the number of years after 1969 when all male freshmen will consider "being very well off financially" essential or very important.

Step 2 Represent other unknown quantities in terms of *x*. There are no other unknown quantities to find, so we can skip this step.

Step 3 Write an equation in *x* that models the conditions.

The 1969 percentage	increased by	0.6 each year for *x* years	equals	100% of the male freshmen.
52	+	0.6*x*	=	100

Step 4 Solve the equation and answer the question.

$$52 + 0.6x = 100 \qquad \text{This is the equation that models the problem's conditions.}$$

$$52 - 52 + 0.6x = 100 - 52 \qquad \text{Subtract 52 from both sides.}$$

$$0.6x = 48 \qquad \text{Simplify.}$$

$$\frac{0.6x}{0.6} = \frac{48}{0.6} \qquad \text{Divide both sides by 0.6.}$$

$$x = 80 \qquad \text{Simplify.}$$

Using current trends, by 80 years after 1969, or in 2049, all male freshmen will consider "being very well off financially" essential or very important. (Do you agree with this projection that extends so far into the future? Are there unexpected events that might cause model breakdown to occur?)

Step 5 Check the proposed solution in the original wording of the problem. The problem states that all men (100%, represented by 100 using the model) will consider the objective essential or very important. Does this occur if we increase the 1969 percentage, 52%, by 0.6 each year for 80 years, our proposed solution?

$$52 + 0.6(80) = 52 + 48 = 100$$

This verifies that using trends shown in **Figure 1.16**, all first-year college men will consider the objective essential or very important 80 years after 1969. ●

⊘ Check Point **2** **Figure 1.16** shows that the freshmen class of 2006 was less interested in developing a philosophy of life than the freshmen of 1969 had been. In 1969, 88% of the women considered this objective essential or very important. Since then, this percentage has decreased by approximately 1.1 each year. If this trend continues, by which year will only 33% of female freshmen consider "developing a meaningful philosophy of life" essential or very important?

(**EXAMPLE 3**) **Selecting a Long-Distance Carrier**

You are choosing between two long-distance telephone plans. Plan A has a monthly fee of $20 with a charge of $0.05 per minute for all long-distance calls. Plan B has a monthly fee of $5 with a charge of $0.10 per minute for all long-distance calls. For how many minutes of long-distance calls will the costs for the two plans be the same?

Solution

Step 1 Let x represent one of the unknown quantities. Let

$$x = \text{the number of minutes of long-distance calls}$$
$$\text{for which the two plans cost the same.}$$

Step 2 Represent other unknown quantities in terms of x. There are no other unknown quantities, so we can skip this step.

Step 3 Write an equation in x that models the conditions. The monthly cost for plan A is the monthly fee, $20, plus the per minute charge, $0.05, times the number of minutes of long-distance calls, x. The monthly cost for plan B is the monthly fee, $5, plus the per-minute charge, $0.10, times the number of minutes of long-distance calls, x.

The monthly cost for plan A	must equal	the monthly cost for plan B.

$$20 + 0.05x \quad = \quad 5 + 0.10x$$

Step 4 Solve the equation and answer the question.

$$20 + 0.05x = 5 + 0.10x \qquad \text{This is the equation that models the problem's conditions.}$$

$$20 = 5 + 0.05x \qquad \text{Subtract 0.05x from both sides.}$$

$$15 = 0.05x \qquad \text{Subtract 5 from both sides.}$$

$$\frac{15}{0.05} = \frac{0.05x}{0.05} \qquad \text{Divide both sides by 0.05.}$$

$$300 = x \qquad \text{Simplify.}$$

Because x represents the number of minutes of long-distance calls for which the two plans cost the same, the costs will be the same for 300 minutes of long-distance calls.

Step 5 Check the proposed solution in the original wording of the problem. The problem states that the costs for the two plans should be the same. Let's see if they are the same with 300 minutes of long-distance calls:

$$\text{Cost for plan A} = \$20 + \$0.05(300) = \$20 + \$15 = \$35$$

Monthly fee	Per-minute charge

$$\text{Cost for plan B} = \$5 + \$0.10(300) = \$5 + \$30 = \$35.$$

With 300 minutes, or 5 hours, of long-distance chatting, both plans cost $35 for the month. Thus, the proposed solution, 300 minutes, satisfies the problem's conditions.

Technology

Numeric and Graphic Connections

We can use a graphing utility to numerically or graphically verify our work in Example 3.

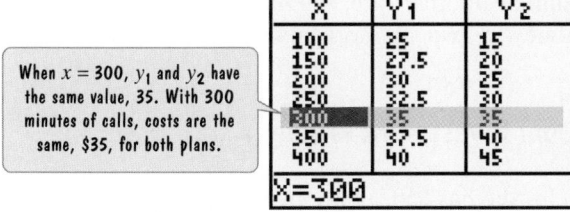

$$20 + 0.05x = 5 + 0.10x$$

Enter $y_1 = 20 + .05x$. Enter $y_2 = 5 + .10x$.

Numeric Check

Display a table for y_1 and y_2.

When $x = 300$, y_1 and y_2 have the same value, 35. With 300 minutes of calls, costs are the same, $35, for both plans.

X	Y₁	Y₂
100	25	15
150	27.5	20
200	30	25
250	32.5	30
300	35	35
350	37.5	40
400	40	45

X=300

Graphic Check

Display graphs for y_1 and y_2. Use the intersection feature.

$y_1 = 20 + 0.05x$

Graphs intersect at (300, 35). With 300 minutes of calls, costs are the same, $35, for both plans.

$y_2 = 5 + 0.10x$

Intersection
X=300 Y=35

[0, 500, 100] by [0, 50, 5]

✓ Check Point **3** You are choosing between two long-distance telephone plans. Plan A has a monthly fee of $15 with a charge of $0.08 per minute for all long-distance calls. Plan B has a monthly fee of $3 with a charge of $0.12 per minute for all long-distance calls. For how many minutes of long-distance calls will the costs for the two plans be the same?

(**EXAMPLE 4**) **A Price Reduction on a Digital Camera**

Your local computer store is having a terrific sale on digital cameras. After a 40% price reduction, you purchase a digital camera for $276. What was the camera's price before the reduction?

Solution

Step 1 Let x represent one of the unknown quantities. We will let
x = the original price of the digital camera prior to the reduction.

Step 2 Represent other unknown quantities in terms of x. There are no other unknown quantities to find, so we can skip this step.

Step 3 Write an equation in x that models the conditions. The camera's original price minus the 40% reduction is the reduced price, $276.

Original price	minus	the reduction (40% of the original price)	is	the reduced price, $276.
x	−	$0.4x$	=	276

Study Tip

Observe that the original price, x, reduced by 40% is $x - 0.4x$ and *not* $x - 0.4$.

Step 4 Solve the equation and answer the question.

$x - 0.4x = 276$ This is the equation that models the problem's conditions.

$0.6x = 276$ Combine like terms: $x - 0.4x = 1x - 0.4x = 0.6x$.

$\dfrac{0.6x}{0.6} = \dfrac{276}{0.6}$ Divide both sides by 0.6.

$x = 460$ Simplify: $0.6\overline{)276.0}$ = 460.

The digital camera's price before the reduction was $460.

Step 5 Check the proposed solution in the original wording of the problem. The price before the reduction, $460, minus the 40% reduction should equal the reduced price given in the original wording, $276:

$$460 - 40\% \text{ of } 460 = 460 - 0.4(460) = 460 - 184 = 276.$$

This verifies that the digital camera's price before the reduction was $460. ⬤

⊘ Check Point **4** After a 30% price reduction, you purchase a new computer for $840. What was the computer's price before the reduction?

Our next example is about simple interest. Simple interest involves interest calculated only on the amount of money that we invest, called the **principal**. The formula $I = Pr$ is used to find the simple interest, I, earned for one year when the principal, P, is invested at an annual interest rate, r. Dual investment problems involve different amounts of money in two or more investments, each paying a different rate.

(**EXAMPLE 5**) **Solving a Dual Investment Problem**

Your grandmother needs your help. She has $50,000 to invest. Part of this money is to be invested in noninsured bonds paying 15% annual interest. The rest of this money is to be invested in a government-insured certificate of deposit paying 7% annual interest. She told you that she requires $6000 per year in extra income from the combination of these investments. How much money should be placed in each investment?

Solution

Step 1 Let x represent one of the unknown quantities. We will let

$$x = \text{the amount invested in the noninsured bonds at 15\%.}$$

Step 2 Represent other unknown quantities in terms of x. The other quantity that we seek is the amount invested at 7% in the certificate of deposit. Because the total amount Grandma has to invest is $50,000 and we already used up x,

$$50,000 - x = \text{the amount invested in the certificate of deposit at 7\%.}$$

Step 3 Write an equation in x that models the conditions. Because Grandma requires $6000 in total interest, the interest for the two investments combined must be $6000. Interest is Pr or rP for each investment.

Interest from the 15% investment	plus	interest from the 7% investment	is	$6000.
$0.15x$	$+$	$0.07(50,000 - x)$	$=$	6000
rate times principal		rate times principal		

Step 4 Solve the equation and answer the question.

$$0.15x + 0.07(50,000 - x) = 6000 \qquad \text{This is the equation that models the problem's conditions.}$$

$$0.15x + 3500 - 0.07x = 6000 \qquad \text{Use the distributive property.}$$

$$0.08x + 3500 = 6000 \qquad \text{Combine like terms.}$$

$$0.08x = 2500 \qquad \text{Subtract 3500 from both sides.}$$

$$\frac{0.08x}{0.08} = \frac{2500}{0.08} \qquad \text{Divide both sides by 0.08.}$$

$$x = 31,250 \qquad \text{Simplify.}$$

Thus,

the amount invested at 15% $= x = 31{,}250$.

the amount invested at 7% $= 50{,}000 - 31{,}250 = 18{,}750$.

Grandma should invest \$31,250 at 15% and \$18,750 at 7%.

Step 5 Check the proposed solution in the original wording of the problem. The problem states that the total interest from the dual investments should be \$6000. Can Grandma count on \$6000 interest? The interest earned on \$31,250 at 15% is (\$31,250) (0.15), or \$4687.50. The interest earned on \$18,750 at 7% is (\$18,750) (0.07), or \$1312.50. The total interest is \$4687.50 + \$1312.50, or \$6000, exactly as it should be. You've made your grandmother happy. (Now if you would just visit her more often …) ●

⏀ Check Point **5** You inherited \$5000 with the stipulation that for the first year the money had to be invested in two funds paying 9% and 11% annual interest. How much did you invest at each rate if the total interest earned for the year was \$487?

Solving geometry problems usually requires a knowledge of basic geometric ideas and formulas. Formulas for area, perimeter, and volume are given in **Table 1.1**.

Table 1.1 Common Formulas for Area, Perimeter, and Volume

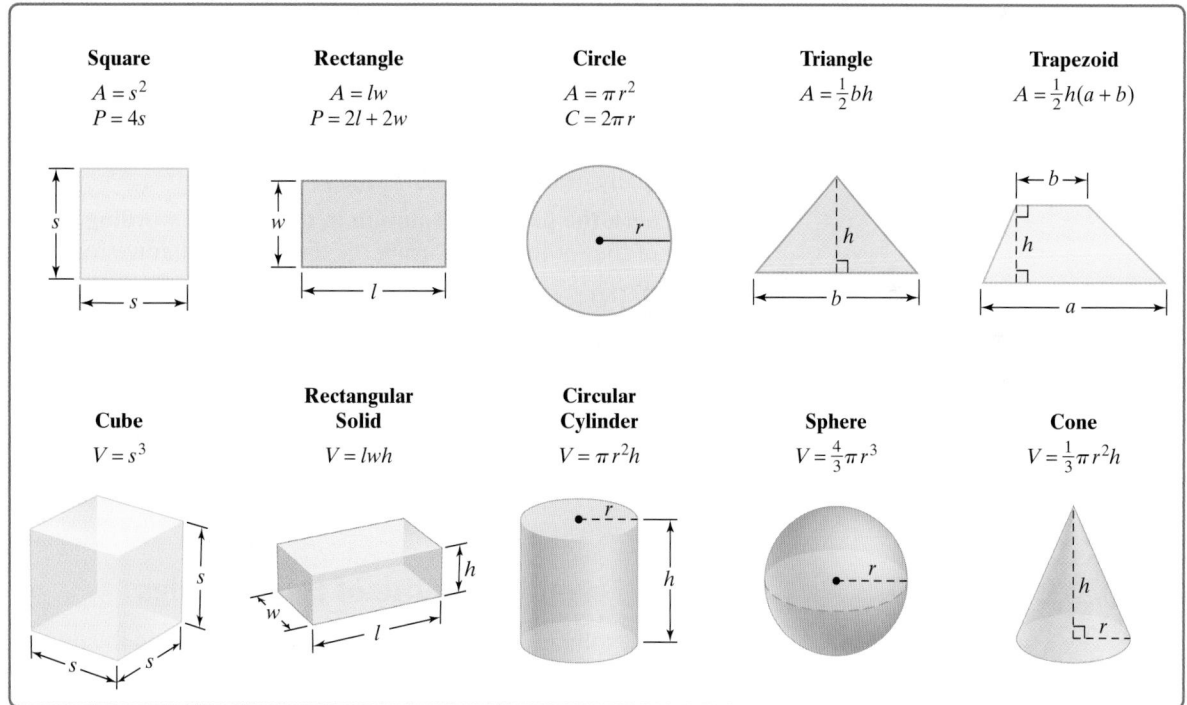

We will be using the formula for the perimeter of a rectangle, $P = 2l + 2w$, in our next example. The formula states that a rectangle's perimeter is the sum of twice its length and twice its width.

(**EXAMPLE 6**) **Finding the Dimensions of an American Football Field**

The length of an American football field is 200 feet more than the width. If the perimeter of the field is 1040 feet, what are its dimensions?

Solution

Step 1 Let x represent one of the unknown quantities. We know something about the length; the length is 200 feet more than the width. We will let

$$x = \text{the width.}$$

Figure 1.17 An American football field

Step 2 Represent other unknown quantities in terms of _x_. Because the length is 200 feet more than the width, we add 200 to the width to represent the length. Thus,

$$x + 200 = \text{the length.}$$

Figure 1.17 illustrates an American football field and its dimensions.

Step 3 Write an equation in _x_ that models the conditions. Because the perimeter of the field is 1040 feet,

Twice the length	plus	twice the width	is	the perimeter.
$2(x + 200)$	$+$	$2x$	$=$	$1040.$

Step 4 Solve the equation and answer the question.

$$2(x + 200) + 2x = 1040 \quad \text{This is the equation that models the}$$
$$\text{problem's conditions.}$$
$$2x + 400 + 2x = 1040 \quad \text{Apply the distributive property.}$$
$$4x + 400 = 1040 \quad \text{Combine like terms: } 2x + 2x = 4x.$$
$$4x = 640 \quad \text{Subtract 400 from both sides.}$$
$$x = 160 \quad \text{Divide both sides by 4.}$$

Thus,

$$\text{width} = x = 160.$$
$$\text{length} = x + 200 = 160 + 200 = 360.$$

The dimensions of an American football field are 160 feet by 360 feet. (The 360-foot length is usually described as 120 yards.)

Step 5 Check the proposed solution in the original wording of the problem. The perimeter of the football field using the dimensions that we found is

$$2(160 \text{ feet}) + 2(360 \text{ feet}) = 320 \text{ feet} + 720 \text{ feet} = 1040 \text{ feet.}$$

Because the problem's wording tells us that the perimeter is 1040 feet, our dimensions are correct.

✓ Check Point **6** The length of a rectangular basketball court is 44 feet more than the width. If the perimeter of the basketball court is 288 feet, what are its dimensions?

② Solve a formula for a variable.

Solving a Formula for One of Its Variables

We know that solving an equation is the process of finding the number (or numbers) that make the equation a true statement. All of the equations we have solved contained only one letter, _x_.

By contrast, formulas contain two or more letters, representing two or more variables. An example is the formula for the perimeter of a rectangle:

$$P = 2l + 2w.$$

We say that this formula is solved for the variable _P_ because _P_ is alone on one side of the equation and the other side does not contain a _P_.

Solving a formula for a variable means rewriting the formula so that the variable is isolated on one side of the equation. It does not mean obtaining a numerical value for that variable.

To solve a formula for one of its variables, treat that variable as if it were the only variable in the equation. Think of the other variables as if they were numbers. Isolate all terms with the specified variable on one side of the equation and all terms without the specified variable on the other side. Then divide both sides by the same nonzero quantity to get the specified variable alone. The next two examples show how to do this.

EXAMPLE 7 **Solving a Formula for a Variable**

Solve the formula $P = 2l + 2w$ for l.

Solution First, isolate $2l$ on the right by subtracting $2w$ from both sides. Then solve for l by dividing both sides by 2.

> We need to isolate l.

$$P = 2l + 2w$$ This is the given formula.

$$P - 2w = 2l + 2w - 2w$$ Isolate $2l$ by subtracting $2w$ from both sides.

$$P - 2w = 2l$$ Simplify.

$$\frac{P - 2w}{2} = \frac{2l}{2}$$ Solve for l by dividing both sides by 2.

$$\frac{P - 2w}{2} = l$$ Simplify.

Equivalently,

$$l = \frac{P - 2w}{2}.$$

● Check Point **7** Solve the formula $P = 2l + 2w$ for w.

EXAMPLE 8 **Solving a Formula for a Variable That Occurs Twice**

The formula

$$A = P + Prt$$

describes the amount, A, that a principal of P dollars is worth after t years when invested at a simple annual interest rate, r. Solve this formula for P.

Solution Notice that all the terms with P already occur on the right side of the formula.

> We need to isolate P.

$$A = P + Prt$$

We can factor P from the two terms on the right to convert the two occurrences of P into one.

$$A = P + Prt$$ This is the given formula.

$$A = P(1 + rt)$$ Factor out P on the right side of the equation.

$$\frac{A}{1 + rt} = \frac{P(1 + rt)}{1 + rt}$$ Divide both sides by $1 + rt$.

$$\frac{A}{1 + rt} = P$$ Simplify: $\dfrac{P\cancel{(1 + rt)}}{1\cancel{(1 + rt)}} = \dfrac{P}{1} = P.$

Study Tip

You cannot solve $A = P + Prt$ for P by subtracting Prt from both sides and writing

$$A - Prt = P.$$

When a formula is solved for a specified variable, that variable must be isolated on one side. The variable P occurs on both sides of

$$A - Prt = P.$$

Equivalently,

$$P = \frac{A}{1 + rt}.$$

● Check Point **8** Solve the formula $P = C + MC$ for C.

Exercise Set 1.3

Practice Exercises

Use the five-step strategy for solving word problems to find the number or numbers described in Exercises 1–10.

1. When five times a number is decreased by 4, the result is 26. What is the number?
2. When two times a number is decreased by 3, the result is 11. What is the number?
3. When a number is decreased by 20% of itself, the result is 20. What is the number?
4. When a number is decreased by 30% of itself, the result is 28. What is the number?
5. When 60% of a number is added to the number, the result is 192. What is the number?
6. When 80% of a number is added to the number, the result is 252. What is the number?
7. 70% of what number is 224?
8. 70% of what number is 252?
9. One number exceeds another by 26. The sum of the numbers is 64. What are the numbers?
10. One number exceeds another by 24. The sum of the numbers is 58. What are the numbers?

Practice Plus

In Exercises 11–18, find all values of x satisfying the given conditions.

11. $y_1 = 13x - 4$, $y_2 = 5x + 10$, and y_1 exceeds y_2 by 2.
12. $y_1 = 10x + 6$, $y_2 = 12x - 7$, and y_1 exceeds y_2 by 3.
13. $y_1 = 10(2x - 1)$, $y_2 = 2x + 1$, and y_1 is 14 more than 8 times y_2.
14. $y_1 = 9(3x - 5)$, $y_2 = 3x - 1$, and y_1 is 51 less than 12 times y_2.
15. $y_1 = 2x + 6$, $y_2 = x + 8$, $y_3 = x$, and the difference between 3 times y_1 and 5 times y_2 is 22 less than y_3.
16. $y_1 = 2.5$, $y_2 = 2x + 1$, $y_3 = x$, and the difference between 2 times y_1 and 3 times y_2 is 8 less than 4 times y_3.
17. $y_1 = \dfrac{1}{x}$, $y_2 = \dfrac{1}{2x}$, $y_3 = \dfrac{1}{x-1}$, and the sum of 3 times y_1 and 4 times y_2 is the product of 4 and y_3.
18. $y_1 = \dfrac{1}{x}$, $y_2 = \dfrac{1}{x^2 - x}$, $y_3 = \dfrac{1}{x-1}$, and the difference between 6 times y_1 and 3 times y_2 is the product of 7 and y_3.

Application Exercises

19. The bar graph shows the time Americans spent using various media in 2007.

Average Number of Hours Americans Used Various Media in 2007

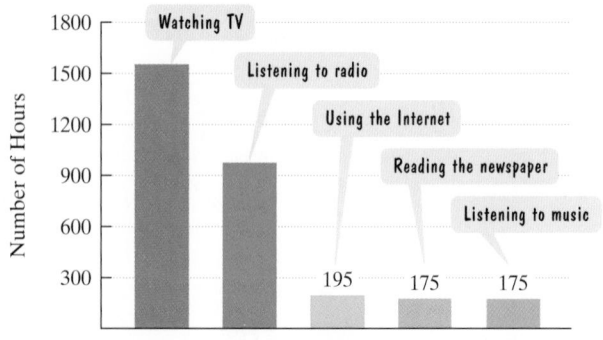

Source: Communication Industry Forecast and Report

Time spent watching TV exceeded time spent listening to the radio by 581 hours. The combined time devoted to these two media was 2529 hours. In 2007, how many hours did Americans spend listening to the radio and how many hours were spent watching TV?

20. Compared with Europeans, American employees use less vacation time.

Average Vacation Time for Europeans and Americans

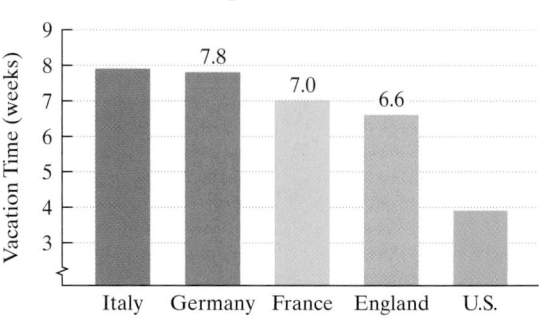

Source: The State of Working America 2006/2007

The average time Italians spend on vacation exceeds the average American vacation time by 4 weeks. The combined average vacation time for Americans and Italians is 11.8 weeks. On average, how many weeks do Americans spend on vacation and how many weeks do Italians spend on vacation?

Exercises 21–22 involve the average salaries represented by the bar graph.

Average Salaries for Various Jobs

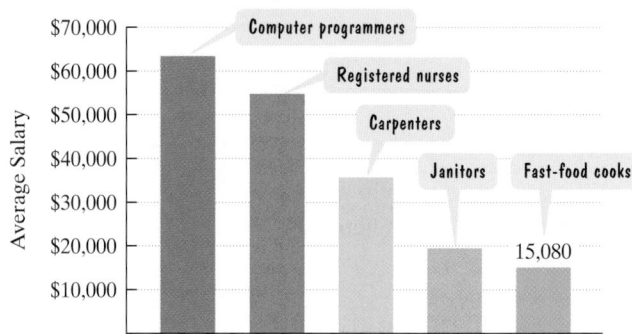

Source: 2007 data from salary.com

21. The average salary for computer programmers is $7740 less than twice the average salary for carpenters. Combined, their average salaries are $99,000. Determine the average salary for each of these jobs.

22. The average salary for registered nurses is $3500 less than three times the average salary for janitors. Combined, their average salaries are $74,060. Determine the average salary for each of these jobs.

The bar graph indicates that American attitudes have become more tolerant over two decades on a variety of issues. Exercises 23–24 are based on the data displayed by the graph.

Changing Attitudes in the United States

Source: USA Today

23. In 1983, 43% of U.S. adults approved of marriage between blacks and whites. For the period from 1983 through 2007, the percentage approving of interracial marriage increased on average by 1.5 each year. If this trend continues, by which year will all American adults approve of interracial marriage?

24. In 1986, 43% of U.S. adults approved of men and women living together without being married. For the period from 1986 through 2007, the percentage approving of cohabitation increased on average by approximately 0.6 each year. If this trend continues, by which year will 61% of all American adults approve of cohabitation?

25. A new car worth $24,000 is depreciating in value by $3000 per year.

 a. Write a formula that models the car's value, y, in dollars, after x years.

 b. Use the formula from part (a) to determine after how many years the car's value will be $9000.

 c. Graph the formula from part (a) in the first quadrant of a rectangular coordinate system. Then show your solution to part (b) on the graph.

26. A new car worth $45,000 is depreciating in value by $5000 per year.

 a. Write a formula that models the car's value, y, in dollars, after x years.

 b. Use the formula from part (a) to determine after how many years the car's value will be $10,000.

 c. Graph the formula from part (a) in the first quadrant of a rectangular coordinate system. Then show your solution to part (b) on the graph.

27. You are choosing between two health clubs. Club A offers membership for a fee of $40 plus a monthly fee of $25. Club B offers membership for a fee of $15 plus a monthly fee of $30. After how many months will the total cost at each health club be the same? What will be the total cost for each club?

28. Video Store A charges $9 to rent a video game for one week. Although only members can rent from the store, membership is free. Video Store B charges only $4 to rent a video game for one week. Only members can rent from the store and membership is $50 per year. After how many video-game rentals will the total amount spent at each store be the same? What will be the total amount spent at each store?

29. The bus fare in a city is $1.25. People who use the bus have the option of purchasing a monthly discount pass for $15.00. With the discount pass, the fare is reduced to $0.75. Determine the number of times in a month the bus must be used so that the total monthly cost without the discount pass is the same as the total monthly cost with the discount pass.

30. A discount pass for a bridge costs $30 per month. The toll for the bridge is normally $5.00, but it is reduced to $3.50 for people who have purchased the discount pass. Determine the number of times in a month the bridge must be crossed so that the total monthly cost without the discount pass is the same as the total monthly cost with the discount pass.

31. In 2005, there were 13,300 students at college A, with a projected enrollment increase of 1000 students per year. In the same year, there were 26,800 students at college B, with a projected enrollment decline of 500 students per year.

 a. According to these projections, when will the colleges have the same enrollment? What will be the enrollment in each college at that time?

 b. Use the following table to numerically check your work in part (a). What equations were entered for Y_1 and Y_2 to obtain this table?

X	Y₁	Y₂
7	20300	23300
8	21300	22800
9	22300	22300
10	23300	21800
11	24300	21300
12	25300	20800
13	26300	20300

X=7

32. In 2000, the population of Greece was 10,600,000, with projections of a population decrease of 28,000 people per year. In the same year, the population of Belgium was 10,200,000, with projections of a population decrease of 12,000 people per year. (Source: United Nations) According to these projections, when will the two countries have the same population? What will be the population at that time?

33. After a 20% reduction, you purchase a television for $336. What was the television's price before the reduction?

34. After a 30% reduction, you purchase a dictionary for $30.80. What was the dictionary's price before the reduction?

35. Including 8% sales tax, an inn charges $162 per night. Find the inn's nightly cost before the tax is added.

36. Including 5% sales tax, an inn charges $252 per night. Find the inn's nightly cost before the tax is added.

Exercises 37–38 involve markup, the amount added to the dealer's cost of an item to arrive at the selling price of that item.

37. The selling price of a refrigerator is $584. If the markup is 25% of the dealer's cost, what is the dealer's cost of the refrigerator?

38. The selling price of a scientific calculator is $15. If the markup is 25% of the dealer's cost, what is the dealer's cost of the calculator?

39. You invested $7000 in two accounts paying 6% and 8% annual interest. If the total interest earned for the year was $520, how much was invested at each rate?

40. You invested $11,000 in two accounts paying 5% and 8% annual interest. If the total interest earned for the year was $730, how much was invested at each rate?

41. Things did not go quite as planned. You invested $8000, part of it in stock that paid 12% annual interest. However, the rest of the money suffered a 5% loss. If the total annual income from both investments was $620, how much was invested at each rate?

42. Things did not go quite as planned. You invested $12,000, part of it in stock that paid 14% annual interest. However, the rest of the money suffered a 6% loss. If the total annual income from both investments was $680, how much was invested at each rate?

43. A rectangular soccer field is twice as long as it is wide. If the perimeter of the soccer field is 300 yards, what are its dimensions?

44. A rectangular swimming pool is three times as long as it is wide. If the perimeter of the pool is 320 feet, what are its dimensions?

45. The length of the rectangular tennis court at Wimbledon is 6 feet longer than twice the width. If the court's perimeter is 228 feet, what are the court's dimensions?

46. The length of a rectangular pool is 6 meters less than twice the width. If the pool's perimeter is 126 meters, what are its dimensions?

47. The rectangular painting in the figure shown measures 12 inches by 16 inches and is surrounded by a frame of uniform width around the four edges. The perimeter of the rectangle formed by the painting and its frame is 72 inches. Determine the width of the frame.

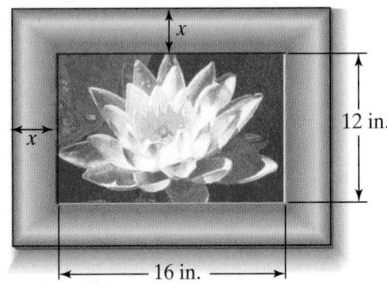

48. The rectangular swimming pool in the figure shown measures 40 feet by 60 feet and is surrounded by a path of uniform width around the four edges. The perimeter of the rectangle formed by the pool and the surrounding path is 248 feet. Determine the width of the path.

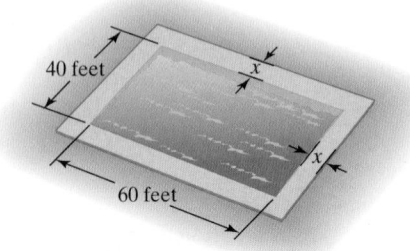

49. An automobile repair shop charged a customer $448, listing $63 for parts and the remainder for labor. If the cost of labor is $35 per hour, how many hours of labor did it take to repair the car?

50. A repair bill on a sailboat came to $1603, including $532 for parts and the remainder for labor. If the cost of labor is $63 per hour, how many hours of labor did it take to repair the sailboat?

51. An HMO pamphlet contains the following recommended weight for women: "Give yourself 100 pounds for the first 5 feet plus 5 pounds for every inch over 5 feet tall." Using this description, what height corresponds to a recommended weight of 135 pounds?

52. A job pays an annual salary of $33,150, which includes a holiday bonus of $750. If paychecks are issued twice a month, what is the gross amount for each paycheck?

53. Answer the question in the following *Peanuts* cartoon strip. (*Note:* You may not use the answer given in the cartoon!)

PEANUTS reprinted by permission of United Feature Syndicate, Inc.

54. The rate for a particular international person-to-person telephone call is $0.43 for the first minute, $0.32 for each additional minute, and a $2.10 service charge. If the cost of a call is $5.73, how long did the person talk?

In Exercises 55–74, solve each formula for the specified variable. Do you recognize the formula? If so, what does it describe?

55. $A = lw$ for w

56. $D = RT$ for R

57. $A = \frac{1}{2}bh$ for b

58. $V = \frac{1}{3}Bh$ for B

59. $I = Prt$ for P

60. $C = 2\pi r$ for r

61. $E = mc^2$ for m

62. $V = \pi r^2 h$ for h

63. $T = D + pm$ for p

64. $P = C + MC$ for M

65. $A = \frac{1}{2}h(a + b)$ for a

66. $A = \frac{1}{2}h(a + b)$ for b

67. $S = P + Prt$ for r

68. $S = P + Prt$ for t

69. $B = \dfrac{F}{S - V}$ for S

70. $S = \dfrac{C}{1 - r}$ for r

71. $IR + Ir = E$ for I

72. $A = 2lw + 2lh + 2wh$ for h

73. $\dfrac{1}{p} + \dfrac{1}{q} = \dfrac{1}{f}$ for f

74. $\dfrac{1}{R} = \dfrac{1}{R_1} + \dfrac{1}{R_2}$ for R_1

Writing in Mathematics

75. In your own words, describe a step-by-step approach for solving algebraic word problems.

76. Write an original word problem that can be solved using a linear equation. Then solve the problem.

77. Explain what it means to solve a formula for a variable.

78. Did you have difficulties solving some of the problems that were assigned in this exercise set? Discuss what you did if this happened to you. Did your course of action enhance your ability to solve algebraic word problems?

Technology Exercises

79. Use a graphing utility to numerically or graphically verify your work in any one exercise from Exercises 27–30. For assistance on how to do this, refer to the Technology box on page 121.

80. A tennis club offers two payment options. Members can pay a monthly fee of $30 plus $5 per hour for court rental time. The second option has no monthly fee, but court time costs $7.50 per hour.
 a. Write a mathematical model representing total monthly costs for each option for x hours of court rental time.
 b. Use a graphing utility to graph the two models in a $[0, 15, 1]$ by $[0, 120, 20]$ viewing rectangle.
 c. Use your utility's trace or intersection feature to determine where the two graphs intersect. Describe what the coordinates of this intersection point represent in practical terms.
 d. Verify part (c) using an algebraic approach by setting the two models equal to one another and determining how many hours one has to rent the court so that the two plans result in identical monthly costs.

Critical Thinking Exercises

Make Sense? *In Exercises 81–84, determine whether each statement makes sense or does not make sense, and explain your reasoning.*

81. By modeling attitudes of college freshmen from 1969 through 2006, I can make precise predictions about the attitudes of the freshman class of 2020.

82. I find the hardest part in solving a word problem is writing the equation that models the verbal conditions.

83. I solved the formula for one of its variables, so now I have a numerical value for that variable.

84. After a 35% reduction, a computer's price is $780, so I determined the original price, x, by solving $x - 0.35 = 780$.

85. At the north campus of a performing arts school, 10% of the students are music majors. At the south campus, 90% of the students are music majors. The campuses are merged into one east campus. If 42% of the 1000 students at the east campus are music majors, how many students did the north and south campuses have before the merger?

86. The price of a dress is reduced by 40%. When the dress still does not sell, it is reduced by 40% of the reduced price. If the price of the dress after both reductions is $72, what was the original price?

87. In a film, the actor Charles Coburn plays an elderly "uncle" character criticized for marrying a woman when he is 3 times her age. He wittily replies, "Ah, but in 20 years time I shall only be twice her age." How old is the "uncle" and the woman?

88. Suppose that we agree to pay you 8¢ for every problem in this chapter that you solve correctly and fine you 5¢ for every problem done incorrectly. If at the end of 26 problems we do not owe each other any money, how many problems did you solve correctly?

89. It was wartime when the Ricardos found out Mrs. Ricardo was pregnant. Ricky Ricardo was drafted and made out a will, deciding that $14,000 in a savings account was to be divided between his wife and his child-to-be. Rather strangely, and certainly with gender bias, Ricky stipulated that if the child were a boy, he would get twice the amount of the mother's portion. If it were a girl, the mother would get twice the amount the girl was to receive. We'll never know what Ricky was thinking of, for (as fate would have it) he did not return from war. Mrs. Ricardo gave birth to twins—a boy and a girl. How was the money divided?

90. A thief steals a number of rare plants from a nursery. On the way out, the thief meets three security guards, one after another. To each security guard, the thief is forced to give one-half the plants that he still has, plus 2 more. Finally, the thief leaves the nursery with 1 lone palm. How many plants were originally stolen?

91. Solve for C: $V = C - \dfrac{C - S}{L} N.$

Group Exercise

92. One of the best ways to learn how to *solve* a word problem in algebra is to *design* word problems of your own. Creating a word problem makes you very aware of precisely how much information is needed to solve the problem. You must also focus on the best way to present information to a reader and on how much information to give. As you write your problem, you gain skills that will help you solve problems created by others.

 The group should design five different word problems that can be solved using linear equations. All of the problems should be on different topics. For example, the group should not have more than one problem on simple interest. The group should turn in both the problems and their algebraic solutions.

 (If you're not sure where to begin, consider the graph for Exercises 23–24 and the data that we did not use regarding attitudes about women in combat.)

Preview Exercises

Exercises 93–95 will help you prepare for the material covered in the next section.

93. Multiply: $(7 - 3x)(-2 - 5x)$.

94. Simplify: $\sqrt{18} - \sqrt{8}$.

95. Rationalize the denominator: $\dfrac{7 + 4\sqrt{2}}{2 - 5\sqrt{2}}$.

Section **1.4**

Objectives

① Add and subtract complex numbers.

② Multiply complex numbers.

③ Divide complex numbers.

④ Perform operations with square roots of negative numbers.

Complex Numbers

Who is this kid warning us about our eyeballs turning black if we attempt to find the square root of −9? Don't believe what you hear on the street. Although square roots of negative numbers are not real numbers, they do play a significant role in algebra. In this section, we move beyond the real numbers and discuss square roots with negative radicands.

The Imaginary Unit *i*

In the next section, we will study equations whose solutions may involve the square roots of negative numbers. Because the square of a real number is never negative, there is no real number x such that $x^2 = -1$. To provide a setting in which such equations have solutions, mathematicians have invented an expanded system of numbers, the complex numbers. The *imaginary number i*, defined to be a solution of the equation $x^2 = -1$, is the basis of this new number system.

> ### The Imaginary Unit *i*
>
> The **imaginary unit *i*** is defined as
> $$i = \sqrt{-1}, \quad \text{where } i^2 = -1.$$

Using the imaginary unit i, we can express the square root of any negative number as a real multiple of i. For example,

$$\sqrt{-25} = \sqrt{-1}\sqrt{25} = i\sqrt{25} = 5i.$$

We can check this result by squaring $5i$ and obtaining -25.

$$(5i)^2 = 5^2 i^2 = 25(-1) = -25$$

A new system of numbers, called *complex numbers*, is based on adding multiples of i, such as $5i$, to real numbers.

Complex Numbers and Imaginary Numbers

The set of all numbers in the form

$$a + bi,$$

with real numbers a and b, and i, the imaginary unit, is called the set of **complex numbers**. The real number a is called the **real part** and the real number b is called the **imaginary part** of the complex number $a + bi$. If $b \neq 0$, then the complex number is called an **imaginary number** (**Figure 1.18**). An imaginary number in the form bi is called a **pure imaginary number**.

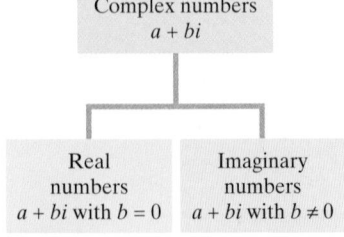

Figure 1.18 The complex number system

Here are some examples of complex numbers. Each number can be written in the form $a + bi$.

$$-4 + 6i \qquad\qquad 2i = 0 + 2i \qquad\qquad 3 = 3 + 0i$$

a, the real part, is -4.	b, the imaginary part, is 6.	a, the real part, is 0.	b, the imaginary part, is 2.	a, the real part, is 3.	b, the imaginary part, is 0.

Can you see that b, the imaginary part, is not zero in the first two complex numbers? Because $b \neq 0$, these complex numbers are imaginary numbers. Furthermore, the imaginary number $2i$ is a pure imaginary number. By contrast, the imaginary part of the complex number on the right is zero. This complex number is not an imaginary number. The number 3, or $3 + 0i$, is a real number.

A complex number is said to be **simplified** if it is expressed in the **standard form** $a + bi$. If b contains a radical, we usually write i before the radical. For example, we write $7 + 3i\sqrt{5}$ rather than $7 + 3\sqrt{5}i$, which could easily be confused with $7 + 3\sqrt{5i}$.

Expressed in standard form, two complex numbers are equal if and only if their real parts are equal and their imaginary parts are equal.

Equality of Complex Numbers

$a + bi = c + di$ if and only if $a = c$ and $b = d$.

① Add and subtract complex numbers.

Operations with Complex Numbers

The form of a complex number $a + bi$ is like the binomial $a + bx$. Consequently, we can add, subtract, and multiply complex numbers using the same methods we used for binomials, remembering that $i^2 = -1$.

Adding and Subtracting Complex Numbers

1. $(a + bi) + (c + di) = (a + c) + (b + d)i$
 In words, this says that you add complex numbers by adding their real parts, adding their imaginary parts, and expressing the sum as a complex number.

2. $(a + bi) - (c + di) = (a - c) + (b - d)i$
 In words, this says that you subtract complex numbers by subtracting their real parts, subtracting their imaginary parts, and expressing the difference as a complex number.

EXAMPLE 1 Adding and Subtracting Complex Numbers

Perform the indicated operations, writing the result in standard form:

a. $(5 - 11i) + (7 + 4i)$ **b.** $(-5 + i) - (-11 - 6i)$.

Solution

a. $(5 - 11i) + (7 + 4i)$
$= 5 - 11i + 7 + 4i$ Remove the parentheses.
$= 5 + 7 - 11i + 4i$ Group real and imaginary terms.
$= (5 + 7) + (-11 + 4)i$ Add real parts and add imaginary parts.
$= 12 - 7i$ Simplify.

b. $(-5 + i) - (-11 - 6i)$
$= -5 + i + 11 + 6i$ Remove the parentheses. Change signs of real and imaginary parts in the complex number being subtracted.
$= -5 + 11 + i + 6i$ Group real and imaginary terms.
$= (-5 + 11) + (1 + 6)i$ Add real parts and add imaginary parts.
$= 6 + 7i$ Simplify.

Study Tip

The following examples, using the same integers as in Example 1, show how operations with complex numbers are just like operations with polynomials.

a. $(5 - 11x) + (7 + 4x)$
$= 12 - 7x$

b. $(-5 + x) - (-11 - 6x)$
$= -5 + x + 11 + 6x$
$= 6 + 7x$

⊘ Check Point **1** Perform the indicated operations, writing the result in standard form:

 a. $(5 - 2i) + (3 + 3i)$ **b.** $(2 + 6i) - (12 - i)$.

Multiplication of complex numbers is performed the same way as multiplication of polynomials, using the distributive property and the FOIL method. After completing the multiplication, we replace any occurrences of i^2 with -1. This idea is illustrated in the next example.

② Multiply complex numbers.

> **EXAMPLE 2** **Multiplying Complex Numbers**

Find the products:

 a. $4i(3 - 5i)$ **b.** $(7 - 3i)(-2 - 5i)$.

Solution

 a. $4i(3 - 5i)$

$= 4i \cdot 3 - 4i \cdot 5i$	Distribute $4i$ throughout the parentheses.
$= 12i - 20i^2$	Multiply.
$= 12i - 20(-1)$	Replace i^2 with -1.
$= 20 + 12i$	Simplify to $12i + 20$ and write in standard form.

 b. $(7 - 3i)(-2 - 5i)$

 F O I L

$= -14 - 35i + 6i + 15i^2$	Use the FOIL method.
$= -14 - 35i + 6i + 15(-1)$	$i^2 = -1$
$= -14 - 15 - 35i + 6i$	Group real and imaginary terms.
$= -29 - 29i$	Combine real and imaginary terms.

⊘ Check Point **2** Find the products:

 a. $7i(2 - 9i)$ **b.** $(5 + 4i)(6 - 7i)$.

③ Divide complex numbers.

Complex Conjugates and Division

It is possible to multiply imaginary numbers and obtain a real number. This occurs when we multiply $a + bi$ and $a - bi$.

 F O I L

$(a + bi)(a - bi) = a^2 - abi + abi - b^2i^2$	Use the FOIL method.
$= a^2 - b^2(-1)$	$i^2 = -1$
$= a^2 + b^2$	Notice that this product eliminates i.

For the complex number $a + bi$, we define its *complex conjugate* to be $a - bi$. The multiplication of complex conjugates results in a real number.

> ### Conjugate of a Complex Number
>
> The **complex conjugate** of the number $a + bi$ is $a - bi$, and the complex conjugate of $a - bi$ is $a + bi$. The multiplication of complex conjugates gives a real number.
>
> $$(a + bi)(a - bi) = a^2 + b^2$$
> $$(a - bi)(a + bi) = a^2 + b^2$$

Complex conjugates are used to divide complex numbers. The goal of the division procedure is to obtain a real number in the denominator. This real number becomes the denominator of a and b in the quotient $a + bi$. By multiplying the numerator and the denominator of the division by the complex conjugate of the denominator, you will obtain this real number in the denominator.

(EXAMPLE 3) **Using Complex Conjugates to Divide Complex Numbers**

Divide and express the result in standard form: $\dfrac{7 + 4i}{2 - 5i}$.

Solution The complex conjugate of the denominator, $2 - 5i$, is $2 + 5i$. Multiplication of both the numerator and the denominator by $2 + 5i$ will eliminate i from the denominator while maintaining the value of the expression.

$\dfrac{7 + 4i}{2 - 5i} = \dfrac{(7 + 4i)}{(2 - 5i)} \cdot \dfrac{(2 + 5i)}{(2 + 5i)}$
 Multiply the numerator and the denominator by the complex conjugate of the denominator.

F O I L

$= \dfrac{14 + 35i + 8i + 20i^2}{2^2 + 5^2}$
 Use the FOIL method in the numerator and $(a - bi)(a + bi) = a^2 + b^2$ in the denominator.

$= \dfrac{14 + 43i + 20(-1)}{29}$
 Combine imaginary terms and replace i^2 with -1.

$= \dfrac{-6 + 43i}{29}$
 Combine real terms in the numerator: $14 + 20(-1) = 14 - 20 = -6$.

$= -\dfrac{6}{29} + \dfrac{43}{29}i$
 Express the answer in standard form.

Observe that the quotient is expressed in the standard form $a + bi$, with $a = -\frac{6}{29}$ and $b = \frac{43}{29}$.

⊘ Check Point **3** Divide and express the result in standard form: $\dfrac{5 + 4i}{4 - i}$.

4 Perform operations with square roots of negative numbers.

Roots of Negative Numbers

The square of $4i$ and the square of $-4i$ both result in -16:

$$(4i)^2 = 16i^2 = 16(-1) = -16 \qquad (-4i)^2 = 16i^2 = 16(-1) = -16.$$

Consequently, in the complex number system -16 has two square roots, namely, $4i$ and $-4i$. We call $4i$ the **principal square root** of -16.

Principal Square Root of a Negative Number

For any positive real number b, the **principal square root** of the negative number $-b$ is defined by

$$\sqrt{-b} = i\sqrt{b}.$$

Consider the multiplication problem

$$5i \cdot 2i = 10i^2 = 10(-1) = -10.$$

This problem can also be given in terms of principal square roots of negative numbers:

$$\sqrt{-25} \cdot \sqrt{-4}.$$

Because the product rule for radicals only applies to real numbers, multiplying radicands is incorrect. **When performing operations with square roots of negative numbers, begin by expressing all square roots in terms of i.** Then perform the indicated operation.

Correct:

$$\sqrt{-25} \cdot \sqrt{-4} = i\sqrt{25} \cdot i\sqrt{4}$$
$$= 5i \cdot 2i$$
$$= 10i^2 = 10(-1) = -10$$

Incorrect:

$$\sqrt{-25} \cdot \sqrt{-4} = \sqrt{(-25)(-4)}$$
$$= \sqrt{100}$$
$$= 10$$

EXAMPLE 4 **Operations Involving Square Roots of Negative Numbers**

Perform the indicated operations and write the result in standard form:

a. $\sqrt{-18} - \sqrt{-8}$ **b.** $\left(-1 + \sqrt{-5}\right)^2$ **c.** $\dfrac{-25 + \sqrt{-50}}{15}.$

Solution Begin by expressing all square roots of negative numbers in terms of i.

a. $\sqrt{-18} - \sqrt{-8} = i\sqrt{18} - i\sqrt{8} = i\sqrt{9 \cdot 2} - i\sqrt{4 \cdot 2}$
$$= 3i\sqrt{2} - 2i\sqrt{2} = i\sqrt{2}$$

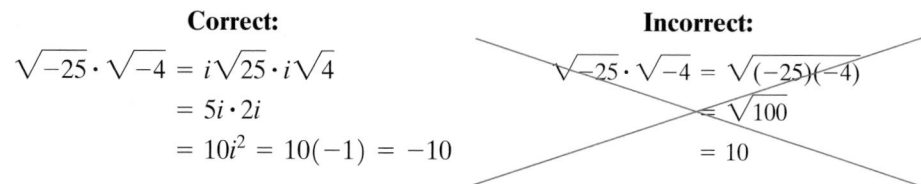
$$(A + B)^2 = A^2 + 2AB + B^2$$

b. $\left(-1 + \sqrt{-5}\right)^2 = \left(-1 + i\sqrt{5}\right)^2 = (-1)^2 + 2(-1)(i\sqrt{5}) + (i\sqrt{5})^2$
$$= 1 - 2i\sqrt{5} + 5i^2$$
$$= 1 - 2i\sqrt{5} + 5(-1)$$
$$= -4 - 2i\sqrt{5}$$

c. $\dfrac{-25 + \sqrt{-50}}{15}$

$= \dfrac{-25 + i\sqrt{50}}{15}$ $\sqrt{-b} = i\sqrt{b}$

$= \dfrac{-25 + 5i\sqrt{2}}{15}$ $\sqrt{50} = \sqrt{25 \cdot 2} = 5\sqrt{2}$

$= \dfrac{-25}{15} + \dfrac{5i\sqrt{2}}{15}$ Write the complex number in standard form.

$= -\dfrac{5}{3} + i\dfrac{\sqrt{2}}{3}$ Simplify.

⊘ **Check Point 4** Perform the indicated operations and write the result in standard form:

a. $\sqrt{-27} + \sqrt{-48}$ **b.** $\left(-2 + \sqrt{-3}\right)^2$ **c.** $\dfrac{-14 + \sqrt{-12}}{2}.$

Exercise Set 1.4

Practice Exercises

In Exercises 1–8, add or subtract as indicated and write the result in standard form.

1. $(7 + 2i) + (1 - 4i)$ **2.** $(-2 + 6i) + (4 - i)$

3. $(3 + 2i) - (5 - 7i)$ **4.** $(-7 + 5i) - (-9 - 11i)$

5. $6 - (-5 + 4i) - (-13 - i)$

6. $7 - (-9 + 2i) - (-17 - i)$

7. $8i - (14 - 9i)$ **8.** $15i - (12 - 11i)$

In Exercises 9–20, find each product and write the result in standard form.

9. $-3i(7i - 5)$ **10.** $-8i(2i - 7)$

11. $(-5 + 4i)(3 + i)$ **12.** $(-4 - 8i)(3 + i)$

13. $(7 - 5i)(-2 - 3i)$ **14.** $(8 - 4i)(-3 + 9i)$

15. $(3 + 5i)(3 - 5i)$ **16.** $(2 + 7i)(2 - 7i)$

17. $(-5 + i)(-5 - i)$ **18.** $(-7 - i)(-7 + i)$

19. $(2 + 3i)^2$ **20.** $(5 - 2i)^2$

In Exercises 21–28, divide and express the result in standard form.

21. $\dfrac{2}{3 - i}$ **22.** $\dfrac{3}{4 + i}$

23. $\dfrac{2i}{1 + i}$ **24.** $\dfrac{5i}{2 - i}$

25. $\dfrac{8i}{4 - 3i}$ **26.** $\dfrac{-6i}{3 + 2i}$

27. $\dfrac{2 + 3i}{2 + i}$ **28.** $\dfrac{3 - 4i}{4 + 3i}$

In Exercises 29–44, perform the indicated operations and write the result in standard form.

29. $\sqrt{-64} - \sqrt{-25}$ **30.** $\sqrt{-81} - \sqrt{-144}$

31. $5\sqrt{-16} + 3\sqrt{-81}$ **32.** $5\sqrt{-8} + 3\sqrt{-18}$

33. $\left(-2 + \sqrt{-4}\right)^2$ **34.** $\left(-5 - \sqrt{-9}\right)^2$

35. $\left(-3 - \sqrt{-7}\right)^2$ **36.** $\left(-2 + \sqrt{-11}\right)^2$

37. $\dfrac{-8 + \sqrt{-32}}{24}$ **38.** $\dfrac{-12 + \sqrt{-28}}{32}$

39. $\dfrac{-6 - \sqrt{-12}}{48}$ **40.** $\dfrac{-15 - \sqrt{-18}}{33}$

41. $\sqrt{-8}\left(\sqrt{-3} - \sqrt{5}\right)$ **42.** $\sqrt{-12}\left(\sqrt{-4} - \sqrt{2}\right)$

43. $\left(3\sqrt{-5}\right)\left(-4\sqrt{-12}\right)$ **44.** $\left(3\sqrt{-7}\right)\left(2\sqrt{-8}\right)$

Practice Plus

In Exercises 45–50, perform the indicated operation(s) and write the result in standard form.

45. $(2 - 3i)(1 - i) - (3 - i)(3 + i)$

46. $(8 + 9i)(2 - i) - (1 - i)(1 + i)$

47. $(2 + i)^2 - (3 - i)^2$

48. $(4 - i)^2 - (1 + 2i)^2$

49. $5\sqrt{-16} + 3\sqrt{-81}$

50. $5\sqrt{-8} + 3\sqrt{-18}$

51. Evaluate $x^2 - 2x + 2$ for $x = 1 + i$.

52. Evaluate $x^2 - 2x + 5$ for $x = 1 - 2i$.

53. Evaluate $\dfrac{x^2 + 19}{2 - x}$ for $x = 3i$.

54. Evaluate $\dfrac{x^2 + 11}{3 - x}$ for $x = 4i$.

Application Exercises

Complex numbers are used in electronics to describe the current in an electric circuit. Ohm's law relates the current in a circuit, I, in amperes, the voltage of the circuit, E, in volts, and the resistance of the circuit, R, in ohms, by the formula $E = IR$. Use this formula to solve Exercises 55–56.

55. Find E, the voltage of a circuit, if $I = (4 - 5i)$ amperes and $R = (3 + 7i)$ ohms.

56. Find E, the voltage of a circuit, if $I = (2 - 3i)$ amperes and $R = (3 + 5i)$ ohms.

57. The mathematician Girolamo Cardano is credited with the first use (in 1545) of negative square roots in solving the now-famous problem, "Find two numbers whose sum is 10 and whose product is 40." Show that the complex numbers $5 + i\sqrt{15}$ and $5 - i\sqrt{15}$ satisfy the conditions of the problem. (Cardano did not use the symbolism $i\sqrt{15}$ or even $\sqrt{-15}$. He wrote R.m 15 for $\sqrt{-15}$, meaning "radix minus 15." He regarded the numbers $5 + $ R.m 15 and $5 - $ R.m 15 as "fictitious" or "ghost numbers," and considered the problem "manifestly impossible." But in a mathematically adventurous spirit, he exclaimed, "Nevertheless, we will operate.")

Writing in Mathematics

58. What is i?

59. Explain how to add complex numbers. Provide an example with your explanation.

60. Explain how to multiply complex numbers and give an example.

61. What is the complex conjugate of $2 + 3i$? What happens when you multiply this complex number by its complex conjugate?

62. Explain how to divide complex numbers. Provide an example with your explanation.

63. Explain each of the three jokes in the cartoon on page 130.

64. A stand-up comedian uses algebra in some jokes, including one about a telephone recording that announces "You have just reached an imaginary number. Please multiply by i and dial again." Explain the joke.

Explain the error in Exercises 65–66.

65. $\sqrt{-9} + \sqrt{-16} = \sqrt{-25} = i\sqrt{25} = 5i$

66. $\left(\sqrt{-9}\right)^2 = \sqrt{-9} \cdot \sqrt{-9} = \sqrt{81} = 9$

Critical Thinking Exercises

Make Sense? *In Exercises 67–70, determine whether each statement makes sense or does not make sense, and explain your reasoning.*

67. The humor in this cartoon is based on the fact that "rational" and "real" have different meanings in mathematics and in everyday speech.

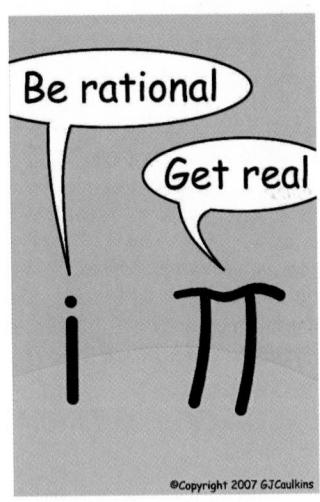

© 2007 GJ Caulkins

68. The word *imaginary* in imaginary numbers tells me that these numbers are undefined.

69. By writing the imaginary number $5i$, I can immediately see that 5 is the constant and i is the variable.

70. When I add or subtract complex numbers, I am basically combining like terms.

In Exercises 71–74, determine whether each statement is true or false. If the statement is false, make the necessary change(s) to produce a true statement.

71. Some irrational numbers are not complex numbers.

72. $(3 + 7i)(3 - 7i)$ is an imaginary number.

73. $\dfrac{7 + 3i}{5 + 3i} = \dfrac{7}{5}$

74. In the complex number system, $x^2 + y^2$ (the sum of two squares) can be factored as $(x + yi)(x - yi)$.

In Exercises 75–77, perform the indicated operations and write the result in standard form.

75. $\dfrac{4}{(2 + i)(3 - i)}$

76. $\dfrac{1 + i}{1 + 2i} + \dfrac{1 - i}{1 - 2i}$

77. $\dfrac{8}{1 + \dfrac{2}{i}}$

Preview Exercises

Exercises 78–80 will help you prepare for the material covered in the next section.

78. Factor: $2x^2 + 7x - 4$.

79. Factor: $x^2 - 6x + 9$.

80. Evaluate

$$\frac{-b - \sqrt{b^2 - 4ac}}{2a}$$

for $a = 2$, $b = 9$, and $c = -5$.

Section 1.5 Quadratic Equations

Objectives

1. Solve quadratic equations by factoring.
2. Solve quadratic equations by the square root property.
3. Solve quadratic equations by completing the square.
4. Solve quadratic equations using the quadratic formula.
5. Use the discriminant to determine the number and type of solutions.
6. Determine the most efficient method to use when solving a quadratic equation.
7. Solve problems modeled by quadratic equations.

Math tattoos. Who knew? Do you recognize the significance of this tattoo? The algebraic expression gives the solutions of a *quadratic equation*.

In this section, we study a number of methods for solving quadratic equations. We also look at applications of these equations.

Definition of a Quadratic Equation

A **quadratic equation** in x is an equation that can be written in the **general form**

$$ax^2 + bx + c = 0,$$

where a, b, and c are real numbers, with $a \neq 0$. A quadratic equation in x is also called a **second-degree polynomial equation** in x.

① Solve quadratic equations by factoring.

Solving Quadratic Equations by Factoring

Here is an example of a quadratic equation in general form:

$$x^2 - 7x + 10 = 0.$$

$a = 1 \qquad b = -7 \qquad c = 10$

We can factor the left side of this equation. We obtain $(x - 5)(x - 2) = 0$. If a quadratic equation has zero on one side and a factored expression on the other side, it can be solved using the **zero-product principle**.

The Zero-Product Principle

If the product of two algebraic expressions is zero, then at least one of the factors is equal to zero.

$$\text{If } AB = 0, \text{ then } A = 0 \text{ or } B = 0.$$

For example, consider the equation $(x - 5)(x - 2) = 0$. According to the zero-product principle, this product can be zero only if at least one of the factors is zero. We set each individual factor equal to zero and solve each resulting equation for x.

$$(x - 5)(x - 2) = 0$$
$$x - 5 = 0 \quad \text{or} \quad x - 2 = 0$$
$$x = 5 \qquad\qquad x = 2$$

We can check each of these proposed solutions, 5 and 2, in the original quadratic equation, $x^2 - 7x + 10 = 0$. Substitute each one separately for x in the equation.

Check 5:	**Check 2:**
$x^2 - 7x + 10 = 0$	$x^2 - 7x + 10 = 0$
$5^2 - 7 \cdot 5 + 10 \stackrel{?}{=} 0$	$2^2 - 7 \cdot 2 + 10 \stackrel{?}{=} 0$
$25 - 35 + 10 \stackrel{?}{=} 0$	$4 - 14 + 10 \stackrel{?}{=} 0$
$0 = 0, \ \text{true}$	$0 = 0, \ \text{true}$

The resulting true statements indicate that the solutions are 2 and 5. The solution set is $\{2, 5\}$. Note that with a quadratic equation, we can have two solutions, compared to the conditional linear equation that had one.

Solving a Quadratic Equation by Factoring

1. If necessary, rewrite the equation in the general form $ax^2 + bx + c = 0$, moving all nonzero terms to one side, thereby obtaining zero on the other side.
2. Factor completely.
3. Apply the zero-product principle, setting each factor containing a variable equal to zero.
4. Solve the equations in step 3.

EXAMPLE 1 Solving Quadratic Equations by Factoring

Solve by factoring:

a. $4x^2 - 2x = 0$ **b.** $2x^2 + 7x = 4.$

Solution

a. We begin with $4x^2 - 2x = 0$.

Step 1 Move all nonzero terms to one side and obtain zero on the other side. All nonzero terms are already on the left and zero is on the other side, so we can skip this step.

Step 2 Factor. We factor out $2x$ from the two terms on the left side.

$$4x^2 - 2x = 0 \qquad \text{This is the given equation.}$$
$$2x(2x - 1) = 0 \qquad \text{Factor.}$$

Steps 3 and 4 Set each factor equal to zero and solve the resulting equations.

$$2x = 0 \quad \text{or} \quad 2x - 1 = 0$$
$$x = 0 \qquad\qquad 2x = 1$$
$$x = \tfrac{1}{2}$$

Step 5 Check the solutions in the original equation.

Check 0:	**Check $\tfrac{1}{2}$:**
$4x^2 - 2x = 0$	$4x^2 - 2x = 0$
$4 \cdot 0^2 - 2 \cdot 0 \overset{?}{=} 0$	$4\left(\tfrac{1}{2}\right)^2 - 2\left(\tfrac{1}{2}\right) \overset{?}{=} 0$
$0 - 0 \overset{?}{=} 0$	$4\left(\tfrac{1}{4}\right) - 2\left(\tfrac{1}{2}\right) \overset{?}{=} 0$
$0 = 0, \quad$ true	$1 - 1 \overset{?}{=} 0$
	$0 = 0, \quad$ true

The solution set is $\left\{0, \tfrac{1}{2}\right\}$.

b. Next, we solve $2x^2 + 7x = 4$.

Step 1 Move all nonzero terms to one side and obtain zero on the other side. Subtract 4 from both sides and write the equation in general form.

$$2x^2 + 7x = 4 \qquad \text{This is the given equation.}$$
$$2x^2 + 7x - 4 = 4 - 4 \qquad \text{Subtract 4 from both sides.}$$
$$2x^2 + 7x - 4 = 0 \qquad \text{Simplify.}$$

Step 2 Factor.

$$2x^2 + 7x - 4 = 0$$
$$(2x - 1)(x + 4) = 0$$

Steps 3 and 4 Set each factor equal to zero and solve the resulting equations.

$$2x - 1 = 0 \quad \text{or} \quad x + 4 = 0$$
$$2x = 1 \qquad\qquad x = -4$$
$$x = \tfrac{1}{2}$$

Step 5 Check the solutions in the original equation.

Check $\tfrac{1}{2}$:	**Check -4:**
$2x^2 + 7x = 4$	$2x^2 + 7x = 4$
$2\left(\tfrac{1}{2}\right)^2 + 7\left(\tfrac{1}{2}\right) \overset{?}{=} 4$	$2(-4)^2 + 7(-4) \overset{?}{=} 4$
$\tfrac{1}{2} + \tfrac{7}{2} \overset{?}{=} 4$	$32 + (-28) \overset{?}{=} 4$
$4 = 4, \quad$ true	$4 = 4, \quad$ true

The solution set is $\left\{-4, \tfrac{1}{2}\right\}$.

✓ Check Point **1** Solve by factoring:

a. $3x^2 - 9x = 0$ **b.** $2x^2 + x = 1$.

Technology

Graphic Connections

You can use a graphing utility to check the real solutions of a quadratic equation. **The real solutions of $ax^2 + bx + c = 0$ correspond to the x-intercepts of the graph of $y = ax^2 + bx + c$.** For example, to check the solutions of $2x^2 + 7x = 4$, or $2x^2 + 7x - 4 = 0$, graph $y = 2x^2 + 7x - 4$. The U-shaped, bowl-like, graph is shown on the right. Note that it is important to have all nonzero terms on one side of the quadratic equation before entering it into the graphing utility. The x-intercepts are -4 and $\frac{1}{2}$, and the graph of $y = 2x^2 + 7x - 4$ passes through $(-4, 0)$ and $\left(\frac{1}{2}, 0\right)$. This verifies that $\left\{-4, \frac{1}{2}\right\}$ is the solution set of $2x^2 + 7x - 4 = 0$, or equivalently, $2x^2 + 7x = 4$.

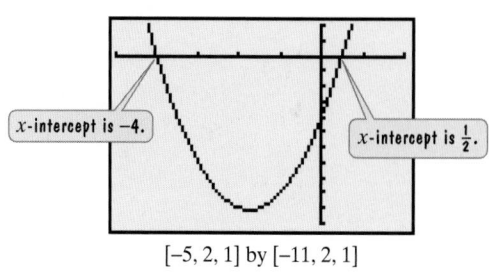

$[-5, 2, 1]$ by $[-11, 2, 1]$

② Solve quadratic equations by the square root property.

Solving Quadratic Equations by the Square Root Property

Quadratic equations of the form $u^2 = d$, where u is an algebraic expression and d is a nonzero real number, can be solved by the *square root property*. First, isolate the squared expression u^2 on one side of the equation and the number d on the other side. Then take the square root of both sides. Remember, there are two numbers whose square is d. One number is \sqrt{d} and one is $-\sqrt{d}$.

We can use factoring to verify that $u^2 = d$ has these two solutions.

$$u^2 = d \qquad \text{This is the given equation.}$$

$$u^2 - d = 0 \qquad \text{Move all terms to one side and obtain zero on the other side.}$$

$$\left(u + \sqrt{d}\right)\left(u - \sqrt{d}\right) = 0 \qquad \text{Factor.}$$

$$u + \sqrt{d} = 0 \quad \text{or} \quad u - \sqrt{d} = 0 \qquad \text{Set each factor equal to zero.}$$

$$u = -\sqrt{d} \qquad\qquad u = \sqrt{d} \qquad \text{Solve the resulting equations.}$$

Because the solutions differ only in sign, we can write them in abbreviated notation as $u = \pm\sqrt{d}$. We read this as "u equals positive or negative the square root of d" or "u equals plus or minus the square root of d."

Now that we have verified these solutions, we can solve $u^2 = d$ directly by taking square roots. This process is called the **square root property**.

The Square Root Property

If u is an algebraic expression and d is a nonzero real number, then $u^2 = d$ has exactly two solutions:

$$\text{If } u^2 = d, \text{ then } u = \sqrt{d} \text{ or } u = -\sqrt{d}.$$

Equivalently,

$$\text{If } u^2 = d, \text{ then } u = \pm\sqrt{d}.$$

Before you can apply the square root property, a squared expression must be isolated on one side of the equation.

EXAMPLE 2 **Solving Quadratic Equations by the Square Root Property**

Solve by the square root property:

a. $3x^2 - 15 = 0$ **b.** $9x^2 + 25 = 0$ **c.** $(x - 2)^2 = 6$.

Solution To apply the square root property, we need a squared expression by itself on one side of the equation.

$$3x^2 - 15 = 0 \qquad 9x^2 + 25 = 0 \qquad (x - 2)^2 = 6$$

We want x^2 by itself. We want x^2 by itself. The squared expression is by itself.

a. $3x^2 - 15 = 0$ This is the original equation.

$3x^2 = 15$ Add 15 to both sides.

$x^2 = 5$ Divide both sides by 3.

$x = \sqrt{5}$ or $x = -\sqrt{5}$ Apply the square root property.

Equivalently, $x = \pm\sqrt{5}$.

By checking both proposed solutions in the original equation, we can confirm that the solution set is $\left\{-\sqrt{5}, \sqrt{5}\right\}$ or $\left\{\pm\sqrt{5}\right\}$.

b. $9x^2 + 25 = 0$ This is the original equation.

$9x^2 = -25$ Subtract 25 from both sides.

$x^2 = -\dfrac{25}{9}$ Divide both sides by 9.

$x = \pm\sqrt{-\dfrac{25}{9}}$ Apply the square root property.

$x = \pm i\sqrt{\dfrac{25}{9}} = \pm\dfrac{5}{3}i$ Express solutions in terms of i.

Because the equation has an x^2-term and no x-term, we can check both proposed solutions, $\pm\dfrac{5}{3}i$, at once.

Check $\dfrac{5}{3}i$ and $-\dfrac{5}{3}i$:

$$9x^2 + 25 = 0$$

$$9\left(\pm\dfrac{5}{3}i\right)^2 + 25 \overset{?}{=} 0$$

$$9\left(\dfrac{25}{9}i^2\right) + 25 \overset{?}{=} 0$$

$$25i^2 + 25 \overset{?}{=} 0$$

$i^2 = -1$

$$25(-1) + 25 \overset{?}{=} 0$$

$$0 = 0, \quad \text{true}$$

The solutions are $-\dfrac{5}{3}i$ and $\dfrac{5}{3}i$. The solution set is $\left\{-\dfrac{5}{3}i, \dfrac{5}{3}i\right\}$ or $\left\{\pm\dfrac{5}{3}i\right\}$.

c. $(x - 2)^2 = 6$ This is the original equation.

$x - 2 = \pm\sqrt{6}$ Apply the square root property.

$x = 2 \pm \sqrt{6}$ Add 2 to both sides.

By checking both values in the original equation, we can confirm that the solution set is $\left\{2 + \sqrt{6}, 2 - \sqrt{6}\right\}$ or $\left\{2 \pm \sqrt{6}\right\}$.

⊘ Check Point **2** Solve by the square root property:

a. $3x^2 - 21 = 0$ **b.** $5x^2 + 45 = 0$ **c.** $(x + 5)^2 = 11$.

❸ Solve quadratic equations by completing the square.

Completing the Square

How do we solve an equation in the form $ax^2 + bx + c = 0$ if the trinomial $ax^2 + bx + c$ cannot be factored? We cannot use the zero-product principle in such a case. However, we can convert the equation into an equivalent equation that can be solved using the square root property. This is accomplished by **completing the square**.

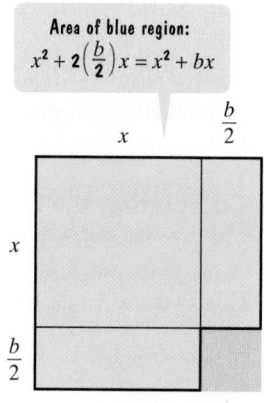

Area of blue region:

$$x^2 + 2\left(\frac{b}{2}\right)x = x^2 + bx$$

Adding this red square of area $\left(\frac{b}{2}\right)^2$ completes the larger square.

Figure 1.19 Visualizing completing the square

Completing the Square

If $x^2 + bx$ is a binomial, then by adding $\left(\dfrac{b}{2}\right)^2$, which is the square of half the coefficient of x, a perfect square trinomial will result. That is,

$$x^2 + bx + \left(\frac{b}{2}\right)^2 = \left(x + \frac{b}{2}\right)^2.$$

Squares and rectangles make it possible to visualize completing the square, as shown in **Figure 1.19**.

EXAMPLE 3 **Completing the Square**

What term should be added to each binomial so that it becomes a perfect square trinomial? Write and factor the trinomial.

a. $x^2 + 8x$ **b.** $x^2 - 7x$ **c.** $x^2 + \dfrac{3}{5}x$

Solution To complete the square, we must add a term to each binomial. The term that should be added is the square of half the coefficient of x.

$$x^2 + 8x \qquad x^2 - 7x \qquad x^2 + \frac{3}{5}x$$

Add $\left(\frac{8}{2}\right)^2 = 4^2$. Add 16 to complete the square.

Add $\left(\frac{-7}{2}\right)^2$, or $\frac{49}{4}$, to complete the square.

Add $\left(\frac{1}{2} \cdot \frac{3}{5}\right)^2 = \left(\frac{3}{10}\right)^2$. Add $\frac{9}{100}$ to complete the square.

a. The coefficient of the x-term in $x^2 + 8x$ is 8. Half of 8 is 4, and $4^2 = 16$. Add 16. The result is a perfect square trinomial.

$$x^2 + 8x + 16 = (x + 4)^2$$

b. The coefficient of the x-term in $x^2 - 7x$ is -7. Half of -7 is $-\dfrac{7}{2}$, and $\left(-\dfrac{7}{2}\right)^2 = \dfrac{49}{4}$. Add $\dfrac{49}{4}$. The result is a perfect square trinomial.

$$x^2 - 7x + \frac{49}{4} = \left(x - \frac{7}{2}\right)^2$$

c. The coefficient of the x-term in $x^2 + \dfrac{3}{5}x$ is $\dfrac{3}{5}$. Half of $\dfrac{3}{5}$ is $\dfrac{1}{2} \cdot \dfrac{3}{5}$, or $\dfrac{3}{10}$, and $\left(\dfrac{3}{10}\right)^2 = \dfrac{9}{100}$. Add $\dfrac{9}{100}$. The result is a perfect square trinomial.

$$x^2 + \frac{3}{5}x + \frac{9}{100} = \left(x + \frac{3}{10}\right)^2$$

Study Tip

You may not be accustomed to factoring perfect square trinomials in which fractions are involved. The constant in the factorization is always half the coefficient of x.

$$x^2 - 7x + \frac{49}{4} = \left(x - \frac{7}{2}\right)^2 \qquad\qquad x^2 + \frac{3}{5}x + \frac{9}{100} = \left(x + \frac{3}{10}\right)^2$$

Half the coefficient of x, -7, is $-\dfrac{7}{2}$.

Half the coefficient of x, $\dfrac{3}{5}$, is $\dfrac{3}{10}$.

Check Point 3 What term should be added to each binomial so that it becomes a perfect square trinomial? Write and factor the trinomial.

a. $x^2 + 6x$ **b.** $x^2 - 5x$ **c.** $x^2 + \dfrac{2}{3}x$

We can solve *any* quadratic equation by completing the square. If the coefficient of the x^2-term is one, we add the square of half the coefficient of x to both sides of the equation. **When you add a constant term to one side of the equation to complete the square, be certain to add the same constant to the other side of the equation.** These ideas are illustrated in Example 4.

(**EXAMPLE 4**) **Solving a Quadratic Equation by Completing the Square**

Solve by completing the square: $x^2 - 6x + 4 = 0$.

Solution We begin by subtracting 4 from both sides. This is done to isolate the binomial $x^2 - 6x$, so that we can complete the square.

$$x^2 - 6x + 4 = 0 \qquad \text{This is the original equation.}$$
$$x^2 - 6x = -4 \qquad \text{Subtract 4 from both sides.}$$

Next, we work with $x^2 - 6x = -4$ and complete the square. Find half the coefficient of the x-term and square it. The coefficient of the x-term is -6. Half of -6 is -3 and $(-3)^2 = 9$. Thus, we add 9 to both sides of the equation.

$$x^2 - 6x + 9 = -4 + 9 \qquad \text{Add 9 to both sides to complete the square.}$$

$$(x - 3)^2 = 5 \qquad \text{Factor and simplify.}$$

$$x - 3 = \sqrt{5} \quad \text{or} \quad x - 3 = -\sqrt{5} \qquad \text{Apply the square root property.}$$
$$x = 3 + \sqrt{5} \qquad x = 3 - \sqrt{5} \qquad \text{Add 3 to both sides in each equation.}$$

The solutions are $3 \pm \sqrt{5}$ and the solution set is $\{3 + \sqrt{5}, 3 - \sqrt{5}\}$, or $\{3 \pm \sqrt{5}\}$.

Study Tip

When you complete the square for the binomial expression $x^2 + bx$, you obtain a different polynomial. When you solve a quadratic equation by completing the square, you obtain an equation with the same solution set because the constant needed to complete the square is added to *both* sides.

☑ **Check Point 4** Solve by completing the square: $x^2 + 4x - 1 = 0$.

If the coefficient of the x^2-term in a quadratic equation is not 1, you must divide each side of the equation by this coefficient before completing the square. For example, to solve $9x^2 - 6x - 4 = 0$ by completing the square, first divide every term by 9:

$$\frac{9x^2}{9} - \frac{6x}{9} - \frac{4}{9} = \frac{0}{9}$$

$$x^2 - \frac{6}{9}x - \frac{4}{9} = 0$$

$$x^2 - \frac{2}{3}x - \frac{4}{9} = 0.$$

Now that the coefficient of the x^2-term is 1, we can solve by completing the square.

(**EXAMPLE 5**) **Solving a Quadratic Equation by Completing the Square**

Solve by completing the square: $9x^2 - 6x - 4 = 0$.

Solution

$$9x^2 - 6x - 4 = 0 \qquad \text{This is the original equation.}$$

$$x^2 - \frac{2}{3}x - \frac{4}{9} = 0 \qquad \text{Divide both sides by 9.}$$

$$x^2 - \frac{2}{3}x = \frac{4}{9} \qquad \text{Add } \tfrac{4}{9} \text{ to both sides to isolate the binomial.}$$

$$x^2 - \frac{2}{3}x + \frac{1}{9} = \frac{4}{9} + \frac{1}{9} \qquad \text{Complete the square: Half of } -\tfrac{2}{3} \text{ is } -\tfrac{2}{6}, \text{ or } -\tfrac{1}{3}, \text{ and } \left(-\tfrac{1}{3}\right)^2 = \tfrac{1}{9}.$$

$$\left(x - \frac{1}{3}\right)^2 = \frac{5}{9} \qquad \text{Factor and simplify.}$$

Technology

Graphic Connections

Obtain a decimal approximation for each solution of
$$9x^2 - 6x - 4 = 0,$$
the equation in Example 5.
$$\frac{1 + \sqrt{5}}{3} \approx 1.1; \quad \frac{1 - \sqrt{5}}{3} \approx -0.4$$

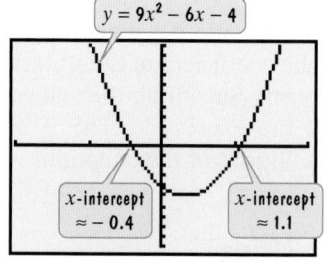

$y = 9x^2 - 6x - 4$

x-intercept ≈ -0.4

x-intercept ≈ 1.1

$[-2, 2, 1]$ by $[-10, 10, 1]$

The x-intercepts of $y = 9x^2 - 6x - 4$ verify the solutions.

$$x - \frac{1}{3} = \sqrt{\frac{5}{9}} \quad \text{or} \quad x - \frac{1}{3} = -\sqrt{\frac{5}{9}} \qquad \text{Apply the square root property.}$$

$$x - \frac{1}{3} = \frac{\sqrt{5}}{3} \qquad\qquad x - \frac{1}{3} = -\frac{\sqrt{5}}{3} \qquad \sqrt{\frac{5}{9}} = \frac{\sqrt{5}}{\sqrt{9}} = \frac{\sqrt{5}}{3}$$

$$x = \frac{1}{3} + \frac{\sqrt{5}}{3} \qquad\qquad x = \frac{1}{3} - \frac{\sqrt{5}}{3} \qquad \text{Add } \tfrac{1}{3} \text{ to both sides and solve for } x.$$

$$x = \frac{1 + \sqrt{5}}{3} \qquad\qquad x = \frac{1 - \sqrt{5}}{3} \qquad \text{Express solutions with a common denominator.}$$

The solutions are $\dfrac{1 \pm \sqrt{5}}{3}$ and the solution set is $\left\{ \dfrac{1 \pm \sqrt{5}}{3} \right\}$.

⊘ **Check Point 5** Solve by completing the square: $2x^2 + 3x - 4 = 0$.

Solving Quadratic Equations Using the Quadratic Formula

We can use the method of completing the square to derive a formula that can be used to solve all quadratic equations. The derivation given below also shows a particular quadratic equation, $3x^2 - 2x - 4 = 0$, to specifically illustrate each of the steps.

Deriving the Quadratic Formula

General Form of a Quadratic Equation	Comment	A Specific Example
$ax^2 + bx + c = 0, a > 0$	This is the given equation.	$3x^2 - 2x - 4 = 0$
$x^2 + \dfrac{b}{a}x + \dfrac{c}{a} = 0$	Divide both sides by the coefficient of x^2.	$x^2 - \dfrac{2}{3}x - \dfrac{4}{3} = 0$
$x^2 + \dfrac{b}{a}x = -\dfrac{c}{a}$	Isolate the binomial by adding $-\dfrac{c}{a}$ on both sides of the equation.	$x^2 - \dfrac{2}{3}x = \dfrac{4}{3}$
$x^2 + \dfrac{b}{a}x + \left(\dfrac{b}{2a}\right)^2 = -\dfrac{c}{a} + \left(\dfrac{b}{2a}\right)^2$ $\underset{\text{(half)}^2}{\underbrace{\qquad}}$ $x^2 + \dfrac{b}{a}x + \dfrac{b^2}{4a^2} = -\dfrac{c}{a} + \dfrac{b^2}{4a^2}$	Complete the square. Add the square of half the coefficient of x to both sides.	$x^2 - \dfrac{2}{3}x + \left(-\dfrac{1}{3}\right)^2 = \dfrac{4}{3} + \left(-\dfrac{1}{3}\right)^2$ $\underset{\text{(half)}^2}{\underbrace{\qquad}}$ $x^2 - \dfrac{2}{3}x + \dfrac{1}{9} = \dfrac{4}{3} + \dfrac{1}{9}$
$\left(x + \dfrac{b}{2a}\right)^2 = -\dfrac{c}{a} \cdot \dfrac{4a}{4a} + \dfrac{b^2}{4a^2}$	Factor on the left side and obtain a common denominator on the right side.	$\left(x - \dfrac{1}{3}\right)^2 = \dfrac{4}{3} \cdot \dfrac{3}{3} + \dfrac{1}{9}$
$\left(x + \dfrac{b}{2a}\right)^2 = \dfrac{-4ac + b^2}{4a^2}$ $\left(x + \dfrac{b}{2a}\right)^2 = \dfrac{b^2 - 4ac}{4a^2}$	Add fractions on the right side.	$\left(x - \dfrac{1}{3}\right)^2 = \dfrac{12 + 1}{9}$ $\left(x - \dfrac{1}{3}\right)^2 = \dfrac{13}{9}$
$x + \dfrac{b}{2a} = \pm\sqrt{\dfrac{b^2 - 4ac}{4a^2}}$	Apply the square root property.	$x - \dfrac{1}{3} = \pm\sqrt{\dfrac{13}{9}}$
$x + \dfrac{b}{2a} = \pm\dfrac{\sqrt{b^2 - 4ac}}{2a}$	Take the square root of the quotient, simplifying the denominator.	$x - \dfrac{1}{3} = \pm\dfrac{\sqrt{13}}{3}$
$x = \dfrac{-b}{2a} \pm \dfrac{\sqrt{b^2 - 4ac}}{2a}$	Solve for x by subtracting $\dfrac{b}{2a}$ from both sides.	$x = \dfrac{1}{3} \pm \dfrac{\sqrt{13}}{3}$
$x = \dfrac{-b \pm \sqrt{b^2 - 4ac}}{2a}$	Combine fractions on the right side.	$x = \dfrac{1 \pm \sqrt{13}}{3}$

The formula shown at the bottom of the left column is called the *quadratic formula*. A similar proof shows that the same formula can be used to solve quadratic equations if a, the coefficient of the x^2-term, is negative.

④ Solve quadratic equations using the quadratic formula.

The Quadratic Formula

The solutions of a quadratic equation in general form $ax^2 + bx + c = 0$, with $a \neq 0$, are given by the **quadratic formula**:

$$x = \frac{-b \pm \sqrt{b^2 - 4ac}}{2a}.$$

> *x* equals negative *b* plus or minus the square root of $b^2 - 4ac$, all divided by 2*a*.

To use the quadratic formula, rewrite the quadratic equation in general form if necessary. Then determine the numerical values for a (the coefficient of the x^2-term), b (the coefficient of the x-term), and c (the constant term). Substitute the values of a, b, and c into the quadratic formula and evaluate the expression. The \pm sign indicates that there are two (not necessarily distinct) solutions of the equation.

EXAMPLE 6 **Solving a Quadratic Equation Using the Quadratic Formula**

Solve using the quadratic formula: $2x^2 - 6x + 1 = 0$.

Solution The given equation is in general form. Begin by identifying the values for a, b, and c.

$$2x^2 - 6x + 1 = 0$$

$a = 2 \qquad b = -6 \qquad c = 1$

Substituting these values into the quadratic formula and simplifying gives the equation's solutions.

$$x = \frac{-b \pm \sqrt{b^2 - 4ac}}{2a} \qquad \text{Use the quadratic formula.}$$

$$= \frac{-(-6) \pm \sqrt{(-6)^2 - 4(2)(1)}}{2 \cdot 2} \qquad \begin{array}{l} \text{Substitute the values for } a, b, \text{ and } c: \\ a = 2, b = -6, \text{ and } c = 1. \end{array}$$

$$= \frac{6 \pm \sqrt{36 - 8}}{4} \qquad \begin{array}{l} -(-6) = 6, (-6)^2 = (-6)(-6) = 36, \text{ and} \\ 4(2)(1) = 8. \end{array}$$

$$= \frac{6 \pm \sqrt{28}}{4} \qquad \text{Complete the subtraction under the radical.}$$

$$= \frac{6 \pm 2\sqrt{7}}{4} \qquad \sqrt{28} = \sqrt{4 \cdot 7} = \sqrt{4}\sqrt{7} = 2\sqrt{7}$$

$$= \frac{2(3 \pm \sqrt{7})}{4} \qquad \text{Factor out 2 from the numerator.}$$

$$= \frac{3 \pm \sqrt{7}}{2} \qquad \text{Divide the numerator and denominator by 2.}$$

The solution set is $\left\{ \dfrac{3 + \sqrt{7}}{2}, \dfrac{3 - \sqrt{7}}{2} \right\}$ or $\left\{ \dfrac{3 \pm \sqrt{7}}{2} \right\}$.

Technology

You can use a graphing utility to verify that the solutions of $2x^2 - 6x + 1 = 0$ are $\dfrac{3 \pm \sqrt{7}}{2}$. Begin by entering $y_1 = 2x^2 - 6x + 1$ in the $\boxed{Y=}$ screen. Then evaluate this equation at each of the proposed solutions.

Y₁((3+√(7))/2)
 0
Y₁((3-√(7))/2)
 0
■

> In each case, the value is 0, verifying that the solutions satisfy $2x^2 - 6x + 1 = 0$.

Study Tip

Many students use the quadratic formula correctly until the last step, where they make an error in simplifying the solutions. Be sure to factor the numerator before dividing the numerator and denominator by the greatest common factor:

$$\frac{6 \pm 2\sqrt{7}}{4} = \frac{2(3 \pm \sqrt{7})}{4} = \frac{\overset{1}{\cancel{2}}(3 \pm \sqrt{7})}{\underset{2}{\cancel{4}}} = \frac{3 \pm \sqrt{7}}{2}.$$

Factor first Then divide by the GCF.

You cannot divide just one term in the numerator and the denominator by their greatest common factor.

Incorrect!

$$\frac{6 \pm 2\sqrt{7}}{4} = \frac{\overset{3}{\cancel{6}} \pm 2\sqrt{7}}{\underset{2}{\cancel{4}}} = \frac{3 \pm 2\sqrt{7}}{2} \qquad \frac{6 \pm 2\sqrt{7}}{4} = \frac{6 \pm \overset{1}{\cancel{2}}\sqrt{7}}{\underset{2}{\cancel{4}}} = \frac{6 \pm \sqrt{7}}{2}$$

Can all irrational solutions of quadratic equations be simplified? No. The following solutions cannot be simplified.

$$\frac{5 \pm 2\sqrt{7}}{2} \qquad \frac{-4 \pm 3\sqrt{7}}{2}$$

Other than 1, terms in each numerator have no common factor.

☑ **Check Point 6** Solve using the quadratic formula:
$$2x^2 + 2x - 1 = 0.$$

(EXAMPLE 7) **Solving a Quadratic Equation Using the Quadratic Formula**

Solve using the quadratic formula: $3x^2 - 2x + 4 = 0$.

Solution The given equation is in general form. Begin by identifying the values for a, b, and c.

$$3x^2 - 2x + 4 = 0$$

$a = 3$ $b = -2$ $c = 4$

Study Tip

Checking irrational and imaginary solutions can be time-consuming. The solutions given by the quadratic formula are always correct, unless you have made a careless error. Checking for computational errors or errors in simplification is sufficient.

$$x = \frac{-b \pm \sqrt{b^2 - 4ac}}{2a}$$
Use the quadratic formula.

$$= \frac{-(-2) \pm \sqrt{(-2)^2 - 4(3)(4)}}{2(3)}$$
Substitute the values for a, b, and c: $a = 3$, $b = -2$, and $c = 4$.

$$= \frac{2 \pm \sqrt{4 - 48}}{6}$$
$-(-2) = 2$ and $(-2)^2 = (-2)(-2) = 4$.

$$= \frac{2 \pm \sqrt{-44}}{6}$$
Subtract under the radical. Because the number under the radical sign is negative, the solutions will not be real numbers.

$$= \frac{2 \pm 2i\sqrt{11}}{6}$$
$\sqrt{-44} = \sqrt{4(11)(-1)} = 2i\sqrt{11}$

$$= \frac{2(1 \pm i\sqrt{11})}{6}$$
Factor 2 from the numerator.

$$= \frac{1 \pm i\sqrt{11}}{3}$$
Divide the numerator and denominator by 2.

$$= \frac{1}{3} \pm i\frac{\sqrt{11}}{3}$$
Write the complex numbers in standard form.

The solutions are complex conjugates, and the solution set is
$$\left\{ \frac{1}{3} + i\frac{\sqrt{11}}{3}, \frac{1}{3} - i\frac{\sqrt{11}}{3} \right\} \text{ or } \left\{ \frac{1}{3} \pm i\frac{\sqrt{11}}{3} \right\}.$$

If $ax^2 + bx + c = 0$ has imaginary solutions, the graph of $y = ax^2 + bx + c$ will not have x-intercepts. This is illustrated by the imaginary solutions of $3x^2 - 2x + 4 = 0$ in Example 7 and the graph of $y = 3x^2 - 2x + 4$ in **Figure 1.20**.

$[-2, 2, 1]$ by $[-1, 10, 1]$

Figure 1.20 This graph has no x-intercepts.

⊘ Check Point **7** Solve using the quadratic formula:

$$x^2 - 2x + 2 = 0.$$

⑤ Use the discriminant to determine the number and type of solutions.

The Discriminant

The quantity $b^2 - 4ac$, which appears under the radical sign in the quadratic formula, is called the **discriminant**. **Table 1.2** shows how the discriminant of the quadratic equation $ax^2 + bx + c = 0$ determines the number and type of solutions.

Table 1.2 The Discriminant and the Kinds of Solutions to $ax^2 + bx + c = 0$

Discriminant $b^2 - 4ac$	Kinds of Solutions to $ax^2 + bx + c = 0$	Graph of $y = ax^2 + bx + c$
$b^2 - 4ac > 0$	**Two unequal real solutions:** If a, b, and c are rational numbers and the discriminant is a perfect square, the solutions are *rational*. If the discriminant is not a perfect square, the solutions are *irrational* conjugates.	Two x-intercepts
$b^2 - 4ac = 0$	**One solution (a repeated solution) that is a real number:** If a, b, and c are rational numbers, the repeated solution is also a rational number.	One x-intercept
$b^2 - 4ac < 0$	**No real solution; two imaginary solutions:** The solutions are complex conjugates.	No x-intercepts

EXAMPLE 8 Using the Discriminant

For each equation, compute the discriminant. Then determine the number and type of solutions:

a. $3x^2 + 4x - 5 = 0$ **b.** $9x^2 - 6x + 1 = 0$ **c.** $3x^2 - 8x + 7 = 0$.

Solution Begin by identifying the values for a, b, and c in each equation. Then compute $b^2 - 4ac$, the discriminant.

Study Tip

The discriminant is $b^2 - 4ac$. It is not $\sqrt{b^2 - 4ac}$, so do not give the discriminant as a radical.

a. $3x^2 + 4x - 5 = 0$

$a = 3$ $b = 4$ $c = -5$

Substitute and compute the discriminant:

$$b^2 - 4ac = 4^2 - 4 \cdot 3(-5) = 16 - (-60) = 16 + 60 = 76.$$

The discriminant, 76, is a positive number that is not a perfect square. Thus, there are two irrational solutions. (These solutions are conjugates of each other.)

b. $9x^2 - 6x + 1 = 0$

$a = 9 \qquad b = -6 \qquad c = 1$

Substitute and compute the discriminant:

$$b^2 - 4ac = (-6)^2 - 4 \cdot 9 \cdot 1 = 36 - 36 = 0.$$

The discriminant, 0, shows that there is only one real solution. This real solution is a rational number.

c. $3x^2 - 8x + 7 = 0$

$a = 3 \qquad b = -8 \qquad c = 7$

$$b^2 - 4ac = (-8)^2 - 4 \cdot 3 \cdot 7 = 64 - 84 = -20$$

The negative discriminant, -20, shows that there are two imaginary solutions. (These solutions are complex conjugates of each other.) ●

⏀ Check Point **8** For each equation, compute the discriminant. Then determine the number and type of solutions:

a. $x^2 + 6x + 9 = 0$ **b.** $2x^2 - 7x - 4 = 0$ **c.** $3x^2 - 2x + 4 = 0.$

⑥ Determine the most efficient method to use when solving a quadratic equation.

Determining Which Method to Use

All quadratic equations can be solved by the quadratic formula. However, if an equation is in the form $u^2 = d$, such as $x^2 = 5$ or $(2x + 3)^2 = 8$, it is faster to use the square root property, taking the square root of both sides. If the equation is not in the form $u^2 = d$, write the quadratic equation in general form $(ax^2 + bx + c = 0)$. Try to solve the equation by factoring. If $ax^2 + bx + c$ cannot be factored, then solve the quadratic equation by the quadratic formula.

Because we used the method of completing the square to derive the quadratic formula, we no longer need it for solving quadratic equations. However, we will use completing the square later in the book to help graph circles and other kinds of equations.

Table 1.3 summarizes our observations about which technique to use when solving a quadratic equation.

Table 1.3 Determining the Most Efficient Technique to Use when Solving a Quadratic Equation

Description and Form of the Quadratic Equation	Most Efficient Solution Method	Example
$ax^2 + bx + c = 0$ and $ax^2 + bx + c$ can be factored easily.	Factor and use the zero-product principle.	$3x^2 + 5x - 2 = 0$ $(3x - 1)(x + 2) = 0$ $3x - 1 = 0$ or $x + 2 = 0$ $x = \dfrac{1}{3}$ $x = -2$
$ax^2 + bx = 0$ The quadratic equation has no constant term. $(c = 0)$	Factor and use the zero-product principle.	$6x^2 + 9x = 0$ $3x(2x + 3) = 0$ $3x = 0$ or $2x + 3 = 0$ $x = 0$ $2x = -3$ $x = -\frac{3}{2}$
$ax^2 + c = 0$ The quadratic equation has no x-term. $(b = 0)$	Solve for x^2 and apply the square root property.	$7x^2 - 4 = 0$ $7x^2 = 4$ $x^2 = \dfrac{4}{7}$ $x = \pm\sqrt{\dfrac{4}{7}}$ $= \pm\dfrac{2}{\sqrt{7}} = \pm\dfrac{2}{\sqrt{7}} \cdot \dfrac{\sqrt{7}}{\sqrt{7}} = \pm\dfrac{2\sqrt{7}}{7}$
$u^2 = d$; u is a first-degree polynomial.	Use the square root property.	$(x + 4)^2 = 5$ $x + 4 = \pm\sqrt{5}$ $x = -4 \pm \sqrt{5}$
$ax^2 + bx + c = 0$ and $ax^2 + bx + c$ cannot be factored or the factoring is too difficult.	Use the quadratic formula: $x = \dfrac{-b \pm \sqrt{b^2 - 4ac}}{2a}.$	$x^2 - 2x - 6 = 0$ $a = 1$ $b = -2$ $c = -6$ $x = \dfrac{-(-2) \pm \sqrt{(-2)^2 - 4(1)(-6)}}{2(1)}$ $= \dfrac{2 \pm \sqrt{4 + 24}}{2(1)}$ $= \dfrac{2 \pm \sqrt{28}}{2} = \dfrac{2 \pm \sqrt{4}\sqrt{7}}{2}$ $= \dfrac{2 \pm 2\sqrt{7}}{2} = \dfrac{2(1 \pm \sqrt{7})}{2}$ $= 1 \pm \sqrt{7}$

7 Solve problems modeled by quadratic equations.

Applications

(**EXAMPLE 9**) **Blood Pressure and Age**

The graphs in **Figure 1.21** illustrate that a person's normal systolic blood pressure, measured in millimeters of mercury (mm Hg), depends on his or her age. (The symbol ⨍ on the vertical axis shows there is a break in values between 0 and 100. Thus, the first tick mark on the vertical axis represents a blood pressure of 100 mm Hg.) The formula

$$P = 0.006A^2 - 0.02A + 120$$

models a man's normal systolic pressure, P, at age A.

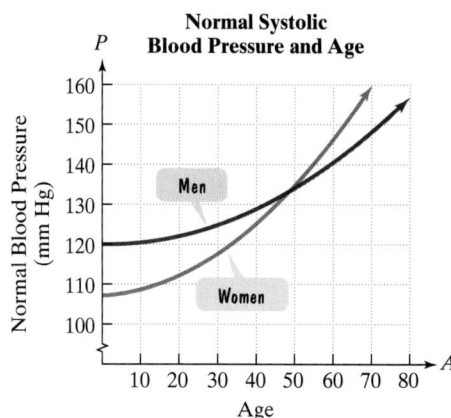

Figure 1.21

a. Find the age, to the nearest year, of a man whose normal systolic blood pressure is 125 mm Hg.

b. Use the graphs in **Figure 1.21** to describe the differences between the normal systolic blood pressures of men and women as they age.

Solution

a. We are interested in the age of a man with a normal systolic blood pressure of 125 millimeters of mercury. Thus, we substitute 125 for P in the given formula for men. Then we solve for A, the man's age.

$$P = 0.006A^2 - 0.02A + 120 \qquad \text{This is the given formula for men.}$$

$$125 = 0.006A^2 - 0.02A + 120 \qquad \text{Substitute 125 for } P.$$

$$0 = 0.006A^2 - 0.02A - 5 \qquad \text{Subtract 125 from both sides and write the quadratic equation in}$$

$$\boxed{a = 0.006} \quad \boxed{b = -0.02} \quad \boxed{c = -5} \qquad \text{general form.}$$

Because the trinomial on the right side of the equation is prime, we solve using the quadratic formula.

Notice that the variable is A, rather than the usual x.

$$A = \frac{-b \pm \sqrt{b^2 - 4ac}}{2a} \qquad \text{Use the quadratic formula.}$$

$$= \frac{-(-0.02) \pm \sqrt{(-0.02)^2 - 4(0.006)(-5)}}{2(0.006)} \qquad \begin{array}{l}\text{Substitute the values} \\ \text{for } a, b, \text{ and } c\text{:} \\ a = 0.006, \\ b = -0.02, \text{ and} \\ c = -5.\end{array}$$

$$= \frac{0.02 \pm \sqrt{0.1204}}{0.012} \qquad \begin{array}{l}\text{Use a calculator to} \\ \text{simplify the radicand.}\end{array}$$

$$\approx \frac{0.02 + 0.347}{0.012} \qquad \begin{array}{l}\text{Use a calculator:} \\ \sqrt{0.1204} \approx 0.347.\end{array}$$

$$A \approx \frac{0.02 + 0.347}{0.012} \qquad \text{or} \qquad A \approx \frac{0.02 - 0.347}{0.012}$$

$$A \approx 31 \qquad\qquad\qquad\qquad A \approx -27 \qquad \begin{array}{l}\text{Use a calculator and} \\ \text{round to the nearest} \\ \text{integer.}\end{array}$$

Reject this solution. Age cannot be negative.

Technology

On most calculators, here is how to approximate

$$\frac{0.02 + \sqrt{0.1204}}{0.012}.$$

Many Scientific Calculators

(.02 + .1204 √)

÷ .012 =

Many Graphing Calculators

(.02 + √ .1204)

÷ .012 ENTER

If your calculator displays an open parenthesis after √ , you'll need to enter another closed parenthesis here.

The positive solution, $A \approx 31$, indicates that 31 is the approximate age of a man whose normal systolic blood pressure is 125 mm Hg. This is illustrated by the black lines with the arrows on the red graph representing men in **Figure 1.22**.

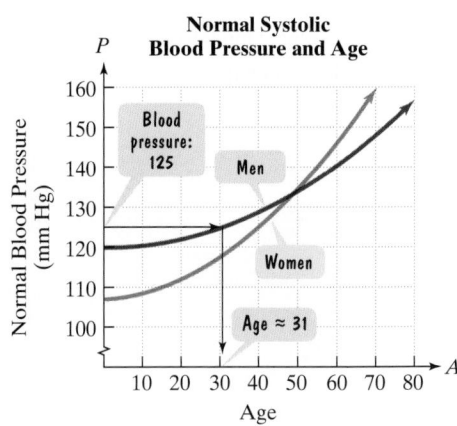

Figure 1.22

b. Take a second look at the graphs in **Figure 1.22**. Before approximately age 50, the blue graph representing women's normal systolic blood pressure lies below the red graph representing men's normal systolic blood pressure. Thus, up to age 50, women's normal systolic blood pressure is lower than men's, although it is increasing at a faster rate. After age 50, women's normal systolic blood pressure is higher than men's.

⊘ Check Point **9** The formula $P = 0.01A^2 + 0.05A + 107$ models a woman's normal systolic blood pressure, P, at age A. Use this formula to find the age, to the nearest year, of a woman whose normal systolic blood pressure is 115 mm Hg. Use the blue graph in **Figure 1.22** to verify your solution.

In our next example, we will be using the *Pythagorean Theorem* to obtain a mathematical model. The ancient Greek philosopher and mathematician Pythagoras (approximately 582–500 B.C.) founded a school whose motto was "All is number." Pythagoras is best remembered for his work with the **right triangle**, a triangle with one angle measuring 90°. The side opposite the 90° angle is called the **hypotenuse**. The other sides are called **legs**. Pythagoras found that if he constructed squares on each of the legs, as well as a larger square on the hypotenuse, the sum of the areas of the smaller squares is equal to the area of the larger square. This is illustrated in **Figure 1.23**.

This relationship is usually stated in terms of the lengths of the three sides of a right triangle and is called the **Pythagorean Theorem**.

Figure 1.23 The area of the large square equals the sum of the areas of the smaller squares.

The Pythagorean Theorem

The sum of the squares of the lengths of the legs of a right triangle equals the square of the length of the hypotenuse.

If the legs have lengths a and b, and the hypotenuse has length c, then

$$a^2 + b^2 = c^2.$$

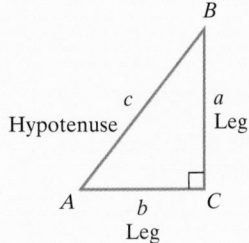

(EXAMPLE 10) **Using the Pythagorean Theorem**

a. A wheelchair ramp with a length of 122 inches has a horizontal distance of 120 inches. What is the ramp's vertical distance?

b. Construction laws are very specific when it comes to access ramps for the disabled. Every vertical rise of 1 inch requires a horizontal run of 12 inches. Does this ramp satisfy the requirement?

Solution

a. **Figure 1.24** shows the right triangle that is formed by the ramp, the wall, and the ground. We can find x, the ramp's vertical distance, using the Pythagorean Theorem.

Figure 1.24

(leg)²	plus	(leg)²	equals	(hypotenuse)²

$$x^2 \quad + \quad 120^2 \quad = \quad 122^2$$

We solve this equation using the square root property.

$$x^2 + 120^2 = 122^2$$ This is the equation resulting from the Pythagorean Theorem.

$$x^2 + 14{,}400 = 14{,}884$$ Square 120 and 122.

$$x^2 = 484$$ Isolate x^2 by subtracting 14,400 from both sides.

$$x = \sqrt{484} \quad \text{or} \quad x = -\sqrt{484}$$ Apply the square root property.

$$x = 22 \qquad\qquad x = -22$$

Because x represents the ramp's vertical distance, we reject the negative value. Thus, the ramp's vertical distance is 22 inches.

b. Every vertical rise of 1 inch requires a horizontal run of 12 inches. Because the ramp has a vertical distance of 22 inches, it requires a horizontal distance of 22(12) inches, or 264 inches. The horizontal distance is only 120 inches, so this ramp does not satisfy construction laws for access ramps for the disabled. ●

⊘ Check Point **10** In a 25-inch television set, the length of the screen's diagonal is 25 inches. If the screen's height is 15 inches, what is its width?

Art, Nature, and Quadratic Equations

A **golden rectangle** can be a rectangle of any size, but its long side must be Φ times as long as its short side, where $\Phi \approx 1.6$. Artists often use golden rectangles in their work because they are considered to be more visually pleasing than other rectangles.

In *The Bathers at Asnieres,* by the French impressionist Georges Seurat (1859–1891), the artist positions parts of the painting as though they were inside golden rectangles.

Georges Seurat, "The Bathers at Asnieres," 1883–1884. Oil on canvas, $79\frac{1}{2} \times 118\frac{1}{2}$ in. Erich Lessing/Art Resource, NY.

If a golden rectangle is divided into a square and a rectangle, as in **Figure 1.25(a)**, the smaller rectangle is a golden rectangle. If the smaller golden rectangle is divided again, the same is true of the yet smaller rectangle, and so on. The process of repeatedly dividing each golden rectangle in this manner is illustrated in **Figure 1.25(b)**. We've also created a spiral by connecting the opposite corners of all the squares with a smooth curve. This spiral matches the spiral shape of the chambered nautilus shell shown in **Figure 1.25(c)**. The shell spirals out at an ever-increasing rate that is governed by this geometry.

Golden Rectangle *A*

Square	Golden Rectangle *B*

Figure 1.25(a)

Figure 1.25(b)

Figure 1.25(c)

In the Exercise Set that follows, you will use the golden rectangles in **Figure 1.25(a)** to obtain an exact value for Φ, the ratio of the long side to the short side in a golden rectangle of any size. Your model will involve a quadratic equation that can be solved by the quadratic formula. (See Exercise 137.)

Exercise Set 1.5

Practice Exercises

Solve each equation in Exercises 1–14 by factoring.

1. $x^2 - 3x - 10 = 0$ **2.** $x^2 - 13x + 36 = 0$

3. $x^2 = 8x - 15$ **4.** $x^2 = -11x - 10$

5. $6x^2 + 11x - 10 = 0$ **6.** $9x^2 + 9x + 2 = 0$

7. $3x^2 - 2x = 8$ **8.** $4x^2 - 13x = -3$

9. $3x^2 + 12x = 0$ **10.** $5x^2 - 20x = 0$

11. $2x(x - 3) = 5x^2 - 7x$ **12.** $16x(x - 2) = 8x - 25$

13. $7 - 7x = (3x + 2)(x - 1)$ **14.** $10x - 1 = (2x + 1)^2$

Solve each equation in Exercises 15–34 by the square root property.

15. $3x^2 = 27$ **16.** $5x^2 = 45$

17. $5x^2 + 1 = 51$ **18.** $3x^2 - 1 = 47$

19. $2x^2 - 5 = -55$ **20.** $2x^2 - 7 = -15$

21. $(x + 2)^2 = 25$ **22.** $(x - 3)^2 = 36$

23. $3(x - 4)^2 = 15$ **24.** $3(x + 4)^2 = 21$

25. $(x + 3)^2 = -16$ **26.** $(x - 1)^2 = -9$

27. $(x - 3)^2 = -5$ **28.** $(x + 2)^2 = -7$

29. $(3x + 2)^2 = 9$ **30.** $(4x - 1)^2 = 16$

31. $(5x - 1)^2 = 7$ **32.** $(8x - 3)^2 = 5$

33. $(3x - 4)^2 = 8$ **34.** $(2x + 8)^2 = 27$

In Exercises 35–46, determine the constant that should be added to the binomial so that it becomes a perfect square trinomial. Then write and factor the trinomial.

35. $x^2 + 12x$ **36.** $x^2 + 16x$

37. $x^2 - 10x$ **38.** $x^2 - 14x$

39. $x^2 + 3x$ **40.** $x^2 + 5x$

41. $x^2 - 7x$ **42.** $x^2 - 9x$

43. $x^2 - \dfrac{2}{3}x$ **44.** $x^2 + \dfrac{4}{5}x$

45. $x^2 - \dfrac{1}{3}x$ **46.** $x^2 - \dfrac{1}{4}x$

Solve each equation in Exercises 47–64 by completing the square.

47. $x^2 + 6x = 7$ **48.** $x^2 + 6x = -8$

49. $x^2 - 2x = 2$ **50.** $x^2 + 4x = 12$

51. $x^2 - 6x - 11 = 0$ **52.** $x^2 - 2x - 5 = 0$

53. $x^2 + 4x + 1 = 0$ **54.** $x^2 + 6x - 5 = 0$

55. $x^2 - 5x + 6 = 0$ **56.** $x^2 + 7x - 8 = 0$

57. $x^2 + 3x - 1 = 0$ **58.** $x^2 - 3x - 5 = 0$

59. $2x^2 - 7x + 3 = 0$ **60.** $2x^2 + 5x - 3 = 0$

61. $4x^2 - 4x - 1 = 0$ **62.** $2x^2 - 4x - 1 = 0$

63. $3x^2 - 2x - 2 = 0$ **64.** $3x^2 - 5x - 10 = 0$

Solve each equation in Exercises 65–74 using the quadratic formula.

65. $x^2 + 8x + 15 = 0$ **66.** $x^2 + 8x + 12 = 0$

67. $x^2 + 5x + 3 = 0$ **68.** $x^2 + 5x + 2 = 0$

69. $3x^2 - 3x - 4 = 0$ **70.** $5x^2 + x - 2 = 0$

71. $4x^2 = 2x + 7$ **72.** $3x^2 = 6x - 1$

73. $x^2 - 6x + 10 = 0$ **74.** $x^2 - 2x + 17 = 0$

In Exercises 75–82, compute the discriminant. Then determine the number and type of solutions for the given equation.

75. $x^2 - 4x - 5 = 0$ **76.** $4x^2 - 2x + 3 = 0$

77. $2x^2 - 11x + 3 = 0$ **78.** $2x^2 + 11x - 6 = 0$

79. $x^2 - 2x + 1 = 0$ **80.** $3x^2 = 2x - 1$

81. $x^2 - 3x - 7 = 0$ **82.** $3x^2 + 4x - 2 = 0$

Solve each equation in Exercises 83–108 by the method of your choice.

83. $2x^2 - x = 1$ **84.** $3x^2 - 4x = 4$

85. $5x^2 + 2 = 11x$ **86.** $5x^2 = 6 - 13x$

87. $3x^2 = 60$ **88.** $2x^2 = 250$

89. $x^2 - 2x = 1$ **90.** $2x^2 + 3x = 1$

91. $(2x + 3)(x + 4) = 1$ **92.** $(2x - 5)(x + 1) = 2$

93. $(3x - 4)^2 = 16$ **94.** $(2x + 7)^2 = 25$

95. $3x^2 - 12x + 12 = 0$ **96.** $9 - 6x + x^2 = 0$

97. $4x^2 - 16 = 0$ **98.** $3x^2 - 27 = 0$

99. $x^2 - 6x + 13 = 0$ **100.** $x^2 - 4x + 29 = 0$

101. $x^2 = 4x - 7$ **102.** $5x^2 = 2x - 3$

103. $2x^2 - 7x = 0$ **104.** $2x^2 + 5x = 3$

105. $\dfrac{1}{x} + \dfrac{1}{x + 2} = \dfrac{1}{3}$ **106.** $\dfrac{1}{x} + \dfrac{1}{x + 3} = \dfrac{1}{4}$

107. $\dfrac{2x}{x - 3} + \dfrac{6}{x + 3} = -\dfrac{28}{x^2 - 9}$

108. $\dfrac{3}{x - 3} + \dfrac{5}{x - 4} = \dfrac{x^2 - 20}{x^2 - 7x + 12}$

In Exercises 109–114, find the x-intercept(s) of the graph of each equation. Use the x-intercepts to match the equation with its graph. The graphs are shown in $[-10, 10, 1]$ by $[-10, 10, 1]$ viewing rectangles and labeled (a) through (f).

109. $y = x^2 - 4x - 5$ **110.** $y = x^2 - 6x + 7$

111. $y = -(x + 1)^2 + 4$ **112.** $y = -(x + 3)^2 + 1$

113. $y = x^2 - 2x + 2$ **114.** $y = x^2 + 6x + 9$

a.

b.

c.

d.

e.

f.

In Exercises 115–122, find all values of x satisfying the given conditions.

115. $y = 2x^2 - 3x$ and $y = 2$.

116. $y = 5x^2 + 3x$ and $y = 2$.

117. $y_1 = x - 1$, $y_2 = x + 4$, and $y_1 y_2 = 14$.

118. $y_1 = x - 3$, $y_2 = x + 8$, and $y_1 y_2 = -30$.

119. $y_1 = \dfrac{2x}{x + 2}$, $y_2 = \dfrac{3}{x + 4}$, and $y_1 + y_2 = 1$.

120. $y_1 = \dfrac{3}{x - 1}$, $y_2 = \dfrac{8}{x}$, and $y_1 + y_2 = 3$.

121. $y_1 = 2x^2 + 5x - 4$, $y_2 = -x^2 + 15x - 10$, and $y_1 - y_2 = 0$.

122. $y_1 = -x^2 + 4x - 2$, $y_2 = -3x^2 + x - 1$, and $y_1 - y_2 = 0$.

Practice Plus

In Exercises 123–124, list all numbers that must be excluded from the domain of each rational expression.

123. $\dfrac{3}{2x^2 + 4x - 9}$ **124.** $\dfrac{7}{2x^2 - 8x + 5}$

125. When the sum of 6 and twice a positive number is subtracted from the square of the number, 0 results. Find the number.

126. When the sum of 1 and twice a negative number is subtracted from twice the square of the number, 0 results. Find the number.

In Exercises 127–130, solve each equation by the method of your choice.

127. $\dfrac{1}{x^2 - 3x + 2} = \dfrac{1}{x + 2} + \dfrac{5}{x^2 - 4}$

128. $\dfrac{x - 1}{x - 2} + \dfrac{x}{x - 3} = \dfrac{1}{x^2 - 5x + 6}$

129. $\sqrt{2}x^2 + 3x - 2\sqrt{2} = 0$

130. $\sqrt{3}x^2 + 6x + 7\sqrt{3} = 0$

Application Exercises

In a round-robin chess tournament, each player is paired with every other player once. The formula

$$N = \frac{x^2 - x}{2}$$

models the number of chess games, N, that must be played in a round-robin tournament with x chess players. Use this formula to solve Exercises 131–132.

131. In a round-robin chess tournament, 21 games were played. How many players were entered in the tournament?

132. In a round-robin chess tournament, 36 games were played. How many players were entered in the tournament?

The graph of the formula in Exercises 131–132 is shown. Use the graph to solve Exercises 133–134.

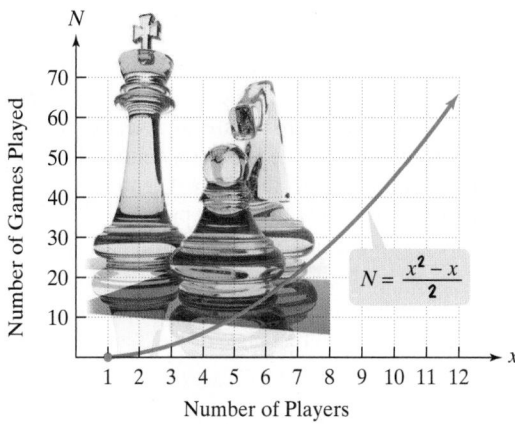

133. Identify your solution to Exercise 131 as a point on the graph.

134. Identify your solution to Exercise 132 as a point on the graph.

Throwing events in track and field include the shot put, the discus throw, the hammer throw, and the javelin throw. The distance that an athlete can achieve depends on the initial velocity of the object thrown and the angle above the horizontal at which the object leaves the hand.

In Exercises 135–136, an athlete whose event is the shot put releases the shot with the same initial velocity, but at different angles.

135. When the shot is released at an angle of 35°, its path can be modeled by the formula

$$y = -0.01x^2 + 0.7x + 6.1,$$

in which x is the shot's horizontal distance, in feet, and y is its height, in feet. This formula is shown by one of the graphs, (a) or (b), in the figure. Use the formula to determine the shot's maximum distance. Use a calculator and round to the nearest tenth of a foot. Which graph, (a) or (b), shows the shot's path?

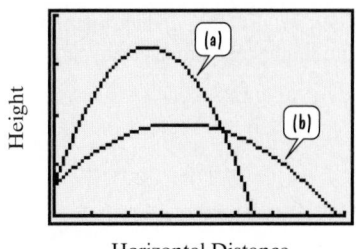

Horizontal Distance
[0, 80, 10] by [0, 40, 10]

136. (Refer to the information on the previous page and the graphs shown in Exercise 135.) When the shot is released at an angle of 65°, its path can be modeled by the formula

$$y = -0.04x^2 + 2.1x + 6.1,$$

in which x is the shot's horizontal distance, in feet, and y is its height, in feet. This formula is shown by one of the graphs, (a) or (b), in the figure in Exercise 135. Use the formula to determine the shot's maximum distance. Use a calculator and round to the nearest tenth of a foot. Which graph, (a) or (b), shows the shot's path?

137. If you have not yet done so, read the essay on page 151. In this exercise, you will use the golden rectangles shown to obtain an exact value for Φ, the ratio of the long side to the short side in a golden rectangle of any size.

Golden Rectangle A

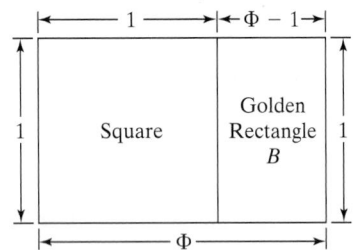

a. The golden ratio in rectangle A, or the ratio of the long side to the short side, can be modeled by $\dfrac{\Phi}{1}$. Write a fractional expression that models the golden ratio in rectangle B.

b. Set the expression for the golden ratio in rectangle A equal to the expression for the golden ratio in rectangle B. Multiply both sides of the equation by the least common denominator and solve the resulting quadratic equation using the quadratic formula. Express Φ as an exact value in simplified radical form.

c. Use your solution from part (b) to complete this statement: The ratio of the long side to the short side in a golden rectangle of any size is _____ to 1.

Use the Pythagorean Theorem and the square root property to solve Exercises 138–141. Express answers in simplified radical form. Then find a decimal approximation to the nearest tenth.

138. A rectangular park is 6 miles long and 3 miles wide. How long is a pedestrian route that runs diagonally across the park?

139. A rectangular park is 4 miles long and 2 miles wide. How long is a pedestrian route that runs diagonally across the park?

140. The base of a 30-foot ladder is 10 feet from a building. If the ladder reaches the flat roof, how tall is the building?

141. A baseball diamond is actually a square with 90-foot sides. What is the distance from home plate to second base?

142. An **isosceles right triangle** has legs that are the same length and acute angles each measuring 45°.

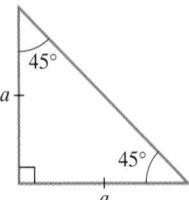

a. Write an expression in terms of a that represents the length of the hypotenuse.

b. Use your result from part (a) to write a sentence that describes the length of the hypotenuse of an isosceles right triangle in terms of the length of a leg.

143. The length of a rectangular sign is 3 feet longer than the width. If the sign's area is 54 square feet, find its length and width.

144. A rectangular parking lot has a length that is 3 yards greater than the width. The area of the parking lot is 180 square yards. Find the length and the width.

145. Each side of a square is lengthened by 3 inches. The area of this new, larger square is 64 square inches. Find the length of a side of the original square.

146. Each side of a square is lengthened by 2 inches. The area of this new, larger square is 36 square inches. Find the length of a side of the original square.

147. A pool measuring 10 meters by 20 meters is surrounded by a path of uniform width, as shown in the figure. If the area of the pool and the path combined is 600 square meters, what is the width of the path?

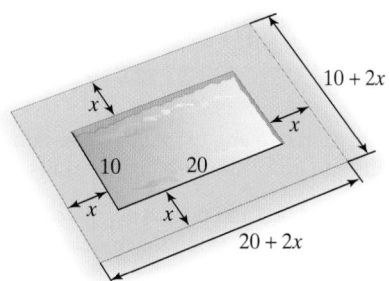

148. A vacant rectangular lot is being turned into a community vegetable garden measuring 15 meters by 12 meters. A path of uniform width is to surround the garden, as shown in the figure. If the area of the garden and path combined is 378 square meters, find the width of the path.

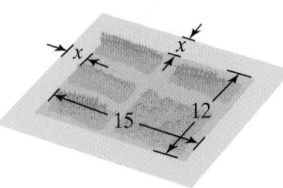

149. A machine produces open boxes using square sheets of metal. The figure illustrates that the machine cuts equal-sized squares measuring 2 inches on a side from the corners and then shapes the metal into an open box by turning up the sides. If each box must have a volume of 200 cubic inches, find the length and width of the open box.

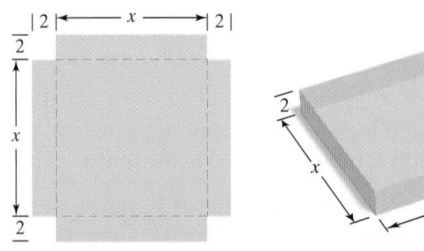

150. A machine produces open boxes using square sheets of metal. The machine cuts equal-sized squares measuring 3 inches on a side from the corners and then shapes the metal into an open box by turning up the sides. If each box must have a volume of 75 cubic inches, find the length and width of the open box.

151. A rain gutter is made from sheets of aluminum that are 20 inches wide. As shown in the figure, the edges are turned up to form right angles. Determine the depth of the gutter that will allow a cross-sectional area of 13 square inches. Show that there are two different solutions to the problem. Round to the nearest tenth of an inch.

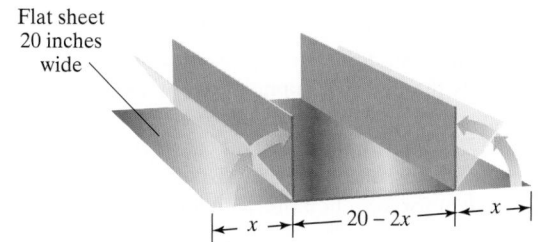

152. A piece of wire is 8 inches long. The wire is cut into two pieces and then each piece is bent into a square. Find the length of each piece if the sum of the areas of these squares is to be 2 square inches.

Writing in Mathematics

153. What is a quadratic equation?

154. Explain how to solve $x^2 + 6x + 8 = 0$ using factoring and the zero-product principle.

155. Explain how to solve $x^2 + 6x + 8 = 0$ by completing the square.

156. Explain how to solve $x^2 + 6x + 8 = 0$ using the quadratic formula.

157. How is the quadratic formula derived?

158. What is the discriminant and what information does it provide about a quadratic equation?

159. If you are given a quadratic equation, how do you determine which method to use to solve it?

160. Describe the relationship between the real solutions of $ax^2 + bx + c = 0$ and the graph of $y = ax^2 + bx + c$.

161. If a quadratic equation has imaginary solutions, how is this shown on the graph of $y = ax^2 + bx + c$?

Technology Exercises

162. Use a graphing utility and x-intercepts to verify any of the real solutions that you obtained for three of the quadratic equations in Exercises 65–74.

163. Use a graphing utility to graph $y = ax^2 + bx + c$ related to any five of the quadratic equations, $ax^2 + bx + c = 0$, in Exercises 75–82. How does each graph illustrate what you determined algebraically using the discriminant?

Critical Thinking Exercises

Make Sense? *In Exercises 164–167, determine whether each statement makes sense or does not make sense, and explain your reasoning.*

164. Because I want to solve $25x^2 - 169 = 0$ fairly quickly, I'll use the quadratic formula.

165. I'm looking at a graph with one x-intercept, so it must be the graph of a linear equation.

166. I obtained -17 for the discriminant, so there are two imaginary irrational solutions.

167. When I use the square root property to determine the length of a right triangle's side, I don't even bother to list the negative square root.

In Exercises 168–171, determine whether each statement is true or false. If the statement is false, make the necessary change(s) to produce a true statement.

168. The equation $(2x - 3)^2 = 25$ is equivalent to $2x - 3 = 5$.

169. Any quadratic equation that can be solved by completing the square can be solved by the quadratic formula.

170. The quadratic formula is developed by applying factoring and the zero-product principle to the quadratic equation $ax^2 + bx + c = 0$.

171. In using the quadratic formula to solve the quadratic equation $5x^2 = 2x - 7$, we have $a = 5$, $b = 2$, and $c = -7$.

172. Write a quadratic equation in general form whose solution set is $\{-3, 5\}$.

173. Solve for t: $s = -16t^2 + v_0t$.

174. A rectangular swimming pool is 12 meters long and 8 meters wide. A tile border of uniform width is to be built around the pool using 120 square meters of tile. The tile is from a discontinued stock (so no additional materials are available) and all 120 square meters are to be used. How wide should the border be? Round to the nearest tenth of a meter. If zoning laws require at least a 2-meter-wide border around the pool, can this be done with the available tile?

Preview Exercises

Exercises 175–177 will help you prepare for the material covered in the next section.

175. Factor completely: $x^3 + x^2 - 4x - 4$.

176. Use the special product $(A + B)^2 = A^2 + 2AB + B^2$ to multiply: $\left(\sqrt{x + 4} + 1\right)^2$.

177. If -8 is substituted for x in the equation $5x^{\frac{2}{3}} + 11x^{\frac{1}{3}} + 2 = 0$, is the resulting statement true or false?

Chapter **1** **Mid-Chapter Check Point**

What You Know: We used the rectangular coordinate system to represent ordered pairs of real numbers and to graph equations in two variables. We saw that linear equations can be written in the form $ax + b = 0$, $a \neq 0$, and quadratic equations can be written in the general form $ax^2 + bx + c = 0$, $a \neq 0$. We solved linear equations and saw that some linear equations have no solution, whereas others have all real numbers as solutions. We solved quadratic equations using factoring, the square root property, completing the square, and the quadratic formula. We saw that the discriminant of $ax^2 + bx + c = 0$, $b^2 - 4ac$, determines the number and type of solutions. We performed operations with complex numbers and used the imaginary unit i ($i = \sqrt{-1}$, where $i^2 = -1$) to represent solutions of quadratic equations with negative discriminants. Only real solutions correspond to x-intercepts. We also solved rational equations by multiplying both sides by the least common denominator and clearing fractions. We developed a strategy for solving a variety of applied problems, using equations to model verbal conditions.

In Exercises 1–12, solve each equation.

1. $-5 + 3(x + 5) = 2(3x - 4)$ **2.** $5x^2 - 2x = 7$

3. $\dfrac{x-3}{5} - 1 = \dfrac{x-5}{4}$ **4.** $3x^2 - 6x - 2 = 0$

5. $4x - 2(1 - x) = 3(2x + 1) - 5$

6. $5x^2 + 1 = 37$ **7.** $x(2x - 3) = -4$

8. $\dfrac{3x}{4} - \dfrac{x}{3} + 1 = \dfrac{4x}{5} - \dfrac{3}{20}$ **9.** $(x + 3)^2 = 24$

10. $\dfrac{1}{x^2} - \dfrac{4}{x} + 1 = 0$

11. $3x + 1 - (x - 5) = 2x - 4$

12. $\dfrac{2x}{x^2 + 6x + 8} = \dfrac{x}{x+4} - \dfrac{2}{x+2}$

In Exercises 13–17, find the x-intercepts of the graph of each equation.

13. $y = x^2 + 6x + 2$

14. $y = 4(x + 1) - 3x - (6 - x)$

15. $y = 2x^2 + 26$

16. $y = \dfrac{x^2}{3} + \dfrac{x}{2} - \dfrac{2}{3}$

17. $y = x^2 - 5x + 8$

In Exercises 18–19, find all values of x satisfying the given conditions.

18. $y_1 = 3(2x - 5) - 2(4x + 1)$, $y_2 = -5(x + 3) - 2$, and $y_1 = y_2$.

19. $y_1 = 2x + 3$, $y_2 = x + 2$, and $y_1 y_2 = 10$.

20. Solve by completing the square: $x^2 + 10x - 3 = 0$.

In Exercises 21–22, without solving the equation, determine the number and type of solutions.

21. $2x^2 + 5x + 4 = 0$ **22.** $10x(x + 4) = 15x - 15$

In Exercises 23–25, graph each equation in a rectangular coordinate system.

23. $y = 2x - 1$ **24.** $y = 1 - |x|$

25. $y = x^2 + 2$

26. Solve for n: $L = a + (n - 1)d$.

27. Solve for l: $A = 2lw + 2lh + 2wh$.

28. Solve for f_1: $f = \dfrac{f_1 f_2}{f_1 + f_2}$.

29. The bar graph represents the average credit card debt for U.S. college students. The average credit card debt for juniors exceeds the debt for sophomores by $421, and the average credit card debt for seniors exceeds the debt for sophomores by $1265. The combined credit card debt for a sophomore, a junior, and a senior is $6429. Determine the average credit card debt for a sophomore, a junior, and a senior.

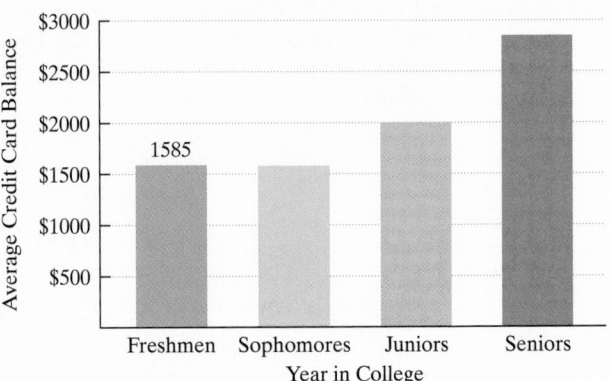

Average Credit Card Debt for United States College Students

Source: Nellie Mae

30. The Disappearing Pay Phone The bar graph shows the number of pay phones in the United States from 2000 through 2006.

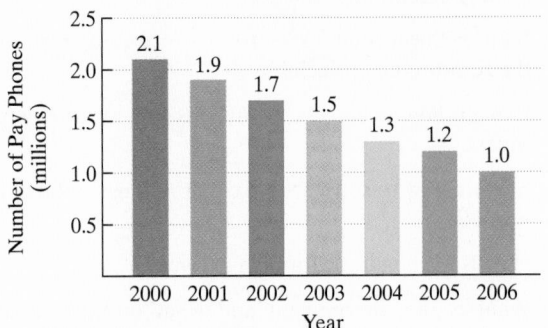

Number of Pay Phones in the United States

Source: Federal Communications Commission

The graph shows that in 2000, there were 2.1 million pay phones. For the period from 2000 through 2006, this decreased by approximately 0.18 million pay phones per year. If this trend continues, when will there be no pay phones in the United States? Round to the nearest year.

31. You invested \$25,000 in two accounts paying 8% and 9% annual interest. At the end of the year, the total interest from these investments was \$2135. How much was invested at each rate?

32. Photo Shop A charges \$1.60 to develop a roll of film plus \$0.11 for each print. Photo Shop B charges \$1.20 to develop a roll of film plus \$0.13 per print. For how many prints will the amount spent at each photo shop be the same? What will be that amount?

33. After a 40% price reduction, you purchase a camcorder for \$468. What was the camcorder's price before the reduction?

34. You invested \$4000. On part of this investment, you earned 4% interest. On the remainder of the investment, you lost 3%. Combining earnings and losses, the annual income from these investments was \$55. How much was invested at each rate?

In Exercises 35–36, find the dimensions of each rectangle.

35. The rectangle's length exceeds twice its width by 5 feet. The perimeter is 46 feet.

36. The rectangle's length is 1 foot shorter than twice its width. The area is 28 square feet.

37. A vertical pole is supported by three wires. Each wire is 13 yards long and is anchored in the ground 5 yards from the base of the pole. How far up the pole will the wires be attached?

38. a. The formula

$$S = 2x^2 - 12x + 82$$

models spending by international travelers to the United States, S, in billions of dollars, x years after 2000. In which years did international travelers spend \$72 billion?

b. The graph of the formula modeling spending by international traveler's is shown below. Identify your solutions from part (a) as points on the graph.

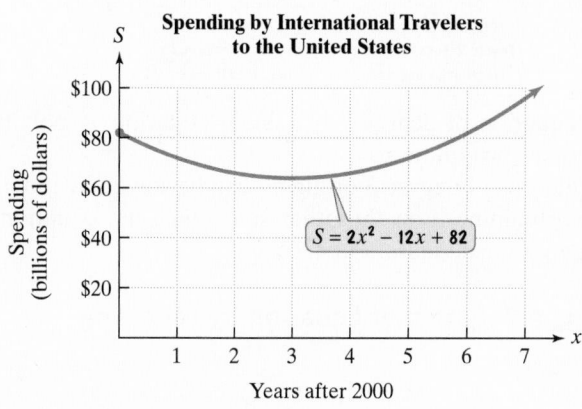

Spending by International Travelers to the United States

$S = 2x^2 - 12x + 82$

Source: Travel Industry Association of America

39. A substantial percentage of the United States population is foreign-born. The bar graph shows the percentage of foreign-born Americans for selected years from 1920 through 2006.

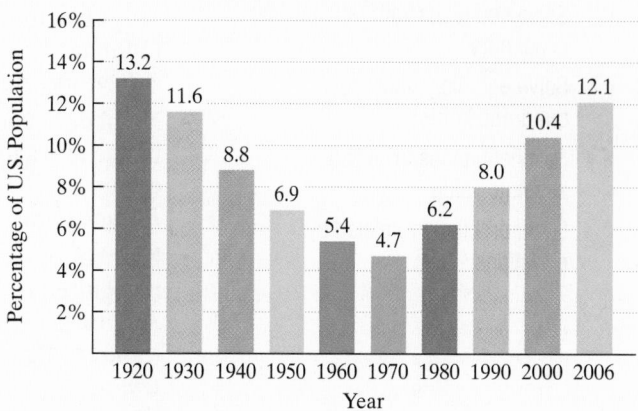

Percentage of the United States Population That Was Foreign-Born, 1920–2006

Source: U.S. Census Bureau

The percentage, p, of the United States population that was foreign-born x years after 1920 can be modeled by the formula

$$p = 0.004x^2 - 0.37x + 14.1.$$

According to this model, in which year will 25% of the United States population be foreign-born? Round to the nearest year.

In Exercises 40–45, perform the indicated operations and write the result in standard form.

40. $(6 - 2i) - (7 - i)$

41. $3i(2 + i)$

42. $(1 + i)(4 - 3i)$

43. $\dfrac{1 + i}{1 - i}$

44. $\sqrt{-75} - \sqrt{-12}$

45. $\left(2 - \sqrt{-3}\right)^2$

Section 1.6 Other Types of Equations

Objectives

① Solve polynomial equations by factoring.

② Solve radical equations.

③ Solve equations with rational exponents.

④ Solve equations that are quadratic in form.

⑤ Solve equations involving absolute value.

⑥ Solve problems modeled by equations.

A few advertising factoids:

- Top ad-spending categories: cars, drugs, and movies (*Source: Advertising Age*)

- Number of commercials watched by the average American child each year: 20,000 (*Source: Broadcasting and Cable*)

- Number of brands recognized by the average American 3-year-old: 100 (*Source: Albany Times Union*)

- Portion of every prime-time cable TV hour devoted to advertising: 14.6 minutes (*Source:* Nielsen Monitor-Plus)

What does algebra have to say about advertising? In particular, what sorts of mathematical models can be used to describe the number of minutes of commercial clutter on prime-time television? In this section, we answer the question after studying procedures for solving a variety of different types of equations.

① Solve polynomial equations by factoring.

Polynomial Equations

A **polynomial equation** is the result of setting two polynomials equal to each other. The equation is in **general form** if one side is 0 and the polynomial on the other side is in descending powers of the variable. The **degree of a polynomial equation** is the same as the highest degree of any term in the equation. Here are examples of three polynomial equations:

$$3x + 5 = 14 \qquad 2x^2 + 7x = 4 \qquad x^3 + x^2 = 4x + 4.$$

| This equation is of degree 1 because 1 is the highest degree. | This equation is of degree 2 because 2 is the highest degree. | This equation is of degree 3 because 3 is the highest degree. |

Notice that a polynomial equation of degree 1 is a linear equation. A polynomial equation of degree 2 is a quadratic equation.

Some polynomial equations of degree 3 or higher can be solved by moving all terms to one side, thereby obtaining 0 on the other side. Once the equation is in general form, factor and then set each factor equal to 0.

EXAMPLE 1 Solving a Polynomial Equation by Factoring

Solve by factoring: $3x^4 = 27x^2$.

Solution

Step 1 Move all nonzero terms to one side and obtain zero on the other side. Subtract $27x^2$ from both sides.

$$3x^4 = 27x^2 \qquad \text{This is the given equation.}$$
$$3x^4 - 27x^2 = 27x^2 - 27x^2 \qquad \text{Subtract } 27x^2 \text{ from both sides.}$$
$$3x^4 - 27x^2 = 0 \qquad \text{Simplify.}$$

Step 2 Factor. We can factor $3x^2$ from each term.

$$3x^4 - 27x^2 = 0$$
$$3x^2(x^2 - 9) = 0$$

Steps 3 and 4 Set each factor equal to zero and solve the resulting equations.

$$3x^2 = 0 \qquad \text{or} \qquad x^2 - 9 = 0$$
$$x^2 = 0 \qquad\qquad\qquad x^2 = 9$$
$$x = \pm\sqrt{0} \qquad\qquad\quad x = \pm\sqrt{9}$$
$$x = 0 \qquad\qquad\qquad x = \pm 3$$

Step 5 Check the solutions in the original equation. Check the three solutions, $0, -3$, and 3, by substituting them into the original equation. Can you verify that the solution set is $\{-3, 0, 3\}$? ⬤

✓ **Check Point 1** Solve by factoring: $4x^4 = 12x^2$.

(EXAMPLE 2) Solving a Polynomial Equation by Factoring

Solve by factoring: $x^3 + x^2 = 4x + 4$.

Solution

Step 1 Move all nonzero terms to one side and obtain zero on the other side. Subtract $4x$ and subtract 4 from both sides.

$$x^3 + x^2 = 4x + 4 \qquad\qquad \textit{This is the given equation.}$$
$$x^3 + x^2 - 4x - 4 = 4x + 4 - 4x - 4 \qquad \textit{Subtract 4x and 4 from both sides.}$$
$$x^3 + x^2 - 4x - 4 = 0 \qquad\qquad \textit{Simplify.}$$

Step 2 Factor. Use factoring by grouping. Group terms that have a common factor.

$$\boxed{x^3 + x^2} + \boxed{-4x - 4} = 0$$

Common factor is x^2. Common factor is -4.

$$x^2(x + 1) - 4(x + 1) = 0 \qquad \textit{Factor } x^2 \textit{ from the first two terms and } -4 \textit{ from the last two terms.}$$
$$(x + 1)(x^2 - 4) = 0 \qquad \textit{Factor out the common binomial factor, } x + 1, \textit{ from each term.}$$

Steps 3 and 4 Set each factor equal to zero and solve the resulting equations.

$$x + 1 = 0 \qquad \text{or} \qquad x^2 - 4 = 0$$
$$x = -1 \qquad\qquad\qquad x^2 = 4$$
$$x = \pm\sqrt{4} = \pm 2$$

Step 5 Check the solutions in the original equation. Check the three solutions, $-1, -2$, and 2, by substituting them into $x^3 + x^2 = 4x + 4$, the original equation. Can you verify that the solution set is $\{-2, -1, 2\}$? ⬤

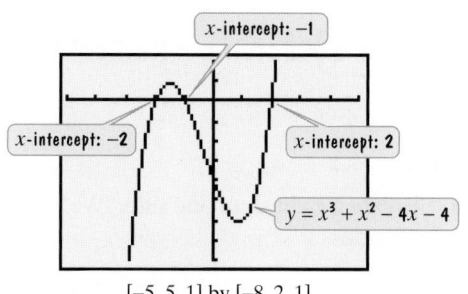

⊘ Check Point **2** Solve by factoring: $2x^3 + 3x^2 = 8x + 12$.

② Solve radical equations.

Radical Equations

A **radical equation** is an equation in which the variable occurs in a square root, cube root, or any higher root. An example of a radical equation is

$$\sqrt{x} = 9.$$

We solve this equation by squaring both sides:

Squaring both sides eliminates the square root.
$$\left(\sqrt{x}\right)^2 = 9^2$$
$$x = 81.$$

The proposed solution, 81, can be checked in the original equation, $\sqrt{x} = 9$. Because $\sqrt{81} = 9$, the solution is 81 and the solution set is $\{81\}$.

In general, we solve radical equations with square roots by squaring both sides of the equation. We solve radical equations with nth roots by raising both sides of the equation to the nth power. Unfortunately, if n is even, all the solutions of the equation raised to the even power may not be solutions of the original equation. Consider, for example, the equation

$$x = 4.$$

If we square both sides, we obtain

$$x^2 = 16.$$

Solving this equation using the square root property, we obtain

$$x = \pm\sqrt{16} = \pm 4.$$

The new equation $x^2 = 16$ has two solutions, -4 and 4. By contrast, only 4 is a solution of the original equation, $x = 4$. For this reason, **when raising both sides of an equation to an even power, always check proposed solutions in the original equation.**

Here is a general method for solving radical equations with nth roots:

Solving Radical Equations Containing *n*th Roots

1. If necessary, arrange terms so that one radical is isolated on one side of the equation.
2. Raise both sides of the equation to the nth power to eliminate the isolated nth root.
3. Solve the resulting equation. If this equation still contains radicals, repeat steps 1 and 2.
4. Check all proposed solutions in the original equation.

Extra solutions may be introduced when you raise both sides of a radical equation to an even power. Such solutions, which are not solutions of the given equation, are called **extraneous solutions** or **extraneous roots**.

(**EXAMPLE 3**) **Solving a Radical Equation**

Solve: $\sqrt{2x - 1} + 2 = x$.

Solution

Step 1 Isolate a radical on one side. We isolate the radical, $\sqrt{2x - 1}$, by subtracting 2 from both sides.

$$\sqrt{2x - 1} + 2 = x \qquad \text{This is the given equation.}$$
$$\sqrt{2x - 1} = x - 2 \qquad \text{Subtract 2 from both sides.}$$

Study Tip

Be sure to square *both sides* of an equation. Do *not* square each term.

Correct:

$$\left(\sqrt{2x-1}\right)^2 = (x-2)^2$$

Incorrect!

Step 2 **Raise both sides to the *n*th power.** Because *n*, the index, is 2, we square both sides.

$$\left(\sqrt{2x-1}\right)^2 = (x-2)^2$$

$$2x - 1 = x^2 - 4x + 4$$

Simplify. Use the formula $(A - B)^2 = A^2 - 2AB + B^2$ on the right side.

Step 3 **Solve the resulting equation.** Because of the x^2-term, the resulting equation is a quadratic equation. We can obtain 0 on the left side by subtracting $2x$ and adding 1 on both sides.

$$2x - 1 = x^2 - 4x + 4$$ The resulting equation is quadratic.

$$0 = x^2 - 6x + 5$$ Write in general form, subtracting $2x$ and adding 1 on both sides.

$$0 = (x - 1)(x - 5)$$ Factor.

$$x - 1 = 0 \quad \text{or} \quad x - 5 = 0$$ Set each factor equal to 0.

$$x = 1 \qquad\qquad x = 5$$ Solve the resulting equations.

Step 4 **Check the proposed solutions in the original equation.**

Check 1:

$$\sqrt{2x-1} + 2 = x$$
$$\sqrt{2 \cdot 1 - 1} + 2 \stackrel{?}{=} 1$$
$$\sqrt{1} + 2 \stackrel{?}{=} 1$$
$$1 + 2 \stackrel{?}{=} 1$$
$$3 = 1, \quad \text{false}$$

Check 5:

$$\sqrt{2x-1} + 2 = x$$
$$\sqrt{2 \cdot 5 - 1} + 2 \stackrel{?}{=} 5$$
$$\sqrt{9} + 2 \stackrel{?}{=} 5$$
$$3 + 2 \stackrel{?}{=} 5$$
$$5 = 5, \quad \text{true}$$

Thus, 1 is an extraneous solution. The only solution is 5, and the solution set is $\{5\}$.

Technology

Numeric Connections

A graphing utility's $\boxed{\text{TABLE}}$ feature provides a numeric check that 1 is not a solution and 5 is a solution of $\sqrt{2x-1} + 2 = x$.

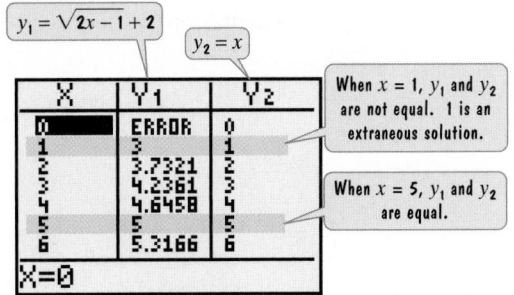

Ø Check Point **3** Solve: $\sqrt{x+3} + 3 = x$.

Solving a radical equation with two or more square root expressions involves isolating a radical, squaring both sides, and then repeating this process. Let's consider an equation containing two square root expressions.

EXAMPLE 4 **Solving an Equation That Has Two Radicals**

Solve: $\sqrt{3x + 1} - \sqrt{x + 4} = 1$.

Solution

Step 1 Isolate a radical on one side. We can isolate the radical $\sqrt{3x + 1}$ by adding $\sqrt{x + 4}$ to both sides. We obtain

$$\sqrt{3x + 1} = \sqrt{x + 4} + 1.$$

Step 2 Square both sides.

$$\left(\sqrt{3x + 1}\right)^2 = \left(\sqrt{x + 4} + 1\right)^2$$

Squaring the expression on the right side of the equation can be a bit tricky. We have to use the formula

$$(A + B)^2 = A^2 + 2AB + B^2.$$

Focusing on just the right side, here is how the squaring is done:

$$\underset{(A+B)^2}{} = \underset{A^2}{} + \underset{2}{} \cdot \underset{A}{} \cdot \underset{B}{} + \underset{B^2}{}$$

$$\left(\sqrt{x + 4} + 1\right)^2 = \left(\sqrt{x + 4}\right)^2 + 2 \cdot \sqrt{x + 4} \cdot 1 + 1^2 = x + 4 + 2\sqrt{x + 4} + 1.$$

Now let's return to squaring both sides.

$$\left(\sqrt{3x + 1}\right)^2 = \left(\sqrt{x + 4} + 1\right)^2 \qquad \text{Square both sides of the equation with an isolated radical.}$$

$$3x + 1 = x + 4 + 2\sqrt{x + 4} + 1 \qquad \left(\sqrt{3x + 1}\right)^2 = 3x + 1; \text{ square the right side using the formula for } (A + B)^2.$$

$$3x + 1 = x + 5 + 2\sqrt{x + 4} \qquad \text{Combine numerical terms on the right side: } 4 + 1 = 5.$$

Can you see that the resulting equation still contains a radical, namely $\sqrt{x + 4}$? Thus, we need to repeat the first two steps.

Repeat Step 1 Isolate a radical on one side. We isolate $2\sqrt{x + 4}$, the radical term, by subtracting $x + 5$ from both sides. We obtain

$$3x + 1 = x + 5 + 2\sqrt{x + 4} \qquad \text{This is the equation from our last step.}$$

$$2x - 4 = 2\sqrt{x + 4}. \qquad \text{Subtract } x \text{ and subtract 5 from both sides.}$$

Although we can simplify the equation by dividing both sides by 2, this sort of simplification is not always helpful. Thus, we will work with the equation in this form.

Repeat Step 2 Square both sides.

> Be careful in squaring both sides. Use $(A - B)^2 = A^2 - 2AB + B^2$ to square the left side. Use $(AB)^2 = A^2B^2$ to square the right side.

$$(2x - 4)^2 = \left(2\sqrt{x + 4}\right)^2 \qquad \text{Square both sides.}$$

$$4x^2 - 16x + 16 = 4(x + 4) \qquad \text{Square both 2 and } \sqrt{x + 4} \text{ on the right side.}$$

Step 3 Solve the resulting equation. We solve this quadratic equation by writing it in general form.

$$4x^2 - 16x + 16 = 4x + 16 \qquad \text{Use the distributive property.}$$

$$4x^2 - 20x = 0 \qquad \text{Subtract } 4x + 16 \text{ from both sides.}$$

$$4x(x - 5) = 0 \qquad \text{Factor.}$$

$$4x = 0 \quad \text{or} \quad x - 5 = 0 \qquad \text{Set each factor equal to zero.}$$

$$x = 0 \qquad\qquad x = 5 \qquad \text{Solve for } x.$$

Technology

Graphic Connections

The graph of

$$y = \sqrt{3x + 1} - \sqrt{x + 4} - 1$$

has only one *x*-intercept at 5. This verifies that the solution set of $\sqrt{3x + 1} - \sqrt{x + 4} = 1$ is $\{5\}$.

$[0, 7, 1]$ by $[-1, 1, 1]$

Step 4 Check the proposed solutions in the original equation.

Check 0:

$$\sqrt{3x + 1} - \sqrt{x + 4} = 1$$
$$\sqrt{3 \cdot 0 + 1} - \sqrt{0 + 4} \stackrel{?}{=} 1$$
$$\sqrt{1} - \sqrt{4} \stackrel{?}{=} 1$$
$$1 - 2 \stackrel{?}{=} 1$$
$$-1 = 1, \quad \text{false}$$

Check 5:

$$\sqrt{3x + 1} - \sqrt{x + 4} = 1$$
$$\sqrt{3 \cdot 5 + 1} - \sqrt{5 + 4} \stackrel{?}{=} 1$$
$$\sqrt{16} - \sqrt{9} \stackrel{?}{=} 1$$
$$4 - 3 \stackrel{?}{=} 1$$
$$1 = 1, \quad \text{true}$$

The check indicates that 0 is not a solution. It is an extraneous solution brought about by squaring each side of the equation. The only solution is 5 and the solution set is $\{5\}$. ●

✓ Check Point **4** Solve: $\sqrt{x + 5} - \sqrt{x - 3} = 2$.

③ Solve equations with rational exponents.

Equations with Rational Exponents

We know that expressions with rational exponents represent radicals:

$$a^{\frac{m}{n}} = \left(\sqrt[n]{a} \right)^m = \sqrt[n]{a^m}.$$

For example, the radical equation $3\sqrt[4]{x^3} - 6 = 0$ can be expressed as $3x^{\frac{3}{4}} - 6 = 0$. A radical equation with rational exponents can be solved by

1. isolating the expression with the rational exponent, and

2. raising both sides of the equation to a power that is the reciprocal of the rational exponent.

Solving Radical Equations of the Form $x^{\frac{m}{n}} = k$

Assume that *m* and *n* are positive integers, $\frac{m}{n}$ is in lowest terms, and *k* is a real number.

1. Isolate the expression with the rational exponent.
2. Raise both sides of the equation to the $\frac{n}{m}$ power.

If *m* is even:

$$x^{\frac{m}{n}} = k$$
$$\left(x^{\frac{m}{n}} \right)^{\frac{n}{m}} = \pm k^{\frac{n}{m}}$$
$$x = \pm k^{\frac{n}{m}}$$

If *m* is odd:

$$x^{\frac{m}{n}} = k$$
$$\left(x^{\frac{m}{n}} \right)^{\frac{n}{m}} = k^{\frac{n}{m}}$$
$$x = k^{\frac{n}{m}}$$

It is incorrect to insert the \pm symbol when the numerator of the exponent is odd. An odd index has only one root.

3. Check all proposed solutions in the original equation to find out if they are actual solutions or extraneous solutions.

(**EXAMPLE 5**) **Solving Equations Involving Rational Exponents**

Solve:

a. $3x^{\frac{3}{4}} - 6 = 0$ **b.** $x^{\frac{2}{3}} - \frac{3}{4} = -\frac{1}{2}$.

Solution

a. To solve $3x^{\frac{3}{4}} - 6 = 0$, our goal is to isolate $x^{\frac{3}{4}}$. Then we raise both sides of the equation to the $\frac{4}{3}$ power because $\frac{4}{3}$ is the reciprocal of $\frac{3}{4}$.

$$3x^{\frac{3}{4}} - 6 = 0 \qquad \text{This is the given equation; we will isolate } x^{\frac{3}{4}}.$$

$$3x^{\frac{3}{4}} = 6 \qquad \text{Add 6 to both sides.}$$

$$\frac{3x^{\frac{3}{4}}}{3} = \frac{6}{3} \qquad \text{Divide both sides by 3.}$$

$$x^{\frac{3}{4}} = 2 \qquad \text{Simplify.}$$

$$\left(x^{\frac{3}{4}}\right)^{\frac{4}{3}} = 2^{\frac{4}{3}} \qquad \begin{array}{l}\text{Raise both sides to the } \frac{4}{3} \text{ power. Because } \frac{m}{n} = \frac{3}{4} \text{ and } m \text{ is} \\ \text{odd, we do not use the } \pm \text{ symbol.}\end{array}$$

$$x = 2^{\frac{4}{3}} \qquad \text{Simplify the left side: } \left(x^{\frac{3}{4}}\right)^{\frac{4}{3}} = x^{\frac{3 \cdot 4}{4 \cdot 3}} = x^{\frac{12}{12}} = x^1 = x.$$

The proposed solution is $2^{\frac{4}{3}}$. Complete the solution process by checking this value in the given equation.

$$3x^{\frac{3}{4}} - 6 = 0 \qquad \text{This is the original equation.}$$

$$3\left(2^{\frac{4}{3}}\right)^{\frac{3}{4}} - 6 \overset{?}{=} 0 \qquad \text{Substitute the proposed solution.}$$

$$3 \cdot 2 - 6 \overset{?}{=} 0 \qquad \left(2^{\frac{4}{3}}\right)^{\frac{3}{4}} = 2^{\frac{4 \cdot 3}{3 \cdot 4}} = 2^{\frac{12}{12}} = 2^1 = 2$$

$$0 = 0, \quad \text{true} \qquad 3 \cdot 2 - 6 = 6 - 6 = 0$$

The solution is $2^{\frac{4}{3}} = \sqrt[3]{2^4} \approx 2.52$. The solution set is $\left\{2^{\frac{4}{3}}\right\}$.

b. To solve $x^{\frac{2}{3}} - \frac{3}{4} = -\frac{1}{2}$, our goal is to isolate $x^{\frac{2}{3}}$. Then we raise both sides of the equation to the $\frac{3}{2}$ power because $\frac{3}{2}$ is the reciprocal of $\frac{2}{3}$.

$$x^{\frac{2}{3}} - \frac{3}{4} = -\frac{1}{2} \qquad \text{This is the given equation.}$$

$$x^{\frac{2}{3}} = \frac{1}{4} \qquad \text{Add } \frac{3}{4} \text{ to both sides. } \frac{3}{4} - \frac{1}{2} = \frac{3}{4} - \frac{2}{4} = \frac{1}{4}.$$

$$\left(x^{\frac{2}{3}}\right)^{\frac{3}{2}} = \pm\left(\frac{1}{4}\right)^{\frac{3}{2}} \qquad \begin{array}{l}\text{Raise both sides to the } \frac{3}{2} \text{ power. Because } \frac{m}{n} = \frac{2}{3} \\ \text{and } m \text{ is even, the } \pm \text{ symbol is necessary.}\end{array}$$

$$x = \pm\frac{1}{8} \qquad \left(\frac{1}{4}\right)^{\frac{3}{2}} = \left(\sqrt{\frac{1}{4}}\right)^3 = \left(\frac{1}{2}\right)^3 = \frac{1}{8}$$

Take a moment to verify that the solution set is $\left\{-\frac{1}{8}, \frac{1}{8}\right\}$.

⊘ **Check Point 5** Solve:

a. $5x^{\frac{3}{2}} - 25 = 0$ **b.** $x^{\frac{2}{3}} - 8 = -4.$

④ Solve equations that are quadratic in form.

Equations That Are Quadratic in Form

Some equations that are not quadratic can be written as quadratic equations using an appropriate substitution. Here are some examples:

Given Equation	Substitution	New Equation
$x^4 - 10x^2 + 9 = 0$ or $(x^2)^2 - 10x^2 + 9 = 0$	$u = x^2$	$u^2 - 10u + 9 = 0$
$5x^{\frac{2}{3}} + 11x^{\frac{1}{3}} + 2 = 0$ or $5\left(x^{\frac{1}{3}}\right)^2 + 11x^{\frac{1}{3}} + 2 = 0$	$u = x^{\frac{1}{3}}$	$5u^2 + 11u + 2 = 0$

An equation that is **quadratic in form** is one that can be expressed as a quadratic equation using an appropriate substitution. Both of the preceding given equations are quadratic in form.

Equations that are quadratic in form contain an expression to a power, the same expression to that power squared, and a constant term. By letting u equal the expression to the power, a quadratic equation in u will result. Now it's easy. Solve this quadratic equation for u. Finally, use your substitution to find the values for the variable in the given equation. Example 6 shows how this is done.

(EXAMPLE 6) Solving an Equation Quadratic in Form

Solve: $x^4 - 8x^2 - 9 = 0$.

Solution Notice that the equation contains an expression to a power, x^2, the same expression to that power squared, x^4 or $(x^2)^2$, and a constant term, -9. We let u equal the expression to the power. Thus,

$$\text{let } u = x^2.$$

Now we write the given equation as a quadratic equation in u and solve for u.

$x^4 - 8x^2 - 9 = 0$	*This is the given equation.*
$(x^2)^2 - 8x^2 - 9 = 0$	*The given equation contains x^2 and x^2 squared.*
$u^2 - 8u - 9 = 0$	*Replace x^2 with u.*
$(u - 9)(u + 1) = 0$	*Factor.*
$u - 9 = 0 \quad \text{or} \quad u + 1 = 0$	*Apply the zero-product principle.*
$u = 9 \qquad\qquad u = -1$	*Solve for u.*

We're not done! Why not? We were asked to solve for x and we have values for u. We use the original substitution, $u = x^2$, to solve for x. Replace u with x^2 in each equation shown, namely $u = 9$ and $u = -1$.

$u = 9$	$u = -1$	*These are the equations in u.*
$x^2 = 9$	$x^2 = -1$	*Replace u with x^2.*
$x = \pm\sqrt{9}$	$x = \pm\sqrt{-1}$	*Apply the square root property.*
$x = \pm 3$	$x = \pm i$	*Simplify.*

The solution set is $\{-3, 3, -i, i\}$. The graph in the technology box shows that only the real solutions, -3 and 3, appear as x-intercepts. ●

Technology

Graphic Connections

The graph of
$$y = x^4 - 8x^2 - 9$$
has x-intercepts at -3 and 3. This verifies that the real solutions of
$$x^4 - 8x^2 - 9 = 0$$
are -3 and 3. The imaginary solutions, $-i$ and i, are not shown as intercepts.

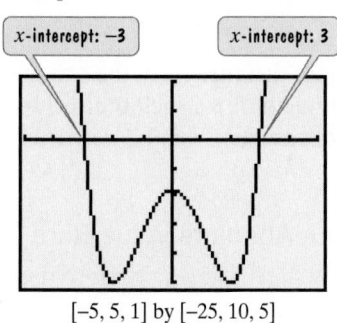

x-intercept: −3 x-intercept: 3

$[-5, 5, 1]$ by $[-25, 10, 5]$

✓ Check Point **6** Solve: $x^4 - 5x^2 + 6 = 0$.

(EXAMPLE 7) **Solving an Equation Quadratic in Form**

Solve: $5x^{\frac{2}{3}} + 11x^{\frac{1}{3}} + 2 = 0$.

Solution Notice that the equation contains an expression to a power, $x^{\frac{1}{3}}$, the same expression to that power squared, $x^{\frac{2}{3}}$ or $\left(x^{\frac{1}{3}}\right)^2$, and a constant term, 2. We let u equal the expression to the power. Thus,

$$\text{let } u = x^{\frac{1}{3}}.$$

Now we write the given equation as a quadratic equation in u and solve for u.

$5x^{\frac{2}{3}} + 11x^{\frac{1}{3}} + 2 = 0$	This is the given equation.
$5\left(x^{\frac{1}{3}}\right)^2 + 11x^{\frac{1}{3}} + 2 = 0$	The given equation contains $x^{\frac{1}{3}}$ and $x^{\frac{1}{3}}$ squared.
$5u^2 + 11u + 2 = 0$	Let $u = x^{\frac{1}{3}}$.
$(5u + 1)(u + 2) = 0$	Factor.
$5u + 1 = 0 \quad$ or $\quad u + 2 = 0$	Set each factor equal to 0.
$5u = -1 \qquad\qquad u = -2$	Solve for u.
$u = -\dfrac{1}{5}$	

Use the original substitution, $u = x^{\frac{1}{3}}$, to solve for x. Replace u with $x^{\frac{1}{3}}$ in each of the preceding equations, namely $u = -\frac{1}{5}$ and $u = -2$.

$u = -\dfrac{1}{5}$	$u = -2$	These are the equations in u.
$x^{\frac{1}{3}} = -\dfrac{1}{5}$	$x^{\frac{1}{3}} = -2$	Replace u with $x^{\frac{1}{3}}$.
$\left(x^{\frac{1}{3}}\right)^3 = \left(-\dfrac{1}{5}\right)^3$	$\left(x^{\frac{1}{3}}\right)^3 = (-2)^3$	Solve for x by cubing both sides of each equation.
$x = -\dfrac{1}{125}$	$x = -8$	Simplify.

We did not raise both sides of an equation to an even power. A check will show that both -8 and $-\frac{1}{125}$ are solutions of the original equation. The solution set is $\left\{-8, -\frac{1}{125}\right\}$. ●

✓ Check Point **7** Solve: $3x^{\frac{2}{3}} - 11x^{\frac{1}{3}} - 4 = 0$.

⑤ Solve equations involving absolute value.

Equations Involving Absolute Value

We have seen that the absolute value of x, denoted $|x|$, describes the distance of x from zero on a number line. Now consider an **absolute value equation**, such as

$$|x| = 2.$$

This means that we must determine real numbers whose distance from the origin on a number line is 2. **Figure 1.26** shows that there are two numbers such that $|x| = 2$, namely, 2 and -2. We write $x = 2$ or $x = -2$. This observation can be generalized as follows:

Figure 1.26

Rewriting an Absolute Value Equation without Absolute Value Bars

If c is a positive real number and u represents any algebraic expression, then $|u| = c$ is equivalent to $u = c$ or $u = -c$.

Technology

Graphic Connections

You can use a graphing utility to verify the solution of an absolute value equation. Consider, for example,

$$|2x - 3| = 11.$$

Graph $y_1 = |2x - 3|$ and $y_2 = 11$. The graphs are shown in a $[-10, 10, 1]$ by $[-1, 15, 1]$ viewing rectangle. The x-coordinates of the intersection points are -4 and 7, verifying that $\{-4, 7\}$ is the solution set.

$[-10, 10, 1]$ by $[-1, 15, 1]$

EXAMPLE 8 Solving an Equation Involving Absolute Value

Solve: $|2x - 3| = 11$.

Solution

$\|2x - 3\| = 11$	This is the given equation.
$2x - 3 = 11$ or $2x - 3 = -11$	Rewrite the equation without absolute value bars: $\|u\| = c$ is equivalent to $u = c$ or $u = -c$.
$2x = 14 \qquad\qquad 2x = -8$	Add 3 to both sides of each equation.
$x = 7 \qquad\qquad\; x = -4$	Divide both sides of each equation by 2.

Check 7:	**Check -4:**	
$\|2x - 3\| = 11$	$\|2x - 3\| = 11$	This is the original equation.
$\|2(7) - 3\| \overset{?}{=} 11$	$\|2(-4) - 3\| \overset{?}{=} 11$	Substitute the proposed solutions.
$\|14 - 3\| \overset{?}{=} 11$	$\|-8 - 3\| \overset{?}{=} 11$	Perform operations inside the absolute value bars.
$\|11\| \overset{?}{=} 11$	$\|-11\| \overset{?}{=} 11$	
$11 = 11$, true	$11 = 11$, true	These true statements indicate that 7 and -4 are solutions.

The solution set is $\{-4, 7\}$.

⊘ Check Point **8** Solve: $|2x - 1| = 5$.

EXAMPLE 9 Solving an Equation Involving Absolute Value

Solve: $5|1 - 4x| - 15 = 0$.

Solution

$5\|1 - 4x\| - 15 = 0$	This is the given equation.

We need to isolate $|1 - 4x|$, the absolute value expression.

$5\|1 - 4x\| = 15$	Add 15 to both sides.
$\|1 - 4x\| = 3$	Divide both sides by 5.
$1 - 4x = 3$ or $1 - 4x = -3$	Rewrite $\|u\| = c$ as $u = c$ or $u = -c$.
$-4x = 2 \qquad\qquad -4x = -4$	Subtract 1 from both sides of each equation.
$x = -\dfrac{1}{2} \qquad\qquad x = 1$	Divide both sides of each equation by -4.

Take a moment to check $-\frac{1}{2}$ and 1, the proposed solutions, in the original equation, $5|1 - 4x| - 15 = 0$. In each case, you should obtain the true statement $0 = 0$. The solution set is $\left\{-\frac{1}{2}, 1\right\}$. These solutions appear as x-intercepts for the graph of $y = 5|1 - 4x| - 15$, as shown in **Figure 1.27**.

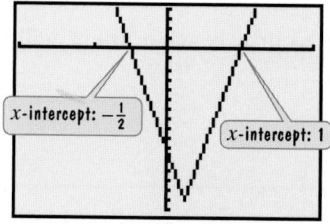

$[-2, 2, 1]$ by $[-16, 4, 1]$

Figure 1.27 The graph of $y = 5|1 - 4x| - 15$

⊘ Check Point **9** Solve: $4|1 - 2x| - 20 = 0$.

[−2, 6, 1] by [−2, 15, 1]

Figure 1.28 An absolute value equation whose graph has no x-intercepts

The absolute value of a number is never negative. Thus, if u is an algebraic expression and c is a negative number, then $|u| = c$ has no solution. For example, the equation $|3x - 6| = -2$ has no solution because $|3x - 6|$ cannot be negative. The solution set is \varnothing, the empty set. The graph of $y = |3x - 6| + 2$, shown in **Figure 1.28**, lies above the x-axis and has no x-intercepts.

The absolute value of 0 is 0. Thus, if u is an algebraic expression and $|u| = 0$, the solution is found by solving $u = 0$. For example, the solution of $|x - 2| = 0$ is obtained by solving $x - 2 = 0$. The solution is 2 and the solution set is $\{2\}$.

⑥ Solve problems modeled by equations.

Applications

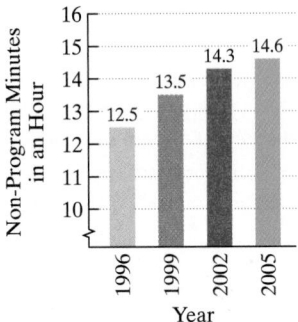

Figure 1.29
Source: Nielsen Monitor-Plus

(**EXAMPLE 10**) **Commercial Clutter**

By 2005, the amount of "clutter," including commercials and plugs for other shows, had increased to the point where an "hour-long" drama on cable TV was 45.4 minutes. The graph in **Figure 1.29** shows the average number of nonprogram minutes in an hour of prime-time cable television. Although the minutes of clutter grew from 1996 through 2005, the growth was leveling off. The data can be modeled by the formula

$$M = 0.7\sqrt{x} + 12.5,$$

where M is the average number of nonprogram minutes in an hour of prime-time cable x years after 1996. Assuming the trend from 1996 through 2005 continues, use the model to project when there will be 15.1 cluttered minutes in every prime-time cable TV hour.

Solution To find when there will be 15.1 cluttered minutes in every prime-time cable TV hour, substitute 15.1 for M in the given model. Then solve for x, the number of years after 1996.

$M = 0.7\sqrt{x} + 12.5$	This is the given formula.
$15.1 = 0.7\sqrt{x} + 12.5$	Substitute 15.1 for M.
$2.6 = 0.7\sqrt{x}$	Subtract 12.5 from both sides.
$\dfrac{2.6}{0.7} = \sqrt{x}$	Divide both sides by 0.7.
$\left(\dfrac{2.6}{0.7}\right)^2 = (\sqrt{x})^2$	Square both sides.
$14 \approx x$	Use a calculator.

The model indicates that there will be 15.1 cluttered minutes in an hour approximately 14 years after 1996. Because 1996 + 14 = 2010, this is projected to occur in 2010. ●

⊘ Check Point **10** Use the model in Example 10 to project when there will be 16 cluttered minutes in a prime-time cable TV hour.

Exercise Set 1.6

Practice Exercises

Solve each polynomial equation in Exercises 1–10 by factoring and then using the zero-product principle.

1. $3x^4 - 48x^2 = 0$

2. $5x^4 - 20x^2 = 0$

3. $3x^3 + 2x^2 = 12x + 8$

4. $4x^3 - 12x^2 = 9x - 27$

5. $2x - 3 = 8x^3 - 12x^2$

6. $x + 1 = 9x^3 + 9x^2$

7. $4y^3 - 2 = y - 8y^2$

8. $9y^3 + 8 = 4y + 18y^2$

9. $2x^4 = 16x$

10. $3x^4 = 81x$

Solve each radical equation in Exercises 11–30. Check all proposed solutions.

11. $\sqrt{3x + 18} = x$

12. $\sqrt{20 - 8x} = x$

13. $\sqrt{x + 3} = x - 3$

14. $\sqrt{x + 10} = x - 2$

15. $\sqrt{2x + 13} = x + 7$

16. $\sqrt{6x + 1} = x - 1$

17. $x - \sqrt{2x + 5} = 5$

18. $x - \sqrt{x + 11} = 1$

19. $\sqrt{2x + 19} - 8 = x$

20. $\sqrt{2x + 15} - 6 = x$

21. $\sqrt{3x + 10} = x + 4$

22. $\sqrt{x} - 3 = x - 9$

23. $\sqrt{x + 8} - \sqrt{x - 4} = 2$

24. $\sqrt{x + 5} - \sqrt{x - 3} = 2$

25. $\sqrt{x - 5} - \sqrt{x - 8} = 3$

26. $\sqrt{2x - 3} - \sqrt{x - 2} = 1$

27. $\sqrt{2x + 3} + \sqrt{x - 2} = 2$

28. $\sqrt{x + 2} + \sqrt{3x + 7} = 1$

29. $\sqrt{3\sqrt{x + 1}} = \sqrt{3x - 5}$

30. $\sqrt{1 + 4\sqrt{x}} = 1 + \sqrt{x}$

Solve each equation with rational exponents in Exercises 31–40. Check all proposed solutions.

31. $x^{\frac{3}{2}} = 8$

32. $x^{\frac{3}{2}} = 27$

33. $(x - 4)^{\frac{3}{2}} = 27$

34. $(x + 5)^{\frac{3}{2}} = 8$

35. $6x^{\frac{5}{2}} - 12 = 0$

36. $8x^{\frac{5}{3}} - 24 = 0$

37. $(x - 4)^{\frac{2}{3}} = 16$

38. $(x + 5)^{\frac{2}{3}} = 4$

39. $(x^2 - x - 4)^{\frac{3}{4}} - 2 = 6$

40. $(x^2 - 3x + 3)^{\frac{3}{2}} - 1 = 0$

Solve each equation in Exercises 41–60 by making an appropriate substitution.

41. $x^4 - 5x^2 + 4 = 0$

42. $x^4 - 13x^2 + 36 = 0$

43. $9x^4 = 25x^2 - 16$

44. $4x^4 = 13x^2 - 9$

45. $x - 13\sqrt{x} + 40 = 0$

46. $2x - 7\sqrt{x} - 30 = 0$

47. $x^{-2} - x^{-1} - 20 = 0$

48. $x^{-2} - x^{-1} - 6 = 0$

49. $x^{\frac{2}{3}} - x^{\frac{1}{3}} - 6 = 0$

50. $2x^{\frac{2}{3}} + 7x^{\frac{1}{3}} - 15 = 0$

51. $x^{\frac{3}{2}} - 2x^{\frac{3}{4}} + 1 = 0$

52. $x^{\frac{2}{5}} + x^{\frac{1}{5}} - 6 = 0$

53. $2x - 3x^{\frac{1}{2}} + 1 = 0$

54. $x + 3x^{\frac{1}{2}} - 4 = 0$

55. $(x - 5)^2 - 4(x - 5) - 21 = 0$

56. $(x + 3)^2 + 7(x + 3) - 18 = 0$

57. $(x^2 - x)^2 - 14(x^2 - x) + 24 = 0$

58. $(x^2 - 2x)^2 - 11(x^2 - 2x) + 24 = 0$

59. $\left(y - \frac{8}{y}\right)^2 + 5\left(y - \frac{8}{y}\right) - 14 = 0$

60. $\left(y - \frac{10}{y}\right)^2 + 6\left(y - \frac{10}{y}\right) - 27 = 0$

In Exercises 61–78, solve each absolute value equation or indicate that the equation has no solution.

61. $|x| = 8$

62. $|x| = 6$

63. $|x - 2| = 7$

64. $|x + 1| = 5$

65. $|2x - 1| = 5$

66. $|2x - 3| = 11$

67. $2|3x - 2| = 14$

68. $3|2x - 1| = 21$

69. $7|5x| + 2 = 16$

70. $7|3x| + 2 = 16$

71. $2\left|4 - \frac{5}{2}x\right| + 6 = 18$

72. $4\left|1 - \frac{3}{4}x\right| + 7 = 10$

73. $|x + 1| + 5 = 3$

74. $|x + 1| + 6 = 2$

75. $|2x - 1| + 3 = 3$

76. $|3x - 2| + 4 = 4$

Hint for Exercises 77–78: Absolute value expressions are equal when the expressions inside the absolute value bars are equal to or opposites of each other.

77. $|3x - 1| = |x + 5|$

78. $|2x - 7| = |x + 3|$

In Exercises 79–84, find the x-intercepts of the graph of each equation. Then use the x-intercepts to match the equation with its graph. [The graphs are labeled (a) through (f).]

79. $y = \sqrt{x + 2} + \sqrt{x - 1} - 3$

80. $y = \sqrt{x - 4} + \sqrt{x + 4} - 4$

81. $y = x^{\frac{1}{3}} + 2x^{\frac{1}{6}} - 3$

82. $y = x^{-2} - x^{-1} - 6$

83. $y = (x + 2)^2 - 9(x + 2) + 20$

84. $y = 2(x + 2)^2 + 5(x + 2) - 3$

a.

$[-1, 10, 1]$ by $[-3, 3, 1]$

b.

$[-3, 3, 1]$ by $[-10, 10, 1]$

c.

$[-1, 10, 1]$ by $[-4, 4, 1]$

d.

$[-6, 3, 1]$ by $[-10, 10, 1]$

e.

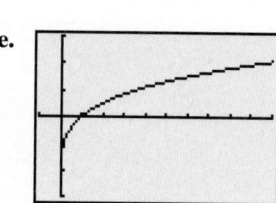

$[-1, 10, 1]$ by $[-3, 3, 1]$

f.

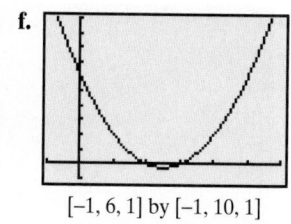

$[-1, 6, 1]$ by $[-1, 10, 1]$

In Exercises 85–94, find all values of x satisfying the given conditions.

85. $y = |5 - 4x|$ and $y = 11$.

86. $y = |2 - 3x|$ and $y = 13$.

87. $y = x + \sqrt{x + 5}$ and $y = 7$.

88. $y = x - \sqrt{x - 2}$ and $y = 4$.

89. $y = 2x^3 + x^2 - 8x + 2$ and $y = 6$.

90. $y = x^3 + 4x^2 - x + 6$ and $y = 10$.

91. $y = (x + 4)^{\frac{3}{2}}$ and $y = 8$.

92. $y = (x - 5)^{\frac{3}{2}}$ and $y = 125$.

93. $y_1 = (x^2 - 1)^2$, $y_2 = 2(x^2 - 1)$, and y_1 exceeds y_2 by 3.

94. $y_1 = 6\left(\dfrac{2x}{x - 3}\right)^2$, $y_2 = 5\left(\dfrac{2x}{x - 3}\right)$, and y_1 exceeds y_2 by 6.

Practice Plus

In Exercises 95–98, solve each equation.

95. $|x^2 + 2x - 36| = 12$

96. $|x^2 + 6x + 1| = 8$

97. $x(x + 1)^3 - 42(x + 1)^2 = 0$

98. $x(x - 2)^3 - 35(x - 2)^2 = 0$

99. If 5 times a number is decreased by 4, the principal square root of this difference is 2 less than the number. Find the number(s).

100. If a number is decreased by 3, the principal square root of this difference is 5 less than the number. Find the number(s).

101. Solve for V: $r = \sqrt{\dfrac{3V}{\pi h}}$.

102. Solve for A: $r = \sqrt{\dfrac{A}{4\pi}}$.

In Exercises 103–104, list all numbers that must be excluded from the domain of each expression.

103. $\dfrac{|x - 1| - 3}{|x + 2| - 14}$

104. $\dfrac{x^3 - 2x^2 - 9x + 18}{x^3 + 3x^2 - x - 3}$

Application Exercises

A basketball player's hang time is the time spent in the air when shooting a basket. The formula

$$t = \frac{\sqrt{d}}{2}$$

models hang time, t, in seconds, in terms of the vertical distance of a player's jump, d, in feet. Use this formula to solve Exercises 105–106.

105. When Michael Wilson of the Harlem Globetrotters slamdunked a basketball, his hang time for the shot was approximately 1.16 seconds. What was the vertical distance of his jump, rounded to the nearest tenth of a foot?

106. If hang time for a shot by a professional basketball player is 0.85 second, what is the vertical distance of the jump, rounded to the nearest tenth of a foot?

Use the graph of the formula for hang time to solve Exercises 107–108.

107. How is your answer to Exercise 105 shown on the graph?

108. How is your answer to Exercise 106 shown on the graph?

The bar graph shows the percentage of full-time college students in the United States who had jobs for four selected years. The data can be described by the mathematical model

$$J = 2.6\sqrt{x} + 35,$$

where J is the percentage of full-time college students with jobs x years after 1975. Use this information to solve Exercises 109–110.

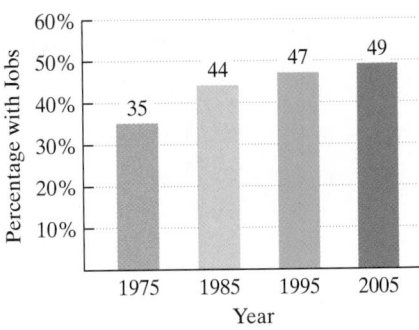

Percentage of Full-Time College Students with Jobs

Source: Department of Education

109. Use the formula to project when 50.6% of full-time college students will have jobs.

110. Use the formula to project when 53.2% of full-time college students will have jobs.

The graph of the model for the percentage of full-time college students with jobs is shown in a rectangular coordinate system. Use the graph to solve Exercises 111–112.

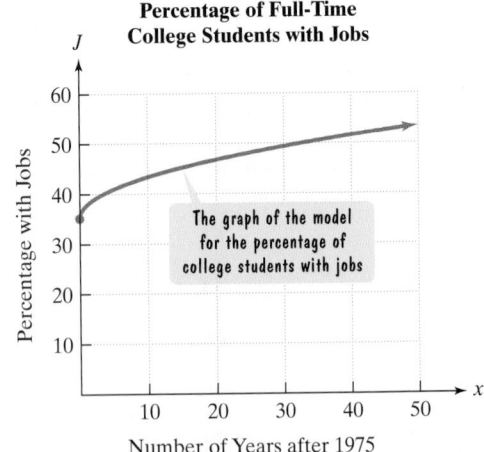

Percentage of Full-Time College Students with Jobs

111. a. Identify your solution from Exercise 109 as a point on the graph at the bottom of the previous page.

b. Use the graph to estimate the percentage of full-time college students who will have jobs in 2015. Give your estimate to the nearest percent.

112. a. Identify your solution from Exercise 110 as a point on the graph at the bottom of the previous page.

b. Use the graph to estimate the percentage of full-time college students who will have jobs in 2025. Give your estimate to the nearest percent.

For each planet in our solar system, its year is the time it takes the planet to revolve once around the sun. The formula

$$E = 0.2x^{\frac{3}{2}}$$

models the number of Earth days in a planet's year, E, where x is the average distance of the planet from the sun, in millions of kilometers. Use the equation to solve Exercises 113–114.

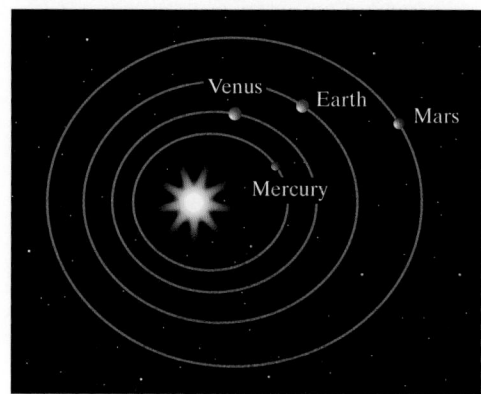

113. We, of course, have 365 Earth days in our year. What is the average distance of Earth from the sun? Use a calculator and round to the nearest million kilometers.

114. There are approximately 88 Earth days in the year of the planet Mercury. What is the average distance of Mercury from the sun? Use a calculator and round to the nearest million kilometers.

Use the Pythagorean Theorem to solve Exercises 115–116.

115. Two vertical poles of lengths 6 feet and 8 feet stand 10 feet apart. A cable reaches from the top of one pole to some point on the ground between the poles and then to the top of the other pole. Where should this point be located to use 18 feet of cable?

116. Towns A and B are located 6 miles and 3 miles, respectively, from a major expressway. The point on the expressway closest to town A is 12 miles from the point on the expressway closest to town B. Two new roads are to be built from A to the expressway and then to B.

a. Express the combined lengths of the new roads in terms of x as shown in the figure.

b. If the combined lengths of the new roads is 15 miles, what distance does x represent?

Writing in Mathematics

117. Without actually solving the equation, give a general description of how to solve $x^3 - 5x^2 - x + 5 = 0$.

118. In solving $\sqrt{3x + 4} - \sqrt{2x + 4} = 2$, why is it a good idea to isolate a radical term? What if we don't do this and simply square each side? Describe what happens.

119. What is an extraneous solution to a radical equation?

120. Explain how to recognize an equation that is quadratic in form. Provide two original examples with your explanation.

121. Describe two methods for solving this equation: $x - 5\sqrt{x} + 4 = 0$.

122. Explain how to solve an equation involving absolute value.

123. Explain why the procedure that you explained in Exercise 122 does not apply to the equation $|x - 2| = -3$. What is the solution set for this equation?

Technology Exercises

In Exercises 124–126, use a graphing utility and the graph's x-intercepts to solve each equation. Check by direct substitution. A viewing rectangle is given.

124. $x^3 + 3x^2 - x - 3 = 0$

$[-6, 6, 1]$ by $[-6, 6, 1]$

125. $-x^4 + 4x^3 - 4x^2 = 0$

$[-6, 6, 1]$ by $[-9, 2, 1]$

126. $\sqrt{2x + 13} - x - 5 = 0$

$[-5, 5, 1]$ by $[-5, 5, 1]$

Critical Thinking Exercises

Make Sense? *In Exercises 127–130, determine whether each statement makes sense or does not make sense, and explain your reasoning.*

127. When checking a radical equation's proposed solution, I can substitute into the original equation or any equation that is part of the solution process.

128. After squaring both sides of a radical equation, the only solution that I obtained was extraneous, so \varnothing must be the solution set of the original equation.

129. The equation $5x^{\frac{2}{3}} + 11x^{\frac{1}{3}} + 2 = 0$ is quadratic in form, but when I reverse the variable terms and obtain $11x^{\frac{1}{3}} + 5x^{\frac{2}{3}} + 2 = 0$, the resulting equation is no longer quadratic in form.

130. When I solve an equation that is quadratic in form, it's important to write down the substitution that I am making.

In Exercises 131–134, determine whether each statement is true or false. If the statement is false, make the necessary change(s) to produce a true statement.

131. The first step in solving $\sqrt{x + 6} = x + 2$ is to square both sides, obtaining $x + 6 = x^2 + 4$.

132. The equations $\sqrt{x + 4} = -5$ and $x + 4 = 25$ have the same solution set.

133. To solve $x - 9\sqrt{x} + 14 = 0$, we let $\sqrt{u} = x$.

134. The equation $|x| = -6$ is equivalent to $x = 6$ or $x = -6$.

135. Solve: $\sqrt{6x - 2} = \sqrt{2x + 3} - \sqrt{4x - 1}$.

136. Solve without squaring both sides:
$$5 - \frac{2}{x} = \sqrt{5 - \frac{2}{x}}.$$

137. Solve for x: $\sqrt[3]{x\sqrt{x}} = 9$.

138. Solve for x: $x^{\frac{5}{6}} + x^{\frac{2}{3}} - 2x^{\frac{1}{2}} = 0$.

Preview Exercises

Exercises 139–141 will help you prepare for the material covered in the next section.

139. Is -1 a solution of $3 - 2x \le 11$?

140. Solve: $-2x - 4 = x + 5$.

141. Solve: $\dfrac{x + 3}{4} = \dfrac{x - 2}{3} + \dfrac{1}{4}$.

Section 1.7

Linear Inequalities and Absolute Value Inequalities

Objectives

1. Use interval notation.
2. Find intersections and unions of intervals.
3. Solve linear inequalities.
4. Recognize inequalities with no solution or all real numbers as solutions.
5. Solve compound inequalities.
6. Solve absolute value inequalities.

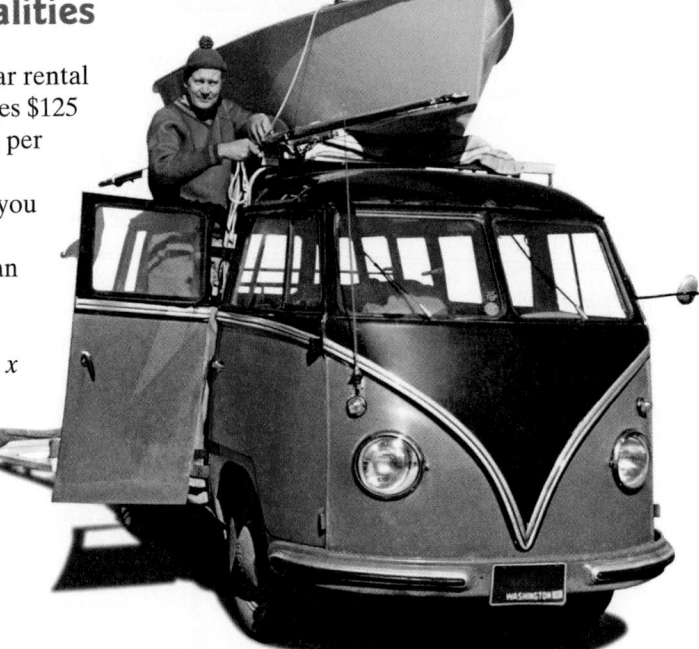

Rent-a-Heap, a car rental company, charges \$125 per week plus \$0.20 per mile to rent one of their cars. Suppose you are limited by how much money you can spend for the week: You can spend at most \$335. If we let x represent the number of miles you drive the heap in a week, we can write an inequality that models the given conditions:

The weekly charge of \$125	plus	the charge of \$0.20 per mile for x miles	must be less than or equal to	\$335.
125	+	$0.20x$	\le	335.

Placing an inequality symbol between a polynomial of degree 1 and a constant results in a *linear inequality in one variable*. In this section, we will study how to solve linear inequalities such as $125 + 0.20x \leq 335$. **Solving an inequality** is the process of finding the set of numbers that make the inequality a true statement. These numbers are called the **solutions** of the inequality and we say that they **satisfy** the inequality. The set of all solutions is called the **solution set** of the inequality. Set-builder notation and a new notation, called *interval notation*, are used to represent these solution sets. We begin this section by looking at interval notation.

① Use interval notation.

Interval Notation

Some sets of real numbers can be represented using **interval notation**. Suppose that a and b are two real numbers such that $a < b$.

Interval Notation	Graph
The **open interval** (a, b) represents the set of real numbers between, but not including, a and b. $$(a, b) = \{x \mid a < x < b\}$$ *x is greater than a (a < x)* and *x is less than b (x < b).*	a (a, b) b → x The parentheses in the graph and in interval notation indicate that a and b, the endpoints, are excluded from the interval.
The **closed interval** $[a, b]$ represents the set of real numbers between, and including, a and b. $$[a, b] = \{x \mid a \leq x \leq b\}$$ *x is greater than or equal to a (a ≤ x)* and *x is less than or equal to b (x ≤ b).*	a $[a, b]$ b → x The square brackets in the graph and in interval notation indicate that a and b, the endpoints, are included in the interval.
The **infinite interval** (a, ∞) represents the set of real numbers that are greater than a. $$(a, \infty) = \{x \mid x > a\}$$ The infinity symbol does not represent a real number. It indicates that the interval extends indefinitely to the right.	a (a, ∞) → x The parenthesis indicates that a is excluded from the interval.
The **infinite interval** $(-\infty, b]$ represents the set of real numbers that are less than or equal to b. $$(-\infty, b] = \{x \mid x \leq b\}$$ The negative infinity symbol indicates that the interval extends indefinitely to the left.	$(-\infty, b]$ b → x The square bracket indicates that b is included in the interval.

Parentheses and Brackets in Interval Notation

Parentheses indicate endpoints that are not included in an interval. Square brackets indicate endpoints that are included in an interval. Parentheses are always used with ∞ or $-\infty$.

Table 1.4 lists nine possible types of intervals used to describe subsets of real numbers.

Table 1.4 Intervals on the Real Number Line

Let a and b be real numbers such that $a < b$.		
Interval Notation	**Set-Builder Notation**	**Graph**
(a,b)	$\{x\mid a < x < b\}$	
$[a,b]$	$\{x\mid a \le x \le b\}$	
$[a,b)$	$\{x\mid a \le x < b\}$	
$(a,b]$	$\{x\mid a < x \le b\}$	
(a,∞)	$\{x\mid x > a\}$	
$[a,\infty)$	$\{x\mid x \ge a\}$	
$(-\infty,b)$	$\{x\mid x < b\}$	
$(-\infty,b]$	$\{x\mid x \le b\}$	
$(-\infty, \infty)$	$\{x\mid x \text{ is a real number}\}$ or \mathbb{R} (set of all real numbers)	

(**EXAMPLE 1**) **Using Interval Notation**

Express each interval in set-builder notation and graph:

 a. $(-1, 4]$ **b.** $[2.5, 4]$ **c.** $(-4, \infty)$.

Solution

 a. $(-1, 4] = \{x\mid -1 < x \le 4\}$

 b. $[2.5, 4] = \{x\mid 2.5 \le x \le 4\}$

 c. $(-4, \infty) = \{x\mid x > -4\}$

⊘ **Check Point 1** Express each interval in set-builder notation and graph:

 a. $[-2, 5)$ **b.** $[1, 3.5]$ **c.** $(-\infty, -1)$.

② Find intersections and unions of intervals.

Intersections and Unions of Intervals

In Chapter P, we learned how to find intersections and unions of sets. Recall that $A \cap B$ (A intersection B) is the set of elements common to both set A and set B. By contrast, $A \cup B$ (A union B) is the set of elements in set A or in set B or in both sets.

Because intervals represent sets, it is possible to find their intersections and unions. Graphs are helpful in this process.

Finding Intersections and Unions of Two Intervals

1. Graph each interval on a number line.

2. a. To find the intersection, take the portion of the number line that the two graphs have in common.

 b. To find the union, take the portion of the number line representing the total collection of numbers in the two graphs.

EXAMPLE 2 **Finding Intersections and Unions of Intervals**

Use graphs to find each set:

 a. $(1, 4) \cap [2, 8]$ **b.** $(1, 4) \cup [2, 8]$.

Solution

 a. $(1, 4) \cap [2, 8]$, the intersection of the intervals $(1, 4)$ and $[2, 8]$, consists of the numbers that are in both intervals.

Graph of $(1, 4)$: $\{x \mid 1 < x < 4\}$

Graph of $[2, 8]$: $\{x \mid 2 \leq x \leq 8\}$

To find $(1, 4) \cap [2, 8]$, take the portion of the number line that the two graphs have in common.

Numbers in both
$(1, 4)$ and $[2, 8]$: $\{x \mid 1 < x < 4$ and $2 \leq x \leq 8\}$

The numbers common to both intervals are those that are greater than or equal to 2 and less than 4: [2, 4).

Thus, $(1, 4) \cap [2, 8] = [2, 4)$.

 b. $(1, 4) \cup [2, 8]$, the union of the intervals $(1, 4)$ and $[2, 8]$, consists of the numbers that are in either one interval or the other (or both).

Graph of $(1, 4)$: $\{x \mid 1 < x < 4\}$

Graph of $[2, 8]$: $\{x \mid 2 \leq x \leq 8\}$

To find $(1, 4) \cup [2, 8]$, take the portion of the number line representing the total collection of numbers in the two graphs.

Numbers in either
$(1, 4)$ or $[2, 8]$ or both: $\{x \mid 1 < x < 4$ or $2 \leq x \leq 8\}$

The numbers in either one interval or the other (or both) are those that are greater than 1 and less than or equal to 8: (1, 8].

Thus, $(1, 4) \cup [2, 8] = (1, 8]$.

⊘ **Check Point 2** Use graphs to find each set:

 a. $[1, 3] \cap (2, 6)$ **b.** $[1, 3] \cup (2, 6)$.

③ Solve linear inequalities.

Solving Linear Inequalities in One Variable

We know that a linear equation in x can be expressed as $ax + b = 0$. A **linear inequality in x** can be written in one of the following forms:

$$ax + b < 0, \, ax + b \leq 0, \, ax + b > 0, \, ax + b \geq 0.$$

In each form, $a \neq 0$.

Back to our question that opened this section: How many miles can you drive your Rent-a-Heap car if you can spend at most $335? We answer the question by solving

$$0.20x + 125 \leq 335$$

for x. The solution procedure is nearly identical to that for solving

$$0.20x + 125 = 335.$$

Our goal is to get x by itself on the left side. We do this by subtracting 125 from both sides to isolate $0.20x$:

$0.20x + 125 \leq 335$	This is the given inequality.
$0.20x + 125 - 125 \leq 335 - 125$	Subtract 125 from both sides.
$0.02x \leq 210.$	Simplify.

Finally, we isolate x from $0.20x$ by dividing both sides of the inequality by 0.20:

$\dfrac{0.20x}{0.20} \leq \dfrac{210}{0.20}$	Divide both sides by 0.20.
$x \leq 1050.$	Simplify.

With at most $335 to spend, you can travel at most 1050 miles.

We started with the inequality $0.20x + 125 \leq 335$ and obtained the inequality $x \leq 1050$ in the final step. These inequalities have the same solution set, namely $\{x | x \leq 1050\}$. Inequalities such as these, with the same solution set, are said to be **equivalent**.

We isolated x from $0.20x$ by dividing both sides of $0.20x \leq 210$ by 0.20, a positive number. Let's see what happens if we divide both sides of an inequality by a negative number. Consider the inequality $10 < 14$. Divide 10 and 14 by -2:

$$\frac{10}{-2} = -5 \quad \text{and} \quad \frac{14}{-2} = -7.$$

Because -5 lies to the right of -7 on the number line, -5 is greater than -7:

$$-5 > -7.$$

Notice that the direction of the inequality symbol is reversed:

$$10 < 14$$
$$-5 > -7.$$

Dividing by -2 changes the direction of the inequality symbol.

In general, **when we multiply or divide both sides of an inequality by a negative number, the direction of the inequality symbol is reversed.** When we reverse the direction of the inequality symbol, we say that we change the *sense* of the inequality.

We can isolate a variable in a linear inequality in the same way we isolate a variable in a linear equation. The properties on the next page are used to create equivalent inequalities.

Study Tip

English phrases such as "at least" and "at most" can be modeled by inequalities.

English Sentence	Inequality
x is at least 5.	$x \geq 5$
x is at most 5.	$x \leq 5$
x is between 5 and 7.	$5 < x < 7$
x is no more than 5.	$x \leq 5$
x is no less than 5.	$x \geq 5$

Properties of Inequalities

Property	The Property in Words	Example
The Addition Property of Inequality If $a < b$, then $a + c < b + c$. If $a < b$, then $a - c < b - c$.	If the same quantity is added to or subtracted from both sides of an inequality, the resulting inequality is equivalent to the original one.	$2x + 3 < 7$ Subtract 3: $2x + 3 - 3 < 7 - 3$. Simplify: $2x < 4$.
The Positive Multiplication Property of Inequality If $a < b$ and c is positive, then $ac < bc$. If $a < b$ and c is positive, then $\dfrac{a}{c} < \dfrac{b}{c}$.	If we multiply or divide both sides of an inequality by the same positive quantity, the resulting inequality is equivalent to the original one.	$2x < 4$ Divide by 2: $\dfrac{2x}{2} < \dfrac{4}{2}$. Simplify: $x < 2$.
The Negative Multiplication Property of Inequality If $a < b$ and c is negative, then $ac > bc$. If $a < b$ and c is negative, $\dfrac{a}{c} > \dfrac{b}{c}$.	If we multiply or divide both sides of an inequality by the same negative quantity and reverse the direction of the inequality symbol, the resulting inequality is equivalent to the original one.	$-4x < 20$ Divide by -4 and change the sense of the inequality: $\dfrac{-4x}{-4} > \dfrac{20}{-4}$. Simplify: $x > -5$.

EXAMPLE 3 **Solving a Linear Inequality**

Solve and graph the solution set on a number line:

$$3 - 2x \le 11.$$

Solution

$3 - 2x \le 11$	This is the given inequality.
$3 - 2x - 3 \le 11 - 3$	Subtract 3 from both sides.
$-2x \le 8$	Simplify.
$\dfrac{-2x}{-2} \ge \dfrac{8}{-2}$	Divide both sides by -2 and change the sense of the inequality.
$x \ge -4$	Simplify.

Discovery

As a partial check, select one number from the solution set of $3 - 2x \le 11$. Substitute that number into the original inequality. Perform the resulting computations. You should obtain a true statement.

Is it possible to perform a partial check using a number that is not in the solution set? What should happen in this case? Try doing this.

The solution set consists of all real numbers that are greater than or equal to -4, expressed as $\{x \mid x \ge -4\}$ in set-builder notation. The interval notation for this solution set is $[-4, \infty)$. The graph of the solution set is shown as follows:

Check Point 3 Solve and graph the solution set on a number line:

$$2 - 3x \le 5.$$

EXAMPLE 4 **Solving a Linear Inequality**

Solve and graph the solution set on a number line:

$$-2x - 4 > x + 5.$$

Solution

Step 1 Simplify each side. Because each side is already simplified, we can skip this step.

Study Tip

You can solve

$$-2x - 4 > x + 5$$

by isolating x on the right side. Add $2x$ to both sides.

$$-2x - 4 + 2x > x + 5 + 2x$$
$$-4 > 3x + 5$$

Now subtract 5 from both sides.

$$-4 - 5 > 3x + 5 - 5$$
$$-9 > 3x$$

Finally, divide both sides by 3.

$$\frac{-9}{3} > \frac{3x}{3}$$
$$-3 > x$$

This last inequality means the same thing as $x < -3$.

Step 2 Collect variable terms on one side and constant terms on the other side. We will collect variable terms of $-2x - 4 > x + 5$ on the left and constant terms on the right.

$-2x - 4 > x + 5$	This is the given inequality.
$-2x - 4 - x > x + 5 - x$	Subtract x from both sides.
$-3x - 4 > 5$	Simplify.
$-3x - 4 + 4 > 5 + 4$	Add 4 to both sides.
$-3x > 9$	Simplify.

Step 3 Isolate the variable and solve. We isolate the variable, x, by dividing both sides by -3. Because we are dividing by a negative number, we must reverse the inequality symbol.

$\dfrac{-3x}{-3} < \dfrac{9}{-3}$	Divide both sides by -3 and change the sense of the inequality.
$x < -3$	Simplify.

Step 4 Express the solution set in set-builder or interval notation and graph the set on a number line. The solution set consists of all real numbers that are less than -3, expressed in set-builder notation as $\{x \mid x < -3\}$. The interval notation for this solution set is $(-\infty, -3)$. The graph of the solution set is shown as follows:

Technology

Numeric and Graphic Connections

You can use a graphing utility to check the solution set of a linear inequality. Enter each side of the inequality separately under y_1 and y_2. Then use the table or the graphs. To use the table, first locate the x-value for which the y-values are the same. Then scroll up or down to locate x values for which y_1 is greater than y_2 or for which y_1 is less than y_2. To use the graphs, locate the intersection point and then find the x-values for which the graph of y_1 lies above the graph of y_2 $(y_1 > y_2)$ or for which the graph of y_1 lies below the graph of y_2 $(y_1 < y_2)$.

Let's verify our work in Example 4 and show that $(-\infty, -3)$ is the solution set of

$$-2x - 4 > x + 5.$$

Enter $y_1 = -2x - 4$ in the $\boxed{y=}$ screen. Enter $y_2 = x + 5$ in the $\boxed{y=}$ screen.

We are looking for values of x for which y_1 is greater than y_2.

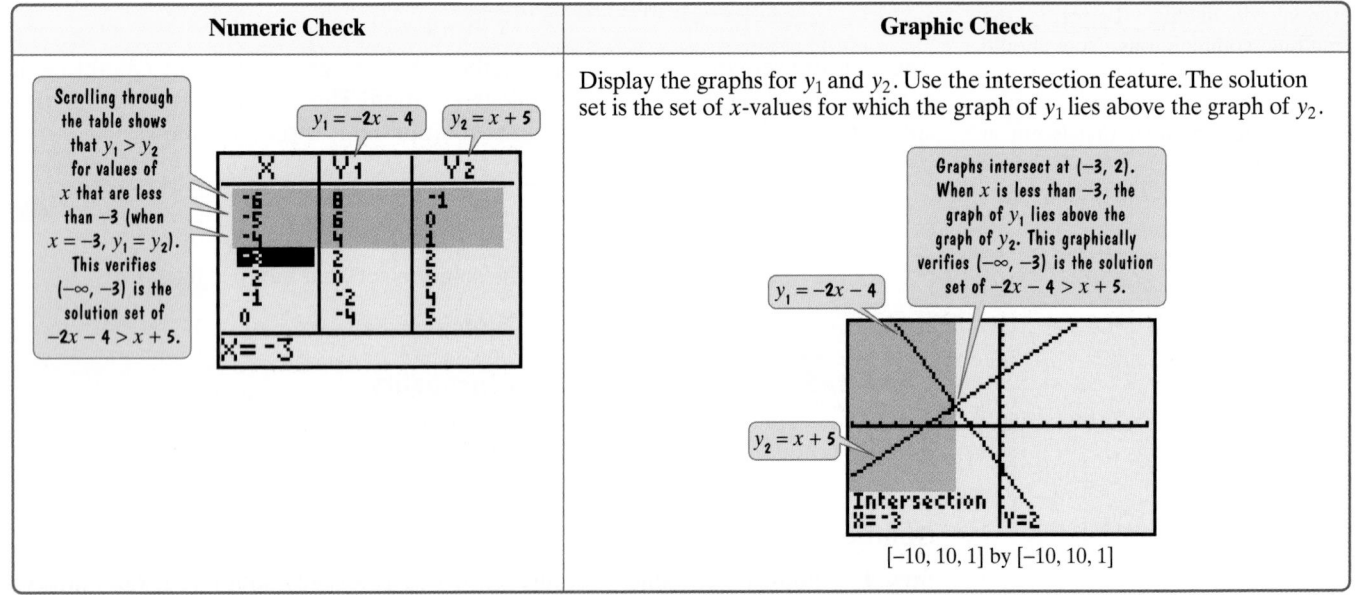

Numeric Check	Graphic Check
Scrolling through the table shows that $y_1 > y_2$ for values of x that are less than -3 (when $x = -3$, $y_1 = y_2$). This verifies $(-\infty, -3)$ is the solution set of $-2x - 4 > x + 5$.	Display the graphs for y_1 and y_2. Use the intersection feature. The solution set is the set of x-values for which the graph of y_1 lies above the graph of y_2. Graphs intersect at $(-3, 2)$. When x is less than -3, the graph of y_1 lies above the graph of y_2. This graphically verifies $(-\infty, -3)$ is the solution set of $-2x - 4 > x + 5$.

$[-10, 10, 1]$ by $[-10, 10, 1]$

⊘ Check Point **4** Solve and graph the solution set on a number line: $3x + 1 > 7x - 15$.

If an inequality contains fractions with constants in the denominators, begin by multiplying both sides by the least common denominator. This will clear the inequality of fractions.

(EXAMPLE 5) **Solving a Linear Inequality Containing Fractions**

Solve and graph the solution set on a number line:

$$\frac{x + 3}{4} \geq \frac{x - 2}{3} + \frac{1}{4}.$$

Solution The denominators are 4, 3, and 4. The least common denominator is 12. We begin by multiplying both sides of the inequality by 12.

$$\frac{x + 3}{4} \geq \frac{x - 2}{3} + \frac{1}{4}$$ This is the given inequality.

$$12\left(\frac{x + 3}{4}\right) \geq 12\left(\frac{x - 2}{3} + \frac{1}{4}\right)$$ Multiply both sides by 12. Multiplying by a positive number preserves the sense of the inequality.

$$\frac{12}{1} \cdot \frac{x + 3}{4} \geq \frac{12}{1} \cdot \frac{x - 2}{3} + \frac{12}{1} \cdot \frac{1}{4}$$ Multiply each term by 12. Use the distributive property on the right side.

$$\frac{\overset{3}{\cancel{12}}}{1} \cdot \frac{x + 3}{\underset{1}{\cancel{4}}} \geq \frac{\overset{4}{\cancel{12}}}{1} \cdot \frac{x - 2}{\underset{1}{\cancel{3}}} + \frac{\overset{3}{\cancel{12}}}{1} \cdot \frac{1}{\underset{1}{\cancel{4}}}$$ Divide out common factors in each multiplication.

$$3(x + 3) \geq 4(x - 2) + 3$$ The fractions are now cleared.

Now that the fractions have been cleared, we follow the four steps that we used in the previous example.

Step 1 Simplify each side.

$$3(x + 3) \geq 4(x - 2) + 3$$ This is the inequality with the fractions cleared.

$$3x + 9 \geq 4x - 8 + 3$$ Use the distributive property.

$$3x + 9 \geq 4x - 5$$ Simplify.

Step 2 Collect variable terms on one side and constant terms on the other side. We will collect variable terms on the left and constant terms on the right.

$$3x + 9 - 4x \geq 4x - 5 - 4x$$ Subtract 4x from both sides.

$$-x + 9 \geq -5$$ Simplify.

$$-x + 9 - 9 \geq -5 - 9$$ Subtract 9 from both sides.

$$-x \geq -14$$ Simplify.

Step 3 Isolate the variable and solve. To isolate x, we must eliminate the negative sign in front of the x. Because $-x$ means $-1x$, we can do this by multiplying (or dividing) both sides of the inequality by -1. We are multiplying by a negative number. Thus, we must reverse the direction of the inequality symbol.

$$(-1)(-x) \leq (-1)(-14)$$ Multiply both sides by -1 and change the sense of the inequality.

$$x \leq 14$$ Simplify.

Step 4 Express the solution set in set-builder or interval notation and graph the set on a number line. The solution set consists of all real numbers that are less than or

equal to 14, expressed in set-builder notation as $\{x \mid x \le 14\}$. The interval notation for this solution set is $(-\infty, 14]$. The graph of the solution set is shown as follows:

⊘ Check Point **5** Solve and graph the solution set on a number line:

$$\frac{x-4}{2} \ge \frac{x-2}{3} + \frac{5}{6}.$$

④ Recognize inequalities with no solution or all real numbers as solutions.

Inequalities with Unusual Solution Sets

We have seen that some equations have no solution. This is also true for some inequalities. An example of such an inequality is

$$x > x + 1.$$

There is no number that is greater than itself plus 1. This inequality has no solution and its solution set is \varnothing, the empty set.

By contrast, some inequalities are true for all real numbers. An example of such an inequality is

$$x < x + 1.$$

Every real number is less than itself plus 1. The solution set is $\{x \mid x \text{ is a real number}\}$ or \mathbb{R}. In interval notation, the solution set is $(-\infty, \infty)$.

If you attempt to solve an inequality that has no solution, you will eliminate the variable and obtain a false statement, such as $0 > 1$. If you attempt to solve an inequality that is true for all real numbers, you will eliminate the variable and obtain a true statement, such as $0 < 1$.

(**EXAMPLE 6**) **Solving Linear Inequalities**

Solve each inequality:

 a. $2(x + 4) > 2x + 3$ **b.** $x + 7 \le x - 2.$

Solution

Technology

Graphic Connections

The graphs of

 $y_1 = 2(x + 4)$ and $y_2 = 2x + 3$

are parallel lines.

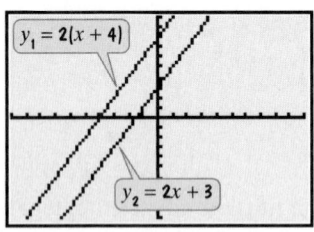

[−10, 10, 1] by [−10, 10, 1]

The graph of y_1 is always above the graph of y_2. Every value of x satisfies the inequality $y_1 > y_2$. Thus, the solution set of the inequality

 $2(x + 4) > 2x + 3$

is $(-\infty, \infty)$.

a.

$2(x + 4) > 2x + 3$	This is the given inequality.
$2x + 8 > 2x + 3$	Apply the distributive property.
$2x + 8 - 2x > 2x + 3 - 2x$	Subtract 2x from both sides.
$8 > 3$	Simplify. The statement $8 > 3$ is true.

The inequality $8 > 3$ is true for all values of x. Because this inequality is equivalent to the original inequality, the original inequality is true for all real numbers. The solution set is

$$\{x \mid x \text{ is a real number}\} \text{ or } \mathbb{R} \text{ or } (-\infty, \infty).$$

b.

$x + 7 \le x - 2$	This is the given inequality.
$x + 7 - x \le x - 2 - x$	Subtract x from both sides.
$7 \le -2$	Simplify. The statement $7 \le -2$ is false.

The inequality $7 \le -2$ is false for all values of x. Because this inequality is equivalent to the original inequality, the original inequality has no solution. The solution set is \varnothing.

⊘ Check Point **6** Solve each inequality:

 a. $3(x + 1) > 3x + 2$ **b.** $x + 1 \le x - 1.$

⑤ Solve compound inequalities.

Solving Compound Inequalities

We now consider two inequalities such as

$$-3 < 2x + 1 \quad \text{and} \quad 2x + 1 \le 3,$$

expressed as a **compound inequality**

$$-3 < 2x + 1 \le 3.$$

The word *and* does not appear when the inequality is written in the shorter form, although intersection is implied. The shorter form enables us to solve both inequalities at once. By performing each operation on all three parts of the inequality, our goal is to **isolate *x* in the middle**.

(**EXAMPLE 7**) **Solving a Compound Inequality**

Solve and graph the solution set on a number line:

$$-3 < 2x + 1 \le 3.$$

Solution We would like to isolate *x* in the middle. We can do this by first subtracting 1 from all three parts of the compound inequality. Then we isolate *x* from $2x$ by dividing all three parts of the inequality by 2.

$-3 < 2x + 1 \le 3$	This is the given inequality.
$-3 - 1 < 2x + 1 - 1 \le 3 - 1$	Subtract 1 from all three parts.
$-4 < 2x \le 2$	Simplify.
$\dfrac{-4}{2} < \dfrac{2x}{2} \le \dfrac{2}{2}$	Divide each part by 2.
$-2 < x \le 1$	Simplify.

The solution set consists of all real numbers greater than -2 and less than or equal to 1, represented by $\{x \mid -2 < x \le 1\}$ in set-builder notation and $(-2, 1]$ in interval notation. The graph is shown as follows:

⊘ Check Point **7** Solve and graph the solution set on a number line: $1 \le 2x + 3 < 11.$

Technology

Numeric and Graphic Connections

Let's verify our work in Example 7 and show that $(-2, 1]$ is the solution set of $-3 < 2x + 1 \le 3.$

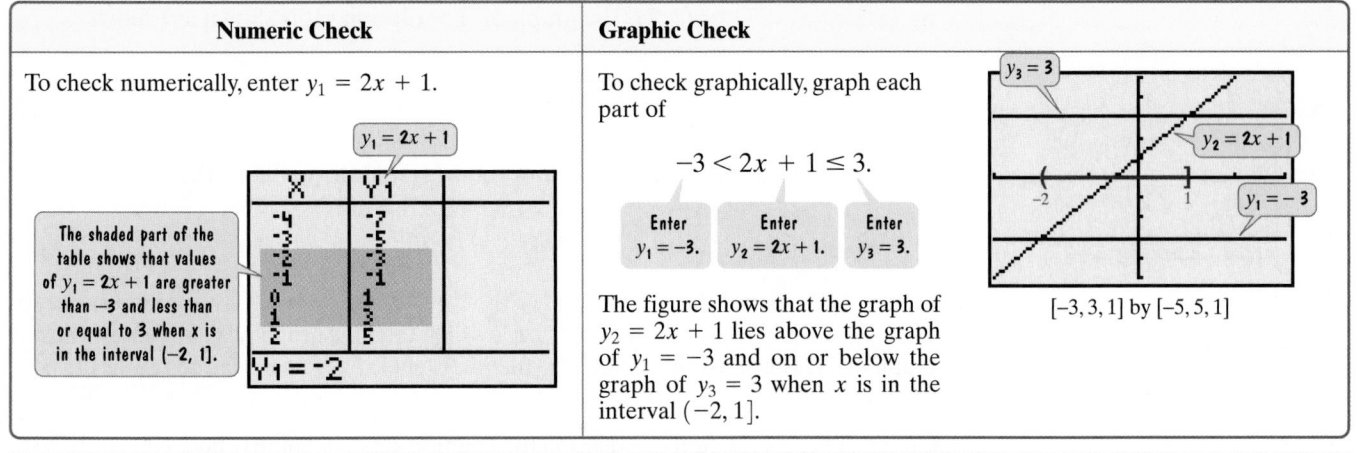

Numeric Check	Graphic Check
To check numerically, enter $y_1 = 2x + 1$.	To check graphically, graph each part of
	$$-3 < 2x + 1 \le 3.$$
The shaded part of the table shows that values of $y_1 = 2x + 1$ are greater than -3 and less than or equal to 3 when *x* is in the interval $(-2, 1]$.	Enter $y_1 = -3$. Enter $y_2 = 2x + 1$. Enter $y_3 = 3$.
	The figure shows that the graph of $y_2 = 2x + 1$ lies above the graph of $y_1 = -3$ and on or below the graph of $y_3 = 3$ when *x* is in the interval $(-2, 1]$.

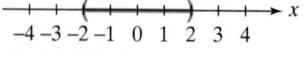 Solve absolute value inequalities.

Solving Inequalities with Absolute Value

We know that $|x|$ describes the distance of x from zero on a real number line. We can use this geometric interpretation to solve an inequality such as

$$|x| < 2.$$

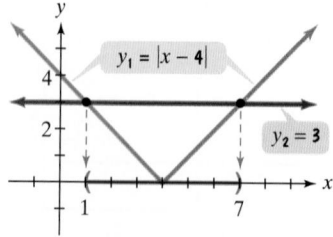

Figure 1.30 $|x| < 2$, so $-2 < x < 2$.

This means that the distance of x from 0 is *less than* 2, as shown in **Figure 1.30**. The interval shows values of x that lie less than 2 units from 0. Thus, x can lie between -2 and 2. That is, x is greater than -2 and less than 2. We write $(-2, 2)$ or $\{x | -2 < x < 2\}$.

Some absolute value inequalities use the "greater than" symbol. For example, $|x| > 2$ means that the distance of x from 0 is *greater than* 2, as shown in **Figure 1.31**. Thus, x can be less than -2 *or* greater than 2. We write $x < -2$ or $x > 2$. This can be expressed in interval notation as $(-\infty, -2) \cup (2, \infty)$.

Figure 1.31 $|x| > 2$, so $x < -2$ or $x > 2$.

These observations suggest the following principles for solving inequalities with absolute value.

Study Tip

In the $|u| < c$ case, we have one compound inequality to solve. In the $|u| > c$ case, we have two separate inequalities to solve.

Solving an Absolute Value Inequality

If u is an algebraic expression and c is a positive number,

1. The solutions of $|u| < c$ are the numbers that satisfy $-c < u < c$.
2. The solutions of $|u| > c$ are the numbers that satisfy $u < -c$ or $u > c$.

These rules are valid if $<$ is replaced by \le and $>$ is replaced by \ge.

EXAMPLE 8 Solving an Absolute Value Inequality

Solve and graph the solution set on a number line: $|x - 4| < 3$.

Solution We rewrite the inequality without absolute value bars.

$$|u| < c \text{ means } -c < u < c.$$

$$|x - 4| < 3 \quad \text{means} \quad -3 < x - 4 < 3.$$

We solve the compound inequality by adding 4 to all three parts.

$$-3 < x - 4 < 3$$
$$-3 + 4 < x - 4 + 4 < 3 + 4$$
$$1 < x < 7$$

The solution set consists of all real numbers greater than 1 and less than 7, denoted by $\{x | 1 < x < 7\}$ or $(1, 7)$. The graph of the solution set is shown as follows:

We can use the rectangular coordinate system to visualize the solution set of

$$|x - 4| < 3.$$

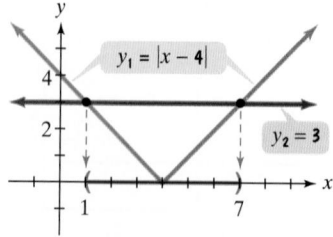

Figure 1.32 The solution set of $|x - 4| < 3$ is $(1, 7)$.

Figure 1.32 shows the graphs of $y_1 = |x - 4|$ and $y_2 = 3$. The solution set of $|x - 4| < 3$ consists of all values of x for which the blue graph of y_1 lies below the red graph of y_2. These x-values make up the interval $(1, 7)$, which is the solution set.

 Check Point **8** Solve and graph the solution set on a number line: $|x - 2| < 5$.

EXAMPLE 9 **Solving an Absolute Value Inequality**

Solve and graph the solution set on a number line: $-2|3x + 5| + 7 \geq -13$.

Solution

$$-2|3x + 5| + 7 \geq -13$$ This is the given inequality.

> We need to isolate $|3x + 5|$, the absolute value expression.

$$-2|3x + 5| + 7 - 7 \geq -13 - 7$$ Subtract 7 from both sides.

$$-2|3x + 5| \geq -20$$ Simplify.

$$\frac{-2|3x + 5|}{-2} \leq \frac{-20}{-2}$$ Divide both sides by -2 and change the sense of the inequality.

$$|3x + 5| \leq 10$$ Simplify.

$$-10 \leq 3x + 5 \leq 10$$ Rewrite without absolute value bars: $|u| \leq c$ means $-c \leq u \leq c$.

> Now we need to isolate x in the middle.

$$-10 - 5 \leq 3x + 5 - 5 \leq 10 - 5$$ Subtract 5 from all three parts.

$$-15 \leq 3x \leq 5$$ Simplify.

$$\frac{-15}{3} \leq \frac{3x}{3} \leq \frac{5}{3}$$ Divide each part by 3.

$$-5 \leq x \leq \frac{5}{3}$$ Simplify.

The solution set is $\left\{ x \mid -5 \leq x \leq \frac{5}{3} \right\}$ in set-builder notation and $\left[-5, \frac{5}{3} \right]$ in interval notation. The graph is shown as follows:

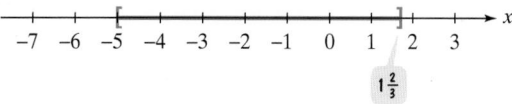

$1\frac{2}{3}$

Check Point 9 Solve and graph the solution set on a number line: $-3|5x - 2| + 20 \geq -19$.

EXAMPLE 10 **Solving an Absolute Value Inequality**

Solve and graph the solution set on a number line: $7 < |5 - 2x|$.

Solution We begin by expressing the inequality with the absolute value expression on the left side:

$$|5 - 2x| > 7.$$ $c < |u|$ means the same thing as $|u| > c$. In both cases, the inequality symbol points to c.

We rewrite this inequality without absolute value bars.

$$|u| > c \quad \text{means} \quad u < -c \quad \text{or} \quad u > c.$$

$|5 - 2x| > 7$ means $5 - 2x < -7$ or $5 - 2x > 7.$

Because $|5 - 2x| > 7$ means $5 - 2x < -7$ or $5 - 2x > 7$, we solve $5 - 2x < -7$ and $5 - 2x > 7$ separately. Then we take the union of their solution sets.

$5 - 2x < -7$ or $5 - 2x > 7$		These are the inequalities without absolute value bars.
$5 - 5 - 2x < -7 - 5$ $5 - 5 - 2x > 7 - 5$		Subtract 5 from both sides.
$-2x < -12$ $-2x > 2$		Simplify.
$\dfrac{-2x}{-2} > \dfrac{-12}{-2}$ $\dfrac{-2x}{-2} < \dfrac{2}{-2}$		Divide both sides by -2 and change the sense of each inequality.
$x > 6$ $x < -1$		Simplify.

The solution set consists of all numbers that are less than -1 or greater than 6. The solution set is $\{x \mid x < -1 \text{ or } x > 6\}$, or, in interval notation $(-\infty, -1) \cup (6, \infty)$. The graph of the solution set is shown as follows:

Study Tip

The graph of the solution set for $|u| > c$ will be divided into two intervals whose union cannot be represented as a single interval. The graph of the solution set for $|u| < c$ will be a single interval. Avoid the common error of rewriting $|u| > c$ as $-c < u > c$.

⊘ **Check Point 10** Solve and graph the solution set on a number line: $18 < |6 - 3x|$.

Applications

Our next example shows how to use an inequality to select the better deal between two pricing options. We use our strategy for solving word problems, modeling the verbal conditions of the problem with a linear inequality.

(**EXAMPLE 11**) **Selecting the Better Deal**

Acme Car rental agency charges \$4 a day plus \$0.15 per mile, whereas Interstate rental agency charges \$20 a day and \$0.05 per mile. How many miles must be driven to make the daily cost of an Acme rental a better deal than an Interstate rental?

Solution

Step 1 Let x represent one of the unknown quantities. We are looking for the number of miles that must be driven in a day to make Acme the better deal. Thus,

let $x = $ the number of miles driven in a day.

Step 2 Represent other unknown quantities in terms of x. We are not asked to find another quantity, so we can skip this step.

Step 3 Write an inequality in x that models the conditions. Acme is a better deal than Interstate if the daily cost of Acme is less than the daily cost of Interstate.

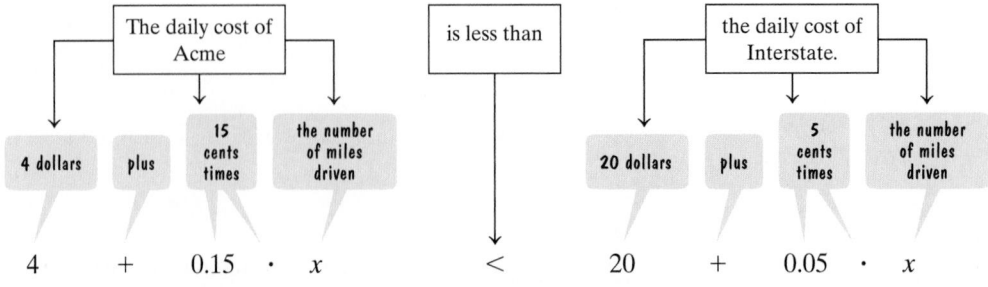

Technology

Graphic Connections

The graphs of the daily cost models for the car rental agencies

$$y_1 = 4 + 0.15x$$
$$\text{and } y_2 = 20 + 0.05x$$

are shown in a $[0, 300, 10]$ by $[0, 40, 4]$ viewing rectangle. The graphs intersect at $(160, 28)$.

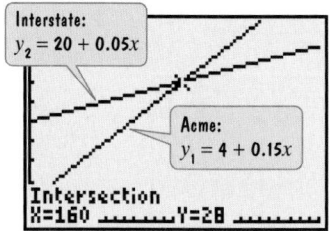

To the left of $x = 160$, the graph of Acme's daily cost lies below that of Interstate's daily cost. This shows that for fewer than 160 miles per day, Acme offers the better deal.

Step 4 Solve the inequality and answer the question.

$$4 + 0.15x < 20 + 0.05x \qquad \text{This is the inequality that models the verbal conditions.}$$

$$4 + 0.15x - 0.05x < 20 + 0.05x - 0.05x \qquad \text{Subtract 0.05x from both sides.}$$

$$4 + 0.1x < 20 \qquad \text{Simplify.}$$

$$4 + 0.1x - 4 < 20 - 4 \qquad \text{Subtract 4 from both sides.}$$

$$0.1x < 16 \qquad \text{Simplify.}$$

$$\frac{0.1x}{0.1} < \frac{16}{0.1} \qquad \text{Divide both sides by 0.1.}$$

$$x < 160 \qquad \text{Simplify.}$$

Thus, driving fewer than 160 miles per day makes Acme the better deal.

Step 5 Check the proposed solution in the original wording of the problem. One way to do this is to take a mileage less than 160 miles per day to see if Acme is the better deal. Suppose that 150 miles are driven in a day.

$$\text{Cost for Acme} = 4 + 0.15(150) = 26.50$$

$$\text{Cost for Interstate} = 20 + 0.05(150) = 27.50$$

Acme has a lower daily cost, making Acme the better deal. ●

☑ Check Point **11** A car can be rented from Basic Rental for $260 per week with no extra charge for mileage. Continental charges $80 per week plus 25 cents for each mile driven to rent the same car. How many miles must be driven in a week to make the rental cost for Basic Rental a better deal than Continental's?

Exercise Set 1.7

Practice Exercises

In Exercises 1–14, express each interval in set-builder notation and graph the interval on a number line.

1. $(1, 6]$
2. $(-2, 4]$
3. $[-5, 2)$
4. $[-4, 3)$
5. $[-3, 1]$
6. $[-2, 5]$
7. $(2, \infty)$
8. $(3, \infty)$
9. $[-3, \infty)$
10. $[-5, \infty)$
11. $(-\infty, 3)$
12. $(-\infty, 2)$
13. $(-\infty, 5.5)$
14. $(-\infty, 3.5]$

In Exercises 15–26, use graphs to find each set.

15. $(-3, 0) \cap [-1, 2]$
16. $(-4, 0) \cap [-2, 1]$
17. $(-3, 0) \cup [-1, 2]$
18. $(-4, 0) \cup [-2, 1]$
19. $(-\infty, 5) \cap [1, 8]$
20. $(-\infty, 6) \cap [2, 9)$
21. $(-\infty, 5) \cup [1, 8]$
22. $(-\infty, 6) \cup [2, 9)$
23. $[3, \infty) \cap (6, \infty)$
24. $[2, \infty) \cap (4, \infty)$
25. $[3, \infty) \cup (6, \infty)$
26. $[2, \infty) \cup (4, \infty)$

In all exercises, other than \varnothing, use interval notation to express solution sets and graph each solution set on a number line.

In Exercises 27–50, solve each linear inequality.

27. $5x + 11 < 26$
28. $2x + 5 < 17$
29. $3x - 7 \geq 13$
30. $8x - 2 \geq 14$
31. $-9x \geq 36$
32. $-5x \leq 30$

33. $8x - 11 \leq 3x - 13$
34. $18x + 45 \leq 12x - 8$
35. $4(x + 1) + 2 \geq 3x + 6$
36. $8x + 3 > 3(2x + 1) + x + 5$
37. $2x - 11 < -3(x + 2)$
38. $-4(x + 2) > 3x + 20$
39. $1 - (x + 3) \geq 4 - 2x$
40. $5(3 - x) \leq 3x - 1$
41. $\dfrac{x}{4} - \dfrac{3}{2} \leq \dfrac{x}{2} + 1$
42. $\dfrac{3x}{10} + 1 \geq \dfrac{1}{5} - \dfrac{x}{10}$
43. $1 - \dfrac{x}{2} > 4$
44. $7 - \dfrac{4}{5}x < \dfrac{3}{5}$
45. $\dfrac{x - 4}{6} \geq \dfrac{x - 2}{9} + \dfrac{5}{18}$
46. $\dfrac{4x - 3}{6} + 2 \geq \dfrac{2x - 1}{12}$
47. $4(3x - 2) - 3x < 3(1 + 3x) - 7$
48. $3(x - 8) - 2(10 - x) > 5(x - 1)$
49. $5(x - 2) - 3(x + 4) \geq 2x - 20$
50. $6(x - 1) - (4 - x) \geq 7x - 8$

In Exercises 51–58, solve each compound inequality.

51. $6 < x + 3 < 8$
52. $7 < x + 5 < 11$
53. $-3 \leq x - 2 < 1$
54. $-6 < x - 4 \leq 1$
55. $-11 < 2x - 1 \leq -5$
56. $3 \leq 4x - 3 < 19$
57. $-3 \leq \dfrac{2}{3}x - 5 < -1$
58. $-6 \leq \dfrac{1}{2}x - 4 < -3$

In Exercises 59–94, solve each absolute value inequality.

59. $|x| < 3$
60. $|x| < 5$

61. $|x - 1| \le 2$

62. $|x + 3| \le 4$

63. $|2x - 6| < 8$

64. $|3x + 5| < 17$

65. $|2(x - 1) + 4| \le 8$

66. $|3(x - 1) + 2| \le 20$

67. $\left|\dfrac{2x + 6}{3}\right| < 2$

68. $\left|\dfrac{3(x - 1)}{4}\right| < 6$

69. $|x| > 3$

70. $|x| > 5$

71. $|x - 1| \ge 2$

72. $|x + 3| \ge 4$

73. $|3x - 8| > 7$

74. $|5x - 2| > 13$

75. $\left|\dfrac{2x + 2}{4}\right| \ge 2$

76. $\left|\dfrac{3x - 3}{9}\right| \ge 1$

77. $\left|3 - \dfrac{2}{3}x\right| > 5$

78. $\left|3 - \dfrac{3}{4}x\right| > 9$

79. $3|x - 1| + 2 \ge 8$

80. $5|2x + 1| - 3 \ge 9$

81. $-2|x - 4| \ge -4$

82. $-3|x + 7| \ge -27$

83. $-4|1 - x| < -16$

84. $-2|5 - x| < -6$

85. $3 \le |2x - 1|$

86. $9 \le |4x + 7|$

87. $5 > |4 - x|$

88. $2 > |11 - x|$

89. $1 < |2 - 3x|$

90. $4 < |2 - x|$

91. $12 < \left|-2x + \dfrac{6}{7}\right| + \dfrac{3}{7}$

92. $1 < \left|x - \dfrac{11}{3}\right| + \dfrac{7}{3}$

93. $4 + \left|3 - \dfrac{x}{3}\right| \ge 9$

94. $\left|2 - \dfrac{x}{2}\right| - 1 \le 1$

In Exercises 95–102, use interval notation to represent all values of x satisfying the given conditions.

95. $y_1 = \dfrac{x}{2} + 3$, $y_2 = \dfrac{x}{3} + \dfrac{5}{2}$, and $y_1 \le y_2$.

96. $y_1 = \dfrac{2}{3}(6x - 9) + 4$, $y_2 = 5x + 1$, and $y_1 > y_2$.

97. $y = 1 - (x + 3) + 2x$ and y is at least 4.

98. $y = 2x - 11 + 3(x + 2)$ and y is at most 0.

99. $y = |3x - 4| + 2$ and $y < 8$.

100. $y = |2x - 5| + 1$ and $y > 9$.

101. $y = 7 - \left|\dfrac{x}{2} + 2\right|$ and y is at most 4.

102. $y = 8 - |5x + 3|$ and y is at least 6.

Practice Plus

In Exercises 103–104, use the graph of $y = |4 - x|$ to solve each inequality.

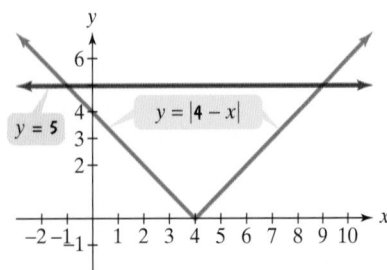

103. $|4 - x| < 5$

104. $|4 - x| \ge 5$

In Exercises 105–106, use the table to solve each inequality.

105. $-2 \le 5x + 3 < 13$

106. $-3 < 2x - 5 \le 3$

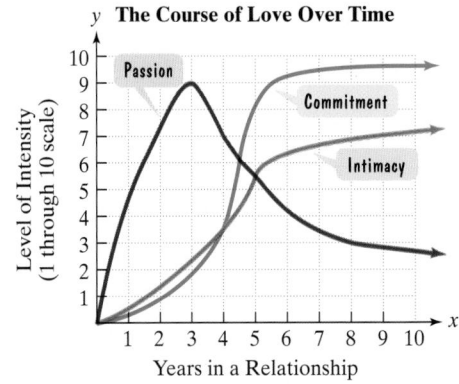

107. When 3 times a number is subtracted from 4, the absolute value of the difference is at least 5. Use interval notation to express the set of all numbers that satisfy this condition.

108. When 4 times a number is subtracted from 5, the absolute value of the difference is at most 13. Use interval notation to express the set of all numbers that satisfy this condition.

Application Exercises

The graphs show that the three components of love, namely passion, intimacy, and commitment, progress differently over time. Passion peaks early in a relationship and then declines. By contrast, intimacy and commitment build gradually. Use the graphs to solve Exercises 109–116.

The Course of Love Over Time

Source: R. J. Sternberg. A Triangular Theory of Love, *Psychological Review*, 93, 119–135.

109. Use interval notation to write an inequality that expresses for which years in a relationship intimacy is greater than commitment.

110. Use interval notation to write an inequality that expresses for which years in a relationship passion is greater than or equal to intimacy.

111. What is the relationship between passion and intimacy on the interval $[5, 7)$?

112. What is the relationship between intimacy and commitment on the interval $[4, 7)$?

113. What is the relationship between passion and commitment for $\{x | 6 < x < 8\}$?

114. What is the relationship between passion and commitment for $\{x | 7 < x < 9\}$?

115. What is the maximum level of intensity for passion? After how many years in a relationship does this occur?

116. After approximately how many years do levels of intensity for commitment exceed the maximum level of intensity for passion?

117. The percentage, P, of U.S. voters who used electronic voting systems, such as optical scans, in national elections can be modeled by the formula

$$P = 3.1x + 25.8,$$

where x is the number of years after 1994. In which years will more than 63% of U.S. voters use electronic systems?

118. The percentage, P, of U.S. voters who used punch cards or lever machines in national elections can be modeled by the formula

$$P = -2.5x + 63.1,$$

where x is the number of years after 1994. In which years will fewer than 38.1% of U.S. voters use punch cards or lever machines?

119. A basic cellular phone plan costs $20 per month for 60 calling minutes. Additional time costs $0.40 per minute. The formula

$$C = 20 + 0.40(x - 60)$$

gives the monthly cost for this plan, C, for x calling minutes, where $x > 60$. How many calling minutes are possible for a monthly cost of at least $28 and at most $40?

120. The formula for converting Fahrenheit temperature, F, to Celsius temperature, C, is

$$C = \frac{5}{9}(F - 32).$$

If Celsius temperature ranges from 15° to 35°, inclusive, what is the range for the Fahrenheit temperature? Use interval notation to express this range.

121. If a coin is tossed 100 times, we would expect approximately 50 of the outcomes to be heads. It can be demonstrated that a coin is unfair if h, the number of outcomes that result in heads, satisfies $\left| \dfrac{h - 50}{5} \right| \geq 1.645$. Describe the number of outcomes that determine an unfair coin that is tossed 100 times.

In Exercises 122–133, use the strategy for solving word problems, modeling the verbal conditions of the problem with a linear inequality.

122. A truck can be rented from Basic Rental for $50 per day plus $0.20 per mile. Continental charges $20 per day plus $0.50 per mile to rent the same truck. How many miles must be driven in a day to make the rental cost for Basic Rental a better deal than Continental's?

123. You are choosing between two long-distance telephone plans. Plan A has a monthly fee of $15 with a charge of $0.08 per minute for all long-distance calls. Plan B has a monthly fee of $3 with a charge of $0.12 per minute for all long-distance calls. How many minutes of long-distance calls in a month make plan A the better deal?

124. A city commission has proposed two tax bills. The first bill requires that a homeowner pay $1800 plus 3% of the assessed home value in taxes. The second bill requires taxes of $200 plus 8% of the assessed home value. What price range of home assessment would make the first bill a better deal?

125. A local bank charges $8 per month plus 5¢ per check. The credit union charges $2 per month plus 8¢ per check. How many checks should be written each month to make the credit union a better deal?

126. A company manufactures and sells blank audiocassette tapes. The weekly fixed cost is $10,000 and it costs $0.40 to produce each tape. The selling price is $2.00 per tape. How many tapes must be produced and sold each week for the company to generate a profit?

127. A company manufactures and sells personalized stationery. The weekly fixed cost is $3000 and it costs $3.00 to produce each package of stationery. The selling price is $5.50 per package. How many packages of stationery must be produced and sold each week for the company to generate a profit?

128. An elevator at a construction site has a maximum capacity of 2800 pounds. If the elevator operator weighs 265 pounds and each cement bag weighs 65 pounds, how many bags of cement can be safely lifted on the elevator in one trip?

129. An elevator at a construction site has a maximum capacity of 3000 pounds. If the elevator operator weighs 245 pounds and each cement bag weighs 95 pounds, how many bags of cement can be safely lifted on the elevator in one trip?

130. To earn an A in a course, you must have a final average of at least 90%. On the first four examinations, you have grades of 86%, 88%, 92%, and 84%. If the final examination counts as two grades, what must you get on the final to earn an A in the course?

131. On two examinations, you have grades of 86 and 88. There is an optional final examination, which counts as one grade. You decide to take the final in order to get a course grade of A, meaning a final average of at least 90.

 a. What must you get on the final to earn an A in the course?

 b. By taking the final, if you do poorly, you might risk the B that you have in the course based on the first two exam grades. If your final average is less than 80, you will lose your B in the course. Describe the grades on the final that will cause this to happen.

132. Parts for an automobile repair cost $175. The mechanic charges $34 per hour. If you receive an estimate for at least $226 and at most $294 for fixing the car, what is the time interval that the mechanic will be working on the job?

133. The toll to a bridge is $3.00. A three-month pass costs $7.50 and reduces the toll to $0.50. A six-month pass costs $30 and permits crossing the bridge for no additional fee. How many crossings per three-month period does it take for the three-month pass to be the best deal?

Writing in Mathematics

134. When graphing the solutions of an inequality, what does a parenthesis signify? What does a square bracket signify?

135. Describe ways in which solving a linear inequality is similar to solving a linear equation.

136. Describe ways in which solving a linear inequality is different than solving a linear equation.

137. What is a compound inequality and how is it solved?

138. Describe how to solve an absolute value inequality involving the symbol $<$. Give an example.

139. Describe how to solve an absolute value inequality involving the symbol $>$. Give an example.

140. Explain why $|x| < -4$ has no solution.

141. Describe the solution set of $|x| > -4$.

Technology Exercises

In Exercises 142–143, solve each inequality using a graphing utility. Graph each side separately. Then determine the values of x for which the graph for the left side lies above the graph for the right side.

142. $-3(x - 6) > 2x - 2$ **143.** $-2(x + 4) > 6x + 16$

144. Use a graphing utility's [TABLE] feature to verify your work in Exercises 142–143.

145. A bank offers two checking account plans. Plan A has a base service charge of $4.00 per month plus 10¢ per check. Plan B charges a base service charge of $2.00 per month plus 15¢ per check.

 a. Write models for the total monthly costs for each plan if x checks are written.

 b. Use a graphing utility to graph the models in the same [0, 50, 10] by [0, 10, 1] viewing rectangle.

 c. Use the graphs (and the intersection feature) to determine for what number of checks per month plan A will be better than plan B.

 d. Verify the result of part (c) algebraically by solving an inequality.

Critical Thinking Exercises

Make Sense? *In Exercises 146–149, determine whether each statement makes sense or does not make sense, and explain your reasoning.*

146. I prefer interval notation over set-builder notation because it takes less space to write solution sets.

147. I can check inequalities by substituting 0 for the variable: When 0 belongs to the solution set, I should obtain a true statement, and when 0 does not belong to the solution set, I should obtain a false statement.

148. In an inequality such as $5x + 4 < 8x - 5$, I can avoid division by a negative number depending on which side I collect the variable terms and on which side I collect the constant terms.

149. I'll win the contest if I can complete the crossword puzzle in 20 minutes plus or minus 5 minutes, so my winning time, x, is modeled by $|x - 20| \le 5$.

In Exercises 150–153, determine whether each statement is true or false. If the statement is false, make the necessary change(s) to produce a true statement.

150. $(-\infty, -1] \cap [-4, \infty) = [-4, -1]$

151. $(-\infty, 3) \cup (-\infty, -2) = (-\infty, -2)$

152. The inequality $3x > 6$ is equivalent to $2 > x$.

153. All irrational numbers satisfy $|x - 4| > 0$.

154. What's wrong with this argument? Suppose x and y represent two real numbers, where $x > y$.

$2 > 1$	This is a true statement.
$2(y - x) > 1(y - x)$	Multiply both sides by $y - x$.
$2y - 2x > y - x$	Use the distributive property.
$y - 2x > -x$	Subtract y from both sides.
$y > x$	Add $2x$ to both sides.

The final inequality, $y > x$, is impossible because we were initially given $x > y$.

155. Write an absolute value inequality for which the interval shown is the solution.

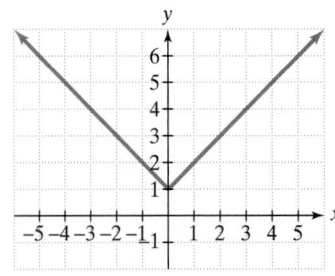

Group Exercise

156. Each group member should research one situation that provides two different pricing options. These can involve areas such as public transportation options (with or without discount passes), cell phone plans, long-distance telephone plans, or anything of interest. Be sure to bring in all the details for each option. At a second group meeting, select the two pricing situations that are most interesting and relevant. Using each situation, write a word problem about selecting the better of the two options. The word problem should be one that can be solved using a linear inequality. The group should turn in the two problems and their solutions.

Preview Exercises

Exercises 157–159 will help you prepare for the material covered in the first section of the next chapter.

157. Here are two sets of ordered pairs:

$$\text{set 1: } \{(1, 5), (2, 5)\}$$
$$\text{set 2: } \{(5, 1), (5, 2)\}.$$

In which set is each x-coordinate paired with only one y-coordinate?

158. Graph $y = 2x$ and $y = 2x + 4$ in the same rectangular coordinate system. Select integers for x, starting with -2 and ending with 2.

159. Use the following graph to solve this exercise.

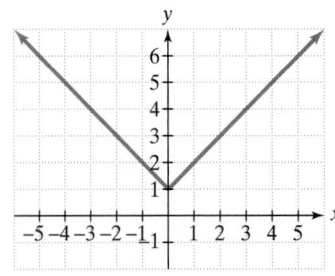

 a. What is the y-coordinate when the x-coordinate is 2?

 b. What are the x-coordinates when the y-coordinate is 4?

 c. Describe the x-coordinates of all points on the graph.

 d. Describe the y-coordinates of all points on the graph.

Chapter 1 Summary, Review, and Test

DEFINITIONS AND CONCEPTS	EXAMPLES

1.1 Graphs and Graphing Utilities

a. The rectangular coordinate system consists of a horizontal number line, the x-axis, and a vertical number line, the y-axis, intersecting at their zero points, the origin. Each point in the system corresponds to an ordered pair of real numbers (x, y). The first number in the pair is the x-coordinate; the second number is the y-coordinate. See Figure 1.1 on page 90.

Ex. 1, p. 91

b. An ordered pair is a solution of an equation in two variables if replacing the variables by the corresponding coordinates results in a true statement. The ordered pair is said to satisfy the equation. The graph of the equation is the set of all points whose coordinates satisfy the equation. One method for graphing an equation is to plot ordered-pair solutions and connect them with a smooth curve or line.

Ex. 2, p. 92;
Ex. 3, p. 92

c. An x-intercept of a graph is the x-coordinate of a point where the graph intersects the x-axis. The y-coordinate corresponding to an x-intercept is always zero.

A y-intercept of a graph is the y-coordinate of a point where the graph intersects the y-axis. The x-coordinate corresponding to a y-intercept is always zero.

Ex. 5, p. 95

1.2 Linear Equations and Rational Equations

a. A linear equation in one variable x can be written in the form $ax + b = 0, a \neq 0$.

b. The procedure for solving a linear equation is given in the box on page 104.

Ex. 1, p. 103;
Ex. 2, p. 104

c. If an equation contains fractions, begin by multiplying both sides by the least common denominator, thereby clearing fractions.

Ex. 3, p. 105

d. A rational equation is an equation containing one or more rational expressions. If an equation contains rational expressions with variable denominators, avoid in the solution set any values of the variable that make a denominator zero.

Ex. 4, p. 107;
Ex. 5, p. 107;
Ex. 6, p. 108

e. An identity is an equation that is true for all real numbers for which both sides are defined. A conditional equation is not an identity and is true for at least one real number. An inconsistent equation is an equation that is not true for even one real number.

Ex. 7, p. 110

1.3 Models and Applications

a. A five-step procedure for solving word problems using equations that model verbal conditions is given in the box on page 117.

Ex. 1, p. 117;
Ex. 2, p. 118;
Ex. 3, p. 120;
Ex. 4, p. 121;
Ex. 5, p. 122;
Ex. 6, p. 123

b. Solving a formula for a variable means rewriting the formula so that the specified variable is isolated on one side of the equation.

Ex. 7, p. 125;
Ex. 8, p. 125

1.4 Complex Numbers

a. The imaginary unit i is defined as

$$i = \sqrt{-1}, \text{ where } i^2 = -1.$$

The set of numbers in the form $a + bi$ is called the set of complex numbers; a is the real part and b is the imaginary part. If $b = 0$, the complex number is a real number. If $b \neq 0$, the complex number is an imaginary number. Complex numbers in the form bi are called pure imaginary numbers.

b. Rules for adding and subtracting complex numbers are given in the box on page 131.

Ex. 1, p. 131

c. To multiply complex numbers, multiply as if they are polynomials. After completing the multiplication, replace i^2 with -1 and simplify.

Ex. 2, p. 132

DEFINITIONS AND CONCEPTS	EXAMPLES

d. The complex conjugate of $a + bi$ is $a - bi$ and vice versa. The multiplication of complex conjugates gives a real number:

$$(a + bi)(a - bi) = a^2 + b^2.$$

e. To divide complex numbers, multiply the numerator and the denominator by the complex conjugate of the denominator.	Ex. 3, p. 133
f. When performing operations with square roots of negative numbers, begin by expressing all square roots in terms of i. The principal square root of $-b$ is defined by $$\sqrt{-b} = i\sqrt{b}.$$	Ex. 4, p. 134

1.5 Quadratic Equations

a. A quadratic equation in x can be written in the general form $ax^2 + bx + c = 0, a \neq 0$.	
b. The procedure for solving a quadratic equation by factoring and the zero-product principle is given in the box on page 137.	Ex. 1, p. 137
c. The procedure for solving a quadratic equation by the square root property is given in the box on page 139.	Ex. 2, p. 139
d. All quadratic equations can be solved by completing the square. Isolate the binomial with the two variable terms on one side of the equation. If the coefficient of the x^2-term is not one, divide each side of the equation by this coefficient. Then add the square of half the coefficient of x to both sides.	Ex. 4, p. 142; Ex. 5, p. 142
e. All quadratic equations can be solved by the quadratic formula $$x = \frac{-b \pm \sqrt{b^2 - 4ac}}{2a}.$$ The formula is derived by completing the square of the equation $ax^2 + bx + c = 0$.	Ex. 6, p. 144; Ex. 7, p. 145
f. The discriminant, $b^2 - 4ac$, indicates the number and type of solutions to the quadratic equation $ax^2 + bx + c = 0$, shown in Table 1.2 on page 146.	Ex. 8, p. 146
g. Table 1.3 on page 148 shows the most efficient technique to use when solving a quadratic equation.	Ex. 9, p. 149; Ex. 10, p. 150

1.6 Other Types of Equations

a. Some polynomial equations of degree 3 or greater can be solved by moving all terms to one side, obtaining zero on the other side, factoring, and using the zero-product principle. Factoring by grouping is often used.	Ex. 1, p. 158; Ex. 2, p. 159		
b. A radical equation is an equation in which the variable occurs in a square root, a cube root, and so on. A radical equation can be solved by isolating the radical and raising both sides of the equation to a power equal to the radical's index. When raising both sides to an even power, check all proposed solutions in the original equation. Eliminate extraneous solutions from the solution set.	Ex. 3, p. 160; Ex. 4, p. 162		
c. A radical equation with a rational exponent can be solved by isolating the expression with the rational exponent and raising both sides of the equation to a power that is the reciprocal of the rational exponent. See the details in the box on page 163.	Ex. 5, p. 163		
d. An equation is quadratic in form if it can be written in the form $au^2 + bu + c = 0$, where u is an algebraic expression and $a \neq 0$. Solve for u and use the substitution that resulted in this equation to find the values for the variable in the given equation.	Ex. 6, p. 165; Ex. 7, p. 166		
e. Absolute value equations in the form $	u	= c, c > 0$, can be solved by rewriting the equation without absolute value bars: $u = c$ or $u = -c$.	Ex. 8, p. 167; Ex. 9, p. 167

1.7 Linear Inequalities and Absolute Value Inequalities

a. Solution sets of inequalities are expressed using set-builder notation and interval notation. In interval notation, parentheses indicate endpoints that are not included in an interval. Square brackets indicate endpoints that are included in an interval. See Table 1.4 on page 174.	Ex. 1, p. 174

DEFINITIONS AND CONCEPTS	EXAMPLES
b. A procedure for finding intersections and unions of intervals is given in the box on page 175.	Ex. 2, p. 175
c. A linear inequality in one variable x can be expressed as $ax + b \le 0, ax + b < 0, ax + b \ge 0,$ or $ax + b > 0, a \ne 0.$	
d. A linear inequality is solved using a procedure similar to solving a linear equation. However, when multiplying or dividing by a negative number, change the sense of the inequality.	Ex. 3, p. 177; Ex. 4, p. 177; Ex. 5, p. 179
e. A compound inequality with three parts can be solved by isolating the variable in the middle.	Ex. 7, p. 181
f. Inequalities involving absolute value can be solved by rewriting the inequalities without absolute value bars. The ways to do this are shown in the box on page 182.	Ex. 8, p. 182; Ex. 9, p. 183; Ex. 10, p. 183

Review Exercises

1.1

Graph each equation in Exercises 1–4. Let $x = -3, -2, -1, 0, 1, 2,$ and 3.

1. $y = 2x - 2$　　　　　**2.** $y = x^2 - 3$

3. $y = x$　　　　　　　**4.** $y = |x| - 2$

5. What does a $[-20, 40, 10]$ by $[-5, 5, 1]$ viewing rectangle mean? Draw axes with tick marks and label the tick marks to illustrate this viewing rectangle.

In Exercises 6–8, use the graph and determine the x-intercepts, if any, and the y-intercepts, if any. For each graph, tick marks along the axes represent one unit each.

6.

7.

8.

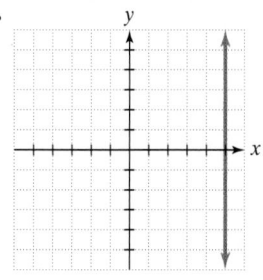

The line graph shows the top marginal income tax rates in the United States from 1925 through 2005. Use the graph to solve Exercises 9–14.

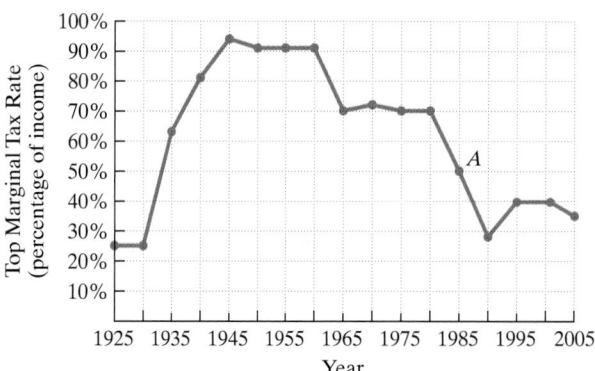

Top United States Marginal Tax Rates, 1925–2005

Source: National Taxpayers Union

9. What are the coordinates of point A? What does this mean in terms of the information given by the graph?

10. Estimate the top marginal tax rate in 2005.

11. For the period shown, during which year did the United States have the highest marginal tax rate? Estimate, to the nearest percent, the tax rate for that year.

12. For the period from 1950 through 2005, during which year did the United States have the lowest marginal tax rate? Estimate, to the nearest percent, the tax rate for that year.

13. For the period shown, during which ten-year period did the top marginal tax rate remain constant? Estimate, to the nearest percent, the tax rate for that period.

14. For the period shown, during which five-year period did the top marginal tax rate increase most rapidly? Estimate, to the nearest percent, the increase in the top tax rate for that period.

1.2

In Exercises 15–35, solve each equation. Then state whether the equation is an identity, a conditional equation, or an inconsistent equation.

15. $2x - 5 = 7$　　　　　**16.** $5x + 20 = 3x$

17. $7(x - 4) = x + 2$ **18.** $1 - 2(6 - x) = 3x + 2$

19. $2(x - 4) + 3(x + 5) = 2x - 2$

20. $2x - 4(5x + 1) = 3x + 17$

21. $7x + 5 = 5(x + 3) + 2x$

22. $7x + 13 = 2(2x - 5) + 3x + 23$

23. $\dfrac{2x}{3} = \dfrac{x}{6} + 1$ **24.** $\dfrac{x}{2} - \dfrac{1}{10} = \dfrac{x}{5} + \dfrac{1}{2}$

25. $\dfrac{2x}{3} = 6 - \dfrac{x}{4}$ **26.** $\dfrac{x}{4} = 2 - \dfrac{x - 3}{3}$

27. $\dfrac{3x + 1}{3} - \dfrac{13}{2} = \dfrac{1 - x}{4}$ **28.** $\dfrac{9}{4} - \dfrac{1}{2x} = \dfrac{4}{x}$

29. $\dfrac{7}{x - 5} + 2 = \dfrac{x + 2}{x - 5}$ **30.** $\dfrac{1}{x - 1} - \dfrac{1}{x + 1} = \dfrac{2}{x^2 - 1}$

31. $\dfrac{5}{x + 3} + \dfrac{1}{x - 2} = \dfrac{8}{x^2 + x - 6}$

32. $\dfrac{1}{x + 5} = 0$ **33.** $\dfrac{4}{x + 2} + \dfrac{3}{x} = \dfrac{10}{x^2 + 2x}$

34. $3 - 5(2x + 1) - 2(x - 4) = 0$

35. $\dfrac{x + 2}{x + 3} + \dfrac{1}{x^2 + 2x - 3} - 1 = 0$

1.3

In Exercises 36–43, use the five-step strategy for solving word problems.

36. The bar graph represents the millions of barrels of oil consumed each day by the countries with the greatest oil consumption.

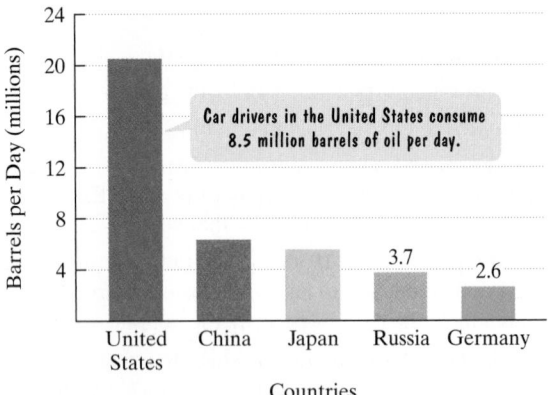

Countries with the Greatest Oil Consumption

Source: U.S. Energy Information Administration

Oil consumption in China exceeds Japan's by 0.8 million barrels per day, and oil consumption in the United States exceeds Japan's by 15 million barrels per day. Of the 82 million barrels of oil used by the world every day, the combined consumption for the United States, China, and Japan is 32.3 million barrels. Determine the daily oil consumption, in millions of barrels, for the United States, China, and Japan.

37. The line graph indicates that in 2000, 17.5% of people in the United States spoke a language other than English at home. For the period from 2000 through 2005, this had been increasing by approximately 0.4% per year. If this trend continues, by which year will 25.1% of people in the United States speak a language other than English at home?

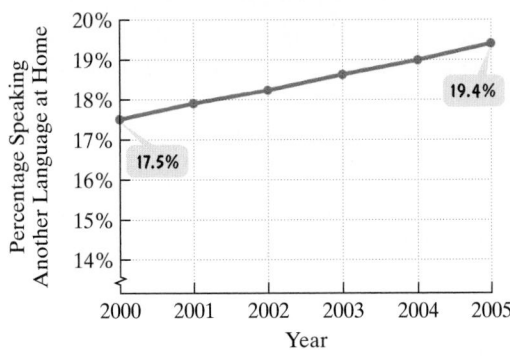

Percentage of People in the United States Speaking a Language Other Than English at Home

Source: U.S. Census Bureau

38. You are choosing between two long-distance telephone plans. One plan has a monthly fee of $15 with a charge of $0.05 per minute. The other plan has a monthly fee of $5 with a charge of $0.07 per minute. For how many minutes of long-distance calls will the costs for the two plans be the same?

39. After a 20% price reduction, a cordless phone sold for $48. What was the phone's price before the reduction?

40. A salesperson earns $300 per week plus 5% commission of sales. How much must be sold to earn $800 in a week?

41. You invested $9000 in two funds paying 4% and 7% annual interest. At the end of the year, the total interest from these investments was $555. How much was invested at each rate?

42. You invested $8000 in two funds paying 2% and 5% annual interest. At the end of the year, the interest from the 5% investment exceeded the interest from the 2% investment by $85. How much money was invested at each rate?

43. The length of a rectangular field is 6 yards less than triple the width. If the perimeter of the field is 340 yards, what are its dimensions?

44. In 2009, there were 14,100 students at college A, with a projected enrollment increase of 1500 students per year. In the same year, there were 41,700 students at college B, with a projected enrollment decline of 800 students per year.

a. Let x represent the number of years after 2009. Write, but do not solve, an equation that can be used to find how many years after 2009 the colleges will have the same enrollment.

b. The following table is based on your equation in part (a). Y_1 represents one side of the equation and Y_2 represents

the other side of the equation. Use the table to answer the following questions: In which year will the colleges have the same enrollment? What will be the enrollment in each college at that time?

X	Y₁	Y₂
7	24600	36100
8	26100	35300
9	27600	34500
10	29100	33700
11	30600	32900
12	32100	32100
13	33600	31300

X=7

In Exercises 45–47, solve each formula for the specified variable.

45. $vt + gt^2 = s$ for g **46.** $T = gr + gvt$ for g

47. $T = \dfrac{A - P}{Pr}$ for P

1.4

In Exercises 48–57, perform the indicated operations and write the result in standard form.

48. $(8 - 3i) - (17 - 7i)$ **49.** $4i(3i - 2)$

50. $(7 - i)(2 + 3i)$ **51.** $(3 - 4i)^2$

52. $(7 + 8i)(7 - 8i)$ **53.** $\dfrac{6}{5 + i}$

54. $\dfrac{3 + 4i}{4 - 2i}$ **55.** $\sqrt{-32} - \sqrt{-18}$

56. $\left(-2 + \sqrt{-100}\right)^2$ **57.** $\dfrac{4 + \sqrt{-8}}{2}$

1.5

Solve each equation in Exercises 58–59 by factoring.

58. $2x^2 + 15x = 8$ **59.** $5x^2 + 20x = 0$

Solve each equation in Exercises 60–63 by the square root property.

60. $2x^2 - 3 = 125$ **61.** $\dfrac{x^2}{2} + 5 = -3$

62. $(x + 3)^2 = -10$ **63.** $(3x - 4)^2 = 18$

In Exercises 64–65, determine the constant that should be added to the binomial so that it becomes a perfect square trinomial. Then write and factor the trinomial.

64. $x^2 + 20x$ **65.** $x^2 - 3x$

Solve each equation in Exercises 66–67 by completing the square.

66. $x^2 - 12x + 27 = 0$ **67.** $3x^2 - 12x + 11 = 0$

Solve each equation in Exercises 68–70 using the quadratic formula.

68. $x^2 = 2x + 4$ **69.** $x^2 - 2x + 19 = 0$

70. $2x^2 = 3 - 4x$

In Exercises 71–72, without solving the given quadratic equation, determine the number and type of solutions.

71. $x^2 - 4x + 13 = 0$ **72.** $9x^2 = 2 - 3x$

Solve each equation in Exercises 73–81 by the method of your choice.

73. $2x^2 - 11x + 5 = 0$ **74.** $(3x + 5)(x - 3) = 5$

75. $3x^2 - 7x + 1 = 0$ **76.** $x^2 - 9 = 0$

77. $(x - 3)^2 - 25 = 0$ **78.** $3x^2 - x + 2 = 0$

79. $3x^2 - 10x = 8$ **80.** $(x + 2)^2 + 4 = 0$

81. $\dfrac{5}{x + 1} + \dfrac{x - 1}{4} = 2$

82. The formula $W = 3t^2$ models the weight of a human fetus, W, in grams, after t weeks, where $0 \leq t \leq 39$. After how many weeks does the fetus weigh 588 grams?

83. By 2007, cellphones with 2-gigabyte storage cards could hold 2000 songs. The bar graph shows the percentage of new cellphones that played music from 2005 through 2007, with projections for 2008 and 2009.

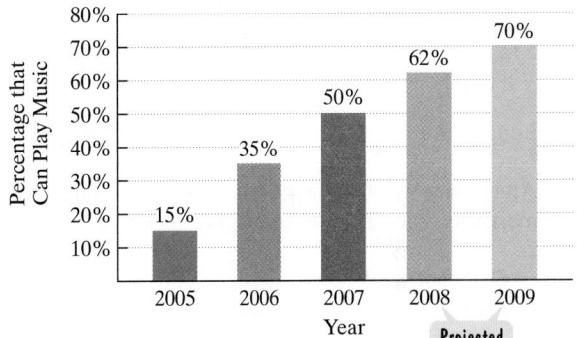

Percentage of New Cellphones That Play Music

Source: Ovum

The formula

$$M = -1.8x^2 + 21x + 15$$

models the percentage of new cellphones that play music, M, x years after 2005.

a. Use the formula to find the percentage of new cellphones that will play music in 2009. Does this overestimate or underestimate the percentage shown by the graph? By how much?

b. Use the formula to determine the first year in which 75% of new cellphones will play music.

84. An architect is allowed 15 square yards of floor space to add a small bedroom to a house. Because of the room's design in relationship to the existing structure, the width of the rectangular floor must be 7 yards less than two times the length. Find the length and width of the rectangular floor that the architect is permitted.

85. A building casts a shadow that is double the height of the building. If the distance from the end of the shadow to the top of the building is 300 meters, how high is the building? Round to the nearest meter.

1.6

Solve each polynomial equation in Exercises 86–87.

86. $2x^4 = 50x^2$

87. $2x^3 - x^2 - 18x + 9 = 0$

Solve each radical equation in Exercises 88–89.

88. $\sqrt{2x - 3} + x = 3$

89. $\sqrt{x - 4} + \sqrt{x + 1} = 5$

Solve the equations with rational exponents in Exercises 90–91.

90. $3x^{\frac{3}{4}} - 24 = 0$

91. $(x - 7)^{\frac{2}{3}} = 25$

Solve each equation in Exercises 92–93 by making an appropriate substitution.

92. $x^4 - 5x^2 + 4 = 0$

93. $x^{\frac{1}{2}} + 3x^{\frac{1}{4}} - 10 = 0$

Solve the equations containing absolute value in Exercises 94–95.

94. $|2x + 1| = 7$

95. $2|x - 3| - 6 = 10$

Solve each equation in Exercises 96–102 by the method of your choice.

96. $3x^{\frac{4}{3}} - 5x^{\frac{2}{3}} + 2 = 0$

97. $2\sqrt{x - 1} = x$

98. $|2x - 5| - 3 = 0$

99. $x^3 + 2x^2 = 9x + 18$

100. $\sqrt{2x + 3} - x = 0$

101. $x^3 + 3x^2 - 2x - 6 = 0$

102. $-4|x + 1| + 12 = 0$

103. Long before the passage of laws prohibiting marriage between people of the same sex, a substantial percentage of Americans were in favor of laws prohibiting interracial marriage. Since 1972, the General Social Survey has asked

> Do you think that there should be laws against marriages between negroes/blacks/African Americans and whites?

In 1972, 39.3% of the adult U.S. population was in favor of such laws. The bar graph shows the percentage of Americans in favor of legislation prohibiting interracial marriage for five selected years from 1993 through 2002.

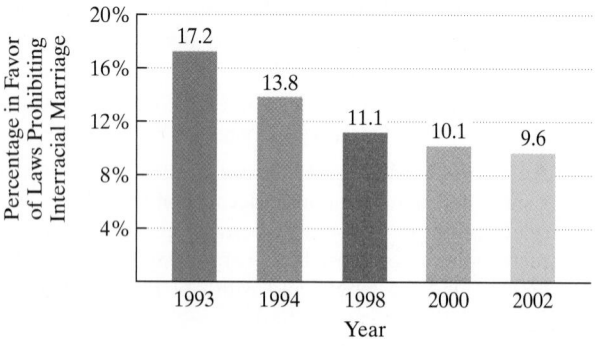

Percentage of Americans in Favor of Laws Prohibiting Interracial Marriage

Source: Ben Schott, *Schott's Almanac 2007,* Donnelley and Sons

The formula

$$p = -2.5\sqrt{t} + 17$$

models the percentage of Americans, p, in favor of laws prohibiting interracial marriage t years after 1993. If trends indicated by this model continue, in what year will the percentage favoring such legislation decrease to 7%?

1.7

In Exercises 104–106, express each interval in set-builder notation and graph the interval on a number line.

104. $[-3, 5)$

105. $(-2, \infty)$

106. $(-\infty, 0]$

In Exercises 107–110, use graphs to find each set.

107. $(-2, 1] \cap [-1, 3)$

108. $(-2, 1] \cup [-1, 3)$

109. $[1, 3) \cap (0, 4)$

110. $[1, 3) \cup (0, 4)$

In Exercises 111–121, solve each inequality. Other than \varnothing, use interval notation to express solution sets and graph each solution set on a number line.

111. $-6x + 3 \le 15$

112. $6x - 9 \ge -4x - 3$

113. $\dfrac{x}{3} - \dfrac{3}{4} - 1 > \dfrac{x}{2}$

114. $6x + 5 > -2(x - 3) - 25$

115. $3(2x - 1) - 2(x - 4) \ge 7 + 2(3 + 4x)$

116. $5(x - 2) - 3(x + 4) \ge 2x - 20$

117. $7 < 2x + 3 \le 9$

118. $|2x + 3| \le 15$

119. $\left| \dfrac{2x + 6}{3} \right| > 2$

120. $|2x + 5| - 7 \ge -6$

121. $-4|x + 2| + 5 \le -7$

In Exercises 122–123, use interval notation to represent all values of x satisfying the given conditions.

122. $y_1 = -10 - 3(2x + 1)$, $y_2 = 8x + 1$, and $y_1 > y_2$.

123. $y = 3 - |2x - 5|$ and y is at least -6.

124. A car rental agency rents a certain car for $40 per day with unlimited mileage or $24 per day plus $0.20 per mile. How far can a customer drive this car per day for the $24 option to cost no more than the unlimited mileage option?

125. To receive a B in a course, you must have an average of at least 80% but less than 90% on five exams. Your grades on the first four exams were 95%, 79%, 91%, and 86%. What range of grades on the fifth exam will result in a B for the course?

126. A retiree requires an annual income of at least $9000 from an investment paying 7.5% annual interest. How much should the retiree invest to achieve the desired return?

Chapter 1 TEST

In Exercises 1–23, solve each equation or inequality. Other than \varnothing, use interval notation to express solution sets of inequalities and graph these solution sets on a number line.

1. $7(x - 2) = 4(x + 1) - 21$

2. $-10 - 3(2x + 1) - 8x - 1 = 0$

3. $\dfrac{2x - 3}{4} = \dfrac{x - 4}{2} - \dfrac{x + 1}{4}$

4. $\dfrac{2}{x - 3} - \dfrac{4}{x + 3} = \dfrac{8}{x^2 - 9}$

5. $2x^2 - 3x - 2 = 0$ **6.** $(3x - 1)^2 = 75$

7. $(x + 3)^2 + 25 = 0$ **8.** $x(x - 2) = 4$

9. $4x^2 = 8x - 5$ **10.** $x^3 - 4x^2 - x + 4 = 0$

11. $\sqrt{x - 3} + 5 = x$ **12.** $\sqrt{8 - 2x} - x = 0$

13. $\sqrt{x + 4} + \sqrt{x - 1} = 5$ **14.** $5x^{\frac{3}{2}} - 10 = 0$

15. $x^{\frac{2}{3}} - 9x^{\frac{1}{3}} + 8 = 0$ **16.** $\left| \dfrac{2}{3}x - 6 \right| = 2$

17. $-3|4x - 7| + 15 = 0$ **18.** $\dfrac{1}{x^2} - \dfrac{4}{x} + 1 = 0$

19. $\dfrac{2x}{x^2 + 6x + 8} + \dfrac{2}{x + 2} = \dfrac{x}{x + 4}$

20. $3(x + 4) \geq 5x - 12$ **21.** $\dfrac{x}{6} + \dfrac{1}{8} \leq \dfrac{x}{2} - \dfrac{3}{4}$

22. $-3 \leq \dfrac{2x + 5}{3} < 6$ **23.** $|3x + 2| \geq 3$

In Exercises 24–25, use interval notation to represent all values of x satisfying the given conditions.

24. $y = 2x - 5$, and y is at least -3 and no more than 7.

25. $y = \left| \dfrac{2 - x}{4} \right|$ and y is at least 1.

In Exercises 26–27, use graphs to find each set.

26. $[-1, 2) \cup (0, 5]$ **27.** $[-1, 2) \cap (0, 5]$

In Exercises 28–29, solve each formula for the specified variable.

28. $V = \dfrac{1}{3}lwh$ for h **29.** $y - y_1 = m(x - x_1)$ for x

In Exercises 30–31, graph each equation in a rectangular coordinate system.

30. $y = 2 - |x|$ **31.** $y = x^2 - 4$

In Exercises 32–34, perform the indicated operations and write the result in standard form.

32. $(6 - 7i)(2 + 5i)$ **33.** $\dfrac{5}{2 - i}$

34. $2\sqrt{-49} + 3\sqrt{-64}$

The graphs show the amount being paid in Social Security benefits and the amount going into the system. All data are expressed in billions of dollars. Amounts from 2008 through 2024 are projections.

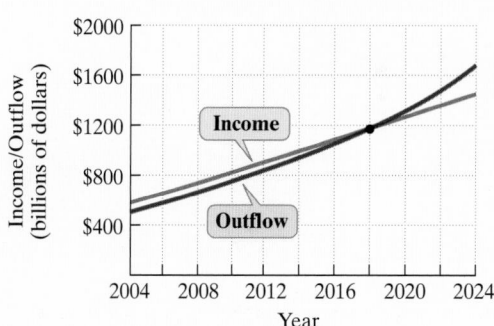

Social Insecurity: Income and Outflow of the Social Security System

Source: 2004 Social Security Trustees Report

Exercises 35–37 are based on the data shown by the graphs.

35. In 2004, the system's income was \$575 billion, projected to increase at an average rate of \$43 billion per year. In which year will the system's income be \$1177 billion?

36. The data for the system's outflow can be modeled by the formula

$$B = 0.07x^2 + 47.4x + 500,$$

where B represents the amount paid in benefits, in billions of dollars, x years after 2004. According to this model, when will the amount paid in benefits be \$1177 billion? Round to the nearest year.

37. How well do your answers to Exercises 35 and 36 model the data shown by the graphs?

38. For every one million U.S. residents, the number of movie theaters exceeds the number of drive-in theaters by 16 and the number of video rental stores exceeds the number of drive-in theaters by 64. Combined, there are 83 drive-in theaters, movie theaters, and video rental stores per one million U.S. residents. How many of each of these establishments are there per one million residents? (*Source:* U.S. Census Bureau)

39. The costs for two different kinds of heating systems for a small home are given in the following table. After how many years will total costs for solar heating and electric heating be the same? What will be the cost at that time?

System	Cost to Install	Operating Cost/Year
Solar	$29,700	$150
Electric	$5000	$1100

40. You invested $10,000 in two accounts paying 8% and 10% annual interest. At the end of the year, the total interest from these investments was $940. How much was invested at each rate?

41. The length of a rectangular carpet is 4 feet greater than twice its width. If the area is 48 square feet, find the carpet's length and width.

42. A vertical pole is to be supported by a wire that is 26 feet long and anchored 24 feet from the base of the pole. How far up the pole should the wire be attached?

43. After a 60% reduction, a jacket sold for $20. What was the jacket's price before the reduction?

44. You are choosing between two telephone plans for local calls. Plan A charges $25 per month for unlimited calls. Plan B has a monthly fee of $13 with a charge of $0.06 per local call. How many local telephone calls in a month make plan A the better deal?

Functions and Graphs

A vast expanse of open water at the top of our world was once covered with ice. The melting of the Arctic ice caps has forced polar bears to swim as far as 40 miles, causing them to drown in significant numbers. Such deaths were rare in the past. There is strong scientific consensus that human activities are changing the Earth's climate. Scientists now believe that there is a striking correlation between atmospheric carbon dioxide concentration and global temperature. As both of these variables increase at significant rates, there are warnings of a planetary emergency that threatens to condemn coming generations to a catastrophically diminished future.*

In this chapter, you'll learn to approach our climate crisis mathematically by creating formulas, called functions, that model data for average global temperature and carbon dioxide concentration over time. Understanding the concept of a function will give you a new perspective on many situations, ranging from global warming to using mathematics in a way that is similar to making a movie.

A mathematical model involving global warming is developed in Example 9 in Section 2.3. Using mathematics in a way that is similar to making a movie is discussed in the essay on page 250.

Sources: Al Gore, *An Inconvenient Truth*, Rodale, 2006; *Time*, April 3, 2006

Section 2.1 Basics of Functions and Their Graphs

Objectives

1. Find the domain and range of a relation.
2. Determine whether a relation is a function.
3. Determine whether an equation represents a function.
4. Evaluate a function.
5. Graph functions by plotting points.
6. Use the vertical line test to identify functions.
7. Obtain information about a function from its graph.
8. Identify the domain and range of a function from its graph.
9. Identify intercepts from a function's graph.

Magnified 6000 times, this color-scanned image shows a T-lymphocyte blood cell (green) infected with the HIV virus (red). Depletion of the number of T cells causes destruction of the immune system.

The average number of T cells in a person with HIV is a *function* of time after infection. In this section, you will be introduced to the basics of functions and their graphs. We will analyze the graph of a function using an example that illustrates the progression of HIV and T cell count. Much of our work in this course will be devoted to the important topic of functions and how they model your world.

1. Find the domain and range of a relation.

Table 2.1 Top U.S. Last Names

Name	% of All Names
Smith	1.006%
Johnson	0.810%
Williams	0.699%
Brown	0.621%
Jones	0.621%

Source: Russell Ash, *The Top 10 of Everything*

Relations

The top five U.S. last names shown in **Table 2.1** account for nearly 4% of the entire population. The table indicates a correspondence between a last name and the percentage of Americans who share that name. We can write this correspondence using a set of ordered pairs:

$$\{(\text{Smith}, 1.006\%), (\text{Johnson}, 0.810\%), (\text{Williams}, 0.699\%),$$
$$(\text{Brown}, 0.621\%), (\text{Jones}, 0.621\%)\}.$$

These braces indicate we are representing a set.

The mathematical term for a set of ordered pairs is a *relation*.

Definition of a Relation

A **relation** is any set of ordered pairs. The set of all first components of the ordered pairs is called the **domain** of the relation and the set of all second components is called the **range** of the relation.

EXAMPLE 1 Finding the Domain and Range of a Relation

Find the domain and range of the relation:

$$\{(\text{Smith}, 1.006\%), (\text{Johnson}, 0.810\%), (\text{Williams}, 0.699\%),$$
$$(\text{Brown}, 0.621\%), (\text{Jones}, 0.621\%)\}.$$

Solution The domain is the set of all first components. Thus, the domain is

$$\{\text{Smith, Johnson, Williams, Brown, Jones}\}.$$

The range is the set of all second components. Thus, the range is

$$\{1.006\%, 0.810\%, 0.699\%, 0.621\%\}.$$

> Although Brown and Jones are both shared by 0.621% of the U.S. population, it is not necessary to list 0.621% twice.

⊘ Check Point **|** Find the domain and range of the relation:

$$\{(0, 9.1), (10, 6.7), (20, 10.7), (30, 13.2), (36, 17.4)\}.$$

As you worked Check Point 1, did you wonder if there was a rule that assigned the "inputs" in the domain to the "outputs" in the range? For example, for the ordered pair (30, 13.2), how does the output 13.2 depend on the input 30? The ordered pair is based on the data in **Figure 2.1(a)**, which shows the percentage of first-year U.S. college students claiming no religious affiliation.

Figure 2.1(a) Data for women and men
Source: John Macionis, *Sociology*, Twelfth Edition, Prentice Hall, 2008

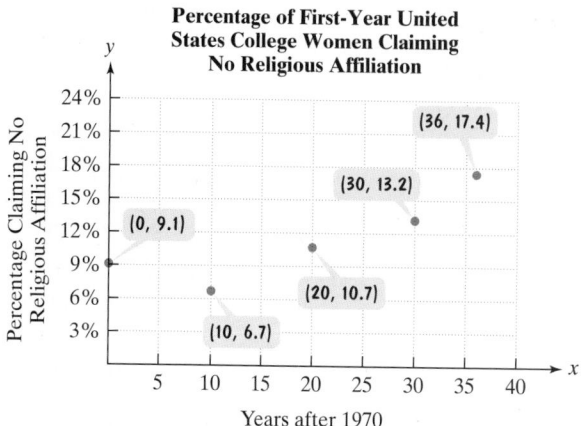

Figure 2.1(b) Visually representing the relation for the women's data

In **Figure 2.1(b)**, we used the data for college women to create the following ordered pairs:

$$\left(\text{years after 1970,} \quad \begin{matrix} \text{percentage of first-year college} \\ \text{women claiming no religious} \\ \text{affiliation} \end{matrix} \right).$$

Consider, for example, the ordered pair (30, 13.2).

$$(30, 13.2)$$

> 30 years after 1970, or in 2000,

> 13.2% of first-year college women claimed no religious affiliation.

The five points in **Figure 2.1(b)** visually represent the relation formed from the women's data. Another way to visually represent the relation is as follows:

Domain Range

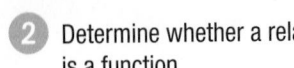
② Determine whether a relation is a function.

Functions

Table 2.1, repeated in the margin, shows the top five U.S. last names and the percentage of Americans who share those names. We've used this information to define two relations. **Figure 2.2(a)** shows a correspondence between last names and percents sharing those names. **Figure 2.2(b)** shows a correspondence between percents sharing last names and those last names.

Table 2.1 Top U.S. Last Names

Name	% of All Names
Smith	1.006%
Johnson	0.810%
Williams	0.699%
Brown	0.621%
Jones	0.621%

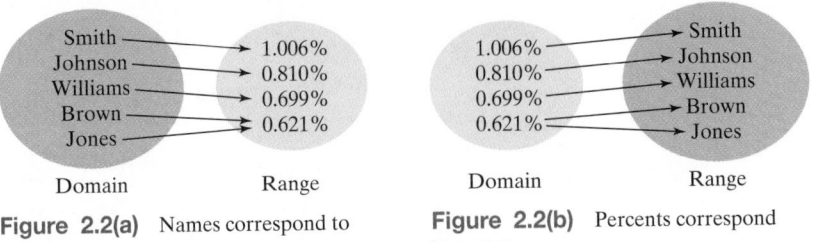

Figure 2.2(a) Names correspond to percents.

Figure 2.2(b) Percents correspond to names.

A relation in which each member of the domain corresponds to exactly one member of the range is a **function**. Can you see that the relation in **Figure 2.2(a)** is a function? Each last name in the domain corresponds to exactly one percent in the range. If we know the last name, we can be sure of the percentage of Americans sharing that name. Notice that more than one element in the domain can correspond to the same element in the range: Brown and Jones are both shared by 0.621% of Americans.

Is the relation in **Figure 2.2(b)** a function? Does each member of the domain correspond to precisely one member of the range? This relation is not a function because there is a member of the domain that corresponds to two different members of the range:

$$(0.621\%, \text{Brown}) \quad (0.621\%, \text{Jones}).$$

The member of the domain 0.621% corresponds to both Brown and Jones in the range. If we know that the percentage of Americans sharing a last name is 0.621%, we cannot be sure of that last name. Because **a function is a relation in which no two ordered pairs have the same first component and different second components**, the ordered pairs (0.621%, Brown) and (0.621%, Jones) are not ordered pairs of a function.

> Same first component

$$(0.621\%, \text{Brown}) \quad (0.621\%, \text{Jones})$$

> Different second components

Definition of a Function

A **function** is a correspondence from a first set, called the **domain**, to a second set, called the **range**, such that each element in the domain corresponds to *exactly one* element in the range.

In Check Point 1, we considered a relation that gave a correspondence between years after 1970 and the percentage of first-year college women claiming no religious affiliation. Can you see that this relation is a function?

> Each element in the domain

$$\{(0, 9.1), (10, 6.7), (20, 10.7), (30, 13.2), (36, 17.4)\}$$

> corresponds to exactly one element in the range.

However, Example 2 illustrates that not every correspondence between sets is a function.

EXAMPLE 2 **Determining Whether a Relation Is a Function**

Determine whether each relation is a function:

a. $\{(1, 6), (2, 6), (3, 8), (4, 9)\}$ **b.** $\{(6, 1), (6, 2), (8, 3), (9, 4)\}$.

Solution We begin by making a figure for each relation that shows the domain and the range (**Figure 2.3**).

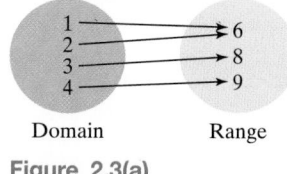

Domain Range

Figure 2.3(a)

a. **Figure 2.3(a)** shows that every element in the domain corresponds to exactly one element in the range. The element 1 in the domain corresponds to the element 6 in the range. Furthermore, 2 corresponds to 6, 3 corresponds to 8, and 4 corresponds to 9. No two ordered pairs in the given relation have the same first component and different second components. Thus, the relation is a function.

b. **Figure 2.3(b)** shows that 6 corresponds to both 1 and 2. If any element in the domain corresponds to more than one element in the range, the relation is not a function. This relation is not a function; two ordered pairs have the same first component and different second components.

Domain Range

Figure 2.3(b)

Same first component

$(6, 1)$ $(6, 2)$

Different second components

Study Tip

If a relation is a function, reversing the components in each of its ordered pairs may result in a relation that is not a function.

Look at **Figure 2.3(a)** again. The fact that 1 and 2 in the domain correspond to the same number, 6, in the range does not violate the definition of a function. **A function can have two different first components with the same second component.** By contrast, a relation is not a function when two different ordered pairs have the same first component and different second components. Thus, the relation in **Figure 2.3(b)** is not a function.

✓ Check Point **2** Determine whether each relation is a function:

a. $\{(1, 2), (3, 4), (5, 6), (5, 8)\}$ **b.** $\{(1, 2), (3, 4), (6, 5), (8, 5)\}$.

3 Determine whether an equation represents a function.

Functions as Equations

Functions are usually given in terms of equations rather than as sets of ordered pairs. For example, here is an equation that models the percentage of first-year college women claiming no religious affiliation as a function of time:

$$y = 0.013x^2 - 0.21x + 8.7.$$

The variable x represents the number of years after 1970. The variable y represents the percentage of first-year college women claiming no religious affiliation. The variable y is a function of the variable x. For each value of x, there is one and only one value of y. The variable x is called the **independent variable** because it can be assigned any value from the domain. Thus, x can be assigned any nonnegative integer representing the number of years after 1970. The variable y is called the **dependent variable** because its value depends on x. The percentage claiming no religious affiliation depends on the number of years after 1970. The value of the dependent variable, y, is calculated after selecting a value for the independent variable, x.

We have seen that not every set of ordered pairs defines a function. Similarly, not all equations with the variables x and y define functions. If an equation is solved for y and more than one value of y can be obtained for a given x, then the equation does not define y as a function of x.

EXAMPLE 3 Determining Whether an Equation Represents a Function

Determine whether each equation defines y as a function of x:

a. $x^2 + y = 4$ **b.** $x^2 + y^2 = 4$.

Solution Solve each equation for y in terms of x. If two or more values of y can be obtained for a given x, the equation is not a function.

a.
$$x^2 + y = 4 \qquad \text{This is the given equation.}$$
$$x^2 + y - x^2 = 4 - x^2 \qquad \text{Solve for y by subtracting } x^2 \text{ from both sides.}$$
$$y = 4 - x^2 \qquad \text{Simplify.}$$

From this last equation we can see that for each value of x, there is one and only one value of y. For example, if $x = 1$, then $y = 4 - 1^2 = 3$. The equation defines y as a function of x.

b.
$$x^2 + y^2 = 4 \qquad \text{This is the given equation.}$$
$$x^2 + y^2 - x^2 = 4 - x^2 \qquad \text{Isolate } y^2 \text{ by subtracting } x^2 \text{ from both sides.}$$
$$y^2 = 4 - x^2 \qquad \text{Simplify.}$$
$$y = \pm\sqrt{4 - x^2} \qquad \text{Apply the square root property: If } u^2 = d,$$
$$\text{then } u = \pm\sqrt{d}.$$

The \pm in this last equation shows that for certain values of x (all values between -2 and 2), there are two values of y. For example, if $x = 1$, then $y = \pm\sqrt{4 - 1^2} = \pm\sqrt{3}$. For this reason, the equation does not define y as a function of x. ●

⊘ **Check Point 3** Solve each equation for y and then determine whether the equation defines y as a function of x:

a. $2x + y = 6$ **b.** $x^2 + y^2 = 1$.

④ **Evaluate a function.**

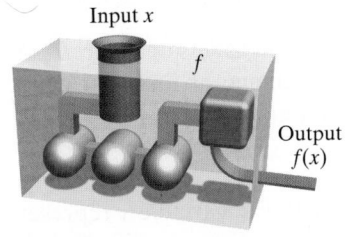

Figure 2.4 A "function machine" with inputs and outputs

Function Notation

If an equation in x and y gives one and only one value of y for each value of x, then the variable y is a function of the variable x. When an equation represents a function, the function is often named by a letter such as $f, g, h, F, G,$ or H. Any letter can be used to name a function. Suppose that f names a function. Think of the domain as the set of the function's inputs and the range as the set of the function's outputs. As shown in **Figure 2.4**, input is represented by x and the output by $f(x)$. The special notation $f(x)$, read "f of x" or "f at x," represents the **value of the function at the number** x.

Let's make this clearer by considering a specific example. We know that the equation

$$y = 0.013x^2 - 0.21x + 8.7$$

defines y as a function of x. We'll name the function f. Now, we can apply our new function notation.

Study Tip

The notation $f(x)$ does *not* mean "f times x." The notation describes the value of the function at x.

We read this equation as "f of x equals $0.013x^2 - 0.21x + 8.7$."

Input	Output	Equation
x	$f(x)$	$f(x) = 0.013x^2 - 0.21x + 8.7$

Suppose we are interested in finding $f(30)$, the function's output when the input is 30. To find the value of the function at 30, we substitute 30 for x. We are **evaluating the function** at 30.

$f(x) = 0.013x^2 - 0.21x + 8.7$	*This is the given function.*
$f(30) = 0.013(30)^2 - 0.21(30) + 8.7$	*Replace each occurrence of x with 30.*
$\quad\quad = 0.013(900) - 0.21(30) + 8.7$	*Evaluate the exponential expression: $30^2 = 30 \cdot 30 = 900$.*
$\quad\quad = 11.7 - 6.3 + 8.7$	*Perform the multiplications.*
$f(30) = 14.1$	*Subtract and add from left to right.*

The statement $f(30) = 14.1$, read "f of 30 equals 14.1," tells us that the value of the function at 30 is 14.1. When the function's input is 30, its output is 14.1. **Figure 2.5** illustrates the input and output in terms of a function machine.

$$f(30) = 14.1$$

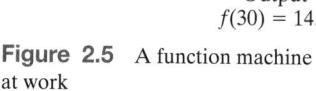

30 years after 1970, or in 2000, | **14.1% of first-year college women claimed no religious affiliation.**

Figure 2.5 A function machine at work

We have seen that in 2000, 13.2% actually claimed nonaffiliation, so our function that models the data slightly overestimates the percent for 2000.

Technology

Graphing utilities can be used to evaluate functions. The screens below show the evaluation of

$$f(x) = 0.013x^2 - 0.21x + 8.7$$

at 30 on a TI-84 Plus graphing calculator. The function f is named Y_1.

```
Plot1 Plot2 Plot3
\Y1■.013X²-.21X+
8.7
\Y2=
\Y3=
\Y4=
\Y5=
\Y6=
```

```
Y1(30)
           14.1
```

We used $f(x) = 0.013x^2 - 0.21x + 8.7$ to find $f(30)$. To find other function values, such as $f(40)$ or $f(55)$, substitute the specified input value, 40 or 55, for x in the function's equation.

If a function is named f and x represents the independent variable, the notation $f(x)$ corresponds to the y-value for a given x. Thus,

$$f(x) = 0.013x^2 - 0.21x + 8.7 \quad \text{and} \quad y = 0.013x^2 - 0.21x + 8.7$$

define the same function. This function may be written as

$$y = f(x) = 0.013x^2 - 0.21x + 8.7.$$

EXAMPLE 4 **Evaluating a Function**

If $f(x) = x^2 + 3x + 5$, evaluate each of the following:

a. $f(2)$ **b.** $f(x + 3)$ **c.** $f(-x)$.

Solution We substitute 2, $x + 3$, and $-x$ for x in the equation for f. When replacing x with a variable or an algebraic expression, you might find it helpful to think of the function's equation as

$$f(\boxed{x}) = \boxed{x}^2 + 3\boxed{x} + 5.$$

$$f(x) = x^2 + 3x + 5$$

The function's equation (repeated)

a. We find $f(2)$ by substituting 2 for x in the equation.

$$f(2) = 2^2 + 3 \cdot 2 + 5 = 4 + 6 + 5 = 15$$

Thus, $f(2) = 15$.

b. We find $f(x + 3)$ by substituting $x + 3$ for x in the equation.

$$f(x + 3) = (x + 3)^2 + 3(x + 3) + 5$$

Equivalently,

$$f(x + 3) = (x + 3)^2 + 3(x + 3) + 5$$
$$= x^2 + 6x + 9 + 3x + 9 + 5 \quad \text{Square } x + 3 \text{ using}$$
$$(A + B)^2 = A^2 + 2AB + B^2.$$
$$\text{Distribute 3 throughout the parentheses.}$$
$$= x^2 + 9x + 23. \quad \text{Combine like terms.}$$

c. We find $f(-x)$ by substituting $-x$ for x in the equation.

$$f(-x) = (-x)^2 + 3(-x) + 5$$

Equivalently,

$$f(-x) = (-x)^2 + 3(-x) + 5$$
$$= x^2 - 3x + 5.$$

Discovery

Using $f(x) = x^2 + 3x + 5$ and the answers in parts (b) and (c):

1. Is $f(x + 3)$ equal to $f(x) + f(3)$?

2. Is $f(-x)$ equal to $-f(x)$?

✓ Check Point 4 If $f(x) = x^2 - 2x + 7$, evaluate each of the following:

 a. $f(-5)$ **b.** $f(x + 4)$ **c.** $f(-x)$.

⑤ Graph functions by plotting points.

Graphs of Functions

The **graph of a function** is the graph of its ordered pairs. For example, the graph of $f(x) = 2x$ is the set of points (x, y) in the rectangular coordinate system satisfying $y = 2x$. Similarly, the graph of $g(x) = 2x + 4$ is the set of points (x, y) in the rectangular coordinate system satisfying the equation $y = 2x + 4$. In the next example, we graph both of these functions in the same rectangular coordinate system.

(EXAMPLE 5) Graphing Functions

Graph the functions $f(x) = 2x$ and $g(x) = 2x + 4$ in the same rectangular coordinate system. Select integers for x, starting with -2 and ending with 2.

Solution We begin by setting up a partial table of coordinates for each function. Then, we plot the five points in each table and connect them, as shown in **Figure 2.6**. The graph of each function is a straight line. Do you see a relationship between the two graphs? The graph of g is the graph of f shifted vertically up by 4 units.

x	$f(x) = 2x$	(x, y) or $(x, f(x))$
-2	$f(-2) = 2(-2) = -4$	$(-2, -4)$
-1	$f(-1) = 2(-1) = -2$	$(-1, -2)$
0	$f(0) = 2 \cdot 0 = 0$	$(0, 0)$
1	$f(1) = 2 \cdot 1 = 2$	$(1, 2)$
2	$f(2) = 2 \cdot 2 = 4$	$(2, 4)$

x	$g(x) = 2x + 4$	(x, y) or $(x, g(x))$
-2	$g(-2) = 2(-2) + 4 = 0$	$(-2, 0)$
-1	$g(-1) = 2(-1) + 4 = 2$	$(-1, 2)$
0	$g(0) = 2 \cdot 0 + 4 = 4$	$(0, 4)$
1	$g(1) = 2 \cdot 1 + 4 = 6$	$(1, 6)$
2	$g(2) = 2 \cdot 2 + 4 = 8$	$(2, 8)$

Choose x. Compute $f(x)$ by evaluating f at x. Form the ordered pair. Choose x. Compute $g(x)$ by evaluating g at x. Form the ordered pair.

Figure 2.6

The graphs in Example 5 are straight lines. All functions with equations of the form $f(x) = mx + b$ graph as straight lines. Such functions, called **linear functions**, will be discussed in detail in Section 2.3.

Technology

We can use a graphing utility to check the tables and the graphs in Example 5 for the functions

$$f(x) = 2x \quad \text{and} \quad g(x) = 2x + 4.$$

Enter $y_1 = 2x$ in the $\boxed{y=}$ screen.

Enter $y_2 = 2x + 4$ in the $\boxed{y=}$ screen.

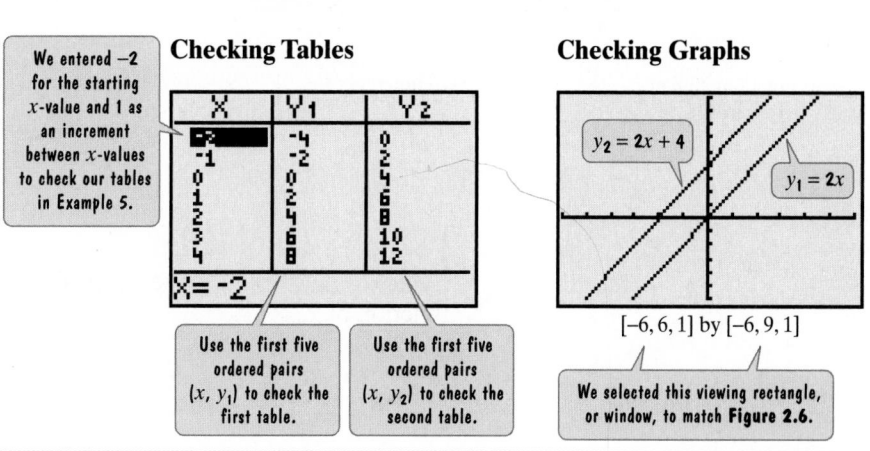

Checking Tables

We entered −2 for the starting x-value and 1 as an increment between x-values to check our tables in Example 5.

Use the first five ordered pairs (x, y_1) to check the first table.

Use the first five ordered pairs (x, y_2) to check the second table.

Checking Graphs

$y_2 = 2x + 4$

$y_1 = 2x$

$[-6, 6, 1]$ by $[-6, 9, 1]$

We selected this viewing rectangle, or window, to match **Figure 2.6**.

✓ Check Point **5** Graph the functions $f(x) = 2x$ and $g(x) = 2x - 3$ in the same rectangular coordinate system. Select integers for x, starting with -2 and ending with 2. How is the graph of g related to the graph of f?

⑥ Use the vertical line test to identify functions.

The Vertical Line Test

Not every graph in the rectangular coordinate system is the graph of a function. The definition of a function specifies that no value of x can be paired with two or more different values of y. Consequently, if a graph contains two or more different points with the same first coordinate, the graph cannot represent a function. This is illustrated in **Figure 2.7**. Observe that points sharing a common first coordinate are vertically above or below each other.

This observation is the basis of a useful test for determining whether a graph defines y as a function of x. The test is called the **vertical line test**.

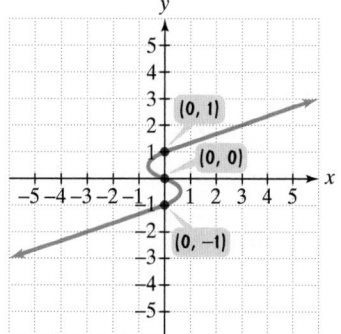

Figure 2.7 y is not a function of x because 0 is paired with three values of y, namely, 1, 0, and -1.

The Vertical Line Test for Functions

If any vertical line intersects a graph in more than one point, the graph does not define y as a function of x.

(**EXAMPLE 6**) **Using the Vertical Line Test**

Use the vertical line test to identify graphs in which y is a function of x.

a.

b.

c.

d.
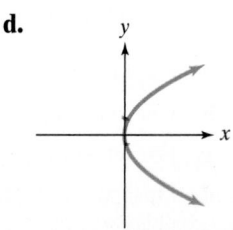

Solution y is a function of x for the graphs in (b) and (c).

a.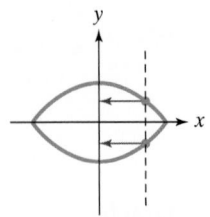

y is **not a function of** x.
Two values of y
correspond to an x-value.

b.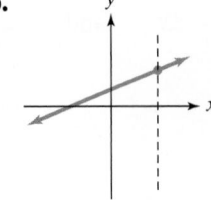

y is **a function of** x.

c.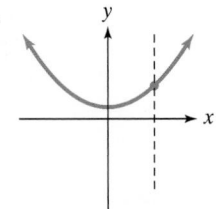

y is **a function of** x.

d.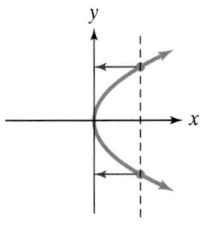

y is **not a function of** x.
Two values of y
correspond to an x-value.

⬤

⊘ Check Point **6** Use the vertical line test to identify graphs in which y is a function of x.

a.

b.

c.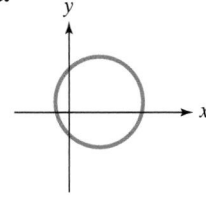

⑦ Obtain information about a function from its graph.

Obtaining Information from Graphs

You can obtain information about a function from its graph. At the right or left of a graph, you will find closed dots, open dots, or arrows.

- A closed dot indicates that the graph does not extend beyond this point and the point belongs to the graph.
- An open dot indicates that the graph does not extend beyond this point and the point does not belong to the graph.
- An arrow indicates that the graph extends indefinitely in the direction in which the arrow points.

⬭ EXAMPLE 7 ⬭ **Analyzing the Graph of a Function**

The human immunodeficiency virus, or HIV, infects and kills helper T cells. Because T cells stimulate the immune system to produce antibodies, their destruction disables the body's defenses against other pathogens. By counting the number of T cells that remain active in the body, the progression of HIV can be monitored. The fewer helper T cells, the more advanced the disease. **Figure 2.8** shows a graph that is used to monitor the average progression of the disease. The average number of T cells, $f(x)$, is a function of time after infection, x.

a. Explain why f represents the graph of a function.
b. Use the graph to find $f(8)$.
c. For what value of x is $f(x) = 350$?
d. Describe the general trend shown by the graph.

Figure 2.8
Source: B. E. Pruitt et al., *Human Sexuality*, Prentice Hall, 2007

Solution

a. No vertical line can be drawn that intersects the graph of f more than once. By the vertical line test, f represents the graph of a function.

b. To find $f(8)$, or f of 8, we locate 8 on the x-axis. **Figure 2.9** shows the point on the graph of f for which 8 is the first coordinate. From this point, we look to the y-axis to find the corresponding y-coordinate. We see that the y-coordinate is 200. Thus,

$$f(8) = 200.$$

When the time after infection is 8 years, the average T cell count is 200 cells per milliliter of blood. (AIDS clinical diagnosis is given at a T cell count of 200 or below.)

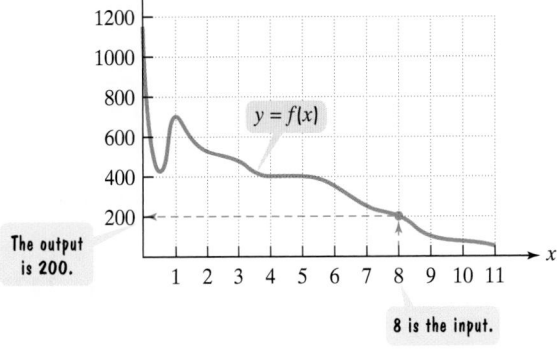

Figure 2.9 Finding $f(8)$

c. To find the value of x for which $f(x) = 350$, we find the approximate location of 350 on the y-axis. **Figure 2.10** shows that there is one point on the graph of f for which 350 is the second coordinate. From this point, we look to the x-axis to find the corresponding x-coordinate. We see that the x-coordinate is 6. Thus,

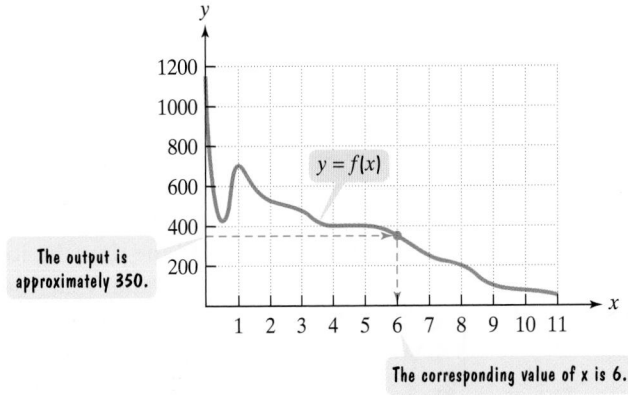

Figure 2.10 Finding x for which $f(x) = 350$

$$f(x) = 350 \text{ for } x = 6.$$

An average T cell count of 350 occurs 6 years after infection.

d. **Figure 2.11** uses voice balloons to describe the general trend shown by the graph.

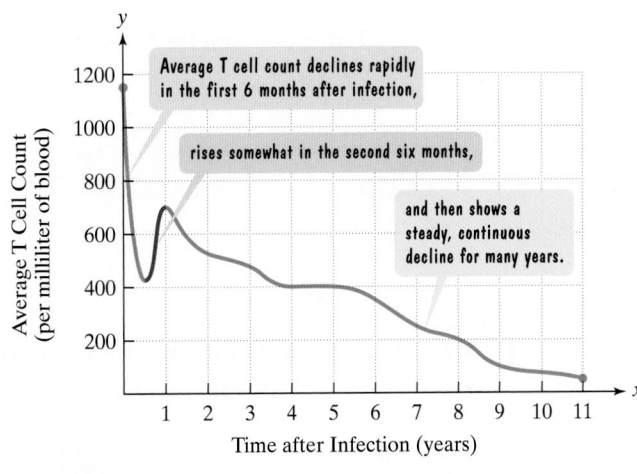

Figure 2.11 Describing changing T cell count over time in a person infected with HIV

⊘ Check Point 7

> **a.** Use the graph of f in **Figure 2.8** on page 206 to find $f(5)$.
>
> **b.** For what value of x is $f(x) = 100$?
>
> **c.** Estimate the minimum average T cell count during the asymptomatic stage.

⑧ Identify the domain and range of a function from its graph.

Identifying Domain and Range from a Function's Graph

Study Tip

Throughout this discussion, we will be using interval notation. Recall that square brackets indicate endpoints that are included in an interval. Parentheses indicate endpoints that are not included in an interval. Parentheses are always used with ∞ or $-\infty$. For more detail on interval notation, see Section 1.7, pages 173–174.

Figure 2.12 illustrates how the graph of a function is used to determine the function's domain and its range.

Domain: set of inputs

> Found on the x-axis

Range: set of outputs

> Found on the y-axis

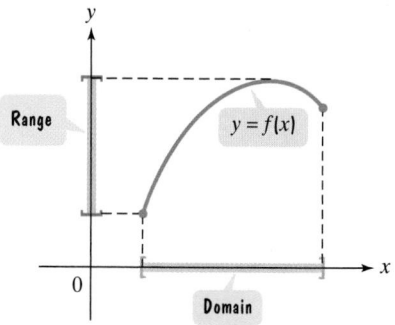

Figure 2.12 Domain and range of f

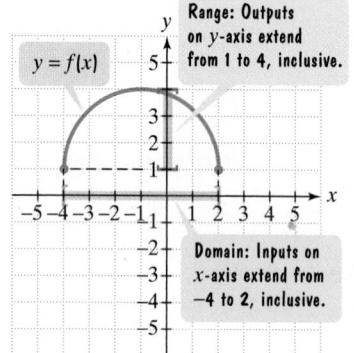

Figure 2.13 Domain and range of f

Let's apply these ideas to the graph of the function shown in **Figure 2.13**. To find the domain, look for all the inputs on the x-axis that correspond to points on the graph. Can you see that they extend from -4 to 2, inclusive? The function's domain can be represented as follows:

Using Set-Builder Notation **Using Interval Notation**

$$\{\, x \mid -4 \leq x \leq 2 \,\}$$ $$[-4, 2].$$

> The set of all x — such that — x is greater than or equal to -4 and less than or equal to 2.

> The square brackets indicate -4 and 2 are included. Note the square brackets on the x-axis in **Figure 2.13**.

To find the range, look for all the outputs on the y-axis that correspond to points on the graph. They extend from 1 to 4, inclusive. The function's range can be represented as follows:

Using Set-Builder Notation **Using Interval Notation**

$$\{\, y \mid 1 \leq y \leq 4 \,\}$$ $$[1, 4].$$

> The set of all y — such that — y is greater than or equal to 1 and less than or equal to 4.

> The square brackets indicate 1 and 4 are included. Note the square brackets on the y-axis in **Figure 2.13**.

(**EXAMPLE 8**) **Identifying the Domain and Range of a Function from Its Graph**

Use the graph of each function to identify its domain and its range.

a.

b.

c.

d.

e.

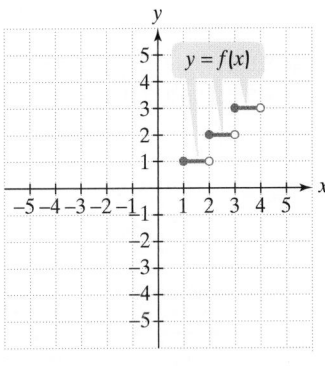

Solution For the graph of each function, the domain is highlighted in purple on the x-axis and the range is highlighted in green on the y-axis.

a.

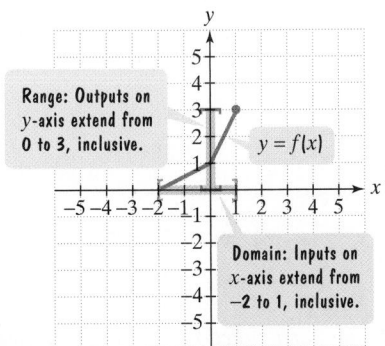

Domain = $\{x \mid -2 \le x \le 1\}$ or $[-2, 1]$
Range = $\{y \mid 0 \le y \le 3\}$ or $[0, 3]$

b.

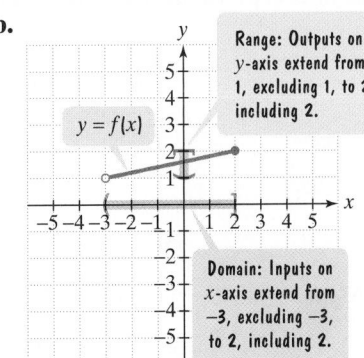

Domain = $\{x \mid -3 < x \le 2\}$ or $(-3, 2]$
Range = $\{y \mid 1 < y \le 2\}$ or $(1, 2]$

c.

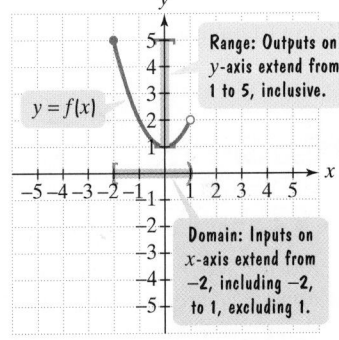

Domain = $\{x \mid -2 \le x < 1\}$ or $[-2, 1)$
Range = $\{y \mid 1 \le y \le 5\}$ or $[1, 5]$

d.

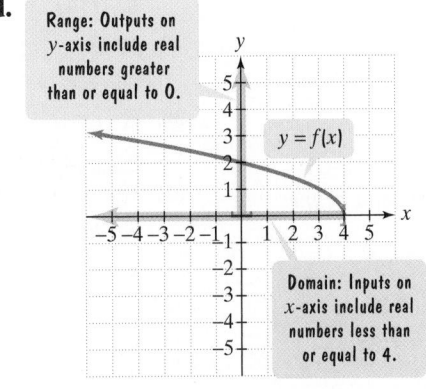

Domain = $\{x \mid x \le 4\}$ or $(-\infty, 4]$
Range = $\{y \mid y \ge 0\}$ or $[0, \infty)$

e.

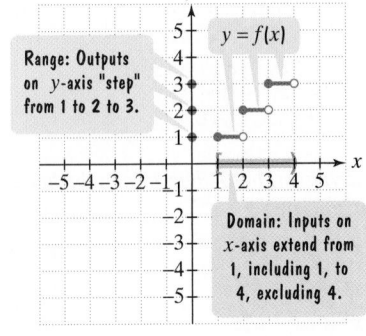

Domain = $\{x \mid 1 \le x < 4\}$ or $[1, 4)$
Range = $\{y \mid y = 1, 2, 3\}$

☑ Check Point **8** Use the graph of each function to identify its domain and its range.

a.

b.

c.

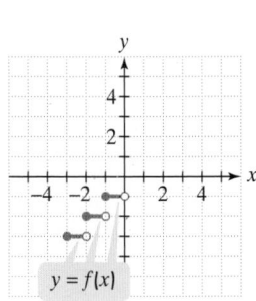

⑨ Identify intercepts from a function's graph.

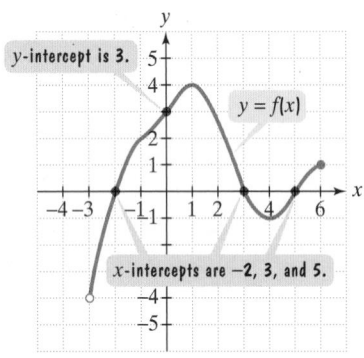

Figure 2.14 Identifying intercepts

Identifying Intercepts from a Function's Graph

Figure 2.14 illustrates how we can identify intercepts from a function's graph. To find the x-intercepts, look for the points at which the graph crosses the x-axis. There are three such points: $(-2, 0)$, $(3, 0)$, and $(5, 0)$. Thus, the x-intercepts are -2, 3, and 5. We express this in function notation by writing $f(-2) = 0$, $f(3) = 0$, and $f(5) = 0$. We say that -2, 3, and 5 are the *zeros of the function*. The **zeros of a function** f are the x-values for which $f(x) = 0$. Thus, the real zeros are the x-intercepts.

To find the y-intercept, look for the point at which the graph crosses the y-axis. This occurs at $(0, 3)$. Thus, the y-intercept is 3. We express this in function notation by writing $f(0) = 3$.

By the definition of a function, for each value of x we can have at most one value for y. What does this mean in terms of intercepts? **A function can have more than one x-intercept but at most one y-intercept.**

Exercise Set 2.1

Practice Exercises

In Exercises 1–10, determine whether each relation is a function. Give the domain and range for each relation.

1. $\{(1, 2), (3, 4), (5, 5)\}$ **2.** $\{(4, 5), (6, 7), (8, 8)\}$

3. $\{(3, 4), (3, 5), (4, 4), (4, 5)\}$

4. $\{(5, 6), (5, 7), (6, 6), (6, 7)\}$

5. $\{(3, -2), (5, -2), (7, 1), (4, 9)\}$

6. $\{(10, 4), (-2, 4), (-1, 1), (5, 6)\}$

7. $\{(-3, -3), (-2, -2), (-1, -1), (0, 0)\}$

8. $\{(-7, -7), (-5, -5), (-3, -3), (0, 0)\}$

9. $\{(1, 4), (1, 5), (1, 6)\}$

10. $\{(4, 1), (5, 1), (6, 1)\}$

In Exercises 11–26, determine whether each equation defines y as a function of x.

11. $x + y = 16$ **12.** $x + y = 25$

13. $x^2 + y = 16$ **14.** $x^2 + y = 25$

15. $x^2 + y^2 = 16$ **16.** $x^2 + y^2 = 25$

17. $x = y^2$ **18.** $4x = y^2$

19. $y = \sqrt{x + 4}$ **20.** $y = -\sqrt{x + 4}$

21. $x + y^3 = 8$ **22.** $x + y^3 = 27$

23. $xy + 2y = 1$ **24.** $xy - 5y = 1$

25. $|x| - y = 2$ **26.** $|x| - y = 5$

In Exercises 27–38, evaluate each function at the given values of the independent variable and simplify.

27. $f(x) = 4x + 5$
 a. $f(6)$ **b.** $f(x + 1)$ **c.** $f(-x)$

28. $f(x) = 3x + 7$
 a. $f(4)$ **b.** $f(x + 1)$ **c.** $f(-x)$

29. $g(x) = x^2 + 2x + 3$
 a. $g(-1)$ **b.** $g(x + 5)$ **c.** $g(-x)$

30. $g(x) = x^2 - 10x - 3$
 a. $g(-1)$ **b.** $g(x + 2)$ **c.** $g(-x)$

31. $h(x) = x^4 - x^2 + 1$
 a. $h(2)$ **b.** $h(-1)$
 c. $h(-x)$ **d.** $h(3a)$

32. $h(x) = x^3 - x + 1$
 a. $h(3)$ **b.** $h(-2)$
 c. $h(-x)$ **d.** $h(3a)$

33. $f(r) = \sqrt{r + 6} + 3$
 a. $f(-6)$ **b.** $f(10)$ **c.** $f(x - 6)$

34. $f(r) = \sqrt{25 - r} - 6$

 a. $f(16)$ **b.** $f(-24)$ **c.** $f(25 - 2x)$

35. $f(x) = \dfrac{4x^2 - 1}{x^2}$

 a. $f(2)$ **b.** $f(-2)$ **c.** $f(-x)$

36. $f(x) = \dfrac{4x^3 + 1}{x^3}$

 a. $f(2)$ **b.** $f(-2)$ **c.** $f(-x)$

37. $f(x) = \dfrac{x}{|x|}$

 a. $f(6)$ **b.** $f(-6)$ **c.** $f(r^2)$

38. $f(x) = \dfrac{|x + 3|}{x + 3}$

 a. $f(5)$ **b.** $f(-5)$ **c.** $f(-9 - x)$

In Exercises 39–50, graph the given functions, f and g, in the same rectangular coordinate system. Select integers for x, starting with −2 and ending with 2. Once you have obtained your graphs, describe how the graph of g is related to the graph of f.

39. $f(x) = x, g(x) = x + 3$

40. $f(x) = x, g(x) = x - 4$

41. $f(x) = -2x, g(x) = -2x - 1$

42. $f(x) = -2x, g(x) = -2x + 3$

43. $f(x) = x^2, g(x) = x^2 + 1$

44. $f(x) = x^2, g(x) = x^2 - 2$

45. $f(x) = |x|, g(x) = |x| - 2$

46. $f(x) = |x|, g(x) = |x| + 1$

47. $f(x) = x^3, g(x) = x^3 + 2$

48. $f(x) = x^3, g(x) = x^3 - 1$

49. $f(x) = 3, g(x) = 5$

50. $f(x) = -1, g(x) = 4$

In Exercises 51–54, graph the given square root functions, f and g, in the same rectangular coordinate system. Use the integer values of x given to the right of each function to obtain ordered pairs. Because only nonnegative numbers have square roots that are real numbers, be sure that each graph appears only for values of x that cause the expression under the radical sign to be greater than or equal to zero. Once you have obtained your graphs, describe how the graph of g is related to the graph of f.

51. $f(x) = \sqrt{x}$ $(x = 0, 1, 4, 9)$ and
 $g(x) = \sqrt{x} - 1$ $(x = 0, 1, 4, 9)$

52. $f(x) = \sqrt{x}$ $(x = 0, 1, 4, 9)$ and
 $g(x) = \sqrt{x} + 2$ $(x = 0, 1, 4, 9)$

53. $f(x) = \sqrt{x}$ $(x = 0, 1, 4, 9)$ and
 $g(x) = \sqrt{x - 1}$ $(x = 1, 2, 5, 10)$

54. $f(x) = \sqrt{x}$ $(x = 0, 1, 4, 9)$ and
 $g(x) = \sqrt{x + 2}$ $(x = -2, -1, 2, 7)$

In Exercises 55–64, use the vertical line test to identify graphs in which y is a function of x.

55. **56.**

57. **58.**

59. **60.**

61. **62.**

63. **64.**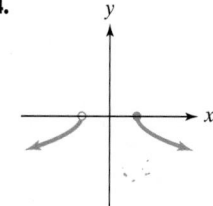

In Exercises 65–70, use the graph of f to find each indicated function value.

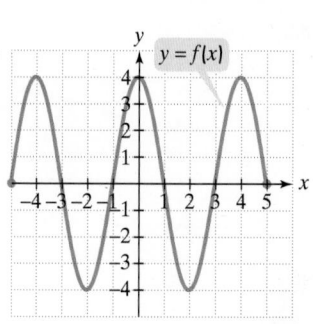

65. $f(-2)$

66. $f(2)$

67. $f(4)$

68. $f(-4)$

69. $f(-3)$

70. $f(-1)$

Use the graph of g to solve Exercises 71–76.

71. Find $g(-4)$.

72. Find $g(2)$.

73. Find $g(-10)$.

74. Find $g(10)$.

75. For what value of x is $g(x) = 1$?

76. For what value of x is $g(x) = -1$?

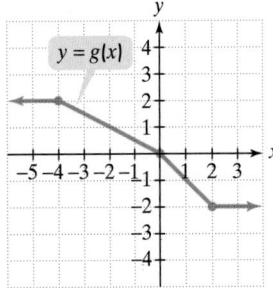

In Exercises 77–92, use the graph to determine **a.** *the function's domain;* **b.** *the function's range;* **c.** *the x-intercepts, if any;* **d.** *the y-intercept, if any; and* **e.** *the missing function values, indicated by question marks, below each graph.*

77.

$f(-2) = ?$ $f(2) = ?$

78.

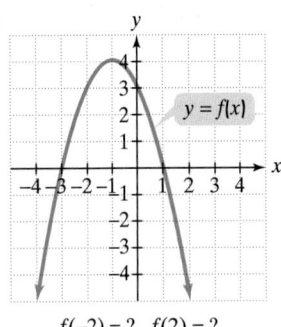

$f(-2) = ?$ $f(2) = ?$

79.

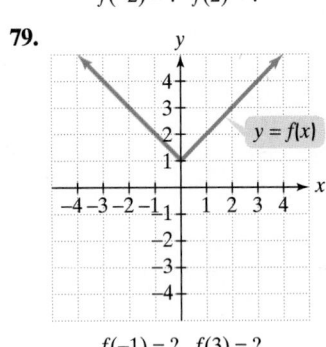

$f(-1) = ?$ $f(3) = ?$

80.

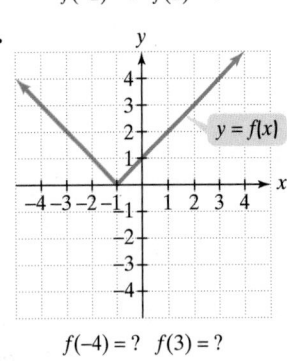

$f(-4) = ?$ $f(3) = ?$

81.

$f(3) = ?$

82.

$f(-5) = ?$

83.

$f(4) = ?$

84.

$f(3) = ?$

85.

$f(-1) = ?$

86.

$f(-2) = ?$

87.

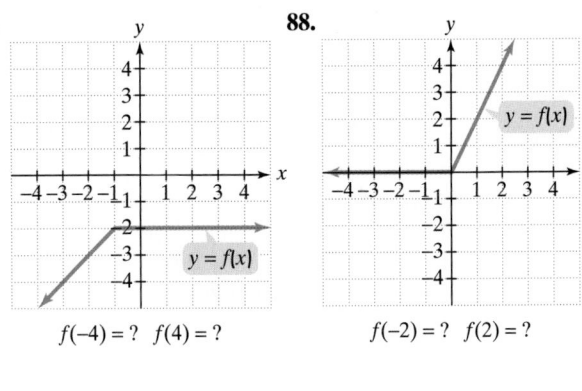

$f(-4) = ?$ $f(4) = ?$

88.

$f(-2) = ?$ $f(2) = ?$

89.

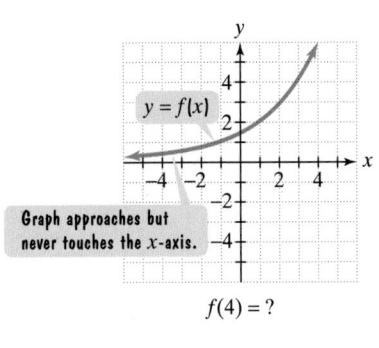

Graph approaches but never touches the *x*-axis.

$f(4) = ?$

90.

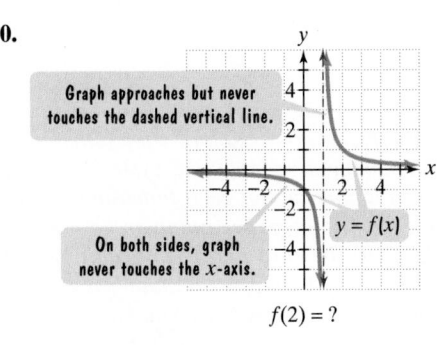

Graph approaches but never touches the dashed vertical line.

On both sides, graph never touches the *x*-axis.

$f(2) = ?$

91.

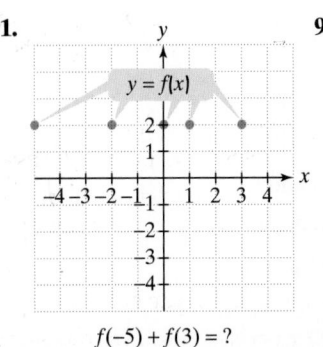

$f(-5) + f(3) = ?$

92.

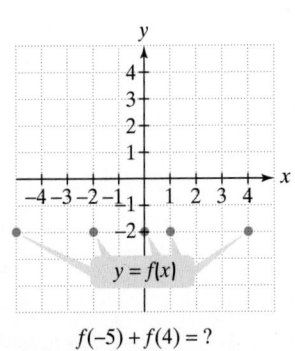

$f(-5) + f(4) = ?$

Practice Plus

In Exercises 93–94, let $f(x) = x^2 - x + 4$ and $g(x) = 3x - 5$.

93. Find $g(1)$ and $f(g(1))$. **94.** Find $g(-1)$ and $f(g(-1))$.

In Exercises 95–96, let f and g be defined by the following table:

x	$f(x)$	$g(x)$
-2	6	0
-1	3	4
0	-1	1
1	-4	-3
2	0	-6

95. Find $\sqrt{f(-1) - f(0)} - [g(2)]^2 + f(-2) \div g(2) \cdot g(-1)$.

96. Find $|f(1) - f(0)| - [g(1)]^2 + g(1) \div f(-1) \cdot g(2)$.

In Exercises 97–98, find $f(-x) - f(x)$ for the given function f. Then simplify the expression.

97. $f(x) = x^3 + x - 5$ **98.** $f(x) = x^2 - 3x + 7$

Application Exercises

The Corruption Perceptions Index uses perceptions of the general public, business people, and risk analysts to rate countries by how likely they are to accept bribes. The ratings are on a scale from 0 to 10, where higher scores represent less corruption. The graph shows the corruption ratings for the world's least corrupt and most corrupt countries. (The rating for the United States is 7.6.) Use the graph to solve Exercises 99–100.

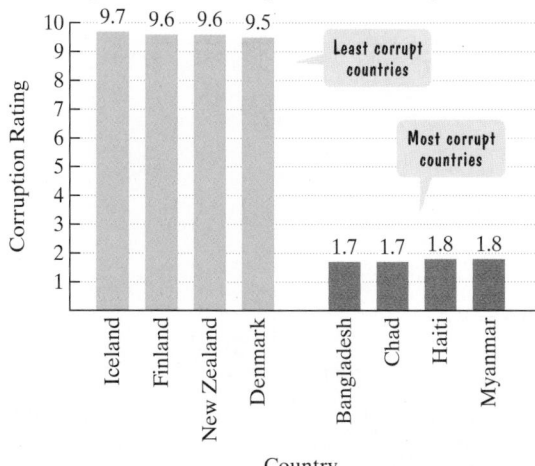

Top Four Least Corrupt and Most Corrupt Countries

Source: Transparency International, *Corruption Perceptions Index*

99. Use the four least corrupt countries to solve this exercise.

 a. Write a set of four ordered pairs in which countries correspond to corruption ratings. Each ordered pair should be in the form

 (country, corruption rating).

 b. Is the relation in part (a) a function? Explain your answer.

 c. Write a set of four ordered pairs in which corruption ratings correspond to countries. Each ordered pair should be in the form

 (corruption rating, country).

 d. Is the relation in part (c) a function? Explain your answer.

100. Repeat parts (a) through (d) in Exercise 99 using the four most corrupt countries.

The bar graph shows your chances of surviving to various ages once you reach 60.

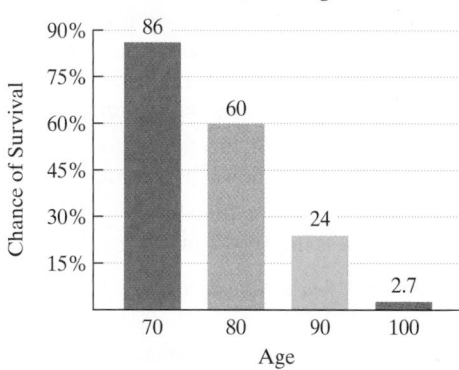

Chances of 60-Year-Olds Surviving to Various Ages

Source: National Center for Health Statistics

The functions

$$f(x) = -2.9x + 286$$
$$\text{and} \quad g(x) = 0.01x^2 - 4.9x + 370$$

model the chance, as a percent, that a 60-year-old will survive to age x. Use this information to solve Exercises 101–102.

101. **a.** Find and interpret $f(70)$. **b.** Find and interpret $g(70)$.

 c. Which function serves as a better model for the chance of surviving to age 70?

102. **a.** Find and interpret $f(90)$. **b.** Find and interpret $g(90)$.

 c. Which function serves as a better model for the chance of surviving to age 90?

To go, please. The graphs show that more Americans are ordering their food to go, instead of dining inside restaurants. A quadratic function models the average number of meals per person that Americans ordered for takeout and a linear function models the average number of meals ordered for eating in restaurants. In each model, x represents the number of years after 1984. Use the graphs and the displayed equations to solve Exercises 103–104.

Models for Average Number of Meals per Person Americans Ordered from 1984 through 2005

Takeout $T(x) = -0.125x^2 + 5.25x + 72$

In restaurants $R(x) = -0.6x + 94$

Source: NPD Group

(In Exercises 103–104, refer to the graphs and their equations at the bottom of the previous page.)

103. a. Use the equation for function T to find and interpret $T(20)$. How is this shown on the graph of T?

b. Use the equation for function R to find and interpret $R(0)$. How is this shown on the graph of R?

c. According to the graphs, in which year did the average number of takeout orders approximately equal the average number of in-restaurant orders? Use the equations for T and R to find the average number of meals per person for each kind of order in that year.

104. a. Use the equation for function T to find and interpret $T(18)$. How is this shown on the graph of T?

b. Use the equation for function R to find and interpret $R(20)$. How is this shown on the graph of R?

In Exercises 105–108, you will be developing functions that model given conditions.

105. A company that manufactures bicycles has a fixed cost of $100,000. It costs $100 to produce each bicycle. The total cost for the company is the sum of its fixed cost and variable costs. Write the total cost, C, as a function of the number of bicycles produced, x. Then find and interpret $C(90)$.

106. A car was purchased for $22,500. The value of the car decreased by $3200 per year for the first six years. Write a function that describes the value of the car, V, after x years, where $0 \leq x \leq 6$. Then find and interpret $V(3)$.

107. You commute to work a distance of 40 miles and return on the same route at the end of the day. Your average rate on the return trip is 30 miles per hour faster than your average rate on the outgoing trip. Write the total time, T, in hours, devoted to your outgoing and return trips as a function of your rate on the outgoing trip, x. Then find and interpret $T(30)$. Hint:

$$\text{Time traveled} = \frac{\text{Distance traveled}}{\text{Rate of travel}}.$$

108. A chemist working on a flu vaccine needs to mix a 10% sodium-iodine solution with a 60% sodium-iodine solution to obtain a 50-milliliter mixture. Write the amount of sodium iodine in the mixture, S, in milliliters, as a function of the number of milliliters of the 10% solution used, x. Then find and interpret $S(30)$.

Writing in Mathematics

109. What is a relation? Describe what is meant by its domain and its range.

110. Explain how to determine whether a relation is a function. What is a function?

111. How do you determine if an equation in x and y defines y as a function of x?

112. Does $f(x)$ mean f times x when referring to a function f? If not, what does $f(x)$ mean? Provide an example with your explanation.

113. What is the graph of a function?

114. Explain how the vertical line test is used to determine whether a graph represents a function.

115. Explain how to identify the domain and range of a function from its graph.

116. For people filing a single return, federal income tax is a function of adjusted gross income because for each value of adjusted gross income there is a specific tax to be paid. By contrast, the price of a house is not a function of the lot size on which the house sits because houses on same-sized lots can sell for many different prices.

a. Describe an everyday situation between variables that is a function.

b. Describe an everyday situation between variables that is not a function.

Technology Exercise

117. Use a graphing utility to verify any five pairs of graphs that you drew by hand in Exercises 39–54.

Critical Thinking Exercises

Make Sense? *In Exercises 118–121, determine whether each statement makes sense or does not make sense, and explain your reasoning.*

118. My body temperature is a function of the time of day.

119. Using $f(x) = 3x + 2$, I found $f(50)$ by applying the distributive property to $(3x + 2)50$.

120. I graphed a function showing how paid vacation days depend on the number of years a person works for a company. The domain was the number of paid vacation days.

121. I graphed a function showing how the average number of annual physician visits depends on a person's age. The domain was the average number of annual physician visits.

Use the graph of f to determine whether each statement in Exercises 122–125 is true or false.

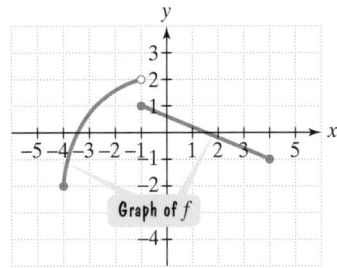

122. The domain of f is $[-4, -1) \cup (-1, 4]$.

123. The range of f is $[-2, 2]$.

124. $f(-1) - f(4) = 2$

125. $f(0) = 2.1$

126. If $f(x) = 3x + 7$, find $\dfrac{f(a + h) - f(a)}{h}$.

127. Give an example of a relation with the following characteristics: The relation is a function containing two ordered pairs. Reversing the components in each ordered pair results in a relation that is not a function.

128. If $f(x + y) = f(x) + f(y)$ and $f(1) = 3$, find $f(2), f(3)$, and $f(4)$. Is $f(x + y) = f(x) + f(y)$ for all functions?

Preview Exercises

Exercises 129–131 will help you prepare for the material covered in the next section.

129. The function $C(t) = 20 + 0.40(t - 60)$ describes the monthly cost, $C(t)$, in dollars, for a cellular phone plan for t calling minutes, where $t > 60$. Find and interpret $C(100)$.

130. Use point plotting to graph $f(x) = x + 2$ if $x \leq 1$.

131. Simplify: $2(x + h)^2 + 3(x + h) + 5 - (2x^2 + 3x + 5)$.

Section 2.2

More on Functions and Their Graphs

Objectives

1. Identify intervals on which a function increases, decreases, or is constant.
2. Use graphs to locate relative maxima or minima.
3. Identify even or odd functions and recognize their symmetries.
4. Understand and use piecewise functions.
5. Find and simplify a function's difference quotient.

"For a while we pondered whether to take a vacation or get a divorce. We decided that a trip to Bermuda is over in two weeks, but a divorce is something you always have."
—*Woody Allen*

The *Comedy Thesaurus* (Quirk Books, 2005) contains 23 jokes on the subject of divorce. This section opens with a graph on the subject, intended less for hilarious observations and more for an informal understanding of how we describe graphs of functions. The graph in **Figure 2.15** shows the percent distribution of divorces in the United States by number of years of marriage.

Figure 2.15
Source: Divorce Center

You are probably familiar with the words and phrases used to describe the graph in **Figure 2.15**:

 increasing decreasing maximum slowing rate of decrease

In this section, you will enhance your intuitive understanding of ways of describing graphs by viewing these descriptions from the perspective of functions.

1. Identify intervals on which a function increases, decreases, or is constant.

Increasing and Decreasing Functions

Too late for that flu shot now! It's only 8 A.M. and you're feeling lousy. Your temperature is 101°F. Fascinated by the way that algebra models the world (your author is projecting a bit here), you decide to construct graphs showing your body temperature as a function of the time of day. You decide to let x represent the number of hours after 8 A.M. and $f(x)$ your temperature at time x.

At 8 A.M. your temperature is 101°F and you are not feeling well. However, your temperature starts to decrease. It reaches normal (98.6°F) by 11 A.M. Feeling energized, you construct the graph shown on the right, indicating decreasing temperature for $\{x \mid 0 < x < 3\}$, or on the interval $(0, 3)$.

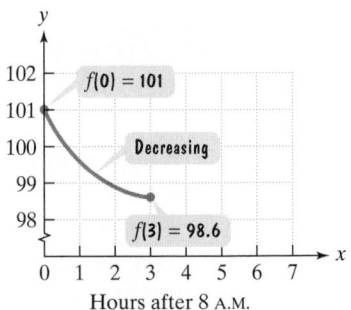

Temperature decreases on $(0, 3)$, reaching 98.6° by 11 A.M.

Did creating that first graph drain you of your energy? Your temperature starts to rise after 11 A.M. By 1 P.M., 5 hours after 8 A.M., your temperature reaches 100°F. However, you keep plotting points on your graph. At the right, we can see that your temperature increases for $\{x \mid 3 < x < 5\}$, or on the interval $(3, 5)$.

The graph of f is decreasing to the left of $x = 3$ and increasing to the right of $x = 3$. Thus, your temperature 3 hours after 8 A.M. was at its lowest point. Your relative minimum temperature was 98.6°.

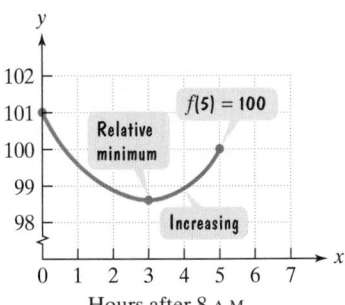

Temperature increases on $(3, 5)$.

By 3 P.M., your temperature is no worse than it was at 1 P.M.: It is still 100°F. (Of course, it's no better, either.) Your temperature remained the same, or constant, for $\{x \mid 5 < x < 7\}$, or on the interval $(5, 7)$.

The time-temperature flu scenario illustrates that a function f is increasing when its graph rises from left to right, decreasing when its graph falls from left to right, and remains constant when it neither rises nor falls. Let's now provide a more precise algebraic description for these intuitive concepts.

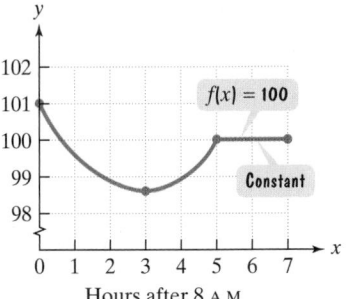

Temperature remains constant at 100° on $(5, 7)$.

Increasing, Decreasing, and Constant Functions

1. A function is **increasing** on an open interval, I, if $f(x_1) < f(x_2)$ whenever $x_1 < x_2$ for any x_1 and x_2 in the interval.

2. A function is **decreasing** on an open interval, I, if $f(x_1) > f(x_2)$ whenever $x_1 < x_2$ for any x_1 and x_2 in the interval.

3. A function is **constant** on an open interval, I, if $f(x_1) = f(x_2)$ for any x_1 and x_2 in the interval.

Increasing	**Decreasing**	**Constant**
		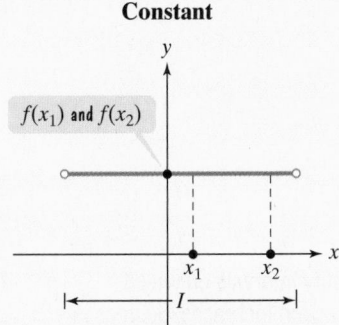
(1) For $x_1 < x_2$ in I, $f(x_1) < f(x_2)$; f is increasing on I.	**(2)** For $x_1 < x_2$ in I, $f(x_1) > f(x_2)$; f is decreasing on I.	**(3)** For x_1 and x_2 in I, $f(x_1) = f(x_2)$; f is constant on I.

EXAMPLE 1 Intervals on Which a Function Increases, Decreases, or Is Constant

State the intervals on which each given function is increasing, decreasing, or constant.

a.

b.
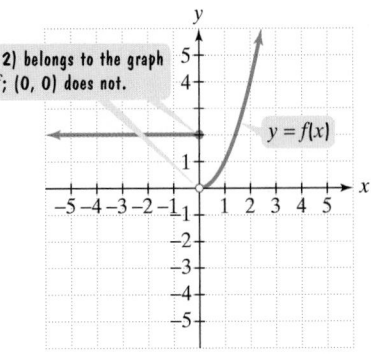

Solution

a. The function is decreasing on the interval $(-\infty, 0)$, increasing on the interval $(0, 2)$, and decreasing on the interval $(2, \infty)$.

b. Although the function's equations are not given, the graph indicates that the function is defined in two pieces. The part of the graph to the left of the *y*-axis shows that the function is constant on the interval $(-\infty, 0)$. The part to the right of the *y*-axis shows that the function is increasing on the interval $(0, \infty)$. ●

○ Check Point 1 State the intervals on which the given function is increasing, decreasing, or constant.

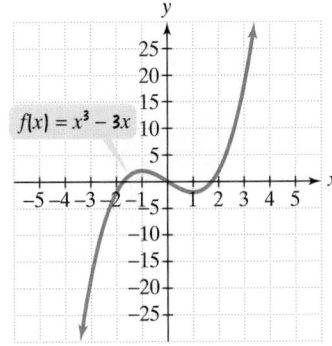

② Use graphs to locate relative maxima or minima.

Relative Maxima and Relative Minima

The points at which a function changes its increasing or decreasing behavior can be used to find the *relative maximum* or *relative minimum* values of the function.

Definitions of Relative Maximum and Relative Minimum

1. A function value $f(a)$ is a **relative maximum** of *f* if there exists an open interval containing *a* such that $f(a) > f(x)$ for all $x \neq a$ in the open interval.

2. A function value $f(b)$ is a **relative minimum** of *f* if there exists an open interval containing *b* such that $f(b) < f(x)$ for all $x \neq b$ in the open interval.

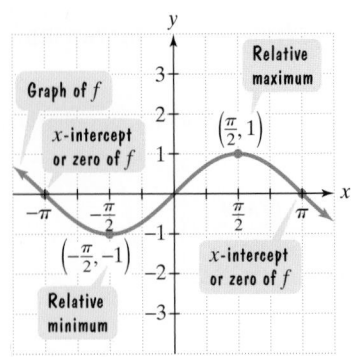

Figure 2.16 Using a graph to locate where a function has a relative maximum or minimum

③ Identify even or odd functions and recognize their symmetries.

Figure 2.17 To most people, an attractive face is one in which each half is an almost perfect mirror image of the other half.

If the graph of a function is given, we can often visually locate the number(s) at which the function has a relative maximum or a relative minimum. For example, the graph of f in **Figure 2.16** shows that

- f has a relative maximum at $\dfrac{\pi}{2}$.

 The relative maximum is $f\left(\dfrac{\pi}{2}\right) = 1$.

- f has a relative minimum at $-\dfrac{\pi}{2}$.

 The relative minimum is $f\left(-\dfrac{\pi}{2}\right) = -1$.

Notice that f does not have a relative maximum or minimum at $-\pi$ and π, the x-intercepts, or zeros, of the function.

Even and Odd Functions and Symmetry

Is beauty in the eye of the beholder? Or are there certain objects (or people) that are so well balanced and proportioned that they are universally pleasing to the eye? What constitutes an attractive human face? In **Figure 2.17**, we've drawn lines between paired features and marked the midpoints. Notice how the features line up almost perfectly. Each half of the face is a mirror image of the other half through the white vertical line.

Did you know that graphs of some equations exhibit exactly the kind of symmetry shown by the attractive face in **Figure 2.17**? The word *symmetry* comes from the Greek *symmetria*, meaning "the same measure." We can identify graphs with symmetry by looking at a function's equation and determining if the function is *even* or *odd*.

Definitions of Even and Odd Functions

The function f is an **even function** if

$$f(-x) = f(x) \quad \text{for all } x \text{ in the domain of } f.$$

The right side of the equation of an even function does not change if x is replaced with $-x$.

The function f is an **odd function** if

$$f(-x) = -f(x) \quad \text{for all } x \text{ in the domain of } f.$$

Every term on the right side of the equation of an odd function changes its sign if x is replaced with $-x$.

EXAMPLE 2 **Identifying Even or Odd Functions**

Determine whether each of the following functions is even, odd, or neither:

a. $f(x) = x^3 - 6x$ **b.** $g(x) = x^4 - 2x^2$ **c.** $h(x) = x^2 + 2x + 1$.

Solution In each case, replace x with $-x$ and simplify. If the right side of the equation stays the same, the function is even. If every term on the right side changes sign, the function is odd.

a. We use the given function's equation, $f(x) = x^3 - 6x$, to find $f(-x)$.

Use $f(x) = x^3 - 6x$.

Replace x with $-x$.

$$f(-x) = (-x)^3 - 6(-x) = (-x)(-x)(-x) - 6(-x) = -x^3 + 6x$$

There are two terms on the right side of the given equation, $f(x) = x^3 - 6x$, and each term changed its sign when we replaced x with $-x$. Because $f(-x) = -f(x)$, f is an odd function.

b. We use the given function's equation, $g(x) = x^4 - 2x^2$, to find $g(-x)$.

Use $g(x) = x^4 - 2x^2$.

Replace x with $-x$.

$$g(-x) = (-x)^4 - 2(-x)^2 = (-x)(-x)(-x)(-x) - 2(-x)(-x)$$
$$= x^4 - 2x^2$$

The right side of the equation of the given function, $g(x) = x^4 - 2x^2$, did not change when we replaced x with $-x$. Because $g(-x) = g(x)$, g is an even function.

c. We use the given function's equation, $h(x) = x^2 + 2x + 1$, to find $h(-x)$.

Use $h(x) = x^2 + 2x + 1$.

Replace x with $-x$.

$$h(-x) = (-x)^2 + 2(-x) + 1 = x^2 - 2x + 1$$

The right side of the equation of the given function, $h(x) = x^2 + 2x + 1$, changed when we replaced x with $-x$. Thus, $h(-x) \neq h(x)$, so h is not an even function. The sign of *each* of the three terms in the equation for $h(x)$ did not change when we replaced x with $-x$. Only the second term changed signs. Thus, $h(-x) \neq -h(x)$, so h is not an odd function. We conclude that h is neither an even nor an odd function.

⊘ **Check Point 2** Determine whether each of the following functions is even, odd, or neither:

a. $f(x) = x^2 + 6$ **b.** $g(x) = 7x^3 - x$ **c.** $h(x) = x^5 + 1$.

Now, let's see what even and odd functions tell us about a function's graph. Begin with the even function $f(x) = x^2 - 4$, shown in **Figure 2.18**. The function is even because

$$f(-x) = (-x)^2 - 4 = x^2 - 4 = f(x).$$

Examine the pairs of points shown, such as $(3, 5)$ and $(-3, 5)$. Notice that we obtain the same y-coordinate whenever we evaluate the function at a value of x and the value of its opposite, $-x$. Like the attractive face, each half of the graph is a mirror image of the other half through the y-axis. If we were to fold the paper along the y-axis, the two halves of the graph would coincide. This is what it means for the graph to be *symmetric with respect to the y-axis*. A graph is **symmetric with respect to the y-axis** if, for every point (x, y) on the graph, the point $(-x, y)$ is also on the graph. All even functions have graphs with this kind of symmetry.

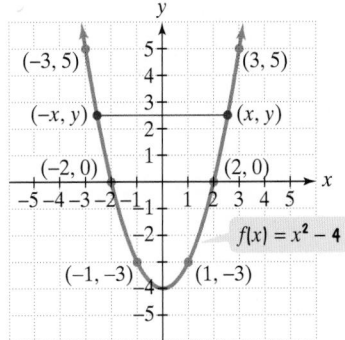

Figure 2.18 y-axis symmetry with $f(-x) = f(x)$

Even Functions and *y*-Axis Symmetry

The graph of an even function in which $f(-x) = f(x)$ is symmetric with respect to the y-axis.

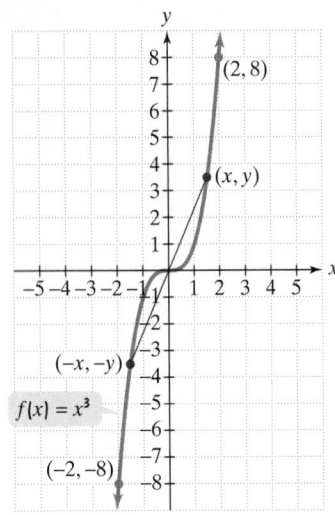

Figure 2.19 Origin symmetry with $f(-x) = -f(x)$

Now, consider the graph of the function $f(x) = x^3$, shown in **Figure 2.19**. The function is odd because

$$f(-x) = (-x)^3 = (-x)(-x)(-x) = -x^3 = -f(x).$$

Although the graph in **Figure 2.19** is not symmetric with respect to the y-axis, it is symmetric in another way. Look at the pairs of points, such as $(2, 8)$ and $(-2, -8)$. For each point (x, y) on the graph, the point $(-x, -y)$ is also on the graph. The points $(2, 8)$ and $(-2, -8)$ are reflections of one another through the origin. This means that the origin is the midpoint of the line segment connecting the points.

A graph is **symmetric with respect to the origin** if, for every point (x, y) on the graph, the point $(-x, -y)$ is also on the graph. Observe that the first- and third-quadrant portions of $f(x) = x^3$ are reflections of one another with respect to the origin. Notice that $f(x)$ and $f(-x)$ have opposite signs, so that $f(-x) = -f(x)$. All odd functions have graphs with origin symmetry.

Odd Functions and Origin Symmetry

The graph of an odd function in which $f(-x) = -f(x)$ is symmetric with respect to the origin.

④ Understand and use piecewise functions.

Piecewise Functions

A cellular phone company offers the following plan:

- $20 per month buys 60 minutes.
- Additional time costs $0.40 per minute.

We can represent this plan mathematically by writing the total monthly cost, C, as a function of the number of calling minutes, t.

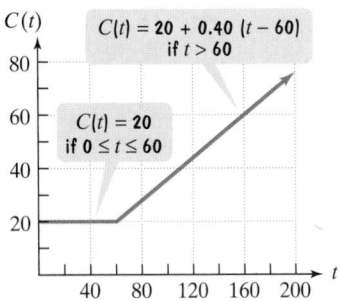

Figure 2.20

$$C(t) = \begin{cases} 20 & \text{if } 0 \leq t \leq 60 \\ 20 + 0.40(t - 60) & \text{if } t > 60 \end{cases}$$

The cost is $20 for up to and including 60 calling minutes.

The cost is $20 plus $0.40 per minute for additional time for more than 60 calling minutes.

$20 for first 60 minutes ・ $0.40 per minute ・ times the number of calling minutes exceeding 60

A function that is defined by two (or more) equations over a specified domain is called a **piecewise function**. Many cellular phone plans can be represented with piecewise functions. The graph of the piecewise function described above is shown in **Figure 2.20**.

EXAMPLE 3 Evaluating a Piecewise Function

Use the function that describes the cellular phone plan

$$C(t) = \begin{cases} 20 & \text{if } 0 \leq t \leq 60 \\ 20 + 0.40(t - 60) & \text{if } t > 60 \end{cases}$$

to find and interpret each of the following:

a. $C(30)$ **b.** $C(100)$.

Solution

a. To find $C(30)$, we let $t = 30$. Because 30 lies between 0 and 60, we use the first line of the piecewise function.

$$C(t) = 20 \qquad \text{This is the function's equation for } 0 \leq t \leq 60.$$
$$C(30) = 20 \qquad \text{Replace } t \text{ with 30. Regardless of this function's input, the constant output is 20.}$$

This means that with 30 calling minutes, the monthly cost is $20. This can be visually represented by the point $(30, 20)$ on the first piece of the graph in **Figure 2.20**.

b. To find $C(100)$, we let $t = 100$. Because 100 is greater than 60, we use the second line of the piecewise function.

$$C(t) = 20 + 0.40(t - 60)$$ This is the function's equation for $t > 60$.

$$C(100) = 20 + 0.40(100 - 60)$$ Replace t with 100.

$$= 20 + 0.40(40)$$ Subtract within parentheses: $100 - 60 = 40$.

$$= 20 + 16$$ Multiply: $0.40(40) = 16$.

$$= 36$$ Add: $20 + 16 = 36$.

Thus, $C(100) = 36$. This means that with 100 calling minutes, the monthly cost is $36. This can be visually represented by the point $(100, 36)$ on the second piece of the graph in **Figure 2.20**.

⊘ Check Point **3** Use the function in Example 2 to find and interpret each of the following:

 a. $C(40)$ **b.** $C(80)$.

Identify your solutions by points on the graph in **Figure 2.20**.

(**EXAMPLE 4**) **Graphing a Piecewise Function**

Graph the piecewise function defined by

$$f(x) = \begin{cases} x + 2 & \text{if} \quad x \le 1 \\ 4 & \text{if} \quad x > 1. \end{cases}$$

Solution We graph f in two parts, using a partial table of coordinates to create each piece. The tables of coordinates and the completed graph are shown in **Figure 2.21**.

Graph $f(x) = x + 2$ for $x \le 1$.
Domain $= (-\infty, 1]$

x ($x \le 1$)	$f(x) = x + 2$	$(x, f(x))$
1	$f(1) = 1 + 2 = 3$	$(1, 3)$
0	$f(0) = 0 + 2 = 2$	$(0, 2)$
−1	$f(-1) = -1 + 2 = 1$	$(-1, 1)$
−2	$f(-2) = -2 + 2 = 0$	$(-2, 0)$
−3	$f(-3) = -3 + 2 = -1$	$(-3, -1)$
−4	$f(-4) = -4 + 2 = -2$	$(-4, -2)$

Graph $f(x) = 4$ for $x > 1$.
Domain $= (1, \infty)$

x ($x > 1$)	$f(x) = 4$	$(x, f(x))$
1.5	$f(1.5) = 4$	$(1.5, 4)$
2	$f(2) = 4$	$(2, 4)$
3	$f(3) = 4$	$(3, 4)$
4	$f(4) = 4$	$(4, 4)$
5	$f(5) = 4$	$(5, 4)$

Figure 2.21 Graphing a piecewise function

We can use the graph of the piecewise function in **Figure 2.21** to find the range of f. The range of the piece on the left is $\{y | y \le 3\}$. The range of the horizontal piece on the right is $\{y | y = 4\}$. Thus, the range of f is

$$\{y | y \le 3\} \cup \{y | y = 4\}, \text{ or } (-\infty, 3] \cup \{4\}.$$

✓ Check Point **4** Graph the piecewise function defined by

$$f(x) = \begin{cases} 3 & \text{if} \quad x \leq -1 \\ x - 2 & \text{if} \quad x > -1. \end{cases}$$

Some piecewise functions are called **step functions** because their graphs form discontinuous steps. One such function is called the **greatest integer function**, symbolized by $\text{int}(x)$ or $[\![x]\!]$, where

$$\text{int}(x) = \text{the greatest integer that is less than or equal to } x.$$

For example,

$$\text{int}(1) = 1, \quad \text{int}(1.3) = 1, \quad \text{int}(1.5) = 1, \quad \text{int}(1.9) = 1.$$

1 is the greatest integer that is less than or equal to 1, 1.3, 1.5, and 1.9.

Here are some additional examples:

$$\text{int}(2) = 2, \quad \text{int}(2.3) = 2, \quad \text{int}(2.5) = 2, \quad \text{int}(2.9) = 2.$$

2 is the greatest integer that is less than or equal to 2, 2.3, 2.5, and 2.9.

Notice how we jumped from 1 to 2 in the function values for $\text{int}(x)$. In particular,

$$\text{If } 1 \leq x < 2, \quad \text{then} \quad \text{int}(x) = 1.$$
$$\text{If } 2 \leq x < 3, \quad \text{then} \quad \text{int}(x) = 2.$$

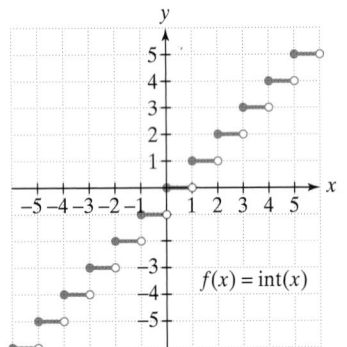

Figure 2.22 The graph of the greatest integer function

The graph of $f(x) = \text{int}(x)$ is shown in **Figure 2.22**. The graph of the greatest integer function jumps vertically one unit at each integer. However, the graph is constant between each pair of consecutive integers. The rightmost horizontal step shown in the graph illustrates that

$$\text{If } 5 \leq x < 6, \quad \text{then} \quad \text{int}(x) = 5.$$

In general,

$$\text{If } n \leq x < n + 1, \text{ where } n \text{ is an integer}, \quad \text{then} \quad \text{int}(x) = n.$$

⑤ Find and simplify a function's difference quotient.

Functions and Difference Quotients

In the next section, we will be studying the average rate of change of a function. A ratio, called the *difference quotient*, plays an important role in understanding the rate at which functions change.

Definition of the Difference Quotient of a Function

The expression

$$\frac{f(x + h) - f(x)}{h}$$

for $h \neq 0$ is called the **difference quotient** of the function f.

(**EXAMPLE 5**) **Evaluating and Simplifying a Difference Quotient**

If $f(x) = 2x^2 - x + 3$, find and simplify each expression:

a. $f(x + h)$ **b.** $\dfrac{f(x + h) - f(x)}{h}, h \neq 0.$

Solution

a. We find $f(x + h)$ by replacing x with $x + h$ each time that x appears in the equation.

$$f(x) = 2x^2 \quad - \quad x \quad + \quad 3$$

Replace x with $x + h$.	Replace x with $x + h$.	Replace x with $x + h$.	Copy the 3. There is no x in this term.

$$f(x + h) = 2(x + h)^2 - (x + h) \quad + \quad 3$$
$$= 2(x^2 + 2xh + h^2) - x - h \ + \ 3$$
$$= 2x^2 + 4xh + 2h^2 - x - h \ + \ 3$$

b. Using our result from part (a), we obtain the following:

This is $f(x + h)$ from part (a).	This is $f(x)$ from the given equation.

$$\frac{f(x + h) - f(x)}{h} = \frac{\boxed{2x^2 + 4xh + 2h^2 - x - h + 3} - (2x^2 - x + 3)}{h}$$

$$= \frac{2x^2 + 4xh + 2h^2 - x - h + 3 - 2x^2 + x - 3}{h} \qquad \text{Remove parentheses and change the sign of each term in the parentheses.}$$

$$= \frac{(2x^2 - 2x^2) + (-x + x) + (3 - 3) + 4xh + 2h^2 - h}{h} \qquad \text{Group like terms.}$$

$$= \frac{4xh + 2h^2 - 1h}{h} \qquad \text{Simplify.}$$

We wrote $-h$ as $-1h$ to avoid possible errors in the next factoring step.

$$= \frac{h(4x + 2h - 1)}{h} \qquad \text{Factor h from the numerator.}$$

$$= 4x + 2h - 1 \qquad \text{Divide out identical factors of h in the numerator and denominator.}$$

⟡ Check Point **5** If $f(x) = -2x^2 + x + 5$, find and simplify each expression:

a. $f(x + h)$ **b.** $\dfrac{f(x + h) - f(x)}{h}, h \neq 0.$

Exercise Set 2.2

Practice Exercises

In Exercises 1–12, use the graph to determine

 a. *intervals on which the function is increasing, if any.*
 b. *intervals on which the function is decreasing, if any.*
 c. *intervals on which the function is constant, if any.*

1.

2.

3.

4.

5.

6.

7.

8.

9.

10.

11.

12.

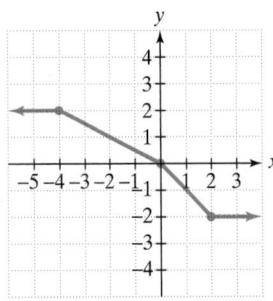

In Exercises 13–16, the graph of a function f is given. Use the graph to find each of the following:

 a. The numbers, if any, at which f has a relative maximum. What are these relative maxima?

 b. The numbers, if any, at which f has a relative minimum. What are these relative minima?

13.

14.

15.

$f(x) = 2x^3 + 3x^2 - 12x + 1$

$[-4, 4, 1]$ by $[-15, 25, 5]$

16.

$f(x) = 2x^3 - 15x^2 + 24x + 19$

$[-2, 6, 1]$ by $[-15, 35, 5]$

In Exercises 17–28, determine whether each function is even, odd, or neither.

17. $f(x) = x^3 + x$

18. $f(x) = x^3 - x$

19. $g(x) = x^2 + x$

20. $g(x) = x^2 - x$

21. $h(x) = x^2 - x^4$

22. $h(x) = 2x^2 + x^4$

23. $f(x) = x^2 - x^4 + 1$

24. $f(x) = 2x^2 + x^4 + 1$

25. $f(x) = \frac{1}{5}x^6 - 3x^2$

26. $f(x) = 2x^3 - 6x^5$

27. $f(x) = x\sqrt{1 - x^2}$

28. $f(x) = x^2\sqrt{1 - x^2}$

In Exercises 29–32, use possible symmetry to determine whether each graph is the graph of an even function, an odd function, or a function that is neither even nor odd.

29.

30.

31.

32.

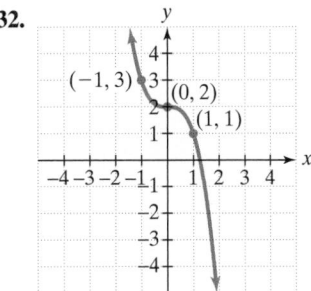

33. Use the graph of f to determine each of the following. Where applicable, use interval notation.

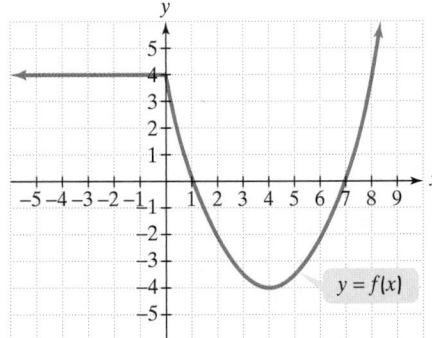

a. the domain of f

b. the range of f

c. the x-intercepts

d. the y-intercept

e. intervals on which f is increasing

f. intervals on which f is decreasing

g. intervals on which f is constant

h. the number at which f has a relative minimum

i. the relative minimum of f

j. $f(-3)$

k. the values of x for which $f(x) = -2$

l. Is f even, odd, or neither?

34. Use the graph of f to determine each of the following. Where applicable, use interval notation.

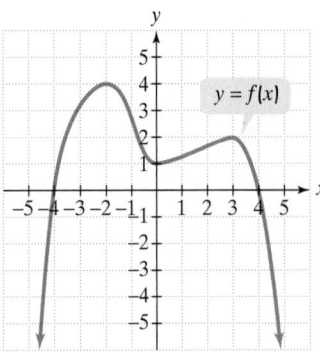

a. the domain of f

b. the range of f

c. the x-intercepts

d. the y-intercept

e. intervals on which f is increasing

f. intervals on which f is decreasing

g. values of x for which $f(x) \leq 0$

h. the numbers at which f has a relative maximum

i. the relative maxima of f

j. $f(-2)$

k. the values of x for which $f(x) = 0$

l. Is f even, odd, or neither?

35. Use the graph of f to determine each of the following. Where applicable, use interval notation.

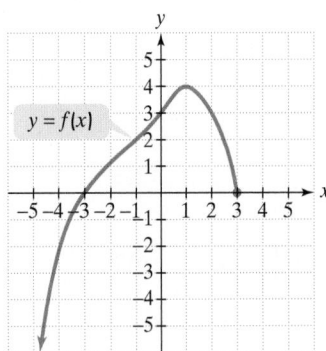

a. the domain of f

b. the range of f

c. the zeros of f

d. $f(0)$

e. intervals on which f is increasing

f. intervals on which f is decreasing

g. values of x for which $f(x) \leq 0$

h. any relative maxima and the numbers at which they occur

i. the value of x for which $f(x) = 4$

j. Is $f(-1)$ positive or negative?

36. Use the graph of f to determine each of the following. Where applicable, use interval notation.

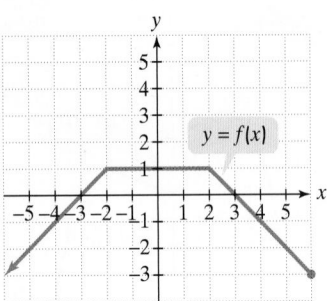

a. the domain of f

b. the range of f

c. the zeros of f

d. $f(0)$

e. intervals on which f is increasing

f. intervals on which f is decreasing

g. intervals on which f is constant

h. values of x for which $f(x) > 0$

i. values of x for which $f(x) = -2$

j. Is $f(4)$ positive or negative?

k. Is f even, odd, or neither?

l. Is $f(2)$ a relative maximum?

In Exercises 37–42, evaluate each piecewise function at the given values of the independent variable.

37. $f(x) = \begin{cases} 3x + 5 & \text{if } x < 0 \\ 4x + 7 & \text{if } x \geq 0 \end{cases}$

 a. $f(-2)$ **b.** $f(0)$ **c.** $f(3)$

38. $f(x) = \begin{cases} 6x - 1 & \text{if } x < 0 \\ 7x + 3 & \text{if } x \geq 0 \end{cases}$

 a. $f(-3)$ **b.** $f(0)$ **c.** $f(4)$

39. $g(x) = \begin{cases} x + 3 & \text{if } x \geq -3 \\ -(x + 3) & \text{if } x < -3 \end{cases}$

 a. $g(0)$ **b.** $g(-6)$ **c.** $g(-3)$

40. $g(x) = \begin{cases} x + 5 & \text{if } x \geq -5 \\ -(x + 5) & \text{if } x < -5 \end{cases}$

 a. $g(0)$ **b.** $g(-6)$ **c.** $g(-5)$

41. $h(x) = \begin{cases} \dfrac{x^2 - 9}{x - 3} & \text{if } x \neq 3 \\ 6 & \text{if } x = 3 \end{cases}$

 a. $h(5)$ **b.** $h(0)$ **c.** $h(3)$

42. $h(x) = \begin{cases} \dfrac{x^2 - 25}{x - 5} & \text{if } x \neq 5 \\ 10 & \text{if } x = 5 \end{cases}$

 a. $h(7)$ **b.** $h(0)$ **c.** $h(5)$

In Exercises 43–54, the domain of each piecewise function is $(-\infty, \infty)$.

 a. *Graph each function.*

 b. *Use your graph to determine the function's range.*

43. $f(x) = \begin{cases} -x & \text{if } x < 0 \\ x & \text{if } x \geq 0 \end{cases}$

44. $f(x) = \begin{cases} x & \text{if } x < 0 \\ -x & \text{if } x \geq 0 \end{cases}$

45. $f(x) = \begin{cases} 2x & \text{if } x \leq 0 \\ 2 & \text{if } x > 0 \end{cases}$

46. $f(x) = \begin{cases} \frac{1}{2}x & \text{if } x \leq 0 \\ 3 & \text{if } x > 0 \end{cases}$

47. $f(x) = \begin{cases} x + 3 & \text{if } x < -2 \\ x - 3 & \text{if } x \geq -2 \end{cases}$

48. $f(x) = \begin{cases} x + 2 & \text{if } x < -3 \\ x - 2 & \text{if } x \geq -3 \end{cases}$

49. $f(x) = \begin{cases} 3 & \text{if } x \leq -1 \\ -3 & \text{if } x > -1 \end{cases}$

50. $f(x) = \begin{cases} 4 & \text{if } x \leq -1 \\ -4 & \text{if } x > -1 \end{cases}$

51. $f(x) = \begin{cases} \frac{1}{2}x^2 & \text{if } x < 1 \\ 2x - 1 & \text{if } x \geq 1 \end{cases}$

52. $f(x) = \begin{cases} -\frac{1}{2}x^2 & \text{if } x < 1 \\ 2x + 1 & \text{if } x \geq 1 \end{cases}$

53. $f(x) = \begin{cases} 0 & \text{if } x < -4 \\ -x & \text{if } -4 \leq x < 0 \\ x^2 & \text{if } x \geq 0 \end{cases}$

54. $f(x) = \begin{cases} 0 & \text{if } x < -3 \\ -x & \text{if } -3 \leq x < 0 \\ x^2 - 1 & \text{if } x \geq 0 \end{cases}$

In Exercises 55–76, find and simplify the difference quotient

$$\frac{f(x + h) - f(x)}{h}, h \neq 0$$

for the given function.

55. $f(x) = 4x$ **56.** $f(x) = 7x$

57. $f(x) = 3x + 7$ **58.** $f(x) = 6x + 1$

59. $f(x) = x^2$ **60.** $f(x) = 2x^2$

61. $f(x) = x^2 - 4x + 3$ **62.** $f(x) = x^2 - 5x + 8$

63. $f(x) = 2x^2 + x - 1$ **64.** $f(x) = 3x^2 + x + 5$

65. $f(x) = -x^2 + 2x + 4$ **66.** $f(x) = -x^2 - 3x + 1$

67. $f(x) = -2x^2 + 5x + 7$ **68.** $f(x) = -3x^2 + 2x - 1$

69. $f(x) = -2x^2 - x + 3$ **70.** $f(x) = -3x^2 + x - 1$

71. $f(x) = 6$

72. $f(x) = 7$

73. $f(x) = \dfrac{1}{x}$

74. $f(x) = \dfrac{1}{2x}$

75. $f(x) = \sqrt{x}$

76. $f(x) = \sqrt{x - 1}$

Practice Plus

In Exercises 77–78, let f be defined by the following graph:

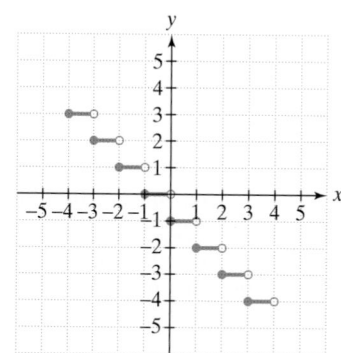

77. Find

$$\sqrt{f(-1.5) + f(-0.9)} - [f(\pi)]^2 + f(-3) \div f(1) \cdot f(-\pi).$$

78. Find

$$\sqrt{f(-2.5) - f(1.9)} - [f(-\pi)]^2 + f(-3) \div f(1) \cdot f(\pi).$$

A cellular phone company offers the following plans. Also given are the piecewise functions that model these plans. Use this information to solve Exercises 79–80.

Plan A

• $30 per month buys 120 minutes.

• Additional time costs $0.30 per minute.

$$C(t) = \begin{cases} 30 & \text{if } 0 \le t \le 120 \\ 30 + 0.30(t - 120) & \text{if } t > 120 \end{cases}$$

Plan B

• $40 per month buys 200 minutes.

• Additional time costs $0.30 per minute.

$$C(t) = \begin{cases} 40 & \text{if } 0 \le t \le 200 \\ 40 + 0.30(t - 200) & \text{if } t > 200 \end{cases}$$

79. Simplify the algebraic expression in the second line of the piecewise function for plan A. Then use point-plotting to graph the function.

80. Simplify the algebraic expression in the second line of the piecewise function for plan B. Then use point-plotting to graph the function.

In Exercises 81–82, write a piecewise function that models each cellular phone billing plan. Then graph the function.

81. $50 per month buys 400 minutes. Additional time costs $0.30 per minute.

82. $60 per month buys 450 minutes. Additional time costs $0.35 per minute.

Application Exercises

With aging, body fat increases and muscle mass declines. The line graphs show the percent body fat in adult women and men as they age from 25 to 75 years. Use the graphs to solve Exercises 83–90.

Percent Body Fat in Adults

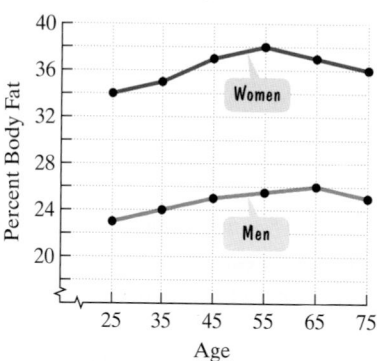

Source: Thompson et al., The Science of Nutrition, Benjamin Cummings, 2008

83. State the intervals on which the graph giving the percent body fat in women is increasing and decreasing.

84. State the intervals on which the graph giving the percent body fat in men is increasing and decreasing.

85. For what age does the percent body fat in women reach a maximum? What is the percent body fat for that age?

86. At what age does the percent body fat in men reach a maximum? What is the percent body fat for that age?

87. Use interval notation to give the domain and the range for the graph of the function for women.

88. Use interval notation to give the domain and the range for the graph of the function for men.

89. The function $p(x) = -0.002x^2 + 0.15x + 22.86$ models percent body fat, $p(x)$, where x is the number of years a person's age exceeds 25. Use the graphs to determine whether this model describes percent body fat in women or in men.

90. The function $p(x) = -0.004x^2 + 0.25x + 33.64$ models percent body fat, $p(x)$, where x is the number of years a person's age exceeds 25. Use the graphs to determine whether this model describes percent body fat in women or in men.

Here is the 2007 Federal Tax Rate Schedule X that specifies the tax owed by a single taxpayer.

If Your Taxable Income Is Over	But Not Over	The Tax You Owe Is	Of the Amount Over
$ 0	$ 7825	10%	$ 0
$ 7825	$ 31,850	$ 782.50 + 15%	$ 7825
$ 31,850	$ 77,100	$ 4386.25 + 25%	$ 31,850
$ 77,100	$160,850	$ 15,698.75 + 28%	$ 77,100
$160,850	$349,700	$ 39,148.75 + 33%	$160,850
$349,700	—	$101,469.25 + 35%	$349,700

The tax table on the previous page can be modeled by a piecewise function, where x represents the taxable income of a single taxpayer and T(x) is the tax owed:

$$T(x) = \begin{cases} 0.10x & \text{if} & 0 < x \le 7825 \\ 782.50 + 0.15(x - 7825) & \text{if} & 7825 < x \le 31,850 \\ 4386.25 + 0.25(x - 31,850) & \text{if} & 31,850 < x \le 77,100 \\ 15,698.75 + 0.28(x - 77,100) & \text{if} & 77,100 < x \le 160,850 \\ \underline{\qquad ? \qquad} & \text{if} & 160,850 < x \le 349,700 \\ \underline{\qquad ? \qquad} & \text{if} & x > 349,700. \end{cases}$$

Use this information to solve Exercises 91–94.

91. Find and interpret $T(20,000)$.

92. Find and interpret $T(50,000)$.

In Exercises 93–94, refer to the tax table on the previous page.

93. Find the algebraic expression for the missing piece of $T(x)$ that models tax owed for the domain $(160,850, 349,700]$.

94. Find the algebraic expression for the missing piece of $T(x)$ that models tax owed for the domain $(349,700, \infty)$.

The figure shows the cost of mailing a first-class letter, $f(x)$, as a function of its weight, x, in ounces, for weights not exceeding 3.5 ounces. Use the graph to solve Exercises 95–98.

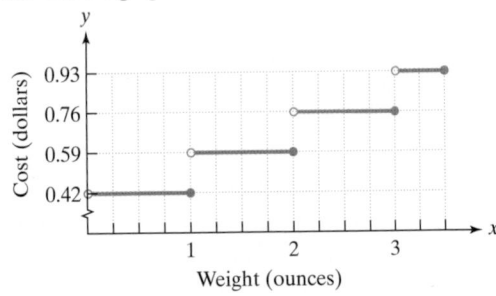

Source: Lynn E. Baring, Postmaster, Inverness, CA

95. Find $f(3)$. What does this mean in terms of the variables in this situation?

96. Find $f(3.5)$. What does this mean in terms of the variables in this situation?

97. What is the cost of mailing a letter that weighs 1.5 ounces?

98. What is the cost of mailing a letter that weighs 1.8 ounces?

99. If $3.5 < x \le 4$, the cost of mailing a first-class letter jumps to $1.34. The cost then increases by $0.17 per ounce for weights not exceeding 13 ounces:

Weight Not Exceeding	Cost
5 ounces	$1.51
6 ounces	$1.68

etc.

Use this information to extend the graph shown above so that the function's domain is $(0, 13]$.

Writing in Mathematics

100. What does it mean if a function f is increasing on an interval?

101. Suppose that a function f whose graph contains no breaks or gaps on (a, c) is increasing on (a, b), decreasing on (b, c), and defined at b. Describe what occurs at $x = b$. What does the function value $f(b)$ represent?

102. If you are given a function's equation, how do you determine if the function is even, odd, or neither?

103. If you are given a function's graph, how do you determine if the function is even, odd, or neither?

104. What is a piecewise function?

105. Explain how to find the difference quotient of a function f, $\dfrac{f(x + h) - f(x)}{h}$, if an equation for f is given.

Technology Exercises

106. The function

$$f(x) = -0.00002x^3 + 0.008x^2 - 0.3x + 6.95$$

models the number of annual physician visits, $f(x)$, by a person of age x. Graph the function in a $[0, 100, 5]$ by $[0, 40, 2]$ viewing rectangle. What does the shape of the graph indicate about the relationship between one's age and the number of annual physician visits? Use the TABLE or minimum function capability to find the coordinates of the minimum point on the graph of the function. What does this mean?

In Exercises 107–112, use a graphing utility to graph each function. Use a $[-5, 5, 1]$ by $[-5, 5, 1]$ viewing rectangle. Then find the intervals on which the function is increasing, decreasing, or constant.

108. $f(x) = x^3 - 6x^2 + 9x + 1$

108. $g(x) = |4 - x^2|$

109. $h(x) = |x - 2| + |x + 2|$

110. $f(x) = x^{\frac{1}{3}}(x - 4)$

111. $g(x) = x^{\frac{2}{3}}$

112. $h(x) = 2 - x^{\frac{2}{5}}$

113. a. Graph the functions $f(x) = x^n$ for $n = 2, 4,$ and 6 in a $[-2, 2, 1]$ by $[-1, 3, 1]$ viewing rectangle.

b. Graph the functions $f(x) = x^n$ for $n = 1, 3,$ and 5 in a $[-2, 2, 1]$ by $[-2, 2, 1]$ viewing rectangle.

c. If n is positive and even, where is the graph of $f(x) = x^n$ increasing and where is it decreasing?

d. If n is positive and odd, what can you conclude about the graph of $f(x) = x^n$ in terms of increasing or decreasing behavior?

e. Graph all six functions in a $[-1, 3, 1]$ by $[-1, 3, 1]$ viewing rectangle. What do you observe about the graphs in terms of how flat or how steep they are?

Critical Thinking Exercises

Make Sense? *In Exercises 114–117, determine whether each statement makes sense or does not make sense, and explain your reasoning.*

114. My graph is decreasing on $(-\infty, a)$ and increasing on (a, ∞), so $f(a)$ must be a relative maximum.

115. This work by artist Scott Kim (1955–) has the same kind of symmetry as an even function.

"DYSLEXIA," 1981

116. I graphed

$$f(x) = \begin{cases} 2 & \text{if} \quad x \neq 4 \\ 3 & \text{if} \quad x = 4 \end{cases}$$

and one piece of my graph is a single point.

117. I noticed that the difference quotient is always zero if $f(x) = c$, where c is any constant.

118. Sketch the graph of f using the following properties. (More than one correct graph is possible.) f is a piecewise function that is decreasing on $(-\infty, 2), f(2) = 0, f$ is increasing on $(2, \infty)$, and the range of f is $[0, \infty)$.

119. Define a piecewise function on the intervals $(-\infty, 2], (2, 5)$, and $[5, \infty)$ that does not "jump" at 2 or 5 such that one piece is a constant function, another piece is an increasing function, and the third piece is a decreasing function.

120. Suppose that $h(x) = \dfrac{f(x)}{g(x)}$. The function f can be even, odd, or neither. The same is true for the function g.

 a. Under what conditions is h definitely an even function?

 b. Under what conditions is h definitely an odd function?

Group Exercise

121. (For assistance with this exercise, refer to the discussion of piecewise functions beginning on page 220, as well as to Exercises 79–80.) Group members who have cellular phone plans should describe the total monthly cost of the plan as follows:

$____$ per month buys $____$ minutes. Additional time costs $\$____$ per minute.

(For simplicity, ignore other charges.) The group should select any three plans, from "basic" to "premier." For each plan selected, write a piecewise function that describes the plan and graph the function. Graph the three functions in the same rectangular coordinate system. Now examine the graphs. For any given number of calling minutes, the best plan is the one whose graph is lowest at that point. Compare the three calling plans. Is one plan always a better deal than the other two? If not, determine the interval of calling minutes for which each plan is the best deal. (You can check out cellular phone plans by visiting www.point.com.)

Preview Exercises

Exercises 122–124 will help you prepare for the material covered in the next section.

122. If $(x_1, y_1) = (-3, 1)$ and $(x_2, y_2) = (-2, 4)$, find $\dfrac{y_2 - y_1}{x_2 - x_1}$.

123. Find the ordered pairs (____, 0) and (0, ____) satisfying $4x - 3y - 6 = 0$.

124. Solve for y: $3x + 2y - 4 = 0$.

Section 2.3 **Linear Functions and Slope**

Objectives

1 Calculate a line's slope.

2 Write the point-slope form of the equation of a line.

3 Write and graph the slope-intercept form of the equation of a line.

4 Graph horizontal or vertical lines.

5 Recognize and use the general form of a line's equation.

6 Use intercepts to graph the general form of a line's equation.

7 Model data with linear functions and make predictions.

Is there a relationship between literacy and child mortality? As the percentage of adult females who are literate increases, does the mortality of children under five decrease? **Figure 2.23** on the next page indicates that this is, indeed, the case. Each point in the figure represents one country.

Literacy and Child Mortality

A scatter plot with *x*-axis labeled "Percentage of Adult Females Who Are Literate" ranging from 0 to 100, and *y*-axis labeled "Under-Five Mortality (per thousand)" ranging from 0 to 350. A regression line passes through the data points with a negative slope.

Figure 2.23
Source: United Nations

Data presented in a visual form as a set of points is called a **scatter plot**. Also shown in **Figure 2.23** is a line that passes through or near the points. A line that best fits the data points in a scatter plot is called a **regression line**. By writing the equation of this line, we can obtain a model for the data and make predictions about child mortality based on the percentage of literate adult females in a country.

Data often fall on or near a line. In this section, we will use functions to model such data and make predictions. We begin with a discussion of a line's steepness.

① Calculate a line's slope.

The Slope of a Line

Mathematicians have developed a useful measure of the steepness of a line, called the *slope* of the line. Slope compares the vertical change (the **rise**) to the horizontal change (the **run**) when moving from one fixed point to another along the line. To calculate the slope of a line, we use a ratio that compares the change in *y* (the rise) to the corresponding change in *x* (the run).

Definition of Slope

The **slope** of the line through the distinct points (x_1, y_1) and (x_2, y_2) is

$$\frac{\text{Change in } y}{\text{Change in } x} = \frac{\text{Rise}}{\text{Run}} \quad \text{Vertical change} \atop \text{Horizontal change}$$

$$= \frac{y_2 - y_1}{x_2 - x_1},$$

where $x_2 - x_1 \neq 0$.

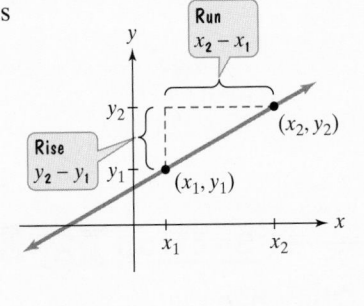

It is common notation to let the letter *m* represent the slope of a line. The letter *m* is used because it is the first letter of the French verb *monter*, meaning "to rise" or "to ascend."

EXAMPLE 1 Using the Definition of Slope

Find the slope of the line passing through each pair of points:

a. $(-3, -1)$ and $(-2, 4)$ **b.** $(-3, 4)$ and $(2, -2)$.

Solution

a. Let $(x_1, y_1) = (-3, -1)$ and $(x_2, y_2) = (-2, 4)$. We obtain the slope as follows:

$$m = \frac{\text{Change in } y}{\text{Change in } x} = \frac{y_2 - y_1}{x_2 - x_1} = \frac{4 - (-1)}{-2 - (-3)} = \frac{5}{1} = 5.$$

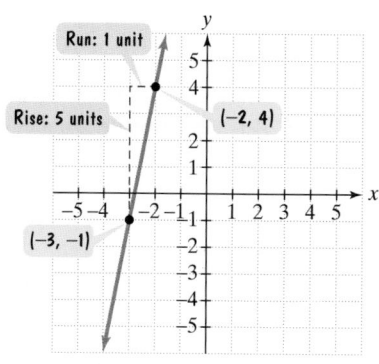

Figure 2.24 Visualizing a slope of 5

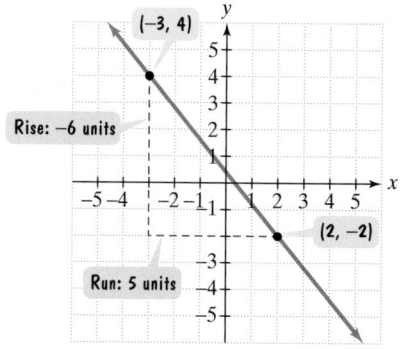

Figure 2.25 Visualizing a slope of $-\frac{6}{5}$

Study Tip

Always be clear in the way you use language, especially in mathematics. For example, it's not a good idea to say that a line has "no slope." This could mean that the slope is zero or that the slope is undefined.

The situation is illustrated in **Figure 2.24**. The slope of the line is 5. For every vertical change, or rise, of 5 units, there is a corresponding horizontal change, or run, of 1 unit. The slope is positive and the line rises from left to right.

Study Tip

When computing slope, it makes no difference which point you call (x_1, y_1) and which point you call (x_2, y_2). If we let $(x_1, y_1) = (-2, 4)$ and $(x_2, y_2) = (-3, -1)$, the slope is still 5:

$$m = \frac{\text{Change in } y}{\text{Change in } x} = \frac{y_2 - y_1}{x_2 - x_1} = \frac{-1 - 4}{-3 - (-2)} = \frac{-5}{-1} = 5.$$

However, you should not subtract in one order in the numerator $(y_2 - y_1)$ and then in a different order in the denominator $(x_1 - x_2)$.

$$\frac{-1 - 4}{-2 - (-3)} = \frac{-5}{1} = -5. \quad \text{Incorrect! The slope is not } -5.$$

b. To find the slope of the line passing through $(-3, 4)$ and $(2, -2)$, we can let $(x_1, y_1) = (-3, 4)$ and $(x_2, y_2) = (2, -2)$. The slope of the line is computed as follows:

$$m = \frac{\text{Change in } y}{\text{Change in } x} = \frac{y_2 - y_1}{x_2 - x_1} = \frac{-2 - 4}{2 - (-3)} = \frac{-6}{5} = -\frac{6}{5}.$$

The situation is illustrated in **Figure 2.25**. The slope of the line is $-\frac{6}{5}$. For every vertical change of -6 units (6 units down), there is a corresponding horizontal change of 5 units. The slope is negative and the line falls from left to right. ●

⊘ **Check Point 1** Find the slope of the line passing through each pair of points:

a. $(-3, 4)$ and $(-4, -2)$ **b.** $(4, -2)$ and $(-1, 5)$.

Example 1 illustrates that a line with a positive slope is increasing and a line with a negative slope is decreasing. By contrast, a horizontal line is a constant function and has a slope of zero. A vertical line has no horizontal change, so $x_2 - x_1 = 0$ in the formula for slope. Because we cannot divide by zero, the slope of a vertical line is undefined. This discussion is summarized in **Table 2.2**.

Table 2.2 Possibilities for a Line's Slope

Positive Slope	Negative Slope	Zero Slope	Undefined Slope
$m > 0$	$m < 0$	$m = 0$	m is undefined.
Line rises from left to right.	Line falls from left to right.	Line is horizontal.	Line is vertical.

2 Write the point-slope form of the equation of a line.

The Point-Slope Form of the Equation of a Line

We can use the slope of a line to obtain various forms of the line's equation. For example, consider a nonvertical line that has slope m and that contains the point (x_1, y_1).

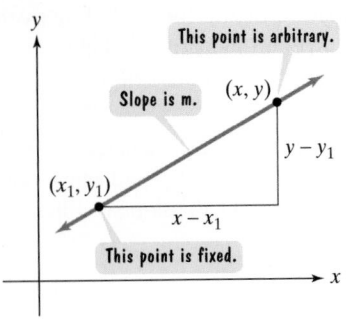

Figure 2.26 A line passing through (x_1, y_1) with slope m

The line in **Figure 2.26** has slope m and contains the point (x_1, y_1). Let (x, y) represent any other point on the line.

Regardless of where the point (x, y) is located, the steepness of the line in **Figure 2.26** remains the same. Thus, the ratio for the slope stays a constant m. This means that for all points (x, y) along the line

$$m = \frac{\text{Change in } y}{\text{Change in } x} = \frac{y - y_1}{x - x_1}.$$

We can clear the fraction by multiplying both sides by $x - x_1$, the least common denominator.

$$m = \frac{y - y_1}{x - x_1} \qquad \text{This is the slope of the line in Figure 2.26.}$$

$$m(x - x_1) = \frac{y - y_1}{x - x_1} \cdot (x - x_1) \qquad \text{Multiply both sides by } x - x_1.$$

$$m(x - x_1) = y - y_1 \qquad \text{Simplify: } \frac{y - y_1}{x - x_1} \cdot (x - x_1) = y - y_1.$$

Now, if we reverse the two sides, we obtain the *point-slope form* of the equation of a line.

Study Tip

When writing the point-slope form of a line's equation, you will never substitute numbers for x and y. You will substitute values for x_1, y_1, and m.

Point-Slope Form of the Equation of a Line

The **point-slope form of the equation** of a nonvertical line with slope m that passes through the point (x_1, y_1) is

$$y - y_1 = m(x - x_1).$$

For example, the point-slope form of the equation of the line passing through $(1, 5)$ with slope 2 $(m = 2)$ is

$$y - 5 = 2(x - 1).$$

We will soon be expressing the equation of a nonvertical line in function notation. To do so, we need to solve the point-slope form of a line's equation for y. Example 2 illustrates how to isolate y on one side of the equal sign.

EXAMPLE 2 **Writing an Equation in Point-Slope Form for a Line**

Write an equation in point-slope form for the line with slope 4 that passes through the point $(-1, 3)$. Then solve the equation for y.

Solution We use the point-slope form of the equation of a line with $m = 4$, $x_1 = -1$, and $y_1 = 3$.

$$y - y_1 = m(x - x_1) \qquad \text{This is the point-slope form of the equation.}$$

$$y - 3 = 4[x - (-1)] \qquad \text{Substitute the given values: } m = 4 \text{ and } (x_1, y_1) = (-1, 3).$$

$$y - 3 = 4(x + 1) \qquad \text{We now have an equation in point-slope form for the given line.}$$

Now we solve this equation for y and write an equivalent equation that can be expressed in function notation.

We need to isolate y.

$$y - 3 = 4(x + 1) \qquad \text{This is the point-slope form of the equation.}$$

$$y - 3 = 4x + 4 \qquad \text{Use the distributive property.}$$

$$y = 4x + 7 \qquad \text{Add 3 to both sides.}$$

⊘ Check Point **2** Write an equation in point-slope form for the line with slope 6 that passes through the point $(2, -5)$. Then solve the equation for y.

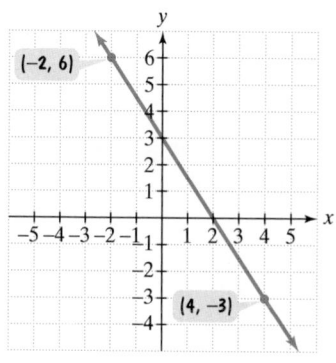

Figure 2.27 Write an equation in point-slope form for this line

Discovery

You can use either point for (x_1, y_1) when you write a point-slope equation for a line. Rework Example 3 using $(-2, 6)$ for (x_1, y_1). Once you solve for y, you should still obtain

$$y = -\frac{3}{2}x + 3.$$

③ Write and graph the slope-intercept form of the equation of a line.

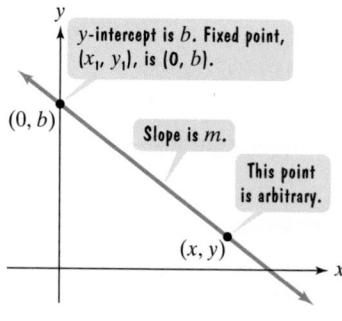

Figure 2.28 A line with slope m and y-intercept b

EXAMPLE 3 Writing an Equation in Point-Slope Form for a Line

Write an equation in point-slope form for the line passing through the points $(4, -3)$ and $(-2, 6)$. (See **Figure 2.27**.) Then solve the equation for y.

Solution To use the point-slope form, we need to find the slope. The slope is the change in the y-coordinates divided by the corresponding change in the x-coordinates.

$$m = \frac{6 - (-3)}{-2 - 4} = \frac{9}{-6} = -\frac{3}{2} \quad \text{This is the definition of slope using } (4, -3) \text{ and } (-2, 6).$$

We can take either point on the line to be (x_1, y_1). Let's use $(x_1, y_1) = (4, -3)$. Now, we are ready to write the point-slope form of the equation.

$$y - y_1 = m(x - x_1) \quad \text{This is the point-slope form of the equation.}$$
$$y - (-3) = -\frac{3}{2}(x - 4) \quad \text{Substitute: } (x_1, y_1) = (4, -3) \text{ and } m = -\frac{3}{2}.$$
$$y + 3 = -\frac{3}{2}(x - 4) \quad \text{Simplify.}$$

We now have an equation in point-slope form for the line shown in **Figure 2.27**. Now, we solve this equation for y.

We need to isolate y.

$$y + 3 = -\frac{3}{2}(x - 4) \quad \text{This is the point-slope form of the equation.}$$
$$y + 3 = -\frac{3}{2}x + 6 \quad \text{Use the distributive property.}$$
$$y = -\frac{3}{2}x + 3 \quad \text{Subtract 3 from both sides.}$$

✓ Check Point 3 Write an equation in point-slope form for the line passing through the points $(-2, -1)$ and $(-1, -6)$. Then solve the equation for y.

The Slope-Intercept Form of the Equation of a Line

Let's write the point-slope form of the equation of a nonvertical line with slope m and y-intercept b. The line is shown in **Figure 2.28**. Because the y-intercept is b, the line passes through $(0, b)$. We use the point-slope form with $x_1 = 0$ and $y_1 = b$.

$$y - y_1 = m(x - x_1)$$

Let $y_1 = b$. Let $x_1 = 0$.

We obtain

$$y - b = m(x - 0).$$

Simplifying on the right side gives us

$$y - b = mx.$$

Finally, we solve for y by adding b to both sides.

$$y = mx + b$$

Thus, if a line's equation is written with y isolated on one side, the coefficient of x is the line's slope and the constant term is the y-intercept. This form of a line's equation is called the *slope-intercept form* of the line.

> **Slope-Intercept Form of the Equation of a Line**
>
> The **slope-intercept form of the equation** of a nonvertical line with slope m and y-intercept b is
>
> $$y = mx + b.$$

The slope-intercept form of a line's equation, $y = mx + b$, can be expressed in function notation by replacing y with $f(x)$:

$$f(x) = mx + b.$$

We have seen that functions in this form are called **linear functions**. Thus, in the equation of a linear function, the coefficient of x is the line's slope and the constant term is the y-intercept. Here are two examples:

$$y = 2x - 4 \qquad\qquad f(x) = \frac{1}{2}x + 2.$$

| The slope is 2. | The y-intercept is −4. | | The slope is $\frac{1}{2}$. | The y-intercept is 2. |

If a linear function's equation is in slope-intercept form, we can use the y-intercept and the slope to obtain its graph.

Graphing $y = mx + b$ Using the Slope and y-Intercept

1. Plot the point containing the y-intercept on the y-axis. This is the point $(0, b)$.
2. Obtain a second point using the slope, m. Write m as a fraction, and use rise over run, starting at the point containing the y-intercept, to plot this point.
3. Use a straightedge to draw a line through the two points. Draw arrowheads at the ends of the line to show that the line continues indefinitely in both directions.

Study Tip

Writing the slope, m, as a fraction allows you to identify the rise (the fraction's numerator) and the run (the fraction's denominator).

EXAMPLE 4 **Graphing Using the Slope and y-Intercept**

Graph the linear function: $f(x) = -\frac{3}{2}x + 2$.

Solution The equation of the line is in the form $f(x) = mx + b$. We can find the slope, m, by identifying the coefficient of x. We can find the y-intercept, b, by identifying the constant term.

$$f(x) = -\frac{3}{2}x + 2$$

| The slope is $-\frac{3}{2}$. | The y-intercept is 2. |

Now that we have identified the slope, $-\frac{3}{2}$, and the y-intercept, 2, we use the three-step procedure to graph the equation.

Step 1 Plot the point containing the y-intercept on the y-axis. The y-intercept is 2. We plot $(0, 2)$, shown in **Figure 2.29**.

Step 2 Obtain a second point using the slope, m. Write m as a fraction, and use rise over run, starting at the point containing the y-intercept, to plot this point. The slope, $-\frac{3}{2}$, is already written as a fraction.

$$m = -\frac{3}{2} = \frac{-3}{2} = \frac{\text{Rise}}{\text{Run}}$$

We plot the second point on the line by starting at $(0, 2)$, the first point. Based on the slope, we move 3 units *down* (the rise) and 2 units to the *right* (the run). This puts us at a second point on the line, $(2, -1)$, shown in **Figure 2.29**.

Step 3 Use a straightedge to draw a line through the two points. The graph of the linear function $f(x) = -\frac{3}{2}x + 2$ is shown as a blue line in **Figure 2.29**. ●

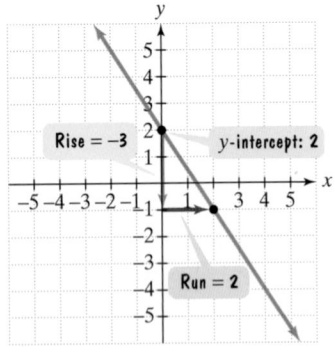

Figure 2.29 The graph of $f(x) = -\frac{3}{2}x + 2$

✓ Check Point **4** Graph the linear function: $f(x) = \frac{3}{5}x + 1$.

④ Graph horizontal or vertical lines.

Equations of Horizontal and Vertical Lines

If a line is horizontal, its slope is zero: $m = 0$. Thus, the equation $y = mx + b$ becomes $y = b$, where b is the y-intercept. All horizontal lines have equations of the form $y = b$.

EXAMPLE 5 **Graphing a Horizontal Line**

Graph $y = -4$ in the rectangular coordinate system.

Solution All ordered pairs that are solutions of $y = -4$ have a value of y that is always -4. Any value can be used for x. In the table on the right, we have selected three of the possible values for x: $-2, 0$, and 3. The table shows that three ordered pairs that are solutions of $y = -4$ are $(-2, -4)$, $(0, -4)$, and $(3, -4)$. Drawing a line that passes through the three points gives the horizontal line shown in **Figure 2.30**.

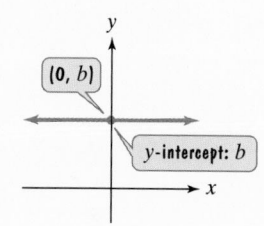

x	$y = -4$	(x, y)
-2	-4	$(-2, -4)$
0	-4	$(0, -4)$
3	-4	$(3, -4)$

For all choices of x, y is a constant -4.

Figure 2.30 The graph of $y = -4$ or $f(x) = -4$

✓ **Check Point 5** Graph $y = 3$ in the rectangular coordinate system.

Equation of a Horizontal Line

A horizontal line is given by an equation of the form

$$y = b,$$

where b is the y-intercept of the line. The slope of a horizontal line is zero.

(0, b)

y-intercept: b

Because any vertical line can intersect the graph of a horizontal line $y = b$ only once, a horizontal line is the graph of a function. Thus, we can express the equation $y = b$ as $f(x) = b$. This linear function is often called a **constant function**.

Next, let's see what we can discover about the graph of an equation of the form $x = a$ by looking at an example.

EXAMPLE 6 **Graphing a Vertical Line**

Graph the linear equation: $x = 2$.

Solution All ordered pairs that are solutions of $x = 2$ have a value of x that is always 2. Any value can be used for y. In the table on the right, we have selected three of the possible values for y: $-2, 0$, and 3. The table shows that three ordered pairs that are solutions of $x = 2$ are $(2, -2)$, $(2, 0)$, and $(2, 3)$. Drawing a line that passes through the three points gives the vertical line shown in **Figure 2.31**.

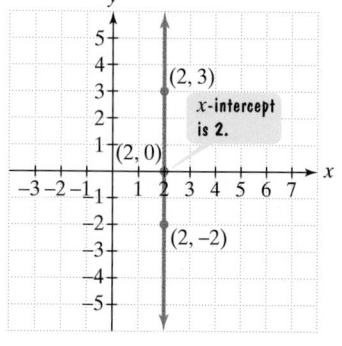

Figure 2.31 The graph of $x = 2$

For all choices of y,

x is always 2.

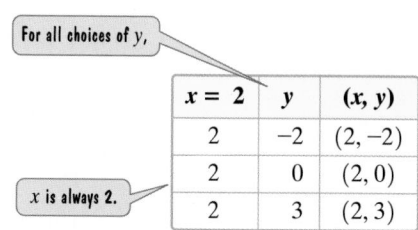

$x = 2$	y	(x, y)
2	-2	$(2, -2)$
2	0	$(2, 0)$
2	3	$(2, 3)$

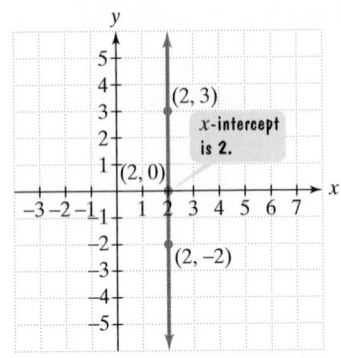

Figure 2.31 (repeated) The graph of $x = 2$

Equation of a Vertical Line

A vertical line is given by an equation of the form

$$x = a,$$

where a is the x-intercept of the line. The slope of a vertical line is undefined.

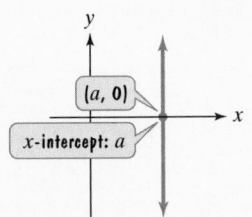

Does a vertical line represent the graph of a linear function? No. Look at the graph of $x = 2$ in **Figure 2.31**. A vertical line drawn through $(2, 0)$ intersects the graph infinitely many times. This shows that infinitely many outputs are associated with the input 2. **No vertical line represents a linear function.**

⊘ Check Point **6** Graph the linear equation: $x = -3$.

The General Form of the Equation of a Line

The vertical line whose equation is $x = 5$ cannot be written in slope-intercept form, $y = mx + b$, because its slope is undefined. However, every line has an equation that can be expressed in the form $Ax + By + C = 0$. For example, $x = 5$ can be expressed as $1x + 0y - 5 = 0$, or $x - 5 = 0$. The equation $Ax + By + C = 0$ is called the *general form* of the equation of a line.

> #### General Form of the Equation of a Line
> Every line has an equation that can be written in the **general form**
> $$Ax + By + C = 0,$$
> where A, B, and C are real numbers, and A and B are not both zero.

If the equation of a line is given in general form, it is possible to find the slope, m, and the y-intercept, b, for the line. We solve the equation for y, transforming it into the slope-intercept form $y = mx + b$. In this form, the coefficient of x is the slope of the line and the constant term is its y-intercept.

(EXAMPLE 7) **Finding the Slope and the y-Intercept**

Find the slope and the y-intercept of the line whose equation is $3x + 2y - 4 = 0$.

Solution The equation is given in general form. We begin by rewriting it in the form $y = mx + b$. We need to solve for y.

Our goal is to isolate y.

$$3x + 2y - 4 = 0$$ This is the given equation.

$$2y = -3x + 4$$ Isolate the term containing y by adding $-3x + 4$ to both sides.

$$\frac{2y}{2} = \frac{-3x + 4}{2}$$ Divide both sides by 2.

$$y = -\frac{3}{2}x + 2$$ On the right, divide each term in the numerator by 2 to obtain slope-intercept form.

slope y-intercept

The coefficient of x, $-\frac{3}{2}$, is the slope and the constant term, 2, is the y-intercept. This is the form of the equation that we graphed in **Figure 2.29** on page 234.

☑ Check Point **7** Find the slope and the *y*-intercept of the line whose equation is $3x + 6y - 12 = 0$. Then use the *y*-intercept and the slope to graph the equation.

⑥ Use intercepts to graph the general form of a line's equation.

Using Intercepts to Graph $Ax + By + C = 0$

Example 7 and Check Point 7 illustrate that one way to graph the general form of a line's equation is to convert to slope-intercept form, $y = mx + b$. Then use the slope and the *y*-intercept to obtain the graph.

A second method for graphing $Ax + By + C = 0$ uses intercepts. This method does not require rewriting the general form in a different form.

> ### Using Intercepts to Graph $Ax + By + C = 0$
>
> **1.** Find the *x*-intercept. Let $y = 0$ and solve for *x*. Plot the point containing the *x*-intercept on the *x*-axis.
>
> **2.** Find the *y*-intercept. Let $x = 0$ and solve for *y*. Plot the point containing the *y*-intercept on the *y*-axis.
>
> **3.** Use a straightedge to draw a line through the two points containing the intercepts. Draw arrowheads at the ends of the line to show that the line continues indefinitely in both directions.

(**EXAMPLE 8**) **Using Intercepts to Graph a Linear Equation**

Graph using intercepts: $4x - 3y - 6 = 0$.

Solution

Step 1 Find the *x*-intercept. Let $y = 0$ and solve for *x*.

$$4x - 3 \cdot 0 - 6 = 0 \qquad \text{Replace } y \text{ with 0 in } 4x - 3y - 6 = 0.$$
$$4x - 6 = 0 \qquad \text{Simplify.}$$
$$4x = 6 \qquad \text{Add 6 to both sides.}$$
$$x = \frac{6}{4} = \frac{3}{2} \qquad \text{Divide both sides by 4.}$$

Figure 2.32 The graph of $4x - 3y - 6 = 0$

The *x*-intercept is $\frac{3}{2}$, so the line passes through $\left(\frac{3}{2}, 0\right)$ or $(1.5, 0)$, as shown in **Figure 2.32**.

Step 2 Find the *y*-intercept. Let $x = 0$ and solve for *y*.

$$4 \cdot 0 - 3y - 6 = 0 \qquad \text{Replace } x \text{ with 0 in } 4x - 3y - 6 = 0.$$
$$-3y - 6 = 0 \qquad \text{Simplify.}$$
$$-3y = 6 \qquad \text{Add 6 to both sides.}$$
$$y = -2 \qquad \text{Divide both sides by } -3.$$

The *y*-intercept is -2, so the line passes through $(0, -2)$, as shown in **Figure 2.32**.

Step 3 Graph the equation by drawing a line through the two points containing the intercepts. The graph of $4x - 3y - 6 = 0$ is shown in **Figure 2.32**. ●

☑ Check Point **8** Graph using intercepts: $3x - 2y - 6 = 0$.

We've covered a lot of territory. Let's take a moment to summarize the various forms for equations of lines.

Equations of Lines

1. Point-slope form	$y - y_1 = m(x - x_1)$
2. Slope-intercept form	$y = mx + b$ or $f(x) = mx + b$
3. Horizontal line	$y = b$
4. Vertical line	$x = a$
5. General form	$Ax + By + C = 0$

⑦ Model data with linear functions and make predictions.

Applications

Linear functions are useful for modeling data that fall on or near a line.

EXAMPLE 9 Modeling Global Warming

The amount of carbon dioxide in the atmosphere, measured in parts per million, has been increasing as a result of the burning of oil and coal. The buildup of gases and particles traps heat and raises the planet's temperature. The bar graph in **Figure 2.33(a)** gives the average atmospheric concentration of carbon dioxide and the average global temperature for six selected years. The data are displayed as a set of six points in a rectangular coordinate system in **Figure 2.33(b)**.

Figure 2.33(a)
Source: National Oceanic and Atmospheric Administration

Figure 2.33(b)

a. Shown on the scatter plot in **Figure 2.33(b)** is a line that passes through or near the six points. Write the slope-intercept form of this equation using function notation.

b. The preindustrial concentration of atmospheric carbon dioxide was 280 parts per million. The United Nation's Intergovernmental Panel on Climate Change predicts global temperatures will rise between 2°F and 5°F if carbon dioxide concentration doubles from the preindustrial level. Compared to the average global temperature of 58.11°F for 2005, how well does the function from part (a) model this prediction?

Solution

a. The line in **Figure 2.33(b)** passes through (326, 57.06) and (377, 58.11). We start by finding its slope.

$$m = \frac{\text{Change in } y}{\text{Change in } x} = \frac{58.11 - 57.06}{377 - 326} = \frac{1.05}{51} \approx 0.02$$

The slope indicates that for each increase of one part per million in carbon dioxide concentration, the average global temperature is increasing by approximately 0.02°F.

Now we write the line's equation in slope-intercept form.

$$y - y_1 = m(x - x_1)$$ Begin with the point-slope form.

$$y - 57.06 = 0.02(x - 326)$$ Either ordered pair can be (x_1, y_1). Let $(x_1, y_1) = (326, 57.06)$. From above, $m \approx 0.02$.

$$y - 57.06 = 0.02x - 6.52$$ Apply the distributive property: $0.02(326) = 6.52$.

$$y = 0.02x + 50.54$$ Add 57.06 to both sides and solve for y.

A linear function that models average global temperature, $f(x)$, for an atmospheric carbon dioxide concentration of x parts per million is

$$f(x) = 0.02x + 50.54.$$

b. If carbon dioxide concentration doubles from its preindustrial level of 280 parts per million, which many experts deem very likely, the concentration will reach 280×2, or 560 parts per million. We use the linear function to predict average global temperature at this concentration.

$$f(x) = 0.02x + 50.54$$ Use the function from part (a).

$$f(560) = 0.02(560) + 50.54$$ Substitute 560 for x.

$$= 11.2 + 50.54 = 61.74$$

Our model projects an average global temperature of 61.74°F for a carbon dioxide concentration of 560 parts per million. Compared to the average global temperature of 58.11° for 2005 shown in **Figure 2.33(a)**, this is an increase of

$$61.74°F - 58.11°F = 3.63°F.$$

This is consistent with a rise between 2°F and 5°F as predicted by the Intergovernmental Panel on Climate Change.

⊘ Check Point **9** Use the data points $(317, 57.04)$ and $(354, 57.64)$, shown, but not labeled, in **Figure 2.33(b)** to obtain a linear function that models average global temperature, $f(x)$, for an atmospheric carbon dioxide concentration of x parts per million. Round m to three decimal places and b to one decimal place. Then use the function to project average global temperature at a concentration of 600 parts per million.

Technology

You can use a graphing utility to obtain a model for a scatter plot in which the data points fall on or near a straight line. After entering the data in **Figure 2.33(a)**, a graphing utility displays a scatter plot of the data and the regression line, that is, the line that best fits the data.

[310, 380, 10] by [56.8, 58.4, 0.2]

Also displayed is the regression line's equation.

Exercise Set 2.3

Practice Exercises

In Exercises 1–10, find the slope of the line passing through each pair of points or state that the slope is undefined. Then indicate whether the line through the points rises, falls, is horizontal, or is vertical.

1. $(4, 7)$ and $(8, 10)$ **2.** $(2, 1)$ and $(3, 4)$

3. $(-2, 1)$ and $(2, 2)$ **4.** $(-1, 3)$ and $(2, 4)$

5. $(4, -2)$ and $(3, -2)$ **6.** $(4, -1)$ and $(3, -1)$

7. $(-2, 4)$ and $(-1, -1)$ **8.** $(6, -4)$ and $(4, -2)$

9. $(5, 3)$ and $(5, -2)$ **10.** $(3, -4)$ and $(3, 5)$

In Exercises 11–38, use the given conditions to write an equation for each line in point-slope form and slope-intercept form.

11. Slope $= 2$, passing through $(3, 5)$

12. Slope $= 4$, passing through $(1, 3)$

13. Slope $= 6$, passing through $(-2, 5)$

14. Slope $= 8$, passing through $(4, -1)$

15. Slope $= -3$, passing through $(-2, -3)$

16. Slope $= -5$, passing through $(-4, -2)$

17. Slope $= -4$, passing through $(-4, 0)$

18. Slope $= -2$, passing through $(0, -3)$

19. Slope $= -1$, passing through $\left(-\frac{1}{2}, -2\right)$

20. Slope $= -1$, passing through $\left(-4, -\frac{1}{4}\right)$

21. Slope $= \frac{1}{2}$, passing through the origin

22. Slope $= \frac{1}{3}$, passing through the origin

23. Slope $= -\frac{2}{3}$, passing through $(6, -2)$

24. Slope $= -\frac{3}{5}$, passing through $(10, -4)$

25. Passing through $(1, 2)$ and $(5, 10)$

26. Passing through $(3, 5)$ and $(8, 15)$

27. Passing through $(-3, 0)$ and $(0, 3)$

28. Passing through $(-2, 0)$ and $(0, 2)$

29. Passing through $(-3, -1)$ and $(2, 4)$

30. Passing through $(-2, -4)$ and $(1, -1)$

31. Passing through $(-3, -2)$ and $(3, 6)$

32. Passing through $(-3, 6)$ and $(3, -2)$

33. Passing through $(-3, -1)$ and $(4, -1)$

34. Passing through $(-2, -5)$ and $(6, -5)$

35. Passing through $(2, 4)$ with x-intercept $= -2$

36. Passing through $(1, -3)$ with x-intercept $= -1$

37. x-intercept $= -\frac{1}{2}$ and y-intercept $= 4$

38. x-intercept $= 4$ and y-intercept $= -2$

In Exercises 39–48, give the slope and y-intercept of each line whose equation is given. Then graph the linear function.

39. $y = 2x + 1$

40. $y = 3x + 2$

41. $f(x) = -2x + 1$

42. $f(x) = -3x + 2$

43. $f(x) = \frac{3}{4}x - 2$

44. $f(x) = \frac{3}{4}x - 3$

45. $y = -\frac{3}{5}x + 7$

46. $y = -\frac{2}{5}x + 6$

47. $g(x) = -\frac{1}{2}x$

48. $g(x) = -\frac{1}{3}x$

In Exercises 49–58, graph each equation in a rectangular coordinate system.

49. $y = -2$

50. $y = 4$

51. $x = -3$

52. $x = 5$

53. $y = 0$

54. $x = 0$

55. $f(x) = 1$

56. $f(x) = 3$

57. $3x - 18 = 0$

58. $3x + 12 = 0$

In Exercises 59–66,

a. *Rewrite the given equation in slope-intercept form.*

b. *Give the slope and y-intercept.*

c. *Use the slope and y-intercept to graph the linear function.*

59. $3x + y - 5 = 0$

60. $4x + y - 6 = 0$

61. $2x + 3y - 18 = 0$

62. $4x + 6y + 12 = 0$

63. $8x - 4y - 12 = 0$

64. $6x - 5y - 20 = 0$

65. $3y - 9 = 0$

66. $4y + 28 = 0$

In Exercises 67–72, use intercepts to graph each equation.

67. $6x - 2y - 12 = 0$

68. $6x - 9y - 18 = 0$

69. $2x + 3y + 6 = 0$

70. $3x + 5y + 15 = 0$

71. $8x - 2y + 12 = 0$

72. $6x - 3y + 15 = 0$

Practice Plus

In Exercises 73–76, find the slope of the line passing through each pair of points or state that the slope is undefined. Assume that all variables represent positive real numbers. Then indicate whether the line through the points rises, falls, is horizontal, or is vertical.

73. $(0, a)$ and $(b, 0)$

74. $(-a, 0)$ and $(0, -b)$

75. (a, b) and $(a, b + c)$

76. $(a - b, c)$ and $(a, a + c)$

In Exercises 77–78, give the slope and y-intercept of each line whose equation is given. Assume that $B \neq 0$.

77. $Ax + By = C$

78. $Ax = By - C$

In Exercises 79–80, find the value of y if the line through the two given points is to have the indicated slope.

79. $(3, y)$ and $(1, 4), m = -3$

80. $(-2, y)$ and $(4, -4), m = \frac{1}{3}$

In Exercises 81–82, graph each linear function.

81. $3x - 4f(x) - 6 = 0$

82. $6x - 5f(x) - 20 = 0$

83. If one point on a line is $(3, -1)$ and the line's slope is -2, find the y-intercept.

84. If one point on a line is $(2, -6)$ and the line's slope is $-\frac{3}{2}$, find the y-intercept.

Use the figure to make the lists in Exercises 85–86.

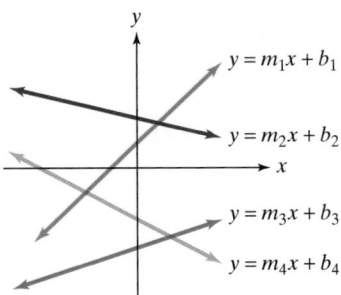

85. List the slopes m_1, m_2, m_3, and m_4 in order of decreasing size.

86. List the y-intercepts b_1, b_2, b_3, and b_4 in order of decreasing size.

Application Exercises

Americans are getting married later in life, or not getting married at all. In 2006, nearly half of Americans ages 25 through 29 were unmarried. The bar graph at the top of the next page shows the percentage of never-married men and women in this age group. The data are displayed as two sets of four points each, one scatter plot for the percentage of never-married American men and one for the percentage of never-married American women. Also shown for each scatter plot is a line that passes through or near the four points. Use these lines to solve Exercises 87–88.

Percentage of United States Population Never Married, Ages 25–29

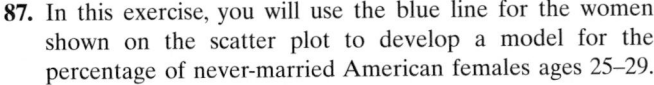

Source: U.S. Census Bureau

87. In this exercise, you will use the blue line for the women shown on the scatter plot to develop a model for the percentage of never-married American females ages 25–29.

 a. Use the two points whose coordinates are shown by the voice balloons to find the point-slope form of the equation of the line that models the percentage of never-married American females ages 25–29, *y*, *x* years after 1980.

 b. Write the equation from part (a) in slope-intercept form. Use function notation.

 c. Use the linear function to predict the percentage of never-married American females, ages 25–29, in 2020.

88. In this exercise, you will use the red line for the men shown on the scatter plot to develop a model for the percentage of never-married American males ages 25–29.

 a. Use the two points whose coordinates are shown by the voice balloons to find the point-slope form of the equation of the line that models the percentage of never-married American males ages 25–29, *y*, *x* years after 1980.

 b. Write the equation from part (a) in slope-intercept form. Use function notation.

 c. Use the linear function to predict the percentage of never-married American males, ages 25–29, in 2015.

The bar graph gives the life expectancy for American men and women born in six selected years. In Exercises 89–90, you will use the data to obtain models for life expectancy and make predictions about how long American men and women will live in the future.

Life Expectancy in the United States, by Year of Birth

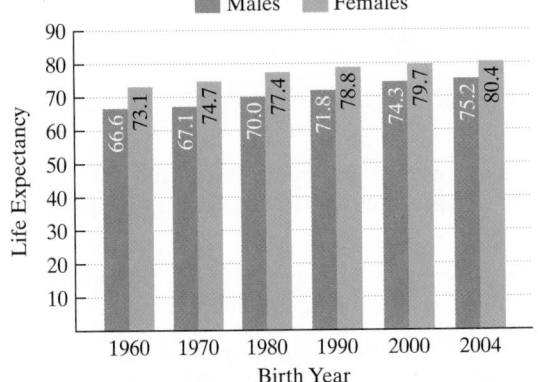

Source: National Center for Health Statistics

89. Use the data for males shown in the bar graph at the bottom of the previous column to solve this exercise.

 a. Let *x* represent the number of birth years after 1960 and let *y* represent male life expectancy. Create a scatter plot that displays the data as a set of six points in a rectangular coordinate system.

 b. Draw a line through the two points that show male life expectancies for 1980 and 2000. Use the coordinates of these points to write a linear function that models life expectancy, $E(x)$, for American men born *x* years after 1960.

 c. Use the function from part (b) to project the life expectancy of American men born in 2020.

90. Use the data for females shown in the bar graph at the bottom of the previous column to solve this exercise.

 a. Let *x* represent the number of birth years after 1960 and let *y* represent female life expectancy. Create a scatter plot that displays the data as a set of six points in a rectangular coordinate system.

 b. Draw a line through the two points that show female life expectancies for 1970 and 2000. Use the coordinates of these points to write a linear function that models life expectancy, $E(x)$, for American women born *x* years after 1960. Round the slope to two decimal places.

 c. Use the function from part (b) to project the life expectancy of American women born in 2020.

91. Shown, again, is the scatter plot that indicates a relationship between the percentage of adult females in a country who are literate and the mortality of children under five. Also shown is a line that passes through or near the points. Find a linear function that models the data by finding the slope-intercept form of the line's equation. Use the function to make a prediction about child mortality based on the percentage of adult females in a country who are literate.

Literacy and Child Mortality

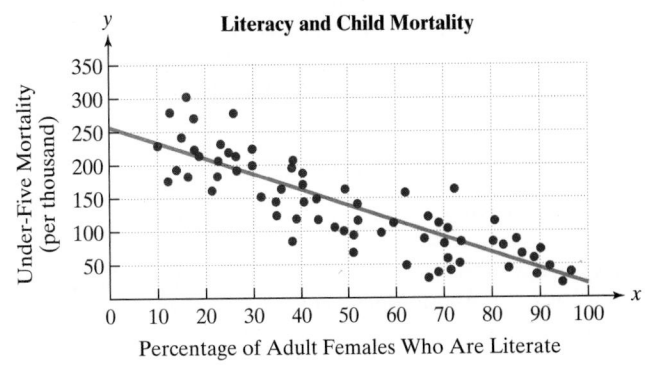

Source: United Nations

92. Just as money doesn't buy happiness for individuals, the two don't necessarily go together for countries either. However, the scatter plot does show a relationship between a country's annual per capita income and the percentage of people in that country who call themselves "happy."

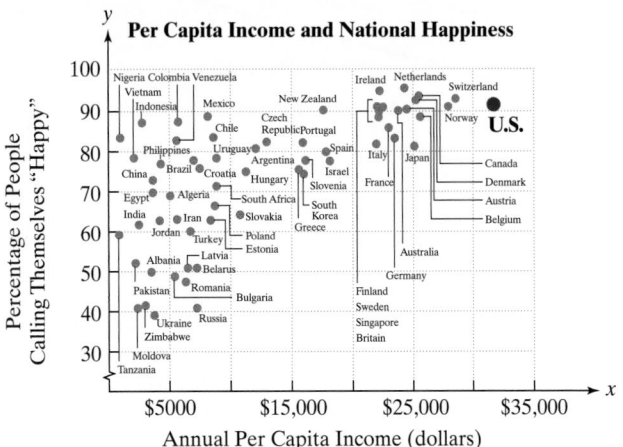

Source: Richard Layard, *Happiness: Lessons from a New Science,* Penguin, 2005

Draw a line that fits the data so that the spread of the data points around the line is as small as possible. Use the coordinates of two points along your line to write the slope-intercept form of its equation. Express the equation in function notation and use the linear function to make a prediction about national happiness based on per capita income.

Writing in Mathematics

93. What is the slope of a line and how is it found?

94. Describe how to write the equation of a line if the coordinates of two points along the line are known.

95. Explain how to derive the slope-intercept form of a line's equation, $y = mx + b$, from the point-slope form
$$y - y_1 = m(x - x_1).$$

96. Explain how to graph the equation $x = 2$. Can this equation be expressed in slope-intercept form? Explain.

97. Explain how to use the general form of a line's equation to find the line's slope and y-intercept.

98. Explain how to use intercepts to graph the general form of a line's equation.

99. Take another look at the scatter plot in Exercise 91. Although there is a relationship between literacy and child mortality, we cannot conclude that increased literacy causes child mortality to decrease. Offer two or more possible explanations for the data in the scatter plot.

Technology Exercises

Use a graphing utility to graph each equation in Exercises 100–103. Then use the TRACE *feature to trace along the line and find the coordinates of two points. Use these points to compute the line's slope. Check your result by using the coefficient of x in the line's equation.*

100. $y = 2x + 4$

101. $y = -3x + 6$

102. $y = -\frac{1}{2}x - 5$

103. $y = \frac{3}{4}x - 2$

104. Is there a relationship between wine consumption and deaths from heart disease? The table gives data from 19 developed countries.

Country		A	B	C	D	E	F	G [France]
Liters of alcohol from drinking wine, per person per year (x)		2.5	3.9	2.9	2.4	2.9	0.8	9.1
Deaths from heart disease, per 100,000 people per year (y)		211	167	131	191	220	297	71

Country	H	I	J	K	L	M	N	O	P	Q	R	S [U.S.]
(x)	0.8	0.7	7.9	1.8	1.9	0.8	6.5	1.6	5.8	1.3	1.2	2.7
(y)	211	300	107	167	266	227	86	207	115	285	199	172

Source: New York Times

a. Use the statistical menu of your graphing utility to enter the 19 ordered pairs of data items shown in the table.

b. Use the scatter plot capability to draw a scatter plot of the data.

c. Select the linear regression option. Use your utility to obtain values for a and b for the equation of the regression line, $y = ax + b$. You may also be given a **correlation coefficient**, r. Values of r close to 1 indicate that the points can be described by a linear relationship and the regression line has a positive slope. Values of r close to -1 indicate that the points can be described by a linear relationship and the regression line has a negative slope. Values of r close to 0 indicate no linear relationship between the variables. In this case, a linear model does not accurately describe the data.

d. Use the appropriate sequence (consult your manual) to graph the regression equation on top of the points in the scatter plot.

Critical Thinking Exercises

Make Sense? *In Exercises 105–108, determine whether each statement makes sense or does not make sense, and explain your reasoning.*

105. The graph of my linear function at first increased, reached a maximum point, and then decreased.

106. A linear function that models tuition and fees at public four-year colleges from 2000 through 2006 has negative slope.

107. Because the variable m does not appear in $Ax + By + C = 0$, equations in this form make it impossible to determine the line's slope.

108. The federal minimum wage was $5.15 per hour from 1997 through 2006, so $f(x) = 5.15$ models the minimum wage, $f(x)$, in dollars, for the domain $\{1997, 1998, 1999, \ldots, 2006\}$.

In Exercises 109–112, determine whether each statement is true or false. If the statement is false, make the necessary change(s) to produce a true statement.

109. The equation $y = mx + b$ shows that no line can have a y-intercept that is numerically equal to its slope.

110. Every line in the rectangular coordinate system has an equation that can be expressed in slope-intercept form.

111. The graph of the linear function $5x + 6y - 30 = 0$ is a line passing through the point $(6, 0)$ with slope $-\frac{5}{6}$.

112. The graph of $x = 7$ in the rectangular coordinate system is the single point $(7, 0)$.

In Exercises 113–114, find the coefficients that must be placed in each shaded area so that the function's graph will be a line satisfying the specified conditions.

113. ▨ $x + $ ▨ $y - 12 = 0$; x-intercept $= -2$; y-intercept $= 4$

114. ▨ $x + $ ▨ $y - 12 = 0$; y-intercept $= -6$; slope $= \frac{1}{2}$

115. Prove that the equation of a line passing through $(a, 0)$ and $(0, b)(a \neq 0, b \neq 0)$ can be written in the form $\frac{x}{a} + \frac{y}{b} = 1$. Why is this called the *intercept form* of a line?

116. Excited about the success of celebrity stamps, post office officials were rumored to have put forth a plan to institute two new types of thermometers. On these new scales, $°E$ represents degrees Elvis and $°M$ represents degrees Madonna. If it is known that $40°E = 25°M$, $280°E = 125°M$, and degrees Elvis is linearly related to degrees Madonna, write an equation expressing E in terms of M.

Group Exercise

117. In Exercises 87–88, we used the data in a bar graph to develop linear functions that modeled the percentage of never-married American females and males, ages 25–29. For this group exercise, you might find it helpful to pattern your work after Exercises 87 and 88. Group members should begin by consulting an almanac, newspaper, magazine, or the Internet to find data that appear to lie approximately on or near a line. Working by hand or using a graphing utility, group members should construct scatter plots for the data that were assembled. If working by hand, draw a line that approximately fits the data in each scatter plot and then write its equation as a function in slope-intercept form. If using a graphing utility, obtain the equation of each regression line. Then use each linear function's equation to make predictions about what might occur in the future. Are there circumstances that might affect the accuracy of the prediction? List some of these circumstances.

Preview Exercises

Exercises 118–120 will help you prepare for the material covered in the next section.

118. Write the slope-intercept form of the equation of the line passing through $(-3, 1)$ whose slope is the same as the line whose equation is $y = 2x + 1$.

119. Write an equation in general form of the line passing through $(3, -5)$ whose slope is the negative reciprocal (the reciprocal with the opposite sign) of $-\frac{1}{4}$.

120. If $f(x) = x^2$, find
$$\frac{f(x_2) - f(x_1)}{x_2 - x_1},$$
where $x_1 = 1$ and $x_2 = 4$.

Section 2.4 **More on Slope**

Objectives

❶ Find slopes and equations of parallel and perpendicular lines.

❷ Interpret slope as rate of change.

❸ Find a function's average rate of change.

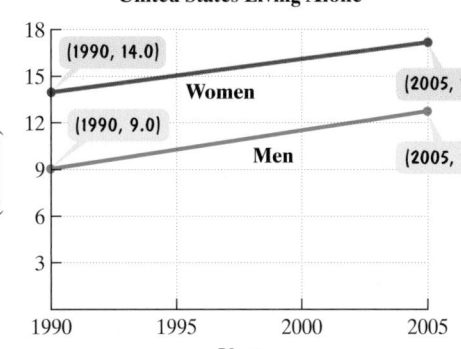

Number of People in the United States Living Alone

(1990, 14.0) Women (2005, 17.2)

(1990, 9.0) Men (2005, 12.7)

Number Living Alone (millions)

Year

Figure 2.34
Source: U.S. Census Bureau

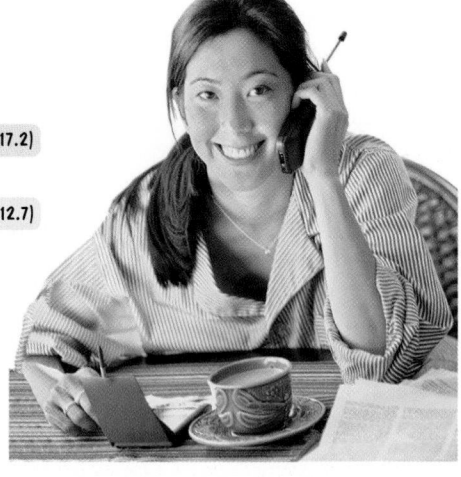

A best guess at the future of our nation indicates that the numbers of men and women living alone will increase each year. **Figure 2.34** shows that in 2005, 12.7 million men and 17.2 million women lived alone, an increase over the numbers displayed in the graph for 1990.

Turn back a page and take a second look at **Figure 2.34**. Can you tell that the green graph representing men has a greater slope than the red graph representing women? This indicates a greater rate of change in the number of men living alone than in the number of women living alone over the period from 1990 through 2005. In this section, you will learn to interpret slope as a rate of change. You will also explore the relationships between slopes of parallel and perpendicular lines.

① Find slopes and equations of parallel and perpendicular lines.

Parallel and Perpendicular Lines

Two nonintersecting lines that lie in the same plane are **parallel**. If two lines do not intersect, the ratio of the vertical change to the horizontal change is the same for both lines. Because two parallel lines have the same "steepness," they must have the same slope.

> ### Slope and Parallel Lines
> **1.** If two nonvertical lines are parallel, then they have the same slope.
> **2.** If two distinct nonvertical lines have the same slope, then they are parallel.
> **3.** Two distinct vertical lines, both with undefined slopes, are parallel.

(EXAMPLE 1) **Writing Equations of a Line Parallel to a Given Line**

Write an equation of the line passing through $(-3, 1)$ and parallel to the line whose equation is $y = 2x + 1$. Express the equation in point-slope form and slope-intercept form.

Solution The situation is illustrated in **Figure 2.35**. We are looking for the equation of the red line shown on the left. How do we obtain this equation? Notice that the line passes through the point $(-3, 1)$. Using the point-slope form of the line's equation, we have $x_1 = -3$ and $y_1 = 1$.

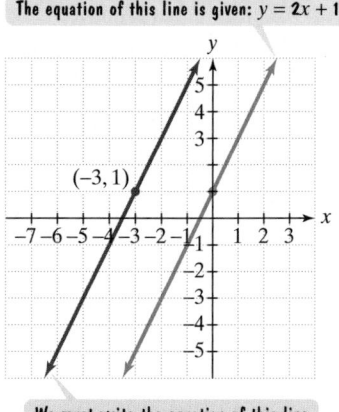

The equation of this line is given: $y = 2x + 1$.

We must write the equation of this line.

Figure 2.35

$$y - y_1 = m(x - x_1)$$

$y_1 = 1$ $x_1 = -3$

With $(x_1, y_1) = (-3, 1)$, the only thing missing from the equation of the red line is m, the slope. Do we know anything about the slope of either line in **Figure 2.35**? The answer is yes; we know the slope of the blue line on the right, whose equation is given.

$$y = 2x + 1$$

The slope of the blue line on the right in **Figure 2.35** is 2.

Parallel lines have the same slope. Because the slope of the blue line is 2, the slope of the red line, the line whose equation we must write, is also 2: $m = 2$. We now have values for x_1, y_1, and m for the red line.

$$y - y_1 = m(x - x_1)$$

$y_1 = 1$ $m = 2$ $x_1 = -3$

The point-slope form of the red line's equation is

$$y - 1 = 2[x - (-3)] \text{ or}$$
$$y - 1 = 2(x + 3).$$

Solving for y, we obtain the slope-intercept form of the equation.

$$y - 1 = 2x + 6 \quad \text{Apply the distributive property.}$$
$$y = 2x + 7 \quad \text{Add 1 to both sides. This is the slope-intercept}$$
$$\text{form, } y = mx + b, \text{ of the equation. Using function}$$
$$\text{notation, the equation is } f(x) = 2x + 7.$$

⦿

⊘ Check Point 1 Write an equation of the line passing through $(-2, 5)$ and parallel to the line whose equation is $y = 3x + 1$. Express the equation in point-slope form and slope-intercept form.

Two lines that intersect at a right angle $(90°)$ are said to be **perpendicular**, shown in **Figure 2.36**. The relationship between the slopes of perpendicular lines is not as obvious as the relationship between parallel lines. **Figure 2.36** shows line AB, with slope $\frac{c}{d}$. Rotate line AB counterclockwise $90°$ to the left to obtain line $A'B'$, perpendicular to line AB. The figure indicates that the rise and the run of the new line are reversed from the original line, but the former rise, the new run, is now negative. This means that the slope of the new line is $-\frac{d}{c}$. Notice that the product of the slopes of the two perpendicular lines is -1:

$$\left(\frac{c}{d}\right)\left(-\frac{d}{c}\right) = -1.$$

This relationship holds for all perpendicular lines and is summarized in the following box:

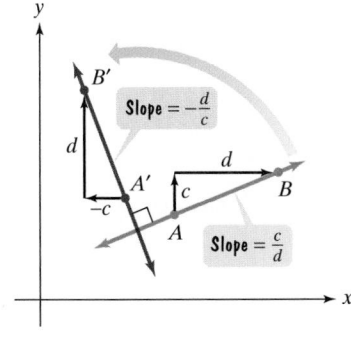

Figure 2.36 Slopes of perpendicular lines

Slope and Perpendicular Lines

1. If two nonvertical lines are perpendicular, then the product of their slopes is -1.

2. If the product of the slopes of two lines is -1, then the lines are perpendicular.

3. A horizontal line having zero slope is perpendicular to a vertical line having undefined slope.

An equivalent way of stating this relationship is to say that **one line is perpendicular to another line if its slope is the *negative reciprocal* of the slope of the other line**. For example, if a line has slope 5, any line having slope $-\frac{1}{5}$ is perpendicular to it. Similarly, if a line has slope $-\frac{3}{4}$, any line having slope $\frac{4}{3}$ is perpendicular to it.

EXAMPLE 2 Writing Equations of a Line Perpendicular to a Given Line

a. Find the slope of any line that is perpendicular to the line whose equation is $x + 4y - 8 = 0$.

b. Write the equation of the line passing through $(3, -5)$ and perpendicular to the line whose equation is $x + 4y - 8 = 0$. Express the equation in general form.

Solution

a. We begin by writing the equation of the given line, $x + 4y - 8 = 0$, in slope-intercept form. Solve for y.

$$x + 4y - 8 = 0 \quad \text{This is the given equation.}$$
$$4y = -x + 8 \quad \text{To isolate the y-term, subtract x and add 8 on both sides.}$$
$$y = -\frac{1}{4}x + 2 \quad \text{Divide both sides by 4.}$$

Slope is $-\frac{1}{4}$.

The given line has slope $-\frac{1}{4}$. Any line perpendicular to this line has a slope that is the negative reciprocal of $-\frac{1}{4}$. Thus, the slope of any perpendicular line is 4.

b. Let's begin by writing the point-slope form of the perpendicular line's equation. Because the line passes through the point $(3, -5)$, we have $x_1 = 3$ and $y_1 = -5$. In part (a), we determined that the slope of any line perpendicular to $x + 4y - 8 = 0$ is 4, so the slope of this particular perpendicular line must also be 4: $m = 4$.

$$y - y_1 = m(x - x_1)$$

$$\underbrace{y_1 = -5} \qquad \underbrace{m = 4} \qquad \underbrace{x_1 = 3}$$

The point-slope form of the perpendicular line's equation is

$$y - (-5) = 4(x - 3) \text{ or}$$
$$y + 5 = 4(x - 3).$$

How can we express this equation in general form $(Ax + By + C = 0)$? We need to obtain zero on one side of the equation. Let's do this and keep A, the coefficient of x, positive.

$y + 5 = 4(x - 3)$	This is the point-slope form of the line's equation.
$y + 5 = 4x - 12$	Apply the distributive property.
$y - y + 5 - 5 = 4x - y - 12 - 5$	To obtain 0 on the left, subtract y and subtract 5 on both sides.
$0 = 4x - y - 17$	Simplify.

In general form, the equation of the perpendicular line is $4x - y - 17 = 0$.

⬤

✓ Check Point **2**

a. Find the slope of any line that is perpendicular to the line whose equation is $x + 3y - 12 = 0$.

b. Write the equation of the line passing through $(-2, -6)$ and perpendicular to the line whose equation is $x + 3y - 12 = 0$. Express the equation in general form.

② Interpret slope as rate of change.

Slope as Rate of Change

Slope is defined as the ratio of a change in y to a corresponding change in x. It describes how fast y is changing with respect to x. For a linear function, slope may be interpreted as the rate of change of the dependent variable per unit change in the independent variable.

Our next example shows how slope can be interpreted as a rate of change in an applied situation. When calculating slope in applied problems, keep track of the units in the numerator and the denominator.

(EXAMPLE 3) Slope as a Rate of Change

The line graphs for the number of women and men living alone are shown again in **Figure 2.37**. Find the slope of the line segment for the women. Describe what this slope represents.

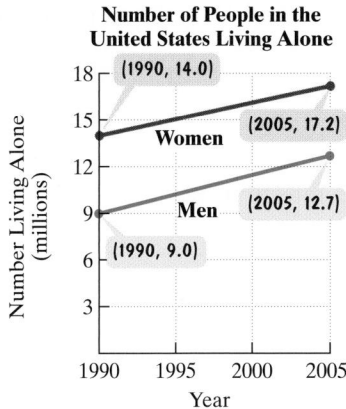

Number of People in the United States Living Alone

Figure 2.37
Source: U.S. Census Bureau

Solution We let *x* represent a year and *y* the number of women living alone in that year. The two points shown on the line segment for women have the following coordinates:

$$(1990, 14.0) \qquad\qquad (2005, 17.2)$$

In 1990, 14 million U.S. women lived alone. In 2005, 17.2 million U.S. women lived alone.

Now we compute the slope:

$$m = \frac{\text{Change in } y}{\text{Change in } x} = \frac{17.2 - 14.0}{2005 - 1990}$$

The unit in the numerator is *million women*.

The unit in the denominator is *year*.

$$= \frac{3.2}{15} \approx \frac{0.21 \text{ million women}}{\text{year}}.$$

The slope indicates that the number of American women living alone increased at a rate of approximately 0.21 million each year for the period from 1990 through 2005. The rate of change is 0.21 million women per year.

Check Point **3** Use the ordered pairs in **Figure 2.37** to find the slope of the green line segment for the men. Express the slope correct to two decimal places and describe what it represents.

In Check Point 3, did you find that the slope of the line segment for the men is different from that of the women? The rate of change for the number of men living alone is greater than the rate of change for the number of women living alone. The green line segment representing men in **Figure 2.37** is steeper than the red line segment representing women. If you extend the line segments far enough, the resulting lines will intersect. They are not parallel.

③ Find a function's average rate of change.

The Average Rate of Change of a Function

If the graph of a function is not a straight line, the **average rate of change** between any two points is the slope of the line containing the two points. This line is called a **secant line**. For example, **Figure 2.38** shows the graph of a particular man's height, in inches, as a function of his age, in years. Two points on the graph are labeled: (13, 57) and (18, 76). At age 13, this man was 57 inches tall and at age 18, he was 76 inches tall.

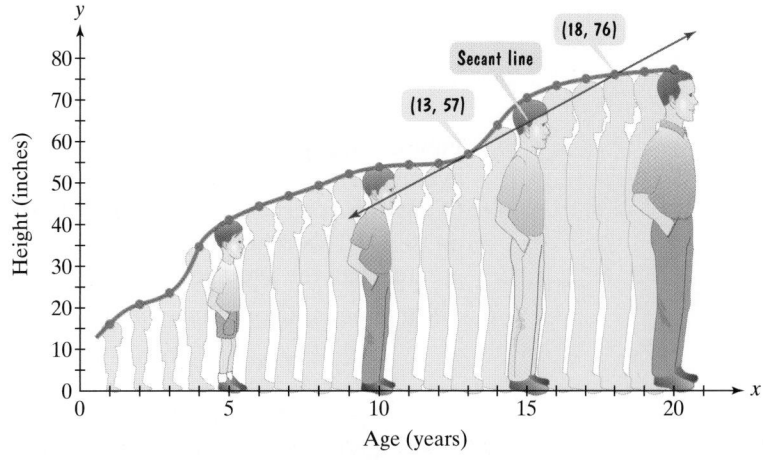

Figure 2.38 Height as a function of age

The man's average growth rate between ages 13 and 18 is the slope of the secant line containing $(13, 57)$ and $(18, 76)$:

$$m = \frac{\text{Change in } y}{\text{Change in } x} = \frac{76 - 57}{18 - 13} = \frac{19}{5} = 3\frac{4}{5}.$$

This man's average rate of change, or average growth rate, from age 13 to age 18 was $3\frac{4}{5}$, or 3.8, inches per year.

The Average Rate of Change of a Function

Let $(x_1, f(x_1))$ and $(x_2, f(x_2))$ be distinct points on the graph of a function f. (See **Figure 2.39**.) The **average rate of change of** f from x_1 to x_2 is

$$\frac{f(x_2) - f(x_1)}{x_2 - x_1}.$$

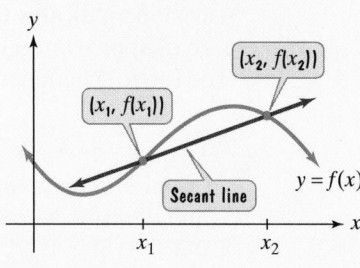

Figure 2.39

(**EXAMPLE 4**) **Finding the Average Rate of Change**

Find the average rate of change of $f(x) = x^2$ from

a. $x_1 = 0$ to $x_2 = 1$ **b.** $x_1 = 1$ to $x_2 = 2$ **c.** $x_1 = -2$ to $x_2 = 0$.

Solution

a. The average rate of change of $f(x) = x^2$ from $x_1 = 0$ to $x_2 = 1$ is

$$\frac{f(x_2) - f(x_1)}{x_2 - x_1} = \frac{f(1) - f(0)}{1 - 0} = \frac{1^2 - 0^2}{1} = 1.$$

Figure 2.40(a) shows the secant line of $f(x) = x^2$ from $x_1 = 0$ to $x_2 = 1$. The average rate of change is positive and the function is increasing on the interval $(0, 1)$.

b. The average rate of change of $f(x) = x^2$ from $x_1 = 1$ to $x_2 = 2$ is

$$\frac{f(x_2) - f(x_1)}{x_2 - x_1} = \frac{f(2) - f(1)}{2 - 1} = \frac{2^2 - 1^2}{1} = 3.$$

Figure 2.40(b) shows the secant line of $f(x) = x^2$ from $x_1 = 1$ to $x_2 = 2$. The average rate of change is positive and the function is increasing on the interval $(1, 2)$. Can you see that the graph rises more steeply on the interval $(1, 2)$ than on $(0, 1)$? This is because the average rate of change from $x_1 = 1$ to $x_2 = 2$ is greater than the average rate of change from $x_1 = 0$ to $x_2 = 1$.

c. The average rate of change of $f(x) = x^2$ from $x_1 = -2$ to $x_2 = 0$ is

$$\frac{f(x_2) - f(x_1)}{x_2 - x_1} = \frac{f(0) - f(-2)}{0 - (-2)} = \frac{0^2 - (-2)^2}{2} = \frac{-4}{2} = -2.$$

Figure 2.40(c) shows the secant line of $f(x) = x^2$ from $x_1 = -2$ to $x_2 = 0$. The average rate of change is negative and the function is decreasing on the interval $(-2, 0)$.

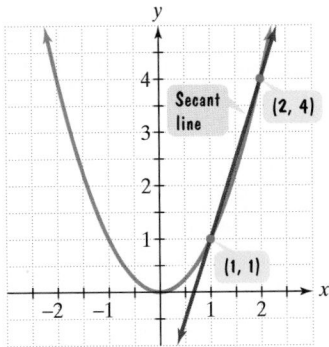

Figure 2.40(a) The secant line of $f(x) = x^2$ from $x_1 = 0$ to $x_2 = 1$

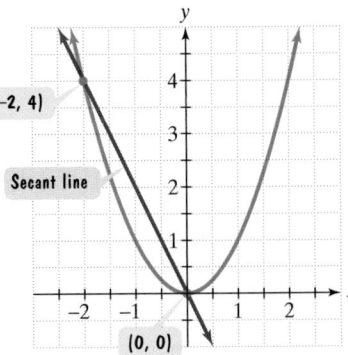

Figure 2.40(b) The secant line of $f(x) = x^2$ from $x_1 = 1$ to $x_2 = 2$

Figure 2.40(c) The secant line of $f(x) = x^2$ from $x_1 = -2$ to $x_2 = 0$

✓ Check Point **4** Find the average rate of change of $f(x) = x^3$ from

a. $x_1 = 0$ to $x_2 = 1$ **b.** $x_1 = 1$ to $x_2 = 2$ **c.** $x_1 = -2$ to $x_2 = 0$.

Suppose we are interested in the average rate of change of f from $x_1 = x$ to $x_2 = x + h$. In this case, the average rate of change is

$$\frac{f(x_2) - f(x_1)}{x_2 - x_1} = \frac{f(x + h) - f(x)}{x + h - x} = \frac{f(x + h) - f(x)}{h}.$$

Do you recognize the last expression? It is the difference quotient that you used in Section 2.2. Thus, the difference quotient gives the average rate of change of a function from x to $x + h$. In the difference quotient, h is thought of as a number very close to 0. In this way, the average rate of change can be found for a very short interval.

EXAMPLE 5 **Finding the Average Rate of Change**

When a person receives a drug injected into a muscle, the concentration of the drug in the body, measured in milligrams per 100 milliliters, is a function of the time elapsed after the injection, measured in hours. **Figure 2.41** shows the graph of such a function, where x represents hours after the injection and $f(x)$ is the drug's concentration at time x. Find the average rate of change in the drug's concentration between 3 and 7 hours.

Solution At 3 hours, the drug's concentration is 0.05 and at 7 hours, the concentration is 0.02. The average rate of change in its concentration between 3 and 7 hours is

$$\frac{f(x_2) - f(x_1)}{x_2 - x_1} = \frac{f(7) - f(3)}{7 - 3} = \frac{0.02 - 0.05}{7 - 3} = \frac{-0.03}{4} = -0.0075.$$

The average rate of change is -0.0075. This means that the drug's concentration is decreasing at an average rate of 0.0075 milligram per 100 milliliters per hour.

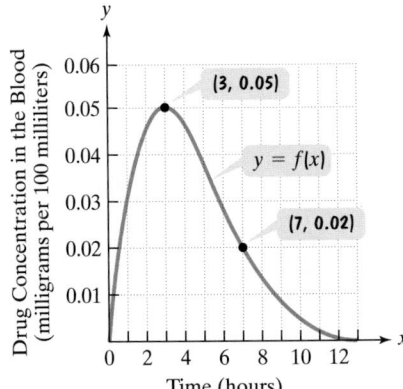

Figure 2.41 Concentration of a drug as a function of time

Study Tip

Units used to describe x and y tend to "pile up" when expressing the rate of change of y with respect to x. The unit used to express the rate of change of y with respect to x is

the unit used to describe y **per** the unit used to describe x.

In **Figure 2.41**, y, or drug concentration, is described in milligrams per 100 milliliters.

In **Figure 2.41**, x, or time, is described in hours.

In **Figure 2.41**, the rate of change is described in terms of milligrams per 100 milliliters per hour.

⊘ Check Point **5** Use **Figure 2.41** on the previous page to find the average rate of change in the drug's concentration between 1 hour and 3 hours.

How Calculus Studies Change

Take a rapid sequence of still photographs of a moving scene and project them onto a screen at thirty shots a second or faster. Our eyes see the results as continuous motion. The small difference between one frame and the next cannot be detected by the human visual system. The idea of calculus likewise regards continuous motion as made up of a sequence of still configurations. Calculus masters the mystery of movement by "freezing the frame" of a continuous changing process, instant by instant. For example, **Figure 2.42** shows a male's changing height over intervals of time. Over the period of time from P to D, his average rate of growth is his change in height—that is, his height at time D minus his height at time P—divided by the change in time from P to D. This is the slope of secant line PD.

The secant lines PD, PC, PB, and PA shown in **Figure 2.42** have slopes that show average growth rates for successively shorter periods of time. Calculus makes these time frames so small that they approach a single point—that is, a single instant in time. This point is shown as point P in **Figure 2.42**. The slope of the line that touches the graph at P gives the male's growth rate at one instant in time, P.

Figure 2.42 Analyzing continuous growth over intervals of time and at an instant in time

Exercise Set 2.4

Practice Exercises

In Exercises 1–4, write an equation for line L in point-slope form and slope-intercept form.

1.

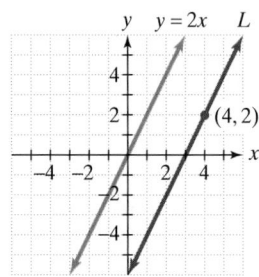

L is parallel to $y = 2x$.

2.

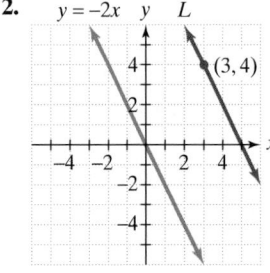

L is parallel to $y = -2x$.

3.

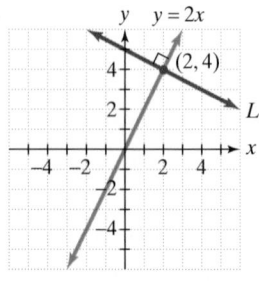

L is perpendicular to $y = 2x$.

4.

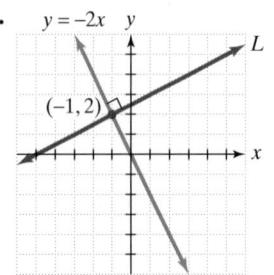

L is perpendicular to $y = -2x$.

In Exercises 5–8, use the given conditions to write an equation for each line in point-slope form and slope-intercept form.

5. Passing through $(-8, -10)$ and parallel to the line whose equation is $y = -4x + 3$

6. Passing through $(-2, -7)$ and parallel to the line whose equation is $y = -5x + 4$

7. Passing through $(2, -3)$ and perpendicular to the line whose equation is $y = \frac{1}{5}x + 6$

8. Passing through $(-4, 2)$ and perpendicular to the line whose equation is $y = \frac{1}{3}x + 7$

In Exercises 9–12, use the given conditions to write an equation for each line in point-slope form and general form.

9. Passing through $(-2, 2)$ and parallel to the line whose equation is $2x - 3y - 7 = 0$

10. Passing through $(-1, 3)$ and parallel to the line whose equation is $3x - 2y - 5 = 0$

11. Passing through $(4, -7)$ and perpendicular to the line whose equation is $x - 2y - 3 = 0$

12. Passing through $(5, -9)$ and perpendicular to the line whose equation is $x + 7y - 12 = 0$

In Exercises 13–18, find the average rate of change of the function from x_1 to x_2.

13. $f(x) = 3x$ from $x_1 = 0$ to $x_2 = 5$

14. $f(x) = 6x$ from $x_1 = 0$ to $x_2 = 4$

15. $f(x) = x^2 + 2x$ from $x_1 = 3$ to $x_2 = 5$

16. $f(x) = x^2 - 2x$ from $x_2 = 3$ to $x_2 = 6$

17. $f(x) = \sqrt{x}$ from $x_1 = 4$ to $x_2 = 9$

18. $f(x) = \sqrt{x}$ from $x_1 = 9$ to $x_2 = 16$

Practice Plus

In Exercises 19–24, write an equation in slope-intercept form of a linear function f whose graph satisfies the given conditions.

19. The graph of f passes through $(-1, 5)$ and is perpendicular to the line whose equation is $x = 6$.

20. The graph of f passes through $(-2, 6)$ and is perpendicular to the line whose equation is $x = -4$.

21. The graph of f passes through $(-6, 4)$ and is perpendicular to the line that has an x-intercept of 2 and a y-intercept of -4.

22. The graph of f passes through $(-5, 6)$ and is perpendicular to the line that has an x-intercept of 3 and a y-intercept of -9.

23. The graph of f is perpendicular to the line whose equation is $3x - 2y - 4 = 0$ and has the same y-intercept as this line.

24. The graph of f is perpendicular to the line whose equation is $4x - y - 6 = 0$ and has the same y-intercept as this line.

Application Exercises

The bar graph shows that as online news has grown, traditional news media have slipped.

Percentage of Americans Who Regularly Use Various News Media

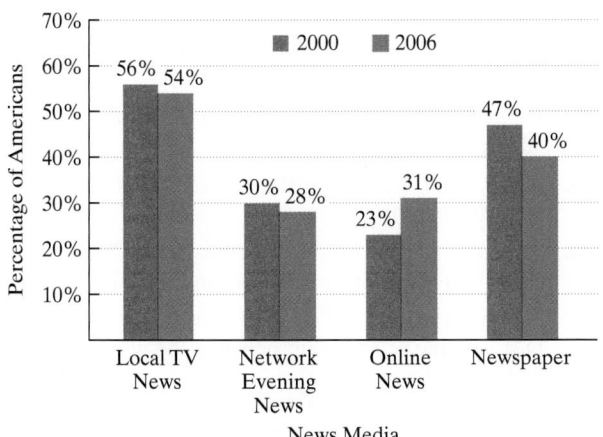

Source: Pew Research Center

In Exercises 25–26, find a linear function in slope-intercept form that models the given description. Each function should model the percentage of Americans, $P(x)$, who regularly used the news outlet x years after 2000.

25. In 2000, 47% of Americans regularly used newspapers for getting news and this has decreased at an average rate of approximately 1.2% per year since then.

26. In 2000, 23% of Americans regularly used online news for getting news and this has increased at an average rate of approximately 1.3% per year since then.

The stated intent of the 1994 "don't ask, don't tell" policy was to reduce the number of discharges of gay men and lesbians from the military. Nearly 12,000 active-duty gay servicemembers have been dismissed under the policy. The line graph shows the number of discharges under "don't ask, don't tell" from 1994 through 2006. Use the data displayed by the graph to solve Exercises 27–28.

Number of Active-Duty Gay Servicemembers Discharged from the Military for Homosexuality

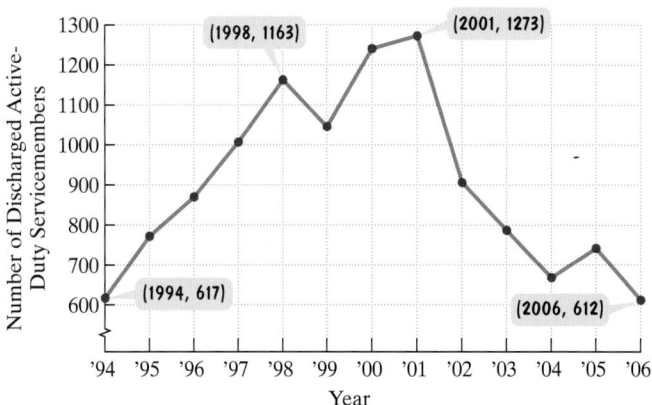

Source: General Accountability Office

27. Find the average rate of change, rounded to the nearest whole number, from 1994 through 1998. Describe what this means.

28. Find the average rate of change, rounded to the nearest whole number, from 2001 through 2006. Describe what this means.

The function $f(x) = 1.1x^3 - 35x^2 + 264x + 557$ models the number of discharges, $f(x)$, under "don't ask, don't tell" x years after 1994. Use this model and its graph, shown on the domain $[0, 12]$ to solve Exercises 29–30.

Graph of a Model for Discharges under "Don't Ask, Don't Tell"

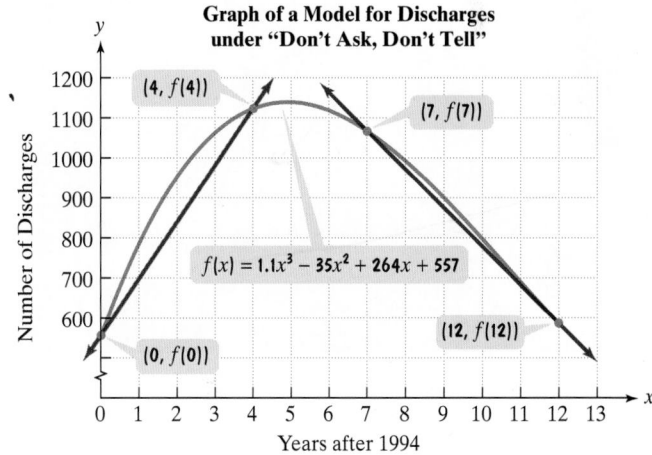

29. a. Find the slope of the secant line, rounded to the nearest whole number, from $x_1 = 0$ to $x_2 = 4$.

b. Does the slope from part (a) underestimate or overestimate the average yearly increase that you determined in Exercise 27? By how much?

30. a. Find the slope of the secant line, rounded to the nearest whole number, from $x_1 = 7$ to $x_2 = 12$.

b. Does the slope from part (b) underestimate or overestimate the average yearly decrease that you determined in Exercise 28? By how much?

Writing in Mathematics

31. If two lines are parallel, describe the relationship between their slopes.

32. If two lines are perpendicular, describe the relationship between their slopes.

33. If you know a point on a line and you know the equation of a line perpendicular to this line, explain how to write the line's equation.

34. A formula in the form $y = mx + b$ models the average retail price, y, of a new car x years after 2000. Would you expect m to be positive, negative, or zero? Explain your answer.

35. What is a secant line?

36. What is the average rate of change of a function?

Technology Exercise

37. a. Why are the lines whose equations are $y = \frac{1}{3}x + 1$ and $y = -3x - 2$ perpendicular?

b. Use a graphing utility to graph the equations in a $[-10, 10, 1]$ by $[-10, 10, 1]$ viewing rectangle. Do the lines appear to be perpendicular?

c. Now use the zoom square feature of your utility. Describe what happens to the graphs. Explain why this is so.

Critical Thinking Exercises

Make Sense? *In Exercises 38–41, determine whether each statement makes sense or does not make sense, and explain your reasoning.*

38. Some of the steel girders in this photo of the Eiffel Tower appear to have slopes that are negative reciprocals of each other.

39. I have linear functions that model changes for men and women over the same time period. The functions have the same slope, so their graphs are parallel lines, indicating that the rate of change for men is the same as the rate of change for women.

40. The graph of my function is not a straight line, so I cannot use slope to analyze its rates of change.

41. According to the essay on page 250, calculus studies change by analyzing slopes of secant lines over successively shorter intervals.

42. What is the slope of a line that is perpendicular to the line whose equation is $Ax + By + C = 0$, $A \neq 0$ and $B \neq 0$?

43. Determine the value of A so that the line whose equation is $Ax + y - 2 = 0$ is perpendicular to the line containing the points $(1, -3)$ and $(-2, 4)$.

Preview Exercises

Exercises 44–46 will help you prepare for the material covered in the next section. In each exercise, graph the functions in parts (a) and (b) in the same rectangular coordinate system.

44. a. Graph $f(x) = |x|$ using the ordered pairs $(-3, f(-3))$, $(-2, f(-2))$, $(-1, f(-1))$, $(0, f(0))$, $(1, f(1))$, $(2, f(2))$, and $(3, f(3))$.

b. Subtract 4 from each y-coordinate of the ordered pairs in part (a). Then graph the ordered pairs and connect them with two linear pieces.

c. Describe the relationship between the graph in part (b) and the graph in part (a).

45. a. Graph $f(x) = x^2$ using the ordered pairs $(-3, f(-3))$, $(-2, f(-2))$, $(-1, f(-1))$, $(0, f(0))$, $(1, f(1))$, $(2, f(2))$, and $(3, f(3))$.

b. Add 2 to each x-coordinate of the ordered pairs in part (a). Then graph the ordered pairs and connect them with a smooth curve.

c. Describe the relationship between the graph in part (b) and the graph in part (a).

46. a. Graph $f(x) = x^3$ using the ordered pairs $(-2, f(-2))$, $(-1, f(-1))$, $(0, f(0))$, $(1, f(1))$, and $(2, f(2))$.

b. Replace each x-coordinate of the ordered pairs in part (a) with its opposite, or additive inverse. Then graph the ordered pairs and connect them with a smooth curve.

c. Describe the relationship between the graph in part (b) and the graph in part (a).

 Chapter **2** **Mid-Chapter Check Point**

What You Know: We learned that a function is a relation in which no two ordered pairs have the same first component and different second components. We represented functions as equations and used function notation. We graphed functions and applied the vertical line test to identify graphs of functions. We determined the domain and range of a function from its graph, using inputs on the x-axis for the domain and outputs on the y-axis for the range. We used graphs to identify intervals on which functions increase, decrease, or are constant, as well as to locate relative maxima or minima. We identified even functions $[f(-x) = f(x)$: y-axis symmetry] and odd functions $[f(-x) = -f(x)$: origin symmetry]. Finally, we studied linear functions and slope, using slope (change in y divided by change in x) to develop various forms for equations of lines:

Point-slope form	Slope-intercept form	Horizontal line	Vertical line	General form
$y - y_1 = m(x - x_1)$	$y = f(x) = mx + b$	$y = f(x) = b$	$x = a$	$Ax + By + C = 0.$

We saw that parallel lines have the same slope and that perpendicular lines have slopes that are negative reciprocals. For linear functions, slope was interpreted as the rate of change of the dependent variable per unit change in the independent variable. For nonlinear functions, the slope of the secant line between $(x_1, f(x_1))$ and $(x_2, f(x_2))$ described the average rate of change of f from x_1 to x_2: $\dfrac{f(x_2) - f(x_1)}{x_2 - x_1}$.

In Exercises 1–6, determine whether each relation is a function. Give the domain and range for each relation.

1. $\{(2, 6), (1, 4), (2, -6)\}$

2. $\{(0, 1), (2, 1), (3, 4)\}$

3.

4.

5.

6.
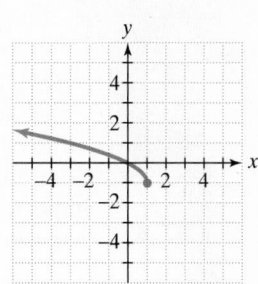

In Exercises 7–8, determine whether each equation defines y as a function of x.

7. $x^2 + y = 5$

8. $x + y^2 = 5$

Use the graph of f to solve Exercises 9–24. Where applicable, use interval notation.

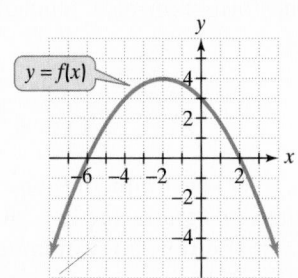

9. Explain why f represents the graph of a function.

10. Find the domain of f.

11. Find the range of f.

12. Find the x-intercept(s).

13. Find the y-intercept.

14. Find the interval(s) on which f is increasing.

15. Find the interval(s) on which f is decreasing.

16. At what number does f have a relative maximum?

17. What is the relative maximum of f?

18. Find $f(-4)$.

19. For what value or values of x is $f(x) = -2$?

20. For what value or values of x is $f(x) = 0$?

21. For what values of x is $f(x) > 0$?

22. Is $f(100)$ positive or negative?

23. Is f even, odd, or neither?

24. Find the average rate of change of f from $x_1 = -4$ to $x_2 = 4$.

In Exercises 25–36, graph each equation in a rectangular coordinate system.

25. $y = -2x$

26. $y = -2$

27. $x + y = -2$

28. $y = \frac{1}{3}x - 2$

29. $x = 3.5$

30. $4x - 2y = 8$

31. $f(x) = x^2 - 4$

32. $f(x) = x - 4$

33. $f(x) = |x| - 4$

34. $5y = -3x$

35. $5y = 20$

36. $f(x) = \begin{cases} -1 & \text{if} & x \le 0 \\ 2x + 1 & \text{if} & x > 0 \end{cases}$

37. Let $f(x) = -2x^2 + x - 5$.

 a. Find $f(-x)$. Is f even, odd, or neither?

 b. Find $\dfrac{f(x + h) - f(x)}{h}$, $h \ne 0$.

38. Let $C(x) = \begin{cases} 30 & \text{if} \quad 0 \le t \le 200 \\ 30 + 0.40(t - 200) & \text{if} \quad t > 200 \end{cases}$.

 a. Find $C(150)$. **b.** Find $C(250)$.

In Exercises 39–42, write a function in slope-intercept form whose graph satisfies the given conditions.

39. Slope $= -2$, passing through $(-4, 3)$

40. Passing through $(-1, -5)$ and $(2, 1)$

41. Passing through $(3, -4)$ and parallel to the line whose equation is $3x - y - 5 = 0$

42. Passing through $(-4, -3)$ and perpendicular to the line whose equation is $2x - 5y - 10 = 0$

43. Determine whether the line through $(2, -4)$ and $(7, 0)$ is parallel to a second line through $(-4, 2)$ and $(1, 6)$.

44. Exercise is useful not only in preventing depression, but also as a treatment. The graphs in the next column show the percentage of patients with depression in remission when exercise (brisk walking) was used as a treatment. (The control group that engaged in no exercise had 11% of the patients in remission.)

 a. Find the slope of the line passing through the two points shown by the voice balloons. Express the slope as a decimal.

Exercise and Percentage of Patients with Depression in Remission

Source: Newsweek, March 26, 2007

 b. Use your answer from part (a) to complete this statement:

 For each minute of brisk walking, the percentage of patients with depression in remission increased by _____ %. The rate of change is _____ % per _____.

45. Find the average rate of change of $f(x) = 3x^2 - x$ from $x_1 = -1$ to $x_2 = 2$.

Section 2.5

Transformations of Functions

Objectives

1. Recognize graphs of common functions.
2. Use vertical shifts to graph functions.
3. Use horizontal shifts to graph functions.
4. Use reflections to graph functions.
5. Use vertical stretching and shrinking to graph functions.
6. Use horizontal stretching and shrinking to graph functions.
7. Graph functions involving a sequence of transformations.

Have you seen *Terminator 2, The Mask*, or *The Matrix*? These were among the first films to use spectacular effects in which a character or object having one shape was transformed in a fluid fashion into a quite different shape. The name for such a transformation is **morphing**. The effect allows a real actor to be seamlessly transformed into a computer-generated animation. The animation can be made to perform impossible feats before it is morphed back to the conventionally filmed image.

Like transformed movie images, the graph of one function can be turned into the graph of a different function. To do this, we need to rely on a function's equation. Knowing that a graph is a transformation of a familiar graph makes graphing easier.

Graphs of Common Functions

① Recognize graphs of common functions.

Table 2.3 on the next page gives names to seven frequently encountered functions in algebra. The table shows each function's graph and lists characteristics of the function. Study the shape of each graph and take a few minutes to verify the function's characteristics from its graph. Knowing these graphs is essential for analyzing their transformations into more complicated graphs.

Table 2.3 Algebra's Common Graphs

Constant Function	Identity Function	Absolute Value Function
$f(x) = c$	$f(x) = x$	$f(x) = \|x\|$
• Domain: $(-\infty, \infty)$ • Range: the single number c • Constant on $(-\infty, \infty)$ • Even function	• Domain: $(-\infty, \infty)$ • Range: $(-\infty, \infty)$ • Increasing on $(-\infty, \infty)$ • Odd function	• Domain: $(-\infty, \infty)$ • Range: $[0, \infty)$ • Decreasing on $(-\infty, 0)$ and increasing on $(0, \infty)$ • Even function

Standard Quadratic Function	Square Root Function	Standard Cubic Function	Cube Root Function
$f(x) = x^2$	$f(x) = \sqrt{x}$	$f(x) = x^3$	$f(x) = \sqrt[3]{x}$
• Domain: $(-\infty, \infty)$ • Range: $[0, \infty)$ • Decreasing on $(-\infty, 0)$ and increasing on $(0, \infty)$ • Even function	• Domain: $[0, \infty)$ • Range: $[0, \infty)$ • Increasing on $(0, \infty)$ • Neither even nor odd	• Domain: $(-\infty, \infty)$ • Range: $(-\infty, \infty)$ • Increasing on $(-\infty, \infty)$ • Odd function	• Domain: $(-\infty, \infty)$ • Range: $(-\infty, \infty)$ • Increasing on $(-\infty, \infty)$ • Odd function

Discovery

The study of how changing a function's equation can affect its graph can be explored with a graphing utility. Use your graphing utility to verify the hand-drawn graphs as you read this section.

② Use vertical shifts to graph functions.

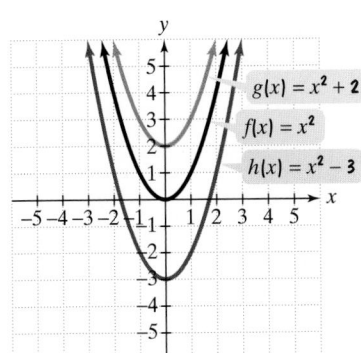

Figure 2.43 Vertical shifts

Vertical Shifts

Let's begin by looking at three graphs whose shapes are the same. **Figure 2.43** shows the graphs. The black graph in the middle is the standard quadratic function, $f(x) = x^2$. Now, look at the blue graph on the top. The equation of this graph, $g(x) = x^2 + 2$, adds 2 to the right side of $f(x) = x^2$. The y-coordinate of each point of g is 2 more than the corresponding y-coordinate of each point of f. What effect does this have on the graph of f? It shifts the graph vertically up by 2 units.

$$g(x) = x^2 + 2 = f(x) + 2$$

The graph of g shifts the graph of f up **2** units.

Finally, look at the red graph on the bottom in **Figure 2.43**. The equation of this graph, $h(x) = x^2 - 3$, subtracts 3 from the right side of $f(x) = x^2$. The y-coordinate of each point of h is 3 less than the corresponding y-coordinate of

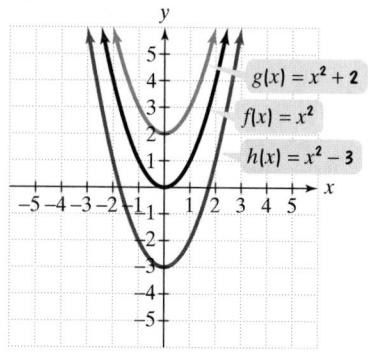

Figure 2.43 (repeated) Vertical shifts

each point of f. What effect does this have on the graph of f? It shifts the graph vertically down by 3 units.

$$h(x) = x^2 - 3 = f(x) - 3$$

The graph of h shifts the graph of f down 3 units.

In general, if c is positive, $y = f(x) + c$ shifts the graph of f upward c units and $y = f(x) - c$ shifts the graph of f downward c units. These are called **vertical shifts** of the graph of f.

Vertical Shifts

Let f be a function and c a positive real number.
- The graph of $y = f(x) + c$ is the graph of $y = f(x)$ shifted c units vertically upward.
- The graph of $y = f(x) - c$ is the graph of $y = f(x)$ shifted c units vertically downward.

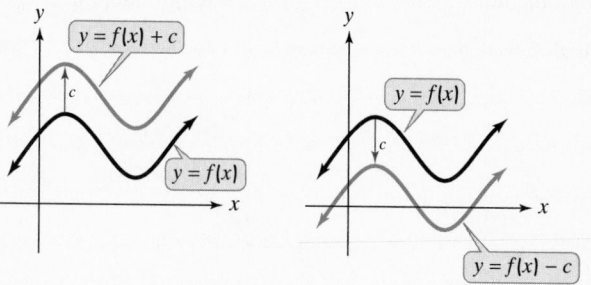

Study Tip

To keep track of transformations, identify a number of points on the given function's graph. Then analyze what happens to the coordinates of these points with each transformation.

EXAMPLE 1 Vertical Shift Downward

Use the graph of $f(x) = |x|$ to obtain the graph of $g(x) = |x| - 4$.

Solution The graph of $g(x) = |x| - 4$ has the same shape as the graph of $f(x) = |x|$. However, it is shifted down vertically 4 units.

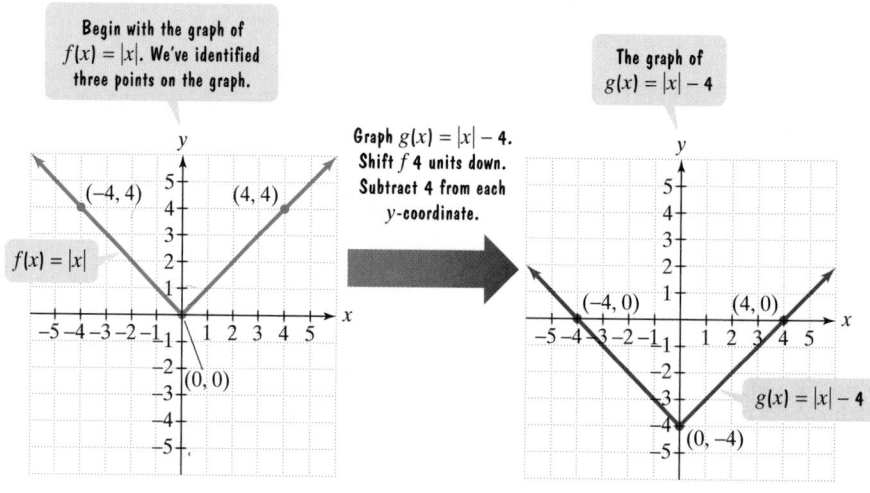

✓ Check Point 1 Use the graph of $f(x) = |x|$ to obtain the graph of $g(x) = |x| + 3$.

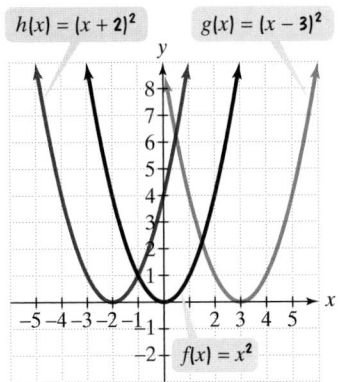

3 Use horizontal shifts to graph functions.

Figure 2.44 Horizontal shifts

Horizontal Shifts

We return to the graph of $f(x) = x^2$, the standard quadratic function. In **Figure 2.44**, the graph of function f is in the middle of the three graphs. By contrast to the vertical shift situation, this time there are graphs to the left and to the right of the graph of f. Look at the blue graph on the right. The equation of this graph, $g(x) = (x - 3)^2$, subtracts 3 from each value of x before squaring it. What effect does this have on the graph of $f(x) = x^2$? It shifts the graph horizontally to the right by 3 units.

$$g(x) = (x - 3)^2 = f(x - 3)$$

The graph of g shifts the graph of f 3 units to the right.

 Does it seem strange that *subtracting* 3 in the domain causes a shift of 3 units to the *right*? Perhaps a partial table of coordinates for each function will numerically convince you of this shift.

x	$f(x) = x^2$
-2	$(-2)^2 = 4$
-1	$(-1)^2 = 1$
0	$0^2 = 0$
1	$1^2 = 1$
2	$2^2 = 4$

x	$g(x) = (x - 3)^2$
1	$(1 - 3)^2 = (-2)^2 = 4$
2	$(2 - 3)^2 = (-1)^2 = 1$
3	$(3 - 3)^2 = \quad 0^2 = 0$
4	$(4 - 3)^2 = \quad 1^2 = 1$
5	$(5 - 3)^2 = \quad 2^2 = 4$

Notice that for the values of $f(x)$ and $g(x)$ to be the same, the values of x used in graphing g must each be 3 units greater than those used to graph f. For this reason, the graph of g is the graph of f shifted 3 units to the right.

 Now, look at the red graph on the left in **Figure 2.44**. The equation of this graph, $h(x) = (x + 2)^2$, adds 2 to each value of x before squaring it. What effect does this have on the graph of $f(x) = x^2$? It shifts the graph horizontally to the left by 2 units.

$$h(x) = (x + 2)^2 = f(x + 2)$$

The graph of h shifts the graph of f 2 units to the left.

 In general, if c is positive, $y = f(x + c)$ shifts the graph of f to the left c units and $y = f(x - c)$ shifts the graph of f to the right c units. These are called **horizontal shifts** of the graph of f.

Horizontal Shifts

Let f be a function and c a positive real number.

- The graph of $y = f(x + c)$ is the graph of $y = f(x)$ shifted to the left c units.
- The graph of $y = f(x - c)$ is the graph of $y = f(x)$ shifted to the right c units.

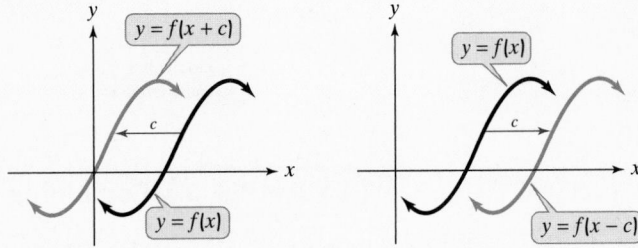

Study Tip

On a number line, if x represents a number and c is positive, then $x + c$ lies c units to the right of x and $x - c$ lies c units to the left of x. This orientation does not apply to horizontal shifts: $f(x + c)$ causes a shift of c units to the left and $f(x - c)$ causes a shift of c units to the right.

EXAMPLE 2 **Horizontal Shift to the Left**

Use the graph of $f(x) = \sqrt{x}$ to obtain the graph of $g(x) = \sqrt{x + 5}$.

Solution Compare the equations for $f(x) = \sqrt{x}$ and $g(x) = \sqrt{x + 5}$. The equation for g adds 5 to each value of x before taking the square root.

$$y = g(x) = \sqrt{x + 5} = f(x + 5)$$

The graph of g shifts the graph of f 5 units to the left.

The graph of $g(x) = \sqrt{x + 5}$ has the same shape as the graph of $f(x) = \sqrt{x}$. However, it is shifted horizontally to the left 5 units.

Study Tip

Notice the difference between $f(x) + c$ and $f(x + c)$.

- $y = f(x) + c$ shifts the graph of $y = f(x)$ c units vertically upward.
- $y = f(x + c)$ shifts the graph of $y = f(x)$ c units horizontally to the left.

There are analogous differences between $f(x) - c$ and $f(x - c)$.

✓ **Check Point 2** Use the graph of $f(x) = \sqrt{x}$ to obtain the graph of $g(x) = \sqrt{x - 4}$.

Some functions can be graphed by combining horizontal and vertical shifts. These functions will be variations of a function whose equation you know how to graph, such as the standard quadratic function, the standard cubic function, the square root function, the cube root function, or the absolute value function.

In our next example, we will use the graph of the standard quadratic function, $f(x) = x^2$, to obtain the graph of $h(x) = (x + 1)^2 - 3$. We will graph three functions:

$$f(x) = x^2 \qquad g(x) = (x + 1)^2 \qquad h(x) = (x + 1)^2 - 3.$$

Start by graphing the standard quadratic function. Shift the graph of f horizontally one unit to the left. Shift the graph of g vertically down 3 units.

EXAMPLE 3 **Combining Horizontal and Vertical Shifts**

Use the graph of $f(x) = x^2$ to obtain the graph of $h(x) = (x + 1)^2 - 3$.

Solution

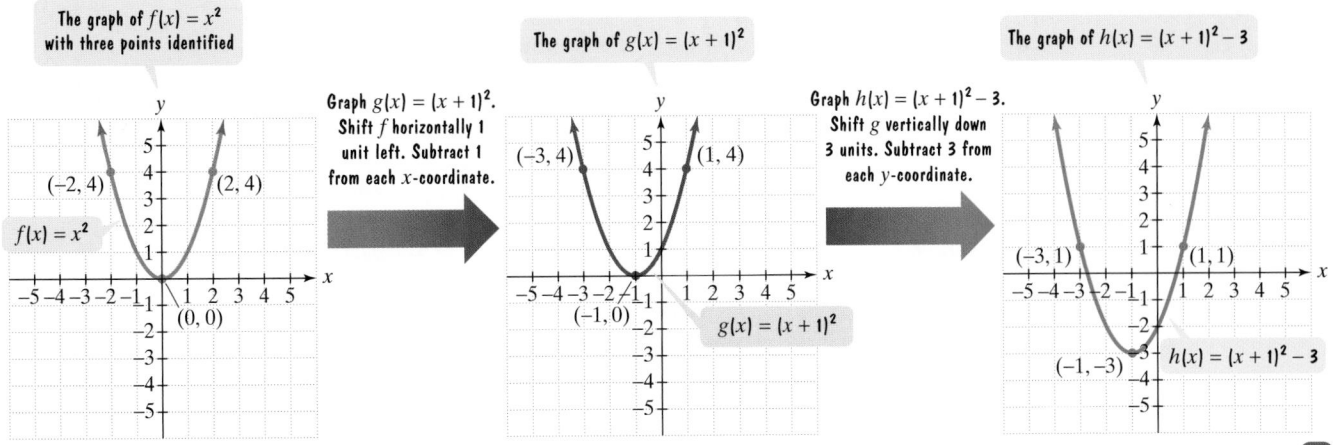

Discovery

Work Example 3 by first shifting the graph of $f(x) = x^2$ three units down, graphing $g(x) = x^2 - 3$. Now, shift this graph one unit left to graph $h(x) = (x + 1)^2 - 3$. Did you obtain the last graph shown in the solution of Example 3? What can you conclude?

⊘ **Check Point 3** Use the graph of $f(x) = \sqrt{x}$ to obtain the graph of $h(x) = \sqrt{x - 1} - 2$.

4 Use reflections to graph functions.

Reflections of Graphs

This photograph shows a reflection of an old bridge in a Maryland river. This perfect reflection occurs because the surface of the water is absolutely still. A mild breeze rippling the water's surface would distort the reflection.

Is it possible for graphs to have mirror-like qualities? Yes. **Figure 2.45** shows the graphs of $f(x) = x^2$ and $g(x) = -x^2$. The graph of g is a **reflection about the x-axis** of the graph of f. For corresponding values of x, the y-coordinates of g are the opposites of the y-coordinates of f. In general, the graph of $y = -f(x)$ reflects the graph of f about the x-axis. Thus, the graph of g is a reflection of the graph of f about the x-axis because

$$g(x) = -x^2 = -f(x).$$

Reflection about the x-Axis

The graph of $y = -f(x)$ is the graph of $y = f(x)$ reflected about the x-axis.

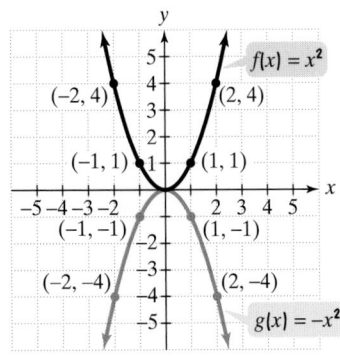

Figure 2.45 Reflection about the x-axis

EXAMPLE 4 Reflection about the x-Axis

Use the graph of $f(x) = \sqrt[3]{x}$ to obtain the graph of $g(x) = -\sqrt[3]{x}$.

Solution Compare the equations for $f(x) = \sqrt[3]{x}$ and $g(x) = -\sqrt[3]{x}$. The graph of g is a reflection about the x-axis of the graph of f because

$$g(x) = -\sqrt[3]{x} = -f(x).$$

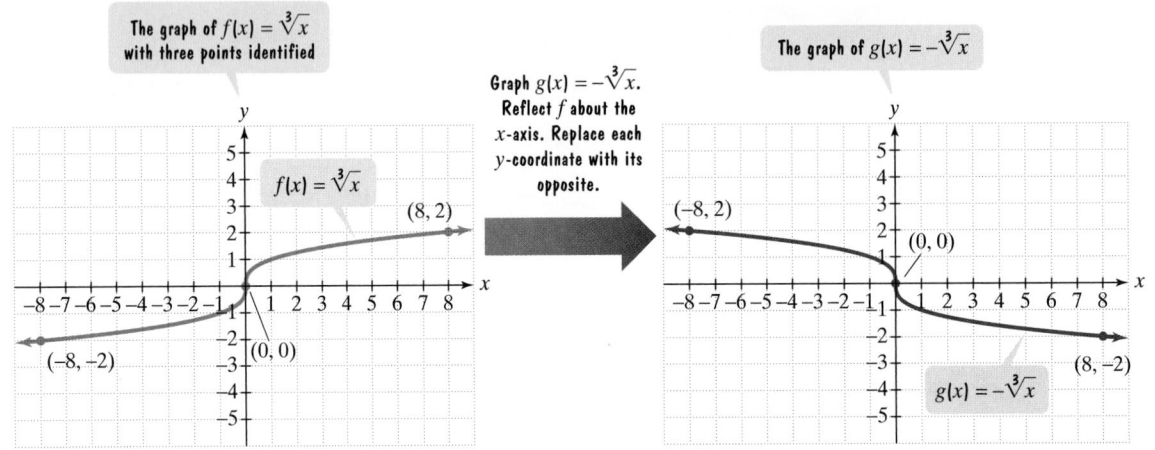

✓ Check Point **4** Use the graph of $f(x) = |x|$ to obtain the graph of $g(x) = -|x|$.

It is also possible to reflect graphs about the y-axis.

Reflection about the y-Axis

The graph of $y = f(-x)$ is the graph of $y = f(x)$ reflected about the y-axis.

For each point (x, y) on the graph of $y = f(x)$, the point $(-x, y)$ is on the graph of $y = f(-x)$.

EXAMPLE 5 Reflection about the y-Axis

Use the graph of $f(x) = \sqrt{x}$ to obtain the graph of $h(x) = \sqrt{-x}$.

Solution Compare the equations for $f(x) = \sqrt{x}$ and $h(x) = \sqrt{-x}$. The graph of h is a reflection about the y-axis of the graph of f because

$$h(x) = \sqrt{-x} = f(-x).$$

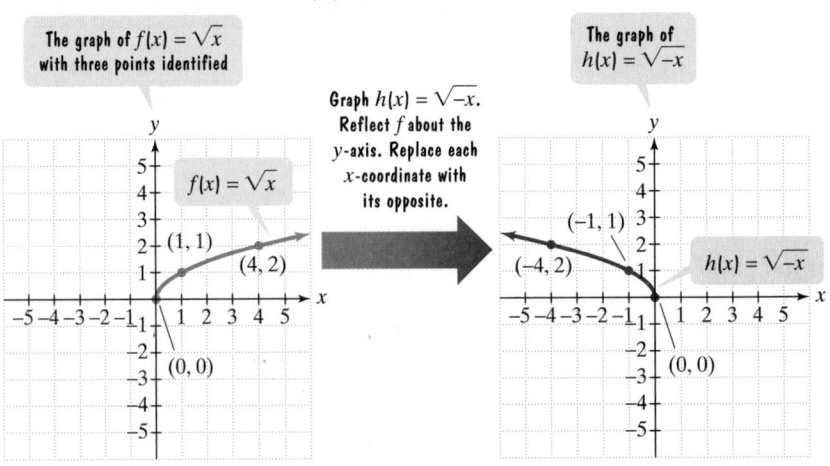

✓ Check Point **5** Use the graph of $f(x) = \sqrt[3]{x}$ to obtain the graph of $h(x) = \sqrt[3]{-x}$.

⑤ Use vertical stretching and shrinking to graph functions.

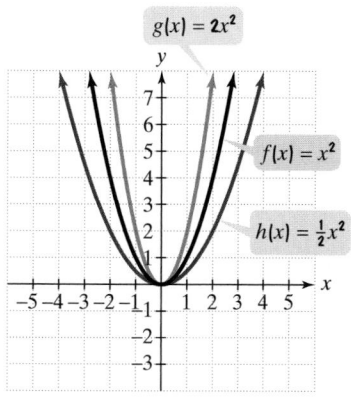

Figure 2.46 Vertically stretching and shrinking $f(x) = x^2$

Vertical Stretching and Shrinking

Morphing does much more than move an image horizontally, vertically, or about an axis. An object having one shape is transformed into a different shape. Horizontal shifts, vertical shifts, and reflections do not change the basic shape of a graph. Graphs remain rigid and proportionally the same when they undergo these transformations. How can we shrink and stretch graphs, thereby altering their basic shapes?

Look at the three graphs in **Figure 2.46**. The black graph in the middle is the graph of the standard quadratic function, $f(x) = x^2$. Now, look at the blue graph on the top. The equation of this graph is $g(x) = 2x^2$, or $g(x) = 2f(x)$. Thus, for each x, the y-coordinate of g is 2 times as large as the corresponding y-coordinate on the graph of f. The result is a narrower graph because the values of y are rising faster. We say that the graph of g is obtained by vertically *stretching* the graph of f. Now, look at the red graph on the bottom. The equation of this graph is $h(x) = \frac{1}{2}x^2$, or $h(x) = \frac{1}{2}f(x)$. Thus, for each x, the y-coordinate of h is one-half as large as the corresponding y-coordinate on the graph of f. The result is a wider graph because the values of y are rising more slowly. We say that the graph of h is obtained by vertically *shrinking* the graph of f.

These observations can be summarized as follows:

Vertically Stretching and Shrinking Graphs

Let f be a function and c a positive real number.

- If $c > 1$, the graph of $y = cf(x)$ is the graph of $y = f(x)$ vertically stretched by multiplying each of its y-coordinates by c.
- If $0 < c < 1$, the graph of $y = cf(x)$ is the graph of $y = f(x)$ vertically shrunk by multiplying each of its y-coordinates by c.

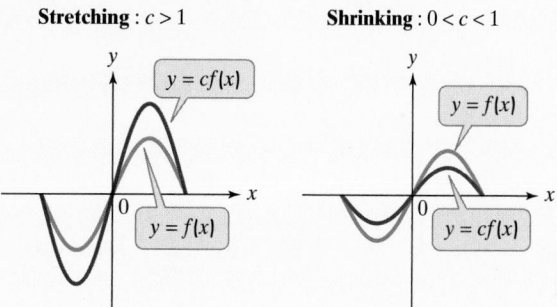

(EXAMPLE 6) **Vertically Shrinking a Graph**

Use the graph of $f(x) = x^3$ to obtain the graph of $h(x) = \frac{1}{2}x^3$.

Solution The graph of $h(x) = \frac{1}{2}x^3$ is obtained by vertically shrinking the graph of $f(x) = x^3$.

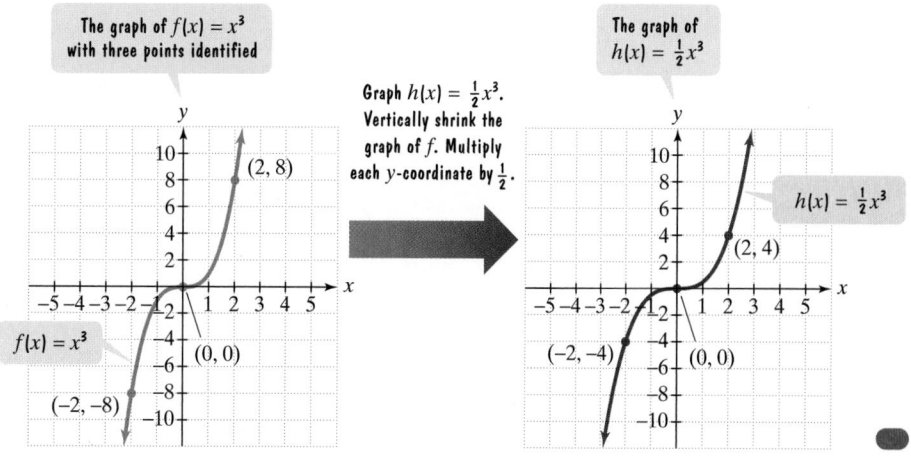

⊘ Check Point **6** Use the graph of $f(x) = |x|$ to obtain the graph of $g(x) = 2|x|$.

6 Use horizontal stretching and shrinking to graph functions.

Horizontal Stretching and Shrinking

It is also possible to stretch and shrink graphs horizontally.

Horizontally Stretching and Shrinking Graphs

Let f be a function and c a positive real number.

- If $c > 1$, the graph of $y = f(cx)$ is the graph of $y = f(x)$ horizontally shrunk by dividing each of its x-coordinates by c.

- If $0 < c < 1$, the graph of $y = f(cx)$ is the graph of $y = f(x)$ horizontally stretched by dividing each of its x-coordinates by c.

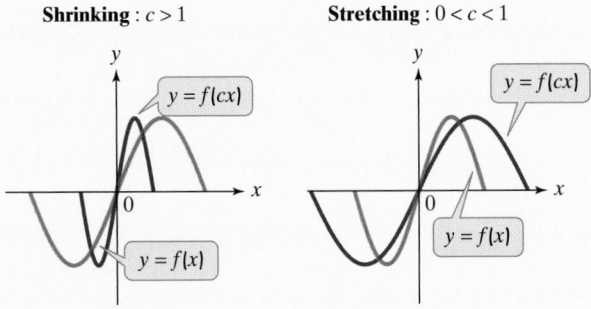

EXAMPLE 7 Horizontally Stretching and Shrinking a Graph

Use the graph of $y = f(x)$ in **Figure 2.47** to obtain each of the following graphs:

a. $g(x) = f(2x)$ **b.** $h(x) = f\left(\frac{1}{2}x\right)$.

Solution

a. The graph of $g(x) = f(2x)$ is obtained by horizontally shrinking the graph of $y = f(x)$.

Figure 2.47

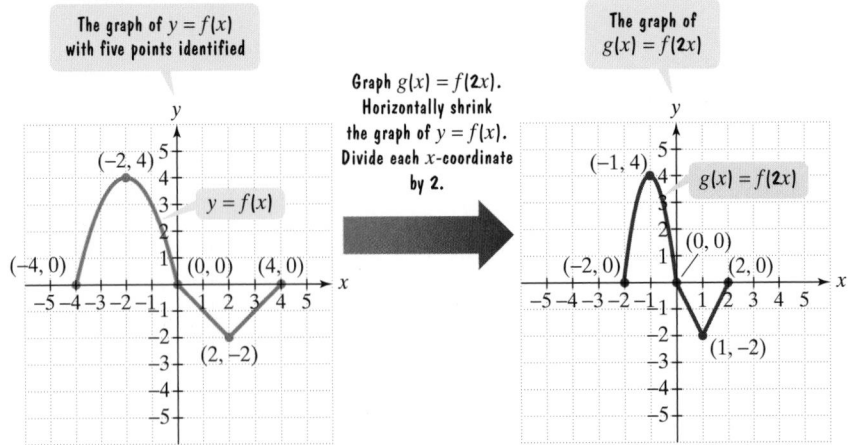

b. The graph of $h(x) = f\left(\frac{1}{2}x\right)$ is obtained by horizontally stretching the graph of $y = f(x)$.

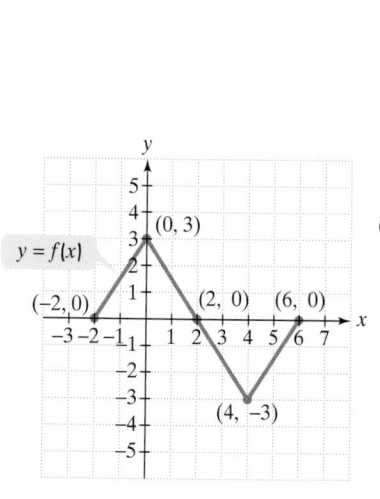

Figure 2.48

⊘ **Check Point 7** Use the graph of $y = f(x)$ in **Figure 2.48** to obtain each of the following graphs:

a. $g(x) = f(2x)$ **b.** $h(x) = f\left(\frac{1}{2}x\right)$.

7 Graph functions involving a sequence of transformations.

Sequences of Transformations

Table 2.4 summarizes the procedures for transforming the graph of $y = f(x)$.

Table 2.4 **Summary of Transformations**

In each case, c represents a positive real number.

To Graph:	Draw the Graph of f and:	Changes in the Equation of $y = f(x)$
Vertical shifts		
$y = f(x) + c$	Raise the graph of f by c units.	c is added to $f(x)$.
$y = f(x) - c$	Lower the graph of f by c units.	c is subtracted from $f(x)$.
Horizontal shifts		
$y = f(x + c)$	Shift the graph of f to the left c units.	x is replaced with $x + c$.
$y = f(x - c)$	Shift the graph of f to the right c units.	x is replaced with $x - c$.
Reflection about the x-axis $y = -f(x)$	Reflect the graph of f about the x-axis.	$f(x)$ is multiplied by -1.
Reflection about the y-axis $y = f(-x)$	Reflect the graph of f about the y-axis.	x is replaced with $-x$.
Vertical stretching or shrinking $y = cf(x), c > 1$	Multiply each y-coordinate of $y = f(x)$ by c, vertically stretching the graph of f.	$f(x)$ is multiplied by $c, c > 1$.
$y = cf(x), 0 < c < 1$	Multiply each y-coordinate of $y = f(x)$ by c, vertically shrinking the graph of f.	$f(x)$ is multiplied by $c, 0 < c < 1$.
Horizontal stretching or shrinking $y = f(cx), c > 1$	Divide each x-coordinate of $y = f(x)$ by c, horizontally shrinking the graph of f.	x is replaced with $cx, c > 1$.
$y = f(cx), 0 < c < 1$	Divide each x-coordinate of $y = f(x)$ by c, horizontally stretching the graph of f.	x is replaced with $cx, 0 < c < 1$.

A function involving more than one transformation can be graphed by performing transformations in the following order:

1. Horizontal shifting
2. Stretching or shrinking
3. Reflecting
4. Vertical shifting

EXAMPLE 8 **Graphing Using a Sequence of Transformations**

Use the graph of $y = f(x)$ given in **Figure 2.47** of Example 7 on page 262, and repeated below, to graph $y = -\frac{1}{2}f(x - 1) + 3$.

Solution Our graphs will evolve in the following order:

1. Horizontal shifting: Graph $y = f(x - 1)$ by shifting the graph of $y = f(x)$ 1 unit to the right.

2. Shrinking: Graph $y = \frac{1}{2}f(x - 1)$ by shrinking the previous graph by a factor of $\frac{1}{2}$.

3. Reflecting: Graph $y = -\frac{1}{2}f(x - 1)$ by reflecting the previous graph about the x-axis.

4. Vertical shifting: Graph $y = -\frac{1}{2}f(x - 1) + 3$ by shifting the previous graph up 3 units.

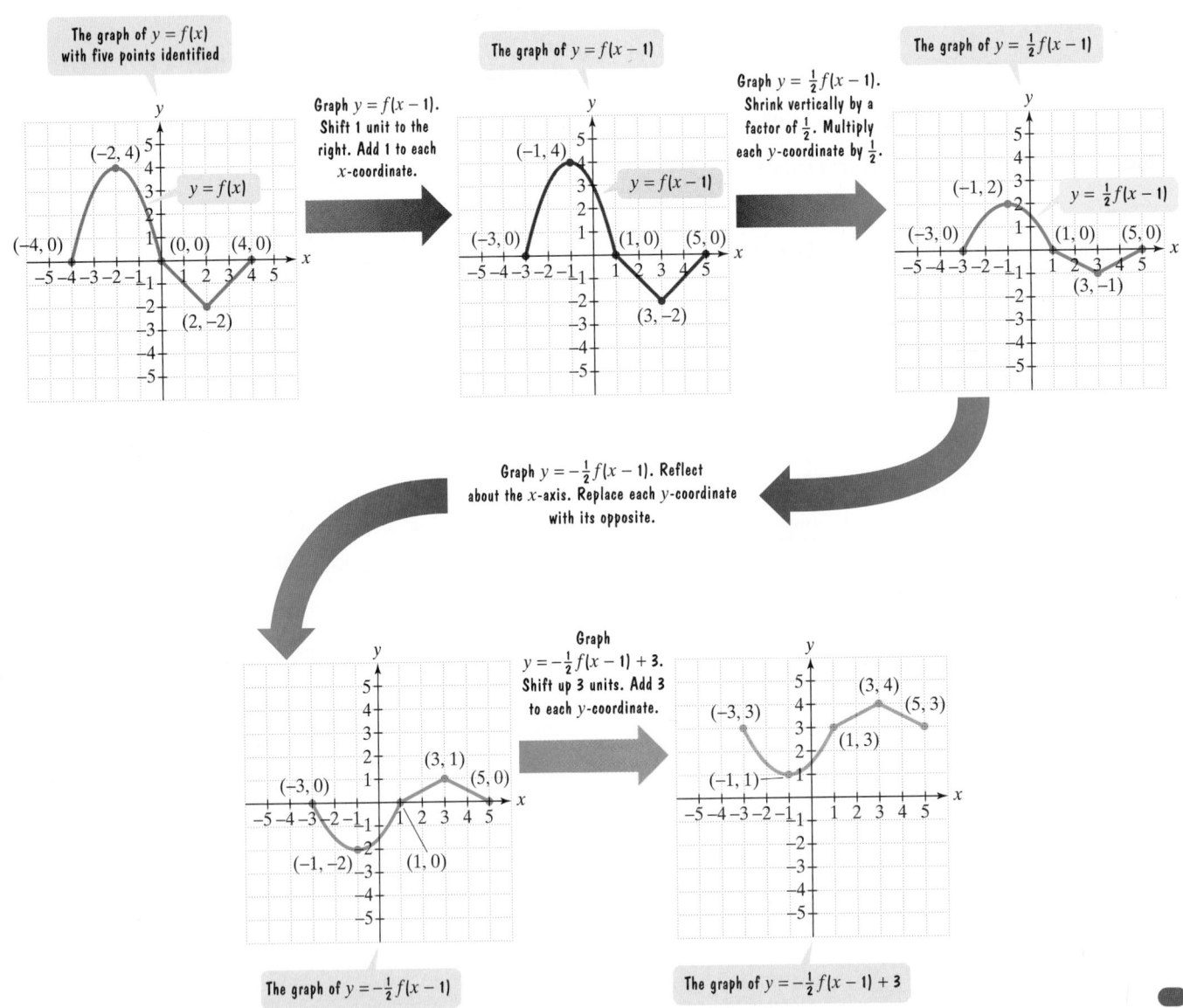

✓ Check Point **8** Use the graph of $y = f(x)$ given in **Figure 2.48** of Check Point 7 on page 263 to graph $y = -\frac{1}{3}f(x + 1) - 2$.

EXAMPLE 9 Graphing Using a Sequence of Transformations

Use the graph of $f(x) = x^2$ to graph $g(x) = 2(x + 3)^2 - 1$.

Solution Our graphs will evolve in the following order:

1. Horizontal shifting: Graph $y = (x + 3)^2$ by shifting the graph of $f(x) = x^2$ three units to the left.
2. Stretching: Graph $y = 2(x + 3)^2$ by stretching the previous graph by a factor of 2.
3. Vertical shifting: Graph $g(x) = 2(x + 3)^2 - 1$ by shifting the previous graph down 1 unit.

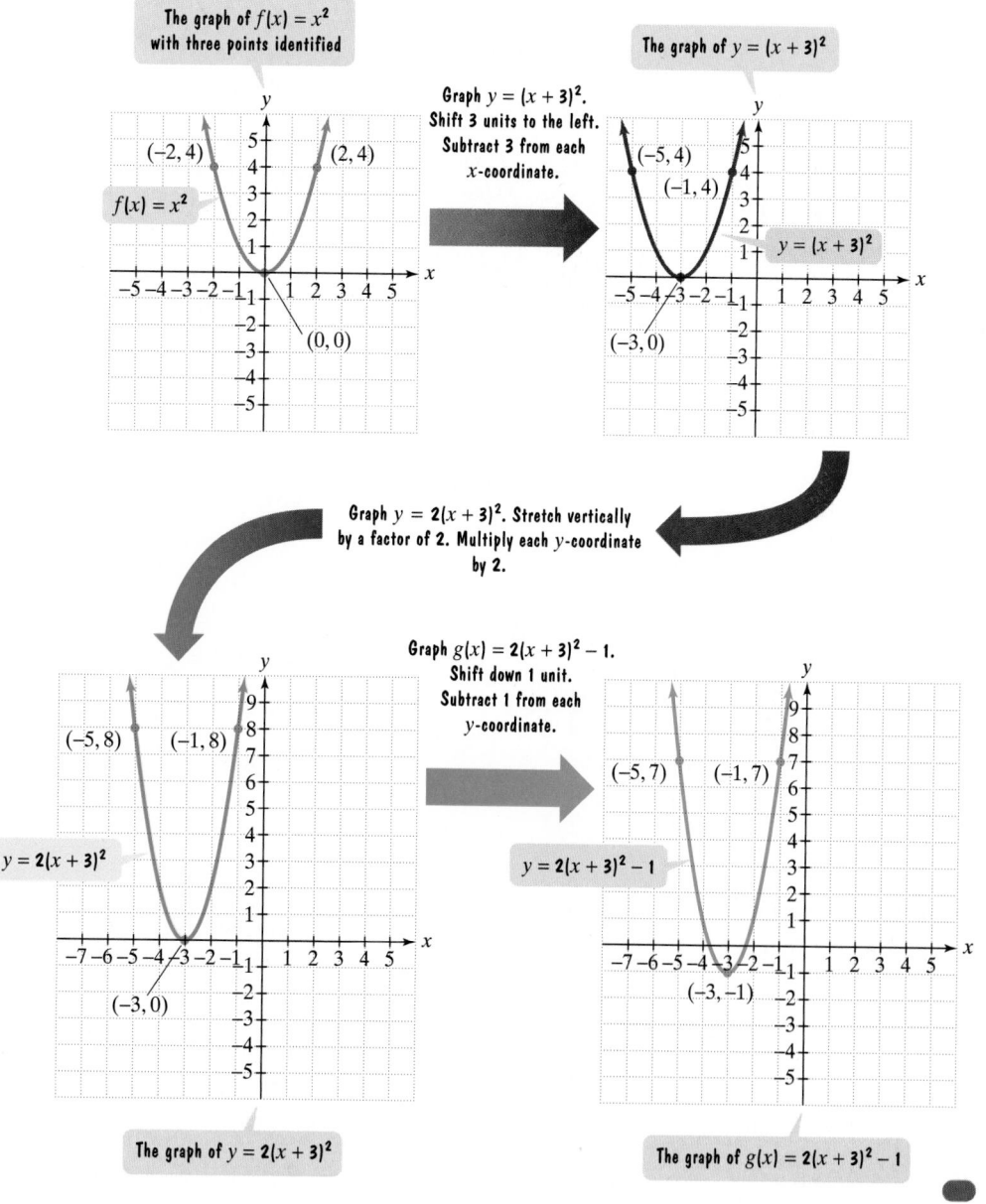

✓ Check Point **9** Use the graph of $f(x) = x^2$ to graph $g(x) = 2(x - 1)^2 + 3$.

Exercise Set 2.5

Practice Exercises

In Exercises 1–16, use the graph of $y = f(x)$ to graph each function g.

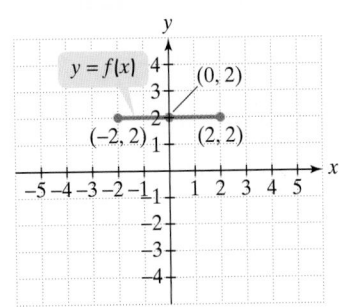

1. $g(x) = f(x) + 1$

2. $g(x) = f(x) - 1$

3. $g(x) = f(x + 1)$

4. $g(x) = f(x - 1)$

5. $g(x) = f(x - 1) - 2$

6. $g(x) = f(x + 1) + 2$

7. $g(x) = f(-x)$

8. $g(x) = -f(x)$

9. $g(x) = -f(x) + 3$

10. $g(x) = f(-x) + 3$

11. $g(x) = \frac{1}{2}f(x)$

12. $g(x) = 2f(x)$

13. $g(x) = f\left(\frac{1}{2}x\right)$

14. $g(x) = f(2x)$

15. $g(x) = -f\left(\frac{1}{2}x\right) + 1$

16. $g(x) = -f(2x) - 1$

In Exercises 17–32, use the graph of $y = f(x)$ to graph each function g.

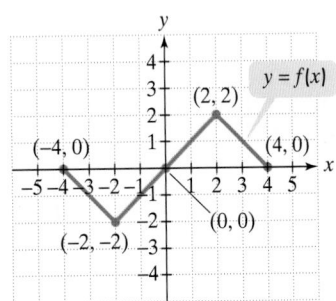

17. $g(x) = f(x) - 1$

18. $g(x) = f(x) + 1$

19. $g(x) = f(x - 1)$

20. $g(x) = f(x + 1)$

21. $g(x) = f(x - 1) + 2$

22. $g(x) = f(x + 1) - 2$

23. $g(x) = -f(x)$

24. $g(x) = f(-x)$

25. $g(x) = f(-x) + 1$

26. $g(x) = -f(x) + 1$

27. $g(x) = 2f(x)$

28. $g(x) = \frac{1}{2}f(x)$

29. $g(x) = f(2x)$

30. $g(x) = f\left(\frac{1}{2}x\right)$

31. $g(x) = 2f(x + 2) + 1$

32. $g(x) = 2f(x + 2) - 1$

In Exercises 33–44, use the graph of $y = f(x)$ to graph each function g.

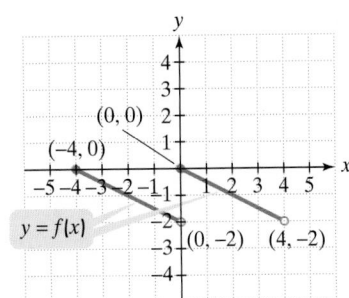

33. $g(x) = f(x) + 2$

34. $g(x) = f(x) - 2$

35. $g(x) = f(x + 2)$

36. $g(x) = f(x - 2)$

37. $g(x) = -f(x + 2)$

38. $g(x) = -f(x - 2)$

39. $g(x) = -\frac{1}{2}f(x + 2)$

40. $g(x) = -\frac{1}{2}f(x - 2)$

41. $g(x) = -\frac{1}{2}f(x + 2) - 2$

42. $g(x) = -\frac{1}{2}f(x - 2) + 2$

43. $g(x) = \frac{1}{2}f(2x)$

44. $g(x) = 2f\left(\frac{1}{2}x\right)$

In Exercises 45–52, use the graph of $y = f(x)$ to graph each function g.

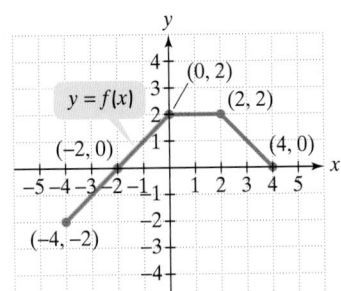

45. $g(x) = f(x - 1) - 1$

46. $g(x) = f(x + 1) + 1$

47. $g(x) = -f(x - 1) + 1$

48. $g(x) = -f(x + 1) - 1$

49. $g(x) = 2f\left(\frac{1}{2}x\right)$

50. $g(x) = \frac{1}{2}f(2x)$

51. $g(x) = \frac{1}{2}f(x + 1)$

52. $g(x) = 2f(x - 1)$

In Exercises 53–66, begin by graphing the standard quadratic function, $f(x) = x^2$. Then use transformations of this graph to graph the given function.

53. $g(x) = x^2 - 2$

54. $g(x) = x^2 - 1$

55. $g(x) = (x - 2)^2$

56. $g(x) = (x - 1)^2$

57. $h(x) = -(x - 2)^2$

58. $h(x) = -(x - 1)^2$

59. $h(x) = (x - 2)^2 + 1$

60. $h(x) = (x - 1)^2 + 2$

61. $g(x) = 2(x - 2)^2$

62. $g(x) = \frac{1}{2}(x - 1)^2$

63. $h(x) = 2(x - 2)^2 - 1$

64. $h(x) = \frac{1}{2}(x - 1)^2 - 1$

65. $h(x) = -2(x + 1)^2 + 1$

66. $h(x) = -2(x + 2)^2 + 1$

In Exercises 67–80, begin by graphing the square root function, $f(x) = \sqrt{x}$. Then use transformations of this graph to graph the given function.

67. $g(x) = \sqrt{x} + 2$ **68.** $g(x) = \sqrt{x} + 1$

69. $g(x) = \sqrt{x + 2}$ **70.** $g(x) = \sqrt{x + 1}$

71. $h(x) = -\sqrt{x + 2}$ **72.** $h(x) = -\sqrt{x + 1}$

73. $h(x) = \sqrt{-x + 2}$ **74.** $h(x) = \sqrt{-x + 1}$

75. $g(x) = \frac{1}{2}\sqrt{x + 2}$ **76.** $g(x) = 2\sqrt{x + 1}$

77. $h(x) = \sqrt{x + 2} - 2$ **78.** $h(x) = \sqrt{x + 1} - 1$

79. $g(x) = 2\sqrt{x + 2} - 2$ **80.** $g(x) = 2\sqrt{x + 1} - 1$

In Exercises 81–94, begin by graphing the absolute value function, $f(x) = |x|$. Then use transformations of this graph to graph the given function.

81. $g(x) = |x| + 4$ **82.** $g(x) = |x| + 3$

83. $g(x) = |x + 4|$ **84.** $g(x) = |x + 3|$

85. $h(x) = |x + 4| - 2$ **86.** $h(x) = |x + 3| - 2$

87. $h(x) = -|x + 4|$ **88.** $h(x) = -|x + 3|$

89. $g(x) = -|x + 4| + 1$ **90.** $g(x) = -|x + 4| + 2$

91. $h(x) = 2|x + 4|$ **92.** $h(x) = 2|x + 3|$

93. $g(x) = -2|x + 4| + 1$ **94.** $g(x) = -2|x + 3| + 2$

In Exercises 95–106, begin by graphing the standard cubic function, $f(x) = x^3$. Then use transformations of this graph to graph the given function.

95. $g(x) = x^3 - 3$ **96.** $g(x) = x^3 - 2$

97. $g(x) = (x - 3)^3$ **98.** $g(x) = (x - 2)^3$

99. $h(x) = -x^3$ **100.** $h(x) = -(x - 2)^3$

101. $h(x) = \frac{1}{2}x^3$ **102.** $h(x) = \frac{1}{4}x^3$

103. $r(x) = (x - 3)^3 + 2$ **104.** $r(x) = (x - 2)^3 + 1$

105. $h(x) = \frac{1}{2}(x - 3)^3 - 2$ **106.** $h(x) = \frac{1}{2}(x - 2)^3 - 1$

In Exercises 107–118, begin by graphing the cube root function, $f(x) = \sqrt[3]{x}$. Then use transformations of this graph to graph the given function.

107. $g(x) = \sqrt[3]{x} + 2$ **108.** $g(x) = \sqrt[3]{x} - 2$

109. $g(x) = \sqrt[3]{x + 2}$ **110.** $g(x) = \sqrt[3]{x - 2}$

111. $h(x) = \frac{1}{2}\sqrt[3]{x + 2}$ **112.** $h(x) = \frac{1}{2}\sqrt[3]{x - 2}$

113. $r(x) = \frac{1}{2}\sqrt[3]{x + 2} - 2$ **114.** $r(x) = \frac{1}{2}\sqrt[3]{x - 2} + 2$

115. $h(x) = -\sqrt[3]{x + 2}$ **116.** $h(x) = -\sqrt[3]{x - 2}$

117. $g(x) = \sqrt[3]{-x - 2}$ **118.** $g(x) = \sqrt[3]{-x + 2}$

Practice Plus

In Exercises 119–122, use transformations of the graph of the greatest integer function, $f(x) = \text{int}(x)$, to graph each function. (The graph of $f(x) = \text{int}(x)$ is shown in **Figure 2.22** on page 222.)

119. $g(x) = 2\,\text{int}\,(x + 1)$ **120.** $g(x) = 3\,\text{int}\,(x - 1)$

121. $h(x) = \text{int}\,(-x) + 1$ **122.** $h(x) = \text{int}\,(-x) - 1$

In Exercises 123–126, write a possible equation for the function whose graph is shown. Each graph shows a transformation of a common function.

123.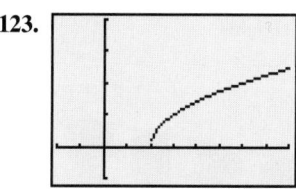
$[-2, 8, 1]$ by $[-1, 4, 1]$

124.
$[-3, 3, 1]$ by $[-6, 6, 1]$

125.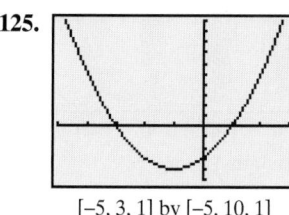
$[-5, 3, 1]$ by $[-5, 10, 1]$

126.
$[-1, 9, 1]$ by $[-1, 5, 1]$

Application Exercises

127. The function $f(x) = 2.9\sqrt{x} + 20.1$ models the median height, $f(x)$, in inches, of boys who are x months of age. The graph of f is shown.

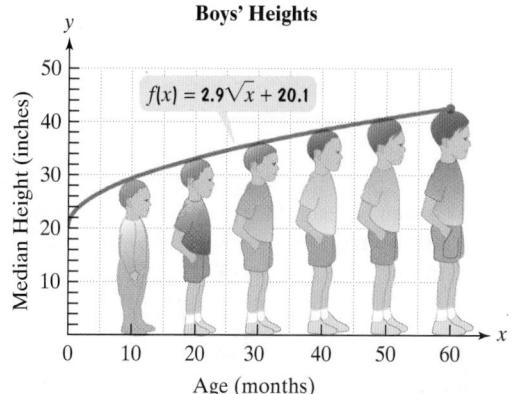

Source: Laura Walther Nathanson, *The Portable Pediatrician for Parents*

a. Describe how the graph can be obtained using transformations of the square root function $f(x) = \sqrt{x}$.

b. According to the model, what is the median height of boys who are 48 months, or four years, old? Use a calculator and round to the nearest tenth of an inch. The actual median height for boys at 48 months is 40.8 inches. How well does the model describe the actual height?

(This exercise continues on the next page.)

c. Use the model to find the average rate of change, in inches per month, between birth and 10 months. Round to the nearest tenth.

d. Use the model to find the average rate of change, in inches per month, between 50 and 60 months. Round to the nearest tenth. How does this compare with your answer in part (c)? How is this difference shown by the graph?

128. The function $f(x) = 3.1\sqrt{x} + 19$ models the median height, $f(x)$, in inches, of girls who are x months of age. The graph of f is shown.

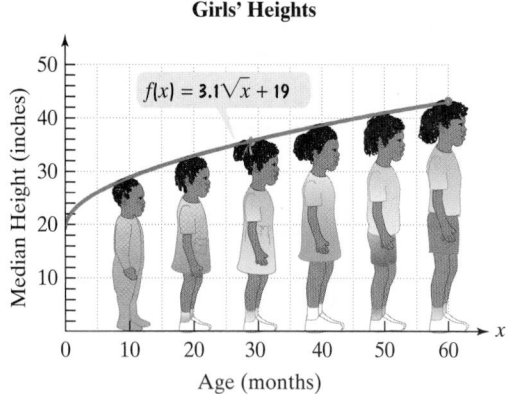

Girls' Heights

$f(x) = 3.1\sqrt{x} + 19$

Median Height (inches) / Age (months)

Source: Laura Walther Nathanson, *The Portable Pediatrician for Parents*

a. Describe how the graph can be obtained using transformations of the square root function $f(x) = \sqrt{x}$.

b. According to the model, what is the median height of girls who are 48 months, or four years, old? Use a calculator and round to the nearest tenth of an inch. The actual median height for girls at 48 months is 40.2 inches. How well does the model describe the actual height?

c. Use the model to find the average rate of change, in inches per month, between birth and 10 months. Round to the nearest tenth.

d. Use the model to find the average rate of change, in inches per month, between 50 and 60 months. Round to the nearest tenth. How does this compare with your answer in part (c)? How is this difference shown by the graph?

Writing in Mathematics

129. What must be done to a function's equation so that its graph is shifted vertically upward?

130. What must be done to a function's equation so that its graph is shifted horizontally to the right?

131. What must be done to a function's equation so that its graph is reflected about the x-axis?

132. What must be done to a function's equation so that its graph is reflected about the y-axis?

133. What must be done to a function's equation so that its graph is stretched vertically?

134. What must be done to a function's equation so that its graph is shrunk horizontally?

Technology Exercises

135. a. Use a graphing utility to graph $f(x) = x^2 + 1$.

b. Graph $f(x) = x^2 + 1$, $g(x) = f(2x)$, $h(x) = f(3x)$, and $k(x) = f(4x)$ in the same viewing rectangle.

c. Describe the relationship among the graphs of f, g, h, and k, with emphasis on different values of x for points on all four graphs that give the same y-coordinate.

d. Generalize by describing the relationship between the graph of f and the graph of g, where $g(x) = f(cx)$ for $c > 1$.

e. Try out your generalization by sketching the graphs of $f(cx)$ for $c = 1$, $c = 2$, $c = 3$, and $c = 4$ for a function of your choice.

136. a. Use a graphing utility to graph $f(x) = x^2 + 1$.

b. Graph $f(x) = x^2 + 1$, $g(x) = f\left(\frac{1}{2}x\right)$, and $h(x) = f\left(\frac{1}{4}x\right)$ in the same viewing rectangle.

c. Describe the relationship among the graphs of f, g, and h, with emphasis on different values of x for points on all three graphs that give the same y-coordinate.

d. Generalize by describing the relationship between the graph of f and the graph of g, where $g(x) = f(cx)$ for $0 < c < 1$.

e. Try out your generalization by sketching the graphs of $f(cx)$ for $c = 1$, and $c = \frac{1}{2}$, and $c = \frac{1}{4}$ for a function of your choice.

Critical Thinking Exercises

Make Sense? *During the winter, you program your home thermostat so that at midnight, the temperature is 55°. This temperature is maintained until 6 A.M. Then the house begins to warm up so that by 9 A.M. the temperature is 65°. At 6 P.M. the house begins to cool. By 9 P.M., the temperature is again 55°. The graph illustrates home temperature, $f(t)$, as a function of hours after midnight, t.*

Home Temperature as a Function of Time

$y = f(t)$

Temperature (°F) / Hours after Midnight

In Exercises 137–140, determine whether each statement makes sense or does not make sense, and explain your reasoning. If the statement makes sense, graph the new function on the domain $[0, 24]$. If the statement does not make sense, correct the function in the statement and graph the corrected function on the domain $[0, 24]$.

137. I decided to keep the house 5° warmer than before, so I reprogrammed the thermostat to $y = f(t) + 5$.

138. I decided to keep the house 5° cooler than before, so I reprogrammed the thermostat to $y = f(t) - 5$.

139. I decided to change the heating schedule to start one hour earlier than before, so I reprogrammed the thermostat to $y = f(t - 1)$.

140. I decided to change the heating schedule to start one hour later than before, so I reprogrammed the thermostat to $y = f(t + 1)$.

In Exercises 141–144, determine whether each statement is true or false. If the statement is false, make the necessary change(s) to produce a true statement.

141. If $f(x) = |x|$ and $g(x) = |x + 3| + 3$, then the graph of g is a translation of the graph of f three units to the right and three units upward.

142. If $f(x) = -\sqrt{x}$ and $g(x) = \sqrt{-x}$, then f and g have identical graphs.

143. If $f(x) = x^2$ and $g(x) = 5(x^2 - 2)$, then the graph of g can be obtained from the graph of f by stretching f five units followed by a downward shift of two units.

144. If $f(x) = x^3$ and $g(x) = -(x - 3)^3 - 4$, then the graph of g can be obtained from the graph of f by moving f three units to the right, reflecting about the x-axis, and then moving the resulting graph down four units.

In Exercises 145–148, functions f and g are graphed in the same rectangular coordinate system. If g is obtained from f through a sequence of transformations, find an equation for g.

145.

146.

147.

148.

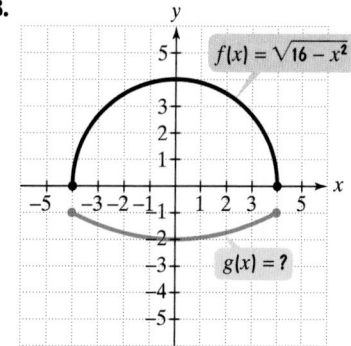

For Exercises 149–152, assume that (a, b) is a point on the graph of f. What is the corresponding point on the graph of each of the following functions?

149. $y = f(-x)$

150. $y = 2f(x)$

151. $y = f(x - 3)$

152. $y = f(x) - 3$

Preview Exercises

Exercises 153–155 will help you prepare for the material covered in the next section.

In Exercises 153–154, perform the indicated operation or operations.

153. $(2x - 1)(x^2 + x - 2)$

154. $(f(x))^2 - 2f(x) + 6$, where $f(x) = 3x - 4$

155. Simplify: $\dfrac{2}{\dfrac{3}{x} - 1}$.

Section 2.6 **Combinations of Functions; Composite Functions**

Objectives

① Find the domain of a function.

② Combine functions using the algebra of functions, specifying domains.

③ Form composite functions.

④ Determine domains for composite functions.

⑤ Write functions as compositions.

We're born. We die. **Figure 2.49** quantifies these statements by showing the numbers of births and deaths in the United States for six selected years.

Study Tip

Throughout this section, we will be using the intersection of sets expressed in interval notation. Recall that the intersection of sets A and B, written $A \cap B$, is the set of elements common to both set A and set B. When sets A and B are in interval notation, to find the intersection, graph each interval and take the portion of the number line that the two graphs have in common. We will also be using notation involving the union of sets A and B, $A \cup B$, meaning the set of elements in A or in B or in both. For more detail, see Section P.1, pages 5–6 and Section 1.7, pages 174–175.

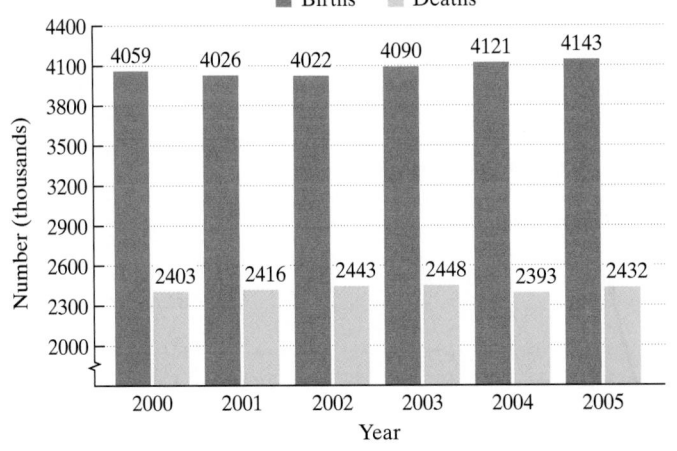

Numbers of Births and Deaths in the United States

Figure 2.49
Source: U.S. Department of Health and Human Services

In this section, we look at these data from the perspective of functions. By considering the yearly change in the U.S. population, you will see that functions can be subtracted using procedures that will remind you of combining algebraic expressions.

① Find the domain of a function.

The Domain of a Function

We begin with two functions that model the data in **Figure 2.49**.

$$B(x) = 7.4x^2 - 15x + 4046 \qquad D(x) = -3.5x^2 + 20x + 2405$$

Number of births, $B(x)$, in thousands, x years after **2000**

Number of deaths, $D(x)$, in thousands, x years after **2000**

The years in **Figure 2.49** extend from 2000 through 2005. Because x represents the number of years after 2000,

$$\text{Domain of } B = \{x \mid x = 0, 1, 2, 3, 4, 5\}$$

and

$$\text{Domain of } D = \{x \mid x = 0, 1, 2, 3, 4, 5\}.$$

Functions that model data often have their domains explicitly given with the function's equation. However, for most functions, only an equation is given and the domain is not specified. In cases like this, the domain of a function f is the largest set of real numbers for which the value of $f(x)$ is a real number. For example, consider the function

$$f(x) = \frac{1}{x - 3}.$$

Because division by 0 is undefined, the denominator, $x - 3$, cannot be 0. Thus, x cannot equal 3. The domain of the function consists of all real numbers other than 3, represented by

Domain of $f = \{x \mid x$ is a real number and $x \neq 3\}$.

Using interval notation,

Domain of $f = (-\infty, 3) \cup (3, \infty)$.

All real numbers less than 3	or	All real numbers greater than 3

Now consider a function involving a square root:

$$g(x) = \sqrt{x - 3}.$$

Because only nonnegative numbers have square roots that are real numbers, the expression under the square root sign, $x - 3$, must be nonnegative. We can use inspection to see that $x - 3 \geq 0$ if $x \geq 3$. The domain of g consists of all real numbers that are greater than or equal to 3:

Domain of $g = \{x \mid x \geq 3\}$ or $[3, \infty)$.

Finding a Function's Domain

If a function f does not model data or verbal conditions, its domain is the largest set of real numbers for which the value of $f(x)$ is a real number. Exclude from a function's domain real numbers that cause division by zero and real numbers that result in a square root of a negative number.

(EXAMPLE 1) **Finding the Domain of a Function**

Find the domain of each function:

a. $f(x) = x^2 - 7x$ **b.** $g(x) = \dfrac{3x + 2}{x^2 - 2x - 3}$ **c.** $h(x) = \sqrt{3x + 12}$.

Solution The domain is the set of all real numbers, $(-\infty, \infty)$, unless x appears in a denominator or a square root.

a. The function $f(x) = x^2 - 7x$ contains neither division nor a square root. For every real number, x, the algebraic expression $x^2 - 7x$ represents a real number. Thus, the domain of f is the set of all real numbers.

Domain of $f = (-\infty, \infty)$

b. The function $g(x) = \dfrac{3x + 2}{x^2 - 2x - 3}$ contains division. Because division by 0 is undefined, we must exclude from the domain the values of x that cause the denominator, $x^2 - 2x - 3$, to be 0. We can identify these values by setting $x^2 - 2x - 3$ equal to 0.

$x^2 - 2x - 3 = 0$	Set the function's denominator equal to 0.
$(x + 1)(x - 3) = 0$	Factor.
$x + 1 = 0$ or $x - 3 = 0$	Set each factor equal to 0.
$x = -1$ $x = 3$	Solve the resulting equations.

We must exclude -1 and 3 from the domain of g.

Domain of $g = (-\infty, -1) \cup (-1, 3) \cup (3, \infty)$

Study Tip

In parts (a) and (b), observe when to factor and when not to factor a polynomial.

• $f(x) = x^2 - 7x$ • $g(x) = \dfrac{3x + 2}{x^2 - 2x - 3}$

Do not factor $x^2 - 7x$ and set it equal to zero. No values of x need be excluded from the domain.

Do factor $x^2 - 2x - 3$ and set it equal to zero. We must exclude values of x that cause this denominator to be zero.

c. The function $h(x) = \sqrt{3x + 12}$ contains an even root. Because only nonnegative numbers have real square roots, the quantity under the radical sign, $3x + 12$, must be greater than or equal to 0.

$[-10, 10, 1]$ by $[-10, 10, 1]$

Figure 2.50

$$3x + 12 \geq 0 \quad \text{Set the function's radicand greater than or equal to 0.}$$
$$3x \geq -12 \quad \text{Subtract 12 from both sides.}$$
$$x \geq -4 \quad \text{Divide both sides by 3. Division by a positive number preserves the sense of the inequality.}$$

The domain of h consists of all real numbers greater than or equal to -4.

Domain of $h = [-4, \infty)$

The domain is highlighted on the x-axis in **Figure 2.50**.

◯ Check Point **I** Find the domain of each function:

a. $f(x) = x^2 + 3x - 17$ **b.** $g(x) = \dfrac{5x}{x^2 - 49}$ **c.** $h(x) = \sqrt{9x - 27}$.

② Combine functions using the algebra of functions, specifying domains.

The Algebra of Functions

We can combine functions using addition, subtraction, multiplication, and division by performing operations with the algebraic expressions that appear on the right side of the equations. For example, the functions $f(x) = 2x$ and $g(x) = x - 1$ can be combined to form the sum, difference, product, and quotient of f and g. Here's how it's done:

For each function, $f(x) = 2x$ and $g(x) = x - 1$.

Sum: $f + g$
$$(f + g)(x) = f(x) + g(x)$$
$$= 2x + (x - 1) = 3x - 1$$

Difference: $f - g$
$$(f - g)(x) = f(x) - g(x)$$
$$= 2x - (x - 1) = 2x - x + 1 = x + 1$$

Product: fg
$$(fg)(x) = f(x) \cdot g(x)$$
$$= 2x(x - 1) = 2x^2 - 2x$$

Quotient: $\dfrac{f}{g}$
$$\left(\dfrac{f}{g}\right)(x) = \dfrac{f(x)}{g(x)} = \dfrac{2x}{x - 1}, x \neq 1.$$

The domain for each of these functions consists of all real numbers that are common to the domains of f and g. In the case of the quotient function $\dfrac{f(x)}{g(x)}$, we must remember not to divide by 0, so we add the further restriction that $g(x) \neq 0$.

The Algebra of Functions: Sum, Difference, Product, and Quotient of Functions

Let f and g be two functions. The **sum** $f + g$, the **difference** $f - g$, the **product** fg, and the **quotient** $\dfrac{f}{g}$ are functions whose domains are the set of all real numbers common to the domains of f and g $(D_f \cap D_g)$, defined as follows:

1. Sum: $(f + g)(x) = f(x) + g(x)$

2. Difference: $(f - g)(x) = f(x) - g(x)$

3. Product: $(fg)(x) = f(x) \cdot g(x)$

4. Quotient: $\left(\dfrac{f}{g}\right)(x) = \dfrac{f(x)}{g(x)}$, provided $g(x) \neq 0$.

EXAMPLE 2 **Combining Functions**

Let $f(x) = 2x - 1$ and $g(x) = x^2 + x - 2$. Find each of the following functions:

a. $(f + g)(x)$ **b.** $(f - g)(x)$ **c.** $(fg)(x)$ **d.** $\left(\dfrac{f}{g}\right)(x)$.

Determine the domain for each function.

Solution

a. $(f + g)(x) = f(x) + g(x)$ *This is the definition of the sum f + g.*

$\qquad\qquad = (2x - 1) + (x^2 + x - 2)$ *Substitute the given functions.*

$\qquad\qquad = x^2 + 3x - 3$ *Remove parentheses and combine like terms.*

b. $(f - g)(x) = f(x) - g(x)$ *This is the definition of the difference f − g.*

$\qquad\qquad = (2x - 1) - (x^2 + x - 2)$ *Substitute the given functions.*

$\qquad\qquad = 2x - 1 - x^2 - x + 2$ *Remove parentheses and change the sign of each term in the second set of parentheses.*

$\qquad\qquad = -x^2 + x + 1$ *Combine like terms and arrange terms in descending powers of x.*

c. $(fg)(x) = f(x) \cdot g(x)$ *This is the definition of the product fg.*

$\qquad\qquad = (2x - 1)(x^2 + x - 2)$ *Substitute the given functions.*

$\qquad\qquad = 2x(x^2 + x - 2) - 1(x^2 + x - 2)$ *Multiply each term in the second factor by 2x and −1, respectively.*

$\qquad\qquad = 2x^3 + 2x^2 - 4x - x^2 - x + 2$ *Use the distributive property.*

$\qquad\qquad = 2x^3 + (2x^2 - x^2) + (-4x - x) + 2$ *Rearrange terms so that like terms are adjacent.*

$\qquad\qquad = 2x^3 + x^2 - 5x + 2$ *Combine like terms.*

d. $\left(\dfrac{f}{g}\right)(x) = \dfrac{f(x)}{g(x)}$ *This is the definition of the quotient $\dfrac{f}{g}$.*

$\qquad\qquad = \dfrac{2x - 1}{x^2 + x - 2}$ *Substitute the given functions. This rational expression cannot be simplified.*

Study Tip

If the function $\frac{f}{g}$ can be simplified, determine the domain *before* simplifying.

Example:

$f(x) = x^2 - 4$ and
$g(x) = x - 2$

$\left(\dfrac{f}{g}\right)(x) = \dfrac{x^2 - 4}{x - 2}$

$x \neq 2$. The domain of $\frac{f}{g}$ is $(-\infty, 2) \cup (2, \infty)$.

$= \dfrac{(x + 2)(x - 2)}{(x - 2)} = x + 2$

Because the equations for f and g do not involve division or contain even roots, the domain of both f and g is the set of all real numbers. Thus, the domain of $f + g, f - g$, and fg is the set of all real numbers, $(-\infty, \infty)$.

The function $\frac{f}{g}$ contains division. We must exclude from its domain values of x that cause the denominator, $x^2 + x - 2$, to be 0. Let's identify these values.

$\qquad x^2 + x - 2 = 0$ *Set the denominator of $\frac{f}{g}$ equal to 0.*

$\qquad (x + 2)(x - 1) = 0$ *Factor.*

$x + 2 = 0$ or $x - 1 = 0$ *Set each factor equal to 0.*

$\qquad x = -2 \qquad\qquad x = 1$ *Solve the resulting equations.*

We must exclude -2 and 1 from the domain of $\frac{f}{g}$.

$$\text{Domain of } \frac{f}{g} = (-\infty, -2) \cup (-2, 1) \cup (1, \infty)$$

⊘ Check Point **2** Let $f(x) = x - 5$ and $g(x) = x^2 - 1$. Find each of the following functions:

 a. $(f + g)(x)$ **b.** $(f - g)(x)$ **c.** $(fg)(x)$ **d.** $\left(\dfrac{f}{g}\right)(x)$.

Determine the domain for each function.

(**EXAMPLE 3**) **Adding Functions and Determining the Domain**

Let $f(x) = \sqrt{x + 3}$ and $g(x) = \sqrt{x - 2}$. Find each of the following:

 a. $(f + g)(x)$ **b.** the domain of $f + g$.

Solution

 a. $(f + g)(x) = f(x) + g(x) = \sqrt{x + 3} + \sqrt{x - 2}$

 b. The domain of $f + g$ is the set of all real numbers that are common to the domain of f and the domain of g. Thus, we must find the domains of f and g before finding their intersection.

$$\bullet \; f(x) = \sqrt{x + 3} \qquad\qquad \bullet \; g(x) = \sqrt{x - 2}$$

$x + 3$ must be nonnegative:	$x - 2$ must be nonnegative:
$x + 3 \geq 0. \; D_f = [-3, \infty)$	$x - 2 \geq 0. \; D_g = [2, \infty)$

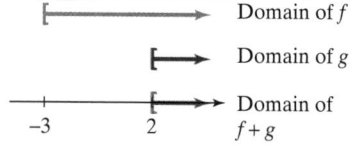

Domain of f

Domain of g

Domain of $f + g$

Figure 2.51 Finding the domain of the sum $f + g$

Now, we can use a number line to determine $D_f \cap D_g$, the domain of $f + g$. **Figure 2.51** shows the domain of f in blue and the domain of g in red. Can you see that all real numbers greater than or equal to 2 are common to both domains? This is shown in purple on the number line. Thus, the domain of $f + g$ is $[2, \infty)$. ●

Technology

Graphic Connections

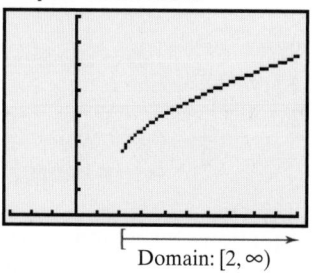

Domain: $[2, \infty)$

The graph on the left is the graph of

$$y = \sqrt{x + 3} + \sqrt{x - 2}$$

in a $[-3, 10, 1]$ by $[0, 8, 1]$ viewing rectangle. The graph reveals what we discovered algebraically in Example 3(b). The domain of this function is $[2, \infty)$.

⊘ Check Point **3** Let $f(x) = \sqrt{x - 3}$ and $g(x) = \sqrt{x + 1}$. Find each of the following:

 a. $(f + g)(x)$ **b.** the domain of $f + g$.

③ Form composite functions.

Composite Functions

There is another way of combining two functions. To help understand this new combination, suppose that your local computer store is having a sale. The models that are on sale cost either $300 less than the regular price or 85% of the regular

price. If x represents the computer's regular price, the discounts can be modeled with the following functions:

$$f(x) = x - 300 \qquad g(x) = 0.85x.$$

> The computer is on sale for $300 less than its regular price.

> The computer is on sale for 85% of its regular price.

At the store, you bargain with the salesperson. Eventually, she makes an offer you can't refuse. The sale price will be 85% of the regular price followed by a $300 reduction:

$$0.85x - 300.$$

> 85% of the regular price

> followed by a $300 reduction

In terms of the functions f and g, this offer can be obtained by taking the output of $g(x) = 0.85x$, namely $0.85x$, and using it as the input of f:

$$f(x) = x - 300$$

> Replace x with $0.85x$, the output of $g(x) = 0.85x$.

$$f(0.85x) = 0.85x - 300.$$

Because $0.85x$ is $g(x)$, we can write this last equation as

$$f(g(x)) = 0.85x - 300.$$

We read this equation as "f of g of x is equal to $0.85x - 300$." We call $f(g(x))$ the **composition of the function f with g**, or a **composite function**. This composite function is written $f \circ g$. Thus,

$$(f \circ g)(x) = f(g(x)) = 0.85x - 300.$$

> This can be read "f of g of x" or "f composed with g of x."

Like all functions, we can evaluate $f \circ g$ for a specified value of x in the function's domain. For example, here's how to find the value of the composite function describing the offer you cannot refuse at 1400:

$$(f \circ g)(x) = 0.85x - 300$$

> Replace x with 1400.

$$(f \circ g)(1400) = 0.85(1400) - 300 = 1190 - 300 = 890.$$

This means that a computer that regularly sells for $1400 is on sale for $890 subject to both discounts. We can use a partial table of coordinates for each of the discount functions, g and f, to numerically verify this result.

Computer's regular price	85% of the regular price		85% of the regular price	$300 reduction
x	$g(x) = 0.85x$		x	$f(x) = x - 300$
1200	1020		1020	720
1300	1105		1105	805
1400	1190		1190	890

Using these tables, we can find $(f \circ g)(1400)$:

Tables for the discount functions
(repeated)

$$(f \circ g)(1400) = f(g(1400)) = f(1190) = 890.$$

The table for g shows that $g(1400) = 1190$.

The table for f shows that $f(1190) = 890$.

This verifies that a computer that regularly sells for \$1400 is on sale for \$890 subject to both discounts.

Before you run out to buy a computer, let's generalize our discussion of the computer's double discount and define the composition of any two functions.

The Composition of Functions

The **composition of the function f with g** is denoted by $f \circ g$ and is defined by the equation

$$(f \circ g)(x) = f(g(x)).$$

The **domain of the composite function $f \circ g$** is the set of all x such that

1. x is in the domain of g and
2. $g(x)$ is in the domain of f.

The composition of f with g, $f \circ g$, is illustrated in **Figure 2.52**.

Step 1 Input x into g. **Step 2** Input $g(x)$ into f.

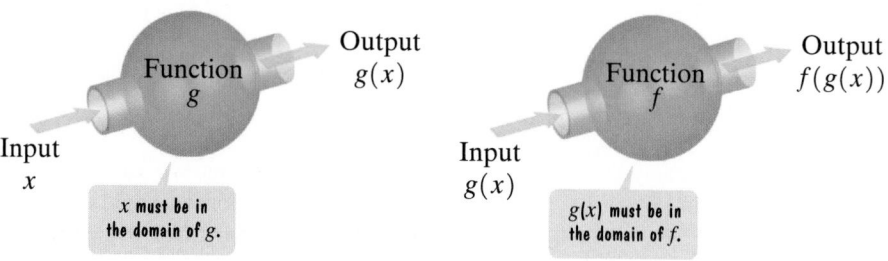

Figure 2.52

The figure reinforces the fact that the inside function g in $f(g(x))$ is done first.

(**EXAMPLE 4**) **Forming Composite Functions**

Given $f(x) = 3x - 4$ and $g(x) = x^2 - 2x + 6$, find each of the following:

a. $(f \circ g)(x)$ **b.** $(g \circ f)(x)$ **c.** $(g \circ f)(1)$.

Solution

a. We begin with $(f \circ g)(x)$, the composition of f with g. Because $(f \circ g)(x)$ means $f(g(x))$, we must replace each occurrence of x in the equation for f with $g(x)$.

$$f(x) = 3x - 4 \qquad \textit{This is the given equation for f.}$$

Replace x with $g(x)$.

$$(f \circ g)(x) = f(g(x)) = 3g(x) - 4$$

$$= 3(x^2 - 2x + 6) - 4 \qquad \begin{array}{l} \textit{Because} \\ g(x) = x^2 - 2x + 6, \\ \textit{replace } g(x) \textit{ with } x^2 - 2x + 6. \end{array}$$

$$= 3x^2 - 6x + 18 - 4 \qquad \textit{Use the distributive property.}$$

$$= 3x^2 - 6x + 14 \qquad \textit{Simplify.}$$

Thus, $(f \circ g)(x) = 3x^2 - 6x + 14$.

b. Next, we find $(g \circ f)(x)$, the composition of g with f. Because $(g \circ f)(x)$ means $g(f(x))$, we must replace each occurrence of x in the equation for g with $f(x)$.

$$g(x) = x^2 - 2x + 6 \qquad \textit{This is the equation for g.}$$

Replace x with $f(x)$.

$$(g \circ f)(x) = g(f(x)) = (f(x))^2 - 2f(x) + 6$$

$$= (3x - 4)^2 - 2(3x - 4) + 6 \qquad \begin{array}{l} \textit{Because f(x) = 3x - 4,} \\ \textit{replace f(x) with 3x - 4.} \end{array}$$

$$= 9x^2 - 24x + 16 - 6x + 8 + 6 \qquad \begin{array}{l} \textit{Use } (A - B)^2 = \\ A^2 - 2AB + B^2 \textit{ to} \\ \textit{square 3x - 4.} \end{array}$$

$$= 9x^2 - 30x + 30 \qquad \begin{array}{l} \textit{Simplify:} \\ -24x - 6x = -30x \\ \textit{and } 16 + 8 + 6 = 30. \end{array}$$

Thus, $(g \circ f)(x) = 9x^2 - 30x + 30$. **Notice that $(f \circ g)(x)$ is not the same function as $(g \circ f)(x)$.**

c. We can use $(g \circ f)(x)$ to find $(g \circ f)(1)$.

$$(g \circ f)(x) = 9x^2 - 30x + 30$$

Replace x with 1.

$$(g \circ f)(1) = 9 \cdot 1^2 - 30 \cdot 1 + 30 = 9 - 30 + 30 = 9$$

It is also possible to find $(g \circ f)(1)$ without determining $(g \circ f)(x)$.

$$(g \circ f)(1) = g(f(1)) = g(-1) = 9$$

First find $f(1)$.
$f(x) = 3x - 4$, so
$f(1) = 3 \cdot 1 - 4 = -1$.

Next find $g(-1)$.
$g(x) = x^2 - 2x + 6$, so
$g(-1) = (-1)^2 - 2(-1) + 6$
$= 1 + 2 + 6 = 9$.

✓ Check Point **4** Given $f(x) = 5x + 6$ and $g(x) = 2x^2 - x - 1$, find each of the following:

a. $(f \circ g)(x)$ **b.** $(g \circ f)(x)$ **c.** $(f \circ g)(-1)$.

④ Determine domains for composite functions.

We need to be careful in determining the domain for a composite function.

Excluding Values from the Domain of $(f \circ g)(x) = f(g(x))$

The following values must be excluded from the input x:

- If x is not in the domain of g, it must not be in the domain of $f \circ g$.
- Any x for which $g(x)$ is not in the domain of f must not be in the domain of $f \circ g$.

EXAMPLE 5 **Forming a Composite Function and Finding Its Domain**

Given $f(x) = \dfrac{2}{x-1}$ and $g(x) = \dfrac{3}{x}$, find each of the following:

a. $(f \circ g)(x)$ **b.** the domain of $f \circ g$.

Solution

a. Because $(f \circ g)(x)$ means $f(g(x))$, we must replace x in $f(x) = \dfrac{2}{x-1}$ with $g(x)$.

$$(f \circ g)(x) = f(g(x)) = \frac{2}{g(x)-1} = \frac{2}{\frac{3}{x}-1} = \frac{2}{\frac{3}{x}-1} \cdot \frac{x}{x} = \frac{2x}{3-x}$$

$g(x) = \frac{3}{x}$

Simplify the complex fraction by multiplying by $\frac{x}{x}$, or 1.

Study Tip

The procedure for simplifying complex fractions can be found in Section P.6, pages 80–82.

Thus, $(f \circ g)(x) = \dfrac{2x}{3-x}$.

b. We determine values to exclude from the domain of $(f \circ g)(x)$ in two steps.

Rules for Excluding Numbers from the Domain of $(f \circ g)(x) = f(g(x))$	Applying the Rules to $f(x) = \dfrac{2}{x-1}$ and $g(x) = \dfrac{3}{x}$
If x is not in the domain of g, it must not be in the domain of $f \circ g$.	Because $g(x) = \dfrac{3}{x}$, 0 is not in the domain of g. Thus, 0 must be excluded from the domain of $f \circ g$.
Any x for which $g(x)$ is not in the domain of f must not be in the domain of $f \circ g$.	Because $f(g(x)) = \dfrac{2}{g(x)-1}$, we must exclude from the domain of $f \circ g$ any x for which $g(x) = 1$. $\dfrac{3}{x} = 1$ Set g(x) equal to 1. $3 = x$ Multiply both sides by x. 3 must be excluded from the domain of $f \circ g$.

We see that 0 and 3 must be excluded from the domain of $f \circ g$. The domain of $f \circ g$ is

$$(-\infty, 0) \cup (0, 3) \cup (3, \infty).$$

✓ **Check Point 5** Given $f(x) = \dfrac{4}{x+2}$ and $g(x) = \dfrac{1}{x}$, find each of the following:

a. $(f \circ g)(x)$ **b.** the domain of $f \circ g$.

⑤ Write functions as compositions.

Decomposing Functions

When you form a composite function, you "compose" two functions to form a new function. It is also possible to reverse this process. That is, you can "decompose" a given function and express it as a composition of two functions. Although there is more than one way to do this, there is often a "natural" selection that comes to mind first. For example, consider the function h defined by

$$h(x) = (3x^2 - 4x + 1)^5.$$

The function h takes $3x^2 - 4x + 1$ and raises it to the power 5. A natural way to write h as a composition of two functions is to raise the function $g(x) = 3x^2 - 4x + 1$ to the power 5. Thus, if we let

$$f(x) = x^5 \text{ and } g(x) = 3x^2 - 4x + 1, \text{ then}$$

$$(f \circ g)(x) = f(g(x)) = f(3x^2 - 4x + 1) = (3x^2 - 4x + 1)^5.$$

$\boxed{\text{EXAMPLE 6}}$ **Writing a Function as a Composition**

Express $h(x)$ as a composition of two functions:

$$h(x) = \sqrt[3]{x^2 + 1}.$$

Study Tip

Suppose the form of function h is $h(x) = (\text{algebraic expression})^{\text{power}}$. Function h can be expressed as a composition, $f \circ g$, using

$f(x) = x^{\text{power}}$

$g(x) = $ algebraic expression.

Solution The function h takes $x^2 + 1$ and takes its cube root. A natural way to write h as a composition of two functions is to take the cube root of the function $g(x) = x^2 + 1$. Thus, we let

$$f(x) = \sqrt[3]{x} \text{ and } g(x) = x^2 + 1.$$

We can check this composition by finding $(f \circ g)(x)$. This should give the original function, namely $h(x) = \sqrt[3]{x^2 + 1}$.

$$(f \circ g)(x) = f(g(x)) = f(x^2 + 1) = \sqrt[3]{x^2 + 1} = h(x) \qquad \bullet$$

☑ Check Point **6** Express $h(x)$ as a composition of two functions:

$$h(x) = \sqrt{x^2 + 5}.$$

Exercise Set 2.6

Practice Exercises

In Exercises 1–30, find the domain of each function.

1. $f(x) = 3(x - 4)$

2. $f(x) = 2(x + 5)$

3. $g(x) = \dfrac{3}{x - 4}$

4. $g(x) = \dfrac{2}{x + 5}$

5. $f(x) = x^2 - 2x - 15$

6. $f(x) = x^2 + x - 12$

7. $g(x) = \dfrac{3}{x^2 - 2x - 15}$

8. $g(x) = \dfrac{2}{x^2 + x - 12}$

9. $f(x) = \dfrac{1}{x + 7} + \dfrac{3}{x - 9}$

10. $f(x) = \dfrac{1}{x + 8} + \dfrac{3}{x - 10}$

11. $g(x) = \dfrac{1}{x^2 + 1} - \dfrac{1}{x^2 - 1}$

12. $g(x) = \dfrac{1}{x^2 + 4} - \dfrac{1}{x^2 - 4}$

13. $h(x) = \dfrac{4}{\dfrac{3}{x} - 1}$

14. $h(x) = \dfrac{5}{\dfrac{4}{x} - 1}$

15. $f(x) = \dfrac{1}{\dfrac{4}{x - 1} - 2}$

16. $f(x) = \dfrac{1}{\dfrac{4}{x - 2} - 3}$

17. $f(x) = \sqrt{x - 3}$

18. $f(x) = \sqrt{x + 2}$

19. $g(x) = \dfrac{1}{\sqrt{x-3}}$ **20.** $g(x) = \dfrac{1}{\sqrt{x+2}}$

21. $g(x) = \sqrt{5x+35}$ **22.** $g(x) = \sqrt{7x-70}$

23. $f(x) = \sqrt{24-2x}$ **24.** $f(x) = \sqrt{84-6x}$

25. $h(x) = \sqrt{x-2} + \sqrt{x+3}$

26. $h(x) = \sqrt{x-3} + \sqrt{x+4}$

27. $g(x) = \dfrac{\sqrt{x-2}}{x-5}$ **28.** $g(x) = \dfrac{\sqrt{x-3}}{x-6}$

29. $f(x) = \dfrac{2x+7}{x^3 - 5x^2 - 4x + 20}$

30. $f(x) = \dfrac{7x+2}{x^3 - 2x^2 - 9x + 18}$

In Exercises 31–48, find $f + g, f - g, fg,$ and $\frac{f}{g}$. Determine the domain for each function.

31. $f(x) = 2x + 3, g(x) = x - 1$

32. $f(x) = 3x - 4, g(x) = x + 2$

33. $f(x) = x - 5, g(x) = 3x^2$

34. $f(x) = x - 6, g(x) = 5x^2$

35. $f(x) = 2x^2 - x - 3, g(x) = x + 1$

36. $f(x) = 6x^2 - x - 1, g(x) = x - 1$

37. $f(x) = 3 - x^2, g(x) = x^2 + 2x - 15$

38. $f(x) = 5 - x^2, g(x) = x^2 + 4x - 12$

39. $f(x) = \sqrt{x}, g(x) = x - 4$

40. $f(x) = \sqrt{x}, g(x) = x - 5$

41. $f(x) = 2 + \dfrac{1}{x}, g(x) = \dfrac{1}{x}$

42. $f(x) = 6 - \dfrac{1}{x}, g(x) = \dfrac{1}{x}$

43. $f(x) = \dfrac{5x+1}{x^2 - 9}, g(x) = \dfrac{4x-2}{x^2 - 9}$

44. $f(x) = \dfrac{3x+1}{x^2 - 25}, g(x) = \dfrac{2x-4}{x^2 - 25}$

45. $f(x) = \sqrt{x+4}, g(x) = \sqrt{x-1}$

46. $f(x) = \sqrt{x+6}, g(x) = \sqrt{x-3}$

47. $f(x) = \sqrt{x-2}, g(x) = \sqrt{2-x}$

48. $f(x) = \sqrt{x-5}, g(x) = \sqrt{5-x}$

In Exercises 49–64, find
 a. $(f \circ g)(x);$ **b.** $(g \circ f)(x);$ **c.** $(f \circ g)(2).$

49. $f(x) = 2x, g(x) = x + 7$

50. $f(x) = 3x, g(x) = x - 5$

51. $f(x) = x + 4, g(x) = 2x + 1$

52. $f(x) = 5x + 2, g(x) = 3x - 4$

53. $f(x) = 4x - 3, g(x) = 5x^2 - 2$

54. $f(x) = 7x + 1, g(x) = 2x^2 - 9$

55. $f(x) = x^2 + 2, g(x) = x^2 - 2$

56. $f(x) = x^2 + 1, g(x) = x^2 - 3$

57. $f(x) = 4 - x, g(x) = 2x^2 + x + 5$

58. $f(x) = 5x - 2, g(x) = -x^2 + 4x - 1$

59. $f(x) = \sqrt{x}, g(x) = x - 1$

60. $f(x) = \sqrt{x}, g(x) = x + 2$

61. $f(x) = 2x - 3, g(x) = \dfrac{x+3}{2}$

62. $f(x) = 6x - 3, g(x) = \dfrac{x+3}{6}$

63. $f(x) = \dfrac{1}{x}, g(x) = \dfrac{1}{x}$

64. $f(x) = \dfrac{2}{x}, g(x) = \dfrac{2}{x}$

In Exercises 65–72, find
 a. $(f \circ g)(x);$ **b.** *the domain of $f \circ g$.*

65. $f(x) = \dfrac{2}{x+3}, g(x) = \dfrac{1}{x}$

66. $f(x) = \dfrac{5}{x+4}, g(x) = \dfrac{1}{x}$

67. $f(x) = \dfrac{x}{x+1}, g(x) = \dfrac{4}{x}$

68. $f(x) = \dfrac{x}{x+5}, g(x) = \dfrac{6}{x}$

69. $f(x) = \sqrt{x}, g(x) = x - 2$

70. $f(x) = \sqrt{x}, g(x) = x - 3$

71. $f(x) = x^2 + 4, g(x) = \sqrt{1-x}$

72. $f(x) = x^2 + 1, g(x) = \sqrt{2-x}$

In Exercises 73–80, express the given function h as a composition of two functions f and g so that $h(x) = (f \circ g)(x)$.

73. $h(x) = (3x - 1)^4$ **74.** $h(x) = (2x - 5)^3$

75. $h(x) = \sqrt[3]{x^2 - 9}$ **76.** $h(x) = \sqrt{5x^2 + 3}$

77. $h(x) = |2x - 5|$ **78.** $h(x) = |3x - 4|$

79. $h(x) = \dfrac{1}{2x - 3}$ **80.** $h(x) = \dfrac{1}{4x + 5}$

Practice Plus

Use the graphs of f and g to solve Exercises 81–88.

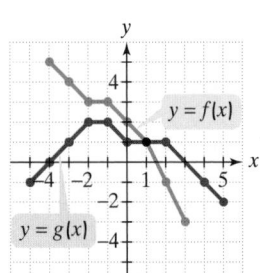

81. Find $(f + g)(-3).$ **82.** Find $(g - f)(-2).$

83. Find $(fg)(2).$ **84.** Find $\left(\dfrac{g}{f}\right)(3).$

85. Find the domain of $f + g.$ **86.** Find the domain of $\dfrac{f}{g}.$

87. Graph $f + g.$ **88.** Graph $f - g.$

In Exercises 89–92, use the graphs of f and g to evaluate each composite function.

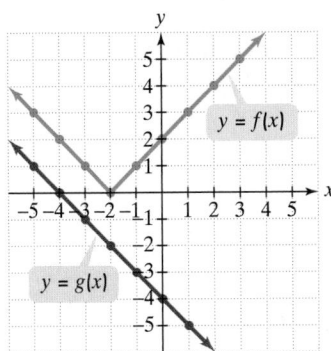

89. $(f \circ g)(-1)$

90. $(f \circ g)(1)$

91. $(g \circ f)(0)$

92. $(g \circ f)(-1)$

In Exercises 93–94, find all values of x satisfying the given conditions.

93. $f(x) = 2x - 5, g(x) = x^2 - 3x + 8,$ and $(f \circ g)(x) = 7.$

94. $f(x) = 1 - 2x, g(x) = 3x^2 + x - 1,$ and $(f \circ g)(x) = -5.$

Application Exercises

We opened the section with functions that model the numbers of births and deaths in the United States from 2000 through 2005:

$$B(x) = 7.4x^2 - 15x + 4046 \qquad D(x) = -3.5x^2 + 20x + 2405.$$

Number of births, $B(x)$, in thousands, x years after 2000

Number of deaths, $D(x)$, in thousands, x years after 2000

Use these functions to solve Exercises 95–96.

95. a. Write a function that models the change in U.S. population for each year from 2000 through 2005.

 b. Use the function from part (a) to find the change in U.S. population in 2003.

 c. Does the result in part (b) overestimate or underestimate the actual population change in 2003 obtained from the data in **Figure 2.49** on page 270? By how much?

96. a. Write a function that models the total number of births and deaths in the United States for each year from 2000 through 2005.

 b. Use the function from part (a) to find the total number of births and deaths in the United States in 2005.

 c. Does the result in part (b) overestimate or underestimate the actual number of total births and deaths in 2005 obtained from the data in **Figure 2.49** on page 270? By how much?

97. A company that sells radios has yearly fixed costs of $600,000. It costs the company $45 to produce each radio. Each radio will sell for $65. The company's costs and revenue are modeled by the following functions, where x represents the number of radios produced and sold:

$$C(x) = 600,000 + 45x \quad \text{This function models the company's costs.}$$

$$R(x) = 65x. \quad \text{This function models the company's revenue.}$$

Find and interpret $(R - C)(20,000), (R - C)(30,000),$ and $(R - C)(40,000).$

98. A department store has two locations in a city. From 2004 through 2008, the profits for each of the store's two branches are modeled by the functions $f(x) = -0.44x + 13.62$ and $g(x) = 0.51x + 11.14.$ In each model, x represents the number of years after 2004, and f and g represent the profit, in millions of dollars.

 a. What is the slope of f? Describe what this means.

 b. What is the slope of g? Describe what this means.

 c. Find $f + g$. What is the slope of this function? What does this mean?

99. The regular price of a computer is x dollars. Let $f(x) = x - 400$ and $g(x) = 0.75x.$

 a. Describe what the functions f and g model in terms of the price of the computer.

 b. Find $(f \circ g)(x)$ and describe what this models in terms of the price of the computer.

 c. Repeat part (b) for $(g \circ f)(x).$

 d. Which composite function models the greater discount on the computer, $f \circ g$ or $g \circ f$? Explain.

100. The regular price of a pair of jeans is x dollars. Let $f(x) = x - 5$ and $g(x) = 0.6x.$

 a. Describe what functions f and g model in terms of the price of the jeans.

 b. Find $(f \circ g)(x)$ and describe what this models in terms of the price of the jeans.

 c. Repeat part (b) for $(g \circ f)(x).$

 d. Which composite function models the greater discount on the jeans, $f \circ g$ or $g \circ f$? Explain.

Writing in Mathematics

101. If a function is defined by an equation, explain how to find its domain.

102. If equations for f and g are given, explain how to find $f - g.$

103. If equations for two functions are given, explain how to obtain the quotient function and its domain.

104. Describe a procedure for finding $(f \circ g)(x).$ What is the name of this function?

105. Describe the values of x that must be excluded from the domain of $(f \circ g)(x).$

Technology Exercises

106. Graph $y_1 = x^2 - 2x, y_2 = x,$ and $y_3 = y_1 \div y_2$ in the same $[-10, 10, 1]$ by $[-10, 10, 1]$ viewing rectangle. Then use the $\boxed{\text{TRACE}}$ feature to trace along y_3. What happens at $x = 0$? Explain why this occurs.

107. Graph $y_1 = \sqrt{2 - x}, y_2 = \sqrt{x},$ and $y_3 = \sqrt{2 - y_2}$ in the same $[-4, 4, 1]$ by $[0, 2, 1]$ viewing rectangle. If y_1 represents f and y_2 represents g, use the graph of y_3 to find the domain of $f \circ g$. Then verify your observation algebraically.

Critical Thinking Exercises

Make Sense? *In Exercises 108–111, determine whether each statement makes sense or does not make sense, and explain your reasoning.*

108. I used a function to model data from 1980 through 2005. The independent variable in my model represented the number of years after 1980, so the function's domain was $\{x \mid x = 0, 1, 2, 3, \ldots, 25\}.$

109. I have two functions. Function f models total world population x years after 2000 and function g models population of the world's more-developed regions x years after 2000. I can use $f - g$ to determine the population of the world's less-developed regions for the years in both function's domains.

110. I must have made a mistake in finding the composite functions $f \circ g$ and $g \circ f$, because I notice that $f \circ g$ is not the same function as $g \circ f$.

111. This diagram illustrates that $f(g(x)) = x^2 + 4$.

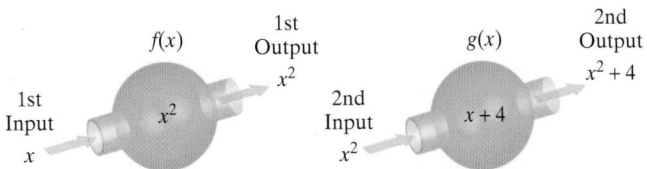

In Exercises 112–115, determine whether each statement is true or false. If the statement is false, make the necessary change(s) to produce a true statement.

112. If $f(x) = x^2 - 4$ and $g(x) = \sqrt{x^2 - 4}$, then $(f \circ g)(x) = -x^2$ and $(f \circ g)(5) = -25$.

113. There can never be two functions f and g, where $f \neq g$, for which $(f \circ g)(x) = (g \circ f)(x)$.

114. If $f(7) = 5$ and $g(4) = 7$, then $(f \circ g)(4) = 35$.

115. If $f(x) = \sqrt{x}$ and $g(x) = 2x - 1$, then $(f \circ g)(5) = g(2)$.

116. Prove that if f and g are even functions, then fg is also an even function.

117. Define two functions f and g so that $f \circ g = g \circ f$.

Preview Exercises

Exercises 118–120 will help you prepare for the material covered in the next section.

118. Consider the function defined by

$$\{(-2, 4), (-1, 1), (1, 1), (2, 4)\}.$$

Reverse the components of each ordered pair and write the resulting relation. Is this relation a function?

119. Solve for y: $\quad x = \dfrac{5}{y} + 4$.

120. Solve for y: $\quad x = y^2 - 1, y \geq 0$.

(Section) **2.7** **Inverse Functions**

Objectives

① Verify inverse functions.

② Find the inverse of a function.

③ Use the horizontal line test to determine if a function has an inverse function.

④ Use the graph of a one-to-one function to graph its inverse function.

⑤ Find the inverse of a function and graph both functions on the same axes.

In most societies, women say they prefer to marry men who are older than themselves, whereas men say they prefer women who are younger. Evolutionary psychologists attribute these preferences to female concern with a partner's material resources and male concern with a partner's fertility (*Source:* David M. Buss, *Psychological Inquiry*, 6, 1–30). When the man is considerably older than the woman, people rarely comment. However, when the woman is older, as in the relationship between actors Ashton Kutcher and Demi Moore, people take notice. **Figure 2.53** on the next page shows the preferred age difference in a mate in five selected countries.

Preferred Age Difference in a Mate

Figure 2.53
Source: Carole Wade and Carol Tavris,
Psychology, 6th Edition, Prentice Hall, 2000

We can focus on the data for the women and define a function. Let the domain of the function be the set of the five countries shown in the graph. Let the range be the set of the average number of years women in each of the respective countries prefer men who are older than themselves. The function can be written as follows:

f: {(Zambia, 4.2), (Colombia, 4.5), (Poland, 3.3), (Italy, 3.3), (U.S., 2.5)}.

Now let's "undo" f by interchanging the first and second components in each of its ordered pairs. Switching the inputs and outputs of f, we obtain the following relation:

Same first component

Undoing f: {(4.2, Zambia), (4.5, Colombia), (3.3, Poland), (3.3, Italy), (2.5, U.S.)}.

Different second components

Can you see that this relation is not a function? Two of its ordered pairs have the same first component and different second components. This violates the definition of a function.

If a function f is a set of ordered pairs, (x, y), then the changes produced by f can be "undone" by reversing the components of all the ordered pairs. The resulting relation, (y, x), may or may not be a function. In this section, we will develop these ideas by studying functions whose compositions have a special "undoing" relationship.

Inverse Functions

Here are two functions that describe situations related to the price of a computer, x:

$$f(x) = x - 300 \qquad g(x) = x + 300.$$

Function f subtracts $300 from the computer's price and function g adds $300 to the computer's price. Let's see what $f(g(x))$ does. Put $g(x)$ into f:

$$f(x) = x - 300 \qquad \text{This is the given equation for f.}$$

Replace x with $g(x)$.

$$f(g(x)) = g(x) - 300$$
$$= x + 300 - 300 \qquad \text{Because } g(x) = x + 300,$$
$$= x. \qquad \text{replace } g(x) \text{ with } x + 300.$$

This is the computer's original price.

Using $f(x) = x - 300$ and $g(x) = x + 300$, we see that $f(g(x)) = x$. By putting $g(x)$ into f and finding $f(g(x))$, the computer's price, x, went through two changes: the first, an increase; the second, a decrease:

$$x + 300 - 300.$$

The final price of the computer, x, is identical to its starting price, x.

In general, if the changes made to x by a function g are undone by the changes made by a function f, then

$$f(g(x)) = x.$$

Assume, also, that this "undoing" takes place in the other direction:

$$g(f(x)) = x.$$

Under these conditions, we say that each function is the *inverse function* of the other. The fact that g is the inverse of f is expressed by renaming g as f^{-1}, read "f-inverse." For example, the inverse functions

$$f(x) = x - 300 \qquad g(x) = x + 300$$

are usually named as follows:

$$f(x) = x - 300 \qquad f^{-1}(x) = x + 300.$$

We can use partial tables of coordinates for f and f^{-1} to gain numerical insight into the relationship between a function and its inverse function.

The tables illustrate that if a function f is the set of ordered pairs (x, y), then its inverse, f^{-1}, is the set of ordered pairs (y, x). Using these tables, we can see how one function's changes to x are undone by the other function:

$$(f^{-1} \circ f)(1300) = f^{-1}(f(1300)) = f^{-1}(1000) = 1300.$$

The table for f shows that $f(1300) = 1000$.

The table for f^{-1} shows that $f^{-1}(1000) = 1300$.

The final price of the computer, $1300, is identical to its starting price, $1300.

With these ideas in mind, we present the formal definition of the inverse of a function:

Definition of the Inverse of a Function

Let f and g be two functions such that

$$f(g(x)) = x \qquad \text{for every } x \text{ in the domain of } g$$

and

$$g(f(x)) = x \qquad \text{for every } x \text{ in the domain of } f.$$

The function g is the **inverse of the function** f and is denoted by f^{-1} (read "f-inverse"). Thus, $f(f^{-1}(x)) = x$ and $f^{-1}(f(x)) = x$. The domain of f is equal to the range of f^{-1}, and vice versa.

Study Tip

The notation f^{-1} represents the inverse function of f. The -1 is *not* an exponent. The notation f^{-1} does *not* mean $\dfrac{1}{f}$:

$$f^{-1} \neq \dfrac{1}{f}.$$

1 Verify inverse functions.

(**EXAMPLE 1**) **Verifying Inverse Functions**

Show that each function is the inverse of the other:

$$f(x) = 3x + 2 \quad \text{and} \quad g(x) = \frac{x - 2}{3}.$$

Solution To show that f and g are inverses of each other, we must show that $f(g(x)) = x$ and $g(f(x)) = x$. We begin with $f(g(x))$.

$$f(x) = 3x + 2 \quad \text{This is the equation for f.}$$

Replace x with $g(x)$.

$$f(g(x)) = 3g(x) + 2 = 3\left(\frac{x - 2}{3}\right) + 2 = x - 2 + 2 = x$$

$$g(x) = \frac{x - 2}{3}$$

Next, we find $g(f(x))$.

$$g(x) = \frac{x - 2}{3} \quad \text{This is the equation for g.}$$

Replace x with $f(x)$.

$$g(f(x)) = \frac{f(x) - 2}{3} = \frac{(3x + 2) - 2}{3} = \frac{3x}{3} = x$$

$$f(x) = 3x + 2$$

Because g is the inverse of f (and vice versa), we can use inverse notation and write

$$f(x) = 3x + 2 \quad \text{and} \quad f^{-1}(x) = \frac{x - 2}{3}.$$

Notice how f^{-1} undoes the changes produced by f: f changes x by *multiplying* by 3 and *adding* 2, and f^{-1} undoes this by *subtracting* 2 and *dividing* by 3. This "undoing" process is illustrated in **Figure 2.54**. ●

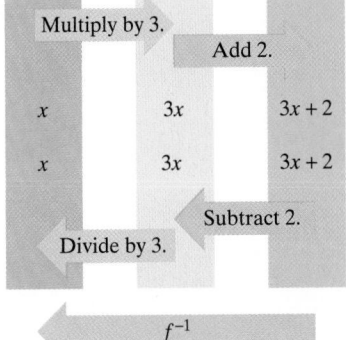

Figure 2.54 f^{-1} undoes the changes produced by f.

✓ Check Point **1** Show that each function is the inverse of the other:

$$f(x) = 4x - 7 \quad \text{and} \quad g(x) = \frac{x + 7}{4}.$$

2 Find the inverse of a function.

Finding the Inverse of a Function

The definition of the inverse of a function tells us that the domain of f is equal to the range of f^{-1}, and vice versa. This means that if the function f is the set of ordered pairs (x, y), then the inverse of f is the set of ordered pairs (y, x). If a function is defined by an equation, we can obtain the equation for f^{-1}, the inverse of f, by interchanging the role of x and y in the equation for the function f.

Finding the Inverse of a Function

The equation for the inverse of a function f can be found as follows:

1. Replace $f(x)$ with y in the equation for $f(x)$.

2. Interchange x and y.

3. Solve for y. If this equation does not define y as a function of x, the function f does not have an inverse function and this procedure ends. If this equation does define y as a function of x, the function f has an inverse function.

4. If f has an inverse function, replace y in step 3 by $f^{-1}(x)$. We can verify our result by showing that $f(f^{-1}(x)) = x$ and $f^{-1}(f(x)) = x$.

Study Tip

The procedure for finding a function's inverse uses a *switch-and-solve* strategy. Switch x and y, and then solve for y.

EXAMPLE 2 Finding the Inverse of a Function

Find the inverse of $f(x) = 7x - 5$.

Solution

Step 1 Replace $f(x)$ with y:

$$y = 7x - 5.$$

Step 2 Interchange x and y:

$$x = 7y - 5. \quad \text{This is the inverse function.}$$

Step 3 Solve for y:

$$x + 5 = 7y \qquad \text{Add 5 to both sides.}$$

$$\frac{x + 5}{7} = y. \qquad \text{Divide both sides by 7.}$$

Step 4 Replace y with $f^{-1}(x)$:

$$f^{-1}(x) = \frac{x + 5}{7}. \qquad \begin{array}{l}\text{The equation is written}\\ \text{with } f^{-1} \text{ on the left.}\end{array}$$

Thus, the inverse of $f(x) = 7x - 5$ is $f^{-1}(x) = \dfrac{x + 5}{7}$.

The inverse function, f^{-1}, undoes the changes produced by f. f changes x by multiplying by 7 and subtracting 5. f^{-1} undoes this by adding 5 and dividing by 7. ●

Discovery

In Example 2, we found that if $f(x) = 7x - 5$, then

$$f^{-1}(x) = \frac{x + 5}{7}.$$

Verify this result by showing that

$$f(f^{-1}(x)) = x$$

and

$$f^{-1}(f(x)) = x.$$

⊘ Check Point **2** Find the inverse of $f(x) = 2x + 7$.

EXAMPLE 3 Finding the Inverse of a Function

Find the inverse of $f(x) = x^3 + 1$.

Solution

Step 1 Replace $f(x)$ with y: $y = x^3 + 1$.

Step 2 Interchange x and y: $x = y^3 + 1$.

Step 3 Solve for y:

> Our goal is to isolate y. Because $\sqrt[3]{y^3} = y$, we will take the cube root of both sides of the equation.

$$x - 1 = y^3 \qquad \text{Subtract 1 from both sides.}$$

$$\sqrt[3]{x - 1} = \sqrt[3]{y^3} \qquad \text{Take the cube root on both sides.}$$

$$\sqrt[3]{x - 1} = y. \qquad \text{Simplify.}$$

Step 4 Replace y with $f^{-1}(x)$: $f^{-1}(x) = \sqrt[3]{x - 1}$.

Thus, the inverse of $f(x) = x^3 + 1$ is $f^{-1}(x) = \sqrt[3]{x - 1}$. ●

⊘ Check Point **3** Find the inverse of $f(x) = 4x^3 - 1$.

(**EXAMPLE 4**) **Finding the Inverse of a Function**

Find the inverse of $f(x) = \dfrac{5}{x} + 4.$

Solution

Step 1 Replace $f(x)$ with y:

$$y = \dfrac{5}{x} + 4.$$

Step 2 Interchange x and y:

$$x = \dfrac{5}{y} + 4.$$

> Our goal is to isolate y. To get y out of the denominator, we will multiply both sides of the equation by y, $y \neq 0$.

Step 3 Solve for y:

$$x = \dfrac{5}{y} + 4 \qquad \text{This is the equation from step 2.}$$

$$xy = \left(\dfrac{5}{y} + 4\right)y \qquad \text{Multiply both sides by } y, y \neq 0.$$

$$xy = \dfrac{5}{y} \cdot y + 4y \qquad \text{Use the distributive property.}$$

$$xy = 5 + 4y \qquad \text{Simplify: } \dfrac{5}{y} \cdot y = 5.$$

$$xy - 4y = 5 \qquad \text{Subtract } 4y \text{ from both sides.}$$

$$y(x - 4) = 5 \qquad \text{Factor out } y \text{ from } xy - 4y \text{ to obtain a single occurrence of } y.$$

$$\dfrac{y(x - 4)}{x - 4} = \dfrac{5}{x - 4} \qquad \text{Divide both sides by } x - 4, x \neq 4.$$

$$y = \dfrac{5}{x - 4}. \qquad \text{Simplify.}$$

Step 4 Replace y with $f^{-1}(x)$:

$$f^{-1}(x) = \dfrac{5}{x - 4}.$$

Thus, the inverse of $f(x) = \dfrac{5}{x} + 4$ is $f^{-1}(x) = \dfrac{5}{x - 4}.$

⬤

\oslash Check Point **4** Find the inverse of $f(x) = \dfrac{3}{x} - 1.$

③ Use the horizontal line test to determine if a function has an inverse function.

The Horizontal Line Test and One-to-One Functions

Let's see what happens if we try to find the inverse of the standard quadratic function, $f(x) = x^2.$

Step 1 Replace $f(x)$ with y: $y = x^2.$

Step 2 Interchange x and y: $x = y^2.$

Step 3 Solve for y: We apply the square root property to solve $y^2 = x$ for $y.$ We obtain

$$y = \pm\sqrt{x}.$$

The \pm in $y = \pm\sqrt{x}$ shows that for certain values of x (all positive real numbers), there are two values of y. Because this equation does not represent y as a function of x, the standard quadratic function $f(x) = x^2$ does not have an inverse function.

We can use a few of the solutions of $y = x^2$ to illustrate numerically that this function does not have an inverse:

A function provides exactly one output for each input. Thus, the ordered pairs in the bottom row do not define a function.

Can we look at the graph of a function and tell if it represents a function with an inverse? Yes. The graph of the standard quadratic function $f(x) = x^2$ is shown in **Figure 2.55**. Four units above the x-axis, a horizontal line is drawn. This line intersects the graph at two of its points, $(-2, 4)$ and $(2, 4)$. Inverse functions have ordered pairs with the coordinates reversed. We just saw what happened when we interchanged x and y. We obtained $(4, -2)$ and $(4, 2)$, and these ordered pairs do not define a function.

If any horizontal line, such as the one in **Figure 2.55**, intersects a graph at two or more points, the set of these points will not define a function when their coordinates are reversed. This suggests the **horizontal line test** for inverse functions.

Figure 2.55 The horizontal line intersects the graph twice.

Discovery

How might you restrict the domain of $f(x) = x^2$, graphed in **Figure 2.55**, so that the remaining portion of the graph passes the horizontal line test?

The Horizontal Line Test For Inverse Functions

A function f has an inverse that is a function, f^{-1}, if there is no horizontal line that intersects the graph of the function f at more than one point.

EXAMPLE 5 **Applying the Horizontal Line Test**

Which of the following graphs represent functions that have inverse functions?

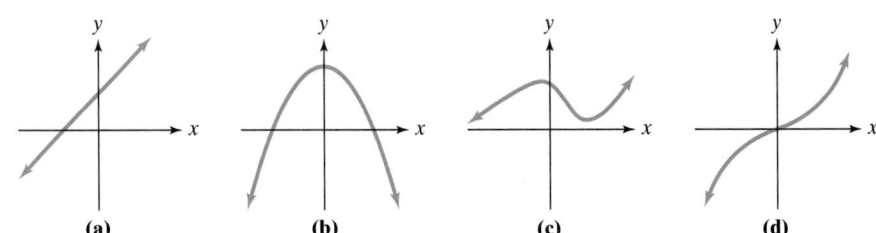

Solution Notice that horizontal lines can be drawn in graphs **(b)** and **(c)** that intersect the graphs more than once. These graphs do not pass the horizontal line test. These are not the graphs of functions with inverse functions. By contrast, no horizontal line can be drawn in graphs **(a)** and **(d)** that intersects the graphs more than once. These graphs pass the horizontal line test. Thus, the graphs in parts **(a)** and **(d)** represent functions that have inverse functions.

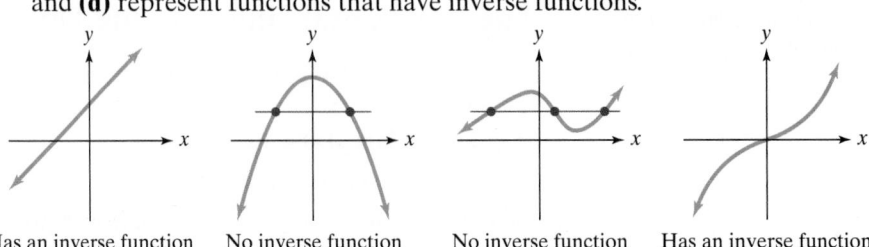

Has an inverse function
(a)

No inverse function
(b)

No inverse function
(c)

Has an inverse function
(d)

⊘ Check Point **5** Which of the following graphs represent functions that have inverse functions?

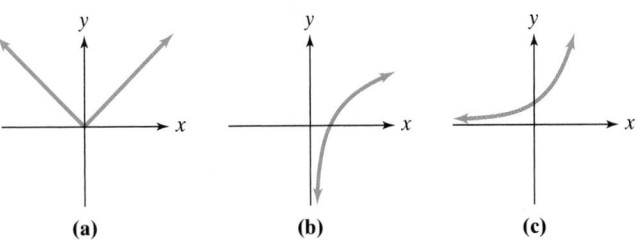

(a) (b) (c)

A function passes the horizontal line test when no two different ordered pairs have the same second component. This means that if $x_1 \neq x_2$, then $f(x_1) \neq f(x_2)$. Such a function is called a **one-to-one function**. Thus, **a one-to-one function is a function in which no two different ordered pairs have the same second component. Only one-to-one functions have inverse functions.** Any function that passes the horizontal line test is a one-to-one function. Any one-to-one function has a graph that passes the horizontal line test.

④ Use the graph of a one-to-one function to graph its inverse function.

Graphs of f and f^{-1}

There is a relationship between the graph of a one-to-one function, f, and its inverse, f^{-1}. Because inverse functions have ordered pairs with the coordinates interchanged, if the point (a, b) is on the graph of f, then the point (b, a) is on the graph of f^{-1}. The points (a, b) and (b, a) are symmetric with respect to the line $y = x$. Thus, **the graph of f^{-1} is a reflection of the graph of f about the line $y = x$**. This is illustrated in **Figure 2.56**.

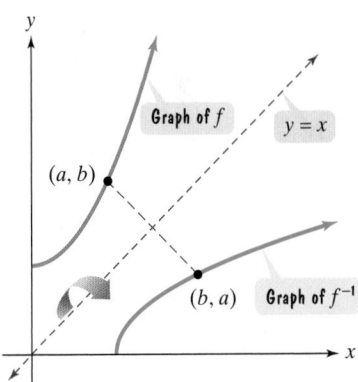

Figure 2.56 The graph of f^{-1} is a reflection of the graph of f about $y = x$.

(EXAMPLE 6) **Graphing the Inverse Function**

Use the graph of f in **Figure 2.57** to draw the graph of its inverse function.

Solution We begin by noting that no horizontal line intersects the graph of f at more than one point, so f does have an inverse function. Because the points $(-3, -2)$, $(-1, 0)$, and $(4, 2)$ are on the graph of f, the graph of the inverse function, f^{-1}, has points with these ordered pairs reversed. Thus, $(-2, -3)$, $(0, -1)$, and $(2, 4)$ are on the graph of f^{-1}. We can use these points to graph f^{-1}. The graph of f^{-1} is shown in green in **Figure 2.58**. Note that the green graph of f^{-1} is the reflection of the blue graph of f about the line $y = x$.

Figure 2.57

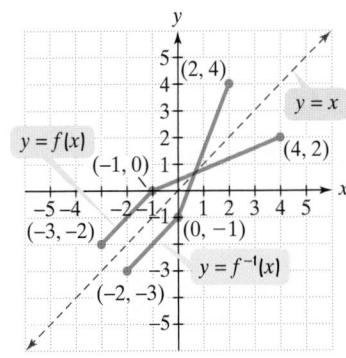

Figure 2.58 The graphs of f and f^{-1}

⊘ Check Point **6** The graph of function f consists of two line segments, one segment from $(-2, -2)$ to $(-1, 0)$ and a second segment from $(-1, 0)$ to $(1, 2)$. Graph f and use the graph to draw the graph of its inverse function.

5 Find the inverse of a function and graph both functions on the same axes.

Figure 2.59

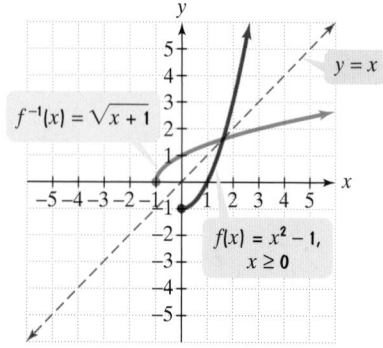

Figure 2.60

In our final example, we will first find f^{-1}. Then we will graph f and f^{-1} in the same rectangular coordinate system.

EXAMPLE 7 Finding the Inverse of a Domain-Restricted Function

Find the inverse of $f(x) = x^2 - 1$ if $x \geq 0$. Graph f and f^{-1} in the same rectangular coordinate system.

Solution The graph of $f(x) = x^2 - 1$ is the graph of the standard quadratic function shifted vertically down 1 unit. **Figure 2.59** shows the function's graph. This graph fails the horizontal line test, so the function $f(x) = x^2 - 1$ does not have an inverse function. By restricting the domain to $x \geq 0$, as given, we obtain a new function whose graph is shown in red in **Figure 2.59**. This red portion of the graph is increasing on the interval $(0, \infty)$ and passes the horizontal line test. This tells us that $f(x) = x^2 - 1$ has an inverse function if we restrict its domain to $x \geq 0$. We use our four-step procedure to find this inverse function. Begin with $f(x) = x^2 - 1, x \geq 0$.

Step 1 Replace $f(x)$ with y: $y = x^2 - 1, x \geq 0$.

Step 2 Interchange x and y: $x = y^2 - 1, y \geq 0$.

Step 3 Solve for y:

$$x = y^2 - 1, y \geq 0 \quad \text{This is the equation from step 2.}$$

$$x + 1 = y^2 \quad \text{Add 1 to both sides.}$$

$$\sqrt{x + 1} = y \quad \text{Apply the square root property.}$$

> Because $y \geq 0$, take only the principal square root and not the negative square root.

Step 4 Replace y with $f^{-1}(x)$: $f^{-1}(x) = \sqrt{x + 1}$.

Thus, the inverse of $f(x) = x^2 - 1, x \geq 0$, is $f^{-1}(x) = \sqrt{x + 1}$. The graphs of f and f^{-1} are shown in **Figure 2.60**. We obtained the graph of $f^{-1}(x) = \sqrt{x + 1}$ by shifting the graph of the square root function, $y = \sqrt{x}$, horizontally to the left 1 unit. Note that the green graph of f^{-1} is the reflection of the red graph of f about the line $y = x$. ●

○ Check Point **7** Find the inverse of $f(x) = x^2 + 1$ if $x \geq 0$. Graph f and f^{-1} in the same rectangular coordinate system.

Exercise Set 2.7

Practice Exercises

In Exercises 1–10, find $f(g(x))$ and $g(f(x))$ and determine whether each pair of functions f and g are inverses of each other.

1. $f(x) = 4x$ and $g(x) = \dfrac{x}{4}$

2. $f(x) = 6x$ and $g(x) = \dfrac{x}{6}$

3. $f(x) = 3x + 8$ and $g(x) = \dfrac{x - 8}{3}$

4. $f(x) = 4x + 9$ and $g(x) = \dfrac{x - 9}{4}$

5. $f(x) = 5x - 9$ and $g(x) = \dfrac{x + 5}{9}$

6. $f(x) = 3x - 7$ and $g(x) = \dfrac{x + 3}{7}$

7. $f(x) = \dfrac{3}{x - 4}$ and $g(x) = \dfrac{3}{x} + 4$

8. $f(x) = \dfrac{2}{x - 5}$ and $g(x) = \dfrac{2}{x} + 5$

9. $f(x) = -x$ and $g(x) = -x$

10. $f(x) = \sqrt[3]{x - 4}$ and $g(x) = x^3 + 4$

The functions in Exercises 11–28 are all one-to-one. For each function,

 a. *Find an equation for $f^{-1}(x)$, the inverse function.*

 b. *Verify that your equation is correct by showing that $f(f^{-1}(x)) = x$ and $f^{-1}(f(x)) = x$.*

11. $f(x) = x + 3$

12. $f(x) = x + 5$

13. $f(x) = 2x$

14. $f(x) = 4x$

15. $f(x) = 2x + 3$

16. $f(x) = 3x - 1$

17. $f(x) = x^3 + 2$

18. $f(x) = x^3 - 1$

19. $f(x) = (x + 2)^3$

20. $f(x) = (x - 1)^3$

21. $f(x) = \dfrac{1}{x}$

22. $f(x) = \dfrac{2}{x}$

23. $f(x) = \sqrt{x}$

24. $f(x) = \sqrt[3]{x}$

25. $f(x) = \dfrac{7}{x} - 3$

26. $f(x) = \dfrac{4}{x} + 9$

27. $f(x) = \dfrac{2x + 1}{x - 3}$

28. $f(x) = \dfrac{2x - 3}{x + 1}$

Which graphs in Exercises 29–34 represent functions that have inverse functions?

29.

30.

31.

32.

33.

34.

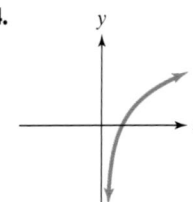

In Exercises 35–38, use the graph of f to draw the graph of its inverse function.

35.

36.

37.

38.

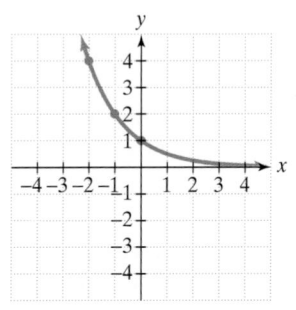

In Exercises 39–52,

 a. *Find an equation for $f^{-1}(x)$.*

 b. *Graph f and f^{-1} in the same rectangular coordinate system.*

 c. *Use interval notation to give the domain and the range of f and f^{-1}.*

39. $f(x) = 2x - 1$

40. $f(x) = 2x - 3$

41. $f(x) = x^2 - 4, x \geq 0$

42. $f(x) = x^2 - 1, x \leq 0$

43. $f(x) = (x - 1)^2, x \leq 1$

44. $f(x) = (x - 1)^2, x \geq 1$

45. $f(x) = x^3 - 1$

46. $f(x) = x^3 + 1$

47. $f(x) = (x + 2)^3$

48. $f(x) = (x - 2)^3$

(Hint for Exercises 49–52: To solve for a variable involving an nth root, raise both sides of the equation to the nth power: $(\sqrt[n]{y})^n = y$.)

49. $f(x) = \sqrt{x - 1}$

50. $f(x) = \sqrt{x + 2}$

51. $f(x) = \sqrt[3]{x} + 1$

52. $f(x) = \sqrt[3]{x - 1}$

Practice Plus

In Exercises 53–58, f and g are defined by the following tables. Use the tables to evaluate each composite function.

x	$f(x)$
-1	1
0	4
1	5
2	-1

x	$g(x)$
-1	0
1	1
4	2
10	-1

53. $f(g(1))$

54. $f(g(4))$

55. $(g \circ f)(-1)$

56. $(g \circ f)(0)$

57. $f^{-1}(g(10))$

58. $f^{-1}(g(1))$

In Exercises 59–64, let

$$f(x) = 2x - 5$$
$$g(x) = 4x - 1$$
$$h(x) = x^2 + x + 2.$$

Evaluate the indicated function without finding an equation for the function.

59. $(f \circ g)(0)$

60. $(g \circ f)(0)$

61. $f^{-1}(1)$

62. $g^{-1}(7)$

63. $g(f[h(1)])$

64. $f(g[h(1)])$

Application Exercises

The bar graph shows the average number of hours that Americans sleep per day, by age group. Use this information to solve Exercises 65–66.

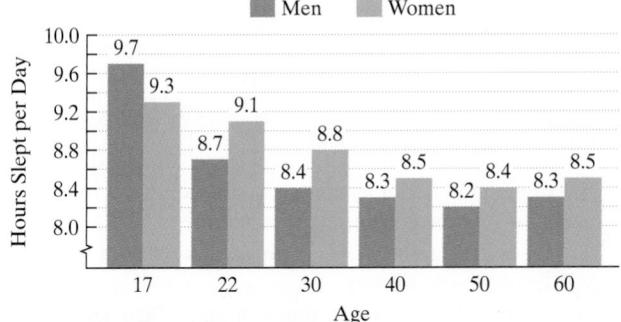

Hours Slept per Day, by Age

Source: ATUS, Bureau of Labor Statistics

(In Exercises 65–66, refer to the graph at the bottom of the previous page.)

65. a. Consider a function, f, whose domain is the set of six ages shown. Let the range be the average number of hours that men sleep per day. Write the function f as a set of ordered pairs.

b. Write the relation that is the inverse of f as a set of ordered pairs. Based on these ordered pairs, is f a one-to-one function? Explain your answer.

66. a. Consider a function, g, whose domain is the set of six ages shown. Let the range be the average number of hours that women sleep per day. Write the function g as a set of ordered pairs.

b. Write the relation that is the inverse of g as a set of ordered pairs. Based on these ordered pairs, is g a one-to-one function? Explain your answer.

67. The graph represents the probability of two people in the same room sharing a birthday as a function of the number of people in the room. Call the function f.

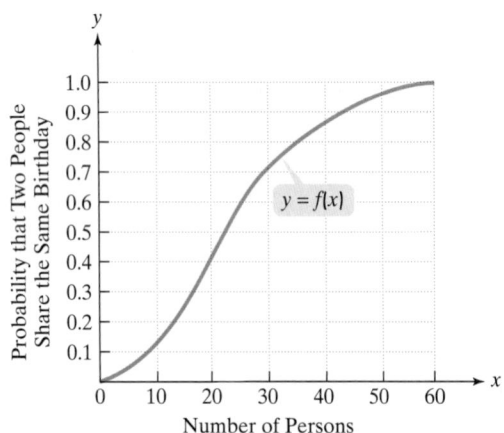

a. Explain why f has an inverse that is a function.

b. Describe in practical terms the meaning of $f^{-1}(0.25)$, $f^{-1}(0.5)$, and $f^{-1}(0.7)$.

68. A study of 900 working women in Texas showed that their feelings changed throughout the day. As the graph indicates,

Average Level of Happiness at Different Times of Day

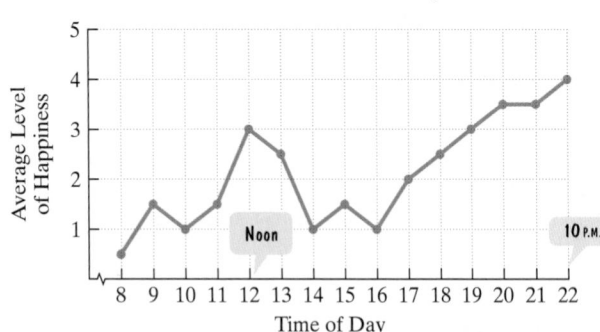

Source: D. Kahneman et al., "A Survey Method for Characterizing Daily Life Experience," *Science.*

the women felt better as time passed, except for a blip (that's slang for relative maximum) at lunchtime.

a. Does the graph have an inverse that is a function? Explain your answer.

b. Identify two or more times of day when the average happiness level is 3. Express your answers as ordered pairs.

c. Do the ordered pairs in part (b) indicate that the graph represents a one-to-one function? Explain your answer.

69. The formula

$$y = f(x) = \frac{9}{5}x + 32$$

is used to convert from x degrees Celsius to y degrees Fahrenheit. The formula

$$y = g(x) = \frac{5}{9}(x - 32)$$

is used to convert from x degrees Fahrenheit to y degrees Celsius. Show that f and g are inverse functions.

Writing in Mathematics

70. Explain how to determine if two functions are inverses of each other.

71. Describe how to find the inverse of a one-to-one function.

72. What is the horizontal line test and what does it indicate?

73. Describe how to use the graph of a one-to-one function to draw the graph of its inverse function.

74. How can a graphing utility be used to visually determine if two functions are inverses of each other?

75. What explanations can you offer for the trends shown by the graph in Exercise 68?

Technology Exercises

In Exercises 76–83, use a graphing utility to graph the function. Use the graph to determine whether the function has an inverse that is a function (that is, whether the function is one-to-one).

76. $f(x) = x^2 - 1$

77. $f(x) = \sqrt[3]{2 - x}$

78. $f(x) = \dfrac{x^3}{2}$

79. $f(x) = \dfrac{x^4}{4}$

80. $f(x) = \text{int}(x - 2)$

81. $f(x) = |x - 2|$

82. $f(x) = (x - 1)^3$

83. $f(x) = -\sqrt{16 - x^2}$

In Exercises 84–86, use a graphing utility to graph f and g in the same viewing rectangle. In addition, graph the line $y = x$ and visually determine if f and g are inverses.

84. $f(x) = 4x + 4$, $g(x) = 0.25x - 1$

85. $f(x) = \dfrac{1}{x} + 2$, $g(x) = \dfrac{1}{x - 2}$

86. $f(x) = \sqrt[3]{x} - 2$, $g(x) = (x + 2)^3$

Critical Thinking Exercises

Make Sense? *In Exercises 87–90, determine whether each statement makes sense or does not make sense, and explain your reasoning.*

87. I found the inverse of $f(x) = 5x - 4$ in my head: The reverse of multiplying by 5 and subtracting 4 is adding 4 and dividing by 5, so $f^{-1}(x) = \dfrac{x + 4}{5}$.

88. I'm working with the linear function $f(x) = 3x + 5$ and I do not need to find f^{-1} in order to determine the value of $(f \circ f^{-1})(17)$.

Exercises 89–90 are based on the following cartoon.

DID YOU KNOW IF YOU COUNT THE CRICKET CHIRPS IN ONE MINUTE, DIVIDE BY FOUR, THEN ADD FORTY IT GIVES YOU THE OUTSIDE TEMPERATURE?

FAHRENHEIT OR CELSIUS?

IS THERE SUCH A THING AS METRIC CRICKETS?

CLUMSY'S BAIT SHOP

B.C. by permission of Johnny Hart and Creators Syndicate, Inc.

89. Assuming that there is no such thing as metric crickets, I modeled the information in the first frame of the cartoon with the function

$$T(n) = \frac{n}{4} + 40,$$

where $T(n)$ is the temperature, in degrees Fahrenheit, and n is the number of cricket chirps per minute.

90. I used the function in Exercise 89 and found an equation for $T^{-1}(n)$, which expresses the number of cricket chirps per minute as a function of Fahrenheit temperature.

In Exercises 91–94, determine whether each statement is true or false. If the statement is false, make the necessary change(s) to produce a true statement.

91. The inverse of $\{(1, 4), (2, 7)\}$ is $\{(2, 7), (1, 4)\}$.

92. The function $f(x) = 5$ is one-to-one.

93. If $f(x) = 3x$, then $f^{-1}(x) = \dfrac{1}{3x}$.

94. The domain of f is the same as the range of f^{-1}.

95. If $f(x) = 3x$ and $g(x) = x + 5$, find $(f \circ g)^{-1}(x)$ and $(g^{-1} \circ f^{-1})(x)$.

96. Show that

$$f(x) = \frac{3x - 2}{5x - 3}$$

is its own inverse.

97. *Freedom 7* was the spacecraft that carried the first American into space in 1961. Total flight time was 15 minutes and the spacecraft reached a maximum height of 116 miles. Consider a function, s, that expresses *Freedom 7*'s height, $s(t)$, in miles, after t minutes. Is s a one-to-one function? Explain your answer.

98. If $f(2) = 6$, and f is one-to-one, find x satisfying $8 + f^{-1}(x - 1) = 10$.

Group Exercise

99. In Tom Stoppard's play *Arcadia*, the characters dream and talk about mathematics, including ideas involving graphing, composite functions, symmetry, and lack of symmetry in things that are tangled, mysterious, and unpredictable. Group members should read the play. Present a report on the ideas discussed by the characters that are related to concepts that we studied in this chapter. Bring in a copy of the play and read appropriate excerpts.

Preview Exercises

Exercises 100–102 will help you prepare for the material covered in the next section.

100. Let $(x_1, y_1) = (7, 2)$ and $(x_2, y_2) = (1, -1)$. Find $\sqrt{(x_2 - x_1)^2 + (y_2 - y_1)^2}$. Express the answer in simplified radical form.

101. Use a rectangular coordinate system to graph the circle with center $(1, -1)$ and radius 1.

102. Solve by completing the square: $y^2 - 6y - 4 = 0$.

Section **2.8** ## Distance and Midpoint Formulas; Circles

Objectives

① Find the distance between two points.

② Find the midpoint of a line segment.

③ Write the standard form of a circle's equation.

④ Give the center and radius of a circle whose equation is in standard form.

⑤ Convert the general form of a circle's equation to standard form.

It's a good idea to know your way around a circle. Clocks, angles, maps, and compasses are based on circles. Circles occur everywhere in nature: in ripples on water, patterns on a moth's wings, and cross sections of trees. Some consider the circle to be the most pleasing of all shapes.

The rectangular coordinate system gives us a unique way of knowing a circle. It enables us to translate a circle's geometric definition into an algebraic equation. To do this, we must first develop a formula for the distance between any two points in rectangular coordinates.

① Find the distance between two points.

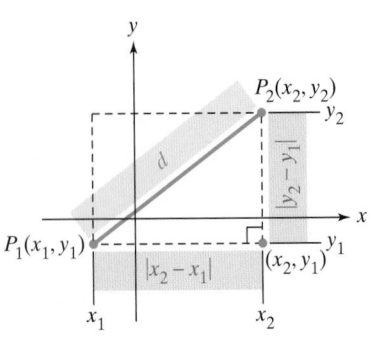

Figure 2.61

The Distance Formula

Using the Pythagorean Theorem, we can find the distance between the two points $P_1(x_1, y_1)$ and $P_2(x_2, y_2)$ in the rectangular coordinate system. The two points are illustrated in **Figure 2.61**.

The distance that we need to find is represented by d and shown in blue. Notice that the distance between the two points on the dashed horizontal line is the absolute value of the difference between the x-coordinates of the points. This distance, $|x_2 - x_1|$, is shown in pink. Similarly, the distance between the two points on the dashed vertical line is the absolute value of the difference between the y-coordinates of the points. This distance, $|y_2 - y_1|$, is also shown in pink.

Because the dashed lines are horizontal and vertical, a right triangle is formed. Thus, we can use the Pythagorean Theorem to find the distance d. Squaring the lengths of the triangle's sides results in positive numbers, so absolute value notation is not necessary.

$$d^2 = (x_2 - x_1)^2 + (y_2 - y_1)^2$$ Apply the Pythagorean Theorem to the right triangle in Figure 2.61.

$$d = \pm\sqrt{(x_2 - x_1)^2 + (y_2 - y_1)^2}$$ Apply the square root property.

$$d = \sqrt{(x_2 - x_1)^2 + (y_2 - y_1)^2}$$ Because distance is nonnegative, write only the principal square root.

This result is called the **distance formula**.

The Distance Formula

The distance, d, between the points (x_1, y_1) and (x_2, y_2) in the rectangular coordinate system is

$$d = \sqrt{(x_2 - x_1)^2 + (y_2 - y_1)^2}.$$

To compute the distance between two points, find the square of the difference between the x-coordinates plus the square of the difference between the y-coordinates. The principal square root of this sum is the distance.

When using the distance formula, it does not matter which point you call (x_1, y_1) and which you call (x_2, y_2).

EXAMPLE 1 **Using the Distance Formula**

Find the distance between $(-1, 4)$ and $(3, -2)$.

Solution We will let $(x_1, y_1) = (-1, 4)$ and $(x_2, y_2) = (3, -2)$.

$$d = \sqrt{(x_2 - x_1)^2 + (y_2 - y_1)^2}$$ Use the distance formula.

$$= \sqrt{[3 - (-1)]^2 + (-2 - 4)^2}$$ Substitute the given values.

$$= \sqrt{4^2 + (-6)^2}$$ Perform operations inside grouping symbols: $3 - (-1) = 3 + 1 = 4$ and $-2 - 4 = -6$.

$$= \sqrt{16 + 36}$$ *Caution: This does not equal $\sqrt{16} + \sqrt{36}$.* Square 4 and -6.

$$= \sqrt{52}$$ Add.

$$= \sqrt{4 \cdot 13} = 2\sqrt{13} \approx 7.21$$ $\sqrt{52} = \sqrt{4 \cdot 13} = \sqrt{4}\sqrt{13} = 2\sqrt{13}$

The distance between the given points is $2\sqrt{13}$ units, or approximately 7.21 units. The situation is illustrated in **Figure 2.62**.

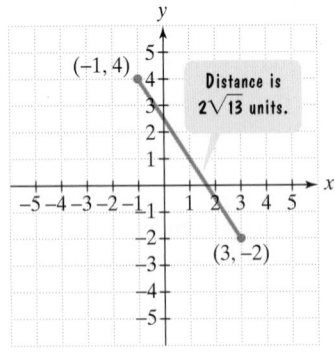

Figure 2.62 Finding the distance between two points

⊘ Check Point **1** Find the distance between $(-4, 9)$ and $(1, -3)$.

② Find the midpoint of a line segment.

The Midpoint Formula

The distance formula can be used to derive a formula for finding the midpoint of a line segment between two given points. The formula is given as follows:

The Midpoint Formula

Consider a line segment whose endpoints are (x_1, y_1) and (x_2, y_2). The coordinates of the segment's midpoint are

$$\left(\frac{x_1 + x_2}{2}, \frac{y_1 + y_2}{2} \right).$$

To find the midpoint, take the average of the two x-coordinates and the average of the two y-coordinates.

Study Tip

The midpoint formula requires finding the *sum* of coordinates. By contrast, the distance formula requires finding the *difference* of coordinates:

Midpoint: Sum of coordinates

Distance: Difference of coordinates

$$\left(\frac{x_1 + x_2}{2}, \frac{y_1 + y_2}{2} \right) \qquad \sqrt{(x_2 - x_1)^2 + (y_2 - y_1)^2}$$

It's easy to confuse the two formulas. Be sure to use addition, not subtraction, when applying the midpoint formula.

(**EXAMPLE 2**) **Using the Midpoint Formula**

Find the midpoint of the line segment with endpoints $(1, -6)$ and $(-8, -4)$.

Solution To find the coordinates of the midpoint, we average the coordinates of the endpoints.

$$\text{Midpoint} = \left(\frac{1 + (-8)}{2}, \frac{-6 + (-4)}{2} \right) = \left(\frac{-7}{2}, \frac{-10}{2} \right) = \left(-\frac{7}{2}, -5 \right)$$

Average the x-coordinates.

Average the y-coordinates.

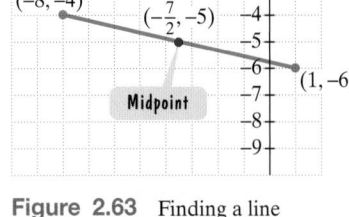

Figure 2.63 Finding a line segment's midpoint

Figure 2.63 illustrates that the point $\left(-\frac{7}{2}, -5 \right)$ is midway between the points $(1, -6)$ and $(-8, -4)$. ●

⊘ Check Point **2** Find the midpoint of the line segment with endpoints $(1, 2)$ and $(7, -3)$.

Circles

Our goal is to translate a circle's geometric definition into an equation. We begin with this geometric definition.

Definition of a Circle

A **circle** is the set of all points in a plane that are equidistant from a fixed point, called the **center**. The fixed distance from the circle's center to any point on the circle is called the **radius**.

Figure 2.64 is our starting point for obtaining a circle's equation. We've placed the circle into a rectangular coordinate system. The circle's center is (h, k) and its radius is r. We let (x, y) represent the coordinates of any point on the circle.

What does the geometric definition of a circle tell us about the point (x, y) in **Figure 2.64**? The point is on the circle if and only if its distance from the center is r. We can use the distance formula to express this idea algebraically:

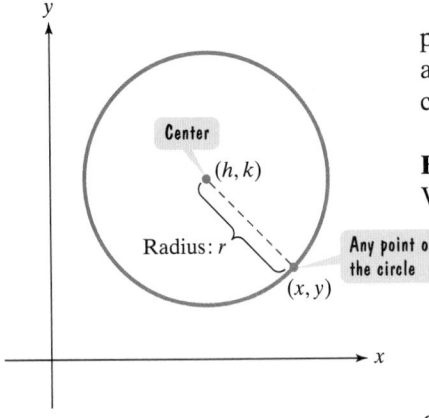

The distance between (x, y) and (h, k) is always r.

$$\sqrt{(x - h)^2 + (y - k)^2} = r.$$

Figure 2.64 A circle centered at (h, k) with radius r

Squaring both sides of $\sqrt{(x - h)^2 + (y - k)^2} = r$ yields the *standard form of the equation of a circle*.

③ Write the standard form of a circle's equation.

The Standard Form of the Equation of a Circle

The **standard form of the equation of a circle** with center (h, k) and radius r is

$$(x - h)^2 + (y - k)^2 = r^2.$$

$\boxed{\text{EXAMPLE 3}}$ **Finding the Standard Form of a Circle's Equation**

Write the standard form of the equation of the circle with center $(0, 0)$ and radius 2. Graph the circle.

Solution The center is $(0, 0)$. Because the center is represented as (h, k) in the standard form of the equation, $h = 0$ and $k = 0$. The radius is 2, so we will let $r = 2$ in the equation.

$$(x - h)^2 + (y - k)^2 = r^2 \qquad \text{This is the standard form of a circle's equation.}$$

$$(x - 0)^2 + (y - 0)^2 = 2^2 \qquad \text{Substitute 0 for } h, \text{ 0 for } k, \text{ and 2 for } r.$$

$$x^2 + y^2 = 4 \qquad \text{Simplify.}$$

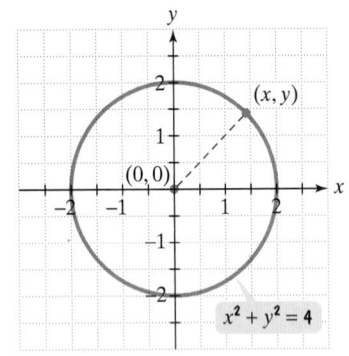

Figure 2.65 The graph of $x^2 + y^2 = 4$

The standard form of the equation of the circle is $x^2 + y^2 = 4$. **Figure 2.65** shows the graph. ●

✓ Check Point **3** Write the standard form of the equation of the circle with center $(0, 0)$ and radius 4.

Technology

$y_1 = \sqrt{4 - x^2}$

$y_2 = -\sqrt{4 - x^2}$

To graph a circle with a graphing utility, first solve the equation for y.

$$x^2 + y^2 = 4$$
$$y^2 = 4 - x^2$$
$$y = \pm\sqrt{4 - x^2} \quad \boxed{\text{y is not a function of x.}}$$

Graph the two equations

$$y_1 = \sqrt{4 - x^2} \quad \text{and} \quad y_2 = -\sqrt{4 - x^2}$$

in the same viewing rectangle. The graph of $y_1 = \sqrt{4 - x^2}$ is the top semicircle because y is always positive. The graph of $y_2 = -\sqrt{4 - x^2}$ is the bottom semicircle because y is always negative. Use a $\boxed{\text{ZOOM SQUARE}}$ setting so that the circle looks like a circle. (Many graphing utilities have problems connecting the two semicircles because the segments directly to the left and to the right of the center become nearly vertical.)

Example 3 and Check Point 3 involved circles centered at the origin. The standard form of the equation of all such circles is $x^2 + y^2 = r^2$, where r is the circle's radius. Now, let's consider a circle whose center is not at the origin.

(EXAMPLE 4) **Finding the Standard Form of a Circle's Equation**

Write the standard form of the equation of the circle with center $(-2, 3)$ and radius 4.

Solution The center is $(-2, 3)$. Because the center is represented as (h, k) in the standard form of the equation, $h = -2$ and $k = 3$. The radius is 4, so we will let $r = 4$ in the equation.

$$(x - h)^2 + (y - k)^2 = r^2 \quad \text{This is the standard form of a circle's equation.}$$
$$[x - (-2)]^2 + (y - 3)^2 = 4^2 \quad \text{Substitute -2 for h, 3 for k, and 4 for r.}$$
$$(x + 2)^2 + (y - 3)^2 = 16 \quad \text{Simplify.}$$

The standard form of the equation of the circle is $(x + 2)^2 + (y - 3)^2 = 16$. ●

⊘ Check Point **4** Write the standard form of the equation of the circle with center $(0, -6)$ and radius 10.

④ Give the center and radius of a circle whose equation is in standard form.

(EXAMPLE 5) **Using the Standard Form of a Circle's Equation to Graph the Circle**

a. Find the center and radius of the circle whose equation is
$$(x - 2)^2 + (y + 4)^2 = 9.$$

b. Graph the equation.

c. Use the graph to identify the relation's domain and range.

Solution

a. We begin by finding the circle's center, (h, k), and its radius, r. We can find the values for h, k, and r by comparing the given equation to the standard form of the equation of a circle, $(x - h)^2 + (y - k)^2 = r^2$.

$$(x - 2)^2 + (y + 4)^2 = 9$$

$$(x - 2)^2 + (y - (-4))^2 = 3^2$$

| This is $(x - h)^2$, with $h = 2$. | This is $(y - k)^2$, with $k = -4$. | This is r^2, with $r = 3$. |

We see that $h = 2$, $k = -4$, and $r = 3$. Thus, the circle has center $(h, k) = (2, -4)$ and a radius of 3 units.

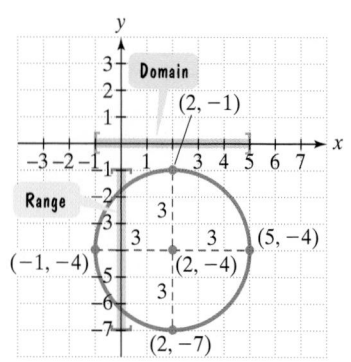

Figure 2.66 The graph of $(x - 2)^2 + (y + 4)^2 = 9$

b. To graph this circle, first locate the center $(2, -4)$. Because the radius is 3, you can locate at least four points on the circle by going out three units to the right, to the left, up, and down from the center.

The points three units to the right and to the left of $(2, -4)$ are $(5, -4)$ and $(-1, -4)$, respectively. The points three units up and down from $(2, -4)$ are $(2, -1)$ and $(2, -7)$, respectively.

Using these points, we obtain the graph in **Figure 2.66**.

c. The four points that we located on the circle can be used to determine the relation's domain and range. The points $(-1, -4)$ and $(5, -4)$ show that values of x extend from -1 to 5, inclusive:

$$\text{Domain} = [-1, 5].$$

The points $(2, -7)$ and $(2, -1)$ show that values of y extend from -7 to -1, inclusive:

$$\text{Range} = [-7, -1]. \qquad \bullet$$

Study Tip

It's easy to make sign errors when finding h and k, the coordinates of a circle's center, (h, k). Keep in mind that h and k are the numbers that *follow the subtraction signs* in a circle's equation:

$$(x - 2)^2 + (y + 4)^2 = 9$$
$$(x - 2)^2 + (y - (-4))^2 = 9.$$

The number *after the* subtraction is 2: $h = 2$.

The number *after the* subtraction is -4: $k = -4$.

⊘ **Check Point 5**

a. Find the center and radius of the circle whose equation is

$$(x + 3)^2 + (y - 1)^2 = 4.$$

b. Graph the equation.

c. Use the graph to identify the relation's domain and range.

If we square $x - 2$ and $y + 4$ in the standard form of the equation in Example 5, we obtain another form for the circle's equation.

$$(x - 2)^2 + (y + 4)^2 = 9 \quad \text{This is the standard form of the equation in Example 5.}$$
$$x^2 - 4x + 4 + y^2 + 8y + 16 = 9 \quad \text{Square } x - 2 \text{ and } y + 4.$$
$$x^2 + y^2 - 4x + 8y + 20 = 9 \quad \text{Combine constants and rearrange terms.}$$
$$x^2 + y^2 - 4x + 8y + 11 = 0 \quad \text{Subtract 9 from both sides.}$$

This result suggests that an equation in the form $x^2 + y^2 + Dx + Ey + F = 0$ can represent a circle. This is called the *general form of the equation of a circle*.

The General Form of the Equation of a Circle

The **general form of the equation of a circle** is

$$x^2 + y^2 + Dx + Ey + F = 0,$$

where D, E, and F are real numbers.

⑤ Convert the general form of a circle's equation to standard form.

We can convert the general form of the equation of a circle to the standard form $(x - h)^2 + (y - k)^2 = r^2$. We do so by completing the square on x and y. Let's see how this is done.

EXAMPLE 6 Converting the General Form of a Circle's Equation to Standard Form and Graphing the Circle

Study Tip

To review completing the square, see Section 1.5, pages 140–142.

Write in standard form and graph: $x^2 + y^2 + 4x - 6y - 23 = 0$.

Solution Because we plan to complete the square on both x and y, let's rearrange the terms so that x-terms are arranged in descending order, y-terms are arranged in descending order, and the constant term appears on the right.

$$x^2 + y^2 + 4x - 6y - 23 = 0 \qquad \text{This is the given equation.}$$

$$(x^2 + 4x) + (y^2 - 6y) = 23 \qquad \begin{array}{l}\text{Rewrite in anticipation of} \\ \text{completing the square.}\end{array}$$

$$(x^2 + 4x + 4) + (y^2 - 6y + 9) = 23 + 4 + 9 \qquad \begin{array}{l}\text{Complete the square on } x: \frac{1}{2} \cdot 4 = 2 \\ \text{and } 2^2 = 4, \text{ so add 4 to both} \\ \text{sides. Complete the square on} \\ y: \frac{1}{2}(-6) = -3 \text{ and } (-3)^2 = 9, \\ \text{so add 9 to both sides.}\end{array}$$

> Remember that numbers added on the left side must also be added on the right side.

$$(x + 2)^2 + (y - 3)^2 = 36 \qquad \begin{array}{l}\text{Factor on the left and add on} \\ \text{the right.}\end{array}$$

This last equation is in standard form. We can identify the circle's center and radius by comparing this equation to the standard form of the equation of a circle, $(x - h)^2 + (y - k)^2 = r^2$.

$$(x + 2)^2 + (y - 3)^2 = 36$$

$$(x - (-2))^2 + (y - 3)^2 = 6^2$$

> This is $(x - h)^2$, with $h = -2$.

> This is $(y - k)^2$, with $k = 3$.

> This is r^2, with $r = 6$.

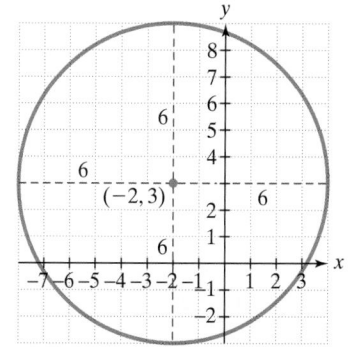

Figure 2.67 The graph of $(x + 2)^2 + (y - 3)^2 = 36$

We use the center, $(h, k) = (-2, 3)$, and the radius, $r = 6$, to graph the circle. The graph is shown in **Figure 2.67**. ●

Technology

To graph $x^2 + y^2 + 4x - 6y - 23 = 0$, the general form of the circle's equation given in Example 6, rewrite the equation as a quadratic equation in y.

$$y^2 - 6y + (x^2 + 4x - 23) = 0$$

Now solve for y using the quadratic formula, with $a = 1$, $b = -6$, and $c = x^2 + 4x - 23$.

$$y = \frac{-b \pm \sqrt{b^2 - 4ac}}{2a} = \frac{-(-6) \pm \sqrt{(-6)^2 - 4 \cdot 1(x^2 + 4x - 23)}}{2 \cdot 1} = \frac{6 \pm \sqrt{36 - 4(x^2 + 4x - 23)}}{2}$$

Because we will enter these equations, there is no need to simplify. Enter

$$y_1 = \frac{6 + \sqrt{36 - 4(x^2 + 4x - 23)}}{2}$$

and

$$y_2 = \frac{6 - \sqrt{36 - 4(x^2 + 4x - 23)}}{2}.$$

Use a ZOOM SQUARE setting. The graph is shown on the right.

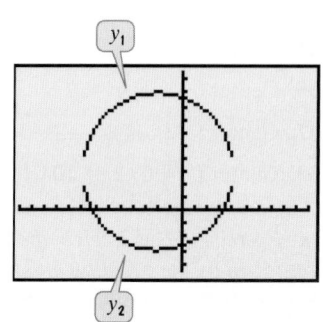

⊘ Check Point **6** Write in standard form and graph:

$$x^2 + y^2 + 4x - 4y - 1 = 0.$$

Exercise Set 2.8

Practice Exercises

In Exercises 1–18, find the distance between each pair of points. If necessary, round answers to two decimals places.

1. $(2, 3)$ and $(14, 8)$ **2.** $(5, 1)$ and $(8, 5)$

3. $(4, -1)$ and $(-6, 3)$ **4.** $(2, -3)$ and $(-1, 5)$

5. $(0, 0)$ and $(-3, 4)$ **6.** $(0, 0)$ and $(3, -4)$

7. $(-2, -6)$ and $(3, -4)$ **8.** $(-4, -1)$ and $(2, -3)$

9. $(0, -3)$ and $(4, 1)$ **10.** $(0, -2)$ and $(4, 3)$

11. $(3.5, 8.2)$ and $(-0.5, 6.2)$ **12.** $(2.6, 1.3)$ and $(1.6, -5.7)$

13. $\left(0, -\sqrt{3}\right)$ and $\left(\sqrt{5}, 0\right)$

14. $\left(0, -\sqrt{2}\right)$ and $\left(\sqrt{7}, 0\right)$

15. $\left(3\sqrt{3}, \sqrt{5}\right)$ and $\left(-\sqrt{3}, 4\sqrt{5}\right)$

16. $\left(2\sqrt{3}, \sqrt{6}\right)$ and $\left(-\sqrt{3}, 5\sqrt{6}\right)$

17. $\left(\dfrac{7}{3}, \dfrac{1}{5}\right)$ and $\left(\dfrac{1}{3}, \dfrac{6}{5}\right)$ **18.** $\left(-\dfrac{1}{4}, -\dfrac{1}{7}\right)$ and $\left(\dfrac{3}{4}, \dfrac{6}{7}\right)$

In Exercises 19–30, find the midpoint of each line segment with the given endpoints.

19. $(6, 8)$ and $(2, 4)$ **20.** $(10, 4)$ and $(2, 6)$

21. $(-2, -8)$ and $(-6, -2)$ **22.** $(-4, -7)$ and $(-1, -3)$

23. $(-3, -4)$ and $(6, -8)$ **24.** $(-2, -1)$ and $(-8, 6)$

25. $\left(-\dfrac{7}{2}, \dfrac{3}{2}\right)$ and $\left(-\dfrac{5}{2}, -\dfrac{11}{2}\right)$

26. $\left(-\dfrac{2}{5}, \dfrac{7}{15}\right)$ and $\left(-\dfrac{2}{5}, -\dfrac{4}{15}\right)$

27. $\left(8, 3\sqrt{5}\right)$ and $\left(-6, 7\sqrt{5}\right)$

28. $\left(7\sqrt{3}, -6\right)$ and $\left(3\sqrt{3}, -2\right)$

29. $\left(\sqrt{18}, -4\right)$ and $\left(\sqrt{2}, 4\right)$ **30.** $\left(\sqrt{50}, -6\right)$ and $\left(\sqrt{2}, 6\right)$

In Exercises 31–40, write the standard form of the equation of the circle with the given center and radius.

31. Center $(0, 0), r = 7$ **32.** Center $(0, 0), r = 8$

33. Center $(3, 2), r = 5$ **34.** Center $(2, -1), r = 4$

35. Center $(-1, 4), r = 2$ **36.** Center $(-3, 5), r = 3$

37. Center $(-3, -1), r = \sqrt{3}$ **38.** Center $(-5, -3), r = \sqrt{5}$

39. Center $(-4, 0), r = 10$ **40.** Center $(-2, 0), r = 6$

In Exercises 41–52, give the center and radius of the circle described by the equation and graph each equation. Use the graph to identify the relation's domain and range.

41. $x^2 + y^2 = 16$ **42.** $x^2 + y^2 = 49$

43. $(x - 3)^2 + (y - 1)^2 = 36$

44. $(x - 2)^2 + (y - 3)^2 = 16$

45. $(x + 3)^2 + (y - 2)^2 = 4$

46. $(x + 1)^2 + (y - 4)^2 = 25$

47. $(x + 2)^2 + (y + 2)^2 = 4$

48. $(x + 4)^2 + (y + 5)^2 = 36$

49. $x^2 + (y - 1)^2 = 1$ **50.** $x^2 + (y - 2)^2 = 4$

51. $(x + 1)^2 + y^2 = 25$ **52.** $(x + 2)^2 + y^2 = 16$

In Exercises 53–64, complete the square and write the equation in standard form. Then give the center and radius of each circle and graph the equation.

53. $x^2 + y^2 + 6x + 2y + 6 = 0$

54. $x^2 + y^2 + 8x + 4y + 16 = 0$

55. $x^2 + y^2 - 10x - 6y - 30 = 0$

56. $x^2 + y^2 - 4x - 12y - 9 = 0$

57. $x^2 + y^2 + 8x - 2y - 8 = 0$

58. $x^2 + y^2 + 12x - 6y - 4 = 0$

59. $x^2 - 2x + y^2 - 15 = 0$ **60.** $x^2 + y^2 - 6y - 7 = 0$

61. $x^2 + y^2 - x + 2y + 1 = 0$ **62.** $x^2 + y^2 + x + y - \frac{1}{2} = 0$

63. $x^2 + y^2 + 3x - 2y - 1 = 0$

64. $x^2 + y^2 + 3x + 5y + \frac{9}{4} = 0$

Practice Plus

In Exercises 65–66, a line segment through the center of each circle intersects the circle at the points shown.

 a. Find the coordinates of the circle's center.

 b. Find the radius of the circle.

 c. Use your answers from parts (a) and (b) to write the standard form of the circle's equation.

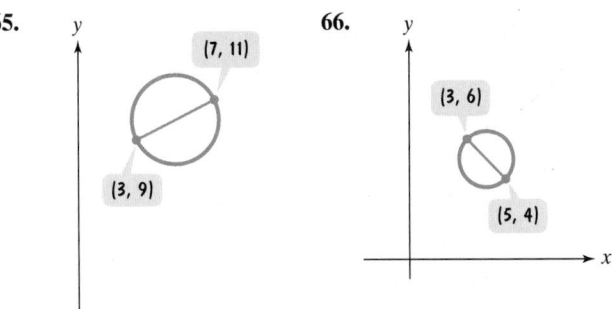

In Exercises 67–70, graph both equations in the same rectangular coordinate system and find all points of intersection. Then show that these ordered pairs satisfy the equations.

67. $x^2 + y^2 = 16$
$\quad x - y = 4$

68. $x^2 + y^2 = 9$
$\quad x - y = 3$

69. $(x - 2)^2 + (y + 3)^2 = 4$
$\qquad\qquad\quad y = x - 3$

70. $(x - 3)^2 + (y + 1)^2 = 9$
$\qquad\qquad\quad y = x - 1$

Application Exercises

The cell phone screen shows coordinates of six cities from a rectangular coordinate system placed on North America by long-distance telephone companies. Each unit in this system represents $\sqrt{0.1}$ mile.

Source: Peter H. Dana

In Exercises 71–72, use this information to find the distance, to the nearest mile, between each pair of cities.

71. Boston and San Francisco

72. New Orleans and Houston

73. A rectangular coordinate system with coordinates in miles is placed with the origin at the center of Los Angeles. The figure indicates that the University of Southern California is located 2.4 miles west and 2.7 miles south of central Los Angeles. A seismograph on the campus shows that a small earthquake occurred. The quake's epicenter is estimated to be approximately 30 miles from the university. Write the standard form of the equation for the set of points that could be the epicenter of the quake.

74. The Ferris wheel in the figure has a radius of 68 feet. The clearance between the wheel and the ground is 14 feet. The rectangular coordinate system shown has its origin on the ground directly below the center of the wheel. Use the coordinate system to write the equation of the circular wheel.

Writing in Mathematics

75. In your own words, describe how to find the distance between two points in the rectangular coordinate system.

76. In your own words, describe how to find the midpoint of a line segment if its endpoints are known.

77. What is a circle? Without using variables, describe how the definition of a circle can be used to obtain a form of its equation.

78. Give an example of a circle's equation in standard form. Describe how to find the center and radius for this circle.

79. How is the standard form of a circle's equation obtained from its general form?

80. Does $(x - 3)^2 + (y - 5)^2 = 0$ represent the equation of a circle? If not, describe the graph of this equation.

81. Does $(x - 3)^2 + (y - 5)^2 = -25$ represent the equation of a circle? What sort of set is the graph of this equation?

82. Write and solve a problem about the flying time between a pair of cities shown on the cell phone screen for Exercises 71–72. Do not use the pairs in Exercise 71 or Exercise 72. Begin by determining a reasonable average speed, in miles per hour, for a jet flying between the cities.

Technology Exercises

In Exercises 83–85, use a graphing utility to graph each circle whose equation is given.

83. $x^2 + y^2 = 25$

84. $(y + 1)^2 = 36 - (x - 3)^2$

85. $x^2 + 10x + y^2 - 4y - 20 = 0$

Critical Thinking Exercises

Make Sense? *In Exercises 86–89, determine whether each statement makes sense or does not make sense, and explain your reasoning.*

86. I've noticed that in mathematics, one topic often leads logically to a new topic:

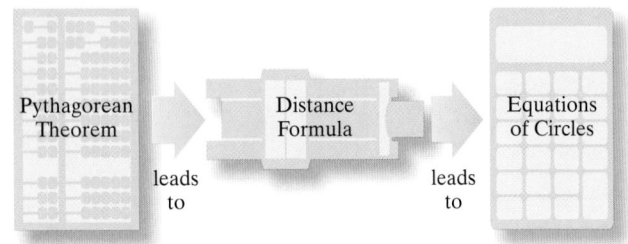

| Pythagorean Theorem | leads to | Distance Formula | leads to | Equations of Circles |

87. To avoid sign errors when finding h and k, I place parentheses around the numbers that follow the subtraction signs in a circle's equation.

88. I used the equation $(x + 1)^2 + (y - 5)^2 = -4$ to identify the circle's center and radius.

89. My graph of $(x - 2)^2 + (y + 1)^2 = 16$ is my graph of $x^2 + y^2 = 16$ translated two units right and one unit down.

In Exercises 90–93, determine whether each statement is true or false. If the statement is false, make the necessary change(s) to produce a true statement.

90. The equation of the circle whose center is at the origin with radius 16 is $x^2 + y^2 = 16$.

91. The graph of $(x - 3)^2 + (y + 5)^2 = 36$ is a circle with radius 6 centered at $(-3, 5)$.

92. The graph of $(x - 4) + (y + 6) = 25$ is a circle with radius 5 centered at $(4, -6)$.

93. The graph of $(x - 3)^2 + (y + 5)^2 = -36$ is a circle with radius 6 centered at $(3, -5)$.

94. Show that the points $A(1, 1 + d)$, $B(3, 3 + d)$, and $C(6, 6 + d)$ are collinear (lie along a straight line) by showing that the distance from A to B plus the distance from B to C equals the distance from A to C.

95. Prove the midpoint formula by using the following procedure.

 a. Show that the distance between (x_1, y_1) and $\left(\dfrac{x_1 + x_2}{2}, \dfrac{y_1 + y_2}{2}\right)$ is equal to the distance between (x_2, y_2) and $\left(\dfrac{x_1 + x_2}{2}, \dfrac{y_1 + y_2}{2}\right)$.

 b. Use the procedure from Exercise 94 and the distances from part (a) to show that the points (x_1, y_1), $\left(\dfrac{x_1 + x_2}{2}, \dfrac{y_1 + y_2}{2}\right)$, and (x_2, y_2) are collinear.

96. Find the area of the donut-shaped region bounded by the graphs of $(x - 2)^2 + (y + 3)^2 = 25$ and $(x - 2)^2 + (y + 3)^2 = 36$.

97. A **tangent line** to a circle is a line that intersects the circle at exactly one point. The tangent line is perpendicular to the radius of the circle at this point of contact. Write an equation in point-slope form for the line tangent to the circle whose equation is $x^2 + y^2 = 25$ at the point $(3, -4)$.

Preview Exercises

Exercises 98–100 will help you prepare for the material covered in the first section of the next chapter.

In Exercises 98–99, solve each quadratic equation by the method of your choice.

98. $0 = -2(x - 3)^2 + 8$ **99.** $-x^2 - 2x + 1 = 0$

100. Use the graph of $f(x) = x^2$ to graph $g(x) = (x + 3)^2 + 1$.

Chapter 2 Summary, Review, and Test

Summary

DEFINITIONS AND CONCEPTS	EXAMPLES
2.1 Basics of Functions and Their Graphs	
a. A relation is any set of ordered pairs. The set of first components is the domain of the relation and the set of second components is the range.	Ex. 1, p. 198
b. A function is a correspondence from a first set, called the domain, to a second set, called the range, such that each element in the domain corresponds to exactly one element in the range. If any element in a relation's domain corresponds to more than one element in the range, the relation is not a function.	Ex. 2, p. 201
c. Functions are usually given in terms of equations involving x and y, in which x is the independent variable and y is the dependent variable. If an equation is solved for y and more than one value of y can be obtained for a given x, then the equation does not define y as a function of x. If an equation defines a function, the value of the function at x, $f(x)$, often replaces y.	Ex. 3, p. 202; Ex. 4, p. 203
d. The graph of a function is the graph of its ordered pairs.	Ex. 5, p. 204
e. The vertical line test for functions: If any vertical line intersects a graph in more than one point, the graph does not define y as a function of x.	Ex. 6, p. 205

DEFINITIONS AND CONCEPTS	**EXAMPLES**

f. The graph of a function can be used to determine the function's domain and its range. To find the domain, look for all the inputs on the x-axis that correspond to points on the graph. To find the range, look for all the outputs on the y-axis that correspond to points on the graph. — Ex. 8, p. 208

g. The zeros of a function, f, are the values of x for which $f(x) = 0$. At the real zeros, the graph of f has x-intercepts. A function can have more than one x-intercept but at most one y-intercept. — Figure 2.14, p. 210

2.2 More on Functions and Their Graphs

a. A function is increasing on intervals where its graph rises, decreasing on intervals where it falls, and constant on intervals where it neither rises nor falls. Precise definitions are given in the box on page 216. — Ex. 1, p. 217

b. If the graph of a function is given, we can often visually locate the number(s) at which the function has a relative maximum or relative minimum. Precise definitions are given in the box on page 217. — Figure 2.16, p. 218

c. The graph of an even function in which $f(-x) = f(x)$ is symmetric with respect to the y-axis. The graph of an odd function in which $f(-x) = -f(x)$ is symmetric with respect to the origin. — Ex. 2, p. 218

d. Piecewise functions are defined by two (or more) equations over a specified domain. Some piecewise functions are called step functions because their graphs form discontinuous steps. An example is $f(x) = \text{int}(x)$, where $\text{int}(x)$ is the greatest integer that is less than or equal to x. — Ex. 3, p. 220; Ex. 4, p. 221; Figure 2.22, p. 222

e. The difference quotient of a function f is
$$\frac{f(x + h) - f(x)}{h}, h \neq 0.$$
— Ex. 5, p. 222

2.3 Linear Functions and Slope

a. The slope, m, of the line through (x_1, y_1) and (x_2, y_2) is $m = \dfrac{y_2 - y_1}{x_2 - x_1}$. — Ex. 1, p. 230

b. Equations of lines include point-slope form, $y - y_1 = m(x - x_1)$, slope-intercept form, $y = mx + b$, and general form, $Ax + By + C = 0$. The equation of a horizontal line is $y = b$; a vertical line is $x = a$. A vertical line is not a linear function. — Ex. 2, p. 232; Ex. 3, p. 233; Ex. 5, p. 235; Ex. 6, p. 235

c. Linear functions in the form $f(x) = mx + b$ can be graphed using the slope, m, and the y-intercept, b. (See the box on page 234.) Linear equations in the general form $Ax + By + C = 0$ can be solved for y and graphed using the slope and the y-intercept. Intercepts can also be used to graph $Ax + By + C = 0$. (See the box on page 237.) — Ex. 4, p. 234; Ex. 7, p. 236; Ex. 8, p. 237

2.4 More on Slope

a. Parallel lines have equal slopes. Perpendicular lines have slopes that are negative reciprocals. — Ex. 1, p. 244; Ex. 2, p. 245

b. The slope of a linear function is the rate of change of the dependent variable per unit change of the independent variable. — Ex. 3, p. 246

c. The average rate of change of f from x_1 to x_2 is
$$\frac{f(x_2) - f(x_1)}{x_2 - x_1}.$$
— Ex. 4, p. 248; Ex. 5, p. 249

2.5 Transformations of Functions

a. Table 2.3 on page 255 shows the graphs of the constant function, $f(x) = c$, the identity function, $f(x) = x$, the absolute value function, $f(x) = |x|$, the standard quadratic function, $f(x) = x^2$, the square root function, $f(x) = \sqrt{x}$, the standard cubic function, $f(x) = x^3$, and the cube root function, $f(x) = \sqrt[3]{x}$. The table also lists characteristics of each function.

b. Table 2.4 on page 263 summarizes how to graph a function using vertical shifts, $y = f(x) \pm c$, horizontal shifts, $y = f(x \pm c)$, reflections about the x-axis, $y = -f(x)$, reflections about the y-axis, $y = f(-x)$, vertical stretching, $y = cf(x), c > 1$, vertical shrinking, $y = cf(x), 0 < c < 1$, horizontal shrinking, $y = f(cx), c > 1$, and horizontal stretching, $y = f(cx), 0 < c < 1$. — Ex. 1, p. 256; Ex. 2, p. 258; Ex. 3, p. 258; Ex. 4, p. 260; Ex. 5, p. 260; Ex. 6, p. 261; Ex. 7, p. 262

DEFINITIONS AND CONCEPTS	**EXAMPLES**
c. A function involving more than one transformation can be graphed in the following order: (1) horizontal shifting; (2) stretching or shrinking; (3) reflecting; (4) vertical shifting.	Ex. 8, p. 264; Ex. 9, p. 265

2.6 Combinations of Functions; Composite Functions

a. If a function f does not model data or verbal conditions, its domain is the largest set of real numbers for which the value of $f(x)$ is a real number. Exclude from a function's domain real numbers that cause division by zero and real numbers that result in a square root of a negative number.	Ex. 1, p. 271
b. When functions are given as equations, they can be added, subtracted, multiplied, or divided by performing operations with the algebraic expressions that appear on the right side of the equations. Definitions for the sum $f + g$, the difference $f - g$, the product fg, and the quotient $\frac{f}{g}$ functions, with domains $D_f \cap D_g$, and $g(x) \neq 0$ for the quotient function, are given in the box on page 272.	Ex. 2, p. 273; Ex. 3, p. 274
c. The composition of functions f and $g, f \circ g$, is defined by $(f \circ g)(x) = f(g(x))$. The domain of the composite function $f \circ g$ is given in the box on page 276. This composite function is obtained by replacing each occurrence of x in the equation for f with $g(x)$.	Ex. 4, p. 276; Ex. 5, p. 278

2.7 Inverse Functions

a. If $f(g(x)) = x$ and $g(f(x)) = x$, function g is the inverse of function f, denoted f^{-1} and read "f–inverse." Thus, to show that f and g are inverses of each other, one must show that $f(g(x)) = x$ and $g(f(x)) = x$.	Ex. 1, p. 285
b. The procedure for finding a function's inverse uses a switch-and-solve strategy. Switch x and y, and then solve for y. The procedure is given in the box on page 285.	Ex. 2, p. 286; Ex. 3, p. 286; Ex. 4, p. 287
c. The horizontal line test for inverse functions: A function f has an inverse that is a function, f^{-1}, if there is no horizontal line that intersects the graph of the function f at more than one point.	Ex. 5, p. 288
d. A one-to-one function is one in which no two different ordered pairs have the same second component. Only one-to-one functions have inverse functions.	
e. If the point (a, b) is on the graph of f, then the point (b, a) is on the graph of f^{-1}. The graph of f^{-1} is a reflection of the graph of f about the line $y = x$.	Ex. 6, p. 289; Ex. 7, p. 290

2.8 Distance and Midpoint Formulas; Circles

a. The distance, d, between the points (x_1, y_1) and (x_2, y_2) is given by $d = \sqrt{(x_2 - x_1)^2 + (y_2 - y_1)^2}$.	Ex. 1, p. 294
b. The midpoint of the line segment whose endpoints are (x_1, y_1) and (x_2, y_2) is the point with coordinates $\left(\dfrac{x_1 + x_2}{2}, \dfrac{y_1 + y_2}{2} \right)$.	Ex. 2, p. 295
c. The standard form of the equation of a circle with center (h, k) and radius r is $(x - h)^2 + (y - k)^2 = r^2$.	Ex. 3, p. 296; Ex. 4, p. 297; Ex. 5, p. 297
d. The general form of the equation of a circle is $x^2 + y^2 + Dx + Ey + F = 0$.	
e. To convert from the general form to the standard form of a circle's equation, complete the square on x and y.	Ex. 6, p. 299

Review Exercises

2.1 and 2.2

In Exercises 1–3, determine whether each relation is a function. Give the domain and range for each relation.

1. $\{(2, 7), (3, 7), (5, 7)\}$　　**2.** $\{(1, 10), (2, 500), (13, \pi)\}$

3. $\{(12, 13), (14, 15), (12, 19)\}$

In Exercises 4–6, determine whether each equation defines y as a function of x.

4. $2x + y = 8$　　　　　　**5.** $3x^2 + y = 14$

6. $2x + y^2 = 6$

In Exercises 7–10, evaluate each function at the given values of the independent variable and simplify.

7. $f(x) = 5 - 7x$

　　a. $f(4)$　　　　**b.** $f(x + 3)$　　　　**c.** $f(-x)$

8. $g(x) = 3x^2 - 5x + 2$

　　a. $g(0)$　　　　**b.** $g(-2)$

　　c. $g(x - 1)$　　**d.** $g(-x)$

9. $g(x) = \begin{cases} \sqrt{x - 4} & \text{if } x \geq 4 \\ 4 - x & \text{if } x < 4 \end{cases}$

　　a. $g(13)$　　　　**b.** $g(0)$　　　　**c.** $g(-3)$

10. $f(x) = \begin{cases} \dfrac{x^2 - 1}{x - 1} & \text{if } x \neq 1 \\ 12 & \text{if } x = 1 \end{cases}$

 a. $f(-2)$ **b.** $f(1)$ **c.** $f(2)$

In Exercises 11–16, use the vertical line test to identify graphs in which y is a function of x.

11.

12.

13.

14.

15.

16.
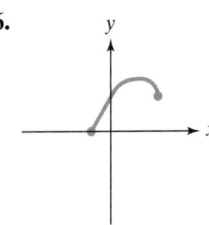

In Exercises 17–19, use the graph to determine **a.** *the function's domain;* **b.** *the function's range;* **c.** *the x-intercepts, if any;* **d.** *the y-intercept, if there is one;* **e.** *intervals on which the function is increasing, decreasing, or constant; and* **f.** *the missing function values, indicated by question marks, below each graph.*

17.
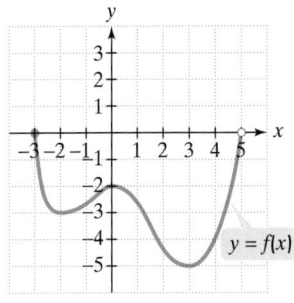

$f(-2) = ?$ $f(3) = ?$

18.
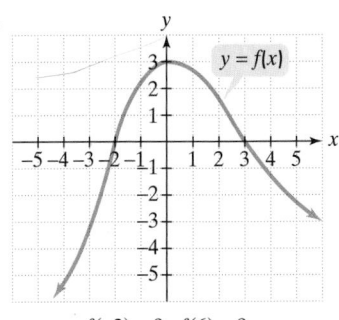

$f(-2) = ?$ $f(6) = ?$

19.
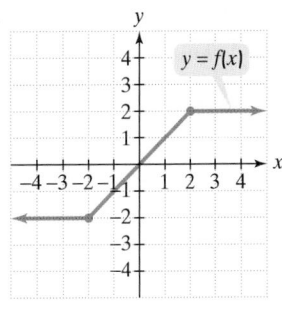

$f(-9) = ?$ $f(14) = ?$

In Exercises 20–21, find each of the following:

 a. *The numbers, if any, at which f has a relative maximum. What are these relative maxima?*

 b. *The numbers, if any, at which f has a relative minimum. What are these relative minima?*

20. Use the graph in Exercise 17.

21. Use the graph in Exercise 18.

In Exercises 22–24, determine whether each function is even, odd, or neither. State each function's symmetry. If you are using a graphing utility, graph the function and verify its possible symmetry.

22. $f(x) = x^3 - 5x$ **23.** $f(x) = x^4 - 2x^2 + 1$

24. $f(x) = 2x\sqrt{1 - x^2}$

In Exercises 25–26, the domain of each piecewise function is $(-\infty, \infty)$.

 a. *Graph each function.*

 b. *Use the graph to determine the function's range.*

25. $f(x) = \begin{cases} 5 & \text{if } x \leq -1 \\ -3 & \text{if } x > -1 \end{cases}$

26. $f(x) = \begin{cases} 2x & \text{if } x < 0 \\ -x & \text{if } x \geq 0 \end{cases}$

In Exercises 27–28, find and simplify the difference quotient

$$\frac{f(x + h) - f(x)}{h}, \quad h \neq 0$$

for the given function.

27. $f(x) = 8x - 11$ **28.** $f(x) = -2x^2 + x + 10$

29. The graph shows the height, in meters, of an eagle in terms of its time, in seconds, in flight.

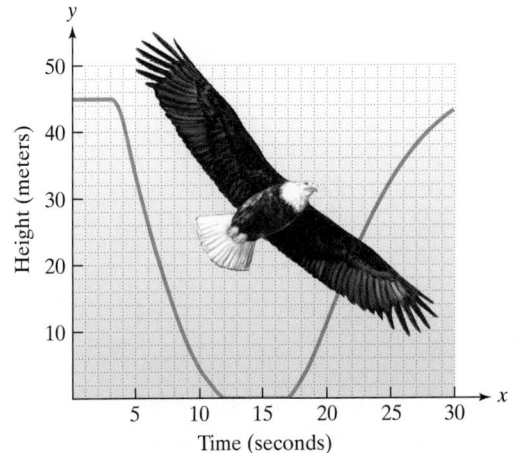

(Be sure to refer to the graph at the bottom of the previous page.)

a. Is the eagle's height a function of time? Use the graph to explain why or why not.

b. On which interval is the function decreasing? Describe what this means in practical terms.

c. On which intervals is the function constant? What does this mean for each of these intervals?

d. On which interval is the function increasing? What does this mean?

30. A cargo service charges a flat fee of $5 plus $1.50 for each pound or fraction of a pound. Graph shipping cost, $C(x)$, in dollars, as a function of weight, x, in pounds, for $0 < x \leq 5$.

2.3 and 2.4

In Exercises 31–34, find the slope of the line passing through each pair of points or state that the slope is undefined. Then indicate whether the line through the points rises, falls, is horizontal, or is vertical.

31. $(3, 2)$ and $(5, 1)$
32. $(-1, -2)$ and $(-3, -4)$
33. $\left(-3, \frac{1}{4}\right)$ and $\left(6, \frac{1}{4}\right)$
34. $(-2, 5)$ and $(-2, 10)$

In Exercises 35–38, use the given conditions to write an equation for each line in point-slope form and slope-intercept form.

35. Passing through $(-3, 2)$ with slope -6

36. Passing through $(1, 6)$ and $(-1, 2)$

37. Passing through $(4, -7)$ and parallel to the line whose equation is $3x + y - 9 = 0$

38. Passing through $(-3, 6)$ and perpendicular to the line whose equation is $y = \frac{1}{3}x + 4$

39. Write an equation in general form for the line passing through $(-12, -1)$ and perpendicular to the line whose equation is $6x - y - 4 = 0$.

In Exercises 40–43, give the slope and y-intercept of each line whose equation is given. Then graph the line.

40. $y = \frac{2}{5}x - 1$
41. $f(x) = -4x + 5$
42. $2x + 3y + 6 = 0$
43. $2y - 8 = 0$

44. Graph using intercepts: $2x - 5y - 10 = 0$.

45. Graph: $2x - 10 = 0$.

46. The points in the scatter plot show the number of firearms per 100 persons and the number of deaths per 100,000 persons for industrialized countries with the highest death rates.

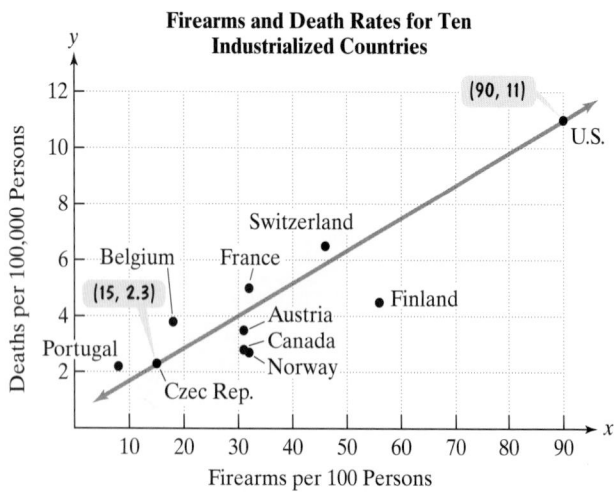

Firearms and Death Rates for Ten Industrialized Countries

Source: International Action Network on Small Arms

a. Use the two points whose coordinates are shown by the voice balloons to find an equation in point-slope form for the line that models deaths per 100,000 persons, y, as a function of firearms per 100 persons, x.

b. Write the equation in part (a) in slope-intercept form. Use function notation.

c. France has 32 firearms per 100 persons. Use the appropriate point in the scatter plot to estimate that country's deaths per 100,000 persons.

d. Use the function from part (b) to find the number of deaths per 100,000 persons for France. Round to one decimal place. Does the function underestimate or overestimate the deaths per 100,000 persons that you estimated in part (c)? How is this shown by the line in the scatter plot?

47. The bar graph shows the growth in corporate profits, in billions of dollars, from 2002 through 2006.

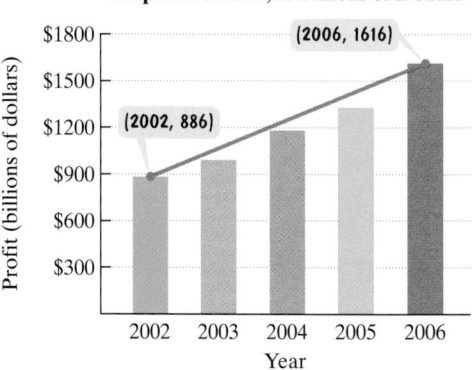

Corporate Profits, in Billions of Dollars

Source: Bureau of Economic Analysis

Find the slope of the line passing through the two points shown by the voice balloons. Then express the slope as a rate of change with the proper units attached.

48. Find the average rate of change of $f(x) = x^2 - 4x$ from $x_1 = 5$ to $x_2 = 9$.

2.5

In Exercises 49–53, use the graph of $y = f(x)$ to graph each function g.

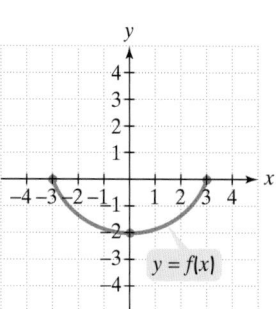

49. $g(x) = f(x + 2) + 3$
50. $g(x) = \frac{1}{2}f(x - 1)$
51. $g(x) = -f(2x)$
52. $g(x) = 2f\left(\frac{1}{2}x\right)$
53. $g(x) = -f(-x) - 1$

In Exercises 54–57, begin by graphing the standard quadratic function, $f(x) = x^2$. Then use transformations of this graph to graph the given function.

54. $g(x) = x^2 + 2$

55. $h(x) = (x + 2)^2$

56. $r(x) = -(x + 1)^2$

57. $y(x) = \frac{1}{2}(x - 1)^2 + 1$

In Exercises 58–60, begin by graphing the square root function, $f(x) = \sqrt{x}$. Then use transformations of this graph to graph the given function.

58. $g(x) = \sqrt{x + 3}$

59. $h(x) = \sqrt{3 - x}$

60. $r(x) = 2\sqrt{x + 2}$

In Exercises 61–63, begin by graphing the absolute value function, $f(x) = |x|$. Then use transformations of this graph to graph the given function.

61. $g(x) = |x + 2| - 3$

62. $h(x) = -|x - 1| + 1$

63. $r(x) = \frac{1}{2}|x + 2|$

In Exercises 64–66, begin by graphing the standard cubic function, $f(x) = x^3$. Then use transformations of this graph to graph the given function.

64. $g(x) = \frac{1}{2}(x - 1)^3$

65. $h(x) = -(x + 1)^3$

66. $r(x) = \frac{1}{4}x^3 - 1$

In Exercises 67–69, begin by graphing the cube root function, $f(x) = \sqrt[3]{x}$. Then use transformations of this graph to graph the given function.

67. $g(x) = \sqrt[3]{x + 2} - 1$

68. $h(x) = -\sqrt[3]{2x}$

69. $r(x) = -2\sqrt[3]{-x}$

2.6

In Exercises 70–75, find the domain of each function.

70. $f(x) = x^2 + 6x - 3$

71. $g(x) = \dfrac{4}{x - 7}$

72. $h(x) = \sqrt{8 - 2x}$

73. $f(x) = \dfrac{x}{x^2 + 4x - 21}$

74. $g(x) = \dfrac{\sqrt{x - 2}}{x - 5}$

75. $f(x) = \sqrt{x - 1} + \sqrt{x + 5}$

In Exercises 76–78, find $f + g, f - g, fg,$ and $\frac{f}{g}$. Determine the domain for each function.

76. $f(x) = 3x - 1, \quad g(x) = x - 5$

77. $f(x) = x^2 + x + 1, \quad g(x) = x^2 - 1$

78. $f(x) = \sqrt{x + 7}, \quad g(x) = \sqrt{x - 2}$

In Exercises 79–80, find **a.** $(f \circ g)(x)$; **b.** $(g \circ f)(x)$; **c.** $(f \circ g)(3)$.

79. $f(x) = x^2 + 3, \quad g(x) = 4x - 1$

80. $f(x) = \sqrt{x}, \quad g(x) = x + 1$

In Exercises 81–82, find **a.** $(f \circ g)(x)$; **b.** the domain of $(f \circ g)$.

81. $f(x) = \dfrac{x + 1}{x - 2}, \quad g(x) = \dfrac{1}{x}$

82. $f(x) = \sqrt{x - 1}, \quad g(x) = x + 3$

In Exercises 83–84, express the given function h as a composition of two functions f and g so that $h(x) = (f \circ g)(x)$.

83. $h(x) = (x^2 + 2x - 1)^4$

84. $h(x) = \sqrt[3]{7x + 4}$

2.7

In Exercises 85–86, find $f(g(x))$ and $g(f(x))$ and determine whether each pair of functions f and g are inverses of each other.

85. $f(x) = \dfrac{3}{5}x + \dfrac{1}{2}$ and $g(x) = \dfrac{5}{3}x - 2$

86. $f(x) = 2 - 5x$ and $g(x) = \dfrac{2 - x}{5}$

The functions in Exercises 87–89 are all one-to-one. For each function,

a. Find an equation for $f^{-1}(x)$, the inverse function.

b. Verify that your equation is correct by showing that $f(f^{-1}(x)) = x$ and $f^{-1}(f(x)) = x$.

87. $f(x) = 4x - 3$

88. $f(x) = 8x^3 + 1$

89. $f(x) = \dfrac{2}{x} + 5$

Which graphs in Exercises 90–93 represent functions that have inverse functions?

90.

91.

92.

93.

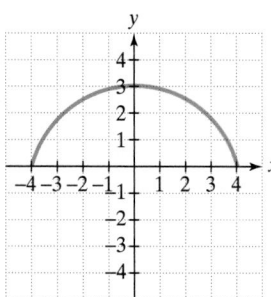

94. Use the graph of f in the figure shown to draw the graph of its inverse function.

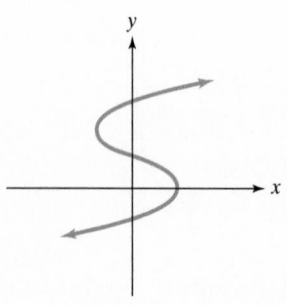

In Exercises 95–96, find an equation for $f^{-1}(x)$. Then graph f and f^{-1} in the same rectangular coordinate system.

95. $f(x) = 1 - x^2, x \geq 0$ **96.** $f(x) = \sqrt{x} + 1$

2.8

In Exercises 97–98, find the distance between each pair of points. If necessary, round answers to two decimal places.

97. $(-2, 3)$ and $(3, -9)$ **98.** $(-4, 3)$ and $(-2, 5)$

In Exercises 99–100, find the midpoint of each line segment with the given endpoints.

99. $(2, 6)$ and $(-12, 4)$ **100.** $(4, -6)$ and $(-15, 2)$

In Exercises 101–102, write the standard form of the equation of the circle with the given center and radius.

101. Center $(0, 0), r = 3$ **102.** Center $(-2, 4), r = 6$

In Exercises 103–105, give the center and radius of each circle and graph its equation. Use the graph to identify the relation's domain and range.

103. $x^2 + y^2 = 1$ **104.** $(x + 2)^2 + (y - 3)^2 = 9$

105. $x^2 + y^2 - 4x + 2y - 4 = 0$

CHAPTER
Test Prep
VIDEOS

Chapter 2 Test

1. List by letter all relations that are not functions.

a. $\{(7, 5), (8, 5), (9, 5)\}$ **d.** $x^2 + y^2 = 100$

b. $\{(5, 7), (5, 8), (5, 9)\}$ **e.**

c.

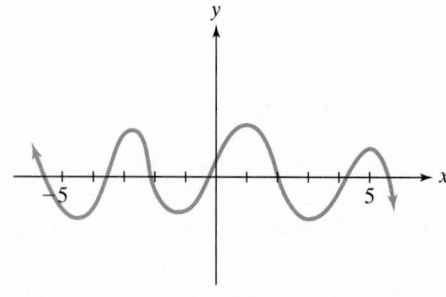

2. Use the graph of $y = f(x)$ to solve this exercise.

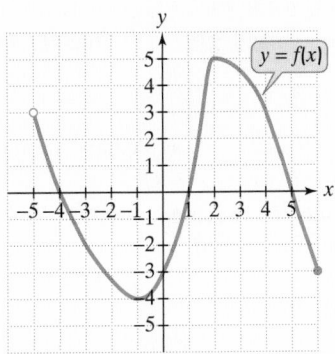

a. What is $f(4) - f(-3)$?

b. What is the domain of f?

c. What is the range of f?

d. On which interval or intervals is f increasing?

e. On which interval or intervals is f decreasing?

f. For what number does f have a relative maximum? What is the relative maximum?

g. For what number does f have a relative minimum? What is the relative minimum?

h. What are the x-intercepts?

i. What is the y-intercept?

3. Use the graph of $y = f(x)$ to solve this exercise.

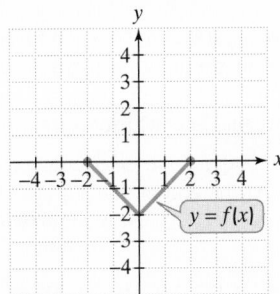

a. What are the zeros of f?

b. Find the value(s) of x for which $f(x) = -1$.

c. Find the value(s) of x for which $f(x) = -2$.

d. Is f even, odd, or neither?

e. Does f have an inverse function?

f. Is $f(0)$ a relative maximum, a relative minimum, or neither?

g. Graph $g(x) = f(x + 1) - 1$.

h. Graph $h(x) = \frac{1}{2}f\left(\frac{1}{2}x\right)$.

i. Graph $r(x) = -f(-x) + 1$.

j. Find the average rate of change of f from $x_1 = -2$ to $x_2 = 1$.

In Exercises 4–15, graph each equation in a rectangular coordinate system. If two functions are indicated, graph both in the same system. Then use your graphs to identify each relation's domain and range.

4. $x + y = 4$

5. $x^2 + y^2 = 4$

6. $f(x) = 4$

7. $f(x) = -\frac{1}{3}x + 2$

8. $(x + 2)^2 + (y - 1)^2 = 9$

9. $f(x) = \begin{cases} 2 & \text{if } x \le 0 \\ -1 & \text{if } x > 0 \end{cases}$

10. $x^2 + y^2 + 4x - 6y - 3 = 0$

11. $f(x) = |x|$ and $g(x) = \frac{1}{2}|x + 1| - 2$

12. $f(x) = x^2$ and $g(x) = -(x - 1)^2 + 4$

13. $f(x) = 2x - 4$ and f^{-1}

14. $f(x) = x^3 - 1$ and f^{-1}

15. $f(x) = x^2 - 1, x \ge 0$, and f^{-1}

In Exercises 16–23, let $f(x) = x^2 - x - 4$ and $g(x) = 2x - 6$.

16. Find $f(x - 1)$.

17. Find $\dfrac{f(x + h) - f(x)}{h}$.

18. Find $(g - f)(x)$.

19. Find $\left(\dfrac{f}{g}\right)(x)$ and its domain.

20. Find $(f \circ g)(x)$.

21. Find $(g \circ f)(x)$.

22. Find $g(f(-1))$.

23. Find $f(-x)$. Is f even, odd, or neither?

In Exercises 24–25, use the given conditions to write an equation for each line in point-slope form and slope-intercept form.

24. Passing through $(2, 1)$ and $(-1, -8)$

25. Passing through $(-4, 6)$ and perpendicular to the line whose equation is $y = -\frac{1}{4}x + 5$

26. Write an equation in general form for the line passing through $(-7, -10)$ and parallel to the line whose equation is $4x + 2y - 5 = 0$.

27. The scatter plot shows the number of sentenced inmates in the United States per 100,000 residents from 2001 through 2005. Also shown is a line that passes through or near the data points.

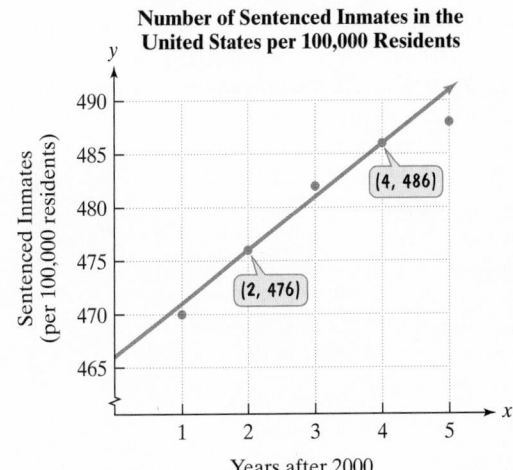

Number of Sentenced Inmates in the United States per 100,000 Residents

Source: U.S. Justice Department

a. Use the two points whose coordinates are shown by the voice balloons to find the point-slope form of the equation of the line that models the number of inmates per 100,000 residents, y, x years after 2000.

b. Write the equation from part (a) in slope-intercept form. Use function notation.

c. Use the linear function to predict the number of sentenced inmates in the United States per 100,000 residents in 2010.

28. Find the average rate of change of $f(x) = 3x^2 - 5$ from $x_1 = 6$ to $x_2 = 10$.

29. If $g(x) = \begin{cases} \sqrt{x - 3} & \text{if } x \geq 3 \\ 3 - x & \text{if } x < 3 \end{cases}$, find $g(-1)$ and $g(7)$.

In Exercises 30–31, find the domain of each function.

30. $f(x) = \dfrac{3}{x + 5} + \dfrac{7}{x - 1}$

31. $f(x) = 3\sqrt{x + 5} + 7\sqrt{x - 1}$

32. If $f(x) = \dfrac{7}{x - 4}$ and $g(x) = \dfrac{2}{x}$, find $(f \circ g)(x)$ and the domain of $f \circ g$.

33. Express $h(x) = (2x + 3)^7$ as a composition of two functions f and g so that $h(x) = (f \circ g)(x)$.

34. Find the length and the midpoint of the line segment whose endpoints are $(2, -2)$ and $(5, 2)$.

Cumulative Review Exercises (Chapters 1–2)

Use the graph of $y = f(x)$ to solve Exercises 1–5.

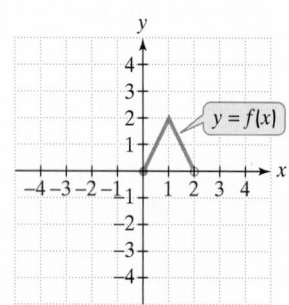

1. Find the domain and the range of f.

2. For what value(s) of x is $f(x) = 1$?

3. Find the relative maximum.

4. Graph $g(x) = f(x - 1) + 1$.

5. Graph $h(x) = -2f\left(\frac{1}{2}x\right)$.

In Exercises 6–10, solve each equation or inequality.

6. $(x + 3)(x - 4) = 8$

7. $3(4x - 1) = 4 - 6(x - 3)$

8. $\sqrt{x} + 2 = x$

9. $x^{\frac{2}{3}} - x^{\frac{1}{3}} - 6 = 0$

10. $\dfrac{x}{2} - 3 \leq \dfrac{x}{4} + 2$

In Exercises 11–14, graph each equation in a rectangular coordinate system. If two functions are indicated, graph both in the same system. Then use your graphs to identify each relation's domain and range.

11. $3x - 6y - 12 = 0$

12. $(x - 2)^2 + (y + 1)^2 = 4$

13. $f(x) = \sqrt[3]{x}$ and $g(x) = \sqrt[3]{x - 3} + 4$

14. $f(x) = \sqrt{x - 3} + 2$ and f^{-1}

In Exercises 15–16, let $f(x) = 4 - x^2$ and $g(x) = x + 5$.

15. Find $\dfrac{f(x + h) - f(x)}{h}$ and simplify.

16. Find all values of x satisfying $(f \circ g)(x) = 0$.

17. Write equations in point-slope form, slope-intercept form, and general form for the line passing through $(-2, 5)$ and perpendicular to the line whose equation is $y = -\frac{1}{4}x + \frac{1}{3}$.

18. You invested $6000 in two accounts paying 7% and 9% annual interest. At the end of the year, the total interest from these investments was $510. How much was invested at each rate?

19. For a summer sales job, you are choosing between two pay arrangements: a weekly salary of $200 plus 5% commission on sales, or a straight 15% commission. For how many dollars of sales will the earnings be the same regardless of the pay arrangement?

20. The length of a rectangular garden is 2 feet more than twice its width. If 22 feet of fencing is needed to enclose the garden, what are its dimensions?

Polynomial and Rational Functions

3

We are surrounded by evidence that the world is profoundly mathematical. After turning a somersault, a diver's path can be modeled by a quadratic function, $f(x) = ax^2 + bx + c$, as can the path of a football tossed from quarterback to receiver or the path of a flipped coin. Even if you throw an object directly upward, although its path is straight and vertical, its changing height over time is described by a quadratic function. And tailgaters beware: whether you're driving a car, a motorcycle, or a truck on dry or wet roads, an array of quadratic functions that model your required stopping distances at various speeds are available to help you become a safer driver.

The quadratic functions surrounding our long history of throwing things appear throughout the chapter, including Example 5 in Section 3.1 and Example 4 in Section 3.6. Tailgaters should pay close attention to the Section 3.6 opener, Exercises 77–78 and 92–93 in Exercise Set 3.6, and Exercise 75 in the Chapter Review Exercises.

311

Section 3.1 **Quadratic Functions**

Objectives

1. Recognize characteristics of parabolas.
2. Graph parabolas.
3. Determine a quadratic function's minimum or maximum value.
4. Solve problems involving a quadratic function's minimum or maximum value.

Many sports involve objects that are thrown, kicked, or hit, and then proceed with no additional force of their own. Such objects are called **projectiles**. Paths of projectiles, as well as their heights over time, can be modeled by quadratic functions. We have seen that a **quadratic function** is any function of the form

$$f(x) = ax^2 + bx + c,$$

where a, b, and c are real numbers, with $a \neq 0$. A quadratic function is a polynomial function whose greatest exponent is 2. In this section, you will learn to use graphs of quadratic functions to gain a visual understanding of the algebra that describes football, baseball, basketball, the shot put, and other projectile sports.

1. Recognize characteristics of parabolas.

Graphs of Quadratic Functions

The graph of any quadratic function is called a **parabola**. Parabolas are shaped like bowls or inverted bowls, as shown in **Figure 3.1**. If the coefficient of x^2 (the value of a in $ax^2 + bx + c$) is positive, the parabola opens upward. If the coefficient of x^2 is negative, the parabola opens downward. The **vertex** (or turning point) of the parabola is the lowest point on the graph when it opens upward and the highest point on the graph when it opens downward.

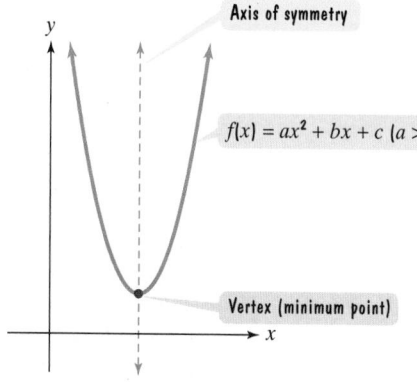

$a > 0$: Parabola opens upward.

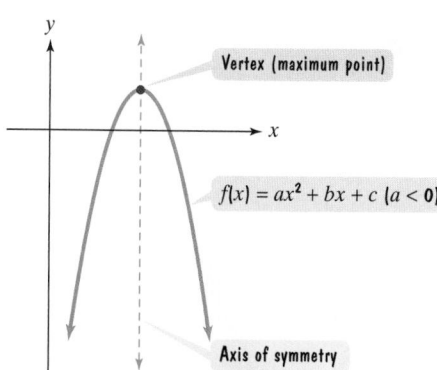

$a < 0$: Parabola opens downward.

Figure 3.1 Characteristics of graphs of quadratic functions

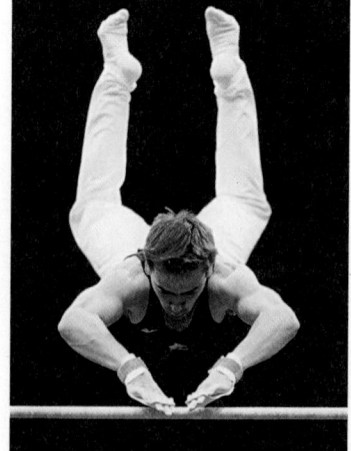

Look at the unusual image of the word *mirror* shown below. The artist, Scott Kim, has created the image so that the two halves of the whole are mirror images of each other. A parabola shares this kind of symmetry, in which a vertical line through the vertex divides the figure in half. Parabolas are symmetric with respect to this line, called the **axis of symmetry**. If a parabola is folded along its axis of symmetry, the two halves match exactly.

② Graph parabolas.

Graphing Quadratic Functions in Standard Form

In our earlier work with transformations, we applied a series of transformations to the graph of $f(x) = x^2$. The graph of this function is a parabola. The vertex for this parabola is $(0, 0)$. In **Figure 3.2(a)**, the graph of $f(x) = ax^2$ for $a > 0$ is shown in black; it opens *upward*. In **Figure 3.2(b)**, the graph of $f(x) = ax^2$ for $a < 0$ is shown in black; it opens *downward*.

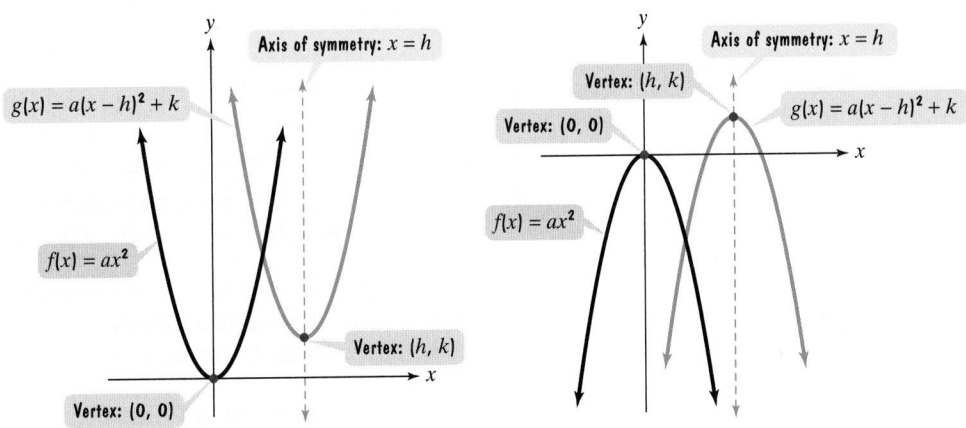

Figure 3.2(a) $a > 0$: Parabola opens upward. Figure 3.2(b) $a < 0$: Parabola opens downward.

Transformations of $f(x) = ax^2$

Figures 3.2(a) and **3.2(b)** also show the graph of $g(x) = a(x - h)^2 + k$ in blue. Compare these graphs to those of $f(x) = ax^2$. Observe that h determines a horizontal shift and k determines a vertical shift of the graph of $f(x) = ax^2$:

$$g(x) = a(x - h)^2 + k.$$

| If $h > 0$, the graph of $f(x) = ax^2$ is shifted h units to the right. | If $k > 0$, the graph of $y = a(x - h)^2$ is shifted k units up. |

Consequently, the vertex $(0, 0)$ on the black graph of $f(x) = ax^2$ moves to the point (h, k) on the blue graph of $g(x) = a(x - h)^2 + k$. The axis of symmetry is the vertical line whose equation is $x = h$.

The form of the expression for g is convenient because it immediately identifies the vertex of the parabola as (h, k). This is the **standard form** of a quadratic function.

The Standard Form of a Quadratic Function

The quadratic function

$$f(x) = a(x - h)^2 + k, \quad a \neq 0$$

is in **standard form**. The graph of f is a parabola whose vertex is the point (h, k). The parabola is symmetric with respect to the line $x = h$. If $a > 0$, the parabola opens upward; if $a < 0$, the parabola opens downward.

The sign of a in $f(x) = a(x - h)^2 + k$ determines whether the parabola opens upward or downward. Furthermore, if $|a|$ is small, the parabola opens more flatly than if $|a|$ is large. Here is a general procedure for graphing parabolas whose equations are in standard form:

Graphing Quadratic Functions with Equations in Standard Form

To graph $f(x) = a(x - h)^2 + k$,

1. Determine whether the parabola opens upward or downward. If $a > 0$, it opens upward. If $a < 0$, it opens downward.
2. Determine the vertex of the parabola. The vertex is (h, k).
3. Find any x-intercepts by solving $f(x) = 0$. The function's real zeros are the x-intercepts.
4. Find the y-intercept by computing $f(0)$.
5. Plot the intercepts, the vertex, and additional points as necessary. Connect these points with a smooth curve that is shaped like a bowl or an inverted bowl.

In the graphs that follow, we will show each axis of symmetry as a dashed vertical line. Because this vertical line passes through the vertex, (h, k), its equation is $x = h$. The line is dashed because it is not part of the parabola.

EXAMPLE 1 **Graphing a Quadratic Function in Standard Form**

Graph the quadratic function $f(x) = -2(x - 3)^2 + 8$.

Solution We can graph this function by following the steps in the preceding box. We begin by identifying values for a, h, and k.

Standard form
$$f(x) = a(x - h)^2 + k$$
$$a = -2 \quad h = 3 \quad k = 8$$
Given function
$$f(x) = -2(x - 3)^2 + 8$$

Step 1 Determine how the parabola opens. Note that a, the coefficient of x^2, is -2. Thus, $a < 0$; this negative value tells us that the parabola opens downward.

Step 2 Find the vertex. The vertex of the parabola is at (h, k). Because $h = 3$ and $k = 8$, the parabola has its vertex at $(3, 8)$.

Step 3 Find the x-intercepts by solving $f(x) = 0$. Replace $f(x)$ with 0 in $f(x) = -2(x - 3)^2 + 8$.

$$0 = -2(x - 3)^2 + 8 \qquad \text{Find x-intercepts, setting f(x) equal to 0.}$$
$$2(x - 3)^2 = 8 \qquad \text{Solve for x. Add } 2(x - 3)^2 \text{ to both sides of the equation.}$$
$$(x - 3)^2 = 4 \qquad \text{Divide both sides by 2.}$$
$$x - 3 = \sqrt{4} \quad \text{or} \quad x - 3 = -\sqrt{4} \qquad \text{Apply the square root property.}$$
$$x - 3 = 2 \qquad\qquad x - 3 = -2 \qquad \sqrt{4} = 2$$
$$x = 5 \qquad\qquad\quad x = 1 \qquad \text{Add 3 to both sides in each equation.}$$

The x-intercepts are 1 and 5. The parabola passes through $(1, 0)$ and $(5, 0)$.

Step 4 Find the y-intercept by computing $f(0)$. Replace x with 0 in $f(x) = -2(x - 3)^2 + 8$.

$$f(0) = -2(0 - 3)^2 + 8 = -2(-3)^2 + 8 = -2(9) + 8 = -10$$

The y-intercept is -10. The parabola passes through $(0, -10)$.

Step 5 Graph the parabola. With a vertex at $(3, 8)$, x-intercepts at 5 and 1, and a y-intercept at -10, the graph of f is shown in **Figure 3.3**. The axis of symmetry is the vertical line whose equation is $x = 3$.

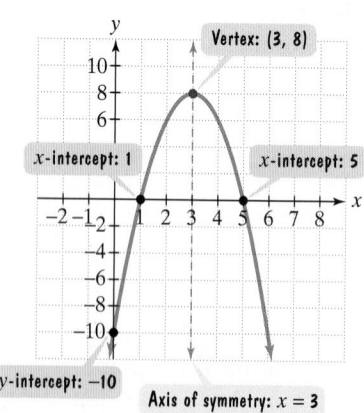

Figure 3.3 The graph of $f(x) = -2(x - 3)^2 + 8$

⬤ Check Point **1** Graph the quadratic function $f(x) = -(x - 1)^2 + 4$.

(**EXAMPLE 2**) **Graphing a Quadratic Function in Standard Form**

Graph the quadratic function $f(x) = (x + 3)^2 + 1$.

Solution We begin by finding values for a, h, and k.

$$f(x) = a(x - h)^2 + k \qquad \text{Standard form of quadratic function}$$
$$f(x) = (x + 3)^2 + 1 \qquad \text{Given function}$$
$$f(x) = 1(x - (-3))^2 + 1$$

$$\boxed{a = 1} \quad \boxed{h = -3} \quad \boxed{k = 1}$$

Step 1 Determine how the parabola opens. Note that a, the coefficient of x^2, is 1. Thus, $a > 0$; this positive value tells us that the parabola opens upward.

Step 2 Find the vertex. The vertex of the parabola is at (h, k). Because $h = -3$ and $k = 1$, the parabola has its vertex at $(-3, 1)$.

Step 3 Find the x-intercepts by solving $f(x) = 0$. Replace $f(x)$ with 0 in $f(x) = (x + 3)^2 + 1$. Because the vertex is at $(-3, 1)$, which lies above the x-axis, and the parabola opens upward, it appears that this parabola has no x-intercepts. We can verify this observation algebraically.

$$0 = (x + 3)^2 + 1 \qquad \text{Find possible x-intercepts, setting } f(x) \text{ equal to 0.}$$

$$-1 = (x + 3)^2 \qquad \text{Solve for x. Subtract 1 from both sides.}$$

$$x + 3 = \sqrt{-1} \quad \text{or} \quad x + 3 = -\sqrt{-1} \qquad \text{Apply the square root property.}$$

$$x + 3 = i \qquad\qquad x + 3 = -i \qquad \sqrt{-1} = i$$

$$x = -3 + i \qquad\qquad x = -3 - i \qquad \text{The solutions are } -3 \pm i.$$

Because this equation has no real solutions, the parabola has no x-intercepts.

Step 4 Find the y-intercept by computing $f(0)$. Replace x with 0 in $f(x) = (x + 3)^2 + 1$.

$$f(0) = (0 + 3)^2 + 1 = 3^2 + 1 = 9 + 1 = 10$$

The y-intercept is 10. The parabola passes through $(0, 10)$.

Step 5 Graph the parabola. With a vertex at $(-3, 1)$, no x-intercepts, and a y-intercept at 10, the graph of f is shown in **Figure 3.4**. The axis of symmetry is the vertical line whose equation is $x = -3$. ⬤

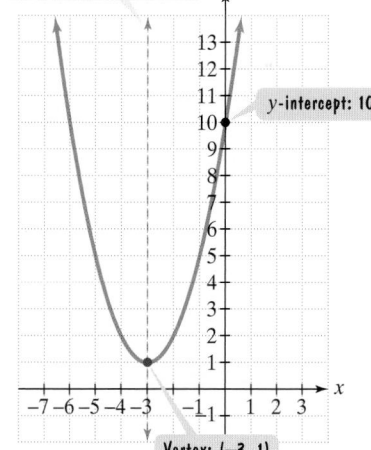

Figure 3.4 The graph of $f(x) = (x + 3)^2 + 1$

⬤ Check Point **2** Graph the quadratic function $f(x) = (x - 2)^2 + 1$.

Graphing Quadratic Functions in the Form $f(x) = ax^2 + bx + c$

Quadratic functions are frequently expressed in the form $f(x) = ax^2 + bx + c$. How can we identify the vertex of a parabola whose equation is in this form? Completing the square provides the answer to this question.

$$f(x) = ax^2 + bx + c$$

$$= a\left(x^2 + \frac{b}{a}x\right) + c \qquad \text{Factor out } a \text{ from } ax^2 + bx.$$

$$= a\left(x^2 + \frac{b}{a}x + \frac{b^2}{4a^2}\right) + c - a\left(\frac{b^2}{4a^2}\right)$$

> Complete the square by adding the square of half the coefficient of x.

> By completing the square, we added $a \cdot \dfrac{b^2}{4a^2}$. To avoid changing the function's equation, we must subtract this term.

$$= a\left(x + \frac{b}{2a}\right)^2 + c - \frac{b^2}{4a}$$

Write the trinomial as the square of a binomial and simplify the constant term.

Compare this form of the equation with a quadratic function's **standard form**.

Standard form $\qquad f(x) = a(x - h)^2 + k$

$$h = -\frac{b}{2a} \qquad k = c - \frac{b^2}{4a}$$

Equation under discussion $\qquad f(x) = a\left(x - \left(-\frac{b}{2a}\right)\right)^2 + c - \frac{b^2}{4a}$

The important part of this observation is that h, the x-coordinate of the vertex, is $-\dfrac{b}{2a}$. The y-coordinate can be found by evaluating the function at $-\dfrac{b}{2a}$.

The Vertex of a Parabola Whose Equation Is $f(x) = ax^2 + bx + c$

Consider the parabola defined by the quadratic function $f(x) = ax^2 + bx + c$. The parabola's vertex is $\left(-\dfrac{b}{2a}, f\left(-\dfrac{b}{2a}\right)\right)$. The x-coordinate is $-\dfrac{b}{2a}$. The y-coordinate is found by substituting the x-coordinate into the parabola's equation and evaluating the function at this value of x.

We can apply our five-step procedure to graph parabolas in the form $f(x) = ax^2 + bx + c$.

Graphing Quadratic Functions with Equations in the Form $f(x) = ax^2 + bx + c$

To graph $f(x) = ax^2 + bx + c$,

1. Determine whether the parabola opens upward or downward. If $a > 0$, it opens upward. If $a < 0$, it opens downward.

2. Determine the vertex of the parabola. The vertex is $\left(-\dfrac{b}{2a}, f\left(-\dfrac{b}{2a}\right)\right)$.

3. Find any x-intercepts by solving $f(x) = 0$. The real solutions of $ax^2 + bx + c = 0$ are the x-intercepts.

4. Find the y-intercept by computing $f(0)$. Because $f(0) = c$ (the constant term in the function's equation), the y-intercept is c and the parabola passes through $(0, c)$.

5. Plot the intercepts, the vertex, and additional points as necessary. Connect these points with a smooth curve.

EXAMPLE 3 **Graphing a Quadratic Function in the Form**
$$f(x) = ax^2 + bx + c$$

Graph the quadratic function $f(x) = -x^2 - 2x + 1$. Use the graph to identify the function's domain and its range.

Solution

Step 1 Determine how the parabola opens. Note that a, the coefficient of x^2, is -1. Thus, $a < 0$; this negative value tells us that the parabola opens downward.

Step 2 Find the vertex. We know that the x-coordinate of the vertex is $x = -\dfrac{b}{2a}$. We identify a, b, and c in $f(x) = ax^2 + bx + c$.

$$f(x) = -x^2 - 2x + 1$$

$$\boxed{a = -1} \quad \boxed{b = -2} \quad \boxed{c = 1}$$

Substitute the values of a and b into the equation for the x-coordinate:

$$x = -\frac{b}{2a} = -\frac{-2}{2(-1)} = -\left(\frac{-2}{-2}\right) = -1.$$

The x-coordinate of the vertex is -1. We substitute -1 for x in the equation of the function, $f(x) = -x^2 - 2x + 1$, to find the y-coordinate:

$$f(-1) = -(-1)^2 - 2(-1) + 1 = -1 + 2 + 1 = 2.$$

The vertex is at $(-1, 2)$.

Step 3 Find the x-intercepts by solving $f(x) = 0$. Replace $f(x)$ with 0 in $f(x) = -x^2 - 2x + 1$. We obtain $0 = -x^2 - 2x + 1$. This equation cannot be solved by factoring. We will use the quadratic formula to solve it.

$$-x^2 - 2x + 1 = 0$$

$$\boxed{a = -1} \quad \boxed{b = -2} \quad \boxed{c = 1}$$

$$x = \frac{-b \pm \sqrt{b^2 - 4ac}}{2a} = \frac{-(-2) \pm \sqrt{(-2)^2 - 4(-1)(1)}}{2(-1)} = \frac{2 \pm \sqrt{4 - (-4)}}{-2}$$

> To locate the x-intercepts, we need decimal approximations. Thus, there is no need to simplify the radical form of the solutions.

$$x = \frac{2 + \sqrt{8}}{-2} \approx -2.4 \quad \text{or} \quad x = \frac{2 - \sqrt{8}}{-2} \approx 0.4$$

The x-intercepts are approximately -2.4 and 0.4. The parabola passes through $(-2.4, 0)$ and $(0.4, 0)$.

Step 4 Find the y-intercept by computing $f(0)$. Replace x with 0 in $f(x) = -x^2 - 2x + 1$.

$$f(0) = -0^2 - 2 \cdot 0 + 1 = 1$$

The y-intercept is 1, which is the constant term in the function's equation. The parabola passes through $(0, 1)$.

Step 5 Graph the parabola. With a vertex at $(-1, 2)$, x-intercepts at approximately -2.4 and 0.4, and a y-intercept at 1, the graph of f is shown in **Figure 3.5(a)**. The axis of symmetry is the vertical line whose equation is $x = -1$.

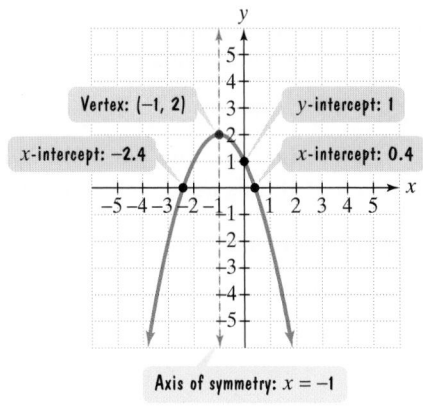

Figure 3.5(a) The graph of $f(x) = -x^2 - 2x + 1$

Figure 3.5(b) Determining the domain and range of $f(x) = -x^2 - 2x + 1$

Study Tip

The domain of any quadratic function includes all real numbers. If the vertex is the graph's highest point, the range includes all real numbers at or below the y-coordinate of the vertex. If the vertex is the graph's lowest point, the range includes all real numbers at or above the y-coordinate of the vertex.

Now we are ready to determine the domain and range of $f(x) = -x^2 - 2x + 1$. We can use the parabola, shown again in **Figure 3.5(b)**, to do so. To find the domain, look for all the inputs on the x-axis that correspond to points on the graph. As the graph widens and continues to fall at both ends, can you see that these inputs include all real numbers?

Domain of f is $\{x \mid x$ is a real number$\}$ or $(-\infty, \infty)$.

To find the range, look for all the outputs on the y-axis that correspond to points on the graph. **Figure 3.5(b)** shows that the parabola's vertex, $(-1, 2)$, is the highest point on the graph. Because the y-coordinate of the vertex is 2, outputs on the y-axis fall at or below 2.

Range of f is $\{y \mid y \le 2\}$ or $(-\infty, 2]$.

⊘ **Check Point 3** Graph the quadratic function $f(x) = -x^2 + 4x + 1$. Use the graph to identify the function's domain and its range.

③ Determine a quadratic function's minimum or maximum value.

Minimum and Maximum Values of Quadratic Functions

Consider the quadratic function $f(x) = ax^2 + bx + c$. If $a > 0$, the parabola opens upward and the vertex is its lowest point. If $a < 0$, the parabola opens downward and the vertex is its highest point. The x-coordinate of the vertex is $-\dfrac{b}{2a}$. Thus, we can find the minimum or maximum value of f by evaluating the quadratic function at $x = -\dfrac{b}{2a}$.

Minimum and Maximum: Quadratic Functions

Consider the quadratic function $f(x) = ax^2 + bx + c$.

1. If $a > 0$, then f has a minimum that occurs at $x = -\dfrac{b}{2a}$. This minimum value is $f\left(-\dfrac{b}{2a}\right)$.

2. If $a < 0$, then f has a maximum that occurs at $x = -\dfrac{b}{2a}$. This maximum value is $f\left(-\dfrac{b}{2a}\right)$.

In each case, the value of x gives the location of the minimum or maximum value. The value of y, or $f\left(-\dfrac{b}{2a}\right)$, gives that minimum or maximum value.

EXAMPLE 4 Obtaining Information about a Quadratic Function from Its Equation

Consider the quadratic function $f(x) = -3x^2 + 6x - 13$.

a. Determine, without graphing, whether the function has a minimum value or a maximum value.

b. Find the minimum or maximum value and determine where it occurs.

c. Identify the function's domain and its range.

Solution We begin by identifying a, b, and c in the function's equation:

$$f(x) = -3x^2 + 6x - 13.$$

$a = -3$ $b = 6$ $c = -13$

a. Because $a < 0$, the function has a maximum value.

b. The maximum value occurs at

$$x = -\frac{b}{2a} = -\frac{6}{2(-3)} = -\frac{6}{-6} = -(-1) = 1.$$

The maximum value occurs at $x = 1$ and the maximum value of $f(x) = -3x^2 + 6x - 13$ is

$$f(1) = -3 \cdot 1^2 + 6 \cdot 1 - 13 = -3 + 6 - 13 = -10.$$

We see that the maximum is -10 at $x = 1$.

c. Like all quadratic functions, the domain is $(-\infty, \infty)$. Because the function's maximum value is -10, the range includes all real numbers at or below -10. The range is $(-\infty, -10]$.

We can use the graph of $f(x) = -3x^2 + 6x - 13$ to visualize the results of Example 4. **Figure 3.6** shows the graph in a $[-6, 6, 1]$ by $[-50, 20, 10]$ viewing rectangle. The maximum function feature verifies that the function's maximum is -10 at $x = 1$. Notice that x gives the location of the maximum and y gives the maximum value. Notice, too, that the maximum value is -10 and not the ordered pair $(1, -10)$.

Range is $(-\infty, -10]$.

Maximum
X=1 Y=-10

$[-6, 6, 1]$ by $[-50, 20, 10]$

Figure 3.6

✓ Check Point 4 Repeat parts (a) through (c) of Example 4 using the quadratic function $f(x) = 4x^2 - 16x + 1000$.

④ Solve problems involving a quadratic function's minimum or maximum value.

Applications of Quadratic Functions

Many applied problems involve finding the maximum or minimum value of a quadratic function, as well as where this value occurs.

EXAMPLE 5 The Parabolic Path of a Punted Football

Figure 3.7 shows that when a football is kicked, the nearest defensive player is 6 feet from the point of impact with the kicker's foot. The height of the punted football, $f(x)$, in feet, can be modeled by

$$f(x) = -0.01x^2 + 1.18x + 2,$$

where x is the ball's horizontal distance, in feet, from the point of impact with the kicker's foot.

a. What is the maximum height of the punt and how far from the point of impact does this occur?

b. How far must the nearest defensive player, who is 6 feet from the kicker's point of impact, reach to block the punt?

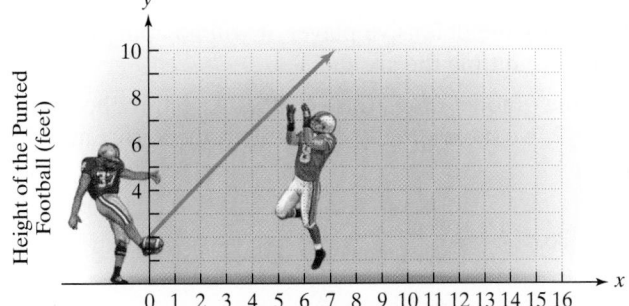

Height of the Punted Football (feet)

Distance from the Point of Impact (feet)

Figure 3.7

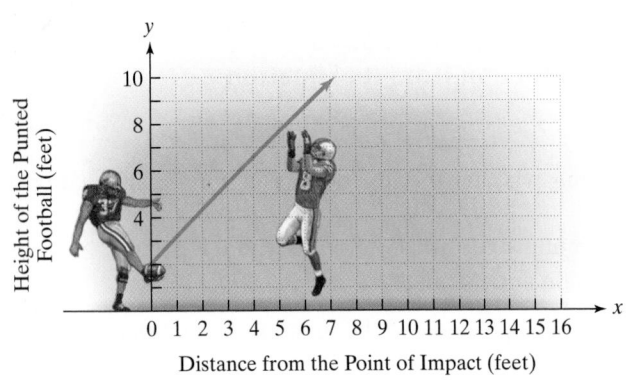

Height of the Punted Football (feet)

Distance from the Point of Impact (feet)

Figure 3.7 (repeated)

c. If the ball is not blocked by the defensive player, how far down the field will it go before hitting the ground?

d. Graph the function that models the football's parabolic path.

Solution

a. We begin by identifying the numbers $a, b,$ and c in the function's equation.

$$f(x) = -0.01x^2 + 1.18x + 2$$

$a = -0.01 \qquad b = 1.18 \qquad c = 2$

Because $a < 0$, the function has a maximum that occurs at $x = -\dfrac{b}{2a}$.

$$x = -\frac{b}{2a} = -\frac{1.18}{2(-0.01)} = -(-59) = 59$$

This means that the maximum height of the punt occurs 59 feet from the kicker's point of impact. The maximum height of the punt is

$$f(59) = -0.01(59)^2 + 1.18(59) + 2 = 36.81,$$

or 36.81 feet.

b. **Figure 3.7** shows that the defensive player is 6 feet from the kicker's point of impact. To block the punt, he must touch the football along its parabolic path. This means that we must find the height of the ball 6 feet from the kicker. Replace x with 6 in the given function, $f(x) = -0.01x^2 + 1.18x + 2$.

$$f(6) = -0.01(6)^2 + 1.18(6) + 2 = -0.36 + 7.08 + 2 = 8.72$$

The defensive player must reach 8.72 feet above the ground to block the punt.

c. Assuming that the ball is not blocked by the defensive player, we are interested in how far down the field it will go before hitting the ground. We are looking for the ball's horizontal distance, x, when its height above the ground, $f(x)$, is 0 feet. To find this x-intercept, replace $f(x)$ with 0 in $f(x) = -0.01x^2 + 1.18x + 2$. We obtain $0 = -0.01x^2 + 1.18x + 2$, or $-0.01x^2 + 1.18x + 2 = 0$. The equation cannot be solved by factoring. We will use the quadratic formula to solve it.

$-0.01x^2 + 1.18x + 2 = 0$

$a = -0.01 \qquad b = 1.18 \qquad c = 2$

The equation for determining the ball's maximum horizontal distance

Use a calculator to evaluate the radicand.

$$x = \frac{-b \pm \sqrt{b^2 - 4ac}}{2a} = \frac{-1.18 \pm \sqrt{(1.18)^2 - 4(-0.01)(2)}}{2(-0.01)} = \frac{-1.18 \pm \sqrt{1.4724}}{-0.02}$$

$$x = \frac{-1.18 + \sqrt{1.4724}}{-0.02} \qquad \text{or} \qquad x = \frac{-1.18 - \sqrt{1.4724}}{-0.02}$$

$$x \approx -1.7 \qquad\qquad\qquad x \approx 119.7 \qquad \text{Use a calculator and round to the nearest tenth.}$$

Reject this value. We are interested in the football's height corresponding to horizontal distances from its point of impact onward, or $x \geq 0$.

If the football is not blocked by the defensive player, it will go approximately 119.7 feet down the field before hitting the ground.

d. In terms of graphing the model for the football's parabolic path, $f(x) = -0.01x^2 + 1.18x + 2$, we have already determined the vertex and the approximate x-intercept.

vertex: $(59, 36.81)$

The ball's maximum height, 36.81 feet, occurs at a horizontal distance of 59 feet.

x-intercept: 119.7

The ball's maximum horizontal distance is approximately 119.7 feet.

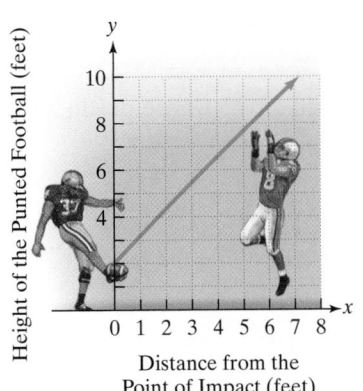

Figure 3.7 (partly repeated)

Figure 3.7 indicates that the y-intercept is 2, meaning that the ball is kicked from a height of 2 feet. Let's verify this value by replacing x with 0 in $f(x) = -0.01x^2 + 1.18x + 2$.

$$f(0) = -0.01 \cdot 0^2 + 1.18 \cdot 0 + 2 = 0 + 0 + 2 = 2$$

Using the vertex, $(59, 36.81)$, the x-intercept, 119.7, and the y-intercept, 2, the graph of the equation that models the football's parabolic path is shown in **Figure 3.8**. The graph is shown only for $x \geq 0$, indicating horizontal distances that begin at the football's impact with the kicker's foot and end with the ball hitting the ground.

Figure 3.8 The parabolic path of a punted football

Ø Check Point **5** An archer's arrow follows a parabolic path. The height of the arrow, $f(x)$, in feet, can be modeled by

$$f(x) = -0.005x^2 + 2x + 5,$$

where x is the arrow's horizontal distance, in feet.

a. What is the maximum height of the arrow and how far from its release does this occur?

b. Find the horizontal distance the arrow travels before it hits the ground. Round to the nearest foot.

c. Graph the function that models the arrow's parabolic path.

Quadratic functions can also be modeled from verbal conditions. Once we have obtained a quadratic function, we can then use the x-coordinate of the vertex to determine its maximum or minimum value. Here is a step-by-step strategy for solving these kinds of problems:

Strategy for Solving Problems Involving Maximizing or Minimizing Quadratic Functions

1. Read the problem carefully and decide which quantity is to be maximized or minimized.

2. Use the conditions of the problem to express the quantity as a function in one variable.

3. Rewrite the function in the form $f(x) = ax^2 + bx + c$.

4. Calculate $-\dfrac{b}{2a}$. If $a > 0$, f has a minimum at $x = -\dfrac{b}{2a}$. This minimum value is $f\left(-\dfrac{b}{2a}\right)$. If $a < 0$, f has a maximum at $x = -\dfrac{b}{2a}$. This maximum value is $f\left(-\dfrac{b}{2a}\right)$.

5. Answer the question posed in the problem.

(EXAMPLE 6) **Minimizing a Product**

Among all pairs of numbers whose difference is 10, find a pair whose product is as small as possible. What is the minimum product?

Solution

Step 1 Decide what must be maximized or minimized. We must minimize the product of two numbers. Calling the numbers x and y, and calling the product P, we must minimize

$$P = xy.$$

Step 2 Express this quantity as a function in one variable. In the formula $P = xy$, P is expressed in terms of two variables, x and y. However, because the difference of the numbers is 10, we can write

$$x - y = 10.$$

We can solve this equation for y in terms of x (or vice versa), substitute the result into $P = xy$, and obtain P as a function of one variable.

$$-y = -x + 10 \quad \text{Subtract x from both sides of } x - y = 10.$$

$$y = x - 10 \quad \text{Multiply both sides of the equation by } -1 \text{ and solve for y.}$$

Now we substitute $x - 10$ for y in $P = xy$.

$$P = xy = x(x - 10)$$

Because P is now a function of x, we can write

$$P(x) = x(x - 10)$$

Step 3 Write the function in the form $f(x) = ax^2 + bx + c$. We apply the distributive property to obtain

$$P(x) = x(x - 10) = x^2 - 10x.$$

$$\boxed{a = 1} \quad \boxed{b = -10}$$

Technology

Numeric Connections

The TABLE feature of a graphing utility can be used to verify our work in Example 6.

Enter $y_1 = x^2 - 10x$, the function for the product, when one of the numbers is x.

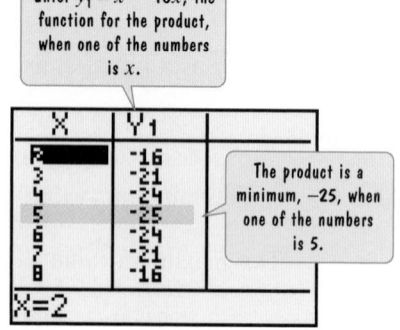

The product is a minimum, −25, when one of the numbers is 5.

$X=2$

Step 4 Calculate $-\dfrac{b}{2a}$. If $a > 0$, the function has a minimum at this value. The voice balloons show that $a = 1$ and $b = -10$.

$$x = -\frac{b}{2a} = -\frac{-10}{2(1)} = -(-5) = 5$$

This means that the product, P, of two numbers whose difference is 10 is a minimum when one of the numbers, x, is 5.

Step 5 Answer the question posed by the problem. The problem asks for the two numbers and the minimum product. We found that one of the numbers, x, is 5. Now we must find the second number, y.

$$y = x - 10 = 5 - 10 = -5$$

The number pair whose difference is 10 and whose product is as small as possible is 5, −5. The minimum product is $5(-5)$, or −25. ●

⊘ Check Point **6** Among all pairs of numbers whose difference is 8, find a pair whose product is as small as possible. What is the minimum product?

(**EXAMPLE 7**) **Maximizing Area**

You have 100 yards of fencing to enclose a rectangular region. Find the dimensions of the rectangle that maximize the enclosed area. What is the maximum area?

Solution

Step 1 Decide what must be maximized or minimized. We must maximize area. What we do not know are the rectangle's dimensions, x and y.

Step 2 Express this quantity as a function in one variable. Because we must maximize the area of a rectangle, we have $A = xy$. We need to transform this into a function in which A is represented by one variable. Because you have 100 yards of fencing, the perimeter of the rectangle is 100 yards. This means that

$$2x + 2y = 100.$$

We can solve this equation for y in terms of x, substitute the result into $A = xy$, and obtain A as a function in one variable. We begin by solving for y.

$$2y = 100 - 2x \quad \text{Subtract 2x from both sides of 2x + 2y = 100.}$$

$$y = \frac{100 - 2x}{2} \quad \text{Divide both sides by 2.}$$

$$y = 50 - x \quad \text{Divide each term in the numerator by 2.}$$

Now we substitute $50 - x$ for y in $A = xy$.

$$A = xy = x(50 - x)$$

The rectangle and its dimensions are illustrated in **Figure 3.9**. Because A is now a function of x, we can write

$$A(x) = x(50 - x).$$

This function models the area, $A(x)$, of any rectangle whose perimeter is 100 yards in terms of one of its dimensions, x.

Step 3 Write the function in the form $f(x) = ax^2 + bx + c$. We apply the distributive property to obtain

$$A(x) = x(50 - x) = 50x - x^2 = -x^2 + 50x.$$

$a = -1$ $b = 50$

Step 4 Calculate $-\dfrac{b}{2a}$. If $a < 0$, the function has a maximum at this value. The voice balloons show that $a = -1$ and $b = 50$.

$$x = -\frac{b}{2a} = -\frac{50}{2(-1)} = 25$$

This means that the area, $A(x)$, of a rectangle with perimeter 100 yards is a maximum when one of the rectangle's dimensions, x, is 25 yards.

Step 5 Answer the question posed by the problem. We found that $x = 25$. **Figure 3.9** shows that the rectangle's other dimension is $50 - x = 50 - 25 = 25$. The dimensions of the rectangle that maximize the enclosed area are 25 yards by 25 yards. The rectangle that gives the maximum area is actually a square with an area of 25 yards \cdot 25 yards, or 625 square yards. ●

Figure 3.9 What value of x will maximize the rectangle's area?

Technology

Graphic Connections

The graph of the area function

$$A(x) = x(50 - x)$$

was obtained with a graphing utility using a [0, 50, 2] by [0, 700, 25] viewing rectangle. The maximum function feature verifies that a maximum area of 625 square yards occurs when one of the dimensions is 25 yards.

(✓ Check Point **7** You have 120 feet of fencing to enclose a rectangular region. Find the dimensions of the rectangle that maximize the enclosed area. What is the maximum area?

Exercise Set 3.1

Practice Exercises

In Exercises 1–4, the graph of a quadratic function is given. Write the function's equation, selecting from the following options.

$$f(x) = (x + 1)^2 - 1 \qquad g(x) = (x + 1)^2 + 1$$
$$h(x) = (x - 1)^2 + 1 \qquad j(x) = (x - 1)^2 - 1$$

1.

2.

3.

4.

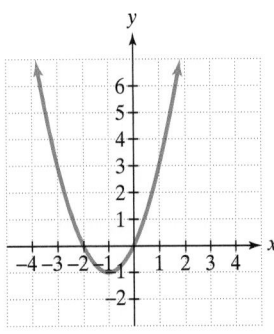

In Exercises 5–8, the graph of a quadratic function is given. Write the function's equation, selecting from the following options.

$$f(x) = x^2 + 2x + 1 \qquad g(x) = x^2 - 2x + 1$$
$$h(x) = x^2 - 1 \qquad j(x) = -x^2 - 1$$

5.

6.

7.

8.

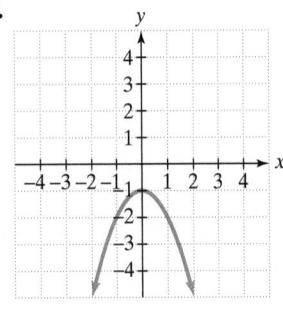

In Exercises 9–16, find the coordinates of the vertex for the parabola defined by the given quadratic function.

9. $f(x) = 2(x - 3)^2 + 1$
10. $f(x) = -3(x - 2)^2 + 12$
11. $f(x) = -2(x + 1)^2 + 5$
12. $f(x) = -2(x + 4)^2 - 8$
13. $f(x) = 2x^2 - 8x + 3$
14. $f(x) = 3x^2 - 12x + 1$
15. $f(x) = -x^2 - 2x + 8$
16. $f(x) = -2x^2 + 8x - 1$

In Exercises 17–38, use the vertex and intercepts to sketch the graph of each quadratic function. Give the equation of the parabola's axis of symmetry. Use the graph to determine the function's domain and range.

17. $f(x) = (x - 4)^2 - 1$
18. $f(x) = (x - 1)^2 - 2$
19. $f(x) = (x - 1)^2 + 2$
20. $f(x) = (x - 3)^2 + 2$
21. $y - 1 = (x - 3)^2$
22. $y - 3 = (x - 1)^2$
23. $f(x) = 2(x + 2)^2 - 1$
24. $f(x) = \frac{5}{4} - \left(x - \frac{1}{2}\right)^2$
25. $f(x) = 4 - (x - 1)^2$
26. $f(x) = 1 - (x - 3)^2$
27. $f(x) = x^2 - 2x - 3$
28. $f(x) = x^2 - 2x - 15$
29. $f(x) = x^2 + 3x - 10$
30. $f(x) = 2x^2 - 7x - 4$
31. $f(x) = 2x - x^2 + 3$
32. $f(x) = 5 - 4x - x^2$
33. $f(x) = x^2 + 6x + 3$
34. $f(x) = x^2 + 4x - 1$
35. $f(x) = 2x^2 + 4x - 3$
36. $f(x) = 3x^2 - 2x - 4$
37. $f(x) = 2x - x^2 - 2$
38. $f(x) = 6 - 4x + x^2$

In Exercises 39–44, an equation of a quadratic function is given.

 a. Determine, without graphing, whether the function has a minimum value or a maximum value.

 b. Find the minimum or maximum value and determine where it occurs.

 c. Identify the function's domain and its range.

39. $f(x) = 3x^2 - 12x - 1$
40. $f(x) = 2x^2 - 8x - 3$
41. $f(x) = -4x^2 + 8x - 3$
42. $f(x) = -2x^2 - 12x + 3$
43. $f(x) = 5x^2 - 5x$
44. $f(x) = 6x^2 - 6x$

Practice Plus

In Exercises 45–48, give the domain and the range of each quadratic function whose graph is described.

45. The vertex is $(-1, -2)$ and the parabola opens up.
46. The vertex is $(-3, -4)$ and the parabola opens down.
47. Maximum $= -6$ at $x = 10$
48. Minimum $= 18$ at $x = -6$

In Exercises 49–52, write an equation in standard form of the parabola that has the same shape as the graph of $f(x) = 2x^2$, but with the given point as the vertex.

49. $(5, 3)$
50. $(7, 4)$
51. $(-10, -5)$
52. $(-8, -6)$

In Exercises 53–56, write an equation in standard form of the parabola that has the same shape as the graph of $f(x) = 3x^2$ or $g(x) = -3x^2$, but with the given maximum or minimum.

53. Maximum $= 4$ at $x = -2$
54. Maximum $= -7$ at $x = 5$
55. Minimum $= 0$ at $x = 11$
56. Minimum $= 0$ at $x = 9$

Application Exercises

An athlete whose event is the shot put releases the shot with the same initial velocity, but at different angles. The figure shows the parabolic paths for shots released at angles of 35° and 65°. Exercises 57–58 are based on the functions that model the parabolic paths.

57. When the shot whose path is shown by the blue graph is released at an angle of 35°, its height, $f(x)$, in feet, can be modeled by

$$f(x) = -0.01x^2 + 0.7x + 6.1,$$

where x is the shot's horizontal distance, in feet, from its point of release. Use this model to solve parts (a) through (c) and verify your answers using the blue graph.

a. What is the maximum height of the shot and how far from its point of release does this occur?

b. What is the shot's maximum horizontal distance, to the nearest tenth of a foot, or the distance of the throw?

c. From what height was the shot released?

58. When the shot whose path is shown by the red graph is released at an angle of 65°, its height, $g(x)$, in feet, can be modeled by

$$g(x) = -0.04x^2 + 2.1x + 6.1,$$

where x is the shot's horizontal distance, in feet, from its point of release. Use this model to solve parts (a) through (c) and verify your answers using the red graph.

a. What is the maximum height, to the nearest tenth of a foot, of the shot and how far from its point of release does this occur?

b. What is the shot's maximum horizontal distance, to the nearest tenth of a foot, or the distance of the throw?

c. From what height was the shot released?

59. The graph at the top of the next column shows U.S. adult wine consumption, in gallons per person, for selected years from 1980 through 2005.

The function

$$f(x) = 0.004x^2 - 0.094x + 2.6$$

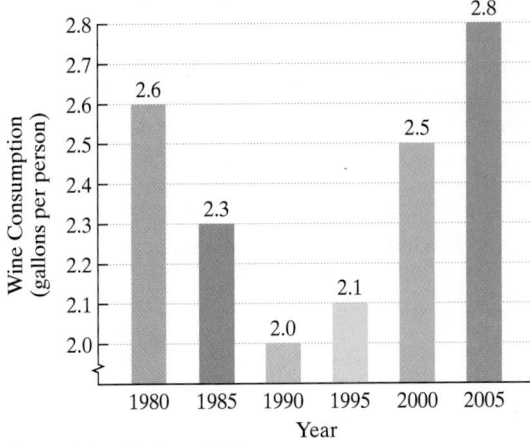

Source: Adams Business Media

models U.S. wine consumption, $f(x)$, in gallons per person, x years after 1980.

a. According to this function, what was U.S. adult wine consumption in 2005? Does this overestimate or underestimate the value shown by the graph? By how much?

b. According to this function, in which year was wine consumption at a minimum? Round to the nearest year. What does the function give for per capita consumption for that year? Does this seem reasonable in terms of the data shown by the graph or has model breakdown occurred?

60. The graph shows the number of movie tickets sold in the United States, in billions, from 2000 through 2005.

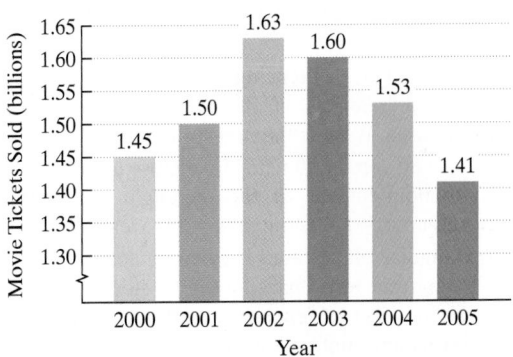

Source: National Association of Theater Owners

The function

$$f(x) = -0.03x^2 + 0.14x + 1.43$$

models U.S. movie attendance, $f(x)$, in billions of tickets sold, x years after 2000.

a. According to this function, how many billions of movie tickets were sold in 2005? Does this overestimate or underestimate the number shown by the graph? By how much?

b. According to this function, in which year was movie attendance at a maximum? Round to the nearest year. What does the function give for the billions of tickets sold for that year? By how much does this differ from the number shown by the graph?

61. Among all pairs of numbers whose sum is 16, find a pair whose product is as large as possible. What is the maximum product?

62. Among all pairs of numbers whose sum is 20, find a pair whose product is as large as possible. What is the maximum product?

63. Among all pairs of numbers whose difference is 16, find a pair whose product is as small as possible. What is the minimum product?

64. Among all pairs of numbers whose difference is 24, find a pair whose product is as small as possible. What is the minimum product?

65. You have 600 feet of fencing to enclose a rectangular plot that borders on a river. If you do not fence the side along the river, find the length and width of the plot that will maximize the area. What is the largest area that can be enclosed?

66. You have 200 feet of fencing to enclose a rectangular plot that borders on a river. If you do not fence the side along the river, find the length and width of the plot that will maximize the area. What is the largest area that can be enclosed?

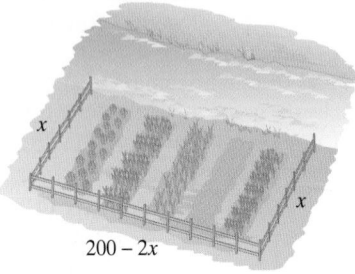

67. You have 50 yards of fencing to enclose a rectangular region. Find the dimensions of the rectangle that maximize the enclosed area. What is the maximum area?

68. You have 80 yards of fencing to enclose a rectangular region. Find the dimensions of the rectangle that maximize the enclosed area. What is the maximum area?

69. A rectangular playground is to be fenced off and divided in two by another fence parallel to one side of the playground. Six hundred feet of fencing is used. Find the dimensions of the playground that maximize the total enclosed area. What is the maximum area?

70. A rectangular playground is to be fenced off and divided in two by another fence parallel to one side of the playground. Four hundred feet of fencing is used. Find the dimensions of the playground that maximize the total enclosed area. What is the maximum area?

71. A rain gutter is made from sheets of aluminum that are 20 inches wide by turning up the edges to form right angles. Determine the depth of the gutter that will maximize its cross-sectional area and allow the greatest amount of water to flow. What is the maximum cross-sectional area?

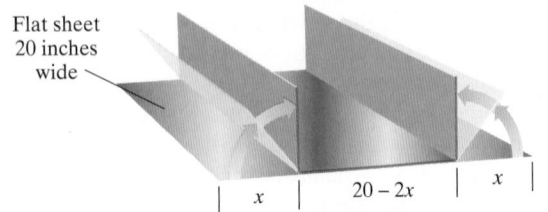

72. A rain gutter is made from sheets of aluminum that are 12 inches wide by turning up the edges to form right angles. Determine the depth of the gutter that will maximize its cross-sectional area and allow the greatest amount of water to flow. What is the maximum cross-sectional area?

73. Hunky Beef, a local sandwich store, has a fixed weekly cost of $525.00, and variable costs for making a roast beef sandwich are $0.55.

 a. Let x represent the number of roast beef sandwiches made and sold each week. Write the weekly cost function, C, for Hunky Beef. (*Hint:* The cost function is the sum of fixed and variable costs.)

 b. The function $R(x) = -0.001x^2 + 3x$ describes the money, in dollars, that Hunky Beef takes in each week from the sale of x roast beef sandwiches. Use this revenue function and the cost function from part (a) to write the store's weekly profit function, P. (*Hint:* The profit function is the difference between revenue and cost functions.)

 c. Use the store's profit function to determine the number of roast beef sandwiches it should make and sell each week to maximize profit. What is the maximum weekly profit?

Writing in Mathematics

74. What is a quadratic function?

75. What is a parabola? Describe its shape.

76. Explain how to decide whether a parabola opens upward or downward.

77. Describe how to find a parabola's vertex if its equation is expressed in standard form. Give an example.

78. Describe how to find a parabola's vertex if its equation is in the form $f(x) = ax^2 + bx + c$. Use $f(x) = x^2 - 6x + 8$ as an example.

79. A parabola that opens upward has its vertex at $(1, 2)$. Describe as much as you can about the parabola based on this information. Include in your discussion the number of x-intercepts (if any) for the parabola.

Technology Exercises

80. Use a graphing utility to verify any five of your hand-drawn graphs in Exercises 17–38.

81. a. Use a graphing utility to graph $y = 2x^2 - 82x + 720$ in a standard viewing rectangle. What do you observe?

 b. Find the coordinates of the vertex for the given quadratic function.

 c. The answer to part (b) is $(20.5, -120.5)$. Because the leading coefficient, 2, of the given function is positive, the vertex is a minimum point on the graph. Use this fact to help find a viewing rectangle that will give a relatively complete picture of the parabola. With an axis of symmetry at $x = 20.5$, the setting for x should extend past this, so try Xmin $= 0$ and Xmax $= 30$. The setting for y should include (and probably go below) the y-coordinate of the graph's minimum y-value, so try Ymin $= -130$. Experiment with Ymax until your utility shows the parabola's major features.

d. In general, explain how knowing the coordinates of a parabola's vertex can help determine a reasonable viewing rectangle on a graphing utility for obtaining a complete picture of the parabola.

In Exercises 82–85, find the vertex for each parabola. Then determine a reasonable viewing rectangle on your graphing utility and use it to graph the quadratic function.

82. $y = -0.25x^2 + 40x$

83. $y = -4x^2 + 20x + 160$

84. $y = 5x^2 + 40x + 600$

85. $y = 0.01x^2 + 0.6x + 100$

86. The following data show fuel efficiency, in miles per gallon, for all U.S. automobiles in the indicated year.

x (Years after 1940)	*y* (Average Number of Miles per Gallon for U.S. Automobiles)
1940: 0	14.8
1950: 10	13.9
1960: 20	13.4
1970: 30	13.5
1980: 40	15.9
1990: 50	20.2
2000: 60	22.0

Source: U.S. Department of Transportation

a. Use a graphing utility to draw a scatter plot of the data. Explain why a quadratic function is appropriate for modeling these data.

b. Use the quadratic regression feature to find the quadratic function that best fits the data.

c. Use the model in part (b) to determine the worst year for automobile fuel efficiency. What was the average number of miles per gallon for that year?

d. Use a graphing utility to draw a scatter plot of the data and graph the quadratic function of best fit on the scatter plot.

Critical Thinking Exercises

Make Sense? *In Exercises 87–90, determine whether each statement makes sense or does not make sense, and explain your reasoning.*

87. I must have made an error when graphing this parabola because its axis of symmetry is the *y*-axis.

88. I like to think of a parabola's vertex as the point where it intersects its axis of symmetry.

89. I threw a baseball vertically upward and its path was a parabola.

90. **Figure 3.7** on page 319 shows that a linear function provides a better description of the football's path than a quadratic function.

In Exercises 91–94, determine whether each statement is true or false. If the statement is false, make the necessary change(s) to produce a true statement.

91. No quadratic functions have a range of $(-\infty, \infty)$.

92. The vertex of the parabola described by $f(x) = 2(x - 5)^2 - 1$ is at $(5, 1)$.

93. The graph of $f(x) = -2(x + 4)^2 - 8$ has one *y*-intercept and two *x*-intercepts.

94. The maximum value of *y* for the quadratic fu. $f(x) = -x^2 + x + 1$ is 1.

In Exercises 95–96, find the axis of symmetry for each parabola whose equation is given. Use the axis of symmetry to find a second point on the parabola whose y-coordinate is the same as the given point.

95. $f(x) = 3(x + 2)^2 - 5$; $(-1, -2)$

96. $f(x) = (x - 3)^2 + 2$; $(6, 11)$

In Exercises 97–98, write the equation of each parabola in standard form.

97. Vertex: $(-3, -4)$; The graph passes through the point $(1, 4)$.

98. Vertex: $(-3, -1)$; The graph passes through the point $(-2, -3)$.

99. A rancher has 1000 feet of fencing to construct six corrals, as shown in the figure. Find the dimensions that maximize the enclosed area. What is the maximum area?

100. The annual yield per lemon tree is fairly constant at 320 pounds when the number of trees per acre is 50 or fewer. For each additional tree over 50, the annual yield per tree for all trees on the acre decreases by 4 pounds due to overcrowding. Find the number of trees that should be planted on an acre to produce the maximum yield. How many pounds is the maximum yield?

Group Exercise

101. Each group member should consult an almanac, newspaper, magazine, or the Internet to find data that initially increase and then decrease, or vice versa, and therefore can be modeled by a quadratic function. Group members should select the two sets of data that are most interesting and relevant. For each data set selected,

a. Use the quadratic regression feature of a graphing utility to find the quadratic function that best fits the data.

b. Use the equation of the quadratic function to make a prediction from the data. What circumstances might affect the accuracy of your prediction?

c. Use the equation of the quadratic function to write and solve a problem involving maximizing or minimizing the function.

Preview Exercises

Exercises 102–104 will help you prepare for the material covered in the next section.

102. Factor: $x^3 + 3x^2 - x - 3$.

103. If $f(x) = x^3 - 2x - 5$, find $f(2)$ and $f(3)$. Then explain why the continuous graph of f must cross the *x*-axis between 2 and 3.

104. Determine whether $f(x) = x^4 - 2x^2 + 1$ is even, odd, or neither. Describe the symmetry, if any, for the graph of f.

Section **3.2** **Polynomial Functions and Their Graphs**

Objectives

① Identify polynomial functions.

② Recognize characteristics of graphs of polynomial functions.

③ Determine end behavior.

④ Use factoring to find zeros of polynomial functions.

⑤ Identify zeros and their multiplicities.

⑥ Use the Intermediate Value Theorem.

⑦ Understand the relationship between degree and turning points.

⑧ Graph polynomial functions.

In 1980, U.S. doctors diagnosed 41 cases of a rare form of cancer, Kaposi's sarcoma, that involved skin lesions, pneumonia, and severe immunological deficiencies. All cases involved gay men ranging in age from 26 to 51. By the end of 2005, more than one million Americans, straight and gay, male and female, old and young, were infected with the HIV virus.

Modeling AIDS-related data and making predictions about the epidemic's havoc is serious business. **Figure 3.10** shows the number of AIDS cases diagnosed in the United States from 1983 through 2005.

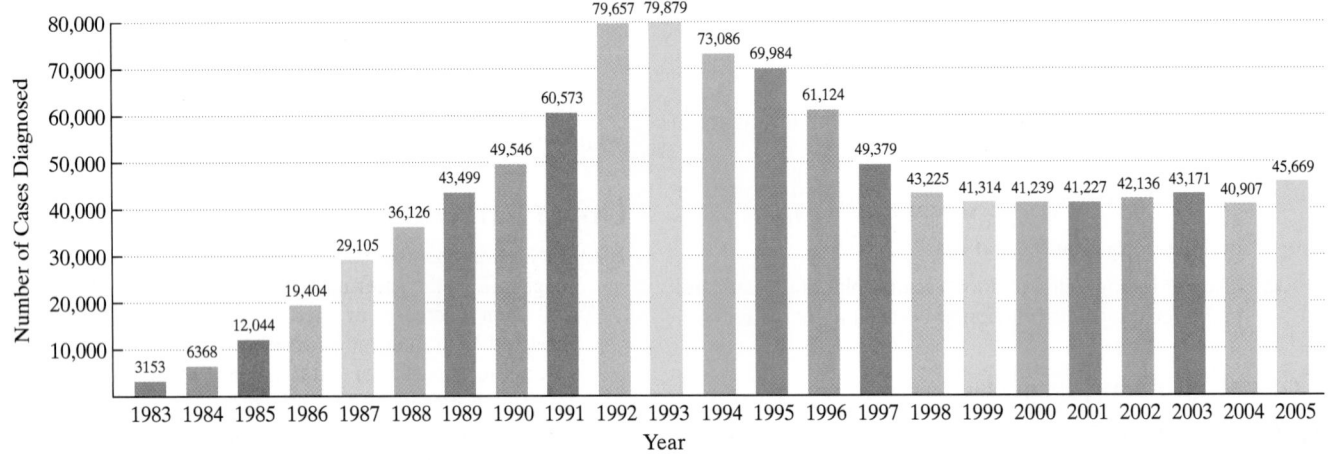

AIDS Cases Diagnosed in the United States, 1983–2005

Figure 3.10
Source: Department of Health and Human Services

① Identify polynomial functions.

Changing circumstances and unforeseen events can result in models for AIDS-related data that are not particularly useful over long periods of time. For example, the function

$$f(x) = -49x^3 + 806x^2 + 3776x + 2503$$

models the number of AIDS cases diagnosed in the United States x years after 1983. The model was obtained using a portion of the data shown in **Figure 3.10**, namely cases diagnosed from 1983 through 1991, inclusive. **Figure 3.11** shows the graph of f from 1983 through 1991. This function is an example of a *polynomial function of degree 3.*

$f(x) = -49x^3 + 806x^2 + 3776x + 2503$

[0, 8, 1] by [0, 60,000, 5000]

Figure 3.11 The graph of a function modeling the number of AIDS diagnoses from 1983 through 1991

Definition of a Polynomial Function

Let n be a nonnegative integer and let $a_n, a_{n-1}, \ldots, a_2, a_1, a_0$ be real numbers, with $a_n \neq 0$. The function defined by

$$f(x) = a_n x^n + a_{n-1}x^{n-1} + \cdots + a_2 x^2 + a_1 x + a_0$$

is called a **polynomial function of degree n**. The number a_n, the coefficient of the variable to the highest power, is called the **leading coefficient**.

Polynomial Functions	**Not Polynomial Functions**

Polynomial Functions

$f(x) = -3x^5 + \sqrt{2}x^2 + 5$

> Polynomial function of degree 5

$g(x) = -3x^4(x - 2)(x + 3)$
$= -3x^4(x^2 + x - 6)$
$= -3x^6 - 3x^5 + 18x^4$

> Polynomial function of degree 6

Not Polynomial Functions

$F(x) = -3\sqrt{x} + \sqrt{2}x^2 + 5$
$\quad = -3x^{\frac{1}{2}} + \sqrt{2}x^2 + 5$

> The exponent on the variable is not an integer.

$G(x) = -\dfrac{3}{x^2} + \sqrt{2}x^2 + 5$
$\quad = -3x^{-2} + \sqrt{2}x^2 + 5$

> The exponent on the variable is not a nonnegative integer.

A constant function $f(x) = c$, where $c \neq 0$, is a polynomial function of degree 0. A linear function $f(x) = mx + b$, where $m \neq 0$, is a polynomial function of degree 1. A quadratic function $f(x) = ax^2 + bx + c$, where $a \neq 0$, is a polynomial function of degree 2. In this section, we focus on polynomial functions of degree 3 or higher.

② Recognize characteristics of graphs of polynomial functions.

Smooth, Continuous Graphs

Polynomial functions of degree 2 or higher have graphs that are *smooth* and *continuous*. By **smooth**, we mean that the graphs contain only rounded curves with no sharp corners. By **continuous**, we mean that the graphs have no breaks and can be drawn without lifting your pencil from the rectangular coordinate system. These ideas are illustrated in **Figure 3.12**.

Graphs of Polynomial Functions

Not Graphs of Polynomial Functions

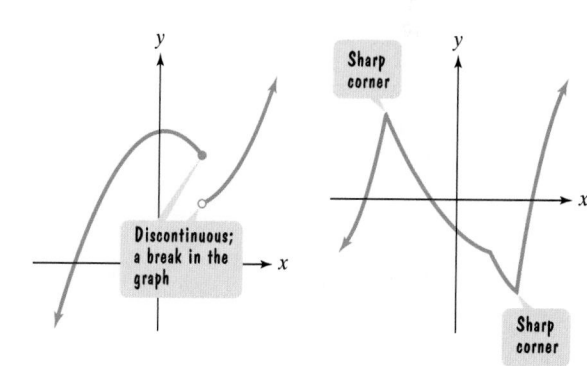

Figure 3.12 Recognizing graphs of polynomial functions

③ Determine end behavior.

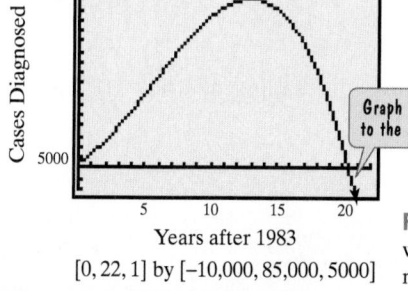

Years after 1983

$[0, 22, 1]$ by $[-10{,}000, 85{,}000, 5000]$

End Behavior of Polynomial Functions

Figure 3.13 shows the graph of the function

$$f(x) = -49x^3 + 806x^2 + 3776x + 2503,$$

which models the number of U.S. AIDS diagnosed from 1983 through 1991. Look what happens to the graph when we extend the year up through 2005. By year 21 (2004), the values of y are negative and the function no longer models AIDS diagnoses. We've added an arrow to the graph at the far right to emphasize that it continues to decrease without bound. It is this far-right *end behavior* of the graph that makes it inappropriate for modeling AIDS cases into the future.

Figure 3.13 By extending the viewing rectangle, we see that y is eventually negative and the function no longer models the number of AIDS cases.

The behavior of the graph of a function to the far left or the far right is called its **end behavior**. Although the graph of a polynomial function may have intervals where it increases or decreases, the graph will eventually rise or fall without bound as it moves far to the left or far to the right.

How can you determine whether the graph of a polynomial function goes up or down at each end? The end behavior of a polynomial function

$$f(x) = a_n x^n + a_{n-1} x^{n-1} + \cdots + a_1 x + a_0$$

depends upon the leading term $a_n x^n$, because when $|x|$ is large, the other terms are relatively insignificant in size. In particular, the sign of the leading coefficient, a_n, and the degree, n, of the polynomial function reveal its end behavior. In terms of end behavior, only the term of highest degree counts, as summarized by the **Leading Coefficient Test**.

The Leading Coefficient Test

As x increases or decreases without bound, the graph of the polynomial function

$$f(x) = a_n x^n + a_{n-1} x^{n-1} + a_{n-2} x^{n-2} + \cdots + a_1 x + a_0 \quad (a_n \neq 0)$$

eventually rises or falls. In particular,

1. For n odd:

If the leading coefficient is positive, the graph falls to the left and rises to the right. (\swarrow, \nearrow)

If the leading coefficient is negative, the graph rises to the left and falls to the right. (\nwarrow, \searrow)

2. For n even:

If the leading coefficient is positive, the graph rises to the left and rises to the right. (\nwarrow, \nearrow)

If the leading coefficient is negative, the graph falls to the left and falls to the right. (\swarrow, \searrow)

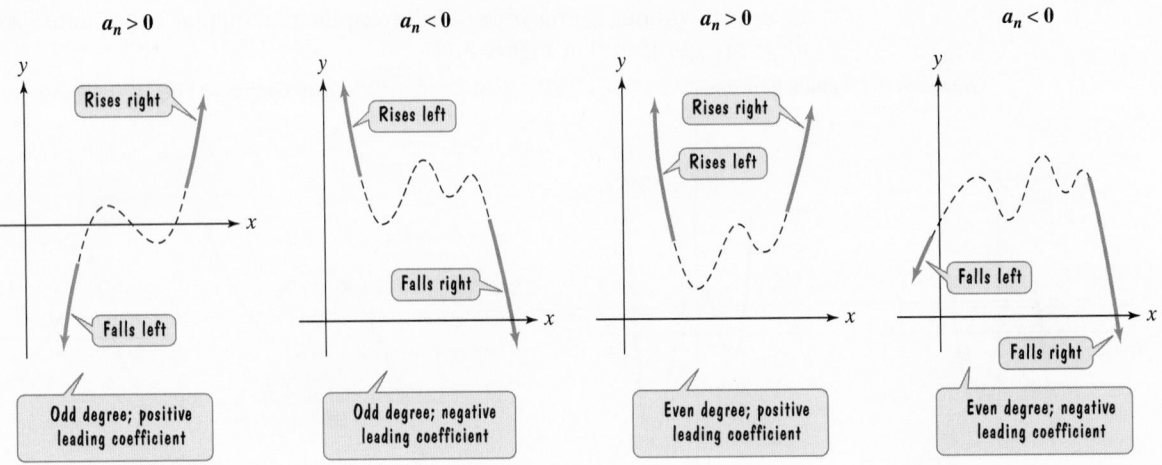

Study Tip

Odd-degree polynomial functions have graphs with opposite behavior at each end. Even-degree polynomial functions have graphs with the same behavior at each end.

EXAMPLE 1 Using the Leading Coefficient Test

Use the Leading Coefficient Test to determine the end behavior of the graph of
$$f(x) = x^3 + 3x^2 - x - 3.$$

Solution We begin by identifying the sign of the leading coefficient and the degree of the polynomial.

$$f(x) = x^3 + 3x^2 - x - 3$$

The leading coefficient, 1, is positive.

The degree of the polynomial, 3, is odd.

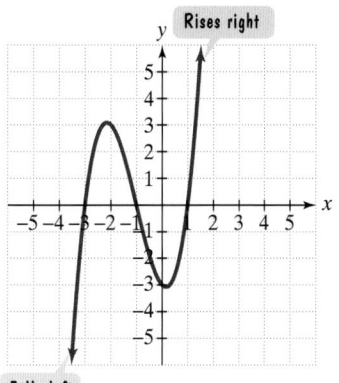

Rises right

Falls left

Figure 3.14 The graph of $f(x) = x^3 + 3x^2 - x - 3$

The degree of the function f is 3, which is odd. Odd-degree poly have graphs with opposite behavior at each end. The leading positive. Thus, the graph falls to the left and rises to the right (\swarrow, is shown in **Figure 3.14**.

⊘ Check Point **1** Use the Leading Coefficient Test to determine the end behavior of the graph of $f(x) = x^4 - 4x^2$.

(**EXAMPLE 2**) **Using the Leading Coefficient Test**

Use the Leading Coefficient Test to determine the end behavior of the graph of
$$f(x) = -4x^3(x - 1)^2(x + 5).$$

Solution Although the equation for f is in factored form, it is not necessary to multiply to determine the degree of the function.

$$f(x) = -4x^3(x - 1)^2(x + 5)$$

Degree of this factor is 3. Degree of this factor is 2. Degree of this factor is 1.

When multiplying exponential expressions with the same base, we add the exponents. This means that the degree of f is $3 + 2 + 1$, or 6, which is even. Even-degree polynomial functions have graphs with the same behavior at each end. Without multiplying out, you can see that the leading coefficient is -4, which is negative. Thus, the graph of f falls to the left and falls to the right (\swarrow, \searrow). ●

⊘ Check Point **2** Use the Leading Coefficient Test to determine the end behavior of the graph of
$$f(x) = 2x^3(x - 1)(x + 5).$$

(**EXAMPLE 3**) **Using the Leading Coefficient Test**

Use end behavior to explain why
$$f(x) = -49x^3 + 806x^2 + 3776x + 2503$$
is only an appropriate model for AIDS diagnoses for a limited time period.

Solution We begin by identifying the sign of the leading coefficient and the degree of the polynomial.

$$f(x) = -49x^3 + 806x^2 + 3776x + 2503$$

The leading coefficient, -49, is negative. The degree of the polynomial, 3, is odd.

The degree of f is 3, which is odd. Odd-degree polynomial functions have graphs with opposite behavior at each end. The leading coefficient, -49, is negative. Thus, the graph rises to the left and falls to the right (\nwarrow, \searrow). The fact that the graph falls to the right indicates that at some point the number of AIDS diagnoses will be negative, an impossibility. If a function has a graph that decreases without bound over time, it will not be capable of modeling nonnegative phenomena over long time periods. Model breakdown will eventually occur. ●

⊘ Check Point **3** The polynomial function
$$f(x) = -0.27x^3 + 9.2x^2 - 102.9x + 400$$
models the ratio of students to computers in U.S. public schools x years after 1980. Use end behavior to determine whether this function could be an appropriate model for computers in the classroom well into the twenty-first century. Explain your answer.

$[-8, 8, 1]$ by $[-10, 10, 1]$

Figure 3.15

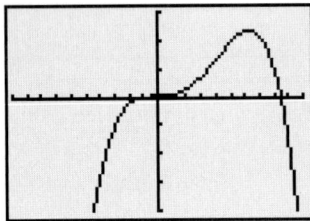

$[-10, 10, 1]$ by $[-1000, 750, 250]$

Figure 3.16

Figure 3.17

④ Use factoring to find zeros of polynomial functions.

If you use a graphing utility to graph a polynomial function, it is important to select a viewing rectangle that accurately reveals the graph's end behavior. If the viewing rectangle, or window, is too small, it may not accurately show a complete graph with the appropriate end behavior.

EXAMPLE 4 Using the Leading Coefficient Test

The graph of $f(x) = -x^4 + 8x^3 + 4x^2 + 2$ was obtained with a graphing utility using a $[-8, 8, 1]$ by $[-10, 10, 1]$ viewing rectangle. The graph is shown in **Figure 3.15**. Is this a complete graph that shows the end behavior of the function?

Solution We begin by identifying the sign of the leading coefficient and the degree of the polynomial.

$$f(x) = -x^4 + 8x^3 + 4x^2 + 2$$

The leading coefficient, -1, is negative.

The degree of the polynomial, 4, is even.

The degree of f is 4, which is even. Even-degree polynomial functions have graphs with the same behavior at each end. The leading coefficient, -1, is negative. Thus, the graph should fall to the left and fall to the right (\swarrow, \searrow). The graph in **Figure 3.15** is falling to the left, but it is not falling to the right. Therefore, the graph is not complete enough to show end behavior. A more complete graph of the function is shown in a larger viewing rectangle in **Figure 3.16**.

☑ Check Point **4** The graph of $f(x) = x^3 + 13x^2 + 10x - 4$ is shown in a standard viewing rectangle in **Figure 3.17**. Use the Leading Coefficient Test to determine whether this is a complete graph that shows the end behavior of the function. Explain your answer.

Zeros of Polynomial Functions

If f is a polynomial function, then the values of x for which $f(x)$ is equal to 0 are called the **zeros** of f. These values of x are the **roots**, or **solutions**, of the polynomial equation $f(x) = 0$. Each real root of the polynomial equation appears as an x-intercept of the graph of the polynomial function.

EXAMPLE 5 Finding Zeros of a Polynomial Function

Find all zeros of $f(x) = x^3 + 3x^2 - x - 3$.

Solution By definition, the zeros are the values of x for which $f(x)$ is equal to 0. Thus, we set $f(x)$ equal to 0:

$$f(x) = x^3 + 3x^2 - x - 3 = 0.$$

We solve the polynomial equation $x^3 + 3x^2 - x - 3 = 0$ for x as follows:

$x^3 + 3x^2 - x - 3 = 0$	This is the equation needed to find the function's zeros.
$x^2(x + 3) - 1(x + 3) = 0$	Factor x^2 from the first two terms and -1 from the last two terms.
$(x + 3)(x^2 - 1) = 0$	A common factor of $x + 3$ is factored from the expression.
$x + 3 = 0$ or $x^2 - 1 = 0$	Set each factor equal to 0.
$x = -3$ $\qquad x^2 = 1$	Solve for x.
$x = \pm 1$	Remember that if $x^2 = d$, then $x = \pm\sqrt{d}$.

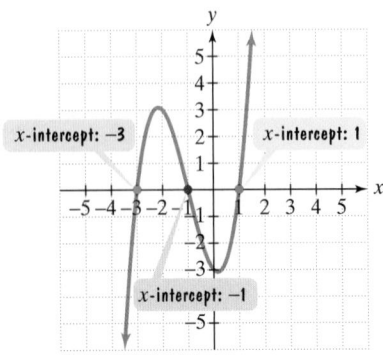

x-intercept: -3 x-intercept: 1

x-intercept: -1

Figure 3.18

The zeros of f are -3, -1, and 1. The graph of f in **Figure 3.18** shows that each zero is an x-intercept. The graph passes through the points $(-3, 0)$, $(-1, 0)$, and $(1, 0)$.

Technology

Graphic and Numeric Connections

A graphing utility can be used to verify that $-3, -1,$ and 1 are the three real zeros of $f(x) = x^3 + 3x^2 - x - 3.$

Numeric Check

Display a table for the function.

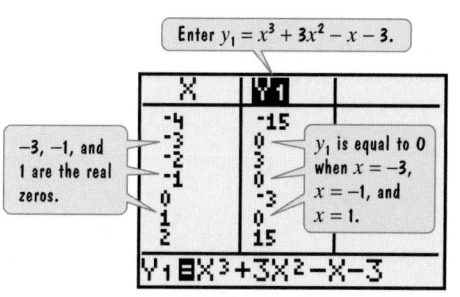

Graphic Check

Display a graph for the function. The x-intercepts indicate that $-3, -1,$ and 1 are the real zeros.

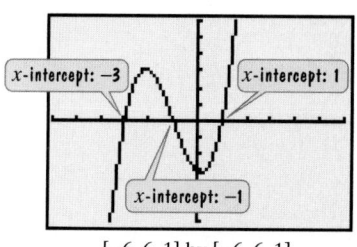

$[-6, 6, 1]$ by $[-6, 6, 1]$

The utility's $\boxed{\text{ZERO}}$ feature on the graph of f also verifies that $-3, -1,$ and 1 are the function's real zeros.

\oslash Check Point **5** Find all zeros of $f(x) = x^3 + 2x^2 - 4x - 8.$

$\boxed{\text{EXAMPLE 6}}$ **Finding Zeros of a Polynomial Function**

Find all zeros of $f(x) = -x^4 + 4x^3 - 4x^2.$

Solution We find the zeros of f by setting $f(x)$ equal to 0 and solving the resulting equation.

$$-x^4 + 4x^3 - 4x^2 = 0 \qquad \text{We now have a polynomial equation.}$$
$$x^4 - 4x^3 + 4x^2 = 0 \qquad \text{Multiply both sides by } -1. \text{ This step is optional.}$$
$$x^2(x^2 - 4x + 4) = 0 \qquad \text{Factor out } x^2.$$
$$x^2(x - 2)^2 = 0 \qquad \text{Factor completely.}$$
$$x^2 = 0 \quad \text{or} \quad (x - 2)^2 = 0 \qquad \text{Set each factor equal to 0.}$$
$$x = 0 \qquad\qquad x = 2 \qquad \text{Solve for x.}$$

The zeros of $f(x) = -x^4 + 4x^3 - 4x^2$ are 0 and 2. The graph of f, shown in **Figure 3.19**, has x-intercepts at 0 and 2. The graph passes through the points $(0, 0)$ and $(2, 0)$. ●

Figure 3.19 The zeros of $f(x) = -x^4 + 4x^3 - 4x^2$, namely 0 and 2, are the x-intercepts for the graph of f.

\oslash Check Point **6** Find all zeros of $f(x) = x^4 - 4x^2.$

⑤ Identify zeros and their multiplicities.

Multiplicities of Zeros

We can use the results of factoring to express a polynomial as a product of factors. For instance, in Example 6, we can use our factoring to express the function's equation as follows:

$$f(x) = -x^4 + 4x^3 - 4x^2 = -(x^4 - 4x^3 + 4x^2) = -x^2(x - 2)^2.$$

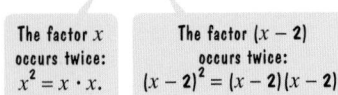

The factor x
occurs twice:
$x^2 = x \cdot x.$

The factor $(x - 2)$
occurs twice:
$(x - 2)^2 = (x - 2)(x - 2).$

Notice that each factor occurs twice. In factoring the equation for the polynomial function f, if the same factor $x - r$ occurs k times, but not $k + 1$ times, we call r a **zero with multiplicity k**. For the polynomial function

$$f(x) = -x^2(x - 2)^2,$$

0 and 2 are both zeros with multiplicity 2.

Multiplicity provides another connection between zeros and graphs. The multiplicity of a zero tells us whether the graph of a polynomial function touches the x-axis at the zero and turns around, or if the graph crosses the x-axis at the zero. For example, look again at the graph of $f(x) = -x^4 + 4x^3 - 4x^2$ in **Figure 3.19**. Each zero, 0 and 2, is a zero with multiplicity 2. The graph of f touches, but does not cross, the x-axis at each of these zeros of even multiplicity. By contrast, a graph crosses the x-axis at zeros of odd multiplicity.

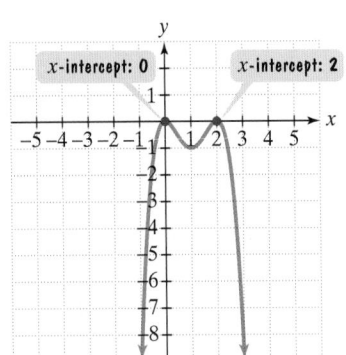

Figure 3.19 (repeated) The graph of $f(x) = -x^4 + 4x^3 - 4x^2$

Multiplicity and x-Intercepts

If r is a zero of **even multiplicity**, then the graph **touches** the x-axis **and turns around** at r. If r is a zero of **odd multiplicity**, then the graph **crosses** the x-axis at r. Regardless of whether the multiplicity of a zero is even or odd, graphs tend to flatten out near zeros with multiplicity greater than one.

If a polynomial function's equation is expressed as a product of linear factors, we can quickly identify zeros and their multiplicities.

EXAMPLE 7 **Finding Zeros and Their Multiplicities**

Find the zeros of $f(x) = \frac{1}{2}(x + 1)(2x - 3)^2$ and give the multiplicity of each zero. State whether the graph crosses the x-axis or touches the x-axis and turns around at each zero.

Solution We find the zeros of f by setting $f(x)$ equal to 0:

$$\frac{1}{2}(x + 1)(2x - 3)^2 = 0.$$

Set each variable factor equal to 0.

$x + 1 = 0$
$x = -1$

$2x - 3 = 0$
$x = \frac{3}{2}$

$$\frac{1}{2}(x + 1)^1(2x - 3)^2 = 0$$

This exponent is 1.
Thus, the multiplicity
of -1 is 1.

This exponent is 2.
Thus, the multiplicity
of $\frac{3}{2}$ is 2.

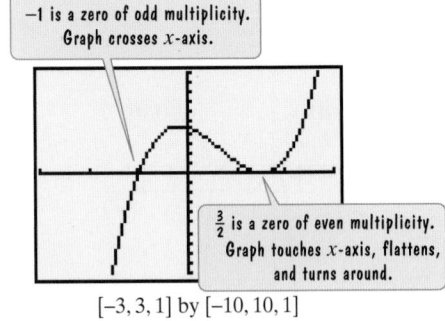

-1 is a zero of odd multiplicity.
Graph crosses x-axis.

$\frac{3}{2}$ is a zero of even multiplicity.
Graph touches x-axis, flattens,
and turns around.

$[-3, 3, 1]$ by $[-10, 10, 1]$

Figure 3.20 The graph of
$f(x) = \frac{1}{2}(x + 1)(2x - 3)^2$

The zeros of $f(x) = \frac{1}{2}(x + 1)(2x - 3)^2$ are -1, with multiplicity 1, and $\frac{3}{2}$, with multiplicity 2. Because the multiplicity of -1 is odd, the graph crosses the x-axis at this zero. Because the multiplicity of $\frac{3}{2}$ is even, the graph touches the x-axis and turns around at this zero. These relationships are illustrated by the graph of f in **Figure 3.20**. ●

🖋 Check Point **7** Find the zeros of $f(x) = -4\left(x + \frac{1}{2}\right)^2 (x - 5)^3$ and give the multiplicity of each zero. State whether the graph crosses the x-axis or touches the x-axis and turns around at each zero.

6 Use the Intermediate Value Theorem.

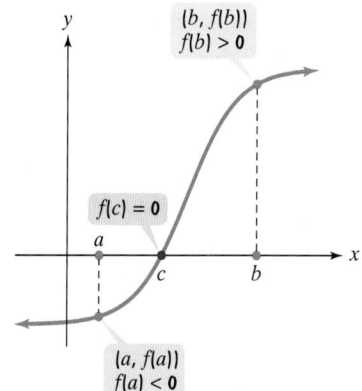

Figure 3.21 The graph must cross the x-axis at some value between a and b.

The Intermediate Value Theorem

The *Intermediate Value Theorem* tells us of the existence of real zeros. The idea behind the theorem is illustrated in **Figure 3.21**. The figure shows that if $(a, f(a))$ lies below the x-axis and $(b, f(b))$ lies above the x-axis, the smooth, continuous graph of the polynomial function f must cross the x-axis at some value c between a and b. This value is a real zero for the function.

These observations are summarized in the **Intermediate Value Theorem**.

The Intermediate Value Theorem for Polynomial Functions

Let f be a polynomial function with real coefficients. If $f(a)$ and $f(b)$ have opposite signs, then there is at least one value of c between a and b for which $f(c) = 0$. Equivalently, the equation $f(x) = 0$ has at least one real root between a and b.

EXAMPLE 8 **Using the Intermediate Value Theorem**

Show that the polynomial function $f(x) = x^3 - 2x - 5$ has a real zero between 2 and 3.

Solution Let us evaluate f at 2 and at 3. If $f(2)$ and $f(3)$ have opposite signs, then there is at least one real zero between 2 and 3. Using $f(x) = x^3 - 2x - 5$, we obtain

$$f(2) = 2^3 - 2 \cdot 2 - 5 = 8 - 4 - 5 = -1$$

> $f(2)$ is negative.

and

$$f(3) = 3^3 - 2 \cdot 3 - 5 = 27 - 6 - 5 = 16.$$

> $f(3)$ is positive.

$[-3, 3, 1]$ by $[-10, 10, 1]$

Figure 3.22

Because $f(2) = -1$ and $f(3) = 16$, the sign change shows that the polynomial function has a real zero between 2 and 3. This zero is actually irrational and is approximated using a graphing utility's ZERO feature as 2.0945515 in **Figure 3.22**.

🖋 Check Point **8** Show that the polynomial function $f(x) = 3x^3 - 10x + 9$ has a real zero between -3 and -2.

7 Understand the relationship between degree and turning points.

Turning Points of Polynomial Functions

The graph of $f(x) = x^5 - 6x^3 + 8x + 1$ is shown in **Figure 3.23** on the next page. The graph has four smooth **turning points**.

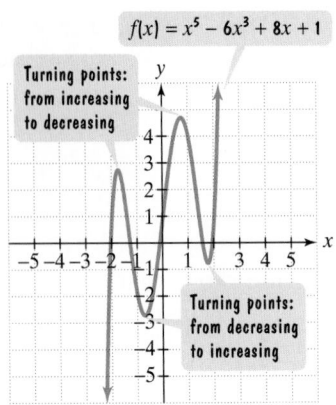

$f(x) = x^5 - 6x^3 + 8x + 1$

Turning points: from increasing to decreasing

Turning points: from decreasing to increasing

Figure 3.23 Graph with four turning points

8 Graph polynomial functions.

At each turning point **Figure 3.23**, the graph changes direction from increasing to decreasing or vice versa. The given equation has 5 as its greatest exponent and is therefore a polynomial function of degree 5. Notice that the graph has four turning points. In general, **if f is a polynomial function of degree n, then the graph of f has at most n − 1 turning points**.

Figure 3.23 illustrates that the y-coordinate of each turning point is either a relative maximum or a relative minimum of f. Without the aid of a graphing utility or a knowledge of calculus, it is difficult and often impossible to locate turning points of polynomial functions with degrees greater than 2. If necessary, test values can be taken between the x-intercepts to get a general idea of how high the graph rises or how low the graph falls. For the purpose of graphing in this section, a general estimate is sometimes appropriate and necessary.

A Strategy for Graphing Polynomial Functions

Here's a general strategy for graphing a polynomial function. A graphing utility is a valuable complement, but not a necessary component, to this strategy. If you are using a graphing utility, some of the steps listed in the following box will help you to select a viewing rectangle that shows the important parts of the graph.

Graphing a Polynomial Function

$$f(x) = a_n x^n + a_{n-1} x^{n-1} + a_{n-2} x^{n-2} + \cdots + a_1 x + a_0, \, a_n \neq 0$$

1. Use the Leading Coefficient Test to determine the graph's end behavior.
2. Find x-intercepts by setting $f(x) = 0$ and solving the resulting polynomial equation. If there is an x-intercept at r as a result of $(x - r)^k$ in the complete factorization of $f(x)$, then
 a. If k is even, the graph touches the x-axis at r and turns around.
 b. If k is odd, the graph crosses the x-axis at r.
 c. If $k > 1$, the graph flattens out near $(r, 0)$.
3. Find the y-intercept by computing $f(0)$.
4. Use symmetry, if applicable, to help draw the graph:
 a. y-axis symmetry: $f(-x) = f(x)$
 b. Origin symmetry: $f(-x) = -f(x)$.
5. Use the fact that the maximum number of turning points of the graph is $n - 1$, where n is the degree of the polynomial function, to check whether it is drawn correctly.

Study Tip

Remember that, without calculus, it is often impossible to give the exact location of turning points. However, you can obtain additional points satisfying the function to estimate how high the graph rises or how low it falls. To obtain these points, use values of x between (and to the left and right of) the x-intercepts.

EXAMPLE 9 **Graphing a Polynomial Function**

Graph: $f(x) = x^4 - 2x^2 + 1$.

Solution

Step 1 Determine end behavior. Identify the sign of a_n, the leading coefficient, and the degree, n, of the polynomial function.

$$f(x) = x^4 - 2x^2 + 1$$

The leading coefficient, 1, is positive.

The degree of the polynomial function, 4, is even.

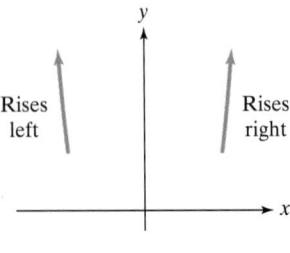

Rises left

Rises right

Because the degree, 4, is even, the graph has the same behavior at each end. The leading coefficient, 1, is positive. Thus, the graph rises to the left and rises to the right.

Step 2 Find x-intercepts (zeros of the function) by setting $f(x) = 0$.

$$x^4 - 2x^2 + 1 = 0 \qquad \text{Set } f(x) \text{ equal to 0.}$$
$$(x^2 - 1)(x^2 - 1) = 0 \qquad \text{Factor.}$$
$$(x + 1)(x - 1)(x + 1)(x - 1) = 0 \qquad \text{Factor completely.}$$
$$(x + 1)^2(x - 1)^2 = 0 \qquad \text{Express the factorization in a more compact form.}$$
$$(x + 1)^2 = 0 \quad \text{or} \quad (x - 1)^2 = 0 \qquad \text{Set each factorization equal to 0.}$$
$$x = -1 \qquad\qquad x = 1 \qquad \text{Solve for } x.$$

We see that -1 and 1 are both repeated zeros with multiplicity 2. Because of the even multiplicity, the graph touches the x-axis at -1 and 1 and turns around. Furthermore, the graph tends to flatten out near these zeros with multiplicity greater than one.

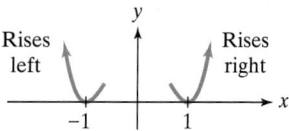

Step 3 Find the y-intercept by computing $f(0)$. We use $f(x) = x^4 - 2x^2 + 1$ and compute $f(0)$.

$$f(0) = 0^4 - 2 \cdot 0^2 + 1 = 1$$

There is a y-intercept at 1, so the graph passes through $(0, 1)$.

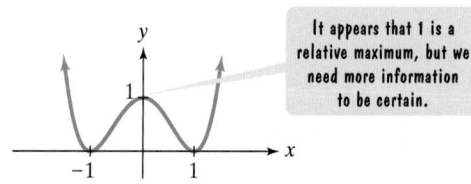

It appears that 1 is a relative maximum, but we need more information to be certain.

Step 4 Use possible symmetry to help draw the graph. Our partial graph suggests y-axis symmetry. Let's verify this by finding $f(-x)$.

$$f(x) = x^4 - 2x^2 + 1$$

Replace x with $-x$.

$$f(-x) = (-x)^4 - 2(-x)^2 + 1 = x^4 - 2x^2 + 1$$

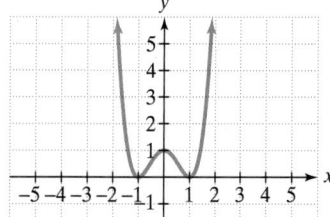

Figure 3.24 The graph of $f(x) = x^4 - 2x^2 + 1$

Because $f(-x) = f(x)$, the graph of f is symmetric with respect to the y-axis. **Figure 3.24** shows the graph of $f(x) = x^4 - 2x^2 + 1$.

Step 5 Use the fact that the maximum number of turning points of the graph is $n - 1$ to check whether it is drawn correctly. Because $n = 4$, the maximum number of turning points is $4 - 1$, or 3. Because the graph in **Figure 3.24** has three turning points, we have not violated the maximum number possible. Can you see how this verifies that 1 is indeed a relative maximum and $(0, 1)$ is a turning point? If the graph rose above 1 on either side of $x = 0$, it would have to rise above 1 on the other side as well because of symmetry. This would require additional turning points to smoothly curve back to the x-intercepts. The graph already has three turning points, which is the maximum number for a fourth-degree polynomial function. ●

☑ Check Point **9** Use the five-step strategy to graph $f(x) = x^3 - 3x^2$.

Exercise Set 3.2

Practice Exercises

In Exercises 1–10, determine which functions are polynomial functions. For those that are, identify the degree.

1. $f(x) = 5x^2 + 6x^3$

2. $f(x) = 7x^2 + 9x^4$

3. $g(x) = 7x^5 - \pi x^3 + \frac{1}{5}x$

4. $g(x) = 6x^7 + \pi x^5 + \frac{2}{3}x$

5. $h(x) = 7x^3 + 2x^2 + \frac{1}{x}$

6. $h(x) = 8x^3 - x^2 + \frac{2}{x}$

7. $f(x) = x^{\frac{1}{2}} - 3x^2 + 5$

8. $f(x) = x^{\frac{1}{3}} - 4x^2 + 7$

9. $f(x) = \dfrac{x^2 + 7}{x^3}$

10. $f(x) = \dfrac{x^2 + 7}{3}$

In Exercises 11–14, identify which graphs are not those of polynomial functions.

11.

12.

13.

14.

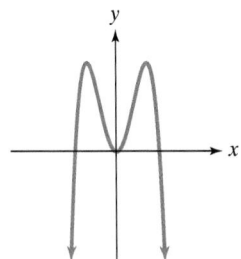

In Exercises 15–18, use the Leading Coefficient Test to determine the end behavior of the graph of the given polynomial function. Then use this end behavior to match the polynomial function with its graph. [The graphs are labeled (a) through (d).]

15. $f(x) = -x^4 + x^2$

16. $f(x) = x^3 - 4x^2$

17. $f(x) = (x - 3)^2$

18. $f(x) = -x^3 - x^2 + 5x - 3$

a.

b.

c.

d.

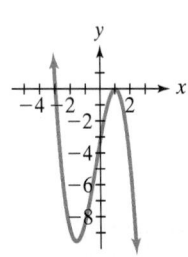

In Exercises 19–24, use the Leading Coefficient Test to determine the end behavior of the graph of the polynomial function.

19. $f(x) = 5x^3 + 7x^2 - x + 9$

20. $f(x) = 11x^3 - 6x^2 + x + 3$

21. $f(x) = 5x^4 + 7x^2 - x + 9$

22. $f(x) = 11x^4 - 6x^2 + x + 3$

23. $f(x) = -5x^4 + 7x^2 - x + 9$

24. $f(x) = -11x^4 - 6x^2 + x + 3$

In Exercises 25–32, find the zeros for each polynomial function and give the multiplicity for each zero. State whether the graph crosses the x-axis, or touches the x-axis and turns around, at each zero.

25. $f(x) = 2(x - 5)(x + 4)^2$

26. $f(x) = 3(x + 5)(x + 2)^2$

27. $f(x) = 4(x - 3)(x + 6)^3$

28. $f(x) = -3\left(x + \frac{1}{2}\right)(x - 4)^3$

29. $f(x) = x^3 - 2x^2 + x$

30. $f(x) = x^3 + 4x^2 + 4x$

31. $f(x) = x^3 + 7x^2 - 4x - 28$

32. $f(x) = x^3 + 5x^2 - 9x - 45$

In Exercises 33–40, use the Intermediate Value Theorem to show that each polynomial has a real zero between the given integers.

33. $f(x) = x^3 - x - 1$; between 1 and 2

34. $f(x) = x^3 - 4x^2 + 2$; between 0 and 1

35. $f(x) = 2x^4 - 4x^2 + 1$; between -1 and 0

36. $f(x) = x^4 + 6x^3 - 18x^2$; between 2 and 3

37. $f(x) = x^3 + x^2 - 2x + 1$; between -3 and -2

38. $f(x) = x^5 - x^3 - 1$; between 1 and 2

39. $f(x) = 3x^3 - 10x + 9$; between -3 and -2

40. $f(x) = 3x^3 - 8x^2 + x + 2$; between 2 and 3

In Exercises 41–64,

 a. Use the Leading Coefficient Test to determine the graph's end behavior.

 b. Find the x-intercepts. State whether the graph crosses the x-axis, or touches the x-axis and turns around, at each intercept.

 c. Find the y-intercept.

 d. Determine whether the graph has y-axis symmetry, origin symmetry, or neither.

 e. If necessary, find a few additional points and graph the function. Use the maximum number of turning points to check whether it is drawn correctly.

41. $f(x) = x^3 + 2x^2 - x - 2$

42. $f(x) = x^3 + x^2 - 4x - 4$

43. $f(x) = x^4 - 9x^2$

44. $f(x) = x^4 - x^2$

45. $f(x) = -x^4 + 16x^2$

46. $f(x) = -x^4 + 4x^2$

47. $f(x) = x^4 - 2x^3 + x^2$

48. $f(x) = x^4 - 6x^3 + 9x^2$

49. $f(x) = -2x^4 + 4x^3$

50. $f(x) = -2x^4 + 2x^3$

51. $f(x) = 6x^3 - 9x - x^5$

52. $f(x) = 6x - x^3 - x^5$

53. $f(x) = 3x^2 - x^3$

54. $f(x) = \frac{1}{2} - \frac{1}{2}x^4$

55. $f(x) = -3(x - 1)^2(x^2 - 4)$

56. $f(x) = -2(x - 4)^2(x^2 - 25)$

57. $f(x) = x^2(x - 1)^3(x + 2)$

58. $f(x) = x^3(x + 2)^2(x + 1)$

59. $f(x) = -x^2(x - 1)(x + 3)$

60. $f(x) = -x^2(x + 2)(x - 2)$

61. $f(x) = -2x^3(x - 1)^2(x + 5)$

62. $f(x) = -3x^3(x - 1)^2(x + 3)$

63. $f(x) = (x - 2)^2(x + 4)(x - 1)$

64. $f(x) = (x + 3)(x + 1)^3(x + 4)$

Practice Plus

In Exercises 65–72, complete graphs of polynomial functions whose zeros are integers are shown.

 a. *Find the zeros and state whether the multiplicity of each zero is even or odd.*

 b. *Write an equation, expressed as the product of factors, of a polynomial function that might have each graph. Use a leading coefficient of 1 or −1, and make the degree of f as small as possible.*

 c. *Use both the equation in part (b) and the graph to find the y-intercept.*

65.

[−5, 5, 1] by [−12, 12, 1]

66.

[−6, 6, 1] by [−40, 40, 10]

67.

[−3, 6, 1] by [−10, 10, 1]

68.

[−3, 3, 1] by [−10, 10, 1]

69.

[−4, 4, 1] by [−40, 4, 4]

70.

[−2, 5, 1] by [−40, 4, 4]

71.

[−3, 3, 1] by [−5, 10, 1]

72.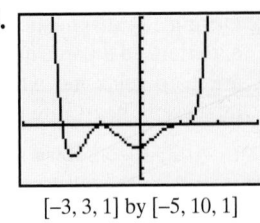

[−3, 3, 1] by [−5, 10, 1]

Application Exercises

The bar graph shows the number of Americans living with HIV and AIDS from 2001 through 2005.

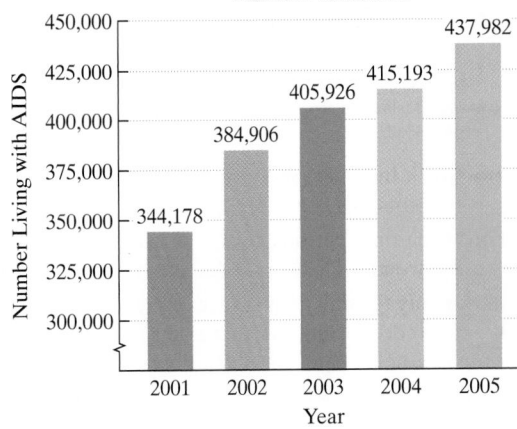

Number of Americans Living with HIV and AIDS

Source: Department of Health and Human Services

The data in the bar graph can be modeled by the following second- and third-degree polynomial functions:

Number living with HIV and AIDS x years after 2000

$$f(x) = -3402x^2 + 42{,}203x + 308{,}453$$
$$g(x) = 2769x^3 - 28{,}324x^2 + 107{,}555x + 261{,}931.$$

Use these functions to solve Exercises 73–74.

73. **a.** Use both functions to find the number of Americans living with HIV and AIDS in 2003. Which function provides a better description for the actual number shown in the bar graph?

 b. Consider the function from part (a) that serves as a better model for 2003. Use the Leading Coefficient Test to determine the end behavior to the right for the graph of this function. Will the function be useful in modeling the number of Americans living with HIV and AIDS over an extended period of time? Explain your answer.

74. **a.** Use both functions to find the number of Americans living with HIV and AIDS in 2005. Which function provides a better description for the actual number shown in the bar graph?

 b. Consider the function from part (a) that serves as a better model for 2005. Use the Leading Coefficient Test to determine the end behavior to the right for the graph of this function. Based on this end behavior, can the function be used to model the number of Americans living with HIV and AIDS over an extended period of time? Explain your answer.

75. During a diagnostic evaluation, a 33-year-old woman experienced a panic attack a few minutes after she had been asked to relax her whole body. The graph shows the rapid increase in heart rate during the panic attack.

Heart Rate before and during a Panic Attack

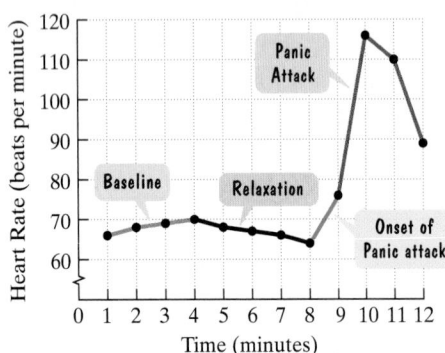

Source: Davis and Palladino, *Psychology*, Fifth Edition, Prentice Hall, 2007

a. For which time periods during the diagnostic evaluation was the woman's heart rate increasing?

b. For which time periods during the diagnostic evaluation was the woman's heart rate decreasing?

c. How many turning points (from increasing to decreasing or from decreasing to increasing) occurred for the woman's heart rate during the first 12 minutes of the diagnostic evaluation?

d. Suppose that a polynomial function is used to model the data displayed by the graph using

(time during the evaluation, heart rate).

Use the number of turning points to determine the degree of the polynomial function of best fit.

e. For the model in part (d), should the leading coefficient of the polynomial function be positive or negative? Explain your answer.

f. Use the graph to estimate the woman's maximum heart rate during the first 12 minutes of the diagnostic evaluation. After how many minutes did this occur?

g. Use the graph to estimate the woman's minimum heart rate during the first 12 minutes of the diagnostic evaluation. After how many minutes did this occur?

76. Even after a campaign to curb grade inflation, 51% of the grades given at Harvard in the 2005 school year were B+ or better. The graph shows the percentage of Harvard students with B+ averages or better for the period from 1960 through 2005.

Percentage of Harvard Students with B+ Averages or Better

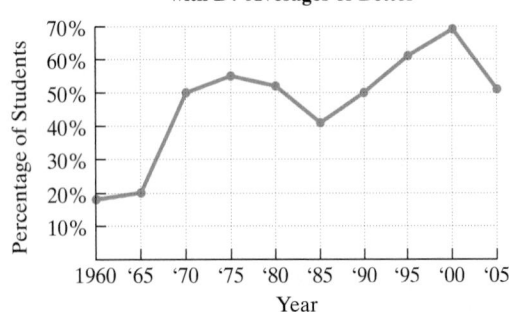

Source: *Mother Jones*, January/February 2008

a. For which years was the percentage of students with B+ averages or better increasing?

b. For which years was the percentage of students with B+ averages or better decreasing?

c. How many turning points (from increasing to decreasing or from decreasing to increasing) does the graph have for the period shown?

d. Suppose that a polynomial function is used to model the data shown in the graph using

(number of years after 1960, percentage of students with B+ averages or better).

Use the number of turning points to determine the degree of the polynomial function of best fit.

e. For the model in part (d), should the leading coefficient of the polynomial function be positive or negative? Explain your answer.

f. Use the graph to estimate the maximum percentage of Harvard students with B+ averages or better. In which year did this occur?

g. Use the graph to estimate the minimum percentage of Harvard students with B+ averages or better. In which year did this occur?

Writing in Mathematics

77. What is a polynomial function?

78. What do we mean when we describe the graph of a polynomial function as smooth and continuous?

79. What is meant by the end behavior of a polynomial function?

80. Explain how to use the Leading Coefficient Test to determine the end behavior of a polynomial function.

81. Why is a third-degree polynomial function with a negative leading coefficient not appropriate for modeling non-negative real-world phenomena over a long period of time?

82. What are the zeros of a polynomial function and how are they found?

83. Explain the relationship between the multiplicity of a zero and whether or not the graph crosses or touches the x-axis at that zero.

84. If f is a polynomial function, and $f(a)$ and $f(b)$ have opposite signs, what must occur between a and b? If $f(a)$ and $f(b)$ have the same sign, does it necessarily mean that this will not occur? Explain your answer.

85. Explain the relationship between the degree of a polynomial function and the number of turning points on its graph.

86. Can the graph of a polynomial function have no x-intercepts? Explain.

87. Can the graph of a polynomial function have no y-intercept? Explain.

88. Describe a strategy for graphing a polynomial function. In your description, mention intercepts, the polynomial's degree, and turning points.

Technology Exercises

89. Use a graphing utility to verify any five of the graphs that you drew by hand in Exercises 41–64.

Write a polynomial function that imitates the end behavior of each graph in Exercises 90–93. The dashed portions of the graphs indicate that you should focus only on imitating the left and right behavior of the graph and can be flexible about what occurs between the left and right ends. Then use your graphing utility to graph the polynomial function and verify that you imitated the end behavior shown in the given graph.

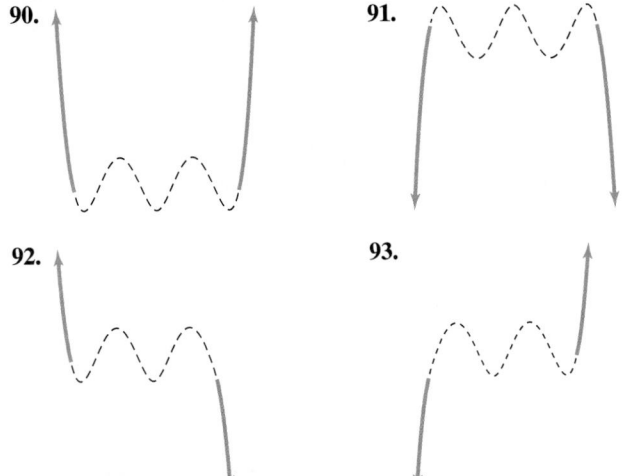

90. **91.**

92. **93.**

In Exercises 94–97, use a graphing utility with a viewing rectangle large enough to show end behavior to graph each polynomial function.

94. $f(x) = x^3 + 13x^2 + 10x - 4$

95. $f(x) = -2x^3 + 6x^2 + 3x - 1$

96. $f(x) = -x^4 + 8x^3 + 4x^2 + 2$

97. $f(x) = -x^5 + 5x^4 - 6x^3 + 2x + 20$

In Exercises 98–99, use a graphing utility to graph f and g in the same viewing rectangle. Then use the ZOOM OUT feature to show that f and g have identical end behavior.

98. $f(x) = x^3 - 6x + 1, \quad g(x) = x^3$

99. $f(x) = -x^4 + 2x^3 - 6x, \quad g(x) = -x^4$

Critical Thinking Exercises

Make Sense? *In Exercises 100–103, determine whether each statement makes sense or does not make sense, and explain your reasoning.*

100. When I'm trying to determine end behavior, it's the coefficient of the leading term of a polynomial function that I should inspect.

101. I graphed $f(x) = (x + 2)^3(x - 4)^2$, and the graph touched the x-axis and turned around at −2.

102. I'm graphing a fourth-degree polynomial function with four turning points.

103. Although I have not yet learned techniques for finding the x-intercepts of $f(x) = x^3 + 2x^2 - 5x - 6$, I can easily determine the y-intercept.

In Exercises 104–107, determine whether each statement is true or false. If the statement is false, make the necessary change(s) to produce a true statement.

104. If $f(x) = -x^3 + 4x$, then the graph of f falls to the left and falls to the right.

105. A mathematical model that is a polynomial of degree n whose leading term is $a_n x^n$, n odd and $a_n < 0$, is ideally suited to describe phenomena that have positive values over unlimited periods of time.

106. There is more than one third-degree polynomial function with the same three x-intercepts.

107. The graph of a function with origin symmetry can rise to the left and rise to the right.

Use the descriptions in Exercises 108–109 to write an equation of a polynomial function with the given characteristics. Use a graphing utility to graph your function to see if you are correct. If not, modify the function's equation and repeat this process.

108. Crosses the x-axis at −4, 0, and 3; lies above the x-axis between −4 and 0; lies below the x-axis between 0 and 3

109. Touches the x-axis at 0 and crosses the x-axis at 2; lies below the x-axis between 0 and 2

Preview Exercises

Exercises 110–112 will help you prepare for the material covered in the next section.

110. Divide 737 by 21 without using a calculator. Write the answer as

$$\text{quotient} + \frac{\text{remainder}}{\text{divisor}}.$$

111. Rewrite $4 - 5x - x^2 + 6x^3$ in descending powers of x.

112. Use

$$\frac{2x^3 - 3x^2 - 11x + 6}{x - 3} = 2x^2 + 3x - 2$$

to factor $2x^3 - 3x^2 - 11x + 6$ completely.

Dividing Polynomials; Remainder and Factor Theorems

Objectives

① Use long division to divide polynomials.

② Use synthetic division to divide polynomials.

③ Evaluate a polynomial using the Remainder Theorem.

④ Use the Factor Theorem to solve a polynomial equation.

A moth has moved into your closet. She appeared in your bedroom at night, but somehow her relatively stout body escaped your clutches. Within a few weeks, swarms of moths in your tattered wardrobe suggest that Mama Moth was in the family way. There must be at least 200 critters nesting in every crevice of your clothing.

Two hundred plus moth-tykes from one female moth—is this possible? Indeed it is. The number of eggs, $f(x)$, in a female moth is a function of her abdominal width, x, in millimeters, modeled by

$$f(x) = 14x^3 - 17x^2 - 16x + 34, \quad 1.5 \le x \le 3.5.$$

Because there are 200 moths feasting on your favorite sweaters, Mama's abdominal width can be estimated by finding the solutions of the polynomial equation

$$14x^3 - 17x^2 - 16x + 34 = 200.$$

How can we solve such an equation? You might begin by subtracting 200 from both sides to obtain zero on one side. But then what? The factoring that we used in the previous section will not work in this situation.

In Section 3.4, we will present techniques for solving certain kinds of polynomial equations. These techniques will further enhance your ability to manipulate algebraically the polynomial functions that model your world. Because these techniques are based on understanding polynomial division, in this section we look at two methods for dividing polynomials. (We'll return to Mama Moth's abdominal width in the exercise set.)

Long Division of Polynomials and the Division Algorithm

① Use long division to divide polynomials.

We begin by looking at division by a polynomial containing more than one term, such as

$$x + 3 \overline{)x^2 + 10x + 21}.$$

> Divisor has two terms and is a binomial.

> The polynomial dividend has three terms and is a trinomial.

When a divisor has more than one term, the four steps used to divide whole numbers—**divide, multiply, subtract, bring down the next term** — form the repetitive procedure for polynomial long division.

EXAMPLE 1 Long Division of Polynomials

Divide $x^2 + 10x + 21$ by $x + 3$.

Solution The following steps illustrate how polynomial division is very similar to numerical division.

$$x + 3 \overline{)x^2 + 10x + 21}$$

Arrange the terms of the dividend $(x^2 + 10x + 21)$ and the divisor $(x + 3)$ in descending powers of x.

$$\begin{array}{r} x \\ x + 3 \overline{)x^2 + 10x + 21} \end{array}$$

Divide x^2 (the first term in the dividend) by x (the first term in the divisor): $\dfrac{x^2}{x} = x$. Align like terms.

$x(x + 3) = x^2 + 3x$

$$\begin{array}{r} x \\ x + 3 \overline{)x^2 + 10x + 21} \\ \underline{x^2 + 3x} \end{array}$$

Multiply each term in the divisor $(x + 3)$ by x, aligning terms of the product under like terms in the dividend.

$$x + 3 \overline{\smash{)}x^2 + 10x + 21}$$
$$\underline{x^2 + 3x}$$
$$7x$$

Change signs of the polynomial being subtracted.

Subtract $x^2 + 3x$ from $x^2 + 10x$ by changing the sign of each term in the lower expression and adding.

$$x + 3 \overline{\smash{)}x^2 + 10x + 21}$$
$$\underline{x^2 + 3x} \quad \downarrow$$
$$7x + 21$$

Bring down 21 from the original dividend and add algebraically to form a new dividend.

$$x + 7$$
$$x + 3 \overline{\smash{)}x^2 + 10x + 21}$$
$$\underline{x^2 + 3x}$$
$$7x + 21$$

Find the second term of the quotient. Divide the first term of $7x + 21$ by x, the first term of the divisor: $\dfrac{7x}{x} = 7$.

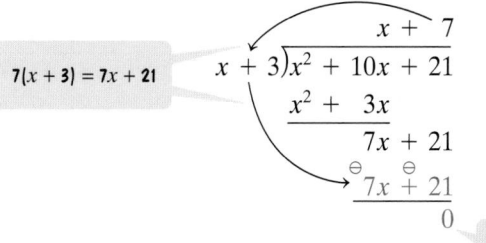

$7(x + 3) = 7x + 21$

$$x + 7$$
$$x + 3 \overline{\smash{)}x^2 + 10x + 21}$$
$$\underline{x^2 + 3x}$$
$$7x + 21$$
$$\underline{7x + 21}$$
$$0$$

Remainder

Multiply the divisor $(x + 3)$ by 7, aligning under like terms in the new dividend. Then subtract to obtain the remainder of 0.

The quotient is $x + 7$. Because the remainder is 0, we can conclude that $x + 3$ is a factor of $x^2 + 10x + 21$ and

$$\frac{x^2 + 10x + 21}{x + 3} = x + 7.$$

✓ **Check Point** | Divide $x^2 + 14x + 45$ by $x + 9$.

Before considering additional examples, let's summarize the general procedure for dividing one polynomial by another.

Long Division of Polynomials

1. Arrange the terms of both the dividend and the divisor in descending powers of any variable.
2. **Divide** the first term in the dividend by the first term in the divisor. The result is the first term of the quotient.
3. **Multiply** every term in the divisor by the first term in the quotient. Write the resulting product beneath the dividend with like terms lined up.
4. **Subtract** the product from the dividend.
5. **Bring down** the next term in the original dividend and write it next to the remainder to form a new dividend.
6. Use this new expression as the dividend and repeat this process until the remainder can no longer be divided. This will occur when the degree of the remainder (the highest exponent on a variable in the remainder) is less than the degree of the divisor.

In our next long division, we will obtain a nonzero remainder.

EXAMPLE 2 Long Division of Polynomials

Divide $4 - 5x - x^2 + 6x^3$ by $3x - 2$.

Solution We begin by writing the dividend in descending powers of x.

$$4 - 5x - x^2 + 6x^3 = 6x^3 - x^2 - 5x + 4$$

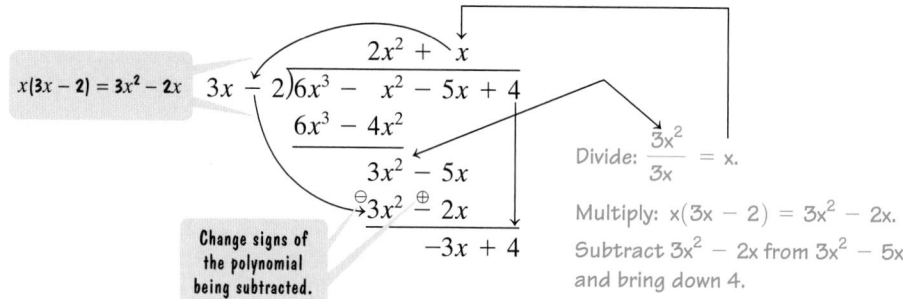

$2x^2(3x - 2) = 6x^3 - 4x^2$

Change signs of the polynomial being subtracted.

Divide: $\dfrac{6x^3}{3x} = 2x^2$.

Multiply: $2x^2(3x - 2) = 6x^3 - 4x^2$.

Subtract $6x^3 - 4x^2$ from $6x^3 - x^2$ and bring down $-5x$.

Now we divide $3x^2$ by $3x$ to obtain x, multiply x and the divisor, and subtract.

$x(3x - 2) = 3x^2 - 2x$

Change signs of the polynomial being subtracted.

Divide: $\dfrac{3x^2}{3x} = x$.

Multiply: $x(3x - 2) = 3x^2 - 2x$.

Subtract $3x^2 - 2x$ from $3x^2 - 5x$ and bring down 4.

Now we divide $-3x$ by $3x$ to obtain -1, multiply -1 and the divisor, and subtract.

$-1(3x - 2) = -3x + 2$

Change signs of the polynomial being subtracted.

Remainder

Divide: $\dfrac{-3x}{3x} = -1$.

Multiply: $-1(3x - 2) = -3x + 2$.

Subtract $-3x + 2$ from $-3x + 4$, leaving a remainder of 2.

The quotient is $2x^2 + x - 1$ and the remainder is 2. When there is a nonzero remainder, as in this example, list the quotient, plus the remainder above the divisor. Thus,

$$\frac{6x^3 - x^2 - 5x + 4}{3x - 2} = \underbrace{2x^2 + x - 1}_{\text{Quotient}} + \underbrace{\frac{2}{3x - 2}}_{\substack{\text{Remainder} \\ \text{above divisor}}}.$$

An important property of division can be illustrated by clearing fractions in the equation that concluded Example 2. Multiplying both sides of this equation by $3x - 2$ results in the following equation:

$$\underbrace{6x^3 - x^2 - 5x + 4}_{\text{Dividend}} = \underbrace{(3x - 2)}_{\text{Divisor}}\underbrace{(2x^2 + x - 1)}_{\text{Quotient}} + \underbrace{2}_{\text{Remainder}}.$$

Polynomial long division is checked by multiplying the divisor with the quotient and then adding the remainder. This should give the dividend. The process illustrates the **Division Algorithm**.

The Division Algorithm

If $f(x)$ and $d(x)$ are polynomials, with $d(x) \neq 0$, and the degree of $d(x)$ is less than or equal to the degree of $f(x)$, then there exist unique polynomials $q(x)$ and $r(x)$ such that

$$\underbrace{f(x)}_{\text{Dividend}} = \underbrace{d(x)}_{\text{Divisor}} \cdot \underbrace{q(x)}_{\text{Quotient}} + \underbrace{r(x)}_{\text{Remainder}}.$$

The remainder, $r(x)$, equals 0 or it is of degree less than the degree of $d(x)$. If $r(x) = 0$, we say that $d(x)$ **divides evenly** into $f(x)$ and that $d(x)$ and $q(x)$ are **factors** of $f(x)$.

Check Point 2 Divide $7 - 11x - 3x^2 + 2x^3$ by $x - 3$. Express the result in the form quotient, plus remainder divided by divisor.

If a power of x is missing in either a dividend or a divisor, add that power of x with a coefficient of 0 and then divide. In this way, like terms will be aligned as you carry out the long division.

EXAMPLE 3 Long Division of Polynomials

Divide $6x^4 + 5x^3 + 3x - 5$ by $3x^2 - 2x$.

Solution We write the dividend, $6x^4 + 5x^3 + 3x - 5$, as $6x^4 + 5x^3 + 0x^2 + 3x - 5$ to keep all like terms aligned.

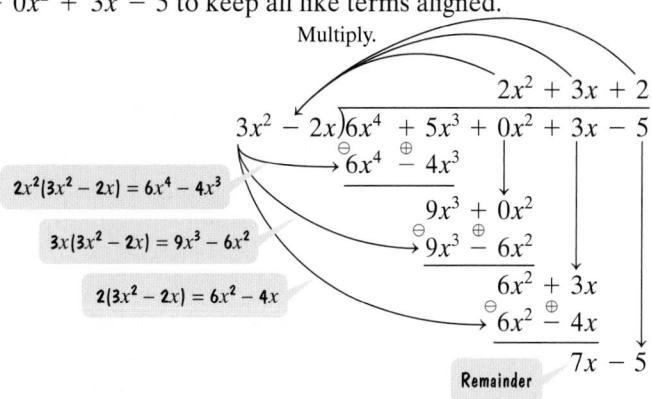

The division process is finished because the degree of $7x - 5$, which is 1, is less than the degree of the divisor $3x^2 - 2x$, which is 2. The answer is

$$\frac{6x^4 + 5x^3 + 3x - 5}{3x^2 - 2x} = 2x^2 + 3x + 2 + \frac{7x - 5}{3x^2 - 2x}.$$

Check Point 3 Divide $2x^4 + 3x^3 - 7x - 10$ by $x^2 - 2x$.

② Use synthetic division to divide polynomials.

Dividing Polynomials Using Synthetic Division

We can use **synthetic division** to divide polynomials if the divisor is of the form $x - c$. This method provides a quotient more quickly than long division. Let's compare the two methods showing $x^3 + 4x^2 - 5x + 5$ divided by $x - 3$.

Long Division **Synthetic Division**

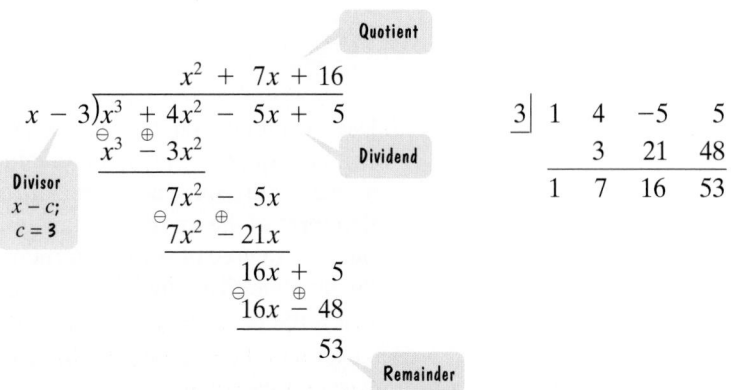

Long Division

$$x - 3\overline{)x^3 + 4x^2 - 5x + 5}$$

Quotient: $x^2 + 7x + 16$

Dividend

Divisor $x - c$; $c = 3$

$$\underline{x^3 - 3x^2}$$
$$7x^2 - 5x$$
$$\underline{7x^2 - 21x}$$
$$16x + 5$$
$$\underline{16x - 48}$$
$$53$$

Remainder

Notice the relationship between the polynomials in the long division process and the numbers that appear in synthetic division.

These are the coefficients of the dividend $x^3 + 4x^2 - 5x + 5$.

The divisor is $x - 3$. This is **3**, or c, in $x - c$.

$$3 \, | \begin{array}{rrrr} 1 & 4 & -5 & 5 \\ & 3 & 21 & 48 \\ \hline 1 & 7 & 16 & 53 \end{array}$$

These are the coefficients of the quotient $x^2 + 7x + 16$.

This is the remainder.

Now let's look at the steps involved in synthetic division.

Synthetic Division

To divide a polynomial by $x - c$:

Example

$$x - 3\overline{)x^3 + 4x^2 - 5x + 5}$$

1. Arrange the polynomial in descending powers, with a 0 coefficient for any missing term.

2. Write c for the divisor, $x - c$. To the right, write the coefficients of the dividend.

$$3 \, | \begin{array}{rrrr} 1 & 4 & -5 & 5 \end{array}$$

3. Write the leading coefficient of the dividend on the bottom row.

$$3 \, | \begin{array}{rrrr} 1 & 4 & -5 & 5 \end{array}$$
↓ Bring down 1.
$$1$$

4. Multiply c (in this case, 3) times the value just written on the bottom row. Write the product in the next column in the second row.

$$3 \, | \begin{array}{rrrr} 1 & 4 & -5 & 5 \\ & 3 & & \\ \hline 1 & & & \end{array}$$

Multiply by 3: $3 \cdot 1 = 3$.

5. Add the values in this new column, writing the sum in the bottom row.

$$3 \, | \begin{array}{rrrr} 1 & 4 & -5 & 5 \\ & 3 & & \\ \hline 1 & 7 & & \end{array}$$ Add.

6. Repeat this series of multiplications and additions until all columns are filled in.

$$3 \, | \begin{array}{rrrr} 1 & 4 & -5 & 5 \\ & 3 & 21 & \\ \hline 1 & 7 & 16 & \end{array}$$ Add.

Multiply by 3: $3 \cdot 7 = 21$.

$$3 \, | \begin{array}{rrrr} 1 & 4 & -5 & 5 \\ & 3 & 21 & 48 \\ \hline 1 & 7 & 16 & 53 \end{array}$$ Add.

Multiply by 3: $3 \cdot 16 = 48$.

7. Use the numbers in the last row to write the quotient, plus the remainder above the divisor. **The degree of the first term of the quotient is one less than the degree of the first term of the dividend.** The final value in this row is the remainder.

Written from
1 7 16 **53**
the last row of the synthetic division

$$1x^2 + 7x + 16 + \frac{53}{x - 3}$$

$$x - 3\overline{)x^3 + 4x^2 - 5x + 5}$$

EXAMPLE 4 **Using Synthetic Division**

Use synthetic division to divide $5x^3 + 6x + 8$ by $x + 2$.

Solution The divisor must be in the form $x - c$. Thus, we write $x + 2$ as $x - (-2)$. This means that $c = -2$. Writing a 0 coefficient for the missing x^2-term in the dividend, we can express the division as follows:

$$x - (-2)\overline{)5x^3 + 0x^2 + 6x + 8}.$$

Now we are ready to set up the problem so that we can use synthetic division.

Use the coefficients of the dividend
$5x^3 + 0x^2 + 6x + 8$ in descending powers of x.

This is c in
$x - (-2)$. $\underline{-2|}$ 5 0 6 8

We begin the synthetic division process by bringing down 5. This is followed by a series of multiplications and additions.

1. Bring down 5.

$$\begin{array}{r|rrrr} -2 & 5 & 0 & 6 & 8 \\ & \downarrow & & & \\ \hline & 5 & & & \end{array}$$

2. Multiply: $-2(5) = -10$.

$$\begin{array}{r|rrrr} -2 & 5 & 0 & 6 & 8 \\ & & -10 & & \\ \hline & 5 & & & \end{array}$$

Multiply 5 by -2.

3. Add: $0 + (-10) = -10$.

$$\begin{array}{r|rrrr} -2 & 5 & 0 & 6 & 8 \\ & & -10 & & \text{Add.} \\ \hline & 5 & -10 & & \end{array}$$

4. Multiply: $-2(-10) = 20$.

$$\begin{array}{r|rrrr} -2 & 5 & 0 & 6 & 8 \\ & & -10 & 20 & \\ \hline & 5 & -10 & & \end{array}$$

Multiply -10 by -2.

5. Add: $6 + 20 = 26$.

$$\begin{array}{r|rrrr} -2 & 5 & 0 & 6 & 8 \\ & & -10 & 20 & \text{Add.} \\ \hline & 5 & -10 & 26 & \end{array}$$

6. Multiply: $-2(26) = -52$.

$$\begin{array}{r|rrrr} -2 & 5 & 0 & 6 & 8 \\ & & -10 & 20 & -52 \\ \hline & 5 & -10 & 26 & \end{array}$$

Multiply 26 by -2.

7. Add: $8 + (-52) = -44$.

$$\begin{array}{r|rrrr} -2 & 5 & 0 & 6 & 8 \\ & & -10 & 20 & -52 & \text{Add.} \\ \hline & 5 & -10 & 26 & -44 \end{array}$$

The numbers in the last row represent the coefficients of the quotient and the remainder. The degree of the first term of the quotient is one less than that of the dividend. Because the degree of the dividend, $5x^3 + 6x + 8$, is 3, the degree of the quotient is 2. This means that the 5 in the last row represents $5x^2$.

$$\begin{array}{r|rrrr} -2 & 5 & 0 & 6 & 8 \\ & & -10 & 20 & -52 \\ \hline & 5 & -10 & 26 & -44 \end{array}$$

The quotient is $5x^2 - 10x + 26$. The remainder is -44.

Thus,

$$x + 2\overline{)5x^3 + 6x + 8} = 5x^2 - 10x + 26 - \frac{44}{x + 2}.$$

⊘ Check Point 4 Use synthetic division to divide $x^3 - 7x - 6$ by $x + 2$.

③ Evaluate a polynomial using the Remainder Theorem.

The Remainder Theorem

Let's consider the Division Algorithm when the dividend, $f(x)$, is divided by $x - c$. In this case, the remainder must be a constant because its degree is less than one, the degree of $x - c$.

$$f(x) = (x - c)q(x) + r$$

Dividend · Divisor · Quotient · The remainder, r, is a constant when dividing by $x - c$.

Now let's evaluate f at c.

$$f(c) = (c - c)q(c) + r \quad \text{Find } f(c) \text{ by letting } x = c \text{ in } f(x) = (x - c)q(x) + r.$$
This will give an expression for r.

$$f(c) = 0 \cdot q(c) + r \quad c - c = 0$$
$$f(c) = r \quad 0 \cdot q(c) = 0 \text{ and } 0 + r = r.$$

What does this last equation mean? If a polynomial is divided by $x - c$, the remainder is the value of the polynomial at c. This result is called the **Remainder Theorem**.

> ## The Remainder Theorem
>
> If the polynomial $f(x)$ is divided by $x - c$, then the remainder is $f(c)$.

Example 5 shows how we can use the Remainder Theorem to evaluate a polynomial function at 2. Rather than substituting 2 for x, we divide the function by $x - 2$. The remainder is $f(2)$.

EXAMPLE 5 **Using the Remainder Theorem to Evaluate a Polynomial Function**

Given $f(x) = x^3 - 4x^2 + 5x + 3$, use the Remainder Theorem to find $f(2)$.

Solution By the Remainder Theorem, if $f(x)$ is divided by $x - 2$, then the remainder is $f(2)$. We'll use synthetic division to divide.

$$
\begin{array}{r|rrrr}
2 & 1 & -4 & 5 & 3 \\
 & & 2 & -4 & 2 \\
\hline
 & 1 & -2 & 1 & 5 \\
\end{array}
$$
Remainder

The remainder, 5, is the value of $f(2)$. Thus, $f(2) = 5$. We can verify that this is correct by evaluating $f(2)$ directly. Using $f(x) = x^3 - 4x^2 + 5x + 3$, we obtain

$$f(2) = 2^3 - 4 \cdot 2^2 + 5 \cdot 2 + 3 = 8 - 16 + 10 + 3 = 5. \qquad \bullet$$

⊘ **Check Point 5** Given $f(x) = 3x^3 + 4x^2 - 5x + 3$, use the Remainder Theorem to find $f(-4)$.

④ Use the Factor Theorem to solve a polynomial equation.

The Factor Theorem

Let's look again at the Division Algorithm when the divisor is of the form $x - c$.

$$f(x) = (x - c)q(x) + r$$

Dividend · Divisor · Quotient · Constant remainder

By the Remainder Theorem, the remainder r is $f(c)$, so we can substitute $f(c)$ for r:

$$f(x) = (x - c)q(x) + f(c).$$

Notice that if $f(c) = 0$, then

$$f(x) = (x - c)q(x)$$

so that $x - c$ is a factor of $f(x)$. This means that for the polynomial function $f(x)$, if $f(c) = 0$, then $x - c$ is a factor of $f(x)$.

Let's reverse directions and see what happens if $x - c$ is a factor of $f(x)$. This means that

$$f(x) = (x - c)q(x).$$

If we replace x in $f(x) = (x - c)q(x)$ with c, we obtain

$$f(c) = (c - c)q(c) = 0 \cdot q(c) = 0.$$

Thus, if $x - c$ is a factor of $f(x)$, then $f(c) = 0$.

We have proved a result known as the **Factor Theorem**.

> ### The Factor Theorem
>
> Let $f(x)$ be a polynomial.
>
> **a.** If $f(c) = 0$, then $x - c$ is a factor of $f(x)$.
>
> **b.** If $x - c$ is a factor of $f(x)$, then $f(c) = 0$.

The example that follows shows how the Factor Theorem can be used to solve a polynomial equation.

(**EXAMPLE 6**) **Using the Factor Theorem**

Solve the equation $2x^3 - 3x^2 - 11x + 6 = 0$ given that 3 is a zero of $f(x) = 2x^3 - 3x^2 - 11x + 6$.

Solution We are given that 3 is a zero of $f(x) = 2x^3 - 3x^2 - 11x + 6$. This means that $f(3) = 0$. Because $f(3) = 0$, the Factor Theorem tells us that $x - 3$ is a factor of $f(x)$. We'll use synthetic division to divide $f(x)$ by $x - 3$.

$$
\begin{array}{r}
3\, |\ \ 2 \ \ -3 \ \ -11 \ \ \ \ 6 \\
\underline{\ \ \ \ \ \ \ \ 6 \ \ \ \ \ 9 \ \ -6} \\
2 \ \ \ \ \ 3 \ \ -2 \ \ \ \ \ 0
\end{array}
\qquad
\begin{array}{l}
\ 2x^2 + \ 3x - 2 \\
x - 3\overline{)2x^3 - 3x^2 - 11x + 6}
\end{array}
$$

The remainder, 0, verifies that $x - 3$ is a factor of $2x^3 - 3x^2 - 11x + 6$.

Equivalently,

$$2x^3 - 3x^2 - 11x + 6 = (x - 3)(2x^2 + 3x - 2).$$

Now we can solve the polynomial equation.

$2x^3 - 3x^2 - 11x + 6 = 0$	This is the given equation.
$(x - 3)(2x^2 + 3x - 2) = 0$	Factor using the result from the synthetic division.
$(x - 3)(2x - 1)(x + 2) = 0$	Factor the trinomial.
$x - 3 = 0$ or $2x - 1 = 0$ or $x + 2 = 0$	Set each factor equal to 0.
$x = 3 \qquad\qquad x = \frac{1}{2} \qquad\qquad x = -2$	Solve for x.

The solution set is $\left\{-2, \frac{1}{2}, 3\right\}$.

Based on the Factor Theorem, the following statements are useful in solving polynomial equations:

1. If $f(x)$ is divided by $x - c$ and the remainder is zero, then c is a zero of f and c is a root of the polynomial equation $f(x) = 0$.

2. If $f(x)$ is divided by $x - c$ and the remainder is zero, then $x - c$ is a factor of $f(x)$.

 Check Point 6 Solve the equation $15x^3 + 14x^2 - 3x - 2 = 0$ given that -1 is a zero of $f(x) = 15x^3 + 14x^2 - 3x - 2$.

Technology

Graphic Connections

Because the solution set of

$$2x^3 - 3x^2 - 11x + 6 = 0$$

is $\left\{-2, \frac{1}{2}, 3\right\}$, this implies that the polynomial function

$$f(x) = 2x^3 - 3x^2 - 11x + 6$$

has x-intercepts (or zeros) at $-2, \frac{1}{2}$, and 3. This is verified by the graph of f.

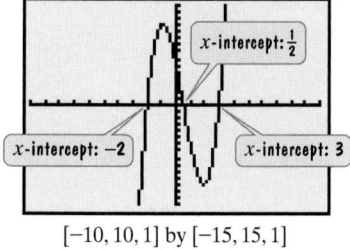

x-intercept: $\frac{1}{2}$

x-intercept: -2

x-intercept: 3

$[-10, 10, 1]$ by $[-15, 15, 1]$

Exercise Set 3.3

Practice Exercises

In Exercises 1–16, divide using long division. State the quotient, $q(x)$, and the remainder, $r(x)$.

1. $(x^2 + 8x + 15) \div (x + 5)$
2. $(x^2 + 3x - 10) \div (x - 2)$
3. $(x^3 + 5x^2 + 7x + 2) \div (x + 2)$
4. $(x^3 - 2x^2 - 5x + 6) \div (x - 3)$
5. $(6x^3 + 7x^2 + 12x - 5) \div (3x - 1)$
6. $(6x^3 + 17x^2 + 27x + 20) \div (3x + 4)$
7. $(12x^2 + x - 4) \div (3x - 2)$
8. $(4x^2 - 8x + 6) \div (2x - 1)$
9. $\dfrac{2x^3 + 7x^2 + 9x - 20}{x + 3}$
10. $\dfrac{3x^2 - 2x + 5}{x - 3}$
11. $\dfrac{4x^4 - 4x^2 + 6x}{x - 4}$
12. $\dfrac{x^4 - 81}{x - 3}$
13. $\dfrac{6x^3 + 13x^2 - 11x - 15}{3x^2 - x - 3}$
14. $\dfrac{x^4 + 2x^3 - 4x^2 - 5x - 6}{x^2 + x - 2}$
15. $\dfrac{18x^4 + 9x^3 + 3x^2}{3x^2 + 1}$
16. $\dfrac{2x^5 - 8x^4 + 2x^3 + x^2}{2x^3 + 1}$

In Exercises 17–32, divide using synthetic division.

17. $(2x^2 + x - 10) \div (x - 2)$ 18. $(x^2 + x - 2) \div (x - 1)$
19. $(3x^2 + 7x - 20) \div (x + 5)$
20. $(5x^2 - 12x - 8) \div (x + 3)$
21. $(4x^3 - 3x^2 + 3x - 1) \div (x - 1)$
22. $(5x^3 - 6x^2 + 3x + 11) \div (x - 2)$
23. $(6x^5 - 2x^3 + 4x^2 - 3x + 1) \div (x - 2)$
24. $(x^5 + 4x^4 - 3x^2 + 2x + 3) \div (x - 3)$
25. $(x^2 - 5x - 5x^3 + x^4) \div (5 + x)$
26. $(x^2 - 6x - 6x^3 + x^4) \div (6 + x)$
27. $\dfrac{x^5 + x^3 - 2}{x - 1}$
28. $\dfrac{x^7 + x^5 - 10x^3 + 12}{x + 2}$
29. $\dfrac{x^4 - 256}{x - 4}$
30. $\dfrac{x^7 - 128}{x - 2}$
31. $\dfrac{2x^5 - 3x^4 + x^3 - x^2 + 2x - 1}{x + 2}$
32. $\dfrac{x^5 - 2x^4 - x^3 + 3x^2 - x + 1}{x - 2}$

In Exercises 33–40, use synthetic division and the Remainder Theorem to find the indicated function value.

33. $f(x) = 2x^3 - 11x^2 + 7x - 5$; $f(4)$
34. $f(x) = x^3 - 7x^2 + 5x - 6$; $f(3)$
35. $f(x) = 3x^3 - 7x^2 - 2x + 5$; $f(-3)$
36. $f(x) = 4x^3 + 5x^2 - 6x - 4$; $f(-2)$
37. $f(x) = x^4 + 5x^3 + 5x^2 - 5x - 6$; $f(3)$
38. $f(x) = x^4 - 5x^3 + 5x^2 + 5x - 6$; $f(2)$
39. $f(x) = 2x^4 - 5x^3 - x^2 + 3x + 2$; $f\left(-\dfrac{1}{2}\right)$
40. $f(x) = 6x^4 + 10x^3 + 5x^2 + x + 1$; $f\left(-\dfrac{2}{3}\right)$

41. Use synthetic division to divide
$$f(x) = x^3 - 4x^2 + x + 6 \text{ by } x + 1.$$
Use the result to find all zeros of f.

42. Use synthetic division to divide
$$f(x) = x^3 - 2x^2 - x + 2 \text{ by } x + 1.$$
Use the result to find all zeros of f.

43. Solve the equation $2x^3 - 5x^2 + x + 2 = 0$ given that 2 is a zero of $f(x) = 2x^3 - 5x^2 + x + 2$.

44. Solve the equation $2x^3 - 3x^2 - 11x + 6 = 0$ given that -2 is a zero of $f(x) = 2x^3 - 3x^2 - 11x + 6$.

45. Solve the equation $12x^3 + 16x^2 - 5x - 3 = 0$ given that $-\frac{3}{2}$ is a root.

46. Solve the equation $3x^3 + 7x^2 - 22x - 8 = 0$ given that $-\frac{1}{3}$ is a root.

Practice Plus

In Exercises 47–50, use the graph or the table to determine a solution of each equation. Use synthetic division to verify that this number is a solution of the equation. Then solve the polynomial equation.

47. $x^3 + 2x^2 - 5x - 6 = 0$

$[0, 4, 1]$ by $[-25, 25, 5]$

48. $2x^3 + x^2 - 13x + 6 = 0$

$[-4, 0, 1]$ by $[-25, 25, 5]$

49. $6x^3 - 11x^2 + 6x - 1 = 0$

50. $2x^3 + 11x^2 - 7x - 6 = 0$

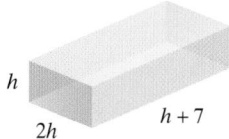

Application Exercises

51. a. Use synthetic division to show that 3 is a solution of the polynomial equation

$$14x^3 - 17x^2 - 16x - 177 = 0.$$

b. Use the solution from part (a) to solve this problem. The number of eggs, $f(x)$, in a female moth is a function of her abdominal width, x, in millimeters, modeled by

$$f(x) = 14x^3 - 17x^2 - 16x + 34.$$

What is the abdominal width when there are 211 eggs?

52. a. Use synthetic division to show that 2 is a solution of the polynomial equation

$$2h^3 + 14h^2 - 72 = 0.$$

b. Use the solution from part (a) to solve this problem. The width of a rectangular box is twice the height and the length is 7 inches more than the height. If the volume is 72 cubic inches, find the dimensions of the box.

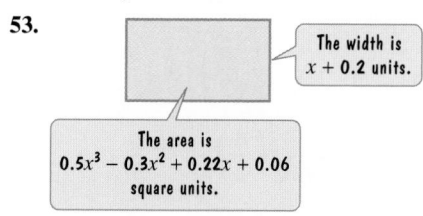

In Exercises 53–54, write a polynomial that represents the length of each rectangle.

53.

54.

During the 1980s, the controversial economist Arthur Laffer promoted the idea that tax increases lead to a reduction in government revenue. Called supply-side economics, the theory uses functions such as

$$f(x) = \frac{80x - 8000}{x - 110}, \quad 30 \le x \le 100.$$

This function models the government tax revenue, $f(x)$, in tens of billions of dollars, in terms of the tax rate, x. The graph of the function is shown. It illustrates tax revenue decreasing quite dramatically as the tax rate increases. At a tax rate of (gasp) 100%, the government takes all our money and no one has an incentive to work. With no income earned, zero dollars in tax revenue is generated.

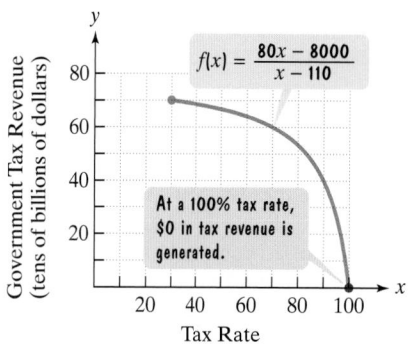

Use function f and its graph to solve Exercises 55–56.

55. a. Find and interpret $f(30)$. Identify the solution as a point on the graph of the function.

b. Rewrite the function by using long division to perform

$$(80x - 8000) \div (x - 110).$$

Then use this new form of the function to find $f(30)$. Do you obtain the same answer as you did in part (a)?

c. Is f a polynomial function? Explain your answer.

56. a. Find and interpret $f(40)$. Identify the solution as a point on the graph of the function.

b. Rewrite the function by using long division to perform

$$(80x - 8000) \div (x - 110).$$

Then use this new form of the function to find $f(40)$. Do you obtain the same answer as you did in part (a)?

c. Is f a polynomial function? Explain your answer.

Writing in Mathematics

57. Explain how to perform long division of polynomials. Use $2x^3 - 3x^2 - 11x + 7$ divided by $x - 3$ in your explanation.

58. In your own words, state the Division Algorithm.

59. How can the Division Algorithm be used to check the quotient and remainder in a long division problem?

60. Explain how to perform synthetic division. Use the division problem in Exercise 57 to support your explanation.

61. State the Remainder Theorem.

62. Explain how the Remainder Theorem can be used to find $f(-6)$ if $f(x) = x^4 + 7x^3 + 8x^2 + 11x + 5$. What advantage is there to using the Remainder Theorem in this situation rather than evaluating $f(-6)$ directly?

63. How can the Factor Theorem be used to determine if $x - 1$ is a factor of $x^3 - 2x^2 - 11x + 12$?

64. If you know that -2 is a zero of

$$f(x) = x^3 + 7x^2 + 4x - 12,$$

explain how to solve the equation

$$x^3 + 7x^2 + 4x - 12 = 0.$$

Technology Exercise

65. For each equation that you solved in Exercises 43–46, use a graphing utility to graph the polynomial function defined by the left side of the equation. Use end behavior to obtain a complete graph. Then use the graph's x-intercepts to verify your solutions.

Critical Thinking Exercises

Make Sense? *In Exercises 66–69, determine whether each statement makes sense or does not make sense, and explain your reasoning.*

66. When performing the division $(x^5 + 1) \div (x + 1)$, there's no need for me to follow all the steps involved in polynomial long division because I can work the problem in my head and see that the quotient must be $x^4 + 1$.

67. Every time I divide polynomials using synthetic division, I am using a highly condensed form of the long division procedure where omitting the variables and exponents does not involve the loss of any essential data.

68. The only nongraphic method that I have for evaluating a function at a given value is to substitute that value into the function's equation.

69. I found the zeros of function f, but I still need to find the solutions of the equation $f(x) = 0$.

In Exercises 70–73, determine whether each statement is true or false. If the statement is false, make the necessary change(s) to produce a true statement.

70. If a trinomial in x of degree 6 is divided by a trinomial in x of degree 3, the degree of the quotient is 2.

71. Synthetic division can be used to find the quotient of $10x^3 - 6x^2 + 4x - 1$ and $x - \frac{1}{2}$.

72. Any problem that can be done by synthetic division can also be done by the method for long division of polynomials.

73. If a polynomial long-division problem results in a remainder that is a whole number, then the divisor is a factor of the dividend.

74. Find k so that $4x + 3$ is a factor of
$$20x^3 + 23x^2 - 10x + k.$$

75. When $2x^2 - 7x + 9$ is divided by a polynomial, the quotient is $2x - 3$ and the remainder is 3. Find the polynomial.

76. Find the quotient of $x^{3n} + 1$ and $x^n + 1$.

77. Synthetic division is a process for dividing a polynomial by $x - c$. The coefficient of x in the divisor is 1. How might synthetic division be used if you are dividing by $2x - 4$?

78. Use synthetic division to show that 5 is a solution of
$$x^4 - 4x^3 - 9x^2 + 16x + 20 = 0.$$
Then solve the polynomial equation.

Preview Exercises

Exercises 79–81 will help you prepare for the material covered in the next section.

79. Solve: $x^2 + 4x - 1 = 0$.

80. Solve: $x^2 + 4x + 6 = 0$.

81. Let $f(x) = a_n(x^4 - 3x^2 - 4)$. If $f(3) = -150$, determine the value of a_n.

Section 3.4 Zeros of Polynomial Functions

Objectives

1. Use the Rational Zero Theorem to find possible rational zeros.
2. Find zeros of a polynomial function.
3. Solve polynomial equations.
4. Use the Linear Factorization Theorem to find polynomials with given zeros.
5. Use Descartes's Rule of Signs.

AVTORIS CARMEN.

Non me terra teget, cœlo sed raptus in alto
Illuftris uiuam docta per ora uirûm.
Quicquid uenturis fpectabit Phœbus in annis,
Cardanos nofcet, nomen & ufcg meum.

You stole my formula!

Tartaglia's Secret Formula for One Solution of
$$x^3 + mx = n$$

$$x = \sqrt[3]{\sqrt{\left(\frac{n}{2}\right)^2 + \left(\frac{m}{3}\right)^3} + \frac{n}{2}} - \sqrt[3]{\sqrt{\left(\frac{n}{2}\right)^2 + \left(\frac{m}{3}\right)^3} - \frac{n}{2}}$$

Popularizers of mathematics are sharing bizarre stories that are giving math a secure place in popular culture. One episode, able to compete with the wildest fare served up by television talk shows and the tabloids, involves three Italian mathematicians and, of all things, zeros of polynomial functions.

Tartaglia (1499–1557), poor and starving, has found a formula that gives a root for a third-degree polynomial equation. Cardano (1501–1576) begs Tartaglia to reveal the secret formula, wheedling it from him with the promise he will find the impoverished Tartaglia a patron. Then Cardano publishes his famous work *Ars Magna*, in which he presents Tartaglia's formula as his own. Cardano uses his most talented student, Ferrari (1522–1565), who derived a formula for a root of a

fourth-degree polynomial equation, to falsely accuse Tartaglia of plagiarism. The dispute becomes violent and Tartaglia is fortunate to escape alive.

The noise from this "You Stole My Formula" episode is quieted by the work of French mathematician Evariste Galois (1811–1832). Galois proved that there is no general formula for finding roots of polynomial equations of degree 5 or higher. There are, however, methods for finding roots. In this section, we study methods for finding zeros of polynomial functions. We begin with a theorem that plays an important role in this process.

Study Tip

Be sure you are familiar with the various kinds of zeros of polynomial functions. Here's a quick example:

$$f(x) = (x + 3)(2x - 1)(x + \sqrt{2})(x - \sqrt{2})(x - 4 + 5i)(x - 4 - 5i).$$

Zeros: $-3, \quad \dfrac{1}{2}, \quad -\sqrt{2}, \quad \sqrt{2}, \quad 4 - 5i, \quad 4 + 5i$

Rational zeros Irrational zeros Complex imaginary zeros

Real zeros Nonreal zeros

① Use the Rational Zero Theorem to find possible rational zeros.

The Rational Zero Theorem

The Rational Zero Theorem provides us with a tool that we can use to make a list of all possible rational zeros of a polynomial function. Equivalently, the theorem gives all possible rational roots of a polynomial equation. Not every number in the list will be a zero of the function, but every rational zero of the polynomial function will appear somewhere in the list.

The Rational Zero Theorem

If $f(x) = a_n x^n + a_{n-1} x^{n-1} + \cdots + a_1 x + a_0$ has *integer* coefficients and $\dfrac{p}{q}$ (where $\dfrac{p}{q}$ is reduced to lowest terms) is a rational zero of f, then p is a factor of the constant term, a_0, and q is a factor of the leading coefficient, a_n.

You can explore the "why" behind the Rational Zero Theorem in Exercise 92 of Exercise Set 3.4. For now, let's see if we can figure out what the theorem tells us about possible rational zeros. To use the theorem, list all the integers that are factors of the constant term, a_0. Then list all the integers that are factors of the leading coefficient, a_n. Finally, list all possible rational zeros:

$$\text{Possible rational zeros} = \frac{\text{Factors of the constant term}}{\text{Factors of the leading coefficient}}.$$

(**EXAMPLE 1**) **Using the Rational Zero Theorem**

List all possible rational zeros of $f(x) = -x^4 + 3x^2 + 4$.

Solution The constant term is 4. We list all of its factors: $\pm 1, \pm 2, \pm 4$. The leading coefficient is -1. Its factors are ± 1.

Factors of the constant term, 4: $\pm 1, \quad \pm 2, \quad \pm 4$
Factors of the leading coefficient, -1: ± 1

Because

$$\text{Possible rational zeros} = \frac{\text{Factors of the constant term}}{\text{Factors of the leading coefficient}},$$

we must take each number in the first row, $\pm 1, \pm 2, \pm 4$, and divide by each number in the second row, ± 1.

$$\text{Possible rational zeros} = \frac{\text{Factors of 4}}{\text{Factors of } -1} = \frac{\pm 1, \pm 2, \pm 4}{\pm 1} = \pm 1, \quad \pm 2, \quad \pm 4$$

Divide ±1 by ±1. Divide ±2 by ±1. Divide ±4 by ±1.

Study Tip

Always keep in mind the relationship among zeros, roots, and x-intercepts. The zeros of a function f are the roots, or solutions, of the equation $f(x) = 0$. Furthermore, the real zeros, or real roots, are the x-intercepts of the graph of f.

There are six possible rational zeros. The graph of $f(x) = -x^4 + 3x^2 + 4$ is shown in **Figure 3.25**. The x-intercepts are -2 and 2. Thus, -2 and 2 are the actual rational zeros. ●

○ Check Point **1** List all possible rational zeros of

$$f(x) = x^3 + 2x^2 - 5x - 6.$$

−2 is a rational zero. 2 is a rational zero.

Figure 3.25 The graph of $f(x) = -x^4 + 3x^2 + 4$ shows that -2 and 2 are rational zeros.

(**EXAMPLE 2**) **Using the Rational Zero Theorem**

List all possible rational zeros of $f(x) = 15x^3 + 14x^2 - 3x - 2$.

Solution The constant term is -2 and the leading coefficient is 15.

$$\text{Possible rational zeros} = \frac{\text{Factors of the constant term, } -2}{\text{Factors of the leading coefficient, } 15} = \frac{\pm 1, \pm 2}{\pm 1, \pm 3, \pm 5, \pm 15}$$

$$= \pm 1, \quad \pm 2, \quad \pm \frac{1}{3}, \quad \pm \frac{2}{3}, \quad \pm \frac{1}{5}, \quad \pm \frac{2}{5}, \quad \pm \frac{1}{15}, \quad \pm \frac{2}{15}$$

Divide ±1 and ±2 by ±1. Divide ±1 and ±2 by ±3. Divide ±1 and ±2 by ±5. Divide ±1 and ±2 by ±15.

There are 16 possible rational zeros. The actual solution set of
$$15x^3 + 14x^2 - 3x - 2 = 0$$
is $\left\{-1, -\frac{1}{3}, \frac{2}{5}\right\}$, which contains three of the 16 possible zeros. ●

○ Check Point **2** List all possible rational zeros of

$$f(x) = 4x^5 + 12x^4 - x - 3.$$

2 Find zeros of a polynomial function.

How do we determine which (if any) of the possible rational zeros are rational zeros of the polynomial function? To find the first rational zero, we can use a trial-and-error process involving synthetic division: If $f(x)$ is divided by $x - c$ and the remainder is zero, then c is a zero of f. After we identify the first rational zero, we use the result of the synthetic division to factor the original polynomial. Then we set each factor equal to zero to identify any additional rational zeros.

(**EXAMPLE 3**) **Finding Zeros of a Polynomial Function**

Find all zeros of $f(x) = x^3 + 2x^2 - 5x - 6$.

Solution We begin by listing all possible rational zeros.
Possible rational zeros

$$= \frac{\text{Factors of the constant term, } -6}{\text{Factors of the leading coefficient, } 1} = \frac{\pm 1, \pm 2, \pm 3, \pm 6}{\pm 1} = \pm 1, \pm 2, \pm 3, \pm 6$$

Divide the eight numbers in the numerator by ±1.

Now we will use synthetic division to see if we can find a rational zero among the possible rational zeros $\pm1, \pm2, \pm3, \pm6$. Keep in mind that if $f(x)$ is divided by $x - c$ and the remainder is zero, then c is a zero of f. Let's start by testing 1. If 1 is not a rational zero, then we will test other possible rational zeros.

Test 1.

Possible rational zero

Coefficients of
$f(x) = x^3 + 2x^2 - 5x - 6$

$$\begin{array}{c|rrrr} 1 & 1 & 2 & -5 & -6 \\ & & 1 & 3 & -2 \\ \hline & 1 & 3 & -2 & -8 \end{array}$$

The nonzero remainder shows that 1 is not a zero.

Test 2.

Possible rational zero

Coefficients of
$f(x) = x^3 + 2x^2 - 5x - 6$

$$\begin{array}{c|rrrr} 2 & 1 & 2 & -5 & -6 \\ & & 2 & 8 & 6 \\ \hline & 1 & 4 & 3 & 0 \end{array}$$

The zero remainder shows that 2 is a zero.

The zero remainder tells us that 2 is a zero of the polynomial function $f(x) = x^3 + 2x^2 - 5x - 6$. Equivalently, 2 is a solution, or root, of the polynomial equation $x^3 + 2x^2 - 5x - 6 = 0$. Thus, $x - 2$ is a factor of the polynomial. The first three numbers in the bottom row of the synthetic division on the right, 1, 4, and 3, give the coefficients of the other factor. This factor is $x^2 + 4x + 3$.

$$x^3 + 2x^2 - 5x - 6 = 0 \qquad \text{Finding the zeros of } f(x) = x^3 + 2x^2 - 5x - 6$$
$$\text{is the same as finding the roots of this}$$
$$\text{equation.}$$

$$(x - 2)(x^2 + 4x + 3) = 0 \qquad \text{Factor using the result from the}$$
$$\text{synthetic division.}$$

$$(x - 2)(x + 3)(x + 1) = 0 \qquad \text{Factor completely.}$$

$$x - 2 = 0 \quad \text{or} \quad x + 3 = 0 \quad \text{or} \quad x + 1 = 0 \qquad \text{Set each factor equal to zero.}$$
$$x = 2 \qquad\qquad x = -3 \qquad\qquad x = -1 \qquad \text{Solve for } x.$$

The solution set is $\{-3, -1, 2\}$. The zeros of f are $-3, -1$, and 2. ●

⬜ **Check Point** **3** Find all zeros of

$$f(x) = x^3 + 8x^2 + 11x - 20.$$

Our work in Example 3 involved finding zeros of a third-degree polynomial function. The Rational Zero Theorem is a tool that allows us to rewrite such functions as products of two factors, one linear and one quadratic. Zeros of the quadratic factor are found by factoring, the quadratic formula, or the square root property.

EXAMPLE 4 **Finding Zeros of a Polynomial Function**

Find all zeros of $f(x) = x^3 + 7x^2 + 11x - 3$.

Solution We begin by listing all possible rational zeros.

$$\text{Possible rational zeros} = \frac{\text{Factors of the constant term}, -3}{\text{Factors of the leading coefficient}, 1} = \frac{\pm1, \pm3}{\pm1} = \pm1, \pm3$$

Now we will use synthetic division to see if we can find a rational zero among the four possible rational zeros.

Test 1.	Test -1.	Test 3.	Test -3.
$\begin{array}{c\|rrrr} 1 & 1 & 7 & 11 & -3 \\ & & 1 & 8 & 19 \\ \hline & 1 & 8 & 19 & 16 \end{array}$	$\begin{array}{c\|rrrr} -1 & 1 & 7 & 11 & -3 \\ & & -1 & -6 & -5 \\ \hline & 1 & 6 & 5 & -8 \end{array}$	$\begin{array}{c\|rrrr} 3 & 1 & 7 & 11 & -3 \\ & & 3 & 30 & 123 \\ \hline & 1 & 10 & 41 & 120 \end{array}$	$\begin{array}{c\|rrrr} -3 & 1 & 7 & 11 & -3 \\ & & -3 & -12 & 3 \\ \hline & 1 & 4 & -1 & 0 \end{array}$

Test −3. (repeated)

$$\begin{array}{r|rrrr} -3 & 1 & 7 & 11 & -3 \\ & & -3 & -12 & 3 \\ \hline & 1 & 4 & -1 & 0 \end{array}$$

The zero remainder when testing −3, repeated in the margin, tells us that −3 is a zero of the polynomial function $f(x) = x^3 + 7x^2 + 11x - 3$. To find all zeros of f, we proceed as follows:

$$x^3 + 7x^2 + 11x - 3 = 0$$ Finding the zeros of f is the same thing as finding the roots of $f(x) = 0$.

$$(x + 3)(x^2 + 4x - 1) = 0$$ This result is from the last synthetic division, repeated in the margin. The first three numbers in the bottom row, 1, 4, and −1, give the coefficients of the second factor.

$$x + 3 = 0 \quad \text{or} \quad x^2 + 4x - 1 = 0$$ Set each factor equal to 0.
$$x = -3.$$ Solve the linear equation.

We can use the quadratic formula to solve $x^2 + 4x - 1 = 0$.

$$x = \frac{-b \pm \sqrt{b^2 - 4ac}}{2a}$$ We use the quadratic formula because $x^2 + 4x - 1$ cannot be factored.

$$= \frac{-4 \pm \sqrt{4^2 - 4(1)(-1)}}{2(1)}$$ Let $a = 1$, $b = 4$, and $c = -1$.

$$= \frac{-4 \pm \sqrt{20}}{2}$$ Multiply and subtract under the radical: $4^2 - 4(1)(-1) = 16 - (-4) = 16 + 4 = 20$.

$$= \frac{-4 \pm 2\sqrt{5}}{2}$$ $\sqrt{20} = \sqrt{4 \cdot 5} = 2\sqrt{5}$

$$= -2 \pm \sqrt{5}$$ Divide the numerator and the denominator by 2.

The solution set is $\left\{-3, -2 - \sqrt{5}, -2 + \sqrt{5}\right\}$. The zeros of $f(x) = x^3 + 7x^3 + 11x - 3$ are $-3, -2 - \sqrt{5}$, and $-2 + \sqrt{5}$. Among these three real zeros, one zero is rational and two are irrational. ●

⊘ **Check Point 4** Find all zeros of $f(x) = x^3 + x^2 - 5x - 2$.

If the degree of a polynomial function or equation is 4 or higher, it is often necessary to find more than one linear factor by synthetic division.

One way to speed up the process of finding the first zero is to graph the function. Any x-intercept is a zero.

❸ Solve polynomial equations.

EXAMPLE 5 **Solving a Polynomial Equation**

Solve: $x^4 - 6x^2 - 8x + 24 = 0$.

Solution Recall that we refer to the *zeros* of a polynomial function and the *roots* of a polynomial equation. Because we are given an equation, we will use the word "roots," rather than "zeros," in the solution process. We begin by listing all possible rational roots.

$$\text{Possible rational roots} = \frac{\text{Factors of the constant term, 24}}{\text{Factors of the leading coefficient, 1}}$$

$$= \frac{\pm 1, \pm 2, \pm 3, \pm 4, \pm 6, \pm 8, \pm 12, \pm 24}{\pm 1}$$

$$= \pm 1, \pm 2, \pm 3, \pm 4, \pm 6, \pm 8, \pm 12, \pm 24$$

Part of the graph of $f(x) = x^4 - 6x^2 - 8x + 24$ is shown in **Figure 3.26**. Because the x-intercept is 2, we will test 2 by synthetic division and show that it is a root of the given equation. Without the graph, the procedure would be to start the trial-and-error synthetic division with 1 and proceed until a zero remainder is found, as we did in Example 4.

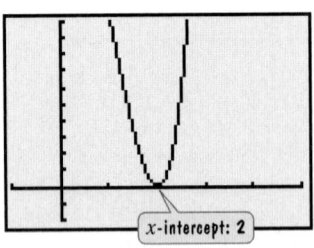

Figure 3.26 The graph of $f(x) = x^4 - 6x^2 - 8x + 24$ in a $[-1, 5, 1]$ by $[-2, 10, 1]$ viewing rectangle

x-intercept: 2

$$\begin{array}{r|rrrrr} 2 & 1 & 0 & -6 & -8 & 24 \\ & & 2 & 4 & -4 & -24 \\ \hline & 1 & 2 & -2 & -12 & 0 \end{array}$$

Careful!
$x^4 - 6x^2 - 8x + 24 = x^4 + 0x^3 - 6x^2 - 8x + 24$

The zero remainder indicates that 2 is a root of
$x^4 - 6x^2 - 8x + 24 = 0$.

Now we can rewrite the given equation in factored form.

$$x^4 - 6x^2 - 8x + 24 = 0 \qquad \text{This is the given equation.}$$

$$(x - 2)(x^3 + 2x^2 - 2x - 12) = 0 \qquad \text{This is the result obtained from the synthetic division. The first four numbers in the bottom row, 1, 2, -2, and -12, give the coefficients of the second factor.}$$

$$x - 2 = 0 \quad \text{or} \quad x^3 + 2x^2 - 2x - 12 = 0 \qquad \text{Set each factor equal to 0.}$$

We can use the same approach to look for rational roots of the polynomial equation $x^3 + 2x^2 - 2x - 12 = 0$, listing all possible rational roots. Without the graph in **Figure 3.26**, the procedure would be to start testing possible rational roots by trial-and-error synthetic division. However, take a second look at the graph in **Figure 3.26**. Because the graph turns around at 2, this means that 2 is a root of even multiplicity. Thus, 2 must also be a root of $x^3 + 2x^2 - 2x - 12 = 0$, confirmed by the following synthetic division.

$$
\begin{array}{r|rrrr}
2 & 1 & 2 & -2 & -12 \\
 & & 2 & 8 & 12 \\
\hline
 & 1 & 4 & 6 & 0
\end{array}
$$

These are the coefficients of $x^3 + 2x^2 - 2x - 12 = 0.$

The zero remainder indicates that **2** is a root of $x^3 + 2x^2 - 2x - 12 = 0.$

Now we can solve the original equation as follows:

$$x^4 - 6x^2 - 8x + 24 = 0 \qquad \text{This is the given equation.}$$

$$(x - 2)(x^3 + 2x^2 - 2x - 12) = 0 \qquad \text{This factorization was obtained from the first synthetic division.}$$

$$(x - 2)(x - 2)(x^2 + 4x + 6) = 0 \qquad \text{This factorization was obtained from the second synthetic division. The first three numbers in the bottom row, 1, 4, and 6, give the coefficients of the third factor.}$$

$$x - 2 = 0 \quad \text{or} \quad x - 2 = 0 \quad \text{or} \quad x^2 + 4x + 6 = 0 \qquad \text{Set each factor equal to 0.}$$

$$x = 2 \qquad\qquad x = 2. \qquad\qquad\qquad \text{Solve the linear equations.}$$

We can use the quadratic formula to solve $x^2 + 4x + 6 = 0$.

$$x = \frac{-b \pm \sqrt{b^2 - 4ac}}{2a} \qquad \text{We use the quadratic formula because } x^2 + 4x + 6 \text{ cannot be factored.}$$

$$= \frac{-4 \pm \sqrt{4^2 - 4(1)(6)}}{2(1)} \qquad \text{Let } a = 1, b = 4, \text{ and } c = 6.$$

$$= \frac{-4 \pm \sqrt{-8}}{2} \qquad \text{Multiply and subtract under the radical: } 4^2 - 4(1)(6) = 16 - 24 = -8.$$

$$= \frac{-4 \pm 2i\sqrt{2}}{2} \qquad \sqrt{-8} = \sqrt{4(2)(-1)} = 2i\sqrt{2}$$

$$= -2 \pm i\sqrt{2} \qquad \text{Simplify.}$$

The solution set of the original equation, $x^4 - 6x^2 - 8x + 24 = 0$, is $\{2, -2 - i\sqrt{2}, -2 + i\sqrt{2}\}$. A graphing utility does not reveal the two imaginary roots.

In Example 5, 2 is a repeated root of the equation with multiplicity 2. Counting this multiple root separately, the fourth-degree equation $x^4 - 6x^2 - 8x + 24 = 0$ has four roots: $2, 2, -2 + i\sqrt{2}$, and $-2 - i\sqrt{2}$. The equation and its roots illustrate two general properties:

Properties of Roots of Polynomial Equations

1. If a polynomial equation is of degree n, then counting multiple roots separately, the equation has n roots.
2. If $a + bi$ is a root of a polynomial equation with real coefficients $(b \neq 0)$, then the imaginary number $a - bi$ is also a root. Imaginary roots, if they exist, occur in conjugate pairs.

⊘ Check Point **5** Solve: $x^4 - 6x^3 + 22x^2 - 30x + 13 = 0$.

The Fundamental Theorem of Algebra

The fact that a polynomial equation of degree n has n roots is a consequence of a theorem proved in 1799 by a 22-year-old student named Carl Friedrich Gauss in his doctoral dissertation. His result is called the **Fundamental Theorem of Algebra**.

Study Tip

As you read the Fundamental Theorem of Algebra, don't confuse *complex root* with *imaginary root* and conclude that every polynomial equation has at least one imaginary root. Recall that complex numbers, $a + bi$, include both real numbers $(b = 0)$ and imaginary numbers $(b \neq 0)$.

The Fundamental Theorem of Algebra

If $f(x)$ is a polynomial of degree n, where $n \geq 1$, then the equation $f(x) = 0$ has at least one complex root.

Suppose, for example, that $f(x) = 0$ represents a polynomial equation of degree n. By the Fundamental Theorem of Algebra, we know that this equation has at least one complex root; we'll call it c_1. By the Factor Theorem, we know that $x - c_1$ is a factor of $f(x)$. Therefore, we obtain

$$(x - c_1)q_1(x) = 0 \quad \text{The degree of the polynomial } q_1(x) \text{ is } n - 1.$$
$$x - c_1 = 0 \quad \text{or} \quad q_1(x) = 0. \quad \text{Set each factor equal to 0.}$$

If the degree of $q_1(x)$ is at least 1, by the Fundamental Theorem of Algebra, the equation $q_1(x) = 0$ has at least one complex root. We'll call it c_2. The Factor Theorem gives us

$$q_1(x) = 0 \quad \text{The degree of } q_1(x) \text{ is } n - 1.$$
$$(x - c_2)q_2(x) = 0 \quad \text{The degree of } q_2(x) \text{ is } n - 2.$$
$$x - c_2 = 0 \quad \text{or} \quad q_2(x) = 0. \quad \text{Set each factor equal to 0.}$$

Let's see what we have up to this point and then continue the process.

$$f(x) = 0 \quad \text{This is the original polynomial equation of degree } n.$$
$$(x - c_1)q_1(x) = 0 \quad \text{This is the result from our first application of the Fundamental Theorem.}$$
$$(x - c_1)(x - c_2)q_2(x) = 0 \quad \text{This is the result from our second application of the Fundamental Theorem.}$$

By continuing this process, we will obtain the product of n linear factors. Setting each of these linear factors equal to zero results in n complex roots. Thus, if $f(x)$ is a polynomial of degree n, where $n \geq 1$, then $f(x) = 0$ has exactly n roots, where roots are counted according to their multiplicity.

④ Use the Linear Factorization Theorem to find polynomials with given zeros.

The Linear Factorization Theorem

In Example 5, we found that $x^4 - 6x^2 - 8x + 24 = 0$ has $\{2, -2 \pm i\sqrt{2}\}$ as a solution set, where 2 is a repeated root with multiplicity 2. The polynomial can be factored over the complex nonreal numbers as follows:

$$f(x) = x^4 - 6x^2 - 8x + 24$$

These are the four zeros.

$$= [x - (-2 + i\sqrt{2})][x - (-2 - i\sqrt{2})](x - 2)(x - 2).$$

These are the linear factors.

This fourth-degree polynomial has four linear factors. Just as an nth-degree polynomial equation has n roots, an nth-degree polynomial has n linear factors. This is formally stated as the **Linear Factorization Theorem**.

The Linear Factorization Theorem

If $f(x) = a_n x^n + a_{n-1} x^{n-1} + \cdots + a_1 x + a_0$, where $n \geq 1$ and $a_n \neq 0$, then

$$f(x) = a_n (x - c_1)(x - c_2) \cdots (x - c_n),$$

where c_1, c_2, \ldots, c_n are complex numbers (possibly real and not necessarily distinct). In words: An nth-degree polynomial can be expressed as the product of a nonzero constant and n linear factors, where each linear factor has a leading coefficient of 1.

Many of our problems involving polynomial functions and polynomial equations dealt with the process of finding zeros and roots. The Linear Factorization Theorem enables us to reverse this process, finding a polynomial function when the zeros are given.

EXAMPLE 6 **Finding a Polynomial Function with Given Zeros**

Find a fourth-degree polynomial function $f(x)$ with real coefficients that has $-2, 2,$ and i as zeros and such that $f(3) = -150$.

Solution Because i is a zero and the polynomial has real coefficients, the conjugate, $-i$, must also be a zero. We can now use the Linear Factorization Theorem.

$f(x) = a_n(x - c_1)(x - c_2)(x - c_3)(x - c_4)$	This is the linear factorization for a fourth-degree polynomial.
$= a_n(x + 2)(x - 2)(x - i)(x + i)$	Use the given zeros: $c_1 = -2, c_2 = 2, c_3 = i$, and, from above, $c_4 = -i$.
$= a_n(x^2 - 4)(x^2 + 1)$	Multiply: $(x - i)(x + i) = x^2 - i^2 = x^2 - (-1) = x^2 + 1$.
$f(x) = a_n(x^4 - 3x^2 - 4)$	Complete the multiplication.
$f(3) = a_n(3^4 - 3 \cdot 3^2 - 4) = -150$	To find a_n, use the fact that $f(3) = -150$.
$a_n(81 - 27 - 4) = -150$	Solve for a_n.
$50a_n = -150$	Simplify: $81 - 27 - 4 = 50$.
$a_n = -3$	Divide both sides by 50.

Substituting -3 for a_n in the formula for $f(x)$, we obtain

$$f(x) = -3(x^4 - 3x^2 - 4).$$

Equivalently,

$$f(x) = -3x^4 + 9x^2 + 12.$$

Technology

Graphic Connections

The graph of $f(x) = -3x^4 + 9x^2 + 12$, shown in a $[-3, 3, 1]$ by $[-200, 20, 20]$ viewing rectangle, verifies that -2 and 2 are real zeros. By tracing along the curve, we can check that $f(3) = -150$.

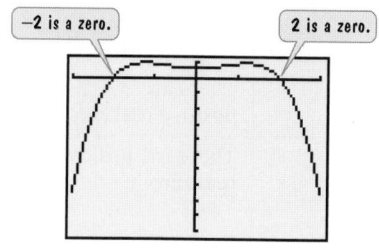

-2 is a zero. 2 is a zero.

⊘ **Check Point 6** Find a third-degree polynomial function $f(x)$ with real coefficients that has -3 and i as zeros and such that $f(1) = 8$.

⑤ Use Descartes's Rule of Signs.

Descartes's Rule of Signs

Because an nth-degree polynomial equation might have roots that are imaginary numbers, we should note that such an equation can have *at most n real roots*. **Descartes's Rule of Signs** provides even more specific information about the number of real zeros that a polynomial can have. The rule is based on considering *variations in sign* between consecutive coefficients. For example, the function $f(x) = 3x^7 - 2x^5 - x^4 + 7x^2 + x - 3$ has three sign changes:

$$f(x) = 3x^7 - 2x^5 - x^4 + 7x^2 + x - 3.$$

sign change sign change sign change

"An equation can have as many true [positive] roots as it contains changes of sign, from plus to minus or from minus to plus." René Descartes (1596–1650) in *La Géométrie* (1637)

Descartes's Rule of Signs

Let $f(x) = a_n x^n + a_{n-1} x^{n-1} + \cdots + a_2 x^2 + a_1 x + a_0$ be a polynomial with real coefficients.

1. The number of *positive real zeros* of f is either
 a. the same as the number of sign changes of $f(x)$

 or

 b. less than the number of sign changes of $f(x)$ by a positive even integer. If $f(x)$ has only one variation in sign, then f has exactly one positive real zero.

2. The number of *negative real zeros* of f is either
 a. the same as the number of sign changes of $f(-x)$

 or

 b. less than the number of sign changes of $f(-x)$ by a positive even integer. If $f(-x)$ has only one variation in sign, then f has exactly one negative real zero.

Study Tip

The number of real zeros given by Descartes's Rule of Signs includes rational zeros from a list of possible rational zeros, as well as irrational zeros not on the list. It does not include any imaginary zeros.

Table 3.1 illustrates what Descartes's Rule of Signs tells us about the positive real zeros of various polynomial functions.

Table 3.1 Descartes's Rule of Signs and Positive Real Zeros

Polynomial Function	Sign Changes	Conclusion
$f(x) = 3x^7 - 2x^5 - x^4 + 7x^2 + x - 3$ sign change sign change sign change	3	There are 3 positive real zeros. or There is $3 - 2 = 1$ positive real zero.
$f(x) = 4x^5 + 2x^4 - 3x^2 + x + 5$ sign change sign change	2	There are 2 positive real zeros. or There are $2 - 2 = 0$ positive real zeros.
$f(x) = -7x^6 - 5x^4 + x + 9$ sign change	1	There is 1 positive real zero.

Study Tip

Be sure that the polynomial function is written in descending powers of x when counting sign changes.

(EXAMPLE 7) Using Descartes's Rule of Signs

Determine the possible numbers of positive and negative real zeros of $f(x) = x^3 + 2x^2 + 5x + 4$.

Solution

1. To find possibilities for positive real zeros, count the number of sign changes in the equation for $f(x)$. Because all the coefficients are positive, there are no variations in sign. Thus, there are no positive real zeros.

2. To find possibilities for negative real zeros, count the number of sign changes in the equation for $f(-x)$. We obtain this equation by replacing x with $-x$ in the given function.

$$f(x) = x^3 + 2x^2 + 5x + 4$$

Replace x with $-x$.

$$f(-x) = (-x)^3 + 2(-x)^2 + 5(-x) + 4$$
$$= -x^3 + 2x^2 - 5x + 4$$

Now count the sign changes.

$$f(-x) = -x^3 + 2x^2 - 5x + 4$$

sign change **sign change** **sign change**

There are three variations in sign. The number of negative real zeros of f is either equal to the number of sign changes, 3, or is less than this number by an even integer. This means that either there are 3 negative real zeros or there is $3 - 2 = 1$ negative real zero.

What do the results of Example 7 mean in terms of solving

$$x^3 + 2x^2 + 5x + 4 = 0?$$

Without using Descartes's Rule of Signs, we list the possible rational roots as follows:

Possible rational roots

$$= \frac{\text{Factors of the constant term, 4}}{\text{Factors of the leading coefficient, 1}} = \frac{\pm 1, \pm 2, \pm 4}{\pm 1} = \pm 1, \pm 2, \pm 4.$$

However, Descartes's Rule of Signs informed us that $f(x) = x^3 + 2x^2 + 5x + 4$ has no positive real zeros. Thus, the polynomial equation $x^3 + 2x^2 + 5x + 4 = 0$ has no positive real roots. This means that we can eliminate the positive numbers from our list of possible rational roots. Possible rational roots include only -1, -2, and -4. We can use synthetic division and test the first of these three possible rational roots of $x^3 + 2x^2 + 5x + 4 = 0$ as follows:

Test -1.

$$\underline{-1}\,|\;\; 1 \quad 2 \quad 5 \quad 4$$
$$\qquad\quad -1 \;\; -1 \;\; -4$$
$$\overline{\quad\quad 1 \quad 1 \quad 4 \quad 0.}$$

The zero remainder shows that -1 is a root.

By solving the equation $x^3 + 2x^2 + 5x + 4 = 0$, you will find that this equation of degree 3 has three roots. One root is -1 and the other two roots are imaginary numbers in a conjugate pair. Verify this by completing the solution process.

⊘ **Check Point 7** Determine the possible numbers of positive and negative real zeros of $f(x) = x^4 - 14x^3 + 71x^2 - 154x + 120$.

Exercise Set 3.4

Practice Exercises

In Exercises 1–8, use the Rational Zero Theorem to list all possible rational zeros for each given function.

1. $f(x) = x^3 + x^2 - 4x - 4$

2. $f(x) = x^3 + 3x^2 - 6x - 8$

3. $f(x) = 3x^4 - 11x^3 - x^2 + 19x + 6$

4. $f(x) = 2x^4 + 3x^3 - 11x^2 - 9x + 15$

5. $f(x) = 4x^4 - x^3 + 5x^2 - 2x - 6$

6. $f(x) = 3x^4 - 11x^3 - 3x^2 - 6x + 8$

7. $f(x) = x^5 - x^4 - 7x^3 + 7x^2 - 12x - 12$

8. $f(x) = 4x^5 - 8x^4 - x + 2$

In Exercises 9–16,

 a. *List all possible rational zeros.*

 b. *Use synthetic division to test the possible rational zeros and find an actual zero.*

 c. *Use the quotient from part (b) to find the remaining zeros of the polynomial function.*

9. $f(x) = x^3 + x^2 - 4x - 4$

10. $f(x) = x^3 - 2x^2 - 11x + 12$

11. $f(x) = 2x^3 - 3x^2 - 11x + 6$

12. $f(x) = 2x^3 - 5x^2 + x + 2$

13. $f(x) = x^3 + 4x^2 - 3x - 6$

14. $f(x) = 2x^3 + x^2 - 3x + 1$

15. $f(x) = 2x^3 + 6x^2 + 5x + 2$

16. $f(x) = x^3 - 4x^2 + 8x - 5$

In Exercises 17–24,

 a. *List all possible rational roots.*

 b. *Use synthetic division to test the possible rational roots and find an actual root.*

 c. *Use the quotient from part (b) to find the remaining roots and solve the equation.*

17. $x^3 - 2x^2 - 11x + 12 = 0$

18. $x^3 - 2x^2 - 7x - 4 = 0$

19. $x^3 - 10x - 12 = 0$

20. $x^3 - 5x^2 + 17x - 13 = 0$

21. $6x^3 + 25x^2 - 24x + 5 = 0$

22. $2x^3 - 5x^2 - 6x + 4 = 0$

23. $x^4 - 2x^3 - 5x^2 + 8x + 4 = 0$

24. $x^4 - 2x^2 - 16x - 15 = 0$

In Exercises 25–32, find an nth-degree polynomial function with real coefficients satisfying the given conditions. If you are using a graphing utility, use it to graph the function and verify the real zeros and the given function value.

25. $n = 3$; 1 and $5i$ are zeros; $f(-1) = -104$

26. $n = 3$; 4 and $2i$ are zeros; $f(-1) = -50$

27. $n = 3$; -5 and $4 + 3i$ are zeros; $f(2) = 91$

28. $n = 3$; 6 and $-5 + 2i$ are zeros; $f(2) = -636$

29. $n = 4$; i and $3i$ are zeros; $f(-1) = 20$

30. $n = 4$; $-2, -\frac{1}{2}$, and i are zeros; $f(1) = 18$

31. $n = 4$; $-2, 5$, and $3 + 2i$ are zeros; $f(1) = -96$

32. $n = 4$; $-4, \frac{1}{3}$, and $2 + 3i$ are zeros; $f(1) = 100$

In Exercises 33–38, use Descartes's Rule of Signs to determine the possible number of positive and negative real zeros for each given function.

33. $f(x) = x^3 + 2x^2 + 5x + 4$

34. $f(x) = x^3 + 7x^2 + x + 7$

35. $f(x) = 5x^3 - 3x^2 + 3x - 1$

36. $f(x) = -2x^3 + x^2 - x + 7$

37. $f(x) = 2x^4 - 5x^3 - x^2 - 6x + 4$

38. $f(x) = 4x^4 - x^3 + 5x^2 - 2x - 6$

In Exercises 39–52, find all zeros of the polynomial function or solve the given polynomial equation. Use the Rational Zero Theorem, Descartes's Rule of Signs, and possibly the graph of the polynomial function shown by a graphing utility as an aid in obtaining the first zero or the first root.

39. $f(x) = x^3 - 4x^2 - 7x + 10$

40. $f(x) = x^3 + 12x^2 + 21x + 10$

41. $2x^3 - x^2 - 9x - 4 = 0$

42. $3x^3 - 8x^2 - 8x + 8 = 0$

43. $f(x) = x^4 - 2x^3 + x^2 + 12x + 8$

44. $f(x) = x^4 - 4x^3 - x^2 + 14x + 10$

45. $x^4 - 3x^3 - 20x^2 - 24x - 8 = 0$

46. $x^4 - x^3 + 2x^2 - 4x - 8 = 0$

47. $f(x) = 3x^4 - 11x^3 - x^2 + 19x + 6$

48. $f(x) = 2x^4 + 3x^3 - 11x^2 - 9x + 15$

49. $4x^4 - x^3 + 5x^2 - 2x - 6 = 0$

50. $3x^4 - 11x^3 - 3x^2 - 6x + 8 = 0$

51. $2x^5 + 7x^4 - 18x^2 - 8x + 8 = 0$

52. $4x^5 + 12x^4 - 41x^3 - 99x^2 + 10x + 24 = 0$

Practice Plus

Exercises 53–60, show incomplete graphs of given polynomial functions.

 a. *Find all the zeros of each function.*

 b. *Without using a graphing utility, draw a complete graph of the function.*

53. $f(x) = -x^3 + x^2 + 16x - 16$

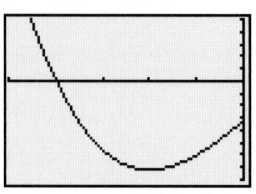

$[-5, 0, 1]$ by $[-40, 25, 5]$

54. $f(x) = -x^3 + 3x^2 - 4$

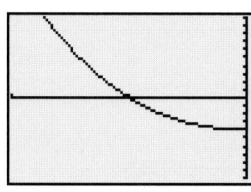

$[-2, 0, 1]$ by $[-10, 10, 1]$

55. $f(x) = 4x^3 - 8x^2 - 3x + 9$

$[-2, 0, 1]$ by $[-10, 10, 1]$

56. $f(x) = 3x^3 + 2x^2 + 2x - 1$

$[0, 2, \frac{1}{6}]$ by $[-3, 15, 1]$

57. $f(x) = 2x^4 - 3x^3 - 7x^2 - 8x + 6$

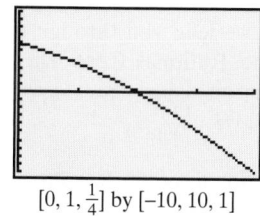

$[0, 1, \frac{1}{4}]$ by $[-10, 10, 1]$

58. $f(x) = 2x^4 + 2x^3 - 22x^2 - 18x + 36$

$[0, 4, 1]$ by $[-50, 50, 10]$

59. $f(x) = 3x^5 + 2x^4 - 15x^3 - 10x^2 + 12x + 8$

$[0, 4, 1]$ by $[-20, 25, 5]$

60. $f(x) = -5x^4 + 4x^3 - 19x^2 + 16x + 4$

$[0, 2, 1]$ by $[-10, 10, 1]$

Application Exercises

A popular model of carry-on luggage has a length that is 10 inches greater than its depth. Airline regulations require that the sum of the length, width, and depth cannot exceed 40 inches. These conditions, with the assumption that this sum is 40 inches, can be modeled by a function that gives the volume of the luggage, V, in cubic inches, in terms of its depth, x, in inches.

| Volume | = | depth | · | length | · | width: 40 − (depth + length) |

$$V(x) = x \cdot (x + 10) \cdot [40 - (x + x + 10)]$$
$$V(x) = x(x + 10)(30 - 2x)$$

Use function V to solve Exercises 61–62.

61. If the volume of the carry-on luggage is 2000 cubic inches, determine two possibilities for its depth. Where necessary, round to the nearest tenth of an inch.

62. If the volume of the carry-on luggage is 1500 cubic inches, determine two possibilities for its depth. Where necessary, round to the nearest tenth of an inch.

Use the graph of the function modeling the volume of the carry-on luggage to solve Exercises 63–64.

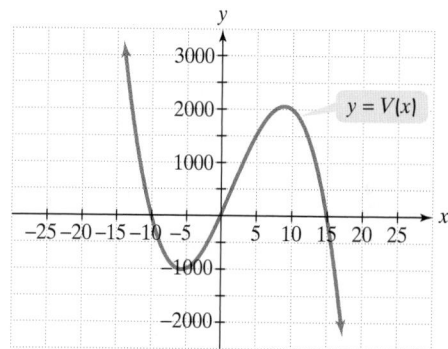

63. a. Identify your answers from Exercise 61 as points on the graph.

b. Use the graph to describe a realistic domain, x, for the volume function, where x represents the depth of the carry-on luggage.

64. a. Identify your answers from Exercise 62 as points on the graph.

b. Use the graph to describe a realistic domain, x, for the volume function, where x represents the depth of the carry-on luggage.

Writing in Mathematics

65. Describe how to find the possible rational zeros of a polynomial function.

66. How does the linear factorization of $f(x)$, that is,

$$f(x) = a_n(x - c_1)(x - c_2) \cdots (x - c_n),$$

show that a polynomial equation of degree n has n roots?

67. Describe how to use Descartes's Rule of Signs to determine the possible number of positive real zeros of a polynomial function.

68. Describe how to use Descartes's Rule of Signs to determine the possible number of negative roots of a polynomial equation.

69. Why must every polynomial equation with real coefficients of degree 3 have at least one real root?

70. Explain why the equation $x^4 + 6x^2 + 2 = 0$ has no rational roots.

71. Suppose $\frac{3}{4}$ is a root of a polynomial equation. What does this tell us about the leading coefficient and the constant term in the equation?

Technology Exercises

The equations in Exercises 72–75 have real roots that are rational. Use the Rational Zero Theorem to list all possible rational roots. Then graph the polynomial function in the given viewing rectangle to determine which possible rational roots are actual roots of the equation.

72. $2x^3 - 15x^2 + 22x + 15 = 0; [-1, 6, 1]$ by $[-50, 50, 10]$

73. $6x^3 - 19x^2 + 16x - 4 = 0; [0, 2, 1]$ by $[-3, 2, 1]$

74. $2x^4 + 7x^3 - 4x^2 - 27x - 18 = 0; [-4, 3, 1]$ by $[-45, 45, 15]$

75. $4x^4 + 4x^3 + 7x^2 - x - 2 = 0; [-2, 2, 1]$ by $[-5, 5, 1]$

76. Use Descartes's Rule of Signs to determine the possible number of positive and negative real zeros of $f(x) = 3x^4 + 5x^2 + 2$. What does this mean in terms of the graph of f? Verify your result by using a graphing utility to graph f.

77. Use Descartes's Rule of Signs to determine the possible number of positive and negative real zeros of $f(x) = x^5 - x^4 + x^3 - x^2 + x - 8$. Verify your result by using a graphing utility to graph f.

78. Write equations for several polynomial functions of odd degree and graph each function. Is it possible for the graph to have no real zeros? Explain. Try doing the same thing for polynomial functions of even degree. Now is it possible to have no real zeros?

Use a graphing utility to obtain a complete graph for each polynomial function in Exercises 79–82. Then determine the number of real zeros and the number of imaginary zeros for each function.

79. $f(x) = x^3 - 6x - 9$

80. $f(x) = 3x^5 - 2x^4 + 6x^3 - 4x^2 - 24x + 16$

81. $f(x) = 3x^4 + 4x^3 - 7x^2 - 2x - 3$

82. $f(x) = x^6 - 64$

Critical Thinking Exercises

Make Sense? *In Exercises 83–86, determine whether each statement makes sense or does not make sense, and explain your reasoning.*

83. I've noticed that $f(-x)$ is used to explore the number of negative real zeros of a polynomial function, as well as to determine whether a function is even, odd, or neither.

84. By using the quadratic formula, I do not need to bother with synthetic division when solving polynomial equations of degree 3 or higher.

85. I'm working with a fourth-degree polynomial function with integer coefficients and zeros at 1 and $3 + \sqrt{5}$. I'm certain that $3 + \sqrt{2}$ cannot also be a zero of this function.

86. I'm working with the polynomial function $f(x) = x^4 + 3x^2 + 2$ that has four possible rational zeros but no actual rational zeros.

In Exercises 87–90, determine whether each statement is true or false. If the statement is false, make the necessary change(s) to produce a true statement.

87. The equation $x^3 + 5x^2 + 6x + 1 = 0$ has one positive real root.

88. Descartes's Rule of Signs gives the exact number of positive and negative real roots for a polynomial equation.

89. Every polynomial equation of degree 3 with integer coefficients has at least one rational root.

90. Every polynomial equation of degree n has n distinct solutions.

91. If the volume of the solid shown in the figure is 208 cubic inches, find the value of x.

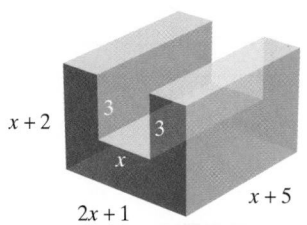

92. In this exercise, we lead you through the steps involved in the proof of the Rational Zero Theorem. Consider the polynomial equation

$$a_n x^n + a_{n-1} x^{n-1} + a_{n-2} x^{n-2} + \cdots + a_1 x + a_0 = 0,$$

and let $\dfrac{p}{q}$ be a rational root reduced to lowest terms..

a. Substitute $\dfrac{p}{q}$ for x in the equation and show that the equation can be written as

$$a_n p^n + a_{n-1} p^{n-1} q + a_{n-2} p^{n-2} q^2 + \cdots + a_1 p q^{n-1} = -a_0 q^n.$$

b. Why is p a factor of the left side of the equation?

c. Because p divides the left side, it must also divide the right side. However, because $\dfrac{p}{q}$ is reduced to lowest terms, p and q have no common factors other than -1 and 1. Because p does divide the right side and has no factors in common with q^n, what can you conclude?

d. Rewrite the equation from part (a) with all terms containing q on the left and the term that does not have a factor of q on the right. Use an argument that parallels parts (b) and (c) to conclude that q is a factor of a_n.

In Exercises 93–96, the graph of a polynomial function is given. What is the smallest degree that each polynomial could have?

93.

94.

95.

96.

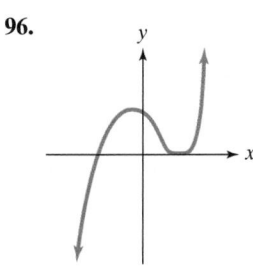

97. Explain why a polynomial function of degree 20 cannot cross the x-axis exactly once.

Preview Exercises

Exercises 98–100 will help you prepare for the material covered in the next section. Use the graph of function f to solve each exercise.

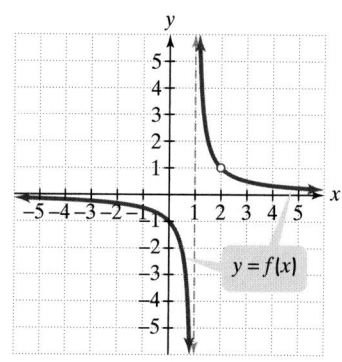

$y = f(x)$

98. For what values of x is the function undefined?

99. Write the equation of the vertical asymptote, or the vertical line that the graph of f approaches but does not touch.

100. Write the equation of the horizontal asymptote, or the horizontal line that the graph of f approaches but does not touch.

Chapter 3 Mid-Chapter Check Point

What You Know: We graphed quadratic functions using vertices, intercepts, and additional points, as necessary. We learned that the vertex of $f(x) = a(x - h)^2 + k$ is (h, k) and the vertex of $f(x) = ax^2 + bx + c$ is $\left(-\frac{b}{2a}, f\left(-\frac{b}{2a}\right)\right)$. We used the vertex to solve problems that involved minimizing or maximizing quadratic functions. We learned a number of techniques for finding the zeros of a polynomial function f of degree 3 or higher or, equivalently, finding the roots, or solutions, of the equation $f(x) = 0$. For some functions, the zeros were found by factoring $f(x)$. For other functions, we listed possible rational zeros and used synthetic division and the Factor Theorem to determine the zeros. We saw that graphs cross the x-axis at zeros of odd multiplicity and touch the x-axis and turn around at zeros of even multiplicity. We learned to graph polynomial functions using zeros, the Leading Coefficient Test, intercepts, and symmetry. We checked graphs using the fact that a polynomial function of degree n has a graph with at most $n - 1$ turning points. After finding zeros of polynomial functions, we reversed directions by using the Linear Factorization Theorem to find functions with given zeros.

In Exercises 1–4, graph the given quadratic function. Give each function's domain and range.

1. $f(x) = (x - 3)^2 - 4$

2. $f(x) = 5 - (x + 2)^2$

3. $f(x) = -x^2 - 4x + 5$

4. $f(x) = 3x^2 - 6x + 1$

In Exercises 5–13, find all zeros of each polynomial function. Then graph the function.

5. $f(x) = (x - 2)^2(x + 1)^3$

6. $f(x) = -(x - 2)^2(x + 1)^2$

7. $f(x) = x^3 - x^2 - 4x + 4$

8. $f(x) = x^4 - 5x^2 + 4$

9. $f(x) = -(x + 1)^6$

10. $f(x) = -6x^3 + 7x^2 - 1$

11. $f(x) = 2x^3 - 2x$

12. $f(x) = x^3 - 2x^2 + 26x$

13. $f(x) = -x^3 + 5x^2 - 5x - 3$

In Exercises 14–19, solve each polynomial equation.

14. $x^3 - 3x + 2 = 0$

15. $6x^3 - 11x^2 + 6x - 1 = 0$

16. $(2x + 1)(3x - 2)^3(2x - 7) = 0$

17. $2x^3 + 5x^2 - 200x - 500 = 0$

18. $x^4 - x^3 - 11x^2 = x + 12$

19. $2x^4 + x^3 - 17x^2 - 4x + 6 = 0$

20. A company manufactures and sells bath cabinets. The function
$$P(x) = -x^2 + 150x - 4425$$
models the company's daily profit, $P(x)$, when x cabinets are manufactured and sold per day. How many cabinets should be manufactured and sold per day to maximize the company's profit? What is the maximum daily profit?

21. Among all pairs of numbers whose sum is -18, find a pair whose product is as large as possible. What is the maximum product?

22. The base of a triangle measures 40 inches minus twice the measure of its height. For what measure of the height does the triangle have a maximum area? What is the maximum area?

In Exercises 23–24, divide, using synthetic division if possible.

23. $(6x^4 - 3x^3 - 11x^2 + 2x + 4) \div (3x^2 - 1)$

24. $(2x^4 - 13x^3 + 17x^2 + 18x - 24) \div (x - 4)$

In Exercises 25–26, find an nth-degree polynomial function with real coefficients satisfying the given conditions.

25. $n = 3$; 1 and i are zeros; $f(-1) = 8$

26. $n = 4$; 2 (with multiplicity 2) and $3i$ are zeros; $f(0) = 36$

27. Does $f(x) = x^3 - x - 5$ have a real zero between 1 and 2?

Rational Functions and Their Graphs

Your grandmother appears to be slowing down. Enter … Mega-Grandma! Japanese researchers have developed the robotic exoskeleton shown here to help the elderly and disabled walk and even lift heavy objects like the three 22-pound bags of rice in the photo. It's called the Hybrid Assistive Limb, or HAL. (The inventor has obviously never seen *2001: A Space Odyssey*.) HAL's brain is a computer housed in a back-pack that learns to mimic the wearer's gait and posture. Bioelectric sensors pick up signals transmitted from the brain to the muscles, so it can anticipate movements the moment the wearer thinks of them. A commercial version is available at a hefty cost ranging between $14,000 and $20,000. (*Source*: sanlab.kz.tsukuba.ac.jp)

The cost of manufacturing robotic exoskeletons can be modeled by rational functions. In this section, you will see that high production levels of HAL can eventually make this amazing invention more affordable for the elderly and people with disabilities.

1. Find the domains of rational functions.

Rational Functions

Rational functions are quotients of polynomial functions. This means that rational functions can be expressed as

$$f(x) = \frac{p(x)}{q(x)},$$

where p and q are polynomial functions and $q(x) \neq 0$. The **domain** of a rational function is the set of all real numbers except the x-values that make the denominator zero. For example, the domain of the rational function

$$f(x) = \frac{x^2 + 7x + 9}{x(x - 2)(x + 5)}$$

This is $p(x)$.

This is $q(x)$.

is the set of all real numbers except $0, 2,$ and -5.

EXAMPLE 1 **Finding the Domain of a Rational Function**

Find the domain of each rational function:

a. $f(x) = \dfrac{x^2 - 9}{x - 3}$ **b.** $g(x) = \dfrac{x}{x^2 - 9}$ **c.** $h(x) = \dfrac{x + 3}{x^2 + 9}$.

Solution Rational functions contain division. Because division by 0 is undefined, we must exclude from the domain of each function values of x that cause the polynomial function in the denominator to be 0.

a. The denominator of $f(x) = \dfrac{x^2 - 9}{x - 3}$ is 0 if $x = 3$. Thus, x cannot equal 3.

The domain of f consists of all real numbers except 3. We can express the domain in set-builder or interval notation:

Domain of $f = \{x | x \neq 3\}$

Domain of $f = (-\infty, 3) \cup (3, \infty)$.

Study Tip

Because the domain of a rational function is the set of all real numbers except those for which the denominator is 0, you can identify such numbers by setting the denominator equal to 0 and solving for x. Exclude the resulting real values of x from the domain.

b. The denominator of $g(x) = \dfrac{x}{x^2 - 9}$ is 0 if $x = -3$ or $x = 3$. Thus, the domain of g consists of all real numbers except -3 and 3. We can express the domain in set-builder or interval notation:

$$\text{Domain of } g = \{x \,|\, x \neq -3, x \neq 3\}$$
$$\text{Domain of } g = (-\infty, -3) \cup (-3, 3) \cup (3, \infty).$$

c. No real numbers cause the denominator of $h(x) = \dfrac{x + 3}{x^2 + 9}$ to equal 0. The domain of h consists of all real numbers.

$$\text{Domain of } h = (-\infty, \infty)$$

⬤

⊘ Check Point 1 Find the domain of each rational function:

a. $f(x) = \dfrac{x^2 - 25}{x - 5}$　　　**b.** $g(x) = \dfrac{x}{x^2 - 25}$　　　**c.** $h(x) = \dfrac{x + 5}{x^2 + 25}$.

② Use arrow notation.

The most basic rational function is the **reciprocal function**, defined by $f(x) = \dfrac{1}{x}$. The denominator of the reciprocal function is zero when $x = 0$, so the domain of f is the set of all real numbers except 0.

Let's look at the behavior of f near the excluded value 0. We start by evaluating $f(x)$ to the left of 0.

x approaches 0 from the left.

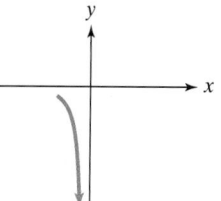

x	-1	-0.5	-0.1	-0.01	-0.001
$f(x) = \dfrac{1}{x}$	-1	-2	-10	-100	-1000

Mathematically, we say that "x approaches 0 from the left." From the table and the accompanying graph, it appears that as x approaches 0 from the left, the function values, $f(x)$, decrease without bound. We say that "$f(x)$ approaches negative infinity." We use a special arrow notation to describe this situation symbolically:

As $x \to 0^-$, $f(x) \to -\infty$.　　As x approaches 0 from the left, $f(x)$ approaches negative infinity (that is, the graph falls).

Observe that the minus $(-)$ superscript on the 0 $(x \to 0^-)$ is read "from the left."

Next, we evaluate $f(x)$ to the right of 0.

x approaches 0 from the right.

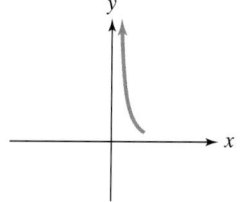

x	0.001	0.01	0.1	0.5	1
$f(x) = \dfrac{1}{x}$	1000	100	10	2	1

Mathematically, we say that "x approaches 0 from the right." From the table and the accompanying graph, it appears that as x approaches 0 from the right, the function values, $f(x)$, increase without bound. We say that "$f(x)$ approaches infinity." We again use a special arrow notation to describe this situation symbolically:

As $x \to 0^+$, $f(x) \to \infty$.　　As x approaches 0 from the right, $f(x)$ approaches infinity (that is, the graph rises).

Observe that the plus $(+)$ superscript on the 0 $(x \to 0^+)$ is read "from the right."

Now let's see what happens to the function values of $f(x) = \dfrac{1}{x}$ as x gets farther away from the origin. The following tables suggest what happens to $f(x)$ as x increases or decreases without bound.

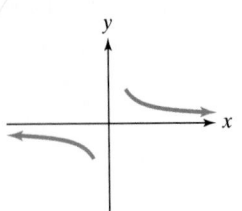

Figure 3.27 $f(x)$ approaches 0 as x increases or decreases without bound.

x increases without bound:				
x	1	10	100	1000
$f(x) = \dfrac{1}{x}$	1	0.1	0.01	0.001

x decreases without bound:				
x	-1	-10	-100	-1000
$f(x) = \dfrac{1}{x}$	-1	-0.1	-0.01	-0.001

It appears that as x increases or decreases without bound, the function values, $f(x)$, are getting progressively closer to 0.

Figure 3.27 illustrates the end behavior of $f(x) = \dfrac{1}{x}$ as x increases or decreases without bound. The graph shows that the function values, $f(x)$, are approaching 0. This means that as x increases or decreases without bound, the graph of f is approaching the horizontal line $y = 0$ (that is, the x-axis). We use arrow notation to describe this situation:

$$\text{As } x \to \infty,\ f(x) \to 0 \qquad \text{and} \qquad \text{as } x \to -\infty,\ f(x) \to 0.$$

As x approaches infinity (that is, increases without bound), $f(x)$ approaches 0.

As x approaches negative infinity (that is, decreases without bound), $f(x)$ approaches 0.

Thus, as x approaches infinity $(x \to \infty)$ or as x approaches negative infinity $(x \to -\infty)$, the function values are approaching zero: $f(x) \to 0$.

The graph of the reciprocal function $f(x) = \dfrac{1}{x}$ is shown in **Figure 3.28**. Unlike the graph of a polynomial function, the graph of the reciprocal function has a break and is composed of two distinct branches.

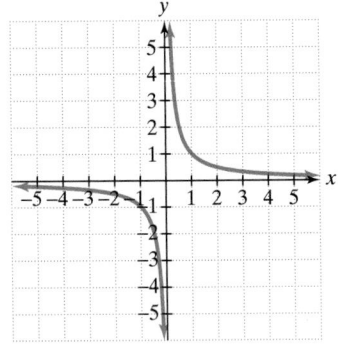

Figure 3.28 The graph of the reciprocal function $f(x) = \dfrac{1}{x}$

Study Tip

If x is far from 0, then $\dfrac{1}{x}$ is close to 0. By contrast, if x is close to 0, then $\dfrac{1}{x}$ is far from 0.

The Reciprocal Function as a Knuckle Tattoo

"I got the tattoo because I like the idea of math not being well behaved. That sounds lame and I really don't mean that in some kind of anarchy-type way. I just think that it's kind of nice that something as perfectly functional as math can kink up around the edges."

Kink up around the edges? On the next page, we'll describe the graphic behavior of the reciprocal function using *asymptotes* rather than kink. Asymptotes are lines that graphs approach but never touch. *Asymptote* comes from the Greek word *asymptotos*, meaning "not meeting."

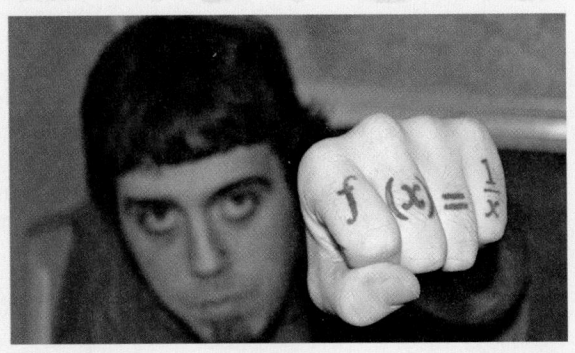

The arrow notation used throughout our discussion of the reciprocal function is summarized in the following box:

Arrow Notation

Symbol	Meaning
$x \to a^+$	x approaches a from the right.
$x \to a^-$	x approaches a from the left.
$x \to \infty$	x approaches infinity; that is, x increases without bound.
$x \to -\infty$	x approaches negative infinity; that is, x decreases without bound.

Another basic rational function is $f(x) = \dfrac{1}{x^2}$. The graph of this even function, with y-axis symmetry and positive function values, is shown in **Figure 3.29**. Like the reciprocal function, the graph has a break and is composed of two distinct branches.

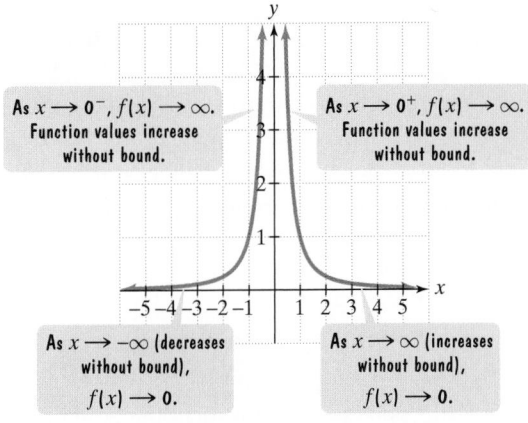

As $x \longrightarrow 0^-$, $f(x) \longrightarrow \infty$.
Function values increase without bound.

As $x \longrightarrow 0^+$, $f(x) \longrightarrow \infty$.
Function values increase without bound.

As $x \longrightarrow -\infty$ (decreases without bound), $f(x) \longrightarrow 0$.

As $x \longrightarrow \infty$ (increases without bound), $f(x) \longrightarrow 0$.

Figure 3.29 The graph of $f(x) = \dfrac{1}{x^2}$

③ Identify vertical asymptotes.

Vertical Asymptotes of Rational Functions

Look again at the graph of $f(x) = \dfrac{1}{x^2}$ in **Figure 3.29**. The curve approaches, but does not touch, the y-axis. The y-axis, or $x = 0$, is said to be a *vertical asymptote* of the graph. A rational function may have no vertical asymptotes, one vertical asymptote, or several vertical asymptotes. The graph of a rational function never intersects a vertical asymptote. We will use dashed lines to show asymptotes.

Definition of a Vertical Asymptote

The line $x = a$ is a **vertical asymptote** of the graph of a function f if $f(x)$ increases or decreases without bound as x approaches a.

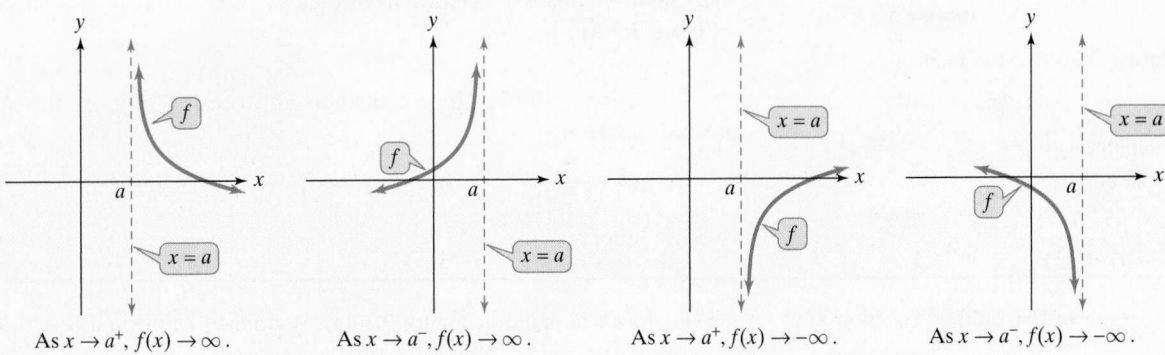

As $x \to a^+$, $f(x) \to \infty$.

As $x \to a^-$, $f(x) \to \infty$.

As $x \to a^+$, $f(x) \to -\infty$.

As $x \to a^-$, $f(x) \to -\infty$.

Thus, as x approaches a from either the left or the right, $f(x) \to \infty$ or $f(x) \to -\infty$.

If the graph of a rational function has vertical asymptotes, they can be located using the following theorem:

Locating Vertical Asymptotes

If $f(x) = \dfrac{p(x)}{q(x)}$ is a rational function in which $p(x)$ and $q(x)$ have no common factors and a is a zero of $q(x)$, the denominator, then $x = a$ is a vertical asymptote of the graph of f.

(EXAMPLE 2) **Finding the Vertical Asymptotes of a Rational Function**

Find the vertical asymptotes, if any, of the graph of each rational function:

a. $f(x) = \dfrac{x}{x^2 - 9}$ 　　**b.** $g(x) = \dfrac{x + 3}{x^2 - 9}$ 　　**c.** $h(x) = \dfrac{x + 3}{x^2 + 9}$.

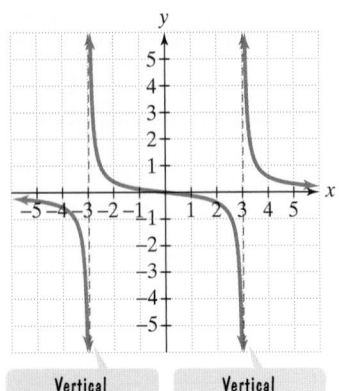

Figure 3.30(a) The graph of $f(x) = \dfrac{x}{x^2 - 9}$ has two vertical asymptotes.

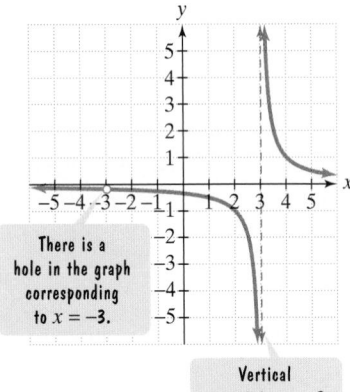

There is a hole in the graph corresponding to $x = -3$.

Vertical asymptote: $x = 3$

Figure 3.30(b) The graph of $g(x) = \dfrac{x + 3}{x^2 - 9}$ has one vertical asymptote.

Solution Factoring is usually helpful in identifying zeros of denominators and any common factors in the numerators and denominators.

a. $f(x) = \dfrac{x}{x^2 - 9} = \dfrac{x}{(x + 3)(x - 3)}$

This factor is 0 if $x = -3$. This factor is 0 if $x = 3$.

There are no common factors in the numerator and the denominator. The zeros of the denominator are -3 and 3. Thus, the lines $x = -3$ and $x = 3$ are the vertical asymptotes for the graph of f. [See **Figure 3.30(a)**.]

b. We will use factoring to see if there are common factors.

$$g(x) = \dfrac{x + 3}{x^2 - 9} = \dfrac{(x + 3)}{(x + 3)(x - 3)} = \dfrac{1}{x - 3}, \text{ provided } x \neq -3$$

There is a common factor, $x + 3$, so simplify. This denominator is 0 if $x = 3$.

The only zero of the denominator of $g(x)$ in simplified form is 3. Thus, the line $x = 3$ is the only vertical asymptote of the graph of g. [See **Figure 3.30(b)**.]

c. We cannot factor the denominator of $h(x)$ over the real numbers.

$$h(x) = \dfrac{x + 3}{x^2 - 9}$$

No real numbers make this denominator 0.

The denominator has no real zeros. Thus, the graph of h has no vertical asymptotes. [See **Figure 3.30(c)**.]

Figure 3.30(c) The graph of $h(x) = \dfrac{x + 3}{x^2 + 9}$ has no vertical asymptotes.

⊘ Check Point **2** Find the vertical asymptotes, if any, of the graph of each rational function:

a. $f(x) = \dfrac{x}{x^2 - 1}$ **b.** $g(x) = \dfrac{x - 1}{x^2 - 1}$ **c.** $h(x) = \dfrac{x - 1}{x^2 + 1}$.

Technology

The graph of the rational function $f(x) = \dfrac{x}{x^2 - 9}$, drawn by hand in **Figure 3.30(a)**, is graphed below in a $[-5, 5, 1]$ by $[-4, 4, 1]$ viewing rectangle. The graph is shown in connected mode and in dot mode. In connected mode, the graphing utility plots many points and connects the points with curves. In dot mode, the utility plots the same points, but does not connect them.

Connected Mode

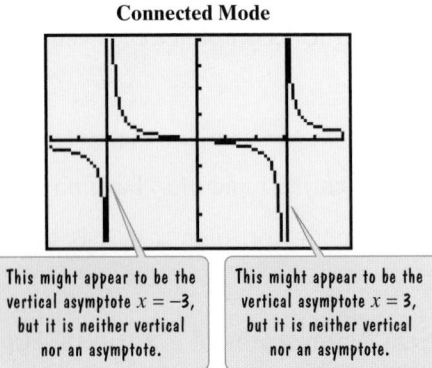

This might appear to be the vertical asymptote $x = -3$, but it is neither vertical nor an asymptote.

This might appear to be the vertical asymptote $x = 3$, but it is neither vertical nor an asymptote.

Dot Mode

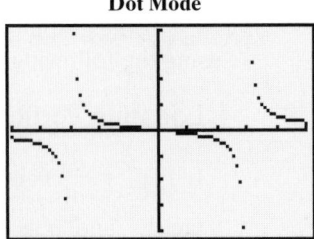

The steep lines in connected mode that are "almost" the vertical asymptotes $x = -3$ and $x = 3$ are not part of the graph and do not represent the vertical asymptotes. The graphing utility has incorrectly connected the last point to the left of $x = -3$ with the first point to the right of $x = -3$. It has also incorrectly connected the last point to the left of $x = 3$ with the first point to the right of $x = 3$. The effect is to create two near-vertical segments that look like asymptotes. This erroneous effect does not appear using dot mode.

Study Tip

It is essential to factor the numerator and the denominator of a rational function to identify possible vertical asymptotes or holes.

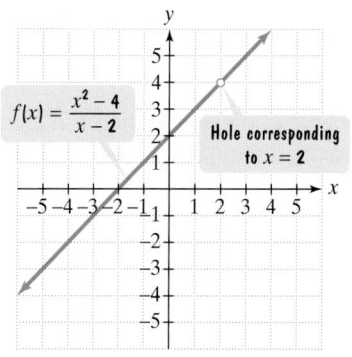

$$f(x) = \frac{x^2 - 4}{x - 2}$$

Hole corresponding to x = 2

Figure 3.31 A graph with a hole corresponding to the denominator's zero

④ Identify horizontal asymptotes.

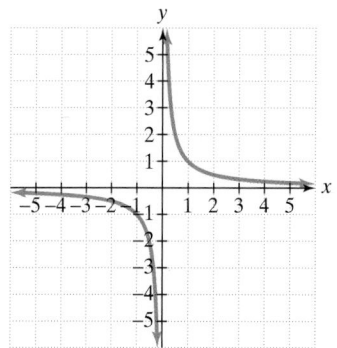

Figure 3.28 The graph of $f(x) = \dfrac{1}{x}$

(repeated)

A value where the denominator of a rational function is zero does not necessarily result in a vertical asymptote. There is a hole corresponding to $x = a$, and not a vertical asymptote, in the graph of a rational function under the following conditions: The value a causes the denominator to be zero, but there is a reduced form of the function's equation in which a does not cause the denominator to be zero.

Consider, for example, the function

$$f(x) = \frac{x^2 - 4}{x - 2}.$$

Because the denominator is zero when $x = 2$, the function's domain is all real numbers except 2. However, there is a reduced form of the equation in which 2 does not cause the denominator to be zero:

$$f(x) = \frac{x^2 - 4}{x - 2} = \frac{(x + 2)(x - 2)}{x - 2} = x + 2, \ x \neq 2.$$

Denominator is zero at x = 2.

In this reduced form, 2 does not result in a zero denominator.

Figure 3.31 shows that the graph has a hole corresponding to $x = 2$. Graphing utilities do not show this feature of the graph.

Horizontal Asymptotes of Rational Functions

Figure 3.28, repeated, shows the graph of the reciprocal function $f(x) = \dfrac{1}{x}$. As $x \to \infty$ and as $x \to -\infty$, the function values are approaching 0: $f(x) \to 0$. The line $y = 0$ (that is, the x-axis) is a *horizontal asymptote* of the graph. Many, but not all, rational functions have horizontal asymptotes.

Definition of a Horizontal Asymptote

The line $y = b$ is a **horizontal asymptote** of the graph of a function f if $f(x)$ approaches b as x increases or decreases without bound.

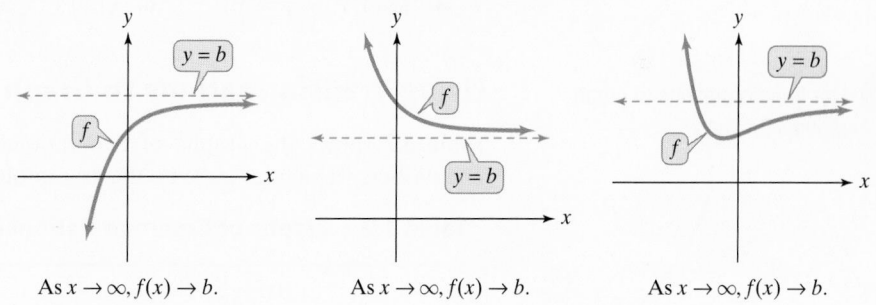

As $x \to \infty, f(x) \to b$. As $x \to \infty, f(x) \to b$. As $x \to \infty, f(x) \to b$.

Recall that a rational function may have several vertical asymptotes. By contrast, it can have at most one horizontal asymptote. Although a graph can never intersect a vertical asymptote, it may cross its horizontal asymptote.

If the graph of a rational function has a horizontal asymptote, it can be located using the following theorem:

Study Tip

Unlike identifying possible vertical asymptotes or holes, we do not use factoring to determine a possible horizontal asymptote.

Locating Horizontal Asymptotes

Let f be the rational function given by

$$f(x) = \frac{a_n x^n + a_{n-1} x^{n-1} + \cdots + a_1 x + a_0}{b_m x^m + b_{m-1} x^{m-1} + \cdots + b_1 x + b_0}, \quad a_n \neq 0, b_m \neq 0.$$

The degree of the numerator is n. The degree of the denominator is m.

1. If $n < m$, the x-axis, or $y = 0$, is the horizontal asymptote of the graph of f.
2. If $n = m$, the line $y = \dfrac{a_n}{b_m}$ is the horizontal asymptote of the graph of f.
3. If $n > m$, the graph of f has no horizontal asymptote.

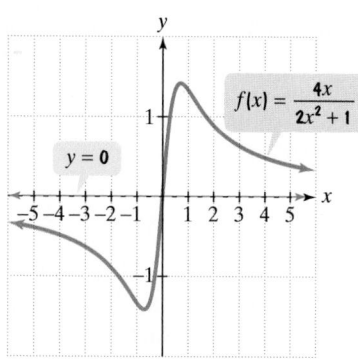

Figure 3.32(a) The horizontal asymptote of the graph is $y = 0$.

EXAMPLE 3 Finding the Horizontal Asymptote of a Rational Function

Find the horizontal asymptote, if any, of the graph of each rational function:

a. $f(x) = \dfrac{4x}{2x^2 + 1}$ **b.** $g(x) = \dfrac{4x^2}{2x^2 + 1}$ **c.** $h(x) = \dfrac{4x^3}{2x^2 + 1}$.

Solution

a. $f(x) = \dfrac{4x}{2x^2 + 1}$

The degree of the numerator, 1, is less than the degree of the denominator, 2. Thus, the graph of f has the x-axis as a horizontal asymptote. [See **Figure 3.32(a)**.] The equation of the horizontal asymptote is $y = 0$.

b. $g(x) = \dfrac{4x^2}{2x^2 + 1}$

The degree of the numerator, 2, is equal to the degree of the denominator, 2. The leading coefficients of the numerator and denominator, 4 and 2, are used to obtain the equation of the horizontal asymptote. The equation of the horizontal asymptote is $y = \frac{4}{2}$ or $y = 2$. [See **Figure 3.32(b)**.]

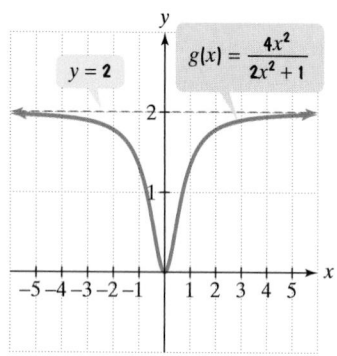

Figure 3.32(b) The horizontal asymptote of the graph is $y = 2$.

c. $h(x) = \dfrac{4x^3}{2x^2 + 1}$

The degree of the numerator, 3, is greater than the degree of the denominator, 2. Thus, the graph of h has no horizontal asymptote. [See **Figure 3.32(c)**.]

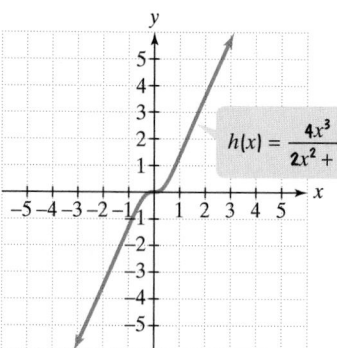

Figure 3.32(c) The graph has no horizontal asymptote.

✓ Check Point **3** Find the horizontal asymptote, if any, of the graph of each rational function:

a. $f(x) = \dfrac{9x^2}{3x^2 + 1}$ **b.** $g(x) = \dfrac{9x}{3x^2 + 1}$ **c.** $h(x) = \dfrac{9x^3}{3x^2 + 1}$.

⑤ Use transformations to graph rational functions.

Using Transformations to Graph Rational Functions

Table 3.2 shows the graphs of two rational functions, $f(x) = \dfrac{1}{x}$ and $f(x) = \dfrac{1}{x^2}$. The dashed green lines indicate the asymptotes.

Table 3.2 Graphs of Common Rational Functions

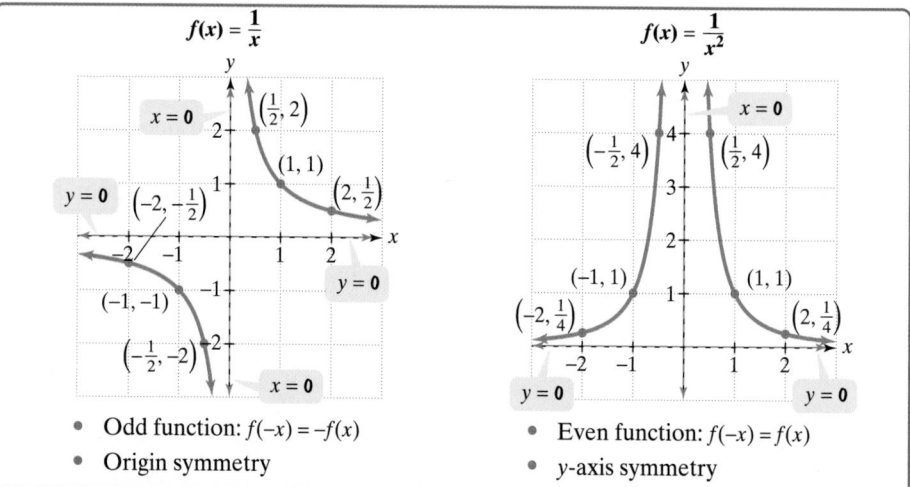

Some rational functions can be graphed using transformations (horizontal shifting, stretching or shrinking, reflecting, vertical shifting) of these two common graphs.

EXAMPLE 4 **Using Transformations to Graph a Rational Function**

Use the graph of $f(x) = \dfrac{1}{x^2}$ to graph $g(x) = \dfrac{1}{(x - 2)^2} + 1$.

Solution

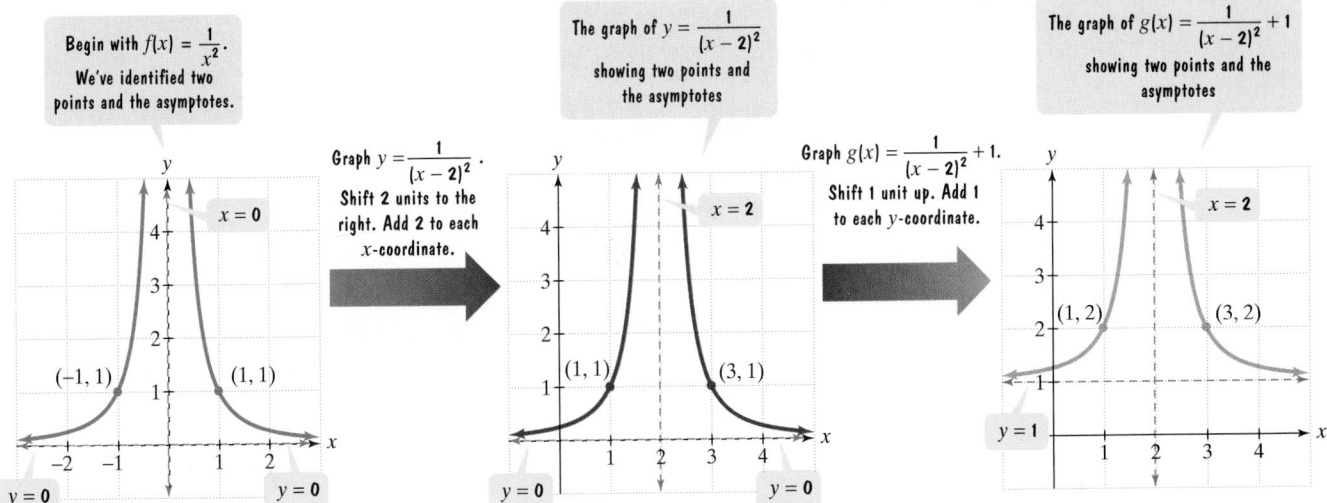

Begin with $f(x) = \dfrac{1}{x^2}$.
We've identified two points and the asymptotes.

Graph $y = \dfrac{1}{(x - 2)^2}$.
Shift 2 units to the right. Add 2 to each x-coordinate.

The graph of $y = \dfrac{1}{(x - 2)^2}$ showing two points and the asymptotes

Graph $g(x) = \dfrac{1}{(x - 2)^2} + 1$.
Shift 1 unit up. Add 1 to each y-coordinate.

The graph of $g(x) = \dfrac{1}{(x - 2)^2} + 1$ showing two points and the asymptotes

☑ **Check Point 4** Use the graph of $f(x) = \dfrac{1}{x}$ to graph $g(x) = \dfrac{1}{x + 2} - 1$.

⑥ Graph rational functions.

Graphing Rational Functions

Rational functions that are not transformations of $f(x) = \dfrac{1}{x}$ or $f(x) = \dfrac{1}{x^2}$ can be graphed using the following procedure:

Strategy for Graphing a Rational Function

The following strategy can be used to graph

$$f(x) = \frac{p(x)}{q(x)},$$

where p and q are polynomial functions with no common factors.

1. Determine whether the graph of f has symmetry.

$$f(-x) = f(x): \qquad y\text{-axis symmetry}$$
$$f(-x) = -f(x): \qquad \text{origin symmetry}$$

2. Find the y-intercept (if there is one) by evaluating $f(0)$.
3. Find the x-intercepts (if there are any) by solving the equation $p(x) = 0$.
4. Find any vertical asymptote(s) by solving the equation $q(x) = 0$.
5. Find the horizontal asymptote (if there is one) using the rule for determining the horizontal asymptote of a rational function.
6. Plot at least one point between and beyond each x-intercept and vertical asymptote.
7. Use the information obtained previously to graph the function between and beyond the vertical asymptotes.

$\boxed{\textbf{EXAMPLE 5}}$ **Graphing a Rational Function**

Graph: $f(x) = \dfrac{2x - 1}{x - 1}$.

Solution

Step 1 Determine symmetry.

$$f(-x) = \frac{2(-x) - 1}{-x - 1} = \frac{-2x - 1}{-x - 1} = \frac{2x + 1}{x + 1}$$

Because $f(-x)$ does not equal either $f(x)$ or $-f(x)$, the graph has neither y-axis symmetry nor origin symmetry.

Step 2 Find the y-intercept. Evaluate $f(0)$.

$$f(0) = \frac{2 \cdot 0 - 1}{0 - 1} = \frac{-1}{-1} = 1$$

The y-intercept is 1, so the graph passes through $(0, 1)$.

Step 3 Find x-intercept(s). This is done by solving $p(x) = 0$, where $p(x)$ is the numerator of $f(x)$.

$$2x - 1 = 0 \qquad \text{Set the numerator equal to 0.}$$
$$2x = 1 \qquad \text{Add 1 to both sides.}$$
$$x = \frac{1}{2} \qquad \text{Divide both sides by 2.}$$

The x-intercept is $\frac{1}{2}$, so the graph passes through $\left(\frac{1}{2}, 0\right)$.

Step 4 Find the vertical asymptote(s). Solve $q(x) = 0$, where $q(x)$ is the denominator of $f(x)$, thereby finding zeros of the denominator. (Note that the numerator and denominator of $f(x) = \dfrac{2x - 1}{x - 1}$ have no common factors.)

$$x - 1 = 0 \qquad \text{Set the denominator equal to 0.}$$
$$x = 1 \qquad \text{Add 1 to both sides.}$$

The equation of the vertical asymptote is $x = 1$.

Step 5 Find the horizontal asymptote. Because the numerator and denominator of $f(x) = \dfrac{2x - 1}{x - 1}$ have the same degree, 1, the leading coefficients of the numerator and denominator, 2 and 1, respectively, are used to obtain the equation of the horizontal asymptote. The equation is

$$y = \frac{2}{1} = 2.$$

The equation of the horizontal asymptote is $y = 2$.

Step 6 Plot points between and beyond each x-intercept and vertical asymptote. With an x-intercept at $\frac{1}{2}$ and a vertical asymptote at $x = 1$, we evaluate the function at $-2, -1, \dfrac{3}{4}, 2$, and 4.

x	-2	-1	$\dfrac{3}{4}$	2	4
$f(x) = \dfrac{2x - 1}{x - 1}$	$\dfrac{5}{3}$	$\dfrac{3}{2}$	-2	3	$\dfrac{7}{3}$

Figure 3.33 shows these points, the y-intercept, the x-intercept, and the asymptotes.

Step 7 Graph the function. The graph of $f(x) = \dfrac{2x - 1}{x - 1}$ is shown in **Figure 3.34**.

Technology

The graph of $y = \dfrac{2x - 1}{x - 1}$, obtained using the dot mode in a $[-6, 6, 1]$ by $[-6, 6\ 1]$ viewing rectangle, verifies that our hand-drawn graph in **Figure 3.34** is correct.

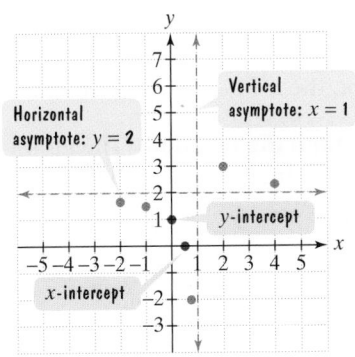

Figure 3.33 Preparing to graph the rational function $f(x) = \dfrac{2x - 1}{x - 1}$

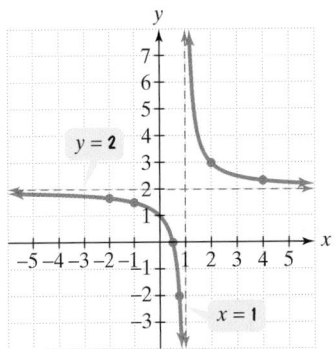

Figure 3.34 The graph of $f(x) = \dfrac{2x - 1}{x - 1}$

✓ **Check Point 5** Graph: $f(x) = \dfrac{3x - 3}{x - 2}$.

(**EXAMPLE 6**) **Graphing a Rational Function**

Graph: $f(x) = \dfrac{3x^2}{x^2 - 4}$.

Solution

Step 1 Determine symmetry. $f(-x) = \dfrac{3(-x)^2}{(-x)^2 - 4} = \dfrac{3x^2}{x^2 - 4} = f(x)$: The graph of f is symmetric with respect to the y-axis.

Step 2 Find the y-intercept. $f(0) = \dfrac{3 \cdot 0^2}{0^2 - 4} = \dfrac{0}{-4} = 0$: The y-intercept is 0, so the graph passes through the origin.

Step 3 Find the x-intercept(s). $3x^2 = 0$, so $x = 0$: The x-intercept is 0, verifying that the graph passes through the origin.

Step 4 Find the vertical asymptote(s). Set $q(x) = 0$. (Note that the numerator and denominator of $f(x) = \dfrac{3x^2}{x^2 - 4}$ have no common factors.)

$$x^2 - 4 = 0 \qquad \text{Set the denominator equal to 0.}$$
$$x^2 = 4 \qquad \text{Add 4 to both sides.}$$
$$x = \pm 2 \qquad \text{Use the square root property.}$$

The vertical asymptotes are $x = -2$ and $x = 2$.

Step 5 Find the horizontal asymptote. Because the numerator and denominator of $f(x) = \dfrac{3x^2}{x^2 - 4}$ have the same degree, 2, their leading coefficients, 3 and 1, are used to determine the equation of the horizontal asymptote. The equation is $y = \dfrac{3}{1} = 3$.

Study Tip

Because the graph has y-axis symmetry, it is not necessary to evaluate the even function at -3 and again at 3.

$$f(-3) = f(3) = \tfrac{27}{5}$$

This also applies to evaluation at -1 and 1.

Step 6 Plot points between and beyond each x-intercept and vertical asymptote. With an x-intercept at 0 and vertical asymptotes at $x = -2$ and $x = 2$, we evaluate the function at $-3, -1, 1, 3,$ and 4.

x	-3	-1	1	3	4
$f(x) = \dfrac{3x^2}{x^2 - 4}$	$\dfrac{27}{5}$	-1	-1	$\dfrac{27}{5}$	4

Technology

The graph of $y = \dfrac{3x^2}{x^2 - 4}$, generated by a graphing utility, verifies that our hand-drawn graph is correct.

$[-6, 6, 1]$ by $[-6, 6, 1]$

Figure 3.35 shows the points $\left(-3, \dfrac{27}{5}\right), (-1, -1), (1, -1), \left(3, \dfrac{27}{5}\right)$, and $(4, 4)$, the y-intercept, the x-intercept, and the asymptotes.

Step 7 Graph the function. The graph of $f(x) = \dfrac{3x^2}{x^2 - 4}$ is shown in **Figure 3.36**. The y-axis symmetry is now obvious.

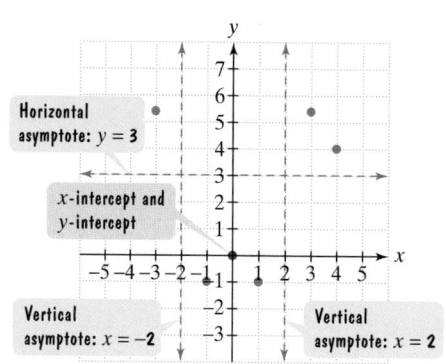

Figure 3.35 Preparing to graph
$f(x) = \dfrac{3x^2}{x^2 - 4}$

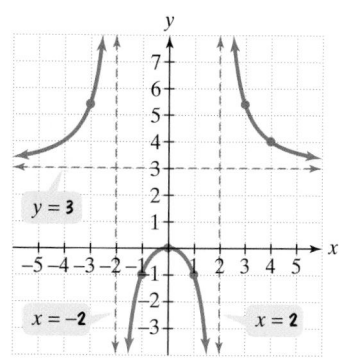

Figure 3.36 The graph of
$f(x) = \dfrac{3x^2}{x^2 - 4}$

Check Point 6 Graph: $f(x) = \dfrac{2x^2}{x^2 - 9}$.

Example 7 illustrates that not every rational function has vertical and horizontal asymptotes.

EXAMPLE 7 **Graphing a Rational Function**

Graph: $f(x) = \dfrac{x^4}{x^2 + 1}$.

Solution

Step 1 Determine symmetry. $f(-x) = \dfrac{(-x)^4}{(-x)^2 + 1} = \dfrac{x^4}{x^2 + 1} = f(x)$

The graph of f is symmetric with respect to the y-axis.

Step 2 Find the y-intercept. $f(0) = \dfrac{0^4}{0^2 + 1} = \dfrac{0}{1} = 0$: The y-intercept is 0.

Step 3 Find the x-intercept(s). $x^4 = 0$, so $x = 0$: The x-intercept is 0.

Step 4 Find the vertical asymptote. Set $q(x) = 0$.

$$x^2 + 1 = 0 \qquad \text{Set the denominator equal to 0.}$$
$$x^2 = -1 \qquad \text{Subtract 1 from both sides.}$$

Although this equation has imaginary roots ($x = \pm i$), there are no real roots. Thus, the graph of f has no vertical asymptotes.

Step 5 Find the horizontal asymptote. Because the degree of the numerator, 4, is greater than the degree of the denominator, 2, there is no horizontal asymptote.

Step 6 Plot points between and beyond each x-intercept and vertical asymptote. With an x-intercept at 0 and no vertical asymptotes, let's look at function values at $-2, -1, 1$, and 2. You can evaluate the function at 1 and 2. Use y-axis symmetry to obtain function values at -1 and -2:

$$f(-1) = f(1) \text{ and } f(-2) = f(2).$$

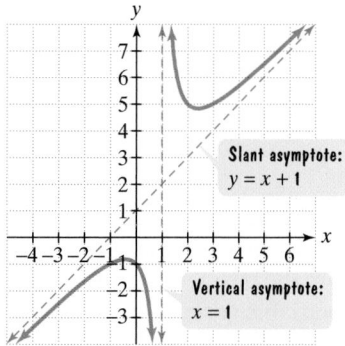

Figure 3.37 The graph of $f(x) = \dfrac{x^4}{x^2 + 1}$

7 Identify slant asymptotes.

x		-2	-1	1	2
$f(x) = \dfrac{x^4}{x^2 + 1}$		$\dfrac{16}{5}$	$\dfrac{1}{2}$	$\dfrac{1}{2}$	$\dfrac{16}{5}$

Step 7 Graph the function. Figure 3.37 shows the graph of f using the points obtained from the table and y-axis symmetry. Notice that as x approaches infinity or negative infinity ($x \rightarrow \infty$ or $x \rightarrow -\infty$), the function values, $f(x)$, are getting larger without bound [$f(x) \rightarrow \infty$]. ●

○ Check Point **7** Graph: $f(x) = \dfrac{x^4}{x^2 + 2}$.

Slant Asymptotes

Examine the graph of

$$f(x) = \frac{x^2 + 1}{x - 1},$$

shown in **Figure 3.38**. Note that the degree of the numerator, 2, is greater than the degree of the denominator, 1. Thus, the graph of this function has no horizontal asymptote. However, the graph has a **slant asymptote,** $y = x + 1$.

The graph of a rational function has a slant asymptote if the degree of the numerator is one more than the degree of the denominator. The equation of the slant asymptote can be found by division. For example, to find the slant asymptote for the graph of $f(x) = \dfrac{x^2 + 1}{x - 1}$, divide $x - 1$ into $x^2 + 1$:

$$\underline{1} \begin{array}{ccc} 1 & 0 & 1 \\ & 1 & 1 \\ \hline 1 & 1 & 2 \end{array}$$

Remainder

$$\begin{array}{r} 1x + 1 + \dfrac{2}{x-1} \\ x - 1 \overline{) x^2 + 0x + 1} \end{array}.$$

Observe that

$$f(x) = \frac{x^2 + 1}{x - 1} = \underbrace{x + 1}_{} + \frac{2}{x - 1}.$$

The equation of the slant asymptote is $y = x + 1$.

As $|x| \rightarrow \infty$, the value of $\dfrac{2}{x - 1}$ is approximately 0. Thus, when $|x|$ is large, the function is very close to $y = x + 1 + 0$. This means that as $x \rightarrow \infty$ or as $x \rightarrow -\infty$, the graph of f gets closer and closer to the line whose equation is $y = x + 1$. The line $y = x + 1$ is a slant asymptote of the graph.

In general, if $f(x) = \dfrac{p(x)}{q(x)}$, p and q have no common factors, and the degree of p is one greater than the degree of q, find the slant asymptote by dividing $q(x)$ into $p(x)$. The division will take the form

$$\frac{p(x)}{q(x)} = mx + b + \frac{\text{remainder}}{q(x)}.$$

Slant asymptote: $y = mx + b$

The equation of the slant asymptote is obtained by dropping the term with the remainder. Thus, the equation of the slant asymptote is $y = mx + b$.

Figure 3.38 The graph of $f(x) = \dfrac{x^2 + 1}{x - 1}$ with a slant asymptote

Slant asymptote: $y = x + 1$

Vertical asymptote: $x = 1$

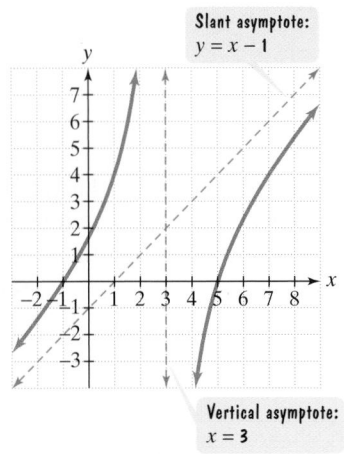

Figure 3.39 The graph of
$f(x) = \dfrac{x^2 - 4x - 5}{x - 3}$

EXAMPLE 8 Finding the Slant Asymptote of a Rational Function

Find the slant asymptote of $f(x) = \dfrac{x^2 - 4x - 5}{x - 3}$.

Solution Because the degree of the numerator, 2, is exactly one more than the degree of the denominator, 1, and $x - 3$ is not a factor of $x^2 - 4x - 5$, the graph of f has a slant asymptote. To find the equation of the slant asymptote, divide $x - 3$ into $x^2 - 4x - 5$:

$$\underline{3}\, \begin{array}{rrr} 1 & -4 & -5 \\ & 3 & -3 \\ \hline 1 & -1 & -8 \end{array}$$

Remainder

$$\begin{array}{r} 1x - 1 - \dfrac{8}{x-3} \\ x - 3\overline{)x^2 - 4x - 5} \end{array}$$

Drop the remainder term and you'll have the equation of the slant asymptote.

The equation of the slant asymptote is $y = x - 1$. Using our strategy for graphing rational functions, the graph of $f(x) = \dfrac{x^2 - 4x - 5}{x - 3}$ is shown in **Figure 3.39**. ●

⊘ Check Point **8** Find the slant asymptote of $f(x) = \dfrac{2x^2 - 5x + 7}{x - 2}$.

⑧ Solve applied problems involving rational functions.

Applications

There are numerous examples of asymptotic behavior in functions that model real-world phenomena. Let's consider an example from the business world. The **cost function**, C, for a business is the sum of its fixed and variable costs:

$$C(x) = (\text{fixed cost}) + cx.$$

Cost per unit times the number of units produced, x

The **average cost** per unit for a company to produce x units is the sum of its fixed and variable costs divided by the number of units produced. The **average cost function** is a rational function that is denoted by \overline{C}. Thus,

Cost of producing x units: fixed plus variable costs

$$\overline{C}(x) = \dfrac{(\text{fixed cost}) + cx}{x}.$$

Number of units produced

EXAMPLE 9 Average Cost for a Business

We return to the robotic exoskeleton described in the section opener. Suppose a company that manufactures this invention has a fixed monthly cost of $1,000,000 and that it costs $5000 to produce each robotic system.

 a. Write the cost function, C, of producing x robotic systems.

 b. Write the average cost function, \overline{C}, of producing x robotic systems.

 c. Find and interpret $\overline{C}(1000), \overline{C}(10{,}000)$, and $\overline{C}(100{,}000)$.

 d. What is the horizontal asymptote for the graph of the average cost function, \overline{C}? Describe what this represents for the company.

Solution

a. The cost function, C, is the sum of the fixed cost and the variable costs.

$$C(x) = 1,000,000 + 5000x$$

> Fixed cost is $1,000,000.

> Variable cost: $5000 for each robotic system produced

b. The average cost function, \overline{C}, is the sum of fixed and variable costs divided by the number of robotic systems produced.

$$\overline{C}(x) = \frac{1,000,000 + 5000x}{x} \quad \text{or} \quad \overline{C}(x) = \frac{5000x + 1,000,000}{x}$$

c. We evaluate \overline{C} at 1000, 10,000, and 100,000, interpreting the results.

$$\overline{C}(1000) = \frac{5000(1000) + 1,000,000}{1000} = 6000$$

The average cost per robotic system of producing 1000 systems per month is $6000.

$$\overline{C}(10,000) = \frac{5000(10,000) + 1,000,000}{10,000} = 5100$$

The average cost per robotic system of producing 10,000 systems per month is $5100.

$$\overline{C}(100,000) = \frac{5000(100,000) + 1,000,000}{100,000} = 5010$$

The average cost per robotic system of producing 100,000 systems per month is $5010. Notice that with higher production levels, the cost of producing each robotic exoskeleton decreases.

d. We developed the average cost function

$$\overline{C}(x) = \frac{5000x + 1,000,000}{x}$$

in which the degree of the numerator, 1, is equal to the degree of the denominator, 1. The leading coefficients of the numerator and denominator, 5000 and 1, are used to obtain the equation of the horizontal asymptote. The equation of the horizontal asymptote is

$$y = \frac{5000}{1} \quad \text{or} \quad y = 5000.$$

The horizontal asymptote is shown in **Figure 3.40**. This means that the more robotic systems produced each month, the closer the average cost per system for the company comes to $5000. The least possible cost per robotic exoskeleton is approaching $5000. Competitively low prices take place with high production levels, posing a major problem for small businesses. ●

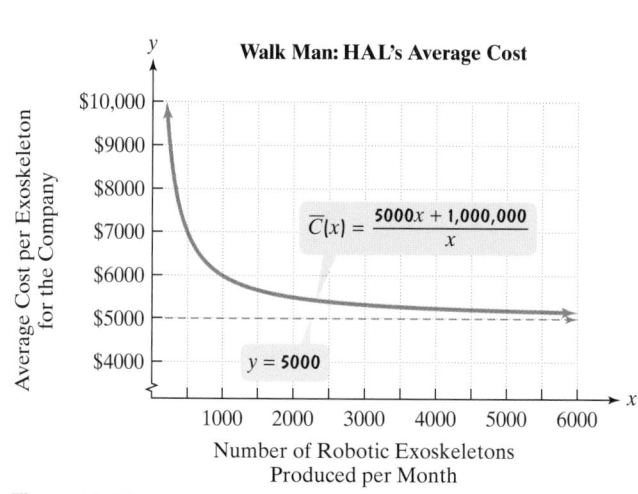

Walk Man: HAL's Average Cost

$\overline{C}(x) = \dfrac{5000x + 1,000,000}{x}$

$y = 5000$

Number of Robotic Exoskeletons Produced per Month

Figure 3.40

⊘ Check Point **9** A company is planning to manufacture wheelchairs that are light, fast, and beautiful. The fixed monthly cost will be $500,000 and it will cost $400 to produce each radically innovative chair.

a. Write the cost function, C, of producing x wheelchairs.

b. Write the average cost function, \overline{C}, of producing x wheelchairs.

c. Find and interpret $\overline{C}(1000), \overline{C}(10,000)$, and $\overline{C}(100,000)$.

d. What is the horizontal asymptote for the graph of the average cost function, \overline{C}? Describe what this represents for the company.

Exercise Set 3.5

Practice Exercises

In Exercises 1–8, find the domain of each rational function.

1. $f(x) = \dfrac{5x}{x - 4}$

2. $f(x) = \dfrac{7x}{x - 8}$

3. $g(x) = \dfrac{3x^2}{(x - 5)(x + 4)}$

4. $g(x) = \dfrac{2x^2}{(x - 2)(x + 6)}$

5. $h(x) = \dfrac{x + 7}{x^2 - 49}$

6. $h(x) = \dfrac{x + 8}{x^2 - 64}$

7. $f(x) = \dfrac{x + 7}{x^2 + 49}$

8. $f(x) = \dfrac{x + 8}{x^2 + 64}$

Use the graph of the rational function in the figure shown to complete each statement in Exercises 9–14.

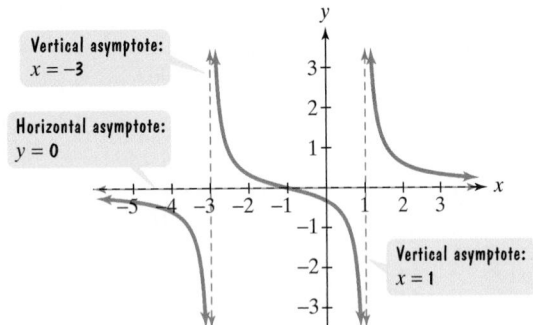

9. As $x \to -3^-$, $f(x) \to$ _____.

10. As $x \to -3^+$, $f(x) \to$ _____.

11. As $x \to 1^-$, $f(x) \to$ _____.

12. As $x \to 1^+$, $f(x) \to$ _____.

13. As $x \to -\infty$, $f(x) \to$ _____.

14. As $x \to \infty$, $f(x) \to$ _____.

Use the graph of the rational function in the figure shown to complete each statement in Exercises 15–20.

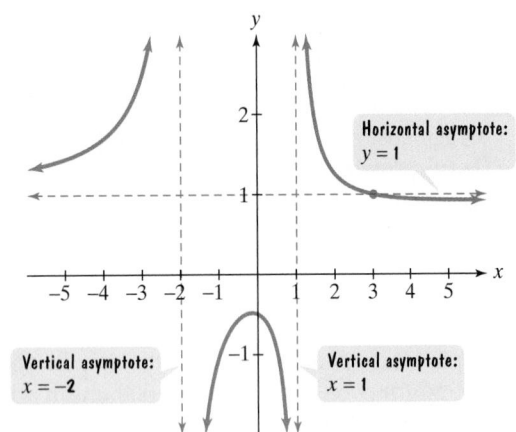

15. As $x \to 1^+$, $f(x) \to$ _____.

16. As $x \to 1^-$, $f(x) \to$ _____.

17. As $x \to -2^+$, $f(x) \to$ _____.

18. As $x \to -2^-$, $f(x) \to$ _____.

19. As $x \to \infty$, $f(x) \to$ _____.

20. As $x \to -\infty$, $f(x) \to$ _____.

In Exercises 21–28, find the vertical asymptotes, if any, of the graph of each rational function.

21. $f(x) = \dfrac{x}{x + 4}$

22. $f(x) = \dfrac{x}{x - 3}$

23. $g(x) = \dfrac{x + 3}{x(x + 4)}$

24. $g(x) = \dfrac{x + 3}{x(x - 3)}$

25. $h(x) = \dfrac{x}{x(x + 4)}$

26. $h(x) = \dfrac{x}{x(x - 3)}$

27. $r(x) = \dfrac{x}{x^2 + 4}$

28. $r(x) = \dfrac{x}{x^2 + 3}$

In Exercises 29–36, find the horizontal asymptote, if any, of the graph of each rational function.

29. $f(x) = \dfrac{12x}{3x^2 + 1}$

30. $f(x) = \dfrac{15x}{3x^2 + 1}$

31. $g(x) = \dfrac{12x^2}{3x^2 + 1}$

32. $g(x) = \dfrac{15x^2}{3x^2 + 1}$

33. $h(x) = \dfrac{12x^3}{3x^2 + 1}$

34. $h(x) = \dfrac{15x^3}{3x^2 + 1}$

35. $f(x) = \dfrac{-2x + 1}{3x + 5}$

36. $f(x) = \dfrac{-3x + 7}{5x - 2}$

In Exercises 37–48, use transformations of $f(x) = \dfrac{1}{x}$ or $f(x) = \dfrac{1}{x^2}$ to graph each rational function.

37. $g(x) = \dfrac{1}{x - 1}$

38. $g(x) = \dfrac{1}{x - 2}$

39. $h(x) = \dfrac{1}{x} + 2$

40. $h(x) = \dfrac{1}{x} + 1$

41. $g(x) = \dfrac{1}{x + 1} - 2$

42. $g(x) = \dfrac{1}{x + 2} - 2$

43. $g(x) = \dfrac{1}{(x + 2)^2}$

44. $g(x) = \dfrac{1}{(x + 1)^2}$

45. $h(x) = \dfrac{1}{x^2} - 4$

46. $h(x) = \dfrac{1}{x^2} - 3$

47. $h(x) = \dfrac{1}{(x - 3)^2} + 1$

48. $h(x) = \dfrac{1}{(x - 3)^2} + 2$

In Exercises 49–70, follow the seven steps on page 373 to graph each rational function.

49. $f(x) = \dfrac{4x}{x - 2}$

50. $f(x) = \dfrac{3x}{x - 1}$

51. $f(x) = \dfrac{2x}{x^2 - 4}$

52. $f(x) = \dfrac{4x}{x^2 - 1}$

53. $f(x) = \dfrac{2x^2}{x^2 - 1}$

54. $f(x) = \dfrac{4x^2}{x^2 - 9}$

55. $f(x) = \dfrac{-x}{x + 1}$

56. $f(x) = \dfrac{-3x}{x + 2}$

57. $f(x) = -\dfrac{1}{x^2 - 4}$

58. $f(x) = -\dfrac{2}{x^2 - 1}$

59. $f(x) = \dfrac{2}{x^2 + x - 2}$

60. $f(x) = \dfrac{-2}{x^2 - x - 2}$

61. $f(x) = \dfrac{2x^2}{x^2 + 4}$

62. $f(x) = \dfrac{4x^2}{x^2 + 1}$

63. $f(x) = \dfrac{x + 2}{x^2 + x - 6}$

64. $f(x) = \dfrac{x - 4}{x^2 - x - 6}$

65. $f(x) = \dfrac{x^4}{x^2 + 2}$

66. $f(x) = \dfrac{2x^4}{x^2 + 1}$

67. $f(x) = \dfrac{x^2 + x - 12}{x^2 - 4}$

68. $f(x) = \dfrac{x^2}{x^2 + x - 6}$

69. $f(x) = \dfrac{3x^2 + x - 4}{2x^2 - 5x}$

70. $f(x) = \dfrac{x^2 - 4x + 3}{(x + 1)^2}$

In Exercises 71–78, **a.** *Find the slant asymptote of the graph of each rational function and* **b.** *Follow the seven-step strategy and use the slant asymptote to graph each rational function.*

71. $f(x) = \dfrac{x^2 - 1}{x}$

72. $f(x) = \dfrac{x^2 - 4}{x}$

73. $f(x) = \dfrac{x^2 + 1}{x}$

74. $f(x) = \dfrac{x^2 + 4}{x}$

75. $f(x) = \dfrac{x^2 + x - 6}{x - 3}$

76. $f(x) = \dfrac{x^2 - x + 1}{x - 1}$

77. $f(x) = \dfrac{x^3 + 1}{x^2 + 2x}$

78. $f(x) = \dfrac{x^3 - 1}{x^2 - 9}$

Practice Plus

In Exercises 79–84, the equation for f is given by the simplified expression that results after performing the indicated operation. Write the equation for f and then graph the function.

79. $\dfrac{5x^2}{x^2 - 4} \cdot \dfrac{x^2 + 4x + 4}{10x^3}$

80. $\dfrac{x - 5}{10x - 2} \div \dfrac{x^2 - 10x + 25}{25x^2 - 1}$

81. $\dfrac{x}{2x + 6} - \dfrac{9}{x^2 - 9}$

82. $\dfrac{2}{x^2 + 3x + 2} - \dfrac{4}{x^2 + 4x + 3}$

83. $\dfrac{1 - \dfrac{3}{x + 2}}{1 + \dfrac{1}{x - 2}}$

84. $\dfrac{x - \dfrac{1}{x}}{x + \dfrac{1}{x}}$

In Exercises 85–88, use long division to rewrite the equation for g in the form

$$\text{quotient} + \frac{\text{remainder}}{\text{divisor}}.$$

Then use this form of the function's equation and transformations of $f(x) = \dfrac{1}{x}$ *to graph g.*

85. $g(x) = \dfrac{2x + 7}{x + 3}$

86. $g(x) = \dfrac{3x + 7}{x + 2}$

87. $g(x) = \dfrac{3x - 7}{x - 2}$

88. $g(x) = \dfrac{2x - 9}{x - 4}$

Application Exercises

89. A company is planning to manufacture mountain bikes. The fixed monthly cost will be $100,000 and it will cost $100 to produce each bicycle.

 a. Write the cost function, C, of producing x mountain bikes.

 b. Write the average cost function, \overline{C}, of producing x mountain bikes.

 c. Find and interpret $\overline{C}(500), \overline{C}(1000), \overline{C}(2000),$ and $\overline{C}(4000)$.

 d. What is the horizontal asymptote for the graph of the average cost function, \overline{C}? Describe what this means in practical terms.

90. A company that manufactures running shoes has a fixed monthly cost of $300,000. It costs $30 to produce each pair of shoes.

 a. Write the cost function, C, of producing x pairs of shoes.

 b. Write the average cost function, \overline{C}, of producing x pairs of shoes.

 c. Find and interpret $\overline{C}(1000), \overline{C}(10,000),$ and $\overline{C}(100,000)$.

 d. What is the horizontal asymptote for the graph of the average cost function, \overline{C}? Describe what this represents for the company.

91. The function

$$f(x) = \frac{6.5x^2 - 20.4x + 234}{x^2 + 36}$$

models the pH level, $f(x)$, of the human mouth x minutes after a person eats food containing sugar. The graph of this function is shown in the figure.

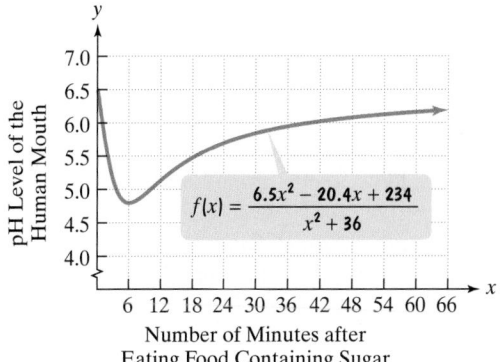

Number of Minutes after
Eating Food Containing Sugar

 a. Use the graph to obtain a reasonable estimate, to the nearest tenth, of the pH level of the human mouth 42 minutes after a person eats food containing sugar.

 b. After eating sugar, when is the pH level the lowest? Use the function's equation to determine the pH level, to the nearest tenth, at this time.

 c. According to the graph, what is the normal pH level of the human mouth?

 d. What is the equation of the horizontal asymptote associated with this function? Describe what this means in terms of the mouth's pH level over time.

 e. Use the graph to describe what happens to the pH level during the first hour.

92. A drug is injected into a patient and the concentration of the drug in the bloodstream is monitored. The drug's concentration, $C(t)$, in milligrams per liter, after t hours is modeled by

$$C(t) = \frac{5t}{t^2 + 1}.$$

The graph of this rational function, obtained with a graphing utility, is shown in the figure.

$[0, 10, 1]$ by $[0, 3, 1]$

a. Use the graph at the bottom of the previous page to obtain a reasonable estimate of the drug's concentration after 3 hours.

b. Use the function's equation displayed in the voice balloon by the graph to determine the drug's concentration after 3 hours.

c. Use the function's equation to find the horizontal asymptote for the graph. Describe what this means about the drug's concentration in the patient's bloodstream as time increases.

Among all deaths from a particular disease, the percentage that are smoking related (21–39 cigarettes per day) is a function of the disease's **incidence ratio**. *The incidence ratio describes the number of times more likely smokers are than nonsmokers to die from the disease. The following table shows the incidence ratios for heart disease and lung cancer for two age groups.*

Incidence Ratios		
	Heart Disease	**Lung Cancer**
Ages 55–64	1.9	10
Ages 65–74	1.7	9

Source: Alexander M. Walker, *Observations and Inference,* Epidemiology Resources Inc., 1991.

For example, the incidence ratio of 9 in the table means that smokers between the ages of 65 and 74 are 9 times more likely than nonsmokers in the same age group to die from lung cancer. The rational function

$$P(x) = \frac{100(x - 1)}{x}$$

models the percentage of smoking-related deaths among all deaths from a disease, P(x), in terms of the disease's incidence ratio, x. The graph of the rational function is shown. Use this function to solve Exercises 93–96.

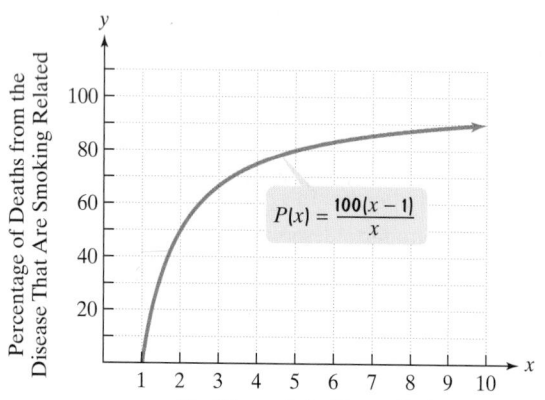

The Disease's Incidence Ratio:
The number of times more likely smokers are
than nonsmokers to die from the disease

93. Find $P(10)$. Describe what this means in terms of the incidence ratio, 10, given in the table. Identify your solution as a point on the graph.

94. Find $P(9)$. Round to the nearest percent. Describe what this means in terms of the incidence ratio, 9, given in the table. Identify your solution as a point on the graph.

95. What is the horizontal asymptote of the graph? Describe what this means about the percentage of deaths caused by smoking with increasing incidence ratios.

96. According to the model and its graph, is there a disease for which all deaths are caused by smoking? Explain your answer.

97. The bar graph shows the amount, in billions of dollars, that the United States government spent on human resources and total budget outlays for six selected years. (Human resources include education, health, Medicare, Social Security, and veterans benefits and services.)

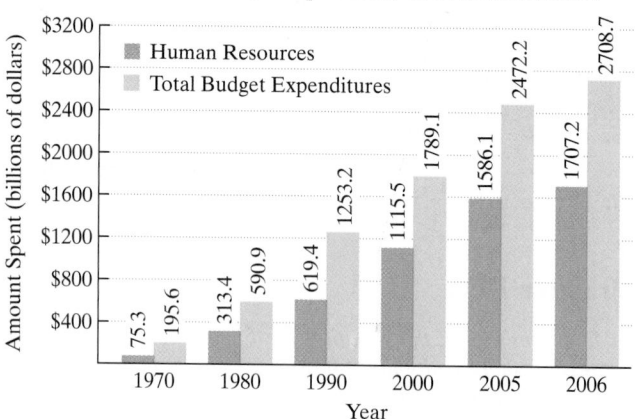

Federal Budget Expenditures on Human Resources

Source: Office of Management and Budget

The function $p(x) = 11x^2 + 40x + 1040$ models the amount, $p(x)$, in billions of dollars, that the United States government spent on human resources x years after 1970. The function $q(x) = 12x^2 + 230x + 2190$ models total budget expenditures, $q(x)$, in billions of dollars, x years after 1970.

a. Use p and q to write a rational function that models the fraction of total budget outlays spent on human resources x years after 1970.

b. Use the data displayed by the bar graph to find the percentage of federal expenditures spent on human resources in 2006. Round to the nearest percent.

c. Use the rational function from part (a) to find the percentage of federal expenditures spent on human resources in 2006. Round to the nearest percent. Does this underestimate or overestimate the actual percent that you found in part (b)? By how much?

d. What is the equation of the horizontal asymptote associated with the rational function in part (a)? If trends modeled by the function continue, what percentage of the federal budget will be spent on human resources over time? Round to the nearest percent. Does this projection seem realistic? Why or why not?

Writing in Mathematics

98. What is a rational function?

99. Use everyday language to describe the graph of a rational function f such that as $x \to -\infty$, $f(x) \to 3$.

100. Use everyday language to describe the behavior of a graph near its vertical asymptote if $f(x) \to \infty$ as $x \to -2^-$ and $f(x) \to -\infty$ as $x \to -2^+$.

101. If you are given the equation of a rational function, explain how to find the vertical asymptotes, if any, of the function's graph.

102. If you are given the equation of a rational function, explain how to find the horizontal asymptote, if any, of the function's graph.

103. Describe how to graph a rational function.

104. If you are given the equation of a rational function, how can you tell if the graph has a slant asymptote? If it does, how do you find its equation?

105. Is every rational function a polynomial function? Why or why not? Does a true statement result if the two adjectives *rational* and *polynomial* are reversed? Explain.

106. Although your friend has a family history of heart disease, he smokes, on average, 25 cigarettes per day. He sees the table showing incidence ratios for heart disease (see Exercises 93–96) and feels comfortable that they are less than 2, compared to 9 and 10 for lung cancer. He claims that all family deaths have been from heart disease and decides not to give up smoking. Use the given function and its graph to describe some additional information not given in the table that might influence his decision.

Technology Exercises

107. Use a graphing utility to verify any five of your hand-drawn graphs in Exercises 37–78.

108. Use a graphing utility to graph $y = \dfrac{1}{x}$, $y = \dfrac{1}{x^3}$, and $\dfrac{1}{x^5}$ in the same viewing rectangle. For odd values of n, how does changing n affect the graph of $y = \dfrac{1}{x^n}$?

109. Use a graphing utility to graph $y = \dfrac{1}{x^2}$, $y = \dfrac{1}{x^4}$, and $y = \dfrac{1}{x^6}$ in the same viewing rectangle. For even values of n, how does changing n affect the graph of $y = \dfrac{1}{x^n}$?

110. Use a graphing utility to graph

$$f(x) = \frac{x^2 - 4x + 3}{x - 2} \quad \text{and} \quad g(x) = \frac{x^2 - 5x + 6}{x - 2}.$$

What differences do you observe between the graph of f and the graph of g? How do you account for these differences?

111. The rational function

$$f(x) = \frac{27,725(x - 14)}{x^2 + 9} - 5x$$

models the number of arrests, $f(x)$, per 100,000 drivers, for driving under the influence of alcohol, as a function of a driver's age, x.

a. Graph the function in a $[0, 70, 5]$ by $[0, 400, 20]$ viewing rectangle.

b. Describe the trend shown by the graph.

c. Use the $\boxed{\text{ZOOM}}$ and $\boxed{\text{TRACE}}$ features or the maximum function feature of your graphing utility to find the age that corresponds to the greatest number of arrests. How many arrests, per 100,000 drivers, are there for this age group?

Critical Thinking Exercises

Make Sense? *In Exercises 112–115, determine whether each statement makes sense or does not make sense, and explain your reasoning.*

112. I've graphed a rational function that has two vertical asymptotes and two horizontal asymptotes.

113. My graph of $y = \dfrac{x - 1}{(x - 1)(x - 2)}$ has vertical asymptotes at $x = 1$ and $x = 2$.

114. The function

$$f(x) = \frac{1.96x + 3.14}{3.04x + 21.79}$$

models the fraction of nonviolent prisoners in New York State prisons x years after 1980. I can conclude from this equation that over time the percentage of nonviolent prisoners will exceed 60%.

115. As production level increases, the average cost for a company to produce each unit of its product also increases.

In Exercises 116–119, determine whether each statement is true or false. If the statement is false, make the necessary change(s) to produce a true statement.

116. The graph of a rational function cannot have both a vertical asymptote and a horizontal asymptote.

117. It is possible to have a rational function whose graph has no y-intercept.

118. The graph of a rational function can have three vertical asymptotes.

119. The graph of a rational function can never cross a vertical asymptote.

In Exercises 120–123, write the equation of a rational function $f(x) = \dfrac{p(x)}{q(x)}$ having the indicated properties, in which the degrees of p and q are as small as possible. More than one correct function may be possible. Graph your function using a graphing utility to verify that it has the required properties.

120. f has a vertical asymptote given by $x = 3$, a horizontal asymptote $y = 0$, y-intercept at -1, and no x-intercept.

121. f has vertical asymptotes given by $x = -2$ and $x = 2$, a horizontal asymptote $y = 2$, y-intercept at $\frac{9}{2}$, x-intercepts at -3 and 3, and y-axis symmetry.

122. f has a vertical asymptote given by $x = 1$, a slant asymptote whose equation is $y = x$, y-intercept at 2, and x-intercepts at -1 and 2.

123. f has no vertical, horizontal, or slant asymptotes, and no x-intercepts.

Preview Exercises

Exercises 124–126 will help you prepare for the material covered in the next section.

124. Solve: $2x^2 + x = 15$.

125. Solve: $x^3 + x^2 = 4x + 4$.

126. Simplify: $\dfrac{x + 1}{x + 3} - 2$.

Section 3.6 **Polynomial and Rational Inequalities**

Objectives

① Solve polynomial inequalities.

② Solve rational inequalities.

③ Solve problems modeled by polynomial or rational inequalities.

© The New Yorker Collection 1995 Warren Miller from cartoonbank.com. All Rights Reserved.

Tailgaters beware: If your car is going 35 miles per hour on dry pavement, your required stopping distance is 160 feet, or the width of a football field. At 65 miles per hour, the distance required is 410 feet, or approximately the length of one and one-tenth football fields. **Figure 3.41** shows stopping distances for cars at various speeds on dry roads and on wet roads.

A car's required stopping distance, $f(x)$, in feet, on dry pavement traveling at x miles per hour can be modeled by the quadratic function

$$f(x) = 0.0875x^2 - 0.4x + 66.6.$$

How can we use this function to determine speeds on dry pavement requiring stopping distances that exceed the length of one and one-half football fields, or 540 feet? We must solve the inequality

$$0.0875x^2 - 0.4x + 66.6 > 540.$$

Required stopping distance exceeds 540 feet.

We begin by subtracting 540 from both sides. This will give us zero on the right:

$$0.0875x^2 - 0.4x + 66.6 - 540 > 540 - 540$$
$$0.0875x^2 - 0.4x - 473.4 > 0.$$

The form of this inequality is $ax^2 + bx + c > 0$. Such a quadratic inequality is called a *polynomial inequality*.

Stopping Distances for Cars at Selected Speeds

■ Dry Pavement ■ Wet Pavement

Figure 3.41
Source: National Highway Traffic Safety Administration

Definition of a Polynomial Inequality

A polynomial inequality is any inequality that can be put into one of the forms

$$f(x) < 0, \quad f(x) > 0, \quad f(x) \le 0, \quad \text{or} \quad f(x) \ge 0,$$

where f is a polynomial function.

In this section, we establish the basic techniques for solving polynomial inequalities. We will also use these techniques to solve inequalities involving rational functions.

Technology

We used the statistical menu of a graphing utility and the quadratic regression program to obtain the quadratic function that models stopping distance on dry pavement. After entering the appropriate data from **Figure 3.41**, namely

$(35, 160), (45, 225), (55, 310),$
$(65, 410),$

we obtained the results shown in the screen.

```
QuadReg
y=ax²+bx+c
a=.0875
b=-.4
c=66.5625
```

Solving Polynomial Inequalities

Graphs can help us visualize the solutions of polynomial inequalities. For example, the graph of $f(x) = x^2 - 7x + 10$ is shown in **Figure 3.42**. The x-intercepts, 2 and 5, are **boundary points** between where the graph lies above the x-axis, shown in blue, and where the graph lies below the x-axis, shown red.

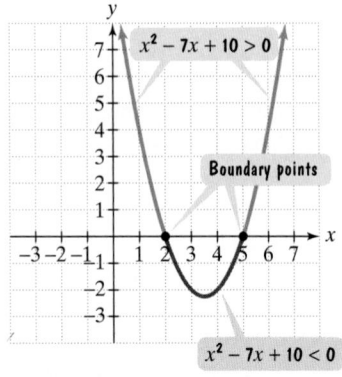

Figure 3.42

Locating the x-intercepts of a polynomial function, f, is an importan finding the solution set for polynomial inequalities in the form $f(x)$ $f(x) > 0$. We use the x-intercepts of f as boundary points that divide the real number line into intervals. On each interval, the graph of f is either above the x-axis $[f(x) > 0]$ or below the x-axis $[f(x) < 0]$. For this reason, x-intercepts play a fundamental role in solving polynomial inequalities. The x-intercepts are found by solving the equation $f(x) = 0$.

① Solve polynomial inequalities.

Procedure for Solving Polynomial Inequalities

1. Express the inequality in the form
$$f(x) < 0 \quad \text{or} \quad f(x) > 0,$$
where f is a polynomial function.

2. Solve the equation $f(x) = 0$. The real solutions are the **boundary points**.

3. Locate these boundary points on a number line, thereby dividing the number line into intervals.

4. Choose one representative number, called a **test value**, within each interval and evaluate f at that number.

 a. If the value of f is positive, then $f(x) > 0$ for all numbers, x, in the interval.

 b. If the value of f is negative, then $f(x) < 0$ for all numbers, x, in the interval.

5. Write the solution set, selecting the interval or intervals that satisfy the given inequality.

This procedure is valid if $<$ is replaced by \leq or $>$ is replaced by \geq. However, if the inequality involves \leq or \geq, include the boundary points [the solutions of $f(x) = 0$] in the solution set.

EXAMPLE 1 **Solving a Polynomial Inequality**

Solve and graph the solution set on a real number line: $2x^2 + x > 15$.

Solution

Step 1 Express the inequality in the form $f(x) < 0$ or $f(x) > 0$. We begin by rewriting the inequality so that 0 is on the right side.

$$2x^2 + x > 15 \qquad \text{This is the given inequality.}$$
$$2x^2 + x - 15 > 15 - 15 \qquad \text{Subtract 15 from both sides.}$$
$$2x^2 + x - 15 > 0 \qquad \text{Simplify.}$$

This inequality is equivalent to the one we wish to solve. It is in the form $f(x) > 0$, where $f(x) = 2x^2 + x - 15$.

Step 2 Solve the equation $f(x) = 0$. We find the x-intercepts of $f(x) = 2x^2 + x - 15$ by solving the equation $2x^2 + x - 15 = 0$.

$$2x^2 + x - 15 = 0 \qquad \text{This polynomial equation is a}$$
$$\qquad\qquad\qquad\qquad \text{quadratic equation.}$$
$$(2x - 5)(x + 3) = 0 \qquad \text{Factor.}$$
$$2x - 5 = 0 \quad \text{or} \quad x + 3 = 0 \qquad \text{Set each factor equal to 0.}$$
$$x = \tfrac{5}{2} \qquad\qquad x = -3 \qquad \text{Solve for x.}$$

The x-intercepts of f are -3 and $\tfrac{5}{2}$. We will use these x-intercepts as boundary points on a number line.

Step 3 Locate the boundary points on a number line and separate the line into intervals. The number line with the boundary points is shown as follows:

The boundary points divide the number line into three intervals:
$$(-\infty, -3) \quad \left(-3, \tfrac{5}{2}\right) \quad \left(\tfrac{5}{2}, \infty\right).$$

Step 4 **Choose one test value within each interval and evaluate f at that number.**

Interval	Test Value	Substitute into $f(x) = 2x^2 + x - 15$	Conclusion
$(-\infty, -3)$	-4	$f(-4) = 2(-4)^2 + (-4) - 15$ $= 13$, positive	$f(x) > 0$ for all x in $(-\infty, -3)$.
$\left(-3, \dfrac{5}{2}\right)$	0	$f(0) = 2 \cdot 0^2 + 0 - 15$ $= -15$, negative	$f(x) < 0$ for all x in $\left(-3, \dfrac{5}{2}\right)$.
$\left(\dfrac{5}{2}, \infty\right)$	3	$f(3) = 2 \cdot 3^2 + 3 - 15$ $= 6$, positive	$f(x) > 0$ for all x in $\left(\dfrac{5}{2}, \infty\right)$.

Technology

Graphic Connections

The solution set for
$$2x^2 + x > 15$$
or, equivalently,
$$2x^2 + x - 15 > 0$$
can be verified with a graphing utility. The graph of $f(x) = 2x^2 + x - 15$ was obtained using a $[-10, 10, 1]$ by $[-16, 6, 1]$ viewing rectangle. The graph lies above the x-axis, representing $>$, for all x in
$(-\infty, -3)$ or $\left(\frac{5}{2}, \infty\right)$.

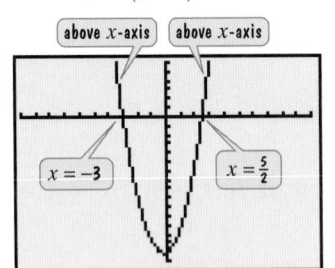

Step 5 **Write the solution set, selecting the interval or intervals that satisfy the given inequality.** We are interested in solving $f(x) > 0$, where $f(x) = 2x^2 + x - 15$. Based on our work in step 4, we see that $f(x) > 0$ for all x in $(-\infty, -3)$ or $\left(\frac{5}{2}, \infty\right)$. Thus, the solution set of the given inequality, $2x^2 + x > 15$, or, equivalently, $2x^2 + x - 15 > 0$, is

$$(-\infty, -3) \cup \left(\tfrac{5}{2}, \infty\right) \text{ or } \left\{x \mid x < -3 \text{ or } x > \tfrac{5}{2}\right\}.$$

The graph of the solution set on a number line is shown as follows:

Check Point 1 Solve and graph the solution set: $x^2 - x > 20$.

EXAMPLE 2 Solving a Polynomial Inequality

Solve and graph the solution set on a real number line: $x^3 + x^2 \le 4x + 4$.

Solution

Step 1 **Express the inequality in the form $f(x) \le 0$ or $f(x) \ge 0$.** We begin by rewriting the inequality so that 0 is on the right side.

$$x^3 + x^2 \le 4x + 4 \qquad \text{This is the given inequality.}$$
$$x^3 + x^2 - 4x - 4 \le 4x + 4 - 4x - 4 \qquad \text{Subtract } 4x + 4 \text{ from both sides.}$$
$$x^3 + x^2 - 4x - 4 \le 0 \qquad \text{Simplify.}$$

This inequality is equivalent to the one we wish to solve. It is in the form $f(x) \le 0$, where $f(x) = x^3 + x^2 - 4x - 4$.

Step 2 **Solve the equation $f(x) = 0$.** We find the x-intercepts of $f(x) = x^3 + x^2 - 4x - 4$ by solving the equation $x^3 + x^2 - 4x - 4 = 0$.

$$x^3 + x^2 - 4x - 4 = 0 \qquad \text{This polynomial equation is of degree 3.}$$
$$x^2(x + 1) - 4(x + 1) = 0 \qquad \text{Factor } x^2 \text{ from the first two terms and } -4 \text{ from the last two terms.}$$
$$(x + 1)(x^2 - 4) = 0 \qquad \text{A common factor of } x + 1 \text{ is factored from the expression.}$$
$$(x + 1)(x + 2)(x - 2) = 0 \qquad \text{Factor completely.}$$
$$x + 1 = 0 \quad \text{or} \quad x + 2 = 0 \quad \text{or} \quad x - 2 = 0 \qquad \text{Set each factor equal to 0.}$$
$$x = -1 \qquad\qquad x = -2 \qquad\qquad x = 2 \qquad \text{Solve for x.}$$

The x-intercepts of f are -2, -1, and 2. We will use these x-intercepts as boundary points on a number line.

Step 3 Locate the boundary points on a number line and separate the line into intervals. The number line with the boundary points is shown as follows:

The boundary points divide the number line into four intervals:

$$(-\infty, -2) \quad (-2, -1) \quad (-1, 2) \quad (2, \infty).$$

Step 4 Choose one test value within each interval and evaluate f at that number.

Interval	Test Value	Substitute into $f(x) = x^3 + x^2 - 4x - 4$	Conclusion
$(-\infty, -2)$	-3	$f(-3) = (-3)^3 + (-3)^2 - 4(-3) - 4$ $= -10$, negative	$f(x) < 0$ for all x in $(-\infty, -2)$.
$(-2, -1)$	-1.5	$f(-1.5) = (-1.5)^3 + (-1.5)^2 - 4(-1.5) - 4$ $= 0.875$, positive	$f(x) > 0$ for all x in $(-2, -1)$.
$(-1, 2)$	0	$f(0) = 0^3 + 0^2 - 4 \cdot 0 - 4$ $= -4$, negative	$f(x) < 0$ for all x in $(-1, 2)$.
$(2, \infty)$	3	$f(3) = 3^3 + 3^2 - 4 \cdot 3 - 4$ $= 20$, positive	$f(x) > 0$ for all x in $(2, \infty)$.

Technology

Graphic Connections

The solution set for
$$x^3 + x^2 \le 4x + 4$$
or, equivalently,
$$x^3 + x^2 - 4x - 4 \le 0$$
can be verified with a graphing utility. The graph of
$f(x) = x^3 + x^2 - 4x - 4$ lies on or below the x-axis, representing \le, for all x in $(-\infty, -2]$ or $[-1, 2]$.

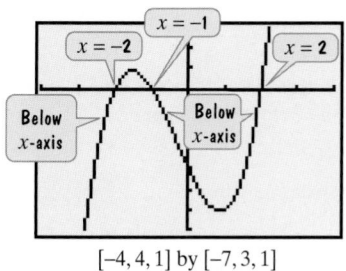

$[-4, 4, 1]$ by $[-7, 3, 1]$

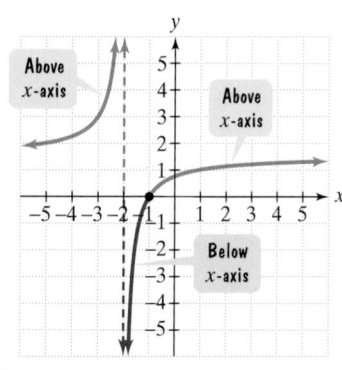

Figure 3.43 The graph of
$$f(x) = \frac{3x + 3}{2x + 4}$$

Step 5 Write the solution set, selecting the interval or intervals that satisfy the given inequality. We are interested in solving $f(x) \le 0$, where $f(x) = x^3 + x^2 - 4x - 4$. Based on our work in step 4, we see that $f(x) < 0$ for all x in $(-\infty, -2)$ or $(-1, 2)$. However, because the inequality involves \le (less than or *equal to*), we must also include the solutions of $x^3 + x^2 - 4x - 4 = 0$, namely -2, -1, and 2, in the solution set. Thus, the solution set of the given inequality, $x^3 + x^2 \le 4x + 4$, or, equivalently, $x^3 + x^2 - 4x - 4 \le 0$, is

$$(-\infty, -2] \cup [-1, 2]$$

or $\{x | x \le -2 \text{ or } -1 \le x \le 2\}$.

The graph of the solution set on a number line is shown as follows:

⊘ **Check Point 2** Solve and graph the solution set on a real number line: $x^3 + 3x^2 \le x + 3$.

Solving Rational Inequalities

A **rational inequality** is any inequality that can be put into one of the forms

$$f(x) < 0, \quad f(x) > 0, \quad f(x) \le 0, \quad \text{or} \quad f(x) \ge 0,$$

where f is a rational function. An example of a rational inequality is

$$\frac{3x + 3}{2x + 4} > 0.$$

This inequality is in the form $f(x) > 0$, where f is the rational function given by

$$f(x) = \frac{3x + 3}{2x + 4}.$$

The graph of f is shown in **Figure 3.43**.

We can find the x-intercept of f by setting the numerator equal to 0:

$$3x + 3 = 0$$
$$3x = -3 \qquad \text{\small f has an x-intercept}$$
$$x = -1. \qquad \text{\small at -1 and passes through $(-1, 0)$.}$$

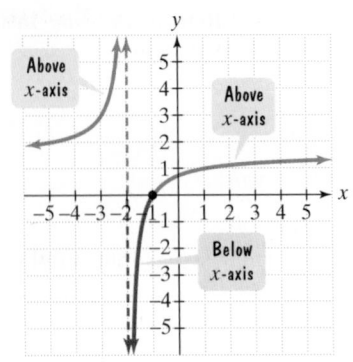

Figure 3.43 The graph of $f(x) = \dfrac{3x + 3}{2x + 4}$ (repeated)

2 Solve rational inequalities.

We can determine where f is undefined by setting the denominator equal to 0:

$$2x + 4 = 0$$
$$2x = -4$$
$$x = -2.$$

> f is undefined at −2. **Figure 3.43** shows that the function's vertical asymptote is $x = -2$.

By setting both the numerator and the denominator of f equal to 0, we obtained -2 and -1. These numbers separate the x-axis into three intervals: $(-\infty, -2), (-2, -1),$ and $(-1, \infty)$. On each interval, the graph of f is either above the x-axis $[f(x) > 0]$ or below the x-axis $[f(x) < 0]$.

Examine the graph in **Figure 3.43** carefully. Can you see that it is above the x-axis for all x in $(-\infty, -2)$ or $(-1, \infty)$, shown in blue? Thus, the solution set of $\dfrac{3x + 3}{2x + 4} > 0$ is $(-\infty, -2) \cup (-1, \infty)$. By contrast, the graph of f lies below the x-axis for all x in $(-2, -1)$, shown in red. Thus, the solution set of $\dfrac{3x + 3}{2x + 4} < 0$ is $(-2, -1)$.

The first step in solving a rational inequality is to bring all terms to one side, obtaining zero on the other side. Then express the rational function on the nonzero side as a single quotient. The second step is to set the numerator and the denominator of f equal to zero. The solutions of these equations serve as boundary points that separate the real number line into intervals. At this point, the procedure is the same as the one we used for solving polynomial inequalities.

EXAMPLE 3 **Solving a Rational Inequality**

Solve and graph the solution set: $\dfrac{x + 1}{x + 3} \geq 2$.

Solution

Step 1 Express the inequality so that one side is zero and the other side is a single quotient. We subtract 2 from both sides to obtain zero on the right.

$$\frac{x + 1}{x + 3} \geq 2 \qquad \text{This is the given inequality.}$$

$$\frac{x + 1}{x + 3} - 2 \geq 0 \qquad \begin{array}{l}\text{Subtract 2 from both sides, obtaining 0}\\ \text{on the right.}\end{array}$$

$$\frac{x + 1}{x + 3} - \frac{2(x + 3)}{x + 3} \geq 0 \qquad \begin{array}{l}\text{The least common denominator is } x + 3.\\ \text{Express 2 in terms of this denominator.}\end{array}$$

$$\frac{x + 1 - 2(x + 3)}{x + 3} \geq 0 \qquad \text{Subtract rational expressions.}$$

$$\frac{x + 1 - 2x - 6}{x + 3} \geq 0 \qquad \text{Apply the distributive property.}$$

$$\frac{-x - 5}{x + 3} \geq 0 \qquad \text{Simplify.}$$

This inequality is equivalent to the one we wish to solve. It is in the form $f(x) \geq 0$, where $f(x) = \dfrac{-x - 5}{x + 3}$.

Step 2 Set the numerator and the denominator of f equal to zero. The real solutions are the boundary points.

$$-x - 5 = 0 \qquad x + 3 = 0 \qquad \begin{array}{l}\text{Set the numerator and denominator equal}\\ \text{to 0. These are the values that make the}\\ \text{previous quotient zero or undefined.}\end{array}$$

$$x = -5 \qquad x = -3 \qquad \text{Solve for x.}$$

We will use these solutions as boundary points on a number line.

Step 3 Locate the boundary points on a number line and separate the line into intervals. The number line with the boundary points is shown as follows:

The boundary points divide the number line into three intervals:

$$(-\infty, -5) \quad (-5, -3) \quad (-3, \infty).$$

Step 4 Choose one test value within each interval and evaluate f at that number.

Interval	Test Value	Substitute into $f(x) = \dfrac{-x - 5}{x + 3}$	Conclusion
$(-\infty, -5)$	-6	$f(-6) = \dfrac{-(-6) - 5}{-6 + 3}$ $= -\frac{1}{3}$, negative	$f(x) < 0$ for all x in $(-\infty, -5)$.
$(-5, -3)$	-4	$f(-4) = \dfrac{-(-4) - 5}{-4 + 3}$ $= 1$, positive	$f(x) > 0$ for all x in $(-5, -3)$.
$(-3, \infty)$	0	$f(0) = \dfrac{-0 - 5}{0 + 3}$ $= -\frac{5}{3}$, negative	$f(x) < 0$ for all x in $(-3, \infty)$.

Step 5 Write the solution set, selecting the interval or intervals that satisfy the given inequality. We are interested in solving $f(x) \geq 0$, where $f(x) = \dfrac{-x - 5}{x + 3}$. Based on our work in step 4, we see that $f(x) > 0$ for all x in $(-5, -3)$. However, because the inequality involves \geq (greater than or *equal to*), we must also include the solution of $f(x) = 0$, namely the value that we obtained when we set the numerator of f equal to zero. Thus, we must include -5 in the solution set. The solution set of the given inequality is

$$[-5, -3) \text{ or } \{x| -5 \leq x < -3\}.$$

> −3 causes the denominator of f to equal zero. It must be excluded from the solution set.

The graph of the solution set on a number line is shown as follows:

The graph of the solution set on a number line.

Technology

Graphic Connections

The solution set for

$$\frac{x + 1}{x + 3} \geq 2$$

or, equivalently,

$$\frac{-x - 5}{x + 3} \geq 0$$

can be verified with a graphing utility. The graph of $f(x) = \dfrac{-x - 5}{x + 3}$ lies on or above the x-axis, representing \geq, for all x in $[-5, -3)$.

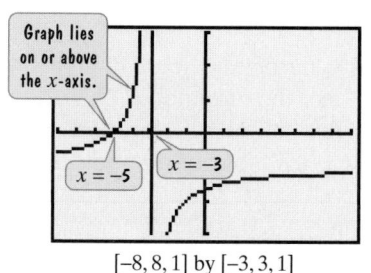

Graph lies on or above the x-axis.

$x = -5$ $x = -3$

$[-8, 8, 1]$ by $[-3, 3, 1]$

⊘ **Check Point 3** Solve and graph the solution set: $\dfrac{2x}{x + 1} \geq 1$.

3 Solve problems modeled by polynomial or rational inequalities.

Applications

If you throw an object directly upward, although its path is straight and vertical, its changing height over time can be described by a quadratic function.

The Position Function for a Free-Falling Object Near Earth's Surface

An object that is falling or vertically projected into the air has its height above the ground, $s(t)$, in feet, given by

$$s(t) = -16t^2 + v_0 t + s_0,$$

where v_0 is the original velocity (initial velocity) of the object, in feet per second, t is the time that the object is in motion, in seconds, and s_0 is the original height (initial height) of the object, in feet.

In Example 4, we solve a polynomial inequality in a problem about the position of a free-falling object.

EXAMPLE 4 **Using the Position Function**

A ball is thrown vertically upward from the top of the Leaning Tower of Pisa (190 feet high) with an initial velocity of 96 feet per second (**Figure 3.44**). During which time period will the ball's height exceed that of the tower?

Solution

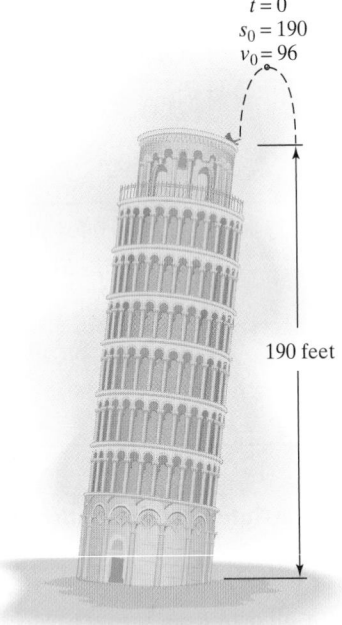

$t = 0$
$s_0 = 190$
$v_0 = 96$

190 feet

Figure 3.44 Throwing a ball from 190 feet with a velocity of 96 feet per second

$s(t) = -16t^2 + v_0 t + s_0$ This is the position function for a free-falling object.

$s(t) = -16t^2 + 96t + 190$ Because v_0 (initial velocity) = 96 and s_0 (initial position) = 190, substitute these values into the formula.

When will $s(t)$, the ball's height, exceed that of the tower?

$$-16t^2 + 96t + 190 > 190$$

$-16t^2 + 96t + 190 > 190$ This is the inequality that models the problem's question. We must find t.

$-16t^2 + 96t > 0$ Subtract 190 from both sides. This inequality is in the form $f(t) > 0$, where $f(t) = -16t^2 + 96t$.

$-16t^2 + 96t = 0$ Solve the equation $f(t) = 0$.

$-16t(t - 6) = 0$ Factor.

$-16t = 0$ or $t - 6 = 0$ Set each factor equal to 0.

$t = 0$ $t = 6$ Solve for t. The boundary points are 0 and 6.

Locate these values on a number line.

The intervals are $(-\infty, 0)$, $(0, 6)$, and $(6, \infty)$. For our purposes, the mathematical model is useful only from $t = 0$ until the ball hits the ground. (By setting $-16t^2 + 96t + 190$ equal to zero, we find $t \approx 7.57$; the ball hits the ground after approximately 7.57 seconds.) Thus, we use $(0, 6)$ and $(6, 7.57)$ for our intervals.

Interval	Test Value	Substitute into $f(t) = -16t^2 + 96t$	Conclusion
$(0, 6)$	1	$f(1) = -16 \cdot 1^2 + 96 \cdot 1$ $= 80$, positive	$f(t) > 0$ for all t in $(0, 6)$.
$(6, 7.57)$	7	$f(7) = -16 \cdot 7^2 + 96 \cdot 7$ $= -112$, negative	$f(t) < 0$ for all t in $(6, 7.57)$.

We are interested in solving $f(t) > 0$, where $f(t) = -16t^2 + 96t$. We see that $f(t) > 0$ for all t in $(0, 6)$. This means that the ball's height exceeds that of the tower between 0 and 6 seconds.

Technology

Graphic Connections

The graphs of

$$y_1 = -16x^2 + 96x + 190$$

and

$$y_2 = 190$$

are shown in a

$$[0, 8, 1] \text{ by } [0, 360, 36]$$

seconds
in motion

height,
in feet

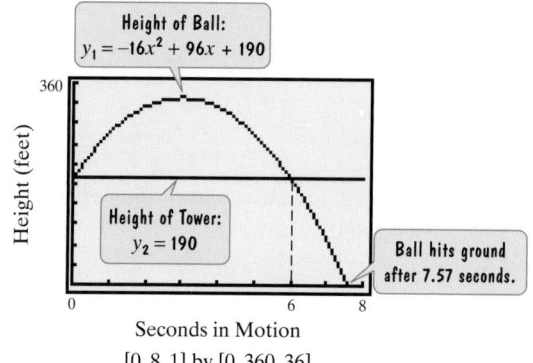

Height of Ball:
$y_1 = -16x^2 + 96x + 190$

360

Height (feet)

Height of Tower:
$y_2 = 190$

Ball hits ground
after 7.57 seconds.

0 6 8
Seconds in Motion
$[0, 8, 1]$ by $[0, 360, 36]$

viewing rectangle. The graphs show that the ball's height exceeds that of the tower between 0 and 6 seconds.

⊘ Check Point **4** An object is propelled straight up from ground level with an initial velocity of 80 feet per second. Its height at time t is modeled by

$$s(t) = -16t^2 + 80t,$$

where the height, $s(t)$, is measured in feet and the time, t, is measured in seconds. In which time interval will the object be more than 64 feet above the ground?

Exercise Set 3.6

Practice Exercises

Solve each polynomial inequality in Exercises 1–42 and graph the solution set on a real number line. Express each solution set in interval notation.

1. $(x - 4)(x + 2) > 0$

2. $(x + 3)(x - 5) > 0$

3. $(x - 7)(x + 3) \le 0$

4. $(x + 1)(x - 7) \le 0$

5. $x^2 - 5x + 4 > 0$

6. $x^2 - 4x + 3 < 0$

7. $x^2 + 5x + 4 > 0$

8. $x^2 + x - 6 > 0$

9. $x^2 - 6x + 9 < 0$

10. $x^2 - 2x + 1 > 0$

11. $3x^2 + 10x - 8 \le 0$

12. $9x^2 + 3x - 2 \ge 0$

13. $2x^2 + x < 15$

14. $6x^2 + x > 1$

15. $4x^2 + 7x < -3$

16. $3x^2 + 16x < -5$

17. $5x \le 2 - 3x^2$

18. $4x^2 + 1 \ge 4x$

19. $x^2 - 4x \ge 0$

20. $x^2 + 2x < 0$

21. $2x^2 + 3x > 0$

22. $3x^2 - 5x \le 0$

23. $-x^2 + x \ge 0$

24. $-x^2 + 2x \ge 0$

25. $x^2 \le 4x - 2$

26. $x^2 \le 2x + 2$

27. $9x^2 - 6x + 1 < 0$

28. $4x^2 - 4x + 1 \ge 0$

29. $(x - 1)(x - 2)(x - 3) \ge 0$

30. $(x + 1)(x + 2)(x + 3) \ge 0$

31. $x(3 - x)(x - 5) \le 0$

32. $x(4 - x)(x - 6) \le 0$

33. $(2 - x)^2\left(x - \dfrac{7}{2}\right) < 0$

34. $(5 - x)^2\left(x - \dfrac{13}{2}\right) < 0$

35. $x^3 + 2x^2 - x - 2 \ge 0$

36. $x^3 + 2x^2 - 4x - 8 \ge 0$

37. $x^3 - 3x^2 - 9x + 27 < 0$

38. $x^3 + 7x^2 - x - 7 < 0$

39. $x^3 + x^2 + 4x + 4 > 0$

40. $x^3 - x^2 + 9x - 9 > 0$

41. $x^3 \ge 9x^2$

42. $x^3 \le 4x^2$

Solve each rational inequality in Exercises 43–60 and graph the solution set on a real number line. Express each solution set in interval notation.

43. $\dfrac{x - 4}{x + 3} > 0$

44. $\dfrac{x + 5}{x - 2} > 0$

45. $\dfrac{x + 3}{x + 4} < 0$

46. $\dfrac{x + 5}{x + 2} < 0$

47. $\dfrac{-x + 2}{x - 4} \ge 0$

48. $\dfrac{-x - 3}{x + 2} \le 0$

49. $\dfrac{4 - 2x}{3x + 4} \le 0$

50. $\dfrac{3x + 5}{6 - 2x} \ge 0$

51. $\dfrac{x}{x - 3} > 0$

52. $\dfrac{x + 4}{x} > 0$

53. $\dfrac{(x + 4)(x - 1)}{x + 2} \le 0$

54. $\dfrac{(x + 3)(x - 2)}{x + 1} \le 0$

55. $\dfrac{x + 1}{x + 3} < 2$

56. $\dfrac{x}{x - 1} > 2$

57. $\dfrac{x + 4}{2x - 1} \le 3$

58. $\dfrac{1}{x - 3} < 1$

59. $\dfrac{x - 2}{x + 2} \le 2$

60. $\dfrac{x}{x + 2} \ge 2$

Practice Plus

In Exercises 61–64, find the domain of each function.

61. $f(x) = \sqrt{2x^2 - 5x + 2}$

62. $f(x) = \dfrac{1}{\sqrt{4x^2 - 9x + 2}}$

63. $f(x) = \sqrt{\dfrac{2x}{x + 1} - 1}$

64. $f(x) = \sqrt{\dfrac{x}{2x - 1} - 1}$

Solve each inequality in Exercises 65–70 and graph the solution set on a real number line.

65. $|x^2 + 2x - 36| > 12$

66. $|x^2 + 6x + 1| > 8$

67. $\dfrac{3}{x + 3} > \dfrac{3}{x - 2}$

68. $\dfrac{1}{x + 1} > \dfrac{2}{x - 1}$

69. $\dfrac{x^2 - x - 2}{x^2 - 4x + 3} > 0$

70. $\dfrac{x^2 - 3x + 2}{x^2 - 2x - 3} > 0$

In Exercises 71–72, use the graph of the polynomial function to solve each inequality.

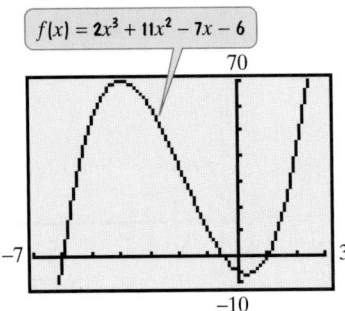

$f(x) = 2x^3 + 11x^2 - 7x - 6$

71. $2x^3 + 11x^2 \geq 7x + 6$

72. $2x^3 + 11x^2 < 7x + 6$

In Exercises 73–74, use the graph of the rational function to solve each inequality.

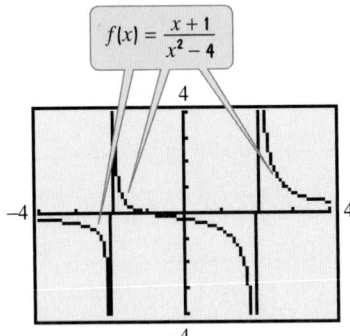

$f(x) = \dfrac{x + 1}{x^2 - 4}$

73. $\dfrac{1}{4(x + 2)} \leq -\dfrac{3}{4(x - 2)}$

74. $\dfrac{1}{4(x + 2)} > -\dfrac{3}{4(x - 2)}$

Application Exercises

Use the position function

$$s(t) = -16t^2 + v_0 t + s_0$$

$(v_0 = \text{initial velocity, } s_0 = \text{initial position, } t = \text{time})$

to answer Exercises 75–76.

75. Divers in Acapulco, Mexico, dive headfirst at 8 feet per second from the top of a cliff 87 feet above the Pacific Ocean. During which time period will the diver's height exceed that of the cliff?

76. You throw a ball straight up from a rooftop 160 feet high with an initial velocity of 48 feet per second. During which time period will the ball's height exceed that of the rooftop?

The functions

$$f(x) = 0.0875x^2 - 0.4x + 66.6$$

Dry pavement

and

Wet pavement

$$g(x) = 0.0875x^2 + 1.9x + 11.6$$

model a car's stopping distance, $f(x)$ or $g(x)$, in feet, traveling at x miles per hour. Function f models stopping distance on dry pavement and function g models stopping distance on wet pavement. The graphs of these functions are shown for $\{x|x \geq 30\}$. Notice that the figure does not specify which graph is the model for dry roads and which is the model for wet roads. Use this information to solve Exercises 77–78.

Graphs of Models for Stopping Distances

77. a. Use the given functions to find the stopping distance on dry pavement and the stopping distance on wet pavement for a car traveling at 35 miles per hour. Round to the nearest foot.

 b. Based on your answers to part (a), which rectangular coordinate graph shows stopping distances on dry pavement and which shows stopping distances on wet pavement?

 c. How well do your answers to part (a) model the actual stopping distances shown in **Figure 3.41** on page 384?

 d. Determine speeds on dry pavement requiring stopping distances that exceed the length of one and one-half football fields, or 540 feet. Round to the nearest mile per hour. How is this shown on the appropriate graph of the models?

78. a. Use the given functions to find the stopping distance on dry pavement and the stopping distance on wet pavement for a car traveling at 55 miles per hour. Round to the nearest foot.

 b. Based on your answers to part (a), which rectangular coordinate graph shows stopping distances on dry pavement and which shows stopping distances on wet pavement?

 c. How well do your answers to part (a) model the actual stopping distances shown in **Figure 3.41** on page 384?

 d. Determine speeds on wet pavement requiring stopping distances that exceed the length of one and one-half football fields, or 540 feet. Round to the nearest mile per hour. How is this shown on the appropriate graph of the models?

79. The perimeter of a rectangle is 50 feet. Describe the possible lengths of a side if the area of the rectangle is not to exceed 114 square feet.

80. The perimeter of a rectangle is 180 feet. Describe the possible lengths of a side if the area of the rectangle is not to exceed 800 square feet.

Writing in Mathematics

81. What is a polynomial inequality?

82. What is a rational inequality?

83. If f is a polynomial or rational function, explain how the graph of f can be used to visualize the solution set of the inequality $f(x) < 0$.

Technology Exercises

84. Use a graphing utility to verify your solution sets to any three of the polynomial inequalities that you solved algebraically in Exercises 1–42.

85. Use a graphing utility to verify your solution sets to any three of the rational inequalities that you solved algebraically in Exercises 43–60.

Solve each inequality in Exercises 86–91 using a graphing utility.

86. $x^2 + 3x - 10 > 0$

87. $2x^2 + 5x - 3 \leq 0$

88. $x^3 + x^2 - 4x - 4 > 0$

89. $\dfrac{x - 4}{x - 1} \leq 0$

90. $\dfrac{x + 2}{x - 3} \leq 2$

91. $\dfrac{1}{x + 1} \leq \dfrac{2}{x + 4}$

The graph shows stopping distances for trucks at various speeds on dry roads and on wet roads. Use this information to solve Exercises 92–93.

Stopping Distances for Trucks at Selected Speeds

Source: National Highway Traffic Safety Administration

92. a. Use the statistical menu of your graphing utility and the quadratic regression program to obtain the quadratic function that models a truck's stopping distance, $f(x)$, in feet, on dry pavement traveling at x miles per hour. Round the x-coefficient and the constant term to one decimal place.

b. Use the function from part (a) to determine speeds on dry pavement requiring stopping distances that exceed 455 feet. Round to the nearest mile per hour.

93. a. Use the statistical menu of your graphing utility and the quadratic regression program to obtain the quadratic function that models a truck's stopping distance, $f(x)$, in feet, on wet pavement traveling at x miles per hour. Round the x-coefficient and the constant term to one decimal place.

b. Use the function from part (a) to determine speeds on wet pavement requiring stopping distances that exceed 446 feet.

Critical Thinking Exercises

Make Sense? *In Exercises 94–97, determine whether each statement makes sense or does not make sense, and explain your reasoning.*

94. When solving $f(x) > 0$, where f is a polynomial function, I only pay attention to the sign of f at each test value and not the actual function value.

95. I'm solving a polynomial inequality that has a value for which the polynomial function is undefined.

96. Because it takes me longer to come to a stop on a wet road than on a dry road, graph (a) for Exercises 77–78 is the model for stopping distances on wet pavement and graph (b) is the model for stopping distances on dry pavement.

97. I began the solution of the rational inequality $\dfrac{x + 1}{x + 3} \geq 2$ by setting both $x + 1$ and $x + 3$ equal to zero.

In Exercises 98–101, determine whether each statement is true or false. If the statement is false, make the necessary change(s) to produce a true statement.

98. The solution set of $x^2 > 25$ is $(5, \infty)$.

99. The inequality $\dfrac{x - 2}{x + 3} < 2$ can be solved by multiplying both sides by $x + 3$, resulting in the equivalent inequality $x - 2 < 2(x + 3)$.

100. $(x + 3)(x - 1) \geq 0$ and $\dfrac{x + 3}{x - 1} \geq 0$ have the same solution set.

101. The inequality $\dfrac{x - 2}{x + 3} < 2$ can be solved by multiplying both sides by $(x + 3)^2, x \neq -3$, resulting in the equivalent inequality $(x - 2)(x + 3) < 2(x + 3)^2$.

102. Write a polynomial inequality whose solution set is $[-3, 5]$.

103. Write a rational inequality whose solution set is $(-\infty, -4) \cup [3, \infty)$.

In Exercises 104–107, use inspection to describe each inequality's solution set. Do not solve any of the inequalities.

104. $(x - 2)^2 > 0$

105. $(x - 2)^2 \leq 0$

106. $(x - 2)^2 < -1$

107. $\dfrac{1}{(x - 2)^2} > 0$

108. The graphing utility screen shows the graph of $y = 4x^2 - 8x + 7$.

$[-2, 6, 1]$ by $[-2, 8, 1]$

a. Use the graph to describe the solution set of $4x^2 - 8x + 7 > 0$.

b. Use the graph to describe the solution set of $4x^2 - 8x + 7 < 0$.

c. Use an algebraic approach to verify each of your descriptions in parts (a) and (b).

109. The graphing utility screen shows the graph of $y = \sqrt{27 - 3x^2}$. Write and solve a quadratic inequality that explains why the graph only appears for $-3 \leq x \leq 3$.

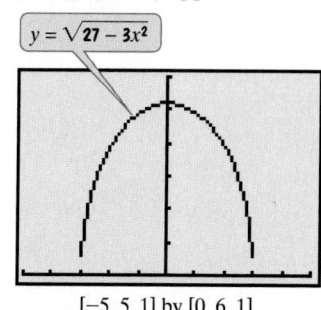

$[-5, 5, 1]$ by $[0, 6, 1]$

Preview Exercises

Exercises 110–112 will help you prepare for the material covered in the next section.

110. a. If $y = kx^2$, find the value of k using $x = 2$ and $y = 64$.

 b. Substitute the value for k into $y = kx^2$ and write the resulting equation.

 c. Use the equation from part (b) to find y when $x = 5$.

111. a. If $y = \dfrac{k}{x}$, find the value of k using $x = 8$ and $y = 12$.

 b. Substitute the value for k into $y = \dfrac{k}{x}$ and write the resulting equation.

 c. Use the equation from part (b) to find y when $x = 3$.

112. If $S = \dfrac{kA}{P}$, find the value of k using $A = 60{,}000$, $P = 40$, and $S = 12{,}000$.

Section 3.7 Modeling Using Variation

Objectives

1. Solve direct variation problems.
2. Solve inverse variation problems.
3. Solve combined variation problems.
4. Solve problems involving joint variation.

Have you ever wondered how telecommunication companies estimate the number of phone calls expected per day between two cities? The formula

$$C = \frac{0.02P_1P_2}{d^2}$$

shows that the daily number of phone calls, C, increases as the populations of the cities, P_1 and P_2, in thousands, increase and decreases as the distance, d, between the cities increases.

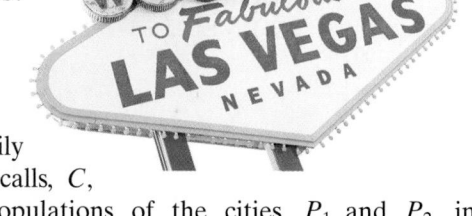

Certain formulas occur so frequently in applied situations that they are given special names. Variation formulas show how one quantity changes in relation to other quantities. Quantities can vary *directly, inversely*, or *jointly*. In this section, we look at situations that can be modeled by each of these kinds of variation. And think of this: The next time you get one of those "all-circuits-are-busy" messages, you will be able to use a variation formula to estimate how many other callers you're competing with for those precious 5-cent minutes.

1 Solve direct variation problems.

Direct Variation

When you swim underwater, the pressure in your ears depends on the depth at which you are swimming. The formula

$$p = 0.43d$$

describes the water pressure, p, in pounds per square inch, at a depth of d feet. We can use this linear function to determine the pressure in your ears at various depths:

If $d = 20$, $p = 0.43(20) = 8.6$. At a depth of 20 feet, water pressure is 8.6 pounds per square inch.

Doubling the depth doubles the pressure.

If $d = 40$, $p = 0.43(40) = 17.2$. At a depth of 40 feet, water pressure is 17.2 pounds per square inch.

Doubling the depth doubles the pressure.

If $d = 80$, $p = 0.43(80) = 34.4$. At a depth of 80 feet, water pressure is 34.4 pounds per square inch.

The formula $p = 0.43d$ illustrates that water pressure is a constant multiple of your underwater depth. If your depth is doubled, the pressure is doubled; if your depth is tripled, the pressure is tripled; and so on. Because of this, the

pressure in your ears is said to **vary directly** as your underwater depth. The **equation of variation** is

$$p = 0.43d.$$

Generalizing our discussion of pressure and depth, we obtain the following statement:

Direct Variation

If a situation is described by an equation in the form

$$y = kx,$$

where k is a nonzero constant, we say that **y varies directly as x** or **y is directly proportional to x**. The number k is called the **constant of variation** or the **constant of proportionality**.

Can you see that **the direct variation equation, $y = kx$, is a special case of the linear function $y = mx + b$**? When $m = k$ and $b = 0$, $y = mx + b$ becomes $y = kx$. Thus, the slope of a direct variation equation is k, the constant of variation. Because b, the y-intercept, is 0, the graph of a direct variation equation is a line passing through the origin. This is illustrated in **Figure 3.45**, which shows the graph of $p = 0.43d$: Water pressure varies directly as depth.

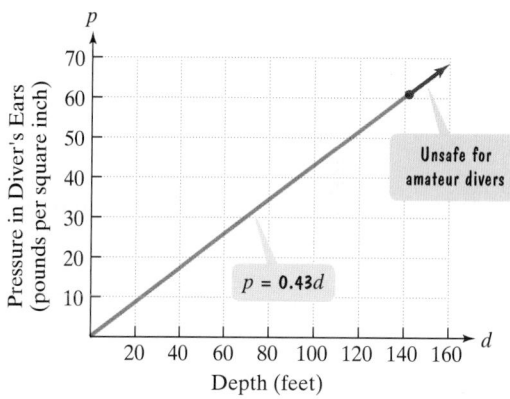

Figure 3.45 Water pressure at various depths

Problems involving direct variation can be solved using the following procedure. This procedure applies to direct variation problems, as well as to the other kinds of variation problems that we will discuss.

Solving Variation Problems

1. Write an equation that models the given English statement.
2. Substitute the given pair of values into the equation in step 1 and solve for k, the constant of variation.
3. Substitute the value of k into the equation in step 1.
4. Use the equation from step 3 to answer the problem's question.

(**EXAMPLE 1**) **Solving a Direct Variation Problem**

The volume of blood, B, in a person's body varies directly as body weight, W. A person who weighs 160 pounds has approximately 5 quarts of blood. Estimate the number of quarts of blood in a person who weighs 200 pounds.

Solution

Step 1 Write an equation. We know that *y varies directly as x* is expressed as

$$y = kx.$$

By changing letters, we can write an equation that models the following English statement: The volume of blood, *B*, varies directly as body weight, *W*.

$$B = kW$$

Step 2 Use the given values to find k. A person who weighs 160 pounds has approximately 5 quarts of blood. Substitute 160 for *W* and 5 for *B* in the direct variation equation. Then solve for *k*.

$B = kW$	The volume of blood varies directly as body weight.
$5 = k \cdot 160$	Substitute 160 for W and 5 for B.
$\dfrac{5}{160} = \dfrac{k \cdot 160}{160}$	Divide both sides by 160.
$0.03125 = k$	Express $\frac{5}{160}$, or $\frac{1}{32}$, in decimal form.

Step 3 Substitute the value of k into the equation.

$B = kW$	Use the equation from step 1.
$B = 0.03125W$	Replace k, the constant of variation, with 0.03125.

Step 4 Answer the problem's question. We are interested in estimating the number of quarts of blood in a person who weighs 200 pounds. Substitute 200 for *W* in $B = 0.03125W$ and solve for *B*.

$B = 0.03125W$	This is the equation from step 3.
$B = 0.03125(200)$	Substitute 200 for W.
$= 6.25$	Multiply.

A person who weighs 200 pounds has approximately 6.25 quarts of blood. ●

⊘ Check Point 1 The number of gallons of water, *W*, used when taking a shower varies directly as the time, *t*, in minutes, in the shower. A shower lasting 5 minutes uses 30 gallons of water. How much water is used in a shower lasting 11 minutes?

The direct variation equation $y = kx$ **is a linear function. If $k > 0$, then the slope of the line is positive. Consequently, as x increases, y also increases.**

A direct variation situation can involve variables to higher powers. For example, *y* can vary directly as x^2 ($y = kx^2$) or as x^3 ($y = kx^3$).

Direct Variation with Powers

y **varies directly as the *n*th power of *x*** if there exists some nonzero constant *k* such that

$$y = kx^n.$$

We also say that *y* **is directly proportional to the *n*th power of *x*.**

Direct variation with whole number powers is modeled by polynomial functions. In our next example, the graph of the variation equation is the familiar parabola.

 EXAMPLE 2 Solving a Direct Variation Problem

The distance, *s*, that a body falls from rest varies directly as the square of the time, *t*, of the fall. If skydivers fall 64 feet in 2 seconds, how far will they fall in 4.5 seconds?

Solution

Step 1 Write an equation. We know that *y varies directly as the square of x* is expressed as

$$y = kx^2.$$

By changing letters, we can write an equation that models the following English statement: Distance, *s*, varies directly as the square of time, *t*, of the fall.

$$s = kt^2$$

Step 2 Use the given values to find *k*. Skydivers fall 64 feet in 2 seconds. Substitute 64 for *s* and 2 for *t* in the direct variation equation. Then solve for *k*.

$$s = kt^2 \qquad \text{Distance varies directly as the square of time.}$$
$$64 = k \cdot 2^2 \qquad \text{Skydivers fall 64 feet in 2 seconds.}$$
$$64 = 4k \qquad \text{Simplify: } 2^2 = 4.$$
$$\frac{64}{4} = \frac{4k}{4} \qquad \text{Divide both sides by 4.}$$
$$16 = k \qquad \text{Simplify.}$$

Step 3 Substitute the value of *k* into the equation.

$$s = kt^2 \qquad \text{Use the equation from step 1.}$$
$$s = 16t^2 \qquad \text{Replace k, the constant of variation, with 16.}$$

Step 4 Answer the problem's question. How far will the skydivers fall in 4.5 seconds? Substitute 4.5 for *t* in $s = 16t^2$ and solve for *s*.

$$s = 16(4.5)^2 = 16(20.25) = 324$$

Thus, in 4.5 seconds, the skydivers will fall 324 feet.

We can express the variation equation from Example 2 in function notation, writing

$$s(t) = 16t^2.$$

The distance that a body falls from rest is a function of the time, *t*, of the fall. The parabola that is the graph of this quadratic function is shown in **Figure 3.46**. The graph increases rapidly from left to right, showing the effects of the acceleration of gravity.

Distance Fallen by Skydivers over Time

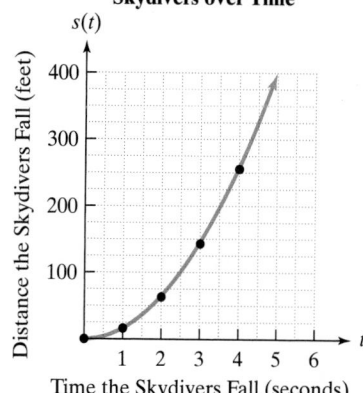

Figure 3.46 The graph of $s(t) = 16t^2$

⊘ Check Point **2** The weight of a great white shark varies directly as the cube of its length. A great white shark caught off Catalina Island, California, was 15 feet long and weighed 2025 pounds. What was the weight of the 25-foot-long shark in the novel *Jaws*?

2 Solve inverse variation problems.

Inverse Variation

The distance from San Francisco to Los Angeles is 420 miles. The time that it takes to drive from San Francisco to Los Angeles depends on the rate at which one drives and is given by

$$\text{Time} = \frac{420}{\text{Rate}}.$$

For example, if you average 30 miles per hour, the time for the drive is

$$\text{Time} = \frac{420}{30} = 14,$$

or 14 hours. If you average 50 miles per hour, the time for the drive is

$$\text{Time} = \frac{420}{50} = 8.4,$$

or 8.4 hours. As your rate (or speed) increases, the time for the trip decreases and vice versa. This is illustrated by the graph in **Figure 3.47**.

We can express the time for the San Francisco–Los Angeles trip using t for time and r for rate:

$$t = \frac{420}{r}.$$

This equation is an example of an **inverse variation** equation. Time, t, **varies inversely** as rate, r. When two quantities vary inversely, one quantity increases as the other decreases and vice versa.

Generalizing, we obtain the following statement:

Figure 3.47

Inverse Variation

If a situation is described by an equation in the form

$$y = \frac{k}{x},$$

where k is a nonzero constant, we say that y **varies inversely as** x or y **is inversely proportional to** x. The number k is called the **constant of variation**.

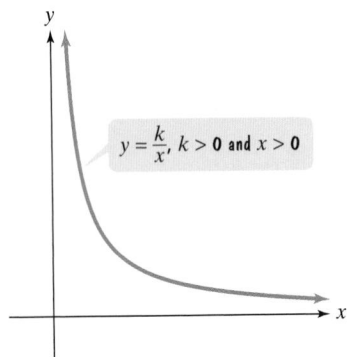

$y = \frac{k}{x}$, $k > 0$ and $x > 0$

Figure 3.48 The graph of the inverse variation equation

Notice that the **inverse variation equation**

$$y = \frac{k}{x}, \quad \text{or} \quad f(x) = \frac{k}{x},$$

is a rational function. For $k > 0$ and $x > 0$, the graph of the function takes on the shape shown in **Figure 3.48**.

We use the same procedure to solve inverse variation problems as we did to solve direct variation problems. Example 3 illustrates this procedure.

(**EXAMPLE 3**) **Solving an Inverse Variation Problem**

When you use a spray can and press the valve at the top, you decrease the pressure of the gas in the can. This decrease of pressure causes the volume of the gas in the can to increase. Because the gas needs more room than is provided in the can, it expands in spray form through the small hole near the valve. In general, if the temperature is constant, the pressure, P, of a gas in a container varies inversely as the volume, V, of the container. The pressure of a gas sample in a container whose volume is 8 cubic inches is 12 pounds per square inch. If the sample expands to a volume of 22 cubic inches, what is the new pressure of the gas?

Solution

Step 1 Write an equation. We know that y *varies inversely as* x is expressed as

$$y = \frac{k}{x}.$$

By changing letters, we can write an equation that models the following English statement: The pressure, P, of a gas in a container varies inversely as the volume, V.

$$P = \frac{k}{V}$$

Step 2 Use the given values to find k. The pressure of a gas sample in a container whose volume is 8 cubic inches is 12 pounds per square inch. Substitute 12 for P and 8 for V in the inverse variation equation. Then solve for k.

Doubling the pressure halves the volume.

$$P = \frac{k}{V} \qquad \text{Pressure varies inversely as volume.}$$

$$12 = \frac{k}{8} \qquad \text{The pressure in an 8 cubic-inch}$$
$$\text{container is 12 pounds per square inch.}$$

$$12 \cdot 8 = \frac{k}{8} \cdot 8 \qquad \text{Multiply both sides by 8.}$$

$$96 = k \qquad \text{Simplify.}$$

Step 3 Substitute the value of k into the equation.

$$P = \frac{k}{V} \qquad \text{Use the equation from step 1.}$$

$$P = \frac{96}{V} \qquad \text{Replace } k, \text{ the constant of variation,}$$
$$\text{with 96.}$$

Step 4 Answer the problem's question. We need to find the pressure when the volume expands to 22 cubic inches. Substitute 22 for V and solve for P.

$$P = \frac{96}{V} = \frac{96}{22} = 4\frac{4}{11}$$

When the volume is 22 cubic inches, the pressure of the gas is $4\frac{4}{11}$ pounds per square inch. ●

⊘ Check Point **3** The length of a violin string varies inversely as the frequency of its vibrations. A violin string 8 inches long vibrates at a frequency of 640 cycles per second. What is the frequency of a 10-inch string?

 Solve combined variation problems.

Combined Variation

In **combined variation**, direct and inverse variation occur at the same time. For example, as the advertising budget, A, of a company increases, its monthly sales, S, also increase. Monthly sales vary directly as the advertising budget:

$$S = kA.$$

By contrast, as the price of the company's product, P, increases, its monthly sales, S, decrease. Monthly sales vary inversely as the price of the product:

$$S = \frac{k}{P}.$$

We can combine these two variation equations into one combined equation:

$$S = \frac{kA}{P}.$$

Monthly sales , S, vary directly as the advertising budget, A, and inversely as the price of the product, P.

The following example illustrates an application of combined variation.

(EXAMPLE 4) **Solving a Combined Variation Problem**

The owners of Rollerblades Plus determine that the monthly sales, S, of its skates vary directly as its advertising budget, A, and inversely as the price of the skates, P. When $60,000 is spent on advertising and the price of the skates is $40, the monthly sales are 12,000 pairs of rollerblades.

 a. Write an equation of variation that describes this situation.

 b. Determine monthly sales if the amount of the advertising budget is increased to $70,000.

Solution

a. Write an equation.

$$S = \frac{kA}{P}$$

> Translate "sales vary directly as the advertising budget and inversely as the skates' price."

Use the given values to find k.

$$12{,}000 = \frac{k(60{,}000)}{40}$$

When $60{,}000 is spent on advertising ($A = 60{,}000$) and the price is $40 ($P = 40$), monthly sales are 12,000 units ($S = 12{,}000$).

$$12{,}000 = k \cdot 1500$$ Divide 60,000 by 40.

$$\frac{12{,}000}{1500} = \frac{k \cdot 1500}{1500}$$ Divide both sides of the equation by 1500.

$$8 = k$$ Simplify.

Therefore, the equation of variation that models monthly sales is

$$S = \frac{8A}{P}.$$ Substitute 8 for k in $S = \frac{kA}{P}$.

b. The advertising budget is increased to $70,000, so $A = 70{,}000$. The skates' price is still $40, so $P = 40$.

$$S = \frac{8A}{P}$$ This is the equation from part (a).

$$S = \frac{8(70{,}000)}{40}$$ Substitute 70,000 for A and 40 for P.

$$S = 14{,}000$$ Simplify.

With a $70,000 advertising budget and $40 price, the company can expect to sell 14,000 pairs of rollerblades in a month (up from 12,000). ●

⊘ Check Point **4** The number of minutes needed to solve an exercise set of variation problems varies directly as the number of problems and inversely as the number of people working to solve the problems. It takes 4 people 32 minutes to solve 16 problems. How many minutes will it take 8 people to solve 24 problems?

④ Solve problems involving joint variation.

Joint Variation

Joint variation is a variation in which a variable varies directly as the product of two or more other variables. Thus, the equation $y = kxz$ is read "y varies jointly as x and z."

Joint variation plays a critical role in Isaac Newton's formula for gravitation:

$$F = G\frac{m_1 m_2}{d^2}.$$

The formula states that the force of gravitation, F, between two bodies varies jointly as the product of their masses, m_1 and m_2, and inversely as the square of the distance between them, d. (G is the gravitational constant.) The formula indicates that gravitational force exists between any two objects in the universe, increasing as the distance between the bodies decreases. One practical result is that the pull of the moon on the oceans is greater on the side of Earth closer to the moon. This gravitational imbalance is what produces tides.

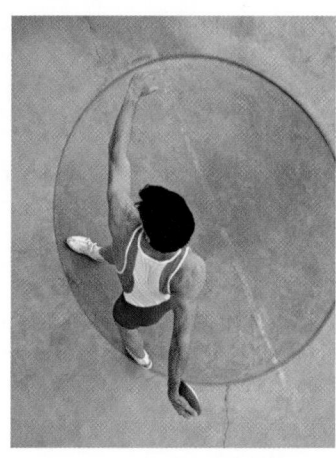

(**EXAMPLE 5**) **Modeling Centrifugal Force**

The centrifugal force, C, of a body moving in a circle varies jointly with the radius of the circular path, r, and the body's mass, m, and inversely with the square of the time, t, it takes to move about one full circle. A 6-gram body moving in a circle with radius 100 centimeters at a rate of 1 revolution in 2 seconds has a centrifugal force of 6000 dynes. Find the centrifugal force of an 18-gram body moving in a circle with radius 100 centimeters at a rate of 1 revolution in 3 seconds.

Solution

$C = \dfrac{krm}{t^2}$	Translate "Centrifugal force, C, varies jointly with radius, r, and mass, m, and inversely with the square of time, t."
$6000 = \dfrac{k(100)(6)}{2^2}$	A 6-gram body ($m = 6$) moving in a circle with radius 100 centimeters ($r = 100$) at 1 revolution in 2 seconds ($t = 2$) has a centrifugal force of 6000 dynes ($C = 6000$).
$6000 = 150k$	Simplify.
$40 = k$	Divide both sides by 150 and solve for k.
$C = \dfrac{40rm}{t^2}$	Substitute 40 for k in the model for centrifugal force.
$C = \dfrac{40(100)(18)}{3^2}$	Find centrifugal force, C, of an 18-gram body ($m = 18$) moving in a circle with radius 100 centimeters ($r = 100$) at 1 revolution in 3 seconds ($t = 3$).
$= 8000$	Simplify.

The centrifugal force is 8000 dynes. ●

⊘ Check Point **5** The volume of a cone, V, varies jointly as its height, h, and the square of its radius, r. A cone with a radius measuring 6 feet and a height measuring 10 feet has a volume of 120π cubic feet. Find the volume of a cone having a radius of 12 feet and a height of 2 feet.

Exercise Set 3.7

Practice Exercises

Use the four-step procedure for solving variation problems given on page 395 to solve Exercises 1–10.

1. y varies directly as x. $y = 65$ when $x = 5$. Find y when $x = 12$.

2. y varies directly as x. $y = 45$ when $x = 5$. Find y when $x = 13$.

3. y varies inversely as x. $y = 12$ when $x = 5$. Find y when $x = 2$.

4. y varies inversely as x. $y = 6$ when $x = 3$. Find y when $x = 9$.

5. y varies directly as x and inversely as the square of z. $y = 20$ when $x = 50$ and $z = 5$. Find y when $x = 3$ and $z = 6$.

6. a varies directly as b and inversely as the square of c. $a = 7$ when $b = 9$ and $c = 6$. Find a when $b = 4$ and $c = 8$.

7. y varies jointly as x and z. $y = 25$ when $x = 2$ and $z = 5$. Find y when $x = 8$ and $z = 12$.

8. C varies jointly as A and T. $C = 175$ when $A = 2100$ and $T = 4$. Find C when $A = 2400$ and $T = 6$.

9. y varies jointly as a and b and inversely as the square root of c. $y = 12$ when $a = 3, b = 2$, and $c = 25$. Find y when $a = 5, b = 3$, and $c = 9$.

10. y varies jointly as m and the square of n and inversely as p. $y = 15$ when $m = 2, n = 1$, and $p = 6$. Find y when $m = 3, n = 4$, and $p = 10$.

Practice Plus

In Exercises 11–20, write an equation that expresses each relationship. Then solve the equation for y.

11. x varies jointly as y and z.

12. x varies jointly as y and the square of z.

13. x varies directly as the cube of z and inversely as y.

14. x varies directly as the cube root of z and inversely as y.

15. x varies jointly as y and z and inversely as the square root of w.

16. x varies jointly as y and z and inversely as the square of w.

17. x varies jointly as z and the sum of y and w.

18. x varies jointly as z and the difference between y and w.

19. x varies directly as z and inversely as the difference between y and w.

20. x varies directly as z and inversely as the sum of y and w.

Application Exercises

Use the four-step procedure for solving variation problems given on page 395 to solve Exercises 21–36.

21. An alligator's tail length, T, varies directly as its body length, B. An alligator with a body length of 4 feet has a tail length of 3.6 feet. What is the tail length of an alligator whose body length is 6 feet?

|← —— Body length, B —— →|← —— Tail length, T —— →|

22. An object's weight on the moon, M, varies directly as its weight on Earth, E. Neil Armstrong, the first person to step on the moon on July 20, 1969, weighed 360 pounds on Earth (with all of his equipment on) and 60 pounds on the moon. What is the moon weight of a person who weighs 186 pounds on Earth?

23. The height that a ball bounces varies directly as the height from which it was dropped. A tennis ball dropped from 12 inches bounces 8.4 inches. From what height was the tennis ball dropped if it bounces 56 inches?

24. The distance that a spring will stretch varies directly as the force applied to the spring. A force of 12 pounds is needed to stretch a spring 9 inches. What force is required to stretch the spring 15 inches?

25. If all men had identical body types, their weight would vary directly as the cube of their height. Shown below is Robert Wadlow, who reached a record height of 8 feet 11 inches (107 inches) before his death at age 22. If a man who is 5 feet 10 inches tall (70 inches) with the same body type as Mr. Wadlow weighs 170 pounds, what was Robert Wadlow's weight shortly before his death?

26. The number of houses that can be served by a water pipe varies directly as the square of the diameter of the pipe. A water pipe that has a 10-centimeter diameter can supply 50 houses.
 a. How many houses can be served by a water pipe that has a 30-centimeter diameter?
 b. What size water pipe is needed for a new subdivision of 1250 houses?

27. The figure shows that a bicyclist tips the cycle when making a turn. The angle B, formed by the vertical direction and the bicycle, is called the banking angle. The banking angle varies inversely as the cycle's turning radius. When the turning radius is 4 feet, the banking angle is 28°. What is the banking angle when the turning radius is 3.5 feet?

$B°$

28. The water temperature of the Pacific Ocean varies inversely as the water's depth. At a depth of 1000 meters, the water temperature is 4.4° Celsius. What is the water temperature at a depth of 5000 meters?

29. Radiation machines, used to treat tumors, produce an intensity of radiation that varies inversely as the square of the distance from the machine. At 3 meters, the radiation intensity is 62.5 milliroentgens per hour. What is the intensity at a distance of 2.5 meters?

30. The illumination provided by a car's headlight varies inversely as the square of the distance from the headlight. A car's headlight produces an illumination of 3.75 footcandles at a distance of 40 feet. What is the illumination when the distance is 50 feet?

31. Body-mass index, or BMI, takes both weight and height into account when assessing whether an individual is underweight or overweight. BMI varies directly as one's weight, in pounds, and inversely as the square of one's height, in inches. In adults, normal values for the BMI are between 20 and 25, inclusive. Values below 20 indicate that an individual is underweight and values above 30 indicate that an individual is obese. A person who weighs 180 pounds and is 5 feet, or 60 inches, tall has a BMI of 35.15. What is the BMI, to the nearest tenth, for a 170-pound person who is 5 feet 10 inches tall. Is this person overweight?

32. One's intelligence quotient, or IQ, varies directly as a person's mental age and inversely as that person's chronological age. A person with a mental age of 25 and a chronological age of 20 has an IQ of 125. What is the chronological age of a person with a mental age of 40 and an IQ of 80?

33. The heat loss of a glass window varies jointly as the window's area and the difference between the outside and inside temperatures. A window 3 feet wide by 6 feet long loses 1200 Btu per hour when the temperature outside is 20° colder than the temperature inside. Find the heat loss through a glass window that is 6 feet wide by 9 feet long when the temperature outside is 10° colder than the temperature inside.

34. Kinetic energy varies jointly as the mass and the square of the velocity. A mass of 8 grams and velocity of 3 centimeters per second has a kinetic energy of 36 ergs. Find the kinetic energy for a mass of 4 grams and velocity of 6 centimeters per second.

35. Sound intensity varies inversely as the square of the distance from the sound source. If you are in a movie theater and you change your seat to one that is twice as far from the speakers, how does the new sound intensity compare to that of your original seat?

36. Many people claim that as they get older, time seems to pass more quickly. Suppose that the perceived length of a period of time is inversely proportional to your age. How long will a year seem to be when you are three times as old as you are now?

37. The average number of daily phone calls, C, between two cities varies jointly as the product of their populations, P_1 and P_2, and inversely as the square of the distance, d, between them.

 a. Write an equation that expresses this relationship.

 b. The distance between San Francisco (population: 777,000) and Los Angeles (population: 3,695,000) is 420 miles. If the average number of daily phone calls between the cities is 326,000, find the value of k to two decimal places and write the equation of variation.

 c. Memphis (population: 650,000) is 400 miles from New Orleans (population: 220,000). Find the average number of daily phone calls, to the nearest whole number, between these cities.

38. The force of wind blowing on a window positioned at a right angle to the direction of the wind varies jointly as the area of the window and the square of the wind's speed. It is known that a wind of 30 miles per hour blowing on a window measuring 4 feet by 5 feet exerts a force of 150 pounds. During a storm with winds of 60 miles per hour, should hurricane shutters be placed on a window that measures 3 feet by 4 feet and is capable of withstanding 300 pounds of force?

39. The table shows the values for the current, I, in an electric circuit and the resistance, R, of the circuit.

I (amperes)	0.5	1.0	1.5	2.0	2.5	3.0	4.0	5.0
R (ohms)	12.0	6.0	4.0	3.0	2.4	2.0	1.5	1.2

 a. Graph the ordered pairs in the table of values, with values of I along the x-axis and values of R along the y-axis. Connect the eight points with a smooth curve.

 b. Does current vary directly or inversely as resistance? Use your graph and explain how you arrived at your answer.

 c. Write an equation of variation for I and R, using one of the ordered pairs in the table to find the constant of variation. Then use your variation equation to verify the other seven ordered pairs in the table.

Writing in Mathematics

40. What does it mean if two quantities vary directly?

41. In your own words, explain how to solve a variation problem.

42. What does it mean if two quantities vary inversely?

43. Explain what is meant by combined variation. Give an example with your explanation.

44. Explain what is meant by joint variation. Give an example with your explanation.

In Exercises 45–46, describe in words the variation shown by the given equation.

45. $z = \dfrac{k\sqrt{x}}{y^2}$ 46. $z = kx^2\sqrt{y}$

47. We have seen that the daily number of phone calls between two cities varies jointly as their populations and inversely as the square of the distance between them. This model, used by telecommunication companies to estimate the line capacities needed among various cities, is called the *gravity model*. Compare the model to Newton's formula for gravitation on page 400 and describe why the name *gravity model* is appropriate.

Technology Exercise

48. Use a graphing utility to graph any three of the variation equations in Exercises 21–30. Then TRACE along each curve and identify the point that corresponds to the problem's solution.

Critical Thinking Exercises

Make Sense? *In Exercises 49–52, determine whether each statement makes sense or does not make sense, and explain your reasoning.*

49. I'm using an inverse variation equation and I need to determine the value of the dependent variable when the independent variable is zero.

50. The graph of this direct variation equation that has a positive constant of variation shows one variable increasing as the other variable decreases.

51. When all is said and done, it seems to me that direct variation equations are special kinds of linear functions and inverse variation equations are special kinds of rational functions.

52. Using the language of variation, I can now state the formula for the area of a trapezoid, $A = \frac{1}{2}h(b_1 + b_2)$, as, "A trapezoid's area varies jointly with its height and the sum of its bases."

53. In a hurricane, the wind pressure varies directly as the square of the wind velocity. If wind pressure is a measure of a hurricane's destructive capacity, what happens to this destructive power when the wind speed doubles?

54. The illumination from a light source varies inversely as the square of the distance from the light source. If you raise a lamp from 15 inches to 30 inches over your desk, what happens to the illumination?

55. The heat generated by a stove element varies directly as the square of the voltage and inversely as the resistance. If the voltage remains constant, what needs to be done to triple the amount of heat generated?

56. Galileo's telescope brought about revolutionary changes in astronomy. A comparable leap in our ability to observe the universe took place as a result of the Hubble Space Telescope. The space telescope was able to see stars and galaxies whose brightness is $\frac{1}{50}$ of the faintest objects observable using ground-based telescopes. Use the fact that the brightness of a point source, such as a star, varies inversely as the square of its distance from an observer to show that the space telescope was able to see about seven times farther than a ground-based telescope.

Group Exercise

57. Begin by deciding on a product that interests the group because you are now in charge of advertising this product. Members were told that the demand for the product varies directly as the amount spent on advertising and inversely as the price of the product. However, as more money is spent on advertising, the price of your product rises. Under what conditions would members recommend an increased expense in advertising? Once you've determined what your product is, write formulas for the given conditions and experiment with hypothetical numbers. What other factors might you take into consideration in terms of your recommendation? How do these factor affect the demand for your product?

Preview Exercises

Exercises 58–60 will help you prepare for the material covered in the first section of the next chapter.

58. Use point plotting to graph $f(x) = 2^x$. Begin by setting up a partial table of coordinates, selecting integers from -3 to 3, inclusive, for x. Because $y = 0$ is a horizontal asymptote, your graph should approach, but never touch, the negative portion of the x-axis.

In Exercises 59–60, use transformations of your graph from Exercise 58 to graph each function.

59. $g(x) = f(-x) = 2^{-x}$ **60.** $h(x) = f(x) + 1 = 2^x + 1$

Chapter 3 Summary, Review, and Test

Summary

DEFINITIONS AND CONCEPTS	EXAMPLES
3.1 Quadratic Functions	
a. A quadratic function is of the form $f(x) = ax^2 + bx + c, a \neq 0$.	
b. The standard form of a quadratic function is $f(x) = a(x - h)^2 + k, a \neq 0$.	
c. The graph of a quadratic function is a parabola. The vertex is (h, k) or $\left(-\dfrac{b}{2a}, f\left(-\dfrac{b}{2a}\right)\right)$. A procedure for graphing a quadratic function in standard form is given in the box on page 314. A procedure for graphing a quadratic function in the form $f(x) = ax^2 + bx + c$ is given in the box on page 316.	Ex. 1, p. 314; Ex. 2, p. 315; Ex. 3, p. 317
d. See the box on page 318 for minimum or maximum values of quadratic functions.	Ex. 4, p. 319; Ex. 5, p. 319
e. A strategy for solving problems involving maximizing or minimizing quadratic functions is given in the box on page 321.	Ex. 6, p. 322; Ex. 7, p. 323
3.2 Polynomial Functions and Their Graphs	
a. Polynomial Function of Degree n: $f(x) = a_n x^n + a_{n-1} x^{n-1} + \cdots + a_2 x^2 + a_1 x + a_0, a_n \neq 0$	
b. The graphs of polynomial functions are smooth and continuous.	Fig. 3.12, p. 329
c. The end behavior of the graph of a polynomial function depends on the leading term, given by the Leading Coefficient Test in the box on page 330.	Ex. 1, p. 330; Ex. 2, p. 331; Ex. 3, p. 331; Ex. 4, p. 332
d. The values of x for which $f(x)$ is equal to 0 are the zeros of the polynomial function f. These values are the roots, or solutions, of the polynomial equation $f(x) = 0$.	Ex. 5, p. 332; Ex. 6, p. 333
e. If $x - r$ occurs k times in a polynomial function's factorization, r is a repeated zero with multiplicity k. If k is even, the graph touches the x-axis and turns around at r. If k is odd, the graph crosses the x-axis at r.	Ex. 7, p. 334
f. The Intermediate Value Theorem: If f is a polynomial function and $f(a)$ and $f(b)$ have opposite signs, there is at least one value of c between a and b for which $f(c) = 0$.	Ex. 8, p. 335

DEFINITIONS AND CONCEPTS	**EXAMPLES**
g. If f is a polynomial of degree n, the graph of f has at most $n - 1$ turning points.	Fig. 3.23, p. 336
h. A strategy for graphing a polynomial function is given in the box on page 336.	Ex. 9, p. 336

3.3 Dividing Polynomials; Remainder and Factor Theorems

a. Long division of polynomials is performed by dividing, multiplying, subtracting, bringing down the next term, and repeating this process until the degree of the remainder is less than the degree of the divisor. The details are given in the box on page 343.	Ex. 1, p. 342; Ex. 2, p. 343; Ex. 3, p. 345
b. The Division Algorithm: $f(x) = d(x)q(x) + r(x)$. The dividend is the product of the divisor and the quotient plus the remainder.	
c. Synthetic division is used to divide a polynomial by $x - c$. The details are given in the box on page 346.	Ex. 4, p. 347
d. The Remainder Theorem: If a polynomial $f(x)$ is divided by $x - c$, then the remainder is $f(c)$.	Ex. 5, p. 348
e. The Factor Theorem: If $x - c$ is a factor of a polynomial function $f(x)$, then c is a zero of f and a root of $f(x) = 0$. If c is a zero of f or a root of $f(x) = 0$, then $x - c$ is a factor of $f(x)$.	Ex. 6, p. 349

3.4 Zeros of Polynomial Functions

a. The Rational Zero Theorem states that the possible rational zeros of a polynomial $$\text{function} = \frac{\text{Factors of the constant term}}{\text{Factors of the leading coefficient}}.$$ The theorem is stated in the box on page 353.	Ex. 1, p. 353; Ex. 2, p. 354; Ex. 3, p. 354; Ex. 4, p. 355; Ex. 5, p. 356
b. Number of roots: If $f(x)$ is a polynomial of degree $n \geq 1$, then, counting multiple roots separately, the equation $f(x) = 0$ has n roots.	
c. If $a + bi$ is a root of $f(x) = 0$ with real coefficients, then $a - bi$ is also a root.	
d. The Linear Factorization Theorem: An nth-degree polynomial can be expressed as the product of n linear factors. Thus, $f(x) = a_n(x - c_1)(x - c_2) \cdots (x - c_n)$.	Ex. 6, p. 359
e. Descartes's Rule of Signs: The number of positive real zeros of f equals the number of sign changes of $f(x)$ or is less than that number by an even integer. The number of negative real zeros of f applies a similar statement to $f(-x)$.	Table 3.1, p. 360; Ex. 7, p. 360

3.5 Rational Functions and Their Graphs

a. Rational function: $f(x) = \dfrac{p(x)}{q(x)}$; p and q are polynomial functions and $q(x) \neq 0$. The domain of f is the set of all real numbers excluding values of x that make $q(x)$ zero.	Ex. 1, p. 366
b. Arrow notation is summarized in the box on page 368.	
c. The line $x = a$ is a vertical asymptote of the graph of f if $f(x)$ increases or decreases without bound as x approaches a. Vertical asymptotes are located using the theorem in the box on page 369.	Ex. 2, p. 369
d. The line $y = b$ is a horizontal asymptote of the graph of f if $f(x)$ approaches b as x increases or decreases without bound. Horizontal asymptotes are located using the theorem in the box on page 371.	Ex. 3, p. 372
e. Table 3.2 on page 372 shows the graphs of $f(x) = \dfrac{1}{x}$ and $f(x) = \dfrac{1}{x^2}$. Some rational functions can be graphed using transformations of these common graphs.	Ex. 4, p. 373
f. A strategy for graphing rational functions is given in the box on page 373.	Ex. 5, p. 374; Ex. 6, p. 375; Ex. 7, p. 376
g. The graph of a rational function has a slant asymptote when the degree of the numerator is one more than the degree of the denominator. The equation of the slant asymptote is found using division and dropping the remainder term.	Ex. 8, p. 378

3.6 Polynomial and Rational Inequalities

a. A polynomial inequality can be expressed as $f(x) < 0, f(x) > 0, f(x) \leq 0$, or $f(x) \geq 0$, where f is a polynomial function. A procedure for solving polynomial inequalities is given in the box on page 385.	Ex. 1, p. 385; Ex. 2, p. 386

DEFINITIONS AND CONCEPTS	EXAMPLES
b. A rational inequality can be expressed as $f(x) < 0, f(x) > 0, f(x) \le 0,$ or $f(x) \ge 0$, where f is a rational function. The procedure for solving such inequalities begins with expressing them so that one side is zero and the other side is a single quotient. Find boundary points by setting the numerator and denominator equal to zero. Then follow a procedure similar to that for solving polynomial inequalities.	Ex. 3, p. 388

3.7 Modeling Using Variation

a. A procedure for solving variation problems is given in the box on page 395.

b.

English Statement	Equation	
y varies directly as x. y is directly proportional to x.	$y = kx$	Ex. 1, p. 395
y varies directly as x^n. y is directly proportional to x^n.	$y = kx^n$	Ex. 2, p. 396
y varies inversely as x. y is inversely proportional to x.	$y = \dfrac{k}{x}$	Ex. 3, p. 398; Ex. 4, p. 399
y varies inversely as x^n. y is inversely proportional to x^n.	$y = \dfrac{k}{x^n}$	
y varies jointly as x and z.	$y = kxz$	Ex. 5, p. 401

Review Exercises

3.1

In Exercises 1–4, use the vertex and intercepts to sketch the graph of each quadratic function. Give the equation for the parabola's axis of symmetry. Use the graph to determine the function's domain and range.

1. $f(x) = -(x + 1)^2 + 4$ **2.** $f(x) = (x + 4)^2 - 2$

3. $f(x) = -x^2 + 2x + 3$ **4.** $f(x) = 2x^2 - 4x - 6$

In Exercises 5–6, use the function's equation, and not its graph, to find

 a. *the minimum or maximum value and where it occurs.*

 b. *the function's domain and its range.*

5. $f(x) = -x^2 + 14x - 106$ **6.** $f(x) = 2x^2 + 12x + 703$

7. A quarterback tosses a football to a receiver 40 yards downfield. The height of the football, $f(x)$, in feet, can be modeled by

$$f(x) = -0.025x^2 + x + 6,$$

where x is the ball's horizontal distance, in yards, from the quarterback.

 a. What is the ball's maximum height and how far from the quarterback does this occur?

 b. From what height did the quarterback toss the football?

 c. If the football is not blocked by a defensive player nor caught by the receiver, how far down the field will it go before hitting the ground? Round to the nearest tenth of a yard.

 d. Graph the function that models the football's parabolic path.

8. A field bordering a straight stream is to be enclosed. The side bordering the stream is not to be fenced. If 1000 yards of fencing material is to be used, what are the dimensions of the largest rectangular field that can be fenced? What is the maximum area?

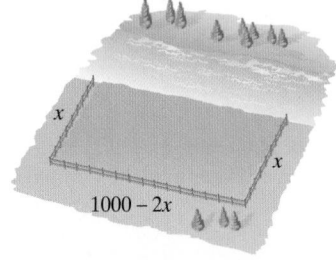

9. Among all pairs of numbers whose difference is 14, find a pair whose product is as small as possible. What is the minimum product?

3.2

In Exercises 10–13, use the Leading Coefficient Test to determine the end behavior of the graph of the given polynomial function. Then use this end behavior to match the polynomial function with its graph. [The graphs are labeled (a) through (d).]

10. $f(x) = -x^3 + x^2 + 2x$ **11.** $f(x) = x^6 - 6x^4 + 9x^2$

12. $f(x) = x^5 - 5x^3 + 4x$ **13.** $f(x) = -x^4 + 1$

a.

b.

c.

d.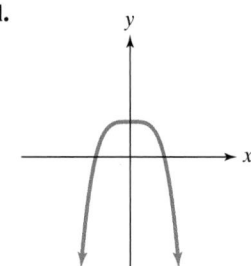

14. The polynomial function

$$f(x) = -0.87x^3 + 0.35x^2 + 81.62x + 7684.94$$

models the number of thefts, $f(x)$, in thousands, in the United States x years after 1987. Will this function be useful in modeling the number of thefts over an extended period of time? Explain your answer.

15. A herd of 100 elk is introduced to a small island. The number of elk, $f(x)$, after x years is modeled by the polynomial function

$$f(x) = -x^4 + 21x^2 + 100.$$

Use the Leading Coefficient Test to determine the graph's end behavior to the right. What does this mean about what will eventually happen to the elk population?

In Exercises 16–17, find the zeros for each polynomial function and give the multiplicity of each zero. State whether the graph crosses the x-axis, or touches the x-axis and turns around, at each zero.

16. $f(x) = -2(x - 1)(x + 2)^2(x + 5)^3$

17. $f(x) = x^3 - 5x^2 - 25x + 125$

18. Show that $f(x) = x^3 - 2x - 1$ has a real zero between 1 and 2.

In Exercises 19–24,

 a. *Use the Leading Coefficient Test to determine the graph's end behavior.*

 b. *Determine whether the graph has y-axis symmetry, origin symmetry, or neither.*

 c. *Graph the function.*

19. $f(x) = x^3 - x^2 - 9x + 9$ **20.** $f(x) = 4x - x^3$

21. $f(x) = 2x^3 + 3x^2 - 8x - 12$ **22.** $f(x) = -x^4 + 25x^2$

23. $f(x) = -x^4 + 6x^3 - 9x^2$ **24.** $f(x) = 3x^4 - 15x^3$

In Exercises 25–26, graph each polynomial function.

25. $f(x) = 2x^2(x - 1)^3(x + 2)$

26. $f(x) = -x^3(x + 4)^2(x - 1)$

3.3

In Exercises 27–29, divide using long division.

27. $(4x^3 - 3x^2 - 2x + 1) \div (x + 1)$

28. $(10x^3 - 26x^2 + 17x - 13) \div (5x - 3)$

29. $(4x^4 + 6x^3 + 3x - 1) \div (2x^2 + 1)$

In Exercises 30–31, divide using synthetic division.

30. $(3x^4 + 11x^3 - 20x^2 + 7x + 35) \div (x + 5)$

31. $(3x^4 - 2x^2 - 10x) \div (x - 2)$

32. Given $f(x) = 2x^3 - 7x^2 + 9x - 3$, use the Remainder Theorem to find $f(-13)$.

33. Use synthetic division to divide $f(x) = 2x^3 + x^2 - 13x + 6$ by $x - 2$. Use the result to find all zeros of f.

34. Solve the equation $x^3 - 17x + 4 = 0$ given that 4 is a root.

3.4

In Exercises 35–36, use the Rational Zero Theorem to list all possible rational zeros for each given function.

35. $f(x) = x^4 - 6x^3 + 14x^2 - 14x + 5$

36. $f(x) = 3x^5 - 2x^4 - 15x^3 + 10x^2 + 12x - 8$

In Exercises 37–38, use Descartes's Rule of Signs to determine the possible number of positive and negative real zeros for each given function.

37. $f(x) = 3x^4 - 2x^3 - 8x + 5$

38. $f(x) = 2x^5 - 3x^3 - 5x^2 + 3x - 1$

39. Use Descartes's Rule of Signs to explain why $2x^4 + 6x^2 + 8 = 0$ has no real roots.

For Exercises 40–46,

 a. *List all possible rational roots or rational zeros.*

 b. *Use Descartes's Rule of Signs to determine the possible number of positive and negative real roots or real zeros.*

 c. *Use synthetic division to test the possible rational roots or zeros and find an actual root or zero.*

 d. *Use the quotient from part (c) to find all the remaining roots or zeros.*

40. $f(x) = x^3 + 3x^2 - 4$ **41.** $f(x) = 6x^3 + x^2 - 4x + 1$

42. $8x^3 - 36x^2 + 46x - 15 = 0$ **43.** $2x^3 + 9x^2 - 7x + 1 = 0$

44. $x^4 - x^3 - 7x^2 + x + 6 = 0$ **45.** $4x^4 + 7x^2 - 2 = 0$

46. $f(x) = 2x^4 + x^3 - 9x^2 - 4x + 4$

In Exercises 47–48, find an nth-degree polynomial function with real coefficients satisfying the given conditions. If you are using a graphing utility, graph the function and verify the real zeros and the given function value.

47. $n = 3$; 2 and $2 - 3i$ are zeros; $f(1) = -10$

48. $n = 4$; i is a zero; -3 is a zero of multiplicity 2; $f(-1) = 16$

In Exercises 49–50, find all the zeros of each polynomial function and write the polynomial as a product of linear factors.

49. $f(x) = 2x^4 + 3x^3 + 3x - 2$

50. $g(x) = x^4 - 6x^3 + x^2 + 24x + 16$

In Exercises 51–54, graphs of fifth-degree polynomial functions are shown. In each case, specify the number of real zeros and the number of imaginary zeros. Indicate whether there are any real zeros with multiplicity other than 1.

51. **52.**

53. **54.**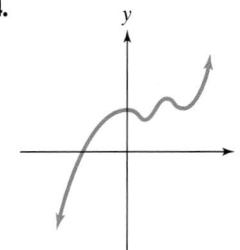

3.5

In Exercises 55–56, use transformations of $f(x) = \dfrac{1}{x}$ or $f(x) = \dfrac{1}{x^2}$ to graph each rational function.

55. $g(x) = \dfrac{1}{(x + 2)^2} - 1$ **56.** $h(x) = \dfrac{1}{x - 1} + 3$

In Exercises 57–64, find the vertical asymptotes, if any, the horizontal asymptote, if one exists, and the slant asymptote, if there is one, of the graph of each rational function. Then graph the rational function.

57. $f(x) = \dfrac{2x}{x^2 - 9}$ **58.** $g(x) = \dfrac{2x - 4}{x + 3}$

59. $h(x) = \dfrac{x^2 - 3x - 4}{x^2 - x - 6}$

60. $r(x) = \dfrac{x^2 + 4x + 3}{(x + 2)^2}$

61. $y = \dfrac{x^2}{x + 1}$

62. $y = \dfrac{x^2 + 2x - 3}{x - 3}$

63. $f(x) = \dfrac{-2x^3}{x^2 + 1}$

64. $g(x) = \dfrac{4x^2 - 16x + 16}{2x - 3}$

65. A company is planning to manufacture affordable graphing calculators. The fixed monthly cost will be \$50,000 and it will cost \$25 to produce each calculator.

 a. Write the cost function, C, of producing x graphing calculators.

 b. Write the average cost function, \overline{C}, of producing x graphing calculators.

 c. Find and interpret $\overline{C}(50)$, $\overline{C}(100)$, $\overline{C}(1000)$, and $\overline{C}(100,000)$.

 d. What is the horizontal asymptote for the graph of this function and what does it represent?

Exercises 66–67 involve rational functions that model the given situations. In each case, find the horizontal asymptote as $x \to \infty$ and then describe what this means in practical terms.

66. $f(x) = \dfrac{150x + 120}{0.05x + 1}$; the number of bass, $f(x)$, after x months in a lake that was stocked with 120 bass

67. $P(x) = \dfrac{72,900}{100x^2 + 729}$; the percentage, $P(x)$, of people in the United States with x years of education who are unemployed

68. The bar graph shows the population of the United States, in millions, for five selected years.

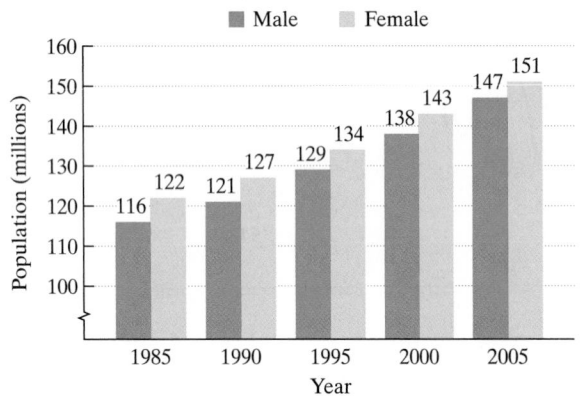

Population of the United States

Source: U.S. Census Bureau

Here are two functions that model the data:

$M(x) = 1.58x + 114.4$ — Male U.S. population, $M(x)$, in millions, x years after 1985

$F(x) = 1.48x + 120.6$ — Female U.S. population, $F(x)$, in millions, x years after 1985

 a. Write a function that models the total U.S. population, $P(x)$, in millions, x years after 1985.

 b. Write a rational function that models the fraction of men in the U.S. population, $R(x)$, x years after 1985.

 c. What is the equation of the horizontal asymptote associated with the function in part (b)? Round to two decimal places. What does this mean about the percentage of men in the U.S. population over time?

3.6

In Exercises 69–74, solve each inequality and graph the solution set on a real number line.

69. $2x^2 + 5x - 3 < 0$

70. $2x^2 + 9x + 4 \geq 0$

71. $x^3 + 2x^2 > 3x$

72. $\dfrac{x - 6}{x + 2} > 0$

73. $\dfrac{(x + 1)(x - 2)}{x - 1} \geq 0$

74. $\dfrac{x + 3}{x - 4} \leq 5$

75. The graph shows stopping distances for motorcycles at various speeds on dry roads and on wet roads.

Stopping Distances for Motorcycles at Selected Speeds

Source: National Highway Traffic Safety Administration

The functions

$$f(x) = 0.125x^2 - 0.8x + 99$$

Dry pavement

and

Wet pavement

$$g(x) = 0.125x^2 + 2.3x + 27$$

model a motorcycle's stopping distance, $f(x)$ or $g(x)$, in feet, traveling at x miles per hour. Function f models stopping distance on dry pavement and function g models stopping distance on wet pavement.

 a. Use function g to find the stopping distance on wet pavement for a motorcycle traveling at 35 miles per hour. Round to the nearest foot. Does your rounded answer overestimate or underestimate the stopping distance shown by the graph? By how many feet?

 b. Use function f to determine speeds on dry pavement requiring stopping distances that exceed 267 feet.

76. Use the position function

$$s(t) = -16t^2 + v_0 t + s_0$$

to solve this problem. A projectile is fired vertically upward from ground level with an initial velocity of 48 feet per second. During which time period will the projectile's height exceed 32 feet?

3.7

Solve the variation problems in Exercises 77–82.

77. Many areas of Northern California depend on the snowpack of the Sierra Nevada mountain range for their water supply. The volume of water produced from melting snow varies directly as the volume of snow. Meteorologists have determined that 250 cubic centimeters of snow will melt to 28 cubic centimeters of water. How much water does 1200 cubic centimeters of melting snow produce?

78. The distance that a body falls from rest is directly proportional to the square of the time of the fall. If skydivers fall 144 feet in 3 seconds, how far will they fall in 10 seconds?

79. The pitch of a musical tone varies inversely as its wavelength. A tone has a pitch of 660 vibrations per second and a wavelength of 1.6 feet. What is the pitch of a tone that has a wavelength of 2.4 feet?

80. The loudness of a stereo speaker, measured in decibels, varies inversely as the square of your distance from the speaker. When you are 8 feet from the speaker, the loudness is 28 decibels. What is the loudness when you are 4 feet from the speaker?

81. The time required to assemble computers varies directly as the number of computers assembled and inversely as the number of workers. If 30 computers can be assembled by 6 workers in 10 hours, how long would it take 5 workers to assemble 40 computers?

82. The volume of a pyramid varies jointly as its height and the area of its base. A pyramid with a height of 15 feet and a base with an area of 35 square feet has a volume of 175 cubic feet. Find the volume of a pyramid with a height of 20 feet and a base with an area of 120 square feet.

83. Heart rates and life spans of most mammals can be modeled using inverse variation. The bar graph shows the average heart rate and the average life span of five mammals.

Heart Rate and Life Span

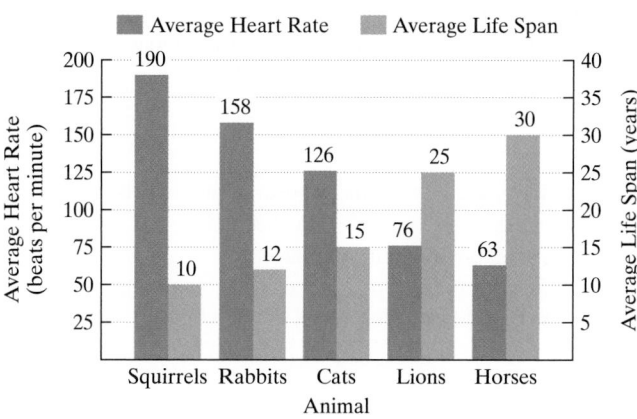

Source: *The Handy Science Answer Book*, Visible Ink Press, 2003

a. A mammal's average life span, L, in years, varies inversely as its average heart rate, R, in beats per minute. Use the data shown for horses to write the equation that models this relationship.

b. Is the inverse variation equation in part (a) an exact model or an approximate model for the data shown for lions?

c. Elephants have an average heart rate of 27 beats per minute. Determine their average life span.

CHAPTER
Test Prep
VIDEOS

Chapter 3 Test

In Exercises 1–2, use the vertex and intercepts to sketch the graph of each quadratic function. Give the equation for the parabola's axis of symmetry. Use the graph to determine the function's domain and range.

1. $f(x) = (x + 1)^2 + 4$

2. $f(x) = x^2 - 2x - 3$

3. Determine, without graphing, whether the quadratic function $f(x) = -2x^2 + 12x - 16$ has a minimum value or a maximum value. Then find

 a. the minimum or maximum value and where it occurs.

 b. the function's domain and its range.

4. The function $f(x) = -x^2 + 46x - 360$ models the daily profit, $f(x)$, in hundreds of dollars, for a company that manufactures x computers daily. How many computers should be manufactured each day to maximize profit? What is the maximum daily profit?

5. Among all pairs of numbers whose sum is 14, find a pair whose product is as large as possible. What is the maximum product?

6. Consider the function $f(x) = x^3 - 5x^2 - 4x + 20$.

 a. Use factoring to find all zeros of f.

 b. Use the Leading Coefficient Test and the zeros of f to graph the function.

7. Use end behavior to explain why the graph at the top of the next column cannot be the graph of $f(x) = x^5 - x$. Then use intercepts to explain why the graph cannot represent $f(x) = x^5 - x$.

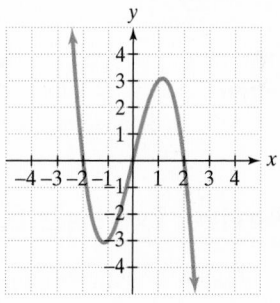

8. The graph of $f(x) = 6x^3 - 19x^2 + 16x - 4$ is shown in the figure.

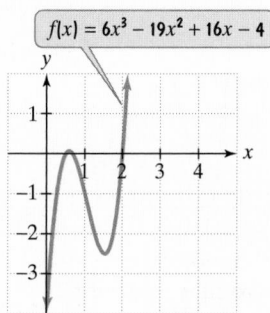

$f(x) = 6x^3 - 19x^2 + 16x - 4$

 a. Based on the graph of f, find the root of the equation $6x^3 - 19x^2 + 16x - 4 = 0$ that is an integer.

 b. Use synthetic division to find the other two roots of $6x^3 - 19x^2 + 16x - 4 = 0$.

9. Use the Rational Zero Theorem to list all possible rational zeros of $f(x) = 2x^3 + 11x^2 - 7x - 6$.

10. Use Descartes's Rule of Signs to determine the possible number of positive and negative real zeros of
$$f(x) = 3x^5 - 2x^4 - 2x^2 + x - 1.$$

11. Solve: $x^3 + 9x^2 + 16x - 6 = 0$.

12. Consider the function whose equation is given by $f(x) = 2x^4 - x^3 - 13x^2 + 5x + 15$.
a. List all possible rational zeros.
b. Use the graph of f in the figure shown and synthetic division to find all zeros of the function.

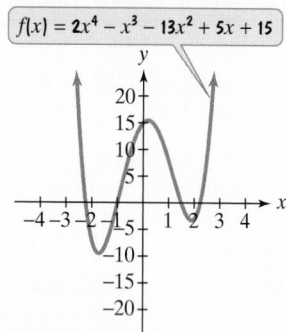

$$f(x) = 2x^4 - x^3 - 13x^2 + 5x + 15$$

13. Use the graph of $f(x) = x^3 + 3x^2 - 4$ in the figure shown to factor $x^3 + 3x^2 - 4$.

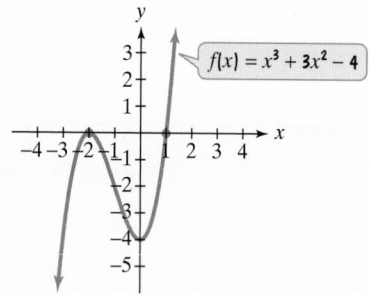

$$f(x) = x^3 + 3x^2 - 4$$

14. Find a fourth-degree polynomial function $f(x)$ with real coefficients that has $-1, 1,$ and i as zeros and such that $f(3) = 160$.

15. The figure shows an incomplete graph of $f(x) = -3x^3 - 4x^2 + x + 2$. Find all the zeros of the function. Then draw a complete graph.

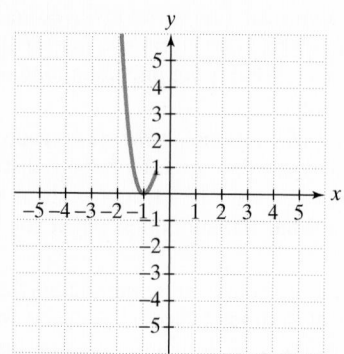

In Exercises 16–21, find the domain of each rational function and graph the function.

16. $f(x) = \dfrac{1}{(x + 3)^2}$

17. $f(x) = \dfrac{1}{x - 1} + 2$

18. $f(x) = \dfrac{x}{x^2 - 16}$

19. $f(x) = \dfrac{x^2 - 9}{x - 2}$

20. $f(x) = \dfrac{x + 1}{x^2 + 2x - 3}$

21. $f(x) = \dfrac{4x^2}{x^2 + 3}$

22. A company is planning to manufacture portable satellite radio players. The fixed monthly cost will be $300,000 and it will cost $10 to produce each player.
a. Write the average cost function, \overline{C}, of producing x players.
b. What is the horizontal asymptote for the graph of this function and what does it represent?

Solve each inequality in Exercises 23–24 and graph the solution set on a real number line. Express each solution set in interval notation.

23. $x^2 < x + 12$

24. $\dfrac{2x + 1}{x - 3} \leq 3$

25. The intensity of light received at a source varies inversely as the square of the distance from the source. A particular light has an intensity of 20 foot-candles at 15 feet. What is the light's intensity at 10 feet?

Cumulative Review Exercises (Chapters 1–3)

Use the graph of $y = f(x)$ to solve Exercises 1–6.

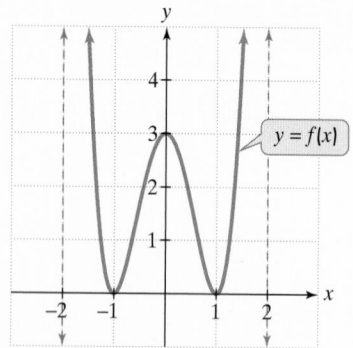

$$y = f(x)$$

1. Find the domain and the range of f.
2. Find the zeros and the least possible multiplicity of each zero.
3. Where does the relative maximum occur?
4. Find $(f \circ f)(-1)$.
5. Use arrow notation to complete this statement: $f(x) \to \infty$ as _____ or as _____.

6. Graph $g(x) = f(x + 2) + 1$.

In Exercises 7–12, solve each equation or inequality.

7. $|2x - 1| = 3$

8. $3x^2 - 5x + 1 = 0$

9. $9 + \dfrac{3}{x} = \dfrac{2}{x^2}$

10. $x^3 + 2x^2 - 5x - 6 = 0$

11. $|2x - 5| > 3$

12. $3x^2 > 2x + 5$

In Exercises 13–18, graph each equation in a rectangular coordinate system. If two functions are given, graph both in the same system.

13. $f(x) = x^3 - 4x^2 - x + 4$

14. $f(x) = x^2 + 2x - 8$

15. $f(x) = x^2(x - 3)$

16. $f(x) = \dfrac{x - 1}{x - 2}$

17. $f(x) = |x|$ and $g(x) = -|x| - 1$

18. $x^2 + y^2 - 2x + 4y - 4 = 0$

In Exercises 19–20, let $f(x) = 2x^2 - x - 1$ and $g(x) = 4x - 1$.

19. Find $(f \circ g)(x)$.

20. Find $\dfrac{f(x + h) - f(x)}{h}$.

Exponential and Logarithmic Functions

4

Can I put aside $25,000 when I'm 20 and wind up sitting on half a million dollars by my early fifties? Will population growth lead to a future without comfort or individual choice? Why did I feel I was walking too slowly on my visit to New York City? Are Californians at greater risk from drunk drivers than from earthquakes? What is the difference between earthquakes measuring 6 and 7 on the Richter scale? And what can possibly be causing merchants at our local shopping mall to grin from ear to ear as they watch the browsers?

The functions that you will be learning about in this chapter will provide you with the mathematics for answering these questions. You will see how these remarkable functions enable us to predict the future and rediscover the past.

You'll be sitting on $500,000 in Example 10 of Section 4.4. Here's where you'll find the other models related to our questions:

- *World population growth: Section 4.5, Example 5*
- *Population and walking speed: Section 4.5, Check Point 4, and Review Exercises, Exercise 82*
- *Alcohol and risk of a car accident: Section 4.4, Example 9*
- *Earthquake intensity: Section 4.2, Example 9.*

We open the chapter with those grinning merchants and the sound of ka-ching!

Section 4.1 **Exponential Functions**

Objectives

① Evaluate exponential functions.

② Graph exponential functions.

③ Evaluate functions with base *e*.

④ Use compound interest formulas.

Just browsing? Take your time. Researchers know, to the dollar, the average amount the typical consumer spends per minute at the shopping mall. And the longer you stay, the more you spend. So if you say you're just browsing, that's just fine with the mall merchants. Browsing is time and, as shown in **Figure 4.1**, time is money.

The data in **Figure 4.1** can be modeled by the function

$$f(x) = 42.2(1.56)^x,$$

where $f(x)$ is the average amount spent, in dollars, at a shopping mall after x hours. Can you see how this function is different from polynomial functions? The

variable x is in the exponent. Functions whose equations contain a variable in the exponent are called **exponential functions**. Many real-life situations, including population growth, growth of epidemics, radioactive decay, and other changes that involve rapid increase or decrease, can be described using exponential functions.

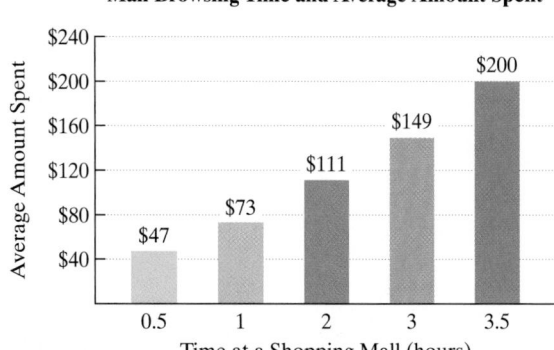

Mall Browsing Time and Average Amount Spent

Figure 4.1
Source: International Council of Shopping Centers Research, 2006

Definition of the Exponential Function

The **exponential function f with base b** is defined by

$$f(x) = b^x \quad \text{or} \quad y = b^x,$$

where b is a positive constant other than 1 ($b > 0$ and $b \neq 1$) and x is any real number.

Here are some examples of exponential functions:

$$f(x) = 2^x \qquad g(x) = 10^x \qquad h(x) = 3^{x+1} \qquad j(x) = \left(\frac{1}{2}\right)^{x-1}.$$

Base is 2.　　　Base is 10.　　　Base is 3.　　　Base is $\frac{1}{2}$.

Each of these functions has a constant base and a variable exponent.

By contrast, the following functions are not exponential functions:

$$F(x) = x^2 \qquad G(x) = 1^x \qquad H(x) = (-1)^x \qquad J(x) = x^x.$$

Variable is the base and not the exponent.　　　The base of an exponential function must be a positive constant other than 1.　　　The base of an exponential function must be positive.　　　Variable is both the base and the exponent.

Why is $G(x) = 1^x$ not classified as an exponential function? The number 1 raised to any power is 1. Thus, the function G can be written as $G(x) = 1$, which is a constant function.

Why is $H(x) = (-1)^x$ not an exponential function? The base of an exponential function must be positive to avoid having to exclude many values of x from the domain that result in nonreal numbers in the range:

$$H(x) = (-1)^x \qquad H\left(\frac{1}{2}\right) = (-1)^{\frac{1}{2}} = \sqrt{-1} = i.$$

Not an exponential function

All values of x resulting in even roots of negative numbers produce nonreal numbers.

① Evaluate exponential functions.

You will need a calculator to evaluate exponential expressions. Most scientific calculators have a $\boxed{y^x}$ key. Graphing calculators have a $\boxed{\wedge}$ key. To evaluate expressions of the form b^x, enter the base b, press $\boxed{y^x}$ or $\boxed{\wedge}$, enter the exponent x, and finally press $\boxed{=}$ or $\boxed{\text{ENTER}}$.

(EXAMPLE 1) Evaluating an Exponential Function

The exponential function $f(x) = 42.2(1.56)^x$ models the average amount spent, $f(x)$, in dollars, at a shopping mall after x hours. What is the average amount spent, to the nearest dollar, after four hours?

Solution Because we are interested in the amount spent after four hours, substitute 4 for x and evaluate the function.

$$f(x) = 42.2(1.56)^x \quad \text{This is the given function.}$$
$$f(4) = 42.2(1.56)^4 \quad \text{Substitute 4 for x.}$$

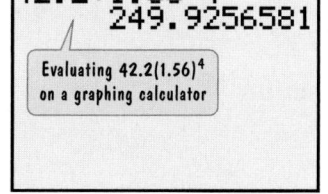

Evaluating $42.2(1.56)^4$ on a graphing calculator

Use a scientific or graphing calculator to evaluate $f(4)$. Press the following keys on your calculator to do this:

Scientific calculator: $42.2 \boxed{\times} 1.56 \boxed{y^x} 4 \boxed{=}$

Graphing calculator: $42.2 \boxed{\times} 1.56 \boxed{\wedge} 4 \boxed{\text{ENTER}}$.

The display should be approximately 249.92566.

$$f(4) = 42.2(1.56)^4 \approx 249.92566 \approx 250$$

Thus, the average amount spent after four hours at a mall is $250. ●

✓ Check Point 1 Use the exponential function in Example 1 to find the average amount spent, to the nearest dollar, after three hours at a shopping mall. Does this rounded function value underestimate or overestimate the amount shown in **Figure 4.1**? By how much?

② Graph exponential functions.

Graphing Exponential Functions

We are familiar with expressions involving b^x, where x is a rational number. For example,

$$b^{1.7} = b^{\frac{17}{10}} = \sqrt[10]{b^{17}} \quad \text{and} \quad b^{1.73} = b^{\frac{173}{100}} = \sqrt[100]{b^{173}}.$$

However, note that the definition of $f(x) = b^x$ includes all real numbers for the domain x. You may wonder what b^x means when x is an irrational number, such as $b^{\sqrt{3}}$ or b^{π}. Using closer and closer approximations for $\sqrt{3}$ ($\sqrt{3} \approx 1.73205$), we can think of $b^{\sqrt{3}}$ as the value that has the successively closer approximations

$$b^{1.7}, b^{1.73}, b^{1.732}, b^{1.73205}, \ldots.$$

In this way, we can graph exponential functions with no holes, or points of discontinuity, at the irrational domain values.

EXAMPLE 2 Graphing an Exponential Function

Graph: $f(x) = 2^x$.

Solution We begin by setting up a table of coordinates.

x	$f(x) = 2^x$
-3	$f(-3) = 2^{-3} = \dfrac{1}{8}$
-2	$f(-2) = 2^{-2} = \dfrac{1}{4}$
-1	$f(-1) = 2^{-1} = \dfrac{1}{2}$
0	$f(0) = 2^0 = 1$
1	$f(1) = 2^1 = 2$
2	$f(2) = 2^2 = 4$
3	$f(3) = 2^3 = 8$

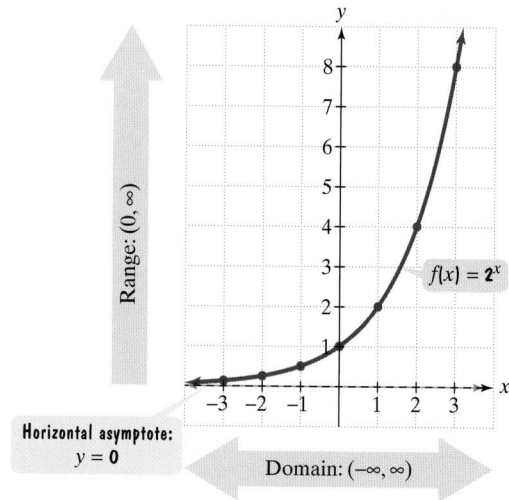

Figure 4.2 The graph of $f(x) = 2^x$

We plot these points, connecting them with a continuous curve. **Figure 4.2** shows the graph of $f(x) = 2^x$. Observe that the graph approaches, but never touches, the negative portion of the x-axis. Thus, the x-axis, or $y = 0$, is a horizontal asymptote. The range is the set of all positive real numbers. Although we used integers for x in our table of coordinates, you can use a calculator to find additional points. For example, $f(0.3) = 2^{0.3} \approx 1.231$ and $f(0.95) = 2^{0.95} \approx 1.932$. The points $(0.3, 1.231)$ and $(0.95, 1.932)$ approximately fit the graph.

⊘ **Check Point 2** Graph: $f(x) = 3^x$.

EXAMPLE 3 Graphing an Exponential Function

Graph: $g(x) = \left(\dfrac{1}{2}\right)^x$.

Solution We begin by setting up a table of coordinates. We compute the function values by noting that

$$g(x) = \left(\frac{1}{2}\right)^x = (2^{-1})^x = 2^{-x}.$$

x	$g(x) = \left(\dfrac{1}{2}\right)^x$ or 2^{-x}
-3	$g(-3) = 2^{-(-3)} = 2^3 = 8$
-2	$g(-2) = 2^{-(-2)} = 2^2 = 4$
-1	$g(-1) = 2^{-(-1)} = 2^1 = 2$
0	$g(0) = 2^{-0} = 1$
1	$g(1) = 2^{-1} = \dfrac{1}{2^1} = \dfrac{1}{2}$
2	$g(2) = 2^{-2} = \dfrac{1}{2^2} = \dfrac{1}{4}$
3	$g(3) = 2^{-3} = \dfrac{1}{2^3} = \dfrac{1}{8}$

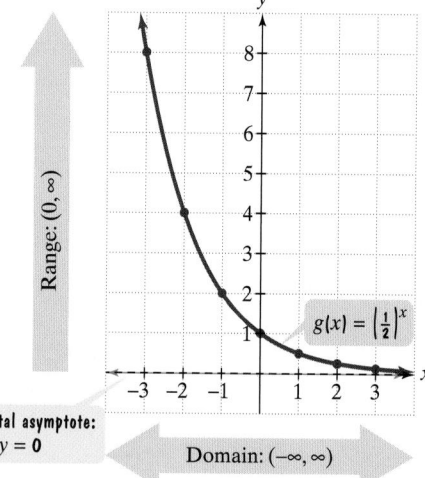

Figure 4.3 The graph of $g(x) = \left(\dfrac{1}{2}\right)^x$

We plot these points, connecting them with a continuous curve. **Figure 4.3** shows the graph of $g(x) = \left(\frac{1}{2}\right)^x$. This time the graph approaches, but never touches, the *positive* portion of the x-axis. Once again, the x-axis, or $y = 0$, is a horizontal asymptote. The range consists of all positive real numbers.

Do you notice a relationship between the graphs of $f(x) = 2^x$ and $g(x) = \left(\frac{1}{2}\right)^x$ in **Figures 4.2** and **4.3**? The graph of $g(x) = \left(\frac{1}{2}\right)^x$ is the graph of $f(x) = 2^x$ reflected about the y-axis:

$$g(x) = \left(\frac{1}{2}\right)^x = 2^{-x} = f(-x).$$

> Recall that the graph of $y = f(-x)$
> is the graph of $y = f(x)$
> reflected about the y-axis.

✓ Check Point **3** Graph: $f(x) = \left(\frac{1}{3}\right)^x$. Note that $f(x) = \left(\frac{1}{3}\right)^x = (3^{-1})^x = 3^{-x}$.

Four exponential functions have been graphed in **Figure 4.4**. Compare the black and green graphs, where $b > 1$, to those in blue and red, where $b < 1$. When $b > 1$, the value of y increases as the value of x increases. When $b < 1$, the value of y decreases as the value of x increases. Notice that all four graphs pass through $(0, 1)$.

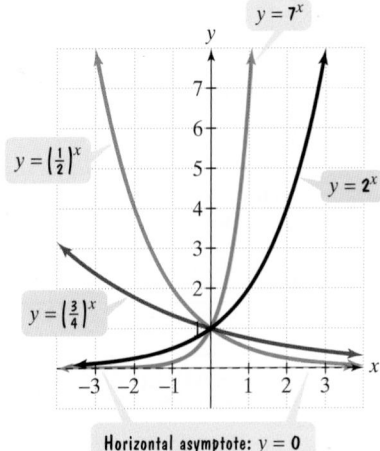

Figure 4.4 Graphs of four exponential functions

These graphs illustrate the following general characteristics of exponential functions:

Characteristics of Exponential Functions of the Form $f(x) = b^x$

1. The domain of $f(x) = b^x$ consists of all real numbers: $(-\infty, \infty)$. The range of $f(x) = b^x$ consists of all positive real numbers: $(0, \infty)$.

2. The graphs of all exponential functions of the form $f(x) = b^x$ pass through the point $(0, 1)$ because $f(0) = b^0 = 1$ $(b \neq 0)$. The y-intercept is 1. There is no x-intercept.

3. If $b > 1$, $f(x) = b^x$ has a graph that goes up to the right and is an increasing function. The greater the value of b, the steeper the increase.

4. If $0 < b < 1$, $f(x) = b^x$ has a graph that goes down to the right and is a decreasing function. The smaller the value of b, the steeper the decrease.

5. $f(x) = b^x$ is one-to-one and has an inverse that is a function.

6. The graph of $f(x) = b^x$ approaches, but does not touch, the x-axis. The x-axis, or $y = 0$, is a horizontal asymptote.

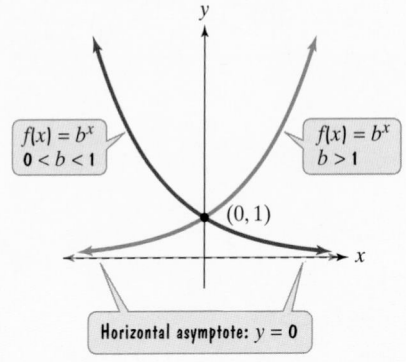

Transformations of Exponential Functions

The graphs of exponential functions can be translated vertically or horizontally, reflected, stretched, or shrunk. These transformations are summarized in **Table 4.1**.

Table 4.1 Transformations Involving Exponential Functions

In each case, c represents a positive real number.

Transformation	Equation	Description
Vertical translation	$g(x) = b^x + c$	• Shifts the graph of $f(x) = b^x$ upward c units.
	$g(x) = b^x - c$	• Shifts the graph of $f(x) = b^x$ downward c units.
Horizontal translation	$g(x) = b^{x+c}$	• Shifts the graph of $f(x) = b^x$ to the left c units.
	$g(x) = b^{x-c}$	• Shifts the graph of $f(x) = b^x$ to the right c units.
Reflection	$g(x) = -b^x$	• Reflects the graph of $f(x) = b^x$ about the x-axis.
	$g(x) = b^{-x}$	• Reflects the graph of $f(x) = b^x$ about the y-axis.
Vertical stretching or shrinking	$g(x) = cb^x$	• Vertically stretches the graph of $f(x) = b^x$ if $c > 1$. • Vertically shrinks the graph of $f(x) = b^x$ if $0 < c < 1$.
Horizontal stretching or shrinking	$g(x) = b^{cx}$	• Horizontally shrinks the graph of $f(x) = b^x$ if $c > 1$ • Horizontally stretches the graph of $f(x) = b^x$ if $0 < c < 1$.

EXAMPLE 4 **Transformations Involving Exponential Functions**

Use the graph of $f(x) = 3^x$ to obtain the graph of $g(x) = 3^{x+1}$.

Solution The graph of $g(x) = 3^{x+1}$ is the graph of $f(x) = 3^x$ shifted 1 unit to the left.

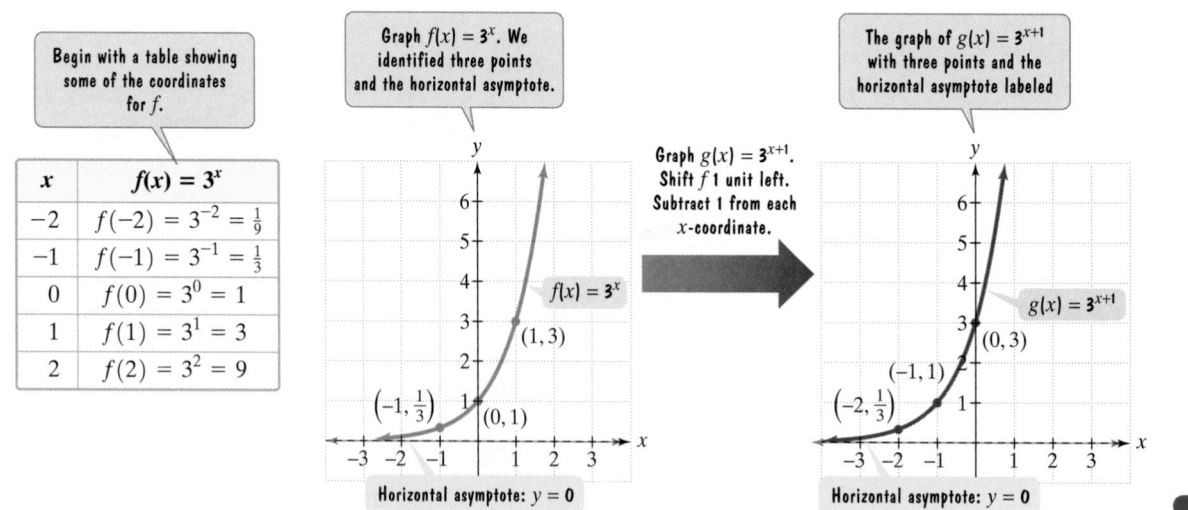

Begin with a table showing some of the coordinates for f.

x	$f(x) = 3^x$
-2	$f(-2) = 3^{-2} = \frac{1}{9}$
-1	$f(-1) = 3^{-1} = \frac{1}{3}$
0	$f(0) = 3^0 = 1$
1	$f(1) = 3^1 = 3$
2	$f(2) = 3^2 = 9$

Graph $f(x) = 3^x$. We identified three points and the horizontal asymptote.

The graph of $g(x) = 3^{x+1}$ with three points and the horizontal asymptote labeled

Graph $g(x) = 3^{x+1}$. Shift f 1 unit left. Subtract 1 from each x-coordinate.

Horizontal asymptote: $y = 0$

✔ **Check Point 4** Use the graph of $f(x) = 3^x$ to obtain the graph of $g(x) = 3^{x-1}$.

If an exponential function is translated upward or downward, the horizontal asymptote is shifted by the amount of the vertical shift.

EXAMPLE 5 Transformations Involving Exponential Functions

Use the graph of $f(x) = 2^x$ to obtain the graph of $g(x) = 2^x - 3$.

Solution The graph of $g(x) = 2^x - 3$ is the graph of $f(x) = 2^x$ shifted down 3 units.

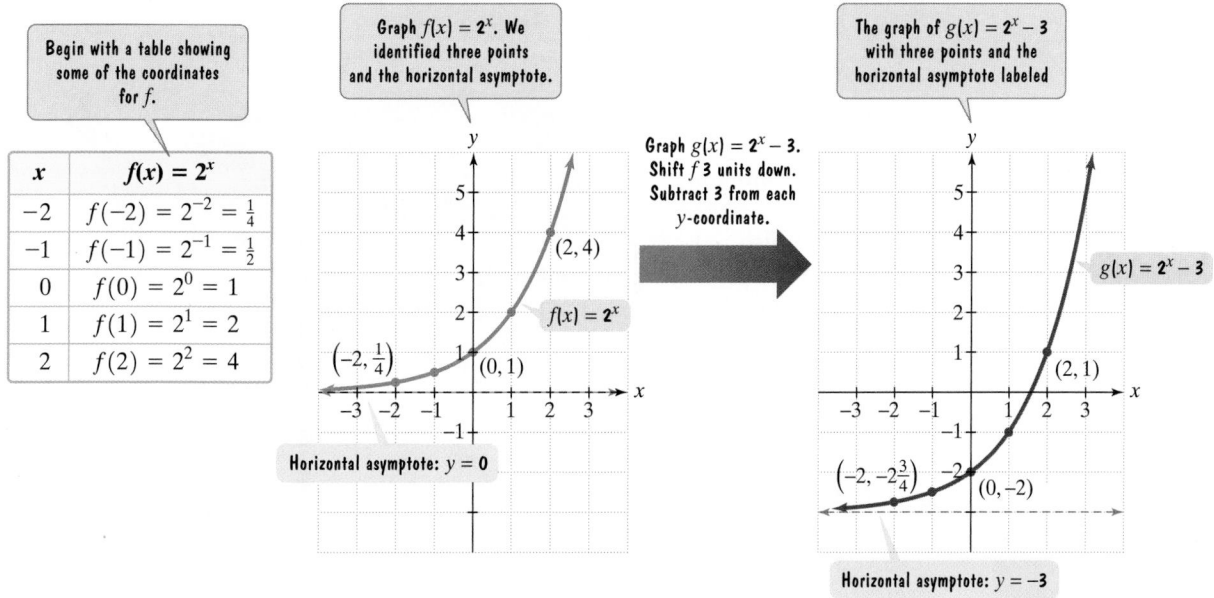

Begin with a table showing some of the coordinates for f.

x	$f(x) = 2^x$
-2	$f(-2) = 2^{-2} = \frac{1}{4}$
-1	$f(-1) = 2^{-1} = \frac{1}{2}$
0	$f(0) = 2^0 = 1$
1	$f(1) = 2^1 = 2$
2	$f(2) = 2^2 = 4$

Graph $f(x) = 2^x$. We identified three points and the horizontal asymptote.

Graph $g(x) = 2^x - 3$. Shift f 3 units down. Subtract 3 from each y-coordinate.

The graph of $g(x) = 2^x - 3$ with three points and the horizontal asymptote labeled

✓ **Check Point 5** Use the graph of $f(x) = 2^x$ to obtain the graph of $g(x) = 2^x + 1$.

③ Evaluate functions with base e.

Graphic Connections

As $n \to \infty$, the graph of $y = \left(1 + \frac{1}{n}\right)^n$ approaches the graph of $y = e$.

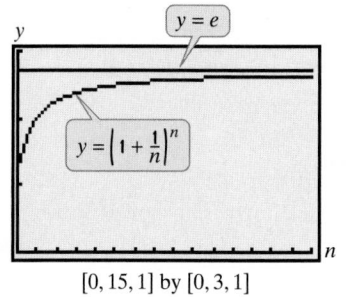

$[0, 15, 1]$ by $[0, 3, 1]$

The Natural Base e

An irrational number, symbolized by the letter e, appears as the base in many applied exponential functions. The number e is defined as the value that $\left(1 + \frac{1}{n}\right)^n$ approaches as n gets larger and larger. **Table 4.2** shows values of $\left(1 + \frac{1}{n}\right)^n$ for increasingly large values of n. As $n \to \infty$, the approximate value of e to nine decimal places is

$$e \approx 2.718281827.$$

The irrational number e, approximately 2.72, is called the **natural base**. The function $f(x) = e^x$ is called the **natural exponential function**.

Use a scientific or graphing calculator with an $\boxed{e^x}$ key to evaluate e to various powers. For example, to find e^2, press the following keys on most calculators:

Scientific calculator: $2 \boxed{e^x}$

Graphing calculator: $\boxed{e^x} \, 2 \, \boxed{\text{ENTER}}$.

The display should be approximately 7.389.

$$e^2 \approx 7.389$$

The number e lies between 2 and 3. Because $2^2 = 4$ and $3^2 = 9$, it makes sense that e^2, approximately 7.389, lies between 4 and 9.

Table 4.2

n	$\left(1 + \dfrac{1}{n}\right)^n$
1	2
2	2.25
5	2.48832
10	2.59374246
100	2.704813829
1000	2.716923932
10,000	2.718145927
100,000	2.718268237
1,000,000	2.718280469
1,000,000,000	2.718281827

As $n \to \infty$, $\left(1 + \dfrac{1}{n}\right)^n \to e$.

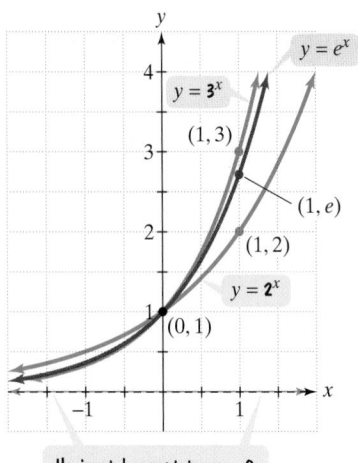

Figure 4.5 Graphs of three exponential functions

Because $2 < e < 3$, the graph of $y = e^x$ is between the graphs of $y = 2^x$ and $y = 3^x$, shown in **Figure 4.5**.

EXAMPLE 6 Gray Wolf Population

Insatiable killer. That's the reputation the gray wolf acquired in the United States in the nineteenth and early twentieth centuries. Although the label was undeserved, an estimated two million wolves were shot, trapped, or poisoned. By 1960, the population was reduced to 800 wolves. **Figure 4.6** shows the rebounding population in two recovery areas after the gray wolf was declared an endangered species and received federal protection.

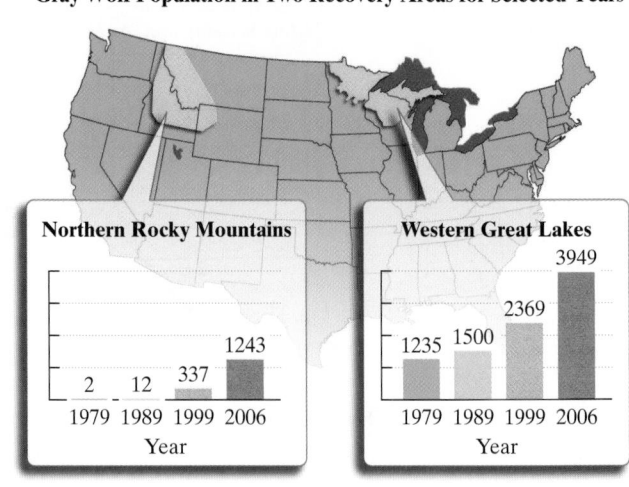

Gray Wolf Population in Two Recovery Areas for Selected Years

Figure 4.6
Source: U.S. Fish and Wildlife Service

The exponential function

$$f(x) = 1.26e^{0.247x}$$

models the gray wolf population of the Northern Rocky Mountains, $f(x)$, x years after 1978. If the wolf is not removed from the endangered species list and trends shown in **Figure 4.6** continue, project its population in the recovery area in 2010.

Solution Because 2010 is 32 years after 1978, we substitute 32 for x in the given function.

$$f(x) = 1.26e^{0.247x} \quad \text{This is the given function.}$$
$$f(32) = 1.26e^{0.247(32)} \quad \text{Substitute 32 for x.}$$

Perform this computation on your calculator.

Scientific calculator: 1.26 \times (.247 \times 32) e^x =

Graphing calculator: 1.26 \times e^x (.247 \times 32) ENTER

The display should be approximately 3412.1973.

Thus, $\qquad f(32) = 1.26e^{0.247(32)} \approx 3412.$

This parenthesis is given on some calculators.

This indicates that the gray wolf population of the Northern Rocky Mountains in the year 2010 is projected to be 3412.

Check Point **6** The exponential function $f(x) = 1066e^{0.042x}$ models the gray wolf population of the Western Great Lakes, $f(x)$, x years after 1978. If trends shown in **Figure 4.6** continue, project the gray wolf's population in the recovery area in 2012.

In 2008, using exponential functions and projections like those in Example 6 and Check Point 6, the U.S. Fish and Wildlife Service removed the gray wolf from the endangered species list, a ruling environmentalists vowed to appeal.

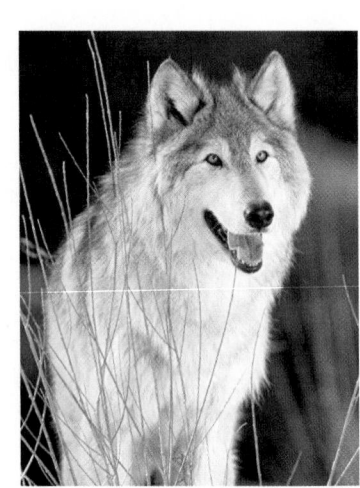

4 Use compound interest formulas.

Compound Interest

We all want a wonderful life with fulfilling work, good health, and loving relationships. And let's be honest: Financial security wouldn't hurt! Achieving this goal depends on understanding how money in savings accounts grows in remarkable ways as a result of *compound interest*. **Compound interest** is interest computed on your original investment as well as on any accumulated interest.

Suppose a sum of money, called the **principal**, P, is invested at an annual percentage rate r, in decimal form, compounded once per year. Because the interest is added to the principal at year's end, the accumulated value, A, is

$$A = P + Pr = P(1 + r).$$

The accumulated amount of money follows this pattern of multiplying the previous principal by $(1 + r)$ for each successive year, as indicated in **Table 4.3**.

Table 4.3

Time in Years	Accumulated Value after Each Compounding
0	$A = P$
1	$A = P(1 + r)$
2	$A = P(1 + r)(1 + r) = P(1 + r)^2$
3	$A = P(1 + r)^2(1 + r) = P(1 + r)^3$
4	$A = P(1 + r)^3(1 + r) = P(1 + r)^4$
⋮	⋮
t	$A = P(1 + r)^t$

This formula gives the balance, A, that a principal, P, is worth after t years at interest rate r, compounded once a year.

Most savings institutions have plans in which interest is paid more than once a year. If compound interest is paid twice a year, the compounding period is six months. We say that the interest is **compounded semiannually**. When compound interest is paid four times a year, the compounding period is three months and the interest is said to be **compounded quarterly**. Some plans allow for monthly compounding or daily compounding.

In general, when compound interest is paid n times a year, we say that there are **n compounding periods per year**. The formula $A = P(1 + r)^t$ can be adjusted to take into account the number of compounding periods in a year. If there are n compounding periods per year, in each time period the interest rate is $\frac{r}{n}$ and there are nt time periods in t years. This results in the following formula for the balance, A, after t years:

$$A = P\left(1 + \frac{r}{n}\right)^{nt}.$$

Some banks use **continuous compounding**, where the number of compounding periods increases infinitely (compounding interest every trillionth of a second, every quadrillionth of a second, etc.). Let's see what happens to the balance, A, as $n \to \infty$.

$$\frac{n}{r} \cdot rt = nt$$

$$A = P\left(1 + \frac{r}{n}\right)^{nt} = P\left[\left(1 + \frac{1}{\frac{n}{r}}\right)^{\frac{n}{r}}\right]^{rt} = P\left[\left(1 + \frac{1}{h}\right)^{h}\right]^{rt} = Pe^{rt}$$

Let $h = \frac{n}{r}$.
As $n \to \infty$, $h \to \infty$.

As $h \to \infty$, by definition $\left(1 + \frac{1}{h}\right)^{h} \to e$.

We see that the formula for continuous compounding is $A = Pe^{rt}$. Although continuous compounding sounds terrific, it yields only a fraction of a percent more interest over a year than daily compounding.

Formulas for Compound Interest

After t years, the balance, A, in an account with principal P and annual interest rate r (in decimal form) is given by the following formulas:

1. For n compoundings per year: $A = P\left(1 + \dfrac{r}{n}\right)^{nt}$

2. For continuous compounding: $A = Pe^{rt}$.

EXAMPLE 7 **Choosing between Investments**

You decide to invest $8000 for 6 years and you have a choice between two accounts. The first pays 7% per year, compounded monthly. The second pays 6.85% per year, compounded continuously. Which is the better investment?

Solution The better investment is the one with the greater balance in the account after 6 years. Let's begin with the account with monthly compounding. We use the compound interest model with $P = 8000, r = 7\% = 0.07, n = 12$ (monthly compounding means 12 compoundings per year), and $t = 6$.

$$A = P\left(1 + \frac{r}{n}\right)^{nt} = 8000\left(1 + \frac{0.07}{12}\right)^{12 \cdot 6} \approx 12{,}160.84$$

The balance in this account after 6 years is $12,160.84.

For the second investment option, we use the model for continuous compounding with $P = 8000, r = 6.85\% = 0.0685$, and $t = 6$.

$$A = Pe^{rt} = 8000e^{0.0685(6)} \approx 12{,}066.60$$

The balance in this account after 6 years is $12,066.60, slightly less than the previous amount. Thus, the better investment is the 7% monthly compounding option. ●

⊘ Check Point 7 A sum of $10,000 is invested at an annual rate of 8%. Find the balance in the account after 5 years subject to **a.** quarterly compounding and **b.** continuous compounding.

Exercise Set 4.1

Practice Exercises

In Exercises 1–10, approximate each number using a calculator. Round your answer to three decimal places.

1. $2^{3.4}$ **2.** $3^{2.4}$ **3.** $3^{\sqrt{5}}$ **4.** $5^{\sqrt{3}}$ **5.** $4^{-1.5}$

6. $6^{-1.2}$ **7.** $e^{2.3}$ **8.** $e^{3.4}$ **9.** $e^{-0.95}$ **10.** $e^{-0.75}$

In Exercises 11–18, graph each function by making a table of coordinates. If applicable, use a graphing utility to confirm your hand-drawn graph.

11. $f(x) = 4^x$ **12.** $f(x) = 5^x$

13. $g(x) = \left(\frac{3}{2}\right)^x$ **14.** $g(x) = \left(\frac{4}{3}\right)^x$

15. $h(x) = \left(\frac{1}{2}\right)^x$ **16.** $h(x) = \left(\frac{1}{3}\right)^x$

17. $f(x) = (0.6)^x$ **18.** $f(x) = (0.8)^x$

In Exercises 19–24, the graph of an exponential function is given. Select the function for each graph from the following options:

$$f(x) = 3^x, g(x) = 3^{x-1}, h(x) = 3^x - 1,$$
$$F(x) = -3^x, G(x) = 3^{-x}, H(x) = -3^{-x}.$$

19.

20.

21.

22.

23.

24.

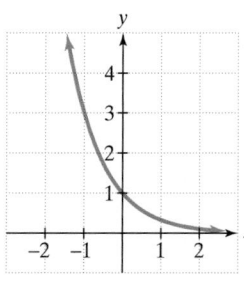

In Exercises 25–34, begin by graphing $f(x) = 2^x$. Then use transformations of this graph to graph the given function. Be sure to graph and give equations of the asymptotes. Use the graphs to determine each function's domain and range. If applicable, use a graphing utility to confirm your hand-drawn graphs.

25. $g(x) = 2^{x+1}$ **26.** $g(x) = 2^{x+2}$

27. $g(x) = 2^x - 1$ **28.** $g(x) = 2^x + 2$

29. $h(x) = 2^{x+1} - 1$ **30.** $h(x) = 2^{x+2} - 1$

31. $g(x) = -2^x$ **32.** $g(x) = 2^{-x}$

33. $g(x) = 2 \cdot 2^x$ **34.** $g(x) = \frac{1}{2} \cdot 2^x$

The figure shows the graph of $f(x) = e^x$. In Exercises 35–46, use transformations of this graph to graph each function. Be sure to give equations of the asymptotes. Use the graphs to determine each function's domain and range. If applicable, use a graphing utility to confirm your hand-drawn graphs.

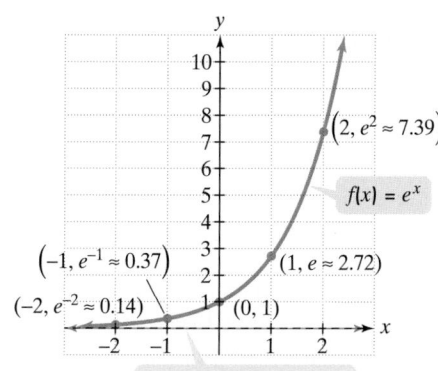

35. $g(x) = e^{x-1}$ **36.** $g(x) = e^{x+1}$

37. $g(x) = e^x + 2$ **38.** $g(x) = e^x - 1$

39. $h(x) = e^{x-1} + 2$ **40.** $h(x) = e^{x+1} - 1$

41. $h(x) = e^{-x}$ **42.** $h(x) = -e^x$

43. $g(x) = 2e^x$ **44.** $g(x) = \frac{1}{2} e^x$

45. $h(x) = e^{2x} + 1$ **46.** $h(x) = e^{\frac{x}{2}} + 2$

In Exercises 47–52, graph functions f and g in the same rectangular coordinate system. Graph and give equations of all asymptotes. If applicable, use a graphing utility to confirm your hand-drawn graphs.

47. $f(x) = 3^x$ and $g(x) = 3^{-x}$

48. $f(x) = 3^x$ and $g(x) = -3^x$

49. $f(x) = 3^x$ and $g(x) = \frac{1}{3} \cdot 3^x$

50. $f(x) = 3^x$ and $g(x) = 3 \cdot 3^x$

51. $f(x) = \left(\frac{1}{2}\right)^x$ and $g(x) = \left(\frac{1}{2}\right)^{x-1} + 1$

52. $f(x) = \left(\frac{1}{2}\right)^x$ and $g(x) = \left(\frac{1}{2}\right)^{x-1} + 2$

Use the compound interest formulas $A = P\left(1 + \dfrac{r}{n}\right)^{nt}$ and $A = Pe^{rt}$ to solve Exercises 53–56. Round answers to the nearest cent.

53. Find the accumulated value of an investment of $10,000 for 5 years at an interest rate of 5.5% if the money is **a.** compounded semiannually; **b.** compounded quarterly; **c.** compounded monthly; **d.** compounded continuously.

54. Find the accumulated value of an investment of $5000 for 10 years at an interest rate of 6.5% if the money is **a.** compounded semiannually; **b.** compounded quarterly; **c.** compounded monthly; **d.** compounded continuously.

55. Suppose that you have $12,000 to invest. Which investment yields the greater return over 3 years: 7% compounded monthly or 6.85% compounded continuously?

56. Suppose that you have $6000 to invest. Which investment yields the greater return over 4 years: 8.25% compounded quarterly or 8.3% compounded semiannually?

Practice Plus

In Exercises 57–58, graph f and g in the same rectangular coordinate system. Then find the point of intersection of the two graphs.

57. $f(x) = 2^x$, $g(x) = 2^{-x}$

58. $f(x) = 2^{x+1}$, $g(x) = 2^{-x+1}$

59. Graph $y = 2^x$ and $x = 2^y$ in the same rectangular coordinate system.

60. Graph $y = 3^x$ and $x = 3^y$ in the same rectangular coordinate system.

In Exercises 61–64, give the equation of each exponential function whose graph is shown.

61.

62.

63.

64.

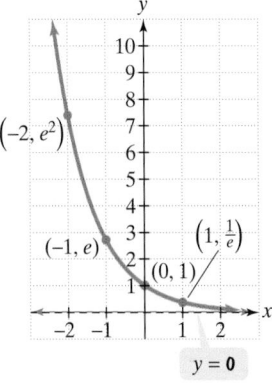

Application Exercises

Use a calculator with a $\boxed{y^x}$ *key or a* $\boxed{\wedge}$ *key to solve Exercises 65–70.*

65. India is currently one of the world's fastest-growing countries. By 2040, the population of India will be larger than the population of China; by 2050, nearly one-third of the world's population will live in these two countries alone. The exponential function $f(x) = 574(1.026)^x$ models the population of India, $f(x)$, in millions, x years after 1974.

 a. Substitute 0 for x and, without using a calculator, find India's population in 1974.

 b. Substitute 27 for x and use your calculator to find India's population, to the nearest million, in the year 2001 as modeled by this function.

 c. Find India's population, to the nearest million, in the year 2028 as predicted by this function.

 d. Find India's population, to the nearest million, in the year 2055 as predicted by this function.

 e. What appears to be happening to India's population every 27 years?

66. The 1986 explosion at the Chernobyl nuclear power plant in the former Soviet Union sent about 1000 kilograms of radioactive cesium-137 into the atmosphere. The function $f(x) = 1000(0.5)^{\frac{x}{30}}$ describes the amount, $f(x)$, in kilograms, of cesium-137 remaining in Chernobyl x years after 1986. If even 100 kilograms of cesium-137 remain in Chernobyl's atmosphere, the area is considered unsafe for human habitation. Find $f(80)$ and determine if Chernobyl will be safe for human habitation by 2066.

The formula $S = C(1 + r)^t$ models inflation, where C = the value today, r = the annual inflation rate, and S = the inflated value t years from now. Use this formula to solve Exercises 67–68. Round answers to the nearest dollar.

67. If the inflation rate is 6%, how much will a house now worth $465,000 be worth in 10 years?

68. If the inflation rate is 3%, how much will a house now worth $510,000 be worth in 5 years?

69. A decimal approximation for $\sqrt{3}$ is 1.7320508. Use a calculator to find $2^{1.7}$, $2^{1.73}$, $2^{1.732}$, $2^{1.73205}$, and $2^{1.7320508}$. Now find $2^{\sqrt{3}}$. What do you observe?

70. A decimal approximation for π is 3.141593. Use a calculator to find 2^3, $2^{3.1}$, $2^{3.14}$, $2^{3.141}$, $2^{3.1415}$, $2^{3.14159}$, and $2^{3.141593}$. Now find 2^{π}. What do you observe?

Use a calculator with an $\boxed{e^x}$ *key to solve Exercises 71–76.*

The graph shows the number of words, in millions, in the U.S. federal tax code for selected years from 1955 through 2005. The data can be modeled by

$$f(x) = 0.15x + 1.44 \quad and \quad g(x) = 1.87e^{0.0344x},$$

in which $f(x)$ and $g(x)$ represent the number of words, in millions, in the federal tax code x years after 1955. Use these functions to solve Exercises 71–72. Round answers to one decimal place.

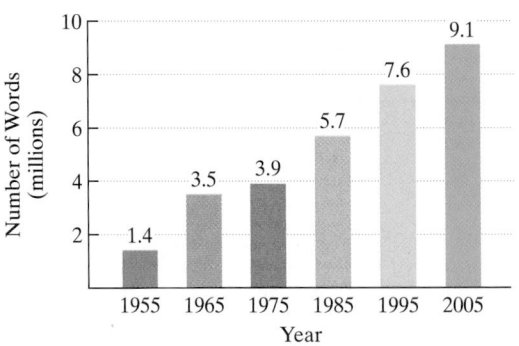

Number of Words, in Millions, in the Federal Tax Code

Source: The Tax Foundation

71. a. According to the linear model, how many millions of words were in the federal tax code in 2005?

 b. According to the exponential model, how many millions of words were in the federal tax code in 2005?

 c. Which function is a better model for the data in 2005?

72. a. According to the linear model, how many millions of words were in the federal tax code in 1975?

 b. According to the exponential model, how many millions of words were in the federal tax code in 1975?

 c. Which function is a better model for the data in 1975?

73. In college, we study large volumes of information—information that, unfortunately, we do not often retain for very long. The function

$$f(x) = 80e^{-0.5x} + 20$$

describes the percentage of information, $f(x)$, that a particular person remembers x weeks after learning the information.

 a. Substitute 0 for x and, without using a calculator, find the percentage of information remembered at the moment it is first learned.

 b. Substitute 1 for x and find the percentage of information that is remembered after 1 week.

 c. Find the percentage of information that is remembered after 4 weeks.

 d. Find the percentage of information that is remembered after one year (52 weeks).

74. In 1626, Peter Minuit convinced the Wappinger Indians to sell him Manhattan Island for $24. If the Native Americans had put the $24 into a bank account paying 5% interest, how much would the investment have been worth in the year 2005 if interest were compounded

 a. monthly? **b.** continuously?

The bar graph shows the percentage of people 25 years of age and older who were college graduates in the United States for seven selected years.

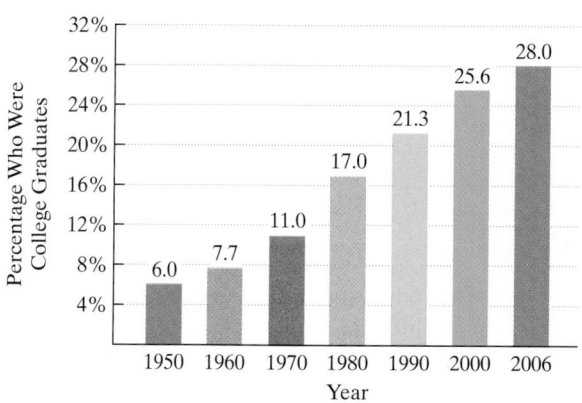

Percentage of College Graduates, Among People Ages 25 and Older, in the United States

Source: U.S. Census Bureau

The functions

$$f(x) = 6.19(1.029)^x \quad \text{and} \quad g(x) = \frac{37.3}{1 + 6.1e^{-0.052x}}$$

model the percentage of. college graduates, among people ages 25 and older, $f(x)$ or $g(x)$, x years after 1950. Use these functions to solve Exercises 75–76.

75. Which function is a better model for the percentage who were college graduates in 2006?

76. Which function is a better model for the percentage who were college graduates in 1990?

Writing in Mathematics

77. What is an exponential function?

78. What is the natural exponential function?

79. Use a calculator to evaluate $\left(1 + \dfrac{1}{x}\right)^x$ for $x = 10, 100, 1000,$ 10,000, 100,000, and 1,000,000. Describe what happens to the expression as x increases.

80. Describe how you could use the graph of $f(x) = 2^x$ to obtain a decimal approximation for $\sqrt{2}$.

Technology Exercises

81. You have \$10,000 to invest. One bank pays 5% interest compounded quarterly and a second bank pays 4.5% interest compounded monthly.

 a. Use the formula for compound interest to write a function for the balance in each bank at any time t.

 b. Use a graphing utility to graph both functions in an appropriate viewing rectangle. Based on the graphs, which bank offers the better return on your money?

82. a. Graph $y = e^x$ and $y = 1 + x + \dfrac{x^2}{2}$ in the same viewing rectangle.

 b. Graph $y = e^x$ and $y = 1 + x + \dfrac{x^2}{2} + \dfrac{x^3}{6}$ in the same viewing rectangle.

 c. Graph $y = e^x$ and $y = 1 + x + \dfrac{x^2}{2} + \dfrac{x^3}{6} + \dfrac{x^4}{24}$ in the same viewing rectangle.

 d. Describe what you observe in parts (a)–(c). Try generalizing this observation.

Critical Thinking Exercises

Make Sense? *In Exercises 83–86, determine whether each statement makes sense or does not make sense, and explain your reasoning.*

83. My graph of $f(x) = 3 \cdot 2^x$ shows that the horizontal asymptote for f is $x = 3$.

84. I'm using a photocopier to reduce an image over and over by 50%, so the exponential function $f(x) = \left(\frac{1}{2}\right)^x$ models the new image size, where x is the number of reductions.

85. I'm looking at data that show the number of Americans who travel outside the United States to get medical care, and a linear function appears to be a better choice than an exponential function for modeling the number of medical tourists from 2004 through 2007.

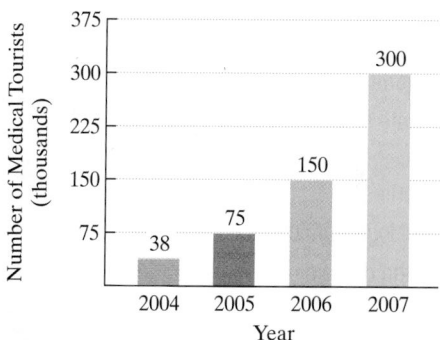

Number of Americans Traveling Abroad for Medical Care

Source: Patients Beyond Borders

86. I use the natural base e when determining how much money I'd have in a bank account that earns compound interest subject to continuous compounding.

In Exercises 87–90, determine whether each statement is true or false. If the statement is false, make the necessary change(s) to produce a true statement.

87. As the number of compounding periods increases on a fixed investment, the amount of money in the account over a fixed interval of time will increase without bound.

88. The functions $f(x) = 3^{-x}$ and $g(x) = -3^x$ have the same graph.

89. If $f(x) = 2^x$, then $f(a + b) = f(a) + f(b)$.

90. The functions $f(x) = \left(\frac{1}{3}\right)^x$ and $g(x) = 3^{-x}$ have the same graph.

91. The graphs labeled (a)–(d) in the figure represent $y = 3^x$, $y = 5^x$, $y = \left(\frac{1}{3}\right)^x$, and $y = \left(\frac{1}{5}\right)^x$, but not necessarily in that order. Which is which? Describe the process that enables you to make this decision.

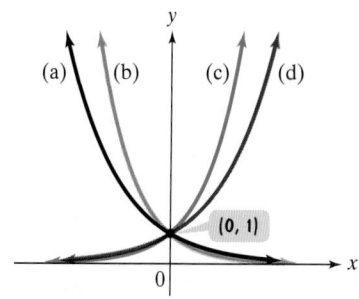

92. Graph $f(x) = 2^x$ and its inverse function in the same rectangular coordinate system.

93. The *hyperbolic cosine* and *hyperbolic sine* functions are defined by

$$\cosh x = \frac{e^x + e^{-x}}{2} \quad \text{and} \quad \sinh x = \frac{e^x - e^{-x}}{2}.$$

a. Show that $\cosh x$ is an even function.
b. Show that $\sinh x$ is an odd function.
c. Prove that $(\cosh x)^2 - (\sinh x)^2 = 1$.

Preview Exercises

Exercises 94–96 will help you prepare for the material covered in the next section.

94. What problem do you encounter when using the switch-and-solve strategy to find the inverse of $f(x) = 2^x$? (The switch-and-solve strategy is described in the box on page 285.)

95. 25 to what power gives 5? ($25^? = 5$)

96. Solve: $(x - 3)^2 > 0$.

Section **4.2** Logarithmic Functions

Objectives

❶ Change from logarithmic to exponential form.

❷ Change from exponential to logarithmic form.

❸ Evaluate logarithms.

❹ Use basic logarithmic properties.

❺ Graph logarithmic functions.

❻ Find the domain of a logarithmic function.

❼ Use common logarithms.

❽ Use natural logarithms.

The earthquake that ripped through northern California on October 17, 1989 measured 7.1 on the Richter scale, killed more than 60 people, and injured more than 2400. Shown here is San Francisco's Marina district, where shock waves tossed houses off their foundations and into the street.

A higher measure on the Richter scale is more devastating than it seems because for each increase in one unit on the scale, there is a tenfold increase in the intensity of an earthquake. In this section, our focus is on the inverse of the exponential function, called the logarithmic function. The logarithmic function will help you to understand diverse phenomena, including earthquake intensity, human memory, and the pace of life in large cities.

Study Tip

The discussion that follows is based on our work with inverse functions in Section 2.7. Here is a summary of what you should already know about functions and their inverses.

1. Only one-to-one functions have inverses that are functions. A function, f, has an inverse function, f^{-1}, if there is no horizontal line that intersects the graph of f at more than one point.

2. If a function is one-to-one, its inverse function can be found by interchanging x and y in the function's equation and solving for y.

3. If $f(a) = b$, then $f^{-1}(b) = a$. The domain of f is the range of f^{-1}. The range of f is the domain of f^{-1}.

4. $f(f^{-1}(x)) = x$ and $f^{-1}(f(x)) = x$.

5. The graph of f^{-1} is the reflection of the graph of f about the line $y = x$.

The Definition of Logarithmic Functions

No horizontal line can be drawn that intersects the graph of an exponential function at more than one point. This means that the exponential function is one-to-one and has an inverse. Let's use our switch-and-solve strategy from Section 2.7 to find the inverse.

> All exponential functions have inverse functions.

$$f(x) = b^x$$

Step 1 Replace $f(x)$ with y: $y = b^x$.
Step 2 Interchange x and y: $x = b^y$.
Step 3 Solve for y: ?

The question mark indicates that we do not have a method for solving $b^y = x$ for y. To isolate the exponent y, a new notation, called *logarithmic notation*, is needed. This notation gives us a way to name the inverse of $f(x) = b^x$. **The inverse function of the exponential function with base b is called the *logarithmic function with base b.***

> ### Definition of the Logarithmic Function
> For $x > 0$ and $b > 0, b \neq 1$,
>
> $$y = \log_b x \text{ is equivalent to } b^y = x.$$
>
> The function $f(x) = \log_b x$ is the **logarithmic function with base b.**

The equations

$$y = \log_b x \quad \text{and} \quad b^y = x$$

are different ways of expressing the same thing. The first equation is in **logarithmic form** and the second equivalent equation is in **exponential form**.

Notice that a **logarithm, y, is an exponent**. You should learn the location of the base and exponent in each form.

Study Tip

To change from logarithmic form to the more familiar exponential form, use this pattern:

$$y = \log_b x \quad \text{means} \quad b^y = x.$$

Location of Base and Exponent in Exponential and Logarithmic Forms

Logarithmic Form: $y = \log_b x$ Exponential Form: $b^y = x$

Exponent
Base

① Change from logarithmic to exponential form.

EXAMPLE 1 Changing from Logarithmic to Exponential Form

Write each equation in its equivalent exponential form:

a. $2 = \log_5 x$ **b.** $3 = \log_b 64$ **c.** $\log_3 7 = y$.

Solution We use the fact that $y = \log_b x$ means $b^y = x$.

a. $2 = \log_5 x$ means $5^2 = x$. **b.** $3 = \log_b 64$ means $b^3 = 64$.

Logarithms are exponents. Logarithms are exponents.

c. $\log_3 7 = y$ or $y = \log_3 7$ means $3^y = 7$.

⊘ Check Point **1** Write each equation in its equivalent exponential form:

a. $3 = \log_7 x$ **b.** $2 = \log_b 25$ **c.** $\log_4 26 = y$.

② Change from exponential to logarithmic form.

EXAMPLE 2 Changing from Exponential to Logarithmic Form

Write each equation in its equivalent logarithmic form:

a. $12^2 = x$ **b.** $b^3 = 8$ **c.** $e^y = 9$.

Solution We use the fact that $b^y = x$ means $y = \log_b x$.

a. $12^2 = x$ means $2 = \log_{12} x$. **b.** $b^3 = 8$ means $3 = \log_b 8$.

Exponents are logarithms. Exponents are logarithms.

c. $e^y = 9$ means $y = \log_e 9$.

✓ Check Point **2** Write each equation in its equivalent logarithmic form:

 a. $2^5 = x$ **b.** $b^3 = 27$ **c.** $e^y = 33.$

③ Evaluate logarithms.

 Remembering that logarithms are exponents makes it possible to evaluate some logarithms by inspection. The logarithm of x with base b, $\log_b x$, is the exponent to which b must be raised to get x. For example, suppose we want to evaluate $\log_2 32$. We ask, 2 to what power gives 32? Because $2^5 = 32$, $\log_2 32 = 5$.

EXAMPLE 3 **Evaluating Logarithms**

Evaluate:

 a. $\log_2 16$ **b.** $\log_7 \frac{1}{49}$ **c.** $\log_{25} 5$ **d.** $\log_2 \sqrt[5]{2}.$

Solution

Logarithmic Expression	Question Needed for Evaluation	Logarithmic Expression Evaluated
a. $\log_2 16$	2 to what power gives 16?	$\log_2 16 = 4$ because $2^4 = 16.$
b. $\log_7 \frac{1}{49}$	7 to what power gives $\frac{1}{49}$?	$\log_7 \frac{1}{49} = -2$ because $7^{-2} = \frac{1}{7^2} = \frac{1}{49}.$
c. $\log_{25} 5$	25 to what power gives 5?	$\log_{25} 5 = \frac{1}{2}$ because $25^{\frac{1}{2}} = \sqrt{25} = 5.$
d. $\log_2 \sqrt[5]{2}$	2 to what power gives $\sqrt[5]{2}$, or $2^{\frac{1}{5}}$?	$\log_2 \sqrt[5]{2} = \frac{1}{5}$ because $= 2^{\frac{1}{5}} = \sqrt[5]{2}.$

✓ Check Point **3** Evaluate:

 a. $\log_{10} 100$ **b.** $\log_5 \frac{1}{125}$ **c.** $\log_{36} 6$ **d.** $\log_3 \sqrt[7]{3}.$

④ Use basic logarithmic properties.

Basic Logarithmic Properties

Because logarithms are exponents, they have properties that can be verified using properties of exponents.

Basic Logarithmic Properties Involving One

 1. $\log_b b = 1$ because 1 is the exponent to which b must be raised to obtain b. $(b^1 = b)$

 2. $\log_b 1 = 0$ because 0 is the exponent to which b must be raised to obtain 1. $(b^0 = 1)$

EXAMPLE 4 **Using Properties of Logarithms**

Evaluate:

 a. $\log_7 7$ **b.** $\log_5 1.$

Solution

 a. Because $\log_b b = 1$, we conclude $\log_7 7 = 1.$ This means that $7^1 = 7.$

 b. Because $\log_b 1 = 0$, we conclude $\log_5 1 = 0.$ This means that $5^0 = 1.$

✓ Check Point **4** Evaluate:

 a. $\log_9 9$ **b.** $\log_8 1$.

Now that we are familiar with logarithmic notation, let's resume and finish the switch-and-solve strategy for finding the inverse of $f(x) = b^x$.

Step 1 **Replace $f(x)$ with y:** $y = b^x$.

Step 2 **Interchange x and y:** $x = b^y$.

Step 3 **Solve for y:** $y = \log_b x$.

Step 4 **Replace y with $f^{-1}(x)$:** $f^{-1}(x) = \log_b x$.

The completed switch-and-solve strategy illustrates that if $f(x) = b^x$, then $f^{-1}(x) = \log_b x$. The inverse of an exponential function is the logarithmic function with the same base.

In Section 2.7, we saw how inverse functions "undo" one another. In particular,

$$f(f^{-1}(x)) = x \quad \text{and} \quad f^{-1}(f(x)) = x.$$

Applying these relationships to exponential and logarithmic functions, we obtain the following **inverse properties of logarithms**:

Inverse Properties of Logarithms

For $b > 0$ and $b \neq 1$,

$\log_b b^x = x$ The logarithm with base b of b raised to a power equals that power.

$b^{\log_b x} = x$. b raised to the logarithm with base b of a number equals that number.

(**EXAMPLE 5**) **Using Inverse Properties of Logarithms**

Evaluate:

 a. $\log_4 4^5$ **b.** $6^{\log_6 9}$.

Solution

 a. Because $\log_b b^x = x$, we conclude $\log_4 4^5 = 5$.

 b. Because $b^{\log_b x} = x$, we conclude $6^{\log_6 9} = 9$. ●

✓ Check Point **5** Evaluate:

 a. $\log_7 7^8$ **b.** $3^{\log_3 17}$.

⑤ Graph logarithmic functions.

Graphs of Logarithmic Functions

How do we graph logarithmic functions? We use the fact that a logarithmic function is the inverse of an exponential function. This means that the logarithmic function reverses the coordinates of the exponential function. It also means that the graph of the logarithmic function is a reflection of the graph of the exponential function about the line $y = x$.

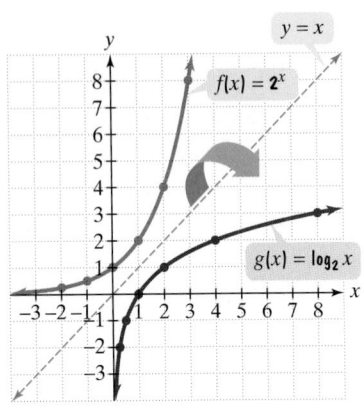

Figure 4.7 The graphs of
$f(x) = 2^x$ and its inverse function

Graphs of Exponential and Logarithmic Functions

Graph $f(x) = 2^x$ and $g(x) = \log_2 x$ in the same rectangular coordinate system.

Solution We first set up a table of coordinates for $f(x) = 2^x$. Reversing these coordinates gives the coordinates for the inverse function $g(x) = \log_2 x$.

x	-2	-1	0	1	2	3
$f(x) = 2^x$	$\frac{1}{4}$	$\frac{1}{2}$	1	2	4	8

x	$\frac{1}{4}$	$\frac{1}{2}$	1	2	4	8
$g(x) = \log_2 x$	-2	-1	0	1	2	3

Reverse
coordinates.

We now plot the ordered pairs from each table, connecting them with smooth curves. **Figure 4.7** shows the graphs of $f(x) = 2^x$ and its inverse function $g(x) = \log_2 x$. The graph of the inverse can also be drawn by reflecting the graph of $f(x) = 2^x$ about the line $y = x$. ●

Study Tip

You can obtain a partial table of coordinates for $g(x) = \log_2 x$ without having to obtain and reverse coordinates for $f(x) = 2^x$. Because $g(x) = \log_2 x$ means $2^{g(x)} = x$, we begin with values for $g(x)$ and compute corresponding values for x:

Use $x = 2^{g(x)}$ to compute x. For example,
if $g(x) = -2$, $x = 2^{-2} = \frac{1}{2^2} = \frac{1}{4}$.

Start with
values for $g(x)$.

x	$\frac{1}{4}$	$\frac{1}{2}$	1	2	4	8
$g(x) = \log_2 x$	-2	-1	0	1	2	3

✓ **Check Point 6** Graph $f(x) = 3^x$ and $g(x) = \log_3 x$ in the same rectangular coordinate system.

Figure 4.8 illustrates the relationship between the graph of an exponential function, shown in blue, and its inverse, a logarithmic function, shown in red, for bases greater than 1 and for bases between 0 and 1. Also shown and labeled are the exponential function's horizontal asymptote ($y = 0$) and the logarithmic function's vertical asymptote ($x = 0$).

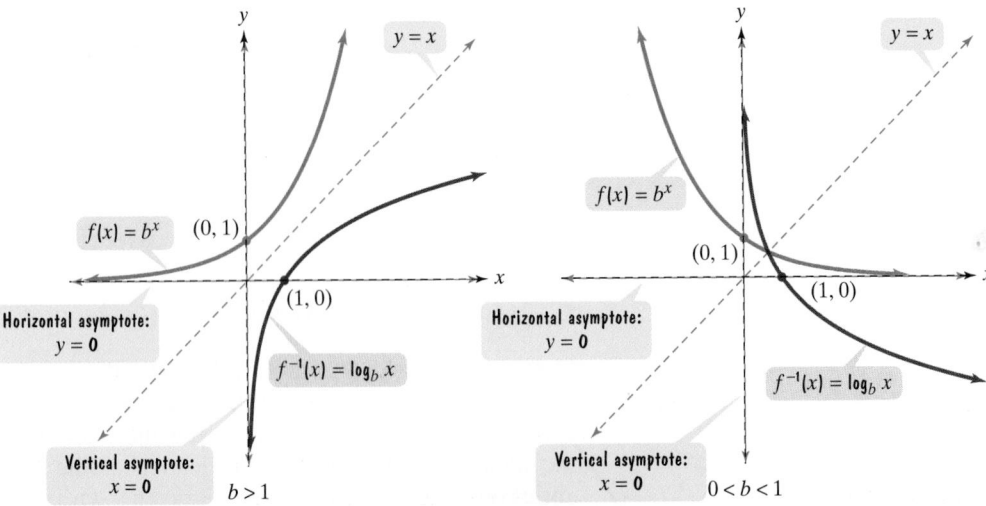

Figure 4.8 Graphs of
exponential and logarithmic
functions

The red graphs in **Figure 4.8** illustrate the following general characteristics of logarithmic functions:

Characteristics of Logarithmic Functions of the Form $f(x) = \log_b x$

1. The domain of $f(x) = \log_b x$ consists of all positive real numbers: $(0, \infty)$. The range of $f(x) = \log_b x$ consists of all real numbers: $(-\infty, \infty)$.

2. The graphs of all logarithmic functions of the form $f(x) = \log_b x$ pass through the point $(1, 0)$ because $f(1) = \log_b 1 = 0$. The x-intercept is 1. There is no y-intercept.

3. If $b > 1$, $f(x) = \log_b x$ has a graph that goes up to the right and is an increasing function.

4. If $0 < b < 1$, $f(x) = \log_b x$ has a graph that goes down to the right and is a decreasing function.

5. The graph of $f(x) = \log_b x$ approaches, but does not touch, the y-axis. The y-axis, or $x = 0$, is a vertical asymptote.

The graphs of logarithmic functions can be translated vertically or horizontally, reflected, stretched, or shrunk. These transformations are summarized in **Table 4.4**.

Table 4.4 **Transformations Involving Logarithmic Functions**

In each case, c represents a positive real number.

Transformation	Equation	Description
Vertical translation	$g(x) = \log_b x + c$ $g(x) = \log_b x - c$	• Shifts the graph of $f(x) = \log_b x$ upward c units. • Shifts the graph of $f(x) = \log_b x$ downward c units.
Horizontal translation	$g(x) = \log_b(x + c)$ $g(x) = \log_b(x - c)$	• Shifts the graph of $f(x) = \log_b x$ to the left c units. Vertical asymptote: $x = -c$ • Shifts the graph of $f(x) = \log_b x$ to the right c units. Vertical asymptote: $x = c$
Reflection	$g(x) = -\log_b x$ $g(x) = \log_b(-x)$	• Reflects the graph of $f(x) = \log_b x$ about the x-axis. • Reflects the graph of $f(x) = \log_b x$ about the y-axis.
Vertical stretching or shrinking	$g(x) = c \log_b x$	• Vertically stretches the graph of $f(x) = \log_b x$ if $c > 1$. • Vertically shrinks the graph of $f(x) = \log_b x$ if $0 < c < 1$.
Horizontal stretching or shrinking	$g(x) = \log_b(cx)$	• Horizontally shrinks the graph of $f(x) = \log_b x$ if $c > 1$. • Horizontally stretches the graph of $f(x) = \log_b x$ if $0 < c < 1$.

For example, **Figure 4.9** illustrates that the graph of $g(x) = \log_2(x - 1)$ is the graph of $f(x) = \log_2 x$ shifted one unit to the right. If a logarithmic function is translated to the left or to the right, both the x-intercept and the vertical asymptote are shifted by the amount of the horizontal shift. In **Figure 4.9**, the x-intercept of f is 1. Because g is shifted one unit to the right, its x-intercept is 2. Also observe that the vertical asymptote for f, the y-axis, or $x = 0$, is shifted one unit to the right for the vertical asymptote for g. Thus, $x = 1$ is the vertical asymptote for g.

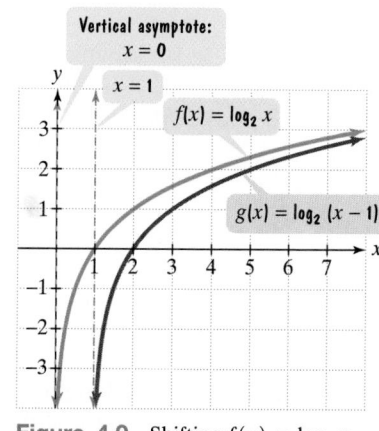

Figure 4.9 Shifting $f(x) = \log_2 x$ one unit to the right

Here are some other examples of transformations of graphs of logarithmic functions:

- The graph of $g(x) = 3 + \log_4 x$ is the graph of $f(x) = \log_4 x$ shifted up three units, shown in **Figure 4.10**.
- The graph of $h(x) = -\log_2 x$ is the graph of $f(x) = \log_2 x$ reflected about the x-axis, shown in **Figure 4.11**.
- The graph of $r(x) = \log_2(-x)$ is the graph of $f(x) = \log_2 x$ reflected about the y-axis, shown in **Figure 4.12**.

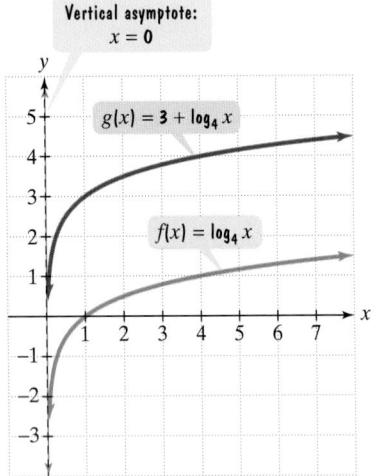

Figure 4.10 Shifting vertically up three units

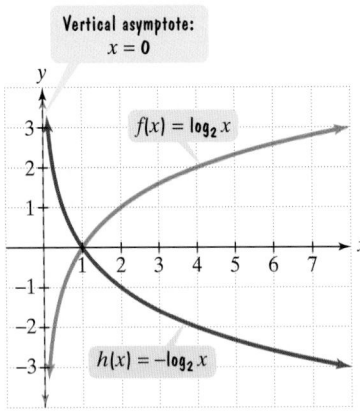

Figure 4.11 Reflection about the x-axis

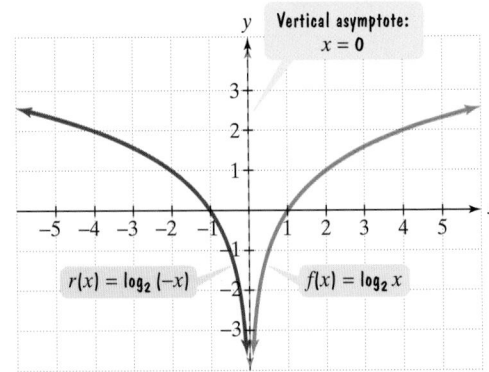

Figure 4.12 Reflection about the y-axis

⑥ Find the domain of a logarithmic function.

The Domain of a Logarithmic Function

In Section 4.1, we learned that the domain of an exponential function of the form $f(x) = b^x$ includes all real numbers and its range is the set of positive real numbers. Because the logarithmic function reverses the domain and the range of the exponential function, the **domain of a logarithmic function of the form $f(x) = \log_b x$ is the set of all positive real numbers**. Thus, $\log_2 8$ is defined because the value of x in the logarithmic expression, 8, is greater than zero and therefore is included in the domain of the logarithmic function $f(x) = \log_2 x$. However, $\log_2 0$ and $\log_2(-8)$ are not defined because 0 and -8 are not positive real numbers and therefore are excluded from the domain of the logarithmic function $f(x) = \log_2 x$. In general, **the domain of $f(x) = \log_b g(x)$ consists of all x for which $g(x) > 0$.**

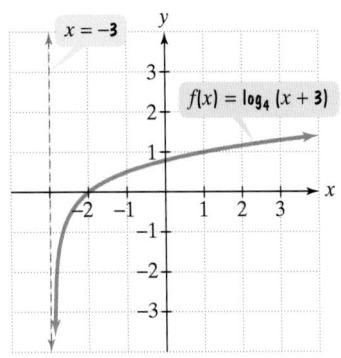

Figure 4.13 The domain of $g(x) = \log_4(x + 3)$ is $(-3, \infty)$.

(**EXAMPLE 7**) **Finding the Domain of a Logarithmic Function**

Find the domain of $f(x) = \log_4(x + 3)$.

Solution The domain of f consists of all x for which $x + 3 > 0$. Solving this inequality for x, we obtain $x > -3$. Thus, the domain of f is $(-3, \infty)$. This is illustrated in **Figure 4.13**. The vertical asymptote is $x = -3$ and all points on the graph of f have x-coordinates that are greater than -3. ●

⊘ Check Point **7** Find the domain of $f(x) = \log_4(x - 5)$.

⑦ Use common logarithms.

Common Logarithms

The logarithmic function with base 10 is called the **common logarithmic function**. The function $f(x) = \log_{10} x$ is usually expressed as $f(x) = \log x$. A calculator with a $\boxed{\text{LOG}}$ key can be used to evaluate common logarithms. Here are some examples:

Logarithm	Most Scientific Calculator Keystrokes	Most Graphing Calculator Keystrokes	Display (or Approximate Display)
log 1000	1000 $\boxed{\text{LOG}}$	$\boxed{\text{LOG}}$ 1000 $\boxed{\text{ENTER}}$	3
$\log\dfrac{5}{2}$	$\boxed{(}$ 5 $\boxed{\div}$ 2 $\boxed{)}$ $\boxed{\text{LOG}}$	$\boxed{\text{LOG}}$ $\boxed{(}$ 5 $\boxed{\div}$ 2 $\boxed{)}$ $\boxed{\text{ENTER}}$	0.39794
$\dfrac{\log 5}{\log 2}$	5 $\boxed{\text{LOG}}$ $\boxed{\div}$ 2 $\boxed{\text{LOG}}$ $\boxed{=}$	$\boxed{\text{LOG}}$ 5 $\boxed{\div}$ $\boxed{\text{LOG}}$ 2 $\boxed{\text{ENTER}}$	2.32193
log(−3)	3 $\boxed{+/-}$ $\boxed{\text{LOG}}$	$\boxed{\text{LOG}}$ $\boxed{(-)}$ 3 $\boxed{\text{ENTER}}$	$\boxed{\text{ERROR}}$

Some graphing calculators display an open parenthesis when the $\boxed{\text{LOG}}$ key is pressed. In this case, remember to close the set of parentheses after entering the function's domain value: $\boxed{\text{LOG}}$ 5 $\boxed{)}$ $\boxed{\div}$ $\boxed{\text{LOG}}$ 2 $\boxed{)}$ $\boxed{\text{ENTER}}$.

The error message or $\boxed{\text{NONREAL ANS}}$ given by many calculators for $\log(-3)$ is a reminder that the domain of the common logarithmic function, $f(x) = \log x$, is the set of positive real numbers. In general, the domain of $f(x) = \log g(x)$ consists of all x for which $g(x) > 0$.

Many real-life phenomena start with rapid growth and then the growth begins to level off. This type of behavior can be modeled by logarithmic functions.

$\boxed{\text{EXAMPLE 8}}$ **Modeling Height of Children**

The percentage of adult height attained by a boy who is x years old can be modeled by

$$f(x) = 29 + 48.8 \log(x + 1),$$

where x represents the boy's age and $f(x)$ represents the percentage of his adult height. Approximately what percentage of his adult height has a boy attained at age eight?

Solution We substitute the boy's age, 8, for x and evaluate the function.

$$\begin{aligned} f(x) &= 29 + 48.8 \log(x + 1) & \text{This is the given function.} \\ f(8) &= 29 + 48.8 \log(8 + 1) & \text{Substitute 8 for x.} \\ &= 29 + 48.8 \log 9 & \text{Graphing calculator keystrokes:} \\ & & 29\ \boxed{+}\ 48.8\ \boxed{\text{LOG}}\ 9\ \boxed{\text{ENTER}} \\ &\approx 76 \end{aligned}$$

Thus, an 8-year-old boy has attained approximately 76% of his adult height. ●

\oslash Check Point **8** Use the function in Example 8 to answer this question: Approximately what percentage of his adult height has a boy attained at age ten?

The basic properties of logarithms that were listed earlier in this section can be applied to common logarithms.

Properties of Common Logarithms

General Properties	Common Logarithms
1. $\log_b 1 = 0$	**1.** $\log 1 = 0$
2. $\log_b b = 1$	**2.** $\log 10 = 1$
3. $\log_b b^x = x$	**3.** $\log 10^x = x$
4. $b^{\log_b x} = x$	**4.** $10^{\log x} = x$

Inverse properties

The property $\log 10^x = x$ can be used to evaluate common logarithms involving powers of 10. For example,

$$\log 100 = \log 10^2 = 2, \quad \log 1000 = \log 10^3 = 3, \quad \text{and} \quad \log 10^{7.1} = 7.1.$$

EXAMPLE 9 **Earthquake Intensity**

The magnitude, R, on the Richter scale of an earthquake of intensity I is given by

$$R = \log\frac{I}{I_0},$$

where I_0 is the intensity of a barely felt zero-level earthquake. The earthquake that destroyed San Francisco in 1906 was $10^{8.3}$ times as intense as a zero-level earthquake. What was its magnitude on the Richter scale?

Solution Because the earthquake was $10^{8.3}$ times as intense as a zero-level earthquake, the intensity, I, is $10^{8.3}\, I_0$.

$$R = \log\frac{I}{I_0} \qquad \text{This is the formula for magnitude on the Richter scale.}$$

$$R = \log\frac{10^{8.3} I_0}{I_0} \qquad \text{Substitute } 10^{8.3} I_0 \text{ for } I.$$

$$= \log 10^{8.3} \qquad \text{Simplify.}$$

$$= 8.3 \qquad \text{Use the property log } 10^x = x.$$

San Francisco's 1906 earthquake registered 8.3 on the Richter scale. ⬤

Check Point 9 Use the formula in Example 9 to solve this problem. If an earthquake is 10,000 times as intense as a zero-level quake ($I = 10{,}000 I_0$), what is its magnitude on the Richter scale?

⑧ Use natural logarithms.

Natural Logarithms

The logarithmic function with base e is called the **natural logarithmic function**. The function $f(x) = \log_e x$ is usually expressed as $f(x) = \ln x$, read "el en of x." A calculator with an ⎡LN⎤ key can be used to evaluate natural logarithms. Keystrokes are identical to those shown for common logarithmic evaluations on page 431.

Like the domain of all logarithmic functions, the domain of the natural logarithmic function $f(x) = \ln x$ is the set of all positive real numbers. Thus, the domain of $f(x) = \ln g(x)$ consists of all x for which $g(x) > 0$.

[−10, 10, 1] by [−10, 10, 1]

Figure 4.14 The domain of $f(x) = \ln(3 - x)$ is $(-\infty, 3)$.

EXAMPLE 10 **Finding Domains of Natural Logarithmic Functions**

Find the domain of each function:

a. $f(x) = \ln(3 - x)$ **b.** $h(x) = \ln(x - 3)^2$.

Solution

a. The domain of f consists of all x for which $3 - x > 0$. Solving this inequality for x, we obtain $x < 3$. Thus, the domain of f is $\{x \mid x < 3\}$ or $(-\infty, 3)$. This is verified by the graph in **Figure 4.14**.

b. The domain of h consists of all x for which $(x - 3)^2 > 0$. It follows that the domain of h is all real numbers except 3. Thus, the domain of h is $\{x \mid x \neq 3\}$ or $(-\infty, 3) \cup (3, \infty)$. This is shown by the graph in **Figure 4.15**. To make it more obvious that 3 is excluded from the domain, we used a ⎡DOT⎤ format. ⬤

[−10, 10, 1] by [−10, 10, 1]

Figure 4.15 3 is excluded from the domain of $h(x) = \ln(x - 3)^2$.

Check Point 10 Find the domain of each function:

a. $f(x) = \ln(4 - x)$ **b.** $h(x) = \ln x^2$.

The basic properties of logarithms that were listed earlier in this section can be applied to natural logarithms.

Properties of Natural Logarithms

General Properties	**Natural Logarithms**
1. $\log_b 1 = 0$	**1.** $\ln 1 = 0$
2. $\log_b b = 1$	**2.** $\ln e = 1$
3. $\log_b b^x = x$	**3.** $\ln e^x = x$
4. $b^{\log_b x} = x$	**4.** $e^{\ln x} = x$

Inverse properties

Examine the inverse properties, $\ln e^x = x$ and $e^{\ln x} = x$. Can you see how \ln and e "undo" one another? For example,

$$\ln e^2 = 2, \quad \ln e^{7x^2} = 7x^2, \quad e^{\ln 2} = 2, \quad \text{and} \quad e^{\ln 7x^2} = 7x^2.$$

EXAMPLE 11 **Dangerous Heat: Temperature in an Enclosed Vehicle**

When the outside air temperature is anywhere from $72°$ to $96°$ Fahrenheit, the temperature in an enclosed vehicle climbs by $43°$ in the first hour. The bar graph in **Figure 4.16** shows the temperature increase throughout the hour. The function

$$f(x) = 13.4 \ln x - 11.6$$

models the temperature increase, $f(x)$, in degrees Fahrenheit, after x minutes. Use the function to find the temperature increase, to the nearest degree, after 50 minutes. How well does the function model the actual increase shown in **Figure 4.16**?

Temperature Increase in an Enclosed Vehicle

Figure 4.16
Source: Professor Jan Null, San Francisco State University

Solution We find the temperature increase after 50 minutes by substituting 50 for x and evaluating the function at 50.

$$f(x) = 13.4 \ln x - 11.6 \qquad \text{This is the given function.}$$
$$f(50) = 13.4 \ln 50 - 11.6 \qquad \text{Substitute 50 for x.}$$
$$\approx 41 \qquad \text{Graphing calculator keystrokes:}$$

13.4 |ln| 50 |−| 11.6 |ENTER| . On some calculators, a parenthesis is needed after 50.

According to the function, the temperature will increase by approximately $41°$ after 50 minutes. Because the increase shown in **Figure 4.16** is $41°$, the function models the actual increase extremely well.

⬤ Check Point **11** Use the function in Example 11 to find the temperature increase, to the nearest degree, after 30 minutes. How well does the function model the actual increase shown in **Figure 4.16**?

The Curious Number e

You will learn more about each curiosity mentioned below if you take calculus.

Figure 4.17

- The number e was named by the Swiss mathematician Leonhard Euler (1707–1783), who proved that it is the limit as $n \to \infty$ of $\left(1 + \dfrac{1}{n}\right)^n$.

- e features in Euler's remarkable relationship $e^{i\pi} = -1$, in which $i = \sqrt{-1}$.

- The first few decimal places of e are fairly easy to remember:
 $e = 2.7\ 1828\ 1828\ 45\ 90\ 45\ldots$

- The best approximation of e using numbers less than 1000 is also easy to remember:
 $e \approx \dfrac{878}{323} \approx 2.71826\ldots$

- Isaac Newton (1642–1727), one of the cofounders of calculus, showed that
 $e^x = 1 + x + \dfrac{x^2}{2!} + \dfrac{x^3}{3!} + \dfrac{x^4}{4!} + \cdots$, from which we obtain $e = 1 + 1 + \dfrac{1}{2!} + \dfrac{1}{3!} + \dfrac{1}{4!} + \cdots$, an infinite sum suitable for calculation because its terms decrease so rapidly. (*Note*: $n!$ (n factorial) is the product of all the consecutive integers from n down to 1: $n! = n(n-1)(n-2)(n-3)\cdot\cdots\cdot3\cdot2\cdot1$.)

- The area of the region bounded by $y = \dfrac{1}{x}$, the x-axis, $x = 1$ and $x = t$ (shaded in **Figure 4.17**) is a function of t, designated by $A(t)$. Grégoire de Saint-Vincent, a Belgian Jesuit (1584–1667), spent his entire professional life attempting to find a formula for $A(t)$. With his student, he showed that $A(t) = \ln t$, becoming one of the first mathematicians to make use of the logarithmic function for something other than a computational device.

Exercise Set 4.2

Practice Exercises

In Exercises 1–8, write each equation in its equivalent exponential form.

1. $4 = \log_2 16$ **2.** $6 = \log_2 64$

3. $2 = \log_3 x$ **4.** $2 = \log_9 x$

5. $5 = \log_b 32$ **6.** $3 = \log_b 27$

7. $\log_6 216 = y$ **8.** $\log_5 125 = y$

In Exercises 9–20, write each equation in its equivalent logarithmic form.

9. $2^3 = 8$ **10.** $5^4 = 625$ **11.** $2^{-4} = \frac{1}{16}$ **12.** $5^{-3} = \frac{1}{125}$

13. $\sqrt[3]{8} = 2$ **14.** $\sqrt[3]{64} = 4$ **15.** $13^2 = x$ **16.** $15^2 = x$

17. $b^3 = 1000$ **18.** $b^3 = 343$ **19.** $7^y = 200$ **20.** $8^y = 300$

In Exercises 21–42, evaluate each expression without using a calculator.

21. $\log_4 16$ **22.** $\log_7 49$ **23.** $\log_2 64$ **24.** $\log_3 27$

25. $\log_5 \frac{1}{5}$ **26.** $\log_6 \frac{1}{6}$ **27.** $\log_2 \frac{1}{8}$ **28.** $\log_3 \frac{1}{9}$

29. $\log_7 \sqrt{7}$ **30.** $\log_6 \sqrt{6}$ **31.** $\log_2 \frac{1}{\sqrt{2}}$ **32.** $\log_3 \frac{1}{\sqrt{3}}$

33. $\log_{64} 8$ **34.** $\log_{81} 9$ **35.** $\log_5 5$ **36.** $\log_{11} 11$

37. $\log_4 1$ **38.** $\log_6 1$ **39.** $\log_5 5^7$ **40.** $\log_4 4^6$

41. $8^{\log_8 19}$ **42.** $7^{\log_7 23}$

43. Graph $f(x) = 4^x$ and $g(x) = \log_4 x$ in the same rectangular coordinate system.

44. Graph $f(x) = 5^x$ and $g(x) = \log_5 x$ in the same rectangular coordinate system.

45. Graph $f(x) = \left(\frac{1}{2}\right)^x$ and $g(x) = \log_{\frac{1}{2}} x$ in the same rectangular coordinate system.

46. Graph $f(x) = \left(\frac{1}{4}\right)^x$ and $g(x) = \log_{\frac{1}{4}} x$ in the same rectangular coordinate system.

In Exercises 47–52, the graph of a logarithmic function is given. Select the function for each graph from the following options:

$$f(x) = \log_3 x,\ g(x) = \log_3(x-1),\ h(x) = \log_3 x - 1,$$
$$F(x) = -\log_3 x,\ G(x) = \log_3(-x),\ H(x) = 1 - \log_3 x.$$

47.

48.

49.

50.

51.

52.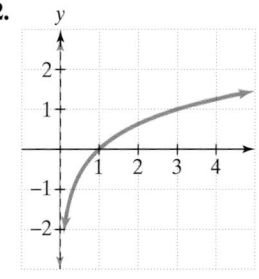

In Exercises 53–58, begin by graphing $f(x) = \log_2 x$. Then use transformations of this graph to graph the given function. What is the vertical asymptote? Use the graphs to determine each function's domain and range.

53. $g(x) = \log_2(x + 1)$

54. $g(x) = \log_2(x + 2)$

55. $h(x) = 1 + \log_2 x$

56. $h(x) = 2 + \log_2 x$

57. $g(x) = \frac{1}{2}\log_2 x$

58. $g(x) = -2\log_2 x$

The figure shows the graph of $f(x) = \log x$. In Exercises 59–64, use transformations of this graph to graph each function. Graph and give equations of the asymptotes. Use the graphs to determine each function's domain and range.

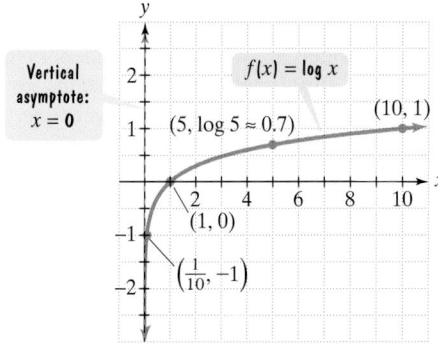

59. $g(x) = \log(x - 1)$

60. $g(x) = \log(x - 2)$

61. $h(x) = \log x - 1$

62. $h(x) = \log x - 2$

63. $g(x) = 1 - \log x$

64. $g(x) = 2 - \log x$

The figure shows the graph of $f(x) = \ln x$. In Exercises 65–74, use transformations of this graph to graph each function. Graph and give equations of the asymptotes. Use the graphs to determine each function's domain and range.

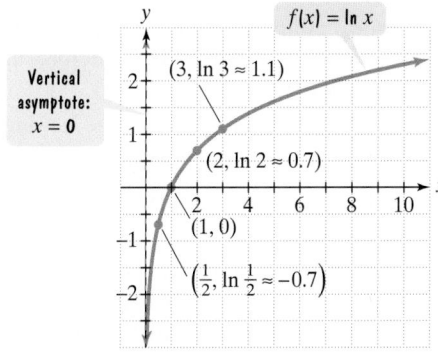

65. $g(x) = \ln(x + 2)$

66. $g(x) = \ln(x + 1)$

67. $h(x) = \ln(2x)$

68. $h(x) = \ln\left(\frac{1}{2}x\right)$

69. $g(x) = 2 \ln x$

70. $g(x) = \frac{1}{2} \ln x$

71. $h(x) = -\ln x$

72. $h(x) = \ln(-x)$

73. $g(x) = 2 - \ln x$

74. $g(x) = 1 - \ln x$

In Exercises 75–80, find the domain of each logarithmic function.

75. $f(x) = \log_5(x + 4)$

76. $f(x) = \log_5(x + 6)$

77. $f(x) = \log(2 - x)$

78. $f(x) = \log(7 - x)$

79. $f(x) = \ln(x - 2)^2$

80. $f(x) = \ln(x - 7)^2$

In Exercises 81–100, evaluate or simplify each expression without using a calculator.

81. $\log 100$

82. $\log 1000$

83. $\log 10^7$

84. $\log 10^8$

85. $10^{\log 33}$

86. $10^{\log 53}$

87. $\ln 1$

88. $\ln e$

89. $\ln e^6$

90. $\ln e^7$

91. $\ln \dfrac{1}{e^6}$

92. $\ln \dfrac{1}{e^7}$

93. $e^{\ln 125}$

94. $e^{\ln 300}$

95. $\ln e^{9x}$

96. $\ln e^{13x}$

97. $e^{\ln 5x^2}$

98. $e^{\ln 7x^2}$

99. $10^{\log\sqrt{x}}$

100. $10^{\log\sqrt[3]{x}}$

Practice Plus

In Exercises 101–104, write each equation in its equivalent exponential form. Then solve for x.

101. $\log_3(x - 1) = 2$

102. $\log_5(x + 4) = 2$

103. $\log_4 x = -3$

104. $\log_{64} x = \dfrac{2}{3}$

In Exercises 105–108, evaluate each expression without using a calculator.

105. $\log_3(\log_7 7)$

106. $\log_5(\log_2 32)$

107. $\log_2(\log_3 81)$

108. $\log(\ln e)$

In Exercises 109–112, find the domain of each logarithmic function.

109. $f(x) = \ln(x^2 - x - 2)$

110. $f(x) = \ln(x^2 - 4x - 12)$

111. $f(x) = \log\left(\dfrac{x + 1}{x - 5}\right)$

112. $f(x) = \log\left(\dfrac{x - 2}{x + 5}\right)$

Application Exercises

The percentage of adult height attained by a girl who is x years old can be modeled by

$$f(x) = 62 + 35 \log(x - 4),$$

where x represents the girl's age (from 5 to 15) and $f(x)$ represents the percentage of her adult height. Use the function to solve Exercises 113–114. Round answers to the nearest tenth of a percent.

113. Approximately what percentage of her adult height has a girl attained at age 13?

114. Approximately what percentage of her adult height has a girl attained at age ten?

The bar graph indicates that the percentage of first-year college students expressing antifeminist views has been declining since 1970. Use this information to solve Exercises 115–116.

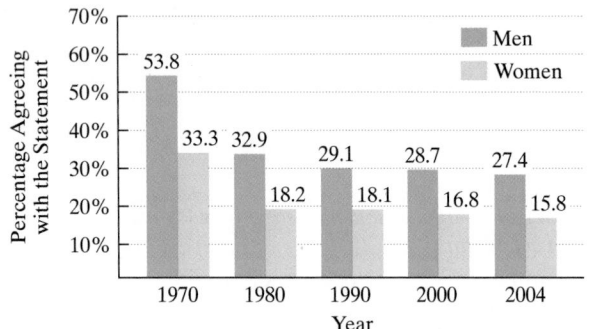

Opposition to Feminism among First-Year United States College Students, 1970–2004

Statement: "The activities of married women are best confined to the home and family."

Source: John Macionis, *Sociology*, Eleventh Edition, Prentice Hall, 2007

115. The function

$$f(x) = -7.49 \ln x + 53$$

models the percentage of first-year college men, $f(x)$, expressing antifeminist views (by agreeing with the statement) x years after 1969.

 a. Use the function to find the percentage of first-year college men expressing antifeminist views in 2004. Round to one decimal place. Does this function value overestimate or underestimate the percentage displayed by the graph? By how much?

 b. Use the function to project the percentage of first-year college men who will express antifeminist views in 2010. Round to one decimal place.

116. The function

$$f(x) = -4.86 \ln x + 32.5$$

models the percentage of first-year college women, $f(x)$, expressing antifeminist views (by agreeing with the statement) x years after 1969.

 a. Use the function to find the percentage of first-year college women expressing antifeminist views in 2004. Round to one decimal place. Does this function value overestimate or underestimate the percentage displayed by the graph? By how much?

 b. Use the function to project the percentage of first-year college women who will express antifeminist views in 2010. Round to one decimal place.

The loudness level of a sound, D, in decibels, is given by the formula

$$D = 10 \log(10^{12} I),$$

where I is the intensity of the sound, in watts per meter². Decibel levels range from 0, a barely audible sound, to 160, a sound resulting in a ruptured eardrum. (Any exposure to sounds of 130 decibels or higher puts a person at immediate risk for hearing damage.) Use the formula to solve Exercises 117–118.

117. The sound of a blue whale can be heard 500 miles away, reaching an intensity of 6.3×10^6 watts per meter². Determine the decibel level of this sound. At close range, can the sound of a blue whale rupture the human eardrum?

118. What is the decibel level of a normal conversation, 3.2×10^{-6} watt per meter²?

119. Students in a psychology class took a final examination. As part of an experiment to see how much of the course content they remembered over time, they took equivalent forms of the exam in monthly intervals thereafter. The average score for the group, $f(t)$, after t months was modeled by the function

$$f(t) = 88 - 15 \ln(t + 1), \qquad 0 \le t \le 12.$$

 a. What was the average score on the original exam?

 b. What was the average score after 2 months? 4 months? 6 months? 8 months? 10 months? one year?

 c. Sketch the graph of f (either by hand or with a graphing utility). Describe what the graph indicates in terms of the material retained by the students.

Writing in Mathematics

120. Describe the relationship between an equation in logarithmic form and an equivalent equation in exponential form.

121. What question can be asked to help evaluate $\log_3 81$?

122. Explain why the logarithm of 1 with base b is 0.

123. Describe the following property using words: $\log_b b^x = x$.

124. Explain how to use the graph of $f(x) = 2^x$ to obtain the graph of $g(x) = \log_2 x$.

125. Explain how to find the domain of a logarithmic function.

126. Logarithmic models are well suited to phenomena in which growth is initially rapid but then begins to level off. Describe something that is changing over time that can be modeled using a logarithmic function.

127. Suppose that a girl is 4 feet 6 inches at age 10. Explain how to use the function in Exercises 113–114 to determine how tall she can expect to be as an adult.

Technology Exercises

In Exercises 128–131, graph f and g in the same viewing rectangle. Then describe the relationship of the graph of g to the graph of f.

128. $f(x) = \ln x, g(x) = \ln(x + 3)$

129. $f(x) = \ln x, g(x) = \ln x + 3$

130. $f(x) = \log x, g(x) = -\log x$

131. $f(x) = \log x, g(x) = \log(x - 2) + 1$

132. Students in a mathematics class took a final examination. They took equivalent forms of the exam in monthly intervals thereafter. The average score, $f(t)$, for the group after t months was modeled by the human memory function $f(t) = 75 - 10 \log(t + 1)$, where $0 \le t \le 12$. Use a graphing utility to graph the function. Then determine how many months will elapse before the average score falls below 65.

133. In parts (a)–(c), graph f and g in the same viewing rectangle.

 a. $f(x) = \ln(3x), g(x) = \ln 3 + \ln x$

 b. $f(x) = \log(5x^2), g(x) = \log 5 + \log x^2$

 c. $f(x) = \ln(2x^3), g(x) = \ln 2 + \ln x^3$

 d. Describe what you observe in parts (a)–(c). Generalize this observation by writing an equivalent expression for $\log_b (MN)$, where $M > 0$ and $N > 0$.

 e. Complete this statement: The logarithm of a product is equal to _____.

134. Graph each of the following functions in the same viewing rectangle and then place the functions in order from the one that increases most slowly to the one that increases most rapidly.

$$y = x,\ y = \sqrt{x},\ y = e^x,\ y = \ln x,\ y = x^x,\ y = x^2$$

Critical Thinking Exercises

Make Sense? *In Exercises 135–138, determine whether each statement makes sense or does not make sense, and explain your reasoning.*

135. I've noticed that exponential functions and logarithmic functions exhibit inverse, or opposite, behavior in many ways. For example, a vertical translation shifts an exponential function's horizontal asymptote and a horizontal translation shifts a logarithmic function's vertical asymptote.

136. I estimate that $\log_8 16$ lies between 1 and 2 because $8^1 = 8$ and $8^2 = 64$.

137. I can evaluate some common logarithms without having to use a calculator.

138. An earthquake of magnitude 8 on the Richter scale is twice as intense as an earthquake of magnitude 4.

In Exercises 139–142, determine whether each statement is true or false. If the statement is false, make the necessary change(s) to produce a true statement.

139. $\dfrac{\log_2 8}{\log_2 4} = \dfrac{8}{4}$

140. $\log(-100) = -2$

141. The domain of $f(x) = \log_2 x$ is $(-\infty, \infty)$.

142. $\log_b x$ is the exponent to which b must be raised to obtain x.

143. Without using a calculator, find the exact value of

$$\frac{\log_3 81 - \log_\pi 1}{\log_{2\sqrt{2}} 8 - \log 0.001}.$$

144. Without using a calculator, find the exact value of $\log_4[\log_3(\log_2 8)]$.

145. Without using a calculator, determine which is the greater number: $\log_4 60$ or $\log_3 40$.

Group Exercise

146. This group exercise involves exploring the way we grow. Group members should create a graph for the function that models the percentage of adult height attained by a boy who is x years old, $f(x) = 29 + 48.8 \log(x + 1)$. Let $x = 1, 2, 3, \ldots, 12$, find function values, and connect the resulting points with a smooth curve. Then create a graph for the function that models the percentage of adult height attained by a girl who is x years old, $g(x) = 62 + 35 \log(x - 4)$. Let $x = 5, 6, 7, \ldots, 15$, find function values, and connect the resulting points with a smooth curve. Group members should then discuss similarities and differences in the growth patterns for boys and girls based on the graphs.

Preview Exercises

Exercises 147–149 will help you prepare for the material covered in the next section. In each exercise, evaluate the indicated logarithmic expressions without using a calculator.

147.
a. Evaluate: $\log_2 32$.
b. Evaluate: $\log_2 8 + \log_2 4$.
c. What can you conclude about $\log_2 32$, or $\log_2(8 \cdot 4)$?

148.
a. Evaluate: $\log_2 16$.
b. Evaluate: $\log_2 32 - \log_2 2$.
c. What can you conclude about

$$\log_2 16,\ \text{or}\ \log_2\!\left(\frac{32}{2}\right)?$$

149.
a. Evaluate: $\log_3 81$.
b. Evaluate: $2 \log_3 9$.
c. What can you conclude about

$$\log_3 81,\ \text{or}\ \log_3 9^2?$$

(Section) **4.3** **Properties of Logarithms**

Objectives

1 Use the product rule.
2 Use the quotient rule.
3 Use the power rule.
4 Expand logarithmic expressions.
5 Condense logarithmic expressions.
6 Use the change-of-base property.

We all learn new things in different ways. In this section, we consider important properties of logarithms. What would be the most effective way for you to learn these properties? Would it be helpful to use your graphing utility and discover one of these properties for yourself? To do so, work Exercise 133 in Exercise Set 4.2 before continuing. Would it be helpful to evaluate certain logarithmic expressions that suggest three of the properties? If this is the case, work Preview Exercises 147–149 in Exercise Set 4.2 before continuing. Would the properties become more meaningful if you could see exactly where they come from? If so, you will find details of the proofs of many of these properties in the appendix. The remainder of our work in this chapter will be based on the properties of logarithms that you learn in this section.

1 Use the product rule.

The Product Rule

Properties of exponents correspond to properties of logarithms. For example, when we multiply with the same base, we add exponents:

$$b^m \cdot b^n = b^{m+n}.$$

This property of exponents, coupled with an awareness that a logarithm is an exponent, suggests the following property, called the **product rule**:

> ### The Product Rule
>
> Let b, M, and N be positive real numbers with $b \neq 1$.
>
> $$\log_b(MN) = \log_b M + \log_b N$$
>
> The logarithm of a product is the sum of the logarithms.

When we use the product rule to write a single logarithm as the sum of two logarithms, we say that we are **expanding a logarithmic expression**. For example, we can use the product rule to expand $\ln(7x)$:

$$\ln(7x) = \ln 7 + \ln x.$$

| The logarithm of a product | is | the sum of the logarithms. |

EXAMPLE 1 **Using the Product Rule**

Use the product rule to expand each logarithmic expression:

a. $\log_4(7 \cdot 5)$ **b.** $\log(10x)$.

Solution

a. $\log_4(7 \cdot 5) = \log_4 7 + \log_4 5$ The logarithm of a product is the sum of the logarithms.

b. $\log(10x) = \log 10 + \log x$ The logarithm of a product is the sum of the logarithms. These are common logarithms with base 10 understood.

$\qquad\qquad = 1 + \log x$ Because $\log_b b = 1$, then log 10 = 1.

Check Point 1 Use the product rule to expand each logarithmic expression:

a. $\log_6(7 \cdot 11)$ **b.** $\log(100x)$.

2 Use the quotient rule.

The Quotient Rule

When we divide with the same base, we subtract exponents:

$$\frac{b^m}{b^n} = b^{m-n}.$$

This property suggests the following property of logarithms, called the **quotient rule**:

> ### The Quotient Rule
>
> Let b, M, and N be positive real numbers with $b \neq 1$.
>
> $$\log_b\left(\frac{M}{N}\right) = \log_b M - \log_b N$$
>
> The logarithm of a quotient is the difference of the logarithms.

When we use the quotient rule to write a single logarithm as the difference of two logarithms, we say that we are **expanding a logarithmic expression**. For example, we can use the quotient rule to expand $\log \dfrac{x}{2}$:

$$\log\left(\frac{x}{2}\right) = \log x - \log 2.$$

The logarithm of a quotient is the difference of the logarithms.

EXAMPLE 2 **Using the Quotient Rule**

Use the quotient rule to expand each logarithmic expression:

a. $\log_7\left(\dfrac{19}{x}\right)$ **b.** $\ln\left(\dfrac{e^3}{7}\right)$.

Solution

a. $\log_7\left(\dfrac{19}{x}\right) = \log_7 19 - \log_7 x$ The logarithm of a quotient is the difference of the logarithms.

b. $\ln\left(\dfrac{e^3}{7}\right) = \ln e^3 - \ln 7$ The logarithm of a quotient is the difference of the logarithms. These are natural logarithms with base e understood.

$\qquad\qquad = 3 - \ln 7$ Because $\ln e^x = x$, then $\ln e^3 = 3$. ●

⊘ Check Point **2** Use the quotient rule to expand each logarithmic expression:

a. $\log_8\left(\dfrac{23}{x}\right)$ **b.** $\ln\left(\dfrac{e^5}{11}\right)$.

③ Use the power rule.

The Power Rule

When an exponential expression is raised to a power, we multiply exponents:

$$(b^m)^n = b^{mn}.$$

This property suggests the following property of logarithms, called the **power rule**:

The Power Rule

Let b and M be positive real numbers with $b \neq 1$, and let p be any real number.

$$\log_b M^p = p \log_b M$$

The logarithm of a number with an exponent is the product of the exponent and the logarithm of that number.

When we use the power rule to "pull the exponent to the front," we say that we are **expanding a logarithmic expression**. For example, we can use the power rule to expand $\ln x^2$:

$$\ln x^2 = 2 \ln x.$$

The logarithm of a number with an exponent is the product of the exponent and the logarithm of that number.

Figure 4.18 shows the graphs of $y = \ln x^2$ and $y = 2 \ln x$ in $[-5, 5, 1]$ by $[-5, 5, 1]$ viewing rectangles. Are $\ln x^2$ and $2 \ln x$ the same? The graphs illustrate that $y = \ln x^2$ and $y = 2 \ln x$ have different domains. The graphs are only the same if $x > 0$. Thus, we should write

$$\ln x^2 = 2 \ln x \text{ for } x > 0.$$

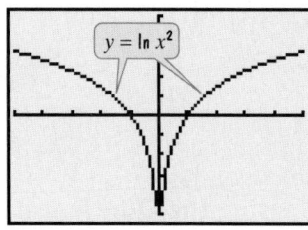
Domain: $(-\infty, 0) \cup (0, \infty)$

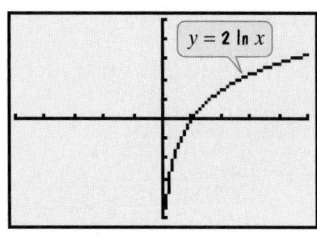
Domain: $(0, \infty)$

Figure 4.18 $\ln x^2$ and $2 \ln x$ have different domains.

When expanding a logarithmic expression, you might want to determine whether the rewriting has changed the domain of the expression. For the rest of this section, assume that all variables and variable expressions represent positive numbers.

EXAMPLE 3 **Using the Power Rule**

Use the power rule to expand each logarithmic expression:

a. $\log_5 7^4$ **b.** $\ln \sqrt{x}$ **c.** $\log(4x)^5$.

Solution

a. $\log_5 7^4 = 4 \log_5 7$ The logarithm of a number with an exponent is the exponent times the logarithm of the number.

b. $\ln \sqrt{x} = \ln x^{\frac{1}{2}}$ Rewrite the radical using a rational exponent.

 $= \frac{1}{2} \ln x$ Use the power rule to bring the exponent to the front.

c. $\log(4x)^5 = 5 \log(4x)$ We immediately apply the power rule because the entire variable expression, 4x, is raised to the 5th power. ⬤

✓ Check Point **3** Use the power rule to expand each logarithmic expression:

 a. $\log_6 3^9$ **b.** $\ln \sqrt[3]{x}$ **c.** $\log(x + 4)^2$.

④ Expand logarithmic expressions.

Expanding Logarithmic Expressions

It is sometimes necessary to use more than one property of logarithms when you expand a logarithmic expression. Properties for expanding logarithmic expressions are as follows:

Properties for Expanding Logarithmic Expressions

For $M > 0$ and $N > 0$:

 1. $\log_b(MN) = \log_b M + \log_b N$ Product rule

 2. $\log_b\left(\dfrac{M}{N}\right) = \log_b M - \log_b N$ Quotient rule

 3. $\log_b M^p = p \log_b M$ Power rule

Study Tip

The graphs show that

$$\ln(x + 3) \neq \ln x + \ln 3.$$

$y = \ln x$ shifted 3 units left	$y = \ln x$ shifted $\ln 3$ units up

In general,

$$\log_b(M + N) \neq \log_b M + \log_b N.$$

$[-4, 5, 1]$ by $[-3, 3, 1]$

Try to avoid the following errors:

Incorrect!

$$\log_b(M + N) = \log_b M + \log_b N$$
$$\log_b(M - N) = \log_b M - \log_b N$$
$$\log_b(M \cdot N) = \log_b M \cdot \log_b N$$
$$\log_b\left(\frac{M}{N}\right) = \frac{\log_b M}{\log_b N}$$
$$\frac{\log_b M}{\log_b N} = \log_b M - \log_b N$$
$$\log_b(MN^p) = p\log_b(MN)$$

EXAMPLE 4 **Expanding Logarithmic Expressions**

Use logarithmic properties to expand each expression as much as possible:

 a. $\log_b(x^2\sqrt{y})$ **b.** $\log_6\left(\dfrac{\sqrt[3]{x}}{36y^4}\right)$.

Solution We will have to use two or more of the properties for expanding logarithms in each part of this example.

a. $\log_b(x^2\sqrt{y}) = \log_b\left(x^2 y^{\frac{1}{2}}\right)$ *Use exponential notation.*

 $\qquad\qquad\quad = \log_b x^2 + \log_b y^{\frac{1}{2}}$ *Use the product rule.*

 $\qquad\qquad\quad = 2\log_b x + \dfrac{1}{2}\log_b y$ *Use the power rule.*

b. $\log_6\left(\dfrac{\sqrt[3]{x}}{36y^4}\right) = \log_6\left(\dfrac{x^{\frac{1}{3}}}{36y^4}\right)$ *Use exponential notation.*

 $\qquad\qquad\qquad = \log_6 x^{\frac{1}{3}} - \log_6(36y^4)$ *Use the quotient rule.*

 $\qquad\qquad\qquad = \log_6 x^{\frac{1}{3}} - (\log_6 36 + \log_6 y^4)$ *Use the product rule on* $\log_6(36y^4)$.

 $\qquad\qquad\qquad = \dfrac{1}{3}\log_6 x - (\log_6 36 + 4\log_6 y)$ *Use the power rule.*

 $\qquad\qquad\qquad = \dfrac{1}{3}\log_6 x - \log_6 36 - 4\log_6 y$ *Apply the distributive property.*

 $\qquad\qquad\qquad = \dfrac{1}{3}\log_6 x - 2 - 4\log_6 y$ *$\log_6 36 = 2$ because 2 is the power to which we must raise 6 to get 36. $(6^2 = 36)$*

Check Point 4 Use logarithmic properties to expand each expression as much as possible:

 a. $\log_b\left(x^4\sqrt[3]{y}\right)$ **b.** $\log_5\left(\dfrac{\sqrt{x}}{25y^3}\right)$.

 Condense logarithmic expressions.

Condensing Logarithmic Expressions

To **condense a logarithmic expression**, we write the sum or difference of two or more logarithmic expressions as a single logarithmic expression. We use the properties of logarithms to do so.

Study Tip

These properties are the same as those in the box on page 440. The only difference is that we've reversed the sides in each property from the previous box.

Properties for Condensing Logarithmic Expressions

For $M > 0$ and $N > 0$:

1. $\log_b M + \log_b N = \log_b(MN)$ Product rule

2. $\log_b M - \log_b N = \log_b\left(\dfrac{M}{N}\right)$ Quotient rule

3. $p \log_b M = \log_b M^p$ Power rule

EXAMPLE 5 **Condensing Logarithmic Expressions**

Write as a single logarithm:

 a. $\log_4 2 + \log_4 32$ **b.** $\log(4x - 3) - \log x.$

Solution

 a. $\log_4 2 + \log_4 32 = \log_4(2 \cdot 32)$ Use the product rule.

 $= \log_4 64$ We now have a single logarithm. However, we can simplify.

 $= 3$ $\log_4 64 = 3$ because $4^3 = 64$.

 b. $\log(4x - 3) - \log x = \log\left(\dfrac{4x - 3}{x}\right)$ Use the quotient rule.

✓ **Check Point 5** Write as a single logarithm:

 a. $\log 25 + \log 4$ **b.** $\log(7x + 6) - \log x.$

Coefficients of logarithms must be 1 before you can condense them using the product and quotient rules. For example, to condense

$$2 \ln x + \ln(x + 1),$$

the coefficient of the first term must be 1. We use the power rule to rewrite the coefficient as an exponent:

> 1. Use the power rule to make the number in front an exponent.

$$2 \ln x + \ln(x + 1) = \ln x^2 + \ln(x + 1) = \ln[x^2(x + 1)].$$

> 2. Use the product rule. The sum of logarithms with coefficients of 1 is the logarithm of the product.

EXAMPLE 6 **Condensing Logarithmic Expressions**

Write as a single logarithm:

 a. $\frac{1}{2}\log x + 4\log(x - 1)$ **b.** $3\ln(x + 7) - \ln x$

 c. $4\log_b x - 2\log_b 6 - \frac{1}{2}\log_b y.$

Solution

a. $\frac{1}{2}\log x + 4\log(x - 1)$

$= \log x^{\frac{1}{2}} + \log(x - 1)^4$ Use the power rule so that all coefficients are 1.

$= \log\left[x^{\frac{1}{2}}(x - 1)^4\right]$ Use the product rule. The condensed form can be expressed as $\log\left[\sqrt{x}(x - 1)^4\right]$.

b. $3\ln(x + 7) - \ln x$

$= \ln(x + 7)^3 - \ln x$ Use the power rule so that all coefficients are 1.

$= \ln\left[\dfrac{(x + 7)^3}{x}\right]$ Use the quotient rule.

c. $4\log_b x - 2\log_b 6 - \frac{1}{2}\log_b y$

$= \log_b x^4 - \log_b 6^2 - \log_b y^{\frac{1}{2}}$ Use the power rule so that all coefficients are 1.

$= \log_b x^4 - \left(\log_b 36 + \log_b y^{\frac{1}{2}}\right)$ Rewrite as a single subtraction.

$= \log_b x^4 - \log_b\left(36y^{\frac{1}{2}}\right)$ Use the product rule.

$= \log_b\left(\dfrac{x^4}{36y^{\frac{1}{2}}}\right)$ or $\log_b\left(\dfrac{x^4}{36\sqrt{y}}\right)$ Use the quotient rule.

⬤

⊘ Check Point **6** Write as a single logarithm:

a. $2\ln x + \frac{1}{3}\ln(x + 5)$ **b.** $2\log(x - 3) - \log x$

c. $\frac{1}{4}\log_b x - 2\log_b 5 - 10\log_b y$.

⑥ Use the change-of-base property.

The Change-of-Base Property

We have seen that calculators give the values of both common logarithms (base 10) and natural logarithms (base e). To find a logarithm with any other base, we can use the following change-of-base property:

The Change-of-Base Property

For any logarithmic bases a and b, and any positive number M,

$$\log_b M = \frac{\log_a M}{\log_a b}.$$

The logarithm of M with base b is equal to the logarithm of M with any new base divided by the logarithm of b with that new base.

In the change-of-base property, base b is the base of the original logarithm. Base a is a new base that we introduce. Thus, the change-of-base property allows us to change from base b to *any* new base a, as long as the newly introduced base is a positive number not equal to 1.

The change-of-base property is used to write a logarithm in terms of quantities that can be evaluated with a calculator. Because calculators contain keys for common (base 10) and natural (base e) logarithms, we will frequently introduce base 10 or base e.

Change-of-Base Property	Introducing Common Logarithms	Introducing Natural Logarithms
$\log_b M = \dfrac{\log_a M}{\log_a b}$	$\log_b M = \dfrac{\log_{10} M}{\log_{10} b}$	$\log_b M = \dfrac{\log_e M}{\log_e b}$
a is the new introduced base.	10 is the new introduced base.	e is the new introduced base.

Using the notations for common logarithms and natural logarithms, we have the following results:

The Change-of-Base Property: Introducing Common and Natural Logarithms

Introducing Common Logarithms	**Introducing Natural Logarithms**
$\log_b M = \dfrac{\log M}{\log b}$	$\log_b M = \dfrac{\ln M}{\ln b}$

EXAMPLE 7 Changing Base to Common Logarithms

Use common logarithms to evaluate $\log_5 140$.

Solution Because $\quad \log_b M = \dfrac{\log M}{\log b}$,

$$\log_5 140 = \frac{\log 140}{\log 5}$$

$$\approx 3.07.$$

Use a calculator: 140 |LOG| |÷| 5 |LOG|
|=| or |LOG| 140 |÷| |LOG| 5 |ENTER| .
On some calculators, parentheses are needed after 140 and 5.

This means that $\log_5 140 \approx 3.07$.

Discovery

Find a reasonable estimate of $\log_5 140$ to the nearest whole number. To what power can you raise 5 in order to get 140? Compare your estimate to the value obtained in Example 7.

☑ **Check Point 7** Use common logarithms to evaluate $\log_7 2506$.

EXAMPLE 8 Changing Base to Natural Logarithms

Use natural logarithms to evaluate $\log_5 140$.

Solution Because $\quad \log_b M = \dfrac{\ln M}{\ln b}$,

$$\log_5 140 = \frac{\ln 140}{\ln 5}$$

$$\approx 3.07.$$

Use a calculator: 140 |LN| |÷| 5 |LN| |=|
or |LN| 140 |÷| |LN| 5 |ENTER| .
On some calculators, parentheses are needed after 140 and 5.

We have again shown that $\log_5 140 \approx 3.07$.

☑ **Check Point 8** Use natural logarithms to evaluate $\log_7 2506$.

Technology

We can use the change-of-base property to graph logarithmic functions with bases other than 10 or e on a graphing utility. For example, **Figure 4.19** shows the graphs of

$$y = \log_2 x \quad \text{and} \quad y = \log_{20} x$$

in a $[0, 10, 1]$ by $[-3, 3, 1]$ viewing rectangle. Because $\log_2 x = \dfrac{\ln x}{\ln 2}$ and $\log_{20} x = \dfrac{\ln x}{\ln 20}$, the functions are entered as

$$y_1 = \boxed{LN}\,x\ \boxed{\div}\boxed{LN}\,2$$

$$\text{and}\quad y_2 = \boxed{LN}\,x\ \boxed{\div}\boxed{LN}\,20.$$

On some calculators, parentheses are needed after x, 2, and 20.

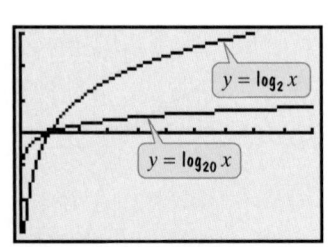

Figure 4.19 Using the change-of-base property to graph logarithmic functions

Exercise Set 4.3

Practice Exercises

In Exercises 1–40, use properties of logarithms to expand each logarithmic expression as much as possible. Where possible, evaluate logarithmic expressions without using a calculator.

1. $\log_5(7 \cdot 3)$ **2.** $\log_8(13 \cdot 7)$ **3.** $\log_7(7x)$

4. $\log_9(9x)$ **5.** $\log(1000x)$ **6.** $\log(10{,}000x)$

7. $\log_7\left(\dfrac{7}{x}\right)$ **8.** $\log_9\left(\dfrac{9}{x}\right)$ **9.** $\log\left(\dfrac{x}{100}\right)$

10. $\log\left(\dfrac{x}{1000}\right)$ **11.** $\log_4\left(\dfrac{64}{y}\right)$ **12.** $\log_5\left(\dfrac{125}{y}\right)$

13. $\ln\left(\dfrac{e^2}{5}\right)$ **14.** $\ln\left(\dfrac{e^4}{8}\right)$ **15.** $\log_b x^3$

16. $\log_b x^7$ **17.** $\log N^{-6}$ **18.** $\log M^{-8}$

19. $\ln \sqrt[5]{x}$ **20.** $\ln \sqrt[7]{x}$ **21.** $\log_b(x^2 y)$

22. $\log_b(xy^3)$ **23.** $\log_4\left(\dfrac{\sqrt{x}}{64}\right)$ **24.** $\log_5\left(\dfrac{\sqrt{x}}{25}\right)$

25. $\log_6\left(\dfrac{36}{\sqrt{x+1}}\right)$ **26.** $\log_8\left(\dfrac{64}{\sqrt{x+1}}\right)$ **27.** $\log_b\left(\dfrac{x^2 y}{z^2}\right)$

28. $\log_b\left(\dfrac{x^3 y}{z^2}\right)$ **29.** $\log\sqrt{100x}$ **30.** $\ln\sqrt{ex}$

31. $\log_3\sqrt[3]{\dfrac{x}{y}}$ **32.** $\log_5\sqrt[5]{\dfrac{x}{y}}$ **33.** $\log_b\left(\dfrac{\sqrt{x}\,y^3}{z^3}\right)$

34. $\log_b\left(\dfrac{\sqrt[3]{x}\,y^4}{z^5}\right)$ **35.** $\log_5\sqrt[3]{\dfrac{x^2 y}{25}}$ **36.** $\log_2\sqrt[5]{\dfrac{xy^4}{16}}$

37. $\ln\left[\dfrac{x^3\sqrt{x^2+1}}{(x+1)^4}\right]$ **38.** $\ln\left[\dfrac{x^4\sqrt{x^2+3}}{(x+3)^5}\right]$

39. $\log\left[\dfrac{10x^2\sqrt[3]{1-x}}{7(x+1)^2}\right]$ **40.** $\log\left[\dfrac{100x^3\sqrt[3]{5-x}}{3(x+7)^2}\right]$

In Exercises 41–70, use properties of logarithms to condense each logarithmic expression. Write the expression as a single logarithm whose coefficient is 1. Where possible, evaluate logarithmic expressions without using a calculator.

41. $\log 5 + \log 2$ **42.** $\log 250 + \log 4$

43. $\ln x + \ln 7$ **44.** $\ln x + \ln 3$

45. $\log_2 96 - \log_2 3$ **46.** $\log_3 405 - \log_3 5$

47. $\log(2x+5) - \log x$ **48.** $\log(3x+7) - \log x$

49. $\log x + 3\log y$ **50.** $\log x + 7\log y$

51. $\frac{1}{2}\ln x + \ln y$ **52.** $\frac{1}{3}\ln x + \ln y$

53. $2\log_b x + 3\log_b y$ **54.** $5\log_b x + 6\log_b y$

55. $5\ln x - 2\ln y$ **56.** $7\ln x - 3\ln y$

57. $3\ln x - \frac{1}{3}\ln y$ **58.** $2\ln x - \frac{1}{2}\ln y$

59. $4\ln(x+6) - 3\ln x$ **60.** $8\ln(x+9) - 4\ln x$

61. $3\ln x + 5\ln y - 6\ln z$ **62.** $4\ln x + 7\ln y - 3\ln z$

63. $\frac{1}{2}(\log x + \log y)$ **64.** $\frac{1}{3}(\log_4 x - \log_4 y)$

65. $\frac{1}{2}(\log_5 x + \log_5 y) - 2\log_5(x+1)$

66. $\frac{1}{3}(\log_4 x - \log_4 y) + 2\log_4(x+1)$

67. $\frac{1}{3}[2\ln(x+5) - \ln x - \ln(x^2-4)]$

68. $\frac{1}{3}[5\ln(x+6) - \ln x - \ln(x^2-25)]$

69. $\log x + \log(x^2-1) - \log 7 - \log(x+1)$

70. $\log x + \log(x^2-4) - \log 15 - \log(x+2)$

In Exercises 71–78, use common logarithms or natural logarithms and a calculator to evaluate to four decimal places.

71. $\log_5 13$ **72.** $\log_6 17$ **73.** $\log_{14} 87.5$

74. $\log_{16} 57.2$ **75.** $\log_{0.1} 17$ **76.** $\log_{0.3} 19$

77. $\log_\pi 63$ **78.** $\log_\pi 400$

In Exercises 79–82, use a graphing utility and the change-of-base property to graph each function.

79. $y = \log_3 x$ **80.** $y = \log_{15} x$

81. $y = \log_2(x+2)$ **82.** $y = \log_3(x-2)$

Practice Plus

In Exercises 83–88, let $\log_b 2 = A$ and $\log_b 3 = C$. Write each expression in terms of A and C.

83. $\log_b \frac{3}{2}$ **84.** $\log_b 6$ **85.** $\log_b 8$

86. $\log_b 81$ **87.** $\log_b\sqrt{\dfrac{2}{27}}$ **88.** $\log_b\sqrt{\dfrac{3}{16}}$

In Exercises 89–102, determine whether each equation is true or false. Where possible, show work to support your conclusion. If the statement is false, make the necessary change(s) to produce a true statement.

89. $\ln e = 0$ **90.** $\ln 0 = e$

91. $\log_4(2x^3) = 3\log_4(2x)$ **92.** $\ln(8x^3) = 3\ln(2x)$

93. $x\log 10^x = x^2$ **94.** $\ln(x+1) = \ln x + \ln 1$

95. $\ln(5x) + \ln 1 = \ln(5x)$ **96.** $\ln x + \ln(2x) = \ln(3x)$

97. $\log(x+3) - \log(2x) = \dfrac{\log(x+3)}{\log(2x)}$

98. $\dfrac{\log(x+2)}{\log(x-1)} = \log(x+2) - \log(x-1)$

99. $\log_6\left(\dfrac{x-1}{x^2+4}\right) = \log_6(x-1) - \log_6(x^2+4)$

100. $\log_6[4(x+1)] = \log_6 4 + \log_6(x+1)$

101. $\log_3 7 = \dfrac{1}{\log_7 3}$ **102.** $e^x = \dfrac{1}{\ln x}$

Application Exercises

103. The loudness level of a sound can be expressed by comparing the sound's intensity to the intensity of a sound barely audible to the human ear. The formula

$$D = 10(\log I - \log I_0)$$

describes the loudness level of a sound, D, in decibels, where I is the intensity of the sound, in watts per meter2, and I_0 is the intensity of a sound barely audible to the human ear.

a. Express the formula so that the expression in parentheses is written as a single logarithm.

b. Use the form of the formula from part (a) to answer this question: If a sound has an intensity 100 times the intensity of a softer sound, how much larger on the decibel scale is the loudness level of the more intense sound?

104. The formula

$$t = \frac{1}{c}[\ln A - \ln(A - N)]$$

describes the time, t, in weeks, that it takes to achieve mastery of a portion of a task, where A is the maximum learning possible, N is the portion of the learning that is to be achieved, and c is a constant used to measure an individual's learning style.

a. Express the formula so that the expression in brackets is written as a single logarithm.

b. The formula is also used to determine how long it will take chimpanzees and apes to master a task. For example, a typical chimpanzee learning sign language can master a maximum of 65 signs. Use the form of the formula from part (a) to answer this question: How many weeks will it take a chimpanzee to master 30 signs if c for that chimp is 0.03?

Writing in Mathematics

105. Describe the product rule for logarithms and give an example.

106. Describe the quotient rule for logarithms and give an example.

107. Describe the power rule for logarithms and give an example.

108. Without showing the details, explain how to condense $\ln x - 2\ln(x + 1)$.

109. Describe the change-of-base property and give an example.

110. Explain how to use your calculator to find $\log_{14} 283$.

111. You overhear a student talking about a property of logarithms in which division becomes subtraction. Explain what the student means by this.

112. Find $\ln 2$ using a calculator. Then calculate each of the following: $1 - \frac{1}{2}$; $\quad 1 - \frac{1}{2} + \frac{1}{3}$; $\quad 1 - \frac{1}{2} + \frac{1}{3} - \frac{1}{4}$; $1 - \frac{1}{2} + \frac{1}{3} - \frac{1}{4} + \frac{1}{5}$; Describe what you observe.

Technology Exercises

113. a. Use a graphing utility (and the change-of-base property) to graph $y = \log_3 x$.

b. Graph $y = 2 + \log_3 x$, $y = \log_3(x + 2)$, and $y = -\log_3 x$ in the same viewing rectangle as $y = \log_3 x$. Then describe the change or changes that need to be made to the graph of $y = \log_3 x$ to obtain each of these three graphs.

114. Graph $y = \log x$, $y = \log(10x)$, and $y = \log(0.1x)$ in the same viewing rectangle. Describe the relationship among the three graphs. What logarithmic property accounts for this relationship?

115. Use a graphing utility and the change-of-base property to graph $y = \log_3 x$, $y = \log_{25} x$, and $y = \log_{100} x$ in the same viewing rectangle.

a. Which graph is on the top in the interval $(0, 1)$? Which is on the bottom?

b. Which graph is on the top in the interval $(1, \infty)$? Which is on the bottom?

c. Generalize by writing a statement about which graph is on top, which is on the bottom, and in which intervals, using $y = \log_b x$ where $b > 1$.

Disprove each statement in Exercises 116–120 by

a. *letting y equal a positive constant of your choice, and*

b. *using a graphing utility to graph the function on each side of the equal sign. The two functions should have different graphs, showing that the equation is not true in general.*

116. $\log(x + y) = \log x + \log y$

117. $\log\left(\dfrac{x}{y}\right) = \dfrac{\log x}{\log y}$ **118.** $\ln(x - y) = \ln x - \ln y$

119. $\ln(xy) = (\ln x)(\ln y)$ **120.** $\dfrac{\ln x}{\ln y} = \ln x - \ln y$

Critical Thinking Exercises

Make Sense? *In Exercises 121–124, determine whether each statement makes sense or does not make sense, and explain your reasoning.*

121. Because I cannot simplify the expression $b^m + b^n$ by adding exponents, there is no property for the logarithm of a sum.

122. Because logarithms are exponents, the product, quotient, and power rules remind me of properties for operations with exponents.

123. I can use any positive number other than 1 in the change-of-base property, but the only practical bases are 10 and e because my calculator gives logarithms for these two bases.

124. I expanded $\log_4 \sqrt{\dfrac{x}{y}}$ by writing the radical using a rational exponent and then applying the quotient rule, obtaining $\dfrac{1}{2}\log_4 x - \log_4 y$.

In Exercises 125–132, determine whether each statement is true or false. If the statement is false, make the necessary change(s) to produce a true statement.

125. $\ln \sqrt{2} = \dfrac{\ln 2}{2}$

126. $\dfrac{\log_7 49}{\log_7 7} = \log_7 49 - \log_7 7$

127. $\log_b(x^3 + y^3) = 3\log_b x + 3\log_b y$

128. $\log_b(xy)^5 = (\log_b x + \log_b y)^5$

129. Use the change-of-base property to prove that

$$\log e = \frac{1}{\ln 10}.$$

130. If $\log 3 = A$ and $\log 7 = B$, find $\log_7 9$ in terms of A and B.

131. Write as a single term that does not contain a logarithm:

$$e^{\ln 8x^5 - \ln 2x^2}.$$

132. If $f(x) = \log_b x$, show that

$$\frac{f(x + h) - f(x)}{h} = \log_b\left(1 + \frac{h}{x}\right)^{\frac{1}{h}}, h \neq 0.$$

Preview Exercises

Exercises 133–135 will help you prepare for the material covered in the next section.

133. Solve for x:° $a(x - 2) = b(2x + 3)$.

134. Solve: $x(x - 7) = 3$.

135. Solve: $\dfrac{x + 2}{4x + 3} = \dfrac{1}{x}$.

Chapter 4 Mid-Chapter Check Point

What You Know: We evaluated and graphed exponential functions $[f(x) = b^x, b > 0$ and $b \neq 1]$, including the natural exponential function $[f(x) = e^x, e \approx 2.718]$. A function has an inverse that is a function if there is no horizontal line that intersects the function's graph more than once. The exponential function passes this horizontal line test and we called the inverse of the exponential function with base b the logarithmic function with base b. We learned that $y = \log_b x$ is equivalent to $b^y = x$. We evaluated and graphed logarithmic functions, including the common logarithmic function $[f(x) = \log_{10} x$ or $f(x) = \log x]$ and the natural logarithmic function $[f(x) = \log_e x$ or $f(x) = \ln x]$. We learned to use transformations to graph exponential and logarithmic functions. Finally, we used properties of logarithms to expand and condense logarithmic expressions.

In Exercises 1–5, graph f and g in the same rectangular coordinate system. Graph and give equations of all asymptotes. Give each function's domain and range.

1. $f(x) = 2^x$ and $g(x) = 2^x - 3$

2. $f(x) = \left(\frac{1}{2}\right)^x$ and $g(x) = \left(\frac{1}{2}\right)^{x-1}$

3. $f(x) = e^x$ and $g(x) = \ln x$

4. $f(x) = \log_2 x$ and $g(x) = \log_2(x - 1) + 1$

5. $g(x) = \log_{\frac{1}{2}} x$ and $g(x) = -2 \log_{\frac{1}{2}} x$

In Exercises 6–9, find the domain of each function.

6. $f(x) = \log_3(x + 6)$

7. $g(x) = \log_3 x + 6$

8. $h(x) = \log_3(x + 6)^2$

9. $f(x) = 3^{x+6}$

In Exercises 10–20, evaluate each expression without using a calculator. If evaluation is not possible, state the reason.

10. $\log_2 8 + \log_5 25$

11. $\log_3 \frac{1}{9}$

12. $\log_{100} 10$

13. $\log \sqrt[3]{10}$

14. $\log_2(\log_3 81)$

15. $\log_3\left(\log_2 \frac{1}{8}\right)$

16. $6^{\log_6 5}$

17. $\ln e^{\sqrt{7}}$

18. $10^{\log 13}$

19. $\log_{100} 0.1$

20. $\log_\pi \pi^{\sqrt{\pi}}$

In Exercises 21–22, expand and evaluate numerical terms.

21. $\log\left(\dfrac{\sqrt{xy}}{1000}\right)$

22. $\ln(e^{19} x^{20})$

In Exercises 23–25, write each expression as a single logarithm.

23. $8 \log_7 x - \frac{1}{3}\log_7 y$

24. $7 \log_5 x + 2 \log_5 x$

25. $\frac{1}{2}\ln x - 3 \ln y - \ln(z - 2)$

26. Use the formulas

$$A = P\left(1 + \frac{r}{n}\right)^{nt} \quad \text{and} \quad A = Pe^{rt}$$

to solve this exercise. You decide to invest $8000 for 3 years at an annual rate of 8%. How much more is the return if the interest is compounded continuously than if it is compounded monthly? Round to the nearest dollar.

Section 4.4 Exponential and Logarithmic Equations

Objectives

1 Use like bases to solve exponential equations.

2 Use logarithms to solve exponential equations.

3 Use the definition of a logarithm to solve logarithmic equations.

4 Use the one-to-one property of logarithms to solve logarithmic equations.

5 Solve applied problems involving exponential and logarithmic equations.

At age 20, you inherit $30,000. You'd like to put aside $25,000 and eventually have over half a million dollars for early retirement. Is this possible? In this section, you will see how techniques for solving equations with variable exponents provide an answer to this question.

Exponential Equations

An **exponential equation** is an equation containing a variable in an exponent. Examples of exponential equations include

$$2^{3x-8} = 16, \quad 4^x = 15, \quad \text{and} \quad 40e^{0.6x} = 240.$$

1 Use like bases to solve exponential equations.

Some exponential equations can be solved by expressing each side of the equation as a power of the same base. All exponential functions are one-to-one— that is, no two different ordered pairs have the same second component. Thus, if b is a positive number other than 1 and $b^M = b^N$, then $M = N$.

Solving Exponential Equations by Expressing Each Side as a Power of the Same Base

$$\text{If } b^M = b^N, \text{ then } M = N.$$

| Express each side as a power of the same base. | Set the exponents equal to each other. |

1. Rewrite the equation in the form $b^M = b^N$.
2. Set $M = N$.
3. Solve for the variable.

Technology

Graphic Connections

The graphs of

$$y_1 = 2^{3x-8}$$
$$\text{and} \quad y_2 = 16$$

have an intersection point whose x-coordinate is 4. This verifies that $\{4\}$ is the solution set of $2^{3x-8} = 16$.

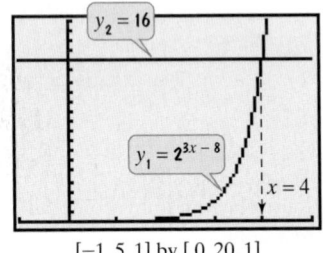

$[-1, 5, 1]$ by $[0, 20, 1]$

EXAMPLE 1 Solving Exponential Equations

Solve: **a.** $2^{3x-8} = 16$ **b.** $27^{x+3} = 9^{x-1}$.

Solution In each equation, express both sides as a power of the same base. Then set the exponents equal to each other and solve for the variable.

a. Because 16 is 2^4, we express each side of $2^{3x-8} = 16$ in terms of base 2.

$2^{3x-8} = 16$	This is the given equation.
$2^{3x-8} = 2^4$	Write each side as a power of the same base.
$3x - 8 = 4$	If $b^M = b^N$, $b > 0$ and $b \neq 1$, then $M = N$.
$3x = 12$	Add 8 to both sides.
$x = 4$	Divide both sides by 3.

Substituting 4 for x into the original equation produces the true statement $16 = 16$. The solution set is $\{4\}$.

b. Because $27 = 3^3$ and $9 = 3^2$, we can express both sides of $27^{x+3} = 9^{x-1}$ in terms of base 3.

$27^{x+3} = 9^{x-1}$	This is the given equation.
$(3^3)^{x+3} = (3^2)^{x-1}$	Write each side as a power of the same base.
$3^{3(x+3)} = 3^{2(x-1)}$	When an exponential expression is raised to a power, multiply exponents.
$3(x + 3) = 2(x - 1)$	If two powers of the same base are equal, then the exponents are equal.
$3x + 9 = 2x - 2$	Apply the distributive property.
$x + 9 = -2$	Subtract 2x from both sides.
$x = -11$	Subtract 9 from both sides.

Substituting -11 for x into the original equation produces $27^{-8} = 9^{-12}$, which simplifies to the true statement $3^{-24} = 3^{-24}$. The solution set is $\{-11\}$.

 Check Point 1 Solve: **a.** $5^{3x-6} = 125$ **b.** $8^{x+2} = 4^{x-3}$.

2 Use logarithms to solve exponential equations.

Most exponential equations cannot be rewritten so that each side has the same base. Here are two examples:

$$4^x = 15 \qquad\qquad 10^x = 120{,}000.$$

| We cannot rewrite both sides in terms of base 2 or base 4. | We cannot rewrite both sides in terms of base 10. |

Logarithms are extremely useful in solving these equations. The solution begins with isolating the exponential expression. Notice that the exponential expression is already isolated in both $4^x = 15$ and $10^x = 120{,}000$. Then we take the logarithm on both sides. Why can we do this? All logarithmic relations are functions. Thus, if M and N are positive real numbers and $M = N$, then $\log_b M = \log_b N$.

The base that is used when taking the logarithm on both sides of an equation can be any base at all. If the exponential equation involves base 10, as in $10^x = 120{,}000$, we'll take the common logarithm on both sides. If the exponential equation involves any other base, as in $4^x = 15$, we'll take the natural logarithm on both sides.

Using Logarithms to Solve Exponential Equations

1. Isolate the exponential expression.

2. Take the natural logarithm on both sides of the equation for bases other than 10. Take the common logarithm on both sides of the equation for base 10.

3. Simplify using one of the following properties:

$$\ln b^x = x \ln b \quad \text{or} \quad \ln e^x = x \quad \text{or} \quad \log 10^x = x.$$

4. Solve for the variable.

(**EXAMPLE 2**) **Solving Exponential Equations**

Solve: **a.** $4^x = 15$ **b.** $10^x = 120{,}000$.

Solution We will use the natural logarithmic function to solve $4^x = 15$ and the common logarithmic function to solve $10^x = 120{,}000$.

a. Because the exponential expression, 4^x, is already isolated on the left side of $4^x = 15$, we begin by taking the natural logarithm on both sides of the equation.

$$4^x = 15 \qquad \text{This is the given equation.}$$
$$\ln 4^x = \ln 15 \qquad \text{Take the natural logarithm on both sides.}$$
$$x \ln 4 = \ln 15 \qquad \text{Use the power rule and bring the variable exponent to the front: } \ln b^x = x \ln b.$$
$$x = \frac{\ln 15}{\ln 4} \qquad \text{Solve for x by dividing both sides by ln 4.}$$

Discovery

Keep in mind that the base used when taking the logarithm on both sides of an equation can be any base at all. Solve $4^x = 15$ by taking the common logarithm on both sides. Solve again, this time taking the logarithm with base 4 on both sides. Use the change-of-base property to show that the solutions are the same as the one obtained in Example 2(a).

We now have an exact value for x. We use the exact value for x in the equation's solution set. Thus, the equation's solution is $\dfrac{\ln 15}{\ln 4}$ and the solution set is $\left\{ \dfrac{\ln 15}{\ln 4} \right\}$. We can obtain a decimal approximation by using a calculator: $x \approx 1.95$. Because $4^2 = 16$, it seems reasonable that the solution to $4^x = 15$ is approximately 1.95.

b. Because the exponential expression, 10^x, is already isolated on the left side of $10^x = 120{,}000$, we begin by taking the common logarithm on both sides of the equation.

$$10^x = 120{,}000 \qquad \text{This is the given equation.}$$
$$\log 10^x = \log 120{,}000 \qquad \text{Take the common logarithm on both sides.}$$
$$x = \log 120{,}000 \qquad \text{Use the inverse property } \log 10^x = x \text{ on the left.}$$

The equation's solution is $\log 120{,}000$ and the solution set is $\{\log 120{,}000\}$. We can obtain a decimal approximation by using a calculator: $x \approx 5.08$. Because $10^5 = 100{,}000$, it seems reasonable that the solution to $10^x = 120{,}000$ is approximately 5.08.

⊘ Check Point **2** Solve: **a.** $5^x = 134$ **b.** $10^x = 8000$.

Find each solution set and then use a calculator to obtain a decimal approximation to two decimal places for the solution.

EXAMPLE 3 **Solving an Exponential Equation**

Solve: $40e^{0.6x} - 3 = 237$.

Solution We begin by adding 3 to both sides and dividing both sides by 40 to isolate the exponential expression, $e^{0.6x}$. Then we take the natural logarithm on both sides of the equation.

$40e^{0.6x} - 3 = 237$	This is the given equation.
$40e^{0.6x} = 240$	Add 3 to both sides.
$e^{0.6x} = 6$	Isolate the exponential factor by dividing both sides by 40.
$\ln e^{0.6x} = \ln 6$	Take the natural logarithm on both sides.
$0.6x = \ln 6$	Use the inverse property $\ln e^x = x$ on the left.
$x = \dfrac{\ln 6}{0.6} \approx 2.99$	Divide both sides by 0.6 and solve for x.

Thus, the solution of the equation is $\dfrac{\ln 6}{0.6} \approx 2.99$. Try checking this approximate solution in the original equation to verify that $\left\{ \dfrac{\ln 6}{0.6} \right\}$ is the solution set. ●

✓ **Check Point 3** Solve: $7e^{2x} - 5 = 58$. Find the solution set and then use a calculator to obtain a decimal approximation to two decimal places for the solution.

EXAMPLE 4 **Solving an Exponential Equation**

Solve: $5^{x-2} = 4^{2x+3}$.

Solution Because each exponential expression is isolated on one side of the equation, we begin by taking the natural logarithm on both sides.

$5^{x-2} = 4^{2x+3}$	This is the given equation.
$\ln 5^{x-2} = \ln 4^{2x+3}$	Take the natural logarithm on both sides.

Be sure to insert parentheses around the binomials.

$(x - 2)\ln 5 = (2x + 3)\ln 4$	Use the power rule and bring the variable exponents to the front: $\ln b^x = x \ln b$.

Remember that ln 5 and ln 4 are constants, not variables.

$x \ln 5 - 2 \ln 5 = 2x \ln 4 + 3 \ln 4$	Use the distributive property to distribute ln 5 and ln 4 to both terms in parentheses.
$x \ln 5 - 2x \ln 4 = 2 \ln 5 + 3 \ln 4$	Collect variable terms involving x on the left by subtracting 2x ln 4 and adding 2 ln 5 on both sides.
$x(\ln 5 - 2 \ln 4) = 2 \ln 5 + 3 \ln 4$	Factor out x from the two terms on the left.
$x = \dfrac{2 \ln 5 + 3 \ln 4}{\ln 5 - 2 \ln 4}$	Isolate x by dividing both sides by $\ln 5 - 2 \ln 4$.

Discovery

Use properties of logarithms to show that the solution in Example 4 can be expressed as

$$\frac{\ln 1600}{\ln\left(\frac{5}{16}\right)}.$$

The solution set is $\left\{ \dfrac{2 \ln 5 + 3 \ln 4}{\ln 5 - 2 \ln 4} \right\}$. The solution is approximately -6.34. ●

✓ **Check Point 4** Solve: $3^{2x-1} = 7^{x+1}$. Find the solution set and then use a calculator to obtain a decimal approximation to two decimal places for the solution.

<table><tr><td>EXAMPLE 5</td><td>Solving an Exponential Equation</td></tr></table>

Solve: $e^{2x} - 4e^x + 3 = 0$.

Solution The given equation is quadratic in form. If $u = e^x$, the equation can be expressed as $u^2 - 4u + 3 = 0$. Because this equation can be solved by factoring, we factor to isolate the exponential term.

$e^{2x} - 4e^x + 3 = 0$	This is the given equation.
$(e^x - 3)(e^x - 1) = 0$	Factor on the left. Notice that if $u = e^x$, $u^2 - 4u + 3 = (u - 3)(u - 1)$.
$e^x - 3 = 0$ or $e^x - 1 = 0$	Set each factor equal to 0.
$e^x = 3$ $e^x = 1$	Solve for e^x.
$\ln e^x = \ln 3$ $x = 0$	Take the natural logarithm on both sides of the first equation. The equation on the right can be solved by inspection.
$x = \ln 3$	$\ln e^x = x$

The solution set is $\{0, \ln 3\}$. The solutions are 0 and $\ln 3$, which is approximately 1.10.

Technology

Graphic Connections

Shown below is the graph of $y = e^{2x} - 4e^x + 3$. There are two x-intercepts, one at 0 and one at approximately 1.10. These intercepts verify our algebraic solution.

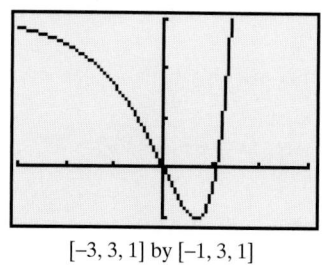

$[-3, 3, 1]$ by $[-1, 3, 1]$

⊘ Check Point **5** Solve: $e^{2x} - 8e^x + 7 = 0$. Find the solution set and then use a calculator to obtain a decimal approximation to two decimal places, if necessary, for the solutions.

3 Use the definition of a logarithm to solve logarithmic equations.

Logarithmic Equations

A **logarithmic equation** is an equation containing a variable in a logarithmic expression. Examples of logarithmic equations include

$$\log_4(x + 3) = 2 \quad \text{and} \quad \ln(x + 2) - \ln(4x + 3) = \ln\left(\frac{1}{x}\right).$$

Some logarithmic equations can be expressed in the form $\log_b M = c$. We can solve such equations by rewriting them in exponential form.

Using the Definition of a Logarithm to Solve Logarithmic Equations

1. Express the equation in the form $\log_b M = c$.

2. Use the definition of a logarithm to rewrite the equation in exponential form:

$$\log_b M = c \quad \text{means} \quad b^c = M.$$

Logarithms are exponents.

3. Solve for the variable.

4. Check proposed solutions in the original equation. Include in the solution set only values for which $M > 0$.

<table><tr><td>EXAMPLE 6</td><td>Solving Logarithmic Equations</td></tr></table>

Solve: **a.** $\log_4(x + 3) = 2$ **b.** $3 \ln(2x) = 12$.

Solution The form $\log_b M = c$ involves a single logarithm whose coefficient is 1 on one side and a constant on the other side. Equation (a) is already in this form. We will need to divide both sides of equation (b) by 3 to obtain this form.

Technology

Graphic Connections

The graphs of

$$y_1 = \log_4(x + 3) \text{ and } y_2 = 2$$

have an intersection point whose x-coordinate is 13. This verifies that $\{13\}$ is the solution set for $\log_4(x + 3) = 2$.

$[-3, 17, 1]$ by $[-2, 3, 1]$

a. $\log_4(x + 3) = 2$ This is the given equation.

 $4^2 = x + 3$ Rewrite in exponential form: $\log_b M = c$ means $b^c = M$.

 $16 = x + 3$ Square 4.

 $13 = x$ Subtract 3 from both sides.

Check 13:

 $\log_4(x + 3) = 2$ This is the given logarithmic equation.

 $\log_4(13 + 3) \overset{?}{=} 2$ Substitute 13 for x.

 $\log_4 16 \overset{?}{=} 2$

 $2 = 2,$ true $\log_4 16 = 2$ because $4^2 = 16$.

This true statement indicates that the solution set is $\{13\}$.

b. $3 \ln(2x) = 12$ This is the given equation.

 $\ln(2x) = 4$ Divide both sides by 3.

 $\log_e(2x) = 4$ Rewrite the natural logarithm showing base e. This step is optional.

 $e^4 = 2x$ Rewrite in exponential form: $\log_b M = c$ means $b^c = M$.

 $\dfrac{e^4}{2} = x$ Divide both sides by 2.

Check $\dfrac{e^4}{2}$:

 $3 \ln(2x) = 12$ This is the given logarithmic equation.

 $3 \ln\left[2\left(\dfrac{e^4}{2}\right)\right] \overset{?}{=} 12$ Substitute $\dfrac{e^4}{2}$ for x.

 $3 \ln e^4 \overset{?}{=} 12$ Simplify: $\dfrac{\cancel{2}}{1} \cdot \dfrac{e^4}{\cancel{2}} = e^4$.

 $3 \cdot 4 \overset{?}{=} 12$ Because $\ln e^x = x$, we conclude $\ln e^4 = 4$.

 $12 = 12,$ true

This true statement indicates that the solution set is $\left\{\dfrac{e^4}{2}\right\}$.

○ **Check Point 6**

 Solve: **a.** $\log_2(x - 4) = 3$ **b.** $4 \ln(3x) = 8$.

Logarithmic expressions are defined only for logarithms of positive real numbers. **Always check proposed solutions of a logarithmic equation in the original equation. Exclude from the solution set any proposed solution that produces the logarithm of a negative number or the logarithm of 0.**

To rewrite the logarithmic equation $\log_b M = c$ in the equivalent exponential form $b^c = M$, we need a single logarithm whose coefficient is one. It is sometimes necessary to use properties of logarithms to condense logarithms into a single logarithm. In the next example, we use the product rule for logarithms to obtain a single logarithmic expression on the left side.

EXAMPLE 7 Solving a Logarithmic Equation

Solve: $\log_2 x + \log_2(x - 7) = 3$.

Solution

 $\log_2 x + \log_2(x - 7) = 3$ This is the given equation.

 $\log_2[x(x - 7)] = 3$ Use the product rule to obtain a single logarithm: $\log_b M + \log_b N = \log_b(MN)$.

$$2^3 = x(x - 7)$$ Rewrite in exponential form: $\log_b M = c$ means $b^c = M$.

$$8 = x^2 - 7x$$ Evaluate 2^3 on the left and apply the distributive property on the right.

$$0 = x^2 - 7x - 8$$ Set the equation equal to 0.

$$0 = (x - 8)(x + 1)$$ Factor.

$$x - 8 = 0 \quad \text{or} \quad x + 1 = 0$$ Set each factor equal to 0.

$$x = 8 \qquad\qquad x = -1$$ Solve for x.

Check 8:	**Check −1:**
$\log_2 x + \log_2(x - 7) = 3$	$\log_2 x + \log_2(x - 7) = 3$
$\log_2 8 + \log_2(8 - 7) \overset{?}{=} 3$	$\log_2(-1) + \log_2(-1 - 7) \overset{?}{=} 3$
$\log_2 8 + \log_2 1 \overset{?}{=} 3$	The number −1 does not check.
$3 + 0 \overset{?}{=} 3$	Negative numbers do not have logarithms.
$3 = 3, \text{ true}$	

The solution set is $\{8\}$.

⊘ Check Point 7 Solve: $\log x + \log(x - 3) = 1$.

4 Use the one-to-one property of logarithms to solve logarithmic equations.

Some logarithmic equations can be expressed in the form $\log_b M = \log_b N$, where the bases on both sides of the equation are the same. Because all logarithmic functions are one-to-one, we can conclude that $M = N$.

> **Using the One-to-One Property of Logarithms to Solve Logarithmic Equations**
>
> 1. Express the equation in the form $\log_b M = \log_b N$. This form involves a single logarithm whose coefficient is 1 on each side of the equation.
> 2. Use the one-to-one property to rewrite the equation without logarithms: If $\log_b M = \log_b N$, then $M = N$.
> 3. Solve for the variable.
> 4. Check proposed solutions in the original equation. Include in the solution set only values for which $M > 0$ and $N > 0$.

EXAMPLE 8 Solving a Logarithmic Equation

Solve: $\ln(x + 2) - \ln(4x + 3) = \ln\left(\dfrac{1}{x}\right)$.

Solution In order to apply the one-to-one property of logarithms, we need a single logarithm whose coefficient is 1 on each side of the equation. The right side is already in this form. We can obtain a single logarithm on the left side by applying the quotient rule.

$$\ln(x + 2) - \ln(4x + 3) = \ln\left(\frac{1}{x}\right)$$ This is the given equation.

$$\ln\left(\frac{x + 2}{4x + 3}\right) = \ln\left(\frac{1}{x}\right)$$ Use the quotient rule to obtain a single logarithm on the left side: $\log_b M - \log_b N = \log_b\left(\dfrac{M}{N}\right)$.

$$\frac{x + 2}{4x + 3} = \frac{1}{x}$$ Use the one-to-one property: If $\log_b M = \log_b N$, then $M = N$.

Technology

Numeric Connections

A graphing utility's TABLE feature can be used to verify that $\{3\}$ is the solution set of

$$\ln(x + 2) - \ln(4x + 3) = \ln\left(\frac{1}{x}\right).$$

$y_1 = \ln(x + 2) - \ln(4x + 3)$ $y_2 = \ln\left(\frac{1}{x}\right)$

X	Y₁	Y₂
-2	ERROR	ERROR
-1	ERROR	ERROR
0	-.4055	ERROR
1	-.8473	0
2	-1.012	-.6931
3	-1.099	-1.099
4	-1.153	-1.386

X = -2

y_1 and y_2 are equal when $x = 3$.

⑤ Solve applied problems involving exponential and logarithmic equations.

$$x(4x + 3)\left(\frac{x + 2}{4x + 3}\right) = x(4x + 3)\left(\frac{1}{x}\right) \qquad \text{Multiply both sides by } x(4x + 3), \text{ the LCD.}$$

$$x(x + 2) = 4x + 3 \qquad \text{Simplify.}$$

$$x^2 + 2x = 4x + 3 \qquad \text{Apply the distributive property.}$$

$$x^2 - 2x - 3 = 0 \qquad \begin{array}{l}\text{Subtract } 4x + 3 \text{ from both sides and set} \\ \text{the equation equal to 0.}\end{array}$$

$$(x - 3)(x + 1) = 0 \qquad \text{Factor.}$$

$$x - 3 = 0 \quad \text{or} \quad x + 1 = 0 \qquad \text{Set each factor equal to 0.}$$

$$x = 3 \qquad\qquad x = -1 \qquad \text{Solve for x.}$$

Substituting 3 for x into $\ln(x + 2) - \ln(4x + 3) = \ln\left(\frac{1}{x}\right)$ produces the true statement $\ln\left(\frac{1}{3}\right) = \ln\left(\frac{1}{3}\right)$. However, substituting -1 produces logarithms of negative numbers. Thus, -1 is not a solution. The solution set is $\{3\}$. ●

⊘ Check Point 8 Solve: $\ln(x - 3) = \ln(7x - 23) - \ln(x + 1)$.

Applications

Our first applied example provides a mathematical perspective on the old slogan "Alcohol and driving don't mix." In California, where 38% of fatal traffic crashes involve drinking drivers, it is illegal to drive with a blood alcohol concentration of 0.08 or higher. At these levels, drivers may be arrested and charged with driving under the influence.

EXAMPLE 9 **Alcohol and Risk of a Car Accident**

Medical research indicates that the risk of having a car accident increases exponentially as the concentration of alcohol in the blood increases. The risk is modeled by

$$R = 6e^{12.77x},$$

where x is the blood alcohol concentration and R, given as a percent, is the risk of having a car accident. What blood alcohol concentration corresponds to a 17% risk of a car accident? How is this shown on the graph of R in **Figure 4.20**?

Solution For a risk of 17%, we let $R = 17$ in the equation and solve for x, the blood alcohol concentration.

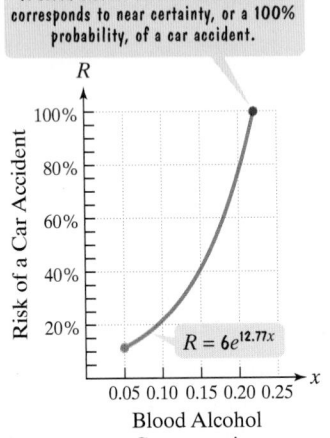

A blood alcohol concentration of 0.22 corresponds to near certainty, or a 100% probability, of a car accident.

$R = 6e^{12.77x}$

Figure 4.20

$$R = 6e^{12.77x} \qquad \text{This is the given equation.}$$

$$6e^{12.77x} = 17 \qquad \begin{array}{l}\text{Substitute 17 for R and (optional) reverse the two} \\ \text{sides of the equation.}\end{array}$$

$$e^{12.77x} = \frac{17}{6} \qquad \begin{array}{l}\text{Isolate the exponential factor by dividing both} \\ \text{sides by 6.}\end{array}$$

$$\ln e^{12.77x} = \ln\left(\frac{17}{6}\right) \qquad \text{Take the natural logarithm on both sides.}$$

$$12.77x = \ln\left(\frac{17}{6}\right) \qquad \text{Use the inverse property } \ln e^x = x \text{ on the left side.}$$

$$x = \frac{\ln\left(\frac{17}{6}\right)}{12.77} \approx 0.08 \qquad \text{Divide both sides by 12.77.}$$

For a blood alcohol concentration of 0.08, the risk of a car accident is 17%. This is shown on the graph of R in **Figure 4.20** by the point (0.08, 17) that lies on the blue curve. Take a moment to locate this point on the curve. In many states, it is illegal to drive with a blood alcohol concentration of 0.08. ●

✓ Check Point **9** Use the formula in Example 9 to answer this question: What blood alcohol concentration corresponds to a 7% risk of a car accident? (In many states, drivers under the age of 21 can lose their licenses for driving at this level.)

Suppose that you inherit $30,000 at age 20. Is it possible to invest $25,000 and have over half a million dollars for early retirement? Our next example illustrates the power of compound interest.

(EXAMPLE 10) **Revisiting the Formula for Compound Interest**

The formula

$$A = P\left(1 + \frac{r}{n}\right)^{nt}$$

describes the accumulated value, A, of a sum of money, P, the principal, after t years at annual percentage rate r (in decimal form) compounded n times a year. How long will it take $25,000 to grow to $500,000 at 9% annual interest compounded monthly?

Solution

$$A = P\left(1 + \frac{r}{n}\right)^{nt}$$

This is the given formula.

$$500,000 = 25,000\left(1 + \frac{0.09}{12}\right)^{12t}$$

A(the desired accumulated value) = $500,000,
P(the principal) = $25,000,
r(the interest rate) = 9% = 0.09, and n = 12 (monthly compounding).

> Because of the exponent, 12*t*, do not distribute 25,000 over the terms in parentheses.

Playing Doubles: Interest Rates and Doubling Time

One way to calculate what your savings will be worth at some point in the future is to consider doubling time. The following table shows how long it takes for your money to double at different annual interest rates subject to continuous compounding.

Annual Interest Rate	Years to Double
5%	13.9 years
7%	9.9 years
9%	7.7 years
11%	6.3 years

Of course, the first problem is collecting some money to invest. The second problem is finding a reasonably safe investment with a return of 9% or more.

Our goal is to solve the equation for t. Let's reverse the two sides of the equation and then simplify within parentheses.

$$25,000\left(1 + \frac{0.09}{12}\right)^{12t} = 500,000$$

Reverse the two sides of the previous equation.

$$25,000(1 + 0.0075)^{12t} = 500,000$$

Divide within parentheses: $\frac{0.09}{12} = 0.0075$.

$$25,000(1.0075)^{12t} = 500,000$$

Add within parentheses.

$$(1.0075)^{12t} = 20$$

Divide both sides by 25,000.

$$\ln(1.0075)^{12t} = \ln 20$$

Take the natural logarithm on both sides.

$$12t \ln(1.0075) = \ln 20$$

Use the power rule to bring the exponent to the front: $\ln b^x = x \ln b$.

$$t = \frac{\ln 20}{12 \ln 1.0075}$$

Solve for t, dividing both sides by 12 ln 1.0075.

$$\approx 33.4$$

Use a calculator.

After approximately 33.4 years, the $25,000 will grow to an accumulated value of $500,000. If you set aside the money at age 20, you can begin enjoying a life of leisure at about age 53. ●

✓ Check Point **10** How long, to the nearest tenth of a year, will it take $1000 to grow to $3600 at 8% annual interest compounded quarterly?

(EXAMPLE 11) **Fair or Poor Health, by Annual Income**

The bar graph in **Figure 4.21** shows people with lower incomes are more likely to report that their health is fair or poor. The function

$$f(x) = 54.8 - 12.3 \ln x$$

models the percentage of Americans reporting fair or poor health, $f(x)$, in terms of annual income, x, in thousands of dollars. According to the model, what annual income corresponds to 10% reporting fair or poor health? Round to the nearest thousand dollars.

Americans Reporting Fair or Poor Health, by Annual Income

Figure 4.21
Source: William Kornblum and Joseph Julian, *Social Problems*, Twelfth Edition, Prentice Hall, 2007

Solution To find what annual income corresponds to 10% reporting fair or poor health, we substitute 10 for $f(x)$ and solve for x, the annual income.

$f(x) = 54.8 - 12.3 \ln x$	This is the given function.
$10 = 54.8 - 12.3 \ln x$	Substitute 10 for f(x).

Our goal is to isolate ln x and then rewrite the equation in exponential form.

$-44.8 = -12.3 \ln x$	Subtract 54.8 from both sides.
$\dfrac{44.8}{12.3} = \ln x$	Divide both sides by −12.3.
$\dfrac{44.8}{12.3} = \log_e x$	Rewrite the natural logarithm showing base e. This step is optional.
$e^{\frac{44.8}{12.3}} = x$	Rewrite in exponential form.
$38 \approx x$	Use a calculator.

An annual income of approximately $38,000 corresponds to 10% of Americans reporting fair or poor health.

⊘ Check Point **11** According to the function in Example 11, what annual income corresponds to 25% reporting fair or poor health? Round to the nearest thousand dollars.

Exercise Set 4.4

Practice Exercises

Solve each exponential equation in Exercises 1–22 by expressing each side as a power of the same base and then equating exponents.

1. $2^x = 64$

2. $3^x = 81$

3. $5^x = 125$

4. $5^x = 625$

5. $2^{2x-1} = 32$

6. $3^{2x+1} = 27$

7. $4^{2x-1} = 64$

8. $5^{3x-1} = 125$

9. $32^x = 8$

10. $4^x = 32$

11. $9^x = 27$

12. $125^x = 625$

13. $3^{1-x} = \frac{1}{27}$

14. $5^{2-x} = \frac{1}{125}$

15. $6^{\frac{x-3}{4}} = \sqrt{6}$

16. $7^{\frac{x-2}{6}} = \sqrt{7}$

17. $4^x = \dfrac{1}{\sqrt{2}}$

18. $9^x = \dfrac{1}{\sqrt[3]{3}}$

19. $8^{x+3} = 16^{x-1}$

20. $8^{1-x} = 4^{x+2}$

21. $e^{x+1} = \dfrac{1}{e}$

22. $e^{x+4} = \dfrac{1}{e^{2x}}$

Solve each exponential equation in Exercises 23–48. Express the solution set in terms of natural logarithms. Then use a calculator to obtain a decimal approximation, correct to two decimal places, for the solution.

23. $10^x = 3.91$

24. $10^x = 8.07$

25. $e^x = 5.7$

26. $e^x = 0.83$

27. $5^x = 17$

28. $19^x = 143$

29. $5e^x = 23$

30. $9e^x = 107$

31. $3e^{5x} = 1977$

32. $4e^{7x} = 10{,}273$

33. $e^{1-5x} = 793$

34. $e^{1-8x} = 7957$

35. $e^{5x-3} - 2 = 10{,}476$

36. $e^{4x-5} - 7 = 11{,}243$

37. $7^{x+2} = 410$

38. $5^{x-3} = 137$

39. $7^{0.3x} = 813$

40. $3^{\frac{x}{7}} = 0.2$

41. $5^{2x+3} = 3^{x-1}$

42. $7^{2x+1} = 3^{x+2}$

43. $e^{2x} - 3e^x + 2 = 0$

44. $e^{2x} - 2e^x - 3 = 0$

45. $e^{4x} + 5e^{2x} - 24 = 0$

46. $e^{4x} - 3e^{2x} - 18 = 0$

47. $3^{2x} + 3^x - 2 = 0$

48. $2^{2x} + 2^x - 12 = 0$

Solve each logarithmic equation in Exercises 49–90. Be sure to reject any value of x that is not in the domain of the original logarithmic expressions. Give the exact answer. Then, where necessary, use a calculator to obtain a decimal approximation, correct to two decimal places, for the solution.

49. $\log_3 x = 4$

50. $\log_5 x = 3$

51. $\ln x = 2$

52. $\ln x = 3$

53. $\log_4(x + 5) = 3$

54. $\log_5(x - 7) = 2$

55. $\log_3(x - 4) = -3$

56. $\log_7(x + 2) = -2$

57. $\log_4(3x + 2) = 3$

58. $\log_2(4x + 1) = 5$

59. $5 \ln(2x) = 20$

60. $6 \ln(2x) = 30$

61. $6 + 2 \ln x = 5$

62. $7 + 3 \ln x = 6$

63. $\ln \sqrt{x + 3} = 1$

64. $\ln \sqrt{x + 4} = 1$

65. $\log_5 x + \log_5(4x - 1) = 1$

66. $\log_6(x + 5) + \log_6 x = 2$

67. $\log_3(x - 5) + \log_3(x + 3) = 2$

68. $\log_2(x - 1) + \log_2(x + 1) = 3$

69. $\log_2(x + 2) - \log_2(x - 5) = 3$

70. $\log_4(x + 2) - \log_4(x - 1) = 1$

71. $2 \log_3(x + 4) = \log_3 9 + 2$

72. $3 \log_2(x - 1) = 5 - \log_2 4$

73. $\log_2(x - 6) + \log_2(x - 4) - \log_2 x = 2$

74. $\log_2(x - 3) + \log_2 x - \log_2(x + 2) = 2$

75. $\log(x + 4) = \log x + \log 4$

76. $\log(5x + 1) = \log(2x + 3) + \log 2$

77. $\log(3x - 3) = \log(x + 1) + \log 4$

78. $\log(2x - 1) = \log(x + 3) + \log 3$

79. $2 \log x = \log 25$

80. $3 \log x = \log 125$

81. $\log(x + 4) - \log 2 = \log(5x + 1)$

82. $\log(x + 7) - \log 3 = \log(7x + 1)$

83. $2 \log x - \log 7 = \log 112$

84. $\log(x - 2) + \log 5 = \log 100$

85. $\log x + \log(x + 3) = \log 10$

86. $\log(x + 3) + \log(x - 2) = \log 14$

87. $\ln(x - 4) + \ln(x + 1) = \ln(x - 8)$

88. $\log_2(x - 1) - \log_2(x + 3) = \log_2\left(\dfrac{1}{x}\right)$

89. $\ln(x - 2) - \ln(x + 3) = \ln(x - 1) - \ln(x + 7)$

90. $\ln(x - 5) - \ln(x + 4) = \ln(x - 1) - \ln(x + 2)$

Practice Plus

In Exercises 91–100, solve each equation.

91. $5^{2x} \cdot 5^{4x} = 125$

92. $3^{x+2} \cdot 3^x = 81$

93. $2 |\ln x| - 6 = 0$

94. $3 |\log x| - 6 = 0$

95. $3^{x^2} = 45$

96. $5^{x^2} = 50$

97. $\ln(2x + 1) + \ln(x - 3) - 2 \ln x = 0$

98. $\ln 3 - \ln(x + 5) - \ln x = 0$

99. $5^{x^2-12} = 25^{2x}$

100. $3^{x^2-12} = 9^{2x}$

Application Exercises

101. The formula $A = 36.1e^{0.0126t}$ models the population of California, A, in millions, t years after 2005.

 a. What was the population of California in 2005?

 b. When will the population of California reach 40 million?

102. The formula $A = 22.9e^{0.0183t}$ models the population of Texas, A, in millions, t years after 2005.

 a. What was the population of Texas in 2005?

 b. When will the population of Texas reach 27 million?

The function $f(x) = 20(0.975)^x$ models the percentage of surface sunlight, $f(x)$, that reaches a depth of x feet beneath the surface of the ocean. The figure shows the graph of this function. Use this information to solve Exercises 103–104.

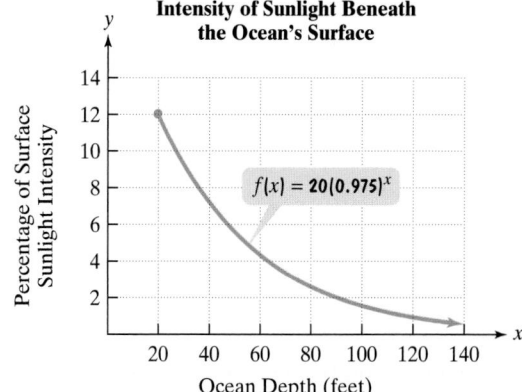

Intensity of Sunlight Beneath the Ocean's Surface

$f(x) = 20(0.975)^x$

Ocean Depth (feet)

Percentage of Surface Sunlight Intensity

103. Use the function to determine at what depth, to the nearest foot, there is 1% of surface sunlight. How is this shown on the graph of f?

104. Use the function to determine at what depth, to the nearest foot, there is 3% of surface sunlight. How is this shown on the graph of f?

In Exercises 105–108, complete the table for a savings account subject to n compoundings yearly $\left[A = P\left(1 + \dfrac{r}{n}\right)^{nt}\right]$. *Round answers to one decimal place.*

	Amount Invested	Number of Compounding Periods	Annual Interest Rate	Accumulated Amount	Time t in Years
105.	$12,500	4	5.75%	$20,000	
106.	$7250	12	6.5%	$15,000	
107.	$1000	360		$1400	2
108.	$5000	360		$9000	4

In Exercises 109–112, complete the table for a savings account subject to continuous compounding $(A = Pe^{rt})$. *Round answers to one decimal place.*

	Amount Invested	Annual Interest Rate	Accumulated Amount	Time t in Years
109.	$8000	8%	Double the amount invested	
110.	$8000		$12,000	2
111.	$2350		Triple the amount invested	7
112.	$17,425	4.25%	$25,000	

The days when something happens and it's not captured on camera appear to be over. The bar graph shows that by 2007, 68% of cellphones sold in the United States were equipped with cameras.

Percentage of New Cellphones with Cameras

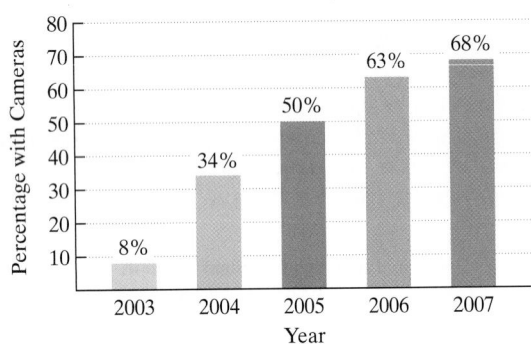

Source: Strategy Analytics Inc.

The data can be modeled by the function $f(x) = 8 + 38 \ln x$, *where* $f(x)$ *is the percentage of new cellphones with cameras* x *years after 2002. Use this information to solve Exercises 113–114.*

113. a. Use the function to determine the percentage of new cellphones with cameras in 2007. Round to the nearest whole percent. Does this overestimate or underestimate the percent displayed by the graph? By how much?

 b. If trends shown from 2003 through 2007 continue, use the function to determine by which year 87% of new cellphones will be equipped with cameras.

114. a. Use the function to determine the percentage of new cellphones with cameras in 2006. Round to the nearest whole percent. Does this overestimate or underestimate the percent displayed by the graph? By how much?

b. If trends shown from 2003 through 2007 continue, use the function to determine by which year all new cellphones will be equipped with cameras.

The function $P(x) = 95 - 30 \log_2 x$ *models the percentage,* $P(x)$, *of students who could recall the important features of a classroom lecture as a function of time, where* x *represents the number of days that have elapsed since the lecture was given. The figure shows the graph of the function. Use this information to solve Exercises 115–116. Round answers to one decimal place.*

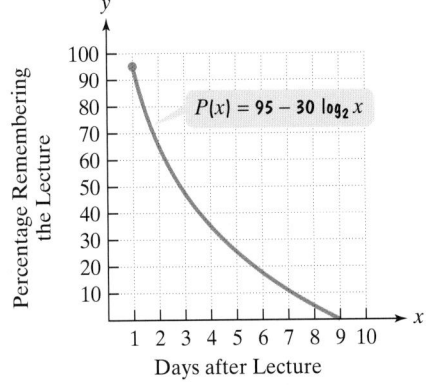

115. After how many days do only half the students recall the important features of the classroom lecture? (Let $P(x) = 50$ and solve for x.) Locate the point on the graph that conveys this information.

116. After how many days have all students forgotten the important features of the classroom lecture? (Let $P(x) = 0$ and solve for x.) Locate the point on the graph that conveys this information.

The pH scale is used to measure the acidity or alkalinity of a solution. The scale ranges from 0 to 14. A neutral solution, such as pure water, has a pH of 7. An acid solution has a pH less than 7 and an alkaline solution has a pH greater than 7. The lower the pH below 7, the more acidic is the solution. Each whole-number decrease in pH represents a tenfold increase in acidity.

The pH Scale

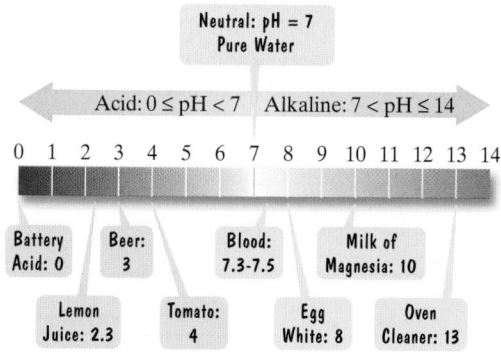

The pH of a solution is given by

$$pH = -\log x,$$

where x represents the concentration of the hydrogen ions in the solution, in moles per liter. Use the formula to solve Exercises 117–118. Express answers as powers of 10.

117. a. Normal, unpolluted rain has a pH of about 5.6. What is the hydrogen ion concentration?

b. An environmental concern involves the destructive effects of acid rain. The most acidic rainfall ever had a pH of 2.4. What was the hydrogen ion concentration?

c. How many times greater is the hydrogen ion concentration of the acidic rainfall in part (b) than the normal rainfall in part (a)?

118. a. The figure indicates that lemon juice has a pH of 2.3. What is the hydrogen ion concentration?

b. Stomach acid has a pH that ranges from 1 to 3. What is the hydrogen ion concentration of the most acidic stomach?

c. How many times greater is the hydrogen ion concentration of the acidic stomach in part (b) than the lemon juice in part (a)?

Writing in Mathematics

119. Explain how to solve an exponential equation when both sides can be written as a power of the same base.

120. Explain how to solve an exponential equation when both sides cannot be written as a power of the same base. Use $3^x = 140$ in your explanation.

121. Explain the differences between solving $\log_3(x - 1) = 4$ and $\log_3(x - 1) = \log_3 4$.

122. In many states, a 17% risk of a car accident with a blood alcohol concentration of 0.08 is the lowest level for charging a motorist with driving under the influence. Do you agree with the 17% risk as a cutoff percentage, or do you feel that the percentage should be lower or higher? Explain your answer. What blood alcohol concentration corresponds to what you believe is an appropriate percentage?

Technology Exercises

In Exercises 123–130, use your graphing utility to graph each side of the equation in the same viewing rectangle. Then use the x-coordinate of the intersection point to find the equation's solution set. Verify this value by direct substitution into the equation.

123. $2^{x+1} = 8$

124. $3^{x+1} = 9$

125. $\log_3(4x - 7) = 2$

126. $\log_3(3x - 2) = 2$

127. $\log(x + 3) + \log x = 1$

128. $\log(x - 15) + \log x = 2$

129. $3^x = 2x + 3$

130. $5^x = 3x + 4$

Hurricanes are one of nature's most destructive forces. These low-pressure areas often have diameters of over 500 miles. The function $f(x) = 0.48 \ln(x + 1) + 27$ models the barometric air pressure, $f(x)$, in inches of mercury, at a distance of x miles from the eye of a hurricane. Use this function to solve Exercises 131–132.

131. Graph the function in a [0, 500, 50] by [27, 30, 1] viewing rectangle. What does the shape of the graph indicate about barometric air pressure as the distance from the eye increases?

132. Use an equation to answer this question: How far from the eye of a hurricane is the barometric air pressure 29 inches of mercury? Use the TRACE and ZOOM features or the intersect command of your graphing utility to verify your answer.

133. The function $P(t) = 145e^{-0.092t}$ models a runner's pulse, $P(t)$, in beats per minute, t minutes after a race, where $0 \le t \le 15$. Graph the function using a graphing utility. TRACE along the graph and determine after how many minutes the runner's pulse will be 70 beats per minute. Round to the nearest tenth of a minute. Verify your observation algebraically.

134. The function $W(t) = 2600(1 - 0.51e^{-0.075t})^3$ models the weight, $W(t)$, in kilograms, of a female African elephant at age t years. (1 kilogram ≈ 2.2 pounds) Use a graphing utility to graph the function. Then TRACE along the curve to estimate the age of an adult female elephant weighing 1800 kilograms.

Critical Thinking Exercises

Make Sense? In Exercises 135–138, determine whether each statement makes sense or does not make sense, and explain your reasoning.

135. Because the equations $2^x = 15$ and $2^x = 16$ are similar, I solved them using the same method.

136. Because the equations

$$\log(3x + 1) = 5 \text{ and } \log(3x + 1) = \log 5$$

are similar, I solved them using the same method.

137. I can solve $4^x = 15$ by writing the equation in logarithmic form.

138. It's important for me to check that the proposed solution of an equation with logarithms gives only logarithms of positive numbers in the original equation.

In Exercises 139–142, determine whether each statement is true or false. If the statement is false, make the necessary change(s) to produce a true statement.

139. If $\log(x + 3) = 2$, then $e^2 = x + 3$.

140. If $\log(7x + 3) - \log(2x + 5) = 4$, then the equation in exponential form is $10^4 = (7x + 3) - (2x + 5)$.

141. If $x = \dfrac{1}{k}\ln y$, then $y = e^{kx}$.

142. Examples of exponential equations include $10^x = 5.71$, $e^x = 0.72$, and $x^{10} = 5.71$.

143. If \$4000 is deposited into an account paying 3% interest compounded annually and at the same time \$2000 is deposited into an account paying 5% interest compounded annually, after how long will the two accounts have the same balance? Round to the nearest year.

Solve each equation in Exercises 144–146. Check each proposed solution by direct substitution or with a graphing utility.

144. $(\ln x)^2 = \ln x^2$

145. $(\log x)(2 \log x + 1) = 6$

146. $\ln(\ln x) = 0$

Group Exercise

147. Research applications of logarithmic functions as mathematical models and plan a seminar based on your group's research. Each group member should research one of the following areas or any other area of interest: pH (acidity of solutions), intensity of sound (decibels), brightness of stars, human memory, progress over time in a sport, profit over time. For the area that you select, explain how logarithmic functions are used and provide examples.

Preview Exercises

Exercises 148–150 will help you prepare for the material covered in the next section.

148. The formula $A = 10e^{-0.003t}$ models the population of Hungary, A, in millions, t years after 2006.
 a. Find Hungary's population, in millions, for 2006, 2007, 2008, and 2009. Round to two decimal places.
 b. Is Hungary's population increasing or decreasing?

149. The table shows the average amount that Americans paid for a gallon of gasoline from 2002 through 2006. Create a scatter plot for the data. Based on the shape of the scatter plot, would a logarithmic function, an exponential function, or a linear function be the best choice for modeling the data?

Average Gas Price in the U.S.

Year	Average Price per Gallon
2002	\$1.40
2003	\$1.60
2004	\$1.92
2005	\$2.30
2006	\$2.91

Source: Oil Price Information Service

150. a. Simplify: $e^{\ln 3}$.
 b. Use your simplification from part (a) to rewrite 3^x in terms of base e.

Section 4.5

Exponential Growth and Decay; Modeling Data

Objectives

1 Model exponential growth and decay.

2 Use logistic growth models.

3 Choose an appropriate model for data.

4 Express an exponential model in base e.

The most casual cruise on the Internet shows how people disagree when it comes to making predictions about the effects of the world's growing population. Some argue that there is a recent slowdown in the growth rate, economies remain robust, and famines in North Korea and Ethiopia are aberrations rather than signs of the future. Others say that the 6.8 billion people on Earth is twice as many as can be supported in middle-class comfort, and the world is running out of arable land and fresh water. Debates about entities that are growing exponentially can be approached mathematically: We can create functions that model data and use these functions to make predictions. In this section, we will show you how this is done.

1 Model exponential growth and decay.

Exponential Growth and Decay

One of algebra's many applications is to predict the behavior of variables. This can be done with *exponential growth* and *decay models*. With exponential growth or decay, quantities grow or decay at a rate directly proportional to their size.

Populations that are growing exponentially grow extremely rapidly as they get larger because there are more adults to have offspring. For example, world population is increasing at approximately 1.2% per year. This means that each year world population is 1.2% more than what it was in the previous year. In 2007, world population was 6.6 billion. Thus, we compute the world population in 2008 as follows:

$$6.6 \text{ billion} + 1.2\% \text{ of } 6.6 \text{ billion} = 6.6 + (0.012)(6.6) = 6.6792.$$

This computation indicates that 6.6792 billion people populated the world in 2008. The 0.0792 billion represents an increase of 79.2 million people from 2007 to 2008, the equivalent of the population of Germany. Using 1.2% as the annual rate of increase, world population for 2009 is found in a similar manner:

$$6.6792 + 1.2\% \text{ of } 6.6792 = 6.6792 + (0.012)(6.6792) \approx 6.759.$$

This computation indicates that approximately 6.759 billion people will populate the world in 2009.

The explosive growth of world population may remind you of the growth of money in an account subject to compound interest. The balance in an account subject to continuous compounding and world population are special cases of *exponential growth models*.

Study Tip

You have seen the formula for exponential growth before, but with different letters. It is the formula for compound interest with continous compounding.

$$A = Pe^{rt}$$

| Amount at time t | Principal is the original amount. | Interest rate is the growth rate. |

$$A = A_0e^{kt}$$

Exponential Growth and Decay Models

The mathematical model for **exponential growth** or **decay** is given by

$$f(t) = A_0e^{kt} \quad \text{or} \quad A = A_0e^{kt}.$$

- **If $k > 0$, the function models the amount, or size, of a *growing* entity.** A_0 is the original amount, or size, of the growing entity at time $t = 0$, A is the amount at time t, and k is a constant representing the growth rate.

- **If $k < 0$, the function models the amount, or size, of a *decaying* entity.** A_0 is the original amount, or size, of the decaying entity at time $t = 0$, A is the amount at time t, and k is a constant representing the decay rate.

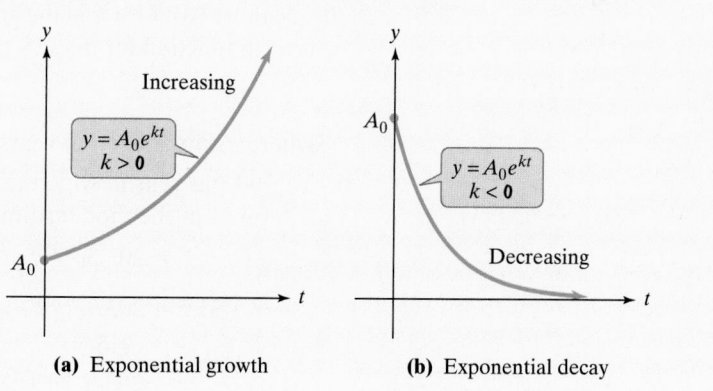

(a) Exponential growth **(b)** Exponential decay

Sometimes we need to use given data to determine k, the rate of growth or decay. After we compute the value of k, we can use the formula $A = A_0e^{kt}$ to make predictions. This idea is illustrated in our first two examples.

EXAMPLE 1 **Modeling the Growth of the U.S. Population**

The graph in **Figure 4.22** shows the U.S. population, in millions, for five selected years from 1970 through 2007. In 1970, the U.S. population was 203.3 million. By 2007, it had grown to 300.9 million.

a. Find an exponential growth function that models the data for 1970 through 2007.

b. By which year will the U.S. population reach 315 million?

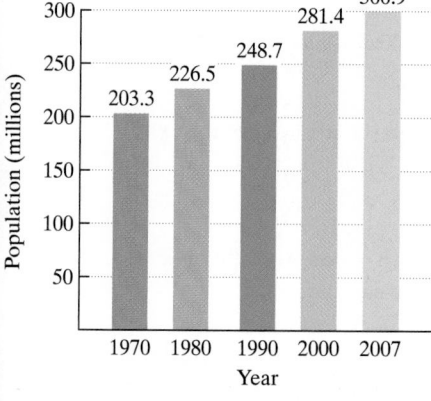

Figure 4.22 *Source:* U.S. Census Bureau

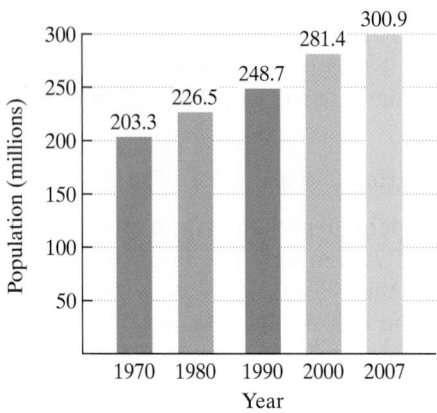

U.S. Population, 1970–2007

Figure 4.22 (repeated)

Solution

a. We use the exponential growth model

$$A = A_0 e^{kt}$$

in which t is the number of years after 1970. This means that 1970 corresponds to $t = 0$. At that time the U.S. population was 203.3 million, so we substitute 203.3 for A_0 in the growth model:

$$A = 203.3 e^{kt}.$$

We are given that 300.9 million was the population in 2007. Because 2007 is 37 years after 1970, when $t = 37$ the value of A is 300.9. Substituting these numbers into the growth model will enable us to find k, the growth rate. We know that $k > 0$ because the problem involves growth.

$A = 203.3 e^{kt}$	Use the growth model with $A_0 = 203.3$.
$300.9 = 203.3 e^{k \cdot 37}$	When $t = 37$, $A = 300.9$. Substitute these numbers into the model.
$e^{37k} = \dfrac{300.9}{203.3}$	Isolate the exponential factor by dividing both sides by 203.3. We also reversed the sides.
$\ln e^{37k} = \ln\left(\dfrac{300.9}{203.3}\right)$	Take the natural logarithm on both sides.
$37k = \ln\left(\dfrac{300.9}{203.3}\right)$	Simplify the left side using $\ln e^x = x$.
$k = \dfrac{\ln\left(\dfrac{300.9}{203.3}\right)}{37} \approx 0.011$	Divide both sides by 37 and solve for k. Then use a calculator.

The value of k, approximately 0.011, indicates a growth rate of about 1.1%. We substitute 0.011 for k in the growth model, $A = 203.3 e^{kt}$, to obtain an exponential growth function for the U.S. population. It is

$$A = 203.3 e^{0.011t},$$

where t is measured in years after 1970.

b. To find the year in which the U.S. population will reach 315 million, substitute 315 for A in the model from part (a) and solve for t.

$A = 203.3 e^{0.011t}$	This is the model from part (a).
$315 = 203.3 e^{0.011t}$	Substitute 315 for A.
$e^{0.011t} = \dfrac{315}{203.3}$	Divide both sides by 203.3. We also reversed the sides.
$\ln e^{0.011t} = \ln\left(\dfrac{315}{203.3}\right)$	Take the natural logarithm on both sides.
$0.011t = \ln\left(\dfrac{315}{203.3}\right)$	Simplify on the left using $\ln e^x = x$.
$t = \dfrac{\ln\left(\dfrac{315}{203.3}\right)}{0.011} \approx 40$	Divide both sides by 0.011 and solve for t. Then use a calculator.

Because t represents the number of years after 1970, the model indicates that the U.S. population will reach 315 million by $1970 + 40$, or in the year 2010.

In Example 1, we used only two data values, the population for 1970 and the population for 2007, to develop a model for U.S. population growth from 1970 through 2007. By not using data for any other years, have we created a model that inaccurately describes both the existing data and future population projections given by the U.S. Census Bureau? Something else to think about: Is an exponential model the best choice for describing U.S. population growth, or might a linear model provide a better description? We return to these issues in Exercises 64–68 in the exercise set.

⊘ Check Point **1** In 1990, the population of Africa was 643 million and by 2006 it had grown to 906 million.

 a. Use the exponential growth model $A = A_0 e^{kt}$, in which t is the number of years after 1990, to find the exponential growth function that models the data.

 b. By which year will Africa's population reach 2000 million, or two billion?

Our next example involves exponential decay and its use in determining the age of fossils and artifacts. The method is based on considering the percentage of carbon-14 remaining in the fossil or artifact. Carbon-14 decays exponentially with a *half-life* of approximately 5715 years. The **half-life** of a substance is the time required for half of a given sample to disintegrate. Thus, after 5715 years a given amount of carbon-14 will have decayed to half the original amount. Carbon dating is useful for artifacts or fossils up to 80,000 years old. Older objects do not have enough carbon-14 left to determine age accurately.

Carbon Dating and Artistic Development

The artistic community was electrified by the discovery in 1995 of spectacular cave paintings in a limestone cavern in France. Carbon dating of the charcoal from the site showed that the images, created by artists of remarkable talent, were 30,000 years old, making them the oldest cave paintings ever found. The artists seemed to have used the cavern's natural contours to heighten a sense of perspective. The quality of the painting suggests that the art of early humans did not mature steadily from primitive to sophisticated in any simple linear fashion.

(**EXAMPLE 2**) **Carbon-14 Dating: The Dead Sea Scrolls**

 a. Use the fact that after 5715 years a given amount of carbon-14 will have decayed to half the original amount to find the exponential decay model for carbon-14.

 b. In 1947, earthenware jars containing what are known as the Dead Sea Scrolls were found by an Arab Bedouin herdsman. Analysis indicated that the scroll wrappings contained 76% of their original carbon-14. Estimate the age of the Dead Sea Scrolls.

Solution

 a. We begin with the exponential decay model $A = A_0 e^{kt}$. We know that $k < 0$ because the problem involves the decay of carbon-14. After 5715 years ($t = 5715$), the amount of carbon-14 present, A, is half the original amount, A_0.

Thus, we can substitute $\dfrac{A_0}{2}$ for A in the exponential decay model. This will enable us to find k, the decay rate.

$$A = A_0 e^{kt}$$ Begin with the exponential decay model.

$$\frac{A_0}{2} = A_0 e^{k5715}$$ After 5715 years ($t = 5715$), $A = \dfrac{A_0}{2}$ (because the amount present, A, is half the original amount, A_0).

$$\frac{1}{2} = e^{5715k}$$ Divide both sides of the equation by A_0.

$$\ln\left(\frac{1}{2}\right) = \ln e^{5715k}$$ Take the natural logarithm on both sides.

$$\ln\left(\frac{1}{2}\right) = 5715k$$ Simplify the right side using $\ln e^x = x$.

$$k = \frac{\ln\left(\dfrac{1}{2}\right)}{5715} \approx -0.000121$$ Divide both sides by 5715 and solve for k.

Substituting -0.000121 for k in the decay model, $A = A_0 e^{kt}$, the model for carbon-14 is

$$A = A_0 e^{-0.000121t}.$$

b. In 1947, the Dead Sea Scrolls contained 76% of their original carbon-14. To find their age in 1947, substitute $0.76A_0$ for A in the model from part (a) and solve for t.

$A = A_0 e^{-0.000121t}$	This is the decay model for carbon-14.
$0.76A_0 = A_0 e^{-0.000121t}$	A, the amount present, is 76% of the original amount, so $A = 0.76A_0$.
$0.76 = e^{-0.000121t}$	Divide both sides of the equation by A_0.
$\ln 0.76 = \ln e^{-0.000121t}$	Take the natural logarithm on both sides.
$\ln 0.76 = -0.000121t$	Simplify the right side using $\ln e^x = x$.
$t = \dfrac{\ln 0.76}{-0.000121} \approx 2268$	Divide both sides by -0.000121 and solve for t.

The Dead Sea Scrolls are approximately 2268 years old plus the number of years between 1947 and the current year. ●

Ø Check Point **2** Strontium-90 is a waste product from nuclear reactors. As a consequence of fallout from atmospheric nuclear tests, we all have a measurable amount of strontium-90 in our bones.

a. The half-life of strontium-90 is 28 years, meaning that after 28 years a given amount of the substance will have decayed to half the original amount. Find the exponential decay model for strontium-90.

b. Suppose that a nuclear accident occurs and releases 60 grams of strontium-90 into the atmosphere. How long will it take for strontium-90 to decay to a level of 10 grams?

❷ Use logistic growth models.

Logistic Growth Models

From population growth to the spread of an epidemic, nothing on Earth can grow exponentially indefinitely. Growth is always limited. This is shown in **Figure 4.23** by the horizontal asymptote. The *logistic growth model* is a function used to model situations of this type.

Logistic Growth Model

The mathematical model for limited logistic growth is given by

$$f(t) = \frac{c}{1 + ae^{-bt}} \quad \text{or} \quad A = \frac{c}{1 + ae^{-bt}},$$

where $a, b,$ and c are constants, with $c > 0$ and $b > 0$.

Figure 4.23 The logistic growth curve has a horizontal asymptote that identifies the limit of the growth of A over time.

As time increases $(t \to \infty)$, the expression ae^{-bt} in the model approaches 0, and A gets closer and closer to c. This means that $y = c$ is a horizontal asymptote for the graph of the function. Thus, the value of A can never exceed c and c represents the limiting size that A can attain.

EXAMPLE 3 **Modeling the Spread of the Flu**

The function

$$f(t) = \frac{30,000}{1 + 20e^{-1.5t}}$$

describes the number of people, $f(t)$, who have become ill with influenza t weeks after its initial outbreak in a town with 30,000 inhabitants.

a. How many people became ill with the flu when the epidemic began?

b. How many people were ill by the end of the fourth week?

c. What is the limiting size of $f(t)$, the population that becomes ill?

Solution

a. The time at the beginning of the flu epidemic is $t = 0$. Thus, we can find the number of people who were ill at the beginning of the epidemic by substituting 0 for t.

$$f(t) = \frac{30,000}{1 + 20e^{-1.5t}} \qquad \text{This is the given logistic growth function.}$$

$$f(0) = \frac{30,000}{1 + 20e^{-1.5(0)}} \qquad \text{When the epidemic began, } t = 0.$$

$$= \frac{30,000}{1 + 20} \qquad e^{-1.5(0)} = e^0 = 1$$

$$\approx 1429$$

Approximately 1429 people were ill when the epidemic began.

b. We find the number of people who were ill at the end of the fourth week by substituting 4 for t in the logistic growth function.

$$f(t) = \frac{30,000}{1 + 20e^{-1.5t}} \qquad \text{Use the given logistic growth function.}$$

$$f(4) = \frac{30,000}{1 + 20e^{-1.5(4)}} \qquad \text{To find the number of people ill by the end of week four, let } t = 4.$$

$$\approx 28,583 \qquad \text{Use a calculator.}$$

Approximately 28,583 people were ill by the end of the fourth week. Compared with the number of people who were ill initially, 1429, this illustrates the virulence of the epidemic.

c. Recall that in the logistic growth model, $f(t) = \dfrac{c}{1 + ae^{-bt}}$, the constant c represents the limiting size that $f(t)$ can attain. Thus, the number in the numerator, 30,000, is the limiting size of the population that becomes ill. ●

Technology

The graph of the logistic growth function for the flu epidemic

$$y = \frac{30,000}{1 + 20e^{-1.5x}}$$

can be obtained using a graphing utility. We started x at 0 and ended at 10. This takes us to week 10. (In Example 3, we found that by week 4 approximately 28,583 people were ill.) We also know that 30,000 is the limiting size, so we took values of y up to 30,000. Using a [0, 10, 1] by [0, 30,000, 3000] viewing rectangle, the graph of the logistic growth function is shown below.

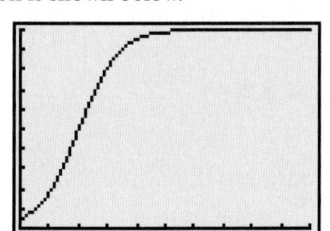

⟟ Check Point **3** In a learning theory project, psychologists discovered that

$$f(t) = \frac{0.8}{1 + e^{-0.2t}}$$

is a model for describing the proportion of correct responses, $f(t)$, after t learning trials.

a. Find the proportion of correct responses prior to learning trials taking place.

b. Find the proportion of correct responses after 10 learning trials.

c. What is the limiting size of $f(t)$, the proportion of correct responses, as continued learning trials take place?

③ Choose an appropriate model for data.

Modeling Data

Throughout this chapter, we have been working with models that were given. However, we can create functions that model data by observing patterns in scatter plots. **Figure 4.24** shows scatter plots for data that are exponential or logarithmic.

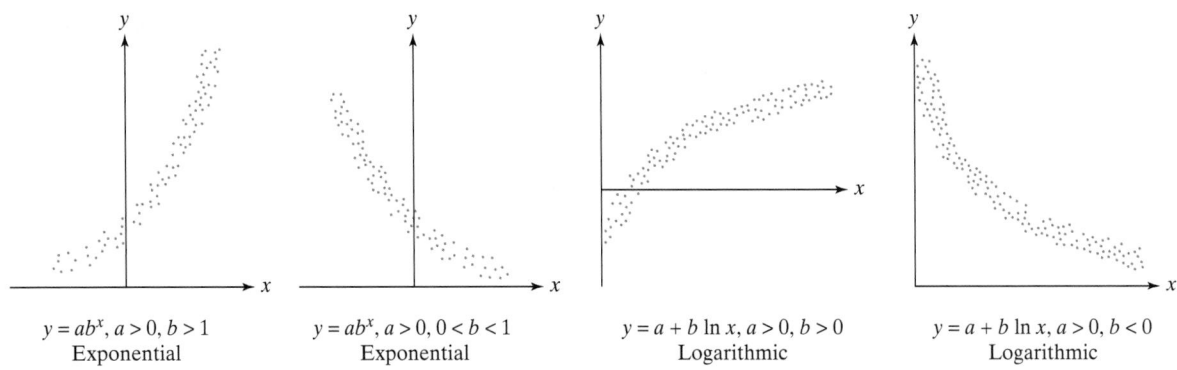

$y = ab^x, a > 0, b > 1$
Exponential

$y = ab^x, a > 0, 0 < b < 1$
Exponential

$y = a + b \ln x, a > 0, b > 0$
Logarithmic

$y = a + b \ln x, a > 0, b < 0$
Logarithmic

Figure 4.24 Scatter plots for exponential or logarithmic models

(**EXAMPLE 4**) **Choosing a Model for Data**

The bar graph in **Figure 4.25(a)** indicates that for the period from 2002 through 2006, an increasing number of Americans had weight-loss surgery. A scatter plot is shown in **Figure 4.25(b)**. What type of function would be a good choice for modeling the data?

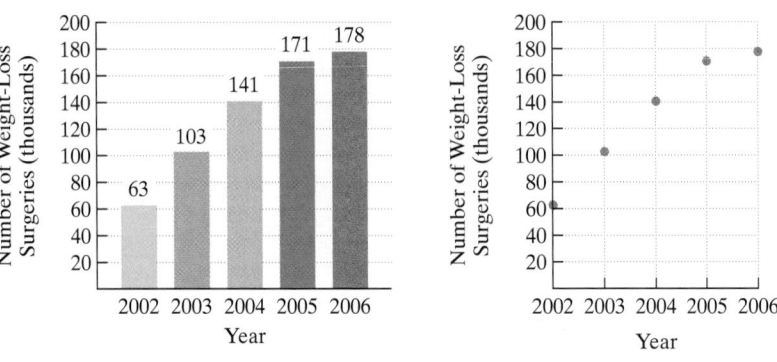

Number of Weight-Loss Surgeries in the United States

Figure 4.25(a)
Source: American Society for Bariatric Surgery

Figure 4.25(b)

Solution Because the data in the scatter plot increase rapidly at first and then begin to level off a bit, the shape suggests that a logarithmic function is a good choice for modeling the data.

Table 4.5 Population and Walking Speed

Population (thousands)	Walking Speed (feet per second)
5.5	0.6
14	1.0
71	1.6
138	1.9
342	2.2

Source: Mark and Helen Bornstein, "The Pace of Life"

⊘ Check Point **4** **Table 4.5** shows the populations of various cities, in thousands, and the average walking speed, in feet per second, of a person living in the city. Create a scatter plot for the data. Based on the scatter plot, what function would be a good choice for modeling the data?

How can we obtain a logarithmic function that models the data for the number of weight-loss surgeries, in thousands, shown in **Figure 4.25(a)**? A graphing utility can be used to obtain a logarithmic model of the form $y = a + b \ln x$. **Because the domain of the logarithmic function is the set of positive numbers, zero must not be a value for x.** What does this mean for the number of weight-loss surgeries that begin in

the year 2002? We must start values of *x* after 0. Thus, we'll assign *x* to represent the number of years after 2001. This gives us the data shown in **Table 4.6**. Using the logarithmic regression option, we obtain the equation in **Figure 4.26**.

Table 4.6

x, Number of Years after 2001	*y*, Number of Weight-Loss Surgeries (thousands)
1 (2002)	63
2 (2003)	103
3 (2004)	141
4 (2005)	171
5 (2006)	178

Figure 4.26 A logarithmic model for the data in **Table 4.6**

From **Figure 4.26**, we see that the logarithmic model of the data, with numbers rounded to three decimal places, is

$$y = 59.059 + 75.343 \ln x.$$

The number *r* that appears in **Figure 4.26** is called the **correlation coefficient** and is a measure of how well the model fits the data. The value of *r* is such that $-1 \le r \le 1$. A positive *r* means that as the *x*-values increase, so do the *y*-values. A negative *r* means that as the *x*-values increase, the *y*-values decrease. **The closer that *r* is to −1 or 1, the better the model fits the data.** Because *r* is approximately 0.992, the model fits the data very well.

EXAMPLE 5 **Choosing a Model for Data**

Figure 4.27(a) shows world population, in billions, for seven selected years from 1950 through 2006. A scatter plot is shown in **Figure 4.27(b)**. Suggest two types of functions that would be good choices for modeling the data.

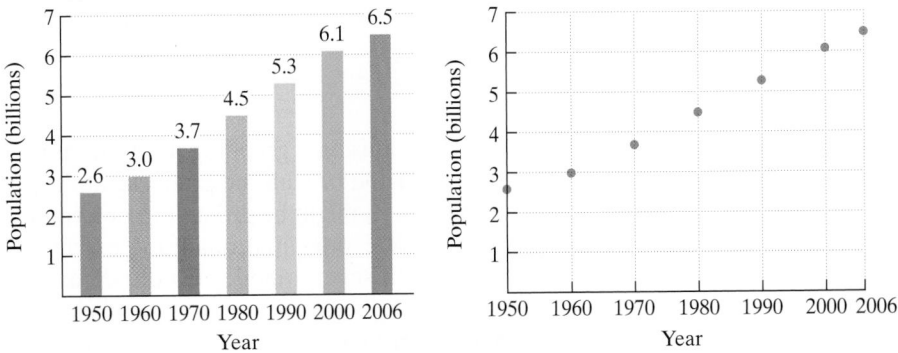

World Population, 1950–2006

Figure 4.27(a)

Figure 4.27(b)

Source: U.S. Census Bureau, International Database

Solution Because the data in the scatter plot appear to increase more and more rapidly, the shape suggests that an exponential model might be a good choice. Furthermore, we can probably draw a line that passes through or near the seven points. Thus, a linear function would also be a good choice for modeling the data.

The data for world population are shown in **Table 4.7**. Using a graphing utility's linear regression feature and exponential regression feature, we enter the data and obtain the models shown in **Figure 4.28**.

Table 4.7

> Although the domain of $y = ab^x$ is the set of all real numbers, some graphing utilities only accept positive values for x. That's why we assigned x to represent the number of years after 1949.

x, Number of Years after 1949	y, World Population (billions)
1 (1950)	2.6
11 (1960)	3.0
21 (1970)	3.7
31 (1980)	4.5
41 (1990)	5.3
51 (2000)	6.1
57 (2006)	6.5

```
LinReg
 y=ax+b
 a=.0727020426
 b=2.316352131
 r²=.9933771692
 r=.9966830836
ExpReg
 y=a*b^x
 a=2.568733848
 b=1.017094896
 r²=.9938074127
 r=.9968988979
```

Figure 4.28 A linear model and an exponential model for the data in Table 4.7

Study Tip

Once you have obtained one or more models for data, you can use a graphing utility's TABLE feature to numerically see how well each model describes the data. Enter the models as y_1, y_2, and so on. Create a table, scroll through the table, and compare the table values given by the models to the actual data.

Using **Figure 4.28** and rounding to three decimal places, the functions

$$f(x) = 0.073x + 2.316 \quad \text{and} \quad g(x) = 2.569(1.017)^x$$

model world population, in billions, x years after 1949. We named the linear function f and the exponential function g, although any letters can be used. Because r, the correlation coefficient, is close to 1 in each screen in **Figure 4.28**, the models fit the data very well.

⊘ Check Point **5** It's a new dawn for technology, appealing to people who have just hung that huge plasma in the home theater: the era of high-definition television. **Table 4.8** shows the percentage of households in the United States with HDTV sets for four selected years from 2001 through 2009. Create a scatter plot for the data. Based on the scatter plot, what function would be a good choice for modeling the data?

Table 4.8 Percentage of U.S. Households with HDTV sets

Year	Percentage of Households
2001	1%
2004	10%
2006	26%
2009	47%

Source: Consumer Electronics Association

When using a graphing utility to model data, begin with a scatter plot, drawn either by hand or with the graphing utility, to obtain a general picture for the shape of the data. It might be difficult to determine which model best fits the data—linear, logarithmic, exponential, quadratic, or something else. If necessary, use your graphing utility to fit several models to the data. The best model is the one that yields the value of r, the correlation coefficient, closest to 1 or -1. Finding a proper fit for data can be almost as much art as it is mathematics. In this era of technology, the process of creating models that best fit data is one that involves more decision making than computation.

④ Express an exponential model in base e.

Expressing $y = ab^x$ in Base e

Graphing utilities display exponential models in the form $y = ab^x$. However, our discussion of exponential growth involved base e. Because of the inverse property $b = e^{\ln b}$, we can rewrite any model in the form $y = ab^x$ in terms of base e.

Expressing an Exponential Model in Base *e*

$y = ab^x$ is equivalent to $y = ae^{(\ln b) \cdot x}$.

EXAMPLE 6 **Rewriting the Model for World Population in Base *e***

We have seen that the function

$$g(x) = 2.569(1.017)^x$$

models world population, $g(x)$, in billions, x years after 1949. Rewrite the model in terms of base *e*.

Solution We use the two equivalent equations shown in the voice balloons to rewrite the model in terms of base *e*.

$y = ab^x$ $\qquad\qquad\qquad\qquad\qquad\qquad\qquad\qquad y = ae^{(\ln b)\,\cdot\,x}$

$g(x) = 2.569(1.017)^x$ is equivalent to $g(x) = 2.569e^{(\ln 1.017)\,\cdot\,x}$.

Using $\ln 1.017 \approx 0.017$, the exponential growth model for world population, $g(x)$, in billions, x years after 1949 is

$$g(x) = 2.569e^{0.017x}.$$

In Example 6, we can replace $g(x)$ with A and x with t so that the model has the same letters as those in the exponential growth model $A = A_0e^{kt}$.

$A =$ A_o e^{kt} This is the exponential growth model.

$A = 2.569e^{0.017t}$ This is the model for world population.

The value of k, 0.017, indicates a growth rate of 1.7% per year. Although this is an excellent model for the data, we must be careful about making projections about world population using this growth function. Why? World population growth rate is now 1.2%, not 1.7%, so our model will overestimate future populations.

✓ Check Point **6** Rewrite $y = 4(7.8)^x$ in terms of base *e*. Express the answer in terms of a natural logarithm and then round to three decimal places.

Exercise Set 4.5

Practice Exercises and Application Exercises

The exponential models describe the population of the indicated country, A, in millions, t years after 2006. Use these models to solve Exercises 1–6.

India — $A = 1095.4e^{0.014t}$

Iraq — $A = 26.8e^{0.027t}$

Japan — $A = 127.5e^{0.001t}$

Russia — $A = 142.9e^{-0.004t}$

1. What was the population of Japan in 2006?

2. What was the population of Iraq in 2006?

3. Which country has the greatest growth rate? By what percentage is the population of that country increasing each year?

4. Which country has a decreasing population? By what percentage is the population of that country decreasing each year?

5. When will India's population be 1238 million?

6. When will India's population be 1416 million?

About the size of New Jersey, Israel has seen its population soar to more than 6 million since it was established. With the help of U.S. aid, the country now has a diversified economy rivaling those of other developed Western nations. By contrast, the Palestinians, living under Israeli occupation and a corrupt regime, endure bleak conditions. The graphs show that by 2050, Palestinians in the West Bank, Gaza Strip, and East Jerusalem will outnumber Israelis. Exercises 7–8 involve the projected growth of these two populations.

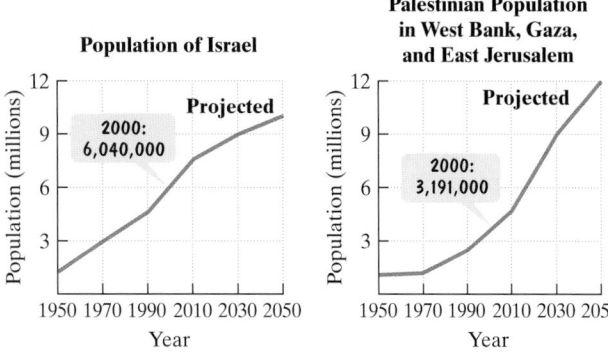

Source: *Newsweek*

7. a. In 2000, the population of Israel was approximately 6.04 million and by 2050 it is projected to grow to 10 million. Use the exponential growth model $A = A_0e^{kt}$, in which t is the number of years after 2000, to find an exponential growth function that models the data.

 b. In which year will Israel's population be 9 million?

8. a. In 2000, the population of the Palestinians in the West Bank, Gaza Strip, and East Jerusalem was approximately 3.2 million and by 2050 it is projected to grow to 12 million. Use the exponential growth model $A = A_0e^{kt}$, in which t is the number of years after 2000, to find the exponential growth function that models the data.

 b. In which year will the Palestinian population be 9 million?

In Exercises 9–14, complete the table. Round projected populations to one decimal place and values of k to four decimal places.

	Country	2007 Population (millions)	Projected 2025 Population (millions)	Projected Growth Rate, k
9.	Philippines	91.1		0.0147
10.	Pakistan	164.7		0.0157
11.	Colombia	44.4	55.2	
12.	Madagascar	19.4	32.4	
13.	South Africa	44.0	40.0	
14.	Bulgaria	7.3	6.3	

Source: International Programs Center, U.S. Census Bureau

An artifact originally had 16 grams of carbon-14 present. The decay model $A = 16e^{-0.000121t}$ describes the amount of carbon-14 present after t years. Use this model to solve Exercises 15–16.

15. How many grams of carbon-14 will be present in 5715 years?

16. How many grams of carbon-14 will be present in 11,430 years?

17. The half-life of the radioactive element krypton-91 is 10 seconds. If 16 grams of krypton-91 are initially present, how many grams are present after 10 seconds? 20 seconds? 30 seconds? 40 seconds? 50 seconds?

18. The half-life of the radioactive element plutonium-239 is 25,000 years. If 16 grams of plutonium-239 are initially present, how many grams are present after 25,000 years? 50,000 years? 75,000 years? 100,000 years? 125,000 years?

Use the exponential decay model for carbon-14, $A = A_0e^{-0.000121t}$, to solve Exercises 19–20.

19. Prehistoric cave paintings were discovered in a cave in France. The paint contained 15% of the original carbon-14. Estimate the age of the paintings.

20. Skeletons were found at a construction site in San Francisco in 1989. The skeletons contained 88% of the expected amount of carbon-14 found in a living person. In 1989, how old were the skeletons?

In Exercises 21–26, complete the table. Round half-lives to one decimal place and values of k to six decimal places.

	Radioactive Substance	Half-Life	Decay Rate, k
21.	Tritium		5.5% per year = −0.055
22.	Krypton-85		6.3% per year = −0.063
23.	Radium-226	1620 years	
24.	Uranium-238	4560 years	
25.	Arsenic-74	17.5 days	
26.	Calcium-47	113 hours	

27. The August 1978 issue of *National Geographic* described the 1964 find of bones of a newly discovered dinosaur weighing 170 pounds, measuring 9 feet, with a 6-inch claw on one toe of each hind foot. The age of the dinosaur was estimated using potassium-40 dating of rocks surrounding the bones.

 a. Potassium-40 decays exponentially with a half-life of approximately 1.31 billion years. Use the fact that after 1.31 billion years a given amount of potassium-40 will have decayed to half the original amount to show that the decay model for potassium-40 is given by $A = A_0e^{-0.52912t}$, where t is in billions of years.

 b. Analysis of the rocks surrounding the dinosaur bones indicated that 94.5% of the original amount of potassium-40 was still present. Let $A = 0.945A_0$ in the model in part (a) and estimate the age of the bones of the dinosaur.

Use the exponential decay model, $A = A_0e^{kt}$, to solve Exercises 28–31. Round answers to one decimal place.

28. The half-life of thorium-229 is 7340 years. How long will it take for a sample of this substance to decay to 20% of its original amount?

29. The half-life of lead is 22 years. How long will it take for a sample of this substance to decay to 80% of its original amount?

30. The half-life of aspirin in your bloodstream is 12 hours. How long will it take for the aspirin to decay to 70% of the original dosage?

31. Xanax is a tranquilizer used in the short-term relief of symptoms of anxiety. Its half-life in the bloodstream is 36 hours. How long will it take for Xanax to decay to 90% of the original dosage?

32. A bird species in danger of extinction has a population that is decreasing exponentially ($A = A_0e^{kt}$). Five years ago the population was at 1400 and today only 1000 of the birds are alive. Once the population drops below 100, the situation will be irreversible. When will this happen?

33. Use the exponential growth model, $A = A_0e^{kt}$, to show that the time it takes a population to double (to grow from A_0 to $2A_0$) is given by $t = \dfrac{\ln 2}{k}$.

34. Use the exponential growth model, $A = A_0e^{kt}$, to show that the time it takes a population to triple (to grow from A_0 to $3A_0$) is given by $t = \dfrac{\ln 3}{k}$.

Use the formula $t = \dfrac{\ln 2}{k}$ that gives the time for a population with a growth rate k to double to solve Exercises 35–36. Express each answer to the nearest whole year.

35. The growth model $A = 4.1e^{0.01t}$ describes New Zealand's population, A, in millions, t years after 2006.

 a. What is New Zealand's growth rate?

 b. How long will it take New Zealand to double its population?

36. The growth model $A = 107.4e^{0.012t}$ describes Mexico's population, A, in millions, t years after 2006.

 a. What is Mexico's growth rate?

 b. How long will it take Mexico to double its population?

37. The logistic growth function

$$f(t) = \frac{100{,}000}{1 + 5000e^{-t}}$$

describes the number of people, $f(t)$, who have become ill with influenza t weeks after its initial outbreak in a particular community.

 a. How many people became ill with the flu when the epidemic began?

 b. How many people were ill by the end of the fourth week?

 c. What is the limiting size of the population that becomes ill?

Shown, again, at the top of the next column is world population, in billions, for seven selected years from 1950 through 2006. Using a graphing utility's logistic regression option, we obtain the equation shown on the screen.

x, Number of Years after 1949	y, World Population (billions)
1 (1950)	2.6
11 (1960)	3.0
21 (1970)	3.7
31 (1980)	4.5
41 (1990)	5.3
51 (2000)	6.1
57 (2006)	6.5

We see from the calculator screen that a logistic growth model for world population, $f(x)$, in billions, x years after 1949 is

$$f(x) = \frac{11.82}{1 + 3.81e^{-0.027x}}.$$

Use this function to solve Exercises 38–42.

38. How well does the function model the data for 2000?

39. How well does the function model the data for 2006?

40. When will world population reach 7 billion?

41. When will world population reach 8 billion?

42. According to the model, what is the limiting size of the population that Earth will eventually sustain?

The logistic growth function

$$P(x) = \frac{90}{1 + 271e^{-0.122x}}$$

models the percentage, $P(x)$, of Americans who are x years old with some coronary heart disease. Use the function to solve Exercises 43–46.

43. What percentage of 20-year-olds have some coronary heart disease?

44. What percentage of 80-year-olds have some coronary heart disease?

45. At what age is the percentage of some coronary heart disease 50%?

46. At what age is the percentage of some coronary heart disease 70%?

Exercises 47–50 present data in the form of tables. For each data set shown by the table,

 a. *Create a scatter plot for the data.*

 b. *Use the scatter plot to determine whether an exponential function or a logarithmic function is the best choice for modeling the data. (If applicable, in Exercise 70, you will use your graphing utility to obtain these functions.)*

47. Percent of Miscarriages, by Age

Woman's Age	Percent of Miscarriages
22	9%
27	10%
32	13%
37	20%
42	38%
47	52%

Source: Time

48. Savings Needed for Health-Care Expenses during Retirement

Age at Death	Savings Needed
80	$219,000
85	$307,000
90	$409,000
95	$524,000
100	$656,000

Source: Employee Benefit Research Institute

49. Intensity and Loudness Level of Various Sounds

Intensity (watts per meter2)	Loudness Level (decibels)
0.1 (loud thunder)	110
1 (rock concert, 2 yd from speakers)	120
10 (jackhammer)	130
100 (jet takeoff, 40 yd away)	140

50. Temperature Increase in an Enclosed Vehicle

Minutes	Temperature Increase (°F)
10	19°
20	29°
30	34°
40	38°
50	41°
60	43°

In Exercises 51–54, rewrite the equation in terms of base e. Express the answer in terms of a natural logarithm and then round to three decimal places.

51. $y = 100(4.6)^x$ **52.** $y = 1000(7.3)^x$

53. $y = 2.5(0.7)^x$ **54.** $y = 4.5(0.6)^x$

Writing in Mathematics

55. Nigeria has a growth rate of 0.025 or 2.5%. Describe what this means.

56. How can you tell whether an exponential model describes exponential growth or exponential decay?

57. Suppose that a population that is growing exponentially increases from 800,000 people in 2003 to 1,000,000 people in 2006. Without showing the details, describe how to obtain the exponential growth function that models the data.

58. What is the half-life of a substance?

59. Describe a difference between exponential growth and logistic growth.

60. Describe the shape of a scatter plot that suggests modeling the data with an exponential function.

61. You take up weightlifting and record the maximum number of pounds you can lift at the end of each week. You start off with rapid growth in terms of the weight you can lift from week to week, but then the growth begins to level off. Describe how to obtain a function that models the number of pounds you can lift at the end of each week. How can you use this function to predict what might happen if you continue the sport?

62. Would you prefer that your salary be modeled exponentially or logarithmically? Explain your answer.

63. One problem with all exponential growth models is that nothing can grow exponentially forever. Describe factors that might limit the size of a population.

Technology Exercises

In Example 1 on page 461, we used two data points and an exponential function to model the population of the United States from 1970 through 2007. The data are shown again in the table. Use all five data points to solve Exercises 64–68.

x, Number of Years after 1969	y, U.S. Population (millions)
1 (1970)	203.3
11 (1980)	226.5
21 (1990)	248.7
31 (2000)	281.4
38 (2007)	300.9

64. a. Use your graphing utility's exponential regression option to obtain a model of the form $y = ab^x$ that fits the data. How well does the correlation coefficient, r, indicate that the model fits the data?

 b. Rewrite the model in terms of base e. By what percentage is the population of the United States increasing each year?

65. Use your graphing utility's logarithmic regression option to obtain a model of the form $y = a + b \ln x$ that fits the data. How well does the correlation coefficient, r, indicate that the model fits the data?

66. Use your graphing utility's linear regression option to obtain a model of the form $y = ax + b$ that fits the data. How well does the correlation coefficient, r, indicate that the model fits the data?

67. Use your graphing utility's power regression option to obtain a model of the form $y = ax^b$ that fits the data. How well does the correlation coefficient, r, indicate that the model fits the data?

68. Use the values of r in Exercises 64–67 to select the two models of best fit. Use each of these models to predict by which year the U.S. population will reach 315 million. How do these answers compare to the year we found in Example 1, namely 2010? If you obtained different years, how do you account for this difference?

69. The figure shows the number of people in the United States age 65 and over, with projected figures for the year 2010 and beyond.

United States Population Age 65 and Over

Source: U.S. Census Bureau

a. Let *x* represent the number of years after 1899 and let *y* represent the U.S. population age 65 and over, in millions. Use your graphing utility to find the model that best fits the data in the bar graph.

b. Rewrite the model in terms of base *e*. By what percentage is the 65 and over population increasing each year?

70. In Exercises 47–50, you determined the best choice for the kind of function that modeled the data in the table. For each of the exercises that you worked, use a graphing utility to find the actual function that best fits the data. Then use the model to make a reasonable prediction for a value that exceeds those shown in the table's first column.

Critical Thinking Exercises

Make Sense? *In Exercises 71–74, determine whether each statement makes sense or does not make sense, and explain your reasoning.*

71. I used an exponential model with a positive growth rate to describe the depreciation in my car's value over four years.

72. After 100 years, a population whose growth rate is 3% will have three times as many people as a population whose growth rate is 1%.

73. When I used an exponential function to model Russia's declining population, the growth rate *k* was negative.

74. Because carbon-14 decays exponentially, carbon dating can determine the ages of ancient fossils.

The exponential growth models describe the population of the indicated country, A, in millions, t years after 2006.

Canada $A = 33.1e^{0.009t}$

Uganda $A = 28.2e^{0.034t}$

In Exercises 75–78, use this information to determine whether each statement is true or false. If the statement is false, make the necessary change(s) to produce a true statement.

75. In 2006, Canada's population exceeded Uganda's by 4.9 million.

76. By 2009, the models indicate that Canada's population will exceed Uganda's by approximately 2.8 million.

77. The models indicate that in 2013, Uganda's population will exceed Canada's.

78. Uganda's growth rate is approximately 3.8 times that of Canada's.

79. Over a period of time, a hot object cools to the temperature of the surrounding air. This is described mathematically by Newton's Law of Cooling:

$$T = C + (T_0 - C)e^{-kt},$$

where *t* is the time it takes for an object to cool from temperature T_0 to temperature T, C is the surrounding air temperature, and *k* is a positive constant that is associated with the cooling object. A cake removed from the oven has a temperature of 210°F and is left to cool in a room that has a temperature of 70°F. After 30 minutes, the temperature of the cake is 140°F. What is the temperature of the cake after 40 minutes?

Group Exercise

80. Each group member should consult an almanac, newspaper, magazine, or the Internet to find data that can be modeled by exponential or logarithmic functions. Group members should select the two sets of data that are most interesting and relevant. For each set selected, find a model that best fits the data. Each group member should make one prediction based on the model and then discuss a consequence of this prediction. What factors might change the accuracy of the prediction?

Preview Exercises

Exercises 81–83 will help you prepare for the material covered in the first section of the next chapter.

81. a. Does (4, −1) satisfy $x + 2y = 2$?

b. Does (4, −1) satisfy $x − 2y = 6$?

82. Graph $x + 2y = 2$ and $x − 2y = 6$ in the same rectangular coordinate system. At what point do the graphs intersect?

83. Solve: $5(2x − 3) − 4x = 9$.

Chapter 4 Summary, Review, and Test

Summary

DEFINITIONS AND CONCEPTS	**EXAMPLES**
4.1 Exponential Functions	
a. The exponential function with base b is defined by $f(x) = b^x$, where $b > 0$ and $b \neq 1$.	Ex. 1, p. 413
b. Characteristics of exponential functions and graphs for $0 < b < 1$ and $b > 1$ are shown in the box on page 415.	Ex. 2, p. 414; Ex. 3, p. 414
c. Transformations involving exponential functions are summarized in Table 4.1 on page 416.	Ex. 4, p. 416; Ex. 5, p. 417
d. The natural exponential function is $f(x) = e^x$. The irrational number e is called the natural base, where $e \approx 2.7183$. e is the value that $\left(1 + \dfrac{1}{n}\right)^n$ approaches as $n \to \infty$.	Ex. 6, p. 418
e. Formulas for compound interest: After t years, the balance, A, in an account with principal P and annual interest rate r (in decimal form) is given by one of the following formulas: **1.** For n compoundings per year: $A = P\left(1 + \dfrac{r}{n}\right)^{nt}$ **2.** For continuous compounding: $A = Pe^{rt}$.	Ex. 7, p. 420
4.2 Logarithmic Functions	
a. Definition of the logarithmic function: For $x > 0$ and $b > 0$, $b \neq 1$, $y = \log_b x$ is equivalent to $b^y = x$. The function $f(x) = \log_b x$ is the logarithmic function with base b. This function is the inverse function of the exponential function with base b.	Ex. 1, p. 425; Ex. 2, p. 425; Ex. 3, p. 426
b. Graphs of logarithmic functions for $b > 1$ and $0 < b < 1$ are shown in Figure 4.8 on page 428. Characteristics of the graphs are summarized in the box on page 429.	Ex. 6, p. 428
c. Transformations involving logarithmic functions are summarized in Table 4.4 on page 429.	Figures 4.9–4.12, pp. 429–430
d. The domain of a logarithmic function of the form $f(x) = \log_b x$ is the set of all positive real numbers. The domain of $f(x) = \log_b g(x)$ consists of all x for which $g(x) > 0$.	Ex. 7, p. 430; Ex. 10, p. 432
e. Common and natural logarithms: $f(x) = \log x$ means $f(x) = \log_{10} x$ and is the common logarithmic function. $f(x) = \ln x$ means $f(x) = \log_e x$ and is the natural logarithmic function.	Ex. 8, p. 431; Ex. 9, p. 432; Ex. 11, p. 433

f. Basic Logarithmic Properties

Base b ($b > 0$, $b \neq 1$)	Base 10 (Common Logarithms)	Base e (Natural Logarithms)	
$\log_b 1 = 0$	$\log 1 = 0$	$\ln 1 = 0$	
$\log_b b = 1$	$\log 10 = 1$	$\ln e = 1$	Ex. 4, p. 426
$\log_b b^x = x$	$\log 10^x = x$	$\ln e^x = x$	
$b^{\log_b x} = x$	$10^{\log x} = x$	$e^{\ln x} = x$	Ex. 5, p. 427

4.3 Properties of Logarithms	
a. *The Product Rule:* $\log_b(MN) = \log_b M + \log_b N$	Ex. 1, p. 438
b. *The Quotient Rule:* $\log_b\left(\dfrac{M}{N}\right) = \log_b M - \log_b N$	Ex. 2, p. 439
c. *The Power Rule:* $\log_b M^p = p \log_b M$	Ex. 3, p. 440

DEFINITIONS AND CONCEPTS	EXAMPLES

d. *The Change-of-Base Property:*

The General Property	Introducing Common Logarithms	Introducing Natural Logarithms
$\log_b M = \dfrac{\log_a M}{\log_a b}$	$\log_b M = \dfrac{\log M}{\log b}$	$\log_b M = \dfrac{\ln M}{\ln b}$

Ex. 7, p. 444;
Ex. 8, p. 444

e. Properties for expanding logarithmic expressions are given in the box on page 440. Ex. 4, p. 441

f. Properties for condensing logarithmic expressions are given in the box on page 442. Ex. 5, p. 442;
Ex. 6, p. 442

4.4 Exponential and Logarithmic Equations

a. An exponential equation is an equation containing a variable in an exponent. Some exponential equations can be solved by expressing each side as a power of the same base: If $b^M = b^N$, then $M = N$. Details are in the box on page 448. Ex. 1, p. 448

b. The procedure for using logarithms to solve exponential equations is given in the box on page 449. The solution procedure involves isolating the exponential expression. Take the natural logarithm on both sides for bases other than 10 and take the common logarithm on both sides for base 10. Simplify using

$$\ln b^x = x \ln b \quad \text{or} \quad \ln e^x = x \quad \text{or} \quad \log 10^x = x.$$

Ex. 2, p. 449;
Ex. 3, p. 450;
Ex. 4, p. 450;
Ex. 5, p. 451

c. A logarithmic equation is an equation containing a variable in a logarithmic expression. Some logarithmic equations can be expressed in the form $\log_b M = c$. The definition of a logarithm is used to rewrite the equation in exponential form: $b^c = M$. See the box on page 451. When checking logarithmic equations, reject proposed solutions that produce the logarithm of a negative number or the logarithm of 0 in the original equation. Ex. 6, p. 451;
Ex. 7, p. 452

d. Some logarithmic equations can be expressed in the form $\log_b M = \log_b N$. Use the one-to-one property to rewrite the equation without logarithms: $M = N$. See the box on page 453. Ex. 8, p. 453

4.5 Exponential Growth and Decay; Modeling Data

a. Exponential growth and decay models are given by $A = A_0 e^{kt}$ in which t represents time, A_0 is the amount present at $t = 0$, and A is the amount present at time t. If $k > 0$, the model describes growth and k is the growth rate. If $k < 0$, the model describes decay and k is the decay rate. Ex. 1, p. 461;
Ex. 2, p. 463

b. The logistic growth model, given by $A = \dfrac{c}{1 + ae^{-bt}}$, describes situations in which growth is limited. $y = c$ is a horizontal asymptote for the graph, and growth, A, can never exceed c. Ex. 3, p. 465

c. Scatter plots for exponential and logarithmic models are shown in Figure 4.24 on page 466. When using a graphing utility to model data, the closer that the correlation coefficient, r, is to -1 or 1, the better the model fits the data. Ex. 4, p. 466;
Ex. 5, p. 467

d. Expressing an Exponential Model in Base e: $y = ab^x$ is equivalent to $y = ae^{(\ln b)\cdot x}$. Ex. 6, p. 469

Review Exercises

4.1

In Exercises 1–4, the graph of an exponential function is given. Select the function for each graph from the following options:

$$f(x) = 4^x, g(x) = 4^{-x},$$
$$h(x) = -4^{-x}, r(x) = -4^{-x} + 3.$$

1.

2.

3.

4.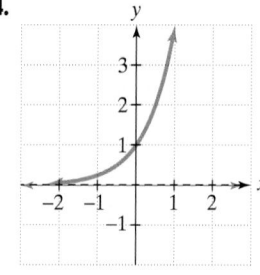

In Exercises 5–9, graph f and g in the same rectangular coordinate system. Use transformations of the graph of f to obtain the graph of g. Graph and give equations of all asymptotes. Use the graphs to determine each function's domain and range.

5. $f(x) = 2^x$ and $g(x) = 2^{x-1}$

6. $f(x) = 3^x$ and $g(x) = 3^x - 1$

7. $f(x) = 3^x$ and $g(x) = -3^x$

8. $f(x) = \left(\frac{1}{2}\right)^x$ and $g(x) = \left(\frac{1}{2}\right)^{-x}$

9. $f(x) = e^x$ and $g(x) = 2e^{\frac{x}{2}}$

Use the compound interest formulas to solve Exercises 10–11.

10. Suppose that you have $5000 to invest. Which investment yields the greater return over 5 years: 5.5% compounded semiannually or 5.25% compounded monthly?

11. Suppose that you have $14,000 to invest. Which investment yields the greater return over 10 years: 7% compounded monthly or 6.85% compounded continuously?

12. A cup of coffee is taken out of a microwave oven and placed in a room. The temperature, T, in degrees Fahrenheit, of the coffee after t minutes is modeled by the function $T = 70 + 130e^{-0.04855t}$. The graph of the function is shown in the figure.

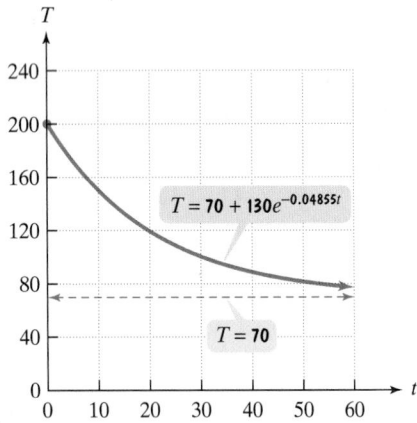

Use the graph to answer each of the following questions.

a. What was the temperature of the coffee when it was first taken out of the microwave?

b. What is a reasonable estimate of the temperature of the coffee after 20 minutes? Use your calculator to verify this estimate.

c. What is the limit of the temperature to which the coffee will cool? What does this tell you about the temperature of the room?

4.2

In Exercises 13–15, write each equation in its equivalent exponential form.

13. $\frac{1}{2} = \log_{49} 7$ **14.** $3 = \log_4 x$ **15.** $\log_3 81 = y$

In Exercises 16–18, write each equation in its equivalent logarithmic form.

16. $6^3 = 216$ **17.** $b^4 = 625$ **18.** $13^y = 874$

In Exercises 19–29, evaluate each expression without using a calculator. If evaluation is not possible, state the reason.

19. $\log_4 64$ **20.** $\log_5 \frac{1}{25}$ **21.** $\log_3(-9)$

22. $\log_{16} 4$ **23.** $\log_{17} 17$ **24.** $\log_3 3^8$

25. $\ln e^5$ **26.** $\log_3 \frac{1}{\sqrt{3}}$ **27.** $\ln \frac{1}{e^2}$

28. $\log \frac{1}{1000}$ **29.** $\log_3(\log_8 8)$

30. Graph $f(x) = 2^x$ and $g(x) = \log_2 x$ in the same rectangular coordinate system. Use the graphs to determine each function's domain and range.

31. Graph $f(x) = \left(\frac{1}{3}\right)^x$ and $g(x) = \log_{\frac{1}{3}} x$ in the same rectangular coordinate system. Use the graphs to determine each function's domain and range.

In Exercises 32–35, the graph of a logarithmic function is given. Select the function for each graph from the following options:

$$f(x) = \log x, g(x) = \log(-x),$$
$$h(x) = \log(2 - x), r(x) = 1 + \log(2 - x).$$

32.

33.

34.

35.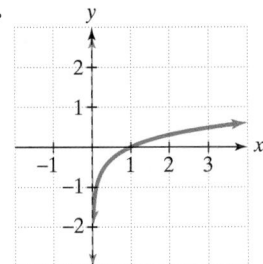

In Exercises 36–38, begin by graphing $f(x) = \log_2 x$. Then use transformations of this graph to graph the given function. What is the graph's x-intercept? What is the vertical asymptote? Use the graphs to determine each function's domain and range.

36. $g(x) = \log_2(x - 2)$ **37.** $h(x) = -1 + \log_2 x$

38. $r(x) = \log_2(-x)$

In Exercises 39–40, graph f and g in the same rectangular coordinate system. Use transformations of the graph of f to obtain the graph of g. Graph and give equations of all asymptotes. Use the graphs to determine each function's domain and range.

39. $f(x) = \log x$ and $g(x) = -\log(x + 3)$

40. $f(x) = \ln x$ and $g(x) = -\ln(2x)$

In Exercises 41–43, find the domain of each logarithmic function.

41. $f(x) = \log_8(x + 5)$ **42.** $f(x) = \log(3 - x)$

43. $f(x) = \ln(x - 1)^2$

In Exercises 44–46, use inverse properties of logarithms to simplify each expression.

44. $\ln e^{6x}$ **45.** $e^{\ln \sqrt{x}}$ **46.** $10^{\log 4x^2}$

47. On the Richter scale, the magnitude, R, of an earthquake of intensity I is given by $R = \log \dfrac{I}{I_0}$, where I_0 is the intensity of a barely felt zero-level earthquake. If the intensity of an earthquake is $1000I_0$, what is its magnitude on the Richter scale?

48. Students in a psychology class took a final examination. As part of an experiment to see how much of the course content they remembered over time, they took equivalent forms of the exam in monthly intervals thereafter. The average score, $f(t)$, for the group after t months is modeled by the function $f(t) = 76 - 18\log(t + 1)$, where $0 \le t \le 12$.

 a. What was the average score when the exam was first given?

 b. What was the average score after 2 months? 4 months? 6 months? 8 months? one year?

 c. Use the results from parts (a) and (b) to graph f. Describe what the shape of the graph indicates in terms of the material retained by the students.

49. The formula

$$t = \frac{1}{c}\ln\left(\frac{A}{A - N}\right)$$

describes the time, t, in weeks, that it takes to achieve mastery of a portion of a task. In the formula, A represents maximum learning possible, N is the portion of the learning that is to be achieved, and c is a constant used to measure an individual's learning style. A 50-year-old man decides to start running as a way to maintain good health. He feels that the maximum rate he could ever hope to achieve is 12 miles per hour. How many weeks will it take before the man can run 5 miles per hour if $c = 0.06$ for this person?

4.3

In Exercises 50–53, use properties of logarithms to expand each logarithmic expression as much as possible. Where possible, evaluate logarithmic expressions without using a calculator.

50. $\log_6(36x^3)$

51. $\log_4\left(\dfrac{\sqrt{x}}{64}\right)$

52. $\log_2\left(\dfrac{xy^2}{64}\right)$

53. $\ln\sqrt[3]{\dfrac{x}{e}}$

In Exercises 54–57, use properties of logarithms to condense each logarithmic expression. Write the expression as a single logarithm whose coefficient is 1.

54. $\log_b 7 + \log_b 3$

55. $\log 3 - 3\log x$

56. $3\ln x + 4\ln y$

57. $\frac{1}{2}\ln x - \ln y$

In Exercises 58–59, use common logarithms or natural logarithms and a calculator to evaluate to four decimal places.

58. $\log_6 72,348$

59. $\log_4 0.863$

In Exercises 60–63, determine whether each equation is true or false. Where possible, show work to support your conclusion. If the statement is false, make the necessary change(s) to produce a true statement.

60. $(\ln x)(\ln 1) = 0$

61. $\log(x + 9) - \log(x + 1) = \dfrac{\log(x + 9)}{\log(x + 1)}$

62. $(\log_2 x)^4 = 4\log_2 x$

63. $\ln e^x = x\ln e$

4.4

In Exercises 64–73, solve each exponential equation. Where necessary, express the solution set in terms of natural or common logarithms and use a calculator to obtain a decimal approximation, correct to two decimal places, for the solution.

64. $2^{4x-2} = 64$

65. $125^x = 25$

66. $10^x = 7000$

67. $9^{x+2} = 27^{-x}$

68. $8^x = 12,143$

69. $9e^{5x} = 1269$

70. $e^{12-5x} - 7 = 123$

71. $5^{4x+2} = 37,500$

72. $3^{x+4} = 7^{2x-1}$

73. $e^{2x} - e^x - 6 = 0$

In Exercises 74–79, solve each logarithmic equation.

74. $\log_4(3x - 5) = 3$

75. $3 + 4\ln(2x) = 15$

76. $\log_2(x + 3) + \log_2(x - 3) = 4$

77. $\log_3(x - 1) - \log_3(x + 2) = 2$

78. $\ln(x + 4) - \ln(x + 1) = \ln x$

79. $\log_4(2x + 1) = \log_4(x - 3) + \log_4(x + 5)$

80. The function $P(x) = 14.7e^{-0.21x}$ models the average atmospheric pressure, $P(x)$, in pounds per square inch, at an altitude of x miles above sea level. The atmospheric pressure at the peak of Mt. Everest, the world's highest mountain, is 4.6 pounds per square inch. How many miles above sea level, to the nearest tenth of a mile, is the peak of Mt. Everest?

81. The amount of carbon dioxide in the atmosphere, measured in parts per million, has been increasing as a result of the burning of oil and coal. The buildup of gases and particles traps heat and raises the planet's temperature, a phenomenon called the greenhouse effect. Carbon dioxide accounts for about half of the warming. The function $f(t) = 364(1.005)^t$ projects carbon dioxide concentration, $f(t)$, in parts per million, t years after 2000. Using the projections given by the function, when will the carbon dioxide concentration be double the preindustrial level of 280 parts per million?

82. The function $W(x) = 0.37\ln x + 0.05$ models the average walking speed, $W(x)$, in feet per second, of residents in a city whose population is x thousand. Visitors to New York City frequently feel they are moving too slowly to keep pace with New Yorkers' average walking speed of 3.38 feet per second. What is the population of New York City? Round to the nearest thousand.

83. Use the formula for compound interest with n compoundings per year to solve this problem. How long, to the nearest tenth of a year, will it take $12,500 to grow to $20,000 at 6.5% annual interest compounded quarterly?

Use the formula for continuous compounding to solve Exercises 84–85.

84. How long, to the nearest tenth of a year, will it take $50,000 to triple in value at 7.5% annual interest compounded continuously?

85. What interest rate, to the nearest percent, is required for an investment subject to continuous compounding to triple in 5 years?

4.5

86. According to the U.S. Bureau of the Census, in 1990 there were 22.4 million residents of Hispanic origin living in the United States. By 2000, the number had increased to 35.3 million. The exponential growth function $A = 22.4e^{kt}$ describes the U.S. Hispanic population, A, in millions, t years after 1990.

 a. Find k, correct to three decimal places.

 b. Use the resulting model to project the Hispanic resident population in 2010.

 c. In which year will the Hispanic resident population reach 60 million?

87. Use the exponential decay model, $A = A_0e^{kt}$, to solve this exercise. The half-life of polonium-210 is 140 days. How long will it take for a sample of this substance to decay to 20% of its original amount?

88. The function

$$f(t) = \frac{500{,}000}{1 + 2499e^{-0.92t}}$$

models the number of people, $f(t)$, in a city who have become ill with influenza t weeks after its initial outbreak.

 a. How many people became ill with the flu when the epidemic began?

 b. How many people were ill by the end of the sixth week?

 c. What is the limiting size of $f(t)$, the population that becomes ill?

Exercises 89–90 present data in the form of tables. For each data set shown by the table,

 a. *Create a scatter plot for the data.*

 b. *Use the scatter plot to determine whether an exponential function or a logarithmic function is the better choice for modeling the data.*

89. **Growth of the Human Brain**

Age	Percentage of Adult Size Brain
1	30%
2	50%
4	78%
6	88%
8	92%
10	95%
11	99%

Source: Gerrig and Zimbardo, *Psychology and Life*, Eighteenth Edition, Allyn and Bacon, 2008

90. **Text Messaging in the U.S.**

Year	Monthly Text Messages (billions)
2002	0.9
2003	1.0
2004	2.1
2005	8.3
2006	14.2
2007	28.9

Source: CTIA

In Exercises 91–92, rewrite the equation in terms of base e. Express the answer in terms of a natural logarithm and then round to three decimal places.

91. $y = 73(2.6)^x$

92. $y = 6.5(0.43)^x$

93. The figure shows world population projections through the year 2150. The data are from the United Nations Family Planning Program and are based on optimistic or pessimistic expectations for successful control of human population growth. Suppose that you are interested in modeling these data using exponential, logarithmic, linear, and quadratic functions. Which function would you use to model each of the projections? Explain your choices. For the choice corresponding to a quadratic model, would your formula involve one with a positive or negative leading coefficient? Explain.

Source: U.N.

1. Graph $f(x) = 2^x$ and $g(x) = 2^{x+1}$ in the same rectangular coordinate system.

2. Graph $f(x) = \log_2 x$ and $g(x) = \log_2(x - 1)$ in the same rectangular coordinate system.

3. Write in exponential form: $\log_5 125 = 3$.

4. Write in logarithmic form: $\sqrt{36} = 6$.

5. Find the domain: $f(x) = \ln(3 - x)$.

In Exercises 6–7, use properties of logarithms to expand each logarithmic expression as much as possible. Where possible, evaluate logarithmic expressions without using a calculator.

6. $\log_4(64x^5)$

7. $\log_3\left(\dfrac{\sqrt[3]{x}}{81}\right)$

In Exercises 8–9, write each expression as a single logarithm.

8. $6 \log x + 2 \log y$

9. $\ln 7 - 3 \ln x$

10. Use a calculator to evaluate $\log_{15} 71$ to four decimal places.

In Exercises 11–18, solve each equation.

11. $3^{x-2} = 9^{x+4}$

12. $5^x = 1.4$

13. $400e^{0.005x} = 1600$

14. $e^{2x} - 6e^x + 5 = 0$

15. $\log_6(4x - 1) = 3$

16. $2 \ln(3x) = 8$

17. $\log x + \log(x + 15) = 2$

18. $\ln(x - 4) - \ln(x + 1) = \ln 6$

19. On the decibel scale, the loudness of a sound, D, in decibels, is given by $D = 10 \log \dfrac{I}{I_0}$, where I is the intensity of the sound, in watts per meter2, and I_0 is the intensity of a sound barely audible to the human ear. If the intensity of a sound is $10^{12}I_0$, what is its loudness in decibels? (Such a sound is potentially damaging to the ear.)

In Exercises 20–22, simplify each expression.

20. $\ln e^{5x}$

21. $\log_b b$

22. $\log_6 1$

Use the compound interest formulas to solve Exercises 23–25.

23. Suppose you have $3000 to invest. Which investment yields the greater return over 10 years: 6.5% compounded semiannually or 6% compounded continuously? How much more (to the nearest dollar) is yielded by the better investment?

24. How long, to the nearest tenth of a year, will it take $4000 to grow to $8000 at 5% annual interest compounded quarterly?

25. What interest rate, to the nearest tenth of a percent, is required for an investment subject to continuous compounding to double in 10 years?

26. The function
$$A = 82.4e^{-0.002t}$$
models the population of Germany, A, in millions, t years after 2006.
 a. What was the population of Germany in 2006?
 b. Is the population of Germany increasing or decreasing? Explain.
 c. In which year will the population of Germany be 81.5 million?

27. The 1990 population of Europe was 509 million; in 2000, it was 729 million. Write the exponential growth function that describes the population of Europe, in millions, t years after 1990.

28. Use the exponential decay model, $A = A_0 e^{kt}$, to solve this exercise. The half-life of iodine-131 is 7.2 days. How long will it take for a sample of this substance to decay to 30% of its original amount? Round to one decimal place.

29. The logistic growth function
$$f(t) = \frac{140}{1 + 9e^{-0.165t}}$$
describes the population, $f(t)$, of an endangered species of elk t years after they were introduced to a nonthreatening habitat.
 a. How many elk were initially introduced to the habitat?
 b. How many elk are expected in the habitat after 10 years?
 c. What is the limiting size of the elk population that the habitat will sustain?

In Exercises 30–33, determine whether the values in each table belong to an exponential function, a logarithmic function, a linear function, or a quadratic function.

30.

x	y
0	3
1	1
2	−1
3	−3
4	−5

31.

x	y
$\frac{1}{3}$	−1
1	0
3	1
9	2
27	3

32.

x	y
0	1
1	5
2	25
3	125
4	625

33.

x	y
0	12
1	3
2	0
3	3
4	12

34. Rewrite $y = 96(0.38)^x$ in terms of base e. Express the answer in terms of a natural logarithm and then round to three decimal places.

Cumulative Review Exercises (Chapters 1–4)

In Exercises 1–8, solve each equation or inequality.

1. $|3x - 4| = 2$
2. $\sqrt{2x - 5} - \sqrt{x - 3} = 1$
3. $x^4 + x^3 - 3x^2 - x + 2 = 0$
4. $e^{5x} - 32 = 96$
5. $\log_2(x + 5) + \log_2(x - 1) = 4$
6. $\ln(x + 4) + \ln(x + 1) = 2\ln(x + 3)$
7. $14 - 5x \geq -6$
8. $|2x - 4| \leq 2$

In Exercises 9–14, graph each equation in a rectangular coordinate system. If two functions are indicated, graph both in the same system.

9. $(x - 3)^2 + (y + 2)^2 = 4$
10. $f(x) = (x - 2)^2 - 1$
11. $f(x) = \dfrac{x^2 - 1}{x^2 - 4}$
12. $f(x) = (x - 2)^2(x + 1)$
13. $f(x) = 2x - 4$ and $f^{-1}(x)$
14. $f(x) = \ln x$ and $g(x) = \ln(x - 2) + 1$

15. Write the point-slope form and the slope-intercept form of the line passing through $(1, 3)$ and $(3, -3)$.

16. If $f(x) = x^2$ and $g(x) = x + 2$, find $(f \circ g)(x)$ and $(g \circ f)(x)$.

17. You discover that the number of hours you sleep each night varies inversely as the square of the number of cups of coffee consumed during the early evening. If 2 cups of coffee are consumed, you get 8 hours of sleep. If the number of cups of coffee is doubled, how many hours should you expect to sleep?

A baseball player hits a pop fly into the air. The function

$$s(t) = -16t^2 + 64t + 5$$

models the ball's height above the ground, $s(t)$, in feet, t seconds after it is hit. Use the function to solve Exercises 18–19.

18. When does the baseball reach its maximum height? What is that height?

19. After how many seconds does the baseball hit the ground? Round to the nearest tenth of a second.

20. You are paid time-and-a-half for each hour worked over 40 hours a week. Last week you worked 50 hours and earned $660. What is your normal hourly salary?

Systems of Equations and Inequalities

5

Television, movies, and magazines place great emphasis on physical beauty. Our culture emphasizes physical appearance to such an extent that it is a central factor in the perception and judgment of others. The modern emphasis on thinness as the ideal body shape has been suggested as a major cause of eating disorders among adolescent women.

Cultural values of physical attractiveness change over time. During the 1950s, actress Jayne Mansfield embodied the postwar ideal: curvy, buxom, and big-hipped. Men, too, have been caught up in changes of how they "ought" to look. The 1960s ideal was the soft and scrawny hippie. Today's ideal man is tough and muscular.

Given the importance of culture in setting standards of attractiveness, how can you establish a healthy weight range for your age and height? In this chapter, we will use systems of inequalities to explore these skin-deep issues.

You'll find a weight that fits you using the models (mathematical, not fashion) in Example 5 of Section 5.5 and Exercises 77–80 in Exercise Set 5.5. Exercises 85–86 use graphs and a formula for body-mass index to indicate whether you are obese, overweight, borderline overweight, normal weight, or underweight.

Section 5.1

Systems of Linear Equations in Two Variables

Objectives

1. Decide whether an ordered pair is a solution of a linear system.
2. Solve linear systems by substitution.
3. Solve linear systems by addition.
4. Identify systems that do not have exactly one ordered-pair solution.
5. Solve problems using systems of linear equations.

Researchers identified college students who generally were procrastinators or nonprocrastinators. The students were asked to report throughout the semester how many symptoms of physical illness they had experienced. **Figure 5.1** shows that by late in the semester, all students experienced increases in symptoms. Early in the semester, procrastinators reported fewer symptoms, but late in the semester, as work came due, they reported more symptoms than their nonprocrastinating peers.

The data in **Figure 5.1** can be analyzed using a pair of linear models in two variables. The figure shows that by week 6, both groups reported the same number of symptoms of illness, an average of approximately 3.5 symptoms per group. In this section, you will learn two algebraic methods, called *substitution* and *addition*, that will reinforce this graphic observation, verifying (6, 3.5) as the point of intersection.

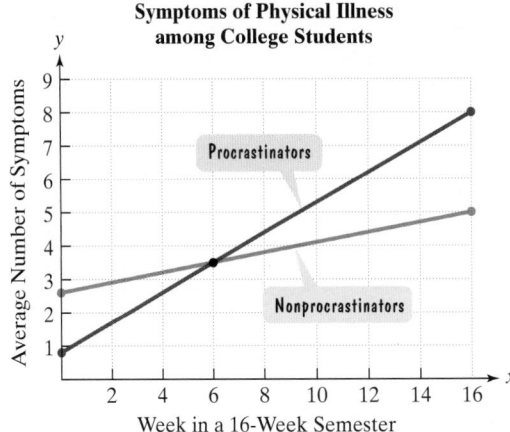

Symptoms of Physical Illness among College Students

Figure 5.1
Source: Gerrig and Zimbardo, *Psychology and Life*, 18th Edition, Allyn and Bacon, 2008

1. Decide whether an ordered pair is a solution of a linear system.

Systems of Linear Equations and Their Solutions

All equations in the form $Ax + By = C$ are straight lines when graphed. Two such equations are called a **system of linear equations** or a **linear system**. **A solution to a system of linear equations in two variables** is an ordered pair that satisfies both equations in the system. For example, (3, 4) satisfies the system

$$\begin{cases} x + y = 7 & \text{(3 + 4 is, indeed, 7.)} \\ x - y = -1. & \text{(3 - 4 is, indeed, -1.)} \end{cases}$$

Thus, (3, 4) satisfies both equations and is a solution of the system. The solution can be described by saying that $x = 3$ and $y = 4$. The solution can also be described using set notation. The solution set to the system is $\{(3, 4)\}$ – that is, the set consisting of the ordered pair (3, 4).

A system of linear equations can have exactly one solution, no solution, or infinitely many solutions. We begin with systems that have exactly one solution.

EXAMPLE 1 Determining Whether Ordered Pairs Are Solutions of a System

Consider the system:

$$\begin{cases} x + 2y = 2 \\ x - 2y = 6. \end{cases}$$

Determine if each ordered pair is a solution of the system:

a. $(4, -1)$ **b.** $(-4, 3)$.

Solution

a. We begin by determining whether $(4, -1)$ is a solution. Because 4 is the x-coordinate and -1 is the y-coordinate of $(4, -1)$, we replace x with 4 and y with -1.

$$
\begin{array}{ll}
x + 2y = 2 & \qquad x - 2y = 6 \\
4 + 2(-1) \stackrel{?}{=} 2 & \qquad 4 - 2(-1) \stackrel{?}{=} 6 \\
4 + (-2) \stackrel{?}{=} 2 & \qquad 4 - (-2) \stackrel{?}{=} 6 \\
2 = 2, \quad \text{true} & \qquad 4 + 2 \stackrel{?}{=} 6 \\
& \qquad 6 = 6, \quad \text{true}
\end{array}
$$

The pair $(4, -1)$ satisfies both equations: It makes each equation true. Thus, the ordered pair is a solution of the system.

b. To determine whether $(-4, 3)$ is a solution, we replace x with -4 and y with 3.

$$
\begin{array}{ll}
x + 2y = 2 & \qquad x - 2y = 6 \\
-4 + 2 \cdot 3 \stackrel{?}{=} 2 & \qquad -4 - 2 \cdot 3 \stackrel{?}{=} 6 \\
-4 + 6 \stackrel{?}{=} 2 & \qquad -4 - 6 \stackrel{?}{=} 6 \\
2 = 2, \quad \text{true} & \qquad -10 = 6, \quad \text{false}
\end{array}
$$

The pair $(-4, 3)$ fails to satisfy *both* equations: It does not make both equations true. Thus, the ordered pair is not a solution of the system. ●

Study Tip

When solving linear systems by graphing, neatly drawn graphs are essential for determining points of intersection.

- Use rectangular coordinate graph paper.
- Use a ruler or straightedge.
- Use a pencil with a sharp point.

The solution of a system of linear equations can sometimes be found by graphing both of the equations in the same rectangular coordinate system. For a system with one solution, the **coordinates of the point of intersection give the system's solution**. For example, the system in Example 1,

$$
\begin{cases}
x + 2y = 2 \\
x - 2y = 6,
\end{cases}
$$

is graphed in **Figure 5.2**. The solution of the system, $(4, -1)$, corresponds to the point of intersection of the lines.

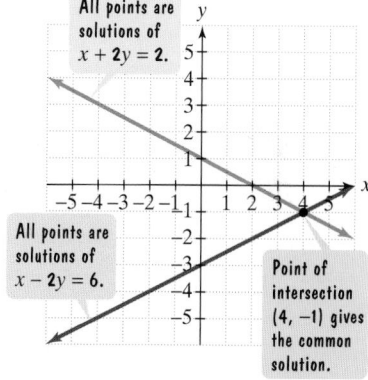

Figure 5.2 Visualizing a system's solution

⊘ Check Point **1** Consider the system:

$$
\begin{cases}
2x - 3y = -4 \\
2x + y = 4.
\end{cases}
$$

Determine if each ordered pair is a solution of the system:

a. $(1, 2)$ **b.** $(7, 6)$.

② Solve linear systems by substitution.

Eliminating a Variable Using the Substitution Method

Finding the solution to a linear system by graphing equations may not be easy to do. For example, a solution of $\left(-\frac{2}{3}, \frac{157}{29}\right)$ would be difficult to "see" as an intersection point on a graph.

Let's consider a method that does not depend on finding a system's solution visually: the substitution method. This method involves converting the system to one equation in one variable by an appropriate substitution.

Solving Linear Systems by Substitution

1. Solve either of the equations for one variable in terms of the other. (If one of the equations is already in this form, you can skip this step.)
2. Substitute the expression found in step 1 into the *other* equation. This will result in an equation in one variable.
3. Solve the equation containing one variable.
4. Back-substitute the value found in step 3 into one of the original equations. Simplify and find the value of the remaining variable.
5. Check the proposed solution in both of the system's given equations.

EXAMPLE 2 **Solving a System by Substitution**

Solve by the substitution method:

$$\begin{cases} 5x - 4y = 9 \\ x - 2y = -3. \end{cases}$$

Solution

Step 1 Solve either of the equations for one variable in terms of the other. We begin by isolating one of the variables in either of the equations. By solving for x in the second equation, which has a coefficient of 1, we can avoid fractions.

$$x - 2y = -3 \qquad \text{This is the second equation in the given system.}$$
$$x = 2y - 3 \qquad \text{Solve for x by adding 2y to both sides.}$$

Step 2 Substitute the expression from step 1 into the other equation. We substitute $2y - 3$ for x in the first equation.

$$x = \boxed{2y - 3} \qquad 5\boxed{x} - 4y = 9$$

This gives us an equation in one variable, namely

$$5(2y - 3) - 4y = 9.$$

The variable x has been eliminated.

Step 3 Solve the resulting equation containing one variable.

$$5(2y - 3) - 4y = 9 \qquad \text{This is the equation containing one variable.}$$
$$10y - 15 - 4y = 9 \qquad \text{Apply the distributive property.}$$
$$6y - 15 = 9 \qquad \text{Combine like terms.}$$
$$6y = 24 \qquad \text{Add 15 to both sides.}$$
$$y = 4 \qquad \text{Divide both sides by 6.}$$

Step 4 Back-substitute the obtained value into one of the original equations. Now that we have the y-coordinate of the solution, we back-substitute 4 for y into one of the original equations to find x. Let's use both equations to show that we obtain the same value for x in either case.

Using the first equation:	**Using the second equation:**
$5x - 4y = 9$	$x - 2y = -3$
$5x - 4(4) = 9$	$x - 2(4) = -3$
$5x - 16 = 9$	$x - 8 = -3$
$5x = 25$	$x = 5$
$x = 5$	

With $x = 5$ and $y = 4$, the proposed solution is $(5, 4)$.

Step 5 Check. Take a moment to show that $(5, 4)$ satisfies both given equations. The solution set is $\{(5, 4)\}$.

Technology

Graphic Connections

A graphing utility can be used to solve the system in Example 2. Solve each equation for y, graph the equations, and use the intersection feature. The utility displays the solution $(5, 4)$ as $x = 5$, $y = 4$.

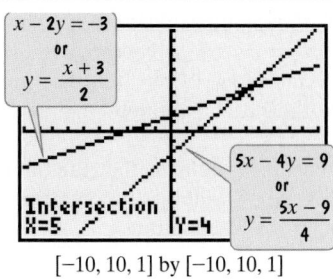

$[-10, 10, 1]$ by $[-10, 10, 1]$

⊘ Check Point **2** Solve by the substitution method:

$$\begin{cases} 3x + 2y = 4 \\ 2x + y = 1. \end{cases}$$

③ Solve linear systems by addition.

Eliminating a Variable Using the Addition Method

The substitution method is most useful if one of the given equations has an isolated variable. A second, and frequently the easiest, method for solving a linear system is the addition method. Like the substitution method, the addition method involves eliminating a variable and ultimately solving an equation containing only one variable. However, this time we eliminate a variable by adding the equations.

For example, consider the following system of linear equations:

$$\begin{cases} 3x - 4y = 11 \\ -3x + 2y = -7. \end{cases}$$

When we add these two equations, the x-terms are eliminated. This occurs because the coefficients of the x-terms, 3 and -3, are opposites (additive inverses) of each other:

$$\begin{cases} 3x - 4y = 11 \\ \underline{-3x + 2y = -7} \end{cases}$$

$$-2y = 4 \qquad \boxed{\text{The sum is an equation in one variable.}}$$

$$y = -2. \qquad \text{Divide both sides by } -2 \text{ and solve for } y.$$

Now we can back-substitute -2 for y into one of the original equations to find x. It does not matter which equation you use; you will obtain the same value for x in either case. If we use either equation, we can show that $x = 1$ and the solution $(1, -2)$ satisfies both equations in the system.

When we use the addition method, we want to obtain two equations whose sum is an equation containing only one variable. The key step is to **obtain, for one of the variables, coefficients that differ only in sign**. To do this, we may need to multiply one or both equations by some nonzero number so that the coefficients of one of the variables, x or y, become opposites. Then when the two equations are added, this variable is eliminated.

Study Tip

Although the addition method is also known as the *elimination method*, variables are eliminated when using both the substitution and addition methods. The name *addition method* specifically tells us that the elimination of a variable is accomplished by adding two equations.

Solving Linear Systems by Addition

1. If necessary, rewrite both equations in the form $Ax + By = C$.
2. If necessary, multiply either equation or both equations by appropriate nonzero numbers so that the sum of the x-coefficients or the sum of the y-coefficients is 0.
3. Add the equations in step 2. The sum is an equation in one variable.
4. Solve the equation in one variable.
5. Back-substitute the value obtained in step 4 into either of the given equations and solve for the other variable.
6. Check the solution in both of the original equations.

EXAMPLE 3 Solving a System by the Addition Method

Solve by the addition method:

$$\begin{cases} 3x + 2y = 48 \\ 9x - 8y = -24. \end{cases}$$

Solution

Step 1 Rewrite both equations in the form $Ax + By = C$. Both equations are already in this form. Variable terms appear on the left and constants appear on the right.

Step 2 If necessary, multiply either equation or both equations by appropriate numbers so that the sum of the x-coefficients or the sum of the y-coefficients is 0. We can eliminate x or y. Let's eliminate x. Consider the terms in x in each equation, that is, $3x$ and $9x$. To eliminate x, we can multiply each term of the first equation by -3 and then add the equations.

$$\begin{cases} 3x + 2y = 48 \\ 9x - 8y = -24 \end{cases} \quad \xrightarrow[\text{No change}]{\text{Multiply by } -3.} \quad \begin{cases} -9x - 6y = -144 \\ \underline{9x - 8y = -24} \end{cases}$$

Step 3 Add the equations. Add: $-14y = -168$

Step 4 Solve the equation in one variable. We solve $-14y = -168$ by dividing both sides by -14.

$$\frac{-14y}{-14} = \frac{-168}{-14} \quad \text{Divide both sides by } -14.$$
$$y = 12 \quad \text{Simplify.}$$

Step 5 Back-substitute and find the value for the other variable. We can back-substitute 12 for y into either one of the given equations. We'll use the first one.

$$3x + 2y = 48 \quad \text{This is the first equation in the given system.}$$
$$3x + 2(12) = 48 \quad \text{Substitute 12 for } y.$$
$$3x + 24 = 48 \quad \text{Multiply.}$$
$$3x = 24 \quad \text{Subtract 24 from both sides.}$$
$$x = 8 \quad \text{Divide both sides by 3.}$$

We found that $y = 12$ and $x = 8$. The proposed solution is $(8, 12)$.

Step 6 Check. Take a few minutes to show that $(8, 12)$ satisfies both of the original equations in the system. The solution set is $\{(8, 12)\}$.

✓ Check Point **3** Solve by the addition method:

$$\begin{cases} 4x + 5y = 3 \\ 2x - 3y = 7. \end{cases}$$

Some linear systems have solutions that are not integers. If the value of one variable turns out to be a "messy" fraction, back-substitution might lead to cumbersome arithmetic. If this happens, you can return to the original system and use the addition method to find the value of the other variable.

(**EXAMPLE 4**) **Solving a System by the Addition Method**

Solve by the addition method:

$$\begin{cases} 2x = 7y - 17 \\ 5y = 17 - 3x. \end{cases}$$

Solution

Step 1 Rewrite both equations in the form $Ax + By = C$. We first arrange the system so that variable terms appear on the left and constants appear on the right. We obtain

$$\begin{cases} 2x - 7y = -17 \\ 3x + 5y = 17. \end{cases}$$ Subtract 7y from both sides of the first equation.
Add 3x to both sides of the second equation.

Step 2 If necessary, multiply either equation or both equations by appropriate numbers so that the sum of the x-coefficients or the sum of the y-coefficients is 0. We can eliminate x or y. Let's eliminate x by multiplying the first equation by 3 and the second equation by -2.

$$\begin{cases} 2x - 7y = -17 \\ 3x + 5y = 17 \end{cases} \quad \begin{array}{l} \text{Multiply by 3.} \\ \text{Multiply by } -2. \end{array} \quad \begin{cases} 6x - 21y = -51 \\ -6x - 10y = -34 \end{cases}$$

Step 3 Add the equations. Add: $-31y = -85$

Step 4 Solve the equation in one variable. We solve $-31y = -85$ by dividing both sides by -31.

$$\frac{-31y}{-31} = \frac{-85}{-31} \qquad \text{Divide both sides by } -31.$$

$$y = \frac{85}{31} \qquad \text{Simplify.}$$

Step 5 Back-substitute and find the value for the other variable. Back-substitution of $\frac{85}{31}$ for y into either of the given equations results in cumbersome arithmetic. Instead, let's use the addition method on the given system in the form $Ax + By = C$ to find the value for x. Thus, we eliminate y by multiplying the first equation by 5 and the second equation by 7.

$$\begin{cases} 2x - 7y = -17 \\ 3x + 5y = 17 \end{cases} \quad \begin{array}{l} \text{Multiply by 5.} \\ \text{Multiply by 7.} \end{array} \quad \begin{cases} 10x - 35y = -85 \\ 21x + 35y = 119 \end{cases}$$

Add: $31x = 34$

$$x = \frac{34}{31} \qquad \text{Divide both sides by 31.}$$

We found that $y = \dfrac{85}{31}$ and $x = \dfrac{34}{31}$. The proposed solution is $\left(\dfrac{34}{31}, \dfrac{85}{31} \right)$.

Step 6 Check. For this system, a calculator is helpful in showing that $\left(\frac{34}{31}, \frac{85}{31} \right)$ satisfies both of the original equations in the system. The solution set is $\left\{ \left(\frac{34}{31}, \frac{85}{31} \right) \right\}$.

⊘ Check Point **4** Solve by the addition method:

$$\begin{cases} 2x = 9 + 3y \\ 4y = 8 - 3x. \end{cases}$$

④ Identify systems that do not have exactly one ordered-pair solution.

Linear Systems Having No Solution or Infinitely Many Solutions

We have seen that a system of linear equations in two variables represents a pair of lines. The lines either intersect at one point, are parallel, or are identical. Thus, there are three possibilities for the number of solutions to a system of two linear equations in two variables.

The Number of Solutions to a System of Two Linear Equations

The number of solutions to a system of two linear equations in two variables is given by one of the following. (See **Figure 5.3**.)

Number of Solutions	What This Means Graphically
Exactly one ordered-pair solution	The two lines intersect at one point.
No solution	The two lines are parallel.
Infinitely many solutions	The two lines are identical.

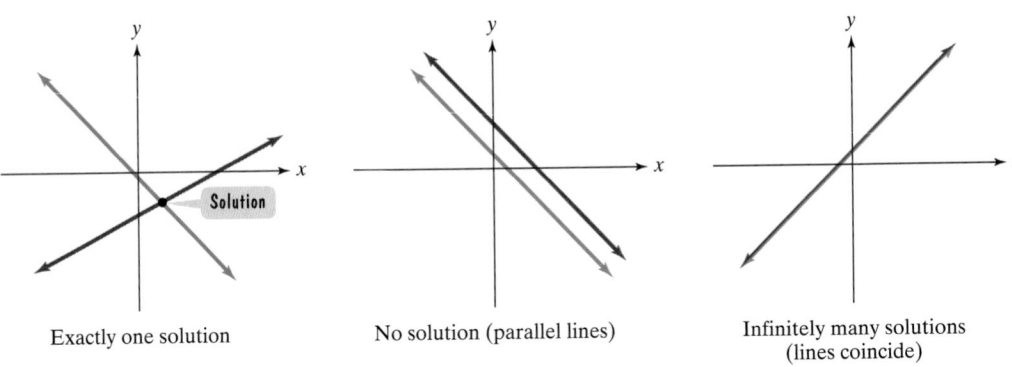

| Exactly one solution | No solution (parallel lines) | Infinitely many solutions (lines coincide) |

Figure 5.3 Possible graphs for a system of two linear equations in two variables

A linear system with no solution is called an **inconsistent system**. If you attempt to solve such a system by substitution or addition, you will eliminate both variables. A false statement, such as $0 = 12$, will be the result.

(**EXAMPLE 5**) **A System with No Solution**

Solve the system:

$$\begin{cases} 4x + 6y = 12 \\ 6x + 9y = 12. \end{cases}$$

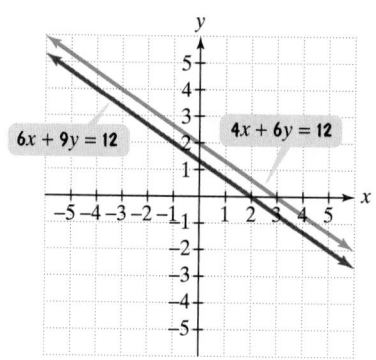

Figure 5.4 The graph of an inconsistent system

Solution Because no variable is isolated, we will use the addition method. To obtain coefficients of x that differ only in sign, we multiply the first equation by 3 and multiply the second equation by -2.

$$\begin{cases} 4x + 6y = 12 \\ 6x + 9y = 12 \end{cases}$$

Multiply by 3.

Multiply by -2.

$$\begin{cases} 12x + 18y = 36 \\ -12x - 18y = -24 \end{cases}$$

Add: $\qquad\qquad\quad 0 = 12$

> There are no values of x and y for which $0 = 12$. No values of x and y satisfy $0x + 0y = 12$.

The false statement $0 = 12$ indicates that the system is inconsistent and has no solution. The solution set is the empty set, \varnothing.

The lines corresponding to the two equations in Example 5 are shown in **Figure 5.4**. The lines are parallel and have no point of intersection.

Discovery

Show that the graphs of $4x + 6y = 12$ and $6x + 9y = 12$ must be parallel lines by solving each equation for y. What is the slope and y-intercept for each line? What does this mean? If a linear system is inconsistent, what must be true about the slopes and y-intercepts for the system's graphs?

⊘ **Check Point 5** Solve the system:

$$\begin{cases} 5x - 2y = 4 \\ -10x + 4y = 7. \end{cases}$$

A linear system that has at least one solution is called a **consistent system**. Lines that intersect and lines that coincide both represent consistent systems. If the lines coincide, then the consistent system has infinitely many solutions, represented by every point on either line.

The equations in a linear system with infinitely many solutions are called **dependent**. If you attempt to solve such a system by substitution or addition, you will eliminate both variables. However, a true statement, such as $10 = 10$, will be the result.

(**EXAMPLE 6**) **A System with Infinitely Many Solutions**

Solve the system:

$$\begin{cases} y = 3x - 2 \\ 15x - 5y = 10. \end{cases}$$

Solution Because the variable y is isolated in $y = 3x - 2$, the first equation, we can use the substitution method. We substitute the expression for y into the second equation.

$y = \boxed{3x - 2} \qquad 15x - 5\boxed{y} = 10$ Substitute $3x - 2$ for y.

$15x - 5(3x - 2) = 10$ The substitution results in an equation in one variable.

$15x - 15x + 10 = 10$ Apply the distributive property.

> This statement is true for all values of x and y.

$10 = 10$ Simplify.

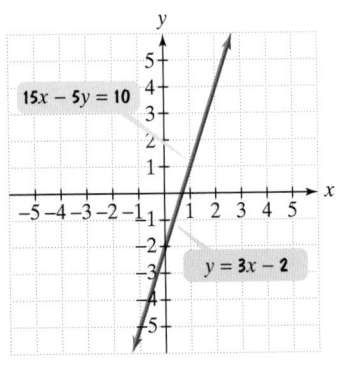

Figure 5.5 The graph of a system with infinitely many solutions

In our final step, both variables have been eliminated and the resulting statement, $10 = 10$, is true. This true statement indicates that the system has infinitely many solutions. The solution set consists of all points (x, y) lying on either of the coinciding lines, $y = 3x - 2$ or $15x - 5y = 10$, as shown in **Figure 5.5**.

We express the solution set for the system in one of two equivalent ways:

$$\{(x, y) \mid y = 3x - 2\} \quad \text{or} \quad \{(x, y) \mid 15x - 5y = 10\}.$$

> The set of all ordered pairs (x, y) such that $y = 3x - 2$

> The set of all ordered pairs (x, y) such that $15x - 5y = 10$

Study Tip

Although the system in Example 6 has infinitely many solutions, this does not mean that any ordered pair of numbers you can form will be a solution. The ordered pair (x, y) must satisfy one of the system's equations, $y = 3x - 2$ or $15x - 5y = 10$, and there are infinitely many such ordered pairs. Because the graphs are coinciding lines, the ordered pairs that are solutions of one of the equations are also solutions of the other equation.

✓ Check Point **6** Solve the system:

$$\begin{cases} x = 4y - 8 \\ 5x - 20y = -40. \end{cases}$$

⑤ Solve problems using systems of linear equations.

Functions of Business: Break-Even Analysis

Suppose that a company produces and sells x units of a product. Its *revenue* is the money generated by selling x units of the product. Its *cost* is the cost of producing x units of the product.

Revenue and Cost Functions

A company produces and sells x units of a product.

Revenue Function

$$R(x) = (\text{price per unit sold})x$$

Cost Function

$$C(x) = \text{fixed cost} + (\text{cost per unit produced})x$$

The point of intersection of the graphs of the revenue and cost functions is called the **break-even point**. The x-coordinate of the point reveals the number of units that a company must produce and sell so that money coming in, the revenue, is equal to money going out, the cost. The y-coordinate of the break-even point gives the amount of money coming in and going out. Example 7 illustrates the use of the substitution method in determining a company's break-even point.

(**EXAMPLE 7**) **Finding a Break-Even Point**

Technology is now promising to bring light, fast, and beautiful wheelchairs to millions of disabled people. A company is planning to manufacture these radically different wheelchairs. Fixed cost will be \$500,000 and it will cost \$400 to produce each wheelchair. Each wheelchair will be sold for \$600.

 a. Write the cost function, C, of producing x wheelchairs.

 b. Write the revenue function, R, from the sale of x wheelchairs.

 c. Determine the break-even point. Describe what this means.

Solution

a. The cost function is the sum of the fixed cost and variable cost.

> Fixed cost of $500,000 plus Variable cost: $400 for each chair produced

$$C(x) = 500,000 + 400x$$

b. The revenue function is the money generated from the sale of x wheelchairs.

> Revenue per chair, $600, times the number of chairs sold

$$R(x) = 600x$$

c. The break-even point occurs where the graphs of C and R intersect. Thus, we find this point by solving the system

$$\begin{cases} C(x) = 500,000 + 400x \\ R(x) = 600x \end{cases} \quad \text{or} \quad \begin{cases} y = 500,000 + 400x \\ y = 600x. \end{cases}$$

Using substitution, we can substitute $600x$ for y in the first equation:

$$600x = 500,000 + 400x \qquad \text{Substitute 600x for y in } y = 500,000 + 400x.$$

$$200x = 500,000 \qquad \text{Subtract 400x from both sides.}$$

$$x = 2500. \qquad \text{Divide both sides by 200.}$$

Back-substituting 2500 for x in either of the system's equations (or functions), we obtain

$$R(2500) = 600(2500) = 1,500,000.$$

> We used $R(x) = 600x$.

The break-even point is (2500, 1,500,000). This means that the company will break even if it produces and sells 2500 wheelchairs. At this level, the money coming in is equal to the money going out: $1,500,000. ●

Figure 5.6 shows the graphs of the revenue and cost functions for the wheelchair business. Similar graphs and models apply no matter how small or large a business venture may be.

The intersection point confirms that the company breaks even by producing and selling 2500 wheelchairs. Can you see what happens for $x < 2500$? The red cost graph lies above the blue revenue graph. The cost is greater than the revenue and the business is losing money. Thus, if they sell fewer than 2500 wheelchairs, the result is a *loss*. By contrast, look at what happens for $x > 2500$. The blue revenue graph lies above the red cost graph. The revenue is greater than the cost and the business is making money. Thus, if they sell more than 2500 wheelchairs, the result is a *gain*.

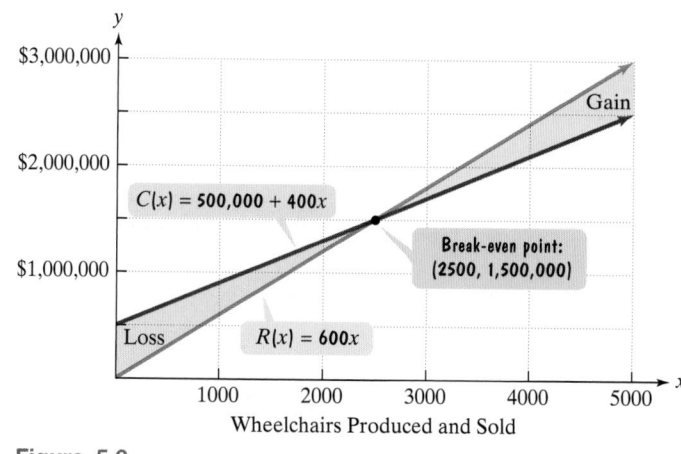

Figure 5.6

☑ Check Point **7** A company that manufactures running shoes has a fixed cost of $300,000. Additionally, it costs $30 to produce each pair of shoes. They are sold at $80 per pair.

a. Write the cost function, C, of producing x pairs of running shoes.
b. Write the revenue function, R, from the sale of x pairs of running shoes.
c. Determine the break-even point. Describe what this means.

What does every entrepreneur, from a kid selling lemonade to Donald Trump, want to do? Generate profit, of course. The *profit* made is the money taken in, or the revenue, minus the money spent, or the cost. This relationship between revenue and cost allows us to define the *profit function*, $P(x)$.

The Profit Function

The profit, $P(x)$, generated after producing and selling x units of a product is given by the **profit function**

$$P(x) = R(x) - C(x),$$

where R and C are the revenue and cost functions, respectively.

The profit function for the wheelchair business in Example 7 is

$$P(x) = R(x) - C(x)$$
$$= 600x - (500,000 + 400x)$$
$$= 200x - 500,000.$$

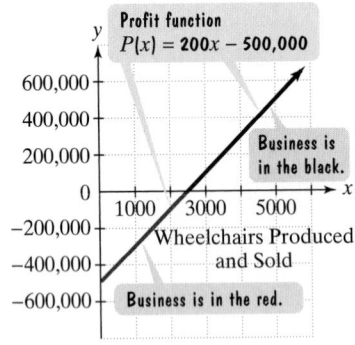

Figure 5.7

The graph of this profit function is shown in **Figure 5.7**. The red portion lies below the x-axis and shows a loss when fewer than 2500 wheelchairs are sold. The business is "in the red." The black portion lies above the x-axis and shows a gain when more than 2500 wheelchairs are sold. The wheelchair business is "in the black."

Exercise Set 5.1

Practice Exercises

In Exercises 1–4, determine whether the given ordered pair is a solution of the system.

1. $(2, 3)$
$$\begin{cases} x + 3y = 11 \\ x - 5y = -13 \end{cases}$$

2. $(-3, 5)$
$$\begin{cases} 9x + 7y = 8 \\ 8x - 9y = -69 \end{cases}$$

3. $(2, 5)$
$$\begin{cases} 2x + 3y = 17 \\ x + 4y = 16 \end{cases}$$

4. $(8, 5)$
$$\begin{cases} 5x - 4y = 20 \\ 3y = 2x + 1 \end{cases}$$

In Exercises 5–18, solve each system by the substitution method.

5. $\begin{cases} x + y = 4 \\ y = 3x \end{cases}$

6. $\begin{cases} x + y = 6 \\ y = 2x \end{cases}$

7. $\begin{cases} x + 3y = 8 \\ y = 2x - 9 \end{cases}$

8. $\begin{cases} 2x - 3y = -13 \\ y = 2x + 7 \end{cases}$

9. $\begin{cases} x = 4y - 2 \\ x = 6y + 8 \end{cases}$

10. $\begin{cases} x = 3y + 7 \\ x = 2y - 1 \end{cases}$

11. $\begin{cases} 5x + 2y = 0 \\ x - 3y = 0 \end{cases}$

12. $\begin{cases} 4x + 3y = 0 \\ 2x - y = 0 \end{cases}$

13. $\begin{cases} 2x + 5y = -4 \\ 3x - y = 11 \end{cases}$

14. $\begin{cases} 2x + 5y = 1 \\ -x + 6y = 8 \end{cases}$

15. $\begin{cases} 2x - 3y = 8 - 2x \\ 3x + 4y = x + 3y + 14 \end{cases}$

16. $\begin{cases} 3x - 4y = x - y + 4 \\ 2x + 6y = 5y - 4 \end{cases}$

17. $\begin{cases} y = \dfrac{1}{3}x + \dfrac{2}{3} \\ y = \dfrac{5}{7}x - 2 \end{cases}$

18. $\begin{cases} y = -\dfrac{1}{2}x + 2 \\ y = \dfrac{3}{4}x + 7 \end{cases}$

In Exercises 19–30, solve each system by the addition method.

19. $\begin{cases} x + y = 1 \\ x - y = 3 \end{cases}$

20. $\begin{cases} x + y = 6 \\ x - y = -2 \end{cases}$

21. $\begin{cases} 2x + 3y = 6 \\ 2x - 3y = 6 \end{cases}$

22. $\begin{cases} 3x + 2y = 14 \\ 3x - 2y = 10 \end{cases}$

23. $\begin{cases} x + 2y = 2 \\ -4x + 3y = 25 \end{cases}$

24. $\begin{cases} 2x - 7y = 2 \\ 3x + y = -20 \end{cases}$

25. $\begin{cases} 4x + 3y = 15 \\ 2x - 5y = 1 \end{cases}$

26. $\begin{cases} 3x - 7y = 13 \\ 6x + 5y = 7 \end{cases}$

27. $\begin{cases} 3x - 4y = 11 \\ 2x + 3y = -4 \end{cases}$

28. $\begin{cases} 2x + 3y = -16 \\ 5x - 10y = 30 \end{cases}$

29. $\begin{cases} 3x = 4y + 1 \\ 3y = 1 - 4x \end{cases}$

30. $\begin{cases} 5x = 6y + 40 \\ 2y = 8 - 3x \end{cases}$

In Exercises 31–42, solve by the method of your choice. Identify systems with no solution and systems with infinitely many solutions, using set notation to express their solution sets.

31. $\begin{cases} x = 9 - 2y \\ x + 2y = 13 \end{cases}$

32. $\begin{cases} 6x + 2y = 7 \\ y = 2 - 3x \end{cases}$

33. $\begin{cases} y = 3x - 5 \\ 21x - 35 = 7y \end{cases}$

34. $\begin{cases} 9x - 3y = 12 \\ y = 3x - 4 \end{cases}$

35. $\begin{cases} 3x - 2y = -5 \\ 4x + y = 8 \end{cases}$

36. $\begin{cases} 2x + 5y = -4 \\ 3x - y = 11 \end{cases}$

37. $\begin{cases} x + 3y = 2 \\ 3x + 9y = 6 \end{cases}$

38. $\begin{cases} 4x - 2y = 2 \\ 2x - y = 1 \end{cases}$

39. $\begin{cases} \dfrac{x}{4} - \dfrac{y}{4} = -1 \\ x + 4y = -9 \end{cases}$

40. $\begin{cases} \dfrac{x}{6} - \dfrac{y}{2} = \dfrac{1}{3} \\ x + 2y = -3 \end{cases}$

41. $\begin{cases} 2x = 3y + 4 \\ 4x = 3 - 5y \end{cases}$

42. $\begin{cases} 4x = 3y + 8 \\ 2x = -14 + 5y \end{cases}$

In Exercises 43–46, let x represent one number and let y represent the other number. Use the given conditions to write a system of equations. Solve the system and find the numbers.

43. The sum of two numbers is 7. If one number is subtracted from the other, their difference is −1. Find the numbers.

44. The sum of two numbers is 2. If one number is subtracted from the other, their difference is 8. Find the numbers.

45. Three times a first number decreased by a second number is 1. The first number increased by twice the second number is 12. Find the numbers.

46. The sum of three times a first number and twice a second number is 8. If the second number is subtracted from twice the first number, the result is 3. Find the numbers.

Practice Plus

In Exercises 47–48, solve each system by the method of your choice.

47. $\begin{cases} \dfrac{x+2}{2} - \dfrac{y+4}{3} = 3 \\ \dfrac{x+y}{5} = \dfrac{x-y}{2} - \dfrac{5}{2} \end{cases}$

48. $\begin{cases} \dfrac{x-y}{3} = \dfrac{x+y}{2} - \dfrac{1}{2} \\ \dfrac{x+2}{2} - 4 = \dfrac{y+4}{3} \end{cases}$

In Exercises 49–50, solve each system for x and y, expressing either value in terms of a or b, if necessary. Assume that $a \neq 0$ and $b \neq 0$.

49. $\begin{cases} 5ax + 4y = 17 \\ ax + 7y = 22 \end{cases}$

50. $\begin{cases} 4ax + by = 3 \\ 6ax + 5by = 8 \end{cases}$

51. For the linear function $f(x) = mx + b, f(-2) = 11$ and $f(3) = -9$. Find m and b.

52. For the linear function $f(x) = mx + b, f(-3) = 23$ and $f(2) = -7$. Find m and b.

Use the graphs of the linear functions to solve Exercises 53–54.

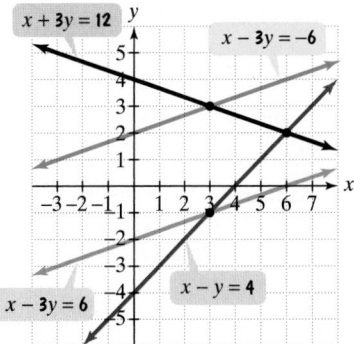

53. Write the linear system whose solution set is $\{(6, 2)\}$. Express each equation in the system in slope-intercept form.

54. Write the linear system whose solution set is \varnothing. Express each equation in the system in slope-intercept form.

Application Exercises

The figure shows the graphs of the cost and revenue functions for a company that manufactures and sells small radios. Use the information in the figure to solve Exercises 55–60.

Radios Produced and Sold

55. How many radios must be produced and sold for the company to break even?

56. More than how many radios must be produced and sold for the company to have a profit?

57. Use the formulas shown in the voice balloons to find $R(200) - C(200)$. Describe what this means for the company.

58. Use the formulas shown in the voice balloons to find $R(300) - C(300)$. Describe what this means for the company.

59. a. Use the formulas shown in the voice balloons to write the company's profit function, P, from producing and selling x radios.

 b. Find the company's profit if 10,000 radios are produced and sold.

60. a. Use the formulas shown in the voice balloons to write the company's profit function, P, from producing and selling x radios.

 b. Find the company's profit if 20,000 radios are produced and sold.

Exercises 61–64 describe a number of business ventures. For each exercise,

 a. *Write the cost function, C.*

 b. *Write the revenue function, R.*

 c. *Determine the break-even point. Describe what this means.*

61. A company that manufactures small canoes has a fixed cost of $18,000. It costs $20 to produce each canoe. The selling price is $80 per canoe. (In solving this exercise, let x represent the number of canoes produced and sold.)

62. A company that manufactures bicycles has a fixed cost of $100,000. It costs $100 to produce each bicycle. The selling price is $300 per bike. (In solving this exercise, let x represent the number of bicycles produced and sold.)

63. You invest in a new play. The cost includes an overhead of $30,000, plus production costs of $2500 per performance. A sold-out performance brings in $3125. (In solving this exercise, let x represent the number of sold-out performances.)

64. You invested $30,000 and started a business writing greeting cards. Supplies cost 2¢ per card and you are selling each card for 50¢. (In solving this exercise, let x represent the number of cards produced and sold.)

An important application of systems of equations arises in connection with supply and demand. As the price of a product increases, the demand for that product decreases. However, at higher prices, suppliers are willing to produce greater quantities of the product. The price at which supply and demand are equal is called the **equilibrium price.** *The quantity supplied and demanded at that price is called the* **equilibrium quantity.** *Exercises 65–66 involve supply and demand.*

65. The following models describe wages for low-skilled labor.

Demand Model	**Supply Model**
$p = -0.325x + 5.8$	$p = 0.375x + 3$
Price of labor (per hour) Millions of workers employers will hire	Price of labor (per hour) Millions of available workers

Source: O'Sullivan and Sheffrin, *Economics*, Prentice Hall, 2007

 a. Solve the system and find the equilibrium number of workers, in millions, and the equilibrium hourly wage.

 b. Use your answer from part (a) to complete this statement:

 If workers are paid _____ per hour, there will be ___ million available workers and ___ million workers will be hired.

 c. In 2007, the federal minimum wage was set at $5.15 per hour. Substitute 5.15 for p in the demand model, $p = -0.325x + 5.8$, and determine the millions of workers employers will hire at this price.

 d. At a minimum wage of $5.15 per hour, use the supply model, $p = 0.375x + 3$, to determine the millions of available workers. Round to one decimal place.

 e. At a minimum wage of $5.15 per hour, use your answers from parts (c) and (d) to determine how many more people are looking for work than employers are willing to hire.

66. The following models describe demand and supply for three-bedroom rental apartments.

Demand Model	**Supply Model**
$p = -50x + 2000$	$p = 50x$
Monthly rental price Number of apartments demanded, in thousands	Monthly rental price Number of apartments supplied, in thousands

 a. Solve the system and find the equilibrium quantity and the equilibrium price.

 b. Use your answer from part (a) to complete this statement:

 When rents are _____ per month, consumers will demand _____ apartments and suppliers will offer _____ apartments for rent.

67. In each of the 1996, 2000, and 2004 presidential elections, 37% of voters believed abortion should be "always legal" or "always illegal." The bar graph shows the breakdown of these abortion "polars" as a percentage of voters in each election.

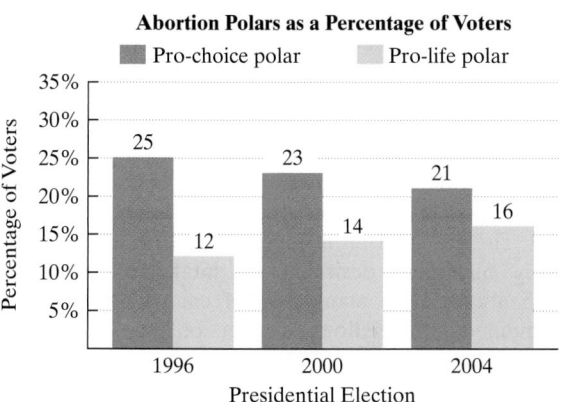

Abortion Polars as a Percentage of Voters

Source: Newsweek

The data can be modeled by the following system of equations:

$$\begin{cases} x + 2y = 50 \\ -x + 2y = 24. \end{cases}$$

The percentage of pro-choice polars, y, x years after 1996

The percentage of pro-life polars, y, x years after 1996

In which year will the percentage of voters who are pro-choice polars be the same as the percentage of voters who are pro-life polars? For that year, what percent will be pro-choice and what percent will be pro-life?

68. The bar graph shows the percentage of Americans for and against the death penalty for a person convicted of murder.

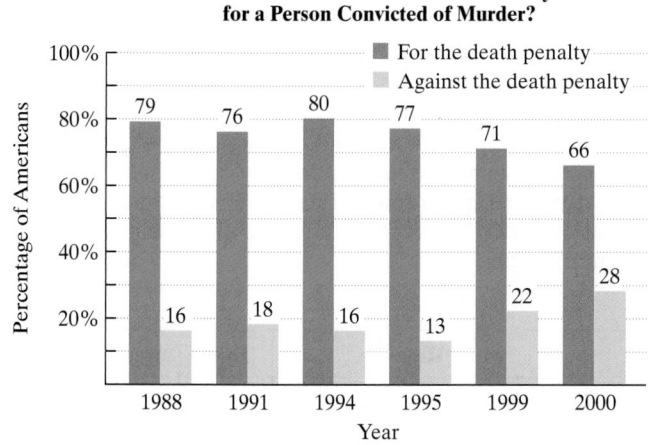

Are You in Favor of the Death Penalty for a Person Convicted of Murder?

Source: Newsweek poll

The data can be modeled by the following system of equations:

$$\begin{cases} 13x + 12y = 992 \\ -x + y = 16. \end{cases}$$

The percent, y, in favor of the death penalty x years after 1988

The percent, y, against the death penalty x years after 1988

In which year will the percentage of Americans in favor of the death penalty be the same as the percentage of Americans who oppose it? For that year, what percent will be for the death penalty and what percent will be against it?

69. We opened this section with a study showing that late in the semester, procrastinating students reported more symptoms of physical illness than their nonprocrastinating peers.

 a. At the beginning of the semester, procrastinators reported an average of 0.8 symptoms, increasing at a rate of 0.45 symptoms per week. Write a function that models the average number of symptoms after x weeks.

 b. At the beginning of the semester, nonprocrastinators reported an average of 2.6 symptoms, increasing at a rate of 0.15 symptoms per week. Write a function that models the average number of symptoms after x weeks.

 c. By which week in the semester did both groups report the same number of symptoms of physical illness? For that week, how many symptoms were reported by each group? How is this shown in **Figure 5.1** on page 482?

70. Although Social Security is a problem, some projections indicate that there's a much bigger time bomb ticking in the federal budget, and that's Medicare. In 2000, the cost of Social Security was 5.48% of the gross domestic product, increasing by 0.04% of the GDP per year. In 2000, the cost of Medicare was 1.84% of the gross domestic product, increasing by 0.17% of the GDP per year.

(*Source:* Congressional Budget Office)

 a. Write a function that models the cost of Social Security as a percentage of the GDP x years after 2000.

 b. Write a function that models the cost of Medicare as a percentage of the GDP x years after 2000.

 c. In which year will the cost of Medicare and Social Security be the same? For that year, what will be the cost of each program as a percentage of the GDP? Which program will have the greater cost after that year?

The bar graph shows the percentage of Americans who used cigarettes, by ethnicity, in 1985 and 2005. For each of the groups shown, cigarette use has been linearly decreasing. Use this information to solve Exercises 71–72.

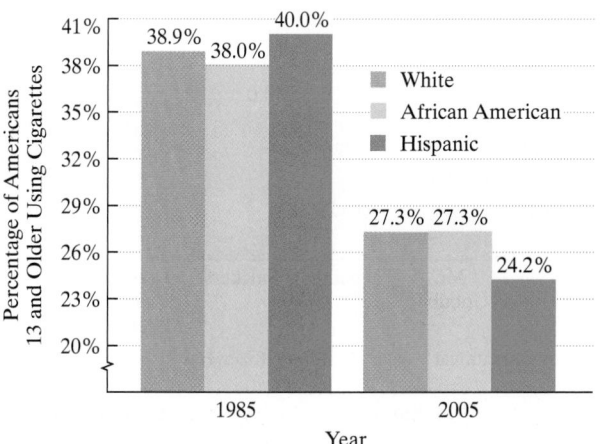

Cigarette Use in the United States

Source: Department of Health and Human Services

(Exercises 71–72 are based on the bar graph at the bottom of the previous page.)

71. In this exercise, let x represent the number of years after 1985 and let y represent the percentage of Americans in one of the groups shown who used cigarettes.

a. Use the data points $(0, 38)$ and $(20, 27.3)$ to find the slope-intercept equation of the line that models the percentage of African Americans who used cigarettes, y, x years after 1985. Round the value of the slope m to two decimal places.

b. Use the data points $(0, 40)$ and $(20, 24.2)$ to find the slope-intercept equation of the line that models the percentage of Hispanics who used cigarettes, y, x years after 1985.

c. Use the models from parts (a) and (b) to find the year during which cigarette use was the same for African Americans and Hispanics. What percentage of each group used cigarettes during that year?

72. In this exercise, let x represent the number of years after 1985 and let y represent the percentage of Americans in one of the groups shown who used cigarettes.

a. Use the data points $(0, 38.9)$ and $(20, 27.3)$ to find the slope-intercept equation of the line that models the percentage of whites who used cigarettes, y, x years after 1985.

b. Use the data points $(0, 40)$ and $(20, 24.2)$ to find the slope-intercept equation of the line that models the percentage of Hispanics who used cigarettes, y, x years after 1985.

c. Use the models from parts (a) and (b) to find the year, to the nearest whole year, during which cigarette use was the same for whites and Hispanics. What percentage of each group, to the nearest percent, used cigarettes during that year?

Use a system of linear equations to solve Exercises 73–84.

Looking for Mr. Goodbar? It's probably not a good idea if you want to look like Mr. Universe or Julia Roberts. The graph shows the four candy bars with the highest fat content, representing grams of fat and calories in each bar. Exercises 73–76 are based on the graph.

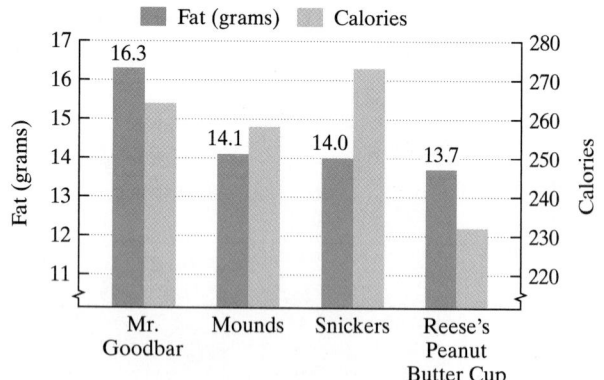

Candy Bars with the Highest Fat Content

Source: Krantz and Sveum, *The World's Worsts*, HarperCollins, 2005

73. One Mr. Goodbar and two Mounds bars contain 780 calories. Two Mr. Goodbars and one Mounds bar contain 786 calories. Find the caloric content of each candy bar.

74. One Snickers bar and two Reese's Peanut Butter Cups contain 737 calories. Two Snickers bars and one Reese's Peanut Butter Cup contain 778 calories. Find the caloric content of each candy bar.

75. A collection of Halloween candy contains a total of five Mr. Goodbars and Mounds bars. Chew on this: The grams of fat in these candy bars exceed the daily maximum desirable fat intake of 70 grams by 7.1 grams. How many bars of each kind of candy are contained in the Halloween collection?

76. A collection of Halloween candy contains a total of 12 Snickers bars and Reese's Peanut Butter Cups. Chew on this: The grams of fat in these candy bars exceed twice the daily maximum desirable fat intake of 70 grams by 26.5 grams. How many bars of each kind of candy are contained in the Halloween collection?

77. A hotel has 200 rooms. Those with kitchen facilities rent for $100 per night and those without kitchen facilities rent for $80 per night. On a night when the hotel was completely occupied, revenues were $17,000. How many of each type of room does the hotel have?

78. A new restaurant is to contain two-seat tables and four-seat tables. Fire codes limit the restaurant's maximum occupancy to 56 customers. If the owners have hired enough servers to handle 17 tables of customers, how many of each kind of table should they purchase?

79. A rectangular lot whose perimeter is 360 feet is fenced along three sides. An expensive fencing along the lot's length costs $20 per foot and an inexpensive fencing along the two side widths costs only $8 per foot. The total cost of the fencing along the three sides comes to $3280. What are the lot's dimensions?

80. A rectangular lot whose perimeter is 320 feet is fenced along three sides. An expensive fencing along the lot's length costs $16 per foot and an inexpensive fencing along the two side widths costs only $5 per foot. The total cost of the fencing along the three sides comes to $2140. What are the lot's dimensions?

81. When a crew rows with the current, it travels 16 miles in 2 hours. Against the current, the crew rows 8 miles in 2 hours. Let x = the crew's rowing rate in still water and let y = the rate of the current. The following chart summarizes this information:

	Rate	×	Time	=	Distance
Rowing with current	$x + y$		2		16
Rowing against current	$x - y$		2		8

Find the rate of rowing in still water and the rate of the current.

82. When an airplane flies with the wind, it travels 800 miles in 4 hours. Against the wind, it takes 5 hours to cover the same distance. Find the plane's rate in still air and the rate of the wind.

In Exercises 83–84, an isosceles triangle containing two angles with equal measure is shown. The degree measure of each triangle's three interior angles and an exterior angle is represented with variables. Find the measure of the three interior angles.

83.

84.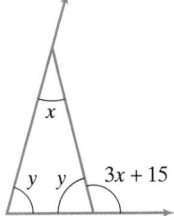

Writing in Mathematics

85. What is a system of linear equations? Provide an example with your description.

86. What is the solution of a system of linear equations?

87. Explain how to solve a system of equations using the substitution method. Use $y = 3 - 3x$ and $3x + 4y = 6$ to illustrate your explanation.

88. Explain how to solve a system of equations using the addition method. Use $3x + 5y = -2$ and $2x + 3y = 0$ to illustrate your explanation.

89. When is it easier to use the addition method rather than the substitution method to solve a system of equations?

90. When using the addition or substitution method, how can you tell if a system of linear equations has infinitely many solutions? What is the relationship between the graphs of the two equations?

91. When using the addition or substitution method, how can you tell if a system of linear equations has no solution? What is the relationship between the graphs of the two equations?

92. Describe the break-even point for a business.

Technology Exercise

93. Verify your solutions to any five exercises in Exercises 5–42 by using a graphing utility to graph the two equations in the system in the same viewing rectangle. Then use the intersection feature to display the solution.

Critical Thinking Exercises

Make Sense? *In Exercises 94–97, determine whether each statement makes sense or does not make sense, and explain your reasoning.*

94. Even if a linear system has a solution set involving fractions, such as $\left\{\left(\frac{8}{11}, \frac{43}{11}\right)\right\}$, I can use graphs to determine if the solution set is reasonable.

95. Each equation in a system of linear equations has infinitely many ordered-pair solutions.

96. Every linear system has infinitely many ordered-pair solutions.

97. If I know the perimeter of this rectangle and triangle, each in the same unit of measure, I can use a system of linear equations to determine values for x and y.

 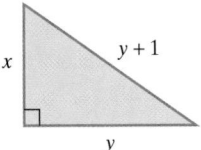

98. Write a system of equations having $\{(-2, 7)\}$ as a solution set. (More than one system is possible.)

99. Solve the system for x and y in terms of $a_1, b_1, c_1, a_2, b_2,$ and c_2:

$$a_1x + b_1y = c_1$$
$$a_2x + b_2y = c_2.$$

100. Two identical twins can only be distinguished by the characteristic that one always tells the truth and the other always lies. One twin tells you of a lucky number pair: "When I multiply my first lucky number by 3 and my second lucky number by 6, the addition of the resulting numbers produces a sum of 12. When I add my first lucky number and twice my second lucky number, the sum is 5." Which twin is talking?

101. A marching band has 52 members, and there are 24 in the pom-pom squad. They wish to form several hexagons and squares like those diagrammed below. Can it be done with no people left over?

B = Band Member
P = Pom-pom Person

Group Exercise

102. The group should write four different word problems that can be solved using a system of linear equations in two variables. All of the problems should be on different topics. The group should turn in the four problems and their algebraic solutions.

Preview Exercises

Exercises 103–105 will help you prepare for the material covered in the next section.

103. If $x = 3, y = 2,$ and $z = -3,$ does the ordered triple (x, y, z) satisfy the equation $2x - y + 4z = -8$?

104. Consider the following equations:

$$\begin{cases} 5x - 2y - 4z = 3 & \text{Equation 1} \\ 3x + 3y + 2z = -3. & \text{Equation 2} \end{cases}$$

Use these equations to eliminate z. Copy Equation 1 and multiply Equation 2 by 2. Then add the equations.

105. Write an equation involving $a, b,$ and c based on the following description:

When the value of x in $y = ax^2 + bx + c$ is 4, the value of y is 1682.

Section 5.2

Systems of Linear Equations in Three Variables

Objectives

1 Verify the solution of a system of linear equations in three variables.

2 Solve systems of linear equations in three variables.

3 Solve problems using systems in three variables.

All animals sleep, but the length of time they sleep varies widely: Cattle sleep for only a few minutes at a time. We humans seem to need more sleep than other animals, up to eight hours a day. Without enough sleep, we have difficulty concentrating, make mistakes in routine tasks, lose energy, and feel bad-tempered. There is a relationship between hours of sleep and death rate per year per 100,000 people. How many hours of sleep will put you in the group with the minimum death rate? In this section, we will answer this question by solving a system of linear equations with more than two variables.

1 Verify the solution of a system of linear equations in three variables.

Systems of Linear Equations in Three Variables and Their Solutions

An equation such as $x + 2y - 3z = 9$ is called a *linear equation in three variables*. In general, any equation of the form

$$Ax + By + Cz = D,$$

where A, B, C, and D are real numbers such that A, B, and C are not all 0, is a **linear equation in three variables: x, y, and z**. The graph of this linear equation in three variables is a plane in three-dimensional space.

The process of solving a system of three linear equations in three variables is geometrically equivalent to finding the point of intersection (assuming that there is one) of three planes in space. (See **Figure 5.8**.) A **solution** of a system of linear equations in three variables is an ordered triple of real numbers that satisfies all equations of the system. The **solution set** of the system is the set of all its solutions.

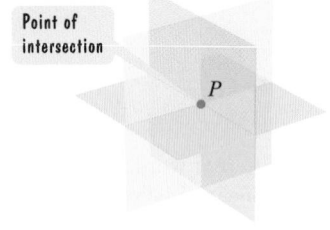

Point of intersection

P

Figure 5.8

EXAMPLE 1 Determining Whether an Ordered Triple Satisfies a System

Show that the ordered triple $(-1, 2, -2)$ is a solution of the system:

$$\begin{cases} x + 2y - 3z = 9 \\ 2x - y + 2z = -8 \\ -x + 3y - 4z = 15. \end{cases}$$

Solution Because -1 is the x-coordinate, 2 is the y-coordinate, and -2 is the z-coordinate of $(-1, 2, -2)$, we replace x with -1, y with 2, and z with -2 in each of the three equations.

$$x + 2y - 3z = 9$$

$$-1 + 2(2) - 3(-2) \overset{?}{=} 9$$

$$-1 + 4 + 6 \overset{?}{=} 9$$

$$9 = 9, \quad \text{true}$$

$$2x - y + 2z = -8$$

$$2(-1) - 2 + 2(-2) \overset{?}{=} -8$$

$$-2 - 2 - 4 \overset{?}{=} -8$$

$$-8 = -8, \quad \text{true}$$

$$-x + 3y - 4z = 15$$

$$-(-1) + 3(2) - 4(-2) \overset{?}{=} 15$$

$$1 + 6 + 8 \overset{?}{=} 15$$

$$15 = 15, \quad \text{true}$$

The ordered triple $(-1, 2, -2)$ satisfies the three equations: It makes each equation true. Thus, the ordered triple is a solution of the system.

Check Point **1** Show that the ordered triple $(-1, -4, 5)$ is a solution of the system:

$$\begin{cases} x - 2y + 3z = 22 \\ 2x - 3y - z = 5 \\ 3x + y - 5z = -32. \end{cases}$$

 Solve systems of linear equations in three variables.

Solving Systems of Linear Equations in Three Variables by Eliminating Variables

The method for solving a system of linear equations in three variables is similar to that used on systems of linear equations in two variables. We use addition to eliminate any variable, reducing the system to two equations in two variables. Once we obtain a system of two equations in two variables, we use addition or substitution to eliminate a variable. The result is a single equation in one variable. We solve this equation to get the value of the remaining variable. Other variable values are found by back-substitution.

Study Tip

It does not matter which variable you eliminate, as long as you do it in two different pairs of equations.

Solving Linear Systems in Three Variables by Eliminating Variables

1. Reduce the system to two equations in two variables. This is usually accomplished by taking two different pairs of equations and using the addition method to eliminate the same variable from both pairs.

2. Solve the resulting system of two equations in two variables using addition or substitution. The result is an equation in one variable that gives the value of that variable.

3. Back-substitute the value of the variable found in step 2 into either of the equations in two variables to find the value of the second variable.

4. Use the values of the two variables from steps 2 and 3 to find the value of the third variable by back-substituting into one of the original equations.

5. Check the proposed solution in each of the original equations.

EXAMPLE 2 **Solving a System in Three Variables**

Solve the system:

$$\begin{cases} 5x - 2y - 4z = 3 & \text{Equation 1} \\ 3x + 3y + 2z = -3 & \text{Equation 2} \\ -2x + 5y + 3z = 3. & \text{Equation 3} \end{cases}$$

$$\begin{cases} 5x - 2y - 4z = 3 & \text{Equation 1} \\ 3x + 3y + 2z = -3 & \text{Equation 2} \\ -2x + 5y + 3z = 3 & \text{Equation 3} \end{cases}$$

The given system (repeated)

Solution There are many ways to proceed. Because our initial goal is to reduce the system to two equations in two variables, **the central idea is to take two different pairs of equations and eliminate the same variable from both pairs.**

Step 1 Reduce the system to two equations in two variables. We choose any two equations and use the addition method to eliminate a variable. Let's eliminate z using Equations 1 and 2. We do so by multiplying Equation 2 by 2. Then we add equations.

(Equation 1) $\begin{cases} 5x - 2y - 4z = 3 \\ 3x + 3y + 2z = -3 \end{cases}$ $\xrightarrow{\text{No change}}$ $\xrightarrow{\text{Multiply by 2.}}$ $\begin{cases} 5x - 2y - 4z = 3 \\ 6x + 6y + 4z = -6 \end{cases}$
(Equation 2)

Add: $11x + 4y \quad\quad = -3$ Equation 4

Now we must eliminate the *same* variable using another pair of equations. We can eliminate z from Equations 2 and 3. First, we multiply Equation 2 by -3. Next, we multiply Equation 3 by 2. Finally, we add equations.

(Equation 2) $\begin{cases} 3x + 3y + 2z = -3 \\ -2x + 5y + 3z = 3 \end{cases}$ $\xrightarrow{\text{Multiply by }-3.}$ $\xrightarrow{\text{Multiply by 2.}}$ $\begin{cases} -9x - 9y - 6z = 9 \\ -4x + 10y + 6z = 6 \end{cases}$
(Equation 3)

Add: $-13x + \quad y \quad\quad = 15$ Equation 5

Equations 4 and 5 give us a system of two equations in two variables:

$$\begin{cases} 11x + 4y = -3 & \text{Equation 4} \\ -13x + y = 15. & \text{Equation 5} \end{cases}$$

Step 2 Solve the resulting system of two equations in two variables. We will use the addition method to solve Equations 4 and 5 for x and y. To do so, we multiply Equation 5 on both sides by -4 and add this to Equation 4.

(Equation 4) $\begin{cases} 11x + 4y = -3 \\ -13x + y = 15 \end{cases}$ $\xrightarrow{\text{No change}}$ $\xrightarrow{\text{Multiply by }-4.}$ $\begin{cases} 11x + 4y = -3 \\ 52x - 4y = -60 \end{cases}$
(Equation 5)

$63x \quad\quad = -63$

Add: $x \quad\quad = -1$ Divide both sides by 63.

Step 3 Use back-substitution in one of the equations in two variables to find the value of the second variable. We back-substitute -1 for x in either Equation 4 or 5 to find the value of y.

$$-13x + y = 15 \qquad \text{Equation 5}$$
$$-13(-1) + y = 15 \qquad \text{Substitute } -1 \text{ for x.}$$
$$13 + y = 15 \qquad \text{Multiply.}$$
$$y = 2 \qquad \text{Subtract 13 from both sides.}$$

Step 4 Back-substitute the values found for two variables into one of the original equations to find the value of the third variable. We can now use any one of the original equations and back-substitute the values of x and y to find the value for z. We will use Equation 2.

$$3x + 3y + 2z = -3 \qquad \text{Equation 2}$$
$$3(-1) + 3(2) + 2z = -3 \qquad \text{Substitute } -1 \text{ for x and 2 for y.}$$
$$3 + 2z = -3 \qquad \begin{array}{l}\text{Multiply and then add:} \\ 3(-1) + 3(2) = -3 + 6 = 3.\end{array}$$
$$2z = -6 \qquad \text{Subtract 3 from both sides.}$$
$$z = -3 \qquad \text{Divide both sides by 2.}$$

With $x = -1$, $y = 2$, and $z = -3$, the proposed solution is the ordered triple $(-1, 2, -3)$.

Step 5 Check. Check the proposed solution, $(-1, 2, -3)$, by substituting the values for x, y, and z into each of the three original equations. These substitutions yield three true statements. Thus, the solution set is $\{(-1, 2, -3)\}$. ●

⊘ Check Point **2** Solve the system:

$$\begin{cases} x + 4y - z = 20 \\ 3x + 2y + z = 8 \\ 2x - 3y + 2z = -16. \end{cases}$$

In some examples, one of the variables is already eliminated from a given equation. In this case, the missing variable should be eliminated from the other two equations, thereby making it possible to omit one of the elimination steps. We illustrate this idea in Example 3.

(**EXAMPLE 3**) **Solving a System of Equations with a Missing Term**

Solve the system:

$$\begin{cases} x + \quad\ z = 8 \qquad \text{Equation 1} \\ x + y + 2z = 17 \qquad \text{Equation 2} \\ x + 2y + z = 16. \qquad \text{Equation 3} \end{cases}$$

Solution

Step 1 Reduce the system to two equations in two variables. Because Equation 1 contains only x and z, we could omit one of the elimination steps by eliminating y using Equations 2 and 3. This will give us two equations in x and z. To eliminate y using Equations 2 and 3, we multiply Equation 2 by -2 and add Equation 3.

(Equation 2) $\begin{cases} x + y + 2z = 17 \end{cases}$ $\xrightarrow{\text{Multiply by } -2.}$ $\begin{cases} -2x - 2y - 4z = -34 \end{cases}$
(Equation 3) $\begin{cases} x + 2y + z = 16 \end{cases}$ $\xrightarrow{\text{No change}}$ $\underline{\begin{cases} x + 2y + z = 16 \end{cases}}$

Add: $-x \qquad\quad - 3z = -18$ Equation 4

Equation 4 and the given Equation 1 provide us with a system of two equations in two variables:

$$\begin{cases} x + \ z = 8 \qquad \text{Equation 1} \\ -x - 3z = -18. \quad \text{Equation 4} \end{cases}$$

Step 2 Solve the resulting system of two equations in two variables. We will solve Equations 1 and 4 for x and z.

$$\begin{cases} x + \ z = \quad 8 \quad \text{Equation 1} \\ \underline{-x - 3z = -18} \quad \text{Equation 4} \end{cases}$$

Add: $-2z = -10$
$z = \quad 5$ Divide both sides by -2.

Step 3 Use back-substitution in one of the equations in two variables to find the value of the second variable. To find x, we back-substitute 5 for z in either Equation 1 or 4. We will use Equation 1.

$x + z = 8$ Equation 1
$x + 5 = 8$ Substitute 5 for z.
$x = 3$ Subtract 5 from both sides.

$$\begin{cases} x + z = 8 & \text{Equation 1} \\ x + y + 2z = 17 & \text{Equation 2} \\ x + 2y + z = 16 & \text{Equation 3} \end{cases}$$

The given system (repeated)

Step 4 Back-substitute the values found for two variables into one of the original equations to find the value of the third variable. To find y, we back-substitute 3 for x and 5 for z into Equation 2 or 3. We cannot use Equation 1 because y is missing in this equation. We will use Equation 2.

$$x + y + 2z = 17 \qquad \text{Equation 2}$$
$$3 + y + 2(5) = 17 \qquad \text{Substitute 3 for x and 5 for z.}$$
$$y + 13 = 17 \qquad \text{Multiply and add.}$$
$$y = 4 \qquad \text{Subtract 13 from both sides.}$$

We found that $z = 5$, $x = 3$, and $y = 4$. Thus, the proposed solution is the ordered triple $(3, 4, 5)$.

Step 5 Check. Substituting 3 for x, 4 for y, and 5 for z into each of the three original equations yields three true statements. Consequently, the solution set is $\{(3, 4, 5)\}$. ●

⊘ Check Point **3** Solve the system:

$$\begin{cases} 2y - z = 7 \\ x + 2y + z = 17 \\ 2x - 3y + 2z = -1. \end{cases}$$

A system of linear equations in three variables represents three planes. The three planes may not always intersect at one point. The planes may have no common point of intersection and represent an inconsistent system with no solution. By contrast, the planes may coincide or intersect along a line. In these cases, the planes have infinitely many points in common and represent systems with infinitely many solutions. Systems of linear equations in three variables that are inconsistent or that contain dependent equations will be discussed in Chapter 6.

③ Solve problems using systems in three variables.

Applications

Systems of equations may allow us to find models for data without using a graphing utility. Three data points that do not lie on or near a line determine the graph of a quadratic function of the form $y = ax^2 + bx + c, a \neq 0$. Quadratic functions often model situations in which values of y are decreasing and then increasing, suggesting the bowl-like shape of a parabola.

(**EXAMPLE 4**) **Modeling Data Relating Sleep and Death Rate**

In a study relating sleep and death rate, the following data were obtained. Use the function $y = ax^2 + bx + c$ to model the data.

x (Average Number of Hours of Sleep)	y (Death Rate per Year per 100,000 Males)
4	1682
7	626
9	967

Solution We need to find values for a, b, and c in $y = ax^2 + bx + c$. We can do so by solving a system of three linear equations in a, b, and c. We obtain the three equations by using the values of x and y from the data as follows:

$y = ax^2 + bx + c$ *Use the quadratic function to model the data.*

When $x = 4$, $y = 1682$: $\begin{cases} 1682 = a \cdot 4^2 + b \cdot 4 + c \\ 626 = a \cdot 7^2 + b \cdot 7 + c \\ 967 = a \cdot 9^2 + b \cdot 9 + c \end{cases}$ or $\begin{cases} 16a + 4b + c = 1682 \\ 49a + 7b + c = 626 \\ 81a + 9b + c = 967. \end{cases}$

When $x = 7$, $y = 626$:

When $x = 9$, $y = 967$:

Technology

The graph of

$$y = 104.5x^2 - 1501.5x + 6016$$

is displayed in a $[3, 12, 1]$ by $[500, 2000, 100]$ viewing rectangle. The minimum function feature shows that the lowest point on the graph, the vertex, is approximately $(7.2, 622.5)$. Men who average 7.2 hours of sleep are in the group with the lowest death rate, approximately 622.5 deaths per 100,000 males.

Minimum
X=7.212766 Y=622.53916

The easiest way to solve this system is to eliminate c from two pairs of equations, obtaining two equations in a and b. Solving this system gives $a = 104.5$, $b = -1501.5$, and $c = 6016$. We now substitute the values for a, b, and c into $y = ax^2 + bx + c$. The function that models the given data is

$$y = 104.5x^2 - 1501.5x + 6016.$$

We can use the model that we obtained in Example 4 to find the death rate of males who average, say, 6 hours of sleep. First, write the model in function notation:

$$f(x) = 104.5x^2 - 1501.5x + 6016.$$

Substitute 6 for x:

$$f(6) = 104.5(6)^2 - 1501.5(6) + 6016 = 769.$$

According to the model, the death rate for males who average 6 hours of sleep is 769 deaths per 100,000 males.

⊘ Check Point **4** Find the quadratic function $y = ax^2 + bx + c$ whose graph passes through the points $(1, 4)$, $(2, 1)$, and $(3, 4)$.

Exercise Set 5.2

Practice Exercises

In Exercises 1–4, determine if the given ordered triple is a solution of the system.

1. $(2, -1, 3)$
$\begin{cases} x + y + z = 4 \\ x - 2y - z = 1 \\ 2x - y - 2z = -1 \end{cases}$

2. $(5, -3, -2)$
$\begin{cases} x + y + z = 0 \\ x + 2y - 3z = 5 \\ 3x + 4y + 2z = -1 \end{cases}$

3. $(4, 1, 2)$
$\begin{cases} x - 2y = 2 \\ 2x + 3y = 11 \\ y - 4z = -7 \end{cases}$

4. $(-1, 3, 2)$
$\begin{cases} x - 2z = -5 \\ y - 3z = -3 \\ 2x - z = -4 \end{cases}$

Solve each system in Exercises 5–18.

5. $\begin{cases} x + y + 2z = 11 \\ x + y + 3z = 14 \\ x + 2y - z = 5 \end{cases}$

6. $\begin{cases} 2x + y - 2z = -1 \\ 3x - 3y - z = 5 \\ x - 2y + 3z = 6 \end{cases}$

7. $\begin{cases} 4x - y + 2z = 11 \\ x + 2y - z = -1 \\ 2x + 2y - 3z = -1 \end{cases}$

8. $\begin{cases} x - y + 3z = 8 \\ 3x + y - 2z = -2 \\ 2x + 4y + z = 0 \end{cases}$

9. $\begin{cases} 3x + 2y - 3z = -2 \\ 2x - 5y + 2z = -2 \\ 4x - 3y + 4z = 10 \end{cases}$

10. $\begin{cases} 2x + 3y + 7z = 13 \\ 3x + 2y - 5z = -22 \\ 5x + 7y - 3z = -28 \end{cases}$

11. $\begin{cases} 2x - 4y + 3z = 17 \\ x + 2y - z = 0 \\ 4x - y - z = 6 \end{cases}$

12. $\begin{cases} x + z = 3 \\ x + 2y - z = 1 \\ 2x - y + z = 3 \end{cases}$

13. $\begin{cases} 2x + y = 2 \\ x + y - z = 4 \\ 3x + 2y + z = 0 \end{cases}$

14. $\begin{cases} x + 3y + 5z = 20 \\ y - 4z = -16 \\ 3x - 2y + 9z = 36 \end{cases}$

15. $\begin{cases} x + y = -4 \\ y - z = 1 \\ 2x + y + 3z = -21 \end{cases}$

16. $\begin{cases} x + y = 4 \\ x + z = 4 \\ y + z = 4 \end{cases}$

17. $\begin{cases} 3(2x + y) + 5z = -1 \\ 2(x - 3y + 4z) = -9 \\ 4(1 + x) = -3(z - 3y) \end{cases}$

18. $\begin{cases} 7z - 3 = 2(x - 3y) \\ 5y + 3z - 7 = 4x \\ 4 + 5z = 3(2x - y) \end{cases}$

In Exercises 19–22, find the quadratic function $y = ax^2 + bx + c$ whose graph passes through the given points.

19. $(-1, 6), (1, 4), (2, 9)$ **20.** $(-2, 7), (1, -2), (2, 3)$

21. $(-1, -4), (1, -2), (2, 5)$ **22.** $(1, 3), (3, -1), (4, 0)$

In Exercises 23–24, let x represent the first number, y the second number, and z the third number. Use the given conditions to write a system of equations. Solve the system and find the numbers.

23. The sum of three numbers is 16. The sum of twice the first number, 3 times the second number, and 4 times the third number is 46. The difference between 5 times the first number and the second number is 31. Find the three numbers.

24. The following is known about three numbers: Three times the first number plus the second number plus twice the third number is 5. If 3 times the second number is subtracted from the sum of the first number and 3 times the third number, the result is 2. If the third number is subtracted from 2 times the first number and 3 times the second number, the result is 1. Find the numbers.

Practice Plus

Solve each system in Exercises 25–26.

25. $\begin{cases} \dfrac{x+2}{6} - \dfrac{y+4}{3} + \dfrac{z}{2} = 0 \\ \dfrac{x+1}{2} + \dfrac{y-1}{2} - \dfrac{z}{4} = \dfrac{9}{2} \\ \dfrac{x-5}{4} + \dfrac{y+1}{3} + \dfrac{z-2}{2} = \dfrac{19}{4} \end{cases}$

26. $\begin{cases} \dfrac{x+3}{2} - \dfrac{y-1}{2} + \dfrac{z+2}{4} = \dfrac{3}{2} \\ \dfrac{x-5}{2} + \dfrac{y+1}{3} - \dfrac{z}{4} = -\dfrac{25}{6} \\ \dfrac{x-3}{4} - \dfrac{y+1}{2} + \dfrac{z-3}{2} = -\dfrac{5}{2} \end{cases}$

In Exercises 27–28, find the equation of the quadratic function $y = ax^2 + bx + c$ whose graph is shown. Select three points whose coordinates appear to be integers.

27.

28.
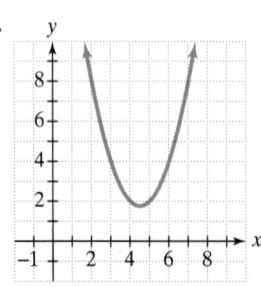

In Exercises 29–30, solve each system for (x, y, z) in terms of the nonzero constants a, b, and c.

29. $\begin{cases} ax - by - 2cz = 21 \\ ax + by + cz = 0 \\ 2ax - by + cz = 14 \end{cases}$ **30.** $\begin{cases} ax - by + 2cz = -4 \\ ax + 3by - cz = 1 \\ 2ax + by + 3cz = 2 \end{cases}$

Application Exercises

31. You throw a ball straight up from a rooftop. The ball misses the rooftop on its way down and eventually strikes the ground. A mathematical model can be used to describe the relationship for the ball's height above the ground, y, after x seconds. Consider the following data:

x, seconds after the ball is thrown	y, ball's height, in feet, above the ground
1	224
3	176
4	104

a. Find the quadratic function $y = ax^2 + bx + c$ whose graph passes through the given points.

b. Use the function in part (a) to find the value for y when $x = 5$. Describe what this means.

32. A mathematical model can be used to describe the relationship between the number of feet a car travels once the brakes are applied, y, and the number of seconds the car is in motion after the brakes are applied, x. A research firm collects the following data:

x, seconds in motion after brakes are applied	y, feet car travels once the brakes are applied
1	46
2	84
3	114

a. Find the quadratic function $y = ax^2 + bx + c$ whose graph passes through the given points.

b. Use the function in part (a) to find the value for y when $x = 6$. Describe what this means.

Use a system of linear equations in three variables to solve Exercises 33–39.

The bar graph compares the body composition of a 160-pound adult male and a 135-pound adult female. Exercises 33–34 are based on the data displayed by the graph.

Source: Thompson et al., *The Science of Nutrition*, Benjamin Cummings, 2008

33. This exercise refers to the body composition of a 135-pound adult female, shown by the graph on the previous page. Ninety-five percent of her total body weight consists of water, fat, and protein. The difference between the percentage of body weight consisting of water and fat is 35%. The difference between the percentage of body weight consisting of fat and protein is 9%. Find the percentage of total body weight consisting of water, of fat, and of protein.

34. This exercise refers to the body composition of a 160-pound adult male, shown by the graph on the previous page. Ninety-four percent of his total body weight consists of water, fat, and protein. The difference between the percentage of body weight consisting of water and fat is 47%. The difference between the percentage of body weight consisting of protein and fat is 2%. Find the percentage of total body weight consisting of water, of fat, and of protein.

35. At a college production of *Streetcar Named Desire*, 400 tickets were sold. The ticket prices were $8, $10, and $12, and the total income from ticket sales was $3700. How many tickets of each type were sold if the combined number of $8 and $10 tickets sold was 7 times the number of $12 tickets sold?

36. A certain brand of razor blades comes in packages of 6, 12, and 24 blades, costing $2, $3, and $4 per package, respectively. A store sold 12 packages containing a total of 162 razor blades and took in $35. How many packages of each type were sold?

37. A person invested $6700 for one year, part at 8%, part at 10%, and the remainder at 12%. The total annual income from these investments was $716. The amount of money invested at 12% was $300 more than the amount invested at 8% and 10% combined. Find the amount invested at each rate.

38. A person invested $17,000 for one year, part at 10%, part at 12%, and the remainder at 15%. The total annual income from these investments was $2110. The amount of money invested at 12% was $1000 less than the amount invested at 10% and 15% combined. Find the amount invested at each rate.

39. In the following triangle, the degree measures of the three interior angles and two of the exterior angles are represented with variables. Find the measure of each interior angle.

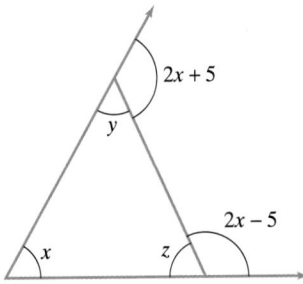

Writing in Mathematics

40. What is a system of linear equations in three variables?

41. How do you determine whether a given ordered triple is a solution of a system in three variables?

42. Describe in general terms how to solve a system in three variables.

43. AIDS is taking a deadly toll on southern Africa. Describe how to use the techniques that you learned in this section to obtain a model for African life span using projections with AIDS, shown by the red graph in the figure. Let x represent the number of years after 1985 and let y represent African life span in that year.

African Life Span

Source: United Nations

Technology Exercises

44. Does your graphing utility have a feature that allows you to solve linear systems by entering coefficients and constant terms? If so, use this feature to verify the solutions to any five exercises that you worked by hand from Exercises 5–16.

45. Verify your results in Exercises 19–22 by using a graphing utility to graph the resulting parabola. Trace along the curve and convince yourself that the three points given in the exercise lie on the parabola.

Critical Thinking Exercises

Make Sense? *In Exercises 46–49, determine whether each statement makes sense or does not make sense, and explain your reasoning.*

46. Solving a system in three variables, I found that $x = 3$ and $y = -1$. Because z represents a third variable, z cannot equal 3 or -1.

47. A system of linear equations in three variables, x, y, and z, cannot contain an equation in the form $y = mx + b$.

48. I'm solving a three-variable system in which one of the given equations has a missing term, so it will not be necessary to use any of the original equations twice when I reduce the system to two equations in two variables.

49. Because the percentage of the U.S. population that was foreign-born decreased from 1910 through 1970 and then increased after that, a quadratic function of the form $f(x) = ax^2 + bx + c$, rather than a linear function of the form $f(x) = mx + b$, should be used to model the data.

50. Describe how the system

$$\begin{cases} x + y - z - 2w = -8 \\ x - 2y + 3z + w = 18 \\ 2x + 2y + 2z - 2w = 10 \\ 2x + y - z + w = 3 \end{cases}$$

could be solved. Is it likely that in the near future a graphing utility will be available to provide a geometric solution (using intersecting graphs) to this system? Explain.

51. A modernistic painting consists of triangles, rectangles, and pentagons, all drawn so as to not overlap or share sides. Within each rectangle are drawn 2 red roses and each pentagon contains 5 carnations. How many triangles, rectangles, and pentagons appear in the painting if the painting contains a total of 40 geometric figures, 153 sides of geometric figures, and 72 flowers?

Group Exercise

52. Group members should develop appropriate functions that model each of the projections shown in Exercise 43.

Preview Exercises

Exercises 53–55 will help you prepare for the material covered in the next section.

53. Subtract: $\dfrac{3}{x - 4} - \dfrac{2}{x + 2}$.

54. Add: $\dfrac{5x - 3}{x^2 + 1} + \dfrac{2x}{(x^2 + 1)^2}$.

55. Solve:
$$\begin{cases} A + B = 3 \\ 2A - 2B + C = 17 \\ 4A - 2C = 14. \end{cases}$$

Section 5.3 **Partial Fractions**

Objectives

1 Decompose $\dfrac{P}{Q}$, where Q has only distinct linear factors.

2 Decompose $\dfrac{P}{Q}$, where Q has repeated linear factors.

3 Decompose $\dfrac{P}{Q}$, where Q has a nonrepeated prime quadratic factor.

4 Decompose $\dfrac{P}{Q}$, where Q has a prime, repeated quadratic factor.

The rising and setting of the sun suggest the obvious: Things change over time. Calculus is the study of rates of change, allowing the motion of the rising sun to be measured by "freezing the frame" at one instant in time. If you are given a function, calculus reveals its rate of change at any "frozen" instant. In this section, you will learn an algebraic technique used in calculus to find a function if its rate of change is known. The technique involves expressing a given function in terms of simpler functions.

The Idea behind Partial Fraction Decomposition

We know how to use common denominators to write a sum or difference of rational expressions as a single rational expression. For example,

$$\frac{3}{x - 4} - \frac{2}{x + 2} = \frac{3(x + 2) - 2(x - 4)}{(x - 4)(x + 2)}$$

$$= \frac{3x + 6 - 2x + 8}{(x - 4)(x + 2)} = \frac{x + 14}{(x - 4)(x + 2)}.$$

For solving the kind of calculus problem described in the section opener, we must reverse this process:

Partial fraction Partial fraction

$\dfrac{x + 14}{(x - 4)(x + 2)}$ is expressed as the sum of two simpler fractions.

$$\frac{x + 14}{(x - 4)(x + 2)} = \frac{3}{x - 4} + \frac{-2}{x + 2}.$$

This is the partial fraction decomposition of $\dfrac{x + 14}{(x - 4)(x + 2)}$.

Each of the two fractions on the right is called a **partial fraction**. The sum of these fractions is called the **partial fraction decomposition** of the rational expression on the left-hand side.

Partial fraction decompositions can be written for rational expressions of the form $\dfrac{P(x)}{Q(x)}$, where P and Q have no common factors and the highest power in the numerator is less than the highest power in the denominator. In this section, we will show you how to write the partial fraction decompositions for each of the following rational expressions:

$$\dfrac{9x^2 - 9x + 6}{(2x - 1)(x + 2)(x - 2)}$$

> $P(x) = 9x^2 - 9x + 6$; highest power = 2
>
> $Q(x) = (2x - 1)(x + 2)(x - 2)$; multiplying factors, highest power = 3.

$$\dfrac{5x^3 - 3x^2 + 7x - 3}{(x^2 + 1)^2}.$$

> $P(x) = 5x^3 - 3x^2 + 7x - 3$; highest power = 3
>
> $Q(x) = (x^2 + 1)^2$; squaring the expression, highest power = 4.

The partial fraction decomposition of a rational expression depends on the factors of the denominator. We consider four cases involving different kinds of factors in the denominator:

1. The denominator is a product of distinct linear factors.
2. The denominator is a product of linear factors, some of which are repeated.
3. The denominator has prime quadratic factors, none of which is repeated.
4. The denominator has a repeated prime quadratic factor.

1 Decompose $\dfrac{P}{Q}$, where Q has only distinct linear factors.

The Partial Fraction Decomposition of a Rational Expression with Distinct Linear Factors in the Denominator

If the denominator of a rational expression has a linear factor of the form $ax + b$, then the partial fraction decomposition will contain a term of the form

$$\dfrac{A}{ax + b}.$$

> Constant
>
> Linear factor

Each distinct linear factor in the denominator produces a partial fraction of the form *constant over linear factor*. For example,

$$\dfrac{9x^2 - 9x + 6}{(2x - 1)(x + 2)(x - 2)} = \dfrac{A}{2x - 1} + \dfrac{B}{x + 2} + \dfrac{C}{x - 2}.$$

> We write a constant over each linear factor in the denominator.

The Partial Fraction Decomposition of $\dfrac{P(x)}{Q(x)}$: $Q(x)$ Has Distinct Linear Factors

The form of the partial fraction decomposition for a rational expression with distinct linear factors in the denominator is

$$\dfrac{P(x)}{(a_1 x + b_1)(a_2 x + b_2)(a_3 x + b_3) \cdots (a_n x + b_n)}$$

$$= \dfrac{A_1}{a_1 x + b_1} + \dfrac{A_2}{a_2 x + b_2} + \dfrac{A_3}{a_3 x + b_3} + \cdots + \dfrac{A_n}{a_n x + b_n}.$$

(EXAMPLE 1) **Partial Fraction Decomposition with Distinct Linear Factors**

Find the partial fraction decomposition of

$$\frac{x + 14}{(x - 4)(x + 2)}.$$

Solution We begin by setting up the partial fraction decomposition with the unknown constants. Write a constant over each of the two distinct linear factors in the denominator.

$$\frac{x + 14}{(x - 4)(x + 2)} = \frac{A}{x - 4} + \frac{B}{x + 2}$$

Our goal is to find A and B. We do this by multiplying both sides of the equation by the least common denominator, $(x - 4)(x + 2)$.

$$(x - 4)(x + 2)\frac{x + 14}{(x - 4)(x + 2)} = (x - 4)(x + 2)\left(\frac{A}{x - 4} + \frac{B}{x + 2}\right)$$

We use the distributive property on the right side.

$$(x - 4)(x + 2)\frac{x + 14}{(x - 4)(x + 2)}$$

$$= (x - 4)(x + 2)\frac{A}{(x - 4)} + (x - 4)(x + 2)\frac{B}{(x + 2)}$$

Dividing out common factors in numerators and denominators, we obtain

$$x + 14 = A(x + 2) + B(x - 4).$$

To find values for A and B that make both sides equal, we'll express the sides in exactly the same form by writing the variable x-terms and then writing the constant terms. Apply the distributive property on the right side.

$x + 14 = Ax + 2A + Bx - 4B$	Distribute A and B over the parentheses.
$x + 14 = Ax + Bx + 2A - 4B$	Rearrange terms.
$1x + 14 = (A + B)x + (2A - 4B)$	Rewrite to identify the coefficient of x and the constant term.

As shown by the arrows, if two polynomials are equal, coefficients of like powers of x must be equal $(A + B = 1)$ and their constant terms must be equal $(2A - 4B = 14)$. Consequently, A and B satisfy the following two equations:

$$\begin{cases} A + B = 1 \\ 2A - 4B = 14. \end{cases}$$

We can use the addition method to solve this linear system in two variables. By multiplying the first equation by -2 and adding equations, we obtain $A = 3$ and $B = -2$. Thus,

$$\frac{x + 14}{(x - 4)(x + 2)} = \frac{A}{x - 4} + \frac{B}{x + 2} = \frac{3}{x - 4} + \frac{-2}{x + 2} \left(\text{or } \frac{3}{x - 4} - \frac{2}{x + 2} \right).$$

Steps in Partial Fraction Decomposition

1. Set up the partial fraction decomposition with the unknown constants A, B, C, etc., in the numerators of the decomposition.
2. Multiply both sides of the resulting equation by the least common denominator.
3. Simplify the right side of the equation.
4. Write both sides in descending powers, equate coefficients of like powers of x, and equate constant terms.
5. Solve the resulting linear system for A, B, C, etc.
6. Substitute the values for A, B, C, etc., into the equation in step 1 and write the partial fraction decomposition.

Study Tip

You will encounter some examples in which the denominator of the given rational expression is not already factored. If necessary, begin by factoring the denominator. Then apply the six steps needed to obtain the partial fraction decomposition.

✓ **Check Point** ❘ Find the partial fraction decomposition of $\dfrac{5x - 1}{(x - 3)(x + 4)}$.

② Decompose $\dfrac{P}{Q}$, where Q has repeated linear factors.

The Partial Fraction Decomposition of a Rational Expression with Linear Factors in the Denominator, Some of Which Are Repeated

Suppose that $(ax + b)^n$ is a factor of the denominator. This means that the linear factor $ax + b$ is repeated n times. When this occurs, the partial fraction decomposition will contain a sum of n fractions for this factor of the denominator.

The Partial Fraction Decomposition of $\dfrac{P(x)}{Q(x)}$: $Q(x)$ Has Repeated Linear Factors

The form of the partial fraction decomposition for a rational expression containing the linear factor $ax + b$ occurring n times as its denominator is

$$\frac{P(x)}{(ax + b)^n} = \frac{A_1}{ax + b} + \frac{A_2}{(ax + b)^2} + \frac{A_3}{(ax + b)^3} + \cdots + \frac{A_n}{(ax + b)^n}.$$

> Include one fraction with a constant numerator for each power of $ax + b$.

EXAMPLE 2 **Partial Fraction Decomposition with Repeated Linear Factors**

Find the partial fraction decomposition of $\dfrac{x - 18}{x(x - 3)^2}$.

Study Tip

Avoid this common error:

$$\frac{x - 18}{x(x - 3)^2} = \frac{A}{x} + \frac{B}{x - 3} + \frac{C}{x - 3}$$

Listing $x - 3$ twice does not take into account $(x - 3)^2$.

Solution

Step 1 Set up the partial fraction decomposition with the unknown constants. Because the linear factor $x - 3$ occurs twice, we must include one fraction with a constant numerator for each power of $x - 3$.

$$\frac{x - 18}{x(x - 3)^2} = \frac{A}{x} + \frac{B}{x - 3} + \frac{C}{(x - 3)^2}$$

Step 2 Multiply both sides of the resulting equation by the least common denominator. We clear fractions, multiplying both sides by $x(x - 3)^2$, the least common denominator.

$$x(x - 3)^2 \left[\frac{x - 18}{x(x - 3)^2} \right] = x(x - 3)^2 \left[\frac{A}{x} + \frac{B}{x - 3} + \frac{C}{(x - 3)^2} \right]$$

We use the distributive property on the right side.

$$x\,(x - 3)^2 \cdot \frac{x - 18}{x\,(x - 3)^2} = x(x - 3)^2 \cdot \frac{A}{x} + x(x - 3)^2 \cdot \frac{B}{(x - 3)} + x(x - 3)^2 \cdot \frac{C}{(x - 3)^2}$$

Dividing out common factors in numerators and denominators, we obtain

$$x - 18 = A(x - 3)^2 + Bx(x - 3) + Cx.$$

Step 3 Simplify the right side of the equation. Square $x - 3$. Then apply the distributive property.

$$x - 18 = A(x^2 - 6x + 9) + Bx(x - 3) + Cx \qquad \text{Square } x - 3 \text{ using } (A - B)^2 = A^2 - 2AB + B^2.$$

$$x - 18 = Ax^2 - 6Ax + 9A + Bx^2 - 3Bx + Cx \qquad \text{Apply the distributive property.}$$

Step 4 Write both sides in descending powers, equate coefficients of like powers of x, and equate constant terms. The left side, $x - 18$, is in descending powers of x: $x - 18x^0$. We will write the right side in descending powers of x.

$$x - 18 = Ax^2 + Bx^2 - 6Ax - 3Bx + Cx + 9A \qquad \text{Rearrange terms on the right side.}$$

Express both sides in the same form.

$$0x^2 + 1x - 18 = (A + B)x^2 + (-6A - 3B + C)x + 9A \qquad \text{Rewrite to identify coefficients and the constant term.}$$

Equating coefficients of like powers of x and equating constant terms results in the following system of linear equations:

$$\begin{cases} A + B = 0 \\ -6A - 3B + C = 1 \\ 9A = -18. \end{cases}$$

Step 5 Solve the resulting system for A, B, and C. Dividing both sides of the last equation by 9, we obtain $A = -2$. Substituting -2 for A in the first equation, $A + B = 0$, gives $-2 + B = 0$, so $B = 2$. We find C by substituting -2 for A and 2 for B in the middle equation, $-6A - 3B + C = 1$. We obtain $C = -5$.

Step 6 Substitute the values of A, B, and C, and write the partial fraction decomposition. With $A = -2$, $B = 2$, and $C = -5$, the required partial fraction decomposition is

$$\frac{x - 18}{x(x - 3)^2} = \frac{A}{x} + \frac{B}{x - 3} + \frac{C}{(x - 3)^2} = -\frac{2}{x} + \frac{2}{x - 3} - \frac{5}{(x - 3)^2}.$$

⦿ Check Point **2** Find the partial fraction decomposition of $\dfrac{x + 2}{x(x - 1)^2}$.

❸ Decompose $\dfrac{P}{Q}$, where Q has a nonrepeated prime quadratic factor.

The Partial Fraction Decomposition of a Rational Expression with Prime, Nonrepeated Quadratic Factors in the Denominator

Our final two cases of partial fraction decomposition involve prime quadratic factors of the form $ax^2 + bx + c$. Based on our work with the discriminant, we know that $ax^2 + bx + c$ is prime and cannot be factored over the integers if $b^2 - 4ac < 0$ or if $b^2 - 4ac$ is not a perfect square.

The Partial Fraction Decomposition of $\dfrac{P(x)}{Q(x)}$: $Q(x)$ Has a Nonrepeated, Prime Quadratic Factor

If $ax^2 + bx + c$ is a prime quadratic factor of $Q(x)$, the partial fraction decomposition will contain a term of the form

$$\frac{Ax + B}{ax^2 + bx + c}.$$

Linear numerator

Quadratic factor

The voice balloons in the box show that each distinct prime quadratic factor in the denominator produces a partial fraction of the form *linear numerator over quadratic factor*. For example,

$$\frac{3x^2 + 17x + 14}{(x - 2)(x^2 + 2x + 4)} = \frac{A}{x - 2} + \frac{Bx + C}{x^2 + 2x + 4}.$$

We write a constant over the linear factor in the denominator.

We write a linear numerator over the prime quadratic factor in the denominator.

Our next example illustrates how a linear system in three variables is used to determine values for A, B, and C.

(EXAMPLE 3) **Partial Fraction Decomposition**

Find the partial fraction decomposition of

$$\frac{3x^2 + 17x + 14}{(x - 2)(x^2 + 2x + 4)}.$$

Solution

Step 1 Set up the partial fraction decomposition with the unknown constants. We put a constant (A) over the linear factor and a linear expression $(Bx + C)$ over the prime quadratic factor.

$$\frac{3x^2 + 17x + 14}{(x - 2)(x^2 + 2x + 4)} = \frac{A}{x - 2} + \frac{Bx + C}{x^2 + 2x + 4}$$

Step 2 Multiply both sides of the resulting equation by the least common denominator. We clear fractions, multiplying both sides by $(x - 2)(x^2 + 2x + 4)$, the least common denominator.

$$(x - 2)(x^2 + 2x + 4)\left[\frac{3x^2 + 17x + 14}{(x - 2)(x^2 + 2x + 4)}\right] = (x - 2)(x^2 + 2x + 4)\left[\frac{A}{x - 2} + \frac{Bx + C}{x^2 + 2x + 4}\right]$$

We use the distributive property on the right side.

$$(x - 2)(x^2 + 2x + 4) \cdot \frac{3x^2 + 17x + 14}{(x - 2)(x^2 + 2x + 4)}$$

$$= (x - 2)(x^2 + 2x + 4) \cdot \frac{A}{x - 2} + (x - 2)(x^2 + 2x + 4) \cdot \frac{Bx + C}{x^2 + 2x + 4}$$

Dividing out common factors in numerators and denominators, we obtain

$$3x^2 + 17x + 14 = A(x^2 + 2x + 4) + (Bx + C)(x - 2).$$

Step 3 Simplify the right side of the equation. We simplify on the right side by distributing A over each term in parentheses and multiplying $(Bx + C)(x - 2)$ using the FOIL method.

$$3x^2 + 17x + 14 = Ax^2 + 2Ax + 4A + Bx^2 - 2Bx + Cx - 2C$$

Step 4 Write both sides in descending powers, equate coefficients of like powers of x, and equate constant terms. The left side, $3x^2 + 17x + 14$, is in descending powers of x. We write the right side in descending powers of x

$$3x^2 + 17x + 14 = Ax^2 + Bx^2 + 2Ax - 2Bx + Cx + 4A - 2C$$

and express both sides in the same form.

$$3x^2 + 17x + 14 = (A + B)x^2 + (2A - 2B + C)x + (4A - 2C)$$

Equating coefficients of like powers of x and equating constant terms results in the following system of linear equations:

$$\begin{cases} A + B = 3 \\ 2A - 2B + C = 17 \\ 4A - 2C = 14. \end{cases}$$

Step 5 Solve the resulting system for $A, B,$ and C. Because the first equation involves A and B, we can obtain another equation in A and B by eliminating C from the second and third equations. Multiply the second equation by 2 and add equations. Solving in this manner, we obtain $A = 5, B = -2,$ and $C = 3$.

Step 6 Substitute the values of $A, B,$ and C, and write the partial fraction decomposition. With $A = 5, B = -2,$ and $C = 3$, the required partial fraction decomposition is

$$\frac{3x^2 + 17x + 14}{(x - 2)(x^2 + 2x + 4)} = \frac{A}{x - 2} + \frac{Bx + C}{x^2 + 2x + 4} = \frac{5}{x - 2} + \frac{-2x + 3}{x^2 + 2x + 4}.$$

Technology

Numeric Connections

You can use the $\boxed{\text{TABLE}}$ feature of a graphing utility to check a partial fraction decomposition. To check the result of Example 3, enter the given rational function and its partial fraction decomposition:

$$y_1 = \frac{3x^2 + 17x + 14}{(x - 2)(x^2 + 2x + 4)}$$

$$y_2 = \frac{5}{x - 2} + \frac{-2x + 3}{x^2 + 2x + 4}.$$

X	Y1	Y2
-3	.28571	.28571
-2	.5	.5
-1	0	0
0	-1.75	-1.75
1	-4.857	-4.857
2	ERROR	ERROR
3	4.8421	4.8421

X=-3

No matter how far up or down we scroll, $y_1 = y_2$, so the decomposition appears to be correct.

☑ Check Point **3** Find the partial fraction decomposition of

$$\frac{8x^2 + 12x - 20}{(x + 3)(x^2 + x + 2)}.$$

④ Decompose $\dfrac{P}{Q}$, where Q has a prime, repeated quadratic factor.

The Partial Fraction Decomposition of a Rational Expression with a Prime, Repeated Quadratic Factor in the Denominator

Suppose that $(ax^2 + bx + c)^n$ is a factor of the denominator and that $ax^2 + bx + c$ cannot be factored further. This means that the quadratic factor $ax^2 + bx + c$ occurs n times. When this occurs, the partial fraction decomposition will contain a linear numerator for each power of $ax^2 + bx + c$.

The Partial Fraction Decomposition of $\dfrac{P(x)}{Q(x)}$: $Q(x)$ Has a Prime, Repeated Quadratic Factor

The form of the partial fraction decomposition for a rational expression containing the prime factor $ax^2 + bx + c$ occurring n times as its denominator is

$$\frac{P(x)}{(ax^2 + bx + c)^n} = \frac{A_1x + B_1}{ax^2 + bx + c} + \frac{A_2x + B_2}{(ax^2 + bx + c)^2} + \frac{A_3x + B_3}{(ax^2 + bx + c)^3} + \cdots + \frac{A_nx + B_n}{(ax^2 + bx + c)^n}.$$

Include one fraction with a linear numerator for each power of $ax^2 + bx + c$.

EXAMPLE 4 **Partial Fraction Decomposition with a Repeated Quadratic Factor**

Find the partial fraction decomposition of

$$\frac{5x^3 - 3x^2 + 7x - 3}{(x^2 + 1)^2}.$$

Solution

Step 1 Set up the partial fraction decomposition with the unknown constants. Because the quadratic factor $x^2 + 1$ occurs twice, we must include one fraction with a linear numerator for each power of $x^2 + 1$.

$$\frac{5x^3 - 3x^2 + 7x - 3}{(x^2 + 1)^2} = \frac{Ax + B}{x^2 + 1} + \frac{Cx + D}{(x^2 + 1)^2}$$

Step 2 Multiply both sides of the resulting equation by the least common denominator. We clear fractions, multiplying both sides by $(x^2 + 1)^2$, the least common denominator.

$$(x^2 + 1)^2 \left[\frac{5x^3 - 3x^2 + 7x - 3}{(x^2 + 1)^2} \right] = (x^2 + 1)^2 \left[\frac{Ax + B}{x^2 + 1} + \frac{Cx + D}{(x^2 + 1)^2} \right]$$

Now we multiply and simplify.

$$5x^3 - 3x^2 + 7x - 3 = (x^2 + 1)(Ax + B) + Cx + D$$

Step 3 Simplify the right side of the equation. We multiply $(x^2 + 1)(Ax + B)$ using the FOIL method.

$$5x^3 - 3x^2 + 7x - 3 = Ax^3 + Bx^2 + Ax + B + Cx + D$$

Step 4 Write both sides in descending powers, equate coefficients of like powers of x, and equate constant terms.

$$5x^3 - 3x^2 + 7x - 3 = Ax^3 + Bx^2 + Ax + Cx + B + D$$

$$5x^3 - 3x^2 + 7x - 3 = Ax^3 + Bx^2 + (A + C)x + (B + D)$$

Equating coefficients of like powers of x and equating constant terms results in the following system of linear equations:

$$\begin{cases} A = 5 \\ B = -3 \\ A + C = 7 \\ B + D = -3. \end{cases}$$

With $A = 5$, we immediately obtain $C = 2$.

With $B = -3$, we immediately obtain $D = 0$.

Study Tip

When the denominator of a rational expression contains a **power of a linear factor**, set up the partial fraction decomposition with **constant numerators** (A, B, C, etc.). When the denominator of a rational expression contains a **power of a prime quadratic factor**, set up the partial fraction decomposition with **linear numerators** ($Ax + B$, $Cx + D$, etc.).

Step 5 Solve the resulting system for $A, B, C,$ and D. Based on our observations in step 4, $A = 5, B = -3, C = 2,$ and $D = 0.$

Step 6 Substitute the values of $A, B, C,$ and D, and write the partial fraction decomposition.

$$\frac{5x^3 - 3x^2 + 7x - 3}{(x^2 + 1)^2} = \frac{Ax + B}{x^2 + 1} + \frac{Cx + D}{(x^2 + 1)^2} = \frac{5x - 3}{x^2 + 1} + \frac{2x}{(x^2 + 1)^2}$$ ●

 Check Point **4** Find the partial fraction decomposition of $\dfrac{2x^3 + x + 3}{(x^2 + 1)^2}$.

Study Tip

When a rational expression contains a power of a factor in the denominator, be sure to set up the partial fraction decomposition to allow for every natural-number power of that factor less than or equal to the power. Example:

$$\frac{2x + 1}{(x - 5)^2 x^3}$$

$$= \frac{A}{x - 5} + \frac{B}{(x - 5)^2} + \frac{C}{x} + \frac{D}{x^2} + \frac{E}{x^3}$$

Although $(x - 5)^2$ and x^2 are quadratic, they are still expressed as powers of linear factors, $x - 5$ and $x.$ Thus, the numerators are constant.

Exercise Set 5.3

Practice Exercises

In Exercises 1–8, write the form of the partial fraction decomposition of the rational expression. It is not necessary to solve for the constants.

1. $\dfrac{11x - 10}{(x - 2)(x + 1)}$

2. $\dfrac{5x + 7}{(x - 1)(x + 3)}$

3. $\dfrac{6x^2 - 14x - 27}{(x + 2)(x - 3)^2}$

4. $\dfrac{3x + 16}{(x + 1)(x - 2)^2}$

5. $\dfrac{5x^2 - 6x + 7}{(x - 1)(x^2 + 1)}$

6. $\dfrac{5x^2 - 9x + 19}{(x - 4)(x^2 + 5)}$

7. $\dfrac{x^3 + x^2}{(x^2 + 4)^2}$

8. $\dfrac{7x^2 - 9x + 3}{(x^2 + 7)^2}$

In Exercises 9–42, write the partial fraction decomposition of each rational expression.

9. $\dfrac{x}{(x - 3)(x - 2)}$

10. $\dfrac{1}{x(x - 1)}$

11. $\dfrac{3x + 50}{(x - 9)(x + 2)}$

12. $\dfrac{5x - 1}{(x - 2)(x + 1)}$

13. $\dfrac{7x - 4}{x^2 - x - 12}$

14. $\dfrac{9x + 21}{x^2 + 2x - 15}$

15. $\dfrac{4}{2x^2 - 5x - 3}$

16. $\dfrac{x}{x^2 + 2x - 3}$

17. $\dfrac{4x^2 + 13x - 9}{x(x - 1)(x + 3)}$

18. $\dfrac{4x^2 - 5x - 15}{x(x + 1)(x - 5)}$

19. $\dfrac{4x^2 - 7x - 3}{x^3 - x}$

20. $\dfrac{2x^2 - 18x - 12}{x^3 - 4x}$

21. $\dfrac{6x - 11}{(x - 1)^2}$

22. $\dfrac{x}{(x + 1)^2}$

23. $\dfrac{x^2 - 6x + 3}{(x - 2)^3}$

24. $\dfrac{2x^2 + 8x + 3}{(x + 1)^3}$

25. $\dfrac{x^2 + 2x + 7}{x(x - 1)^2}$

26. $\dfrac{3x^2 + 49}{x(x + 7)^2}$

27. $\dfrac{x^2}{(x - 1)^2(x + 1)}$

28. $\dfrac{x^2}{(x - 1)^2(x + 1)^2}$

29. $\dfrac{5x^2 - 6x + 7}{(x - 1)(x^2 + 1)}$

30. $\dfrac{5x^2 - 9x + 19}{(x - 4)(x^2 + 5)}$

31. $\dfrac{5x^2 + 6x + 3}{(x + 1)(x^2 + 2x + 2)}$

32. $\dfrac{9x + 2}{(x - 2)(x^2 + 2x + 2)}$

33. $\dfrac{x + 4}{x^2(x^2 + 4)}$

34. $\dfrac{10x^2 + 2x}{(x - 1)^2(x^2 + 2)}$

35. $\dfrac{6x^2 - x + 1}{x^3 + x^2 + x + 1}$

36. $\dfrac{3x^2 - 2x + 8}{x^3 + 2x^2 + 4x + 8}$

37. $\dfrac{x^3 + x^2 + 2}{(x^2 + 2)^2}$

38. $\dfrac{x^2 + 2x + 3}{(x^2 + 4)^2}$

39. $\dfrac{x^3 - 4x^2 + 9x - 5}{(x^2 - 2x + 3)^2}$

40. $\dfrac{3x^3 - 6x^2 + 7x - 2}{(x^2 - 2x + 2)^2}$

41. $\dfrac{4x^2 + 3x + 14}{x^3 - 8}$

42. $\dfrac{3x - 5}{x^3 - 1}$

Practice Plus

In Exercises 43–46, perform each long division and write the partial fraction decomposition of the remainder term.

43. $\dfrac{x^5 + 2}{x^2 - 1}$

44. $\dfrac{x^5}{x^2 - 4x + 4}$

45. $\dfrac{x^4 - x^2 + 2}{x^3 - x^2}$

46. $\dfrac{x^4 + 2x^3 - 4x^2 + x - 3}{x^2 - x - 2}$

In Exercises 47–50, write the partial fraction decomposition of each rational expression.

47. $\dfrac{1}{x^2 - c^2}$ $\quad (c \neq 0)$

48. $\dfrac{ax + b}{x^2 - c^2}$ $\quad (c \neq 0)$

49. $\dfrac{ax + b}{(x - c)^2}$ $\quad (c \neq 0)$

50. $\dfrac{1}{x^2 - ax - bx + ab}$ $\quad (a \neq b)$

Application Exercises

51. Find the partial fraction decomposition for $\dfrac{1}{x(x + 1)}$ and use the result to find the following sum:

$$\frac{1}{1 \cdot 2} + \frac{1}{2 \cdot 3} + \frac{1}{3 \cdot 4} + \cdots + \frac{1}{99 \cdot 100}.$$

52. Find the partial fraction decomposition for $\dfrac{2}{x(x + 2)}$ and use the result to find the following sum:

$$\frac{2}{1 \cdot 3} + \frac{2}{3 \cdot 5} + \frac{2}{5 \cdot 7} + \cdots + \frac{2}{99 \cdot 101}.$$

Writing in Mathematics

53. Explain what is meant by the partial fraction decomposition of a rational expression.

54. Explain how to find the partial fraction decomposition of a rational expression with distinct linear factors in the denominator.

55. Explain how to find the partial fraction decomposition of a rational expression with a repeated linear factor in the denominator.

56. Explain how to find the partial fraction decomposition of a rational expression with a prime quadratic factor in the denominator.

57. Explain how to find the partial fraction decomposition of a rational expression with a repeated, prime quadratic factor in the denominator.

58. How can you verify your result for the partial fraction decomposition for a given rational expression without using a graphing utility?

Technology Exercise

59. Use the $\boxed{\text{TABLE}}$ feature of a graphing utility to verify any three of the decompositions that you obtained in Exercises 9–42.

Critical Thinking Exercises

Make Sense? *In Exercises 60–63, determine whether each statement makes sense or does not make sense, and explain your reasoning.*

60. Partial fraction decomposition involves finding a single rational expression for a given sum or difference of rational expressions.

61. I apply partial fraction decompositions for rational expressions of the form $\dfrac{P(x)}{Q(x)}$, where P and Q have no common factors and the degree of P is greater than the degree of Q.

62. Because $x + 5$ is linear and $x^2 - 3x + 2$ is quadratic, I set up the following partial fraction decomposition:

$$\frac{7x^2 + 9x + 3}{(x + 5)(x^2 - 3x + 2)} = \frac{A}{x + 5} + \frac{Bx + C}{x^2 - 3x + 2}.$$

63. Because $(x + 3)^2$ consists of two factors of $x + 3$, I set up the following partial fraction decomposition:

$$\frac{5x + 2}{(x + 3)^2} = \frac{A}{x + 3} + \frac{B}{x + 3}.$$

64. Use an extension of the Study Tip on page 514 to describe how to set up the partial fraction decomposition of a rational expression that contains powers of a prime cubic factor in the denominator. Give an example of such a decomposition.

65. Find the partial fraction decomposition of

$$\frac{4x^2 + 5x - 9}{x^3 - 6x - 9}.$$

Preview Exercises

Exercises 66–68 will help you prepare for the material covered in the next section.

66. Solve by the substitution method:

$$4x + 3y = 4$$
$$y = 2x - 7.$$

67. Solve by the addition method:

$$2x + 4y = -4$$
$$3x + 5y = -3.$$

68. Graph $x - y = 3$ and $(x - 2)^2 + (y + 3)^2 = 4$ in the same rectangular coordinate system. What are the two intersection points? Show that each of these ordered pairs satisfies both equations.

(Section) **5.4** # Systems of Nonlinear Equations in Two Variables

Objectives

1 Recognize systems of nonlinear equations in two variables.

2 Solve nonlinear systems by substitution.

3 Solve nonlinear systems by addition.

4 Solve problems using systems of nonlinear equations.

Scientists debate the probability that a "doomsday rock" will collide with Earth. It has been estimated that an asteroid, a tiny planet that revolves around the sun, crashes into Earth about once every 250,000 years, and that such a collision would have disastrous results. In 1908, a small fragment struck Siberia, leveling thousands of acres of trees. One theory about the extinction of dinosaurs 65 million years ago involves Earth's collision with a large asteroid and the resulting drastic changes in Earth's climate.

Understanding the path of Earth and the path of a comet is essential to detecting threatening space debris. Orbits about the sun are not described by linear equations in the form $Ax + By = C$. The ability to solve systems that contain nonlinear equations provides NASA scientists watching for troublesome asteroids with a way to locate possible collision points with Earth's orbit.

1 Recognize systems of nonlinear equations in two variables.

Systems of Nonlinear Equations and Their Solutions

A **system of** two **nonlinear equations** in two variables, also called a **nonlinear system**, contains at least one equation that cannot be expressed in the form $Ax + By = C$. Here are two examples:

$$\begin{cases} x^2 = 2y + 10 \\ 3x - y = 9 \end{cases}$$

Not in the form $Ax + By = C$. The term x^2 is not linear.

$$\begin{cases} y = x^2 + 3 \\ x^2 + y^2 = 9. \end{cases}$$

Neither equation is in the form $Ax + By = C$. The terms x^2 and y^2 are not linear.

A **solution** of a nonlinear system in two variables is an ordered pair of real numbers that satisfies both equations in the system. The **solution set** of the system is the set of all such ordered pairs. As with linear systems in two variables, the solution of a nonlinear system (if there is one) corresponds to the intersection point(s) of the graphs of the equations in the system. Unlike linear systems, the graphs can be circles, parabolas, or anything other than two lines. We will solve nonlinear systems using the substitution method and the addition method.

② Solve nonlinear systems by substitution.

Eliminating a Variable Using the Substitution Method

The substitution method involves converting a nonlinear system into one equation in one variable by an appropriate substitution. The steps in the solution process are exactly the same as those used to solve a linear system by substitution. However, when you obtain an equation in one variable, this equation may not be linear. In our first example, this equation is quadratic.

EXAMPLE 1 **Solving a Nonlinear System by the Substitution Method**

Solve by the substitution method:

$$\begin{cases} x^2 = 2y + 10 & \text{(The graph is a parabola.)} \\ 3x - y = 9. & \text{(The graph is a line.)} \end{cases}$$

Solution

Step 1 Solve one of the equations for one variable in terms of the other. We begin by isolating one of the variables raised to the first power in either of the equations. By solving for y in the second equation, which has a coefficient of -1, we can avoid fractions.

$$3x - y = 9 \qquad \text{This is the second equation in the given system.}$$
$$3x = y + 9 \qquad \text{Add y to both sides.}$$
$$3x - 9 = y \qquad \text{Subtract 9 from both sides.}$$

Step 2 Substitute the expression from step 1 into the other equation. We substitute $3x - 9$ for y in the first equation.

$$y = \boxed{3x - 9} \qquad x^2 = 2\boxed{y} + 10$$

This gives us an equation in one variable, namely

$$x^2 = 2(3x - 9) + 10.$$

The variable y has been eliminated.

Step 3 Solve the resulting equation containing one variable.

$$x^2 = 2(3x - 9) + 10 \qquad \text{This is the equation containing one variable.}$$
$$x^2 = 6x - 18 + 10 \qquad \text{Use the distributive property.}$$
$$x^2 = 6x - 8 \qquad \text{Combine numerical terms on the right.}$$
$$x^2 - 6x + 8 = 0 \qquad \text{Move all terms to one side and set the quadratic equation equal to 0.}$$
$$(x - 4)(x - 2) = 0 \qquad \text{Factor.}$$
$$x - 4 = 0 \text{ or } x - 2 = 0 \qquad \text{Set each factor equal to 0.}$$
$$x = 4 \qquad\qquad x = 2 \qquad \text{Solve for x.}$$

Step 4 Back-substitute the obtained values into the equation from step 1. Now that we have the x-coordinates of the solutions, we back-substitute 4 for x and 2 for x into the equation $y = 3x - 9$.

If x is 4, $\quad y = 3(4) - 9 = 3, \quad$ so $(4, 3)$ is a solution.

If x is 2, $\quad y = 3(2) - 9 = -3, \quad$ so $(2, -3)$ is a solution.

Step 5 Check the proposed solutions in both of the system's given equations. We begin by checking $(4, 3)$. Replace x with 4 and y with 3.

$x^2 = 2y + 10$	$3x - y = 9$	These are the given equations.
$4^2 \overset{?}{=} 2(3) + 10$	$3(4) - 3 \overset{?}{=} 9$	Let x = 4 and y = 3.
$16 \overset{?}{=} 6 + 10$	$12 - 3 \overset{?}{=} 9$	Simplify.
$16 = 16,$ true	$9 = 9,$ true	True statements result.

The ordered pair $(4, 3)$ satisfies both equations. Thus, $(4, 3)$ is a solution of the system. Now let's check $(2, -3)$. Replace x with 2 and y with -3 in both given equations.

$x^2 = 2y + 10$	$3x - y = 9$	These are the given equations.
$2^2 \overset{?}{=} 2(-3) + 10$	$3(2) - (-3) \overset{?}{=} 9$	Let x = 2 and y = -3.
$4 \overset{?}{=} -6 + 10$	$6 + 3 \overset{?}{=} 9$	Simplify.
$4 = 4,$ true	$9 = 9,$ true	True statements result.

The ordered pair $(2, -3)$ also satisfies both equations and is a solution of the system. The solutions are $(4, 3)$ and $(2, -3)$, and the solution set is $\{(4, 3), (2, -3)\}$.

 Figure 5.9 shows the graphs of the equations in the system and the solutions as intersection points.

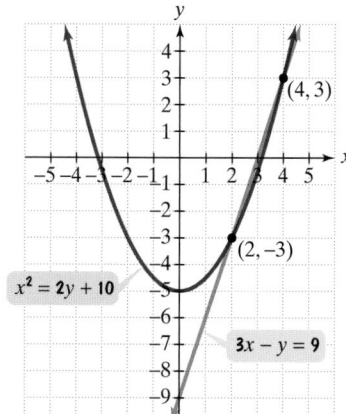

Figure 5.9 Points of intersection illustrate the nonlinear system's solutions.

☑ Check Point **1** Solve by the substitution method:

$$\begin{cases} x^2 = y - 1 \\ 4x - y = -1. \end{cases}$$

(**EXAMPLE 2**) **Solving a Nonlinear System by the Substitution Method**

Study Tip

Recall that

$$(x - h)^2 + (y - k)^2 = r^2$$

describes a circle with center (h, k) and radius r.

Solve by the substitution method:

$$\begin{cases} x - y = 3 & \text{(The graph is a line.)} \\ (x - 2)^2 + (y + 3)^2 = 4. & \text{(The graph is a circle.)} \end{cases}$$

Solution Graphically, we are finding the intersection of a line and a circle with center $(2, -3)$ and radius 2.

Step 1 Solve one of the equations for one variable in terms of the other. We will solve for x in the linear equation—that is, the first equation. (We could also solve for y.)

$x - y = 3$	This is the first equation in the given system.
$x = y + 3$	Add y to both sides.

Step 2 Substitute the expression from step 1 into the other equation. We substitute $y + 3$ for x in the second equation.

$$x = \boxed{y + 3} \qquad (\boxed{x} - 2)^2 + (y + 3)^2 = 4$$

This gives an equation in one variable, namely

$$(y + 3 - 2)^2 + (y + 3)^2 = 4.$$

The variable x has been eliminated.

Step 3 Solve the resulting equation containing one variable.

$$(y + 3 - 2)^2 + (y + 3)^2 = 4 \qquad \text{This is the equation containing one variable.}$$

$$(y + 1)^2 + (y + 3)^2 = 4 \qquad \text{Combine numerical terms in the first parentheses.}$$

$$y^2 + 2y + 1 + y^2 + 6y + 9 = 4 \qquad \text{Use the formula } (A + B)^2 = A^2 + 2AB + B^2 \text{ to square } y + 1 \text{ and } y + 3.$$

$$2y^2 + 8y + 10 = 4 \qquad \text{Combine like terms on the left.}$$

$$2y^2 + 8y + 6 = 0 \qquad \text{Subtract 4 from both sides and set the quadratic equation equal to 0.}$$

$$2(y^2 + 4y + 3) = 0 \qquad \text{Factor out 2.}$$

$$2(y + 3)(y + 1) = 0 \qquad \text{Factor completely.}$$

$$y + 3 = 0 \quad \text{or} \quad y + 1 = 0 \qquad \text{Set each variable factor equal to 0.}$$

$$y = -3 \qquad\qquad y = -1 \qquad \text{Solve for y.}$$

Step 4 Back-substitute the obtained values into the equation from step 1. Now that we have the y-coordinates of the solutions, we back-substitute -3 for y and -1 for y in the equation $x = y + 3$.

If $y = -3$: $\quad x = -3 + 3 = 0$, \quad so $(0, -3)$ is a solution.

If $y = -1$: $\quad x = -1 + 3 = 2$, \quad so $(2, -1)$ is a solution.

Step 5 Check the proposed solutions in both of the system's given equations. Take a moment to show that each ordered pair satisfies both given equations, $x - y = 3$ and $(x - 2)^2 + (y + 3)^2 = 4$. The solutions are $(0, -3)$ and $(2, -1)$, and the solution set of the given system is $\{(0, -3), (2, -1)\}$.

Figure 5.10 shows the graphs of the equations in the system and the solutions as intersection points. ⬤

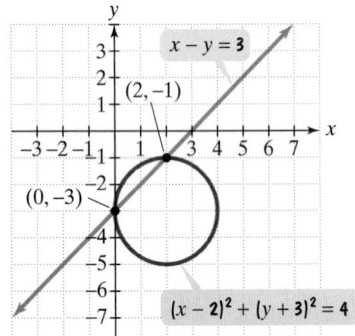

Figure 5.10 Points of intersection illustrate the nonlinear system's solutions.

✓ Check Point **2** Solve by the substitution method:

$$\begin{cases} x + 2y = 0 \\ (x - 1)^2 + (y - 1)^2 = 5. \end{cases}$$

③ Solve nonlinear systems by addition.

Eliminating a Variable Using the Addition Method

In solving linear systems with two variables, we learned that the addition method works well when each equation is in the form $Ax + By = C$. For nonlinear systems, the addition method can be used when each equation is in the form $Ax^2 + By^2 = C$. If necessary, we will multiply either equation or both equations by appropriate numbers so that the coefficients of x^2 or y^2 will have a sum of 0. We then add equations. The sum will be an equation in one variable.

(**EXAMPLE 3**) **Solving a Nonlinear System by the Addition Method**

Solve the system:

$$\begin{cases} 4x^2 + y^2 = 13 & \text{Equation 1} \\ x^2 + y^2 = 10. & \text{Equation 2} \end{cases}$$

Solution We can use the same steps that we did when we solved linear systems by the addition method.

Step 1 Write both equations in the form $Ax^2 + By^2 = C$. Both equations are already in this form, so we can skip this step.

Step 2 If necessary, multiply either equation or both equations by appropriate numbers so that the sum of the x^2-coefficients or the sum of the y^2-coefficients is 0. We can eliminate y^2 by multiplying Equation 2 by -1.

$$\begin{cases} 4x^2 + y^2 = 13 \\ x^2 + y^2 = 10 \end{cases} \xrightarrow[\text{Multiply by } -1.]{\text{No change}} \begin{cases} 4x^2 + y^2 = 13 \\ -x^2 - y^2 = -10 \end{cases}$$

Steps 3 and 4 Add equations and solve for the remaining variable.

$$\begin{cases} 4x^2 + y^2 = 13 \\ \underline{-x^2 - y^2 = -10} \end{cases}$$

$$3x^2 = 3 \qquad \text{Add equations.}$$

$$x^2 = 1 \qquad \text{Divide both sides by 3.}$$

$$x = \pm 1 \qquad \text{Use the square root property:}$$
$$\qquad\qquad\qquad \text{If } x^2 = c, \text{ then } x = \pm\sqrt{c}.$$

Step 5 Back-substitute and find the values for the other variable. We must back-substitute each value of x into either one of the original equations. Let's use $x^2 + y^2 = 10$, Equation 2. If $x = 1$,

$$1^2 + y^2 = 10 \qquad \text{Replace x with 1 in Equation 2.}$$

$$y^2 = 9 \qquad \text{Subtract 1 from both sides.}$$

$$y = \pm 3. \qquad \text{Apply the square root property.}$$

$(1, 3)$ and $(1, -3)$ are solutions. If $x = -1$,

$$(-1)^2 + y^2 = 10 \qquad \text{Replace x with } -1 \text{ in Equation 2.}$$

$$y^2 = 9 \qquad \text{The steps are the same as before.}$$

$$y = \pm 3.$$

$(-1, 3)$ and $(-1, -3)$ are solutions.

Step 6 Check. Take a moment to show that each of the four ordered pairs satisfies the given equations, $4x^2 + y^2 = 13$ and $x^2 + y^2 = 10$. The solution set of the given system is $\{(1, 3), (1, -3), (-1, 3), (-1, -3)\}$.

Figure 5.11 shows the graphs of the equations in the system and the solutions as intersection points. ●

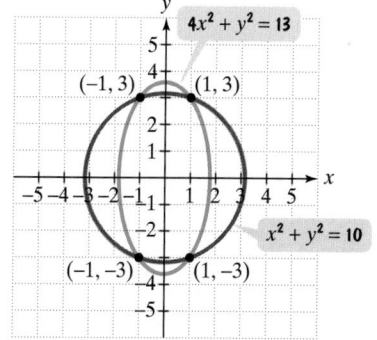

Figure 5.11 A system with four solutions

✓ Check Point **3** Solve the system:

$$\begin{cases} 3x^2 + 2y^2 = 35 \\ 4x^2 + 3y^2 = 48. \end{cases}$$

In solving nonlinear systems, we include only ordered pairs with real numbers in the solution set. We have seen that each of these ordered pairs corresponds to a point of intersection of the system's graphs.

Study Tip

When solving nonlinear systems, extra solutions may be introduced that do not satisfy both equations in the system. Therefore, you should get into the habit of checking all proposed pairs in each of the system's two equations.

EXAMPLE 4 Solving a Nonlinear System by the Addition Method

Solve the system:

$$\begin{cases} y = x^2 + 3 & \text{Equation 1 (The graph is a parabola.)} \\ x^2 + y^2 = 9. & \text{Equation 2 (The graph is a circle.)} \end{cases}$$

Solution We could use substitution because Equation 1, $y = x^2 + 3$, has y expressed in terms of x, but substituting $x^2 + 3$ for y in $x^2 + y^2 = 9$ would result in a fourth-degree equation. However, we can rewrite Equation 1 by subtracting x^2 from both sides and adding the equations to eliminate the x^2-terms.

Notice how like terms are arranged in columns.

$$\begin{cases} -x^2 + y \quad\;\; = \;\; 3 & \text{Subtract } x^2 \text{ from both sides of Equation 1.} \\ x^2 \quad\;\; + y^2 = \;\; 9 & \text{This is Equation 2.} \end{cases}$$
$$\overline{\quad\;\; y + y^2 = 12} \quad \text{Add the equations.}$$

We now solve this quadratic equation.

$$y + y^2 = 12 \quad \text{This is the equation containing one variable.}$$

$$y^2 + y - 12 = 0 \quad \text{Subtract 12 from both sides and set the quadratic equation equal to 0.}$$

$$(y + 4)(y - 3) = 0 \quad \text{Factor.}$$

$$y + 4 = 0 \quad \text{or} \quad y - 3 = 0 \quad \text{Set each factor equal to 0.}$$

$$y = -4 \qquad\qquad y = 3 \quad \text{Solve for } y.$$

To complete the solution, we must back-substitute each value of y into either one of the original equations. We will use $y = x^2 + 3$, Equation 1. First, we substitute -4 for y.

$$-4 = x^2 + 3$$

$$-7 = x^2 \quad \text{Subtract 3 from both sides.}$$

Because the square of a real number cannot be negative, the equation $x^2 = -7$ does not have real-number solutions. We will not include the imaginary solutions, $x = \pm\sqrt{-7}$, or $i\sqrt{7}$ and $-i\sqrt{7}$, in the ordered pairs that make up the solution set. Thus, we move on to our other value for y, 3, and substitute this value into Equation 1.

$$y = x^2 + 3 \quad \text{This is Equation 1.}$$

$$3 = x^2 + 3 \quad \text{Back-substitute 3 for } y.$$

$$0 = x^2 \quad \text{Subtract 3 from both sides.}$$

$$0 = x \quad \text{Solve for } x.$$

We showed that if $y = 3$, then $x = 0$. Thus, $(0, 3)$ is the solution with a real ordered pair. Take a moment to show that $(0, 3)$ satisfies the given equations, $y = x^2 + 3$ and $x^2 + y^2 = 9$. The solution set of the system is $\{(0, 3)\}$. **Figure 5.12** shows the system's graphs and the solution as an intersection point.

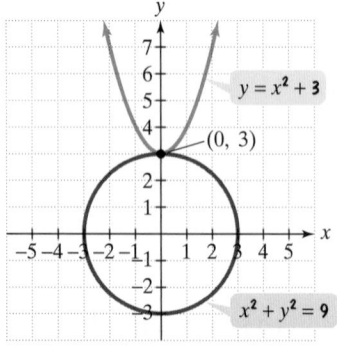

Figure 5.12 A system with one real solution

⊘ Check Point **4** Solve the system:

$$\begin{cases} y = x^2 + 5 \\ x^2 + y^2 = 25. \end{cases}$$

④ Solve problems using systems of nonlinear equations.

Applications

Many geometric problems can be modeled and solved by the use of systems of nonlinear equations. We will use our step-by-step strategy for solving problems using mathematical models that are created from verbal conditions.

EXAMPLE 5 **An Application of a Nonlinear System**

You have 36 yards of fencing to build the enclosure in **Figure 5.13**. Some of this fencing is to be used to build an internal divider. If you'd like to enclose 54 square yards, what are the dimensions of the enclosure?

Figure 5.13 Building an enclosure

Solution

Step 1 Use variables to represent unknown quantities. Let x = the enclosure's length and y = the enclosure's width. These variables are shown in **Figure 5.13**.

Step 2 Write a system of equations modeling the problem's conditions. The first condition is that you have 36 yards of fencing.

Fencing along both lengths	plus	fencing along both widths	plus	fencing for the internal divider	equals	36 yards.
$2x$	$+$	$2y$	$+$	y	$=$	36

Adding like terms, we can express the equation that models the verbal conditions for the fencing as $2x + 3y = 36$.

The second condition is that you'd like to enclose 54 square yards. The rectangle's area, the product of its length and its width, must be 54 square yards.

Length	times	width	is	54 square yards.
x	\cdot	y	$=$	54

Step 3 Solve the system and answer the problem's question. We must solve the system

$$\begin{cases} 2x + 3y = 36 & \text{Equation 1} \\ \quad\quad\; xy = 54. & \text{Equation 2} \end{cases}$$

We will use substitution. Because Equation 1 has no coefficients of 1 or -1, we will work with Equation 2 and solve for y. Dividing both sides of $xy = 54$ by x, we obtain

$$y = \frac{54}{x}.$$

Now we substitute $\dfrac{54}{x}$ for y in Equation 1 and solve for x.

$$2x + 3y = 36 \quad \text{This is Equation 1.}$$
$$2x + 3 \cdot \frac{54}{x} = 36 \quad \text{Substitute } \frac{54}{x} \text{ for } y.$$
$$2x + \frac{162}{x} = 36 \quad \text{Multiply.}$$

$$x\left(2x + \frac{162}{x}\right) = 36 \cdot x \qquad \textit{Clear fractions by multiplying both sides by x.}$$

$$2x^2 + 162 = 36x \qquad \textit{Use the distributive property on the left side.}$$

$$2x^2 - 36x + 162 = 0 \qquad \textit{Subtract 36x from both sides and set the quadratic equation equal to 0.}$$

$$2(x^2 - 18x + 81) = 0 \qquad \textit{Factor out 2.}$$

$$2(x - 9)^2 = 0 \qquad \textit{Factor completely using } A^2 - 2AB + B^2 = (A - B)^2.$$

$$x - 9 = 0 \qquad \textit{Set the repeated factor equal to zero.}$$

$$x = 9 \qquad \textit{Solve for x.}$$

We back-substitute this value of x into $y = \dfrac{54}{x}$.

$$\text{If } x = 9, \quad y = \frac{54}{9} = 6.$$

This means that the dimensions of the enclosure in **Figure 5.13** are 9 yards by 6 yards.

Step 4 Check the proposed solution in the original wording of the problem. Take a moment to check that a length of 9 yards and a width of 6 yards results in 36 yards of fencing and an area of 54 square yards. ●

Figure 5.13 (repeated)

✓ Check Point **5** Find the length and width of a rectangle whose perimeter is 20 feet and whose area is 21 square feet.

Exercise Set 5.4

Practice Exercises

In Exercises 1–18, solve each system by the substitution method.

1. $\begin{cases} x + y = 2 \\ y = x^2 - 4 \end{cases}$

2. $\begin{cases} x - y = -1 \\ y = x^2 + 1 \end{cases}$

3. $\begin{cases} x + y = 2 \\ y = x^2 - 4x + 4 \end{cases}$

4. $\begin{cases} 2x + y = -5 \\ y = x^2 + 6x + 7 \end{cases}$

5. $\begin{cases} y = x^2 - 4x - 10 \\ y = -x^2 - 2x + 14 \end{cases}$

6. $\begin{cases} y = x^2 + 4x + 5 \\ y = x^2 + 2x - 1 \end{cases}$

7. $\begin{cases} x^2 + y^2 = 25 \\ x - y = 1 \end{cases}$

8. $\begin{cases} x^2 + y^2 = 5 \\ 3x - y = 5 \end{cases}$

9. $\begin{cases} xy = 6 \\ 2x - y = 1 \end{cases}$

10. $\begin{cases} xy = -12 \\ x - 2y + 14 = 0 \end{cases}$

11. $\begin{cases} y^2 = x^2 - 9 \\ 2y = x - 3 \end{cases}$

12. $\begin{cases} x^2 + y = 4 \\ 2x + y = 1 \end{cases}$

13. $\begin{cases} xy = 3 \\ x^2 + y^2 = 10 \end{cases}$

14. $\begin{cases} xy = 4 \\ x^2 + y^2 = 8 \end{cases}$

15. $\begin{cases} x + y = 1 \\ x^2 + xy - y^2 = -5 \end{cases}$

16. $\begin{cases} x + y = -3 \\ x^2 + 2y^2 = 12y + 18 \end{cases}$

17. $\begin{cases} x + y = 1 \\ (x - 1)^2 + (y + 2)^2 = 10 \end{cases}$

18. $\begin{cases} 2x + y = 4 \\ (x + 1)^2 + (y - 2)^2 = 4 \end{cases}$

In Exercises 19–28, solve each system by the addition method.

19. $\begin{cases} x^2 + y^2 = 13 \\ x^2 - y^2 = 5 \end{cases}$

20. $\begin{cases} 4x^2 - y^2 = 4 \\ 4x^2 + y^2 = 4 \end{cases}$

21. $\begin{cases} x^2 - 4y^2 = -7 \\ 3x^2 + y^2 = 31 \end{cases}$

22. $\begin{cases} 3x^2 - 2y^2 = -5 \\ 2x^2 - y^2 = -2 \end{cases}$

23. $\begin{cases} 3x^2 + 4y^2 - 16 = 0 \\ 2x^2 - 3y^2 - 5 = 0 \end{cases}$

24. $\begin{cases} 16x^2 - 4y^2 - 72 = 0 \\ x^2 - y^2 - 3 = 0 \end{cases}$

25. $\begin{cases} x^2 + y^2 = 25 \\ (x - 8)^2 + y^2 = 41 \end{cases}$ **26.** $\begin{cases} x^2 + y^2 = 5 \\ x^2 + (y - 8)^2 = 41 \end{cases}$

27. $\begin{cases} y^2 - x = 4 \\ x^2 + y^2 = 4 \end{cases}$ **28.** $\begin{cases} x^2 - 2y = 8 \\ x^2 + y^2 = 16 \end{cases}$

In Exercises 29–42, solve each system by the method of your choice.

29. $\begin{cases} 3x^2 + 4y^2 = 16 \\ 2x^2 - 3y^2 = 5 \end{cases}$ **30.** $\begin{cases} x + y^2 = 4 \\ x^2 + y^2 = 16 \end{cases}$

31. $\begin{cases} 2x^2 + y^2 = 18 \\ xy = 4 \end{cases}$ **32.** $\begin{cases} x^2 + 4y^2 = 20 \\ xy = 4 \end{cases}$

33. $\begin{cases} x^2 + 4y^2 = 20 \\ x + 2y = 6 \end{cases}$ **34.** $\begin{cases} 3x^2 - 2y^2 = 1 \\ 4x - y = 3 \end{cases}$

35. $\begin{cases} x^3 + y = 0 \\ x^2 - y = 0 \end{cases}$ **36.** $\begin{cases} x^3 + y = 0 \\ 2x^2 - y = 0 \end{cases}$

37. $\begin{cases} x^2 + (y - 2)^2 = 4 \\ x^2 - 2y = 0 \end{cases}$ **38.** $\begin{cases} x^2 - y^2 - 4x + 6y - 4 = 0 \\ x^2 + y^2 - 4x - 6y + 12 = 0 \end{cases}$

39. $\begin{cases} y = (x + 3)^2 \\ x + 2y = -2 \end{cases}$ **40.** $\begin{cases} (x - 1)^2 + (y + 1)^2 = 5 \\ 2x - y = 3 \end{cases}$

41. $\begin{cases} x^2 + y^2 + 3y = 22 \\ 2x + y = -1 \end{cases}$ **42.** $\begin{cases} x - 3y = -5 \\ x^2 + y^2 - 25 = 0 \end{cases}$

In Exercises 43–46, let x represent one number and let y represent the other number. Use the given conditions to write a system of nonlinear equations. Solve the system and find the numbers.

43. The sum of two numbers is 10 and their product is 24. Find the numbers.

44. The sum of two numbers is 20 and their product is 96. Find the numbers.

45. The difference between the squares of two numbers is 3. Twice the square of the first number increased by the square of the second number is 9. Find the numbers.

46. The difference between the squares of two numbers is 5. Twice the square of the second number subtracted from three times the square of the first number is 19. Find the numbers.

Practice Plus

In Exercises 47–52, solve each system by the method of your choice.

47. $\begin{cases} 2x^2 + xy = 6 \\ x^2 + 2xy = 0 \end{cases}$ **48.** $\begin{cases} 4x^2 + xy = 30 \\ x^2 + 3xy = -9 \end{cases}$

49. $\begin{cases} -4x + y = 12 \\ y = x^3 + 3x^2 \end{cases}$ **50.** $\begin{cases} -9x + y = 45 \\ y = x^3 + 5x^2 \end{cases}$

51. $\begin{cases} \dfrac{3}{x^2} + \dfrac{1}{y^2} = 7 \\ \dfrac{5}{x^2} - \dfrac{2}{y^2} = -3 \end{cases}$ **52.** $\begin{cases} \dfrac{2}{x^2} + \dfrac{1}{y^2} = 11 \\ \dfrac{4}{x^2} - \dfrac{2}{y^2} = -14 \end{cases}$

In Exercises 53–54, make a rough sketch in a rectangular coordinate system of the graphs representing the equations in each system.

53. The system, whose graphs are a line with positive slope and a parabola whose equation has a positive leading coefficient, has two solutions.

54. The system, whose graphs are a line with negative slope and a parabola whose equation has a negative leading coefficient, has one solution.

Application Exercises

55. A planet's orbit follows a path described by $16x^2 + 4y^2 = 64$. A comet follows the parabolic path $y = x^2 - 4$. Where might the comet intersect the orbiting planet?

56. A system for tracking ships indicates that a ship lies on a path described by $2y^2 - x^2 = 1$. The process is repeated and the ship is found to lie on a path described by $2x^2 - y^2 = 1$. If it is known that the ship is located in the first quadrant of the coordinate system, determine its exact location.

57. Find the length and width of a rectangle whose perimeter is 36 feet and whose area is 77 square feet.

58. Find the length and width of a rectangle whose perimeter is 40 feet and whose area is 96 square feet.

Use the formula for the area of a rectangle and the Pythagorean Theorem to solve Exercises 59–60.

59. A small television has a picture with a diagonal measure of 10 inches and a viewing area of 48 square inches. Find the length and width of the screen.

60. The area of a rug is 108 square feet and the length of its diagonal is 15 feet. Find the length and width of the rug.

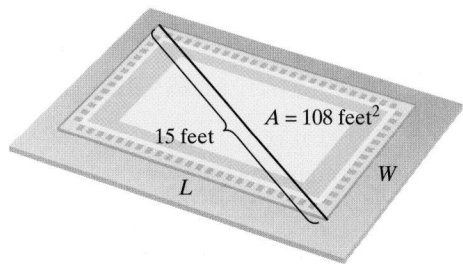

61. The figure shows a square floor plan with a smaller square area that will accommodate a combination fountain and pool. The floor with the fountain-pool area removed has an area of 21 square meters and a perimeter of 24 meters. Find the dimensions of the floor and the dimensions of the square that will accommodate the pool.

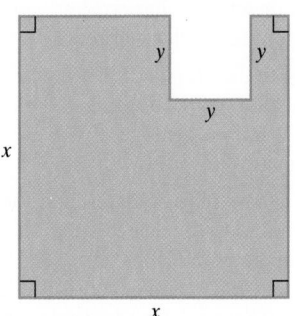

62. The area of the rectangular piece of cardboard shown below is 216 square inches. The cardboard is used to make an open box by cutting a 2-inch square from each corner and turning up the sides. If the box is to have a volume of 224 cubic inches, find the length and width of the cardboard that must be used.

63. The bar graph shows that compared to a century ago, work in the United States now involves mostly white-collar service jobs.

The Changing Pattern of Work in the United States, 1900–2005

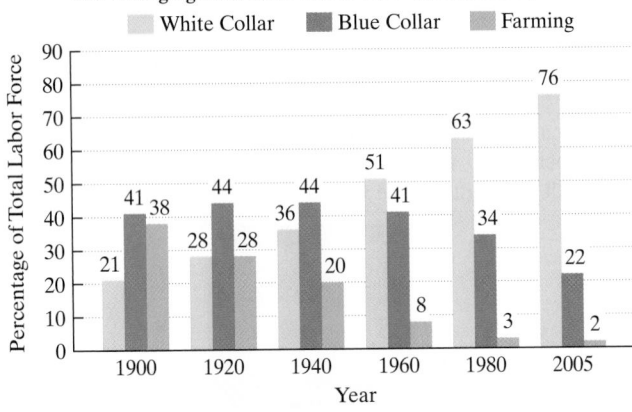

Source: U.S. Department of Labor

The data can be modeled by linear and quadratic functions.

White collar $0.5x - y = -18$

Blue collar $y = -0.004x^2 + 0.23x + 41$

Farming $0.4x + y = 35$

In each function, x represents the number of years after 1900 and y represents the percentage of the total U.S. labor force.

a. Based on the information in the graph, it appears that there was a year when the percentage of white-collar workers in the labor force was the same as the percentage of blue-collar workers in the labor force. According to the graph, between which two decades did this occur?

b. Solve a nonlinear system to determine the year described in part (a). Round to the nearest year. What percentage of the labor force, to the nearest percent, consisted of white-collar workers and what percentage consisted of blue-collar workers?

c. According to the graph, for which year was the percentage of white-collar workers the same as the percentage of farmers? What percentage of U.S. workers were in each of these groups?

d. Solve a linear system to determine the year described in part (c). Round to the nearest year. Use the models to find the percentage of the labor force consisting of white-collar workers and the percentage consisting of farmers. How well do your answers model the actual data specified in part (c)?

Writing in Mathematics

64. What is a system of nonlinear equations? Provide an example with your description.

65. Explain how to solve a nonlinear system using the substitution method. Use $x^2 + y^2 = 9$ and $2x - y = 3$ to illustrate your explanation.

66. Explain how to solve a nonlinear system using the addition method. Use $x^2 - y^2 = 5$ and $3x^2 - 2y^2 = 19$ to illustrate your explanation.

Technology Exercises

67. Verify your solutions to any five exercises from Exercises 1–42 by using a graphing utility to graph the two equations in the system in the same viewing rectangle. Then use the intersection feature to verify the solutions.

68. Write a system of equations, one equation whose graph is a line and the other whose graph is a parabola, that has no ordered pairs that are real numbers in its solution set. Graph the equations using a graphing utility and verify that you are correct.

Critical Thinking Exercises

Make Sense? *In Exercises 69–72, determine whether each statement makes sense or does not make sense, and explain your reasoning.*

69. I use the same steps to solve nonlinear systems as I did to solve linear systems, although I don't obtain linear equations when a variable is eliminated.

70. I graphed a nonlinear system that modeled the orbits of Earth and Mars, and the graphs indicated the system had a solution with a real ordered pair.

71. Without using any algebra, it's obvious that the nonlinear system consisting of $x^2 + y^2 = 4$ and $x^2 + y^2 = 25$ does not have real-number solutions.

72. I think that the nonlinear system consisting of $x^2 + y^2 = 36$ and $y = (x - 2)^2 - 3$ is easier to solve graphically than by using the substitution method or the addition method.

In Exercises 73–76, determine whether each statement is true or false. If the statement is false, make the necessary change(s) to produce a true statement.

73. A system of two equations in two variables whose graphs are a circle and a line can have four real ordered-pair solutions.

74. A system of two equations in two variables whose graphs are a parabola and a circle can have four real ordered-pair solutions.

75. A system of two equations in two variables whose graphs are two circles must have at least two real ordered-pair solutions.

76. A system of two equations in two variables whose graphs are a parabola and a circle cannot have only one real ordered-pair solution.

77. The points of intersection of the graphs of $xy = 20$ and $x^2 + y^2 = 41$ are joined to form a rectangle. Find the area of the rectangle.

78. Find a and b in this figure.

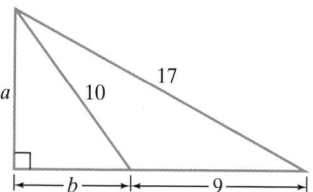

Solve the systems in Exercises 79–80.

79. $\log_y x = 3$
$\log_y(4x) = 5$

80. $\log x^2 = y + 3$
$\log x = y - 1$

Preview Exercises

Exercises 81–83 will help you prepare for the material covered in the next section. In each exercise, graph the linear function.

81. $2x - 3y = 6$

82. $f(x) = -\frac{2}{3}x$

83. $f(x) = -2$

Chapter 5 **Mid-Chapter Check Point**

What You Know: We learned to solve systems of equations. We solved linear and nonlinear systems in two variables by the substitution method and by the addition method. We solved linear systems in three variables by eliminating a variable, reducing the system to two equations in two variables. We saw that some linear systems, called inconsistent systems, have no solution, whereas other linear systems, called dependent systems, have infinitely many solutions. We applied systems to a variety of situations, including finding the break-even point for a business, finding a quadratic function from three points on its graph, and finding a rational function's partial fraction decomposition.

In Exercises 1–12, solve each system by the method of your choice.

1. $\begin{cases} x = 3y - 7 \\ 4x + 3y = 2 \end{cases}$

2. $\begin{cases} 3x + 4y = -5 \\ 2x - 3y = 8 \end{cases}$

3. $\begin{cases} \dfrac{2x}{3} + \dfrac{y}{5} = 6 \\ \dfrac{x}{6} - \dfrac{y}{2} = -4 \end{cases}$

4. $\begin{cases} y = 4x - 5 \\ 8x - 2y = 10 \end{cases}$

5. $\begin{cases} 2x + 5y = 3 \\ 3x - 2y = 1 \end{cases}$

6. $\begin{cases} \dfrac{x}{12} - y = \dfrac{1}{4} \\ 4x - 48y = 16 \end{cases}$

7. $\begin{cases} 2x - y + 2z = -8 \\ x + 2y - 3z = 9 \\ 3x - y - 4z = 3 \end{cases}$

8. $\begin{cases} x - 3z = -5 \\ 2x - y + 2z = 16 \\ 7x - 3y - 5z = 19 \end{cases}$

9. $\begin{cases} x^2 + y^2 = 9 \\ x + 2y - 3 = 0 \end{cases}$

10. $\begin{cases} 3x^2 + 2y^2 = 14 \\ 2x^2 - y^2 = 7 \end{cases}$

11. $\begin{cases} y = x^2 - 6 \\ x^2 + y^2 = 8 \end{cases}$

12. $\begin{cases} x - 2y = 4 \\ 2y^2 + xy = 8 \end{cases}$

In Exercises 13–16, write the partial fraction decomposition of each rational expression.

13. $\dfrac{x^2 - 6x + 3}{(x - 2)^3}$

14. $\dfrac{10x^2 + 9x - 7}{(x + 2)(x^2 - 1)}$

15. $\dfrac{x^2 + 4x - 23}{(x + 3)(x^2 + 4)}$

16. $\dfrac{x^3}{(x^2 + 4)^2}$

17. A company is planning to manufacture PDAs (personal digital assistants). The fixed cost will be $400,000 and it will cost $20 to produce each PDA. Each PDA will be sold for $100.

 a. Write the cost function, C, of producing x PDAs.

 b. Write the revenue function, R, from the sale of x PDAs.

 c. Write the profit function, P, from producing and selling x PDAs.

 d. Determine the break-even point. Describe what this means.

18. Roses sell for $3 each and carnations for $1.50 each. If a mixed bouquet of 20 flowers consisting of roses and carnations costs $39, how many of each type of flower is in the bouquet?

19. Find the measure of each angle whose degree measure is represented with a variable.

20. Find the quadratic function $y = ax^2 + bx + c$ whose graph passes through the points $(-1, 0)$, $(1, 4)$, and $(2, 3)$.

21. Find the length and width of a rectangle whose perimeter is 21 meters and whose area is 20 square meters.

(Section) **5.5** **Systems of Inequalities**

Objectives

1. Graph a linear inequality in two variables.

2. Graph a nonlinear inequality in two variables.

3. Use mathematical models involving linear inequalities.

4. Graph a system of inequalities.

We opened the chapter noting that the modern emphasis on thinness as the ideal body shape has been suggested as a major cause of eating disorders. In this section, as well as in the exercise set, we use systems of linear inequalities in two variables that will enable you to establish a healthy weight range for your height and age.

Linear Inequalities in Two Variables and Their Solutions

We have seen that equations in the form $Ax + By = C$ are straight lines when graphed. If we change the symbol = to $>$, $<$, \geq, or \leq, we obtain a **linear inequality in two variables**. Some examples of linear inequalities in two variables are $x + y > 2$, $3x - 5y \leq 15$, and $2x - y < 4$.

A **solution of an inequality in two variables**, x and y, is an ordered pair of real numbers with the following property: When the x-coordinate is substituted for x and the y-coordinate is substituted for y in the inequality, we obtain a true statement. For example, $(3, 2)$ is a solution of the inequality $x + y > 1$. When 3 is substituted for x and 2 is substituted for y, we obtain the true statement $3 + 2 > 1$, or $5 > 1$. Because there are infinitely many pairs of numbers that have a sum greater than 1, the inequality $x + y > 1$ has infinitely many solutions. Each ordered-pair solution is said to **satisfy** the inequality. Thus, $(3, 2)$ satisfies the inequality $x + y > 1$.

1. Graph a linear inequality in two variables.

The Graph of a Linear Inequality in Two Variables

We know that the graph of an equation in two variables is the set of all points whose coordinates satisfy the equation. Similarly, the **graph of an inequality in two variables** is the set of all points whose coordinates satisfy the inequality.

Let's use **Figure 5.14** to get an idea of what the graph of a linear inequality in two variables looks like. Part of the figure shows the graph of the linear equation $x + y = 2$. The line divides the points in the rectangular coordinate system into three sets. First, there is the set of points along the line, satisfying $x + y = 2$. Next, there is the set of points in the green region above the line. Points in the green region satisfy the linear inequality $x + y > 2$. Finally, there is the set of points in the purple region below the line. Points in the purple region satisfy the linear inequality $x + y < 2$.

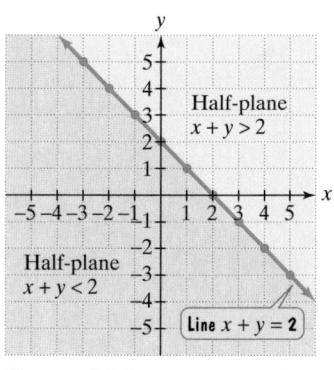

Figure 5.14

A **half-plane** is the set of all the points on one side of a line. In **Figure 5.14**, the green region is a half-plane. The purple region is also a half-plane. A half-plane is the graph of a linear inequality that involves $>$ or $<$. The graph of an inequality that involves \geq or \leq is a half-plane and a line. A solid line is used to show that a line is part of a graph. A dashed line is used to show that a line is not part of a graph.

Graphing a Linear Inequality in Two Variables

1. Replace the inequality symbol with an equal sign and graph the corresponding linear equation. Draw a solid line if the original inequality contains a \leq or \geq symbol. Draw a dashed line if the original inequality contains a $<$ or $>$ symbol.

2. Choose a test point from one of the half-planes. (Do not choose a point on the line.) Substitute the coordinates of the test point into the inequality.

3. If a true statement results, shade the half-plane containing this test point. If a false statement results, shade the half-plane not containing this test point.

EXAMPLE 1 **Graphing a Linear Inequality in Two Variables**

Graph: $2x - 3y \geq 6$.

Solution

Step 1 Replace the inequality symbol by = and graph the linear equation. We need to graph $2x - 3y = 6$. We can use intercepts to graph this line.

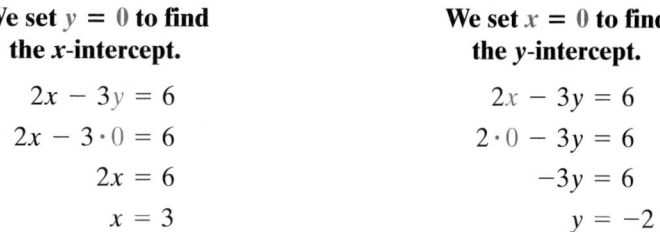

We set $y = 0$ to find the x-intercept.	We set $x = 0$ to find the y-intercept.
$2x - 3y = 6$	$2x - 3y = 6$
$2x - 3 \cdot 0 = 6$	$2 \cdot 0 - 3y = 6$
$2x = 6$	$-3y = 6$
$x = 3$	$y = -2$

The x-intercept is 3, so the line passes through $(3, 0)$. The y-intercept is -2, so the line passes through $(0, -2)$. Using the intercepts, the line is shown in **Figure 5.15** as a solid line. This is because the inequality $2x - 3y \geq 6$ contains a \geq symbol, in which equality is included.

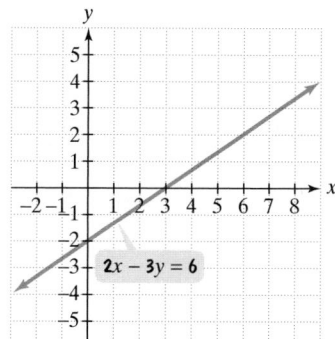

Figure 5.15 Preparing to graph $2x - 3y \geq 6$

Step 2 Choose a test point from one of the half-planes and not from the line. Substitute its coordinates into the inequality. The line $2x - 3y = 6$ divides the plane into three parts – the line itself and two half-planes. The points in one half-plane satisfy $2x - 3y > 6$. The points in the other half-plane satisfy $2x - 3y < 6$. We need to find which half-plane belongs to the solution of $2x - 3y \geq 6$. To do so, we test a point from either half-plane. The origin, $(0, 0)$, is the easiest point to test.

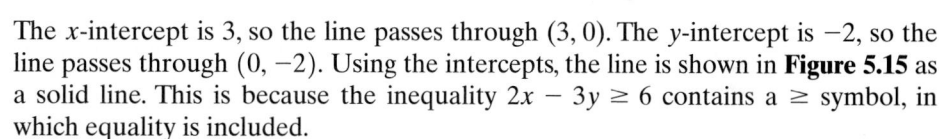

$$2x - 3y \geq 6 \qquad \text{This is the given inequality.}$$
$$2 \cdot 0 - 3 \cdot 0 \overset{?}{\geq} 6 \qquad \text{Test } (0, 0) \text{ by substituting 0 for x and 0 for y.}$$
$$0 - 0 \overset{?}{\geq} 6 \qquad \text{Multiply.}$$
$$0 \geq 6 \qquad \text{This statement is false.}$$

Step 3 If a false statement results, shade the half-plane not containing the test point. Because 0 is not greater than or equal to 6, the test point, $(0, 0)$, is not part of the solution set. Thus, the half-plane below the solid line $2x - 3y = 6$ is part of the solution set. The solution set is the line and the half-plane that does not contain the point $(0, 0)$, indicated by shading this half-plane. The graph is shown using green shading and a blue line in **Figure 5.16**.

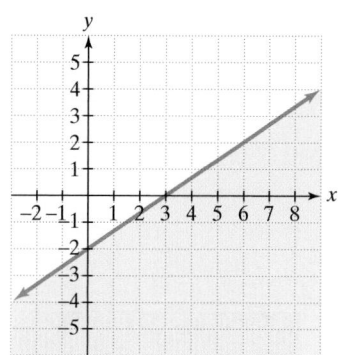

Figure 5.16 The graph of $2x - 3y \geq 6$

✓ Check Point **1** Graph: $4x - 2y \geq 8$.

When graphing a linear inequality, choose a test point that lies in one of the half-planes and *not on the line dividing the half-planes*. The test point $(0, 0)$ is convenient because it is easy to calculate when 0 is substituted for each variable. However, if $(0, 0)$ lies on the dividing line and not in a half-plane, a different test point must be selected.

(**EXAMPLE 2**) **Graphing a Linear Inequality in Two Variables**

Graph: $y > -\dfrac{2}{3}x$.

Solution

Step 1 Replace the inequality symbol by $=$ and graph the linear equation. Because we are interested in graphing $y > -\frac{2}{3}x$, we begin by graphing $y = -\frac{2}{3}x$. We can use the slope and the y-intercept to graph this linear function.

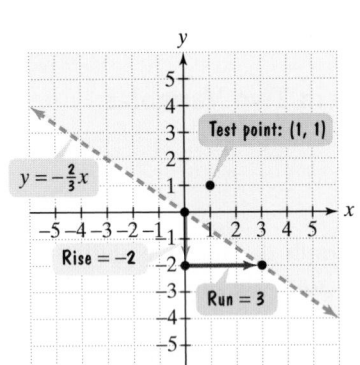

Figure 5.17 The graph of $y > -\frac{2}{3}x$

$$y = -\frac{2}{3}x + 0$$

$$\text{Slope} = \frac{-2}{3} = \frac{\text{rise}}{\text{run}} \qquad y\text{-intercept} = 0$$

The y-intercept is 0, so the line passes through $(0, 0)$. Using the y-intercept and the slope, the line is shown in **Figure 5.17** as a dashed line. This is because the inequality $y > -\frac{2}{3}x$ contains a $>$ symbol, in which equality is not included.

Step 2 Choose a test point from one of the half-planes and not from the line. Substitute its coordinates into the inequality. We cannot use $(0, 0)$ as a test point because it lies on the line and not in a half-plane. Let's use $(1, 1)$, which lies in the half-plane above the line.

$$y > -\frac{2}{3}x \qquad \text{This is the given inequality.}$$

$$1 \overset{?}{>} -\frac{2}{3} \cdot 1 \qquad \text{Test (1, 1) by substituting 1 for x and 1 for y.}$$

$$1 > -\frac{2}{3} \qquad \text{This statement is true.}$$

Step 3 If a true statement results, shade the half-plane containing the test point. Because 1 is greater than $-\frac{2}{3}$, the test point $(1, 1)$ is part of the solution set. All the points on the same side of the line $y = -\frac{2}{3}x$ as the point $(1, 1)$ are members of the solution set. The solution set is the half-plane that contains the point $(1, 1)$, indicated by shading this half-plane. The graph is shown using green shading and a dashed blue line in **Figure 5.17**.

Technology

Most graphing utilities can graph inequalities in two variables with the $^{\circ}\boxed{\text{SHADE}}^{\circ}$ feature. The procedure varies by model, so consult your manual. For most graphing utilities, you must first solve for y if it is not already isolated. The figure shows the graph of $y > -\frac{2}{3}x$. Most displays do not distinguish between dashed and solid boundary lines.

✓ **Check Point 2** Graph: $y > -\dfrac{3}{4}x.$

Graphing Linear Inequalities without Using Test Points

You can graph inequalities in the form $y > mx + b$ or $y < mx + b$ without using test points. The inequality symbol indicates which half-plane to shade.

- If $y > mx + b$, shade the half-plane above the line $y = mx + b$.
- If $y < mx + b$, shade the half-plane below the line $y = mx + b$.

Observe how this is illustrated in **Figure 5.17** in the margin on the previous page. The graph of $y > -\frac{2}{3}x$ is the half-plane above the line $y = -\frac{2}{3}x$.

It is also not necessary to use test points when graphing inequalities involving half-planes on one side of a vertical or a horizontal line.

For the Vertical Line $x = a$:	For the Horizontal Line $y = b$:
• If $x > a$, shade the half-plane to the right of $x = a$.	• If $y > b$, shade the half-plane above $y = b$.
• If $x < a$, shade the half-plane to the left of $x = a$.	• If $y < b$, shade the half-plane below $y = b$.

Study Tip

Continue using test points to graph inequalities in the form $Ax + By > C$ or $Ax + By < C$. The graph of $Ax + By > C$ can lie above or below the line given by $Ax + By = C$, depending on the value of B. The same comment applies to the graph of $Ax + By < C$.

$x < a$ in the yellow region. $x > a$ in the green region.

$x = a$

$y = b$ $y > b$ in the green region.

$y < b$ in the yellow region.

EXAMPLE 3 **Graphing Inequalities without Using Test Points**

Graph each inequality in a rectangular coordinate system:

 a. $y \le -3$ **b.** $x > 2$.

Solution

 a. $y \le -3$ **b.** $x > 2$

Graph $y = -3$, a horizontal line with y-intercept -3. The line is solid because equality is included in $y \le -3$. Because of the less than part of \le, shade the half-plane below the horizontal line.

Graph $x = 2$, a vertical line with x-intercept **2**. The line is dashed because equality is not included in $x > 2$. Because of $>$, the greater than symbol, shade the half-plane to the right of the vertical line.

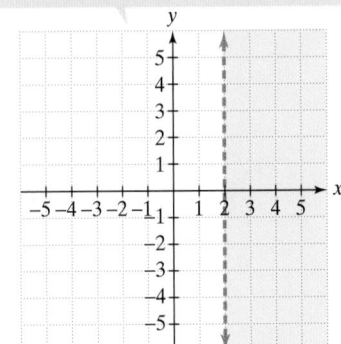

☑ Check Point **3** Graph each inequality in a rectangular coordinate system:

 a. $y > 1$ **b.** $x \leq -2$.

② Graph a nonlinear inequality in two variables.

Graphing a Nonlinear Inequality in Two Variables

Example 4 illustrates that a nonlinear inequality in two variables is graphed in the same way that we graph a linear inequality.

(**EXAMPLE 4**) **Graphing a Nonlinear Inequality in Two Variables**

Graph: $x^2 + y^2 \leq 9$.

Solution

Step 1 Replace the inequality symbol with = and graph the nonlinear equation. We need to graph $x^2 + y^2 = 9$. The graph is a circle of radius 3 with its center at the origin. The graph is shown in **Figure 5.18** as a solid circle because equality is included in the \leq symbol.

Step 2 Choose a test point from one of the regions and not from the circle. Substitute its coordinates into the inequality. The circle divides the plane into three parts—the circle itself, the region inside the circle, and the region outside the circle. We need to determine whether the region inside or outside the circle is included in the solution. To do so, we will use the test point $(0, 0)$ from inside the circle.

$$x^2 + y^2 \leq 9 \qquad \text{This is the given inequality.}$$

$$0^2 + 0^2 \overset{?}{\leq} 9 \qquad \text{Test } (0, 0) \text{ by substituting 0 for } x \text{ and 0 for } y.$$

$$0 + 0 \overset{?}{\leq} 9 \qquad \text{Square 0: } 0^2 = 0.$$

$$0 \leq 9 \qquad \text{Add. This statement is true.}$$

Step 3 If a true statement results, shade the region containing the test point. The true statement tells us that all the points inside the circle satisfy $x^2 + y^2 \leq 9$. The graph is shown using green shading and a solid blue circle in **Figure 5.19**.

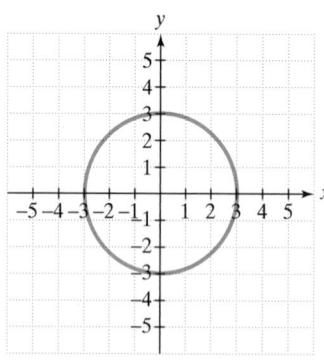

Figure 5.18 Preparing to graph $x^2 + y^2 \leq 9$

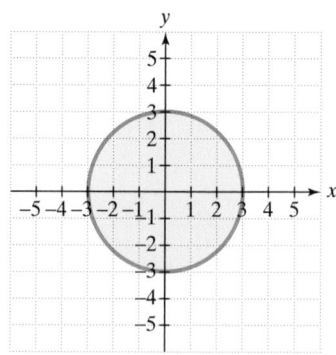

Figure 5.19 The graph of $x^2 + y^2 \leq 9$

☑ Check Point **4** Graph: $x^2 + y^2 \geq 16$.

③ Use mathematical models involving linear inequalities.

Modeling with Systems of Linear Inequalities

Just as two or more linear equations make up a system of linear equations, two or more linear inequalities make up a **system of linear inequalities**. A **solution of a system of linear inequalities** in two variables is an ordered pair that satisfies each inequality in the system.

EXAMPLE 5 **Does Your Weight Fit You?**

The latest guidelines, which apply to both men and women, give healthy weight ranges, rather than specific weights, for your height. **Figure 5.20** shows the healthy weight region for various heights for people between the ages of 19 and 34, inclusive.

Figure 5.20
Source: U.S. Department of Health and Human Services

If x represents height, in inches, and y represents weight, in pounds, the healthy weight region in **Figure 5.20** can be modeled by the following system of linear inequalities:

$$\begin{cases} 4.9x - y \geq 165 \\ 3.7x - y \leq 125. \end{cases}$$

Show that point A in **Figure 5.20** is a solution of the system of inequalities that describes healthy weight.

Solution Point A has coordinates $(70, 170)$. This means that if a person is 70 inches tall, or 5 feet 10 inches, and weighs 170 pounds, then that person's weight is within the healthy weight region. We can show that $(70, 170)$ satisfies the system of inequalities by substituting 70 for x and 170 for y in each inequality in the system.

$4.9x - y \geq 165$	$3.7x - y \leq 125$
$4.9(70) - 170 \overset{?}{\geq} 165$	$3.7(70) - 170 \overset{?}{\leq} 125$
$343 - 170 \overset{?}{\geq} 165$	$259 - 170 \overset{?}{\leq} 125$
$173 \geq 165,$ true	$89 \leq 125,$ true

The coordinates $(70, 170)$ make each inequality true. Thus, $(70, 170)$ satisfies the system for the healthy weight region and is a solution of the system. ⬤

✓ **Check Point 5** Show that point B in **Figure 5.20** is a solution of the system of inequalities that describes healthy weight.

④ Graph a system of inequalities.

Graphing Systems of Linear Inequalities

The **solution set of a system of linear inequalities in two variables** is the set of all ordered pairs that satisfy each inequality in the system. Thus, to graph a system of inequalities in two variables, begin by graphing each individual inequality in the same rectangular coordinate system. Then find the region, if there is one, that is common to every graph in the system. This region of intersection gives a picture of the system's solution set.

(**EXAMPLE 6**) **Graphing a System of Linear Inequalities**

Graph the solution set of the system:

$$\begin{cases} x - y < 1 \\ 2x + 3y \geq 12. \end{cases}$$

Solution Replacing each inequality symbol with an equal sign indicates that we need to graph $x - y = 1$ and $2x + 3y = 12$. We can use intercepts to graph these lines.

$x - y = 1$

x-intercept: $x - 0 = 1$ | Set $y = 0$ in each equation.
$x = 1$
The line passes through $(1, 0)$.

y-intercept: $0 - y = 1$ | Set $x = 0$ in each equation.
$-y = 1$
$y = -1$
The line passes through $(0, -1)$.

$2x + 3y = 12$

x-intercept: $2x + 3 \cdot 0 = 12$
$2x = 12$
$x = 6$
The line passes through $(6, 0)$.

y-intercept: $2 \cdot 0 + 3y = 12$
$3y = 12$
$y = 4$
The line passes through $(0, 4)$.

Now we are ready to graph the solution set of the system of linear inequalities.

Graph $x - y < 1$. The blue line, $x - y = 1$, is dashed: Equality is not included in $x - y < 1$. Because $(0, 0)$ makes the inequality true $(0 - 0 < 1$, or $0 < 1$, is true), shade the half-plane containing $(0, 0)$ in yellow.

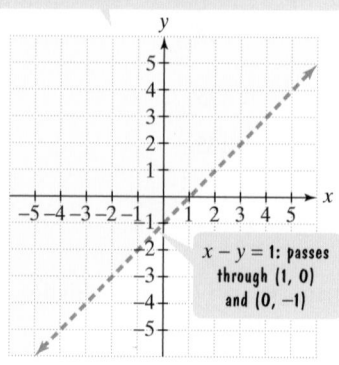

The graph of $x - y < 1$

Add the graph of $2x + 3y \geq 12$. The red line, $2x + 3y = 12$, is solid: Equality is included in $2x + 3y \geq 12$. Because $(0, 0)$ makes the inequality false $(2 \cdot 0 + 3 \cdot 0 \geq 12$, or $0 \geq 12$, is false), shade the half-plane not containing $(0, 0)$ using green vertical shading.

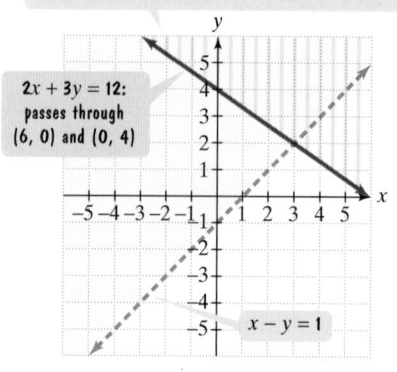

$2x + 3y = 12$: passes through $(6, 0)$ and $(0, 4)$

Adding the graph of $2x + 3y \geq 12$

The solution set of the system is graphed as the intersection (the overlap) of the two half-planes. This is the region in which the yellow shading and the green vertical shading overlap.

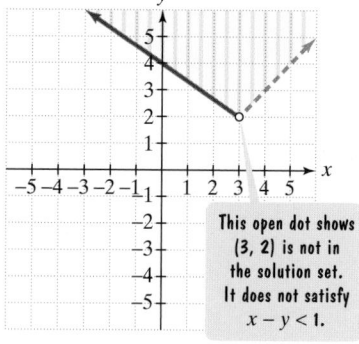

This open dot shows $(3, 2)$ is not in the solution set. It does not satisfy $x - y < 1$.

The graph of $x - y < 1$ and $2x + 3y \geq 12$

⊘ Check Point **6** Graph the solution set of the system:

$$\begin{cases} x - 3y < 6 \\ 2x + 3y \geq -6. \end{cases}$$

EXAMPLE 7 **Graphing a System of Inequalities**

Graph the solution set of the system:

$$\begin{cases} y \geq x^2 - 4 \\ x - y \geq 2. \end{cases}$$

Solution We begin by graphing $y \geq x^2 - 4$. Because equality is included in \geq, we graph $y = x^2 - 4$ as a solid parabola. Because $(0, 0)$ makes the inequality $y \geq x^2 - 4$ true (we obtain $0 \geq -4$), we shade the interior portion of the parabola containing $(0, 0)$, shown in yellow in **Figure 5.21**.

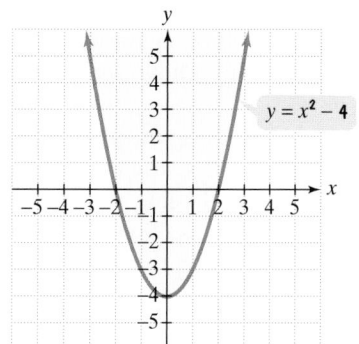

Figure 5.21 The graph of $y \geq x^2 - 4$

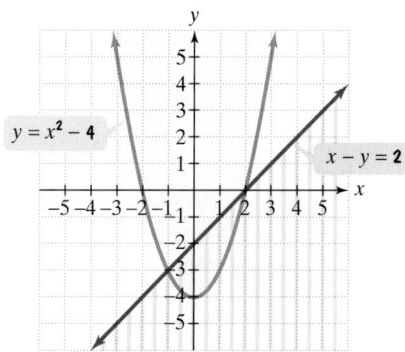

Figure 5.22 Adding the graph of $x - y \geq 2$

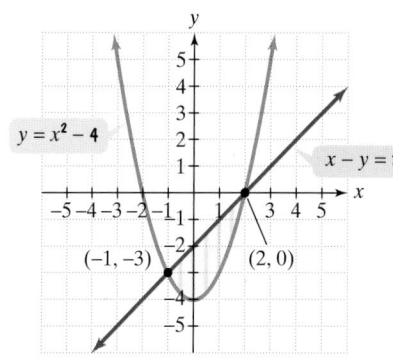

Figure 5.23 The graph of $y \geq x^2 - 4$ and $x - y \geq 2$

Now we graph $x - y \geq 2$ in the same rectangular coordinate system. First we graph the line $x - y = 2$ using its x-intercept, 2, and its y-intercept, -2. Because $(0, 0)$ makes the inequality $x - y \geq 2$ false (we obtain $0 \geq 2$), we shade the half-plane below the line. This is shown in **Figure 5.22** using green vertical shading.

The solution of the system is shown in **Figure 5.23** by the intersection (the overlap) of the solid yellow and green vertical shadings. The graph of the system's solution set consists of the region enclosed by the parabola and the line. To find the points of intersection of the parabola and the line, use the substitution method to solve the nonlinear system

$$\begin{cases} y = x^2 - 4 \\ x - y = 2. \end{cases}$$

Take a moment to show that the solutions are $(-1, -3)$ and $(2, 0)$, as shown in **Figure 5.23**.

⊘ Check Point **7** Graph the solution set of the system:

$$\begin{cases} y \geq x^2 - 4 \\ x + y \leq 2. \end{cases}$$

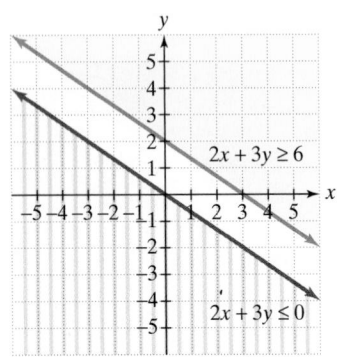

Figure 5.24 A system of inequalities with no solution

A system of inequalities has no solution if there are no points in the rectangular coordinate system that simultaneously satisfy each inequality in the system. For example, the system

$$\begin{cases} 2x + 3y \geq 6 \\ 2x + 3y \leq 0, \end{cases}$$

whose separate graphs are shown in **Figure 5.24**, has no overlapping region. Thus, the system has no solution. The solution set is \varnothing, the empty set.

EXAMPLE 8 Graphing a System of Inequalities

Graph the solution set of the system:

$$\begin{cases} x - y < 2 \\ -2 \leq x < 4 \\ y < 3. \end{cases}$$

Solution We begin by graphing $x - y < 2$, the first given inequality. The line $x - y = 2$ has an x-intercept of 2 and a y-intercept of -2. The test point $(0, 0)$ makes the inequality $x - y < 2$ true, and its graph is shown in **Figure 5.25**.

Now, let's consider the second given inequality, $-2 \leq x < 4$. Replacing the inequality symbols by $=$, we obtain $x = -2$ and $x = 4$, graphed as red vertical lines in **Figure 5.26**. The line of $x = 4$ is not included. Because x is between -2 and 4, we shade the region between the vertical lines. We must intersect this region with the yellow region in **Figure 5.25**. The resulting region is shown in yellow and green vertical shading in **Figure 5.26**.

Finally, let's consider the third given inequality, $y < 3$. Replacing the inequality symbol by $=$, we obtain $y = 3$, which graphs as a horizontal line. Because of the less than symbol in $y < 3$, the graph consists of the half-plane below the line $y = 3$. We must intersect this half-plane with the region in **Figure 5.26**. The resulting region is shown in yellow and green vertical shading in **Figure 5.27**. This region represents the graph of the solution set of the given system.

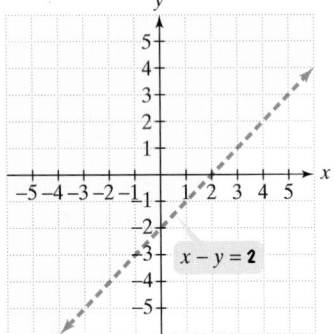

Figure 5.25 The graph of $x - y < 2$

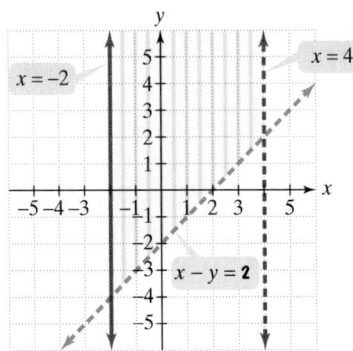

Figure 5.26 The graph of $x - y < 2$ and $-2 \leq x < 4$

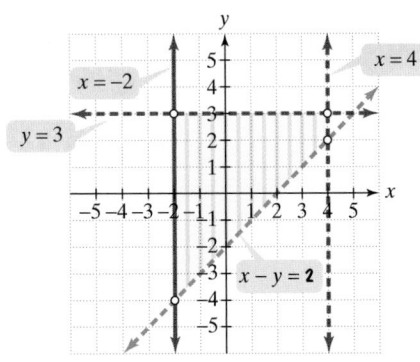

Figure 5.27 The graph of $x - y < 2$ and $-2 \leq x < 4$ and $y < 3$

In **Figure 5.27** it may be difficult to tell where the graph of $x - y = 2$ intersects the vertical line $x = 4$. Using the substitution method, it can be determined that this intersection point is $(4, 2)$. Take a moment to verify that the four intersection points in **Figure 5.27** are, clockwise from upper left, $(-2, 3)$, $(4, 3)$, $(4, 2)$, and $(-2, -4)$. These points are shown as open dots because none satisfies all three of the system's inequalities.

⊘ Check Point **8** Graph the solution set of the system:

$$\begin{cases} x + y < 2 \\ -2 \leq x < 1 \\ y > -3. \end{cases}$$

Exercise Set 5.5

Practice Exercises

In Exercises 1–26, graph each inequality.

1. $x + 2y \le 8$

2. $3x - 6y \le 12$

3. $x - 2y > 10$

4. $2x - y > 4$

5. $y \le \frac{1}{3}x$

6. $y \le \frac{1}{4}x$

7. $y > 2x - 1$

8. $y > 3x + 2$

9. $x \le 1$

10. $x \le -3$

11. $y > 1$

12. $y > -3$

13. $x^2 + y^2 \le 1$

14. $x^2 + y^2 \le 4$

15. $x^2 + y^2 > 25$

16. $x^2 + y^2 > 36$

17. $(x - 2)^2 + (y + 1)^2 < 9$

18. $(x + 2)^2 + (y - 1)^2 < 16$

19. $y < x^2 - 1$

20. $y < x^2 - 9$

21. $y \ge x^2 - 9$

22. $y \ge x^2 - 1$

23. $y > 2^x$

24. $y \le 3^x$

25. $y \ge \log_2(x + 1)$

26. $y \ge \log_3(x - 1)$

In Exercises 27–62, graph the solution set of each system of inequalities or indicate that the system has no solution.

27. $\begin{cases} 3x + 6y \le 6 \\ 2x + y \le 8 \end{cases}$

28. $\begin{cases} x - y \ge 4 \\ x + y \le 6 \end{cases}$

29. $\begin{cases} 2x - 5y \le 10 \\ 3x - 2y > 6 \end{cases}$

30. $\begin{cases} 2x - y \le 4 \\ 3x + 2y > -6 \end{cases}$

31. $\begin{cases} y > 2x - 3 \\ y < -x + 6 \end{cases}$

32. $\begin{cases} y < -2x + 4 \\ y < x - 4 \end{cases}$

33. $\begin{cases} x + 2y \le 4 \\ y \ge x - 3 \end{cases}$

34. $\begin{cases} x + y \le 4 \\ y \ge 2x - 4 \end{cases}$

35. $\begin{cases} x \le 2 \\ y \ge -1 \end{cases}$

36. $\begin{cases} x \le 3 \\ y \le -1 \end{cases}$

37. $-2 \le x < 5$

38. $-2 < y \le 5$

39. $\begin{cases} x - y \le 1 \\ x \ge 2 \end{cases}$

40. $\begin{cases} 4x - 5y \ge -20 \\ x \ge -3 \end{cases}$

41. $\begin{cases} x + y > 4 \\ x + y < -1 \end{cases}$

42. $\begin{cases} x + y > 3 \\ x + y < -2 \end{cases}$

43. $\begin{cases} x + y > 4 \\ x + y > -1 \end{cases}$

44. $\begin{cases} x + y > 3 \\ x + y > -2 \end{cases}$

45. $\begin{cases} y \ge x^2 - 1 \\ x - y \ge -1 \end{cases}$

46. $\begin{cases} y \ge x^2 - 4 \\ x - y \ge 2 \end{cases}$

47. $\begin{cases} x^2 + y^2 \le 16 \\ x + y > 2 \end{cases}$

48. $\begin{cases} x^2 + y^2 \le 4 \\ x + y > 1 \end{cases}$

49. $\begin{cases} x^2 + y^2 > 1 \\ x^2 + y^2 < 16 \end{cases}$

50. $\begin{cases} x^2 + y^2 > 1 \\ x^2 + y^2 < 9 \end{cases}$

51. $\begin{cases} (x - 1)^2 + (y + 1)^2 < 25 \\ (x - 1)^2 + (y + 1)^2 \ge 16 \end{cases}$

52. $\begin{cases} (x + 1)^2 + (y - 1)^2 < 16 \\ (x + 1)^2 + (y - 1)^2 \ge 4 \end{cases}$

53. $\begin{cases} x^2 + y^2 \le 1 \\ y - x^2 > 0 \end{cases}$

54. $\begin{cases} x^2 + y^2 < 4 \\ y - x^2 \ge 0 \end{cases}$

55. $\begin{cases} x^2 + y^2 < 16 \\ y \ge 2^x \end{cases}$

56. $\begin{cases} x^2 + y^2 \le 16 \\ y < 2^x \end{cases}$

57. $\begin{cases} x - y \le 2 \\ x > -2 \\ y \le 3 \end{cases}$

58. $\begin{cases} 3x + y \le 6 \\ x > -2 \\ y \le 4 \end{cases}$

59. $\begin{cases} x \ge 0 \\ y \ge 0 \\ 2x + 5y < 10 \\ 3x + 4y \le 12 \end{cases}$

60. $\begin{cases} x \ge 0 \\ y \ge 0 \\ 2x + y < 4 \\ 2x - 3y \le 6 \end{cases}$

61. $\begin{cases} 3x + y \le 6 \\ 2x - y \le -1 \\ x > -2 \\ y < 4 \end{cases}$

62. $\begin{cases} 2x + y \le 6 \\ x + y > 2 \\ 1 \le x \le 2 \\ y < 3 \end{cases}$

Practice Plus

In Exercises 63–64, write each sentence as an inequality in two variables. Then graph the inequality.

63. The y-variable is at least 4 more than the product of −2 and the x-variable.

64. The y-variable is at least 2 more than the product of −3 and the x-variable.

In Exercises 65–68, write the given sentences as a system of inequalities in two variables. Then graph the system.

65. The sum of the x-variable and the y-variable is at most 4. The y-variable added to the product of 3 and the x-variable does not exceed 6.

66. The sum of the x-variable and the y-variable is at most 3. The y-variable added to the product of 4 and the x-variable does not exceed 6.

67. The sum of the x-variable and the y-variable is no more than 2. The y-variable is no less than the difference between the square of the x-variable and 4.

68. The sum of the squares of the x-variable and the y-variable is no more than 25. The sum of twice the y-variable and the x-variable is no less than 5.

In Exercises 69–70, rewrite each inequality in the system without absolute value bars. Then graph the rewritten system in rectangular coordinates.

69. $\begin{cases} |x| \leq 2 \\ |y| \leq 3 \end{cases}$ **70.** $\begin{cases} |x| \leq 1 \\ |y| \leq 2 \end{cases}$

*The graphs of solution sets of systems of inequalities involve finding the intersection of the solution sets of two or more inequalities. By contrast, in Exercises 71–72, you will be graphing the **union** of the solution sets of two inequalities.*

71. Graph the union of $y > \frac{3}{2}x - 2$ and $y < 4$.

72. Graph the union of $x - y \geq -1$ and $5x - 2y \leq 10$.

Without graphing, in Exercises 73–76, determine if each system has no solution or infinitely many solutions.

73. $\begin{cases} 3x + y < 9 \\ 3x + y > 9 \end{cases}$

74. $\begin{cases} 6x - y \leq 24 \\ 6x - y > 24 \end{cases}$

75. $\begin{cases} (x + 4)^2 + (y - 3)^2 \leq 9 \\ (x + 4)^2 + (y - 3)^2 \geq 9 \end{cases}$

76. $\begin{cases} (x - 4)^2 + (y + 3)^2 \leq 24 \\ (x - 4)^2 + (y + 3)^2 \geq 24 \end{cases}$

Application Exercises

The figure shows the healthy weight region for various heights for people ages 35 and older.

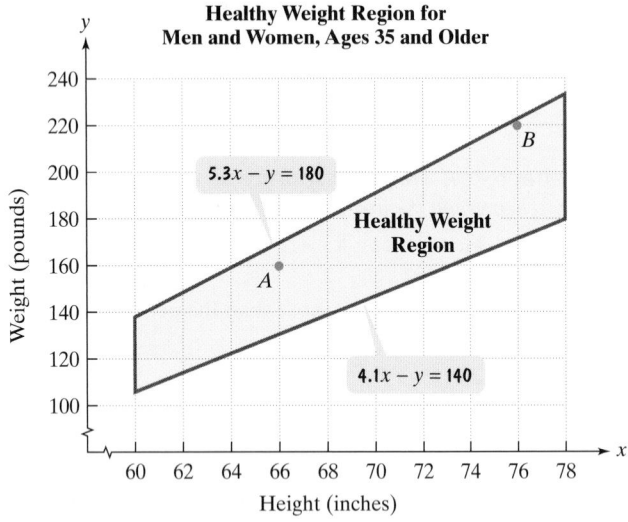

Healthy Weight Region for Men and Women, Ages 35 and Older

Source: U.S. Department of Health and Human Services

If x represents height, in inches, and y represents weight, in pounds, the healthy weight region can be modeled by the following system of linear inequalities:

$$\begin{cases} 5.3x - y \geq 180 \\ 4.1x - y \leq 140. \end{cases}$$

Use this information to solve Exercises 77–80.

77. Show that point A is a solution of the system of inequalities that describes healthy weight for this age group.

78. Show that point B is a solution of the system of inequalities that describes healthy weight for this age group.

79. Is a person in this age group who is 6 feet tall weighing 205 pounds within the healthy weight region?

80. Is a person in this age group who is 5 feet 8 inches tall weighing 135 pounds within the healthy weight region?

81. Many elevators have a capacity of 2000 pounds.

 a. If a child averages 50 pounds and an adult 150 pounds, write an inequality that describes when x children and y adults will cause the elevator to be overloaded.

 b. Graph the inequality. Because x and y must be positive, limit the graph to quadrant I only.

 c. Select an ordered pair satisfying the inequality. What are its coordinates and what do they represent in this situation?

82. A patient is not allowed to have more than 330 milligrams of cholesterol per day from a diet of eggs and meat. Each egg provides 165 milligrams of cholesterol. Each ounce of meat provides 110 milligrams.

 a. Write an inequality that describes the patient's dietary restrictions for x eggs and y ounces of meat.

 b. Graph the inequality. Because x and y must be positive, limit the graph to quadrant I only.

 c. Select an ordered pair satisfying the inequality. What are its coordinates and what do they represent in this situation?

83. On your next vacation, you will divide lodging between large resorts and small inns. Let x represent the number of nights spent in large resorts. Let y represent the number of nights spent in small inns.

 a. Write a system of inequalities that models the following conditions:

 You want to stay at least 5 nights. At least one night should be spent at a large resort. Large resorts average $200 per night and small inns average $100 per night. Your budget permits no more than $700 for lodging.

 b. Graph the solution set of the system of inequalities in part (a).

 c. Based on your graph in part (b), what is the greatest number of nights you could spend at a large resort and still stay within your budget?

84. A person with no more than $15,000 to invest plans to place the money in two investments. One investment is high risk, high yield; the other is low risk, low yield. At least $2000 is to be placed in the high-risk investment. Furthermore, the amount invested at low risk should be at least three times the amount invested at high risk. Find and graph a system of inequalities that describes all possibilities for placing the money in the high- and low-risk investments.

The graph of an inequality in two variables is a region in the rectangular coordinate system. Regions in coordinate systems have numerous applications. For example, the regions in the following two graphs indicate whether a person is obese, overweight, borderline overweight, normal weight, or underweight.

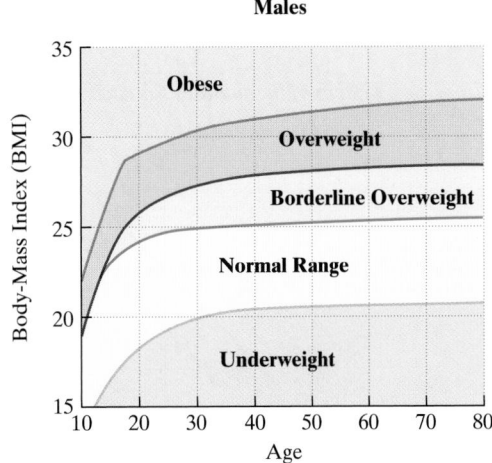

Source: Centers for Disease Control and Prevention

The horizontal axis shows a person's age. The vertical axis shows that person's body-mass index (BMI), computed using the following formula:

$$BMI = \frac{703W}{H^2}.$$

The variable W represents weight, in pounds. The variable H represents height, in inches. Use this information to solve Exercises 85–86.

85. A man is 20 years old, 72 inches (6 feet) tall, and weighs 200 pounds.

 a. Compute the man's BMI. Round to the nearest tenth.

 b. Use the man's age and his BMI to locate this information as a point in the coordinate system for males. Is this person obese, overweight, borderline overweight, normal weight, or underweight?

86. A woman is 25 years old, 66 inches (5 feet, 6 inches) tall, and weighs 105 pounds.

 a. Compute the woman's BMI. Round to the nearest tenth.

 b. Use the woman's age and her BMI to locate this information as a point in the coordinate system for females. Is this person obese, overweight, borderline overweight, normal weight, or underweight?

Writing in Mathematics

87. What is a linear inequality in two variables? Provide an example with your description.

88. How do you determine if an ordered pair is a solution of an inequality in two variables, x and y?

89. What is a half-plane?

90. What does a solid line mean in the graph of an inequality?

91. What does a dashed line mean in the graph of an inequality?

92. Compare the graphs of $3x - 2y > 6$ and $3x - 2y \leq 6$. Discuss similarities and differences between the graphs.

93. What is a system of linear inequalities?

94. What is a solution of a system of linear inequalities?

95. Explain how to graph the solution set of a system of inequalities.

96. What does it mean if a system of linear inequalities has no solution?

Technology Exercises

Graphing utilities can be used to shade regions in the rectangular coordinate system, thereby graphing an inequality in two variables. Read the section of the user's manual for your graphing utility that describes how to shade a region. Then use your graphing utility to graph the inequalities in Exercises 97–102.

97. $y \leq 4x + 4$

98. $y \geq \frac{2}{3}x - 2$

99. $y \geq x^2 - 4$

100. $y \geq \frac{1}{2}x^2 - 2$

101. $2x + y \leq 6$

102. $3x - 2y \geq 6$

103. Does your graphing utility have any limitations in terms of graphing inequalities? If so, what are they?

104. Use a graphing utility with a $\boxed{\text{SHADE}}$ feature to verify any five of the graphs that you drew by hand in Exercises 1–26.

105. Use a graphing utility with a $\boxed{\text{SHADE}}$ feature to verify any five of the graphs that you drew by hand for the systems in Exercises 27–62.

Critical Thinking Exercises

Make Sense? *In Exercises 106–109, determine whether each statement makes sense or does not make sense, and explain your reasoning.*

106. When graphing a linear inequality, I should always use $(0, 0)$ as a test point because it's easy to perform the calculations when 0 is substituted for each variable.

107. When graphing $3x - 4y < 12$, it's not necessary for me to graph the linear equation $3x - 4y = 12$ because the inequality contains a $<$ symbol, in which equality is not included.

108. The reason that systems of linear inequalities are appropriate for modeling healthy weight is because guidelines give healthy weight ranges, rather than specific weights, for various heights.

109. I graphed the solution set of $y \geq x + 2$ and $x \geq 1$ without using test points.

In Exercises 110–113, write a system of inequalities for each graph.

110.

111.

112.

113.

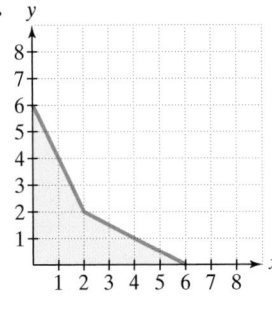

114. Write a system of inequalities whose solution set includes every point in the rectangular coordinate system.

115. Sketch the graph of the solution set for the following system of inequalities:

$$\begin{cases} y \geq nx + b \ (n < 0, b > 0) \\ y \leq mx + b \ (m > 0, b > 0). \end{cases}$$

Preview Exercises

Exercises 116–118 will help you prepare for the material covered in the next section.

116. a. Graph the solution set of the system:

$$\begin{cases} x + y \geq 6 \\ x \leq 8 \\ y \geq 5. \end{cases}$$

b. List the points that form the corners of the graphed region in part (a).

c. Evaluate $3x + 2y$ at each of the points obtained in part (b).

117. a. Graph the solution set of the system:

$$\begin{cases} x \geq 0 \\ y \geq 0 \\ 3x - 2x \leq 6 \\ y \leq -x + 7. \end{cases}$$

b. List the points that form the corners of the graphed region in part (a).

c. Evaluate $2x + 5y$ at each of the points obtained in part (b).

118. Bottled water and medical supplies are to be shipped to survivors of an earthquake by plane. The bottled water weighs 20 pounds per container and medical kits weigh 10 pounds per kit. Each plane can carry no more than 80,000 pounds. If x represents the number of bottles of water to be shipped per plane and y represents the number of medical kits per plane, write an inequality that models each plane's 80,000-pound weight restriction.

Section 5.6 **Linear Programming**

Objectives

1 Write an objective function describing a quantity that must be maximized or minimized.

2 Use inequalities to describe limitations in a situation.

3 Use linear programming to solve problems.

West Berlin children at Tempelhof airport watch fleets of U.S. airplanes bringing in supplies to circumvent the Soviet blockade. The airlift began June 28, 1948 and continued for 15 months.

The Berlin Airlift (1948 – 1949) was an operation by the United States and Great Britain in response to military action by the former Soviet Union: Soviet troops closed all roads and rail lines between West Germany and Berlin, cutting off supply routes to the city. The Allies used a mathematical technique developed during World

War II to maximize the amount of supplies transported. During the 15-month airlift, 278,228 flights provided basic necessities to blockaded Berlin, saving one of the world's great cities.

In this section, we will look at an important application of systems of linear inequalities. Such systems arise in **linear programming**, a method for solving problems in which a particular quantity that must be maximized or minimized is limited by other factors. Linear programming is one of the most widely used tools in management science. It helps businesses allocate resources to manufacture products in a way that will maximize profit. Linear programming accounts for more than 50% and perhaps as much as 90% of all computing time used for management decisions in business. The Allies used linear programming to save Berlin.

① Write an objective function describing a quantity that must be maximized or minimized.

Objective Functions in Linear Programming

Many problems involve quantities that must be maximized or minimized. Businesses are interested in maximizing profit. An operation in which bottled water and medical kits are shipped to earthquake survivors needs to maximize the number of survivors helped by this shipment. An **objective function** is an algebraic expression in two or more variables describing a quantity that must be maximized or minimized.

(EXAMPLE I) Writing an Objective Function

Bottled water and medical supplies are to be shipped to survivors of an earthquake by plane. Each container of bottled water will serve 10 people and each medical kit will aid 6 people. If x represents the number of bottles of water to be shipped and y represents the number of medical kits, write the objective function that models the number of people that can be helped.

Solution Because each bottle of water serves 10 people and each medical kit aids 6 people, we have

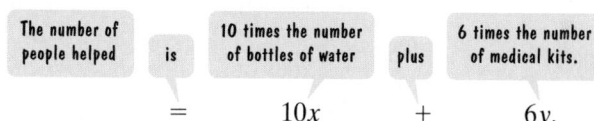

| The number of people helped | is | 10 times the number of bottles of water | plus | 6 times the number of medical kits. |

$$= \qquad 10x \qquad + \qquad 6y.$$

Using z to represent the number of people helped, the objective function is

$$z = 10x + 6y.$$

Unlike the functions that we have seen so far, the objective function is an equation in three variables. For a value of x and a value of y, there is one and only one value of z. Thus, z is a function of x and y. ●

⊘ Check Point **I** A company manufactures bookshelves and desks for computers. Let x represent the number of bookshelves manufactured daily and y the number of desks manufactured daily. The company's profits are $25 per bookshelf and $55 per desk. Write the objective function that models the company's total daily profit, z, from x bookshelves and y desks. (Check Points 2 through 4 are related to this situation, so keep track of your answers.)

② Use inequalities to describe limitations in a situation.

Constraints in Linear Programming

Ideally, the number of earthquake survivors helped in Example 1 should increase without restriction so that every survivor receives water and medical kits. However, the planes that ship these supplies are subject to weight and volume restrictions. In linear programming problems, such restrictions are called **constraints**. Each

constraint is expressed as a linear inequality. The list of constraints forms a system of linear inequalities.

EXAMPLE 2) Writing a Constraint

Each plane can carry no more than 80,000 pounds. The bottled water weighs 20 pounds per container and each medical kit weighs 10 pounds. Let x represent the number of bottles of water to be shipped and y the number of medical kits. Write an inequality that models this constraint.

Solution Because each plane can carry no more than 80,000 pounds, we have

The total weight of the water bottles	plus	the total weight of the medical kits	must be less than or equal to	80,000 pounds.
$20x$	$+$	$10y$	\leq	80,000.

Each bottle weighs 20 pounds. Each kit weighs 10 pounds.

The plane's weight constraint is modeled by the inequality

$$20x + 10y \leq 80,000.$$

Ø Check Point **2** To maintain high quality, the company in Check Point 1 should not manufacture more than a total of 80 bookshelves and desks per day. Write an inequality that models this constraint.

In addition to a weight constraint on its cargo, each plane has a limited amount of space in which to carry supplies. Example 3 demonstrates how to express this constraint.

EXAMPLE 3) Writing a Constraint

Each plane can carry a total volume of supplies that does not exceed 6000 cubic feet. Each water bottle is 1 cubic foot and each medical kit also has a volume of 1 cubic foot. With x still representing the number of water bottles and y the number of medical kits, write an inequality that models this second constraint.

Solution Because each plane can carry a volume of supplies that does not exceed 6000 cubic feet, we have

The total volume of the water	plus	the total volume of the medical kits	must be less than or equal to	6000 cubic feet.
$1x$	$+$	$1y$	\leq	6000.

Each bottle is 1 cubic foot. Each kit is 1 cubic foot.

The plane's volume constraint is modeled by the inequality $x + y \leq 6000$.

In summary, here's what we have described so far in this aid-to-earthquake-victims situation:

$$z = 10x + 6y$$

This is the objective function modeling the number of people helped with x bottles of water and y medical kits.

$$\begin{cases} 20x + 10y \leq 80,000 \\ x + y \leq 6000. \end{cases}$$

These are the constraints based on each plane's weight and volume limitations.

Ø Check Point **3** To meet customer demand, the company in Check Point 1 must manufacture between 30 and 80 bookshelves per day, inclusive. Furthermore, the company must manufacture at least 10 and no more than 30 desks per day. Write an inequality that models each of these sentences. Then summarize what you have described about this company by writing the objective function for its profits and the three constraints.

③ Use linear programming to solve problems.

Solving Problems with Linear Programming

The problem in the earthquake situation described previously is to maximize the number of survivors who can be helped, subject to each plane's weight and volume constraints. The process of solving this problem is called *linear programming*, based on a theorem that was proven during World War II.

Solving a Linear Programming Problem

Let $z = ax + by$ be an objective function that depends on x and y. Furthermore, z is subject to a number of constraints on x and y. If a maximum or minimum value of z exists, it can be determined as follows:

1. Graph the system of inequalities representing the constraints.
2. Find the value of the objective function at each corner, or **vertex**, of the graphed region. The maximum and minimum of the objective function occur at one or more of the corner points.

EXAMPLE 4 **Solving a Linear Programming Problem**

Determine how many bottles of water and how many medical kits should be sent on each plane to maximize the number of earthquake victims who can be helped.

Solution We must maximize $z = 10x + 6y$ subject to the following constraints:

$$\begin{cases} 20x + 10y \le 80,000 \\ x + y \le 6000. \end{cases}$$

Step 1 Graph the system of inequalities representing the constraints. Because x (the number of bottles of water per plane) and y (the number of medical kits per plane) must be nonnegative, we need to graph the system of inequalities in quadrant I and its boundary only.

To graph the inequality $20x + 10y \le 80,000$, we graph the equation $20x + 10y = 80,000$ as a solid blue line (**Figure 5.28**). Setting $y = 0$, the x-intercept is 4000 and setting $x = 0$, the y-intercept is 8000. Using $(0, 0)$ as a test point, the inequality is satisfied, so we shade below the blue line, as shown in yellow in **Figure 5.28**.

Now we graph $x + y \le 6000$ by first graphing $x + y = 6000$ as a solid red line. Setting $y = 0$, the x-intercept is 6000. Setting $x = 0$, the y-intercept is 6000. Using $(0, 0)$ as a test point, the inequality is satisfied, so we shade below the red line, as shown using green vertical shading in **Figure 5.28**.

We use the addition method to find where the lines $20x + 10y = 80,000$ and $x + y = 6000$ intersect.

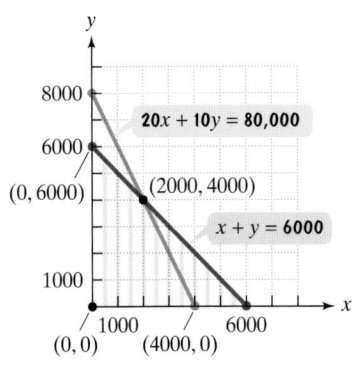

Figure 5.28 The region in quadrant I representing the constraints $20x + 10y \le 80,000$ and $x + y \le 6000$

$$\begin{cases} 20x + 10y = 80,000 \\ x + y = 6000 \end{cases} \xrightarrow[\text{Multiply by } -10.}{\text{No change}} \begin{cases} 20x + 10y = 80,000 \\ -10x - 10y = -60,000 \end{cases}$$

$$\text{Add:} \quad 10x \qquad = 20,000$$
$$x \qquad = 2000$$

Back-substituting 2000 for x in $x + y = 6000$, we find $y = 4000$, so the intersection point is $(2000, 4000)$.

The system of inequalities representing the constraints is shown by the region in which the yellow shading and the green vertical shading overlap in **Figure 5.28**. The graph of the system of inequalities is shown again in **Figure 5.29**. The red and blue line segments are included in the graph.

Figure 5.29

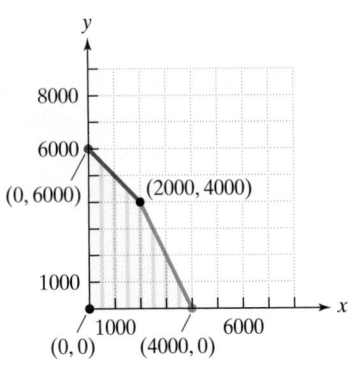

Figure 5.29 (repeated)

Step 2 Find the value of the objective function at each corner of the graphed region. The maximum and minimum of the objective function occur at one or more of the corner points. We must evaluate the objective function, $z = 10x + 6y$, at the four corners, or vertices, of the region in **Figure 5.29**.

Corner (x, y)	Objective Function $z = 10x + 6y$
$(0, 0)$	$z = 10(0) + 6(0) = 0$
$(4000, 0)$	$z = 10(4000) + 6(0) = 40{,}000$
$(2000, 4000)$	$z = 10(2000) + 6(4000) = 44{,}000$ ← maximum
$(0, 6000)$	$z = 10(0) + 6(6000) = 36{,}000$

Thus, the maximum value of z is 44,000 and this occurs when $x = 2000$ and $y = 4000$. In practical terms, this means that the maximum number of earthquake survivors who can be helped with each plane shipment is 44,000. This can be accomplished by sending 2000 water bottles and 4000 medical kits per plane.

✓ Check Point **4** For the company in Check Points 1–3, how many bookshelves and how many desks should be manufactured per day to obtain maximum profit? What is the maximum daily profit?

(EXAMPLE 5) Solving a Linear Programming Problem

Find the maximum value of the objective function

$$z = 2x + y$$

subject to the following constraints:

$$\begin{cases} x \geq 0,\ y \geq 0 \\ x + 2y \leq 5 \\ x - y \leq 2. \end{cases}$$

Solution We begin by graphing the region in quadrant I ($x \geq 0$, $y \geq 0$) formed by the constraints. The graph is shown in **Figure 5.30**.

Now we evaluate the objective function at the four vertices of this region.

Objective function: $z = 2x + y$

At $(0, 0)$: $z = 2 \cdot 0 + 0 = 0$

At $(2, 0)$: $z = 2 \cdot 2 + 0 = 4$

At $(3, 1)$: $z = 2 \cdot 3 + 1 = 7$ **Maximum value of z**

At $(0, 2.5)$: $z = 2 \cdot 0 + 2.5 = 2.5$

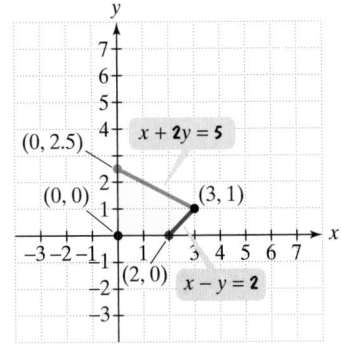

Figure 5.30 The graph of $x + 2y \leq 5$ and $x - y \leq 2$ in quadrant I

Thus, the maximum value of z is 7, and this occurs when $x = 3$ and $y = 1$.

We can see why the objective function in Example 5 has a maximum value that occurs at a vertex by solving the equation for y.

$z = 2x + y$ This is the objective function of Example 5.

$y = -2x + z$ Solve for y. Recall that the slope-intercept form of a line is $y = mx + b$.

Slope $= -2$ y-intercept $= z$

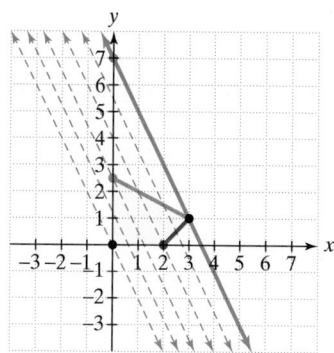

Figure 5.31 The line with slope −2 with the greatest y-intercept that intersects the shaded region passes through one of its vertices.

In this form, z represents the y-intercept of the objective function. The equation describes infinitely many parallel lines, each with slope −2. The process in linear programming involves finding the maximum z-value for all lines that intersect the region determined by the constraints. Of all the lines whose slope is −2, we're looking for the one with the greatest y-intercept that intersects the given region. As we see in **Figure 5.31**, such a line will pass through one (or possibly more) of the vertices of the region.

⊘ Check Point **5** Find the maximum value of the objective function $z = 3x + 5y$ subject to the constraints $x \geq 0, y \geq 0, x + y \geq 1, x + y \leq 6$.

Exercise Set 5.6

Practice Exercises

In Exercises 1–4, find the value of the objective function at each corner of the graphed region. What is the maximum value of the objective function? What is the minimum value of the objective function?

1. Objective Function
$z = 5x + 6y$

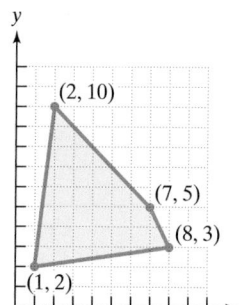

2. Objective Function
$z = 3x + 2y$

3. Objective Function
$z = 40x + 50y$

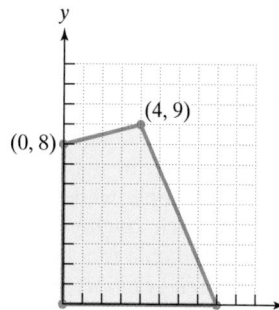

4. Objective Function
$z = 30x + 45y$

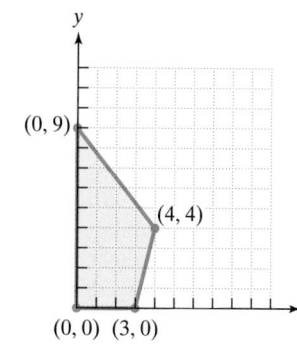

In Exercises 5–14, an objective function and a system of linear inequalities representing constraints are given.

a. *Graph the system of inequalities representing the constraints.*

b. *Find the value of the objective function at each corner of the graphed region.*

c. *Use the values in part (b) to determine the maximum value of the objective function and the values of x and y for which the maximum occurs.*

5. Objective Function
Constraints

$z = 3x + 2y$
$$\begin{cases} x \geq 0, y \geq 0 \\ 2x + y \leq 8 \\ x + y \geq 4 \end{cases}$$

6. Objective Function
Constraints

$z = 2x + 3y$
$$\begin{cases} x \geq 0, y \geq 0 \\ 2x + y \leq 8 \\ 2x + 3y \leq 12 \end{cases}$$

7. Objective Function
Constraints

$z = 4x + y$
$$\begin{cases} x \geq 0, y \geq 0 \\ 2x + 3y \leq 12 \\ x + y \geq 3 \end{cases}$$

8. Objective Function
Constraints

$z = x + 6y$
$$\begin{cases} x \geq 0, y \geq 0 \\ 2x + y \leq 10 \\ x - 2y \geq -10 \end{cases}$$

9. Objective Function
Constraints

$z = 3x - 2y$
$$\begin{cases} 1 \leq x \leq 5 \\ y \geq 2 \\ x - y \geq -3 \end{cases}$$

10. Objective Function
Constraints

$z = 5x - 2y$
$$\begin{cases} 0 \leq x \leq 5 \\ 0 \leq y \leq 3 \\ x + y \geq 2 \end{cases}$$

11. Objective Function
Constraints

$z = 4x + 2y$
$$\begin{cases} x \geq 0, y \geq 0 \\ 2x + 3y \leq 12 \\ 3x + 2y \leq 12 \\ x + y \geq 2 \end{cases}$$

12. Objective Function

Constraints

$z = 2x + 4y$

$$\begin{cases} x \geq 0, y \geq 0 \\ x + 3y \geq 6 \\ x + y \geq 3 \\ x + y \leq 9 \end{cases}$$

13. Objective Function

Constraints

$z = 10x + 12y$

$$\begin{cases} x \geq 0, y \geq 0 \\ x + y \leq 7 \\ 2x + y \leq 10 \\ 2x + 3y \leq 18 \end{cases}$$

14. Objective Function

Constraints

$z = 5x + 6y$

$$\begin{cases} x \geq 0, y \geq 0 \\ 2x + y \geq 10 \\ x + 2y \geq 10 \\ x + y \leq 10 \end{cases}$$

Application Exercises

15. A television manufacturer makes rear-projection and plasma televisions. The profit per unit is $125 for the rear-projection televisions and $200 for the plasma televisions.

 a. Let $x =$ the number of rear-projection televisions manufactured in a month and let $y =$ the number of plasma televisions manufactured in a month. Write the objective function that models the total monthly profit.

 b. The manufacturer is bound by the following constraints:

 • Equipment in the factory allows for making at most 450 rear-projection televisions in one month.

 • Equipment in the factory allows for making at most 200 plasma televisions in one month.

 • The cost to the manufacturer per unit is $600 for the rear-projection televisions and $900 for the plasma televisions. Total monthly costs cannot exceed $360,000.

 Write a system of three inequalities that models these constraints.

 c. Graph the system of inequalities in part (b). Use only the first quadrant and its boundary, because x and y must both be nonnegative.

 d. Evaluate the objective function for total monthly profit at each of the five vertices of the graphed region. [The vertices should occur at $(0, 0)$, $(0, 200)$, $(300, 200)$, $(450, 100)$, and $(450, 0)$.]

 e. Complete the missing portions of this statement: The television manufacturer will make the greatest profit by manufacturing _____ rear-projection televisions each month and _____ plasma televisions each month. The maximum monthly profit is $ _____.

16. a. A student earns $10 per hour for tutoring and $7 per hour as a teacher's aid. Let $x =$ the number of hours each week spent tutoring and let $y =$ the number of hours each week spent as a teacher's aid. Write the objective function that models total weekly earnings.

 b. The student is bound by the following constraints:

 • To have enough time for studies, the student can work no more than 20 hours per week.

 • The tutoring center requires that each tutor spend at least three hours per week tutoring.

 • The tutoring center requires that each tutor spend no more than eight hours per week tutoring.

 Write a system of three inequalities that models these constraints.

 c. Graph the system of inequalities in part (b). Use only the first quadrant and its boundary, because x and y are nonnegative.

 d. Evaluate the objective function for total weekly earnings at each of the four vertices of the graphed region. [The vertices should occur at $(3, 0)$, $(8, 0)$, $(3, 17)$, and $(8, 12)$.]

 e. Complete the missing portions of this statement: The student can earn the maximum amount per week by tutoring for _____ hours per week and working as a teacher's aid for _____ hours per week. The maximum amount that the student can earn each week is $ _____.

Use the two steps for solving a linear programming problem, given in the box on page 543, to solve the problems in Exercises 17–23.

17. A manufacturer produces two models of mountain bicycles. The times (in hours) required for assembling and painting each model are given in the following table:

	Model A	Model B
Assembling	5	4
Painting	2	3

The maximum total weekly hours available in the assembly department and the paint department are 200 hours and 108 hours, respectively. The profits per unit are $25 for model A and $15 for model B. How many of each type should be produced to maximize profit?

18. A large institution is preparing lunch menus containing foods A and B. The specifications for the two foods are given in the following table:

Food	Units of Fat per Ounce	Units of Carbohydrates per Ounce	Units of Protein per Ounce
A	1	2	1
B	1	1	1

Each lunch must provide at least 6 units of fat per serving, no more than 7 units of protein, and at least 10 units of carbohydrates. The institution can purchase food A for $0.12 per ounce and food B for $0.08 per ounce. How many ounces of each food should a serving contain to meet the dietary requirements at the least cost?

19. Food and clothing are shipped to survivors of a natural disaster. Each carton of food will feed 12 people, while each carton of clothing will help 5 people. Each 20-cubic-foot box of food weighs 50 pounds and each 10-cubic-foot box of clothing weighs 20 pounds. The commercial carriers transporting food and clothing are bound by the following constraints:

 • The total weight per carrier cannot exceed 19,000 pounds.

 • The total volume must be less than 8000 cubic feet.

 How many cartons of food and clothing should be sent with each plane shipment to maximize the number of people who can be helped?

20. On June 24, 1948, the former Soviet Union blocked all land and water routes through East Germany to Berlin. A gigantic airlift was organized using American and British planes to bring food, clothing, and other supplies to the more than 2 million people in West Berlin. The cargo capacity was 30,000 cubic feet for an American plane and 20,000 cubic feet for a British plane. To break the Soviet blockade, the Western Allies had to maximize cargo capacity, but were subject to the following restrictions:

- No more than 44 planes could be used.

- The larger American planes required 16 personnel per flight, double that of the requirement for the British planes. The total number of personnel available could not exceed 512.

- The cost of an American flight was $9000 and the cost of a British flight was $5000. Total weekly costs could not exceed $300,000.

Find the number of American and British planes that were used to maximize cargo capacity.

21. A theater is presenting a program for students and their parents on drinking and driving. The proceeds will be donated to a local alcohol information center. Admission is $2.00 for parents and $1.00 for students. However, the situation has two constraints: The theater can hold no more than 150 people and every two parents must bring at least one student. How many parents and students should attend to raise the maximum amount of money?

22. You are about to take a test that contains computation problems worth 6 points each and word problems worth 10 points each. You can do a computation problem in 2 minutes and a word problem in 4 minutes. You have 40 minutes to take the test and may answer no more than 12 problems. Assuming you answer all the problems attempted correctly, how many of each type of problem must you answer to maximize your score? What is the maximum score?

23. In 1978, a ruling by the Civil Aeronautics Board allowed Federal Express to purchase larger aircraft. Federal Express's options included 20 Boeing 727s that United Airlines was retiring and/or the French-built Dassault Fanjet Falcon 20. To aid in their decision, executives at Federal Express analyzed the following data:

	Boeing 727	Falcon 20
Direct Operating Cost	$1400 per hour	$500 per hour
Payload	42,000 pounds	6000 pounds

Federal Express was faced with the following constraints:

- Hourly operating cost was limited to $35,000.

- Total payload had to be at least 672,000 pounds.

- Only twenty 727s were available.

Given the constraints, how many of each kind of aircraft should Federal Express have purchased to maximize the number of aircraft?

Writing in Mathematics

24. What kinds of problems are solved using the linear programming method?

25. What is an objective function in a linear programming problem?

26. What is a constraint in a linear programming problem? How is a constraint represented?

27. In your own words, describe how to solve a linear programming problem.

28. Describe a situation in your life in which you would really like to maximize something, but you are limited by at least two constraints. Can linear programming be used in this situation? Explain your answer.

Critical Thinking Exercises

Make Sense? *In Exercises 29–32, determine whether each statement makes sense or does not make sense, and explain your reasoning.*

29. In order to solve a linear programming problem, I use the graph representing the constraints and the graph of the objective function.

30. I use the coordinates of each vertex from my graph representing the constraints to find the values that maximize or minimize an objective function.

31. I need to be able to graph systems of linear inequalities in order to solve linear programming problems.

32. An important application of linear programming for businesses involves maximizing profit.

33. Suppose that you inherit $10,000. The will states how you must invest the money. Some (or all) of the money must be invested in stocks and bonds. The requirements are that at least $3000 be invested in bonds, with expected returns of $0.08 per dollar, and at least $2000 be invested in stocks, with expected returns of $0.12 per dollar. Because the stocks are medium risk, the final stipulation requires that the investment in bonds should never be less than the investment in stocks. How should the money be invested so as to maximize your expected returns?

34. Consider the objective function $z = Ax + By$ $(A > 0$ and $B > 0)$ subject to the following constraints: $2x + 3y \le 9$, $x - y \le 2$, $x \ge 0$, and $y \ge 0$. Prove that the objective function will have the same maximum value at the vertices $(3, 1)$ and $(0, 3)$ if $A = \frac{2}{3}B$.

Group Exercises

35. Group members should choose a particular field of interest. Research how linear programming is used to solve problems in that field. If possible, investigate the solution of a specific practical problem. Present a report on your findings, including the contributions of George Dantzig, Narendra Karmarkar, and L. G. Khachion to linear programming.

36. Members of the group should interview a business executive who is in charge of deciding the product mix for a business. How are production policy decisions made? Are other methods used in conjunction with linear programming? What are these methods? What sort of academic background, particularly in mathematics, does this executive have? Present a group report addressing these questions, emphasizing the role of linear programming for the business.

Preview Exercises

Exercises 37–39 will help you prepare for the material covered in the first section of the next chapter.

37. Solve the system:

$$\begin{cases} x + y + 2z = 19 \\ y + 2z = 13 \\ z = 5. \end{cases}$$

What makes it fairly easy to find the solution?

38. Solve the system:

$$\begin{cases} w - x + 2y - 2z = -1 \\ x - \frac{1}{3}y + z = \frac{8}{3} \\ y - z = 1 \\ z = 3. \end{cases}$$

Express the solution set in the form $\{(w, x, y, z)\}$. What makes it fairly easy to find the solution?

39. Consider the following array of numbers:

$$\begin{bmatrix} 1 & 2 & -1 \\ 4 & -3 & -15 \end{bmatrix}.$$

Rewrite the array as follows: Multiply each number in the top row by -4 and add this product to the corresponding number in the bottom row. Do not change the numbers in the top row.

Chapter 5 Summary, Review, and Test

Summary

DEFINITIONS AND CONCEPTS	EXAMPLES
5.1 Systems of Linear Equations in Two Variables	
a. Two equations in the form $Ax + By = C$ are called a system of linear equations. A solution of the system is an ordered pair that satisfies both equations in the system.	Ex. 1, p. 482
b. Systems of linear equations in two variables can be solved by eliminating a variable, using the substitution method (see the box on page 484) or the addition method (see the box on page 486).	Ex. 2, p. 484; Ex. 3, p. 486; Ex. 4, p. 487
c. Some linear systems have no solution and are called inconsistent systems; others have infinitely many solutions. The equations in a linear system with infinitely many solutions are called dependent. For details, see the box on page 488.	Ex. 5, p. 488; Ex. 6, p. 489
d. Functions of Business **Revenue Function** $$R(x) = (\text{price per unit sold})x$$ **Cost Function** $$C(x) = \text{fixed cost} + (\text{cost per unit produced})x$$ **Profit Function** $$P(x) = R(x) - C(x)$$ The point of intersection of the graphs of R and C is the break-even point. The x-coordinate of the point reveals the number of units that a company must produce and sell so that the money coming in, the revenue, is equal to the money going out, the cost. The y-coordinate gives the amount of money coming in and going out.	Ex. 7, p. 490; Figure 5.7, p. 492
5.2 Systems of Linear Equations in Three Variables	
a. Three equations in the form $Ax + By + Cz = D$ are called a system of linear equations in three variables. A solution of the system is an ordered triple that satisfies all three equations in the system.	Ex. 1, p. 498
b. A system of linear equations in three variables can be solved by eliminating variables. Use the addition method to eliminate any variable, reducing the system to two equations in two variables. Use substitution or the addition method to solve the resulting system in two variables. Details are found in the box on page 499.	Ex. 2, p. 499; Ex. 3, p. 501
c. Three points that do not lie on a line determine the graph of a quadratic function $y = ax^2 + bx + c$. Use the three given points to create a system of three equations. Solve the system to find a, b, and c.	Ex. 4, p. 502

DEFINITIONS AND CONCEPTS **EXAMPLES**

5.3 Partial Fractions

a. Partial fraction decomposition is used on rational expressions in which the numerator and denominator have no common factors and the highest power in the numerator is less than the highest power in the denominator. The steps in partial fraction decomposition are given in the box on page 509.

b. Include one partial fraction with a constant numerator for each distinct linear factor in the denominator. Include one partial fraction with a constant numerator for each power of a repeated linear factor in the denominator.

Ex. 1, p. 508;
Ex. 2, p. 510

c. Include one partial fraction with a linear numerator for each distinct prime quadratic factor in the denominator. Include one partial fraction with a linear numerator for each power of a prime, repeated quadratic factor in the denominator.

Ex. 3, p. 512;
Ex. 4, p. 514

5.4 Systems of Nonlinear Equations in Two Variables

a. A system of two nonlinear equations in two variables contains at least one equation that cannot be expressed as $Ax + By = C$.

b. Systems of nonlinear equations in two variables can be solved algebraically by eliminating all occurrences of one of the variables by the substitution or addition methods.

Ex. 1, p. 518;
Ex. 2, p. 519;
Ex. 3, p. 520;
Ex. 4, p. 522

5.5 Systems of Inequalities

a. A linear inequality in two variables can be written in the form
$Ax + By > C, Ax + By \geq C, Ax + By < C,$ or $Ax + By \leq C$.

b. The procedure for graphing a linear inequality in two variables is given in the box on page 529. A nonlinear inequality in two variables is graphed using the same procedure.

Ex. 1, p. 529;
Ex. 2, p. 530;
Ex. 3, p. 531;
Ex. 4, p. 532

c. To graph the solution set of a system of inequalities, graph each inequality in the system in the same rectangular coordinate system. Then find the region, if there is one, that is common to every graph in the system.

Ex. 6, p. 534;
Ex. 7, p. 535;
Ex. 8, p. 536

5.6 Linear Programming

a. An objective function is an algebraic expression in three variables describing a quantity that must be maximized or minimized.

Ex. 1, p. 541

b. Constraints are restrictions, expressed as linear inequalities.

Ex. 2, p. 542;
Ex. 3, p. 542

c. Steps for solving a linear programming problem are given in the box on page 543.

Ex. 4, p. 543;
Ex. 5, p. 544

Review Exercises

5.1

In Exercises 1–5, solve by the method of your choice. Identify systems with no solution and systems with infinitely many solutions, using set notation to express their solution sets.

1. $\begin{cases} y = 4x + 1 \\ 3x + 2y = 13 \end{cases}$

2. $\begin{cases} x + 4y = 14 \\ 2x - y = 1 \end{cases}$

3. $\begin{cases} 5x + 3y = 1 \\ 3x + 4y = -6 \end{cases}$

4. $\begin{cases} 2y - 6x = 7 \\ 3x - y = 9 \end{cases}$

5. $\begin{cases} 4x - 8y = 16 \\ 3x - 6y = 12 \end{cases}$

6. A company is planning to manufacture computer desks. The fixed cost will be $60,000 and it will cost $200 to produce each desk. Each desk will be sold for $450.
 a. Write the cost function, C, of producing x desks.
 b. Write the revenue function, R, from the sale of x desks.
 c. Determine the break-even point. Describe what this means.

7.

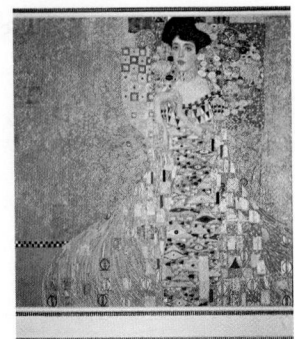

Gustav Klimt (1826–1918) "Mrs. Adele Bloch-Bauer, I", 1907. Oil on canvas, 138 × 138 cm. Private Collection. Photo: Erich Lessing/Art Resource, NY

Pablo Picasso (1881–1973) "Boy with a Pipe", 1905 (oil on canvas). Collection of Mr. and Mrs. John Hay Whitney, New York, USA. © DACS/The Bridgeman Art Library. © 2008 Estate of Pablo Picasso/Artists Rights Society (ARS), New York

Talk about paintings by numbers: In 2007, this glittering Klimt set the record for the most ever paid for a painting, a title that had been held by Picasso's *Boy with a Pipe*. Combined, the two paintings sold for $239 million. The difference between the selling price for Klimt's work and the selling price for Picasso's work was $31 million. Find the amount paid for each painting.

8. The graph shows that from 2000 through 2006, Americans unplugged land lines and switched to cellphones.

Number of Cellphone and Land-Line Customers in the United States

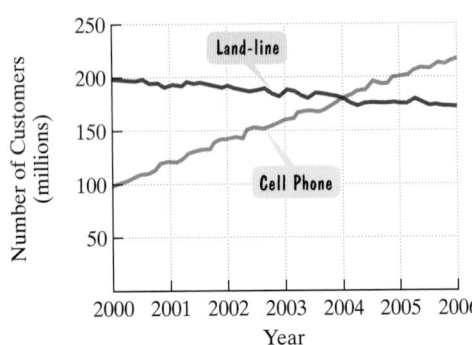

Source: Federal Communications Commission

a. Use the graphs to estimate the point of intersection. In what year was the number of cellphone and land-line customers the same? How many millions of customers were there for each?

b. In 2000, there were 98 million cellphone customers. For the period shown by the graph, this has increased at an average rate of 19.8 million customers per year. Write a function that models the number of cellphone customers, y, in millions, x years after 2000.

c. The function $4.3x + y = 198$ models the number of land-line customers, y, in millions, x years after 2000. Use this model and the model you obtained in part (b) to determine the year, rounded to the nearest year, when the number of cellphone and land-line customers was the

same. According to the models, how many millions of customers, rounded to the nearest ten million, were there for each?

d. How well do the models in parts (b) and (c) describe the point of intersection of the graphs that you estimated in part (a)?

9. The perimeter of a rectangular table top is 34 feet. The difference between 4 times the length and 3 times the width is 33 feet. Find the dimensions.

10. A travel agent offers two package vacation plans. The first plan costs $360 and includes 3 days at a hotel and a rental car for 2 days. The second plan costs $500 and includes 4 days at a hotel and a rental car for 3 days. The daily charge for the hotel is the same under each plan, as is the daily charge for the car. Find the cost per day for the hotel and for the car.

11. The calorie-nutrient information for an apple and an avocado is given in the table. How many of each should be eaten to get exactly 1000 calories and 100 grams of carbohydrates?

	One Apple	**One Avocado**
Calories	100	350
Carbohydrates (grams)	24	14

5.2

Solve each system in Exercises 12–13.

12. $\begin{cases} 2x - y + z = 1 \\ 3x - 3y + 4z = 5 \\ 4x - 2y + 3z = 4 \end{cases}$

13. $\begin{cases} x + 2y - z = 5 \\ 2x - y + 3z = 0 \\ 2y + z = 1 \end{cases}$

14. Find the quadratic function $y = ax^2 + bx + c$ whose graph passes through the points $(1, 4), (3, 20),$ and $(-2, 25)$.

15. The bar graph shows the average debt in the United States, not including real estate mortgages, by age group. The difference between the average debt for the 30–39 age group and the 18–29 age group is $8100. The difference between the average debt for the 40–49 age group and the 30–39 age group is $3100. The combined average debt for these three age groups is $44,200. Find the average debt for each of these age groups.

Average Debt by Age

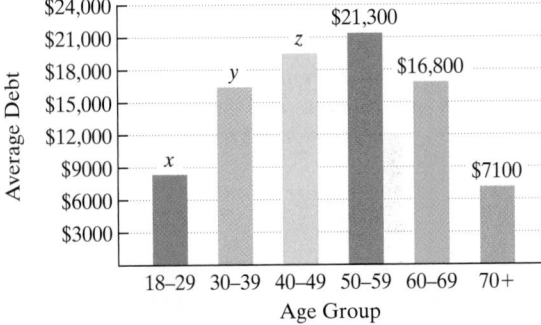

Source: Experian

5.3

In Exercises 16–24, write the partial fraction decomposition of each rational expression.

16. $\dfrac{x}{(x-3)(x+2)}$

17. $\dfrac{11x-2}{x^2-x-12}$

18. $\dfrac{4x^2-3x-4}{x(x+2)(x-1)}$

19. $\dfrac{2x+1}{(x-2)^2}$

20. $\dfrac{2x-6}{(x-1)(x-2)^2}$

21. $\dfrac{3x}{(x-2)(x^2+1)}$

22. $\dfrac{7x^2-7x+23}{(x-3)(x^2+4)}$

23. $\dfrac{x^3}{(x^2+4)^2}$

24. $\dfrac{4x^3+5x^2+7x-1}{(x^2+x+1)^2}$

5.4

In Exercises 25–35, solve each system by the method of your choice.

25. $\begin{cases} 5y = x^2 - 1 \\ x - y = 1 \end{cases}$

26. $\begin{cases} y = x^2 + 2x + 1 \\ x + y = 1 \end{cases}$

27. $\begin{cases} x^2 + y^2 = 2 \\ x + y = 0 \end{cases}$

28. $\begin{cases} 2x^2 + y^2 = 24 \\ x^2 + y^2 = 15 \end{cases}$

29. $\begin{cases} xy - 4 = 0 \\ y - x = 0 \end{cases}$

30. $\begin{cases} y^2 = 4x \\ x - 2y + 3 = 0 \end{cases}$

31. $\begin{cases} x^2 + y^2 = 10 \\ y = x + 2 \end{cases}$

32. $\begin{cases} xy = 1 \\ y = 2x + 1 \end{cases}$

33. $\begin{cases} x + y + 1 = 0 \\ x^2 + y^2 + 6y - x = -5 \end{cases}$

34. $\begin{cases} x^2 + y^2 = 13 \\ x^2 - y = 7 \end{cases}$

35. $\begin{cases} 2x^2 + 3y^2 = 21 \\ 3x^2 - 4y^2 = 23 \end{cases}$

36. The perimeter of a rectangle is 26 meters and its area is 40 square meters. Find its dimensions.

37. Find the coordinates of all points (x, y) that lie on the line whose equation is $2x + y = 8$, so that the area of the rectangle shown in the figure is 6 square units.

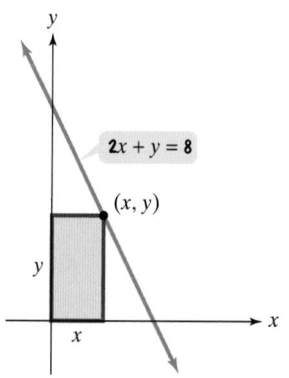

38. Two adjoining square fields with an area of 2900 square feet are to be enclosed with 240 feet of fencing. The situation is represented in the figure. Find the length of each side where a variable appears.

5.5

In Exercises 39–45, graph each inequality.

39. $3x - 4y > 12$

40. $y \le -\dfrac{1}{2}x + 2$

41. $x < -2$

42. $y \ge 3$

43. $x^2 + y^2 > 4$

44. $y \le x^2 - 1$

45. $y \le 2^x$

In Exercises 46–55, graph the solution set of each system of inequalities or indicate that the system has no solution.

46. $\begin{cases} 3x + 2y \ge 6 \\ 2x + y \ge 6 \end{cases}$

47. $\begin{cases} 2x - y \ge 4 \\ x + 2y < 2 \end{cases}$

48. $\begin{cases} y < x \\ y \le 2 \end{cases}$

49. $\begin{cases} x + y \le 6 \\ y \ge 2x - 3 \end{cases}$

50. $\begin{cases} 0 \le x \le 3 \\ y > 2 \end{cases}$

51. $\begin{cases} 2x + y < 4 \\ 2x + y > 6 \end{cases}$

52. $\begin{cases} x^2 + y^2 \le 16 \\ x + y < 2 \end{cases}$

53. $\begin{cases} x^2 + y^2 \le 9 \\ y < -3x + 1 \end{cases}$

54. $\begin{cases} y > x^2 \\ x + y < 6 \\ y < x + 6 \end{cases}$

55. $\begin{cases} y \ge 0 \\ 3x + 2y \ge 4 \\ x - y \le 3 \end{cases}$

5.6

56. Find the value of the objective function $z = 2x + 3y$ at each corner of the graphed region shown. What is the maximum value of the objective function? What is the minimum value of the objective function?

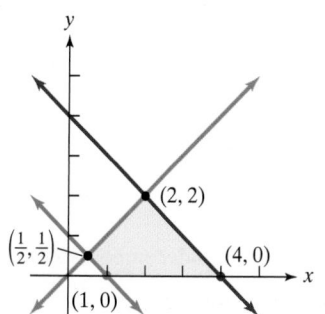

In Exercises 57–59, graph the region determined by the constraints. Then find the maximum value of the given objective function, subject to the constraints.

57. Objective Function $\qquad z = 2x + 3y$

Constraints

$$\begin{cases} x \geq 0, y \geq 0 \\ x + y \leq 8 \\ 3x + 2y \geq 6 \end{cases}$$

58. Objective Function $\qquad z = x + 4y$

Constraints

$$\begin{cases} 0 \leq x \leq 5, 0 \leq y \leq 7 \\ x + y \geq 3 \end{cases}$$

59. Objective Function $\qquad z = 5x + 6y$

Constraints

$$\begin{cases} x \geq 0, y \geq 0 \\ y \leq x \\ 2x + y \leq 12 \\ 2x + 3y \geq 6 \end{cases}$$

60. A paper manufacturing company converts wood pulp to writing paper and newsprint. The profit on a unit of writing paper is $500 and the profit on a unit of newsprint is $350.

a. Let x represent the number of units of writing paper produced daily. Let y represent the number of units of newsprint produced daily. Write the objective function that models total daily profit.

b. The manufacturer is bound by the following constraints:

• Equipment in the factory allows for making at most 200 units of paper (writing paper and newsprint) in a day.

• Regular customers require at least 10 units of writing paper and at least 80 units of newsprint daily.

Write a system of inequalities that models these constraints.

c. Graph the inequalities in part (b). Use only the first quadrant, because x and y must both be positive. (*Suggestion:* Let each unit along the x- and y-axes represent 20.)

d. Evaluate the objective function at each of the three vertices of the graphed region.

e. Complete the missing portions of this statement: The company will make the greatest profit by producing _____ units of writing paper and _____ units of newsprint each day. The maximum daily profit is $ _____.

61. A manufacturer of lightweight tents makes two models whose specifications are given in the following table:

	Cutting Time per Tent	Assembly Time per Tent
Model A	0.9 hour	0.8 hour
Model B	1.8 hours	1.2 hours

On a monthly basis, the manufacturer has no more than 864 hours of labor available in the cutting department and at most 672 hours in the assembly division. The profits come to $25 per tent for model A and $40 per tent for model B. How many of each should be manufactured monthly to maximize the profit?

CHAPTER

Test Prep

VIDEOS

Chapter 5 Test

In Exercises 1–5, solve the system.

1. $\begin{cases} x = y + 4 \\ 3x + 7y = -18 \end{cases}$

2. $\begin{cases} 2x + 5y = -2 \\ 3x - 4y = 20 \end{cases}$

3. $\begin{cases} x + y + z = 6 \\ 3x + 4y - 7z = 1 \\ 2x - y + 3z = 5 \end{cases}$

4. $\begin{cases} x^2 + y^2 = 25 \\ x + y = 1 \end{cases}$

5. $\begin{cases} 2x^2 - 5y^2 = -2 \\ 3x^2 + 2y^2 = 35 \end{cases}$

6. Find the partial fraction decomposition for $\dfrac{x}{(x+1)(x^2+9)}$.

In Exercises 7–10, graph the solution set of each inequality or system of inequalities.

7. $x - 2y < 8$

8. $\begin{cases} x \geq 0, y \geq 0 \\ 3x + y \leq 9 \\ 2x + 3y \geq 6 \end{cases}$

9. $\begin{cases} x^2 + y^2 > 1 \\ x^2 + y^2 < 4 \end{cases}$

10. $\begin{cases} y \leq 1 - x^2 \\ x^2 + y^2 \leq 9 \end{cases}$

11. Find the maximum value of the objective function $z = 3x + 5y$ subject to the following constraints: $x \geq 0, y \geq 0, x + y \leq 6, x \geq 2$.

12. Health experts agree that cholesterol intake should be limited to 300 mg or less each day. Three ounces of shrimp and 2 ounces of scallops contain 156 mg of cholesterol. Five ounces of shrimp and 3 ounces of scallops contain 45 mg of cholesterol less than the suggested maximum daily intake. Determine the cholesterol content in an ounce of each item.

13. A company is planning to produce and sell a new line of computers. The fixed cost will be $360,000 and it will cost $850 to produce each computer. Each computer will be sold for $1150.

 a. Write the cost function, C, of producing x computers.

 b. Write the revenue function, R, from the sale of x computers.

 c. Determine the break-even point. Describe what this means.

14. Find the quadratic function whose graph passes through the points $(-1, -2)$, $(2, 1)$, and $(-2, 1)$.

15. The rectangular plot of land shown in the figure is to be fenced along three sides using 39 feet of fencing. No fencing is to be placed along the river's edge. The area of the plot is 180 square feet. What are its dimensions?

16. A manufacturer makes two types of jet skis, regular and deluxe. The profit on a regular jet ski is $200 and the profit on the deluxe model is $250. To meet customer demand, the company must manufacture at least 50 regular jet skis per week and at least 75 deluxe models. To maintain high quality, the total number of both models of jet skis manufactured by the company should not exceed 150 per week. How many jet skis of each type should be manufactured per week to obtain maximum profit? What is the maximum weekly profit?

Cumulative Review Exercises (Chapters 1–5)

The figure shows the graph of $y = f(x)$ and its two vertical asymptotes. Use the graph to solve Exercises 1–10.

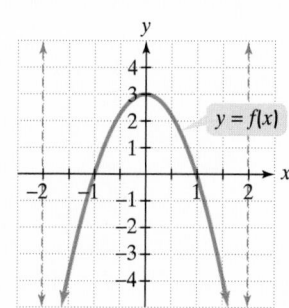

1. Find the domain and the range of f.

2. Find the zeros.

3. What is the relative maximum and where does it occur?

4. Find the interval(s) on which f is decreasing.

5. Is $f(-0.7)$ positive or negative?

6. Find $(f \circ f)(-1)$.

7. Use arrow notation to complete this statement:

 $f(x) \to -\infty$ as _____ or as _____ .

8. Does f appear to be even, odd, or neither?

9. Graph $g(x) = f(x + 2) - 1$.

10. Graph $h(x) = \frac{1}{2}f\left(\frac{1}{2}x\right)$.

In Exercises 11–21, solve each equation, inequality, or system of equations.

11. $\sqrt{x^2 - 3x} = 2x - 6$

12. $4x^2 = 8x - 7$

13. $\left|\dfrac{x}{3} + 2\right| < 4$

14. $\dfrac{x + 5}{x - 1} > 2$

15. $2x^3 + x^2 - 13x + 6 = 0$

16. $6x - 3(5x + 2) = 4(1 - x)$

17. $\log(x + 3) + \log x = 1$

18. $3^{x+2} = 11$

19. $x^{\frac{1}{2}} - 2x^{\frac{1}{4}} - 15 = 0$

20. $\begin{cases} 3x - y = -2 \\ 2x^2 - y = 0 \end{cases}$

21. $\begin{cases} x + 2y + 3z = -2 \\ 3x + 3y + 10z = -2 \\ 2y - 5z = 6 \end{cases}$

In Exercises 22–28, graph each equation, function, or inequality in a rectangular coordinate system. If two functions are indicated, graph both in the same system.

22. $f(x) = (x + 2)^2 - 4$

23. $2x - 3y \le 6$

24. $y = 3^{x-2}$

25. $f(x) = \dfrac{x^2 - x - 6}{x + 1}$

26. $f(x) = 2x - 4$ and f^{-1}

27. $(x - 2)^2 + (y - 4)^2 > 9$

28. $f(x) = |x|$ and $g(x) = -|x - 2|$

In Exercises 29–30, let $f(x) = 2x^2 - x - 1$ *and* $g(x) = 1 - x$.

29. Find $(f \circ g)(x)$ and $(g \circ f)(x)$.

30. Find $\dfrac{f(x + h) - f(x)}{h}$ and simplify.

In Exercises 31–32, write the linear function in slope-intercept form satisfying the given conditions.

31. Graph of f passes through $(2, 4)$ and $(4, -2)$.

32. Graph of g passes through $(-1, 0)$ and is perpendicular to the line whose equation is $x + 3y - 6 = 0$.

33. You invested $4000 in two stocks paying 12% and 14% annual interest. At the end of the year, the total interest from these investments was $508. How much was invested at each rate?

34. The length of a rectangle is 1 meter more than twice the width. If the rectangle's area is 36 square meters, find its dimensions.

35. What interest rate is required for an investment of $6000 subject to continuous compounding to grow to $18,000 in 10 years?

Matrices and Determinants

6

You are being drawn deeper into cyberspace, spending more time online each week. With constantly improving high-resolution images, cyberspace is reshaping your life by nourishing shared enthusiasms. The people who built your computer talk of bandwidth that will give you the visual experience, in high-definition 3-D format, of being in the same room with a person who is actually in another city. Rectangular arrays of numbers, called matrices, play a central role in representing computer images and in the forthcoming technology of tele-immersion.

The use of rectangular arrays of numbers in the digital representation of images and the manipulation of images on a computer screen is discussed in Examples 8 and 9 in Section 6.3.

Section 6.1 **Matrix Solutions to Linear Systems**

Objectives

1 Write the augmented matrix for a linear system.
2 Perform matrix row operations.
3 Use matrices and Gaussian elimination to solve systems.
4 Use matrices and Gauss-Jordan elimination to solve systems.

The data below show that we spend a lot of time sprucing up.

Average Number of Minutes per Day Americans Spend on Grooming

	Ages 15–19	Ages 20–24	Ages 45–54	Ages 65+	Married	Single
Men	37	37	34	28	31	34
Women	59	49	46	46	44	50

Source: Bureau of Labor Statistics' American Time-Use Survey

The 12 numbers inside the brackets are arranged in two rows and six columns. This rectangular array of 12 numbers, arranged in rows and columns and placed in brackets, is an example of a **matrix** (plural: **matrices**). The numbers inside the brackets are called **elements** of the matrix. Matrices are used to display information and to solve systems of linear equations. Because systems involving two equations in two variables can easily be solved by substitution or addition, we will focus on matrix solutions to systems of linear equations in three or more variables.

1 Write the augmented matrix for a linear system.

Augmented Matrices

A matrix gives us a shortened way of writing a system of equations. The first step in solving a system of linear equations using matrices is to write the *augmented matrix*. An **augmented matrix** has a vertical bar separating the columns of the matrix into two groups. The coefficients of each variable are placed to the left of the vertical line and the constants are placed to the right. If any variable is missing, its coefficient is 0. Here are two examples:

System of Linear Equations

$$\begin{cases} 3x + y + 2z = 31 \\ x + y + 2z = 19 \\ x + 3y + 2z = 25 \end{cases}$$

$$\begin{cases} x + 2y - 5z = -19 \\ y + 3z = 9 \\ z = 4 \end{cases}$$

Augmented Matrix

$$\begin{bmatrix} 3 & 1 & 2 & | & 31 \\ 1 & 1 & 2 & | & 19 \\ 1 & 3 & 2 & | & 25 \end{bmatrix}$$

$$\begin{bmatrix} 1 & 2 & -5 & | & -19 \\ 0 & 1 & 3 & | & 9 \\ 0 & 0 & 1 & | & 4 \end{bmatrix}.$$

Our goal in solving a system of linear equations in three variables using matrices is to produce a matrix with 1s down the diagonal from upper left to lower right on the left side of the vertical bar, called the **main diagonal**, and 0s below the 1s. In general, the matrix will be of the form

$$\left[\begin{array}{ccc|c} 1 & a & b & c \\ 0 & 1 & d & e \\ 0 & 0 & 1 & f \end{array}\right],$$

where a through f represent real numbers. The third row of this matrix gives us the value of one variable. The other variables can then be found by back-substitution.

② Perform matrix row operations.

Matrix Row Operations

A matrix with 1s down the main diagonal and 0s below the 1s is said to be in **row-echelon form**. How do we produce a matrix in this form? We use **row operations** on the augmented matrix. These row operations are just like what you did when solving a linear system by the addition method. The difference is that we no longer write the variables, usually represented by x, y, and z.

Matrix Row Operations

The following row operations produce matrices that represent systems with the same solution set:

1. Two rows of a matrix may be interchanged. This is the same as interchanging two equations in a linear system.

2. The elements in any row may be multiplied by a nonzero number. This is the same as multiplying both sides of an equation by a nonzero number.

3. The elements in any row may be multiplied by a nonzero number, and these products may be added to the corresponding elements in any other row. This is the same as multiplying both sides of an equation by a nonzero number and then adding equations to eliminate a variable.

Two matrices are **row equivalent** if one can be obtained from the other by a sequence of row operations.

Study Tip

When performing the row operation

$$kR_i + R_j$$

you use row i to find the products. However, **elements in row i do not change. It is the elements in row j that change:** Add k times the elements in row i to the corresponding elements in row j. Replace elements in row j by these sums.

Each matrix row operation in the preceding box can be expressed symbolically as follows:

1. Interchange the elements in the ith and jth rows: $R_i \leftrightarrow R_j$.

2. Multiply each element in the ith row by k: kR_i.

3. Add k times the elements in row i to the corresponding elements in row j: $kR_i + R_j$.

(**EXAMPLE 1**) **Performing Matrix Row Operations**

Use the matrix

$$\left[\begin{array}{ccc|c} 3 & 18 & -12 & 21 \\ 1 & 2 & -3 & 5 \\ -2 & -3 & 4 & -6 \end{array}\right]$$

and perform each indicated row operation:

a. $R_1 \leftrightarrow R_2$ **b.** $\frac{1}{3}R_1$ **c.** $2R_2 + R_3$.

$$\begin{bmatrix} 3 & 18 & -12 & | & 21 \\ 1 & 2 & -3 & | & 5 \\ -2 & -3 & 4 & | & -6 \end{bmatrix}$$

The given matrix (repeated)

Solution

a. The notation $R_1 \leftrightarrow R_2$ means to interchange the elements in row 1 and row 2. This results in the row-equivalent matrix

$$\begin{bmatrix} 1 & 2 & -3 & | & 5 \\ 3 & 18 & -12 & | & 21 \\ -2 & -3 & 4 & | & -6 \end{bmatrix}.$$

This was row 2; now it's row 1.

This was row 1; now it's row 2.

b. The notation $\frac{1}{3}R_1$ means to multiply each element in row 1 by $\frac{1}{3}$. This results in the row-equivalent matrix

$$\begin{bmatrix} \frac{1}{3}(3) & \frac{1}{3}(18) & \frac{1}{3}(-12) & | & \frac{1}{3}(21) \\ 1 & 2 & -3 & | & 5 \\ -2 & -3 & 4 & | & -6 \end{bmatrix} = \begin{bmatrix} 1 & 6 & -4 & | & 7 \\ 1 & 2 & -3 & | & 5 \\ -2 & -3 & 4 & | & -6 \end{bmatrix}.$$

c. The notation $2R_2 + R_3$ means to add 2 times the elements in row 2 to the corresponding elements in row 3. Replace the elements in row 3 by these sums. First, we find 2 times the elements in row 2, namely, $1, 2, -3$, and 5:

$$2(1) \text{ or } 2, \qquad 2(2) \text{ or } 4, \qquad 2(-3) \text{ or } -6, \qquad 2(5) \text{ or } 10.$$

Now we add these products to the corresponding elements in row 3. Although we use row 2 to find the products, row 2 does not change. It is the elements in row 3 that change, resulting in the row-equivalent matrix

Replace row 3 by the sum of itself and 2 times row 2.

$$\begin{bmatrix} 3 & 18 & -12 & | & 21 \\ 1 & 2 & -3 & | & 5 \\ -2+2=0 & -3+4=1 & 4+(-6)=-2 & | & -6+10=4 \end{bmatrix} = \begin{bmatrix} 3 & 18 & -12 & | & 21 \\ 1 & 2 & -3 & | & 5 \\ 0 & 1 & -2 & | & 4 \end{bmatrix}.$$

⊘ **Check Point** ┃ Use the matrix

$$\begin{bmatrix} 4 & 12 & -20 & | & 8 \\ 1 & 6 & -3 & | & 7 \\ -3 & -2 & 1 & | & -9 \end{bmatrix}$$

and perform each indicated row operation:

a. $R_1 \leftrightarrow R_2$ **b.** $\frac{1}{4}R_1$ **c.** $3R_2 + R_3$.

③ Use matrices and Gaussian elimination to solve systems.

Solving Linear Systems Using Gaussian Elimination

The process that we use to solve linear systems using matrix row operations is called **Gaussian elimination**, after the German mathematician Carl Friedrich Gauss (1777–1855). Here are the steps used in Gaussian elimination:

Solving Linear Systems of Three Equations with Three Variables Using Gaussian Elimination

1. Write the augmented matrix for the system.

2. Use matrix row operations to simplify the matrix to a row-equivalent matrix in row-echelon form, with 1s down the main diagonal from upper left to lower right, and 0s below the 1s in the first and second columns.

$$\begin{bmatrix} 1 & * & * & | & * \\ * & * & * & | & * \\ * & * & * & | & * \end{bmatrix} \rightarrow \begin{bmatrix} 1 & * & * & | & * \\ 0 & * & * & | & * \\ 0 & * & * & | & * \end{bmatrix} \rightarrow \begin{bmatrix} 1 & * & * & | & * \\ 0 & 1 & * & | & * \\ 0 & * & * & | & * \end{bmatrix} \rightarrow \begin{bmatrix} 1 & * & * & | & * \\ 0 & 1 & * & | & * \\ 0 & 0 & * & | & * \end{bmatrix} \rightarrow \begin{bmatrix} 1 & * & * & | & * \\ 0 & 1 & * & | & * \\ 0 & 0 & 1 & | & * \end{bmatrix}$$

Get 1 in the upper left-hand corner.

Use the 1 in the first column to get 0s below it.

Get 1 in the second row, second column position.

Use the 1 in the second column to get 0 below it.

Get 1 in the third row, third column position.

3. Write the system of linear equations corresponding to the matrix in step 2 and use back-substitution to find the system's solution.

(EXAMPLE 2) **Gaussian Elimination with Back-Substitution**

Use matrices to solve the system:

$$\begin{cases} 3x + y + 2z = 31 \\ x + y + 2z = 19 \\ x + 3y + 2z = 25. \end{cases}$$

Solution

Step 1 Write the augmented matrix for the system.

Linear System **Augmented Matrix**

$$\begin{cases} 3x + y + 2z = 31 \\ x + y + 2z = 19 \\ x + 3y + 2z = 25 \end{cases} \qquad \begin{bmatrix} 3 & 1 & 2 & | & 31 \\ 1 & 1 & 2 & | & 19 \\ 1 & 3 & 2 & | & 25 \end{bmatrix}$$

Step 2 Use matrix row operations to simplify the matrix to row-echelon form, with 1s down the main diagonal from upper left to lower right, and 0s below the 1s in the first and second columns. Our first step in achieving this goal is to get 1 in the top position of the first column.

We want 1 in this position. $\begin{bmatrix} 3 & 1 & 2 & | & 31 \\ 1 & 1 & 2 & | & 19 \\ 1 & 3 & 2 & | & 25 \end{bmatrix}$

To get 1 in this position, we interchange row 1 and row 2: $R_1 \leftrightarrow R_2$. (We could also interchange row 1 and row 3 to attain our goal.)

$$\begin{bmatrix} 1 & 1 & 2 & | & 19 \\ 3 & 1 & 2 & | & 31 \\ 1 & 3 & 2 & | & 25 \end{bmatrix}$$

This was row 2; now it's row 1.

This was row 1; now it's row 2.

Now we want to get 0s below the 1 in the first column.

We want 0 in these positions. $\begin{bmatrix} 1 & 1 & 2 & | & 19 \\ 3 & 1 & 2 & | & 31 \\ 1 & 3 & 2 & | & 25 \end{bmatrix}$

To get a 0 where there is now a 3, multiply the top row of numbers by -3 and add these products to the second row of numbers: $-3R_1 + R_2$. To get a 0 where there is now a 1, multiply the top row of numbers by -1 and add these products to the third row of numbers: $-1R_1 + R_3$. Although we are using row 1 to find the products, the numbers in row 1 do not change.

Replace row 2 by $-3R_1 + R_2$.

Replace row 3 by $-1R_1 + R_3$.

$$\begin{bmatrix} 1 & 1 & 2 & | & 19 \\ -3(1)+3 & -3(1)+1 & -3(2)+2 & | & -3(19)+31 \\ -1(1)+1 & -1(1)+3 & -1(2)+2 & | & -1(19)+25 \end{bmatrix} = \begin{bmatrix} 1 & 1 & 2 & | & 19 \\ 0 & -2 & -4 & | & -26 \\ 0 & 2 & 0 & | & 6 \end{bmatrix}$$

We want 1 in this position.

We move on to the second column. To get 1 in the desired position, we multiply -2 by its reciprocal, $-\frac{1}{2}$. Therefore, we multiply all the numbers in the second row by $-\frac{1}{2}$: $-\frac{1}{2}R_2$.

$-\frac{1}{2}R_2$

$$\begin{bmatrix} 1 & 1 & 2 & | & 19 \\ -\frac{1}{2}(0) & -\frac{1}{2}(-2) & -\frac{1}{2}(-4) & | & -\frac{1}{2}(-26) \\ 0 & 2 & 0 & | & 6 \end{bmatrix} = \begin{bmatrix} 1 & 1 & 2 & | & 19 \\ 0 & 1 & 2 & | & 13 \\ 0 & 2 & 0 & | & 6 \end{bmatrix}.$$

We want 0 in this position.

$$\begin{bmatrix} 1 & 1 & 2 & | & 19 \\ 0 & 1 & 2 & | & 13 \\ 0 & 2 & 0 & | & 6 \end{bmatrix}$$

We want 0 in this position.

The matrix from the bottom of the previous page (repeated)

So far, our matrix row operations have resulted in the matrix that we repeated in the margin. We are not yet done with the second column. The voice balloon shows that we want to get a 0 where there is now a 2. If we multiply the second row of numbers by -2 and add these products to the third row of numbers, we will get 0 in this position: $-2R_2 + R_3$. Although we are using the numbers in row 2 to find the products, the numbers in row 2 do not change.

Replace row 3 by $-2R_2 + R_3$.

$$\begin{bmatrix} 1 & 1 & 2 & | & 19 \\ 0 & 1 & 2 & | & 13 \\ -2(0)+0 & -2(1)+2 & -2(2)+0 & | & -2(13)+6 \end{bmatrix} = \begin{bmatrix} 1 & 1 & 2 & | & 19 \\ 0 & 1 & 2 & | & 13 \\ 0 & 0 & -4 & | & -20 \end{bmatrix}$$

We want 1 in this position.

We move on to the third column. To get 1 in the desired position, we multiply -4 by its reciprocal, $-\frac{1}{4}$. Therefore, we multiply all the numbers in the third row by $-\frac{1}{4}$: $-\frac{1}{4}R_3$.

$$-\frac{1}{4}R_3 \quad \begin{bmatrix} 1 & 1 & 2 & | & 19 \\ 0 & 1 & 2 & | & 13 \\ -\frac{1}{4}(0) & -\frac{1}{4}(0) & -\frac{1}{4}(-4) & | & -\frac{1}{4}(-20) \end{bmatrix} = \begin{bmatrix} 1 & 1 & 2 & | & 19 \\ 0 & 1 & 2 & | & 13 \\ 0 & 0 & 1 & | & 5 \end{bmatrix}$$

We now have the desired matrix in row-echelon form, with 1s down the main diagonal and 0s below the 1s in the first and second columns.

Step 3 Write the system of linear equations corresponding to the matrix in step 2 and use back-substitution to find the system's solution. The system represented by the matrix in step 2 is

$$\begin{bmatrix} 1 & 1 & 2 & | & 19 \\ 0 & 1 & 2 & | & 13 \\ 0 & 0 & 1 & | & 5 \end{bmatrix} \rightarrow \begin{cases} 1x + 1y + 2z = 19 \\ 0x + 1y + 2z = 13 \\ 0x + 0y + 1z = 5 \end{cases} \text{or} \begin{cases} x + y + 2z = 19 & (1) \\ y + 2z = 13. & (2) \\ z = 5 & (3) \end{cases}$$

We immediately see from equation (3) that the value for z is 5. To find y, we back-substitute 5 for z in the second equation.

$$y + 2z = 13 \quad \text{Equation (2)}$$
$$y + 2(5) = 13 \quad \text{Substitute 5 for z.}$$
$$y + 10 = 13 \quad \text{Multiply.}$$
$$y = 3 \quad \text{Subtract 10 from both sides and solve for y.}$$

Finally, back-substitute 3 for y and 5 for z in the first equation.

$$x + y + 2z = 19 \quad \text{Equation (1)}$$
$$x + 3 + 2(5) = 19 \quad \text{Substitute 3 for y and 5 for z.}$$
$$x + 13 = 19 \quad \text{Multiply and add.}$$
$$x = 6 \quad \text{Subtract 13 from both sides and solve for x.}$$

With $z = 5$, $y = 3$, and $x = 6$, the solution set of the original system is $\{(6, 3, 5)\}$. Check to see that the solution satisfies all three equations in the given system.

Technology

Most graphing utilities can convert an augmented matrix to row-echelon form, with 1s down the main diagonal and 0s below the 1s. However, row-echelon form is not unique. Your graphing utility might give a row-echelon form different from the one you obtained by hand. However, all row-echelon forms for a given system's augmented matrix produce the same solution to the system. Enter the augmented matrix and name it A. Then use the [REF] (row-echelon form) command on matrix A.

⊘ Check Point **2** Use matrices to solve the system:

$$\begin{cases} 2x + y + 2z = 18 \\ x - y + 2z = 9 \\ x + 2y - z = 6. \end{cases}$$

Modern supercomputers are capable of solving systems with more than 600,000 variables. The augmented matrices for such systems are huge, but the solution using matrices is exactly like what we did in Example 2. Work with the augmented matrix,

one column at a time. Get 1s down the main diagonal from upper left to lower right and 0s below the 1s. Let's see how this works for a linear system involving four equations in four variables.

(**EXAMPLE 3**) **Gaussian Elimination with Back-Substitution**

Use matrices to solve the system:

$$\begin{cases} 2w + x + 3y - z = 6 \\ w - x + 2y - 2z = -1 \\ w - x - y + z = -4 \\ -w + 2x - 2y - z = -7. \end{cases}$$

Solution

Step 1 Write the augmented matrix for the system.

Linear System

$$\begin{cases} 2w + x + 3y - z = 6 \\ w - x + 2y - 2z = -1 \\ w - x - y + z = -4 \\ -w + 2x - 2y - z = -7 \end{cases}$$

Augmented Matrix

$$\left[\begin{array}{rrrr|r} 2 & 1 & 3 & -1 & 6 \\ 1 & -1 & 2 & -2 & -1 \\ 1 & -1 & -1 & 1 & -4 \\ -1 & 2 & -2 & -1 & -7 \end{array}\right]$$

Step 2 Use matrix row operations to simplify the matrix to row-echelon form, with 1s down the main diagonal from upper left to lower right, and 0s below the 1s in the first, second, and third columns. Our first step in achieving this goal is to get 1 in the top position of the first column. To do this, we interchange row 1 and row 2: $R_1 \leftrightarrow R_2$.

We want
0s in these
positions.

$$\left[\begin{array}{rrrr|r} 1 & -1 & 2 & -2 & -1 \\ 2 & 1 & 3 & -1 & 6 \\ 1 & -1 & -1 & 1 & -4 \\ -1 & 2 & -2 & -1 & -7 \end{array}\right]$$

This was row 2; now it's row 1.

This was row 1; now it's row 2.

Now we use the 1 at the top of the first column to get 0s below it.

Use the previous matrix and:
Replace row 2 by $-2R_1 + R_2$.
Replace row 3 by $-1R_1 + R_3$.
Replace row 4 by $1R_1 + R_4$.

$$\left[\begin{array}{rrrr|r} 1 & -1 & 2 & -2 & -1 \\ 0 & 3 & -1 & 3 & 8 \\ 0 & 0 & -3 & 3 & -3 \\ 0 & 1 & 0 & -3 & -8 \end{array}\right]$$

We want
1 in this
position.

We move on to the second column. We can obtain 1 in the desired position by multiplying the numbers in the second row by $\frac{1}{3}$, the reciprocal of 3.

$$\left[\begin{array}{rrrr|r} 1 & -1 & 2 & -2 & -1 \\ \frac{1}{3}(0) & \frac{1}{3}(3) & \frac{1}{3}(-1) & \frac{1}{3}(3) & \frac{1}{3}(8) \\ 0 & 0 & -3 & 3 & -3 \\ 0 & 1 & 0 & -3 & -8 \end{array}\right] = \left[\begin{array}{rrrr|r} 1 & -1 & 2 & -2 & -1 \\ 0 & 1 & -\frac{1}{3} & 1 & \frac{8}{3} \\ 0 & 0 & -3 & 3 & -3 \\ 0 & 1 & 0 & -3 & -8 \end{array}\right]$$

$\frac{1}{3}R_2$

We want 0s in these positions.
The top position already has a 0.

$$\begin{bmatrix} 1 & -1 & 2 & -2 & | & -1 \\ 0 & 1 & -\frac{1}{3} & 1 & | & \frac{8}{3} \\ 0 & 0 & -3 & 3 & | & -3 \\ 0 & 1 & 0 & -3 & | & -8 \end{bmatrix}$$

We want 0s in these positions. The top position already has a 0.

The matrix from the bottom of the previous page (repeated)

So far, our matrix row operations have resulted in the matrix that we repeated in the margin. Now we use the 1 in the second row, second column position to get 0s below it.

Replace row 4 in the previous matrix by $-1R_2 + R_4$.

$$\begin{bmatrix} 1 & -1 & 2 & -2 & | & -1 \\ 0 & 1 & -\frac{1}{3} & 1 & | & \frac{8}{3} \\ 0 & 0 & -3 & 3 & | & -3 \\ 0 & 0 & \frac{1}{3} & -4 & | & -\frac{32}{3} \end{bmatrix}$$ **We want 1 in this position.**

We move on to the third column. We can obtain 1 in the desired position by multiplying the numbers in the third row by $-\frac{1}{3}$, the reciprocal of -3.

$$\begin{bmatrix} 1 & -1 & 2 & -2 & | & -1 \\ 0 & 1 & -\frac{1}{3} & 1 & | & \frac{8}{3} \\ -\frac{1}{3}(0) & -\frac{1}{3}(0) & -\frac{1}{3}(-3) & -\frac{1}{3}(3) & | & -\frac{1}{3}(-3) \\ 0 & 0 & \frac{1}{3} & -4 & | & -\frac{32}{3} \end{bmatrix} = \begin{bmatrix} 1 & -1 & 2 & -2 & | & -1 \\ 0 & 1 & -\frac{1}{3} & 1 & | & \frac{8}{3} \\ 0 & 0 & 1 & -1 & | & 1 \\ 0 & 0 & \frac{1}{3} & -4 & | & -\frac{32}{3} \end{bmatrix}$$ $-\frac{1}{3}R_3$

We want 0 in this position.

Now we use the 1 in the third column to get 0 below it.

Replace row 4 in the previous matrix by $-\frac{1}{3}R_3 + R_4$.

$$\begin{bmatrix} 1 & -1 & 2 & -2 & | & -1 \\ 0 & 1 & -\frac{1}{3} & 1 & | & \frac{8}{3} \\ 0 & 0 & 1 & -1 & | & 1 \\ 0 & 0 & 0 & -\frac{11}{3} & | & -11 \end{bmatrix}$$ **We want 1 in this position.**

We move on to the fourth column. Because we want 1s down the diagonal from upper left to lower right, we want 1 where there is now $-\frac{11}{3}$. We can obtain 1 in this position by multiplying the numbers in the fourth row by $-\frac{3}{11}$.

$$\begin{bmatrix} 1 & -1 & 2 & -2 & | & -1 \\ 0 & 1 & -\frac{1}{3} & 1 & | & \frac{8}{3} \\ 0 & 0 & 1 & -1 & | & 1 \\ -\frac{3}{11}(0) & -\frac{3}{11}(0) & -\frac{3}{11}(0) & -\frac{3}{11}(-\frac{11}{3}) & | & -\frac{3}{11}(-11) \end{bmatrix}$$

$$= \begin{bmatrix} 1 & -1 & 2 & -2 & | & -1 \\ 0 & 1 & -\frac{1}{3} & 1 & | & \frac{8}{3} \\ 0 & 0 & 1 & -1 & | & 1 \\ 0 & 0 & 0 & 1 & | & 3 \end{bmatrix}$$ $-\frac{3}{11}R_4$

We now have the desired matrix in row-echelon form, with 1s down the main diagonal and 0s below the 1s. An equivalent row-echelon matrix can be obtained using a graphing utility and the $\boxed{\text{REF}}$ command on the augmented matrix.

Step 3 Write the system of linear equations corresponding to the matrix in step 2 and use back-substitution to find the system's solution. The system represented by the matrix in step 2 is

$$\begin{bmatrix} 1 & -1 & 2 & -2 & | & -1 \\ 0 & 1 & -\frac{1}{3} & 1 & | & \frac{8}{3} \\ 0 & 0 & 1 & -1 & | & 1 \\ 0 & 0 & 0 & 1 & | & 3 \end{bmatrix} \rightarrow \begin{cases} 1w - 1x + 2y - 2z = -1 \\ 0w + 1x - \frac{1}{3}y + 1z = \frac{8}{3} \\ 0w + 0x + 1y - 1z = 1 \\ 0w + 0x + 0y + 1z = 3 \end{cases}$$ or $$\begin{cases} w - x + 2y - 2z = -1 \\ x - \frac{1}{3}y + z = \frac{8}{3} \\ y - z = 1 \\ z = 3. \end{cases}$$

We immediately see that the value for z is 3. We can now use back-substitution to find the values for y, x, and w.

These are the four equations from the last column.

$$z = 3 \quad\bigg|\quad y - z = 1 \quad\bigg|\quad x - \frac{1}{3}y + z = \frac{8}{3} \quad\bigg|\quad w - x + 2y -$$

$$y - 3 = 1 \quad\bigg|\quad x - \frac{1}{3}(4) + 3 = \frac{8}{3} \quad\bigg|\quad w - 1 + 2(4) - 2(3) = -1$$

$$y = 4 \quad\bigg|\quad x + \frac{5}{3} = \frac{8}{3} \quad\bigg|\quad w - 1 + 8 - 6 = -1$$

$$x = 1 \quad\bigg|\quad w + 1 = -1$$

$$w = -2$$

Let's agree to write the solution for the system in the alphabetical order of the variables from left to right, namely (w, x, y, z). Thus, the solution set is $\{(-2, 1, 4, 3)\}$. We can verify the solution by substituting the value for each variable into the original system of equations and obtaining four true statements.

⦿ **Check Point 3** Use matrices to solve the system:

$$\begin{cases} w - 3x - 2y + z = -3 \\ 2w - 7x - y + 2z = 1 \\ 3w - 7x - 3y + 3z = -5 \\ 5w + x + 4y - 2z = 18. \end{cases}$$

④ Use matrices and Gauss-Jordan elimination to solve systems.

Solving Linear Systems Using Gauss-Jordan Elimination

Using Gaussian elimination, we obtain a matrix in row-echelon form, with 1s down the main diagonal and 0s below the 1s. A second method, called **Gauss-Jordan elimination**, after Carl Friedrich Gauss and Wilhelm Jordan (1842–1899), continues the process until a matrix with 1s down the main diagonal and 0s in every position *above and below* each 1 is found. Such a matrix is said to be in **reduced row-echelon form**. For a system of three linear equations in three variables, x, y, and z, we must get the augmented matrix into the form

$$\begin{bmatrix} 1 & 0 & 0 & | & a \\ 0 & 1 & 0 & | & b \\ 0 & 0 & 1 & | & c \end{bmatrix}.$$

Based on this matrix, we conclude that $x = a$, $y = b$, and $z = c$.

Solving Linear Systems Using Gauss-Jordan Elimination

1. Write the augmented matrix for the system.

2. Use matrix row operations to simplify the matrix to a row-equivalent matrix in reduced row-echelon form, with 1s down the main diagonal from upper left to lower right, and 0s above and below the 1s.

 a. Get 1 in the upper left-hand corner.

 b. Use the 1 in the first column to get 0s below it.

 c. Get 1 in the second row, second column.

 d. Use the 1 in the second column to make the remaining entries in the second column 0.

 e. Get 1 in the third row, third column.

 f. Use the 1 in the third column to make the remaining entries in the third column 0.

 g. Continue this procedure as far as possible.

3. Use the reduced row-echelon form of the matrix in step 2 to write the system's solution set. (Back-substitution is not necessary.)

Technology

Most graphing utilities can convert a matrix to reduced row-echelon form. Enter the system's augmented matrix and name it A. Then use the $\boxed{\text{RREF}}$ (reduced row-echelon form) command on matrix A.

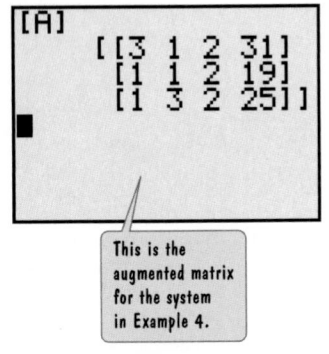

This is the augmented matrix for the system in Example 4.

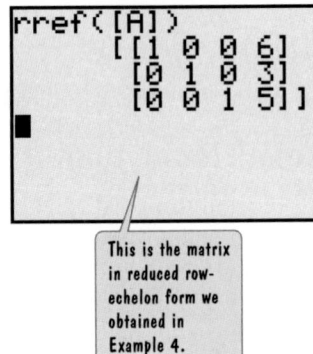

This is the matrix in reduced row-echelon form we obtained in Example 4.

EXAMPLE 4 **Using Gauss-Jordan Elimination**

Use Gauss-Jordan elimination to solve the system:

$$\begin{cases} 3x + y + 2z = 31 \\ x + y + 2z = 19 \\ x + 3y + 2z = 25. \end{cases}$$

Solution In Example 2, we used Gaussian elimination to obtain the following matrix:

We want
0s in these
positions.
$$\begin{bmatrix} 1 & 1 & 2 & | & 19 \\ 0 & 1 & 2 & | & 13 \\ 0 & 0 & 1 & | & 5 \end{bmatrix}.$$

To use Gauss-Jordan elimination, we need 0s both above and below the 1s in the main diagonal. We use the 1 in the second row, second column to get a 0 above it.

Replace row 1 in the previous matrix by $-1R_2 + R_1$.
$$\begin{bmatrix} 1 & 0 & 0 & | & 6 \\ 0 & 1 & 2 & | & 13 \\ 0 & 0 & 1 & | & 5 \end{bmatrix}$$
We want 0s in these positions.

We use the 1 in the third column to get 0s above it.

$$\begin{bmatrix} 1 & 0 & 0 & | & 6 \\ 0 & 1 & 0 & | & 3 \\ 0 & 0 & 1 & | & 5 \end{bmatrix}$$
Replace row 2 in the previous matrix by $-2R_3 + R_2$.

This last matrix corresponds to

$$x = 6, \quad y = 3, \quad z = 5.$$

As we found in Example 2, the solution set is $\{(6, 3, 5)\}$.

✓ Check Point **4** Solve the system in Check Point 2 using Gauss-Jordan elimination. Begin by working with the matrix that you obtained in Check Point 2.

Exercise Set 6.1

Practice Exercises

In Exercises 1–8, write the augmented matrix for each system of linear equations.

1. $\begin{cases} 2x + y + 2z = 2 \\ 3x - 5y - z = 4 \\ x - 2y - 3z = -6 \end{cases}$

2. $\begin{cases} 3x - 2y + 5z = 31 \\ x + 3y - 3z = -12 \\ -2x - 5y + 3z = 11 \end{cases}$

3. $\begin{cases} x - y + z = 8 \\ y - 12z = -15 \\ z = 1 \end{cases}$

4. $\begin{cases} x - 2y + 3z = 9 \\ y + 3z = 5 \\ z = 2 \end{cases}$

5. $\begin{cases} 5x - 2y - 3z = 0 \\ x + y = 5 \\ 2x - 3z = 4 \end{cases}$

6. $\begin{cases} x - 2y + z = 10 \\ 3x + y = 5 \\ 7x + 2z = 2 \end{cases}$

7. $\begin{cases} 2w + 5x - 3y + z = 2 \\ 3x + y = 4 \\ w - x + 5y = 9 \\ 5w - 5x - 2y = 1 \end{cases}$

8. $\begin{cases} 4w + 7x - 8y + z = 3 \\ 5x + y = 5 \\ w - x - y = 17 \\ 2w - 2x + 11y = 4 \end{cases}$

In Exercises 9–12, write the system of linear equations represented by the augmented matrix. Use x, y, and z, or, if necessary, w, x, y, and z, for the variables.

9. $\begin{bmatrix} 5 & 0 & 3 & | & -11 \\ 0 & 1 & -4 & | & 12 \\ 7 & 2 & 0 & | & 3 \end{bmatrix}$

10. $\begin{bmatrix} 7 & 0 & 4 & | & -13 \\ 0 & 1 & -5 & | & 11 \\ 2 & 7 & 0 & | & 6 \end{bmatrix}$

11. $\begin{bmatrix} 1 & 1 & 4 & 1 & | & 3 \\ -1 & 1 & -1 & 0 & | & 7 \\ 2 & 0 & 0 & 5 & | & 11 \\ 0 & 0 & 12 & 4 & | & 5 \end{bmatrix}$

12. $\begin{bmatrix} 4 & 1 & 5 & 1 & | & 6 \\ 1 & -1 & 0 & -1 & | & 8 \\ 3 & 0 & 0 & 7 & | & 4 \\ 0 & 0 & 11 & 5 & | & 3 \end{bmatrix}$

In Exercises 13–18, perform each matrix row operation and write the new matrix.

13. $\begin{bmatrix} 2 & -6 & 4 & | & 10 \\ 1 & 5 & -5 & | & 0 \\ 3 & 0 & 4 & | & 7 \end{bmatrix} \frac{1}{2}R_1$

14. $\begin{bmatrix} 3 & -12 & 6 & | & 9 \\ 1 & -4 & 4 & | & 0 \\ 2 & 0 & 7 & | & 4 \end{bmatrix} \quad \frac{1}{3}R_1$

15. $\begin{bmatrix} 1 & -3 & 2 & | & 0 \\ 3 & 1 & -1 & | & 7 \\ 2 & -2 & 1 & | & 3 \end{bmatrix} \quad -3R_1 + R_2$

16. $\begin{bmatrix} 1 & -1 & 5 & | & -6 \\ 3 & 3 & -1 & | & 10 \\ 1 & 3 & 2 & | & 5 \end{bmatrix} \quad -3R_1 + R_2$

17. $\begin{bmatrix} 1 & -1 & 1 & 1 & | & 3 \\ 0 & 1 & -2 & -1 & | & 0 \\ 2 & 0 & 3 & 4 & | & 11 \\ 5 & 1 & 2 & 4 & | & 6 \end{bmatrix} \quad \begin{matrix} \\ \\ -2R_1 + R_3 \\ -5R_1 + R_4 \end{matrix}$

18. $\begin{bmatrix} 1 & -5 & 2 & -2 & | & 4 \\ 0 & 1 & -3 & -1 & | & 0 \\ 3 & 0 & 2 & -1 & | & 6 \\ -4 & 1 & 4 & 2 & | & -3 \end{bmatrix} \quad \begin{matrix} \\ \\ -3R_1 + R_3 \\ 4R_1 + R_4 \end{matrix}$

In Exercises 19–20, a few steps in the process of simplifying the given matrix to row-echelon form, with 1s down the diagonal from upper left to lower right, and 0s below the 1s, are shown. Fill in the missing numbers in the steps that are shown.

19. $\begin{bmatrix} 1 & -1 & 1 & | & 8 \\ 2 & 3 & -1 & | & -2 \\ 3 & -2 & -9 & | & 9 \end{bmatrix} \rightarrow \begin{bmatrix} 1 & -1 & 1 & | & 8 \\ 0 & 5 & \square & | & \square \\ 0 & 1 & \square & | & \square \end{bmatrix}$

$\rightarrow \begin{bmatrix} 1 & -1 & 1 & | & 8 \\ 0 & 1 & \square & | & \square \\ 0 & 1 & \square & | & \square \end{bmatrix}$

20. $\begin{bmatrix} 1 & -2 & 3 & | & 4 \\ 2 & 1 & -4 & | & 3 \\ -3 & 4 & -1 & | & -2 \end{bmatrix} \rightarrow \begin{bmatrix} 1 & -2 & 3 & | & 4 \\ 0 & 5 & \square & | & \square \\ 0 & -2 & \square & | & \square \end{bmatrix}$

$\rightarrow \begin{bmatrix} 1 & -2 & 3 & | & 4 \\ 0 & 1 & \square & | & \square \\ 0 & -2 & \square & | & \square \end{bmatrix}$

In Exercises 21–38, solve each system of equations using matrices. Use Gaussian elimination with back-substitution or Gauss-Jordan elimination.

21. $\begin{cases} x + y - z = -2 \\ 2x - y + z = 5 \\ -x + 2y + 2z = 1 \end{cases}$

22. $\begin{cases} x - 2y - z = 2 \\ 2x - y + z = 4 \\ -x + y - 2z = -4 \end{cases}$

23. $\begin{cases} x + 3y = 0 \\ x + y + z = 1 \\ 3x - y - z = 11 \end{cases}$

24. $\begin{cases} 3y - z = -1 \\ x + 5y - z = -4 \\ -3x + 6y + 2z = 11 \end{cases}$

25. $\begin{cases} 2x - y - z = 4 \\ x + y - 5z = -4 \\ x - 2y = 4 \end{cases}$

26. $\begin{cases} x - 3z = -2 \\ 2x + 2y + z = 4 \\ 3x + y - 2z = 5 \end{cases}$

27. $\begin{cases} x + y + z = 4 \\ x - y - z = 0 \\ x - y + z = 2 \end{cases}$

28. $\begin{cases} 3x + y - z = 0 \\ x + y + 2z = 6 \\ 2x + 2y + 3z = 10 \end{cases}$

29. $\begin{cases} x + 2y = z - 1 \\ x = 4 + y - z \\ x + y - 3z = -2 \end{cases}$

30. $\begin{cases} 2x + y = z + 1 \\ 2x = 1 + 3y - z \\ x + y + z = 4 \end{cases}$

31. $\begin{cases} 3a - b - 4c = 3 \\ 2a - b + 2c = -8 \\ a + 2b - 3c = 9 \end{cases}$

32. $\begin{cases} 3a + b - c = 0 \\ 2a + 3b - 5c = 1 \\ a - 2b + 3c = -4 \end{cases}$

33. $\begin{cases} 2x + 2y + 7z = -1 \\ 2x + y + 2z = 2 \\ 4x + 6y + z = 15 \end{cases}$

34. $\begin{cases} 3x + 2y + 3z = 3 \\ 4x - 5y + 7z = 1 \\ 2x + 3y - 2z = 6 \end{cases}$

35. $\begin{cases} w + x + y + z = 4 \\ 2w + x - 2y - z = 0 \\ w - 2x - y - 2z = -2 \\ 3w + 2x + y + 3z = 4 \end{cases}$

36. $\begin{cases} w + x + y + z = 5 \\ w + 2x - y - 2z = -1 \\ w - 3x - 3y - z = -1 \\ 2w - x + 2y - z = -2 \end{cases}$

37. $\begin{cases} 3w - 4x + y + z = 9 \\ w + x - y - z = 0 \\ 2w + x + 4y - 2z = 3 \\ -w + 2x + y - 3z = 3 \end{cases}$

38. $\begin{cases} 2w + y - 3z = 8 \\ w - x + 4z = -10 \\ 3w + 5x - y - z = 20 \\ w + x - y - z = 6 \end{cases}$

Practice Plus

39. Find the quadratic function $f(x) = ax^2 + bx + c$ for which $f(-2) = -4, f(1) = 2$, and $f(2) = 0$.

40. Find the quadratic function $f(x) = ax^2 + bx + c$ for which $f(-1) = 5, f(1) = 3$, and $f(2) = 5$.

41. Find the cubic function $f(x) = ax^3 + bx^2 + cx + d$ for which $f(-1) = 0, f(1) = 2, f(2) = 3$, and $f(3) = 12$.

42. Find the cubic function $f(x) = ax^3 + bx^2 + cx + d$ for which $f(-1) = 3, f(1) = 1, f(2) = 6$, and $f(3) = 7$.

43. Solve the system:

$$\begin{cases} 2\ln w + \ln x + 3\ln y - 2\ln z = -6 \\ 4\ln w + 3\ln x + \ln y - \ln z = -2 \\ \ln w + \ln x + \ln y + \ln z = -5 \\ \ln w + \ln x - \ln y - \ln z = 5. \end{cases}$$

(*Hint:* Let $A = \ln w, B = \ln x, C = \ln y$, and $D = \ln z$. Solve the system for A, B, C, and D. Then use the logarithmic equations to find w, x, y, and z.)

44. Solve the system:

$$\begin{cases} \ln w + \ln x + \ln y + \ln z = -1 \\ -\ln w + 4\ln x + \ln y - \ln z = 0 \\ \ln w - 2\ln x + \ln y - 2\ln z = 11 \\ -\ln w - 2\ln x + \ln y + 2\ln z = -3. \end{cases}$$

(*Hint:* Let $A = \ln w, B = \ln x, C = \ln y$, and $D = \ln z$. Solve the system for A, B, C, and D. Then use the logarithmic equations to find w, x, y, and z.)

Application Exercises

45. A ball is thrown straight upward. A position function

$$s(t) = \frac{1}{2}at^2 + v_0t + s_0$$

can be used to describe the ball's height, $s(t)$, in feet, after t seconds.

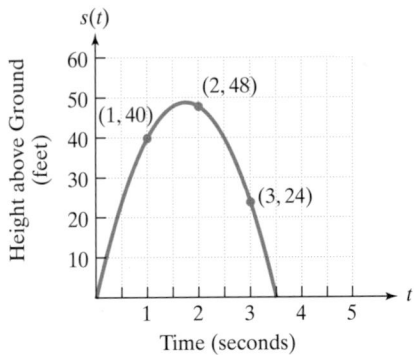

a. Use the points labeled in the graph to find the values of a, v_0, and s_0. Solve the system of linear equations involving a, v_0, and s_0 using matrices.

b. Find and interpret $s(3.5)$. Identify your solution as a point on the graph shown.

c. After how many seconds does the ball reach its maximum height? What is its maximum height?

46. A football is kicked straight upward. A position function

$$s(t) = \frac{1}{2}at^2 + v_0t + s_0$$

can be used to describe the ball's height, $s(t)$, in feet, after t seconds.

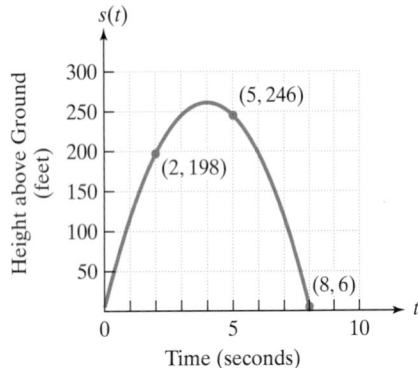

a. Use the points labeled in the graph to find the values of a, v_0, and s_0. Solve the system of linear equations involving a, v_0, and s_0 using matrices.

b. Find and interpret $s(7)$. Identify your solution as a point on the graph shown.

c. After how many seconds does the ball reach its maximum height? What is its maximum height?

Write a system of linear equations in three or four variables to solve Exercises 47–50. Then use matrices to solve the system.

47. Three foods have the following nutritional content per ounce.

	Calories	Protein (in grams)	Vitamin C (in milligrams)
Food A	40	5	30
Food B	200	2	10
Food C	400	4	300

If a meal consisting of the three foods allows exactly 660 calories, 25 grams of protein, and 425 milligrams of vitamin C, how many ounces of each kind of food should be used?

48. A furniture company produces three types of desks: a children's model, an office model, and a deluxe model. Each desk is manufactured in three stages: cutting, construction, and finishing. The time requirements for each model and manufacturing stage are given in the following table.

	Children's model	Office model	Deluxe model
Cutting	2 hr	3 hr	2 hr
Construction	2 hr	1 hr	3 hr
Finishing	1 hr	1 hr	2 hr

Each week the company has available a maximum of 100 hours for cutting, 100 hours for construction, and 65 hours for finishing. If all available time must be used, how many of each type of desk should be produced each week?

49. Imagine the entire global population as a village of precisely 200 people. The bar graph shows some numeric observations based on this scenario.

Earth's Population as a Village of 200 People

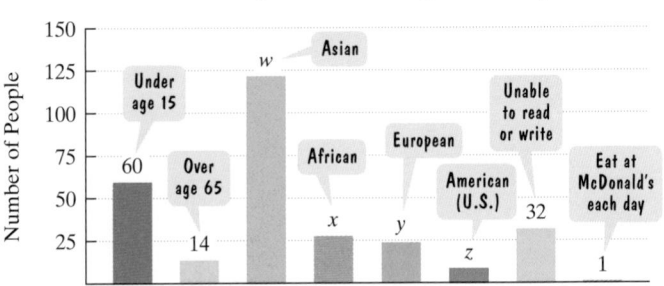

Source: Gary Rimmer, *Number Freaking*, The Disinformation Company Ltd., 2006

Combined, there are 183 Asians, Africans, Europeans, and Americans in the village. The number of Asians exceeds the number of Africans and Europeans by 70. The difference between the number of Europeans and Americans is 15. If the number of Africans is doubled, their population exceeds the number of Europeans and Americans by 23. Determine the number of Asians, Africans, Europeans, and Americans in the global village.

50. The bar graph shows the number of rooms, bathrooms, fireplaces, and elevators in the U.S. White House.

The U.S. White House by the Numbers

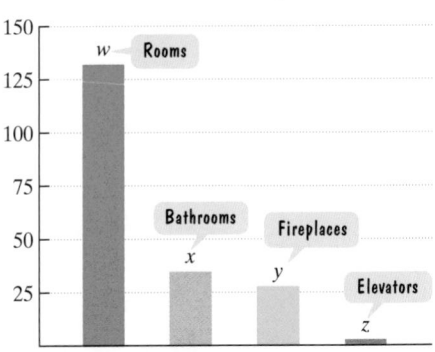

Source: The White House

Combined, there are 198 rooms, bathrooms, fireplaces, and elevators. The number of rooms exceeds the number of bathrooms and fireplaces by 69. The difference between the number of fireplaces and elevators is 25. If the number of bathrooms is doubled, it exceeds the number of fireplaces and elevators by 39. Determine the number of rooms, bathrooms, fireplaces, and elevators in the U.S. White House.

Writing in Mathematics

51. What is a matrix?

52. Describe what is meant by the augmented matrix of a system of linear equations.

53. In your own words, describe each of the three matrix row operations. Give an example with each of the operations.

54. Describe how to use row operations and matrices to solve a system of linear equations.

55. What is the difference between Gaussian elimination and Gauss-Jordan elimination?

Technology Exercises

56. Most graphing utilities can perform row operations on matrices. Consult the owner's manual for your graphing utility to learn proper keystrokes for performing these operations. Then duplicate the row operations of any three exercises that you solved from Exercises 13–18.

57. If your graphing utility has a $\boxed{\text{REF}}$ (row-echelon form) command or a $\boxed{\text{RREF}}$ (reduced row-echelon form) command, use this feature to verify your work with any five systems that you solved from Exercises 21–38.

58. Solve using a graphing utility's $\boxed{\text{REF}}$ or $\boxed{\text{RREF}}$ command:

$$\begin{cases} 2x_1 - 2x_2 + 3x_3 - x_4 & = 12 \\ x_1 + 2x_2 - x_3 + 2x_4 - x_5 = -7 \\ x_1 + x_3 + x_4 - 5x_5 = 1 \\ -x_1 + x_2 - x_3 - 2x_4 - 3x_5 = 0 \\ x_1 - x_2 - x_4 + x_5 = 4. \end{cases}$$

Critical Thinking Exercises

Make Sense? *In Exercises 59–62, determine whether each statement makes sense or does not make sense, and explain your reasoning.*

59. Matrix row operations remind me of what I did when solving a linear system by the addition method, although I no longer write the variables.

60. When I use matrices to solve linear systems, the only arithmetic involves multiplication or a combination of multiplication and addition.

61. When I use matrices to solve linear systems, I spend most of my time using row operations to express the system's augmented matrix in row-echelon form.

62. Using row operations on an augmented matrix, I obtain a row in which 0s appear to the left of the vertical bar, but 6 appears on the right, so the system I'm working with has no solution.

In Exercises 63–66, determine whether each statement is true or false. If the statement is false, make the necessary change(s) to produce a true statement.

63. A matrix row operation such as $-\frac{4}{5}R_1 + R_2$ is not permitted because of the negative fraction.

64. The augmented matrix for the system

$$\begin{array}{rcl} x - 3y & = & 5 \\ y - 2z & = & 7 \\ 2x + z & = & 4 \end{array} \quad \text{is} \quad \left[\begin{array}{ccc|c} 1 & -3 & & 5 \\ 1 & -2 & & 7 \\ 2 & & 1 & 4 \end{array}\right].$$

65. In solving a linear system of three equations in three variables, we begin with the augmented matrix and use row operations to obtain a row-equivalent matrix with 0s down the diagonal from left to right and 1s below each 0.

66. The row operation $kR_i + R_j$ indicates that it is the elements in row i that change.

67. The table shows the daily production level and profit for a business.

x (Number of Units Produced Daily)	30	50	100
y (Daily Profit)	$5900	$7500	$4500

Use the quadratic function $y = ax^2 + bx + c$ to determine the number of units that should be produced each day for maximum profit. What is the maximum daily profit?

Preview Exercises

Exercises 68–70 will help you prepare for the material covered in the next section. In each exercise, refer to the following system:

$$\begin{cases} 3x - 4y + 4z = 7 \\ x - y - 2z = 2 \\ 2x - 3y + 6z = 5. \end{cases}$$

68. Show that $(12z + 1, 10z - 1, z)$ satisfies the system for $z = 0$.

69. Show that $(12z + 1, 10z - 1, z)$ satisfies the system for $z = 1$.

70. a. Select a value for z other than 0 or 1 and show that $(12z + 1, 10z - 1, z)$ satisfies the system.

 b. Based on your work in Exercises 68–70(a), how does this system differ from those in Exercises 21–34?

Inconsistent and Dependent Systems and Their Applications

Objectives

1. Apply Gaussian elimination to systems without unique solutions.

2. Apply Gaussian elimination to systems with more variables than equations.

3. Solve problems involving systems without unique solutions.

Traffic jams getting you down? Powerful computers, able to solve systems with hundreds of thousands of variables in a single bound, may promise a gridlock-free future. The computer in your car could be linked to a central computer that manages traffic flow by controlling traffic lights, rerouting you away from raffic congestion, issuing weather reports, and selecting the best route to your destination. New technologies could eventually drive your car at a steady 75 miles per hour along automated highways as you comfortably nap. In this section, we look at the role of linear systems without unique solutions in a future free of traffic jams.

1. Apply Gaussian elimination to systems without unique solutions.

Linear systems can have one solution, no solution, or infinitely many solutions. We can use Gaussian elimination on systems with three or more variables to determine how many solutions such systems may have. In the case of systems with no solution or infinitely many solutions, it is impossible to rewrite the augmented matrix in the desired form with 1s down the main diagonal from upper left to lower right, and 0s below the 1s. Let's see what this means by looking at a system that has no solution.

EXAMPLE 1 A System with No Solution

Use Gaussian elimination to solve the system:

$$\begin{cases} x - y - 2z = 2 \\ 2x - 3y + 6z = 5 \\ 3x - 4y + 4z = 12. \end{cases}$$

Solution

Step 1 Write the augmented matrix for the system.

Discovery

Use the addition method to solve Example 1. Describe what happens. Why does this mean that there is no solution?

Linear System

$$\begin{cases} x - y - 2z = 2 \\ 2x - 3y + 6z = 5 \\ 3x - 4y + 4z = 12 \end{cases}$$

Augmented Matrix

$$\begin{bmatrix} 1 & -1 & -2 & | & 2 \\ 2 & -3 & 6 & | & 5 \\ 3 & -4 & 4 & | & 12 \end{bmatrix}$$

Step 2 Attempt to simplify the matrix to row-echelon form, with 1s down the main diagonal and 0s below the 1s. Notice that the augmented matrix already has a 1 in the top position of the first column. Now we want 0s below the 1. To get the first 0, multiply row 1 by −2 and add these products to row 2. To get the second 0, multiply

row 1 by -3 and add these products to row 3. Performing these operations, we obtain the following matrix:

We want 1 in this position.

$$\begin{bmatrix} 1 & -1 & -2 & | & 2 \\ 0 & -1 & 10 & | & 1 \\ 0 & -1 & 10 & | & 6 \end{bmatrix}$$

Use the augmented matrix and:
Replace row 2 by $-2R_1 + R_2$.
Replace row 3 by $-3R_1 + R_3$.

Moving on to the second column, we obtain 1 in the desired position by multiplying row 2 by -1.

$$\begin{bmatrix} 1 & -1 & -2 & | & 2 \\ -1(0) & -1(-1) & -1(10) & | & -1(1) \\ 0 & -1 & 10 & | & 6 \end{bmatrix} = \begin{bmatrix} 1 & -1 & -2 & | & 2 \\ 0 & 1 & -10 & | & -1 \\ 0 & -1 & 10 & | & 6 \end{bmatrix} \quad {}_{-1R_2}$$

We want 0 in this position.

Now we want a 0 below the 1 in column 2. To get the 0, multiply row 2 by 1 and add these products to row 3. (Equivalently, add row 2 to row 3.) We obtain the following matrix:

$$\begin{bmatrix} 1 & -1 & -2 & | & 2 \\ 0 & 1 & -10 & | & -1 \\ 0 & 0 & 0 & | & 5 \end{bmatrix}$$

Replace row 3 in the previous matrix by $1R_2 + R_3$.

It is impossible to convert this last matrix to the desired form of 1s down the main diagonal. If we translate the last row back into equation form, we get

$$0x + 0y + 0z = 5,$$

There are no values of x, y, and z for which $0 = 5$.

which is false. Regardless of which values we select for x, y, and z, the last equation can never be a true statement. Consequently, the system has no solution. The solution set is \varnothing, the empty set. ●

Ø Check Point **1** Use Gaussian elimination to solve the system:

$$\begin{cases} x - 2y - z = -5 \\ 2x - 3y - z = 0 \\ 3x - 4y - z = 1. \end{cases}$$

Recall that the graph of a system of three linear equations in three variables consists of three planes. When these planes intersect in a single point, the system has precisely one ordered-triple solution. When the planes have no point in common, the system has no solution, like the one in Example 1. **Figure 6.1** illustrates some of the geometric possibilities for these inconsistent systems.

Three planes are parallel with no common intersection point.

Two planes are parallel with no common intersection point.

Planes intersect two at a time. There is no intersection point common to all three planes.

Figure 6.1 Three planes may have no common point of intersection.

Now let's see what happens when we apply Gaussian elimination to a system with infinitely many solutions. Representing the solution set for these systems can be a bit tricky.

> **EXAMPLE 2** **A System with an Infinite Number of Solutions**

Use Gaussian elimination to solve the following system:

$$\begin{cases} 3x - 4y + 4z = 7 \\ x - y - 2z = 2 \\ 2x - 3y + 6z = 5. \end{cases}$$

Solution As always, we start with the augmented matrix.

$$\begin{bmatrix} 3 & -4 & 4 & | & 7 \\ 1 & -1 & -2 & | & 2 \\ 2 & -3 & 6 & | & 5 \end{bmatrix} \quad \begin{array}{c} R_1 \leftrightarrow R_2 \\ \hline \text{Interchange rows} \\ \text{1 and 2.} \end{array} \quad \begin{bmatrix} 1 & -1 & -2 & | & 2 \\ 3 & -4 & 4 & | & 7 \\ 2 & -3 & 6 & | & 5 \end{bmatrix} \quad \begin{array}{l} \text{Replace row 2} \\ \text{by } -3R_1 + R_2. \\ \text{Replace row 3} \\ \text{by } -2R_1 + R_3. \end{array}$$

$$\begin{bmatrix} 1 & -1 & -2 & | & 2 \\ 0 & -1 & 10 & | & 1 \\ 0 & -1 & 10 & | & 1 \end{bmatrix} \quad \begin{array}{c} -1R_2 \\ \hline \text{Multiply row} \\ \text{2 by } -1. \end{array} \quad \begin{bmatrix} 1 & -1 & -2 & | & 2 \\ 0 & 1 & -10 & | & -1 \\ 0 & -1 & 10 & | & 1 \end{bmatrix} \quad \begin{array}{l} \text{Replace row 3} \\ \text{by } 1R_2 + R_3. \end{array}$$

$$\begin{bmatrix} 1 & -1 & -2 & | & 2 \\ 0 & 1 & -10 & | & -1 \\ 0 & 0 & 0 & | & 0 \end{bmatrix}$$

If we translate row 3 of the matrix into equation form, we obtain

$$0x + 0y + 0z = 0$$

or

$$0 = 0.$$

This equation results in a true statement regardless of which values we select for $x, y,$ and z. Consequently, the equation $0x + 0y + 0z = 0$ is *dependent* on the other two equations in the system in the sense that it adds no new information about the variables. Thus, we can drop it from the system, which can now be expressed in the form

$$\begin{bmatrix} 1 & -1 & -2 & | & 2 \\ 0 & 1 & -10 & | & -1 \end{bmatrix}. \qquad \begin{array}{l} \text{This is the last matrix from} \\ \text{above with row 3 omitted.} \end{array}$$

The original system is equivalent to the system

$$\begin{cases} x - y - 2z = 2 \\ y - 10z = -1. \end{cases} \qquad \begin{array}{l} \text{This is the system represented} \\ \text{by the above matrix.} \end{array}$$

Although neither of these equations gives a value for z, we can use them to express x and y in terms of z. From the last equation, we obtain

$$y = 10z - 1. \qquad \text{Add 10z to both sides and isolate y.}$$

Back-substituting for y into the first equation obtained from the final matrix, we can find x in terms of z.

$$x - y - 2z = 2 \qquad \begin{array}{l} \text{This is the first equation} \\ \text{obtained from the final matrix.} \end{array}$$

$$x - (10z - 1) - 2z = 2 \qquad \begin{array}{l} \text{Because } y = 10z - 1, \\ \text{substitute } 10z - 1 \text{ for y.} \end{array}$$

$$x - 10z + 1 - 2z = 2 \qquad \text{Apply the distributive property.}$$

$$x - 12z + 1 = 2 \qquad \text{Combine like terms.}$$

$$x = 12z + 1 \qquad \text{Solve for x in terms of z.}$$

We have now found two equations expressing x and y in terms of z:

$$x = 12z + 1$$
$$y = 10z - 1.$$

Because no value is determined for z, we can find a solution of the system by letting z equal any real number and then using these equations to obtain x and y. For example, if $z = 1$, then

$$x = 12z + 1 = 12(1) + 1 = 13 \text{ and}$$
$$y = 10z - 1 = 10(1) - 1 = 9.$$

Consequently, $(13, 9, 1)$ is a solution of the system. On the other hand, if we let $z = -1$, then

$$x = 12z + 1 = 12(-1) + 1 = -11 \text{ and}$$
$$y = 10z - 1 = 10(-1) - 1 = -11.$$

Thus, $(-11, -11, -1)$ is another solution of the system.

We see that for any arbitrary choice of z, every ordered triple of the form $(12z + 1, 10z - 1, z)$ is a solution of the system. The solution set of this system with dependent equations is

$$\{(12z + 1, 10z - 1, z)\}.$$

We have seen that when three planes have no point in common, the corresponding system has no solution. When the system has infinitely many solutions, like the one in Example 2, the three planes intersect in more than one point. **Figure 6.2** illustrates geometric possibilities for systems with dependent equations.

The planes intersect
along a common line.

The planes coincide.

Figure 6.2 Three planes may intersect at infinitely many points.

⊘ Check Point **2** Use Gaussian elimination to solve the following system:

$$\begin{cases} x - 2y - z = 5 \\ 2x - 5y + 3z = 6 \\ x - 3y + 4z = 1. \end{cases}$$

② Apply Gaussian elimination to systems with more variables than equations.

Nonsquare Systems

Up to this point, we have encountered only *square* systems in which the number of equations is equal to the number of variables. In a **nonsquare system**, the number of variables differs from the number of equations. In Example 3, we have two equations and three variables.

(**EXAMPLE 3**) **A System with Fewer Equations Than Variables**

Use Gaussian elimination to solve the system:

$$\begin{cases} 3x + 7y + 6z = 26 \\ x + 2y + z = 8. \end{cases}$$

Solution We begin with the augmented matrix.

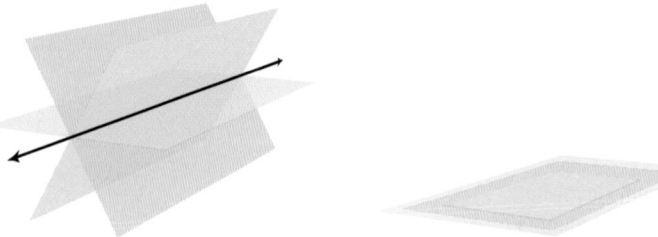

Because the matrix $\begin{bmatrix} 1 & 2 & 1 & | & 8 \\ 0 & 1 & 3 & | & 2 \end{bmatrix}$ has 1s down the diagonal that begins with the upper-left entry and a 0 below the leading 1, we translate this matrix back into equation form.

$$\begin{cases} x + 2y + z = 8 & \text{Equation 1} \\ y + 3z = 2 & \text{Equation 2} \end{cases}$$

We can let z equal any real number and use back-substitution to express x and y in terms of z.

Equation 2

$$y + 3z = 2$$
$$y = -3z + 2$$

Equation 1

$$x + 2y + z = 8$$
$$x + 2(-3z + 2) + z = 8$$
$$x - 6z + 4 + z = 8$$
$$x - 5z + 4 = 8$$
$$x = 5z + 4$$

For any arbitrary choice of z, every ordered triple of the form $(5z + 4, -3z + 2, z)$ is a solution of the system. We can express the system's solution set as

$$\{(5z + 4, -3z + 2, z)\}.$$

○ **Check Point 3** Use Gaussian elimination to solve the system:

$$\begin{cases} x + 2y + 3z = 70 \\ x + y + z = 60. \end{cases}$$

Applications

How will computers be programmed to control traffic flow and avoid congestion? They will be required to solve systems continually based on the following premise: If traffic is to keep moving, during any period of time the number of cars entering an intersection must equal the number of cars leaving that intersection. Let's see what this means by looking at the intersections of four one-way city streets.

(**EXAMPLE 4**) **Traffic Control**

Figure 6.3 shows the intersections of four one-way streets. As you study the figure, notice that 300 cars per hour want to enter intersection I_1 from the north on 27th Avenue. Also, 200 cars per hour want to head east from intersection I_2 on Palm Drive. The letters w, x, y, and z stand for the number of cars passing between the intersections.

a. If the traffic is to keep moving, at each intersection the number of cars entering per hour must equal the number of cars leaving per hour. Use this idea to set up a linear system of equations involving w, x, y, and z.

b. Use Gaussian elimination to solve the system.

c. If construction on 27th Avenue limits z to 50 cars per hour, how many cars per hour must pass between the other intersections to keep traffic flowing?

Solution

a. Set up the system by considering one intersection at a time, referring to **Figure 6.3**.

For Intersection I_1: Because $300 + 700 = 1000$ cars enter I_1 and $w + z$ cars leave the intersection, then $w + z = 1000$.

For Intersection I_2: Because $w + x$ cars enter the intersection and $200 + 900 = 1100$ cars leave I_2, then $w + x = 1100$.

For Intersection I_3: **Figure 6.3** indicates that $300 + 400 = 700$ cars enter and $x + y$ leave, so $x + y = 700$.

For Intersection I_4: With $y + z$ cars entering and $200 + 400 = 600$ cars exiting, traffic will keep flowing if $y + z = 600$.

Discovery

Let $z = 1$ for the solution

$$(5z + 4, -3z + 2, z).$$

What solution do you obtain? Substitute these three values in the two original equations:

$$\begin{cases} 3x + 7y + 6z = 26 \\ x + 2y + z = 8. \end{cases}$$

Show that each equation is satisfied. Repeat this process for two other values of z.

③ Solve problems involving systems without unique solutions.

Figure 6.3 The intersections of four one-way streets

700 Cars/hr → I_1 — w → I_2 → 200 Cars/hr

300 Cars/hr ↓ ↑ 900 Cars/hr

Palm Drive

27th Ave z 37th Ave x

N W—E S

200 Cars/hr ← I_4 — y → I_3 ← 400 Cars/hr

Sunset Drive

400 Cars/hr 300 Cars/hr

The system of equations that models this situation is given by

$$\begin{cases} w + z = 1000 \\ w + x = 1100 \\ x + y = 700 \\ y + z = 600. \end{cases}$$

b. To solve this system using Gaussian elimination, we begin with the augmented matrix.

**System of Linear Equations
(showing missing variables
with 0 coefficients)**

Augmented Matrix

$$\begin{cases} 1w + 0x + 0y + 1z = 1000 \\ 1w + 1x + 0y + 0z = 1100 \\ 0w + 1x + 1y + 0z = 700 \\ 0w + 0x + 1y + 1z = 600 \end{cases} \qquad \begin{bmatrix} 1 & 0 & 0 & 1 & | & 1000 \\ 1 & 1 & 0 & 0 & | & 1100 \\ 0 & 1 & 1 & 0 & | & 700 \\ 0 & 0 & 1 & 1 & | & 600 \end{bmatrix}$$

We can now use row operations to obtain the following matrix:

$$\begin{bmatrix} 1 & 0 & 0 & 1 & | & 1000 \\ 0 & 1 & 0 & -1 & | & 100 \\ 0 & 0 & 1 & 1 & | & 600 \\ 0 & 0 & 0 & 0 & | & 0 \end{bmatrix}.$$

$w + z = 1000$
$x - z = 100$
$y + z = 600$

The last row of the matrix shows that the system in the voice balloons has dependent equations and infinitely many solutions. To write the solution set containing these infinitely many solutions, let z equal any real number. Use the three equations in the voice balloons to express w, x, and y in terms of z:

$$w = 1000 - z, \quad x = 100 + z, \quad \text{and} \quad y = 600 - z.$$

With z arbitrary, the alphabetically ordered solution (w, x, y, z) enables us to express the system's solution set as

$$\{(1000 - z, 100 + z, 600 - z, z)\}.$$

c. We are given that construction limits z to 50 cars per hour. Because $z = 50$, we substitute 50 for z in the system's ordered solution:

$(1000 - z, 100 + z, 600 - z, z)$ Use the system's solution.
$= (1000 - 50, 100 + 50, 600 - 50, 50)$ $z = 50$
$= (950, 150, 550, 50)$.

Thus, $w = 950$, $x = 150$, and $y = 550$. (See **Figure 6.4**.) With construction on 27th Avenue, this means that to keep traffic flowing, 950 cars per hour must be routed between I_1 and I_2, 150 per hour between I_3 and I_2, and 550 per hour between I_3 and I_4.

Figure 6.4 With z limited to 50 cars per hour, values for w, x, and y are determined.

✓ Check Point **4** **Figure 6.5** shows a system of four one-way streets. The numbers in the figure denote the number of cars per minute that travel in the direction shown.

a. Use the requirement that the number of cars entering each of the intersections per minute must equal the number of cars leaving per minute to set up a system of equations in w, x, y, and z.

b. Use Gaussian elimination to solve the system.

c. If construction limits z to 10 cars per minute, how many cars per minute must pass between the other intersections to keep traffic flowing?

Figure 6.5

Exercise Set 6.2

Practice Exercises

In Exercises 1–24, use Gaussian elimination to find the complete solution to each system of equations, or show that none exists.

1. $\begin{cases} 5x + 12y + z = 10 \\ 2x + 5y + 2z = -1 \\ x + 2y - 3z = 5 \end{cases}$

2. $\begin{cases} 2x - 4y + z = 3 \\ x - 3y + z = 5 \\ 3x - 7y + 2z = 12 \end{cases}$

3. $\begin{cases} 5x + 8y - 6z = 14 \\ 3x + 4y - 2z = 8 \\ x + 2y - 2z = 3 \end{cases}$

4. $\begin{cases} 5x - 11y + 6z = 12 \\ -x + 3y - 2z = -4 \\ 3x - 5y + 2z = 4 \end{cases}$

5. $\begin{cases} 3x + 4y + 2z = 3 \\ 4x - 2y - 8z = -4 \\ x + y - z = 3 \end{cases}$

6. $\begin{cases} 2x - y - z = 0 \\ x + 2y + z = 3 \\ 3x + 4y + 2z = 8 \end{cases}$

7. $\begin{cases} 8x + 5y + 11z = 30 \\ -x - 4y + 2z = 3 \\ 2x - y + 5z = 12 \end{cases}$

8. $\begin{cases} x + y - 10z = -4 \\ x - 7z = -5 \\ 3x + 5y - 36z = -10 \end{cases}$

9. $\begin{cases} w - 2x - y - 3z = -9 \\ w + x - y = 0 \\ 3w + 4x + z = 6 \\ 2x - 2y + z = 3 \end{cases}$

10. $\begin{cases} 2w + x - 2y - z = 3 \\ w - 2x + y + z = 4 \\ -w - 8x + 7y + 5z = 13 \\ 3w + x - 2y + 2z = 6 \end{cases}$

11. $\begin{cases} 2w + x - y = 3 \\ w - 3x + 2y = -4 \\ 3w + x - 3y + z = 1 \\ w + 2x - 4y - z = -2 \end{cases}$

12. $\begin{cases} 2w - x + 3y + z = 0 \\ 3w + 2x + 4y - z = 0 \\ 5w - 2x - 2y - z = 0 \\ 2w + 3x - 7y - 5z = 0 \end{cases}$

13. $\begin{cases} w - 3x + y - 4z = 4 \\ -2w + x + 2y = -2 \\ 3w - 2x + y - 6z = 2 \\ -w + 3x + 2y - z = -6 \end{cases}$

14. $\begin{cases} 3w + 2x - y + 2z = -12 \\ 4w - x + y + 2z = 1 \\ w + x + y + z = -2 \\ -2w + 3x + 2y - 3z = 10 \end{cases}$

15. $\begin{cases} 2x + y - z = 2 \\ 3x + 3y - 2z = 3 \end{cases}$

16. $\begin{cases} 3x + 2y - z = 5 \\ x + 2y - z = 1 \end{cases}$

17. $\begin{cases} x + 2y + 3z = 5 \\ y - 5z = 0 \end{cases}$

18. $\begin{cases} 3x - y + 4z = 8 \\ y + 2z = 1 \end{cases}$

19. $\begin{cases} x + y - 2z = 2 \\ 3x - y - 6z = -7 \end{cases}$

20. $\begin{cases} -2x - 5y + 10z = 19 \\ x + 2y - 4z = 12 \end{cases}$

21. $\begin{cases} w + x - y + z = -2 \\ 2w - x + 2y - z = 7 \\ -w + 2x + y + 2z = -1 \end{cases}$

22. $\begin{cases} 2w - 3x + 4y + z = 7 \\ w - x + 3y - 5z = 10 \\ 3w + x - 2y - 2z = 6 \end{cases}$

23. $\begin{cases} w + 2x + 3y - z = 7 \\ 2x - 3y + z = 4 \\ w - 4x + y = 3 \end{cases}$

24. $\begin{cases} w - x + z = 0 \\ w - 4x + y + 2z = 0 \\ 3w - y + 2z = 0 \end{cases}$

Practice Plus

In Exercises 25–28, the first screen shows the augmented matrix, A, for a nonsquare linear system of three equations in four variables, w, x, y, and z. The second screen shows the reduced row-echelon form of matrix A. For each exercise,

 a. *Write the system represented by A.*

 b. *Use the reduced row-echelon form of A to find the system's complete solution.*

25.

26.

27.

28.

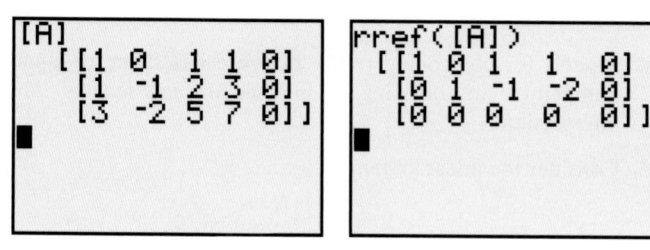

Application Exercises

The figure for Exercises 29–32 shows the intersections of three one-way streets. To keep traffic moving, the number of cars per minute entering an intersection must equal the number exiting that intersection. For intersection I_1, $x + 10$ cars enter and $y + 14$ cars exit per minute. Thus, $x + 10 = y + 14$.

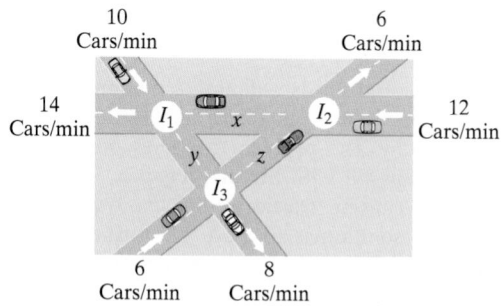

29. Write an equation for intersection I_2 that keeps traffic moving.

30. Write an equation for intersection I_3 that keeps traffic moving.

31. Use Gaussian elimination to solve the system formed by the equation given prior to Exercise 29 and the two equations that you obtained in Exercises 29–30.

32. Use your ordered solution obtained in Exercise 31 to solve this exercise. If construction limits z to 4 cars per minute, how many cars per minute must pass between the other intersections to keep traffic flowing?

33. The figure shows the intersections of four one-way streets.

a. Set up a system of equations that keeps traffic moving.

b. Use Gaussian elimination to solve the system.

c. If construction limits z to 50 cars per hour, how many cars per hour must pass between the other intersections to keep traffic moving?

34. The vitamin content per ounce for three foods is given in the following table.

	Milligrams per Ounce		
	Thiamin	Riboflavin	Niacin
Food A	3	7	1
Food B	1	5	3
Food C	3	8	2

a. Use matrices to show that no combination of these foods can provide exactly 14 mg of thiamin, 32 mg of riboflavin, and 9 mg of niacin.

b. Use matrices to describe in practical terms what happens if the riboflavin requirement is increased by 5 mg and the other requirements stay the same.

35. Three foods have the following nutritional content per ounce.

	Units per Ounce		
	Vitamin A	Iron	Calcium
Food 1	20	20	10
Food 2	30	10	10
Food 3	10	10	30

a. A diet must consist precisely of 220 units of vitamin A, 180 units of iron, and 340 units of calcium. However, the dietician runs out of Food 1. Use a matrix approach to show that under these conditions the dietary requirements cannot be met.

b. Now suppose that all three foods are available. Use matrices to give two possible ways to meet the iron and calcium requirements with the three foods.

36. A company that manufactures products A, B, and C does both manufacturing and testing. The hours needed to manufacture and test each product are shown in the table.

	Hours Needed Weekly to Manufacture	Hours Needed Weekly to Test
Product A	7	2
Product B	6	2
Product C	3	1

The company has exactly 67 hours per week available for manufacturing and 20 hours per week available for testing. Give two different combinations for the number of products that can be manufactured and tested weekly.

Writing in Mathematics

37. Describe what happens when Gaussian elimination is used to solve an inconsistent system.

38. Describe what happens when Gaussian elimination is used to solve a system with dependent equations.

39. In solving a system of dependent equations in three variables, one student simply said that there are infinitely many solutions. A second student expressed the solution set as $\{(4z + 3, 5z - 1, z)\}$. Which is the better form of expressing the solution set and why?

Technology Exercise

40. a. The figure shows the intersections of a number of one-way streets. The numbers given represent traffic flow at a peak period (from 4 P.M. to 5:30 P.M.). Use the figure to write a linear system of six equations in seven variables based on the idea that at each intersection the number of cars entering must equal the number of cars leaving.

b. Use a graphing utility with a [REF] or [RREF] command to find the complete solution to the system.

Critical Thinking Exercises

Make Sense? *In Exercises 41–44, determine whether each statement makes sense or does not make sense, and explain your reasoning.*

41. I omitted row 3 from $\begin{bmatrix} 1 & -1 & -2 & | & 2 \\ 0 & 1 & -10 & | & -1 \\ 0 & 0 & 0 & | & 5 \end{bmatrix}$ and expressed

the system in the form $\begin{bmatrix} 1 & -1 & -2 & | & 2 \\ 0 & 1 & -10 & | & -1 \end{bmatrix}$.

42. I omitted row 3 from $\begin{bmatrix} 1 & -1 & -2 & | & 2 \\ 0 & 1 & -10 & | & -1 \\ 0 & 0 & 0 & | & 0 \end{bmatrix}$ and expressed

the system in the form $\begin{bmatrix} 1 & -1 & -2 & | & 2 \\ 0 & 1 & -10 & | & -1 \end{bmatrix}$.

43. I solved a nonsquare system in which the number of equations was the same as the number of variables.

44. Models for controlling traffic flow are based on an equal number of cars entering an intersection and leaving that intersection.

45. Consider the linear system

$$
\begin{aligned}
x + 3y + \quad z &= a^2 \\
2x + 5y + 2az &= 0 \\
x + \quad y + a^2z &= -9.
\end{aligned}
$$

For which values of a will the system be inconsistent?

Group Exercise

46. Before beginning this exercise, the group needs to read and solve Exercise 40.

a. A political group is planning a demonstration on 95th Street between 113th Place and 117th Court for 5 P.M. Wednesday. The problem becomes one of minimizing traffic flow on 95th Street (between 113th and 117th) without causing traffic tie-ups on other streets. One possible solution is to close off traffic on 95th Street between 113th and 117th (let $x_6 = 0$). What can group members conclude about x_7 under these conditions?

b. Working with a matrix allows us to simplify the problem caused by the political demonstration, but it did not actually solve the problem. There are an infinite number of solutions; each value of x_7 we choose gives us a new picture. We also assumed x_6 was equal to 0; changing that assumption would also lead to different solutions. With your group, design another solution to the traffic flow problem caused by the political demonstration.

Preview Exercises

Exercises 47–49 will help you prepare for the material covered in the next section. In each exercise, perform the indicated operation or operations.

47. $-6 - (-5)$

48. $1(-4) + 2(5) + 3(-6)$

49. $\frac{1}{2}[8 - (-8)]$

Matrix Operations and Their Applications

Objectives

1. Use matrix notation.
2. Understand what is meant by equal matrices.
3. Add and subtract matrices.
4. Perform scalar multiplication.
5. Solve matrix equations.
6. Multiply matrices.
7. Model applied situations with matrix operations.

Turn on your computer and read your e-mail or write a paper. When you need to do research, use the Internet to browse through art museums and photography exhibits. When you need a break, load a flight simulator program and fly through a photorealistic computer world. As different as these experiences may be, they all share one thing— you're looking at images based on matrices. Matrices have applications in numerous fields, including the new technology of digital photography in which pictures are represented by numbers rather than film. In this section, we turn our attention to matrix algebra and some of its applications.

1. Use matrix notation.

Notations for Matrices

We have seen that an array of numbers, arranged in rows and columns and placed in brackets, is called a matrix. We can represent a matrix in two different ways.

- A capital letter, such as A, B, or C, can denote a matrix.
- A lowercase letter enclosed in brackets, such as that shown below, can denote a matrix.

$$A = [a_{ij}]$$

Matrix A with elements a_{ij}

A general element in matrix A is denoted by a_{ij}. This refers to the element in the ith row and jth column. For example, a_{32} is the element of A located in the third row, second column.

A matrix of **order $m \times n$** has m rows and n columns. If $m = n$, a matrix has the same number of rows as columns and is called a **square matrix.**

EXAMPLE 1 Matrix Notation

Let

$$A = \begin{bmatrix} 3 & 2 & 0 \\ -4 & -5 & -\frac{1}{5} \end{bmatrix}.$$

a. What is the order of A?

b. If $A = [a_{ij}]$, identify a_{23} and a_{12}.

Solution

a. The matrix has 2 rows and 3 columns, so it is of order 2×3.

b. The element a_{23} is in the second row and third column. Thus, $a_{23} = -\frac{1}{5}$. The element a_{12} is in the first row and second column. Consequently, $a_{12} = 2$.

⊘ Check Point **1** Let

$$A = \begin{bmatrix} 5 & -2 \\ -3 & \pi \\ 1 & 6 \end{bmatrix}.$$

a. What is the order of A? **b.** Identify a_{12} and a_{31}.

② Understand what is meant by equal matrices.

Equality of Matrices

Two matrices are **equal** if and only if they have the same order and corresponding elements are equal.

> ### Definition of Equality of Matrices
> Two matrices A and B are **equal** if and only if they have the same order $m \times n$ and $a_{ij} = b_{ij}$ for $i = 1, 2, \ldots, m$ and $j = 1, 2, \ldots, n$.

For example, if $A = \begin{bmatrix} x & y+1 \\ z & 6 \end{bmatrix}$ and $B = \begin{bmatrix} 1 & 5 \\ 3 & 6 \end{bmatrix}$, then $A = B$ if and only if $x = 1$, $y + 1 = 5$ (so $y = 4$), and $z = 3$.

③ Add and subtract matrices.

Matrix Addition and Subtraction

Table 6.1 shows that matrices of the same order can be added or subtracted by simply adding or subtracting corresponding elements.

Table 6.1 Adding and Subtracting Matrices

Let $A = [a_{ij}]$ and $B = [b_{ij}]$ be matrices of order $m \times n$.

Definition	The Definition in Words	Example
Matrix Addition $$A + B = [a_{ij} + b_{ij}]$$	Matrices of the same order are added by adding the elements in corresponding positions.	$\begin{bmatrix} 1 & -2 \\ 3 & 5 \end{bmatrix} + \begin{bmatrix} -1 & 6 \\ 0 & 4 \end{bmatrix}$ $= \begin{bmatrix} 1 + (-1) & -2 + 6 \\ 3 + 0 & 5 + 4 \end{bmatrix} = \begin{bmatrix} 0 & 4 \\ 3 & 9 \end{bmatrix}$
Matrix Subtraction $$A - B = [a_{ij} - b_{ij}]$$	Matrices of the same order are subtracted by subtracting the elements in corresponding positions.	$\begin{bmatrix} 1 & -2 \\ 3 & 5 \end{bmatrix} - \begin{bmatrix} -1 & 6 \\ 0 & 4 \end{bmatrix}$ $= \begin{bmatrix} 1 - (-1) & -2 - 6 \\ 3 - 0 & 5 - 4 \end{bmatrix} = \begin{bmatrix} 2 & -8 \\ 3 & 1 \end{bmatrix}$

The sum or difference of two matrices of different orders is undefined. For example, consider the matrices

$$A = \begin{bmatrix} 0 & 3 \\ 4 & 3 \end{bmatrix} \quad \text{and} \quad B = \begin{bmatrix} 1 & 9 \\ 4 & 5 \\ 2 & 3 \end{bmatrix}.$$

The order of A is 2×2; the order of B is 3×2. These matrices are of different orders and cannot be added or subtracted.

Technology

Graphing utilities can add and subtract matrices. Enter the matrices and name them $[A]$ and $[B]$. Then use a keystroke sequence similar to

$$\boxed{[A]}\,\boxed{+}\,\boxed{[B]}\,\boxed{\text{ENTER}}$$

$$\boxed{[A]}\,\boxed{-}\,\boxed{[B]}\,\boxed{\text{ENTER}}$$

Consult your manual and verify the results in Example 2.

EXAMPLE 2 **Adding and Subtracting Matrices**

Perform the indicated matrix operations:

a. $\begin{bmatrix} 0 & 5 & 3 \\ -2 & 6 & -8 \end{bmatrix} + \begin{bmatrix} -2 & 3 & 5 \\ 7 & -9 & 6 \end{bmatrix}$

b. $\begin{bmatrix} -6 & 7 \\ 2 & -3 \end{bmatrix} - \begin{bmatrix} -5 & 6 \\ 0 & -4 \end{bmatrix}.$

Solution

a. $\begin{bmatrix} 0 & 5 & 3 \\ -2 & 6 & -8 \end{bmatrix} + \begin{bmatrix} -2 & 3 & 5 \\ 7 & -9 & 6 \end{bmatrix}$

$= \begin{bmatrix} 0 + (-2) & 5 + 3 & 3 + 5 \\ -2 + 7 & 6 + (-9) & -8 + 6 \end{bmatrix}$ Add the corresponding elements in the 2 × 3 matrices.

$= \begin{bmatrix} -2 & 8 & 8 \\ 5 & -3 & -2 \end{bmatrix}$ Simplify.

b. $\begin{bmatrix} -6 & 7 \\ 2 & -3 \end{bmatrix} - \begin{bmatrix} -5 & 6 \\ 0 & -4 \end{bmatrix}$

$= \begin{bmatrix} -6 - (-5) & 7 - 6 \\ 2 - 0 & -3 - (-4) \end{bmatrix}$ Subtract the corresponding elements in the 2 × 2 matrices.

$= \begin{bmatrix} -1 & 1 \\ 2 & 1 \end{bmatrix}$ Simplify. ●

⊘ **Check Point 2** Perform the indicated matrix operations:

a. $\begin{bmatrix} -4 & 3 \\ 7 & -6 \end{bmatrix} + \begin{bmatrix} 6 & -3 \\ 2 & -4 \end{bmatrix}$ **b.** $\begin{bmatrix} 5 & 4 \\ -3 & 7 \\ 0 & 1 \end{bmatrix} - \begin{bmatrix} -4 & 8 \\ 6 & 0 \\ -5 & 3 \end{bmatrix}.$

A matrix whose elements are all equal to 0 is called a **zero matrix**. If A is an $m \times n$ matrix and 0 is the $m \times n$ zero matrix, then $A + 0 = A$. For example,

$$\begin{bmatrix} -5 & 2 \\ 3 & 6 \end{bmatrix} + \begin{bmatrix} 0 & 0 \\ 0 & 0 \end{bmatrix} = \begin{bmatrix} -5 & 2 \\ 3 & 6 \end{bmatrix}.$$

The $m \times n$ zero matrix is called the **additive identity** for $m \times n$ matrices.

For any matrix A, the **additive inverse** of A, written $-A$, is the matrix with the same order as A such that every element of $-A$ is the opposite of the corresponding element of A. Because corresponding elements are added in matrix addition, $A + (-A)$ is a zero matrix. For example,

$$\begin{bmatrix} -5 & 2 \\ 3 & 6 \end{bmatrix} + \begin{bmatrix} 5 & -2 \\ -3 & -6 \end{bmatrix} = \begin{bmatrix} 0 & 0 \\ 0 & 0 \end{bmatrix}.$$

Properties of matrix addition are similar to properties for adding real numbers.

Properties of Matrix Addition

If A, B, and C are $m \times n$ matrices and 0 is the $m \times n$ zero matrix, then the following properties are true.

1. $A + B = B + A$ — Commutative property of addition
2. $(A + B) + C = A + (B + C)$ — Associative property of addition
3. $A + 0 = 0 + A = A$ — Additive identity property
4. $A + (-A) = (-A) + A = 0$ — Additive inverse property

④ Perform scalar multiplication.

Scalar Multiplication

A matrix of order 1×1, such as $[6]$, contains only one entry. To distinguish this matrix from the number 6, we refer to 6 as a **scalar**. In general, in our work with matrices, we will refer to real numbers as scalars.

To multiply a matrix A by a scalar c, we multiply each entry in A by c. For example,

$$4\begin{bmatrix} 2 & 5 \\ -3 & 0 \end{bmatrix} = \begin{bmatrix} 4(2) & 4(5) \\ 4(-3) & 4(0) \end{bmatrix} = \begin{bmatrix} 8 & 20 \\ -12 & 0 \end{bmatrix}.$$

Scalar Matrix

Definition of Scalar Multiplication

If $A = [a_{ij}]$ is a matrix of order $m \times n$ and c is a scalar, then the matrix cA is the $m \times n$ matrix given by

$$cA = [ca_{ij}].$$

This matrix is obtained by multiplying each element of A by the real number c. We call cA a **scalar multiple** of A.

EXAMPLE 3 Scalar Multiplication

If $A = \begin{bmatrix} -1 & 4 \\ 3 & 0 \end{bmatrix}$ and $B = \begin{bmatrix} 2 & -3 \\ 5 & -6 \end{bmatrix}$, find the following matrices:

a. $-5B$ **b.** $2A + 3B$.

Solution

a. $-5B = -5\begin{bmatrix} 2 & -3 \\ 5 & -6 \end{bmatrix} = \begin{bmatrix} -5(2) & -5(-3) \\ -5(5) & -5(-6) \end{bmatrix} = \begin{bmatrix} -10 & 15 \\ -25 & 30 \end{bmatrix}$

Multiply each element by −5.

b. $2A + 3B = 2\begin{bmatrix} -1 & 4 \\ 3 & 0 \end{bmatrix} + 3\begin{bmatrix} 2 & -3 \\ 5 & -6 \end{bmatrix}$

$= \begin{bmatrix} 2(-1) & 2(4) \\ 2(3) & 2(0) \end{bmatrix} + \begin{bmatrix} 3(2) & 3(-3) \\ 3(5) & 3(-6) \end{bmatrix}$

Multiply each element in A by 2. Multiply each element in B by 3.

$= \begin{bmatrix} -2 & 8 \\ 6 & 0 \end{bmatrix} + \begin{bmatrix} 6 & -9 \\ 15 & -18 \end{bmatrix} = \begin{bmatrix} -2 + 6 & 8 + (-9) \\ 6 + 15 & 0 + (-18) \end{bmatrix}$

Perform the addition of these 2 x 2 matrices by adding corresponding elements.

$= \begin{bmatrix} 4 & -1 \\ 21 & -18 \end{bmatrix}$

Technology

You can verify the algebraic solution in Example 3(b) by first entering the matrices $[A]$ and $[B]$ into your graphing utility. The screen below shows the required computation.

```
2[A]+3[B]
     [[4   -1 ]
      [21  -18]]
■
```

⊘ Check Point **3** If $A = \begin{bmatrix} -4 & 1 \\ 3 & 0 \end{bmatrix}$ and $B = \begin{bmatrix} -1 & -2 \\ 8 & 5 \end{bmatrix}$, find the following matrices:

 a. $-6B$ **b.** $3A + 2B$.

Discovery

Verify each of the four properties listed in the box using

$$A = \begin{bmatrix} 2 & -4 \\ -5 & 3 \end{bmatrix},$$

$$B = \begin{bmatrix} 4 & 0 \\ 1 & -6 \end{bmatrix},$$

$c = 4$, and $d = 2$.

Properties of scalar multiplication are similar to properties for multiplying real numbers.

Properties of Scalar Multiplication

If A and B are $m \times n$ matrices, and c and d are scalars, then the following properties are true.

1. $(cd)A = c(dA)$ Associative property of scalar multiplication

2. $1A = A$ Scalar identity property

3. $c(A + B) = cA + cB$ Distributive property

4. $(c + d)A = cA + dA$ Distributive property

⑤ Solve matrix equations.

Have you noticed the many similarities between addition of real numbers and matrix addition, subtraction of real numbers and matrix subtraction, and multiplication of real numbers and scalar multiplication? Example 4 shows how these similarities can be used to solve matrix equations involving matrix addition, matrix subtraction, and scalar multiplication.

(**EXAMPLE 4**) **Solving a Matrix Equation**

Solve for X in the matrix equation

$$2X + A = B,$$

where $A = \begin{bmatrix} 1 & -5 \\ 0 & 2 \end{bmatrix}$ and $B = \begin{bmatrix} -6 & 5 \\ 9 & 1 \end{bmatrix}$.

Solution We begin by solving the matrix equation for X.

$$2X + A = B$$ This is the given matrix equation.

$$2X = B - A$$ Subtract matrix A from both sides.

We multiply both sides by $\frac{1}{2}$ rather than divide both sides by 2. This is in anticipation of performing scalar multiplication.

$$X = \frac{1}{2}(B - A)$$ Multiply both sides by $\frac{1}{2}$ and solve for matrix X.

Now we use the matrices A and B to find the matrix X.

$$X = \frac{1}{2}\left(\begin{bmatrix} -6 & 5 \\ 9 & 1 \end{bmatrix} - \begin{bmatrix} 1 & -5 \\ 0 & 2 \end{bmatrix} \right)$$ Substitute the matrices into $X = \frac{1}{2}(B - A)$.

$$= \frac{1}{2} \begin{bmatrix} -7 & 10 \\ 9 & -1 \end{bmatrix}$$ Subtract matrices by subtracting corresponding elements.

$$= \begin{bmatrix} -\dfrac{7}{2} & 5 \\ \dfrac{9}{2} & -\dfrac{1}{2} \end{bmatrix}$$ Perform the scalar multiplication by multiplying each element by $\frac{1}{2}$.

Take a few minutes to show that this matrix satisfies the given equation $2X + A = B$. Substitute the matrix for X and the given matrices for A and B into the equation. The matrices on each side of the equal sign, $2X + A$ and B, should be equal. ●

✓ Check Point **4** Solve for X in the matrix equation $3X + A = B$, where

$$A = \begin{bmatrix} 2 & -8 \\ 0 & 4 \end{bmatrix} \quad \text{and} \quad B = \begin{bmatrix} -10 & 1 \\ -9 & 17 \end{bmatrix}.$$

⑥ Multiply matrices.

Matrix Multiplication

We do not multiply two matrices by multiplying the corresponding entries of the matrices. Instead, we must think of matrix multiplication as *row-by-column multiplication*. To better understand how this works, let's begin with the definition of matrix multiplication for matrices of order 2×2.

Definition of Matrix Multiplication: 2×2 Matrices

$$AB = \begin{bmatrix} a & b \\ c & d \end{bmatrix}\begin{bmatrix} e & f \\ g & h \end{bmatrix} = \begin{bmatrix} ae + bg & af + bh \\ ce + dg & cf + dh \end{bmatrix}$$

Row 1 of A × Column 1 of B | Row 1 of A × Column 2 of B

Row 2 of A × Column 1 of B | Row 2 of A × Column 2 of B

Notice that we obtain the element in the ith row and jth column in AB by performing computations with elements in the ith row of A and the jth column of B. For example, we obtain the element in the first row and first column of AB by performing computations with elements in the first row of A and the first column of B.

First row of A | First column of B

$$\begin{bmatrix} a & b \end{bmatrix}\begin{bmatrix} e \\ g \end{bmatrix} = \begin{bmatrix} ae + bg & \end{bmatrix}$$

1. Multiply each element in row 1 of A by the corresponding element in column 1 of B.
2. Add these products.
3. Record the sum as the element in row 1, column 1 of the product matrix.

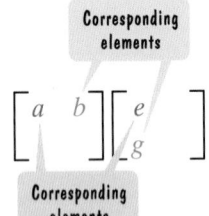

Corresponding elements

$$\begin{bmatrix} a & b \end{bmatrix}\begin{bmatrix} e \\ g \end{bmatrix}$$

Corresponding elements

Figure 6.6 Finding corresponding elements when multiplying matrices

You may wonder how to find the corresponding elements in step 1 in the voice balloon. The element at the far left of row 1 corresponds to the element at the top of column 1. The second element from the left of row 1 corresponds to the second element from the top of column 1. This is illustrated in **Figure 6.6**.

(EXAMPLE 5) **Multiplying Matrices**

Find AB, given

$$A = \begin{bmatrix} 2 & 3 \\ 4 & 7 \end{bmatrix} \quad \text{and} \quad B = \begin{bmatrix} 0 & 1 \\ 5 & 6 \end{bmatrix}.$$

Solution We will perform a row-by-column computation.

$$AB = \begin{bmatrix} 2 & 3 \\ 4 & 7 \end{bmatrix}\begin{bmatrix} 0 & 1 \\ 5 & 6 \end{bmatrix}$$

Row 1 of A × Column 1 of B Row 1 of A × Column 2 of B

$$= \begin{bmatrix} 2(0) + 3(5) & 2(1) + 3(6) \\ 4(0) + 7(5) & 4(1) + 7(6) \end{bmatrix} = \begin{bmatrix} 15 & 20 \\ 35 & 46 \end{bmatrix}$$

Row 2 of A × Column 1 of B Row 2 of A × Column 2 of B

✓ **Check Point 5** Find AB, given $A = \begin{bmatrix} 1 & 3 \\ 2 & 5 \end{bmatrix}$ and $B = \begin{bmatrix} 4 & 6 \\ 1 & 0 \end{bmatrix}$.

We can generalize the process of Example 5 to multiply an $m \times n$ matrix and an $n \times p$ matrix. **For the product of two matrices to be defined, the number of columns of the first matrix must equal the number of rows of the second matrix.**

First Matrix Second Matrix

$m \times n$ $n \times p$

The number of columns in the first matrix must be the same as the number of rows in the second matrix.

Study Tip

The following diagram illustrates the first sentence in the box defining matrix multiplication. The diagram is helpful in determining the order of the product AB.

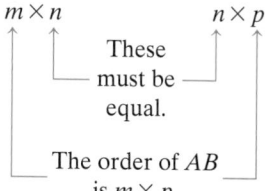

Matrix A Matrix B

$m \times n$ $n \times p$

These must be equal.

The order of AB is $m \times p$.

Definition of Matrix Multiplication

The **product** of an $m \times n$ matrix, A, and an $n \times p$ matrix, B, is an $m \times p$ matrix, AB, whose elements are found as follows: The element in the ith row and jth column of AB is found by multiplying each element in the ith row of A by the corresponding element in the jth column of B and adding the products.

To find a product AB, each row of A must have the same number of elements as each column of B. We obtain p_{ij}, the element in the ith row and jth column in AB, by performing computations with elements in the ith row of A and the jth column of B:

ith row of A jth column of B Element in the ith row and jth column of AB

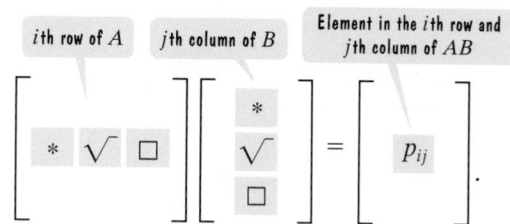

When multiplying corresponding elements, keep in mind that the element at the far left of row i corresponds to the element at the top of column j. The element second from the left in row i corresponds to the element second from the top in column j. Likewise, the element third from the left in row i corresponds to the element third from the top in column j, and so on.

EXAMPLE 6 **Multiplying Matrices**

Matrices A and B are defined as follows:

$$A = \begin{bmatrix} 1 & 2 & 3 \end{bmatrix} \qquad B = \begin{bmatrix} 4 \\ 5 \\ 6 \end{bmatrix}.$$

Find each product: **a.** AB **b.** BA.

Solution

a. Matrix A is a 1×3 matrix and matrix B is a 3×1 matrix. Thus, the product AB is a 1×1 matrix.

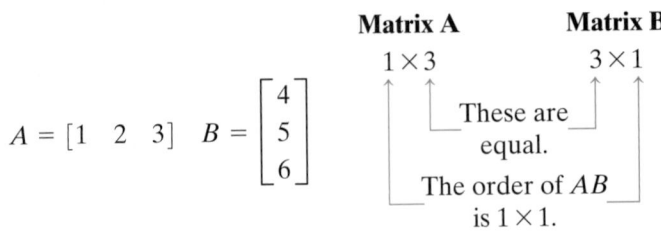

$$AB = [1 \quad 2 \quad 3] \begin{bmatrix} 4 \\ 5 \\ 6 \end{bmatrix}$$ We will perform a row-by-column computation.

$$= [(1)(4) + (2)(5) + (3)(6)]$$ Multiply elements in row 1 of A by corresponding elements in column 1 of B and add the products.

$$= [4 + 10 + 18]$$ Perform the multiplications.

$$= [32]$$ Add.

b. Matrix B is a 3×1 matrix and matrix A is a 1×3 matrix. Thus, the product BA is a 3×3 matrix.

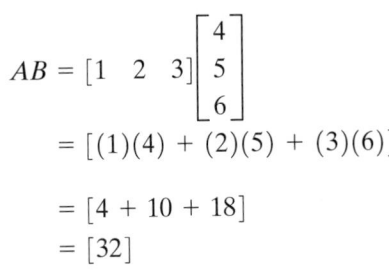

$$BA = \begin{bmatrix} 4 \\ 5 \\ 6 \end{bmatrix} [1 \quad 2 \quad 3]$$ We perform a row-by-column computation.

Technology

The screens illustrate the solution of Example 6 using a graphing utility.

$$= \begin{bmatrix} 4 & 8 & 12 \\ 5 & 10 & 15 \\ 6 & 12 & 18 \end{bmatrix}$$ Simplify.

In Example 6, did you notice that AB and BA are different matrices? For most matrices A and B, $AB \neq BA$. Because **matrix multiplication is not commutative**, be careful about the order in which matrices appear when performing this operation.

⏀ Check Point **6** If $A = \begin{bmatrix} 2 & 0 & 4 \end{bmatrix}$ and $B = \begin{bmatrix} 1 \\ 3 \\ 7 \end{bmatrix}$, find AB and BA.

Arthur Cayley

The Granger Collection

Matrices were first studied intensively by the English mathematician Arthur Cayley (1821–1895). Before reaching the age of 25, he published 25 papers, setting a pattern of prolific creativity that lasted throughout his life. Cayley was a lawyer, painter, mountaineer, and Cambridge professor whose greatest invention was that of matrices and matrix theory. Cayley's matrix algebra, especially the noncommutativity of multiplication ($AB \neq BA$), opened up a new area of mathematics called abstract algebra.

(EXAMPLE 7) Multiplying Matrices

Where possible, find each product:

a. $\begin{bmatrix} 4 & 2 \\ 1 & 3 \end{bmatrix}\begin{bmatrix} 1 & 2 & 3 & 4 \\ 0 & 2 & -1 & 6 \end{bmatrix}$ **b.** $\begin{bmatrix} 1 & 2 & 3 & 4 \\ 0 & 2 & -1 & 6 \end{bmatrix}\begin{bmatrix} 4 & 2 \\ 1 & 3 \end{bmatrix}$.

Solution

a. The first matrix is a 2×2 matrix and the second is a 2×4 matrix. The product will be a 2×4 matrix.

First Matrix **Second Matrix**
2×2 2×4

These are equal.

The order of the product is 2×4.

$\begin{bmatrix} 4 & 2 \\ 1 & 3 \end{bmatrix}\begin{bmatrix} 1 & 2 & 3 & 4 \\ 0 & 2 & -1 & 6 \end{bmatrix}$ *We perform a row-by-column computation.*

Row 1 × Column 1 Row 1 × Column 2 Row 1 × Column 3 Row 1 × Column 4

$= \begin{bmatrix} 4(1) + 2(0) & 4(2) + 2(2) & 4(3) + 2(-1) & 4(4) + 2(6) \\ 1(1) + 3(0) & 1(2) + 3(2) & 1(3) + 3(-1) & 1(4) + 3(6) \end{bmatrix}$

Row 2 × Column 1 Row 2 × Column 2 Row 2 × Column 3 Row 2 × Column 4

$= \begin{bmatrix} 4 + 0 & 8 + 4 & 12 - 2 & 16 + 12 \\ 1 + 0 & 2 + 6 & 3 - 3 & 4 + 18 \end{bmatrix}$

$= \begin{bmatrix} 4 & 12 & 10 & 28 \\ 1 & 8 & 0 & 22 \end{bmatrix}$

b. $\begin{bmatrix} 1 & 2 & 3 & 4 \\ 0 & 2 & -1 & 6 \end{bmatrix}\begin{bmatrix} 4 & 2 \\ 1 & 3 \end{bmatrix}$ First matrix Second matrix
2×4 2×2

These numbers must be the same to multiply the matrices.

The number of columns in the first matrix does not equal the number of rows in the second matrix. Thus, the product of these two matrices is undefined. ⬤

⏀ Check Point **7** Where possible, find each product:

a. $\begin{bmatrix} 1 & 3 \\ 0 & 2 \end{bmatrix}\begin{bmatrix} 2 & 3 & -1 & 6 \\ 0 & 5 & 4 & 1 \end{bmatrix}$ **b.** $\begin{bmatrix} 2 & 3 & -1 & 6 \\ 0 & 5 & 4 & 1 \end{bmatrix}\begin{bmatrix} 1 & 3 \\ 0 & 2 \end{bmatrix}$.

Although matrix multiplication is not commutative, it does obey many of the properties of real numbers.

Properties of Matrix Multiplication

If A, B, and C are matrices and c is a scalar, then the following properties are true. (Assume the order of each matrix is such that all operations in these properties are defined.)

1. $(AB)C = A(BC)$ *Associative Property of Matrix Multiplication*
2. $A(B + C) = AB + AC$ *Distributive Properties of Matrix*
 $(A + B)C = AC + BC$ *Multiplication*
3. $c(AB) = (cA)B$ *Associative Property of Scalar Multiplication*

⑦ Model applied situations with matrix operations.

Applications

All of the still images that you see on the Web have been created or manipulated on a computer in a digital format—made up of hundreds of thousands, or even millions, of tiny squares called **pixels**. Pixels are created by dividing an image into a grid. The computer can change the brightness of every square or pixel in this grid. A digital camera captures photos in this digital format. Also, you can scan pictures to convert them into digital format. Example 8 illustrates the role that matrices play in this new technology.

(**EXAMPLE 8**) **Matrices and Digital Photography**

The letter L in **Figure 6.7** is shown using 9 pixels in a 3×3 grid. The colors possible in the grid are shown in **Figure 6.8**. Each color is represented by a specific number: 0, 1, 2, or 3.

Figure 6.7 The letter L

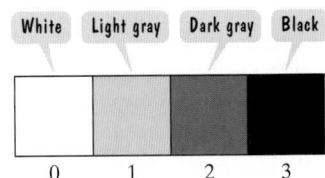

Figure 6.8 Color levels

a. Find a matrix that represents a digital photograph of this letter L.

b. Increase the contrast of the letter L by changing the dark gray to black and the light gray to white. Use matrix addition to accomplish this.

Solution

a. Look at the L and the background in **Figure 6.7**. Because the L is dark gray, color level 2, and the background is light gray, color level 1, a digital photograph of **Figure 6.7** can be represented by the matrix

$$\begin{bmatrix} 2 & 1 & 1 \\ 2 & 1 & 1 \\ 2 & 2 & 1 \end{bmatrix}.$$

b. We can make the L black, color level 3, by increasing each 2 in the above matrix to 3. We can make the background white, color level 0, by decreasing each 1 in the above matrix to 0. This is accomplished using the following matrix addition:

$$\begin{bmatrix} 2 & 1 & 1 \\ 2 & 1 & 1 \\ 2 & 2 & 1 \end{bmatrix} + \begin{bmatrix} 1 & -1 & -1 \\ 1 & -1 & -1 \\ 1 & 1 & -1 \end{bmatrix} = \begin{bmatrix} 3 & 0 & 0 \\ 3 & 0 & 0 \\ 3 & 3 & 0 \end{bmatrix}.$$

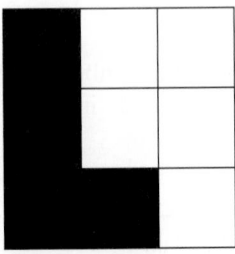

Figure 6.9 Changing contrast: the letter L

The picture corresponding to the matrix sum to the right of the equal sign is shown in **Figure 6.9**.

⊘ Check Point **8** Change the contrast of the letter L in **Figure 6.7** on the previous page by making the L light gray and the background black. Use matrix addition to accomplish this.

Images of space

Photographs sent back from space use matrices with thousands of pixels. Each pixel is assigned a number from 0 to 63 representing its color–0 for pure white and 63 for pure black. In the image of Saturn shown here, matrix operations provide false colors that emphasize the banding of the planet's upper atmosphere.

We have seen how functions can be transformed using translations, reflections, stretching, and shrinking. In a similar way, matrix operations are used to transform and manipulate computer graphics.

(**EXAMPLE 9**) **Transformations of an Image**

The quadrilateral in **Figure 6.10** can be represented by the matrix

$$A = \begin{bmatrix} -2 & -1 & 3 & 1 \\ -3 & 2 & 4 & -2 \end{bmatrix}.$$

Coordinates of vertices

x-coordinates
y-coordinates

Each column in the matrix gives the coordinates of a vertex, or corner, of the quadrilateral. Use matrix operations to perfom the following transformations:

a. Move the quadrilateral 4 units to the right and 1 unit down.

b. Shrink the quadrilateral to half its perimeter.

c. Let $B = \begin{bmatrix} -1 & 0 \\ 0 & 1 \end{bmatrix}$. Find BA. What effect does this have on the quadrilateral in **Figure 6.10**?

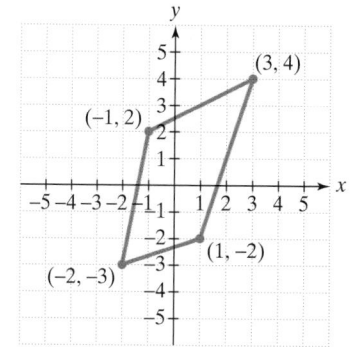

Figure 6.10

Solution

a. We translate the quadrilateral 4 units right and 1 unit down by adding 4 to each *x*-coordinate and subtracting 1 from each *y*-coordinate. This is accomplished using the following matrix addition:

$$\begin{bmatrix} -2 & -1 & 3 & 1 \\ -3 & 2 & 4 & -2 \end{bmatrix} + \begin{bmatrix} 4 & 4 & 4 & 4 \\ -1 & -1 & -1 & -1 \end{bmatrix} = \begin{bmatrix} 2 & 3 & 7 & 5 \\ -4 & 1 & 3 & -3 \end{bmatrix}.$$

This matrix represents the original quadrilateral.

Shift 4 units to the right and 1 unit down.

This matrix represents the translated quadrilateral.

Each column in the matrix on the right gives the coordinates of a vertex of the translated quadrilateral. The original quadrilateral and the translated image are shown in **Figure 6.11**.

Figure 6.11 Shifting the quadrilateral 4 units right and 1 unit down

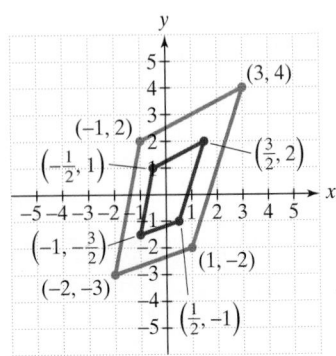

Figure 6.12 Shrinking the quadrilateral to half the original perimeter

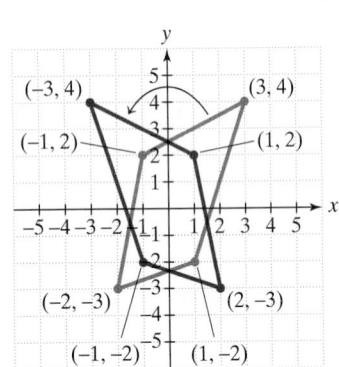

Figure 6.13

b. We shrink the quadrilateral in **Figure 6.10**, shown in blue in **Figure 6.12**, to half its perimeter by multiplying each x-coordinate and each y-coordinate by $\frac{1}{2}$. This is accomplished using the following scalar multiplication:

$$\frac{1}{2}\begin{bmatrix} -2 & -1 & 3 & 1 \\ -3 & 2 & 4 & -2 \end{bmatrix} = \begin{bmatrix} -1 & -\frac{1}{2} & \frac{3}{2} & \frac{1}{2} \\ -\frac{3}{2} & 1 & 2 & -1 \end{bmatrix}.$$

> This matrix represents the original quadrilateral.

> This matrix represents the quadrilateral with half the original perimeter.

Each column in the matrix on the right gives the coordinates of a vertex of the reduced quadrilateral. The original quadrilateral and the reduced image are shown in **Figure 6.12**.

c. We begin by finding BA. Keep in mind that A represents the original quadrilateral, shown in blue in **Figure 6.13**.

$$BA = \begin{bmatrix} -1 & 0 \\ 0 & 1 \end{bmatrix}\begin{bmatrix} -2 & -1 & 3 & 1 \\ -3 & 2 & 4 & -2 \end{bmatrix}$$

$$= \begin{bmatrix} (-1)(-2) + 0(-3) & (-1)(-1) + 0(2) & (-1)(3) + 0(4) & (-1)(1) + 0(-2) \\ 0(-2) + 1(-3) & 0(-1) + 1(2) & 0(3) + 1(4) & 0(1) + 1(-2) \end{bmatrix}$$

$$= \begin{bmatrix} 2 & 1 & -3 & -1 \\ -3 & 2 & 4 & -2 \end{bmatrix}$$

Each column in the matrix multiplication gives the coordinates of a vertex of the transformed image. The original quadrilateral and this transformed image are shown in **Figure 6.13**. Notice that each x-coordinate on the original blue image is replaced with its opposite on the transformed red image.

We can conclude that multiplication by $\begin{bmatrix} -1 & 0 \\ 0 & 1 \end{bmatrix}$ reflected the blue quadrilateral about the y-axis. ●

⊘ **Check Point 9** Consider the triangle represented by the matrix

$$A = \begin{bmatrix} 0 & 3 & 4 \\ 0 & 5 & 2 \end{bmatrix}.$$

Use matrix operations to perform the following transformations:

a. Move the triangle 3 units to the left and 1 unit down.

b. Enlarge the triangle to twice its original perimeter.

Illustrate your results in parts (a) and (b) by showing the original triangle and the transformed image in a rectangular coordinate system.

c. Let $B = \begin{bmatrix} 1 & 0 \\ 0 & -1 \end{bmatrix}$. Find BA. What effect does this have on the original triangle?

Exercise Set 6.3

Practice Exercises

In Exercises 1–4,

a. *Give the order of each matrix.*

b. *If $A = [a_{ij}]$, identify a_{32} and a_{23}, or explain why identification is not possible.*

1. $\begin{bmatrix} 4 & -7 & 5 \\ -6 & 8 & -1 \end{bmatrix}$ **2.** $\begin{bmatrix} -6 & 4 & -1 \\ -9 & 0 & \frac{1}{2} \end{bmatrix}$

3. $\begin{bmatrix} 1 & -5 & \pi & e \\ 0 & 7 & -6 & -\pi \\ -2 & \frac{1}{2} & 11 & -\frac{1}{5} \end{bmatrix}$ **4.** $\begin{bmatrix} -4 & 1 & 3 & -5 \\ 2 & -1 & \pi & 0 \\ 1 & 0 & -e & \frac{1}{5} \end{bmatrix}$

In Exercises 5–8, find values for the variables so that the matrices in each exercise are equal.

5. $\begin{bmatrix} x \\ 4 \end{bmatrix} = \begin{bmatrix} 6 \\ y \end{bmatrix}$ **6.** $\begin{bmatrix} x \\ 7 \end{bmatrix} = \begin{bmatrix} 11 \\ y \end{bmatrix}$

7. $\begin{bmatrix} x & 2y \\ z & 9 \end{bmatrix} = \begin{bmatrix} 4 & 12 \\ 3 & 9 \end{bmatrix}$ **8.** $\begin{bmatrix} x & y+3 \\ 2z & 8 \end{bmatrix} = \begin{bmatrix} 12 & 5 \\ 6 & 8 \end{bmatrix}$

In Exercises 9–16, find the following matrices:

a. $A + B$ **b.** $A - B$

c. $-4A$ **d.** $3A + 2B.$

9. $A = \begin{bmatrix} 4 & 1 \\ 3 & 2 \end{bmatrix}$, $B = \begin{bmatrix} 5 & 9 \\ 0 & 7 \end{bmatrix}$

10. $A = \begin{bmatrix} -2 & 3 \\ 0 & 1 \end{bmatrix}$, $B = \begin{bmatrix} 8 & 1 \\ 5 & 4 \end{bmatrix}$

11. $A = \begin{bmatrix} 1 & 3 \\ 3 & 4 \\ 5 & 6 \end{bmatrix}$, $B = \begin{bmatrix} 2 & -1 \\ 3 & -2 \\ 0 & 1 \end{bmatrix}$

12. $A = \begin{bmatrix} 3 & 1 & 1 \\ -1 & 2 & 5 \end{bmatrix}$, $B = \begin{bmatrix} 2 & -3 & 6 \\ -3 & 1 & -4 \end{bmatrix}$

13. $A = \begin{bmatrix} 2 \\ -4 \\ 1 \end{bmatrix}$, $B = \begin{bmatrix} -5 \\ 3 \\ -1 \end{bmatrix}$

14. $A = \begin{bmatrix} 6 & 2 & -3 \end{bmatrix}$, $B = \begin{bmatrix} 4 & -2 & 3 \end{bmatrix}$

15. $A = \begin{bmatrix} 2 & -10 & -2 \\ 14 & 12 & 10 \\ 4 & -2 & 2 \end{bmatrix}$, $B = \begin{bmatrix} 6 & 10 & -2 \\ 0 & -12 & -4 \\ -5 & 2 & -2 \end{bmatrix}$

16. $A = \begin{bmatrix} 6 & -3 & 5 \\ 6 & 0 & -2 \\ -4 & 2 & -1 \end{bmatrix}$, $B = \begin{bmatrix} -3 & 5 & 1 \\ -1 & 2 & -6 \\ 2 & 0 & 4 \end{bmatrix}$

In Exercises 17–26, let

$$A = \begin{bmatrix} -3 & -7 \\ 2 & -9 \\ 5 & 0 \end{bmatrix} \quad and \quad B = \begin{bmatrix} -5 & -1 \\ 0 & 0 \\ 3 & -4 \end{bmatrix}.$$

Solve each matrix equation for X.

17. $X - A = B$

18. $X - B = A$

19. $2X + A = B$

20. $3X + A = B$

21. $3X + 2A = B$

22. $2X + 5A = B$

23. $B - X = 4A$

24. $A - X = 4B$

25. $4A + 3B = -2X$

26. $4B + 3A = -2X$

In Exercises 27–36, find (if possible) the following matrices:

 a. AB **b.** BA.

27. $A = \begin{bmatrix} 1 & 3 \\ 5 & 3 \end{bmatrix}$, $B = \begin{bmatrix} 3 & -2 \\ -1 & 6 \end{bmatrix}$

28. $A = \begin{bmatrix} 3 & -2 \\ 1 & 5 \end{bmatrix}$, $B = \begin{bmatrix} 0 & 0 \\ 5 & -6 \end{bmatrix}$

29. $A = \begin{bmatrix} 1 & 2 & 3 & 4 \end{bmatrix}$, $B = \begin{bmatrix} 1 \\ 2 \\ 3 \\ 4 \end{bmatrix}$

30. $A = \begin{bmatrix} -1 \\ -2 \\ -3 \end{bmatrix}$, $B = \begin{bmatrix} 1 & 2 & 3 \end{bmatrix}$

31. $A = \begin{bmatrix} 1 & -1 & 4 \\ 4 & -1 & 3 \\ 2 & 0 & -2 \end{bmatrix}$, $B = \begin{bmatrix} 1 & 1 & 0 \\ 1 & 2 & 4 \\ 1 & -1 & 3 \end{bmatrix}$

32. $A = \begin{bmatrix} 1 & -1 & 1 \\ 5 & 0 & -2 \\ 3 & -2 & 2 \end{bmatrix}$, $B = \begin{bmatrix} 1 & 1 & 0 \\ 1 & -4 & 5 \\ 3 & -1 & 2 \end{bmatrix}$

33. $A = \begin{bmatrix} 4 & 2 \\ 6 & 1 \\ 3 & 5 \end{bmatrix}$, $B = \begin{bmatrix} 2 & 3 & 4 \\ -1 & -2 & 0 \end{bmatrix}$

34. $A = \begin{bmatrix} 2 & 4 \\ 3 & 1 \\ 4 & 2 \end{bmatrix}$, $B = \begin{bmatrix} 3 & 2 & 0 \\ -1 & -3 & 5 \end{bmatrix}$

35. $A = \begin{bmatrix} 2 & -3 & 1 & -1 \\ 1 & 1 & -2 & 1 \end{bmatrix}$, $B = \begin{bmatrix} 1 & 2 \\ -1 & 1 \\ 5 & 4 \\ 10 & 5 \end{bmatrix}$

36. $A = \begin{bmatrix} 2 & -1 & 3 & 2 \\ 1 & 0 & -2 & 1 \end{bmatrix}$, $B = \begin{bmatrix} -1 & 2 \\ 1 & 1 \\ 3 & -4 \\ 6 & 5 \end{bmatrix}$

In Exercises 37–44, perform the indicated matrix operations given that A, B, and C are defined as follows. If an operation is not defined, state the reason.

$$A = \begin{bmatrix} 4 & 0 \\ -3 & 5 \\ 0 & 1 \end{bmatrix} \quad B = \begin{bmatrix} 5 & 1 \\ -2 & -2 \end{bmatrix} \quad C = \begin{bmatrix} 1 & -1 \\ -1 & 1 \end{bmatrix}$$

37. $4B - 3C$

38. $5C - 2B$

39. $BC + CB$

40. $A(B + C)$

41. $A - C$

42. $B - A$

43. $A(BC)$

44. $A(CB)$

Practice Plus

In Exercises 45–50, let

$$A = \begin{bmatrix} 1 & 0 \\ 0 & 1 \end{bmatrix}, \quad B = \begin{bmatrix} 1 & 0 \\ 0 & -1 \end{bmatrix}, \quad C = \begin{bmatrix} -1 & 0 \\ 0 & 1 \end{bmatrix},$$

$$D = \begin{bmatrix} -1 & 0 \\ 0 & -1 \end{bmatrix}.$$

45. Find the product of the sum of A and B and the difference between C and D.

46. Find the product of the difference between A and B and the sum of C and D.

47. Use any three of the matrices to verify a distributive property.

48. Use any three of the matrices to verify an associative property.

In Exercises 49–50, suppose that the vertices of a computer graphic are points, (x, y), represented by the matrix

$$Z = \begin{bmatrix} x \\ y \end{bmatrix}.$$

49. Find BZ and explain why this reflects the graphic about the x-axis.

50. Find CZ and explain why this reflects the graphic about the y-axis.

Application Exercises

The + sign in the figure is shown using 9 pixels in a 3 × 3 grid. The color levels are given to the right of the figure. Each color is represented by a specific number: 0, 1, 2, or 3. Use this information to solve Exercises 51–52.

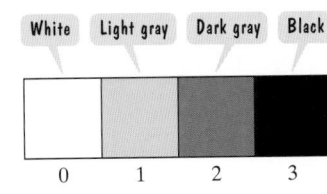

51. **a.** Find a matrix that represents a digital photograph of the + sign.

 b. Adjust the contrast by changing the black to dark gray and the light gray to white. Use matrix addition to accomplish this.

 c. Adjust the contrast by changing the black to light gray and the light gray to dark gray. Use matrix addition to accomplish this.

52. **a.** Find a matrix that represents a digital photograph of the + sign.

 b. Adjust the contrast by changing the black to dark gray and the light gray to black. Use matrix addition to accomplish this.

 c. Adjust the contrast by leaving the black alone and changing the light gray to white. Use matrix addition to accomplish this.

The figure shows the letter L in a rectangular coordinate system.

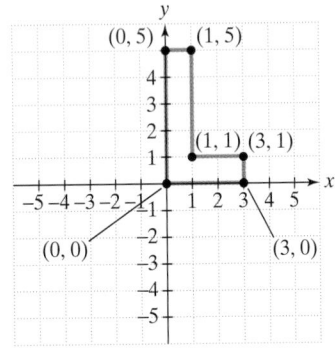

The figure can be represented by the matrix

$$B = \begin{bmatrix} 0 & 3 & 3 & 1 & 1 & 0 \\ 0 & 0 & 1 & 1 & 5 & 5 \end{bmatrix}.$$

Each column in the matrix describes a point on the letter. The order of the columns shows the direction in which a pencil must move to draw the letter. The L is completed by connecting the last point in the matrix, (0, 5), to the starting point, (0, 0). Use these ideas to solve Exercises 53–60.

53. Use matrix operations to move the L 2 units to the left and 3 units down. Then graph the letter and its transformation in a rectangular coordinate system.

54. Use matrix operations to move the L 2 units to the right and 3 units down. Then graph the letter and its transformation in a rectangular coordinate system.

55. Reduce the L to half its perimeter and move the reduced image 1 unit up. Then graph the letter and its transformation.

56. Reduce the L to half its perimeter and move the reduced image 2 units up. Then graph the letter and its transformation.

57. **a.** If $A = \begin{bmatrix} 1 & 0 \\ 0 & -1 \end{bmatrix}$, find AB.

 b. Graph the object represented by matrix AB. What effect does the matrix multiplication have on the letter L represented by matrix B?

58. **a.** If $A = \begin{bmatrix} -1 & 0 \\ 0 & 1 \end{bmatrix}$, find AB.

 b. Graph the object represented by matrix AB. What effect does the matrix multiplication have on the letter L represented by matrix B?

59. **a.** If $A = \begin{bmatrix} 0 & -1 \\ 1 & 0 \end{bmatrix}$, find AB.

 b. Graph the object represented by matrix AB. What effect does the matrix multiplication have on the letter L represented by matrix B?

60. **a.** If $A = \begin{bmatrix} 2 & 0 \\ 0 & 1 \end{bmatrix}$, find AB.

 b. Graph the object represented by matrix AB. What effect does the matrix multiplication have on the letter L represented by matrix B?

61. Completing the transition to adulthood is measured by one or more of the following: leaving home, finishing school, getting married, having a child, or being financially independent. The bar graph shows the percentage of Americans, ages 20 and 30, who had completed the transition to adulthood in 1960 and in 2000.

Percentage Having Completed the Transition to Adulthood

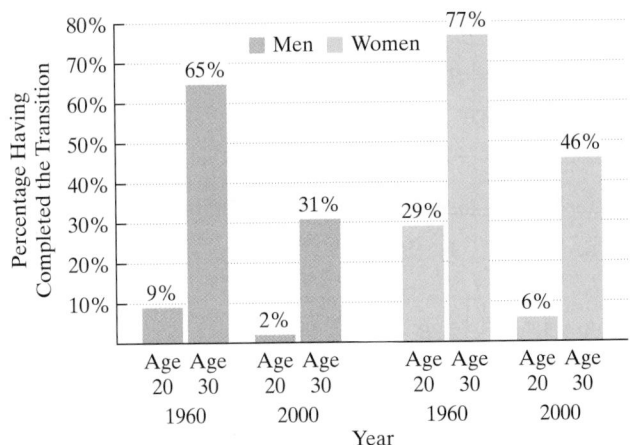

Source: James M. Henslin, *Sociology*, Eighth Edition, Allyn and Bacon, 2007

a. Use a 2 × 2 matrix to represent the data for 2000. Entries in the matrix should be percents that are organized as follows:

$$\begin{array}{c} \\ \text{Age 20} \\ \text{Age 30} \end{array} \begin{array}{cc} \text{Men} & \text{Women} \\ \left[\begin{array}{cc} & \\ & \end{array} \right]. \end{array}$$

Call this matrix A.

b. Use a 2 × 2 matrix to represent the data for 1960. Call this matrix B.

c. Find $B - A$. What does this matrix represent?

Section 6.3 Matrix Operations and Their Applications **591**

62. The table gives an estimate of basic caloric needs for different age groups and activity levels.

Age Range	Sedentary		Moderately Active		Active	
19 – 30	2400	2000	2700	2100	3000	2400
31 – 50	2200	1800	2500	2000	2900	2200
51 +	2000	1600	2300	1800	2600	2100
	Men	Women	Men	Women	Men	Women

Source: USA Today

a. Use a 3×3 matrix to represent the daily caloric needs, by age and activity level, for men. Call this matrix M.

b. Use a 3×3 matrix to represent the daily caloric needs, by age and activity level, for women. Call this matrix W.

c. Find $M - W$. What does this matrix represent?

63. The final grade in a particular course is determined by grades on the midterm and final. The grades for five students and the two grading systems are modeled by the following matrices. Call the first matrix A and the second B.

$$\begin{array}{cc} & \text{Midterm} \quad \text{Final} \\ \begin{array}{c} \text{Student 1} \\ \text{Student 2} \\ \text{Student 3} \\ \text{Student 4} \\ \text{Student 5} \end{array} & \begin{bmatrix} 76 & 92 \\ 74 & 84 \\ 94 & 86 \\ 84 & 62 \\ 58 & 80 \end{bmatrix} \end{array} \quad \begin{array}{cc} & \text{System} \quad \text{System} \\ & \quad 1 \qquad \quad 2 \\ \begin{array}{c} \text{Midterm} \\ \text{Final} \end{array} & \begin{bmatrix} 0.5 & 0.3 \\ 0.5 & 0.7 \end{bmatrix} \end{array}$$

a. Describe the grading system that is represented by matrix B.

b. Compute the matrix AB and assign each of the five students a final course grade first using system 1 and then using system 2. ($89.5 - 100 = A, 79.5 - 89.4 = B,$ $69.5 - 79.4 = C, 59.5 - 69.4 = D$, below $59.5 = F$)

64. In a certain county, the proportion of voters in each age group registered as Republicans, Democrats, or Independents is given by the following matrix, which we'll call A.

$$\begin{array}{cc} & \qquad \qquad \text{Age} \\ & \begin{array}{ccc} \text{18–30} & \text{31–50} & \text{Over 50} \end{array} \\ \begin{array}{c} \text{Republicans} \\ \text{Democrats} \\ \text{Independents} \end{array} & \begin{bmatrix} 0.40 & 0.30 & 0.70 \\ 0.30 & 0.60 & 0.25 \\ 0.30 & 0.10 & 0.05 \end{bmatrix} \end{array}$$

The distribution, by age and gender, of this county's voting population is given by the following matrix, which we'll call B.

$$\begin{array}{cc} & \quad \text{Male} \qquad \text{Female} \\ \begin{array}{cc} & \text{18–30} \\ \text{Age} & \text{31–50} \\ & \text{Over 50} \end{array} & \begin{bmatrix} 6000 & 8000 \\ 12,000 & 14,000 \\ 14,000 & 16,000 \end{bmatrix} \end{array}$$

a. Calculate the product AB.

b. How many female Democrats are there?

c. How many male Republicans are there?

Writing in Mathematics

65. What is meant by the order of a matrix? Give an example with your explanation.

66. What does a_{ij} mean?

67. What are equal matrices?

68. How are matrices added?

69. Describe how to subtract matrices.

70. Describe matrices that cannot be added or subtracted.

71. Describe how to perform scalar multiplication. Provide an example with your description.

72. Describe how to multiply matrices.

73. Describe when the multiplication of two matrices is not defined.

74. If two matrices can be multiplied, describe how to determine the order of the product.

75. Low-resolution digital photographs use 262,144 pixels in a 512×512 grid. If you enlarge a low-resolution digital photograph enough, describe what will happen.

Technology Exercise

76. Use the matrix feature of a graphing utility to verify each of your answers to Exercises 37–44.

Critical Thinking Exercises

Make Sense? *In Exercises 77–80, determine whether each statement makes sense or does not make sense, and explain your reasoning.*

77. I added matrices of the same order by adding corresponding elements.

78. I multiplied an $m \times n$ matrix and an $n \times p$ matrix by multiplying corresponding elements.

79. I'm working with two matrices that can be added but not multiplied.

80. I'm working with two matrices that can be multiplied but not added.

81. Find two matrices A and B such that $AB = BA$.

82. Consider a square matrix such that each element that is not on the diagonal from upper left to lower right is zero. Experiment with such matrices (call each matrix A) by finding AA. Then write a sentence or two describing a method for multiplying this kind of matrix by itself.

83. If $AB = -BA$, then A and B are said to be anticommutative. Are $A = \begin{bmatrix} 0 & -1 \\ 1 & 0 \end{bmatrix}$ and $B = \begin{bmatrix} 1 & 0 \\ 0 & -1 \end{bmatrix}$ anticommutative?

Group Exercise

84. The interesting and useful applications of matrix theory are nearly unlimited. Applications of matrices range from representing digital photographs to predicting long-range trends in the stock market. Members of the group should research an application of matrices that they find intriguing. The group should then present a seminar to the class about this application.

Preview Exercises

Exercises 85–87 will help you prepare for the material covered in the next section.

85. Multiply:

$$\begin{bmatrix} a_{11} & a_{12} \\ a_{21} & a_{22} \end{bmatrix} \begin{bmatrix} 1 & 0 \\ 0 & 1 \end{bmatrix}.$$

After performing the multiplication, describe what happens to the elements in the first matrix.

86. Use Gauss-Jordan elimination to solve the system:

$$\begin{cases} -x - y - z = 1 \\ 4x + 5y \quad\quad = 0 \\ \quad\quad y - 3z = 0. \end{cases}$$

87. Multiply and write the linear system represented by the following matrix multiplication:

$$\begin{bmatrix} a_1 & b_1 & c_1 \\ a_2 & b_2 & c_2 \\ a_3 & b_3 & c_3 \end{bmatrix} \begin{bmatrix} x \\ y \\ z \end{bmatrix} = \begin{bmatrix} d_1 \\ d_2 \\ d_3 \end{bmatrix}.$$

Chapter 6 Mid-Chapter Check Point

What You Know: We learned to use matrices to solve systems of linear equations. Gaussian elimination required simplifying the augmented matrix to one with 1s down the main diagonal and 0s below the 1s. Gauss-Jordan elimination simplified the augmented matrix to one with 1s down the main diagonal and 0s above and below each 1. Such a matrix, in reduced row-echelon form, did not require back-substitution to solve the system. We applied Gaussian elimination to systems with no solution, as well as to represent the solution set for systems with infinitely many solutions, including nonsquare systems. We learned how to perform operations with matrices, including matrix addition, matrix subtraction, scalar multiplication, and matrix multiplication.

In Exercises 1–5, use matrices to find the complete solution to each system of equations, or show that none exists.

1. $\begin{cases} x + 2y - 3z = -7 \\ 3x - y + 2z = 8 \\ 2x - y + z = 5 \end{cases}$

2. $\begin{cases} 2x + 4y + 5z = 2 \\ x + y + 2z = 1 \\ 3x + 5y + 7z = 4 \end{cases}$

3. $\begin{cases} x - 2y + 2z = -2 \\ 2x + 3y - z = 1 \end{cases}$

4. $\begin{cases} w + x + y + z = 6 \\ w - x + 3y + z = -14 \\ w + 2x \quad\quad - 3z = 12 \\ 2w + 3x + 6y + z = 1 \end{cases}$

5. $\begin{cases} 2x - 2y + 2z = 5 \\ x - y + z = 2 \\ 2x + y - z = 1 \end{cases}$

In Exercises 6–10, perform the indicated matrix operations or solve the matrix equation for X given that A, B, and C are defined as follows. If an operation is not defined, state the reason.

$$A = \begin{bmatrix} 0 & 2 \\ -1 & 3 \\ 1 & 0 \end{bmatrix} \quad B = \begin{bmatrix} 4 & 1 \\ -6 & -2 \end{bmatrix} \quad C = \begin{bmatrix} -1 & 0 \\ 0 & 1 \end{bmatrix}$$

6. $2C - \frac{1}{2}B$ **7.** $A(B + C)$ **8.** $A(BC)$

9. $A + C$ **10.** $2X - 3C = B$

Section 6.4 Multiplicative Inverses of Matrices and Matrix Equations

Objectives

1. Find the multiplicative inverse of a square matrix.
2. Use inverses to solve matrix equations.
3. Encode and decode messages.

This 1941 RCA radiogram shows an encoded message from the Japanese government.

In 1939, Britain's secret service hired top chess players, mathematicians, and other masters of logic to break the code used by the Nazis in communications between headquarters and troops. The project, which employed over 10,000 people, broke the code less than a year later, providing the Allies with information about Nazi troop movements throughout World War II.

Messages must often be sent in such a way that the real meaning is hidden from everyone but the sender and the recipient. In this section, we will look at the role that matrices and their inverses play in this process.

The Multiplicative Identity Matrix

For the real numbers, we know that 1 is the multiplicative identity because $a \cdot 1 = 1 \cdot a = a$. Is there a similar property for matrix multiplication? That is, is there a matrix I such that $AI = A$ and $IA = A$? The answer is yes. A square matrix with 1s down the main diagonal from upper left to lower right and 0s elsewhere does not change the elements in a matrix in products with that matrix. In the case of 2×2 matrices,

$$\begin{bmatrix} a_{11} & a_{12} \\ a_{21} & a_{22} \end{bmatrix} \begin{bmatrix} 1 & 0 \\ 0 & 1 \end{bmatrix} = \begin{bmatrix} a_{11} & a_{12} \\ a_{21} & a_{22} \end{bmatrix}$$

The elements in the matrix do not change.

and $\begin{bmatrix} 1 & 0 \\ 0 & 1 \end{bmatrix} \begin{bmatrix} a_{11} & a_{12} \\ a_{21} & a_{22} \end{bmatrix} = \begin{bmatrix} a_{11} & a_{12} \\ a_{21} & a_{22} \end{bmatrix}.$

The elements in the matrix do not change.

The $n \times n$ square matrix with 1s down the main diagonal from upper left to lower right and 0s elsewhere is called the **multiplicative identity matrix of order n**. This matrix is designated by I_n. For example,

$$I_2 = \begin{bmatrix} 1 & 0 \\ 0 & 1 \end{bmatrix}, \quad I_3 = \begin{bmatrix} 1 & 0 & 0 \\ 0 & 1 & 0 \\ 0 & 0 & 1 \end{bmatrix},$$

and so on.

① Find the multiplicative inverse of a square matrix.

The Multiplicative Inverse of a Matrix

The multiplicative identity matrix, I_n, will help us to define a new concept: the multiplicative inverse of a matrix. To do so, let's consider a similar concept, the multiplicative inverse of a nonzero number, a. Recall that the multiplicative inverse of a is $\frac{1}{a}$. The multiplicative inverse has the following property:

$$a \cdot \frac{1}{a} = 1 \quad \text{and} \quad \frac{1}{a} \cdot a = 1.$$

We can define the multiplicative inverse of a square matrix in a similar manner.

Definition of the Multiplicative Inverse of a Square Matrix

Let A be an $n \times n$ matrix. If there exists an $n \times n$ matrix A^{-1} (read: "A inverse") such that

$$AA^{-1} = I_n \quad \text{and} \quad A^{-1}A = I_n,$$

then A^{-1} is the **multiplicative inverse** of A.

We have seen that matrix multiplication is not commutative. Thus, to show that a matrix B is the multiplicative inverse of the matrix A, find both AB and BA. If B is the multiplicative inverse of A, both products (AB and BA) will be the multiplicative identity matrix, I_n.

EXAMPLE 1 **The Multiplicative Inverse of a Matrix**

Show that B is the multiplicative inverse of A, where

$$A = \begin{bmatrix} -1 & 3 \\ 2 & -5 \end{bmatrix} \quad \text{and} \quad B = \begin{bmatrix} 5 & 3 \\ 2 & 1 \end{bmatrix}.$$

Solution To show that B is the multiplicative inverse of A, we must find the products AB and BA. If B is the multiplicative inverse of A, then AB will be the

multiplicative identity matrix and BA will be the multiplicative identity matrix. Because A and B are 2×2 matrices, $n = 2$. Thus, we denote the multiplicative identity matrix as I_2; it is also a 2×2 matrix. We must show that

- $AB = I_2 = \begin{bmatrix} 1 & 0 \\ 0 & 1 \end{bmatrix}$ and

- $BA = I_2 = \begin{bmatrix} 1 & 0 \\ 0 & 1 \end{bmatrix}.$

Let's first show $AB = I_2$.

$$AB = \begin{bmatrix} -1 & 3 \\ 2 & -5 \end{bmatrix} \begin{bmatrix} 5 & 3 \\ 2 & 1 \end{bmatrix}$$

$$= \begin{bmatrix} -1(5) + 3(2) & -1(3) + 3(1) \\ 2(5) + (-5)(2) & 2(3) + (-5)(1) \end{bmatrix} = \begin{bmatrix} 1 & 0 \\ 0 & 1 \end{bmatrix}$$

Let's now show $BA = I_2$.

$$BA = \begin{bmatrix} 5 & 3 \\ 2 & 1 \end{bmatrix} \begin{bmatrix} -1 & 3 \\ 2 & -5 \end{bmatrix}$$

$$= \begin{bmatrix} 5(-1) + 3(2) & 5(3) + 3(-5) \\ 2(-1) + 1(2) & 2(3) + 1(-5) \end{bmatrix} = \begin{bmatrix} 1 & 0 \\ 0 & 1 \end{bmatrix}$$

Both products give the multiplicative identity matrix. Thus, B is the multiplicative inverse of A and we can designate B as $A^{-1} = \begin{bmatrix} 5 & 3 \\ 2 & 1 \end{bmatrix}.$ ●

⊘ Check Point **1** Show that B is the multiplicative inverse of A, where

$$A = \begin{bmatrix} 2 & 1 \\ 1 & 1 \end{bmatrix} \quad \text{and} \quad B = \begin{bmatrix} 1 & -1 \\ -1 & 2 \end{bmatrix}.$$

One method for finding the multiplicative inverse of a matrix A is to begin by denoting the elements in A^{-1} with variables. Using the equation $AA^{-1} = I_n$, we can find a value for each element in the multiplicative inverse that is represented by a variable. Example 2 shows how this is done.

(**EXAMPLE 2**) **Finding the Multiplicative Inverse of a Matrix**

Find the multiplicative inverse of

$$A = \begin{bmatrix} 2 & 1 \\ 5 & 3 \end{bmatrix}.$$

Solution Let us denote the multiplicative inverse by

$$A^{-1} = \begin{bmatrix} w & x \\ y & z \end{bmatrix}.$$

Because A is a 2×2 matrix, we use the equation $AA^{-1} = I_2$ to find values for w, x, y, and z.

$$\overset{A}{\begin{bmatrix} 2 & 1 \\ 5 & 3 \end{bmatrix}} \overset{A^{-1}}{\begin{bmatrix} w & x \\ y & z \end{bmatrix}} = \overset{I_2}{\begin{bmatrix} 1 & 0 \\ 0 & 1 \end{bmatrix}}$$

$$\begin{bmatrix} 2w + y & 2x + z \\ 5w + 3y & 5x + 3z \end{bmatrix} = \begin{bmatrix} 1 & 0 \\ 0 & 1 \end{bmatrix}$$

Use row-by-column matrix multiplication on the left side of $\begin{bmatrix} 2 & 1 \\ 5 & 3 \end{bmatrix} \begin{bmatrix} w & x \\ y & z \end{bmatrix} = \begin{bmatrix} 1 & 0 \\ 0 & 1 \end{bmatrix}.$

We now equate corresponding elements to obtain the following two systems of linear equations:

$$\begin{cases} 2w + y = 1 \\ 5w + 3y = 0 \end{cases} \quad \text{and} \quad \begin{cases} 2x + z = 0 \\ 5x + 3z = 1. \end{cases}$$

Technology

You can use a graphing utility to find the inverse of the matrix in Example 2. Enter the matrix and name it A. The screens show A and A^{-1}. Verify that this is correct by showing that

$$AA^{-1} = I_2 \quad \text{and} \quad A^{-1}A = I_2.$$

Each of these systems can be solved using the addition method.

$$\begin{cases} 2w + y = 1 \\ 5w + 3y = 0 \end{cases} \xrightarrow[\text{No change}]{\text{Multiply by } -3.}$$

$$\begin{array}{r} -6w - 3y = -3 \\ 5w + 3y = 0 \\ \hline -w = -3 \end{array}$$

Add:

$$\begin{aligned} w &= 3 \\ y &= -5 \end{aligned}$$

Use back-substitution.

$$\begin{cases} 2x + z = 0 \\ 5x + 3z = 1 \end{cases} \xrightarrow[\text{No change}]{\text{Multiply by } -3.}$$

$$\begin{array}{r} -6x - 3z = 0 \\ 5x + 3z = 1 \\ \hline -x = 1 \end{array}$$

Add:

$$\begin{aligned} x &= -1 \\ z &= 2 \end{aligned}$$

Use back-substitution.

Using these values, we have

$$A^{-1} = \begin{bmatrix} w & x \\ y & z \end{bmatrix} = \begin{bmatrix} 3 & -1 \\ -5 & 2 \end{bmatrix}.$$

⊘ **Check Point 2** Find the multiplicative inverse of $A = \begin{bmatrix} 5 & 7 \\ 2 & 3 \end{bmatrix}$.

Only square matrices of order $n \times n$ have multiplicative inverses, but not every square matrix possesses a multiplicative inverse. For example, suppose that you apply the procedure of Example 2 to $A = \begin{bmatrix} -6 & 4 \\ -3 & 2 \end{bmatrix}$:

This is A. This represents A^{-1}. This is the multiplicative identity matrix.

$$\begin{bmatrix} -6 & 4 \\ -3 & 2 \end{bmatrix} \begin{bmatrix} w & x \\ y & z \end{bmatrix} = \begin{bmatrix} 1 & 0 \\ 0 & 1 \end{bmatrix}.$$

Multiplying matrices on the left and equating corresponding elements results in inconsistent systems with no solutions. There are no values for w, x, y, and z. This shows that matrix A does not have a multiplicative inverse.

A nonsquare matrix, one with a different number of rows than columns, cannot have a multiplicative inverse. If A is an $m \times n$ matrix and B is an $n \times m$ matrix ($n \neq m$), then the products AB and BA are of different orders. This means that they could not be equal to each other, so that AB and BA could not both equal the multiplicative identity matrix.

If a square matrix has a multiplicative inverse, that inverse is unique. This means that the square matrix has no more than one inverse. If a square matrix has a multiplicative inverse, it is said to be **invertible** or **nonsingular.** If a square matrix has no multiplicative inverse, it is called **singular.**

A Quick Method for Finding the Multiplicative Inverse of a 2 × 2 Matrix

The same method used in Example 2 can be used to develop the general form of the multiplicative inverse of a 2 × 2 matrix. The following rule enables us to calculate the multiplicative inverse, if there is one:

Study Tip

To find the matrix that appears as the second factor for the inverse of

$$A = \begin{bmatrix} a & b \\ c & d \end{bmatrix}:$$

- Reverse a and d, the numbers in the diagonal from upper left to lower right.
- Negate b and c, the numbers in the other diagonal.

Multiplicative Inverse of a 2 × 2 Matrix

If $A = \begin{bmatrix} a & b \\ c & d \end{bmatrix}$, then $A^{-1} = \dfrac{1}{ad - bc}\begin{bmatrix} d & -b \\ -c & a \end{bmatrix}$.

The matrix A is invertible if and only if $ad - bc \neq 0$. If $ad - bc = 0$, then A does not have a multiplicative inverse.

(**EXAMPLE 3**) **Using the Quick Method to Find a Multiplicative Inverse**

Find the multiplicative inverse of

$$A = \begin{bmatrix} -1 & -2 \\ 3 & 4 \end{bmatrix}.$$

Solution

Study Tip

When using the formula to find the multiplicative inverse, start by computing $ad - bc$. If the computed value is 0, there is no need to continue. The given matrix is singular—that is, it does not have a multiplicative inverse.

$$A = \begin{bmatrix} -1 & -2 \\ 3 & 4 \end{bmatrix}$$

This is the given matrix. We've designated the elements a, b, c, and d.

$$A^{-1} = \frac{1}{ad - bc}\begin{bmatrix} d & -b \\ -c & a \end{bmatrix}$$

This is the formula for the inverse of $\begin{bmatrix} a & b \\ c & d \end{bmatrix}$.

$$= \frac{1}{(-1)(4) - (-2)(3)}\begin{bmatrix} 4 & -(-2) \\ -3 & -1 \end{bmatrix}$$

Apply the formula with $a = -1$, $b = -2$, $c = 3$, and $d = 4$.

$$= \frac{1}{2}\begin{bmatrix} 4 & 2 \\ -3 & -1 \end{bmatrix}$$

Simplify.

$$= \begin{bmatrix} 2 & 1 \\ -\frac{3}{2} & -\frac{1}{2} \end{bmatrix}$$

Perform the scalar multiplication by multiplying each element in the matrix by $\frac{1}{2}$.

The inverse of $A = \begin{bmatrix} -1 & -2 \\ 3 & 4 \end{bmatrix}$ is $A^{-1} = \begin{bmatrix} 2 & 1 \\ -\frac{3}{2} & -\frac{1}{2} \end{bmatrix}$.

We can verify this result by showing that $AA^{-1} = I_2$ and $A^{-1}A = I_2$. ●

⏺ Check Point **3** Find the multiplicative inverse of

$$A = \begin{bmatrix} 3 & -2 \\ -1 & 1 \end{bmatrix}.$$

Finding Multiplicative Inverses of $n \times n$ Matrices with n Greater Than 2

To find the multiplicative inverse of a 3×3 invertible matrix, we begin by denoting the elements in the multiplicative inverse with variables. Here is an example:

$$\begin{bmatrix} -1 & -1 & -1 \\ 4 & 5 & 0 \\ 0 & 1 & -3 \end{bmatrix} \begin{bmatrix} x_1 & x_2 & x_3 \\ y_1 & y_2 & y_3 \\ z_1 & z_2 & z_3 \end{bmatrix} = \begin{bmatrix} 1 & 0 & 0 \\ 0 & 1 & 0 \\ 0 & 0 & 1 \end{bmatrix}.$$

This is matrix A whose inverse we wish to find. | This represents A^{-1}. | This is the multiplicative identity matrix, I_3.

We multiply the matrices on the left, using the row-by-column definition of matrix multiplication.

$$\begin{bmatrix} -x_1 - y_1 - z_1 & -x_2 - y_2 - z_2 & -x_3 - y_3 - z_3 \\ 4x_1 + 5y_1 + 0z_1 & 4x_2 + 5y_2 + 0z_2 & 4x_3 + 5y_3 + 0z_3 \\ 0x_1 + 1y_1 - 3z_1 & 0x_2 + 1y_2 - 3z_2 & 0x_3 + 1y_3 - 3z_3 \end{bmatrix} = \begin{bmatrix} 1 & 0 & 0 \\ 0 & 1 & 0 \\ 0 & 0 & 1 \end{bmatrix}$$

We now equate corresponding entries to obtain the following three systems of linear equations:

$$\begin{cases} -x_1 - y_1 - z_1 = 1 \\ 4x_1 + 5y_1 + 0z_1 = 0 \\ 0x_1 + y_1 - 3z_1 = 0 \end{cases} \qquad \begin{cases} -x_2 - y_2 - z_2 = 0 \\ 4x_2 + 5y_2 + 0z_2 = 1 \\ 0x_2 + y_2 - 3z_2 = 0 \end{cases} \qquad \begin{cases} -x_3 - y_3 - z_3 = 0 \\ 4x_3 + 5y_3 + 0z_3 = 0 \\ 0x_3 + y_3 - 3z_3 = 1. \end{cases}$$

Notice that the variables on the left of the equal signs have the same coefficients in each system. We can use Gauss-Jordan elimination to solve all three systems at once. Form an augmented matrix that contains the coefficients of the three systems to the left of the vertical line and the constants for the systems to the right.

$$\left[\begin{array}{ccc|ccc} -1 & -1 & -1 & 1 & 0 & 0 \\ 4 & 5 & 0 & 0 & 1 & 0 \\ 0 & 1 & -3 & 0 & 0 & 1 \end{array}\right]$$

Coefficients of the three systems | Constants on the right in each of the three systems

To solve all three systems using Gauss-Jordan elimination, we must obtain $\begin{bmatrix} 1 & 0 & 0 \\ 0 & 1 & 0 \\ 0 & 0 & 1 \end{bmatrix}$ to the left of the vertical line. Use matrix row operations, working one column at a time. Obtain 1 in the required position. Then obtain 0s in the other two positions. Using these operations, we obtain the matrix

$$\left[\begin{array}{ccc|ccc} 1 & 0 & 0 & 15 & 4 & -5 \\ 0 & 1 & 0 & -12 & -3 & 4 \\ 0 & 0 & 1 & -4 & -1 & 1 \end{array}\right].$$

This augmented matrix provides the solutions to the three systems of equations. They are given by

$$\left[\begin{array}{ccc|c} 1 & 0 & 0 & 15 \\ 0 & 1 & 0 & -12 \\ 0 & 0 & 1 & -4 \end{array}\right] \qquad \begin{array}{l} x_1 = 15 \\ y_1 = -12 \\ z_1 = -4 \end{array}$$

and $\left[\begin{array}{ccc|c} 1 & 0 & 0 & 4 \\ 0 & 1 & 0 & -3 \\ 0 & 0 & 1 & -1 \end{array}\right] \quad \begin{array}{l} x_2 = 4 \\ y_2 = -3 \\ z_2 = -1 \end{array} \quad$ and $\left[\begin{array}{ccc|c} 1 & 0 & 0 & -5 \\ 0 & 1 & 0 & 4 \\ 0 & 0 & 1 & 1 \end{array}\right] \quad \begin{array}{l} x_3 = -5 \\ y_3 = 4 \\ z_3 = 1. \end{array}$

Using the nine values from the previous page, the inverse matrix is

$$\begin{bmatrix} x_1 & x_2 & x_3 \\ y_1 & y_2 & y_3 \\ z_1 & z_2 & z_3 \end{bmatrix} = \begin{bmatrix} 15 & 4 & -5 \\ -12 & -3 & 4 \\ -4 & -1 & 1 \end{bmatrix}.$$

Take a second look at the matrix obtained at the point where Gauss-Jordan elimination was completed. This matrix is shown, again, below. Notice that the 3×3 matrix to the right of the vertical bar is the multiplicative inverse of A. Also notice that the multiplicative identity matrix, I_3 is the matrix that appears to the left of the vertical bar.

$$\left[\begin{array}{ccc|ccc} 1 & 0 & 0 & 15 & 4 & -5 \\ 0 & 1 & 0 & -12 & -3 & 4 \\ 0 & 0 & 1 & -4 & -1 & 1 \end{array} \right].$$

This is the multiplicative identity, I_3.

This is the multiplicative inverse of A.

The observations in the voice balloons and the procedures followed above give us a general method for finding the multiplicative inverse of an invertible matrix.

Study Tip

Because we have a quick method for finding the multiplicative inverse of a 2×2 matrix, the procedure on the right is recommended for matrices of order 3×3 or greater when a graphing utility is not being used.

Procedure for Finding the Multiplicative Inverse of an Invertible Matrix

To find A^{-1} for any $n \times n$ matrix A for which A^{-1} exists,

1. Form the augmented matrix $[A|I_n]$, where I_n is the multiplicative identity matrix of the same order as the given matrix A.

2. Perform row operations on $[A|I_n]$ to obtain a matrix of the form $[I_n|B]$. This is equivalent to using Gauss-Jordan elimination to change A into the identity matrix.

3. Matrix B is A^{-1}.

4. Verify the result by showing that $AA^{-1} = I_n$ and $A^{-1}A = I_n$.

(**EXAMPLE 4**) **Finding the Multiplicative Inverse of a 3 \times 3 Matrix**

Find the multiplicative inverse of

$$A = \begin{bmatrix} 1 & -1 & 1 \\ 0 & -2 & 1 \\ -2 & -3 & 0 \end{bmatrix}.$$

Solution

Step 1 Form the augmented matrix $[A|I_3]$.

$$\left[\begin{array}{ccc|ccc} 1 & -1 & 1 & 1 & 0 & 0 \\ 0 & -2 & 1 & 0 & 1 & 0 \\ -2 & -3 & 0 & 0 & 0 & 1 \end{array} \right]$$

This is matrix A.

This is I_3, the multiplicative identity matrix, with 1s down the main diagonal and 0s elsewhere.

Step 2 Perform row operations on $[A|I_3]$ to obtain a matrix of the form $[I_3|B]$. To the left of the vertical dividing line, we want 1s down the diagonal from upper left to lower right and 0s elsewhere.

$$\left[\begin{array}{ccc|ccc} 1 & -1 & 1 & 1 & 0 & 0 \\ 0 & -2 & 1 & 0 & 1 & 0 \\ -2 & -3 & 0 & 0 & 0 & 1 \end{array}\right]$$

Replace row 3
by $2R_1 + R_3$.
→

$$\left[\begin{array}{ccc|ccc} 1 & -1 & 1 & 1 & 0 & 0 \\ 0 & -2 & 1 & 0 & 1 & 0 \\ 0 & -5 & 2 & 2 & 0 & 1 \end{array}\right]$$
$-\frac{1}{2}R_2$ →

$$\left[\begin{array}{ccc|ccc} 1 & -1 & 1 & 1 & 0 & 0 \\ 0 & 1 & -\frac{1}{2} & 0 & -\frac{1}{2} & 0 \\ 0 & -5 & 2 & 2 & 0 & 1 \end{array}\right]$$

Replace row 1 by $1R_2 + R_1$.
Replace row 3 by $5R_2 + R_3$.
→

$$\left[\begin{array}{ccc|ccc} 1 & 0 & \frac{1}{2} & 1 & -\frac{1}{2} & 0 \\ 0 & 1 & -\frac{1}{2} & 0 & -\frac{1}{2} & 0 \\ 0 & 0 & -\frac{1}{2} & 2 & -\frac{5}{2} & 1 \end{array}\right]$$
$-2R_3$ →

$$\left[\begin{array}{ccc|ccc} 1 & 0 & \frac{1}{2} & 1 & -\frac{1}{2} & 0 \\ 0 & 1 & -\frac{1}{2} & 0 & -\frac{1}{2} & 0 \\ 0 & 0 & 1 & -4 & 5 & -2 \end{array}\right]$$

Replace row 1 by $-\frac{1}{2}R_3 + R_1$.
Replace row 2 by $\frac{1}{2}R_3 + R_2$.
→

$$\left[\begin{array}{ccc|ccc} 1 & 0 & 0 & 3 & -3 & 1 \\ 0 & 1 & 0 & -2 & 2 & -1 \\ 0 & 0 & 1 & -4 & 5 & -2 \end{array}\right]$$

This is the multiplicative identity, I_3.

This is the multiplicative inverse of A.

Technology

We can use a graphing utility to verify the inverse matrix we found in Example 4. Enter the elements in matrix A and press $\boxed{x^{-1}}$ to display A^{-1}.

```
[A]
      [[1  -1  1]
       [0  -2  1]
       [-2 -3  0]]
[A]-1
      [[3  -3  1 ]
       [-2 2  -1]
       [-4 5  -2]]
```

Step 3 Matrix B is A^{-1}. The last matrix shown is in the form $[I_3 | B]$. The multiplicative identity matrix is on the left of the vertical bar. Matrix B, the multiplicative inverse of A, is on the right. Thus, the multiplicative inverse of A is

$$A^{-1} = \left[\begin{array}{ccc} 3 & -3 & 1 \\ -2 & 2 & -1 \\ -4 & 5 & -2 \end{array}\right].$$

Step 4 Verify the result by showing that $AA^{-1} = I_3$ and $A^{-1}A = I_3$. Try confirming the result by multiplying A and A^{-1} to obtain I_3. Do you obtain I_3 if you reverse the order of the multiplication?

We have seen that not all square matrices have multiplicative inverses. If the row operations in step 2 result in all zeros in a row or column to the left of the vertical line, the given matrix does not have a multiplicative inverse.

Technology

The matrix

$$A = \left[\begin{array}{cc} 4 & 6 \\ 2 & 3 \end{array}\right] = \left[\begin{array}{cc} a & b \\ c & d \end{array}\right]$$

has no multiplicative inverse because

$$ad - bc = 4 \cdot 3 - 6 \cdot 2$$
$$= 12 - 12 = 0.$$

When we try to find the inverse with a graphing utility, an ERROR message occurs, indicating the matrix is singular.

```
[A]
        [[4 6]
         [2 3]]
[A]-1
■
```

```
ERR:SINGULAR MAT
1■Quit
2:Goto
```

✓ **Check Point 4** Find the multiplicative inverse of

$$A = \left[\begin{array}{ccc} 1 & 0 & 2 \\ -1 & 2 & 3 \\ 1 & -1 & 0 \end{array}\right].$$

Summary: Finding Multiplicative Inverses for Invertible Matrices

Use a graphing utility with matrix capabilities, or

a. If the matrix is 2×2: The inverse of $A = \left[\begin{array}{cc} a & b \\ c & d \end{array}\right]$ is

$$A^{-1} = \frac{1}{ad - bc}\left[\begin{array}{cc} d & -b \\ -c & a \end{array}\right].$$

b. If the matrix A is $n \times n$ where $n > 2$: Use the procedure on page 598. Form $[A | I_n]$ and use row transformations to obtain $[I_n | B]$. Then $A^{-1} = B$.

Solving Systems of Equations Using Multiplicative Inverses of Matrices

Matrix multiplication can be used to represent a system of linear equations.

| **Linear System** | **Matrix Form of the System** |

$$\begin{cases} a_1x + b_1y + c_1z = d_1 \\ a_2x + b_2y + c_2z = d_2 \\ a_3x + b_3y + c_3z = d_3 \end{cases} \qquad \begin{bmatrix} a_1 & b_1 & c_1 \\ a_2 & b_2 & c_2 \\ a_3 & b_3 & c_3 \end{bmatrix} \begin{bmatrix} x \\ y \\ z \end{bmatrix} = \begin{bmatrix} d_1 \\ d_2 \\ d_3 \end{bmatrix}$$

> The matrix contains the system's coefficients. The matrix contains the system's variables. The matrix contains the system's constants.

You can work with the matrix form of the system and obtain the form of the linear system on the left. To do so, perform the matrix multiplication on the left side of the matrix equation. Then equate the corresponding elements.

The matrix equation

$$\underset{A}{\begin{bmatrix} a_1 & b_1 & c_1 \\ a_2 & b_2 & c_2 \\ a_3 & b_3 & c_3 \end{bmatrix}} \underset{X}{\begin{bmatrix} x \\ y \\ z \end{bmatrix}} = \underset{B}{\begin{bmatrix} d_1 \\ d_2 \\ d_3 \end{bmatrix}}$$

is abbreviated as $AX = B$, where A is the **coefficient matrix** of the system, and X and B are matrices containing one column, called **column matrices**. The matrix B is called the **constant matrix**.

Here is a specific example of a linear system and its matrix form:

| **Linear System** | **Matrix Form** |

$$\begin{cases} x - y + z = 2 \\ - 2y + z = 2 \\ -2x - 3y = \frac{1}{2} \end{cases} \qquad \underset{\substack{A,\ \text{the} \\ \text{coefficent} \\ \text{matrix}}}{\begin{bmatrix} 1 & -1 & 1 \\ 0 & -2 & 1 \\ -2 & -3 & 0 \end{bmatrix}} \underset{X}{\begin{bmatrix} x \\ y \\ z \end{bmatrix}} = \underset{\substack{B,\ \text{the} \\ \text{constant} \\ \text{matrix}}}{\begin{bmatrix} 2 \\ 2 \\ \frac{1}{2} \end{bmatrix}}$$

Coefficients Constants

The matrix equation $AX = B$ can be solved using A^{-1} if it exists.

$$AX = B \qquad \text{This is the matrix equation.}$$

$$A^{-1}AX = A^{-1}B \qquad \text{Multiply both sides by } A^{-1}. \text{ Because matrix multiplication is not commutative, put } A^{-1} \text{ in the same left position on both sides.}$$

$$I_nX = A^{-1}B \qquad \text{The multiplicative inverse property tells us that } A^{-1}A = I_n.$$

$$X = A^{-1}B \qquad \text{Because } I_n \text{ is the multiplicative identity, } I_nX = X.$$

We see that if $AX = B$, then $X = A^{-1}B$.

② Use inverses to solve matrix equations.

Solving a System Using A^{-1}

If $AX = B$ has a unique solution, then $X = A^{-1}B$. To solve a linear system of equations, multiply A^{-1} and B to find X.

EXAMPLE 5 Using the Inverse of a Matrix to Solve a System

Solve the system by using A^{-1}, the inverse of the coefficient matrix:

$$\begin{cases} x - y + z = 2 \\ -2y + z = 2 \\ -2x - 3y = \frac{1}{2}. \end{cases}$$

Technology

We can use a graphing utility to solve a linear system with a unique solution by entering the elements in A, the coefficient matrix, and B, the column matrix. Then find the product of A^{-1} and B. The screen below verifies our solution in Example 5.

This verifies that
$x = .5$, or $\frac{1}{2}$,
$y = -.5$, or $-\frac{1}{2}$,
and $z = 1$.

Solution The linear system can be written as

$$\underbrace{\begin{bmatrix} 1 & -1 & 1 \\ 0 & -2 & 1 \\ -2 & -3 & 0 \end{bmatrix}}_{A} \underbrace{\begin{bmatrix} x \\ y \\ z \end{bmatrix}}_{X} = \underbrace{\begin{bmatrix} 2 \\ 2 \\ \frac{1}{2} \end{bmatrix}}_{B}.$$

The solution is given by $X = A^{-1}B$. Consequently, we must find A^{-1}. We found the inverse of matrix A in Example 4. Using this result,

$$X = A^{-1}B = \begin{bmatrix} 3 & -3 & 1 \\ -2 & 2 & -1 \\ -4 & 5 & -2 \end{bmatrix} \begin{bmatrix} 2 \\ 2 \\ \frac{1}{2} \end{bmatrix} = \begin{bmatrix} 3\cdot 2 + (-3)\cdot 2 + 1\cdot\frac{1}{2} \\ -2\cdot 2 + 2\cdot 2 + (-1)\cdot\frac{1}{2} \\ -4\cdot 2 + 5\cdot 2 + (-2)\cdot\frac{1}{2} \end{bmatrix} = \begin{bmatrix} \frac{1}{2} \\ -\frac{1}{2} \\ 1 \end{bmatrix}.$$

Thus, $x = \frac{1}{2}$, $y = -\frac{1}{2}$, and $z = 1$. The solution set is $\left\{\left(\frac{1}{2}, -\frac{1}{2}, 1\right)\right\}$. ●

✓ Check Point **5** Solve the system by using A^{-1}, the inverse of the coefficient matrix that you found in Check Point 4:

$$\begin{cases} x + 2z = 6 \\ -x + 2y + 3z = -5 \\ x - y = 6. \end{cases}$$

③ Encode and decode messages.

Applications of Matrix Inverses to Coding

A **cryptogram** is a message written so that no one other than the intended recipient can understand it. To encode a message, we begin by assigning a number to each letter in the alphabet: $A = 1, B = 2, C = 3, \ldots, Z = 26$, and a space $= 0$. For example, the numerical equivalent of the word MATH is 13, 1, 20, 8. The numerical equivalent of the message is then converted into a matrix. Finally, an invertible matrix can be used to convert the message into code. The multiplicative inverse of this matrix can be used to decode the message.

> ### Encoding a Word or Message
>
> 1. Express the word or message numerically.
> 2. List the numbers in step 1 by columns and form a square matrix. If you do not have enough numbers to form a square matrix, put zeros in any remaining spaces in the last column.
> 3. Select any square invertible matrix, called the **coding matrix**, the same size as the matrix in step 2. Multiply the coding matrix by the square matrix that expresses the message numerically. The resulting matrix is the **coded matrix**.
> 4. Use the numbers, by columns, from the coded matrix in step 3 to write the encoded message.

$(\text{EXAMPLE } 6)$ **Encoding a Word**

Use matrices to encode the word MATH.

Solution

Step 1 Express the word numerically. As shown previously, the numerical equivalent of MATH is 13, 1, 20, 8.

Step 2 List the numbers in step 1 by columns and form a square matrix. The 2×2 matrix for the numerical equivalent of MATH, 13, 1, 20, 8, is

$$\begin{bmatrix} 13 & 20 \\ 1 & 8 \end{bmatrix}.$$

Step 3 Multiply the matrix in step 2 by a square invertible matrix. We will use $\begin{bmatrix} -2 & -3 \\ 3 & 4 \end{bmatrix}$ as the coding matrix.

$$\begin{bmatrix} -2 & -3 \\ 3 & 4 \end{bmatrix} \begin{bmatrix} 13 & 20 \\ 1 & 8 \end{bmatrix} = \begin{bmatrix} -2(13) - 3(1) & -2(20) - 3(8) \\ 3(13) + 4(1) & 3(20) + 4(8) \end{bmatrix}$$

Coding matrix Numerical representation of MATH

$$= \begin{bmatrix} -29 & -64 \\ 43 & 92 \end{bmatrix}$$

Coded matrix

Step 4 Use the numbers, by columns, from the coded matrix in step 3 to write the encoded message. The encoded message is $-29, \ 43, -64, \ 92$. ●

\oslash Check Point **6** Use the coding matrix in Example 6, $\begin{bmatrix} -2 & -3 \\ 3 & 4 \end{bmatrix}$, to encode the word BASE.

The inverse of a coding matrix can be used to decode a word or message that was encoded.

Decoding a Word or Message That Was Encoded

1. Find the multiplicative inverse of the coding matrix.
2. Multiply the multiplicative inverse of the coding matrix and the coded matrix.
3. Express the numbers, by columns, from the matrix in step 2 as letters.

$(\text{EXAMPLE } 7)$ **Decoding a Word**

Decode $-29, 43, -64, 92$ from Example 6.

Solution

Step 1 Find the inverse of the coding matrix. The coding matrix in Example 6 was $\begin{bmatrix} -2 & -3 \\ 3 & 4 \end{bmatrix}$. We use the formula for the multiplicative inverse of a 2×2 matrix to find the multiplicative inverse of this matrix. It is $\begin{bmatrix} 4 & 3 \\ -3 & -2 \end{bmatrix}$.

Step 2 Multiply the multiplicative inverse of the coding matrix and the coded matrix.

$$\underbrace{\begin{bmatrix} 4 & 3 \\ -3 & -2 \end{bmatrix}}_{\substack{\text{Multiplicative inverse} \\ \text{of the coding matrix}}} \underbrace{\begin{bmatrix} -29 & -64 \\ 43 & 92 \end{bmatrix}}_{\substack{\text{Coded} \\ \text{matrix}}} = \begin{bmatrix} 4(-29) + 3(43) & 4(-64) + 3(92) \\ -3(-29) - 2(43) & -3(-64) - 2(92) \end{bmatrix}$$

$$= \begin{bmatrix} 13 & 20 \\ 1 & 8 \end{bmatrix}$$

Step 3 Express the numbers, by columns, from the matrix in step 2 as letters. The numbers are 13, 1, 20, and 8. Using letters, the decoded message is MATH. ●

✓ Check Point **7** Decode the word that you encoded in Check Point 6.

Decoding is simple for an authorized receiver who knows the coding matrix. Because any invertible matrix can be used for the coding matrix, decoding a cryptogram for an unauthorized receiver who does not know this matrix is extremely difficult.

Exercise Set 6.4

Practice Exercises

In Exercises 1–12, find the products AB and BA to determine whether B is the multiplicative inverse of A.

1. $A = \begin{bmatrix} 4 & -3 \\ -5 & 4 \end{bmatrix}$, $B = \begin{bmatrix} 4 & 3 \\ 5 & 4 \end{bmatrix}$

2. $A = \begin{bmatrix} -2 & -1 \\ -1 & 1 \end{bmatrix}$, $B = \begin{bmatrix} 1 & 1 \\ 1 & 2 \end{bmatrix}$

3. $A = \begin{bmatrix} -4 & 0 \\ 1 & 3 \end{bmatrix}$, $B = \begin{bmatrix} -2 & 4 \\ 0 & 1 \end{bmatrix}$

4. $A = \begin{bmatrix} -2 & 4 \\ 1 & -2 \end{bmatrix}$, $B = \begin{bmatrix} 1 & 2 \\ -1 & -2 \end{bmatrix}$

5. $A = \begin{bmatrix} -2 & 1 \\ \frac{3}{2} & -\frac{1}{2} \end{bmatrix}$, $B = \begin{bmatrix} 1 & 2 \\ 3 & 4 \end{bmatrix}$

6. $A = \begin{bmatrix} 4 & 5 \\ 2 & 3 \end{bmatrix}$, $B = \begin{bmatrix} \frac{3}{2} & -\frac{5}{2} \\ -1 & 2 \end{bmatrix}$

7. $A = \begin{bmatrix} 0 & 1 & 0 \\ 0 & 0 & 1 \\ 1 & 0 & 0 \end{bmatrix}$, $B = \begin{bmatrix} 0 & 0 & 1 \\ 1 & 0 & 0 \\ 0 & 1 & 0 \end{bmatrix}$

8. $A = \begin{bmatrix} -2 & 1 & -1 \\ -5 & 2 & -1 \\ 3 & -1 & 1 \end{bmatrix}$, $B = \begin{bmatrix} 1 & 0 & 1 \\ 2 & 1 & 3 \\ -1 & 1 & 1 \end{bmatrix}$

9. $A = \begin{bmatrix} 1 & 2 & 3 \\ 1 & 3 & 4 \\ 1 & 4 & 3 \end{bmatrix}$, $B = \begin{bmatrix} \frac{7}{2} & -3 & \frac{1}{2} \\ -\frac{1}{2} & 0 & \frac{1}{2} \\ -\frac{1}{2} & 1 & -\frac{1}{2} \end{bmatrix}$

10. $A = \begin{bmatrix} 0 & 2 & 0 \\ 3 & 3 & 2 \\ 2 & 5 & 1 \end{bmatrix}$, $B = \begin{bmatrix} -3.5 & -1 & 2 \\ 0.5 & 0 & 0 \\ 4.5 & 2 & -3 \end{bmatrix}$

11. $A = \begin{bmatrix} 0 & 0 & -2 & 1 \\ -1 & 0 & 1 & 1 \\ 0 & 1 & -1 & 0 \\ 1 & 0 & 0 & -1 \end{bmatrix}$, $B = \begin{bmatrix} 1 & 2 & 0 & 3 \\ 0 & 1 & 1 & 1 \\ 0 & 1 & 0 & 1 \\ 1 & 2 & 0 & 2 \end{bmatrix}$

12. $A = \begin{bmatrix} 1 & -2 & 1 & 0 \\ 0 & 1 & -2 & 1 \\ 0 & 0 & 1 & -2 \\ 0 & 0 & 0 & 1 \end{bmatrix}$, $B = \begin{bmatrix} 1 & 2 & 3 & 4 \\ 0 & 1 & 2 & 3 \\ 0 & 0 & 1 & 2 \\ 0 & 0 & 0 & 1 \end{bmatrix}$

In Exercises 13–18, use the fact that if $A = \begin{bmatrix} a & b \\ c & d \end{bmatrix}$, then

$A^{-1} = \dfrac{1}{ad - bc}\begin{bmatrix} d & -b \\ -c & a \end{bmatrix}$ *to find the inverse of each matrix, if possible. Check that $AA^{-1} = I_2$ and $A^{-1}A = I_2$.*

13. $A = \begin{bmatrix} 2 & 3 \\ -1 & 2 \end{bmatrix}$

14. $A = \begin{bmatrix} 0 & 3 \\ 4 & -2 \end{bmatrix}$

15. $A = \begin{bmatrix} 3 & -1 \\ -4 & 2 \end{bmatrix}$

16. $A = \begin{bmatrix} 2 & -6 \\ 1 & -2 \end{bmatrix}$

17. $A = \begin{bmatrix} 10 & -2 \\ -5 & 1 \end{bmatrix}$

18. $A = \begin{bmatrix} 6 & -3 \\ -2 & 1 \end{bmatrix}$

In Exercises 19–28, find A^{-1} by forming $[A|I]$ and then using row operations to obtain $[I|B]$, where $A^{-1} = [B]$. Check that $AA^{-1} = I$ and $A^{-1}A = I$.

19. $A = \begin{bmatrix} 2 & 0 & 0 \\ 0 & 4 & 0 \\ 0 & 0 & 6 \end{bmatrix}$

20. $A = \begin{bmatrix} 3 & 0 & 0 \\ 0 & 6 & 0 \\ 0 & 0 & 9 \end{bmatrix}$

21. $A = \begin{bmatrix} 1 & 2 & -1 \\ -2 & 0 & 1 \\ 1 & -1 & 0 \end{bmatrix}$

22. $A = \begin{bmatrix} 1 & -1 & 1 \\ 0 & 2 & -1 \\ 2 & 3 & 0 \end{bmatrix}$

23. $A = \begin{bmatrix} 2 & 2 & -1 \\ 0 & 3 & -1 \\ -1 & -2 & 1 \end{bmatrix}$

24. $A = \begin{bmatrix} 2 & 4 & -4 \\ 1 & 3 & -4 \\ 2 & 4 & -3 \end{bmatrix}$

25. $A = \begin{bmatrix} 5 & 0 & 2 \\ 2 & 2 & 1 \\ -3 & 1 & -1 \end{bmatrix}$

26. $A = \begin{bmatrix} 3 & 2 & 6 \\ 1 & 1 & 2 \\ 2 & 2 & 5 \end{bmatrix}$

27. $A = \begin{bmatrix} 1 & 0 & 0 & 0 \\ 0 & -1 & 0 & 0 \\ 0 & 0 & 3 & 0 \\ 1 & 0 & 0 & 1 \end{bmatrix}$

28. $A = \begin{bmatrix} 2 & 0 & 0 & 1 \\ 0 & 1 & 0 & 0 \\ 0 & 0 & -1 & 0 \\ 0 & 0 & 0 & 2 \end{bmatrix}$

In Exercises 29–32, write each linear system as a matrix equation in the form $AX = B$, where A is the coefficient matrix and B is the constant matrix.

29. $\begin{cases} 6x + 5y = 13 \\ 5x + 4y = 10 \end{cases}$

30. $\begin{cases} 7x + 5y = 23 \\ 3x + 2y = 10 \end{cases}$

31. $\begin{cases} x + 3y + 4z = -3 \\ x + 2y + 3z = -2 \\ x + 4y + 3z = -6 \end{cases}$

32. $\begin{cases} x + 4y - z = 3 \\ x + 3y - 2z = 5 \\ 2x + 7y - 5z = 12 \end{cases}$

In Exercises 33–36, write each matrix equation as a system of linear equations without matrices.

33. $\begin{bmatrix} 4 & -7 \\ 2 & -3 \end{bmatrix} \begin{bmatrix} x \\ y \end{bmatrix} = \begin{bmatrix} -3 \\ 1 \end{bmatrix}$

34. $\begin{bmatrix} 3 & 0 \\ -3 & 1 \end{bmatrix} \begin{bmatrix} x \\ y \end{bmatrix} = \begin{bmatrix} 6 \\ -7 \end{bmatrix}$

35. $\begin{bmatrix} 2 & 0 & -1 \\ 0 & 3 & 0 \\ 1 & 1 & 0 \end{bmatrix} \begin{bmatrix} x \\ y \\ z \end{bmatrix} = \begin{bmatrix} 6 \\ 9 \\ 5 \end{bmatrix}$

36. $\begin{bmatrix} -1 & 0 & 1 \\ 0 & -1 & 0 \\ 0 & 1 & 1 \end{bmatrix} \begin{bmatrix} x \\ y \\ z \end{bmatrix} = \begin{bmatrix} -4 \\ 2 \\ 4 \end{bmatrix}$

In Exercises 37–42,

 a. *Write each linear system as a matrix equation in the form $AX = B$.*

 b. *Solve the system using the inverse that is given for the coefficient matrix.*

37. $\begin{cases} 2x + 6y + 6z = 8 \\ 2x + 7y + 6z = 10 \\ 2x + 7y + 7z = 9 \end{cases}$

The inverse of

$\begin{bmatrix} 2 & 6 & 6 \\ 2 & 7 & 6 \\ 2 & 7 & 7 \end{bmatrix}$ is $\begin{bmatrix} \frac{7}{2} & 0 & -3 \\ -1 & 1 & 0 \\ 0 & -1 & 1 \end{bmatrix}$.

38. $\begin{cases} x + 2y + 5z = 2 \\ 2x + 3y + 8z = 3 \\ -x + y + 2z = 3 \end{cases}$

The inverse of

$\begin{bmatrix} 1 & 2 & 5 \\ 2 & 3 & 8 \\ -1 & 1 & 2 \end{bmatrix}$ is $\begin{bmatrix} 2 & -1 & -1 \\ 12 & -7 & -2 \\ -5 & 3 & 1 \end{bmatrix}$.

39. $\begin{cases} x - y + z = 8 \\ 2y - z = -7 \\ 2x + 3y = 1 \end{cases}$

The inverse of

$\begin{bmatrix} 1 & -1 & 1 \\ 0 & 2 & -1 \\ 2 & 3 & 0 \end{bmatrix}$ is $\begin{bmatrix} 3 & 3 & -1 \\ -2 & -2 & 1 \\ -4 & -5 & 2 \end{bmatrix}$.

40. $\begin{cases} x - 6y + 3z = 11 \\ 2x - 7y + 3z = 14 \\ 4x - 12y + 5z = 25 \end{cases}$

The inverse of

$\begin{bmatrix} 1 & -6 & 3 \\ 2 & -7 & 3 \\ 4 & -12 & 5 \end{bmatrix}$ is $\begin{bmatrix} 1 & -6 & 3 \\ 2 & -7 & 3 \\ 4 & -12 & 5 \end{bmatrix}$.

41. $\begin{cases} w - x + 2y = -3 \\ x - y + z = 4 \\ -w + x - y + 2z = 2 \\ -x + y - 2z = -4 \end{cases}$

The inverse of

$\begin{bmatrix} 1 & -1 & 2 & 0 \\ 0 & 1 & -1 & 1 \\ -1 & 1 & -1 & 2 \\ 0 & -1 & 1 & -2 \end{bmatrix}$ is $\begin{bmatrix} 0 & 0 & -1 & -1 \\ 1 & 4 & 1 & 3 \\ 1 & 2 & 1 & 2 \\ 0 & -1 & 0 & -1 \end{bmatrix}$.

42. $\begin{cases} 2w + y + z = 6 \\ 3w + z = 9 \\ -w + x - 2y + z = 4 \\ 4w - x + y = 6 \end{cases}$

The inverse of

$\begin{bmatrix} 2 & 0 & 1 & 1 \\ 3 & 0 & 0 & 1 \\ -1 & 1 & -2 & 1 \\ 4 & -1 & 1 & 0 \end{bmatrix}$ is $\begin{bmatrix} -1 & 2 & -1 & -1 \\ -4 & 9 & -5 & -6 \\ 0 & 1 & -1 & -1 \\ 3 & -5 & 3 & 3 \end{bmatrix}$.

Practice Plus

In Exercises 43–44, find A^{-1} and check.

43. $A = \begin{bmatrix} e^x & e^{3x} \\ -e^{3x} & e^{5x} \end{bmatrix}$

44. $A = \begin{bmatrix} e^{2x} & -e^x \\ e^{3x} & e^{2x} \end{bmatrix}$

In Exercises 45–46, if I is the multiplicative identity matrix of order 2, find $(I - A)^{-1}$ for the given matrix A.

45. $\begin{bmatrix} 8 & -5 \\ -3 & 2 \end{bmatrix}$

46. $\begin{bmatrix} 7 & -5 \\ -4 & 3 \end{bmatrix}$

In Exercises 47–48, find $(AB)^{-1}$, $A^{-1}B^{-1}$, and $B^{-1}A^{-1}$. What do you observe?

47. $A = \begin{bmatrix} 2 & 1 \\ 3 & 1 \end{bmatrix} \quad B = \begin{bmatrix} 4 & 7 \\ 1 & 2 \end{bmatrix}$

48. $A = \begin{bmatrix} 2 & -9 \\ 1 & -4 \end{bmatrix} \quad B = \begin{bmatrix} 9 & 5 \\ 7 & 4 \end{bmatrix}$

49. Prove the following statement:

If $A = \begin{bmatrix} a & 0 & 0 \\ 0 & b & 0 \\ 0 & 0 & c \end{bmatrix}$, $a \neq 0, b \neq 0, c \neq 0$,

then $A^{-1} = \begin{bmatrix} \frac{1}{a} & 0 & 0 \\ 0 & \frac{1}{b} & 0 \\ 0 & 0 & \frac{1}{c} \end{bmatrix}$.

50. Prove the following statement:

If $A = \begin{bmatrix} a & b \\ c & d \end{bmatrix}$ and $ad - bc \neq 0$,

then $A^{-1} = \dfrac{1}{ad - bc} \begin{bmatrix} d & -b \\ -c & a \end{bmatrix}$.

(*Hint:* Use the method of Example 2 on page 594.)

Application Exercises

In Exercises 51–52, use the coding matrix

$$A = \begin{bmatrix} 4 & -1 \\ -3 & 1 \end{bmatrix} \text{ and its inverse } A^{-1} = \begin{bmatrix} 1 & 1 \\ 3 & 4 \end{bmatrix}$$

to encode and then decode the given message.

51. HELP

52. LOVE

In Exercises 53–54, use the coding matrix

$$A = \begin{bmatrix} 1 & -1 & 0 \\ 3 & 0 & 2 \\ -1 & 0 & -1 \end{bmatrix} \text{ and its inverse}$$

$$A^{-1} = \begin{bmatrix} 0 & 1 & 2 \\ -1 & 1 & 2 \\ 0 & -1 & -3 \end{bmatrix} \text{ to write a cryptogram for each}$$

message. Check your result by decoding the cryptogram.

53. S E N D _ C A S H
 19 5 14 4 0 3 1 19 8

Use $\begin{bmatrix} 19 & 4 & 1 \\ 5 & 0 & 19 \\ 14 & 3 & 8 \end{bmatrix}$.

54. S T A Y _ W E L L
 19 20 1 25 0 23 5 12 12

Use $\begin{bmatrix} 19 & 25 & 5 \\ 20 & 0 & 12 \\ 1 & 23 & 12 \end{bmatrix}$.

Writing in Mathematics

55. What is the multiplicative identity matrix?

56. If you are given two matrices, A and B, explain how to determine if B is the multiplicative inverse of A.

57. Explain why a matrix that does not have the same number of rows and columns cannot have a multiplicative inverse.

58. Explain how to find the multiplicative inverse for a 2×2 invertible matrix.

59. Explain how to find the multiplicative inverse for a 3×3 invertible matrix.

60. Explain how to write a linear system of three equations in three variables as a matrix equation.

61. Explain how to solve the matrix equation $AX = B$.

62. What is a cryptogram?

63. It's January 1, and you've written down your major goal for the year. You do not want those closest to you to see what you've written in case you do not accomplish your objective. Consequently, you decide to use a coding matrix to encode your goal. Explain how this can be accomplished.

64. A year has passed since Exercise 63. (Time flies when you're solving exercises in algebra books.) It's been a terrific year and so many wonderful things have happened that you can't remember your goal from a year ago. You consult your personal journal and you find the encoded message and the coding matrix. How can you use these to find your original goal?

Technology Exercises

In Exercises 65–70, use a graphing utility to find the multiplicative inverse of each matrix. Check that the displayed inverse is correct.

65. $\begin{bmatrix} 3 & -1 \\ -2 & 1 \end{bmatrix}$

66. $\begin{bmatrix} -4 & 1 \\ 6 & -2 \end{bmatrix}$

67. $\begin{bmatrix} -2 & 1 & -1 \\ -5 & 2 & -1 \\ 3 & -1 & 1 \end{bmatrix}$

68. $\begin{bmatrix} 1 & 1 & -1 \\ -3 & 2 & -1 \\ 3 & -3 & 2 \end{bmatrix}$

69. $\begin{bmatrix} 7 & -3 & 0 & 2 \\ -2 & 1 & 0 & -1 \\ 4 & 0 & 1 & -2 \\ -1 & 1 & 0 & -1 \end{bmatrix}$

70. $\begin{bmatrix} 1 & 2 & 0 & 0 \\ 0 & 0 & 1 & 0 \\ 1 & 3 & 0 & 1 \\ 4 & 0 & 0 & 2 \end{bmatrix}$

In Exercises 71–76, write each system in the form $AX = B$. Then solve the system by entering A and B into your graphing utility and computing $A^{-1}B$.

71. $\begin{cases} x - y + z = -6 \\ 4x + 2y + z = 9 \\ 4x - 2y + z = -3 \end{cases}$

72. $\begin{cases} y + 2z = 0 \\ -x + y = 1 \\ 2x - y + z = -1 \end{cases}$

73. $\begin{cases} 3x - 2y + z = -2 \\ 4x - 5y + 3z = -9 \\ 2x - y + 5z = -5 \end{cases}$

74. $\begin{cases} x - y = 1 \\ 6x + y + 20z = 14 \\ y + 3z = 1 \end{cases}$

75. $\begin{cases} v - 3x + z = -3 \\ w + y = -1 \\ x + z = 7 \\ v + w - x + 4y = -8 \\ v + w + x + y + z = 8 \end{cases}$

76. $\begin{cases} w + x + y + z = 4 \\ w + 3x - 2y + 2z = 7 \\ 2w + 2x + y + z = 3 \\ w - x + 2y + 3z = 5 \end{cases}$

In Exercises 77–78, use a coding matrix A of your choice. Use a graphing utility to find the multiplicative inverse of your coding matrix. Write a cryptogram for each message. Check your result by decoding the cryptogram. Use your graphing utility to perform all necessary matrix multiplications.

77. A R R I V E D _ S A F E L Y
 1 18 18 9 22 5 4 0 19 1 6 5 12 25

78. A R T _ E N R I C H E S
 1 18 20 0 5 14 18 9 3 8 5 19

Critical Thinking Exercises

Make Sense? *In Exercises 79–82, determine whether each statement makes sense or does not make sense, and explain your reasoning.*

79. I found the multiplicative inverse of a 2×3 matrix.

80. I used Gauss-Jordan elimination to find the multiplicative inverse of a 3×3 matrix.

81. I used matrix multiplication to represent a system of linear equations.

82. I made an encoding error by selecting the wrong square invertible matrix.

In Exercises 83–88, determine whether each statement is true or false. If the statement is false, make the necessary change(s) to produce a true statement.

83. All square 2×2 matrices have inverses because there is a formula for finding these inverses.

84. Two 2×2 invertible matrices can have a matrix sum that is not invertible.

85. To solve the matrix equation $AX = B$ for X, multiply A and the inverse of B.

86. $(AB)^{-1} = A^{-1}B^{-1}$, assuming A, B, and AB are invertible.

87. $(A + B)^{-1} = A^{-1} + B^{-1}$, assuming A, B, and $A + B$ are invertible.

88. $\begin{bmatrix} 1 & -3 \\ -1 & 3 \end{bmatrix}$ is an invertible matrix.

89. Give an example of a 2×2 matrix that is its own inverse.

90. If $A = \begin{bmatrix} 3 & 5 \\ 2 & 4 \end{bmatrix}$, find $(A^{-1})^{-1}$.

91. Find values of a for which the following matrix is not invertible:

$$\begin{bmatrix} 1 & a + 1 \\ a - 2 & 4 \end{bmatrix}.$$

Group Exercise

92. Each person in the group should work with one partner. Send a coded word or message to each other by giving your partner the coded matrix and the coding matrix that you selected. Once messages are sent, each person should decode the message received.

Preview Exercises

Exercises 93–95 will help you prepare for the material covered in the next section. Simplify the expression in each exercise.

93. $2(-5) - (-3)(4)$

94. $\dfrac{2(-5) - 1(-4)}{5(-5) - 6(-4)}$

95. $2(-30 - (-3)) - 3(6 - 9) + (-1)(1 - 15)$

Section 6.5 — Determinants and Cramer's Rule

Objectives

1. Evaluate a second-order determinant.
2. Solve a system of linear equations in two variables using Cramer's rule.
3. Evaluate a third-order determinant.
4. Solve a system of linear equations in three variables using Cramer's rule.
5. Use determinants to identify inconsistent systems and systems with dependent equations.
6. Evaluate higher-order determinants.

A portion of Charles Babbage's unrealized Difference Engine

As cyberspace absorbs more and more of our work, play, shopping, and socializing, where will it all end? Which activities will still be offline in 2025?

Our technologically transformed lives can be traced back to the English inventor Charles Babbage (1792–1871). Babbage knew of a method for solving linear systems called *Cramer's rule*, in honor of the Swiss geometer Gabriel Cramer (1704–1752). Cramer's rule was simple, but involved numerous multiplications for large systems. Babbage designed a machine, called the "difference engine," that consisted of toothed wheels on shafts for performing these multiplications. Despite the fact that only one-seventh of the functions ever worked, Babbage's invention demonstrated how complex calculations could be handled mechanically. In 1944, scientists at IBM used the lessons of the difference engine to create the world's first computer.

Those who invented computers hoped to relegate the drudgery of repeated computation to a machine. In this section, we look at a method for solving linear systems that played a critical role in this process. The method uses real numbers, called *determinants*, that are associated with arrays of numbers. As with matrix methods, solutions are obtained by writing down the coefficients and constants of a linear system and performing operations with them.

① Evaluate a second-order determinant.

The Determinant of a 2 × 2 Matrix

Associated with every square matrix is a real number, called its **determinant**. The determinant for a 2 × 2 square matrix is defined as follows:

Study Tip

To evaluate a second-order determinant, find the difference of the product of the two diagonals.

$$\begin{vmatrix} a_1 & b_1 \\ a_2 & b_2 \end{vmatrix} = a_1 b_2 - a_2 b_1$$

Definition of the Determinant of a 2 × 2 Matrix

The determinant of the matrix $\begin{bmatrix} a_1 & b_1 \\ a_2 & b_2 \end{bmatrix}$ is denoted by $\begin{vmatrix} a_1 & b_1 \\ a_2 & b_2 \end{vmatrix}$ and is defined by

$$\begin{vmatrix} a_1 & b_1 \\ a_2 & b_2 \end{vmatrix} = a_1 b_2 - a_2 b_1.$$

We also say that the **value** of the **second-order determinant** $\begin{vmatrix} a_1 & b_1 \\ a_2 & b_2 \end{vmatrix}$ is $a_1 b_2 - a_2 b_1$.

Example 1 illustrates that the determinant of a matrix may be positive or negative. A determinant can also have 0 as its value.

EXAMPLE 1 Evaluating the Determinant of a 2 × 2 Matrix

Evaluate the determinant of each of the following matrices:

a. $\begin{bmatrix} 5 & 6 \\ 7 & 3 \end{bmatrix}$ **b.** $\begin{bmatrix} 2 & 4 \\ -3 & -5 \end{bmatrix}$.

Discovery

Write and then evaluate three determinants, one whose value is positive, one whose value is negative, and one whose value is 0.

Solution We multiply and subtract as indicated.

a. $\begin{vmatrix} 5 & 6 \\ 7 & 3 \end{vmatrix} = 5 \cdot 3 - 7 \cdot 6 = 15 - 42 = -27$ *The value of the second-order determinant is -27.*

b. $\begin{vmatrix} 2 & 4 \\ -3 & -5 \end{vmatrix} = 2(-5) - (-3)(4) = -10 + 12 = 2$ *The value of the second-order determinant is 2.*

✓ **Check Point 1** Evaluate the determinant of each of the following matrices:

a. $\begin{bmatrix} 10 & 9 \\ 6 & 5 \end{bmatrix}$ **b.** $\begin{bmatrix} 4 & 3 \\ -5 & -8 \end{bmatrix}$.

② Solve a system of linear equations in two variables using Cramer's rule.

Solving Systems of Linear Equations in Two Variables Using Determinants

Determinants can be used to solve a linear system in two variables. In general, such a system appears as

$$\begin{cases} a_1 x + b_1 y = c_1 \\ a_2 x + b_2 y = c_2. \end{cases}$$

Let's first solve this system for x using the addition method. We can solve for x by eliminating y from the equations. Multiply the first equation by b_2 and the second equation by $-b_1$. Then add the two equations:

$$\begin{cases} a_1 x + b_1 y = c_1 \\ a_2 x + b_2 y = c_2 \end{cases} \xrightarrow[\text{Multiply by } -b_1.]{\text{Multiply by } b_2.} \begin{cases} a_1 b_2 x + b_1 b_2 y = c_1 b_2 \\ -a_2 b_1 x - b_1 b_2 y = -c_2 b_1 \end{cases}$$

Add: $(a_1 b_2 - a_2 b_1)x = c_1 b_2 - c_2 b_1$

$$x = \frac{c_1 b_2 - c_2 b_1}{a_1 b_2 - a_2 b_1}.$$

Because

$$\begin{vmatrix} c_1 & b_1 \\ c_2 & b_2 \end{vmatrix} = c_1 b_2 - c_2 b_1 \quad \text{and} \quad \begin{vmatrix} a_1 & b_1 \\ a_2 & b_2 \end{vmatrix} = a_1 b_2 - a_2 b_1,$$

we can express our answer for x as the quotient of two determinants:

$$x = \frac{c_1 b_2 - c_2 b_1}{a_1 b_2 - a_2 b_1} = \frac{\begin{vmatrix} c_1 & b_1 \\ c_2 & b_2 \end{vmatrix}}{\begin{vmatrix} a_1 & b_1 \\ a_2 & b_2 \end{vmatrix}}.$$

Similarly, we could use the addition method to solve our system for y, again expressing y as the quotient of two determinants. This method of using determinants to solve the linear system, called **Cramer's rule,** is summarized in the box.

> ### Solving a Linear System in Two Variables Using Determinants Cramer's Rule
>
> If
>
> $$\begin{cases} a_1 x + b_1 y = c_1 \\ a_2 x + b_2 y = c_2, \end{cases}$$
>
> then
>
> $$x = \frac{\begin{vmatrix} c_1 & b_1 \\ c_2 & b_2 \end{vmatrix}}{\begin{vmatrix} a_1 & b_1 \\ a_2 & b_2 \end{vmatrix}} \quad \text{and} \quad y = \frac{\begin{vmatrix} a_1 & c_1 \\ a_2 & c_2 \end{vmatrix}}{\begin{vmatrix} a_1 & b_1 \\ a_2 & b_2 \end{vmatrix}},$$
>
> where
>
> $$\begin{vmatrix} a_1 & b_1 \\ a_2 & b_2 \end{vmatrix} \neq 0.$$

Here are some helpful tips when solving

$$\begin{cases} a_1 x + b_1 y = c_1 \\ a_2 x + b_2 y = c_2 \end{cases}$$

using determinants:

1. Three different determinants are used to find x and y. The determinants in the denominators for x and y are identical. The determinants in the numerators for x and y differ. In abbreviated notation, we write

$$x = \frac{D_x}{D} \quad \text{and} \quad y = \frac{D_y}{D}, \text{where } D \neq 0.$$

2. The elements of D, the determinant in the denominator, are the coefficients of the variables in the system.

$$D = \begin{vmatrix} a_1 & b_1 \\ a_2 & b_2 \end{vmatrix}$$

3. D_x, the determinant in the numerator of x, is obtained by replacing the x-coefficients, in D, a_1 and a_2, with the constants on the right sides of the equations, c_1 and c_2.

$$D = \begin{vmatrix} a_1 & b_1 \\ a_2 & b_2 \end{vmatrix} \quad \text{and} \quad D_x = \begin{vmatrix} c_1 & b_1 \\ c_2 & b_2 \end{vmatrix} \qquad \text{Replace the column with } a_1 \text{ and } a_2 \text{ with the constants } c_1 \text{ and } c_2 \text{ to get } D_x.$$

4. D_y, the determinant in the numerator for y, is obtained by replacing the y-coefficients, in D, b_1 and b_2, with the constants on the right sides of the equations, c_1 and c_2.

$$D = \begin{vmatrix} a_1 & b_1 \\ a_2 & b_2 \end{vmatrix} \quad \text{and} \quad D_y = \begin{vmatrix} a_1 & c_1 \\ a_2 & c_2 \end{vmatrix} \qquad \text{Replace the column with } b_1 \text{ and } b_2 \text{ with the constants } c_1 \text{ and } c_2 \text{ to get } D_y.$$

EXAMPLE 2 Using Cramer's Rule to Solve a Linear System

Use Cramer's rule to solve the system:

$$\begin{cases} 5x - 4y = 2 \\ 6x - 5y = 1. \end{cases}$$

Solution Because

$$x = \frac{D_x}{D} \quad \text{and} \quad y = \frac{D_y}{D},$$

we will set up and evaluate the three determinants D, D_x, and D_y.

1. D, the determinant in both denominators, consists of the x- and y-coefficients.

$$D = \begin{vmatrix} 5 & -4 \\ 6 & -5 \end{vmatrix} = (5)(-5) - (6)(-4) = -25 + 24 = -1$$

Because this determinant is not zero, we continue to use Cramer's rule to solve the system.

2. D_x, the determinant in the numerator for x, is obtained by replacing the x-coefficients in D, 5 and 6, by the constants on the right sides of the equations, 2 and 1.

$$D_x = \begin{vmatrix} 2 & -4 \\ 1 & -5 \end{vmatrix} = (2)(-5) - (1)(-4) = -10 + 4 = -6$$

3. D_y, the determinant in the numerator for y, is obtained by replacing the y-coefficients in D, -4 and -5, by the constants on the right sides of the equations, 2 and 1.

$$D_y = \begin{vmatrix} 5 & 2 \\ 6 & 1 \end{vmatrix} = (5)(1) - (6)(2) = 5 - 12 = -7$$

4. Thus,

$$x = \frac{D_x}{D} = \frac{-6}{-1} = 6 \quad \text{and} \quad y = \frac{D_y}{D} = \frac{-7}{-1} = 7.$$

As always, the solution $(6, 7)$ can be checked by substituting these values into the original equations. The solution set is $\{(6, 7)\}$. ●

☑ Check Point **2** Use Cramer's rule to solve the system:

$$\begin{cases} 5x + 4y = 12 \\ 3x + 6y = 24. \end{cases}$$

③ Evaluate a third-order determinant.

The Determinant of a 3 × 3 Matrix

Associated with every square matrix is a real number called its determinant. The determinant for a 3 × 3 matrix is defined as follows:

Definition of a Third-Order Determinant

$$\begin{vmatrix} a_1 & b_1 & c_1 \\ a_2 & b_2 & c_2 \\ a_3 & b_3 & c_3 \end{vmatrix} = a_1 b_2 c_3 + b_1 c_2 a_3 + c_1 a_2 b_3 - a_3 b_2 c_1 - b_3 c_2 a_1 - c_3 a_2 b_1$$

The six terms and the three factors in each term in this complicated evaluation formula, $a_1b_2c_3 + b_1c_2a_3 + c_1a_2b_3 - a_3b_2c_1 - b_3c_2a_1 - c_3a_2b_1$, can be rearranged, and then we can apply the distributive property. We obtain

$$a_1b_2c_3 - a_1b_3c_2 - a_2b_1c_3 + a_2b_3c_1 + a_3b_1c_2 - a_3b_2c_1$$

$$= a_1(b_2c_3 - b_3c_2) - a_2(b_1c_3 - b_3c_1) + a_3(b_1c_2 - b_2c_1)$$

$$= a_1 \begin{vmatrix} b_2 & c_2 \\ b_3 & c_3 \end{vmatrix} - a_2 \begin{vmatrix} b_1 & c_1 \\ b_3 & c_3 \end{vmatrix} + a_3 \begin{vmatrix} b_1 & c_1 \\ b_2 & c_2 \end{vmatrix}.$$

You can evaluate each of the second-order determinants and obtain the three expressions in parentheses in the second step.

In summary, we now have arranged the definition of a third-order determinant as follows:

Definition of the Determinant of a 3 × 3 Matrix

A third-order determinant is defined by

Evaluating the Determinant of a 3 × 3 Matrix

Here are some tips that may be helpful when evaluating the determinant of a 3×3 matrix:

1. Each of the three terms in the definition contains two factors—a numerical factor and a second-order determinant.
2. The numerical factor in each term is an element from the first column of the third-order determinant.
3. The minus sign precedes the second term.
4. The second-order determinant that appears in each term is obtained by crossing out the row and the column containing the numerical factor.

The **minor** of an element is the determinant that remains after deleting the row and column of that element. For this reason, we call this method **expansion by minors**.

(**EXAMPLE 3**) **Evaluating the Determinant of a 3 × 3 Matrix**

Evaluate the determinant of the following matrix:

$$\begin{bmatrix} 4 & 1 & 0 \\ -9 & 3 & 4 \\ -3 & 8 & 1 \end{bmatrix}.$$

Solution We know that each of the three terms in the determinant contains a numerical factor and a second-order determinant. The numerical factors are from the first column of the given matrix. They are highlighted in the following matrix:

$$\begin{bmatrix} 4 & 1 & 0 \\ -9 & 3 & 4 \\ -3 & 8 & 1 \end{bmatrix}.$$

We find the minor for each numerical factor by deleting the row and column of that element:

$$\begin{bmatrix} 4 & 1 & 0 \\ -9 & 3 & 4 \\ -3 & 8 & 1 \end{bmatrix} \quad \begin{bmatrix} 4 & 1 & 0 \\ -9 & 3 & 4 \\ -3 & 8 & 1 \end{bmatrix} \quad \begin{bmatrix} 4 & 1 & 0 \\ -9 & 3 & 4 \\ -3 & 8 & 1 \end{bmatrix}$$

The minor for 4 is $\begin{vmatrix} 3 & 4 \\ 8 & 1 \end{vmatrix}$.

The minor for -9 is $\begin{vmatrix} 1 & 0 \\ 8 & 1 \end{vmatrix}$.

The minor for -3 is $\begin{vmatrix} 1 & 0 \\ 3 & 4 \end{vmatrix}$.

Now we have three numerical factors, 4, −9, and −3, and three second-order determinants. We multiply each numerical factor by its second-order determinant to find the three terms of the third-order determinant:

$$4\begin{vmatrix} 3 & 4 \\ 8 & 1 \end{vmatrix}, \quad -9\begin{vmatrix} 1 & 0 \\ 8 & 1 \end{vmatrix}, \quad -3\begin{vmatrix} 1 & 0 \\ 3 & 4 \end{vmatrix}.$$

Based on the preceding definition, we subtract the second term from the first term and add the third term:

Don't forget to supply the minus sign.

$$\begin{vmatrix} 4 & 1 & 0 \\ -9 & 3 & 4 \\ -3 & 8 & 1 \end{vmatrix} = 4\begin{vmatrix} 3 & 4 \\ 8 & 1 \end{vmatrix} - (-9)\begin{vmatrix} 1 & 0 \\ 8 & 1 \end{vmatrix} - 3\begin{vmatrix} 1 & 0 \\ 3 & 4 \end{vmatrix}$$ *Begin by evaluating the three second-order determinants.*

$$= 4(3\cdot 1 - 8\cdot 4) + 9(1\cdot 1 - 8\cdot 0) - 3(1\cdot 4 - 3\cdot 0)$$

$$= 4(3 - 32) + 9(1 - 0) - 3(4 - 0)$$ *Multiply within parentheses.*

$$= 4(-29) + 9(1) - 3(4)$$ *Subtract within parentheses.*

$$= -116 + 9 - 12$$ *Multiply.*

$$= -119$$ *Add and subtract as indicated.*

Technology

A graphing utility can be used to evaluate the determinant of a matrix. Enter the matrix and call it A. Then use the determinant command. The screen below verifies our result in Example 3.

```
[A]
     [[4   1  0]
      [-9  3  4]
      [-3  8  1]]
det([A])
               -119
■
```

Check Point 3 Evaluate the determinant of the following matrix:

$$\begin{bmatrix} 2 & 1 & 7 \\ -5 & 6 & 0 \\ -4 & 3 & 1 \end{bmatrix}.$$

The six terms in the definition of a third-order determinant can be rearranged and factored in a variety of ways. Thus, it is possible to expand a determinant by minors about any row or any column. *Minus signs must be supplied preceding any element appearing in a position where the sum of its row and its column is an odd number.* For example, expanding about the elements in column 2 gives us

$$\begin{vmatrix} a_1 & b_1 & c_1 \\ a_2 & b_2 & c_2 \\ a_3 & b_3 & c_3 \end{vmatrix} = -b_1\begin{vmatrix} a_2 & c_2 \\ a_3 & c_3 \end{vmatrix} + b_2\begin{vmatrix} a_1 & c_1 \\ a_3 & c_3 \end{vmatrix} - b_3\begin{vmatrix} a_1 & c_1 \\ a_2 & c_2 \end{vmatrix}.$$

Minus sign is supplied because b_1 appears in row 1 and column 2; $1 + 2 = 3$, an odd number.

Minus sign is supplied because b_3 appears in row 3 and column 2; $3 + 2 = 5$, an odd number.

Study Tip

Keep in mind that you can expand a determinant by minors about any row or column. Use alternating plus and minus signs to precede the numerical factors of the minors according to the following sign array:

$$\begin{vmatrix} + & - & + \\ - & + & - \\ + & - & + \end{vmatrix}.$$

Expanding by minors about column 3, we obtain

$$\begin{vmatrix} a_1 & b_1 & c_1 \\ a_2 & b_2 & c_2 \\ a_3 & b_3 & c_3 \end{vmatrix} = c_1 \begin{vmatrix} a_2 & b_2 \\ a_3 & b_3 \end{vmatrix} - c_2 \begin{vmatrix} a_1 & b_1 \\ a_3 & b_3 \end{vmatrix} + c_3 \begin{vmatrix} a_1 & b_1 \\ a_2 & b_2 \end{vmatrix}.$$

> Minus sign must be supplied because c_2 appears in row 2 and column 3; $2 + 3 = 5$, an odd number.

When evaluating a 3×3 determinant using expansion by minors, you can expand about any row or column. To simplify the arithmetic, if a row or column contains one or more 0s, expand about that row or column.

EXAMPLE 4 Evaluating a Third-Order Determinant

Evaluate:

$$\begin{vmatrix} 9 & 5 & 0 \\ -2 & -3 & 0 \\ 1 & 4 & 2 \end{vmatrix}.$$

Solution Note that the last column has two 0s. We will expand the determinant about the elements in that column.

$$\begin{vmatrix} 9 & 5 & 0 \\ -2 & -3 & 0 \\ 1 & 4 & 2 \end{vmatrix} = 0 \begin{vmatrix} -2 & -3 \\ 1 & 4 \end{vmatrix} - 0 \begin{vmatrix} 9 & 5 \\ 1 & 4 \end{vmatrix} + 2 \begin{vmatrix} 9 & 5 \\ -2 & -3 \end{vmatrix}$$

$$= 0 - 0 + 2[9(-3) - (-2)5] \qquad \text{Evaluate the second-order}$$

$$= 2(-27 + 10) \qquad\qquad \text{determinant whose numerical}$$

$$= 2(-17) \qquad\qquad \text{factor is not 0.}$$

$$= -34$$

⏺ Check Point 4 Evaluate:

$$\begin{vmatrix} 6 & 4 & 0 \\ -3 & -5 & 3 \\ 1 & 2 & 0 \end{vmatrix}.$$

④ Solve a system of linear equations in three variables using Cramer's rule.

Solving Systems of Linear Equations in Three Variables Using Determinants

Cramer's rule can be applied to solving systems of linear equations in three variables. The determinants in the numerator and denominator of all variables are third-order determinants.

> **Solving Three Equations in Three Variables Using Determinants Cramer's Rule**
>
> If
>
> $$\begin{cases} a_1 x + b_1 y + c_1 z = d_1 \\ a_2 x + b_2 y + c_2 z = d_2 \\ a_3 x + b_3 y + c_3 z = d_3 \end{cases}$$
>
> then
>
> $$x = \frac{D_x}{D}, \, y = \frac{D_y}{D}, \, \text{and } z = \frac{D_z}{D}, \text{where } D \neq 0.$$

These four third-order determinants are given by

$$D = \begin{vmatrix} a_1 & b_1 & c_1 \\ a_2 & b_2 & c_2 \\ a_3 & b_3 & c_3 \end{vmatrix}$$ These are the coefficients of the variables x, y, and z.

$$D_x = \begin{vmatrix} d_1 & b_1 & c_1 \\ d_2 & b_2 & c_2 \\ d_3 & b_3 & c_3 \end{vmatrix}$$ Replace x-coefficients in D with the constants on the right of the three equations.

$$D_y = \begin{vmatrix} a_1 & d_1 & c_1 \\ a_2 & d_2 & c_2 \\ a_3 & d_3 & c_3 \end{vmatrix}$$ Replace y-coefficients in D with the constants on the right of the three equations.

$$D_z = \begin{vmatrix} a_1 & b_1 & d_1 \\ a_2 & b_2 & d_2 \\ a_3 & b_3 & d_3 \end{vmatrix}$$ Replace z-coefficients in D with the constants on the right of the three equations.

EXAMPLE 5 Using Cramer's Rule to Solve a Linear System in Three Variables

Use Cramer's rule to solve:

$$\begin{cases} x + 2y - z = -4 \\ x + 4y - 2z = -6 \\ 2x + 3y + z = 3. \end{cases}$$

Solution Because

$$x = \frac{D_x}{D}, \quad y = \frac{D_y}{D}, \quad \text{and} \quad z = \frac{D_z}{D},$$

we need to set up and evaluate four determinants.

Step 1 Set up the determinants.

1. D, the determinant in all three denominators, consists of the x-, y-, and z-coefficients.

$$D = \begin{vmatrix} 1 & 2 & -1 \\ 1 & 4 & -2 \\ 2 & 3 & 1 \end{vmatrix}$$

2. D_x, the determinant in the numerator for x, is obtained by replacing the x-coefficients in D, 1, 1, and 2, with the constants on the right sides of the equations, -4, -6, and 3.

$$D_x = \begin{vmatrix} -4 & 2 & -1 \\ -6 & 4 & -2 \\ 3 & 3 & 1 \end{vmatrix}$$

3. D_y, the determinant in the numerator for y, is obtained by replacing the y-coefficients in D, 2, 4, and 3, with the constants on the right sides of the equations, -4, -6, and 3.

$$D_y = \begin{vmatrix} 1 & -4 & -1 \\ 1 & -6 & -2 \\ 2 & 3 & 1 \end{vmatrix}$$

4. D_z, the determinant in the numerator for z, is obtained by replacing the z-coefficients in D, -1, -2, and 1, with the constants on the right sides of the equations, -4, -6, and 3.

$$D_z = \begin{vmatrix} 1 & 2 & -4 \\ 1 & 4 & -6 \\ 2 & 3 & 3 \end{vmatrix}$$

Step 2 Evaluate the four determinants.

$$D = \begin{vmatrix} 1 & 2 & -1 \\ 1 & 4 & -2 \\ 2 & 3 & 1 \end{vmatrix} = 1\begin{vmatrix} 4 & -2 \\ 3 & 1 \end{vmatrix} - 1\begin{vmatrix} 2 & -1 \\ 3 & 1 \end{vmatrix} + 2\begin{vmatrix} 2 & -1 \\ 4 & -2 \end{vmatrix}$$

$$= 1(4 + 6) - 1(2 + 3) + 2(-4 + 4)$$
$$= 1(10) - 1(5) + 2(0) = 5$$

Study Tip

To find D_x, D_y, and D_z, you'll need to apply the evaluation process for a 3×3 determinant three times. The values of D_x, D_y, and D_z cannot be obtained from the numbers that occur in the computation of D.

Using the same technique to evaluate each determinant, we obtain

$$D_x = -10, \quad D_y = 5, \quad \text{and} \quad D_z = 20.$$

Step 3 Substitute these four values and solve the system.

$$x = \frac{D_x}{D} = \frac{-10}{5} = -2$$

$$y = \frac{D_y}{D} = \frac{5}{5} = 1$$

$$z = \frac{D_z}{D} = \frac{20}{5} = 4$$

The solution $(-2, 1, 4)$ can be checked by substitution into the original three equations. The solution set is $\{(-2, 1, 4)\}$. ●

☑ Check Point **5** Use Cramer's rule to solve the system:

$$\begin{cases} 3x - 2y + z = 16 \\ 2x + 3y - z = -9 \\ x + 4y + 3z = 2. \end{cases}$$

⑤ Use determinants to identify inconsistent systems and systems with dependent equations.

Cramer's Rule with Inconsistent and Dependent Systems

If D, the determinant in the denominator, is 0, the variables described by the quotient of determinants are not real numbers. However, when $D = 0$, this indicates that the system is either inconsistent or contains dependent equations. This gives rise to the following two situations:

Determinants: Inconsistent and Dependent Systems

1. If $D = 0$ and at least one of the determinants in the numerator is not 0, then the system is inconsistent. The solution set is \varnothing.

2. If $D = 0$ and all the determinants in the numerators are 0, then the equations in the system are dependent. The system has infinitely many solutions.

Discovery

Write a system of two equations that is inconsistent. Now use determinants and the result boxed above to verify that this is truly an inconsistent system. Repeat the same process for a system with two dependent equations.

Although we have focused on applying determinants to solve linear systems, they have other applications, some of which we consider in the exercise set that follows Example 6.

6 Evaluate higher-order determinants.

The Determinant of Any $n \times n$ Matrix

The determinant of a matrix with n rows and n columns is said to be an ***n*th-order determinant**. The value of an nth-order determinant $(n > 2)$ can be found in terms of determinants of order $n - 1$. For example, we found the value of a third-order determinant in terms of determinants of order 2.

We can generalize this idea for fourth-order determinants and higher. We have seen that the **minor** of the element a_{ij} is the determinant obtained by deleting the ith row and the jth column in the given array of numbers. The **cofactor** of the element a_{ij} is $(-1)^{i+j}$ times the minor of a_{ij}. If the sum of the row and column $(i + j)$ is even, the cofactor is the same as the minor. If the sum of the row and column $(i + j)$ is odd, the cofactor is the opposite of the minor.

Let's see what this means in the case of a fourth-order determinant.

EXAMPLE 6 **Evaluating the Determinant of a 4 \times 4 Matrix**

Evaluate the determinant of the following matrix:

$$A = \begin{bmatrix} 1 & -2 & 3 & 0 \\ -1 & 1 & 0 & 2 \\ 0 & 2 & 0 & -3 \\ 2 & 3 & -4 & 1 \end{bmatrix}.$$

Solution

$$|A| = \begin{vmatrix} 1 & -2 & 3 & 0 \\ -1 & 1 & 0 & 2 \\ 0 & 2 & 0 & -3 \\ 2 & 3 & -4 & 1 \end{vmatrix}$$

With two 0s in the third column, we will expand along the third column.

$$= (-1)^{1+3}(3)\begin{vmatrix} -1 & 1 & 2 \\ 0 & 2 & -3 \\ 2 & 3 & 1 \end{vmatrix} + (-1)^{4+3}(-4)\begin{vmatrix} 1 & -2 & 0 \\ -1 & 1 & 2 \\ 0 & 2 & -3 \end{vmatrix}$$

3 is in row 1, column 3.

−4 is in row 4, column 3.

$$= 3\begin{vmatrix} -1 & 1 & 2 \\ 0 & 2 & -3 \\ 2 & 3 & 1 \end{vmatrix} + 4\begin{vmatrix} 1 & -2 & 0 \\ -1 & 1 & 2 \\ 0 & 2 & -3 \end{vmatrix}$$

The determinant that follows 3 is obtained by crossing out the row and the column (row 1, column 3) in the original determinant. The minor for −4 is obtained in a similar manner.

Evaluate the two third-order determinants to get

$$|A| = 3(-25) + 4(-1) = -79.$$

Check Point 6 Evaluate the determinant of the following matrix:

$$A = \begin{bmatrix} 0 & 4 & 0 & -3 \\ -1 & 1 & 5 & 2 \\ 1 & -2 & 0 & 6 \\ 3 & 0 & 0 & 1 \end{bmatrix}.$$

If a linear system has n equations, Cramer's rule requires you to compute $n + 1$ determinants of nth order. The excessive number of calculations required to perform Cramer's rule for systems with four or more equations makes it an inefficient method for solving large systems.

Exercise Set 6.5

Practice Exercises

Evaluate each determinant in Exercises 1–10.

1. $\begin{vmatrix} 5 & 7 \\ 2 & 3 \end{vmatrix}$

2. $\begin{vmatrix} 4 & 8 \\ 5 & 6 \end{vmatrix}$

3. $\begin{vmatrix} -4 & 1 \\ 5 & 6 \end{vmatrix}$

4. $\begin{vmatrix} 7 & 9 \\ -2 & -5 \end{vmatrix}$

5. $\begin{vmatrix} -7 & 14 \\ 2 & -4 \end{vmatrix}$

6. $\begin{vmatrix} 1 & -3 \\ -8 & 2 \end{vmatrix}$

7. $\begin{vmatrix} -5 & -1 \\ -2 & -7 \end{vmatrix}$

8. $\begin{vmatrix} \frac{1}{5} & \frac{1}{6} \\ -6 & 5 \end{vmatrix}$

9. $\begin{vmatrix} \frac{1}{2} & \frac{1}{2} \\ \frac{1}{8} & -\frac{3}{4} \end{vmatrix}$

10. $\begin{vmatrix} \frac{2}{3} & \frac{1}{3} \\ -\frac{1}{2} & \frac{3}{4} \end{vmatrix}$

For Exercises 11–26, use Cramer's rule to solve each system or to determine that the system is inconsistent or contains dependent equations.

11. $\begin{cases} x + y = 7 \\ x - y = 3 \end{cases}$

12. $\begin{cases} 2x + y = 3 \\ x - y = 3 \end{cases}$

13. $\begin{cases} 12x + 3y = 15 \\ 2x - 3y = 13 \end{cases}$

14. $\begin{cases} x - 2y = 5 \\ 5x - y = -2 \end{cases}$

15. $\begin{cases} 4x - 5y = 17 \\ 2x + 3y = 3 \end{cases}$

16. $\begin{cases} 3x + 2y = 2 \\ 2x + 2y = 3 \end{cases}$

17. $\begin{cases} x + 2y = 3 \\ 5x + 10y = 15 \end{cases}$

18. $\begin{cases} 2x - 9y = 5 \\ 3x - 3y = 11 \end{cases}$

19. $\begin{cases} 3x - 4y = 4 \\ 2x + 2y = 12 \end{cases}$

20. $\begin{cases} 3x = 7y + 1 \\ 2x = 3y - 1 \end{cases}$

21. $\begin{cases} 2x = 3y + 2 \\ 5x = 51 - 4y \end{cases}$

22. $\begin{cases} y = -4x + 2 \\ 2x = 3y + 8 \end{cases}$

23. $\begin{cases} 3x = 2 - 3y \\ 2y = 3 - 2x \end{cases}$

24. $\begin{cases} x + 2y - 3 = 0 \\ 12 = 8y + 4x \end{cases}$

25. $\begin{cases} 4y = 16 - 3x \\ 6x = 32 - 8y \end{cases}$

26. $\begin{cases} 2x = 7 + 3y \\ 4x - 6y = 3 \end{cases}$

Evaluate each determinant in Exercises 27–32.

27. $\begin{vmatrix} 3 & 0 & 0 \\ 2 & 1 & -5 \\ 2 & 5 & -1 \end{vmatrix}$

28. $\begin{vmatrix} 4 & 0 & 0 \\ 3 & -1 & 4 \\ 2 & -3 & 5 \end{vmatrix}$

29. $\begin{vmatrix} 3 & 1 & 0 \\ -3 & 4 & 0 \\ -1 & 3 & -5 \end{vmatrix}$

30. $\begin{vmatrix} 2 & -4 & 2 \\ -1 & 0 & 5 \\ 3 & 0 & 4 \end{vmatrix}$

31. $\begin{vmatrix} 1 & 1 & 1 \\ 2 & 2 & 2 \\ -3 & 4 & -5 \end{vmatrix}$

32. $\begin{vmatrix} 1 & 2 & 3 \\ 2 & 2 & -3 \\ 3 & 2 & 1 \end{vmatrix}$

In Exercises 33–40, use Cramer's rule to solve each system.

33. $\begin{cases} x + y + z = 0 \\ 2x - y + z = -1 \\ -x + 3y - z = -8 \end{cases}$

34. $\begin{cases} x - y + 2z = 3 \\ 2x + 3y + z = 9 \\ -x - y + 3z = 11 \end{cases}$

35. $\begin{cases} 4x - 5y - 6z = -1 \\ x - 2y - 5z = -12 \\ 2x - y = 7 \end{cases}$

36. $\begin{cases} x - 3y + z = -2 \\ x + 2y = 8 \\ 2x - y = 1 \end{cases}$

37. $\begin{cases} x + y + z = 4 \\ x - 2y + z = 7 \\ x + 3y + 2z = 4 \end{cases}$

38. $\begin{cases} 2x + 2y + 3z = 10 \\ 4x - y + z = -5 \\ 5x - 2y + 6z = 1 \end{cases}$

39. $\begin{cases} x + 2z = 4 \\ 2y - z = 5 \\ 2x + 3y = 13 \end{cases}$

40. $\begin{cases} 3x + 2z = 4 \\ 5x - y = -4 \\ 4y + 3z = 22 \end{cases}$

Evaluate each determinant in Exercises 41–44.

41. $\begin{vmatrix} 4 & 2 & 8 & -7 \\ -2 & 0 & 4 & 1 \\ 5 & 0 & 0 & 5 \\ 4 & 0 & 0 & -1 \end{vmatrix}$

42. $\begin{vmatrix} 3 & -1 & 1 & 2 \\ -2 & 0 & 0 & 0 \\ 2 & -1 & -2 & 3 \\ 1 & 4 & 2 & 3 \end{vmatrix}$

43. $\begin{vmatrix} -2 & -3 & 3 & 5 \\ 1 & -4 & 0 & 0 \\ 1 & 2 & 2 & -3 \\ 2 & 0 & 1 & 1 \end{vmatrix}$

44. $\begin{vmatrix} 1 & -3 & 2 & 0 \\ -3 & -1 & 0 & -2 \\ 2 & 1 & 3 & 1 \\ 2 & 0 & -2 & 0 \end{vmatrix}$

Practice Plus

In Exercises 45–46, evaluate each determinant.

45. $\begin{vmatrix} \begin{vmatrix} 3 & 1 \\ -2 & 3 \end{vmatrix} & \begin{vmatrix} 7 & 0 \\ 1 & 5 \end{vmatrix} \\ \begin{vmatrix} 3 & 0 \\ 0 & 7 \end{vmatrix} & \begin{vmatrix} 9 & -6 \\ 3 & 5 \end{vmatrix} \end{vmatrix}$

46. $\begin{vmatrix} \begin{vmatrix} 5 & 0 \\ 4 & -3 \end{vmatrix} & \begin{vmatrix} -1 & 0 \\ 0 & -1 \end{vmatrix} \\ \begin{vmatrix} 7 & -5 \\ 4 & 6 \end{vmatrix} & \begin{vmatrix} 4 & 1 \\ -3 & 5 \end{vmatrix} \end{vmatrix}$

In Exercises 47–48, write the system of linear equations for which Cramer's rule yields the given determinants.

47. $D = \begin{vmatrix} 2 & -4 \\ 3 & 5 \end{vmatrix}$, $D_x = \begin{vmatrix} 8 & -4 \\ -10 & 5 \end{vmatrix}$

48. $D = \begin{vmatrix} 2 & -3 \\ 5 & 6 \end{vmatrix}$, $D_x = \begin{vmatrix} 8 & -3 \\ 11 & 6 \end{vmatrix}$

In Exercises 49–52, solve each equation for x.

49. $\begin{vmatrix} -2 & x \\ 4 & 6 \end{vmatrix} = 32$

50. $\begin{vmatrix} x + 3 & -6 \\ x - 2 & -4 \end{vmatrix} = 28$

51. $\begin{vmatrix} 1 & x & -2 \\ 3 & 1 & 1 \\ 0 & -2 & 2 \end{vmatrix} = -8$

52. $\begin{vmatrix} 2 & x & 1 \\ -3 & 1 & 0 \\ 2 & 1 & 4 \end{vmatrix} = 39$

Application Exercises

Determinants are used to find the area of a triangle whose vertices are given by three points in a rectangular coordinate system. The area of a triangle with vertices (x_1, y_1), (x_2, y_2), and (x_3, y_3) is

$$\text{Area} = \pm \frac{1}{2} \begin{vmatrix} x_1 & y_1 & 1 \\ x_2 & y_2 & 1 \\ x_3 & y_3 & 1 \end{vmatrix},$$

where the \pm symbol indicates that the appropriate sign should be chosen to yield a positive area. Use this information to work Exercises 53–54.

53. Use determinants to find the area of the triangle whose vertices are $(3, -5), (2, 6),$ and $(-3, 5)$.

54. Use determinants to find the area of the triangle whose vertices are $(1, 1), (-2, -3),$ and $(11, -3)$.

Determinants are used to show that three points lie on the same line (are collinear). If

$$\begin{vmatrix} x_1 & y_1 & 1 \\ x_2 & y_2 & 1 \\ x_3 & y_3 & 1 \end{vmatrix} = 0,$$

then the points $(x_1, y_1), (x_2, y_2),$ *and* (x_3, y_3) *are collinear. If the determinant does not equal 0, then the points are not collinear. Use this information to work Exercises 55–56.*

55. Are the points $(3, -1), (0, -3),$ and $(12, 5)$ collinear?

56. Are the points $(-4, -6), (1, 0),$ and $(11, 12)$ collinear?

Determinants are used to write an equation of a line passing through two points. An equation of the line passing through the distinct points (x_1, y_1) *and* (x_2, y_2) *is given by*

$$\begin{vmatrix} x & y & 1 \\ x_1 & y_1 & 1 \\ x_2 & y_2 & 1 \end{vmatrix} = 0.$$

Use this information to work Exercises 57–58.

57. Use the determinant to write an equation of the line passing through $(3, -5)$ and $(-2, 6)$. Then expand the determinant, expressing the line's equation in slope-intercept form.

58. Use the determinant to write an equation of the line passing through $(-1, 3)$ and $(2, 4)$. Then expand the determinant, expressing the line's equation in slope-intercept form.

Writing in Mathematics

59. Explain how to evaluate a second-order determinant.

60. Describe the determinants D_x and D_y in terms of the coefficients and constants in a system of two equations in two variables.

61. Explain how to evaluate a third-order determinant.

62. When expanding a determinant by minors, when is it necessary to supply minus signs?

63. Without going into too much detail, describe how to solve a linear system in three variables using Cramer's rule.

64. In applying Cramer's rule, what does it mean if $D = 0$?

65. The process of solving a linear system in three variables using Cramer's rule can involve tedious computation. Is there a way of speeding up this process, perhaps using Cramer's rule to find the value for only one of the variables? Describe how this process might work, presenting a specific example with your description. Remember that your goal is still to find the value for each variable in the system.

66. If you could use only one method to solve linear systems in three variables, which method would you select? Explain why this is so.

Technology Exercises

67. Use the feature of your graphing utility that evaluates the determinant of a square matrix to verify any five of the determinants that you evaluated by hand in Exercises 1–10, 27–32, or 41–44.

In Exercises 68–69, use a graphing utility to evaluate the determinant for the given matrix.

68. $\begin{bmatrix} 3 & -2 & -1 & 4 \\ -5 & 1 & 2 & 7 \\ 2 & 4 & 5 & 0 \\ -1 & 3 & -6 & 5 \end{bmatrix}$

69. $\begin{bmatrix} 8 & 2 & 6 & -1 & 0 \\ 2 & 0 & -3 & 4 & 7 \\ 2 & 1 & -3 & 6 & -5 \\ -1 & 2 & 1 & 5 & -1 \\ 4 & 5 & -2 & 3 & -8 \end{bmatrix}$

70. What is the fastest method for solving a linear system with your graphing utility?

Critical Thinking Exercises

Make Sense? *In Exercises 71–74, determine whether each statement makes sense or does not make sense, and explain your reasoning.*

71. I'm solving a linear system using a determinant that contains two rows and three columns.

72. I can speed up the tedious computations required by Cramer's rule by using the value of D to determine the value of D_x.

73. When using Cramer's rule to solve a linear system, the number of determinants that I set up and evaluate is the same as the number of variables in the system.

74. Using Cramer's rule to solve a linear system, I found the value of D to be zero, so the system is inconsistent.

75. a. Evaluate: $\begin{vmatrix} a & a \\ 0 & a \end{vmatrix}$.

b. Evaluate: $\begin{vmatrix} a & a & a \\ 0 & a & a \\ 0 & 0 & a \end{vmatrix}$.

c. Evaluate: $\begin{vmatrix} a & a & a & a \\ 0 & a & a & a \\ 0 & 0 & a & a \\ 0 & 0 & 0 & a \end{vmatrix}$.

d. Describe the pattern in the given determinants.

e. Describe the pattern in the evaluations.

76. Evaluate: $\begin{vmatrix} 2 & 0 & 0 & 0 & 0 \\ 0 & 3 & 0 & 0 & 0 \\ 0 & 0 & 2 & 0 & 0 \\ 0 & 0 & 0 & 1 & 0 \\ 0 & 0 & 0 & 0 & 4 \end{vmatrix}$.

77. What happens to the value of a second-order determinant if the two columns are interchanged?

78. Consider the system

$$a_1 x + b_1 y = c_1$$

$$a_2 x + b_2 y = c_2.$$

Use Cramer's rule to prove that if the first equation of the system is replaced by the sum of the two equations, the resulting system has the same solution as the original system.

79. Show that the equation of a line through (x_1, y_1) and (x_2, y_2) is given by the determinant equation in Exercises 57–58.

Group Exercise

80. We have seen that determinants can be used to solve linear equations, give areas of triangles in rectangular coordinates, and determine equations of lines. Not impressed with these applications? Members of the group should research an application of determinants that they find intriguing. The group should then present a seminar to the class about this application.

Preview Exercises

Exercises 81–83 will help you prepare for the material covered in the first section of the next chapter.

81. Consider the equation $\dfrac{x^2}{9} + \dfrac{y^2}{4} = 1$.

 a. Set $y = 0$ and find the x-intercepts.

 b. Set $x = 0$ and find the y-intercepts.

82. Divide both sides of $25x^2 + 16y^2 = 400$ by 400 and simplify.

83. Complete the square and write the circle's equation in standard form:

$$x^2 + y^2 - 2x + 4y = 4.$$

Then give the center and radius of the circle and graph the equation.

Chapter ⑥ Summary, Review, and Test

Summary

DEFINITIONS AND CONCEPTS	EXAMPLES
6.1 Matrix Solutions to Linear Systems	
a. Matrix row operations are described in the box on page 557.	Ex. 1, p. 557
b. To solve a linear system using Gaussian elimination, begin with the system's augmented matrix. Use matrix row operations to get 1s down the main diagonal from upper left to lower right, and 0s below the 1s. Such a matrix is in row-echelon form. Details are in the box on page 558.	Ex. 2, p. 559; Ex. 3, p. 561
c. To solve a linear system using Gauss-Jordan elimination, use the procedure of Gaussian elimination, but obtain 0s above and below the 1s in the main diagonal from upper left to lower right. Such a matrix is in reduced row-echelon form. Details are in the box on page 563.	Ex. 4, p. 564
6.2 Inconsistent and Dependent Systems and Their Applications	
a. If Gaussian elimination results in a matrix with a row containing all 0s to the left of the vertical line and a nonzero number to the right, the system has no solution (is inconsistent).	Ex. 1, p. 568
b. In a square system, if Gaussian elimination results in a matrix with a row with all 0s, but not a row like the one in part (a), the system has an infinite number of solutions (contains dependent equations).	Ex. 2, p. 570
c. In nonsquare systems, the number of variables differs from the number of equations.	Ex. 3, p. 571
6.3 Matrix Operations and Their Applications	
a. A matrix of order $m \times n$ has m rows and n columns. Two matrices are equal if and only if they have the same order and corresponding elements are equal.	Ex. 1, p. 577
b. Matrix Addition and Subtraction: Matrices of the same order are added or subtracted by adding or subtracting corresponding elements. Properties of matrix addition are given in the box on page 580.	Ex. 2, p. 579
c. Scalar Multiplication: If A is a matrix and c is a scalar, then cA is the matrix formed by multiplying each element in A by c. Properties of scalar multiplication are given in the box on page 581.	Ex. 3, p. 580; Ex. 4, p. 581
d. Matrix Multiplication: The product of an $m \times n$ matrix A and an $n \times p$ matrix B is an $m \times p$ matrix AB. The element in the ith row and jth column of AB is found by multiplying each element in the ith row of A by the corresponding element in the jth column of B and adding the products. Matrix multiplication is not commutative: $AB \neq BA$. Properties of matrix multiplication are given in the box on page 586.	Ex. 5, p. 582; Ex. 6, p. 583; Ex. 7, p. 585
6.4 Multiplicative Inverses of Matrices and Matrix Equations	
a. The multiplicative identity matrix I_n is an $n \times n$ matrix with 1s down the main diagonal from upper left to lower right and 0s elsewhere.	
b. Let A be an $n \times n$ square matrix. If there is a square matrix A^{-1} such that $AA^{-1} = I_n$ and $A^{-1}A = I_n$, then A^{-1} is the multiplicative inverse of A.	Ex. 1, p. 593
c. If a square matrix has a multiplicative inverse, it is invertible or nonsingular. Methods for finding multiplicative inverses for invertible matrices, including a formula for 2×2 matrices, are given in the box on page 599.	Ex. 2, p. 594; Ex. 3, p. 596; Ex. 4, p. 598

DEFINITIONS AND CONCEPTS

EXAMPLES

d. Linear systems can be represented by matrix equations of the form $AX = B$ in which A is the coefficient matrix and B is the constant matrix. If $AX = B$ has a unique solution, then $X = A^{-1}B$.

Ex. 5, p. 601

6.5 Determinants and Cramer's Rule

a. Value of a second-order determinant:

$$\begin{vmatrix} a_1 & b_1 \\ a_2 & b_2 \end{vmatrix} = a_1 b_2 - a_2 b_1$$

Ex. 1, p. 607

b. Cramer's rule for solving systems of linear equations in two variables uses three second-order determinants and is stated in the box on page 608.

Ex. 2, p. 609

c. To evaluate an nth-order determinant, where $n > 2$,
1. Select a row or column about which to expand.
2. Multiply each element a_{ij} in the row or column by $(-1)^{i+j}$ times the determinant obtained by deleting the ith row and the jth column in the given array of numbers.
3. The value of the determinant is the sum of the products found in step 2.

Ex. 3, p. 610;
Ex. 4, p. 612;
Ex. 6, p. 615

d. Cramer's rule for solving systems of linear equations in three variables uses four third-order determinants and is stated in the box on page 612.

Ex. 5, p. 613

e. Cramer's rule with inconsistent and dependent systems is summarized by the two situations in the box on page 614.

Review Exercises

6.1

In Exercises 1–2, perform each matrix row operation and write the new matrix.

1. $\begin{bmatrix} 1 & 2 & 2 & | & 2 \\ 0 & 1 & -1 & | & 2 \\ 0 & 5 & 4 & | & 1 \end{bmatrix}$ $-5R_2 + R_3$

2. $\begin{bmatrix} 2 & -2 & 1 & | & -1 \\ 1 & 2 & -1 & | & 2 \\ 6 & 4 & 3 & | & 5 \end{bmatrix}$ $\frac{1}{2}R_1$

In Exercises 3–5, solve each system of equations using matrices. Use Gaussian elimination with back-substitution or Gauss-Jordan elimination.

3. $\begin{cases} x + 2y + 3z = -5 \\ 2x + y + z = 1 \\ x + y - z = 8 \end{cases}$

4. $\begin{cases} x - 2y + z = 0 \\ y - 3z = -1 \\ 2y + 5z = -2 \end{cases}$

5. $\begin{cases} 3x_1 + 5x_2 - 8x_3 + 5x_4 = -8 \\ x_1 + 2x_2 - 3x_3 + x_4 = -7 \\ 2x_1 + 3x_2 - 7x_3 + 3x_4 = -11 \\ 4x_1 + 8x_2 - 10x_3 + 7x_4 = -10 \end{cases}$

6. The table shows the pollutants in the air in a city on a typical summer day.

x (Hours after 6 A.M.)	y (Amount of Pollutants in the Air, in parts per million)
2	98
4	138
10	162

a. Use the function $y = ax^2 + bx + c$ to model the data. Use either Gaussian elimination with back-substitution or Gauss-Jordan elimination to find the values for a, b, and c.

b. Use the function to find the time of day at which the city's air pollution level is at a maximum. What is the maximum level?

7. Sociologists Joseph Kahl and Dennis Gilbert developed a six-tier model to portray the class structure of the United States. The bar graph represents the percentage of Americans who are members of each of the six social classes.

The United States Social Class Ladder

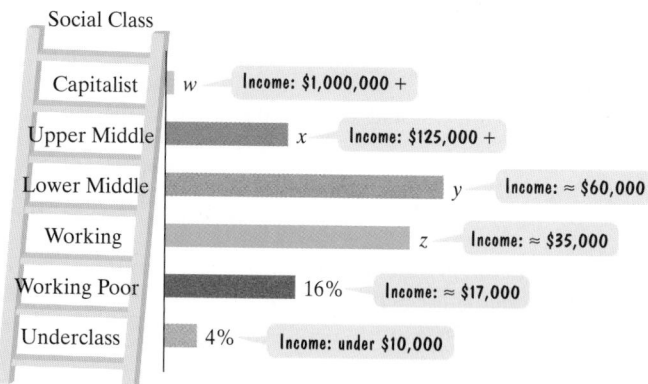

Percentage of the Population

Source: James Henslin, *Sociology*, Eighth Edition, Allyn and Bacon, 2007

Combined, members of the capitalist class, the upper-middle class, the lower-middle class, and the working class make up 80% of the U.S. population. The percentage of the population belonging to the lower-middle class exceeds the percentage belonging to capitalist and upper-middle classes by 18%. The difference between the percentage belonging to the lower-middle class and the working class is 4%. If the percentage belonging to the upper-middle class is tripled, it exceeds the

percentage belonging to the capitalist and lower-middle classes by 10%. Determine the percentage of the U.S. population who are members of the capitalist class, the upper-middle class, the lower-middle class, and the working class.

6.2

In Exercises 8–11, use Gaussian elimination to find the complete solution to each system, or show that none exists.

8. $\begin{cases} 2x - 3y + z = 1 \\ x - 2y + 3z = 2 \\ 3x - 4y - z = 1 \end{cases}$

9. $\begin{cases} x - 3y + z = 1 \\ -2x + y + 3z = -7 \\ x - 4y + 2z = 0 \end{cases}$

10. $\begin{cases} x_1 + 4x_2 + 3x_3 - 6x_4 = 5 \\ x_1 + 3x_2 + x_3 - 4x_4 = 3 \\ 2x_1 + 8x_2 + 7x_3 - 5x_4 = 11 \\ 2x_1 + 5x_2 - 6x_4 = 4 \end{cases}$

11. $\begin{cases} 2x + 3y - 5z = 15 \\ x + 2y - z = 4 \end{cases}$

12. The figure shows the intersections of three one-way streets. The numbers given represent traffic flow, in cars per hour, at a peak period (from 4 P.M. to 6 P.M.).

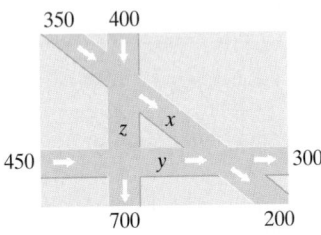

a. Use the idea that the number of cars entering each intersection per hour must equal the number of cars leaving per hour to set up a system of linear equations involving x, y, and z.

b. Use Gaussian elimination to solve the system.

c. If construction limits the value of z to 400, how many cars per hour must pass between the other intersections to keep traffic flowing?

6.3

13. Find values for x, y, and z so that the following matrices are equal:

$$\begin{bmatrix} 2x & y + 7 \\ z & 4 \end{bmatrix} = \begin{bmatrix} -10 & 13 \\ 6 & 4 \end{bmatrix}.$$

In Exercises 14–27, perform the indicated matrix operations given that A, B, C, and D are defined as follows. If an operation is not defined, state the reason.

$$A = \begin{bmatrix} 2 & -1 & 2 \\ 5 & 3 & -1 \end{bmatrix} \quad B = \begin{bmatrix} 0 & -2 \\ 3 & 2 \\ 1 & -5 \end{bmatrix}$$

$$C = \begin{bmatrix} 1 & 2 & 3 \\ -1 & 1 & 2 \\ -1 & 2 & 1 \end{bmatrix} \quad D = \begin{bmatrix} -2 & 3 & 1 \\ 3 & -2 & 4 \end{bmatrix}$$

14. $A + D$ **15.** $2B$ **16.** $D - A$

17. $B + C$ **18.** $3A + 2D$ **19.** $-2A + 4D$

20. $-5(A + D)$ **21.** AB **22.** BA

23. BD **24.** DB **25.** $AB - BA$

26. $(A - D)C$ **27.** $B(AC)$

28. Solve for X in the matrix equation

$$3X + A = B,$$

where $A = \begin{bmatrix} 4 & 6 \\ -5 & 0 \end{bmatrix}$ and $B = \begin{bmatrix} -2 & -12 \\ 4 & 1 \end{bmatrix}$.

In Exercises 29–30, use nine pixels in a 3 × 3 grid and the color levels shown.

29. Write a 3 × 3 matrix that represents a digital photograph of the letter T in dark gray on a light gray background.

30. Find a matrix B so that $A + B$ increases the contrast of the letter T by changing the dark gray to black and the light gray to white.

The figure shows a right triangle in a rectangular coordinate system.

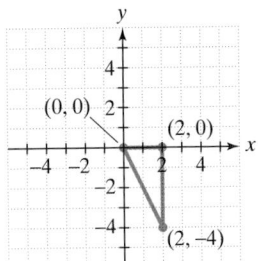

The figure can be represented by the matrix

$$B = \begin{bmatrix} 0 & 2 & 2 \\ 0 & 0 & -4 \end{bmatrix}.$$

Use the triangle and the matrix that represents it to solve Exercises 31–36.

31. Use matrix operations to move the triangle 2 units to the left and 1 unit up. Then graph the triangle and its transformation in a rectangular coordinate system.

32. Use matrix operations to reduce the triangle to half its perimeter and move the reduced image 2 units down. Then graph the triangle and its transformation in a rectangular coordinate system.

In Exercises 33–36, find AB and graph the resulting image. What effect does the multiplication have on the triangle represented by matrix B?

33. $A = \begin{bmatrix} 1 & 0 \\ 0 & -1 \end{bmatrix}$ **34.** $A = \begin{bmatrix} -1 & 0 \\ 0 & 1 \end{bmatrix}$

35. $A = \begin{bmatrix} 0 & -1 \\ 1 & 0 \end{bmatrix}$ **36.** $A = \begin{bmatrix} 2 & 0 \\ 0 & 1 \end{bmatrix}$

6.4

In Exercises 37–38, find the products AB and BA to determine whether B is the multiplicative inverse of A.

37. $A = \begin{bmatrix} 2 & 7 \\ 1 & 4 \end{bmatrix}$, $B = \begin{bmatrix} 4 & -7 \\ -1 & 3 \end{bmatrix}$

38. $A = \begin{bmatrix} 1 & 0 & 0 \\ 0 & 2 & -7 \\ 0 & -1 & 4 \end{bmatrix}$, $B = \begin{bmatrix} 1 & 0 & 0 \\ 0 & 4 & 7 \\ 0 & 1 & 2 \end{bmatrix}$

In Exercises 39–42, find A^{-1}. Check that $AA^{-1} = I$ and $A^{-1}A = I$.

39. $A = \begin{bmatrix} 1 & -1 \\ -2 & 3 \end{bmatrix}$

40. $A = \begin{bmatrix} 0 & 1 \\ 5 & 3 \end{bmatrix}$

41. $A = \begin{bmatrix} 1 & 0 & -2 \\ 2 & 1 & 0 \\ 1 & 0 & -3 \end{bmatrix}$

42. $A = \begin{bmatrix} 1 & 3 & -2 \\ 4 & 13 & -7 \\ 5 & 16 & -8 \end{bmatrix}$

In Exercises 43–44,

 a. Write each linear system as a matrix equation in the form $AX = B$.

 b. Solve the system using the inverse that is given for the coefficient matrix.

43.
$$\begin{cases} x + y + 2z = 7 \\ \phantom{x + {}} y + 3z = -2 \\ 3x \phantom{{}+ y} - 2z = 0 \end{cases}$$
The inverse of $\begin{bmatrix} 1 & 1 & 2 \\ 0 & 1 & 3 \\ 3 & 0 & -2 \end{bmatrix}$ is $\begin{bmatrix} -2 & 2 & 1 \\ 9 & -8 & -3 \\ -3 & 3 & 1 \end{bmatrix}$.

44.
$$\begin{cases} x - y + 2z = 12 \\ \phantom{x {}-{}} y - z = -5 \\ x \phantom{{}- y} + 2z = 10 \end{cases}$$
The inverse of $\begin{bmatrix} 1 & -1 & 2 \\ 0 & 1 & -1 \\ 1 & 0 & 2 \end{bmatrix}$ is $\begin{bmatrix} 2 & 2 & -1 \\ -1 & 0 & 1 \\ -1 & -1 & 1 \end{bmatrix}$.

45. Use the coding matrix $A = \begin{bmatrix} 3 & 2 \\ 4 & 3 \end{bmatrix}$ and its inverse $A^{-1} = \begin{bmatrix} 3 & -2 \\ -4 & 3 \end{bmatrix}$ to encode and then decode the word RULE.

6.5

In Exercises 46–51, evaluate each determinant.

46. $\begin{vmatrix} 3 & 2 \\ -1 & 5 \end{vmatrix}$

47. $\begin{vmatrix} -2 & -3 \\ -4 & -8 \end{vmatrix}$

48. $\begin{vmatrix} 2 & 4 & -3 \\ 1 & -1 & 5 \\ -2 & 4 & 0 \end{vmatrix}$

49. $\begin{vmatrix} 4 & 7 & 0 \\ -5 & 6 & 0 \\ 3 & 2 & -4 \end{vmatrix}$

50. $\begin{vmatrix} 1 & 1 & 0 & 2 \\ 0 & 3 & 2 & 1 \\ 0 & -2 & 4 & 0 \\ 0 & 3 & 0 & 1 \end{vmatrix}$

51. $\begin{vmatrix} 2 & 2 & 2 & 2 \\ 0 & 2 & 2 & 2 \\ 0 & 0 & 2 & 2 \\ 0 & 0 & 0 & 2 \end{vmatrix}$

In Exercises 52–55, use Cramer's rule to solve each system.

52. $\begin{cases} x - 2y = 8 \\ 3x + 2y = -1 \end{cases}$

53. $\begin{cases} 7x + 2y = 0 \\ 2x + y = -3 \end{cases}$

54. $\begin{cases} x + 2y + 2z = 5 \\ 2x + 4y + 7z = 19 \\ -2x - 5y - 2z = 8 \end{cases}$

55. $\begin{cases} 2x + y \phantom{{}- 2z} = -4 \\ \phantom{2x + {}} y - 2z = 0 \\ 3x \phantom{{}+ y} - 2z = -11 \end{cases}$

56. Use the quadratic function $y = ax^2 + bx + c$ to model the following data:

x (Age of a Driver)	y (Average Number of Automobile Accidents per Day in the United States)
20	400
40	150
60	400

Use Cramer's rule to determine values for a, b, and c. Then use the model to write a statement about the average number of automobile accidents in which 30-year-olds and 50-year-olds are involved daily.

CHAPTER

Test Prep
VIDEOS

Chapter 6 Test

In Exercises 1–2, solve each system of equations using matrices.

1. $\begin{cases} x + 2y - z = -3 \\ 2x - 4y + z = -7 \\ -2x + 2y - 3z = 4 \end{cases}$

2. $\begin{cases} x - 2y + z = 2 \\ 2x - y - z = 1 \end{cases}$

In Exercises 3–6, let

$$A = \begin{bmatrix} 3 & 1 \\ 1 & 0 \\ 2 & 1 \end{bmatrix}, \quad B = \begin{bmatrix} 1 & -1 \\ 2 & 1 \end{bmatrix}, \quad \text{and} \quad C = \begin{bmatrix} 1 & 2 \\ -1 & 3 \end{bmatrix}.$$

Carry out the indicated operations.

3. $2B + 3C$

4. AB

5. C^{-1}

6. $BC - 3B$

7. If $A = \begin{bmatrix} 1 & 2 & 2 \\ 2 & 3 & 3 \\ 1 & -1 & -2 \end{bmatrix}$ and $B = \begin{bmatrix} -3 & 2 & 0 \\ 7 & -4 & 1 \\ -5 & 3 & -1 \end{bmatrix}$, show that B is the inverse of A.

8. Consider the system

$$3x + 5y = 9$$

$$2x - 3y = -13.$$

a. Express the system in the form $AX = B$, where A, X, and B are appropriate matrices.

b. Find A^{-1}, the inverse of the coefficient matrix.

c. Use A^{-1} to solve the given system.

9. Evaluate: $\begin{vmatrix} 4 & -1 & 3 \\ 0 & 5 & -1 \\ 5 & 2 & 4 \end{vmatrix}$.

10. Solve for x only using Cramer's rule:

$$\begin{cases} 3x + y - 2z = -3 \\ 2x + 7y + 3z = 9 \\ 4x - 3y - z = 7. \end{cases}$$

Cumulative Review Exercises (Chapters 1–6)

Solve each equation or inequality in Exercises 1–6.

1. $2x^2 = 4 - x$

2. $5x + 8 \le 7(1 + x)$

3. $\sqrt{2x + 4} - \sqrt{x + 3} - 1 = 0$

4. $3x^3 + 8x^2 - 15x + 4 = 0$

5. $e^{2x} - 14e^x + 45 = 0$

6. $\log_3 x + \log_3(x + 2) = 1$

7. Use matrices to solve this system:

$$\begin{cases} x - y + z = 17 \\ 2x + 3y + z = 8 \\ -4x + y + 5z = -2. \end{cases}$$

8. Solve for y using Cramer's rule:

$$\begin{cases} x - 2y + z = 7 \\ 2x + y - z = 0 \\ 3x + 2y - 2z = -2. \end{cases}$$

9. If $f(x) = \sqrt{4x - 7}$, find $f^{-1}(x)$.

10. Graph: $f(x) = \dfrac{x}{x^2 - 16}$.

11. Use the graph of $f(x) = 4x^4 - 4x^3 - 25x^2 + x + 6$ shown in the figure to factor the polynomial completely.

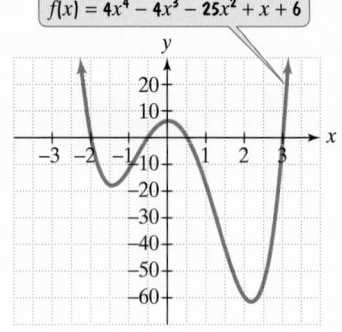

$f(x) = 4x^4 - 4x^3 - 25x^2 + x + 6$

12. Graph $y = \log_2 x$ and $y = \log_2(x + 1)$ in the same rectangular coordinate system.

13. Use the exponential decay model $A = A_0 e^{kt}$ to solve this problem. A radioactive substance has a half-life of 40 days. There are initially 900 grams of the substance.

a. Find the decay model for this substance. Round k to the nearest thousandth.

b. How much of the substance will remain after 10 days? Round to the nearest hundredth of a gram.

14. Multiply the matrices: $\begin{bmatrix} 1 & -1 & 0 \\ 2 & 1 & 3 \end{bmatrix} \begin{bmatrix} 4 & -1 \\ 2 & 0 \\ 1 & 1 \end{bmatrix}$.

15. Find the partial fraction decomposition of

$$\frac{3x^2 + 17x - 38}{(x - 3)(x - 2)(x + 2)}.$$

In Exercises 16–19, graph each equation, function, or inequality in a rectangular coordinate system.

16. $y = -\frac{2}{3}x - 1$

17. $3x - 5y < 15$

18. $f(x) = x^2 - 2x - 3$

19. $(x - 1)^2 + (y + 1)^2 = 9$

20. Use synthetic division to divide $x^3 - 6x + 4$ by $x - 2$.

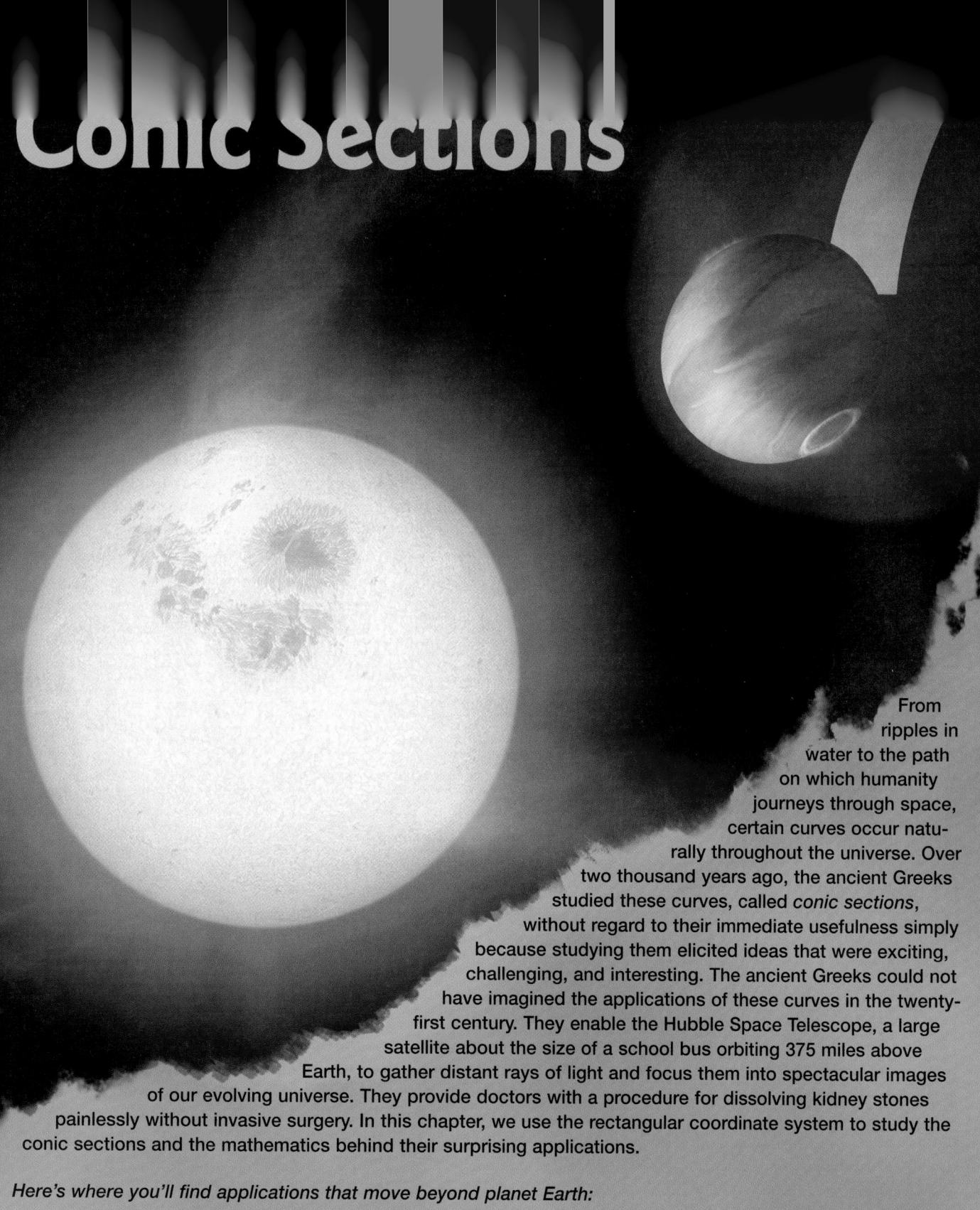

Conic Sections

From ripples in water to the path on which humanity journeys through space, certain curves occur naturally throughout the universe. Over two thousand years ago, the ancient Greeks studied these curves, called *conic sections*, without regard to their immediate usefulness simply because studying them elicited ideas that were exciting, challenging, and interesting. The ancient Greeks could not have imagined the applications of these curves in the twenty-first century. They enable the Hubble Space Telescope, a large satellite about the size of a school bus orbiting 375 miles above Earth, to gather distant rays of light and focus them into spectacular images of our evolving universe. They provide doctors with a procedure for dissolving kidney stones painlessly without invasive surgery. In this chapter, we use the rectangular coordinate system to study the conic sections and the mathematics behind their surprising applications.

Here's where you'll find applications that move beyond planet Earth:

- *Planetary orbits: Section 7.1, page 631; Exercise Set 7.1, Exercise 78*
- *Halley's Comet: Essay on page 632*
- *Hubble Space Telescope: Section 7.3, pages 651 and 659.*

For a kidney stone here on Earth, see Section 7.1, page 632.

Section 7.1 The Ellipse

Objectives

1. Graph ellipses centered at the origin.
2. Write equations of ellipses in standard form.
3. Graph ellipses not centered at the origin.
4. Solve applied problems involving ellipses.

You took on a summer job driving a truck, delivering books that were ordered online. You're an avid reader, so just being around books sounded appealing. However, now you're feeling a bit shaky driving the truck for the first time. It's 10 feet wide and 9 feet high; compared to your compact car, it feels like you're behind the wheel of a tank. Up ahead you see a sign at the semielliptical entrance to a tunnel: Caution! Tunnel is 10 Feet High at Center Peak. Then you see another sign: Caution! Tunnel Is 40 Feet Wide. Will your truck clear the opening of the tunnel's archway?

Mathematics is present in the movements of planets, bridge and tunnel construction, navigational systems used to keep track of a ship's location, manufacture of lenses for telescopes, and even in a procedure for disintegrating kidney stones. The mathematics behind these applications involves conic sections. Conic sections are curves that result from the intersection of a right circular cone and a plane. **Figure 7.1** illustrates the four conic sections: the circle, the ellipse, the parabola, and the hyperbola.

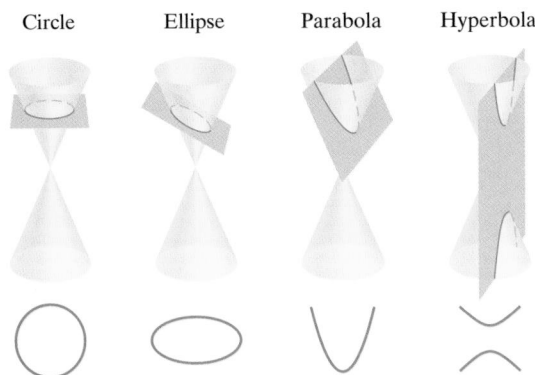

Figure 7.1 Obtaining the conic sections by intersecting a plane and a cone

In this section, we study the symmetric oval-shaped curve known as the ellipse. We will use a geometric definition for an ellipse to derive its equation. With this equation, we will determine if your delivery truck will clear the tunnel's entrance.

Definition of an Ellipse

Figure 7.2 illustrates how to draw an ellipse. Place pins at two fixed points, each of which is called a *focus* (plural: *foci*). If the ends of a fixed length of string are fastened to the pins and we draw the string taut with a pencil, the path traced by the pencil will be an ellipse. Notice that the sum of the distances of the pencil point from the foci remains constant because the length of the string is fixed. This procedure for drawing an ellipse illustrates its geometric definition.

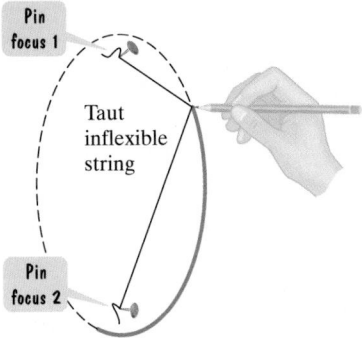

Figure 7.2 Drawing an ellipse

> #### Definition of an Ellipse
>
> An **ellipse** is the set of all points, P, in a plane the sum of whose distances from two fixed points, F_1 and F_2, is constant (see **Figure 7.3**). These two fixed points are called the **foci** (plural of **focus**). The midpoint of the segment connecting the foci is the **center** of the ellipse.

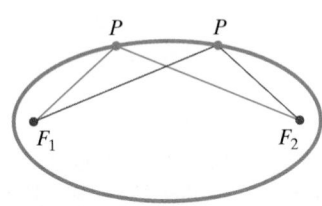

Figure 7.3

Figure 7.4 illustrates that an ellipse can be elongated in any direction. In this section, we will limit our discussion to ellipses that are elongated horizontally or vertically. The line through the foci intersects the ellipse at two points, called the **vertices** (singular: **vertex**). The line segment that joins the vertices is the **major axis**. Notice that the midpoint of the major axis is the center of the ellipse. The line segment whose endpoints are on the ellipse and that is perpendicular to the major axis at the center is called the **minor axis** of the ellipse.

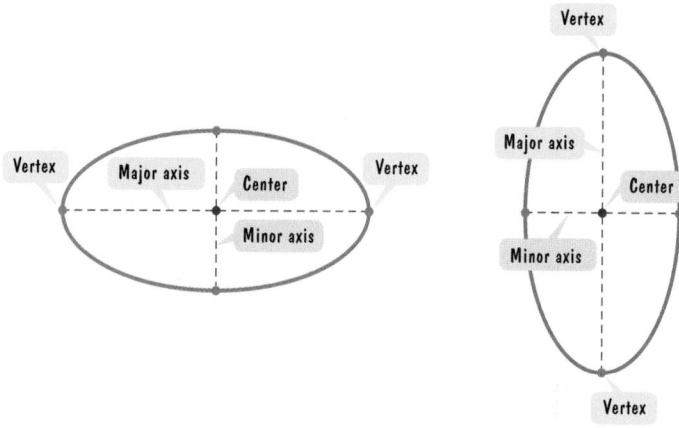

Figure 7.4 Horizontal and vertical elongations of an ellipse

Standard Form of the Equation of an Ellipse

The rectangular coordinate system gives us a unique way of describing an ellipse. It enables us to translate an ellipse's geometric definition into an algebraic equation.

We start with **Figure 7.5** to obtain an ellipse's equation. We've placed an ellipse that is elongated horizontally into a rectangular coordinate system. The foci are on the x-axis at $(-c, 0)$ and $(c, 0)$, as in **Figure 7.5**. In this way, the center of the ellipse is at the origin. We let (x, y) represent the coordinates of any point on the ellipse.

What does the definition of an ellipse tell us about the point (x, y) in **Figure 7.5**? For any point (x, y) on the ellipse, the sum of the distances to the two foci, $d_1 + d_2$, must be constant. As we shall see, it is convenient to denote this constant by $2a$. Thus, the point (x, y) is on the ellipse if and only if

$$d_1 + d_2 = 2a.$$

$$\sqrt{(x + c)^2 + y^2} + \sqrt{(x - c)^2 + y^2} = 2a \quad \text{Use the distance formula.}$$

After eliminating radicals and simplifying, we obtain

$$(a^2 - c^2)x^2 + a^2y^2 = a^2(a^2 - c^2).$$

Look at the triangle in **Figure 7.5**. Notice that the distance from F_1 to F_2 is $2c$. Because the length of any side of a triangle is less than the sum of the lengths of the other two sides, $2c < d_1 + d_2$. Equivalently, $2c < 2a$ and $c < a$. Consequently, $a^2 - c^2 > 0$. For convenience, let $b^2 = a^2 - c^2$. Substituting b^2 for $a^2 - c^2$ in the preceding equation, we obtain

$$b^2x^2 + a^2y^2 = a^2b^2$$

$$\frac{b^2x^2}{a^2b^2} + \frac{a^2y^2}{a^2b^2} = \frac{a^2b^2}{a^2b^2} \quad \text{Divide both sides by } a^2b^2.$$

$$\frac{x^2}{a^2} + \frac{y^2}{b^2} = 1. \quad \text{Simplify.}$$

This last equation is the **standard form of the equation of an ellipse centered at the origin**. There are two such equations, one for a horizontal major axis and one for a vertical major axis.

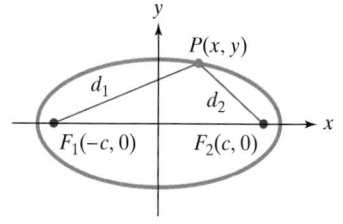

Figure 7.5

Study Tip

The algebraic details behind eliminating the radicals and obtaining the equation shown can be found in the appendix. There you will find a step-by-step derivation of the ellipse's equation.

Standard Forms of the Equations of an Ellipse

The **standard form of the equation of an ellipse** with center at the origin, and major and minor axes of lengths $2a$ and $2b$ (where a and b are positive, and $a^2 > b^2$) is

$$\frac{x^2}{a^2} + \frac{y^2}{b^2} = 1 \quad \text{or} \quad \frac{x^2}{b^2} + \frac{y^2}{a^2} = 1.$$

Study Tip

The form $c^2 = a^2 - b^2$ is the one you should remember. When finding the foci, this form is easy to manipulate.

Figure 7.6 illustrates that the vertices are on the major axis, a units from the center. The foci are on the major axis, c units from the center. For both equations, $b^2 = a^2 - c^2$. Equivalently, $c^2 = a^2 - b^2$.

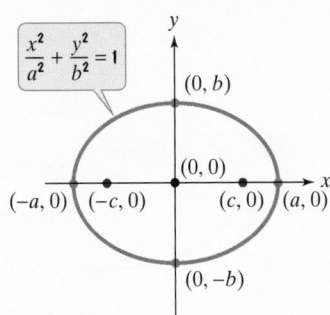

Figure 7.6(a) Major axis is horizontal with length $2a$.

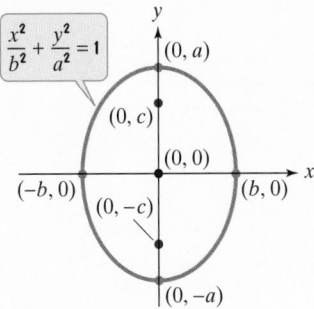

Figure 7.6(b) Major axis is vertical with length $2a$.

The intercepts shown in **Figure 7.6(a)** can be obtained algebraically. Let's do this for

$$\frac{x^2}{a^2} + \frac{y^2}{b^2} = 1.$$

x-intercepts: Set $y = 0$.

$$\frac{x^2}{a^2} = 1$$

$$x^2 = a^2$$

$$x = \pm a$$

x-intercepts are $-a$ and a. The graph passes through $(-a, 0)$ and $(a, 0)$, which are the vertices.

y-intercepts: Set $x = 0$.

$$\frac{y^2}{b^2} = 1$$

$$y^2 = b^2$$

$$y = \pm b$$

y-intercepts are $-b$ and b. The graph passes through $(0, -b)$ and $(0, b)$.

Using the Standard Form of the Equation of an Ellipse

We can use the standard form of an ellipse's equation to graph the ellipse. Although the definition of the ellipse is given in terms of its foci, the foci are not part of the graph. A complete graph of an ellipse can be obtained without graphing the foci.

① Graph ellipses centered at the origin.

EXAMPLE 1) **Graphing an Ellipse Centered at the Origin**

Graph and locate the foci: $\dfrac{x^2}{9} + \dfrac{y^2}{4} = 1$.

Solution The given equation is the standard form of an ellipse's equation with $a^2 = 9$ and $b^2 = 4$.

$$\frac{x^2}{9} + \frac{y^2}{4} = 1$$

$a^2 = 9$. This is the larger of the two denominators.

$b^2 = 4$. This is the smaller of the two denominators.

Technology

We graph $\dfrac{x^2}{9} + \dfrac{y^2}{4} = 1$ with a graphing utility by solving for y.

$$\frac{y^2}{4} = 1 - \frac{x^2}{9}$$

$$y^2 = 4\left(1 - \frac{x^2}{9}\right)$$

$$y = \pm 2\sqrt{1 - \frac{x^2}{9}}$$

Notice that the square root property requires us to define two functions. Enter

$$y_1 = 2\;\boxed{\surd}\;(1\;\boxed{-}\;x\;\boxed{\wedge}\;2\;\boxed{\div}\;9)$$

and

$$y_2 = -y_1.$$

To see the true shape of the ellipse, use the

$$\boxed{\text{ZOOM SQUARE}}$$

feature so that one unit on the y-axis is the same length as one unit on the x-axis.

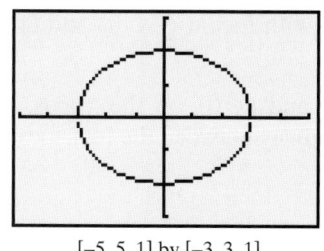

$[-5, 5, 1]$ by $[-3, 3, 1]$

Because the denominator of the x^2-term is greater than the denominator of the y^2-term, the major axis is horizontal. Based on the standard form of the equation, we know the vertices are $(-a, 0)$ and $(a, 0)$. Because $a^2 = 9$, $a = 3$. Thus, the vertices are $(-3, 0)$ and $(3, 0)$, shown in **Figure 7.7**.

Now let us find the endpoints of the vertical minor axis. According to the standard form of the equation, these endpoints are $(0, -b)$ and $(0, b)$. Because $b^2 = 4$, $b = 2$. Thus, the endpoints of the minor axis are $(0, -2)$ and $(0, 2)$. They are shown in **Figure 7.7**.

Finally, we find the foci, which are located at $(-c, 0)$ and $(c, 0)$. We can use the formula $c^2 = a^2 - b^2$ to do so. We know that $a^2 = 9$ and $b^2 = 4$. Thus,

$$c^2 = a^2 - b^2 = 9 - 4 = 5.$$

Because $c^2 = 5$, $c = \sqrt{5}$. The foci, $(-c, 0)$ and $(c, 0)$, are located at $\left(-\sqrt{5}, 0\right)$ and $\left(\sqrt{5}, 0\right)$. They are shown in **Figure 7.7**.

You can sketch the ellipse in **Figure 7.7** by locating endpoints on the major and minor axes.

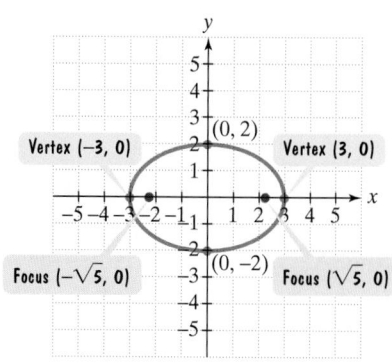

Figure 7.7 The graph of $\dfrac{x^2}{9} + \dfrac{y^2}{4} = 1$

$$\frac{x^2}{3^2} + \frac{y^2}{2^2} = 1$$

Endpoints of the major axis are 3 units to the right and left of the center.

Endpoints of the minor axis are 2 units up and down from the center.

⊘ **Check Point 1** Graph and locate the foci: $\dfrac{x^2}{36} + \dfrac{y^2}{9} = 1$.

EXAMPLE 2 **Graphing an Ellipse Centered at the Origin**

Graph and locate the foci: $25x^2 + 16y^2 = 400$.

Solution We begin by expressing the equation in standard form. Because we want 1 on the right side, we divide both sides by 400.

$$\frac{25x^2}{400} + \frac{16y^2}{400} = \frac{400}{400}$$

$$\frac{x^2}{16} + \frac{y^2}{25} = 1$$

$b^2 = 16$. This is the smaller of the two denominators.

$a^2 = 25$. This is the larger of the two denominators.

The equation is the standard form of an ellipse's equation with $a^2 = 25$ and $b^2 = 16$. Because the denominator of the y^2-term is greater than the denominator of the x^2-term, the major axis is vertical. Based on the standard form of the equation, we know the vertices are $(0, -a)$ and $(0, a)$. Because $a^2 = 25$, $a = 5$. Thus, the vertices are $(0, -5)$ and $(0, 5)$, shown in **Figure 7.8**.

Now let us find the endpoints of the horizontal minor axis. According to the standard form of the equation, these endpoints are $(-b, 0)$ and $(b, 0)$. Because

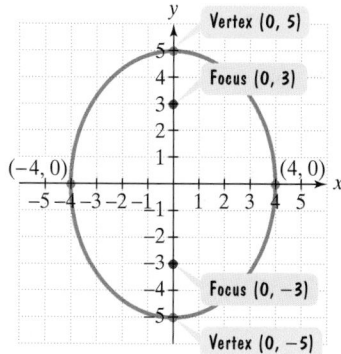

Figure 7.8 The graph of $25x^2 + 16y^2 = 400$, or $\dfrac{x^2}{16} + \dfrac{y^2}{25} = 1$

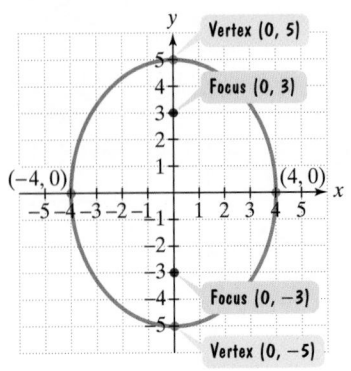

Figure 7.8 (repeated) The graph of $\dfrac{x^2}{16} + \dfrac{y^2}{25} = 1$

② Write equations of ellipses in standard form.

$b^2 = 16$, $b = 4$. Thus, the endpoints of the minor axis are $(-4, 0)$ and $(4, 0)$. They are shown in **Figure 7.8**.

Finally, we find the foci, which are located at $(0, -c)$ and $(0, c)$. We can use the formula $c^2 = a^2 - b^2$ to do so. We know that $a^2 = 25$ and $b^2 = 16$. Thus,

$$c^2 = a^2 - b^2 = 25 - 16 = 9.$$

Because $c^2 = 9$, $c = 3$. The foci, $(0, -c)$ and $(0, c)$, are located at $(0, -3)$ and $(0, 3)$. They are shown in **Figure 7.8**.

You can sketch the ellipse in **Figure 7.8** by locating endpoints on the major and minor axes.

$$\frac{x^2}{4^2} + \frac{y^2}{5^2} = 1$$

> **Endpoints of the minor axis are 4 units to the right and left of the center.**

> **Endpoints of the major axis are 5 units up and down from the center.**

✓ **Check Point 2** Graph and locate the foci: $16x^2 + 9y^2 = 144$.

In Examples 1 and 2, we used the equation of an ellipse to find its foci and vertices. In the next example, we reverse this procedure.

(**EXAMPLE 3**) **Finding the Equation of an Ellipse from Its Foci and Vertices**

Find the standard form of the equation of an ellipse with foci at $(-1, 0)$ and $(1, 0)$ and vertices $(-2, 0)$ and $(2, 0)$.

Solution Because the foci are located at $(-1, 0)$ and $(1, 0)$, on the x-axis, the major axis is horizontal. The center of the ellipse is midway between the foci, located at $(0, 0)$. Thus, the form of the equation is

$$\frac{x^2}{a^2} + \frac{y^2}{b^2} = 1.$$

We need to determine the values for a^2 and b^2. The distance from the center, $(0, 0)$, to either vertex, $(-2, 0)$ or $(2, 0)$, is 2. Thus, $a = 2$.

$$\frac{x^2}{2^2} + \frac{y^2}{b^2} = 1 \qquad \text{or} \qquad \frac{x^2}{4} + \frac{y^2}{b^2} = 1$$

We must still find b^2. The distance from the center, $(0, 0)$, to either focus, $(-1, 0)$ or $(1, 0)$, is 1, so $c = 1$. Using $c^2 = a^2 - b^2$, we have

$$1^2 = 2^2 - b^2$$

and

$$b^2 = 2^2 - 1^2 = 4 - 1 = 3.$$

Substituting 3 for b^2 in $\dfrac{x^2}{4} + \dfrac{y^2}{b^2} = 1$ gives us the standard form of the ellipse's equation. The equation is

$$\frac{x^2}{4} + \frac{y^2}{3} = 1.$$

✓ **Check Point 3** Find the standard form of the equation of an ellipse with foci at $(-2, 0)$ and $(2, 0)$ and vertices $(-3, 0)$ and $(3, 0)$.

③ Graph ellipses not centered at the origin.

Translations of Ellipses

Horizontal and vertical translations can be used to graph ellipses that are not centered at the origin. **Figure 7.9** illustrates that the graphs of

$$\frac{(x - h)^2}{a^2} + \frac{(y - k)^2}{b^2} = 1 \quad \text{and} \quad \frac{x^2}{a^2} + \frac{y^2}{b^2} = 1$$

have the same size and shape. However, the graph of the first equation is centered at (h, k) rather than at the origin.

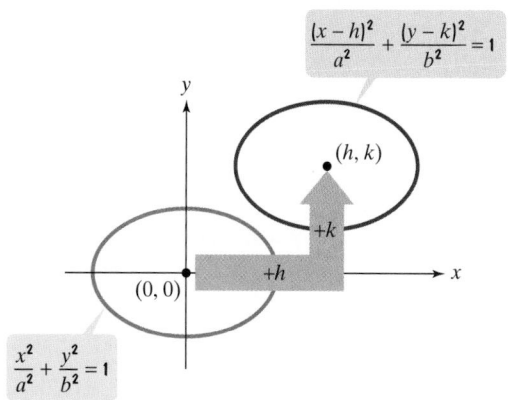

Figure 7.9 Translating an ellipse's graph

Table 7.1 gives the standard forms of equations of ellipses centered at (h, k) and shows their graphs.

Table 7.1 Standard Forms of Equations of Ellipses Centered at (h, k)

Equation	Center	Major Axis	Vertices	Graph
$\dfrac{(x - h)^2}{a^2} + \dfrac{(y - k)^2}{b^2} = 1$ Endpoints of major axis are a units right and a units left of center. $a^2 > b^2$ Foci are c units right and c units left of center, where $c^2 = a^2 - b^2$.	(h, k)	Parallel to the x-axis, horizontal	$(h - a, k)$ $(h + a, k)$	Vertex $(h + a, k)$ Focus $(h - c, k)$ Major axis (h, k) Vertex $(h - a, k)$ Focus $(h + c, k)$
$\dfrac{(x - h)^2}{b^2} + \dfrac{(y - k)^2}{a^2} = 1$ $a^2 > b^2$ Endpoints of the major axis are a units above and a units below the center. Foci are c units above and c units below the center, where $c^2 = a^2 - b^2$.	(h, k)	Parallel to the y-axis, vertical	$(h, k - a)$ $(h, k + a)$	Vertex $(h, k + a)$ Focus $(h, k + c)$ (h, k) Vertex $(h, k - a)$ Focus $(h, k - c)$ Major axis

EXAMPLE 4 **Graphing an Ellipse Centered at** (h, k)

Graph: $\dfrac{(x-1)^2}{4} + \dfrac{(y+2)^2}{9} = 1$. Where are the foci located?

Solution To graph the ellipse, we need to know its center, (h, k). In the standard forms of equations centered at (h, k), h is the number subtracted from x and k is the number subtracted from y.

> This is $(x-h)^2$, with $h = 1$. This is $(y-k)^2$, with $k = -2$.

$$\dfrac{(x-1)^2}{4} + \dfrac{(y-(-2))^2}{9} = 1$$

We see that $h = 1$ and $k = -2$. Thus, the center of the ellipse, (h, k), is $(1, -2)$. We can graph the ellipse by locating endpoints on the major and minor axes. To do this, we must identify a^2 and b^2.

$$\dfrac{(x-1)^2}{4} + \dfrac{(y+2)^2}{9} = 1$$

> $b^2 = 4$. This is the smaller of the two denominators. $a^2 = 9$. This is the larger of the two denominators.

The larger number is under the expression involving y. This means that the major axis is vertical and parallel to the y-axis.

We can sketch the ellipse by locating endpoints on the major and minor axes.

$$\dfrac{(x-1)^2}{2^2} + \dfrac{(y+2)^2}{3^2} = 1$$

> Endpoints of the minor axis are 2 units to the right and left of the center. Endpoints of the major axis (the vertices) are 3 units up and down from the center.

We categorize the observations in the voice balloons as follows:

$\dfrac{(x-1)^2}{4} + \dfrac{(y+2)^2}{9} = 1$

Figure 7.10 The graph of an ellipse centered at $(1, -2)$

For a Vertical Major Axis with Center $(1, -2)$	
Vertices	**Endpoints of Minor Axis**
$(1, -2 + 3) = (1, 1)$	$(1 + 2, -2) = (3, -2)$
$(1, -2 - 3) = (1, -5)$	$(1 - 2, -2) = (-1, -2)$

> 3 units above and below center 2 units right and left of center

Using the center and these four points, we can sketch the ellipse shown in **Figure 7.10**. With $c^2 = a^2 - b^2$, we have $c^2 = 9 - 4 = 5$. So the foci are located $\sqrt{5}$ units above and below the center, at $\left(1, -2 + \sqrt{5}\right)$ and $\left(1, -2 - \sqrt{5}\right)$.

✓ **Check Point 4** Graph: $\dfrac{(x+1)^2}{9} + \dfrac{(y-2)^2}{4} = 1$. Where are the foci located?

In some cases, it is necessary to convert the equation of an ellipse to standard form by completing the square on x and y. For example, suppose that we wish to graph the ellipse whose equation is

$$9x^2 + 4y^2 - 18x + 16y - 11 = 0.$$

Because we plan to complete the square on both x and y, we need to rearrange terms so that

- x-terms are arranged in descending order.
- y-terms are arranged in descending order.
- the constant term appears on the right.

$$9x^2 + 4y^2 - 18x + 16y - 11 = 0$$

This is the given equation.

$$(9x^2 - 18x) + (4y^2 + 16y) = 11$$

Group terms and add 11 to both sides.

$$9(x^2 - 2x + \square) + 4(y^2 + 4y + \square) = 11$$

To complete the square, coefficients of x^2 and y^2 must be 1. Factor out 9 and 4, respectively.

We added 9 · 1, or 9, to the left side.

We also added 4 · 4, or 16, to the left side.

Study Tip

When completing the square, remember that changes made on the left side of the equation must also be made on the right side of the equation.

$$9(x^2 - 2x + 1) + 4(y^2 + 4y + 4) = 11 + 9 + 16$$

Complete each square by adding the square of half the coefficient of x and y, respectively.

9 and 16, added on the left side, must also be added on the right side.

$$9(x - 1)^2 + 4(y + 2)^2 = 36$$

Factor.

$$\frac{9(x-1)^2}{36} + \frac{4(y+2)^2}{36} = \frac{36}{36}$$

Divide both sides by 36.

$$\frac{(x-1)^2}{4} + \frac{(y+2)^2}{9} = 1$$

Simplify.

The equation is now in standard form. This is precisely the form of the equation that we graphed in Example 4.

④ Solve applied problems involving ellipses.

Applications

Ellipses have many applications. German scientist Johannes Kepler (1571–1630) showed that the planets in our solar system move in elliptical orbits, with the sun at a focus. Earth satellites also travel in elliptical orbits, with Earth at a focus.

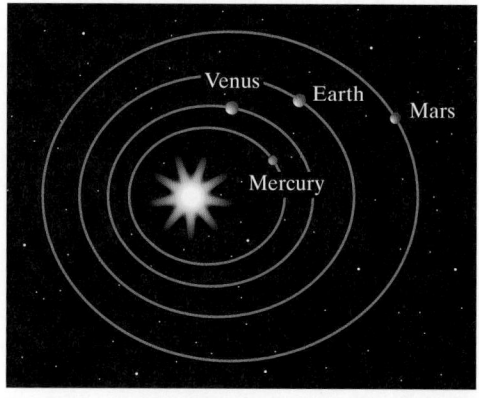

Planets move in elliptical orbits.

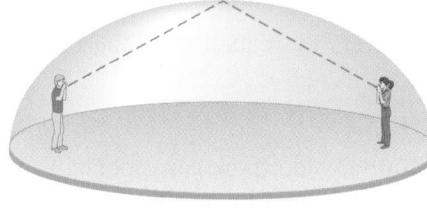

Whispering in an elliptical dome

One intriguing aspect of the ellipse is that a ray of light or a sound wave emanating from one focus will be reflected from the ellipse to exactly the other focus. A whispering gallery is an elliptical room with an elliptical, dome-shaped ceiling. People standing at the foci can whisper and hear each other quite clearly, while persons in other locations in the room cannot hear them. Statuary Hall in the U.S. Capitol Building is elliptical. President John Quincy Adams, while a member of the House of Representatives, was aware of this acoustical phenomenon. He situated his desk at a focal point of the elliptical ceiling, easily eavesdropping on the private conversations of other House members located near the other focus.

The elliptical reflection principle is used in a procedure for disintegrating kidney stones. The patient is placed within a device that is elliptical in shape. The patient is placed so the kidney is centered at one focus, while ultrasound waves from the other focus hit the walls and are reflected to the kidney stone. The convergence of the ultrasound waves at the kidney stone causes vibrations that shatter it into fragments. The small pieces can then be passed painlessly through the patient's system. The patient recovers in days, as opposed to up to six weeks if surgery is used instead.

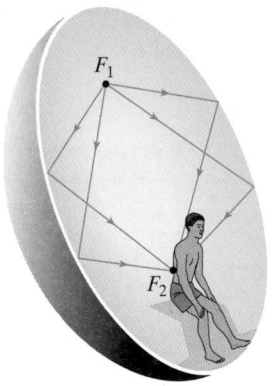

Disintegrating kidney stones

Ellipses are often used for supporting arches of bridges and in tunnel construction. This application forms the basis of our next example.

EXAMPLE 5 **An Application Involving an Ellipse**

A semielliptical archway over a one-way road has a height of 10 feet and a width of 40 feet (see **Figure 7.11**). Your truck has a width of 10 feet and a height of 9 feet. Will your truck clear the opening of the archway?

Figure 7.11
A semielliptical archway

Solution Because your truck's width is 10 feet, to determine the clearance, we must find the height of the archway 5 feet from the center. If that height is 9 feet or less, the truck will not clear the opening.

In **Figure 7.12**, we've constructed a coordinate system with the x-axis on the ground and the origin at the center of the archway. Also shown is the truck, whose height is 9 feet.

Figure 7.12

Using the equation $\dfrac{x^2}{a^2} + \dfrac{y^2}{b^2} = 1$, we can express the equation of the blue archway in **Figure 7.12** as $\dfrac{x^2}{20^2} + \dfrac{y^2}{10^2} = 1$, or $\dfrac{x^2}{400} + \dfrac{y^2}{100} = 1$.

As shown in **Figure 7.12**, the edge of the 10-foot-wide truck corresponds to $x = 5$. We find the height of the archway 5 feet from the center by substituting 5 for x and solving for y.

Halley's Comet

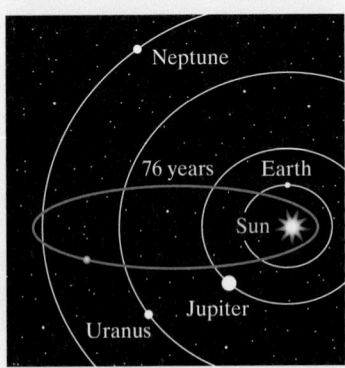

Halley's Comet has an elliptical orbit with the sun at one focus. The comet returns every 76.3 years. The first recorded sighting was in 239 B.C. It was last seen in 1986. At that time, spacecraft went close to the comet, measuring its nucleus to be 7 miles long and 4 miles wide. By 2024, Halley's Comet will have reached the farthest point in its elliptical orbit before returning to be next visible from Earth in 2062.

The elliptical orbit of Halley's Comet

$$\frac{5^2}{400} + \frac{y^2}{100} = 1 \qquad \text{Substitute 5 for x in } \frac{x^2}{400} + \frac{y^2}{100} = 1.$$

$$\frac{25}{400} + \frac{y^2}{100} = 1 \qquad \text{Square 5.}$$

$$400\left(\frac{25}{400} + \frac{y^2}{100}\right) = 400(1) \qquad \text{Clear fractions by multiplying both sides by 400.}$$

$$25 + 4y^2 = 400 \qquad \text{Use the distributive property and simplify.}$$

$$4y^2 = 375 \qquad \text{Subtract 25 from both sides.}$$

$$y^2 = \frac{375}{4} \qquad \text{Divide both sides by 4.}$$

$$y = \sqrt{\frac{375}{4}} \qquad \text{Take only the positive square root. The archway is above the x-axis, so y is nonnegative.}$$

$$\approx 9.68 \qquad \text{Use a calculator.}$$

Thus, the height of the archway 5 feet from the center is approximately 9.68 feet. Because your truck's height is 9 feet, there is enough room for the truck to clear the archway.

✓ Check Point **5** Will a truck that is 12 feet wide and has a height of 9 feet clear the opening of the archway described in Example 5?

Exercise Set 7.1

Practice Exercises

In Exercises 1–18, graph each ellipse and locate the foci.

1. $\dfrac{x^2}{16} + \dfrac{y^2}{4} = 1$

2. $\dfrac{x^2}{25} + \dfrac{y^2}{16} = 1$

3. $\dfrac{x^2}{9} + \dfrac{y^2}{36} = 1$

4. $\dfrac{x^2}{16} + \dfrac{y^2}{49} = 1$

5. $\dfrac{x^2}{25} + \dfrac{y^2}{64} = 1$

6. $\dfrac{x^2}{49} + \dfrac{y^2}{36} = 1$

7. $\dfrac{x^2}{49} + \dfrac{y^2}{81} = 1$

8. $\dfrac{x^2}{64} + \dfrac{y^2}{100} = 1$

9. $\dfrac{x^2}{\frac{9}{4}} + \dfrac{y^2}{\frac{25}{4}} = 1$

10. $\dfrac{x^2}{\frac{81}{4}} + \dfrac{y^2}{\frac{25}{16}} = 1$

11. $x^2 = 1 - 4y^2$

12. $y^2 = 1 - 4x^2$

13. $25x^2 + 4y^2 = 100$

14. $9x^2 + 4y^2 = 36$

15. $4x^2 + 16y^2 = 64$

16. $4x^2 + 25y^2 = 100$

17. $7x^2 = 35 - 5y^2$

18. $6x^2 = 30 - 5y^2$

In Exercises 19–24, find the standard form of the equation of each ellipse and give the location of its foci.

19.

20.

21.

22.

23.

24.

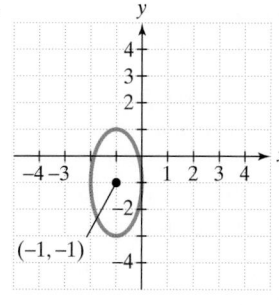

In Exercises 25–36, find the standard form of the equation of each ellipse satisfying the given conditions.

25. Foci: $(-5, 0), (5, 0)$; vertices: $(-8, 0), (8, 0)$

26. Foci: $(-2, 0), (2, 0)$; vertices: $(-6, 0), (6, 0)$

27. Foci: $(0, -4), (0, 4)$; vertices: $(0, -7), (0, 7)$

28. Foci: $(0, -3), (0, 3)$; vertices: $(0, -4), (0, 4)$

29. Foci: $(-2, 0), (2, 0)$; y-intercepts: -3 and 3

30. Foci: $(0, -2), (0, 2)$; x-intercepts: -2 and 2

31. Major axis horizontal with length 8; length of minor axis = 4; center: $(0, 0)$

32. Major axis horizontal with length 12; length of minor axis $= 6$; center: $(0,0)$

33. Major axis vertical with length 10; length of minor axis $= 4$; center: $(-2,3)$

34. Major axis vertical with length 20; length of minor axis $= 10$; center: $(2,-3)$

35. Endpoints of major axis: $(7,9)$ and $(7,3)$
 Endpoints of minor axis: $(5,6)$ and $(9,6)$

36. Endpoints of major axis: $(2,2)$ and $(8,2)$
 Endpoints of minor axis: $(5,3)$ and $(5,1)$

In Exercises 37–50, graph each ellipse and give the location of its foci.

37. $\dfrac{(x-2)^2}{9} + \dfrac{(y-1)^2}{4} = 1$

38. $\dfrac{(x-1)^2}{16} + \dfrac{(y+2)^2}{9} = 1$

39. $(x+3)^2 + 4(y-2)^2 = 16$

40. $(x-3)^2 + 9(y+2)^2 = 18$

41. $\dfrac{(x-4)^2}{9} + \dfrac{(y+2)^2}{25} = 1$

42. $\dfrac{(x-3)^2}{9} + \dfrac{(y+1)^2}{16} = 1$

43. $\dfrac{x^2}{25} + \dfrac{(y-2)^2}{36} = 1$

44. $\dfrac{(x-4)^2}{4} + \dfrac{y^2}{25} = 1$

45. $\dfrac{(x+3)^2}{9} + (y-2)^2 = 1$

46. $\dfrac{(x+2)^2}{16} + (y-3)^2 = 1$

47. $\dfrac{(x-1)^2}{2} + \dfrac{(y+3)^2}{5} = 1$

48. $\dfrac{(x+1)^2}{2} + \dfrac{(y-3)^2}{5} = 1$

49. $9(x-1)^2 + 4(y+3)^2 = 36$

50. $36(x+4)^2 + (y+3)^2 = 36$

In Exercises 51–56, convert each equation to standard form by completing the square on x and y. Then graph the ellipse and give the location of its foci.

51. $9x^2 + 25y^2 - 36x + 50y - 164 = 0$

52. $4x^2 + 9y^2 - 32x + 36y + 64 = 0$

53. $9x^2 + 16y^2 - 18x + 64y - 71 = 0$

54. $x^2 + 4y^2 + 10x - 8y + 13 = 0$

55. $4x^2 + y^2 + 16x - 6y - 39 = 0$

56. $4x^2 + 25y^2 - 24x + 100y + 36 = 0$

Practice Plus

In Exercises 57–62, find the solution set for each system by graphing both of the system's equations in the same rectangular coordinate system and finding points of intersection. Check all solutions in both equations.

57. $\begin{cases} x^2 + y^2 = 1 \\ x^2 + 9y^2 = 9 \end{cases}$

58. $\begin{cases} x^2 + y^2 = 25 \\ 25x^2 + y^2 = 25 \end{cases}$

59. $\begin{cases} \dfrac{x^2}{25} + \dfrac{y^2}{9} = 1 \\ y = 3 \end{cases}$

60. $\begin{cases} \dfrac{x^2}{4} + \dfrac{y^2}{36} = 1 \\ x = -2 \end{cases}$

61. $\begin{cases} 4x^2 + y^2 = 4 \\ 2x - y = 2 \end{cases}$

62. $\begin{cases} 4x^2 + y^2 = 4 \\ x + y = 3 \end{cases}$

In Exercises 63–64, graph each semiellipse.

63. $y = -\sqrt{16 - 4x^2}$

64. $y = -\sqrt{4 - 4x^2}$

Application Exercises

65. Will a truck that is 8 feet wide carrying a load that reaches 7 feet above the ground clear the semielliptical arch on the one-way road that passes under the bridge shown in the figure?

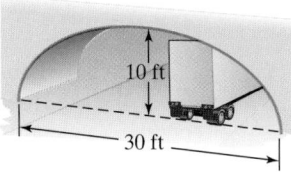

66. A semielliptic archway has a height of 20 feet and a width of 50 feet, as shown in the figure. Can a truck 14 feet high and 10 feet wide drive under the archway without going into the other lane?

67. The elliptical ceiling in Statuary Hall in the U.S. Capitol Building is 96 feet long and 23 feet tall.

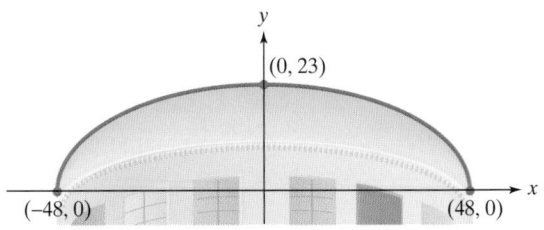

 a. Using the rectangular coordinate system in the figure shown, write the standard form of the equation of the elliptical ceiling.

 b. John Quincy Adams discovered that he could overhear the conversations of opposing party leaders near the left side of the chamber if he situated his desk at the focus at the right side of the chamber. How far from the center of the ellipse along the major axis did Adams situate his desk? (Round to the nearest foot.)

68. If an elliptical whispering room has a height of 30 feet and a width of 100 feet, where should two people stand if they would like to whisper back and forth and be heard?

Writing in Mathematics

69. What is an ellipse?

70. Describe how to graph $\dfrac{x^2}{25} + \dfrac{y^2}{16} = 1$.

71. Describe how to locate the foci for $\dfrac{x^2}{25} + \dfrac{y^2}{16} = 1$.

72. Describe one similarity and one difference between the graphs of $\dfrac{x^2}{25} + \dfrac{y^2}{16} = 1$ and $\dfrac{x^2}{16} + \dfrac{y^2}{25} = 1$.

73. Describe one similarity and one difference between the graphs of $\dfrac{x^2}{25} + \dfrac{y^2}{16} = 1$ and $\dfrac{(x-1)^2}{25} + \dfrac{(y-1)^2}{16} = 1$.

74. An elliptipool is an elliptical pool table with only one pocket. A pool shark places a ball on the table, hits it in what appears to be a random direction, and yet it bounces off the edge, falling directly into the pocket. Explain why this happens.

Technology Exercises

75. Use a graphing utility to graph any five of the ellipses that you graphed by hand in Exercises 1–18.

76. Use a graphing utility to graph any three of the ellipses that you graphed by hand in Exercises 37–50. First solve the given equation for y by using the square root property. Enter each of the two resulting equations to produce each half of the ellipse.

77. Use a graphing utility to graph any one of the ellipses that you graphed by hand in Exercises 51–56. Write the equation as a quadratic equation in y and use the quadratic formula to solve for y. Enter each of the two resulting equations to produce each half of the ellipse.

78. Write an equation for the path of each of the following elliptical orbits. Then use a graphing utility to graph the two ellipses in the same viewing rectangle. Can you see why early astronomers had difficulty detecting that these orbits are ellipses rather than circles?

- Earth's orbit: Length of major axis: 186 million miles

 Length of minor axis: 185.8 million miles

- Mars's orbit: Length of major axis: 283.5 million miles

 Length of minor axis: 278.5 million miles

Critical Thinking Exercises

Make Sense? *In Exercises 79–82, determine whether each statement makes sense or does not make sense, and explain your reasoning.*

79. I graphed an ellipse with a horizontal major axis and foci on the y-axis.

80. I graphed an ellipse that was symmetric about its major axis but not symmetric about its minor axis.

81. You told me that an ellipse centered at the origin has vertices at $(-5, 0)$ and $(5, 0)$, so I was able to graph the ellipse.

82. In a whispering gallery at our science museum, I stood at one focus, my friend stood at the other focus, and we had a clear conversation, very little of which was heard by the 25 museum visitors standing between us.

83. Find the standard form of the equation of an ellipse with vertices at $(0, -6)$ and $(0, 6)$, passing through $(2, -4)$.

84. An Earth satellite has an elliptical orbit described by

$$\frac{x^2}{(5000)^2} + \frac{y^2}{(4750)^2} = 1.$$

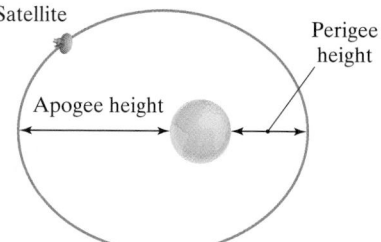

(All units are in miles.) The coordinates of the center of Earth are $(16, 0)$.

 a. The perigee of the satellite's orbit is the point that is nearest Earth's center. If the radius of Earth is approximately 4000 miles, find the distance of the perigee above Earth's surface.

 b. The apogee of the satellite's orbit is the point that is the greatest distance from Earth's center. Find the distance of the apogee above Earth's surface.

85. The equation of the red ellipse in the figure shown is

$$\frac{x^2}{25} + \frac{y^2}{9} = 1.$$

Write the equation for each circle shown in the figure.

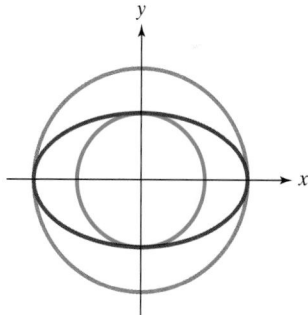

86. What happens to the shape of the graph of $\dfrac{x^2}{a^2} + \dfrac{y^2}{b^2} = 1$ as $\dfrac{c}{a} \to 0$, where $c^2 = a^2 - b^2$?

Preview Exercises

Exercises 87–89 will help you prepare for the material covered in the next section.

87. Divide both sides of $4x^2 - 9y^2 = 36$ by 36 and simplify. How does the simplified equation differ from that of an ellipse?

88. Consider the equation $\dfrac{x^2}{16} - \dfrac{y^2}{9} = 1$.

 a. Find the x-intercepts.

 b. Explain why there are no y-intercepts.

89. Consider the equation $\dfrac{y^2}{9} - \dfrac{x^2}{16} = 1$.

 a. Find the y-intercepts.

 b. Explain why there are no x-intercepts.

Section 7.2 The Hyperbola

Objectives

1. Locate a hyperbola's vertices and foci.
2. Write equations of hyperbolas in standard form.
3. Graph hyperbolas centered at the origin.
4. Graph hyperbolas not centered at the origin.
5. Solve applied problems involving hyperbolas.

St. Mary's Cathedral

Conic sections are often used to create unusual architectural designs. The top of St. Mary's Cathedral in San Francisco is a 2135-cubic-foot dome with walls rising 200 feet above the floor and supported by four massive concrete pylons that extend 94 feet into the ground. Cross sections of the roof are parabolas and hyperbolas. In this section, we study the curve with two parts known as the hyperbola.

Definition of a Hyperbola

Figure 7.13 shows a cylindrical lampshade casting two shadows on a wall. These shadows indicate the distinguishing feature of hyperbolas: Their graphs contain two disjoint parts, called **branches**. Although each branch might look like a parabola, its shape is actually quite different.

The definition of a hyperbola is similar to that of an ellipse. For an ellipse, the *sum* of the distances to the foci is a constant. By contrast, for a hyperbola the *difference* of the distances to the foci is a constant.

Figure 7.13 Casting hyperbolic shadows

> ### Definition of a Hyperbola
> A **hyperbola** is the set of points in a plane the difference of whose distances from two fixed points, called foci, is constant.

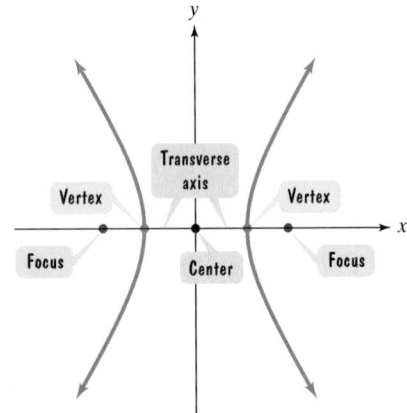

Figure 7.14 The two branches of a hyperbola

Figure 7.14 illustrates the two branches of a hyperbola. The line through the foci intersects the hyperbola at two points, called the **vertices**. The line segment that joins the vertices is the **transverse axis**. The midpoint of the transverse axis is the **center** of the hyperbola. Notice that the center lies midway between the vertices, as well as midway between the foci.

Standard Form of the Equation of a Hyperbola

The rectangular coordinate system enables us to translate a hyperbola's geometric definition into an algebraic equation. **Figure 7.15** is our starting point for obtaining an equation. We place the foci, F_1 and F_2, on the x-axis at the points $(-c, 0)$ and $(c, 0)$. Note that the center of this hyperbola is at the origin. We let (x, y) represent the coordinates of any point, P, on the hyperbola.

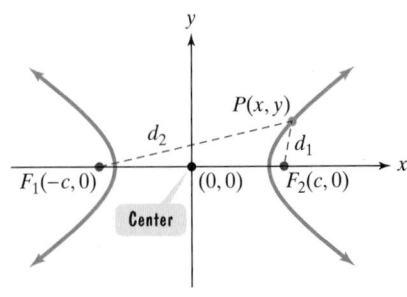

Figure 7.15

What does the definition of a hyperbola tell us about the point (x, y) in **Figure 7.15**? For any point (x, y) on the hyperbola, the absolute value of the difference of the distances from the two foci, $|d_2 - d_1|$, must be constant. We denote this constant by $2a$, just as we did for the ellipse. Thus, the point (x, y) is on the hyperbola if and only if

$$|d_2 - d_1| = 2a.$$

$$\left|\sqrt{(x + c)^2 + (y - 0)^2} - \sqrt{(x - c)^2 + (y - 0)^2}\right| = 2a \quad \text{Use the distance formula.}$$

After eliminating radicals and simplifying, we obtain

$$(c^2 - a^2)x^2 - a^2y^2 = a^2(c^2 - a^2).$$

For convenience, let $b^2 = c^2 - a^2$. Substituting b^2 for $c^2 - a^2$ in the preceding equation, we obtain

$$b^2x^2 - a^2y^2 = a^2b^2.$$

$$\frac{b^2x^2}{a^2b^2} - \frac{a^2y^2}{a^2b^2} = \frac{a^2b^2}{a^2b^2} \quad \text{Divide both sides by } a^2b^2.$$

$$\frac{x^2}{a^2} - \frac{y^2}{b^2} = 1 \quad \text{Simplify.}$$

This last equation is called the **standard form of the equation of a hyperbola centered at the origin**. There are two such equations. The first is for a hyperbola in which the transverse axis lies on the x-axis. The second is for a hyperbola in which the transverse axis lies on the y-axis.

> ### Standard Forms of the Equations of a Hyperbola
>
> The **standard form of the equation of a hyperbola** with center at the origin is
>
> $$\frac{x^2}{a^2} - \frac{y^2}{b^2} = 1 \quad \text{or} \quad \frac{y^2}{a^2} - \frac{x^2}{b^2} = 1.$$

Study Tip

The form $c^2 = a^2 + b^2$ is the one you should remember. When finding the foci, this form is easy to manipulate.

Figure 7.16(a) illustrates that for the equation on the left, the transverse axis lies on the x-axis. **Figure 7.16(b)** illustrates that for the equation on the right, the transverse axis lies on the y-axis. The vertices are a units from the center and the foci are c units from the center. For both equations, $b^2 = c^2 - a^2$. Equivalently, $c^2 = a^2 + b^2$.

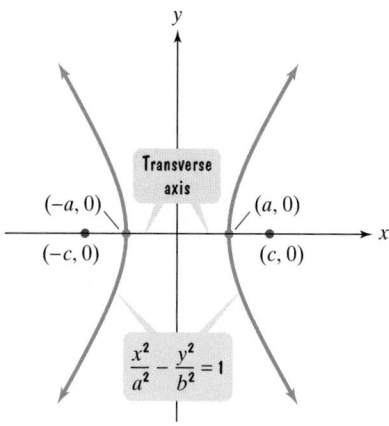

Figure 7.16(a) Transverse axis lies on the x-axis.

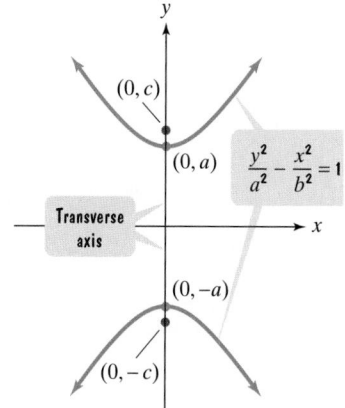

Figure 7.16(b) Transverse axis lies on the y-axis.

Study Tip

When the x^2-term is preceded by a plus sign, the transverse axis is horizontal. When the y^2-term is preceded by a plus sign, the transverse axis is vertical.

1 Locate a hyperbola's vertices and foci.

Study Tip

Notice the sign difference between the following equations:
Finding an ellipse's foci:

$$c^2 = a^2 - b^2$$

Finding a hyperbola's foci:

$$c^2 = a^2 + b^2.$$

Using the Standard Form of the Equation of a Hyperbola

We can use the standard form of the equation of a hyperbola to find its vertices and locate its foci. Because the vertices are a units from the center, begin by identifying a^2 in the equation. In the standard form of a hyperbola's equation, a^2 **is the number under the variable whose term is preceded by a plus sign** $(+)$. If the x^2-term is preceded by a plus sign, the transverse axis lies along the x-axis. Thus, the vertices are a units to the left and right of the origin. If the y^2-term is preceded by a plus sign, the transverse axis lies along the y-axis. Thus, the vertices are a units above and below the origin.

We know that the foci are c units from the center. The substitution that is used to derive the hyperbola's equation, $c^2 = a^2 + b^2$, is needed to locate the foci when a^2 and b^2 are known.

EXAMPLE 1 Finding Vertices and Foci from a Hyperbola's Equation

Find the vertices and locate the foci for each of the following hyperbolas with the given equation:

a. $\dfrac{x^2}{16} - \dfrac{y^2}{9} = 1$ **b.** $\dfrac{y^2}{9} - \dfrac{x^2}{16} = 1.$

Solution Both equations are in standard form. We begin by identifying a^2 and b^2 in each equation.

a. The first equation is in the form $\dfrac{x^2}{a^2} - \dfrac{y^2}{b^2} = 1.$

$$\frac{x^2}{16} - \frac{y^2}{9} = 1$$

$a^2 = 16$. This is the denominator of the term preceded by a plus sign. $b^2 = 9$. This is the denominator of the term preceded by a minus sign.

Because the x^2-term is preceded by a plus sign, the transverse axis lies along the x-axis. Thus, the vertices are a units to the *left* and *right* of the origin. Based on the standard form of the equation, we know the vertices are $(-a, 0)$ and $(a, 0)$. Because $a^2 = 16$, $a = 4$. Thus, the vertices are $(-4, 0)$ and $(4, 0)$, shown in **Figure 7.17**.

We use $c^2 = a^2 + b^2$ to find the foci, which are located at $(-c, 0)$ and $(c, 0)$. We know that $a^2 = 16$ and $b^2 = 9$; we need to find c^2 in order to find c.

$$c^2 = a^2 + b^2 = 16 + 9 = 25$$

Because $c^2 = 25$, $c = 5$. The foci are located at $(-5, 0)$ and $(5, 0)$. They are shown in **Figure 7.17**.

b. The second given equation is in the form $\dfrac{y^2}{a^2} - \dfrac{x^2}{b^2} = 1.$

$$\frac{y^2}{9} - \frac{x^2}{16} = 1$$

$a^2 = 9$. This is the denominator of the term preceded by a plus sign. $b^2 = 16$. This is the denominator of the term preceded by a minus sign.

Because the y^2-term is preceded by a plus sign, the transverse axis lies along the y-axis. Thus, the vertices are a units *above* and *below* the origin. Based on the standard form of the equation, we know the vertices are $(0, -a)$ and $(0, a)$. Because $a^2 = 9$, $a = 3$. Thus, the vertices are $(0, -3)$ and $(0, 3)$, shown in **Figure 7.18**.

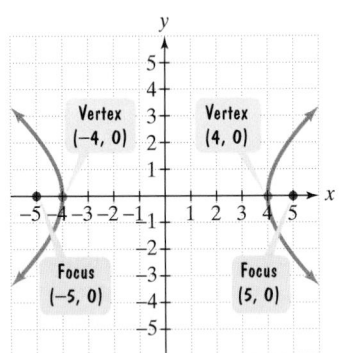

Figure 7.17 The graph of
$\dfrac{x^2}{16} - \dfrac{y^2}{9} = 1$

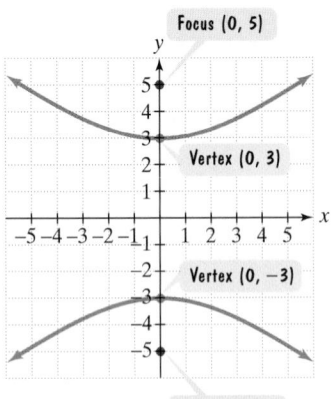

Figure 7.18 The graph of
$\dfrac{y^2}{9} - \dfrac{x^2}{16} = 1$

We use $c^2 = a^2 + b^2$ to find the foci, which are located at $(0, -c)$ and $(0, c)$.

$$c^2 = a^2 + b^2 = 9 + 16 = 25$$

Because $c^2 = 25, c = 5$. The foci are located at $(0, -5)$ and $(0, 5)$. They are shown in **Figure 7.18**.

⬤

Ⓞ Check Point **1** Find the vertices and locate the foci for each of the following hyperbolas with the given equation:

a. $\dfrac{x^2}{25} - \dfrac{y^2}{16} = 1$ **b.** $\dfrac{y^2}{25} - \dfrac{x^2}{16} = 1.$

In Example 1, we used equations of hyperbolas to find their foci and vertices. In the next example, we reverse this procedure.

② Write equations of hyperbolas in standard form.

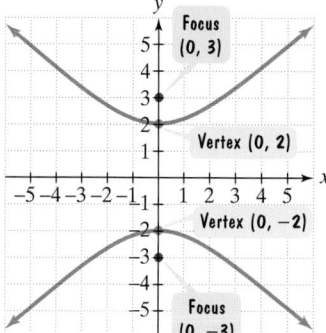

Figure 7.19

(EXAMPLE 2) **Finding the Equation of a Hyperbola from Its Foci and Vertices**

Find the standard form of the equation of a hyperbola with foci at $(0, -3)$ and $(0, 3)$ and vertices $(0, -2)$ and $(0, 2)$, shown in **Figure 7.19**.

Solution Because the foci are located at $(0, -3)$ and $(0, 3)$, on the y-axis, the transverse axis lies on the y-axis. The center of the hyperbola is midway between the foci, located at $(0, 0)$. Thus, the form of the equation is

$$\frac{y^2}{a^2} - \frac{x^2}{b^2} = 1.$$

We need to determine the values for a^2 and b^2. The distance from the center, $(0, 0)$, to either vertex, $(0, -2)$ or $(0, 2)$, is 2, so $a = 2$.

$$\frac{y^2}{2^2} - \frac{x^2}{b^2} = 1 \quad \text{or} \quad \frac{y^2}{4} - \frac{x^2}{b^2} = 1$$

We must still find b^2. The distance from the center, $(0, 0)$, to either focus, $(0, -3)$ or $(0, 3)$, is 3. Thus, $c = 3$. Using $c^2 = a^2 + b^2$, we have

$$3^2 = 2^2 + b^2$$

and

$$b^2 = 3^2 - 2^2 = 9 - 4 = 5.$$

Substituting 5 for b^2 in $\dfrac{y^2}{4} - \dfrac{x^2}{b^2} = 1$ gives us the standard form of the hyperbola's equation. The equation is

$$\frac{y^2}{4} - \frac{x^2}{5} = 1.$$

⬤

Ⓞ Check Point **2** Find the standard form of the equation of a hyperbola with foci at $(0, -5)$ and $(0, 5)$ and vertices $(0, -3)$ and $(0, 3)$.

The Asymptotes of a Hyperbola

As x and y get larger, the two branches of the graph of a hyperbola approach a pair of intersecting straight lines, called **asymptotes**. The asymptotes pass through the center of the hyperbola and are helpful in graphing hyperbolas.

Figure 7.20 shows the asymptotes for the graphs of hyperbolas centered at the origin. The asymptotes pass through the corners of a rectangle. Note that the dimensions of this rectangle are $2a$ by $2b$. The line segment of length $2b$ is the **conjugate axis** of the hyperbola and is perpendicular to the transverse axis through the center of the hyperbola.

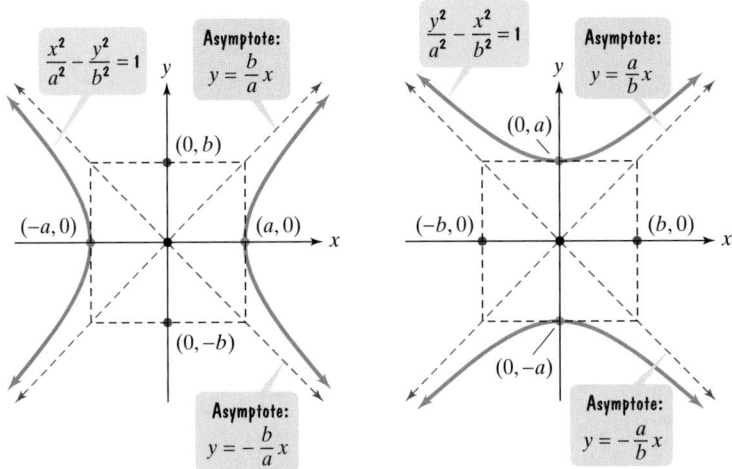

Figure 7.20 Asymptotes of a hyperbola

The Asymptotes of a Hyperbola Centered at the Origin

The hyperbola $\dfrac{x^2}{a^2} - \dfrac{y^2}{b^2} = 1$ has a horizontal transverse axis and two asymptotes

$$y = \frac{b}{a}x \qquad \text{and} \qquad y = -\frac{b}{a}x.$$

The hyperbola $\dfrac{y^2}{a^2} - \dfrac{x^2}{b^2} = 1$ has a vertical transverse axis and two asymptotes

$$y = \frac{a}{b}x \qquad \text{and} \qquad y = -\frac{a}{b}x.$$

Why are $y = \pm\dfrac{b}{a}x$ the asymptotes for a hyperbola whose transverse axis is horizontal? The proof can be found in the appendix.

③ Graph hyperbolas centered at the origin.

Graphing Hyperbolas Centered at the Origin

Hyperbolas are graphed using vertices and asymptotes.

Graphing Hyperbolas

1. Locate the vertices.
2. Use dashed lines to draw the rectangle centered at the origin with sides parallel to the axes, crossing one axis at $\pm a$ and the other at $\pm b$.
3. Use dashed lines to draw the diagonals of this rectangle and extend them to obtain the asymptotes.
4. Draw the two branches of the hyperbola by starting at each vertex and approaching the asymptotes.

EXAMPLE 3 **Graphing a Hyperbola**

Graph and locate the foci: $\dfrac{x^2}{25} - \dfrac{y^2}{16} = 1$. What are the equations of the asymptotes?

Solution

Step 1 Locate the vertices. The given equation is in the form $\dfrac{x^2}{a^2} - \dfrac{y^2}{b^2} = 1$, with $a^2 = 25$ and $b^2 = 16$.

$$\underset{a^2\,=\,25}{\underbrace{}} \dfrac{x^2}{25} - \dfrac{y^2}{16} = 1 \underset{b^2\,=\,16}{\underbrace{}}$$

Based on the standard form of the equation with the transverse axis on the x-axis, we know that the vertices are $(-a, 0)$ and $(a, 0)$. Because $a^2 = 25$, $a = 5$. Thus, the vertices are $(-5, 0)$ and $(5, 0)$, shown in **Figure 7.21**.

Step 2 Draw a rectangle. Because $a^2 = 25$ and $b^2 = 16$, $a = 5$ and $b = 4$. We construct a rectangle to find the asymptotes, using -5 and 5 on the x-axis (the vertices are located here) and -4 and 4 on the y-axis. The rectangle passes through these four points, shown using dashed lines in **Figure 7.21**.

Step 3 Draw extended diagonals for the rectangle to obtain the asymptotes. We draw dashed lines through the opposite corners of the rectangle, shown in **Figure 7.21**, to obtain the graph of the asymptotes. Based on the standard form of the hyperbola's equation, the equations for these asymptotes are

$$y = \pm\dfrac{b}{a}x \qquad \text{or} \qquad y = \pm\dfrac{4}{5}x.$$

Technology

Graph $\dfrac{x^2}{25} - \dfrac{y^2}{16} = 1$ by solving for y:

$$y_1 = \dfrac{\sqrt{16x^2 - 400}}{5}$$

$$y_2 = -\dfrac{\sqrt{16x^2 - 400}}{5} = -y_1.$$

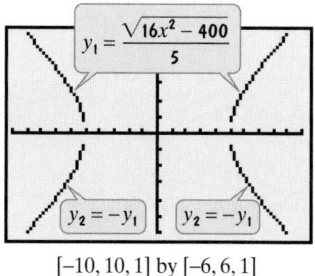

$[-10, 10, 1]$ by $[-6, 6, 1]$

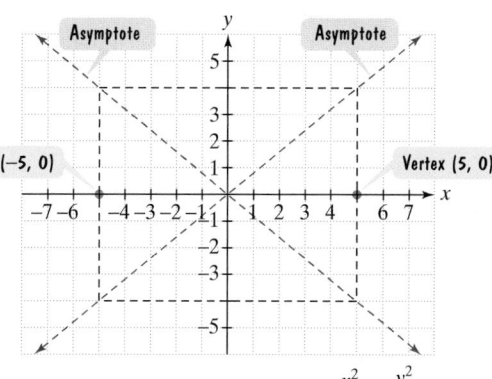

Figure 7.21 Preparing to graph $\dfrac{x^2}{25} - \dfrac{y^2}{16} = 1$

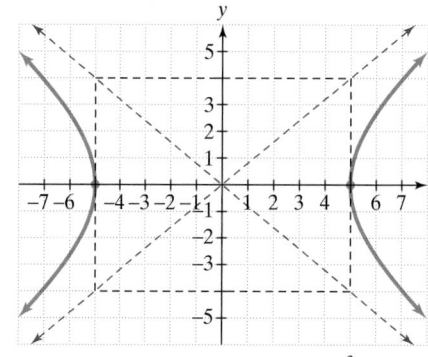

Figure 7.22 The graph of $\dfrac{x^2}{25} - \dfrac{y^2}{16} = 1$

Step 4 Draw the two branches of the hyperbola by starting at each vertex and approaching the asymptotes. The hyperbola is shown in **Figure 7.22**.

We now consider the foci, located at $(-c, 0)$ and $(c, 0)$. We find c using $c^2 = a^2 + b^2$.

$$c^2 = 25 + 16 = 41$$

Because $c^2 = 41$, $c = \sqrt{41}$. The foci are located at $\left(-\sqrt{41}, 0\right)$ and $\left(\sqrt{41}, 0\right)$, approximately $(-6.4, 0)$ and $(6.4, 0)$. ⬤

✓ **Check Point 3** Graph and locate the foci: $\dfrac{x^2}{36} - \dfrac{y^2}{9} = 1$. What are the equations of the asymptotes?

EXAMPLE 4 Graphing a Hyperbola

Graph and locate the foci: $9y^2 - 4x^2 = 36$. What are the equations of the asymptotes?

Solution We begin by writing the equation in standard form. The right side should be 1, so we divide both sides by 36.

$$\frac{9y^2}{36} - \frac{4x^2}{36} = \frac{36}{36}$$

$$\frac{y^2}{4} - \frac{x^2}{9} = 1 \qquad \text{Simplify. The right side is now 1.}$$

Now we are ready to use our four-step procedure for graphing hyperbolas.

Step 1 Locate the vertices. The equation that we obtained is in the form $\frac{y^2}{a^2} - \frac{x^2}{b^2} = 1$, with $a^2 = 4$ and $b^2 = 9$.

$$\frac{y^2}{4} - \frac{x^2}{9} = 1$$

$a^2 = 4$ \qquad $b^2 = 9$

Based on the standard form of the equation with the transverse axis on the y-axis, we know that the vertices are $(0, -a)$ and $(0, a)$. Because $a^2 = 4$, $a = 2$. Thus, the vertices are $(0, -2)$ and $(0, 2)$, shown in **Figure 7.23**.

Step 2 Draw a rectangle. Because $a^2 = 4$ and $b^2 = 9$, $a = 2$ and $b = 3$. We construct a rectangle to find the asymptotes, using -2 and 2 on the y-axis (the vertices are located here) and -3 and 3 on the x-axis. The rectangle passes through these four points, shown using dashed lines in **Figure 7.23**.

Step 3 Draw extended diagonals of the rectangle to obtain the asymptotes. We draw dashed lines through the opposite corners of the rectangle, shown in **Figure 7.23**, to obtain the graph of the asymptotes. Based on the standard form of the hyperbola's equation, the equations of these asymptotes are

$$y = \pm \frac{a}{b}x \qquad \text{or} \qquad y = \pm \frac{2}{3}x.$$

Step 4 Draw the two branches of the hyperbola by starting at each vertex and approaching the asymptotes. The hyperbola is shown in **Figure 7.24**.

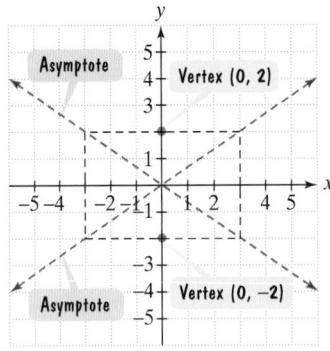

Figure 7.23 Preparing to graph $\frac{y^2}{4} - \frac{x^2}{9} = 1$

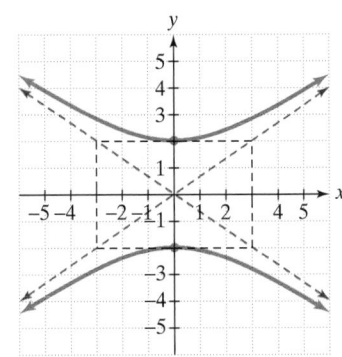

Figure 7.24 The graph of $\frac{y^2}{4} - \frac{x^2}{9} = 1$

We now consider the foci, located at $(0, -c)$ and $(0, c)$. We find c using $c^2 = a^2 + b^2$.

$$c^2 = 4 + 9 = 13$$

Because $c^2 = 13, c = \sqrt{13}$. The foci are located at $\left(0, -\sqrt{13}\right)$ and $\left(0, \sqrt{13}\right)$, approximately $(0, -3.6)$ and $(0, 3.6)$. ●

⊘ Check Point **4** Graph and locate the foci: $y^2 - 4x^2 = 4$. What are the equations of the asymptotes?

④ Graph hyperbolas not centered at the origin.

Translations of Hyperbolas

The graph of a hyperbola can be centered at (h, k), rather than at the origin. Horizontal and vertical translations are accomplished by replacing x with $x - h$ and y with $y - k$ in the standard form of the hyperbola's equation.

Table 7.2 gives the standard forms of equations of hyperbolas centered at (h, k) and shows their graphs.

Table 7.2 Standard Forms of Equations of Hyperbolas Centered at (h, k)

Equation	Center	Transverse Axis	Vertices	Graph
$\dfrac{(x - h)^2}{a^2} - \dfrac{(y - k)^2}{b^2} = 1$ Vertices are a units right and a units left of center. Foci are c units right and c units left of center, where $c^2 = a^2 + b^2$.	(h, k)	Parallel to the x-axis; horizontal	$(h - a, k)$ $(h + a, k)$	
$\dfrac{(y - k)^2}{a^2} - \dfrac{(x - h)^2}{b^2} = 1$ Vertices are a units above and a units below the center. Foci are c units above and c units below the center, where $c^2 = a^2 + b^2$.	(h, k)	Parallel to the y-axis; vertical	$(h, k - a)$ $(h, k + a)$	

(EXAMPLE 5) **Graphing a Hyperbola Centered at (h, k)**

Graph: $\dfrac{(x - 2)^2}{16} - \dfrac{(y - 3)^2}{9} = 1$. Where are the foci located? What are the equations of the asymptotes?

Solution In order to graph the hyperbola, we need to know its center, (h, k). In the standard forms of equations centered at (h, k), h is the number subtracted from x and k is the number subtracted from y.

This is $(x - h)^2$, with $h = 2$.

This is $(y - k)^2$, with $k = 3$.

$$\frac{(x - 2)^2}{16} - \frac{(y - 3)^2}{9} = 1$$

We see that $h = 2$ and $k = 3$. Thus, the center of the hyperbola, (h, k), is $(2, 3)$. We can graph the hyperbola by using vertices, asymptotes, and our four-step graphing procedure.

Step 1 Locate the vertices. To do this, we must identify a^2.

$$\frac{(x - 2)^2}{16} - \frac{(y - 3)^2}{9} = 1 \qquad \text{The form of this equation is } \frac{(x - h)^2}{a^2} - \frac{(y - k)^2}{b^2} = 1.$$

$a^2 = 16$ $\qquad b^2 = 9$

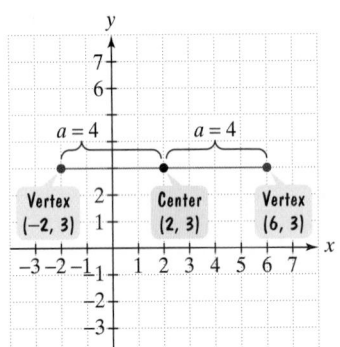

Figure 7.25 Locating a hyperbola's center and vertices

Based on the standard form of the equation with a horizontal transverse axis, the vertices are a units to the left and right of the center. Because $a^2 = 16$, $a = 4$. This means that the vertices are 4 units to the left and right of the center, $(2, 3)$. Four units to the left of $(2, 3)$ puts one vertex at $(2 - 4, 3)$, or $(-2, 3)$. Four units to the right of $(2, 3)$ puts the other vertex at $(2 + 4, 3)$, or $(6, 3)$. The vertices are shown in **Figure 7.25**.

Step 2 Draw a rectangle. Because $a^2 = 16$ and $b^2 = 9$, $a = 4$ and $b = 3$. The rectangle passes through points that are 4 units to the right and left of the center (the vertices are located here) and 3 units above and below the center. The rectangle is shown using dashed lines in **Figure 7.26**.

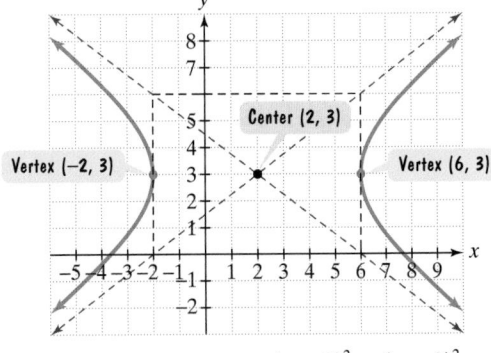

Figure 7.26 The graph of $\dfrac{(x - 2)^2}{16} - \dfrac{(y - 3)^2}{9} = 1$

Step 3 Draw extended diagonals of the rectangle to obtain the asymptotes. We draw dashed lines through the opposite corners of the rectangle, shown in **Figure 7.26**, to obtain the graph of the asymptotes. The equations of the asymptotes of the unshifted hyperbola $\dfrac{x^2}{16} - \dfrac{y^2}{9} = 1$ are $y = \pm \dfrac{b}{a} x$, or $y = \pm \dfrac{3}{4} x$. Thus, the asymptotes for the hyperbola that is shifted two units to the right and three units up, namely

$$\frac{(x - 2)^2}{16} - \frac{(y - 3)^2}{9} = 1$$

have equations that can be expressed as

$$y - 3 = \pm \frac{3}{4}(x - 2).$$

Step 4 Draw the two branches of the hyperbola by starting at each vertex and approaching the asymptotes. The hyperbola is shown in **Figure 7.26**.

We now consider the foci, located c units to the right and left of the center. We find c using $c^2 = a^2 + b^2$.

$$c^2 = 16 + 9 = 25$$

Because $c^2 = 25$, $c = 5$. This means that the foci are 5 units to the left and right of the center, $(2, 3)$. Five units to the left of $(2, 3)$ puts one focus at $(2 - 5, 3)$, or $(-3, 3)$. Five units to the right of $(2, 3)$ puts the other focus at $(2 + 5, 3)$, or $(7, 3)$.

Study Tip

You can also use the point-slope form of a line's equation

$$y - y_1 = m(x - x_1)$$

to find the equations of the asymptotes. The center of the hyperbola, (h, k), is a point on each asymptote, so $x_1 = h$ and $y_1 = k$. The slopes, m, are $\pm \dfrac{b}{a}$ for a horizontal transverse axis and $\pm \dfrac{a}{b}$ for a vertical transverse axis.

☑ Check Point **5** Graph: $\dfrac{(x-3)^2}{4} - \dfrac{(y-1)^2}{1} = 1$. Where are the foci located? What are the equations of the asymptotes?

In our next example, it is necessary to convert the equation of a hyperbola to standard form by completing the square on x and y.

EXAMPLE 6 **Graphing a Hyperbola Centered at** (h, k)

Graph: $4x^2 - 24x - 25y^2 + 250y - 489 = 0$. Where are the foci located? What are the equations of the asymptotes?

Solution We begin by completing the square on x and y.

$4x^2 - 24x - 25y^2 + 250y - 489 = 0$ This is the given equation.

$(4x^2 - 24x) + (-25y^2 + 250y) = 489$ Group terms and add 489 to both sides.

$4(x^2 - 6x + \square) - 25(y^2 - 10y + \square) = 489$ Factor out 4 and -25, respectively, so coefficients of x^2 and y^2 are 1.

$4(x^2 - 6x + 9) - 25(y^2 - 10y + 25) = 489 + 36 + (-625)$ Complete each square by adding the square of half the coefficient of x and y, respectively.

> We added $4 \cdot 9$, or 36, to the left side.

> We added $-25 \cdot 25$, or -625, to the left side.

> Add $36 + (-625)$ to the right side.

$4(x - 3)^2 - 25(y - 5)^2 = -100$ Factor.

$\dfrac{4(x - 3)^2}{-100} - \dfrac{25(y - 5)^2}{-100} = \dfrac{-100}{-100}$ Divide both sides by -100.

$\dfrac{(x - 3)^2}{-25} + \dfrac{(y - 5)^2}{4} = 1$ Simplify.

> This is $(y - k)^2$, with $k = 5$.

> This is $(x - h)^2$, with $h = 3$.

$\dfrac{(y - 5)^2}{4} - \dfrac{(x - 3)^2}{25} = 1$ Write the equation in standard form, $\dfrac{(y - k)^2}{a^2} - \dfrac{(x - h)^2}{b^2} = 1$.

Study Tip

The hyperbola's center is $(3, 5)$ because the last equation shows that 3 is subtracted from x and 5 is subtracted from y. Many students tend to read the equation from left to right and get the center backward. The hyperbola's center is *not* $(5, 3)$.

We see that $h = 3$ and $k = 5$. Thus, the center of the hyperbola, (h, k), is $(3, 5)$. Because the x^2-term is being subtracted, the transverse axis is vertical and the hyperbola opens upward and downward.

We use our four-step procedure to obtain the graph of

$$\dfrac{(y - 5)^2}{4} - \dfrac{(x - 3)^2}{25} = 1.$$

> $a^2 = 4$ $b^2 = 25$

Step 1 Locate the vertices. Based on the standard form of the equation with a vertical transverse axis, the vertices are a units above and below the center. Because $a^2 = 4$, $a = 2$. This means that the vertices are 2 units above and below the center, $(3, 5)$. This puts the vertices at $(3, 7)$ and $(3, 3)$, shown in **Figure 7.27**.

Step 2 Draw a rectangle. Because $a^2 = 4$ and $b^2 = 25$, $a = 2$ and $b = 5$. The rectangle passes through points that are 2 units above and below the center (the vertices are located here) and 5 units to the right and left of the center. The rectangle is shown using dashed lines in **Figure 7.27**.

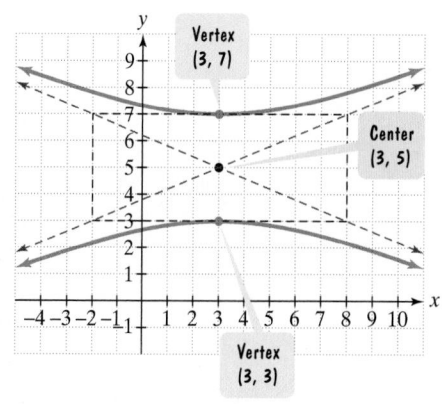

Figure 7.27 The graph of $\dfrac{(y - 5)^2}{4} - \dfrac{(x - 3)^2}{25} = 1$

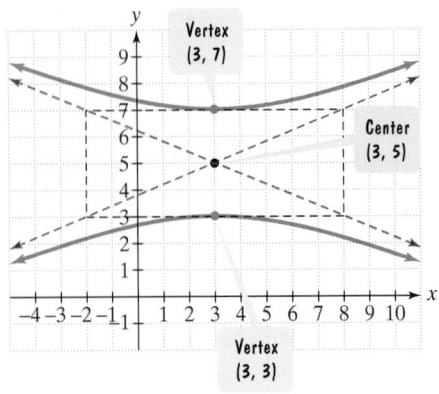

Figure 7.27 (repeated) The graph of
$$\frac{(y-5)^2}{4} - \frac{(x-3)^2}{25} = 1$$

Step 3 Draw extended diagonals of the rectangle to obtain the asymptotes. We draw dashed lines through the opposite corners of the rectangle, shown in **Figure 7.27**, to obtain the graph of the asymptotes. The equations of the asymptotes of the unshifted hyperbola $\frac{y^2}{4} - \frac{x^2}{25} = 1$ are $y = \pm\frac{a}{b}x$, or $y = \pm\frac{2}{5}x$. Thus, the asymptotes for the hyperbola that is shifted three units to the right and five units up, namely

$$\frac{(y-5)^2}{4} - \frac{(x-3)^2}{25} = 1$$

have equations that can be expressed as

$$y - 5 = \pm\frac{2}{5}(x-3).$$

Step 4 Draw the two branches of the hyperbola by starting at each vertex and approaching the asymptotes. The hyperbola is shown in **Figure 7.27**.

We now consider the foci, located c units above and below the center, $(3, 5)$. We find c using $c^2 = a^2 + b^2$.

$$c^2 = 4 + 25 = 29$$

Because $c^2 = 29$, $c = \sqrt{29}$. The foci are located at $\left(3, 5 + \sqrt{29}\right)$ and $\left(3, 5 - \sqrt{29}\right)$.

⬤

∅ **Check Point 6** Graph: $4x^2 - 24x - 9y^2 - 90y - 153 = 0$. Where are the foci located? What are the equations of the asymptotes?

 Solve applied problems involving hyperbolas.

Applications

Hyperbolas have many applications. When a jet flies at a speed greater than the speed of sound, the shock wave that is created is heard as a sonic boom. The wave has the shape of a cone. The shape formed as the cone hits the ground is one branch of a hyperbola.

Halley's Comet, a permanent part of our solar system, travels around the sun in an elliptical orbit. Other comets pass through the solar system only once, following a hyperbolic path with the sun as a focus.

Hyperbolas are of practical importance in fields ranging from architecture to navigation. Cooling towers used in the design for nuclear power plants have cross sections that are both ellipses and hyperbolas. Three-dimensional solids whose cross sections are hyperbolas are used in some rather unique architectural creations, including the TWA building at Kennedy Airport in New York City and the St. Louis Science Center Planetarium.

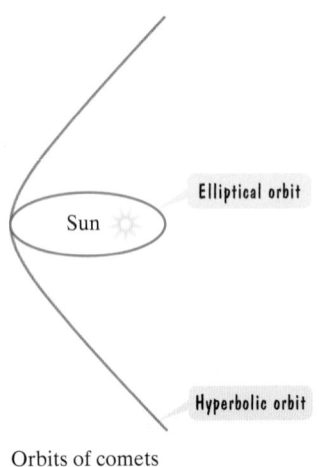

The hyperbolic shape of a sonic boom

Orbits of comets

EXAMPLE 7 **An Application Involving Hyperbolas**

An explosion is recorded by two microphones that are 2 miles apart. Microphone M_1 received the sound 4 seconds before microphone M_2. Assuming sound travels at 1100 feet per second, determine the possible locations of the explosion relative to the location of the microphones.

Solution We begin by putting the microphones in a coordinate system. Because 1 mile = 5280 feet, we place M_1 5280 feet on a horizontal axis to the right of the origin and M_2 5280 feet on a horizontal axis to the left of the origin. **Figure 7.28** illustrates that the two microphones are 2 miles apart.

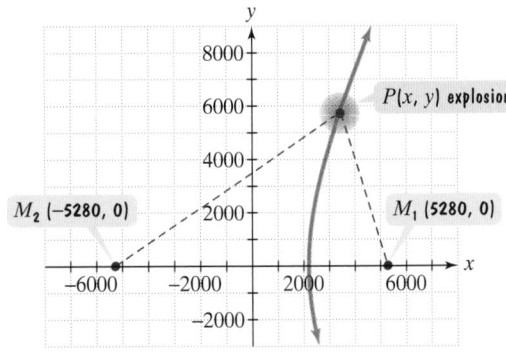

Figure 7.28 Locating an explosion on the branch of a hyperbola

We know that M_2 received the sound 4 seconds after M_1. Because sound travels at 1100 feet per second, the difference between the distance from P to M_1 and the distance from P to M_2 is 4400 feet. The set of all points P (or locations of the explosion) satisfying these conditions fits the definition of a hyperbola, with microphones M_1 and M_2 at the foci.

$$\frac{x^2}{a^2} - \frac{y^2}{b^2} = 1 \qquad \text{Use the standard form of the hyperbola's equation. } P(x, y), \text{ the explosion point, lies on this hyperbola. We must find } a^2 \text{ and } b^2.$$

The difference between the distances, represented by $2a$ in the derivation of the hyperbola's equation, is 4400 feet. Thus, $2a = 4400$ and $a = 2200$.

$$\frac{x^2}{(2200)^2} - \frac{y^2}{b^2} = 1 \qquad \text{Substitute 2200 for } a.$$

$$\frac{x^2}{4,840,000} - \frac{y^2}{b^2} = 1 \qquad \text{Square 2200.}$$

We must still find b^2. We know that $a = 2200$. The distance from the center, $(0, 0)$, to either focus, $(-5280, 0)$ or $(5280, 0)$, is 5280. Thus, $c = 5280$. Using $c^2 = a^2 + b^2$, we have

$$5280^2 = 2200^2 + b^2$$

and

$$b^2 = 5280^2 - 2200^2 = 23,038,400.$$

The equation of the hyperbola with a microphone at each focus is

$$\frac{x^2}{4,840,000} - \frac{y^2}{23,038,400} = 1. \qquad \text{Substitute 23,038,400 for } b^2.$$

We can conclude that the explosion occurred somewhere on the right branch (the branch closer to M_1) of the hyperbola given by this equation. ●

In Example 7, we determined that the explosion occurred somewhere along one branch of a hyperbola, but not exactly where on the hyperbola. If, however, we had received the sound from another pair of microphones, we could locate the sound along a branch of another hyperbola. The exact location of the explosion would be the point where the two hyperbolas intersect.

✓ Check Point **7** Rework Example 7 assuming microphone M_1 receives the sound 3 seconds before microphone M_2.

Exercise Set 7.2

Practice Exercises

In Exercises 1–4, find the vertices and locate the foci of each hyperbola with the given equation. Then match each equation to one of the graphs that are shown and labeled (a)–(d).

1. $\dfrac{x^2}{4} - \dfrac{y^2}{1} = 1$

2. $\dfrac{x^2}{1} - \dfrac{y^2}{4} = 1$

3. $\dfrac{y^2}{4} - \dfrac{x^2}{1} = 1$

4. $\dfrac{y^2}{1} - \dfrac{x^2}{4} = 1$

a.

b.

c.

d.
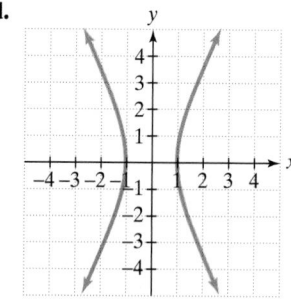

In Exercises 5–12, find the standard form of the equation of each hyperbola satisfying the given conditions.

5. Foci: $(0, -3), (0, 3)$; vertices: $(0, -1), (0, 1)$

6. Foci: $(0, -6), (0, 6)$; vertices: $(0, -2), (0, 2)$

7. Foci: $(-4, 0), (4, 0)$; vertices: $(-3, 0), (3, 0)$

8. Foci: $(-7, 0), (7, 0)$; vertices: $(-5, 0), (5, 0)$

9. Endpoints of transverse axis: $(0, -6), (0, 6)$; asymptote: $y = 2x$

10. Endpoints of transverse axis: $(-4, 0), (4, 0)$; asymptote: $y = 2x$

11. Center: $(4, -2)$; Focus: $(7, -2)$; vertex: $(6, -2)$

12. Center: $(-2, 1)$; Focus: $(-2, 6)$; vertex: $(-2, 4)$

In Exercises 13–26, use vertices and asymptotes to graph each hyperbola. Locate the foci and find the equations of the asymptotes.

13. $\dfrac{x^2}{9} - \dfrac{y^2}{25} = 1$ **14.** $\dfrac{x^2}{16} - \dfrac{y^2}{25} = 1$

15. $\dfrac{x^2}{100} - \dfrac{y^2}{64} = 1$ **16.** $\dfrac{x^2}{144} - \dfrac{y^2}{81} = 1$

17. $\dfrac{y^2}{16} - \dfrac{x^2}{36} = 1$ **18.** $\dfrac{y^2}{25} - \dfrac{x^2}{64} = 1$

19. $4y^2 - x^2 = 1$ **20.** $9y^2 - x^2 = 1$

21. $9x^2 - 4y^2 = 36$ **22.** $4x^2 - 25y^2 = 100$

23. $9y^2 - 25x^2 = 225$ **24.** $16y^2 - 9x^2 = 144$

25. $y = \pm\sqrt{x^2 - 2}$ **26.** $y = \pm\sqrt{x^2 - 3}$

In Exercises 27–32, find the standard form of the equation of each hyperbola.

27.

28.

29.

30.

31.

32.
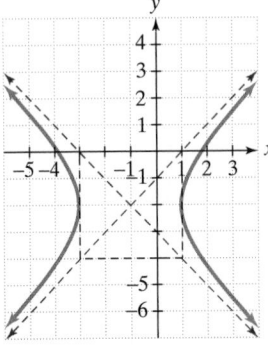

In Exercises 33–42, use the center, vertices, and asymptotes to graph each hyperbola. Locate the foci and find the equations of the asymptotes.

33. $\dfrac{(x + 4)^2}{9} - \dfrac{(y + 3)^2}{16} = 1$ **34.** $\dfrac{(x + 2)^2}{9} - \dfrac{(y - 1)^2}{25} = 1$

35. $\dfrac{(x + 3)^2}{25} - \dfrac{y^2}{16} = 1$ **36.** $\dfrac{(x + 2)^2}{9} - \dfrac{y^2}{25} = 1$

37. $\dfrac{(y + 2)^2}{4} - \dfrac{(x - 1)^2}{16} = 1$

38. $\dfrac{(y - 2)^2}{36} - \dfrac{(x + 1)^2}{49} = 1$

39. $(x - 3)^2 - 4(y + 3)^2 = 4$

40. $(x + 3)^2 - 9(y - 4)^2 = 9$

41. $(x - 1)^2 - (y - 2)^2 = 3$

42. $(y - 2)^2 - (x + 3)^2 = 5$

In Exercises 43–50, convert each equation to standard form by completing the square on x and y. Then graph the hyperbola. Locate the foci and find the equations of the asymptotes.

43. $x^2 - y^2 - 2x - 4y - 4 = 0$

44. $4x^2 - y^2 + 32x + 6y + 39 = 0$

45. $16x^2 - y^2 + 64x - 2y + 67 = 0$

46. $9y^2 - 4x^2 - 18y + 24x - 63 = 0$

47. $4x^2 - 9y^2 - 16x + 54y - 101 = 0$

48. $4x^2 - 9y^2 + 8x - 18y - 6 = 0$

49. $4x^2 - 25y^2 - 32x + 164 = 0$

50. $9x^2 - 16y^2 - 36x - 64y + 116 = 0$

Practice Plus

In Exercises 51–56, graph each relation. Use the relation's graph to determine its domain and range.

51. $\dfrac{x^2}{9} - \dfrac{y^2}{16} = 1$ **52.** $\dfrac{x^2}{25} - \dfrac{y^2}{4} = 1$

53. $\dfrac{x^2}{9} + \dfrac{y^2}{16} = 1$ **54.** $\dfrac{x^2}{25} + \dfrac{y^2}{4} = 1$

55. $\dfrac{y^2}{16} - \dfrac{x^2}{9} = 1$ **56.** $\dfrac{y^2}{4} - \dfrac{x^2}{25} = 1$

In Exercises 57–60, find the solution set for each system by graphing both of the system's equations in the same rectangular coordinate system and finding points of intersection. Check all solutions in both equations.

57. $\begin{cases} x^2 - y^2 = 4 \\ x^2 + y^2 = 4 \end{cases}$ **58.** $\begin{cases} x^2 - y^2 = 9 \\ x^2 + y^2 = 9 \end{cases}$

59. $\begin{cases} 9x^2 + y^2 = 9 \\ y^2 - 9x^2 = 9 \end{cases}$ **60.** $\begin{cases} 4x^2 + y^2 = 4 \\ y^2 - 4x^2 = 4 \end{cases}$

Application Exercises

61. An explosion is recorded by two microphones that are 1 mile apart. Microphone M_1 received the sound 2 seconds before microphone M_2. Assuming sound travels at 1100 feet per second, determine the possible locations of the explosion relative to the location of the microphones.

62. Radio towers A and B, 200 kilometers apart, are situated along the coast, with A located due west of B. Simultaneous radio signals are sent from each tower to a ship, with the signal from B received 500 microseconds before the signal from A.

a. Assuming that the radio signals travel 300 meters per microsecond, determine the equation of the hyperbola on which the ship is located.

b. If the ship lies due north of tower B, how far out at sea is it?

63. An architect designs two houses that are shaped and positioned like a part of the branches of the hyperbola whose equation is $625y^2 - 400x^2 = 250,000$, where x and y are in yards. How far apart are the houses at their closest point?

64. Scattering experiments, in which moving particles are deflected by various forces, led to the concept of the nucleus of an atom. In 1911, the physicist Ernest Rutherford (1871–1937) discovered that when alpha particles are directed toward the nuclei of gold atoms, they are eventually deflected along hyperbolic paths, illustrated in the figure. If a particle gets as close as 3 units to the nucleus along a hyperbolic path with an asymptote given by $y = \frac{1}{2}x$, what is the equation of its path?

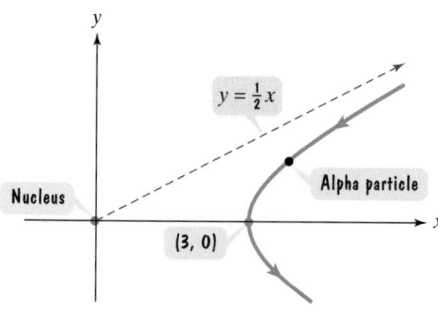

Moiré patterns, such as those shown in Exercises 65–66, can appear when two repetitive patterns overlap to produce a third, sometimes unintended, pattern.

a. *In each exercise, use the name of a conic section to describe the moiré pattern.*

b. *Select one of the following equations that can possibly describe a conic section within the moiré pattern:*

$$x^2 + y^2 = 1; \quad x^2 - y^2 = 1; \quad x^2 + 4y^2 = 4.$$

65.

66.
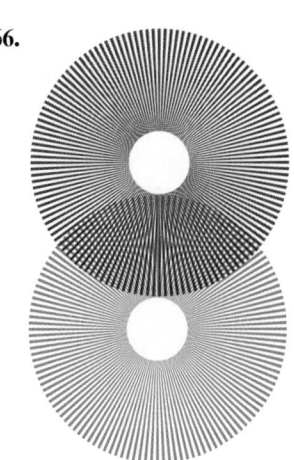

Writing in Mathematics

67. What is a hyperbola?

68. Describe how to graph $\dfrac{x^2}{9} - \dfrac{y^2}{1} = 1$.

69. Describe how to locate the foci of the graph of $\dfrac{x^2}{9} - \dfrac{y^2}{1} = 1$.

70. Describe one similarity and one difference between the graphs of $\dfrac{x^2}{9} - \dfrac{y^2}{1} = 1$ and $\dfrac{y^2}{9} - \dfrac{x^2}{1} = 1$.

71. Describe one similarity and one difference between the graphs of $\dfrac{x^2}{9} - \dfrac{y^2}{1} = 1$ and $\dfrac{(x-3)^2}{9} - \dfrac{(y+3)^2}{1} = 1$.

72. How can you distinguish an ellipse from a hyperbola by looking at their equations?

73. In 1992, a NASA team began a project called Spaceguard Survey, calling for an international watch for comets that might collide with Earth. Why is it more difficult to detect a possible "doomsday comet" with a hyperbolic orbit than one with an elliptical orbit?

Technology Exercises

74. Use a graphing utility to graph any five of the hyperbolas that you graphed by hand in Exercises 13–26.

75. Use a graphing utility to graph any three of the hyperbolas that you graphed by hand in Exercises 33–42. First solve the given equation for y by using the square root property. Enter each of the two resulting equations to produce each branch of the hyperbola.

76. Use a graphing utility to graph any one of the hyperbolas that you graphed by hand in Exercises 43–50. Write the equation as a quadratic equation in y and use the quadratic formula to solve for y. Enter each of the two resulting equations to produce each branch of the hyperbola.

77. Use a graphing utility to graph $\dfrac{x^2}{4} - \dfrac{y^2}{9} = 0$. Is the graph a hyperbola? In general, what is the graph of $\dfrac{x^2}{a^2} - \dfrac{y^2}{b^2} = 0$?

78. Graph $\dfrac{x^2}{a^2} - \dfrac{y^2}{b^2} = 1$ and $\dfrac{x^2}{a^2} - \dfrac{y^2}{b^2} = -1$ in the same viewing rectangle for values of a^2 and b^2 of your choice. Describe the relationship between the two graphs.

79. Write $4x^2 - 6xy + 2y^2 - 3x + 10y - 6 = 0$ as a quadratic equation in y and then use the quadratic formula to express y in terms of x. Graph the resulting two equations using a graphing utility in a $[-50, 70, 10]$ by $[-30, 50, 10]$ viewing rectangle. What effect does the xy-term have on the graph of the resulting hyperbola? What problems would you encounter if you attempted to write the given equation in standard form by completing the square?

80. Graph $\dfrac{x^2}{16} - \dfrac{y^2}{9} = 1$ and $\dfrac{x|x|}{16} - \dfrac{y|y|}{9} = 1$ in the same viewing rectangle. Explain why the graphs are not the same.

Critical Thinking Exercises

Make Sense? *In Exercises 81–84, determine whether each statement makes sense or does not make sense, and explain your reasoning.*

81. I changed the addition in an ellipse's equation to subtraction and this changed its elongation from horizontal to vertical.

82. I noticed that the definition of a hyperbola closely resembles that of an ellipse in that it depends on the distances between a set of points in a plane to two fixed points, the foci.

83. I graphed a hyperbola centered at the origin that had y-intercepts, but no x-intercepts.

84. I graphed a hyperbola centered at the origin that was symmetric with respect to the x-axis and also symmetric with respect to the y-axis.

In Exercises 85–88, determine whether each statement is true or false. If the statement is false, make the necessary change(s) to produce a true statement.

85. If one branch of a hyperbola is removed from a graph, then the branch that remains must define y as a function of x.

86. All points on the asymptotes of a hyperbola also satisfy the hyperbola's equation.

87. The graph of $\dfrac{x^2}{9} - \dfrac{y^2}{4} = 1$ does not intersect the line $y = -\dfrac{2}{3}x$.

88. Two different hyperbolas can never share the same asymptotes.

89. What happens to the shape of the graph of $\dfrac{x^2}{a^2} - \dfrac{y^2}{b^2} = 1$ as $\dfrac{c}{a} \to \infty$, where $c^2 = a^2 + b^2$?

90. Find the standard form of the equation of the hyperbola with vertices $(5, -6)$ and $(5, 6)$, passing through $(0, 9)$.

91. Find the equation of a hyperbola whose asymptotes are perpendicular.

Preview Exercises

Exercises 92–94 will help you prepare for the material covered in the next section.

In Exercises 92–93, graph each parabola with the given equation.

92. $y = x^2 + 4x - 5$

93. $y = -3(x - 1)^2 + 2$

94. Isolate the terms involving y on the left side of the equation:

$$y^2 + 2y + 12x - 23 = 0.$$

Then write the equation in an equivalent form by completing the square on the left side.

Chapter 7 Mid-Chapter Check Point

What You Know: We learned that the four conic sections are the circle, the ellipse, the hyperbola, and the parabola. Prior to this chapter, we graphed circles with center (h, k) and radius r:

$$(x - h)^2 + (y - k)^2 = r^2.$$

In this chapter, you learned to graph ellipses centered at the origin and ellipses centered at (h, k):

$$\frac{(x - h)^2}{a^2} + \frac{(y - k)^2}{b^2} = 1 \text{ or } \frac{(x - h)^2}{b^2} + \frac{(y - k)^2}{a^2} = 1, a^2 > b^2.$$

We saw that the larger denominator (a^2) determines whether the major axis is horizontal or vertical. We used vertices and asymptotes to graph hyperbolas centered at the origin and hyperbolas centered at (h, k):

$$\frac{(x - h)^2}{a^2} - \frac{(y - k)^2}{b^2} = 1 \text{ or } \frac{(y - k)^2}{a^2} - \frac{(x - h)^2}{b^2} = 1.$$

We used $c^2 = a^2 - b^2$ to locate the foci of an ellipse. We used $c^2 = a^2 + b^2$ to locate the foci of a hyperbola.

In Exercises 1–5, graph each ellipse. Give the location of the foci.

1. $\dfrac{x^2}{25} + \dfrac{y^2}{4} = 1$ **2.** $9x^2 + 4y^2 = 36$

3. $\dfrac{(x - 2)^2}{16} + \dfrac{(y + 1)^2}{25} = 1$ **4.** $\dfrac{(x + 2)^2}{25} + \dfrac{(y - 1)^2}{16} = 1$

5. $x^2 + 9y^2 - 4x + 54y + 49 = 0$

In Exercises 6–11, graph each hyperbola. Give the location of the foci and the equations of the asymptotes.

6. $\dfrac{x^2}{9} - y^2 = 1$ **7.** $\dfrac{y^2}{9} - x^2 = 1$

8. $y^2 - 4x^2 = 16$ **9.** $4x^2 - 49y^2 = 196$

10. $\dfrac{(x - 2)^2}{9} - \dfrac{(y + 2)^2}{16} = 1$

11. $4x^2 - y^2 + 8x + 6y + 11 = 0$

In Exercises 12–18, graph each equation.

12. $x^2 + y^2 = 4$ **13.** $x + y = 4$

14. $x^2 - y^2 = 4$ **15.** $x^2 + 4y^2 = 4$

16. $(x + 1)^2 + (y - 1)^2 = 4$

17. $x^2 + 4(y - 1)^2 = 4$

18. $(x - 1)^2 - (y - 1)^2 = 4$

In Exercises 19–22, find the standard form of the equation of the conic section satisfying the given conditions.

19. Ellipse; Foci: $(-4, 0)$, $(4, 0)$; Vertices: $(-5, 0)$, $(5, 0)$

20. Ellipse; Endpoints of major axis: $(-8, 2)$, $(10, 2)$; Foci: $(-4, 2)$, $(6, 2)$

21. Hyperbola; Foci: $(0, -3)$, $(0, 3)$; Vertices: $(0, -2)$, $(0, 2)$

22. Hyperbola; Foci: $(-4, 5)$, $(2, 5)$; Vertices: $(-3, 5)$, $(1, 5)$

23. A semielliptical archway over a one-way road has a height of 10 feet and a width of 30 feet. A truck has a width of 10 feet and a height of 9.5 feet. Will this truck clear the opening of the archway?

24. A lithotriper is used to disintegrate kidney stones. The patient is placed within an elliptical device with the kidney centered at one focus, while ultrasound waves from the other focus hit the walls and are reflected to the kidney stone, shattering the stone. Suppose that the length of the major axis of the ellipse is 40 centimeters and the length of the minor axis is 20 centimeters. How far from the kidney stone should the electrode that sends the ultrasound waves be placed in order to shatter the stone?

25. An explosion is recorded by two forest rangers, one at a primary station and the other at an outpost 6 kilometers away. The ranger at the primary station hears the explosion 6 seconds before the ranger at the outpost.

 a. Assuming sound travels at 0.35 kilometer per second, write an equation in standard form that gives all the possible locations of the explosion. Use a coordinate system with the two ranger stations on the x-axis and the midpoint between the stations at the origin.

 b. Graph the equation that gives the possible locations of the explosion. Show the locations of the ranger stations in your drawing.

Section 7.3

The Parabola

Objectives

① Graph parabolas with vertices at the origin.

② Write equations of parabolas in standard form.

③ Graph parabolas with vertices not at the origin.

④ Solve applied problems involving parabolas.

At first glance, this image looks like columns of smoke rising from a fire into a starry sky. Those are, indeed, stars in the background, but you are not looking at ordinary smoke columns. These stand almost 6 trillion miles high and are 7000 light-years from Earth—more than 400 million times as far away as the sun.

This NASA photograph is one of a series of stunning images captured from the ends of the universe by the Hubble Space Telescope. The image shows infant star systems the size of our solar system emerging from the gas and dust that shrouded their creation. Using a parabolic mirror that is 94.5 inches in diameter, the Hubble has provided answers to many of the profound mysteries of the cosmos: How big and how old is the universe? How did the galaxies come to exist? Do other Earth-like planets orbit other sun-like stars? In this section, we study parabolas and their applications, including parabolic shapes that gather distant rays of light and focus them into spectacular images.

Definition of a Parabola

In Chapter 3, we studied parabolas, viewing them as graphs of quadratic functions in the form

$$y = a(x - h)^2 + k \quad \text{or} \quad y = ax^2 + bx + c.$$

Study Tip

Here is a summary of what you should already know about graphing parabolas.

Graphing $y = a(x - h)^2 + k$ **and** $y = ax^2 + bx + c$

1. If $a > 0$, the graph opens upward. If $a < 0$, the graph opens downward.
2. The vertex of $y = a(x - h)^2 + k$ is (h, k).

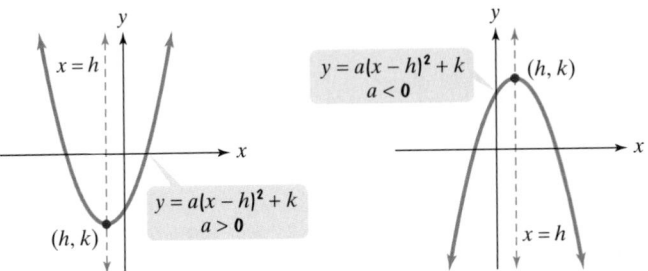

3. The x-coordinate of the vertex of $y = ax^2 + bx + c$ is $x = -\dfrac{b}{2a}$.

Parabolas can be given a geometric definition that enables us to include graphs that open to the left or to the right, as well as those that open obliquely. The definitions of ellipses and hyperbolas involved two fixed points, the foci. By contrast, the definition of a parabola is based on one point and a line.

Definition of a Parabola

A **parabola** is the set of all points in a plane that are equidistant from a fixed line, the **directrix**, and a fixed point, the **focus**, that is not on the line (see **Figure 7.29**).

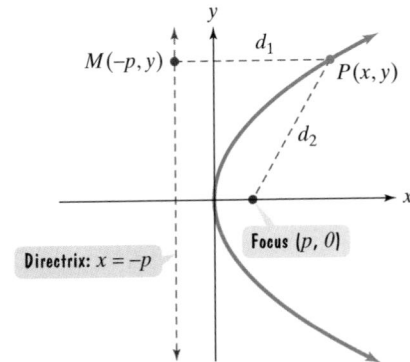

In **Figure 7.29**, find the line passing through the focus and perpendicular to the directrix. This is the **axis of symmetry** of the parabola. The point of intersection of the parabola with its axis of symmetry is called the **vertex**. Notice that the vertex is midway between the focus and the directrix.

Standard Form of the Equation of a Parabola

The rectangular coordinate system enables us to translate a parabola's geometric definition into an algebraic equation. **Figure 7.30** is our starting point for obtaining an equation. We place the focus on the x-axis at the point $(p, 0)$. The directrix has an equation given by $x = -p$. The vertex, located midway between the focus and the directrix, is at the origin.

What does the definition of a parabola tell us about the point (x, y) in **Figure 7.30**? For any point (x, y) on the parabola, the distance d_1 to the directrix is equal to the distance d_2 to the focus. Thus, the point (x, y) is on the parabola if and only if

$$d_1 = d_2.$$

$$\sqrt{(x + p)^2 + (y - y)^2} = \sqrt{(x - p)^2 + (y - 0)^2} \quad \text{Use the distance formula.}$$

$$(x + p)^2 = (x - p)^2 + y^2 \quad \text{Square both sides of the equation.}$$

Figure 7.29

Figure 7.30

$$x^2 + 2px + p^2 = x^2 - 2px + p^2 + y^2 \qquad \text{Square } x + p \text{ and } x - p.$$
$$2px = -2px + y^2 \qquad \text{Subtract } x^2 + p^2 \text{ from both}$$
$$\text{sides of the equation.}$$
$$y^2 = 4px \qquad \text{Solve for } y^2.$$

This last equation is called the **standard form of the equation of a parabola with its vertex at the origin**. There are two such equations, one for a focus on the *x*-axis and one for a focus on the *y*-axis.

> ### Standard Forms of the Equations of a Parabola
> The **standard form of the equation of a parabola** with vertex at the origin is
> $$y^2 = 4px \qquad \text{or} \qquad x^2 = 4py.$$
> **Figure 7.31(a)** illustrates that for the equation on the left, the focus is on the *x*-axis, which is the axis of symmetry. **Figure 7.31(b)** illustrates that for the equation on the right, the focus is on the *y*-axis, which is the axis of symmetry.

Study Tip

It is helpful to think of p as the *directed distance* from the vertex to the focus. If $p > 0$, the focus lies p units to the right of the vertex or p units above the vertex. If $p < 0$, the focus lies $|p|$ units to the left of the vertex or $|p|$ units below the vertex.

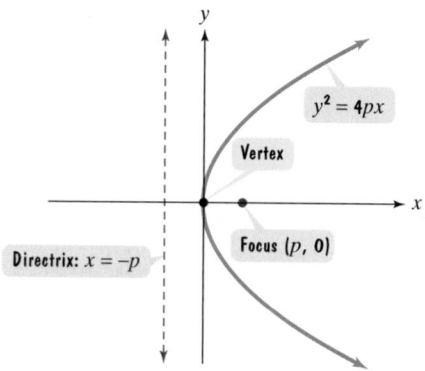

Figure 7.31(a) Parabola with the *x*-axis as the axis of symmetry. If $p > 0$, the graph opens to the right. If $p < 0$, the graph opens to the left.

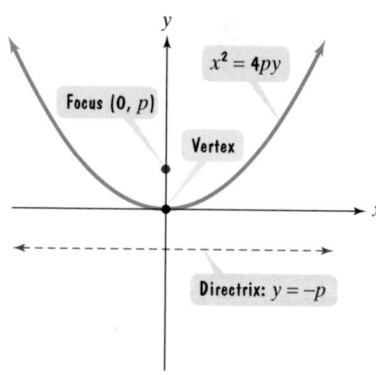

Figure 7.31(b) Parabola with the *y*-axis as the axis of symmetry. If $p > 0$, the graph opens upward. If $p < 0$, the graph opens downward.

① Graph parabolas with vertices at the origin.

Using the Standard Form of the Equation of a Parabola

We can use the standard form of the equation of a parabola to find its focus and directrix. Observing the graph's symmetry from its equation is helpful in locating the focus.

$$y^2 = 4px \qquad\qquad x^2 = 4py$$

> The equation does not change if y is replaced with $-y$. There is *x*-axis symmetry and the focus is on the *x*-axis at $(p, 0)$.

> The equation does not change if x is replaced with $-x$. There is *y*-axis symmetry and the focus is on the *y*-axis at $(0, p)$.

Although the definition of a parabola is given in terms of its focus and its directrix, the focus and directrix are not part of the graph. The vertex, located at the origin, is a point on the graph of $y^2 = 4px$ and $x^2 = 4py$. Example 1 illustrates how you can find two additional points on the parabola.

(EXAMPLE 1) **Finding the Focus and Directrix of a Parabola**

Find the focus and directrix of the parabola given by $y^2 = 12x$. Then graph the parabola.

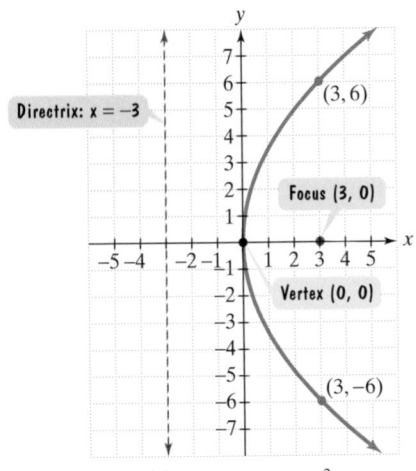

Figure 7.32 The graph of $y^2 = 12x$

Technology

We graph $y^2 = 12x$ with a graphing utility by first solving for y. The screen shows the graphs of $y = \sqrt{12x}$ and $y = -\sqrt{12x}$. The graph fails the vertical line test. Because $y^2 = 12x$ is not a function, you were not familiar with this form of the parabola's equation in Chapter 3.

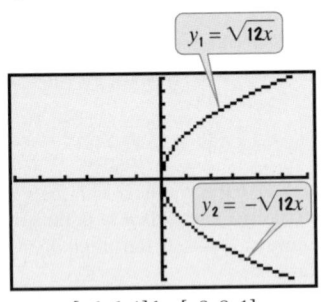

$[-6, 6, 1]$ by $[-8, 8, 1]$

Solution The given equation, $y^2 = 12x$, is in the standard form $y^2 = 4px$, so $4p = 12$.

> No change if y is replaced with $-y$. The parabola has x-axis symmetry.

$$y^2 = 12x$$

> This is $4p$.

We can find both the focus and the directrix by finding p.

$$4p = 12$$
$$p = 3 \quad \text{Divide both sides by 4.}$$

Because p is positive, the parabola, with its x-axis symmetry, opens to the right. The focus is 3 units to the right of the vertex, $(0, 0)$.

Focus: $(p, 0) = (3, 0)$
Directrix: $x = -p; x = -3$

The focus, $(3, 0)$, and directrix, $x = -3$, are shown in **Figure 7.32**.

To graph the parabola, we will use two points on the graph that lie directly above and below the focus. Because the focus is at $(3, 0)$, substitute 3 for x in the parabola's equation, $y^2 = 12x$.

$$y^2 = 12 \cdot 3 \qquad \text{Replace } x \text{ with 3 in } y^2 = 12x.$$
$$y^2 = 36 \qquad \text{Simplify.}$$
$$y = \pm\sqrt{36} = \pm 6 \qquad \text{Apply the square root property.}$$

The points on the parabola above and below the focus are $(3, 6)$ and $(3, -6)$. The graph is sketched in **Figure 7.32**. ●

✓ **Check Point 1** Find the focus and directrix of the parabola given by $y^2 = 8x$. Then graph the parabola.

In general, the points on a parabola $y^2 = 4px$ that lie above and below the focus, $(p, 0)$, are each at a distance $|2p|$ from the focus. This is because if $x = p$, then $y^2 = 4px = 4p^2$, so $y = \pm 2p$. The line segment joining these two points is called the *latus rectum*; its length is $|4p|$.

The Latus Rectum and Graphing Parabolas

The **latus rectum** of a parabola is a line segment that passes through its focus, is parallel to its directrix, and has its endpoints on the parabola. **Figure 7.33** shows that the length of the latus rectum for the graphs of $y^2 = 4px$ and $x^2 = 4py$ is $|4p|$.

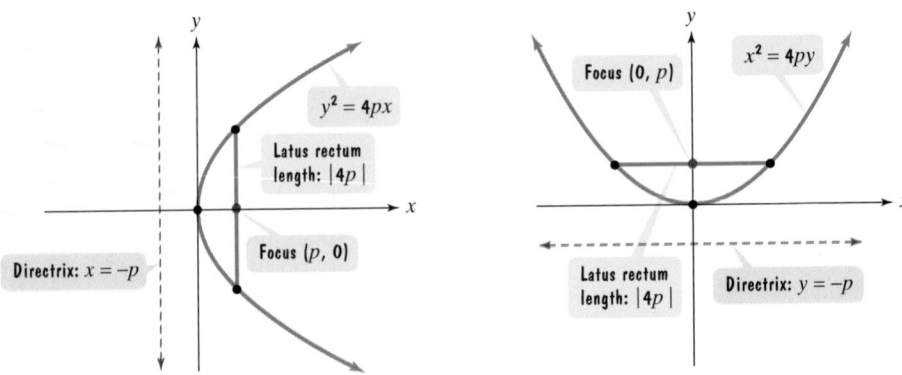

Figure 7.33 Endpoints of the latus rectum are helpful in determining a parabola's "width," or how it opens.

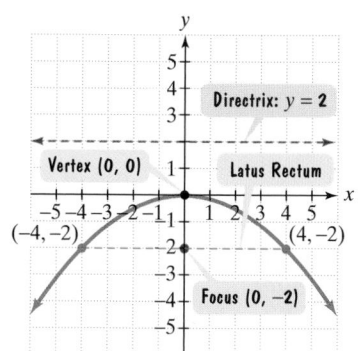

Figure 7.34 The graph of $x^2 = -8y$

Technology

Graph $x^2 = -8y$ by first solving for y: $y = -\dfrac{x^2}{8}$. The graph passes the vertical line test. Because $x^2 = -8y$ is a function, you were familiar with the parabola's alternate algebraic form, $y = -\dfrac{1}{8}x^2$, in Chapter 3. The form is $y = ax^2 + bx + c$, with $a = -\dfrac{1}{8}, b = 0$, and $c = 0$.

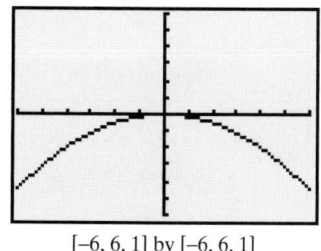

$[-6, 6, 1]$ by $[-6, 6, 1]$

② Write equations of parabolas in standard form.

EXAMPLE 2 Finding the Focus and Directrix of a Parabola

Find the focus and directrix of the parabola given by $x^2 = -8y$. Then graph the parabola.

Solution The given equation, $x^2 = -8y$, is in the standard form $x^2 = 4py$, so $4p = -8$.

> No change if x is replaced with $-x$. The parabola has y-axis symmetry.

$$x^2 = -8y$$

> This is 4p.

We can find both the focus and the directrix by finding p.

$$4p = -8$$
$$p = -2 \quad \text{Divide both sides by 4.}$$

Because p is negative, the parabola, with its y-axis symmetry, opens downward. The focus is 2 units below the vertex, $(0, 0)$.

Focus: $(0, p) = (0, -2)$

Directrix: $y = -p; y = 2$

The focus and directrix are shown in **Figure 7.34**.

To graph the parabola, we will use the vertex, $(0, 0)$, and the two endpoints of the latus rectum. The length of the latus rectum is

$$|4p| = |4(-2)| = |-8| = 8.$$

Because the graph has y-axis symmetry, the latus rectum extends 4 units to the left and 4 units to the right of the focus, $(0, -2)$. The endpoints of the latus rectum are $(-4, -2)$ and $(4, -2)$. Passing a smooth curve through the vertex and these two points, we sketch the parabola, shown in **Figure 7.34**. ●

⊘ Check Point **2** Find the focus and directrix of the parabola given by $x^2 = -12y$. Then graph the parabola.

In Examples 1 and 2, we used the equation of a parabola to find its focus and directrix. In the next example, we reverse this procedure.

EXAMPLE 3 Finding the Equation of a Parabola from Its Focus and Directrix

Find the standard form of the equation of a parabola with focus $(5, 0)$ and directrix $x = -5$, shown in **Figure 7.35**.

Solution The focus is $(5, 0)$. Thus, the focus is on the x-axis. We use the standard form of the equation in which there is x-axis symmetry, namely $y^2 = 4px$.

We need to determine the value of p. **Figure 7.35** shows that the focus is 5 units to the right of the vertex, $(0, 0)$. Thus, p is positive and $p = 5$. We substitute 5 for p in $y^2 = 4px$ to obtain the standard form of the equation of the parabola. The equation is

$$y^2 = 4 \cdot 5x \quad \text{or} \quad y^2 = 20x.$$

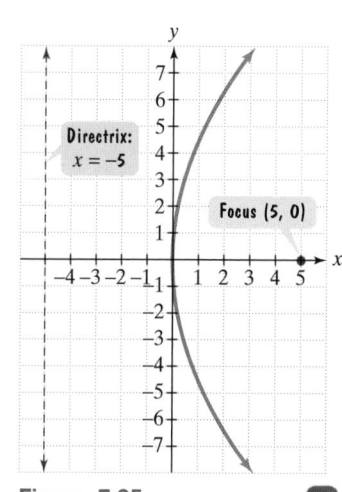

Figure 7.35

⊘ **Check Point 3** Find the standard form of the equation of a parabola with focus $(8, 0)$ and directrix $x = -8$.

③ Graph parabolas with vertices not at the origin.

Translations of Parabolas

The graph of a parabola can have its vertex at (h, k), rather than at the origin. Horizontal and vertical translations are accomplished by replacing x with $x - h$ and y with $y - k$ in the standard form of the parabola's equation.

Table 7.3 gives the standard forms of equations of parabolas with vertex at (h, k). **Figure 7.36** shows their graphs.

Table 7.3 Standard Forms of Equations of Parabolas with Vertex at (h, k)

Equation	Vertex	Axis of Symmetry	Focus	Directrix	Description
$(y - k)^2 = 4p(x - h)$	(h, k)	Horizontal	$(h + p, k)$	$x = h - p$	If $p > 0$, opens to the right. If $p < 0$, opens to the left.
$(x - h)^2 = 4p(y - k)$	(h, k)	Vertical	$(h, k + p)$	$y = k - p$	If $p > 0$, opens upward. If $p < 0$, opens downward.

Study Tip

If y is the squared term, there is horizontal symmetry and the parabola's equation is not a function. If x is the squared term, there is vertical symmetry and the parabola's equation is a function. Continue to think of p as the directed distance from the vertex, (h, k), to the focus.

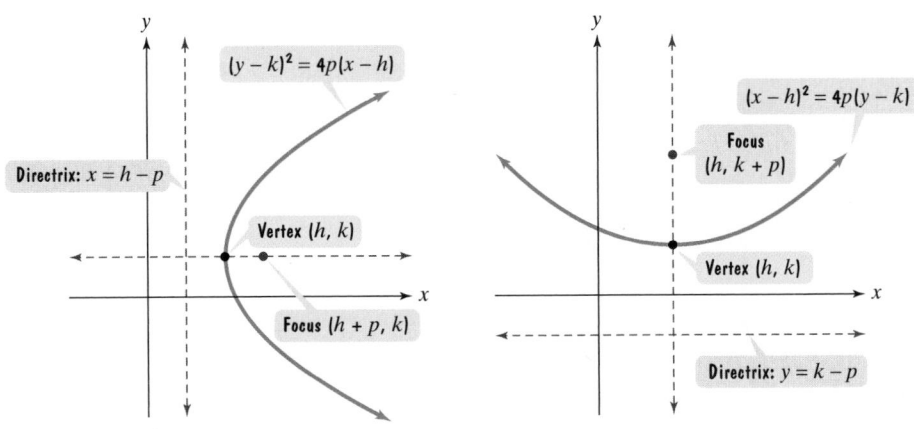

Figure 7.36 Graphs of parabolas with vertex at (h, k) and $p > 0$

The two parabolas shown in **Figure 7.36** illustrate standard forms of equations for $p > 0$. If $p < 0$, a parabola with a horizontal axis of symmetry will open to the left and the focus will lie to the left of the directrix. If $p < 0$, a parabola with a vertical axis of symmetry will open downward and the focus will lie below the directrix.

EXAMPLE 4 **Graphing a Parabola with Vertex at (h, k)**

Find the vertex, focus, and directrix of the parabola given by

$$(x - 3)^2 = 8(y + 1).$$

Then graph the parabola.

Solution In order to find the focus and directrix, we need to know the vertex. In the standard forms of equations with vertex at (h, k), h is the number subtracted from x and k is the number subtracted from y.

$$(x - 3)^2 = 8(y - (-1))$$

This is $(x - h)^2$, with $h = 3$. This is $y - k$, with $k = -1$.

We see that $h = 3$ and $k = -1$. Thus, the vertex of the parabola is $(h, k) = (3, -1)$.

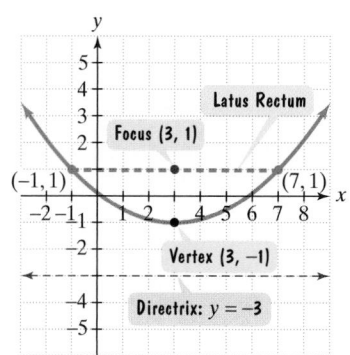

Figure 7.37 The graph of $(x - 3)^2 = 8(y + 1)$

Technology

Graph $(x - 3)^2 = 8(y + 1)$ by first solving for y:

$$\tfrac{1}{8}(x - 3)^2 = y + 1$$

$$y = \tfrac{1}{8}(x - 3)^2 - 1.$$

The graph passes the vertical line test. Because $(x - 3)^2 = 8(y + 1)$ is a function, you were familiar with the parabola's alternate algebraic form, $y = \tfrac{1}{8}(x - 3)^2 - 1$, in Chapter 3. The form is $y = a(x - h)^2 + k$ with $a = \tfrac{1}{8}, h = 3$, and $k = -1$.

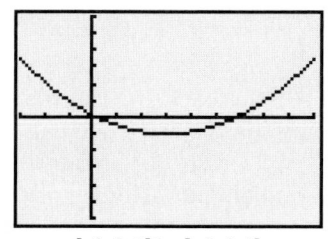

[-3, 9, 1] by [-6, 6, 1]

Now that we have the vertex, we can find both the focus and directrix by finding p.

$$(x - 3)^2 = 8(y + 1)$$

The equation is in the standard form $(x - h)^2 = 4p(y - k)$. Because x is the squared term, there is vertical symmetry and the parabola's equation is a function.

This is $4p$.

Because $4p = 8$, $p = 2$. Based on the standard form of the equation, the axis of symmetry is vertical. With a positive value for p and a vertical axis of symmetry, the parabola opens upward. Because $p = 2$, the focus is located 2 units above the vertex, $(3, -1)$. Likewise, the directrix is located 2 units below the vertex.

Focus: $\qquad (h, k + p) = (3, -1 + 2) = (3, 1)$

The vertex, (h, k), is $(3, -1)$.

The focus is 2 units above the vertex, $(3, -1)$.

Directrix: $\qquad y = k - p$
$\qquad\qquad\quad y = -1 - 2 = -3$

The directrix is 2 units below the vertex, $(3, -1)$.

Thus, the focus is $(3, 1)$ and the directrix is $y = -3$. They are shown in **Figure 7.37**. To graph the parabola, we will use the vertex, $(3, -1)$, and the two endpoints of the latus rectum. The length of the latus rectum is

$$|4p| = |4 \cdot 2| = |8| = 8.$$

Because the graph has vertical symmetry, the latus rectum extends 4 units to the left and 4 units to the right of the focus, $(3, 1)$. The endpoints of the latus rectum are $(3 - 4, 1)$, or $(-1, 1)$, and $(3 + 4, 1)$, or $(7, 1)$. Passing a smooth curve through the vertex and these two points, we sketch the parabola, shown in **Figure 7.37**. ●

⌀ Check Point **4** Find the vertex, focus, and directrix of the parabola given by $(x - 2)^2 = 4(y + 1)$. Then graph the parabola.

In some cases, we need to convert the equation of a parabola to standard form by completing the square on x or y, whichever variable is squared. Let's see how this is done.

(**EXAMPLE 5**) **Graphing a Parabola with Vertex at (h, k)**

Find the vertex, focus, and directrix of the parabola given by

$$y^2 + 2y + 12x - 23 = 0.$$

Then graph the parabola.

Solution We convert the given equation to standard form by completing the square on the variable y. We isolate the terms involving y on the left side.

$$y^2 + 2y + 12x - 23 = 0 \qquad \text{This is the given equation.}$$
$$y^2 + 2y = -12x + 23 \qquad \text{Isolate the terms involving } y.$$
$$y^2 + 2y + 1 = -12x + 23 + 1 \qquad \text{Complete the square by adding the square of half the coefficient of } y.$$
$$(y + 1)^2 = -12x + 24 \qquad \text{Factor.}$$

To express the equation $(y + 1)^2 = -12x + 24$ in the standard form $(y - k)^2 = 4p(x - h)$, we factor out -12 on the right. The standard form of the parabola's equation is

$$(y + 1)^2 = -12(x - 2).$$

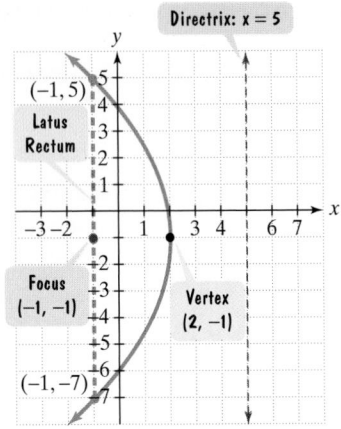

Figure 7.38 The graph of $y^2 + 2y + 12x - 23 = 0$, or $(y + 1)^2 = -12(x - 2)$

Technology

Graph $y^2 + 2y + 12x - 23 = 0$ by solving the equation for y.

$$y^2 + 2y + (12x - 23) = 0$$

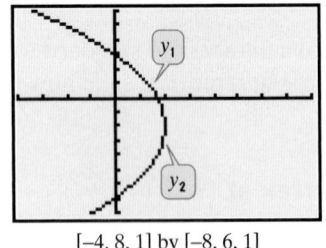

$a = 1 \quad b = 2 \quad c = 12x - 23$

Use the quadratic formula to solve for y and enter the resulting equations.

$$y_1 = \frac{-2 + \sqrt{4 - 4(12x - 23)}}{2}$$

$$y_2 = \frac{-2 - \sqrt{4 - 4(12x - 23)}}{2}$$

[−4, 8, 1] by [−8, 6, 1]

④ Solve applied problems involving parabolas.

We use $(y + 1)^2 = -12(x - 2)$ to identify the vertex, (h, k), and the value for p needed to locate the focus and the directrix.

$$[y - (-1)]^2 = -12(x - 2)$$

This is $(y - k)^2$, with $k = -1$. This is $4p$. This is $x - h$, with $h = 2$.

The equation is in the standard form $(y - k)^2 = 4p(x - h)$. Because y is the squared term, there is horizontal symmetry and the parabola's equation is not a function.

We see that $h = 2$ and $k = -1$. Thus, the vertex of the parabola is $(h, k) = (2, -1)$. Because $4p = -12$, $p = -3$. Based on the standard form of the equation, the axis of symmetry is horizontal. With a negative value for p and a horizontal axis of symmetry, the parabola opens to the left. Because $p = -3$, the focus is located 3 units to the left of the vertex, $(2, -1)$. Likewise, the directrix is located 3 units to the right of the vertex.

Focus: $(h + p, k) = (2 + (-3), -1) = (-1, -1)$

The vertex, (h, k), is $(2, -1)$. The focus is 3 units to the left of the vertex, $(2, -1)$.

Directrix: $x = h - p$
$x = 2 - (-3) = 5$

The directrix is 3 units to the right of the vertex, $(2, -1)$.

Thus, the focus is $(-1, -1)$ and the directrix is $x = 5$. They are shown in **Figure 7.38**.

To graph the parabola, we will use the vertex, $(2, -1)$, and the two endpoints of the latus rectum. The length of the latus rectum is

$$|4p| = |4(-3)| = |-12| = 12.$$

Because the graph has horizontal symmetry, the latus rectum extends 6 units above and 6 units below the focus, $(-1, -1)$. The endpoints of the latus rectum are $(-1, -1 + 6)$, or $(-1, 5)$, and $(-1, -1 - 6)$, or $(-1, -7)$. Passing a smooth curve through the vertex and these two points, we sketch the parabola shown in **Figure 7.38**. ●

✓ Check Point **5** Find the vertex, focus, and directrix of the parabola given by $y^2 + 2y + 4x - 7 = 0$. Then graph the parabola.

Applications

Parabolas have many applications. Cables hung between structures to form suspension bridges form parabolas. Arches constructed of steel and concrete, whose main purpose is strength, are usually parabolic in shape.

Suspension bridge

Arch bridge

We have seen that comets in our solar system travel in orbits that are ellipses and hyperbolas. Some comets follow parabolic paths. Only comets with elliptical orbits, such as Halley's Comet, return to our part of the galaxy.

If a parabola is rotated about its axis of symmetry, a parabolic surface is formed. **Figure 7.39(a)** shows how a parabolic surface can be used to reflect light. Light originates at the focus. Note how the light is reflected by the parabolic surface, so that the outgoing light is parallel to the axis of symmetry. The reflective properties of parabolic surfaces are used in the design of searchlights [see **Figure 7.39(b)**], automobile headlights, and parabolic microphones.

The Hubble Space Telescope

The Hubble Space Telescope

For decades, astronomers hoped to create an observatory above the atmosphere that would provide an unobscured view of the universe. This vision was realized with the 1990 launching of the Hubble Space Telescope. The telescope initially had blurred vision due to problems with its parabolic mirror. The mirror had been ground two millionths of a meter smaller than design specifications. In 1993, astronauts from the Space Shuttle *Endeavor* equipped the telescope with optics to correct the blurred vision. "A small change for a mirror, a giant leap for astronomy," Christopher J. Burrows of the Space Telescope Science Institute said when clear images from the ends of the universe were presented to the public after the repair mission.

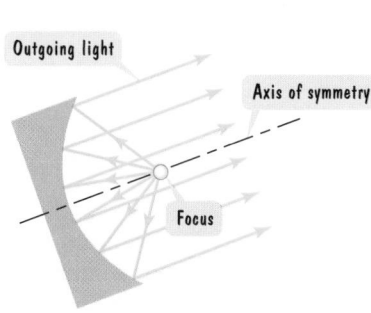

Figure 7.39(a) Parabolic surface reflecting light

Figure 7.39(b) Light from the focus is reflected parallel to the axis of symmetry.

Figure 7.40(a) shows how a parabolic surface can be used to reflect *incoming* light. Note that light rays strike the surface and are reflected *to the focus*. This principle is used in the design of reflecting telescopes, radar, and television satellite dishes. Reflecting telescopes magnify the light from distant stars by reflecting the light from these bodies to the focus of a parabolic mirror [see **Figure 7.40(b)**].

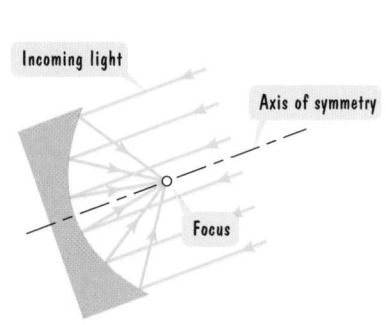

Figure 7.40(a) Parabolic surface reflecting incoming light

Figure 7.40(b) Incoming light rays are reflected to the focus.

EXAMPLE 6 Using the Reflection Property of Parabolas

An engineer is designing a flashlight using a parabolic reflecting mirror and a light source, shown in **Figure 7.41**. The casting has a diameter of 4 inches and a depth of 2 inches. What is the equation of the parabola used to shape the mirror? At what point should the light source be placed relative to the mirror's vertex?

Solution We position the parabola with its vertex at the origin and opening upward (**Figure 7.42**). Thus, the focus is on the y-axis, located at $(0, p)$. We use the

Figure 7.42

Figure 7.41 Designing a flashlight

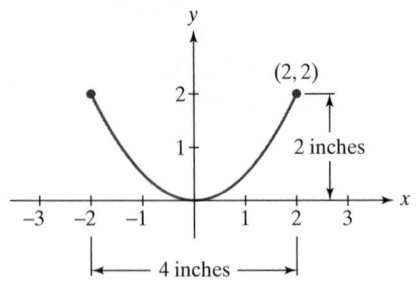

Figure 7.42 (repeated)

standard form of the equation in which there is y-axis symmetry, namely $x^2 = 4py$. We need to find p. Because $(2, 2)$ lies on the parabola, we let $x = 2$ and $y = 2$ in $x^2 = 4py$.

$$2^2 = 4p \cdot 2 \quad \text{Substitute 2 for x and 2 for y in } x^2 = 4py.$$

$$4 = 8p \quad \text{Simplify.}$$

$$p = \tfrac{1}{2} \quad \text{Divide both sides of the equation by 8 and reduce the resulting fraction.}$$

We substitute $\frac{1}{2}$ for p in $x^2 = 4py$ to obtain the standard form of the equation of the parabola. The equation of the parabola used to shape the mirror is

$$x^2 = 4 \cdot \tfrac{1}{2} y \quad \text{or} \quad x^2 = 2y.$$

The light source should be placed at the focus, $(0, p)$. Because $p = \frac{1}{2}$, the light should be placed at $\left(0, \frac{1}{2}\right)$, or $\frac{1}{2}$ inch above the vertex.

⬤

🗹 Check Point **6** In Example 6, suppose that the casting has a diameter of 6 inches and a depth of 4 inches. What is the equation of the parabola used to shape the mirror? At what point should the light source be placed relative to the mirror's vertex?

Degenerate Conic Sections

We opened the chapter by noting that conic sections are curves that result from the intersection of a cone and a plane. However, these intersections might not result in a conic section. Three degenerate cases occur when the cutting plane passes through the vertex. These **degenerate conic sections** are a point, a line, and a pair of intersecting lines, illustrated in **Figure 7.43**.

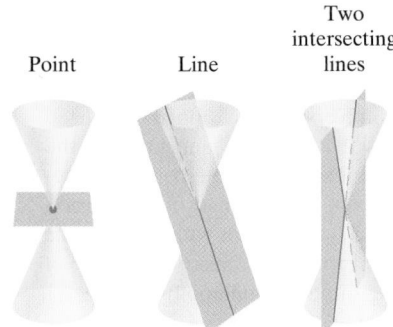

Figure 7.43 Degenerate conics

Exercise Set 7.3

Practice Exercises

In Exercises 1–4, find the focus and directrix of each parabola with the given equation. Then match each equation to one of the graphs that are shown and labeled (a)–(d).

1. $y^2 = 4x$

2. $x^2 = 4y$

3. $x^2 = -4y$

4. $y^2 = -4x$

a.

b.

c.

d.

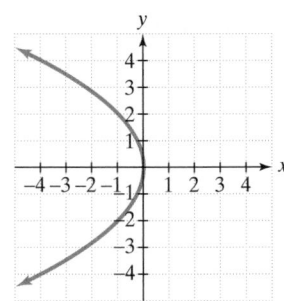

In Exercises 5–16, find the focus and directrix of the parabola with the given equation. Then graph the parabola.

5. $y^2 = 16x$

6. $y^2 = 4x$

7. $y^2 = -8x$

8. $y^2 = -12x$

9. $x^2 = 12y$

10. $x^2 = 8y$

11. $x^2 = -16y$

12. $x^2 = -20y$

13. $y^2 - 6x = 0$

14. $x^2 - 6y = 0$

15. $8x^2 + 4y = 0$

16. $8y^2 + 4x = 0$

In Exercises 17–30, find the standard form of the equation of each parabola satisfying the given conditions.

17. Focus: $(7, 0)$; Directrix: $x = -7$

18. Focus: $(9, 0)$; Directrix: $x = -9$

19. Focus: $(-5, 0)$; Directrix: $x = 5$

20. Focus: $(-10, 0)$; Directrix: $x = 10$

21. Focus: $(0, 15)$; Directrix: $y = -15$

22. Focus: $(0, 20)$; Directrix: $y = -20$

23. Focus: $(0, -25)$; Directrix: $y = 25$

24. Focus: $(0, -15)$; Directrix: $y = 15$

25. Vertex: $(2, -3)$; Focus: $(2, -5)$

26. Vertex: $(5, -2)$; Focus: $(7, -2)$

27. Focus: $(3, 2)$; Directrix: $x = -1$

28. Focus: $(2, 4)$; Directrix: $x = -4$

29. Focus: $(-3, 4)$; Directrix: $y = 2$

30. Focus: $(7, -1)$; Directrix: $y = -9$

In Exercises 31–34, find the vertex, focus, and directrix of each parabola with the given equation. Then match each equation to one of the graphs that are shown and labeled (a)–(d).

31. $(y - 1)^2 = 4(x - 1)$

32. $(x + 1)^2 = 4(y + 1)$

33. $(x + 1)^2 = -4(y + 1)$

34. $(y - 1)^2 = -4(x - 1)$

a.

b.

c.

d.

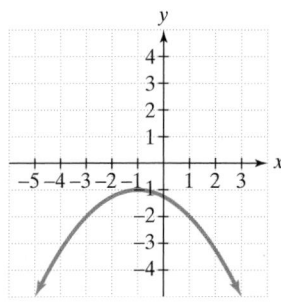

In Exercises 35–42, find the vertex, focus, and directrix of each parabola with the given equation. Then graph the parabola.

35. $(x - 2)^2 = 8(y - 1)$ **36.** $(x + 2)^2 = 4(y + 1)$

37. $(x + 1)^2 = -8(y + 1)$ **38.** $(x + 2)^2 = -8(y + 2)$

39. $(y + 3)^2 = 12(x + 1)$ **40.** $(y + 4)^2 = 12(x + 2)$

41. $(y + 1)^2 = -8x$ **42.** $(y - 1)^2 = -8x$

In Exercises 43–48, convert each equation to standard form by completing the square on x or y. Then find the vertex, focus, and directrix of the parabola. Finally, graph the parabola.

43. $x^2 - 2x - 4y + 9 = 0$ **44.** $x^2 + 6x + 8y + 1 = 0$

45. $y^2 - 2y + 12x - 35 = 0$ **46.** $y^2 - 2y - 8x + 1 = 0$

47. $x^2 + 6x - 4y + 1 = 0$ **48.** $x^2 + 8x - 4y + 8 = 0$

Practice Plus

In Exercises 49–54, use the vertex and the direction in which the parabola opens to determine the relation's domain and range. Is the relation a function?

49. $y^2 + 6y - x + 5 = 0$ **50.** $y^2 - 2y - x - 5 = 0$

51. $y = -x^2 + 4x - 3$ **52.** $y = -x^2 - 4x + 4$

53. $x = -4(y - 1)^2 + 3$ **54.** $x = -3(y - 1)^2 - 2$

In Exercises 55–60, find the solution set for each system by graphing both of the system's equations in the same rectangular coordinate system and finding points of intersection. Check all solutions in both equations.

55. $\begin{cases} (y - 2)^2 = x + 4 \\ \quad y = -\dfrac{1}{2}x \end{cases}$ **56.** $\begin{cases} (y - 3)^2 = x - 2 \\ \quad x + y = 5 \end{cases}$

57. $\begin{cases} x = y^2 - 3 \\ x = y^2 - 3y \end{cases}$ **58.** $\begin{cases} x = y^2 - 5 \\ x^2 + y^2 = 25 \end{cases}$

59. $\begin{cases} x = (y + 2)^2 - 1 \\ (x - 2)^2 + (y + 2)^2 = 1 \end{cases}$ **60.** $\begin{cases} x = 2y^2 + 4y + 5 \\ (x + 1)^2 + (y - 2)^2 = 1 \end{cases}$

Application Exercises

61. The reflector of a flashlight is in the shape of a parabolic surface. The casting has a diameter of 4 inches and a depth of 1 inch. How far from the vertex should the light bulb be placed?

62. The reflector of a flashlight is in the shape of a parabolic surface. The casting has a diameter of 8 inches and a depth of 1 inch. How far from the vertex should the light bulb be placed?

63. A satellite dish, like the one shown below, is in the shape of a parabolic surface. Signals coming from a satellite strike the surface of the dish and are reflected to the focus, where the receiver is located. The satellite dish shown has a diameter of 12 feet and a depth of 2 feet. How far from the base of the dish should the receiver be placed?

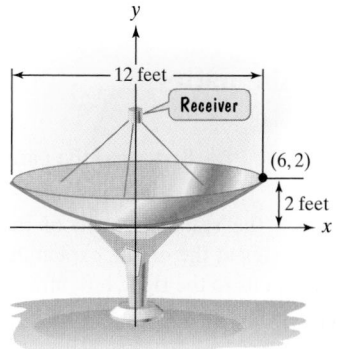

64. In Exercise 63, if the diameter of the dish is halved and the depth stays the same, how far from the base of the smaller dish should the receiver be placed?

65. The towers of the Golden Gate Bridge connecting San Francisco to Marin County are 1280 meters apart and rise 160 meters above the road. The cable between the towers has the shape of a parabola and the cable just touches the sides of the road midway between the towers. What is the height of the cable 200 meters from a tower? Round to the nearest meter.

66. The towers of a suspension bridge are 800 feet apart and rise 160 feet above the road. The cable between the towers has the shape of a parabola and the cable just touches the sides of the road midway between the towers. What is the height of the cable 100 feet from a tower?

67. The parabolic arch shown in the figure is 50 feet above the water at the center and 200 feet wide at the base. Will a boat that is 30 feet tall clear the arch 30 feet from the center?

68. A satellite dish in the shape of a parabolic surface has a diameter of 20 feet. If the receiver is to be placed 6 feet from the base, how deep should the dish be?

Writing in Mathematics

69. What is a parabola?

70. Explain how to use $y^2 = 8x$ to find the parabola's focus and directrix.

71. If you are given the standard form of the equation of a parabola with vertex at the origin, explain how to determine if the parabola opens to the right, left, upward, or downward.

72. Describe one similarity and one difference between the graphs of $y^2 = 4x$ and $(y - 1)^2 = 4(x - 1)$.

73. How can you distinguish parabolas from other conic sections by looking at their equations?

74. Look at the satellite dish shown in Exercise 63. Why must the receiver for a shallow dish be farther from the base of the dish than for a deeper dish of the same diameter?

Technology Exercises

75. Use a graphing utility to graph any five of the parabolas that you graphed by hand in Exercises 5–16.

76. Use a graphing utility to graph any three of the parabolas that you graphed by hand in Exercises 35–42. First solve the given equation for y, possibly using the square root property. Enter each of the two resulting equations to produce the complete graph.

Use a graphing utility to graph the parabolas in Exercises 77–78. Write the given equation as a quadratic equation in y and use the quadratic formula to solve for y. Enter each of the equations to produce the complete graph.

77. $y^2 + 2y - 6x + 13 = 0$

78. $y^2 + 10y - x + 25 = 0$

In Exercises 79–80, write each equation as a quadratic equation in y and then use the quadratic formula to express y in terms of x. Graph the resulting two equations using a graphing utility. What effect does the xy-term have on the graph of the resulting parabola?

79. $16x^2 - 24xy + 9y^2 - 60x - 80y + 100 = 0$

80. $x^2 + 2\sqrt{3}xy + 3y^2 + 8\sqrt{3}x - 8y + 32 = 0$

Critical Thinking Exercises

Make Sense? *In Exercises 81–84, determine whether each statement makes sense or does not make sense, and explain your reasoning.*

81. I graphed a parabola that opened to the right and contained a maximum point.

82. Knowing that a parabola opening to the right has a vertex at $(-1, 1)$ gives me enough information to determine its graph.

83. I noticed that depending on the values for A and B, assuming that they are both not zero, the graph of $Ax^2 + By^2 = C$ can represent any of the conic sections other than a parabola.

84. I'm using a telescope in which light from distant stars is reflected to the focus of a parabolic mirror.

In Exercises 85–88, determine whether each statement is true or false. If the statement is false, make the necessary change(s) to produce a true statement.

85. The parabola whose equation is $x = 2y - y^2 + 5$ opens to the right.

86. If the parabola whose equation is $x = ay^2 + by + c$ has its vertex at $(3, 2)$ and $a > 0$, then it has no y-intercepts.

87. Some parabolas that open to the right have equations that define y as a function of x.

88. The graph of $x = a(y - k) + h$ is a parabola with vertex at (h, k).

89. Find the focus and directrix of a parabola whose equation is of the form $Ax^2 + Ey = 0$, $A \neq 0$, $E \neq 0$.

90. Write the standard form of the equation of a parabola whose points are equidistant from $y = 4$ and $(-1, 0)$.

Group Exercise

91. Consult the research department of your library or the Internet to find an example of architecture that incorporates one or more conic sections in its design. Share this example with other group members. Explain precisely how conic sections are used. Do conic sections enhance the appeal of the architecture? In what ways?

Preview Exercises

Exercises 92–94 will help you prepare for the material covered in the first section of the next chapter.

92. Evaluate $\dfrac{(-1)^n}{3^n - 1}$ for $n = 1, 2, 3$, and 4.

93. Find the product of all positive integers from n down through 1 for $n = 5$.

94. Evaluate $i^2 + 1$ for all consecutive integers from 1 to 6, inclusive. Then find the sum of the six evaluations.

Chapter 7 Summary, Review, and Test

Summary

DEFINITIONS AND CONCEPTS	EXAMPLES

7.1 The Ellipse

a. An ellipse is the set of all points in a plane the sum of whose distances from two fixed points, the foci, is constant.

b. Standard forms of the equations of an ellipse with center at the origin are $\dfrac{x^2}{a^2} + \dfrac{y^2}{b^2} = 1$ [foci: $(-c, 0), (c, 0)$] and $\dfrac{x^2}{b^2} + \dfrac{y^2}{a^2} = 1$ [foci: $(0, -c), (0, c)$], where $c^2 = a^2 - b^2$ and $a^2 > b^2$. See the box on page 626 containing Figure 7.6.

Ex. 1, p. 626; Ex. 2, p. 627; Ex. 3, p. 628

c. Standard forms of the equations of an ellipse centered at (h, k) are $\dfrac{(x - h)^2}{a^2} + \dfrac{(y - k)^2}{b^2} = 1$ and $\dfrac{(x - h)^2}{b^2} + \dfrac{(y - k)^2}{a^2} = 1$, $a^2 > b^2$. See Table 7.1 on page 629.

Ex. 4, p. 630

7.2 The Hyperbola

a. A hyperbola is the set of all points in a plane the difference of whose distances from two fixed points, the foci, is constant.

b. Standard forms of the equations of a hyperbola with center at the origin are $\dfrac{x^2}{a^2} - \dfrac{y^2}{b^2} = 1$ [foci: $(-c, 0), (c, 0)$] and $\dfrac{y^2}{a^2} - \dfrac{x^2}{b^2} = 1$ [foci: $(0, c), (0, -c)$], where $c^2 = a^2 + b^2$. See the box on page 637 and Figure 7.16.

Ex. 1, p. 638; Ex. 2, p. 639

c. Asymptotes for $\dfrac{x^2}{a^2} - \dfrac{y^2}{b^2} = 1$ are $y = \pm \dfrac{b}{a}x$. Asymptotes for $\dfrac{y^2}{a^2} - \dfrac{x^2}{b^2} = 1$ are $y = \pm \dfrac{a}{b}x$.

d. A procedure for graphing hyperbolas is given in the box on page 640.

Ex. 3, p. 641; Ex. 4, p. 642

e. Standard forms of the equations of a hyperbola centered at (h, k) are $\dfrac{(x - h)^2}{a^2} - \dfrac{(y - k)^2}{b^2} = 1$ and $\dfrac{(y - k)^2}{a^2} - \dfrac{(x - h)^2}{b^2} = 1$. See Table 7.2 on page 643.

Ex. 5, p. 643; Ex. 6, p. 645

DEFINITIONS AND CONCEPTS	EXAMPLES		
7.3 The Parabola			
a. A parabola is the set of all points in a plane that are equidistant from a fixed line, the directrix, and a fixed point, the focus.			
b. Standard forms of the equations of parabolas with vertex at the origin are $y^2 = 4px$ [focus: $(p, 0)$] and $x^2 = 4py$ [focus: $(0, p)$]. See the box and Figure 7.31 on page 653.	Ex. 1, p. 653; Ex. 3, p. 655		
c. A parabola's latus rectum is a line segment that passes through its focus, is parallel to its directrix, and has its endpoints on the parabola. The length of the latus rectum for $y^2 = 4px$ and $x^2 = 4py$ is $	4p	$. A parabola can be graphed using the vertex and endpoints of the latus rectum.	Ex. 2, p. 655
d. Standard forms of the equations of a parabola with vertex at (h, k) are $(y - k)^2 = 4p(x - h)$ and $(x - h)^2 = 4p(y - k)$. See Table 7.3 on page 656 and Figure 7.36.	Ex. 4, p. 656; Ex. 5, p. 657		

Review Exercises

7.1

In Exercises 1–8, graph each ellipse and locate the foci.

1. $\dfrac{x^2}{36} + \dfrac{y^2}{25} = 1$ **2.** $\dfrac{y^2}{25} + \dfrac{x^2}{16} = 1$

3. $4x^2 + y^2 = 16$ **4.** $4x^2 + 9y^2 = 36$

5. $\dfrac{(x - 1)^2}{16} + \dfrac{(y + 2)^2}{9} = 1$ **6.** $\dfrac{(x + 1)^2}{9} + \dfrac{(y - 2)^2}{16} = 1$

7. $4x^2 + 9y^2 + 24x - 36y + 36 = 0$

8. $9x^2 + 4y^2 - 18x + 8y - 23 = 0$

In Exercises 9–11, find the standard form of the equation of each ellipse satisfying the given conditions.

9. Foci: $(-4, 0)$, $(4, 0)$; Vertices: $(-5, 0)$, $(5, 0)$

10. Foci: $(0, -3)$, $(0, 3)$; Vertices: $(0, -6)$, $(0, 6)$

11. Major axis horizontal with length 12; length of minor axis $= 4$; center: $(-3, 5)$

12. A semielliptical arch supports a bridge that spans a river 20 yards wide. The center of the arch is 6 yards above the river's center. Write an equation for the ellipse so that the x-axis coincides with the water level and the y-axis passes through the center of the arch.

13. A semielliptic archway has a height of 15 feet at the center and a width of 50 feet, as shown in the figure. The 50-foot width consists of a two-lane road. Can a truck that is 12 feet high and 14 feet wide drive under the archway without going into the other lane?

14. An elliptical pool table has a ball placed at each focus. If one ball is hit toward the edge of the table, explain what will occur.

7.2

In Exercises 15–22, graph each hyperbola. Locate the foci and find the equations of the asymptotes.

15. $\dfrac{x^2}{16} - y^2 = 1$ **16.** $\dfrac{y^2}{16} - x^2 = 1$

17. $9x^2 - 16y^2 = 144$ **18.** $4y^2 - x^2 = 16$

19. $\dfrac{(x - 2)^2}{25} - \dfrac{(y + 3)^2}{16} = 1$

20. $\dfrac{(y + 2)^2}{25} - \dfrac{(x - 3)^2}{16} = 1$

21. $y^2 - 4y - 4x^2 + 8x - 4 = 0$

22. $x^2 - y^2 - 2x - 2y - 1 = 0$

In Exercises 23–24, find the standard form of the equation of each hyperbola satisfying the given conditions.

23. Foci: $(0, -4)$, $(0, 4)$; Vertices: $(0, -2)$, $(0, 2)$

24. Foci: $(-8, 0)$, $(8, 0)$; Vertices: $(-3, 0)$, $(3, 0)$

25. Explain why it is not possible for a hyperbola to have foci at $(0, -2)$ and $(0, 2)$ and vertices at $(0, -3)$ and $(0, 3)$.

26. Radio tower M_2 is located 200 miles due west of radio tower M_1. The situation is illustrated in the figure shown, where a coordinate system has been superimposed. Simultaneous radio signals are sent from each tower to a ship, with the signal from M_2 received 500 microseconds before the signal from M_1. Assuming that radio signals travel at 0.186 mile per microsecond, determine the equation of the hyperbola on which the ship is located.

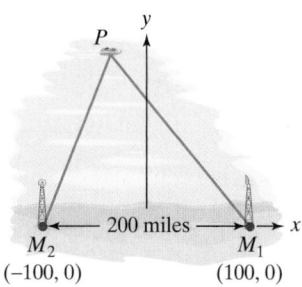

7.3

In Exercises 27–33, find the vertex, focus, and directrix of each parabola with the given equation. Then graph the parabola.

27. $y^2 = 8x$

28. $x^2 + 16y = 0$

29. $(y - 2)^2 = -16x$

30. $(x - 4)^2 = 4(y + 1)$

31. $x^2 + 4y = 4$

32. $y^2 - 4x - 10y + 21 = 0$

33. $x^2 - 4x - 2y = 0$

In Exercises 34–35, find the standard form of the equation of each parabola satisfying the given conditions.

34. Focus: $(12, 0)$; Directrix: $x = -12$

35. Focus: $(0, -11)$; Directrix: $y = 11$

36. An engineer is designing headlight units for automobiles. The unit has a parabolic surface with a diameter of 12 inches and a depth of 3 inches. The situation is illustrated in the figure, where a coordinate system has been superimposed. What is the equation of the parabola in this system? Where should the light source be placed? Describe this placement relative to the vertex.

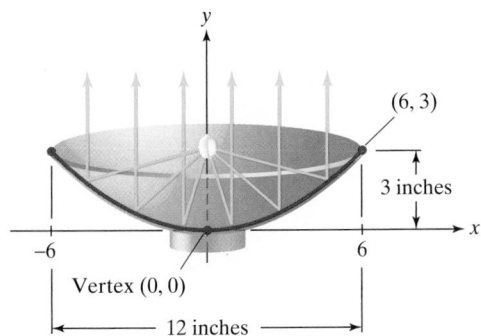

37. The George Washington Bridge spans the Hudson River from New York to New Jersey. Its two towers are 3500 feet apart and rise 316 feet above the road. As shown in the figure, the cable between the towers has the shape of a parabola and the cable just touches the sides of the road midway between the towers. What is the height of the cable 1000 feet from a tower?

38. The giant satellite dish in the figure shown is in the shape of a parabolic surface. Signals strike the surface and are reflected to the focus, where the receiver is located. The diameter of the dish is 300 feet and its depth is 44 feet. How far, to the nearest foot, from the base of the dish should the receiver be placed?

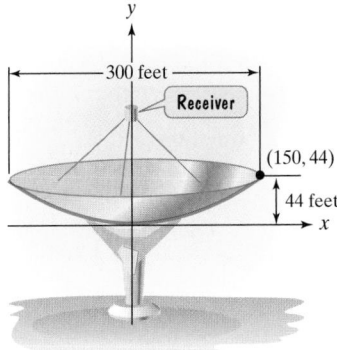

CHAPTER Test Prep VIDEOS Chapter 7 Test

In Exercises 1–5, graph the conic section with the given equation. For ellipses, find the foci. For hyperbolas, find the foci and give the equations of the asymptotes. For parabolas, find the vertex, focus, and directrix.

1. $9x^2 - 4y^2 = 36$

2. $x^2 = -8y$

3. $\dfrac{(x + 2)^2}{25} + \dfrac{(y - 5)^2}{9} = 1$

4. $4x^2 - y^2 + 8x + 2y + 7 = 0$

5. $(x + 5)^2 = 8(y - 1)$

In Exercises 6–8, find the standard form of the equation of the conic section satisfying the given conditions.

6. Ellipse; Foci: $(-7, 0), (7, 0)$; Vertices: $(-10, 0), (10, 0)$

7. Hyperbola; Foci: $(0, -10), (0, 10)$; Vertices: $(0, -7), (0, 7)$

8. Parabola; Focus: $(50, 0)$; Directrix: $x = -50$

9. A sound whispered at one focus of a whispering gallery can be heard at the other focus. The figure shows a whispering gallery whose cross section is a semielliptical arch with a height of 24 feet and a width of 80 feet. How far from the room's center should two people stand so that they can whisper back and forth and be heard?

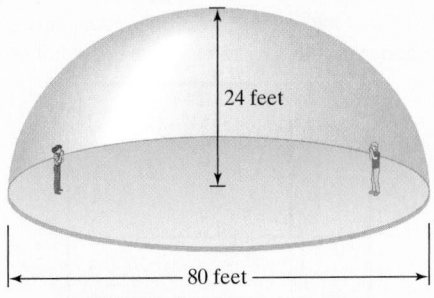

10. An engineer is designing headlight units for cars. The unit shown in the figure has a parabolic surface with a diameter of 6 inches and a depth of 3 inches.

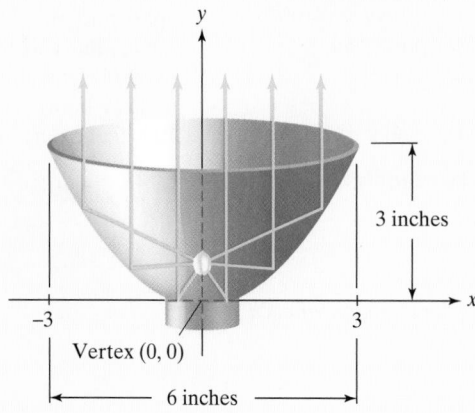

3 inches

–3 3 x

Vertex $(0, 0)$

6 inches

 a. Using the coordinate system that has been positioned on the unit, find the parabola's equation.

 b. If the light source is located at the focus, describe its placement relative to the vertex.

Cumulative Review Exercises (Chapters 1–7)

Solve each equation or inequality in Exercises 1–7.

1. $2(x - 3) + 5x = 8(x - 1)$

2. $-3(2x - 4) > 2(6x - 12)$

3. $x - 5 = \sqrt{x + 7}$ **4.** $(x - 2)^2 = 20$

5. $|2x - 1| \geq 7$ **6.** $3x^3 + 4x^2 - 7x + 2 = 0$

7. $\log_2(x + 1) + \log_2(x - 1) = 3$

Solve each system in Exercises 8–10.

8. $\begin{cases} 3x + 4y = 2 \\ 2x + 5y = -1 \end{cases}$ **9.** $\begin{cases} 2x^2 - y^2 = -8 \\ x - y = 6 \end{cases}$

10. (Use matrices.)

$$\begin{cases} x - y + z = 17 \\ -4x + y + 5z = -2 \\ 2x + 3y + z = 8 \end{cases}$$

In Exercises 11–13, graph each equation, function, or system in a rectangular coordinate system.

11. $f(x) = (x - 1)^2 - 4$ **12.** $\dfrac{x^2}{9} + \dfrac{y^2}{4} = 1$

13. $\begin{cases} 5x + y \leq 10 \\ y \geq \dfrac{1}{4}x + 2 \end{cases}$

14. a. List all possible rational roots of

$$32x^3 - 52x^2 + 17x + 3 = 0.$$

 b. The graph of $f(x) = 32x^3 - 52x^2 + 17x + 3$ is shown in a $[-1, 3, 1]$ by $[-2, 6, 1]$ viewing rectangle. Use the graph of f and synthetic division to solve the equation in part (a).

15. The figure shows the graph of $y = f(x)$ and its two vertical asymptotes.

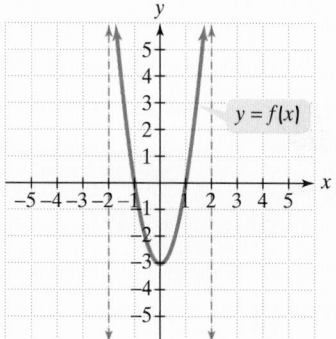

$y = f(x)$

 a. Find the domain and the range of f.

 b. What is the relative minimum and where does it occur?

 c. Find the interval on which f is increasing.

 d. Find $f(-1) - f(0)$.

 e. Find $(f \circ f)(1)$.

 f. Use arrow notation to complete this statement:
$$f(x) \to \infty \text{ as } \underline{\quad} \text{ or as } \underline{\quad}.$$

 g. Graph $g(x) = f(x - 2) + 1$.

 h. Graph $h(x) = -f(2x)$.

16. If $f(x) = x^2 - 4$ and $g(x) = x + 2$, find $(g \circ f)(x)$.

17. Expand using logarithmic properties. Where possible, evaluate logarithmic expressions.

$$\log_5\left(\frac{x^3\sqrt{y}}{125}\right)$$

18. Write the slope-intercept form of the equation of the line passing through $(1, -4)$ and $(-5, 8)$.

19. Rent-a-Truck charges a daily rental rate for a truck of $39 plus $0.16 a mile. A competing agency, Ace Truck Rentals, charges $25 a day plus $0.24 a mile for the same truck. How many miles must be driven in a day to make the daily cost of both agencies the same? What will be the cost?

20. The local cable television company offers two deals. Basic cable service with one movie channel costs $35 per month. Basic service with two movie channels cost $45 per month. Find the charge for the basic cable service and the charge for each movie channel.

Sequences, Induction, and Probability

Something incredible has happened. Your college roommate, a gifted athlete, has been given a six-year contract with a professional baseball team. He will be playing against the likes of Alex Rodriguez and Manny Ramirez. Management offers him three options. One is a beginning salary of $1,700,000 with annual increases of $70,000 per year starting in the second year. A second option is $1,700,000 the first year with an annual increase of 2% per year beginning in the second year. The third option involves less money the first year—$1,500,000—but there is an annual increase of 9% yearly after that. Which option offers the most money over the six-year contract?

A similar problem appears as Exercise 67 in Exercise Set 8.3, and this problem appears as the Group Exercise on page 702.

Section 8.1 Sequences and Summation Notation

Sequences

Many creations in nature involve intricate mathematical designs, including a variety of spirals. For example, the arrangement of the individual florets in the head of a sunflower forms spirals. In some species, there are 21 spirals in the clockwise direction and 34 in the counterclockwise direction. The precise numbers depend on the species of sunflower: 21 and 34, or 34 and 55, or 55 and 89, or even 89 and 144.

This observation becomes even more interesting when we consider a sequence of numbers investigated by Leonardo of Pisa, also known as Fibonacci, an Italian mathematician of the thirteenth century. The **Fibonacci sequence** of numbers is an infinite sequence that begins as follows:

$$1, 1, 2, 3, 5, 8, 13, 21, 34, 55, 89, 144, 233, \ldots .$$

The first two terms are 1. Every term thereafter is the sum of the two preceding terms. For example, the third term, 2, is the sum of the first and second terms: $1 + 1 = 2$. The fourth term, 3, is the sum of the second and third terms: $1 + 2 = 3$, and so on. Did you know that the number of spirals in a daisy or a sunflower, 21 and 34, are two Fibonacci numbers? The number of spirals in a pine cone, 8 and 13, and a pineapple, 8 and 13, are also Fibonacci numbers.

We can think of the Fibonacci sequence as a function. The terms of the sequence

$$1, 1, 2, 3, 5, 8, 13, 21, 34, 55, 89, 144, 233, \ldots$$

are the range values for a function f whose domain is the set of positive integers.

Domain:	1,	2,	3,	4,	5,	6,	7,	...
	↓	↓	↓	↓	↓	↓	↓	
Range:	1,	1,	2,	3,	5,	8,	13,	...

Thus, $f(1) = 1, f(2) = 1, f(3) = 2, f(4) = 3, f(5) = 5, f(6) = 8, f(7) = 13$, and so on.

The letter a with a subscript is used to represent function values of a sequence, rather than the usual function notation. The subscripts make up the domain of the sequence and they identify the location of a term. Thus, a_1 represents the first term of the sequence, a_2 represents the second term, a_3 the third term, and so on. This notation is shown for the first six terms of the Fibonacci sequence:

$$1, \quad 1, \quad 2, \quad 3, \quad 5, \quad 8.$$

$a_1 = 1 \quad a_2 = 1 \quad a_3 = 2 \quad a_4 = 3 \quad a_5 = 5 \quad a_6 = 8$

The notation a_n represents the nth term, or **general term**, of a sequence. The entire sequence is represented by $\{a_n\}$.

Fibonacci Numbers on the Piano Keyboard

One Octave

Numbers in the Fibonacci sequence can be found in an octave on the piano keyboard. The octave contains 2 black keys in one cluster and 3 black keys in another cluster, for a total of 5 black keys. It also has 8 white keys, for a total of 13 keys. The numbers 2, 3, 5, 8, and 13 are the third through seventh terms of the Fibonacci sequence.

Definition of a Sequence

An **infinite sequence** $\{a_n\}$ is a function whose domain is the set of positive integers. The function values, or **terms**, of the sequence are represented by

$$a_1, a_2, a_3, a_4, \ldots, a_n, \ldots .$$

Sequences whose domains consist only of the first n positive integers are called **finite sequences**.

① Find particular terms of a sequence from the general term.

EXAMPLE 1 **Writing Terms of a Sequence from the General Term**

Write the first four terms of the sequence whose nth term, or general term, is given:

a. $a_n = 3n + 4$ **b.** $a_n = \dfrac{(-1)^n}{3^n - 1}$.

Solution

a. We need to find the first four terms of the sequence whose general term is $a_n = 3n + 4$. To do so, we replace n in the formula with $1, 2, 3,$ and 4.

a_1, 1st term $3 \cdot 1 + 4 = 3 + 4 = 7$ a_2, 2nd term $3 \cdot 2 + 4 = 6 + 4 = 10$

a_3, 3rd term $3 \cdot 3 + 4 = 9 + 4 = 13$ a_4, 4th term $3 \cdot 4 + 4 = 12 + 4 = 16$

The first four terms are $7, 10, 13,$ and 16. The sequence defined by $a_n = 3n + 4$ can be written as

$$7, 10, 13, 16, \ldots, 3n + 4, \ldots.$$

Study Tip

The factor $(-1)^n$ in the general term of a sequence causes the signs of the terms to alternate between positive and negative, depending on whether n is even or odd.

b. We need to find the first four terms of the sequence whose general term is $a_n = \dfrac{(-1)^n}{3^n - 1}$. To do so, we replace each occurrence of n in the formula with $1, 2, 3,$ and 4.

a_1, 1st term $\dfrac{(-1)^1}{3^1 - 1} = \dfrac{-1}{3 - 1} = -\dfrac{1}{2}$ a_2, 2nd term $\dfrac{(-1)^2}{3^2 - 1} = \dfrac{1}{9 - 1} = \dfrac{1}{8}$

a_3, 3rd term $\dfrac{(-1)^3}{3^3 - 1} = \dfrac{-1}{27 - 1} = -\dfrac{1}{26}$ a_4, 4th term $\dfrac{(-1)^4}{3^4 - 1} = \dfrac{1}{81 - 1} = \dfrac{1}{80}$

The first four terms are $-\dfrac{1}{2}, \dfrac{1}{8}, -\dfrac{1}{26},$ and $\dfrac{1}{80}$. The sequence defined by $\dfrac{(-1)^n}{3^n - 1}$ can be written as

$$-\frac{1}{2}, \frac{1}{8}, -\frac{1}{26}, \frac{1}{80}, \ldots, \frac{(-1)^n}{3^n - 1}, \ldots.$$

⬤ **Check Point 1** Write the first four terms of the sequence whose nth term, or general term, is given:

a. $a_n = 2n + 5$ **b.** $a_n = \dfrac{(-1)^n}{2^n + 1}$.

Although sequences are usually named with the letter a, any lowercase letter can be used. For example, the first four terms of the sequence $\{b_n\} = \left\{\left(\frac{1}{2}\right)^n\right\}$ are $b_1 = \frac{1}{2}, b_2 = \frac{1}{4}, b_3 = \frac{1}{8},$ and $b_4 = \frac{1}{16}$.

Because a sequence is a function whose domain is the set of positive integers, the **graph of a sequence** is a set of discrete points. For example, consider the sequence whose general term is $a_n = \frac{1}{n}$. How does the graph of this sequence differ

Technology

Graphing utilities can write the terms of a sequence and graph them. For example, to find the first six terms of $\{a_n\} = \left\{\frac{1}{n}\right\}$, enter

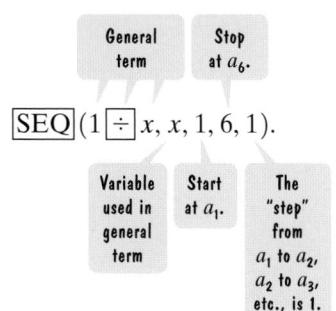

The first few terms of the sequence are shown in the viewing rectangle. By pressing the right arrow key to scroll right, you can see the remaining terms.

from the graph of the function $f(x) = \frac{1}{x}$? The graph of $f(x) = \frac{1}{x}$ is shown in **Figure 8.1(a)** for positive values of x. To obtain the graph of the sequence $\{a_n\} = \left\{\frac{1}{n}\right\}$, remove all the points from the graph of f except those whose x-coordinates are positive integers. Thus, we remove all points except $(1, 1)$, $\left(2, \frac{1}{2}\right)$, $\left(3, \frac{1}{3}\right)$, $\left(4, \frac{1}{4}\right)$, and so on. The remaining points are the graph of the sequence $\{a_n\} = \left\{\frac{1}{n}\right\}$, shown in **Figure 8.1(b)**. Notice that the horizontal axis is labeled n and the vertical axis is labeled a_n.

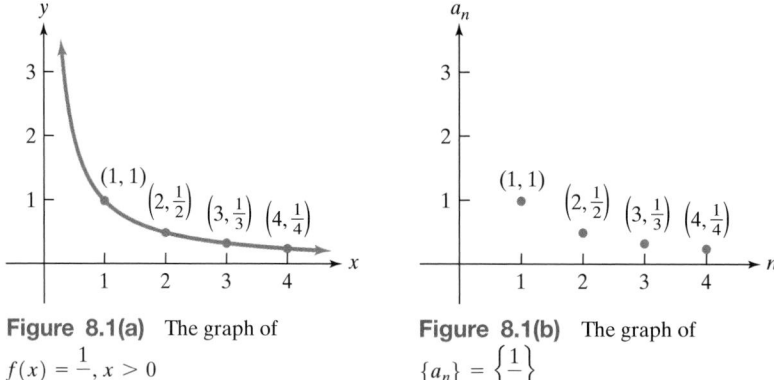

Figure 8.1(a) The graph of
$$f(x) = \frac{1}{x}, x > 0$$

Figure 8.1(b) The graph of
$$\{a_n\} = \left\{\frac{1}{n}\right\}$$

Comparing a continuous graph to the graph of a sequence

Recursion Formulas

In Example 1, the formulas used for the nth term of a sequence expressed the term as a function of n, the number of the term. Sequences can also be defined using **recursion formulas**. A recursion formula defines the nth term of a sequence as a function of the previous term. Our next example illustrates that if the first term of a sequence is known, then the recursion formula can be used to determine the remaining terms.

② Use recursion formulas.

EXAMPLE 2 **Using a Recursion Formula**

Find the first four terms of the sequence in which $a_1 = 5$ and $a_n = 3a_{n-1} + 2$ for $n \geq 2$.

Solution Let's be sure we understand what is given.

$$a_1 = 5 \quad \text{and} \quad a_n = 3a_{n-1} + 2$$

| The first term is 5. | Each term after the first | is | 3 times the previous term | plus 2. |

Now let's write the first four terms of this sequence.

$a_1 = 5$ — This is the given first term.

$a_2 = 3a_1 + 2$ — Use $a_n = 3a_{n-1} + 2$, with $n = 2$. Thus, $a_2 = 3a_{2-1} + 2 = 3a_1 + 2$.

$\quad = 3(5) + 2 = 17$ — Substitute 5 for a_1.

$a_3 = 3a_2 + 2$ — Again use $a_n = 3a_{n-1} + 2$, with $n = 3$.

$\quad = 3(17) + 2 = 53$ — Substitute 17 for a_2.

$a_4 = 3a_3 + 2$ — Notice that a_4 is defined in terms of a_3. We used $a_n = 3a_{n-1} + 2$, with $n = 4$.

$\quad = 3(53) + 2 = 161$ — Use the value of a_3, the third term, obtained above.

The first four terms are $5, 17, 53$, and 161.

⊘ Check Point **2** Find the first four terms of the sequence in which $a_1 = 3$ and $a_n = 2a_{n-1} + 5$ for $n \geq 2$.

③ Use factorial notation.

Factorial Notation

Products of consecutive positive integers occur quite often in sequences. These products can be expressed in a special notation, called **factorial notation**.

Factorials from 0 through 20

0!	1
1!	1
2!	2
3!	6
4!	24
5!	120
6!	720
7!	5040
8!	40,320
9!	362,880
10!	3,628,800
11!	39,916,800
12!	479,001,600
13!	6,227,020,800
14!	87,178,291,200
15!	1,307,674,368,000
16!	20,922,789,888,000
17!	355,687,428,096,000
18!	6,402,373,705,728,000
19!	121,645,100,408,832,000
20!	2,432,902,008,176,640,000

As n increases, $n!$ grows very rapidly. Factorial growth is more explosive than exponential growth discussed in Chapter 4.

Factorial Notation

If n is a positive integer, the notation $n!$ (read "n factorial") is the product of all positive integers from n down through 1.

$$n! = n(n-1)(n-2) \cdots (3)(2)(1)$$

$0!$ (zero factorial), by definition, is 1.

$$0! = 1$$

The values of $n!$ for the first six positive integers are

$$1! = 1$$
$$2! = 2 \cdot 1 = 2$$
$$3! = 3 \cdot 2 \cdot 1 = 6$$
$$4! = 4 \cdot 3 \cdot 2 \cdot 1 = 24$$
$$5! = 5 \cdot 4 \cdot 3 \cdot 2 \cdot 1 = 120$$
$$6! = 6 \cdot 5 \cdot 4 \cdot 3 \cdot 2 \cdot 1 = 720.$$

Factorials affect only the number or variable that they follow unless grouping symbols appear. For example,

$$2 \cdot 3! = 2(3 \cdot 2 \cdot 1) = 2 \cdot 6 = 12$$

whereas

$$(2 \cdot 3)! = 6! = 6 \cdot 5 \cdot 4 \cdot 3 \cdot 2 \cdot 1 = 720.$$

In this sense, factorials are similar to exponents.

EXAMPLE 3 **Finding Terms of a Sequence Involving Factorials**

Write the first four terms of the sequence whose nth term is

$$a_n = \frac{2^n}{(n-1)!}.$$

Solution We need to find the first four terms of the sequence. To do so, we replace each n in $\frac{2^n}{(n-1)!}$ with $1, 2, 3$, and 4.

a_1, 1st term $\quad \dfrac{2^1}{(1-1)!} = \dfrac{2}{0!} = \dfrac{2}{1} = 2$

a_2, 2nd term $\quad \dfrac{2^2}{(2-1)!} = \dfrac{4}{1!} = \dfrac{4}{1} = 4$

a_3, 3rd term $\quad \dfrac{2^3}{(3-1)!} = \dfrac{8}{2!} = \dfrac{8}{2 \cdot 1} = 4$

a_4, 4th term $\quad \dfrac{2^4}{(4-1)!} = \dfrac{16}{3!} = \dfrac{16}{3 \cdot 2 \cdot 1} = \dfrac{16}{6} = \dfrac{8}{3}$

The first four terms are $2, 4, 4$, and $\frac{8}{3}$. ●

Technology

Most calculators have factorial keys. To find 5!, most calculators use one of the following:

Many Scientific Calculators

$$5 \boxed{x!}$$

Many Graphing Calculators

$$5 \boxed{!} \ \boxed{\text{ENTER}}.$$

Because $n!$ becomes quite large as n increases, your calculator will display these larger values in scientific notation.

⊘ Check Point **3** Write the first four terms of the sequence whose *n*th term is

$$a_n = \frac{20}{(n + 1)!}.$$

When evaluating fractions with factorials in the numerator and the denominator, try to reduce the fraction before performing the multiplications. For example, consider $\frac{26!}{21!}$. Rather than write out 26! as the product of all integers from 26 down to 1, we can express 26! as

$$26! = 26 \cdot 25 \cdot 24 \cdot 23 \cdot 22 \cdot 21!.$$

In this way, we can divide both the numerator and the denominator by the common factor, 21!.

$$\frac{26!}{21!} = \frac{26 \cdot 25 \cdot 24 \cdot 23 \cdot 22 \cdot \cancel{21!}}{\cancel{21!}} = 26 \cdot 25 \cdot 24 \cdot 23 \cdot 22 = 7{,}893{,}600$$

EXAMPLE 4 **Evaluating Fractions with Factorials**

Evaluate each factorial expression:

a. $\dfrac{10!}{2!8!}$ **b.** $\dfrac{(n + 1)!}{n!}$.

Solution

a. $\dfrac{10!}{2!8!} = \dfrac{10 \cdot 9 \cdot \cancel{8!}}{2 \cdot 1 \cdot \cancel{8!}} = \dfrac{90}{2} = 45$

b. $\dfrac{(n + 1)!}{n!} = \dfrac{(n + 1) \cdot \cancel{n!}}{\cancel{n!}} = n + 1$

⊘ Check Point **4** Evaluate each factorial expression:

a. $\dfrac{14!}{2!12!}$ **b.** $\dfrac{n!}{(n - 1)!}$.

④ Use summation notation.

Summation Notation

It is sometimes useful to find the sum of the first *n* terms of a sequence. For example, consider the cost of raising a child born in the United States in 2006 to a middle-income ($43,200–$72,600 per year) family, shown in **Table 8.1**.

Table 8.1 The Cost of Raising a Child Born in the U.S. in 2006 to a Middle-Income Family

Year	2006	2007	2008	2009	2010	2011	2012	2013	2014
Average Cost	$10,600	$10,930	$11,270	$11,960	$12,330	$12,710	$12,950	$13,350	$13,760
	Child is under 1.	Child is 1.	Child is 2.	Child is 3.	Child is 4.	Child is 5.	Child is 6.	Child is 7.	Child is 8.

Year	2015	2016	2017	2018	2019	2020	2021	2022	2023
Average Cost	$13,970	$14,400	$14,840	$16,360	$16,860	$17,390	$18,430	$19,000	$19,590
	Child is 9.	Child is 10.	Child is 11.	Child is 12.	Child is 13.	Child is 14.	Child is 15.	Child is 16.	Child is 17.

Source: U.S. Department of Agriculture

We can let a_n represent the cost of raising a child in year n, where $n = 1$ corresponds to 2006, $n = 2$ to 2007, $n = 3$ to 2008, and so on. The terms of the finite sequence in **Table 8.1** are given as follows:

10,600, 10,930, 11,270, 11,960, 12,330, 12,710, 12,950, 13,350, 13,760,

a_1 a_2 a_3 a_4 a_5 a_6 a_7 a_8 a_9

13,970, 14,400, 14,840, 16,360, 16,860, 17,390, 18,430, 19,000, 19,590.

a_{10} a_{11} a_{12} a_{13} a_{14} a_{15} a_{16} a_{17} a_{18}

Why might we want to add the terms of this sequence? We do this to find the total cost of raising a child born in 2006 from birth through age 17. Thus,

$$a_1 + a_2 + a_3 + a_4 + a_5 + a_6 + a_7 + a_8 + a_9 + a_{10} + a_{11} + a_{12} + a_{13} + a_{14} + a_{15} + a_{16} + a_{17} + a_{18}$$
$$= 10{,}600 + 10{,}930 + 11{,}270 + 11{,}960 + 12{,}330 + 12{,}710 + 12{,}950 + 13{,}350 + 13{,}760$$
$$+ 13{,}970 + 14{,}400 + 14{,}840 + 16{,}360 + 16{,}860 + 17{,}390 + 18{,}430 + 19{,}000 + 19{,}590$$
$$= 260{,}700.$$

We see that the total cost of raising a child born in 2006 from birth through age 17 is $260,700.

There is a compact notation for expressing the sum of the first n terms of a sequence. For example, rather than write

$$a_1 + a_2 + a_3 + a_4 + a_5 + a_6 + a_7 + a_8 + a_9 + a_{10} + a_{11} + a_{12} + a_{13} + a_{14} + a_{15} + a_{16} + a_{17} + a_{18},$$

we can use *summation notation* to express the sum as

$$\sum_{i=1}^{18} a_i.$$

We read this expression as "the sum as i goes from 1 to 18 of a_i." The letter i is called the *index of summation* and is not related to the use of i to represent $\sqrt{-1}$.

You can think of the symbol Σ (the uppercase Greek letter sigma) as an instruction to add up the terms of a sequence.

Summation Notation

The sum of the first n terms of a sequence is represented by the **summation notation**

$$\sum_{i=1}^{n} a_i = a_1 + a_2 + a_3 + a_4 + \cdots + a_n,$$

where i is the **index of summation**, n is the **upper limit of summation**, and 1 is the **lower limit of summation**.

Any letter can be used for the index of summation. The letters i, j, and k are used commonly. Furthermore, the lower limit of summation can be an integer other than 1.

When we write out a sum that is given in summation notation, we are **expanding the summation notation**. Example 5 shows how to do this.

(**EXAMPLE 5**) **Using Summation Notation**

Expand and evaluate the sum:

a. $\displaystyle\sum_{i=1}^{6} (i^2 + 1)$ **b.** $\displaystyle\sum_{k=4}^{7} [(-2)^k - 5]$ **c.** $\displaystyle\sum_{i=1}^{5} 3.$

Technology

Graphing utilities can calculate the sum of a sequence. For example, to find the sum of the sequence in Example 5(a), enter

SUM SEQ $(x^2 + 1, x, 1, 6, 1)$.

Then press ENTER ; 97 should be displayed. Use this capability to verify Example 5(b).

```
sum(seq(X²+1,X,1
,6,1)
                97
```

Solution

a. To find $\sum\limits_{i=1}^{6}(i^2 + 1)$, we must replace i in the expression $i^2 + 1$ with all consecutive integers from 1 to 6, inclusive. Then we add.

$$\sum_{i=1}^{6}(i^2 + 1) = (1^2 + 1) + (2^2 + 1) + (3^2 + 1) + (4^2 + 1)$$
$$+ (5^2 + 1) + (6^2 + 1)$$
$$= 2 + 5 + 10 + 17 + 26 + 37$$
$$= 97$$

b. The index of summation in $\sum\limits_{k=4}^{7}[(-2)^k - 5]$ is k. First we evaluate $(-2)^k - 5$ for all consecutive integers from 4 through 7, inclusive. Then we add.

$$\sum_{k=4}^{7}[(-2)^k - 5] = [(-2)^4 - 5] + [(-2)^5 - 5]$$
$$+ [(-2)^6 - 5] + [(-2)^7 - 5]$$
$$= (16 - 5) + (-32 - 5) + (64 - 5) + (-128 - 5)$$
$$= 11 + (-37) + 59 + (-133)$$
$$= -100$$

c. To find $\sum\limits_{i=1}^{5} 3$, we observe that every term of the sum is 3. The notation $i = 1$ through 5 indicates that we must add the first five terms of a sequence in which every term is 3.

$$\sum_{i=1}^{5} 3 = 3 + 3 + 3 + 3 + 3 = 15$$

⬤

✓ Check Point **5** Expand and evaluate the sum:

a. $\sum\limits_{i=1}^{6} 2i^2$ **b.** $\sum\limits_{k=3}^{5} (2^k - 3)$ **c.** $\sum\limits_{i=1}^{5} 4.$

Although the domain of a sequence is the set of positive integers, any integers can be used for the limits of summation. For a given sum, we can vary the upper and lower limits of summation, as well as the letter used for the index of summation. By doing so, we can produce different-looking summation notations for the same sum. For example, the sum of the squares of the first four positive integers, $1^2 + 2^2 + 3^2 + 4^2$, can be expressed in a number of equivalent ways:

$$\sum_{i=1}^{4} i^2 = 1^2 + 2^2 + 3^2 + 4^2 = 30$$

$$\sum_{i=0}^{3} (i + 1)^2 = (0 + 1)^2 + (1 + 1)^2 + (2 + 1)^2 + (3 + 1)^2$$
$$= 1^2 + 2^2 + 3^2 + 4^2 = 30$$

$$\sum_{k=2}^{5} (k - 1)^2 = (2 - 1)^2 + (3 - 1)^2 + (4 - 1)^2 + (5 - 1)^2$$
$$= 1^2 + 2^2 + 3^2 + 4^2 = 30.$$

(**EXAMPLE 6**) **Writing Sums in Summation Notation**

Express each sum using summation notation:

a. $1^3 + 2^3 + 3^3 + \cdots + 7^3$ **b.** $1 + \dfrac{1}{3} + \dfrac{1}{9} + \dfrac{1}{27} + \cdots + \dfrac{1}{3^{n-1}}.$

Solution In each case, we will use 1 as the lower limit of summation and i for the index of summation.

a. The sum $1^3 + 2^3 + 3^3 + \cdots + 7^3$ has seven terms, each of the form i^3, starting at $i = 1$ and ending at $i = 7$. Thus,

$$1^3 + 2^3 + 3^3 + \cdots + 7^3 = \sum_{i=1}^{7} i^3.$$

b. The sum

$$1 + \frac{1}{3} + \frac{1}{9} + \frac{1}{27} + \cdots + \frac{1}{3^{n-1}}$$

has n terms, each of the form $\dfrac{1}{3^{i-1}}$, starting at $i = 1$ and ending at $i = n$. Thus,

$$1 + \frac{1}{3} + \frac{1}{9} + \frac{1}{27} + \cdots + \frac{1}{3^{n-1}} = \sum_{i=1}^{n} \frac{1}{3^{i-1}}.$$ ●

⊘ Check Point **6** Express each sum using summation notation:

a. $1^2 + 2^2 + 3^2 + \cdots + 9^2$ **b.** $1 + \dfrac{1}{2} + \dfrac{1}{4} + \dfrac{1}{8} + \cdots + \dfrac{1}{2^{n-1}}.$

Table 8.2 contains some important properties of sums expressed in summation notation.

Table 8.2 Properties of Sums

Property	Example
1. $\displaystyle\sum_{i=1}^{n} ca_i = c \sum_{i=1}^{n} a_i$, c any real number	$\displaystyle\sum_{i=1}^{4} 3i^2 = 3 \cdot 1^2 + 3 \cdot 2^2 + 3 \cdot 3^2 + 3 \cdot 4^2$ $3 \displaystyle\sum_{i=1}^{4} i^2 = 3(1^2 + 2^2 + 3^2 + 4^2) = 3 \cdot 1^2 + 3 \cdot 2^2 + 3 \cdot 3^2 + 3 \cdot 4^2$ Conclusion: $\displaystyle\sum_{i=1}^{4} 3i^2 = 3 \sum_{i=1}^{4} i^2$
2. $\displaystyle\sum_{i=1}^{n} (a_i + b_i) = \sum_{i=1}^{n} a_i + \sum_{i=1}^{n} b_i$	$\displaystyle\sum_{i=1}^{4} (i + i^2) = (1 + 1^2) + (2 + 2^2) + (3 + 3^2) + (4 + 4^2)$ $\displaystyle\sum_{i=1}^{4} i + \sum_{i=1}^{4} i^2 = (1 + 2 + 3 + 4) + (1^2 + 2^2 + 3^2 + 4^2)$ $\qquad\qquad = (1 + 1^2) + (2 + 2^2) + (3 + 3^2) + (4 + 4^2)$ Conclusion: $\displaystyle\sum_{i=1}^{4} (i + i^2) = \sum_{i=1}^{4} i + \sum_{i=1}^{4} i^2$
3. $\displaystyle\sum_{i=1}^{n} (a_i - b_i) = \sum_{i=1}^{n} a_i - \sum_{i=1}^{n} b_i$	$\displaystyle\sum_{i=3}^{5} (i^2 - i^3) = (3^2 - 3^3) + (4^2 - 4^3) + (5^2 - 5^3)$ $\displaystyle\sum_{i=3}^{5} i^2 - \sum_{i=3}^{5} i^3 = (3^2 + 4^2 + 5^2) - (3^3 + 4^3 + 5^3)$ $\qquad\qquad = (3^2 - 3^3) + (4^2 - 4^3) + (5^2 - 5^3)$ Conclusion: $\displaystyle\sum_{i=3}^{5} (i^2 - i^3) = \sum_{i=3}^{5} i^2 - \sum_{i=3}^{5} i^3$

Exercise Set 8.1

Practice Exercises

In Exercises 1–12, write the first four terms of each sequence whose general term is given.

1. $a_n = 3n + 2$

2. $a_n = 4n - 1$

3. $a_n = 3^n$

4. $a_n = \left(\dfrac{1}{3}\right)^n$

5. $a_n = (-3)^n$

6. $a_n = \left(-\dfrac{1}{3}\right)^n$

7. $a_n = (-1)^n(n + 3)$

8. $a_n = (-1)^{n+1}(n + 4)$

9. $a_n = \dfrac{2n}{n + 4}$

10. $a_n = \dfrac{3n}{n + 5}$

11. $a_n = \dfrac{(-1)^{n+1}}{2^n - 1}$

12. $a_n = \dfrac{(-1)^{n+1}}{2^n + 1}$

The sequences in Exercises 13–18 are defined using recursion formulas. Write the first four terms of each sequence.

13. $a_1 = 7$ and $a_n = a_{n-1} + 5$ for $n \geq 2$

14. $a_1 = 12$ and $a_n = a_{n-1} + 4$ for $n \geq 2$

15. $a_1 = 3$ and $a_n = 4a_{n-1}$ for $n \geq 2$

16. $a_1 = 2$ and $a_n = 5a_{n-1}$ for $n \geq 2$

17. $a_1 = 4$ and $a_n = 2a_{n-1} + 3$ for $n \geq 2$

18. $a_1 = 5$ and $a_n = 3a_{n-1} - 1$ for $n \geq 2$

In Exercises 19–22, the general term of a sequence is given and involves a factorial. Write the first four terms of each sequence.

19. $a_n = \dfrac{n^2}{n!}$

20. $a_n = \dfrac{(n + 1)!}{n^2}$

21. $a_n = 2(n + 1)!$

22. $a_n = -2(n - 1)!$

In Exercises 23–28, evaluate each factorial expression.

23. $\dfrac{17!}{15!}$

24. $\dfrac{18!}{16!}$

25. $\dfrac{16!}{2!14!}$

26. $\dfrac{20!}{2!18!}$

27. $\dfrac{(n + 2)!}{n!}$

28. $\dfrac{(2n + 1)!}{(2n)!}$

In Exercises 29–42, find each indicated sum.

29. $\displaystyle\sum_{i=1}^{6} 5i$

30. $\displaystyle\sum_{i=1}^{6} 7i$

31. $\displaystyle\sum_{i=1}^{4} 2i^2$

32. $\displaystyle\sum_{i=1}^{5} i^3$

33. $\displaystyle\sum_{k=1}^{5} k(k + 4)$

34. $\displaystyle\sum_{k=1}^{4} (k - 3)(k + 2)$

35. $\displaystyle\sum_{i=1}^{4} \left(-\dfrac{1}{2}\right)^i$

36. $\displaystyle\sum_{i=2}^{4} \left(-\dfrac{1}{3}\right)^i$

37. $\displaystyle\sum_{i=5}^{9} 11$

38. $\displaystyle\sum_{i=3}^{7} 12$

39. $\displaystyle\sum_{i=0}^{4} \dfrac{(-1)^i}{i!}$

40. $\displaystyle\sum_{i=0}^{4} \dfrac{(-1)^{i+1}}{(i + 1)!}$

41. $\displaystyle\sum_{i=1}^{5} \dfrac{i!}{(i - 1)!}$

42. $\displaystyle\sum_{i=1}^{5} \dfrac{(i + 2)!}{i!}$

In Exercises 43–54, express each sum using summation notation. Use 1 as the lower limit of summation and i for the index of summation.

43. $1^2 + 2^2 + 3^2 + \cdots + 15^2$

44. $1^4 + 2^4 + 3^4 + \cdots + 12^4$

45. $2 + 2^2 + 2^3 + \cdots + 2^{11}$

46. $5 + 5^2 + 5^3 + \cdots + 5^{12}$

47. $1 + 2 + 3 + \cdots + 30$

48. $1 + 2 + 3 + \cdots + 40$

49. $\dfrac{1}{2} + \dfrac{2}{3} + \dfrac{3}{4} + \cdots + \dfrac{14}{14 + 1}$

50. $\dfrac{1}{3} + \dfrac{2}{4} + \dfrac{3}{5} + \cdots + \dfrac{16}{16 + 2}$

51. $4 + \dfrac{4^2}{2} + \dfrac{4^3}{3} + \cdots + \dfrac{4^n}{n}$

52. $\dfrac{1}{9} + \dfrac{2}{9^2} + \dfrac{3}{9^3} + \cdots + \dfrac{n}{9^n}$

53. $1 + 3 + 5 + \cdots + (2n - 1)$

54. $a + ar + ar^2 + \cdots + ar^{n-1}$

In Exercises 55–60, express each sum using summation notation. Use a lower limit of summation of your choice and k for the index of summation.

55. $5 + 7 + 9 + 11 + \cdots + 31$

56. $6 + 8 + 10 + 12 + \cdots + 32$

57. $a + ar + ar^2 + \cdots + ar^{12}$

58. $a + ar + ar^2 + \cdots + ar^{14}$

59. $a + (a + d) + (a + 2d) + \cdots + (a + nd)$

60. $(a + d) + (a + d^2) + \cdots + (a + d^n)$

Practice Plus

In Exercises 61–68, use the graphs of $\{a_n\}$ and $\{b_n\}$ to find each indicated sum.

The Graph of $\{a_n\}$

The Graph of $\{b_n\}$

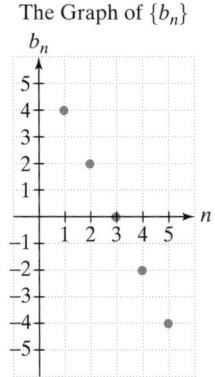

61. $\displaystyle\sum_{i=1}^{5} (a_i^2 + 1)$

62. $\displaystyle\sum_{i=1}^{5} (b_i^2 - 1)$

63. $\displaystyle\sum_{i=1}^{5} (2a_i + b_i)$

64. $\displaystyle\sum_{i=1}^{5} (a_i + 3b_i)$

65. $\sum_{i=4}^{5} \left(\frac{a_i}{b_i}\right)^2$

66. $\sum_{i=4}^{5} \left(\frac{a_i}{b_i}\right)^3$

67. $\sum_{i=1}^{5} a_i^2 + \sum_{i=1}^{5} b_i^2$

68. $\sum_{i=1}^{5} a_i^2 - \sum_{i=3}^{5} b_i^2$

Application Exercises

69. Advertisers don't have to fear that they'll face a sea of "sold out" signs as they rush to the Internet. The growing number of popular sites filled with user-created content, including MySpace.com and YouTube.com, provide plenty of inventory for advertisers who can't find space on top portals such as Yahoo. The bar graph shows U.S. online ad spending, in billions of dollars, from 2000 through 2006.

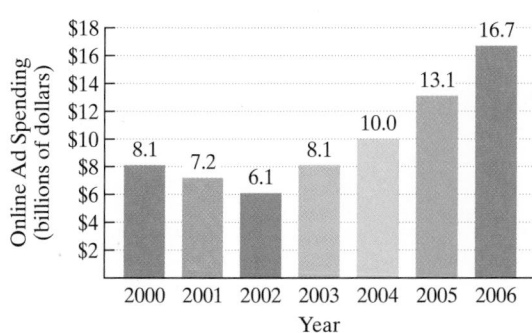

United States Online Ad Spending

Source: eMarketer

Let a_n represent online ad spending, in billions of dollars, n years after 1999.

a. Use the numbers given in the graph to find and interpret

$$\frac{1}{7} \sum_{i=1}^{7} a_i.$$

b. The finite sequence whose general term is

$$a_n = 0.5n^2 - 1.5n + 8,$$

where $n = 1, 2, 3, \ldots, 7$, models online ad spending, a_n, in billions of dollars, n years after 1999. Use the model to find $\frac{1}{7} \sum_{i=1}^{7} a_i$. Does this underestimate or overestimate the actual sum in part (a)? By how much?

70. More and more television commercial time is devoted to drug companies as hucksters for the benefits and risks of their wares. The bar graph shows the amount that drug companies spent on consumer drug ads, in billions of dollars, from 2002 through 2006.

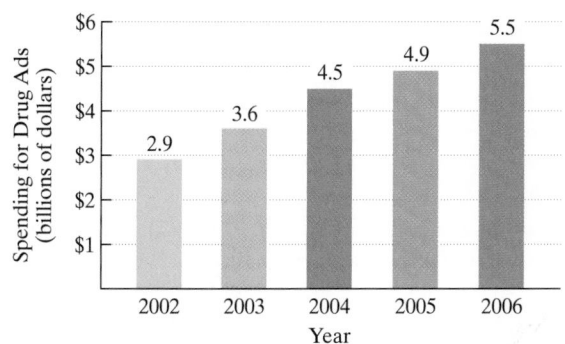

Spending for Consumer Drug Ads

Source: Nielsen Monitor-Plus

Let a_n represent spending for consumer drug ads, in billions of dollars, n years after 2001.

a. Use the numbers given in the graph to find and interpret

$$\frac{1}{5} \sum_{i=1}^{5} a_i.$$

b. The finite sequence whose general term is

$$a_n = 0.65n + 2.3,$$

where $n = 1, 2, 3, 4, 5$, models spending for consumer drug ads, in billions of dollars, n years after 2001. Use the model to find $\frac{1}{5} \sum_{i=1}^{5} a_i$. Does this seem reasonable in terms of the actual sum in part (a), or has model breakdown occurred?

71. A deposit of $6000 is made in an account that earns 6% interest compounded quarterly. The balance in the account after n quarters is given by the sequence

$$a_n = 6000\left(1 + \frac{0.06}{4}\right)^n, \quad n = 1, 2, 3, \ldots.$$

Find the balance in the account after five years. Round to the nearest cent.

72. A deposit of $10,000 is made in an account that earns 8% interest compounded quarterly. The balance in the account after n quarters is given by the sequence

$$a_n = 10,000\left(1 + \frac{0.08}{4}\right)^n, \quad n = 1, 2, 3, \ldots.$$

Find the balance in the account after six years. Round to the nearest cent.

Writing in Mathematics

73. What is a sequence? Give an example with your description.

74. Explain how to write terms of a sequence if the formula for the general term is given.

75. What does the graph of a sequence look like? How is it obtained?

76. What is a recursion formula?

77. Explain how to find $n!$ if n is a positive integer.

78. Explain the best way to evaluate $\frac{900!}{899!}$ without a calculator.

79. What is the meaning of the symbol Σ? Give an example with your description.

80. You buy a new car for $24,000. At the end of n years, the value of your car is given by the sequence

$$a_n = 24,000\left(\frac{3}{4}\right)^n, \quad n = 1, 2, 3, \ldots.$$

Find a_5 and write a sentence explaining what this value represents. Describe the nth term of the sequence in terms of the value of your car at the end of each year.

Technology Exercises

In Exercises 81–85, use a calculator's factorial key to evaluate each expression.

81. $\dfrac{200!}{198!}$

82. $\left(\dfrac{300}{20}\right)!$

83. $\dfrac{20!}{300}$

84. $\dfrac{20!}{(20-3)!}$

85. $\dfrac{54!}{(54-3)!3!}$

86. Use the $\boxed{\text{SEQ}}$ (sequence) capability of a graphing utility to verify the terms of the sequences you obtained for any five sequences from Exercises 1–12 or 19–22.

87. Use the $\boxed{\text{SUM}}$ $\boxed{\text{SEQ}}$ (sum of the sequence) capability of a graphing utility to verify any five of the sums you obtained in Exercises 29–42.

88. As n increases, the terms of the sequence

$$a_n = \left(1 + \frac{1}{n}\right)^n$$

get closer and closer to the number e (where $e \approx 2.7183$). Use a calculator to find $a_{10}, a_{100}, a_{1000}, a_{10,000}$, and $a_{100,000}$, comparing these terms to your calculator's decimal approximation for e.

Many graphing utilities have a sequence-graphing mode that plots the terms of a sequence as points on a rectangular coordinate system. Consult your manual; if your graphing utility has this capability, use it to graph each of the sequences in Exercises 89–92. What appears to be happening to the terms of each sequence as n gets larger?

89. $a_n = \dfrac{n}{n+1}$ n:[0, 10, 1] by a_n:[0, 1, 0.1]

90. $a_n = \dfrac{100}{n}$ n:[0, 1000, 100] by a_n:[0, 1, 0.1]

91. $a_n = \dfrac{2n^2 + 5n - 7}{n^3}$ n:[0, 10, 1] by a_n:[0, 2, 0.2]

92. $a_n = \dfrac{3n^4 + n - 1}{5n^4 + 2n^2 + 1}$ n:[0, 10, 1] by a_n:[0, 1, 0.1]

Critical Thinking Exercises

Make Sense? *In Exercises 93–96, determine whether each statement makes sense or does not make sense, and explain your reasoning.*

93. Now that I've studied sequences, I realize that the joke in this cartoon is based on the fact that you can't have a negative number of sheep.

WHEN MATHEMATICIANS CAN'T SLEEP

94. By writing $a_1, a_2, a_3, a_4, \ldots, a_n, \ldots$, I can see that the range of a sequence is the set of positive integers.

95. It makes a difference whether or not I use parentheses around the expression following the summation symbol, because the value of $\displaystyle\sum_{i=1}^{8}(i+7)$ is 92, but the value of $\displaystyle\sum_{i=1}^{8} i + 7$ is 43.

96. Without writing out the terms, I can see that $(-1)^{2n}$ in $a_n = \dfrac{(-1)^{2n}}{3n}$ causes the terms to alternate in sign.

In Exercises 97–100, determine whether each statement is true or false. If the statement is false, make the necessary change(s) to produce a true statement.

97. $\dfrac{n!}{(n-1)!} = \dfrac{1}{n-1}$

98. The Fibonacci sequence 1, 1, 2, 3, 5, 8, 13, 21, 34, 55, 89, 144, ... can be defined recursively using $a_0 = 1, a_1 = 1$; $a_n = a_{n-2} + a_{n-1}$, where $n \geq 2$.

99. $\displaystyle\sum_{i=1}^{2}(-1)^i 2^i = 0$

100. $\displaystyle\sum_{i=1}^{2} a_i b_i = \sum_{i=1}^{2} a_i \sum_{i=1}^{2} b_i$

101. Write the first five terms of the sequence whose first term is 9 and whose general term is

$$a_n = \begin{cases} \dfrac{a_{n-1}}{2} & \text{if } a_{n-1} \text{ is even} \\ 3a_{n-1} + 5 & \text{if } a_{n-1} \text{ is odd} \end{cases}$$

for $n \geq 2$.

Group Exercise

102. Enough curiosities involving the Fibonacci sequence exist to warrant a flourishing Fibonacci Association, which publishes a quarterly journal. Do some research on the Fibonacci sequence by consulting the Internet or the research department of your library, and find one property that interests you. After doing this research, get together with your group to share these intriguing properties.

Preview Exercises

Exercises 103–105 will help you prepare for the material covered in the next section.

103. Consider the sequence 8, 3, −2, −7, −12, Find $a_2 - a_1$, $a_3 - a_2, a_4 - a_3$, and $a_5 - a_4$. What do you observe?

104. Consider the sequence whose nth term is $a_n = 4n - 3$. Find $a_2 - a_1, a_3 - a_2, a_4 - a_3$, and $a_5 - a_4$. What do you observe?

105. Use the formula $a_n = 4 + (n-1)(-7)$ to find the eighth term of the sequence 4, −3, −10,

Section 8.2 Arithmetic Sequences

Objectives

1. Find the common difference for an arithmetic sequence.
2. Write terms of an arithmetic sequence.
3. Use the formula for the general term of an arithmetic sequence.
4. Use the formula for the sum of the first n terms of an arithmetic sequence.

Your grandmother and her financial counselor are looking at options in case an adult residential facility is needed in the future. The good news is that your grandmother's total assets are $500,000. The bad news is that adult residential community costs average $64,130 annually, increasing by $1800 each year. In this section, we will see how sequences can be used to model your grandmother's situation and help her to identify realistic options.

1. Find the common difference for an arithmetic sequence.

Arithmetic Sequences

The bar graph in **Figure 8.2** shows annual salaries, rounded to the nearest thousand dollars, of U.S. senators from 2000 to 2005. The graph illustrates that each year salaries increased by $4 thousand. The sequence of annual salaries

142, 146, 150, 154, 158, 162, . . .

shows that each term after the first, 142, differs from the preceding term by a constant amount, namely 4. This sequence is an example of an *arithmetic sequence*.

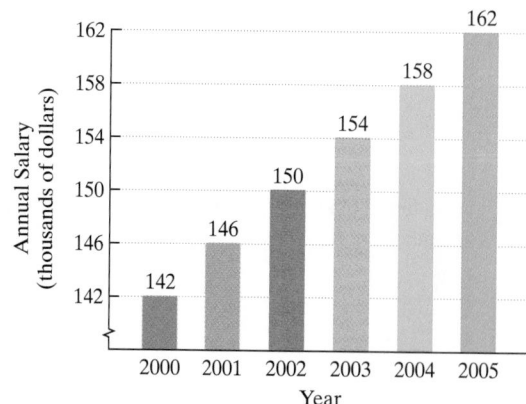

Annual Salaries of U.S. Senators

Figure 8.2 *Source:* U.S. Senate

Definition of an Arithmetic Sequence

An **arithmetic sequence** is a sequence in which each term after the first differs from the preceding term by a constant amount. The difference between consecutive terms is called the **common difference** of the sequence.

The common difference, d, is found by subtracting any term from the term that directly follows it. In the following examples, the common difference is found by subtracting the first term from the second term, $a_2 - a_1$.

Arithmetic Sequence	Common Difference
142, 146, 150, 154, 158, . . .	$d = 146 - 142 = 4$
$-5, -2, 1, 4, 7, . . .$	$d = -2 - (-5) = -2 + 5 = 3$
$8, 3, -2, -7, -12, . . .$	$d = 3 - 8 = -5$

Figure 8.3 shows the graphs of the last two arithmetic sequences in our list. The common difference for the increasing sequence in **Figure 8.3(a)** is 3. The common difference for the decreasing sequence in **Figure 8.3(b)** is −5.

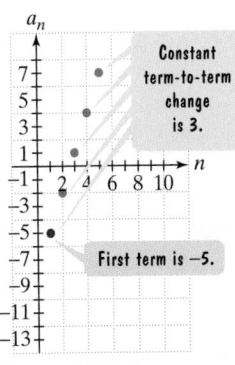

Figure 8.3(a) The graph of $\{a_n\} = -5, -2, 1, 4, 7, \ldots$

Figure 8.3(b) The graph of $\{b_n\} = 8, 3, -2, -7, -12, \ldots$

The graph of each arithmetic sequence in **Figure 8.3** forms a set of discrete points lying on a straight line. This illustrates that **an arithmetic sequence is a linear function whose domain is the set of positive integers**.

If the first term of an arithmetic sequence is a_1, each term after the first is obtained by adding d, the common difference, to the previous term. This can be expressed recursively as follows:

$$a_n = a_{n-1} + d.$$

Add d to the term in any position to get the next term.

To use this recursion formula, we must be given the first term.

② Write terms of an arithmetic sequence.

(**EXAMPLE 1**) **Writing the Terms of an Arithmetic Sequence**

Write the first six terms of the arithmetic sequence in which $a_1 = 6$ and $a_n = a_{n-1} - 2$.

Solution The recursion formula $a_1 = 6$ and $a_n = a_{n-1} - 2$ indicates that each term after the first, 6, is obtained by adding −2 to the previous term.

$a_1 = 6$	This is given.
$a_2 = a_1 - 2 = 6 - 2 = 4$	Use $a_n = a_{n-1} - 2$ with $n = 2$.
$a_3 = a_2 - 2 = 4 - 2 = 2$	Use $a_n = a_{n-1} - 2$ with $n = 3$.
$a_4 = a_3 - 2 = 2 - 2 = 0$	Use $a_n = a_{n-1} - 2$ with $n = 4$.
$a_5 = a_4 - 2 = 0 - 2 = -2$	Use $a_n = a_{n-1} - 2$ with $n = 5$.
$a_6 = a_5 - 2 = -2 - 2 = -4$	Use $a_n = a_{n-1} - 2$ with $n = 6$.

The first six terms are

$$6, 4, 2, 0, -2, \text{ and } -4.$$

⊘ Check Point **1** Write the first six terms of the arithmetic sequence in which $a_1 = 100$ and $a_n = a_{n-1} - 30$.

③ Use the formula for the general term of an arithmetic sequence.

The General Term of an Arithmetic Sequence

Consider an arithmetic sequence whose first term is a_1 and whose common difference is d. We are looking for a formula for the general term, a_n. Let's begin by writing the first six terms. The first term is a_1. The second term is $a_1 + d$. The third term is

$a_1 + d + d$, or $a_1 + 2d$. Thus, we start with a_1 and add d to each successive term. The first six terms are

$$a_1, \quad a_1 + d, \quad a_1 + 2d, \quad a_1 + 3d, \quad a_1 + 4d, \quad a_1 + 5d.$$

| a_1, first term | a_2, second term | a_3, third term | a_4, fourth term | a_5, fifth term | a_6, sixth term |

Compare the coefficient of d and the subscript of a denoting the term number. Can you see that the coefficient of d is 1 less than the subscript of a denoting the term number?

a_3: third term $= a_1 + 2d$ a_4: fourth term $= a_1 + 3d$

One less than 3, or 2, is the coefficient of d.

One less than 4, or 3, is the coefficient of d.

Thus, the formula for the nth term is

$$a_n: n\text{th term} = a_1 + (n - 1)d.$$

One less than n, or $n - 1$, is the coefficient of d.

General Term of an Arithmetic Sequence

The nth term (the general term) of an arithmetic sequence with first term a_1 and common difference d is

$$a_n = a_1 + (n - 1)d.$$

EXAMPLE 2 **Using the Formula for the General Term of an Arithmetic Sequence**

Find the eighth term of the arithmetic sequence whose first term is 4 and whose common difference is -7.

Solution To find the eighth term, a_8, we replace n in the formula with 8, a_1 with 4, and d with -7.

$$a_n = a_1 + (n - 1)d$$
$$a_8 = 4 + (8 - 1)(-7) = 4 + 7(-7) = 4 + (-49) = -45$$

The eighth term is -45. We can check this result by writing the first eight terms of the sequence:

$$4, -3, -10, -17, -24, -31, -38, -45.$$

⊘ Check Point 2 Find the ninth term of the arithmetic sequence whose first term is 6 and whose common difference is -5.

EXAMPLE 3 **Using an Arithmetic Sequence to Model Teachers' Earnings**

According to the National Education Association, teachers in the United States earned an average of \$44,600 in 2002. This amount has increased by approximately \$1130 per year.

a. Write a formula for the nth term of the arithmetic sequence that describes teachers' average earnings n years after 2001.

b. How much will U.S. teachers earn, on average, by the year 2012?

Solution

a. With a yearly increase of $1130, we can express teachers' earnings by the following arithmetic sequence:

$$44,600, \quad 44,600 + 1130 = 45,730, \quad 45,730 + 1130 = 46,860, \dots .$$

a_1: earnings in 2002, 1 year after 2001	a_2: earnings in 2003, 2 years after 2001	a_3: earnings in 2004, 3 years after 2001

In the sequence $44,600, 45,730, 46,860, \dots, a_1$, the first term, represents the amount teachers earned in 2002. Each subsequent year this amount increases by $1130, so $d = 1130$. We use the formula for the general term of an arithmetic sequence to write the nth term of the sequence that describes teachers' earnings n years after 2001.

$$a_n = a_1 + (n - 1)d \qquad \text{This is the formula for the general term of an arithmetic sequence.}$$

$$a_n = 44,600 + (n - 1)1130 \qquad a_1 = 44,600 \text{ and } d = 1130.$$

$$a_n = 44,600 + 1130n - 1130 \qquad \text{Distribute 1130 to each term in parentheses.}$$

$$a_n = 1130n + 43,470 \qquad \text{Simplify.}$$

Thus, teachers' earnings n years after 2001 can be described by $a_n = 1130n + 43,470$.

b. Now we need to project teachers' earnings in 2012. The year 2012 is 11 years after 2001. Thus, $n = 11$. We substitute 11 for n in $a_n = 1130n + 43,470$.

$$a_{11} = 1130 \cdot 11 + 43,470 = 55,900$$

The 11th term of the sequence is 55,900. Thus, U.S. teachers are projected to earn an average of $55,900 by the year 2012. ●

⊘ **Check Point 3** Thanks to drive-thrus and curbside delivery, Americans are eating more meals behind the wheel. In 2004, we averaged 32 à la car meals, increasing by approximately 0.7 meal per year. (*Source: Newsweek*)

a. Write a formula for the nth term of the arithmetic sequence that models the average number of car meals n years after 2003.

b. How many car meals will Americans average by the year 2014?

④ Use the formula for the sum of the first n terms of an arithmetic sequence.

The Sum of the First n Terms of an Arithmetic Sequence

The sum of the first n terms of an arithmetic sequence, denoted by S_n, and called the **nth partial sum**, can be found without having to add up all the terms. Let

$$S_n = a_1 + a_2 + a_3 + \cdots + a_n$$

be the sum of the first n terms of an arithmetic sequence. Because d is the common difference between terms, S_n can be written forward and backward as follows:

Forward: Start with the first term, a_1. Keep adding d.

$$S_n = a_1 \qquad\qquad + (a_1 + d) + (a_1 + 2d) + \cdots + a_n$$

$$S_n = a_n \qquad\qquad + (a_n - d) + (a_n - 2d) + \cdots + a_1$$

Backward: Start with the last term, a_n. Keep subtracting d.

$$\overline{2S_n = (a_1 + a_n) + (a_1 + a_n) + (a_1 + a_n) + \cdots + (a_1 + a_n)}. \qquad \text{Add the two equations.}$$

Because there are n sums of $(a_1 + a_n)$ on the right side, we can express this side as $n(a_1 + a_n)$. Thus, the last equation can be written as follows:

$$2S_n = n(a_1 + a_n)$$

$$S_n = \frac{n}{2}(a_1 + a_n). \quad \text{Solve for } S_n, \text{ dividing both sides by 2.}$$

We have proved the following result:

The Sum of the First n Terms of an Arithmetic Sequence

The sum, S_n, of the first n terms of an arithmetic sequence is given by

$$S_n = \frac{n}{2}(a_1 + a_n),$$

in which a_1 is the first term and a_n is the nth term.

To find the sum of the terms of an arithmetic sequence using $S_n = \frac{n}{2}(a_1 + a_n)$,

we need to know the first term, a_1, the last term, a_n, and the number of terms, n. The following examples illustrate how to use this formula.

EXAMPLE 4 **Finding the Sum of n Terms of an Arithmetic Sequence**

Find the sum of the first 100 terms of the arithmetic sequence: $1, 3, 5, 7, \ldots$.

Solution By finding the sum of the first 100 terms of $1, 3, 5, 7, \ldots$, we are finding the sum of the first 100 odd numbers. To find the sum of the first 100 terms, S_{100}, we replace n in the formula with 100.

$$S_n = \frac{n}{2}(a_1 + a_n)$$

$$S_{100} = \frac{100}{2}(a_1 + a_{100})$$

The first term, a_1, is 1.	We must find a_{100}, the 100th term.

We use the formula for the general term of a sequence to find a_{100}. The common difference, d, of $1, 3, 5, 7, \ldots$, is 2.

$a_n = a_1 + (n - 1)d$ This is the formula for the nth term of an arithmetic sequence. Use it to find the 100th term.

$a_{100} = 1 + (100 - 1) \cdot 2$ Substitute 100 for n, 2 for d, and 1 (the first term) for a_1.

$\phantom{a_{100}} = 1 + 99 \cdot 2$ Perform the subtraction in parentheses.

$\phantom{a_{100}} = 1 + 198 = 199$ Multiply $(99 \cdot 2 = 198)$ and then add.

Now we are ready to find the sum of the 100 terms $1, 3, 5, 7, \ldots, 199$.

$S_n = \frac{n}{2}(a_1 + a_n)$ Use the formula for the sum of the first n terms of an arithmetic sequence. Let $n = 100$, $a_1 = 1$, and $a_{100} = 199$.

$$S_{100} = \frac{100}{2}(1 + 199) = 50(200) = 10{,}000$$

The sum of the first 100 odd numbers is 10,000. Equivalently, the 100th partial sum of the sequence $1, 3, 5, 7, \ldots$ is 10,000. ●

🖉 **Check Point 4** Find the sum of the first 15 terms of the arithmetic sequence: $3, 6, 9, 12, \ldots$.

EXAMPLE 5 Using S_n to Evaluate a Summation

Find the following sum: $\displaystyle\sum_{i=1}^{25}(5i - 9)$.

Technology

To find

$$\sum_{i=1}^{25}(5i - 9)$$

on a graphing utility, enter

SUM SEQ $(5x - 9, x, 1, 25, 1)$.

Then press ENTER .

```
sum(seq(5X-9,X,1
,25,1))
            1400
```

Solution

$$\sum_{i=1}^{25}(5i - 9) = (5\cdot 1 - 9) + (5\cdot 2 - 9) + (5\cdot 3 - 9) + \cdots + (5\cdot 25 - 9)$$

$$= -4 \qquad + 1 \qquad + 6 \qquad + \cdots + 116$$

By evaluating the first three terms and the last term, we see that $a_1 = -4$; d, the common difference, is $1 - (-4)$, or 5; and a_{25}, the last term, is 116.

$$S_n = \frac{n}{2}(a_1 + a_n) \qquad \text{\textit{Use the formula for the sum of the first } n \text{ terms of an}}$$
$$\text{\textit{arithmetic sequence. Let } n = 25, a_1 = -4, \text{ and } a_{25} = 116.}$$

$$S_{25} = \frac{25}{2}(-4 + 116) = \frac{25}{2}(112) = 1400$$

Thus,

$$\sum_{i=1}^{25}(5i - 9) = 1400. \qquad \bullet$$

☑ Check Point **5** Find the following sum: $\displaystyle\sum_{i=1}^{30}(6i - 11)$.

EXAMPLE 6 Modeling Total Residential Community Costs over a Six-Year Period

Your grandmother has assets of $500,000. One option that she is considering involves an adult residential community for a six-year period beginning in 2009. The model

$$a_n = 1800n + 64{,}130$$

describes yearly adult residential community costs n years after 2008. Does your grandmother have enough to pay for the facility?

Solution We must find the sum of an arithmetic sequence whose general term is $a_n = 1800n + 64{,}130$. The first term of the sequence corresponds to the facility's costs in the year 2009. The last term corresponds to costs in the year 2014. Because the model describes costs n years after 2008, $n = 1$ describes the year 2009 and $n = 6$ describes the year 2014.

$$a_n = 1800n + 64{,}130 \qquad \text{\textit{This is the given formula for the general term of the sequence.}}$$

$$a_1 = 1800\cdot 1 + 64{,}130 = 65{,}930 \qquad \text{\textit{Find } a_1 \text{ by replacing } n \text{ with 1.}}$$

$$a_6 = 1800\cdot 6 + 64{,}130 = 74{,}930 \qquad \text{\textit{Find } a_6 \text{ by replacing } n \text{ with 6.}}$$

The first year the facility will cost $65,930. By year six, the facility will cost $74,930. Now we must find the sum of the costs for all six years. We focus on the sum of the first six terms of the arithmetic sequence

$$65{,}930, \; 67{,}730, \; \ldots, \; 74{,}930.$$

$$\underbrace{\phantom{65{,}930}}_{a_1} \qquad \underbrace{\phantom{67{,}730}}_{a_2} \qquad \underbrace{\phantom{74{,}930}}_{a_6}$$

We find this sum using the formula for the sum of the first n terms of an arithmetic sequence. We are adding 6 terms: $n = 6$. The first term is 65,930: $a_1 = 65{,}930$. The last term—that is, the sixth term—is 74,930: $a_6 = 74{,}930$.

$$S_n = \frac{n}{2}(a_1 + a_n)$$

$$S_6 = \frac{6}{2}(65{,}930 + 74{,}930) = 3(140{,}860) = 422{,}580$$

Total adult residential community costs for your grandmother are predicted to be \$422,580. Because your grandmother's assets are \$500,000, she has enough to pay for the facility for the six-year period.

○ Check Point **6** In Example 6, how much would it cost for the adult residential community for a ten-year period beginning in 2009?

Exercise Set 8.2

Practice Exercises

In Exercises 1–14, write the first six terms of each arithmetic sequence.

1. $a_1 = 200, d = 20$
2. $a_1 = 300, d = 50$
3. $a_1 = -7, d = 4$
4. $a_1 = -8, d = 5$
5. $a_1 = 300, d = -90$
6. $a_1 = 200, d = -60$
7. $a_1 = \frac{5}{2}, d = -\frac{1}{2}$
8. $a_1 = \frac{3}{4}, d = -\frac{1}{4}$
9. $a_n = a_{n-1} + 6, a_1 = -9$
10. $a_n = a_{n-1} + 4, a_1 = -7$
11. $a_n = a_{n-1} - 10, a_1 = 30$
12. $a_n = a_{n-1} - 20, a_1 = 50$
13. $a_n = a_{n-1} - 0.4, a_1 = 1.6$
14. $a_n = a_{n-1} - 0.3, a_1 = -1.7$

In Exercises 15–22, find the indicated term of the arithmetic sequence with first term, a_1, and common difference, d.

15. Find a_6 when $a_1 = 13, d = 4$.
16. Find a_{16} when $a_1 = 9, d = 2$.
17. Find a_{50} when $a_1 = 7, d = 5$.
18. Find a_{60} when $a_1 = 8, d = 6$.
19. Find a_{200} when $a_1 = -40, d = 5$.
20. Find a_{150} when $a_1 = -60, d = 5$.
21. Find a_{60} when $a_1 = 35, d = -3$.
22. Find a_{70} when $a_1 = -32, d = 4$.

In Exercises 23–34, write a formula for the general term (the nth term) of each arithmetic sequence. Do not use a recursion formula. Then use the formula for a_n to find a_{20}, the 20th term of the sequence.

23. $1, 5, 9, 13, \ldots$
24. $2, 7, 12, 17, \ldots$
25. $7, 3, -1, -5, \ldots$
26. $6, 1, -4, -9, \ldots$
27. $a_1 = 9, d = 2$
28. $a_1 = 6, d = 3$
29. $a_1 = -20, d = -4$
30. $a_1 = -70, d = -5$
31. $a_n = a_{n-1} + 3, a_1 = 4$
32. $a_n = a_{n-1} + 5, a_1 = 6$
33. $a_n = a_{n-1} - 10, a_1 = 30$
34. $a_n = a_{n-1} - 12, a_1 = 24$

35. Find the sum of the first 20 terms of the arithmetic sequence: $4, 10, 16, 22, \ldots$.
36. Find the sum of the first 25 terms of the arithmetic sequence: $7, 19, 31, 43, \ldots$.
37. Find the sum of the first 50 terms of the arithmetic sequence: $-10, -6, -2, 2, \ldots$.
38. Find the sum of the first 50 terms of the arithmetic sequence: $-15, -9, -3, 3, \ldots$.
39. Find $1 + 2 + 3 + 4 + \cdots + 100$, the sum of the first 100 natural numbers.
40. Find $2 + 4 + 6 + 8 + \cdots + 200$, the sum of the first 100 positive even integers.
41. Find the sum of the first 60 positive even integers.
42. Find the sum of the first 80 positive even integers.
43. Find the sum of the even integers between 21 and 45.
44. Find the sum of the odd integers between 30 and 54.

For Exercises 45–50, write out the first three terms and the last term. Then use the formula for the sum of the first n terms of an arithmetic sequence to find the indicated sum.

45. $\sum_{i=1}^{17}(5i + 3)$
46. $\sum_{i=1}^{20}(6i - 4)$
47. $\sum_{i=1}^{30}(-3i + 5)$
48. $\sum_{i=1}^{40}(-2i + 6)$
49. $\sum_{i=1}^{100} 4i$
50. $\sum_{i=1}^{50}(-4i)$

Practice Plus

Use the graphs of the arithmetic sequences $\{a_n\}$ and $\{b_n\}$ to solve Exercises 51–58.

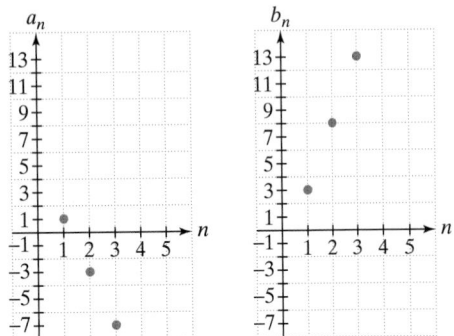

51. Find $a_{14} + b_{12}$.

52. Find $a_{16} + b_{18}$.

53. If $\{a_n\}$ is a finite sequence whose last term is -83, how many terms does $\{a_n\}$ contain?

54. If $\{b_n\}$ is a finite sequence whose last term is 93, how many terms does $\{b_n\}$ contain?

55. Find the difference between the sum of the first 14 terms of $\{b_n\}$ and the sum of the first 14 terms of $\{a_n\}$.

56. Find the difference between the sum of the first 15 terms of $\{b_n\}$ and the sum of the first 15 terms of $\{a_n\}$.

57. Write a linear function $f(x) = mx + b$, whose domain is the set of positive integers, that represents $\{a_n\}$.

58. Write a linear function $g(x) = mx + b$, whose domain is the set of positive integers, that represents $\{b_n\}$.

Use a system of two equations in two variables, a_1 and d, to solve Exercises 59–60.

59. Write a formula for the general term (the nth term) of the arithmetic sequence whose second term, a_2, is 4 and whose sixth term, a_6, is 16.

60. Write a formula for the general term (the nth term) of the arithmetic sequence whose third term, a_3, is 7 and whose eighth term, a_8, is 17.

Application Exercises

The bar graphs show changes that have taken place in the United States over time. Exercises 61–62 involve developing arithmetic sequences that model the data.

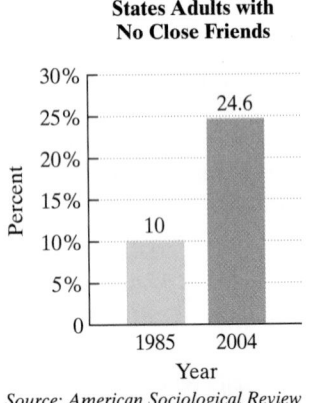

Percentage of United States Adults with No Close Friends

Source: American Sociological Review

Percentage of High School Grades of A+, A, or A− for College Freshmen

Source: www.grade-inflation.com

61. In 1985, 10% of Americans had no close friends. On average, this has increased by approximately 0.77% per year.

 a. Write a formula for the nth term of the arithmetic sequence that models the percentage of Americans with no close friends n years after 1984.

 b. If trends shown by the model in part (a) continue, what percentage of Americans will have no close friends in 2011? Round to one decimal place.

62. In 1968, 17.6% of high school grades for college freshmen consisted of A's (A+, A, or A−). On average, this has increased by approximately 0.83% per year.

 a. Write a formula for the nth term of the arithmetic sequence that models the percentage of high school grades of A for college freshmen n years after 1967.

 b. If trends shown by the model in part (a) continue, what percentage of high school grades for college freshmen will consist of A's in 2018?

63. Company A pays $24,000 yearly with raises of $1600 per year. Company B pays $28,000 yearly with raises of $1000 per year. Which company will pay more in year 10? How much more?

64. Company A pays $23,000 yearly with raises of $1200 per year. Company B pays $26,000 yearly with raises of $800 per year. Which company will pay more in year 10? How much more?

In Exercises 65–67, we revisit the data from Chapter P showing the average cost of tuition and fees at public and private four-year U.S. colleges.

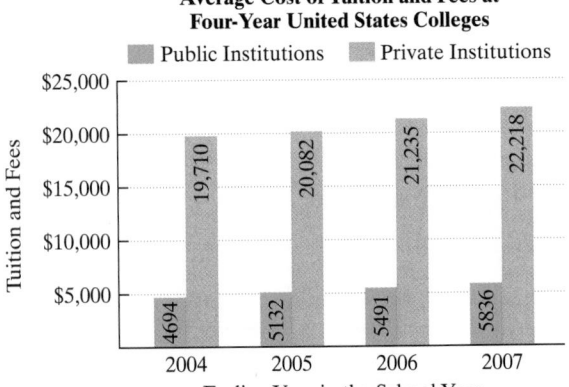

Average Cost of Tuition and Fees at Four-Year United States Colleges

Source: The College Board

65. a. Use the numbers shown in the bar graph to find the total cost of tuition and fees at public colleges for a four-year period from the school year ending in 2004 through the school year ending in 2007.

 b. The model

$$a_n = 379n + 4342$$

describes the cost of tuition and fees at public colleges in academic year n, where $n = 1$ corresponds to the school year ending in 2004, $n = 2$ to the school year ending in 2005, and so on. Use this model and the formula for S_n to find the total cost of tuition and fees at public colleges for a four-year period from the school year ending in 2004 through the school year ending in 2007. Does the model underestimate or overestimate the actual sum you obtained in part (a)? By how much?

66. a. Use the numbers shown in the bar graph to find the total cost of tuition and fees at private colleges for a four-year period from the school year ending in 2004 through the school year ending in 2007.

b. The model

$$a_n = 868n + 18,642$$

describes the cost of tuition and fees at private colleges in academic year n, where $n = 1$ corresponds to the school year ending in 2004, $n = 2$ to the school year ending in 2005, and so on. Use this model and the formula for S_n to find the total cost of tuition and fees at private colleges for a four-year period from the school year ending in 2004 through the school year ending in 2007. Does the model underestimate or overestimate the actual sum that you obtained in part (a)? By how much?

67. Use one of the models in Exercises 65–66 and the formula for S_n to find the total cost of tuition and fees for your undergraduate education. How well does the model describe your anticipated costs?

68. A company offers a starting yearly salary of $33,000 with raises of $2500 per year. Find the total salary over a ten-year period.

69. You are considering two job offers. Company A will start you at $19,000 a year and guarantee a raise of $2600 per year. Company B will start you at a higher salary, $27,000 a year, but will only guarantee a raise of $1200 per year. Find the total salary that each company will pay over a ten-year period. Which company pays the greater total amount?

70. A theater has 30 seats in the first row, 32 seats in the second row, increasing by 2 seats per row for a total of 26 rows. How many seats are there in the theater?

71. A section in a stadium has 20 seats in the first row, 23 seats in the second row, increasing by 3 seats each row for a total of 38 rows. How many seats are in this section of the stadium?

Writing in Mathematics

72. What is an arithmetic sequence? Give an example with your explanation.

73. What is the common difference in an arithmetic sequence?

74. Explain how to find the general term of an arithmetic sequence.

75. Explain how to find the sum of the first n terms of an arithmetic sequence without having to add up all the terms.

Technology Exercises

76. Use the SEQ (sequence) capability of a graphing utility and the formula you obtained for a_n to verify the value you found for a_{20} in any five exercises from Exercises 23–34.

77. Use the capability of a graphing utility to calculate the sum of a sequence to verify any five of your answers to Exercises 45–50.

Critical Thinking Exercises

Make Sense? *In Exercises 78–81, determine whether each statement makes sense or does not make sense, and explain your reasoning.*

78. Rather than performing the addition, I used the formula $S_n = \frac{n}{2}(a_1 + a_n)$ to find the sum of the first thirty terms of the sequence $2, 4, 8, 16, 32, \ldots$.

79. I was able to find the sum of the first fifty terms of an arithmetic sequence even though I did not identify every term.

80. The sequence for the number of seats per row in our movie theater as the rows move toward the back is arithmetic with $d = 1$ so people don't block the view of those in the row behind them.

81. Beginning at 6:45 A.M., a bus stops on my block every 23 minutes, so I used the formula for the nth term of an arithmetic sequence to describe the stopping time for the nth bus of the day.

82. In the sequence $21,700, 23,172, 24,644, 26,116, \ldots$, which term is 314,628?

83. A *degree-day* is a unit used to measure the fuel requirements of buildings. By definition, each degree that the average daily temperature is below 65°F is 1 degree-day. For example, a temperature of 42°F constitutes 23 degree-days. If the average temperature on January 1 was 42°F and fell 2°F for each subsequent day up to and including January 10, how many degree-days are included from January 1 to January 10?

84. Show that the sum of the first n positive odd integers,

$$1 + 3 + 5 + \cdots + (2n - 1),$$

is n^2.

Preview Exercises

Exercises 85–87 will help you prepare for the material covered in the next section.

85. Consider the sequence $1, -2, 4, -8, 16, \ldots$. Find $\dfrac{a_2}{a_1}, \dfrac{a_3}{a_2}, \dfrac{a_4}{a_3},$ and $\dfrac{a_5}{a_4}$. What do you observe?

86. Consider the sequence whose nth term is $a_n = 3 \cdot 5^n$. Find $\dfrac{a_2}{a_1}, \dfrac{a_3}{a_2}, \dfrac{a_4}{a_3},$ and $\dfrac{a_5}{a_4}$. What do you observe?

87. Use the formula $a_n = a_1 3^{n-1}$ to find the 7th term of the sequence $11, 33, 99, 297, \ldots$.

Section 8.3 Geometric Sequences and Series

Objectives

1. Find the common ratio of a geometric sequence.
2. Write terms of a geometric sequence.
3. Use the formula for the general term of a geometric sequence.
4. Use the formula for the sum of the first n terms of a geometric sequence.
5. Find the value of an annuity.
6. Use the formula for the sum of an infinite geometric series.

Here we are at the closing moments of a job interview. You're shaking hands with the manager. You managed to answer all the tough questions without losing your poise, and now you've been offered a job. As a matter of fact, your qualifications are so terrific that you've been offered two jobs—one just the day before, with a rival company in the same field! One company offers $30,000 the first year, with increases of 6% per year for four years after that. The other offers $32,000 the first year, with annual increases of 3% per year after that. Over a five-year period, which is the better offer?

If salary raises amount to a certain percent each year, the yearly salaries over time form a geometric sequence. In this section, we investigate geometric sequences and their properties. After studying the section, you will be in a position to decide which job offer to accept: You will know which company will pay you more over five years.

① Find the common ratio of a geometric sequence.

Geometric Sequences

Figure 8.4 shows a sequence in which the number of squares is increasing. From left to right, the number of squares is 1, 5, 25, 125, and 625. In this sequence, each term after the first, 1, is obtained by multiplying the preceding term by a constant amount, namely 5. This sequence of increasing numbers of squares is an example of a *geometric sequence*.

Figure 8.4 A geometric sequence of squares

Definition of a Geometric Sequence

A **geometric sequence** is a sequence in which each term after the first is obtained by multiplying the preceding term by a fixed nonzero constant. The amount by which we multiply each time is called the **common ratio** of the sequence.

The common ratio, r, is found by dividing any term after the first term by the term that directly precedes it. In the following examples, the common ratio is found by dividing the second term by the first term, $\dfrac{a_2}{a_1}$.

Study Tip

When the common ratio of a geometric sequence is negative, the signs of the terms alternate.

Geometric sequence	Common ratio
$1, 5, 25, 125, 625, \ldots$	$r = \dfrac{5}{1} = 5$
$4, 8, 16, 32, 64, \ldots$	$r = \dfrac{8}{4} = 2$
$6, -12, 24, -48, 96, \ldots$	$r = \dfrac{-12}{6} = -2$
$9, -3, 1, -\dfrac{1}{3}, \dfrac{1}{9}, \ldots$	$r = \dfrac{-3}{9} = -\dfrac{1}{3}$

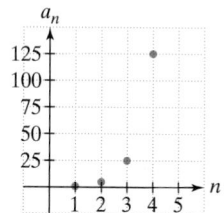

Figure 8.5 The graph of $\{a_n\} = 1, 5, 25, 125, \ldots$

Figure 8.5 shows a partial graph of the first geometric sequence in our list. The graph forms a set of discrete points lying on the exponential function $f(x) = 5^{x-1}$. This illustrates that **a geometric sequence with a positive common ratio other than 1 is an exponential function whose domain is the set of positive integers**.

How do we write out the terms of a geometric sequence when the first term and the common ratio are known? We multiply the first term by the common ratio to get the second term, multiply the second term by the common ratio to get the third term, and so on.

② Write terms of a geometric sequence.

EXAMPLE 1 **Writing the Terms of a Geometric Sequence**

Write the first six terms of the geometric sequence with first term 6 and common ratio $\frac{1}{3}$.

Solution The first term is 6. The second term is $6 \cdot \frac{1}{3}$, or 2. The third term is $2 \cdot \frac{1}{3}$, or $\frac{2}{3}$. The fourth term is $\frac{2}{3} \cdot \frac{1}{3}$, or $\frac{2}{9}$, and so on. The first six terms are

$$6, 2, \frac{2}{3}, \frac{2}{9}, \frac{2}{27}, \text{ and } \frac{2}{81}.$$

⊘ **Check Point 1** Write the first six terms of the geometric sequence with first term 12 and common ratio $\frac{1}{2}$.

③ Use the formula for the general term of a geometric sequence.

The General Term of a Geometric Sequence

Consider a geometric sequence whose first term is a_1 and whose common ratio is r. We are looking for a formula for the general term, a_n. Let's begin by writing the first six terms. The first term is a_1. The second term is $a_1 r$. The third term is $a_1 r \cdot r$, or $a_1 r^2$. The fourth term is $a_1 r^2 \cdot r$, or $a_1 r^3$, and so on. Starting with a_1 and multiplying each successive term by r, the first six terms are

$$a_1, \qquad a_1 r, \qquad a_1 r^2, \qquad a_1 r^3, \qquad a_1 r^4, \qquad a_1 r^5.$$

a_1, first term	a_2, second term	a_3, third term	a_4, fourth term	a_5, fifth term	a_6, sixth term

Can you see that the exponent on r is 1 less than the subscript of a denoting the term number?

a_3: third term $= a_1 r^2$ a_4: fourth term $= a_1 r^3$

One less than 3, or 2, is the exponent on r. One less than 4, or 3, is the exponent on r.

Thus, the formula for the nth term is

$$a_n = a_1 r^{n-1}.$$

One less than n, or $n - 1$, is the exponent on r.

General Term of a Geometric Sequence

The nth term (the general term) of a geometric sequence with first term a_1 and common ratio r is

$$a_n = a_1 r^{n-1}.$$

Study Tip

Be careful with the order of operations when evaluating

$$a_1 r^{n-1}.$$

First find r^{n-1}. Then multiply the result by a_1.

Geometric Population Growth

Economist Thomas Malthus (1766–1834) predicted that population would increase as a geometric sequence and food production would increase as an arithmetic sequence. He concluded that eventually population would exceed food production. If two sequences, one geometric and one arithmetic, are increasing, the geometric sequence will eventually overtake the arithmetic sequence, regardless of any head start that the arithmetic sequence might initially have.

EXAMPLE 2 **Using the Formula for the General Term of a Geometric Sequence**

Find the eighth term of the geometric sequence whose first term is -4 and whose common ratio is -2.

Solution To find the eighth term, a_8, we replace n in the formula with 8, a_1 with -4, and r with -2.

$$a_n = a_1 r^{n-1}$$
$$a_8 = -4(-2)^{8-1} = -4(-2)^7 = -4(-128) = 512$$

The eighth term is 512. We can check this result by writing the first eight terms of the sequence:

$$-4, 8, -16, 32, -64, 128, -256, 512.$$

⊘ **Check Point 2** Find the seventh term of the geometric sequence whose first term is 5 and whose common ratio is -3.

In Chapter 4, we studied exponential functions of the form $f(x) = b^x$ and used an exponential function to model the growth of the U.S. population from 1970 through 2007 (Example 1 on page 461). In our next example, we revisit the country's population growth over a shorter period of time, 2000 through 2006. Because a geometric sequence is an exponential function whose domain is the set of positive integers, geometric and exponential growth mean the same thing.

EXAMPLE 3 **Geometric Population Growth**

The table shows the population of the United States in 2000, with estimates given by the Census Bureau for 2001 through 2006.

Year	2000	2001	2002	2003	2004	2005	2006
Population (millions)	281.4	284.5	287.6	290.8	294.0	297.2	300.5

a. Show that the population is increasing geometrically.

b. Write the general term for the geometric sequence modeling the population of the United States, in millions, n years after 1999.

c. Project the U.S. population, in millions, for the year 2009.

Solution

a. First, we use the sequence of population growth, 281.4, 284.5, 287.6, 290.8, and so on, to divide the population for each year by the population in the preceding year.

$$\frac{284.5}{281.4} \approx 1.011, \quad \frac{287.6}{284.5} \approx 1.011, \quad \frac{290.8}{287.6} \approx 1.011$$

Continuing in this manner, we will keep getting approximately 1.011. This means that the population is increasing geometrically with $r \approx 1.011$. The population of the United States in any year shown in the sequence is approximately 1.011 times the population the year before.

b. The sequence of the U.S. population growth is

$$281.4, 284.5, 287.6, 290.8, 294.0, 297.2, 300.5, \dots.$$

Because the population is increasing geometrically, we can find the general term of this sequence using

$$a_n = a_1 r^{n-1}.$$

In this sequence, $a_1 = 281.4$ and [from part (a)] $r \approx 1.011$. We substitute these values into the formula for the general term. This gives the general term for the geometric sequence modeling the U.S. population, in millions, n years after 1999.

$$a_n = 281.4(1.011)^{n-1}$$

c. We can use the formula for the general term, a_n, in part (b) to project the U.S. population for the year 2009. The year 2009 is 10 years after 1999— that is, $2009 - 1999 = 10$. Thus, $n = 10$. We substitute 10 for n in $a_n = 281.4(1.011)^{n-1}$.

$$a_{10} = 281.4(1.011)^{10-1} = 281.4(1.011)^9 \approx 310.5$$

The model projects that the United States will have a population of approximately 310.5 million in the year 2009.

⬤

Ø Check Point 3 Write the general term for the geometric sequence

$$3, 6, 12, 24, 48, \dots.$$

Then use the formula for the general term to find the eighth term.

④ Use the formula for the sum of the first n terms of a geometric sequence.

The Sum of the First *n* Terms of a Geometric Sequence

The sum of the first n terms of a geometric sequence, denoted by S_n and called the **nth partial sum**, can be found without having to add up all the terms. Recall that the first n terms of a geometric sequence are

$$a_1, a_1 r, a_1 r^2, \dots, a_1 r^{n-2}, a_1 r^{n-1}.$$

We proceed as follows:

$$S_n = a_1 + a_1 r + a_1 r^2 + \cdots + a_1 r^{n-2} + a_1 r^{n-1} \qquad \text{S_n is the sum of the first n terms of the sequence.}$$

$$rS_n = a_1 r + a_1 r^2 + a_1 r^3 + \cdots + a_1 r^{n-1} + a_1 r^n \qquad \text{Multiply both sides of the equation by r.}$$

$$S_n - rS_n = a_1 - a_1 r^n \qquad \text{Subtract the second equation from the first equation.}$$

$$S_n(1 - r) = a_1(1 - r^n) \qquad \text{Factor out S_n on the left and a_1 on the right.}$$

$$S_n = \frac{a_1(1 - r^n)}{1 - r}. \qquad \text{Solve for S_n by dividing both sides by $1 - r$ (assuming that $r \neq 1$).}$$

We have proved the following result:

> **The Sum of the First n Terms of a Geometric Sequence**
>
> The sum, S_n, of the first n terms of a geometric sequence is given by
>
> $$S_n = \frac{a_1(1 - r^n)}{1 - r},$$
>
> in which a_1 is the first term and r is the common ratio ($r \neq 1$).

To find the sum of the terms of a geometric sequence, we need to know the first term, a_1, the common ratio, r, and the number of terms, n. The following examples illustrate how to use this formula.

EXAMPLE 4 **Finding the Sum of the First n Terms of a Geometric Sequence**

Find the sum of the first 18 terms of the geometric sequence: $2, -8, 32, -128, \ldots.$

Solution To find the sum of the first 18 terms, S_{18}, we replace n in the formula with 18.

$$S_n = \frac{a_1(1 - r^n)}{1 - r}$$

$$S_{18} = \frac{a_1(1 - r^{18})}{1 - r}$$

The first term, a_1, is 2. We must find r, the common ratio.

We can find the common ratio by dividing the second term of $2, -8, 32, -128, \ldots$ by the first term.

$$r = \frac{a_2}{a_1} = \frac{-8}{2} = -4$$

Now we are ready to find the sum of the first 18 terms of $2, -8, 32, -128, \ldots.$

$$S_n = \frac{a_1(1 - r^n)}{1 - r} \qquad \text{Use the formula for the sum of the first } n \text{ terms of a geometric sequence.}$$

$$S_{18} = \frac{2[1 - (-4)^{18}]}{1 - (-4)} \qquad a_1 \text{ (the first term)} = 2, r = -4, \text{ and } n = 18 \text{ because we want the sum of the first 18 terms.}$$

$$= -27{,}487{,}790{,}694 \qquad \text{Use a calculator.}$$

The sum of the first 18 terms is $-27{,}487{,}790{,}694$. Equivalently, this number is the 18th partial sum of the sequence $2, -8, 32, -128, \ldots.$ ●

⊘ Check Point **4** Find the sum of the first nine terms of the geometric sequence: $2, -6, 18, -54, \ldots.$

EXAMPLE 5 **Using S_n to Evaluate a Summation**

Find the following sum: $\displaystyle\sum_{i=1}^{10} 6 \cdot 2^i.$

Solution Let's write out a few terms in the sum.

$$\sum_{i=1}^{10} 6 \cdot 2^i = 6 \cdot 2 + 6 \cdot 2^2 + 6 \cdot 2^3 + \cdots + 6 \cdot 2^{10}$$

Technology

To find

$$\sum_{i=1}^{10} 6 \cdot 2^i$$

on a graphing utility, enter

[SUM] [SEQ] $(6 \times 2^x, x, 1, 10, 1)$.

Then press [ENTER].

```
sum(seq(6*2^X,X,
1,10,1))
          12276
```

Do you see that each term after the first is obtained by multiplying the preceding term by 2? To find the sum of the 10 terms ($n = 10$), we need to know the first term, a_1, and the common ratio, r. The first term is $6 \cdot 2$ or 12: $a_1 = 12$. The common ratio is 2.

$$S_n = \frac{a_1(1 - r^n)}{1 - r} \quad \text{Use the formula for the sum of the first } n \text{ terms of a geometric sequence.}$$

$$S_{10} = \frac{12(1 - 2^{10})}{1 - 2} \quad \begin{array}{l} a_1 \text{ (the first term)} = 12, r = 2, \text{ and } n = 10 \\ \text{because we are adding ten terms.} \end{array}$$

$$= 12{,}276 \quad \text{Use a calculator.}$$

Thus,

$$\sum_{i=1}^{10} 6 \cdot 2^i = 12{,}276.$$

⌀ **Check Point 5** Find the following sum: $\displaystyle\sum_{i=1}^{8} 2 \cdot 3^i$.

Some of the exercises in the previous exercise set involved situations in which salaries increased by a fixed amount each year. A more realistic situation is one in which salary raises increase by a certain percent each year. Example 6 shows how such a situation can be modeled using a geometric sequence.

EXAMPLE 6 Computing a Lifetime Salary

A union contract specifies that each worker will receive a 5% pay increase each year for the next 30 years. One worker is paid $20,000 the first year. What is this person's total lifetime salary over a 30-year period?

Solution The salary for the first year is $20,000. With a 5% raise, the second-year salary is computed as follows:

Salary for year 2 $= 20{,}000 + 20{,}000(0.05) = 20{,}000(1 + 0.05) = 20{,}000(1.05)$.

Each year, the salary is 1.05 times what it was in the previous year. Thus, the salary for year 3 is 1.05 times $20{,}000(1.05)$, or $20{,}000(1.05)^2$. The salaries for the first five years are given in the table.

Yearly Salaries

Year 1	Year 2	Year 3	Year 4	Year 5	...
20,000	20,000(1.05)	$20{,}000(1.05)^2$	$20{,}000(1.05)^3$	$20{,}000(1.05)^4$...

The numbers in the bottom row form a geometric sequence with $a_1 = 20{,}000$ and $r = 1.05$. To find the total salary over 30 years, we use the formula for the sum of the first n terms of a geometric sequence, with $n = 30$.

$$S_n = \frac{a_1(1 - r^n)}{1 - r}$$

$$S_{30} = \frac{20{,}000[1 - (1.05)^{30}]}{1 - 1.05}$$

Total salary over 30 years

$$= \frac{20{,}000[1 - (1.05)^{30}]}{-0.05}$$

$$\approx 1{,}328{,}777 \quad \text{Use a calculator.}$$

The total salary over the 30-year period is approximately $1,328,777.

⊘ Check Point **6** A job pays a salary of $30,000 the first year. During the next 29 years, the salary increases by 6% each year. What is the total lifetime salary over the 30-year period?

⑤ Find the value of an annuity.

Annuities

The compound interest formula

$$A = P(1 + r)^t$$

gives the future value, A, after t years, when a fixed amount of money, P, the principal, is deposited in an account that pays an annual interest rate r (in decimal form) compounded once a year. However, money is often invested in small amounts at periodic intervals. For example, to save for retirement, you might decide to place $1000 into an Individual Retirement Account (IRA) at the end of each year until you retire. An **annuity** is a sequence of equal payments made at equal time periods. An IRA is an example of an annuity.

Suppose P dollars is deposited into an account at the end of each year. The account pays an annual interest rate, r, compounded annually. At the end of the first year, the account contains P dollars. At the end of the second year, P dollars is deposited again. At the time of this deposit, the first deposit has received interest earned during the second year. The **value of the annuity** is the sum of all deposits made plus all interest paid. Thus, the value of the annuity after two years is

$$P + P(1 + r).$$

Deposit of P dollars at end of second year	First-year deposit of P dollars with interest earned for a year

The value of the annuity after three years is

$$P \quad + \quad P(1 + r) \quad + \quad P(1 + r)^2.$$

Deposit of P dollars at end of third year	Second-year deposit of P dollars with interest earned for a year	First-year deposit of P dollars with interest earned over two years

The value of the annuity after t years is

$$P + P(1 + r) + P(1 + r)^2 + P(1 + r)^3 + \cdots + P(1 + r)^{t-1}.$$

Deposit of P dollars at end of year t	First-year deposit of P dollars with interest earned over $t - 1$ years

This is the sum of the terms of a geometric sequence with first term P and common ratio $1 + r$. We use the formula

$$S_n = \frac{a_1(1 - r^n)}{1 - r}$$

to find the sum of the terms:

$$S_t = \frac{P[1 - (1 + r)^t]}{1 - (1 + r)} = \frac{P[1 - (1 + r)^t]}{-r} = \frac{P[(1 + r)^t - 1]}{r}.$$

This formula gives the value of an annuity after t years if interest is compounded once a year. We can adjust the formula to find the value of an annuity if equal payments are made at the end of each of n yearly compounding periods.

Value of an Annuity: Interest Compounded n Times per Year

If P is the deposit made at the end of each compounding period for an annuity at r percent annual interest compounded n times per year, the value, A, of the annuity after t years is

$$A = \frac{P\left[\left(1 + \frac{r}{n}\right)^{nt} - 1\right]}{\frac{r}{n}}.$$

Stashing Cash and Making Taxes Less Taxing

As you prepare for your future career, retirement probably seems very far away. Making regular deposits into an IRA may not be fun, but there is a special incentive from Uncle Sam that makes it far more appealing. Traditional IRAs are **tax-deferred savings plans**. This means that you do not pay taxes on deposits and interest until you begin withdrawals, typically at retirement. Before then, yearly deposits count as adjustments to gross income and are not part of your taxable income. Not only do you get a tax break now, but you ultimately earn more. This is because you do not pay taxes on interest from year to year, allowing earnings to accumulate until you start withdrawals. With a tax code that encourages long-term savings, opening an IRA early in your career is a smart way to gain more control over how you will spend a large part of your life.

EXAMPLE 7 **Determining the Value of an Annuity**

At age 25, to save for retirement, you decide to deposit $200 at the end of each month into an IRA that pays 7.5% compounded monthly.

a. How much will you have from the IRA when you retire at age 65?

b. Find the interest.

Solution

a. Because you are 25, the amount that you will have from the IRA when you retire at 65 is its value after 40 years.

$$A = \frac{P\left[\left(1 + \frac{r}{n}\right)^{nt} - 1\right]}{\frac{r}{n}}$$

Use the formula for the value of an annuity.

$$A = \frac{200\left[\left(1 + \frac{0.075}{12}\right)^{12 \cdot 40} - 1\right]}{\frac{0.075}{12}}$$

The annuity involves month-end deposits of $200: $P = 200$. The interest rate is 7.5%: $r = 0.075$. The interest is compounded monthly: $n = 12$. The number of years is 40: $t = 40$.

$$= \frac{200[(1 + 0.00625)^{480} - 1]}{0.00625}$$

Using parentheses keys, this can be performed in a single step on a graphing calculator.

$$= \frac{200[(1.00625)^{480} - 1]}{0.00625}$$

$$\approx \frac{200(19.8989 - 1)}{0.00625}$$

Use a calculator to find $(1.00625)^{480}$:

$1.00625 \boxed{y^x} 480 \boxed{=}$.

$$\approx 604{,}765$$

After 40 years, you will have approximately $604,765 when retiring at age 65.

b. Interest = Value of the IRA − Total deposits

$$\approx \$604{,}765 - \$200 \cdot 12 \cdot 40$$

> $200 per month × 12 months per year × 40 years

$$= \$604{,}765 - \$96{,}000 = \$508{,}765$$

The interest is approximately $508,765, more than five times the amount of your contributions to the IRA. ⬤

⊘ Check Point 7 At age 30, to save for retirement, you decide to deposit $100 at the end of each month into an IRA that pays 9.5% compounded monthly.

 a. How much will you have from the IRA when you retire at age 65?

 b. Find the interest.

⑥ Use the formula for the sum of an infinite geometric series.

Geometric Series

An infinite sum of the form

$$a_1 + a_1 r + a_1 r^2 + a_1 r^3 + \cdots + a_1 r^{n-1} + \cdots$$

with first term a_1 and common ratio r is called an **infinite geometric series**. How can we determine which infinite geometric series have sums and which do not? We look at what happens to r^n as n gets larger in the formula for the sum of the first n terms of this series, namely

$$S_n = \frac{a_1(1 - r^n)}{1 - r}.$$

If r is any number between -1 and 1, that is, $-1 < r < 1$, the term r^n approaches 0 as n gets larger. For example, consider what happens to r^n for $r = \frac{1}{2}$:

$$\left(\frac{1}{2}\right)^1 = \frac{1}{2} \quad \left(\frac{1}{2}\right)^2 = \frac{1}{4} \quad \left(\frac{1}{2}\right)^3 = \frac{1}{8} \quad \left(\frac{1}{2}\right)^4 = \frac{1}{16} \quad \left(\frac{1}{2}\right)^5 = \frac{1}{32} \quad \left(\frac{1}{2}\right)^6 = \frac{1}{64}.$$

These numbers are approaching 0 as n gets larger.

Take another look at the formula for the sum of the first n terms of a geometric sequence.

$$S_n = \frac{a_1(1 - r^n)}{1 - r}$$

If $-1 < r < 1$, r^n approaches 0 as n gets larger.

Let us replace r^n with 0 in the formula for S_n. This change gives us a formula for the sum of an infinite geometric series with a common ratio between -1 and 1.

The Sum of an Infinite Geometric Series

If $-1 < r < 1$ (equivalently, $|r| < 1$), then the sum of the infinite geometric series

$$a_1 + a_1 r + a_1 r^2 + a_1 r^3 + \cdots,$$

in which a_1 is the first term and r is the common ratio, is given by

$$S = \frac{a_1}{1 - r}.$$

If $|r| \geq 1$, the infinite series does not have a sum.

To use the formula for the sum of an infinite geometric series, we need to know the first term and the common ratio. For example, consider

First term, a_1, is $\frac{1}{2}$.

$$\frac{1}{2} + \frac{1}{4} + \frac{1}{8} + \frac{1}{16} + \frac{1}{32} + \cdots.$$

Common ratio, r, is $\frac{a_2}{a_1}$.

$$r = \frac{1}{4} \div \frac{1}{2} = \frac{1}{4} \cdot 2 = \frac{1}{2}$$

With $r = \dfrac{1}{2}$, the condition that $|r| < 1$ is met, so the infinite geometric series has a sum given by $S = \dfrac{a_1}{1-r}$. The sum of the series is found as follows:

$$\frac{1}{2} + \frac{1}{4} + \frac{1}{8} + \frac{1}{16} + \frac{1}{32} + \cdots = \frac{a_1}{1-r} = \frac{\dfrac{1}{2}}{1 - \dfrac{1}{2}} = \frac{\dfrac{1}{2}}{\dfrac{1}{2}} = 1.$$

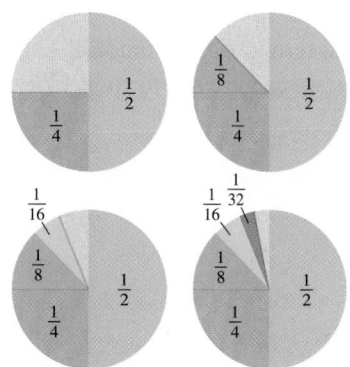

Figure 8.6 The sum $\frac{1}{2} + \frac{1}{4} + \frac{1}{8} + \frac{1}{16} + \frac{1}{32} + \cdots$ is approaching 1.

Thus, the sum of the infinite geometric series is 1. Notice how this is illustrated in **Figure 8.6**. As more terms are included, the sum is approaching the area of one complete circle.

EXAMPLE 8 **Finding the Sum of an Infinite Geometric Series**

Find the sum of the infinite geometric series: $\frac{3}{8} - \frac{3}{16} + \frac{3}{32} - \frac{3}{64} + \cdots$.

Solution Before finding the sum, we must find the common ratio.

$$r = \frac{a_2}{a_1} = \frac{-\dfrac{3}{16}}{\dfrac{3}{8}} = -\frac{3}{16} \cdot \frac{8}{3} = -\frac{1}{2}$$

Because $r = -\frac{1}{2}$, the condition that $|r| < 1$ is met. Thus, the infinite geometric series has a sum.

$$S = \frac{a_1}{1-r}$$

This is the formula for the sum of an infinite geometric series. Let $a_1 = \dfrac{3}{8}$ and $r = -\dfrac{1}{2}$.

$$= \frac{\dfrac{3}{8}}{1 - \left(-\dfrac{1}{2}\right)} = \frac{\dfrac{3}{8}}{\dfrac{3}{2}} = \frac{3}{8} \cdot \frac{2}{3} = \frac{1}{4}$$

Thus, the sum of $\frac{3}{8} - \frac{3}{16} + \frac{3}{32} - \frac{3}{64} + \cdots$ is $\frac{1}{4}$. Put in an informal way, as we continue to add more and more terms, the sum is approximately $\frac{1}{4}$. ●

✓ Check Point **8** Find the sum of the infinite geometric series: $3 + 2 + \frac{4}{3} + \frac{8}{9} + \cdots$.

We can use the formula for the sum of an infinite geometric series to express a repeating decimal as a fraction in lowest terms.

EXAMPLE 9 **Writing a Repeating Decimal as a Fraction**

Express $0.\overline{7}$ as a fraction in lowest terms.

Solution

$$0.\overline{7} = 0.7777\ldots = \frac{7}{10} + \frac{7}{100} + \frac{7}{1000} + \frac{7}{10,000} + \cdots$$

Observe that $0.\overline{7}$ is an infinite geometric series with first term $\frac{7}{10}$ and common ratio $\frac{1}{10}$. Because $r = \frac{1}{10}$, the condition that $|r| < 1$ is met. Thus, we can use our formula to find the sum. Therefore,

$$0.\overline{7} = \frac{a_1}{1-r} = \frac{\frac{7}{10}}{1 - \frac{1}{10}} = \frac{\frac{7}{10}}{\frac{9}{10}} = \frac{7}{10} \cdot \frac{10}{9} = \frac{7}{9}.$$

An equivalent fraction for $0.\overline{7}$ is $\frac{7}{9}$.

⊘ Check Point 9 Express $0.\overline{9}$ as a fraction in lowest terms.

Infinite geometric series have many applications, as illustrated in Example 10.

EXAMPLE 10 **Tax Rebates and the Multiplier Effect**

A tax rebate that returns a certain amount of money to taxpayers can have a total effect on the economy that is many times this amount. In economics, this phenomenon is called the **multiplier effect**. Suppose, for example, that the government reduces taxes so that each consumer has $2000 more income. The government assumes that each person will spend 70% of this (= $1400). The individuals and businesses receiving this $1400 in turn spend 70% of it (= $980), creating extra income for other people to spend, and so on. Determine the total amount spent on consumer goods from the initial $2000 tax rebate.

Solution The total amount spent is given by the infinite geometric series

$$1400 + 980 + 686 + \cdots.$$

70% of 1400	70% of 980

The first term is 1400: $a_1 = 1400$. The common ratio is 70%, or 0.7: $r = 0.7$. Because $r = 0.7$, the condition that $|r| < 1$ is met. Thus, we can use our formula to find the sum. Therefore,

$$1400 + 980 + 686 + \cdots = \frac{a_1}{1-r} = \frac{1400}{1 - 0.7} \approx 4667.$$

This means that the total amount spent on consumer goods from the initial $2000 rebate is approximately $4667.

⊘ Check Point 10 Rework Example 10 and determine the total amount spent on consumer goods with a $1000 tax rebate and 80% spending down the line.

Exercise Set 8.3

Practice Exercises

In Exercises 1–8, write the first five terms of each geometric sequence.

1. $a_1 = 5,° r = 3$
2. $a_1 = 4,° r = 3$

3. $a_1 = 20,° r = \frac{1}{2}$
4. $a_1 = 24,° r = \frac{1}{3}$

5. $a_n = -4a_{n-1},° a_1 = 10$
6. $a_n = -3a_{n-1},° a_1 = 10$

7. $a_n = -5a_{n-1},° a_1 = -6$
8. $a_n = -6a_{n-1},° a_1 = -2$

In Exercises 9–16, use the formula for the general term (the nth term) of a geometric sequence to find the indicated term of each sequence with the given first term, a_1, and common ratio, r.

9. Find a_8 when $a_1 = 6, r = 2$.

10. Find a_8 when $a_1 = 5, r = 3$.

11. Find a_{12} when $a_1 = 5, r = -2$.

12. Find a_{12} when $a_1 = 4, r = -2$.

13. Find a_{40} when $a_1 = 1000, r = -\frac{1}{2}$.

14. Find a_{30} when $a_1 = 8000, r = -\frac{1}{2}$.

15. Find a_8 when $a_1 = 1,000,000, r = 0.1$.

16. Find a_8 when $a_1 = 40,000, r = 0.1$.

In Exercises 17–24, write a formula for the general term (the nth term) of each geometric sequence. Then use the formula for a_n to find a_7, the seventh term of the sequence.

17. $3, 12, 48, 192, \ldots$
18. $3, 15, 75, 375, \ldots$

19. $18, 6, 2, \frac{2}{3}, \ldots$
20. $12, 6, 3, \frac{3}{2}, \ldots$

21. $1.5, -3, 6, -12, \ldots$
22. $5, -1, \frac{1}{5}, -\frac{1}{25}, \ldots$

23. $0.0004, -0.004, 0.04, -0.4, \ldots$

24. $0.0007, -0.007, 0.07, -0.7, \ldots$

Use the formula for the sum of the first n terms of a geometric sequence to solve Exercises 25–30.

25. Find the sum of the first 12 terms of the geometric sequence: $2, 6, 18, 54, \ldots$.

26. Find the sum of the first 12 terms of the geometric sequence: $3, 6, 12, 24, \ldots$.

27. Find the sum of the first 11 terms of the geometric sequence: $3, -6, 12, -24, \ldots$.

28. Find the sum of the first 11 terms of the geometric sequence: $4, -12, 36, -108, \ldots$.

29. Find the sum of the first 14 terms of the geometric sequence: $-\frac{3}{2}, 3, -6, 12, \ldots$.

30. Find the sum of the first 14 terms of the geometric sequence: $-\frac{1}{24}, \frac{1}{12}, -\frac{1}{6}, \frac{1}{3}, \ldots$.

In Exercises 31–36, find the indicated sum. Use the formula for the sum of the first n terms of a geometric sequence.

31. $\sum_{i=1}^{8} 3^i$
32. $\sum_{i=1}^{6} 4^i$
33. $\sum_{i=1}^{10} 5 \cdot 2^i$

34. $\sum_{i=1}^{7} 4(-3)^i$
35. $\sum_{i=1}^{6} \left(\frac{1}{2}\right)^{i+1}$
36. $\sum_{i=1}^{6} \left(\frac{1}{3}\right)^{i+1}$

In Exercises 37–44, find the sum of each infinite geometric series.

37. $1 + \frac{1}{3} + \frac{1}{9} + \frac{1}{27} + \cdots$
38. $1 + \frac{1}{4} + \frac{1}{16} + \frac{1}{64} + \cdots$

39. $3 + \frac{3}{4} + \frac{3}{4^2} + \frac{3}{4^3} + \cdots$
40. $5 + \frac{5}{6} + \frac{5}{6^2} + \frac{5}{6^3} + \cdots$

41. $1 - \frac{1}{2} + \frac{1}{4} - \frac{1}{8} + \cdots$
42. $3 - 1 + \frac{1}{3} - \frac{1}{9} + \cdots$

43. $\sum_{i=1}^{\infty} 8(-0.3)^{i-1}$
44. $\sum_{i=1}^{\infty} 12(-0.7)^{i-1}$

In Exercises 45–50, express each repeating decimal as a fraction in lowest terms.

45. $0.\overline{5} = \frac{5}{10} + \frac{5}{100} + \frac{5}{1000} + \frac{5}{10,000} + \cdots$

46. $0.\overline{1} = \frac{1}{10} + \frac{1}{100} + \frac{1}{1000} + \frac{1}{10,000} + \cdots$

47. $0.\overline{47} = \frac{47}{100} + \frac{47}{10,000} + \frac{47}{1,000,000} + \cdots$

48. $0.\overline{83} = \frac{83}{100} + \frac{83}{10,000} + \frac{83}{1,000,000} + \cdots$

49. $0.\overline{257}$
50. $0.\overline{529}$

In Exercises 51–56, the general term of a sequence is given. Determine whether the sequence is arithmetic, geometric, or neither. If the sequence is arithmetic, find the common difference; if it is geometric, find the common ratio.

51. $a_n = n + 5$
52. $a_n = n - 3$

53. $a_n = 2^n$
54. $a_n = \left(\frac{1}{2}\right)^n$

55. $a_n = n^2 + 5$
56. $a_n = n^2 - 3$

Practice Plus

In Exercises 57–62, let

$$\{a_n\} = -5, 10, -20, 40, \ldots,$$
$$\{b_n\} = 10, -5, -20, -35, \ldots,$$

and

$$\{c_n\} = -2, 1, -\frac{1}{2}, \frac{1}{4}, \ldots.$$

57. Find $a_{10} + b_{10}$.
58. Find $a_{11} + b_{11}$.

59. Find the difference between the sum of the first 10 terms of $\{a_n\}$ and the sum of the first 10 terms of $\{b_n\}$.

60. Find the difference between the sum of the first 11 terms of $\{a_n\}$ and the sum of the first 11 terms of $\{b_n\}$.

61. Find the product of the sum of the first 6 terms of $\{a_n\}$ and the sum of the infinite series containing all the terms of $\{c_n\}$.

62. Find the product of the sum of the first 9 terms of $\{a_n\}$ and the sum of the infinite series containing all the terms of $\{c_n\}$.

In Exercises 63–64, find a_2 and a_3 for each geometric sequence.

63. $8, a_2, a_3, 27$
64. $2, a_2, a_3, -54$

Application Exercises

Use the formula for the general term (the nth term) of a geometric sequence to solve Exercises 65–68.

In Exercises 65–66, suppose you save $1 the first day of a month, $2 the second day, $4 the third day, and so on. That is, each day you save twice as much as you did the day before.

65. What will you put aside for savings on the fifteenth day of the month?

66. What will you put aside for savings on the thirtieth day of the month?

67. A professional baseball player signs a contract with a beginning salary of $3,000,000 for the first year and an annual increase of 4% per year beginning in the second year. That is, beginning in year 2, the athlete's salary will be 1.04 times what it was in the previous year. What is the athlete's salary for year 7 of the contract? Round to the nearest dollar.

68. You are offered a job that pays $30,000 for the first year with an annual increase of 5% per year beginning in the second year. That is, beginning in year 2, your salary will be 1.05 times what it was in the previous year. What can you expect to earn in your sixth year on the job?

In Exercises 69–70, you will develop geometric sequences that model the population growth for California and Texas, the two most-populated U.S. states.

69. The table shows population estimates for California from 2003 through 2006 from the U.S. Census Bureau.

Year	2003	2004	2005	2006
Population in millions	35.48	35.89	36.13	36.46

 a. Divide the population for each year by the population in the preceding year. Round to two decimal places and show that California has a population increase that is approximately geometric.

 b. Write the general term of the geometric sequence modeling California's population, in millions, *n* years after 2002.

 c. Use your model from part (b) to project California's population, in millions, for the year 2010. Round to two decimal places.

70. The table shows population estimates for Texas from 2003 through 2006 from the U.S. Census Bureau.

Year	2003	2004	2005	2006
Population in millions	22.12	22.49	22.86	23.41

 a. Divide the population for each year by the population in the preceding year. Round to two decimal places and show that Texas has a population increase that is approximately geometric.

 b. Write the general term of the geometric sequence modeling Texas's population, in millions, *n* years after 2002.

 c. Use your model from part (b) to project Texas's population, in millions, for the year 2010. Round to two decimal places.

Use the formula for the sum of the first n terms of a geometric sequence to solve Exercises 71–76.

In Exercises 71–72, you save $1 the first day of a month, $2 the second day, $4 the third day, continuing to double your savings each day.

71. What will your total savings be for the first 15 days?

72. What will your total savings be for the first 30 days?

73. A job pays a salary of $24,000 the first year. During the next 19 years, the salary increases by 5% each year. What is the total lifetime salary over the 20-year period? Round to the nearest dollar.

74. You are investigating two employment opportunities. Company A offers $30,000 the first year. During the next four years, the salary is guaranteed to increase by 6% per year. Company B offers $32,000 the first year, with guaranteed annual increases of 3% per year after that. Which company offers the better total salary for a five-year contract? By how much? Round to the nearest dollar.

75. A pendulum swings through an arc of 20 inches. On each successive swing, the length of the arc is 90% of the previous length.

$$20, \quad 0.9(20), \quad 0.9^2(20), \quad 0.9^3(20), \ldots$$

| 1st swing | 2nd swing | 3rd swing | 4th swing |

After 10 swings, what is the total length of the distance the pendulum has swung?

76. A pendulum swings through an arc of 16 inches. On each successive swing, the length of the arc is 96% of the previous length.

$$16, \quad 0.96(16), \quad (0.96)^2(16), \quad (0.96)^3(16), \ldots$$

| 1st swing | 2nd swing | 3rd swing | 4th swing |

After 10 swings, what is the total length of the distance the pendulum has swung?

Use the formula for the value of an annuity to solve Exercises 77–84. Round answers to the nearest dollar.

77. To save money for a sabbatical to earn a master's degree, you deposit $2000 at the end of each year in an annuity that pays 7.5% compounded annually.

 a. How much will you have saved at the end of five years?

 b. Find the interest.

78. To save money for a sabbatical to earn a master's degree, you deposit $2500 at the end of each year in an annuity that pays 6.25% compounded annually.

 a. How much will you have saved at the end of five years?

 b. Find the interest.

79. At age 25, to save for retirement, you decide to deposit $50 at the end of each month in an IRA that pays 5.5% compounded monthly.

 a. How much will you have from the IRA when you retire at age 65?

 b. Find the interest.

80. At age 25, to save for retirement, you decide to deposit $75 at the end of each month in an IRA that pays 6.5% compounded monthly.

 a. How much will you have from the IRA when you retire at age 65?

 b. Find the interest.

81. To offer scholarship funds to children of employees, a company invests $10,000 at the end of every three months in an annuity that pays 10.5% compounded quarterly.

 a. How much will the company have in scholarship funds at the end of ten years?

 b. Find the interest.

82. To offer scholarship funds to children of employees, a company invests $15,000 at the end of every three months in an annuity that pays 9% compounded quarterly.

 a. How much will the company have in scholarship funds at the end of ten years?

 b. Find the interest.

83. Here are two ways of investing $30,000 for 20 years.

Lump-Sum Deposit	Rate	Time
$30,000	5% compounded annually	20 years

Periodic Deposits	Rate	Time
$1500 at the end of each year	5% compounded annually	20 years

After 20 years, how much more will you have from the lump-sum investment than from the annuity?

84. Here are two ways of investing $40,000 for 25 years.

Lump-Sum Deposit	Rate	Time
$40,000	6.5% compounded annually	25 years

Periodic Deposits	Rate	Time
$1600 at the end of each year	6.5% compounded annually	25 years

After 25 years, how much more will you have from the lump-sum investment than from the annuity?

Use the formula for the sum of an infinite geometric series to solve Exercises 85–87.

85. A new factory in a small town has an annual payroll of $6 million. It is expected that 60% of this money will be spent in the town by factory personnel. The people in the town who receive this money are expected to spend 60% of what they receive in the town, and so on. What is the total of all this spending, called the *total economic impact* of the factory, on the town each year?

86. How much additional spending will be generated by a $10 billion tax rebate if 60% of all income is spent?

87. If the shading process shown in the figure is continued indefinitely, what fractional part of the largest square will eventually be shaded?

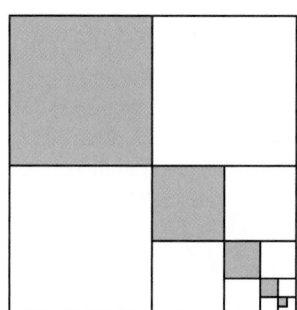

Writing in Mathematics

88. What is a geometric sequence? Give an example with your explanation.

89. What is the common ratio in a geometric sequence?

90. Explain how to find the general term of a geometric sequence.

91. Explain how to find the sum of the first n terms of a geometric sequence without having to add up all the terms.

92. What is an annuity?

93. What is the difference between a geometric sequence and an infinite geometric series?

94. How do you determine if an infinite geometric series has a sum? Explain how to find the sum of such an infinite geometric series.

95. Would you rather have $10,000,000 and a brand new BMW, or 1¢ today, 2¢ tomorrow, 4¢ on day 3, 8¢ on day 4, 16¢ on day 5, and so on, for 30 days? Explain.

96. For the first 30 days of a flu outbreak, the number of students on your campus who become ill is increasing. Which is worse: The number of students with the flu is increasing arithmetically or is increasing geometrically? Explain your answer.

Technology Exercises

97. Use the ⎡SEQ⎤ (sequence) capability of a graphing utility and the formula you obtained for a_n to verify the value you found for a_7 in any three exercises from Exercises 17–24.

98. Use the capability of a graphing utility to calculate the sum of a sequence to verify any three of your answers to Exercises 31–36.

In Exercises 99–100, use a graphing utility to graph the function. Determine the horizontal asymptote for the graph of f and discuss its relationship to the sum of the given series.

99. Function **Series**

$$f(x) = \frac{2\left[1 - \left(\frac{1}{3}\right)^x\right]}{1 - \frac{1}{3}} \qquad 2 + 2\left(\frac{1}{3}\right) + 2\left(\frac{1}{3}\right)^2 + 2\left(\frac{1}{3}\right)^3 + \cdots$$

100. Function Series

$$f(x) = \frac{4[1 - (0.6)^x]}{1 - 0.6} \circ \text{°}4 + 4(0.6) + 4(0.6)^2 + 4(0.6)^3 + \cdots$$

Critical Thinking Exercises

Make Sense? *In Exercises 101–104, determine whether each statement makes sense or does not make sense, and explain your reasoning.*

101. There's no end to the number of geometric sequences that I can generate whose first term is 5 if I pick nonzero numbers r and multiply 5 by each value of r repeatedly.

102. I've noticed that the big difference between arithmetic and geometric sequences is that arithmetic sequences are based on addition and geometric sequences are based on multiplication.

103. I modeled California's population growth with a geometric sequence, so my model is an exponential function whose domain is the set of natural numbers.

104. I used a formula to find the sum of the infinite geometric series $3 + 1 + \frac{1}{3} + \frac{1}{9} + \cdots$ and then checked my answer by actually adding all the terms.

In Exercises 105–108, determine whether each statement is true or false. If the statement is false, make the necessary change(s) to produce a true statement.

105. The sequence $2, 6, 24, 120, \ldots$ is an example of a geometric sequence.

106. The sum of the geometric series $\frac{1}{2} + \frac{1}{4} + \frac{1}{8} + \cdots + \frac{1}{512}$ can only be estimated without knowing precisely what terms occur between $\frac{1}{8}$ and $\frac{1}{512}$.

107. $10 - 5 + \dfrac{5}{2} - \dfrac{5}{4} + \cdots = \dfrac{10}{1 - \dfrac{1}{2}}$

108. If the nth term of a geometric sequence is $a_n = 3(0.5)^{n-1}$, the common ratio is $\frac{1}{2}$.

109. In a pest-eradication program, sterilized male flies are released into the general population each day. Ninety percent of those flies will survive a given day. How many flies should be released each day if the long-range goal of the program is to keep 20,000 sterilized flies in the population?

110. You are now 25 years old and would like to retire at age 55 with a retirement fund of $1,000,000. How much should you deposit at the end of each month for the next 30 years in an IRA paying 10% annual interest compounded monthly to achieve your goal? Round to the nearest dollar.

Group Exercise

111. Group members serve as a financial team analyzing the three options given to the professional baseball player described in the chapter opener on page 667. As a group, determine which option provides the most amount of money over the six-year contract and which provides the least. Describe one advantage and one disadvantage to each option.

Preview Exercises

Exercises 112–114 will help you prepare for the material covered in the next section.

In Exercises 112–113, show that

$$1 + 2 + 3 + \cdots + n = \frac{n(n + 1)}{2}$$

is true for the given value of n.

112. $n = 3$: Show that $1 + 2 + 3 = \dfrac{3(3 + 1)}{2}$.

113. $n = 5$: Show that $1 + 2 + 3 + 4 + 5 = \dfrac{5(5 + 1)}{2}$.

114. Simplify: $\dfrac{k(k + 1)(2k + 1)}{6} + (k + 1)^2$.

Chapter 8 Mid-Chapter Check Point

What You Know: We learned that a sequence is a function whose domain is the set of positive integers. In an arithmetic sequence, each term after the first differs from the preceding term by a constant, the common difference, d. In a geometric sequence, each term after the first is obtained by multiplying the preceding term by a nonzero constant, the common ratio, r. We found the general term of arithmetic sequences $[a_n = a_1 + (n - 1)d]$ and geometric sequences $[a_n = a_1 r^{n-1}]$ and used these formulas to find particular terms. We determined the sum of the first n terms of arithmetic sequences $\left[S_n = \dfrac{n}{2}(a_1 + a_n)\right]$ and geometric sequences $\left[S_n = \dfrac{a_1(1 - r^n)}{1 - r}\right]$. Finally, we determined the sum of an infinite geometric series,

$$a_1 + a_1 r + a_1 r^2 + a_1 r^3 + \cdots, \text{ if } -1 < r < 1 \left(S = \frac{a_1}{1 - r}\right).$$

In Exercises 1–4, write the first five terms of each sequence. Assume that d represents the common difference of an arithmetic sequence and r represents the common ratio of a geometric sequence.

1. $a_n = (-1)^{n+1} \dfrac{n}{(n - 1)!}$ **2.** $a_1 = 5, d = -3$

3. $a_1 = 5, r = -3$ **4.** $a_1 = 3, a_n = -a_{n-1} + 4$

In Exercises 5–7, write a formula for the general term (the nth term) of each sequence. Then use the formula to find the indicated term.

5. $2, 6, 10, 14, \ldots; a_{20}$ **6.** $3, 6, 12, 24, \ldots; a_{10}$

7. $\dfrac{3}{2}, 1, \dfrac{1}{2}, 0, \ldots; a_{30}$

8. Find the sum of the first ten terms of the sequence:

$$5, 10, 20, 40, \ldots.$$

9. Find the sum of the first 50 terms of the sequence:

$$-2, 0, 2, 4, \ldots.$$

10. Find the sum of the first ten terms of the sequence:

$$-20, 40, -80, 160, \ldots.$$

11. Find the sum of the first 100 terms of the sequence:

$$4, -2, -8, -14, \ldots.$$

In Exercises 12–15, find each indicated sum.

12. $\displaystyle\sum_{i=1}^{4} (i + 4)(i - 1)$

13. $\displaystyle\sum_{i=1}^{50} (3i - 2)$

14. $\displaystyle\sum_{i=1}^{6} \left(\frac{3}{2}\right)^i$

15. $\displaystyle\sum_{i=1}^{\infty} \left(-\frac{2}{5}\right)^{i-1}$

16. Express $0.\overline{45}$ as a fraction in lowest terms.

17. Express the sum using summation notation. Use i for the index of summation.

$$\frac{1}{3} + \frac{2}{4} + \frac{3}{5} + \cdots + \frac{18}{20}$$

18. A skydiver falls 16 feet during the first second of a dive, 48 feet during the second second, 80 feet during the third second, 112 feet during the fourth second, and so on. Find the distance that the skydiver falls during the 15th second and the total distance the skydiver falls in 15 seconds.

19. If the average value of a house increases 10% per year, how much will a house costing $120,000 be worth in 10 years? Round to the nearest dollar.

Section 8.4 Mathematical Induction

Objectives

1 Understand the principle of mathematical induction.

2 Prove statements using mathematical induction.

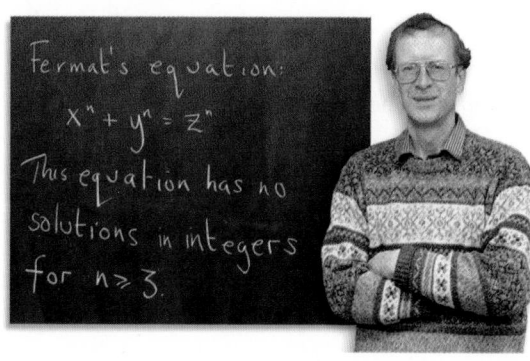

After ten years of work, Princeton University's Andrew Wiles proved Fermat's Last Theorem.

Pierre de Fermat (1601–1665) was a lawyer who enjoyed studying mathematics. In a margin of one of his books, he claimed that no positive integers satisfy

$$x^n + y^n = z^n$$

if n is an integer greater than or equal to 3.

If $n = 2$, we can find positive integers satisfying $x^n + y^n = z^n$, or $x^2 + y^2 = z^2$:

$$3^2 + 4^2 = 5^2.$$

However, Fermat claimed that no positive integers satisfy

$$x^3 + y^3 = z^3, \quad x^4 + y^4 = z^4, \quad x^5 + y^5 = z^5,$$

and so on. Fermat claimed to have a proof of his conjecture, but added, "The margin of my book is too narrow to write it down." Some believe that he never had a proof and intended to frustrate his colleagues.

In 1994, 40-year-old Princeton math professor Andrew Wiles proved Fermat's Last Theorem using a principle called *mathematical induction*. In this section, you will learn how to use this powerful method to prove statements about the positive integers.

1 Understand the principle of mathematical induction.

The Principle of Mathematical Induction

How do we prove statements using mathematical induction? Let's consider an example. We will prove a statement that appears to give a correct formula for the sum of the first n positive integers:

$$S_n: 1 + 2 + 3 + \cdots + n = \frac{n(n + 1)}{2}.$$

We can verify S_n: $1 + 2 + 3 + \cdots + n = \dfrac{n(n + 1)}{2}$ for, say, the first four positive integers. If $n = 1$, the statement S_1 is

Take the first term on the left. $\quad 1 \overset{?}{=} \dfrac{1(1 + 1)}{2}$ \quad Substitute 1 for n on the right.

$$1 \overset{?}{=} \dfrac{1 \cdot 2}{2}$$

$1 = 1$ ✓. This true statement shows that S_1 is true.

If $n = 2$, the statement S_2 is

Add the first two terms on the left. $\quad 1 + 2 \overset{?}{=} \dfrac{2(2 + 1)}{2}$ \quad Substitute 2 for n on the right.

$$3 \overset{?}{=} \dfrac{2 \cdot 3}{2}$$

$3 = 3$ ✓. This true statement shows that S_2 is true.

If $n = 3$, the statement S_3 is

Add the first three terms on the left. $\quad 1 + 2 + 3 \overset{?}{=} \dfrac{3(3 + 1)}{2}$ \quad Substitute 3 for n on the right.

$$6 \overset{?}{=} \dfrac{3 \cdot 4}{2}$$

$6 = 6$ ✓. This true statement shows that S_3 is true.

Finally, if $n = 4$, the statement S_4 is

Add the first four terms on the left. $\quad 1 + 2 + 3 + 4 \overset{?}{=} \dfrac{4(4 + 1)}{2}$ \quad Substitute 4 for n on the right.

$$10 \overset{?}{=} \dfrac{4 \cdot 5}{2}$$

$10 = 10$ ✓. This true statement shows that S_4 is true.

This approach does *not* prove that the given statement S_n is true for every positive integer n. The fact that the formula produces true statements for $n = 1, 2, 3,$ and 4 does not guarantee that it is valid for all positive integers n. Thus, we need to be able to verify the truth of S_n without verifying the statement for each and every one of the positive integers.

A legitimate proof of the given statement S_n involves a technique called **mathematical induction**.

The Principle of Mathematical Induction

Let S_n be a statement involving the positive integer n. If

1. S_1 is true, and

2. the truth of the statement S_k implies the truth of the statement S_{k+1}, for every positive integer k,

then the statement S_n is true for all positive integers n.

Figure 8.7 Falling dominoes illustrate the principle of mathematical induction.

The principle of mathematical induction can be illustrated using an unending line of dominoes, as shown in **Figure 8.7**. If the first domino is pushed over, it knocks down the next, which knocks down the next, and so on, in a chain reaction. To topple all the dominoes in the infinite sequence, two conditions must be satisfied:

1. The first domino must be knocked down.

2. If the domino in position k is knocked down, then the domino in position $k + 1$ must be knocked down.

If the second condition is not satisfied, it does not follow that all the dominoes will topple. For example, suppose the dominoes are spaced far enough apart so that a falling domino does not push over the next domino in the line.

The domino analogy provides the two steps that are required in a proof by mathematical induction.

The Steps in a Proof by Mathematical Induction

Let S_n be a statement involving the positive integer n. To prove that S_n is true for all positive integers n requires two steps.

Step 1 Show that S_1 is true.

Step 2 Show that if S_k is assumed to be true, then S_{k+1} is also true, for every positive integer k.

Notice that to prove S_n, we work only with the statements S_1, S_k, and S_{k+1}. Our first example provides practice in writing these statements.

EXAMPLE 1 Writing S_1, S_k, and S_{k+1}

For the given statement S_n, write the three statements S_1, S_k, and S_{k+1}.

a. S_n: $1 + 2 + 3 + \cdots + n = \dfrac{n(n + 1)}{2}$

b. S_n: $1^2 + 2^2 + 3^2 + \cdots + n^2 = \dfrac{n(n + 1)(2n + 1)}{6}$

Solution

a. We begin with

$$S_n: 1 + 2 + 3 + \cdots + n = \frac{n(n + 1)}{2}.$$

Write S_1 by taking the first term on the left and replacing n with 1 on the right.

$$S_1: 1 = \frac{1(1 + 1)}{2}$$

S_n: $1 + 2 + 3 + \cdots + n = \dfrac{n(n+1)}{2}$

The statement for part (a) (repeated)

Write S_k by taking the sum of the first k terms on the left and replacing n with k on the right.

$$S_k: 1 + 2 + 3 + \cdots + k = \dfrac{k(k+1)}{2}$$

Write S_{k+1} by taking the sum of the first $k + 1$ terms on the left and replacing n with $k + 1$ on the right.

$$S_{k+1}: 1 + 2 + 3 + \cdots + (k+1) = \dfrac{(k+1)[(k+1)+1]}{2}$$

$$S_{k+1}: 1 + 2 + 3 + \cdots + (k+1) = \dfrac{(k+1)(k+2)}{2} \qquad \text{Simplify on the right.}$$

b. We begin with

$$S_n: 1^2 + 2^2 + 3^2 + \cdots + n^2 = \dfrac{n(n+1)(2n+1)}{6}.$$

Write S_1 by taking the first term on the left and replacing n with 1 on the right.

$$S_1: 1^2 = \dfrac{1(1+1)(2 \cdot 1 + 1)}{6}$$

Using S_n: $1^2 + 2^2 + 3^2 + \cdots + n^2 = \dfrac{n(n+1)(2n+1)}{6}$, we write S_k by taking the sum of the first k terms on the left and replacing n with k on the right.

$$S_k: 1^2 + 2^2 + 3^2 + \cdots + k^2 = \dfrac{k(k+1)(2k+1)}{6}$$

Write S_{k+1} by taking the sum of the first $k + 1$ terms on the left and replacing n with $k + 1$ on the right.

$$S_{k+1}: 1^2 + 2^2 + 3^2 + \cdots + (k+1)^2 = \dfrac{(k+1)[(k+1)+1][2(k+1)+1]}{6}$$

$$S_{k+1}: 1^2 + 2^2 + 3^2 + \cdots + (k+1)^2 = \dfrac{(k+1)(k+2)(2k+3)}{6} \qquad \text{Simplify on the right.} \ \bullet$$

⬤ Check Point **I** For the given statement S_n, write the three statements S_1, S_k, and S_{k+1}.

a. $2 + 4 + 6 + \cdots + 2n = n(n+1)$

b. $1^3 + 2^3 + 3^3 + \cdots + n^3 = \dfrac{n^2(n+1)^2}{4}$

Always simplify S_{k+1} before trying to use mathematical induction to prove that S_n is true. For example, consider

$$S_n: 1^2 + 3^2 + 5^2 + \cdots + (2n-1)^2 = \dfrac{n(2n-1)(2n+1)}{3}.$$

Begin by writing S_{k+1} as follows:

$$S_{k+1}: 1^2 + 3^2 + 5^2 + \cdots + [2(k+1) - 1]^2$$

$$= \dfrac{(k+1)[2(k+1)-1][2(k+1)+1]}{3}.$$

The sum of the first $k + 1$ terms

Replace n with $k + 1$ on the right side of S_n.

Now simplify both sides of the equation.

$$S_{k+1}: 1^2 + 3^2 + 5^2 + \cdots + (2k + 2 - 1)^2 = \frac{(k + 1)(2k + 2 - 1)(2k + 2 + 1)}{3}$$

$$S_{k+1}: 1^2 + 3^2 + 5^2 + \cdots + (2k + 1)^2 = \frac{(k + 1)(2k + 1)(2k + 3)}{3}$$

② Prove statements using mathematical induction.

Proving Statements about Positive Integers Using Mathematical Induction

Now that we know how to find $S_1, S_k,$ and S_{k+1}, let's see how we can use these statements to carry out the two steps in a proof by mathematical induction. In Examples 2 and 3, we will use the statements $S_1, S_k,$ and S_{k+1} to prove each of the statements S_n that we worked with in Example 1.

(EXAMPLE 2) **Proving a Formula by Mathematical Induction**

Use mathematical induction to prove that

$$1 + 2 + 3 + \cdots + n = \frac{n(n + 1)}{2}$$

for all positive integers n.

Solution

Step 1 Show that S_1 is true. Statement S_1 is

$$1 = \frac{1(1 + 1)}{2}.$$

Simplifying on the right, we obtain $1 = 1$. This true statement shows that S_1 is true.

Step 2 Show that if S_k is true, then S_{k+1} is true. Using S_k and S_{k+1} from Example 1(a), show that the truth of S_k,

$$1 + 2 + 3 + \cdots + k = \frac{k(k + 1)}{2},$$

implies the truth of S_{k+1},

$$1 + 2 + 3 + \cdots + (k + 1) = \frac{(k + 1)(k + 2)}{2}.$$

We will work with S_k. Because we assume that S_k is true, we add the next consecutive integer after k—namely, $k + 1$—to both sides.

$$1 + 2 + 3 + \cdots + k = \frac{k(k + 1)}{2} \qquad \text{This is } S_k, \text{ which we assume is true.}$$

$$1 + 2 + 3 + \cdots + k + (k + 1) = \frac{k(k + 1)}{2} + (k + 1)$$

> We do not have to write this k because k is understood to be the integer that precedes $k + 1$.

Add $k + 1$ to both sides of the equation.

$$1 + 2 + 3 + \cdots + (k + 1) = \frac{k(k + 1)}{2} + \frac{2(k + 1)}{2} \qquad \text{Write the right side with a common denominator of 2.}$$

$$1 + 2 + 3 + \cdots + (k + 1) = \frac{(k + 1)}{2}(k + 2) \qquad \text{Factor out the common factor } \frac{k + 1}{2} \text{ on the right.}$$

$$1 + 2 + 3 + \cdots + (k + 1) = \frac{(k + 1)(k + 2)}{2} \qquad \text{This final result is the statement } S_{k+1}.$$

We have shown that if we assume that S_k is true and we add $k + 1$ to both sides of S_k, then S_{k+1} is also true. By the principle of mathematical induction, the statement S_n, namely,

$$1 + 2 + 3 + \cdots + n = \frac{n(n + 1)}{2},$$

is true for every positive integer n.

✓ **Check Point 2** Use mathematical induction to prove that

$$2 + 4 + 6 + \cdots + 2n = n(n + 1)$$

for all positive integers n.

(EXAMPLE 3) Proving a Formula by Mathematical Induction

Use mathematical induction to prove that

$$1^2 + 2^2 + 3^2 + \cdots + n^2 = \frac{n(n + 1)(2n + 1)}{6}$$

for all positive integers n.

Solution

Step 1 Show that S_1 is true. Statement S_1 is

$$1^2 = \frac{1(1 + 1)(2 \cdot 1 + 1)}{6}.$$

Simplifying, we obtain $1 = \dfrac{1 \cdot 2 \cdot 3}{6}$. Further simplification on the right gives the statement $1 = 1$. This true statement shows that S_1 is true.

Step 2 Show that if S_k is true, then S_{k+1} is true. Using S_k and S_{k+1} from Example 1(b), show that the truth of

$$S_k: 1^2 + 2^2 + 3^2 + \cdots + k^2 = \frac{k(k + 1)(2k + 1)}{6}$$

implies the truth of

$$S_{k+1}: 1^2 + 2^2 + 3^2 + \cdots + (k + 1)^2 = \frac{(k + 1)(k + 2)(2k + 3)}{6}.$$

We will work with S_k. Because we assume that S_k is true, we add the square of the next consecutive integer after k, namely, $(k + 1)^2$, to both sides of the equation.

$$1^2 + 2^2 + 3^2 + \cdots + k^2 = \frac{k(k + 1)(2k + 1)}{6}$$ This is S_k, assumed to be true. We must work with this and show S_{k+1} is true.

$$1^2 + 2^2 + 3^2 + \cdots + k^2 + (k + 1)^2 = \frac{k(k + 1)(2k + 1)}{6} + (k + 1)^2$$ Add $(k + 1)^2$ to both sides.

$$1^2 + 2^2 + 3^2 + \cdots + (k + 1)^2 = \frac{k(k + 1)(2k + 1)}{6} + \frac{6(k + 1)^2}{6}$$ It is not necessary to write k^2 on the left. Express the right side with the least common denominator, 6.

$$= \frac{(k + 1)}{6}[k(2k + 1) + 6(k + 1)]$$ Factor out the common factor $\dfrac{k + 1}{6}$.

$$= \frac{(k + 1)}{6}(2k^2 + 7k + 6)$$ Multiply and combine like terms.

$$= \frac{(k + 1)}{6}(k + 2)(2k + 3) \quad \text{Factor } 2k^2 + 7k + 6.$$

$$= \frac{(k + 1)(k + 2)(2k + 3)}{6} \quad \text{This final statement is } S_{k+1}.$$

We have shown that if we assume that S_k is true, and we add $(k + 1)^2$ to both sides of S_k, then S_{k+1} is also true. By the principle of mathematical induction, the statement S_n, namely,

$$1^2 + 2^2 + 3^2 + \cdots + n^2 = \frac{n(n + 1)(2n + 1)}{6},$$

is true for every positive integer n.

⬤

Ø Check Point **3** Use mathematical induction to prove that

$$1^3 + 2^3 + 3^3 + \cdots + n^3 = \frac{n^2(n + 1)^2}{4}$$

for all positive integers n.

Example 4 illustrates how mathematical induction can be used to prove statements about positive integers that do not involve sums.

(**EXAMPLE 4**) **Using the Principle of Mathematical Induction**

Prove that 2 is a factor of $n^2 + 5n$ for all positive integers n.

Solution

Step 1 Show that S_1 is true. Statement S_1 reads

2 is a factor of $1^2 + 5 \cdot 1$.

Simplifying the arithmetic, the statement reads

2 is a factor of 6.

This statement is true: that is, $6 = 2 \cdot 3$. This shows that S_1 is true.

Step 2 Show that if S_k is true, then S_{k+1} is true. Let's write S_k and S_{k+1}:

S_k: 2 is a factor of $k^2 + 5k$.

S_{k+1}: 2 is a factor of $(k + 1)^2 + 5(k + 1)$.

We can rewrite statement S_{k+1} by simplifying the algebraic expression in the statement as follows:

$$(k + 1)^2 + 5(k + 1) = k^2 + 2k + 1 + 5k + 5 = k^2 + 7k + 6.$$

Use the formula $(A + B)^2 = A^2 + 2AB + B^2$.

Statement S_{k+1} now reads

2 is a factor of $k^2 + 7k + 6$.

We need to use statement S_k—that is, 2 is a factor of $k^2 + 5k$—to prove statement S_{k+1}. We do this as follows:

$$k^2 + 7k + 6 = (k^2 + 5k) + (2k + 6) = (k^2 + 5k) + 2(k + 3).$$

We assume that 2 is a factor of $k^2 + 5k$ because we assume S_k is true.

Factoring the last two terms shows that 2 is a factor of $2k + 6$.

$$k^2 + 7k + 6 = (k^2 + 5k) + (2k + 6) = (k^2 + 5k) + 2(k + 3)$$

We assume that 2 is a factor of $k^2 + 5k$ because we assume S_k is true.

Factoring the last two terms shows that 2 is a factor of $2k + 6$.

We've repeated the equation from the bottom of the previous page. The voice balloons show that 2 is a factor of $k^2 + 5k$ and of $2(k + 3)$. Thus, if S_k is true, 2 is a factor of the sum $(k^2 + 5k) + 2(k + 3)$, or of $k^2 + 7k + 6$. This is precisely statement S_{k+1}. We have shown that if we assume that S_k is true, then S_{k+1} is also true. By the principle of mathematical induction, the statement S_n, namely 2 is a factor of $n^2 + 5n$, is true for every positive integer n. ●

⊘ **Check Point 4** Prove that 2 is a factor of $n^2 + n$ for all positive integers n.

Exercise Set 8.4

Practice Exercises

In Exercises 1–4, a statement S_n about the positive integers is given. Write statements $S_1, S_2,$ and S_3, and show that each of these statements is true.

1. S_n: $1 + 3 + 5 + \cdots + (2n - 1) = n^2$

2. S_n: $3 + 4 + 5 + \cdots + (n + 2) = \dfrac{n(n + 5)}{2}$

3. S_n: 2 is a factor of $n^2 - n$.

4. S_n: 3 is a factor of $n^3 - n$.

In Exercises 5–10, a statement S_n about the positive integers is given. Write statements S_k and S_{k+1}, simplifying statement S_{k+1} completely.

5. S_n: $4 + 8 + 12 + \cdots + 4n = 2n(n + 1)$

6. S_n: $3 + 4 + 5 + \cdots + (n + 2) = \dfrac{n(n + 5)}{2}$

7. S_n: $3 + 7 + 11 + \cdots + (4n - 1) = n(2n + 1)$

8. S_n: $2 + 7 + 12 + \cdots + (5n - 3) = \dfrac{n(5n - 1)}{2}$

9. S_n: 2 is a factor of $n^2 - n + 2$.

10. S_n: 2 is a factor of $n^2 - n$.

In Exercises 11–24, use mathematical induction to prove that each statement is true for every positive integer n.

11. $4 + 8 + 12 + \cdots + 4n = 2n(n + 1)$

12. $3 + 4 + 5 + \cdots + (n + 2) = \dfrac{n(n + 5)}{2}$

13. $1 + 3 + 5 + \cdots + (2n - 1) = n^2$

14. $3 + 6 + 9 + \cdots + 3n = \dfrac{3n(n + 1)}{2}$

15. $3 + 7 + 11 + \cdots + (4n - 1) = n(2n + 1)$

16. $2 + 7 + 12 + \cdots + (5n - 3) = \dfrac{n(5n - 1)}{2}$

17. $1 + 2 + 2^2 + \cdots + 2^{n-1} = 2^n - 1$

18. $1 + 3 + 3^2 + \cdots + 3^{n-1} = \dfrac{3^n - 1}{2}$

19. $2 + 4 + 8 + \cdots + 2^n = 2^{n+1} - 2$

20. $\dfrac{1}{2} + \dfrac{1}{4} + \dfrac{1}{8} + \cdots + \dfrac{1}{2^n} = 1 - \dfrac{1}{2^n}$

21. $1 \cdot 2 + 2 \cdot 3 + 3 \cdot 4 + \cdots + n(n + 1) = \dfrac{n(n + 1)(n + 2)}{3}$

22. $1 \cdot 3 + 2 \cdot 4 + 3 \cdot 5 + \cdots + n(n + 2) = \dfrac{n(n + 1)(2n + 7)}{6}$

23. $\dfrac{1}{1 \cdot 2} + \dfrac{1}{2 \cdot 3} + \dfrac{1}{3 \cdot 4} + \cdots + \dfrac{1}{n(n + 1)} = \dfrac{n}{n + 1}$

24. $\dfrac{1}{2 \cdot 3} + \dfrac{1}{3 \cdot 4} + \dfrac{1}{4 \cdot 5} + \cdots + \dfrac{1}{(n + 1)(n + 2)} = \dfrac{n}{2n + 4}$

Practice Plus

In Exercises 25–34, use mathematical induction to prove that each statement is true for every positive integer n.

25. 2 is a factor of $n^2 - n$.

26. 2 is a factor of $n^2 + 3n$.

27. 6 is a factor of $n(n + 1)(n + 2)$.

28. 3 is a factor of $n(n + 1)(n - 1)$.

29. $\displaystyle\sum_{i=1}^{n} 5 \cdot 6^i = 6(6^n - 1)$

30. $\displaystyle\sum_{i=1}^{n} 7 \cdot 8^i = 8(8^n - 1)$

31. $n + 2 > n$

32. If $0 < x < 1$, then $0 < x^n < 1$.

33. $(ab)^n = a^n b^n$

34. $\left(\dfrac{a}{b}\right)^n = \dfrac{a^n}{b^n}$

Writing in Mathematics

35. Explain how to use mathematical induction to prove that a statement is true for every positive integer n.

36. Consider the statement S_n given by

$$n^2 - n + 41 \text{ is prime.}$$

Although S_1, S_2, \ldots, S_{40} are true, S_{41} is false. Verify that S_{41} is false. Then describe how this is illustrated by the dominoes in the figure. What does this tell you about a pattern, or formula, that seems to work for several values of n?

Critical Thinking Exercises

Make Sense? *In Exercises 37–40, determine whether each statement makes sense or does not make sense, and explain your reasoning.*

37. I use mathematical induction to prove that statements are true for all real numbers n.

38. I begin proofs by mathematical induction by writing S_k and S_{k+1}, both of which I assume to be true.

39. When a line of falling dominoes is used to illustrate the principle of mathematical induction, it is not necessary for all the dominoes to topple.

40. This triangular arrangement of 36 circles illustrates that

$$1 + 2 + 3 + \cdots + n = \frac{n(n+1)}{2}$$

is true for $n = 8$.

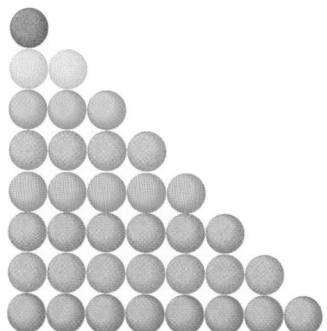

Some statements are false for the first few positive integers, but true for some positive integer m on. In these instances, you can prove S_n for $n \geq m$ by showing that S_m is true and that S_k implies S_{k+1} when $k > m$. Use this extended principle of mathematical induction to prove that each statement in Exercises 41–42 is true.

41. Prove that $n^2 > 2n + 1$ for $n \geq 3$. Show that the formula is true for $n = 3$ and then use step 2 of mathematical induction.

42. Prove that $2^n > n^2$ for $n \geq 5$. Show that the formula is true for $n = 5$ and then use step 2 of mathematical induction.

In Exercises 43–44, find S_1 through S_5 and then use the pattern to make a conjecture about S_n. Prove the conjectured formula for S_n by mathematical induction.

43. $S_n: \dfrac{1}{4} + \dfrac{1}{12} + \dfrac{1}{24} + \cdots + \dfrac{1}{2n(n+1)} = ?$

44. $S_n: \left(1 - \dfrac{1}{2}\right)\left(1 - \dfrac{1}{3}\right)\left(1 - \dfrac{1}{4}\right) \cdots \left(1 - \dfrac{1}{n+1}\right) = ?$

Group Exercise

45. Fermat's most notorious theorem, described in the section opener on page 703, baffled the greatest minds for more than three centuries. In 1994, after ten years of work, Princeton University's Andrew Wiles proved Fermat's Last Theorem. *People* magazine put him on its list of "the 25 most intriguing people of the year," the Gap asked him to model jeans, and Barbara Walters chased him for an interview. "Who's Barbara Walters?" asked the bookish Wiles, who had somehow gone through life without a television.

Using the 1993 PBS documentary "Solving Fermat: Andrew Wiles" or information about Andrew Wiles on the Internet, research and present a group seminar on what Wiles did to prove Fermat's Last Theorem, problems along the way, and the role of mathematical induction in the proof.

Preview Exercises

Exercises 46–48 will help you prepare for the material covered in the next section. Each exercise involves observing a pattern in the expanded form of the binomial expression $(a + b)^n$.

$$(a + b)^1 = a + b$$
$$(a + b)^2 = a^2 + 2ab + b^2$$
$$(a + b)^3 = a^3 + 3a^2b + 3ab^2 + b^3$$
$$(a + b)^4 = a^4 + 4a^3b + 6a^2b^2 + 4ab^3 + b^4$$
$$(a + b)^5 = a^5 + 5a^4b + 10a^3b^2 + 10a^2b^3 + 5ab^4 + b^5$$

46. Describe the pattern for the exponents on a.

47. Describe the pattern for the exponents on b.

48. Describe the pattern for the sum of the exponents on the variables in each term.

Section 8.5 The Binomial Theorem

Objectives

1. Evaluate a binomial coefficient.
2. Expand a binomial raised to a power.
3. Find a particular term in a binomial expansion.

Galaxies are groupings of billions of stars bound together by gravity. Some galaxies, such as the Centaurus galaxy shown here, are elliptical in shape.

Is mathematics discovered or invented? For example, planets revolve in elliptical orbits. Does that mean that the ellipse is out there, waiting for the mind to discover it? Or do people create the definition of an ellipse just as they compose a song? And is it possible for the same mathematics to be discovered/invented by independent researchers separated by time, place, and culture? This is precisely what occurred when mathematicians attempted to find efficient methods for raising binomials to higher and higher powers, such as

$$(x + 2)^3, (x + 2)^4, (x + 2)^5, (x + 2)^6,$$

and so on. In this section, we study higher powers of binomials and a method first discovered/invented by great minds in Eastern and Western cultures working independently.

① Evaluate a binomial coefficient.

Binomial Coefficients

Before turning to powers of binomials, we introduce a special notation that uses factorials.

Definition of a Binomial Coefficient $\binom{n}{r}$

For nonnegative integers n and r, with $n \geq r$, the expression $\binom{n}{r}$ (read "n above r") is called a **binomial coefficient** and is defined by

$$\binom{n}{r} = \frac{n!}{r!(n-r)!}.$$

The symbol $_nC_r$ is often used in place of $\binom{n}{r}$ to denote binomial coefficients.

EXAMPLE 1 Evaluating Binomial Coefficients

Evaluate: **a.** $\binom{6}{2}$ **b.** $\binom{3}{0}$ **c.** $\binom{9}{3}$ **d.** $\binom{4}{4}$.

Solution In each case, we apply the definition of the binomial coefficient.

a. $\binom{6}{2} = \frac{6!}{2!(6-2)!} = \frac{6!}{2!4!} = \frac{6 \cdot 5 \cdot 4!}{2 \cdot 1 \cdot 4!} = 15$

b. $\dbinom{3}{0} = \dfrac{3!}{0!(3-0)!} = \dfrac{3!}{0!3!} = \dfrac{1}{1} = 1$

Remember that $0! = 1$.

c. $\dbinom{9}{3} = \dfrac{9!}{3!(9-3)!} = \dfrac{9!}{3!6!} = \dfrac{9\cdot8\cdot7\cdot6!}{3\cdot2\cdot1\cdot6!} = 84$

d. $\dbinom{4}{4} = \dfrac{4!}{4!(4-4)!} = \dfrac{4!}{4!0!} = \dfrac{1}{1} = 1$

⊘ **Check Point** ❙ Evaluate:

a. $\dbinom{6}{3}$ **b.** $\dbinom{6}{0}$ **c.** $\dbinom{8}{2}$ **d.** $\dbinom{3}{3}$.

Expand a binomial raised to a power.

The Binomial Theorem

When we write out the *binomial expression* $(a+b)^n$, where n is a positive integer, a number of patterns begin to appear.

$$(a+b)^1 = a + b$$
$$(a+b)^2 = a^2 + 2ab + b^2$$
$$(a+b)^3 = a^3 + 3a^2b + 3ab^2 + b^3$$
$$(a+b)^4 = a^4 + 4a^3b + 6a^2b^2 + 4ab^3 + b^4$$
$$(a+b)^5 = a^5 + 5a^4b + 10a^3b^2 + 10a^2b^3 + 5ab^4 + b^5$$

Each expanded form of the binomial expression is a polynomial. Observe the following patterns:

1. The first term in the expansion of $(a+b)^n$ is a^n. The exponents on a decrease by 1 in each successive term.

2. The exponents on b in the expansion of $(a+b)^n$ increase by 1 in each successive term. In the first term, the exponent on b is 0. (Because $b^0 = 1$, b is not shown in the first term.) The last term is b^n.

3. The sum of the exponents on the variables in any term in the expansion of $(a+b)^n$ is equal to n.

4. The number of terms in the polynomial expansion is one greater than the power of the binomial, n. There are $n+1$ terms in the expanded form of $(a+b)^n$.

Using these observations, the variable parts of the expansion of $(a+b)^6$ are

$$a^6, \quad a^5b, \quad a^4b^2, \quad a^3b^3, \quad a^2b^4, \quad ab^5, \quad b^6.$$

The first term is a^6, with the exponents on a decreasing by 1 in each successive term. The exponents on b increase from 0 to 6, with the last term being b^6. The sum of the exponents in each term is equal to 6.

We can generalize from these observations to obtain the variable parts of the expansion of $(a+b)^n$. They are

$$a^n, \quad a^{n-1}b, \quad a^{n-2}b^2, \quad a^{n-3}b^3, \dots, \quad ab^{n-1}, \quad b^n.$$

Exponents on a are decreasing by 1.
Exponents on b are increasing by 1.

Sum of exponents: $n-1+1 = n$

Sum of exponents: $n-3+3 = n$

Sum of exponents: $1+n-1 = n$

If we use binomial coefficients and the pattern for the variable part of each term, a formula called the **Binomial Theorem** can be used to expand any positive integral power of a binomial.

A Formula for Expanding Binomials: The Binomial Theorem

For any positive integer n,

$$(a + b)^n = \binom{n}{0}a^n + \binom{n}{1}a^{n-1}b + \binom{n}{2}a^{n-2}b^2 + \binom{n}{3}a^{n-3}b^3 + \cdots + \binom{n}{n}b^n$$

$$= \sum_{r=0}^{n} \binom{n}{r}a^{n-r}b^r.$$

EXAMPLE 2 **Using the Binomial Theorem**

Expand: $(x + 2)^4$.

Solution We use the Binomial Theorem

$$(a + b)^n = \binom{n}{0}a^n + \binom{n}{1}a^{n-1}b + \binom{n}{2}a^{n-2}b^2 + \binom{n}{3}a^{n-3}b^3 + \cdots + \binom{n}{n}b^n$$

to expand $(x + 2)^4$. In $(x + 2)^4$, $a = x$, $b = 2$, and $n = 4$. In the expansion, powers of x are in descending order, starting with x^4. Powers of 2 are in ascending order, starting with 2^0. (Because $2^0 = 1$, a 2 is not shown in the first term.) The sum of the exponents on x and 2 in each term is equal to 4, the exponent in the expression $(x + 2)^4$.

$$(x + 2)^4 = \binom{4}{0}x^4 + \binom{4}{1}x^3 \cdot 2 + \binom{4}{2}x^2 \cdot 2^2 + \binom{4}{3}x \cdot 2^3 + \binom{4}{4}2^4$$

These binomial coefficients are evaluated using $\binom{n}{r} = \frac{n!}{r!(n-r)!}$.

$$= \frac{4!}{0!4!}x^4 + \frac{4!}{1!3!}x^3 \cdot 2 + \frac{4!}{2!2!}x^2 \cdot 4 + \frac{4!}{3!1!}x \cdot 8 + \frac{4!}{4!0!} \cdot 16$$

$$\frac{4!}{2!2!} = \frac{4 \cdot 3 \cdot 2!}{2! \cdot 2 \cdot 1} = \frac{12}{2} = 6$$

Take a few minutes to verify the other factorial evaluations.

$$= 1 \cdot x^4 + 4x^3 \cdot 2 + 6x^2 \cdot 4 + 4x \cdot 8 + 1 \cdot 16$$

$$= x^4 + 8x^3 + 24x^2 + 32x + 16$$

Technology

You can use a graphing utility's table feature to find the five binomial coefficients in Example 2.

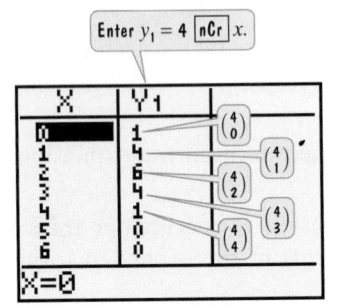

Enter $y_1 = 4 \lfloor nCr \rfloor x$.

Check Point 2 Expand: $(x + 1)^4$.

EXAMPLE 3 **Using the Binomial Theorem**

Expand: $(2x - y)^5$.

Solution Because the Binomial Theorem involves the addition of two terms raised to a power, we rewrite $(2x - y)^5$ as $[2x + (-y)]^5$. We use the Binomial Theorem

$$(a + b)^n = \binom{n}{0}a^n + \binom{n}{1}a^{n-1}b + \binom{n}{2}a^{n-2}b^2 + \binom{n}{3}a^{n-3}b^3 + \cdots + \binom{n}{n}b^n$$

to expand $[2x + (-y)]^5$. In $[2x + (-y)]^5$, $a = 2x$, $b = -y$, and $n = 5$. In the expansion, powers of $2x$ are in descending order, starting with $(2x)^5$. Powers of $-y$ are in ascending order, starting with $(-y)^0$. [Because $(-y)^0 = 1$, a $-y$ is not shown in the first term.] The sum of the exponents on $2x$ and $-y$ in each term is equal to 5, the exponent in the expression $(2x - y)^5$.

$(2x - y)^5 = [2x + (-y)]^5$

$$= \binom{5}{0}(2x)^5 + \binom{5}{1}(2x)^4(-y) + \binom{5}{2}(2x)^3(-y)^2 + \binom{5}{3}(2x)^2(-y)^3 + \binom{5}{4}(2x)(-y)^4 + \binom{5}{5}(-y)^5$$

Evaluate binomial coefficients using $\binom{n}{r} = \frac{n!}{r!(n-r)!}$.

$$= \frac{5!}{0!5!}(2x)^5 + \frac{5!}{1!4!}(2x)^4(-y) + \frac{5!}{2!3!}(2x)^3(-y)^2 + \frac{5!}{3!2!}(2x)^2(-y)^3 + \frac{5!}{4!1!}(2x)(-y)^4 + \frac{5!}{5!0!}(-y)^5$$

$\frac{5!}{2!3!} = \frac{5 \cdot 4 \cdot 3!}{2 \cdot 1 \cdot 3!} = 10$

Take a few minutes to verify the other factorial evaluations.

$$= 1(2x)^5 + 5(2x)^4(-y) + 10(2x)^3(-y)^2 + 10(2x)^2(-y)^3 + 5(2x)(-y)^4 + 1(-y)^5$$

Raise both factors in these parentheses to the indicated powers.

$$= 1(32x^5) + 5(16x^4)(-y) + 10(8x^3)(-y)^2 + 10(4x^2)(-y)^3 + 5(2x)(-y)^4 + 1(-y)^5$$

Now raise $-y$ to the indicated powers.

$$= 1(32x^5) + 5(16x^4)(-y) + 10(8x^3)y^2 + 10(4x^2)(-y^3) + 5(2x)y^4 + 1(-y^5)$$

Multiplying factors in each of the six terms gives us the desired expansion:

$$(2x - y)^5 = 32x^5 - 80x^4y + 80x^3y^2 - 40x^2y^3 + 10xy^4 - y^5.$$

⬤

✓ Check Point **3** Expand: $(x - 2y)^5$.

③ Find a particular term in a binomial expansion.

Finding a Particular Term in a Binomial Expansion

By observing the terms in the formula for expanding binomials, we can find a formula for finding a particular term without writing the entire expansion.

1st term 2nd term 3rd term

$$\binom{n}{0}a^nb^0 \qquad \binom{n}{1}a^{n-1}b^1 \qquad \binom{n}{2}a^{n-2}b^2$$

The exponent on b is 1 less than the term number.

Based on the observation in the bottom voice balloon, the $(r + 1)$st term of the expansion of $(a + b)^n$ is the term that contains b^r.

Finding a Particular Term in a Binomial Expansion

The $(r + 1)$st term of the expansion of $(a + b)^n$ is

$$\binom{n}{r}a^{n-r}b^r.$$

> (EXAMPLE 4) **Finding a Single Term of a Binomial Expansion**

Find the fourth term in the expansion of $(3x + 2y)^7$.

Solution The fourth term in the expansion of $(3x + 2y)^7$ contains $(2y)^3$. To find the fourth term, first note that $4 = 3 + 1$. Equivalently, the fourth term of $(3x + 2y)^7$ is the $(3 + 1)$st term. Thus, $r = 3$, $a = 3x$, $b = 2y$, and $n = 7$. The fourth term is

$$\binom{7}{3}(3x)^{7-3}(2y)^3 = \binom{7}{3}(3x)^4(2y)^3 = \frac{7!}{3!(7-3)!}(3x)^4(2y)^3.$$

> Use the formula for the $(r+1)$st term of $(a+b)^n$: $\binom{n}{r}a^{n-r}b^r$.

> We use $\binom{n}{r} = \frac{n!}{r!(n-r)!}$ to evaluate $\binom{7}{3}$.

Now we need to evaluate the factorial expression and raise $3x$ and $2y$ to the indicated powers. We obtain

$$\frac{7!}{3!4!}(81x^4)(8y^3) = \frac{7 \cdot 6 \cdot 5 \cdot 4!}{3 \cdot 2 \cdot 1 \cdot 4!}(81x^4)(8y^3) = 35(81x^4)(8y^3) = 22{,}680x^4y^3.$$

The fourth term of $(3x + 2y)^7$ is $22{,}680x^4y^3$.

> ⊘ Check Point **4** Find the fifth term in the expansion of $(2x + y)^9$.

The Universality of Mathematics

Pascal's triangle is an array of numbers showing coefficients of the terms in the expansions of $(a + b)^n$. Although credited to French mathematician Blaise Pascal (1623–1662), the triangular array of numbers appeared in a Chinese document printed in 1303. The Binomial Theorem was known in Eastern cultures prior to its discovery in Europe. The same mathematics is often discovered/invented by independent researchers separated by time, place, and culture.

Binomial Expansions	Pascal's Triangle Coefficients in the Expansions	Chinese Document: 1303
$(a + b)^0 = 1$	1	
$(a + b)^1 = a + b$	1 1	
$(a + b)^2 = a^2 + 2ab + b^2$	1 2 1	
$(a + b)^3 = a^3 + 3a^2b + 3ab^2 + b^3$	1 3 3 1	
$(a + b)^4 = a^4 + 4a^3b + 6a^2b^2 + 4ab^3 + b^4$	1 4 6 4 1	
$(a + b)^5 = a^5 + 5a^4b + 10a^3b^2 + 10a^2b^3 + 5ab^4 + b^5$	1 5 10 10 5 1	
	1 6 15 20 15 6 1	
	1 7 21 35 35 21 7 1	
	1 8 28 56 70 56 28 8 1	

Exercise Set 8.5

Practice Exercises

In Exercises 1–8, evaluate the given binomial coefficient.

1. $\binom{8}{3}$ **2.** $\binom{7}{2}$ **3.** $\binom{12}{1}$

4. $\binom{11}{1}$ **5.** $\binom{6}{6}$ **6.** $\binom{15}{2}$

7. $\binom{100}{2}$ **8.** $\binom{100}{98}$

In Exercises 9–30, use the Binomial Theorem to expand each binomial and express the result in simplified form.

9. $(x + 2)^3$ **10.** $(x + 4)^3$

11. $(3x + y)^3$ **12.** $(x + 3y)^3$

13. $(5x - 1)^3$ **14.** $(4x - 1)^3$

15. $(2x + 1)^4$ **16.** $(3x + 1)^4$

17. $(x^2 + 2y)^4$ **18.** $(x^2 + y)^4$

19. $(y - 3)^4$ **20.** $(y - 4)^4$

21. $(2x^3 - 1)^4$ **22.** $(2x^5 - 1)^4$

23. $(c + 2)^5$ **24.** $(c + 3)^5$

25. $(x - 1)^5$ **26.** $(x - 2)^5$

27. $(3x - y)^5$ **28.** $(x - 3y)^5$

29. $(2a + b)^6$ **30.** $(a + 2b)^6$

In Exercises 31–38, write the first three terms in each binomial expansion, expressing the result in simplified form.

31. $(x + 2)^8$ **32.** $(x + 3)^8$

33. $(x - 2y)^{10}$ **34.** $(x - 2y)^9$

35. $(x^2 + 1)^{16}$ **36.** $(x^2 + 1)^{17}$

37. $(y^3 - 1)^{20}$ **38.** $(y^3 - 1)^{21}$

In Exercises 39–48, find the term indicated in each expansion.

39. $(2x + y)^6$; third term **40.** $(x + 2y)^6$; third term

41. $(x - 1)^9$; fifth term **42.** $(x - 1)^{10}$; fifth term

43. $(x^2 + y^3)^8$; sixth term **44.** $(x^3 + y^2)^8$; sixth term

45. $\left(x - \frac{1}{2}\right)^9$; fourth term **46.** $\left(x + \frac{1}{2}\right)^8$; fourth term

47. $(x^2 + y)^{22}$; the term containing y^{14}

48. $(x + 2y)^{10}$; the term containing y^6

Practice Plus

In Exercises 49–52, use the Binomial Theorem to expand each expression and write the result in simplified form.

49. $(x^3 + x^{-2})^4$ **50.** $(x^2 + x^{-3})^4$

51. $\left(x^{\frac{1}{3}} - x^{-\frac{1}{3}}\right)^3$ **52.** $\left(x^{\frac{2}{3}} - \frac{1}{\sqrt[3]{x}}\right)^3$

In Exercises 53–54, find $\dfrac{f(x + h) - f(x)}{h}$ and simplify.

53. $f(x) = x^4 + 7$ **54.** $f(x) = x^5 + 8$

55. Find the middle term in the expansion of $\left(\dfrac{3}{x} + \dfrac{x}{3}\right)^{10}$.

56. Find the middle term in the expansion of $\left(\dfrac{1}{x} - x^2\right)^{12}$.

Application Exercises

The graph shows that U.S. smokers have a greater probability of suffering from some ailments than the general adult population. Exercises 57–58 are based on some of the probabilities, expressed as decimals, shown to the right of the bars. In each exercise, use a calculator to determine the probability, correct to four decimal places.

Probability That United States Adults Suffer from Various Ailments

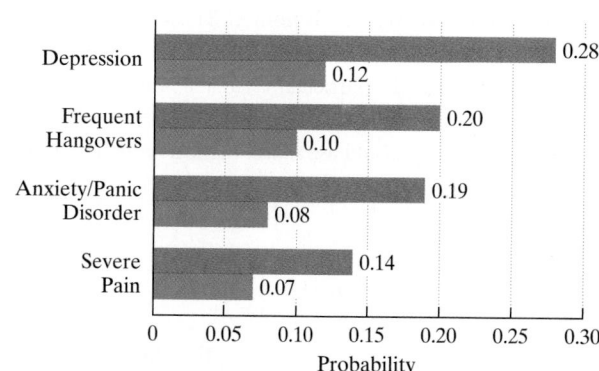

Source: MARS 2005 OTC/DTC

If the probability an event will occur is p and the probability it will not occur is q, then each term in the expansion of $(p + q)^n$ represents a probability.

57. The probability that a smoker suffers from depression is 0.28. If five smokers are randomly selected, the probability that three of them will suffer from depression is the third term of the binomial expansion of

$$(0.28 + 0.72)^5.$$

> 5 smokers are selected.

> Probability a smoker suffers from depression

> Probability a smoker does not suffer from depression

What is this probability?

58. The probability that a person in the general population suffers from depression is 0.12. If five people from the general population are randomly selected, the probability that three of them will suffer from depression is the third term of the binomial expansion of

$(0.12 + 0.88)^5.$

> 5 people from the general population are selected.

> Probability a person in the general population suffers from depression

> Probability a person in the general population does not suffer from depression

What is this probability?

Writing in Mathematics

59. Explain how to evaluate $\binom{n}{r}$. Provide an example with your explanation.

60. Describe the pattern on the exponents on a in the expansion of $(a + b)^n$.

61. Describe the pattern on the exponents on b in the expansion of $(a + b)^n$.

62. What is true about the sum of the exponents on a and b in any term in the expansion of $(a + b)^n$?

63. How do you determine how many terms there are in a binomial expansion?

64. Explain how to use the Binomial Theorem to expand a binomial. Provide an example with your explanation.

65. Explain how to find a particular term in a binomial expansion without having to write out the entire expansion.

66. Describe how you would use mathematical induction to prove

$$(a + b)^n = \binom{n}{0}a^n + \binom{n}{1}a^{n-1}b + \binom{n}{2}a^{n-2}b^2$$

$$+ \cdots + \binom{n}{n-1}ab^{n-1} + \binom{n}{n}b^n.$$

What happens when $n = 1$? Write the statement that we assume to be true. Write the statement that we must prove. What must be done to the left side of the assumed statement to make it look like the left side of the statement that must be proved? (More detail on the actual proof is found in Exercise 85.)

Technology Exercises

67. Use the $\boxed{_nC_r}$ key on a graphing utility to verify your answers in Exercises 1–8.

In Exercises 68–69, graph each of the functions in the same viewing rectangle. Describe how the graphs illustrate the Binomial Theorem.

68. $f_1(x) = (x + 2)^3$ $f_2(x) = x^3$

$f_3(x) = x^3 + 6x^2$ $f_4(x) = x^3 + 6x^2 + 12x$

$f_5(x) = x^3 + 6x^2 + 12x + 8$

Use a $[-10, 10, 1]$ by $[-30, 30, 10]$ viewing rectangle.

69. $f_1(x) = (x + 1)^4$ $f_2(x) = x^4$

$f_3(x) = x^4 + 4x^3$ $f_4(x) = x^4 + 4x^3 + 6x^2$

$f_5(x) = x^4 + 4x^3 + 6x^2 + 4x$

$f_6(x) = x^4 + 4x^3 + 6x^2 + 4x + 1$

Use a $[-5, 5, 1]$ by $[-30, 30, 10]$ viewing rectangle.

In Exercises 70–72, use the Binomial Theorem to find a polynomial expansion for each function. Then use a graphing utility and an approach similar to the one in Exercises 68 and 69 to verify the expansion.

70. $f_1(x) = (x - 1)^3$ **71.** $f_1(x) = (x - 2)^4$

72. $f_1(x) = (x + 2)^6$

Critical Thinking Exercises

Make Sense? *In Exercises 73–76, determine whether each statement makes sense or does not make sense, and explain your reasoning.*

73. In order to expand $(x^3 - y^4)^5$, I find it helpful to rewrite the expression inside the parentheses as $x^3 + (-y^4)$.

74. Without writing the expansion of $(x - 1)^6$, I can see that the terms have alternating positive and negative signs.

75. I use binomial coefficients to expand $(a + b)^n$, where $\binom{n}{1}$ is the coefficient of the first term, $\binom{n}{2}$ is the coefficient of the second term, and so on.

76. One of the terms in my binomial expansion is $\binom{7}{5}x^2y^4$.

In Exercises 77–80, determine whether each statement is true or false. If the statement is false, make the necessary change(s) to produce a true statement.

77. The binomial expansion for $(a + b)^n$ contains n terms.

78. The Binomial Theorem can be written in condensed form as

$$(a + b)^n = \sum_{r=0}^{n} \binom{n}{r}a^{n-r}b^r.$$

79. The sum of the binomial coefficients in $(a + b)^n$ cannot be 2^n.

80. There are no values of a and b such that

$$(a + b)^4 = a^4 + b^4.$$

81. Use the Binomial Theorem to expand and then simplify the result: $(x^2 + x + 1)^3$.

Hint: Write $x^2 + x + 1$ as $x^2 + (x + 1)$.

82. Find the term in the expansion of $(x^2 + y^2)^5$ containing x^4 as a factor.

83. Prove that

$$\binom{n}{r} = \binom{n}{n-r}.$$

84. Show that

$$\binom{n}{r} + \binom{n}{r+1} = \binom{n+1}{r+1}.$$

Hints:

$$(n - r)! = (n - r)(n - r - 1)!$$

$$(r + 1)! = (r + 1)r!$$

85. Follow the outline below and use mathematical induction to prove the Binomial Theorem:

$$(a + b)^n = \binom{n}{0}a^n + \binom{n}{1}a^{n-1}b + \binom{n}{2}a^{n-2}b^2$$

$$+ \cdots + \binom{n}{n-1}ab^{n-1} + \binom{n}{n}b^n.$$

a. Verify the formula for $n = 1$.

b. Replace n with k and write the statement that is assumed true. Replace n with $k + 1$ and write the statement that must be proved.

c. Multiply both sides of the statement assumed to be true by $a + b$. Add exponents on the left. On the right, distribute a and b, respectively.

d. Collect like terms on the right. At this point, you should have

$$(a + b)^{k+1} = \binom{k}{0}a^{k+1} + \left[\binom{k}{0} + \binom{k}{1}\right]a^k b$$

$$+ \left[\binom{k}{1} + \binom{k}{2}\right]a^{k-1}b^2 + \left[\binom{k}{2} + \binom{k}{3}\right]a^{k-2}b^3$$

$$+ \cdots + \left[\binom{k}{k-1} + \binom{k}{k}\right]ab^k + \binom{k}{k}b^{k+1}.$$

e. Use the result of Exercise 84 to add the binomial sums in brackets. For example, because $\binom{n}{r} + \binom{n}{r+1}$

$$= \binom{n+1}{r+1}, \text{ then } \binom{k}{0} + \binom{k}{1} = \binom{k+1}{1} \text{ and }$$

$$\binom{k}{1} + \binom{k}{2} = \binom{k+1}{2}.$$

f. Because $\binom{k}{0} = \binom{k+1}{0}$ (why?) and $\binom{k}{k} = \binom{k+1}{k+1}$ (why?), substitute these results and the results from part (e) into the equation in part (d). This should give the statement that we were required to prove in the second step of the mathematical induction process.

Preview Exercises

Exercises 86–88 will help you prepare for the material covered in the next section.

86. Evaluate $\dfrac{n!}{(n-r)!}$ for $n = 20$ and $r = 3$.

87. Evaluate $\dfrac{n!}{(n-r)!\,r!}$ for $n = 8$ and $r = 3$.

88. You can choose from two pairs of jeans (one blue, one black) and three T-shirts (one beige, one yellow, and one blue), as shown in the diagram.

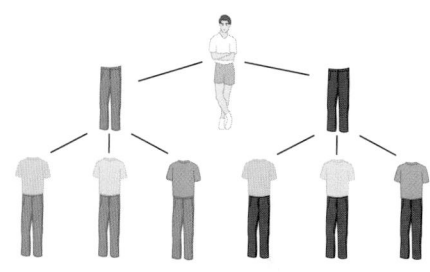

True or false: The diagram shows that you can form 2×3, or 6, different outfits.

Section **8.6** **Counting Principles, Permutations, and Combinations**

Objectives

1. Use the Fundamental Counting Principle.
2. Use the permutations formula.
3. Distinguish between permutation problems and combination problems.
4. Use the combinations formula.

State Lotto

Date January 4

Pay to the Order of Lucky Fellow $ 1,000,000

One Million Dollars 0/100

Have you ever imagined what your life would be like if you won the lottery? What changes would you make? Before you fantasize about becoming a person of leisure with a staff of obedient elves, think about this: The probability of winning top prize in the lottery is about the same as the probability of being struck by lightning. There are millions of possible number combinations in lottery games and only one way of winning the grand prize. Determining the probability of winning involves calculating the chance of getting the winning combination from all possible outcomes. In this section, we begin preparing for the surprising world of probability by looking at methods for counting possible outcomes.

① Use the Fundamental
Counting Principle.

The Fundamental Counting Principle

It's early morning, you're groggy, and you have to select something to wear for your 8 A.M. class. (What *were* you thinking of when you signed up for a class at that hour?!) Fortunately, your "lecture wardrobe" is rather limited—just two pairs of jeans to choose from (one blue, one black), three T-shirts to choose from (one beige, one yellow, and one blue), and two pairs of sneakers to select from (one black pair, one red pair). Your possible outfits are shown in **Figure 8.8**.

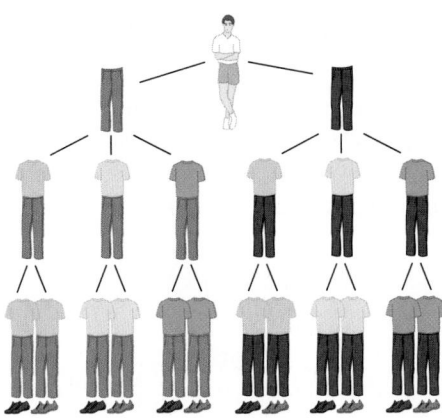

Figure 8.8 Selecting a wardrobe

The **tree diagram**, so named because of its branches, shows that you can form 12 outfits from your two pairs of jeans, three T-shirts, and two pairs of sneakers. Notice that the number of outfits can be obtained by multiplying the number of choices for jeans, 2, the number of choices for the T-shirts, 3, and the number of choices for the sneakers, 2:

$$2 \cdot 3 \cdot 2 = 12.$$

We can generalize this idea to any two or more groups of items—not just jeans, T-shirts, and sneakers—with the **Fundamental Counting Principle**:

The Fundamental Counting Principle

The number of ways in which a series of successive things can occur is found by multiplying the number of ways in which each thing can occur.

For example, if you own 30 pairs of jeans, 20 T-shirts, and 12 pairs of sneakers, you have

$$30 \cdot 20 \cdot 12 = 7200$$

choices for your wardrobe!

EXAMPLE 1 Options in Planning a Course Schedule

Next semester you are planning to take three courses—math, English, and humanities. Based on time blocks and highly recommended professors, there are 8 sections of math, 5 of English, and 4 of humanities that you find suitable. Assuming no scheduling conflicts, how many different three-course schedules are possible?

Solution This situation involves making choices with three groups of items.

The number of possible ways of playing the first four moves on each side in a game of chess is 318,979,564,000.

Running Out of Telephone Numbers

By the year 2020, portable telephones used for business and pleasure will all be videophones. At that time, U.S. population is expected to be 323 million. Faxes, beepers, cell phones, computer phone lines, and business lines may result in certain areas running out of phone numbers. Solution: Add more digits!

With or without extra digits, we expect that the 2020 videophone greeting will still be "hello," a word created by Thomas Edison in 1877. Phone inventor Alexander Graham Bell preferred "ahoy," but "hello" won out, appearing in the *Oxford English Dictionary* in 1883.

(Source: New York Times)

We use the Fundamental Counting Principle to find the number of three-course schedules. Multiply the number of choices for each of the three groups:

$$8 \cdot 5 \cdot 4 = 160.$$

Thus, there are 160 different three-course schedules.

⊘ Check Point **1** A pizza can be ordered with three choices of size (small, medium, or large), four choices of crust (thin, thick, crispy, or regular), and six choices of toppings (ground beef, sausage, pepperoni, bacon, mushrooms, or onions). How many different one-topping pizzas can be ordered?

EXAMPLE 2 A Multiple-Choice Test

You are taking a multiple-choice test that has ten questions. Each of the questions has four answer choices, with one correct answer per question. If you select one of these four choices for each question and leave nothing blank, in how many ways can you answer the questions?

Solution This situation involves making choices with ten questions.

Question 1	Question 2	Question 3	\cdots	Question 9	Question 10
4 choices	4 choices	4 choices		4 choices	4 choices

We use the Fundamental Counting Principle to determine the number of ways that you can answer the questions on the test. Multiply the number of choices, 4, for each of the ten questions.

$$4 \cdot 4 \cdot 4 \cdot 4 \cdot 4 \cdot 4 \cdot 4 \cdot 4 \cdot 4 \cdot 4 = 4^{10} = 1,048,576$$

Thus, you can answer the questions in 1,048,576 different ways.

Are you surprised that there are over one million ways of answering a ten-question multiple-choice test? Of course, there is only one way to answer the test and receive a perfect score. The probability of guessing your way into a perfect score involves calculating the chance of getting a perfect score, just one way from all 1,048,576 possible outcomes. In short, prepare for the test and do not rely on guessing!

⊘ Check Point **2** You are taking a multiple-choice test that has six questions. Each of the questions has three answer choices, with one correct answer per question. If you select one of these three choices for each question and leave nothing blank, in how many ways can you answer the questions?

EXAMPLE 3 Telephone Numbers in the United States

Telephone numbers in the United States begin with three-digit area codes followed by seven-digit local telephone numbers. Area codes and local telephone numbers cannot begin with 0 or 1. How many different telephone numbers are possible?

Solution This situation involves making choices with ten groups of items.

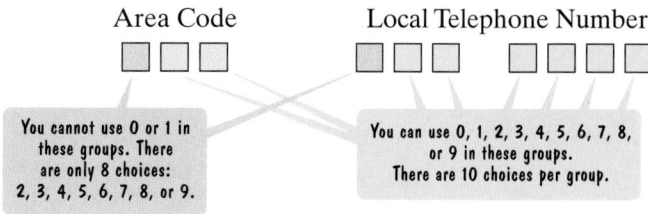

Here are the numbers of choices for each of the ten groups of items:

Area Code
8 10 10

Local Telephone Number
8 10 10 10 10 10 10.

We use the Fundamental Counting Principle to determine the number of different telephone numbers that are possible. The total number of telephone numbers possible is

$$8 \cdot 10 \cdot 10 \cdot 8 \cdot 10 \cdot 10 \cdot 10 \cdot 10 \cdot 10 \cdot 10 = 6,400,000,000.$$

There are six billion four hundred million different telephone numbers that are possible. ●

☑ Check Point **3** License plates in a particular state display two letters followed by three numbers, such as AT-887 or BB-013. How many different license plates can be manufactured?

② Use the permutations formula.

Permutations

You are the coach of a little league baseball team. There are 13 players on the team (and lots of parents hovering in the background, dreaming of stardom for their little "Manny Ramirez"). You need to choose a batting order having 9 players. The order makes a difference, because, for instance, if bases are loaded and "Little Manny" is fourth or fifth at bat, his possible home run will drive in three additional runs. How many batting orders can you form?

You can choose any of 13 players for the first person at bat. Then you will have 12 players from which to choose the second batter, then 11 from which to choose the third batter, and so on. The situation can be shown as follows:

Batter 1	Batter 2	Batter 3	Batter 4	Batter 5	Batter 6	Batter 7	Batter 8	Batter 9
13 choices	12 choices	11 choices	10 choices	9 choices	8 choices	7 choices	6 choices	5 choices

We use the Fundamental Counting Principle to find the number of batting orders. The total number of batting orders is

$$13 \cdot 12 \cdot 11 \cdot 10 \cdot 9 \cdot 8 \cdot 7 \cdot 6 \cdot 5 = 259,459,200.$$

Nearly 260 million batting orders are possible for your 13-player little league team. Each batting order is called a *permutation* of 13 players taken 9 at a time. The number of permutations of 13 players taken 9 at a time is 259,459,200.

A **permutation** is an ordered arrangement of items that occurs when

- No item is used more than once. (Each of the 9 players in the batting order bats exactly once.)
- The order of arrangement makes a difference.

We can obtain a formula for finding the number of permutations of 13 players taken 9 at a time by rewriting our computation:

$$13 \cdot 12 \cdot 11 \cdot 10 \cdot 9 \cdot 8 \cdot 7 \cdot 6 \cdot 5$$

$$= \frac{13 \cdot 12 \cdot 11 \cdot 10 \cdot 9 \cdot 8 \cdot 7 \cdot 6 \cdot 5 \cdot \boxed{4 \cdot 3 \cdot 2 \cdot 1}}{\boxed{4 \cdot 3 \cdot 2 \cdot 1}} = \frac{13!}{4!} = \frac{13!}{(13 - 9)!}.$$

Thus, the number of permutations of 13 things taken 9 at a time is $\frac{13!}{(13 - 9)!}$. The special notation $_{13}P_9$ is used to replace the phrase "the number of permutations of 13 things taken 9 at a time." Using this new notation, we can write

$$_{13}P_9 = \frac{13!}{(13-9)!}.$$

The numerator of this expression is the number of items, 13 team members, expressed as a factorial: 13!. The denominator is also a factorial. It is the factorial of the difference between the number of items, 13, and the number of items in each permutation, 9 batters: $(13-9)!$.

The notation $_nP_r$ means the **number of permutations of n things taken r at a time**. We can generalize from the situation in which 9 batters were taken from 13 players. By generalizing, we obtain the following formula for the number of permutations if r items are taken from n items.

Permutations of n Things Taken r at a Time

The number of possible permutations if r items are taken from n items is

$$_nP_r = \frac{n!}{(n-r)!}.$$

Study Tip

Because all permutation problems are also fundamental counting problems, they can be solved using the formula for $_nP_r$ or using the Fundamental Counting Principle.

Technology

Graphing utilities have a menu item for calculating permutations, usually labeled $\boxed{_nP_r}$. For example, to find $_{20}P_3$, the keystrokes are

20 $\boxed{_nP_r}$ 3 $\boxed{\text{ENTER}}$.

If you are using a scientific calculator, check your manual for the location of the menu item for calculating permutations and the required keystrokes.

(**EXAMPLE 4**) **Using the Formula for Permutations**

You and 19 of your friends have decided to form an Internet marketing consulting firm. The group needs to choose three officers – a CEO, an operating manager, and a treasurer. In how many ways can those offices be filled?

Solution Your group is choosing $r = 3$ officers from a group of $n = 20$ people (you and 19 friends). The order in which the officers are chosen matters because the CEO, the operating manager, and the treasurer each have different responsibilities. Thus, we are looking for the number of permutations of 20 things taken 3 at a time. We use the formula

$$_nP_r = \frac{n!}{(n-r)!}$$

with $n = 20$ and $r = 3$.

$$_{20}P_3 = \frac{20!}{(20-3)!} = \frac{20!}{17!} = \frac{20 \cdot 19 \cdot 18 \cdot 17!}{17!} = \frac{20 \cdot 19 \cdot 18 \cdot \cancel{17!}}{\cancel{17!}} = 20 \cdot 19 \cdot 18 = 6840$$

Thus, there are 6840 different ways of filling the three offices.

✒ **Check Point 4** A corporation has seven members on its board of directors. In how many different ways can it elect a president, vice-president, secretary, and treasurer?

How to Pass the Time for $2\frac{1}{2}$ Million Years

If you were to arrange 15 different books on a shelf and it took you one minute for each permutation, the entire task would take 2,487,965 years.

Source: Isaac Asimov's *Book of Facts.*

(**EXAMPLE 5**) **Using the Formula for Permutations**

You need to arrange seven of your favorite books along a small shelf. How many different ways can you arrange the books, assuming that the order of the books makes a difference to you?

Solution Because you are using all seven of your books in every possible arrangement, you are arranging $r = 7$ books from a group of $n = 7$ books. Thus, we are looking for the number of permutations of 7 things taken 7 at a time. We use the formula

$$_nP_r = \frac{n!}{(n-r)!}$$

with $n = 7$ and $r = 7$.

$$_7P_7 = \frac{7!}{(7-7)!} = \frac{7!}{0!} = \frac{7!}{1} = 5040$$

Thus, you can arrange the books in 5040 ways. There are 5040 different possible permutations.

⏺ **Check Point 5** In how many ways can six books be lined up along a shelf?

③ Distinguish between permutation problems and combination problems.

Combinations

Discussing the tragic death of actor Heath Ledger at age 28, *USA Today* (Jan. 30, 2008) cited five people who had achieved cult-figure status after death. Made iconic by death: Marilyn Monroe (actress, 1927–1962), James Dean (actor, 1931–1955), Jim Morrison (musician and lead singer of The Doors, 1943–1971), Janis Joplin (blues/rock singer, 1943–1970), and Jimi Hendrix (guitar virtuoso, 1943–1970).

Imagine that you ask your friends the following question: "Of these five people, which three would you select to be included in a documentary featuring the best of their work?" You are not asking your friends to rank their three favorite artists in any kind of order—they should merely select the three to be included in the documentary.

One friend answers, "Jim Morrison, Janis Joplin, and Jimi Hendrix." Another responds, "Jimi Hendrix, Janis Joplin, and Jim Morrison." These two people have the same artists in their group of selections, even if they are named in a different order. We are interested *in which artists are named, not the order in which they are named,* for the documentary. Because the items are taken without regard to order, this is not a permutation problem. No ranking of any sort is involved.

Later on, you ask your roommate which three artists she would select for the documentary. She names Marilyn Monroe, James Dean, and Jimi Hendrix. Her selection is different from those of your two other friends because different entertainers are cited.

Mathematicians describe the group of artists given by your roommate as a *combination.* A **combination** of items occurs when

* The items are selected from the same group (the five stars who were made iconic by death).

* No item is used more than once. (You may view Jimi Hendrix as a guitar god, but your three selections cannot be Jimi Hendrix, Jimi Hendrix, and Jimi Hendrix.)

* The order of the items makes no difference. (Morrison, Joplin, Hendrix is the same group in the documentary as Hendrix, Joplin, Morrison.)

Do you see the difference between a permutation and a combination? A permutation is an ordered arrangement of a given group of items. A combination is a group of items taken without regard to their order. **Permutation** problems involve situations in which **order matters**. **Combination** problems involve situations in which the **order of the items makes no difference**.

> (EXAMPLE 6) **Distinguishing between Permutations and Combinations**

For each of the following problems, determine whether the problem is one involving permutations or combinations. (It is not necessary to solve the problem.)

 a. Six students are running for student government president, vice-president, and treasurer. The student with the greatest number of votes becomes the president, the second highest vote-getter becomes vice-president, and the student who gets the third largest number of votes will be treasurer. How many different outcomes are possible for these three positions?

 b. Six people are on the board of supervisors for your neighborhood park. A three-person committee is needed to study the possibility of expanding the park. How many different committees could be formed from the six people?

 c. Baskin-Robbins offers 31 different flavors of ice cream. One of their items is a bowl consisting of three scoops of ice cream, each a different flavor. How many such bowls are possible?

Solution

 a. Students are choosing three student government officers from six candidates. The order in which the officers are chosen makes a difference because each of the offices (president, vice-president, treasurer) is different. Order matters. This is a problem involving permutations.

 b. A three-person committee is to be formed from the six-person board of supervisors. The order in which the three people are selected does not matter because they are not filling different roles on the committee. Because order makes no difference, this is a problem involving combinations.

 c. A three-scoop bowl of three different flavors is to be formed from Baskin-Robbins's 31 flavors. The order in which the three scoops of ice cream are put into the bowl is irrelevant. A bowl with chocolate, vanilla, and strawberry is exactly the same as a bowl with vanilla, strawberry, and chocolate. Different orderings do not change things, and so this is a problem involving combinations. ●

Check Point **6** For each of the following problems, explain if the problem is one involving permutations or combinations. (It is not necessary to solve the problem.)

 a. How many ways can you select 6 free DVDs from a list of 200 DVDs?

 b. In a race in which there are 50 runners and no ties, in how many ways can the first three finishers come in?

④ Use the combinations formula.

A Formula for Combinations

We have seen that the notation $_nP_r$ means the number of permutations of n things taken r at a time. Similarly, the notation $_nC_r$ means the **number of combinations of n things taken r at a time**.

We can develop a formula for $_nC_r$ by comparing permutations and combinations. Consider the letters A, B, C, and D. The number of permutations of these four letters taken three at a time is

$$_4P_3 = \frac{4!}{(4-3)!} = \frac{4!}{1!} = \frac{4 \cdot 3 \cdot 2 \cdot 1}{1} = 24.$$

Here are the 24 permutations:

ABC,	ABD,	ACD,	BCD,
ACB,	ADB,	ADC,	BDC,
BAC,	BAD,	CAD,	CBD,
BCA,	BDA,	CDA,	CDB,
CAB,	DAB,	DAC,	DBC,
CBA,	DBA,	DCA,	DCB.

This column contains only one combination, ABC.

This column contains only one combination, ABD.

This column contains only one combination, ACD.

This column contains only one combination, BCD.

Because the order of items makes no difference in determining combinations, each column of six permutations represents one combination. There is a total of four combinations:

ABC, ABD, ACD, BCD.

Thus, $_4C_3 = 4$: The number of combinations of 4 things taken 3 at a time is 4. With 24 permutations and only four combinations, there are 6, or 3!, times as many permutations as there are combinations.

In general, there are $r!$ times as many permutations of n things taken r at a time as there are combinations of n things taken r at a time. Thus, we find the number of combinations of n things taken r at a time by dividing the number of permutations of n things taken r at a time by $r!$.

$$_nC_r = \frac{_nP_r}{r!} = \frac{\dfrac{n!}{(n-r)!}}{r!} = \frac{n!}{(n-r)!r!}$$

Combinations of n Things Taken r at a Time

The number of possible combinations if r items are taken from n items is

$$_nC_r = \frac{n!}{(n-r)!r!}.$$

Notice that the formula for $_nC_r$ is the same as the formula for the binomial coefficient $\binom{n}{r}$.

EXAMPLE 7 Using the Formula for Combinations

A three-person committee is needed to study ways of improving public transportation. How many committees could be formed from the eight people on the board of supervisors?

Solution The order in which the three people are selected does not matter. This is a problem of selecting $r = 3$ people from a group of $n = 8$ people. We are

Technology

Graphing utilities have a menu item for calculating combinations, usually labeled $_nC_r$. For example, to find $_8C_3$, the keystrokes on most graphing utilities are

$$8 \;\boxed{_nC_r}\; 3 \;\boxed{\text{ENTER}}.$$

If you are using a scientific calculator, check your manual to see whether there is a menu item for calculating combinations.

If you use your calculator's factorial key to find $\frac{8!}{5!3!}$, be sure to enclose the factorials in the denominator with parentheses

$$8\;\boxed{!}\; \boxed{\div}\; \boxed{(}\; 5\;\boxed{!}\; \boxed{\times}\; 3\;\boxed{!}\; \boxed{)}$$

pressing $\boxed{=}$ or $\boxed{\text{ENTER}}$ to obtain the answer.

looking for the number of combinations of eight things taken three at a time. We use the formula

$$_nC_r = \frac{n!}{(n-r)!\,r!}$$

with $n = 8$ and $r = 3$.

$$_8C_3 = \frac{8!}{(8-3)!3!} = \frac{8!}{5!3!} = \frac{8 \cdot 7 \cdot 6 \cdot 5!}{5! \cdot 3 \cdot 2 \cdot 1} = \frac{8 \cdot 7 \cdot 6 \cdot 5!}{5! \cdot 3 \cdot 2 \cdot 1} = 56$$

Thus, 56 committees of three people each can be formed from the eight people on the board of supervisors.

Check Point 7 From a group of 10 physicians, in how many ways can four people be selected to attend a conference on acupuncture?

EXAMPLE 8 **Using the Formula for Combinations**

In poker, a person is dealt 5 cards from a standard 52-card deck. The order in which you are dealt the 5 cards does not matter. How many different 5-card poker hands are possible?

Solution Because the order in which the 5 cards are dealt does not matter, this is a problem involving combinations. We are looking for the number of combinations of $n = 52$ cards dealt $r = 5$ at a time. We use the formula

$$_nC_r = \frac{n!}{(n-r)!\,r!}$$

with $n = 52$ and $r = 5$.

$$_{52}C_5 = \frac{52!}{(52-5)!5!} = \frac{52!}{47!5!} = \frac{52 \cdot 51 \cdot 50 \cdot 49 \cdot 48 \cdot 47!}{47! \cdot 5 \cdot 4 \cdot 3 \cdot 2 \cdot 1} = 2{,}598{,}960$$

Thus, there are 2,598,960 different 5-card poker hands possible. It surprises many people that more than 2.5 million 5-card hands can be dealt from a mere 52 cards.

If you are a card player, it does not get any better than to be dealt the 5-card poker hand shown in **Figure 8.9**. This hand is called a *royal flush*. It consists of an ace, king, queen, jack, and 10, all of the same suit: all hearts, all diamonds, all clubs, or all spades. The probability of being dealt a royal flush involves calculating the number of ways of being dealt such a hand: just 4 of all 2,598,960 possible hands. In the next section, we move from counting possibilities to computing probabilities.

Figure 8.9 A royal flush

Check Point 8 How many different 4-card hands can be dealt from a deck that has 16 different cards?

Exercise Set 8.6

Practice Exercises

In Exercises 1–8, use the formula for $_nP_r$ to evaluate each expression.

1. $_9P_4$

2. $_7P_3$

3. $_8P_5$

4. $_{10}P_4$

5. $_6P_6$

6. $_9P_9$

7. $_8P_0$

8. $_6P_0$

In Exercises 9–16, use the formula for $_nC_r$ to evaluate each expression.

9. $_9C_5$

10. $_{10}C_6$

11. $_{11}C_4$

12. $_{12}C_5$

13. $_7C_7$

14. $_4C_4$

15. $_5C_0$

16. $_6C_0$

In Exercises 17–20, does the problem involve permutations or combinations? Explain your answer. (It is not necessary to solve the problem.)

17. A medical researcher needs 6 people to test the effectiveness of an experimental drug. If 13 people have volunteered for the test, in how many ways can 6 people be selected?

18. Fifty people purchase raffle tickets. Three winning tickets are selected at random. If first prize is $1000, second prize is $500, and third prize is $100, in how many different ways can the prizes be awarded?

19. How many different four-letter passwords can be formed from the letters A, B, C, D, E, F, and G if no repetition of letters is allowed?

20. Fifty people purchase raffle tickets. Three winning tickets are selected at random. If each prize is $500, in how many different ways can the prizes be awarded?

Practice Plus

In Exercises 21–28, evaluate each expression.

21. $\dfrac{_7P_3}{3!} - {_7C_3}$

22. $\dfrac{_{20}P_2}{2!} - {_{20}C_2}$

23. $1 - \dfrac{_3P_2}{_4P_3}$

24. $1 - \dfrac{_5P_3}{_{10}P_4}$

25. $\dfrac{_7C_3}{_5C_4} - \dfrac{98!}{96!}$

26. $\dfrac{_{10}C_3}{_6C_4} - \dfrac{46!}{44!}$

27. $\dfrac{_4C_2 \cdot {_6C_1}}{_{18}C_3}$

28. $\dfrac{_5C_1 \cdot {_7C_2}}{_{12}C_3}$

Application Exercises

Use the Fundamental Counting Principle to solve Exercises 29–40.

29. The model of the car you are thinking of buying is available in nine different colors and three different styles (hatchback, sedan, or station wagon). In how many ways can you order the car?

30. A popular brand of pen is available in three colors (red, green, or blue) and four writing tips (bold, medium, fine, or micro). How many different choices of pens do you have with this brand?

31. An ice cream store sells two drinks (sodas or milk shakes), in four sizes (small, medium, large, or jumbo), and five flavors (vanilla, strawberry, chocolate, coffee, or pistachio). In how many ways can a customer order a drink?

32. A restaurant offers the following lunch menu.

Main Course	Vegetables	Beverages	Desserts
Ham	Potatoes	Coffee	Cake
Chicken	Peas	Tea	Pie
Fish	Green beans	Milk	Ice cream
Beef		Soda	

If one item is selected from each of the four groups, in how many ways can a meal be ordered? Describe two such orders.

33. You are taking a multiple-choice test that has five questions. Each of the questions has three answer choices, with one correct answer per question. If you select one of these three choices for each question and leave nothing blank, in how many ways can you answer the questions?

34. You are taking a multiple-choice test that has eight questions. Each of the questions has three answer choices, with one correct answer per question. If you select one of these three choices for each question and leave nothing blank, in how many ways can you answer the questions?

35. In the original plan for area codes in 1945, the first digit could be any number from 2 through 9, the second digit was either 0 or 1, and the third digit could be any number except 0. With this plan, how many different area codes were possible?

36. How many different four-letter radio station call letters can be formed if the first letter must be W or K?

37. Six performers are to present their comedy acts on a weekend evening at a comedy club. One of the performers insists on being the last stand-up comic of the evening. If this performer's request is granted, how many different ways are there to schedule the appearances?

38. Five singers are to perform at a night club. One of the singers insists on being the last performer of the evening. If this singer's request is granted, how many different ways are there to schedule the appearances?

39. In the *Cambridge Encyclopedia of Language* (Cambridge University Press, 1987), author David Crystal presents five sentences that make a reasonable paragraph regardless of their order. The sentences are as follows:

- Mark had told him about the foxes.
- John looked out the window.
- Could it be a fox?
- However, nobody had seen one for months.
- He thought he saw a shape in the bushes.

How many different five-sentence paragraphs can be formed if the paragraph begins with "He thought he saw a shape in the bushes" and ends with "John looked out of the window"?

40. A television programmer is arranging the order that five movies will be seen between the hours of 6 P.M. and 4 A.M. Two of the movies have a G rating and they are to be shown in the first two time blocks. One of the movies is rated NC-17 and it is to be shown in the last of the time blocks, from 2 A.M. until 4 A.M. Given these restrictions, in how many ways can the five movies be arranged during the indicated time blocks?

Use the formula for $_nP_r$ to solve Exercises 41–48.

41. A club with ten members is to choose three officers – president, vice-president, and secretary-treasurer. If each office is to be held by one person and no person can hold more than one office, in how many ways can those offices be filled?

42. A corporation has ten members on its board of directors. In how many different ways can it elect a president, vice-president, secretary, and treasurer?

43. For a segment of a radio show, a disc jockey can play 7 songs. If there are 13 songs to select from, in how many ways can the program for this segment be arranged?

44. Suppose you are asked to list, in order of preference, the three best movies you have seen this year. If you saw 20 movies during the year, in how many ways can the three best be chosen and ranked?

45. In a race in which six automobiles are entered and there are no ties, in how many ways can the first three finishers come in?

46. In a production of *West Side Story*, eight actors are considered for the male roles of Tony, Riff, and Bernardo. In how many ways can the director cast the male roles?

47. Nine bands have volunteered to perform at a benefit concert, but there is only enough time for five of the bands to play. How many lineups are possible?

48. How many arrangements can be made using four of the letters of the word COMBINE if no letter is to be used more than once?

Use the formula for $_nC_r$ to solve Exercises 49–56.

49. An election ballot asks voters to select three city commissioners from a group of six candidates. In how many ways can this be done?

50. A four-person committee is to be elected from an organization's membership of 11 people. How many different committees are possible?

51. Of 12 possible books, you plan to take 4 with you on vacation. How many different collections of 4 books can you take?

52. There are 14 standbys who hope to get seats on a flight, but only 6 seats are available on the plane. How many different ways can the 6 people be selected?

53. You volunteer to help drive children at a charity event to the zoo, but you can fit only 8 of the 17 children present in your van. How many different groups of 8 children can you drive?

54. Of the 100 people in the U.S. Senate, 18 serve on the Foreign Relations Committee. How many ways are there to select Senate members for this committee (assuming party affiliation is not a factor in selection)?

55. To win at LOTTO in the state of Florida, one must correctly select 6 numbers from a collection of 53 numbers (1 through 53). The order in which the selection is made does not matter. How many different selections are possible?

56. To win in the New York State lottery, one must correctly select 6 numbers from 59 numbers. The order in which the selection is made does not matter. How many different selections are possible?

In Exercises 57–66, solve by the method of your choice.

57. In a race in which six automobiles are entered and there are no ties, in how many ways can the first four finishers come in?

58. A book club offers a choice of 8 books from a list of 40. In how many ways can a member make a selection?

59. A medical researcher needs 6 people to test the effectiveness of an experimental drug. If 13 people have volunteered for the test, in how many ways can 6 people be selected?

60. Fifty people purchase raffle tickets. Three winning tickets are selected at random. If first prize is $1000, second prize is $500, and third prize is $100, in how many different ways can the prizes be awarded?

61. From a club of 20 people, in how many ways can a group of three members be selected to attend a conference?

62. Fifty people purchase raffle tickets. Three winning tickets are selected at random. If each prize is $500, in how many different ways can the prizes be awarded?

63. How many different four-letter passwords can be formed from the letters A, B, C, D, E, F, and G if no repetition of letters is allowed?

64. Nine comedy acts will perform over two evenings. Five of the acts will perform on the first evening and the order in which the acts perform is important. How many ways can the schedule for the first evening be made?

65. Using 15 flavors of ice cream, how many cones with three different flavors can you create if it is important to you which flavor goes on the top, middle, and bottom?

66. Baskin-Robbins offers 31 different flavors of ice cream. One of their items is a bowl consisting of three scoops of ice cream, each a different flavor. How many such bowls are possible?

Exercises 67–72 are based on the following jokes about books:

- *"Outside of a dog, a book is man's best friend. Inside of a dog, it's too dark to read." – Groucho Marx*
- *"I recently bought a book of free verse. For $12." – George Carlin*
- *"If a word in the dictionary was misspelled, how would we know?" – Steven Wright*
- *"Encyclopedia is a Latin term. It means 'to paraphrase a term paper.' " – Greg Ray*
- *"A bookstore is one of the only pieces of evidence we have that people are still thinking." – Jerry Seinfeld*
- *"I honestly believe there is absolutely nothing like going to bed with a good book. Or a friend who's read one." – Phyllis Diller*

67. In how many ways can these six jokes be ranked from best to worst?

68. If Phyllis Diller's joke about books is excluded, in how many ways can the remaining five jokes be ranked from best to worst?

69. In how many ways can people select their three favorite jokes from these comments about books?

70. In how many ways can people select their two favorite jokes from these comments about books?

71. If the order in which these jokes are told makes a difference in terms of how they are received, how many ways can they be delivered if George Carlin's joke is delivered first and Jerry Seinfeld's joke is told last?

72. If the order in which these jokes are told makes a difference in terms of how they are received, how many ways can they be delivered if a joke by a man is told first?

Writing in Mathematics

73. Explain the Fundamental Counting Principle.

74. Write an original problem that can be solved using the Fundamental Counting Principle. Then solve the problem.

75. What is a permutation?

76. Describe what $_nP_r$ represents.

77. Write a word problem that can be solved by evaluating $_7P_3$.

78. What is a combination?

79. Explain how to distinguish between permutation and combination problems.

80. Write a word problem that can be solved by evaluating $_7C_3$.

Technology Exercises

81. Use a graphing utility with an $\boxed{_nP_r}$ menu item to verify your answers in Exercises 1–8.

82. Use a graphing utility with an $\boxed{_nC_r}$ menu item to verify your answers in Exercises 9–16.

Critical Thinking Exercises

Make Sense? *In Exercises 83–86, determine whether each statement makes sense or does not make sense, and explain your reasoning.*

83. I used the Fundamental Counting Principle to determine the number of five-digit ZIP codes that are available to the U.S. Postal Service.

84. I used the permutations formula to determine the number of ways the manager of a baseball team can form a 9-player batting order from a team of 25 players.

85. I used the combinations formula to determine how many different four-note sound sequences can be created from the notes C, D, E, F, G, A, and B.

86. I used the permutations formula to determine the number of ways people can select their 9 favorite baseball players from a team of 25 players.

In Exercises 87–90, determine whether each statement is true or false. If the statement is false, make the necessary change(s) to produce a true statement.

87. The number of ways to choose four questions out of ten questions on an essay test is $_{10}P_4$.

88. If $r > 1$, $_nP_r$ is less than $_nC_r$.

89. $_7P_3 = 3!\,_7C_3$

90. The number of ways to pick a winner and first runner-up in a talent contest with 20 contestants is $_{20}C_2$.

91. Five men and five women line up at a checkout counter in a store. In how many ways can they line up if the first person in line is a woman and the people in line alternate woman, man, woman, man, and so on?

92. How many four-digit odd numbers less than 6000 can be formed using the digits 2, 4, 6, 7, 8, and 9?

93. A mathematics exam consists of 10 multiple-choice questions and 5 open-ended problems in which all work must be shown. If an examinee must answer 8 of the multiple-choice questions and 3 of the open-ended problems, in how many ways can the questions and problems be chosen?

Group Exercise

94. The group should select real-world situations where the Fundamental Counting Principle can be applied. These could involve the number of possible student ID numbers on your campus, the number of possible phone numbers in your community, the number of meal options at a local restaurant, the number of ways a person in the group can select outfits for class, the number of ways a condominium can be purchased in a nearby community, and so on. Once situations have been selected, group members should determine in how many ways each part of the task can be done. Group members will need to obtain menus, find out about telephone-digit requirements in the community, count shirts, pants, shoes in closets, visit condominium sales offices, and so on. Once the group reassembles, apply the Fundamental Counting Principle to determine the number of available options in each situation. Because these numbers may be quite large, use a calculator.

Preview Exercises

Exercises 95–97 will help you prepare for the material covered in the next section.

The figure shows that when a die is rolled, there are six equally likely outcomes: 1, 2, 3, 4, 5, or 6. Use this information to solve each exercise.

95. What fraction of the outcomes are less than 5?

96. What fraction of the outcomes are not less than 5?

97. What fraction of the outcomes are even or greater than 3?

Probability

Objectives

1 Compute empirical probability.

2 Compute theoretical probability.

3 Find the probability that an event will not occur.

4 Find the probability of one event or a second event occurring.

5 Find the probability of one event and a second event occurring.

Possible Values for Probabilities

Table 8.3 The Hours of Sleep Americans Get on a Typical Night

Hours of Sleep	Number of Americans, in millions
4 or less	12
5	27
6	75
7	90
8	81
9	9
10 or more	6
	Total: 300

Source: Discovery Health Media

How many hours of sleep do you typically get each night? **Table 8.3** indicates that 75 million out of 300 million Americans are getting six hours of sleep on a typical night. The *probability* of an American getting six hours of sleep on a typical night is $\frac{75}{300}$. This fraction can be reduced to $\frac{1}{4}$, or expressed as 0.25, or 25%. Thus, 25% of Americans get six hours of sleep each night.

We find a probability by dividing one number by another. Probabilities are assigned to an *event*, such as getting six hours of sleep on a typical night. Events that are certain to occur are assigned probabilities of 1, or 100%. For example, the probability that a given individual will eventually die is 1. Although Woody Allen whined, "I don't want to achieve immortality through my work. I want to achieve it through not dying," death (and taxes) are always certain. By contrast, if an event cannot occur, its probability is 0. Regrettably, the probability that Elvis will return and serenade us with one final reprise of "Don't Be Cruel" (and we hope we're not) is 0.

Probabilities of events are expressed as numbers ranging from 0 to 1, or 0% to 100%. The closer the probability of a given event is to 1, the more likely it is that the event will occur. The closer the probability of a given event is to 0, the less likely it is that the event will occur.

1 Compute empirical probability.

Empirical Probability

Empirical probability applies to situations in which we observe how frequently an event occurs. We use the following formula to compute the empirical probability of an event:

Computing Empirical Probability

The **empirical probability** of event E, denoted by $P(E)$, is

$$P(E) = \frac{\text{observed number of times } E \text{ occurs}}{\text{total number of observed occurrences}}.$$

(**EXAMPLE 1**) **Empirical Probabilities with Real-World Data**

When women turn 40, their gynecologists typically remind them that it is time to undergo mammography screening for breast cancer. The data in **Table 8.4** on the next page are based on 100,000 U.S. women, ages 40 to 50, who participated in mammography screening.

Table 8.4 Mammography Screening on 100,000
U.S. Women, Ages 40 to 50

	Breast Cancer	No Breast Cancer
Positive Mammogram	720	6944
Negative Mammogram	80	92,256

720 + 6944 = 7664 women have positive mammograms.

80 + 92,256 = 92,336 women have negative mammograms.

720 + 80 = 800 women have breast cancer.

6944 + 92,256 = 99,200 women do not have breast cancer.

Source: Gerd Gigerenzer, *Calculated Risks*, Simon and Schuster, 2002

a. Use **Table 8.4** to find the probability that a woman aged 40 to 50 has breast cancer.

b. Among women without breast cancer, find the probability of a positive mammogram.

c. Among women with positive mammograms, find the probability of not having breast cancer.

Solution

a. We begin with the probability that a woman aged 40 to 50 has breast cancer. The probability of having breast cancer is the number of women with breast cancer divided by the total number of women.

$$P(\text{breast cancer}) = \frac{\text{number of women with breast cancer}}{\text{total number of women}}$$

$$= \frac{800}{100,000} = \frac{1}{125} = 0.008$$

The empirical probability that a woman aged 40 to 50 has breast cancer is $\frac{1}{125}$, or 0.008.

b. Now, we find the probability of a positive mammogram among women without breast cancer. Thus, we restrict the data to women without breast cancer:

	No Breast Cancer
Positive Mammogram	6944
Negative Mammogram	92,256

Within the restricted data, the probability of a positive mammogram is the number of women with positive mammograms divided by the total number of women.

$$P(\text{positive mammogram}) = \frac{\text{number of women with positive mammograms}}{\text{total number of women in the restricted data}}$$

$$= \frac{6944}{6944 + 92,256} = \frac{6944}{99,200} = 0.07$$

This is the total number of women without breast cancer.

Among women without breast cancer, the empirical probability of a positive mammogram is $\frac{6944}{99,200}$, or 0.07.

c. Now, we find the probability of not having breast cancer among women with positive mammograms. Thus, we restrict the data to women with positive mammograms:

	Breast Cancer	**No Breast Cancer**
Positive Mammogram	720	6944

Within the restricted data, the probability of not having breast cancer is the number of women with no breast cancer divided by the total number of women.

$$P(\text{no breast cancer}) = \frac{\text{number of women with no breast cancer}}{\text{total number of women in the restricted data}}$$

$$= \frac{6944}{720 + 6944} = \frac{6944}{7664} \approx 0.906$$

This is the total number of women with positive mammograms.

Among women with positive mammograms, the probability of not having breast cancer is $\frac{6944}{7664}$, or approximately 0.906.

\oslash **Check Point 1** Use the data in **Table 8.4** to solve this exercise. Express probabilities as fractions and as decimals rounded to three decimal places.

a. Find the probability that a woman aged 40 to 50 has a positive mammogram.

b. Among women with breast cancer, find the probability of a positive mammogram.

c. Among women with positive mammograms, find the probability of having breast cancer.

② Compute theoretical probability.

Theoretical Probability

You toss a coin. Although it is equally likely to land either heads up, denoted by H, or tails up, denoted by T, the actual outcome is uncertain. Any occurrence for which the outcome is uncertain is called an **experiment**. Thus, tossing a coin is an example of an experiment. The set of all possible outcomes of an experiment is the **sample space** of the experiment, denoted by S. The sample space for the coin-tossing experiment is

$$S = \{H, T\}.$$

Lands heads up Lands tails up

We can define an event more formally using these concepts. An **event**, denoted by E, is any subcollection, or subset, of a sample space. For example, the subset $E = \{T\}$ is the event of landing tails up when a coin is tossed.

Theoretical probability applies to situations like this, in which the sample space only contains equally likely outcomes, all of which are known. To calculate the theoretical probability of an event, we divide the number of outcomes resulting in the event by the number of outcomes in the sample space.

Computing Theoretical Probability

If an event E has $n(E)$ equally likely outcomes and its sample space S has $n(S)$ equally likely outcomes, the **theoretical probability** of event E, denoted by $P(E)$, is

$$P(E) = \frac{\text{number of outcomes in event } E}{\text{number of outcomes in samples space } S} = \frac{n(E)}{n(S)}.$$

The sum of the theoretical probabilities of all possible outcomes in the sample space is 1.

How can we use this formula to compute the probability of a coin landing tails up? We use the following sets:

$$E = \{T\} \qquad S = \{H, T\}.$$

> This is the event of landing tails up.

> This is the sample space with all equally likely outcomes.

The probability of a coin landing tails up is

$$P(E) = \frac{\text{number of outcomes that result in tails up}}{\text{total number of possible outcomes}} = \frac{n(E)}{n(S)} = \frac{1}{2}.$$

Theoretical probability applies to many games of chance, including rolling dice, lotteries, card games, and roulette. The next example deals with the experiment of rolling a die. **Figure 8.10** illustrates that when a die is rolled, there are six equally likely outcomes. The sample space can be shown as

$$S = \{1, 2, 3, 4, 5, 6\}.$$

Figure 8.10 Outcomes when a die is rolled

EXAMPLE 2 **Computing Theoretical Probability**

A die is rolled. Find the probability of getting a number less than 5.

Solution The sample space of equally likely outcomes is $S = \{1, 2, 3, 4, 5, 6\}$. There are six outcomes in the sample space, so $n(S) = 6$.

We are interested in the probability of getting a number less than 5. The event of getting a number less than 5 can be represented by

$$E = \{1, 2, 3, 4\}.$$

There are four outcomes in this event, so $n(E) = 4$.

The probability of rolling a number less than 5 is

$$P(E) = \frac{n(E)}{n(S)} = \frac{4}{6} = \frac{2}{3}.$$

⊘ **Check Point 2** A die is rolled. Find the probability of getting a number greater than 4.

EXAMPLE 3 **Computing Theoretical Probability**

Two ordinary six-sided dice are rolled. What is the probability of getting a sum of 8?

Solution Each die has six equally likely outcomes. By the Fundamental Counting Principle, there are $6 \cdot 6$, or 36, equally likely outcomes in the sample space. That is, $n(S) = 36$. The 36 outcomes are shown below as ordered pairs. The five ways of rolling a sum of 8 appear in the green highlighted diagonal.

		Second Die					
		⚀	⚁	⚂	⚃	⚄	⚅
First Die	⚀	(1,1)	(1,2)	(1,3)	(1,4)	(1,5)	(1,6)
	⚁	(2,1)	(2,2)	(2,3)	(2,4)	(2,5)	(2,6)
	⚂	(3,1)	(3,2)	(3,3)	(3,4)	(3,5)	(3,6)
	⚃	(4,1)	(4,2)	(4,3)	(4,4)	(4,5)	(4,6)
	⚄	(5,1)	(5,2)	(5,3)	(5,4)	(5,5)	(5,6)
	⚅	(6,1)	(6,2)	(6,3)	(6,4)	(6,5)	(6,6)

$S = \{(1, 1), (1, 2), (1, 3), (1, 4),$
$(1, 5), (1, 6), (2, 1), (2, 2),$
$(2, 3), (2, 4), (2, 5), (2, 6),$
$(3, 1), (3, 2), (3, 3), (3, 4),$
$(3, 5), (3, 6), (4, 1), (4, 2),$
$(4, 3), (4, 4), (4, 5), (4, 6),$
$(5, 1), (5, 2), (5, 3), (5, 4),$
$(5, 5), (5, 6), (6, 1), (6, 2),$
$(6, 3), (6, 4), (6, 5), (6, 6)\}$

The phrase "getting a sum of 8" describes the event

$$E = \{(6, 2), (5, 3), (4, 4), (3, 5), (2, 6)\}.$$

This event has 5 outcomes, so $n(E) = 5$. Thus, the probability of getting a sum of 8 is

$$P(E) = \frac{n(E)}{n(S)} = \frac{5}{36}.$$

⊘ Check Point **3** What is the probability of getting a sum of 5 when two six-sided dice are rolled?

Computing Theoretical Probability without Listing an Event and the Sample Space

In some situations, we can compute theoretical probability without having to write out each event and each sample space. For example, suppose you are dealt one card from a standard 52-card deck, illustrated in **Figure 8.11**. The deck has four suits: Hearts and diamonds are red, and clubs and spades are black. Each suit has 13 different face values – A(ace), 2, 3, 4, 5, 6, 7, 8, 9, 10, J(jack), Q(queen), and K(king). Jacks, queens, and kings are called **picture cards** or **face cards**.

Figure 8.11 A standard 52-card bridge deck

EXAMPLE 4 **Probability and a Deck of 52 Cards**

You are dealt one card from a standard 52-card deck. Find the probability of being dealt a heart.

Solution Let E be the event of being dealt a heart. Because there are 13 hearts in the deck, the event of being dealt a heart can occur in 13 ways. The number of outcomes in event E is 13: $n(E) = 13$. With 52 cards in the deck, the total number of possible ways of being dealt a single card is 52. The number of outcomes in the sample space is 52: $n(S) = 52$. The probability of being dealt a heart is

$$P(E) = \frac{n(E)}{n(S)} = \frac{13}{52} = \frac{1}{4}.$$

⊘ Check Point **4** If you are dealt one card from a standard 52-card deck, find the probability of being dealt a king.

If your state has a lottery drawing each week, the probability that someone will win the top prize is relatively high. If there is no winner this week, it is virtually certain that eventually someone will be graced with millions of dollars. So, why are you so unlucky compared to this undisclosed someone? In Example 5, we provide an answer to this question, using the counting principles discussed in Section 8.6.

State lotteries keep 50 cents on the dollar, resulting in $10 billion a year for public funding.
© Damon Higgins/*The Palm Beach Post*

Comparing the Probability of Dying to the Probability of Winning Florida's LOTTO

As a healthy nonsmoking 30-year-old, your probability of dying this year is approximately 0.001. Divide this probability by the probability of winning LOTTO with one ticket:

$$\frac{0.001}{0.0000000436} \approx 22,936.$$

A healthy 30-year-old is nearly 23,000 times more likely to die this year than to win Florida's lottery.

3 Find the probability that an event will not occur.

EXAMPLE 5 Probability and Combinations: Winning the Lottery

Florida's lottery game, LOTTO, is set up so that each player chooses six different numbers from 1 to 53. If the six numbers chosen match the six numbers drawn randomly, the player wins (or shares) the top cash prize. (As of this writing, the top cash prize has ranged from $7 million to $106.5 million.) With one LOTTO ticket, what is the probability of winning this prize?

Solution Because the order of the six numbers does not matter, this is a situation involving combinations. Let E be the event of winning the lottery with one ticket. With one LOTTO ticket, there is only one way of winning. Thus, $n(E) = 1$.

The sample space is the set of all possible six-number combinations. We can use the combinations formula

$$_nC_r = \frac{n!}{(n-r)!\,r!}$$

to find the total number of possible combinations. We are selecting $r = 6$ numbers from a collection of $n = 53$ numbers.

$$_{53}C_6 = \frac{53!}{(53-6)!\,6!} = \frac{53!}{47!\,6!} = \frac{53 \cdot 52 \cdot 51 \cdot 50 \cdot 49 \cdot 48 \cdot \cancel{47!}}{\cancel{47!} \cdot 6 \cdot 5 \cdot 4 \cdot 3 \cdot 2 \cdot 1} = 22,957,480$$

There are nearly 23 million number combinations possible in LOTTO. If a person buys one LOTTO ticket, the probability of winning is

$$P(E) = \frac{n(E)}{n(S)} = \frac{1}{22,957,480} \approx 0.0000000436.$$

The probability of winning the top prize with one LOTTO ticket is $\frac{1}{22,957,480}$, or about 1 in 23 million.

Suppose that a person buys 5000 different tickets in Florida's LOTTO. Because that person has selected 5000 different combinations of the six numbers, the probability of winning is

$$\frac{5000}{22,957,480} \approx 0.000218.$$

The chances of winning top prize are about 218 in a million. At $1 per LOTTO ticket, it is highly probable that our LOTTO player will be $5000 poorer. Knowing a little probability helps a lotto.

⬜ **Check Point 5** People lose interest when they do not win at games of chance, including Florida's LOTTO. With drawings twice weekly instead of once, the game described in Example 5 was brought in to bring back lost players and increase ticket sales. The original LOTTO was set up so that each player chose six different numbers from 1 to 49, rather than from 1 to 53, with a lottery drawing only once a week. With one LOTTO ticket, what was the probability of winning the top cash prize in Florida's original LOTTO? Express the answer as a fraction and as a decimal correct to ten places.

Probability of an Event Not Occurring

If we know $P(E)$, the probability of an event E, we can determine the probability that the event will not occur, denoted by $P(\text{not } E)$. Because the sum of the probabilities of all possible outcomes in any situation is 1,

$$P(E) + P(\text{not } E) = 1.$$

We now solve this equation for $P(\text{not } E)$, the probability that event E will not occur, by subtracting $P(E)$ from both sides. The resulting formula is given in the box on the next page.

The Probability of an Event Not Occurring

The probability that an event E will not occur is equal to 1 minus the probability that it will occur.

$$P(\text{not } E) = 1 - P(E)$$

EXAMPLE 6 **The Probability of an Event Not Occurring**

The circle graph in **Figure 8.12** shows the distribution, by age group, of the 191 million car drivers in the United States, with all numbers rounded to the nearest million. If one driver is randomly selected from this population, find the probability that the person is not in the 20–29 age group. Express the probability as a simplified fraction.

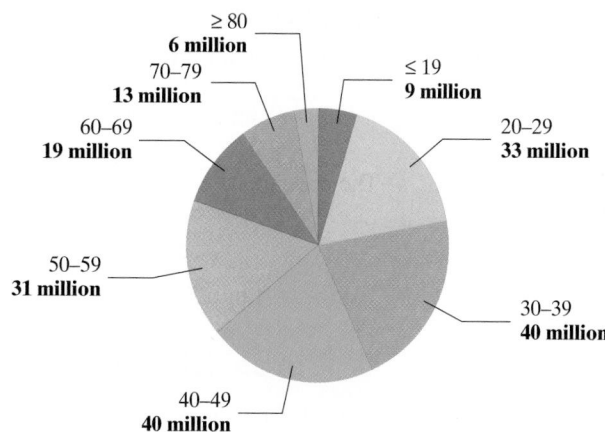

Number of U.S. Car Drivers, by Age Group

Figure 8.12 *Source:* U.S. Census Bureau

Solution We use the probability that the selected person *is* in the 20–29 age group to find the probability that the selected person is not in this age group.

$P(\text{not in 20–29 age group})$

$$= 1 - P(\text{in 20–29 age group})$$

The graph shows 33 million drivers in the 20–29 age group.

$$= 1 - \frac{33}{191}$$

This number, 191 million drivers, was given, but can be obtained by adding the numbers in the eight sectors.

$$= \frac{191}{191} - \frac{33}{191} = \frac{158}{191}$$

The probability that a randomly selected driver is not in the 20–29 age group is $\frac{158}{191}$. ●

⊘ Check Point **6** If one driver is randomly selected from the population represented in **Figure 8.12**, find the probability, expressed as a simplified fraction, that the person is not in the 50–59 age group.

④ Find the probability of one event or a second event occurring.

Or Probabilities with Mutually Exclusive Events

Suppose that you randomly select one card from a deck of 52 cards. Let A be the event of selecting a king and let B be the event of selecting a queen. Only one card is selected, so it is impossible to get both a king and a queen. The events of selecting a king and a queen cannot occur simultaneously. They are called *mutually exclusive events*. If it is impossible for any two events, A and B, to occur simultaneously, they are said to be

mutually exclusive. If A and B are mutually exclusive events, the probability that either A or B will occur is determined by adding their individual probabilities.

Or Probabilities with Mutually Exclusive Events

If A and B are mutually exclusive events, then

$$P(A \text{ or } B) = P(A) + P(B).$$

Using set notation, $P(A \cup B) = P(A) + P(B)$.

(EXAMPLE 7) **The Probability of Either of Two Mutually Exclusive Events Occurring**

If one card is randomly selected from a deck of cards, what is the probability of selecting a king or a queen?

Solution We find the probability that either of these mutually exclusive events will occur by adding their individual probabilities.

$$P(\text{king or queen}) = P(\text{king}) + P(\text{queen}) = \frac{4}{52} + \frac{4}{52} = \frac{8}{52} = \frac{2}{13}$$

The probability of selecting a king or a queen is $\frac{2}{13}$.

⬭

⊘ Check Point **7** If you roll a single, six-sided die, what is the probability of getting either a 4 or a 5?

Or Probabilities with Events That Are Not Mutually Exclusive

Consider the deck of 52 cards shown in **Figure 8.13**. Suppose that these cards are shuffled and you randomly select one card from the deck. What is the probability of selecting a diamond or a picture card (jack, queen, king)? Begin by adding their individual probabilities.

$$P(\text{diamond}) + P(\text{picture card}) = \frac{13}{52} + \frac{12}{52}$$

> There are 13 diamonds in the deck of 52 cards.

> There are 12 picture cards in the deck of 52 cards.

Figure 8.13 A deck of 52 cards

However, this sum is not the probability of selecting a diamond or a picture card. The problem is that there are three cards that are *simultaneously* diamonds and picture cards, shown in **Figure 8.14**. The events of selecting a diamond and selecting a picture card are not mutually exclusive. It is possible to select a card that is both a diamond and a picture card.

Figure 8.14 Three diamonds are picture cards.

The situation is illustrated in the diagram in **Figure 8.15**. Why can't we find the probability of selecting a diamond or a picture card by adding their individual probabilities? The diagram shows that three of the cards, the three diamonds that are picture cards, get counted twice when we add the individual probabilities. First the three cards get counted as diamonds and then they get counted as picture cards. In order to avoid the error of counting the three cards twice, we need to subtract the probability of getting a diamond and a picture card, $\frac{3}{52}$, as follows:

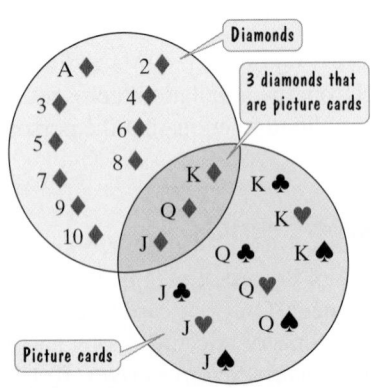

Figure 8.15

$P(\text{diamond or picture card})$

$$= P(\text{diamond}) + P(\text{picture card}) - P(\text{diamond and picture card})$$

$$= \frac{13}{52} + \frac{12}{52} - \frac{3}{52} = \frac{13 + 12 - 3}{52} = \frac{22}{52} = \frac{11}{26}.$$

Thus, the probability of selecting a diamond or a picture card is $\frac{11}{26}$.

In general, if A and B are events that are not mutually exclusive, the probability that A or B will occur is determined by adding their individual probabilities and then subtracting the probability that A and B occur simultaneously.

Or Probabilities with Events That Are Not Mutually Exclusive

If A and B are not mutually exclusive events, then

$$P(A \text{ or } B) = P(A) + P(B) - P(A \text{ and } B).$$

Using set notation,

$$P(A \cup B) = P(A) + P(B) - P(A \cap B).$$

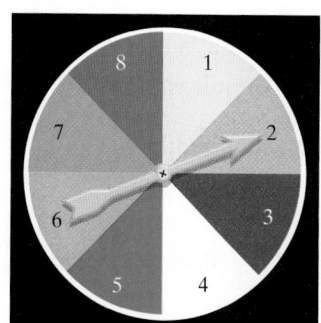

Figure 8.16 It is equally probable that the pointer will land on any one of the eight regions.

EXAMPLE 8 **An *Or* Probability with Events That Are Not Mutually Exclusive**

Figure 8.16 illustrates a spinner. It is equally probable that the pointer will land on any one of the eight regions, numbered 1 through 8. If the pointer lands on a borderline, spin again. Find the probability that the pointer will stop on an even number or a number greater than 5.

Solution It is possible for the pointer to land on a number that is both even and greater than 5. Two of the numbers, 6 and 8, are even and greater than 5. These events are not mutually exclusive. The probability of landing on a number that is even or greater than 5 is calculated as follows:

$$P\left(\begin{array}{c}\text{even or}\\\text{greater than 5}\end{array}\right) = P(\text{even}) + P(\text{greater than 5}) - P\left(\begin{array}{c}\text{even and}\\\text{greater than 5}\end{array}\right)$$

$$= \quad \frac{4}{8} \quad + \quad \frac{3}{8} \quad - \quad \frac{2}{8}$$

Four of the eight numbers, 2, 4, 6, and 8, are even.	Three of the eight numbers, 6, 7, and 8, are greater than 5.	Two of the eight numbers, 6 and 8, are even and greater than 5.

$$= \frac{4 + 3 - 2}{8} = \frac{5}{8}.$$

The probability that the pointer will stop on an even number or a number greater than 5 is $\frac{5}{8}$.

⊘ **Check Point 8** Use **Figure 8.16** to find the probability that the pointer will stop on an odd number or a number less than 5.

EXAMPLE 9 **An *Or* Probability with Real-World Data**

Each year the Internal Revenue Service audits a sample of tax forms to verify their accuracy. **Table 8.5** shows the number of tax returns filed and audited in 2006 by taxable income.

Table 8.5 Tax Returns Filed and Audited, by Taxable Income, 2006

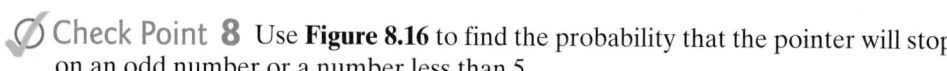

	< \$25,000	\$25,000– \$49,999	\$50,000– \$99,999	≥ \$100,000	Total
Audit	461,729	191,150	163,711	166,839	983,429
No audit	51,509,900	30,637,782	26,300,262	12,726,963	121,174,907
Total	51,971,629	30,828,932	26,463,973	12,893,802	122,158,336

Source: Internal Revenue Service

Table 8.5 Tax Returns Filed and Audited, by Taxable Income (repeated)

	< $25,000	$25,000–$49,999	$50,000–$99,999	≥ $100,000	Total
Audit	461,729	191,150	163,711	166,839	983,429
No audit	51,509,900	30,637,782	26,300,262	12,726,963	121,174,907
Total	51,971,629	30,828,932	26,463,973	12,893,802	122,158,336

Source: Internal Revenue Service

If one person is randomly selected from the population represented in **Table 8.5**, find the probability that

 a. the taxpayer had a taxable income less than $25,000 or was audited.

 b. the taxpayer had a taxable income less than $25,000 or at least $100,000.

Express probabilities as decimals rounded to the nearest hundredth.

Solution

 a. It is possible to select a taxpayer who both earned less than $25,000 and was audited. Thus, these events are not mutually exclusive.

P(less than $25,000 or audited)

$$= P(\text{less than } \$25{,}000) + P(\text{audited}) - P(\text{less than } \$25{,}000 \text{ and audited})$$

$$= \frac{51{,}971{,}629}{122{,}158{,}336} + \frac{983{,}429}{122{,}158{,}336} - \frac{461{,}729}{122{,}158{,}336}$$

> Of the 122,158,336 taxpayers, 51,971,629 had taxable incomes less than $25,000.

> Of the 122,158,336 taxpayers, 983,429 were audited.

> Of the 122,158,336 taxpayers, 461,729 earned less than $25,000 and were audited.

$$= \frac{52{,}493{,}329}{122{,}158{,}336} \approx 0.43$$

The probability that a taxpayer had a taxable income less than $25,000 or was audited is approximately 0.43.

 b. A taxable income of *at least* $100,000 means $100,000 or more. Thus, it is not possible to select a taxpayer with both a taxable income of less than $25,000 and at least $100,000. These events are mutually exclusive.

P(less than $25,000 or at least $100,000)

$$= P(\text{less than } \$25{,}000) + P(\text{at least } \$100{,}000)$$

$$= \frac{51{,}971{,}629}{122{,}158{,}336} + \frac{12{,}893{,}802}{122{,}158{,}336}$$

> Of the 122,158,336 taxpayers, 51,971,629 had taxable incomes less than $25,000.

> Of the 122,158,336 taxpayers, 12,893,802 had taxable incomes of $100,000 or more.

$$= \frac{64{,}865{,}431}{122{,}158{,}336} \approx 0.53$$

The probability that a taxpayer had a taxable income less than $25,000 or at least $100,000 is approximately 0.53.

⊘ Check Point **9** If one person is randomly selected from the population represented in **Table 8.5**, find the probability, expressed as a decimal rounded to the nearest hundredth, that

 a. the taxpayer had a taxable income of at least $100,000 or was not audited.

 b. the taxpayer had a taxable income less than $25,000 or between $50,000 and $99,999, inclusive.

⑤ Find the probability of one event and a second event occurring.

And Probabilities with Independent Events

Suppose that you toss a fair coin two times in succession. The outcome of the first toss, heads or tails, does not affect what happens when you toss the coin a second time. For example, the occurrence of tails on the first toss does not make tails more likely or less likely to occur on the second toss. The repeated toss of a coin produces *independent events* because the outcome of one toss does not influence the outcome of others. Two events are **independent events** if the occurrence of either of them has no effect on the probability of the other.

 If two events are independent, we can calculate the probability of the first occurring and the second occurring by multiplying their probabilities.

> ### *And* Probabilities with Independent Events
> If A and B are independent events, then
> $$P(A \text{ and } B) = P(A) \cdot P(B).$$

(**EXAMPLE 10**) **Independent Events on a Roulette Wheel**

Figure 8.17 shows a U.S. roulette wheel that has 38 numbered slots (1 through 36, 0, and 00). Of the 38 compartments, 18 are black, 18 are red, and two are green. A play has the dealer spin the wheel and a small ball in opposite directions. As the ball slows to a stop, it can land with equal probability on any one of the 38 numbered slots. Find the probability of red occurring on two consecutive plays.

Solution The wheel has 38 equally likely outcomes and 18 are red. Thus, the probability of red occurring on a play is $\frac{18}{38}$, or $\frac{9}{19}$. The result that occurs on each play is independent of all previous results. Thus,

Figure 8.17 A U.S. roulette wheel

$$P(\text{red and red}) = P(\text{red}) \cdot P(\text{red}) = \frac{9}{19} \cdot \frac{9}{19} = \frac{81}{361} \approx 0.224.$$

The probability of red occurring on two consecutive plays is $\frac{81}{361}$. ●

 Some roulette players incorrectly believe that if red occurs on two consecutive plays, then another color is "due." Because the events are independent, the outcomes of previous spins have no effect on any other spins.

⊘ Check Point **10** Find the probability of green occurring on two consecutive plays on a roulette wheel.

 The *and* rule for independent events can be extended to cover three or more events. Thus, if A, B, and C are independent events, then

$$P(A \text{ and } B \text{ and } C) = P(A) \cdot P(B) \cdot P(C).$$

EXAMPLE 11 Independent Events in a Family

The picture in the margin shows a family that has had nine girls in a row. Find the probability of this occurrence.

Solution If two or more events are independent, we can find the probability of them all occurring by multiplying their probabilities. The probability of a baby girl is $\frac{1}{2}$, so the probability of nine girls in a row is $\frac{1}{2}$ used as a factor nine times.

$$P(\text{nine girls in a row}) = \frac{1}{2} \cdot \frac{1}{2} \cdot \frac{1}{2} \cdot \frac{1}{2} \cdot \frac{1}{2} \cdot \frac{1}{2} \cdot \frac{1}{2} \cdot \frac{1}{2} \cdot \frac{1}{2}$$
$$= \left(\frac{1}{2}\right)^9 = \frac{1}{512}$$

The probability of a run of nine girls in a row is $\frac{1}{512}$. (If another child is born into the family, this event is independent of the other nine, and the probability of a girl is still $\frac{1}{2}$.)

◯ Check Point **11** Find the probability of a family having four boys in a row.

Exercise Set 8.7

Practice and Application Exercises

The table shows the distribution, by marital status and gender, of the 212.5 million Americans ages 18 or older. Use the data in the table to solve Exercises 1–10.

Marital Status of the United States Population, Ages 18 or Older, in Millions

	Never Married	Married	Widowed	Divorced	Total
Male	28.6	62.1	2.7	9.0	102.4
Female	23.3	62.8	11.3	12.7	110.1
Total	51.9	124.9	14.0	21.7	212.5

Total male: 28.6 + 62.1 + 2.7 + 9.0 = 102.4

Total female: 23.3 + 62.8 + 11.3 + 12.7 = 110.1

Total never married: 28.6 + 23.3 = 51.9

Total married: 62.1 + 62.8 = 124.9

Total widowed: 2.7 + 11.3 = 14.0

Total divorced: 9.0 + 12.7 = 21.7

Total adult population: 102.4 + 110.1 = 212.5

Source: U.S. Census Bureau

If one person is randomly selected from the population described in the table, find the probability, to the nearest hundredth, that the person

1. is divorced.
2. has never been married.
3. is female.
4. is male.
5. is a widowed male.
6. is a widowed female.
7. Among those who are divorced, find the probability of selecting a woman.
8. Among those who are divorced, find the probability of selecting a man.
9. Among adult men, find the probability of selecting a married person.
10. Among adult women, find the probability of selecting a married person.

In Exercises 11–16, a die is rolled. Find the probability of getting

11. a 4.
12. a 5.
13. an odd number.
14. a number greater than 3.
15. a number greater than 4.
16. a number greater than 7.

In Exercises 17–20, you are dealt one card from a standard 52-card deck. Find the probability of being dealt

17. a queen.
18. a diamond.
19. a picture card.
20. a card greater than 3 and less than 7.

In Exercises 21–22, a fair coin is tossed two times in succession. The sample space of equally likely outcomes is $\{HH, HT, TH, TT\}$. Find the probability of getting

21. two heads.
22. the same outcome on each toss.

In Exercises 23–24, you select a family with three children. If M represents a male child and F a female child, the sample space of equally likely outcomes is $\{MMM, MMF, MFM, MFF, FMM, FMF, FFM, FFF\}$. Find the probability of selecting a family with

23. at least one male child.
24. at least two female children.

In Exercises 25–26, a single die is rolled twice. The 36 equally likely outcomes are shown as follows:

	Second Roll					
	⚀	⚁	⚂	⚃	⚄	⚅
⚀	(1, 1)	(1, 2)	(1, 3)	(1, 4)	(1, 5)	(1, 6)
⚁	(2, 1)	(2, 2)	(2, 3)	(2, 4)	(2, 5)	(2, 6)
⚂	(3, 1)	(3, 2)	(3, 3)	(3, 4)	(3, 5)	(3, 6)
⚃	(4, 1)	(4, 2)	(4, 3)	(4, 4)	(4, 5)	(4, 6)
⚄	(5, 1)	(5, 2)	(5, 3)	(5, 4)	(5, 5)	(5, 6)
⚅	(6, 1)	(6, 2)	(6, 3)	(6, 4)	(6, 5)	(6, 6)

(First Roll shown vertically on the left)

Find the probability of getting

25. two numbers whose sum is 4.

26. two numbers whose sum is 6.

27. To play the California lottery, a person has to select 6 out of 51 numbers, paying $1 for each six-number selection. If you pick six numbers that are the same as the ones drawn by the lottery, you win mountains of money. What is the probability that a person with one combination of six numbers will win? What is the probability of winning if 100 different lottery tickets are purchased?

28. A state lottery is designed so that a player chooses six numbers from 1 to 30 on one lottery ticket. What is the probability that a player with one lottery ticket will win? What is the probability of winning if 100 different lottery tickets are purchased?

Exercises 29–30 involve a deck of 52 cards. If necessary, refer to the picture of a deck of cards, **Figure 8.11** *on page 735.*

29. A poker hand consists of five cards.

 a. Find the total number of possible five-card poker hands.

 b. A diamond flush is a five-card hand consisting of all diamonds. Find the number of possible diamond flushes.

 c. Find the probability of being dealt a diamond flush.

30. If you are dealt 3 cards from a shuffled deck of 52 cards, find the probability that all 3 cards are picture cards.

The table shows the educational attainment of the U.S. population, ages 25 and over. Use the data in the table, expressed in millions, to solve Exercises 31–36.

Educational Attainment, in Millions, of the United States Population, Ages 25 and Over

	Less Than 4 Years High School	4 Years High School Only	Some College [Less than 4 years]	4 Years College [or More]	Total
Male	14	25	20	23	82
Female	15	31	24	22	92
Total	29	56	44	45	174

Source: U.S. Census Bureau

Find the probability, expressed as a simplified fraction, that a randomly selected American, aged 25 or over,

31. has not completed four years (or more) of college.

32. has not completed four years of high school.

33. has completed four years of high school only or less than four years of college.

34. has completed less than four years of high school or four years of high school only.

35. has completed four years of high school only or is a man.

36. has completed four years of high school only or is a woman.

In Exercises 37–42, you are dealt one card from a 52-card deck. Find the probability that

37. you are not dealt a king.

38. you are not dealt a picture card.

39. you are dealt a 2 or a 3.

40. you are dealt a red 7 or a black 8.

41. you are dealt a 7 or a red card.

42. you are dealt a 5 or a black card.

In Exercises 43–44, it is equally probable that the pointer on the spinner shown will land on any one of the eight regions, numbered 1 through 8. If the pointer lands on a borderline, spin again.

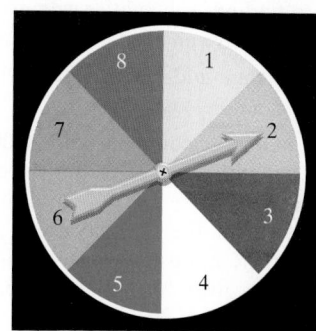

Find the probability that the pointer will stop on

43. an odd number or a number less than 6.

44. an odd number or a number greater than 3.

Use this information to solve Exercises 45–46. The mathematics department of a college has 8 male professors, 11 female professors, 14 male teaching assistants, and 7 female teaching assistants. If a person is selected at random from the group, find the probability that the selected person is

45. a professor or a male.

46. a professor or a female.

In Exercises 47–50, a single die is rolled twice. Find the probability of rolling

47. a 2 the first time and a 3 the second time.

48. a 5 the first time and a 1 the second time.

49. an even number the first time and a number greater than 2 the second time.

50. an odd number the first time and a number less than 3 the second time.

51. If you toss a fair coin six times, what is the probability of getting all heads?

52. If you toss a fair coin seven times, what is the probability of getting all tails?

53. The probability that South Florida will be hit by a major hurricane (category 4 or 5) in any single year is $\frac{1}{16}$. (*Source:* National Hurricane Center)

 a. What is the probability that South Florida will be hit by a major hurricane two years in a row?

 b. What is the probability that South Florida will be hit by a major hurricane in three consecutive years?

 c. What is the probability that South Florida will not be hit by a major hurricane in the next ten years?

 d. What is the probability that South Florida will be hit by a major hurricane at least once in the next ten years?

Writing in Mathematics

54. Describe the difference between theoretical probability and empirical probability.

55. Give an example of an event whose probability must be determined empirically rather than theoretically.

56. Write a probability word problem whose answer is one of the following fractions: $\frac{1}{6}$ or $\frac{1}{4}$ or $\frac{1}{3}$.

57. Explain how to find the probability of an event not occurring. Give an example.

58. What are mutually exclusive events? Give an example of two events that are mutually exclusive.

59. Explain how to find *or* probabilities with mutually exclusive events. Give an example.

60. Give an example of two events that are not mutually exclusive.

61. Explain how to find *or* probabilities with events that are not mutually exclusive. Give an example.

62. Explain how to find *and* probabilities with independent events. Give an example.

63. The president of a large company with 10,000 employees is considering mandatory cocaine testing for every employee. The test that would be used is 90% accurate, meaning that it will detect 90% of the cocaine users who are tested, and that 90% of the nonusers will test negative. This also means that the test gives 10% false positive. Suppose that 1% of the employees actually use cocaine. Find the probability that someone who tests positive for cocaine use is, indeed, a user.

Hint: Find the following probability fraction:

$$\frac{\text{the number of employees who test positive and are cocaine users}}{\text{the number of employees who test positive}}.$$

This fraction is given by

$$\frac{90\% \text{ of } 1\% \text{ of } 10,000}{\text{the number who test positive who actually use cocaine plus the number who test positive who do not use cocaine}}.$$

What does this probability indicate in terms of the percentage of employees who test positive who are not actually users? Discuss these numbers in terms of the issue of mandatory drug testing. Write a paper either in favor of or against mandatory drug testing, incorporating the actual percentage accuracy for such tests.

Critical Thinking Exercises

Make Sense? *In Exercises 64–67, determine whether each statement makes sense or does not make sense, and explain your reasoning.*

64. The probability that Jill will win the election is 0.7 and the probability that she will not win is 0.4.

65. Assuming the next U.S. president will be a Democrat or a Republican, the probability of a Republican president is 0.5.

66. The probability that I will go to graduate school is 1.5.

67. When I toss a coin, the probability of getting heads *or* tails is 1, but the probability of getting heads *and* tails is 0.

68. The target in the figure shown contains four squares. If a dart thrown at random hits the target, find the probability that it will land in a yellow region.

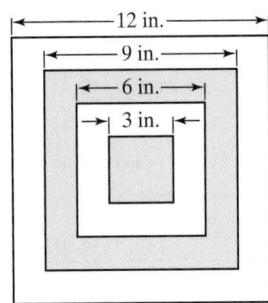

69. Suppose that it is a week in which the cash prize in Florida's LOTTO is promised to exceed $50 million. If a person purchases 22,957,480 tickets in LOTTO at $1 per ticket (all possible combinations), isn't this a guarantee of winning the lottery? Because the probability in this situation is 1, what's wrong with doing this?

70. Some three-digit numbers, such as 101 and 313, read the same forward and backward. If you select a number from all three-digit numbers, find the probability that it will read the same forward and backward.

71. In a class of 50 students, 29 are Democrats, 11 are business majors, and 5 of the business majors are Democrats. If one student is randomly selected from the class, find the probability of choosing

a. a Democrat who is not a business major.

b. a student who is neither a Democrat nor a business major.

72. On New Year's Eve, the probability of a person driving while intoxicated or having a driving accident is 0.35. If the probability of driving while intoxicated is 0.32 and the probability of having a driving accident is 0.09, find the probability of a person having a driving accident while intoxicated.

73. a. If two people are selected at random, the probability that they do not have the same birthday (day and month) is $\frac{365}{365} \cdot \frac{364}{365}$. Explain why this is so. (Ignore leap years and assume 365 days in a year.)

b. If three people are selected at random, find the probability that they all have different birthdays.

c. If three people are selected at random, find the probability that at least two of them have the same birthday.

d. If 20 people are selected at random, find the probability that at least 2 of them have the same birthday.

e. How large a group is needed to give a 0.5 chance of at least two people having the same birthday?

Group Exercise

74. Research and present a group report on state lotteries. Include answers to some or all of the following questions: Which states do not have lotteries? Why not? How much is spent per capita on lotteries? What are some of the lottery games? What is the probability of winning top prize in these games? What income groups spend the greatest amount of money on lotteries? If your state has a lottery, what does it do with the money it makes? Is the way the money is spent what was promised when the lottery first began?

Chapter 8 Summary, Review, and Test

Summary

DEFINITIONS AND CONCEPTS	**EXAMPLES**

8.1 Sequences and Summation Notation

a. An infinite sequence $\{a_n\}$ is a function whose domain is the set of positive integers. The function values, or terms, are represented by

$$a_1, a_2, a_3, a_4, \ldots, a_n, \ldots.$$

Ex. 1, p. 669

b. Sequences can be defined using recursion formulas that define the nth term as a function of the previous term.

Ex. 2, p. 670

c. Factorial Notation:
$$n! = n(n-1)(n-2)\cdots(3)(2)(1) \quad \text{and} \quad 0! = 1$$

Ex. 3, p. 671;
Ex. 4, p. 672

d. Summation Notation:
$$\sum_{i=1}^{n} a_i = a_1 + a_2 + a_3 + a_4 + \cdots + a_n$$

Ex. 5, p. 673;
Ex. 6, p. 675

8.2 Arithmetic Sequences

a. In an arithmetic sequence, each term after the first differs from the preceding term by a constant, the common difference. Subtract any term from the term that directly follows to find the common difference.

List of arithmetic sequences and common differences, p. 679;
Ex. 1, p. 680

b. General term or nth term: $a_n = a_1 + (n-1)d$. The first term is a_1 and the common difference is d.

Ex. 2, p. 681;
Ex. 3, p. 681

c. Sum of the first n terms: $S_n = \dfrac{n}{2}(a_1 + a_n)$

Ex. 4, p. 683;
Ex. 5, p. 684;
Ex. 6, p. 684

8.3 Geometric Sequences and Series

a. In a geometric sequence, each term after the first is obtained by multiplying the preceding term by a nonzero constant, the common ratio. Divide any term after the first by the term that directly precedes it to find the common ratio.

List of geometric sequences and common ratios, p. 689;
Ex. 1, p. 689

b. General term or nth term: $a_n = a_1 r^{n-1}$. The first term is a_1 and the common ratio is r.

Ex. 2, p. 690;
Ex. 3, p. 690

c. Sum of the first n terms: $S_n = \dfrac{a_1(1 - r^n)}{1 - r}, r \neq 1$

Ex. 4, p. 692;
Ex. 5, p. 692;
Ex. 6, p. 693

d. An annuity is a sequence of equal payments made at equal time periods. The value of an annuity, A, is the sum of all deposits made plus all interest paid, given by

$$A = \frac{P\left[\left(1 + \dfrac{r}{n}\right)^{nt} - 1\right]}{\dfrac{r}{n}}.$$

Ex. 7, p. 695

The deposit made at the end of each period is P, the annual interest rate is r, compounded n times per year, and t is the number of years deposits have been made.

DEFINITIONS AND CONCEPTS	EXAMPLES

e. The sum of the infinite geometric series $a_1 + a_1 r + a_1 r^2 + a_1 r^3 + \cdots$ is $S = \dfrac{a_1}{1-r}$; $|r| < 1$. If $|r| \geq 1$, the infinite series does not have a sum.

Ex. 8, p. 697;
Ex. 9, p. 698;
Ex. 10, p. 698

8.4 Mathematical Induction

To prove that S_n is true for all positive integers n,
1. Show that S_1 is true.
2. Show that if S_k is assumed true, then S_{k+1} is also true, for every positive integer k.

Ex. 2, p. 707;
Ex. 3, p. 708;
Ex. 4, p. 709

8.5 The Binomial Theorem

a. Binomial coefficient: $\dbinom{n}{r} = \dfrac{n!}{r!(n-r)!}$

Ex. 1, p. 712

b. Binomial Theorem:

$$(a+b)^n = \binom{n}{0}a^n + \binom{n}{1}a^{n-1}b + \binom{n}{2}a^{n-2}b^2 + \cdots + \binom{n}{n}b^n$$

Ex. 2, p. 714;
Ex. 3, p. 714

c. The $(r+1)$st term in the expansion of $(a+b)^n$ is

$$\binom{n}{r}a^{n-r}b^r.$$

Ex. 4, p. 716

8.6 Counting Principles, Permutations, and Combinations

a. The Fundamental Counting Principle: The number of ways in which a series of successive things can occur is found by multiplying the number of ways in which each thing can occur.

Ex. 1, p. 720;
Ex. 2, p. 721;
Ex. 3, p. 721

b. A permutation from a group of items occurs when no item is used more than once and the order of arrangement makes a difference.

c. Permutations Formula: The number of possible permutations if r items are taken from n items is

$$_nP_r = \frac{n!}{(n-r)!}.$$

Ex. 4, p. 723;
Ex. 5, p. 723

d. A combination from a group of items occurs when no item is used more than once and the order of items makes no difference.

Ex. 6, p. 725

e. Combinations Formula: The number of possible combinations if r items are taken from n items is

$$_nC_r = \frac{n!}{(n-r)!r!}.$$

Ex. 7, p. 726;
Ex. 8, p. 727

8.7 Probability

a. Empirical probability applies to situations in which we observe the frequency of the occurrence of an event. The empirical probability of event E is

$$P(E) = \frac{\text{observed number of times } E \text{ occurs}}{\text{total number of observed occurrences}}.$$

Ex. 1, p. 731

b. Theoretical probability applies to situations in which the sample space of all equally likely outcomes is known. The theoretical probability of event E is

$$P(E) = \frac{\text{number of outcomes in event } E}{\text{number of outcomes in sample space } S} = \frac{n(E)}{n(S)}.$$

Ex. 2, p. 734;
Ex. 3, p. 734;
Ex. 4, p. 735;
Ex. 5, p. 736

c. Probability of an event not occurring: $P(\text{not } E) = 1 - P(E)$.

Ex. 6, p. 737

d. If it is impossible for events A and B to occur simultaneously, the events are mutually exclusive.

DEFINITIONS AND CONCEPTS	EXAMPLES
e. If A and B are mutually exclusive events, then $P(A \text{ or } B) = P(A) + P(B)$.	Ex. 7, p. 738
f. If A and B are not mutually exclusive events, then $$P(A \text{ or } B) = P(A) + P(B) - P(A \text{ and } B).$$	Ex. 8, p. 739; Ex. 9, p. 739
g. Two events are independent if the occurrence of either of them has no effect on the probability of the other.	
h. If A and B are independent events, then $$P(A \text{ and } B) = P(A) \cdot P(B).$$	Ex. 10, p. 741
i. The probability of a succession of independent events is the product of each of their probabilities.	Ex. 11, p. 741

Review Exercises

8.1

In Exercises 1–6, write the first four terms of each sequence whose general term is given.

1. $a_n = 7n - 4$

2. $a_n = (-1)^n \dfrac{n+2}{n+1}$

3. $a_n = \dfrac{1}{(n-1)!}$

4. $a_n = \dfrac{(-1)^{n+1}}{2^n}$

5. $a_1 = 9$ and $a_n = \dfrac{2}{3a_{n-1}}$ for $n \geq 2$

6. $a_1 = 4$ and $a_n = 2a_{n-1} + 3$ for $n \geq 2$

7. Evaluate: $\dfrac{40!}{4!38!}$.

In Exercises 8–9, find each indicated sum.

8. $\displaystyle\sum_{i=1}^{5} (2i^2 - 3)$

9. $\displaystyle\sum_{i=0}^{4} (-1)^{i+1} i!$

In Exercises 10–11, express each sum using summation notation. Use i for the index of summation.

10. $\dfrac{1}{3} + \dfrac{2}{4} + \dfrac{3}{5} + \cdots + \dfrac{15}{17}$

11. $4^3 + 5^3 + 6^3 + \cdots + 13^3$

8.2

In Exercises 12–15, write the first six terms of each arithmetic sequence.

12. $a_1 = 7, d = 4$

13. $a_1 = -4, d = -5$

14. $a_1 = \frac{3}{2}, d = -\frac{1}{2}$

15. $a_{n+1} = a_n + 5, a_1 = -2$

In Exercises 16–18, find the indicated term of the arithmetic sequence with first term, a_1, and common difference, d.

16. Find a_6 when $a_1 = 5, d = 3$.

17. Find a_{12} when $a_1 = -8, d = -2$.

18. Find a_{14} when $a_1 = 14, d = -4$.

In Exercises 19–21, write a formula for the general term (the nth term) of each arithmetic sequence. Do not use a recursion formula. Then use the formula for a_n to find a_{20}, the 20th term of the sequence.

19. $-7, -3, 1, 5, \ldots$

20. $a_1 = 200, d = -20$

21. $a_n = a_{n-1} - 5, a_1 = 3$

22. Find the sum of the first 22 terms of the arithmetic sequence: $5, 12, 19, 26, \ldots$.

23. Find the sum of the first 15 terms of the arithmetic sequence: $-6, -3, 0, 3, \ldots$.

24. Find $3 + 6 + 9 + \cdots + 300$, the sum of the first 100 positive multiples of 3.

In Exercises 25–27, use the formula for the sum of the first n terms of an arithmetic sequence to find the indicated sum.

25. $\displaystyle\sum_{i=1}^{16} (3i + 2)$

26. $\displaystyle\sum_{i=1}^{25} (-2i + 6)$

27. $\displaystyle\sum_{i=1}^{30} (-5i)$

28. The graphic indicates that there are more eyes at school.

Percentage of United States Students Ages 12–18 Seeing Security Cameras at School

2005 58%

2001 39%

35 a

Source: Department of Education

In 2001, 39% of students ages 12–18 reported seeing one or more security cameras at their school. On average, this has increased by approximately 4.75% per year since then.

a. Write a formula for the nth term of the arithmetic sequence that describes the percentage of students ages 12–18 who reported seeing security cameras at school n years after 2000.

b. Use the model to predict the percentage of students ages 12–18 who will report seeing security cameras at school by the year 2013.

29. A company offers a starting salary of $31,500 with raises of $2300 per year. Find the total salary over a ten-year period.

30. A theater has 25 seats in the first row and 35 rows in all. Each successive row contains one additional seat. How many seats are in the theater?

8.3

In Exercises 31–34, write the first five terms of each geometric sequence.

31. $a_1 = 3, r = 2$

32. $a_1 = \frac{1}{2}, r = \frac{1}{2}$

33. $a_1 = 16, r = -\frac{1}{2}$

34. $a_n = -5a_{n-1}, a_1 = -1$

In Exercises 35–37, use the formula for the general term (the nth term) of a geometric sequence to find the indicated term of each sequence.

35. Find a_7 when $a_1 = 2, r = 3$.

36. Find a_6 when $a_1 = 16, r = \frac{1}{2}$.

37. Find a_5 when $a_1 = -3, r = 2$.

In Exercises 38–40, write a formula for the general term (the nth term) of each geometric sequence. Then use the formula for a_n to find a_8, the eighth term of the sequence.

38. $1, 2, 4, 8, \ldots$

39. $100, 10, 1, \frac{1}{10}, \ldots$

40. $12, -4, \frac{4}{3}, -\frac{4}{9}, \ldots$

41. Find the sum of the first 15 terms of the geometric sequence: $5, -15, 45, -135, \ldots$.

42. Find the sum of the first 7 terms of the geometric sequence: $8, 4, 2, 1, \ldots$.

In Exercises 43–45, use the formula for the sum of the first n terms of a geometric sequence to find the indicated sum.

43. $\sum_{i=1}^{6} 5^i$

44. $\sum_{i=1}^{7} 3(-2)^i$

45. $\sum_{i=1}^{5} 2\left(\frac{1}{4}\right)^{i-1}$

In Exercises 46–49, find the sum of each infinite geometric series.

46. $9 + 3 + 1 + \frac{1}{3} + \cdots$

47. $2 - 1 + \frac{1}{2} - \frac{1}{4} + \cdots$

48. $-6 + 4 - \frac{8}{3} + \frac{16}{9} - \cdots$

49. $\sum_{i=1}^{\infty} 5(0.8)^i$

In Exercises 50–51, express each repeating decimal as a fraction in lowest terms.

50. $0.\overline{6}$

51. $0.\overline{47}$

52. Projections for the U.S. population, ages 85 and older, are shown in the following table.

Year	2000	2010	2020	2030	2040	2050
Projected Population in millions	4.2	5.9	8.3	11.6	16.2	22.7

Actual 2000 population

Source: U.S. Census Bureau

a. Show that the U.S. population, ages 85 and older, is projected to increase geometrically.

b. Write the general term of the geometric sequence describing the U.S. population ages 85 and older, in millions, n decades after 2000.

c. Use the model in part (b) to project the U.S. population, ages 85 and older, in 2080.

53. A job pays $32,000 for the first year with an annual increase of 6% per year beginning in the second year. What is the salary in the sixth year? What is the total salary paid over this six-year period? Round answers to the nearest dollar.

In Exercises 54–55, use the formula for the value of an annuity and round to the nearest dollar.

54. You spend $10 per week on lottery tickets, averaging $520 per year. Instead of buying tickets, if you deposited the $520 at the end of each year in an annuity paying 6% compounded annually,

a. How much would you have after 20 years?

b. Find the interest.

55. To save for retirement, you decide to deposit $100 at the end of each month in an IRA that pays 5.5% compounded monthly.

a. How much will you have from the IRA after 30 years?

b. Find the interest.

56. A factory in an isolated town has an annual payroll of $4 million. It is estimated that 70% of this money is spent within the town, that people in the town receiving this money will again spend 70% of what they receive in the town, and so on. What is the total of all this spending in the town each year?

8.4

In Exercises 57–61, use mathematical induction to prove that each statement is true for every positive integer n.

57. $5 + 10 + 15 + \cdots + 5n = \dfrac{5n(n + 1)}{2}$

58. $1 + 4 + 4^2 + \cdots + 4^{n-1} = \dfrac{4^n - 1}{3}$

59. $2 + 6 + 10 + \cdots + (4n - 2) = 2n^2$

60. $1 \cdot 3 + 2 \cdot 4 + 3 \cdot 5 + \cdots + n(n + 2) = \dfrac{n(n + 1)(2n + 7)}{6}$

61. 2 is a factor of $n^2 + 5n$.

8.5

In Exercises 62–63, evaluate the given binomial coefficient.

62. $\binom{11}{8}$

63. $\binom{90}{2}$

In Exercises 64–67, use the Binomial Theorem to expand each binomial and express the result in simplified form.

64. $(2x + 1)^3$

65. $(x^2 - 1)^4$

66. $(x + 2y)^5$

67. $(x - 2)^6$

In Exercises 68–69, write the first three terms in each binomial expansion, expressing the result in simplified form.

68. $(x^2 + 3)^8$

69. $(x - 3)^9$

In Exercises 70–71, find the term indicated in each expansion.

70. $(x + 2)^5$; fourth term

71. $(2x - 3)^6$; fifth term

8.6

In Exercises 72–75, evaluate each expression.

72. $_8P_3$

73. $_9P_5$

74. $_8C_3$

75. $_{13}C_{11}$

In Exercises 76–82, solve by the method of your choice.

76. A popular brand of pen comes in red, green, blue, or black ink. The writing tip can be chosen from extra bold, bold, regular, fine, or micro. How many different choices of pens do you have with this brand?

77. A stock can go up, go down, or stay unchanged. How many possibilities are there if you own five stocks?

78. A club with 15 members is to choose four officers—president, vice-president, secretary, and treasurer. In how many ways can these offices be filled?

79. How many different ways can a director select 4 actors from a group of 20 actors to attend a workshop on performing in rock musicals?

80. From the 20 CDs that you've bought during the past year, you plan to take 3 with you on vacation. How many different sets of three CDs can you take?

81. How many different ways can a director select from 20 male actors and cast the roles of Mark, Roger, Angel, and Collins in the musical *Rent*?

82. In how many ways can five airplanes line up for departure on a runway?

8.7

Suppose that a survey of 350 college students is taken. Each student is asked the type of college attended (public or private) and the family's income level (low, middle, high). Use the data in the table to solve Exercises 83–88. Express probabilities as simplified fractions.

	Public	Private	Total
Low	120	20	140
Middle	110	50	160
High	22	28	50
Total	252	98	350

Find the probability that a randomly selected student in the survey

83. attends a public college.

84. is not from a high-income family.

85. is from a middle-income or a high-income family.

86. attends a private college or is from a high-income family.

87. Among people who attend a public college, find the probability that a randomly selected student is from a low-income family.

88. Among people from a middle-income family, find the probability that a randomly selected student attends a private college.

In Exercises 89–90, a die is rolled. Find the probability of

89. getting a number less than 5.

90. getting a number less than 3 or greater than 4.

In Exercises 91–92, you are dealt one card from a 52-card deck. Find the probability of

91. getting an ace or a king.

92. getting a queen or a red card.

In Exercises 93–95, it is equally probable that the pointer on the spinner shown will land on any one of the six regions, numbered 1 through 6, and colored as shown. If the pointer lands on a border-line, spin again. Find the probability of

93. not stopping on yellow.

94. stopping on red or a number greater than 3.

95. stopping on green on the first spin and stopping on a number less than 4 on the second spin.

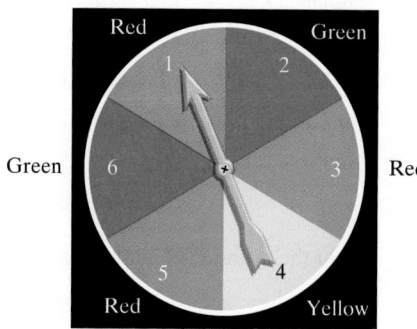

96. A lottery game is set up so that each player chooses five different numbers from 1 to 20. If the five numbers match the five numbers drawn in the lottery, the player wins (or shares) the top cash prize. What is the probability of winning the prize

 a. with one lottery ticket?

 b. with 100 different lottery tickets?

97. What is the probability of a family having five boys born in a row?

98. The probability of a flood in any given year in a region prone to floods is 0.2.

 a. What is the probability of a flood two years in a row?

 b. What is the probability of a flood for three consecutive years?

 c. What is the probability of no flooding for four consecutive years?

CHAPTER
Test Prep
VIDEOS
Chapter 8 Test

1. Write the first five terms of the sequence whose general term is $a_n = \dfrac{(-1)^{n+1}}{n^2}$.

In Exercises 2–4, find each indicated sum.

2. $\displaystyle\sum_{i=1}^{5} (i^2 + 10)$

3. $\displaystyle\sum_{i=1}^{20} (3i - 4)$

4. $\displaystyle\sum_{i=1}^{15} (-2)^i$

In Exercises 5–7, evaluate each expression.

5. $\dbinom{9}{2}$

6. $_{10}P_3$

7. $_{10}C_3$

8. Express the sum using summation notation. Use i for the index of summation.

$$\frac{2}{3} + \frac{3}{4} + \frac{4}{5} + \cdots + \frac{21}{22}$$

In Exercises 9–10, write a formula for the general term (the nth term) of each sequence. Do not use a recursion formula. Then use the formula to find the twelfth term of the sequence.

9. $4, 9, 14, 19, \ldots$

10. $16, 4, 1, \frac{1}{4}, \ldots$

In Exercises 11–12, use a formula to find the sum of the first ten terms of each sequence.

11. $7, -14, 28, -56, \ldots$

12. $-7, -14, -21, -28, \ldots$

13. Find the sum of the infinite geometric series:

$$4 + \frac{4}{2} + \frac{4}{2^2} + \frac{4}{2^3} + \cdots.$$

14. Express $0.\overline{73}$ in fractional notation.

15. A job pays $30,000 for the first year with an annual increase of 4% per year beginning in the second year. What is the total salary paid over an eight-year period? Round to the nearest dollar.

16. Use mathematical induction to prove that for every positive integer n,

$$1 + 4 + 7 + \cdots + (3n - 2) = \frac{n(3n - 1)}{2}.$$

17. Use the Binomial Theorem to expand and simplify: $(x^2 - 1)^5$.

18. Use the Binomial Theorem to write the first three terms in the expansion and simplify: $(x + y^2)^8$.

19. A human resource manager has 11 applicants to fill three different positions. Assuming that all applicants are equally qualified for any of the three positions, in how many ways can this be done?

20. From the ten books that you've recently bought but not read, you plan to take four with you on vacation. How many different sets of four books can you take?

21. How many seven-digit local telephone numbers can be formed if the first three digits are 279?

A class is collecting data on eye color and gender. They organize the data they collected into the table shown. Numbers in the table represent the number of students from the class that belong to each of the categories. Use the data to solve Exercises 22–25. Express probabilities as simplified fractions.

	Brown	Blue	Green
Male	22	18	10
Female	18	20	12

Find the probability that a randomly selected student from this class

22. does not have brown eyes.

23. has brown eyes or blue eyes.

24. is female or has green eyes.

25. Among the students with blue eyes, find the probability of selecting a male.

26. A lottery game is set up so that each player chooses six different numbers from 1 to 15. If the six numbers match the six numbers drawn in the lottery, the player wins (or shares) the top cash prize. What is the probability of winning the prize with 50 different lottery tickets?

27. One card is randomly selected from a deck of 52 cards. Find the probability of selecting a black card or a picture card.

28. A group of students consists of 10 male freshmen, 15 female freshmen, 20 male sophomores, and 5 female sophomores. If one person is randomly selected from the group, find the probability of selecting a freshman or a female.

29. A quiz consisting of four multiple-choice questions has four available options (a, b, c, or d) for each question. If a person guesses at every question, what is the probability of answering all questions correctly?

30. If the spinner shown is spun twice, find the probability that the pointer lands on red on the first spin and blue on the second spin.

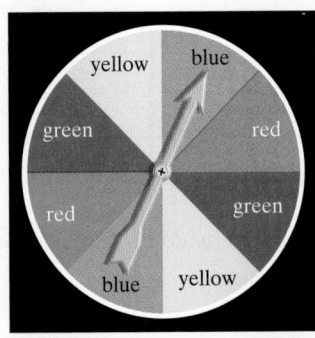

Cumulative Review Exercises (Chapters 1–8)

The figure shows the graph of $y = f(x)$ and its vertical asymptote. Use the graph to solve Exercises 1–9.

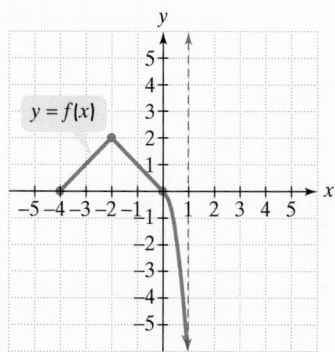

1. Find the domain and the range of f.

2. Does f have a relative maximum or a relative minimum? What is this relative maximum or minimum and where does it occur?

3. Find the interval on which f is decreasing.

4. Is f even, odd, or neither?

5. For what value(s) of x is $f(x) = 1$?

6. Find $(f \circ f)(-4)$.

7. Use arrow notation to complete this statement:

$$f(x) \to -\infty° \text{ as}° \underline{\qquad}.$$

8. Graph $g(x) = f(x - 2) + 1$.

9. Graph $h(x) = -f(2x)$.

In Exercises 10–22, solve each equation, inequality, or system of equations.

10. $-2(x - 5) + 10 = 3(x + 2)$

11. $3x^2 - 6x + 2 = 0$

12. $\log_2 x + \log_2(2x - 3) = 1$

13. $x^{\frac{1}{2}} - 6x^{\frac{1}{4}} + 8 = 0$

14. $\sqrt{2x + 4} - \sqrt{x + 3} - 1 = 0$

15. $|2x + 1| \leq 1$

16. $6x^2 - 6 < 5x$

17. $\dfrac{x - 1}{x + 3} \leq 0$

18. $30e^{0.7x} = 240$

19. $2x^3 + 3x^2 - 8x + 3 = 0$

20. $\begin{cases} 4x^2 + 3y^2 = 48 \\ 3x^2 + 2y^2 = 35 \end{cases}$

21. (Use matrices.)

$$\begin{cases} x - 2y + z = 16 \\ 2x - y - z = 14 \\ 3x + 5y - 4z = -10 \end{cases}$$

22. $\begin{cases} x - y = 1 \\ x^2 - x - y = 1 \end{cases}$

In Exercises 23–29, graph each equation, function, or system in a rectangular coordinate system. If two functions are indicated, graph both in the same system.

23. $100x^2 + y^2 = 25$

24. $4x^2 - 9y^2 - 16x + 54y - 29 = 0$

25. $f(x) = \dfrac{x^2 - 1}{x - 2}$

26. $\begin{cases} 2x - y \geq 4 \\ x \leq 2 \end{cases}$

27. $f(x) = x^2 - 4x - 5$

28. $f(x) = \sqrt[3]{x + 4}$ and f^{-1}

29. $f(x) = \log_2 x$ and $g(x) = -\log_2(x + 1)$

In Exercises 30–31, let $f(x) = -x^2 - 2x + 1$ and $g(x) = x - 1$.

30. Find $(f \circ g)(x)$ and $(g \circ f)(x)$.

31. Find $\dfrac{f(x + h) - f(x)}{h}$ and simplify.

32. If $A = \begin{bmatrix} 4 & 2 \\ 1 & -1 \\ 0 & 5 \end{bmatrix}$ and $B = \begin{bmatrix} 2 & 4 \\ 3 & 1 \end{bmatrix}$, find $AB - 4A$.

33. Find the partial fraction decomposition for

$$\dfrac{2x^2 - 10x + 2}{(x - 2)(x^2 + 2x + 2)}.$$

34. Expand and simplify: $(x^3 + 2y)^5$.

35. Use the formula for the sum of the first n terms of an arithmetic sequence to find $\displaystyle\sum_{i=1}^{50} (4i - 25)$.

In Exercises 36–37, write the linear function in slope-intercept form satisfying the given conditions.

36. Graph of f passes through $(6, 3)$ and $(-2, 1)$.

37. Graph of g passes through $(0, -2)$ and is perpendicular to the line whose equation is $x - 5y - 20 = 0$.

38. For a summer sales job, you are choosing between two pay arrangements: a weekly salary of \$200 plus 5% commission on sales, or a straight 15% commission. For how many dollars of sales will the earnings be the same regardless of the pay arrangement?

39. The perimeter of a soccer field is 300 yards. If the length is 50 yards longer than the width, what are the field's dimensions?

40. If 10 pens and 12 pads cost \$42, and 5 of the same pens and 10 of the same pads cost \$29, find the cost of a pen and a pad.

41. A ball is thrown vertically upward from the top of a 96-foot-tall building with an initial velocity of 80 feet per second. The height of the ball above ground, $s(t)$, in feet, after t seconds is modeled by the position function

$$s(t) = -16t^2 + 80t + 96.$$

a. After how many seconds will the ball strike the ground?

b. When does the ball reach its maximum height? What is the maximum height?

42. The current, I, in amperes, flowing in an electrical circuit varies inversely as the resistance, R, in ohms, in the circuit. When the resistance of an electric percolator is 22 ohms, it draws 5 amperes of current. How much current is needed when the resistance is 10 ohms?

43. The bar graph shows the decline in the percentage of the U.S. adult population that smokes cigarettes. Develop a linear function that models the data. Then use the function to make a projection about what might occur in the future.

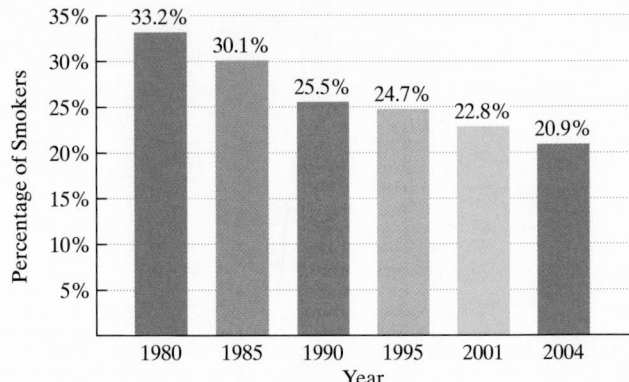

Butt Out: Percentage of Cigarette Smokers Among U.S. Adults

Source: Centers for Disease Control and Prevention

Appendix

Where Did That Come From?

Selected Proofs

Section 4.3 **Properties of Logarithms**

The Product Rule

Let b, M, and N be positive real numbers with $b \neq 1$.

$$\log_b(MN) = \log_b M + \log_b N$$

Proof
We begin by letting $\log_b M = R$ and $\log_b N = S$.
Now we write each logarithm in exponential form.

$$\log_b M = R \quad \text{means} \quad b^R = M.$$
$$\log_b N = S \quad \text{means} \quad b^S = N.$$

By substituting and using a property of exponents, we see that

$$MN = b^R b^S = b^{R+S}.$$

Now we change $MN = b^{R+S}$ to logarithmic form.

$$MN = b^{R+S} \quad \text{means} \quad \log_b(MN) = R + S.$$

Finally, substituting $\log_b M$ for R and $\log_b N$ for S gives us

$$\log_b(MN) = \log_b M + \log_b N,$$

the property that we wanted to prove.

The quotient and power rules for logarithms are proved using similar procedures.

The Change-of-Base Property

For any logarithmic bases a and b, and any positive number M,

$$\log_b M = \frac{\log_a M}{\log_a b}.$$

Proof
To prove the change-of-base property, we let x equal the logarithm on the left side:

$$\log_b M = x.$$

Now we rewrite this logarithm in exponential form.

$$\log_b M = x \quad \text{means} \quad b^x = M.$$

Because b^x and M are equal, the logarithms with base a for each of these expressions must be equal. This means that

$$\log_a b^x = \log_a M$$
$$x \log_a b = \log_a M \qquad \text{Apply the power rule for logarithms on the left side.}$$
$$x = \frac{\log_a M}{\log_a b} \qquad \text{Solve for x by dividing both sides by } \log_a b.$$

In our first step we let x equal $\log_b M$. Replacing x on the left side by $\log_b M$ gives us

$$\log_b M = \frac{\log_a M}{\log_a b},$$

which is the change-of-base property.

<table>
<tr><td>Section</td><td>7.1</td></tr>
</table>

The Ellipse

The Standard Form of the Equation of an Ellipse with a Horizontal Major Axis Centered at the Origin

Proof
Refer to Figure A.1.

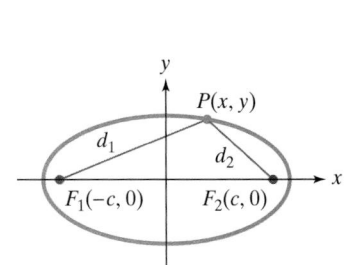

Figure A.1

$d_1 + d_2 = 2a$	The sum of the distances from P to the foci equals a constant, $2a$.
$\sqrt{(x + c)^2 + y^2} + \sqrt{(x - c)^2 + y^2} = 2a$	Use the distance formula.
$\sqrt{(x + c)^2 + y^2} = 2a - \sqrt{(x - c)^2 + y^2}$	Isolate a radical.
$(x + c)^2 + y^2 = 4a^2 - 4a\sqrt{(x - c)^2 + y^2} + (x - c)^2 + y^2$	Square both sides.
$x^2 + 2cx + c^2 + y^2 = 4a^2 - 4a\sqrt{(x - c)^2 + y^2} + x^2 - 2cx + c^2 + y^2$	Square $x + c$ and $x - c$.
$4cx - 4a^2 = -4a\sqrt{(x - c)^2 + y^2}$	Simplify and isolate the radical.
$cx - a^2 = -a\sqrt{(x - c)^2 + y^2}$	Divide both sides by 4.
$(cx - a^2)^2 = a^2[(x - c)^2 + y^2]$	Square both sides.
$c^2x^2 - 2a^2cx + a^4 = a^2(x^2 - 2cx + c^2 + y^2)$	Square $cx - a^2$ and $x - c$.
$c^2x^2 - 2a^2cx + a^4 = a^2x^2 - 2a^2cx + a^2c^2 + a^2y^2$	Use the distributive property.
$c^2x^2 + a^4 = a^2x^2 + a^2c^2 + a^2y^2$	Add $2a^2cx$ to both sides.
$c^2x^2 - a^2x^2 - a^2y^2 = a^2c^2 - a^4$	Rearrange the terms.
$(c^2 - a^2)x^2 - a^2y^2 = a^2(c^2 - a^2)$	Factor out x^2 and a^2, respectively.
$(a^2 - c^2)x^2 + a^2y^2 = a^2(a^2 - c^2)$	Multiply both sides by -1.

Refer to the discussion on page 625 and let $b^2 = a^2 - c^2$ in the preceding equation.

$$b^2x^2 + a^2y^2 = a^2b^2$$

$$\frac{x^2}{a^2} + \frac{y^2}{b^2} = 1 \qquad \text{Divide both sides by } a^2b^2.$$

Section **7.2** **The Hyperbola**

The Asymptotes of a Hyperbola Centered at the Origin

The hyperbola

$$\frac{x^2}{a^2} - \frac{y^2}{b^2} = 1$$

with a horizontal transverse axis has the two asymptotes

$$y = \frac{b}{a}x \quad \text{and} \quad y = -\frac{b}{a}x.$$

Proof

Begin by solving the hyperbola's equation for y.

$$\frac{x^2}{a^2} - \frac{y^2}{b^2} = 1 \qquad \text{This is the standard form of the equation of a hyperbola.}$$

$$\frac{y^2}{b^2} = \frac{x^2}{a^2} - 1 \qquad \text{We isolate the term involving } y^2 \text{ to solve for } y.$$

$$y^2 = \frac{b^2 x^2}{a^2} - b^2 \qquad \text{Multiply both sides by } b^2.$$

$$y^2 = \frac{b^2 x^2}{a^2}\left(1 - \frac{a^2}{x^2}\right) \qquad \text{Factor out } \frac{b^2 x^2}{a^2} \text{ on the right. Verify that this result is correct by multiplying using the distributive property and obtaining the previous step.}$$

$$y = \pm\sqrt{\frac{b^2 x^2}{a^2}\left(1 - \frac{a^2}{x^2}\right)} \qquad \text{Solve for } y \text{ using the square root property: If } u^2 = d, \text{ then } u = \pm\sqrt{d}.$$

$$y = \pm\frac{b}{a}x\sqrt{1 - \frac{a^2}{x^2}} \qquad \text{Simplify.}$$

As $|x| \to \infty$, the value of $\frac{a^2}{x^2}$ approaches 0. Consequently, the value of y can be approximated by

$$y = \pm\frac{b}{a}x.$$

This means that the lines whose equations are $y = \frac{b}{a}x$ and $y = -\frac{b}{a}x$ are asymptotes for the graph of the hyperbola.

Answers to Selected Exercises

CHAPTER P

Section P.1

Check Point Exercises

1. 608 **2.** \$7567 **3.** $\{3, 7\}$ **4.** $\{3, 4, 5, 6, 7, 8, 9\}$ **5. a.** $\sqrt{9}$ **b.** $0, \sqrt{9}$ **c.** $-9, 0, \sqrt{9}$ **d.** $-9, -1.3, 0, 0.\overline{3}, \sqrt{9}$
e. $\frac{\pi}{2}, \sqrt{10}$ **f.** $-9, -1.3, 0, 0.\overline{3}, \frac{\pi}{2}, \sqrt{9}, \sqrt{10}$ **6. a.** $\sqrt{2} - 1$ **b.** $\pi - 3$ **c.** 1 **7.** 9 **8.** $38x^2 + 23x$ **9.** $42 - 4x$

Exercise Set P.1

1. 57 **3.** 10 **5.** 88 **7.** 10 **9.** 44 **11.** 46 **13.** 10 **15.** -8 **17.** 10°C **19.** 60 ft **21.** $\{2, 4\}$ **23.** $\{s, e, t\}$ **25.** \varnothing
27. \varnothing **29.** $\{1, 2, 3, 4, 5\}$ **31.** $\{1, 2, 3, 4, 5, 6, 7, 8, 10\}$ **33.** $\{a, e, i, o, u\}$ **35. a.** $\sqrt{100}$ **b.** $0, \sqrt{100}$ **c.** $-9, 0, \sqrt{100}$
d. $-9, -\frac{4}{5}, 0, 0.25, 9.2, \sqrt{100}$ **e.** $\sqrt{3}$ **f.** $-9, -\frac{4}{5}, 0, 0.25, \sqrt{3}, 9.2, \sqrt{100}$ **37. a.** $\sqrt{64}$ **b.** $0, \sqrt{64}$ **c.** $-11, 0, \sqrt{64}$
d. $-11, -\frac{5}{6}, 0, 0.75, \sqrt{64}$ **e.** $\sqrt{5}, \pi$ **f.** $-11, -\frac{5}{6}, 0, 0.75, \sqrt{5}, \pi, \sqrt{64}$ **39.** 0 **41.** Answers may vary; an example is 2. **43.** true
45. true **47.** true **49.** true **51.** 300 **53.** $12 - \pi$ **55.** $5 - \sqrt{2}$ **57.** -1 **59.** 4 **61.** 3 **63.** 7 **65.** -1
67. $|17 - 2|; 15$ **69.** $|5 - (-2)|; 7$ **71.** $|-4 - (-19)|; 15$ **73.** $|-1.4 - (-3.6)|; 2.2$ **75.** commutative property of addition
77. associative property of addition **79.** commutative property of addition **81.** distributive property of multiplication over addition
83. inverse property of multiplication **85.** $15x + 16$ **87.** $27x - 10$ **89.** $29y - 29$ **91.** $8y - 12$ **93.** $16y - 25$ **95.** $12x^2 + 11$
97. $14x$ **99.** $-2x + 3y + 6$ **101.** x **103.** $>$ **105.** $=$ **107.** $<$ **109.** $=$ **111.** 45 **113.** $\frac{1}{121}$ **115.** 14 **117.** $-\frac{8}{3}$
119. $-\frac{1}{2}$ **121.** $x - (x + 4); -4$ **123.** $6(-5x); -30x$ **125.** $5x - 2x; 3x$ **127.** $8x - (3x + 6); 5x - 6$ **129. a.** 140 beats per minute
b. 160 beats per minute **131. a.** \$22,213 **b.** underestimates by \$5 **c.** \$25,075 **133. a.** $1200 - 0.07x$ **b.** \$780
145. does not make sense **147.** makes sense **149.** false **151.** true **153.** false **155.** false **157.** $<$ **159.** $>$ **160. a.** b^7
b. b^{10} **c.** Add the exponents. **161. a.** b^4 **b.** b^6 **c.** Subtract the exponents. **162.** It moves the decimal point 3 places to the right.

Section P.2

Check Point Exercises

1. a. 3^5 or 243 **b.** $40x^5y^{10}$ **2. a.** $(-3)^3$ or -27 **b.** $9x^{11}y^3$ **3. a.** $\frac{1}{25}$ **b.** $-\frac{1}{27}$ **c.** 16 **d.** $\frac{3y^4}{x^6}$ **4. a.** 3^6 or 729 **b.** $\frac{1}{y^{14}}$
c. b^{12} **5.** $-64x^3$ **6. a.** $-\frac{32}{y^5}$ **b.** $\frac{x^{15}}{27}$ **7. a.** $16x^{12}y^{24}$ **b.** $-18x^3y^8$ **c.** $\frac{5y^6}{x^4}$ **d.** $\frac{y^8}{25x^2}$ **8. a.** $-2,600,000,000$
b. 0.000003017 **9. a.** 5.21×10^9 **b.** -6.893×10^{-8} **10.** 4.1×10^9 **11. a.** 3.55×10^{-1} **b.** 4×10^8 **12.** \$2500

Exercise Set P.2

1. 50 **3.** 64 **5.** -64 **7.** 1 **9.** -1 **11.** $\frac{1}{64}$ **13.** 32 **15.** 64 **17.** 16 **19.** $\frac{1}{9}$ **21.** $\frac{1}{16}$ **23.** $\frac{y}{x^2}$ **25.** y^5 **27.** x^{10}
29. x^5 **31.** x^{21} **33.** $\frac{1}{x^{15}}$ **35.** x^7 **37.** x^{21} **39.** $64x^6$ **41.** $-\frac{64}{x^3}$ **43.** $9x^4y^{10}$ **45.** $6x^{11}$ **47.** $18x^9y^5$ **49.** $4x^{16}$ **51.** $-5a^{11}b$
53. $\frac{2}{b^7}$ **55.** $\frac{1}{16x^6}$ **57.** $\frac{3y^{14}}{4x^4}$ **59.** $\frac{y^2}{25x^6}$ **61.** $-\frac{27\,b^{15}}{a^{18}}$ **63.** 1 **65.** 380 **67.** 0.0006 **69.** $-7,160,000$ **71.** 0.79 **73.** -0.00415
75. $-60,000,100,000$ **77.** 3.2×10^4 **79.** 6.38×10^{17} **81.** -5.716×10^3 **83.** 2.7×10^{-3} **85.** -5.04×10^{-9} **87.** 6.3×10^7
89. 6.4×10^4 **91.** 1.22×10^{-11} **93.** 2.67×10^{13} **95.** 2.1×10^3 **97.** 4×10^5 **99.** 2×10^{-8} **101.** 5×10^3 **103.** 4×10^{15}
105. 9×10^{-3} **107.** 1 **109.** $\frac{y}{16x^8z^6}$ **111.** $\frac{1}{x^{12}y^{16}z^{20}}$ **113.** $\frac{x^{18}y^6}{4}$ **115. a.** 2.52×10^{12} **b.** 3×10^8 **c.** \$8400 **117.** \$9.57 $\times 10^{12}$
119. 1.06×10^{-18} g **121.** 4.064×10^9 **131.** does not make sense **133.** does not make sense **135.** false **137.** false **139.** false
141. false **143.** $\frac{1}{4}$ **145.** about 2.94×10^9 times **147. a.** 8 **b.** 8 **c.** $\sqrt{16} \cdot \sqrt{4} = \sqrt{16 \cdot 4}$ **148. a.** 17.32 **b.** 17.32
c. $\sqrt{300} = 10\sqrt{3}$ **149. a.** $31x$ **b.** $31\sqrt{2}$

Section P.3

Check Point Exercises

1. a. 9 **b.** -3 **c.** $\frac{1}{5}$ **d.** 10 **e.** 14 **2. a.** $5\sqrt{3}$ **b.** $5x\sqrt{2}$ **3. a.** $\frac{5}{4}$ **b.** $5x\sqrt{3}$ **4. a.** $17\sqrt{13}$ **b.** $-19\sqrt{17x}$
5. a. $17\sqrt{3}$ **b.** $10\sqrt{2x}$ **6. a.** $\frac{5\sqrt{3}}{3}$ **b.** $\sqrt{3}$ **7.** $\frac{8(4 - \sqrt{5})}{11}$ or $\frac{32 - 8\sqrt{5}}{11}$ **8. a.** $2\sqrt[3]{5}$ **b.** $2\sqrt[5]{2}$ **c.** $\frac{5}{3}$ **9.** $5\sqrt[3]{3}$
10. a. 5 **b.** 2 **c.** -3 **d.** -2 **e.** $\frac{1}{3}$ **11. a.** 81 **b.** 8 **c.** $\frac{1}{4}$ **12. a.** $10x^4$ **b.** $4x^{5/2}$ **13.** \sqrt{x}

AA1

Exercise Set P.3

1. 6 **3.** -6 **5.** not a real number **7.** 3 **9.** 1 **11.** 13 **13.** $5\sqrt{2}$ **15.** $3|x|\sqrt{5}$ **17.** $2x\sqrt{3}$ **19.** $x\sqrt{x}$ **21.** $2x\sqrt{3x}$
23. $\dfrac{1}{9}$ **25.** $\dfrac{7}{4}$ **27.** $4x$ **29.** $5x\sqrt{2x}$ **31.** $2x^2\sqrt{5}$ **33.** $13\sqrt{3}$ **35.** $-2\sqrt{17x}$ **37.** $5\sqrt{2}$ **39.** $3\sqrt{2x}$ **41.** $34\sqrt{2}$
43. $20\sqrt{2} - 5\sqrt{3}$ **45.** $\dfrac{\sqrt{7}}{7}$ **47.** $\dfrac{\sqrt{10}}{5}$ **49.** $\dfrac{13(3 - \sqrt{11})}{-2}$ **51.** $7(\sqrt{5} + 2)$ **53.** $3(\sqrt{5} - \sqrt{3})$ **55.** 5 **57.** -2
59. not a real number **61.** 3 **63.** -3 **65.** $-\dfrac{1}{2}$ **67.** $2\sqrt[3]{4}$ **69.** $x\sqrt[3]{x}$ **71.** $3\sqrt[3]{2}$ **73.** $2x$ **75.** $7\sqrt[5]{2}$ **77.** $13\sqrt[3]{2}$
79. $-y\sqrt[3]{2x}$ **81.** $\sqrt{2} + 2$ **83.** 6 **85.** 2 **87.** 25 **89.** $\dfrac{1}{16}$ **91.** $14x^{7/12}$ **93.** $4x^{1/4}$ **95.** x^2 **97.** $5x^2|y|^3$ **99.** $27y^{2/3}$
101. $\sqrt{5}$ **103.** x^2 **105.** $\sqrt[3]{x^2}$ **107.** $\sqrt[3]{x^2y}$ **109.** 3 **111.** $\dfrac{x^2}{7y^{3/2}}$ **113.** $\dfrac{x^3}{y^2}$ **115. a.** 67.5%; underestimates by 0.5% **b.** 93.1%
117. $\dfrac{\sqrt{5} + 1}{2}$; 1.62 to 1 **119.** $P = 18\sqrt{5}$ ft; $A = 100$ ft^2 **129.** does not make sense **131.** does not make sense **133.** false
135. false **137.** Let $\square = 3$. **139.** 4 **141. a.** 8 **b.** $\dfrac{1}{4}$ **142.** $10x^7y^9$ **143.** $16x^8 + 6x^5$ **144.** $2x^3 + 11x^2 + 22x + 15$

Section P.4

Check Point Exercises

1. a. $-x^3 + x^2 - 8x - 20$ **b.** $20x^3 - 11x^2 - 2x - 8$ **2.** $15x^3 - 31x^2 + 30x - 8$ **3.** $28x^2 - 41x + 15$ **4. a.** $49x^2 - 64$ **b.** $4y^6 - 25$
5. a. $x^2 + 20x + 100$ **b.** $25x^2 + 40x + 16$ **6. a.** $x^2 - 18x + 81$ **b.** $49x^2 - 42x + 9$ **7.** $2x^2y + 5xy^2 - 2y^3$ **8. a.** $21x^2 - 25xy + 6y^2$
b. $4x^2 + 16xy + 16y^2$

Exercise Set P.4

1. yes; $3x^2 + 2x - 5$ **3.** no **5.** 2 **7.** 4 **9.** $11x^3 + 7x^2 - 12x - 4$; 3 **11.** $12x^3 + 4x^2 + 12x - 14$; 3 **13.** $6x^2 - 6x + 2$; 2
15. $x^3 + 1$ **17.** $2x^3 - 9x^2 + 19x - 15$ **19.** $x^2 + 10x + 21$ **21.** $x^2 - 2x - 15$ **23.** $6x^2 + 13x + 5$ **25.** $10x^2 - 9x - 9$
27. $15x^4 - 47x^2 + 28$ **29.** $8x^5 - 40x^3 + 3x^2 - 15$ **31.** $x^2 - 9$ **33.** $9x^2 - 4$ **35.** $25 - 49x^2$ **37.** $16x^4 - 25x^2$ **39.** $1 - y^{10}$
41. $x^2 + 4x + 4$ **43.** $4x^2 + 12x + 9$ **45.** $x^2 - 6x + 9$ **47.** $16x^4 - 8x^2 + 1$ **49.** $4x^2 - 28x + 49$ **51.** $x^3 + 3x^2 + 3x + 1$
53. $8x^3 + 36x^2 + 54x + 27$ **55.** $x^3 - 9x^2 + 27x - 27$ **57.** $27x^3 - 108x^2 + 144x - 64$ **59.** $7x^2y - 4xy$ is of degree 3
61. $2x^2y + 13xy + 13$ is of degree 3 **63.** $-5x^3 + 8xy - 9y^2$ is of degree 3 **65.** $x^4y^2 + 8x^3y + y - 6x$ is of degree 6
67. $7x^2 + 38xy + 15y^2$ **69.** $2x^2 + xy - 21y^2$ **71.** $15x^2y^2 + xy - 2$ **73.** $49x^2 + 70xy + 25y^2$ **75.** $x^4y^4 - 6x^2y^2 + 9$
77. $x^3 - y^3$ **79.** $9x^2 - 25y^2$ **81.** $49x^2y^4 - 100y^2$ **83.** $48xy$ **85.** $-9x^2 + 3x + 9$ **87.** $16x^4 - 625$ **89.** $4x^2 - 28x + 49$
91. a. \$56,995; underestimates by \$225 **b.** $M - W = -35x^3 + 1373x^2 - 15{,}995x + 63{,}210$ **c.** \$12,348 **d.** \$10,923; overestimates by \$1425
93. $4x^3 - 36x^2 + 80x$ **95.** $6x + 22$ **103.** makes sense **105.** makes sense **107.** false **109.** false **111.** $49x^2 + 70x + 25 - 16y^2$
113. $6x^n - 13$ **115.** 4 **116.** 2 **117.** 3

Mid-Chapter P Check Point

1. $12x^2 - x - 35$ **2.** $-x + 12$ **3.** $10\sqrt{6}$ **4.** $3\sqrt{3}$ **5.** $x + 45$ **6.** $64x^2 - 48x + 9$ **7.** $\dfrac{x^2}{y^3}$ **8.** $\dfrac{3}{4}$ **9.** $-x^2 + 5x - 6$
10. $2x^3 - 11x^2 + 17x - 5$ **11.** $-x^6 + 2x^3$ **12.** $18a^2 - 11ab - 10b^2$ **13.** $\{a, c, d, e, f, h\}$ **14.** $\{c, d\}$ **15.** $5x^2y^3 + 2xy - y^2$
16. $-\dfrac{12y^{15}}{x^3}$ **17.** $\dfrac{6y^3}{x^7}$ **18.** $|\sqrt[3]{x}|$ **19.** 1.2×10^{-2} **20.** $2\sqrt[3]{2}$ **21.** $x^6 - 4$ **22.** $x^4 + 4x^2 + 4$ **23.** $10\sqrt{3}$
24. $\dfrac{77 + 11\sqrt{3}}{46}$ **25.** $\dfrac{11\sqrt{3}}{3}$ **26.** $-11, -\dfrac{3}{7}, 0, 0.45, \sqrt{25}$ **27.** $\sqrt{13} - 2$ **28.** $-x^3$ **29.** \$4.2 $\times 10^{10}$ **30.** 4 times
31. a. model 2 **b.** underestimates by 3 channels **c.** 132

Section P.5

Check Point Exercises

1. a. $2x^2(5x - 2)$ **b.** $(x - 7)(2x + 3)$ **2.** $(x + 5)(x^2 - 2)$ **3.** $(x + 8)(x + 5)$ or $(x + 5)(x + 8)$ **4.** $(x - 7)(x + 2)$ or $(x + 2)(x - 7)$
5. $(3x - 1)(2x + 7)$ or $(2x + 7)(3x - 1)$ **6.** $(3x - y)(x - 4y)$ or $(x - 4y)(3x - y)$ **7. a.** $(x + 9)(x - 9)$ **b.** $(6x + 5)(6x - 5)$
8. $(9x^2 + 4)(3x + 2)(3x - 2)$ **9. a.** $(x + 7)^2$ **b.** $(4x - 7)^2$ **10. a.** $(x + 1)(x^2 - x + 1)$ **b.** $(5x - 2)(25x^2 + 10x + 4)$ **11.** $3x(x - 5)^2$
12. $(x + 10 + 6a)(x + 10 - 6a)$ **13.** $\dfrac{2x - 1}{(x - 1)^{1/2}}$

Exercise Set P.5

1. $9(2x + 3)$ **3.** $3x(x + 2)$ **5.** $9x^2(x^2 - 2x + 3)$ **7.** $(x + 5)(x + 3)$ **9.** $(x - 3)(x^2 + 12)$ **11.** $(x - 2)(x^2 + 5)$ **13.** $(x - 1)(x^2 + 2)$
15. $(3x - 2)(x^2 - 2)$ **17.** $(x + 2)(x + 3)$ **19.** $(x - 5)(x + 3)$ **21.** $(x - 5)(x - 3)$ **23.** $(3x + 2)(x - 1)$ **25.** $(3x - 28)(x + 1)$
27. $(2x - 1)(3x - 4)$ **29.** $(2x + 3)(2x + 5)$ **31.** $(3x - 2)(3x - 1)$ **33.** $(5x + 8)(4x - 1)$ **35.** $(2x + y)(x + y)$ **37.** $(3x + 2y)(2x - 3y)$
39. $(x + 10)(x - 10)$ **41.** $(6x + 7)(6x - 7)$ **43.** $(3x + 5y)(3x - 5y)$ **45.** $(x^2 + 4)(x + 2)(x - 2)$ **47.** $(4x^2 + 9)(2x + 3)(2x - 3)$
49. $(x + 1)^2$ **51.** $(x - 7)^2$ **53.** $(2x + 1)^2$ **55.** $(3x - 1)^2$ **57.** $(x + 3)(x^2 - 3x + 9)$ **59.** $(x - 4)(x^2 + 4x + 16)$
61. $(2x - 1)(4x^2 + 2x + 1)$ **63.** $(4x + 3)(16x^2 - 12x + 9)$ **65.** $3x(x + 1)(x - 1)$ **67.** $4(x + 2)(x - 3)$ **69.** $2(x^2 + 9)(x + 3)(x - 3)$
71. $(x - 3)(x + 3)(x + 2)$ **73.** $2(x - 8)(x + 7)$ **75.** $x(x - 2)(x + 2)$ **77.** prime **79.** $(x - 2)(x + 2)^2$ **81.** $y(y^2 + 9)(y + 3)(y - 3)$

83. $5y^2(2y + 3)(2y - 3)$ **85.** $(x - 6 + 7y)(x - 6 - 7y)$ **87.** $(x + y)(3b + 4)(3b - 4)$ **89.** $(y - 2)(x + 4)(x - 4)$

91. $2x(x + 6 + 2a)(x + 6 - 2a)$ **93.** $x^{1/2}(x - 1)$ **95.** $\dfrac{4(1 + 2x)}{x^{2/3}}$ **97.** $-(x + 3)^{1/2}(x + 2)$ **99.** $\dfrac{x + 4}{(x + 5)^{3/2}}$ **101.** $-\dfrac{4(4x - 1)^{1/2}(x - 1)}{3}$

103. $(x + 1)(5x - 6)(2x + 1)$ **105.** $(x^2 + 6)(6x^2 - 1)$ **107.** $y(y^2 + 1)(y^4 - y^2 + 1)$ **109.** $(x + 2y)(x - 2y)(x + y)(x - y)$

111. $(x - y)^2(x - y + 2)(x - y - 2)$ **113.** $(2x - y^2)(x - 3y^2)$ **115. a.** $(x - 0.4x)(1 - 0.4) = (0.6x)(0.6) = 0.36x$ **b.** no; 36%

117. a. $9x^2 - 16$ **b.** $(3x + 4)(3x - 4)$ **119. a.** $x(x + y) - y(x + y)$ **b.** $(x + y)(x - y)$ **121.** $4a^3 - 4ab^2 = 4a(a + b)(a - b)$

131. makes sense **133.** makes sense **135.** true **137.** false **139.** $-(x + 5)(x - 1)$ **141.** $-\dfrac{10}{(x - 5)^{3/2}(x + 5)^{1/2}}$

143. $b = 0, 3, 4, -c(c + 4)$, where $c > 0$ is an integer **144.** $\dfrac{(x + 5)(x + 1)}{(x + 5)(x - 5)} = \dfrac{x + 1}{x - 5}$ **145.** $\dfrac{2}{3}$ **146.** $\dfrac{7}{6}$

Section P.6

Check Point Exercises

1. a. -5 **b.** $6, -6$ **2. a.** $x^2, x \neq -3$ **b.** $\dfrac{x - 1}{x + 1}, x \neq -1$ **3.** $\dfrac{x - 3}{(x - 2)(x + 3)}, x \neq 2, x \neq -2, x \neq -3$ **4.** $\dfrac{3(x - 1)}{x(x + 2)}, x \neq 1, x \neq 0, x \neq -2$

5. $-2, x \neq -1$ **6.** $\dfrac{2(4x + 1)}{(x + 1)(x - 1)}, x \neq 1, x \neq -1$ **7.** $(x - 3)(x - 3)(x + 3)$ or $(x - 3)^2(x + 3)$ **8.** $\dfrac{-x^2 + 11x - 20}{2(x - 5)^2}, x \neq 5$

9. $\dfrac{2(2 - 3x)}{4 + 3x}, x \neq 0, x \neq -\dfrac{4}{3}$ **10.** $-\dfrac{1}{x(x + 7)}, x \neq 0, x \neq -7$

Exercise Set P.6

1. 3 **3.** $5, -5$ **5.** $-1, -10$ **7.** $\dfrac{3}{x - 3}, x \neq 3$ **9.** $\dfrac{x - 6}{4}, x \neq 6$ **11.** $\dfrac{y + 9}{y - 1}, y \neq 1, 2$ **13.** $\dfrac{x + 6}{x - 6}, x \neq 6, -6$ **15.** $\dfrac{1}{3}, x \neq 2, -3$

17. $\dfrac{(x - 3)(x + 3)}{x(x + 4)}, x \neq 0, -4, 3$ **19.** $\dfrac{x - 1}{x + 2}, x \neq -2, -1, 2, 3$ **21.** $\dfrac{x^2 + 2x + 4}{3x}, x \neq -2, 0, 2$ **23.** $\dfrac{7}{9}, x \neq -1$ **25.** $\dfrac{(x - 2)^2}{x}, x \neq 0, -2, 2$

27. $\dfrac{2(x + 3)}{3}, x \neq 3, -3$ **29.** $\dfrac{x - 5}{2}, x \neq 1, -5$ **31.** $\dfrac{(x + 2)(x + 4)}{x - 5}, x \neq -6, -3, -1, 3, 5$ **33.** $2, x \neq -\dfrac{5}{6}$ **35.** $\dfrac{2x - 1}{x + 3}, x \neq 0, -3$

37. $3, x \neq 2$ **39.** $\dfrac{3}{x - 3}, x \neq 3, -4$ **41.** $\dfrac{9x + 39}{(x + 4)(x + 5)}, x \neq -4, -5$ **43.** $-\dfrac{3}{x(x + 1)}, x \neq -1, 0$ **45.** $\dfrac{3x^2 + 4}{(x + 2)(x - 2)}, x \neq -2, 2$

47. $\dfrac{2x^2 + 50}{(x - 5)(x + 5)}, x \neq -5, 5$ **49.** $\dfrac{13}{6(x + 2)}, x \neq -2$ **51.** $\dfrac{4x + 16}{(x + 3)^2}, x \neq -3$ **53.** $\dfrac{x^2 - x}{(x + 5)(x - 2)(x + 3)}, x \neq -5, 2, -3$

55. $\dfrac{-x^2 - 2x + 1}{(x + 1)(x - 1)}, x \neq -1, 1$ **57.** $\dfrac{x - 1}{x + 2}, x \neq -2, -1$ **59.** $\dfrac{1}{3}, x \neq 3$ **61.** $\dfrac{x + 1}{3x - 1}, x \neq 0, \dfrac{1}{3}$ **63.** $\dfrac{1}{xy}, x \neq 0, y \neq 0, x \neq -y$

65. $\dfrac{x}{x + 3}, x \neq -2, -3$ **67.** $-\dfrac{x - 14}{7}, x \neq -2, 2$ **69.** $\dfrac{x - 3}{x + 2}, x \neq -2, -1, 3$ **71.** $-\dfrac{2x + h}{x^2(x + h)^2}, x \neq 0, h \neq 0, x \neq -h$

73. $\dfrac{x^2 + 5x + 8}{(x + 2)(x + 1)}$ **75.** 2 **77.** $\dfrac{1}{y(y + 5)}$ **79.** $\dfrac{2d}{a^2 + ab + b^2}$ **81. a.** 86.67, 520, 1170; It costs \$86,670,000 to inoculate 40% of the population against this strain of flu, \$520,000,000 to inoculate 80% of the population, and \$1,170,000,000 to inoculate 90% of the population. **b.** $x = 100$
c. The cost increases rapidly; it is impossible to inoculate 100% of the population. **83. a.** 2078; underestimates by 22 calories

b. 2662; underestimates by 38 calories **c.** $\dfrac{-33x^2 + 263x + 515}{-60x^2 + 499x + 295}$ **85.** $\dfrac{4x^2 + 22x}{(x + 5)(x + 6)}$ **99.** does not make sense **101.** makes sense

103. true **105.** false **107.** $\dfrac{x - 1}{x + 3}$ **109.** It cubes x. **110.** $-5; 0; 3; 4; 3; 0; -5$ **111.** $-8; -3; 0; 1; 0; -3; -8$ **112.** $3; 2; 1; 0; 1; 2; 3$

Chapter P Review Exercises

1. 51 **2.** 16 **3.** 124 ft **4.** $\{a, c\}$ **5.** $\{a, b, c, d, e\}$ **6.** $\{a, b, c, d, f, g\}$ **7.** $\{a\}$ **8. a.** $\sqrt{81}$ **b.** $0, \sqrt{81}$ **c.** $-17, 0, \sqrt{81}$
d. $-17, -\dfrac{9}{13}, 0, 0.75, \sqrt{81}$ **e.** $\sqrt{2}, \pi$ **f.** $-17, -\dfrac{9}{13}, 0, 0.75, \sqrt{2}, \pi, \sqrt{81}$ **9.** 103 **10.** $\sqrt{2} - 1$ **11.** $\sqrt{17} - 3$ **12.** $|4 - (-17)|; 21$
13. commutative property of addition **14.** associative property of multiplication **15.** distributive property of multiplication over addition
16. commutative property of multiplication **17.** commutative property of multiplication **18.** commutative property of addition
19. $17x - 15$ **20.** $2x$ **21.** $5y - 17$ **22.** $10x$ **23.** 38.55%; overestimates by 3.55% **24.** -108 **25.** $\dfrac{5}{16}$ **26.** $\dfrac{1}{25}$ **27.** $\dfrac{1}{27}$

28. $-8x^{12}y^9$ **29.** $\dfrac{10}{x^8}$ **30.** $\dfrac{1}{16x^{12}}$ **31.** $\dfrac{y^8}{4x^{10}}$ **32.** 37,400 **33.** 0.0000745 **34.** 3.59×10^6 **35.** 7.25×10^{-3} **36.** 390,000

37. 0.023 **38.** 2.57×10^{11} **39.** 1.75×10^8 **40.** \$1469 **41.** $10\sqrt{3}$ **42.** $2|x|\sqrt{3}$ **43.** $2x\sqrt{5}$ **44.** $r\sqrt{r}$ **45.** $\dfrac{11}{2}$ **46.** $4x\sqrt{3}$

47. $20\sqrt{5}$ **48.** $16\sqrt{2}$ **49.** $24\sqrt{2} - 8\sqrt{3}$ **50.** $6\sqrt{5}$ **51.** $\dfrac{\sqrt{6}}{3}$ **52.** $\dfrac{5(6 - \sqrt{3})}{33}$ **53.** $7(\sqrt{7} + \sqrt{5})$ **54.** 5 **55.** -2

56. not a real number **57.** 5 **58.** $3\sqrt[3]{3}$ **59.** $y\sqrt[3]{y^2}$ **60.** $2\sqrt[4]{5}$ **61.** $13\sqrt[3]{2}$ **62.** $x\sqrt[4]{2}$ **63.** 4 **64.** $\dfrac{1}{5}$ **65.** 5 **66.** $\dfrac{1}{3}$

67. 16 **68.** $\dfrac{1}{81}$ **69.** $20x^{11/12}$ **70.** $3x^{1/4}$ **71.** $25x^4$ **72.** \sqrt{y} **73.** $8x^3 + 10x^2 - 20x - 4$; degree 3 **74.** $8x^4 - 5x^3 + 6$; degree 4
75. $12x^3 + x^2 - 21x + 10$ **76.** $6x^2 - 7x - 5$ **77.** $16x^2 - 25$ **78.** $4x^2 + 20x + 25$ **79.** $9x^2 - 24x + 16$ **80.** $8x^3 + 12x^2 + 6x + 1$

81. $125x^3 - 150x^2 + 60x - 8$ **82.** $-x^2 - 17xy - 3y^2$; degree 2 **83.** $24x^3y^2 + x^2y - 12x^2 + 4$; degree 5 **84.** $3x^2 + 16xy - 35y^2$
85. $9x^2 - 30xy + 25y^2$ **86.** $9x^4 + 12x^2y + 4y^2$ **87.** $49x^2 - 16y^2$ **88.** $a^3 - b^3$ **89.** $3x^2(5x + 1)$ **90.** $(x - 4)(x - 7)$
91. $(3x + 1)(5x - 2)$ **92.** $(8 - x)(8 + x)$ **93.** prime **94.** $3x^2(x - 5)(x + 2)$ **95.** $4x^3(5x^4 - 9)$ **96.** $(x + 3)(x - 3)^2$ **97.** $(4x - 5)^2$
98. $(x^2 + 4)(x + 2)(x - 2)$ **99.** $(y - 2)(y^2 + 2y + 4)$ **100.** $(x + 4)(x^2 - 4x + 16)$ **101.** $3x^2(x - 2)(x + 2)$ **102.** $(3x - 5)(9x^2 + 15x + 25)$
103. $x(x - 1)(x + 1)(x^2 + 1)$ **104.** $(x^2 - 2)(x + 5)$ **105.** $(x + 9 + y)(x + 9 - y)$ **106.** $\dfrac{16(1 + 2x)}{x^{3/4}}$
107. $(x + 2)(x - 2)(x^2 + 3)^{1/2}(-x^4 + x^2 + 13)$ **108.** $\dfrac{6(2x + 1)}{x^{3/2}}$ **109.** $x^2, x \neq -2$ **110.** $\dfrac{x - 3}{x - 6}, x \neq -6, 6$ **111.** $\dfrac{x}{x + 2}, x \neq -2$
112. $\dfrac{(x + 3)^3}{(x - 2)^2(x + 2)}, x \neq 2, -2$ **113.** $\dfrac{2}{x(x + 1)}, x \neq 0, 1, -1, -\dfrac{1}{3}$ **114.** $\dfrac{x + 3}{x - 4}, x \neq -3, 4, 2, 8$ **115.** $\dfrac{1}{x - 3}, x \neq 3, -3$
116. $\dfrac{4x(x - 1)}{(x + 2)(x - 2)}, x \neq 2, -2$ **117.** $\dfrac{2x^2 - 3}{(x - 3)(x + 3)(x - 2)}, x \neq 3, -3, 2$ **118.** $\dfrac{11x^2 - x - 11}{(2x - 1)(x + 3)(3x + 2)}, x \neq \dfrac{1}{2}, -3, -\dfrac{2}{3}$ **119.** $\dfrac{3}{x}, x \neq 0, 2$
120. $\dfrac{3x}{x - 4}, x \neq 0, 4, -4$ **121.** $\dfrac{3x + 8}{3x + 10}, x \neq -3, -\dfrac{10}{3}$

Chapter P Test

1. $6x^2 - 27x$ **2.** $-6x + 17$ **3.** $\{5\}$ **4.** $\{1, 2, 5, a\}$ **5.** $6x^2y^3 + 4xy + 2y^2$ **6.** $\dfrac{5y^8}{x^6}$ **7.** $3r\sqrt{2}$ **8.** $11\sqrt{2}$ **9.** $\dfrac{3(5 - \sqrt{2})}{23}$
10. $2x\sqrt[3]{2x}$ **11.** $\dfrac{x + 3}{x - 2}, x \neq 2, 1$ **12.** 2.5×10^1 **13.** $2x^3 - 13x^2 + 26x - 15$ **14.** $25x^2 + 30xy + 9y^2$ **15.** $\dfrac{2(x + 3)}{x + 1}, x \neq 3, -1, -4, -3$
16. $\dfrac{x^2 + 2x + 15}{(x + 3)(x - 3)}, x \neq 3, -3$ **17.** $\dfrac{11}{(x - 3)(x - 4)}, x \neq 3, 4$ **18.** $\dfrac{3 - x}{3}, x \neq 0$ **19.** $(x - 3)(x - 6)$ **20.** $(x^2 + 3)(x + 2)$
21. $(5x - 3)(5x + 3)$ **22.** $(6x - 7)^2$ **23.** $(y - 5)(y^2 + 5y + 25)$ **24.** $(x + 5 + 3y)(x + 5 - 3y)$ **25.** $\dfrac{2x + 3}{(x + 3)^{3/5}}$
26. $-7, -\dfrac{4}{5}, 0, 0.25, \sqrt{4}, \dfrac{22}{7}$ **27.** commutative property of addition **28.** distributive property of multiplication over addition **29.** 7.6×10^{-4}
30. $\dfrac{1}{243}$ **31.** 1.32×10^{10} **32. a.** 43.08%; overestimates by 0.08% **b.** $R = \dfrac{-0.28n + 47}{0.28n + 53}$ **c.** $\dfrac{2}{3}$; Three women will receive bachelor's degrees for every two men.; It describes the projections exactly.

CHAPTER 1

Section 1.1

Check Point Exercises

1.

2.

$y = 4 - x$

3.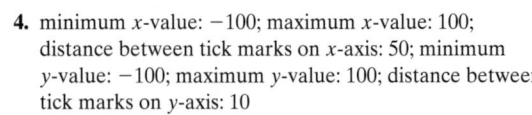

$y = |x + 1|$

4. minimum x-value: -100; maximum x-value: 100; distance between tick marks on x-axis: 50; minimum y-value: -100; maximum y-value: 100; distance between tick marks on y-axis: 10

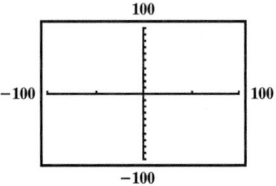

5. a. x-intercept: -3; y-intercept: 5
 b. no x-intercept; y-intercept: 4
 c. x-intercept: 0; y-intercept: 0
6. a. 65% **b.** 60% **c.** overestimates by 5%

Exercise Set 1.1

1.

3.

5.

7.

9.

11.

13.

$y = x^2 - 2$

15.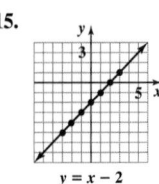

$y = x - 2$

17.

$y = 2x + 1$

19.

$y = -\dfrac{1}{2}x$

21.
$y = 2|x|$

23.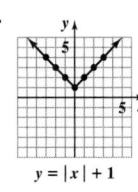
$y = |x| + 1$

25.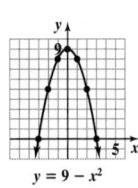
$y = 9 - x^2$

27.
$y = x^3$

29. c **31.** b **33.** c **35.** no **37.** $(2, 0)$ **39.** $(-2, 4)$ and $(1, 1)$ **41. a.** 2 **b.** -4 **43. a.** $1, -2$ **b.** 2 **45. a.** -1 **b.** none

47. $y = 2x + 4$
$y = 2x + 4$

49. $y = 3 - x^2$
$y = 3 - x^2$

51.
$y = 5$

53.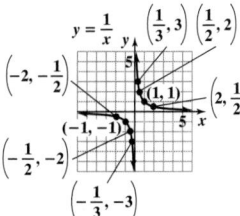
$y = \frac{1}{x}$

55. a. 20% **b.** 18%; underestimates by 2% **c.** Answers will vary.; approximately 45% **d.** 44%; It's less than the estimate. **e.** 1990; 14%
57. 8; 1 **59.** about 1.9 **67.** makes sense **69.** does not make sense **71.** false **73.** true **75.** a **77.** b **79.** b **81.** c
83. true **84.** $-x + 10$ **85.** $9x - 24$

Section 1.2

Check Point Exercises

1. $\{6\}$ **2.** $\{5\}$ **3.** $\{1\}$ **4.** $\{3\}$ **5.** \varnothing **6.** 11 **7.** \varnothing; inconsistent equation **8.** 3.7; by the point $(3.7, 10)$

Exercise Set 1.2

1. $\{11\}$ **3.** $\{7\}$ **5.** $\{13\}$ **7.** $\{2\}$ **9.** $\{9\}$ **11.** $\{-5\}$ **13.** $\{6\}$ **15.** $\{-2\}$ **17.** $\{12\}$ **19.** $\{24\}$ **21.** $\{-15\}$ **23.** $\{5\}$
25. $\left\{\frac{33}{2}\right\}$ **27.** $\{-12\}$ **29.** $\left\{\frac{46}{5}\right\}$ **31. a.** 0 **b.** $\left\{\frac{1}{2}\right\}$ **33. a.** 0 **b.** $\{-2\}$ **35. a.** 0 **b.** $\{2\}$ **37. a.** 0 **b.** $\{4\}$
39. a. 1 **b.** $\{3\}$ **41. a.** -1 **b.** \varnothing **43. a.** 1 **b.** $\{2\}$ **45. a.** $-2, 2$ **b.** \varnothing **47. a.** $-1, 1$ **b.** $\{-3\}$ **49. a.** $-2, 4$ **b.** \varnothing
51. 6 **53.** -7 **55.** 2 **57.** 19 **59.** -1 **61.** identity **63.** inconsistent equation **65.** conditional equation
67. inconsistent equation **69.** $\{-7\}$; conditional equation **71.** \varnothing; inconsistent equation **73.** $\{-4\}$; conditional equation
75. $\{8\}$; conditional equation **77.** $\{-1\}$; conditional equation **79.** \varnothing; inconsistent equation **81.** $3(x - 4) = 3(2 - 2x)$; $\{2\}$
83. $-3(x - 3) = 5(2 - x)$; $\{0.5\}$ **85.** 2 **87.** -7 **89.** $\{-2\}$ **91.** \varnothing or no solution **93.** $\{10\}$ **95.** $\{-2\}$
97. 142 pounds; 13 pounds **99. a.** \$32,000 **b.** \$32,616; \$616 **c.** \$32,597; \$597 **101.** 2013 **103.** 11 learning trials; $(11, 0.95)$ **105.** 125 liters
117. $\{5\}$

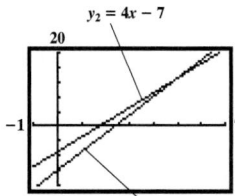
$y_2 = 4x - 7$
$y_1 = 2x + 3(x - 4)$

119. $\{-5\}$

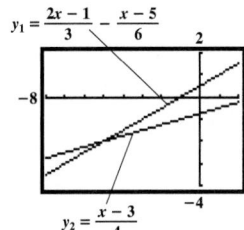
$y_1 = \frac{2x - 1}{3} - \frac{x - 5}{6}$
$y_2 = \frac{x - 3}{4}$

121. makes sense **123.** makes sense **125.** false
127. false **129.** 2 **131.** $x + 150$
132. $20 + 0.05x$ **133.** $4x + 400$

Section 1.3

Check Point Exercises

1. women: \$57,989; men: \$72,026 **2.** by 50 years after 1969, or in 2019 **3.** 300 min **4.** \$1200 **5.** \$3150 at 9%; \$1850 at 11%
6. 50 ft by 94 ft **7.** $w = \dfrac{P - 2l}{2}$ **8.** $C = \dfrac{P}{1 + M}$

Exercise Set 1.3

1. 6 **3.** 25 **5.** 120 **7.** 320 **9.** 19 and 45 **11.** 2 **13.** 8 **15.** all real numbers **17.** 5 **19.** radio: 974 hr; TV: 1555 hr
21. carpenters: \$35,580; computer programmers: \$63,420 **23.** by 38 years after 1983, or in 2021
25. a. $y = 24,000 - 3000x$ **b.** after 5 years
c.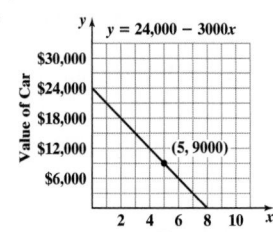
$y = 24,000 - 3000x$
$(5, 9000)$
Value of Car
Years

27. after 5 months; $165 **29.** 30 times **31. a.** 2014; 22,300 students **b.** $y_1 = 13,300 + 1000x$; $y_2 = 26,800 - 500x$ **33.** $420 **35.** $150
37. $467.20 **39.** $2000 at 6%; $5000 at 8% **41.** $6000 at 12%; $2000 at a 5% loss **43.** 50 yd by 100 yd **45.** 36 ft by 78 ft
47. 2 in. **49.** 11 hr **51.** 5 ft 7 in. **53.** 7 oz **55.** $w = \dfrac{A}{l}$ **57.** $b = \dfrac{2A}{h}$ **59.** $P = \dfrac{I}{rt}$ **61.** $m = \dfrac{E}{c^2}$ **63.** $p = \dfrac{T - D}{m}$
65. $a = \dfrac{2A}{h} - b$ **67.** $r = \dfrac{S - P}{Pt}$ **69.** $S = \dfrac{F}{B} + V$ **71.** $I = \dfrac{E}{R + r}$ **73.** $f = \dfrac{pq}{p + q}$ **81.** does not make sense
83. does not make sense **85.** North campus had 600 students; South campus had 400 students. **87.** Coburn $= 60$ years old; woman $= 20$ years old
89. $4000 for the mother; $8000 for the boy; $2000 for the girl **91.** $C = \dfrac{VL - SN}{L - N}$ **93.** $-14 - 29x + 15x^2$ or $15x^2 - 29x - 14$
94. $\sqrt{2}$ **95.** $-\dfrac{54 + 43\sqrt{2}}{46}$

Section 1.4

Check Point Exercises

1. a. $8 + i$ **b.** $-10 + 7i$ **2. a.** $63 + 14i$ **b.** $58 - 11i$ **3.** $\dfrac{16}{17} + \dfrac{21}{17}i$ **4. a.** $7i\sqrt{3}$ **b.** $1 - 4i\sqrt{3}$ **c.** $-7 + i\sqrt{3}$

Exercise Set 1.4

1. $8 - 2i$ **3.** $-2 + 9i$ **5.** $24 - 3i$ **7.** $-14 + 17i$ **9.** $21 + 15i$ **11.** $-19 + 7i$ **13.** $-29 - 11i$ **15.** 34 **17.** 26 **19.** $-5 + 12i$
21. $\dfrac{3}{5} + \dfrac{1}{5}i$ **23.** $1 + i$ **25.** $-\dfrac{24}{25} + \dfrac{32}{25}i$ **27.** $\dfrac{7}{5} + \dfrac{4}{5}i$ **29.** $3i$ **31.** $47i$ **33.** $-8i$ **35.** $2 + 6i\sqrt{7}$ **37.** $-\dfrac{1}{3} + i\dfrac{\sqrt{2}}{6}$ **39.** $-\dfrac{1}{8} - i\dfrac{\sqrt{3}}{24}$
41. $-2\sqrt{6} - 2i\sqrt{10}$ **43.** $24\sqrt{15}$ **45.** $-11 - 5i$ **47.** $-5 + 10i$ **49.** $0 + 47i$ or $47i$ **51.** 0 **53.** $\dfrac{20}{13} + \dfrac{30}{13}i$ **55.** $(47 + 13i)$ volts
57. $(5 + i\sqrt{15}) + (5 - i\sqrt{15}) = 10$; $(5 + i\sqrt{15})(5 - i\sqrt{15}) = 25 - 15i^2 = 25 + 15 = 40$ **67.** makes sense **69.** does not make sense
71. false **73.** false **75.** $\dfrac{14}{25} - \dfrac{2}{25}i$ **77.** $\dfrac{8}{5} + \dfrac{16}{5}i$ **78.** $(2x - 1)(x + 4)$ **79.** $(x - 3)(x - 3)$ or $(x - 3)^2$ **80.** -5

Section 1.5

Check Point Exercises

1. a. $\{0, 3\}$ **b.** $\left\{-1, \dfrac{1}{2}\right\}$ **2. a.** $\{-\sqrt{7}, \sqrt{7}\}$ **b.** $\{-3i, 3i\}$ **c.** $\{-5 + \sqrt{11}, -5 - \sqrt{11}\}$ **3. a.** 9; $x^2 + 6x + 9 = (x + 3)^2$
b. $\dfrac{25}{4}$; $x^2 - 5x + \dfrac{25}{4} = \left(x - \dfrac{5}{2}\right)^2$ **c.** $\dfrac{1}{9}$; $x^2 + \dfrac{2}{3}x + \dfrac{1}{9} = \left(x + \dfrac{1}{3}\right)^2$ **4.** $\{-2 \pm \sqrt{5}\}$ **5.** $\left\{\dfrac{-3 + \sqrt{41}}{4}, \dfrac{-3 - \sqrt{41}}{4}\right\}$ **6.** $\left\{\dfrac{-1 + \sqrt{3}}{2}, \dfrac{-1 - \sqrt{3}}{2}\right\}$
7. $\{1 + i, 1 - i\}$ **8. a.** 0; one real solution that is rational **b.** 81; two rational solutions **c.** -44; two imaginary solutions that
are complex conjugates **9.** approximately 26 years old **10.** 20 in.

Exercise Set 1.5

1. $\{-2, 5\}$ **3.** $\{3, 5\}$ **5.** $\left\{-\dfrac{5}{2}, \dfrac{2}{3}\right\}$ **7.** $\left\{-\dfrac{4}{3}, 2\right\}$ **9.** $\{-4, 0\}$ **11.** $\left\{0, \dfrac{1}{3}\right\}$ **13.** $\{-3, 1\}$ **15.** $\{-3, 3\}$ **17.** $\{-\sqrt{10}, \sqrt{10}\}$
19. $\{\pm 5i\}$ **21.** $\{-7, 3\}$ **23.** $\{4 \pm \sqrt{5}\}$ **25.** $\{-3 \pm 4i\}$ **27.** $\{3 \pm i\sqrt{5}\}$ **29.** $\left\{-\dfrac{5}{3}, \dfrac{1}{3}\right\}$ **31.** $\left\{\dfrac{1 - \sqrt{7}}{5}, \dfrac{1 + \sqrt{7}}{5}\right\}$
33. $\left\{\dfrac{4 - 2\sqrt{2}}{3}, \dfrac{4 + 2\sqrt{2}}{3}\right\}$ **35.** 36; $x^2 + 12x + 36 = (x + 6)^2$ **37.** 25; $x^2 - 10x + 25 = (x - 5)^2$ **39.** $\dfrac{9}{4}$; $x^2 + 3x + \dfrac{9}{4} = \left(x + \dfrac{3}{2}\right)^2$
41. $\dfrac{49}{4}$; $x^2 - 7x + \dfrac{49}{4} = \left(x - \dfrac{7}{2}\right)^2$ **43.** $\dfrac{1}{9}$; $x^2 - \dfrac{2}{3}x + \dfrac{1}{9} = \left(x - \dfrac{1}{3}\right)^2$ **45.** $\dfrac{1}{36}$; $x^2 - \dfrac{1}{3}x + \dfrac{1}{36} = \left(x - \dfrac{1}{6}\right)^2$ **47.** $\{-7, 1\}$
49. $\{1 + \sqrt{3}, 1 - \sqrt{3}\}$ **51.** $\{3 + 2\sqrt{5}, 3 - 2\sqrt{5}\}$ **53.** $\{-2 + \sqrt{3}, -2 - \sqrt{3}\}$ **55.** $\{2, 3\}$ **57.** $\left\{\dfrac{-3 + \sqrt{13}}{2}, \dfrac{-3 - \sqrt{13}}{2}\right\}$
59. $\left\{\dfrac{1}{2}, 3\right\}$ **61.** $\left\{\dfrac{1 + \sqrt{2}}{2}, \dfrac{1 - \sqrt{2}}{2}\right\}$ **63.** $\left\{\dfrac{1 + \sqrt{7}}{3}, \dfrac{1 - \sqrt{7}}{3}\right\}$ **65.** $\{-5, -3\}$ **67.** $\left\{\dfrac{-5 + \sqrt{13}}{2}, \dfrac{-5 - \sqrt{13}}{2}\right\}$
69. $\left\{\dfrac{3 + \sqrt{57}}{6}, \dfrac{3 - \sqrt{57}}{6}\right\}$ **71.** $\left\{\dfrac{1 + \sqrt{29}}{4}, \dfrac{1 - \sqrt{29}}{4}\right\}$ **73.** $\{3 + i, 3 - i\}$ **75.** 36; 2 unequal real solutions that are rational
77. 97; 2 unequal real solutions that are irrational **79.** 0; 1 real solution that is rational **81.** 37; 2 unequal real solutions that are irrational
83. $\left\{-\dfrac{1}{2}, 1\right\}$ **85.** $\left\{\dfrac{1}{5}, 2\right\}$ **87.** $\{-2\sqrt{5}, 2\sqrt{5}\}$ **89.** $\{1 + \sqrt{2}, 1 - \sqrt{2}\}$ **91.** $\left\{\dfrac{-11 + \sqrt{33}}{4}, \dfrac{-11 - \sqrt{33}}{4}\right\}$ **93.** $\left\{0, \dfrac{8}{3}\right\}$ **95.** $\{2\}$
97. $\{-2, 2\}$ **99.** $\{3 + 2i, 3 - 2i\}$ **101.** $\{2 + i\sqrt{3}, 2 - i\sqrt{3}\}$ **103.** $\left\{0, \dfrac{7}{2}\right\}$ **105.** $\{2 + \sqrt{10}, 2 - \sqrt{10}\}$ **107.** $\{-5, -1\}$
109. -1 and 5; d **111.** -3 and 1; f **113.** no x-intercepts; b **115.** $-\dfrac{1}{2}$ and 2 **117.** -6 and 3 **119.** $\dfrac{-5 - \sqrt{33}}{2}$ and $\dfrac{-5 + \sqrt{33}}{2}$
121. $\dfrac{5 - \sqrt{7}}{3}$ and $\dfrac{5 + \sqrt{7}}{3}$ **123.** $\dfrac{-2 - \sqrt{22}}{2}$ and $\dfrac{-2 + \sqrt{22}}{2}$ **125.** $1 + \sqrt{7}$ **127.** $\left\{\dfrac{-1 \pm \sqrt{21}}{2}\right\}$ **129.** $\left\{-2\sqrt{2}, \dfrac{\sqrt{2}}{2}\right\}$ **131.** 7
133. $(7, 21)$ **135.** 77.8 ft; (b) **137. a.** $\dfrac{1}{\Phi - 1}$ **b.** $\Phi = \dfrac{1 + \sqrt{5}}{2}$ **c.** $\dfrac{1 + \sqrt{5}}{2}$ **139.** $2\sqrt{5}$ mi, or about 4.5 mi **141.** $90\sqrt{2}$ ft, or about 127.3 ft
143. length: 9 ft; width: 6 ft **145.** 5 in. **147.** 5 m **149.** 10 in. **151.** 9.3 in. and 0.7 in. **165.** does not make sense **167.** makes sense
169. true **171.** false **173.** $t = \dfrac{v_0 \pm \sqrt{v_0^2 - 64s}}{32}$ **175.** $(x + 1)(x + 2)(x - 2)$ **176.** $x + 5 + 2\sqrt{x + 4}$ **177.** true

Mid-Chapter I Check Point

1. $\{6\}$ **2.** $\left\{-1, \dfrac{7}{5}\right\}$ **3.** $\{-7\}$ **4.** $\left\{\dfrac{3 \pm \sqrt{15}}{3}\right\}$ **5.** all real numbers **6.** $\left\{\pm \dfrac{6\sqrt{5}}{5}\right\}$ **7.** $\left\{\dfrac{3}{4} \pm i\dfrac{\sqrt{23}}{4}\right\}$ **8.** $\{3\}$

9. $\{-3 \pm 2\sqrt{6}\}$ **10.** $\{2 \pm \sqrt{3}\}$ **11.** \varnothing **12.** $\{4\}$ **13.** $-3 - \sqrt{7}$ and $-3 + \sqrt{7}$ **14.** 1 **15.** no x-intercepts

16. $\dfrac{-3 - \sqrt{41}}{4}$ and $\dfrac{-3 + \sqrt{41}}{4}$ **17.** no x-intercepts **18.** 0 **19.** -4 and $\dfrac{1}{2}$ **20.** $\{-5 \pm 2\sqrt{7}\}$

21. two imaginary solutions **22.** two rational solutions **23.** **24.** **25.**

26. $n = \dfrac{L - a}{d} + 1$ **27.** $l = \dfrac{A - 2wh}{2w + 2h}$

$y = 2x - 1$

$y = 1 - |x|$

$y = x^2 + 2$

28. $f_1 = -\dfrac{ff_2}{f - f_2}$ or $f_1 = \dfrac{ff_2}{f_2 - f}$

29. sophomore: \$1581; junior: \$2002; senior: \$2846

30. about 12 years after 2000, or in 2012

31. \$11,500 at 8%; \$13,500 at 9% **32.** 20 prints; \$3.80

33. \$780 **34.** \$2500 at 4%; \$1500 at 3% loss **35.** length: 17 ft; width: 6 ft **36.** length: 7 ft; width: 4 ft **37.** 12 yd

38. a. 1 year and 5 years after 2000, or in 2001 and in 2005 **b.** $(1, 72)$ and $(5, 72)$ **39.** about 116 years after 1920, or in 2036

40. $-1 - i$ **41.** $-3 + 6i$ **42.** $7 + i$ **43.** i **44.** $3i\sqrt{3}$ **45.** $1 - 4i\sqrt{3}$

Section 1.6

Check Point Exercises

1. $\{-\sqrt{3}, 0, \sqrt{3}\}$ **2.** $\left\{-2, -\dfrac{3}{2}, 2\right\}$ **3.** $\{6\}$ **4.** $\{4\}$ **5. a.** $\{\sqrt[3]{25}\}$ or $\{5^{2/3}\}$ **b.** $\{-8, 8\}$ **6.** $\{-\sqrt{3}, -\sqrt{2}, \sqrt{2}, \sqrt{3}\}$

7. $\left\{-\dfrac{1}{27}, 64\right\}$ **8.** $\{-2, 3\}$ **9.** $\{-2, 3\}$ **10.** 25 years after 1996, or 2021

Exercise Set 1.6

1. $\{-4, 0, 4\}$ **3.** $\left\{-2, -\dfrac{2}{3}, 2\right\}$ **5.** $\left\{-\dfrac{1}{2}, \dfrac{1}{2}, \dfrac{3}{2}\right\}$ **7.** $\left\{-2, -\dfrac{1}{2}, \dfrac{1}{2}\right\}$ **9.** $\{0, 2, -1 + i\sqrt{3}, -1 - i\sqrt{3}\}$ **11.** $\{6\}$ **13.** $\{6\}$

15. $\{-6\}$ **17.** $\{10\}$ **19.** $\{-5\}$ **21.** $\{12\}$ **23.** $\{8\}$ **25.** \varnothing **27.** \varnothing **29.** $\left\{\dfrac{13 + \sqrt{105}}{6}\right\}$ **31.** $\{4\}$ **33.** $\{13\}$ **35.** $\{\sqrt[5]{4}\}$

37. $\{-60, 68\}$ **39.** $\{-4, 5\}$ **41.** $\{-2, -1, 1, 2\}$ **43.** $\left\{-\dfrac{4}{3}, -1, 1, \dfrac{4}{3}\right\}$ **45.** $\{25, 64\}$ **47.** $\left\{-\dfrac{1}{4}, \dfrac{1}{5}\right\}$ **49.** $\{-8, 27\}$ **51.** $\{1\}$

53. $\left\{\dfrac{1}{4}, 1\right\}$ **55.** $\{2, 12\}$ **57.** $\{-3, -1, 2, 4\}$ **59.** $\{-8, -2, 1, 4\}$ **61.** $\{-8, 8\}$ **63.** $\{-5, 9\}$ **65.** $\{-2, 3\}$ **67.** $\left\{-\dfrac{5}{3}, 3\right\}$

69. $\left\{-\dfrac{2}{5}, \dfrac{2}{5}\right\}$ **71.** $\left\{-\dfrac{4}{5}, 4\right\}$ **73.** \varnothing **75.** $\left\{\dfrac{1}{2}\right\}$ **77.** $\{-1, 3\}$ **79.** 2; c **81.** 1; e **83.** 2 and 3; f **85.** $-\dfrac{3}{2}$ and 4 **87.** 4

89. $-2, -\dfrac{1}{2},$ and 2 **91.** 0 **93.** $-2, 0,$ and 2 **95.** $\{-8, -6, 4, 6\}$ **97.** $\{-7, -1, 6\}$ **99.** 8 **101.** $V = \dfrac{\pi r^2 h}{3}$ or $\dfrac{1}{3}\pi r^2 h$ **103.** -16 and 12

105. 5.4 ft **107.** $(5.4, 1.16)$ **109.** 36 years after 1975, or in 2011 **111. a.** $(36, 50.6)$ **b.** 51% and 52% are reasonable estimates.

113. 149 million km **115.** either 1.2 feet or 7.5 feet from the base of the 6-foot pole **125.** $\{0, 2\}$ **127.** does not make sense

129. does not make sense **131.** false **133.** false **135.** $\left\{\dfrac{1}{2}\right\}$ **137.** $\{81\}$ **139.** yes **140.** $\{-3\}$ **141.** $\{14\}$

Section 1.7

Check Point Exercises

1. a. $\{x \mid -2 \le x < 5\}$ **b.** $\{x \mid 1 \le x \le 3.5\}$ **c.** $\{x \mid x < -1\}$ **2. a.** $(2, 3]$ **b.** $[1, 6)$

3. $[-1, \infty)$ or $\{x \mid x \ge -1\}$ **4.** $\{x \mid x < 4\}$ or $(-\infty, 4)$ **5.** $\{x \mid x \ge 13\}$ or $[13, \infty)$

6. a. $\{x \mid x$ is a real number$\}$ or \mathbb{R} or $(-\infty, \infty)$ **7.** $[-1, 4)$ or $\{x \mid -1 \le x < 4\}$ **8.** $(-3, 7)$ or $\{x \mid -3 < x < 7\}$
b. \varnothing

9. $\left\{x \mid -\dfrac{11}{5} \le x \le 3\right\}$ or $\left[-\dfrac{11}{5}, 3\right]$ **10.** $\{x \mid x < -4$ or $x > 8\}$ or $(-\infty, -4) \cup (8, \infty)$ **11.** more than 720 mi per week

Exercise Set 1.7

1. $\{x \mid 1 < x \le 6\}$ **3.** $\{x \mid -5 \le x < 2\}$ **5.** $\{x \mid -3 \le x \le 1\}$ **7.** $\{x \mid x > 2\}$

9. $\{x \mid x \geq -3\}$

11. $\{x \mid x < 3\}$

13. $\{x \mid x < 5.5\}$

15. $[-1, 0)$

17. $(-3, 2]$ **19.** $[1, 5)$ **21.** $(-\infty, 8)$ **23.** $(6, \infty)$ **25.** $[3, \infty)$ **27.** $(-\infty, 3)$

29. $\left[\dfrac{20}{3}, \infty\right)$

31. $(-\infty, -4]$

33. $\left(-\infty, -\dfrac{2}{5}\right]$

35. $[0, \infty)$

37. $(-\infty, 1)$

39. $[6, \infty)$

41. $[-10, \infty)$

43. $(-\infty, -6)$

45. $[13, \infty)$

47. $(-\infty, \infty)$

49. \varnothing **51.** $(3, 5)$ **53.** $[-1, 3)$ **55.** $(-5, -2]$ **57.** $[3, 6)$

59. $(-3, 3)$ **61.** $[-1, 3]$ **63.** $(-1, 7)$ **65.** $[-5, 3]$ **67.** $(-6, 0)$ **69.** $(-\infty, -3)$ or $(3, \infty)$ **71.** $(-\infty, -1]$ or $[3, \infty)$

73. $\left(-\infty, \dfrac{1}{3}\right)$ or $(5, \infty)$ **75.** $(-\infty, -5]$ or $[3, \infty)$ **77.** $(-\infty, -3)$ or $(12, \infty)$ **79.** $(-\infty, -1]$ or $[3, \infty)$ **81.** $[2, 6]$

83. $(-\infty, -3) \cup (5, \infty)$ **85.** $(-\infty, -1] \cup [2, \infty)$ **87.** $(-1, 9)$ **89.** $\left(-\infty, \dfrac{1}{3}\right) \cup (1, \infty)$ **91.** $\left(-\infty, -\dfrac{75}{14}\right) \cup \left(\dfrac{87}{14}, \infty\right)$

93. $(-\infty, -6]$ or $[24, \infty)$ **95.** $(-\infty, -3]$ **97.** $[6, \infty)$ **99.** $\left(-\dfrac{2}{3}, \dfrac{10}{3}\right)$ **101.** $(-\infty, -10] \cup [2, \infty)$ **103.** $(-1, 9)$ **105.** $[-1, 2)$

107. $\left(-\infty, -\dfrac{1}{3}\right] \cup [3, \infty)$ **109.** $(0, 4)$ **111.** intimacy \geq passion or passion \leq intimacy **113.** commitment $>$ passion or passion $<$ commitment

115. 9; after 3 years **117.** voting years after 2006 **119.** between 80 and 110 minutes, inclusive **121.** $h \leq 41$ or $h \geq 59$

123. $15 + 0.08x < 3 + 0.12x$; more than 300 min **125.** $2 + 0.08x < 8 + 0.05x$; 199 checks or less **127.** $5.50x > 3000 + 3x$; more than 1200 packages

129. $245 + 95x \leq 3000$; at most 29 bags **131. a.** $\dfrac{86 + 88 + x}{3} \geq 90$; at least a 96 **b.** $\dfrac{86 + 88 + x}{3} < 80$; a grade less than 66

133. more than 3 and less than 15 crossings per three-month period

143.

$\{x \mid x < -3\}$ or $(-\infty, -3)$

145. a. $C = 4 + 0.10x$; $C = 2 + 0.15x$

b.

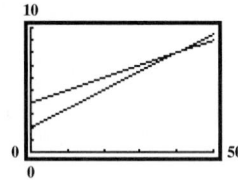

c. 41 or more checks
d. $\{x \mid x > 40\}$ or $(40, \infty)$

147. makes sense **149.** makes sense **151.** false **153.** true **155. a.** $|x - 4| < 3$ **b.** $|x - 4| \geq 3$ **157.** set 1

158.

$y = 2x$
$y = 2x + 4$

159. a. 3 **b.** -3 and 3 **c.** all real numbers **d.** all real numbers greater than or equal to 1

Chapter 1 Review Exercises

1.

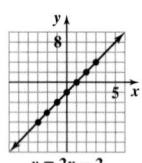

$y = 2x - 2$

2.

$y = x^2 - 3$

3.

$y = x$

4.

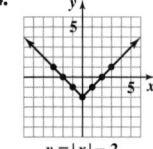

$y = |x| - 2$

5.

6. x-intercept: -2; y-intercept: 2 **7.** x-intercepts: -2, 2; y-intercept: -4 **8.** x-intercept: 5; no y-intercept **9.** $(1985, 50\%)$ **10.** 35%

11. 1945; 94% **12.** 1990; 28% **13.** 1950–1960; 91% **14.** 1930–1935; 38% **15.** $\{6\}$; conditional equation

16. $\{-10\}$; conditional equation **17.** $\{5\}$; conditional equation **18.** $\{-13\}$; conditional equation **19.** $\{-3\}$; conditional equation

20. $\{-1\}$; conditional equation **21.** \varnothing; inconsistent equation **22.** all real numbers; identity **23.** $\{2\}$; conditional equation

24. $\{2\}$; conditional equation **25.** $\left\{\dfrac{72}{11}\right\}$; conditional equation **26.** $\left\{\dfrac{36}{7}\right\}$; conditional equation **27.** $\left\{\dfrac{77}{15}\right\}$; conditional equation

28. $\{2\}$; conditional equation **29.** \varnothing; inconsistent equation **30.** all real numbers except -1 and 1; identity

31. $\left\{\dfrac{5}{2}\right\}$; conditional equation **32.** \varnothing; inconsistent equation **33.** $\left\{\dfrac{4}{7}\right\}$; conditional equation **34.** $\left\{\dfrac{1}{2}\right\}$; conditional equation

35. $\{2\}$; conditional equation **36.** U.S.: 20.5 million barrels; China: 6.3 million barrels; Japan: 5.5 million barrels **37.** by 19 years after 2000, or in 2019

38. 500 min **39.** $60 **40.** $10,000 in sales **41.** $2500 at 4%; $6500 at 7% **42.** $4500 at 2%; $3500 at 5% **43.** 44 yd by 126 yd

44. a. $14,100 + 1500x = 41,700 - 800x$ **b.** 2021; 32,100 **45.** $g = \dfrac{s - vt}{t^2}$ **46.** $g = \dfrac{T}{r + vt}$ **47.** $P = \dfrac{A}{1 + rt}$ **48.** $-9 + 4i$

49. $-12 - 8i$ **50.** $17 + 19i$ **51.** $-7 - 24i$ **52.** 113 **53.** $\dfrac{15}{13} - \dfrac{3}{13}i$ **54.** $\dfrac{1}{5} + \dfrac{11}{10}i$ **55.** $i\sqrt{2}$ **56.** $-96 - 40i$

57. $2 + i\sqrt{2}$ **58.** $\left\{-8, \dfrac{1}{2}\right\}$ **59.** $\{-4, 0\}$ **60.** $\{-8, 8\}$ **61.** $\{-4i, 4i\}$ **62.** $\{-3 - i\sqrt{10}, -3 + i\sqrt{10}\}$ **63.** $\left\{\dfrac{4 - 3\sqrt{2}}{3}, \dfrac{4 + 3\sqrt{2}}{3}\right\}$

64. $100; (x + 10)^2$ **65.** $\dfrac{9}{4}; \left(x - \dfrac{3}{2}\right)^2$ **66.** $\{3, 9\}$ **67.** $\left\{2 + \dfrac{\sqrt{3}}{3}, 2 - \dfrac{\sqrt{3}}{3}\right\}$ **68.** $\{1 + \sqrt{5}, 1 - \sqrt{5}\}$ **69.** $\{1 + 3i\sqrt{2}, 1 - 3i\sqrt{2}\}$

70. $\left\{\dfrac{-2 + \sqrt{10}}{2}, \dfrac{-2 - \sqrt{10}}{2}\right\}$ **71.** 2 complex imaginary solutions **72.** 2 unequal real solutions that are rational **73.** $\left\{\dfrac{1}{2}, 5\right\}$ **74.** $\left\{-2, \dfrac{10}{3}\right\}$

75. $\left\{\dfrac{7 + \sqrt{37}}{6}, \dfrac{7 - \sqrt{37}}{6}\right\}$ **76.** $\{-3, 3\}$ **77.** $\{-2, 8\}$ **78.** $\left\{\dfrac{1}{6} + i\dfrac{\sqrt{23}}{6}, \dfrac{1}{6} - i\dfrac{\sqrt{23}}{6}\right\}$ **79.** $\left\{-\dfrac{2}{3}, 4\right\}$ **80.** $\{-2 - 2i, -2 + 2i\}$

81. $\{4 + \sqrt{5}, 4 - \sqrt{5}\}$ **82.** 14 weeks **83. a.** 70.2%; overestimates by 0.2% **b.** 2010 **84.** length = 5 yd; width = 3 yd

85. approximately 134 m **86.** $\{-5, 0, 5\}$ **87.** $\left\{-3, \dfrac{1}{2}, 3\right\}$ **88.** $\{2\}$ **89.** $\{8\}$ **90.** $\{16\}$ **91.** $\{-118, 132\}$ **92.** $\{-2, -1, 1, 2\}$

93. $\{16\}$ **94.** $\{-4, 3\}$ **95.** $\{-5, 11\}$ **96.** $\left\{-1, -\dfrac{2\sqrt{6}}{9}, \dfrac{2\sqrt{6}}{9}, 1\right\}$ **97.** $\{2\}$ **98.** $\{1, 4\}$ **99.** $\{-3, -2, 3\}$ **100.** $\{3\}$

101. $\{-3, -\sqrt{2}, \sqrt{2}\}$ **102.** $\{-4, 2\}$ **103.** by 16 years after 1993, or in 2009

104. $\{x \mid -3 \le x < 5\}$ **105.** $\{x \mid x > -2\}$ **106.** $\{x \mid x \le 0\}$ **107.** $[-1, 1]$ **108.** $(-2, 3)$

109. $[1, 3)$ **110.** $(0, 4)$

111. $[-2, \infty)$ **112.** $\left[\dfrac{3}{5}, \infty\right)$ **113.** $\left(-\infty, -\dfrac{21}{2}\right)$ **114.** $(-3, \infty)$

115. $(-\infty, -2]$ **116.** \varnothing **117.** $(2, 3]$ **118.** $[-9, 6]$

119. $(-\infty, -6)$ or $(0, \infty)$ **120.** $(-\infty, -3]$ or $[-2, \infty)$ **121.** $(-\infty, -5] \cup [1, \infty)$;

122. $(-\infty, -1)$ **123.** $[-2, 7]$ **124.** no more than 80 miles per day **125.** $[49\%, 99\%)$ **126.** at least $120,000

Chapter 1 Test

1. $\{-1\}$ **2.** $\{-1\}$ **3.** $\{-6\}$ **4.** $\{5\}$ **5.** $\left\{-\dfrac{1}{2}, 2\right\}$ **6.** $\left\{\dfrac{1 - 5\sqrt{3}}{3}, \dfrac{1 + 5\sqrt{3}}{3}\right\}$ **7.** $\{-3 - 5i, -3 + 5i\}$

8. $\{1 - \sqrt{5}, 1 + \sqrt{5}\}$ **9.** $\left\{1 + \dfrac{1}{2}i, 1 - \dfrac{1}{2}i\right\}$ **10.** $\{-1, 1, 4\}$ **11.** $\{7\}$ **12.** $\{2\}$ **13.** $\{5\}$ **14.** $\{\sqrt[3]{4}\}$ **15.** $\{1, 512\}$

16. $\{6, 12\}$ **17.** $\left\{\dfrac{1}{2}, 3\right\}$ **18.** $\{2 - \sqrt{3}, 2 + \sqrt{3}\}$ **19.** $\{4\}$

20. $(-\infty, 12]$ **21.** $\left[\dfrac{21}{8}, \infty\right)$ **22.** $\left[-7, \dfrac{13}{2}\right)$ **23.** $\left(-\infty, -\dfrac{5}{3}\right]$ or $\left[\dfrac{1}{3}, \infty\right)$

24. $[1, 6]$ **25.** $(-\infty, -2] \cup [6, \infty)$ **26.** $[-1, 5]$ **27.** $(0, 2)$ **28.** $h = \dfrac{3V}{lw}$ **29.** $x = \dfrac{y - y_1}{m} + x_1$

30. 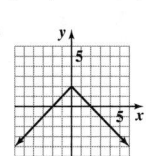 **31.** **32.** $47 + 16i$ **33.** $2 + i$ **34.** $38i$ **35.** 2018 **36.** 2018

37. quite well **38.** drive-in theaters: 1; movie theaters: 17; video rental stores: 65

39. 26 yr; $33,600 **40.** $3000 at 8%; $7000 at 10%

41. length = 12 ft; width = 4 ft **42.** 10 ft **43.** $50

44. more than 200 calls

CHAPTER 2

Section 2.1

Check Point Exercises

1. domain: $\{0, 10, 20, 30, 36\}$; range: $\{9.1, 6.7, 10.7, 13.2, 17.4\}$ **2. a.** not a function **b.** function **3. a.** $y = 6 - 2x$; function
b. $y = \pm\sqrt{1 - x^2}$; not a function **4. a.** 42 **b.** $x^2 + 6x + 15$ **c.** $x^2 + 2x + 7$

5. 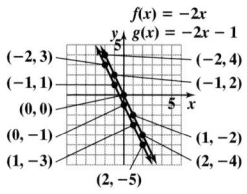 ; The graph of g is the graph of f shifted down by 3 units.

6. a. function **b.** function **c.** not a function **7. a.** 400 **b.** 9 **c.** approximately 425

8. a. domain: $\{x|-2 \le x \le 1\}$; range: $\{y|0 \le y \le 3\}$
b. domain: $\{x|-2 < x \le 1\}$; range: $\{y|-1 \le y < 2\}$
c. domain: $\{x|-3 \le x < 0\}$; range: $\{-3, -2, -1\}$

Exercise Set 2.1

1. function; $\{1, 3, 5\}$; $\{2, 4, 5\}$ **3.** not a function; $\{3, 4\}$; $\{4, 5\}$ **5.** function; $\{3, 4, 5, 7\}$; $\{-2, 1, 9\}$ **7.** function; $\{-3, -2, -1, 0\}$; $\{-3, -2, -1, 0\}$
9. not a function; $\{1\}$; $\{4, 5, 6\}$ **11.** y is a function of x. **13.** y is a function of x. **15.** y is not a function of x. **17.** y is not a function of x.
19. y is a function of x. **21.** y is a function of x. **23.** y is a function of x. **25.** y is a function of x. **27. a.** 29 **b.** $4x + 9$ **c.** $-4x + 5$
29. a. 2 **b.** $x^2 + 12x + 38$ **c.** $x^2 - 2x + 3$ **31. a.** 13 **b.** 1 **c.** $x^4 - x^2 + 1$ **d.** $81a^4 - 9a^2 + 1$ **33. a.** 3 **b.** 7 **c.** $\sqrt{x} + 3$
35. a. $\dfrac{15}{4}$ **b.** $\dfrac{15}{4}$ **c.** $\dfrac{4x^2 - 1}{x^2}$ **37. a.** 1 **b.** -1 **c.** 1

39. **41.** **43.** **45.**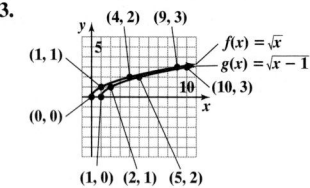

The graph of g is the graph of f shifted up by 3 units. · The graph of g is the graph of f shifted down by 1 unit. · The graph of g is the graph of f shifted up by 1 unit. · The graph of g is the graph of f shifted down by 2 units.

47. **49.** **51.** **53.**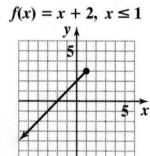

The graph of g is the graph of f shifted up by 2 units. · The graph of g is the graph of f shifted up by 2 units. · The graph of g is the graph of f shifted down by 1 unit. · The graph of g is the graph of f shifted to the right by 1 unit.

55. function **57.** function **59.** not a function **61.** function **63.** function **65.** -4 **67.** 4 **69.** 0 **71.** 2 **73.** 2
75. -2 **77. a.** $(-\infty, \infty)$ **b.** $[-4, \infty)$ **c.** -3 and 1 **d.** -3 **e.** $f(-2) = -3$ and $f(2) = 5$ **79. a.** $(-\infty, \infty)$ **b.** $[1, \infty)$ **c.** none
d. 1 **e.** $f(-1) = 2$ and $f(3) = 4$ **81. a.** $[0, 5)$ **b.** $[-1, 5)$ **c.** 2 **d.** -1 **e.** $f(3) = 1$ **83. a.** $[0, \infty)$ **b.** $[1, \infty)$ **c.** none
d. 1 **e.** $f(4) = 3$ **85. a.** $[-2, 6]$ **b.** $[-2, 6]$ **c.** 4 **d.** 4 **e.** $f(-1) = 5$ **87. a.** $(-\infty, \infty)$ **b.** $(-\infty, -2]$ **c.** none
d. -2 **e.** $f(-4) = -5$ and $f(4) = -2$ **89. a.** $(-\infty, \infty)$ **b.** $(0, \infty)$ **c.** none **d.** 1.5 **e.** $f(4) = 6$ **91. a.** $\{-5, -2, 0, 1, 3\}$
b. $\{2\}$ **c.** none **d.** 2 **e.** $f(-5) + f(3) = 4$ **93.** $-2; 10$ **95.** -38 **97.** $-2x^3 - 2x$
99. a. $\{(\text{Iceland}, 9.7), (\text{Finland}, 9.6), (\text{New Zealand}, 9.6), (\text{Denmark}, 9.5)\}$ **b.** Yes, each country is paired with only one corruption rating.
c. $\{(9.7, \text{Iceland}), (9.6, \text{Finland}), (9.6, \text{New Zealand}), (9.5, \text{Denmark})\}$ **d.** No, the corruption rating 9.6 is paired with two different countries,
Finland and New Zealand. **101. a.** 83; The chance that a 60-year-old will survive to age 70 is 83%. **b.** 76; The chance that a 60-year-old
will survive to age 70 is 76%. **c.** f **103. a.** 127; In 2004, Americans ordered an average of 127 takeout meals per person.; by the point $(20, 127)$
b. 94; In 1984, Americans ordered an average of 94 meals in restaurants per person.; by the point $(0, 94)$ **c.** 1988; 91 takeout meals and 91.6 meals
in restaurants **105.** $C = 100{,}000 + 100x$, where x is the number of bicycles produced; $C(90) = 109{,}000$; It costs \$109,000 to produce 90 bicycles.
107. $T = \dfrac{40}{x} + \dfrac{40}{x + 30}$, where x is the rate on the outgoing trip; $T(30) = 2$; It takes 2 hours, traveling 30 mph outgoing and 60 mph returning.
119. does not make sense **121.** does not make sense **123.** false **125.** false **127.** Answers will vary; an example is $\{(1, 1), (2, 1)\}$.
129. 36; For 100 calling minutes, the monthly cost is \$36.
130. $f(x) = x + 2, x \le 1$ **131.** $4xh + 2h^2 + 3h$

Section 2.2

Check Point Exercises

1. increasing on $(-\infty, -1)$, decreasing on $(-1, 1)$, increasing on $(1, \infty)$ **2. a.** even **b.** odd **c.** neither
3. a. 20; With 40 calling minutes, the cost is \$20.; (40, 20) **b.** 28; With 80 calling minutes, the cost is \$28.; (80, 28)
4. **5. a.** $-2x^2 - 4xh - 2h^2 + x + h + 5$ **b.** $-4x - 2h + 1, h \neq 0$

$$f(x) = \begin{cases} 3 & \text{if } x \leq -1 \\ x - 2 & \text{if } x > -1 \end{cases}$$

Exercise Set 2.2

1. a. $(-1, \infty)$ **b.** $(-\infty, -1)$ **c.** none **3. a.** $(0, \infty)$ **b.** none **c.** none **5. a.** none **b.** $(-2, 6)$ **c.** none **7. a.** $(-\infty, -1)$
b. none **c.** $(-1, \infty)$ **9. a.** $(-\infty, 0)$ or $(1.5, 3)$ **b.** $(0, 1.5)$ or $(3, \infty)$ **c.** none **11. a.** $(-2, 4)$ **b.** none **c.** $(-\infty, -2)$ or $(4, \infty)$
13. a. $0; f(0) = 4$ **b.** $-3, 3; f(-3) = f(3) = 0$ **15. a.** $-2; f(-2) = 21$ **b.** $1; f(1) = -6$ **17.** odd **19.** neither **21.** even **23.** even
25. even **27.** odd **29.** even **31.** odd **33. a.** $(-\infty, \infty)$ **b.** $[-4, \infty)$ **c.** 1 and 7 **d.** 4 **e.** $(4, \infty)$ **f.** $(0, 4)$ **g.** $(-\infty, 0)$
h. 4 **i.** -4 **j.** 4 **k.** 2 and 6 **l.** neither **35. a.** $(-\infty, 3]$ **b.** $(-\infty, 4]$ **c.** -3 and 3 **d.** 3 **e.** $(-\infty, 1)$ **f.** $(1, 3)$
g. $(-\infty, -3]$ **h.** A relative maximum of 4 occurs at 1. **i.** 1 **j.** positive **37. a.** -1 **b.** 7 **c.** 19 **41. a.** 8 **b.** 3 **c.** 6
43. a.

$$f(x) = \begin{cases} -x & \text{if } x < 0 \\ x & \text{if } x \geq 0 \end{cases}$$

b. $[0, \infty)$

45. a.

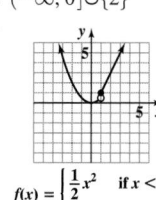

$$f(x) = \begin{cases} 2x & \text{if } x \leq 0 \\ 2 & \text{if } x > 0 \end{cases}$$

b. $(-\infty, 0] \cup \{2\}$

47. a.

$$f(x) = \begin{cases} x + 3 & \text{if } x < -2 \\ x - 3 & \text{if } x \geq -2 \end{cases}$$

b. $(-\infty, \infty)$

49. a.

$$f(x) = \begin{cases} 3 & \text{if } x \leq -1 \\ -3 & \text{if } x > -1 \end{cases}$$

b. $\{-3, 3\}$

51. a.

$$f(x) = \begin{cases} \frac{1}{2}x^2 & \text{if } x < 1 \\ 2x - 1 & \text{if } x \geq 1 \end{cases}$$

b. $[0, \infty)$

53. a.

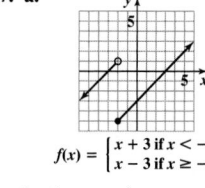

$$f(x) = \begin{cases} 0 & \text{if } x < -4 \\ -x & \text{if } -4 \leq x < 0 \\ x^2 & \text{if } x \geq 0 \end{cases}$$

b. $[0, \infty)$

55. $4, h \neq 0$ **57.** $3, h \neq 0$ **59.** $2x + h, h \neq 0$ **61.** $2x + h - 4, h \neq 0$ **63.** $4x + 2h + 1, h \neq 0$ **65.** $-2x - h + 2, h \neq 0$

67. $-4x - 2h + 5, h \neq 0$ **69.** $-4x - 2h - 1, h \neq 0$ **71.** $0, h \neq 0$ **73.** $-\dfrac{1}{x(x + h)}, h \neq 0$ **75.** $\dfrac{1}{\sqrt{x + h} + \sqrt{x}}, h \neq 0$ **77.** -18

79. $0.30t - 6$ **81.** $C(t) = \begin{cases} 50 & \text{if } 0 \leq t \leq 400 \\ 50 + 0.30(t - 400) & \text{if } t > 400 \end{cases}$

83. increasing: $(25, 55)$; decreasing: $(55, 75)$ **85.** 55 years old; 38% **87.** domain: $[25, 75]$; range: $[34, 38]$ **89.** men
91. 2608.75; A single taxpayer with taxable income of \$20,000 owes \$2608.75. **93.** $39{,}148.75 + 0.33(x - 160{,}850)$
95. 0.76; It costs \$0.76 to mail a 3-ounce first-class letter. **97.** \$0.59
99. **107.** **109.**

increasing: $(-\infty, 1)$ or $(3, \infty)$
decreasing: $(1, 3)$

increasing: $(2, \infty)$
decreasing: $(-\infty, -2)$
constant: $(-2, 2)$

111.

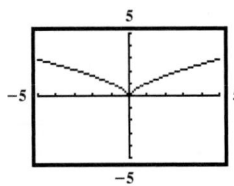

increasing: $(0, \infty)$
decreasing: $(-\infty, 0)$

113. a.

b.

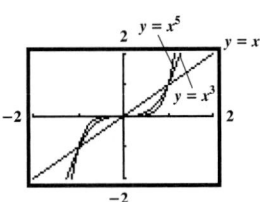

c. increasing: $(0, \infty)$; decreasing: $(-\infty, 0)$

d. $f(x) = x^n$ is increasing for $(-\infty, \infty)$ when n is positive and odd.

e.

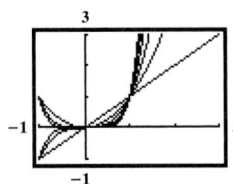

As n increases the steepness increases.

115. makes sense **117.** makes sense **122.** 3 **123.** $\left(\dfrac{3}{2}, 0\right)$ and $(0, -2)$ **124.** $y = \dfrac{-3x + 4}{2}$ or $y = -\dfrac{3}{2}x + 2$

Section 2.3

Check Point Exercises

1. a. 6 **b.** $-\dfrac{7}{5}$ **2.** $y + 5 = 6(x - 2)$; $y = 6x - 17$ **3.** $y + 1 = -5(x + 2)$ or $y + 6 = -5(x + 1)$; $y = -5x - 11$

4.

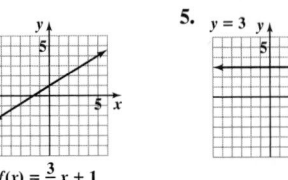

$f(x) = \dfrac{3}{5}x + 1$

5. $y = 3$

6. $x = -3$

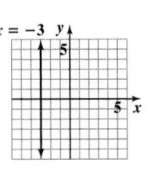

7. slope: $-\dfrac{1}{2}$; y-intercept: 2

$3x + 6y - 12 = 0$

8.

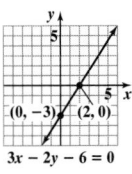

$3x - 2y - 6 = 0$

9. $f(x) = 0.016x + 52.0$; 61.6°F

Exercise Set 2.3

1. $\dfrac{3}{4}$; rises **3.** $\dfrac{1}{4}$; rises **5.** 0; horizontal **7.** -5; falls **9.** undefined; vertical **11.** $y - 5 = 2(x - 3)$; $y = 2x - 1$

13. $y - 5 = 6(x + 2)$; $y = 6x + 17$ **15.** $y + 3 = -3(x + 2)$; $y = -3x - 9$ **17.** $y - 0 = -4(x + 4)$; $y = -4x - 16$

19. $y + 2 = -1\left(x + \dfrac{1}{2}\right)$; $y = -x - \dfrac{5}{2}$ **21.** $y - 0 = \dfrac{1}{2}(x - 0)$; $y = \dfrac{1}{2}x$ **23.** $y + 2 = -\dfrac{2}{3}(x - 6)$; $y = -\dfrac{2}{3}x + 2$

25. using $(1, 2)$, $y - 2 = 2(x - 1)$; $y = 2x$ **27.** using $(-3, 0)$, $y - 0 = 1(x + 3)$; $y = x + 3$ **29.** using $(-3, -1)$, $y + 1 = 1(x + 3)$; $y = x + 2$

31. using $(-3, -2)$, $y + 2 = \dfrac{4}{3}(x + 3)$; $y = \dfrac{4}{3}x + 2$ **33.** using $(-3, -1)$, $y + 1 = 0(x + 3)$; $y = -1$ **35.** using $(2, 4)$, $y - 4 = 1(x - 2)$; $y = x + 2$

37. using $(0, 4)$, $y - 4 = 8(x - 0)$; $y = 8x + 4$

39. $m = 2$; $b = 1$

$y = 2x + 1$

41. $m = -2$; $b = 1$

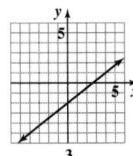

$f(x) = -2x + 1$

43. $m = \dfrac{3}{4}$; $b = -2$

$f(x) = \dfrac{3}{4}x - 2$

45. $m = -\dfrac{3}{5}$; $b = 7$

$y = -\dfrac{3}{5}x + 7$

47. $m = -\dfrac{1}{2}$; $b = 0$

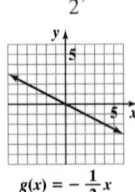

$g(x) = -\dfrac{1}{2}x$

49. $y = -2$

51. $x = -3$

53. $y = 0$

55. $f(x) = 1$

57.

59. a. $y = -3x + 5$
b. $m = -3; b = 5$
c.
$3x + y - 5 = 0$

61. a. $y = -\dfrac{2}{3}x + 6$
b. $m = -\dfrac{2}{3}; b = 6$
c.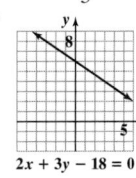
$2x + 3y - 18 = 0$

63. a. $y = 2x - 3$
b. $m = 2; b = -3$
c.
$8x - 4y - 12 = 0$

65. a. $y = 3$
b. $m = 0; b = 3$
c.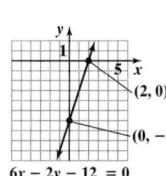
$3y - 9 = 0$

67.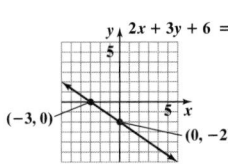
$6x - 2y - 12 = 0$

69.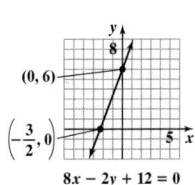
$2x + 3y + 6 = 0$

71.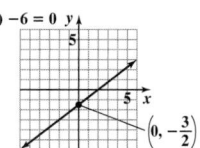
$8x - 2y + 12 = 0$

73. $m = -\dfrac{a}{b}$; falls
75. undefined slope; vertical
77. $m = -\dfrac{A}{B}; b = \dfrac{C}{B}$
79. -2

81.
$3x - 4f(x) - 6 = 0$
$\left(0, -\dfrac{3}{2}\right)$

83. 5
85. m_1, m_3, m_2, m_4
87. a. $y - 31.1 = 0.78(x - 10)$ or $y - 38.9 = 0.78(x - 20)$ **b.** $f(x) = 0.78x + 23.3$ **c.** 54.5%

89. a &b. 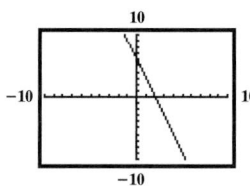 ; $E(x) = 0.215x + 65.7$

91. Answers will vary; an example is $y = -2.3x + 255$, where x is the percentage of adult females who are literate and y is under-five mortality per thousand.; Predictions will vary.

c. 78.6 yr

101. $m = -3$

103. $m = \dfrac{3}{4}$
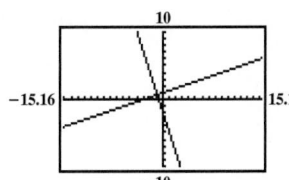

105. does not make sense **107.** does not make sense
109. false **111.** true
113. coefficient of x: -6; coefficient of y: 3
118. $y = 2x + 7$ or $f(x) = 2x + 7$
119. $4x - y - 17 = 0$ **120.** 5

Section 2.4

Check Point Exercises

1. $y - 5 = 3(x + 2)$; $y = 3x + 11$ or $f(x) = 3x + 11$ **2. a.** 3 **b.** $3x - y = 0$ **3.** $m \approx 0.25$; The number of men living alone increased at a rate of 0.25 million per year. The rate of change is 0.25 million men per year. **4. a.** 1 **b.** 7 **c.** 4 **5.** 0.01 mg per 100 ml per hr

Exercise Set 2.4

1. $y - 2 = 2(x - 4)$; $y = 2x - 6$ or $f(x) = 2x - 6$ **3.** $y - 4 = -\dfrac{1}{2}(x - 2)$; $y = -\dfrac{1}{2}x + 5$ or $f(x) = -\dfrac{1}{2}x + 5$

5. $y + 10 = -4(x + 8)$; $y = -4x - 42$ **7.** $y + 3 = -5(x - 2)$; $y = -5x + 7$ **9.** $y - 2 = \dfrac{2}{3}(x + 2)$; $2x - 3y + 10 = 0$

11. $y + 7 = -2(x - 4)$; $2x + y - 1 = 0$ **13.** 3 **15.** 10 **17.** $\dfrac{1}{5}$ **19.** $f(x) = 5$ **21.** $f(x) = -\dfrac{1}{2}x + 1$ **23.** $f(x) = -\dfrac{2}{3}x - 2$

25. $P(x) = -1.2x + 47$ **27.** 137; There was an average increase of approximately 137 discharges per year.
29. a. 142 **b.** overestimates by 5 discharges per year
37. a. The product of their slopes is -1.
b. ; no **c.** 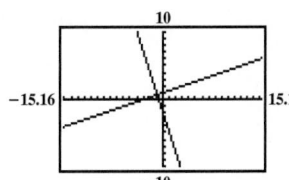 ; The lines now appear to be perpendicular.

39. makes sense **41.** makes sense **43.** $-\dfrac{3}{7}$

45. a.

b.

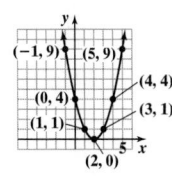

c. The graph in part (b) is the graph in part (a) shifted to the right 2 units.

Mid-Chapter 2 Check Point

1. not a function; domain: $\{1, 2\}$; range: $\{-6, 4, 6\}$ **2.** function; domain: $\{0, 2, 3\}$; range: $\{1, 4\}$ **3.** function; domain: $\{x \mid -2 \le x < 2\}$ or $[-2, 2)$; range: $\{y \mid 0 \le y \le 3\}$ or $[0, 3]$ **4.** not a function; domain: $\{x \mid -3 < x \le 4\}$ or $(-3, 4]$; range: $\{y \mid -1 \le y \le 2\}$ or $[-1, 2]$
5. not a function; domain: $\{-2, -1, 0, 1, 2\}$; range: $\{-2, -1, 1, 3\}$ **6.** function; domain: $\{x \mid x \le 1\}$ or $(-\infty, 1]$; range: $\{y \mid y \ge -1\}$ or $[-1, \infty)$
7. y is a function of x. **8.** y is not a function of x. **9.** No vertical line intersects the graph in more than one point. **10.** $(-\infty, \infty)$
11. $(-\infty, 4]$ **12.** -6 and 2 **13.** 3 **14.** $(-\infty, -2)$ **15.** $(-2, \infty)$ **16.** -2 **17.** 4 **18.** 3 **19.** -7 and 3 **20.** -6 and 2
21. $(-6, 2)$ **22.** negative **23.** neither **24.** -1

25. $y = -2x$

26. $y = -2$

27. $x + y = -2$

28. $y = \dfrac{1}{3}x - 2$

29. $x = 3.5$

30.

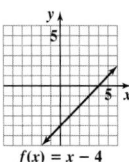

$4x - 2y = 8$

31.

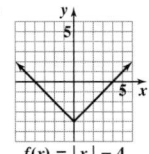

$f(x) = x^2 - 4$

32.

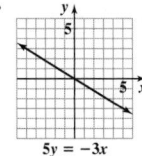

$f(x) = x - 4$

33.

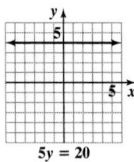

$f(x) = |x| - 4$

34.

$5y = -3x$

35.

$5y = 20$

36.

$f(x) = \begin{cases} -1 \text{ if } x \le 0 \\ 2x + 1 \text{ if } x > 0 \end{cases}$

37. a. $f(-x) = -2x^2 - x - 5$; neither **b.** $-4x - 2h + 1, h \ne 0$ **38. a.** 30 **b.** 50
39. $f(x) = -2x - 5$ **40.** $f(x) = 2x - 3$ **41.** $f(x) = 3x - 13$
42. $f(x) = -\dfrac{5}{2}x - 13$ **43.** The lines are parallel.
44. a. 0.16 **b.** 0.16; 0.16; minute of brisk walking **45.** 2

Section 2.5

Check Point Exercises

1.

2.

3.

4.

5.

6.

7. a.

$g(x) = f(2x)$

b.

$h(x) = f\left(\dfrac{1}{2}x\right)$

8.

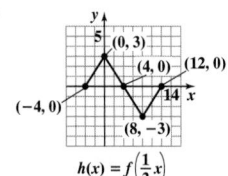

$y = -\dfrac{1}{3}f(x + 1) - 2$

9.

$g(x) = 2(x - 1)^2 + 3$

Exercise Set 2.5

1.

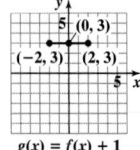

$g(x) = f(x) + 1$

3.

$g(x) = f(x + 1)$

5.

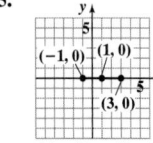

$g(x) = f(x - 1) - 2$

7.

$g(x) = f(-x)$

9.

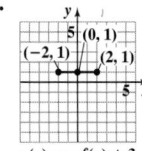

$g(x) = -f(x) + 3$

11.
$g(x) = \frac{1}{2}f(x)$

13. $g(x) = f\left(\frac{1}{2}x\right)$

15.
$g(x) = -f\left(\frac{1}{2}x\right) + 1$

17.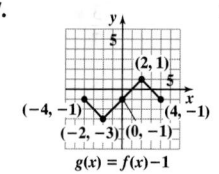
$g(x) = f(x) - 1$

19.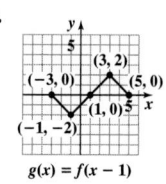
$g(x) = f(x - 1)$

21.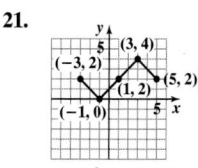
$g(x) = f(x - 1) + 2$

23.
$g(x) = -f(x)$

25.
$g(x) = f(-x) + 1$

27.
$g(x) = 2f(x)$

29.
$g(x) = f(2x)$

31.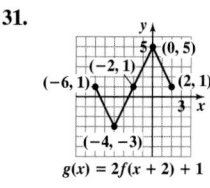
$g(x) = 2f(x + 2) + 1$

33.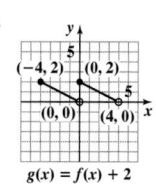
$g(x) = f(x) + 2$

35.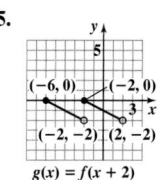
$g(x) = f(x + 2)$

37.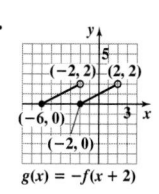
$g(x) = -f(x + 2)$

39.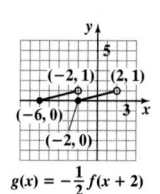
$g(x) = -\frac{1}{2}f(x + 2)$

41.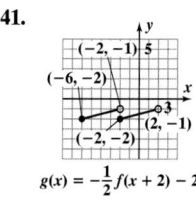
$g(x) = -\frac{1}{2}f(x + 2) - 2$

43.
$g(x) = \frac{1}{2}f(2x)$

45.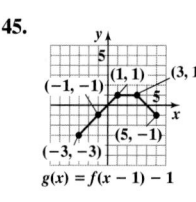
$g(x) = f(x - 1) - 1$

47.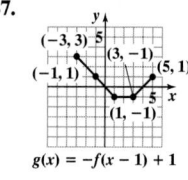
$g(x) = -f(x - 1) + 1$

49.
$g(x) = 2f\left(\frac{1}{2}x\right)$

51.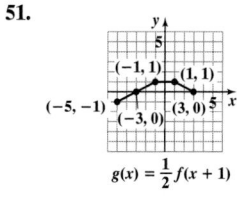
$g(x) = \frac{1}{2}f(x + 1)$

53.

55.

57.

59.

61.

63.

65.

67.

69.

71.

73.

75.

77.

79.

81.

83.

85.

87.

89.

91.

93.

95.

97.

99.

101. **103.** **105.** **107.** **109.**

111. **113.** **115.** **117.** **119.**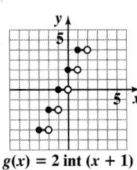

$g(x) = 2$ int $(x + 1)$

121. 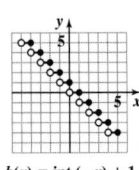 **123.** $y = \sqrt{x - 2}$ **125.** $y = (x + 1)^2 - 4$
127. a. First, vertically stretch the graph of $f(x) = \sqrt{x}$
by the factor 2.9; then, shift the result up 20.1 units. **b.** 40.2 in.; very well
c. 0.9 in. per month **d.** 0.2 in. per month; This is a much smaller rate of change;
The graph is not as steep between 50 and 60 as it is between 0 and 10.

$h(x) = $ int $(-x) + 1$

135. a. **b.**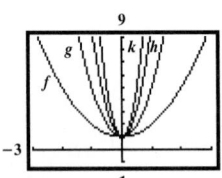

137. makes sense **139.** does not make sense **141.** false **143.** false **145.** $g(x) = -(x + 4)^2$ **147.** $g(x) = -\sqrt{x - 2} + 2$

149. $(-a, b)$ **151.** $(a + 3, b)$ **153.** $2x^3 + x^2 - 5x + 2$ **154.** $9x^2 - 30x + 30$ **155.** $\dfrac{2x}{3 - x}$

Section 2.6

Check Point Exercises

1. a. $(-\infty, \infty)$ **b.** $(-\infty, -7)\cup(-7, 7)\cup(7, \infty)$ **c.** $[3, \infty)$ **2. a.** $(f + g)(x) = x^2 + x - 6; (-\infty, \infty)$ **b.** $(f - g)(x) = -x^2 + x - 4; (-\infty, \infty)$
c. $(fg)(x) = x^3 - 5x^2 - x + 5; (-\infty, \infty)$ **d.** $\left(\dfrac{f}{g}\right)(x) = \dfrac{x - 5}{x^2 - 1}; (-\infty, -1)\cup(-1, 1)\cup(1, \infty)$ **3. a.** $(f + g)(x) = \sqrt{x - 3} + \sqrt{x + 1}$ **b.** $[3, \infty)$
4. a. $(f \circ g)(x) = 10x^2 - 5x + 1$ **b.** $(g \circ f)(x) = 50x^2 + 115x + 65$ **c.** 16 **5. a.** $(f \circ g)(x) = \dfrac{4x}{1 + 2x}$ **b.** $\left(-\infty, -\dfrac{1}{2}\right)\cup\left(-\dfrac{1}{2}, 0\right)\cup(0, \infty)$
6. If $f(x) = \sqrt{x}$ and $g(x) = x^2 + 5$, then $h(x) = (f \circ g)(x)$.

Exercise Set 2.6

1. $(-\infty, \infty)$ **3.** $(-\infty, 4)\cup(4, \infty)$ **5.** $(-\infty, \infty)$ **7.** $(-\infty, -3)\cup(-3, 5)\cup(5, \infty)$ **9.** $(-\infty, -7)\cup(-7, 9)\cup(9, \infty)$
11. $(-\infty, -1)\cup(-1, 1)\cup(1, \infty)$ **13.** $(-\infty, 0)\cup(0, 3)\cup(3, \infty)$ **15.** $(-\infty, 1)\cup(1, 3)\cup(3, \infty)$ **17.** $[3, \infty)$ **19.** $(3, \infty)$ **21.** $[-7, \infty)$
23. $(-\infty, 12]$ **25.** $[2, \infty)$ **27.** $[2, 5)\cup(5, \infty)$ **29.** $(-\infty, -2)\cup(-2, 2)\cup(2, 5)\cup(5, \infty)$

31. $(f + g)(x) = 3x + 2$; domain: $(-\infty, \infty)$; $(f - g)(x) = x + 4$; domain: $(-\infty, \infty)$; $(fg)(x) = 2x^2 + x - 3$; domain: $(-\infty, \infty)$; $\left(\dfrac{f}{g}\right)(x) = \dfrac{2x + 3}{x - 1}$;
domain: $(-\infty, 1)\cup(1, \infty)$ **33.** $(f + g)(x) = 3x^2 + x - 5$; domain: $(-\infty, \infty)$; $(f - g)(x) = -3x^2 + x - 5$; domain: $(-\infty, \infty)$; $(fg)(x) = 3x^3 - 15x^2$;
domain: $(-\infty, \infty)$; $\left(\dfrac{f}{g}\right)(x) = \dfrac{x - 5}{3x^2}$; domain: $(-\infty, 0)\cup(0, \infty)$ **35.** $(f + g)(x) = 2x^2 - 2$; domain: $(-\infty, \infty)$; $(f - g)(x) = 2x^2 - 2x - 4$;
domain: $(-\infty, \infty)$; $(fg)(x) = 2x^3 + x^2 - 4x - 3$; domain: $(-\infty, \infty)$; $\left(\dfrac{f}{g}\right)(x) = 2x - 3$; domain: $(-\infty, -1)\cup(-1, \infty)$
37. $(f + g)(x) = 2x - 12$; domain: $(-\infty, \infty)$; $(f - g)(x) = -2x^2 - 2x + 18$; domain: $(-\infty, \infty)$; $(fg)(x) = -x^4 - 2x^3 + 18x^2 + 6x - 45$;
domain: $(-\infty, \infty)$; $\left(\dfrac{f}{g}\right)(x) = \dfrac{3 - x^2}{x^2 + 2x - 15}$; domain: $(-\infty, -5) \cup (-5, 3)\cup(3, \infty)$
39. $(f + g)(x) = \sqrt{x} + x - 4$; domain: $[0, \infty)$; $(f - g)(x) = \sqrt{x} - x + 4$; domain: $[0, \infty)$; $(fg)(x) = \sqrt{x}(x - 4)$; domain: $[0, \infty)$; $\left(\dfrac{f}{g}\right)(x) = \dfrac{\sqrt{x}}{x - 4}$;
domain: $[0, 4)\cup(4, \infty)$ **41.** $(f + g)(x) = \dfrac{2x + 2}{x}$; domain: $(-\infty, 0)\cup(0, \infty)$; $(f - g)(x) = 2$; domain: $(-\infty, 0)\cup(0, \infty)$; $(fg)(x) = \dfrac{2x + 1}{x^2}$;
domain: $(-\infty, 0)\cup(0, \infty)$; $\left(\dfrac{f}{g}\right)(x) = 2x + 1$; domain: $(-\infty, 0)\cup(0, \infty)$ **43.** $(f + g)(x) = \dfrac{9x - 1}{x^2 - 9}$; domain:
$(-\infty, -3)\cup(-3, 3)\cup(3, \infty)$; $(f - g)(x) = \dfrac{x + 3}{x^2 - 9} = \dfrac{1}{x - 3}$; domain: $(-\infty, -3)\cup(-3, 3)\cup(3, \infty)$; $(fg)(x) = \dfrac{20x^2 - 6x - 2}{(x^2 - 9)^2}$;
domain: $(-\infty, -3)\cup(-3, 3)\cup(3, \infty)$; $\left(\dfrac{f}{g}\right)(x) = \dfrac{5x + 1}{4x - 2}$; domain: $(-\infty, -3)\cup\left(-3, \dfrac{1}{2}\right)\cup\left(\dfrac{1}{2}, 3\right)\cup(3, \infty)$

45. $(f + g)(x) = \sqrt{x + 4} + \sqrt{x - 1}$; domain: $[1, \infty)$; $(f - g)(x) = \sqrt{x + 4} - \sqrt{x - 1}$; domain: $[1, \infty)$; $(fg)(x) = \sqrt{x^2 + 3x - 4}$; domain: $[1, \infty)$; $\left(\dfrac{f}{g}\right)(x) = \dfrac{\sqrt{x + 4}}{\sqrt{x - 1}}$; domain: $(1, \infty)$ **47.** $(f + g)(x) = \sqrt{x - 2} + \sqrt{2 - x}$; domain: $\{2\}$; $(f - g)(x) = \sqrt{x - 2} - \sqrt{2 - x}$; domain: $\{2\}$; $(fg)(x) = \sqrt{x - 2} \cdot \sqrt{2 - x}$; domain: $\{2\}$; $\left(\dfrac{f}{g}\right)(x) = \dfrac{\sqrt{x - 2}}{\sqrt{2 - x}}$; domain: \varnothing **49. a.** $(f \circ g)(x) = 2x + 14$ **b.** $(g \circ f)(x) = 2x + 7$
c. $(f \circ g)(2) = 18$ **51. a.** $(f \circ g)(x) = 2x + 5$ **b.** $(g \circ f)(x) = 2x + 9$ **c.** $(f \circ g)(2) = 9$ **53. a.** $(f \circ g)(x) = 20x^2 - 11$
b. $(g \circ f)(x) = 80x^2 - 120x + 43$ **c.** $(f \circ g)(2) = 69$ **55. a.** $(f \circ g)(x) = x^4 - 4x^2 + 6$ **b.** $(g \circ f)(x) = x^4 + 4x^2 + 2$ **c.** $(f \circ g)(2) = 6$
57. a. $(f \circ g)(x) = -2x^2 - x - 1$ **b.** $(g \circ f)(x) = 2x^2 - 17x + 41$ **c.** -11 **59. a.** $(f \circ g)(x) = \sqrt{x - 1}$ **b.** $(g \circ f)(x) = \sqrt{x} - 1$
c. $(f \circ g)(2) = 1$ **61. a.** $(f \circ g)(x) = x$ **b.** $(g \circ f)(x) = x$ **c.** $(f \circ g)(2) = 2$ **63. a.** $(f \circ g)(x) = x$ **b.** $(g \circ f)(x) = x$ **c.** 2
65. a. $(f \circ g)(x) = \dfrac{2x}{1 + 3x}$ **b.** $\left(-\infty, -\dfrac{1}{3}\right) \cup \left(-\dfrac{1}{3}, 0\right) \cup (0, \infty)$ **67. a.** $(f \circ g)(x) = \dfrac{4}{4 + x}$ **b.** $(-\infty, -4) \cup (-4, 0) \cup (0, \infty)$
69. a. $(f \circ g)(x) = \sqrt{x - 2}$ **b.** $[2, \infty)$ **71. a.** $(f \circ g)(x) = 5 - x$ **b.** $(-\infty, 1]$ **73.** $f(x) = x^4, g(x) = 3x - 1$
75. $f(x) = \sqrt[3]{x}, g(x) = x^2 - 9$ **77.** $f(x) = |x|, g(x) = 2x - 5$ **79.** $f(x) = \dfrac{1}{x}, g(x) = 2x - 3$ **81.** 5 **83.** -1 **85.** $[-4, 3]$

87. **89.** 1 **91.** -6 **93.** 1 and 2
95. a. $(B - D)(x) = 10.9x^2 - 35x + 1641$
b. 1634.1 thousand **c.** overestimates by 0.1 thousand

97. $(R - C)(20,000) = -200,000$; The company loses \$200,000 when 20,000 radios are sold.; $(R - C)(30,000) = 0$; The company breaks even when 30,000 radios are sold.; $(R - C)(40,000) = 200,000$; The company makes a profit of \$200,000 when 40,000 radios are sold. **99. a.** f gives the price of the computer after a \$400 discount. g gives the price of the computer after a 25% discount. **b.** $(f \circ g)(x) = 0.75x - 400$; This models the price of a computer after first a 25% discount and then a \$400 discount. **c.** $(g \circ f)(x) = 0.75(x - 400)$; This models the price of a computer after first a \$400 discount and then a 25% discount. **d.** $f \circ g$ because $0.75x - 400 < 0.75(x - 400)$
107. 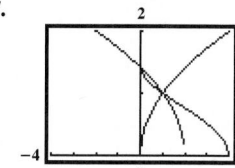 **109.** makes sense **111.** does not make sense **113.** false **115.** true
117. Answers will vary; One possible answer is $f(x) = x + 1$ and $g(x) = x - 1$.

118. $\{(4, -2), (1, -1), (1, 1), (4, 2)\}$; no **119.** $y = \dfrac{5}{x - 4}$ **120.** $y = \sqrt{x + 1}$

Domain: $[0, 4]$

Section 2.7

Check Point Exercises

1. $f(g(x)) = 4\left(\dfrac{x + 7}{4}\right) - 7 = x + 7 - 7 = x$; $g(f(x)) = \dfrac{(4x - 7) + 7}{4} = \dfrac{4x}{4} = x$ **2.** $f^{-1}(x) = \dfrac{x - 7}{2}$ **3.** $f^{-1}(x) = \sqrt[3]{\dfrac{x + 1}{4}}$

4. $f^{-1}(x) = \dfrac{3}{x + 1}$ **5.** (b) and (c)

6. 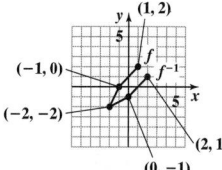 **7.** $f^{-1}(x) = \sqrt{x - 1}$

Exercise Set 2.7

1. $f(g(x)) = x$; $g(f(x)) = x$; f and g are inverses. **3.** $f(g(x)) = x$; $g(f(x)) = x$; f and g are inverses.
5. $f(g(x)) = \dfrac{5x - 56}{9}$; $g(f(x)) = \dfrac{5x - 4}{9}$; f and g are not inverses. **7.** $f(g(x)) = x$; $g(f(x)) = x$; f and g are inverses.

9. $f(g(x)) = x$; $g(f(x)) = x$; f and g are inverses. **11.** $f^{-1}(x) = x - 3$ **13.** $f^{-1}(x) = \dfrac{x}{2}$ **15.** $f^{-1}(x) = \dfrac{x - 3}{2}$ **17.** $f^{-1}(x) = \sqrt[3]{x - 2}$

19. $f^{-1}(x) = \sqrt[3]{x} - 2$ **21.** $f^{-1}(x) = \dfrac{1}{x}$ **23.** $f^{-1}(x) = x^2, x \geq 0$ **25.** $f^{-1}(x) = \dfrac{7}{x + 3}$ **27.** $f^{-1}(x) = \dfrac{3x + 1}{x - 2}; x \neq 2$

29. The function is not one-to-one, so it does not have an inverse function. **31.** The function is not one-to-one, so it does not have an inverse function.
33. The function is one-to-one, so it does have an inverse function.
35. **37.**

39. a. $f^{-1}(x) = \dfrac{x+1}{2}$

b.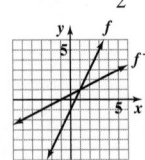

c. domain of f = range of $f^{-1} = (-\infty, \infty)$;
range of f = domain of $f^{-1} = (-\infty, \infty)$

41. a. $f^{-1}(x) = \sqrt{x+4}$

b.

c. domain of f = range of $f^{-1} = [0, \infty)$;
range of f = domain of $f^{-1} = [-4, \infty)$

43. a. $f^{-1}(x) = -\sqrt{x} + 1$

b.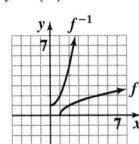

c. domain of f = range of $f^{-1} = (-\infty, 1]$;
range of f = domain of $f^{-1} = [0, \infty)$

45. a. $f^{-1}(x) = \sqrt[3]{x} + 1$

b.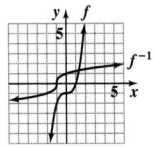

c. domain of f = range of $f^{-1} = (-\infty, \infty)$;
range of f = domain of $f^{-1} = (-\infty, \infty)$

47. a. $f^{-1}(x) = \sqrt[3]{x} - 2$

b.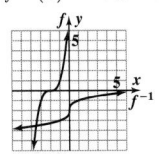

c. domain of f = range of $f^{-1} = (-\infty, \infty)$;
range of f = domain of $f^{-1} = (-\infty, \infty)$

49. a. $f^{-1}(x) = x^2 + 1, x \geq 0$

b.

c. domain of f = range of $f^{-1} = [1, \infty)$;
range of f = domain of $f^{-1} = [0, \infty)$

51. a. $f^{-1}(x) = (x - 1)^3$

b.

c. domain of f = range of $f^{-1} = (-\infty, \infty)$;
range of f = domain of $f^{-1} = (-\infty, \infty)$

53. 5 **55.** 1 **57.** 2 **59.** -7 **61.** 3 **63.** 11

65. a. $\{(17, 9.7), (22, 8.7), (30, 8.4), (40, 8.3), (50, 8.2), (60, 8.3)\}$
b. $\{(9.7, 17), (8.7, 22), (8.4, 30), (8.3, 40), (8.2, 50), (8.3, 60)\}$; no; The inverse of f is not a function.

67. a. f is a one-to-one function. **b.** $f^{-1}(0.25)$ is the number of people in a room for a 25% probability of two people sharing a birthday. $f^{-1}(0.5)$ is the number of people in a room for a 50% probability of two people sharing a birthday. $f^{-1}(0.7)$ is the number of people in a room for a 70% probability of two people sharing a birthday.

69. $f(g(x)) = \dfrac{9}{5}\left[\dfrac{5}{9}(x - 32)\right] + 32 = x$ and $g(f(x)) = \dfrac{5}{9}\left[\left(\dfrac{9}{5}x + 32\right) - 32\right] = x$

77.

one-to-one

79.

not one-to-one

81.

not one-to-one

83.

not one-to-one

85.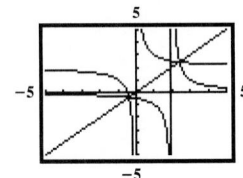

f and g are inverses.

87. makes sense **89.** makes sense **91.** false **93.** false

95. $(f \circ g)^{-1}(x) = \dfrac{x - 15}{3}$; $(g^{-1} \circ f^{-1})(x) = \dfrac{x}{3} - 5 = \dfrac{x - 15}{3}$

97. No; The space craft was at the same height, $s(t)$, for two different values of t-once during the ascent and once again during the descent.

100. $3\sqrt{5}$ **101.** **102.** $\{3 \pm \sqrt{13}\}$

Section 2.8

Check Point Exercises

1. 13 **2.** $\left(4, -\dfrac{1}{2}\right)$ **3.** $x^2 + y^2 = 16$ **4.** $x^2 + (y + 6)^2 = 100$

5. a. center: $(-3, 1)$; radius: 2 **6.** $(x + 2)^2 + (y - 2)^2 = 9$

b.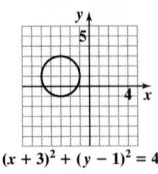

$(x + 3)^2 + (y - 1)^2 = 4$

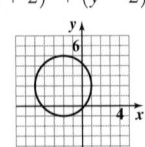

$x^2 + y^2 + 4x - 4y - 1 = 0$

c. domain: $[-5, -1]$
range: $[-1, 3]$

Exercise Set 2.8

1. 13 **3.** $2\sqrt{29} \approx 10.77$ **5.** 5 **7.** $\sqrt{29} \approx 5.39$ **9.** $4\sqrt{2} \approx 5.66$ **11.** $2\sqrt{5} \approx 4.47$ **13.** $2\sqrt{2} \approx 2.83$ **15.** $\sqrt{93} \approx 9.64$

17. $\sqrt{5} \approx 2.24$ **19.** $(4, 6)$ **21.** $(-4, -5)$ **23.** $\left(\dfrac{3}{2}, -6\right)$ **25.** $(-3, -2)$ **27.** $(1, 5\sqrt{5})$ **29.** $(2\sqrt{2}, 0)$ **31.** $x^2 + y^2 = 49$

33. $(x - 3)^2 + (y - 2)^2 = 25$ **35.** $(x + 1)^2 + (y - 4)^2 = 4$ **37.** $(x + 3)^2 + (y + 1)^2 = 3$ **39.** $(x + 4)^2 + y^2 = 100$

41. center: $(0, 0)$
radius: 4
domain: $[-4, 4]$
range: $[-4, 4]$

43. center: $(3, 1)$
radius: 6
domain: $[-3, 9]$
range: $[-5, 7]$

45. center: $(-3, 2)$
radius: 2
domain: $[-5, -1]$
range: $[0, 4]$

47. center: $(-2, -2)$
radius: 2
domain: $[-4, 0]$
range: $[-4, 0]$

49. center: $(0, 1)$
radius: 1
domain: $[-1, 1]$
range: $[0, 2]$

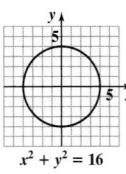

$x^2 + y^2 = 16$ $(x - 3)^2 + (y - 1)^2 = 36$ $(x + 3)^2 + (y - 2)^2 = 4$ $(x + 2)^2 + (y + 2)^2 = 4$ $x^2 + (y - 1)^2 = 1$

51. center: $(-1, 0)$
radius: 5
domain: $[-6, 4]$
range: $[-5, 5]$

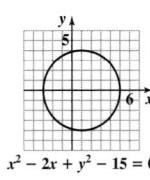

$(x + 1)^2 + y^2 = 25$

53. $(x + 3)^2 + (y + 1)^2 = 4$
center: $(-3, -1)$
radius: 2

$x^2 + y^2 + 6x + 2y + 6 = 0$

55. $(x - 5)^2 + (y - 3)^2 = 64$
center: $(5, 3)$
radius: 8

$x^2 + y^2 - 10x - 6y - 30 = 0$

57. $(x + 4)^2 + (y - 1)^2 = 25$
center: $(-4, 1)$
radius: 5

$x^2 + y^2 + 8x - 2y - 8 = 0$

59. $(x - 1)^2 + y^2 = 16$

center: $(1, 0)$

radius: 4

$x^2 - 2x + y^2 - 15 = 0$

61. $\left(x - \dfrac{1}{2}\right)^2 + (y + 1)^2 = \dfrac{1}{4}$

center: $\left(\dfrac{1}{2}, -1\right)$

radius: $\dfrac{1}{2}$

$x^2 + y^2 - x + 2y + 1 = 0$

63. $\left(x + \dfrac{3}{2}\right)^2 + (y - 1)^2 = \dfrac{17}{4}$

center: $\left(-\dfrac{3}{2}, 1\right)$

radius: $\dfrac{\sqrt{17}}{2}$

$x^2 + y^2 + 3x - 2y - 1 = 0$

65. a. $(5, 10)$ **b.** $\sqrt{5}$
c. $(x - 5)^2 + (y - 10)^2 = 5$
67. $\{(0, -4), (4, 0)\}$

$x^2 + y^2 = 16$
$x - y = 4$
$(4, 0)$
$(0, -4)$

69. $\{(0, -3), (2, -1)\}$

$(x - 2)^2 + (y + 3)^2 = 4$
$y = x - 3$
$(2, -1)$
$(0, -3)$

71. 2693 mi **73.** $(x + 2.4)^2 + (y + 2.7)^2 = 900$

83.

85.

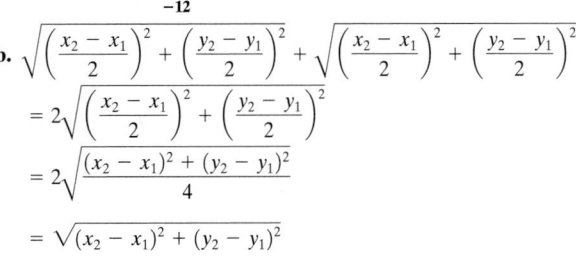

87. makes sense
89. makes sense
91. false
93. false

95. a. Distance between (x_1, y_1) and $\left(\dfrac{x_1 + x_2}{2}, \dfrac{y_1 + y_2}{2}\right)$

$$= \sqrt{\left(\frac{x_1 + x_2}{2} - x_1\right)^2 + \left(\frac{y_1 + y_2}{2} - y_1\right)^2}$$

$$= \sqrt{\left(\frac{x_1 + x_2 - 2x_1}{2}\right)^2 + \left(\frac{y_1 + y_2 - 2y_1}{2}\right)^2}$$

$$= \sqrt{\left(\frac{x_2 - x_1}{2}\right)^2 + \left(\frac{y_2 - y_1}{2}\right)^2}$$

$$= \sqrt{\frac{x_2^2 - 2x_1x_2 + x_1^2}{4} + \frac{y_2^2 - 2y_1y_2 + y_1^2}{4}}$$

$$= \sqrt{\frac{x_1^2 - 2x_1x_2 + x_2^2}{4} + \frac{y_1^2 - 2y_1y_2 + y_2^2}{4}}$$

$$= \sqrt{\left(\frac{x_1 - x_2}{2}\right)^2 + \left(\frac{y_1 - y_2}{2}\right)^2}$$

$$= \sqrt{\left(\frac{x_1 + x_2 - 2x_2}{2}\right)^2 + \left(\frac{y_1 + y_2 - 2y_2}{2}\right)^2}$$

$$= \sqrt{\left(\frac{x_1 + x_2}{2} - x_2\right)^2 + \left(\frac{y_1 + y_2}{2} - y_2\right)^2}$$

$= $ Distance between (x_2, y_2) and $\left(\dfrac{x_1 + x_2}{2}, \dfrac{y_1 + y_2}{2}\right)$

b. $\sqrt{\left(\dfrac{x_2 - x_1}{2}\right)^2 + \left(\dfrac{y_2 - y_1}{2}\right)^2} + \sqrt{\left(\dfrac{x_2 - x_1}{2}\right)^2 + \left(\dfrac{y_2 - y_1}{2}\right)^2}$

$$= 2\sqrt{\left(\frac{x_2 - x_1}{2}\right)^2 + \left(\frac{y_2 - y_1}{2}\right)^2}$$

$$= 2\sqrt{\frac{(x_2 - x_1)^2 + (y_2 - y_1)^2}{4}}$$

$$= \sqrt{(x_2 - x_1)^2 + (y_2 - y_1)^2}$$

$= $ Distance from (x_1, y_1) to (x_2, y_2)

97. $y + 4 = \frac{3}{4}(x - 3)$ **98.** $\{1, 5\}$ **99.** $\{-1 \pm \sqrt{2}\}$ **100.**

$f(x) = x^2$
$g(x) = (x + 3)^2 + 1$

Chapter 2 Review Exercises

1. function; domain: $\{2, 3, 5\}$; range: $\{7\}$ **2.** function; domain: $\{1, 2, 13\}$; range: $\{10, 500, \pi\}$ **3.** not a function; domain: $\{12, 14\}$; range: $\{13, 15, 19\}$
4. y is a function of x. **5.** y is a function of x. **6.** y is not a function of x. **7. a.** $f(4) = -23$ **b.** $f(x + 3) = -7x - 16$
c. $f(-x) = 5 + 7x$ **8. a.** $g(0) = 2$ **b.** $g(-2) = 24$ **c.** $g(x - 1) = 3x^2 - 11x + 10$ **d.** $g(-x) = 3x^2 + 5x + 2$ **9. a.** $g(13) = 3$
b. $g(0) = 4$ **c.** $g(-3) = 7$ **10. a.** -1 **b.** 12 **c.** 3 **11.** not a function **12.** function **13.** function **14.** not a function
15. not a function **16.** function **17. a.** $[-3, 5)$ **b.** $[-5, 0]$ **c.** -3 **d.** -2 **e.** increasing: $(-2, 0)$ or $(3, 5)$; decreasing: $(-3, -2)$
or $(0, 3)$ **f.** $f(-2) = -3$ and $f(3) = -5$ **18. a.** $(-\infty, \infty)$ **b.** $(-\infty, \infty)$ **c.** -2 and 3 **d.** 3 **e.** increasing: $(-5, 0)$;
decreasing: $(-\infty, -5)$ or $(0, \infty)$ **f.** $f(-2) = 0$ and $f(6) = -3$ **19. a.** $(-\infty, \infty)$ **b.** $[-2, 2]$ **c.** 0 **d.** 0 **e.** increasing: $(-2, 2)$;
constant: $(-\infty, -2)$ or $(2, \infty)$ **f.** $f(-9) = -2$ and $f(14) = 2$ **20. a.** 0; $f(0) = -2$ **b.** $-2, 3$; $f(-2) = -3, f(3) = -5$
21. a. 0; $f(0) = 3$ **b.** -5; $f(-5) = -6$ **22.** odd; symmetric with respect to the origin **23.** even; symmetric with respect to the y-axis
24. odd; symmetric with respect to the origin
25. ; $\{-3, 5\}$ **26.** ; $(-\infty, 0]$

$f(x) = \begin{cases} 5 \text{ if } x \le -1 \\ -3 \text{ if } x > -1 \end{cases}$ $f(x) = \begin{cases} 2x \text{ if } x < 0 \\ -x \text{ if } x \ge 0 \end{cases}$

27. 8 **28.** $-4x - 2h + 1$ **29. a.** yes; The graph passes the vertical line test. **b.** $(3, 12)$; The eagle descended.
c. $(0, 3)$ and $(12, 17)$; The eagle's height held steady during the first 3 seconds and the eagle was on the ground for 5 seconds.
d. $(17, 30)$; The eagle was ascending.

30.

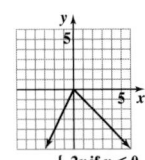

31. $-\frac{1}{2}$; falls **32.** 1; rises **33.** 0; horizontal **34.** undefined; vertical
35. $y - 2 = -6(x + 3)$; $y = -6x - 16$ **36.** using $(1, 6)$, $y - 6 = 2(x - 1)$; $y = 2x + 4$
37. $y + 7 = -3(x - 4)$; $y = -3x + 5$ **38.** $y - 6 = -3(x + 3)$; $y = -3x - 3$ **39.** $x + 6y + 18 = 0$

40. Slope: $\frac{2}{5}$; y-intercept: -1 **41.** Slope: -4; y-intercept: 5 **42.** Slope: $-\frac{2}{3}$; y-intercept: -2 **43.** Slope: 0; y-intercept: 4

$y = \frac{2}{5}x - 1$ $f(x) = -4x + 5$ $2x + 3y + 6 = 0$ $2y - 8 = 0$

44. **45.** $2x - 10 = 0$

$2x - 5y - 10 = 0$

46. a. $y - 2.3 = 0.116(x - 15)$ or $y - 11 = 0.116(x - 90)$ **b.** $f(x) = 0.116x + 0.56$ **c.** approximately 5 deaths per 100,000 persons
d. 4.3 deaths per 100,000 persons; underestimates by 0.7 death per 100,000 persons; The line passes below the point for France.
47. 182.5; Corporate profits increased at a rate of $182.5 billion per year. The rate of change is $182.5 billion per year. **48.** 10

49. $y = g(x)$ **50.** $y = g(x)$ **51.** **52.** $y = g(x)$ **53.**

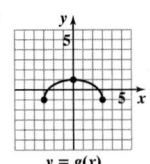

$y = g(x)$ $y = g(x)$

54.

55.

56.

57.

58.

59.

60.

61.

62.

63.

64.

65.

66.

67.

68.

69.

70. $(-\infty, \infty)$ **71.** $(-\infty, 7)\cup(7, \infty)$ **72.** $(-\infty, 4]$ **73.** $(-\infty, -7)\cup(-7, 3)\cup(3, \infty)$
74. $[2, 5)\cup(5, \infty)$ **75.** $[1, \infty)$ **76.** $(f + g)(x) = 4x - 6$; domain: $(-\infty, \infty)$; $(f - g)(x) = 2x + 4$;
domain: $(-\infty, \infty)$; $(fg)(x) = 3x^2 - 16x + 5$; domain: $(-\infty, \infty)$; $\left(\dfrac{f}{g}\right)(x) = \dfrac{3x - 1}{x - 5}$; domain: $(-\infty, 5)\cup(5, \infty)$
77. $(f + g)(x) = 2x^2 + x$; domain: $(-\infty, \infty)$; $(f - g)(x) = x + 2$; domain: $(-\infty, \infty)$; $(fg)(x) = x^4 + x^3 - x - 1$;
domain: $(-\infty, \infty)$; $\left(\dfrac{f}{g}\right)(x) = \dfrac{x^2 + x + 1}{x^2 - 1}$; domain: $(-\infty, -1)\cup(-1, 1)\cup(1, \infty)$

78. $(f + g)(x) = \sqrt{x + 7} + \sqrt{x - 2}$; domain: $[2, \infty)$; $(f - g)(x) = \sqrt{x + 7} - \sqrt{x - 2}$; domain: $[2, \infty)$; $(fg)(x) = \sqrt{x^2 + 5x - 14}$; domain:
$[2, \infty)$; $\left(\dfrac{f}{g}\right)(x) = \dfrac{\sqrt{x + 7}}{\sqrt{x - 2}}$; domain: $(2, \infty)$ **79. a.** $(f \circ g)(x) = 16x^2 - 8x + 4$ **b.** $(g \circ f)(x) = 4x^2 + 11$ **c.** $(f \circ g)(3) = 124$

80. a. $(f \circ g)(x) = \sqrt{x + 1}$ **b.** $(g \circ f)(x) = \sqrt{x} + 1$ **c.** $(f \circ g)(3) = 2$ **81. a.** $(f \circ g)(x) = \dfrac{1 + x}{1 - 2x}$ **b.** $(-\infty, 0)\cup\left(0, \dfrac{1}{2}\right)\cup\left(\dfrac{1}{2}, \infty\right)$

82. a. $(f \circ g)(x) = \sqrt{x + 2}$ **b.** $[-2, \infty)$ **83.** $f(x) = x^4, g(x) = x^2 + 2x - 1$ **84.** $f(x) = \sqrt[3]{x}, g(x) = 7x + 4$ **85.** $f(g(x)) = x - \dfrac{7}{10}$;

$g(f(x)) = x - \dfrac{7}{6}$; f and g are not inverses of each other. **86.** $f(g(x)) = x$; $g(f(x)) = x$; f and g are inverses of each other. **87.** $f^{-1}(x) = \dfrac{x + 3}{4}$

88. $f^{-1}(x) = \sqrt[3]{\dfrac{x - 1}{8}}$ or $\dfrac{\sqrt[3]{x - 1}}{2}$ **89.** $f^{-1}(x) = \dfrac{2}{x - 5}$ **90.** Inverse function exists. **91.** Inverse function does not exist.
92. Inverse function exists. **93.** Inverse function does not exist.

94. **95.** $f^{-1}(x) = \sqrt{1 - x}$ **96.** $f^{-1}(x) = (x - 1)^2, x \geq 1$ **97.** 13 **98.** $2\sqrt{2} \approx 2.83$ **99.** $(-5, 5)$

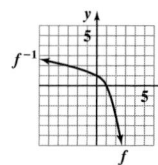

100. $\left(-\dfrac{11}{2}, -2\right)$ **101.** $x^2 + y^2 = 9$

102. $(x + 2)^2 + (y - 4)^2 = 36$

103. center: $(0, 0)$; radius: 1
domain: $[-1, 1]$; range: $[-1, 1]$

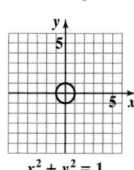

$x^2 + y^2 = 1$

104. center: $(-2, 3)$; radius: 3
domain: $[-5, 1]$; range: $[0, 6]$

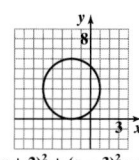

$(x + 2)^2 + (y - 3)^2 = 9$

105. center: $(2, -1)$; radius: 3
domain: $[-1, 5]$; range: $[-4, 2]$

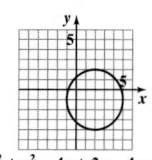

$x^2 + y^2 - 4x + 2y - 4 = 0$

Chapter 2 Test

1. b, c, d **2. a.** $f(4) - f(-3) = 5$ **b.** $(-5, 6]$ **c.** $[-4, 5]$ **d.** $(-1, 2)$ **e.** $(-5, -1)$ or $(2, 6)$ **f.** $2; f(2) = 5$ **g.** $-1; f(-1) = -4$
h. $-4, 1,$ and 5 **i.** -3 **3. a.** -2 and 2 **b.** -1 and 1 **c.** 0 **d.** even **e.** no **f.** relative minimum

g.

h.

i.

j. $-\dfrac{1}{3}$

4. $x + y = 4$

domain: $(-\infty, \infty)$;
range: $(-\infty, \infty)$

5. $x^2 + y^2 = 4$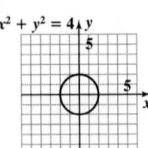

domain: $[-2, 2]$;
range: $[-2, 2]$

6. $f(x) = 4$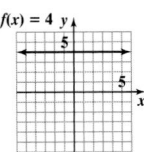

domain: $(-\infty, \infty)$;
range: $\{4\}$

7.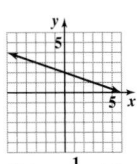

$f(x) = -\frac{1}{3}x + 2$

domain: $(-\infty, \infty)$;
range: $(-\infty, \infty)$

8.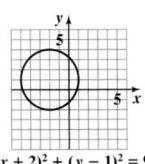

$(x + 2)^2 + (y - 1)^2 = 9$

domain: $[-5, 1]$;
range: $[-2, 4]$

9.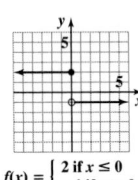

$f(x) = \begin{cases} 2 \text{ if } x \le 0 \\ -1 \text{ if } x > 0 \end{cases}$

domain: $(-\infty, \infty)$;
range: $\{-1, 2\}$

10.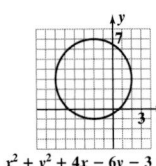

$x^2 + y^2 + 4x - 6y - 3 = 0$

domain: $[-6, 2]$;
range: $[-1, 7]$

11.

domain of $f =$ domain of $g = (-\infty, \infty)$;
range of $f = [0, \infty)$; range of $g = [-2, \infty)$

12.

domain of $f =$ domain of $g = (-\infty, \infty)$;
range of $f = [0, \infty)$; range of $g = (-\infty, 4]$

13.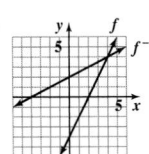

domain of $f =$ range of $f^{-1} = (-\infty, \infty)$;
range of $f =$ domain of $f^{-1} = (-\infty, \infty)$

14.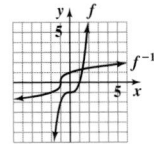

domain of $f =$ range of $f^{-1} = (-\infty, \infty)$;
range of $f =$ domain of $f^{-1} = (-\infty, \infty)$

15.

domain of $f =$ range of $f^{-1} = [0, \infty)$;
range of $f =$ domain of $f^{-1} = [-1, \infty)$

16. $f(x - 1) = x^2 - 3x - 2$　**17.** $2x + h - 1$　**18.** $(g - f)(x) = -x^2 + 3x - 2$

19. $\left(\dfrac{f}{g}\right)(x) = \dfrac{x^2 - x - 4}{2x - 6}; (-\infty, 3) \cup (3, \infty)$　**20.** $(f \circ g)(x) = 4x^2 - 26x + 38$　**21.** $(g \circ f)(x) = 2x^2 - 2x - 14$

22. -10　**23.** $f(-x) = x^2 + x - 4$; neither　**24.** using $(2, 1)$, $y - 1 = 3(x - 2)$; $y = 3x - 5$

25. $y - 6 = 4(x + 4)$; $y = 4x + 22$　**26.** $2x + y + 24 = 0$　**27. a.** $y - 476 = 5(x - 2)$ or $y - 486 = 5(x - 4)$

b. $f(x) = 5x + 466$　**c.** 516 per 100,000 residents　**28.** 48　**29.** $g(-1) = 4; g(7) = 2$　**30.** $(-\infty, -5) \cup (-5, 1) \cup (1, \infty)$

31. $[1, \infty)$　**32.** $\dfrac{7x}{2 - 4x}$; domain: $(-\infty, 0) \cup \left(0, \dfrac{1}{2}\right) \cup \left(\dfrac{1}{2}, \infty\right)$　**33.** $f(x) = x^7, g(x) = 2x + 3$　**34.** $5; (3.5, 0)$

Cumulative Review Exercises (Chapters 1–2)

1. domain: $[0, 2)$; range: $[0, 2]$　**2.** $\dfrac{1}{2}$ and $\dfrac{3}{2}$　**3.** 2

4.

$g(x) = f(x - 1) + 1$

5.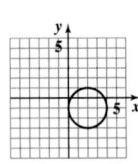

$h(x) = -2f\left(\dfrac{1}{2}x\right)$

6. $\{-4, 5\}$

7. $\left\{\dfrac{25}{18}\right\}$

8. $\{4\}$

9. $\{-8, 27\}$

10. $(-\infty, 20]$

11.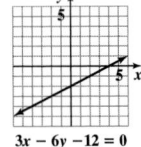

$3x - 6y - 12 = 0$

domain: $(-\infty, \infty)$;
range: $(-\infty, \infty)$

12.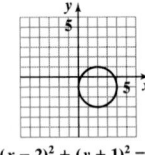

$(x - 2)^2 + (y + 1)^2 = 4$

domain: $[0, 4]$;
range: $[-3, 1]$

13.

domain of $f =$ domain of $g = (-\infty, \infty)$;
range of $f =$ range of $g = (-\infty, \infty)$

14.

domain of $f =$ range of $f^{-1} = [3, \infty)$;
range of $f =$ domain of $f^{-1} = [2, \infty)$

15. $-2x - h$　**16.** -7 and -3　**17.** $y - 5 = 4(x + 2)$; $y = 4x + 13$; $4x - y + 13 = 0$　**18.** \$1500 at 7%; \$4500 at 9%　**19.** \$2000

20. 3 ft by 8 ft

CHAPTER 3

Section 3.1

Check Point Exercises

1.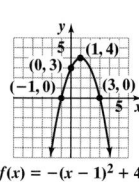
$f(x) = -(x - 1)^2 + 4$

2.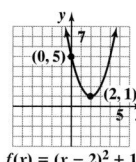
$f(x) = (x - 2)^2 + 1$

3.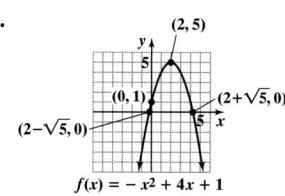
$f(x) = -x^2 + 4x + 1$
domain: $(-\infty, \infty)$; range: $(-\infty, 5]$

4. a. minimum **b.** Minimum is 984 at $x = 2$.
c. domain: $(-\infty, \infty)$; range: $[984, \infty)$

5. a. 205 ft; 200 ft **b.** 402 ft
c.
Arrow's Horizontal Distance (feet)

6. $4, -4; -16$ **7.** 30 ft by 30 ft; 900 sq ft

Exercise Set 3.1

1. $h(x) = (x - 1)^2 + 1$ **3.** $j(x) = (x - 1)^2 - 1$ **5.** $h(x) = x^2 - 1$ **7.** $g(x) = x^2 - 2x + 1$ **9.** $(3, 1)$ **11.** $(-1, 5)$
13. $(2, -5)$ **15.** $(-1, 9)$

17. domain: $(-\infty, \infty)$
range: $[-1, \infty)$
axis of symmetry: $x = 4$
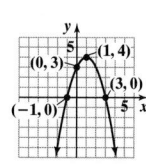
$f(x) = (x - 4)^2 - 1$

19. domain: $(-\infty, \infty)$
range: $[2, \infty)$
axis of symmetry: $x = 1$

$f(x) = (x - 1)^2 + 2$

21. domain: $(-\infty, \infty)$
range: $[1, \infty)$
axis of symmetry: $x = 3$
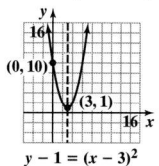
$y - 1 = (x - 3)^2$

23. domain: $(-\infty, \infty)$
range: $[-1, \infty)$
axis of symmetry: $x = -2$

$f(x) = 2(x + 2)^2 - 1$

25. domain: $(-\infty, \infty)$
range: $(-\infty, 4]$
axis of symmetry: $x = 1$
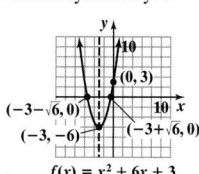
$f(x) = 4 - (x - 1)^2$

27. domain: $(-\infty, \infty)$
range: $[-4, \infty)$
axis of symmetry: $x = 1$
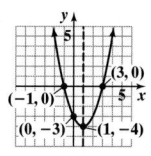
$f(x) = x^2 - 2x - 3$

29. domain: $(-\infty, \infty)$
range: $\left[-\dfrac{49}{4}, \infty\right)$
axis of symmetry: $x = -\dfrac{3}{2}$
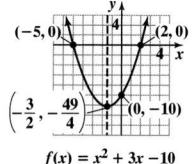
$f(x) = x^2 + 3x - 10$

31. domain: $(-\infty, \infty)$
range: $(-\infty, 4]$
axis of symmetry: $x = 1$

$f(x) = 2x - x^2 + 3$

33. domain: $(-\infty, \infty)$
range: $[-6, \infty)$
axis of symmetry: $x = -3$

$f(x) = x^2 + 6x + 3$

35. domain: $(-\infty, \infty)$
range: $[-5, \infty)$
axis of symmetry: $x = -1$

$f(x) = 2x^2 + 4x - 3$

37. domain: $(-\infty, \infty)$
range: $(-\infty, -1]$
axis of symmetry: $x = 1$

$f(x) = 2x - x^2 - 2$

39. a. minimum **b.** Minimum is -13 at $x = 2$. **c.** domain: $(-\infty, \infty)$; range: $[-13, \infty)$ **41. a.** maximum **b.** Maximum is 1 at $x = 1$.

c. domain: $(-\infty, \infty)$; range: $(-\infty, 1]$ **43. a.** minimum **b.** Minimum is $-\dfrac{5}{4}$ at $x = \dfrac{1}{2}$. **c.** domain: $(-\infty, \infty)$; range: $\left[-\dfrac{5}{4}, \infty\right)$

45. domain: $(-\infty, \infty)$; range: $[-2, \infty)$ **47.** domain: $(-\infty, \infty)$; range: $(-\infty, -6]$ **49.** $f(x) = 2(x - 5)^2 + 3$ **51.** $f(x) = 2(x + 10)^2 - 5$
53. $f(x) = -3(x + 2)^2 + 4$ **55.** $f(x) = 3(x - 11)^2$ **57. a.** 18.35 ft; 35 ft **b.** 77.8 ft **c.** 6.1 ft **59. a.** 2.75 gal per person;
underestimates by 0.05 gal **b.** 1992; 2.048 gal; seems reasonable **61.** 8 and 8; 64 **63.** $8, -8; -64$ **65.** length: 300 ft; width: 150 ft;
maximum area: 45,000 sq ft **67.** 12.5 yd by 12.5 yd; 156.25 sq yd **69.** 150 ft by 100 ft; 15,000 sq ft **71.** 5 in.; 50 sq in.
73. a. $C(x) = 0.55x + 525$ **b.** $P(x) = -0.001x^2 + 2.45x - 525$ **c.** 1225 roast beef sandwiches; $\approx \$975.63$

81. a.

b. $(20.5, -120.5)$
c. Ymax = 750
d. You can choose Xmin and Xmax so the x-value of the vertex is in the center of the graph. Choose Ymin to include the y-value of the vertex.

83. $(2.5, 185)$

85. $(-30, 91)$

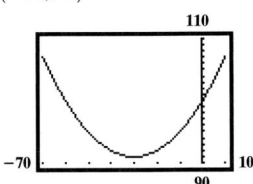

You can only see a little of the parabola.

87. does not make sense **89.** does not make sense **91.** true **93.** false **95.** $x = -2; (-3, -2)$ **97.** $f(x) = \frac{1}{2}(x + 3)^2 - 4$

99. $x = 166\frac{2}{3}$ ft, $y = 125$ ft; approximately 20,833 ft^2 **102.** $(x + 3)(x + 1)(x - 1)$ **103.** $f(2) = -1; f(3) = 16;$ The graph passes through $(2, -1)$, which is below the x-axis, and $(3, 16)$, which is above the x-axis. Since the graph of f is continuous, it must cross the x-axis somewhere between 2 and 3 to get from one of these points to the other. **104.** even; symmetric with respect to the y-axis

Section 3.2

Check Point Exercises

1. The graph rises to the left and to the right. **2.** The graph falls to the left and rises to the right. **3.** Since n is odd and the leading coefficient is negative, the function falls to the right. Since the ratio cannot be negative, the model won't be appropriate. **4.** No; the graph should fall to the left, but doesn't appear to. **5.** $\{-2, 2\}$ **6.** $\{-2, 0, 2\}$ **7.** $-\frac{1}{2}$ with multiplicity 2 and 5 with multiplicity 3; touches and turns at $-\frac{1}{2}$ and crosses at 5
8. $f(-3) = -42; f(-2) = 5$ **9.**

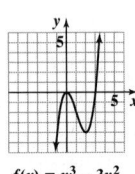

$f(x) = x^3 - 3x^2$

Exercise Set 3.2

1. polynomial function; degree: 3 **3.** polynomial function; degree: 5 **5.** not a polynomial function **7.** not a polynomial function
9. not a polynomial function **11.** could be polynomial function **13.** not a polynomial function **15.** b **17.** a
19. falls to the left and rises to the right **21.** rises to the left and to the right **23.** falls to the left and to the right
25. $x = 5$ has multiplicity 1; The graph crosses the x-axis; $x = -4$ has multiplicity 2; The graph touches the x-axis and turns around.
27. $x = 3$ has multiplicity 1; The graph crosses the x-axis; $x = -6$ has multiplicity 3; The graph crosses the x-axis.
29. $x = 0$ has multiplicity 1; The graph crosses the x-axis; $x = 1$ has multiplicity 2; The graph touches the x-axis and turns around.
31. $x = 2, x = -2$ and $x = -7$ have multiplicity 1; The graph crosses the x-axis. **33.** $f(1) = -1; f(2) = 5; 1.3$ **35.** $f(-1) = -1; f(0) = 1; -0.5$
37. $f(-3) = -11; f(-2) = 1; -2.1$ **39.** $f(-3) = -42; f(-2) = 5; -2.2$
41. a. $f(x)$ rises to the right and falls to the left.
b. $x = -2, x = 1, x = -1;$
 $f(x)$ crosses the x-axis at each.
c. The y-intercept is -2.
d. neither
e.

$f(x) = x^3 + 2x^2 - x - 2$

43. a. $f(x)$ rises to the left and the right.
b. $x = 0, x = 3, x = -3;$
 $f(x)$ crosses the x-axis at -3 and 3;
 $f(x)$ touches the x-axis at 0.
c. The y-intercept is 0.
d. y-axis symmetry
e.

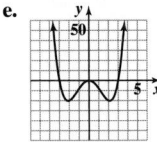

$f(x) = x^4 - 9x^2$

45. a. $f(x)$ falls to the left and the right.
b. $x = 0, x = 4, x = -4;$
 $f(x)$ crosses the x-axis at -4 and 4;
 $f(x)$ touches the x-axis at 0.
c. The y-intercept is 0.
d. y-axis symmetry
e.

$f(x) = -x^4 + 16x^2$

47. a. $f(x)$ rises to the left and the right.
b. $x = 0, x = 1;$
 $f(x)$ touches the x-axis at 0 and 1.
c. The y-intercept is 0.
d. neither
e.

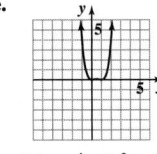

$f(x) = x^4 - 2x^3 + x^2$

49. a. $f(x)$ falls to the left and the right. **51. a.** $f(x)$ rises to the left and falls to the right.

49. a. $f(x)$ falls to the left and the right.
 b. $x = 0, x = 2$;
 $f(x)$ crosses the x-axis at 0 and 2.
 c. The y-intercept is 0.
 d. neither
 e.

$f(x) = -2x^4 + 4x^3$

51. a. $f(x)$ rises to the left and falls to the right.
 b. $x = 0, x = \pm\sqrt{3}$;
 $f(x)$ crosses the x-axis at 0;
 $f(x)$ touches the x-axis at $\sqrt{3}$ and $-\sqrt{3}$.
 c. The y-intercept is 0.
 d. origin symmetry
 e.

$f(x) = 6x^3 - 9x - x^5$

53. a. $f(x)$ rises to the left and falls to the right.
 b. $x = 0, x = 3$;
 $f(x)$ crosses the x-axis at 3;
 $f(x)$ touches the x-axis at 0.
 c. The y-intercept is 0.
 d. neither
 e.

$f(x) = 3x^2 - x^3$

55. a. $f(x)$ falls to the left and the right.
 b. $x = 1, x = -2, x = 2$;
 $f(x)$ crosses the x-axis at -2 and 2;
 $f(x)$ touches the x-axis at 1.
 c. The y-intercept is 12.
 d. neither
 e.

$f(x) = -3(x - 1)^2 (x^2 - 4)$

57. a. $f(x)$ rises to the left and the right.
 b. $x = -2, x = 0, x = 1$;
 $f(x)$ crosses the x-axis at -2 and 1;
 $f(x)$ touches the x-axis at 0.
 c. The y-intercept is 0.
 d. neither
 e.

$f(x) = x^2 (x - 1)^3 (x + 2)$

59. a. $f(x)$ falls to the left and the right.
 b. $x = -3, x = 0, x = 1$;
 $f(x)$ crosses the x-axis at -3 and 1;
 $f(x)$ touches the x-axis at 0.
 c. The y-intercept is 0.
 d. neither
 e.

$f(x) = -x^2 (x - 1)(x + 3)$

61. a. $f(x)$ falls to the left and the right.
 b. $x = -5, x = 0, x = 1$;
 $f(x)$ crosses the x-axis at -5 and 0;
 $f(x)$ touches the x-axis at 1.
 c. The y-intercept is 0.
 d. neither
 e.

$f(x) = -2x^3 (x - 1)^2 (x + 5)$

63. a. $f(x)$ rises to the left and the right.
 b. $x = -4, x = 1, x = 2$;
 $f(x)$ crosses the x-axis at -4 and 1;
 $f(x)$ touches the x-axis at 2.
 c. The y-intercept is -16.
 d. neither
 e.

$f(x) = (x - 2)^2 (x + 4)(x - 1)$

65. a. -2, odd; 1, odd; 4, odd **b.** $f(x) = (x + 2)(x - 1)(x - 4)$ **c.** 8 **67. a.** -1, odd; 3, even **b.** $f(x) = (x + 1)(x - 3)^2$ **c.** 9
69. a. -3, even; 2, even **b.** $f(x) = -(x + 3)^2(x - 2)^2$ **c.** -36 **71. a.** -2, even; -1, odd; 1, odd **b.** $f(x) = (x + 2)^2(x + 1)(x - 1)^3$
c. -4 **73. a.** $f(3) = 404{,}444$; $g(3) = 404{,}443$; function f **b.** falls to the right; No, since the graph falls to the right, the number of people living
with HIV and AIDS will eventually be negative; model breakdown will occur. **75. a.** from 1 through 4 min and from 8 through 10 min
b. from 4 through 8 min and from 10 through 12 min **c.** 3 **d.** 4 **e.** negative; The graph falls to the left and falls to the right.
f. 116 ± 1 beats per min; 10 min **g.** 64 ± 1 beats per min; 8 min

95.

97.

99.

101. does not make sense **103.** makes sense **105.** false **107.** false **109.** $f(x) = x^3 - 2x^2$ **110.** $35\frac{2}{21}$

111. $6x^3 - x^2 - 5x + 4$ **112.** $(x-3)(2x-1)(x+2)$

Section 3.3

Check Point Exercises

1. $x + 5$ **2.** $2x^2 + 3x - 2 + \frac{1}{x-3}$ **3.** $2x^2 + 7x + 14 + \frac{21x - 10}{x^2 - 2x}$ **4.** $x^2 - 2x - 3$ **5.** -105 **6.** $\left\{-1, -\frac{1}{3}, \frac{2}{5}\right\}$

Exercise Set 3.3

1. $x + 3$ **3.** $x^2 + 3x + 1$ **5.** $2x^2 + 3x + 5$ **7.** $4x + 3 + \frac{2}{3x - 2}$ **9.** $2x^2 + x + 6 - \frac{38}{x+3}$ **11.** $4x^3 + 16x^2 + 60x + 246 + \frac{984}{x-4}$

13. $2x + 5$ **15.** $6x^2 + 3x - 1 - \frac{3x-1}{3x^2+1}$ **17.** $2x + 5$ **19.** $3x - 8 + \frac{20}{x+5}$ **21.** $4x^2 + x + 4 + \frac{3}{x-1}$

23. $6x^4 + 12x^3 + 22x^2 + 48x + 93 + \frac{187}{x-2}$ **25.** $x^3 - 10x^2 + 51x - 260 + \frac{1300}{x+5}$ **27.** $x^4 + x^3 + 2x^2 + 2x + 2$ **29.** $x^3 + 4x^2 + 16x + 64$

31. $2x^4 - 7x^3 + 15x^2 - 31x + 64 - \frac{129}{x+2}$ **33.** -25 **35.** -133 **37.** 240 **39.** 1 **41.** $x^2 - 5x + 6; x = -1, x = 2, x = 3$

43. $\left\{-\frac{1}{2}, 1, 2\right\}$ **45.** $\left\{-\frac{3}{2}, -\frac{1}{3}, \frac{1}{2}\right\}$ **47.** 2; The remainder is zero; $\{-3, -1, 2\}$ **49.** 1; The remainder is zero; $\left\{\frac{1}{3}, \frac{1}{2}, 1\right\}$

51. a. The remainder is 0. **b.** 3 mm **53.** $0.5x^2 - 0.4x + 0.3$ **55. a.** 70; When the tax rate is 30%, tax revenue is \$700 billion.; $(30, 70)$

b. $80 + \frac{800}{x - 110}$; $f(30) = 70$; yes **c.** No, f is a rational function because it is a quotient of two polynomials. **67.** makes sense

69. does not make sense **71.** true **73.** false **75.** $x - 2$ **79.** $\{-2 \pm \sqrt{5}\}$ **80.** $\{-2 \pm i\sqrt{2}\}$ **81.** -3

Section 3.4

Check Point Exercises

1. $\pm 1, \pm 2, \pm 3, \pm 6$ **2.** $\pm 1, \pm 3, \pm \frac{1}{2}, \pm \frac{1}{4}, \pm \frac{3}{2}, \pm \frac{3}{4}$ **3.** $\{-5, -4, 1\}$ **4.** $\left\{2, \frac{-3 - \sqrt{5}}{2}, \frac{-3 + \sqrt{5}}{2}\right\}$ **5.** $\{1, 2 - 3i, 2 + 3i\}$

6. $f(x) = x^3 + 3x^2 + x + 3$ **7.** $4, 2,$ or 0 positive zeros, no possible negative zeros

Exercise Set 3.4

1. $\pm 1, \pm 2, \pm 4$ **3.** $\pm 1, \pm 2, \pm 3, \pm 6, \pm \frac{1}{3}, \pm \frac{2}{3}$ **5.** $\pm 1, \pm 2, \pm 3, \pm 6, \pm \frac{1}{2}, \pm \frac{1}{4}, \pm \frac{3}{2}, \pm \frac{3}{4}$ **7.** $\pm 1, \pm 2, \pm 3, \pm 4, \pm 6, \pm 12$ **9. a.** $\pm 1, \pm 2, \pm 4$

b. $-2, -1,$ or 2 **c.** $\{-2, -1, 2\}$ **11. a.** $\pm 1, \pm 2, \pm 3, \pm 6, \pm \frac{1}{2}, \pm \frac{3}{2}$ **b.** $-2, \frac{1}{2},$ or 3 **c.** $\left\{-2, \frac{1}{2}, 3\right\}$ **13. a.** $\pm 1, \pm 2, \pm 3, \pm 6$

b. -1 **c.** $\left\{-1, \frac{-3 - \sqrt{33}}{2}, \frac{-3 + \sqrt{33}}{2}\right\}$ **15. a.** $\pm 1, \pm \frac{1}{2}, \pm 2$ **b.** -2 **c.** $\left\{-2, \frac{-1 + i}{2}, \frac{-1 - i}{2}\right\}$ **17. a.** $\pm 1, \pm 2, \pm 3, \pm 4, \pm 6, \pm 12$

b. $-3, 1,$ or 4 **c.** $\{-3, 1, 4\}$ **19. a.** $\pm 1, \pm 2, \pm 3, \pm 4, \pm 6, \pm 12$ **b.** -2 **c.** $\{-2, 1 + \sqrt{7}, 1 - \sqrt{7}\}$ **21. a.** $\pm 1, \pm 5, \pm \frac{1}{2}, \pm \frac{5}{2}, \pm \frac{1}{3}, \pm \frac{5}{3}, \pm \frac{1}{6}, \pm \frac{5}{6}$

b. $-5, \frac{1}{3},$ or $\frac{1}{2}$ **c.** $\left\{-5, \frac{1}{3}, \frac{1}{2}\right\}$ **23. a.** $\pm 1, \pm 2, \pm 4$ **b.** -2 or 2 **c.** $\{-2, 2, 1 + \sqrt{2}, 1 - \sqrt{2}\}$ **25.** $f(x) = 2x^3 - 2x^2 + 50x - 50$

27. $f(x) = x^3 - 3x^2 - 15x + 125$ **29.** $f(x) = x^4 + 10x^2 + 9$ **31.** $f(x) = x^4 - 9x^3 + 21x^2 + 21x - 130$ **33.** no positive real roots;

3 or 1 negative real roots **35.** 3 or 1 positive real roots; no negative real roots **37.** 2 or 0 positive real roots; 2 or 0 negative real roots

39. $x = -2, x = 5, x = 1$ **41.** $\left\{-\frac{1}{2}, \frac{1 + \sqrt{17}}{2}, \frac{1 - \sqrt{17}}{2}\right\}$ **43.** $-1, 2 + 2i,$ and $2 - 2i$ **45.** $\{-1, -2, 3 + \sqrt{13}, 3 - \sqrt{13}\}$

47. $x = -1, x = 2, x = -\frac{1}{3}, x = 3$ **49.** $\left\{1, -\frac{3}{4}, i\sqrt{2}, -i\sqrt{2}\right\}$ **51.** $\left\{-2, \frac{1}{2}, \sqrt{2}, -\sqrt{2}\right\}$

53. a. $-4, 1,$ and 4 **55. a.** -1 and $\frac{3}{2}$ **57. a.** $\frac{1}{2}, 3, -1 \pm i$ **59. a.** $-2, -1, -\frac{2}{3}, 1,$ and 2

b. **b.** **b.** **b.**

$f(x) = -x^3 + x^2 + 16x - 16$

$f(x) = 4x^3 - 8x^2 - 3x + 9$

$f(x) = 2x^4 - 3x^3 - 7x^2 - 8x + 6$

$f(x) = 3x^5 + 2x^4 - 15x^3 - 10x^2 + 12x + 8$

61. 7.8 in., 10 in. **63. a.** $(7.8, 2000), (10, 2000)$ **b.** $(0, 15)$ **73.** $\left\{\frac{1}{2}, \frac{2}{3}, 2\right\}$ **75.** $\left\{\pm \frac{1}{2}\right\}$ **77.** $5, 3,$ or 1 positive real zeros; no negative real zeros

79.

81.

83. makes sense **85.** makes sense **87.** false
89. true **91.** 3 in. **93.** 3 **95.** 5
98. $x = 1$ and $x = 2$ **99.** $x = 1$ **100.** $y = 0$

1 real zero, 2 nonreal complex zeros

2 real zeros, 2 nonreal complex zeros

Mid-Chapter 3 Check Point

1.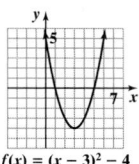
$f(x) = (x - 3)^2 - 4$
domain: $(-\infty, \infty)$
range: $[-4, \infty)$

2.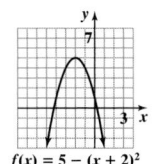
$f(x) = 5 - (x + 2)^2$
domain: $(-\infty, \infty)$
range: $(-\infty, 5]$

3.
$f(x) = -x^2 - 4x + 5$
domain: $(-\infty, \infty)$
range: $(-\infty, 9]$

4.
$f(x) = 3x^2 - 6x + 1$
domain: $(-\infty, \infty)$
range: $[-2, \infty)$

5. -1 and 2
$f(x) = (x - 2)^2 (x + 1)^3$

6. -1 and 2
$f(x) = -(x - 2)^2 (x + 1)^2$

7. $-2, 1$, and 2
$f(x) = x^3 - x^2 - 4x + 4$

8. $-2, -1, 1$, and 2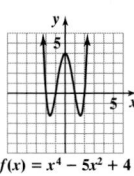
$f(x) = x^4 - 5x^2 + 4$

9. -1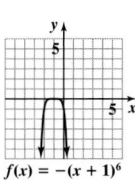
$f(x) = -(x + 1)^6$

10. $-\dfrac{1}{3}, \dfrac{1}{2}$, and 1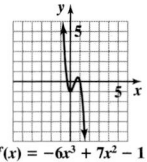
$f(x) = -6x^3 + 7x^2 - 1$

11. $-1, 0$, and 1
$f(x) = 2x^3 - 2x$

12. $0, 1 \pm 5i$
$f(x) = x^3 - 2x^2 + 26x$

13. $3, 1 \pm \sqrt{2}$
$f(x) = -x^3 + 5x^2 - 5x - 3$

14. $\{-2, 1\}$ **15.** $\left\{ \dfrac{1}{3}, \dfrac{1}{2}, 1 \right\}$ **16.** $\left\{ -\dfrac{1}{2}, \dfrac{2}{3}, \dfrac{7}{2} \right\}$ **17.** $\left\{ -10, -\dfrac{5}{2}, 10 \right\}$ **18.** $\{-3, 4, \pm i\}$ **19.** $\left\{ -3, \dfrac{1}{2}, 1 \pm \sqrt{3} \right\}$

20. 75 cabinets per day; \$1200 **21.** $-9, -9; 81$ **22.** 10 in.; 100 sq in. **23.** $2x^2 - x - 3 + \dfrac{x + 1}{3x^2 - 1}$ **24.** $2x^3 - 5x^2 - 3x + 6$

25. $f(x) = -2x^3 + 2x^2 - 2x + 2$ **26.** $f(x) = x^4 - 4x^3 + 13x^2 - 36x + 36$ **27.** yes

Section 3.5

Check Point Exercises

1. a. $\{x | x \neq 5\}$ **b.** $\{x | x \neq -5, x \neq 5\}$ **c.** all real numbers **2. a.** $x = 1, x = -1$ **b.** $x = -1$ **c.** none
3. a. $y = 3$ **b.** $y = 0$ **c.** none

4.
$g(x) = \dfrac{1}{x + 2} - 1$

5.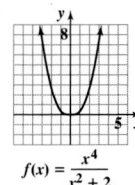
$f(x) = \dfrac{3x - 3}{x - 2}$

6.
$f(x) = \dfrac{2x^2}{x^2 - 9}$

7.
$f(x) = \dfrac{x^4}{x^2 + 2}$

8. $y = 2x - 1$ **9. a.** $C(x) = 500{,}000 + 400x$ **b.** $\overline{C}(x) = \dfrac{500{,}000 + 400x}{x}$ **c.** $\overline{C}(1000) = 900$: The average cost per wheelchair of producing

1000 wheelchairs per month is \$900.; $\overline{C}(10{,}000) = 450$: The average cost per wheelchair of producing 10,000 wheelchairs per month is \$450.;
$\overline{C}(100{,}000) = 405$: The average cost per wheelchair of producing 100,000 wheelchairs per month is \$405. **d.** $y = 400$; The cost per wheelchair
approaches \$400 as more wheelchairs are produced.

Exercise Set 3.5

1. $\{x | x \neq 4\}$ **3.** $\{x | x \neq 5, x \neq -4\}$ **5.** $\{x | x \neq 7, x \neq -7\}$ **7.** all real numbers **9.** $-\infty$ **11.** $-\infty$ **13.** 0 **15.** $+\infty$

17. $-\infty$ **19.** 1 **21.** $x = -4$ **23.** $x = 0, x = -4$ **25.** $x = -4$ **27.** no vertical asymptotes **29.** $y = 0$ **31.** $y = 4$

33. no horizontal asymptote **35.** $y = -\dfrac{2}{3}$

37.

$$g(x) = \frac{1}{x - 1}$$

39.

$$h(x) = \frac{1}{x} + 2$$

41.

$$g(x) = \frac{1}{x + 1} - 2$$

43.

$$g(x) = \frac{1}{(x + 2)^2}$$

45.

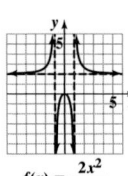

$$h(x) = \frac{1}{x^2} - 4$$

47.

$$h(x) = \frac{1}{(x - 3)^2} + 1$$

49.

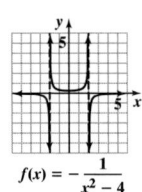

$$f(x) = \frac{4x}{x - 2}$$

51.

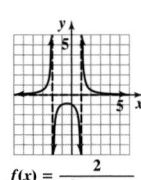

$$f(x) = \frac{2x}{x^2 - 4}$$

53.

$$f(x) = \frac{2x^2}{x^2 - 1}$$

55.

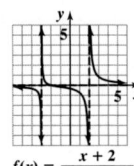

$$f(x) = \frac{-x}{x + 1}$$

57.

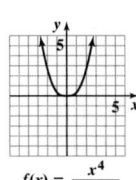

$$f(x) = -\frac{1}{x^2 - 4}$$

59.

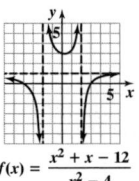

$$f(x) = \frac{2}{x^2 + x - 2}$$

61.

$$f(x) = \frac{2x^2}{x^2 + 4}$$

63.

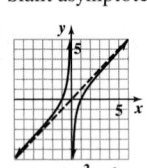

$$f(x) = \frac{x + 2}{x^2 + x - 6}$$

65.

$$f(x) = \frac{x^4}{x^2 + 2}$$

67.

$$f(x) = \frac{x^2 + x - 12}{x^2 - 4}$$

69.

$$f(x) = \frac{3x^2 + x - 4}{2x^2 - 5x}$$

71. a. Slant asymptote: $y = x$
b.

$$f(x) = \frac{x^2 - 1}{x}$$

73. a. Slant asymptote: $y = x$
b.

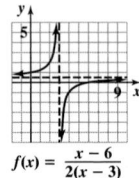

$$f(x) = \frac{x^2 + 1}{x}$$

75. a. Slant asymptote: $y = x + 4$
b.

$$f(x) = \frac{x^2 + x - 6}{x - 3}$$

77. a. Slant asymptote: $y = x - 2$ **79.**
b.

$$f(x) = \frac{x^3 + 1}{x^2 + 2x}$$

$$f(x) = \frac{x + 2}{2x(x - 2)}$$

81.

$$f(x) = \frac{x - 6}{2(x - 3)}$$

83.

$$f(x) = \frac{x - 2}{x + 2}$$

85. $f(x) = \frac{1}{x + 3} + 2$

$$g(x) = \frac{1}{x + 3} + 2$$

87. $f(x) = \frac{-1}{x - 2} + 3$

$$g(x) = \frac{-1}{x - 2} + 3$$

89. a. $C(x) = 100x + 100{,}000$ **b.** $\overline{C}(x) = \dfrac{100x + 100{,}000}{x}$ **c.** $\overline{C}(500) = 300$, when 500 bicycles are produced, it costs $300 to produce each bicycle; $\overline{C}(1000) = 200$, when 1000 bicycles are produced, it costs $200 to produce each bicycle; $\overline{C}(2000) = 150$, when 2000 bicycles are produced, it costs $150 to produce each bicycle; $\overline{C}(4000) = 125$, when 4000 bicycles are produced, it costs $125 to produce each bicycle. **d.** $y = 100$; The cost per bicycle approaches $100 as more bicycles are produced. **91. a.** 6.0 **b.** after 6 minutes; about 4.8 **c.** 6.5 **d.** $y = 6.5$; Over time, the pH level rises back to normal. **e.** It quickly drops below normal and then slowly begins to approach the normal level.

93. 90; An incidence ratio of 10 means 90% of the deaths are smoking related. **95.** $y = 100$; The percentage of deaths cannot exceed 100% as the incidence ratios increase. **97. a.** $f(x) = \dfrac{11x^2 + 40x + 1040}{12x^2 + 230x + 2190}$ **b.** 63% **c.** 64%; overestimates by 1% **d.** $y = \dfrac{11}{12}$; 92%; Answers may vary.

109.

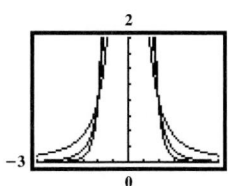

The graph approaches the horizontal asymptote faster and the vertical asymptote slower as n increases.

111. a.

b. The graph increases and reaches a maximum of about 356 arrests per 100,000 drivers at age 25.
c. at age 25, about 356 arrests

113. does not make sense **115.** does not make sense **117.** true **119.** true **124.** $\left\{-3, \dfrac{5}{2}\right\}$ **125.** $\{-2. -1, 2\}$ **126.** $\dfrac{-x - 5}{x + 3}$ or $-\dfrac{x + 5}{x + 3}$

Section 3.6

Check Point Exercises

1. $\{x | x < -4 \text{ or } x > 5\}$ or $(-\infty, -4) \cup (5, \infty)$

2. $\{x | x \le -3 \text{ or } -1 \le x \le 1\}$ or $(-\infty, -3] \cup [-1, 1]$

3. $\{x | x < -1 \text{ or } x \ge 1\}$ or $(-\infty, -1) \cup [1, \infty)$

4. between 1 and 4 seconds, excluding $t = 1$ and $t = 4$

Exercise Set 3.6

1. $(-\infty, -2)$ or $(4, \infty)$

3. $[-3, 7]$

5. $(-\infty, 1)$ or $(4, \infty)$

7. $(-\infty, -4)$ or $(-1, \infty)$

9. \varnothing

11. $\left[-4, \dfrac{2}{3}\right]$

13. $\left(-3, \dfrac{5}{2}\right)$

15. $\left(-1, -\dfrac{3}{4}\right)$

17. $\left[-2, \dfrac{1}{3}\right]$

19. $(-\infty, 0]$ or $[4, \infty)$

21. $\left(-\infty, -\dfrac{3}{2}\right)$ or $(0, \infty)$

23. $[0, 1]$

25. $[2 - \sqrt{2}, 2 + \sqrt{2}]$

27. \varnothing

29. $[1, 2]$ or $[3, \infty)$

31. $[0, 3] \cup [5, \infty)$

33. $(-\infty, 2) \cup \left(2, \dfrac{7}{2}\right)$

35. $[-2, -1]$ or $[1, \infty)$

37. $(-\infty, -3)$

39. $(-1, \infty)$

41. $\{0\}$ or $[9, \infty)$

43. $(-\infty, -3)$ or $(4, \infty)$

45. $(-4, -3)$

47. $[2, 4)$

49. $\left(-\infty, -\dfrac{4}{3}\right)$ or $[2, \infty)$

51. $(-\infty, 0)$ or $(3, \infty)$

53. $(-\infty, -4] \cup (-2, 1]$

55. $(-\infty, -5)$ or $(-3, \infty)$

57. $\left(-\infty, \dfrac{1}{2}\right)$ or $\left[\dfrac{7}{5}, \infty\right)$

59. $(-\infty, -6]$ or $(-2, \infty)$

61. $\left(-\infty, \dfrac{1}{2}\right] \cup [2, \infty)$

63. $(-\infty, -1) \cup [1, \infty)$

65. $(-\infty, -8) \cup (-6, 4) \cup (6, \infty)$

67. $(-3, 2)$

69. $(-\infty, -1) \cup (1, 2) \cup (3, \infty)$

71. $\left[-6, -\dfrac{1}{2}\right] \cup [1, \infty)$ **73.** $(-\infty, -2) \cup [-1, 2)$ **75.** between 0 and $\dfrac{1}{2}$ second **77. a.** dry: 160 ft; wet: 185 ft **b.** dry pavement: graph (b); wet pavement: graph (a) **c.** extremely well; Function values and data are identical **d.** speeds exceeding 76 miles per hour; points on (b) to the right of (76, 540)

79. The sides (in feet) are in $(0, 6]$ or $[19, 25)$. **87.** $\left[-3, \frac{1}{2}\right]$ **89.** $(1, 4]$ **91.** $(-4, -1)\cup[2, \infty)$ **93. a.** $f(x) = 0.1375x^2 - 0.7x + 37.8$

b. speeds exceeding 52 miles per hour **95.** does not make sense **97.** does not make sense **99.** false **101.** true

103. Answers may vary. One possible solution is $\dfrac{x - 3}{x + 4} \geq 0$. **105.** $\{2\}$ **107.** $(-\infty, 2)\cup(2, \infty)$

109.
$$27 - 3x^2 \geq 0$$
$$3x^2 \leq 27$$
$$x^2 \leq 9$$
$$-3 \leq x \leq 3$$

110. a. 16 **b.** $y = 16x^2$ **c.** 400 **111. a.** 96 **b.** $y = \dfrac{96}{x}$ **c.** 32 **112.** 8

Section 3.7

Check Point Exercises

1. 66 gal **2.** 9375 lb **3.** 512 cycles per second **4.** 24 min **5.** 96π cubic feet

Exercise Set 3.7

1. 156 **3.** 30 **5.** $\dfrac{5}{6}$ **7.** 240 **9.** 50 **11.** $x = kyz$; $y = \dfrac{x}{kz}$ **13.** $x = \dfrac{kz^3}{y}$; $y = \dfrac{kz^3}{x}$ **15.** $x = \dfrac{kyz}{\sqrt{w}}$; $y = \dfrac{x\sqrt{w}}{kz}$

17. $x = kz(y + w)$; $y = \dfrac{x - kzw}{kz}$ **19.** $x = \dfrac{kz}{y - w}$; $y = \dfrac{xw + kz}{x}$ **21.** 5.4 ft **23.** 80 in. **25.** about 607 lb **27.** 32°

29. 90 milliroentgens per hour **31.** This person has a BMI of 24.4 and is not overweight. **33.** 1800 Btu per hour

35. $\dfrac{1}{4}$ of what it was originally **37. a.** $C = \dfrac{kP_1P_2}{d^2}$ **b.** $k \approx 0.02$; $C = \dfrac{0.02\,P_1P_2}{d^2}$ **c.** 17,875 daily phone calls

39. a. **b.** Current varies inversely as resistance. **c.** $R = \dfrac{6}{I}$

49. does not make sense **51.** makes sense **53.** The destructive power is four times as much. **55.** Reduce the resistance by a factor of $\dfrac{1}{3}$.

58. **59.** **60.**

Chapter 3 Review Exercises

1. **2.** **3.** **4.**

axis of symmetry; $x = -1$ axis of symmetry: $x = -4$ axis of symmetry: $x = 1$ axis of symmetry: $x = 1$
domain: $(-\infty, \infty)$; range: $(-\infty, 4]$ domain: $(-\infty, \infty)$; range: $[-2, \infty)$ domain: $(-\infty, \infty)$; range: $(-\infty, 4]$ domain: $(-\infty, \infty)$; range: $[-8, \infty)$
5. a. maximum is -57 at $x = 7$ **b.** domain: $(-\infty, \infty)$; range: $(-\infty, -57]$ **6. a.** minimum is 685 at $x = -3$ **b.** domain: $(-\infty, \infty)$; range: $[685, \infty)$
7. a. 16 ft; 20 yd **b.** 6 ft **c.** 45.3 yd **d.** **8.** 250 yd by 500 yd; 125,000 sq yard **9.** -7 and 7; -49

10. c **11.** b **12.** a **13.** d **14.** No; the graph falls to the right, so eventually there would be a negative number of thefts, which is not possible.

15. The graph falls to the right; eventually the elk population will be extinct.

16. $x = 1$, multiplicity 1, crosses; $x = -2$, multiplicity 2, touches; $x = -5$, multiplicity 3, crosses

17. $x = -5$, multiplicity 1, crosses; $x = 5$, multiplicity 2, touches

18. $f(1)$ is negative and $f(2)$ is positive, so by the Intermediate Value Theorem, f has a real zero between 1 and 2.

19. a. The graph falls to the left and rises to the right.
b. no symmetry
c.

$f(x) = x^3 - x^2 - 9x + 9$

20. a. The graph rises to the left and falls to the right.
b. origin symmetry
c.
$f(x) = 4x - x^3$

21. a. The graph falls to the left and rises to the right.
b. no symmetry
c.
$f(x) = 2x^3 + 3x^2 - 8x - 12$

22. a. The graph falls to the left and to the right.
b. y-axis symmetry
c.

$f(x) = -x^4 + 25x^2$

23. a. The graph falls to the left and to the right.
b. no symmetry
c.
$f(x) = -x^4 + 6x^3 - 9x^2$

24. a. The graph rises to the left and to the right.
b. no symmetry
c.
$f(x) = 3x^4 - 15x^3$

25.

$f(x) = 2x^2 (x - 1)^3 (x + 2)$

26.

$f(x) = -x^3 (x + 4)^2 (x - 1)$

27. $4x^2 - 7x + 5 - \dfrac{4}{x + 1}$

28. $2x^2 - 4x + 1 - \dfrac{10}{5x - 3}$

29. $2x^2 + 3x - 1$ **30.** $3x^3 - 4x^2 + 7$

31. $3x^3 + 6x^2 + 10x + 10 + \dfrac{20}{x - 2}$ **32.** -5697

33. $2, \dfrac{1}{2}, -3$ **34.** $\{4, -2\pm\sqrt{5}\}$ **35.** $\pm 1, \pm 5$ **36.** $\pm 1, \pm 2, \pm 4, \pm 8, \pm\dfrac{8}{3}, \pm\dfrac{4}{3}, \pm\dfrac{2}{3}, \pm\dfrac{1}{3}$ **37.** 2 or 0 positive real zeros; no negative real zeros

38. 3 or 1 positive real zeros; 2 or 0 negative real zeros **39.** No sign variations exist for either $f(x)$ or $f(-x)$, so no real roots exist.

40. a. $\pm 1, \pm 2, \pm 4$ **b.** 1 positive real zero; 2 or no negative real zeros **c.** -2 or 1 **d.** $-2, 1$

41. a. $\pm 1, \pm\dfrac{1}{2}, \pm\dfrac{1}{3}, \pm\dfrac{1}{6}$ **b.** 2 or 0 positive real zeros; 1 negative real zero **c.** $-1, \dfrac{1}{3}$, or $\dfrac{1}{2}$ **d.** $-1, \dfrac{1}{3}, \dfrac{1}{2}$

42. a. $\pm 1, \pm 3, \pm 5, \pm 15, \pm\dfrac{1}{2}, \pm\dfrac{1}{4}, \pm\dfrac{1}{8}, \pm\dfrac{3}{2}, \pm\dfrac{3}{4}, \pm\dfrac{3}{8}, \pm\dfrac{5}{2}, \pm\dfrac{5}{4}, \pm\dfrac{5}{8}, \pm\dfrac{15}{2}, \pm\dfrac{15}{4}, \pm\dfrac{15}{8}$ **b.** 3 or 1 positive real solutions; no negative real solutions

c. $\dfrac{1}{2}, \dfrac{3}{2}$, or $\dfrac{5}{2}$ **d.** $\left\{\dfrac{1}{2}, \dfrac{3}{2}, \dfrac{5}{2}\right\}$ **43. a.** $\pm 1, \pm\dfrac{1}{2}$ **b.** 2 or 0 positive real solutions; 1 negative solution **c.** $\dfrac{1}{2}$ **d.** $\left\{\dfrac{1}{2}, \dfrac{-5 - \sqrt{29}}{2}, \dfrac{-5 + \sqrt{29}}{2}\right\}$

44. a. $\pm 1, \pm 2, \pm 3, \pm 6$ **b.** 2 or zero positive real solutions; 2 or zero negative real solutions **c.** $-2, -1, 1$, or 3 **d.** $\{-2, -1, 1, 3\}$

45. a. $\pm 1, \pm 2, \pm\dfrac{1}{2}, \pm\dfrac{1}{4}$ **b.** 1 positive real root; 1 negative real root **c.** $-\dfrac{1}{2}$ or $\dfrac{1}{2}$ **d.** $\left\{-\dfrac{1}{2}, \dfrac{1}{2}, i\sqrt{2}, -i\sqrt{2}\right\}$

46. a. $\pm 1, \pm 2, \pm 4, \pm\dfrac{1}{2}$ **b.** 2 or no positive zeros; 2 or no negative zeros **c.** $-2, -1, \dfrac{1}{2}$, or 2 **d.** $\left\{-2, -1, \dfrac{1}{2}, 2\right\}$

47. $f(x) = x^3 - 6x^2 + 21x - 26$ **48.** $f(x) = 2x^4 + 12x^3 + 20x^2 + 12x + 18$ **49.** $-2, \dfrac{1}{2}, \pm i$; $f(x) = (x - i)(x + i)(x + 2)(2x - 1)$

50. $-1, 4$; $g(x) = (x + 1)^2(x - 4)^2$ **51.** 4 real zeros, one with multiplicity two **52.** 3 real zeros; 2 nonreal complex zeros

53. 2 real zeros, one with multiplicity two; 2 nonreal complex zeros **54.** 1 real zero; 4 nonreal complex zeros

55.

$g(x) = \dfrac{1}{(x + 2)^2} - 1$

56.

$h(x) = \dfrac{1}{x - 1} + 3$

57. Vertical asymptote: $x = 3$ and $x = -3$ horizontal asymptote: $y = 0$
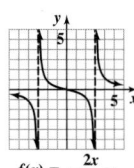
$f(x) = \dfrac{2x}{x^2 - 9}$

58. Vertical asymptote: $x = -3$ horizontal asymptote: $y = 2$

$f(x) = \dfrac{2x - 4}{x + 3}$

59. Vertical asymptotes: $x = 3, -2$ horizontal asymptote: $y = 1$

$h(x) = \dfrac{x^2 - 3x - 4}{x^2 - x - 6}$

60. Vertical asymptote: $x = -2$
horizontal asymptote: $y = 1$

$r(x) = \dfrac{x^2 + 4x + 3}{(x + 2)^2}$

61. Vertical asymptote: $x = -1$
no horizontal asymptote
slant asymptote: $y = x - 1$

$y = \dfrac{x^2}{x + 1}$

62. Vertical asymptote: $x = 3$
no horizontal asymptote
slant asymptote: $y = x + 5$

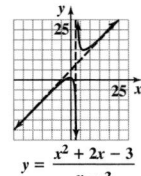

$y = \dfrac{x^2 + 2x - 3}{x - 3}$

63. No vertical asymptote
no horizontal asymptote
slant asymptote: $y = -2x$

$f(x) = \dfrac{-2x^3}{x^2 + 1}$

64. Vertical asymptote: $x = \dfrac{3}{2}$
no horizontal asymptote
slant asymptote: $y = 2x - 5$

$g(x) = \dfrac{4x^2 - 16x + 16}{2x - 3}$

65. a. $C(x) = 25x + 50{,}000$

b. $\overline{C}(x) = \dfrac{25x + 50{,}000}{x}$

c. $\overline{C}(50) = 1025$, when 50 calculators are manufactured, it costs \$1025 to manufacture each; $\overline{C}(100) = 525$, when 100 calculators are manufactured, it costs \$525 to manufacture each; $\overline{C}(1000) = 75$, when 1000 calculators are manufactured, it costs \$75 to manufacture each; $\overline{C}(100{,}000) = 25.5$, when 100,000 calculators are manufactured, it costs \$25.50 to manufacture each.

d. $y = 25$; costs will approach \$25.

66. $y = 3000$; The number of fish in the pond approaches 3000.

67. $y = 0$; As the number of years of education increases the percentage rate of unemployment approaches zero.

68. a. $P(x) = 3.06x + 235$ **b.** $R(x) = \dfrac{1.58x + 114.4}{3.06x + 235}$ **c.** $y = 0.52$; Over time the percentage of men in the U.S. population will approach 52%.

69. $\left(-3, \dfrac{1}{2}\right)$

70. $(-\infty, -4]\cup\left[-\dfrac{1}{2}, \infty\right)$

71. $(-3, 0)\cup(1, \infty)$

72. $(-\infty, -2)\cup(6, \infty)$

73. $[-1, 1)\cup[2, \infty)$

74. $(-\infty, 4)\cup\left[\dfrac{23}{4}, \infty\right)$

75. a. 261 ft; overestimates by 1 ft **b.** speeds exceeding 40 miles per hour **76.** from 1 to 2 sec **77.** 134.4 cm^3 **78.** 1600 ft

79. 440 vibrations per second **80.** 112 decibels **81.** 16 hr **82.** 800 ft^3 **83. a.** $L = \dfrac{1890}{R}$ **b.** an approximate model **c.** 70 yr

Chapter 3 Test

1.

$f(x) = (x + 1)^2 + 4$

axis of symmetry: $x = -1$
domain: $(-\infty, \infty)$; range: $[4, \infty)$

2.

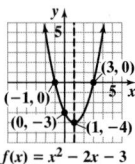

$f(x) = x^2 - 2x - 3$

axis of symmetry: $x = 1$
domain: $(-\infty, \infty)$; range: $[-4, \infty)$

3. a. maximum of 2 at $x = 3$;
b. domain: $(-\infty, \infty)$; range: $(-\infty, 2]$
4. 23 computers;
maximum daily profit $=$ \$16,900
5. 7 and 7; 49

6. a. $5, 2, -2$
b.

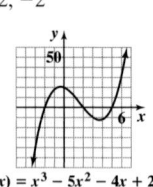

$f(x) = x^3 - 5x^2 - 4x + 20$

7. Since the degree of the polynomial is odd and the leading coefficient is positive, the graph of f should fall to the left and rise to the right. The x-intercepts should be -1, 0, and 1.

8. a. 2 **b.** $\dfrac{1}{2}, \dfrac{2}{3}$ **9.** $\pm 1, \pm 2, \pm 3, \pm 6, \pm\dfrac{1}{2}, \pm\dfrac{3}{2}$

10. 3 or 1 positive real zeros; no negative real zeros.

11. $\{-3, -3 - \sqrt{11}, -3 + \sqrt{11}\}$ **12. a.** $\pm 1, \pm 3, \pm 5, \pm 15, \pm\dfrac{1}{2}, \pm\dfrac{3}{2}, \pm\dfrac{5}{2}, \pm\dfrac{15}{2}$ **b.** $-\sqrt{5}, -1, \dfrac{3}{2}$, and $\sqrt{5}$ **13.** $(x - 1)(x + 2)^2$

14. $f(x) = 2x^4 - 2$ **15.** -1 and $\dfrac{2}{3}$ **16.** $(-\infty, -3)\cup(-3, \infty)$ **17.** $(-\infty, 1)\cup(1, \infty)$

$f(x) = -3x^3 - 4x^2 + x + 2$

$f(x) = \dfrac{1}{(x+3)^2}$

$f(x) = \dfrac{1}{x-1} + 2$

18. domain: $\{x | x \neq 4, x \neq -4\}$ **19.** domain: $\{x | x \neq 2\}$ **20.** domain: $\{x | x \neq -3, x \neq 1\}$ **21.** domain: all real numbers

$f(x) = \dfrac{x}{x^2 - 16}$

$f(x) = \dfrac{x^2 - 9}{x - 2}$

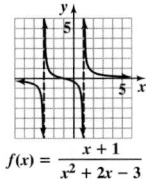

$f(x) = \dfrac{x+1}{x^2 + 2x - 3}$

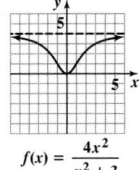

$f(x) = \dfrac{4x^2}{x^2 + 3}$

22. a. $\overline{C}(x) = \dfrac{300,000 + 10x}{x}$ **b.** $y = 10$; As the number of satellite radio players increases, the average cost approaches \$10.

23. $(-3, 4)$ **24.** $(-\infty, 3)\cup[10, \infty)$ **25.** 45 foot-candles

Cumulative Review Exercises (Chapters 1–3)

1. domain: $(-2, 2)$; range: $[0, \infty)$ **2.** -1 and 1, both of multiplicity 2 **3.** 0 **4.** 3 **5.** $x \to -2^+$; $x \to 2^-$

6.

$g(x) = f(x + 2) + 1$

7. $\{2, -1\}$ **8.** $\left\{ \dfrac{5 + \sqrt{13}}{6}, \dfrac{5 - \sqrt{13}}{6} \right\}$ **9.** $\left\{ \dfrac{1}{3}, -\dfrac{2}{3} \right\}$ **10.** $\{-3, -1, 2\}$ **11.** $(-\infty, 1)$ or $(4, \infty)$

12. $(-\infty, -1)$ or $\left(\dfrac{5}{3}, \infty \right)$ **13.**

$f(x) = x^3 - 4x^2 - x + 4$

14.

$f(x) = x^2 + 2x - 8$

15.

$f(x) = x^2(x - 3)$

16.

$f(x) = \dfrac{x-1}{x-2}$

17.

18.

$x^2 + y^2 - 2x + 4y - 4 = 0$

19. $(f \circ g)(x) = 32x^2 - 20x + 2$ **20.** $4x + 2h - 1$

CHAPTER 4

Section 4.1

Check Point Exercises

1. approximately \$160; overestimates by \$11

2.

$f(x) = 3^x$

3.

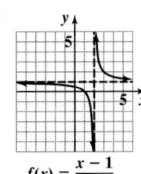

$f(x) = \left(\dfrac{1}{3} \right)^x$

4.

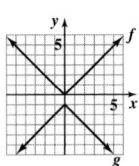

$f(x) = 3^x$
$g(x) = 3^{x-1}$

5.

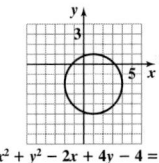

$f(x) = 2^x$
$g(x) = 2^x + 1$

6. approximately 4446 **7. a.** \$14,859.47 **b.** \$14,918.25

Exercise Set 4.1

1. 10.556 **3.** 11.665 **5.** 0.125 **7.** 9.974 **9.** 0.387

11.

$f(x) = 4^x$

13.

$g(x) = \left(\dfrac{3}{2}\right)^x$

15.

$h(x) = \left(\dfrac{1}{2}\right)^x$

17.

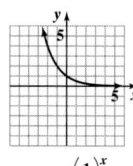

$f(x) = (0.6)^x$

19. $H(x) = -3^{-x}$
21. $F(x) = -3^x$
23. $h(x) = 3^x - 1$

25.

$f(x) = 2^x$
$g(x) = 2^{x+1}$

asymptote: $y = 0$
domain: $(-\infty, \infty)$
range: $(0, \infty)$

27.

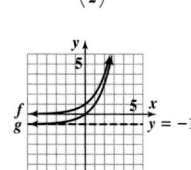

$f(x) = 2^x$
$g(x) = 2^x - 1$

asymptote: $y = -1$
domain: $(-\infty, \infty)$
range: $(-1, \infty)$

29.

$f(x) = 2^x$
$h(x) = 2^{x+1} - 1$

asymptote: $y = -1$
domain: $(-\infty, \infty)$
range: $(-1, \infty)$

31.

$f(x) = 2^x$
$g(x) = -2^x$

asymptote: $y = 0$
domain: $(-\infty, \infty)$
range: $(-\infty, 0)$

33.

$f(x) = 2^x$
$g(x) = 2 \cdot 2^x$

asymptote: $y = 0$
domain: $(-\infty, \infty)$
range: $(0, \infty)$

35.

$g(x) = e^{x-1}$

asymptote: $y = 0$
domain: $(-\infty, \infty)$
range: $(0, \infty)$

37.

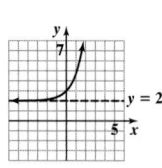

$g(x) = e^x + 2$

asymptote: $y = 2$
domain: $(-\infty, \infty)$
range: $(2, \infty)$

39.

$h(x) = e^{x-1} + 2$

asymptote: $y = 2$
domain: $(-\infty, \infty)$
range: $(2, \infty)$

41.

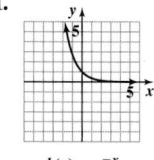

$h(x) = e^{-x}$

asymptote: $y = 0$
domain: $(-\infty, \infty)$
range: $(0, \infty)$

43.

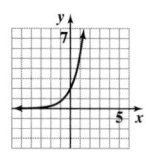

$g(x) = 2e^x$

asymptote: $y = 0$
domain: $(-\infty, \infty)$
range: $(0, \infty)$

45.

$h(x) = e^{2x} + 1$

asymptote: $y = 1$
domain: $(-\infty, \infty)$
range: $(1, \infty)$

47.

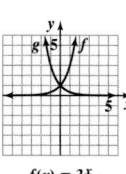

$f(x) = 3^x$
$g(x) = 3^{-x}$

asymptote of f: $y = 0$
asymptote of g: $y = 0$

49.

$f(x) = 3^x$
$g(x) = \dfrac{1}{3} \cdot 3^x$

asymptote of f: $y = 0$
asymptote of g: $y = 0$

51.

$f(x) = \left(\dfrac{1}{2}\right)^x$

$g(x) = \left(\dfrac{1}{2}\right)^{x-1} + 1$

asymptote of f: $y = 0$
asymptote of g: $y = 1$

53. a. \$13,116.51
b. \$13,140.67
c. \$13,157.04
d. \$13,165.31
55. 7% compounded monthly

57. $(0, 1)$

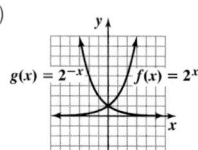

$g(x) = 2^{-x}$ $f(x) = 2^x$

59.

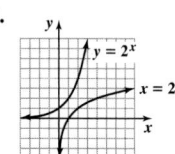

$y = 2^x$
$x = 2^y$

61. $y = 4^x$ **63.** $y = -e^x$ **65. a.** 574 million **b.** 1148 million **c.** 2295 million **d.** 4590 million **e.** It appears to double.
67. \$832,744 **69.** 3.249009585; 3.317278183; 3.321880096; 3.321995226; 3.321997068; $2^{\sqrt{3}} \approx 3.321997085$; The closer the exponent is to $\sqrt{3}$,
the closer the value is to $2^{\sqrt{3}}$. **71. a.** approximately 8.9 million words **b.** approximately 10.4 million words **c.** linear model
73. a. 100% **b.** $\approx 68.5\%$ **c.** $\approx 30.8\%$ **d.** $\approx 20\%$ **75.** the function g

81. a. $A = 10,000\left(1 + \dfrac{0.05}{4}\right)^{4t}$; $A = 10,000\left(1 + \dfrac{0.045}{12}\right)^{12t}$

b.

5% interest compounded quarterly

83. does not make sense **85.** does not make sense **87.** false **89.** false

91. $y = 3^x$ is (d); $y = 5^x$ is (c); $y = \left(\dfrac{1}{3}\right)^x$ is (a); $y = \left(\dfrac{1}{5}\right)^x$ is (b).

93. a. $\cosh(-x) = \dfrac{e^{-x} + e^{-(-x)}}{2} = \dfrac{e^{-x} + e^{x}}{2} = \dfrac{e^{x} + e^{-x}}{2} = \cosh x$ 　　**c.** $\left(\dfrac{e^{x} + e^{-x}}{2}\right)^{2} - \left(\dfrac{e^{x} - e^{-x}}{2}\right)^{2} \overset{?}{=} 1$

b. $\sinh(-x) = \dfrac{e^{-x} - e^{-(-x)}}{2} = \dfrac{e^{-x} - e^{x}}{2} = -\dfrac{e^{x} - e^{-x}}{2} = -\sinh x$ 　　$\dfrac{e^{2x} + 2 + e^{-2x}}{4} - \dfrac{e^{2x} - 2 + e^{-2x}}{4} \overset{?}{=} 1$

$$\dfrac{e^{2x} + 2 + e^{-2x} - e^{2x} + 2 - e^{-2x}}{4} \overset{?}{=} 1$$

$$\dfrac{4}{4} \overset{?}{=} 1$$

$$1 = 1$$

94. We don't know how to solve $x = 2^{y}$ for y. 　　**95.** $\dfrac{1}{2}$ 　　**96.** $(-\infty, 3) \cup (3, \infty)$

Section 4.2

Check Point Exercises

1. a. $7^{3} = x$ 　**b.** $b^{2} = 25$ 　**c.** $4^{y} = 26$ 　**2. a.** $5 = \log_{2} x$ 　**b.** $3 = \log_{b} 27$ 　**c.** $y = \log_{e} 33$ 　**3. a.** 2 　**b.** -3 　**c.** $\dfrac{1}{2}$ 　**d.** $\dfrac{1}{7}$

4. a. 1 　**b.** 0 　**5. a.** 8 　**b.** 17 　**6.**

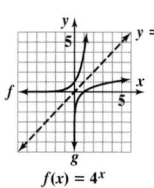

$f(x) = 3^{x}$
$g(x) = \log_{3} x$

7. $(5, \infty)$ 　**8.** 80% 　**9.** 4.0 　**10. a.** $(-\infty, 4)$ 　**b.** $(-\infty, 0) \cup (0, \infty)$

11. 34°; quite well

Exercise Set 4.2

1. $2^{4} = 16$ 　**3.** $3^{2} = x$ 　**5.** $b^{5} = 32$ 　**7.** $6^{y} = 216$ 　**9.** $\log_{2} 8 = 3$ 　**11.** $\log_{2} \dfrac{1}{16} = -4$ 　**13.** $\log_{8} 2 = \dfrac{1}{3}$ 　**15.** $\log_{13} x = 2$

17. $\log_{b} 1000 = 3$ 　**19.** $\log_{7} 200 = y$ 　**21.** 2 　**23.** 6 　**25.** -1 　**27.** -3 　**29.** $\dfrac{1}{2}$ 　**31.** $-\dfrac{1}{2}$ 　**33.** $\dfrac{1}{2}$ 　**35.** 1 　**37.** 0 　**39.** 7 　**41.** 19

43.

$f(x) = 4^{x}$
$g(x) = \log_{4} x$

45.

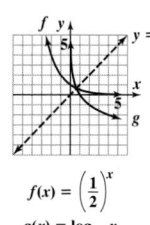

$f(x) = \left(\dfrac{1}{2}\right)^{x}$
$g(x) = \log_{1/2} x$

47. $H(x) = 1 - \log_{3} x$ 　**49.** $h(x) = \log_{3} x - 1$ 　**51.** $g(x) = \log_{3}(x - 1)$

53.

$f(x) = \log_{2} x$
$g(x) = \log_{2}(x+1)$
vertical asymptote: $x = -1$
domain: $(-1, \infty)$
range: $(-\infty, \infty)$

55.

$f(x) = \log_{2} x$
$h(x) = 1 + \log_{2} x$
vertical asymptote: $x = 0$
domain: $(0, \infty)$
range: $(-\infty, \infty)$

57.

$f(x) = \log_{2} x$
$g(x) = \dfrac{1}{2} \log_{2} x$
vertical asymptote: $x = 0$
domain: $(0, \infty)$
range: $(-\infty, \infty)$

59.

$g(x) = \log(x - 1)$
asymptote: $x = 1$
domain: $(1, \infty)$
range: $(-\infty, \infty)$

61.

$h(x) = \log x - 1$
asymptote: $x = 0$
domain: $(0, \infty)$
range: $(-\infty, \infty)$

63.

$g(x) = 1 - \log x$
asymptote: $x = 0$
domain: $(0, \infty)$
range: $(-\infty, \infty)$

65.

$g(x) = \ln(x + 2)$
asymptote: $x = -2$
domain: $(-2, \infty)$
range: $(-\infty, \infty)$

67.

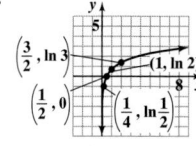

$h(x) = \ln(2x)$
asymptote: $x = 0$
domain: $(0, \infty)$
range: $(-\infty, \infty)$

69.

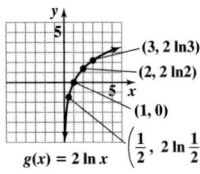

asymptote: $x = 0$
domain: $(0, \infty)$
range: $(-\infty, \infty)$

71.

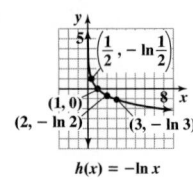

asymptote: $x = 0$
domain: $(0, \infty)$
range: $(-\infty, \infty)$

73.

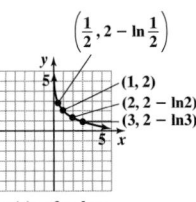

asymptote: $x = 0$
domain: $(0, \infty)$
range: $(-\infty, \infty)$

75. $(-4, \infty)$ **77.** $(-\infty, 2)$ **79.** $(-\infty, 2) \cup (2, \infty)$ **81.** 2 **83.** 7 **85.** 33 **87.** 0 **89.** 6 **91.** -6 **93.** 125 **95.** $9x$

97. $5x^2$ **99.** \sqrt{x} **101.** $3^2 = x - 1; \{10\}$ **103.** $4^{-3} = x; \left\{\dfrac{1}{64}\right\}$ **105.** 0 **107.** 2 **109.** $(-\infty, -1) \cup (2, \infty)$ **111.** $(-\infty, -1) \cup (5, \infty)$

113. 95.4% **115. a.** 26.4%; underestimates by 1% **b.** 25.2% **117.** ≈ 188 db; yes

119. a. 88 **129.** **131.**

b. 71.5; 63.9; 58.8; 55; 52; 49.5

c.

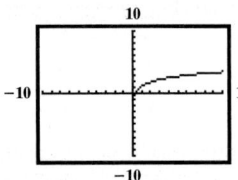

Material retention decreases
as time passes.

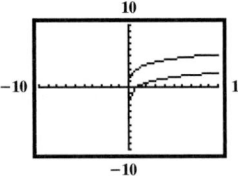

$g(x)$ is $f(x)$ shifted upward
3 units.

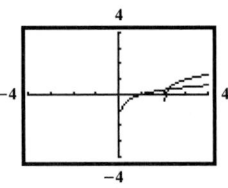

$g(x)$ is $f(x)$ shifted right 2 units
and upward 1 unit.

133. a.

b.

c.

d. They are the same.
$\log_b M + \log_b N$
e. the sum of the logarithms
of its factors

135. makes sense **137.** makes sense **139.** false **141.** false **143.** $\dfrac{4}{5}$ **145.** $\log_3 40 > \log_4 60$

147. a. 5 **b.** 5 **c.** $\log_2 (8 \cdot 4) = \log_2 8 + \log_2 2$ **148. a.** 4 **b.** 4 **c.** $\log_2 \left(\dfrac{32}{2}\right) = \log_2 32 - \log_2 2$

149. a. 4 **b.** 4 **c.** $\log_3 9^2 = 2\log_3 9$

Section 4.3

Check Point Exercises

1. a. $\log_6 7 + \log_6 11$ **b.** $2 + \log x$ **2. a.** $\log_8 23 - \log_8 x$ **b.** $5 - \ln 11$ **3. a.** $9 \log_6 3$ **b.** $\dfrac{1}{3} \ln x$ **c.** $2 \log(x + 4)$

4. a. $4 \log_b x + \dfrac{1}{3} \log_b y$ **b.** $\dfrac{1}{2} \log_5 x - 2 - 3 \log_5 y$ **5. a.** $\log 100 = 2$ **b.** $\log \dfrac{7x + 6}{x}$ **6. a.** $\ln x^2 \sqrt[3]{x + 5}$ **b.** $\log \dfrac{(x - 3)^2}{x}$

c. $\log_b \dfrac{\sqrt[4]{x}}{25 y^{10}}$ **7.** 4.02 **8.** 4.02

Exercise Set 4.3

1. $\log_5 7 + \log_5 3$ **3.** $1 + \log_7 x$ **5.** $3 + \log x$ **7.** $1 - \log_7 x$ **9.** $\log x - 2$ **11.** $3 - \log_4 y$ **13.** $2 - \ln 5$ **15.** $3 \log_b x$

17. $-6 \log N$ **19.** $\dfrac{1}{5} \ln x$ **21.** $2 \log_b x + \log_b y$ **23.** $\dfrac{1}{2} \log_4 x - 3$ **25.** $2 - \dfrac{1}{2} \log_6(x + 1)$ **27.** $2 \log_b x + \log_b y - 2 \log_b z$

29. $1 + \dfrac{1}{2} \log x$ **31.** $\dfrac{1}{3} \log x - \dfrac{1}{3} \log y$ **33.** $\dfrac{1}{2} \log_b x + 3 \log_b y - 3 \log_b z$ **35.** $\dfrac{2}{3} \log_5 x + \dfrac{1}{3} \log_5 y - \dfrac{2}{3}$ **37.** $3 \ln x + \dfrac{1}{2} \ln(x^2 + 1) - 4 \ln(x + 1)$

39. $1 + 2 \log x + \dfrac{1}{3} \log(1 - x) - \log 7 - 2 \log(x + 1)$ **41.** 1 **43.** $\ln(7x)$ **45.** 5 **47.** $\log \left(\dfrac{2x + 5}{x}\right)$ **49.** $\log(xy^3)$

51. $\ln(x^{1/2}y)$ or $\ln(y\sqrt{x})$ **53.** $\log_b(x^2y^3)$ **55.** $\ln\left(\dfrac{x^5}{y^2}\right)$ **57.** $\ln\left(\dfrac{x^3}{y^{1/3}}\right)$ or $\ln\left(\dfrac{x^3}{\sqrt[3]{y}}\right)$ **59.** $\ln\dfrac{(x+6)^4}{x^3}$ **61.** $\ln\left(\dfrac{x^3y^5}{z^6}\right)$ **63.** $\log\sqrt{xy}$

65. $\log_5\left(\dfrac{\sqrt{xy}}{(x+1)^2}\right)$ **67.** $\ln\sqrt[3]{\dfrac{(x+5)^2}{x(x^2-4)}}$ **69.** $\log\dfrac{x(x^2-1)}{7(x+1)} = \log\dfrac{x(x-1)}{7}$ **71.** 1.5937 **73.** 1.6944 **75.** -1.2304 **77.** 3.6193

79. **81.**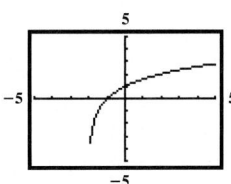

83. $C - A$ **85.** $3A$ **87.** $\dfrac{1}{2}A - \dfrac{3}{2}C$ **89.** false; $\ln e = 1$ **91.** false; $\log_4(2x)^3 = 3\log_4(2x)$ **93.** true **95.** true

97. false; $\log(x+3) - \log(2x) = \log\left(\dfrac{x+3}{2x}\right)$ **99.** true **101.** true **103. a.** $D = 10\log\dfrac{I}{I_0}$ **b.** 20 decibels louder

113. a. **b.** 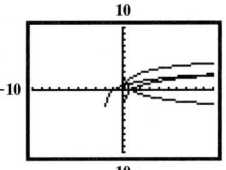 $y = 2 + \log_3 x$ shifts the graph of $y = \log_3 x$ two units upward; $y = \log_3(x+2)$ shifts the graph of $y = \log_3 x$ two units left; $y = -\log_3 x$ reflects the graph of $y = \log_3 x$ about the x-axis.

115. 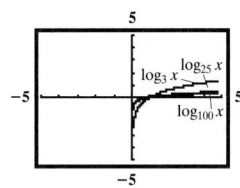 **a.** top graph: $y = \log_{100} x$; bottom graph: $y = \log_3 x$
b. top graph: $y = \log_3 x$; bottom graph: $y = \log_{100} x$
c. The graph of the equation with the largest b will be on the top in the interval $(0, 1)$ and on the bottom in the interval $(1, \infty)$.

121. makes sense **123.** makes sense **125.** true **127.** false **129.** $\log e = \log_{10} e = \dfrac{\ln e}{\ln 10} = \dfrac{1}{\ln 10}$ **131.** $4x^3$ **133.** $x = \dfrac{2a + 3b}{a - 2b}$

134. $\left\{\dfrac{7 \pm \sqrt{61}}{2}\right\}$ **135.** $\{-1, 3\}$

Mid-Chapter 4 Check Point

1.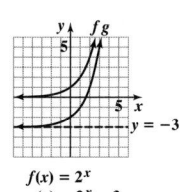

$f(x) = 2^x$
$g(x) = 2^x - 3$

asymptote of f: $y = 0$
asymptote of g: $y = -3$
domain of f = domain of g = $(-\infty, \infty)$
range of f = $(0, \infty)$; range of g = $(-3, \infty)$

2.

$f(x) = \left(\dfrac{1}{2}\right)^x$

$g(x) = \left(\dfrac{1}{2}\right)^{x-1}$

asymptote of f: $y = 0$
asymptote of g: $y = 0$
domain of f = domain of g = $(-\infty, \infty)$
range of f = range of g = $(0, \infty)$

3.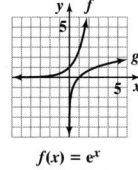

$f(x) = e^x$
$g(x) = \ln x$

asymptote of f: $y = 0$
asymptote of g: $x = 0$
domain of f = range of g = $(-\infty, \infty)$
range of f = domain of g = $(0, \infty)$

4.

$f(x) = \log_2 x$
$g(x) = \log_2(x-1) + 1$

asymptote of f: $x = 0$
asymptote of g: $x = 1$
domain of f = $(0, \infty)$; domain of g = $(1, \infty)$
range of f = range of g = $(-\infty, \infty)$

5.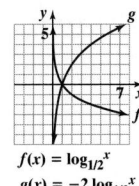

$f(x) = \log_{1/2} x$
$g(x) = -2\log_{1/2} x$

asymptote of f: $x = 0$
asymptote of g: $x = 0$
domain of f = domain of g = $(0, \infty)$
range of f = range of g = $(-\infty, \infty)$

6. $(-6, \infty)$ **7.** $(0, \infty)$ **8.** $(-\infty, -6) \cup (-6, \infty)$ **9.** $(-\infty, \infty)$ **10.** 5 **11.** -2 **12.** $\frac{1}{2}$ **13.** $\frac{1}{3}$ **14.** 2

15. Evaluation not possible; $\log_2 \frac{1}{8} = -3$ and $\log_3(-3)$ is undefined. **16.** 5 **17.** $\sqrt{7}$ **18.** 13 **19.** $-\frac{1}{2}$ **20.** $\sqrt{\pi}$

21. $\frac{1}{2}\log x + \frac{1}{2}\log y - 3$ **22.** $19 + 20 \ln x$ **23.** $\log_7\left(\frac{x^8}{\sqrt[3]{y}}\right)$ **24.** $\log_5 x^9$ **25.** $\ln\left[\frac{\sqrt{x}}{y^3(z-2)}\right]$ **26.** \$8

Section 4.4

Check Point Exercises

1. a. $\{3\}$ **b.** $\{-12\}$ **2. a.** $\left\{\frac{\ln 134}{\ln 5}\right\}; \approx 3.04$ **b.** $\{\log 8000\}; \approx 3.90$ **3.** $\left\{\frac{\ln 9}{2}\right\}; \approx 1.10$ **4.** $\left\{\frac{\ln 3 + \ln 7}{2\ln 3 - \ln 7}\right\}; \approx 12.11$

5. $\{0, \ln 7\}; \ln 7 \approx 1.95$ **6. a.** $\{12\}$ **b.** $\left\{\frac{e^2}{3}\right\}$ **7.** $\{5\}$ **8.** $\{4, 5\}$ **9.** 0.01 **10.** 16.2 yr **11.** \$11,000

Exercise Set 4.4

1. $\{6\}$ **3.** $\{3\}$ **5.** $\{3\}$ **7.** $\{2\}$ **9.** $\left\{\frac{3}{5}\right\}$ **11.** $\left\{\frac{3}{2}\right\}$ **13.** $\{4\}$ **15.** $\{5\}$ **17.** $\left\{-\frac{1}{4}\right\}$ **19.** $\{13\}$ **21.** $\{-2\}$

23. $\left\{\frac{\ln 3.91}{\ln 10}\right\}; \approx 0.59$ **25.** $\{\ln 5.7\}; \approx 1.74$ **27.** $\left\{\frac{\ln 17}{\ln 5}\right\}; \approx 1.76$ **29.** $\left\{\ln \frac{23}{5}\right\}; \approx 1.53$ **31.** $\left\{\frac{\ln 659}{5}\right\}; \approx 1.30$

33. $\left\{\frac{\ln 793 - 1}{-5}\right\}; \approx -1.14$ **35.** $\left\{\frac{\ln 10{,}478 + 3}{5}\right\}; \approx 2.45$ **37.** $\left\{\frac{\ln 410}{\ln 7} - 2\right\}; \approx 1.09$ **39.** $\left\{\frac{\ln 813}{0.3 \ln 7}\right\}; \approx 11.48$ **41.** $\left\{\frac{3\ln 5 + \ln 3}{\ln 3 - 2\ln 5}\right\}; \approx -2.80$

43. $\{0, \ln 2\}; \ln 2 \approx 0.69$ **45.** $\left\{\frac{\ln 3}{2}\right\}; \approx 0.55$ **47.** $\{0\}$ **49.** $\{81\}$ **51.** $\{e^2\}; \approx 7.39$ **53.** $\{59\}$ **55.** $\left\{\frac{109}{27}\right\}$ **57.** $\left\{\frac{62}{3}\right\}$

59. $\left\{\frac{e^4}{2}\right\}; \approx 27.30$ **61.** $\{e^{-1/2}\}; \approx 0.61$ **63.** $\{e^2 - 3\}; \approx 4.39$ **65.** $\left\{\frac{5}{4}\right\}$ **67.** $\{6\}$ **69.** $\{6\}$ **71.** $\{5\}$ **73.** $\{12\}$ **75.** $\left\{\frac{4}{3}\right\}$ **77.** \varnothing

79. $\{5\}$ **81.** $\left\{\frac{2}{9}\right\}$ **83.** $\{28\}$ **85.** $\{2\}$ **87.** \varnothing **89.** $\left\{\frac{11}{3}\right\}$ **91.** $\left\{\frac{1}{2}\right\}$ **93.** $\{e^3, e^{-3}\}$ **95.** $\left\{\pm\sqrt{\frac{\ln 45}{\ln 3}}\right\}$ **97.** $\left\{\frac{5 + \sqrt{37}}{2}\right\}$

99. $\{-2, 6\}$ **101. a.** 36.1 million **b.** 2013 **103.** 118 ft; by the point $(118, 1)$ **105.** 8.2 yr **107.** 16.8% **109.** 8.7 yr **111.** 15.7%
113. a. 69%; overestimates by 1% **b.** 2010 **115.** 2.8 days; $(2.8, 50)$ **117. a.** $10^{-5.6}$ mole per liter **b.** $10^{-2.4}$ mole per liter **c.** $10^{3.2}$ times greater
123. $\{2\}$ **125.** $\{4\}$ **127.** $\{2\}$ **129.** $\{-1.391606, 1.6855579\}$

131.

As distance from eye increases, barometric air pressure increases.

133.

about 7.9 min

135. does not make sense **137.** makes sense **139.** false **141.** true **143.** after 36 yr **145.** $\{10^{-2}, 10^{3/2}\}, 10^{3/2} = 10\sqrt{10} \approx 31.62$
148. a. 10 million; 9.97 million; 9.94 million; 9.91 million **b.** decreasing
149.

; exponential function **150. a.** 3 **b.** $e^{(\ln 3)x}$

Section 4.5

Check Point Exercises

1. a. $A = 643\,e^{0.021t}$ **b.** 2044 **2. a.** $A = A_0 e^{-0.0248t}$ **b.** about 72 yr **3. a.** 0.4 correct responses **b.** 0.7 correct responses
c. 0.8 correct responses
4.

; logarithmic function **5.**

; exponential **6.** $y = 4e^{(\ln 7.8)x}; y = 4e^{2.054x}$

Exercise Set 4.5

1. 127.5 million **3.** Iraq; 2.7% **5.** 2015 **7. a.** $A = 6.04e^{0.01t}$ **b.** 2040 **9.** 118.7 million **11.** 0.0121 **13.** -0.0053
15. approximately 8 grams **17.** 8 grams after 10 seconds; 4 grams after 20 seconds; 2 grams after 30 seconds; 1 gram after 40 seconds; 0.5 gram after 50 seconds **19.** approximately 15,679 years old **21.** 12.6 yr **23.** -0.000428; 0.0428% per year **25.** -0.039608; 3.9608% per day

27. a. $\dfrac{1}{2} = e^{1.31k}$ yields $k = \dfrac{\ln\left(\dfrac{1}{2}\right)}{1.31} \approx -0.52912.$ **b.** about 0.1069 billion or 106,900,000 years old **29.** 7.1 yr **31.** 5.5 hr

33. $2A_0 = A_0e^{kt}$; $2 = e^{kt}$; $\ln 2 = \ln e^{kt}$; $\ln 2 = kt$; $\dfrac{\ln 2}{k} = t$ **35. a.** 1% **b.** about 69 yr **37. a.** about 20 people **b.** about 1080 people
c. 100,000 people **39.** quite well **41.** 2026 **43.** about 3.7% **45.** about 48 years old

47. a.

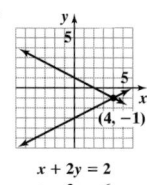

b. exponential function

49. a.

b. logarithmic function

51. $y = 100e^{(\ln 4.6)x}$; $y = 100e^{1.526x}$
53. $y = 2.5e^{(\ln 0.7)x}$; $y = 2.5e^{-0.357x}$

65. $y = 193.1 + 23.574 \ln x$; $r \approx 0.878$; Fit is ok, but not great. **67.** $y = 195.871x^{0.097}$; $r \approx 0.901$; Fits data fairly well. **69. a.** $y = 3.46(1.02)^x$
b. $y = 3.46e^{(\ln 1.02)x}$; $y = 3.46e^{0.02x}$; by approximately 2% **71.** does not make sense **73.** makes sense **75.** true **77.** true
79. about 126° F **81. a.** yes **b.** yes **82.** ; $(4, -1)$ **83.** $\{4\}$

$x + 2y = 2$
$x - 2y = 6$

Chapter 4 Review Exercises

1. $g(x) = 4^{-x}$ **2.** $h(x) = -4^{-x}$ **3.** $r(x) = -4^{-x} + 3$ **4.** $f(x) = 4^x$
5.

$f(x) = 2^x$
$g(x) = 2^{x-1}$

asymptote of f: $y = 0$
asymptote of g: $y = 0$
domain of f = domain of $g = (-\infty, \infty)$
range of f = range of $g = (0, \infty)$

6.

$f(x) = 3^x$
$g(x) = 3^x - 1$

asymptote of f: $y = 0$
asymptote of g: $y = -1$
domain of f = domain of $g = (-\infty, \infty)$
range of $f = (0, \infty)$; range of $g = (-1, \infty)$

7.

$f(x) = 3^x$
$g(x) = -3^x$

asymptote of f: $y = 0$
asymptote of g: $y = 0$
domain of f = domain of $g = (-\infty, \infty)$
range of $f = (0, \infty)$; range of $g = (-\infty, 0)$

8.

$f(x) = \left(\dfrac{1}{2}\right)^x$

$g(x) = \left(\dfrac{1}{2}\right)^{-x}$

asymptote of f: $y = 0$
asymptote of g: $y = 0$
domain of f = domain of $g = (-\infty, \infty)$
range of f = range of $g = (0, \infty)$

9.

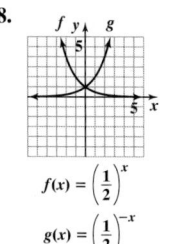

$f(x) = e^x$
$g(x) = 2e^{x/2}$

asymptote of f: $y = 0$
asymptote of g: $y = 0$
domain of f = domain of $g = (-\infty, \infty)$
range of f = range of $g = (0, \infty)$

10. 5.5% compounded semiannually **11.** 7% compounded monthly **12. a.** 200° **b.** 120°; 119° **c.** 70°; The temperature in the room is 70°.
13. $49^{1/2} = 7$ **14.** $4^3 = x$ **15.** $3^y = 81$ **16.** $\log_6 216 = 3$ **17.** $\log_b 625 = 4$ **18.** $\log_{13} 874 = y$ **19.** 3 **20.** -2 **21.** undefined;
$\log_b x$ is defined only for $x > 0$. **22.** $\dfrac{1}{2}$ **23.** 1 **24.** 8 **25.** 5 **26.** $-\dfrac{1}{2}$ **27.** -2 **28.** -3 **29.** 0

30.

$f(x) = 2^x$
$g(x) = \log_2 x$

domain of f = range of g = $(-\infty, \infty)$
range of f = domain of g = $(0, \infty)$

31.

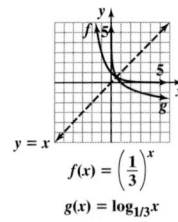

$f(x) = \left(\dfrac{1}{3}\right)^x$

$g(x) = \log_{1/3} x$

domain of f = range of g = $(-\infty, \infty)$
range of f = domain of g = $(0, \infty)$

32. $g(x) = \log(-x)$
33. $r(x) = 1 + \log(2 - x)$
34. $h(x) = \log(2 - x)$
35. $f(x) = \log x$

36.

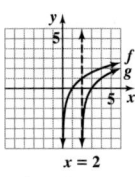

$x = 2$
$f(x) = \log_2 x$
$g(x) = \log_2(x - 2)$

x-intercept: $(3, 0)$
vertical asymptote: $x = 2$
domain: $(2, \infty)$; range: $(-\infty, \infty)$

37.

$f(x) = \log_2 x$
$h(x) = -1 + \log_2 x$

x-intercept: $(2, 0)$
vertical asymptote: $x = 0$
domain: $(0, \infty)$; range: $(-\infty, \infty)$

38.

$f(x) = \log_2 x$
$r(x) = \log_2(-x)$

x-intercept: $(-1, 0)$
vertical asymptote: $x = 0$
domain: $(-\infty, 0)$; range: $(-\infty, \infty)$

39.

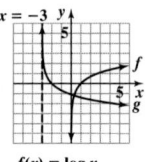

$f(x) = \log x$
$g(x) = -\log(x + 3)$

asymptote of f: $x = 0$
asymptote of g: $x = -3$
domain of f = $(0, \infty)$; domain of g = $(-3, \infty)$
range of f = range of g = $(-\infty, \infty)$

40.

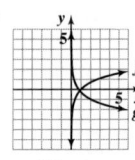

$f(x) = \ln x$
$g(x) = -\ln(2x)$

asymptote of f: $x = 0$
asymptote of g: $x = 0$
domain of f = domain of g = $(0, \infty)$
range of f = range of g = $(-\infty, \infty)$

41. $(-5, \infty)$
42. $(-\infty, 3)$
43. $(-\infty, 1) \cup (1, \infty)$
44. $6x$
45. \sqrt{x}
46. $4x^2$
47. 3.0

48. a. 76 **b.** $\approx 67, \approx 63, \approx 61, \approx 59, \approx 56$
c.

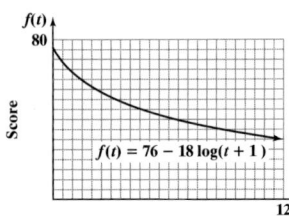

$f(t) = 76 - 18\log(t + 1)$

Time (months)

49. about 9 weeks **50.** $2 + 3\log_6 x$ **51.** $\dfrac{1}{2}\log_4 x - 3$

52. $\log_2 x + 2\log_2 y - 6$ **53.** $\dfrac{1}{3}\ln x - \dfrac{1}{3}$ **54.** $\log_b 21$ **55.** $\log\dfrac{3}{x^3}$

56. $\ln(x^3 y^4)$ **57.** $\ln\dfrac{\sqrt{x}}{y}$ **58.** 6.2448 **59.** -0.1063

60. true **61.** false; $\log(x + 9) - \log(x + 1) = \log\left(\dfrac{x + 9}{x + 1}\right)$

62. false; $4\log_2 x = \log_2 x^4$ **63.** true **64.** $\{2\}$ **65.** $\left\{\dfrac{2}{3}\right\}$ **66.** $\{\log 7000\}; \approx 3.85$

67. $\left\{-\dfrac{4}{5}\right\}$ **68.** $\left\{\dfrac{\ln 12{,}143}{\ln 8}\right\}; \approx 4.52$ **69.** $\left\{\dfrac{1}{5}\ln 141\right\}; \approx 0.99$ **70.** $\left\{\dfrac{12 - \ln 130}{5}\right\}; \approx 1.43$ **71.** $\left\{\dfrac{\ln 37{,}500 - 2\ln 5}{4\ln 5}\right\}; \approx 1.14$

72. $\left\{\dfrac{\ln 7 + 4\ln 3}{2\ln 7 - \ln 3}\right\}; \approx 2.27$ **73.** $\{\ln 3\}; \approx 1.10$ **74.** $\{23\}$ **75.** $\left\{\dfrac{e^3}{2}\right\}; \approx 10.04$ **76.** $\{5\}$ **77.** \varnothing **78.** $\{2\}$ **79.** $\{4\}$

80. 5.5 mi **81.** approximately 2086 **82.** approximately 8103 thousand or 8,103,000 **83.** 7.3 yr **84.** 14.6 yr **85.** about 22%

86. a. 0.045 **b.** 55.1 million **c.** 2012 **87.** 325 days **88. a.** 200 people **b.** about 45,411 people **c.** 500,000 people

89. a.

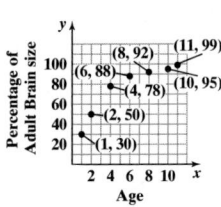

(8, 92) (11, 99)
(6, 88) (10, 95)
(4, 78)
(2, 50)
(1, 30)

Percentage of Adult Brain size
Age

b. logarithmic function

90. a.

(7, 28.9)
(3, 1.0) (6, 14.2)
(5, 8.3)
(4, 2.1)
(2, 0.9)

Monthly Text Messages (billions)
Years after 2000

b. exponential function

91. $y = 73e^{(\ln 2.6)x}; y = 73e^{0.956x}$ **92.** $y = 6.5e^{(\ln 0.43)x}; y = 6.5e^{-0.844x}$

Chapter 4 Test

1.

$f(x) = 2^x$
$g(x) = 2^x + 1$

2.

$x = 1$
$f(x) = \log_2 x$
$g(x) = \log_2(x - 1)$

3. $5^3 = 125$ **4.** $\log_{36} 6 = \dfrac{1}{2}$ **5.** $(-\infty, 3)$ **6.** $3 + 5 \log_4 x$

7. $\dfrac{1}{3} \log_3 x - 4$ **8.** $\log(x^6 y^2)$ **9.** $\ln \dfrac{7}{x^3}$ **10.** 1.5741 **11.** $\{-10\}$

12. $\left\{ \dfrac{\ln 1.4}{\ln 5} \right\}$ **13.** $\left\{ \dfrac{\ln 4}{0.005} \right\}$ **14.** $\{0, \ln 5\}$ **15.** $\{54.25\}$

16. $\left\{ \dfrac{e^4}{3} \right\}$ **17.** $\{5\}$ **18.** \varnothing **19.** 120 db **20.** $5x$ **21.** 1 **22.** 0

23. 6.5% compounded semiannually; $221 more **24.** 13.9 years **25.** about 6.9%

26. a. 82.3 million **b.** decreasing; The growth rate, -0.002, is negative. **c.** 2008 **27.** $A = 509e^{0.036t}$ **28.** 12.5 days **29. a.** 14 elk

b. about 51 elk **c.** 140 elk **30.** linear **31.** logarithmic **32.** exponential **33.** quadratic **34.** $y = 96e^{(\ln 0.38)x}$; $y = 96e^{-0.968x}$

Cumulative Review Exercises (Chapters 1–4)

1. $\left\{ \dfrac{2}{3}, 2 \right\}$ **2.** $\{3, 7\}$ **3.** $\{-2, -1, 1\}$ **4.** $\left\{ \dfrac{\ln 128}{5} \right\}$ **5.** $\{3\}$ **6.** \varnothing **7.** $(-\infty, 4]$ **8.** $[1, 3]$

9.

$(x - 3)^2 + (y + 2)^2 = 4$

10.
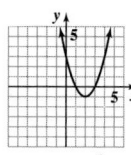
$f(x) = (x - 2)^2 - 1$

11.
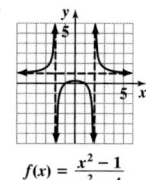
$f(x) = \dfrac{x^2 - 1}{x^2 - 4}$

12.

$f(x) = (x - 2)^2(x + 1)$

13.

$f(x) = 2x - 4$
$f^{-1}(x) = \dfrac{x + 4}{2}$

14.
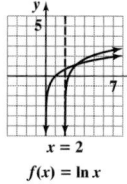
$x = 2$
$f(x) = \ln x$
$g(x) = \ln (x - 2) + 1$

15. using $(1, 3)$, $y - 3 = -3(x - 1)$; $y = -3x + 6$
16. $(f \circ g)(x) = (x + 2)^2$; $(g \circ f)(x) = x^2 + 2$
17. You can expect to sleep 2 hours.
18. after 2 sec; 69 ft
19. 4.1 sec
20. $12 per hr

CHAPTER 5

Section 5.1

Check Point Exercises

1. a. solution **b.** not a solution **2.** $\{(-2, 5)\}$ **3.** $\{(2, -1)\}$ **4.** $\left\{ \left(\dfrac{60}{17}, -\dfrac{11}{17} \right) \right\}$ **5.** no solution or \varnothing

6. $\{(x, y) | x = 4y - 8\}$ or $\{(x, y) | 5x - 20y = -40\}$ **7. a.** $C(x) = 300,000 + 30x$ **b.** $R(x) = 80x$ **c.** $(6000, 480,000)$; The company will break even if it produces and sells 6000 pairs of shoes.

Exercise Set 5.1

1. solution **3.** not a solution **5.** $\{(1, 3)\}$ **7.** $\{(5, 1)\}$ **9.** $\{(-22, -5)\}$ **11.** $\{(0, 0)\}$ **13.** $\{(3, -2)\}$ **15.** $\{(5, 4)\}$ **17.** $\{(7, 3)\}$

19. $\{(2, -1)\}$ **21.** $\{(3, 0)\}$ **23.** $\{(-4, 3)\}$ **25.** $\{(3, 1)\}$ **27.** $\{(1, -2)\}$ **29.** $\left\{ \left(\dfrac{7}{25}, -\dfrac{1}{25} \right) \right\}$ **31.** \varnothing **33.** $\{(x, y) | y = 3x - 5\}$

35. $\{(1, 4)\}$ **37.** $\{(x, y) | x + 3y = 2\}$ **39.** $\{(-5, -1)\}$ **41.** $\left\{ \left(\dfrac{29}{22}, -\dfrac{5}{11} \right) \right\}$ **43.** $x + y = 7$; $x - y = -1$; 3 and 4

45. $3x - y = 1$; $x + 2y = 12$; 2 and 5 **47.** $\{(6, -1)\}$ **49.** $\left\{ \left(\dfrac{1}{a}, 3 \right) \right\}$ **51.** $m = -4, b = 3$ **53.** $y = x - 4$; $y = -\dfrac{1}{3}x + 4$

55. 500 radios **57.** -6000; When the company produces and sells 200 radios, the loss is $6000. **59. a.** $P(x) = 20x - 10,000$ **b.** $190,000

61. a. $C(x) = 18,000 + 20x$ **b.** $R(x) = 80x$ **c.** $(300, 24,000)$; When 300 canoes are produced and sold, both revenue and cost are $24,000.

63. a. $C(x) = 30,000 + 2500x$ **b.** $R(x) = 3125x$ **c.** $(48, 150,000)$; For 48 sold-out performances, both cost and revenue are $150,000.

65. a. 4 million workers; $4.50 per hour **b.** $4.50; 4; 4 **c.** 2 million **d.** 5.7 million **e.** 3.7 million **67.** 2009; 18.5% pro-choice and

18.5% pro-life **69. a.** $y = 0.45x + 0.8$ **b.** $y = 0.15x + 2.6$ **b.** week 6; 3.5 symptoms; by the intersection point $(6, 3.5)$ **71. a.** $y = -0.54x + 38$

b. $y = -0.79x + 40$ **c.** 1993; 33.68% **73.** Mr. Goodbar: 264 cal; Mounds: 258 cal **75.** 3 Mr. Goodbars and 2 Mounds bars

77. 50 rooms with kitchen facilities, 150 rooms without kitchen facilities **79.** 100 ft long by 80 ft wide **81.** rate rowing in still water: 6 mph;

rate of the current: 2 mph **83.** 80°, 50°, 50° **95.** makes sense **97.** makes sense **99.** $y = \dfrac{a_1 c_2 - a_2 c_1}{a_1 b_2 - a_2 b_1}$; $x = \dfrac{b_2 c_1 - b_1 c_2}{a_1 b_2 - a_2 b_1}$

101. Yes; 8 hexagons and 4 squares **103.** yes **104.** $11x + 4y = -3$ **105.** $1682 = 16a + 4b + c$

Section 5.2

Check Point Exercises

1. $(-1) - 2(-4) + 3(5) = 22; 2(-1) - 3(-4) - 5 = 5; 3(-1) + (-4) - 5(5) = -32$ **2.** $\{(1, 4, -3)\}$ **3.** $\{(4, 5, 3)\}$ **4.** $y = 3x^2 - 12x + 13$

Exercise Set 5.2

1. solution **3.** solution **5.** $\{(2, 3, 3)\}$ **7.** $\{(2, -1, 1)\}$ **9.** $\{(1, 2, 3)\}$ **11.** $\{(3, 1, 5)\}$ **13.** $\{(1, 0, -3)\}$ **15.** $\{(1, -5, -6)\}$

17. $\left\{\left(\frac{1}{2}, \frac{1}{3}, -1\right)\right\}$ **19.** $y = 2x^2 - x + 3$ **21.** $y = 2x^2 + x - 5$ **23.** 7, 4, and 5 **25.** $\{(4, 8, 6)\}$ **27.** $y = -\frac{3}{4}x^2 + 6x - 11$

29. $\left\{\left(\frac{8}{a}, -\frac{3}{b}, -\frac{5}{c}\right)\right\}$ **31. a.** $y = -16x^2 + 40x + 200$ **b.** $y = 0$ when $x = 5$; The ball hits the ground after 5 seconds.

33. water: 58%; fat: 23%; protein: 14% **35.** 200 $8 tickets; 150 $10 tickets; 50 $12 tickets **37.** $1200 at 8%, $2000 at 10%, and $3500 at 12%

39. $x = 60, y = 55, z = 65$ **47.** does not make sense **49.** makes sense **51.** 13 triangles, 21 rectangles, and 6 pentagons

53. $\dfrac{x + 14}{(x - 4)(x + 2)}$ **54.** $\dfrac{5x^3 - 3x^2 + 7x - 3}{(x^2 + 1)^2}$ **55.** $\{(5, -2, 3)\}$

Section 5.3

Check Point Exercises

1. $\dfrac{2}{x - 3} + \dfrac{3}{x + 4}$ **2.** $\dfrac{2}{x} - \dfrac{2}{x - 1} + \dfrac{3}{(x - 1)^2}$ **3.** $\dfrac{2}{x + 3} + \dfrac{6x - 8}{x^2 + x + 2}$ **4.** $\dfrac{2x}{x^2 + 1} + \dfrac{-x + 3}{(x^2 + 1)^2}$

Exercise Set 5.3

1. $\dfrac{A}{x - 2} + \dfrac{B}{x + 1}$ **3.** $\dfrac{A}{x + 2} + \dfrac{B}{x - 3} + \dfrac{C}{(x - 3)^2}$ **5.** $\dfrac{A}{x - 1} + \dfrac{Bx + C}{x^2 + 1}$ **7.** $\dfrac{Ax + B}{x^2 + 4} + \dfrac{Cx + D}{(x^2 + 4)^2}$ **9.** $\dfrac{3}{x - 3} - \dfrac{2}{x - 2}$

11. $\dfrac{7}{x - 9} - \dfrac{4}{x + 2}$ **13.** $\dfrac{24}{7(x - 4)} + \dfrac{25}{7(x + 3)}$ **15.** $\dfrac{4}{7(x - 3)} - \dfrac{8}{7(2x + 1)}$ **17.** $\dfrac{3}{x} + \dfrac{2}{x - 1} - \dfrac{1}{x + 3}$ **19.** $\dfrac{3}{x} + \dfrac{4}{x + 1} - \dfrac{3}{x - 1}$

21. $\dfrac{6}{x - 1} - \dfrac{5}{(x - 1)^2}$ **23.** $\dfrac{1}{x - 2} - \dfrac{2}{(x - 2)^2} - \dfrac{5}{(x - 2)^3}$ **25.** $\dfrac{7}{x} - \dfrac{6}{x - 1} + \dfrac{10}{(x - 1)^2}$ **27.** $\dfrac{1}{4(x + 1)} + \dfrac{3}{4(x - 1)} + \dfrac{1}{2(x - 1)^2}$

29. $\dfrac{3}{x - 1} + \dfrac{2x - 4}{x^2 + 1}$ **31.** $\dfrac{2}{x + 1} + \dfrac{3x - 1}{x^2 + 2x + 2}$ **33.** $\dfrac{1}{4x} + \dfrac{1}{x^2} - \dfrac{x + 4}{4(x^2 + 4)}$ **35.** $\dfrac{4}{x + 1} + \dfrac{2x - 3}{x^2 + 1}$ **37.** $\dfrac{x + 1}{x^2 + 2} - \dfrac{2x}{(x^2 + 2)^2}$

39. $\dfrac{x - 2}{x^2 - 2x + 3} + \dfrac{2x + 1}{(x^2 - 2x + 3)^2}$ **41.** $\dfrac{3}{x - 2} + \dfrac{x - 1}{x^2 + 2x + 4}$ **43.** $x^3 + x - \dfrac{1}{2(x + 1)} + \dfrac{3}{2(x - 1)}$ **45.** $x + 1 - \dfrac{2}{x} - \dfrac{2}{x^2} + \dfrac{2}{x - 1}$

47. $\dfrac{\frac{1}{2c}}{x - c} - \dfrac{\frac{1}{2c}}{x + c}$ **49.** $\dfrac{a}{x - c} + \dfrac{ac + b}{(x - c)^2}$ **51.** $\dfrac{1}{x} - \dfrac{1}{x + 1}; \dfrac{99}{100}$ **61.** does not make sense **63.** does not make sense

65. $\dfrac{2}{x - 3} + \dfrac{2x + 5}{x^2 + 3x + 3}$ **66.** $\{(2.5, -2)\}$ **67.** $\{(4, -3)\}$

68. ; $(0, -3)$ and $(2, -1)$; $0 - (-3) = 3$ and $(0 - 2)^2 + (-3 + 3)^2 = 4$ are true; $2 - (-1) = 3$ and $(2 - 2)^2 + (-1 + 3)^2 = 4$ are true.

$x - y = 3$
$(x - 2)^2 + (y + 3)^2 = 4$

Section 5.4

Check Point Exercises

1. $\{(0, 1), (4, 17)\}$ **2.** $\left\{\left(-\frac{6}{5}, \frac{3}{5}\right), (2, -1)\right\}$ **3.** $\{(3, 2), (3, -2), (-3, 2), (-3, -2)\}$ **4.** $\{(0, 5)\}$ **5.** length: 7 ft; width: 3 ft or length: 3 ft; width: 7 ft

Exercise Set 5.4

1. $\{(-3, 5), (2, 0)\}$ **3.** $\{(1, 1), (2, 0)\}$ **5.** $\{(4, -10), (-3, 11)\}$ **7.** $\{(4, 3), (-3, -4)\}$ **9.** $\left\{\left(-\frac{3}{2}, -4\right), (2, 3)\right\}$ **11.** $\{(-5, -4), (3, 0)\}$

13. $\{(3, 1), (-3, -1), (1, 3), (-1, -3)\}$ **15.** $\{(4, -3), (-1, 2)\}$ **17.** $\{(0, 1), (4, -3)\}$ **19.** $\{(3, 2), (3, -2), (-3, 2), (-3, -2)\}$

21. $\{(3, 2), (3, -2), (-3, 2), (-3, -2)\}$ **23.** $\{(2, 1), (2, -1), (-2, 1), (-2, -1)\}$ **25.** $\{(3, 4), (3, -4)\}$

27. $\{(0, 2), (0, -2), (-1, \sqrt{3}), (-1, -\sqrt{3})\}$ **29.** $\{(2, 1), (2, -1), (-2, 1), (-2, -1)\}$ **31.** $\{(-2\sqrt{2}, -\sqrt{2}), (-1, -4), (1, 4), (2\sqrt{2}, \sqrt{2})\}$

33. $\{(2, 2), (4, 1)\}$ **35.** $\{(0, 0), (-1, 1)\}$ **37.** $\{(0, 0), (-2, 2), (2, 2)\}$ **39.** $\left\{(-4, 1), \left(-\frac{5}{2}, \frac{1}{4}\right)\right\}$ **41.** $\left\{\left(\frac{12}{5}, -\frac{29}{5}\right), (-2, 3)\right\}$

43. 4 and 6 **45.** 2 and 1, 2 and -1, -2 and 1, or -2 and -1

47. $\{(2, -1), (-2, 1)\}$ **49.** $\{(2, 20), (-2, 4), (-3, 0)\}$ **51.** $\left\{\left(-1, -\frac{1}{2}\right), \left(-1, \frac{1}{2}\right), \left(1, -\frac{1}{2}\right), \left(1, \frac{1}{2}\right)\right\}$

53.

$y = x^2 - 4$
$y = x$

55. $(0, -4), (-2, 0), (2, 0)$ **57.** 11 ft and 7 ft **59.** width: 6 in.; length: 8 in.
61. $x = 5$ m, $y = 2$ m

63. a. between the 1940s and the 1960s **b.** 1949; 43%; 43% **c.** 1920; 28% **d.** 1919; white collar: 27.5%; farmers: 27.4%; fairly well,
although answers may vary. **69.** makes sense **71.** makes sense **73.** false **75.** false **77.** 18 sq units **79.** $\{(8, 2)\}$

81.

$2x - 3y = 6$

82.

$f(x) = -\frac{2}{3}x$

83.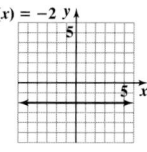

$f(x) = -2$

Mid-Chapter 5 Check Point

1. $\{(-1, 2)\}$ **2.** $\{(1, -2)\}$ **3.** $\{(6, 10)\}$ **4.** $\{(x, y) | y = 4x - 5\}$ or $\{(x, y) | 8x - 2y = 10\}$ **5.** $\left\{\left(\frac{11}{19}, \frac{7}{19}\right)\right\}$ **6.** \varnothing **7.** $\{(-1, 2, -2)\}$

8. $\{(4, -2, 3)\}$ **9.** $\left\{\left(-\frac{9}{5}, \frac{12}{5}\right), (3, 0)\right\}$ **10.** $\{(-2, -1), (-2, 1), (2, -1), (2, 1)\}$ **11.** $\{(-\sqrt{7}, 1), (-2, -2), (2, -2), (\sqrt{7}, 1)\}$

12. $\{(0, -2), (6, 1)\}$ **13.** $\frac{1}{x - 2} - \frac{2}{(x - 2)^2} - \frac{5}{(x - 2)^3}$ **14.** $\frac{5}{x + 2} + \frac{3}{x + 1} + \frac{2}{x - 1}$ **15.** $-\frac{2}{x + 3} + \frac{3x - 5}{x^2 + 4}$ **16.** $\frac{x}{x^2 + 4} - \frac{4x}{(x^2 + 4)^2}$

17. a. $C(x) = 400{,}000 + 20x$ **b.** $R(x) = 100x$ **c.** $P(x) = 80x - 400{,}000$ **d.** $(5000, 500{,}000)$; The company will break even when it
produces and sells 5000 PDAs. At this level, both revenue and cost are \$500,000. **18.** 6 roses and 14 carnations **19.** $x = 55°, y = 35°$
20. $y = -x^2 + 2x + 3$ **21.** length: 8 m; width: 2.5 m

Section 5.5

Check Point Exercises

1.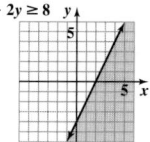
$4x - 2y \geq 8$

2.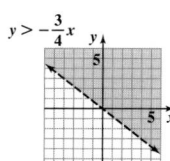
$y > -\frac{3}{4}x$

3. a.
$y > 1$

b.
$x \leq -2$

4.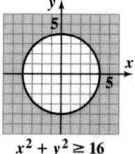
$x^2 + y^2 \geq 16$

5. Point $B = (66, 130)$; $4.9(66) - 130 \geq 165$, or $193.4 \geq 165$, is true; $3.7(66) - 130 \leq 125$, or $114.2 \leq 125$, is true.

6.
$x - 3y < 6$
$2x + 3y \geq -6$

7.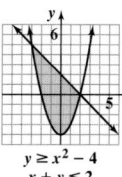
$y \geq x^2 - 4$
$x + y \leq 2$

8.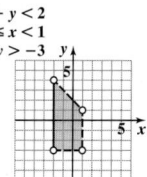
$x + y < 2$
$-2 \leq x < 1$
$y > -3$

Exercise Set 5.5

1.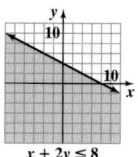
$x + 2y \leq 8$

3.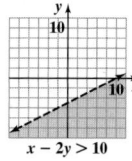
$x - 2y > 10$

5.
$y \leq \frac{1}{3}x$

7.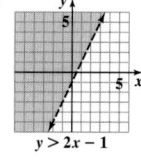
$y > 2x - 1$

9.
$x \leq 1$

11.
$y > 1$

13.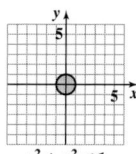
$x^2 + y^2 \leq 1$

15.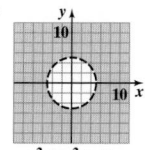
$x^2 + y^2 > 25$

17.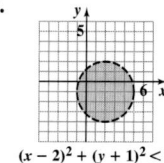
$(x - 2)^2 + (y + 1)^2 < 9$

19.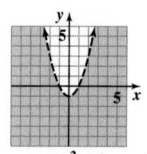
$y < x^2 - 1$

21.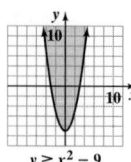
$y \geq x^2 - 9$

23.
$y > 2^x$

25.
$y \geq \log_2 (x + 1)$

27. $3x + 6y \leq 6$
$2x + y \leq 8$

29. $2x - 5y \leq 10$
$3x - 2y > 6$

31. $y > 2x - 3$
$y < -x + 6$

33. $x + 2y \leq 4$
$y \geq x - 3$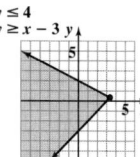

35. $x \leq 2$
$y \geq -1$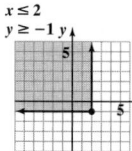

37. $-2 \leq x < 5$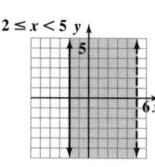

39. $x - y \leq 1$
$x \geq 2$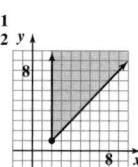

41. \varnothing

43. $x + y > 4$
$x + y > -1$

45.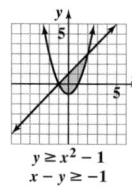
$y \geq x^2 - 1$
$x - y \geq -1$

47.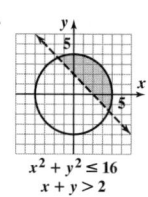
$x^2 + y^2 \leq 16$
$x + y > 2$

49.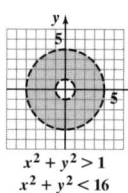
$x^2 + y^2 > 1$
$x^2 + y^2 < 16$

51.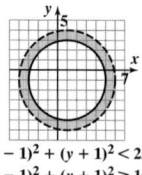
$(x - 1)^2 + (y + 1)^2 < 25$
$(x - 1)^2 + (y + 1)^2 \geq 16$

53.
$x^2 + y^2 \leq 1$
$y - x^2 > 0$

55.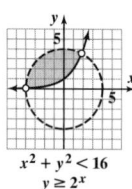
$x^2 + y^2 < 16$
$y \geq 2^x$

57. $x - y \leq 2$
$x > -2$
$y \leq 3$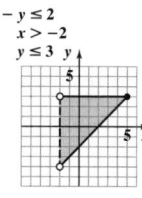

59. $x \geq 0$
$y \geq 0$
$2x + 5y < 10$
$3x + 4y \leq 12$

61. $3x + y \leq 6$
$2x - y \leq -1$
$x > -2$
$y < 4$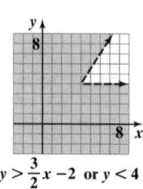

63. $y \geq -2x + 4$

65. $x + y \leq 4$
$3x + y \leq 6$

67.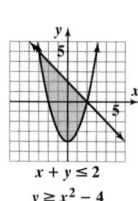
$x + y \leq 2$
$y \geq x^2 - 4$

69. $-2 \leq x \leq 2$
$-3 \leq y \leq 3$

71.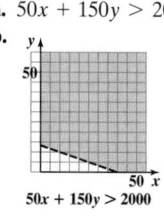
$y > \frac{3}{2}x - 2$ or $y < 4$

73. no solution

75. infinitely many solutions

77. Point $A = (66, 160)$; $5.3(66) - 160 \geq 180$, or $189.8 \geq 180$, is true; $4.1(66) - 160 \leq 140$, or $110.6 \leq 140$, is true.

79. no

81. a. $50x + 150y > 2000$
 b.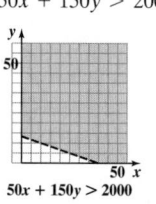
$50x + 150y > 2000$

 c. Answers may vary. Example:
 $(20, 20)$: 20 children and 20 adults
 will cause the elevator to be overloaded.

83. a. $y \geq 0$; $x + y \geq 5$; $x \geq 1$; $200x + 100y \leq 700$
 b. $y \geq 0$
 $x + y \geq 5$
 $x \geq 1$
 $200x + 100y \leq 700$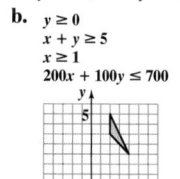
 c. 2 nights

85. a. 27.1 **b.** overweight

97. **99.** **101.**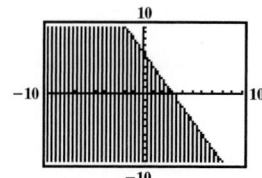

107. does not make sense **109.** makes sense **111.** $y > x - 3$; $y \le x$ **113.** $x + 2y \le 6$ or $2x + y \le 6$

115. $y \ge nx + b$

116. a. 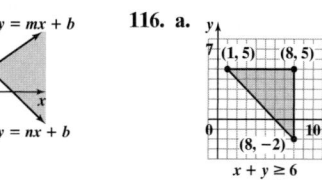 **b.** $(1, 5), (8, 5), (8, -2)$ **117. a.** 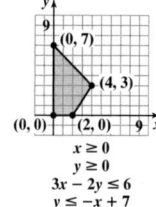 **b.** $(0, 0), (2, 0), (4, 3), (0, 7)$

c. at $(1, 5)$: 13; at $(8, 5)$: 34; at $(8, -2)$: 20 **c.** at $(0, 0)$: 0; at $(2, 0)$: 4; at $(4, 3)$: 23; $(0, 7)$: 35

118. $20x + 10y \le 80{,}000$

Section 5.6

Check Point Exercises

1. $z = 25x + 55y$ **2.** $x + y \le 80$ **3.** $30 \le x \le 80$; $10 \le y \le 30$; objective function: $z = 25x + 55y$; constraints:
$x + y \le 80$; $30 \le x \le 80$; $10 \le y \le 30$ **4.** 50 bookshelves and 30 desks; $2900 **5.** 30

Exercise Set 5.6

1. $(1, 2)$: 17; $(2, 10)$: 70; $(7, 5)$: 65; $(8, 3)$: 58; maximum: $z = 70$; minimum: $z = 17$
3. $(0, 0)$: 0; $(0, 8)$: 400; $(4, 9)$: 610; $(8, 0)$: 320; maximum: $z = 610$; minimum: $z = 0$
5. a. **7. a.**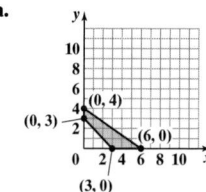

b. $(0, 8)$: 16; $(0, 4)$: 8; $(4, 0)$: 12 **b.** $(0, 4)$: 4; $(0, 3)$: 3; $(3, 0)$: 12; $(6, 0)$: 24
c. maximum value: 16 at $x = 0$ **c.** maximum value: 24 at $x = 6$ and
and $y = 8$ $y = 0$

9. a. **11. a.** **13. a.**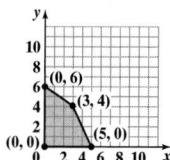

b. $(1, 2)$: -1; $(1, 4)$: -5; $(5, 8)$: -1; $(5, 2)$: 11 **b.** $(0, 4)$: 8; $(0, 2)$: 4; $(2, 0)$: 8; $(4, 0)$: 16; **b.** $(0, 6)$: 72; $(0, 0)$: 0; $(5, 0)$: 50; $(3, 4)$: 78

c. maximum value: 11 at $x = 5$ and $y = 2$ $\left(\dfrac{12}{5}, \dfrac{12}{5}\right)$: $\dfrac{72}{5}$ **c.** maximum value: 78 at $x = 3$ and $y = 4$

c. maximum value: 16 at $x = 4$ and $y = 0$

15. a. $z = 125x + 200y$ **b.** $x \le 450$; $y \le 200$; $600x + 900y \le 360{,}000$ **17.** 40 model A bicycles and no model B bicycles
c. **d.** $(0, 0)$: 0; $(0, 200)$: 40,000; **19.** 300 cartons of food and 200 cartons of clothing
$(300, 200)$: 77,500; $(450, 100)$: 76,250; **21.** 50 students and 100 parents
$(450, 0)$: 56,250 **23.** 10 Boeing 727s and 42 Falcon 20s
e. 300; 200; $77,500

29. does not make sense **31.** makes sense **33.** $5000 in stocks and $5000 in bonds **37.** $\{(6, 3, 5)\}$; Answers may vary.
38. $\{(-2, 1, 4, 3)\}$; Answers may vary. **39.** $\begin{bmatrix} 1 & 2 & -1 \\ 0 & -11 & -11 \end{bmatrix}$

Chapter 5 Review Exercises

1. $\{(1,5)\}$ **2.** $\{(2,3)\}$ **3.** $\{(2,-3)\}$ **4.** \varnothing **5.** $\{(x,y)|3x-6y=12\}$ **6. a.** $C(x)=60,000+200x$ **b.** $R(x)=450x$

c. $(240, 108,000)$; This means the company will break even if it produces and sells 240 desks. **7.** Klimt: \$135 million; Picasso: \$104 million

8. a. Answers will vary; approximately $(2004, 180)$; 2004; 180 million **b.** $y=19.8x+98$ **c.** 2004; 180 million **d.** Answers will vary from "quite well" to "extremely well." **9.** 12 ft by 5 ft **10.** \$80 per day for the room, \$60 per day for the car **11.** 3 apples and 2 avocados

12. $\{(0,1,2)\}$ **13.** $\{(2,1,-1)\}$ **14.** $y=3x^2-4x+5$ **15.** 18–29: \$8300; 30–39: \$16,400; 40–49: \$19,500

16. $\dfrac{3}{5(x-3)}+\dfrac{2}{5(x+2)}$ **17.** $\dfrac{6}{x-4}+\dfrac{5}{x+3}$ **18.** $\dfrac{2}{x}+\dfrac{3}{x+2}-\dfrac{1}{x-1}$ **19.** $\dfrac{2}{x-2}+\dfrac{5}{(x-2)^2}$ **20.** $-\dfrac{4}{x-1}+\dfrac{4}{x-2}-\dfrac{2}{(x-2)^2}$

21. $\dfrac{6}{5(x-2)}+\dfrac{-6x+3}{5(x^2+1)}$ **22.** $\dfrac{5}{x-3}+\dfrac{2x-1}{x^2+4}$ **23.** $\dfrac{x}{x^2+4}-\dfrac{4x}{(x^2+4)^2}$ **24.** $\dfrac{4x+1}{x^2+x+1}+\dfrac{2x-2}{(x^2+x+1)^2}$ **25.** $\{(4,3),(1,0)\}$

26. $\{(0,1),(-3,4)\}$ **27.** $\{(1,-1),(-1,1)\}$ **28.** $\{(3,\sqrt6),(3,-\sqrt6),(-3,\sqrt6),(-3,-\sqrt6)\}$ **29.** $\{(2,2),(-2,-2)\}$ **30.** $\{(9,6),(1,2)\}$

31. $\{(-3,-1),(1,3)\}$ **32.** $\left\{\left(\dfrac{1}{2},2\right),(-1,-1)\right\}$ **33.** $\left\{\left(\dfrac{5}{2},-\dfrac{7}{2}\right),(0,-1)\right\}$ **34.** $\{(2,-3),(-2,-3),(3,2),(-3,2)\}$

35. $\{(3,1),(3,-1),(-3,1),(-3,-1)\}$ **36.** 8 m and 5 m **37.** $(1,6),(3,2)$ **38.** $x=46$ and $y=28$ or $x=50$ and $y=20$

39.
$3x-4y>12$

40.
$y\le-\dfrac{1}{2}x+2$

41.
$x<-2$

42.
$y\ge3$

43.
$x^2+y^2>4$

44.
$y\le x^2-1$

45.
$y\le2^x$

46.
$3x+2y\ge6$
$2x+y\ge6$

47.
$2x-y\ge4$
$x+2y<2$

48.
$y<x$
$y\le2$

49.
$x+y\le6$
$y\ge2x-3$

50.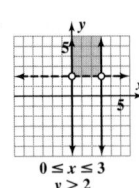
$0\le x\le3$
$y>2$

51. no solution

52.
$x^2+y^2\le16$
$x+y<2$

53.
$x^2+y^2\le9$
$y<-3x+1$

54.
$y>x^2$
$x+y<6$
$y<x+6$

55.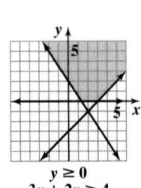
$y\ge0$
$3x+2y\ge4$
$x-y\le3$

56. $(2,2)$: 10; $(4,0)$: 8; $\left(\dfrac{1}{2},\dfrac{1}{2}\right)$: $\dfrac{5}{2}$; $(1,0)$: 2; maximum value: 10; minimum value: 2

57.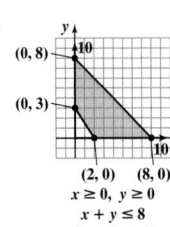
$(0,8)$ $(0,3)$ $(2,0)$ $(8,0)$
$x\ge0,\ y\ge0$
$x+y\le8$
$3x+2y\ge6$
Maximum is 24 at $x=0$, $y=8$.

58.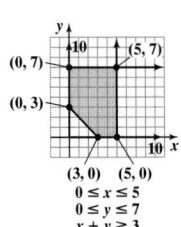
$(0,7)$ $(5,7)$ $(0,3)$ $(3,0)$ $(5,0)$
$0\le x\le5$
$0\le y\le7$
$x+y\ge3$
Maximum is 33 at $x=5$, $y=7$.

59.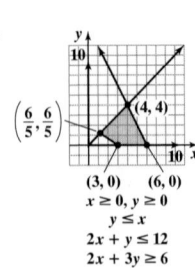
$\left(\dfrac{6}{5},\dfrac{6}{5}\right)$ $(4,4)$ $(3,0)$ $(6,0)$
$x\ge0,\ y\ge0$
$y\le x$
$2x+y\le12$
$2x+3y\ge6$
Maximum is 44 at $x=y=4$.

60. a. $z=500x+350y$
b. $x+y\le200;\ x\ge10;\ y\ge80$
c. (10, 190) 200 (120, 80) (10, 80)
$x+y\le200$
$x\ge10,\ y\ge80$
d. $(10, 80)$: 33,000; $(10, 190)$: 71,500; $(120, 80)$: 88,000
e. 120; 80; 88,000

61. 480 of model A and 240 of model B

Chapter 5 Test

1. $\{(1, -3)\}$ **2.** $\{(4, -2)\}$ **3.** $\{(1, 3, 2)\}$ **4.** $\{(4, -3), (-3, 4)\}$ **5.** $\{(3, 2), (3, -2), (-3, 2), (-3, -2)\}$ **6.** $\dfrac{-1}{10(x + 1)} + \dfrac{x + 9}{10(x^2 + 9)}$

7.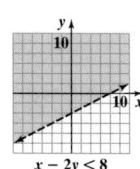

$x - 2y < 8$

8.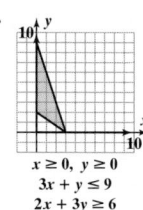

$x \geq 0, \ y \geq 0$
$3x + y \leq 9$
$2x + 3y \geq 6$

9.

$x^2 + y^2 > 1$
$x^2 + y^2 < 4$

10.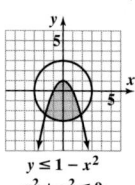

$y \leq 1 - x^2$
$x^2 + y^2 \leq 9$

11. 26 **12.** shrimp: 42 mg; scallops: 15mg **13. a.** $C(x) = 360,000 + 850x$ **b.** $R(x) = 1150x$ **c.** $(1200, 1,380,000)$; The company will break even if it produces and sells 1200 computers. **14.** $y = x^2 - 3$ **15.** $x = 7.5$ ft and $y = 24$ ft or $x = 12$ ft and $y = 15$ ft
16. 50 regular and 100 deluxe jet skis; $35,000

Cumulative Review Exercises (Chapters 1–5)

1. domain: $(-2, 2)$; range: $(-\infty, 3]$ **2.** -1 and 1 **3.** maximum of 3 at $x = 0$ **4.** $(0, 2)$
5. positive **6.** 3 **7.** $x \to -2^+; x \to 2^-$ **8.** even

9.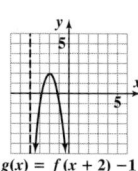

$g(x) = f(x + 2) - 1$

10.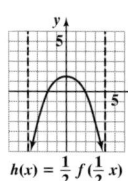

$h(x) = \frac{1}{2} f(\frac{1}{2}x)$

11. $\{3, 4\}$ **12.** $\left\{\dfrac{2 + i\sqrt{3}}{2}, \dfrac{2 - i\sqrt{3}}{2}\right\}$
13. $(-18, 6)$ **14.** $(1, 7)$
15. $\left\{-3, \dfrac{1}{2}, 2\right\}$ **16.** $\{-2\}$
17. $\{2\}$ **18.** $\{-2 + \log_3 11\}$
19. $\{625\}$ **20.** $\left\{\left(-\dfrac{1}{2}, \dfrac{1}{2}\right), (2, 8)\right\}$ **21.** $\{(8, -2, -2)\}$

22.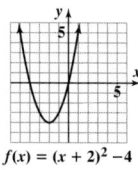

$f(x) = (x + 2)^2 - 4$

23.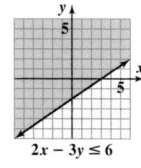

$2x - 3y \leq 6$

24.

$y = 3^{x-2}$

25.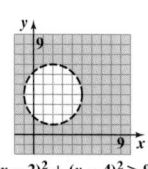

$f(x) = \dfrac{x^2 - x - 6}{x + 1}$

26.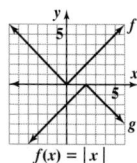

$f(x) = 2x - 4$
$f^{-1}(x) = \dfrac{x + 4}{2}$

27.

$(x - 2)^2 + (y - 4)^2 > 9$

28.

$f(x) = |x|$
$g(x) = -|x - 2|$

29. $(f \circ g)(x) = 2x^2 - 3x$;
$(g \circ f)(x) = -2x^2 + x + 2$
30. $4x + 2h - 1$
31. $y = -3x + 10$
32. $y = 3x + 3$
33. $2600 at 12%; $1400 at 14%
34. 4 m by 9 m
35. 10.99%

CHAPTER 6

Section 6.1

Check Point Exercises

1. a. $\begin{bmatrix} 1 & 6 & -3 & | & 7 \\ 4 & 12 & -20 & | & 8 \\ -3 & -2 & 1 & | & -9 \end{bmatrix}$ **b.** $\begin{bmatrix} 1 & 3 & -5 & | & 2 \\ 1 & 6 & -3 & | & 7 \\ -3 & -2 & 1 & | & -9 \end{bmatrix}$ **c.** $\begin{bmatrix} 4 & 12 & -20 & | & 8 \\ 1 & 6 & -3 & | & 7 \\ 0 & 16 & -8 & | & 12 \end{bmatrix}$ **2.** $\{(5, 2, 3)\}$ **3.** $\{(1, -1, 2, -3)\}$ **4.** $\{(5, 2, 3)\}$

Exercise Set 6.1

1. $\begin{bmatrix} 2 & 1 & 2 & | & 2 \\ 3 & -5 & -1 & | & 4 \\ 1 & -2 & -3 & | & -6 \end{bmatrix}$ **3.** $\begin{bmatrix} 1 & -1 & 1 & | & 8 \\ 0 & 1 & -12 & | & -15 \\ 0 & 0 & 1 & | & 1 \end{bmatrix}$ **5.** $\begin{bmatrix} 5 & -2 & -3 & | & 0 \\ 1 & 1 & 0 & | & 5 \\ 2 & 0 & -3 & | & 4 \end{bmatrix}$

7. $\begin{bmatrix} 2 & 5 & -3 & 1 & | & 2 \\ 0 & 3 & 1 & 0 & | & 4 \\ 1 & -1 & 5 & 0 & | & 9 \\ 5 & -5 & -2 & 0 & | & 1 \end{bmatrix}$ **9.** $5x + 3z = -11$
$y - 4z = 12$
$7x + 2y = 3$

11. $w + x + 4y + z = 3$
$\qquad -w + x - y = 7$
$\qquad 2w + 5z = 11$
$\qquad 12y + 4z = 5$

13. $\begin{bmatrix} 1 & -3 & 2 & | & 5 \\ 1 & 5 & -5 & | & 0 \\ 3 & 0 & 4 & | & 7 \end{bmatrix}$

15. $\begin{bmatrix} 1 & -3 & 2 & | & 0 \\ 0 & 10 & -7 & | & 7 \\ 2 & -2 & 1 & | & 3 \end{bmatrix}$

17. $\begin{bmatrix} 1 & -1 & 1 & 1 & | & 3 \\ 0 & 1 & -2 & -1 & | & 0 \\ 0 & 2 & 1 & 2 & | & 5 \\ 0 & 6 & -3 & -1 & | & -9 \end{bmatrix}$

19. $R_2: -3, -18; R_3: -12, -15; R_2: -\dfrac{3}{5}, -\dfrac{18}{5}; R_3: -12, -15$ **21.** $\{(1, -1, 2)\}$ **23.** $\{(3, -1, -1)\}$ **25.** $\{(2, -1, 1)\}$ **27.** $\{(2, 1, 1)\}$

29. $\{(2, -1, 1)\}$ **31.** $\{(-1, 2, -2)\}$ **33.** $\{(1, 2, -1)\}$ **35.** $\{(1, 2, 3, -2)\}$

37. $\{(0, -3, 0, -3)\}$ **39.** $f(x) = -x^2 + x + 2$ **41.** $f(x) = x^3 - 2x^2 + 3$

43. $\{(e^{-1}, e, e^{-3}, e^{-2})\}$ **45. a.** $a = -32, v_0 = 56, s_0 = 0$ **b.** 0; The ball hits the ground 3.5 seconds after it it thrown. **c.** 1.75 sec; 49 ft

47. $40x + 200y + 400z = 660$; 4 oz of Food A; $\dfrac{1}{2}$ oz of Food B; 1 oz of Food C
$\qquad 5x + 2y + 4z = 25$
$\qquad 30x + 10y + 300z = 425$

49. Asians: 122; Africans: 28; Europeans: 24; Americans: 9 **59.** makes sense **61.** makes sense **63.** false **65.** false **67.** 60 units: $7700
68. For $z = 0, (12z + 1, 10z - 1, z)$ is $(1, -1, 0)$; $3(1) - 4(-1) + 4(0) = 7$ is true; $1 - (-1) - 2(0) = 2$ is true; $2(1) - 3(-1) + 6(0) = 5$ is true.
69. For $z = 1, (12z + 1, 10z - 1, z)$ is $(13, 9, 1)$; $3(13) - 4(9) + 4(1) = 7$ is true; $13 - 9 - 2(1) = 2$ is true; $2(13) - 3(9) + 6(1) = 5$ is true.
70. a. Answers may vary. **b.** This system has more than one solution.

Section 6.2

Check Point Exercises

1. \varnothing **2.** $\{(11t + 13, 5t + 4, t)\}$ **3.** $\{(t + 50, -2t + 10, t)\}$
4. a. $w + z = 15$ **b.** $\{(-t + 15, t + 15, -t + 30, t)\}$ **c.** $w = 5; x = 25; y = 20$
$\qquad w + x = 30$
$\qquad x + y = 45$
$\qquad y + z = 30$

Exercise Set 6.2

1. \varnothing **3.** $\left\{ \left(-2t + 2, 2t + \dfrac{1}{2}, t \right) \right\}$ **5.** $\{(-3, 4, -2)\}$ **7.** $\{(5 - 2t, -2 + t, t)\}$ **9.** $\{(-1, 2, 1, 1)\}$ **11.** $\{(1, 3, 2, 1)\}$

13. $\{(1, -2, 1, 1)\}$ **15.** $\left\{ \left(1 + \dfrac{1}{3}t, \dfrac{1}{3}t, t \right) \right\}$ **17.** $\{(-13t + 5, 5t, t)\}$ **19.** $\left\{ \left(2t - \dfrac{5}{4}, \dfrac{13}{4}, t \right) \right\}$ **21.** $\{(1, -t - 1, 2, t)\}$

23. $\left\{ \left(-\dfrac{2}{11}t + \dfrac{81}{11}, \dfrac{1}{22}t + \dfrac{10}{11}, \dfrac{4}{11}t - \dfrac{8}{11}, t \right) \right\}$

25. a. $4w - 2x + 2y - 3z = 0; 7w - x - y - 3z = 0; w + x + y - z = 0$ **b.** $\{(0.5t, 0, 0.5t, t)\}$
27. a. $w + 2x + 5y + 5z = -3; w + x + 3y + 4z = -1; w - x - y + 2z = 3$ **b.** $\{(1 - 3s - t, -2 - s - 2t, t, s)\}$
29. $z + 12 = x + 6$ **31.** $\{(t + 6, t + 2, t)\}$
33. a. $w + z = 380$ **b.** $\{(380 - t, 220 + t, 50 + t, t)\}$ **c.** $w = 330, x = 270, y = 100$
$\qquad w + x = 600$
$\qquad x - y = 170$
$\qquad y - z = 50$
35. a. The system has no solution, so there is no way to satisfy these dietary requirements with no Food 1 available.
\qquad **b.** 4 oz of Food 1, 0 oz of Food 2, 10 oz of Food 3; 2 oz of Food 1, 5 oz of Food 2, 9 oz of Food 3 (other answers are possible).
41. does not make sense **43.** does not make sense **45.** $a = 1$ or $a = 3$ **47.** -1 **48.** -12 **49.** 8

Section 6.3

Check Point Exercises

1. a. 3×2 **b.** $a_{12} = -2; a_{31} = 1$ **2. a.** $\begin{bmatrix} 2 & 0 \\ 9 & -10 \end{bmatrix}$ **b.** $\begin{bmatrix} 9 & -4 \\ -9 & 7 \\ 5 & -2 \end{bmatrix}$ **3. a.** $\begin{bmatrix} 6 & 12 \\ -48 & -30 \end{bmatrix}$ **b.** $\begin{bmatrix} -14 & -1 \\ 25 & 10 \end{bmatrix}$ **4.** $\begin{bmatrix} -4 & 3 \\ -3 & \dfrac{13}{3} \end{bmatrix}$

5. $\begin{bmatrix} 7 & 6 \\ 13 & 12 \end{bmatrix}$ **6.** $[30]$; $\begin{bmatrix} 2 & 0 & 4 \\ 6 & 0 & 12 \\ 14 & 0 & 28 \end{bmatrix}$ **7. a.** $\begin{bmatrix} 2 & 18 & 11 & 9 \\ 0 & 10 & 8 & 2 \end{bmatrix}$ **b.** The product is undefined.

8. $\begin{bmatrix} 2 & 1 & 1 \\ 2 & 1 & 1 \\ 2 & 2 & 1 \end{bmatrix} + \begin{bmatrix} -1 & 2 & 2 \\ -1 & 2 & 2 \\ -1 & -1 & 2 \end{bmatrix} = \begin{bmatrix} 1 & 3 & 3 \\ 1 & 3 & 3 \\ 1 & 1 & 3 \end{bmatrix}$

9. a. $\begin{bmatrix} 0 & 3 & 4 \\ 0 & 5 & 2 \end{bmatrix} + \begin{bmatrix} -3 & -3 & -3 \\ -1 & -1 & -1 \end{bmatrix} = \begin{bmatrix} -3 & 0 & 1 \\ -1 & 4 & 1 \end{bmatrix}$ **b.** $2\begin{bmatrix} 0 & 3 & 4 \\ 0 & 5 & 2 \end{bmatrix} = \begin{bmatrix} 0 & 6 & 8 \\ 0 & 10 & 4 \end{bmatrix}$

 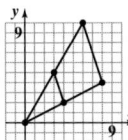

c. $\begin{bmatrix} 0 & 3 & 4 \\ 0 & -5 & -2 \end{bmatrix}$; Multiplying by B reflects the triangle over the x-axis.

Exercise Set 6.3

1. a. 2×3 **b.** a_{32} does not exist; $a_{23} = -1$ **3. a.** 3×4 **b.** $a_{32} = \dfrac{1}{2}$; $a_{23} = -6$ **5.** $x = 6$; $y = 4$ **7.** $x = 4$; $y = 6$; $z = 3$

9. a. $\begin{bmatrix} 9 & 10 \\ 3 & 9 \end{bmatrix}$ **b.** $\begin{bmatrix} -1 & -8 \\ 3 & -5 \end{bmatrix}$ **c.** $\begin{bmatrix} -16 & -4 \\ -12 & -8 \end{bmatrix}$ **d.** $\begin{bmatrix} 22 & 21 \\ 9 & 20 \end{bmatrix}$ **11. a.** $\begin{bmatrix} 3 & 2 \\ 6 & 2 \\ 5 & 7 \end{bmatrix}$ **b.** $\begin{bmatrix} -1 & 4 \\ 0 & 6 \\ 5 & 5 \end{bmatrix}$ **c.** $\begin{bmatrix} -4 & -12 \\ -12 & -16 \\ -20 & -24 \end{bmatrix}$ **d.** $\begin{bmatrix} 7 & 7 \\ 15 & 8 \\ 15 & 20 \end{bmatrix}$

13. a. $\begin{bmatrix} -3 \\ -1 \\ 0 \end{bmatrix}$ **b.** $\begin{bmatrix} 7 \\ -7 \\ 2 \end{bmatrix}$ **c.** $\begin{bmatrix} -8 \\ 16 \\ -4 \end{bmatrix}$ **d.** $\begin{bmatrix} -4 \\ -6 \\ 1 \end{bmatrix}$ **15. a.** $\begin{bmatrix} 8 & 0 & -4 \\ 14 & 0 & 6 \\ -1 & 0 & 0 \end{bmatrix}$ **b.** $\begin{bmatrix} -4 & -20 & 0 \\ 14 & 24 & 14 \\ 9 & -4 & 4 \end{bmatrix}$ **c.** $\begin{bmatrix} -8 & 40 & 8 \\ -56 & -48 & -40 \\ -16 & 8 & -8 \end{bmatrix}$ **d.** $\begin{bmatrix} 18 & -10 & -10 \\ 42 & 12 & 22 \\ 2 & -2 & 2 \end{bmatrix}$

17. $\begin{bmatrix} -8 & -8 \\ 2 & -9 \\ 8 & -4 \end{bmatrix}$ **19.** $\begin{bmatrix} -1 & 3 \\ -1 & \dfrac{9}{2} \\ -1 & -2 \end{bmatrix}$ **21.** $\begin{bmatrix} \dfrac{1}{3} & \dfrac{13}{3} \\ -\dfrac{4}{3} & 6 \\ -\dfrac{7}{3} & -\dfrac{4}{3} \end{bmatrix}$ **23.** $\begin{bmatrix} 7 & 27 \\ -8 & 36 \\ -17 & -4 \end{bmatrix}$ **25.** $\begin{bmatrix} \dfrac{27}{2} & \dfrac{31}{2} \\ -4 & 18 \\ -\dfrac{29}{2} & 6 \end{bmatrix}$ **27. a.** $\begin{bmatrix} 0 & 16 \\ 12 & 8 \end{bmatrix}$ **b.** $\begin{bmatrix} -7 & 3 \\ 29 & 15 \end{bmatrix}$

29. a. $\begin{bmatrix} 30 \end{bmatrix}$ **b.** $\begin{bmatrix} 1 & 2 & 3 & 4 \\ 2 & 4 & 6 & 8 \\ 3 & 6 & 9 & 12 \\ 4 & 8 & 12 & 16 \end{bmatrix}$ **31. a.** $\begin{bmatrix} 4 & -5 & 8 \\ 6 & -1 & 5 \\ 0 & 4 & -6 \end{bmatrix}$ **b.** $\begin{bmatrix} 5 & -2 & 7 \\ 17 & -3 & 2 \\ 3 & 0 & -5 \end{bmatrix}$ **33. a.** $\begin{bmatrix} 6 & 8 & 16 \\ 11 & 16 & 24 \\ 1 & -1 & 12 \end{bmatrix}$ **b.** $\begin{bmatrix} 38 & 27 \\ -16 & -4 \end{bmatrix}$

35. a. $\begin{bmatrix} 0 & 0 \\ 0 & 0 \end{bmatrix}$ **b.** $\begin{bmatrix} 4 & -1 & -3 & 1 \\ -1 & 4 & -3 & 2 \\ 14 & -11 & -3 & -1 \\ 25 & -25 & 0 & -5 \end{bmatrix}$ **37.** $\begin{bmatrix} 17 & 7 \\ -5 & -11 \end{bmatrix}$ **39.** $\begin{bmatrix} 11 & -1 \\ -7 & -3 \end{bmatrix}$

41. $A - C$ is not defined because A is 3×2 and C is 2×2. **43.** $\begin{bmatrix} 16 & -16 \\ -12 & 12 \\ 0 & 0 \end{bmatrix}$ **45.** $\begin{bmatrix} 0 & 0 \\ 0 & 0 \end{bmatrix}$

47. Answers will vary.; Example:

$A(B + C) = \begin{bmatrix} 1 & 0 \\ 0 & 1 \end{bmatrix}\left(\begin{bmatrix} 1 & 0 \\ 0 & -1 \end{bmatrix} + \begin{bmatrix} -1 & 0 \\ 0 & 1 \end{bmatrix}\right) = \begin{bmatrix} 1 & 0 \\ 0 & 1 \end{bmatrix}\begin{bmatrix} 0 & 0 \\ 0 & 0 \end{bmatrix} = \begin{bmatrix} 0 & 0 \\ 0 & 0 \end{bmatrix}$

$AB + AC = \begin{bmatrix} 1 & 0 \\ 0 & 1 \end{bmatrix}\begin{bmatrix} 1 & 0 \\ 0 & -1 \end{bmatrix} + \begin{bmatrix} 1 & 0 \\ 0 & 1 \end{bmatrix}\begin{bmatrix} -1 & 0 \\ 0 & 1 \end{bmatrix} = \begin{bmatrix} 1 & 0 \\ 0 & -1 \end{bmatrix} + \begin{bmatrix} -1 & 0 \\ 0 & 1 \end{bmatrix} = \begin{bmatrix} 0 & 0 \\ 0 & 0 \end{bmatrix}$

So, $A(B + C) = AB + AC$.

49. $\begin{bmatrix} x \\ -y \end{bmatrix}$; It changes the sign of the y-coordinate.

51. a. $\begin{bmatrix} 1 & 3 & 1 \\ 3 & 3 & 3 \\ 1 & 3 & 1 \end{bmatrix}$ **b.** $\begin{bmatrix} 1 & 3 & 1 \\ 3 & 3 & 3 \\ 1 & 3 & 1 \end{bmatrix} + \begin{bmatrix} -1 & -1 & -1 \\ -1 & -1 & -1 \\ -1 & -1 & -1 \end{bmatrix} = \begin{bmatrix} 0 & 2 & 0 \\ 2 & 2 & 2 \\ 0 & 2 & 0 \end{bmatrix}$ **c.** $\begin{bmatrix} 1 & 3 & 1 \\ 3 & 3 & 3 \\ 1 & 3 & 1 \end{bmatrix} + \begin{bmatrix} 1 & -2 & 1 \\ -2 & -2 & -2 \\ 1 & -2 & 1 \end{bmatrix} = \begin{bmatrix} 2 & 1 & 2 \\ 1 & 1 & 1 \\ 2 & 1 & 2 \end{bmatrix}$

53. $\begin{bmatrix} -2 & 1 & 1 & -1 & -1 & -2 \\ -3 & -3 & -2 & -2 & 2 & 2 \end{bmatrix}$ **55.** $\begin{bmatrix} 0 & \dfrac{3}{2} & \dfrac{3}{2} & \dfrac{1}{2} & \dfrac{1}{2} & 0 \\ 1 & 1 & \dfrac{3}{2} & \dfrac{3}{2} & \dfrac{7}{2} & \dfrac{7}{2} \end{bmatrix}$ **57. a.** $\begin{bmatrix} 0 & 3 & 3 & 1 & 1 & 0 \\ 0 & 0 & -1 & -1 & -5 & -5 \end{bmatrix}$

b. The effect is a reflection across the x-axis.

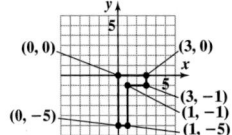

59. a. $\begin{bmatrix} 0 & 0 & -1 & -1 & -5 & -5 \\ 0 & 3 & 3 & 1 & 1 & 0 \end{bmatrix}$

b.

The effect is a 90° counterclockwise rotation about the origin.

61. a. $A = \begin{bmatrix} 2 & 6 \\ 31 & 46 \end{bmatrix}$ **b.** $B = \begin{bmatrix} 9 & 29 \\ 65 & 77 \end{bmatrix}$

c. $B - A = \begin{bmatrix} 7 & 23 \\ 34 & 31 \end{bmatrix}$

The difference between the percentage of people completing the transition to adulthood in 1960 and 2000 by age and gender

63. a. System 1: The midterm and final both count for 50% of the course grade. System 2: The midterm counts for 30% of the course grade and the final counts for 70%.

b. $\begin{bmatrix} 84 & 87.2 \\ 79 & 81 \\ 90 & 88.4 \\ 73 & 68.6 \\ 69 & 73.4 \end{bmatrix}$ System 1 grades are listed first (if different). Student 1: B; Student 2: C or B; Student 3: A or B; Student 4: C or D; Student 5: D or C

77. makes sense **79.** makes sense **83.** $AB = -BA$ so they are anticommutative.

85. $\begin{bmatrix} a_{11} & a_{12} \\ a_{21} & a_{22} \end{bmatrix}$; Nothing happens to the elements in the first matrix. **86.** $\{(15, -12, -4)\}$ **87.** $\begin{cases} a_1 x + b_1 y + c_1 z = d_1 \\ a_2 x + b_2 y + c_2 z = d_2 \\ a_3 x + b_3 y + c_3 z = d_3 \end{cases}$

Mid-Chapter 6 Check Point

1. $\{(1, -1, 2)\}$ **2.** \varnothing **3.** $\left\{\left(-\dfrac{4}{7}-\dfrac{4}{7}t, \dfrac{5}{7}+\dfrac{5}{7}t, t\right)\right\}$ **4.** $\{(3, 6, -4, 1)\}$ **5.** \varnothing **6.** $\begin{bmatrix} -4 & -\dfrac{1}{2} \\ 3 & 3 \end{bmatrix}$ **7.** $\begin{bmatrix} -12 & -2 \\ -21 & -4 \\ 3 & 1 \end{bmatrix}$ **8.** $\begin{bmatrix} 12 & -4 \\ 22 & -7 \\ -4 & 1 \end{bmatrix}$

9. $A + C$ does not exist because A is 3×2 and C is 2×2. **10.** $\begin{bmatrix} \dfrac{1}{2} & \dfrac{1}{2} \\ -3 & \dfrac{1}{2} \end{bmatrix}$

Section 6.4

Check Point Exercises

1. $AB = I_2; BA = I_2$ **2.** $\begin{bmatrix} 3 & -7 \\ -2 & 5 \end{bmatrix}$ **3.** $\begin{bmatrix} 1 & 2 \\ 1 & 3 \end{bmatrix}$ **4.** $\begin{bmatrix} 3 & -2 & -4 \\ 3 & -2 & -5 \\ -1 & 1 & 2 \end{bmatrix}$ **5.** $\{(4, -2, 1)\}$ **6.** The encoded message is $-7, 10, -53, 77$.

7. The decoded message is 2, 1, 19, 5 or BASE.

Exercise Set 6.4

1. $AB = I_2; BA = I_2; B = A^{-1}$ **3.** $AB = \begin{bmatrix} 8 & -16 \\ -2 & 7 \end{bmatrix}; BA = \begin{bmatrix} 12 & 12 \\ 1 & 3 \end{bmatrix}; B \neq A^{-1}$ **5.** $AB = I_2; BA = I_2; B = A^{-1}$

7. $AB = I_3; BA = I_3; B = A^{-1}$ **9.** $AB = I_3; BA = I_3; B = A^{-1}$ **11.** $AB = I_4; BA = I_4; B = A^{-1}$

13. $\begin{bmatrix} \dfrac{2}{7} & -\dfrac{3}{7} \\ \dfrac{1}{7} & \dfrac{2}{7} \end{bmatrix}$ **15.** $\begin{bmatrix} 1 & \dfrac{1}{2} \\ 2 & \dfrac{3}{2} \end{bmatrix}$ **17.** A does not have an inverse. **19.** $\begin{bmatrix} \dfrac{1}{2} & 0 & 0 \\ 0 & \dfrac{1}{4} & 0 \\ 0 & 0 & \dfrac{1}{6} \end{bmatrix}$ **21.** $\begin{bmatrix} 1 & 1 & 2 \\ 1 & 1 & 1 \\ 2 & 3 & 4 \end{bmatrix}$ **23.** $\begin{bmatrix} 1 & 0 & 1 \\ 1 & 1 & 2 \\ 3 & 2 & 6 \end{bmatrix}$

25. $\begin{bmatrix} -3 & 2 & -4 \\ -1 & 1 & -1 \\ 8 & -5 & 10 \end{bmatrix}$ **27.** $\begin{bmatrix} 1 & 0 & 0 & 0 \\ 0 & -1 & 0 & 0 \\ 0 & 0 & \dfrac{1}{3} & 0 \\ -1 & 0 & 0 & 1 \end{bmatrix}$ **29.** $\begin{bmatrix} 6 & 5 \\ 5 & 4 \end{bmatrix}\begin{bmatrix} x \\ y \end{bmatrix} = \begin{bmatrix} 13 \\ 10 \end{bmatrix}$ **31.** $\begin{bmatrix} 1 & 3 & 4 \\ 1 & 2 & 3 \\ 1 & 4 & 3 \end{bmatrix}\begin{bmatrix} x \\ y \\ z \end{bmatrix} = \begin{bmatrix} -3 \\ -2 \\ -6 \end{bmatrix}$ **33.** $\begin{aligned} 4x - 7y &= -3 \\ 2x - 3y &= 1 \end{aligned}$

35. $\begin{aligned} 2x - z &= 6 \\ 3y &= 9 \\ x + y &= 5 \end{aligned}$ **37. a.** $\begin{bmatrix} 2 & 6 & 6 \\ 2 & 7 & 6 \\ 2 & 7 & 7 \end{bmatrix}\begin{bmatrix} x \\ y \\ z \end{bmatrix} = \begin{bmatrix} 8 \\ 10 \\ 9 \end{bmatrix}$ **b.** $\{(1, 2, -1)\}$ **39. a.** $\begin{bmatrix} 1 & -1 & 1 \\ 0 & 2 & -1 \\ 2 & 3 & 0 \end{bmatrix}\begin{bmatrix} x \\ y \\ z \end{bmatrix} = \begin{bmatrix} 8 \\ -7 \\ 1 \end{bmatrix}$ **b.** $\{(2, -1, 5)\}$

41. a. $\begin{bmatrix} 1 & -1 & 2 & 0 \\ 0 & 1 & -1 & 1 \\ -1 & 1 & -1 & 2 \\ 0 & -1 & 1 & -2 \end{bmatrix}\begin{bmatrix} w \\ x \\ y \\ z \end{bmatrix} = \begin{bmatrix} -3 \\ 4 \\ 2 \\ -4 \end{bmatrix}$ **b.** $\{(2, 3, -1, 0)\}$ **43.** $\begin{bmatrix} \dfrac{1}{2}e^{-x} & -\dfrac{1}{2}e^{-3x} \\ \dfrac{1}{2}e^{-3x} & \dfrac{1}{2}e^{-5x} \end{bmatrix}$ **45.** $\begin{bmatrix} \dfrac{1}{8} & \dfrac{5}{8} \\ \dfrac{3}{8} & \dfrac{7}{8} \end{bmatrix}$

47. $(AB)^{-1} = \begin{bmatrix} -23 & 16 \\ 13 & -9 \end{bmatrix}$; $A^{-1}B^{-1} = \begin{bmatrix} -3 & 11 \\ 8 & -29 \end{bmatrix}$; $B^{-1}A^{-1} = \begin{bmatrix} -23 & 16 \\ 13 & -9 \end{bmatrix}$; $(AB)^{-1} = B^{-1}A^{-1}$ **49.** $AA^{-1} = I_3$ and $A^{-1}A = I_3$

51. The encoded message is 27, -19, 32, -20.; The decoded message is 8, 5, 12, 16 or HELP.
53. The encoded message is 14, 85, -33, 4, 18, -7, -18, 19, -9.

65. $\begin{bmatrix} 1 & 1 \\ 2 & 3 \end{bmatrix}$ **67.** $\begin{bmatrix} 1 & 0 & 1 \\ 2 & 1 & 3 \\ -1 & 1 & 1 \end{bmatrix}$ **69.** $\begin{bmatrix} 0 & -1 & 0 & 1 \\ -1 & -5 & 0 & 3 \\ -2 & -4 & 1 & -2 \\ -1 & -4 & 0 & 1 \end{bmatrix}$ **71.** $\{(2, 3, -5)\}$ **73.** $\{(1, 2, -1)\}$ **75.** $\{(2, 1, 3, -2, 4)\}$

79. does not make sense **81.** makes sense **83.** false **85.** false **87.** false **91.** $a = 3$ or $a = -2$ **93.** 2 **94.** 6 **95.** -31

Section 6.5

Check Point Exercises

1. a. -4 **b.** -17 **2.** $\{(4, -2)\}$ **3.** 80 **4.** -24 **5.** $\{(2, -3, 4)\}$ **6.** -250

Exercise Set 6.5

1. 1 **3.** -29 **5.** 0 **7.** 33 **9.** $-\dfrac{7}{16}$ **11.** $\{(5, 2)\}$ **13.** $\{(2, -3)\}$ **15.** $\{(3, -1)\}$ **17.** The system is dependent. **19.** $\{(4, 2)\}$

21. $\{(7, 4)\}$ **23.** The system is inconsistent. **25.** The system is dependent. **27.** 72 **29.** -75 **31.** 0 **33.** $\{(-5, -2, 7)\}$

35. $\{(2, -3, 4)\}$ **37.** $\{(3, -1, 2)\}$ **39.** $\{(2, 3, 1)\}$ **41.** -200 **43.** 195 **45.** -42 **47.** $2x - 4y = 8; 3x + 5y = -10$

49. -11 **51.** 4 **53.** 28 sq units **55.** yes **57.** The equation of the line is $y = -\dfrac{11}{5}x + \dfrac{8}{5}$. **69.** 13,200 **71.** does not make sense

73. does not make sense **75. a.** a^2 **b.** a^3 **c.** a^4 **d.** Each determinant has zeros below the main diagonal and a's everywhere else.
e. Each determinant equals a raised to the power equal to the order of the determinant. **77.** The sign of the value is changed when
2 columns are interchanged in a 2nd order determinant.

79. $\begin{vmatrix} x & y & 1 \\ x_1 & y_1 & 1 \\ x_2 & y_2 & 1 \end{vmatrix} = x(y_1 - y_2) - y(x_1 - x_2) + (x_1y_2 - x_2y_1) = 0$; solving for y, $y = \dfrac{y_1 - y_2}{x_1 - x_2}x + \dfrac{x_1y_2 - x_2y_1}{x_1 - x_2}$, and $m = \dfrac{y_1 - y_2}{x_1 - x_2}$ and $b = \dfrac{x_1y_2 - x_2y_1}{x_1 - x_2}$.

81. a. -3 and 3 **b.** -2 and 2 **82.** $\dfrac{x^2}{16} + \dfrac{y^2}{25} = 1$ **83.** $(x - 1)^2 + (y + 2)^2 = 9$; center: $(1, -2)$; radius: 3;

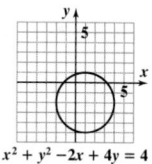

$x^2 + y^2 - 2x + 4y = 4$

Chapter 6 Review Exercises

1. $\begin{bmatrix} 1 & 2 & 2 & | & 2 \\ 0 & 1 & -1 & | & 2 \\ 0 & 0 & 9 & | & -9 \end{bmatrix}$ **2.** $\begin{bmatrix} 1 & -1 & \frac{1}{2} & | & -\frac{1}{2} \\ 1 & 2 & -1 & | & 2 \\ 6 & 4 & 3 & | & 5 \end{bmatrix}$ **3.** $\{(1, 3, -4)\}$ **4.** $\{(-2, -1, 0)\}$ **5.** $\{(2, -2, 3, 4)\}$

6. a. $a = -2; b = 32; c = 42$ **b.** 2:00 p.m.; 170 parts per million **7.** capitalist: 1%; upper middle: 15%; lower middle: 34%; working: 30%
8. \varnothing **9.** $\{(2t + 4, t + 1, t)\}$ **10.** $\{(-37t + 2, 16t, -7t + 1, t)\}$ **11.** $\{(7t + 18, -3t - 7, t)\}$

12. a. $x + z = 750$ **b.** $\{(-t + 750, t - 250, t)\}$ **c.** $x = 350; y = 150$ **13.** $x = -5; y = 6; z = 6$ **14.** $\begin{bmatrix} 0 & 2 & 3 \\ 8 & 1 & 3 \end{bmatrix}$ **15.** $\begin{bmatrix} 0 & -4 \\ 6 & 4 \\ 2 & -10 \end{bmatrix}$
$\ y - z = -250$
$\ x + y = 500$

16. $\begin{bmatrix} -4 & 4 & -1 \\ -2 & -5 & 5 \end{bmatrix}$ **17.** Not possible since B is 3×2 and C is 3×3. **18.** $\begin{bmatrix} 2 & 3 & 8 \\ 21 & 5 & 5 \end{bmatrix}$ **19.** $\begin{bmatrix} -12 & 14 & 0 \\ 2 & -14 & 18 \end{bmatrix}$ **20.** $\begin{bmatrix} 0 & -10 & -15 \\ -40 & -5 & -15 \end{bmatrix}$

21. $\begin{bmatrix} -1 & -16 \\ 8 & 1 \end{bmatrix}$ **22.** $\begin{bmatrix} -10 & -6 & 2 \\ 16 & 3 & 4 \\ -23 & -16 & 7 \end{bmatrix}$ **23.** $\begin{bmatrix} -6 & 4 & -8 \\ 0 & 5 & 11 \\ -17 & 13 & -19 \end{bmatrix}$ **24.** $\begin{bmatrix} 10 & 5 \\ -2 & -30 \end{bmatrix}$ **25.** Not possible since AB is 2×2 and BA is 3×3.

26. $\begin{bmatrix} 7 & 6 & 5 \\ 2 & -1 & 11 \end{bmatrix}$ **27.** $\begin{bmatrix} -6 & -22 & -40 \\ 9 & 43 & 58 \\ -14 & -48 & -94 \end{bmatrix}$ **28.** $\begin{bmatrix} -2 & -6 \\ 3 & \frac{1}{3} \end{bmatrix}$ **29.** $\begin{bmatrix} 2 & 2 & 2 \\ 1 & 2 & 1 \\ 1 & 2 & 1 \end{bmatrix}$ **30.** $\begin{bmatrix} 1 & 1 & 1 \\ -1 & 1 & -1 \\ -1 & 1 & -1 \end{bmatrix}$

31. $\begin{bmatrix} -2 & 0 & 0 \\ 1 & 1 & -3 \end{bmatrix}$

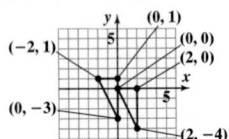

32. $\begin{bmatrix} 0 & 1 & 1 \\ -2 & -2 & -4 \end{bmatrix}$

33. $\begin{bmatrix} 0 & 2 & 2 \\ 0 & 0 & 4 \end{bmatrix}$

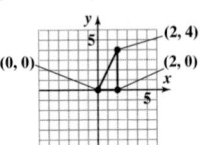

The effect is a reflection over the x-axis

34. $\begin{bmatrix} 0 & -2 & -2 \\ 0 & 0 & -4 \end{bmatrix}$

The effect is a reflection over the y-axis

35. $\begin{bmatrix} 0 & 0 & 4 \\ 0 & 2 & 2 \end{bmatrix}$

The effect is a 90° counterclockwise rotation about the origin

36. $\begin{bmatrix} 0 & 4 & 4 \\ 0 & 0 & -4 \end{bmatrix}$

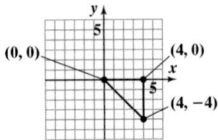

The effect is a horizontal stretch by a factor of 2.

37. $AB = \begin{bmatrix} 1 & 7 \\ 0 & 5 \end{bmatrix}$; $BA = \begin{bmatrix} 1 & 0 \\ 1 & 5 \end{bmatrix}$; $B \neq A^{-1}$ **38.** $AB = I_3$; $BA = I_3$; $B = A^{-1}$ **39.** $\begin{bmatrix} 3 & 1 \\ 2 & 1 \end{bmatrix}$ **40.** $\begin{bmatrix} -\frac{3}{5} & \frac{1}{5} \\ 1 & 0 \end{bmatrix}$ **41.** $\begin{bmatrix} 3 & 0 & -2 \\ -6 & 1 & 4 \\ 1 & 0 & -1 \end{bmatrix}$

42. $\begin{bmatrix} 8 & -8 & 5 \\ -3 & 2 & -1 \\ -1 & -1 & 1 \end{bmatrix}$ **43. a.** $\begin{bmatrix} 1 & 1 & 2 \\ 0 & 1 & 3 \\ 3 & 0 & -2 \end{bmatrix}\begin{bmatrix} x \\ y \\ z \end{bmatrix} = \begin{bmatrix} 7 \\ -2 \\ 0 \end{bmatrix}$ **b.** $\{(-18, 79, -27)\}$ **44. a.** $\begin{bmatrix} 1 & -1 & 2 \\ 0 & 1 & -1 \\ 1 & 0 & 2 \end{bmatrix}\begin{bmatrix} x \\ y \\ z \end{bmatrix} = \begin{bmatrix} 12 \\ -5 \\ 10 \end{bmatrix}$

b. $\{(4, -2, 3)\}$ **45.** The encoded message is 96, 135, 46, 63; The decoded message is 18, 21, 12, 5 or RULE. **46.** 17 **47.** 4

48. -86 **49.** -236 **50.** 4 **51.** 16 **52.** $\left\{\left(\frac{7}{4}, -\frac{25}{8}\right)\right\}$ **53.** $\{(2, -7)\}$ **54.** $\{(23, -12, 3)\}$ **55.** $\{(-3, 2, 1)\}$

56. $a = \frac{5}{8}$; $b = -50$; $c = 1150$; 30- and 50-year-olds are involved in an average of 212.5 automobile accidents per day.

Chapter 6 Test

1. $\left\{\left(-3, \frac{1}{2}, 1\right)\right\}$ **2.** $\{(t, t - 1, t)\}$ **3.** $\begin{bmatrix} 5 & 4 \\ 1 & 11 \end{bmatrix}$ **4.** $\begin{bmatrix} 5 & -2 \\ 1 & -1 \\ 4 & -1 \end{bmatrix}$ **5.** $\begin{bmatrix} \frac{3}{5} & -\frac{2}{5} \\ \frac{1}{5} & \frac{1}{5} \end{bmatrix}$ **6.** $\begin{bmatrix} -1 & 2 \\ -5 & 4 \end{bmatrix}$ **7.** $AB = I_3$; $BA = I_3$

8. a. $\begin{bmatrix} 3 & 5 \\ 2 & -3 \end{bmatrix}\begin{bmatrix} x \\ y \end{bmatrix} = \begin{bmatrix} 9 \\ -13 \end{bmatrix}$ **b.** $\begin{bmatrix} \frac{3}{19} & \frac{5}{19} \\ \frac{2}{19} & -\frac{3}{19} \end{bmatrix}$ **c.** $\{(-2, 3)\}$ **9.** 18 **10.** $x = 2$

Cumulative Review Exercises (Chapters 1–6)

1. $\left\{\frac{-1 + \sqrt{33}}{4}, \frac{-1 - \sqrt{33}}{4}\right\}$ **2.** $\left[\frac{1}{2}, \infty\right)$ **3.** $\{6\}$ **4.** $\left\{-4, \frac{1}{3}, 1\right\}$ **5.** $\{\ln 5, \ln 9\}$ **6.** $\{1\}$ **7.** $\{(7, -4, 6)\}$

8. $y = -1$ **9.** $f^{-1}(x) = \frac{x^2 + 7}{4}$ $(x \geq 0)$

10.

$f(x) = \dfrac{x}{x^2 - 16}$

11. $f(x) = (x + 2)(x - 3)(2x + 1)(2x - 1)$ **13. a.** $A = 900e^{-0.017t}$ **b.** 759.30 g

12.

$y = \log_2(x + 1)$

$y = \log_2 x$

$x = -1$

14. $\begin{bmatrix} 2 & -1 \\ 13 & 1 \end{bmatrix}$ **15.** $\dfrac{8}{x - 3} + \dfrac{-2}{x - 2} + \dfrac{-3}{x + 2}$

16.

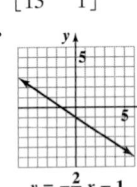

$y = -\frac{2}{3}x - 1$

17.

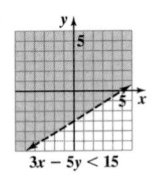

$3x - 5y < 15$

18.

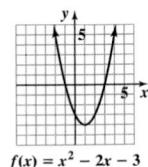

$f(x) = x^2 - 2x - 3$

19.

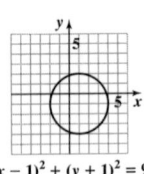

$(x - 1)^2 + (y + 1)^2 = 9$

20. $x^2 + 2x - 2$

CHAPTER 7

Section 7.1

Check Point Exercises

1. foci at $(-3\sqrt{3}, 0)$ and $(3\sqrt{3}, 0)$ **2.** foci at $(0, -\sqrt{7})$ and $(0, \sqrt{7})$ **3.** $\dfrac{x^2}{9} + \dfrac{y^2}{5} = 1$ **4.** foci at $(-1 - \sqrt{5}, 2)$ and $(-1 + \sqrt{5}, 2)$

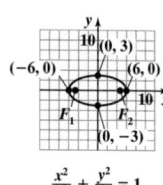

$$\dfrac{x^2}{36} + \dfrac{y^2}{9} = 1$$

$$16x^2 + 9y^2 = 144$$

$$\dfrac{(x + 1)^2}{9} + \dfrac{(y - 2)^2}{4} = 1$$

5. Yes

Exercise Set 7.1

1. foci at $(-2\sqrt{3}, 0)$ and $(2\sqrt{3}, 0)$ **3.** foci at $(0, -3\sqrt{3})$ and $(0, 3\sqrt{3})$ **5.** foci at $(0, -\sqrt{39})$ and $(0, \sqrt{39})$

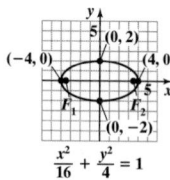

$$\dfrac{x^2}{16} + \dfrac{y^2}{4} = 1$$

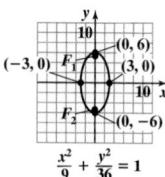

$$\dfrac{x^2}{9} + \dfrac{y^2}{36} = 1$$

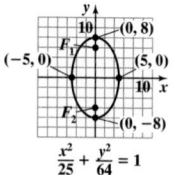

$$\dfrac{x^2}{25} + \dfrac{y^2}{64} = 1$$

7. foci at $(0, -4\sqrt{2})$ and $(0, 4\sqrt{2})$ **9.** foci at $(0, -2)$ and $(0, 2)$ **11.** foci at $\left(-\dfrac{\sqrt{3}}{2}, 0\right)$ and $\left(\dfrac{\sqrt{3}}{2}, 0\right)$

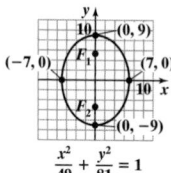

$$\dfrac{x^2}{49} + \dfrac{y^2}{81} = 1$$

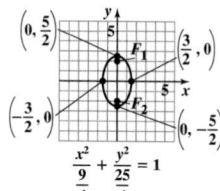

$$\dfrac{x^2}{\frac{9}{4}} + \dfrac{y^2}{\frac{25}{4}} = 1$$

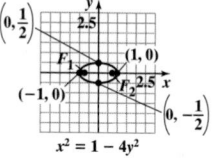

$$x^2 = 1 - 4y^2$$

13. foci at $(0, -\sqrt{21})$ and $(0, \sqrt{21})$ **15.** foci at $(-2\sqrt{3}, 0)$ and $(2\sqrt{3}, 0)$ **17.** foci at $(0, -\sqrt{2})$ and $(0, \sqrt{2})$

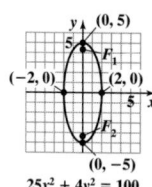

$$25x^2 + 4y^2 = 100$$

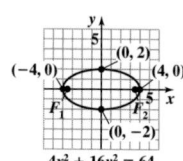

$$4x^2 + 16y^2 = 64$$

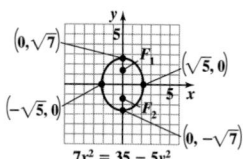

$$7x^2 = 35 - 5y^2$$

19. $\dfrac{x^2}{4} + \dfrac{y^2}{1} = 1$; foci at $(-\sqrt{3}, 0)$ and $(\sqrt{3}, 0)$ **21.** $\dfrac{x^2}{1} + \dfrac{y^2}{4} = 1$; foci at $(0, \sqrt{3})$ and $(0, -\sqrt{3})$

23. $\dfrac{(x + 1)^2}{4} + \dfrac{(y - 1)^2}{1} = 1$; foci at $(-1 - \sqrt{3}, 1)$ and $(-1 + \sqrt{3}, 1)$ **25.** $\dfrac{x^2}{64} + \dfrac{y^2}{39} = 1$ **27.** $\dfrac{x^2}{33} + \dfrac{y^2}{49} = 1$

29. $\dfrac{x^2}{13} + \dfrac{y^2}{9} = 1$ **31.** $\dfrac{x^2}{16} + \dfrac{y^2}{4} = 1$ **33.** $\dfrac{(x + 2)^2}{4} + \dfrac{(y - 3)^2}{25} = 1$ **35.** $\dfrac{(x - 7)^2}{4} + \dfrac{(y - 6)^2}{9} = 1$

37. foci at $(2 - \sqrt{5}, 1)$ and $(2 + \sqrt{5}, 1)$

$$\frac{(x - 2)^2}{9} + \frac{(y - 1)^2}{4} = 1$$

39. foci at $(-3 - 2\sqrt{3}, 2)$ and $(-3 + 2\sqrt{3}, 2)$

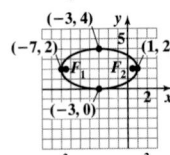

$$(x + 3)^2 + 4(y - 2)^2 = 16$$

41. foci at $(4, 2)$ and $(4, -6)$

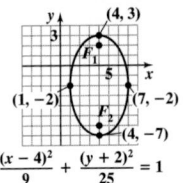

$$\frac{(x - 4)^2}{9} + \frac{(y + 2)^2}{25} = 1$$

43. foci at $(0, 2 + \sqrt{11}), (0, 2 - \sqrt{11})$

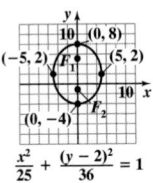

$$\frac{x^2}{25} + \frac{(y - 2)^2}{36} = 1$$

45. foci at $(-3 - 2\sqrt{2}, 2)$ and $(-3 + 2\sqrt{2}, 2)$

$$\frac{(x + 3)^2}{9} + (y - 2)^2 = 1$$

47. foci at $(1, -3 + \sqrt{3})$ and $(1, -3 - \sqrt{3})$

$$\frac{(x - 1)^2}{2} + \frac{(y + 3)^2}{5} = 1$$

49. foci at $(1, -3 + \sqrt{5})$ and $(1, -3 - \sqrt{5})$

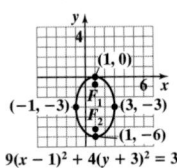

$$9(x - 1)^2 + 4(y + 3)^2 = 36$$

51. $\dfrac{(x - 2)^2}{25} + \dfrac{(y + 1)^2}{9} = 1$

foci at $(-2, -1)$ and $(6, -1)$

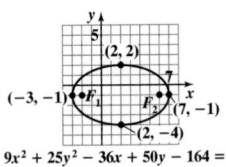

$$9x^2 + 25y^2 - 36x + 50y - 164 = 0$$

53. $\dfrac{(x - 1)^2}{16} + \dfrac{(y + 2)^2}{9} = 1$

foci at $(1 - \sqrt{7}, -2)$ and $(1 + \sqrt{7}, -2)$

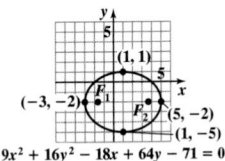

$$9x^2 + 16y^2 - 18x + 64y - 71 = 0$$

55. $\dfrac{(x + 2)^2}{16} + \dfrac{(y - 3)^2}{64} = 1$

foci at $(-2, 3 + 4\sqrt{3})$ and $(-2, 3 - 4\sqrt{3})$

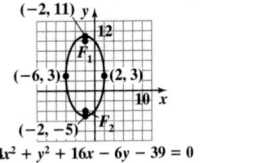

$$4x^2 + y^2 + 16x - 6y - 39 = 0$$

57. $\{(0, -1), (0, 1)\}$　**59.** $\{(0, 3)\}$　**61.** $\{(0, -2), (1, 0)\}$　**63.**

$$y = -\sqrt{16 - 4x^2}$$

65. Yes　**67. a.** $\dfrac{x^2}{2304} + \dfrac{y^2}{529} = 1$　**b.** about 42 feet

79. does not make sense　**81.** does not make sense　**83.** $\dfrac{x^2}{\frac{36}{5}} + \dfrac{y^2}{36} = 1$

85. large circle: $x^2 + y^2 = 25$; small circle: $x^2 + y^2 = 9$　**87.** $\dfrac{x^2}{9} - \dfrac{y^2}{4} = 1$; Terms are separated by subtraction rather than addition.

88. a. -4 and 4　**b.** The equation $y^2 = -9$ has no real solutions.

89. a. -3 and 3　**b.** The equation $x^2 = -16$ has no real solutions.

Section 7.2

Check Point Exercises

1. a. vertices at $(5, 0)$ and $(-5, 0)$; foci at $(\sqrt{41}, 0)$ and $(-\sqrt{41}, 0)$　**b.** vertices at $(0, 5)$ and $(0, -5)$; foci at $(0, \sqrt{41})$ and $(0, -\sqrt{41})$

2. $\dfrac{y^2}{9} - \dfrac{x^2}{16} = 1$

3. foci at $(-3\sqrt{5}, 0)$ and $(3\sqrt{5}, 0)$

asymptotes: $y = \pm\dfrac{1}{2}x$

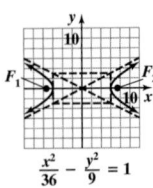

$$\frac{x^2}{36} - \frac{y^2}{9} = 1$$

4. foci at $(0, \sqrt{5})$ and $(0, -\sqrt{5})$

asymptotes: $y = \pm 2x$

$$y^2 - 4x^2 = 4$$

5. foci at $(3 - \sqrt{5}, 1)$ and $(3 + \sqrt{5}, 1)$

asymptotes: $(y - 1) = \pm\dfrac{1}{2}(x - 3)$

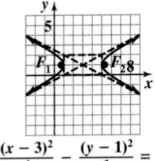

$$\frac{(x - 3)^2}{4} - \frac{(y - 1)^2}{1} = 1$$

6. foci at $(3, -5 + \sqrt{13})$ and $(3, -5 - \sqrt{13})$

asymptotes: $(y + 5) = \pm\frac{2}{3}(x - 3)$

7. $\dfrac{x^2}{2,722,500} - \dfrac{y^2}{25,155,900} = 1$

$4x^2 - 24x - 9y^2 - 90y - 153 = 0$

Exercise Set 7.2

1. vertices at $(2, 0)$ and $(-2, 0)$; foci at $(\sqrt{5}, 0)$ and $(-\sqrt{5}, 0)$; graph (b) **3.** vertices at $(0, 2)$ and $(0, -2)$; foci at $(0, \sqrt{5})$ and $(0, -\sqrt{5})$; graph (a)

5. $y^2 - \dfrac{x^2}{8} = 1$ **7.** $\dfrac{x^2}{9} - \dfrac{y^2}{7} = 1$ **9.** $\dfrac{y^2}{36} - \dfrac{x^2}{9} = 1$ **11.** $\dfrac{(x-4)^2}{4} - \dfrac{(y+2)^2}{5} = 1$

13. foci: $(\pm\sqrt{34}, 0)$

asymptotes: $y = \pm\frac{5}{3}x$

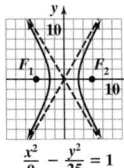

$\dfrac{x^2}{9} - \dfrac{y^2}{25} = 1$

15. foci: $(\pm2\sqrt{41}, 0)$

asymptotes: $y = \pm\frac{4}{5}x$

$\dfrac{x^2}{100} - \dfrac{y^2}{64} = 1$

17. foci: $(0, \pm2\sqrt{13})$

asymptotes: $y = \pm\frac{2}{3}x$

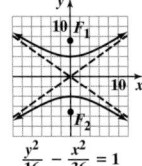

$\dfrac{y^2}{16} - \dfrac{x^2}{36} = 1$

19. foci: $\left(0, \pm\dfrac{\sqrt{5}}{2}\right)$

asymptotes: $y = \pm\frac{1}{2}x$

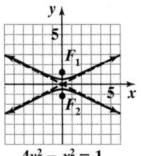

$4y^2 - x^2 = 1$

21. foci: $(\pm\sqrt{13}, 0)$

asymptotes: $y = \pm\frac{3}{2}x$

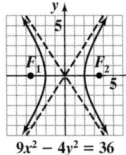

$9x^2 - 4y^2 = 36$

23. foci: $(0, \pm\sqrt{34})$

asymptotes: $y = \pm\frac{5}{3}x$

$9y^2 - 25x^2 = 225$

25. foci: $(\pm2, 0)$

asymptotes: $y = \pm x$

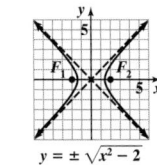

$y = \pm\sqrt{x^2 - 2}$

27. $\dfrac{x^2}{9} - \dfrac{y^2}{25} = 1$

29. $\dfrac{y^2}{4} - \dfrac{x^2}{9} = 1$

31. $\dfrac{(x-2)^2}{4} - \dfrac{(y+3)^2}{9} = 1$

33. foci: $(-9, -3), (1, -3)$

asymptotes: $(y + 3) = \pm\frac{4}{3}(x + 4)$

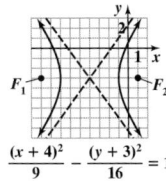

$\dfrac{(x+4)^2}{9} - \dfrac{(y+3)^2}{16} = 1$

35. foci: $(-3 \pm \sqrt{41}, 0)$

asymptotes: $y = \pm\frac{4}{5}(x + 3)$

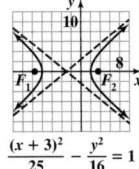

$\dfrac{(x+3)^2}{25} - \dfrac{y^2}{16} = 1$

37. foci: $(1, -2 \pm 2\sqrt{5})$

asymptotes: $(y + 2) = \pm\frac{1}{2}(x - 1)$

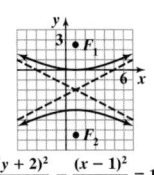

$\dfrac{(y+2)^2}{4} - \dfrac{(x-1)^2}{16} = 1$

39. foci: $(3 \pm \sqrt{5}, -3)$

asymptotes: $(y + 3) = \pm\frac{1}{2}(x - 3)$

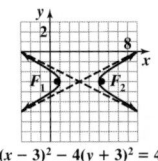

$(x-3)^2 - 4(y+3)^2 = 4$

41. foci: $(1 \pm \sqrt{6}, 2)$

asymptotes: $(y - 2) = \pm(x - 1)$

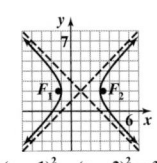

$(x-1)^2 - (y-2)^2 = 3$

43. $(x - 1)^2 - (y + 2)^2 = 1$

foci: $(1 \pm \sqrt{2}, -2)$

asymptotes: $(y + 2) = \pm(x - 1)$

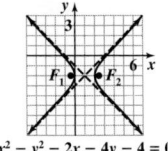

$x^2 - y^2 - 2x - 4y - 4 = 0$

45. $\dfrac{(y+1)^2}{4} - \dfrac{(x+2)^2}{0.25} = 1$
foci: $(-2, -1 \pm \sqrt{4.25})$
asymptotes: $(y+1) = \pm 4(x+2)$

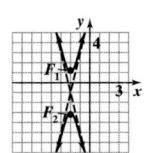

$16x^2 - y^2 + 64x - 2y + 67 = 0$

47. $\dfrac{(x-2)^2}{9} - \dfrac{(y-3)^2}{4} = 1$
foci: $(2 \pm \sqrt{13}, 3)$
asymptotes: $(y-3) = \pm \dfrac{2}{3}(x-2)$

$4x^2 - 9y^2 - 16x + 5y - 101 = 0$

49. $\dfrac{y^2}{4} - \dfrac{(x-4)^2}{25} = 1$
foci: $(4, \pm\sqrt{29})$
asymptotes: $y = \pm \dfrac{2}{5}(x-4)$

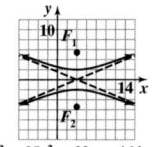

$4x^2 - 25y^2 - 32x + 164 = 0$

51. domain: $(-\infty, -3] \cup [3, \infty)$
range: $(-\infty, \infty)$

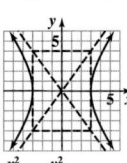

$\dfrac{x^2}{9} - \dfrac{y^2}{16} = 1$

53. domain: $[-3, 3]$
range: $[-4, 4]$

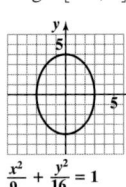

$\dfrac{x^2}{9} + \dfrac{y^2}{16} = 1$

55. domain: $(-\infty, \infty)$
range: $(-\infty, -4] \cup [4, \infty)$

$\dfrac{y^2}{16} - \dfrac{x^2}{9} = 1$

57. $\{(-2, 0), (2, 0)\}$ **59.** $\{(0, -3), (0, 3)\}$

61. If M_1 is located 2640 feet to the right of the origin on the x-axis, the explosion is located on the right branch of the hyperbola given by the equation $\dfrac{x^2}{1{,}210{,}000} - \dfrac{y^2}{5{,}759{,}600} = 1$.

63. 40 yd **65. a.** ellipse **b.** $x^2 + 4y^2 = 4$

77.

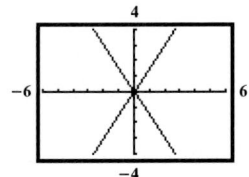

; no; two intersecting lines

79. $2y^2 + (10 - 6x)y + (4x^2 - 3x - 6) = 0$
$$y = \dfrac{3x - 5 \pm \sqrt{x^2 - 24x + 37}}{2}$$

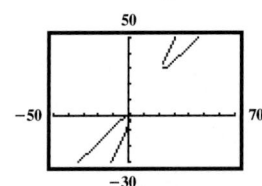

The xy-term rotates the hyperbola.

81. does not make sense **83.** makes sense **85.** false **87.** true **89.** $\dfrac{c}{a}$ will be large when a is small. When this happens, the asymptotes will be nearly vertical. **91.** Any hyperbola where $a = b$, such as $\dfrac{x^2}{4} - \dfrac{y^2}{4} = 1$, has perpendicular asymptotes.

92.

93.

$\left(1 - \dfrac{\sqrt{6}}{3}, 0\right)$ $(1, 2)$ $\left(1 + \dfrac{\sqrt{6}}{3}, 0\right)$ $(0, -1)$ $y = -3(x-1)^2 + 2$ $x = 1$

94. $(y+1)^2 = -12x + 24$

Mid-Chapter 7 Check Point

1. foci: $(\pm\sqrt{21}, 0)$

$\dfrac{x^2}{25} + \dfrac{y^2}{4} = 1$

2. foci: $(0, \pm\sqrt{5})$

$9x^2 + 4y^2 = 36$

3. foci: $(2, 2), (2, -4)$

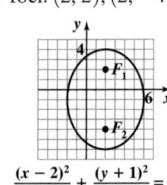

$\dfrac{(x-2)^2}{16} + \dfrac{(y+1)^2}{25} = 1$

4. foci: $(-5, 1), (1, 1)$

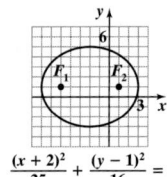

$\dfrac{(x+2)^2}{25} + \dfrac{(y-1)^2}{16} = 1$

5. foci: $(2 \pm 4\sqrt{2}, -3)$

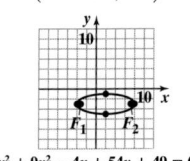

$x^2 + 9y^2 - 4x + 54y + 49 = 0$

6. foci: $(\pm \sqrt{10}, 0)$
asymptotes: $y = \pm \dfrac{1}{3}x$

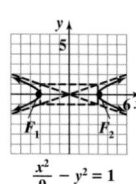

$\dfrac{x^2}{9} - y^2 = 1$

7. foci: $(0, \pm \sqrt{10})$
asymptotes: $y = \pm 3x$

$\dfrac{y^2}{9} - x^2 = 1$

8. foci: $(0, \pm 2\sqrt{5})$
asymptotes: $y = \pm 2x$

$y^2 - 4x^2 = 16$

9. foci: $(\pm \sqrt{53}, 0)$
asymptotes: $y = \pm \dfrac{2}{7}x$

$4x^2 - 49y^2 = 196$

10. foci: $(-3, -2), (7, -2)$
asymptotes: $(y + 2) = \pm \dfrac{4}{3}(x - 2)$

$\dfrac{(x - 2)^2}{9} - \dfrac{(y + 2)^2}{16} = 1$

11. foci: $(-1, 3 \pm 2\sqrt{5})$
asymptotes:
$(y - 3) = \pm 2(x + 1)$

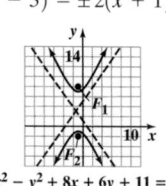

$4x^2 - y^2 + 8x + 6y + 11 = 0$

12.

$x^2 + y^2 = 4$

13.

$x + y = 4$

14.

$x^2 - y^2 = 4$

15.

$x^2 + 4y^2 = 4$

16.

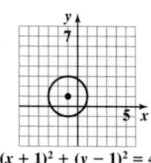

$(x + 1)^2 + (y - 1)^2 = 4$

17.

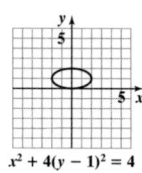

$x^2 + 4(y - 1)^2 = 4$

18.

$(x - 1)^2 - (y - 1)^2 = 4$

19. $\dfrac{x^2}{25} + \dfrac{y^2}{9} = 1$

20. $\dfrac{(x - 1)^2}{81} + \dfrac{(y - 2)^2}{56} = 1$

21. $\dfrac{y^2}{4} - \dfrac{x^2}{5} = 1$

22. $\dfrac{(x + 1)^2}{4} - \dfrac{(y - 5)^2}{5} = 1$

23. no

24. $20\sqrt{3}$ cm

25. a. $\dfrac{x^2}{1.1025} - \dfrac{y^2}{7.8975} = 1$ **b.**

outpost (3, 0)
(−3, 0) primary station

Section 7.3

Check Point Exercises

1. focus: $(2, 0)$
directrix: $x = -2$

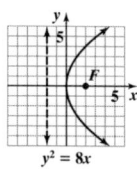

$y^2 = 8x$

2. focus: $(0, -3)$
directrix: $y = 3$

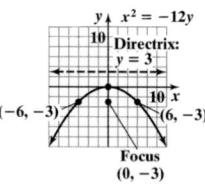

$x^2 = -12y$
Directrix: $y = 3$
$(-6, -3)$ $(6, -3)$
Focus
$(0, -3)$

3. $y^2 = 32x$

4. vertex: $(2, -1)$; focus: $(2, 0)$
directrix: $y = -2$

$(x - 2)^2 = 4(y + 1)$

5. vertex: $(2, -1)$; focus: $(1, -1)$
directrix: $x = 3$

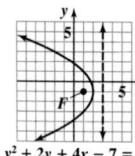

$y^2 + 2y + 4x - 7 = 0$

6. $x^2 = \dfrac{9}{4}y$; The light should be placed at $\left(0, \dfrac{9}{16}\right)$, or $\dfrac{9}{16}$ inch above the vertex.

Exercise Set 7.3

1. focus: $(1, 0)$; directrix: $x = -1$; graph (c)
3. focus: $(0, -1)$, directrix: $y = 1$; graph (b)
5. focus: $(4, 0)$; directrix: $x = -4$

7. focus: $(-2, 0)$; directrix: $x = 2$

9. focus: $(0, 3)$; directrix: $y = -3$

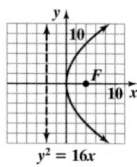

$y^2 = 16x$

$y^2 = -8x$

$x^2 = 12y$

11. focus: $(0, -4)$; directrix: $y = 4$

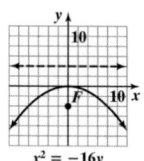

$x^2 = -16y$

13. focus: $\left(\dfrac{3}{2}, 0\right)$; directrix: $x = -\dfrac{3}{2}$

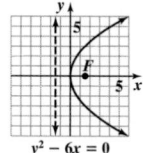

$y^2 - 6x = 0$

15. focus: $\left(0, -\dfrac{1}{8}\right)$; directrix: $y = \dfrac{1}{8}$

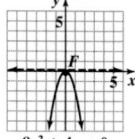

$8x^2 + 4y = 0$

17. $y^2 = 28x$ **19.** $y^2 = -20x$ **21.** $x^2 = 60y$ **23.** $x^2 = -100y$ **25.** $(x - 2)^2 = -8(y + 3)$ **27.** $(y - 2)^2 = 8(x - 1)$

29. $(x + 3)^2 = 4(y - 3)$ **31.** vertex: $(1, 1)$; focus: $(2, 1)$; directrix: $x = 0$; graph (c) **33.** vertex: $(-1, -1)$; focus: $(-1, -2)$; directrix: $y = 0$; graph (d)

35. vertex: $(2, 1)$; focus: $(2, 3)$;
directrix: $y = -1$

$(x - 2)^2 = 8(y - 1)$

37. vertex: $(-1, -1)$; focus: $(-1, -3)$;
directrix: $y = 1$

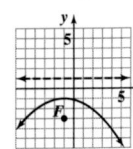

$(x + 1)^2 = -8(y + 1)$

39. vertex: $(-1, -3)$; focus: $(2, -3)$;
directrix: $x = -4$

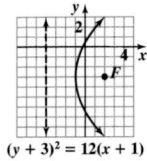

$(y + 3)^2 = 12(x + 1)$

41. vertex: $(0, -1)$; focus: $(-2, -1)$;
directrix: $x = 2$

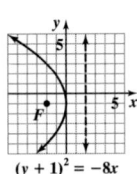

$(y + 1)^2 = -8x$

43. $(x - 1)^2 = 4(y - 2)$; vertex: $(1, 2)$;
focus: $(1, 3)$; directrix: $y = 1$

$x^2 - 2x - 4y + 9 = 0$

45. $(y - 1)^2 = -12(x - 3)$;
vertex: $(3, 1)$; focus: $(0, 1)$;
directrix: $x = 6$

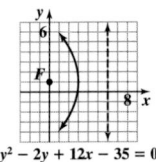

$y^2 - 2y + 12x - 35 = 0$

47. $(x + 3)^2 = 4(y + 2)$;
vertex: $(-3, -2)$; focus: $(-3, -1)$;
directrix: $y = -3$

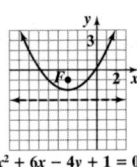

$x^2 + 6x - 4y + 1 = 0$

49. domain: $[-4, \infty)$
range: $(-\infty, \infty)$; not a function
51. domain: $(-\infty, \infty)$
range: $(-\infty, 1]$; function
53. domain: $(-\infty, 3]$
range: $(-\infty, \infty)$; not a function

55. $\{(-4, 2), (0, 0)\}$

57. $\{(-2, 1)\}$

59. \varnothing

61. 1 inch above the vertex **63.** 4.5 feet from the base of the dish **65.** 76 m **67.** yes

77. $y = -1 \pm \sqrt{6x - 12}$

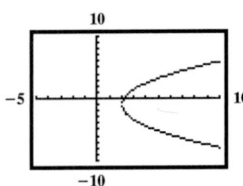

79. $9y^2 + (-24x - 80)y + 16x^2 - 60x + 100 = 0$

$$y = \frac{12x + 40 \pm 10\sqrt{15x + 7}}{9}$$

81. does not make sense

83. makes sense

85. false

87. false

89. focus: $\left(0, -\dfrac{E}{4A}\right)$; directrix: $y = \dfrac{E}{4A}$

92. $-\dfrac{1}{2}; \dfrac{1}{8}; -\dfrac{1}{26}; \dfrac{1}{80}$

93. 120 **94.** 2; 5; 10; 17; 26; 37; Sum is 97.

Chapter 7 Review Exercises

1. foci: $(\pm\sqrt{11}, 0)$

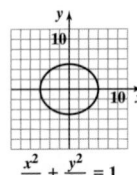

$\dfrac{x^2}{36} + \dfrac{y^2}{25} = 1$

2. foci: $(0, \pm 3)$

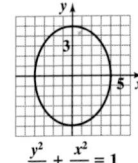

$\dfrac{y^2}{25} + \dfrac{x^2}{16} = 1$

3. foci: $(0, \pm 2\sqrt{3})$

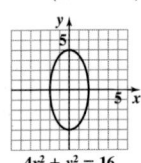

$4x^2 + y^2 = 16$

4. foci: $(\pm\sqrt{5}, 0)$

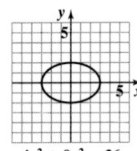

$4x^2 + 9y^2 = 36$

5. foci: $(1 \pm \sqrt{7}, -2)$ **6.** foci: $(-1, 2 \pm \sqrt{7})$ **7.** foci: $(-3 \pm \sqrt{5}, 2)$ **8.** foci: $(1, -1 \pm \sqrt{5})$

5. foci: $(1 \pm \sqrt{7}, -2)$

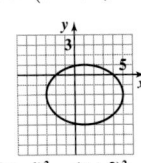

$$\frac{(x-1)^2}{16} + \frac{(y+2)^2}{9} = 1$$

6. foci: $(-1, 2 \pm \sqrt{7})$

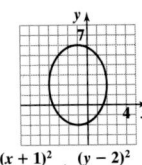

$$\frac{(x+1)^2}{9} + \frac{(y-2)^2}{16} = 1$$

7. foci: $(-3 \pm \sqrt{5}, 2)$

$$4x^2 + 9y^2 + 24x - 36y + 36 = 0$$

8. foci: $(1, -1 \pm \sqrt{5})$

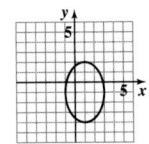

$$9x^2 + 4y^2 - 18x + 8y - 23 = 0$$

9. $\frac{x^2}{25} + \frac{y^2}{9} = 1$ **10.** $\frac{x^2}{27} + \frac{y^2}{36} = 1$ **11.** $\frac{(x+3)^2}{36} + \frac{(y-5)^2}{4} = 1$ **12.** $\frac{x^2}{100} + \frac{y^2}{36} = 1$ **13.** yes

14. The hit ball will collide with the other ball.

15. foci: $(\pm\sqrt{17}, 0)$; $y = \pm\frac{1}{4}x$ **16.** foci: $(0, \pm\sqrt{17})$; $y = \pm 4x$ **17.** foci: $(\pm 5, 0)$; $y = \pm\frac{3}{4}x$ **18.** foci: $(0, \pm 2\sqrt{5})$; $y = \pm\frac{1}{2}x$

$$\frac{x^2}{16} - y^2 = 1$$

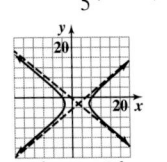

$$\frac{y^2}{16} - x^2 = 1$$

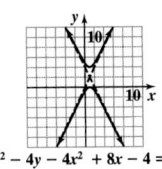

$$9x^2 - 16y^2 = 144$$

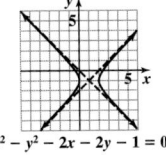

$$4y^2 - x^2 = 16$$

19. foci: $(2 \pm \sqrt{41}, -3)$
$y + 3 = \pm\frac{4}{5}(x-2)$

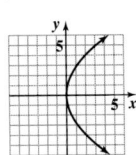

$$\frac{(x-2)^2}{25} - \frac{(y+3)^2}{16} = 1$$

20. foci: $(3, -2 \pm \sqrt{41})$
$y + 2 = \pm\frac{5}{4}(x-3)$

$$\frac{(y+2)^2}{25} - \frac{(x-3)^2}{16} = 1$$

21. foci: $(1, 2 \pm \sqrt{5})$
$y - 2 = \pm 2(x - 1)$

$$y^2 - 4y - 4x^2 + 8x - 4 = 0$$

22. foci: $(1 \pm \sqrt{2}, -1)$
$y + 1 = \pm(x - 1)$

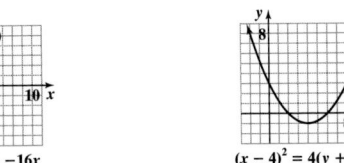

$$x^2 - y^2 - 2x - 2y - 1 = 0$$

23. $\frac{y^2}{4} - \frac{x^2}{12} = 1$ **24.** $\frac{x^2}{9} - \frac{y^2}{55} = 1$ **25.** c must be greater than a. **26.** $\frac{x^2}{2162.25} - \frac{y^2}{7837.75} = 1$

27. vertex: $(0, 0)$; focus: $(2, 0)$
directrix: $x = -2$

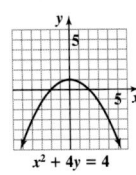

$$y^2 = 8x$$

28. vertex: $(0, 0)$; focus: $(0, -4)$
directrix: $y = 4$

$$x^2 + 16y = 0$$

29. vertex: $(0, 2)$; focus: $(-4, 2)$
directrix: $x = 4$

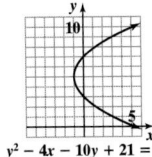

$$(y - 2)^2 = -16x$$

30. vertex: $(4, -1)$; focus: $(4, 0)$
directrix: $y = -2$

$$(x - 4)^2 = 4(y + 1)$$

31. vertex: $(0, 1)$; focus: $(0, 0)$
directrix: $y = 2$

$$x^2 + 4y = 4$$

32. vertex: $(-1, 5)$; focus: $(0, 5)$
directrix: $x = -2$

$$y^2 - 4x - 10y + 21 = 0$$

33. vertex: $(2, -2)$; focus: $\left(2, -\frac{3}{2}\right)$; directrix: $y = -\frac{5}{2}$

$$x^2 - 4x - 2y = 0$$

34. $y^2 = 48x$ **35.** $x^2 = -44y$ **36.** $x^2 = 12y$; Place the light 3 inches from the vertex at $(0, 3)$. **37.** approximately 58 ft

38. approximately 128 ft

Chapter 7 Test

1. foci: $(\pm\sqrt{13}, 0)$
asymptotes: $y = \pm\frac{3}{2}x$

$$9x^2 - 4y^2 = 36$$

2. vertex: $(0, 0)$; focus: $(0, -2)$
directrix: $y = 2$

$$x^2 = -8y$$

3. foci: $(-6, 5), (2, 5)$

$$\frac{(x+2)^2}{25} + \frac{(y-5)^2}{9} = 1$$

4. foci: $(-1, 1 \pm \sqrt{5})$
asymptotes: $y - 1 = \pm 2(x + 1)$

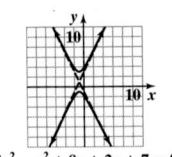

$$4x^2 - y^2 + 8x + 2y + 7 = 0$$

5. vertex: $(-5, 1)$; focus: $(-5, 3)$ **6.** $\dfrac{x^2}{100} + \dfrac{y^2}{51} = 1$ **7.** $\dfrac{y^2}{49} - \dfrac{x^2}{51} = 1$ **8.** $y^2 = 200x$ **9.** 32 ft

directrix: $y = -1$

10. a. $x^2 = 3y$ **b.** Light is placed $\dfrac{3}{4}$ inch above the vertex.

$(x + 5)^2 = 8(y - 1)$

Cumulative Review Exercises (Chapters 1–7)

1. $\{2\}$ **2.** $\{x | x < 2\}$ or $(-\infty, 2)$ **3.** $\{9\}$ **4.** $\{2 + 2\sqrt{5}, 2 - 2\sqrt{5}\}$ **5.** $\{x | x \geq 4 \text{ or } x \leq -3\}$ or $(-\infty, -3] \cup [4, \infty)$ **6.** $\left\{\dfrac{2}{3}, -1 \pm \sqrt{2}\right\}$

7. $\{3\}$ **8.** $\{(2, -1)\}$ **9.** $\{(2, -4), (-14, -20)\}$ **10.** $\{(7, -4, 6)\}$

11. **12.** **13.**

$f(x) = (x - 1)^2 - 4$ $\dfrac{x^2}{9} + \dfrac{y^2}{4} = 1$

14. a. $\pm 1, \pm 3, \pm\dfrac{1}{2}, \pm\dfrac{3}{2}, \pm\dfrac{1}{4}, \pm\dfrac{3}{4}, \pm\dfrac{1}{8}, \pm\dfrac{3}{8}, \pm\dfrac{1}{16}, \pm\dfrac{3}{16}, \pm\dfrac{1}{32}, \pm\dfrac{3}{32}$ **b.** $\left\{-\dfrac{1}{8}, \dfrac{3}{4}, 1\right\}$

15. a. domain: $(-2, 2)$; range: $[-3, \infty)$ **b.** minimum of -3 at $x = 0$ **c.** $(0, 2)$ **d.** 3 **e.** -3 **f.** $x \to -2^+; x \to 2^-$

g. **h.** **16.** $(g \circ f)(x) = x^2 - 2$ **17.** $3 \log_5 x + \dfrac{1}{2}\log_5 y - 3$ **18.** $y = -2x - 2$

$g(x) = f(x - 2) + 1$ $h(x) = -f(2x)$

19. The costs will be the same when the number of miles driven is 175 miles. The cost will be $67

20. $25 for basic cable service and $10 for each movie channel

CHAPTER 8

Section 8.1

Check Point Exercises

1. a. $7, 9, 11, 13$ **b.** $-\dfrac{1}{3}, \dfrac{1}{5}, -\dfrac{1}{9}, \dfrac{1}{17}$ **2.** $3, 11, 27, 59$ **3.** $10, \dfrac{10}{3}, \dfrac{5}{6}, \dfrac{1}{6}$ **4. a.** 91 **b.** n **5. a.** 182 **b.** 47 **c.** 20

6. a. $\displaystyle\sum_{i=1}^{9} i^2$ **b.** $\displaystyle\sum_{i=1}^{n} \dfrac{1}{2^{i-1}}$

Exercise Set 8.1

1. $5, 8, 11, 14$ **3.** $3, 9, 27, 81$ **5.** $-3, 9, -27, 81$ **7.** $-4, 5, -6, 7$ **9.** $\dfrac{2}{5}, \dfrac{2}{3}, \dfrac{6}{7}, 1$ **11.** $1, -\dfrac{1}{3}, \dfrac{1}{7}, -\dfrac{1}{15}$ **13.** $7, 12, 17, 22$

15. $3, 12, 48, 192$ **17.** $4, 11, 25, 53$ **19.** $1, 2, \dfrac{3}{2}, \dfrac{2}{3}$ **21.** $4, 12, 48, 240$ **23.** 272 **25.** 120 **27.** $(n + 2)(n + 1)$ **29.** 105 **31.** 60

33. 115 **35.** $-\dfrac{5}{16}$ **37.** 55 **39.** $\dfrac{3}{8}$ **41.** 15 **43.** $\displaystyle\sum_{i=1}^{15} i^2$ **45.** $\displaystyle\sum_{i=1}^{11} 2^i$ **47.** $\displaystyle\sum_{i=1}^{30} i$ **49.** $\displaystyle\sum_{i=1}^{14} \dfrac{i}{i+1}$ **51.** $\displaystyle\sum_{i=1}^{n} \dfrac{4^i}{i}$ **53.** $\displaystyle\sum_{i=1}^{n} (2i - 1)$

55. $\displaystyle\sum_{k=1}^{14} (2k + 3)$ **57.** $\displaystyle\sum_{k=0}^{12} ar^k$ **59.** $\displaystyle\sum_{k=0}^{n} (a + kd)$ **61.** 45 **63.** 0

65. 2 **67.** 80 **69. a.** 9.9; Online ad spending averaged $9.9 billion per year from 2000 through 2006. **71.** $8081.13 **81.** $39,800$

83. 8.109673361 E15 **85.** $24,804$

89. **91.**

As n gets larger, a_n approaches 1. As n gets larger, a_n approaches 0.

93. does not make sense **95.** makes sense **97.** false **99.** false **101.** $9, 32, 16, 8, 4$ **103.** $-5; -5; -5; -5$; The difference between consecutive terms is always -5. **104.** $4; 4; 4; 4$; The difference between consecutive terms is always 4. **105.** -45

Section 8.2

Check Point Exercises

1. $100, 70, 40, 10, -20, -50$ **2.** -34 **3. a.** $a_n = 0.7n + 31.3$ **b.** 39 **4.** 360 **5.** 2460 **6.** $\$740{,}300$

Exercise Set 8.2

1. $200, 220, 240, 260, 280, 300$ **3.** $-7, -3, 1, 5, 9, 13$ **5.** $300, 210, 120, 30, -60, -150$ **7.** $\frac{5}{2}, 2, \frac{3}{2}, 1, \frac{1}{2}, 0$ **9.** $-9, -3, 3, 9, 15, 21$
11. $30, 20, 10, 0, -10, -20$ **13.** $1.6, 1.2, 0.8, 0.4, 0, -0.4$ **15.** 33 **17.** 252 **19.** 955 **21.** -142 **23.** $a_n = 4n - 3; a_{20} = 77$
25. $a_n = 11 - 4n; a_{20} = -69$ **27.** $a_n = 7 + 2n; a_{20} = 47$ **29.** $a_n = -16 - 4n; a_{20} = -96$ **31.** $a_n = 1 + 3n; a_{20} = 61$
33. $a_n = 40 - 10n; a_{20} = -160$ **35.** 1220 **37.** 4400 **39.** 5050 **41.** 3660 **43.** 396 **45.** $8 + 13 + 18 + \cdots + 88; 816$
47. $2 - 1 - 4 - \cdots - 85; -1245$ **49.** $4 + 8 + 12 + \cdots + 400; 20{,}200$ **51.** 7 **53.** 22 **55.** 847 **57.** $f(x) = -4x + 5$
59. $a_n = 3n - 2$ **61. a.** $a_n = 0.77n + 9.23$ **b.** 30.0% **63.** Company A will pay $\$1400$ more in year 10. **65. a.** $\$21{,}153$
b. $\$21{,}158$; overestimates by $\$5$ **69.** Company A: $\$307{,}000$; Company B: $\$324{,}000$; Company B pays the greater total amount.
71. 2869 seats **79.** makes sense **81.** makes sense **83.** 320 degree-days **85.** $-2; -2; -2; -2$; The ratio of a term to the term that directly
precedes it is always -2. **86.** $5; 5; 5; 5$; The ratio of a term to the term that directly precedes it is always 5. **87.** 8019

Section 8.3

Check Point Exercises

1. $12, 6, 3, \frac{3}{2}, \frac{3}{4}, \frac{3}{8}$ **2.** 3645 **3.** $a_n = 3(2)^{n-1}; a_8 = 384$ **4.** 9842 **5.** $19{,}680$ **6.** $\$2{,}371{,}746$ **7. a.** $\$333{,}946$ **b.** $\$291{,}946$
8. 9 **9.** 1 **10.** $\$4000$

Exercise Set 8.3

1. $5, 15, 45, 135, 405$ **3.** $20, 10, 5, \frac{5}{2}, \frac{5}{4}$ **5.** $10, -40, 160, -640, 2560$ **7.** $-6, 30, -150, 750, -3750$ **9.** $a_8 = 768$ **11.** $a_{12} = -10{,}240$
13. $a_{40} \approx -0.000000002$ **15.** $a_8 = 0.1$ **17.** $a_n = 3(4)^{n-1}; a_7 = 12{,}288$ **19.** $a_n = 18\left(\frac{1}{3}\right)^{n-1}; a_7 = \frac{2}{81}$ **21.** $a_n = 1.5(-2)^{n-1}; a_7 = 96$
23. $a_n = 0.0004(-10)^{n-1}; a_7 = 400$ **25.** $531{,}440$ **27.** 2049 **29.** $\frac{16{,}383}{2}$ **31.** 9840 **33.** $10{,}230$ **35.** $\frac{63}{128}$ **37.** $\frac{3}{2}$ **39.** 4
41. $\frac{2}{3}$ **43.** $\frac{80}{13} \approx 6.15385$ **45.** $\frac{5}{9}$ **47.** $\frac{47}{99}$ **49.** $\frac{257}{999}$ **51.** arithmetic, $d = 1$ **53.** geometric, $r = 2$ **55.** neither
57. 2435 **59.** 2280 **61.** -140 **63.** $a_2 = 12, a_3 = 18$ **65.** $\$16{,}384$ **67.** $\$3{,}795{,}957$ **69. a.** approximately 1.01 for each division
b. $a_n = 35.48(1.01)^{n-1}$ **c.** approximately 38.04 million **71.** $\$32{,}767$ **73.** $\$793{,}583$ **75.** 130.26 in. **77. a.** $\$11{,}617$ **b.** $\$1617$
79. a. $\$87{,}052$ **b.** $\$63{,}052$ **81. a.** $\$693{,}031$ **b.** $\$293{,}031$ **83.** $\$30{,}000$ **85.** $\$9$ million **87.** $\frac{1}{3}$ **99.**
101. makes sense **103.** makes sense **105.** false **107.** false **109.** Release 2000 flies each day.
112. $6 = 6$ **113.** $15 = 15$ **114.** $\dfrac{(k + 1)(k + 2)(2k + 3)}{6}$

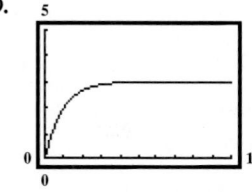

horizontal asymptote: $y = 3$;
sum of series: 3

Mid-Chapter 8 Check Point

1. $1, -2, \frac{3}{2}, -\frac{2}{3}, \frac{5}{24}$ **2.** $5, 2, -1, -4, -7$ **3.** $5, -15, 45, -135, 405$ **4.** $3, 1, 3, 1, 3$ **5.** $a_n = 4n - 2; a_{20} = 78$
6. $a_n = 3(2)^{n-1}; a_{10} = 1536$ **7.** $a_n = -\frac{1}{2}n + 2; a_{30} = -13$ **8.** 5115 **9.** 2350 **10.** 6820 **11.** $-29{,}300$ **12.** 44 **13.** 3725
14. $\frac{1995}{64}$ **15.** $\frac{5}{7}$ **16.** $\frac{5}{11}$ **17.** Answers will vary. An example is $\displaystyle\sum_{i=1}^{18} \frac{i}{i + 2}$. **18.** 464 ft; 3600 ft **19.** $\$311{,}249$

Section 8.4

Check Point Exercises

1. a. $S_1: 2 = 1(1 + 1); S_k: 2 + 4 + 6 + \cdots + 2k = k(k + 1); S_{k+1}: 2 + 4 + 6 + \cdots + 2(k + 1) = (k + 1)(k + 2)$
 b. $S_1: 1^3 = \dfrac{1^2(1 + 1)^2}{4}; S_k: 1^3 + 2^3 + 3^3 + \cdots + k^3 = \dfrac{k^2(k + 1)^2}{4}; S_{k+1}: 1^3 + 2^3 + 3^3 + \cdots + (k + 1)^3 = \dfrac{(k + 1)^2(k + 2)^2}{4}$

2. $S_1: 2 = 1(1 + 1); S_k: 2 + 4 + 6 + \cdots + 2k = k(k + 1); S_{k+1}: 2 + 4 + 6 + \cdots + 2k + 2(k + 1) = (k + 1)(k + 2); S_{k+1}$ can be obtained by
 adding $2k + 2$ to both sides of S_k.
3. $S_1: 1^3 = \dfrac{1^2(1 + 1)^2}{4}; S_k: 1^3 + 2^3 + 3^3 + \cdots + k^3 = \dfrac{k^2(k + 1)^2}{4}; S_{k+1}: 1^3 + 2^3 + 3^3 + \cdots + k^3 + (k + 1)^3 = \dfrac{(k + 1)^2(k + 2)^2}{4}; S_{k+1}$ can
 be obtained by adding $k^3 + 3k^2 + 3k + 1$ to both sides of S_k.
4. $S_1: 2$ is a factor of $1^2 + 1; S_k: 2$ is a factor of $k^2 + k; S_{k+1}: 2$ is a factor of $(k + 1)^2 + (k + 1) = k^2 + 3k + 2; S_{k+1}$ can be obtained from S_k by
 writing $k^2 + 3k + 2$ as $(k^2 + k) + 2(k + 1)$.

Exercise Set 8.4

1. $S_1: 1 = 1^2; S_2: 1 + 3 = 2^2; S_3: 1 + 3 + 5 = 3^2$ **3.** $S_1:$ 2 is a factor of $1 - 1 = 0; S_2:$ 2 is a factor of $2^2 - 2 = 2; S_3:$ 2 is a factor of $3^2 - 3 = 6$.

5. $S_k: 4 + 8 + 12 + \cdots + 4k = 2k(k + 1); S_{k+1}: 4 + 8 + 12 + \cdots + (4k + 4) = 2(k + 1)(k + 2)$

7. $S_k: 3 + 7 + 11 + \cdots + (4k - 1) = k(2k + 1); S_{k+1}: 3 + 7 + 11 + \cdots + (4k + 3) = (k + 1)(2k + 3)$

9. $S_k:$ 2 is a factor of $k^2 - k + 2; S_{k+1}:$ 2 is a factor of $k^2 + k + 2$.

11. $S_1: 4 = 2(1)(1 + 1); S_k: 4 + 8 + 12 + \cdots + 4k = 2k(k + 1); S_{k+1}: 4 + 8 + 12 + \cdots + 4(k + 1) = 2(k + 1)(k + 2); S_{k+1}$ can be obtained by adding $4k + 4$ to both sides of S_k.

13. $S_1: 1 = 1^2; S_k: 1 + 3 + 5 + \cdots + (2k - 1) = k^2; S_{k+1}: 1 + 3 + 5 + \cdots + (2k + 1) = (k + 1)^2; S_{k+1}$ can be obtained by adding $2k + 1$ to both sides of S_k.

15. $S_1: 3 = 1[2(1) + 1]; S_k: 3 + 7 + 11 + \cdots + (4k - 1) = k(2k + 1); S_{k+1}: 3 + 7 + 11 + \cdots + (4k + 3) = (k + 1)(2k + 3); S_{k+1}$ can be obtained by adding $4k + 3$ to both sides of S_k.

17. $S_1: 1 = 2^1 - 1; S_k: 1 + 2 + 2^2 + \cdots + 2^{k-1} = 2^k - 1; S_{k+1}: 1 + 2 + 2^2 + \cdots + 2^k = 2^{k+1} - 1; S_{k+1}$ can be obtained by adding 2^k to both sides of S_k.

19. $S_1: 2 = 2^{1+1} - 2; S_k: 2 + 4 + 8 + \cdots + 2^k = 2^{k+1} - 2; S_{k+1}: 2 + 4 + 8 + \cdots + 2^{k+1} = 2^{k+2} - 2; S_{k+1}$ can be obtained by adding 2^{k+1} to both sides of S_k.

21. $S_1: 1 \cdot 2 = \dfrac{1(1 + 1)(1 + 2)}{3}; S_k: 1 \cdot 2 + 2 \cdot 3 + 3 \cdot 4 + \cdots + k(k + 1) = \dfrac{k(k + 1)(k + 2)}{3};$

$S_{k+1}: 1 \cdot 2 + 2 \cdot 3 + 3 \cdot 4 + \cdots + (k + 1)(k + 2) = \dfrac{(k + 1)(k + 2)(k + 3)}{3}; S_{k+1}$ can be obtained by adding $(k + 1)(k + 2)$ to both sides of S_k.

23. $S_1: \dfrac{1}{1 \cdot 2} = \dfrac{1}{1 + 1}; S_k: \dfrac{1}{1 \cdot 2} + \dfrac{1}{2 \cdot 3} + \dfrac{1}{3 \cdot 4} + \cdots + \dfrac{1}{k(k + 1)} = \dfrac{k}{k + 1}; S_{k+1}: \dfrac{1}{1 \cdot 2} + \dfrac{1}{2 \cdot 3} + \dfrac{1}{3 \cdot 4} + \cdots + \dfrac{1}{(k + 1)(k + 2)} = \dfrac{k + 1}{k + 2}; S_{k+1}$ can

be obtained by adding $\dfrac{1}{(k + 1)(k + 2)}$ to both sides of S_k.

25. $S_1:$ 2 is a factor of 0; $S_k:$ 2 is a factor of $k^2 - k; S_{k+1}:$ 2 is a factor of $k^2 + k; S_{k+1}$ can be obtained from S_k by rewriting $k^2 + k$ as $(k^2 - k) + 2k$.

27. $S_1:$ 6 is a factor of 6; $S_k:$ 6 is a factor of $k(k + 1)(k + 2); S_{k+1}:$ 6 is a factor of $(k + 1)(k + 2)(k + 3); S_{k+1}$ can be obtained from S_k by rewriting $(k + 1)(k + 2)(k + 3)$ as $k(k + 1)(k + 2) + 3(k + 1)(k + 2)$ and noting that either $k + 1$ or $k + 2$ is even, so 6 is a factor of $3(k + 1)(k + 2)$.

29. $S_1: 5 \cdot 6^1 = 6(6^1 - 1); S_k: \sum\limits_{i=1}^{k} 5 \cdot 6^i = 6(6^k - 1); S_{k+1}: \sum\limits_{i=1}^{k+1} 5 \cdot 6^i = 6(6^{k+1} - 1); S_{k+1}$ can be obtained by adding $5 \cdot 6^{k+1}$ to both sides of S_k.

31. $S_1: 1 + 2 > 1; S_k: k + 2 > k; S_{k+1}: k + 3 > k + 1; S_{k+1}$ can be obtained by adding 1 to both sides of S_k.

33. $S_1: (ab)^1 = a^1b^1; S_k: (ab)^k = a^kb^k; S_{k+1}: (ab)^{k+1} = a^{k+1}b^{k+1}; S_{k+1}$ can be obtained by multiplying both sides of S_k by (ab).

37. does not make sense **39.** does not make sense

41. $S_3: 3^2 > 2(3) + 1; S_k: k^2 > 2k + 1$ for $k \geq 3; S_{k+1}: (k + 1)^2 > 2(k + 1) + 1$ or $k^2 + 2k + 1 > 2k + 3; S_{k+1}$ can be obtained from S_k by noting that S_{k+1} is the same as $k^2 > 2$ which is true for $k \geq 3$.

43. $S_1: \dfrac{1}{4}; S_2: \dfrac{1}{3}; S_3: \dfrac{3}{8}; S_4: \dfrac{2}{5}; S_5: \dfrac{5}{12}; S_n: \dfrac{n}{2n + 2};$ Use S_k to obtain the conjectured formula.

46. The exponents begin with the exponent on $a + b$ and decrease by 1 in each successive term. **47.** The exponents begin with 0, increase by 1 in each successive term, and end with the exponent on $a + b$. **48.** The sum of the exponents is the exponent on $a + b$.

Section 8.5

Check Point Exercises

1. a. 20 **b.** 1 **c.** 28 **d.** 1 **2.** $x^4 + 4x^3 + 6x^2 + 4x + 1$ **3.** $x^5 - 10x^4y + 40x^3y^2 - 80x^2y^3 + 80xy^4 - 32y^5$ **4.** $4032x^5y^4$

Exercise Set 8.5

1. 56 **3.** 12 **5.** 1 **7.** 4950 **9.** $x^3 + 6x^2 + 12x + 8$ **11.** $27x^3 + 27x^2y + 9xy^2 + y^3$ **13.** $125x^3 - 75x^2 + 15x - 1$

15. $16x^4 + 32x^3 + 24x^2 + 8x + 1$ **17.** $x^8 + 8x^6y + 24x^4y^2 + 32x^2y^3 + 16y^4$ **19.** $y^4 - 12y^3 + 54y^2 - 108y + 81$

21. $16x^{12} - 32x^9 + 24x^6 - 8x^3 + 1$ **23.** $c^5 + 10c^4 + 40c^3 + 80c^2 + 80c + 32$ **25.** $x^5 - 5x^4 + 10x^3 - 10x^2 + 5x - 1$

27. $243x^5 - 405x^4y + 270x^3y^2 - 90x^2y^3 + 15xy^4 - y^5$ **29.** $64a^6 + 192a^5b + 240a^4b^2 + 160a^3b^3 + 60a^2b^4 + 12ab^5 + b^6$

31. $x^8 + 16x^7 + 112x^6 + \cdots$ **33.** $x^{10} - 20x^9y + 180x^8y^2 - \cdots$ **35.** $x^{32} + 16x^{30} + 120x^{28} + \cdots$ **37.** $y^{60} - 20y^{57} + 190y^{54} - \cdots$

39. $240x^4y^2$ **41.** $126x^5$ **43.** $56x^6y^{15}$ **45.** $-\dfrac{21}{2}x^6$ **47.** $319{,}770x^{16}y^{14}$ **49.** $x^{12} + 4x^7 + 6x^2 + \dfrac{4}{x^3} + \dfrac{1}{x^8}$ **51.** $x - 3x^{1/3} + \dfrac{3}{x^{1/3}} - \dfrac{1}{x}$

53. $4x^3 + 6x^2h + 4xh^2 + h^3$ **55.** 252 **57.** 0.1138 **69.** **71.** $f_1(x) = x^4 - 8x^3 + 24x^2 - 32x + 16$

73. makes sense **75.** does not make sense

77. false **79.** false

81. $x^6 + 3x^5 + 6x^4 + 7x^3 + 6x^2 + 3x + 1$

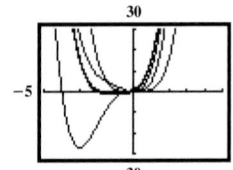

$f_2, f_3, f_4,$ and f_5 are approaching $f_1 = f_6$.

83. $\dbinom{n}{r} = \dfrac{n!}{r!(n - r)!} = \dfrac{n!}{(n - r)!r!} = \dfrac{n!}{(n - r)![n - (n - r)]!} = \dbinom{n}{n - r}$

85. a. $(a + b)^1 = a + b = \binom{1}{0}a^1 + \binom{1}{1}b^1$ **b.** Assume: $(a + b)^k = \binom{k}{0}a^k + \binom{k}{1}a^{k-1}b + \binom{k}{2}a^{k-2}b^2 + \cdots + \binom{k}{k-1}ab^{k-1}$

$+ \binom{k}{k}b^k$; Prove: $(a + b)^{k+1} = \binom{k+1}{0}a^{k+1} + \binom{k+1}{1}a^{k+1-1}b + \binom{k+1}{2}a^{k+1-2}b^2 + \cdots + \binom{k+1}{k+1-1}ab^{k+1-1} + \binom{k+1}{k+1}b^{k+1}$

c. $(a + b)(a + b)^k = (a + b)\left[\binom{k}{0}a^k + \binom{k}{1}a^{k-1}b + \binom{k}{2}a^{k-2}b^2 + \cdots + \binom{k}{k-1}ab^{k-1} + \binom{k}{k}b^k\right]$ or $(a + b)^{k+1} = \binom{k}{0}a^{k+1}$

$+ \binom{k}{0}a^k b + \binom{k}{1}a^k b + \binom{k}{1}a^{k-1}b^2 + \binom{k}{2}a^{k-1}b^2 + \binom{k}{2}a^{k-2}b^3 + \cdots + \binom{k}{k-1}a^2 b^{k-1} + \binom{k}{k-1}ab^k + \binom{k}{k}ab^k + \binom{k}{k}b^{k+1}$

d. $(a + b)^{k+1} = \binom{k}{0}a^{k+1} + \left[\binom{k}{0} + \binom{k}{1}\right]a^k b + \left[\binom{k}{1} + \binom{k}{2}\right]a^{k-1}b^2 + \left[\binom{k}{2} + \binom{k}{3}\right]a^{k-2}b^3 + \cdots + \left[\binom{k}{k-1} + \binom{k}{k}\right]ab^k + \binom{k}{k}b^{k+1}$

e. $(a + b)^{k+1} = \binom{k}{0}a^{k+1} + \binom{k+1}{1}a^k b + \binom{k+1}{2}a^{k-1}b^2 + \binom{k+1}{3}a^{k-2}b^3 + \cdots + \binom{k+1}{k}ab^k + \binom{k}{k}b^{k+1}$

f. $(a + b)^{k+1} = \binom{k+1}{0}a^{k+1} + \binom{k+1}{1}a^k b + \binom{k+1}{2}a^{k-1}b^2 + \binom{k+1}{3}a^{k-2}b^3 + \cdots + \binom{k+1}{k}ab^k + \binom{k+1}{k+1}b^{k+1}$

86. 6840 **87.** 56 **88.** true

Section 8.6

Check Point Exercises

1. 72 **2.** 729 **3.** 676,000 **4.** 840 **5.** 720 **6. a.** combinations **b.** permutations **7.** 210 **8.** 1820

Exercise Set 8.6

1. 3024 **3.** 6720 **5.** 720 **7.** 1 **9.** 126 **11.** 330 **13.** 1 **15.** 1 **17.** combinations **19.** permutations **21.** 0 **23.** $\frac{3}{4}$

25. -9499 **27.** $\frac{3}{68}$ **29.** 27 ways **31.** 40 ways **33.** 243 ways **35.** 144 area codes **37.** 120 ways **39.** 6 paragraphs

41. 720 ways **43.** 8,648,640 ways **45.** 120 ways **47.** 15,120 lineups **49.** 20 ways **51.** 495 collections **53.** 24,310 groups
55. 22,957,480 selections **57.** 360 ways **59.** 1716 ways **61.** 1140 ways **63.** 840 passwords **65.** 2730 cones **67.** 720 **69.** 20
71. 24 **83.** makes sense **85.** does not make sense **87.** false **89.** true **91.** 14,400 ways **93.** 450 ways **95.** $\frac{2}{3}$ **96.** $\frac{1}{3}$ **97.** $\frac{2}{3}$

Section 8.7

Check Point Exercises

1. a. $\frac{7664}{100,000}$ or $\frac{479}{6250} \approx 0.077$ **b.** $\frac{720}{800}$ or $\frac{9}{10} = 0.9$ **c.** $\frac{720}{7664}$ or $\frac{45}{479} \approx 0.094$ **2.** $\frac{1}{3}$ **3.** $\frac{1}{9}$ **4.** $\frac{1}{13}$ **5.** $\frac{1}{13,983,816} \approx 0.0000000715$

6. $\frac{160}{191}$ **7.** $\frac{1}{3}$ **8.** $\frac{3}{4}$ **9. a.** 0.99 **b.** 0.64 **10.** $\frac{1}{361} \approx 0.00277$ **11.** $\frac{1}{16}$

Exercise Set 8.7

1. 0.10 **3.** 0.52 **5.** 0.01 **7.** 0.59 **9.** 0.61 **11.** $\frac{1}{6}$ **13.** $\frac{1}{2}$ **15.** $\frac{1}{3}$ **17.** $\frac{1}{13}$ **19.** $\frac{3}{13}$ **21.** $\frac{1}{4}$ **23.** $\frac{7}{8}$ **25.** $\frac{1}{12}$

27. $\frac{1}{18,009,460}$; $\frac{5}{900,473}$ **29. a.** 2,598,960 **b.** 1287 **c.** $\frac{1287}{2,598,960} \approx 0.0005$ **31.** $\frac{43}{58}$ **33.** $\frac{50}{87}$ **35.** $\frac{113}{174}$ **37.** $\frac{12}{13}$ **39.** $\frac{2}{13}$

41. $\frac{7}{13}$ **43.** $\frac{3}{4}$ **45.** $\frac{33}{40}$ **47.** $\frac{1}{36}$ **49.** $\frac{1}{3}$ **51.** $\frac{1}{64}$ **53. a.** $\frac{1}{256}$ **b.** $\frac{1}{4096}$ **c.** $\left(\frac{15}{16}\right)^{10} \approx 0.524$ **d.** $1 - \left(\frac{15}{16}\right)^{10} \approx 0.476$

65. does not make sense **67.** makes sense **71. a.** $\frac{12}{25}$ **b.** $\frac{3}{10}$ **73. a.** The first person can have any birthday in the year. The second

person can have all but one birthday. **b.** $\frac{365}{365} \cdot \frac{364}{365} \cdot \frac{363}{365} \approx 0.99$ **c.** ≈ 0.01 **d.** ≈ 0.41 **e.** 23 people

Chapter 8 Review Exercises

1. $a_1 = 3$; $a_2 = 10$; $a_3 = 17$; $a_4 = 24$ **2.** $a_1 = -\frac{3}{2}$; $a_2 = \frac{4}{3}$; $a_3 = -\frac{5}{4}$; $a_4 = \frac{6}{5}$ **3.** $a_1 = 1$; $a_2 = 1$; $a_3 = \frac{1}{2}$; $a_4 = \frac{1}{6}$

4. $a_1 = \frac{1}{2}$; $a_2 = -\frac{1}{4}$; $a_3 = \frac{1}{8}$; $a_4 = -\frac{1}{16}$ **5.** $a_1 = 9$; $a_2 = \frac{2}{27}$; $a_3 = 9$; $a_4 = \frac{2}{27}$ **6.** $a_1 = 4$; $a_2 = 11$; $a_3 = 25$; $a_4 = 53$ **7.** 65 **8.** 95

9. -20 **10.** $\sum_{i=1}^{15} \frac{i}{i + 2}$ **11.** $\sum_{i=4}^{13} i^3$ or $\sum_{i=1}^{10} (i + 3)^3$ **12.** 7, 11, 15, 19, 23, 27 **13.** $-4, -9, -14, -19, -24, -29$ **14.** $\frac{3}{2}, 1, \frac{1}{2}, 0, -\frac{1}{2}, -1$
15. $-2, 3, 8, 13, 18, 23$ **16.** $a_6 = 20$ **17.** $a_{12} = -30$ **18.** $a_{14} = -38$ **19.** $a_n = 4n - 11$; $a_{20} = 69$ **20.** $a_n = 220 - 20n$; $a_{20} = -180$
21. $a_n = 8 - 5n$; $a_{20} = -92$ **22.** 1727 **23.** 225 **24.** 15,150 **25.** 440 **26.** -500 **27.** -2325 **28. a.** $a_n = 4.75n + 34.25$ **b.** 96%
29. \$418,500 **30.** 1470 seats **31.** 3, 6, 12, 24, 48 **32.** $\frac{1}{2}, \frac{1}{4}, \frac{1}{8}, \frac{1}{16}, \frac{1}{32}$ **33.** 16, -8, 4, -2, 1 **34.** $-1, 5, -25, 125, -625$

35. $a_7 = 1458$ **36.** $a_6 = \frac{1}{2}$ **37.** $a_5 = -48$ **38.** $a_n = 2^{n-1}$; $a_8 = 128$ **39.** $a_n = 100\left(\frac{1}{10}\right)^{n-1}$; $a_8 = \frac{1}{100,000}$

40. $a_n = 12\left(-\frac{1}{3}\right)^{n-1}$; $a_8 = -\frac{4}{729}$ **41.** 17,936,135 **42.** $\frac{127}{8}$ **43.** 19,530 **44.** -258 **45.** $\frac{341}{128}$ **46.** $\frac{27}{2}$ **47.** $\frac{4}{3}$ **48.** $-\frac{18}{5}$

49. 20 **50.** $\dfrac{2}{3}$ **51.** $\dfrac{47}{99}$ **52. a.** $\dfrac{5.9}{4.2} \approx 1.4; \dfrac{8.3}{5.9} \approx 1.4; \dfrac{11.6}{8.3} \approx 1.4; \dfrac{16.2}{11.6} \approx 1.4; \dfrac{22.7}{16.2} \approx 1.4$ **b.** $a_n = 4.2(1.4)^n$ **c.** 62.0 million

53. \$42,823; \$223,210 **54. a.** \$19,129 **b.** \$8729 **55. a.** \$91,361 **b.** \$55,361 **56.** \$$9\dfrac{1}{3}$$million

57. $S_1: 5 = \dfrac{5(1)(1 + 1)}{2}$; $S_k: 5 + 10 + 15 + \cdots + 5k = \dfrac{5k(k + 1)}{2}$; $S_{k+1}: 5 + 10 + 15 + \cdots + 5(k + 1) = \dfrac{5(k + 1)(k + 2)}{2}$; S_{k+1}

can be obtained by adding $5(k + 1)$ to both sides of S_k.

58. $S_1: 1 = \dfrac{4^1 - 1}{3}$; $S_k: 1 + 4 + 4^2 + \cdots + 4^{k-1} = \dfrac{4^k - 1}{3}$; $S_{k+1}: 1 + 4 + 4^2 + \cdots + 4^k = \dfrac{4^{k+1} - 1}{3}$; S_{k+1} can be obtained by adding 4^k

to both sides of S_k.

59. $S_1: 2 = 2(1)^2$; $S_k: 2 + 6 + 10 + \cdots + (4k - 2) = 2k^2$; $S_{k+1}: 2 + 6 + 10 + \cdots + (4k + 2) = 2k^2 + 4k + 2$; S_{k+1} can be obtained by adding $4k + 2$ to both sides of S_k.

60. $S_1: 1 \cdot 3 = \dfrac{1(1 + 1)[2(1) + 7]}{6}$; $S_k: 1 \cdot 3 + 2 \cdot 4 + 3 \cdot 5 + \cdots + k(k + 2) = \dfrac{k(k + 1)(2k + 7)}{6}$;

$S_{k+1}: 1 \cdot 3 + 2 \cdot 4 + 3 \cdot 5 + \cdots + (k + 1)(k + 3) = \dfrac{(k + 1)(k + 2)(2k + 9)}{6}$; S_{k+1} can be obtained by adding $(k + 1)(k + 3)$ to both sides of S_k.

61. $S_1: 2$ is a factor of 6; $S_k: 2$ is a factor of $k^2 + 5k$; $S_{k+1}: 2$ is a factor of $k^2 + 7k + 6$; S_{k+1} can be obtained from S_k by rewriting $k^2 + 7k + 6$ as $(k^2 + 5k) + 2(k + 3)$.

62. 165 **63.** 4005 **64.** $8x^3 + 12x^2 + 6x + 1$ **65.** $x^8 - 4x^6 + 6x^4 - 4x^2 + 1$ **66.** $x^5 + 10x^4y + 40x^3y^2 + 80x^2y^3 + 80xy^4 + 32y^5$
67. $x^6 - 12x^5 + 60x^4 - 160x^3 + 240x^2 - 192x + 64$ **68.** $x^{16} + 24x^{14} + 252x^{12} + \cdots$ **69.** $x^9 - 27x^8 + 324x^7 - \cdots$ **70.** $80x^2$
71. $4860x^2$ **72.** 336 **73.** 15,120 **74.** 56 **75.** 78 **76.** 20 choices **77.** 243 possibilities **78.** 32,760 ways **79.** 4845 ways
80. 1140 sets **81.** 116,280 ways **82.** 120 ways **83.** $\dfrac{18}{25}$ **84.** $\dfrac{6}{7}$ **85.** $\dfrac{3}{5}$ **86.** $\dfrac{12}{35}$ **87.** $\dfrac{10}{21}$ **88.** $\dfrac{5}{16}$ **89.** $\dfrac{2}{3}$ **90.** $\dfrac{2}{3}$
91. $\dfrac{2}{13}$ **92.** $\dfrac{7}{13}$ **93.** $\dfrac{5}{6}$ **94.** $\dfrac{5}{6}$ **95.** $\dfrac{1}{6}$ **96. a.** $\dfrac{1}{15,504}$ **b.** $\dfrac{25}{3876}$ **97.** $\dfrac{1}{32}$ **98. a.** 0.04 **b.** 0.008 **c.** 0.4096

Chapter 8 Test

1. $a_1 = 1; a_2 = -\dfrac{1}{4}; a_3 = \dfrac{1}{9}; a_4 = -\dfrac{1}{16}; a_5 = \dfrac{1}{25}$ **2.** 105 **3.** 550 **4.** $-21,846$ **5.** 36 **6.** 720 **7.** 120 **8.** $\displaystyle\sum_{i=1}^{20} \dfrac{i + 1}{i + 2}$

9. $a_n = 5n - 1; a_{12} = 59$ **10.** $a_n = 16\left(\dfrac{1}{4}\right)^{n-1}; a_{12} = \dfrac{1}{262,144}$ **11.** -2387 **12.** -385 **13.** 8 **14.** $\dfrac{73}{99}$ **15.** \$276,427

16. $S_1: 1 = \dfrac{1[3(1) - 1]}{2}$; $S_k: 1 + 4 + 7 + \cdots + (3k - 2) = \dfrac{k(3k - 1)}{2}$; $S_{k+1}: 1 + 4 + 7 + \cdots + (3k + 1) = \dfrac{(k + 1)(3k + 2)}{2}$; S_{k+1}

can be obtained by adding $3k + 1$ to both sides of S_k.

17. $x^{10} - 5x^8 + 10x^6 - 10x^4 + 5x^2 - 1$ **18.** $x^8 + 8x^7y^2 + 28x^6y^4$ **19.** 990 ways **20.** 210 sets **21.** $10^4 = 10,000$ **22.** $\dfrac{3}{5}$ **23.** $\dfrac{39}{50}$
24. $\dfrac{3}{5}$ **25.** $\dfrac{9}{19}$ **26.** $\dfrac{10}{1001}$ **27.** $\dfrac{8}{13}$ **28.** $\dfrac{3}{5}$ **29.** $\dfrac{1}{256}$ **30.** $\dfrac{1}{16}$

Cumulative Review Exercises (Chapters 1–8)

1. domain: $[-4, 1)$; range: $(-\infty, 2]$ **2.** maximum of 2 at $x = -2$ **3.** $(-2, 1)$ **4.** neither **5.** -3 and -1 **6.** 0 **7.** $x \to 1^-$

8.

$g(x) = f(x - 2) + 1$

9.
$h(x) = -f(2x)$

10. $\left\{\dfrac{14}{5}\right\}$ **11.** $\left\{\dfrac{3 + \sqrt{3}}{3}, \dfrac{3 - \sqrt{3}}{3}\right\}$ **12.** $\{2\}$

13. $\{16,256\}$ **14.** $\{6\}$ **15.** $-1 \le x \le 0$ or $[-1, 0]$

16. $\left(-\dfrac{2}{3}, \dfrac{3}{2}\right)$ **17.** $(-3, 1]$ **18.** $\{2.9706\}$ **19.** $\left\{1, \dfrac{1}{2}, -3\right\}$

20. $\{(3, 2), (3, -2), (-3, 2), (-3, -2)\}$ **21.** $\{(6, -4, 2)\}$
22. $\{(0, -1), (2, 1)\}$

23. $100x^2 + y^2 = 25$ **24.** $4x^2 - 9y^2 - 16x + 54y - 29 = 0$ **25.** $f(x) = \dfrac{x^2 - 1}{x - 2}$ **26.** $2x - y \ge 4$, $x \le 2$ **27.** $f(x) = x^2 - 4x - 5$

28.
f^{-1}, f

29.
f, g

30. $(f \circ g)(x) = -x^2 + 2; (g \circ f)(x) = -x^2 - 2x$
31. $-2x - h - 2$
32. $\begin{bmatrix} -2 & 10 \\ -5 & 7 \\ 15 & -15 \end{bmatrix}$ **33.** $\dfrac{-1}{x - 2} + \dfrac{3x - 2}{x^2 + 2x + 2}$
34. $x^{15} + 10x^{12}y + 40x^9y^2 + 80x^6y^3 + 80x^3y^4 + 32y^5$ **35.** 3850

36. $y = \dfrac{1}{4}x + \dfrac{3}{2}$ **37.** $y = -5x - 2$ **38.** \$2000 **39.** length: 100 yd; width: 50 yd **40.** pen: \$1.80; pad: \$2 **41. a.** 6 sec
b. 2.5 sec; 196 ft **42.** 11 amps **43.** Answer will vary. An example is: $y = -0.88x + 33.2$ where x is the number of years after 1980. Eventually there may be no smokers among U.S. adults.

Subject Index

Chapter Test Prep Video CD

System Requirements
Windows® Users:
- Pentium II 300 MHz processor
- Windows XP Service Pack 2 or Vista
- In addition to the minimum RAM required by the operating system, this CD-ROM requires 64 MB RAM
- 71 MB available hard drive space (optional - for minimum QuickTime installation if necessary)
- 800 x 600 resolution
- 8x or faster CD-ROM drive
- QuickTime 7.x (for best performance we recommend version 7.4 or higher)
- Sound card

Macintosh® Users:
- Mac OS 10.x
 - In addition to the minimum RAM required by the operating system, this CD-ROM requires 64 MB RAM
- 25 MB available hard drive space (optional - for minimum QuickTime installation if necessary)
- 800 x 600 resolution
- 8x or faster CD-ROM drive
- QuickTime 7.x (for best performance we recommend version 7.4 or higher)

The QuickTime player may already be installed on your computer, but if it is not, you can download it from Apple's website:
* Go to http/www.apple.com/quicktime/download
* Select your operating system and follow the on-screen instructions to download the free player.

How to get started with the Chapter Test Prep Video CD:
Insert the CD into your CD-ROM drive. For Windows users, the program should launch automatically. If it does not, or if you have auto-launch turned off, you will need to open the program manually.

To open the Chapter Test Prep Video CD manually:
<u>Windows Users:</u> **(1)** Double-click on "My Computer" and locate your CD-ROM drive. It is usually the D: drive. **(2)** Right-click on the CD-ROM drive and select "Open" to view the contents of the CD. **(3)** Double-click on the "START" file to open the Home page of the Chapter Test Prep program. **(4)** From the Home page you can select any of the available resources by clicking on the buttons in the top menu bar.

<u>Macintosh Users:</u> **(1)** Locate the CD-ROM Icon on your desktop and double-click it to view the contents of the CD. **(2)** Double-click on the "START" file to open the Home page of the Pass the Test program. **(3)** From the Home page you can select any of the available resources by clicking on the buttons in the top menu bar.

For Pearson's technical support:
- Visit us online anytime at http://247pearsoned.custhelp.com/, where you can search our knowledgebase for common solutions, view product alerts, and review all options for additional assistance. NOTE: Pearson does not support and/or assist with third-party software. For technical assistance with the QuickTime player, please visit Apple's website at http://www.info.apple.com/usen/quicktime

Apple, Macintosh, and QuickTime are trademarks of Apple, Inc., registered in the U.S. and other countries.

Photo Credits

Definitions, Rules, and Formulas

THE REAL NUMBERS

Natural Numbers: $\{1, 2, 3, \ldots\}$
Whole Numbers: $\{0, 1, 2, 3, \ldots\}$
Integers: $\{\ldots, -3, -2, -1, 0, 1, 2, 3, \ldots\}$
Rational Numbers: $\{\frac{a}{b} \mid a$ and b are integers, $b \neq 0\}$
Irrational Numbers: $\{x \mid x$ is real and not rational$\}$

PROPERTIES OF ADDITION AND MULTIPLICATION

Commutative: $a + b = b + a; ab = ba$
Associative: $(a + b) + c = a + (b + c);$
$\qquad (ab)c = a(bc)$
Distributive: $a(b + c) = ab + ac; a(b - c) = ab - ac$
Identity: $a + 0 = a; a \cdot 1 = a$
Inverse: $a + (-a) = 0; a \cdot \frac{1}{a} = 1 \ (a \neq 0)$
Multiplication Properties: $(-1)a = -a;$
$(-1)(-a) = a; a \cdot 0 = 0; (-a)(b) = (a)(-b) = -ab;$
$(-a)(-b) = ab$

EXPONENTS

Definitions of Rational Exponents

1. $a^{\frac{1}{n}} = \sqrt[n]{a}$

2. $a^{\frac{m}{n}} = \left(\sqrt[n]{a}\right)^m$ or $\sqrt[n]{a^m}$

3. $a^{-\frac{m}{n}} = \dfrac{1}{a^{\frac{m}{n}}}$

Properties of Rational Exponents

If m and n are rational exponents, and a and b are real numbers for which the following expressions are defined, then

1. $b^m \cdot b^n = b^{m+n}$

2. $\dfrac{b^m}{b^n} = b^{m-n}$

3. $\left(b^m\right)^n = b^{mn}$

4. $(ab)^n = a^n b^n$

5. $\left(\dfrac{a}{b}\right)^n = \dfrac{a^n}{b^n}$

RADICALS

If $\sqrt[n]{a}$ and $\sqrt[n]{b}$ are real numbers, then

1. If n is even, then $\sqrt[n]{a^n} = |a|$.

2. If n is odd, then $\sqrt[n]{a^n} = a$.

3. The product rule: $\sqrt[n]{a} \cdot \sqrt[n]{b} = \sqrt[n]{ab}$

4. The quotient rule: $\dfrac{\sqrt[n]{a}}{\sqrt[n]{b}} = \sqrt[n]{\dfrac{a}{b}}$

INTERVAL NOTATION, SET-BUILDER NOTATION, AND GRAPHS

$(a, b) = \{x \mid a < x < b\}$

$[a, b) = \{x \mid a \leq x < b\}$

$(a, b] = \{x \mid a < x \leq b\}$

$[a, b] = \{x \mid a \leq x \leq b\}$

$(-\infty, b) = \{x \mid x < b\}$

$(-\infty, b] = \{x \mid x \leq b\}$

$(a, \infty) = \{x \mid x > a\}$

$[a, \infty) = \{x \mid x \geq a\}$

$(-\infty, \infty) = \{x \mid x$ is a real number$\} = \{x \mid x \in R\}$

SLOPE FORMULA

$$\text{slope } (m) = \frac{\text{change in } y}{\text{change in } x} = \frac{y_2 - y_1}{x_2 - x_1} \quad (x_1 \neq x_2)$$

EQUATIONS OF LINES

1. *Slope-intercept form:* $y = mx + b$
m is the line's slope and b is its y-intercept.

2. *General form:* $Ax + By + C = 0$

3. *Point-slope form:* $y - y_1 = m(x - x_1)$
m is the line's slope and (x_1, y_1) is a fixed point on the line.

4. *Horizontal line parallel to the x-axis:* $y = b$

5. *Vertical line parallel to the y-axis:* $x = a$

ABSOLUTE VALUE

1. $|x| = \begin{cases} x & \text{if } x \geq 0 \\ -x & \text{if } x < 0 \end{cases}$

2. If $|x| = c$, then $x = c$ or $x = -c$. $(c > 0)$

3. If $|x| < c$, then $-c < x < c$. $(c > 0)$

4. If $|x| > c$, then $x < -c$ or $x > c$. $(c > 0)$

SPECIAL FACTORIZATIONS

1. *Difference of two squares:*
$$A^2 - B^2 = (A + B)(A - B)$$

2. *Perfect square trinomials:*
$$A^2 + 2AB + B^2 = (A + B)^2$$
$$A^2 - 2AB + B^2 = (A - B)^2$$

3. *Sum of two cubes:*
$$A^3 + B^3 = (A + B)(A^2 - AB + B^2)$$

4. *Difference of two cubes:*
$$A^3 - B^3 = (A - B)(A^2 + AB + B^2)$$

ALGEBRA'S COMMON GRAPHS

Identity Function

Absolute Value Function

Standard Quadratic Function

Square Root Function

Standard Cubic Function

Cube Root Function

Greatest Integer Function

Reciprocal Function

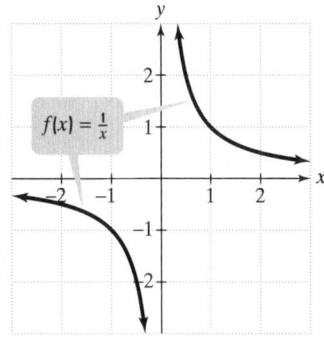

TRANSFORMATIONS

In each case, c represents a positive real number.

Function		Draw the graph of f and:
Vertical translations	$\begin{cases} y = f(x) + c \\ y = f(x) - c \end{cases}$	Shift f upward c units. Shift f downward c units.
Horizontal translations	$\begin{cases} y = f(x - c) \\ y = f(x + c) \end{cases}$	Shift f to the right c units. Shift f to the left c units.
Reflections	$\begin{cases} y = -f(x) \\ y = f(-x) \end{cases}$	Reflect f about the x-axis. Reflect f about the y-axis.
Vertical Stretching or Shrinking	$\begin{cases} y = cf(x); c > 1 \\ y = cf(x); 0 < c < 1 \end{cases}$	Vertically stretch f, multiplying each of its y-coordinates by c. Vertically shrink f, multiplying each of its y-coordinates by c.
Horizontal Stretching or Shrinking	$\begin{cases} y = f(cx); c > 1 \\ y = f(cx); 0 < c < 1 \end{cases}$	Horizontally shrink f, dividing each of its x-coordinates by c. Horizontally stretch f, dividing each of its x-coordinates by c.

DISTANCE AND MIDPOINT FORMULAS

1. The distance from (x_1, y_1) to (x_2, y_2) is

$$\sqrt{(x_2 - x_1)^2 + (y_2 - y_1)^2}.$$

2. The midpoint of the line segment with endpoints (x_1, y_1) and (x_2, y_2) is

$$\left(\frac{x_1 + x_2}{2}, \frac{y_1 + y_2}{2} \right).$$

QUADRATIC FORMULA

The solutions of $ax^2 + bx + c = 0$ with $a \neq 0$ are

$$x = \frac{-b \pm \sqrt{b^2 - 4ac}}{2a}.$$

FUNCTIONS

1. Linear Function: $f(x) = mx + b$

Graph is a line with slope m and y-intercept b.

2. Quadratic Function: $f(x) = ax^2 + bx + c, a \neq 0$

Graph is a parabola with vertex at $x = -\dfrac{b}{2a}$.

Quadratic Function: $f(x) = a(x - h)^2 + k$
In this form, the parabola's vertex is (h, k).

3. nth-Degree Polynomial Function:
$f(x) = a_n x^n + a_{n-1} x^{n-1} + a_{n-2} x^{n-2} + \cdots + a_1 x + a_0, a_n \neq 0$
For n odd and $a_n > 0$, graph falls to the left and rises to the right.
For n odd and $a_n < 0$, graph rises to the left and falls to the right.
For n even and $a_n > 0$, graph rises to the left and rises to the right.
For n even and $a_n < 0$, graph falls to the left and falls to the right.

4. Rational Function: $f(x) = \dfrac{p(x)}{q(x)}$, $p(x)$ and $q(x)$ are polynomials, $q(x) \neq 0$

5. Exponential Function: $f(x) = b^x, b > 0, b \neq 1$
Graphs:

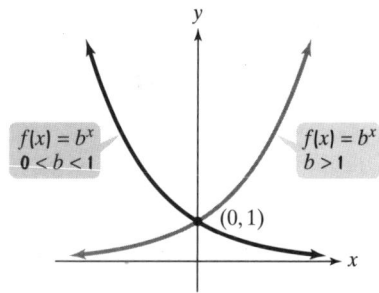

PROPERTIES OF LOGARITHMS

6. Logarithmic Function: $f(x) = \log_b x, b > 0, b \neq 1$
$y = \log_b x$ is equivalent to $x = b^y$.

Graph:

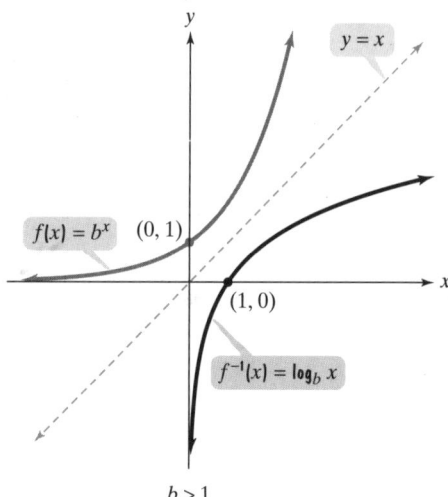

$b > 1$

PROPERTIES OF LOGARITHMS

1. $\log_b(MN) = \log_b M + \log_b N$

2. $\log_b\left(\dfrac{M}{N}\right) = \log_b M - \log_b N$

3. $\log_b M^p = p \log_b M$

4. $\log_b M = \dfrac{\log_a M}{\log_a b} = \dfrac{\ln M}{\ln b} = \dfrac{\log M}{\log b}$

5. $\log_b b^x = x; \quad \ln e^x = x$

6. $b^{\log_b x} = x; \quad e^{\ln x} = x$

INVERSE OF A 2 × 2 MATRIX

If $A = \begin{bmatrix} a & b \\ c & d \end{bmatrix}$, then $A^{-1} = \dfrac{1}{ad - bc} \begin{bmatrix} d & -b \\ -c & a \end{bmatrix}$, where $ad - bc \neq 0$.

CRAMER'S RULE

If

$$a_{11}x_1 + a_{12}x_2 + a_{13}x_3 + \cdots + a_{1n}x_n = b_1$$
$$a_{21}x_1 + a_{22}x_2 + a_{23}x_3 + \cdots + a_{2n}x_n = b_2$$
$$a_{31}x_1 + a_{32}x_2 + a_{33}x_3 + \cdots + a_{3n}x_n = b_3$$
$$\vdots$$
$$a_{n1}x_1 + a_{n2}x_2 + a_{n3}x_3 + \cdots + a_{nn}x_n = b_n$$

then $x_i = \dfrac{D_i}{D}, D \neq 0.$

D: determinant of the system's coefficients

D_i: determinant in which coefficients of x_i are replaced by $b_1, b_2, b_3, \ldots, b_n$.

Country Crafts

TIME-LIFE BOOKS

Alexandria, Virginia

Country Crafts

*creative craft
projects, from sewing
to woodworking*

A19,926

A REBUS BOOK

C O N T E N T S

Painting

Crafting Natural Materials

Working with your hands can be an immensely satisfying experience. Craft projects like those featured on the following pages offer an opportunity for personal expression and individual achievement that is particularly welcome in this age of technology. You will find there is pleasure to be had in the entire process—in choosing the materials, in settling on a particular color or design, in doing the work itself, and, finally, in enjoying the finished piece. Moreover, if you are on a tight decorating budget, learning a craft may allow you to copy antique pieces, such as grain-painted boxes or Pennsylvania-German hand towels, which you might not otherwise be able to afford. Indeed, virtually all the crafts in this book, represented by such varied projects as a primitive hooked rug, a twig picture frame, and a log cabin doll quilt, take their inspiration from the past, recalling America's rich artistic heritage.

Designed to appeal to everyone from beginners to experienced craftspeople, the twenty-eight projects on the following pages involve sewing, embroidery, rugmaking, working with paper, painting, woodworking, and flower crafting. Even if you have never sewn a stitch or held a paintbrush, you should be able to find a project that suits your level of expertise. And, in learning many of these crafts, such as embroidery and rug-hooking, you can try a practice piece to see if you enjoy a particular technique.

For the best results, it is important to read the directions completely before beginning a project. Each craft features a section called Important Information that offers useful background on materials, equipment, and procedures. Following the Important Information section are step-by-step directions, which are keyed to helpful illustrations, diagrams, charts, and patterns. For your convenience, all but one of the patterns in the book are full size, so you will not have to spend time enlarging them.

Throughout the book you will also find practical information on such topics as selecting paints and brushes, dyeing fabric, and drying flowers. While nearly all the materials you will need for the projects are available at crafts and hardware stores, or at sewing, needlework, or florist shops, you can also consult the yellow pages of your telephone book for additional resources. Be sure to buy quality materials and equipment.

As you gain confidence and develop your skills by doing these projects, you may want to adapt the specified techniques, colors, and designs to your own taste. Once you have made the game board on page 134, for example, you could copy one of the colorful antique boards on pages 138-139. But whether you choose to experiment or not, it is important that you get started. While craft projects can be time consuming, you will soon realize that the rewards—and the unique pieces that result—are well worth the effort.

8

Sewing

*easy projects for
needle and thread*

Of all the needlecrafts, sewing is perhaps the most versatile. Fabric and thread can be combined to make an almost limitless variety of accessories and toys, and you need not be an accomplished seamstress to explore the possibilities. There are several projects in this chapter that would suit a beginner: a yo-yo coverlet that requires no machine stitching, a set of small fabric-covered sewing boxes also produced by hand, and some fast-to-sew pillow shams stitched from purchased napkins so that no pattern is necessary.

There are also a number of projects to make for children, including three stuffed toys—a floppy frog bean bag, a topsy-turvy doll, and a handsome cat pieced from crazy patchwork—as well as a colorful log cabin doll quilt. While some require purchasing a few simple materials, most can be created by merely turning to your scrap basket or by selecting colorful remnants at your local fabric shop.

Sewing frog bean bags from easy-to-cut patterns is a simple project that can be done by hand or machine (see pages 44-47).

Victorian Sewing Boxes

In Victorian times, it was customary for women to keep their embroidery tools in a small sewing box that could be carried easily from room to room. Patterns for making fabric-covered sewing boxes like those shown here were published in late-19th-century ladies' magazines. Very possibly, such colorful ribbon-trimmed boxes were made to be sold at the "fancy fairs" or bazaars that were commonly held to raise money for charitable causes. The boxes can make distinctive Christmas tree ornaments or pretty packaging for small gifts.

◆ IMPORTANT INFORMATION

Each box is made from three identical cardboard sections; the box opens when the pointed ends are gently pressed together. The sections are covered individually with fabric. Although you can use any medium-weight fabric, chintz, velveteen, moiré, or antique satin will lend the boxes a particularly Victorian look. Full-size patterns are given for three box sizes: 8½ inches, 6⅝ inches, and 5½ inches long. Stitch all seams with a ¼-inch seam allowance.

◆ MATERIALS AND EQUIPMENT

For each box:

1 piece medium-weight fabric, 10 x 17 inches (for outer covering)
1 piece medium-weight fabric, 10 x 17 inches (for lining)
Lightweight cardboard
1 ball pearl cotton or 1 skein 6-strand embroidery floss

Ribbon and fabric flowers (optional)
Thread
Tracing paper
Scissors
Sewing needle
Darning needle
Dressmaker's pins

◆ DIRECTIONS

1. *Making the pattern:* Using a pencil, trace a Sewing Box Pattern on page 13 in the size of your choice onto the tracing paper and cut out.

2. *Making the cardboard sections:* Place the paper pattern on the cardboard, draw around it, and cut out along the line. Repeat twice to make three cardboard sections.

3. *Cutting the fabric and lining:* If your outer fabric does not have a one-way design or dominant motif, place it with the wrong side up on a worktable. With the wrong side up, lay the lining fabric over it. Place a cardboard section on the fabric layers

A-1

A-2

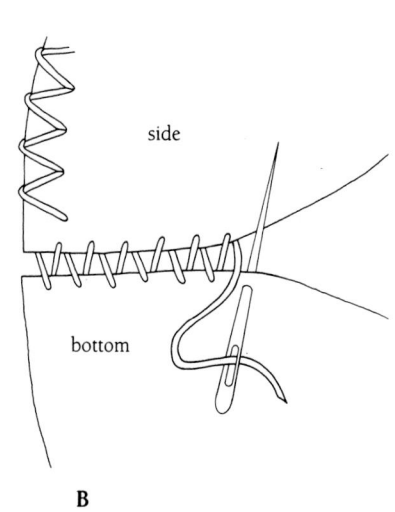

side

bottom

B

and draw a line around it ¼ inch outside the pattern to make a seam allowance. Pin through both layers within the marked line and cut on the line. Mark one edge with an X to be the top of the section. Repeat twice to make three outer covering pieces and three lining pieces.

4. *Positioning the fabric design:* If your outer fabric has a one-way design or dominant motif, follow Step 3, but cut the lining pieces only. After cutting the lining pieces, place the fabric for the outer covering on the worktable with the right side up. Using a lining piece as a placement pattern, lay it over the outer fabric with the wrong side up and the straight grain aligned, adjusting it until you like the way the fabric design works with the shape. Pin the lining piece to the outer fabric and cut around the edge. Mark one edge with an X to be the top of the section. Repeat twice to make three outer covering pieces.

5. *Covering the cardboard sections:* Stitch along the top edge of one lining and outer covering piece. Trim the seam to ⅛ inch. On the lining only, press ¼ inch to the wrong side along the raw edge. Turn the pieces right side out and press the seamed edge. Slide a cardboard section between the lining and the outer covering, keeping the seam allowance on the lining side of the cardboard. Fold the outer fabric over the edge of the cardboard and pin the lining to it, pulling both fabric pieces taut. On the lining side of the cardboard, slipstitch the two fabric pieces together. Remove the pins. Repeat for the remaining two sections.

6. *Embellishing the top edges:* Using the darning needle and the pearl cotton or three strands of the embroidery floss, embellish the top edge of one of the sections with whipstitching. To whipstitch, hold the section with the outer covering facing you. Starting at the right-hand point of the section, bring the needle up from the lining side ¼ inch from the top edge, slide it over the top edge, and bring it up from the lining side again ¼ inch to the left; continue working to the left, placing the stitches ¼ inch apart (Illustration A-1). When you reach the left-hand point of the section, reverse direction and, working from the left to the right in the same manner, sew through the same holes (Illustration A-2). Repeat for the top edge of one more box section. These two sections will be the box sides; the remaining section will be the box bottom.

7. *Joining the sections:* Using the darning needle and the pearl cotton or three strands of the embroidery floss, join one edge of the box bottom to the lower edge of one box side with weaving stitch. To do weaving stitch, take a small stitch, through the lining only, at one point of the box side to secure the thread. Referring to Illustration B, hold the box side against the box bottom with the outer sides up. Bring the needle up between the two sections and over the edge of the box bottom, piercing the cardboard ⅛ inch from the edge. Pass the needle between the sections again, bring it up over the edge of the box side, and insert it down through the box side ⅛ inch from the edge and ¼ inch from the previous stitch. Repeat, gently shaping the box curve until the other point is reached. Place the remaining box side against the other edge of the box bottom, and weave together in the same manner. Reinforce the ends with a few tiny overcast stitches. Trim with ribbon bows and flowers if desired. ◆

SEWING BOX PATTERNS

straight grain

PRETTY PINCUSHIONS

Ever since they originated in the 16th century, pincushions have not only been made as utilitarian sewing accessories; they have also been presented as elegant little gifts intended to be enjoyed for their fanciful designs. Pincushions like the 19th- and early-20th-century examples shown here were traditionally pieced from fabric scraps, and often resemble fruits, vegetables, animals, and birds. They might be elaborately embroidered, encrusted with beads, or covered in cotton-thread crochet. In her 1928 book on needlework tools, Gertrude Whiting suggested making "dainty gift cushions" of graduated, scented, pastel-colored hearts. "Each should be edged…with delicate lace and a bit of ribbon of its own hue…," she advised.

As small labors of love, decorative pincushions can still be charming accessories and gifts. Making one is a good way to experiment with a variety of needlework techniques. Let the past inspire you and try replicating a vintage pincushion. Or use the scraps, ribbons, and buttons in your own sewing box to create a new and personal design.

The pincushions shown here date from the 1880s to the 1940s. The crocheted examples at far left were designed to hang on a wall. The Victorian sewing box at near right has a pincushion inside the lid; a bird perches on top.

15

Napkin Pillow Shams

Cloth napkins are a good fabric choice for pillow shams because they eliminate the need for measuring and cutting pattern pieces. Moreover, many napkins come with a centered pattern or a decorative border that offers the pillow-maker a ready-made design. The shams shown here are made with a back envelope closure so that the case can be easily slipped over a pillow—and just as easily removed for laundering. If desired, the closure can be secured with a button.

◆ IMPORTANT INFORMATION

Choose good-quality cotton or cotton-blend napkins—those shown here are a jacquard cotton—and be sure to preshrink them before you begin sewing. Three matching napkins are used for each pillow sham. Two of them overlap to make the sham back, and the third napkin is used for the sham front. You will need to open the hems on all edges of the front napkin, as well as on the top and bottom edges of the napkins used for the back of the sham; the finished pillow sham will measure the size of one napkin (with the hems opened) less a ½-inch seam allowance.

A tailored hem, or flange, is made by topstitching a 2½-inch border inside the finished edge of the sham. Your pillow should be the same size as the area inside this tailored hem. Ready-made pillows come in many different sizes, but if you cannot find one in the size dictated by the napkins you choose, you can easily make one from polyester stuffing and muslin.

◆ MATERIALS AND EQUIPMENT

For each pillow:
3 cloth napkins, in size desired
1 pillow (see Important Information
 above for size)
Button (optional)

Thread
Scissors
Dressmaker's pins
Dressmaker's chalk
Ruler

◆ DIRECTIONS

1. *Marking the napkin top:* Decide which way you want the napkin pattern to run on your pillow sham. Using a pencil, mark the top edge of each napkin on the wrong side.

2. *Making the sham back:* Remove the hems from the top and bottom edges of two napkins. Press the opened hems. With the wrong side up and the top edge away from you, place one of the two napkins on a worktable. Fold up the left hemmed edge

A

B

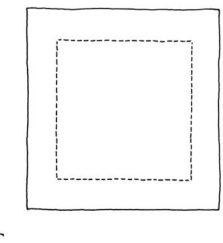

C

1½ inches and press. Topstitch 1¼ inches from the folded edge. This 1½-inch hem will be at the back opening of the sham.

3. *Making the buttonhole (optional):* If the back opening of the sham measures more than 18 inches long, you may want to fasten it with a button. The buttonhole should be made at this time. Find the center of the edge with the 1½-inch hem and mark it for a buttonhole sized to your button. The buttonhole should be perpendicular to the hemmed edge. Make the buttonhole by machine, following the instructions in your operator's manual.

4. *Continuing the sham back:* With the right sides up, place the two napkins for the back on the work surface so that the 1½-inch hem of the first napkin overlaps the left edge of the second napkin. Pin through all the layers and stitch across both ends of the overlap ⅜ inch from the raw edges (Illustration A). Remove the pins and, with the right side up, place the sham back on the worktable in the same position as before.

5. *Making the sham front:* Remove all the hems from the third napkin. Press the opened hems well. With the right sides together, fold the napkin in half to find the center. Using the pencil, mark the center line from top to bottom on the wrong side of the napkin.

6. *Joining the sham front and back:* With the right sides together, place the sham front over the sham back, aligning the center line with the left edge of the lower back napkin (Illustration B). Pin the sham front to the sham back through all the layers around all four edges of the front. Trim the sham back even with the sham front. Stitch a seam with a ½-inch seam allowance along all four edges. Remove the pins and trim the corner seam allowances diagonally.Turn the sham right side out and, using a knitting needle or other blunt-tipped instrument, push out the corners. Press carefully to make the seamed edges sharp.

7. *Making the tailored hem:* With the back facing up, place the sham on the worktable. Pin the back opening closed. Turn the sham over. With the ruler and chalk, measure and mark a line 2½ inches in from the outer edges of the sham. Topstitch along this marked line (Illustration C). Remove the pins from the back opening. Sew on the button, if appropriate. Press the sham. Insert the pillow through the back opening. ◆

THE CRAFTY BUTTON

Much more than utilitarian fasteners, buttons are effective decorations. Selected with care for their colors, shapes, and materials, they can be used to accent the theme of a craft or add a whimsical touch. Round buttons, of course, make good eyes for a stuffed animal or doll, but don't be limited by convention. Treated as imaginative details, unusual buttons—tiny animals, flowers, thimbles, or fish, perhaps—will transform an ordinary sewing project into a work of art.

Yo-Yo Coverlet

Especially popular in the 1930s, yo-yo coverlets—which are pieced from hundreds of puffed fabric circles—offer a good way to take advantage of sewing-basket scraps. They are also easy to make, requiring little sewing experience. Each circle, or yo-yo, is simply basted along the edge, pulled into a puff, and then flattened with an iron. The arrangement of the yo-yos is usually random, as in the coverlet shown here. All the needlework can be done by hand, and no batting, backing, or quilting is necessary; when the yo-yos are joined, the coverlet is finished.

◆ IMPORTANT INFORMATION

The coverlet shown here measures 72 x 108 inches. To figure the coverlet size you would like to make, first measure the length and width of your mattress top. Next, figure the measurement for the side overhang. (This measurement is usually 13 inches to 15 inches for a standard mattress, but it depends on the style of the bed frame and whether or not you use a dust ruffle.) Double this measurement and add the number to the mattress width. Next, figure the measurement for the overhang at the foot of the bed and the amount you need to tuck under the pillows (be generous). Add these two measurements to the mattress length.

You can use scraps, or yardage that you have purchased specifically for the coverlet, but be sure to choose medium-weight, firmly woven cottons that are not overly crisp. If the fabric is too stiff, the edges of the yo-yos will not turn attractively, and if it is too soft, the yo-yos will not hold their shape. Preshrink your fabrics, and avoid mixing fabrics that have a markedly different drape or weight.

The yo-yo circles are traced from a template 4 inches in diameter; after the circles are cut, gathered, and flattened, they measure just under two inches in diameter. You will need 361 circles for each square yard, which will be arranged in 19 rows of 19 yo-yos. A yard of 45-inch-wide fabric should yield 99 four-inch circles. The fabrics can be layered so that you are able to cut several circles at once; you will need to test how many layers your scissors will cut through with ease. Alternating the steps—cutting, gathering, and joining just enough yo-yos to make a small portion of the coverlet at one time—will make the process more fun.

◆ MATERIALS AND EQUIPMENT

Assorted cotton fabric, 22 yards total,
 45 inches wide
Lightweight cardboard
Thread

Tracing paper
Scissors
Sewing needle

A

B

C

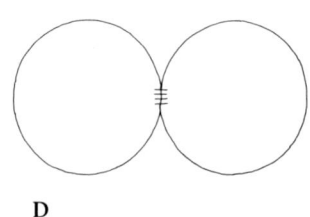

D

◆ DIRECTIONS

1. *Making the template:* Using a pencil, trace the Yo-Yo Pattern below onto the tracing paper and cut out. Place the paper pattern on the cardboard, draw around it, and cut out along the line.

2. *Cutting the fabric:* With the wrong sides up, stack the fabrics on a worktable. Place the template on the stack and draw around it, moving the template along until you have covered the surface with circles. Remove the template, pin the layers together, and cut out the circles along the line through all the layers.

3. *Making the yo-yos:* Press a generous ⅛ inch around the edge of a fabric circle to the wrong side. Using a double thread, baste all around through the folded edge (Illustration A). Pull the stitching, forming gathers, until the circle closes (right side out) and forms a puff (Illustration B). Knot the thread to secure the gathers. Flatten the puff into a yo-yo (Illustration C) and press to keep flat. Repeat to make more yo-yos.

4. *Joining the yo-yos:* With the gathered sides down, place two of the yo-yos side by side. Begin sewing by passing the needle through one yo-yo opening, to hide the knot, and bringing it up at the side of the yo-yo. Where the sides touch, sew the yo-yos together with three or four tiny overcast stitches (Illustration D). Continue joining the yo-yos in this manner to form a row that measures the desired width of the coverlet. Make several rows, then join the rows, matching the sides of the yo-yos in the same manner as above, until the coverlet is the desired length. ◆

YO-YO PATTERN

Log Cabin Doll Quilt

In the 19th century, young girls who were learning to sew often tried their hand at a doll quilt because the small size made it less daunting to a novice seamstress than a full-size bed quilt. The doll quilt shown above is worked in the Log Cabin pattern, an American favorite named for the familiar log structures associated with pioneer days. Each quilt block is composed of fabric strips, or "logs," which are "built" around a central square; tradition holds that the square represents the chimney or hearth. Graduated in length, the strips in a Log Cabin pattern block are sewn on one at a time,

with each end butting against the side of the previous strip so that the block grows outward in a kind of squared-off spiral.

One half of the strips in each block are traditionally light in color and the other half are dark; the light and dark areas divide the block diagonally into triangles. As the Log Cabin blocks are assembled to make the overall design, the light and dark triangular halves of the blocks can be juxtaposed in a number of ways to create different effects. Here, the blocks are arranged in the Straight Furrows pattern, a Log Cabin variation characterized by diagonal stripes.

Along with varied household hints, Lydia Maria Child, the author of the 1833 volume **The Girl's Own Book,** *offered sage advice to young folk. Little girls "often have a great many small bits of cloth, and large remnants of time," she wrote, "which they don't know what to do with; and I think it is better for them to make cradle quilts for their dolls, or their baby brothers, than to be standing around, wishing they had something to do."*

◆ IMPORTANT INFORMATION

This doll quilt is composed of four Log Cabin blocks. The blocks are pieced separately, then sewn together to create a larger square that is set off by a solid-color border. The quilt, backed with contrasting fabric and finished with bias binding, measures about 14 inches square. Like many traditional Log Cabin quilts, it has no batting and is not actually quilted.

Each Log Cabin block is made with strips of fabric in six dark and five light colors. The directions that follow explain how to arrange the strips for one block. When you are making your quilt, you can piece all four blocks in the same fabrics, or vary the colors slightly, as in the quilt shown here. Choose tightly woven cotton fabrics in a variety of prints and solids and preshrink them before cutting. To avoid mixing up the strips for the different blocks, cut the strips for one block at a time and keep them in separate plastic bags.

Before you begin, be sure to read all the directions. Note that the full-size Log Cabin Block Patterns on page 27 include a ¼-inch seam allowance on all sides. The numbers on the Piecing Diagram on page 25 indicate the order in which the pattern pieces are joined; the repeating letters indicate strips to be cut from the same fabric. Pin and stitch all the pieces with the right sides together. When piecing the blocks, backstitch the ends of each seam to make them stronger. Remove the pins after stitching each seam and press the seam allowance toward the darker fabric whenever possible so that it will not show through the finished quilt top.

◆ MATERIALS AND EQUIPMENT

Assorted cotton fabric remnants, 8 inches x 24 inches each (6 dark colors and 5 light colors)
1 piece cotton fabric, 16 x 16 inches (for backing)
½ yard cotton fabric, 45 inches wide (for border and bias binding)
Thread

Lightweight cardboard
Plastic food storage bags
Tracing paper
Scissors
Dressmaker's pins
Dressmaker's chalk
Ruler

◆ DIRECTIONS

1. *Making the patterns:* Using a pencil, trace the Log Cabin Block Patterns on page 27 onto the tracing paper and cut out. Place the paper patterns on the cardboard, draw around them, and cut out along the lines. Transfer all the numbers to the cardboard patterns.

2. *Cutting the fabric:* Separate the dark and light fabrics. Using the chalk or a pencil, label the dark fabrics A, C, E, G, I, and K, and label the light fabrics B, D, F, H, and J. Refer to the Piecing Diagram below to be sure you understand the way in which the light and dark colors go together: pieces 1A and 2B are the same size, pieces 2B and 3B are the same color, and so on. With the wrong side up, place each piece of fabric on a worktable. Place the appropriate cardboard pattern on top and draw around it to mark the cutting lines. From fabric A, cut and label piece 1A. From fabric B, cut and label pieces 2B and 3B. From fabric C, cut and label pieces 4C and 5C. Continuing to refer to the Piecing Diagram, cut and label all the pieces for one block and place them in a plastic bag. Repeat for the remaining three blocks.

3. *Sewing the quilt blocks:* To begin making the quilt block, stitch piece 1A (the dark center square) to piece 2B. Referring to the Piecing Diagram, continue to join the pieces in numerical order. Stitch piece 3B to pieces 1A and 2B so that a square is formed. Then stitch piece 4C in place as shown in the Piecing Diagram. Continue to join the pieces in numerical order, working outward and counterclockwise from the center piece until you have used all the pieces for the block. Repeat to make the remaining three quilt blocks. Press all the blocks carefully on both sides.

4. *Assembling the quilt top:* With the right sides up, lay the four blocks out on the worktable with the dark and light halves arranged according to the Assembly Diagram below. Stitch the two upper blocks together and press the seam to the left.

Piecing Diagram

Assembly Diagram

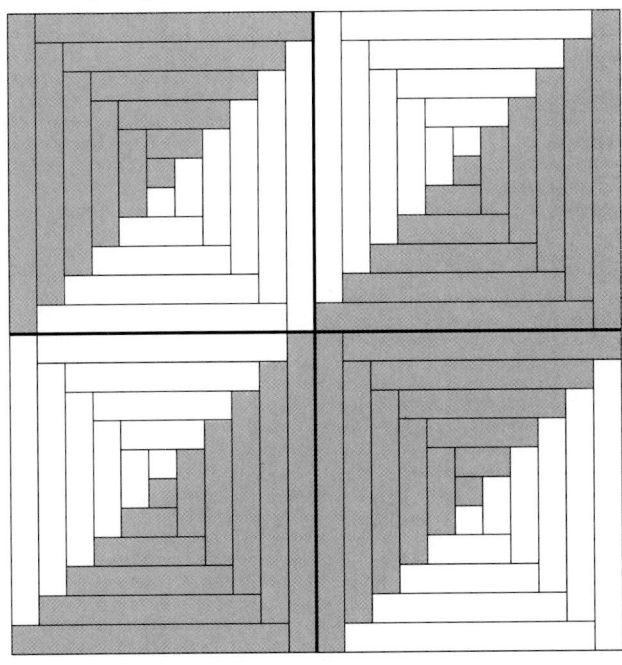

Stitch the two lower blocks together and press the seam to the right. Referring to the Assembly Diagram, stitch the two 2-block units together, matching the center seams carefully. Press the seam to one side; press the four-block square carefully on both sides.

5. *Making the border:* Measure one side of the four-block square. From the border fabric, cut two strips, 1½ inches wide, to this measurement. Stitch the strips to the opposite sides of the four-block square and press the seams toward the border strips. Measure the remaining sides of the four-block square across the ends of the border strips you have already added. Cut two border strips, 1½ inches wide, to this measurement. Stitch the border strips to the remaining two sides of the four-block square and press the seams toward the border strips. Press the entire square carefully on both sides.

6. *Adding the backing:* With the wrong side up, lay the backing fabric on the worktable. With the right side up, center the four-block square on the backing, aligning the grain lines, and pin. Using the ruler and a pencil, mark a square on the backing fabric ¼ inch outside the four-block square. Cut out the backing along this line. Baste the four-block square to the backing along all sides. Remove the pins.

7. *Making the bias binding:* Trim the binding fabric into a rectangle with all four edges cut on the straight grain. Fold the rectangle diagonally so that the crosswise grain aligns with the lengthwise grain (Illustration A). Crease along the fold (bias) line, unfold the fabric, and mark the bias line with the pencil and ruler. Draw lines parallel to this bias line at 2-inch intervals to mark the bias strips; mark enough strips to total 64 inches in length and cut them out. To join two bias strips, place them at right angles to each other with the right sides together and stitch across the end with a ¼-inch seam allowance (Illustration B). Repeat until all the strips are joined. Press the seams open.

8. *Binding the quilt:* Square off one end of the bias binding strip and fold ¼ inch to the wrong side; press. With the right sides together, place the folded end of the bias strip at the center of one edge of the quilt top, aligning the raw edges of the binding and quilt backing. With a ½-inch seam allowance, stitch the binding to the quilt around all sides, allowing for mitered corners as you go. When you reach the point where you started, cut off any excess binding, leaving a small overlap.

9. *Finishing the binding:* Hold the quilt with the right side up and press the binding toward the edges, folding the pleats at the corners into neat miters. Fold the binding over the edge of the quilt, mitering the corners on the back. Fold under the raw edge of the binding ⅜ inch and pin to the backing. Slipstitch the folded edge against the stitching line and slipstitch the mitered corners. Remove the pins and press both sides of the quilt. ◆

crosswise grain

A

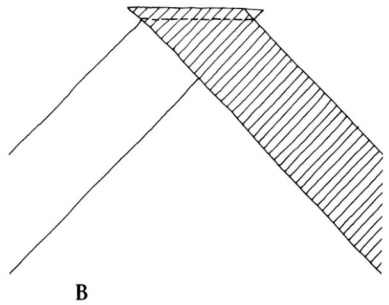

B

LOG CABIN BLOCK PATTERNS

1-2

3-4

5-6

7-8

11-12

17-18

19-20

9-10

15-16

13-14

21

TEA-DYEING FABRIC

Tea-dyeing is a good way to give the mellowed appearance of age to the fabric and trimmings you plan to use for handcrafted folk toys and quilts. The light, warm tint produced by the tea helps tone down the bright colors in new fabrics and does the same for pure whites.

Dyeing with tea is very simple to do. The process works best on 100 percent cotton or linen; cotton blends can also be used, but they generally take longer to absorb color. Be sure to prewash your cloth to remove any sizing, and test-dye a small sample of fabric to see how the color takes before putting all of it in the tea.

The amount of tea you need will vary according to the amount of fabric you are dyeing. For half a yard of 45-inch-wide cotton, three to five tea bags steeped in a quart of water should suffice (use more tea bags if you want a deeper color).

To begin, put the tea bags in a stain-resistant bowl or pan and add boiling water. After ten to twenty minutes, remove the tea bags and swirl the water to mix. To help ensure an evenly dyed color, soak the fabric in clear water and wring it out thoroughly before adding it to the tea; it should be wet but not dripping. Immerse the fabric and leave it in the tea, stirring it from time to time, until the cloth appears slightly darker than the color you desire; the color will lighten when the cloth dries. Remove the fabric, rinse it in cool water, and dry. Press to set the color.

Crazy Cat

This jaunty stuffed cat is made from wool crazy patchwork, which you can easily piece and embroider yourself. Sewn from fabric scraps, crazy patchwork was particularly popular in the late 19th century. The name refers to the haphazard manner in which the scraps were put together. Because the piecing followed no rule, crazy patchwork was faster to make than a geometric pieced pattern.

Crazy patchwork could be very elaborate and was often distinguished by decorative stitching on the piecing seams. The patches themselves might also be embroidered with small bouquets, butterflies, or other decorative motifs; such fancy embroidery was intended to show off the skill of the maker. Most crazy patchwork was made into decorative throws that were used on a piano or sofa. Patchwork toys sewn from fragments of worn-out throws probably first appeared in this century.

Considered quite fashionable, crazy patchwork was generally made by well-to-do ladies with plenty of leisure time. The materials were usually elegant; bits of silk, satin, ribbon, and even lace found their way from scrap baskets (or purchased kits) into the finished work. Occasionally, crazy patchwork was pieced in wool or cotton, but woolen patchwork tended to be utilitarian rather than showy. Wool makes a good choice for a patchwork toy, however, because it holds up well.

◆ IMPORTANT INFORMATION

Choose wool fabric scraps that are similar in weight, and avoid coat fabrics. (You may use silks and satins if you wish to make a fancier cat.) The scraps should be at least 1½ inches and not more than 3½ inches in width for this project; this will ensure that each pattern piece will consist of at least two different fabrics and that the seams will not be so close together that the patchwork becomes bulky.

For this 11-inch-tall cat, you will need enough scraps to piece together a 20 x 40-inch rectangle. You can piece the rectangle first and then cut all the full-size cat patterns from it, or you can piece a number of smaller sections and cut the patterns a few at a time. The larger the piece of "crazy" fabric you make, the more flexibility you will have in planning the way the patches fall in the patterns. If you use smaller patchwork sections, each one should be large enough to accommodate the same pattern twice (each pattern is cut in reverse to make the left and right sides of the cat).

Once the fabric is pieced, it is fused to interfacing to stabilize the grain lines and keep the seams from splitting when the pattern pieces are cut out. After the pattern pieces are cut from the patchwork, the seams are embellished with embroidery. Here, buttons are used for the eyes, but if you are making the cat for a small child the eyes should be embroidered or painted on with acrylic paint.

Pin and stitch all the pieces, right sides together, with a ¼-inch seam allowance. Backstitch the beginning and end of each seam and press the seams open as you work.

In 1864, during the crazy quilt craze, the editors of Godey's Lady's Book *reminded readers that their fancywork projects were "not* Trifles *but arts that, elevating human feeling above animal instincts, make men and women better and families happier."*

◆ MATERIALS AND EQUIPMENT

Assorted fabric scraps

1½ yards fusible interfacing

One 12-ounce package polyester stuffing

1 yard ribbon, ¾ to 1 inch wide

2 buttons, about ½ inch in diameter

1 skein 6-strand embroidery floss in
desired color

Thread

Tracing paper

Scissors

Embroidery needle

Sewing needle

Dressmaker's chalk

◆ DIRECTIONS

1. *Making the patterns:* Using a pencil, trace the Crazy Cat Patterns on pages 34-37 onto the tracing paper. Mark all the dots, letters, notches, and numbers. Cut out the paper patterns along the lines, cutting the notches outward.

2. *Making the crazy patchwork:* Begin the crazy piecing by trimming two fabric scraps so that they have straight edges where you wish to join them. The seams need not be on the straight grain, but bear in mind that bias edges tend to stretch, so plan to join a bias edge to an edge on the straight grain. With right sides together, stitch two pieces together. Decide where you wish to join the next piece, and trim an edge there. Continue joining pieces in this manner to make an interesting "crazy" pattern.

3. *Fusing the interfacing:* When you have pieced the crazy patchwork to the desired size, fuse the interfacing to the fabric following the manufacturer's directions.

4. *Cutting the fabric:* With the right side up, lay the pieced, fused fabric on a worktable. Place one paper pattern on the fabric, adjusting it until you like the way it falls on the piecing. Pin and cut around it, cutting the notches outward. Mark all dots and letters onto the wrong side of the cut piece. Remove the pins. Reverse the pattern and lay it on the right side of the fabric again. Pin, cut, and mark as above. Repeat for all the patterns, being sure to reverse the patterns as you go. (Copy the markings for the face onto only one of the two head pieces.)

5. *Embellishing the seams:* Using the embroidery needle and three strands of the embroidery floss, embellish the seams of the crazy patchwork in the body pieces with herringbone stitch. To work herringbone stitch (Illustration A), hold the fabric right side up and bring the needle up from the wrong side at point 1 about ⅛ inch to the right side of the seam. Make a ¾-inch stitch diagonally across the seam, inserting the needle at point 2. Bring the needle up at point 3 to make a small stitch. Make a ¾-inch stitch diagonally across the seam to point 4. Continue, spacing the stitches evenly so that the diagonals are parallel, until the seam is decorated. In this manner, decorate as many seams as you wish.

6. *Making the cat front:* On the left Upper Front/Paw (Pattern 1), reinforce the corner marked A with a short angled line of machine stitching and clip the corner to

Herringbone Stitch

A

the dot. Stitch the left Upper Front/Paw to the left Paw Back (Pattern 2) between dots A and B, stitching around the paw and up to the neck edge. On the left Lower Front (Pattern 3), reinforce the corner marked A with a short angled line of machine stitching and clip the corner to the dot. Stitch the left Upper Front/Paw to the left Lower Front between dots A and C, then stitch the left Lower Front to the left Paw Back between dots A and D. Repeat to make the right front section of the cat. Stitch the left front section to the right front section along the center front seam between dots E and F.

7. *Making the cat back:* Stitch together the Back pieces (Pattern 4) along the center back seam between dots G and H.

8. *Joining the cat front and back:* Stitch the front and back together at the side seams from the neck edge at dot J around the back haunch to dot K, leaving the lower edge open between the K dots.

9. *Embroidering the cat face:* On one Head piece (Pattern 5), embroider the cat face using the embroidery needle and floss. Use four long stitches for the nose and six lines of stem stitching for the whiskers. To work stem stitch (Illustrations B-1 and B-2), hold the fabric right side up and bring the needle up from the wrong side at point 1. Making a ¼-inch stitch, insert the needle at point 2. Bring the needle up at point 3 halfway between points 1 and 2 and draw through, holding the floss to the left of the needle. Making a ¼-inch stitch, put the needle in at point 4. Bring the needle up again at point 2 in the hole made by the floss going in previously, and draw through, still holding the floss to the left of the needle. Continue in this manner until you have stitched whiskers about an inch long. Sew on the buttons for eyes.

10. *Making the cat head:* Stitch the head front to the head back, up from one dot L, around the ears, and to the other dot L. Clip the corners between the ears and turn the head right side out.

11. *Joining the head and the body:* With the right sides together (the body wrong side out), pin the head to the body, matching the center chin at the notch to the center front seam at dot E, and matching the center back nape at the notch to the center back seam at dot G, aligning the raw edges and easing the body to fit. Stitch and remove the pins.

12. *Making the tail:* Stitch together the Tail pieces (Pattern 6), leaving the straight end open between dots H and M. Turn the tail right side out, using the eraser end of the pencil to push the fabric through the opening. Using some of the polyester stuffing, pack the tail firmly, but leave the open end empty enough to flatten and stitch closed.

13. *Attaching the tail:* Place the tail in the center back seam, matching dots H and M so that the tail curves down. Stitch the center back seam closed through the tail to the end of the seam.

14. *Stuffing the cat:* Turn the cat body right side out. Using the stuffing, pack firmly, starting with the paws, then filling the ears, the head, and the body. Pin closed the opening at the bottom, checking to see that the cat sits well. Stitch closed by hand. Remove the pins. Tie the ribbon in a bow around the neck. ◆

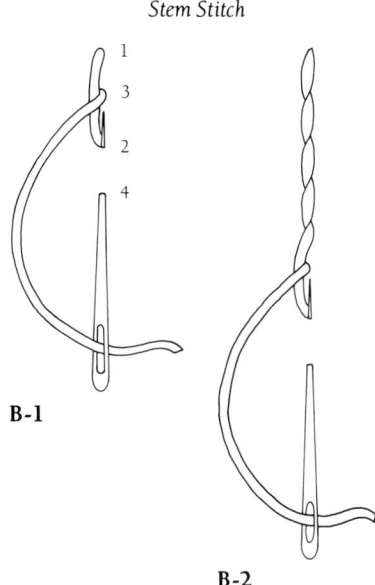

Stem Stitch

B-1

B-2

CRAZY CAT PATTERNS

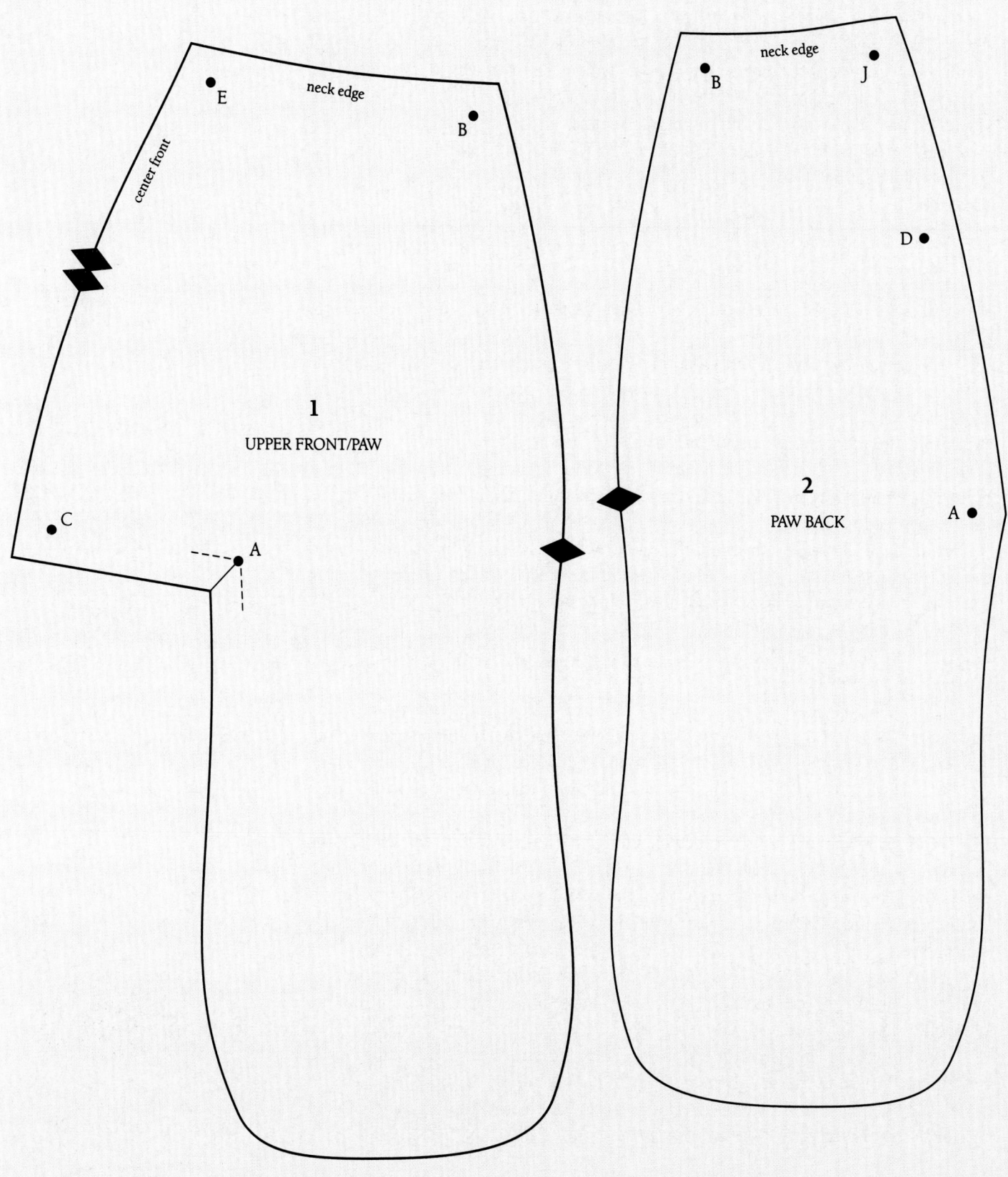

center front

neck edge

• E

B •

1

UPPER FRONT/PAW

• C

• A

neck edge

B •

J •

D •

2

PAW BACK

A •

neck edge

J

G

D

4

BACK

center back

H

M

K

CRAZY CAT PATTERNS

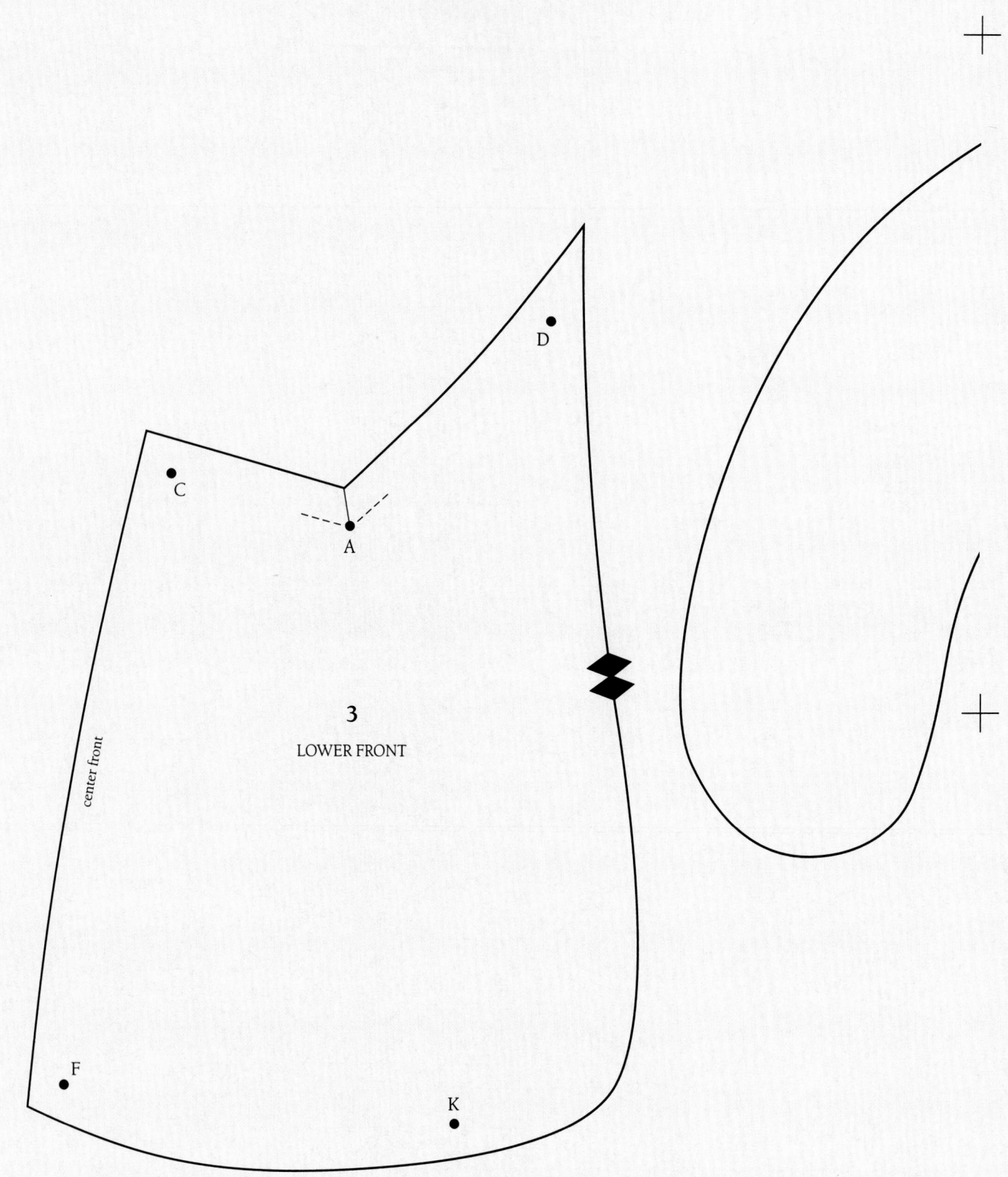

center front

3

LOWER FRONT

C

D

A

F

K

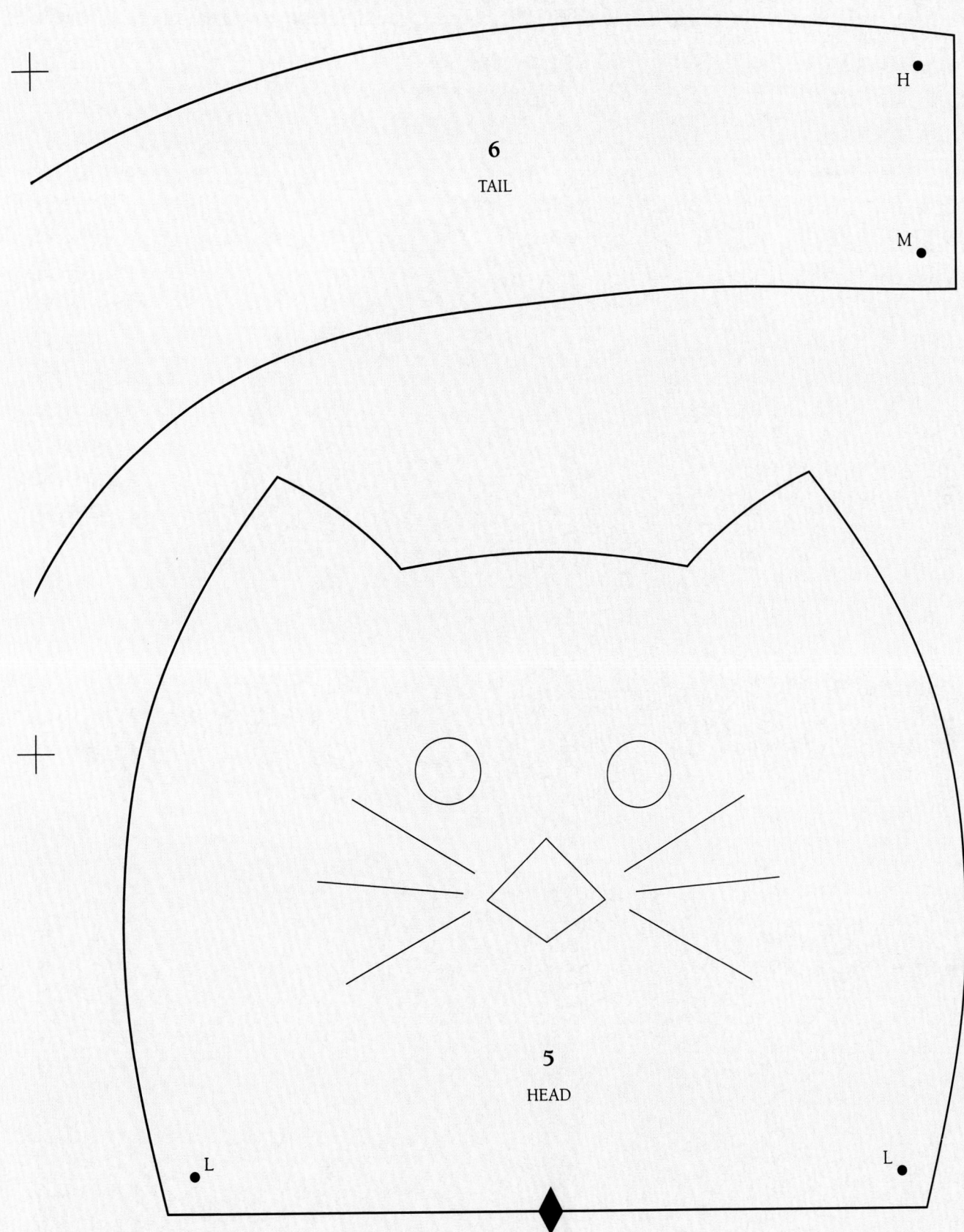

6

TAIL

H

M

5

HEAD

L

L

Topsy-Turvy Doll

Topsy-turvy dolls have delighted children since the 1800s. These unusual cloth toys are composed of two half dolls that are joined together at the waist (a reversible skirt flips to reveal one head and torso at a time). Much of the appeal of the dolls is found in the playful ways their makers chose to highlight the idea of "opposites," varying the types of figures depicted and choosing fabrics in contrasting colors or prints for the doll clothes. The doll to be made here is a contemporary adaptation of one of the most popular topsy-turvy combinations, a black girl and a white girl. (For more information on topsy-turvy dolls, see pages 42-43.)

◆ IMPORTANT INFORMATION

This topsy-turvy doll is about 11 inches tall from head to hem. You will need solid black cotton and natural-colored muslin for the bodies, two different calico prints for the reversible skirt, and striped cottons in contrasting colors for the waistbands. Both halves of the doll are made from the same full-size pattern. A simple skirt is gathered from a two-sided rectangle of cloth; a heart embroidered in red forms the bodice. Stitch all seams with a ¼-inch seam allowance.

◆ MATERIALS AND EQUIPMENT

2 pieces muslin fabric, 9 x 9 inches each
2 pieces black cotton fabric, 9 x 9 inches each
2 pieces calico fabric, 9 x 20½ inches each
 (for reversible skirt)
2 pieces striped cotton fabric, 1½ x 6¼ inches
 each in contrasting colors (for waistbands)
6-strand embroidery floss, 1 skein each
 in red, black, and rust
Thread
One 12-ounce package polyester stuffing

Acrylic paint in white and brown
6-inch embroidery hoop
Tracing paper
Dressmaker's carbon paper in white and
 blue
Scissors
Sewing needle
Embroidery needle
Fine-tipped paintbrush

◆ DIRECTIONS

1. *Making the pattern:* Using a pencil, trace the Topsy-Turvy Doll Pattern on page 41 onto the tracing paper; cut out. Mark the grain line, heart, eyes, and mouth.

2. *Marking the fabric:* With the wrong side up, place one of the two muslin pieces on a worktable. Place the paper pattern on the muslin, aligning the grain lines, and draw around it. Holding the pattern in place, slide the blue carbon face-up under

the muslin and transfer the heart, eyes, and mouth to the right side of the fabric by drawing over them with the pencil. Repeat for one of the black cotton fabric pieces, using the white carbon.

3. *Embroidering the hearts:* With the marked side up, place the muslin in the embroidery hoop, centering the heart. Using the embroidery needle and three strands of the red embroidery floss, bring the needle up from the wrong side at the heart point. Insert the needle at the center of the notch of the heart. Bring the needle up from the wrong side as close as possible to the left of the first stitch at the bottom of the heart and reinsert it as close as possible to the left of the first stitch at the top of the heart. Continue in this manner until the left half of the heart is filled, keeping the stitches straight and smooth. Embroider the right half of the heart in the same manner. Repeat to make the heart on the black cotton fabric piece.

4. *Cutting out the doll bodies:* With the right sides together, place the embroidered muslin piece on the unembroidered muslin piece and pin the two layers together inside the pattern outline. Cut out the doll body along the line, remove the pins, and separate the pieces. Repeat for the black cotton fabric pieces. With the right sides together, pin the embroidered muslin body front to the embroidered black body front at the waist edge only and stitch together. Repeat for the body backs. Remove the pins.

5. *Adding the hair:* With the right sides up, place the pair of doll backs on the worktable (Illustration A). Cut six 3-inch lengths of the black embroidery floss and lay three lengths at each temple of the black doll head, aligning the ends with the raw edge. Baste in place ¼ inch from the raw edge. Cut about thirty 3-inch lengths of the rust embroidery floss and lay them at even intervals around the white doll head, aligning the ends with the raw edge. Baste in place ¼ inch from the raw edge.

6. *Joining the doll bodies:* With the right sides together, lay the pair of doll fronts carefully over the pair of doll backs and pin. Stitch all the way around, leaving a 2-inch opening on one side of the waist for turning and stuffing. Remove the pins and trim the seams to ⅛ inch; clip the inner curves at ¼-inch intervals. Turn the bodies right side out. Pack tightly with the polyester stuffing, using the end of the paintbrush to poke the stuffing into the arms first. Slipstitch the opening in the side closed.

7. *Finishing the heads:* Braid the floss on the black head into two braids, and tie with bows of red floss. Trim the rust floss on the white head evenly, tie it into a ponytail, and add a bow of black floss. Using the brush and brown paint, mark the eyes and mouth on the white face. Using the white paint, repeat for the black face.

8. *Making the skirt:* Baste two rows along one long edge of one calico fabric piece ¼ inch and ⅛ inch in from the raw edge. Repeat for the other calico piece. With the right sides together, lay one calico piece over the other, aligning the basted edges. Stitch on the edge opposite the basting. Press the pieces open. With the right sides together, refold perpendicular to the seam. Stitch along the long edges opposite the fold 2 inches in from each end to make a tube (Illustration B). Press this seam open. Turn the tube right side out.

9. *Making the waistbands:* Fold under ¼ inch on one end of one waistband strip and press. Press under ¼ inch on the long sides. Bring the long sides together, folded edges in, and press again. Repeat for the other waistband.

A

B

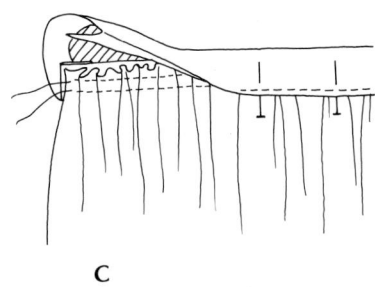

10. *Attaching the waistbands:* On one basted skirt edge, pull the stitching to form gathers until the edge measures 6 inches. Insert one raw edge into one folded waistband, pin, and topstitch through all the layers along the bottom edge of the waistband (Illustration C). Repeat for the other basted skirt edge. Remove the pins. Invert the tube halfway, wrong sides together, to align both waistbands. Press, and topstitch along the bottom edge of the skirt.

11. *Attaching the skirt:* Place the skirt on the doll, tightening each waistband under the arms by overlapping the ends and slipstitching each waistband closed. ◆

C

TOPSY-TURVY DOLL PATTERN

straight grain

Topsy-Turvy Variations

Like many folk toys, topsy-turvy dolls are obscure in origin. It is thought that these two-headed dolls with reversible skirts first became popular just after the Civil War. The unusual form may have derived from 18th-century Pennsylvania hex dolls, which had two heads (usually one animal and one human) and were used for casting spells. Because topsy-turvy dolls typically combine black and white figures, the name is frequently associated with Topsy, the slave child in Harriet Beecher Stowe's 1852 novel, *Uncle Tom's Cabin*. However, the term had been used to mean upside down long before the book was ever written.

While many examples were homemade, topsy-turvys were also mass-produced, beginning in 1899. Marketed under such names as Dolly Double and Tu-N-One, they were available at major toy stores as well as through mail-order companies like Montgomery Ward. There were many variations on the black-and-white combination: one version featured Red Riding Hood, whose skirt doubled back to reveal the hungry wolf; another combined the Goddess of Liberty with Uncle Sam. Some dolls could be purchased as kits that included lithographed cotton body pieces and prestamped dress fabric ready to be cut and assembled. (To make your own topsy-turvy doll, see page 39.)

Seen "topsy" above and "turvy" below, this black-white doll was manufactured around 1900. The fabric faces were printed and molded and then stitched on like masks to imitate more expensive china dolls.

Although the two characters in the c. 1900 topsy-turvy doll above and below wear different outfits, their full skirts and aprons are made of matching fabric. The hats and aprons are removable; the dresses are not.

The homemade topsy-turvy doll above and below is a well-loved toy. What the doll lacks in elegance it makes up for in character. Interestingly, the doll's two dresses are sewn from different versions of the same printed fabric.

This doll was probably made from a kit. The chromolithographed faces depict a happy baby, above, and a crying baby, below. The glad-sad combination is one of the several variations popularized by manufacturers.

Relatively new, this homemade doll combines Goldilocks, above, with the Three Bears, below. Storybook characters have long been favorite subjects for both manufactured and hand-crafted topsy-turvy dolls.

Bean Bag Frogs

Bean bag toys, typically stuffed with grains, bran, flaxseed, or beans—inexpensive materials that would have been on hand at any farm—have been favorites with children for generations. These malleable toys are great for tossing and can assume countless positions as the filling shifts.

◆ IMPORTANT INFORMATION

Different fabrics give the frogs different personalities; try calico, plaid, and elegant velveteen. If you are making the frogs for small children, do not use buttons; embroider or paint the eyes on instead. The full-size patterns are for three frog sizes: about 6 inches, 5½ inches, and 4 inches long. Stitch all seams with a ¼-inch seam allowance.

◆ MATERIALS AND EQUIPMENT

For each frog:

1/3 yard fabric, 45 inches wide

1½ cups rice or
 small beans

Thread

2 novelty buttons

Small funnel

Tracing paper

Scissors

Sewing needle

Dressmaker's pins

Dressmaker's chalk

◆ DIRECTIONS

1. *Making the pattern:* Using a pencil, trace the Bean Bag Frog Patterns on pages 46-47 in the size of your choice onto the tracing paper and cut out.

2. *Cutting and marking the fabric:* With the right sides together, fold the fabric in half, aligning the selvages. Place the fabric on a worktable and lay the paper patterns on top, with the straight grain aligned. Pin the patterns in place and cut out. Remove the pins. Reverse the patterns for the arms and legs and repeat so that you have two of each. Using the chalk, transfer the X and the dots from the paper body pattern to the wrong side of the frog body fabric pieces.

3. *Making the legs and arms:* With the right sides together, place one pair of the leg pieces together and pin, leaving the upper ends open. Stitch. Remove the pins and trim the seams to ⅛ inch; clip at ¼-inch intervals on the inward curves and between the toes. Turn the leg right side out and press. Repeat for the other leg and for both arms.

4. *Filling the legs and arms:* Using the funnel, fill the legs and the arms with the rice or beans. Do not overfill them; they should be floppy, not stiff. Tuck in the seam allowance at the leg ends and slipstitch tightly closed. Baste the arms closed. To make the joints in the arms and legs, hand-stitch across each where indicated by the broken lines on the pattern, using double thread and running stitches.

5. *Making the body:* Holding one body piece, bring the raw edges for the dart together with the right sides facing and pin; stitch from the X to the raw edge to make the dart. Press the seam open. Repeat for the other body piece. With the right sides together, pin the two body pieces together; stitch all the way around, leaving openings between the dots for the arms. Trim the seams to ⅛ inch and clip the inner curve at ¼-inch intervals. Turn the body right side out and press.

6. *Attaching the arms:* Insert one arm in an arm opening on the body with the toes curving toward the face. Stitch in place securely by hand. Through the other arm opening, fill the body with rice or beans, adjusting the amount as desired. Insert the other arm into the opening and stitch in place securely by hand.

7. *Attaching the legs and finishing:* Sew the legs by hand to the underside of the body on either side of the dart (Illustration A). Secure the legs to the underside of the body through the first joint. Sew the buttons in place for the eyes. ◆

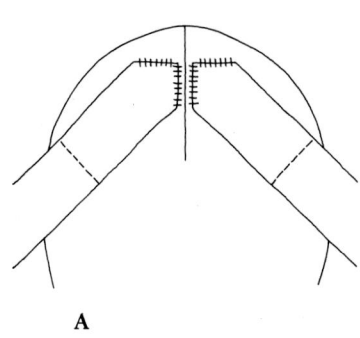

A

BEAN BAG FROG PATTERNS

BODY

straight grain

dart

straight grain

straight grain

ARM

LEG

Embroidery

traditional canvas work and counted-thread stitchery

Although embroidery, the embellishment of a textile with ornamental stitches, requires practice and patience, most of the techniques are not difficult to learn. Depending on your level of skill and creativity, the stitches you make can be simple or complex, and the designs that result, monochromatic or richly hued.

This chapter offers the opportunity to try four embroidery projects. Three of the pieces—the traditional cross-stitch sampler, the easy Irish-stitch footstool cover, and the more complicated needlepoint bellpull—are worked in different forms of counted-thread stitchery, in which you follow a chart to stitch a design onto unmarked fabric. The fourth project, an outline-work hand towel, involves tracing a design onto a cloth and then embroidering it.

If you are new to embroidery, plan to practice the stitches until you feel comfortable with them. You will find that once such handwork is mastered, it can be a satisfying pastime.

Irish stitch, or bargello, makes an attractive covering for a footstool (see pages 64-67). The cardboard horseshoe at center is a needlecase.

Cross-Stitch Sampler

In the 18th and early 19th centuries, a mastery of needlework was considered an important part of a young lady's education. At an early age, she was taught to stitch letters and numerals into a sampler; when older, she would use this skill for marking her household linens. Some samplers served as a kind of personal pattern reference, while others were used as practice pieces on which the needleworker might work to perfect a particular stitch or to experiment with a new motif. The more elaborate samplers included verses and intricate pictorial scenes.

The sampler shown here is worked entirely in cross-stitch, among the simplest of the many stitches that might be incorporated into a sampler. The design has been adapted from a sampler made around 1820 by a Pennsylvania girl named Ruth Hide, who was probably about twelve years old when she worked it. The strawberry vine border and alphabets are typical of motifs found on many American samplers of the period.

Not every little girl who embroidered a sampler enjoyed the task. Around 1800, ten-year-old Patty Polk, of Kent County, Maryland, stitched a piece with the words, "Patty Polk did this and she hated every stitch she did in it. She loves to read much more."

◆ IMPORTANT INFORMATION

Cross-stitch is a type of counted-thread embroidery in which the needleworker follows a chart, placing the stitches by counting threads in the background fabric; the design is not transferred to the fabric before it is stitched. The embroidery is worked on an even-weave fabric, which has the same number of threads running lengthwise and crosswise in each square inch. Any even-weave fabric in a count of from six to over thirty threads per inch can be used. The count of the fabric determines the number of stitches in one inch—the lower the count, the larger the stitch—which in turn determines the size of the finished embroidered design.

This sampler is worked on 25-count linen. Each stitch is made over the intersection of two lengthwise and two crosswise threads, and the design area measures 9½ x 13½ inches. (If you were to stitch over a single-thread intersection, the design area would measure half that size.) To make the sampler, you will need to follow the Design Chart on pages 54-55. Each square in the grid represents one cross-stitch. The different symbols in the squares represent the different colors in the Color Key on page 55.

When working cross-stitch, you will find it easier to keep an even stitch tension with the linen firmly secured in an embroidery hoop. To prevent permanent creases from forming in the linen, remove the embroidery from the hoop when you are not actually cross-stitching. Separate the embroidery floss into two-strand pieces—use 18-inch lengths—and work with two strands throughout. Never knot the floss; instead, leave a 1-inch tail at the back that will be secured as you stitch. To secure the other end of the floss when you are finished, slide the needle under several stitches on the back of the work and trim the floss. If you do not know how to do cross-stitch, refer to the section Learning to Cross-Stitch on page 52 and practice on a scrap of linen.

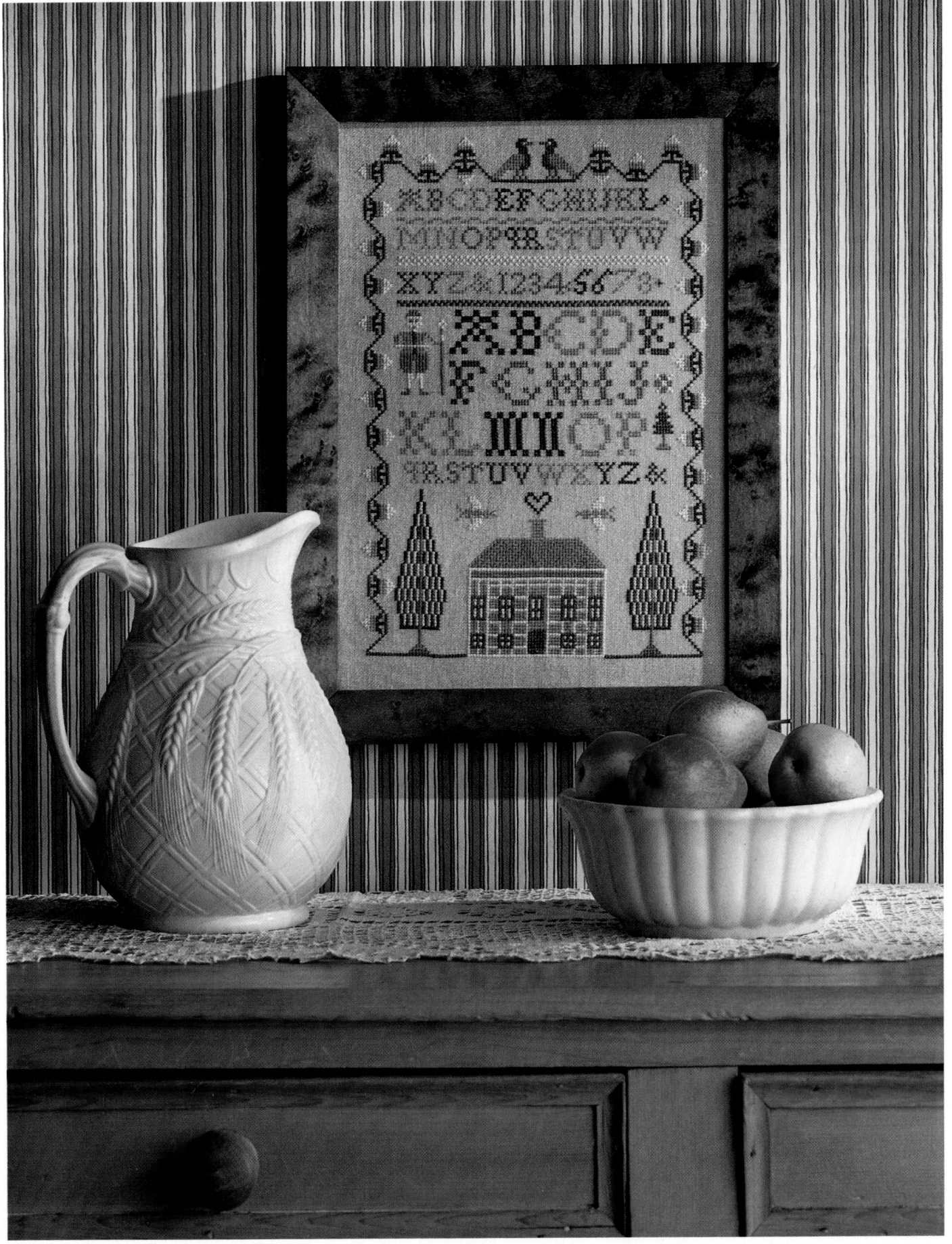

◆MATERIALS AND EQUIPMENT

1 piece 25-count linen, 13½ x 17½ inches
6-strand embroidery floss, 1 skein each in
 forest green, ecru, dark taupe, dark
 green, rose pink, colonial blue, and gold
Thread

6-inch embroidery hoop
Scissors
Tapestry needle
Sewing needle
Dressmaker's pins

◆LEARNING TO CROSS-STITCH

1. *Getting started:* Secure a scrap of linen in the embroidery hoop.

2. *Working cross-stitch:* Each cross-stitch is worked in an X over the intersection of two lengthwise and two crosswise threads in the weave of the linen. Always pass the needle between threads, not through a thread. Referring to Illustration A-1, begin by bringing the needle up near the center of the linen from the back at point 1. Counting two threads to the right and two threads up from point 1, insert the needle at point 2. Counting two threads down, bring the needle up at point 3. Counting two threads to the right and two threads up from point 3, insert the needle at point 4. Continue for a few more stitches, then reverse the process, working back across the row in the same manner, crossing all the stitches as you go (Illustration A-2). When you are making adjacent stitches, the needle will pass through a single hole more than once. You can work in any direction, but all the stitches on your piece should cross in the same way; bear this in mind if you turn the fabric as you stitch.

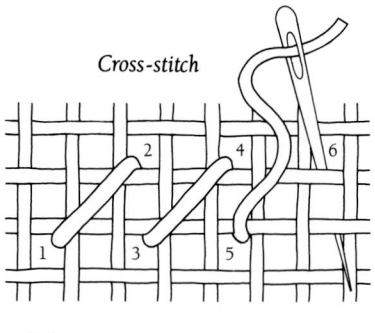

Cross-stitch

A-1

A-2

◆SAMPLER DIRECTIONS

1. *Preparing the linen:* To prevent the edges of the linen from raveling, secure them with zigzag or overcast stitching. Fold the fabric in half lengthwise and hand-baste along the fold; this basting will serve as a reference line as you stitch.

2. *Finding the starting point:* You can stitch the sampler design in any order you like, but always work outward from the reference line; this way, if you make a mistake in your counting you will catch it sooner. A good starting point is the middle of the vine between the birds in the top border; to find it, measure 3½ inches down from the middle of the top edge of the linen along the reference line and mark the spot with a pin.

3. *Beginning the sampler:* Secure the linen in the embroidery hoop with the pin-marked spot to the left of center. Referring to the Design Chart on pages 54-55, begin cross-stitching the vine from the pin to the right top corner; then work back to the pin, crossing the stitches. Continuing to refer to the chart, stitch the strawberries. (Always work all the same-color stitches in one direction, then cross them.)

4. *Completing the sampler:* Still following the chart, continue stitching the sampler. You may want to work the entire right-hand side of the sampler first, moving

your hoop down as needed. The beaks of the flying birds are worked in straight stitches. When you have completed all the cross-stitching, remove the basted reference line.

5. *Washing the sampler:* If the sampler has become soiled from handling, wash it in mild soapy water; rinse it, and roll it in a towel. Spread the sampler on a dry towel. When it is nearly dry, press it.

6. *Sizing the border:* Before framing the sampler, you will need to decide upon the width of the linen border that you would like to see extending beyond the stitching; remember that the frame will overlap the linen slightly. (A 1-inch visible border was allowed for the sampler shown.) Mark the perimeter with hand basting.

7. *Framing:* Frame as desired. Bear in mind that glass should not rest directly against the embroidery. Choose a frame deep enough to allow a spacer, which can be cut from mat board, to fit unseen between the glass and the sampler. ◆

Design Chart

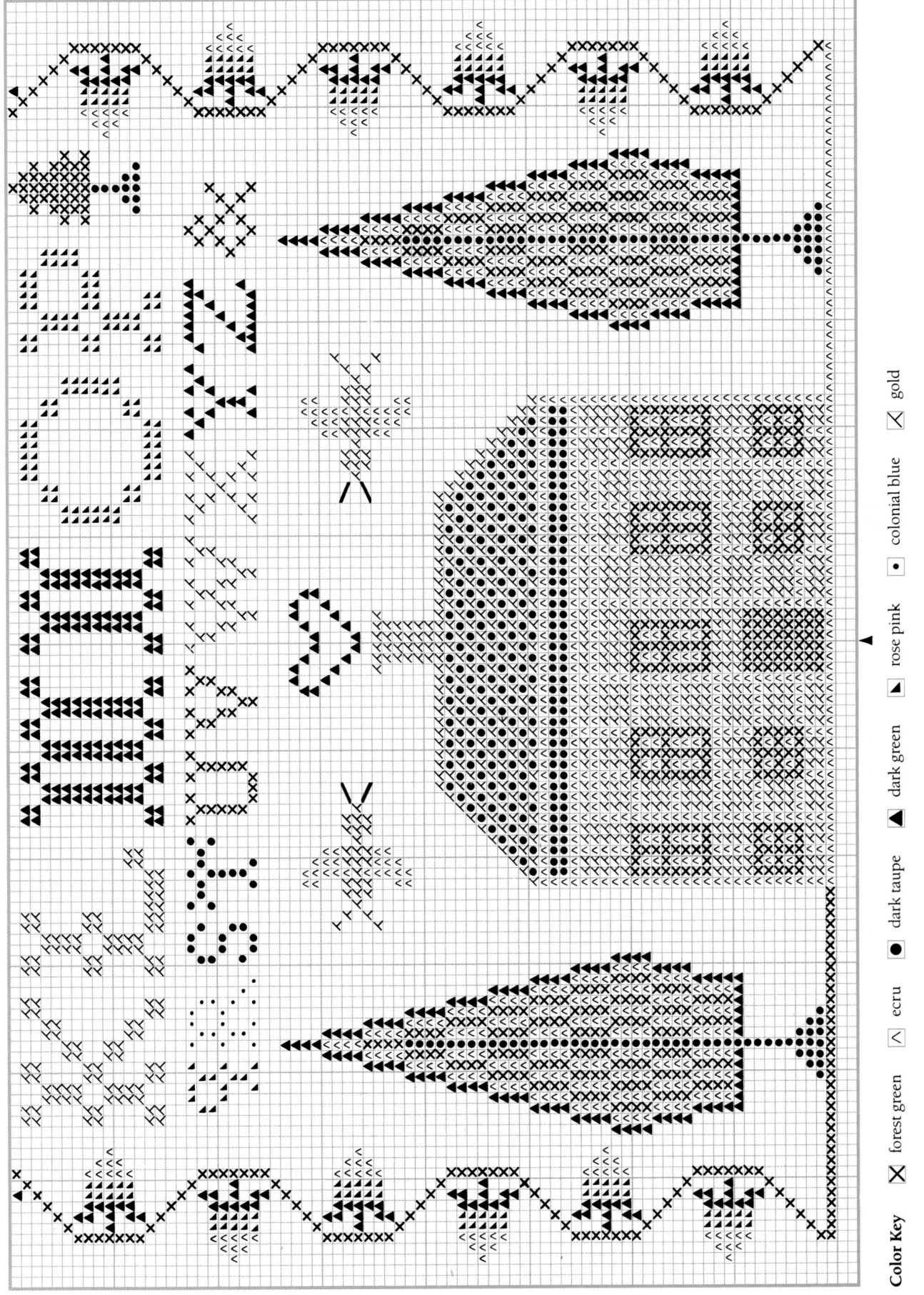

Color Key $\boxed{\times}$ forest green $\boxed{\wedge}$ ecru $\boxed{\bullet}$ dark taupe $\boxed{\blacktriangle}$ dark green $\boxed{\blacktriangle}$ rose pink $\boxed{\bullet}$ colonial blue $\boxed{\diagup}$ gold

STITCHES
IN TIME

Although the tradition of stitching embroidered samplers was introduced to the colonies in the 1600s by English and European settlers, many distinctively American styles of samplers developed. Genealogical samplers like those shown here, for example, are believed to have originated in this country, first appearing in the 1770s. It was not until the mid-19th century that similar types were made in England.

Sometimes called family registers or family records, genealogical samplers were particularly popular between about 1800 and 1830. Intended to be displayed on a wall as decoration, they are typically distinguished by ambitious designs of flowers or landscapes, and those conceived as memorials often feature willows and neoclassical columns and urns. (Following the death of George Washington in 1799, expressions of mourning became fashionable.)

For the most part, genealogical samplers were the products of pri-

The floral vine on Elizabeth Dana's "family register" above was a popular style of border for New England samplers. Lorenza Fisk's family-tree sampler at right displays golden apples; it is one of twenty similar works known to have been made in the Lexington-Concord area of Massachusetts.

vate academies in New England and in Pennsylvania, where schoolgirls studied needle arts, reading, and music. A teacher might draw the designs on linen for her students to stitch in silk or linen thread, or the girls themselves would copy borders and pictures from engravings or from existing needlework pieces. Because the samplers made in a particular academy were often very similar to one another, it is sometimes possible to trace a sampler's origin even if the name of the school or town does not appear on the work. The stitched words—arranged in neat columns, placed in tidy boxes, or worked on apples growing from the "family tree"—generally record a couple's wedding date and the names and birth dates of their children. Some samplers also contain plaintive references to childhood deaths or verses that read as pious reminders of the passing of time. "Perhaps what goodness gives to-day," warns one, "Tomorrow goodness takes away."

Azubah G. Capen was about sixteen when she made the "family record" above at Miss Glover's school in Stoughton, Massachusetts. Elizabeth Newman's sampler at left combines genealogical information with the weeping willows and funerary urns that appeared in 19th-century mourning pictures.

Decorated Hand Towels

The hand towels shown here are embellished with outline work, a style of embroidery that resembles line drawing. Outline work can be sewn in a variety of stitches, but is always done in one color—usually red. Easy and quick, it became popular in America around 1880, and was favored for decorating bed and table linens.

Outline work was considered a particularly artistic form of embroidery because the designs, which were worked from printed patterns, relied upon well-drawn images. Pictures by Kate Greenaway, a well-known 19th-century British book illustrator, were frequently reproduced as patterns for outline work. Other designs were inspired by the type of linens they embellished: the words "good night" and "good morning" might be worked on a pillowcase, or pictures of chinaware stitched onto place mats.

◆ IMPORTANT INFORMATION

These fringed towels measure 18 x 36 inches and are made from white linen, although any firmly woven, lightweight (but not sheer) fabric can be used. To stitch the floral border, you will need to trace the full-size Border Pattern on pages 60-61 onto the fabric. Use a fabric-marking pen with nonpermanent ink that disappears when dampened (such pens are available in the notions department of most variety stores). Test the pen on a scrap of your fabric before tracing the pattern onto the towel.

Three stitches are used for the border: chain stitch for the round buds, stem stitch for the stem, leaf, and petal outlines, and French knots for the dots. You will find it easier to keep an even stitch tension with the linen firmly secured in an embroidery hoop. To prevent permanent creases from forming in the linen, remove the embroidery from the hoop when you are not stitching. Separate the embroidery floss into three-strand pieces—use 18-inch lengths—and stitch with three strands throughout. Never knot the floss; instead, leave a 1-inch tail at the back that will be secured as you stitch. To secure the other end of the floss when you are finished, slide the needle under several stitches on the back of the work and trim the thread. If you do not know how to do the three stitches, refer to the section Learning the Stitches on page 60 and practice on a scrap of fabric before beginning a towel.

◆ MATERIALS AND EQUIPMENT

1 piece lightweight white linen, 22 x 36 inches *Embroidery needle*
2 skeins red 6-strand embroidery floss *Tracing paper*
6-inch embroidery hoop *Nonpermanent-ink fabric-marking pen*
Thread *Black fine-point marking pen*
Scissors *Dressmaker's pins*

Chain Stitch

A

Stem Stitch

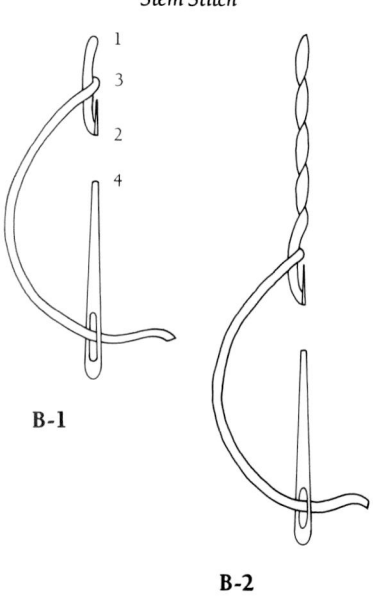

B-1

B-2

◆ LEARNING THE STITCHES

1. *Getting started:* Secure a scrap of linen in the embroidery hoop.

2. *Working chain stitch:* Referring to Illustration A, bring the needle up from the back of the linen at point 1. Form a loop with the floss and insert the needle again at point 1, holding the loop against the linen with a finger; in the same motion, bring the needle up ¹/₁₆ inch away at point 2, and draw the floss through, catching the loop on the surface. Continue in this manner, always inserting the needle back into the hole just made, to make a chain of "links." Anchor the last link with a small stitch.

3. *Working stem stitch:* Referring to Illustration B-1, bring the needle up from the back of the linen at point 1. Making a ¹/₈-inch stitch, insert the needle at point 2. Bring the needle up at point 3 halfway between points 1 and 2, and draw the floss through, holding it to the left of the needle. Making a ¹/₈-inch stitch, insert the needle at point 4 and bring it up again at point 2 in the hole made by the previous stitch. Draw the floss through, still holding it to the left of the needle. Continue to work in this manner (Illustration B-2).

4. *Working French knots:* Referring to Illustration C-1, bring the needle up from the back of the linen at point 1. Holding the needle parallel to the linen and just above the fabric, wrap the floss around it once. Holding the floss so that it fits closely around the point of the needle, insert the needle back into the linen again at point 1 (Illustration C-2). Pull the needle through to the wrong side to finish the knot (Illustration C-3). Bring the needle up again where you wish to make another French knot, and repeat.

BORDER PATTERN

crosswise grain

◆ TOWEL DIRECTIONS

French Knot

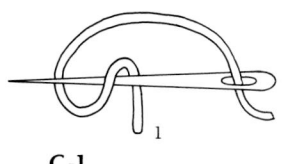

C-1

1. *Preparing the linen:* To prevent the edges of the linen from raveling, secure them with zigzag or overcast stitching.

2. *Making the register marks:* Fold the linen in half lengthwise. Measure 3 inches in from one end and make a mark with the nonpermanent-ink pen on the fold, then measure in another 3¼ inches and make a second mark on the fold.

3. *Making the pattern:* Using a pencil, trace the Border Pattern below onto the tracing paper, aligning the two halves of the design in the middle according to the register marks. Also trace the register marks and the grain line. With the fine-point marking pen, go over the pencil lines to darken them so that you will be able to see them when the linen is placed over the pattern.

4. *Marking the linen:* Place the pattern on a worktable. Unfold the linen and place it over the pattern with the crosswise grain aligned, matching the register marks on the linen with those on the pattern. Pin. Using the nonpermanent-ink pen, trace the design onto the linen. Remove the pins.

C-2

5. *Embroidering the border:* Place the linen in the embroidery hoop, centering one end of the marked border design. Starting at this end, stitch over the marked lines, embroidering the entire design in a logical order. Work the round buds in chain stitch, the stem, leaf, and petal outlines in stem stitch (plan your stitches to meet neatly at the points of the leaves), and the dots in French knots. It is not necessary to cut the floss when changing stitches, but you should avoid carrying the floss from one design area to another on the back of the work.

6. *Hemming the long edges:* When all the embroidery is finished, press the

C-3

Buttonhole Stitch

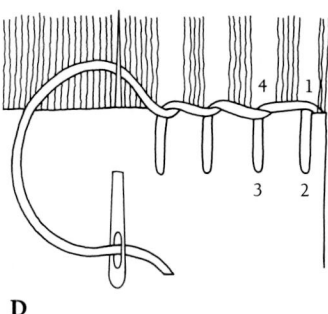

D

towel. With the design centered, trim the towel to be 18 inches wide. On each 36-inch edge, press ½ inch to the wrong side and stitch close to the fold with a small zigzag stitch. Trim the raw edge close to the stitching.

7. *Removing the ink markings:* Following the pen manufacturer's instructions, remove the ink markings. Press the towel again.

8. *Squaring the ends and making the fringe:* Trim the zigzag or overcast stitching from both ends of the towel. To square the towel, loosen the first thread along one cut edge and pull it free. If the thread you have pulled away did not run all the way across the end, keep pulling threads away until one does. The remaining crosswise threads will now be square with the sides of the towel. Trim the towel along the outermost thread, then pull away threads until you have made a ¾-inch-long fringe. Repeat at the other end of the towel.

9. *Securing the fringe with buttonhole stitch:* Referring to Illustration D, hold the towel with the right side up. At the right-hand edge of one fringed end, make a tiny stitch on the wrong side of the towel to secure the floss. Bring the needle up at point 1, passing it through the fringe but not the linen. Insert the needle into the linen ¼ inch from the woven edge, at point 2. Bring the needle up through the fringe again at point 1. Insert the needle into the linen ¼ inch from the woven edge at point 3, holding the floss in a loop against the fringe. Bring the needle through the fringe directly above point 3 at point 4, passing it through the loop of floss under the needle. Pull the floss through, forming a bar of floss along the woven edge. Continue in this manner, working across the end of the towel. When you run out of floss, knot it neatly on the wrong side, then begin a new strand, passing the needle through the fringe and under the bar of the previous stitch. Repeat at the opposite end of the towel.

10. *Finishing the towel:* When you have finished the buttonhole stitching, wash the towel in mild soapy water, rinse, and hang it to dry. When it is nearly dry, place the towel face down and press, spray-starching if desired. ◆

An Embroidered Past

Embroidered hand towels, or *Handdicher,* like the three 19th-century pieces above, are a distinctive Pennsylvania-German folk art. Such handsome decorated linens were particularly popular from about 1820 to 1850. The long, narrow towels, which might be made from one to as many as six pieces of linen, were embroidered by adolescent girls, then set aside for their dowries. No two pieces are quite alike: the girls created their own designs, working them in counted cross-stitch, outline and herringbone stitches, and drawn work. The towels were often signed and dated, and a husband's name or initials might be added at the time of marriage. Most girls stitched only one towel.

Such *Handdicher* were intended for decoration rather than use, and loops or tabs were attached at the top so that the handiwork could be prominently displayed—traditionally on a door between the sitting room and the kitchen.

Irish-Stitch Footstool

Particularly popular in the 18th century in both Europe and America, Irish stitch was a favored form of embroidery for decorating upholstered furnishings. Now known variously as bargello, Hungarian stitch, flame stitch, or Florentine embroidery (all 20th-century terms), Irish stitch is characterized by straight, vertical stitches worked in multicolor zigzag patterns. The patterns vary widely; the footstool cover shown here is worked in a simple, randomly colored zigzag repeat.

◆ IMPORTANT INFORMATION

Irish stitch is a type of counted-thread embroidery in which the needleworker follows a chart, placing the stitches by counting threads in the background fabric; the design is not transferred to the fabric before it is stitched. The embroidery is worked on an even-weave fabric, which has the same number of threads running lengthwise and crosswise in each square inch. For Irish stitch, this fabric is most commonly an open canvas. The mesh count, or the number of threads per inch, determines the size of the stitch and the weight of the yarn to be used. The embroidery for this footstool is worked on 13-mesh bargello canvas. It is stitched with Persian wool, which is usually sold in 5-yard skeins. One skein will cover approximately 4 square inches of 13-mesh bargello canvas. To estimate the number of skeins you need, determine the number of square inches on your canvas and divide by four.

Many needlework shops sell footstools that are ready to be covered. You will need to cut your canvas to the size of the stool (see Step 1 in the Footstool Directions on page 66). To work the cover in the zigzag Irish-stitch pattern, you will need to follow the Design Chart on page 67, which represents a 33-stitch repeat. Each blue line in the grid represents one thread on the canvas; each vertical stitch is made over four horizontal threads of the canvas. The cover for the footstool shown measures 10 x 15 inches, but the 33 stitches can be repeated to cover a canvas of any dimension. It does not matter how the pattern breaks at the edge of the footstool, nor does it matter where or when you change colors. You can use as many colors as you like; change them often.

Separate the wool into two-ply pieces—use 18-inch lengths—and work with two plies throughout. Never knot the wool; instead, leave a 1-inch tail at the back that will be secured as you stitch. To secure the other end of the wool when you are finished, slide the needle under several stitches on the back of the work and trim. You may find it easier to control the stitch tension if you place the canvas in a frame. The stitches should lie evenly on the canvas; they should not be so loose that they will snag, or so tight that the canvas puckers. If you do not know how to do Irish-stitch embroidery, refer to the section Learning Irish Stitch on page 66 and practice on a scrap of canvas.

In 1755, Elizabeth Hinche advertised in the Boston Weekly News-Letter *that she "doth teach plain Sewing, Irish Stitch, Tent Stitch, Sampler Work, Embroidery, and other Sorts of Needle Work, if any Person sees fit to send their Children from the Country...."*

Irish Stitch

A

B

◆ MATERIALS AND EQUIPMENT

Footstool with removable top
1 piece 13-mesh bargello canvas large
 enough for your stool
3-ply Persian wool in assorted colors (see
 Important Information on page 64 for
 quantities)
Staple gun and staples
Scissors
Tapestry needle

Masking tape
Permanent marking pen

For blocking:
Wooden board large enough to
 accommodate canvas
Brown wrapping paper
T-square
Pushpins (aluminum)

◆ LEARNING IRISH STITCH

1. *Working Irish stitch:* Referring to Illustration A, bring the needle up near the center of the canvas from the back at point 1. Count four threads down on the canvas and insert the needle at point 2. Count one thread to the right and four threads up and bring the needle up at point 3. Count four threads down and insert the needle at point 4. (You have now made two stitches.) Working in this manner, stagger the stitches, following the Design Chart opposite, until you have completed the 33-stitch repeat shown in the chart.

2. *Making a second row of stitches:* The first row of stitches establishes the pattern. To continue the pattern, repeat it, following the Design Chart, in a row immediately above or below the first row, bringing the needle up in the same hole through which the stitch above or below it was previously made (Illustration B).

◆ FOOTSTOOL DIRECTIONS

1. *Preparing the canvas:* Measure the length and width of your footstool top, including any curved edges. Add 4 inches to each dimension. Trim the canvas to these larger dimensions. Bind the edges of the canvas with the tape to keep them from fraying. Using the permanent marking pen, draw a border 2 inches inside the edges, marking along the threads in the mesh.

2. *Marking the centering lines:* Draw a line from side to side across the center of the canvas, marking along a row of holes. Draw a line from top to bottom at the center, marking along one thread.

3. *Beginning the embroidery:* Referring to the Design Chart, begin stitching to the right of the canvas center. Work a row of the pattern across the right half of your canvas; repeat the pattern (indicated between A and B on the chart) as necessary, changing colors as you like. Stop stitching at the marked border. Finish off your wool and start again at the center. Still reading the chart from A to B, but in mirror image, stitch across the left half of the canvas.

4. *Completing the embroidery:* Fill in the remaining area of the canvas inside the marked border. Because the first complete row of Irish stitch establishes the pattern, it is not necessary to begin at the middle of the canvas when stitching the subsequent rows; you must, however, always stitch directly above or below the row you have just completed.

5. *Blocking the embroidery:* Using the permanent marking pen and the T-square, mark a rectangle the same size as the canvas on the brown paper. Cut out the paper a few inches beyond this rectangle. Center the paper on the wooden board. Lay the canvas right side down on the paper, aligning it with the marks, and pin to the board with the pushpins (take care to insert the pins between the stitches). Pin first at the corners, then at the center of each side, then at ¾-inch intervals. Spritz the canvas with cold water and allow it to dry for at least twenty-four hours. When it is dry, unpin the canvas from the board and remove the masking tape.

6. *Covering the footstool top:* Center the embroidery on the footstool top and secure it temporarily with a few pushpins around the sides. Turn the top over and wrap the canvas to the back. Holding the canvas snug, staple it to the underside of the footsool top at the middle of each edge. Remove the pushpins and fold the excess canvas diagonally across each corner and staple it to the underside of the top. Check the fit of the top in the footstool. Make sure that no canvas shows at the edges and that the bargello appears square to the edges; adjust, if necessary. Continue stapling until the canvas is secure. ◆

Design Chart

A B

Needlepoint Bellpull

The 19th-century bellpull opposite is stitched in Berlin work, a type of needlepoint made from printed patterns, which originated in Germany in the early 1800s. The craze for Berlin work developed concurrently with the introduction of zephyr wools—soft, smooth, easy-to-dye tapestry wools spun from the fleece of merino sheep. Although both the patterns and the wools were manufactured in Germany, the popularity of Berlin work was international.

Berlin-work patterns were available for embroidering all manner of household furnishings, including rugs, upholstery, cushions, and bellpulls. In the Victorian era, bellpulls were a symbol of social standing; they not only allowed family members to ring for their servants, but also indicated to guests that servants were employed. Today, a needlepoint bellpull makes a handsome wall decoration.

◆ IMPORTANT INFORMATION

Needlepoint is a type of counted-thread embroidery in which the needleworker follows a chart, placing the stitches by counting threads in the background fabric; the design is not transferred to the fabric before it is stitched. The embroidery is worked on an even-weave fabric, which has the same number of threads running lengthwise and crosswise in each square inch. In needlepoint, this fabric is most commonly an open canvas. The mesh count, or the number of threads per inch, determines the size of the stitch and the weight of the yarn to be used. The embroidery for this bellpull is stitched with tapestry wool on 10-mesh needlepoint canvas.

To copy the bellpull opposite, you will need to refer to the Design Chart on pages 72-73. The bellpull measures 6¾ x 59 inches; the 14¾-inch floral design represented by the chart is done four times, worked from bottom to top. Each square in the grid represents one stitch; each stitch is made over a single-thread intersection on the canvas. The symbols represent the colors in the Color Key on page 73; the blank squares represent the taupe background.

This bellpull is embroidered with two basic needlepoint stitches. Basketweave (also called diagonal) stitch is used to fill in the background. This stitch creates a woven pattern on the wrong side of the work, which helps to stabilize the canvas, and is recommended for larger areas. Continental stitch is used for the symboled design. This stitch is not woven on the wrong side and is easier to work in smaller areas than basketweave stitch. The two stitches look identical on the right side of the work.

Never knot the wool; instead, leave a 1-inch tail at the back that will be secured as you stitch. To secure the other end of the wool, slide the needle under several stitches on the back and trim. The stitches should lie evenly; they should not be so tight that the canvas puckers, or so loose that the canvas threads show. If you do not know how to do needlepoint, refer to the section Learning Needlepoint on page 70 and practice on a scrap of canvas. Bellpull hangers are available at needlework shops.

♦ MATERIALS AND EQUIPMENT

1 piece 10-mesh needlepoint canvas, 10 x 64 inches

1 piece cotton flannel, approximately 8 x 60 inches

1 piece taffeta, approximately 8 x 60 inches

91 skeins tapestry wools (see Color Key on page 73 for colors and quantities)

1 pair bellpull hangers with 7-inch bars

Thread

Scissors

Tapestry needle

Sewing needle

Dressmaker's pins

Masking tape

For blocking:

Wooden board, 1 x 6 feet

Brown wrapping paper

T-square

Permanent marking pen

Pushpins (aluminum)

Continental Stitch

A

Basketweave Stitch

B

♦ LEARNING NEEDLEPOINT

1. *Working continental stitch:* This stitch is worked in horizontal rows from right to left; you must turn the canvas 180 degrees before beginning each new row. Referring to Illustration A, bring the needle up near the center of the canvas from the back at point 1. Make a diagonal stitch, inserting the needle at point 2 and sliding it in the same motion under the canvas to the left and up at point 3. Insert the needle again at point 4, bringing it up at point 5. Continue in this manner until you have made four practice stitches. Turn the canvas 180 degrees, and work another row in the same manner, again stitching from right to left.

2. *Working basketweave stitch:* This stitch is worked in diagonal rather than horizontal rows; you do not turn the canvas when stitching each new row. Referring to Illustration B, bring the needle up near the upper right corner of the canvas at point 1. Make a diagonal stitch, inserting the needle at point 2, and bring it up to the left at point 3. Insert the needle at point 4, sliding it in the same motion down under two horizontal canvas threads and bringing it up at point 5. Make a diagonal stitch, inserting the needle at point 6. (You have now made three stitches, creating two short diagonal rows.) Bring the needle up at point 7. Make a diagonal stitch, inserting the needle at point 8, and slide it in the same motion to the left under two vertical canvas threads and up at point 9. Make a diagonal stitch, inserting the needle at point 10, and bring it up at point 11. Insert the needle at point 12. (You have now made three more stitches, completing a third diagonal row.) In this manner, continue to practice the basketweave stitch, beginning the next row at point 13, inserting the needle at point 14, and coming up at point 15. If you must interrupt your stitching, always do so in the middle of a row; this will identify the direction in which you should continue.

◆ BELLPULL DIRECTIONS

1. *Preparing the canvas:* Bind the edges of the canvas with the tape to keep them from fraying. Baste a line down the entire length of the canvas through the central row of holes. Always count out from this reference line to keep your place.

2. *Finding the starting point:* To find the first row (the base) of the symboled design, measure 3 inches in from one end of the canvas along the reference line and mark with a pin. This will be the center of row X on the Design Chart on pages 72-73. (Row Y marks the top of the symboled repeat.)

3. *Beginning the needlepoint:* Referring to the chart, begin stitching in continental stitch at the center of row X, counting out from the reference line to keep your place. Start with the right-hand leaf motif. Begin with the dark olive color and work all of it before changing to the light olive. Work all of the light olive before changing to the medium olive.

4. *Continuing the needlepoint:* Counting the chart symbols as you stitch and working in a logical manner through each color area, continue stitching, always finishing one color area before beginning another. Stitch the symboled design from row X all the way up to row Y. Repeat the symboled design (row X to row Y) three more times. You can fill in the taupe basketweave background around the design as you progress up the canvas or, alternatively, after all the symboled stitching is complete. When stitching the background, work twelve stitches beyond the outline indicated on the chart for the entire length of the canvas, and work four stitches beyond the charted design area across each end of the canvas.

5. *Blocking the needlepoint:* With the pen and T-square, mark a rectangle measuring 10 x 62 inches on a piece of brown paper. Cut out the paper a few inches beyond this rectangle. Center the paper on the piece of wood. Lay the canvas right side down on the paper, matching the edges to the marked rectangle, and pin to the wood with the pushpins (take care to insert the pins between the stitches). Pin first at the corners, then at the center of each side, then at ¾-inch intervals. Spritz the canvas with cold water and let it dry for at least twenty-four hours. When it is dry, unpin the canvas and remove the masking tape. Trim the excess canvas, leaving a 1-inch border of mesh around the needlepoint.

6. *Backing the canvas:* Measure the length and width of the stitched area and cut the flannel to these measurements. Place the needlepoint wrong side up on a worktable and lay the flannel over the stitched area. Pin the two layers together 1½ inches inside the edges of the flannel. On the long edges, fold the unstitched canvas borders to the wrong side, and pin to the flannel. With a single strand of thread, join the canvas to the flannel with herringbone stitch. Referring to Illustration.C, make a small stitch to secure the thread in the flannel at the top of the bellpull, then bring the needle up at point 1 about ⅛ inch to the right of the trimmed canvas edge. Make a ¼-inch stitch diagonally across the edge, inserting the needle at point 2. Bring the needle up at point 3 to make a stitch, then make a ¼-inch stitch diagonally across the edge to point 4. In this manner, finish stitching the canvas to the flannel along one long edge, then repeat for the other side of the bellpull.

Herringbone Stitch

C

7. *Attaching the hangers:* Slide one end of the needlepoint through one hanger and fold four rows of background stitching to the back. Pin the fold to the flannel and secure with herringbone stitch as in Step 6. Repeat to secure a hanger at the other end of the bellpull.

8. *Lining the bellpull:* Measure the length and width of the wrong side of the bellpull. Add 1½ inches to each dimension and cut the taffeta to these dimensions. Press ¾ inch of the taffeta to the wrong side on all edges and pin to the back of the needlepoint. Slipstitch the taffeta in place. ◆

Design Chart

Color Key

☐	taupe	· 42
O	light olive	· 4
T	medium olive	· 3
Z	dark olive	· 4
◁	sage green	· 3
+	forest green	· 3
∴	light wheat	· 4
—	medium wheat	· 4
⊐	toast	· 4
▼	dark brown	· 4
V	light teal	· 2
N	medium teal	· 1
●	dark teal	· 1
⊓	light maroon	· 1
Y	medium maroon	· 1
■	dark maroon	· 1
•	light beige	· 2
∧	medium beige	· 1
‖	light rust	· 3
⊖	medium rust	· 1
⊺	dark rust	· 2

The number following the color indicates the number of skeins of wool needed.

Rugmaking

*time-honored methods
for crafting colorful carpets*

Braiding, hooking, and appliqué are rugmaking techniques that were commonly used during the 19th century. At that time, textiles were among the most valuable household possessions, and woolen scraps and worn clothing were saved and used to make rugs that were placed on tables as well as on floors.

Provided in this chapter are directions for all three techniques. To make a traditional braided rug, you cut and sew fabric strips, braid them, and then lace the braids together. For a hooked rug, you mark a design on a fabric foundation and then fill it in by pulling narrow loops of fabric through the foundation with a simple hook. And to craft a penny rug, you layer multicolored circles and stitch them to a backing. All of these rugmaking methods are easy enough for a beginner to master—even a child can help—and each yields a different effect, producing a rug with a distinctive look of its own.

Bright wool circles, layered and stitched to a woolen backing, will yield
a handsome new penny rug (see pages 90-93).

Braided Wool Rug

Although braided straw and cornhusk mats are mentioned in colonial records, there is very little documentation of braided fabric rugs before the 19th century, when they appeared on display at agricultural fairs. In 1826, Miss Lydia Hunt of Cranston, Rhode Island, was awarded a two-dollar prize at the state's Agricultural Society Fair for her innovative rag carpet. The admiring judges recorded that it "was manufactured from bits and odds and ends of every thing that would otherwise have been wholly useless, braided together, and its substantial fabric as well as economy was deemed worthy a premium." Apparently, many thrifty women used scraps for braiding rugs, but as factory-made fabrics became more readily available toward the middle of the century, rugmakers also began to purchase yard goods for braiding.

Braided rugs can be made in a variety of shapes. The most common—and easiest to braid—are circles and ovals. The directions that follow explain how to make an oval wool rug like the one in the center of the photograph at right; they can be adapted for an oval rug of any size.

◆ IMPORTANT INFORMATION

For ease in handling, a braided rug is assembled in interrelated steps. First, the fabric is cut into strips; the strips are then folded and braided, and the braids are laced together in stages. Before you begin, be sure to read all the directions so that you understand how the work progresses. While the steps may seem complicated, once you get started you will find the process quite simple.

In an oval rug, the length of the center braid determines the shape of the finished oval; the longer the center braid, the more elongated the oval shape will be. To determine the length of the center braid, first decide on the proportions of the rug you would like to make. Subtract the width from the length; to this measurement add 1 inch for each foot of width. The exact proportions of your finished rug may vary, depending on the weight of the fabric you are braiding.

When you are selecting the fabric for your rug, choose medium-weight, tightly woven woolens in harmonious colors. To determine the fabric yardage you will need, use this loose rule of thumb: 1 yard of medium-weight 54-inch-wide wool will equal about 1 square foot when braided. The rug featured here measures $4\frac{1}{2}$ feet at its longest and $2\frac{1}{2}$ feet at its widest, or approximately 11 square feet, and requires about 11 yards of 54-inch-wide wool to make. The weight of the fabric will dictate how wide you need to cut the strips, and thus the thickness of the braid. In general, the heavier the fabric, the wider the strip will need to be. (A strip width of between 2 and 3 inches is common.) You will need to make a sample braid to determine the correct strip width for your fabric. Do not use strips cut from fabrics of different weights because they will form uneven braids that are difficult to handle.

A

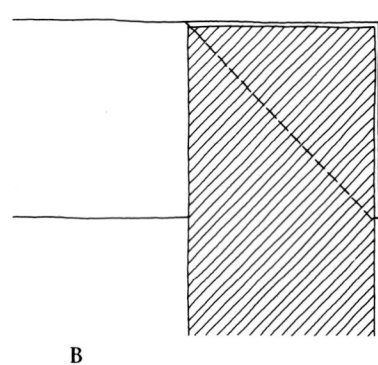

B

Once you have established the strip width for your rug, you will be ready to cut all your wool into strips; cut on the straight grain of the fabric so that the strips do not stretch when braided. Using a transparent graphed ruler and dressmaker's chalk will make the measuring and cutting easy. Cut strips into 3-yard lengths, and coil them into wheels preparatory to braiding. If your fabric will not produce 3-yard lengths, join same-color sections to make the strips. (If your strips are longer, the wheels will be awkward to handle.) Be sure to join the strips along the bias of the fabric so that the seam runs diagonally across them; this distributes the seam bulk when the strips are folded for braiding. Keep your work flat on a worktable, right side up, and anchor the braid you are working on with a C-clamp. To conceal the raw edges, you need to fold each strip lengthwise as it is braided. You can do this by hand or you can use braid folders, which are available from crafts stores and rugmaking suppliers. As you work, place a spring clamp or clothespin on the braid to keep the area just finished from loosening.

The rug is made with one continuous braid that keeps coiling around itself; new strips are added as necessary. When you have braided the center braid to the length you want, you will need to turn a neat corner (see Step 4). As you work around and the rug grows, you will also need to ease in the cables, or loops, of the braids at the curved ends to keep the rug lying flat (see Step 8). Plan to change colors where a curve begins to straighten out. The rug is braided with one side facing up, then turned over for lacing. To lace, you will need to secure the thread with a darning needle, and switch to a blunt lacing needle to join the cables in one braid to the cables in the adjacent braid.

C-1

◆ MATERIALS AND EQUIPMENT

Medium-weight wool fabric, 11 yards total, 54 inches wide
Linen lacing thread or buttonhole thread
Sewing thread
3 braid folders (optional)
C-clamp
Spring clamp or clothespin
Scissors

Darning needle
Lacing needle
Crochet hook
Sewing needle
Transparent graphed ruler
Rubber bands
Safety pins
Dressmaker's chalk

C-2

◆ DIRECTIONS

1. *Making a sample braid:* Measure, mark, and cut three strips of wool, each 3 feet long and 2½ inches wide. Fold the edges of each strip to the wrong side almost to the center, then fold the strip in half lengthwise; the folded strip will be approximately one-quarter the width of the unfolded strip, and the raw edges will be concealed (Illustration A). If you are using braid folders to do this, follow the manufacturer's directions, sliding the folders along the strips so that they remain about 1 to 2 inches below your fingers. Pin the ends of the three strips together and clamp with the

C-clamp to a worktable. To braid, bring the left folded strip over the middle folded strip, then bring the right folded strip over the middle folded strip, keeping the open folded edge of each strip facing to the right. Repeat these two motions, braiding tightly and evenly, making sure the strips stay folded as you move along. After braiding 6 or 7 inches, secure the braid with the spring clamp or clothespin. If you stop braiding to adjust your strips or to take a break, move the spring clamp or clothespin to the point where you have stopped. Finish braiding the three strips. If you are pleased with the weight of the braid—it should be plump and tight—go on to Step 2; if not, keep testing with strips of different widths until you are satisfied.

2. *Preparing the strips:* Once you have decided on a strip width, measure, mark, and cut strips of the desired width from your fabric. To join strips of the same color into 3-yard lengths, place the ends to be joined at right angles to each other with the right sides together, and stitch a seam on the bias, sewing across the corner at a 45-degree angle (Illustration B). Trim the seam allowance to ¼ inch and press the seam open. When the joined lengths measure 3 yards, roll them into a wheel and secure with a rubber band. Repeat for all the fabric colors.

3. *Forming the braid stub and center braid:* Select three different-color wheels for the center braid of the rug. Join the free ends of two of the wheels together on the bias as in Step 2. Over the seam you have just made, fold the edges of the strip to the wrong side almost to the center of the strip and press. With the wrong sides up, place the joined strips on a worktable, unrolling the wheels about 6 inches. At the free end of the third wheel, fold the edges of the strip to the wrong side almost to the center, then fold in half lengthwise for 2 inches down the strip; press and secure with overcast stitching using the sewing needle and sewing thread. Center the end of the overcast strip on the seamed area of the first two strips with the stitched side to the right, forming a T (Illustration C-1). Fold the top strips in half lengthwise over the end of the overcast strip and secure them by slipstitching through all the layers (Illustration C-2). Braid the strips until you reach the length you have determined for your center braid and stop with the right-hand strip over the middle strip.

4. *Making the first turn:* To turn the corner neatly, bring the left strip over the middle strip, then bring the middle strip over the left strip (Illustration D-1); pull the right strip tightly over the middle strip (Illustration D-2); repeat these steps to turn the braid completely (Illustration D-3). Reposition the spring clamp or clothespin to secure the corner. Continue braiding in the normal manner until the outer braid extends 8 inches beyond the center braid.

5. *Beginning the lacing:* Turn the braids over and place them on the worktable. Using the darning needle with a 24-inch length of the lacing thread or buttonhole thread, insert the needle through an open fold in a corner cable to bury the knot. Transfer the thread to the lacing needle. Pass the needle under an inner cable in the center braid, then under an inner cable in the outer braid, being careful not to pierce the fabric with the needle. Continue to pass the needle from braid to braid under alternate cables (Illustration E), pulling the thread very tight as you work, until you reach the stub end of the center braid. When you begin to run out of thread, switch back to the darning needle, take a few small stitches inside a cable, and trim the

D-1

D-2

D-3

E

excess thread to finish. Rethread the same needle, bury the new knot inside the nearest cable, then switch the thread back to the lacing needle to continue.

6. *Joining the braid around the stub end:* Switch the thread back to the darning needle (since the stub end is a fold, not a cable, you cannot lace through it, but must sew the outer braid around it). Wrap the braid around the stub end smoothly, noting the extra cables that will have to be eased in. Stitch through one cable on the stub, then through one on the outer braid, then stitch again through the same two cables. Repeat so that each cable on the stub is attached to the second braid with two stitches, skipping cables on the outer braid as necessary to keep the turn smooth.

7. *Continuing the braid:* Turn the braided work right side up and continue braiding until the braid is long enough to wrap around the other end. Join additional wheels of strips to the working strips as necessary (be sure to sew the seams on the bias, as in Step 2). Switch the thread to the lacing needle and lace the braids together as in Step 5, stopping 4 inches short of the braided corner. Never make the braids more than 3 yards long before lacing them together or they will be too unwieldy to handle.

8. *Easing the braid around the curved ends:* Wrap the braid around the braided corner, noting the extra cables that will have be eased in. Ease in four cables at regular intervals, two on each side of the braided corner, by passing the lacing needle under two consecutive cables on the outer braid. Mark the eased cables with safety pins. Continue to braid and lace the rug until the braid is long enough to wrap around the next turn. Lace as in Step 7. Ease around the turn as above and continue braiding. When you are ready to ease around the next turn, space the extra cables so that they are not adjacent to those marked with the pins in the previous round and ease in six cables at regular intervals. Continue braiding, and ease around the next turn in the same manner, marking the eased cables with safety pins. Continue to braid and ease in the same manner, easing five cables at each end in the next round, and easing three cables at each end in the round after that. Continue to braid and lace, repeating the easing pattern of six, five, and three cables; reposition the safety pins as necessary. As the curves grow larger and shallower, the eased cables will be spaced farther and farther apart. This pattern will produce a flat, even rug with edges that will not ripple or roll up.

9. *Finishing the rug:* Continue braiding and lacing as in Step 8 until the rug is the desired size. Lace around one end of the rug and stop where the curve meets the side. Cut the strips from the wheels about 8 inches beyond this point. Remove the braid folders if you are using them. Unfold the strip ends, and cut them so that they gradually taper to nothing. Fold in the raw edges of the tapered strips, and using the sewing thread and sewing needle, stitch the folds in place. Braid the tapered strips, leaving the last 2 inches free, and lace to the rug, easing as necessary. Using the crochet hook, pull the loose ends into the cables on the wrong side and slipstitch with a few stitches to secure. ◆

OVERDYEING FABRICS

Above, wool strips have been overdyed in graduated shades of four different colors. The palest strips in each color group show the fabric before it was dyed.

To achieve the subtle shadings that give rug designs extra interest, rugmakers often recolor their fabrics by a process known as overdyeing. A particularly effective method of overdyeing is called shading. In shading, the fabric is cut into pieces and dyed in different strengths of the same color to produce varied but related tones. Braided together or hooked into the same area of a rug— traditionally the background—the shaded fabrics create an illusion of dimension that cannot be achieved with fabrics in a single color.

For the best results, overdyeing should be used only on pure wool fabrics. Choose a light-colored fabric and a dye color that is related to the fabric color. Any commercial fabric dye is appropriate, and one package is more than enough for overdyeing one yard of fabric. When dyeing, it is wise to wear rubber gloves and to cover the surfaces of your working area with newspaper. You will also need an enameled pot, a wooden spoon for stirring, and metal tongs for lifting the strips out of the dye.

To begin, prepare the dye in the pot full strength according to the manufacturer's directions. Cut your fabrics into pieces that are a manageable size—four or five inches wide— and cut a scrap for testing the strength of the dye. If you want an even color, you should wet the wool before dyeing it. Test the color, re-membering that the fabric will dry slightly lighter. Dilute the dye with boiling water if needed until you are satisfied with the strength—this will make your darkest color. Add some pieces of fabric. When the pieces are slightly darker than the color you desire, remove them from the dye, rinse them in cool water, and hang them to dry on a clothesline or rack. Dilute the dye to the next shade you want, then add more pieces. In this manner, continue diluting and dyeing until you have pieces in several graduated shades. Don't be overly concerned with achieving perfect results; the varied tones that can occur in dyeing will simply add character to your finished rug.

Black Cats Hooked Rug

Indigenous to North America, rug hooking is believed to have developed in the area of Maine and eastern Canada in the first half of the 19th century. Hooked rugs, made by pulling strips of fabric through a loosely woven backing, probably originated as inexpensive substitutes for the imported carpets that were fashionable at the time. The introduction of burlap bags, used by transatlantic shipping companies for transporting goods during this period, provided an ample supply of backing material for the rugmakers. Rug hooking eventually spread south and west, and by the late 19th century the craft had become so popular that a healthy market for pre-stamped designs had developed.

The rug opposite features a cat design adapted from a late-19th-century hooked rug from Lancaster County, Pennsylvania. It is very easy to hook and has an appealing naive quality that results from the simple pattern and the wide strips of fabric used. If you like, you can adapt the directions that follow to hook any simple, linear design—perhaps a child's drawing or a quilt pattern.

◆ IMPORTANT INFORMATION

This 24½ x 33½-inch rug is a traditional hooked rug, worked in the primitive style. In rugmaking, the term "traditional" refers to a method of hooking in which a simple hook is used to pull strips of fabric to form a looped pile. (This differs from latch hooking, in which cut lengths of yarn are knotted onto a backing with a special ratcheting hook.) The term "primitive" refers to a rug in which the strips of fabric used are at least ¼ inch wide.

The rug should be hooked on a durable foundation; the primitive burlap specified is a sturdy, even-weave cloth, which is woven with the same number of threads running lengthwise and crosswise in each square inch. This type of burlap, which has an open mesh large enough to accommodate the ¼-inch fabric strips, is available from rugmaking suppliers; it is not the same as the burlap you can purchase at a variety store, which is neither evenly woven nor durable. If you wish to practice hooking to see whether you enjoy it before you invest in the primitive burlap, you can work a sample on burlap of any quality. Rug hooks are available at crafts stores and the notions department of most variety stores.

When selecting the fabric for your rug, choose medium-weight wool. The yardage specified in the materials list on page 84 is the approximate amount of fabric you will need, the exact amount will depend on the fabric weight, the frequency with which you change colors, and your hooking density. The strips must be cut on the straight grain so that they do not stretch when the fabric is hooked. Using a transparent graphed ruler will make measuring and cutting the strips easy.

Most of the fabrics used in this rug are solid-color; some plaids, however, were chosen to create an interesting pattern in the border blocks. You might consider

An entry in an 1839 issue of the **Farmer's Monthly Visitor** *prompted women to make good use of their fabric scraps. "After old coats, pantaloons, etc. have been cut up for boys, and are no longer capable of being converted into garments," advised the author, "cut them into strips, and employ the leisure moments of children or domestics in sewing and braiding them for door-mats."*

experimenting with tweeds, checks, and stripes as well. You may also want to vary the shades of your fabrics in the larger, same-color areas. You can mix different fabrics of the same color, or try overdyeing the same fabric to produce a variety of related shades (for information on overdyeing, see page 81).

Before hooking the rug, you will need to enlarge the Scaled Cat Pattern on page 87. Then, referring to the Scaled Schematic Diagram opposite, mark the diagram in full scale onto the burlap. Use a permanent marking pen so that the marks will not bleed and spoil your work if the rug becomes wet. After you mark the burlap, you will need to stretch it on a rug frame. (If you do not have access to a rug frame, which is self-supporting and adjustable, make a 32 x 40-inch frame from canvas stretchers, available at art supply stores.) The burlap must be taut in the frame to ensure an even loop tension. Before cutting the burlap, make sure that it is large enough to fit in your rug frame. If it is not, baste some muslin to the edges to extend them.

The arrows in the Scaled Schematic Diagram indicate the direction in which to hook the rows of loops within different areas; the broken lines indicate a directional area, but not a change in color. These directional changes help create visual interest within a large, single-color space. Small areas should be filled with rows of contour hooking that follow the shape of the area. When outlining, always hook directly over the diagram outline drawn on the burlap. Before you begin, be sure to read all the directions. If you have never hooked a rug, refer to Step 5 in the directions and practice the technique in the burlap border after the burlap is stretched in the frame.

◆MATERIALS AND EQUIPMENT

1 yard 10-ounce primitive burlap, 45 inches wide

1 yard green wool fabric, 54 inches wide (for background)

¾ yard black wool fabric, 54 inches wide (for cats)

Scraps of wool fabric in assorted colors, approximately 2 square yards total (for border blocks)

Scraps of wool fabric in tan and white (for bench and cat details)

10 yards green knitting worsted

3¼ yards twill tape, 2 inches wide

Carpet thread

Rug frame, or canvas stretchers to make 32 x 40-inch frame

Strip cutter with #8 blade (optional)

#2 primitive rug hook

Clear plastic bags

1 piece graph paper, 11 x 14 inches

Yarn needle

Sewing needle

Transparent graphed ruler

Scissors

Permanent marking pen

Dressmaker's chalk

Dressmaker's pins

Pushpins

◆ DIRECTIONS

1. *Cutting the wool strips:* Cut the wool into strips that measure ¼ inch wide and 15 inches long. If you are using a strip cutter (a rugmaking tool designed for cutting the strips in bulk), follow the manufacturer's directions. If you are cutting strips one at a time with scissors, use the ruler and chalk to mark the fabric and cut the strips on the marked lines. Separate the strips according to color and place them in clear plastic bags.

2. *Enlarging the cat pattern:* Using the transparent ruler and a pencil, measure and mark a grid of 1-inch squares onto the graph paper. Referring to the grid in the Scaled Cat Pattern on page 87, mark the outline of the cat in full scale onto your ruled paper. Cut out the cat pattern, and the eyes, nose, and mouth, along the lines.

3. *Marking the burlap:* Using the permanent marking pen, mark a 24 x 33-inch rectangle on the burlap, leaving a generous margin all around. Referring to the measurements in the Scaled Schematic Diagram below, mark the rug pattern within this rectangle. Begin by marking the border of squares, then mark the bench outline. Still referring to the diagram, position the paper cat pattern on the burlap so that the

Scaled Schematic Diagram

cat sits near the right end of the bench, and trace around the cat. Reverse the paper cat pattern and position it so that the cat sits near the left end of the bench; trace again.

4. *Attaching the burlap to the frame:* Following the manufacturer's directions, attach the burlap to the rug frame, marked side up. If you are using canvas stretchers, attach the burlap with pushpins placed at 1-inch intervals.

5. *Learning to hook:* If you do not know how to hook, practice in a border area of the burlap. Hold the end of one wool strip against the wrong side of the burlap with one hand. Hold the hook in your other hand and, from the right side, insert it through one opening in the weave; grasp the strip and pull the cut end through about ½ inch. Skip two threads on the burlap, insert the hook, and again pull up the strip, making a ¼-inch loop; remove the hook. In this manner, continue to pull loops to the right side of the burlap firmly and evenly (Illustration A). The loops will be held in place by their own density. When you reach the end of a strip, pull it to the right side of the work and trim the excess about ½ inch above the loops.

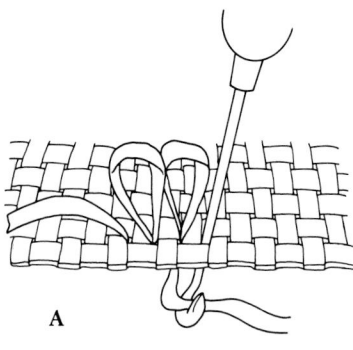

A

6. *Beginning the rug:* Begin by hooking the facial features of the cats with white. Then outline the cats with a row of white loops. Hook a row of black loops just inside the white outlines, then fill in the cats with black, contouring your hooking around the faces, tails, and legs, and hooking the rest of the cats in blocks of horizontal and vertical rows as indicated by the arrows in the Scaled Schematic Diagram. Hook the bench with tan wool.

7. *Filling in the background:* Outline the background area with a row of green loops. Then fill in the green background, as indicated by the arrows in the Scaled Schematic Diagram. Contour your hooking around the legs and tails of the cats.

8. *Hooking the border:* Hook an outline row of green loops all along the outer edge of the rug, then hook a row of green loops between each of the border blocks. Select a color for the upper left block and hook the block in horizontal rows. Select another color for the block immediately below it and hook the block in vertical rows. Hook the remaining blocks, continuing to alternate the direction in which you work, and using any colors you wish.

B

9. *Finishing the right side of the rug:* Trim all the cut ends of the strips even with the loops. Remove the rug from the frame. Trim the burlap, leaving a 1½-inch margin around the hooked area. Fold 1¼ inches of the margin to the wrong side and press. With the right side of the rug facing up, and starting wherever you wish, overcast the folded edge, using the yarn needle and a 24-inch length of the knitting worsted. Bring the needle up from the back as close as possible to the outer row of hooking, leaving a 2-inch tail of yarn at the back. Pass the needle over the edge and bring it up again as close as possible to the first stitch; continue in this manner. To end a length of yarn as you overcast, slide the needle under a few stitches on the back and leave a 2-inch tail. (When the entire edge is overcast, turn the rug over and tie together adjacent loose yarn ends; do not trim the excess yarn.)

10. *Hemming the rug:* With the wrong side up, place the rug on a worktable. Fold in the burlap margin at each corner and miter; trim the bulk from under the fold and stitch the fold closed with the carpet thread. Starting anywhere along one side, place the twill tape over the burlap margin and pin in place with one edge against

the overcasting. Tuck the loose ends of the yarn under the tape. Fold the twill tape at each corner, miter, and slipstitch. Overlap the ends of the twill tape 1 inch; trim the excess and fold under the end of the upper piece. Slipstitch both edges of the twill tape to the burlap all the way around the rug and remove the pins (Illustration B). ◆

SCALED CAT PATTERN

one square = one inch

GRENFELL RUGS

In 1892, Dr Wilfred Grenfell, an English medical missionary and writer, arrived in Labrador, Newfoundland, on a hospital ship. He found that the people in the desolate settlements—icebound most of the year—were dependent entirely on trapping and fishing for their livelihood, and living conditions were bleak. Grenfell decided to stay on, establishing a mission and hospitals, and encouraging the development of local crafts into cottage industries that would generate income for the inhabitants.

Rug hooking became one of the most successful of these industries. Grenfell not only encouraged individuals to create their own designs, but also made kits available to rug hookers through the mission. Much of the fabric used in the rugs was cut from discarded clothing that was gathered and sent to Labrador by English and American volunteers; often the shipments included cotton-knit underwear and silk stockings. The rich dye colors and tight hooking of Grenfell rugs gave them an effect similar to needlepoint.

Production thrived from about 1912 to about 1940, and the rugs hooked in the area during this period were sold widely throughout the United States and England in hotels, resorts, and mission stores. Now known as Grenfell rugs, these rugs (as well as Grenfell mats and bags) are characterized by crisply outlined designs, and typically feature subjects with northern themes, such as polar bears, puffins, and sled-dog teams.

Penny Rug

Probably developed as a way to use wool scraps that were too small to go into braided rugs, penny rugs became fashionable in the middle of the 19th century and continued to be made into the early 1900s. The "pennies"—layered fabric circles—were usually organized into a regular color pattern, and the rugs were made in a variety of geometric shapes; circles, rectangles, octagons, and hexagons were all common. Small rugs, like the antique woolen piece opposite, were often used as table coverings.

◆ IMPORTANT INFORMATION

Each penny in this design is made of three circles of fabric layered concentrically and stitched together with buttonhole stitching. The design requires a total of 205 pennies made from eleven colors and layered in six different combinations. Once assembled, the pennies are sewn to a backing in a concentric pattern.

The pennies can be made from medium-weight, firmly woven wool fabrics or from good-quality felt. You can alter the colors on the charts to reflect your own color preferences. When cutting, you can layer the wool to cut several circles at once—but before doing so, test how many layers your scissors will cut through with ease.

To make the pennies, you will need to cut circular templates using the full-size Penny Patterns on page 92, which are labeled with the numbers 3, 2, and 1. In the directions that follow, you will find references to two important charts, a Cutting Chart and a Color Combination Chart; both charts refer to the circle sizes by number, so be sure to label your templates. The Cutting Chart on page 93 indicates how many of each circle you will need to cut from each color, as well as how much fabric is required to do so. The Color Combination Chart on page 93 indicates how to layer the circles in the correct color combinations; the six combinations are designated with the letters A, B, C, D, E, and F. As you make the rug, refer to the Schematic Diagram on page 93 to cut the rug backing and to lay out the pennies. You can work the buttonhole stitch with carpet thread, buttonhole twist, pearl cotton, or embroidery floss. If you plan to use your rug on a floor, carpet thread is recommended.

◆ MATERIALS AND EQUIPMENT

Assorted wool fabrics or felt, for pennies
(see Cutting Chart on page 93 for amounts)
1 piece wool, 22 x 38 inches, for backing
Carpet thread, buttonhole twist, pearl
cotton, or embroidery floss
Tracing paper

Lightweight cardboard
T-square
Scissors
Embroidery needle
Dressmaker's pins

Buttonhole Stitch

A-1

A-2

◆ DIRECTIONS

1. *Making the templates:* Trace the Penny Patterns below onto the tracing paper; cut out. Place the patterns on the cardboard, draw around them, label, and cut out.

2. *Cutting the fabric circles:* Refer to the Cutting Chart opposite to determine how many circles to cut in each size from each color. With the wrong sides up, lay the fabrics on a worktable. Place a circle template on the appropriate fabric, draw around it and cut out. Repeat until you have cut all the circles.

3. *Assembling the pennies:* Refer to the Color Combination chart opposite to assemble the pennies. Center a small circle (Pattern 3) on the appropriately colored medium circle (Pattern 2) and pin. Referring to Illustration A-1, sew the circles together with buttonhole stitch, using the embroidery needle and your choice of thread. To work buttonhole stitch, bring the needle up from the back through the medium circle at the edge of the small circle at point 1. Insert the needle at point 2, ⅛ inch inside the edge of the small circle, and bring it up again in the medium circle at point 3, just to the right of the first stitch. Insert the needle at point 4; as you pull it through, catch a loop of thread with your thumb. Bring the needle back up through the medium circle ⅛ inch to the left of the first stitch, passing it through the loop of thread (Illustration A-2), and pull taut. Continue in this manner around the circle. Remove the pin. Center the stitched double circle on the appropriately colored large circle (Pattern 1); pin and stitch in the same manner. Repeat to make all the pennies.

4. *Preparing the backing:* Using the T-square and a pencil, mark a 21 x 36-inch rectangle on the wrong side of the fabric. Mark a point 6 inches in from each end on each long side. Mark the midpoints of the short sides. Join these points across the four corners. Cut, following the angled lines. Overcast the raw edges of the backing with zigzag or overcast stitching. Baste a center line both lengthwise and crosswise.

5. *Attaching the pennies:* Referring to the Schematic Diagram opposite, pin one F penny onto the center of the backing and stitch it in place using buttonhole stitch; remove the pin. Stitch three F pennies to either side of the center penny on the 36-inch basted line. Stitch an E penny to each end of the row. Position and stitch the remaining E pennies above and below this row, fitting them snugly between the F pennies. Referring to the diagram, continue attaching the pennies in this manner. For the outer band of pennies, start by centering a penny over each corner, then fill in the rest. ◆

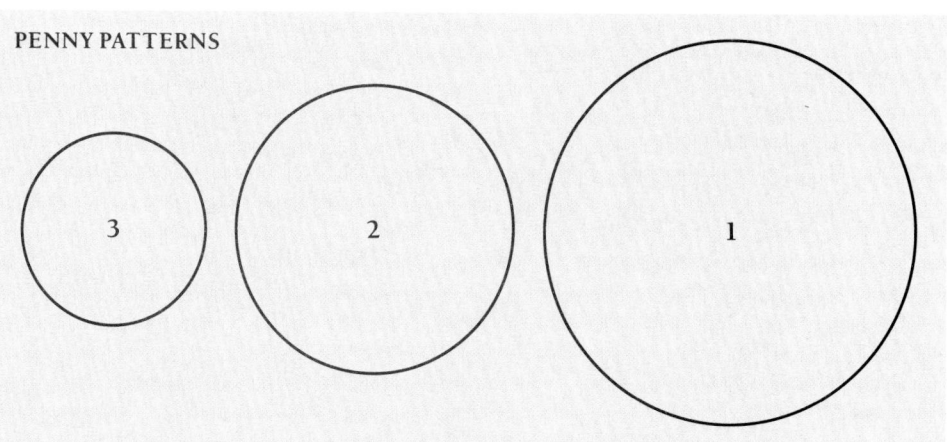

PENNY PATTERNS

Cutting Chart

color	moss green	dark taupe	light slate	cadet blue	beige	caramel	plum	black	forest green	olive	wine
fabric (inches)	25 x 25	16 x 18	12 x 12	16 x 18	14 x 17	9 x 11	9 x 9	12 x 13	8 x 8	7 x 7	5 x 7
pattern 1	126	54	25								
pattern 2				90	50	30	25				
pattern 3					37			90	36	24	18

Color Combination Chart

penny key	A	B	C	D	E	F
quantity	90	36	30	24	18	7
pattern 1	moss green	moss green	dark taupe	dark taupe	light slate	light slate
pattern 2	cadet blue	beige	caramel	beige	plum	plum
pattern 3	black	forest green	beige	olive	wine	beige

Schematic Diagram

Paper Crafting

decorative cutting,
pasting, and painting

Paper is a marvelously adaptable material. It comes in many weights, textures, and colors. It can be painted, cut, or used as a covering. And it is also relatively inexpensive, so it is a good medium to work in if you are new to handicrafts.

This chapter shows you how to cut a plain piece of paper into a Pennsylvania-German scherenshnitt picture, and how to cut and pierce paper to produce delicate, translucent lampshade panels. If you fancy cutting up pretty printed papers, you might be interested in the project for making decoupage dresser accessories; in decoupage, imaginatively arranged graphic images can capture a particular mood or sentiment—and you don't have to be able to draw or paint to convey it. Colorful printed papers can also be used to cover bandboxes. And if it is decorated paper that intrigues you, try the project for marbling; the process is tricky, but once you master it, you will be able to produce papers that are works of art in themselves.

Decorative and useful bandboxes are crafted by putting together simple chipboard
forms and covering them with pretty wallpaper (see pages 110-114).

Cut-and-Pierced Lampshade

The delicate floral pattern in the paper lampshade opposite is made by the traditional method of cutting and piercing. While the patterns produced by this craft can be quite intricate, the process is very easy to learn. The paper is simply pierced, then cut and curled away from the surface so that the cut-out areas can be clearly seen; none of the paper is cut completely away. You can make a lampshade in the pattern shown here or devise your own pattern, perhaps adapting a design from your wallpaper or upholstery fabrics.

◆ IMPORTANT INFORMATION

To make this lampshade, you will need to transfer the full-size Lampshade Pattern on page 99 to heavy paper panels. Before the shade is assembled, the panels are pierced, cut, and curled; they are then backed with lining paper and mounted on a wire frame. Don't try using a purchased paper lampshade; it would be awkward to pierce and not worth the trouble, since attaching the paper to a frame is easy. The only special equipment you will need is a lampshade piercer. The piercer has a handle with a different-size piercing needle at each end; the larger needle is used to pierce the large dots in the design, the smaller needle is used to pierce the lines of closely spaced dots.

Before you begin, study the pattern so that you understand the design elements. All the cutting, piercing, and curling is done on the marked side of the paper, which will be the inner side of the shade; as a result, the design you trace will appear in reverse on the finished shade. The six-paneled lampshade shown here measures 5 inches across the top, 12 inches across the bottom, and 7 inches high. The pattern, however, can be adapted for a lampshade of any size. Lampshade piercers, lining paper, and frames are available from lampshade-making suppliers and some crafts stores.

◆ MATERIALS AND EQUIPMENT

6-paneled wire lampshade frame, 7 inches high
1 sheet ecru lampshade paper, 26 x 38 inches
1 sheet white lining paper, 26 x 38 inches
1½ yards ecru grosgrain ribbon, ⅝ inch wide
1½ yards ecru grosgrain ribbon, ⅛ inch wide
1½ yards blue grosgrain ribbon, ⅛ inch wide
Lampshade piercer

Craft knife
Cutting mat
Tracing paper
Artist's transfer paper
Terry cloth towel
Clear-drying craft glue
Scissors
Clothespins

A

B

◆ DIRECTIONS

1. *Preparing the pattern:* Using a pencil, trace the Lampshade Pattern opposite onto the tracing paper. Place the tracing on a worktable. With one panel down, place the lampshade frame on the paper and adjust the frame so that the design is centered. Draw around the *outside* of the panel (Illustration A) to mark the panel outline.

2. *Cutting the paper panels:* Place the lampshade paper on the worktable. Place the lampshade frame on it and mark the outline of one panel as in Step 1. Repeat to draw all six panels. Cut out the panels on the marked lines.

3. *Marking the design onto the panels:* Place one paper panel on the worktable. Place the paper pattern over it, aligning the panel outlines, and slide the transfer paper, carbon side down, between the two layers. Carefully transfer the design to the panel by drawing over it with a sharp pencil. Repeat to mark all six panels.

4. *Piercing the dots:* Fold the towel in half and place it on the worktable. With the marked side up, place one panel on it. Using the lampshade piercer, pierce the marked dots—use the smaller needle for the small, closely spaced dots and the larger needle for the larger dots. Be sure to hold the piercer straight when inserting it and pulling it out. Repeat to pierce all six panels. Remove the towel.

5. *Cutting the leaves and petals:* With the marked side up, place a paper panel on the cutting mat. Using the craft knife, cut the vein lines. Then cut the leaf and petal outlines, being very careful not to cut beyond the points of the leaves. Repeat to cut the veins, leaves, and petals in all six panels.

6. *Opening the leaf veins:* With the marked side up, hold a panel in one hand; insert the piercer into a vein and move it gently from one end to the other to open the vein. Repeat to open all the veins in all six panels.

7. *Sculpting the cut design:* With the marked side up, hold a paper panel on the worktable. Using your fingers, or rolling the leaves and petals against the piercer handle, gently curl the leaves and petals up from the surface of the paper. Repeat, to curve all the leaves and petals in all six panels.

8. *Lining the panels:* Place the sheet of lining paper on the worktable. Apply a fine bead of glue around the edge of the marked side of one paper panel. With the glue side down, place the panel on the lining paper and press in place around the edges only. Let the glue dry, then cut away the excess lining paper. Repeat to line all six panels.

9. *Attaching the panels to the lampshade frame:* Apply a fine bead of glue around the edge of the lined side of one panel. Place the panel over one opening in the frame. Apply light pressure with your fingertips on the center of the panel and smooth the paper so that it lies flat on the frame. Secure with clothespins placed close together. Repeat for alternate frame openings. Let the glue dry and cut away any excess paper, then glue on the three remaining panels. For these, you will be able to use clothespins only at the top and bottom of the frame, so press the paper against the frame occasionally with your fingers as the glue dries. Let the glue dry, then cut away any excess lampshade paper.

10. *Trimming the panel joints:* Measure the length of a panel joint and cut six pieces of the ⅛-inch-wide ecru ribbon to this length. Apply glue to one piece of the

ribbon, and press the ribbon over one of the joints. Repeat to glue the ribbon over all six joints. Let the glue dry and cut away any excess ribbon.

11. *Trimming the top and bottom of the frame:* Measure around the perimeter of the shade top and cut a piece of the ⅝-inch-wide ecru ribbon to this measurement. Apply glue to one side of the ribbon. Center the ribbon width along the outside edge of the shade top, placing the cut end in the center of one panel (Illustration B). Press the ribbon in place. Roll the remaining width over the top of the frame to the inside of the shade, clipping the corners almost to the wire. Seal the ends of the ribbon with a little glue. In the same manner, trim the bottom of the frame with the ⅝-inch-wide ecru ribbon.

12. *Adding the blue ribbon trim:* Measure and cut a piece of blue ribbon to fit just below the ecru ribbon trim at the top of the shade, and glue in place. Measure and cut a piece of blue ribbon to fit just above the ecru ribbon at the bottom of the shade, and glue in place. Seal the ribbon ends with a little glue. ◆

LAMPSHADE PATTERN

Scherenschnitt

Scherenschnitt, which means "scissors-cutting" in German, is the technique of cutting a piece of paper in an unbroken design. The craft was brought to this country by Swiss and German immigrants, and it was traditionally used for decorating family records, love letters, valentines, and paper doilies. The directions that follow are for the doves-and-garland cutout shown above, in which the symmetrical design is cut from folded paper. Pieces can also be elaborately painted, like the framed scherenschnitt above, which was cut from unfolded paper.

◆ IMPORTANT INFORMATION

To make the doves-and-garland design, you will need to transfer the full-size Scherenschnitt Pattern opposite to folded writing paper, then cut it out with small sharp scissors, cutting through both layers of paper at once.

◆ MATERIALS AND EQUIPMENT

1 sheet writing paper
Contrasting paper (for mounting)
Tracing paper
Artist's transfer paper

Cuticle or embroidery scissors
White craft glue
Tape

◆ DIRECTIONS

1. *Preparing the pattern:* Using a pencil, trace the Scherenschnitt Pattern below onto tracing paper.

2. *Preparing the paper:* Fold the sheet of writing paper in half and close the open edges with small pieces of tape. Place the paper on a worktable. Center the paper pattern over it, aligning the dotted line with the fold. Slide the transfer paper, carbon side down, between the paper pattern and the writing paper. Carefully transfer the design to the folded writing paper by drawing over the pattern with the pencil.

3. *Cutting the design:* With the tip of the scissors, pierce a hole through both layers of writing paper in an interior area that is to be cut out, and carefully cut along the outline of the design. Repeat for the remaining interior areas to be cut out, then cut around the outside of the design.

4. *Pressing the design:* Carefully unfold the cutout and lay it, marked side up, on a worktable. Place a large book over it and leave it overnight, or until the cutout is flattened.

5. *Mounting the design:* Apply drops of glue around the edges of the marked side of the cutout, and glue it to the contrasting paper backing. Frame as desired. ◆

SCHERENSCHNITT PATTERN

ABOUT PAPER

The word "paper" comes from *Cyperus papyrus*, the name of a water reed that was used to make a paperlike product in ancient Egypt and, later, in Greece and Rome. The reed was cut into long strips, which were laid out in several layers crossing at right angles, and then soaked in water. When the strips had softened, the layers were hammered flat and then dried in the sun, forming a sheet.

A distant relative of papyrus, paper as it is known today is made from plant or cloth fibers that are macerated and mixed with water until they form a fibrous pulp. When the pulp is lifted from the water on screens and allowed to drain, a matted mass remains: when flattened and dried, it becomes a sheet of paper.

Most papers—everything from gift wrap to newsprint—are now made from wood pulp. However, fine grass and fiber, or "rag," papers have been made for centuries from many different plants, including flax, cotton, and hemp, as well as the inner bark of certain trees. In fact, nearly all plant and cloth fibers can produce some sort of paper.

The Chinese are credited with inventing the first "true" paper, made from silk pulp, around the 2nd century A.D. They later found that paper could also be made from bamboo and mulberry. Knowledge of Chinese techniques gradually spread westward along the trade routes to Europe, reaching Spain by the 12th century, and England by the 1400s. Lacking silk and other Oriental plant materials, the Europeans introduced the use of cotton and linen rags for fibers. Cotton is now the fiber most commonly used for rag paper.

Depending on the materials they are made from, papers differ in texture, strength, and absorbency, as well as in color. In some, such as mulberry and cotton papers, leaves, flowers, or long fibers are often added to the pulp for decorative effect. The papers at left, displayed on a sheet of papyrus, are made from the five traditional fibers listed below.

1. Mulberry The soft inner bark of the paper-mulberry tree is traditionally used by the Japanese to make a handsome, fibrous paper. The long mulberry fibers not only are decorative, but give the thin paper strength.

2. Daphne A shrub native to the mountains of Nepal and Bhutan, daphne is used to produce lightweight but strong papers.

3. Linen Linen papers, made from flax fibers, are less absorbent than other types of paper. The crisp surface of the thin, nearly transparent, linen papers is sometimes compared to that of parchment.

4. Cotton The most commonly used fiber for handmade papers is cotton. Tea leaves, sugar cane, feathers, and flowers were mixed into the cotton pulp of these papers to add texture and color.

5. Hemp Hemp-fiber papers, which can range from very thin to a cardboardlike thickness, are extremely strong and absorbent, and surprisingly silky to the touch.

Paper Marbling

Traditionally used in bookbinding, paper marbling, in which paper is decorated with intricate patterns through the use of floating colors, originated in Persia in the 15th century. By the end of the 16th century, the technique was known in Turkey, where finely marbled papers were used for official documents (if the writing was tampered with, the marbling would be disturbed and the fraud revealed). At this time, marbled papers were being exported from the Middle East to Europe, but they were not actually produced there until a hundred years later. France and Germany were the primary Western makers of marbled papers until the middle of the 19th century, when English marblers mastered the art. Loath to reveal the details of the technique, marblers worked in secrecy and their craft was long shrouded in mystery. While the technique is now well known, the patterns, which were developed in prescribed colors and given names, have changed very little over the centuries.

Today, marbled papers are still used in bookbinding as well as to decorate accessories such as picture mats, lampshades, and stationery. They may also be substituted for wallpaper when making the bandboxes shown on pages 110-111.

◆ IMPORTANT INFORMATION

Paper marbling is an unpredictable process and you should expect your first marbling attempts to have mixed results; experience will give you a true understanding of the materials and techniques. The outcome is affected by room temperature and humidity, dust, water quality, and the brand of colors used. For best results, the temperature in your workroom should be about 65 degrees and should remain constant. (If the air is very dry, you may need to use a humidifier.) Be sure to read all the directions before starting so that you understand how the work progresses, and set aside plenty of time. The materials and equipment mentioned are available from marbling suppliers and some art supply stores.

In paper marbling, paints or colored inks are dropped onto a viscous bath to create a pattern, and a piece of paper treated with alum (aluminum potassium sulfate) is then laid onto the floating colors; when the paper is lifted away, the pattern adheres to it. The bath, called size, is made from a mixture of water and carrageenin, a thickening agent. The size should be mixed in a proportion of 2 tablespoons of carrageenin per gallon of water and poured into a trough to a depth of about 1 inch. As the size sits, a skin tends to form on its surface and must be skimmed off just before the colors are dropped on.

For the colors, you can use marbling ink, acrylic paint, or gouache—a type of opaque watercolor. Each of these is water-soluble; gouache, however, may be tricky to use. The colors are mixed with ox gall, a dispersing agent, before they are dropped onto the size; the ox gall allows the colors to spread and keeps them from blending together, while the viscosity of the size supports the colors.

The directions opposite explain how to prepare the inks or paints; if you use paints, you will need to experiment to find the correct pigment-to-water proportion for your brand. Some marbling inks come premixed with ox gall. If you use inks that do not contain ox gall, you will have to add it to them; ox gall must also be added to any paints used in the process. The strength of the ox gall varies with the brand, so you will need to find the correct proportions when preparing your colors. If the prepared ink forms large (2-inch) circles when dropped on the size, it contains too much ox gall; add more color. If the circles are so small that they sink down through the size, the ink solution does not contain enough ox gall; add another drop.

You can use the marbling technique successfully on many kinds of paper. Unsized 70-pound offset printing paper, available from a printing shop, will give the best results; writing paper and good-quality construction paper can also be used. While you are learning, cut the paper into 8 x 10-inch sheets; they will be easy to handle and your experiments will not be too costly.

Professional equipment is available from marbling suppliers, but you can use readily available substitutes; you will need a trough, a skimming board, a press board, a rinse board, and a drying rack or clothesline. A professional marbling trough is separated into two parts; one holds the size, the other holds a rinse board and any discarded ink. You can, however, use a rectangular metal roasting pan to hold the size (disposable foil pans are ideal). Plastic is not recommended because it may react with the size. A professional skimming board (used to clean the surface of the size before applying the colors) is a strip of wood that fits the width of the trough; 3-inch strips of newspaper cut to the width of your pan will also work well, but be sure to have plenty of these strips on hand. Use a ¾-inch-thick piece of plywood as a press board to weight down the alum-treated paper; it should be large enough to cover several sheets of paper. Use a second piece of plywood as a rinse board; it should be as big as your largest sheet of paper and must fit into your sink. In addition, you will need enough worktable space to set up the trough, treat and press the paper, and mix the colors. (Cover the tables and floor with newspaper or with plastic sheeting.) You will also need widemouthed jars to hold the prepared colors, a metal bucket, a small metal mixing bowl, an electric blender, and straw whisks for dropping the inks onto the size. You should be able to marble seventy-five to a hundred 8 x 10-inch sheets of paper with 1 gallon of size.

The pattern shown in the photograph on pages 104-105 is called Stone Marbling. This is a simple, basic pattern; while you are learning it, do not try to work with more than four colors at once. From this pattern, more sophisticated patterns can be created when a stylus or other pointed tool is passed through the colors (for information on how to do this, see page 109).

◆ MATERIALS AND EQUIPMENT

Unsized 70-pound offset printing paper,
* writing paper, or construction paper*
Marbling inks, acrylic paints, or gouache
½ ounce liquid ox gall
2 ounces carrageenin instant blender powder
2 ounces alum powder
Distilled water
Marbling trough
Press board
Skimming board or newspaper strips
Rinse board

2-quart electric blender
1-quart saucepan
1-quart metal mixing bowl
Metal bucket
1-quart pitcher or bottle
Widemouthed jars, one for each color
Sponge
Newspaper or plastic sheeting
Straw whisks, one for each color
Drying rack, or clothesline and
* clothespins*

◆ DIRECTIONS

1. *Making the size:* Determine the amount of size you will need for a 1-inch depth in your trough. To mix the size, fill the blender with 2 quarts of hot water (if your tap water is hard, use distilled water). With the blender on slow speed, add 1 level tablespoon of the carrageenin; cover and blend at high speed for fifteen seconds, then pour the mixture into the bucket. Repeat the procedure, maintaining the same proportions, until you have made enough size. Cover the bucket and let the size sit at least two hours, and preferably overnight.

2. *Treating the paper with alum:* Place 2 level tablespoons of alum and 2 cups of water in the saucepan (if your tap water is hard, use distilled water); heat slowly until the alum is dissolved. Let the solution cool, and pour it into the 1-quart mixing bowl. Dip the sponge into the alum solution and squeeze once. Carefully sponge one side of several sheets of paper with alum, wetting the sponge as necessary; the paper should be damp but not wet. Place the paper sheets under the press board for five to ten minutes (they should be partially, but not completely, dry for marbling).

3. *Preparing the colors:* If you are using marbling inks, shake each color well and pour ¼ cup of each into separate jars. If the inks do not contain ox gall, add 1 drop to each jar and mix with separate whisks. If you are using acrylic paints or gouache, pour ¼ cup of distilled water into a jar, add 1 squirt of color and 1 drop of ox gall, and mix with a whisk; repeat to prepare each color you wish to use.

4. *Skimming the size:* Pour the size from the bucket into your trough. Hold the skimming board or newspaper strip at the far end of the trough and, with the edge about ¼ inch below the surface of the size, pull the skimmer toward you with both hands to remove the skin and any dust (Illustration A).

5. *Dropping the color on the size:* Stir one prepared color with a whisk and tap the whisk on the lip of the jar so that the excess falls back into the jar. With the wet end pointed down, hold the whisk at least 1 foot above the trough and lightly tap it on the forefinger of your other hand with even taps; the color will fall from the whisk onto the

A

B

size and spread to form circles. Refilling the whisk as necessary, continue in this manner until the surface is dotted with circles of color. (One or two whisk refills of each color should be enough.) Repeat the process for each marbling color you wish to use.

6. *Marbling the paper:* When you are satisfied with the way the pattern and colors look on the size, take a sheet of alum-coated paper from under the press board. Holding it alum side down by diagonally opposite corners, place one corner on the size at one end of the trough and, in one continuous motion, slowly roll the paper down the length of the trough (Illustration B). Remove the paper from the trough and place it, inked side up, on the rinse board. Stand the rinse board on end in the sink and, using the pitcher or bottle, gently pour water over the paper to remove the excess size. Drape the paper over a rack or clip it to a clothesline with clothespins to dry. Remove any color residues from the trough by skimming as in Step 4. Repeat Steps 5 and 6 to marble the next sheet of paper. Continue in this manner until all of your alum-coated papers have been marbled. Refill the marbling trough with fresh size and color, if necessary.

◆ COMMON MARBLING PROBLEMS

Listed below are some problems commonly experienced by beginning marblers, followed by the probable causes and some possible solutions.

Irregularly shaped voids, or places where no color adhered to the paper: Caused by air bubbles caught between the paper and the size because the paper was laid down too quickly. Lay the paper with a slow, smooth, continuous rolling motion.

Diagonal streaks: Caused by hesitation when laying the paper on the size. Lay the paper with a slow, smooth, continuous rolling motion.

Round voids: Caused by hair, dust, or too much ox gall. Be sure the surface of the size is clean and the color is the right consistency.

Colors run off when the paper is removed from the size: Caused by the untreated side of the paper being placed on the size. Make a pencil mark on the untreated side of the paper to identify it.

Difficulty in laying the paper down on the size: Caused by uneven drying under the press board or low humidity in the workroom. Be sure you apply the alum in a smooth, thin layer; use a humidifier.

Colors are grainy: Caused by improperly dissolved size, contaminated colors, or colors improperly mixed with ox gall. Skim the size. Make sure that the whisks and colors are dust free. Wash and dry your hands and do not use hand lotion. Remix the size and colors, if necessary. ◆

MORE MARBLING PATTERNS

Once you have mastered the basic technique of marbling, you may want to experiment with manipulating the colors to create different marbled patterns.

Shown here are four variations on the Stone Marbling pattern (for information and directions, see pages 104-108). These are created by pulling a stylus, or another pointed instrument such as a knitting needle or thin paintbrush handle, through the drops of color as they lie on the size. The four patterns can be worked in endless color combinations.

FREEFORM

Apply the colors as you would for the Stone Marbling pattern. Use an eyedropper to drop a second color on top of some of the larger circles to make bull's-eyes. Pull the stylus through the bull's-eyes to make freeform shapes. You can make a heart shape by pulling the stylus once across a bull's-eye, or create a star shape by pulling five or six radiating lines from the center of a bull's-eye to its edge. Experiment with different strokes of the stylus to learn how to exaggerate the free forms to achieve a wide variety of effects.

FRENCH CURL

Apply the colors as you would for the Stone Marbling pattern. Beginning in one corner of the trough, pull the stylus through the colors in a circular motion to create a spiral about 4 inches in diameter; pull the stylus from the outside of the spiral and end in the center (the result should look like a cresting wave). Repeat to make spirals in orderly rows over the entire surface of the trough. To achieve different effects, experiment with spirals in different sizes or with different repeated patterns.

FRENCH SHELL

Apply the colors as you would for the Stone Marbling pattern, but before you apply the last color, use an eyedropper to add one drop of good-quality olive oil to the final color and mix thoroughly. The oil will create a soft halo effect in the marbling pattern. Try experimenting with inks from one color; several similar shades used together will produce the subtle variations that characterize this pattern.

GHOST MARBLING

Ghost marbling is used to add an overlay of pattern to a paper that has already been marbled. The marbled paper must be re-treated with alum so that the second ink pattern will adhere (see Step 2 on page 107, but to keep the first pattern from smudging, gently pat the alum-dipped sponge on the paper instead of wiping it across). Apply the ink to the size sparsely, using only one or two colors; then draw the stylus through the inks as you wish. The ghost effect will be most subtle if you use colors that are similar to those already on the paper, but ones that are darker or lighter in value.

Bandboxes

During the first half of the 19th century, bandboxes like those at left were particularly popular in America and were commonly used both as luggage and as storage for a varied assortment of personal effects. These versatile containers were made of wood or cardboard, and were invariably covered with bright, block-printed wallpapers. Many of the distinctive paper designs, which might depict landmarks, famous people, classical motifs, or floral patterns, were created by manufacturers specifically for the box exteriors; the interiors, by contrast, were usually lined with bits and pieces of discarded newspaper. These handsome and colorful boxes are easy to make and can serve as pretty storage containers for all manner of treasures.

◆ IMPORTANT INFORMATION

The bandboxes shown here are made from chipboard—a thin paper board similar to poster board—and then covered with wallpaper and lined with newspaper. Each bandbox is made from four chipboard pieces: the box bottom, the box body, the lid top, and the lid lip. The size of the bottom determines the sizes of the three other pieces and of the wallpaper covering. Chipboard, available at art supply stores, is sold in single, double, and triple thicknesses; use the double-thickness board to make the box bottom and lid top, and the single-thickness board, which is more flexible, to make the box body and lid lip.

When marking the pattern onto the wallpaper, be sure to consider the position of any one-way designs or dominant motifs; double-check their placement when pasting the paper onto the box. You will need approximately 1 square yard of wallpaper; the exact amount will depend on the scale of the designs or motifs. Using a transparent graphed ruler will make measuring the pieces easy.

To cover the box, you can use regular wallpaper and wallpaper paste, or prepasted wallpaper. In either case, follow the manufacturer's directions; if you are using prepasted paper, dampen it when the directions on pages 112-113 specify to apply paste. To prevent the chipboard from warping, be careful not to overdampen the wallpaper. Be sure to smooth out any air bubbles with your fingers when applying the paper to the chipboard. Before assembling the pieces, you should paste a scrap of wallpaper to a scrap of the chipboard so that you can get a feel for the process. Always let the paper set for at least one hour before handling.

The directions that follow are for making a bandbox measuring 9 x 7 x 6¾ inches using the largest of the oval Bandbox Bottom Patterns on page 114. The two smaller patterns are provided for your convenience, should you desire to make smaller bandboxes. To make these smaller boxes, simply follow the same procedure you would for making the large bandbox; the height of the box, however, can vary as you choose. To make a round box, draw a circular pattern with a compass.

◆ MATERIALS AND EQUIPMENT

1 sheet single-thickness chipboard, 30 x 40 inches

1 sheet double-thickness chipboard, 15 x 20 inches

1 piece wallpaper, approximately 36 x 36 inches, regular or prepasted

Wallpaper paste (if using regular wallpaper)

2 flat paintbrushes, ½ and 1½ inches

Craft knife

Scissors

Cutting mat

Tracing paper

Newspaper

Transparent ruler

Metal straightedge

White masking tape

White craft glue

◆ DIRECTIONS

1. *Making the pattern:* Using a pencil, trace the largest of the full-size Bandbox Bottom Patterns on page 114 onto the tracing paper and cut out.

2. *Cutting the chipboard pieces:* Place the double-thickness chipboard on the cutting mat. Place the paper pattern on the chipboard and draw around it; remove the pattern. Mark this oval "B" for the bottom of the box and, using the craft knife, cut it out on the drawn line. Using the paper pattern, draw a second oval on the chipboard; remove the pattern. Using the ruler, measure and mark a line ⅛ inch outside the pattern line. Mark this oval "L" for the lid and cut it out on the outer line. Place the single-thickness chipboard on the cutting mat. On it, for the box body, draw a rectangle 27¼ inches long (2 inches greater than the circumference of the bottom) x 6¾ inches high. For the lid lip, draw another rectangle 28¼ inches long (2 inches greater than the circumference of the lid) x 1½ inches high. Using the metal straightedge as a guide, cut out both rectangles.

3. *Cutting the wallpaper:* With the wrong side up, place the wallpaper on a worktable. Place the lid board on the wallpaper, draw around it and remove. Measure and mark a second oval line ½ inch outside the first. Using the scissors, cut out on the outer line. Place the bottom board on the wallpaper, draw around it and remove. Measure and mark a second oval line ⅛ inch inside the first and cut out on the inner line. Place the lid lip board on the wallpaper, draw around it and remove. Measure and mark a parallel line 1 inch outside one short end and ½ inch outside one long side, and cut out the enlarged rectangle on the outer lines. Place the body board on the wallpaper, draw around it and remove. Measure and mark a parallel line 1 inch outside one short end and 1 inch outside each long side, and cut out the enlarged rectangle on the outer lines.

4. *Forming the body of the box:* Bend the body board into an oval, overlapping the ends by 2 inches, and secure temporarily with the masking tape (Illustration A). Place the body around the bottom board, and adjust the overlap if necessary so that the fit is snug. Remove the body from the bottom and secure the overlap permanently with the masking tape.

A

B

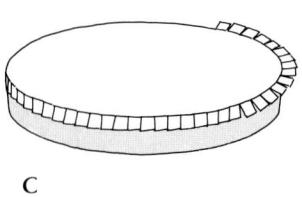

C

5. *Forming the lid lip:* As in Step 4 for the body, fit the lid lip board to the lid board and secure the overlap.

6. *Assembling the lid:* Using the 1½-inch paintbrush, apply wallpaper paste to the oval lid paper, leaving the ½-inch extension dry. Center the lid board on the paper; turn the lid over and smooth the paper. Let dry. Using the scissors, clip the extending paper at ½-inch intervals, cutting from the edge nearly to the lid board (Illustration B). With the clipped edge extending all around, set the lid board onto the lid lip. Using the ½-inch paintbrush, apply wallpaper paste to the underside of the clipped sections one at a time, folding each down over the lip as you move along (Illustration C). Turn the lid over and apply a thin line of craft glue to the seam. Let dry.

7. *Completing the lid:* Apply paste to the smaller wallpaper rectangle, leaving the ½-inch extension dry. Beginning at the seam, wrap the pasted area of the paper around the lid lip, keeping the edge flush with the top (Illustration D), and overlap the ends. Smooth the paper and let dry. Using the scissors, clip the extending paper at ½-inch intervals from the edge of the paper nearly to the lip board. Paste and fold the clipped sections to the inside of the lip as in Step 6. Let dry.

8. *Covering the body of the box:* Apply paste to the remaining wallpaper rectangle, leaving the two 1-inch extensions along the sides dry. Beginning at the seam, center the pasted area over the curved body board; wrap it around and overlap the ends. Smooth the paper and let dry. Clip the extending paper at the top and bottom at ½-inch intervals, cutting from the edge of the paper nearly to the body board. On the top edge only, paste and fold the clipped sections to the inside (Illustration E) as in Step 6. Let dry.

9. *Attaching the body to the bottom:* Set the bottom oval into the body so that the bottom is flush with the edge of the board and the clipped paper extends beyond it. Turn the box over and fold and paste the clipped sections onto the bottom (Illustration F) as in Step 6. On the inside, apply a thin line of craft glue at the seam. Let dry. Apply wallpaper paste to the remaining wallpaper oval and center it on the box bottom. Smooth the paper and let dry.

10. *Lining the inside of the box:* Cut small pieces of newspaper, and glue or paste them to the inside of the box and lid to form a collage; be sure to cover the surfaces completely. ◆

D

E

F

BANDBOX BOTTOM PATTERNS

Decoupage Dresser Set

Decoupage is the craft of cutting out printed images and gluing them to a surface in attractive arrangements, then coating them with a protective sealer. A vogue for decoupage was started in 18th-century France by Marie Antoinette, who amused herself by cutting up engravings by popular contemporary artists and pasting the pieces onto boxes, fans, and screens. In the Victorian era, the fad spread to England, where pasting cutouts into scrapbooks was already fashionable. The instructions on the following pages are for decorating dressing table accessories like those above, but it is not necessary to limit the craft to small objects; it can be used effectively on folding screens, lamps, and furniture. The color of the surface to which the cutouts are applied can change the way the finished piece looks, so you should experiment.

◆ IMPORTANT INFORMATION

In this project, decoupage has been used to decorate accessories made of wood; these were painted ivory, then embellished with pale blue bands before the cutouts were applied. Be sure to sand all articles before painting them. When mixing the paints, use plastic containers with tight-fitting lids so that the paints can be stored and, if necessary, used later for touchups.

Almost any printed paper images will work for decoupage. Some art supply and crafts stores carry books with pictures specifically intended for decoupage. Seed catalogs, old illustrations, and wrapping paper (Victorian-style wrapping paper was used here) are also good sources.

The images should be cut out with small sharp scissors (cuticle or embroidery scissors work best) and they must be cut neatly and cleanly, as any mistakes will show when the piece is finished. After they are cut out, the images are arranged as desired on the surface of the object to be decorated, then fixed in place one at a time with acrylic gel medium. Once the images are fixed, the decorated surfaces should be sealed with an acrylic sealer. You can use either a brush-on or a spray sealer; the brush-on type offers more protection but may cause images cut from thin paper to buckle. Test the sealer on the paper before applying it.

◆ MATERIALS AND EQUIPMENT

Dresser set pieces to be decorated	¼-inch stencil brush
Acrylic paint in ivory and baby blue	Compass
Paper images to cut out	Cuticle or embroidery scissors
Acrylic gel medium	Plastic containers with lids
Clear acrylic sealer	Masking tape
1-inch sponge paintbrush	Ruler
½-inch flat paintbrush	Kneadable eraser

◆ DIRECTIONS

1. *Painting the main color:* Using the sponge brush, paint each dresser set piece with one coat of ivory. Let dry. Repeat twice.

2. *Preparing the bands:* Determine a band width that will be suitable for each piece. Using the ruler and a pencil, mark the placement of the bands on each piece (use a compass if you wish to mark the placement of a round band). Using the masking tape, mask along the pencil marks, rubbing the edges of the tape with a finger to seal.

3. *Painting the bands:* Mix the baby blue paint with the ivory paint to make a color you like. Using the flat paintbrush, paint the exposed bands blue. Let dry thoroughly, and repeat. Remove the tape.

4. *Arranging the images:* Using the cuticle or embroidery scissors, cut out the

images you have chosen. To secure the images in position temporarily, place a tiny ball of kneadable eraser under each image and press into place. Position the most important images first, then layer the remaining cutouts. When your design is complete, lightly outline the images with a pencil.

5. *Attaching the images:* Remove the images, noting the ways they are layered, and remove the kneadable eraser. Using the stencil brush, apply the acrylic gel medium to the backs of the images, starting with the lowest layer and working with one image at a time. Follow the penciled guidelines to position each image and press it with your finger to remove any air bubbles and make it lie flat. Attach the remaining images in the same manner to complete the arrangement. Let all the decoupage dry thoroughly. Erase any pencil marks that show on the surface. Repeat Steps 4 and 5 for all the pieces you wish to decorate.

6. *Sealing the decoupage:* Following the manufacturer's directions, coat the surface of each object with the acrylic sealer and let dry. Repeat twice. ◆

Painting

colorful treatments for boxes,
game boards, a tablecloth,
and more

Painting can be a fast and nearly foolproof way to add a decorative pattern to almost any object. In this chapter, paint is used to stencil a pretty border onto a tablecloth, to turn a plain piece of canvas into a boldly patterned floor cloth, to replicate an old-fashioned game board, and to embellish unfinished boxes with fanciful graining patterns.

You need not be a fine artist to use paint creatively; the graphic look of most of the finished projects presented here is achieved by using stencils or simply by following a marked design. If you are unfamiliar with the properties of the various paints and brushes specified in the directions, read the following special sections devoted to these materials. Often, more than one type of paint is appropriate for a project, so you may be able to use paints you already own. Choose the supplies that work best for you, and remember that paint colors can be mixed—it is your chance to customize your work.

With its design marked out, this game board is ready for painting (see pages 134-137).

UNDERSTANDING PAINT

A wide selection of paints is available for craft projects; along with old standards like artists' oil colors, new types, such as alkyd paints, are also being produced. While the paints may differ in properties and characteristics, their applications often overlap—some paints can be used interchangeably. Consequently, choosing paint can be confusing. To help, the chart at right outlines the properties of four of the most common paint types used in crafts.

When purchasing paint, keep in mind that different brands of the same type of paint are not identical in quality and characteristics. Acrylic craft paint made by one company, for example, may be quicker drying or thicker than an acrylic craft paint produced by another manufacturer. Colors of the same name also vary in appearance.

Composition and Characteristics

OIL Artists' oil colors are composed of pigments or dyes that are mixed with binders such as linseed or poppy-seed oil. They come in tubes and have a buttery consistency. Because of their oil content, these paints dry slowly, making subtle blending and color gradations possible. Used full strength, they produce extremely opaque and permanent color that normally has a sheen; when thinned, they become transparent and dry to a matte finish.

ACRYLIC Acrylic paints are composed of pigments that are mixed with a plastic resin binder. Two types are available: acrylic artists' colors and acrylic craft paints. Acrylic artists' colors come in tubes and can easily be mixed for a versatile range of colors. Acrylic craft paints come in small jars and are more liquid than acrylic artists' colors; some brands are available premixed in "country" colors. Both types produce a permanent and relatively opaque color; when mixed with water, they become transparent.

ALKYD Alkyd artists' colors are composed of pigments that are mixed with an alkyd (alcohol and acid) resin and an oil binder. They come in tubes, have the consistency of oil colors, and can be mixed with oil colors. Alkyd paints dry more quickly than oil paints but more slowly than acrylic paints, and they produce a permanent color that is brighter than either.

JAPAN Japan colors are composed of ground pigments that are mixed in a resinous varnish containing little or no oil. The paints come in both tubes and jars, and are available in a wide variety of colors. For an even broader color range, they can be mixed with oil paint, but the oil will slow down the drying time. Japan colors dry with a flat, opaque appearance.

Uses	Advantages	Disadvantages
◆ Oil colors can be used on many materials, including canvas, wood, metal, porcelain, and glass. They are generally not recommended for stenciling because they dry slowly.	◆ Oil colors are excellent for small-scale, decorative painting because they are opaque and fine textured. Oils can be mixed to produce a wide range of colors.	◆ Oil colors can take days to dry (different colors dry at different rates), and require the use of flammable solvents such as turpentine for thinning and cleanup. Some oil colors contain lead.
◆ Acrylic paints can be used on canvas, wood, paper, and metal; sand and prime metal surfaces before painting. Acrylic craft paints are the easiest acrylic paints to use for stenciling.	◆ Acrylic paints dry in a few minutes and require only water for thinning and cleanup. Once dry, the paints remain flexible, so painted fabrics can be rolled or folded without cracking the colors.	◆ Subtle blending of colors is difficult because acrylics dry quickly. Although they are water-soluble when wet, the paints are extremely hard to remove from brushes if allowed to dry.
◆ Alkyd artists' colors can be used on canvas, wood, glass, metal, and porcelain. They can also be used for wall stenciling.	◆ Alkyd artists' colors dry thoroughly in less than a day, but remain mixable on a palette for several hours. All alkyd artists' colors dry at the same rate and to the same degree of gloss.	◆ Alkyd colors require the use of flammable solvents such as turpentine or mineral spirits for thinning and cleanup.
◆ Japan colors have traditionally been used for American decorative painting. They are especially suitable for stenciling on furniture and walls, and for detailed work on wood or metal.	◆ The varnish base makes Japan colors extremely quick drying. The paints produce a flat color that can be shaded or glazed for a wide variety of effects.	◆ Japan colors can be difficult to find. They require flammable solvents such as turpentine and mineral spirits for thinning and cleanup.

UNDERSTANDING BRUSHES

Brushes are designed for dozens of specific uses. In addition to a wide range of artists' brushes, there are brushes created especially for particular projects like grain-painting and stenciling. Shown here are some of the basic brushes used in crafts. Most are available with either natural or synthetic bristles in various grades. Synthetic brushes are used with acrylic paints because the medium can erode natural bristles.

Brushes like those listed are often made with high-quality materials and they can be expensive. It is best to start out with only the basic brushes required for a project: purchase others only as you become more advanced and are ready to experiment with new techniques. Buy the best quality brush you can afford. A well-made brush will provide better control, and properly cared for, it should last for years.

1. Brights Characterized by flat, short bristles with squared ends, these brushes can be used with buttery paints such as oils, and fluid paints like watercolors. In decorative painting, brights are used for filling in areas of color.

2. Stencil brushes Made with blunt-cut natural hog bristles, stencil brushes are used for applying paint through a stencil. The brushes produce a softly textured, stippled effect, and the blunt bristles help prevent the paint from seeping under the edge of the stencil.

3. Badger softeners Large badger-hair brushes are used dry to soften colors and blend brushstrokes in oil and watercolor painting. They are also used in grain-painting to produce thin washes of color and grain-like striations.

4. Rounds Round brushes, available in a wide range of sizes, are best used with fluid paints. The flexible bristles and pointed tip can produce fine lines, as well as the "comma strokes" often used in decorative painting.

5. Fans Fan brushes are used dry to blend colors in oil and acrylic painting. A variety of large fan brushes is also available for similar use in grain-painting.

6. Overgrainers Overgrainers are used for applying a dark "wood grain" or other precise detail on a dry, previously grained surface.

7. Liners Liners are designed to make smooth, flowing brushstrokes such as those used for scrollwork and script. The long, tapered bristles hold a lot of paint and therefore require less dipping than other brushes.

8. Sponge brushes Inexpensive, disposable brushes made of sponge are adequate for applying a base color to a surface. They can be used with all paint types but will dissolve if cleaned in turpentine or mineral spirits.

9. Brights See (1) above.

10. Stipplers Stipplers are used for making decorative finishes. Used dry on a freshly painted surface, the bristles lift flecks of color to create a freckled or lightly mottled surface.

Stenciled Tablecloth

By the 1820s, the "theorematical system of painting," now known as stenciling, had caught on in America as an inexpensive means for decorating floors, walls, and furniture—and for eliminating the labor and time required in embroidering household linens. Linen bed hangings, coverlets, and tablecloths embellished with stenciled designs began appearing in New England and New York as early as 1825. In many cases, the same stencils were used for both walls and linens. The strawberry design that appears on the tablecloth shown opposite was adapted from an early wall stencil seen in a 19th-century New England house.

In a letter dated 1850, a New York painting instructor offered advice to a student on how to copy a stencil design from an engraving. "I generally give extra lessons in fruits. But if you have practiced as I hope you have, I can give you written instructions on fruit or flowers....You must shade just as the engraver had shaded, let your lights fall where his fall in every instant throughout the pieces."

◆ IMPORTANT INFORMATION

The strawberry vine is applied to the cloth with acrylic craft paint; two stencils are used—one for the red strawberries and stems, the other for the green leaves, stems, and hulls. You can make the stencils by tracing the full-size Stencil Pattern on pages 126-127 onto stencil acetate, a clear plastic film. The 7-inch pattern is stenciled four times to make a continuous border along each side of the tablecloth, and a 2¾-inch space is allowed for filling in at each corner. The cloth shown here measures 38 inches square; if you wish to make a tablecloth in a different size, be sure to keep the length of the repeat and the corner allowance in mind. Any medium-weight cotton or cotton-blend fabric that does not have a polished surface is appropriate for the tablecloth. To preshrink the fabric and remove any sizing, wash and dry it before beginning the project. Before you stencil, you will need to mark a guideline around the cloth; use a fabric-marking pen with nonpermanent ink that disappears when dampened (such pens are available in the notions department of most variety stores).

Acrylic paint dries quickly, so you do not need to wait more than a few moments before moving the stencils, but be sure the paint is dry to the touch before applying the second color. The materials and equipment you will need are available at art supply and crafts stores. Use disposable plastic dishes to hold your paints.

◆ MATERIALS AND EQUIPMENT

1¼ yards cotton or cotton-blend fabric, 45 inches wide
Acrylic craft paint, one 8-ounce container each in red and green
2 pieces stencil acetate, 5½ x 10 inches each
Stencil brush, ½ inch in diameter
Craft knife
Cutting mat

Cloth for pressing
Tracing paper
Nonpermanent-ink fabric-marking pen
Permanent-ink marking pen
Disposable plastic dishes
Paper towels
Masking tape

◆DIRECTIONS

1. *Preparing the fabric:* Cut the preshrunk fabric into a 38-inch square (be sure to cut all four edges on the straight grain). To make a guideline, mark a 33½-inch square centered 2¼ inches inside the fabric square using the nonpermanent-ink pen. Find the middle of each side of the guideline square and mark.

2. *Marking the stencils:* Using a pencil, trace the Stencil Pattern below onto the tracing paper, aligning the two halves of the design in the center according to the register marks. Also trace all the letters, register marks, and broken lines. Place the pattern on a worktable and center one of the two pieces of the stencil acetate over it. Using the permanent-ink marking pen, trace the pattern, including the letters, register marks, and broken lines, onto the acetate. Repeat to mark the second piece of acetate.

3. *Cutting the stencils:* Place one piece of acetate on the cutting mat and, using the craft knife, cut out the two shaded strawberries and the two shaded stems; change blades as necessary. (If you make a mistake and cut into the acetate, you can mend it with a piece of masking tape.) Mark this stencil "R." In the same manner, cut out the second piece of acetate, except for the stem and hull marked X and Y (they will be used for aligning the pattern repeat but not for stenciling). Mark this stencil "G."

4. *Testing the stencil and paints:* Place a scrap of fabric on the worktable. Dip the stencil brush into the green paint, then pounce the brush on paper towels to remove any excess paint. Place the G stencil over the fabric and hold it in place with one hand. If desired, you can tape the corners of the stencil to the fabric. Place the brush at the edge of a cutout; with a circular motion, pounce the brush toward the center. To keep the stencil flat, place your free hand near the edge of the cutout as you paint. Practice your stenciling technique until you are happy with the effect.

5. *Stenciling in green:* With the marked side up, spread the fabric square flat on

STENCIL PATTERN

X

left

the worktable and tape it to keep it flat. Place the G stencil on one edge of the guideline so that the register mark labeled "left" is directly over the center mark. The other bottom register marks must also be on the guideline. Hold the stencil and apply the green paint as in Step 4, painting in all the cut-out areas. Let the paint set, then lift the stencil and move it to the right. With the register marks on the guideline, align the uncut stem (X) over the right-hand green stem that you have just painted. Apply paint as before and let it set. Starting again at the center mark, repeat the process, now moving the stencil to the left and aligning the uncut hull (Y) over the left-hand hull previously painted. Repeat until all four sides of the cloth are stenciled.

6. *Filling in the corners:* Choose a portion of the design to repeat in the corner space. Using the G stencil, place the chosen area of the stencil in one corner of the tablecloth (position the design so that it fits comfortably in the space). Apply green paint over the cut-out areas and let the paint set. Repeat until all four corners of the tablecloth are stenciled. Let dry.

7. *Stenciling in red:* Place the R stencil over the green-painted design, aligning the pattern; it does not matter where you begin. Apply the red paint, moving the stencil as in Step 5. Still using the R stencil, stencil the corners as in Step 6.

8. *Setting the paint:* With the painted side up, place the cloth on an ironing board. Cover one area of the painted border with a clean cloth and, with your iron on the cotton setting, press for three minutes. Repeat for the entire design.

9. *Finishing the tablecloth:* Loosen the parallel thread on one cut edge and pull it free. Continue to pull threads until you have made a 1-inch fringe. Repeat on the opposite edge of the cloth, then on the two remaining edges. Secure the fringe with a line of zigzag stitching at the woven edge of the fabric on all four sides of the tablecloth. Remove the ink markings following the pen manufacturer's directions. ◆

Country Floor Cloth

Painted canvas cloths were probably among the first types of floor coverings used in this country. Whether they were store-bought or made at home, such cloths had many attributes: they provided good insulation, they were washable, and they were durable, requiring only an occasional coat of varnish for upkeep. Easy to make, they are still popular today. (For more floor cloth design ideas, see pages 132-133.)

◆ IMPORTANT INFORMATION

This floor cloth, which measures about 33 x 41 inches, is made of cotton duck canvas. After the canvas is primed with gesso, it is marked in pencil with a 2-inch grid. By referring to the Scaled Schematic Diagram on page 130, you will be able to mark the diamond and checkerboard pattern directly onto this grid.

The design is applied in acrylic craft paint and is sealed with polyurethane for protection. Before painting, the yellow and teal diamonds are masked off with tape, which is sealed with acrylic matte medium to prevent bleeding. The checkerboard border is painted with two simple stencils cut from stencil acetate, a clear plastic film.

After priming the canvas, let the gesso dry for at least two hours. Let the acrylic paint set a few moments before moving the stencils, and be sure the paint is dry to the touch before masking over it or applying adjacent colors. When you seal the tape, let the acrylic matte medium dry for half an hour before painting over it. Use disposable plastic dishes to hold your paints, and choose an appropriate-size brush for the area you are painting; change or clean brushes when changing colors. The materials and equipment you will need are available at art supply and crafts stores.

The first canvas floor cloths in this country were imported from England, but Americans were manufacturing their own by the late 18th century. In 1793, Joseph Barrell, a wealthy Bostonian, wrote to his London agent and canceled his order for floor cloths "as I find I can supply myself better here."

◆ MATERIALS AND EQUIPMENT

1 piece #10 cotton duck canvas, 36 x 44 inches
1 pint gesso
Acrylic craft paint, one 8-ounce container
 each in cream, yellow, teal, black, and red
1 quart clear polyurethane
Assorted flat paintbrushes, ¾ to 3 inches
Stencil brushes, 1½ and ½ inches in
 diameter
Acrylic matte medium
White craft glue
1 sheet stencil acetate, 8½ x 11 inches
2-quart mixing bowl

Rolling pin
Craft knife
Cutting mat
Scissors
Graph paper
T-square
Masking tape, 1 inch wide
Disposable plastic dishes
Paper towels
Sandpaper, 150 grit
Marking pen
Ruler

Scaled Schematic Diagram

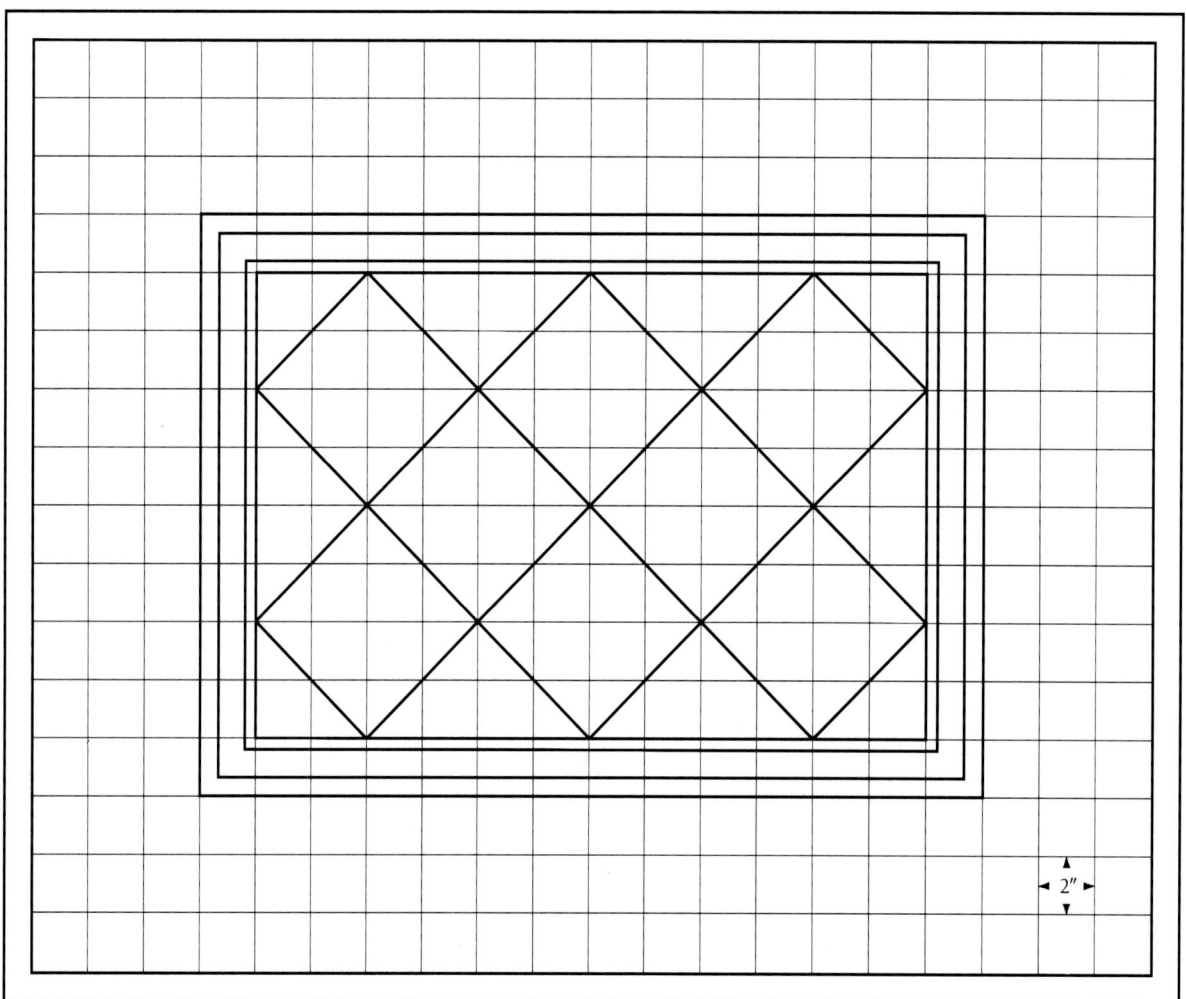

2"

◆DIRECTIONS

1. *Getting started:* In the mixing bowl, mix the gesso with 1 cup of water. Prime one side of the canvas with the gesso and let dry. Turn the canvas over and prime the other side. Let dry. Paint one side of the canvas in cream.

2. *Making the border stencils:* Using a pencil, mark a row of three 2-inch squares on a piece of the graph paper. Place the stencil acetate on the cutting mat and, using the craft knife, cut a rectangle measuring 4 x 8 inches from the acetate and center it over the marked squares. Using the marking pen, trace the row of three squares onto the acetate. Cut out the first and third squares. Mark this stencil "A." Cut a 2-inch square from the remaining acetate. Using the marking pen, divide the 2-inch square into four 1-inch squares. Mark a ¼-inch square on a piece of graph paper and place the paper under the acetate diagonally, so that each corner of the ¼-inch square touches one of the quartering lines (Illustration A). Trace the ¼-inch square onto the acetate and cut it out. Mark this stencil "B."

3. *Marking the pattern:* Measure and mark a 32 x 40-inch rectangle centered on the canvas. Measure and mark a grid of 2-inch squares inside the rectangle; there will be 16 squares on the ends and 20 squares on the sides (320 squares total).

4. *Marking and painting the diamond pattern:* Referring to the Scaled Schematic Diagram opposite and following the 2-inch grid, use the masking tape to mask off a central 16 x 24-inch rectangle (8 x 12 squares). Using the ruler and pencil, mark the diamonds. Mask along the outside edges of the six diamonds to be painted in yellow. Brush the matte medium over the edges of the tape and let dry. Paint the diamonds in yellow and let dry. Remove the tape from around the diamonds only. Mask and seal the outside edges of the remaining diamonds and the triangles, paint them in teal, and let dry. Remove all the tape.

5. *Marking and painting the black border:* Mask along the inside edge of the 16 x 24-inch central rectangle with the masking tape. Measure and mark another rectangle ¼ inch outside it and mask to expose a ¼-inch border. Brush the matte medium over the edges of the tape and let dry. Paint the border in black and let dry. Remove the tape.

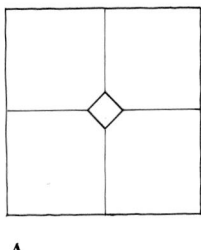

A

6. *Painting the checkerboard border:* Beginning in one corner of the floor cloth, place the A stencil on the canvas, aligning it with any three squares in the 2-inch grid. Dip the 1½-inch stencil brush into the black paint and pounce off any excess paint onto paper towels. Hold the stencil steady with one hand and place the brush at the edge of one cut-out square, and, using a circular motion, work the brush toward the center of the cutout. Repeat in the second cut-out square. Let the paint set a few moments, then reposition the stencil and paint two more squares. Repeat until all the black squares are painted.

7. *Painting the small teal squares:* Place the B stencil on the canvas, aligning it with a cream square. Using the ½-inch stencil brush, paint the cut-out square in teal. Let the paint set a few moments. Remove the stencil and repeat on each cream square. Let dry.

B

8. *Marking and painting the red borders:* Measure and mark a ¾-inch border along both the outside and inside edges of the checkerboard, and mask to expose both ¾-inch borders. Brush the matte medium over the edges of the tape and let dry. Paint the borders in red. Let dry and remove the tape.

9. *Removing paint bumps:* Sand the painted surface lightly. Wipe the canvas with a damp cloth.

10. *Gluing the edges:* With the painted side of the canvas up, measure and mark a line 1¾ inches inside the cut edge of the canvas in the red border. Trim the corners of the canvas diagonally (Illustration B). Turn the canvas over. Apply a 2-inch border of white glue along one edge of the canvas; fold the border over so that the marked line in the red border just shows on the wrong side. Press the folded edge flat with a rolling pin. Repeat for the three remaining sides of the canvas (Illustration C). Let the glue dry overnight.

C

11. *Sealing the floor cloth:* Brush the painted side of the canvas with the acrylic sealer; let dry overnight. Sand the canvas lightly and repeat, giving the canvas at least one more coat of sealer. ◆

FLOOR CLOTH DESIGNS

In the 18th and 19th centuries, canvas floor cloths were often painted to imitate costly tiling or Oriental carpets. In making your own floor cloth, you may want to reproduce a traditional tile or carpet design, or take a cue from the past to devise a new pattern of your own.

The new floor cloths shown here—painted both freehand and with stencils—were inspired by many different sources, including a Baby Blocks quilt pattern, an antique hooked rug, and the familiar rabbit motif that appears on Dedham pottery. The trompe l'oeil cat on the "Oriental" rug is a contemporary twist on a traditional idea. Let these designs spark your imagination once you have learned how to paint the country floor cloth on page 128.

133

Pachisi Board

Board games have a long and colorful history. Pachisi, for instance, originated in ancient India, where it was traditionally played on elaborately embroidered cloths. (The Indian nobility also conducted a version of the game in marble-paved courtyards, using dancing girls from their harems as playing pieces.) By the Middle Ages, the game had become popular in Europe and England, and knowledge of it was brought to America as early as the 17th century. In making game boards, colonial craftsmen often relied on their memory of how the game was played rather than copying an existing board. There were many variations on the basic design, which was composed of four starting corners, four alleyways, and a central "home" area. Antique or new, such game boards can be distinctive works of art; the piece at left is designed to be displayed on a wall. (For more game-board design ideas, see pages 138-139.)

◆ IMPORTANT INFORMATION

This game board is made from Masonite (a type of fiberboard) and framed with square-cut pine molding; both are available at lumberyards. If you do not have a saw, ask the lumberyard to cut the pieces to the dimensions listed below. (If you are cutting the wood yourself, use a crosscut handsaw.) The board is painted in acrylic craft paint and sanded for an aged look.

After the Masonite is primed with a base coat, the pattern is marked in pencil onto the board following the Scaled Schematic Diagram on page 137. Using a transparent graphed ruler will make it easy to mark. You will need a steady hand to paint the board. To help keep the design lines clean when painting, you can mask the edges with masking tape. Be sure the colors are dry to the touch before you apply the tape or start to paint an adjacent color. Use an appropriate-size brush for the area you are painting; change or clean brushes when changing colors.

◆ MATERIALS AND EQUIPMENT

1 piece ¼-inch Masonite, 18½ x 18½ inches
4 strips pine molding, ½ x ¾ x 19 inches each
Acrylic craft paint, one 4-ounce container
 each in ocher, teal, orange, red, yellow,
 and black
Wood glue
Finishing nails, ½ or ¾ inch
Crosscut handsaw (optional)
Tack hammer

Sandpaper, 120 and 220 grit
Assorted flat artists' brushes, ⅛ to 3
 inches
T-square
Ruler
Disposable plastic dishes
1-pound coffee can, 4 inches in diameter
1 quarter
1 dime

◆DIRECTIONS

1. *Preparing the board:* Using the 120-grit sandpaper, sand all rough edges on the Masonite and molding strips.

2. *Painting the base coat:* Paint the smoothest side of the board, as well as all surfaces of the molding strips, in ocher. When dry, lightly sand the painted surfaces with the 220-grit sandpaper. Set the molding strips aside.

3. *Marking the nine-block pattern onto the board:* With the painted side up, place the board on a worktable. Referring to the Scaled Schematic Diagram opposite, use a pencil to mark an 18 x 18-inch square ¼ inch inside the edges. Measure and mark this square into nine 6-inch blocks. Using the ruler, draw diagonal lines from corner to corner in the 18-inch square. Then draw diagonal lines between the remaining corners in the four corner blocks.

4. *Marking the corner blocks:* In one corner block, make a mark 2 inches from the center on each diagonal line. Center the coffee can on these marks and draw around it. Mark a small circle in the center of this large circle by drawing around the quarter. Repeat for the three remaining corner blocks.

5. *Marking the alleyway blocks:* Referring to the Scaled Schematic Diagram, mark the alleyways in the four remaining outer blocks by dividing each of the blocks into eight ¾ x 6-inch strips running parallel to the outer edge. In each of these blocks, divide all but the outer strip into three columns. Each column should contain seven rectangles and each rectangle should measure ¾ x 2 inches. Mark the circle where indicated in each alleyway and in each outer strip by drawing around the dime. Connect the alleyway blocks with a short diagonal line through each corner block.

6. *Marking the central block:* Measure and mark the central block into four 3-inch squares. To mark the star, measure and mark a dot 3½ inches in from a corner on each diagonal line. On each vertical and horizontal line, measure and mark a dot 1 inch in from the sides. Mark lines to connect these eight dots, forming the star. Place the coffee can on one corner of the central block so that the curve connects two outer alleyways, and draw around it to mark a quarter-round. Repeat for the other three corners of the central block.

7. *Painting the corner blocks:* Referring to the photograph on pages 134-135, paint the background and center circle of each corner block in teal. Let dry. Paint the ring shapes in ocher. Let dry.

8. *Painting the star and the alleyways:* Paint the central star and the ¾ x 2-inch rectangles in the middle column of each alleyway block in orange. Let dry. Paint the remaining columns and the ¾ x 6-inch outer strip in each of the alleyway blocks and the connecting triangles in red. Let dry.

9. *Finishing the painting:* Paint the quarter-rounds of the central block in yellow. Paint the background around the star, the dime-size circles, and the ¼-inch border of the board in black. Paint the molding strips in teal. Let all the paint dry overnight.

10. *Aging the game board:* Using the 220-grit sandpaper, sand the game board and molding strips lightly. Sand some areas again, so that the base coat of ocher shows through here and there. Retrace the lines on the alleyway blocks with a pencil.

The game of pachisi was so popular in ancient India that women sometimes included hand-decorated silk or cotton "boards" in their dowries. Men kept the pachisi "boards" rolled up in their turbans, always at the ready for an impromptu game.

11. *Glueing on the molding strips:* With the painted side up, place the board on the worktable. Carefully apply the wood glue along one edge of the board. With one end of one molding strip extending ½ inch beyond the corner of the board, glue the ¾-inch-wide side of the strip to the board edge. Turn the board 90 degrees and repeat, butting one end of the second molding strip against the extended portion of the first strip. Repeat for the two remaining edges. Using the tack hammer, nail two finishing nails through each molding strip into the end of the adjacent strip to reinforce the corners. ◆

Scaled Schematic Diagram

GRAPHIC GAME BOARDS

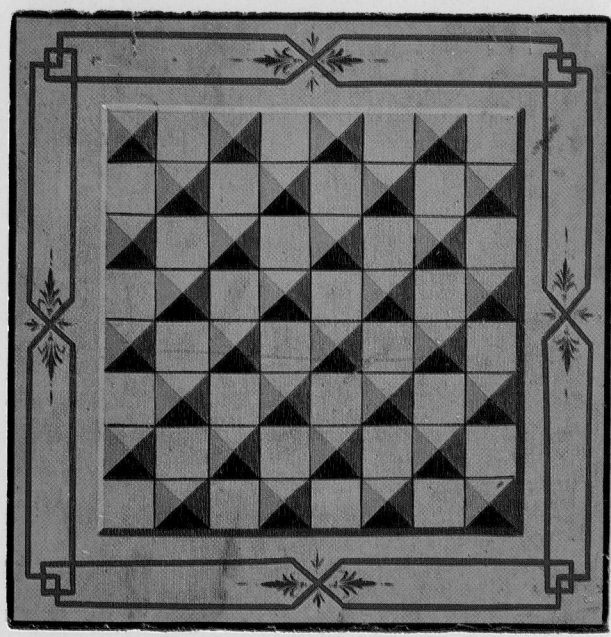

The checkerboards above include, clockwise from top left, a c. 1850 board with a sawtooth border, a late-1800s piece with a grain-painted grid, a c. 1880 board painted for a three-dimensional effect, and a Victorian board with gold detailing.

In the days before radio and television, handmade game boards like those designed for checkers, above, and for pachisi, opposite, could be found in almost any household. While some game boards were simply painted, others were distinguished by ingenious graphics and beautifully rendered images; carefully designed and decorated, the finest boards are now considered true folk art by collectors.

Part of the pleasure of looking at early game boards lies in discover-

ing the small details that the makers thought to include. Pachisi boards, for instance, sometimes display an elaborate painted landscape or compass rose in the center. Many checkerboards feature trompe l'oeil painting and intricate borders. On some examples, the squares were numbered so that players could carry on a game long distance by penny postcard. The boards shown here date from the 19th and early 20th centuries. Let their striking designs inspire you to create your own.

The pachisi boards above include, clockwise from top left, a late-1800s board with a compass rose motif, a late-1800s two-piece board, an early-1900s board with a checkerboard on the back, and a 1915 piece from Kennebunk, Maine.

Grain-Painted Boxes

Intended to simulate the look of fancy woods, grain-painting appeared in the colonies as early as 1700 and was used to decorate furnishings and woodwork. An ornamental effect was commonly considered more important than an exact replication of a particular wood grain, and many rich, abstract patterns emerged as craftsmen manipulated paints and glazes with all manner of tools—brushes, graining combs, sponges, wads of paper or cloth, and their fingers. Boxes like those shown opposite were often grain-painted because their broad, flat surfaces were easy to work on and yielded the showiest results. You will find that much of the pleasure in this craft lies in experimenting; there are no set rules for colors or designs.

◆ IMPORTANT INFORMATION

The directions that follow explain two techniques for grain-painting. In one, a surface is covered with a solid-color base coat and a tinted glaze is applied over the base color and then marked with the fingers, wadded paper towels, or a comb while still wet to create a pattern. The glaze consists of vinegar, corn syrup, and paint pigments; it is simple to mix and dries in about twenty minutes. If you are using this method, choose vivid base colors and tint your glaze a darker color than the base. In the other method, a second paint color is applied over the base coat with a sponge to create a pattern.

Most crafts stores carry inexpensive, unfinished boxes like those used here. You should sand and prime the boxes before you begin. In both graining techniques, acrylic paint is applied as a base coat. When applying the contrasting color, work on the lid first, then the sides. To protect your pieces, finish them with acrylic sealer. Use disposable plastic dishes to hold your paints and glazes and choose an appropriate-size brush for the area you are painting. The directions that follow are for the four different patterns shown on pages 142-143. The first three patterns are worked in a tinted glaze. The fourth pattern is sponge-painted; no glaze is needed.

Rufus Porter, a well-known American decorative painter, recorded these directions in 1825 for imitating bird's-eye maple: "The birds' eyes and curls are formed by removing the staining from the ground with a piece of stiff leather, the edges of which are cut in notches so that several points will touch the work at the same time."

◆ MATERIALS AND EQUIPMENT

Unfinished wooden boxes
Latex primer
Acrylic paints
Clear polyurethane
Assorted flat paintbrushes, ¾ to 3 inches
Natural sponge
Paper towels
Assorted graining combs or lightweight
 cardboard

Sandpaper, 220 grit
Disposable plastic dishes
Scissors

For glaze:
Light corn syrup
Distilled white vinegar
Dry pigments or poster paints
Pint jars, one for each color

◆ DIRECTIONS

If you choose to make one of the first three patterns shown above, you will need to begin by preparing the glaze. To make enough glaze to cover an 8 x 8 x 4-inch box, mix in a jar ¼ teaspoon of corn syrup and ½ teaspoon of dry pigment in the desired color; blend well. Stir in 1 tablespoon of vinegar. The glaze will have the consistency of skim milk. Use a paintbrush to apply the glaze over the acrylic base coat color. Following either method one, two, or three below, manipulate the glaze on the surface; work quickly while the glaze is still wet. If the glaze becomes too dry, or if you don't like the pattern, go over it with a brush dampened with vinegar and start again. When you are satisfied, let the glaze dry before moving to an adjacent area. Let the glaze dry thoroughly before sealing.

1. *Painting the ocher and sepia pattern:* Paint the base coat in ocher. To make a comb, cut from lightweight cardboard a rectangle that is 3 inches wide and as long as the diameter of your box lid; cut the teeth at ⅛-inch intervals. Mix the glaze using sepia pigment and apply to the lid. Hold the comb near one edge of the lid; in two motions, pivot it in an S-shaped curve. Lift the comb, put it down right next to the S shape and repeat the motions. Repeat across the top of the box. Apply glaze to the lid lip and pivot the comb in a series of small curves around the lid. Apply glaze to

the side of the box. Pivot the comb in a small arc; then, without lifting the comb, pivot it from the bottom of the box side in another small arc. Repeat around the box.

2. *Painting the blue and olive pattern:* Paint the base coat in light blue. Mix the glaze using olive pigment and apply to the box lid. Using the tip of your little finger, press a random pattern of dots into the center of the lid. With your index finger, press a circle of finger marks around the dots. Press another circle of finger marks around the first. Press a band of finger marks around the edge of the lid. Apply glaze to one side of the box. Press concentric arcs of finger marks onto the lower part of the box side. Press a band of finger marks across the top of the box side. Repeat for the remaining sides of the box.

3. *Painting the maroon and black pattern:* Paint the base coat in maroon. Mix the glaze using black pigment and apply to the box lid. Using a wadded piece of paper towel, wipe the surface of the lid in diagonal stripes. In the same manner, glaze and wipe the sides of the box and the lid lip.

4. *Painting the rust and ocher pattern:* Paint the base coat in rust. Using the scissors, cut a piece of sponge measuring about 1 inch square by ½ inch thick. Dip the square side of the sponge into ocher paint and press off the excess paint onto paper towels. Use a rhythmic up-and-down motion to sponge the box in diagonal rows, leaving about ¾ inch between the rows. With the edge of the sponge, paint diagonal stripes between the rows. ◆

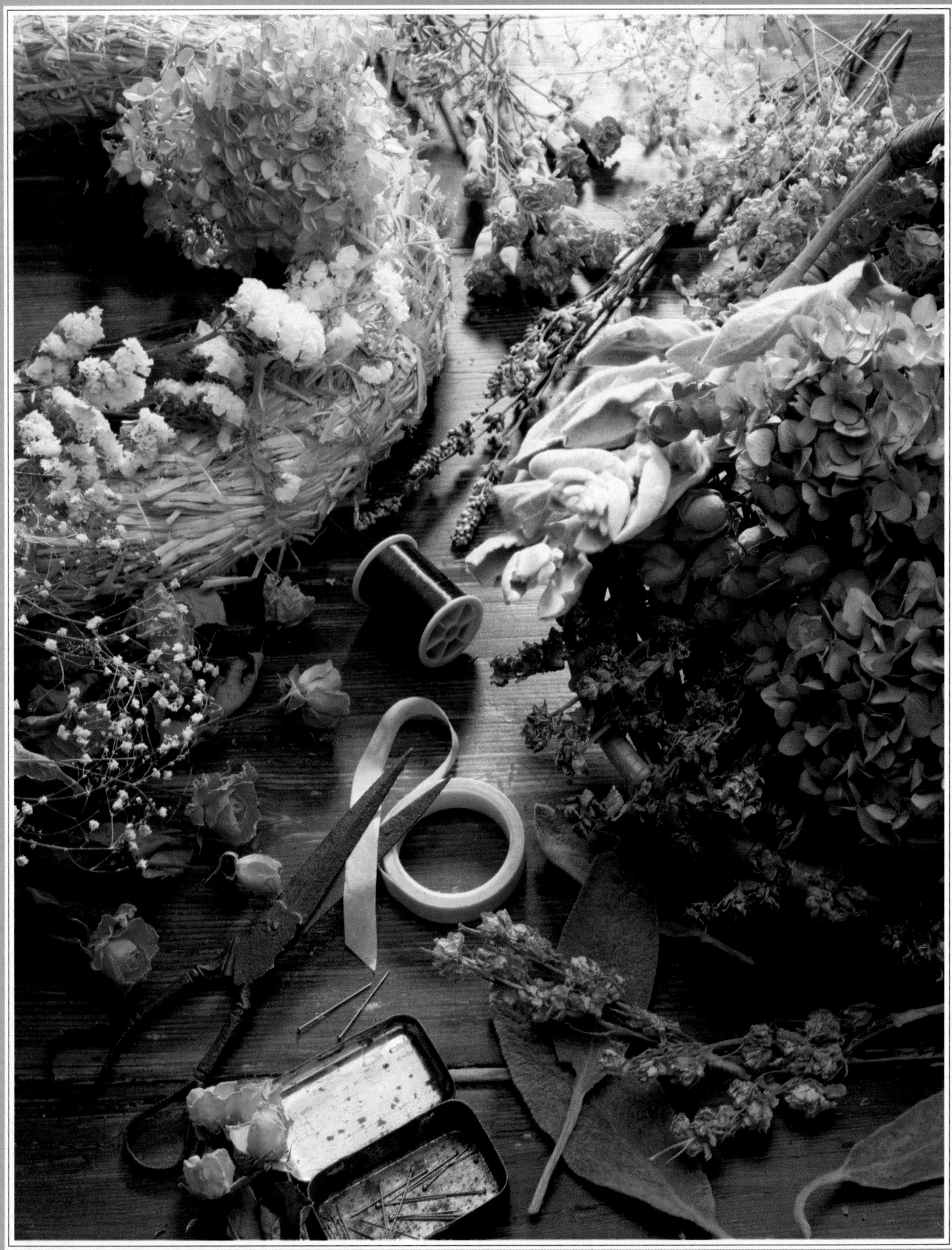

Crafting Natural Materials

*working with wood, flowers,
and foliage*

Whether collected on walks through the countryside or purchased through florists or lumberyards, natural materials like those used for the craft projects in this chapter are appealing because they provide a link to the out-of-doors. There is also something very fulfilling in working with these materials: in enjoying the scent of wood and flowers, and in fashioning branches into rustic accessories.

You might want to begin with the dried-flower wreath; it is an easy project that makes a lovely gift. You can purchase flowers already dried or learn to dry them yourself following the directions provided. Or, look to your back yard or nearby woods for branches and twigs suitable for making the twig picture frame; this frame looks just right with a vintage print or photograph. The three other woodworking projects include a bird feeder, a Shaker-style peg-rack shelf, and a primitive Noah's ark that is sure to please the young at heart. While the feeder and ark require some woodworking experience, the shelf is a good project on which to begin learning this skill.

Dried flowers, taped into bunches, are attached to a wreath form (see pages 158-161).

Twig Picture Frame

The picture frame opposite recalls the twig pieces used to furnish the "great camps" and cottages that proliferated in the Adirondack Mountain region of New York State from the 1870s into the 1930s. As America became increasingly industrialized in the decades following the Civil War, many city dwellers yearned for a simpler life and fled to the Adirondacks each summer to pursue the pleasures of nature. Here, rustic resort homes were built from rough-hewn logs and the rooms appointed with furniture and accessories crafted locally from twigs and branches.

"To the modern man in the Adirondacks, the roar of the rapids, the gaunt dead trees around the lake....are sources of joy and refreshment unspeakable," wrote Henry Beers in the article "The Modern Feeling for Nature," published in 1904 in Points at Issue. "He sees in them the unconsciousness, the spontaneity, the coarse health of the great mother from whom we all are sprung, to whom we all return, but whose existence we have forgotten in the cities."

◆ IMPORTANT INFORMATION

The directions that follow are for a frame with an opening that measures 13½ inches wide and 16½ inches high, but they can be adapted to any size frame. You will need small branches and twigs in a variety of diameters; refer to the Cutting Chart on page 149 for the sizes that were used for this frame. (If you make a frame that is considerably larger or smaller, adjust the branch and twig sizes accordingly.)

Making a frame out of branches and twigs is by necessity an inexact and creative process. Since no two branches or twigs are identical, just try to find pieces that have approximately the same diameters as the pieces specified in the Cutting Chart. When you gather your wood, choose pieces that appeal to you, and don't look for perfection; the knobs, knots, and bark will give the finished frame character. This frame was made from birch, but beech, ash, oak, ironwood, maple, and hickory would also be good choices, as all of them have pretty bark.

You will need to refer to the Assembly Diagram on page 149 to put the pieces together. The main section of the frame is made of four branches, measuring about 1½ inches in diameter, that are notched to fit together where they cross. After the main section is assembled, a lower bar is added, then decorative twig fretwork is applied to the bottom, sides, and top of the frame. Do not cut the fretwork pieces until the main frame and lower bar are assembled. Be sure to fit all the fretwork pieces for each section before you attach any of them, adjusting until you like the overall effect.

To prevent the pieces from splitting as they are nailed together, you will need to predrill holes through the intersecting pieces. Keep an assortment of galvanized nails on hand; as you work, select a nail for each notched joint that is just a little shorter than the combined thickness of the two pieces being joined. Use a drill bit the same size as the nail you plan to use, and drill each hole to a depth that measures about three-quarters of the length of the nail.

You will need only a few tools to make the frame. Use a crosscut handsaw to cut the branches. Use a coping saw to taper the branch ends, to cut the smaller twigs, and to bevel the ends of the angled twigs.

◆MATERIALS AND EQUIPMENT

Assorted small branches and twigs (see *Crosscut handsaw*
 Cutting Chart on page 149 for *Coping saw*
 approximate dimensions) *Wood chisel*
Galvanized flathead nails, #4p, #6p, *Drill with selection of bits*
 #8p, and #12p *Hammer*
Stain or paint of your choice *Ruler*

◆DIRECTIONS

1. *Cutting the branches:* Referring to the Cutting Chart and the Assembly Diagram opposite, cut two branch pieces for the two side bars (pieces #1), and three branch pieces for the top bar and two bottom bars (pieces #2).

2. *Laying out the main frame:* Arrange the two side bars (pieces #1) and a top and bottom bar (pieces #2) so that they frame an opening that measures 13½ inches wide and 16½ inches long. Using a pencil, on the side, top, and bottom branches make marks for notches where the branches cross.

3. *Cutting the notches:* Using the crosscut handsaw, cut a notch between the markings on each branch piece and chisel out with the hammer and chisel; each notch should be as deep as half the diameter of the branch. Fit the pieces together (Illustration A), adjusting the size of the notches if necessary.

4. *Tapering the branch ends:* Choose one side of the frame to be the front, and place the frame with the front side up on a worktable. Center the lower bar (the remaining, unnotched piece #2) across the bottom of the frame, abutting the ends of the side bars. On the front side of the five framing pieces, make a pencil mark 2 inches in from each exposed branch end. Disassemble the frame and, using the coping saw, taper each piece from the pencil marks to the ends.

5. *Assembling the main frame:* Reassemble the notched pieces and, with the back side up, place the frame on the worktable. Drill a hole through a notched intersection; do not penetrate more than halfway through the lower branch. Hammer a nail into the hole. Repeat for the three other notched intersections.

6. *Attaching the lower bar:* Reposition the lower bar across the bottom of the frame. Drill a hole through the lower bar into the end of each side bar. Hammer a nail into each drill hole.

7. *Cutting, fitting, and laying out the lower fretwork:* With the front side up, place the frame on the worktable. Referring to the Cutting Chart and the Assembly Diagram, cut, fit, and lay out the fretwork twigs between the lower bars of the frame, beveling the ends as needed. For each end of each twig, select a nail long enough to go through the adjacent bar and a short way into the twig. To find the best place to make the drill hole, lay the nail perpendicularly across the bar and over the intersecting twig, and mark the corresponding spot on the bar with a pencil dot.

8. *Attaching the lower fretwork:* Referring to the Assembly Diagram, stand the

A

frame upright, hold the center twig (piece #3) in place and drill down through the upper bar into it. Hammer a nail into the hole. Turn the frame over and drill through the lower bar into the other end of the twig. In the same manner, attach the diagonal twigs (pieces #4 and #5) to the bars.

9. *Cutting, fitting, laying out, and attaching the upper fretwork:* Referring to the Cutting Chart and the Assembly Diagram, cut, fit, and lay out the fretwork twigs at the top of the frame, beveling the ends as needed. Mark the pieces for nail placement as in Step 7. Start with the center twig (piece #6), then fit in the diagonal twigs (pieces #7 and #8); drill and nail up through the top bar into the bottoms of the twigs. Fit in the horizontal twigs (pieces #9); from the top, drill and nail them at an angle to the center diagonal twigs (pieces #7). Drill and nail through the side bars into the tops of the end diagonal twigs (pieces #8) and into the ends of the horizontal twigs (pieces #9).

10. *Cutting, fitting, laying out, and attaching the side fretwork:* Referring to the Cutting Chart and the Assembly Diagram, cut, fit, and lay out the fretwork twigs (pieces #10, #11, and #12) at the sides of the frame, beveling the ends as needed. Mark the pieces for nail placement as in Step 7. Working from the center twig out, attach the twigs to one side of the frame, drilling and nailing through them into the bars. Repeat for the other side. Stain or paint the tapered ends of the branches. ◆

Cutting Chart

piece #	quantity required	approximate diameter and length			
		½" d.	¾" d.	1" d.	1½" d.
1	2				31"
2	3				26½"
3	1			5"	
4	2		6"		
5	2		6½"		
6	1			7½"	
7	2		10½"		
8	2	3½"			
9	2		5½"		
10	2	3"			
11	4	6"			
12	4	4"			

Assembly Diagram

Rustic Tray Bird Feeder

This rustic tray bird feeder is not only simple to build, but is also practical: the wide seed tray makes it easy for birds to land, and they can grip the rough bark to establish a good perch while feeding. Ideally, feeders should be placed on the south or east side of a house, out of the path of cold north and northwest winds. (For more information on feeding feathered friends, see page 153.)

◆ IMPORTANT INFORMATION

This bird feeder, which measures about 6 inches wide, 10 inches long, and 8 inches high, is made from slabs of wood cut from firewood logs, small branches, and a piece of ½-inch pine for the floor. Since no two logs or branches are identical, just try to find pieces that have approximately the same diameters as the pieces specified in the materials list below. Choose logs with thick, sculptural bark for the sides and roof, and small branches with smooth bark for the roof supports.

You will need to refer to the Assembly Diagram on page 152 as you cut and construct the bird feeder. You will need a band saw to "rip" (cut with the grain) the wood to the proper size. (A band saw is a potentially dangerous tool and should only be used by someone who knows how to operate it safely.) To prevent the pieces from splitting as they are screwed together, you will need to predrill holes through the intersecting pieces. Use galvanized drywall screws to attach the pieces. Do not stain, paint, or varnish the interior of the bird feeder.

*A contributor to **Good Housekeeping's Discovery Book**, published in 1905, suggested scattering crusts and scraps to feed birds, who "congregate each morning, and if breakfast is tardy announce by impatient twitterings that they at least have kept their engagement."*

◆ MATERIALS AND EQUIPMENT

A few pieces firewood, 5½ and 8 inches in diameter, cut into 10-inch lengths
A few branches, 1¼ inches in diameter (enough to cut four 5-inch lengths)
1 branch, 1¾ inches in diameter, 10 inches long
1 branch, ¾ inch in diameter, 10 inches long

1 piece ½-inch pine board, 4½ x 8¾ inches
Band saw
Drill with bits, ⅛ inch and #2 Phillips
Galvanized drywall screws, #6 x 1⅝ inches
Large screw eye
Ruler

◆ DIRECTIONS

1. *Cutting the tray sides and ends:* Referring to Illustration A, use the ruler and a pencil to mark a 4-inch line across one end of one of the 5½-inch-diameter logs. Using the band saw, rip down the length of the log at this mark to make a 10-inch-long section that measures about ¾ inch high at its center. Mark the center of the 4-inch edge on

one end and rip down the length of the piece at this mark; these two pieces will be the tray sides (pieces #1). Rip down the log to make another section in the same measurements, and cut a 4½-inch-long piece from it. Rip this section in half lengthwise in the same manner as for the sides; these two pieces will be the tray ends (pieces #2).

A

2. *Assembling the tray:* Referring to the Assembly Diagram below, place the piece of pine for the tray bottom (piece #3) on a worktable. With the bark side out and the wider edge down, place one of the tray ends (piece #2) at one end of the tray bottom. On the tray end, make a mark 1 inch in from each end and ¼ inch up from the bottom edge. Using the ⅛-inch bit, drill through the tray end into the tray bottom at each mark. Using the #2 Phillips bit, insert a screw into each hole. Repeat to attach the other tray end. In the same manner, attach the tray sides to the bottom, drilling and inserting screws at the centers and the ends.

3. *Making and attaching the roof supports:* From the 1¼-inch-diameter branches, cut four 5-inch-long pieces for the roof supports (pieces #4). Turn the tray on its side and place one support in one corner of the inside of the tray. Drill through the bottom of the tray into the center of the support and insert a screw into the hole. Repeat to attach a roof support at each of the three remaining corners of the tray bottom.

4. *Cutting the triangular roof braces:* Use the ruler and pencil to mark a 1¼-inch line across one end of the 1¾-inch-diameter branch. Using the band saw, rip down the length of the branch at this mark and discard the smaller piece. Cut the remaining section into two 5-inch-long pieces (pieces #5). On the bark side of one piece, mark the center and cut at an angle from the mark out to each end of the piece. Repeat for the other piece.

5. *Cutting the roof:* Referring to Illustration A, use the ruler and pencil to mark a 6-inch line across one end of one of the 7½-inch-diameter logs. Using the band saw, rip down the length of the log at this mark to make a 10-inch-long section that measures about 1½ inches high at its center. Mark the center of the 6-inch edge on one end of the section and rip down the length of the section at this mark to make two quarter-round pieces for the roof (pieces #6).

Assembly Diagram

6. *Attaching the roof braces:* Referring to the Assembly Diagram, place the tray on the worktable with the bottom down. At one end, place the flat bottom side of one triangular roof brace across the roof supports. Drill through the top of the roof brace into each support and insert a screw into each hole. Repeat to attach the second roof brace.

7. *Attaching the roof and ridgepole:* Referring to the Assembly Diagram, slant one of the roof pieces over the roof braces with the 3-inch flat side down and the tapered edge out. Drill a hole through the roof into the center of each brace and insert a screw into each hole. Repeat to attach the second roof piece. Using the ¾-inch-diameter branch for a ridgepole (piece #7), place it in the space between the two roof pieces. At each end, drill a hole through the ridgepole into the top of the roof brace and insert a screw into the hole. Screw the screw eye into the center of the ridgepole. ◆

FOR THE BIRDS

While nature offers birds an ample food supply, putting out seed and other treats in your yard will provide a welcome supplement to their diet. From one part of the country to another, nearly all birds of the same species eat the same foods. By understanding what certain species like to eat, you may be able to attract a wide variety of birds to your yard—and derive hours of pleasure from watching them dine at your bird feeder.

Among the most nutritious and popular bird feeds are black-stripe—and the smaller black-oil—sunflower seeds. Sunflower seeds are particular favorites of cardinals, nuthatches, grosbeaks, finches, and chickadees. (Because some birds will scatter other seeds out of a feeder in favor of sunflower seeds, you may want to put your sunflower seeds in a separate feeder.)

Niger (thistle) seed will attract redpolls, goldfinches, and siskins. Peanut hearts are favored by blue jays and tufted titmice. Ground-feeding species, such as juncos, sparrows, doves, pheasants, and quail, prefer cracked corn and white proso millet.

In the winter, suet, and peanut butter mixed with seed, will help add necessary calories to a bird's diet. Suet is especially appealing to nuthatches, woodpeckers, and chickadees. Chopped apples, oranges, and raisins are regarded as treats by tanagers, mockingbirds, orioles, and robins.

Keep in mind that water is also essential to birds. If you feed them, you should provide them with a source of fresh, clean water to quench their thirst.

HOME-DRIED FLOWERS

By drying flowers and foliage yourself, you can take advantage of the widest possible range of plants for use in projects like the dried-flower wreath on pages 158-161. Flowers suitable for drying can be picked from your garden or from along the roadside throughout the growing season. Look for plants that have not yet reached peak bloom; if the blossoms are fully opened, they are likely to lose their petals as they dry. Flowers should be picked on dry days, and they should be examined for insects before being brought indoors.

You should always preserve more flowers than you think you will need, since dried flowers are brittle and can break when handled. Dried flowers also fade readily, so they should be stored away from daylight; they can be packed loosely in layers in covered boxes with tissue between the layers until you are ready to use them. Even in the best of circumstances, however, dried flowers will fade once they are displayed, so plan to replace them with a freshly dried supply about once a year.

The following two pages describe four of the most popular methods for drying flowers at home. Although many types of flowers can be preserved successfully with any of the four methods, others respond better to one technique than to another. A little trial-and-error testing may be necessary before you achieve satisfactory results.

FLOWER DRYING METHODS

AIR-DRYING (I)

Hanging flowers upside down to air-dry is a simple procedure that is suitable for a wide variety of plants, and it is particularly useful if you need to dry large quantities of flowers. The most important requirement is a warm, dark, well-ventilated place in which to hang the plants. Attics and closets are ideal; kitchens should be avoided because moisture and grease would cause dust to stick to the flowers. Well-lit rooms can be used if the flowers are carefully wrapped with paper or enclosed in paper bags to prevent fading. The flowers can be hung from rafters, closet poles, blanket racks, or even coat hangers.

When you cut flowers for hanging, remove any thorns, as well as the lower leaves on the stalks, while the plants are fresh and still easy to strip: once the flowers are tied into bunches and hung to dry, the lower leaves can trap moisture and cause mildew to form on the stems.

Flowers dry at different rates of time, depending on their thickness and moisture content, so similar types should be grouped together when hung. For flowers with many layers of petals, such as roses, limit each bunch to three to five stems; smaller, less dense flowers, like lavender or statice, can be gathered in bunches of eight to ten stems. (The larger the bunch, the longer it will take to dry.) As you form each bunch, stagger the arrangement of stems so that the flower heads will not press together. Bind the stems loosely with a rubber band, then gently fan them apart so that air can circulate around the leaves and flower heads. Attach a loop of string or wire to the bound end and hang the bunches, upside down, leaving at least six inches between them. Most flowers will air-dry in two to five weeks; when the plants are thoroughly dried, the petals and stems will be crisp to the touch.

Because dried flowers are fragile it is best to handle them as little as possible: if space allows, leave the flowers hanging until you are ready to use them.

AIR-DRYING (II)

Air-drying flowers on a flat surface is a straightforward technique that is especially good for preserving varieties that have broad, flat flower heads—Queen Anne's lace, zinnias, and daisies, for example. It is also the most convenient way to dry petals and buds for potpourri. (You will need a warm, dry, well-ventilated place to work.)

A window screen suspended between two chairs makes a good surface for drying the small flower heads and petals for potpourri. When spreading the flowers and petals on the screen be careful not to let them overlap, or moisture will be trapped, causing rot. For large flowers, use screening with an open mesh and pull the stems through (the mesh should still be fine enough to fully support the petals on the surface).

If you do not have room to lay the flowers out flat, try air-drying small flowers on a piece of cheesecloth or muslin that has been hung like a hammock. For large flowers, insert the stems through a caned chair seat or the open weave of a hanging basket. Plants and grasses with sturdy stalks and small flower heads can also be dried upright, supported in a vase or other container.

SAND OR CORNMEAL

Drying flowers in sand or a mixture of cornmeal and borax produces fresher-looking blossoms than the air-drying methods. However, it also requires some patience and practice.

With this technique, flowers are buried in the drying medium, which supports the petals in natural positions while they dry. If you use sand, it must be extremely fine and clean. Fine beach sand should be rinsed well to remove any salt, and thoroughly dried before use. Cornmeal mixtures used for drying can vary; a combination of three parts cornmeal to one part borax is reliable. You will also need sturdy, open containers such as shoe boxes or baking pans. It is best to use a

separate container for each type of flower since drying times differ for the various blossoms.

When using this method, roses and other flowers with dense layers of petals should be dried with the heads upward; their stems, therefore, must be trimmed while the flowers are still fresh. You will need a pair of scissors, and some 22- or 24-gauge florist's wire cut into 6- to 8-inch lengths. Trim each stem to within an inch of the flower, then insert a wire, taking care not to let it poke through the flower head. (The flowers can later be given longer stems with additional wire and florist's tape.) Pour an inch or two of the sand or cornmeal mixture into your drying container and settle the flowers on top, leaving some space between the flowers. Slowly add more sand or cornmeal mixture, lifting the petals with a toothpick to ensure that each petal is supported by the mixture. The flowers should be completely covered when you finish.

Flowers with a flat arrangement of petals can be dried with the heads down. Pour an inch or two of the sand or cornmeal mixture into your container and position the flowers so that they do not overlap. Once they are in place, slowly pour in more of the drying medium until the flower heads are completely covered; the stems will stick out of the sand.

Most flowers will dry in three to five weeks, but they can stay in the sand or the cornmeal mixture indefinitely without harm. To check on the drying progress, carefully remove a flower from the container periodically. When the flowers are dry, tilt the container slightly and let the drying medium fall away slowly, or gently scoop the flowers out with a slotted spoon. Dusty residue can be removed from the petals with a watercolor brush. Both the sand and the cornmeal mixture can be used repeatedly, just be sure they are thoroughly dry beforehand.

SILICA-GEL

Drying with a chemical desiccant made from sandlike silica-gel crystals produces the most vivid, natural-color flowers. This method is also fast: silica gel, which actually draws the moisture from petals, dries plants in days rather than weeks. It can be used with many flowers, including orchids and lilies, that become discolored and shriveled when dried by other means.

However, silica gel also has certain drawbacks. Flowers will disintegrate if left in the medium for too long and must be checked regularly during the drying process. Flowers dried in silica gel are also extremely brittle and require careful handling while they are being placed in arrangements. Once dried, the flowers must be kept in conditions with very low humidity, or they will reabsorb moisture and become limp. (Chemical desiccants are also expensive relative to other drying methods.)

Silica gel is available from florists and garden-supply companies, and is used in exactly the same way as the sand and cornmeal mixtures described above. However, the drying must be done in airtight containers, such as cookie tins, to prevent the silica gel from drawing moisture from the air. The drying time is usually two or three days for flowers with a single row of petals, and five to seven days for fuller flowers.

The silica gel can be used repeatedly, but must be dried out each time. Before reuse, pour the crystals into a baking pan and place the pan in a 250° oven for several minutes, until the crystals are fully dried. Store the silica gel in airtight tins between uses.

Dried-Flower Wreath

Wreaths of dried flowers can be enjoyed all year long; they are pretty additions to almost any decor and make welcome gifts. The pastel colors and dainty feeling of the roses, baby's-breath, and other flowers in the wreath opposite give it an old-fashioned country charm. You can, of course, combine plants in a wreath in any way that suits your taste and imagination. You might try making a thematic arrangement, using dried spring flowers perhaps, or mix flowers that have different blooming seasons, using varied colors and sizes. (To learn how to dry your own flowers, see pages 156-157.)

The flowers used in making a wreath can be chosen to convey a particular sentiment or message. Roses, for example, symbolize love, while red and white roses together represent unity. Violets stand for faithfulness, and bluebells constancy. Pansies will tell someone, "I'm thinking of you."

◆ IMPORTANT INFORMATION

The instructions that follow are for the wreath shown here, but they can easily be adapted to a varied choice of flowers, herbs, and leaves. The wreath is assembled on a ready-made straw base that is marked into five equal sections before being covered. Each section is covered with overlapping layers of flowers and leaves that are bound to the straw base with transparent nylon sewing thread (available in the notions department of most variety stores).

Before you arrange the flowers and leaves, you will need to cluster and tape them into small, manageable bunches; refer to the section Preparing the Flowers and Leaves on page 160 to learn how to make the bunches. To arrange the flowers and leaves on each section of the wreath base, refer to the Schematic Diagram on page 161. To achieve the fullness of the wreath shown here, be sure to overlap the bunches generously.

◆ MATERIALS AND EQUIPMENT

Dried materials:
6 stems sea lavender
5 stems baby's-breath
5 stems white statice
25 pink rose blossoms
15 rose-pink carnation blossoms
15 lamb's-ear leaves
5 small or 2 large white hydrangea blossoms
15 stems bunnytail grass
10 stems pink larkspur
10 stems lavender

1 straw wreath base, 12 inches in
 diameter
Transparent nylon sewing thread
Small pruning shears
Wire cutters
2 T-pins
1 roll florist's tape, white or green
Florist's wire
Measuring tape
Black marking pen

◆ PREPARING THE FLOWERS AND LEAVES

Using the pruning shears, cut all the stems about 3 inches below the blossoms or leaves. Make up bunches of flowers as specified below, taping the ends of the stems together for about 2 inches with florist's tape.

Sea lavender (20 bunches): Use three 3-inch-wide clusters per bunch.

Baby's-breath (20 bunches): Use three 3-inch-wide clusters per bunch.

White statice (5 bunches): Use three 3-inch-wide clusters per bunch.

Roses (5 bunches): Use 5 blossoms per bunch.

Carnations (5 bunches): Use 3 blossoms per bunch.

Lamb's-ears (5 bunches): Use 3 leaves per bunch.

Hydrangea (5 bunches): Use one 3-inch-wide blossom per bunch or break apart larger blossoms to make 3-inch-wide bunches.

Bunnytail grass (5 bunches): Use 3 stems per bunch.

Pink larkspur (5 bunches): Use 2 stems per bunch.

Lavender (5 bunches): Use 2 stems per bunch.

◆ DIRECTIONS

1. *Preparing the wreath base:* Pass a piece of florist's wire through the center of the wreath base and wrap it around to the back, twisting it to make a hanging loop. The design of the wreath has no particular top or bottom, so the placement of the loop will not affect the steps that follow. With the marking pen, mark lines on the base to divide it into five equal sections.

2. *Attaching the thread:* Place the base on a worktable with one section centered as if at "twelve o'clock." Push the tip of one T-pin into the base about 2 inches in from the right-hand marking line of this section. With the nylon thread still attached to its spool, wrap the end of the thread around the pin several times, then push the pin completely into the base. Wind the thread several times around base to secure. Place the base on the worktable as before.

3. *Covering the first section of the wreath base:* Referring to the Schematic Diagram opposite, overlap the prepared bunches, positioning them in numerical order. All the heads should point clockwise and be angled toward the inner or outer edges of the wreath base, resulting in all the stems pointing counterclockwise and angling toward the middle of the section (Illustration A). As you work, bind each bunch to the wreath base by wrapping the spool and thread around the base and over the stems several times before positioning the next bunch.

A

4. *Covering the second section of the base:* Attach the flowers and leaves in the same order as in the first section, but reverse the inside/outside positioning of the white statice and the roses (bunches #4 and #5), the carnations and the bunnytail grass (bunches #7 and #13), and the pink larkspur and the lavender (bunches #12 and #16). For example, where in the first section you placed white statice to the outside of the base, in the second section you will angle it to the inside.

5. *Covering the remainder of the base:* Cover the third section in the same manner as the first. Cover the fourth section in the same manner as the second. For the fifth section, judge the placement of the bunches by eye, and try not to duplicate the arrangement that appears in the section on either side. When you reach the beginning of the first section, slide the ends of the stems under the heads of the first-section flowers and bind them carefully so that the thread does not show.

6. *Finishing the wreath:* When the wreath base is completely covered, push the tip of the second T-pin into the base at the end of the last section, wind the thread around it several times, and push the pin into the base. Snip the thread. Look over the finished wreath; if you notice any holes or gaps, make a few more bunches of sea lavender, baby's-breath, lamb's-ears, or bunnytail grass and tuck them in. ◆

Schematic Diagram

1 · sea lavender

2 · sea lavender

3 · baby's-breath

4 · white statice

5 · roses

6 · baby's-breath

7 · carnations

8 · lamb's-ears

9 · sea lavender

10 · sea lavender

11 · hydrangea

12 · pink larkspur

13 · bunnytail grass

14 · baby's-breath

15 · baby's-breath

16 · lavender

A Country Shelf

Shaker craftsmanship inspired the design of the painted peg-rack shelf opposite. Shaker dwellings were models of cleanliness, and the Shakers themselves devised many ways to make housekeeping efficient. While rooms were typically devoid of moldings or woodwork where dust might settle, peg racks were often mounted on walls so that chairs could be hung out of the way when a room was being swept. (Buckets, bonnets, and tools might also be neatly stored on a peg rack.) The Shaker pegs were unique in design: they were lobed at one end to keep things from sliding off, and threaded at the other so that they could be screwed into the wooden rail or board.

◆ IMPORTANT INFORMATION

This peg-rack shelf is made from two pieces of 1 x 4 pine. Three edges of each piece are beveled, then the two pieces are glued and screwed together. Although it is easiest to bevel the edges with a table saw or router, you can achieve the same effect using a hand plane. After the shelf is assembled, it is painted, then heavily sanded for a timeworn appearance. The Shaker-style pegs can be found at hobby stores or lumberyards.

◆ MATERIALS AND EQUIPMENT

1 piece 1 x 4 pine board, 4 feet long	Wood screws, #6 x 1¾ inches
3 Shaker pegs with ½-inch base	Wood glue
Flat latex paint in white and dark blue	Wood filler
Table saw	Sandpaper, 100 grit
Drill with 7/16- and ⅛-inch bits and	Screwdriver
countersink bit	Hammer
Router or hand plane	Metal straightedge
2-inch flat paintbrush	Paper towels

◆ DIRECTIONS

1. *Cutting the wood:* Using the table saw, square off one end of the pine board. Using the straightedge and a pencil, measure and mark a line 24 inches in from the square end. Cut on the marked line. Mark this piece "S," for the shelf board. Measure and mark a line 22¾ inches in from the cut end of the remaining board. Cut on the marked line. Mark this piece "P," for the peg board.

2. *Beveling the boards:* With the table saw set at a 45-degree angle, bevel one long side of the shelf board, leaving the lower ⅛ inch unbeveled. Bevel both short ends of the board in the same manner. Repeat to bevel the peg board.

According to the Shaker Millennial Laws, "Fancy articles of any kind…superfluously finished, trimmed, or ornamented are not suitable for Believers. Whatever is fashioned, let it be plain and simple, unembellished by superfluities which add nothing to its goodness and durability."

3. *Marking the peg placements:* With the beveled side up, place the peg board on a worktable. Measure and mark a line 1½ inches in along the unbeveled edge. Find the middle of this line and mark. Measure along the line and make a mark 7½ inches to either side of the first mark.

4. *Drilling the peg holes:* Using the 7/16-inch bit, drill a hole 5/8 inch deep at each of the three marks. Then, using the 1/8-inch bit, drill the two outer holes all the way through the board.

5. *Marking the shelf board for screws:* With the beveled side up, place the shelf board on the worktable. Measure and mark a line ½ inch in along the unbeveled edge. Find the middle of this line and mark. Measure along the line and make a mark 10 inches to either side of the first mark.

6. *Drilling the screw holes:* Using the 1/8-inch bit, drill through the shelf board at each mark. Turn the board over and, using the countersink bit, countersink the holes.

7. *Attaching the shelf board to the peg board:* With the beveled side up, place the shelf board on the worktable so that the edge with the screw holes is nearest to you. Apply glue along the top edge of the peg board and center the peg board over the screw holes on the shelf board; the back of the peg board should be flush with the back edge of the shelf board, forming a right angle. Turn the unit over and screw the shelf board to the peg board through the holes, countersinking the screws 1/16 inch.

8. *Preparing for painting:* Fill the screw holes with the wood filler. Glue a peg into the middle hole. Let the glue and wood filler dry. Sand all the surfaces lightly.

9. *Painting:* Prime the boards and pegs with one coat of white paint. Let dry. Paint the boards and pegs in dark blue. Let dry. Sand through the paint to round all the sharp edges and to give the wood a timeworn appearance.

10. *Mounting:* Screw the shelf to the wall through the outer peg holes, using screws and anchors appropriate to the wall type. Using a scrap of wood or a folded towel to protect the peg heads, carefully tap the remaining pegs into the board with a hammer. ◆

Noah's Ark

From the 1600s to the early 20th century, Noah's ark toys like the one above were among the most popular children's playthings on both sides of the Atlantic. During the 1800s in America, the arks were considered appropriate "Sunday" toys—as instructional as they were fun—that could be played with quietly on the day of rest. While many Noah's ark toys were imported from Europe (entire towns in Germany were devoted to producing arks, animals, and the small figures of Noah and his family), they were also produced in America; some particularly distinctive examples were crafted and painted by woodcarvers in Pennsylvania and New England. Nearly all arks include a deck for the animals and a dove perched on the roof.

◆ IMPORTANT INFORMATION

You will need a table saw to cut the ark, and a band saw or scroll saw to cut the animals. (These are potentially dangerous tools and should only be used by someone who understands how to operate them safely.) The ark is cut out following the Scaled Schematic Diagrams on page 168. The patterns for the animals shown here are full size; you can paint them freehand or trace the details onto them using artist's transfer paper. Use an appropriate-size brush for the area you are painting.

◆ MATERIALS AND EQUIPMENT

1 piece ½-inch pine board, 8 inches x 12 feet
1 piece ¼-inch pine board or plywood, 6 x 12 inches
1 piece wood dowel, ⅛ inch in diameter, 1½ inches long
Acrylic craft paints: 8 ounces each in white, cream, barn red, and black; 2 ounces each in pink, light brown, gold, green, and gray
Wooden kitchen matches
Table saw
Band saw or scroll saw
Drill with ⅛- and 1/16-inch bits
Wire nails, #18 x 1 inch

Assorted flat paintbrushes, ¼ to 2 inches
Small, fine-pointed paintbrush
Tracing paper
Artist's transfer paper (optional)
Wood glue
Wood filler
Putty knife
Hammer
Mat knife
Sandpaper, 100 grit
Masking tape
T-square
Ruler

◆ CUTTING THE ANIMALS

Using a pencil, trace the full-size Animal Patterns opposite onto the tracing paper and cut out. One at a time, place the paper patterns (except for the dove) on the ½-inch pine, draw around them with the pencil, and cut out, using the band saw or scroll saw. (Draw and cut one lion and lioness and one bull and cow; draw and cut two of each of the other animals.) Draw the dove on the ¼-inch pine or plywood and cut out.

ANIMAL PATTERNS

Scaled Schematic Diagrams

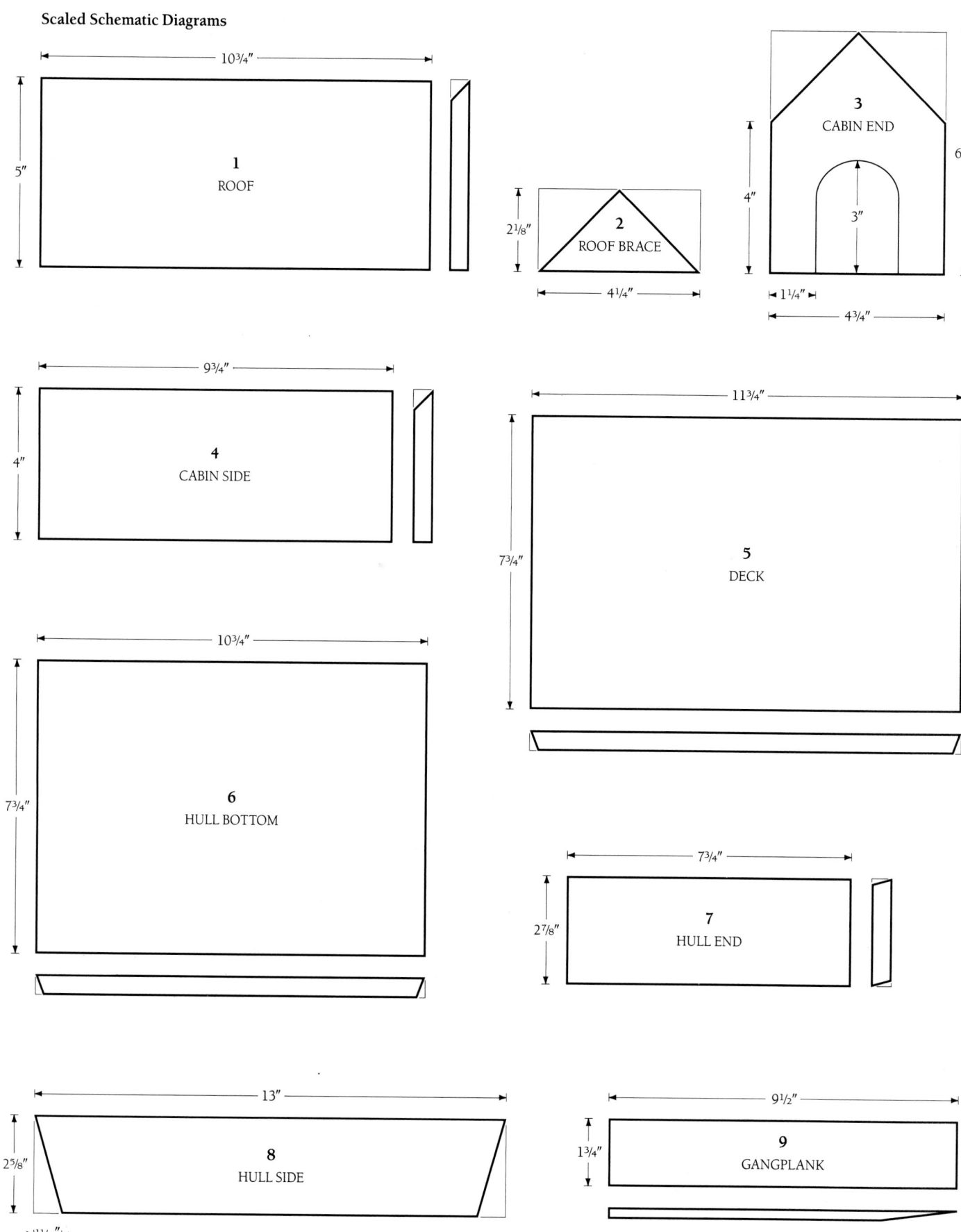

1
ROOF

10¾"

5"

2
ROOF BRACE

2⅛"

4¼"

3
CABIN END

6⅜"

4"

3"

1¼"

4¾"

4
CABIN SIDE

9¾"

4"

5
DECK

11¾"

7¾"

6
HULL BOTTOM

10¾"

7¾"

7
HULL END

7¾"

2⅞"

8
HULL SIDE

13"

2⅝"

11/16"

9
GANGPLANK

9½"

1¾"

2"

◆ CUTTING THE ARK

Using the table saw, cut the pieces listed below from the ½-inch pine. Refer to the Scaled Schematic Diagrams opposite for the dimensions. Mark all the pieces with the appropriate number for quick reference. Do not sand any of the pieces.

Roof (*piece #1*): Cut two; on each piece, bevel one long edge at a 45-degree angle.

Roof brace (*piece #2*): Cut two.

Cabin end (*piece #3*): Cut two; in one piece, cut the doorway arch, using the band saw or scroll saw.

Cabin side (*piece #4*): Cut two; on each piece, bevel one long edge at a 45-degree angle.

Deck (*piece #5*): Cut one; bevel each short edge at a 15-degree angle.

Hull bottom (*piece #6*): Cut one; bevel each short edge at a 15-degree angle.

Hull end (*piece #7*): Cut two; on each piece, bevel each long edge at a 15-degree angle.

Hull side (*piece #8*): Cut two.

Cut the following pieces from the ¼-inch pine or plywood:

Gangplank (*piece #9*): Cut one; taper 2 inches at one end.

Gangplank lip: Cut one piece ¼ x ¼ x 1¾ inches.

◆ASSEMBLING THE ARK

A

B

C

1. *Assembling the roof:* Apply glue to the 45-degree edge of each of the roof pieces (pieces #1). Place the glued edges together and secure with four evenly spaced nails. Using the ruler and pencil, make a mark 1⅛ inches in from each end of the peak on the inside of the roof. Apply glue to the 3-inch edges of each of the roof braces (pieces #2). Place one brace to the inside of a mark at the peak and secure with three evenly spaced nails hammered into it through the roof (Illustration A). Repeat to position and secure the second brace.

2. *Assembling the cabin:* Apply glue to the side edges of one cabin end (piece #3). With the beveled edges up, stand both cabin side pieces (pieces #4) on a worktable parallel to each other and insert one cabin end between them so that the edges are flush and square. Secure each corner with a nail hammered from the cabin side into the end (Illustration B). Repeat for the other cabin end. With the beveled side down, place the deck (piece #5) on the worktable. Using the ruler and pencil, draw a rectangle 1 inch in from the edges. Apply glue to the bottom edge of the cabin and position the cabin on the marked rectangle. Secure the cabin to the deck with a nail toenailed (hammered at an angle) through the side of the cabin into the deck at each corner.

3. *Assembling the hull:* Apply glue to the beveled ends of the hull bottom (piece #6) and, with the unbeveled side up, place it on the worktable. Place one hull end (piece #7) against a glued edge so that the bottom edges are flush, and secure with two evenly spaced nails hammered through the end into the bottom. Repeat to attach the other hull end. On one side of the hull, apply glue to the edge of the hull bottom and to the edge of the hull ends. With the edges flush, place one hull side (piece #8) against the glued edges, and secure with seven evenly spaced nails hammered through it into the adjacent pieces. Repeat to attach the other hull side.

4. *Putting the ark together:* Apply glue along all four edges of the deck. Lower it into the hull, making sure that it is level. Secure with a nail hammered through the center of each hull side and end (Illustration C). Using the putty knife, fill all the nail holes with the wood filler. Let it dry, then sand flush with the wood.

5. *Making the gangplank:* Using the ruler and pencil, measure and mark ½-inch intervals across the length of the untapered side of the gangplank (piece #9). Turn it over, and glue the lip across the untapered end; let the glue set for a few minutes. Turn the gangplank over again. Glue a matchstick across it at each pencil mark, and at each end, keeping all the match heads to the same side. Let the glue dry completely. Using the mat knife, cut the match heads off flush with the plank.

6. *Finishing the dove:* Using the ⅛-inch bit, drill a hole in the bottom edge of the dove. Dip one end of the dowel in glue, then insert it into the hole. Using the ruler and pencil, measure and mark a dot on the roof peak 2¾ inches in from one end. Using the ³⁄₁₆-inch bit, drill a hole at the mark, for the placement of the dove.

◆ PAINTING

1. *Priming the ark and animals:* Paint the ark, roof, and gangplank in white. Paint the edges and one side of the animals in white; let dry. Turn them over; paint the other sides. Let all the paint dry completely.

2. *Painting the ark:* Paint the gangplank, the inside of the cabin, the deck, and the inner edge of the rail around the hull in cream; let dry. To protect the deck while painting the cabin exterior, mask it with tape all along the cabin edges. Paint the cabin and the top of the ark rail in barn red. Let dry. Paint the hull and all the roof surfaces in black. With masking tape, outline two 1-inch-square windows on each side of the cabin and paint them in black. Remove all the tape when the paint is dry.

3. *Painting the animals:* Paint the animals as shown in the photograph on page 165; let the background colors dry before painting the details. (If you do not wish to paint the details freehand, slide a small piece of transfer paper, carbon side down, between each pattern and the corresponding animal and trace over the detail on the pattern with a pencil to transfer it to the wooden animal. Reverse the patterns to trace the details onto the other side of the animals.) Let all the paint dry completely.

4. *Sanding the ark and animals:* Sand through the paint to round all sharp edges. To give a well-worn look to the pieces, sand again in areas that would logically receive the most use, such as the doorway, roof, and hull edges. ◆

Credits

CRAFTS (see also PROPS, below): **Cover**: see specific craft projects. **Pages 10-11**: all sewing boxes adapted from a Victorian design and, except velvet box, executed by Linda Mason, The Watermelon Patch, Manhasset, NY. **Pages 23, 30, 38, 39, 44**: all crafts by Linda Mason, The Watermelon Patch, Manhasset, NY. **Page 51**: sampler by The Scarlet Letter, Sullivan, WI. Frames and catalog available. **Pages 58-59**: hand towels adapted and embroidered by Stephanie Gildersleeve, Brooklyn, NY, from a 1930s towel provided by Abby Ruoff, Shady, NY. **Page 65**: Irish-stitch footstool, Rita Klein Needlepoint, NYC. **Pages 68, 69**: Victorian bellpull, Sally Orent, Simply Lace, Huntington, NY. **Pages 76-77**: large oval braided rug by Polly Whitehorn, Great Neck, NY. **Page 82**: hooked rug by Pat Hornafius, Elizabethtown, PA. Catalog and videotape available. **Pages 90, 91**: antique penny rug, Betty Martin Studio, Northport, NY. **Page 97**: cut-and-pierced lampshade designed and executed by Judy Tripp, Mainely Shades, Falmouth, ME. Books available. **Page 100**: scherenschnitt doves by Claudia Hopf, Kennebunk, ME. Books available. **Pages 104-105**: marbled papers by Faith Harrison, East Hampton, MA. Marbling supplies available. **Pages 110-111**: bandboxes by A Touch of Ivy, NYC. Catalog available. **Page 115**: decoupage dresser set by Ginger Hansen Shafer, NYC. **Page 125**: stenciled tablecloth by Marjorie Yoder, Morgantown, PA. **Page 128**: floor cloth by Dee Shapiro, Great Neck, NY; consultants—Nancy Ferrari, Huntington, NY, and Nancy Good Cayford, Amherst, NH. **Pages 134-135**: game board by Dee Shapiro, Great Neck, NY; consultant—Beverly Stessel, Milford, ME. **Pages 140, 142-143**: all grain-painted boxes by Rubens Teles, Jay Johnson's America's Folk Heritage Gallery, NYC, except pale green sponged box behind oval box, page 140, courtesy of Abby Ruoff, Shady, NY. **Page 147**: twig frame by Abby Ruoff, Shady, NY. **Page 150**: bird feeder by Tom Ames, Olde Ways, Forest, VA. **Page**

159: floral wreath by Betsy Williams, A Proper Season, Andover, MA. Catalog available. **Pages 162, 165**: shelf and Noah's ark by Tom Ames, Olde Ways, Forest, VA. PHOTOGRAPHY: Cover and pages 10-11, 17, 20-21, 23, 30, 38, 51, 58-59, 65, 68, 69, 90, 97, 110-111, 115, 147, 165: George Ross. Frontispiece and pages 8, 19, 28-29, 42-43, 48, 74, 76-77, 81, 88-89, 94, 100, 104-105, 109, 118, 120-121, 125, 128, 134-135, 140, 142-143, 144, 150, 153, 154-155, 156-157, 159: Steven Mays. Pages 14-15, 102-103, 122-123, 132-133: Stephen Donelian. Pages 39, 44, 82, 91, 162: Rob Whitcomb. Page 56: (top) courtesy of Old Sturbridge Village, Sturbridge, MA, photo by Henry E. Peach; (bottom) courtesy of The Henry Francis duPont Winterthur Museum, Wilmington, DE. Page 57: (top) courtesy of Old Sturbridge Village, photo by Henry E. Peach; (bottom) America Hurrah, NYC. Page 63: courtesy of The Pennsylvania German Society, Birdsboro, PA. Pages 138, 139: Schecter Lee. ILLUSTRATIONS: Pages 12, 18, 26, 32, 33, 45, 52, 54-55, 60 (top), 61 (top), 62, 66, 67, 70, 71, 72-73, 78, 79, 86, 92 (left), 148, 152, 170: Patrick J. O'Brien. Pages 22 (left), 40, 41 (top), 98, 107, 108, 112, 113, 131, 160: Ray Skibinski. Pages 13, 22 (right bottom), 25, 27, 34-35, 36-37, 41 (bottom), 46-47, 60-61 (bottom), 85, 87, 92 (bottom), 93, 99, 101, 114, 126-127, 130, 137, 149, 161, 167, 168: computer drawings by Timothy Jeffs. PROPS (see also CRAFTS, above): The Editors would like to thank the following for their courtesy in lending items for photography. Items not listed below are privately owned. **Frontispiece**: bandboxes—A Touch of Ivy, NYC; hand towel—Abby Ruoff, Shady, NY. **Page 8**: buttons—Renaissance Buttons, Evanston, IL; fabric—The Watermelon Patch, Manhasset, NY; thimble—Primrose Lane, Manhasset, NY.; needlecase and sewing machine—Sara Bowman. **Pages 10-11**: velvet sewing box—Waltzing Matilda, Huntington, NY; wallcovering, "Rouen," from *Victoria Mor-*

land's Through the Looking Glass—Raintree Designs, Inc., NYC; small thimble case and thimbles—Primrose Lane, Manhasset, NY; basket—Watermelon Patch, Manhasset, NY. **Pages 14-15**: pincushions—Judy Awrylo. **Page 17**: napkins and place mats—Le Jacquard Français from Palais Royal, Charlottesville, VA. **Page 19**: all buttons—Tender Buttons, NYC. **Pages 20-21**: pillow forms—The Company Store, La Crosse, WI; Laura Ashley lace throw pillow—J. P. Stevens, NYC. **Page 23**: pillow—Linda Mason, Manhasset, NY; teddy bear—Anneliese Rapp, NYC; antique bed and chair—Jones Road Antiques, NYC. **Pages 28-29**: fabric, tea-dyed stuffed animals, heart chain—The Watermelon Patch, Manhasset, NY. **Page 30**: wicker chair—Wicker Garden, NYC; pillow and blanket—Sweet Nellie, NYC. **Page 38**: lace pillow—Gear, NYC; coverlet and pillowcases—Laura Fisher/Antique Quilts and Americana, NYC. **Pages 42-43**: topsy-turvy dolls—Elizabeth DeBarto Skinner, Southampton, NY; Mrs. Lenon Hoyte, Aunt Len's Doll and Toy Museum, NYC. **Page 44**: marbles—The Watermelon Patch, Manhasset, NY. **Page 48**: needles and Persian wool—DMC Corp., South Kearny, NJ; thimble and needlecase—Primrose Lane, Manhasset, NY; embroidery hoop—Watermelon Patch, Manhasset, NY; scissors—Sara Bowman; bargello canvas—Zweigart Canvas ® courtesy Joan Toggitt, Ltd., West Caldwell, NJ; **Page 51**: frame—The Scarlet Letter, Sullivan, WI; wallcovering, "Agatha Wade," from the American Collection—Stroheim & Romann, NYC. **Page 63**: hand towels—private collection, courtesy The Pennsylvania German Society, Birdsboro, PA. **Page 74**: covered basket and thread—Watermelon Patch, Manhasset, NY. **Pages 76-77**: braided rugs—Polly Whitehorn, Great Neck, NY; Roslyn House Antiques, Roslyn, NY; ABC Carpet, NYC. **Page 82**: table, hogscraper candlesticks, painted Shaker box—Roslyn House Antiques, Roslyn, NY; candles—Candlewick, Portland, MI. **Pages 88-89**: Grenfell mats, rugs, purse—Mr. and Mrs. Robert Meltzer,

NYC. **Page 90**: candles—Candlewick, Portland, MI. **Page 94**: wallpaper and bandboxes—A Touch of Ivy, NYC. **Page 97**: lamp base—Judy Tripp, Mainely Shades, Falmouth, ME. **Page 100**: painted scherenschnitt—Claudia Hopf, courtesy of The Watermelon Patch, Manhasset, NY. **Pages 102-103**: all papers—New York Central Art Supply, NYC. **Pages 104-105**: marbleized paper and supplies—Faith Harrison, East Hampton, MA; enamel pitcher—Bonnie Slotnick, NYC. **Page 109**: marbleized papers—Faith Harrison. **Page 118**: brushes—Winsor & Newton, Secaucus, NJ; also available at New York Central Art Supply, NYC. **Pages 120-121**: paintbrushes, acrylic artists' colors—Binney & Smith, Inc., Easton, PA; japan paints—H. Behlen & Bros., Amsterdam, NY; alkyd and oil artists' colors, palette, palette knife, cup—Winsor & Newton, Secaucus, NJ; paints and accessories also available at New York Central Art Supply, NYC. **Pages 122-123**: fans, liners, rounds, brights—Winsor & Newton, Secaucus, NJ; also available at New York Central Art Supply; badger softener, overgrainer, stippler—Whistler Collection; stencil and sponge brushes—New York Central Art Supply, NYC. **Page 128**: painted cupboard—made by John Dossett and painted by Weldine Dossett, Campbelltown, PA. **Pages 132-133**: handcrafted floor cloths, top row: Philadelphia Floorcloths, Inc., Narberth, PA; second row, all: Good & Co. Floorclothmakers, Amherst, NH; third row, all but third from left: Philadelphia Floorcloths; third from left: Good & Co.; fourth row, left: Philadelphia Floorcloths; right: Good & Co.; bottom row: Good & Co. **Page 144**: wreath form and dried flowers—Betsy Williams, A Proper Season, Andover, MA; dried flowers—Primrose Lane, Manhasset, NY; tin box—Bonnie Slotnick, NYC. **Page 147**: Pendleton blanket—Laura Fisher/Antique Quilts & Americana, NYC. **Page 153**: selected seeds, cracked corn, peanut hearts—Duncraft, Pencook, NH. **Pages 154-157**: folding drying rack, #25-333088—Gardener's Eden catalog, San Francisco, CA; all dried flowers—Galerie Felix Flower, NYC. **Page 162**: wallcovering, "Burnett," #5563, from Designers Signature Collection—Greeff Fabrics, Garden City, NY; rag balls, basket, apron—Kathy Wilson, Apple Valley, MN. **Page 165**: table runner—The Watermelon Patch, Manhasset, NY.

Index

Acknowledgments

Our thanks to Sara Bowman, Nancy Good Cayford, Weldine and John Dossett, Jane Fitzpatrick, Stephanie Gildersleeve, Susan and Jack Hale, Claudia and Carroll Hopf, Pat Hornafius, Carter G. Houck, Christina and Michael Kearney, Paula Laverty, Linda Lefko, Sarah Mandell, Karen Marton, Linda Mason, Barbara Meltzer, Frances Beck Reynolds, Eleanor Schrumm, Jeanne Shapiro, Gloria Shattil, Carol Spier, Donna and Peter Steffen, Steve Steinberg, The Watermelon Patch, Frederick Weiser, and Ivy Weitzman for their help on this book.

Second printing
Published simultaneously in Canada
School and library distribution by Silver Burdett Company,
Morristown, New Jersey

TIME-LIFE is a trademark of Time Incorporated U.S.A.

Production by Giga Communications, Inc.
Printed in U.S.A.

Library of Congress Cataloging-in-Publication Data

Country crafts. (American country)
Includes index.
1. Handicraft—United States.
I. Time-Life Books. II. Series.
TT23.C67 1989 745.5 89.4638
ISBN 0-8094-6770-4
ISBN 0-8094-6771-2 (lib. bdg.)

American Country was created by Rebus, Inc., and published by Time-Life Books.

REBUS, INC.

Publisher: RODNEY FRIEDMAN • Editor: MARYA DALRYMPLE
Executive Editor: RACHEL D. CARLEY • Managing Editor: BRENDA SAVARD • Consulting Editor: CHARLES L. MEE, JR.
Associate Editor: SARA COLLINS MEDINA • Copy Editors: ALEXA BARRE, HELEN SCOTT-HARMAN
Writers: JUDITH CRESSY, ROSEMARY G. RENNICKE
Design Editors: NANCY MERNIT, CATHRYN SCHWING
Test Kitchen Director: GRACE YOUNG • Editor, The Country Letter: BONNIE J. SLOTNICK
Editorial Assistants: SANTHA CASSELL, LEE CUTRONE • Contributing Editor: ANNE MOFFAT
Indexer: MARILYN FLAIG

Art Director: JUDITH HENRY • Associate Art Director: SARA REYNOLDS
Designers: AMY BERNIKER, TIMOTHY JEFFS
Photographer: STEVEN MAYS • Photo Editor: SUE ISRAEL
Photo Assistant: ROB WHITCOMB • Freelance Photographers: STEPHEN DONELIAN, GEORGE ROSS
Freelance Photo Stylists: VALORIE FISHER, DEE SHAPIRO

Series Consultants: BOB CAHN, HELAINE W. FENDELMAN, LINDA C. FRANKLIN, GLORIA GALE,
KATHLEEN EAGEN JOHNSON, JUNE SPRIGG, CLAIRE WHITCOMB

Time-Life Books Inc. is a wholly owned subsidiary of TIME INCORPORATED.

Editor-in-Chief: JASON McMANUS • Chairman and Chief Executive Officer: J. RICHARD MUNRO
President and Chief Operating Officer: N. J. NICHOLAS JR. • Editorial Director: RICHARD B. STOLLEY

THE TIME INC. BOOK COMPANY

President and Chief Executive Officer: KELSO F. SUTTON
President, Time Inc. Books Direct: CHRISTOPHER T. LINEN

TIME-LIFE BOOKS INC.

Editor: GEORGE CONSTABLE • Executive Editor: ELLEN PHILLIPS
Director of Design: LOUIS KLEIN • Director of Editorial Resources: PHYLLIS K. WISE
Editorial Board: RUSSELL B. ADAMS JR., DALE M. BROWN, ROBERTA CONLAN, THOMAS H. FLAHERTY,
LEE HASSIG, DONIA ANN STEELE, ROSALIND STUBENBERG
Director of Photography and Research: JOHN CONRAD WEISER
Assistant Director of Editorial Resources: ELISE RITTER GIBSON

President: JOHN M. FAHEY JR.
Senior Vice Presidents: ROBERT M. DeSENA, JAMES L. MERCER, PAUL R. STEWART, JOSEPH J. WARD
Vice Presidents: STEPHEN L. BAIR, STEPHEN L. GOLDSTEIN, JUANITA T. JAMES,
ANDREW P. KAPLAN, CAROL KAPLAN, SUSAN J. MARUYAMA, ROBERT H. SMITH
Supervisor of Quality Control: JAMES KING
Publisher: JOSEPH J. WARD

For information about any Time-Life book please call 1-800-621-7026, or write:
Reader Information, Time-Life Customer Service
P.O. Box C-32068, Richmond, Virginia 23261-2068

Time-Life Books Inc. offers a wide range of fine recordings, including a Rock 'n' Roll Era series.
For subscription information, call 1-800-621-7026, or write TIME-LIFE MUSIC,
P.O. Box C-32068, Richmond, Virginia 23261-2068.

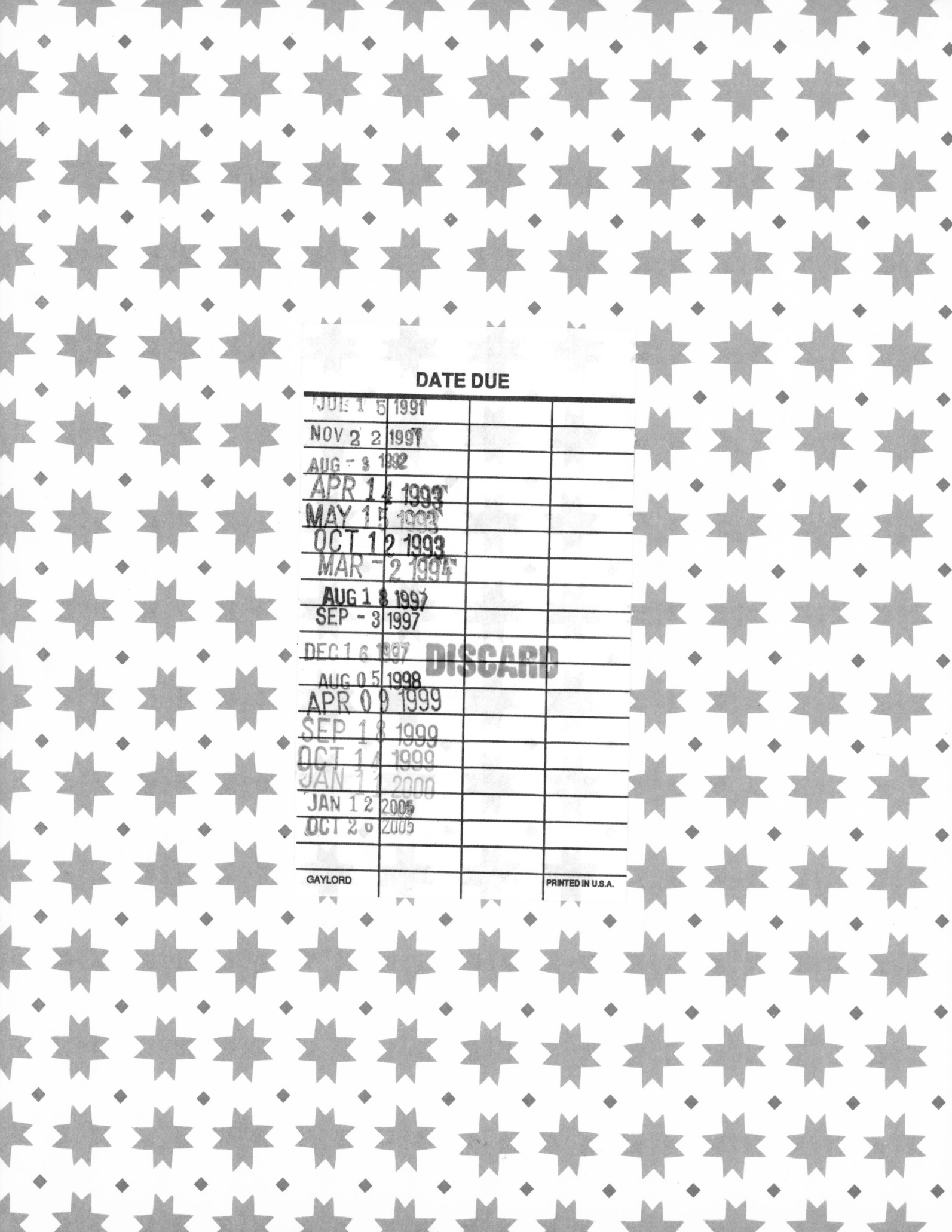